CHILTON'S

CHEVROLET BLAZER/JIMMY/BRAVADA 1982-91 REPAIR MANUAL

CHILTON BOOK COMPANY

ONE OF THE **ABC PUBLISHING COMPANIES,**
A PART OF **CAPITAL CITIES/ABC, INC.**

Manufactured in USA

Chilton Way, Radnor, PA 19089
ISBN 0-8019-8139-5
Library of Congress Catalog Card No. 90-056129
4567890123 4321098765

Contents

Contents

SAFETY NOTICE

Proper service and repair procedures are vital to the safe, reliable operation of all motor vehicles, as well as the personal safety of those performing repairs. This manual outlines procedures for servicing and repairing vehicles using safe, effective methods. The procedures contain many NOTES, CAUTIONS and WARNINGS which should be followed along with standard safety procedures to eliminate the possibility of personal injury or improper service which could damage the vehicle or compromise its safety.

It is important to note that the repair procedures and techniques, tools and parts for servicing motor vehicles, as well as the skill and experience of the individual performing the work vary widely. It is not possible to anticipate all of the conceivable ways or conditions under which vehicles may be serviced, or to provide cautions as to all of the possible hazards that may result. Standard and accepted safety precautions and equipment should be used when handling toxic or flammable fluids, and safety goggles or other protection should be used during cutting, grinding, chiseling, prying, or any other process that can cause material removal or projectiles.

Some procedures require the use of tools specially designed for a specific purpose. Before substituting another tool or procedure, you must be completely satisfied that neither your personal safety, nor the performance of the vehicle will be endangered

Although information in this manual is based on industry sources and is complete as possible at the time of publication, the possibility exists that some car manufacturers made later changes which could not be included here. While striving for total accuracy, Chilton Book Company cannot assume responsibility for any errors, changes or omissions that may occur in the compilation of this data.

PART NUMBERS

Part numbers listed in this reference are not recommendations by Chilton for any product by brand name. They are references that can be used with interchange manuals and aftermarket supplier catalogs to locate each brand supplier's discrete part number.

SPECIAL TOOLS

Special tools are recommended by the vehicle manufacturer to perform their specific job. Use has been kept to a minimum, but where absolutely necessary, they are referred to in the text by the part number of the tool manufacturer. These tools can be purchased under the appropriate part number, from your Chevrolet or GMC dealer or regional distributor or an equivalent tool can be purchased locally from a tool supplier or parts outlet. Before substituting any tool for the recommended one, read the SAFETY NOTICE at the top of this page.

ACKNOWLEDGMENTS

The Chilton Book Company expresses its appreciation to Chevrolet Motor Division, General Motors Corporation, Detroit, Michigan for their generous assistance.

1 General Information and Maintenance

QUICK REFERENCE INDEX

GENERAL INDEX

HOW TO USE THIS BOOK

Chilton's Total Car Care Guide for the S-10 Blazer, S-15 Jimmy and Bravada is intended to help you learn more about the inner working of your vehicle and save you money in it's upkeep.

The first 2 sections will be the most used, since they contain maintenance and tune-up information and procedures. Studies have shown that a properly tuned and maintained vehicle can get at least 10 percent better gas mileage (which translates into lower operating costs) and periodic maintenance will catch minor problems before they turn into major repair bills. The other sections deal with the more complex systems of your vehicle. Operating systems from engine through brakes are covered. It will give you detailed instructions to help you change your own brake pads and shoes, tune-up the engine, replace sparkplugs and filters and do many more jobs that will save you money, give you personal satisfaction and help you avoid expensive problems.

A secondary purpose of this book is a reference for owners who want to understand their vehicle and/or their mechanics better. In this case, no tools at all are required. Knowing just what a particular repair job requires in parts and labor time will allow you to evaluate whether or not you're getting a fair price quote and help decipher itemized bills from a repair shop.

Before attempting any repairs or service on your vehicle, read through the entire procedure outlined in the appropriate Section. This will give you the overall view of what tools and supplies will be required. There is nothing more frustrating than having to walk to the bus stop on Monday morning because you were short one bolt on Sunday afternoon. So read ahead and plan ahead. Each operation should be approached logically and all procedures thoroughly understood before attempting any work. Some special tools that may be required can often be rented from local automotive jobbers or places specializing in renting tools and equipment. Check the yellow pages of your phone book.

All sections contain adjustments, maintenance, removal and installation procedures and overhaul procedures. When overhaul is not considered practical, we tell you how to remove the part and then how to install the new or rebuilt replacement. In this way, you at least save the labor costs. Backyard repair of such components (such as the alternator or water pump) is just not practical but the removal and installation procedure is often simple and well within the capabilities of the averge vehicle owner.

Two basic mechanic's rules should be mentioned: First, whenever the LEFT side of the vehicle or engine is referred to, it is meant to specify the DRIVER'S side of the vehicle. Conversely, the RIGHT side of the vehicle means the PASSENGER'S side. Second, all screws and bolts are removed by turning them counterclockwise and tightened by turning them clockwise.

Safety is always the most important rule. Constantly be aware of the dangers involved in working on a vehicle and take the proper precautions to avoid the risk of personal injury or damage to the vehicle. See the entry in this section, Servicing Your Vehicle Safely and the SAFETY NOTICE on the acknowledgment page before attempting any service procedures and pay attention to the instructions provided. There are 3 common mistakes in mechanical work:

1. Incorrect order of assembly, disassembly or adjustment. When taking something apart or putting it together, doing things in the wrong order usually costs extra time, however, it CAN break something. Read the entire procedure before beginning the disassembly. Do everything in the order in which the instructions say you should do it, even if you can't immediately see a reason for it. When you're taking something apart that is very intricate (for example, a carburetor), you might want to draw a picture of how it looks when assembled at one point, in order to make sure you get everything back in its proper position. We will supply exploded views whenever possible but sometimes the job requires more attention to detail than an illustration provides. When making adjustments, especially tune-up adjustments, do them in order. One adjustment often affects another and you cannot expect satisfactory results unless each adjustment is made only when it cannot be changed by any other.

2. Overtorquing (or undertorquing). While it is more common for overtorquing to cause damage, undertorquing can cause a fastener to vibrate loose causing serious damage, especially, when dealing with aluminum parts. Pay attention to torque specifications and utilize a torque wrench in assembly. If a torque figure is not available, remember that if you are using the right tool to do the job, you will probably not have to strain yourself to get a fastener tight enough. The pitch of most threads is so slight that the tension you put on the wrench will be multiplied many times in actual force on what you are tightening. A good example of how critical torque is can be seen in the case of spark plug installation, especially where you are putting the plug into an aluminum cylinder head. Too little torque can fail to crush the gasket, causing leakage of combustion gases and consequent overheating of the plug and engine parts. Too much torque can damage the threads or distort the plug, which changes the spark gap at the electrode. Since more and more manufacturers are using aluminum in their engine and chassis parts to save weight, a torque wrench should be in any serious do-it-yourselfer's tool box.

There are many commercial products available for ensuring that fasteners won't come loose, even if they are not torqued just right (a very common brand is Loctite®). If you're worried about getting something together tight enough to hold but loose enough to avoid mechanical damage during assembly, one of these products might offer substantial insurance. Read the label on the package and make sure the product is compatible with the materials, fluids and etc. involved before choosing one.

3. Crossthreading. This occurs when a part such as a bolt is screwed into a nut or casting at the wrong angle and forced, causing the threads to become damaged. Crossthreading is more likely to occur if access is difficult. It helps to clean and lubricate the fasteners, then start threading with the part to be installed going straight in, using your fingers. If you encounter resistance, unscrew the part and start over again at a different angle until it can be inserted and turned several turns without much effort. Keep in mind that many parts, especially spark plugs, use tapered threads, so gentle turning will automatically bring the part you're threading to the proper angle if you don't force it or resist a change in angle. Don't put a wrench on the part until it's been turned a couple of turns by hand. If you suddenly encounter resistance and the part has not seated fully, don't force it. Pull it back out and make sure it's clean and threading properly. Always take your time and be patient, once you have some experience working on your vehicle, it will become an enjoyable hobby.

TOOLS AND EQUIPMENT

Naturally, without the proper tools and equipment, it is impossible to properly service your vehicle. It would be impossible to catalog each tool that you would need to perform each or any operation in this book. It would also be unwise for the amateur to rush out and buy an expensive set of tools on the theory that he may need one or more of them at sometime.

The best approach is to proceed slowly, gathering a good quality set of tools that are used most frequently. Don't be misled by the low cost of bargain tools. It is far better to spend a little more for better quality. Forged wrenches, 6- or 12-point sockets and fine tooth ratchets are by far preferable to their less expensive counterparts. As any good mechanic can tell you, there are few worse experiences than trying to work on a vehicle with bad tools. Your monetary savings will be far outweighed by frustration and mangled knuckles.

Begin accumulating tools that are used most frequently; those associated with routine maintenance and tune-up.

In addition to the normal assortment of screwdrivers and pliers, you should have the following tools for routine maintenance jobs:

1. SAE (or Metric) or SAE/Metric wrenches—sockets and combination open end/box end wrenches in sizes from 1/8–3/4 in. (6–19mm) and a spark plug socket (13/16 in. or 5/8 in. depending on plug type).

NOTE: If possible, buy various length socket drive extensions. One break in this department is that the metric sockets available in the U.S. will all fit the ratchet handles and extensions you may already have (1/4 in., 3/8 in. and 1/2 in. drive).

2. Jackstands, for support
3. Oil filter wrench
4. Oil filler spout, for pouring oil
5. Grease gun, for chassis lubrication
6. Hydrometer, for checking the battery
7. A container for draining oil
8. Many rags for wiping up the inevitable mess.

In addition to the above items there are several others that are not absolutely necessary but handy to have around. These include absorbent gravel, a transmission funnel and an usual

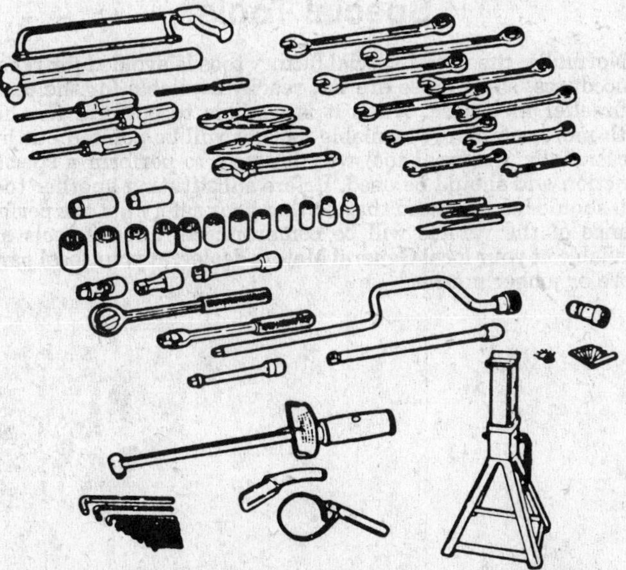

A basic collection of hand tools is necessary for automotive service

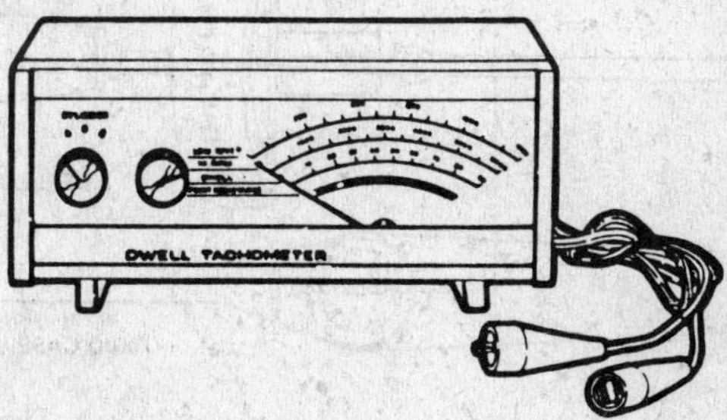

A dwell/tachometer is useful for tune-up work; the dwell function is not necessary if the vehicle has electronic ignition

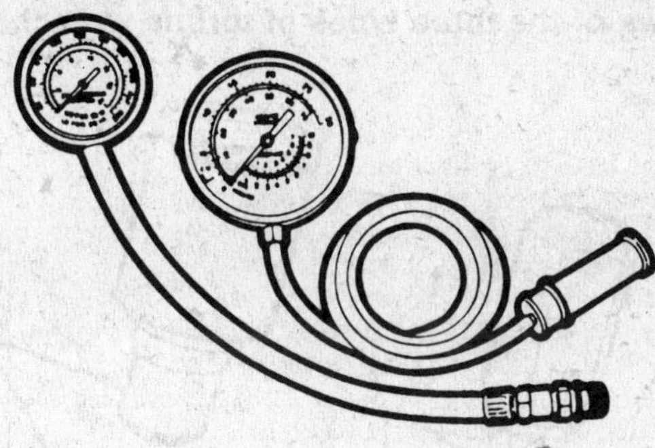

A compression gauge and a combination vacuum/fuel pressure gauge are handy for troubleshooting and tune-up work

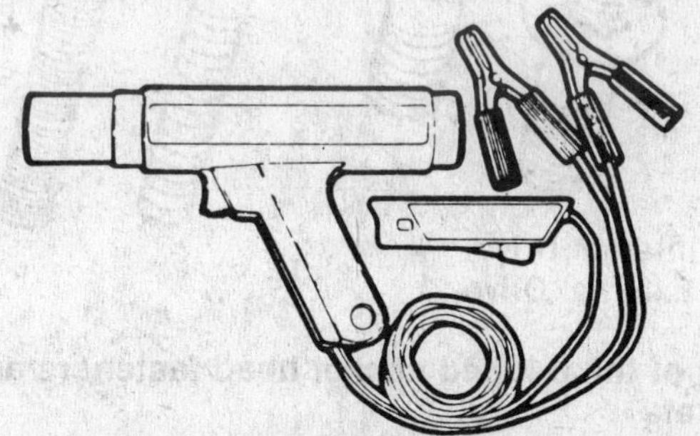

An inductive pickup simplifies timing light connections to the spark plug wire

supply of lubricants, antifreeze and fluids, although these can be purchased as needed. This is a basic list for routine maintenance but only your personal needs and desires can accurately determine your list of tools. If you are serious about maintaining your own vehicle, then a floor jack is as necessary as a spark plug socket. The greatly increased utility, strength and safety of a hydraulic floor jack makes it pay for itself many times over throughout the years.

The second list of tools is for tune-ups. While the tools involved here are slightly more sophisticated, they need not be outrageously expensive. There are several inexpensive tach/dwell meters on the market that are every bit as good for the average mechanic as an expensive professional model. Just be sure it goes to at least 1,200–1,500 rpm on the tach scale and that it works on 4- or 6-cylinder engines. A basic list of tune-up equipment could include:

1. Tach/dwell meter.

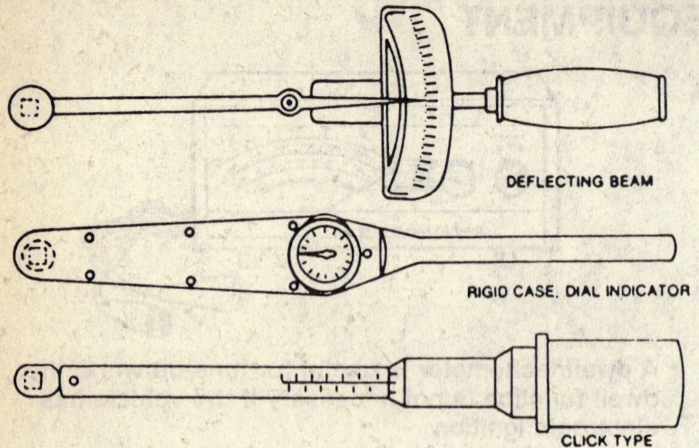

Views of the three types of torque wrenches

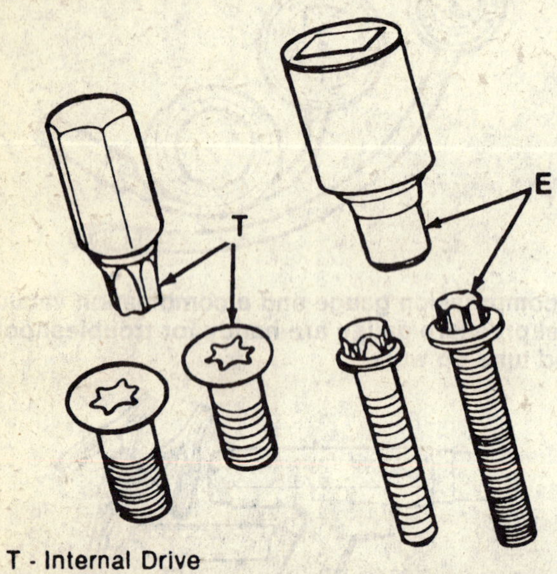

View of the 6 lobed socket head fasteners and sockets

2. Spark plug wrench.
3. Timing light (a DC light that works from the vehicle's battery is best, although an AC light that plugs into 110V house current will suffice at some sacrifice in brightness).
4. Wire spark plug gauge/adjusting tools.
5. Set of feeler blades.

In addition to these basic tools, there are several other tools and gauges you may find useful. These include:

1. A compression gauge. The screw-in type is slower to use but eliminates the possibility of a faulty reading due to escaping pressure.
2. A manifold vacuum gauge.
3. A test light, volt/ohmmeter.
4. An induction meter. This is used for determining whether or not there is current in a wire. These are handy for use if a wire is broken somewhere in a wiring harness.

As a final note, you will find a torque wrench necessary for all but the most basic work. There are 3 types of torque wrenches available; deflecting beam type, dial indicator and click type. The beam type models are perfectly adequate, although the click type models are more precise and allow the user to reach the required torque without having tto assume a sometimes awkward position in reading a scale. No matter what type of torque wrench you purchase, have it calibrated periodically to ensure accuracy.

NOTE: Special tools are occasionally necessary to perform a specific job or are recommended to make a job easier. Their use has been kept to a minimum. When a special tool is indicated, it will be referred to by manufacturer's part number, and, where possible, an illustration of the tool will be provided so an equivalent tool may be used. A list of tool manufacturers and their addresses follows:

In the United States, contact:

Service Tool Division
Kent-Moore Corporation
29784 Little Mack
Roseville, MI 48066-2298

In Canada, contact:

Kent-Moore of Canada, Ltd.
2395 Cawthra Mississauga
Ontario, Canada L5A 3P2.

Special Tools

Normally, the use of special factory toos is avoided for repair procedures, since these are not readily available for the do-it-yourselfer mechanic. When it is possible to perform the hob with more commonly available tools, it will be pointed out but occasionally, a special tool was desigend to perform a specific function and should be used. Before substituting another tool, you should be convinced that neither your safety not the performance of the vehicle will be compromised. Special tools are available at your local General Motors dealer, at your local parts store or jobber market.

SERVICING YOUR VEHICLE SAFELY

It is virtually impossible to anticipate all of the hazards involved with automotive maintenance and service but care and common sense will prevent most accidents.

The rules of safety for mechanics range from "don't smoke around gasoline," to "use the proper tool for the job." The trick to avoiding injuries is to develop safe work habits and take every possible precaution.

Do's

- Do keep a fire extinguisher and first aid kit within easy reach.
- Do wear safety glasses or goggles when cutting, drilling, grinding or prying. If you wear glasses for the sake of vision, then they should be made of hardened glass that can serve also as safety glasses or wear safety goggles over your regular glasses.
- Do shield your eyes whenever you work around the battery. Batteries contain sulphuric acid. In case of contact with the eyes or skin, flush the area with water or a mixture of water and baking soda, then get medical attention immediately.
- Do use safety stands for any under-vehicle service. Jacks are for raising the vehicle; safety stands are for making sure the vehicle stays raised until you want it to come down. Whenever the vehicle is raised, block the wheels remaining on the ground and set the parking brake.
- Do use adequate ventilation when working with any chemicals. Asbestos dust resulting from brake lining wear causes cancer.
- Do disconnect the negative battery cable when working on the electrical system.
- Do follow the manufacturer's directions whenever working with potentially hazardous materials. Both brake fluid and antifreeze are poisonous if taken internally.
- Do properly maintain your tools. Loose hammer heads, mushroomed punches and chisels, frayed or poorly grounded electrical cords, excessively worn screwdrivers, spread wrenches (open end), cracked sockets, slipping ratchets or faulty droplight sockets cause accidents.
- Do use the proper size and type of tool for the job being done.
- Do when possible, pull on a wrench handle rather than push on it and adjust your stance to prevent a fall.
- Do be sure adjustable wrenches are tightly adjusted on the nut or bolt and pulled so the face is on the side of the fixed jaw.
- Do select a wrench or socket that fits the nut or bolt. The wrench or socket should sit straight, not cocked.
- Do strike squarely with a hammer—avoid glancing blows.
- Do set the parking brake and block the drive wheels if the work requires that the engine be running.

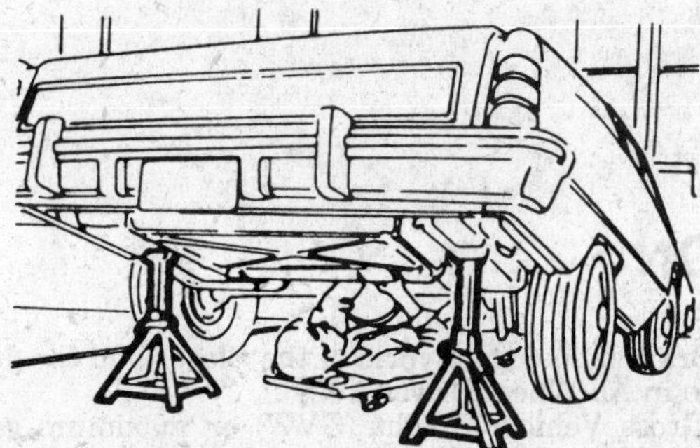

Always use jackstands when working under the vehicle

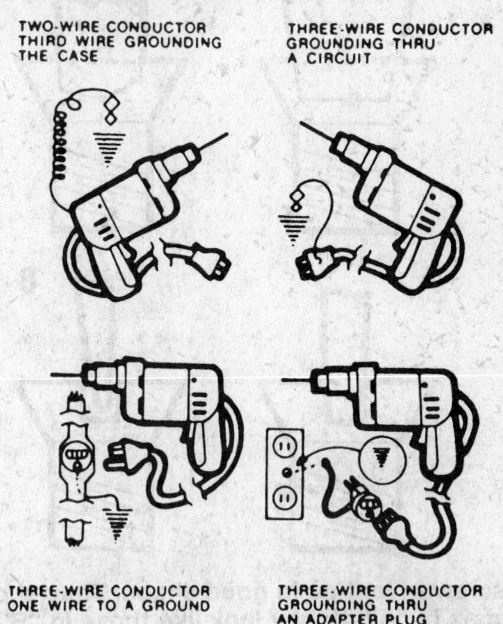

When using electrical tools, make sure they are properly grounded

When using an open end wrench, make sure it is the correct size

Dont's

- Don't run an engine in a garage or anywhere else without proper ventilation—EVER! Carbon monoxide is poisonous. It is absorbed by the body 400 times faster than oxygen. Carbon monoxide is odorless and colorless. Your senses cannot detect its presence. Early symptoms of monoxide poisoning include headache, irritability, improper vision (blurred or hard to focus) and/or drowsiness. When you notice any of these symptons in yourself or your helpers, stop working immediately and get to fresh, outside air. Ventilate the work area thoroughly before returning to the vehicle. It takes a long time to leave the body and can build up a deadly supply of it in your system by simply breathing in a little every day. You may not realize you are slowly poisoning yourself. Always use power vents, windows, fans or open the garage doors.
- Don't work around moving parts while wearing a necktie or other loose clothing. Short sleeves are much safer than long,

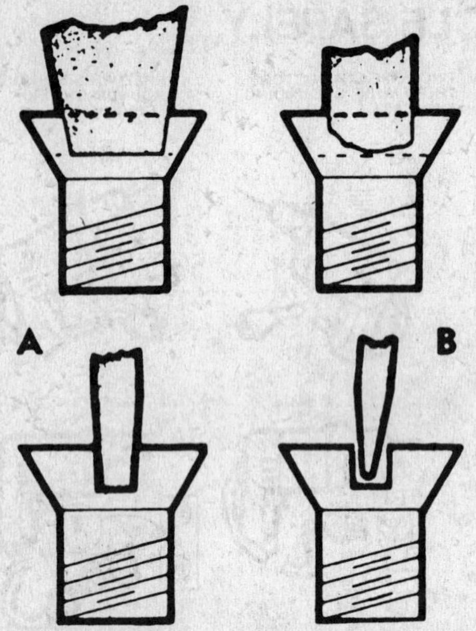

Keep screwdriver tips in good shape. They should fit the slot as in "A". If they look like those in "B", they need grinding or replacing

loose sleeves. Hard-toed shoes with neoprene soles protect your toes and give a better grip on slippery surfaces. Jewelry such as watches, fancy belt buckles, beads or body adornment or any kind is not safe working around a vehicle. Long hair should be hidden under a hat or cap.

- Don't use pockets for tool boxes. A fall or bump can drive a screwdriver deep into your body. Even a wiping cloth hanging from the back pocket can wrap around a spinning shaft, pulley or fan.

- Don't smoke when working around gasoline, cleaning solvent or other flammable material.

- Don't smoke when working around the battery. When the battery is being charged, it gives off explosive hydrogen gas.

- Don't use gasoline to wash your hands. There are excellent soaps available. Gasoline may contain lead, and lead can enter the body through a cut, accumulating in the body until you are very ill. Gasoline also removes all the natural oils from the skin so bone dry hands will suck up oil and grease.

- Don't service the air conditioning system unless you are equipped with the necessary tools and training. The refrigerant, R-12, is extremely cold and when exposed to the air, will instantly freeze any surface it comes in contact with, including your eyes. Although the refrigerant is normally non-toxic, R-12 becomes a deadly poisonous gas in the presence of an open flame. One good whiff of the vapors from burning refrigerant can be fatal.

HISTORY

In 1983, the S-10 Chevy Blazer and the S-15 GMC Jimmy were introduced into the S-10 Pick-Up line. During 1983–85, the S-15 GMC Jimmy, 2 Wheel Drive (2WD), was available with the 2.2L Diesel engine made by Isuzu.

In 1991, the Oldsmobile Bravada was introduced but only as an All Wheel Drive (AWD) vehicle.

IDENTIFICATION

Model

The S-10 Chevy Blazer and the S-15 GMC Jimmy models are available in 2-Wheel Drive (2WD) and 4-Wheel Drive (4WD). Any model with an "S" indication is known as a 2-wheel drive; any model with a "T" indication is known as a 4-wheel drive.

The Bravada, being a hybrid of the Blazer and the Jimmy, is available in All Wheel Drive (AWD).

The Gross Vehicle Weight (GVW) or maximum safe total weight of the vehicle, cargo, extra equipment and occupants. The GVW must not exceed the Gross Vehicle Weight Rating (GVWR) of your vehicle.

ENGINE IDENTIFICATION

Year	Model	Engine Displacement cu. in. (liter)	Engine Series Identification (VIN)	No. of Cylinders	Engine Type
1983	S10/15 Blazer/Jimmy 2WD	119 (1.9)	A	4	OHC
	S10/15 Blazer/Jimmy 2WD	121 (2.0)	Y	4	OHV
	S10/15 Blazer/Jimmy 2WD	173 (2.8)	B	6	OHV
	S10/15 Blazer/Jimmy 4WD	119 (1.9)	A	4	OHC
	S10/15 Blazer/Jimmy 4WD	121 (2.0)	Y	4	OHV
	S10/15 Blazer/Jimmy 4WD	173 (2.8)	B	6	OHV
	S/15 Jimmy 2WD	136 (2.2)	S	4	OHV
1984	S10/15 Blazer/Jimmy 2WD	119 (1.9)	A	4	OHC
	S10/15 Blazer/Jimmy 2WD	121 (2.0)	Y	4	OHV
	S10/15 Blazer/Jimmy 2WD	173 (2.8)	B	6	OHV
	S10/15 Blazer/Jimmy 4WD	119 (1.9)	A	4	OHC
	S10/15 Blazer/Jimmy 4WD	121 (2.0)	Y	4	OHV
	S10/15 Blazer/Jimmy 4WD	173 (2.8)	B	6	OHV
	S/15 Jimmy 2WD	136 (2.2)	S	4	OHV
1985	S10/15 Blazer/Jimmy 2WD	119 (1.9)	A	4	OHC
	S10/15 Blazer/Jimmy 2WD	151 (2.5)	E	4	OHV
	S10/15 Blazer/Jimmy 2WD	173 (2.8)	B	6	OHV
	S10/15 Blazer/Jimmy 4WD	119 (1.9)	A	4	OHC
	S10/15 Blazer/Jimmy 4WD	151 (2.5)	E	4	OHV
	S10/15 Blazer/Jimmy 4WD	173 (2.8)	B	6	OHV
	S/15 Jimmy 2WD	136 (2.2)	S	4	OHV
1986	S10/15 Blazer/Jimmy 2WD	151 (2.5)	E	4	OHV
	S10/15 Blazer/Jimmy 2WD	173 (2.8)	R	6	OHV
	S10/15 Blazer/Jimmy 4WD	151 (2.5)	E	4	OHV
	S10/15 Blazer/Jimmy 4WD	173 (2.8)	R	6	OHV
1987	S10/15 Blazer/Jimmy 2WD	151 (2.5)	E	4	OHV
	S10/15 Blazer/Jimmy 2WD	173 (2.8)	R	6	OHV
	S10/15 Blazer/Jimmy 4WD	151 (2.5)	E	4	OHV
	S10/15 Blazer/Jimmy 4WD	173 (2.8)	R	6	OHV
1988	S10/15 Blazer/Jimmy 2WD	151 (2.5)	E	4	OHV
	S10/15 Blazer/Jimmy 2WD	173 (2.8)	R	6	OHV
	S10/15 Blazer/Jimmy 4WD	173 (2.8)	R	6	OHV
	S10/15 Blazer/Jimmy 4WD	262 (4.3)	Z	6	OHV
1989	S10/15 Blazer/Jimmy 2WD	151 (2.5)	E	4	OHV
	S10/15 Blazer/Jimmy 2WD	173 (2.8)	R	6	OHV
	S10/15 Blazer/Jimmy 2WD	262 (4.3)	Z	6	OHV
	S10/15 Blazer/Jimmy 4WD	173 (2.8)	R	6	OHV
	S10/15 Blazer/Jimmy 4WD	262 (4.3)	Z	6	OHV
1990	S10/15 Blazer/Jimmy 2WD	262 (4.3)	Z	6	OHV
	S10/15 Blazer/Jimmy 4WD	262 (4.3)	Z	6	OHV
1991	S10/15 Blazer/Jimmy 2WD	262 (4.3)	Z	6	OHV
	S10/15 Blazer/Jimmy 4WD	262 (4.3)	Z	6	OHV
	Bravada	262 (4.3)	Z	6	OHV

OHV—Over Head Valves
OHC—Over Head Cam

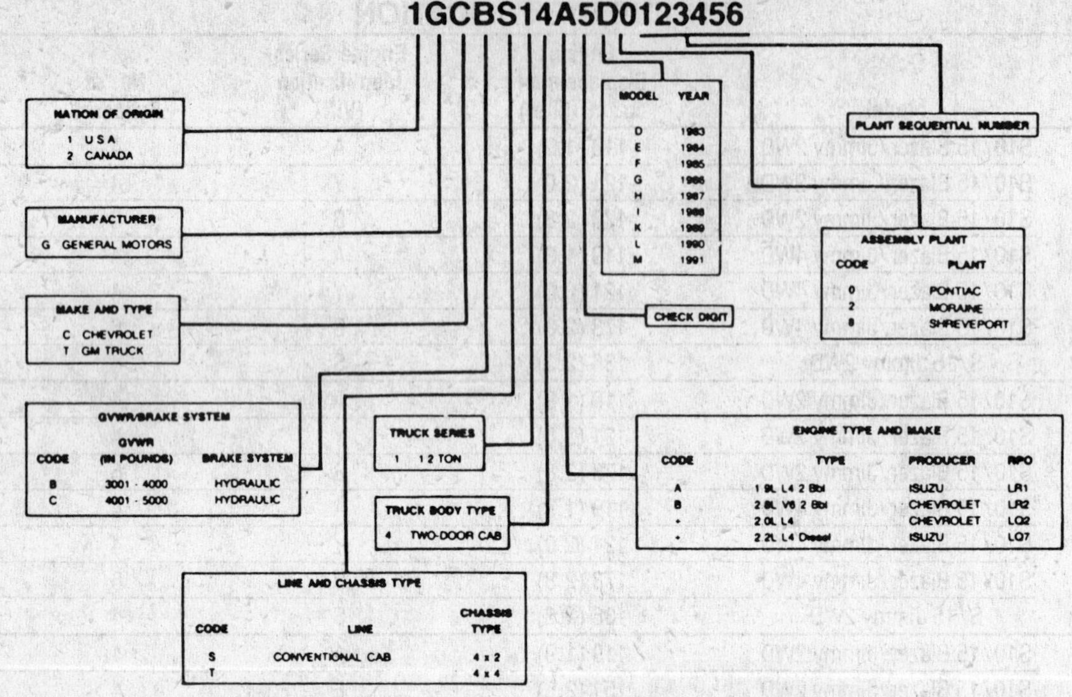

Explanation of the Vehicle Identification Number (VIN)

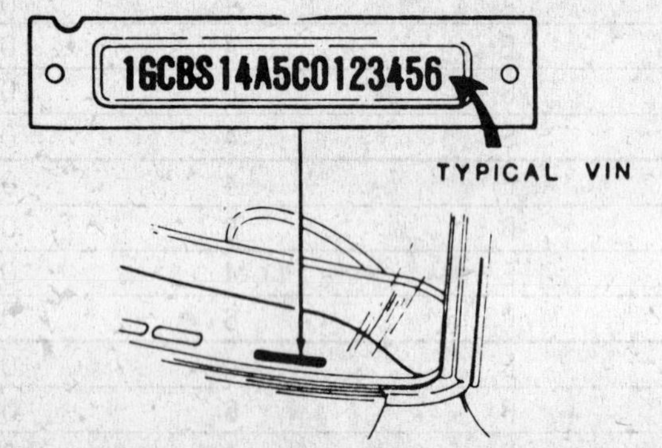

Location of the Vehicle Identification Number (VIN)

Vehicle

The Vehicle Identification Number (VIN) is on a plate attached to the left hand top of the instrument panel, visible through the windshield. The Gross Vehicle Weight (GVW) or maximum safe total weight of the vehicle, cargo and passengers, is also given on the plate.

Engine

1.9L Engine

The engine identification number is on a machined flat surface, on the lower left side of the block, near the flywheel.

2.0L Engine

The engine identification number is stamped on a flat, machined surface, facing forward, on the front of the engine block, just below the head.

2.2L Diesel Engine

The engine identification number is stamped on a flat, machined surface, facing forward, on the left-front of the engine block, just below the water pump.

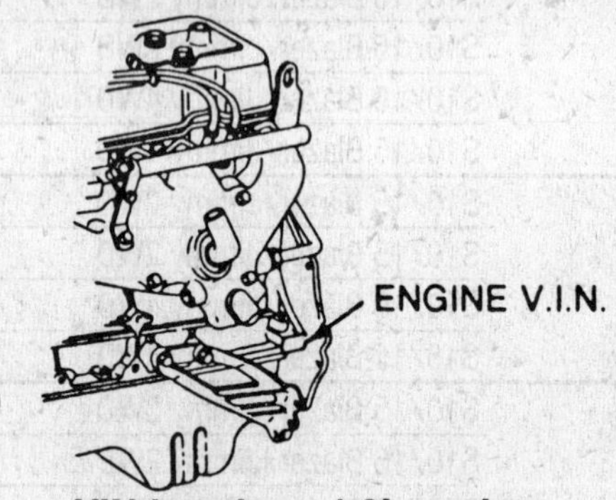

VIN location—1.9L engine

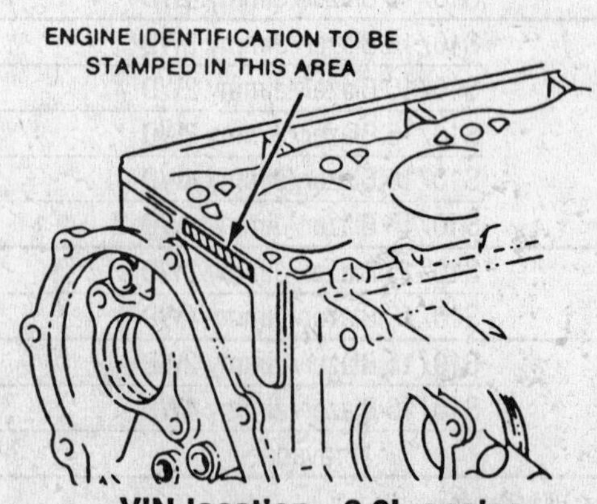

VIN location—2.0L engine

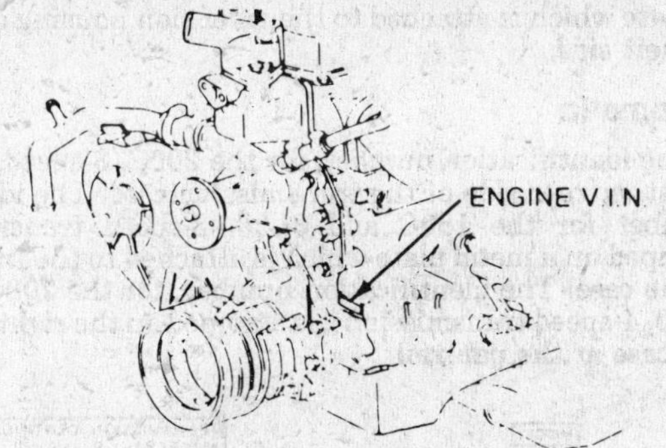

VIN location—2.2L diesel engine

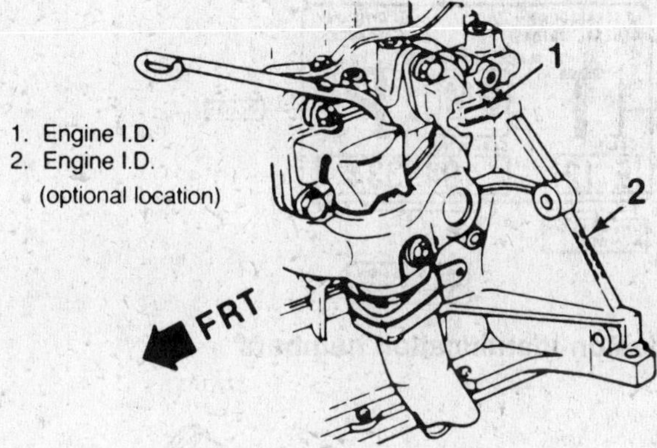

VIN location—2.5L engine

2.5L Engine

The engine identification number is stamped on a flat, machined surface, on the left rear side of the engine block, near the flywheel.

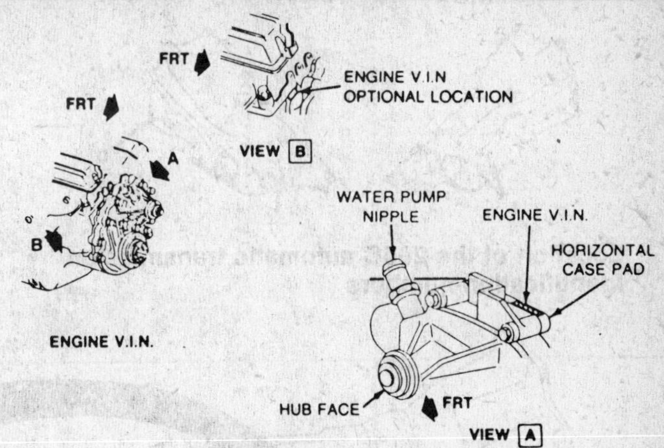

VIN location—2.8L engine

2.8L Engine

The engine identification code is stamped in 2 places. One on an upward facing, machined surface on the left front of the block, just below the head and above the water pump. The other on the right front of the engine, directly under the exhaust manifold.

4.3L Engine

The engine identification code is stamped in 2 places. One on an upward facing, machined surface on the right front of the block, just below the valve cover and above the water pump. The other, on the left rear of the engine, near the exhaust manifold.

Transmission

Manual

The transmission identification number is stamped on a met-

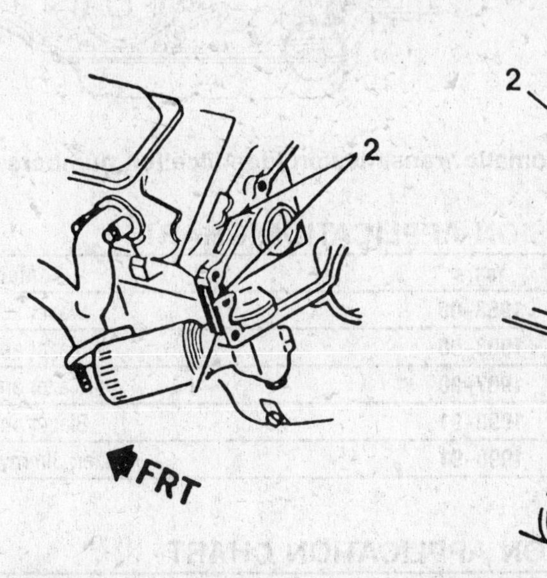

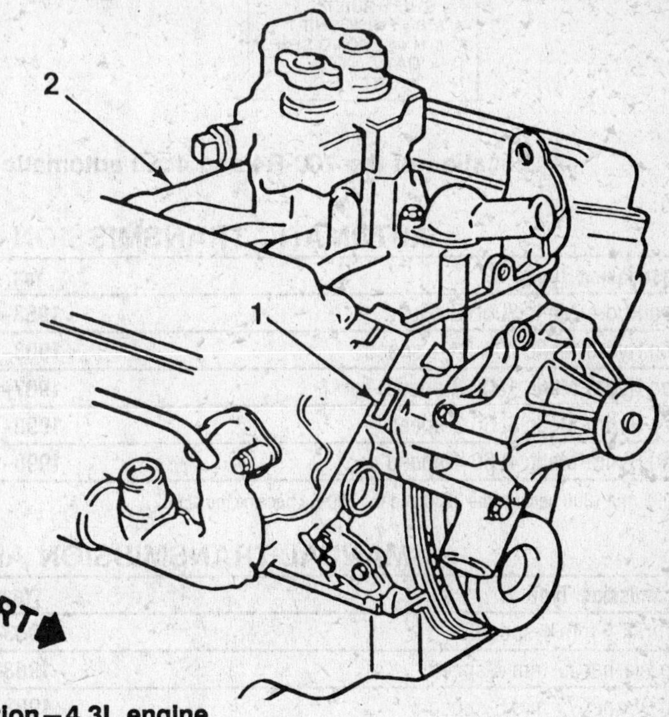

1. Engine I.D. Number Location
2. Optional Engine I.D. Location

VIN location—4.3L engine

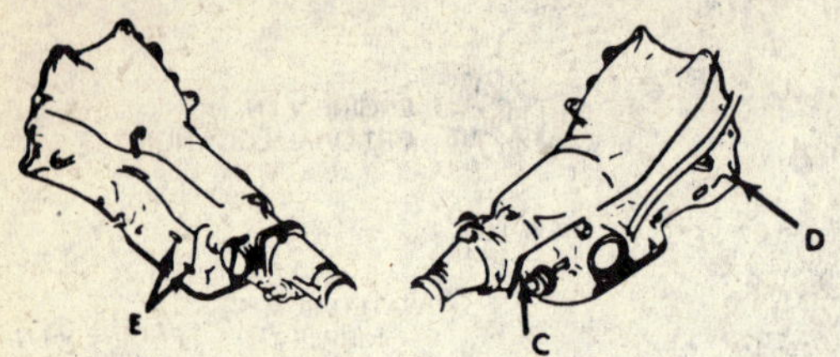

Location of the 200C automatic transmission identification numbers

al plate which is attached to the extension housing case bolt, on the left side.

Automatic

The identification number, for the 200C, 3-speed, is stamped on either rear side of the transmission case. The identification number for the 180C and 3L30, 3-speed transmissions, is stamped on a metal plate which is attached to the front left side of the case. The identification number, for the 700-R4 and the 4L60, 4-speed transmissions, is stamped on the right rear side of the case at the pan rail.

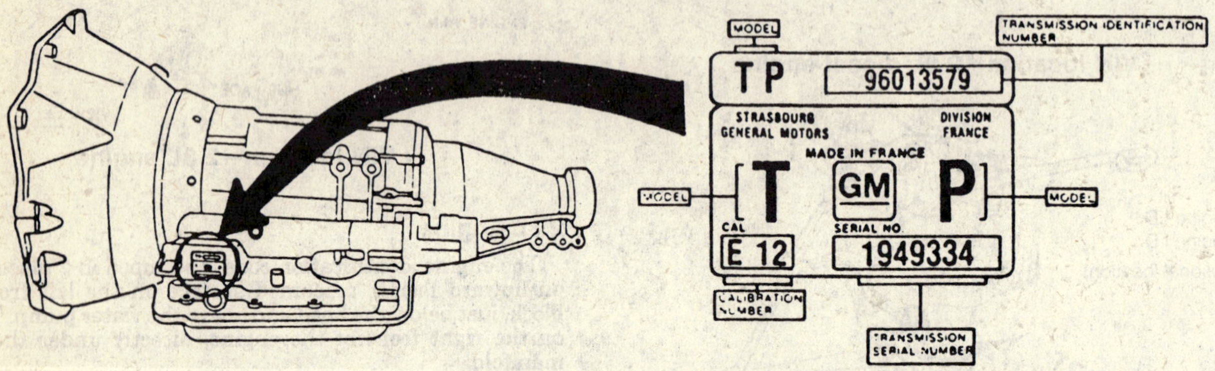

Location of the 180C and 3L30 automatic transmission identification numbers

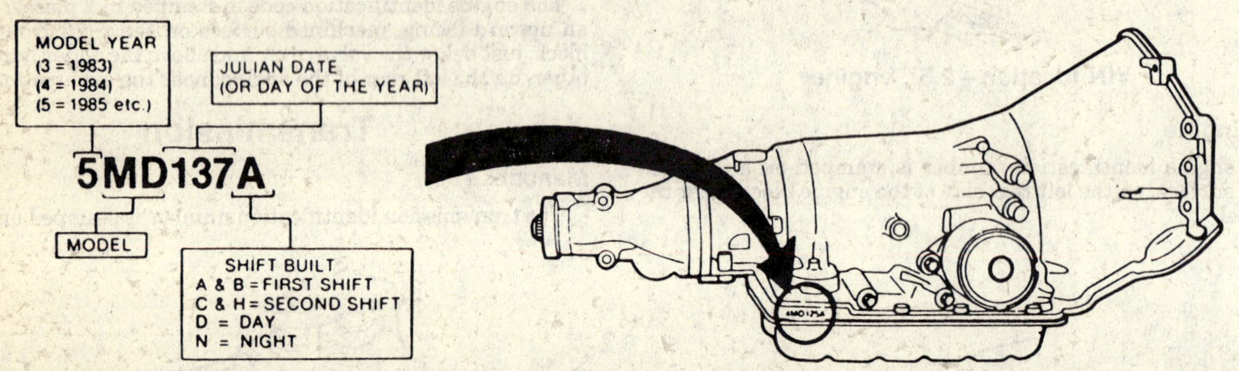

Location of the 700-R4 and 4L60 automatic transmission identification numbers

AUTOMATIC TRANSMISSION APPLICATION CHART

Transmission Type	Years	Models
Turbo Hydra-Matic 200C 3-speed	1983-85	Blazer and Jimmy
Turbo Hydra-Matic 700-R4 4-speed	1983-90	Blazer and Jimmy
Turbo Hydra-Matic 180C 3-speed	1987-90	Blazer and Jimmy
Turbo Hydra-Matic 3L30 3-speed	1990-91	Blazer and Jimmy
Turbo Hydra-Matic 4L60 4-speed	1990-91	Blazer, Jimmy and Bravada

In 1990, the 180C became the 3L30 and the 700-R4 became the 4L60

MANUAL TRANSMISSION APPLICATION CHART

Transmission Type	Years	Models
Isuzu 77.5 mm 4-speed	1983-87	Blazer and Jimmy
Borg Warner 77 mm 4-speed	1983-87	Blazer and Jimmy
Borg Warner 77 mm 5-speed	1983-91	Blazer and Jimmy

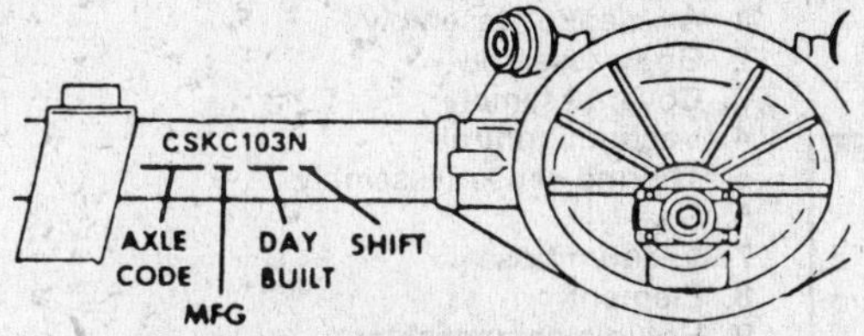

Location and explanation of the rear axle identification number

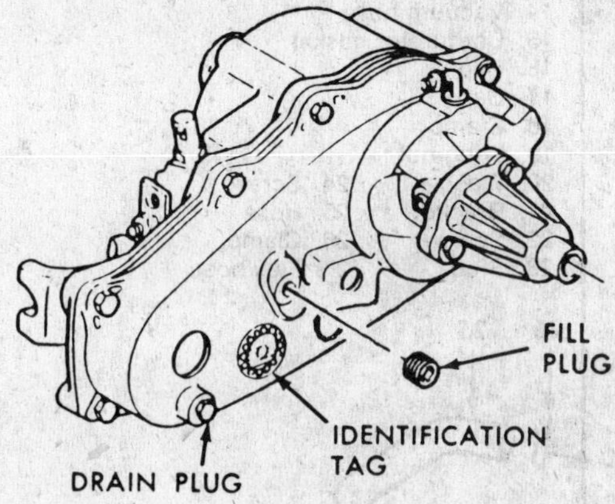

Location of the transfer case (Model 207) identification tag—Blazer and Jimmy

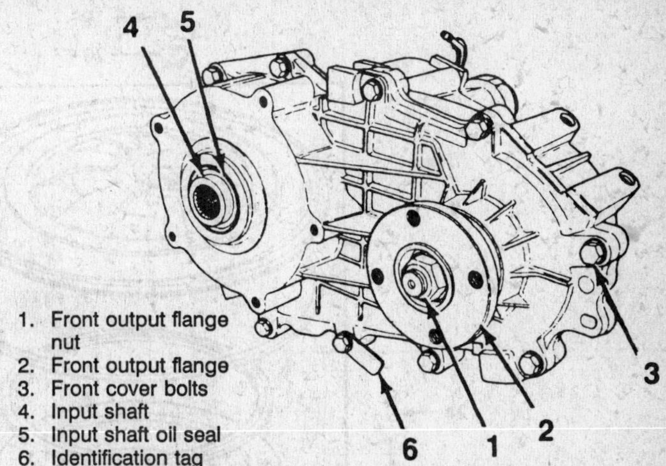

1. Front output flange nut
2. Front output flange
3. Front cover bolts
4. Input shaft
5. Input shaft oil seal
6. Identification tag

Location of the transfer case (Model 207) identification tag—Bravada

Drive Axle

On rear axles, the identification number is stamped on the front right side of the axle tube, next to the differential. On front axles, the ID number is tamped on a tag, under one of the differential cover bolts.

Transfer Case

Blazer and Jimmy

The model 207 and 231 transfer cases are equipped with a identification tag which is attached to the low rear half of the case; the tag gives the model number, the low range reduction ratio and the assembly number. If, for some reason it becomes dislodged or removed, reattach it with an adhesive sealant.

Bravada

The Borg Warner Model 4472 transfer case is equipped with an aluminum identification tag which is attached to 1 of the self tapping case bolts. The tag provides the Borg Warner part number, the General Motors part number, the serial number and the build date. If the tag becomes dislodged or removed, reattach it to the unit.

TRANSFER CASE APPLICATION CHART

Transmission Case Type	Years	Models
New Process 207	1983-88	Blazer and Jimmy
New Process 231	1989-91	Blazer and Jimmy
Borg Warner 4472	1991	Bravada

ROUTINE MAINTENANCE

Air Cleaner

The air cleaner element is a paper cartridge type, it should be replaced every year or 30,000 miles; if the vehicle is operated in heavy traffic or under dusty conditions, replace the element at more frequent intervals.

REMOVAL AND INSTALLATION

1. Remove the top of the air cleaner.
2. Remove and discard the paper element.
3. Using a new element, reverse the removal procedures.

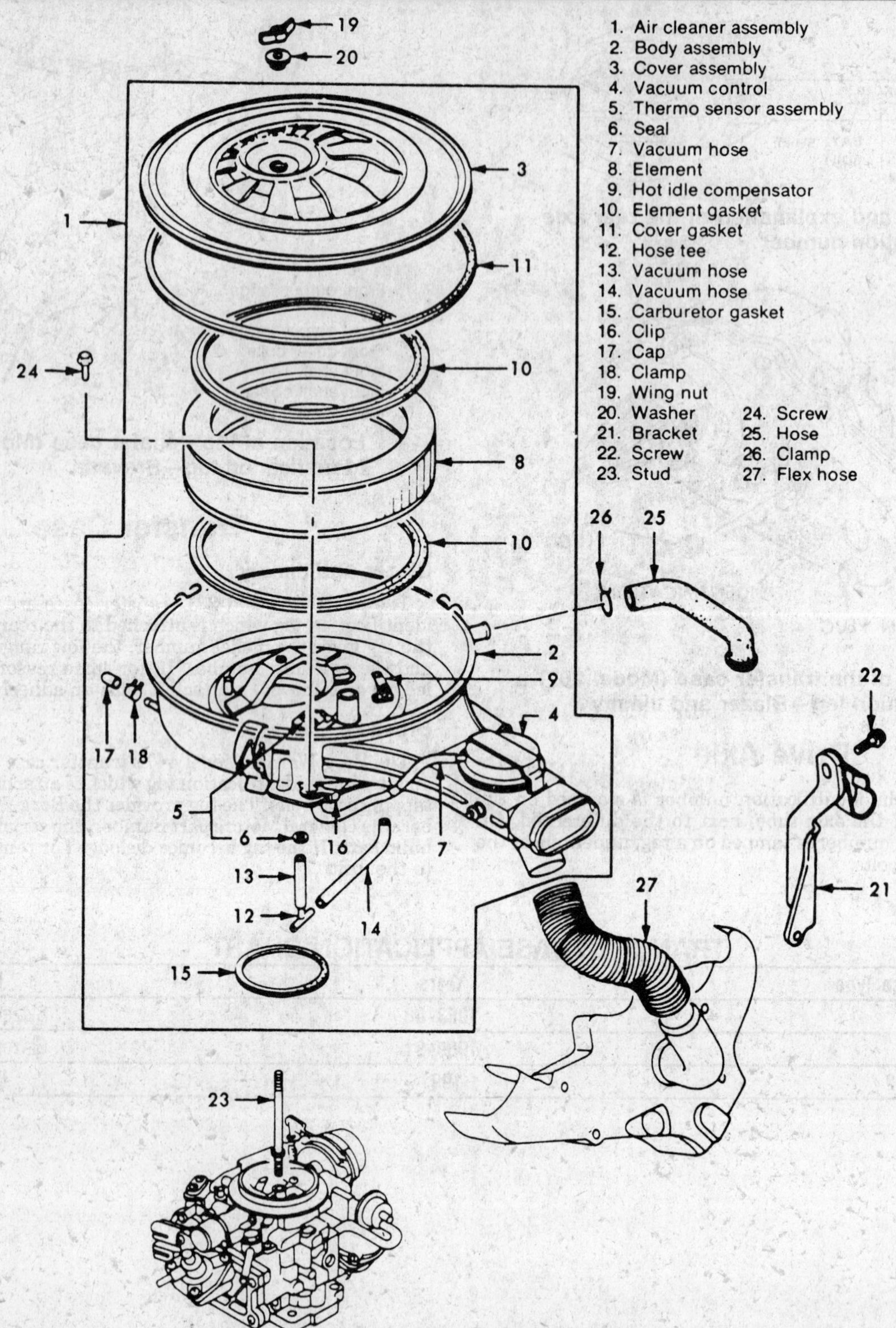

Exploded view of the air cleaner assembly

Gasoline Fuel Filter

The fuel filter should be serviced every 15,000 miles; if operated under severe conditions, change it more often. Three types of fuel filters are used, a pleated-paper element type (with a internal check valve), an inline type and an in-tank type.

NOTE: If an in-line fuel filter is used on an engine which has a filter installed in the carburetor body, be sure to change both at the same time.

CAUTION

Filter replacement should not be attempted when the engine is HOT. Additionally, it is a good idea to place some absorbent rags under the fuel fittings to catch the gasoline which will spill out when the lines are loosened.

REMOVAL AND INSTALLATION

There are three types of fuel filters: Internal (in the carburetor fitting), inline (in the fuel line) and in-tank (the sock on the fuel pickup tube).

Internal Filter

1. Disconnect the fuel line connection at the fuel inlet filter nut on the carburetor.
2. Remove the fuel inlet filter nut from the carburetor.
3. Remove the filter and the spring.

NOTE: If a check valve is not present with the filter, one must be installed when the filter is replaced.

4. Install the spring, filter and check valve (must face the fuel line), then reverse the removal procedures. Torque the filter nut-to-carburetor to 25 ft. lbs. and the fuel line-to-connector to 18 ft. lbs.; do not overtighten.
5. Start the engine and check for leaks.

Inline Filter

CAUTION

Before disconnecting any component of the fuel system, release the fuel pressure.

1. Remove the fuel filler cap to relieve the pressure in the fuel tank.
2. Disconnect the fuel lines from the filter.

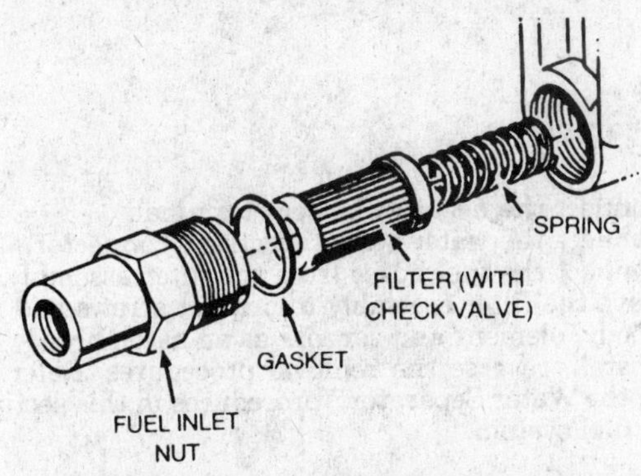

Exploded view of the carburetor internal fuel filter; check valve facing the fuel inlet nut

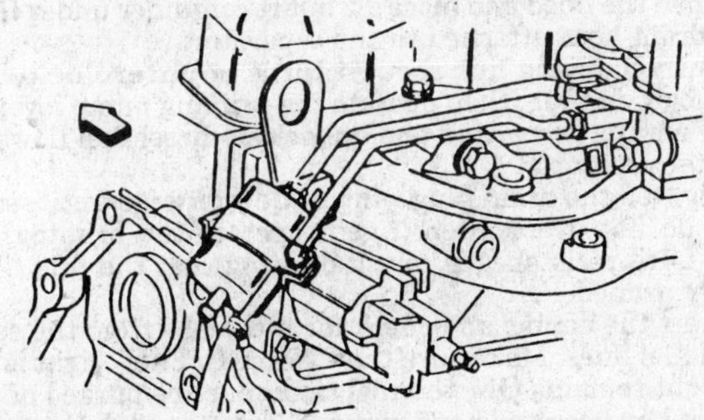

View of the in-line fuel filter—2.5L TBI engine

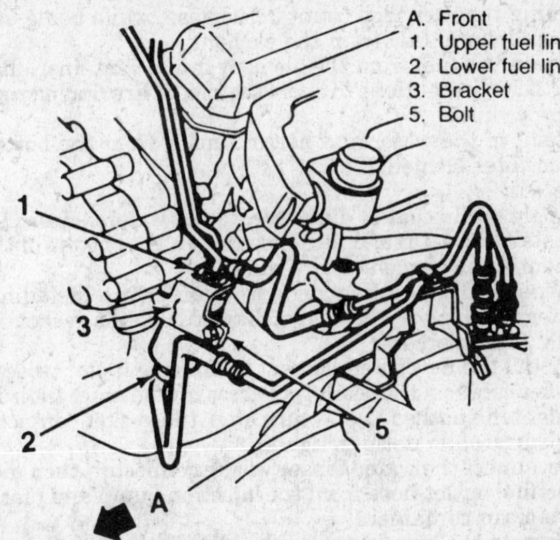

View of the in-line fuel filter—2.8L TBI engine

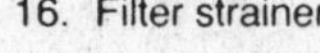

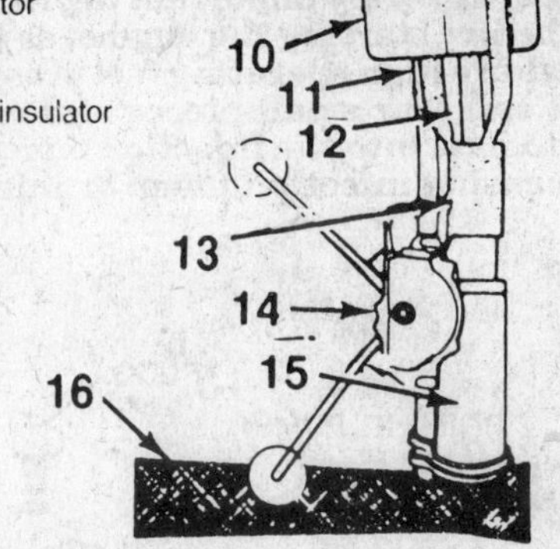

View of the in-tank filter—electric fuel pump ONLY

3. Remove the fuel filter from the retainer or mounting bolt.
4. To install, reverse the removal procedures. Start the engine and check for leaks.

NOTE: The filter has an arrow (fuel flow direction) on the side of the case, be sure to install it correctly in the system, with the arrow facing away from the fuel tank.

In-Tank Filter

To service the in-tank fuel filter, refer to the "Electric Fuel Pump Removal and Installation" procedures in Section 5.

Diesel Fuel Filter

REMOVAL AND INSTALLATION

Filter Element

1. Disconnect the negative battery terminal.
2. Disconnect the water sensor wire connector from the filter assembly.
3. Disconnect the water sensor-to-main body hose.
4. Using a filter band wrench, remove the fuel filter element

by turning the cartridge counterclockwise, while being careful not to spill diesel fuel from the element.

5. Drain the fuel from the element into a container and discard it. Take precautions to avoid the risk of fire during replacement procedures.

6. Remove the water and heater sensor from the bottom of the used filter element.

To install:

7. Apply a thin coat of diesel fuel to the water sensor O-ring, then install the water and heater sensor on the bottom of the replacement filter element and tighten.

8. Wipe all filter sealing surfaces clean before installing the new filter and apply a thin coat of diesel fuel to the gasket on the new fuel filter element.

9. Install the new filter element by turning it clockwise until the gasket contacts the sealing surfaces on the main filter body. Hand tighten another ⅔ of a turn after the gasket contacts the sealing surface; do not overtighten.

10. Reconnect the water sensor wiring connector, then disconnect the fuel outlet hose from the injection pump and place the end in a clean container.

11. Operate the priming pump handle on the injection pump several times to fill the new filter with fuel, until fuel flows from the outlet hose. Reconnect the outlet hose to the injection pump when priming is complete.

12. Start the engine and check for leaks.

NOTE: It is very important to prime the new filter element before starting the engine, as the shock of the diesel engine's high operating fuel pressure hitting a dry element can tear small pieces of debris away and allow them to pass into the injection pump and injectors, possibly causing injection pump or injector damage.

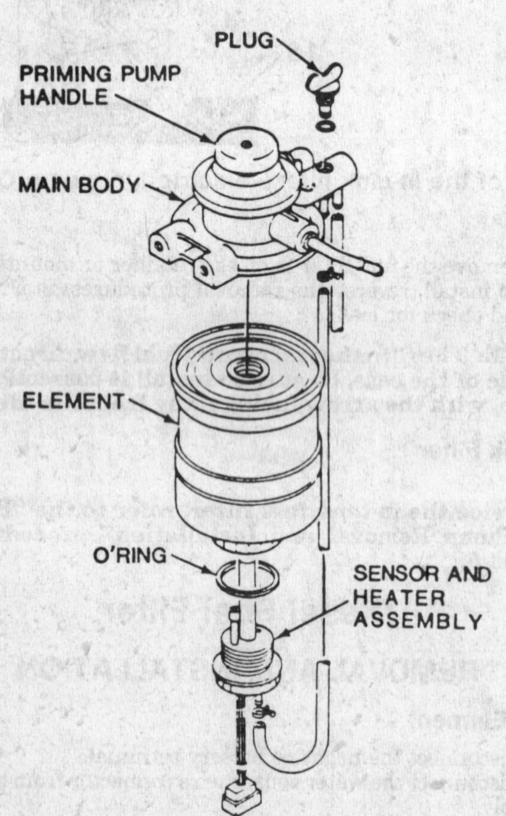

Exploded view of the diesel fuel filter assembly

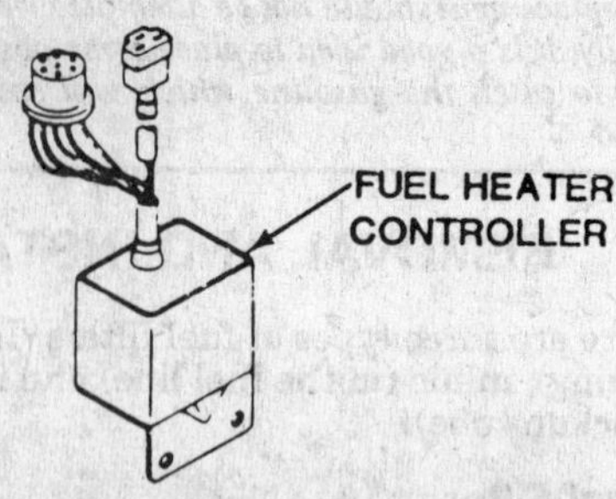

View of the diesel fuel heater controller

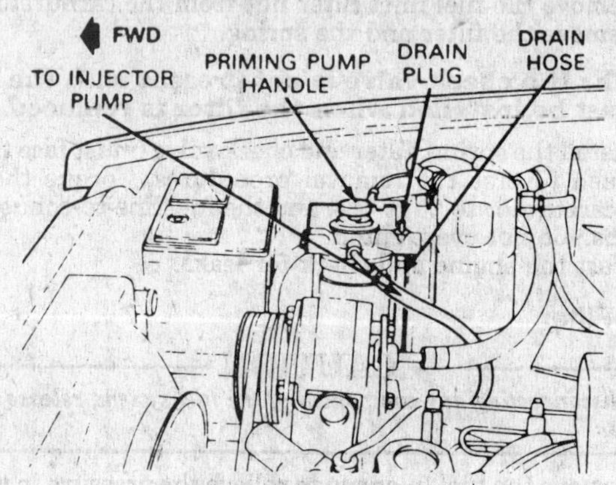

Assembled view of the diesel fuel filter assembly

Filter Assembly

1. Disconnect the negative battery terminal.
2. Disconnect the water sensor electrical connector.
3. Disconnect the fuel hoses from the filter assembly.
4. Remove the filter assembly-to-bracket screws and the filter main body, element and sensors as an assembly.
5. To install, reverse the removal procedures. Refer to the "Draining the Water Separator" procedures in this section and prime the fuel system.

Draining the Water Separator

1. Turn the engine **OFF** and allow it to cool.
2. Open the hood and place a 2 quart container under the end of the drain hose attached to the separator.
3. Turn the wing nut about 4 turns **counterclockwise** to open the drain plug, then operate the priming pump lever until all of the water is drained and only clean diesel fuel flows from the water separator.
4. Tighten the drain plug wing nut **clockwise** until securely closed; do not overtighten. Again operate the priming pump handle until resistance is felt, indicating that the fuel filter is properly primed.
5. Start the engine and check for fuel leaks from the separator and fuel lines. Make sure the "Water In Fuel" light is OFF; if the light remains ON, the fuel tank must be purged of water with a siphon hose and hand pump fed into the tank through the fuel filter.

CAUTION

Do not attempt to siphon any fuel tank contents by using mouth suction to start the siphon effect. Diesel fuel is poisonous and is by far the worst tasting stuff you can imagine. Use a hand siphon pump or power drill attachment to pull the water from the fuel tank.

Positive Crankcase Ventilation (PCV)

The PCV valve is attached to the valve cover by a rubber grommet and connected to the intake manifold through a ventilation hose. Replace the PCV valve and the PCV filter (located in the air cleaner) every 30,000 miles under severe usage or 60,000 miles under light usage.

REMOVAL AND INSTALLATION

1. Pull the PCV from the valve cover grommet and disconnect it from the ventilation hose(s).
2. Inspect the valve for operation: (1) Shake it to see if the valve is free; (2) Blow through it (air should pass in one direction only).

NOTE: When replacing the PCV valve, it is recommended to use a new one.

3. To install, reverse the removal procedures.

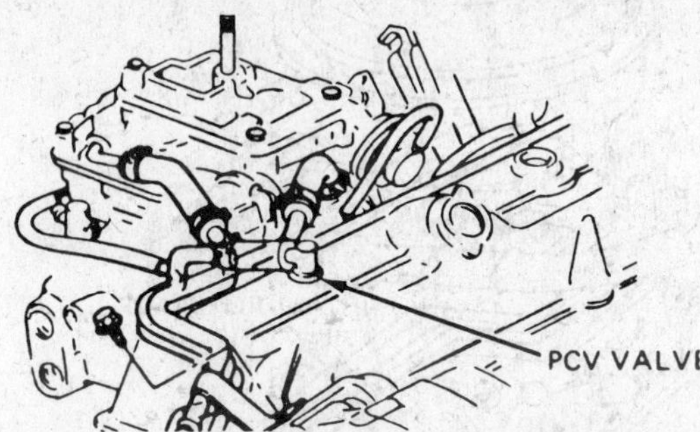

View of a typical PCV valve location

Evaporative Canister

To limit gasoline vapor discharge into the air, this system is designed to trap fuel vapors, which normally escape from the fuel tank and the intake manifold. Vapor arrest is accomplished through the use of the charcoal canister. This canister absorbs fuel vapors and stores them until they can be removed to be burned in the engine. Removal of the vapors from the canister to the engine is accomplished by a canister mounted purge valve, the throttle valve position, a Thermostatic Vacuum Switch (TVS) or a computer controlled canister purge solenoid.

In addition to the modifications and the canister, the fuel tank requires a non-vented gas cap. The domed fuel tank positions a vent high enough above the fuel to keep the vent pipe in the vapor at all times. The single vent pipe is routed directly to the canister. From the canister, the vapors are routed to the intake system, where they will be burned during normal combustion.

SERVICING

Every 30,000 miles or 24 months, check all fuel, vapor lines and hoses for proper hookup, routing and condition. If equipped, check that the bowl vent and purge valves work properly. Remove the canister and check for cracks or damage, then replace, if necessary.

REMOVAL AND INSTALLATION

1. Disconnect and mark the charcoal canister vent hoses.
2. Remove the canister-to-bracket bolt.
3. Lift the canister from the bracket.
4. To install, reverse the removal procedures.

CHARCOAL CANISTER SOLENOID REPLACEMENT

1. Disconnect the negative battery cable.
2. Remove the solenoid retaining bolt, the cover and the solenoid.

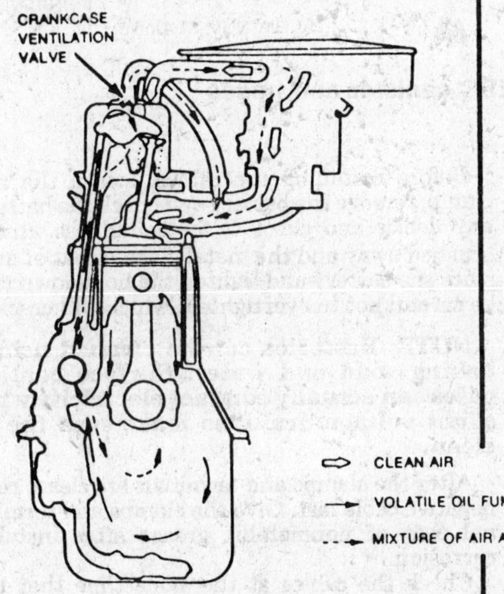

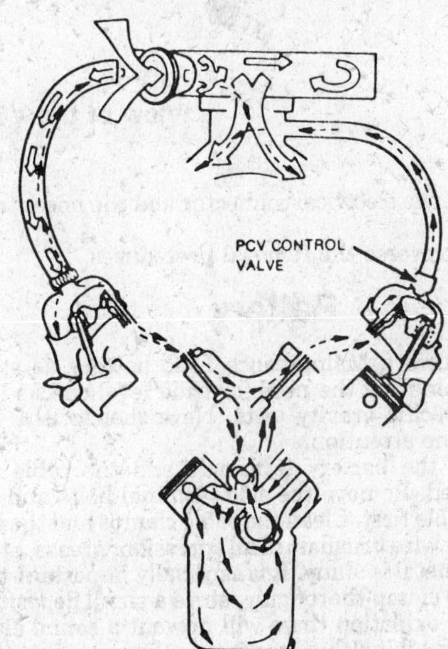

View of the typical gas flow in a PCV system

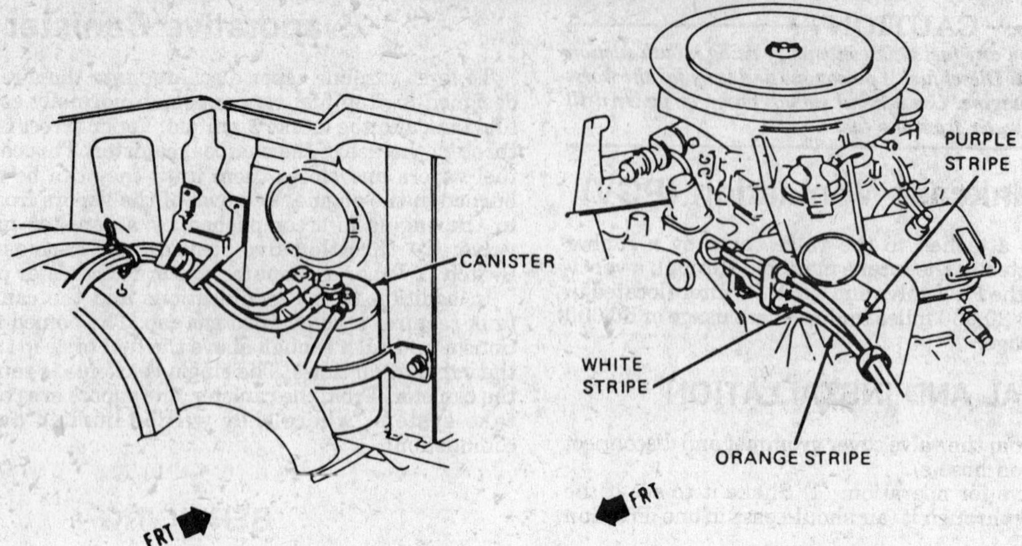

View of the 4 cylinder engine ESC canister and hoses

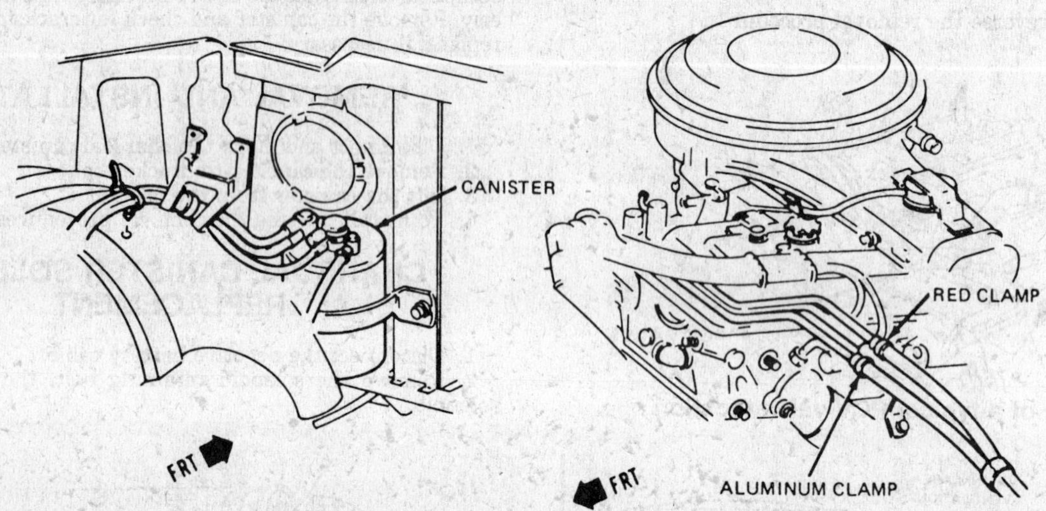

View of the V6 engine ESC canister and hoses

3. Disconnect the electrical connector and the hoses from the solenoid.
4. To install, reverse the removal procedures.

Battery

All vehicles have a Maintenance Free battery as standard equipment, eliminating the need for fluid level checks and the possibility of specific gravity tests. Nevertheless, the battery does require some attention.

Once a year, the battery terminals and the cable clamps should be cleaned. Remove the side terminal bolts and the cables, negative cable first. Clean the cable clamps and the battery terminals with a wire brush until all corrosion, grease, etc. is removed and the metal is shiny. It is especially important to clean the inside of the clamp thoroughly, since a small deposit of foreign material or oxidation there will prevent a sound electrical connection and inhibit either starting or charging. Special tools are available for cleaning the side terminal clamps and terminals.

Before installing the cables, loosen the battery hold-down clamp, remove the battery and check the battery tray. Clear it of any debris and check it for soundness. Rust should be wire brushed away and the metal given a coat of anti-rust paint. Replace the battery and tighten the hold-down clamp securely but be careful not to overtighten, which will crack the battery case.

NOTE: Batteries can be cleaned using a solution of baking soda and water. Surface coatings on battery cases can actually conduct electricity which will cause a slight voltage drain, so make sure the battery case is clean.

After the clamps and terminals are clean, reinstall the cables, negative cable last. Give the clamps and terminals a thin external coat of nonmetallic grease after installation, to retard corrosion.

Check the cables at the same time that the terminals are cleaned. If the cable insulation is cracked, broken or the ends are frayed, the cable should be replaced with a new one of the same length and gauge.

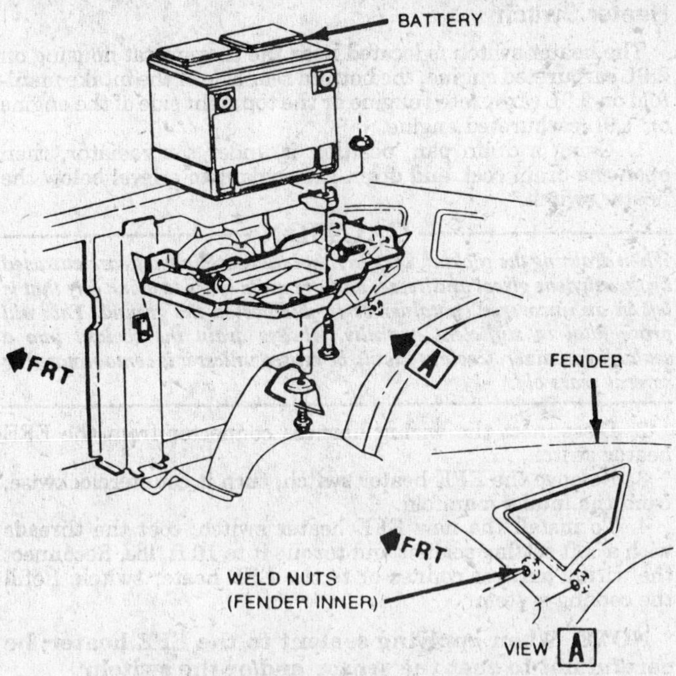

View of a typical battery installation

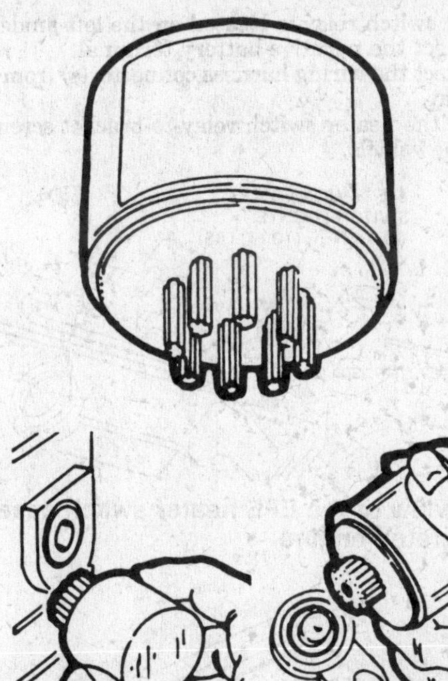

Special tools are also available for cleaning the posts and clamps on side terminal batteries

CAUTION

Keep flames or sparks away from the battery. It gives off explosive hydrogen gas. The battery electrolyte contains sulphuric acid. If you should get any on your skin or in your eyes, flush the affected areas with plenty of clear water. If it lands in your eyes, seek medical help immediately.

Testing the Maintenance Free Battery

Maintenance free batteries, do not require normal attention as far as fluid level checks are concerned. However, the terminals require periodic cleaning, which should be performed at least once a year.

The sealed top battery cannot be checked for charge in the normal manner, since there is no provision for access to the electrolyte. To check the condition of the battery:

1. If the indicator eye on top of the battery is dark, the battery has enough fluid. If the eye is lit, the electrolyte fluid is too low and the battery must be replaced.
2. If a green dot appears in the middle of the eye, the battery is sufficiently charged. Proceed to Step 4. If no green dot is visible, charge the battery as in Step 3.
3. Charge the battery at this rate:

NOTE: Do not charge the battery for more than 50 amp-hours. If the green dot appears or if the electrolyte squirts out of the vent hole, stop the charge and proceed to Step 4.

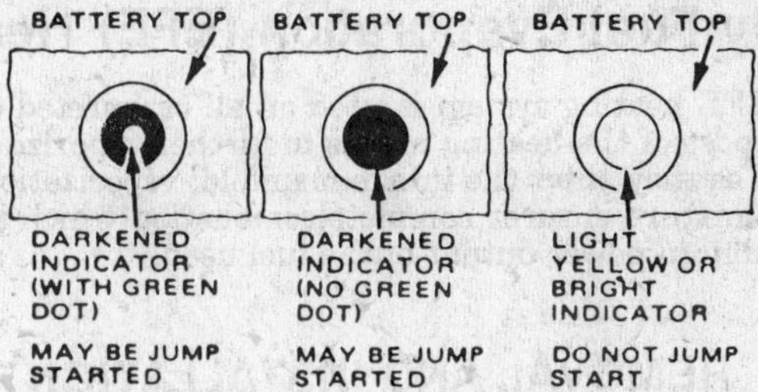

Some maintenance free batteries contain their own built in hydrometer

Charging Rate Amps	Time
75	40 min
50	1 hr
25	2 hr
10	5 hr

Battery	Test Load (Amps)
83–50	150
83-60	180
85A-60	170
87A-60	230
89A-60	270
1981103	200
1981104	250
1981105	270
1981577	260

Temperature (°F)	Minimum Voltage
70 or above	9.6
60	9.5
50	9.4
40	9.3
30	9.1
20	8.9
10	8.7
0	8.5

It may be necessary to tip the battery from side-to-side to get the green dot to appear after charging.

CAUTION

When charging the battery, the electrical system and control unit can be quickly damaged by improper connections, high output battery chargers or incorrect service procedures.

4. Connect a battery load tester and a voltmeter across the battery terminals (the battery cables should be disconnected from the battery). Apply a 300 amp load to the battery for 15 seconds to remove the surface charge. Remove the load.
5. Wait 15 seconds to allow the battery to recover. Apply the appropriate test load, as specified in the following chart:
Apply the load for 15 seconds while reading the voltage. Disconnect the load.
6. Check the results against the following chart. If the battery voltage is at or above the specified voltage for the temperature listed, the battery is good. It the voltage falls below what's listed, the battery should be replaced.

Early Fuel Evaporation (EFE) Heater

The EFE heating system is used on all carbureted engines. The purpose of the heating unit is to further vaporize the fuel droplets as they enter the intake manifold; vaporization of the air/fuel mixture ensures complete combustion which provides the maximum power output of the fuel used.

REMOVAL AND INSTALLATION

Heater Unit

The EFE heater unit is located directly under the carburetor and is electrically operated.

1. Disconnect the negative battery terminal. Remove the air cleaner.
2. From the carburetor, disconnect the vacuum hoses, electrical connectors and fuel hoses. Disconnect the EFE Heater electrical connector from the wiring harness.
3. Remove the carburetor-to-intake manifold nuts and the carburetor from the manifold. Lift the EFE Heater from the intake manifold.
4. Using a putty knife, clean the gasket mounting surfaces.
5. To install, use new gaskets and reverse the removal procedures. Torque the carburetor-to-intake manifold nuts to 13 ft. lbs.

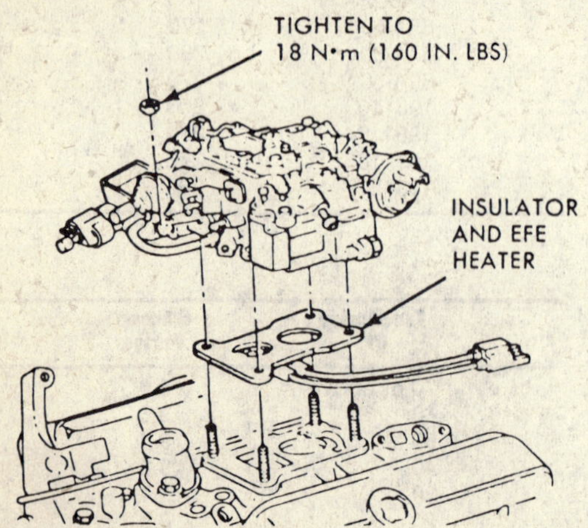

Exploded view of the EFE heater assembly—2.8L carbureted engine

Heater Switch

The heater switch is located near the thermostat housing on 2.8L carbureted engine, the bottom rear side of the intake manifold on 2.0L carbureted engine or the top right side of the engine on 1.9L carbureted engine.

1. Using a drain pan, position it under the radiator, then open the drain cock and drain the coolant to a level below the heater switch.

CAUTION

When draining the coolant, keep in mind that cats and dogs are attracted by the ethylene glycol antifreeze, and are quite likely to drink any that is left in an uncovered container or in puddles on the ground. This will prove fatal in sufficient quantity. Always drain the coolant into a sealable container. Coolant should be reused unless it is contaminated or several years old.

2. Disconnect the wiring harness connector from the EFE heater switch.
3. Remove the EFE heater switch, turn it counterclockwise, from the intake manifold.
4. To install the new EFE heater switch, coat the threads with a soft setting sealant and torque it to 10 ft. lbs. Reconnect the wiring harness connector to the EFE heater switch. Refill the cooling system.

NOTE: When applying sealant to the EFE heater, be careful not to coat the sensor and/or the switch.

Heater Switch Relay

The heater switch relay is located on the left-fender.

1. Disconnect the negative battery terminal.
2. Disconnect the wiring harness connector(s) from the heater switch relay.
3. Remove the heater switch relay-to-bracket screw and the relay from the vehicle.

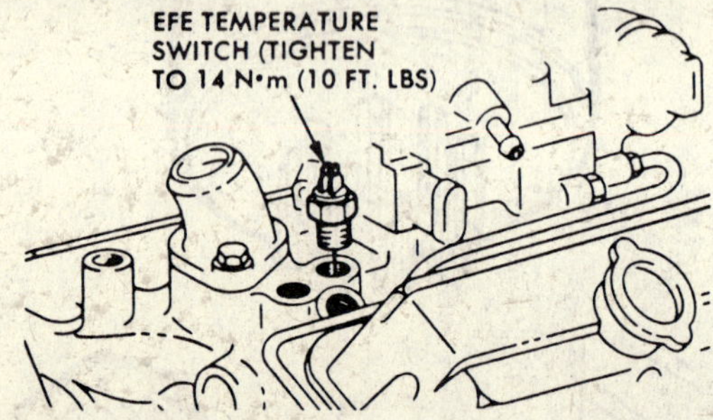

Exploded view of the EFE heater switch assembly—2.8L carbureted engine

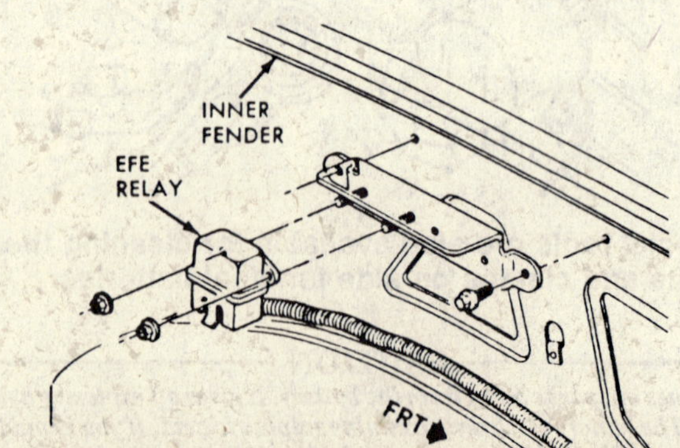

Exploded view of the EFE heater switch relay—1982-83, others similar

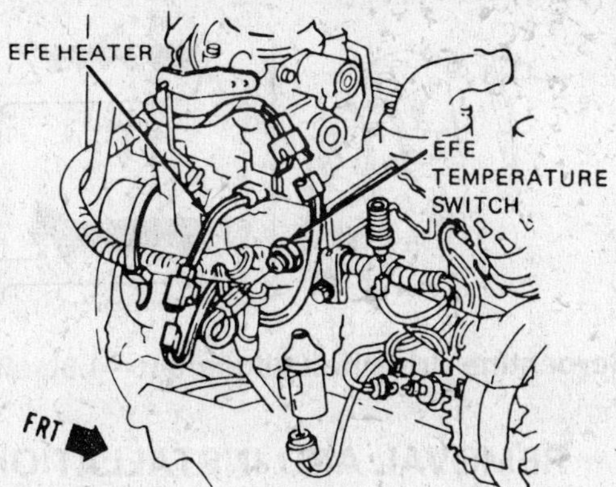

View of the EFE heater and heater switch assembly—1.9L engine

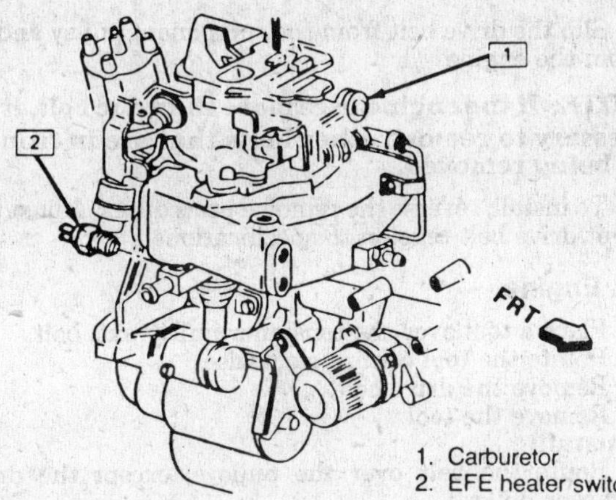

Exploded view of the EFE heater switch—2.0L engine

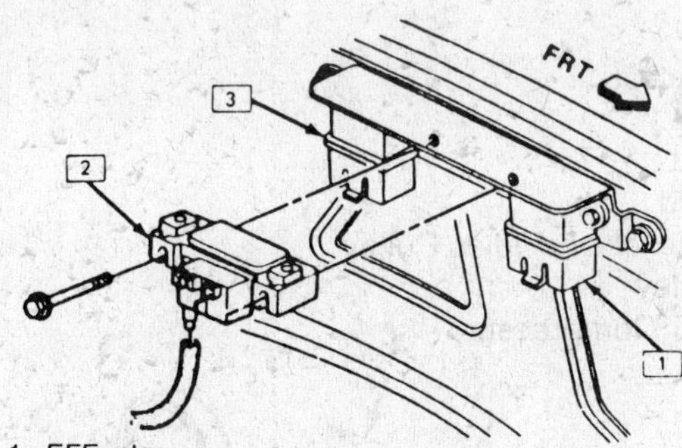

Exploded view of the EFE heater switch relay—1984–85, others similar

4. To install, use a new relay and reverse the removal procedures.

TESTING

1. Disconnect the wiring harness connector from the EFE heater switch, located near the thermostat housing on 2.8L carbureted engine, on the bottom rear side of the intake manifold on 2.0L carbureted engine or on the top right side of the engine on 1.9L carbureted engine.

NOTE: To perform the following inspection, the engine temperature must be below 140°F (60°C).

2. Using a 12 volt test lamp, connect it across the EFE wiring harness connector terminals. Turn the ignition switch **ON** with the engine is OFF, the lamp should glow; if the lamp glows, the EFE heater is good.
3. If the lamp does not glow, reconnect the wiring harness connector to the EFE heater switch.
4. Using a DC voltmeter, place it on the 0–15 volt scale, insert the test probes into the rear of the wiring harness connector body (the black wire is to be grounded) and measure the voltage; it should read 11–13 volts.
5. If the voltage is not 11–13 volts, insure that the black wire is grounded; if the voltage is not 0 volt, the black (grounded) wire is an open circuit, repair it.
6. If the voltage is 0 volts, check for voltage-to-ground at each heater switch terminal—the voltage at each switch terminal should be 11–13 volts.
7. If 1 terminal measures 11–13 volts and the other is low or 0 volts, check the connector for deformed terminals and repair, as necessary.
8. If the electrical connector is making proper contact, replace the EFE heater switch.
9. If the voltage is not 11–13 volts at each switch terminal, check the wiring harness circuit between the heater switch and the ignition switch, then repair, as necessary.
10. Start the engine, allow it to warm to 170°F (76.7°C), then check the voltage across the EFE heater terminals; it should be 0 volts. If the voltage is not 0 volts, replace the EFE heater switch.

Drive Belts

INSPECTION

On 1983–86 vehicles, check the drive belt(s) every 15,000 miles/12 months (heavy usage) or 30,000 miles/24 months (light usage) for evidence of wear such as cracking, fraying and incorrect tension. On 1987–91 vehicles, check the drive belts every 12,000 miles (heavy usage) or 60,000 miles (light usage).

On the 1983–86 vehicles, determine the belt tension at a point halfway between the pulleys by pressing on the belt with moderate thumb pressure. The belt should deflect about 1/4 in. (6mm) over a 7–10 in. (178–254mm) span, or 1/2 in. (12.7mm) over a 13–16 in. (330–406mm) span, at this point. If the deflection is found to be too much or too little, perform the tension adjustments.

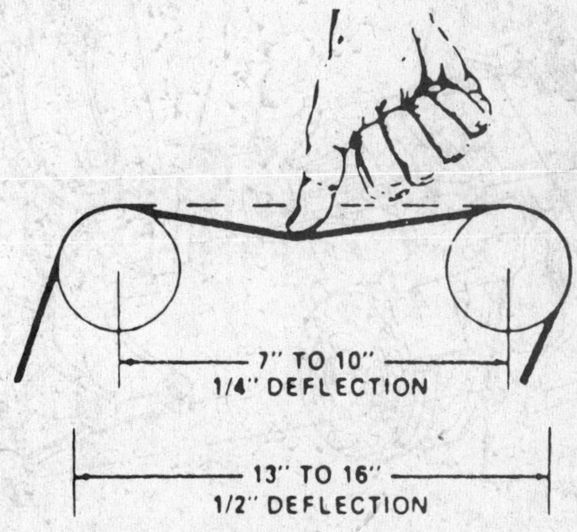

A gauge is recommended but you can check the belt tension with thumb pressure

ADJUSTING TENSION

Except 4.3L Engine

NOTE: The following procedures require the use of GM Belt Tension Gauge No. BT-33-95-ACBN (regular V-belts), BT-33-97M (poly V-belts) or equivalent.

1. If the belt is cold, operate the engine (at idle speed) for 15 minutes; the belt will seat itself in the pulleys allowing the belt fibers to relax or stretch. If the belt is hot, allow it to cool, until it is warm to the touch.

NOTE: A used belt is one that has been rotated at least one complete revolution on the pulleys. This begins the belt seating process and it must never be tensioned to the new belt specifications.

2. Loosen the component-to-mounting bracket bolts.
3. Using a GM Belt Tension Gauge No. BT-33-95-ACBN (standard V-belts), BT-33-97M (poly V-belts) or equivalent, place the tension gauge at the center of the belt between the longest span.
4. Applying belt tension pressure on the component, adjust the drive belt tension to the correct specifications.
5. While holding the correct tension on the component, tighten the component-to-mounting bracket bolt.
6. When the belt tension is correct, remove the tension gauge.

NOTE: It is better to have belts too loose than too tight, because overtight belts will lead to bearing failure, particularly in the water pump and alternator. However, loose belts place an extremely high impact load on the driven components due to the whipping action of the belt.

4.3 L Engine

The belt tensioner is spring loaded and the dirve belt will return to the tensioner position, provided the grooves in the belt match the grooves in the pulley.

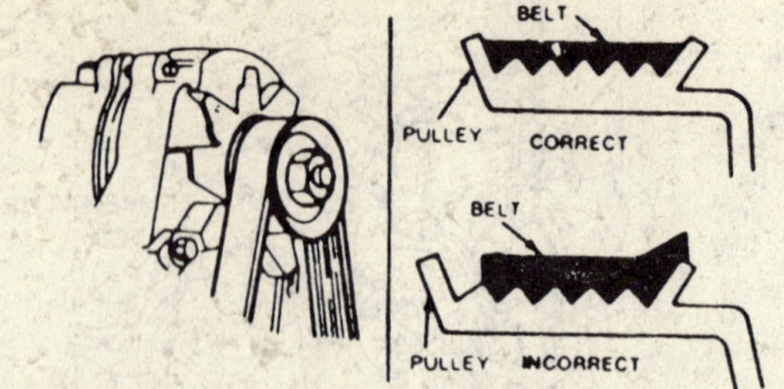

Serpentine drive belt alignment—4.3L engine

REMOVAL AND INSTALLATION

Except 4.3L Engine

1. Loosen the component-to-mounting bracket bolts.
2. Rotate the component to relieve the tension on the drive belt.
3. Slip the drive belt from the component pulley and remove it from the engine.

NOTE: If the engine uses more than one belt, it may be necessary to remove other belts that are in front of the one being removed.

4. To install, reverse the removal procedures. Adjust the component drive belt tension to specifications.

4.3L Engine

1. Place a tool over the tensioner pulley axis bolt.
2. Rotate the tool counterclockwise
3. Remove the drive belt.
4. Remove the tool.

To install:

5. Route the belt over the pulleys, except the drive belt tensionser pulley.

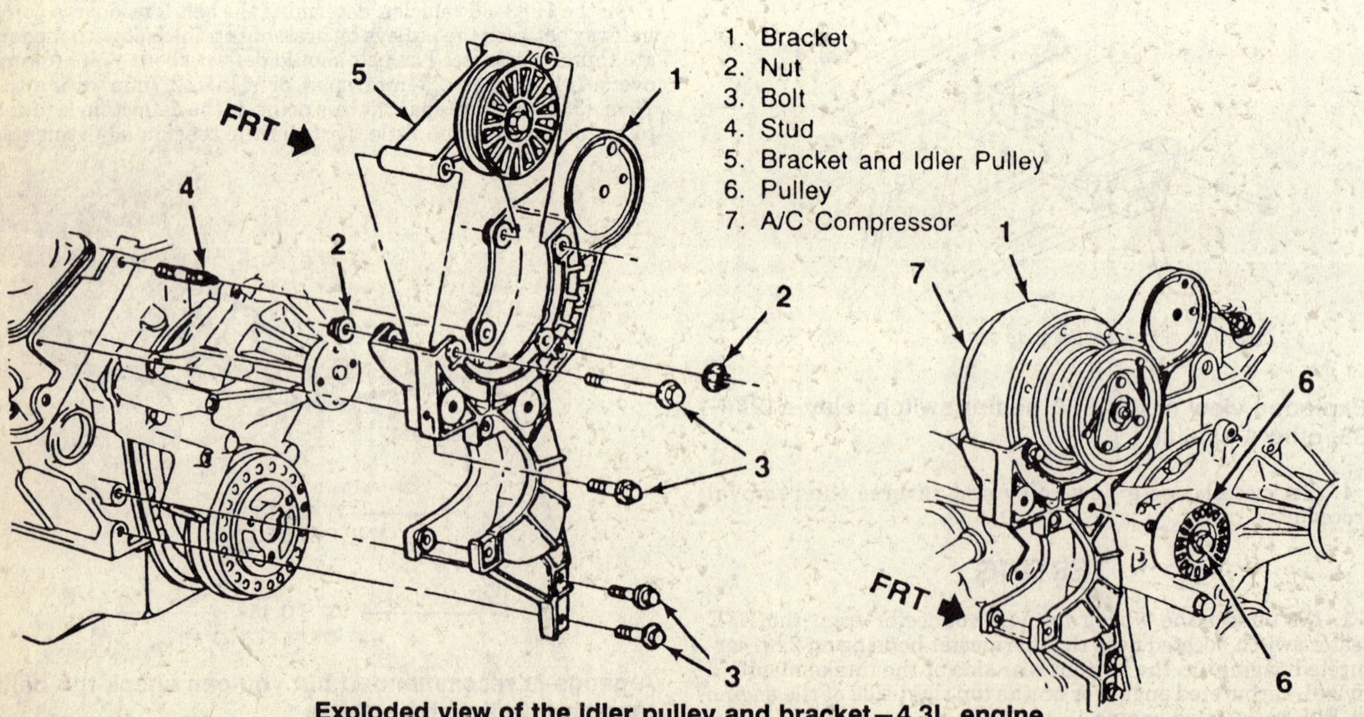

Exploded view of the idler pulley and bracket—4.3L engine

HOW TO SPOT WORN V-BELTS

V–Belts are vital to efficient engine operation – they drive the fan, water pump and other accessories. They require little maintenance (occasional tightening) but they will not last forever. Slipping or failure of the V–belt will lead to overheating. If your V–belt looks like any of these, it should be replaced.

Cracking or Weathering

This belt has deep cracks, which cause it to flex. Too much flexing leads to heat build–up and premature failure. These cracks can be caused by using the belt on a pulley that is too small. Notched belts are available for small diameter pulleys.

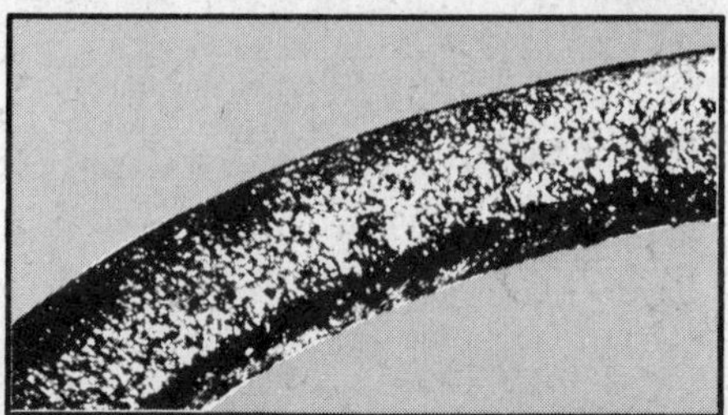

Softening (Grease and Oil)

Oil and grease on a belt can cause the belt's rubber compounds to soften and separate from the reinforcing cords that hold the belt together. The belt will first slip, then finally fail altogether.

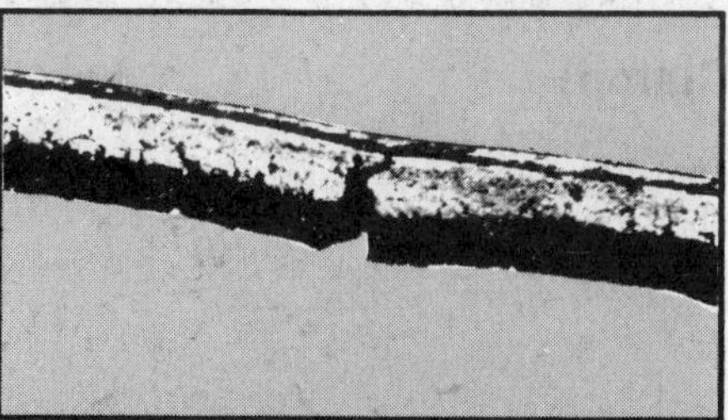

Glazing

Glazing is caused by a belt that is slipping. A slipping belt can cause a run-down battery, erratic power steering, overheating or poor accessory performance. The more the belt slips, the more glazing will be built up on the surface of the belt. The more the belt is glazed, the more it will slip. If the glazing is light, tighten the belt.

Worn Cover

The cover of this belt is worn off and is peeling away. The reinforcing cords will begin to wear and the belt will shortly break. When the belt cover wears in spots or has a rough jagged appearance, check the pulley grooves for roughness.

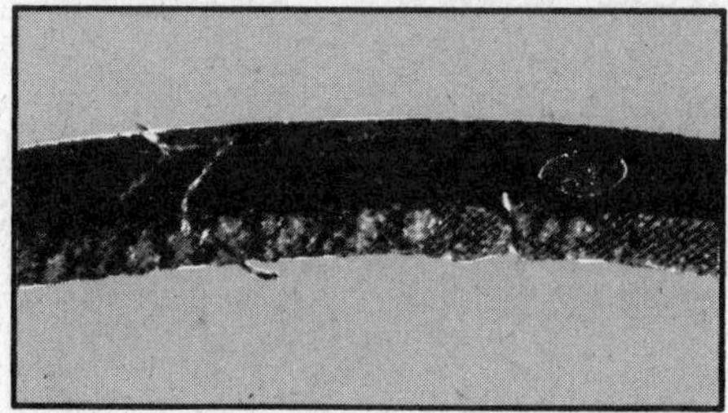

Separation

This belt is on the verge of breaking and leaving you stranded. The layers of the belt are separating and the reinforcing cords are exposed. It's just a matter of time before it breaks completely.

HOW TO SPOT BAD HOSES

Both the upper and lower radiator hoses are called upon to perform difficult jobs in an inhospitable environment. They are subject to nearly 18 psi at under hood temperatures often over 280°F, and must circulate nearly 7500 gallons of coolant an hour—3 good reasons to have good hoses.

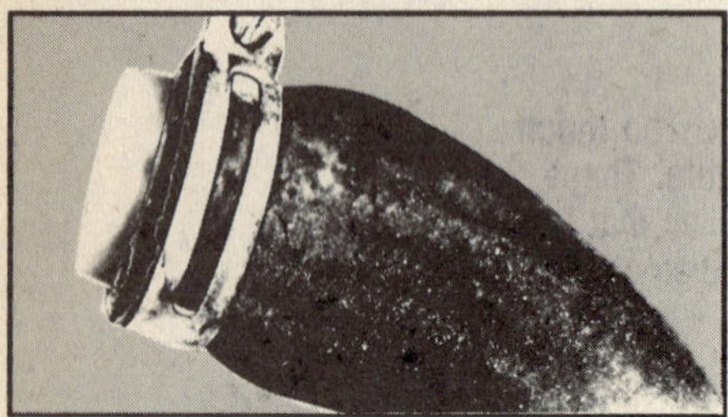

Swollen Hose

A good test for any hose is to feel it for soft or spongy spots. Frequently these will appear as swollen areas of the hose. The most likely cause is oil soaking. This hose could burst at any time, when hot or under pressure.

Cracked Hose

Cracked hoses can usually be seen but feel the hoses to be sure they have not hardened; a prime cause of cracking. This hose has cracked down to the reinforcing cords and could split at any of the cracks.

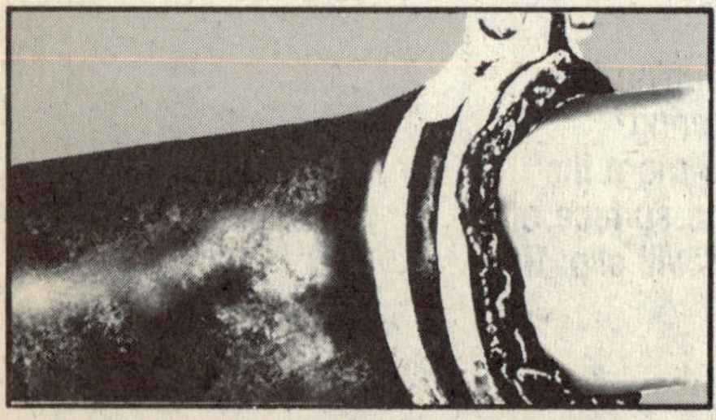

Frayed Hose End (Due to Weak Clamp)

Weakened clamps frequently are the cause of hose and cooling system failure. The connection between the pipe and hose has deteriorated enough to allow coolant to escape when the engine is hot.

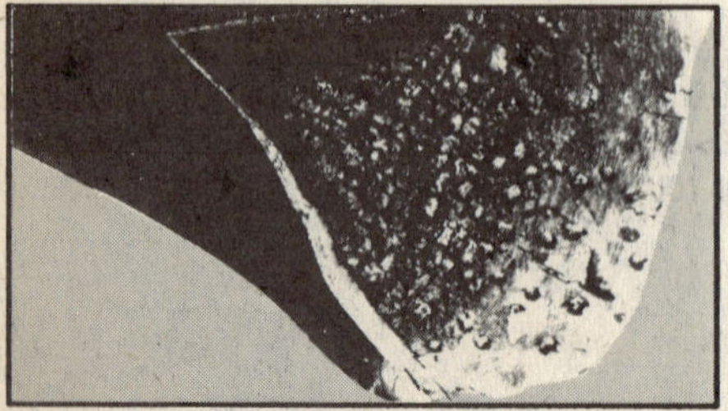

Debris in Cooling System

Debris, rust and scale in the cooling system can cause the inside of a hose to weaken. This can usually be felt on the outside of the hose as soft or thinner areas.

6. Place a tool over the tensioner pulley axis bolt.
7. Rotate the tool counterclockwise.
8. Install the drive belt over the belt tensioner pulley.
9. Remove the tool and check the belt for correct tracking.

Hoses

The upper/lower radiator hoses and all heater hoses should be checked for deterioration, leaks and loose hose clamps every 15,000 miles or 12 months.

REMOVAL AND INSTALLATION

1. Drain the cooling system.

CAUTION

When draining the coolant, keep in mind that cats and dogs are attracted by the ethylene glycol antifreeze, and are quite likely to drink any that is left in an uncovered container or in puddles on the ground. This will prove fatal in sufficient quantity. Always drain the coolant into a sealable container. Coolant should be reused unless it is contaminated or several years old.

2. Loosen the hose clamps at each end of the hose.
3. Working the hose back and forth, slide it off it's connection and then install a new hose, if necessary.

NOTE: When replacing the heater hoses, maintain a 1½ in. (38mm) clearance between the hose clip-to-upper control arm and between the rear overhead heater core lines-to-exhaust pipe.

4. To install, reverse the removal procedures. Refill the cooling system.

NOTE: Draw the hoses tight to prevent sagging or rubbing against other components; route the hoses through the clamps as installed originally. Always make sure the hose clamps are beyond the component bead and placed in the center of the clamping surface before tightening them.

Air Conditioning

SAFETY WARNINGS

Because of the importance of the necessary safety precautions that must be exercised when working with air conditioning systems and R-12 refrigerant, a recap of the safety precautions are outlined.

- Avoid contact with a charged refrigeration system, even when working on another part of the air conditioning system or vehicle. If a heavy tool comes into contact with a section of copper tubing or a heat exchanger, it can easily cause the relatively soft material to rupture.
- When it is necessary to apply force to a fitting which contains refrigerant, as when checking that all system couplings are securely tightened, use a wrench on both parts of the fitting involved, if possible. This will avoid putting torque on the refrigerant tubing. It is advisable, when possible, to use tube or line wrenches when tightening these flare nut fittings.
- Do not attempt to discharge the system by merely loosening a fitting or removing the service valve caps and cracking these valves. Precise control is possible only when using the service gauges. Place a rag under the open end of the center charging hose while discharging the system to catch any drops of liquid that might escape. Wear protective gloves when connecting or disconnecting service gauge hoses.
- Discharge the system only in a well ventilated area, as high concentrations of the gas can exclude oxygen and act as an anaesthetic. When leak testing or soldering, this is particularly important, as toxic gas is formed when R-12 contacts any flame.
- Never start a system without first verifying that both service valves are back-seated, if equipped, and that all fittings throughout the system are snugly connected.
- Avoid applying heat to any refrigerant line or storage vessel. Charging may be aided by using water heated to less than

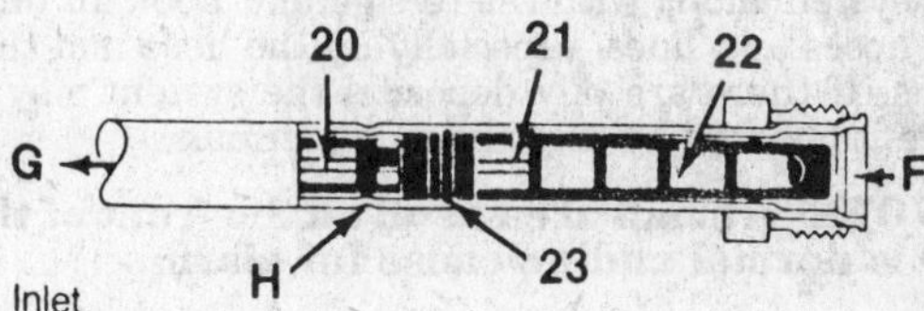

F. Inlet
G. Outlet (to evaporator)
H. Dent on tube (retains the expansion tube)
20. Outlet Screen
21. Expansion tube
22. Inlet screen
23. Seal

Sectional view of the orifice tube—air conditioning system

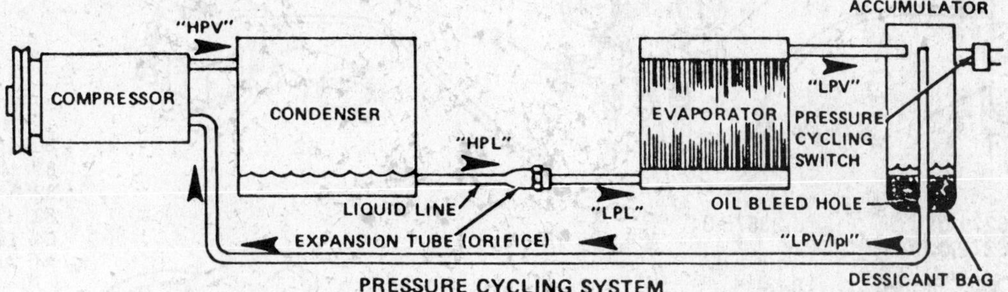

"HPV" – HIGH PRESSURE VAPOR LEAVING COMPRESSOR.

"HPL" – VAPOR IS COOLED DOWN BY CONDENSER, AIR FLOW AND LEAVES AS HIGH PRESSURE LIQUID.

"LPL" – ORIFICE METERS THE LIQUID R-12, INTO EVAPORATOR, REDUCING ITS PRESSURE, AND WARM BLOWER AIR ACROSS EVAPORATOR CORE CAUSES BOILING OFF OF LIQUID INTO VAPOR.

"LPV" – LEAVES EVAPORATOR AS LOW PRESSURE VAPOR AND RETURNS WITH THE SMALL AMOUNT OF . . .

"lpl" – . . . LOW PRESSURE LIQUID THAT DIDN'T BOIL OFF COMPLETELY BACK TO THE COMPRESSOR TO BE COMPRESSED AGAIN.

Typical air conditioning system layout

125°F (52°C) to warm the refrigerant container. Never allow a refrigerant storage container to sit out in the sun or near any other heat source, such as a radiator.

- Always wear goggles when working on a system to protect the eyes. If refrigerant contacts the eyes, it is advisable in all cases to see a physician as soon as possible.
- Frostbite from liquid refrigerant should be treated by first gradually warming the area with cool water and then gently applying petroleum jelly. A physician should be consulted.
- Always keep the refrigerant drum fittings capped when not in use. Avoid any sudden shock to the drum, which might occur from dropping it or from banging a heavy tool against it. Never carry a drum in the passenger compartment of a vehicle.
- Always completely discharge the system before painting the vehicle (if the paint is to be baked on), or before welding anywhere near the refrigerant lines.

NOTE: Any repair work to an air conditioning system should be left to a professional. Do not, under any circumstances, attempt to loosen or tighten any fittings or perform any work other than that outlined here.

SYSTEM INSPECTION

NOTE: The Cycling Clutch Orfice (CCOT) tube air conditioning system does not use a sight glass.

Checking For Oil Leaks

Refrigerant leaks show up as oily areas on the various components because the compressor oil is transported around the entire system along with the refrigerant. Look for oily spots on all the hoses and lines, especially on the hose and tubing connections. If there are oily deposits, the system may have a leak, have it checked by a qualified repairman.

NOTE: A small area of oil on the front of the compressor is normal and no cause for alarm.

Checking The Compressor Belt

Refer to the Drive Belts section in this section.

Keep The Condenser Clear

Periodically inspect the front of the condenser for bent fins or foreign material (dirt, buts, leaves, etc.). If any cooling fins are bent, straighten them carefully with needle-nose pliers. You can remove any debris with a stiff bristle brush or hose.

Operate The A/C System Periodically

A lot of air conditioning problems can be avoided by simply running the air conditioner at least once a week regardless of the season. Simply let the system run for at least 5 minutes a week (even in the winter) and you'll keep the internal parts lubricated as well as preventing the hoses from hardening.

Leak Testing the System

There are several methods of detecting leaks in an air conditioning system; among them, the 2 most popular are (1) halide leak detection or the open flame method and (2) electronic leak detector.

The Halide Leak Detection tool J-6084 or equivalent, is a torch like device which produces a yellow-green color when refrigerant is introduced into the flame at the burner. A purple or violet color indicates the presence of large amounts of refrigerant at the burner.

An Autobalance Refrigerant Leak Detector tool J-29547 or equivalent, is a small portable electronic device with an extended probe. With the unit activated, the probe is passed along those components of the system which contain refrigerant. If a leak is detected, the unit will sound an alarm signal or activate a display signal depending on the manufacturer's design. It is advisable to follow the manufacturer's instructions as the design and function of the detection may vary significantly.

CAUTION

Care should be taken to operate either type of detector in well ventilated areas, so as to reduce the chance of personal injury, which may result from coming in contact with poisonous gases produced when R-12 is exposed to flame or electric spark.

GAUGE SETS (USE)

Most of the service work performed in air conditioning requires the use of a set of 2 gauges, one for the high (head) pressure side of the system, the other for the low (suction) side.

The low side gauge records both pressure and vacuum. Vacu-

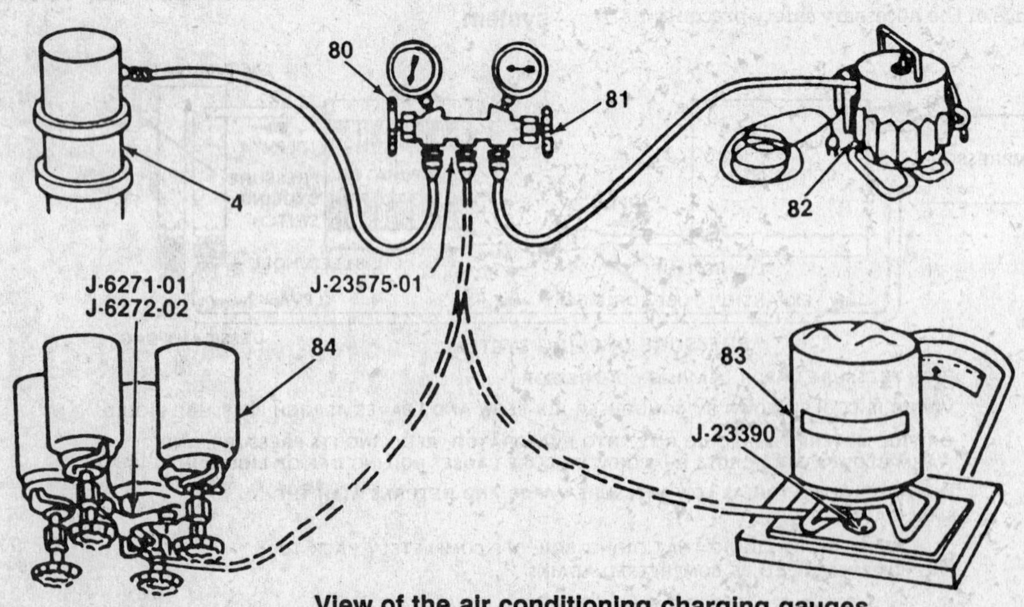

View of the air conditioning charging gauges

um readings are calibrated from 0–30 in. Hg vacuum, and the pressure graduations read from 0–60 psi.

The high side gauge measures pressure from 0–600 psi.

Both gauges are threaded into a manifold that contains 2 hand shut-off valves. Proper manipulation of these valves and the use of the attached test hoses allow the user to perform the following services:

1. Test high and low side pressures.
2. Remove air, moisture and/or contaminated refrigerant.
3. Purge the system of refrigerant.
4. Charge the system with refrigerant.

The manifold valves are designed so they have no direct effect on the gauge readings but serve only to provide for or cut off the flow of refrigerant through the manifold. During all testing and hook-up operations, the valves are kept in a closed position to avoid disturbing the refrigeration system. The valves are Opened ONLY to purge the system of refrigerant or to charge it.

When purging the system, the center hose is uncapped at the lower end and both valves are cracked (opened) slightly. This allows the refrigerant pressure to force the entire contents of the system out through the center hose. During charging, the valve on the high side of the manifold is closed and the valve on the low side is cracked (opened). Under these conditions, the low pressure in the evaporator will draw refrigerant from the relatively warm refrigerant storage container into the system.

Service Valves

For the user to diagnose an air conditioning system he or she must gain entrance to the system in order to observe the pressures; the type of terminal for this purpose is the familiar Schrader valve.

The Schrader valve is similar to a tire valve stem and the process of connecting the test hoses is the same as threading a hand pump outlet hose to a bicycle tire. As the test hose is threaded to the service port the valve core is depressed, allowing the refrigerant to enter the test hose outlet. Removal of the test hose automatically closes the system.

Extreme caution must be observed when removing test hoses from the Schrader valves as some refrigerant will normally escape, usually under high pressure; observe safety precautions.

Using The Manifold Gauges

The following are step-by-step procedures to guide the user to the correct gauge usage.

CAUTION

Wear goggles or face shield during all testing operations. Backseat hand shut-off type service valves.

1. Remove the caps from the high and low side service ports. Make sure both gauge valves are closed.

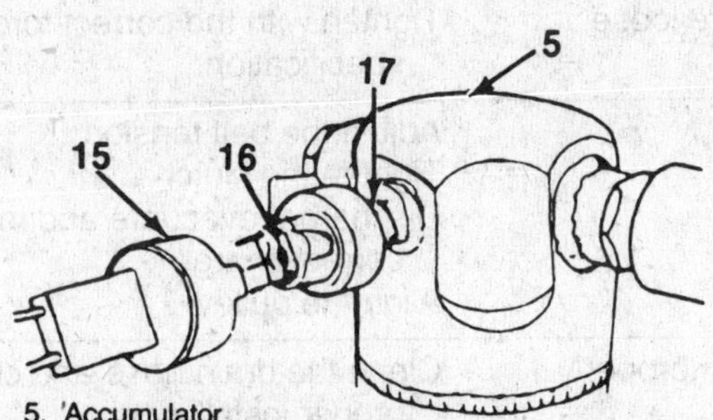

5. Accumulator
15. Electrical connector
16. Pressure cycling switch adjusting screw
17. "Schrader" type valve

View of the air conditioning with the Schrader valve

2. Connect the low side test hose to the service valve that leads to the evaporator (located between the evaporator outlet and the compressor).
3. Attach the high side test hose to the service valve that leads to the condenser.
4. Mid-position the hand shutoff type service valves.
5. Start the engine and allow it to warm-up. All testing and charging of the system should be done after the engine and system has reached normal operating temperatures, except when using certain the charging stations.
6. Adjust the air conditioner controls to Max. cold.
7. Observe the gauge readings.

When the gauges are not being used it is a good idea to:

a. Keep both hand valves in the closed position.
b. Attach both ends of the high and low service hoses to the manifold, if extra outlets are present on the manifold or plug them, if not.
c. Keep the center charging hose attached to an empty refrigerant can. This extra precaution will reduce the possibility of moisture entering the gauges. If the air and moisture have gotten into the gauges, purge the hoses by supplying refrigerant under pressure to the center hose with both gauge valves open and all openings unplugged.

DISCHARGING THE SYSTEM

R-12 refrigerant is a chlorofluorocarbon which, when released into the atmosphere, can contribute to the depletion on the ozone layer in the upper atmosphere. Ozone filters out harmful radiation from the sun. In order to protect the ozone layer, an approved R-12 Recovery/Recycling machine that meets SAE standards should be employed when discharging the system. Follow the operating instructions provided with the approved equipment exactly to properly discharge the system.

EVACUATING

If the air conditioning system has been opened to the atmosphere, it should be air and moisture free before being recharged with refrigerant. Moisture and air mixed with refrigerant will raise the compressor head pressure, possibly damage the system's components and will reduce the performance of the system. In addition, air and moisture in the system can lead to internal corrosion of the system components. Moisture will boil at normal room temperature when exposed to a vacuum. To evacuate or rid the system of air and moisture:

1. Leak test the system and repair any leaks found.
2. Connect an approved charging station, recovery/recycling machine or manifold gauge set and vacuum pump to the discharge and suction ports. The red hose is normally connected to the discharge (high pressure) line. The blue hose is connected to the suction (low pressure) line. If using a manifold gauge set, the center (usually yellow) hose is connected to the charging station or recovery/recycling machine.
3. Open the discharge and suction ports and start the vacuum pump. If the pump is not able to pull at least 26 in. Hg of vacuum there is a leak that must be repaired before evacuation can occur.
4. Once the system has reached at least 26 in. Hg of vacuum, allow the system to evacuate for at least 10 minutes. The longer the system is evacuated, the more moisture will be removed.
5. Close all valves and turn the pump off. If the system loses more than 2 in. Hg of vacuum after 15 minutes, there is a leak that should be repaired.

Troubleshooting Basic Air Conditioning Problems

Problem	Cause	Solution
There's little or no air coming from the vents (and you're sure it's on)	• The A/C fuse is blown • Broken or loose wires or connections • The on/off switch is defective	• Check and/or replace fuse • Check and/or repair connections • Replace switch
The air coming from the vents is not cool enough	• Windows and air vent wings open • The compressor belt is slipping • Heater is on • Condenser is clogged with debris • Refrigerant has escaped through a leak in the system • Receiver/drier is plugged	• Close windows and vent wings • Tighten or replace compressor belt • Shut heater off • Clean the condenser • Check system • Service system
The air has an odor	• Vacuum system is disrupted • Odor producing substances on the evaporator case • Condensation has collected in the bottom of the evaporator housing	• Have the system checked/repaired • Clean the evaporator case • Clean the evaporator housing drains
System is noisy or vibrating	• Compressor belt or mountings loose • Air in the system	• Tighten or replace belt; tighten mounting bolts • Have the system serviced
Sight glass condition		
Constant bubbles, foam or oil streaks	• Undercharged system	• Charge the system
Clear sight glass, but no cold air	• No refrigerant at all	• Check and charge the system
Clear sight glass, but air is cold	• System is OK	
Clouded with milky fluid	• Receiver drier is leaking dessicant	• Have system checked
Large difference in temperature of lines	• System undercharged	• Charge and leak test the system
Compressor noise	• Broken valves • Overcharged • Incorrect oil level • Piston slap • Broken rings • Drive belt pulley bolts are loose	• Replace the valve plate • Discharge, evacuate and install the correct charge • Isolate the compressor and check the oil level. Correct as necessary. • Replace the compressor • Replace the compressor • Tighten with the correct torque specification
Excessive vibration	• Incorrect belt tension • Clutch loose • Overcharged • Pulley is misaligned	• Adjust the belt tension • Tighten the clutch • Discharge, evacuate and install the correct charge • Align the pulley
Condensation dripping in the passenger compartment	• Drain hose plugged or improperly positioned • Insulation removed or improperly installed	• Clean the drain hose and check for proper installation • Replace the insulation on the expansion valve and hoses

Troubleshooting Basic Air Conditioning Problems (cont.)

Problem	Cause	Solution
Frozen evaporator coil	· Faulty thermostat · Thermostat capillary tube improperly installed · Thermostat not adjusted properly	· Replace the thermostat · Install the capillary tube correctly · Adjust the thermostat
Low side low—high side low	· System refrigerant is low · Expansion valve is restricted	· Evacuate, leak test and charge the system · Replace the expansion valve
Low side high—high side low	· Internal leak in the compressor—worn	· Remove the compressor cylinder head and inspect the compressor. Replace the valve plate assembly if necessary. If the compressor pistons, rings or
Low side high—high side low (cont.)		cylinders are excessively worn or scored replace the compressor
	· Cylinder head gasket is leaking · Expansion valve is defective · Drive belt slipping	· Install a replacement cylinder head gasket · Replace the expansion valve · Adjust the belt tension
Low side high—high side high	· Condenser fins obstructed · Air in the system · Expansion valve is defective · Loose or worn fan belts	· Clean the condenser fins · Evacuate, leak test and charge the system · Replace the expansion valve · Adjust or replace the belts as necessary
Low side low—high side high	· Expansion valve is defective · Restriction in the refrigerant hose	· Replace the expansion valve · Check the hose for kinks—replace if necessary
Low side low—high side high	· Restriction in the receiver/drier · Restriction in the condenser	· Replace the receiver/drier · Replace the condenser
Low side and high normal (inadequate cooling)	**· Air in the system** **· Moisture in the system**	**· Evacuate, leak test and charge the system** **· Evacuate, leak test and charge the system**

System Sweep

An efficient vacuum pump can remove all the air contained in a contaminated air conditioning system very quickly, because of its vapor state. Moisture, however, is far more difficult to remove because the vacuum must force the liquid to evaporate before it will be able to be removed from the system. If the system has become severely contaminated, as it might become after all the charge was lost in conjunction with vehicle accident damage, moisture removal is extremely time consuming. A vacuum pump could remove all of the moisture only if it were operated for 12 hours or more.

Under these conditions, sweeping the system with refrigerant will speed the process of moisture removal considerably. To sweep, follow the following procedure:

1. Connect the vacuum pump to the gauges, operate it until the vacuum ceases to increase, then continue the operation for ten more minutes.
2. Charge the system with 50 percent of its rated refrigerant capacity.
3. Operate the system at fast idle for ten minutes.
4. Discharge the system.
5. Repeat (twice) the process of charging to 50 percent capacity, running the system for ten minutes, then discharging it for a total of three sweeps.
6. Replace the drier.
7. Pump the system down as in Step 1.
8. Charge the system.

CHARGING SYSTEM

CAUTION

Never attempt to charge the system by opening the high pressure gauge control while the compressor is operating. The compressor accumulating pressure can burst the refrigerant container, causing sever personal injuries.

1. Start the engine, operate it with the choke Open and normal idle speed, then position the air conditioning control lever on the Off.
2. Using drum or 14 oz. cans of refrigerant, in the inverted position, allow about 1 lb. of refrigerant to enter the system through the low side service fitting on the accumulator.
3. After 1 lb. of refrigerant enters the system, position the control lever on Norm (the compressor will engage) and the blower motor on Hi speed; this operation will draw the remainder of the refrigerant into the system.

NOTE: To speed up the operation, position a fan in front of the condenser; the lowering of the condenser temperature will allow refrigerant to enter the system faster.

4. When the system is charged, turn Off the refrigerant source and allow the engine to run for 30 seconds to clear the lines and gauges.
5. With the engine running, remove the hose adapter from the accumulator service fitting (unscrew the hose quickly to prevent refrigerant from escaping).

CAUTION

Never remove the gauge line from the adapter when the line is connected to the system; always remove the line adapter from the service fitting first.

6. Replace the accumulator protective caps and turn the engine Off.
7. Using a leak detector, inspect the air conditioning system for leaks. If a leak is present, repair it.

Windshield Wipers

For maximum effectiveness and longest element life, the windshield and wiper blades should be kept clean. Dirt, tree sap, road tar and so on will cause streaking, smearing and blade deterioration if left on the glass. It is advisable to wash the windshield carefully with a commercial glass cleaner at least once a month. Wipe off the rubber blades with the wet rag, afterwards.

If the blades are found to be cracked, broken or torn, they should be replaced immediately. Replacement intervals will vary with usage, although ozone deterioration usually limits blade life to about one year. If the wiper pattern is smeared, streaked or if the blade chatters across the glass, the elements should be replaced. It is easiest and most sensible to replace the elements in pairs.

BLADE REPLACEMENT

1. Lift the wiper arm assembly from the windshield.

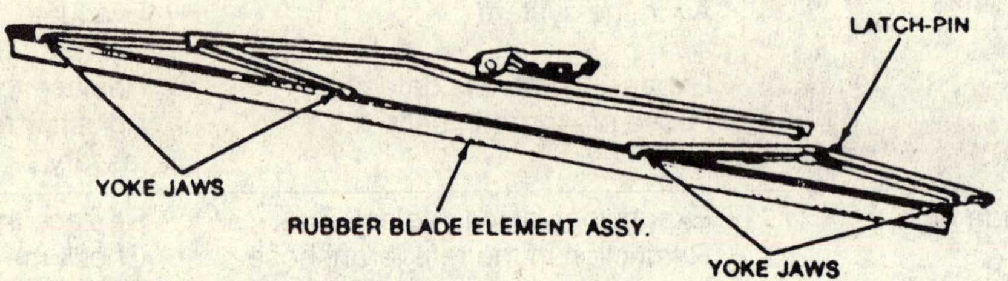

View of the windshield wiper blade assembly

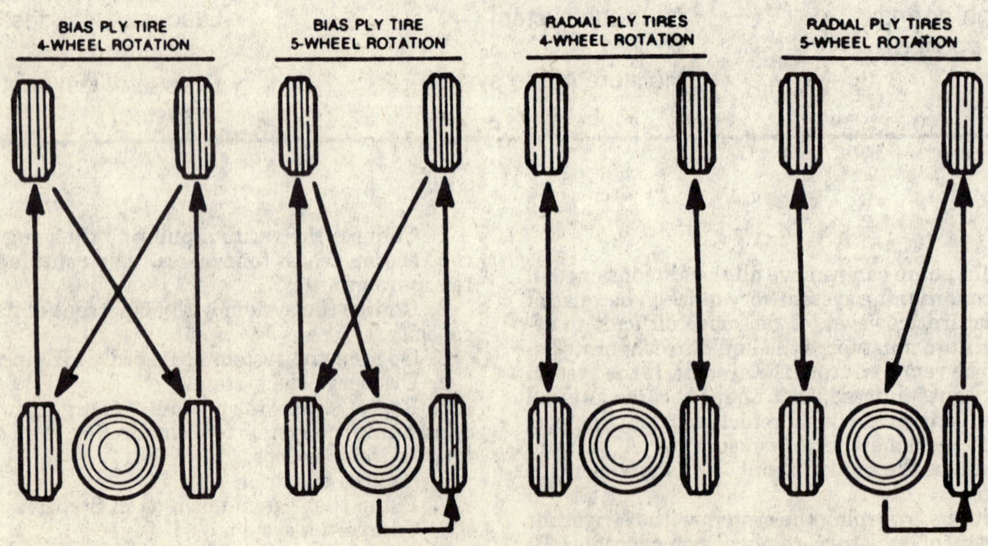

Tire rotation patterns

2. Depress the wiper arm-to-blade assembly pin to disconnect the blade assembly from the wiper arm.
3. To install, use new blade assemblies and reverse the removal procedures.

Tires and Wheels

TIRE DESIGN

Tire Types

For maximum satisfaction, tires should be used in sets of five. Mixing of different types (radial, bias-belted, fiberglass belted) should be avoided. Conventional bias tires are constructed so the cords run bead-to-bead at an angle. This type of construction gives rigidity to both tread and sidewall. Bias-belted tires are similar in construction to conventional bias ply tires. Belts run at an angle and also at a 90 degree angle to the bead, as in the radial tire. Tread life is improved considerably over the conventional bias tire. The radial tire differs in construction, but instead of the carcass plies running are an angle of 90 degree to each other, they run at an angle of 90 degree to the bead. This gives the tread a great deal of rigidity and the sidewall a great deal of flexibility and accounts for the characteristic bulge associated with radial tires.

The vehicles are capable of using radial tires and they are recommended. If they are used, tire sizes and wheel diameters should be selected to maintain ground clearance and tire load capacity equivalent to the minimum specified tire. Radial tires should always be used in sets of five, but in an emergency, radial tires can be used with caution on the rear axle only. If this is done, both tires on the rear should be of radial design.

NOTE: Radial tires should never be used on only the front axle.

Snow tires should not be operated at sustained speeds over 70 mph.

On 4-wheel drive vehicles, all tires must be of the same size, type, and tread pattern, to provide even traction on loose surfaces, to prevent driveline bind when conventional four wheel drive is used, and to prevent excessive wear on the center differential with full time four wheel drive.

Tread Depth

All tires have built-in tread wear indicator bars that show up as ½ in. (12.7mm) wide smooth bands across the tire when $\frac{1}{16}$ in. (1.5mm) of tread remains. The appearance of tread wear indicators means that the tires should be replaced. In fact, many states have laws prohibiting the use of tires with less than $\frac{1}{16}$ in. (1.5mm) tread.

You can check your own tread depth with an inexpensive gauge or by using a Lincoln head penny. Slip the Lincoln penny into several into several tread grooves. If you can see the top of Lincoln's head in 2 adjacent grooves, the tires have less than $\frac{1}{16}$ in. (1.5mm) tread left and should be replaced. You can measure snow tires in the same manner by using the tails side of the Lincoln penny. If you can see the top of the Lincoln memorial, it's time to replace the snow tires.

Thread wear indicators appear when the tire is worn out

TIRE STORAGE

Store the tires at proper inflation pressures if they are mounted on wheels. All tires should be kept in a cool, dry place. If they are stored in the garage or basement, do not let them stand on a concrete floor, set them on strips of wood.

Aluminum Wheels

NOTE: If your vehicle has aluminum wheels, be very careful when using any type of cleaner on either the wheels or the tires. Read the label on the package of the cleaner to make sure it will not damage aluminum.

TIRE INFLATION

The inflation is the most ignored item of auto maintenance. Gasoline mileage can drop as much as 0.8 percent for every 1 pound/square inch (psi) of under inflation.

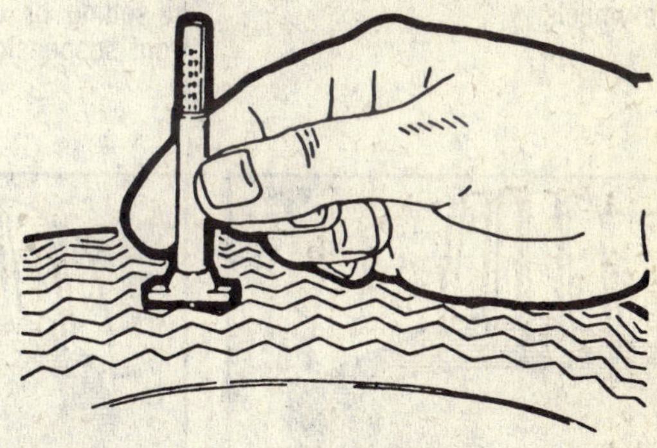

Thread depth an be checked with an inexpensive gauge

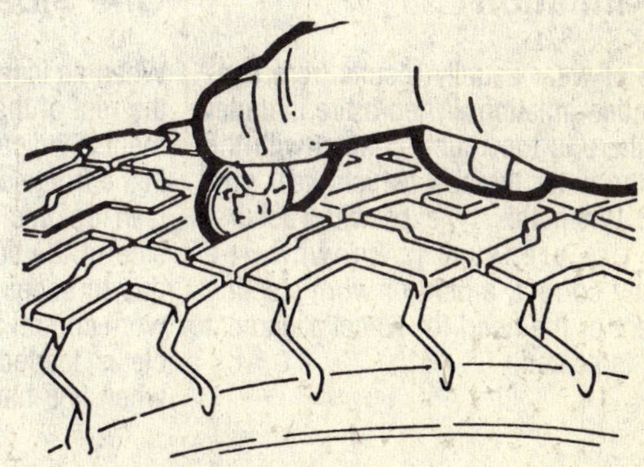

If all of Lincoln's head is visible into two or more adjacent grooves, the tire should be replaced

HOW TO READ TIRE WEAR

The way your tires wear is a good indicator of other parts of your car. Abnormal wear patterns are often caused by the need for simple tire maintenance, or for front end alignment.

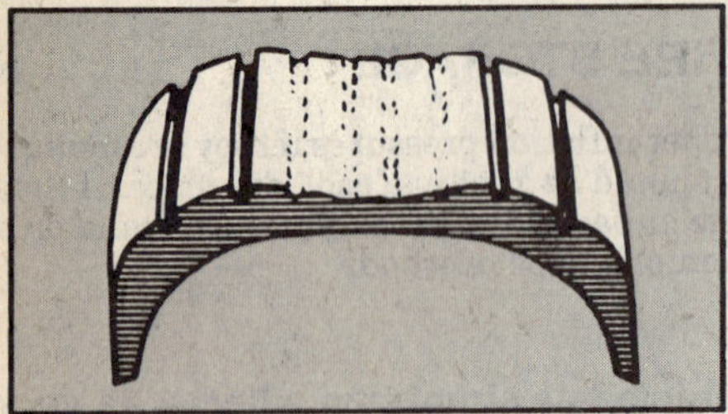

Over-Inflation

Excessive wear at the center of the tread indicates that the air pressure in the tire is consistently too high. The tire is riding on the center of the tread and wearing it prematurely. Occasionally, this wear pattern can result from outrageously wide tires on narrow rims. The cure for this is to replace either the tires or the wheels.

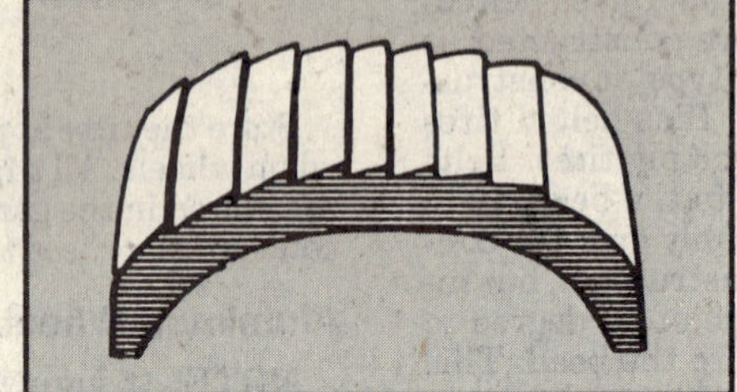

Feathering

Feathering is a condition when the edge of each tread rib develops a slightly rounded edge on one side and a sharp edge on the other. By running your hand over the tire, you can usually feel the sharper edges before you'll be able to see them. The most common causes of feathering are incorrect toe–in setting or deteriorated bushings in the front suspension.

Cupping

Cups or scalloped dips appearing around the edge of the tread almost always indicate worn (sometimes bent) suspension parts. Adjustment of wheel alignment alone will seldom cure the problem. Any worn component that connects the wheel to the vehicle can cause this type of wear. Occasionally, wheels that are out of balance will wear like this, but wheel imbalance usually shows up as bald spots between the outside edges and center of the tread.

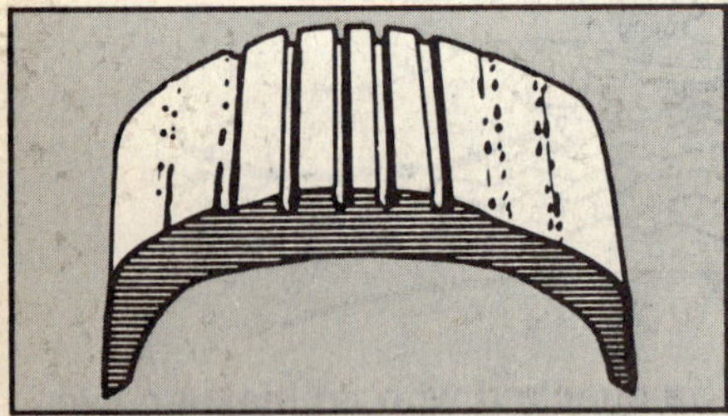

Under-Inflation

This type of wear usually results from consistent under–inflation. When a tire is under inflated, there is too much contact with the road by the outer threads, which wear prematurely. When this type of wear occurs, and the tire pressure is known to be consistenly correct, a bent or worn steering component or the need for wheel alignment could be indicated.

One Side Wear

When an inner or outer rib wears faster than the rest of the tire, the need for wheel alignment is indicated. There is excessive camber in the front suspension, causing the wheel to lean too much, putting excessive load on one side of the tire. Misalignment could also be due to sagging springs, worn ball joints, or worn control arm bushings. Be sure the vehicle is loaded the way it's normally driven when you have the wheels aligned.

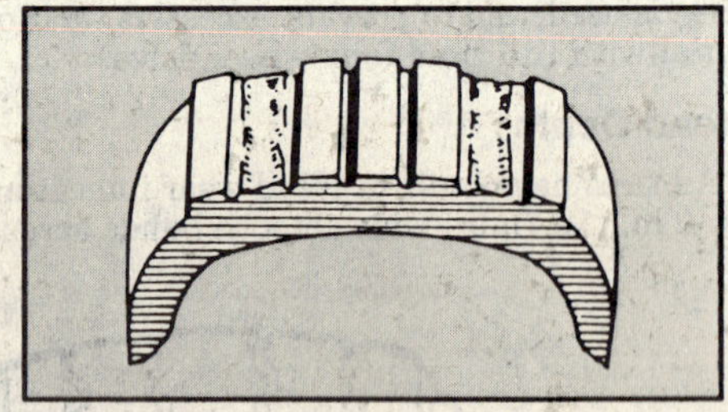

Second-Rib Wear

Second-rib wear is normally found only in radial tires, and appears where the steel belts end in relation to the tread. Normally, it can be kept to a minimum by paying careful attention to tire pressure and frequently rotation the tires. This is often considered normal wear but excessive amounts indicate that the tires are too wide for the wheels.

Two items should be a permanent fixture in every glove compartment: a tire pressure gauge and a tread depth gauge. Check the tire air pressure (including the spare) regularly with a pocket type gauge. Kicking the tires won't tell you a thing and the gauge on the service station air hose is notoriously inaccurate.

The tire pressures recommended for your vehicle are usually found on the glove box door or in the owner's manual. Ideally, inflation pressure should be checked when the tires are cool. When the air becomes heated it expands and the pressure increases. Every 10°F rise (or drop) in temperature means a difference of 1 psi, which also explains why the tire appears to lose air on a very cold night. When it is impossible to check the tires cold, allow for pressure build-up due to heat. If the hot pressure exceeds the cold pressure by more than 15 psi, reduce your speed, load or both. Otherwise internal heat is created in the tire. When the heat approaches the temperature at which the tire was cured, during manufacture, the tread can separate from the body.

CAUTION

Never counteract excessive pressure build-up by bleeding off air pressure (letting some air out). This will only further raise the tire operating temperature.

Before starting a long trip with lots of luggage, you can add about 2–4 psi to the tires to make them run cooler but never exceed the maximum inflation pressure on the side of the tire.

Factory installed wheels and tires are designed to handle loads up to and including their rated load capacity when inflated to the recommended inflation pressures. Correct tire pressures and driving techniques have an important influence on tire life. Heavy cornering, excessively rapid acceleration and unnecessary braking increase tire wear. Underinflated tires can cause handling problems, poor fuel economy, shortened tire life and tire overloading.

Maximum axle load must never exceed the value shown on the side of the tire. The inflation pressure should never exceed 35 psi (standard tires) or 60 psi (compact tire).

Troubleshooting Basic Wheel Problems

Problem	Cause	Solution
The car's front end vibrates at high speed	· The wheels are out of balance · Wheels are out of alignment	· Have wheels balanced · Have wheel alignment checked/adjusted
Car pulls to either side	· Wheels are out of alignment · Unequal tire pressure · Different size tires or wheels	· Have wheel alignment checked/adjusted · Check/adjust tire pressure · Change tires or wheels to same size
The car's wheel(s) wobbles	· Loose wheel lug nuts · Wheels out of balance · Damaged wheel · Wheels are out of alignment · Worn or damaged ball joint · Excessive play in the steering linkage (usually due to worn parts) · Defective shock absorber	· Tighten wheel lug nuts · Have tires balanced · Raise car and spin the wheel. If the wheel is bent, it should be replaced · Have wheel alignment checked/adjusted · Check ball joints · Check steering linkage · Check shock absorbers
Tires wear unevenly or prematurely	· Incorrect wheel size · Wheels are out of balance · Wheels are out of alignment	· Check if wheel and tire size are compatible · Have wheels balanced · Have wheel alignment checked/adjusted

Troubleshooting Basic Tire Problems

Problem	Cause	Solution
The car's front end vibrates at high speeds and the steering wheel shakes	• Wheels out of balance • Front end needs aligning	• Have wheels balanced • Have front end alignment checked
The car pulls to one side while cruising	• Unequal tire pressure (car will usually pull to the low side) • Mismatched tires • Front end needs aligning	• Check/adjust tire pressure • Be sure tires are of the same type and size • Have front end alignment checked
Abnormal, excessive or uneven tire wear See "How to Read Tire Wear"	• Infrequent tire rotation • Improper tire pressure • Sudden stops/starts or high speed on curves	• Rotate tires more frequently to equalize wear • Check/adjust pressure • Correct driving habits
Tire squeals	• Improper tire pressure • Front end needs aligning	• Check/adjust tire pressure • Have front end alignment checked

Tire Size Comparison Chart

"Letter" sizes			Inch Sizes	Metric-inch Sizes		
"60 Series"	**"70 Series"**	**"78 Series"**	**1965–77**	**"60 Series"**	**"70 Series"**	**"80 Series"**
			5.50-12, 5.60-12	165/60-12	165/70-12	155-12
		Y78-12	6.00-12			
		W78-13	5.20-13	165/60-13	145/70-13	135-13
		Y78-13	5.60-13	175/60-13	155/70-13	145-13
			6.15-13	185/60-13	165/70-13	155-13, P155/80-13
A60-13	A70-13	A78-13	6.40-13	195/60-13	175/70-13	165-13
B60-13	B70-13	B78-13	6.70-13	205/60-13	185/70-13	175-13
			6.90-13			
C60-13	C70-13	C78-13	7.00-13	215/60-13	195/70-13	185-13
D60-13	D70-13	D78-13	7.25-13			
E60-13	E70-13	E78-13	7.75-13			195-13
			5.20-14	165/60-14	145/70-14	135-14
			5.60-14	175/60-14	155/70-14	145-14
			5.90-14			
A60-14	A70-14	A78-14	6.15-14	185/60-14	165/70-14	155-14
	B70-14	B78-14	6.45-14	195/60-14	175/70-14	165-14
	C70-14	C78-14	6.95-14	205/60-14	185/70-14	175-14
D60-14	D70-14	D78-14				
E60-14	E70-14	E78-14	7.35-14	215/60-14	195/70-14	185-14
F60-14	F70-14	F78-14, F83-14	7.75-14	225/60-14	200/70-14	195-14
G60-14	G70-14	G77-14, G78-14	8.25-14	235/60-14	205/70-14	205-14
H60-14	H70-14	H78-14	8.55-14	245/60-14	215/70-14	215-14
J60-14	J70-14	J78-14	8.85-14	255/60-14	225/70-14	225-14
L60-14	L70-14		9.15-14	265/60-14	235/70-14	

Tire Size Comparison Chart

"Letter" sizes			Inch Sizes	Metric-inch Sizes		
"60 Series"	"70 Series"	"78 Series"	1965–77	"60 Series"	"70 Series"	"80 Series"
	A70-15	A78-15	5.60-15	185/60-15	165/70-15	155-15
B60-15	B70-15	B78-15	6.35-15	195/60-15	175/70-15	165-15
C60-15	C70-15	C78-15	6.85-15	205/60-15	185/70-15	175-15
	D70-15	D78-15				
E60-15	E70-15	E78-15	7.35-15	215/60-15	195/70-15	185-15
F60-15	F70-15	F78-15	7.75-15	225/60-15	205/70-15	195-15
G60-15	G70-15	G78-15	8.15-15/8.25-15	235/60-15	215/70-15	205-15
H60-15	H70-15	H78-15	8.45-15/8.55-15	245/60-15	225/70-15	215-15
J60-15	J70-15	J78-15	8.85-15/8.90-15	255/60-15	235/70-15	225-15
	K70-15		9.00-15	265/60-15	245/70-15	230-15
L60-15	L70-15	L78-15, L84-15	9.15-15			235-15
	M70-15	M78-15				255-15
		N78-15				

NOTE: Every size tire is not listed and many size comaprisons are approximate, based on load ratings. Wider tires than those supplied new with the vehicle should always be checked for clearance

FLUIDS AND LUBRICANTS

Fuel and Engine Oil Recommendations

ENGINE OIL

Use ONLY SG/CC or SG/CD rated oils of the recommended viscosity. Under the classification system developed by the American Petroleum Institute, the SG rating designates the highest quality oil for use in passenger vehicles. In addition, Chevrolet recommends the use of an SG/Energy Conserving oil. Oils labeled Energy Conserving (or Saving), Fuel (Gas or Gasoline) Saving, etc. are recommended due to their superior lubricating qualities (less friction – easier engine operation) and fuel saving characteristics. Pick your oil viscosity with regard to the anticipated temperatures during the period before your next oil change. Using the accompanying chart, choose the oil viscosity for the lowest expected temperature. You will be assured of easy cold starting and sufficient engine protection.

FUEL

Gasoline

NOTE: Some fuel additives contain chemicals that can damage the catalytic converter and/or oxygen sensor. Read all of the labels carefully before using any additive in the engine or fuel system.

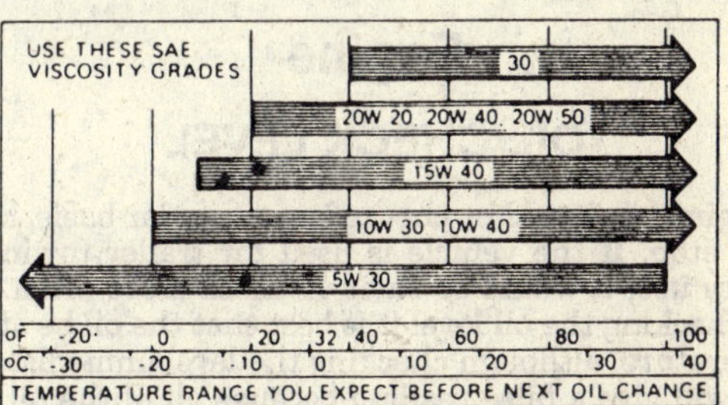

Gasoline engine oil selection chart

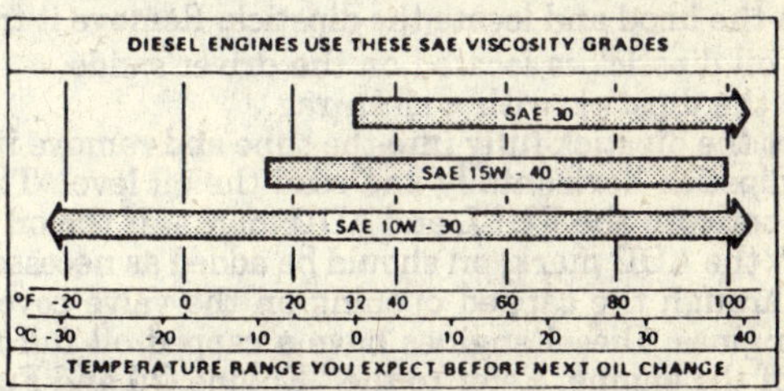

Diesel engine oil selection chart

Fuel should be selected for the brand and octane which performs best with your engine. Judge a gasoline by its ability to prevent pinging, it's engine starting capabilities (cold and hot) and general all weather performance. As far as the octane rating is concerned, refer to the General Engine Specifications chart in Section 3 to find your engine and its compression ratio.

If the compression ratio is 9.0:1 or lower, in most cases a regular unleaded grade of gasoline can be used. If the compression ratio is 9.0:1–9.3:1, use a premium grade of unleaded fuel.

NOTE: Your vehicle's engine fuel requirement can change with time, due to carbon buildup, which changes the compression ratio. If your vehicle's engine knocks, pings or runs on, switch to a higher grade of fuel, if possible, and check the ignition timing. Sometimes changing brands of gasoline will cure the problem. If it is necessary to retard the timing from specifications, don't change it more than a few degrees. Retarded timing will reduce the power output and the fuel mileage, plus it will increase the engine temperature.

Diesel

A diesel-engined vehicle requires the use of diesel fuel. Two grades are manufactured, No. 1 and No. 2, although No. 2 grade is generally the only grade available. Better fuel economy results from the use of No. 2 grade fuel. In some northern parts of the USA, and in most parts of Canada, No. 1 grade fuel is available in winter, or a winterized blend of No. 2 grade is supplied in winter months. If No. 1 grade is available, it should be used whenever temperatures fall below 20°F (−7°C). Winterized No. 2 grade may also be used at these temperatures. However, unwinterized No. 2 grade should not be used below 20°F (−7°C). Cold temperatures cause unwinterized No. 2 grade to thicken (it actually gels), blocking the fuel lines and preventing the engine from running.

Do not use home heating oil or gasoline in the diesel vehicle. Do not attempt to "thin" unwinterized No. 2 diesel fuel with gasoline. Gasoline or home heating oil will damage the engine and void the manufacturer's warranty.

CAUTION

A mixture of gasoline and diesel fuel produces an extremely potent explosive that is more volatile than gasoline alone.

Engine

OIL CHECK LEVEL

The engine oil should be checked on a regular basis, ideally at each fuel stop. If the vehicle is used for trailer towing or for heavy-duty use, it would be safer to check more often.

When checking the oil level it is best that the oil be at operating temperature, although checking the level immediately after stopping will give a false reading because all of the oil will not have drained back into the crankcase. Be sure the vehicle is resting on a level surface, allowing time for the oil to drain back into the crankcase.

1. Open the hood and locate the dipstick. Remove it from the tube. The oil dipstick is located on the driver's side.
2. Wipe the dipstick with a clean rag.
3. Insert the dipstick fully into the tube and remove it again. Hold the dipstick horizontally and read the oil level. The level should be between the FULL and ADD marks. If the oil level is at or below the ADD mark, oil should be added as necessary. Oil is added through the capped opening on the valve cover(s) on gasoline engines. Diesel engines have a capped oil full tube at the front of the engine. Refer to the "Engine Oil and Fuel Recommendations" in this section for the proper viscosity oil to use.
4. Replace the dipstick and check the level after adding oil. Be careful not to overfill the crankcase. Approximately 1 quart of oil will raise the level from ADD to FULL.

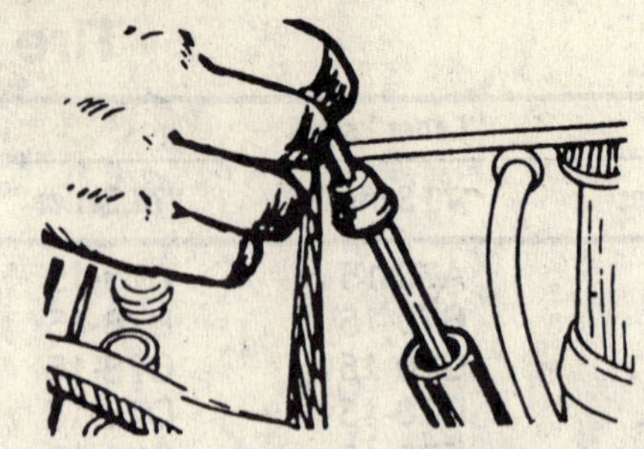

The oil level is checked with the dipstick

The oil level should be between the ADD and FULL marks on the dipstick

OIL AND FILTER CHANGE

Engine oil should be changed every 6000 miles for 1983–87 or 7500 miles for 1988–91 on gasoline engines and every 3000 miles on diesel engines. The oil change and filter replacement interval should be cut in half under conditions such as:

- Driving in dusty conditions.
- Continuous trailer pulling or RV use.
- Extensive or prolonged idling.
- Extensive short trip operation in freezing temperatures (when the engine is not thoroughly warmed-up).
- Frequent long runs at high speed and high ambient temperatures.
- Stop-and-go service such as delivery vehicles.

Operation of the engine in severe conditions such as a dust storm may require an immediate oil and filter change.

Chevrolet and GMC recommend changing both the oil and filter during the first oil change and the filter every other oil change thereafter. For the small price of an oil filter, it's cheap insurance to replace the filter at every oil change. One of the larger filter manufacturers points out in its advertisements that not changing the filter leaves one quart of dirty oil in the engine. This claim is true and should be kept in mind when changing your oil.

NOTE: The oil filter on the diesel engine must be changed every oil change.

To change the oil, the vehicle should be on a level surface and the engine should be at operating temperature. This is to ensure that the foreign matter will be drained away along with the oil and not left in the engine to form sludge. You should have available a container that will hold a minimum of 8 quarts of liquid, a wrench to fit the old drain plug, a spout for pouring in new oil and a rag or 2, which you will always need. If the filter is being replaced, you will also need a band wrench or filter wrench to fit the end of the filter.

NOTE: If the engine is equipped with an oil cooler, this will also have to be drained, using the drain plug. Be sure to add enough oil to fill the cooler in addition to the engine.

1. Position the vehicle on a level surface and set the parking brake or block the wheels. Slide a drain pan under the oil drain plug.

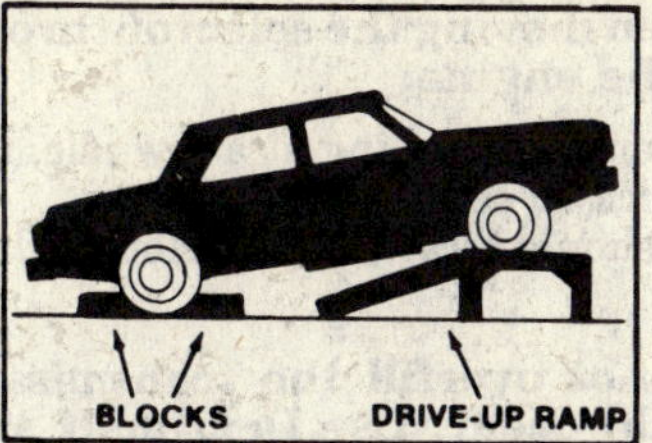

1. Warm the car up before changing your oil. Raise the front end of the car and support it on drive-on ramps or jackstands.

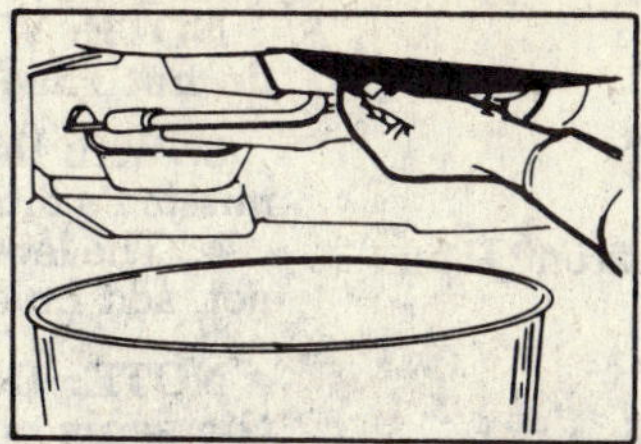

2. Locate the drain plug on the bottom of the oil pan and slide a low flat pan of sufficient capacity under the engine to catch the oil. Loosen the plug with a wrench and turn it out the last few turns by hand. Keep a steady inward pressure on the plug to avoid hot oil from running down your arm.

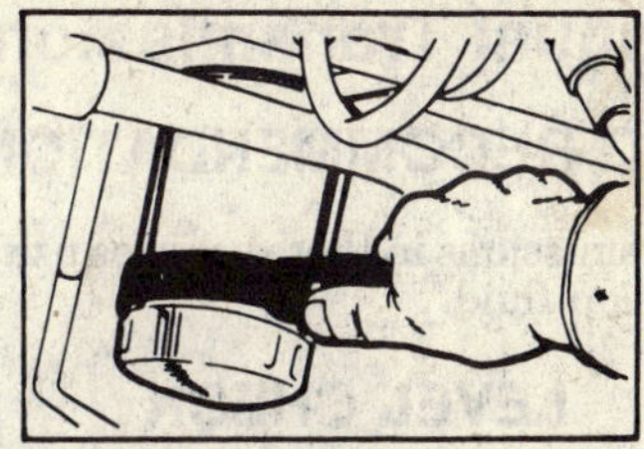

3. Remove the oil filter with a filter wrench. The filter can hold more than a quart of oil, which will be hot. Be sure the gasket comes off with the filter and clean the mounting base on the engine.

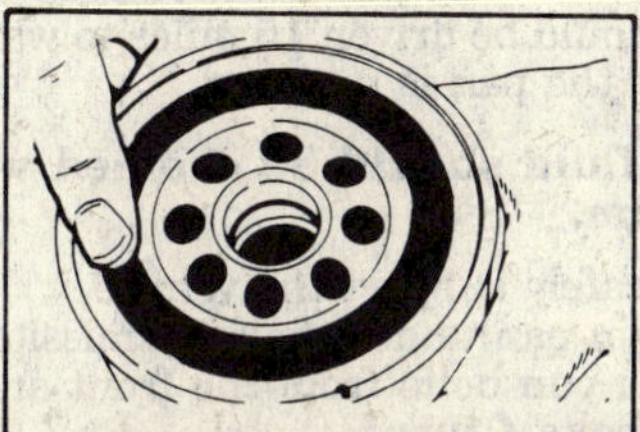

4. Lubricate the gasket on the new filter with clean engine oil. A dry gasket may not make a good seal and will allow the filter to leak.

5. Position a new filter on the mounting base and spin it on by hand. Do not use a wrench. When the gasket contacts the engine, tighten it another ½–1 turn by hand.

6. Using a rag, clean the drain plug and the area around the drain hole in the oil pan.

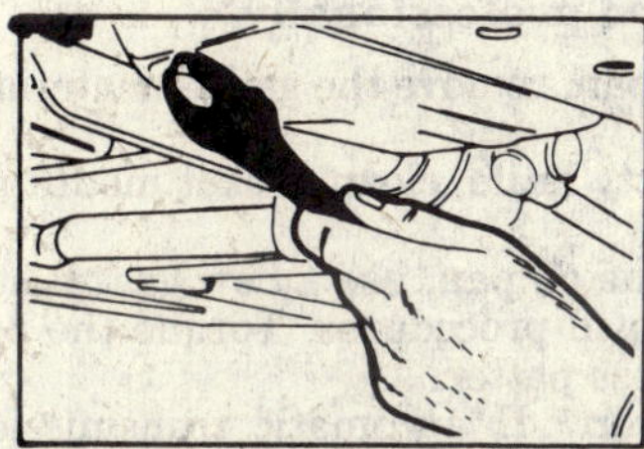

7. Install the drain plug and tighten it finger-tight. If you feel resistance, stop and be sure you are not cross-threading the plug. Finally, tighten the plug with a wrench.

8. Locate the oil cap on the valve cover. An oil spout is the easiest way to add oil, but a funnel will do just as well.

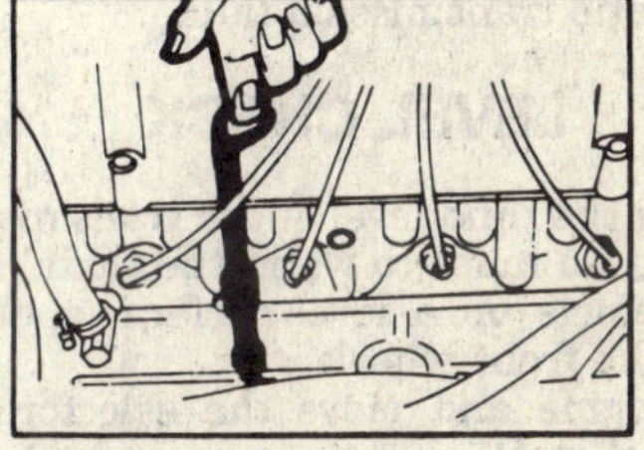

9. Start the engine and check for leaks. The oil pressure warning light will remain on for a few seconds; when it goes out, stop the engine and check the level on the dipstick.

Changing the oil and the filter

2. From under the vehicle, loosen, but do not remove the oil drain plug. Cover your hand with a rag or glove and slowly unscrew the drain plug.

CAUTION

The engine oil will be HOT. Keep your arms, face and hands clear of the oil as it drains out.

3. Remove the plug and let the oil drain into the pan. Do not drop the plug into the drain pan.
4. When all of the oil has drained, clean off the drain plug and reinstall it into pan. Torque the drain plug to 20 ft. lbs. for gasoline or 30 ft. lbs. for diesel engines.
5. Using an oil filter wrench, loosen the oil filter. On most Chevrolet engines, especially the V6s, the oil filter is next to the exhaust pipes. Stay clear of these, since even a passing contact will result in a painful burn.

NOTE: If equipped with catalytic converters stay clear of the converter. The outside temperature of a hot catalytic converter can approach 1200°F (650°C).

6. Cover your hand with a rag and spin the filter off by hand; turn it slowly.
7. Coat the rubber gasket on a new filter with a light film of clean engine oil. Screw the filter onto the mounting stud and tighten it according to the directions on the filter, usually hand-tight one turn past the point where the gasket contacts the mounting base; do not overtighten the filter.
8. Refill the engine with the specified amount of clean engine oil.
9. Run the engine for several minutes, checking for leaks. Check the level of the oil and add oil, if necessary.

When you have finished this job, you will notice that you now possess 4–5 quarts of dirty oil. The best thing to do with it is to pour it into plastic jugs, such as milk or antifreeze containers. Then, locate a service station where you can pour it into their used oil tank for recycling.

NOTE: Pouring used motor oil into a storm drain not only pollutes the environment, it violates Federal law. Dispose of waste oil properly.

Manual Transmission

FLUID RECOMMENDATIONS

All manual transmissions in these vehicles use Dexron® II automatic transmission fluid.

LEVEL CHECK

Remove the filler plug from the passenger's side of the transmission; the upper plug, if the transmission has 2 plugs. The oil should be level with the bottom edge of the filler hole. This should be checked at least once every 6000 miles or more often if any leakage or seepage is observed.

DRAIN AND REFILL

Under normal conditions, the transmission fluid should not be changed. However, if the vehicle is driven in deep water, replace the fluid.

1. Raise and safely support the vehicle.
2. Place a fluid catch pan under the transmission.
3. Remove the bottom plug and drain the fluid.
4. Install the bottom plug and refill the transmission housing.

Automatic Transmission

FLUID RECOMMENDATIONS

When adding fluid or refilling the transmission, use Dexron®II automatic transmission fluid.

LEVEL CHECK

Before checking the fluid level of the transmission, drive the vehicle for at least 15 miles to warm the fluid.

1. Place the vehicle on a level surface, apply the parking brake and block the front wheels.
2. Start the engine and move the selector through each range, then place it in **P**.

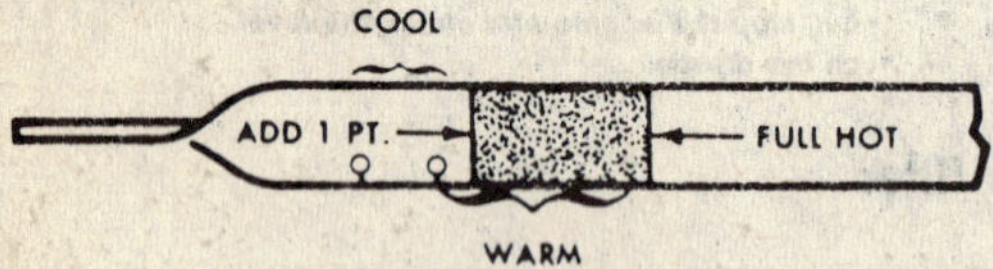

Automatic transmission fluid dipstick

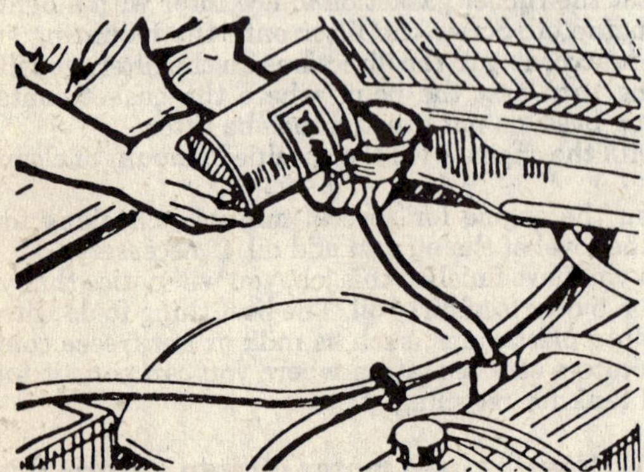

Adding automatic transmission fluid

NOTE: When moving the selector through each range, do not race the engine.

3. With the engine running at a low idle, remove the transmission's dipstick to check the fluid level.
4. The level should be at the Full Hot mark of the dipstick. If not, add fluid.

NOTE: Do not overfill the transmission, damage to the seals could occur. Use Dexron®II automatic transmission fluid. One pint raises the level from ADD to FULL.

DRAIN AND REFILL

The fluid should be changed at 15,000 mile intervals for severe usage or 30,000 mile intervals for light usage.

The vehicle should be driven 15 miles to warm the transmission fluid before the pan is removed.

NOTE: The fluid should be drained while the transmission is warm.

1. Raise and safely support the vehicle.
2. Place a drain pan under the transmission pan.
3. Remove the pan bolts from the front and the sides, then loosen the rear bolts 4 turns.
4. Using a small prybar, pry the pan from the transmission. This will allow the pan to partially drain. Remove the remaining pan bolts and lower the pan from the transmission.

NOTE: If the transmission fluid is dark or has a burnt smell, transmission damage is indicated. Have the transmission checked professionally.

5. Empty the pan, remove the gasket material and clean with a solvent.
6. Using a putty knife, clean gasket mounting surfaces.

To install:

7. To install the oil pan, use a new gasket and sealant, then reverse the removal procedures. Torque the pan bolts to 8 ft. lbs. in a criss-cross pattern.
8. Using Dexron® II automatic transmission fluid, add it through the filler tube. See the Capacities Chart to determine the proper amount of fluid to be added.

NOTE: Do not overfill the transmission. Foaming of the fluid and subsequent transmission damage due to slippage will result.

9. With the gearshift lever in **P**, start the engine and let it idle. Do not race the engine.
10. Apply the parking brake and move the gearshift lever through each position. Return the lever to **Pk** and check the fluid level with the engine idling. The level should be between the 2 dimples on the dipstick, about ¼ in. (6mm) below the ADD mark. Add fluid, if necessary.
11. Check the fluid level after the vehicle has been driven enough to thoroughly warm the transmission.

PAN AND FILTER SERVICE

1. Refer to the Drain and Refill procedures in this section and remove the oil pan.
2. Remove the screen and the filter from the valve body.
3. Install a new filter using a new gasket or O-ring.

NOTE: If the transmission uses a filter having a fully exposed screen, it may be cleaned and reused.

4. To install the oil pan, use a new gasket and sealant, then reverse the removal procedures. Torque the pan bolts to 8 ft. lbs. in a criss-cross pattern. Refill the transmission.

Transfer Case

FLUID RECOMMENDATIONS

When adding fluid or refilling the transfer case, use Dexron®II automatic transmission fluid.

LEVEL CHECK

The transfer case should be checked every 12 months, at 15,000 mile intervals for severe usage or 30,000 mile intervals for light usage, whichever occurs first.

1. Raise and safely support the vehicle (level).
2. At the rear side of the transfer case, remove the filler plug.
3. Using your finger, check the fluid level, it should be level with the bottom of the filler hole.
4. If the fluid level is low, use Dexron®II automatic transmission fluid to bring the fluid up to the proper level.
5. On all except Bravada, install the filler plug and torque it to 30–40 ft. lbs. On Bravada, apply Loctite® to the filler plug and torque it to 80 inch lbs. (9 Nm).

DRAIN AND REFILL

1. Raise and safely support the vehicle.
2. Position drain pan under transfer case.
3. Remove drain and filler plugs, then drain the lubricant into the drain pan.
4. Install drain plug. Except for Bravada, torque the plug to 30–40 ft. lbs. On Bravada, apply Loctite® to the drain plug and torque it to 80 inch lbs. (9 Nm).
5. Remove the drain pan and dump the fluid into a used oil storage tank, for recycling purposes.
6. Using Dexron® II automatic transmission fluid, fill transfer case to edge of filler plug opening.
7. Except for Bravada, install filler plug and torque it to 30–40 ft. lbs. On Bravada, apply Loctite® to the filler plug and torque it to 80 inch lbs. (9 Nm).
8. Lower vehicle and check the operation of the transfer case.

Drive Axle

At least once every 2 years or 30,000 miles, the drive axle(s) should be inspected and refilled with fluid.

No draining of the axle fluid is recommended; be sure to maintain a Full fluid level of ⅜ in. below the filler plug hole.

FLUID RECOMMENDATIONS

Standard Axle

Always use SAE-80W or SAE 80W-90 GL5. Drain and refill the differential at first oil fill, then at every other oil fill.

Locking Axle

NOTE: Never use standard differential lubricant in a positraction differential.

Always use GM part 1052271 gear lubricant. Before refilling the rear axle, add 4 ounces of GM Fluid 1052358. Drain and refill the differential at first oil fill, then at every other oil fill.

LEVEL CHECK

The lubricant level should be checked at each chassis lubrication and maintained at ⅜ in. below the bottom of the filler plug hole.

1. Raise and safely support the vehicle; be sure the vehicle is level.
2. Remove the filler plug, located at the side of the differential carrier.
3. Check the fluid level, it should be ⅜ in. below the bottom of the filler plug hole, add fluid, if necessary.
4. Replace the filler plug.

DRAIN AND REFILL

Refer to Fluid Recommendations in this section for information on when to change the fluid.

Rear Axle

1. Run the vehicle until the lubricant reaches operating temperature.
2. Raise and safely support the vehicle; be sure the vehicle is level.
3. Using a floor jack, support the drive axle. Position a drain pan under the rear axle.
4. Remove the cover from the rear of the drive axle and drain the lubricant.
5. Using a putty knife, clean the gasket mounting surfaces.
6. To install, use a new gasket, sealant and reverse the removal procedures.
7. Torque the cover-to-rear axle bolts in a criss-cross pattern to 20 ft. lbs. Using a suction gun or a squeeze bulb, install the fluid through the filler plug hole. Install the filler plug.

Front Axle

1. Run the vehicle until the lubricant reaches operating temperature.
2. Raise and safely support the vehicle; be sure the vehicle is level.
3. Using a floor jack, support the front axle. Position a drain pan under the front axle.
4. Remove the drain plug from the right side of the front axle and drain the lubricant.
5. Remove the filler plug.
6. To install the drain plug, use a sealant and torque the plug to 24 ft. lbs. (33 Nm).
7. Using a suction gun or a squeeze bulb, install the fluid through the filler plug hole.
8. Using sealant, coat the filler plug threads and torque the plug to 24 ft. lbs. (33 Nm).

Cooling System

At least once every 2 years or 30,000 miles, the engine cooling system should be inspected, flushed and refilled with fresh coolant. If the coolant is left in the system too long, it loses its ability to prevent rust and corrosion. If the coolant has too much water, it won't protect against freezing.

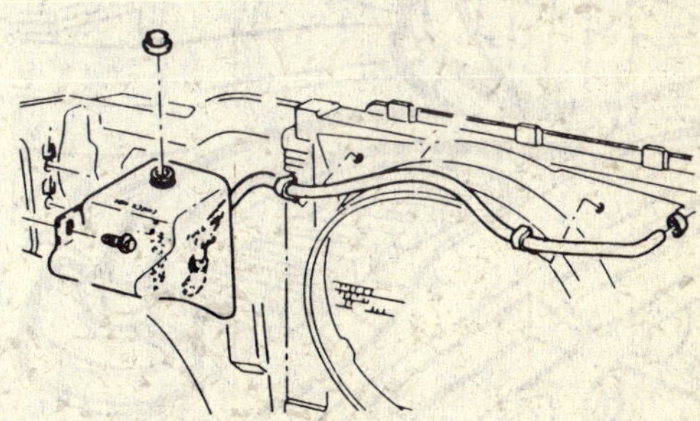

View of the (see through) coolant recovery tank—cooling system

FLUID RECOMMENDATIONS

Using a good quality of ethylene glycol antifreeze (one that will not effect aluminum), mix it with water until a 50–50 antifreeze solution is attained.

LEVEL CHECK

NOTE: When checking the coolant level, the radiator need not be removed, simply check the coolant tank.

Check the coolant recovery bottle (see through plastic bottle). With the engine Cold, the coolant should be at the ADD mark (recovery tank ¼ full). With the engine warm, the coolant should be at the FULL mark (recovery tank ½ full). If necessary, add fluid to the recovery bottle.

DRAIN AND REFILL

CAUTION

To avoid injuries from scalding fluid and steam, do not remove the radiator cap while the engine and radiator are still HOT.

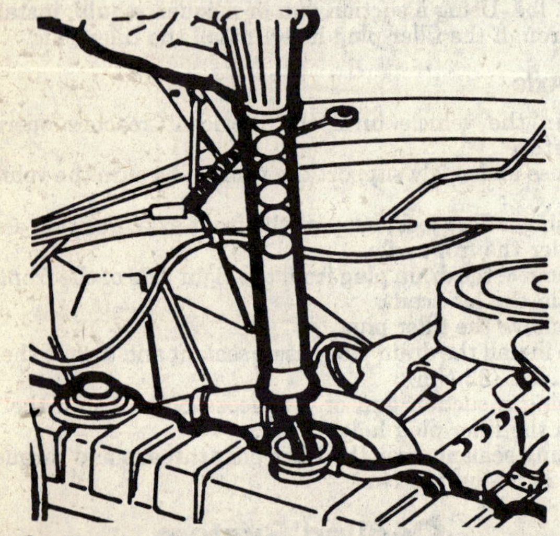

Coolant protection can be checked with a simple, float-type tester

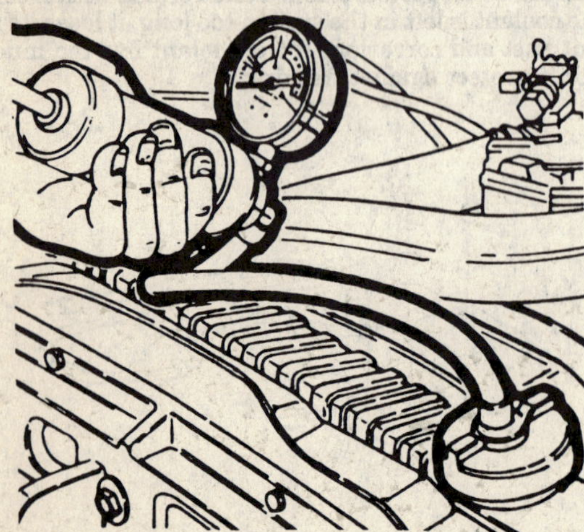

The system should be pressure tested at least once a year

1. When the engine is cool, remove the radiator cap using the following procedures.
   a. Slowly rotate the cap counterclockwise to the detent.
   b. If any residual pressure is present, WAIT until the hissing noise stops.
   c. After the hissing noise has ceased, press down on the cap and continue rotating it counterclockwise to remove it.
2. Place a fluid catch pan under the radiator, open the radiator drain valve and the engine drain plugs, then drain the coolant.

CAUTION

When draining the coolant, keep in mind that cats and dogs are attracted by the ethylene glycol antifreeze, and are quite likely to drink any that is left in an uncovered container or in puddles on the ground. This will prove fatal in sufficient quantity. Always drain the coolant into a sealable container. Coolant should be reused unless it is contaminated or several years old.

3. Close the drain valve and install the engine drain plugs.
4. Empty the coolant reservoir and flush it.
5. Using the correct mixture of antifreeze, fill the radiator to the bottom of the filler neck and the coolant tank to the FULL mark.
6. Install the radiator cap; make sure the arrows align with the overflow tube.
7. Run the engine until it reaches the operating temperatures, allow it to cool, then check the fluid level and add fluid, if necessary.

FLUSHING AND CLEANING THE SYSTEM

1. Refer to the Drain and Refill procedures in this section, then drain the cooling system.

NOTE: Always drain the coolant into a sealable container. Coolant should be reused unless it is contaminated or several years old.

2. Close the drain valve and install the engine drain plugs, then add sufficient water to the cooling system.
3. Run the engine, then drain and refill the system. Perform this procedure several times, until the fluid (drained from the system) is clear.
4. Empty the coolant reservoir and flush it.
5. Using the correct mixture of antifreeze, fill the radiator to the bottom of the filler neck and the coolant tank to the FULL mark.
6. Install the radiator cap; make sure the arrows align with the overflow tube.

Master Cylinder

The vehicles are equipped with a dual braking system, allowing a vehicle to be brought to a safe stop in the event of failure in either the front or rear brakes. The dual master cylinder has 2 entirely separate reservoirs, one connected to the front brakes and the other connected to the rear brakes. In the event of failure in either portion, the remaining part is not affected.

FLUID RECOMMENDATIONS

Use only heavy-duty Delco Supreme 11 or DOT-3 brake fluid.

NOTE: Brake fluid damages paint. It also absorbs moisture from the air; never leave a container or the master cylinder uncovered any longer than necessary. All parts in contact with the brake fluid (master cylinder, hoses, plunger assemblies and etc.) must be kept clean, since any contamination of the brake fluid will adversely affect braking performance.

View of the master cylinder reservoir

LEVEL CHECK

The brake fluid level should be inspected every 6 months.
1. Remove the master cylinder reservoir cap.

NOTE: If equipped with a see through reservoir, it is not necessary to remove the reservoir cap unless you are adding fluid.

2. The fluid should be ¼ in. (6mm) from top of the reservoir, if necessary, add fluid.
3. Replace the reservoir caps.

Hydraulic Clutch

NOTE: The clutch master cylinder is mounted on the firewall next to the brake master cylinder.

FLUID RECOMMENDATIONS

Use heavy duty Delco Supreme 11 or any brand-name DOT-3 brake fluid.

LEVEL CHECK

The hydraulic clutch reservoir should be checked at least every 6 months. Fill to the line on the reservoir.

Power Steering Pump

The power steering pump reservoir is located at the front left-side of the engine.

FLUID RECOMMENDATIONS

Use GM Power Steering Fluid No. 1050017 or equivalent.

NOTE: Avoid using automatic transmission fluid in the power steering unit, except in an emergency.

LEVEL CHECK

The power steering fluid should be checked at least every 6 months. There is a COLD and a HOT mark on the dipstick. The fluid should be checked when the engine is warm and turned OFF. If necessary, add fluid to the power steering pump reservoir.

NOTE: On models equipped with a remote reservoir, the fluid level should be ½–1 in. (25.4mm) from the top when the wheels are turned to the extreme left position.

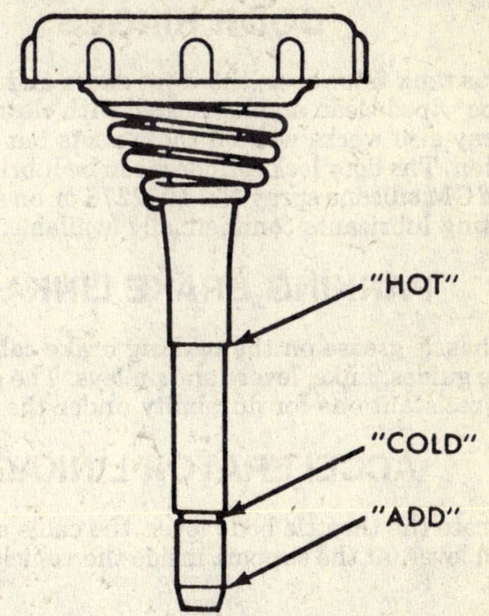

View of the power steering dipstick

Manual Steering Gear

The steering gear is factory-filled with a lubricant which does not require seasonal change. The housing should not be drained; no lubrication is required for the life of the gear.

FLUID RECOMMENDATIONS

Use GM steering gear lubricant No. 1052182 or equivalent.

LEVEL CHECK

The steering lubricant should be checked every 6 months or 7500 miles.

The gear should be inspected for seal leakage when specified in the "Maintenance" chart. Look for solid grease, not an oily film. If a seal is replaced or the gear overhauled, it should be refilled with lubricant.

Chassis Greasing

Chassis greasing should be performed every 6 months or 7500 miles, it can be performed with a commercial pressurized grease gun or at home by using a hand operated grease gun. Wipe the grease fittings clean before greasing in order to prevent the possibility of forcing any dirt into the component.

The 4-wheel drive front driveshaft requires special attention for lubrication. The large constant velocity joint at the front of the transfer case has a special grease fitting in the centering ball; a special needle nose adapter for a flush type fitting is required, as well as a special lubricant, GM part No. 1050679. You can only get at this fitting when it is facing up toward the floorboard, so you need a flexible hose, too.

Water resistant EP chassis lubricant (grease) conforming to GM specification 6031-M should be used for all chassis grease points.

Body Lubrication and Maintenance

HOOD LATCH AND HINGES

Clean the latch surfaces and apply clean engine oil to the latch pilot bolts and the spring anchor. Use the engine oil to lubricate the hood hinges as well. Use a chassis grease to lubricate all the pivot points in the latch release mechanism.

DOOR HINGES

The gas tank filler door, the front doors and rear door hinges should be wiped clean and lubricated with clean engine oil. Silicone spray also works well on these parts but must be applied more often. The door lock cylinders can be lubricated easily with a shot of GM silicone spray No. 1052276 or one of the many dry penetrating lubricants commercially available.

PARKING BRAKE LINKAGE

Use chassis grease on the parking brake cable where it contacts the guides, links, levers and pulleys. The grease should be a water resistant one for durability under the vehicle.

ACCELERATOR LINKAGE

Lubricate the throttle body lever, the cable and the accelerator pedal lever (at the support inside the vehicle) with clean engine oil.

TRANSMISSION SHIFT LINKAGE

Lubricate the shift linkage with water resistant chassis grease which meets GM specification No. 6031M or equivalent.

Front Wheel Bearings—2WD Only

Once every 30,000 miles, clean and repack wheel bearings with a GM Wheel Bearing Grease No. 1051344 or equivalent. Use only enough grease to completely coat the rollers. Remove any excess grease from the exposed surface of the hub and seal.

REMOVAL, PACKING AND INSTALLATION

NOTE: The following procedures require the use of GM tools No. J-29117, J-8092, J-8850, J-8457, J-9746-02 or equivalent.

1. Raise and support the vehicle on jackstands.
2. Remove the tire/wheel assembly.
3. Remove the caliper-to-steering knuckle bolts and the caliper from the steering knuckle. Using a wire, support the caliper from the vehicle; do not disconnect the brake line.
4. From the hub/disc assembly, remove the dust cap, the cotter pin, the spindle nut, the thrust washer and the outer bearing.
5. Grasping the hub/disc assembly firmly, pull the assembly from the axle spindle.
6. Using a small prybar, pry the grease seal from the rear of the hub/disc assembly, then remove the inner bearing.

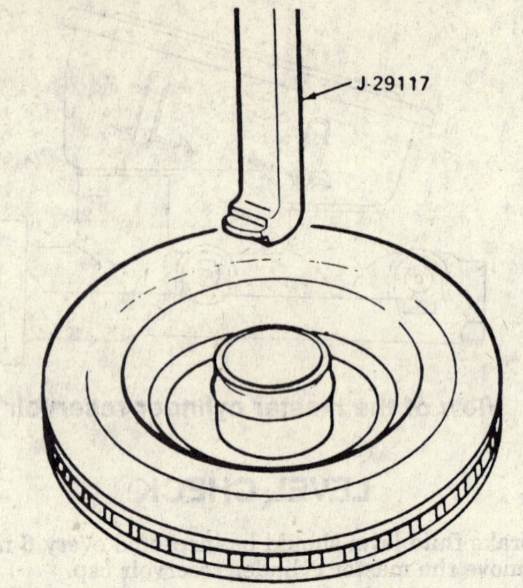

Removing the bearing race from the front wheel hub—2WD

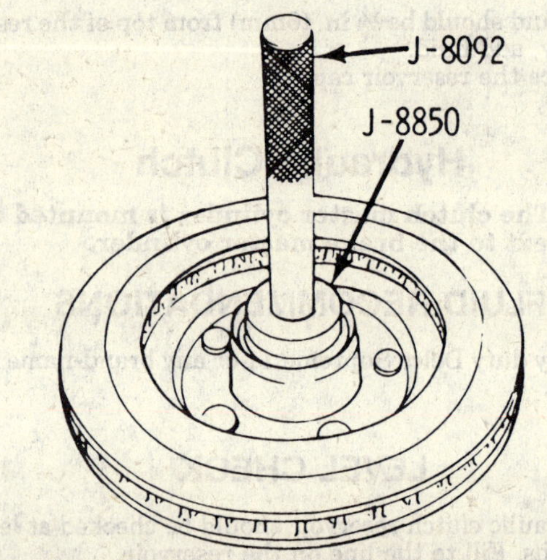

Installing the inner bearing outer race—2WD

NOTE: Do not remove the bearing races from the hub, unless they show signs of damage.

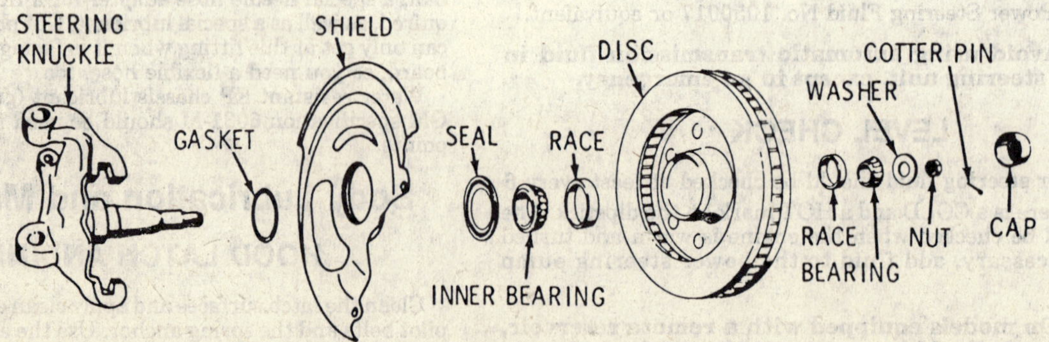

Exploded view of the front wheel bearing assembly— 2WD

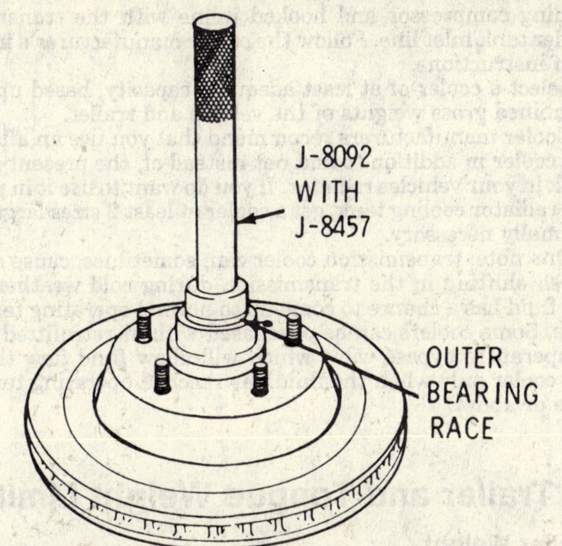

Install the outer bearing outer race—2WD

7. If it is necessary to remove the wheel bearing races, use the GM front bearing race removal tool J-29117 or equivalent, to drive the races from the hub/disc assembly.
8. Using solvent, clean the grease from all of the parts, then blow them dry with compressed air.
9. Inspect all of the parts for scoring, pitting or cracking, replace the parts, if necessary.

To install:

10. If the bearing races were removed, perform the following procedures to the install the them:
    a. Using grease, lightly lubricate the inside of the hub/disc assembly.
    b. Using the GM seal installation tools J-8092 and J-8850 or equivalent, drive the inner bearing race into the hub/disc assembly until it seats.

NOTE: When installing the bearing races, be sure to support the hub/disc assembly with GM tool J-9746-02 or equivalent.

    c. Using the GM seal installation tools J-8092 and J-8457 or equivalent, drive the outer race into the hub/disc assembly until it seats.
11. Using wheel bearing grease, lubricate the bearings, the races and the spindle; be sure to place a gob of grease (inside the hub/disc assembly) between the races to provide an ample supply of lubricant.

NOTE: To lubricate each bearing, place a gob of grease in the palm of the hand, then roll the bearing through the grease until it is well lubricated.

12. Place the inner wheel bearing into the hub/disc assembly. Using a flat plate, drive the new grease seal into the rear of the hub/disc assembly until it is flush with the outer surface.
13. Onto the spindle, install the hub/disc assembly, the thrust washer and the hub nut. While turning the wheel, torque the hub nut to 16 ft. lbs. until the bearings seat. Loosen the nut, retighten it and back it off until the nearest nut slot aligns with a spindle hole (not more than a ½ turn).
14. Install a new cotter pin through the nut and the spindle, then bend the ends and cut off the excess pin. Install the grease cap.
15. If necessary, use a dial indicator to the check the rotor endplay. The endplay should be 0.001–0.005 in. (0.025–0.127mm); if not, readjust the hub/disc assembly.
16. Install the caliper onto the steering knuckle and torque the bolts to 37 ft. lbs. Road test the vehicle.

TRAILER TOWING

These vehicles are popular as trailer towing vehicles. Their strong construction and variety of power train combinations make them ideal for towing campers, boat trailers and utility trailers.

Factory trailer towing packages are available on most vehicles. However, if you are installing a trailer hitch and wiring on your vehicle, there are a few things you ought to know.

General Recommendations

Wiring

Wiring the vehicle for towing is fairly easy. There are a number of good wiring kits available and these should be used, rather than trying to design your own. All trailers will need brake lights, turn signals, tail lights and side marker lights. Most states require extra marker lights for overwide trailers. Also, most states have recently required back-up lights for trailers and most trailer manufacturers have been building trailers with back-up lights for several years.

Additionally, some Class I, most Class II and just about all Class III trailers will have electric brakes.

Add to this number an accessories wire, to operate the trailer internal equipment or to charge the trailer's battery and you can have as many as seven wires in the harness.

Determine the equipment on your trailer and buy the wiring kit necessary. The kit will contain all the wires needed, plus a plug adapter set which included the female plug, mounted on the bumper or hitch and the male plug, wired into or plugged into the trailer harness.

When installing the kit, follow the manufacturer's instructions. The color coding of the wires is standard throughout the industry.

One point to note: some domestic vehicles and most imported vehicles, have separate turn signals. On most domestic vehicles, the brake lights and rear turn signals operate with the same bulb. For those vehicles with separate turn signals, you can purchase an isolation unit so the brake lights won't blink whenever the turn signals are operated or you can go to your local electronics supply house and buy 4 diodes to wire in series with the brake and turn signal bulbs. Diodes will isolate the brake and turn signals. The choice is yours. The isolation units are simple and quick to install but far more expensive than the diodes. The diodes, however, require more work to install properly, since they require the cutting of each bulb's wire and soldering in place of the diode.

One, final point, the best kits are those with a spring loaded cover on the vehicle mounted socket. This cover prevents dirt and moisture from corroding the terminals. Never let the vehicle socket hang loosely; always mount it securely to the bumper or hitch.

Cooling

ENGINE

One of the most common, if not the most common, problems associated with trailer towing is engine overheating.

With factory installed trailer towing packages, a heavy duty cooling system is usually included. Heavy duty cooling systems are available as optional equipment on most vehicles, with or without a trailer package. If you have one of these extra capacity systems, you shouldn't have overheating problems.

If you have a standard cooling system, without an expansion tank, you'll definitely need to get an aftermarket expansion tank kit, preferably one with at least a 2 quart capacity. These kits are easily installed on the radiator's overflow hose and come with a pressure cap designed for expansion tanks.

Another helpful accessory is a Flex Fan. These fan are large diameter units are designed to provide more air flow at low speeds, with blades that have deeply cupped surfaces. The blades then flex or flatten out, at high speed, when less cooling air is needed. These fans are far lighter in weight than stock fans, requiring less horsepower to drive them. Also, they are far quieter than stock fans.

If you do decide to replace your stock fan with a flex fan, note that if your vehicle has a fan clutch, a spacer between the flex fan and water pump hub will be needed.

Aftermarket engine oil coolers are helpful for prolonging engine oil life and reducing overall engine temperatures. Both of these factors increase engine life.

While not absolutely necessary in towing Class I and some Class II trailers, they are recommended for heavier Class II and all Class III towing.

Engine oil cooler systems consist of an adapter, screwed on in place of the oil filter, a remote filter mounting and a multi-tube, a finned heat exchanger, which is mounted in front of the radiator or air conditioning condenser.

TRANSMISSION

An automatic transmission is usually recommended for trailer towing. Modern automatics have proven reliable and, of course, easy to operate, in trailer towing.

The increased load of a trailer, however, causes an increase in the temperature of the automatic transmission fluid. Heat is the worst enemy of an automatic transmission. As the temperature of the fluid increases, the life of the fluid decreases.

It is essential, therefore, that you install an automatic transmission cooler.

The cooler, which consists of a multi-tube, finned heat exchanger, is usually installed in front of the radiator or air conditioning compressor and hooked inline with the transmission cooler tank inlet line. Follow the cooler manufacturer's installation instructions.

Select a cooler of at least adequate capacity, based upon the combined gross weights of the vehicle and trailer.

Cooler manufacturers recommend that you use an aftermarket cooler in addition to and not instead of, the present cooling tank in your vehicles radiator. If you do want to use it in place of the radiator cooling tank, get a cooler at least 2 sizes larger than normally necessary.

One note: transmission cooler can, sometimes, cause slow or harsh shifting in the transmission during cold weather, until the fluid has a chance to come up to normal operating temperature. Some coolers can be purchased with or retrofitted with a temperature bypass valve which will allow fluid flow through the cooler only when the fluid has reached operating temperature or above.

Trailer and Tongue Weight Limits

Trailer Weight

Trailer weight is the first, and most important, factor in determining whether or not your vehicle is suitable for towing the trailer you have in mind. The horsepower-to-weight ratio should be calculated. The basic standard is a ratio of 35:1. That is, 35 lbs. of GVW for every horsepower.

To calculate this ratio, multiply you engine's rated horsepower by 35, then subtract the weight of the vehicle, including passengers and luggage. The resulting figure is the ideal maximum trailer weight that you can tow. One point to consider: a numerically higher axle ratio can offset what appears to be a low trailer weight. If the weight of the trailer that you have in mind is somewhat higher than the weight you just calculated, you might consider changing your rear axle ratio to compensate.

Hitch Weight

There are 3 kinds of hitches: bumper mounted, frame mounted and load equalizing.

Bumper mounted hitches are those which attach solely to the vehicle's bumper. Many states prohibit towing with this type of hitch, when it attaches to the vehicle's stock bumper, since it subjects the bumper to stresses for which it was not designed. After market rear step bumpers, designed for trailer towing, are acceptable for use with bumper mounted hitches.

Frame mounted hitches can be of the type which bolts to 2 or more points on the frame, plus the bumper or just to several points on the frame. Frame mounted hitches can also be of the tongue type, for Class I towing or of the receiver type, for classes II and III.

Load equalizing hitches are usually used for large trailers. Most equalizing hitches are welded in place, they use equalizing bars and chains to level the vehicle after the trailer is connected.

The bolt-on hitches are the most common, since they are relatively easy to install.

Check the gross weight rating of your trailer. Tongue weight is usually figured as 10 percent of gross trailer weight. Therefore, a trailer with a maximum gross weight of 2000 lbs. will have a maximum tongue weight of 200 lbs. Class I trailers fall into this category. Class II trailers are those with a gross weight rating of 2000–3500 lbs., while Class III trailers fall into the 3500–6000 lbs. category. Class IV trailers are those over 6000 lbs. and are for use with 5th wheel vehicles, only.

When you've determined the hitch that you'll need, follow the manufacturer's installation instructions, exactly, especially when it comes to fastener torques. The hitch will subjected to a lot of stress and good hitches come with hardened bolts. Never substitute an inferior bolt for a hardened bolt.

PUSHING AND TOWING

CAUTION

Pushing or tow your vehicle to start it may result in unusually high catalytic converter and exhaust system temperatures, which under extreme conditions may ignite the interior floor covering material above the converter.

Pushing

Vehicles with manual transmissions can be push started.

To push start, make sure both bumpers are in reasonable alignment. Turn the ignition switch ON and engage High gear. Depress the clutch pedal. When a speed of about 10 mph is reached, slightly depress the gas pedal and slowly release the clutch. The engine should start.

NOTE: Automatic transmission equipped vehicles cannot be started by pushing.

Towing

The vehicles can be towed on all 4 wheels (flat towed) at speeds of less than 35 mph for distances less than 50 miles, providing that the axle, driveline and engine/transmission are operable. The transmission should be in Neutral, the engine should be OFF, the steering column unlocked, and the parking brake released.

Do not attach chains to the bumpers or bracketing. All attachments must be made to the structural members. Safety chains should be used. it should also be remembered that power steering and brake assists will not be working with the engine off.

The rear wheels must be raised off the ground or the driveshaft disconnected when the transmission is not operating properly or when speeds or over 35 mph will be used or when towing more than 50 miles.

CAUTION

If a vehicle is towed on its front wheels only, the steering wheel must be secured with the wheels in a straight ahead position.

JUMP STARTING

The following procedure is recommended by the manufacturer. Be sure the booster battery is 12 volt with negative ground. Follow this procedure exactly to avoid possible damage to the electrical system, especially on models equipped with computerized engine controls.

CAUTION

Do not attempt this procedure on a frozen battery; it will probably explode. Do not attempt it on a sealed Delco Freedom battery showing a light color in the charge indicator. Be certain to observe correct polarity connections. Failure to do so will result in almost immediate computer, alternator and regulator destruction. Never allow the jumper cable ends to touch each other.

1. Position the vehicles so they are not touching. Set the parking brake and place automatic transmission in **P** and manual transmission in Neutral. Turn OFF the lights, heater and other electrical loads. Turn both ignition switches OFF.
2. Remove the vent caps from both the booster and discharged battery. Lay a cloth over the open vent cells of each battery. This isn't necessary on batteries equipped with sponge type flame arrestor caps and it isn't possible on sealed batteries.
3. Attach one cable to the positive terminal of the booster battery and the other end to the positive terminal of the discharged battery.

NOTE: If you are attempting to start a vehicle with the diesel engine, it is suggested that this connection be made to the battery on the driver's side of the vehicle, because this battery is closer to the starter and thus the resistance of the electrical cables is lower. From this point on, ignore the other battery in the vehicle.

CAUTION

Do not attempt to jump start the vehicle with a 24 volt power source.

4. Attach one end of the remaining cable to the negative terminal of the booster battery and the other end to a good ground. Do not attach to the negative terminal of discharged batteries. Do not lean over the battery when making this last connection.
5. Start the engine of the vehicle with the booster battery. Start the engine of the vehicle with the discharged battery. If the engine will not start, disconnect the batteries as soon as possible. If this is not done, the 2 batteries will soon reach a state of equilibrium, with both too weak to start an engine. This will not be a problem of the engine of the booster vehicle is kept running fast enough. Lengthy cranking can also overheat and damage the starter.
6. Reverse the above steps to disconnect the booster and discharge batteries. Be certain to remove negative connections first.
7. Reinstall the vent caps. Dispose of the cloths; they may have battery acid on them.

CAUTION

The use of any "hot shot" type of jumper system in excess of 12 volts can damage the electronic control units or cause the discharged battery to explode.

JUMP STARTING A DEAD BATTERY

The chemical reaction in a battery produces explosive hydrogen gas. This is the safe way to jump start a dead battery, reducing the chances of an accidental spark that could cause an explosion.

Jump Starting Precautions

1. Be sure both batteries are of the same voltage.
2. Be sure both batteries are of the same polarity (have the same grounded terminal).
3. Be sure the vehicles are not touching.
4. Be sure the vent cap holes are not obstructed.
5. Do not smoke or allow sparks around the battery.
6. In cold weather, check for frozen electrolyte in the battery. Do not jump start a frozen battery.
7. Do not allow electrolyte on your skin or clothing.
8. Be sure the electrolyte is not frozen.

CAUTION: Make certin that the ignition key, in the vehicle with the dead battery, is in the OFF position. Connecting cables to vehicles with on-board computers will result in computer destruction if the key is not in the OFF position.

Jump Starting Procedure

1. Determine voltages of the two batteries; they must be the same.
2. Bring the starting vehicle close (they must not touch) so that the batteries can be reached easily.
3. Turn off all accessories and both engines. Put both vehicles in Neutral or Park and set the handbrake.
4. Cover the cell caps with a rag—do not cover terminals.
5. If the terminals on the run-down battery are heavily corroded, clean them.
6. Identify the positive and negative posts on both batteries and connect the cables in the order shown.
7. Start the engine of the starting vehicle and run it at fast idle. Try to start the car with the dead battery. Crank it for no more than 10 seconds at a time and let it cool for 20 seconds in between tries.
8. If it doesn't start in 3 tries, there is something else wrong.
9. Disconnect the cables in the reverse order.
10. Replace the cell covers and dispose of the rags.

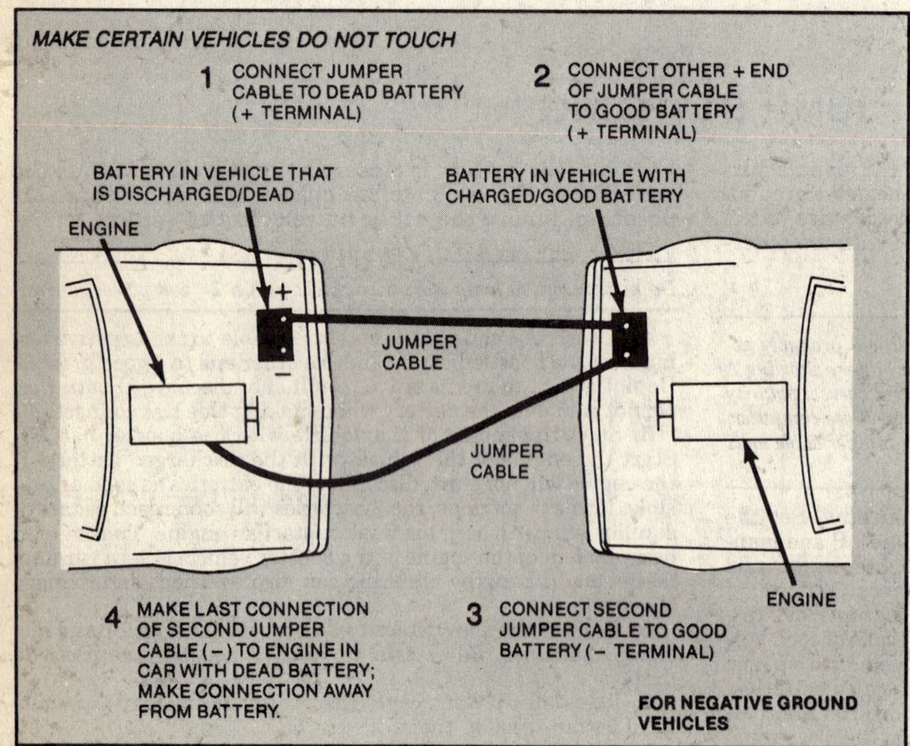

Side terminal batteries occasionally pose a problem when connecting jumper cables. There frequently isn't enough room to clamp the cables without touching sheet metal. Side terminal adaptors are available to alleviate this problem and should be removed after use

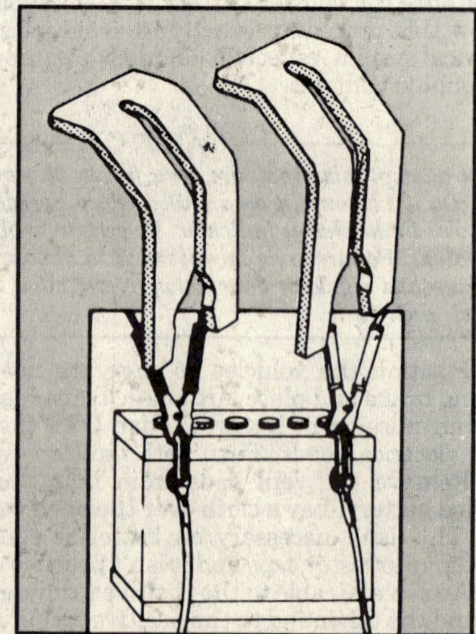

JACKING

The jack supplied with the vehicle is meant for changing tires. It was not meant to support the vehicle while you crawl under it and work. Whenever it is necessary to get under a vehicle to perform service operations, always be sure it is adequately supported, by jackstands at the proper points. Always block the wheels when changing tires.

If your vehicle is equipped with a Positraction rear axle, do not run the engine for any reason with one rear wheel off the ground. Power will be transmitted through the rear wheel remaining on the ground, possibly causing the vehicle to drive itself off the jack.

Some of the service operations in this book require that one or both ends of the vehicle be raised and supported safely. The best arrangement for this, of course, is a grease pit or a vehicle lift but these items are seldom found in the home garage. However, small hydraulic, screw, or scissors jacks are satisfactory for raising the vehicle.

Heavy wooden blocks or adjustable jackstands should be used to support the vehicle while it is being worked on. Drive-on trestles or ramps are also a handy and a safe way to raise the vehicle, assuming their capacity is adequate. These can be bought or constructed from suitable heavy timbers or steel.

In any case, it is always best to spend a little extra time to make sure your vehicle is lifted and supported safely.

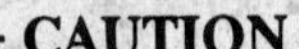

CAUTION

Concrete blocks are not recommended. They may crumble if the load is not evenly distributed. Boxes and milk crates of any description must not be used. Shake the vehicle a few times to make sure the jackstands are securely supporting the weight before crawling under.

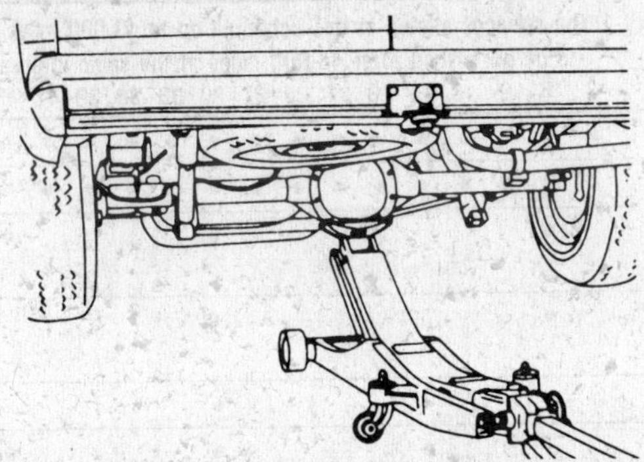

Using the rear axle to lift the rear of the vehicle

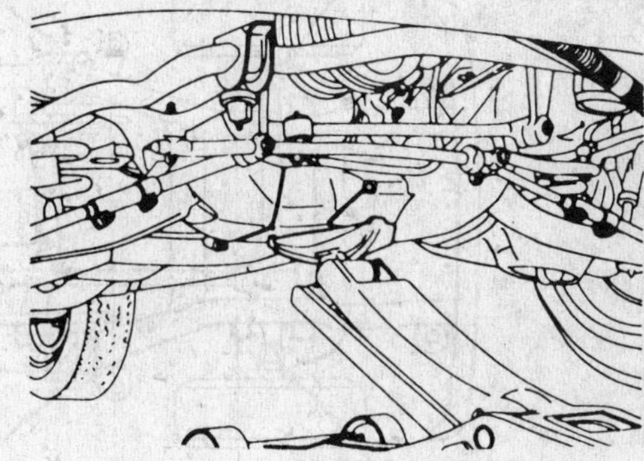

Using the crossmember to lift the front of the vehicle

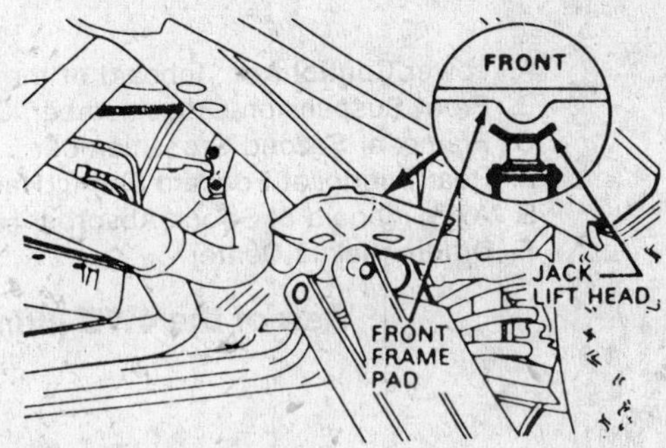

Using the front frame pad to lift the side of the vehicle

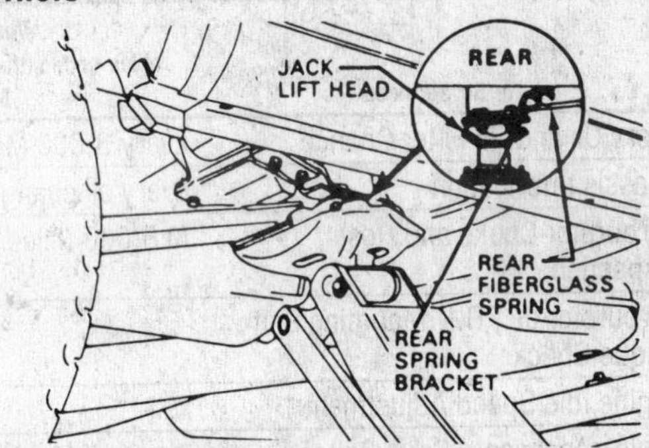

Using the rear spring bracket to lift the side of the vehicle

A. Lower Control Arm; Inboard of the Lower Ball Joint
B. Front Suspension Crossmember; Center
C. Frame; at Second Crossmember
D. Rear Spring; at Forward Spring Hanger
E. Axle; Inboard of Shock Absorber Hanger
F. Differential; at Center

Vehicle Jack or Floor Jack

Floor Jack

Hoist

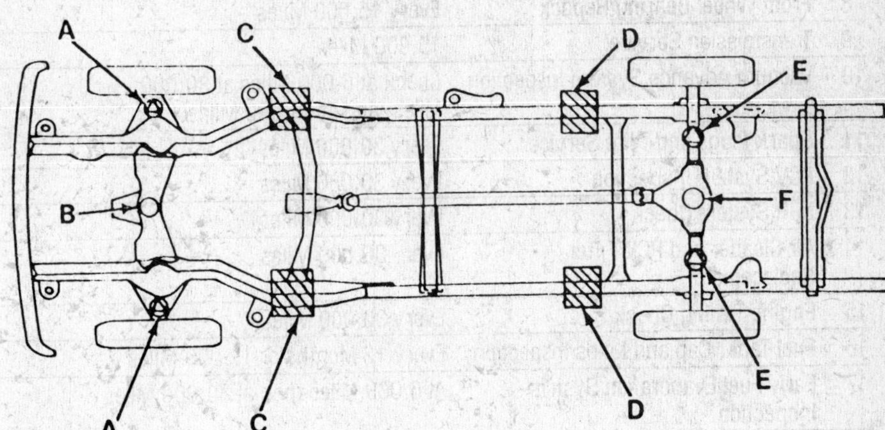

View of the 2WD lifting points—Blazer and Jimmy

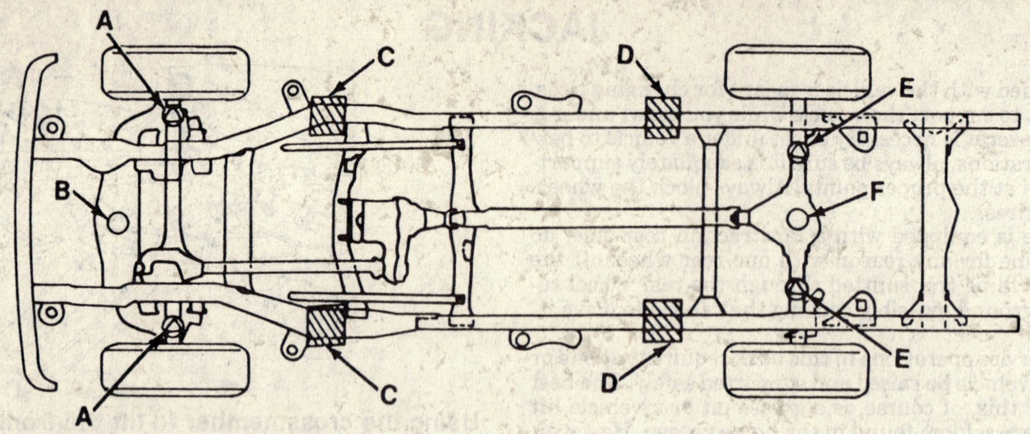

A. Lower Control Arm; Inboard of the Lower Ball Joint
B. Front Suspension Crossmember; Center
C. Frame; at Second Crossmember
D. Rear Spring; at Forward Spring Hanger
E. Axle; Inboard of Shock Absorber Hanger
F. Differential; at Center

△ Vehicle Jack or Floor Jack
○ Floor Jack
 Hoist

View of the 4WD lifting points—Blazer, Bravada and Jimmy

MAINTENANCE INTERVALS SCHEDULE I ①

Item No.	To Be Serviced	When to Perform Miles or Months, Whichever Occurs First Miles (000)	The services shown in this schedule up to 48,000 miles are to be performed after 48,000 miles at the same intervals															
			3	6	9	12	15	18	21	24	27	30	33	36	39	42	45	48
1	Every Oil and Oil Filter Change	Every 3,000 Miles or 3 Months	•	•	•	•	•	•	•	•	•	•	•	•	•	•	•	•
2	Chassis Lubrication	Every oil change	•	•	•	•	•	•	•	•	•	•	•	•	•	•	•	•
3	Carburetor Choke and Hose Inspection	At 6,000 Miles, then at 30,000 Miles		•								•					•	
4	Carburetor or T.B.I. Mounting Bolt Torque Check			•								•						
5	Engine Idle Speed Adjustment			•								•						
6	Engine Accessory Drive Belts Inspection	Every 12 Months or 15,000 Miles					•					•					•	
7	Cooling System Service	Every 24 Months or 30,000 Miles										•						
8	Front Wheel Bearing Repack	Every 15,000 Miles					•					•					•	
9	Transmission Service	15,000 Miles					•					•						
10	Vacuum Advance System Inspection	Check at 6,000 Miles at 30,000 Miles, and at 45,000 Miles		•								•					•	
11	Spark Plugs and Wire Service	Every 30,000 Miles										•						
12	PCV System Inspection	Every 30,000 Miles										•						
13	EGR System Check	Every 30,000 Miles										•						
14	Air Cleaner and PCV Filter Replacement	Every 30,000 Miles										•						
15	Engine Timing Check	Every 30,000 Miles										•						
16	Fuel Tank, Cap and Lines Inspection	Every 12 Months or 15,000 Miles					•					•					•	
17	Early Fuel Evaporation System Inspection	At 6,000 Miles then at 30,000 Miles		•								•						

MAINTENANCE INTERVALS SCHEDULE I ①

Item No.	To Be Serviced	When to Perform Miles or Months, Whichever Occurs First Miles (000)	The services shown in this schedule up to 48,000 miles are to be performed after 48,000 miles at the same intervals															
			3	6	9	12	15	18	21	24	27	30	33	36	39	42	45	48
18	Evaporative Control System Inspection	At 30,000 Miles										•						
19	Fuel Filter Replacement	Every 15,000 Miles					•					•					•	
20	Valve Lash Adjustment	Every 15,000 Miles					•					•					•	
21	Thermostatically Controlled Air Cleaner Inspection	Every 30,000 Miles										•						

SCHEDULE II ②

Item No.	To Be Serviced	When to Perform Miles or Months, Whichever Occurs First Miles (000)	The services shown in this schedule up to 60,000 miles are to be performed after 60,000 miles at the same intervals							
			7.5	15	22.5	30	37.5	45	52.5	60
1	Engine Oil Change	Every 7,500 Miles or 12 Months	•	•	•	•	•	•	•	•
	Oil Filter Change	At First and Every Other Oil Change or 12 Months	•		•		•		•	
2	Chassis Lubrication	Every oil change	•	•	•	•	•	•	•	•
3	Carburetor Choke and Hoses Inspection	At 6 Months or 7,500 Miles and at 60,000 Miles	•			•				•
4	Carburetor or T.B.I. Mounting Bolt Torque Check	At 6 Months or 7,500 Miles and at 60,000 Miles	•							•
5	Engine Idle Speed Adjustment	At 6 Months or 7,500 Miles and at 60,000 Miles	•							•
6	Engine Accessory Drive Belts Inspection	Every 24 Months or 30,000 Miles				•				•
7	Cooling System Service	Every 24 Months or 30,000 Miles				•				•
8	Front Wheel Bearing Repack	Every 30,000 Miles				•				•
9	Transmission Service	30,000 Miles				•				•
10	Vacuum Advance System Inspection	Check at 6 Months or 7,500 Miles, then at 30,000 Miles, and then at 15,000 Mile intervals.	•			•		•		•
11	Spark Plugs and Wire Service	Every 30,000 Miles				•				•
12	PCV System Inspection	Every 30,000 Miles				•				•
13	ERG System Check	Every 30,000 Miles				•				•
14	Air Cleaner and PCV Filter Replacement	Every 30,000 Miles				•				•
15	Engine Timing Check	Every 30,000 Miles				•				•
16	Fuel Tank, Cap and Lines Inspection	Every 24 Months or 30,000 Miles				•				•
17	Early Fuel Evaporation System Inspection	At 7,500 Miles and at 30,000 Miles then at 30,000 Mile intervals.	•			•				•
18	Evaporative Control System Inspection	Every 30,000 Miles				•				•
19	Fuel Filter Replacement	Every 30,000 Miles				•				•
20	Valve Lash Adjustment	Every 15,000 Miles		•		•		•		•
21	Thermostatically Controlled Air Cleaner Inspection	Every 30,000 Miles				•				•

① Severe service
② Normal service

CAPACITIES CHART

Year	Engine No. Cyl. Liters	Crankcase Includes Filter (qt)	Transmission (pts) 4-sp	5-sp	Auto	Transfer Case (pts)	Drive Axle (pts) Front	Rear	Fuel Tank (gal)	Cooling System (qt) w/AC	wo/AC
1983	4-1.9L	4.0	2.5	2.2	10.0①	5.2	3.0	3.5	13.5②	9.5	9.4
	4-2.0L	4.0	2.5	2.2	10.0①	5.2	3.0	3.5	13.5②	9.7	9.6
	4-2.2L	5.0	2.5	2.2	10.0①	—	—	3.5	13.5②	10.0	10.0
	6-2.8L	4.0	2.5	2.2	10.0①	5.2	3.0	3.5	13.5②	12.0	12.0
1984	4-1.9L	4.0	2.5	2.2	10.0①	5.2	3.0	3.5	13.5②	9.5	9.4
	4-2.0L	4.0	2.5	2.2	10.0①	5.2	3.0	3.5	13.5②	9.7	9.6
	4-2.2L	5.0	2.5	2.2	10.0①	—	—	3.5	13.5②	10.0	10.0
	6-2.8L	4.0	2.5	2.2	10.0①	5.2	3.0	3.5	13.5②	12.0	12.0
1985	4-1.9L	4.0	2.5	2.2	10.0①	4.6	2.6	3.8	13.5②	9.5	9.5
	4-2.2L	5.5	2.5	2.2	10.0①	—	—	3.8	13.5②	11.5	11.5
	4-2.5L	3.0	2.5	2.2	10.0①	4.6	2.6	3.8	13.5②	12.0	12.0
	6-2.8L	4.0	2.5	2.2	10.0①	4.6	2.6	3.8	13.5②	12.0	12.0
1986	4-2.5L	3.0	2.5	2.2	10.0	4.6	2.6	3.8	13.5②	10.5	10.5
	6-2.8L	4.0	2.5	2.2	10.0	4.6	2.6	3.8	13.5②	11.6	11.6
1987	4-2.5L	3.0	2.5	2.2	10.0③	4.6	2.6	3.9	13.5②	10.5	10.5
	6-2.8L	4.0	2.5	2.2	10.0③	4.6	2.6	3.9	13.5②	11.5	11.5
1988	4-2.5L	3.0	—	2.2	10.0③	4.6④	2.6	3.9	13.0②	11.5	11.5
	6-2.8L	4.0	—	2.2	10.0③	4.6④	2.6	3.9	13.0②	10.5	10.5
	6-4.3L	4.0	—	2.2	10.0③	4.6④	2.6	3.9	13.0②	13.5	13.5
1989	4-2.5L	3.0	—	2.2	10.0③	4.4	2.6	3.9	13.0②	11.5	11.5
	6-2.8L	4.0	—	2.2	10.0③	4.4	2.6	3.9	13.0②	10.5	10.5
	6-4.3L	4.0	—	2.2	10.0③	4.4	2.6	3.9	13.0②	13.5	13.5
1990	6-4.3L	4.0	—	2.2	⑤	4.4	2.6	3.9	13.0②	13.5	13.5
1991	6-4.3L	4.0	—	2.2	⑤ ⑨	4.4⑧	2.6	3.9	20.0⑦	12.1⑥	12.1⑥

① If equipped with a 200C: 7.0 pts.
② Optional: 20.0 gal.
③ If equipped with a 180C, 3-speed: 3 pts.
④ If equipped with a 231: 2.2 pts.
⑤ 180C and 3L30: 3.0 pts.
700-R4 and 4L60: 10.0 pts.
⑥ Bravada without rear heater: 13.5 qts.
Bravada with rear heater: 16.5 qts.
⑦ Bravada: 27 gals.
⑧ Bravada: 3.0 pts.
⑨ Bravada is only equipped with a 4L60: 10 pts.

2 Engine Performance and Tune-Up

QUICK REFERENCE INDEX

GENERAL INDEX

Diagnosis of Spark Plugs

Problem	Possible Cause	Correction
Brown to grayish-tan deposits and slight electrode wear.	• Normal wear.	• Clean, regap, reinstall.
Dry, fluffy black carbon deposits.	• Poor ignition output.	• Check distributor to coil connections.
Wet, oily deposits with very little electrode wear.	• "Break-in" of new or recently overhauled engine. • Excessive valve stem guide clearances. • Worn intake valve seals.	• Degrease, clean and reinstall the plugs. • Refer to Section 3. • Replace the seals.
Red, brown, yellow and white colored coatings on the insulator. Engine misses intermittently under severe operating conditions.	• By-products of combustion.	• Clean, regap, and reinstall. If heavily coated, replace.
Colored coatings heavily deposited on the portion of the plug projecting into the chamber and on the side facing the intake valve.	• Leaking seals if condition is found in only one or two cylinders.	• Check the seals. Replace if necessary. Clean, regap, and reinstall the plugs.
Shiny yellow glaze coating on the insulator.	• Melted by-products of combustion.	• Avoid sudden acceleration with wide-open throttle after long periods of low speed driving. Replace the plugs.
Burned or blistered insulator tips and badly eroded electrodes.	• Overheating.	• Check the cooling system. • Check for sticking heat riser valves. Refer to Section 1. • Lean air-fuel mixture. • Check the heat range of the plugs. May be too hot. • Check ignition timing. May be over-advanced. • Check the torque value of the plugs to ensure good plug-engine seat contact.
Broken or cracked insulator tips.	• Heat shock from sudden rise in tip temperature under severe operating conditions. Improper gapping of plugs.	• Replace the plugs. Gap correctly.

GASOLINE ENGINE TUNE-UP SPECIFICATIONS

Years	VIN	Engine No. Cyl. cc (cu. in.)	Spark Plugs Type	Spark Plugs Gap (in.)	Ignition Time (deg.) Man. Trans.	Ignition Time (deg.) Auto. Trans.	Idle Speed Man. Trans.	Idle Speed Auto Trans.	Valve Clearance In.	Valve Clearance Exh.
1983	A	4-1950 (119)	R42XLS	0.040	6B	6B	800	900	0.006	0.010
	B	6-2800 (173)	R42TS	0.040	6B	10B	1000	750	Hyd.	Hyd.
	Y	4-2000 (121)	R42CTS	0.035	12B	12B	750	700	Hyd.	Hyd.
1984	A	4-1950 (119)	R42XLS	0.040	6B	6B	800	900	0.006	0.010
	B	6-2800 (173)	R42TS	0.040	6B	10B	1000	750	Hyd.	Hyd.
	Y	4-2000 (121)	R42CTS	0.035	12B	12B	750	700	Hyd.	Hyd.
1985	A	4-1950 (119)	R42XLS	0.040	6B	6B	800	900	0.006	0.010
	B	6-2800 (173)	R42TS	0.040	6B	10B	1000	750	Hyd.	Hyd.
	E	4-2500 (151)	R43CTS6	①	①	①	②	②	Hyd.	Hyd.
1986	E	4-2500 (151)	R43CTS6	①	①	①	②	②	Hyd.	Hyd.
	R	6-2800 (173)	R42CTS	①	①	①	②	②	Hyd.	Hyd.
1987	E	4-2500 (151)	R43CTS6	①	①	①	②	②	Hyd.	Hyd.
	R	6-2800 (173)	R43CTS	①	①	①	②	②	Hyd.	Hyd.
1988	E	4-2500 (151)	R43CTS6	①	①	①	②	②	Hyd.	Hyd.
	R	6-2800 (173)	R43CTS	①	①	①	②	②	Hyd.	Hyd.
	Z	6-4300 (262)	R43CTS	0.040	①	①	②	②	Hyd.	Hyd.
1989	E	4-2500 (151)	R43CTS6	①	①	①	②	②	Hyd.	Hyd.
	R	6-2800 (173)	R43CTS	①	①	①	②	②	Hyd.	Hyd.
	Z	6-4300 (262)	CR43TS	0.045	①	①	②	②	Hyd.	Hyd.
1990	Z	6-4300 (262)	CR43TS	0.045	①	①	②	②	Hyd.	Hyd.
1991	Z	6-4300 (262)	CR43TS	0.045	①	①	②	②	Hyd.	Hyd.

① See underhood sticker
② This function is controlled by the ECU; No adjustment is necessary.

DIESEL ENGINE TUNE-UP SPECIFICATIONS

Year	VIN	Eng. No. Cyl. Displ. cc (Cu. In.)	Injection Timing (deg.)	Intake Valve Opens (deg.)	Low Idle (rpm)	Compression Pressure (psi)	Valve Clearance (in.) Intake	Valve Clearance (in.) Exhaust	Firing Order
1983	S	4-2238 (136.6)	15B	16B	750	441 ①	0.016C	0.16C	1-3-4-2
1984	S	4-2238 (136.6)	15B	16B	750	441 ①	0.016C	0.16C	1-3-4-2
1985	S	4-2238 (136.6)	15B	16B	750	441 ①	0.016C	0.16C	1-3-4-2

NOTE: The underhood specifications sticker often reflects tune-up specification changes made in production. Sticker figures must be used if they disagree with those in this chart.
① @ 200 rpm

TUNE-UP PROCEDURES

In order to extract the full measure of performance and economy from your engine, it is essential that it is properly tuned at regular intervals. A regular tune-up will keep your vehicle's engine running smoothly and will prevent the annoying breakdowns and poor performance associated with an untuned engine.

A complete tune-up should be performed every 30,000 miles. This interval should be halved if the vehicle is operated under severe conditions such as trailer towing, prolonged idling, start-and-stop driving, or if starting or running problems are noticed. It is assumed that the routine maintenance described in Chapter 1 has been kept up, as this will have a decided effect on the results of a tune-up. All of the applicable steps of a tune-up should be followed in order, as the result is a cumulative one.

NOTE: Diesel engines do not require tune-ups, as there is not an ignition system.

If the specifications on the underhood tune-up sticker in the engine compartment disagree with the Tune-Up Specifications chart in this Section, the figures on the sticker must be used. The sticker often reflects changes made during the production run.

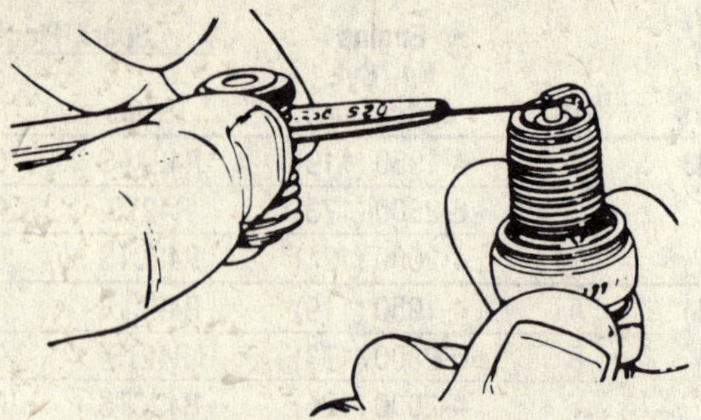

Checking the spark plug gap

Spark Plugs

Normally, a set of spark plugs requires replacement about every 20,000–30,000 miles on vehicles equipped with an High Energy Ignition (HEI) system. Any vehicle which is subjected to severe conditions will need more frequent plug replacement.

Under normal operation, the plug gap increases about 0.001 in. (0.0254mm) for every 1000–2000 miles. As the gap increases, the plug's voltage requirement also increases. It requires a greater voltage to jump the wider gap and about 2–3 times as much voltage to fire a plug at high speeds than at idle.

When you are removing the spark plugs, work on 1 at a time. Don't start by removing the plug wires all at once, for unless you number them, they may become mixed up. Take a minute before you begin and number the wires with tape. The best location for numbering the wires is near the distributor cap.

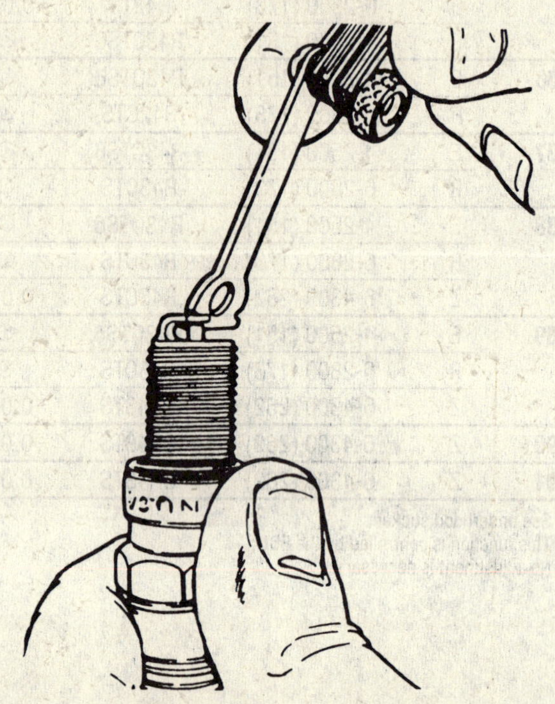

Bending the side electride to adjust the spark plug gap

REMOVAL

When removing the spark plugs, work on 1 at a time. Don't start by removing the plug wire all at once because unless you number them, they're going to get mixed up. On some models though, it will be more convenient for you to remove all of the wires before you start to work on the plugs. If this is necessary, take a minute before you begin and number the wires with tape before you take them off. The time you spend here will pay off later on.

1. Twist the spark plug boot ½ turn and remove the boot from the plug. You may also use a plug wire removal tool designed especially for this purpose. *do not pull on the wire itself.* When the wire has been removed, take a wire brush and clean the area around the plug. Make sure all the grime is removed so none will enter the cylinder after the plug has been removed.
2. Remove the plug using the proper size socket, extensions and universals as necessary.
3. If removing the plug is difficult, drip some penetrating oil (Liquid Wrench®, WD-40® or etc.) on the plug threads, allow it to work, then remove the plug. Also, be sure the socket is straight on the plug, especially on those hard to reach plugs.

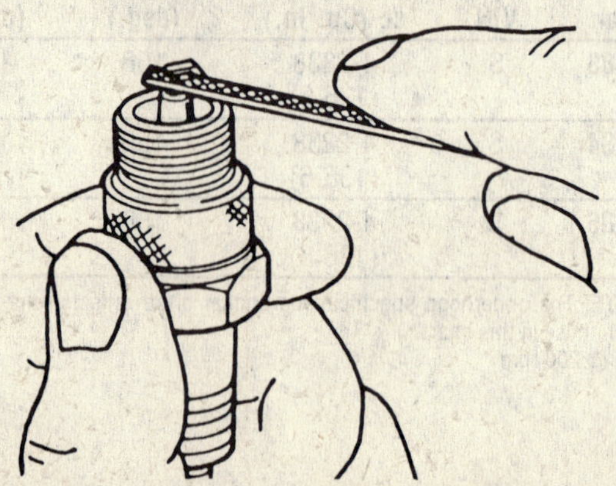

Plugs that are in good condition can be cleaned with a file and reused

INSPECTION

Check the plugs for deposits and wear. If they are not going to be replaced, clean the plugs thoroughly. Remember, any kind of

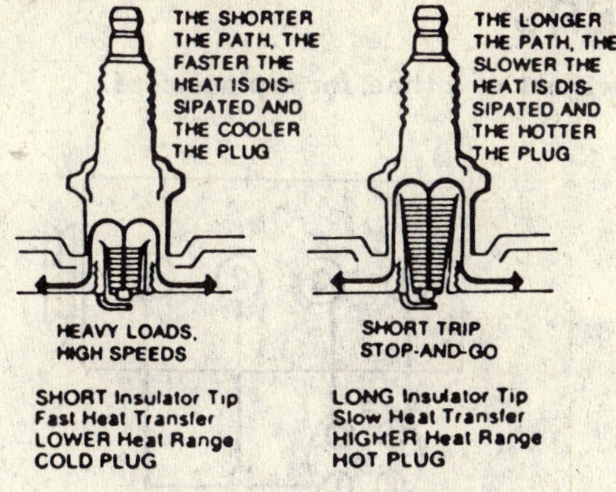

Spark plug heat range

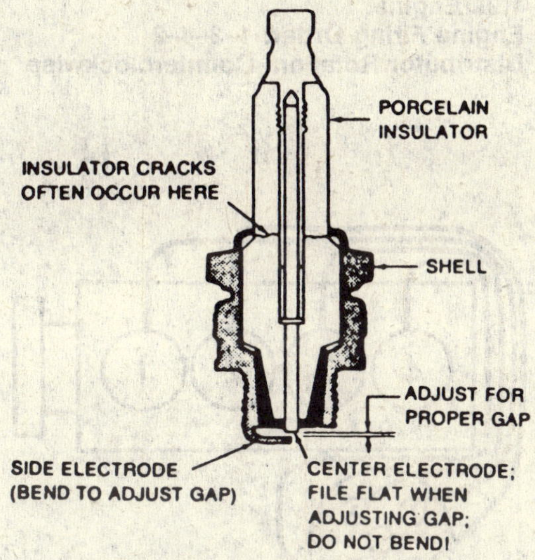

Cross-section of a spark plug

deposit will decrease the efficiency of the plug. Plugs can be cleaned on a spark plug cleaning machine, which can sometimes be found in service stations or you can do an acceptable job of cleaning with a stiff brush. If the plugs are cleaned, the electrodes must be filed flat. Use an ignition points file, not an emery board or the like, which will leave deposits. The electrodes must be filed perfectly flat with sharp edges; rounded edges reduce the spark plug voltage by as much as 50 percent.

Check the spark plug gap before installation. The ground electrode (the L-shaped 1 connected to the body of the plug) must be parallel to the center electrode and the specified size wire gauge (see Tune-Up Specifications) should pass through the gap with a slight drag. Always check the gap on the new plugs, they are not always set correctly at the factory. Do not use a flat feeler gauge when measuring the gap, because the reading will be inaccurate.

Heat range is a term used to describe the cooling characteristics of spark plugs. Plugs with longer nosed insulators take a longer time to dissipate heat than plugs with shorter nosed insulators. These are termed "hot" or "cold" plugs, respectively. It is generally advisable to use the factory recommended plugs. However, in conditions of extremely hard use (cross-country driving in summer) going to the next cooler heat range may be advisable. If most driving is done in the city or over short distances, go to the next hotter heat range plug to eliminate fouling. If in doubt concerning the substitution of spark plugs, consult your Chevrolet, GMC or Oldsmobile dealer.

Wire gapping tools usually have a bending tool attached; use that to adjust the side electrode until the proper distance is obtained. **Absolutely, never bend the center electrode.** Also, be careful not to bend the side electrode too far or too often; it may weaken and break off within the engine, requiring removal of the cylinder head to retrieve it.

INSTALLATION

1. Lubricate the threads of the spark plugs with a drop of oil. Install the plugs and tighten them hand tight. Take care not to cross-thread them.
2. Tighten the spark plugs with the socket. Do not apply the same amount of force you would use for a bolt; just snug them in. If a torque wrench is available, tighten to 11–15 ft. lbs.
3. Install the wire on their respective plugs. Make sure the wires are firmly connected, you will be able to feel them click into place.

Spark Plug Wires

Every 15,000 miles, visually inspect the spark plug cables for burns, cuts or breaks in the insulation. Check the spark plug boots and the nipples on the distributor cap and coil. Replace any damaged wiring.

Every 30,000 miles or so, the resistance of the wires should be checked with an ohmmeter. Wires with excessive resistance will cause misfiring and may make the engine difficult to start in damp weather. Generally, the useful life of the cables is 30,000–45,000 miles.

To check the resistance, remove the distributor cap, leaving the wires in place. Connect 1 lead of an ohmmeter to an electrode within the cap; connect the other lead to the corresponding spark plug terminal (remove it from the spark plug for this test). Replace any wire which shows a resistance over 30,000 ohms. Generally speaking, however, resistance should not be over 25,000 ohms and 30,000 ohms must be considered the outer limit of acceptability.

It should be remembered that resistance is also a function of length; the longer the wire the greater the resistance. Thus, if the wires on your van are longer than the factory originals, resistance will be higher, quite possibly outside these limits.

When installing a new set of spark plug wires, replace the wires 1 at a time, so there will be no mixup. Start by replacing the longest cable first. Install the boot firmly over the spark plug. Route the wire exactly the same as the original. Insert the distributor end of the wire firmly into the distributor cap tower, then seat the boot over the tower. Repeat the process for each wire.

Wire Length	Minimum	Maximum
0–15 inches	3000 ohms	10,000 ohms
15–25 inches	4000 ohms	15,000 ohms
25–35 inches	6000 ohms	20,000 ohms
Over 35 inches	6000 ohms	25,000 ohms

HEI plug wire resistance chart

FIRING ORDERS

NOTE: To avoid confusion, remove and tag the wires 1 at a time, for replacement.

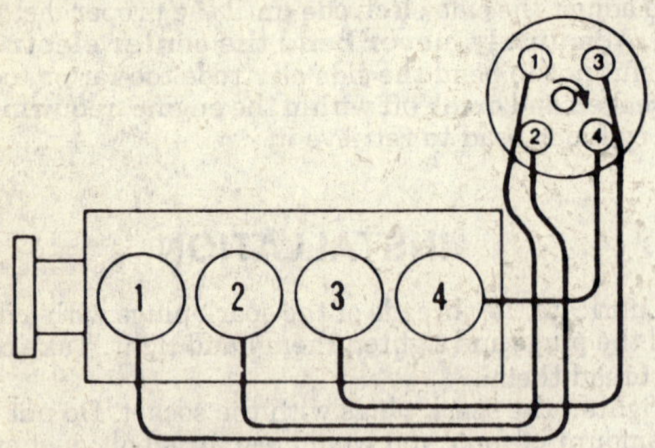

2.0L Engine
Engine Firing Order: 1–3–4–2
Distributor Rotation: Clockwise

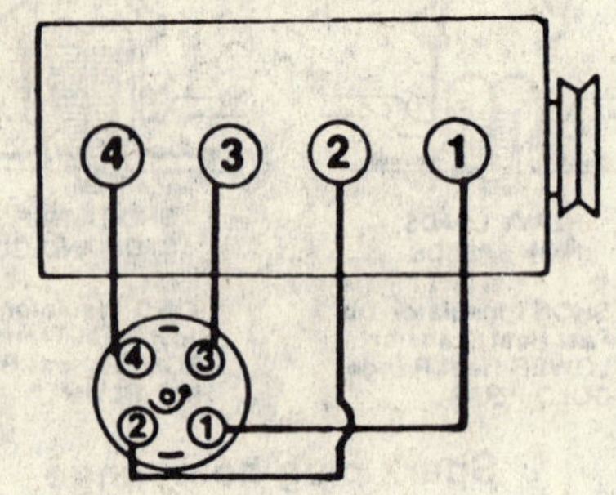

1.9L Engine
Engine Firing Order: 1–3–4–2
Distributor Rotation: Counterclockwise

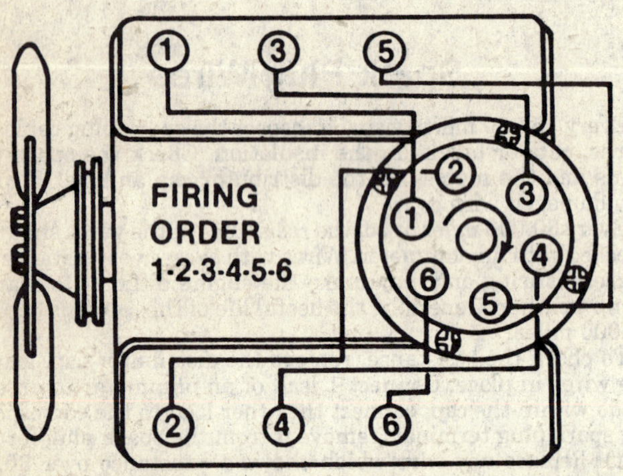

2.8L Engine
Engine Firing Order: 1–2–3–4–5–6
Distributor Rotation: Clockwise

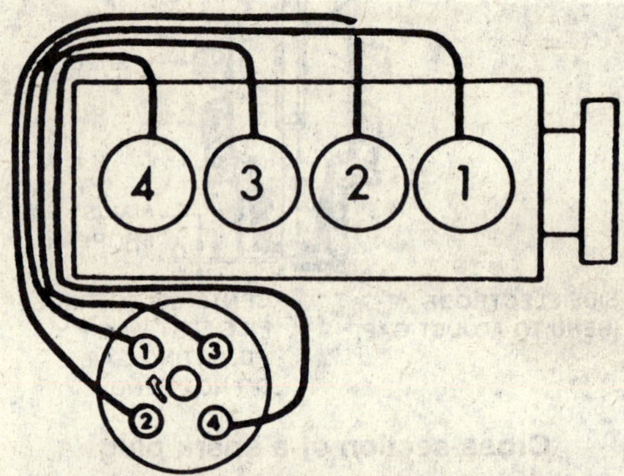

2.5L Engine
Engine Firing Order: 1–3–4–2
Distributor Rotation: Clockwise

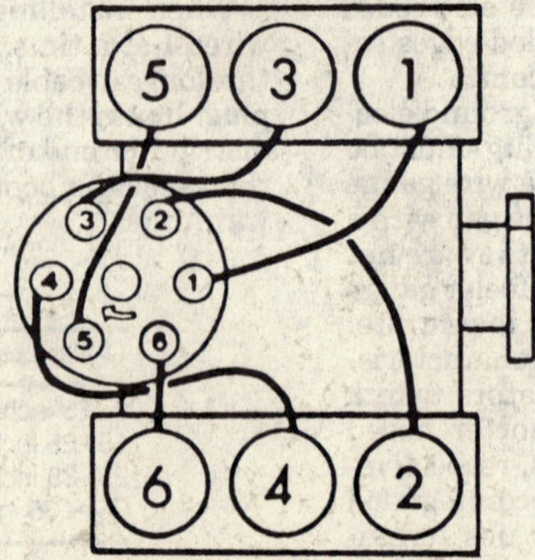

4.3L Engine
Engine Firing Order: 1–6–5–4–3–2
Distributor Rotation: Clockwise

ELECTRONIC IGNITION

GENERAL INFORMATION

The High Energy Ignition (HEI) distributor is used on all gasoline engines. The ignition coil is either mounted to the top of the distributor cap or is externally mounted on the engine, using a secondary circuit high tension wire to connect the coil to the distributor cap. Interconnecting primary wiring is routed through the engine harness.

The HEI distributor is equipped to aid in spark timing changes, necessary for emissions, economy and performance. This system is called the Electronic Spark Timing Control (EST). HEI(EST) distributors use a magnetic pick-up assembly, located inside the distributor containing a permanent magnet, a pole piece with internal teeth and a pick-up coil. When the teeth of the rotating timer core and pole piece align, an induced voltage in the pick-up coil signals the electronic module to open the coil primary circuit. As the primary current decreases, a high voltage is induced in the secondary windings of the ignition coil, directing a spark through the rotor and high voltage leads to fire the spark plugs. The dwell period is automatically controlled by the electronic module and is increased with increasing engine rpm. The HEI system features a longer spark duration which is instrumental in firing lean and EGR (Exhaust Gas Recirculation) diluted fuel/air mixtures. The condenser (capacitor) located within the HEI distributor is provided for noise (static) suppression purposes only and is not a regularly replaced ignition system component.

All spark timing changes in the HEI(EST) distributors are performed electronically by the Electronic Control Module (ECM), which monitors information from the various engine

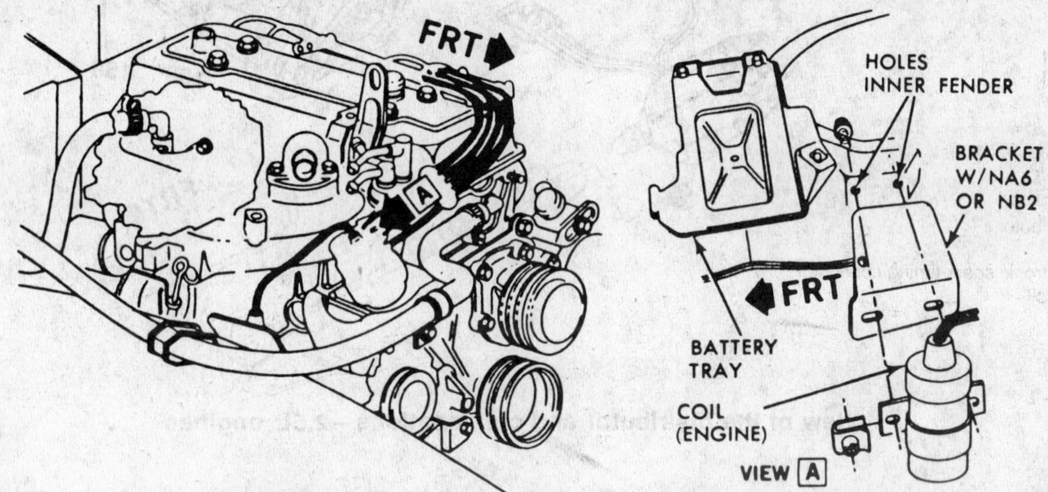

View of the distributor and coil locations—1.9L and 2.0L engines

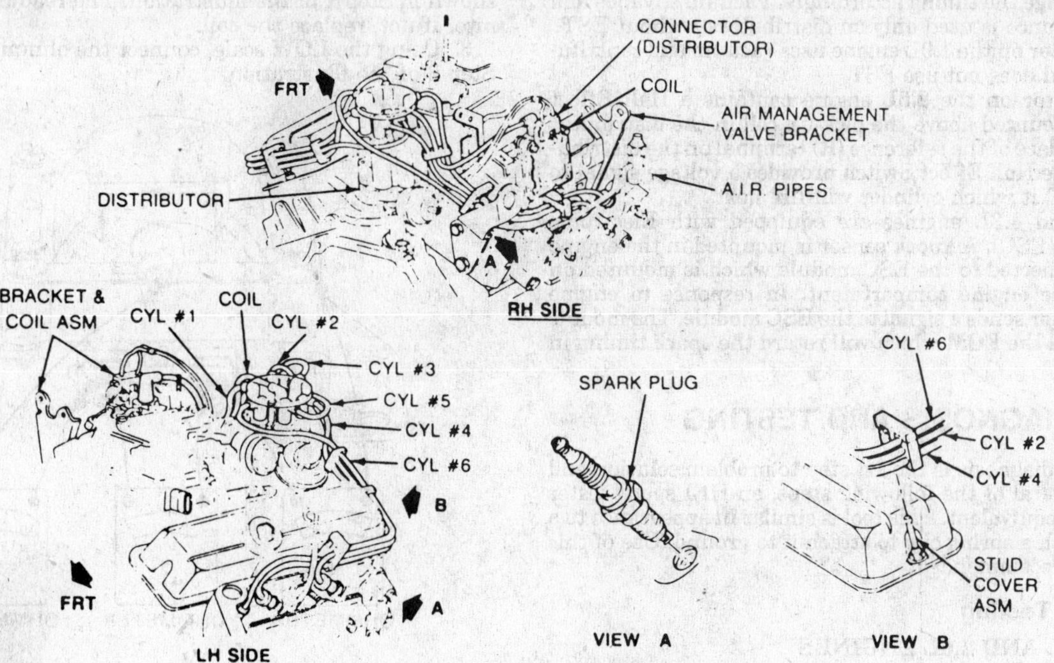

View of the distributor and coil locations—2.8L engines

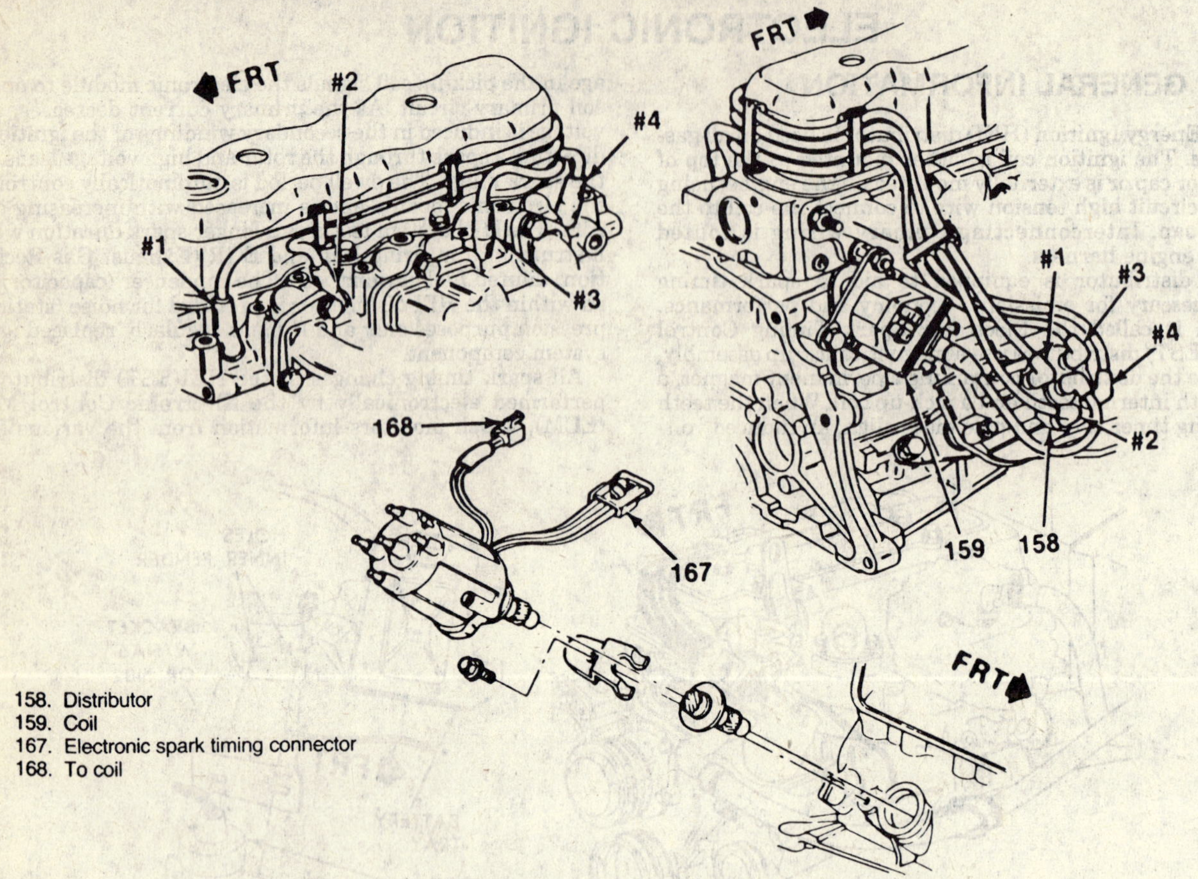

View of the distributor and coil locations—2.5L engines

sensors, computes the desired spark timing and signals the distributor to change the timing accordingly. Vacuum advance and centrifugal advance is used only on distributors without EST.

The distributor on the 1.9L engine uses vacuum and centrifugal advance and does not use EST.

The distributor on the 2.5L engine contains a Hall Effect Switch. It is mounted above the pick-up coil in the distributor and takes the place of the reference (R) terminal on the distributor module. The Hall Effect Switch provides a voltage signal to the ECM to tell it which cylinder will fire next.

The 2.8L and 4.3L engines are equipped with Electronic Spark Control (ESC). A knock sensor is mounted in the engine block. It is connected to the ESC module which is mounted on the cowl in the engine compartment. In response to engine knock, the sensor sends a signal to the ESC module. The module will then signal the ECM which will retard the spark timing in the distributor.

DIAGNOSIS AND TESTING

An accurate diagnosis is the 1st step to problem solution and repair. For several of the following steps, an HEI spark tester tool ST 125 or equivalent. This tool is similar in appearance to a spark plug, with a spring clip to attach it to ground. Use of this tool is highly recommended.

Ignition Coil Testing

EXCEPT 1.9L AND 2.0L ENGINES

1. Disconnect the distributor lead and wiring from the coil.
2. Using the HIGH scale, connect an ohmmeter to the coil as shown in Step 1 of the illustration. The reading should be infinite. If not, replace the coil.
3. Using the LOW scale, connect the ohmmeter as shown in Step 2 of the illustration.

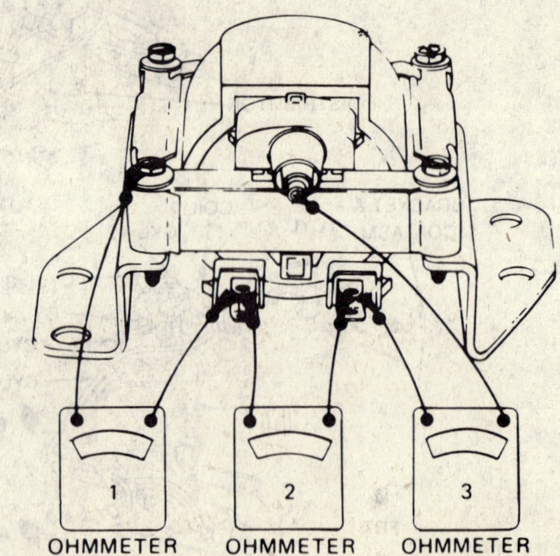

Testing the ignition coil—2.5L and 2.8L engines

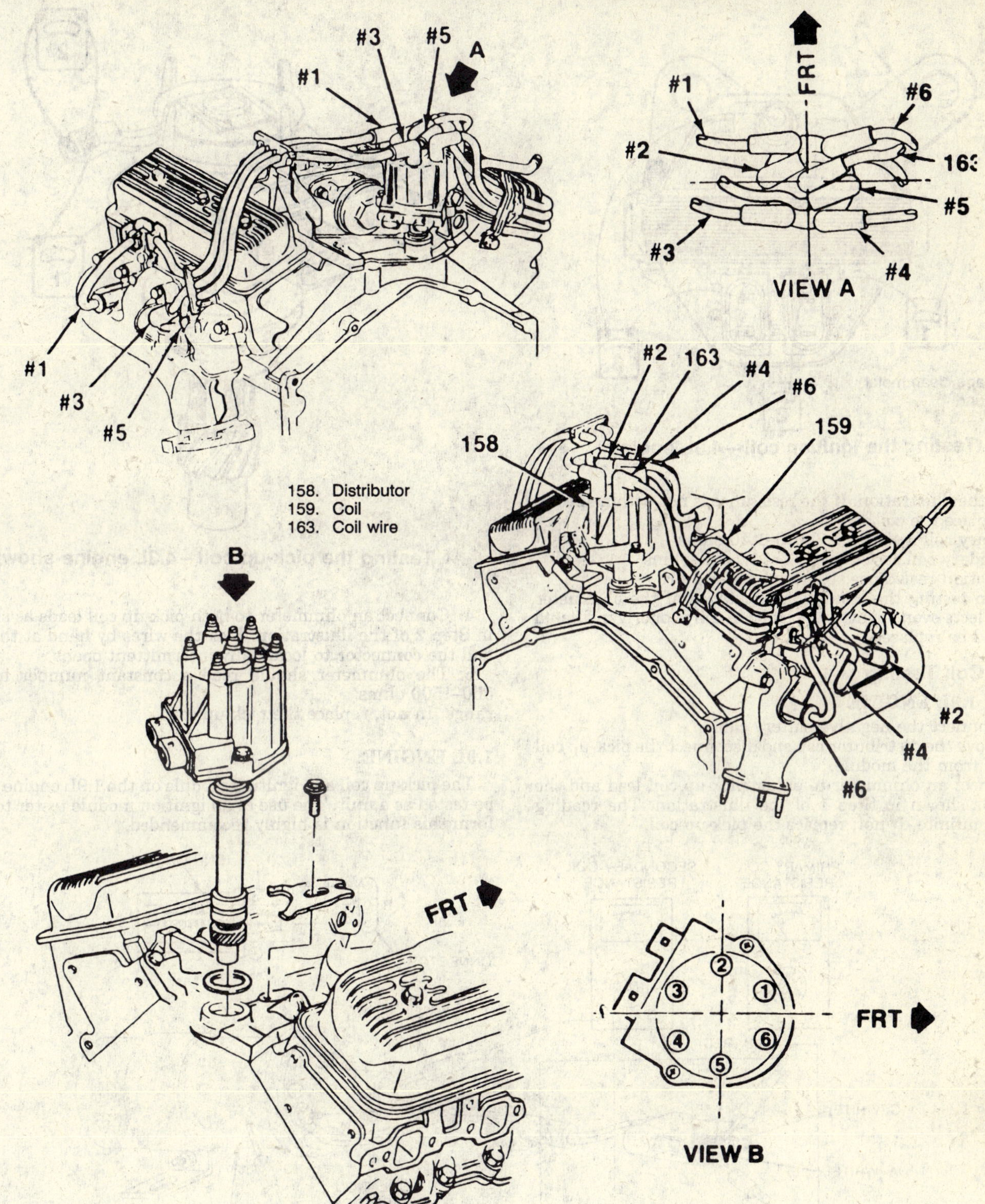

View of the distributor and coil locations—4.3L engine

4. The reading should be very low or zero. If not, replace the coil.
5. Using the HIGH scale, connect the ohmmeter as shown in Step 3 of the illustration.
6. The ohmmeter should not read infinite. If it does, replace the coil.
7. Reconnect the distributor lead and wiring to the coil.

1.9L AND 2.0L ENGINES

1. Check the outer face of the ignition coil for cracking, rust or damage.
2. Check the resistance of the primary and secondary coils as

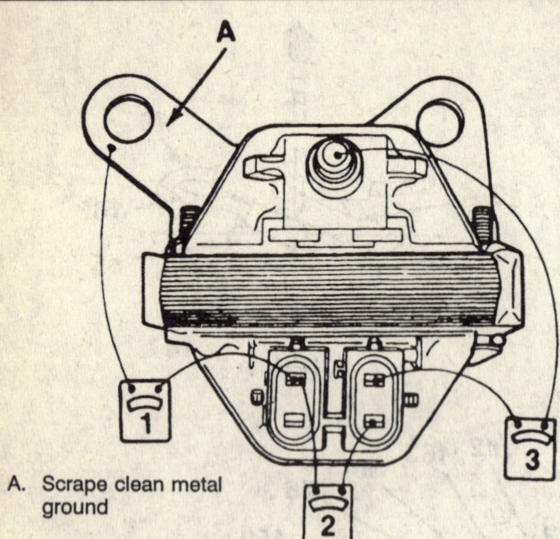

Testing the ignition coil—4.3L engine

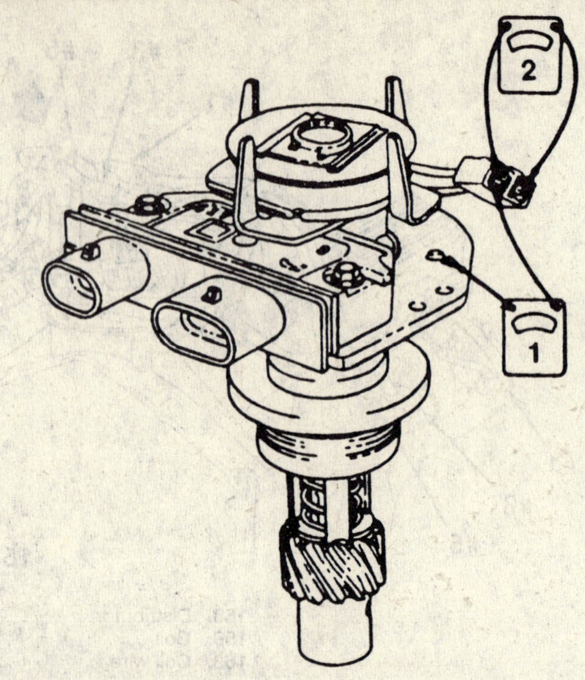

Testing the pick-up coil—4.3L engine shown

shown in the illustration. If the resistance is not within specification, replace the coil.

- Primary coil resistance: 0.090–1.40 ohms
- Secondary coil resistance: 7.3–11.1 kilo-ohms
- Insulation resistance: 10 megohms or more

3. When testing the insulation resistance, if the ohmmeter needle deflects even slightly, the ignition coil is poorly insulated and should be replaced.

Pick-Up Coil Testing

EXCEPT 1.9L ENGINE

1. Disconnect the negative battery cable.
2. Remove the distributor cap and disconnect the pick-up coil connector from the module.
3. Connect an ohmmeter to either pick-up coil lead and the housing as shown in Step 1 of the illustration. The reading should be infinite. If not, replace the pick-up coil.
4. Connect an ohmmeter to both pick-up coil leads as shown in Step 2 of the illustration. Flex the wires by hand at the coil and the connector to locate any intermittent opens.
5. The ohmmeter should read a constant number in the 500–1500 ohms
range. In not, replace the pick-up coil.

1.9L ENGINE

The pick-up coil and ignition module on the 1.9L engine must be tested as a unit. The use of an ignition module tester to perform this function is highly recommended.

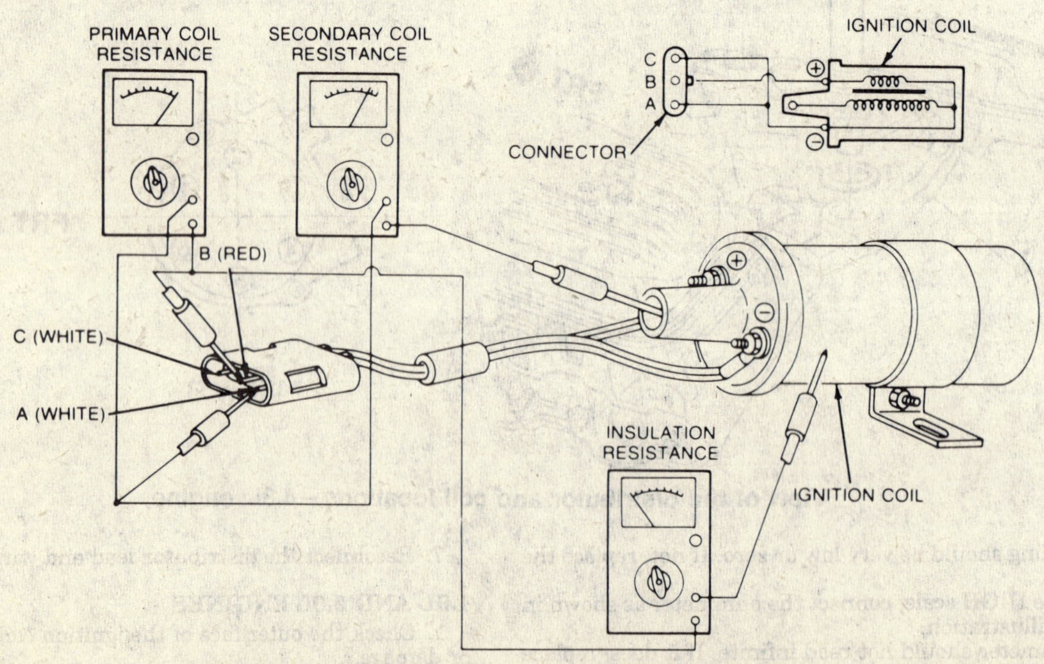

Testing the ignition coil—1.9L and 2.0L engines

Electronic Spark Timing (EST) System

The High Energy Ignition (HEI) system controls fuel combustion by providing the spark to ignite the compressed air/fuel mixture in the combustion chamber at the correct time. To provide improved engine performance, fuel economy and control of the exhaust emissions, the ECM controls distributor spark advance (timing) using the Electronic Spark Timing (EST) system.

OPERATION

The HEI (EST) distributor uses a modified module. The module has 7 terminals instead of the 4 used without EST. Two terminal arrangements are used, depending upon engine application.

To properly control ignition/combustion timing, the ECM needs to know the following information:

- Crankshaft position
- Engine speed (rpm)
- Engine load (manifold pressure or vacuum)
- Atmospheric (barometric) pressure
- Engine temperature
- Transmission gear position (certain models)

The ECM uses information from the MAP and coolant sensors in addition to rpm to calculate spark advance as follows:

- Low MAP output voltage would require MORE spark advance.
- Cold engine would require MORE spark advance.
- High MAP output voltage would require LESS spark advance.
- Hot engine would require LESS spark advance.

Incorrect operation of the EST system can cause the following:

- Detonation—low MAP output or high resistance in the coolant sensor circuit.
- Poor performance—high MAP output or low resistance in the coolant sensor circuit.

The EST system consists of the distributor module, ECM and its connecting wires. The distributor has 4 wires from the HEI module connected to a 4 terminal connector, which mates with a 4 wire connector from the ECM.

Except 2.5L Engine

The distributor 4-terminal connector is labeled A, B, C, D. Circuit functions for these terminals, except the 2.5L Hall Effect Switch model, are as follows:

1. Reference ground—Terminal A—This wire is grounded in the distributor and makes sure the ground circuit has no voltage drop, which could affect performance. If this circuit is open, it could cause poor performance.
2. Bypass—Terminal B—At approximately 400 rpm, the ECM applies 5 volts to this circuit to switch the spark timing control from the HEI module to the ECM. An open or grounded bypass circuit will set a Code 42 and the engine will run at base timing, plus a small amount of advance built into the HEI module.
3. Distributor reference—Terminal C—This provides the ECM with rpm and crankshaft position information.
4. EST—Terminal D—This triggers the HEI module. The ECM does not know what the actual timing is, but it does know when it gets its reference signal. It then advances or retards the spark timing from that point. Therefore, if the base timing is set incorrectly, the entire spark curve will be incorrect.

2.5L Engine With Hall Effect Switch

Circuit functions for the 2.5L Hall Effect Switch distributor are as follows:

1. EST—Terminal A—This triggers the HEI module. The ECM does not know what the actual timing is but it does know when it gets its reference signal. It then advances or retards the spark timing from that point. Therefore, if the base timing is set incorrectly, the entire spark curve will be incorrect.
2. Distributor reference—Terminal B—This provides the ECM with rpm and crankshaft position information.
3. Bypass—Terminal C—At approximately 400 rpm, the ECM applies 5 volts to this circuit to switch the spark timing control from the HEI module to the ECM. An open or grounded bypass circuit will set a Code 42 and the engine will run at base timing, plus a small amount of advance built into the HEI module.
4. Reference ground—Terminal D—This wire is grounded in the distributor and makes sure the ground circuit has no voltage drop, which could affect performance. If this circuit is open, it could cause poor performance.

DIAGNOSIS

Perform the following ignition system check before attempting to diagnose EST system failures.

EST Performance Test

The EST system will usually set a Code 42 when a fault is detected in the system. See Computer Command Control System, in this section, to determine how to retrieve codes from the ECM and for further diagnostic procedures.

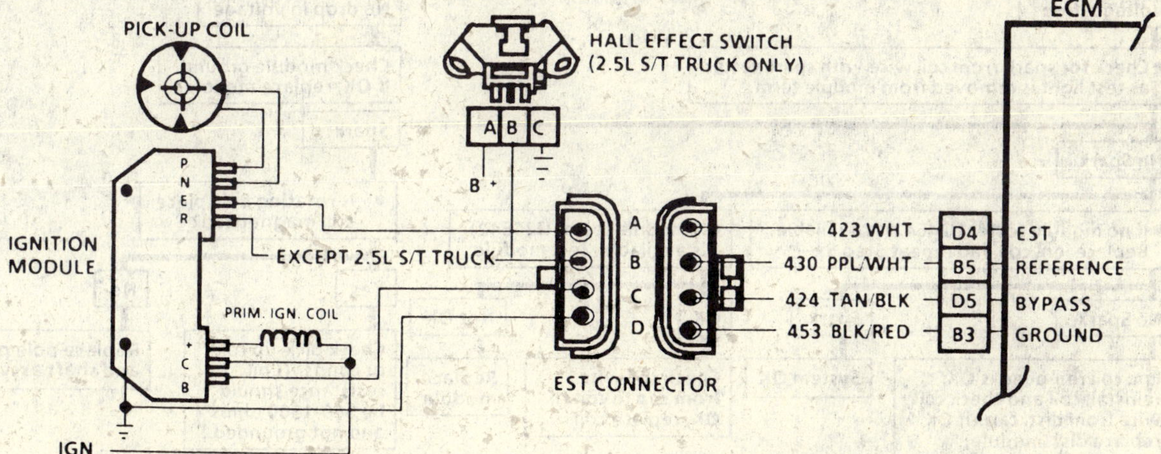

Wiring schematic of the Electronic Spark Timing (EST) system—except 4.3L engine

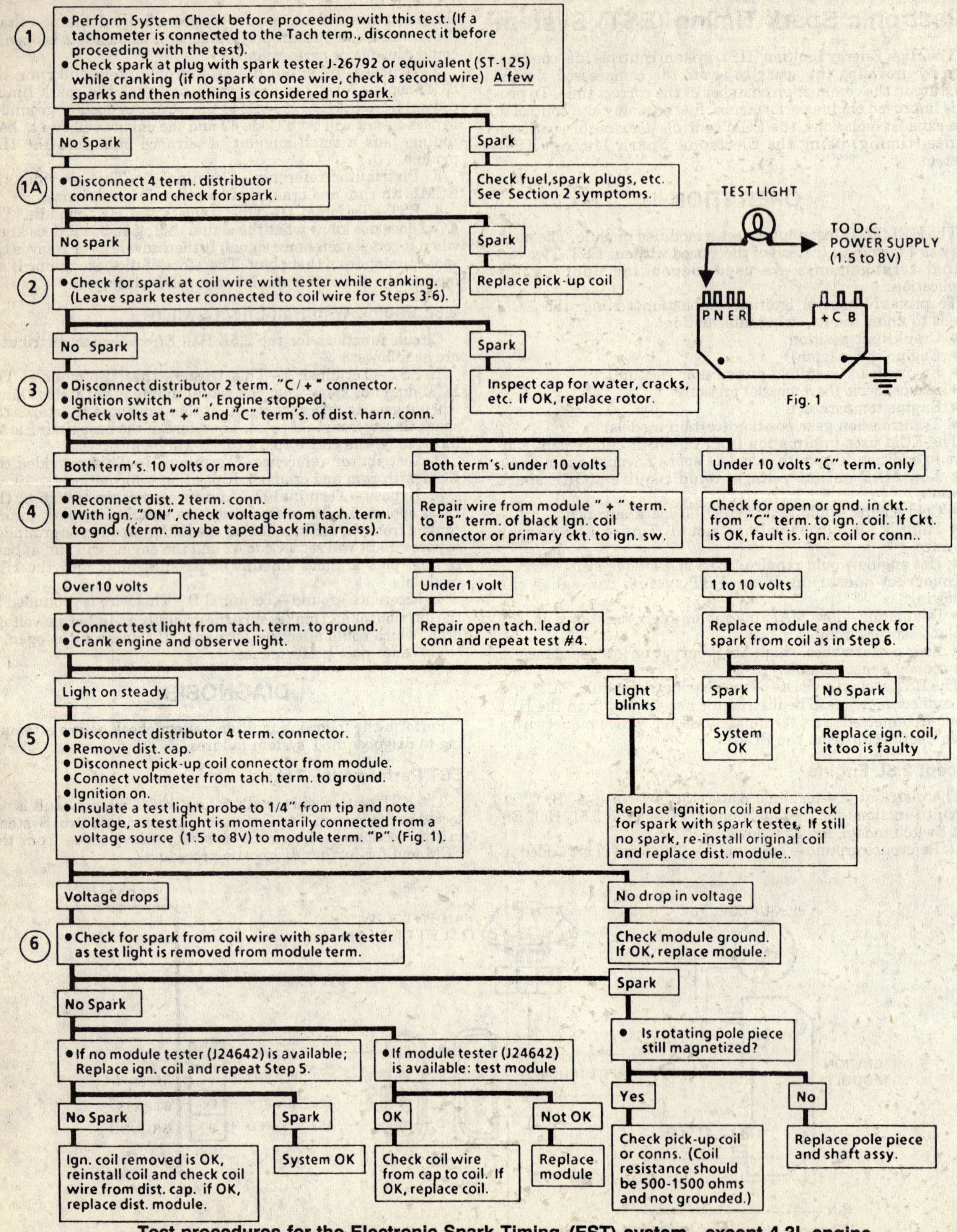

Test procedures for the Electronic Spark Timing (EST) system—except 4.3L engine

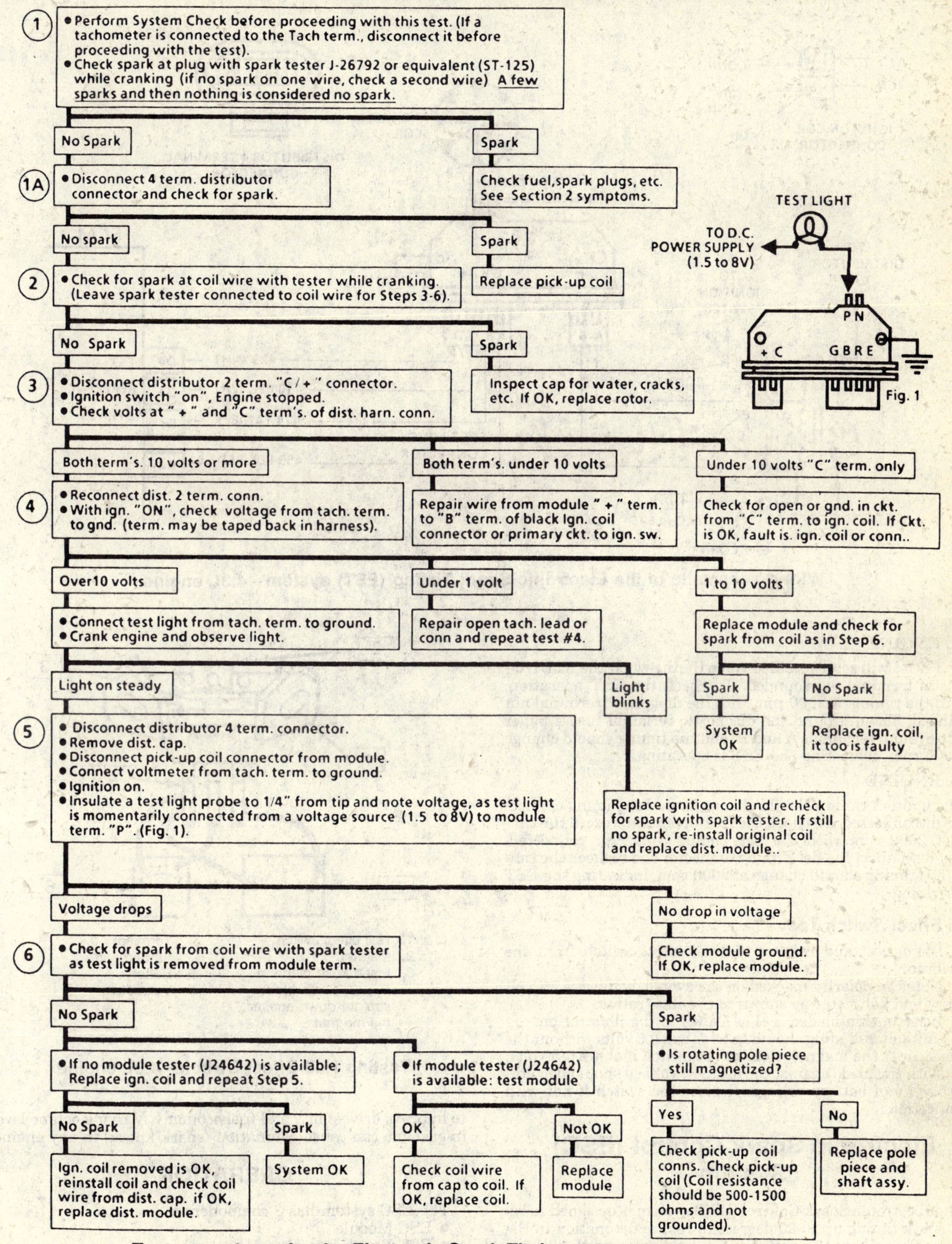

Test procedures for the Electronic Spark Timing (EST) system—4.3L engine

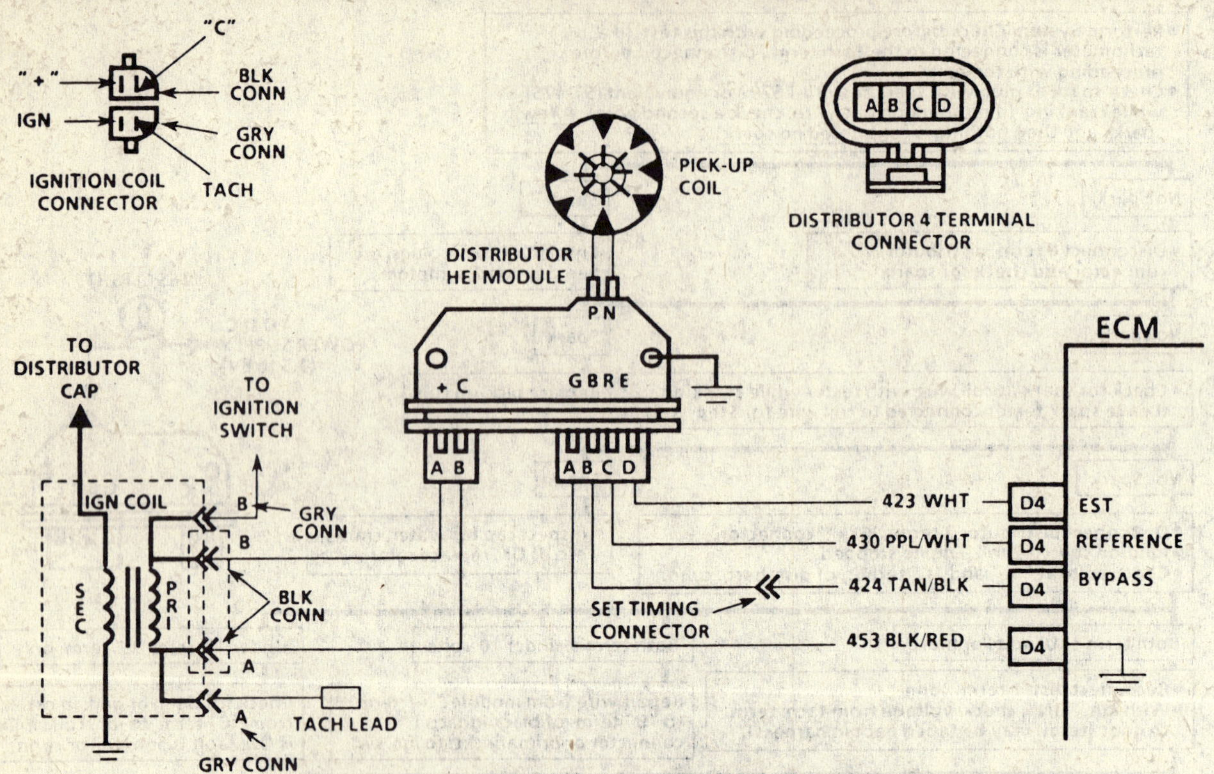

Wiring schematic of the Electronic Spark Timing (EST) system—4.3L engine

2.5L ENGINE

The ECM will set a specified value timing when the ALDL diagnostic terminal is grounded. To check the EST operation, record the timing at 2000 rpm with the diagnostic terminal not grounded. Then, ground the diagnostic terminal (use a paper clip to ground terminals A and B) and the timing should change at 2000 rpm, indicating the EST is operating.

2.5L ENGINE

The ignition timing should change if the Set Timing connector is disconnected. To check the EST operation, record the timing at 2000 rpm with the Set Timing connector connected. Then, disconnect the Set Timing connector and recheck the timing. The timing should change at 2000 rpm, indicating the EST is operating.

Hall Effect Switch Test

1. Disconnect and remove the hall effect switch from the distributor.
2. Note the polarity marked on the switch, connect a 12 volt battery and voltmeter as shown in the illustration.
3. Insert a thin bladed tool as shown in the illustration.
4. Voltmeter reading should be less than 0.5 volts without the blade against the magnet. Replace the switch if above 0.5 volts.
5. With the blade against the magnet, voltage should be within 0.5 volts of battery voltage. Replace the switch if not with specification.

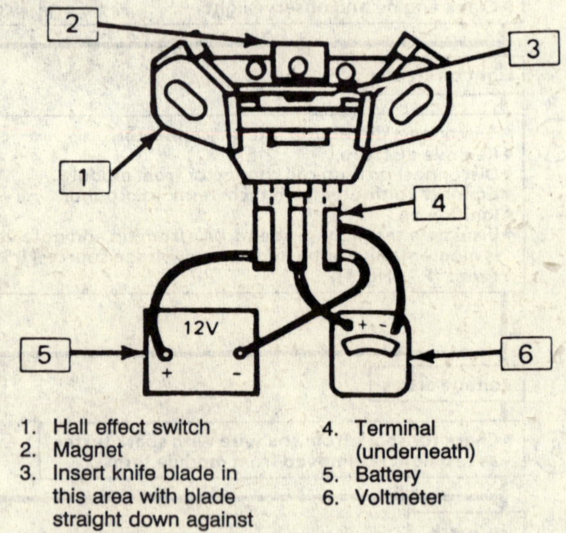

1. Hall effect switch
2. Magnet
3. Insert knife blade in this area with blade straight down against the magnet
4. Terminal (underneath)
5. Battery
6. Voltmeter

Testing Hall Effect Switch—4.3L engine

Electronic Spark Control (ESC) System

The Electronic Spark Control (ESC) system is designed to retard spark timing up to 20 degrees to reduce detonation in the engine. This allows the engine to use maximum spark advance to improve driveability and fuel economy. Varying octane levels in gasoline can cause detonation (spark knock) in any engine.

OPERATION

The ESC system has 3 components:

- ESC Module
- ESC Knock Sensor

• ECM

The knock sensor detects abnormal vibration in the engine. The sensor is mounted in the engine block near the cylinders. The ESC module receives the knock sensor information and sends a signal to the ECM. The ECM then adjusts the Electronic Spark Timing (EST) to reduce spark knocking.

The ESC module sends a voltage signal to the ECM when no spark knocking is detected by the ESC knock sensor, and the ECM provides normal spark advance. When the knock sensor detects spark knock, the module turns off the circuit to the ECM. The ECM then retards EST to reduce spark knock.

DIAGNOSIS

Loss of the ESC knock sensor signal or loss of ground at the ESC module would cause the signal to the ECM to remain high. This condition would cause the ECM to control EST as if there was no spark knock. No retard would occur and spark knocking could become severe under heavy engine load.

Spark retard without the knock sensor connected could indicate a noise signal on the wire to the ECM or a malfunctioning ESC module.

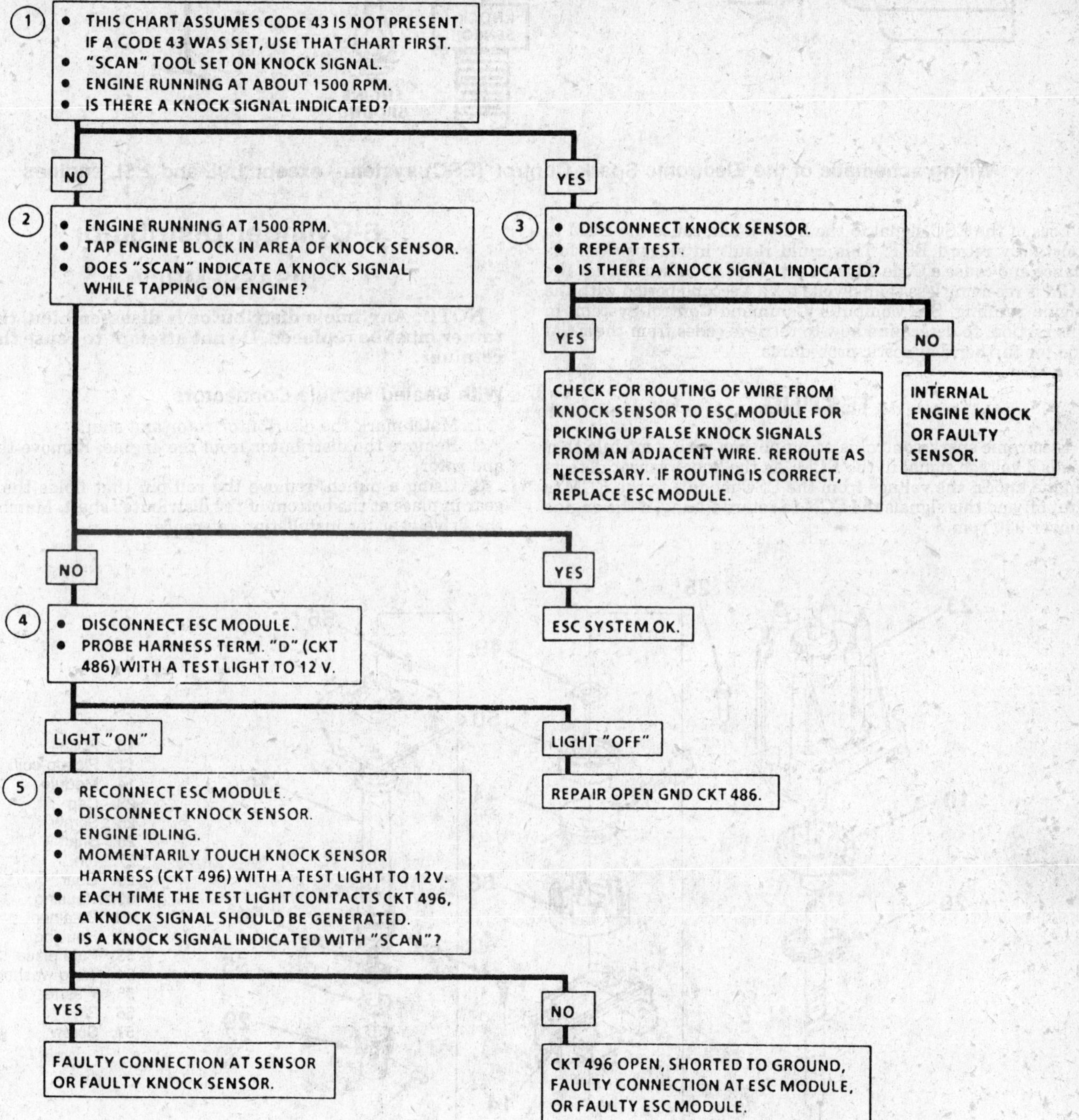

Test procedures for the Electronic Spark Control (ESC) system—except 1.9L and 2.5L engines

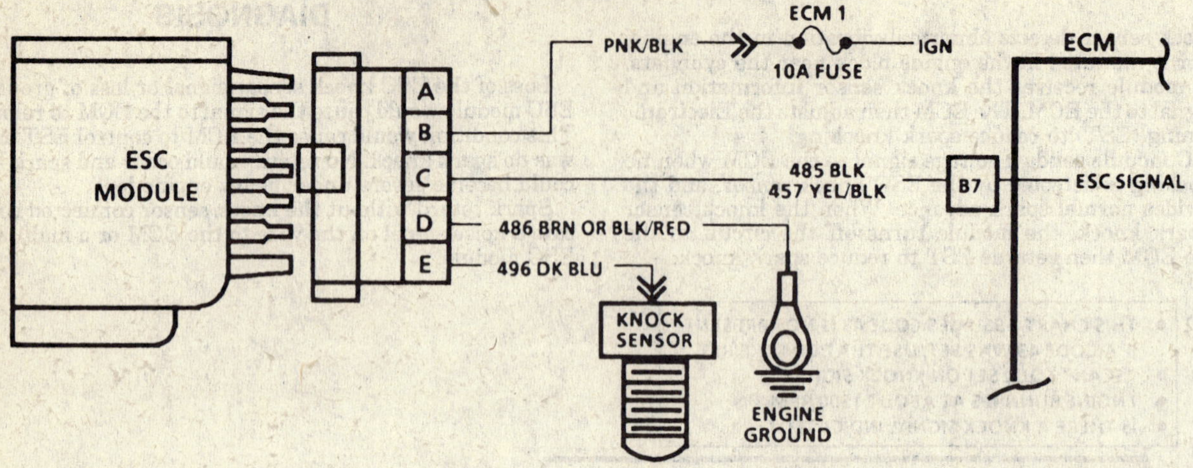

Wiring schematic of the Electronic Spark Control (ESC) system—except 1.9L and 2.5L engines

Loss of the ESC signal to the ECM would cause the ECM to constantly retard EST. This could result in sluggish performance and cause a Code 43 to be set. Code 43 indicates that the ECM is receiving less than 6 volts for a 4 second period with the engine running. See Computer Command Control System, in this section, to determine how to retrieve codes from the ECM and for further diagnostic procedures.

TESTING

Electronic spark control is accomplished with a module that sends a voltage signal to the ECM. As the knock sensor detects engine knock, the voltage from the ESC module to the ECM is shut off and this signals the ECM to retard timing, if the engine is over 900 rpm.

6-Cylinder Distributor

DISASSEMBLY

NOTE: Anytime a distributor is disassembled, the retainer must be replaced. Do not attempt to reuse the old retainer.

With Sealed Module Connectors

1. Matchmark the distributor rotor and shaft.
2. Remove the distributor from the engine. Remove the cap and rotor.
3. Using a punch, remove the roll pin that holds the drive gear in place at the bottom of the distributor shaft. Matchmark the drive gear for installation reference.

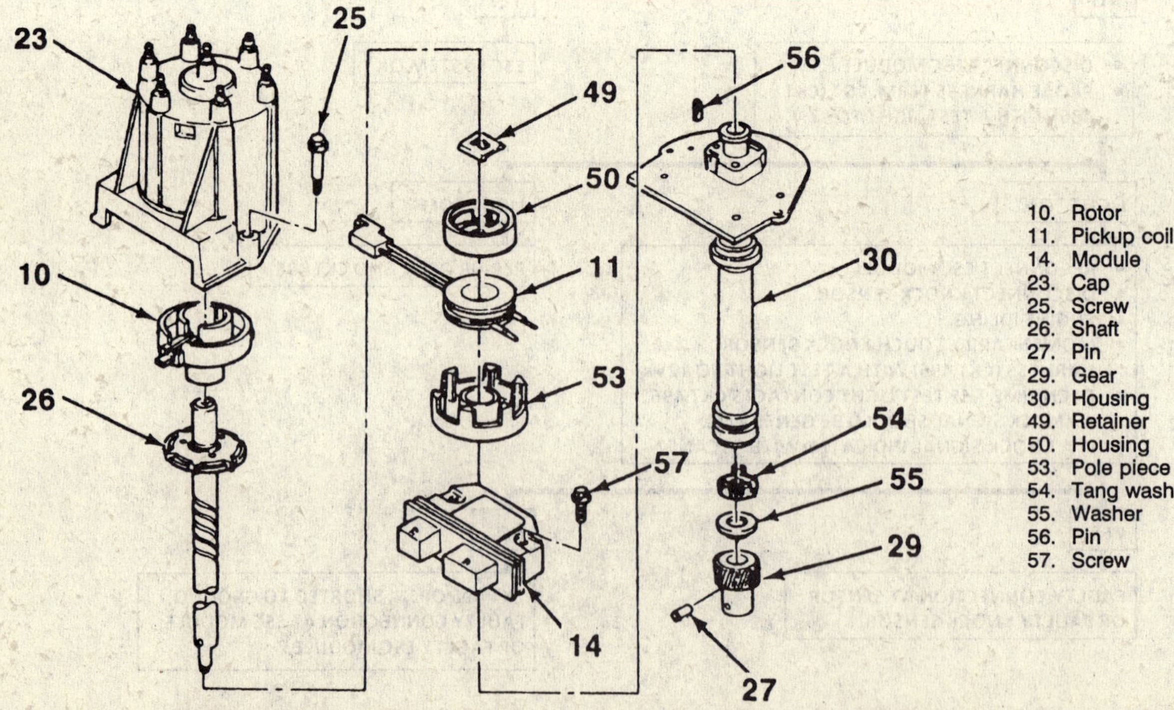

Exploded view of the sealed module distributor—4.3L engine

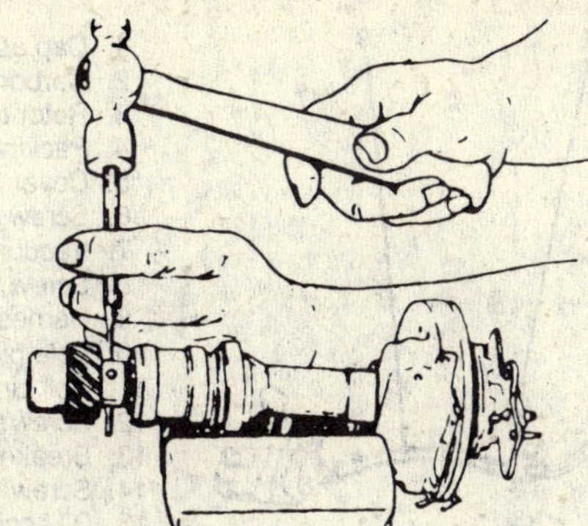

Removing the roll pin—4.3L engine

4. Remove the drive gear, washer or spring and spring retainer or tan washer.
5. Remove the distributor shaft with the pole piece and plate from the housing.
6. Remove the retainer from the housing by prying gently with a prybar. Remove the shield.
7. Remove the pick-up coil connector by lifting the locktab. Remove the pick-up coil.
8. Remove both screws holding the ignition module to the housing and remove the module.

Without Sealed Module Connectors

1. Matchmark the distributor rotor and shaft.
2. Remove the distributor from the engine. Remove the cap and rotor.
3. If equipped, remove both bolts holding the Hall Effect Switch to the housing. Lift away the locking tab of the connector to the switch, then remove the switch by lifting straight up.
4. Using a punch, remove the roll pin that holds the drive gear in place at the bottom of the distributor shaft. Matchmark the drive gear for installation reference.
5. Remove the drive gear, washer or spring and spring retainer, or tan washer.
6. Remove the distributor shaft from the housing by prying straight up.
7. Remove the "C" retaining washer from inside the pick-up coil assembly.
8. Remove the pick-up coil connector by lifting the locktab. Remove the pick-up coil.
9. Remove the wiring harness connectors from the module.
10. Remove both screws holding the ignition module to the housing and remove the module.
11. Remove the bolt holding the wiring harness to the housing and remove the harness.

INSPECTION

1. Inspect the following:
   a. Distributor cap for cracks or tiny holes. Replace the cap if damaged.
   b. Metal terminals in the cap for corrosion. Scrape terminals clean or replace the cap.
   c. Rotor for wear or burning at the outer terminal. The presence of carbon on the terminal indicates rotor wear and the need for replacement.
   d. Distributor shaft for shaft-to-housing looseness. Insert the shaft in the housing. If the shaft wobbles, replace the distributor as an assembly.
   e. Distributor housing for cracks or damage. If the housing is cracked or damaged, replace the distributor as an assembly.
2. Refer to the procedures above and measure the the following:
   a. Voltage of the Hall Effect Switch.
   b. Resistance of the pick-up coil.
   c. Electrical performance of the ignition module.
   d. Resistance of the ignition coil.

ASSEMBLY

With Sealed Module Connectors

NOTE: Be sure to thoroughly coat the bottom of the ignition module with silicone lubricant. Failure to do so could result in heat damage to the module.

1. Install the module to the housing with both screws.
2. Install the pick-up coil. Fit the tab on the bottom of the coil into the anchor hole in the housing. Install the wiring connector and lock into place.
3. Install the shield, retainer and shaft into the housing.
4. Install the spring retainer, spring, washer and driven gear onto the bottom of the housing.
5. Align the matchmarks and install the roll pin into the gear. Spin the shaft and make sure the teeth on the shaft assembly do not touch the pole piece.
6. Install the rotor and cap.

Without Sealed Module Connectors

NOTE: Be sure to thoroughly coat the bottom of the ignition module with silicone lubricant. Failure to do so could result in heat damage to the module.

1. Install the module to the housing with both screws.
2. Install the wiring harness into the housing and attach the wiring harness mounting tabs with the attaching bolt. Ensure the locking tabs are in place.
3. Install the pick-up coil. Fit the tab on the bottom of the coil into the anchor hole in the housing.
4. Install the pick-up coil wiring connector to the module.
5. Install the "C" washer into the coil and the shaft into the housing.
6. Install the tan washer, spring retainer, spring and drive gear onto the shaft. Align the matchmarks on the drive gear and shaft.
7. Install the roll pin into the gear. Turn the shaft by hand to check tooth clearance between the shaft and pick-up coil assembly. If clearance needs adjustment, loosen and retighten the three pick-up coil bolts.
8. If equipped, install the wiring connector for the Hall Effect Switch and install the switch with both attaching bolts. The teeth of the switch should rotate between the back plate and the magnet of the switch without touching.
9. Install the rotor and cap.

4-Cylinder Distributor

DISASSEMBLY

1. Remove the cap, rotor, packing and cover.
2. Remove the screws attaching the vacuum controller then remove the vacuum controller from the housing.
3. Remove the screws attaching the harness assembly.
4. Disconnect connectors of harness assembly from the igniter unit, then remove the harness assembly from the housing.
5. Remove the reluctor from the rotor shaft by prying up.
6. Remove the screws attaching the breaker plate assembly, then remove the breaker plate assembly from the housing.
7. Remove the module from the breaker plate assembly. The module is an integral construction and cannot be disassembled.
8. Drive out the roll pin using a punch.
9. Remove the governor shaft assembly from the housing.

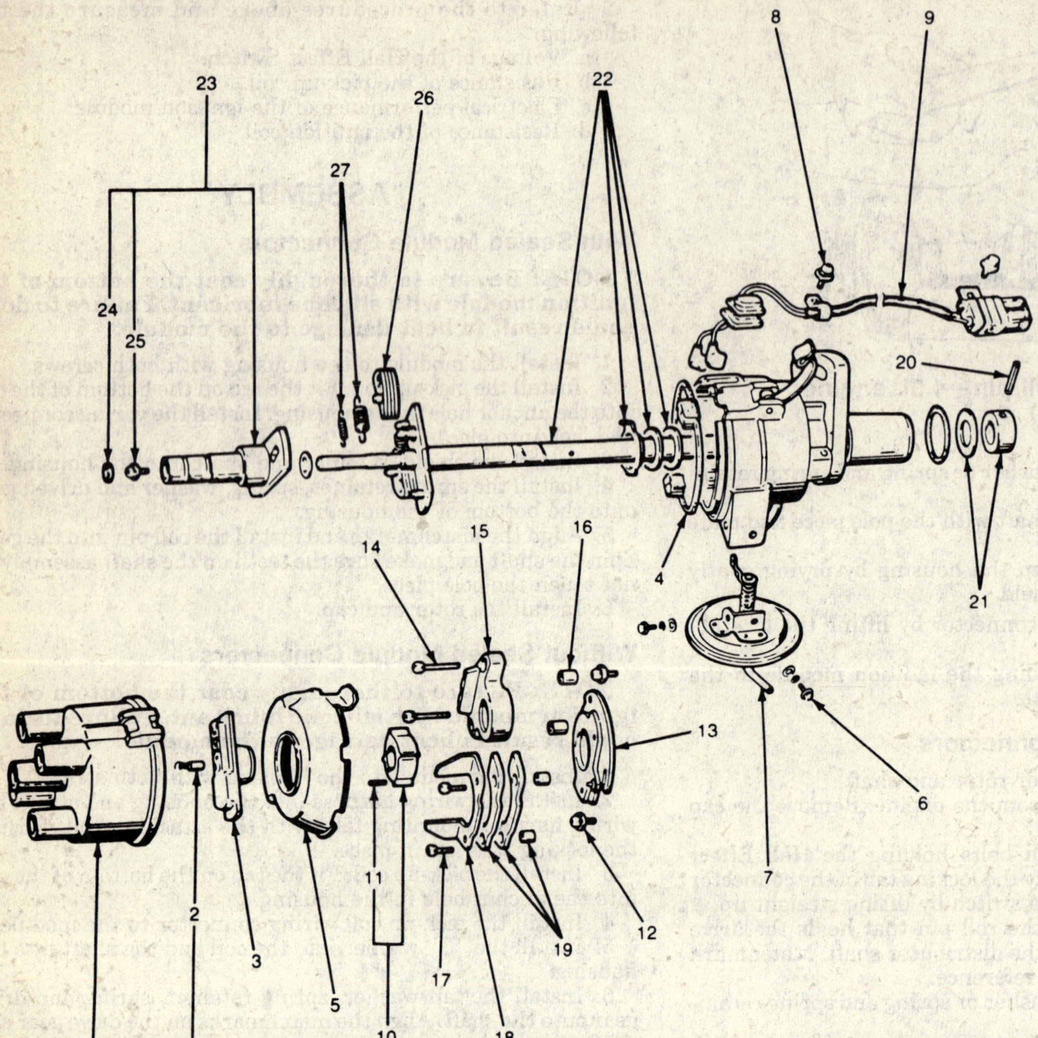

1. Cap assembly
2. Carbon point
3. Rotor head
4. Packing
5. Cover
6. Screw
7. Vacuum control assembly
8. Screw
9. Harness assembly
10. Pole piece
11. Roll pin
12. Screw
13. Breaker plate assembly
14. Screw
15. P/U coil module assembly
16. Spacer
17. Screw
18. Stator
19. Magnet set
20. Roll pin
21. Collar
22. Shaft assembly
23. Rotor shaft assembly
24. Packing
25. Screw
26. Governor weight
27. Governor spring

Exploded view of the distributor—1.9L and 2.0L engines

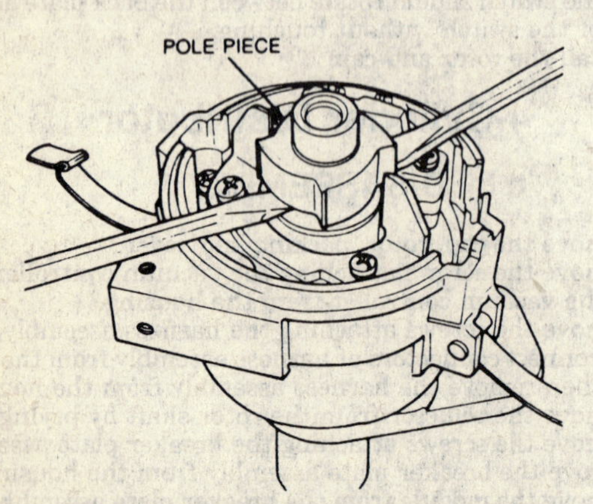

Using 2 prybars to remove the pole piece from the distributor shaft—1.9L and 2.0L engines

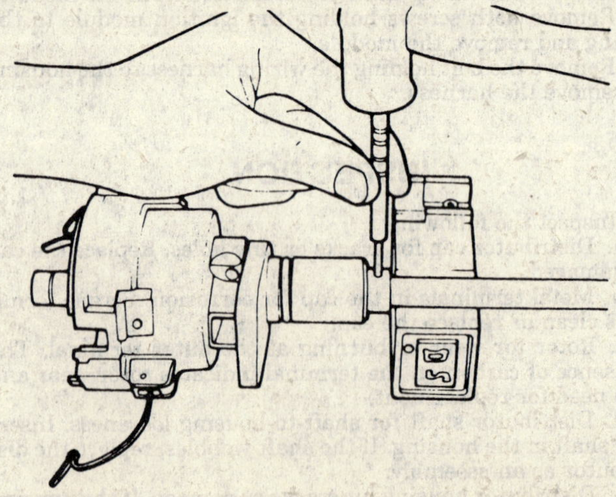

Removing the roll pin—1.9L and 2.0L engines

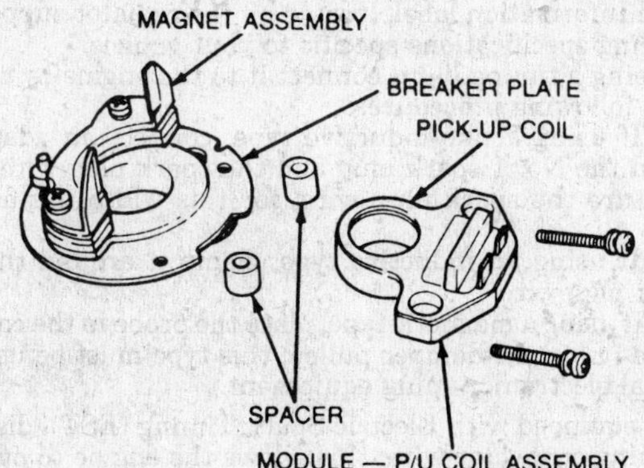

Exploded view of the ignition module and the breaker plate assembly—1.9L and 2.0L engines

NOTE: Matchmark the rotor shaft and governor shaft before disassembly.

10. Remove the packing from the governor shaft and remove the screw attaching the rotor shaft assembly. Remove the rotor shaft assembly from the governor shaft.
11. Remove the governor weights and springs from the shaft assembly.

INSPECTION

Clean disassembled parts in solvent and check for wear or damage. Inspect the distributor cap for cracks or corrosion on terminals. Replace components as necessary.

ADJUSTMENT

Air Gap

Using a non-magnetic feeler gauge, measure the air gap between the pole piece and the stator. Air gap should be 0.3–0.5mm. Adjust by loosening both screws and moving the pole piece until the gap is correct. Tighten the screws and recheck the air gap. Screws are made of non-magnetic stainless steel.

Govenor Advance

Normal operation is indicated if the rotor shaft returns to normal state when released after turning it counterclockwise by hand.

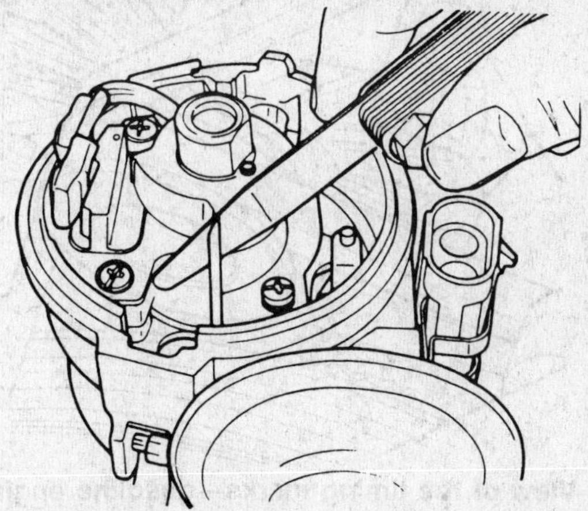

Using a non-magnetic feeler gauge to check the air gap between the pole piece and the breaker plate—1.9L and 2.0L engines

Vacuum Advance

Check vacuum controller for leaks by testing with a hand vacuum pump. Apply vacuum to the controller and test for proper operation. Hold vacuum for a few minutes to test the diaphragm. If the controller holds vacuum, it is good.

ASSEMBLY

Reassemble the distributor by following the disassembly procedure in reverse order. Note the following:

1. The governor springs should be fitted to the spring hanger pin on the shaft assembly with the smaller hook end turned downward.
2. The relation between the cutaway portion of the rotor shaft and the offset of projection at the end of the governor shaft should be carefully noted when install the rotor shaft to the housing.
3. Use a new roll pin when installing the collar.
4. The edge at the cutaway portion of the base must be flush with the edge of the base fixing screw slot when installing the breaker plate assembly.
5. The roller pin should be installed so the slot is in parallel with the cutaway portion of the reluctor as viewed from above.

IGNITION TIMING ADJUSTMENT

The following procedure requires the use of a distributor wrench and a timing light. When using a timing light, be sure to consult the manufacturer's recommendations for installation and usage.

Gasoline Engine

On 2.5L engine, ground the **A** and **B** terminals on the ALDL connector under the dash before adjusting the timing.

View of the timing marks—gasoline engine

On all except 2.5L engine with an EST distributor, disconnect the timing connector wire, located below the heater case in the engine compartment or coming out of the the wiring harness near the distributor, before adjusting the timing.

1. Timing specifications are listed on the Vehicle Emissions Control Information label, located on the radiator support. Use the timing specifications specific to your vehicle.
2. Using a timing light, connect it to the engine by performing the following procedures:
   a. If using a non-inductive type, connect an adapter between the No. 1 spark plug and the spark plug wire; do not puncture the spark plug wire, for this will cause a voltage leak.
   b. If using an inductive type, clamp it around the No. 1 spark plug wire.
   c. If using a magnetic type, place the probe in the connector located near the damper pulley; this type must be used with special electronic timing equipment.
3. If equipped with Electric Spark Timing (EST), disconnect the timing connector wire; this allows the engine to operate in the bypass timing mode.
4. Start the engine aim the timing light at the timing mark on the damper pulley; a line on the damper pulley will align the timing mark. If necessary to adjust the timing, loosen the distributor hold-down clamp and slowly turn the distributor slightly to align the marks. When the alignment is correct, tighten the hold-down bolt.
5. Turn the engine **OFF**. Remove the timing light and reconnect the timing connector wire, if disconnected.

DIESEL ENGINE INJECTION TIMING

NOTE: This procedure requires the use of a static timing gauge tool J-29763 or equivalent; do not attempt any injection timing adjustments without this tool.

1. Check that notched line on the injection pump flange is in alignment with notched line on the injection pump front bracket.
2. Bring the piston in No. 1 cylinder to top dear center on compression stroke by turning the crankshaft as necessary.
3. With the timing pulley housing cover removed, check that the timing belt is properly tensioned and that timing marks are aligned.
4. Disconnect the injection pipe(s) from the injection pump, then remove the distributor head screw and washer. Using the static timing gauge tool J-29763 or equivalent, install it into the distributor head screw hole and set the lift to approximately 0.04 in. (1mm) from the plunger.
5. Use a wrench to hold the delivery holder when loosening the sleeve nuts on the injection pump side.
6. Bring the piston in No. 1 cylinder to a point 45–60 degrees before top dead center (BTDC) by turning the crankshaft, then calibrate the dial indicator to zero.
7. Turn the crankshaft pulley slightly in both directions and check that gauge indication is stable.
8. Turn the crankshaft in the normal direction of rotation, then record the reading of the dial indicator when the timing mark (15 degrees) on the crankshaft pulley is in alignment with the pointer; the reading should be 0.020 in. (0.5mm).

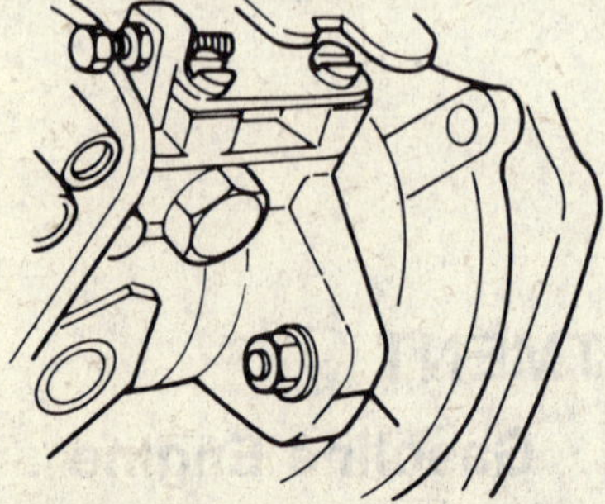
Injection pump and flange alignment—diesel engine

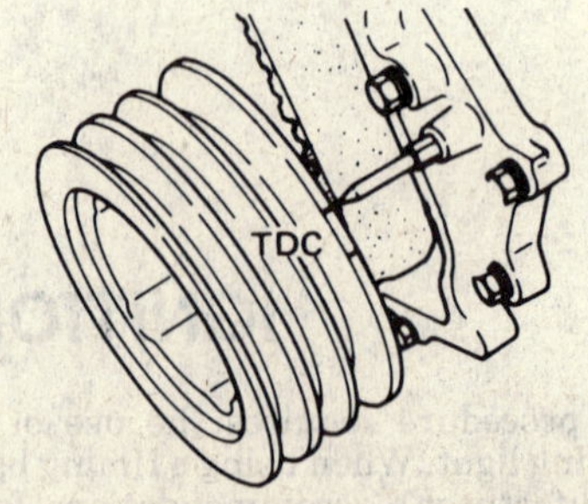

Number 1 piston at TDC—diesel engine

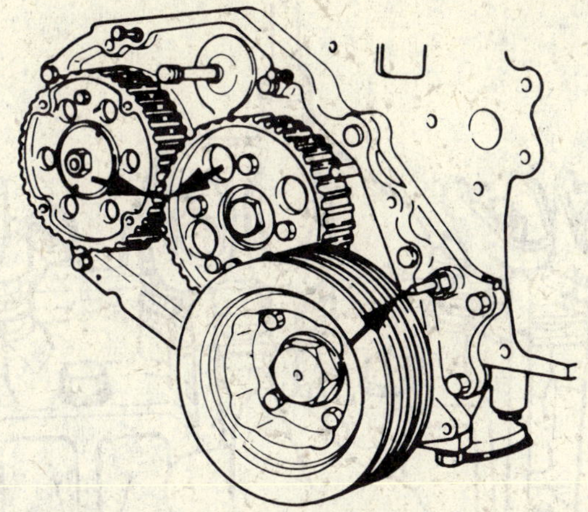
Aligning the timing marks – diesel engine

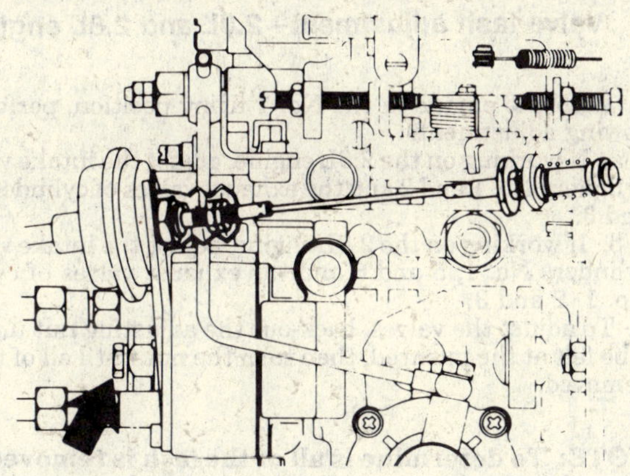
Removing the distributor screw – diesel engine

9. If the reading of dial indicator deviates from the specified range, hold the crankshaft in position 15 degrees BTDC and loosen 2 nuts on injection pump flange.

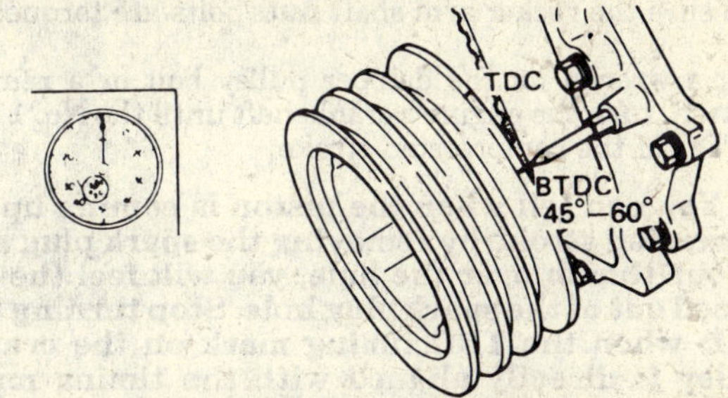

No. 1 piston 45–60 degrees BTDC – diesel engine

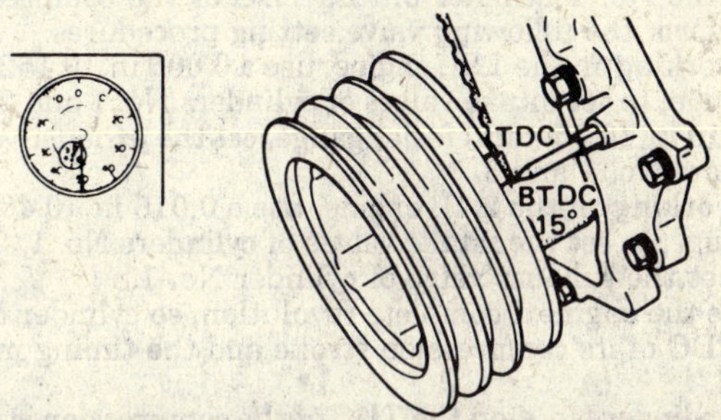

No. 1 piston 15 degrees BTDC – diesel engine

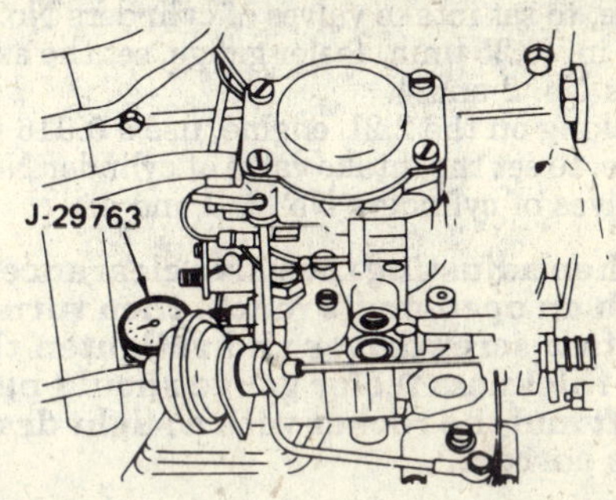

Static timing gauge installed – diesel engine

10. Move the injection pump to a point where dial indicator gives reading of 0.020 in. (0.5mm), then tighten pump flange nuts.

VALVE LASH

Valve adjustment determines how far the valves enter the cylinder and how long they stay open and/or closed.

NOTE: While all valve adjustments must be made as accurately as possible, it is better to have the valve adjustment slightly loose than slightly tight, as a burned valve may result from overly tight adjustments.

ADJUSTMENT

1.9L and 2.2L Diesel

NOTE: The valves are adjusted with the engine Cold.

1. Remove the rocker arm cover.

2. Make sure the rocker arm shaft nuts/bolts are torqued to 16 ft. lbs.
3. Using a wrench on the damper pulley bolt or a remote starter button, turn the engine's crankshaft until the No. 1 piston is at TDC of the compression stroke.

NOTE: You can tell when the piston is coming up on the compression stroke by removing the spark plug and placing your thumb over the hole, you will feel the air being forced out of the spark plug hole. Stop turning the crankshaft when the TDC timing mark on the crankshaft pulley is directly aligned with the timing mark pointer.

4. With the No. 1 cylinder on the TDC of the compression stroke, perform the following valve setting procedures:
   a. If working on the 1.9L engine, use a 0.006 in. (0.152mm) feeler gauge, to set intake valves of cylinders No. 1 and 2. Using a 0.010 in. (0.254mm) feeler gauge, set the exhaust valves of cylinders No. 1 and 3.
   b. If working on the 2.2L engine, use a 0.016 in. (0.40mm) feeler gauge, to set the intake valves of cylinders No. 1, 2 and 3, then set the exhaust valve of cylinder No. 1.
5. Rotate the engine 1 complete revolution, so cylinder No. 4 is on the TDC of its compression stroke and the timing marks are aligned.
6. With cylinder No. 4 on the TDC of the compression stroke, perform the following valve setting procedures:
   a. If working on the 1.9L engine, use a 0.006 in. (0.152mm) feeler gauge, to set intake valves of cylinders No. 3 and 4. Using a 0.010 in. (0.254mm) feeler gauge, set the exhaust valves of cylinders No. 2 and 4.
   b. If working on the 2.2L engine, use a 0.016 in. (0.40mm) feeler gauge, to set the intake valve of cylinder No. 4, then the exhaust valves of cylinders No. 2, 3 and 4.

NOTE: When adjusting the valve clearance, loosen the locknut with an open-end wrench, then turn the adjuster screw with a screwdriver and retighten the locknut. The proper thickness feeler gauge should pass between the camshaft and the rocker with a slight drag when the clearance is correct.

2.0L and 2.8L Engines

1. Remove the air cleaner and the rocker arm cover(s).
2. Rotate the crankshaft until the mark on the crankshaft pulley aligns with the **0** mark on the timing plate. Make sure the No. 1 cylinder is positioned on the compression stroke.

NOTE: To determine the compression stroke, place your fingers on the No. 1 rocker arms, as the mark on the crankshaft pulley comes near the 0 mark on the timing plate. If the valves move, the engine is on the No. 4 firing position; rotate the crankshaft 1 complete revolution and realign the pulley mark with the timing plate **0** mark.

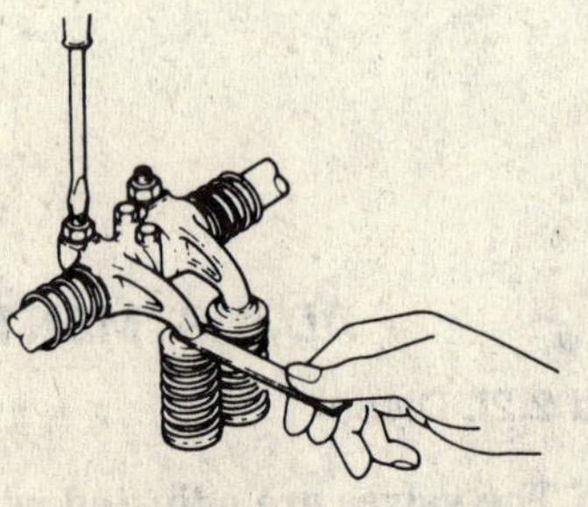

Valve clearance adjustment—1.9L and 2.2L engines

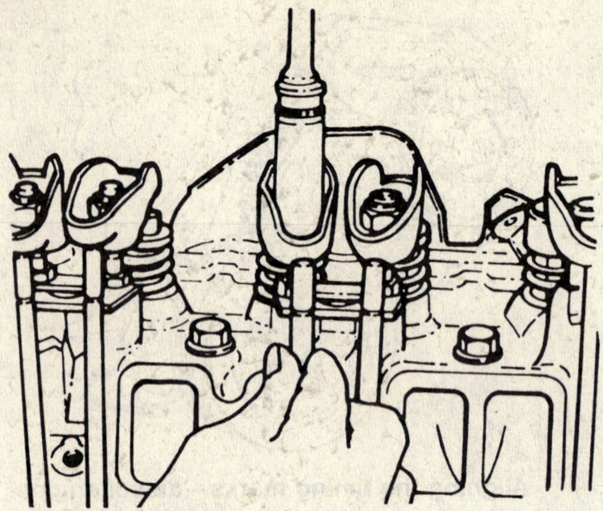

Valve lash adjustment—2.0L and 2.8L engine

3. With the engine in the No. 1 firing position, perform the following adjustments:
   a. If working on the 2.0L engine, adjust the intake valves of cylinders No. 1 and 2 and the exhaust valves of cylinders No. 1 and 3.
   b. If working on the 2.8L engine, adjust the intake valves of cylinders No. 1, 5 and 6 and the exhaust valves of cylinders No. 1, 2 and 3.
4. To adjust the valves, back-out the adjusting nut until lash can be felt at the pushrod, then turn the nut until all of the lash is removed.

NOTE: To determine is all of the lash is removed, turn the pushrod with your fingers until the movement is removed.

5. When all of the lash has been removed, turn the adjusting an additional 1½ turns; this will center the lifter plunger.
6. Rotate the crankshaft 1 complete revolution and realign the timing marks; the engine is now positioned on the No. 4 firing position.
7. With the engine in the No. 4 firing position, perform the following procedures:
   a. If working on the 2.0L engine, adjust the intake valves of cylinders No. 3 and 4 and the exhaust valves of cylinders No. 2 and 4.
   b. If working on the 2.8L engine, adjust the intake valves of cylinders No. 2, 3 and 4 and the exhaust valves of cylinders No. 4, 5 and 6.
8. To compete the installation, reverse the removal procedures.

2.5L Engine

Valve lash is not adjustable on the 2.5L engine. Check that the rocker arm bolts are tightened to 22 ft. lbs. When valve lash falls out of specification (valve tap is heard), replace the rocker arm, pushrod and hydraulic lifter on the offending cylinder.

4.3L Engine

1. To prepare the engine for valve adjustment, rotate the crankshaft until the mark on the damper pulley aligns with the 0 degree mark on the timing plate and the No. 1 cylinder is on the compression stroke.

NOTE: You can tell when the piston is coming up on the compression stroke by removing the spark plug and placing your thumb over the hole, you will feel the air being forced out of the spark plug hole. Stop turning the crankshaft when the TDC timing mark on the crankshaft pulley is directly aligned with the timing mark pointer.

2. With the engine on the compression stroke, adjust the exhaust valves of cylinders No. 1, 5 and 6 and the intake valves of cylinders No. 1, 2 and 3 by performing the following procedures:
   a. Back out the adjusting nut until lash can be felt at the pushrod.
   b. While rotating the pushrod, turn the adjusting nut inward until all of the lash is removed.
   c. When the play has disappeared, turn the adjusting nut inward 1 additional turn.
3. Rotate the crankshaft 1 complete revolution and align the mark on the damper pulley with the **0** degree mark on the timing plate; this is TDC of the compression stroke for the No. 4 cylinder. With the engine on the compression stroke, adjust the exhaust valves of cylinders No. 2, 3 and 4 and the intake valves of cylinders No. 4, 5 and 6, by performing the following procedures:
   a. Back out the adjusting nut until lash can be felt at the pushrod.
   b. While rotating the pushrod, turn the adjusting nut inward until all of the lash is removed.
   c. When the play has disappeared, turn the adjusting nut inward 1 additional turn.
4. To complete the installation, reverse the removal procedures. Start the engine, the check for oil leaks and engine operation.

VALVE ARRANGEMENT

1.9L
E–I–I–E–E–I–I–E (front-to-rear)
2.0L
E–I–I–E–E–I–I–E (front-to-rear)
2.2L
E–I–I–E–E–I–I–E (front-to-rear)
2.5L
I–E–I–E–E–I–E–I (front-to-rear)
2.8L
E–I–I–E–I–E (left bank – front-to-rear)
E–I–E–I–I–E (right bank – front-to-rear)
4.3L
E–I–E–I–I–E (left bank – front-to-rear)
E–I–I–E–I–E (right bank – front-to-rear)

IDLE SPEED AND MIXTURE ADJUSTMENTS

Carbureted Engines

1.9L Engine

In order to adjust the idle mixture, first remove the plug that covers the mixture screw.

1. Set the parking brake, block the drive wheels and place the transmission in Neutral.
2. Remove the carburetor from the engine, place it on a work bench and turn it upside down.
3. Using a punch and a hammer, carefully drive the idle mixture screw metal plug from the base of the carburetor.
4. Reinstall the carburetor onto the engine. Start the engine and adjust the idle speed.
5. Allow the engine to reach normal operating temperatures, the choke must be Open and the air conditioning, if equipped, turned **OFF**. Disconnect and plug the distributor vacuum line, the EGR vacuum line and the idle compensator vacuum lines.
6. Turn the mixture screw all the way in, then back it out 1½ turns.

NOTE: After adjustment, reconnect the vacuum lines.

7. Adjust the throttle speed screw to 850 rpm for manual transmission or 950 rpm for automatic transmission.
8. Adjust the idle mixture screw to achieve the maximum speed.
9. Reset the throttle adjusting screw to 850 rpm for manual transmission or 950 rpm for automatic transmission.

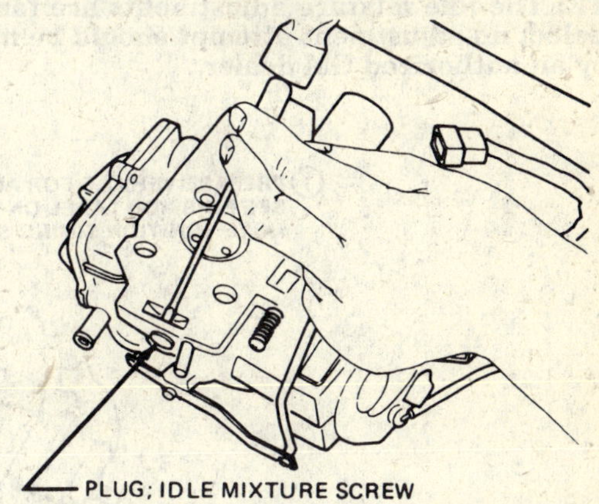

Removing the mixture screw plug – 1.9L engine

10. Turn the idle mixture screw (clockwise) until the engine speed is reduced to 800 rpm for manual transmission or 900 rpm for automatic transmission.
11. If equipped with air conditioning, perform the following procedures:
    a. Turn the air conditioning to **MAX** Cold and the blower to **HIGH**.

Adjusting the idle speed—1.9L engine

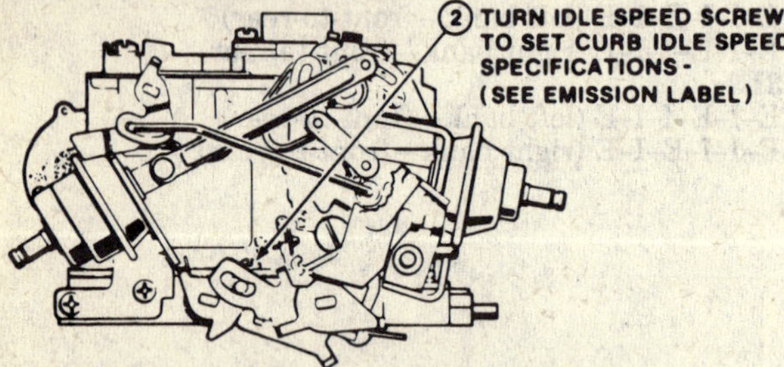

Adjusting the idle speed on the 2SE carburetor without air conditioning—2.0L and 2.8L engines

b. Open the throttle to ⅓ and allow it to close; this allows the speed-up solenoid to reach full travel.

c. Adjust the speed-up controller adjusting screw to set the idle to 900 rpm.

2.0L and 2.8L Engines

NOTE: The idle mixture adjustments are factory set and sealed; no adjustment attempt should be made, except by an authorized GM dealer.

WITHOUT AIR CONDITIONING

1. Refer to the emission control label on the vehicle and prepare the engine for adjustments.
2. Remove the air cleaner, set the parking brake and block the drive wheels.
3. Connect a tachometer to the distributor connector.
4. Place the transmission in **D** for automatic transmission or Neutral for manual transmission; make sure the solenoid is energized.
5. Open the throttle slightly to allow the solenoid plunger to extend. Adjust the curb idle speed to the specified rpm by turning the solenoid screw.
6. Deenergize the solenoid by disconnecting the electrical lead.
7. Set the basic idle speed rpm by turning the idle speed screw. After adjustment, reconnect the solenoid electrical lead.
8. Remove the tachometer and install the air cleaner.

WITH AIR CONDITIONING

1. Refer to the emission label on the vehicle and prepare the engine for adjustments.
2. Remove the air cleaner, set the parking brake and block the drive wheels.
3. Connect a tachometer to the distributor connector.
4. Place the transmission in **D** for automatic transmission or Neutral for manual transmission; make sure the solenoid is energized.
5. Turn the air conditioning **OFF** and set the curb idle speed by turning the idle speed screw.
6. Disconnect the air conditioning lead from the air conditioning compressor; make sure the solenoid is energized. Open the throttle slightly to allow the solenoid plunger to extend.
7. Turn the solenoid screw to adjust to the specified rpm. After adjustment, reconnect the air conditioning compressor lead, remove the tachometer and install the air cleaner.

Throttle Body Engines

2.5L EFI Engine

NOTE: The following procedures require the use a tachometer, GM tool J-33047, BT-8207 or equivalent, GM Torx Bit 20, silicone sealant, a $^{5}/_{32}$ in. drill bit, a prick punch and a $^{1}/_{16}$ in. pin punch.

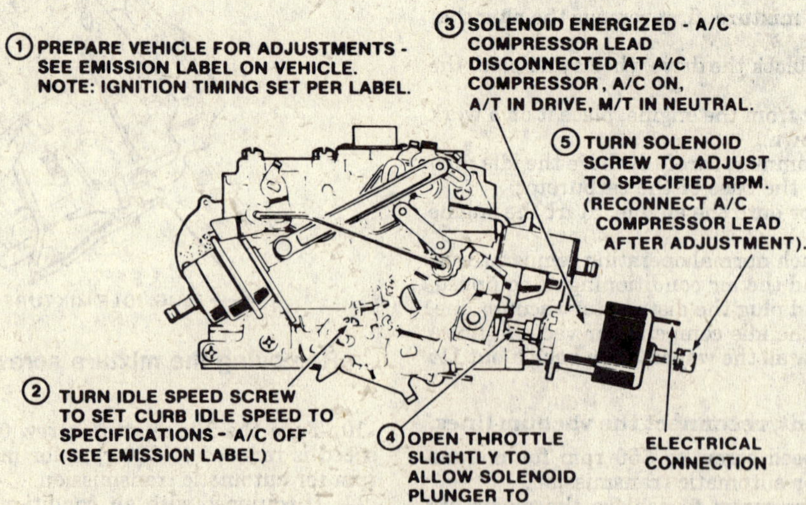

Adjusting the idle speed on E2SE carburetors with air conditioning—2.0L and 2.8L engines

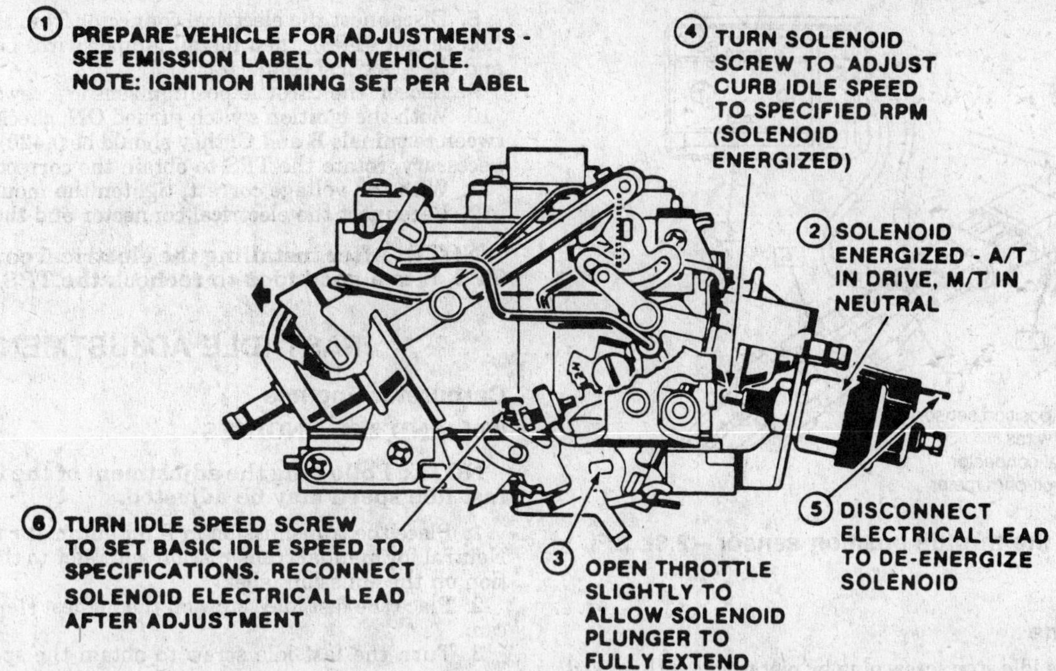

Adjusting the idle speed on E2SE carburetors without air conditioning—2.0L and 2.8L engines

The throttle stop screw, used in regulating the minimum idle speed, is adjusted at the factory and is not necessary to perform. This adjustment should be performed ONLY when the throttle body has been replaced.

NOTE: The replacement of the complete throttle body assembly will have the minimum idle adjusted at the factory.

1. Remove the air cleaner and the gasket. Be sure to plug the THERMAC vacuum port (air cleaner vacuum line-to-throttle body) on the throttle body.
2. Remove the throttle valve cable from the throttle control bracket to provide access to the minimum air adjustment screw.
3. Using the manufacturer's instructions, connect a tachometer to the engine.
4. Remove the electrical connector from the Idle Air Control (IAC) valve, located on the throttle body.
5. To remove the throttle stop screw cover, perform the following procedures:
   a. Using a prick punch, mark the housing at the top over the center line of the throttle stop screw.
   b. Using a $^{5}/_{32}$ in. drill bit, drill (on an angle) a hole through the casting to the hardened cover.
   c. Using a $^{1}/_{16}$ in. pin punch, place it through the hole and drive out the cover to expose the throttle stop screw.
6. Place the transmission in **P** for automatic transmission or Neutral for manual transmission, start the engine and allow the idle speed to stabilize.
7. Using the GM tool J-33047, BT-8207 or equivalent, install it into the idle air passage of the throttle body; be sure the tool is fully seated in the opening and no air leaks exist.
8. Using the GM Torx Bit 20, turn the throttle stop screw until the engine speed is 475–525 rpm for automatic transmission in **P** or 750–800 rpm for manual transmission in Neutral.
9. With the idle speed adjusted, stop the engine, remove the tool J-33047, BT-8207 or equivalent, from the throttle body.
10. Reconnect the Idle Air Control (IAC) electrical connector.
11. Using silicone sealant or equivalent, cover the throttle stop screw.
12. Reinstall the gasket and the air cleaner assembly.

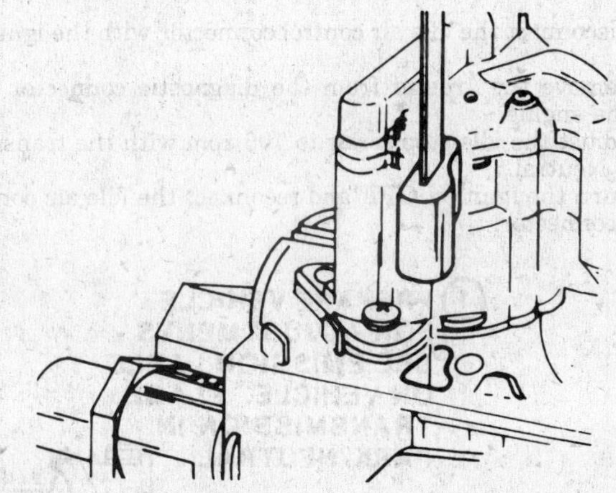
Plug the idle passages of each throttle body as shown

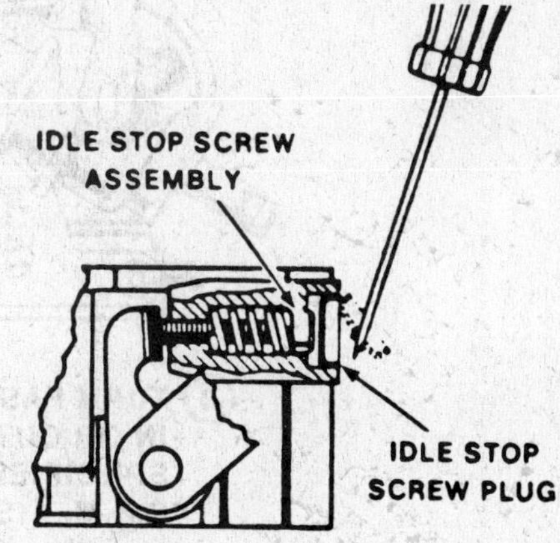

Removing the idle stop screw plug—2.8L EFI engine

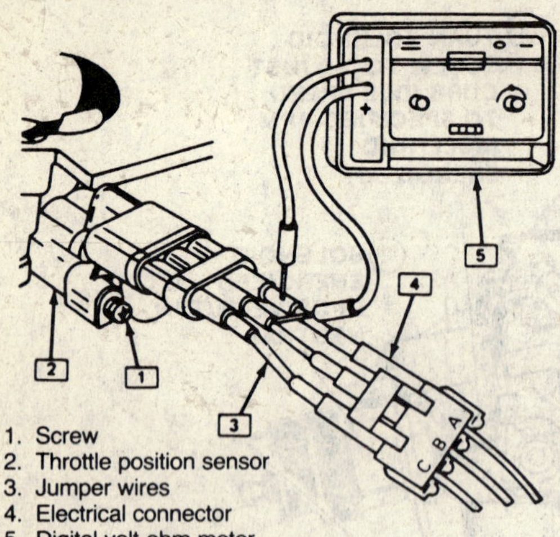

1. Screw
2. Throttle position sensor
3. Jumper wires
4. Electrical connector
5. Digital volt-ohm meter

Adjusting the throttle position sensor—2.8L EFI engine

2.8L EFI Engine

1. Remove the idle stop screw plug by piercing it with an awl.
2. With the idle air control motor connected, ground the diagnostic connector.
3. Turn the ignition **ON** and wait 30 seconds, do not start the engine.
4. Disconnect the idle air control connector with the ignition **ON**.
5. Remove the ground from the diagnostic connector and start the engine.
6. Adjust the idle stop screw to 700 rpm with the transmission in Neutral.
7. Turn the ignition **OFF** and reconnect the idle air control motor connector.
8. Disconnect the electrical connector from the throttle position sensor (TPS), then install jumper wires between the TPS and the electrical connector.
9. Loosen the throttle position sensor screws.
10. With the ignition switch turned **ON**, check the voltage between terminals **B** and **C**; they should be 0.420V and 0.450V. If necessary, rotate the TPS to obtain the correct voltage.
11. With the voltage correct, tighten the mounting screws.
12. Reconnect the electrical connector and the air cleaner.

NOTE: After installing the electrical connector to the TPS, it is a good idea to recheck the TPS voltage.

FAST IDLE ADJUSTMENT

Carburetor Engines

2.0L AND 2.8L ENGINES

NOTE: Following the adjustment of the idle speed, the fast idle speed may be adjusted.

1. Place the transmission in **P** for automatic transmission or Neutral for manual transmission and refer to the recommendation on the emission label.
2. Place the fast idle screw on the highest step of the fast idle cam.
3. Turn the fast idle screw to obtain the specified fast idle rpm.

Diesel Engine

SLOW IDLE SPEED ADJUSTMENT

1. Set parking brake and block drive wheels.
2. Place transmission in Neutral.
3. Start and warm up the engine. Engine coolant temperature above 176°F (80°C).
4. Connect a diesel tachometer according to the manufacturer's instructions.

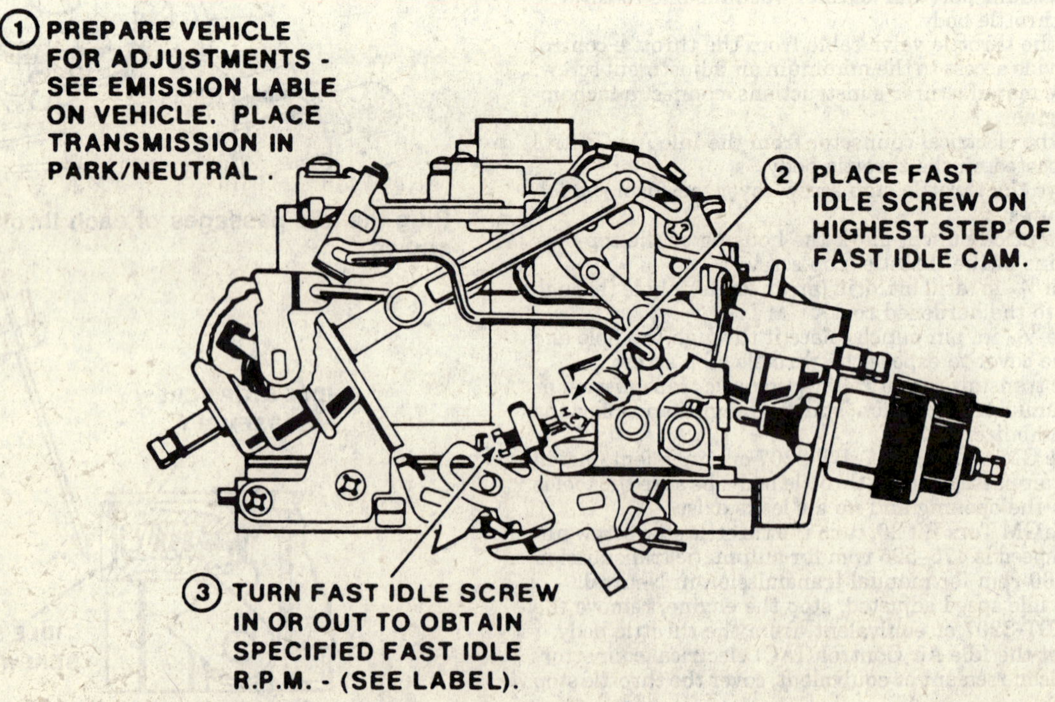

Fast idle adjustment procedure—2.0L and 2.8L engines

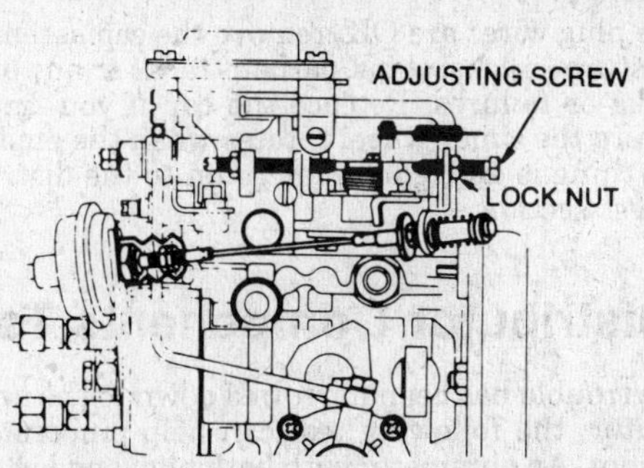

Idle speed adjustment points—1983 2.2L diesel engine

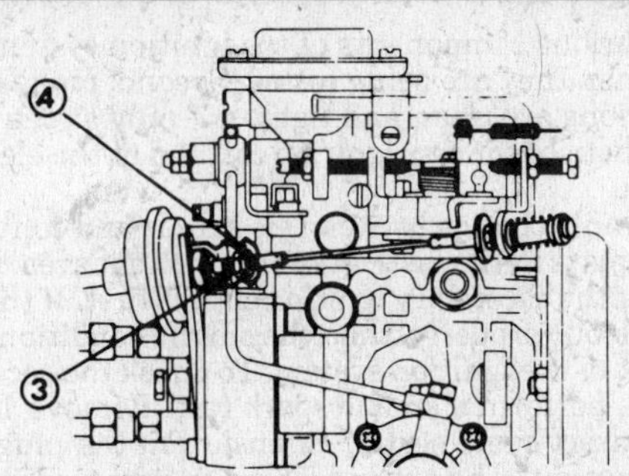

Fast idle adjustment—1983 2.2L diesel engine

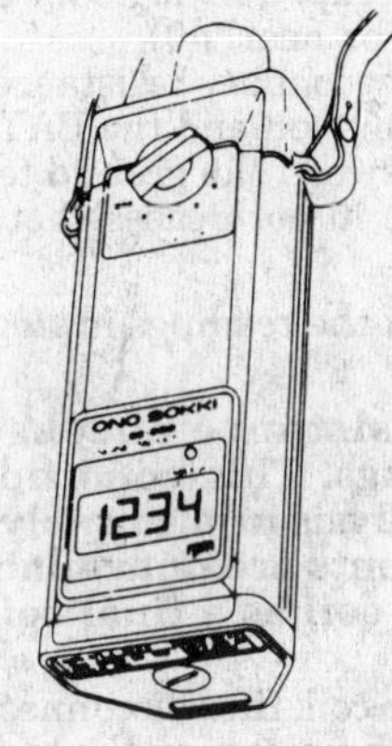

Diesel tachometer

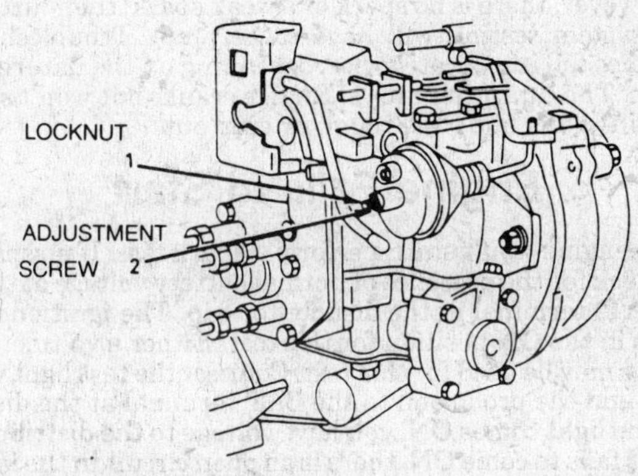

Fast idle adjustment—1984–85 2.2L diesel engine

5. If the idle speed deviates from the specified range of 700–800 rpm, loosen the idle speed adjusting screw locknut.
6. Turn the adjusting screw in or out until the idle speed is in the correct range. After tightening the locknut, lock it in place.

FAST IDLE SPEED ADJUSTMENT

1. Start and warm up the engine. Engine coolant temperature above 176°F (80°).
2. Connect a diesel tachometer according to the manufacturer's instructions.
3. Disconnect the hoses from the vacuum switch valve, then connect a pipe (4mm dia.) in position between the hoses.
4. Loosen adjust nut and adjust engine idle speed by moving the nut. Fast idle should be 900–950 rpm.
5. Tighten the locknut.
6. Remove engine tachometer.

IGNITION SYSTEM

Troubleshooting the HEI System

The symptoms of a defective component within the HEI system are exactly the same as those you would encounter in a conventional system. Some of these symptoms are:

- Hard or no Starting
- Rough Idle
- Poor Fuel Economy
- Engine misses under load or while accelerating

If you suspect a problem in the ignition system, there are certain preliminary checks which you should carry out before you begin to check the electronic portions of the system. First, it is extremely important to make sure the vehicle battery is in as good state of charge. A defective or poorly charged battery will cause the various components of the ignition system to read incorrectly when they are being tested. Second, make sure all wiring connections are clean and tight, not only at the battery but also at the distributor cap, ignition coil and at the electronic control module.

Since the only change between electronic and conventional ignition systems is in the distributor component area, it is imperative to check the secondary ignition circuit first. If the secondary circuit check out properly, then the engine condition is probably not the fault of the ignition system. To check the secondary ignition system, perform a simple spark test. Remove 1 of the plug wires and insert some sort of extension in the plug socket. An old spark plug with the ground electrode removed makes a good extension. Using insulated pliers, hold the wire and extension about ¼ in. away from the block and crank the engine. If a normal spark occurs, then the problem is most likely not in the ignition system. Check for fuel system problems or fouled spark plugs.

If, however, there is no spark or a weak spark, then further ignition system testing will have to be done. Troubleshooting techniques fall into 2 categories, depending on the nature of the problem. The categories are (1) Engine cranks but won't start or (2) Engine runs but runs rough or cuts out.

Engine Fails to Start

If the engine won't start, perform a spark test. If no spark occurs, check for the presence of normal battery voltage at the battery (BAT) terminal in the distributor cap. The ignition switch must be in the **ON** position for this test. Either a voltmeter or a test light may be used for this test. Connect the test light wire to ground and the probe end to the BAT terminal at the distributor. If the light comes ON, you have voltage to the distributor. If the light fails to come ON, there is an open circuit in the ignition primary wiring leading to the distributor. In this case, you will have to check wiring continuity back to the ignition switch using a test light. If there is battery voltage at the BAT terminal but no spark at the plugs, then the problem lies within the distributor assembly. Go to the the distributor components test procedure.

Engine Runs but Runs Rough or Cuts Out

Make sure the plug wires are in good shape first. There should be no obvious cracks or breaks. You can check the plug wires with an ohmmeter but do not pierce the wires with a probe. Check the chart for the correct plug wire resistance.

If the plug wires are OK, remove the cap assembly and check for moisture, cracks, chips, carbon tracks or any other high voltage leaks or failures. Replace the cap if you find any defects. Make sure the timer wheel rotates when the engine is cranked. If everything is all right so far go on to the distributor components test section.

Distributor Components Testing

If the trouble has been narrowed down to the units within the distributor, the following test can help pinpoint the defective component. An ohmmeter with both high and low ranges should be used. These test are made with the cap assembly removed and the battery wire disconnected.

1. Connect an ohmmeter between the TACH and BAT terminals in the distributor cap. The primary coil resistance should be less than 1 ohm (0 or nearly 0).
2. To check the coil secondary resistance, connect an ohmmeter between the rotor button and the BAT terminal. Then connect the ohmmeter between the ground terminal and the rotor button. The resistance in both cases should be between 6000–30,000 ohms.
3. Replace the coil, if the readings in step 1 and 2 are infinite.

NOTE: These resistance checks will not disclose shorted coil windings. This condition can be detected only with scope analysis or a suitably designed coil tester. If these instruments are unavailable, replace the coil with a known good coil as a final coil test.

4. To test the pickup coil, first disconnect the white and green module leads. Set the ohmmeter on the high scale and connect it between a ground and either the white or green lead. Any resistance measurement less than infinity requires replacement of the pickup coil.
5. Pickup coil continuity is tested by connecting the ohmmeter (on low range) between the white and green leads. Normal resistance is between 500–1500 ohms. Move the vacuum advance arm while performing this test. This will detect any break in coil continuity. Such a condition can cause intermittent misfiring. Replace the pickup coil, if the reading is outside the specific limits.
6. If no defects have been found at this time and you still have a problem, then the module will have to be checked. If you do not have access to a module tester, the only possible alternative is a substitution test. If the module fails the substitution test, replace it.

3 Engine and Engine Overhaul

QUICK REFERENCE INDEX

GENERAL INDEX

ENGINE ELECTRICAL

The engine electrical system can be broken down into 3 separate and distinct systems

1. The ignition system.
2. The charging system.
3. The starting system.

High Energy Ignition (HEI) System

The HEI system operates in basically the same manner as the conventional ignition system, with the exception of the type of switching device used. A toothed iron timer core is mounted on the distributor shaft which rotates inside of an electronic pole piece. The pole piece has internal teeth (corresponding to those on the timer core) which contains a permanent magnet and pick-up coil (not to be confused with the ignition coil). The pole piece senses the magnetic field of the timer core teeth and sends a signal to the ignition module which electronically controls the primary coil voltage. The ignition coil operates in basically the same manner as a conventional ignition coil (though the ignition coils do not interchange).

NOTE: The HEI systems uses a capacitor within the distributor which is primarily used for radio interference purposes.

None of the electrical components used in the HEI systems are adjustable. If a component is found to be defective, it must be replaced.

PRECAUTIONS

Before troubleshooting the systems, it might be a good idea to take note of the following precautions:

Timing Light Use

Inductive pick-up timing lights are the best kind to use. Timing lights which connect between the spark plug and the spark plug wire occasionally give false readings.

Some engines incorporate a magnetic timing probe terminal (at the damper pulley) for use of special electronic timing equipment. Refer to the manufacturer's instructions when using this equipment.

Spark Plug Wires

The plug wires are of a different construction than conventional wires. When replacing them, make sure to use the correct wires, since conventional wires won't carry the higher voltage. Also, handle them carefully to avoid cracking or splitting them and never pierce them.

Tachometer Use

Not all tachometers will operate or indicate correctly. While some tachometers may give a reading, this does not necessarily mean the reading is correct. In addition, some tachometers connect differently than others. If you can't figure out whether or not your tachometer will work on your vehicle, check with the tachometer manufacturer.

System Testers

Instruments designed specifically for testing the HEI system are available from several tool manufacturers. Some of these will even test the module.

The Charging System

The charging system provides electrical power for operation of the vehicle's ignition, starting system and all of the electrical accessories. The battery serves as an electrical surge or storage tank, storing (in chemical form) the energy originally produced by the alternator. The system also provides a means of regulating the alternator output to protect the battery from being overcharged and the accessories from being destroyed.

The storage battery is a chemical device incorporating parallel lead plates in a tank containing a sulfuric acid-water solution. Adjacent plates are slightly dissimilar and the chemical reaction of the 2 dissimilar plates produces electrical energy when the battery is connected to a load such as the starter motor. The chemical reaction is reversible, so when the alternator is producing a voltage (electrical pressure) greater than that produced by the battery, electricity is forced into the battery and it is returned to it's fully charged state.

Todays alternators are lighter, more efficient, rotate at higher speeds and have fewer brush problems. In an alternator, the field rotates while all of the current produced passes only through the stator windings. The brushes bear against the continuous slip rings; this causes the current produced to periodically reverse the direction of it's flow. Diodes (electrical one-way switches) block the flow of current from traveling in the wrong direction. A series of diodes are wired together to permit the alternating flow of the stator to be converted to a pulsating but unidirectional flow at the alternator output. The alternator's field is wired in series with the voltage regulator.

Battery and Starting System

The battery is the first link in the chain of mechanisms which work together to provide cranking of the engine. In most modern vehicles, the battery is a lead-acid electrochemical device consisting of six 2 volt (2V) subsections connected in series so the unit is capable of producing approximately 12V of electrical pressure. Each subsection (cell) consists of a series of positive and negative plates held a short distance apart in a solution of sulfuric acid and water. The 2 types of plates are of dissimilar metals. A chemical reaction takes place which produces current flow from the battery, when it's positive and negative terminals are connected to an electrical appliance such as a lamp or motor. The continued transfer of electrons would eventually convert the sulfuric acid in the electrolyte to water and make the 2 plates identical in chemical composition. As electrical energy is removed from the battery, it's voltage output tends to drop. Thus, measuring battery voltage and battery electrolyte composition are 2 ways of checking the ability of the unit to supply power. During the starting of the engine, electrical energy is removed from the battery. However, if the charging circuit is in good condition and the operating conditions are normal, the power removed from the battery will be replaced by the alternator which will force electrons back into the battery, reversing the normal flow and restoring the battery to it's original chemical state.

The battery and starting motor are linked by very heavy electrical cables designed to minimize resistance to the flow of current. Generally, the major power supply cable that leaves the battery goes directly to the starter, while other electrical system needs are supplied by a smaller cable. During the starter operation, power flows from the battery to the starter, then is grounded through the vehicle's frame and the battery's negative ground strap.

The starting motor is a specially designed, direct current electric motor capable of producing a very great amount of power for it's size. One thing that allows the motor to produce a great deal of power is it's tremendous rotating speed. It drives the engine through a tiny pinion gear (attached to the starter's armature), which drives the very large flywheel ring gear at a greatly reduced speed. Another factor allowing it to produce so much power is that only intermittent operation is required of it. Thus, little allowance for air circulation is required and the windings can be built into a very small space.

The starter solenoid is a magnetic device which employs the small current supplied by the starting switch circuit of the ignition switch. This magnetic action moves a plunger, which mechanically engages the starter and electrically closes the heavy switch which connects it to the battery. The starting switch circuit consists of the starting switch (contained within the ignition switch), a transmission neutral safety switch or clutch pedal switch and wiring necessary to connect these with the starter solenoid or relay.

The pinion (small gear) is mounted to a one-way drive clutch. This clutch is splined to the starter armature shaft. When the ignition switch is moved to the Start position, the solenoid plunger slides the pinion toward the flywheel ring rear via a collar and spring. If the teeth on the pinion and flywheel match properly, the pinion will engage the flywheel immediately. If the gear teeth butt one another, the spring will be compressed and will force the gears to mesh as soon as the starter turns far enough to allow them to do so. As the solenoid plunger reaches the end of its travel, it closes the contacts that connect the battery to the starter, then the engine is cranked.

As soon as the engine starts, the flywheel ring gear begins turning fast enough to drive the pinion at an extremely high rate of speed. At this point, the one-way clutch allows the pinion to spin faster than the starter shaft so the starter will not operate at excessive speed(s). When the ignition switch is released from the starter position, the solenoid is de-energized, the spring (contained within the solenoid assembly) pulls the pinion out of mesh and interrupts the current flow to the starter.

Ignition Coil

The ignition coil on the 1.9L and 2.0L engines, are attached to bracket on the inner fender, located on the right side of the engine compartment; on the 2.5L engine, it is attached to the cylinder head, located on the right rear side of the engine; on the 2.8L engine, it is attached to a valve cover bracket, located on the right rear side of the engine; on the 4.3L engine, it is mounted on a bracket, attached to the rear of the intake mainfold in front of the distributor.

TESTING

NOTE: The following procedures require the use of an ohmmeter.

1.9L and 2.0L Engines

For this procedure, the ignition coil may be removed from the vehicle or simply remove the electrical connectors and test it in the vehicle.

1. Remove the ignition coil from the vehicle.
2. Inspect the outer face of the coil for cracking, rusting and/or damage; be sure to inspect the high tension socket.
3. Using an ohmmeter, place one probe on the outer terminal of the electrical connector and the other probe on the center terminal of the electrical connector, then inspect the primary coil resistance, it should be between 0.090–1.40 ohms.
4. Using an ohmmeter, place one probe on the outer terminal of the electrical connector and the other probe on the center terminal of the coil, then inspect the secondary coil resistance, it should be between 7,300–11,100 ohms.
5. Using an ohmmeter, place one probe on the outer terminal of the electrical connector and the other probe on the outer shell of the coil, then inspect the insulation resistance of the coil, it should be less than 1,000,000 ohms.
6. If the coil does not conform to these inspections, replace the coil.

2.5L, 2.8L and 4.3L Engines

For this procedure, the ignition coil may be removed from the engine or simply remove the electrical connectors and test it on the engine.

1. Using an ohmmeter (on the high scale), connect the probes between the primary (low voltage) terminal and coil ground; the reading should be very high or infinity, if not, replace the coil.
2. Using an ohmmeter (on the low scale), connect the probes

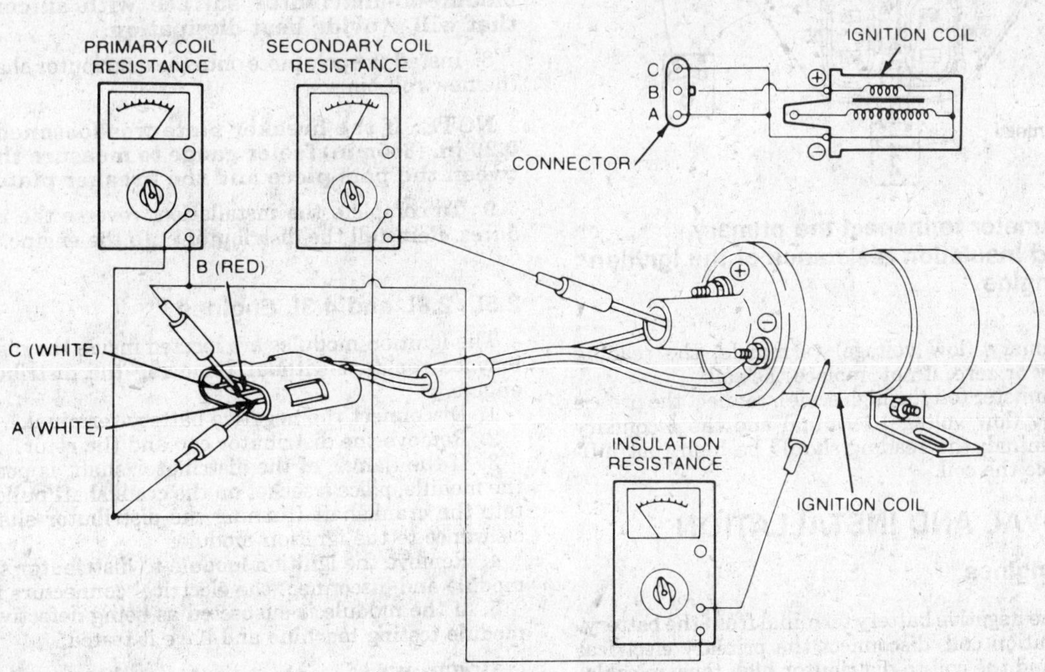

Using an ohmmeter to inspect the primary, secondary and insulation resistance of the ignition coil — 1.9L and 2.0L engines

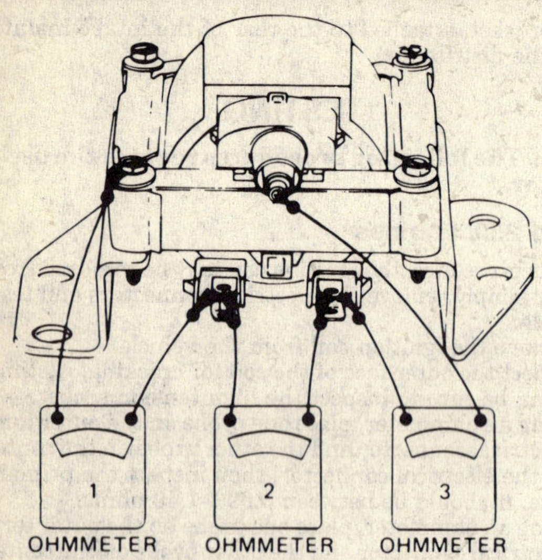

Using an ohmmeter to inspect the primary, secondary and insulation resistance of the ignition coil — 2.5L and 2.8L engines

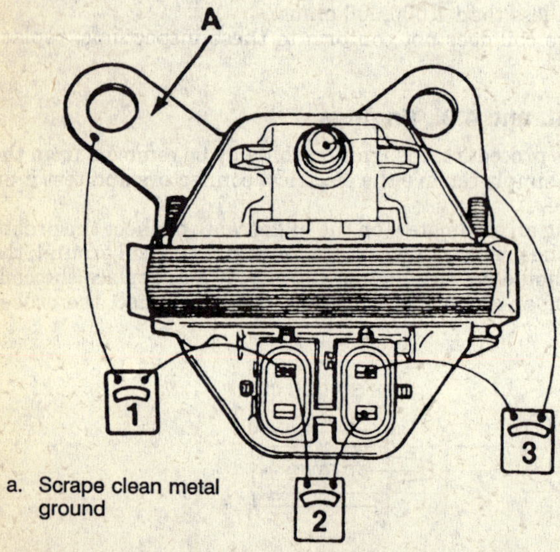

Using an ohmmeter to inspect the primary, secondary and insulation resistance of the ignition coil — 4.3L engine

between both primary (low voltage) terminals; the reading should be very low or zero, if not, replace the coil.

3. Using an ohmmeter (on the high scale), connect the probes between a primary (low voltage) terminal and the secondary (high voltage) terminal; the reading should be high (not infinite), if not, replace the coil.

REMOVAL AND INSTALLATION

1.9L and 2.0L Engines

1. Disconnect the negative battery terminal from the battery.
2. From the ignition coil, disconnect the primary electrical wiring connector and the coil-to-distributor high tension cable.
3. Remove the ignition coil-to-fender screws and the coil from the vehicle.
4. If necessary, test or replace the ignition coil.
5. To install, reverse the removal procedures. Reinstall the wires and the battery terminal.

2.5L, 2.8L and 4.3L Engines

1. Disconnect the negative battery terminal from the battery.
2. At the ignition coil, disconnect the ignition switch-to-coil wire and the distributor-to-coil wires.
3. Remove the coil-to-engine nuts/bolts and the coil from the engine.
4. If necessary, test or replace the ignition coil.
5. To install, reverse the removal procedures. Reinstall the wires and the battery terminal.

Ignition Module

REMOVAL AND INSTALLATION

1.9L and 2.0L Engines

1. Remove the distributor from the engine and place it on a work bench.
2. Remove the distributor cap, the rotor, the packing ring and the cover.
3. Remove the electrical harness-to-distributor screw, then disconnect the electrical harness connectors from the ignition module.
4. Using 2 medium prybars, pry the pole piece from the distributor shaft, then remove the roll pin.
5. Using a Phillips Head screwdriver, remove the ignition module-to-breaker plate screws and lift the module from the distributor; be sure to remove the spacers from the module.
6. If the module is suspected as being defective, take it to a module testing machine and have it tested.
7. To install, replace the ignition module, spacers and screws onto the breaker plate.

NOTE: When replacing the module, sure to coat the module-to-distributor surface with silicone lubricant that will provide heat dissipation.

8. Install the pole piece onto the distributor shaft, followed by the new roll pin.

NOTE: If the breaker plate was loosened, use a 0.12–0.20 in. (3–5mm) feeler gauge to measure the air gap between the pole piece and the breaker plate stator.

9. To complete the installation, reverse the removal procedures. Reinstall the distributor onto the engine.

2.5L, 2.8L and 4.3L Engines

The ignition modules are located inside the distributor; they may be replaced without removing the distributor from the engine.

1. Disconnect the negative battery terminal.
2. Remove the distributor cap and the rotor.
3. If the flange, of the distributor shaft, is positioned above the module, place a socket on the crankshaft pulley bolt and rotate the crankshaft (turning the distributor shaft) to provide clearance to the ignition module.
4. Remove the ignition module-to-distributor screws, lift the module and disconnect the electrical connectors from it.
5. If the module is suspected as being defective, take it to a module testing machine and have it tested.

NOTE: When replacing the module, sure to coat the module-to-distributor surface with silicone lubricant that will provide heat dissipation.

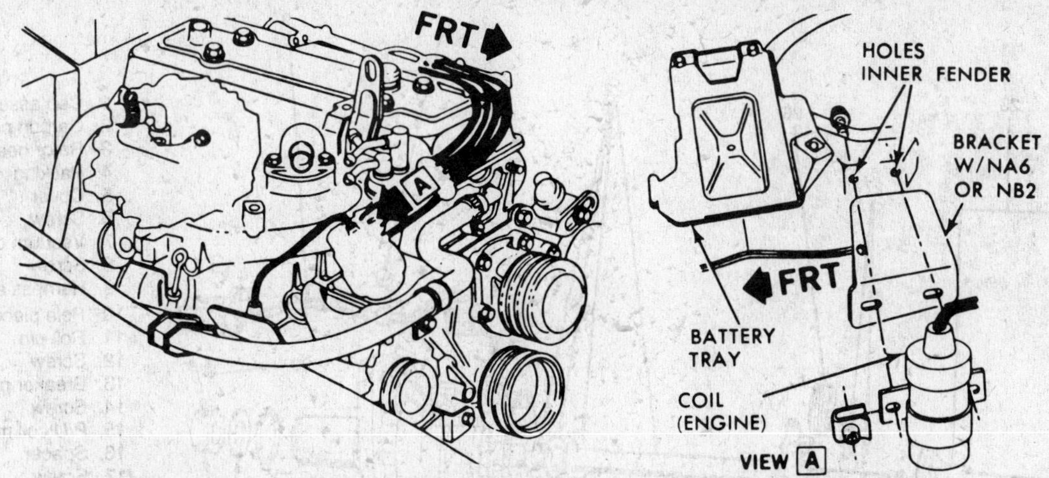

View of the ignition coil and distributor — 1.9L and 2.0L engines

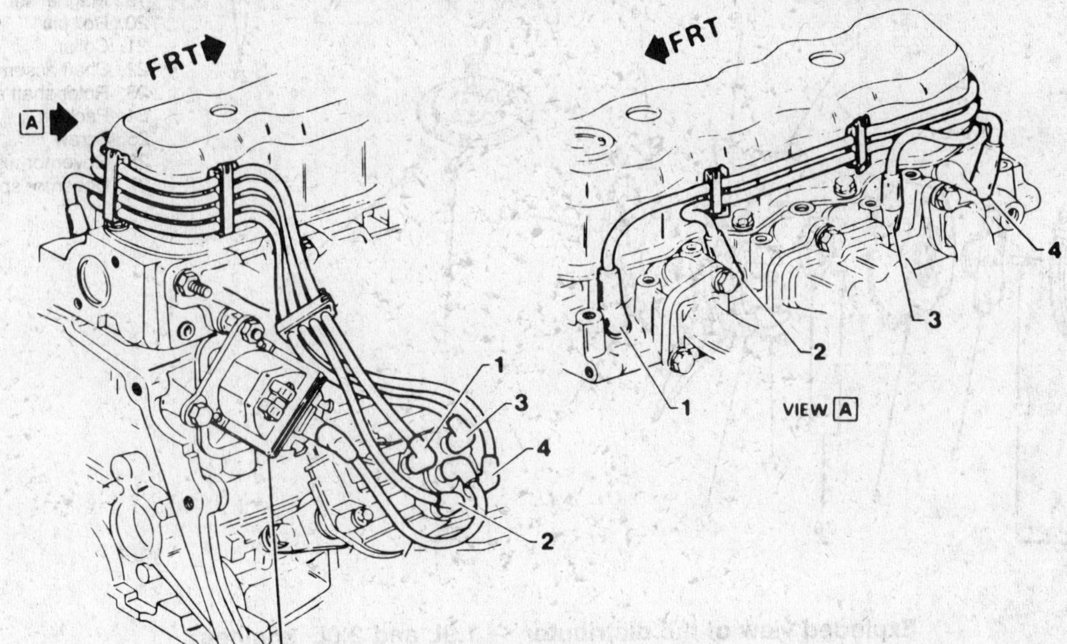

View of the ignition coil, distributor and wiring — 2.5L engine

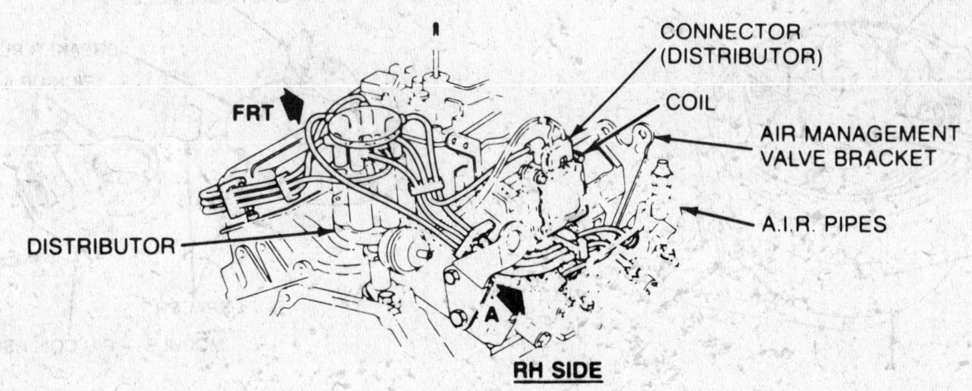

View of the ignition coil, distributor and wiring — 2.8L engine — 4.3L is similar

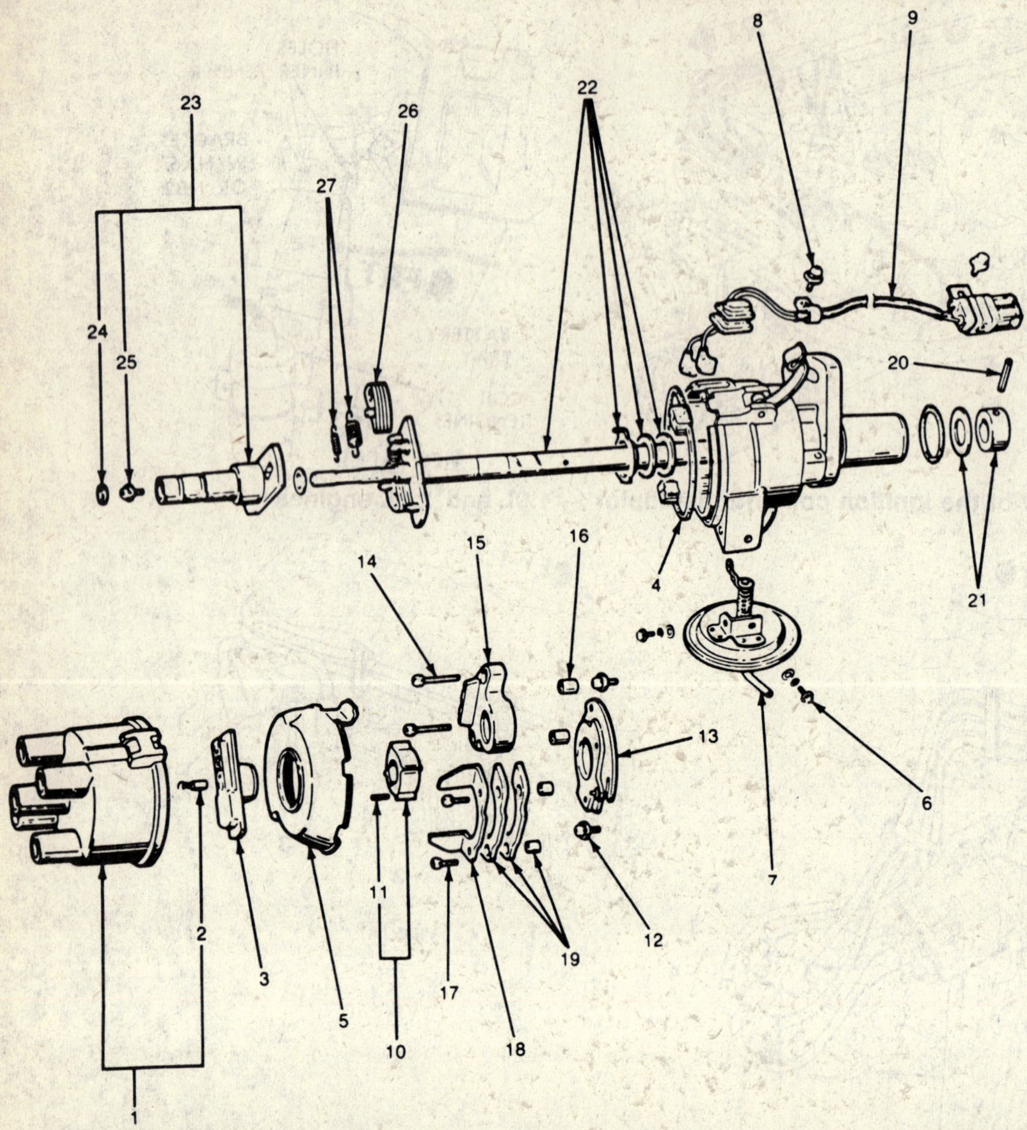

1. Cap assembly
2. Carbon point
3. Rotor head
4. Packing
5. Cover
6. Screw
7. Vacuum control assembly
8. Screw
9. Harness assembly
10. Pole piece
11. Roll pin
12. Screw
13. Breaker plate assembly
14. Screw
15. P/U coil module assembly
16. Spacer
17. Screw
18. Stator
19. Magnet set
20. Roll pin
21. Collar
22. Shaft assembly
23. Rotor shaft assembly
24. Packing
25. Screw
26. Governor weight
27. Governor spring

Exploded view of the distributor — 1.9L and 2.0L engines

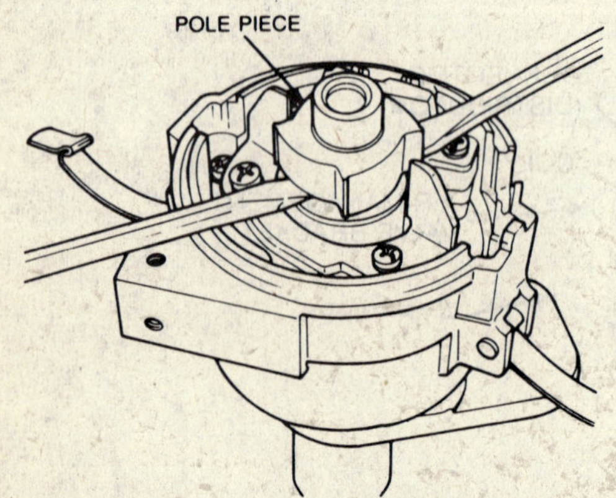

Using 2 prybars to remove the pole piece from the distributor shaft — 1.9L and 2.0L engines

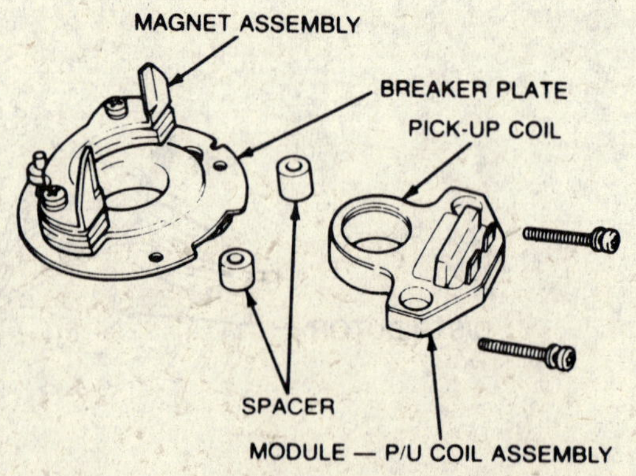

Exploded view of the ignition module and the breaker plate assembly — 1.9L and 2.0L engines

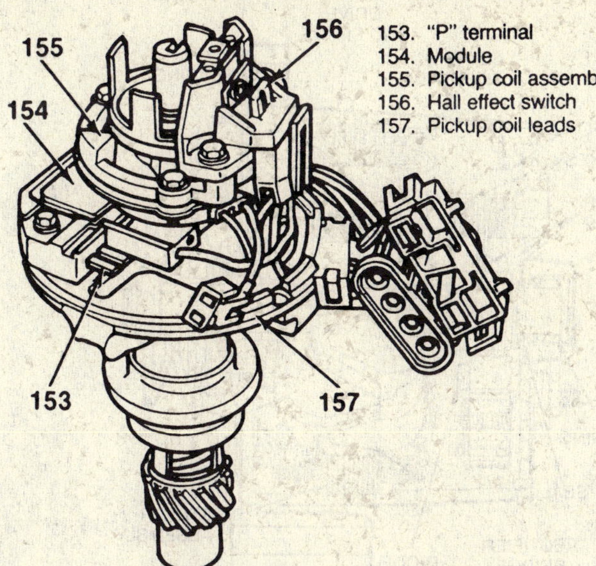

View of the distributor – typical

6. To install, apply silicone lubricant to the module mounting area of the distributor and reverse the removal procedures. Install the rotor, the distributor cap and the negative battery terminal.

Distributor

REMOVAL AND INSTALLATION

Undisturbed Engine

This condition exists if the engine has not been rotated with the distributor removed.

1. Disconnect the negative battery terminal from the battery.
2. Tag and disconnect the electrical connector(s) from the distributor.
3. Remove the distributor cap (do not remove the ignition wires) from the distributor and move it aside.
4. Using a crayon or chalk, make locating marks (for installation purposes) on the rotor, the ignition module, the distributor housing and the engine.
5. Loosen and remove the distributor clamp bolt and clamp, then lift the distributor from the engine.

NOTE: Noting the relative position of the rotor and the module alignment marks, make a second mark on the rotor to align it with the one mark on the module.

To install:

6. Install a new O-ring on the distributor housing.
7. Align the second mark on the rotor with the mark on the module, then install the distributor, taking care to align the mark on the housing with the one on the engine.

NOTE: It may be necessary to lift the distributor and turn the rotor slightly to align the gears and the oil pump driveshaft.

8. With the respective marks aligned, install the clamp and bolt finger-tight.
9. Install and secure the distributor cap.
10. Connect the electrical connector(s) to the distributor.
11. Connect a timing light to the engine (following the manufacturer's instructions). Start the engine, then check and/or adjust the timing.
12. Turn the engine **OFF**, tighten the distributor clamp bolt and remove the timing light.

Disturbed Engine

This condition exists when the engine has been rotated with the distributor removed.

1. Disconnect the negative battery terminal from the battery.
2. Tag and disconnect the electrical connector(s) from the distributor.
3. Remove the distributor cap (do not remove the ignition wires) from the distributor and move it aside.
4. Using a crayon or chalk, make locating marks (for installation purposes) on the rotor, the ignition module, the distributor housing and the engine.
5. Loosen and remove the distributor clamp bolt and clamp, then lift the distributor from the engine.

NOTE: Noting the relative position of the rotor and the module alignment marks, make a second mark on the rotor to align it with the one mark on the module.

To install:

6. Install a new O-ring on the distributor housing.
7. Rotate the crankshaft to position the No. 1 cylinder on the TDC of it's compression stroke. This may be determined by inserting a rag into the No. 1 spark plug hole and slowly turn the engine crankshaft. When the timing mark on the crankshaft pulley aligns with the **0** degree mark on the timing scale and the rag is blown out by the compression, the No. 1 piston is at Top Dead Center (TDC).
8. Turn the rotor so it will point to the No. 1 terminal of the distributor cap.
9. Install the distributor into the engine block. It may be necessary to turn the rotor, a little in either direction, in order to engage the gears.
10. Tap the starter a few times to ensure that the oil pump shaft is mated to the distributor shaft.
11. Bring the engine to No. 1 TDC again and check to see that the rotor is indeed pointing toward the No. 1 terminal of the cap.
12. With the respective marks aligned, install the clamp and bolt finger-tight.
13. Install and secure the distributor cap.
14. Connect the electrical connector(s) to the distributor.

NOTE: If equipped with a vacuum line, reconnect it.

15. Connect a timing light to the engine (following the manufacturer's instructions). Start the engine, then check and/or adjust the timing.
16. Turn the engine **OFF**, tighten the distributor clamp bolt and remove the timing light.

Alternator

The alternating current generator (alternator) supplies a continuous output of electrical energy at all engine speeds. The alternator generates electrical energy and recharges the battery by supplying it with electrical current. This unit consists of 4 main assemblies: 2 end-frame assemblies, a rotor assembly and a stator assembly. The rotor assembly is supported in the drive end-frame by a roller bearing. These bearings are lubricated during assembly and require no maintenance. There are 6 diodes in the end-frame assembly. These diodes are electrical check valves that also change the alternating current developed within the stator windings to a direct current (DC) at the output (BAT) terminal. Three of these diodes are negative and are mounted flush with the end-frame, while the other 3 are positive and are mounted into a strip called a heat sink. The positive diodes are easily identified as the ones within the small cavities or depressions.

The alternators, used on the 1986–91 2.8L and 1988–91 4.3L engines, experienced engineering changes, which are: The elimi-

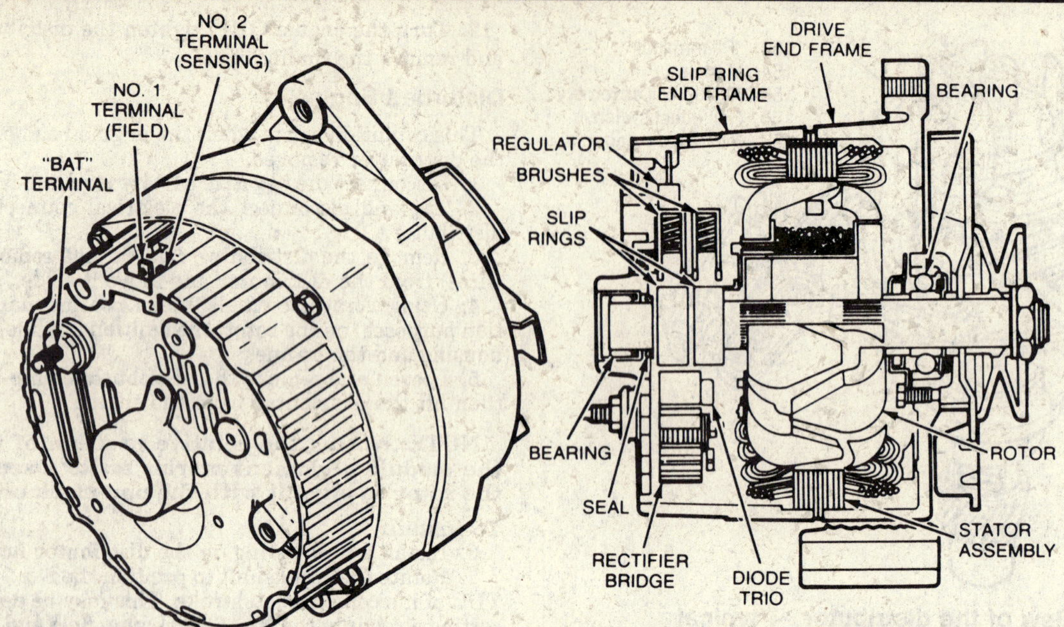

Sectional view of the 10SI alternator – all except 1986–91 2.8L and 1988–91 4.3L engines

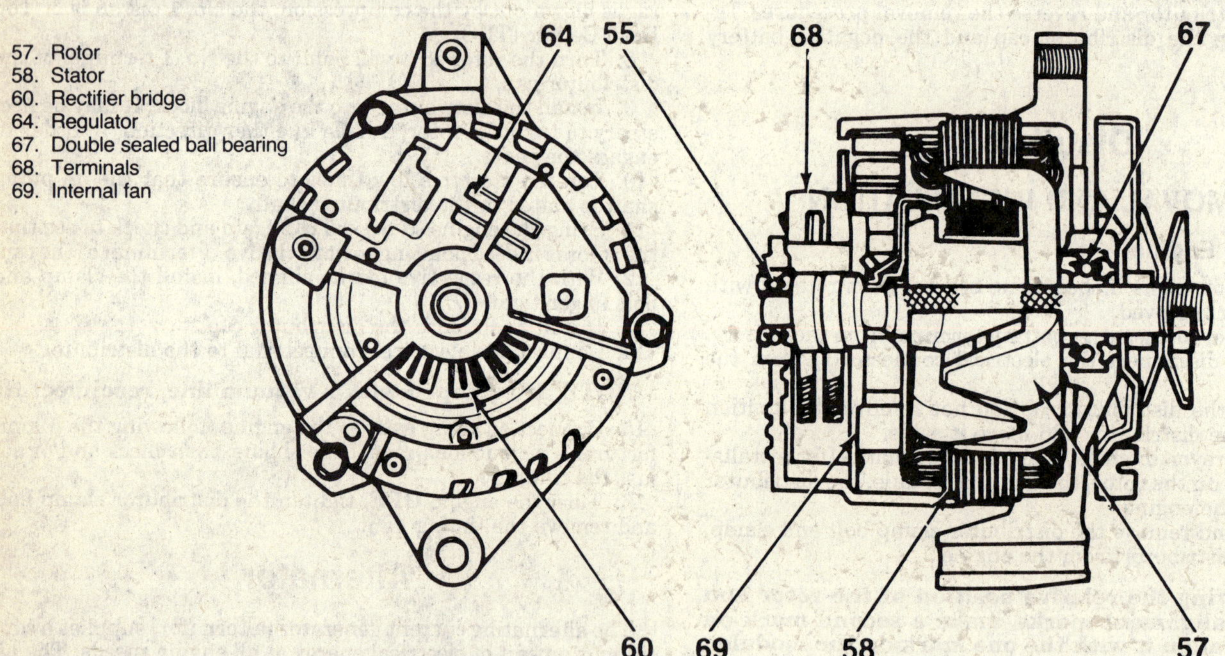

Sectional view of the CS-130 alternator – 1986–91 2.8L and 1988–91 4.3L engines

nation of the diode trio and the reduction of the external wiring connectors from 3-to-2 wires.

NOTE: The new alternators are not serviceable and no periodic maintenance is required.

ALTERNATOR PRECAUTIONS

To prevent damage to the on-board computer, alternator and regulator, the following precautionary measures must be taken when working with the electrical system.

- Never reverse the battery connections. Always check the battery polarity visually. This is to be done before any connections are made to be sure all of the connections correspond to the battery ground polarity.
- Booster batteries for starting must be connected properly. Make sure the positive cable of the booster battery is connected to the positive terminal of the battery that is getting the boost. This applies to both negative and ground cables.
- Make sure the ignition switch is OFF when connecting or disconnecting any electrical component, especially on trucks equipped with an on-board computer control system.
- Disconnect the battery cables before using a fast charger; the charger has a tendency to force current through the diodes

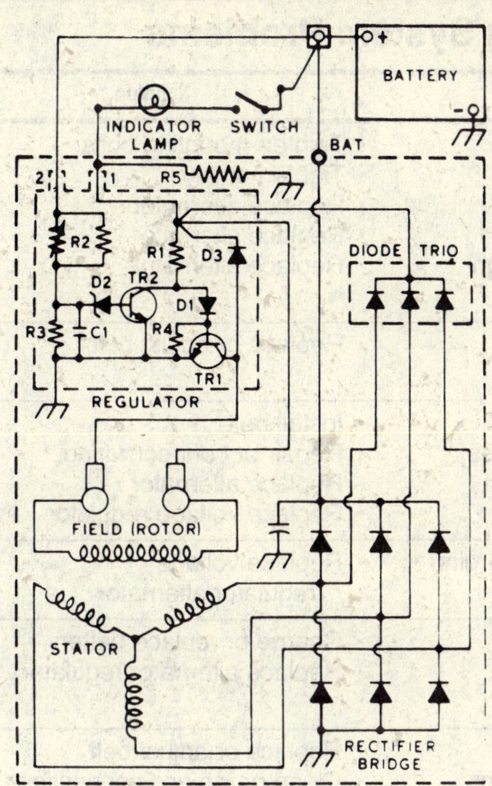

Electrical schematic of the 10SI alternator

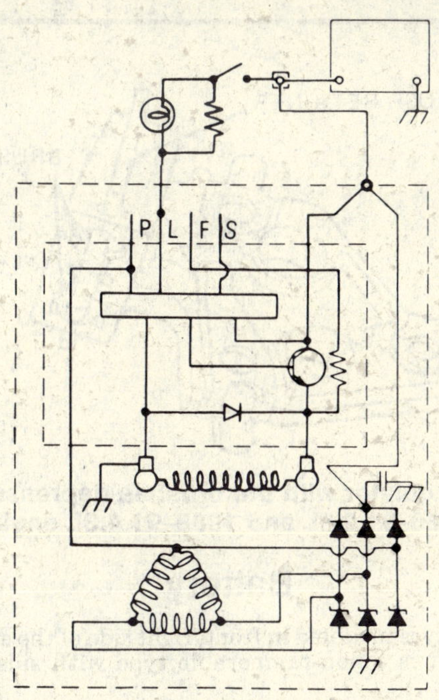

Electrical schematic of the CS-130 alternator – 1986–91 2.8L and 1988–91 4.3L engines

in the opposite direction for which they were designed. This burns out the diodes.

- Never use a fast charger as a booster for starting the vehicle.
- Never disconnect the voltage regulator while the engine is running.
- Do not ground the alternator output terminal.
- Do not operated the alternator on an open circuit with the field energized.
- Do not attempt to polarize an alternator.

REMOVAL AND INSTALLATION

NOTE: The following procedures require the use of GM belt tension gauge BT-33-95-ACBN (regular V-belts) or BT-33-97M (poly V-belts). The belt should deflect about 1/4 in. (6mm) over a 7–10 in. (178–254mm) span or 1/2 in. (12.7mm) over a 13–16 in. (330–406mm) span at this point.

1. Disconnect the negative battery terminal from the battery.
2. If equipped, remove the air pump to gain access to the alternator.
3. Label and disconnect the alternator's electrical connectors.
4. Remove the alternator brace bolt and the drive belt.
5. Support the alternator, then remove the mounting bolts and the unit from the vehicle.

To install:

6. To install, reverse the removal procedures and adjust the drive belt tension. Torque the top mounting bolt to 22 ft. lbs. and the lower mounting bolt to 24–35 ft. lbs. Reconnect the negative battery terminal.
7. To adjust the drive belt, perform the following procedures:
   a. If the belt is Cold, operate the engine (at idle speed) for 15 minutes; the belt will seat itself in the pulleys allowing the belt fibers to relax or stretch. If the belt is hot, allow it to cool, until it is warm to the touch.

NOTE: A used belt is one that has been rotated at least one complete revolution on the pulleys. This begins the belt seating process and it must never be tensioned to the new belt specifications.

   b. Loosen the component-to-mounting bracket bolts.
   c. Using a GM belt tension gauge BT-33-95-ACBN (standard V-belts) or BT-33-97M (poly V-belts), place the tension gauge at the center of the belt between the longest span.
   d. Applying belt tension pressure on the component, adjust the drive belt tension to the correct specifications.
   e. While holding the correct tension on the component, tighten the component-to-mounting bracket bolt.
   f. When the belt tension is correct, remove the tension gauge.

Regulator

The voltage regulators are sealed units mounted within the alternator body and are are nonadjustable.

REMOVAL AND INSTALLATION

NOTE: This procedure is to be performed with the alternator removed from the vehicle. The new alternators – CS-130 models – on 1986–89 2.8L and 1988–91 4.3L engines, are non-servicable; if the alternator proves to be defective, simply replace it.

1. Mark scribe lines on the end-frames to make the reassembly easier.
2. Remove the 4 through-bolts and separate the drive end-frame assembly from the rectifier end-frame assembly.
3. Remove the 3 diode trio attaching nuts and the 3 regulator attaching screws.
4. Remove the diode trio and the regulator from the end frame.

Troubleshooting Basic Charging System Problems

Problem	Cause	Solution
Noisy alternator	• Loose mountings • Loose drive pulley • Worn bearings • Brush noise • Internal circuits shorted (High pitched whine)	• Tighten mounting bolts • Tighten pulley • Replace alternator • Replace alternator • Replace alternator
Squeal when starting engine or accelerating	• Glazed or loose belt	• Replace or adjust belt
Indicator light remains on or ammeter indicates discharge (engine running)	• Broken fan belt • Broken or disconnected wires • Internal alternator problems • Defective voltage regulator	• Install belt • Repair or connect wiring • Replace alternator • Replace voltage regulator
Car light bulbs continually burn out—battery needs water continually	• Alternator/regulator overcharging	• Replace voltage regulator/alternator
Car lights flare on acceleration	• Battery low • Internal alternator/regulator problems	• Charge or replace battery • Replace alternator/regulator
Low voltage output (alternator light flickers continually or ammeter needle wanders)	• Loose or worn belt • Dirty or corroded connections • Internal alternator/regulator problems	• Replace or adjust belt • Clean or replace connections • Replace alternator or regulator

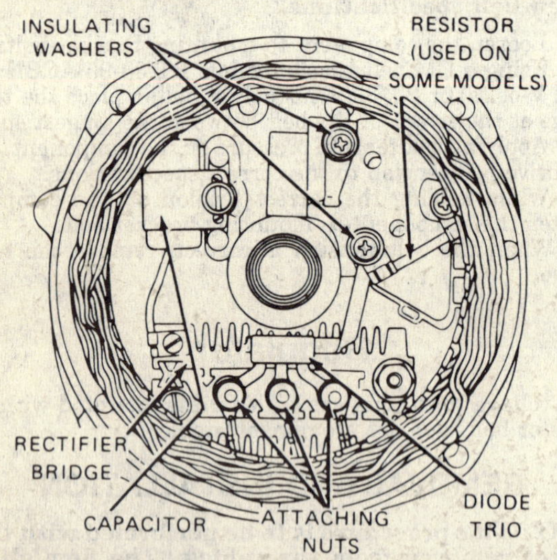

View of the alternator end frame — all except 1986–91 2.8L and 1988–91 4.3L engines

NOTE: Before installing the regulator, push the brushes into the brush holder and install a brush retainer or a tooth pick to hold the brushes in place.

5. To install the regulator, reverse the removal procedures. After the alternator is assembled, remove the brush retainer.

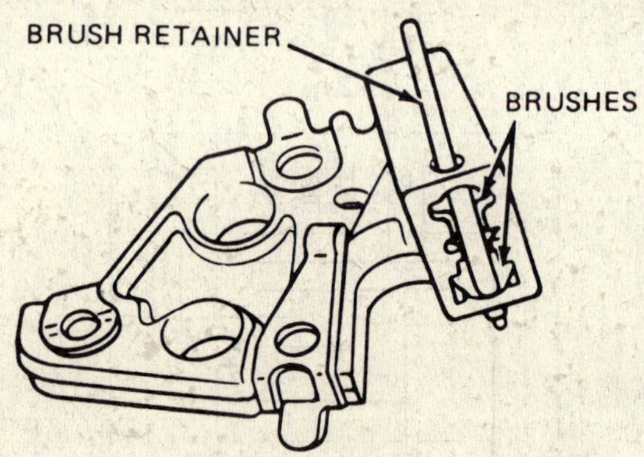

Voltage regulator with the brushes depressed — all except 1986–91 2.8L and 1988–91 4.3L engines

Battery

The battery is mounted in front, right side of the engine compartment. It is a non-tamperable type with side mounted terminals.

REMOVAL AND INSTALLATION

1. Disconnect the negative battery terminal, then the positive battery terminal.
2. Remove the battery hold-down retainer.
3. Remove the battery from the vehicle.
4. Inspect the battery, the cables and the battery carrier for damage.

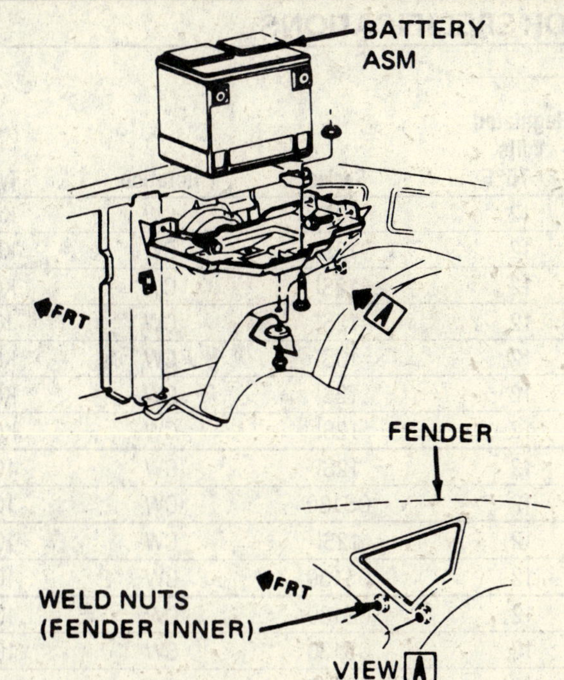

Replacing the battery at the front right side inner fender

5. To install, reverse the removal procedures. Torque the battery retainer to 11 ft. lbs., the top bar to 8 ft. lbs., if equipped, and the battery cable terminals to 10 ft. lbs.

ADJUSTMENTS

No adjustments are necessary or possible. If the battery is determined to be defective (other than charging), discard it.

Starter

The gasoline starter is located on the lower right side (gasoline engines) or on the lower left side (diesel engine). The diesel engine starter is a gear reduction type.

REMOVAL AND INSTALLATION

1983–86

1. Disconnect the negative battery terminal from the battery.
2. Raise and safely support the vehicle.
3. If equipped, remove any starter braces or shields that may be in the way.
4. Label and disconnect the electrical connectors from the starter solenoid.
5. Remove the starter-to-engine bolts, nuts, washers and shims. Allow the starter to drop, then remove it from the engine.

ALTERNATOR AND REGULATOR SPECIFICATIONS

Years	Engine No. Cyl. (cu. in.) L	Alternator Field Current @ 12v (amps)	Alternator Output (amps)	Regulated Volts @ 75°F	Series	Rotation	Type
1983	4 (119) 1.9	4.0–5.0	37	12	10SI	CW	K85
		4.0–5.0	66	12	12SI	CW	K81
		4.0–5.0	78	12	12SI	CW	K64
	4 (121) 2.0	4.0–5.0	37	12	10SI	CW	K85
		4.0–5.0	66	12	12SI	CW	K81
		4.0–5.0	78	12	12SI	CW	K64
	6 (173) 2.8	4.0–5.0	37	12	10SI	CW	K85
		4.0–5.0	66	12	12SI	CW	K81
		4.0–5.0	78	12	12SI	CW	K64
1984	4 (119) 1.9	4.0–5.0	37	12	10SI	CW	K85
		4.0–5.0	66	12	12SI	CW	K81
		4.0–5.0	78	12	12SI	CW	K64
	4 (121) 2.0	4.0–5.0	37	12	10SI	CW	K85
		4.0–5.0	66	12	12SI	CW	K81
		4.0–5.0	78	12	12SI	CW	K64
	6 (173) 2.8	4.0–5.0	37	12	10SI	CW	K85
		4.0–5.0	66	12	12SI	CW	K81
		4.0–5.0	78	12	12SI	CW	K64

ALTERNATOR AND REGULATOR SPECIFICATIONS

Years	Engine No. Cyl. (cu. in.) L	Alternator Field Current @ 12v (amps)	Alternator Output (amps)	Regulated Volts @ 75°F	Series	Rotation	Type
1985	4 (119) 1.9	4.0–5.0	37	12	10SI	CW	K85
		4.0–5.0	66	12	12SI	CW	K81
		4.0–5.0	78	12	12SI	CW	K64
	4 (151) 2.5	4.0–5.0	78	12	12SI	CW	100
	6 (173) 2.8	4.0–5.0	37	12	10SI	CW	K85
		4.0–5.0	66	12	12SI	CW	K81
		4.0–5.0	78	12	12SI	CW	K64
1986	4 (151) 2.5	4.0–5.0	78	12	12SI	CW	100
	6 (173) 2.8	5.4–6.4	85	12	CS130	CW	100
1987	4 (151) 2.5	4.0–5.0	78	12	12SI	CW	100
	6 (173) 2.8	5.4–6.4	85	12	CS130	CW	100
1988	4 (151) 2.5	4.8–5.7	85	12	CS130	CW	100
	6 (173) 2.8	4.8–5.7	85	12	CS130	CW	100
	6 (262) 4.3	5.7–7.1	85	12	CS130	CW	100
1989	4 (151) 2.5	6.0–7.5	96	12	CS130	CW	100
	6 (173) 2.8	4.8–5.7	85	12	CS130	CW	100
	6 (262) 4.3	5.7–7.1	85	12	CS130	CW	100
1990	6 (262) 4.3	5.7–7.1	85	12	CS130	CW	100
1991	6 (262) 4.3	5.7–7.1	85	12	CS130	CW	100
		6.0–7.5	100	12	CS130	CW	100

Troubleshooting Basic Starting System Problems

Problem	Cause	Solution
Starter motor rotates engine slowly	• Battery charge low or battery defective	• Charge or replace battery
	• Defective circuit between battery and starter motor	• Clean and tighten, or replace cables
	• Low load current	• Bench-test starter motor. Inspect for worn brushes and weak brush springs.
	• High load current	• Bench-test starter motor. Check engine for friction, drag or coolant in cylinders. Check ring gear-to-pinion gear clearance.
Starter motor will not rotate engine	• Battery charge low or battery defective	• Charge or replace battery
	• Faulty solenoid	• Check solenoid ground. Repair or replace as necessary.
	• Damage drive pinion gear or ring gear	• Replace damaged gear(s)
	• Starter motor engagement weak	• Bench-test starter motor
	• Starter motor rotates slowly with high load current	• Inspect drive yoke pull-down and point gap, check for worn end bushings, check ring gear clearance
	• Engine seized	• Repair engine

Troubleshooting Basic Starting System Problems

Problem	Cause	Solution
Starter motor drive will not engage (solenoid known to be good)	• Defective contact point assembly • Inadequate contact point assembly ground • Defective hold-in coil	• Repair or replace contact point assembly • Repair connection at ground screw • Replace field winding assembly
Starter motor drive will not disengage	• Starter motor loose on flywheel housing • Worn drive end busing • Damaged ring gear teeth • Drive yoke return spring broken or missing	• Tighten mounting bolts • Replace bushing • Replace ring gear or driveplate • Replace spring
Starter motor drive disengages prematurely	• Weak drive assembly thrust spring • Hold-in coil defective	• Replace drive mechanism • Replace field winding assembly
Low load current	• Worn brushes • Weak brush springs	• Replace brushes • Replace springs

NOTE: Be sure to keep the shims in order so they may be reinstalled in the same order.

6. To install, reverse the removal procedures. Torque the starter-to-engine bolts to 30 ft. lbs. Connect the wires to the starter solenoid and the negative battery cable.

1987–91

1. Disconnect the negative battery terminal.
2. If equipped with a 4.3L engine, raise the vehicle half way, reach through the right wheel well and disconnect the electrical connectors from the starter.
3. Raise and safely support the vehicle.
4. If equipped with 4WD, perform the following procedures:
   a. Remove the skid plate-to-chassis bolts and the skid plate.
   b. Remove the brake line-to-crossmember bracket bolts and both brackets.
   c. Remove the crossmember-to-chassis bolts and the crossmember; there are 3 bolts on each side.
   d. Remove the transmission cooler lines-to-flywheel housing brace, rod-to-flywheel housing brace and the lower flywheel housing, if necessary.
5. If not equipped with a 4.3L engine, label and disconnect the electrical connectors from the starter solenoid.

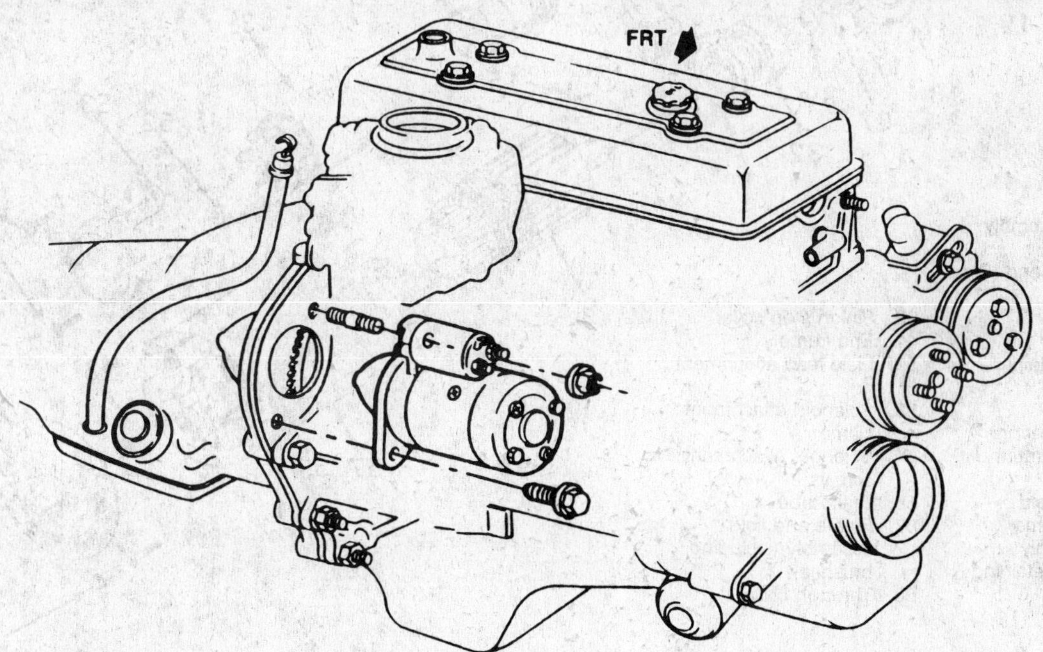

Replacing the starter — 1.9L and 2.0L engines — 2.2L engine is on the left side

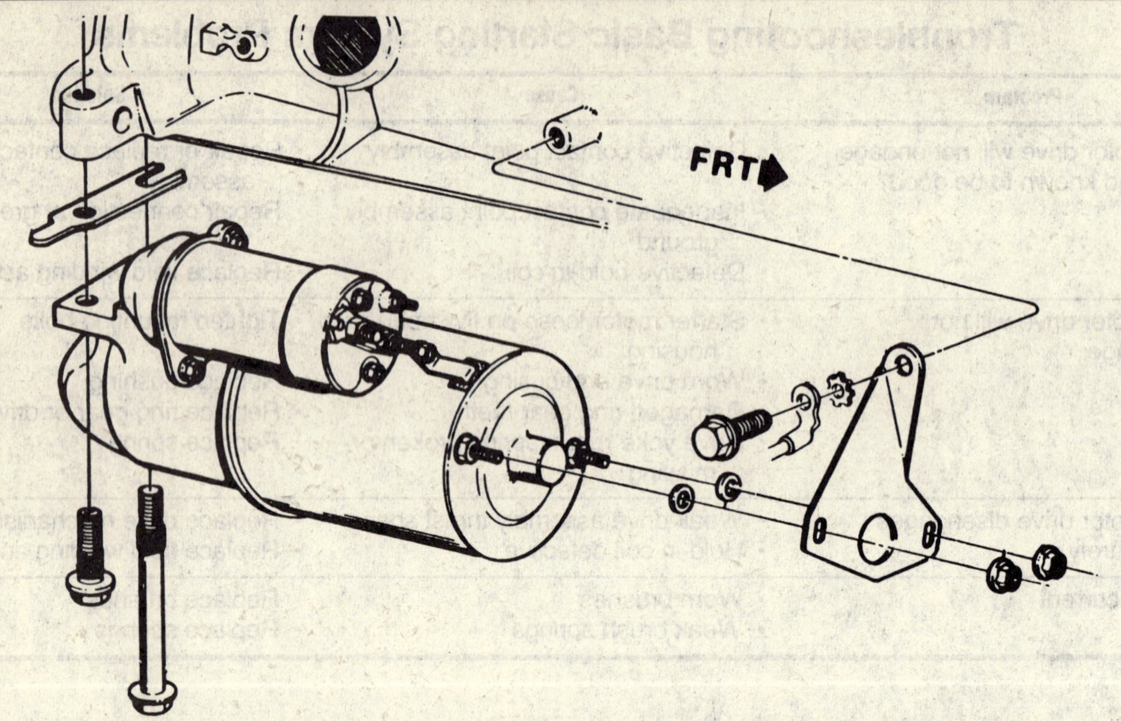

Replacing the starter — 2.5L engine — 2.8L and 4.3L engines are similar

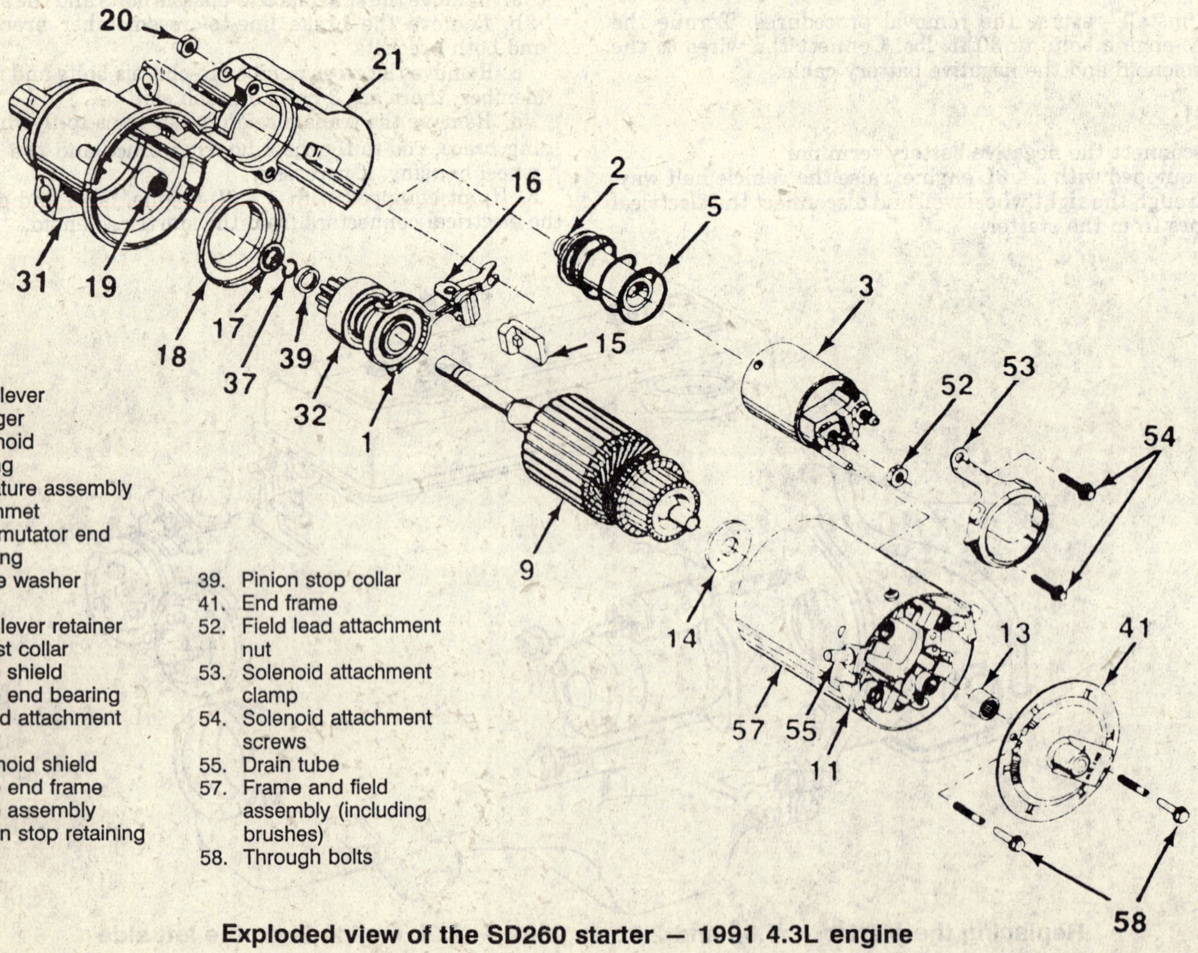

1. Shift lever
2. Plunger
3. Solenoid
5. Spring
9. Armature assembly
11. Grommet
13. Commutator end bearing
14. Brake washer
15. Plug
16. Shift lever retainer
17. Thrust collar
18. Drive shield
19. Drive end bearing
20. Shield attachment nut
21. Solenoid shield
31. Drive end frame
32. Drive assembly
37. Pinion stop retaining ring
39. Pinion stop collar
41. End frame
52. Field lead attachment nut
53. Solenoid attachment clamp
54. Solenoid attachment screws
55. Drain tube
57. Frame and field assembly (including brushes)
58. Through bolts

Exploded view of the SD260 starter — 1991 4.3L engine

6. Remove the starter-to-engine bolts, nuts, washers and shim(s). Allow the starter to drop, then remove it from the engine.

NOTE: Be sure to keep the shims in order so they may be reinstalled in the same order.

7. To install, reverse the removal procedures. Torque the starter-to-engine bolts to 31 ft. lbs. for 2.5L engine or 33 ft. lbs. for 2.8L and 4.3L engines. Connect the wires to the starter solenoid and the negative battery cable.

SOLENOID REPLACEMENT

Direct Drive

1. Remove the starter, then place it on a workbench.
2. Remove the screw and the washer from the motor connector strap terminal.
3. Remove the 2 solenoid retaining screws.
4. Twist the solenoid housing clockwise to remove the flange key from the keyway in the housing, then remove the housing.
5. To install the unit, place the return spring on the plunger and place the solenoid body on the drive housing. Turn it counterclockwise to engage the flange key. Place the 2 retaining screws in position, then install the screw and washer which secures the strap terminal. Install the unit on the starter.

OVERHAUL

Starter Drive Replacement

DIRECT DRIVE

1. Disconnect the field coil straps from the solenoid.
2. Remove the through-bolts, then separate the commutator end-frame, the field frame assembly, the drive housing and the armature assembly, from each other.
3. Slide the 2 piece thrust collar off the end of the armature shaft.
4. Slide a suitably sized metal cylinder, such as a standard ½ in. (12.7mm) pipe coupling or an old pinion, onto the shaft so the end of the coupling or pinion butts against the edge of the pinion retainer.
5. Support the lower end of the armature securely on a soft surface, such as a wooden block and tap the end of the coupling or pinion, driving the retainer towards the armature end of the snapring.
6. Using a pair of pliers, remove the snapring from the groove in the armature shaft. Then, slide the retainer and the starter drive from the shaft.
7. To assemble, lubricate the drive end of the armature shaft with silicone lubricant and slide the starter drive onto the shaft *with the pinion facing outward.* Slide the retainer onto the shaft *with the cupped surface facing outward.*
8. Again, support the armature on a soft surface, with the pinion at the upper end. Center the snapring on top of the shaft (use a new snapring if the original was damaged during removal). Gently place a block of wood flat on top of the snapring , so as not to move it from a centered position. Tap the wooden block with a hammer in order to force the snapring around the shaft. Then, slide the ring down into the snapring groove.
9. Lay the armature down flat on the surface you're working on. Slide the retainer close, up on the shaft, then position it and the thrust collar next to the snapring. Using 2 pairs of pliers, on opposite sides of the shaft, squeeze the thrust collar and the retainer together until the snapring is forced into the retainer.
10. Lubricate the drive housing bushing with a silicone lubricant. Then, install the armature and the clutch assembly into the drive housing, engaging the solenoid shift lever yoke with the clutch and positioning the front of the armature shaft into the bushing.
11. Apply a sealing compound, approved for this application onto the drive housing, then, position the field frame around the armature's shaft and against the drive housing. *Work slowly and carefully to prevent damaging the starter brushes.*
12. Lubricate the bushing in the commutator end-frame with a silicone lubricant, place the leather brake washer onto the ar-

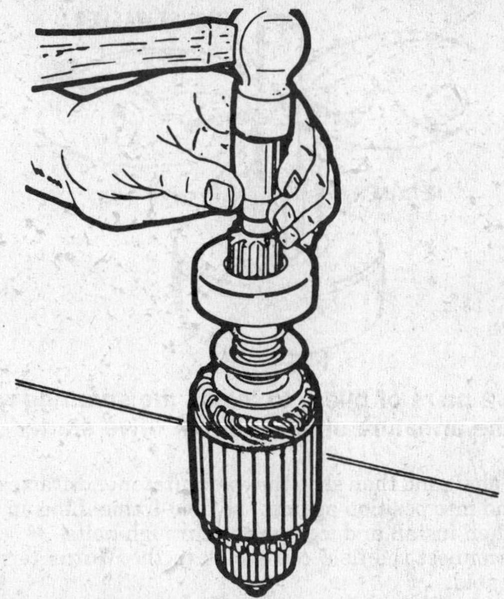

Using a deep socket to drive the retainer from the snapring — direct drive starter

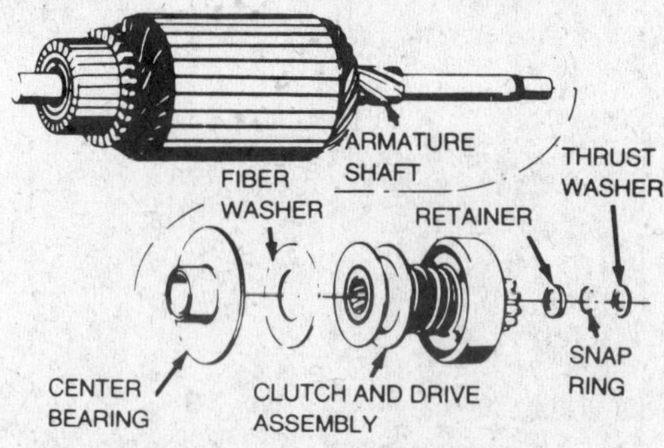

Starter and drive assembly removed

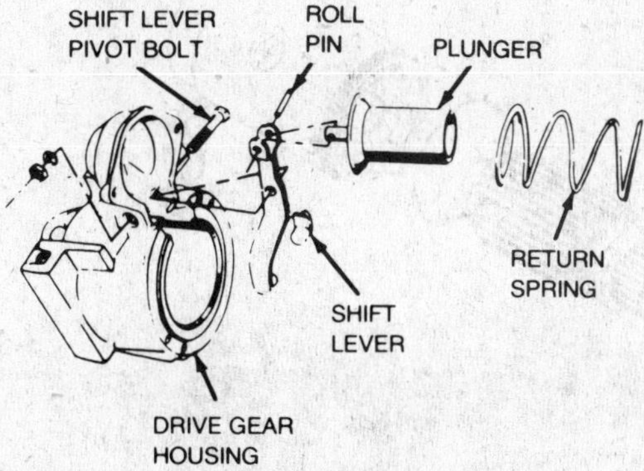

Removing the shaft lever and plunger from the starter

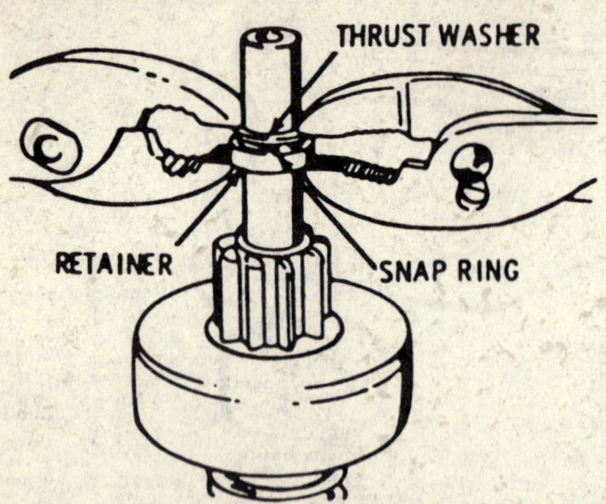

Using 2 pairs of pliers to install the snapring retainer onto the armature shaft — direct drive starter

mature shaft and then slide the commutator end-frame over the shaft and into position against the field frame. Line up the bolt holes, then install and tighten the through-bolts.

13. Reconnect the field coil straps to the **Motor** terminal of the solenoid.

NOTE: If replacement of the starter drive fails to cure the improper engagement of the starter pinion to flywheel, there are probably defective parts in the solenoid and/or the shift lever. The best procedure would probably be to take the assembly to a shop where a pinion clearance check can be made by energizing the solenoid on a test bench. If the pinion clearance is incorrect, disassemble the solenoid and the shift lever, then inspect and replace the worn parts.

GEAR REDUCTION

1. With the starter motor removed from the vehicle, remove the solenoid from the stater.
2. Remove the 2 through-bolts and separate the gear case from the yoke housing.
3. Remove the pinion stopper clip and the pinion stopper.
4. Slide the starter drive off the armature shaft.
5. To install, reverse the removal procedures.

Brush Replacement

1. Remove the armature from the starter housing.
2. Replace the brushes, one at a time, to avoid having to mark the wiring. For each brush, remove the brush holding screw and the old brush, then position the new brush in the same direction (large end toward the center of the field frame), position the wire connector on top of the brush, line up the holes and reinstall the screw. Make sure the screw is snug enough to ensure good contact.
3. To complete the assembly, reverse the disassembly procedures.

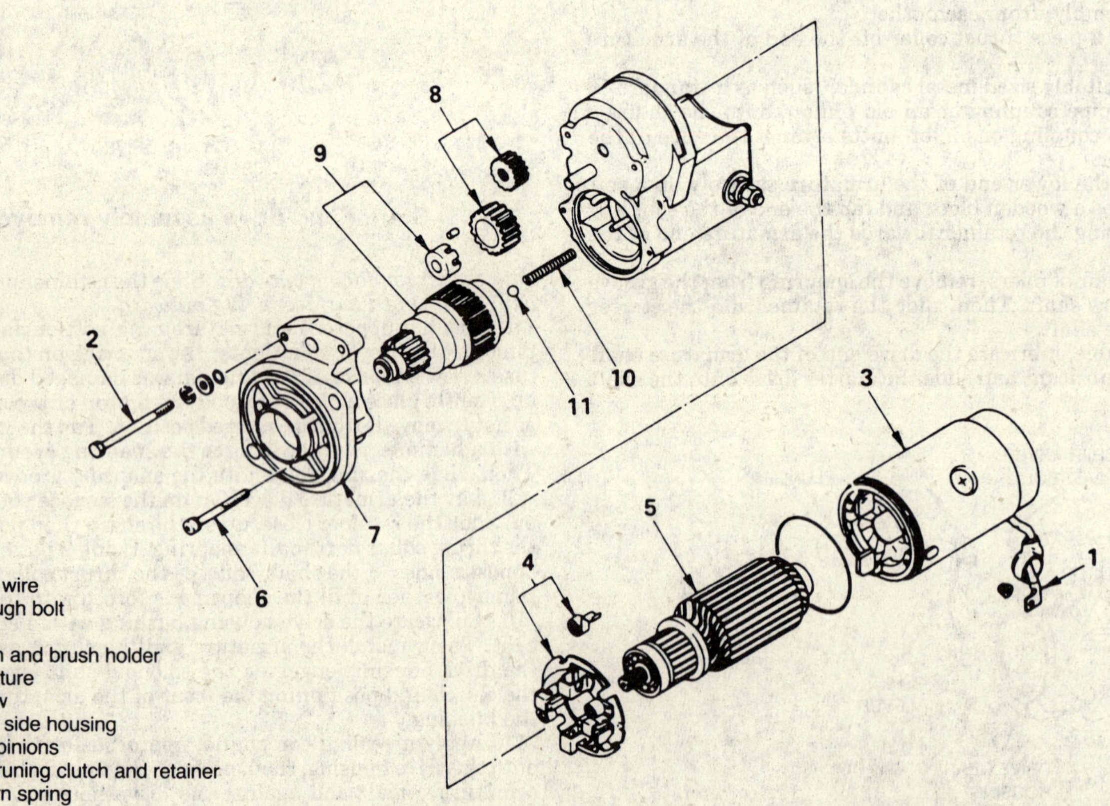

Exploded view of the gear reduction starter — 2.2L diesel engine

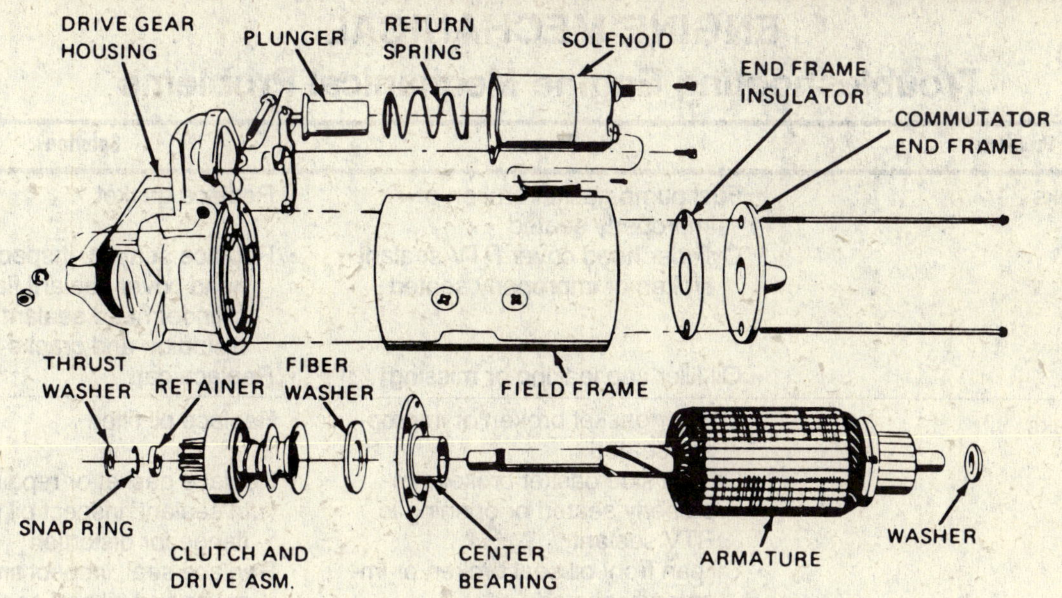

Exploded view of the 5MT starter — gasoline engines, except 4.3L engine

STARTER SPECIFICATIONS

Years	Engine No. Cyl. (cu. in.) L	Series	Type	Amps	No-Load Test Volts	RPM
1983	4 (121) 2.0	5MT	—	50–75	10	6,000–11,900
	6 (173) 2.8	5MT	—	45–70	10	7,000–11,900
1984	4 (121) 2.0	5MT	—	50–75	10	6,000–11,900
	6 (173) 2.8	5MT	—	50–75	10	6,000–11,900
1985	4 (121) 2.0	5MT	—	50–75	10	6,000–11,900
	6 (173) 2.8	5MT	—	50–75	10	6,000–11,900
1986	4 (151) 2.5	5MT	101	50–75	10	6,000–11,900
	6 (173) 2.8	5MT	101	50–75	10	6,000–11,900
1987	4 (151) 2.5	5MT	101	50–75	10	6,000–11,900
	6 (173) 2.8	5MT	101	50–75	10	6,000–11,900
1988	4 (151) 2.5	5MT	101	50–75	10	6,000–11,900
	6 (173) 2.8	5MT	101	50–75	10	6,000–11,900
	6 (262) 4.3	PG-200	—	50–90	10	2,330–2,660
1989	4 (151) 2.5	SD200	—	50–75	10	6,000–11,900
	6 (173) 2.8	SD200	—	50–75	10	6,000–11,900
	6 (262) 4.3	PG-200	—	45–90	10	2,150–2,660
1990	6 (262) 4.3	PG-200	—	45–90	10	2,150–2,660
1991	6 (262) 4.3	SD260	—	50–62	10	8,500–10,700

ENGINE MECHANICAL

Troubleshooting Engine Mechanical Problems

Problem	Cause	Solution
External oil leaks	• Fuel pump gasket broken or improperly seated	• Replace gasket
	• Cylinder head cover RTV sealant broken or improperly seated	• Replace sealant; inspect cylinder head cover sealant flange and cylinder head sealant surface for distortion and cracks
	• Oil filler cap leaking or missing	• Replace cap
External oil leaks	• Oil filter gasket broken or improperly seated	• Replace oil filter
	• Oil pan side gasket broken, improperly seated or opening in RTV sealant	• Replace gasket or repair opening in sealant; inspect oil pan gasket flange for distortion
	• Oil pan front oil seal broken or improperly seated	• Replace seal; inspect timing case cover and oil pan seal flange for distortion
	• Oil pan rear oil seal broken or improperly seated	• Replace seal; inspect oil pan rear oil seal flange; inspect rear main bearing cap for cracks, plugged oil return channels, or distortion in seal groove
	• Timing case cover oil seal broken or improperly seated	• Replace seal
	• Excess oil pressure because of restricted PCV valve	• Replace PCV valve
	• Oil pan drain plug loose or has stripped threads	• Repair as necessary and tighten
	• Rear oil gallery plug loose	• Use appropriate sealant on gallery plug and tighten
	• Rear camshaft plug loose or improperly seated	• Seat camshaft plug or replace and seal, as necessary
	• Distributor base gasket damaged	• Replace gasket
Excessive oil consumption	• Oil level too high	• Drain oil to specified level
	• Oil with wrong viscosity being used	• Replace with specified oil
	• PCV valve stuck closed	• Replace PCV valve
	• Valve stem oil deflectors (or seals) are damaged, missing, or incorrect type	• Replace valve stem oil deflectors
	• Valve stems or valve guides worn	• Measure stem-to-guide clearance and repair as necessary
	• Poorly fitted or missing valve cover baffles	• Replace valve cover
	• Piston rings broken or missing	• Replace broken or missing rings
	• Scuffed piston	• Replace piston
	• Incorrect piston ring gap	• Measure ring gap, repair as necessary
	• Piston rings sticking or excessively loose in grooves	• Measure ring side clearance, repair as necessary
	• Compression rings installed upside down	• Repair as necessary
	• Cylinder walls worn, scored, or glazed	• Repair as necessary

Troubleshooting Engine Mechanical Problems (cont.)

Problem	Cause	Solution
	• Piston ring gaps not properly staggered	• Repair as necessary
	• Excessive main or connecting rod bearing clearance	• Measure bearing clearance, repair as necessary
No oil pressure	• Low oil level	• Add oil to correct level
	• Oil pressure gauge, warning lamp or sending unit inaccurate	• Replace oil pressure gauge or warning lamp
	• Oil pump malfunction	• Replace oil pump
	• Oil pressure relief valve sticking	• Remove and inspect oil pressure relief valve assembly
	• Oil passages on pressure side of pump obstructed	• Inspect oil passages for obstruction
	• Oil pickup screen or tube obstructed	• Inspect oil pickup for obstruction
	• Loose oil inlet tube	• Tighten or seal inlet tube
Low oil pressure	• Low oil level	• Add oil to correct level
	• Inaccurate gauge, warning lamp or sending unit	• Replace oil pressure gauge or warning lamp
	• Oil excessively thin because of dilution, poor quality, or improper grade	• Drain and refill crankcase with recommended oil
	• Excessive oil temperature	• Correct cause of overheating engine
	• Oil pressure relief spring weak or sticking	• Remove and inspect oil pressure relief valve assembly
	• Oil inlet tube and screen assembly has restriction or air leak	• Remove and inspect oil inlet tube and screen assembly. (Fill inlet tube with lacquer thinner to locate leaks.)
	• Excessive oil pump clearance	• Measure clearances
	• Excessive main, rod, or camshaft bearing clearance	• Measure bearing clearances, repair as necessary
High oil pressure	• Improper oil viscosity	• Drain and refill crankcase with correct viscosity oil
	• Oil pressure gauge or sending unit inaccurate	• Replace oil pressure gauge
	• Oil pressure relief valve sticking closed	• Remove and inspect oil pressure relief valve assembly
Main bearing noise	• Insufficient oil supply	• Inspect for low oil level and low oil pressure
	• Main bearing clearance excessive	• Measure main bearing clearance, repair as necessary
	• Bearing insert missing	• Replace missing insert
	• Crankshaft end play excessive	• Measure end play, repair as necessary
	• Improperly tightened main bearing cap bolts	• Tighten bolts with specified torque
	• Loose flywheel or drive plate	• Tighten flywheel or drive plate attaching bolts
	• Loose or damaged vibration damper	• Repair as necessary

Troubleshooting Engine Mechanical Problems (cont.)

Problem	Cause	Solution
Connecting rod bearing noise	• Insufficient oil supply	• Inspect for low oil level and low oil pressure
	• Carbon build-up on piston	• Remove carbon from piston crown
	• Bearing clearance excessive or bearing missing	• Measure clearance, repair as necessary
	• Crankshaft connecting rod journal out-of-round	• Measure journal dimensions, repair or replace as necessary
	• Misaligned connecting rod or cap	• Repair as necessary
	• Connecting rod bolts tightened improperly	• Tighten bolts with specified torque
Piston noise	• Piston-to-cylinder wall clearance excessive (scuffed piston)	• Measure clearance and examine piston
	• Cylinder walls excessively tapered or out-of-round	• Measure cylinder wall dimensions, rebore cylinder
	• Piston ring broken	• Replace all rings on piston
	• Loose or seized piston pin	• Measure piston-to-pin clearance, repair as necessary
	• Connecting rods misaligned	• Measure rod alignment, straighten or replace
	• Piston ring side clearance excessively loose or tight	• Measure ring side clearance, repair as necessary
	• Carbon build-up on piston is excessive	• Remove carbon from piston
Valve actuating component noise	• Insufficient oil supply	• Check for: (a) Low oil level (b) Low oil pressure (c) Plugged push rods (d) Wrong hydraulic tappets (e) Restricted oil gallery (f) Excessive tappet to bore clearance
	• Push rods worn or bent	• Replace worn or bent push rods
	• Rocker arms or pivots worn	• Replace worn rocker arms or pivots
	• Foreign objects or chips in hydraulic tappets	• Clean tappets
	• Excessive tappet leak-down	• Replace valve tappet
	• Tappet face worn	• Replace tappet; inspect corresponding cam lobe for wear
	• Broken or cocked valve springs	• Properly seat cocked springs; replace broken springs
	• Stem-to-guide clearance excessive	• Measure stem-to-guide clearance, repair as required
	• Valve bent	• Replace valve
	• Loose rocker arms	• Tighten bolts with specified torque
	• Valve seat runout excessive	• Regrind valve seat/valves
	• Missing valve lock	• Install valve lock
	• Push rod rubbing or contacting cylinder head	• Remove cylinder head and remove obstruction in head
	• Excessive engine oil (four-cylinder engine)	• Correct oil level

Troubleshooting the Cooling System

Problem	Cause	Solution
High temperature gauge indication—overheating	• Coolant level low	• Replenish coolant
	• Fan belt loose	• Adjust fan belt tension
	• Radiator hose(s) collapsed	• Replace hose(s)
	• Radiator airflow blocked	• Remove restriction (bug screen, fog lamps, etc.)
	• Faulty radiator cap	• Replace radiator cap
	• Ignition timing incorrect	• Adjust ignition timing
	• Idle speed low	• Adjust idle speed
	• Air trapped in cooling system	• Purge air
	• Heavy traffic driving	• Operate at fast idle in neutral intermittently to cool engine
	• Incorrect cooling system component(s) installed	• Install proper component(s)
	• Faulty thermostat	• Replace thermostat
	• Water pump shaft broken or impeller loose	• Replace water pump
	• Radiator tubes clogged	• Flush radiator
	• Cooling system clogged	• Flush system
	• Casting flash in cooling passages	• Repair or replace as necessary. Flash may be visible by removing cooling system components or removing core plugs.
	• Brakes dragging	• Repair brakes
	• Excessive engine friction	• Repair engine
	• Antifreeze concentration over 68%	• Lower antifreeze concentration percentage
	• Missing air seals	• Replace air seals
	• Faulty gauge or sending unit	• Repair or replace faulty component
	• Loss of coolant flow caused by leakage or foaming	• Repair or replace leaking component, replace coolant
	• Viscous fan drive failed	• Replace unit
Low temperature indication—undercooling	• Thermostat stuck open	• Replace thermostat
	• Faulty gauge or sending unit	• Repair or replace faulty component
Coolant loss—boilover	• Overfilled cooling system	• Reduce coolant level to proper specification
	• Quick shutdown after hard (hot) run	• Allow engine to run at fast idle prior to shutdown
	• Air in system resulting in occasional "burping" of coolant	• Purge system
	• Insufficient antifreeze allowing coolant boiling point to be too low	• Add antifreeze to raise boiling point
	• Antifreeze deteriorated because of age or contamination	• Replace coolant
	• Leaks due to loose hose clamps, loose nuts, bolts, drain plugs, faulty hoses, or defective radiator	• Pressure test system to locate source of leak(s) then repair as necessary

Troubleshooting the Cooling System (cont.)

Problem	Cause	Solution
Coolant loss—boilover	• Faulty head gasket • Cracked head, manifold, or block • Faulty radiator cap	• Replace head gasket • Replace as necessary • Replace cap
Coolant entry into crankcase or cylinder(s)	• Faulty head gasket • Crack in head, manifold or block	• Replace head gasket • Replace as necessary
Coolant recovery system inoperative	• Coolant level low • Leak in system • Pressure cap not tight or seal missing, or leaking • Pressure cap defective • Overflow tube clogged or leaking • Recovery bottle vent restricted	• Replenish coolant to FULL mark • Pressure test to isolate leak and repair as necessary • Repair as necessary • Replace cap • Repair as necessary • Remove restriction
Noise	• Fan contacting shroud • Loose water pump impeller • Glazed fan belt • Loose fan belt • Rough surface on drive pulley • Water pump bearing worn • Belt alignment	• Reposition shroud and inspect engine mounts • Replace pump • Apply silicone or replace belt • Adjust fan belt tension • Replace pulley • Remove belt to isolate. Replace pump. • Check pulley alignment. Repair as necessary.
No coolant flow through heater core	• Restricted return inlet in water pump • Heater hose collapsed or restricted • Restricted heater core • Restricted outlet in thermostat housing • Intake manifold bypass hole in cylinder head restricted • Faulty heater control valve • Intake manifold coolant passage restricted	• Remove restriction • Remove restriction or replace hose • Remove restriction or replace core • Remove flash or restriction • Remove restriction • Replace valve • Remove restriction or replace intake manifold

NOTE: *Immediately after shutdown, the engine enters a condition known as heat soak. This is caused by the cooling system being inoperative while engine temperature is still high. If coolant temperature rises above boiling point, expansion and pressure may push some coolant out of the radiator overflow tube. If this does not occur frequently it is considered normal.*

Troubleshooting the Serpentine Drive Belt

Problem	Cause	Solution
Tension sheeting fabric failure (woven fabric on outside circumference of belt has cracked or separated from body of belt)	• Grooved or backside idler pulley diameters are less than minimum recommended	• Replace pulley(s) not conforming to specification
	• Tension sheeting contacting (rubbing) stationary object	• Correct rubbing condition
	• Excessive heat causing woven fabric to age	• Replace belt
	• Tension sheeting splice has fractured	• Replace belt
Noise (objectional squeal, squeak, or rumble is heard or felt while drive belt is in operation)	• Belt slippage	• Adjust belt
	• Bearing noise	• Locate and repair
	• Belt misalignment	• Align belt/pulley(s)
	• Belt-to-pulley mismatch	• Install correct belt
	• Driven component inducing vibration	• Locate defective driven component and repair
	• System resonant frequency inducing vibration	• Vary belt tension within specifications. Replace belt.
Rib chunking (one or more ribs has separated from belt body)	• Foreign objects imbedded in pulley grooves	• Remove foreign objects from pulley grooves
	• Installation damage	• Replace belt
	• Drive loads in excess of design specifications	• Adjust belt tension
	• Insufficient internal belt adhesion	• Replace belt
Rib or belt wear (belt ribs contact bottom of pulley grooves)	• Pulley(s) misaligned	• Align pulley(s)
	• Mismatch of belt and pulley groove widths	• Replace belt
	• Abrasive environment	• Replace belt
	• Rusted pulley(s)	• Clean rust from pulley(s)
	• Sharp or jagged pulley groove tips	• Replace pulley
	• Rubber deteriorated	• Replace belt
Longitudinal belt cracking (cracks between two ribs)	• Belt has mistracked from pulley groove	• Replace belt
	• Pulley groove tip has worn away rubber-to-tensile member	• Replace belt
Belt slips	• Belt slipping because of insufficient tension	• Adjust tension
	• Belt or pulley subjected to substance (belt dressing, oil, ethylene glycol) that has reduced friction	• Replace belt and clean pulleys
	• Driven component bearing failure	• Replace faulty component bearing
	• Belt glazed and hardened from heat and excessive slippage	• Replace belt
"Groove jumping" (belt does not maintain correct position on pulley, or turns over and/or runs off pulleys)	• Insufficient belt tension	• Adjust belt tension
	• Pulley(s) not within design tolerance	• Replace pulley(s)
	• Foreign object(s) in grooves	• Remove foreign objects from grooves

Troubleshooting the Serpentine Drive Belt (cont.)

Problem	Cause	Solution
"Groove jumping" (belt does not maintain correct position on pulley, or turns over and/or runs off pulleys)	• Excessive belt speed • Pulley misalignment • Belt-to-pulley profile mismatched • Belt cordline is distorted	• Avoid excessive engine acceleration • Align pulley(s) • Install correct belt • Replace belt
Belt broken (Note: identify and correct problem before replacement belt is installed)	• Excessive tension • Tensile members damaged during belt installation • Belt turnover • Severe pulley misalignment • Bracket, pulley, or bearing failure	• Replace belt and adjust tension to specification • Replace belt • Replace belt • Align pulley(s) • Replace defective component and belt
Cord edge failure (tensile member exposed at edges of belt or separated from belt body)	• Excessive tension • Drive pulley misalignment • Belt contacting stationary object • Pulley irregularities • Improper pulley construction • Insufficient adhesion between tensile member and rubber matrix	• Adjust belt tension • Align pulley • Correct as necessary • Replace pulley • Replace pulley • Replace belt and adjust tension to specifications
Sporadic rib cracking (multiple cracks in belt ribs at random intervals)	• Ribbed pulley(s) diameter less than minimum specification • Backside bend flat pulley(s) diameter less than minimum • Excessive heat condition causing rubber to harden • Excessive belt thickness • Belt overcured • Excessive tension	• Replace pulley(s) • Replace pulley(s) • Correct heat condition as necessary • Replace belt • Replace belt • Adjust belt tension

Six engines and 3 fuel systems are used to power your S-10/S-15 vehicle, they are:

- 1983–85 Isuzu built 1.9L (118.9 cu. in.) 2-bbl.
- 1983–85 Chevy built 2.8L (173 cu. in.) 2-bbl.
- 1983–84 Chevy built 2.0L (121 cu. in.) 2-bbl.
- 1983–85 Isuzu built 2.2L (136.6 cu. in.) Diesel.
- 1985–89 Pontiac built 2.5L (151 cu. in.) TBI.
- 1986–89 Chevy built 2.8L (173 cu. in.) TBI.
- 1988–91 Chevy built 4.3L (262 cu. in.) TBI.

On the 1985, 2.5L EFI engine, the cylinder head and engine block are both constructed of cast iron. The valve guides are integral with the cylinder head and the rocker arms are retained by individual threaded shoulder bolts. Hydraulic roller lifters are incorporated to reduce the friction between the valve lifters and the camshaft lobes.

On the 1986–89, 2.5L EFI engine, a few changes appeared, such as: (1) the pistons were replaced with hypereutectic types (pistons embedded with silicone nodules in the walls to reduce the cylinder wall friction), (2) a reduced weight, high efficiency alternator and (3) a variable ratio air conditioner compressor.

The 2.8L engine utilizes a 2-bbl carburetor for 1983–85 or an EFI system for 1986–89 and the use of swirl chamber heads (to increase power and fuel efficiency). The engine block and cylinder heads are constructed of cast iron. Other major features are: a wider oil pan flange, raised rails inside the cylinder heads (to improve oil return control), machined rocker cover seal surfaces, a trough along the rocker cover rails (to channel oil away from the gasket) and even distribution of the clamping loads, to make this engine one of the most leak-resistant on the road today.

The 1988–91, 4.3L engine utilizes an EFI system and incorporates many of the design features used the 1986–89, 2.8L EFI engine. The engine is equipped with roller valve lifters instead of the standard flat bottom lifters. The roller lifter is still hydraulic, requiring no valve adjustment. The roller lifter incorporates a roller that rides along the cam lobe reducing friction and component wear. A roller lifter restrictor and retainer is needed to keep the lifter from turning in the bore while the enigne is running.

Engine Overhaul Tips

Most engine overhaul procedures are fairly standard. In addition to specific parts replacement procedures and complete specifications for your individual engine, this Section also is a guide to accept rebuilding procedures. Examples of standard rebuilding practice are shown and should be used along with specific details concerning your particular engine.

Competent and accurate machine shop services will ensure maximum performance, reliability and engine life. Choose your machinist carefully. If the engine is not machined properly, engine failure will result within a short time period after installation.

On most instances it is more profitable for the do-it-yourself mechanic to remove, clean and inspect the component(s), buy the necessary parts and deliver these to a shop for actual machine work.

On the other hand, much of the rebuilding work (crankshaft, block, bearings, piston rods, and other components) is well within the scope of the do-it-yourself mechanic.

TOOLS

The tools required for an engine overhaul or parts replacement will depend on the depth of your involvement. With a few exceptions, they will be the tools found in a mechanic's tool kit (see Section 1). More in-depth work will require any or all of the following:

- A dial indicator (reading in thousandths) mounted on a universal base
- Micrometers and telescope gauges
- Jaw and screw-type pullers
- Scraper
- Valve spring compressor
- Ring groove cleaner
- Piston ring expander and compressor
- Ridge reamer
- Cylinder hone or glaze breaker
- Plastigage®
- Engine stand

Use of most of these tools is illustrated in this Section. Many can be rented for a one-time use from a local parts jobber or tool supply house specializing in automotive work.

Occasionally, the use of special tools is called for. See the information on Special Tools and Safety Notice in the front of this book before substituting another tool.

INSPECTION TECHNIQUES

Procedures and specifications are given in this Section for inspecting, cleaning and assessing the wear limits of most major components. Other procedures such as Magnaflux® and Zyglo® can be used to locate material flaws and stress cracks.

Magnaflux® is a magnetic process applicable only to ferrous materials. The Zyglo® process coats the material with a fluorescent dye penetrant and can be used on any material. Check for suspected surface cracks can be more readily made using spot check dye. The dye is sprayed onto the suspected area, wiped off and the area sprayed with a developer. Cracks will show up brightly.

OVERHAUL TIPS

Aluminum has become extremely popular for use in engines, due to its low weight. Observe the following precautions when handling aluminum parts:

- Never hot tank aluminum parts (the caustic hot tank solution will eat the aluminum.
- Remove all aluminum parts (identification tag, etc.) from engine parts prior to the tanking.
- Always coat threads lightly with engine oil or anti-seize compounds before installation, to prevent seizure.
- Never over-torque bolts or spark plugs especially in aluminum for you may strip the threads.

Stripped threads in any component can be repaired using any of several commercial repair kits (Heli-Coil®, Microdot®, Keenserts®, etc.).

When assembling the engine, any parts that will have frictional contact must be prelubed to provide lubrication at initial start-up. Any product specifically formulated for this purpose can be used, but engine oil is not recommended as a prelube.

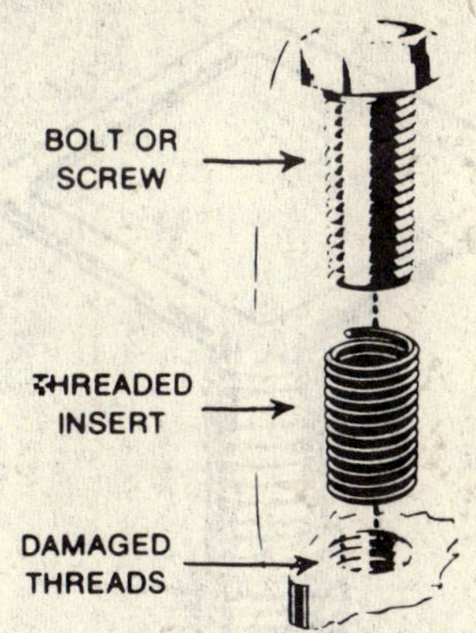

Using the tread repair insert to fix a damaged hole

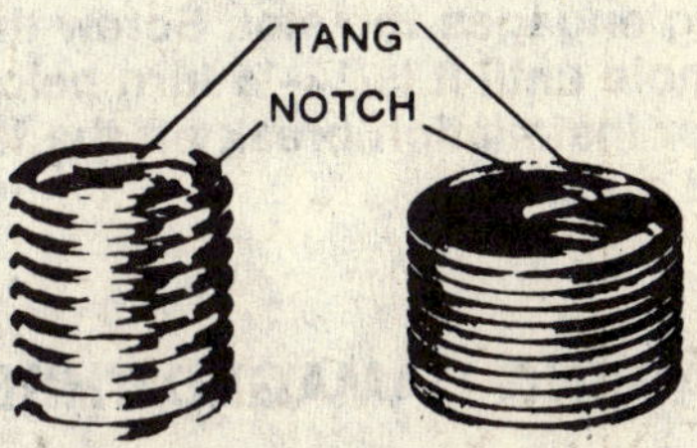

Standard thread repair insert (left) and the spark plug repair insert (right)

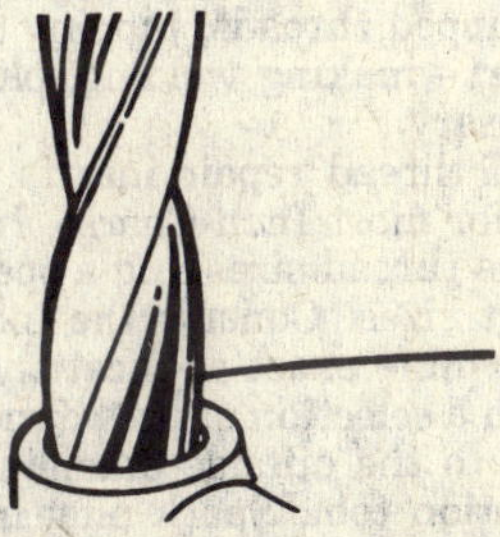

Using a specified drill to drill out the damaged thread. Drill competely through the hole or to the bottom of the blind hole

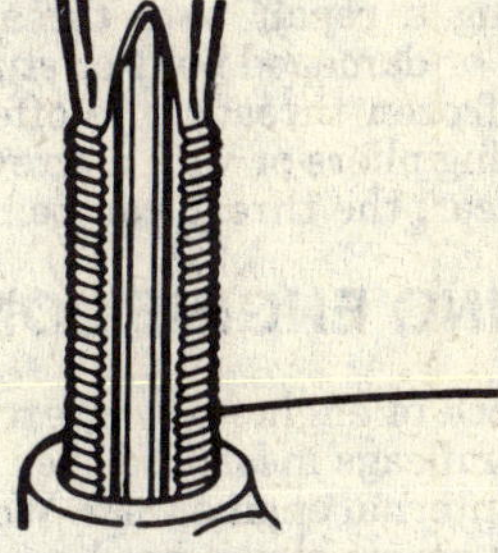

With the tap supplied, tap the hole to receive the thread insert. Keep the tap well oiled and back it out frequently to avoid clogging threads

When semi-permanent (locked, but removable) installation of bolts or nuts is desired, threads should be cleaned and coated with Loctite® or other similar, commercial non-hardening sealant.

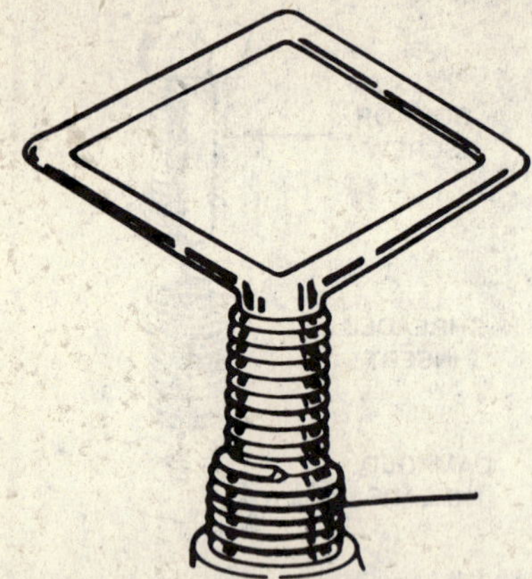

Screw the threaded insert onto the installation tool until the tang engages the slot. Screw the insert into the tapped hole until it is ¼–½ turn below the top surface. After installation break off the tang with a hammer and a punch

REPAIRING DAMAGED THREADS

Several methods of repairing damaged threads are available. Heli-Coil® (shown here), Keenserts® and Microdot® are among the most widely used. All involve basically the same principle—drilling out stripped threads, tapping the hole and installing a prewound insert—making welding, plugging and oversize fasteners unnecessary.

Two types of thread repair inserts are usually supplied—a standard type for most Inch Coarse, Inch Fine, Metric Course and Metric Fine thread sizes and a spark plug type to fit most spark plug port sizes. Consult the individual manufacturer's catalog to determine exact applications. Typical thread repair kits will contain a selection of prewound threaded inserts, a tap (corresponding to the outside diameter threads of the insert) and an installation tool. Spark plug inserts usually differ because they require a tap equipped with pilot threads and a combined reamer/tap section. Most manufacturers also supply blister-packed thread repair inserts separately in addition to a master kit containing a variety of taps and inserts plus installation tools.

Before effecting a repair to a threaded hole, remove any snapped, broken or damaged bolts or studs. Penetrating oil can be used to free frozen threads; the offending item can be removed with locking pliers or with a screw or stud extractor. After the hole is clear, the thread can be repaired, as follows:

CHECKING ENGINE COMPRESSION

A noticeable lack of engine power, excessive oil consumption and/or poor fuel mileage measured over an extended period are all indicators of internal engine wear. Worn piston rings, scored or worn cylinder bores, blown head gaskets, sticking or burnt valves and worn valve seats are all possible culprits here. A check of each cylinder's compression will help you locate the problems.

As mentioned in the Tools and Equipment part of Section 1, a screw-in type compression gauge is more accurate that the type you simply hold against the spark plug hole, although it takes slightly longer to use. It's worth it to obtain a more accurate reading. Follow the procedures below.

Gasoline Engines

1. Warm up the engine to normal operating temperature.

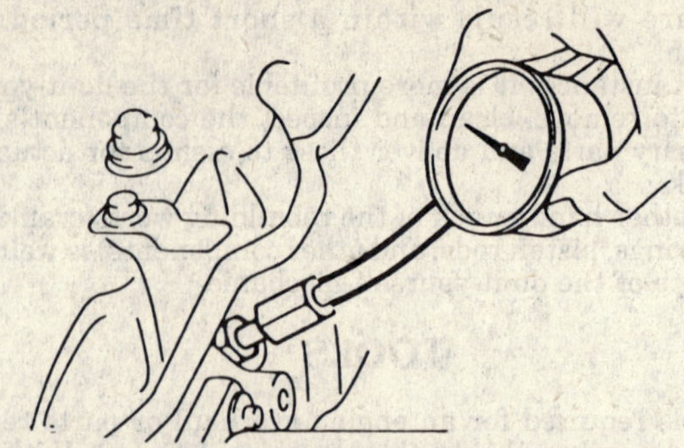

The screw-in type compression gauge is more accurate

2. Remove all spark plugs.
3. Disconnect the high tension lead from the ignition coil.
4. Fully open the throttle, either by operating the carburetor throttle linkage by hand or by having an assistant floor the accelerator pedal.
5. Screw the compression gauge into the No. 1 spark plug hole until the fitting is snug.

NOTE: Be careful not to crossthread the plug hole. On aluminum cylinder heads use extra care, as the threads in these heads are easily ruined.

6. Ask an assistant to depress the accelerator pedal fully on both carbureted and fuel injected vehicles. Then, while reading the compression gauge, ask the assistant to crank the engine 2–3 times in short bursts using the ignition switch.
7. Read the compression gauge at the end of each series of cranks and record the highest of these readings. Repeat this procedure for each of the engine's cylinders. Compare the highest reading of each cylinder to the compression pressure specification in the Tune-Up Specifications chart in Section 2. The specs in this chart are maximum values.

NOTE: A cylinder's compression pressure is usually acceptable, if it is not less than 80 percent of maximum. The difference between each cylinder should be no more than 12–14 pounds.

8. If a cylinder is unusually low, pour a tablespoon of clean engine oil into the cylinder through the spark plug hole and repeat the compression test. If the compression rises after adding the oil, it appears that the cylinder's piston rings or bore are damaged or worn. If the pressure remains low, the valves may not be seating properly (a valve job is needed) or the head gasket may be blown near that cylinder. If compression in any 2 adjacent cylinders is low and if the addition of oil doesn't help the compression, there is leakage past the head gasket. Oil and coolant water in the combustion chamber can result from this problem. There may be evidence of water droplets on the engine dipstick when a head gasket has blown.

NORMAL—Compression builds up quickly and evenly to the specified compression on each cylinder.

PISTON RINGS—Compression low on the first stroke, then tends to build up on the following strokes but does not reach normal. This reading should be tested with the addition of a few shots of engine oil into the cylinders. If the compression increases considerably, the rings are leaking compression.

VALVES—Low on the first stroke, does not tend to build up on following strokes. This reading will stay around the same with a few shots of engine oil in the cylinder.

HEAD GASKET—The compression reading is low between 2 adjacent cylinders. The head gasket between the 2 cylinders may be blown. If there are signs of white smoke coming from the exhaust, while the engine is running, this may indicate water leaking into the cylinder and being converted into steam. Check

Standard Torque Specifications and Fastener Markings

In the absence of specific torques, the following chart can be used as a guide to the maximum safe torque of a particular size/grade of fastener.

- There is no torque difference for fine or coarse threads.
- Torque values are based on clean, dry threads. Reduce the value by 10% if threads are oiled prior to assembly.
- The torque required for aluminum components or fasteners is considerably less.

U.S. Bolts

SAE Grade Number	1 or 2			5			6 or 7		
Number of lines always 2 less than the grade number.									
	Maximum Torque			Maximum Torque			Maximum Torque		
Bolt Size (Inches)—(Thread)	Ft./Lbs.	Kgm	Nm	Ft./Lbs.	Kgm	Nm	Ft./Lbs.	Kgm	Nm
¼—20	5	0.7	6.8	8	1.1	10.8	10	1.4	13.5
—28	6	0.8	8.1	10	1.4	13.6			
5/16—18	11	1.5	14.9	17	2.3	23.0	19	2.6	25.8
—24	13	1.8	17.6	19	2.6	25.7			
⅜—16	18	2.5	24.4	31	4.3	42.0	34	4.7	46.0
—24	20	2.75	27.1	35	4.8	47.5			
7/16—14	28	3.8	37.0	49	6.8	66.4	55	7.6	74.5
—20	30	4.2	40.7	55	7.6	74.5			
½—13	39	5.4	52.8	75	10.4	101.7	85	11.75	115.2
—20	41	5.7	55.6	85	11.7	115.2			
9/16—12	51	7.0	69.2	110	15.2	149.1	120	16.6	162.7
—18	55	7.6	74.5	120	16.6	162.7			
⅝—11	83	11.5	112.5	150	20.7	203.3	167	23.0	226.5
—18	95	13.1	128.8	170	23.5	230.5			
¾—10	105	14.5	142.3	270	37.3	366.0	280	38.7	379.6
—16	115	15.9	155.9	295	40.8	400.0			
⅞— 9	160	22.1	216.9	395	54.6	535.5	440	60.9	596.5
—14	175	24.2	237.2	435	60.1	589.7			
1— 8	236	32.5	318.6	590	81.6	799.9	660	91.3	894.8
—14	250	34.6	338.9	660	91.3	849.8			

Metric Bolts

Relative Strength Marking	4.6, 4.8			8.8		
Bolt Markings						
	Maximum Torque			Maximum Torque		
Bolt Size Thread Size x Pitch (mm)	Ft./Lbs.	Kgm	Nm	Ft./Lbs.	Kgm	Nm
6 x 1.0	2–3	.2–.4	3–4	3–6	.4–.8	5–8
8 x 1.25	6–8	.8–1	8–12	9–14	1.2–1.9	13–19
10 x 1.25	12–17	1.5–2.3	16–23	20–29	2.7–4.0	27–39
12 x 1.25	21–32	2.9–4.4	29–43	35–53	4.8–7.3	47–72
14 x 1.5	35–52	4.8–7.1	48–70	57–85	7.8–11.7	77–110
16 x 1.5	51–77	7.0–10.6	67–100	90–120	12.4–16.5	130–160
18 x 1.5	74–110	10.2–15.1	100–150	130–170	17.9–23.4	180–230
20 x 1.5	110–140	15.1–19.3	150–190	190–240	26.2–46.9	160–320
22 x 1.5	150–190	22.0–26.2	200–260	250–320	34.5–44.1	340–430
24 x 1.5	190–240	26.2–46.9	260–320	310–410	42.7–56.5	420–550

around the cylinder head-to-cylinder block area for signs of coolant and oil leakage, indicating a leaking head gasket.

Diesel Engines

Checking the cylinder compression on diesel engines is basically the same procedures as on gasoline engines, except for the following:

1. A special compression gauge adaptor suitable for diesel engines (because these engines have much greater compression pressures) must be used.
2. Remove the injector tubes and the injectors from each cylinder.

NOTE: Don't forget to remove the washer beneath each injector; otherwise, it may get lost when the engine is cranked.

3. When fitting the compression gauge adaptor to the cylinder head, make sure the bleeder of the gauge, if equipped, is closed.

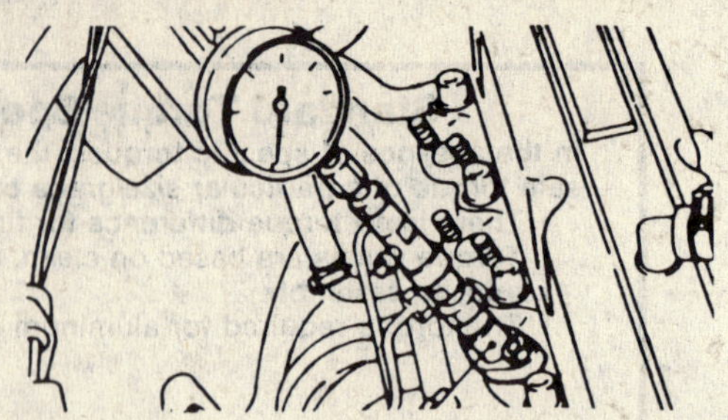

Diesel engines require a special compression gauge adaptor

4. When reinstalling the injector assemblies, install new washers under each injector.

NOTE: The following procedures require the use of an engine hoist with sufficient capacity to safely lift and support 500–1000 lbs.

GENERAL ENGINE SPECIFICATIONS

Year	VIN	No. Cylinder Displacement cu. in. (liter)	Fuel System Type	Net Horsepower @ rpm	Net Torque @ rpm (ft. lbs.)	Bore × Stroke (in.)	Compression Ratio	Oil Pressure @ rpm
1983	A	4-119 (1.9)	2bbl	84 @ 4600	101 @ 3000	3.43 × 3.23	8.4:1	57 @ 2000
	B	6-173 (2.8)	2bbl	110 @ 4800	148 @ 2000	3.50 × 2.99	8.5:1	45 @ 2000
	Y	4-121 (2.0)	2bbl	83 @ 4600	108 @ 2400	3.50 × 3.15	9.3:1	45 @ 2000
	S	4-136 (2.2)	Diesel	58 @ 4300	93 @ 2200	3.46 × 3.62	21.0:1	56 @ 2000
1984	A	4-119 (1.9)	2bbl	84 @ 4600	101 @ 3000	3.43 × 3.23	8.4:1	57 @ 2000
	B	6-173 (2.8)	2bbl	110 @ 4800	148 @ 2000	3.50 × 2.99	8.5:1	45 @ 2000
	Y	4-121 (2.0)	2bbl	83 @ 4600	108 @ 2400	3.50 × 3.15	9.3:1	45 @ 2000
	S	4-136 (2.2)	Diesel	58 @ 4300	93 @ 2200	3.46 × 3.62	21.0:1	56 @ 2000
1985	A	4-119 (1.9)	2bbl	84 @ 4600	101 @ 3000	3.43 × 3.23	8.4:1	57 @ 2000
	B	6-173 (2.8)	2bbl	110 @ 4800	148 @ 2000	3.50 × 2.99	8.5:1	45 @ 2000
	E	4-151 (2.5)	EFI	92 @ 4400	134 @ 2800	4.00 × 3.00	9.0:1	45 @ 2000
	S	4-136 (2.2)	Diesel	58 @ 4300	93 @ 2200	3.46 × 3.62	21.0:1	56 @ 2000
1986	E	4-151 (2.5)	EFI	92 @ 4400	134 @ 2800	4.00 × 3.00	9.0:1	45 @ 2000
	R	6-173 (2.8)	EFI	125 @ 4800	150 @ 2200	3.56 × 3.04	8.5:1	50 @ 2000
1987	E	4-151 (2.5)	EFI	92 @ 4400	134 @ 2800	4.00 × 3.00	9.0:1	45 @ 2000
	R	6-173 (2.8)	EFI	125 @ 4800	150 @ 2200	3.56 × 3.04	8.5:1	50 @ 2000
1988	E	4-151 (2.5)	EFI	92 @ 4400	130 @ 3200	4.00 × 3.00	8.3:1	41 @ 2000
	R	6-173 (2.8)	EFI	125 @ 4800	150 @ 2400	3.56 × 3.04	8.9:1	50 @ 2000
	Z	6-262 (4.3)	EFI	150 @ 4000	230 @ 2400	4.00 × 3.48	9.3:1	30 @ 2000
1989	E	4-151 (2.5)	EFI	92 @ 4400	130 @ 3200	4.00 × 3.00	8.3:1	41 @ 2000
	R	6-173 (2.8)	EFI	125 @ 4800	150 @ 2400	3.56 × 3.04	8.9:1	50 @ 2000
	Z	6-262 (4.3)	EFI	160 @ 4000	230 @ 2800	4.00 × 3.48	9.3:1	18 @ 2000
1990	Z	6-262 (4.3)	EFI	160 @ 4000	230 @ 2800	4.00 × 3.48	9.3:1	18 @ 2000
1991	Z	6-262 (4.3)	EFI	160 @ 4000	230 @ 2800	4.00 × 3.48	9.3:1	18 @ 2000

EFI—Electronic Fuel Injection

VALVE SPECIFICATIONS

All measurements given in inches.

Year	VIN	No. Cylinder Displacement cu. in. (liter)	Seat Angle (deg.)	Face Angle (deg.)	Spring Test Pressure (lbs.)	Spring Installed Height (in.)	Stem-to-Guide Clearance (in.) Intake	Stem-to-Guide Clearance (in.) Exhaust	Stem Diameter (in.) Intake	Stem Diameter (in.) Exhaust
1983	A	4-119 (1.9)	45	45	①	NA	0.0009–0.0022	0.0015–0.0031	0.3102 min.	0.3091 min.
	B	6-173 (2.8)	46	45	195 @ 1.180	1.5748	0.0010–0.0027	0.0010–0.0027	0.3410–0.3416	0.3410–0.3416
	Y	4-121 (2.0)	46	45	182 @ 1.330	1.5984	0.0011–0.0026	0.0014–0.0031	0.3410–0.3416	0.3410–0.3416
	S	4-136 (2.2)	45	45	②	NA	0.0015–0.0027	0.0025–0.0037	0.3150–0.3100	0.3150–0.3090
1984	A	4-119 (1.9)	45	45	①	NA	0.0009–0.0022	0.0015–0.0031	0.3102 min.	0.3091 min.
	B	6-173 (2.8)	46	45	195 @ 1.180	1.5748	0.0010–0.0027	0.0010–0.0027	0.3410–0.3416	0.3410–0.3416
	Y	4-121 (2.0)	46	45	182 @ 1.330	1.5984	0.0011–0.0026	0.0014–0.0031	0.3410–0.3416	0.3410–0.3416
	S	4-136 (2.2)	45	45	②	NA	0.0015–0.0027	0.0025–0.0037	0.3150–0.3100	0.3150–0.3091
1985	A	4-119 (1.9)	45	45	①	NA	0.0009–0.0022	0.0015–0.0031	0.3102 min.	0.3091 min.
	B	6-173 (2.8)	46	45	195 @ 1.180	1.5748	0.0010–0.0027	0.0010–0.0027	0.3410–0.3416	0.3410–0.3416
	E	4-151 (2.5)	46	45	175 @ 1.26	1.69	0.0010–0.0025	0.0013–0.0030	0.3430–0.3420	0.3420–0.3430
	S	4-136 (2.2)	45	45	②	NA	0.0015–0.0027	0.0025–0.0037	0.3100–0.3150	0.3091–0.3150
1986	E	4-151 (2.5)	46	45	175 @ 1.26	1.69	0.0010–0.0025	0.0013–0.0030	0.3430–0.3420	0.3420–0.3430
	R	4-173 (2.8)	46	45	175 @ 1.26	1.94	0.0010–0.0002	0.0010–0.0002	0.3410–0.3420	0.3410–0.3420
1987	E	4-151 (2.5)	46	45	175 @ 1.26	1.69	0.0010–0.0025	0.0013–0.0030	0.3430–0.3420	0.3420–0.3430
	R	6-173 (2.8)	46	45	175 @ 1.26	1.94	0.0010–0.0002	0.0010–0.0002	0.3410–0.3420	0.3410–0.3420
1988	E	4-151 (2.5)	46	45	175 @ 1.26	1.69	0.0010–0.0025	0.0013–0.0030	0.3430–0.3420	0.3420–0.3430
	R	6-173 (2.8)	46	45	175 @ 1.26	1.94	0.0010–0.0002	0.0010–0.0002	0.3410–0.3420	0.3410–0.3420
	Z	6-262 (4.3)	46	45	194 @ 1.25	1.39	0.0010–0.0027	0.0010–0.0027	0.3410–0.3420	0.3410–0.3420
1989	Z	6-262 (4.3)	46	45	194 @ 1.25	1.39	0.0010–0.0027	0.0010–0.0027	0.3410–0.3420	0.3410–0.3420
1990	Z	6-262 (4.3)	46	45	194 @ 1.25	1.39	0.0010–0.0027	0.0010–0.0027	NA	NA
1991	Z	6-262 (4.3)	46	45	194 @ 1.25	1.39	0.0010–0.0027	0.0010–0.0027	NA	NA

NA—Not Available

① Outer: 35 @ 1.814
Inner: 20 @ 1.516

② Outer: 145 @ 1.535
Inner: 44 @ 1.457

CAMSHAFT SPECIFICATIONS

All measurements given in inches.

Year	VIN	No. Cylinder Displacement cu. in. (liter)	Journal Diameter 1	2	3	4	5	Lobe Lift In.	Lobe Lift Ex.	Bearing Clearance	Camshaft End Play
1983	A	4-119 (1.9)	1.3362– 1.3370	1.3362– 1.3370	1.3362– 1.3370	1.3362– 1.3370	1.3362– 1.3370	NA	NA	0.0016– 0.0035	0.0020– 0.0059
	B	6-173 (2.8)	1.8677– 1.8696	1.8677– 1.8696	1.8677– 1.8696	1.8677– 1.8696	—	0.231	0.262	0.0010– 0.0039	NA
	Y	4-121 (2.0)	1.8677– 1.8696	1.8677– 1.8696	1.8677– 1.8696	1.8677– 1.8696	1.8677– 1.8696	0.262	0.262	0.0010– 0.0039	NA
	S	4-136 (2.2)	1.8741– 1.8898	1.8741– 1.8898	1.8741– 1.8898	—	—	NA	NA	0.0020– 0.0097	0.0032– 0.0079
1984	A	4-119 (1.9)	1.3362– 1.3370	1.3362– 1.3370	1.3362– 1.3370	1.3362– 1.3370	1.3362– 1 3370	NA	NA	0.0016– 0.0035	0.0020– 0.0059
	B	6-173 (2.8)	1.8677– 1.8696	1.8677– 1.8696	1.8677– 1.8696	1.8677– 1.8696	—	0.231	0.262	0.0010– 0.0039	NA
	Y	4-121 (2.0)	1.8677– 1.8696	1.8677– 1.8696	1.8677– 1.8696	1.8677– 1.8696	1.8677– 1.8696	0.262	0.262	0.0010– 0.0039	NA
	S	4-136 (2.2)	1.8741– 1.8898	1.8741– 1.8898	1.8741– 1.8898	—	—	NA	NA	0.0020– 0.0097	0.0032– 0.0079
1985	A	4-119 (1.9)	1.3362– 1.3370	1.3362– 1.3370	1.3362– 1.3370	1.3362– 1.3370	1.3362– 1.3370	NA	NA	0.0016– 0.0035	0.0020– 0.0059
	B	6-173 (2.8)	1.8677– 1.8696	1.8677– 1.8696	1.8677– 1.8696	1.8677– 1.8696	—	0.231	0.262	0.0010– 0.0039	NA
	E	4-151 (2.5)	1.8690	1.8690	1.8690	—	—	0.398	0.398	0.0007– 0.0027	0.0015– 0.0050
	S	4-136 (2.2)	1.8741– 1.8898	1.8741– 1.8898	1.8741– 1.8898	—	—	NA	NA	0.0020– 0.0097	0.0032– 0.0079
1986	E	4-151 (2.5)	1.8690	1.8690	1.8690	—	—	0.398	0.398	0.0007– 0.0027	0.0015– 0.0050
	R	6-173 (2.8)	1.8970– 1.8990	1.8970– 1.8990	1.8970– 1.8990	1.8970– 1.8990	—	0.234	0.266	0.0010– 0.0040	—
1987	E	4-151 (2.5)	1.8690	1.8690	1.8690	—	—	0.398	0.398	0.0007– 0.0027	0.0015– 0.0050
	R	6-173 (2.8)	1.8970– 1.8990	1.8970– 1.8990	1.8970– 1.8990	1.8970– 1.8990	—	0.234	0.266	0.0010– 0.0040	—
1988	E	4-151 (2.5)	1.8690	1.8690	1.8690	—	—	0.398	0.398	0.0007– 0.0027	0.0015– 0.0050
	R	6-173 (2.8)	1.8970– 1.8990	1.8970– 1.8990	1.8970– 1.8990	1.8970– 1.8990	—	0.234	0.266	0.0010– 0.0040	—
	Z	6-262 (4.3)	1.8682– 1.8692	1.8682– 1.8692	1.8682– 1.8692	1.8682– 1.8692	—	0.357	0.390	0.0010– 0.0030	0.004– 0.012
1989	E	4-151 (2.5)	1.8690	1.8690	1.8690	—	—	0.232	0.232	0.0007– 0.0027	0.0015– 0.0050
	R	6-173 (2.8)	1.8970– 1.8990	1.8970– 1.8990	1.8970– 1.8990	1.8970– 1.8990	—	0.266	0.277	0.0010– 0.0040	—
	Z	6-262 (4.3)	1.8682– 1.8692	1.8682– 1.8692	1.8682– 1.8692	1.8682– 1.8692	—	0.357	0.390	0.0010– 0.0030	0.004– 0.012
1990	Z	6-262 (4.3)	1.8682– 1.8692	1.8682– 1.8692	1.8682– 1.8692	1.8682– 1.8692	—	0.357	0.390	0.0010– 0.0030	0.004– 0.012
1991	Z	6-262 (4.3)	1.8682– 1.8692	1.8682– 1.8692	1.8682– 1.8692	1.8682– 1.8692	—	0.357 ①	0.390 ②	0.0010– 0.0030	0.004– 0.012

NA—Not Available ① 0.234—Bravada ② 0.257—Bravada

CRANKSHAFT AND CONNECTING ROD SPECIFICATIONS

All measurements are given in inches.

		No.	Crankshaft				Connecting Rod		
Year	VIN	Cylinder Displacement cu. in. (liter)	Main Brg. Journal Dia.	Main Brg. Oil Clearance	Shaft End-play	Thrust on No.	Journal Diameter	Oil Clearance	Side Clearance
1983	A	4-119 (1.9)	2.2050	0.0008–0.0025	0.0117 max.	3	1.9290	0.0007–0.0030	0.0137 max.
	B	6-173 (2.8)	2.4940	0.0017–0.0030	0.0020–0.0067	3	1.9980	0.0014–0.0032	0.0062–0.0173
	Y	4-121 (2.0)	④	⑤	0.0020–0.0071	3	1.9990	0.0010–0.0031	0.0034–0.0240
	S	4-136 (2.2)	2.3590	0.0011–0.0033	0.0018	3	2.0837	0.0016–0.0047	0.0024
1984	A	4-119 (1.9)	2.2050	0.0008–0.0025	0.0117 max.	3	1.9290	0.0007–0.0030	0.0137 max.
	B	6-173 (2.8)	2.4940	0.0017–0.0030	0.0020–0.0067	3	1.9980	0.0014–0.0032	0.0063–0.0173
	Y	4-121 (2.0)	④	⑤	0.0020–0.0071	3	1.9990	0.0010–0.0031	0.0034–0.0240
	S	4-136 (2.2)	2.3590	0.0011–0.0033	0.0018	3	2.0837	0.0016–0.0047	0.0024
1985	A	4-119 (1.9)	2.2050	0.0008–0.0025	0.0117 max.	3	1.9290	0.0007–0.0030	0.0137 max.
	B	6-173 (2.8)	2.4940	0.0017–0.0030	0.0020–0.0067	3	1.9980	0.0014–0.0032–	0.0063–0.0173
	E	4-151 (2.5)	2.3000	0.0005–0.0022	0.0035–0.0085	5	2.000	0.0005–0.0026	0.0060–0.0220
	S	4-136 (2.2)	2.3590	0.0011–0.0033	0.0018	3	2.0837	0.0016–0.0047	0.0024
1986	E	4-151 (2.5)	2.3000	0.0005–0.0022	0.0035–0.0085	5	2.000	0.0005–0.0026	0.0060–0.0220
	R	6-173 (2.8)	①	0.0016–0.0032	0.0020–0.0070	3	1.9983–1.9993	0.0014–0.0035	0.0063–0.0173
1987	E	4-151 (2.5)	2.3000	0.0005–0.0022	0.0035–0.0085	5	2.000	0.0005–0.0026	0.0060–0.0220
	R	6-173 (2.8)	①	0.0016–0.0032	0.0020–0.0070	3	1.9983–1.9993	0.0014–0.0035	0.0063–0.0173
1988	E	4-151 (2.5)	2.3000	0.0005–0.0022	0.0035–0.0085	5	2.000	0.0005–0.0026	0.0060–0.0220
	R	6-173 (2.8)	①	0.0016–0.0032	0.0020–0.0070	3	1.9983–1.9993	0.0014–0.0035	0.0063–0.0173
	Z	6-262 (4.3)	②	③	0.0020–0.0060	3	2.2487–2.2497	0.0013–0.0035	0.0060–0.0140
1989	E	4-151 (2.5)	2.3000	0.0005–0.0022	0.0035–0.0085	5	2.000	0.0005–0.0026	0.0060–0.0220
	R	6-173 (2.8)	①	0.0016–0.0032	0.0020–0.0070	3	1.9983–1.9993	0.0014–0.0035	0.0063–0.0173
	Z	6-262 (4.3)	②	③	0.0020–0.0060	3	2.2487–2.2497	0.0013–0.0035	0.0060–0.0140
1990	Z	6-262 (4.3)	②	③	0.0020–0.0060	3	2.2487–2.2497	0.0013–0.0035	0.0060–0.0140

CRANKSHAFT AND CONNECTING ROD SPECIFICATIONS

All measurements are given in inches.

Year	VIN	No. Cylinder Displacement cu. in. (liter)	Crankshaft Main Brg. Journal Dia.	Crankshaft Main Brg. Oil Clearance	Crankshaft Shaft End-play	Crankshaft Thrust on No.	Connecting Rod Journal Diameter	Connecting Rod Oil Clearance	Connecting Rod Side Clearance
1991	Z	6-262 (4.3)	②	③	0.0020–0.0060	3	2.2487–2.2497	0.0013–0.0035	0.0060–0.0140

① Journals 1, 2, 4: 2.5336–2.5345
Journal 3: 2.5332–2.5340

② Journal 1: 2.4484–2.4493
Journal 2, 3: 2.4481–2.4490
Journal 4: 2.4479–2.4488

③ Journal 1: 0.0008–0.0020
Journal 2, 3: 0.0011–0.0023
Journal 4: 0.0017–0.0032

④ Journals 1, 2, 3, 4: 2.4940–2.4950
Journal 5: 2.4930–2.4950

⑤ Journals 1, 2, 3, 4: 0.0006–0.0019
Journal 5: 0.0014–0.0027

PISTON AND RING SPECIFICATIONS

All measurements are given in inches.

Year	VIN	No. Cylinder Displacement cu. in. (liter)	Piston Clearance	Ring Gap Top Compression	Ring Gap Bottom Compression	Ring Gap Oil Control	Ring Side Clearance Top Compression	Ring Side Clearance Bottom Compression	Ring Side Clearance Oil Control
1983	A	4-119 (1.9)	0.0018–0.0026	0.012–0.020	0.008–0.016	0.008–0.035	0.0059 max.	0.0059 max.	0.0059 max.
	B	6-173 (2.8)	0.0017–0.0027	0.010–0.020	0.010–0.020	0.020–0.055	0.0012–0.0028	0.0016–0.0037	0.0078 max.
	Y	4-121 (2.0)	0.0008–0.0018	0.010–0.020	0.010–0.020	0.020–0.055	0.0012–0.0027	0.0012–0.0038	0.0078 max.
	S	4-136 (2.2)	0.0062–0.0070	0.008–0.016	0.008–0.016	0.008–0.016	0.0018–0.0028	0.0012–0.0021	0.0008–0.0021
1984	A	4-119 (1.9)	0.0018–0.0026	0.012–0.020	0.008–0.016	0.008–0.035	0.0059 max.	0.0059 max.	0.0059 max.
	B	6-173 (2.8)	0.0017–0.0027	0.010–0.020	0.010–0.020	0.020–0.055	0.0012–0.0028	0.0016–0.0037	0.0078 max.
	Y	4-121 (2.0)	0.0008–0.0018	0.010–0.020	0.010–0.020	0.020–0.055	0.0012–0.0027	0.0012–0.0038	0.0078 max.
	S	4-136 (2.2)	0.0062–0.0070	0.008–0.016	0.008–0.016	0.008–0.016	0.0018–0.0028	0.0012–0.0021	0.0008–0.0021
1985	A	4-119 (1.9)	0.0018–0.0026	0.012–0.020	0.008–0.016	0.008–0.035	0.0059 max.	0.0059 max.	0.0059 max.
	B	6-173 (2.8)	0.0017–0.0027	0.010–0.020	0.010–0.020	0.020–0.055	0.0012–0.0028	0.0016–0.0037	0.0078 max.
	E	4-151 (2.5)	0.0014–0.0022	0.010–0.020	0.010–0.020	0.020–0.060	0.0020–0.0030	0.0010–0.0030	0.0015–0.0055
	S	4-136 (2.2)	0.0062–0.0070	0.008–0.016	0.008–0.016	0.008–0.016	0.0018–0.0028	0.0012–0.0021	0.0008–0.0021
1986	E	4-151 (2.5)	0.0014–0.0022	0.010–0.020	0.010–0.020	0.020–0.060	0.0020–0.0030	0.0010–0.0030	0.0150–0.0550
	R	6-173 (2.8)	0.0007–0.0017	0.010–0.022	0.010–0.022	0.020–0.055	0.0012–0.0027	0.0015–0.0037	0.0078
1987	E	4-151 (2.5)	0.0014–0.0022	0.010–0.020	0.010–0.020	0.020–0.060	0.0020–0.0030	0.0010–0.0030	0.0150–0.0550
	R	6-173 (2.8)	0.0007–0.0017	0.010–0.022	0.010–0.022	0.020–0.055	0.0012–0.0027	0.0015–0.0037	0.0078

PISTON AND RING SPECIFICATIONS

All measurements are given in inches.

Year	VIN	No. Cylinder Displacement cu. in. (liter)	Piston Clearance	Ring Gap			Ring Side Clearance		
				Top Compression	Bottom Compression	Oil Control	Top Compression	Bottom Compression	Oil Control
1988	E	4-151 (2.5)	0.0014–0.0022	0.010–0.020	0.010–0.020	0.020–0.060	0.0020–0.0030	0.0010–0.0030	0.0150–0.0550
	R	6-173 (2.8)	0.0007–0.0017	0.010–0.022	0.010–0.022	0.020–0.055	0.0012–0.0027	0.0015–0.0037	0.0078
	Z	6-262 (4.3)	0.0007–0.0017	0.010–0.020	0.010–0.025	0.015–0.055	0.0012–0.0032	0.0012–0.0032	0.0020–0.0070
1989	E	4-151 (2.5)	0.0010–0.0022	0.010–0.020	0.010–0.020	0.020–0.060	0.0020–0.0030	0.0010–0.0030	0.0150–0.0550
	R	6-173 (2.8)	0.0007–0.0017	0.010–0.022	0.010–0.022	0.020–0.055	0.0012–0.0027	0.0015–0.0037	0.078
	Z	6-262 (4.3)	0.0007–0.0017	0.010–0.020	0.010–0.025	0.015–0.055	0.0012–0.0032	0.0012–0.0032	0.0020–0.0070
1990	Z	6-262 (4.3)	0.0007–0.0017	0.010–0.020	0.010–0.025	0.015–0.055	0.0012–0.0032	0.0012–0.0032	0.0020–0.0070
1991	Z	6-262 (4.3)	0.0007–0.0017	0.010–0.020	0.010–0.025	0.015–0.055	0.0012–0.0032	0.0012–0.0032	0.0020–0.0070

TORQUE SPECIFICATIONS

All readings in ft. lbs.

Year	VIN	No. Cylinder Displacement cu. in. (liter)	Cylinder Head Bolts	Main Bearing Bolts	Rod Bearing Bolts	Crankshaft Pulley Bolts	Flywheel Bolts	Manifold		Spark Plugs
								Intake	Exhaust	
1983	A	4-119 (1.9)	72	75	43	87	76	17	16	18
	B	6-173 (2.8)	70	70	37	75	50	23	25	7–15
	Y	4-121 (2.0)	70	70	37	75	50	23	25	7–15
	S	4-136 (2.2)	60	116–130	65	125–150	70	15	15	22
1984	A	4-119 (1.9)	72	75	43	87	76	17	16	18
	B	6-173 (2.8)	70	70	37	75	50	23	25	7–15
	Y	4-121 (2.0)	70	70	37	75	50	23	25	7–15
	S	4-136 (2.2)	60	116–130	65	125–150	70	15	15	22
1985	A	4-119 (1.9)	72	75	43	87	76	17	16	18
	B	6-173 (2.8)	70	70	37	75	50	23	25	7–15
	E	4-151 (2.5)	90	70	39	160	55	30	①	7–15
	S	4-136 (2.2)	60	116–130	65	125–150	70	15	15	22
1986	E	4-151 (2.5)	90	70	32	160	55	30	①	7–15
	R	6-173 (2.8)	70	70	39	70	52	23	25	11
1987	E	4-151 (2.5)	90	70	32	160	55	30	①	7–15
	R	6-173 (2.8)	70	70	39	70	52	23	25	11
1988	E	4-151 (2.5)	③	70	32	160	55④	30	①	7–15
	R	6-173 (2.8)	⑤	70	39	70	52	23	25	11
	Z	6-262 (4.3)	65	80	45	70	75	35	②	11

TORQUE SPECIFICATIONS

All readings in ft. lbs.

Year	VIN	No. Cylinder Displacement cu. in. (liter)	Cylinder Head Bolts	Main Bearing Bolts	Rod Bearing Bolts	Crankshaft Pulley Bolts	Flywheel Bolts	Manifold Intake	Manifold Exhaust	Spark Plugs
1989	E	4-151 (2.5)	③	70	32	160	55④	30	①	7–15
	R	6-173 (2.8)	⑤	70	39	70	52	23	25	11
	Z	6-262 (4.3)	65	80	45	70	75	35	②	11
1990	Z	6-262 (4.3)	65	80	45	70	75	35	②	11
1991	Z	6-262 (4.3)	65	80	45	70	75	35	②	11

① Inner bolts: 36 ft. lbs.
Outer bolts: 32 ft. lbs.
② Center bolts: 26 ft.lbs.
Outer bolts: 20 ft. lbs.
③ Tighten in 3 stages:
1st to 18 ft. lbs.
2nd to 26 ft. lbs. (except studs—tighten to 18 ft. lbs.)
3rd an additional 90 degrees (1/4 turn)
④ With manual transmission 65 ft. lbs.
⑤ Tighten in 2 stages:
1st to 40 ft. lbs.
2nd an additional 90 degrees (1/4 turn)

Gasoline Engine

REMOVAL AND INSTALLATION

Except 4.3L Engine

1. Disconnect the negative battery terminal from the battery.
2. Using a scribing tool, mark the outline of the hood hinges on the hood, then remove the hinge bolts and the hood from the vehicle.
3. If equipped with power steering, disconnect the power steering reservoir from the fan shroud, then disconnect the power steering pump from it's brackets and lay it aside.
4. Remove the upper fan shroud and the fan. If equipped with an automatic transmission, disconnect the transmission oil cooler lines from the radiator.
5. Position a drain pan under the radiator, open the drain cock and drain the cooling system. Disconnect the upper and lower radiator hoses from the radiator, then remove the radiator from the vehicle.

CAUTION

When draining the coolant, keep in mind that cats and dogs are attracted by the ethylene glycol antifreeze, and are quite likely to drink any that is left in an uncovered container or in puddles on the ground. This will prove fatal in sufficient quantity. Always drain the coolant into a sealable container. Coolant should be reused unless it is contaminated or several years old.

6. If equipped with air conditioning, remove the compressor from the engine and move it aside; do not disconnect the pressure lines from the compressor.
7. Remove the air cleaner, the fuel line bracket at the filter, the fuel line and the vacuum hoses from the engine.
8. Disconnect the accelerator, the TV and the cruise control cables from the engine. Disconnect the heater hoses from the engine.
9. Label and disconnect the electrical connectors from the O_2 sensor and other necessary electrical components.
10. Raise and support the front of the vehicle on jackstands.
11. On the 2WD models, disconnect the strut rod. On the 4WD models, disconnect the brake line clip from the crossmember, then remove the crossmember, the front drive shaft from the front axle and the automatic transmission cooler lines from the flywheel cover.
12. Disconnect the exhaust pipe from the catalytic converter hanger and the exhaust manifold(s).
13. Remove the drive belt splash shield, if equipped, and the starter. If equipped with an automatic transmission, remove the lower bell housing cover and the torque converter-to-flywheel bolts.
14. Remove the 2 left side outer air dam bolts, the lower fan shroud and the left side body (cab) mounting bolts, then raise and support (block) the left side of the body with wooden blocks.
15. Remove the upper transmission-to-engine bolts and the body-to-chassis wooden blocks, then lower the body.
16. Remove the lower transmission-to-engine bolts and engine-to-mount through bolts. Lower the vehicle and support the transmission.
17. Using a vertical lifting device, connect it to the engine, raise it slightly and move it forward.
18. From the rear of the engine, remove the wiring harness clips and the ground straps.
19. Lift the engine from the vehicle.

To install:

20. Lower the engine into the vehicle. Install the wiring harness clips and ground straps to the rear of the engine.
21. Install the upper transmission-to-engine bolts.
22. Raise and safely support the vehicle. Install the lower transmission-to-engine bolts and engine-to-mount through bolts. Torque the engine mount through bolts to 50 ft. lbs. for 4 cylinder engines or 85 ft. lbs. for V6 engines and the rear engine mount-to-crossmember nut to 24 ft. lbs.
23. Install the 2 left side outer air dam bolts, the lower fan shroud and the left side body (cab) mounting bolts.
24. If equipped with an automatic transmission, install the torque converter-to-flywheel bolts and the lower bellhousing cover.
25. Install the drive belt splash shield, if equipped, and the starter.
26. Connect the exhaust pipe to the catalytic converter hanger and the exhaust manifold(s).
27. On the 2WD models, connect the strut rod. On the 4WD models, connect the automatic transmission cooler lines to the flywheel cover, the front driveshaft to the front differential. Install the crossmember and connect the brake line clip to the crossmember.
28. Lower the vehicle.
29. Connect the electrical connectors to the O_2 sensor and other necessary electrical components.
30. Connect the accelerator, the TV and the cruise control cables to the engine. Connect the heater hoses to the engine.
31. Install the air cleaner, the fuel line bracket at the filter, the fuel line and the vacuum hoses to the engine.
32. If equipped with air conditioning, install the compressor from the engine.

33. Install the radiator and connect the upper and lower radiator hoses to the radiator.
34. Install the upper fan shroud and the fan. If equipped with an automatic transmission, connect the transmission oil cooler lines to the radiator.
35. If equipped with power steering, connect the power steering reservoir to the fan shroud, then connect the power steering pump to it's brackets.
36. Install the hood. Connect the negative battery cable to the battery.
37. Start the engine, allow it to reach normal operating temperatures and check for leaks.

4.3L Engine

BRAVADA

1. Disconnect the negative battery cable.
2. Remove the underhood light.
3. Raise and safely support the vehicle. Drain the cooling system and the engine oil.

CAUTION

When draining the coolant, keep in mind that cats and dogs are attracted by the ethylene glycol antifreeze, and are quite likely to drink any that is left in an uncovered container or in puddles on the ground. This will prove fatal in sufficient quantity. Always drain the coolant into a sealable container. Coolant should be reused unless it is contaminated or several years old.

4. Disconnect the exhaust pipes from the exhaust manifold.

CAUTION

The EPA warns that prolonged contact with used engine oil may cause a number of skin disorders, including cancer! You should make every effort to minimize your exposure to used engine oil. Protective gloves should be worn when changing the oil. Wash your hands and any other exposed skin areas as soon as possible after exposure to used engine oil. Soap and water, or waterless hand cleaner should be used.

5. Remove the front driveshaft from the front differential.
6. Disconnect the electrical connectors from the starter. Remove the starter.
7. Remove the torque converter cover bolts and the cover. Matchmark the torque converter to flywheel. Remove the torque converter-to-flywheel bolts; it will be necessary to rotate the flywheel to access the other bolts.
8. Remove the engine mount through bolts.
9. Remove the oil filter adapter from the engine.
10. Remove the transmission-to-engine bolt at the strut rod, the transfer case bolt at the strut rod and the strut rod.
11. Remove the transmission-to-engine bolts. Disconnect the transmission cooler lines from the engine clips and lower the vehicle.
12. Remove the air cleaner assembly.
13. Remove the upper fan shroud and the accessory drive belt.
14. Remove the fan and fan clutch assembly. Remove the upper cooling inlet hose from the radiator and the engine.
15. Remove the air conditioner compressor and lay it aside; do not disconnect the air conditioning hoses.
16. Remove the lower cooling outlet hose from the radiator and the engine.
17. Disconnect and drain the transmission and engine oil cooler lines from the radiator.
18. Disconnect the heater hoses from the engine. Remove the radiator-to-chassis bolts and the radiator.
19. Disconnect and plug the power steering hoses from the pump.
20. Label and disconnect the necessary electrical connectors from the engine.
21. Label and disconnect the necessary vacuum connectors from the engine.
22. Disconnect the accelerator cable, the TV cable and the cruise control cable from the engine.
23. Disconnect the electrical connectors and remove the alternator from the engine.
24. Disconnect and plug the fuel lines from the throttle body and remove the left side bracket.
25. Label and disconnect the wiring from the distributor cap and remove the distributor cap.
26. Using a floor jack, support the transmission.
27. Remove the oil bracket from the oil cooler.
28. Connect a vertical lifting device to the engine and lift the engine from the vehicle.
29. If necessary, remove the flywheel-to-crankshaft bolts and the flywheel.

To install:

30. If the flywheel was removed, install it and torque the bolts to 75 ft. lbs. (100 Nm).
31. Lower the engine into the vehicle, install the engine-to-engine mount bolts and torque the **A** bolts to 42 ft. lbs. (57 Nm) or nuts to 35 ft. lbs. (47 Nm), the **B** bolts to 35 ft. lbs. (47 Nm) and the **C** nut/bolt to 52 ft. lbs. (70 Nm).
32. Install the oil bracket from the oil cooler.
33. Install the distributor cap and connect the wiring to the distributor cap.
34. Install the left side bracket and connect and the fuel lines to the throttle body.
35. Install the alternator and connect the electrical connectors.
36. Connect the accelerator cable, the TV cable and the cruise control cable to the engine.
37. Connect the necessary vacuum connectors to the engine.

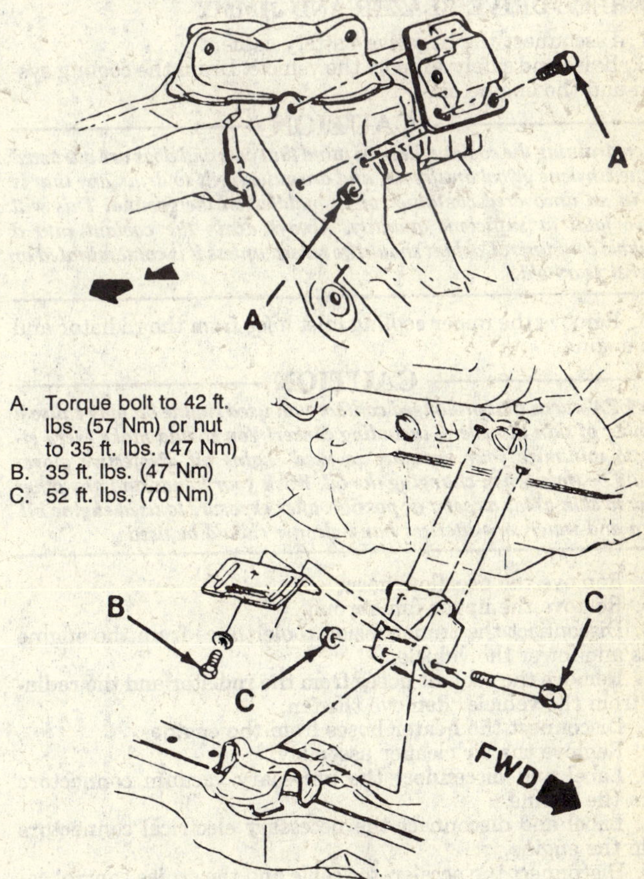

Install the engine mount bolts and nuts — 4.3L engine

38. Connect the necessary electrical connectors to the engine.
39. Connect the power steering hoses to the pump.
40. Install the radiator and connect the heater hoses to the engine.
41. Connect the transmission and engine oil cooler lines to the engine.
42. Connect the lower cooling outlet hose to the radiator and the engine.
43. Install the air conditioner compressor.
44. Install the upper cooling inlet hose to the radiator and the engine. Install the fan clutch assembly and the fan.
45. Install the upper fan shroud and the accessory drive belt.
46. Install the air cleaner assembly.
47. Remove the floor jack from the transmission. Connect the transmission cooler lines to the engine clips. Raise and safely support the vehicle.
48. Install the transmission-to-engine bolts.
49. Install the strut rod, the transfer case bolt to strut rod and the transmission-to-engine bolt at the strut rod.
50. Install the oil filter adapter to the engine.
51. Align the flywheel to torque converter matchmarks and install the bolts.
52. Install the starter and connect the electrical connectors.
53. Install the front driveshaft to the front differential.
54. Connect the exhaust pipes to the exhaust manifold.
55. Lower the vehicle. Refill the cooling system and the engine crankcase.
56. Install the underhood light. Connect the negative battery cable.
57. Start the engine, allow it to reach normal operating temperatures and check for leaks.

2-WHEEL DRIVE BLAZER AND JIMMY

1. Disconnect the negative battery cable.
2. Raise and safely support the vehicle. Drain the cooling system and the engine oil.

CAUTION

When draining the coolant, keep in mind that cats and dogs are attracted by the ethylene glycol antifreeze, and are quite likely to drink any that is left in an uncovered container or in puddles on the ground. This will prove fatal in sufficient quantity. Always drain the coolant into a sealable container. Coolant should be reused unless it is contaminated or several years old.

3. Remove the upper cooling inlet hose from the radiator and the engine.

CAUTION

The EPA warns that prolonged contact with used engine oil may cause a number of skin disorders, including cancer! You should make every effort to minimize your exposure to used engine oil. Protective gloves should be worn when changing the oil. Wash your hands and any other exposed skin areas as soon as possible after exposure to used engine oil. Soap and water, or waterless hand cleaner should be used.

4. Remove the overflow hose.
5. Remove the upper fan shroud.
6. Disconnect the transmission cooler lines from the engine clips and lower the vehicle.
7. Remove the coolant hoses from the radiator and the radiator from the vehicle. Remove the fan.
8. Disconnect the heater hoses from the engine.
9. Remove the air cleaner assembly.
10. Label and disconnect the necessary vacuum connectors from the engine.
11. Label and disconnect the necessary electrical connectors from the engine.
12. Disconnect the accelerator cable and the cruise control cable from the engine.
13. Label and disconnect the wiring from the distributor cap and remove the distributor cap.
14. Raise and safely support the vehicle. Disconnect the converter-to-exhaust pipe bolts and the exhaust pipes from the exhaust manifold.
15. Remove the strut rods from the bellhousing.
16. If equipped with an automatic transmission, remove the torque converter cover bolts and the cover. Matchmark the torque converter to flywheel. Remove the torque converter-to-flywheel bolts; it will be necessary to rotate the flywheel to access the other bolts.
17. Remove the shield from the rear of the catalytic converter.
18. Remove the converter hanger at the exhaust pipe.
19. Remove the lower fan shroud.
20. Disconnect and plug the fuel lines from the throttle body and remove the left side bracket.
21. Remove the 2 outer dam bolts.
22. Raise and safely support the vehicle. Remove the left body mounting bolts.
23. Lower the vehicle and remove the bellhousing-to-engine bolts.
24. Remove the engine mount through bolts.
25. If equipped with air conditioning, remove the air conditioner compressor and lay it aside; do not disconnect the air conditioning hoses.
26. If equipped with power steering, remove the power steering pump and move it aside; do not disconnect the pressure hoses.
27. Using a floor jack, support the transmission.
28. Connect a vertical lifting device to the engine and lift the engine from the vehicle.

To install:

29. Lower the engine into the vehicle, install the engine-to-engine mount bolts and torque the **A** bolts to 42 ft. lbs. (57 Nm) or nuts to 35 ft. lbs. (47 Nm), the **B** bolts to 35 ft. lbs. (47 Nm) and the **C** nut/bolt to 52 ft. lbs. (70 Nm).
30. Raise and safely support the vehicle. Install the lower bellhousing bolts.
31. Lower the vehicle and install the upper bellhousing bolts.
32. Install the body mount bolts.
33. If equipped with power steering, install the power steering pump.
34. If equipped with air conditioning, install the air conditioner compressor.
35. Install the 2 outer dam bolts.
36. Install the fuel lines to the throttle body.
37. Install the lower fan shroud.
38. Install the converter hanger to the exhaust pipe. Install the shield to the rear of the catalytic converter.
39. If equipped with an automatic transmission, align the flywheel to torque converter matchmarks and install the bolts.
40. Install the strut rods to the bellhousing.
41. Connect the exhaust pipes to the exhaust manifold. Connect the converter to the exhaust pipe and lower the vehicle.
42. Install the distributor cap.
43. Connect the accelerator cable and the cruise control cable to the engine.
44. Connect the necessary vacuum connectors to the engine.
45. Connect the necessary electrical connectors to the engine.
46. Install the air cleaner assembly.
47. Connect the heater hoses to the engine. Install the radiator.
48. If equipped with an automatic transmission, connect the transmission and engine oil cooler lines to the engine.
49. Connect the lower cooling outlet hose to the radiator and the engine.
50. Install the upper cooling inlet hose to the radiator and the engine. Install the fan.
51. Install the upper fan shroud.
52. Lower the vehicle. Refill the cooling system and the engine crankcase.
53. Connect the negative battery cable.

54. Start the engine, allow it to reach normal operating temperatures and check for leaks.

4-WHEEL DRIVE

1. Disconnect the negative battery cable.
2. Remove the underhood light.
3. Raise and safely support the vehicle.
4. Remove the front air dam end bolts.
5. Remove the upper transmission-to-engine bolts and lower the vehicle.
6. Remove the remaining transmission-to-engine bolts.
7. Remove the 2nd crossmember.
8. Disconnect the exhaust pipes from the exhaust manifold.
9. Remove the catalytic converter hanger.
10. Remove the torque converter cover bolts and the cover. Matchmark the torque converter to flywheel. Remove the torque converter-to-flywheel bolts; it will be necessary to rotate the flywheel to access the other bolts.
11. Remove the front driveshaft from the front differential.
12. Disconnect the transmission cooler lines from the engine clips and lower the vehicle. Disconnect, drain and plug the transmission lines from the radiator.
13. Remove the engine mount through bolts. Remove the front splash shield-to-chassis bolts and the shield.
14. Remove the lower fan shroud bolts, lower the vehicle and drain the cooling system.

CAUTION

When draining the coolant, keep in mind that cats and dogs are attracted by the ethylene glycol antifreeze, and are quite likely to drink any that is left in an uncovered container or in puddles on the ground. This will prove fatal in sufficient quantity. Always drain the coolant into a sealable container. Coolant should be reused unless it is contaminated or several years old.

15. Remove the upper fan shroud bolts and the shroud.
16. Remove the radiator hoses from the radiator.
17. Remove the oil filter pipe and the remote oil filter.
18. Remove the radiator-to-chassis bolts and the radiator.
19. Remove the fan.
20. Remove the air cleaner assembly.
21. If equipped with air conditioning, remove the air conditioner compressor and lay it aside; do not disconnect the air conditioning hoses.
22. If equipped with power steering, the power steering pump and move it aside; do not disconnect the power steering hoses.
23. Disconnect and plug the fuel lines from the throttle body.
24. Label and disconnect the necessary electrical connectors from the engine.
25. Label and disconnect the necessary vacuum connectors from the engine.
26. Disconnect the accelerator cable, the TV cable and the cruise control cable from the engine.
27. Remove the electrical wiring harness from the bulkhead connector.
28. Disconnect the heater hoses from the engine. Using a floor jack, support the transmission.
29. Connect a vertical lifting device to the engine and lift the engine from the vehicle.

To install:

30. Lower the engine into the vehicle, install the engine-to-engine mount bolts and torque the **A** bolts to 42 ft. lbs. (57 Nm) or nuts to 35 ft. lbs. (47 Nm), the **B** bolts to 35 ft. lbs. (47 Nm) and the **C** nut/bolt to 52 ft. lbs. (70 Nm).
32. Install the rear engine mount-to-crossmember bolts and torque the **A** bolts to 45 ft. lbs. (60 Nm), the **B** bolts to 24 ft. lbs. (32 Nm), the **C** bolts to 40 ft. lbs. (55 Nm) and the **E** bolts to 22 ft. lbs. (30 Nm).
33. Install the transmission-to-engine bolts.
34. Align the flywheel to torque converter matchmarks and install the bolts.

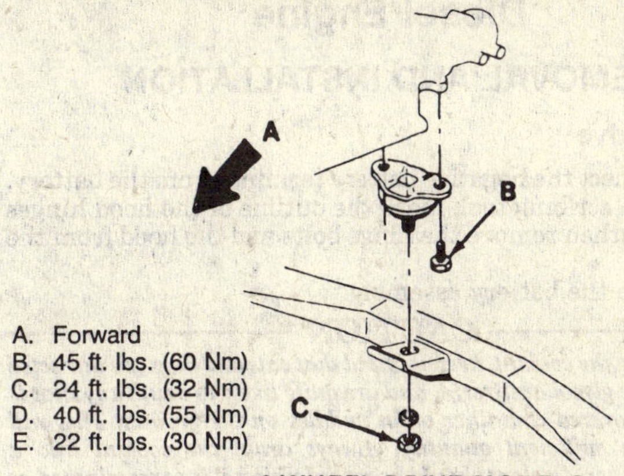

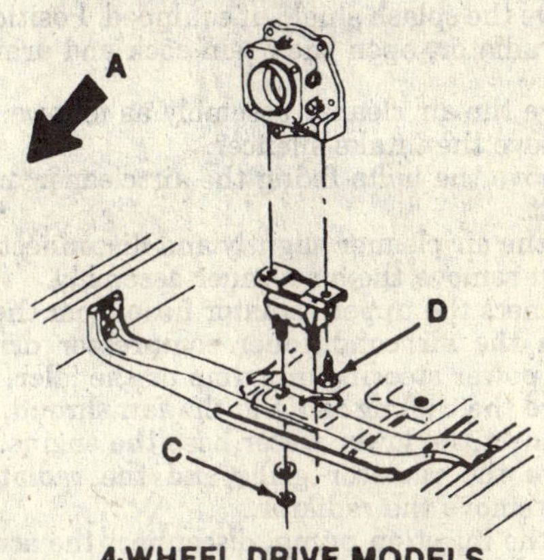

Exploded view of the rear engine mount — 4.3L engine

35. Install the front driveshaft to the front differential.
36. Install the catalytic converter to the hanger.
37. Connect the exhaust pipes to the exhaust manifolds.
38. Install the 2nd crossmember.
39. Install the lower fan shroud bolts and the splash shield.
40. Connect the transmission cooler lines to the engine clips.
41. Lower the vehicle and install the front air dam bolts.
42. Connect the electrical wiring harness to the bulkhead connector.
43. Connect the accelerator cable, the TV cable and the cruise control cable to the engine.
44. Connect the heater hoses to the engine.
45. Connect the necessary vacuum connectors to the engine.
46. Connect the necessary electrical connectors to the engine.
47. Connect and the fuel lines to the throttle body.
48. If equipped with power steering, connect the power steering pump.
49. If equipped with air conditioning, install the air conditioner compressor.
50. Install the fan and the radiator.
51. Using a new O-ring, install the oil filter pipe at the remote oil filter.
52. Install the radiator hoses.
53. Install the drive belts.
54. Install the fan shroud.
55. Lower the vehicle. Refill the cooling system.
56. Install the underhood light. Connect the negative battery cable.
57. Start the engine, allow it to reach normal operating temperatures and check for leaks.

Diesel Engine

REMOVAL AND INSTALLATION

2-Wheel Drive

1. Disconnect the negative battery terminal from the battery.
2. Using a scribing tool, mark the outline of the hood hinges on the hood, then remove the hinge bolts and the hood from the vehicle.
3. Remove the battery assembly.

CAUTION

When draining the coolant, keep in mind that cats and dogs are attracted by the ethylene glycol antifreeze, and are quite likely to drink any that is left in an uncovered container or in puddles on the ground. This will prove fatal in sufficient quantity. Always drain the coolant into a sealable container. Coolant should be reused unless it is contaminated or several years old.

4. Remove the splash shield, if equipped. Position a drain pan under the radiator, open the drain cock and drain the cooling system.
5. Remove the air cleaner assembly as follows:
   a. Remove the intake silencer.
   b. Remove the bolts fixing the air cleaner and loosen the clamp bolt.
   c. Lift the air cleaner slightly and disconnect the breather hose, then remove the air cleaner assembly.
6. Disconnect the upper radiator hose from the engine.
7. Loosen the air conditioner compressor drive belt(s) by moving the power steering oil pump or the idler, if equipped.
8. Remove the cooling fan and the fan shroud.
9. Disconnect the lower water hose the engine.
10. Remove the radiator grille and the radiator mounting bolts, then remove the radiator.
11. From the injection pump, disconnect the accelerator control cable and the fuel lines.
12. Disconnect the air conditioner compressor control cable, if equipped.

NOTE: See the Fuel Section for precautions and service procedures on the diesel engine injection pump and lines.

13. Disconnect the battery cable from the cylinder block.
14. Disconnect the electrical connectors from the transmission, the fuel cut solenoid and the air conditioning compressor.
15. Disconnect the vacuum hose from the fast idle actuator.
16. From the cowl, disconnect the heater hoses at the heater unit.
17. If equipped with a vacuum pump, disconnect the master-vac hose and the vacuum hoses from the vacuum pump.
18. From the alternator, disconnect the electrical wiring connector(s).
19. From the exhaust manifold, disconnect the exhaust pipe. From the engine back plate, remove the exhaust pipe mounting brake.
20. Disconnect the electrical wiring connectors from the starter.
21. At the gearshift lever, slide the boot upwards, then remove the 2 gearshift lever mounting bolts and the lever.
22. Position an oil catch pan under the transmission, then remove the drain plug for manual transmission or the oil cooling lines for automatic transmission and drain the fluid from the transmission.
23. From the transmission, disconnect the speedometer cable and the ground cable.
24. Disconnect the drive shaft at differential side, then slide the driveshaft from the transmission and remove it from the vehicle.
25. If equipped with a manual transmission, remove the return spring from clutch fork and disconnect the clutch cable from the hooked portion of the clutch fork and pull it forward out through stiffener bracket.
26. Remove the transmission-to-rear bracket mount bolts and nuts.
27. Raise the engine/transmission assembly, as required, and remove the crossmember-to-frame bolts. Remove the mounting nuts from the transmission rear extension.
28. Disconnect the electrical connectors from the CRS switch and back-up lamp switch.
29. Be sure the engine is slightly lifted, then remove the engine mount nuts/bolts.
30. To remove the engine, perform the following procedures:
    a. Check that all of the parts have been removed or disconnected from the engine that are fastened to the frame side.
    b. Remove the engine toward the front of the vehicle, maneuvering the hose, so front part of the engine is lifted slightly.
31. To install, reverse the removal procedures. Torque engine mounting bolts to the following:
    - Engine mount-to-engine: 35 ft. lbs.
    - Engine mount-to-frame mount: 52 ft. lbs.
    - Transmission mount-to-transmission: 45 ft. lbs.
    - Transmission mount-to-crossmember: 24 ft. lbs.

4-Wheel Drive

1. Disconnect the negative battery terminal from the battery.
2. Using a scribing tool, mark the outline of the hood hinges on the hood, then remove the hinge bolts and the hood from the vehicle.
3. Remove the battery and the tray.
4. Remove the splash shield, if equipped. Position a drain pan under the radiator, open the drain cock and drain the cooling system.

CAUTION

When draining the coolant, keep in mind that cats and dogs are attracted by the ethylene glycol antifreeze, and are quite likely to drink any that is left in an uncovered container or in puddles on the ground. This will prove fatal in sufficient quantity. Always drain the coolant into a sealable container. Coolant should be reused unless it is contaminated or several years old.

5. Remove the air cleaner as follows:
   a. Remove the intake silencer.
   b. Remove the bolts fixing the air cleaner and loosen the clamp bolt.
   c. Lift the air cleaner slightly and disconnect the breather hose, then remove the air cleaner assembly.
6. From the engine, disconnect the upper radiator hose.
7. Loosen the compressor drive belts by moving the power steering oil pump or idler, if equipped.
8. Remove the cooling fan and fan shroud.
9. From the engine, disconnect the lower radiator hose.
10. Remove the radiator grille, the radiator mounting bolts and the radiator.
11. From the fuel injection pump, disconnect the accelerator control cable and the fuel hoses.
12. If equipped, disconnect the air conditioning compressor control cable.
13. Disconnect the battery cable from the cylinder block.
14. Disconnect the electrical wiring connectors from the transmission, the fuel cut solenoid and the air conditioning compressor.
15. Disconnect the vacuum hose(s) from the fast idle actuator and the master-vac hose from the vacuum pump.
16. At the cowl, disconnect the heater hoses from the heater unit.
17. From the alternator, disconnect the electrical wiring connectors.
18. From the exhaust manifold, disconnect the exhaust pipe,

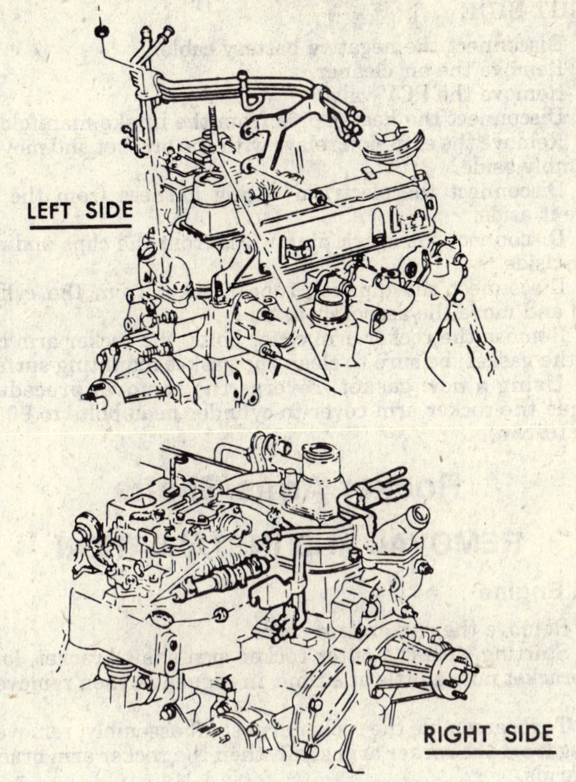

Removing the fuel evaporation tubes — 2.0L engine

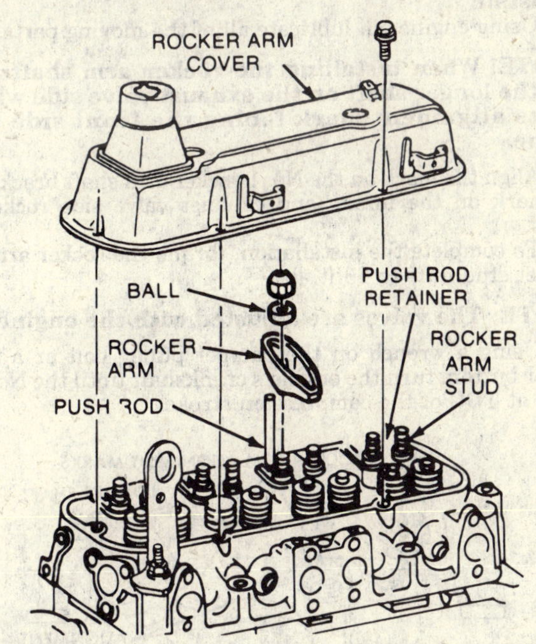

Exploded view of the rocker arm cover — 2.0L engine

then remove the exhaust pipe mounting brake from the engine back plate.

19. From the starter, disconnect the electrical wiring connectors.

20. Slide the transmission and transfer gearshift lever boot upwards on each lever, remove the gearshift lever attaching bolts.

21. From the transfer case gearshift lever, remove the return spring, then the levers.

22. Remove the transmission.

23. Remove the engine mounting nuts/bolts; make sure the engine is slightly lifted before removing the mounting nuts/bolts.

24. To remove the engine, perform the following procedures:

a. Check that all the parts have been removed or disconnected from the engine that are fastened to the frame side.

b. Move the engine toward the front of the vehicle by maneuvering the hoist, so front part of the engine is lifted slightly, then remove the engine.

25. To install the engine, reverse the removal procedures. Torque engine mounting bolts to the following:

- Engine mount-to-engine: 35 ft. lbs.
- Engine mount-to-frame mount: 52 ft. lbs.
- Transmission mount-to-transmission: 45 ft. lbs.
- Transmission mount-to-crossmember: 24 ft. lbs.

Rocker Arm Cover

REMOVAL AND INSTALLATION

1.9L Engine

1. Disconnect the negative battery terminal from the battery.
2. Remove the air cleaner assembly.
3. From the rocker arm cover, remove the spark plug wires, the evaporator pipe from the intake manifold-to-engine lift bracket.
4. Remove the rocker arm cover-to-engine nuts/washers.
5. Remove the rocker arm cover.
6. Using a putty knife, clean the gasket mounting surfaces.
7. To install, use a new gasket and reverse the removal procedures.

2.0L Engine

1. Disconnect the negative battery terminal from the battery.
2. Remove the air cleaner assembly and the distributor cap.
3. Remove the fuel vapor canister harness tubes from the rocker arm cover.
4. Remove the accelerator cable and the PCV valve.
5. Remove the rocker arm cover-to-cylinder head bolts and the cover.

NOTE: If the cover sticks, use a rubber mallet to bump it or a prying tool to lift it from the cylinder head.

6. Using a putty knife, clean the gasket mounting surfaces.
7. To install, use a new gasket, an ⅛ in. bead of RTV sealant and reverse the removal procedures. Torque the rocker arm cover-to-cylinder head bolts to 8 ft. lbs.

2.2L Diesel Engine

1. Disconnect the negative battery terminal from the battery.
2. Remove the PCV valve from the rocker arm cover and the PCV valve hose.
3. Remove the air cleaner.
4. Remove the rocker arm cover-to-cylinder head bolts and the cover from the engine.
5. Using a putty knife, clean the gasket mounting surfaces.
6. To install, use a new gasket and reverse the removal procedures. Torque the rocker arm cover-to-cylinder head bolts to 9–13 ft. lbs.

2.5L Engine

1. Disconnect the negative battery cable from the battery.
2. Remove the air cleaner.
3. Disconnect the Positive Crankcase Ventilation (PCV) valve hose, the ignition wires from the rocker arm cover.

4. Remove the Exhaust Gas Recirculation (EGR) valve.
5. From the intake manifold stud, label and disconnect the vacuum hoses.
6. Remove the rocker arm cover-to-cylinder head bolts and the cover.
7. Using a putty knife, clean the gasket mounting surfaces.

NOTE: Be sure to use solvent to remove any oil or grease that may remain on the sealing surfaces.

8. To install, use a new gasket, a $^3/_{16}$ in. (5mm) continuous bead of RTV sealant and reverse the removal procedures. Torque the valve cover-to-cylinder head bolts to 6 ft. lbs.

2.8L Engine

LEFT SIDE

1. Disconnect the negative battery terminal from the battery.
2. Disconnect the air management hose, the vacuum hose(s), the electrical wires and the pipe bracket. Remove the spark plug wires and clips from the retaining stubs.
3. Disconnect the fuel line(s) from the carburetor or throttle body.
4. Remove the rocker arm cover-to-cylinder head bolts/studs and the cover from the engine.

NOTE: If the cover will not lift, use a rubber mallet to bump it loose from the cylinder head or use a small prybar to lift the cover.

5. Using a putty knife, clean the gasket mounting surfaces.
6. To install, use a new gasket, a ⅛ in. bead of RTV sealant and reverse the removal procedures. Torque the rocker arm cover-to-cylinder head bolts/studs to 8 ft. lbs.

RIGHT SIDE

1. Disconnect the negative battery terminal from the battery.
2. Remove the air management and coil brackets.
3. Disconnect the air management hose, the vacuum hose(s), the electrical wires and the pipe bracket. Remove the spark plug wires and clips from the retaining stubs.
4. Disconnect the carburetor or throttle body controls and the brackets.
5. Remove the rocker arm cover-to-cylinder head bolts/studs and the cover from the engine.

NOTE: If the cover will not lift, use a rubber mallet to bump it loose from the cylinder head or use a small prybar to lift the cover.

6. Using a putty knife, clean the gasket mounting surfaces.
7. To install, use a new gasket, a ⅛ in. bead of RTV sealant and reverse the removal procedures. Torque the rocker arm cover-to-cylinder head bolts/studs to 8 ft. lbs.

4.3L Engine

LEFT SIDE

1. Disconnect the negative battery cable.
2. Remove the air cleaner and the heat stove tube.
3. Remove the crankcase ventilation pipe.
4. Disconnect the fuel lines from the TBI and the retaining clips and move them aside.
5. Remove the alternator rear bracket.
6. Disconnect the spark plug wires from the clips and move them aside.
7. Disconnect the power brake vacuum line from the intake manifold and move it aside.
8. Remove the rocker arm cover bolts, the rocker arm cover and the gasket; be sure to clean the gasket mounting surfaces.
9. Using a new gasket, reverse the removal procedures. Torque the rocker arm cover-to-cylinder head bolts to 90 inch lbs. (10 Nm).

RIGHT SIDE

1. Disconnect the negative battery cable.
2. Remove the air cleaner.
3. Remove the PCV valve.
4. Disconnect the heater pipe from the intake manifold.
5. Remove the emission relays with the bracket and move the assembly aside.
6. Disconnect the electrical wiring harness from the clips move it aside.
7. Disconnect the spark plug wires from the clips and move them aside.
8. Disconnect the dipstick tube bracket from the cylinder head and move the assembly aside.
9. Remove the rocker arm cover bolts, the rocker arm cover and the gasket; be sure to clean the gasket mounting surfaces.
10. Using a new gasket, reverse the removal procedures. Torque the rocker arm cover-to-cylinder head bolts to 90 inch lbs. (10 Nm).

Rocker Arms/Shafts

REMOVAL AND INSTALLATION

1.9L Engine

1. Remove the rocker arm cover.
2. Starting with the outer rocker arm shaft bracket, loosen the bracket nuts a little at a time, in sequence, then remove the nuts.
3. To disassemble the rocker arm shaft assembly, remove the spring from the rocker arm shaft, then the rocker arm brackets and arms.
4. Inspect the rocker arm shafts for runnout, wear and/or damage, if necessary, replace the rocker arm shafts.

To install:

5. Using engine oil, lubricate all of the moving parts.

NOTE: When installing the rocker arm shafts, position the longer shaft on the exhaust valve side with the shafts alignment mark facing the front side of the engine.

6. Align the mark on the No. 1 rocker arm shaft bracket with the mark on the intake and exhaust valve side rocker arm shafts.
7. To complete the installation, torque the rocker arm shaft bracket stud nuts to 16 ft. lbs.

NOTE: The valves are adjusted with the engine Cold.

8. Using a wrench on the damper pulley bolt or a remote starter button, turn the engine's crankshaft until the No. 1 piston is at TDC of the compression stroke.

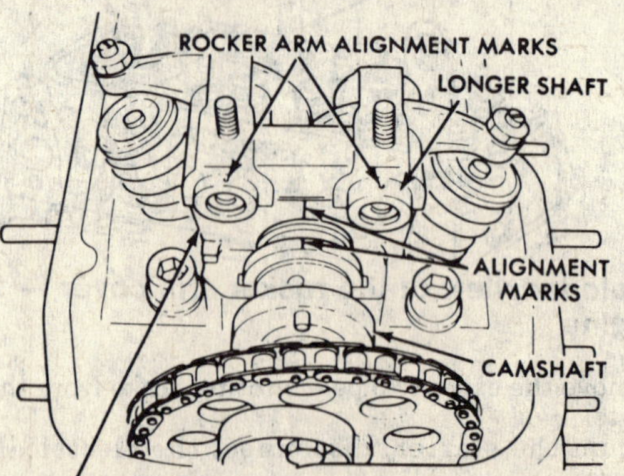

View of the rocker arm installation — 1.9L engine

NOTE: You can tell when the piston is coming up on the compression stroke by removing the spark plug and placing your thumb over the hole, then you will feel the air being forced out of the spark plug hole. Stop turning the crankshaft when the TDC timing mark on the crankshaft pulley is directly aligned with the timing mark pointer.

9. Using a 0.006 in. (0.152mm) feeler gauge, set intake valves of cylinders No. 1 and 2. Using a 0.010 in. (0.254mm) feeler gauge, set the exhaust valves of cylinders No. 1 and 3.
10. Rotate the engine one complete revolution, so cylinder No. 4 is on the TDC of its compression stroke and the timing marks are aligned.
11. Using a 0.006 in. (0.152mm) feeler gauge, set intake valves of cylinders No. 3 and 4. Using a 0.010 in. (0.254mm) feeler gauge, set the exhaust valves of cylinders No. 2 and 4.

NOTE: When adjusting the valve clearance, loosen the locknut with an open-end wrench, then turn the adjuster screw with a screwdriver and retighten the locknut. The proper thickness feeler gauge should pass between the camshaft and the rocker with a slight drag when the clearance is correct.

12. To complete the installation, reverse the removal procedures.

2.0L Engine

1. Remove the rocker arm cover.
2. Remove the rocker arm nuts, the ball washers and the rocker arms off the studs, then lift out the pushrods.

NOTE: Always keep the rocker arm assemblies together and install them on the same stud.

To install:

3. Coat the bearing surfaces of the rocker arms and the rocker arm ball washers with Molykote® or its equivalent.

NOTE: At time of installation, flanges must be free of oil. A bead of sealant must be applied to flanges and sealant must be wet to touch when bolts are torqued.

4. Install the pushrods making sure they seat properly in the lifter.

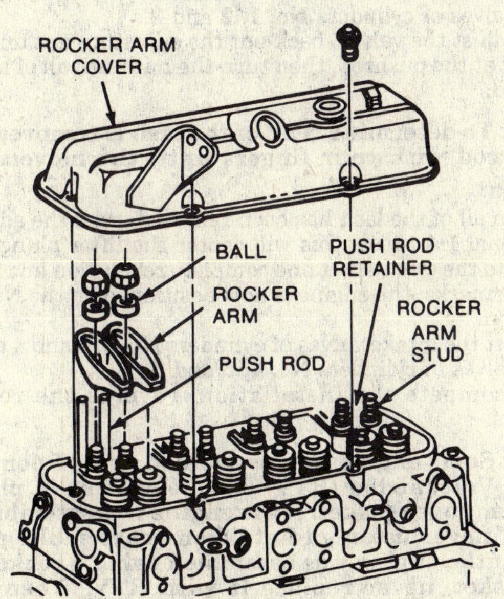

View of the rocker arm assembly — 2.0L engine

5. Install the rocker arms, the ball washers and the nuts. Tighten the rocker arm nuts until all lash is eliminated.
6. Adjust the valves when the lifter is on the base circle of a camshaft lobe:
   a. Crank the engine until the mark on the crankshaft pulley lines up with the **0** degree mark on the timing tab. Make sure the engine is in the No. 1 firing position. Place your fingers on the No. 1 rocker arms as the mark on the crank pulley comes near the **0** degree mark.

NOTE: If the valves are not moving, the engine is in the No. 1 firing position. If the valves move, the engine is in the No. 4 firing position; rotate the engine one complete revolution and it will be in the No. 1 position.

   b. When the engine is on the No. 1 firing position, adjust the following valves:
- Exhaust – 1, 3
- Intake – 1, 2

   c. Back the adjusting nut out until lash can be felt at the pushrod, then turn the nut until all lash is removed (this can be determined by rotating the pushrod while turning the adjusting nut). When all lash has been removed, turn the nut in 1½ additional turns, this will center the lifter plunger.
   d. Crank the engine one complete revolution until the timing tab (**0** degree mark) and the crankshaft pulley mark are again in alignment. Now the engine is in the No. 4 firing position. Adjust the following valves:
- Exhaust – 2, 4
- Intake – 3, 4

7. After adjusting the valves, reverse the removal procedures. Start the engine, then check the timing and the idle speed.

2.2L Diesel Engine

1. Remove the rocker cover.
2. Remove the rocker arm bracket-to-cylinder head bolts in sequence, commencing with the outer ones.
3. Remove the rocker arm, the bracket and shaft assembly.
4. To disassemble, remove the snapring, the rocker arms, the springs and the brackets.

NOTE: Always keep the rocker arm assemblies together and install them on the same stud.

To install:

5. Inspect the rocker arm shafts for runnout, wear and/or damage, if necessary, replace the rocker arm shafts or components.
6. Using engine oil, lubricate all of the moving parts.

To install:

7. To install, position the brackets with the **F** marks facing the front of the engine. Torque the bracket-to-cylinder head bolts to 9–17 ft. lbs., working from the center and working outward.

NOTE: The valves are adjusted with the engine Cold.

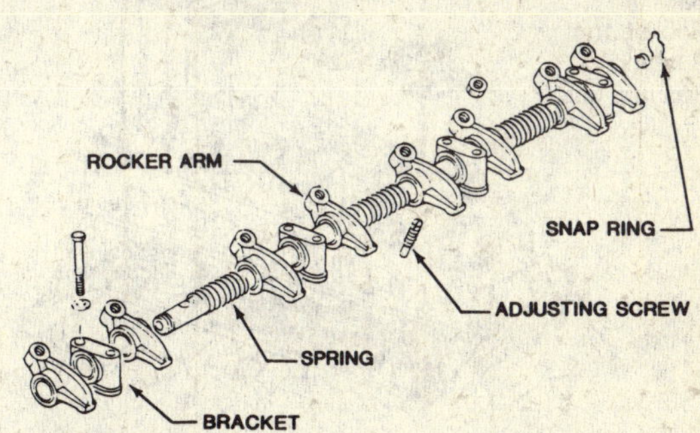

Exploded view of the rocker arm assembly — 2.2L diesel engine

8. Using a wrench on the damper pulley bolt or a remote starter button, turn the engine's crankshaft until the No. 1 piston is at TDC of the compression stroke.

NOTE: You can tell when the piston is coming up on the compression stroke by removing the spark plug and placing your thumb over the hole, then you will feel the air being forced out of the spark plug hole. Stop turning the crankshaft when the TDC timing mark on the crankshaft pulley is directly aligned with the timing mark pointer.

9. Using a 0.016 in. (0.4mm) feeler gauge, set the intake valves of cylinders No. 1, 2 and 3, then set the exhaust valve of cylinder No. 1.
10. Rotate the engine one complete revolution, so cylinder No. 4 is on the TDC of its compression stroke and the timing marks are aligned.
11. Using a 0.016 in. (0.4mm) feeler gauge, set the intake valve of cylinder No. 4, then the exhaust valves of cylinders No. 2, 3 and 4.

NOTE: When adjusting the valve clearance, loosen the locknut with an open-end wrench, then turn the adjuster screw with a screwdriver and retighten the locknut. The proper thickness feeler gauge should pass between the camshaft and the rocker with a slight drag when the clearance is correct.

12. To complete the installation, reverse the removal procedures.

2.5L Engine

The rocker arm opens and closes the valves through a very simple ball pivot type operation.

1. Remove the rocker arm cover.
2. Using a socket wrench, remove the rocker arm bolts, the ball washer and the rocker arm.

NOTE: If only the pushrod is to be removed, back off the rocker arm bolt, swing the rocker arm aside and remove the pushrod. When removing more than one assembly, at the same time, be sure to keep them in order for reassembly purposes.

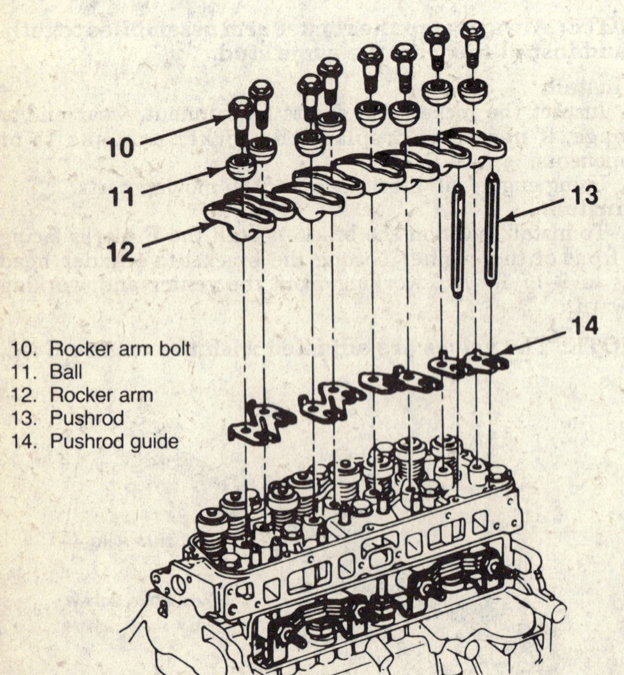

Exploded view of the rocker arm assembly — 2.5L engine

To install:

3. Inspect the rocker arms and ball washers for scoring and/or other damage, replace them, if necessary.

NOTE: If replacing worn components with new ones, be sure to coat the new parts with Molykote® before installation.

4. Torque the rocker arm-to-cylinder head bolts to 20 ft. lbs.; do not overtighten.
5. To complete the installation, reverse the removal procedures. Start the engine, the check for oil leaks and engine operation.

2.8L Engine

1. Remove the rocker arm cover.
2. Remove the rocker arm nut, the rocker arm and the ball washer.

NOTE: If only the pushrod is to be removed, loosen the rocker arm nut, swing the rocker arm to the side and remove the pushrod.

To install:

3. Inspect the part for damage, wear and/or scoring; if necessary, replace the damaged parts.
4. Before installation, coat all of the working parts with Molykote®.
5. To adjust the valves, rotate the crankshaft until the mark on the crankshaft pulley aligns with the **0** mark on the timing plate. Make sure the No. 1 cylinder is positioned on the compression stroke.

NOTE: To determine the compression stroke, place your fingers on the No. 1 rocker arms, as the mark on the crankshaft pulley comes near the 0 mark on the timing plate. If the valves move, the engine is on the No. 4 firing position; rotate the crankshaft one complete revolution and realign the pulley mark with the timing plate **0** mark.

6. Adjust the intake valves of cylinders No. 1, 5 and 6 and the exhaust valves of cylinders No. 1, 2 and 3.
7. To adjust the valves, back-out the adjusting nut until lash can be felt at the pushrod, then turn the nut until all of the lash is removed.

NOTE: To determine is all of the lash is removed, turn the pushrod with your fingers until the movement is removed.

8. When all of the lash has been removed, turn the adjusting an additional 1½ turns; this will center the lifter plunger.
9. Rotate the crankshaft one complete revolution and realign the timing marks; the engine is now positioned on the No. 4 firing position.
10. Adjust the intake valves of cylinders No. 2, 3 and 4 and the exhaust valves of cylinders No. 4, 5 and 6.
11. To compete the installation, reverse the removal procedures.

NOTE: Some engines are assembled using Room Temperature Vulcanizing (RTV) silcone sealant in place of rocker arm cover gasket. If the engine was assembled using RTV, never use a gasket when reassembling. Conversely, if the engine was assembled using a rocker arm cover gasket, never replace it with RTV. When using RTV, an ⅛ in. (3mm) inch bead is sufficient. Always run the bead on the inside of the bolt holes.

Cylinder heads use threaded rocker arm studs. If the threads in the head are damaged or stripped, the head can be retapped and a helical type insert installed.

NOTE: If the engine is equipped with the AIR exhaust emission control system, the interfering components of the system must be removed. Disconnect the lines of the air injection nozzles in the exhaust manifolds.

4.3L Engine

1. Remove the rocker arm cover.
2. Remove the rocker arm nut, the rocker arm and the ball washer.

NOTE: If only the pushrod is to be removed, loosen the rocker arm nut, swing the rocker arm to the side and remove the pushrod.

To install:

3. Inspect the part for damage, wear and/or scoring; if necessary, replace the damaged parts.
4. Before installation, coat all of the working parts with Molykote®.
5. To adjust the valves, rotate the crankshaft until the mark on the crankshaft pulley aligns with the **0** mark on the timing plate. Make sure the No. 1 cylinder is positioned on the compression stroke.

NOTE: To determine the compression stroke, place your fingers on the No. 1 rocker arms, as the mark on the crankshaft pulley comes near the "0" mark on the timing plate. If the valves move, the engine is on the No. 4 firing position; rotate the crankshaft one complete revolution and realign the pulley mark with the timing plate "0" mark.

6. Adjust the exhaust valves of cylinders No. 1, 5 and 6 and the intake valves of cylinders No. 1, 2 and 3.
7. To adjust the valves, back-out the adjusting nut until lash can be felt at the pushrod, then turn the nut until all of the lash is removed.

NOTE: To determine is all of the lash is removed, turn the pushrod with your fingers until the movement is removed.

8. When all of the lash has been removed, turn the adjusting an additional 1 turn; this will center the lifter plunger.
9. Rotate the crankshaft 1 complete revolution and realign the timing marks; the engine is now positioned on the No. 4 firing position.
10. Adjust the exhaust valves of cylinders No. 2, 3 and 4 and the intake valves of cylinders No. 4, 5 and 6.
11. To compete the installation, reverse the removal procedures.

NOTE: Some engines are assembled using Room Temperature Vulcanizing (RTV) silcone sealant in place of rocker arm cover gasket. If the engine was assembled using RTV, never use a gasket when reassembling. Conversely, if the engine was assembled using a rocker arm cover gasket, never replace it with RTV. When using RTV, an ⅛ in. (3mm) inch bead is sufficient. Always run the bead on the inside of the bolt holes.

Cylinder heads use threaded rocker arm studs. If the threads in the head are damaged or stripped, the head can be retapped and a helical type insert installed.

NOTE: If the engine is equipped with the AIR exhaust emission control system, the interfering components of the system must be removed. Disconnect the lines of the air injection nozzles in the exhaust manifolds.

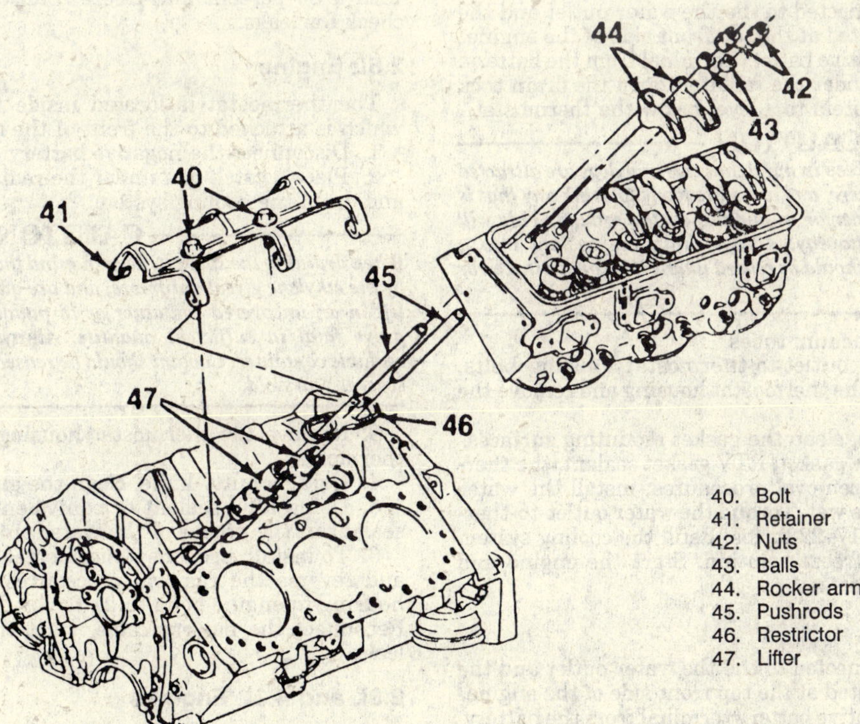

40. Bolt
41. Retainer
42. Nuts
43. Balls
44. Rocker arms
45. Pushrods
46. Restrictor
47. Lifter

Exploded view of the rocker arm assembly — 4.3L engine

Thermostat

REMOVAL AND INSTALLATION

1.9L Engine

1. Place a drain pan under the radiator, open the drain cock and drain the cooling system to a level below the thermostat.

CAUTION

When draining the coolant, keep in mind that cats and dogs are attracted by the ethylene glycol antifreeze, and are quite likely to drink any that is left in an uncovered container or in puddles on the ground. This will prove fatal in sufficient quantity. Always drain the coolant into a sealable container. Coolant should be reused unless it is contaminated or several years old.

2. Disconnect the PCV hose, the ECS hose, the Air hose and the TCA hose.
3. Remove the air cleaner-to-carburetor bolts and loosen the clamp bolts, then lift the air cleaner and disconnect the TCA hose from the thermosenser (on the intake manifold). Remove the rubber hoses from the air cleaner-to-carburetor slow actuator and the air cleaner-to-vacuum control (California), then remove the air cleaner assembly.
4. Remove the outlet pipe-to-inlet mainfold bolts, the outlet pipe (with the radiator hose attached) and the thermostat from the engine.
5. Using a putty knife, clean the gasket mounting surfaces.
6. To install, use a new gasket, RTV gasket sealant, the thermostat and reverse the removal procedures; install the outlet pipe while the sealant is wet. Torque the outlet pipe-to-intake manifold bolts to 21 ft. lbs. (28 Nm). Refill the cooling system with a 50 percent anti-freeze solution. Start the engine and check for leaks.

2.0L Engine

The thermostat is connected to the the water outlet and the thermostat housing, located at the top front side of the engine.

1. Disconnect the negative battery terminal from the battery.
2. Place a drain pan under the radiator, open the drain cock and drain the cooling system to a level below the thermostat.

CAUTION

When draining the coolant, keep in mind that cats and dogs are attracted by the ethylene glycol antifreeze, and are quite likely to drink any that is left in an uncovered container or in puddles on the ground. This will prove fatal in sufficient quantity. Always drain the coolant into a sealable container. Coolant should be reused unless it is contaminated or several years old.

3. Remove the steel vacuum tubes.
4. Remove the water outlet-to-thermostat housing bolts, then lift the outlet from the thermostat housing and remove the thermostat.
5. Using a putty knife, clean the gasket mounting surfaces.
6. To install, use a new gasket, RTV gasket sealant, the thermostat and reverse the removal procedures; install the water outlet while the sealant is wet. Torque the water outlet-to-thermostat housing bolts to 17–22 ft. lbs. Refill the cooling system with a 50 percent anti-freeze solution. Start the engine and check for leaks.

2.2L Diesel Engine

The thermostat is connected to the the water outlet and the thermostat housing, located at the top front side of the engine.

1. Disconnect the negative battery terminal from the battery.
2. Place a drain pan under the radiator, open the drain cock and drain the cooling system to a level below the thermostat.

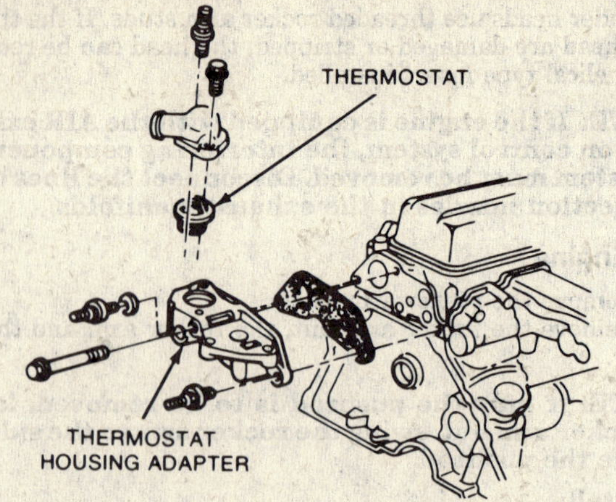

Exploded view of the thermostat and housing – 2.0L engine

CAUTION

When draining the coolant, keep in mind that cats and dogs are attracted by the ethylene glycol antifreeze, and are quite likely to drink any that is left in an uncovered container or in puddles on the ground. This will prove fatal in sufficient quantity. Always drain the coolant into a sealable container. Coolant should be reused unless it is contaminated or several years old.

3. Disconnect the electrical wiring.
4. Remove the water outlet-to-thermostat housing bolts, then lift the outlet from the thermostat housing and remove the thermostat.
5. Using a putty knife, clean the gasket mounting surfaces.
6. To install, use a new gasket, RTV gasket sealant, the thermostat and reverse the removal procedures; install the water outlet while the sealant is wet. Torque the water outlet-to-thermostat housing bolts to 10–17 ft. lbs. Refill the cooling system with a 50 percent anti-freeze solution. Start the engine and check for leaks.

2.5L Engine

The thermostat is located inside the thermostat housing, which is attached to the front of the cylinder head.

1. Disconnect the negative battery cable from the battery.
2. Place a catch pan under the radiator, open the drain cock and drain the cooling system.

CAUTION

When draining the coolant, keep in mind that cats and dogs are attracted by the ethylene glycol antifreeze, and are quite likely to drink any that is left in an uncovered container or in puddles on the ground. This will prove fatal in sufficient quantity. Always drain the coolant into a sealable container. Coolant should be reused unless it is contaminated or several years old.

3. Remove the thermostat housing-to-engine bolts and the thermostat.
4. Using a putty knife, clean the gasket mounting surfaces.
5. Using RTV sealant or equivalent, place an ⅛ in. bead of sealant in the groove of the water outlet.
6. To install, use a new thermostat, if possible, a new gasket and reverse the removal procedures. Torque the thermostat housing-to-engine bolts to 21 ft. lbs. Refill the cooling system. Reconnect the battery cable, start the engine and check for leaks.

2.8L and 4.3L Engines

The thermostat is located between the water outlet and the front of the intake manifold.

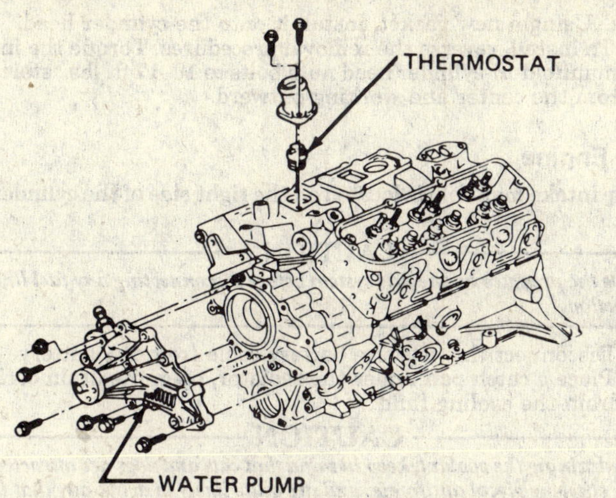

Exploded view of the thermostat and housing — 2.8L and 4.3L engines

1. Disconnect the negative battery terminal from the battery.
2. Place a drain pan under the radiator, open the drain cock and drain the cooling system to a level below the thermostat.

CAUTION

When draining the coolant, keep in mind that cats and dogs are attracted by the ethylene glycol antifreeze, and are quite likely to drink any that is left in an uncovered container or in puddles on the ground. This will prove fatal in sufficient quantity. Always drain the coolant into a sealable container. Coolant should be reused unless it is contaminated or several years old.

3. Remove the water outlet-to-intake manifold bolts, then lift the outlet from the intake manifold and remove the thermostat.
4. Using a putty knife, clean the gasket mounting surfaces.
5. To install, use RTV gasket sealant (place an ⅛ in. bead in the groove on the outlet housing), the thermostat and reverse the removal procedures; install the water outlet housing while the sealant is wet. Torque the water outlet-to-intake manifold bolts to 21 ft. lbs. (28 Nm). Refill the cooling system with a 50 percent anti-freeze solution. Start the engine and check for leaks.

Intake Manifold

REMOVAL AND INSTALLATION

1.9L Engine

1. Disconnect the negative battery terminal from the battery. Remove the air cleaner assembly.
2. Position a drain pan under the radiator, open the drain cock and drain the cooling system to a level below the intake manifold.

CAUTION

When draining the coolant, keep in mind that cats and dogs are attracted by the ethylene glycol antifreeze, and are quite likely to drink any that is left in an uncovered container or in puddles on the ground. This will prove fatal in sufficient quantity. Always drain the coolant into a sealable container. Coolant should be reused unless it is contaminated or several years old.

3. From the intake manifold, disconnect the upper radiator hose, the vacuum hose, the heater hose (from the rear of the intake manifold).
4. From the carburetor, disconnect the accelerator control cable, then the automatic choke and the solenoid electrical connectors.
5. From the distributor, disconnect the vacuum advance hose and the thermo-unit wiring electrical connector.
6. Disconnect the PCV valve from the rocker arm cover, then remove the oil level gauge guide tube-to-intake manifold bolt.
7. Disconnect the EGR pipe from the EGR valve adapter, the EGR valve and the adapter. Remove the nut from under the EGR valve.
8. Disconnect the AIR vacuum hose from the 3-way connector.
9. Remove the intake manifold-to-cylinder head nuts and the intake manifold from the engine.
10. Using a putty knife, clean the gasket mounting surfaces. Inspect the manifold for cracks, damage or distortion; if necessary, replace the intake manifold.
11. To install, use a new gasket and reverse the removal procedures.

2.0L Engine

1. Disconnect the negative battery terminal from the battery.
2. Remove the air cleaner, then the distributor cap, the distributor hold-down nut and clamp.
3. Raise and support the vehicle on jackstands.
4. Position a drain pan under the radiator, open the drain cock and drain the cooling system to a level below the intake manifold.

CAUTION

When draining the coolant, keep in mind that cats and dogs are attracted by the ethylene glycol antifreeze, and are quite likely to drink any that is left in an uncovered container or in puddles on the ground. This will prove fatal in sufficient quantity. Always drain the coolant into a sealable container. Coolant should be reused unless it is contaminated or several years old.

5. Tag and disconnect the vacuum hose and the primary wires from the coil.
6. Remove the fuel pump-to-engine bolts and allow the pump to hang.
7. Remove the jackstands and lower the vehicle.
8. Disconnect the accelerator cable, the fuel inlet line, then the necessary vacuum hoses and wires. Remove the carburetor-to-intake manifold nuts, the carburetor and lift off the Early Fuel Evaporation (EFE) heater grid..
9. Disconnect the fuel vapor harness pipes from the cylinder head.
10. From the intake manifold, disconnect the heater hose, the bypass hose, the necessary hoses and wires. Remove the intake manifold-to-cylinder head nuts/bolts, the intake manifold and the gasket.
11. Using a putty knife, clean the gasket mounting surfaces.

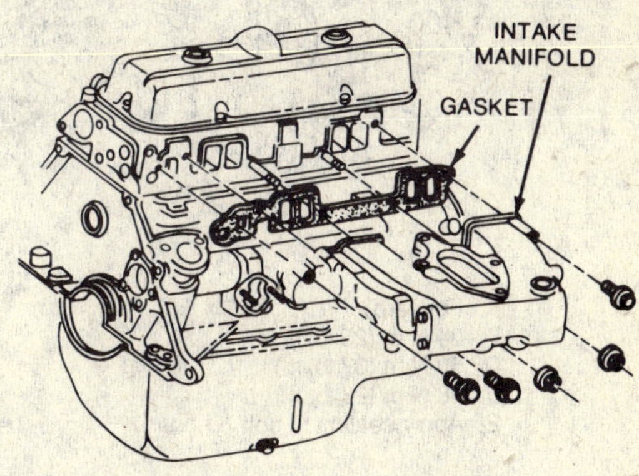

Exploded view of the intake manifold — 2.0L engine

Inspect the manifold for cracks, damage or distortion; if necessary, replace the intake manifold.

12. To install, use a new gasket and reverse the removal procedures. Torque the intake manifold-to-cylinder head nuts/bolts to 25 ft. lbs. Refill the cooling system. Adjust the drive belts. Check and/or adjust the engine timing and idle speed.

2.2L Diesel Engine

1. Disconnect the negative battery terminal from the battery.
2. Remove the air cleaner.
3. Disconnect the heater pipe bracket, the PCV valve hose, the necessary wires and clips from the intake manifold.
4. Remove the intake manifold-to-cylinder head bolts and the intake manifold.

NOTE: If removing the intake/exhaust manifold gasket, it will be necessary to remove the exhaust manifold.

5. If the exhaust manifold has been removed, perform the following procedures:
   a. Using a putty knife, clean the gasket mounting surfaces.
   b. Inspect the manifold for cracks, damage or distortion; if necessary, replace the intake manifold.
   c. Using a new gasket, install it onto the cylinder head.
6. To install, reverse the removal procedures. Torque the intake manifold-to-cylinder head nuts/bolts to 10–17 ft. lbs., starting from the center and working outward.

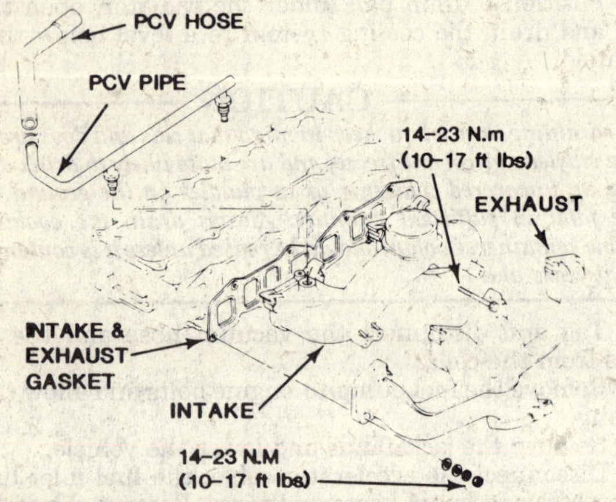

Exploded view of the intake manifold — 2.2L engine

2.5L Engine

The intake manifold is located on the right side of the cylinder head.

CAUTION

Relieve the pressure on the fuel system before disconnecting any fuel line connection.

1. Disconnect the negative battery cable from the battery.
2. Place a catch pan under the radiator, open the drain cock and drain the cooling fluid.

CAUTION

When draining the coolant, keep in mind that cats and dogs are attracted by the ethylene glycol antifreeze, and are quite likely to drink any that is left in an uncovered container or in puddles on the ground. This will prove fatal in sufficient quantity. Always drain the coolant into a sealable container. Coolant should be reused unless it is contaminated or several years old.

3. Remove the air cleaner assembly. Label and disconnect the vacuum hoses from the exhaust manifold, thermostat housing and etc.
4. Label and disconnect the electrical connectors that may be in the way. Disconnect the accelerator, the cruise control and TV cables.
5. Remove the coolant hoses from the intake manifold. Remove and plug the fuel line at the throttle body.
6. Remove the alternator bracket-to-engine bolts and move the alternator/bracket aside.
7. Remove the ignition coil-to-cylinder head/intake manifold bolts and the coil from the engine.
8. Remove the intake manifold-to-engine bolts and the manifold from the engine.
9. Using a putty knife, clean the gasket mounting surfaces.
10. To install, use a new gasket, sealant (for some bolts) and reverse the removal procedures. Torque the intake manifold-to-engine bolts to 25–37 ft. lbs. Refill the cooling system. Start the engine and check for leaks.

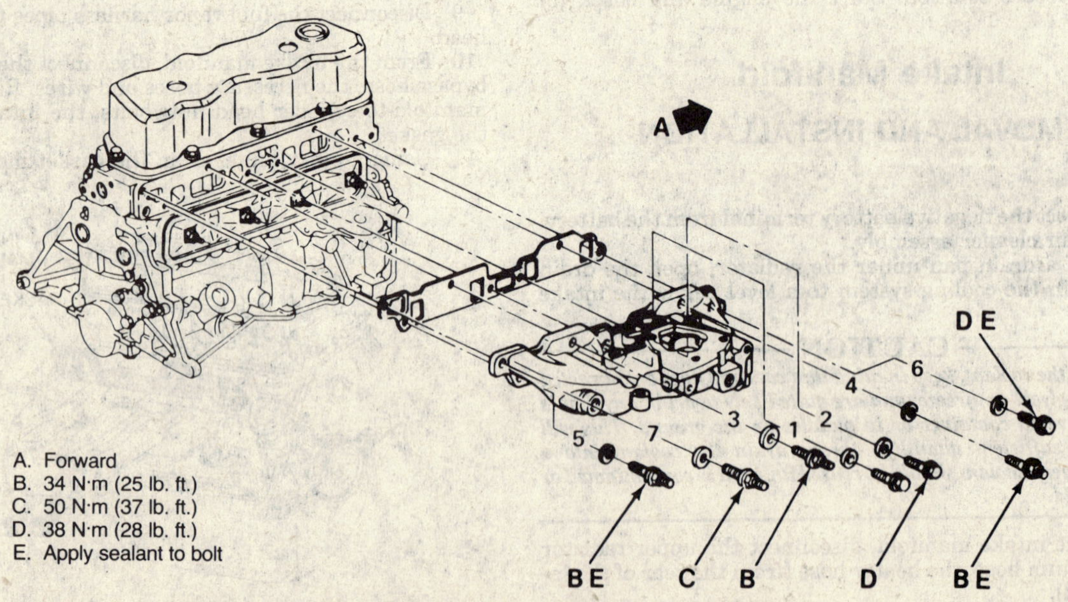

Exploded view of the intake manifold — 2.5L engine

2.8L Engine

1. Position a drain pan under the radiator, open the drain cock and drain the cooling system to a level below the intake manifold.

CAUTION

When draining the coolant, keep in mind that cats and dogs are attracted by the ethylene glycol antifreeze, and are quite likely to drink any that is left in an uncovered container or in puddles on the ground. This will prove fatal in sufficient quantity. Always drain the coolant into a sealable container. Coolant should be reused unless it is contaminated or several years old.

2. Disconnect the negative battery terminal from the battery.
3. Remove the air cleaner. Remove the electrical connectors, the vacuum hoses, the fuel lines and the accelerator cables from the carburetor or TBI unit.
4. If equipped with an AIR management system, remove the hose and the mounting bracket.
5. Label and disconnect the spark plug wires from the spark plugs and the electrical connectors from the ignition coil. Disconnect the coolant switch electrical connectors on the intake manifold.
6. Remove the distributor cap (with the wires connected). Mark the position of the rotor-to-distributor body and the the distributor body-to-engine relationships, then remove the distributor from the engine; do not crank the engine with the distributor removed.
7. Remove the heater and upper radiator hoses from the intake manifold.
8. If equipped, remove the evaporative canister and the power brake vacuum hoses from the intake manifold; remove the emission canister pipe bracket(s) from the rear of the rocker arm covers.
9. Remove the rocker arm covers.
10. Remove the intake manifold-to-engine nuts and bolts, then the intake manifold from the engine.
11. Using a putty knife, remove and discard the gaskets, then clean the gasket mounting surfaces. Since the manifold is made from aluminum, be sure to inspect it for warpage and/or cracks; if necessary, replace it.
12. To install, use new intake mainfold-to-cylinder head gaskets, a $^3/_{16}$ in. (5mm) bead of RTV sealant, applied to the front and rear of the engine block.

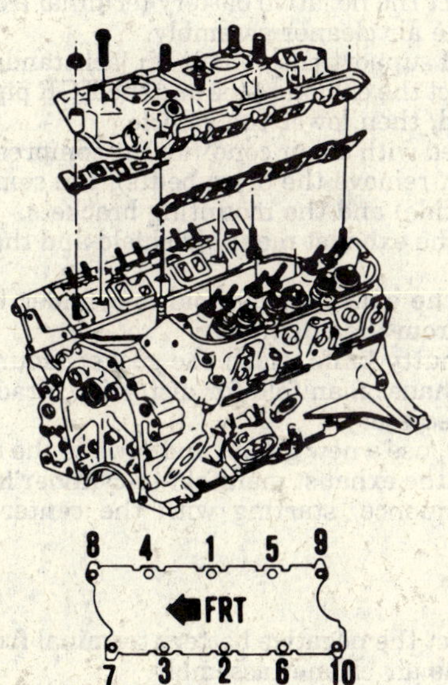

Exploded view of the intake manifold — 2.8L engine

NOTE: The gaskets are marked "Right Side" and "Left Side"; do not interchange them. The gaskets will have to be cut slightly to fit past the center pushrods; do not cut any more material than necessary. Hold the gaskets in place by extending the ridge bead of sealer ¼ in. onto the gasket ends.

13. To complete the installation, reverse the removal procedures. Torque the intake manifold-to-cylinder head nuts and bolts, in sequence, to 23 ft. lbs. Refill the cooling system with a 50 percent solution of ethylene glycol anti-freeze. Adjust the ignition timing, the idle speed, if possible, and check the coolant level after the engine has warmed up.

4.3L Engine

1. Position a drain pan under the radiator, open the drain cock and drain the cooling system to a level below the intake manifold.

CAUTION

When draining the coolant, keep in mind that cats and dogs are attracted by the ethylene glycol antifreeze, and are quite likely to drink any that is left in an uncovered container or in puddles on the ground. This will prove fatal in sufficient quantity. Always drain the coolant into a sealable container. Coolant should be reused unless it is contaminated or several years old.

2. Disconnect the negative battery cable from the battery.
3. Remove the air cleaner and the heat stove.
4. Remove the 2 braces from the rear of the fan belt tensioner.
5. Remove the radiator inlet hose.
6. Disconnect and remove the emission relays with the bracket.
7. Disconnect the electrical wiring harnesses from the clips and move them aside.
8. Disconnect the ground cable from the intake manifold stud.
9. Remove the power brake vacuum pipe from the intake manifold.
10. Remove the heater hose from the intake manifold.
11. Disconnect and plug the fuel lines from the TBI.
12. Label and disconnect the electrical connectors from the ignition coil and remove the coil.
13. Label and disconnect the electrical connectors from the sensors on the manifold.
14. Label and disconnect the electrical connectors from the distributor and remove the distributor.
15. Label and disconnect the electrical connectors from the TBI unit.
16. Disconnect the EGR hose.
17. Disconnect the throttle cable, the TVS cable and the cruise control cable.
18. Remove the intake manifold-to-cylinder head bolts and the intake manifold.
19. Remove and discard the gaskets; be sure to clean the gasket mounting surfaces. Inspect the manifold for warpage and/or cracks; if necessary, replace it.

To install:

20. Using new gaskets, install the intake manifold. Apply a $^3/_{16}$ in. (5mm) bead of RTV sealant, applied to the front and rear of the engine block.
21. Torque the intake manifold-to-cylinder head nuts and bolts, in sequence, to 35 ft. lbs. (47 Nm), except for the rear left bolt which is 41 ft. lbs. (56 Nm).
22. Connect the throttle cable, the TVS and the cruise control cables.
23. Connect the EGR hose.
24. Connect the electrical connectors and hoses to the TBI unit.
25. Install the distributor.

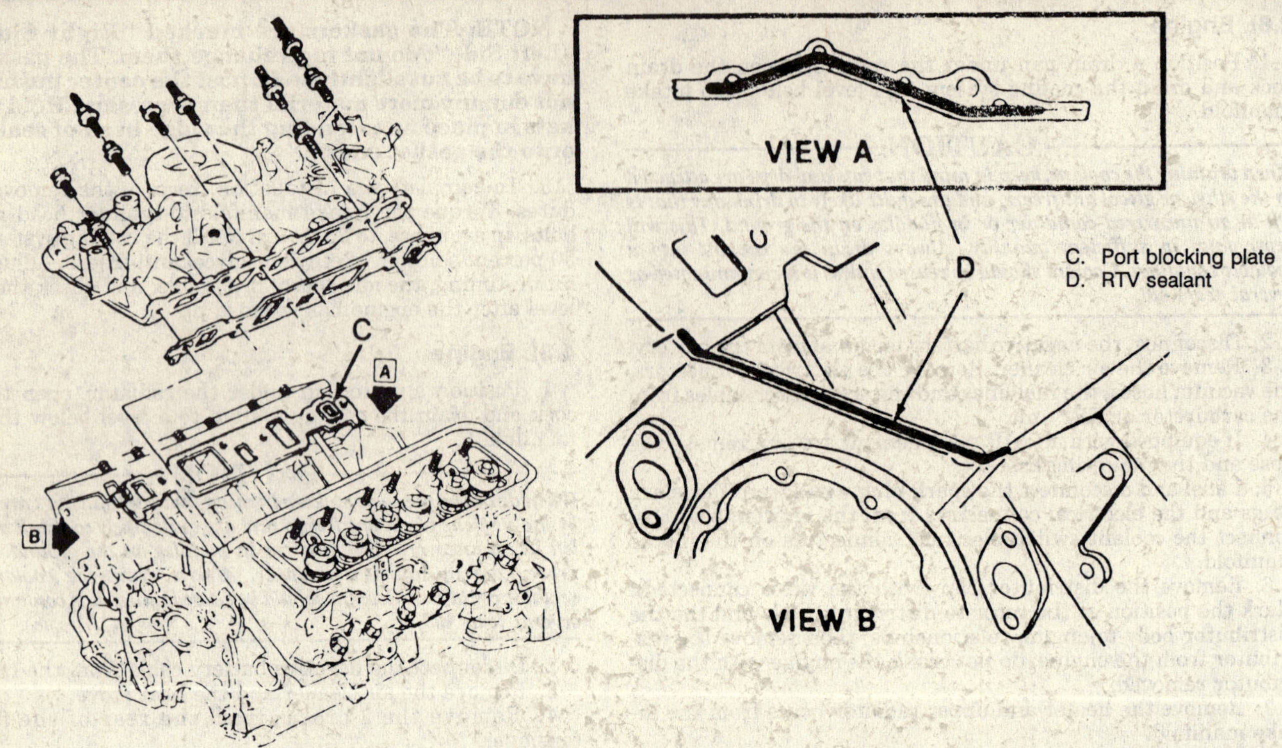

Exploded view of the intake manifold — 4.3L engine

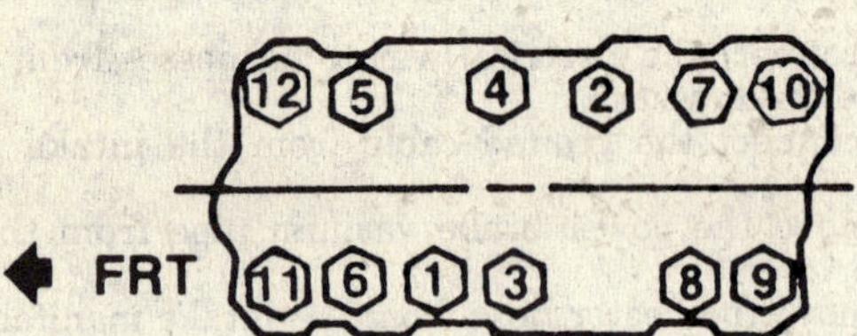

INITIAL TIGHTENING SEQUENCE

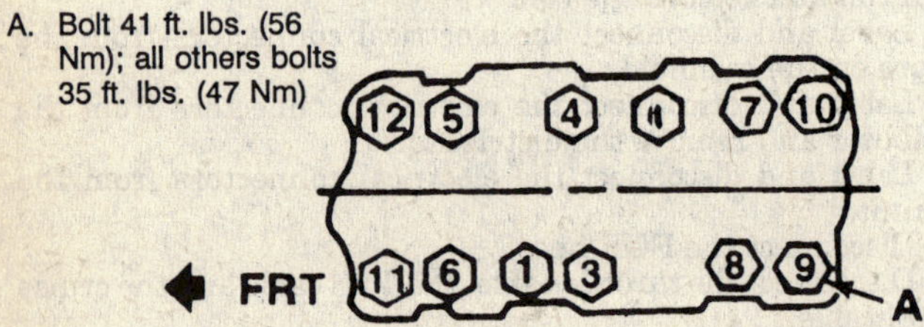

FINAL TIGHTENING SEQUENCE

View of the intake manifold torque sequence — 4.3L engine

26. Connect the electrical connectors to the sensors on the intake manifold.
27. Install the ignition coil and connect the electrical connectors to it.
28. Connect the fuel lines. Connect the heater hoses.
29. Connect the power brake vacuum line. Connect the ground cable to the manifold stud.
30. Connect the electrical wiring harness to the clips. Install the emission relays with the bracket and connect the electrical connectors.
31. Install the radiator inlet hose and refill the cooling system.
32. Install the rear braces of the fan belt tensioner.
33. Install the air cleaner and the heat stove tube.
34. Connect the negative battery cable. Start the engine, allow it to reach normal operating temperatures and check for leaks. Adjust the ignition timing, the idle speed, if possible, and check the coolant level after the engine has warmed up.

Exhaust Manifold

REMOVAL AND INSTALLATION

1.9L Engine

1. Disconnect the negative battery terminal from the battery and remove the air cleaner assembly.
2. Raise and support the vehicle on jackstands.
3. Disconnect the exhaust pipe and the EGR pipe from the exhaust manifold, then lower the vehicle.
4. If equipped with an air conditioning compressor or a power steering pump, remove the drive belt(s), the compressor/pump (move them aside) and the mounting brackets.
5. Remove the exhaust manifold shield and the heat stove, if equipped.
6. Remove the exhaust manifold-to-cylinder head nuts and the manifold from the engine.
7. Using a putty knife, clean the gasket mounting surfaces. Inspect the exhaust manifold for distortion, cracks or damage; replace it, if necessary.
8. To install, use a new gasket and reverse the removal procedures. Torque the exhaust manifold-to-cylinder head nuts to 16 ft. lbs., in sequence, starting with the center and working outwards.

2.0L Engine

1. Disconnect the negative battery terminal from the battery and remove the air cleaner assembly.
2. Raise and support the vehicle on jackstands.
3. Disconnect the exhaust pipe from the exhaust manifold.

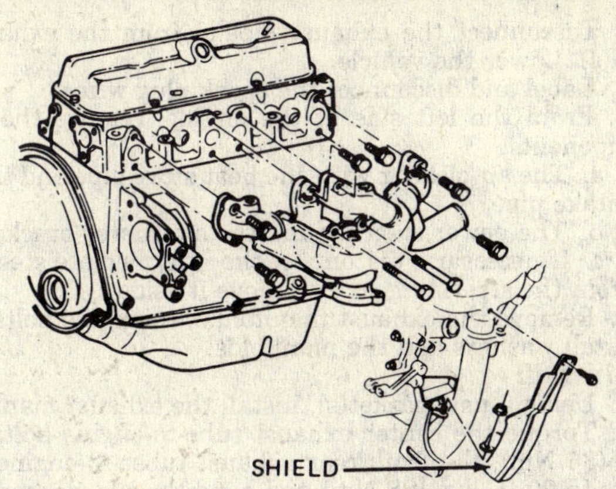

Exploded view of the exhaust manifold — 2.0L engine

4. If equipped with an Air Injection Reaction (AIR) system, remove the AIR hose, the AIR pipe bracket bolt and the dipstick tube bracket.
5. From the front of the engine, remove the fuel vapor canister harness (steel) pipes.
6. Remove the exhaust manifold-to-cylinder head bolts and the manifold from the engine.
7. Using a putty knife, clean the gasket mounting surfaces. Inspect the exhaust manifold for distortion, cracks or damage; replace it, if necessary.
8. To install, use a new gasket and reverse the removal procedures. Torque the exhaust manifold-to-cylinder head bolts to 26 ft. lbs., in sequence, starting with the center and working outwards.

2.2L Diesel Engine

1. Disconnect the negative battery terminal from the battery.
2. Remove the air cleaner, then the PCV valve from the rocker arm cover.
3. Disconnect the exhaust pipe from the exhaust manifold at the flange.
4. Remove the exhaust manifold-to-cylinder head nuts and the exhaust manifold from the engine.
5. If the intake manifold has been removed, perform the following procedures:
   a. Using a putty knife, clean the gasket mounting surfaces.
   b. Inspect the manifold for cracks, damage or distortion; if necessary, replace the intake manifold.
   c. Using a new gasket, install it onto the cylinder head.
6. To install, reverse the removal procedures. Torque the exhaust manifold-to-cylinder head nuts/bolts to 10–17 ft. lbs., starting from the center and working outward.

2.5L Engine

The exhaust manifold is located on the left side of the engine.

1. Disconnect the negative battery terminal from the battery.
2. At the air conditioning compressor, if equipped, remove the drive belt, the compressor (lay it aside) and the rear adjusting bracket, if used.
3. Disconnect the exhaust pipe from the exhaust manifold, then lower the vehicle.
4. Remove the air cleaner and disconnect the electrical connector from the oxygen sensor.
5. Remove the exhaust manifold-to-engine bolts/washers and the manifold from the engine.
6. Using a putty knife, clean the gasket mounting surfaces.
7. To install, use a new gasket and reverse the removal procedures. Torque the exhaust manifold-to-engine bolts to 36 ft. lbs. (center bolts) or 32 ft. lbs. (outer bolts).

2.8L Engine

LEFT SIDE

1. Disconnect the negative battery terminal from the battery.
2. Raise and support the vehicle on jackstands.
3. Disconnect the exhaust pipe from the exhaust manifold.
4. Remove the rear exhaust manifold-to-cylinder head bolts, then lower the vehicle.
5. Disconnect the air management hoses and wiring.
6. If equipped, remove the power steering pump and bracket; do not disconnect the power steering hoses.
7. Remove the front exhaust manifold-to-cylinder head bolts.
8. Using a putty knife, clean the gasket mounting surfaces. Inspect the exhaust manifold for distortion, cracks or damage; replace it, if necessary.
9. To install, use a new gasket and reverse the removal procedures. Torque the exhaust manifold-to-cylinder head bolts to 25 ft. lbs., in a circular pattern, working from the center to the outer ends.

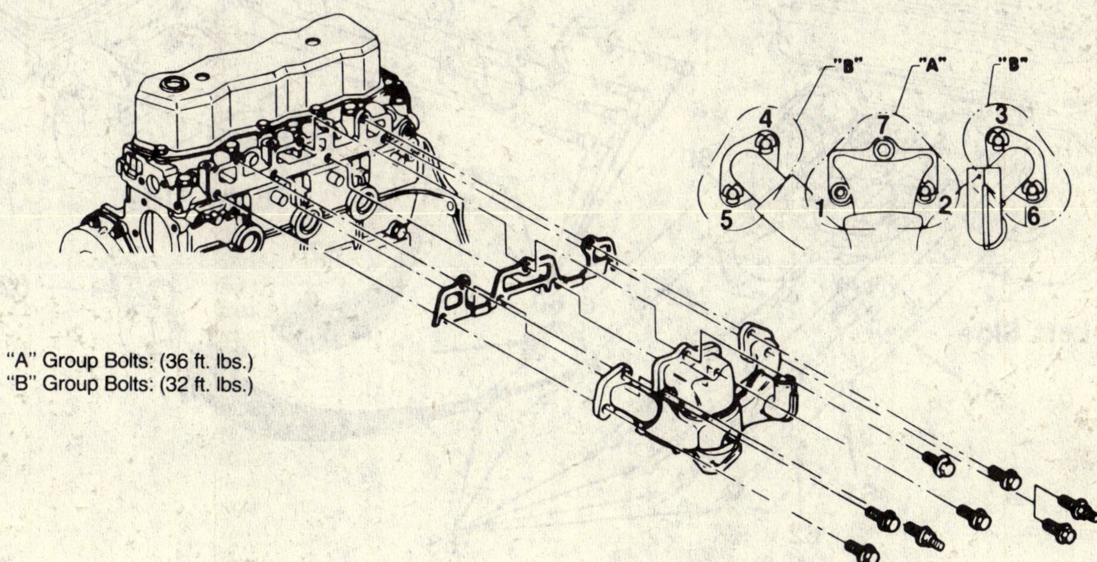

Exploded view of the exhaust manifold — 2.5L engine

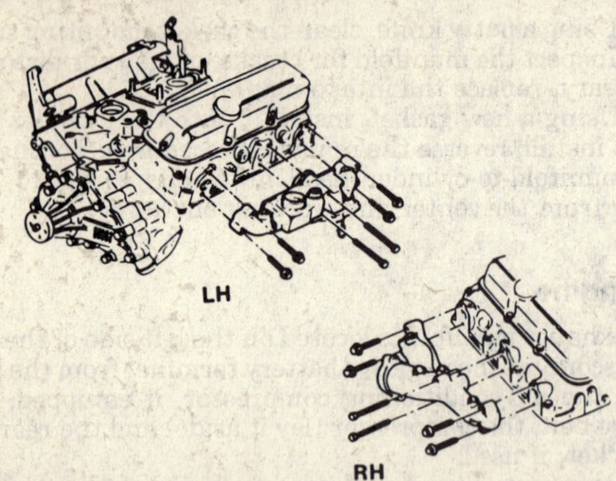

Exploded view of the exhaust manifold — 2.8L engine

RIGHT SIDE

1. Disconnect the negative battery terminal from the battery.
2. Raise and support the vehicle on jackstands.
3. Disconnect the exhaust pipe from the exhaust manifold.
4. Disconnect the air management hoses and wiring, then lower the vehicle.
5. Remove the exhaust manifold-to-cylinder head bolts.
6. Using a putty knife, clean the gasket mounting surfaces. Inspect the exhaust manifold for distortion, cracks or damage; replace it, if necessary.
7. To install, use a new gasket and reverse the removal procedures. Torque the exhaust manifold-to-cylinder head bolts to 25 ft. lbs., in a circular pattern, working from the center to the outer ends.

4.3L Engine

1. Disconnect the negative battery cable.
2. Raise and safely support the vehicle.
3. Disconnect the exhaust pipe(s) from the exhaust manifold(s). Lower the vehicle.
4. Label and disconnect the spark plug wires.
5. From the left side of the engine, remove the following components:
   a. The air cleaner with the heat stove pipe and the cold air intake pipe.
   b. The power steering and the alternator brackets.
   c. If necessary, disconnect the intermediate steering shaft from the steering gear and move it aside.
6. Remove the exhaust manifold(s)-to-engine bolts, washers and tab washers and the manifolds.

To install:

7. Using a new gasket(s), install the exhaust manifold(s).
8. Torque the center exhaust tube-to-engine bolts to 26 ft. lbs. (36 Nm), the front/rear exhaust tubes-to-engine manifold bolts to 20 ft. lbs. (28 Nm) and bend the tab washers over the bolt heads.
9. On the left side of the engine; perform the following procedures:
   a. If the intermediate steering shaft was separated from the steering gear, connect it.
   b. Install the alternator and power steering brackets.
   c. Install the air cleaner with the heat stove pipe and the cold air intake pipe.
10. Install the spark plug wires.
11. Raise and safely support the vehicle.
12. Connect the exhaust pipes to the exhaust manifold.
13. Lower the vehicle and connect the negative battery cable.

Air Conditioning Compressor

REMOVAL AND INSTALLATION

4-Cylinder Engines

1. Refer to Discharging The Air Conditioning System in Section 1 and discharge the air conditioning system.

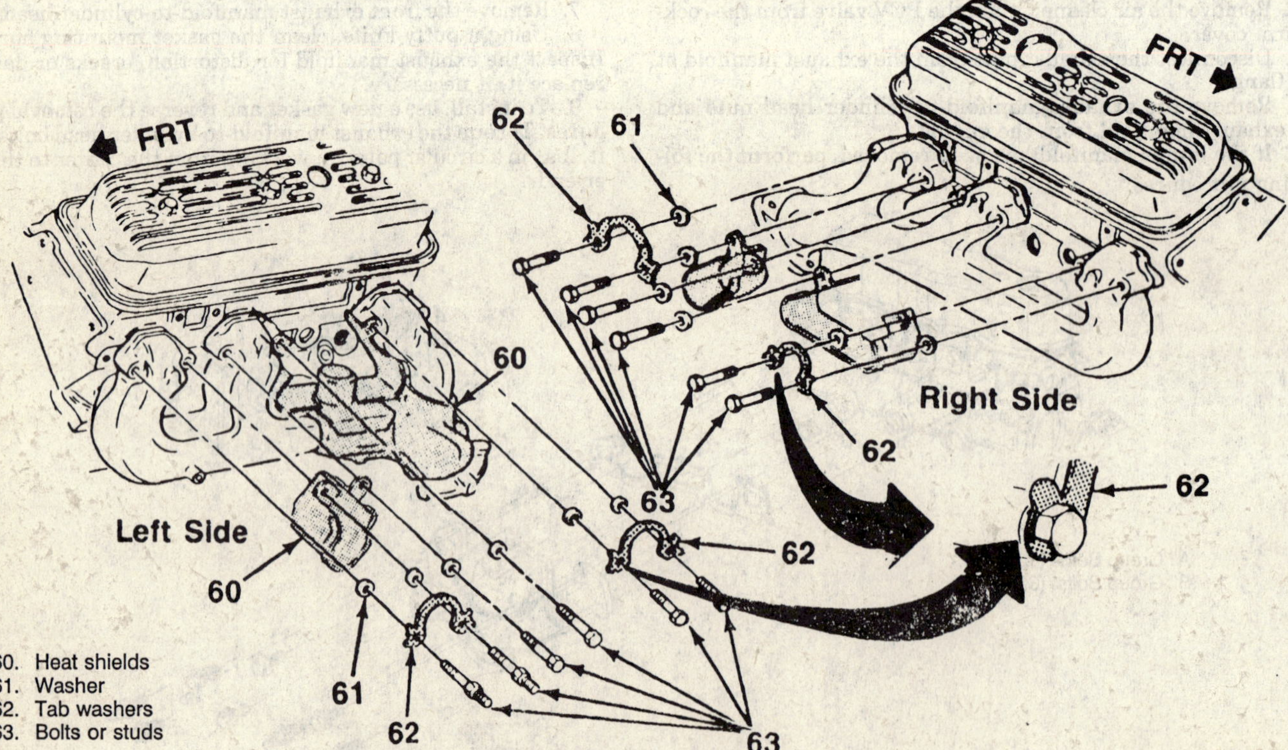

Exploded view of the exhaust manifold — 4.3L engine

2. Disconnect the negative battery terminal from the battery.
3. Disconnect the electrical connectors from the compressor.
4. At the rear of the compressor, remove the bracket from the exhaust manifold. If equipped, remove the power steering pump bracket.
5. Remove the compressor-to-front bracket bolts, the drive belt and the compressor from the vehicle.
6. To install, reverse the removal procedures. Torque the compressor-to-front bracket bolts to 68 ft. lbs., the manifold-to-rear compressor bolt to 47 ft. lbs. and the engine brace-to-compressor nut to 37 ft. lbs.
7. Refer to the Drive Belt Adjusting procedures in Section 1 and adjust the air conditioning drive belt.
8. Refer to Charging The Air Conditioning System in Section 1 and charge the air conditioning system.

V6 Engines

1. Refer to Discharging The Air Conditioning System in Section 1 and discharge the air conditioning system.
2. Disconnect the negative battery terminal from the battery.
3. Disconnect the electrical connectors from the compressor.
4. From the rear of the compressor, remove the intake manifold-to-compressor support bracket.

NOTE: If the engine is equipped with a carburetor, disconnect the vacuum brake from the carburetor for access.

5. Remove the drive belt idler bracket-to-intake manifold bolts, the drive belt and the bracket from the vehicle.
6. Remove the compressor-to-mounting bracket bolts and the compressor from the vehicle.
7. To install, reverse the removal procedures. Torque the compressor-to-front bracket bolts to 68 ft. lbs. and the manifold-to-compressor bolt to 47 ft. lbs.
8. Refer to the, Drive Belt Adjusting procedures in Section 1 and adjust the air conditioning drive belt.
9. Refer to Charging The Air Conditioning System in Section 1 and charge the air conditioning system.

Radiator

DIAGNOSIS

Test for restrictions in the radiator by warming the engine to operating temperature and then turning the engine off. Feel the radiator, it should be hot along the left side and warm along the right side. The temperature should rise evenly from right to left. If cold spots are felt, have the radiator tested for clogged sections.

REMOVAL AND INSTALLATION

1. Disconnect the negative battery terminal.

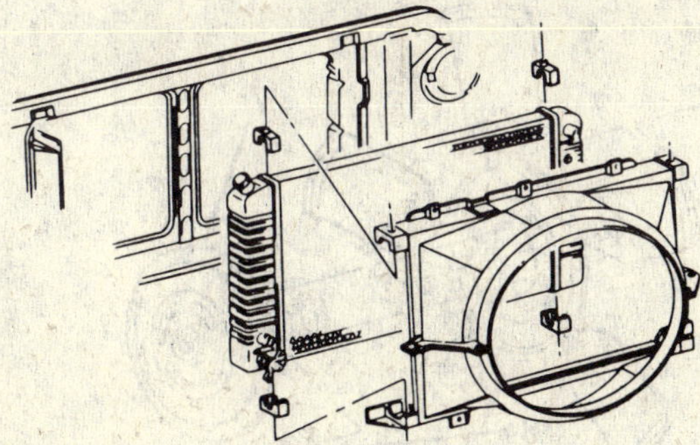

Exploded view of a typical radiator and shroud assembly

2. Using a drain pan, position it under the radiator, open the drain cock and drain the cooling system.

CAUTION

When draining the coolant, keep in mind that cats and dogs are attracted by the ethylene glycol antifreeze, and are quite likely to drink any that is left in an uncovered container or in puddles on the ground. This will prove fatal in sufficient quantity. Always drain the coolant into a sealable container. Coolant should be reused unless it is contaminated or several years old.

3. From the radiator, remove the upper and lower radiator hoses, then the overflow hose.
4. If equipped with an automatic transmission, disconnect and plug the oil cooler lines at the radiator.
5. If equipped with air conditioning, remove the air conditioning hose retaining clip.
6. Remove the upper fan shroud, the radiator to chassis screws and the radiator.
7. To install, reverse the removal procedures. Refill the cooling system with a 50 percent solution of anti-freeze. Start the engine, allow it to reach normal operating temperatures and check for leaks.

Oil Cooler – Diesel Engine

REMOVAL AND INSTALLATION

1. Disconnect the negative battery terminal.
2. Using a drain pan, position it under the radiator, open the drain cock and drain the cooling system.

CAUTION

When draining the coolant, keep in mind that cats and dogs are attracted by the ethylene glycol antifreeze, and are quite likely to drink any that is left in an uncovered container or in puddles on the ground. This will prove fatal in sufficient quantity. Always drain the coolant into a sealable container. Coolant should be reused unless it is contaminated or several years old.

3. Remove the oil filter.
4. Disconnect the coolant hoses from the oil cooler.
5. Remove oil cooler nut and the cooler from the vehicle.
6. To install, reverse the removal procedures. Refill the cooling system with a 50 percent solution of anti-freeze. Start the engine, allow it to reach normal operating temperatures and check for leaks.

Air Conditioning Condenser

REMOVAL AND INSTALLATION

NOTE: Refer to Air Conditioning Charging and Discharging in Section 1 when performing refrigerant service.

1. Discharge the air conditioning system.
2. Drain the cooling system.

CAUTION

When draining the coolant, keep in mind that cats and dogs are attracted by the ethylene glycol antifreeze, and are quite likely to drink any that is left in an uncovered container or in puddles on the ground. This will prove fatal in sufficient quantity. Always drain the coolant into a sealable container. Coolant should be reused unless it is contaminated or several years old.

3. Remove the upper and lower radiator hoses.
4. Disconnect all coolant lines leading to the radiator.
5. Remove the radiator.
6. Remove the shields at both sides of the radiator support.

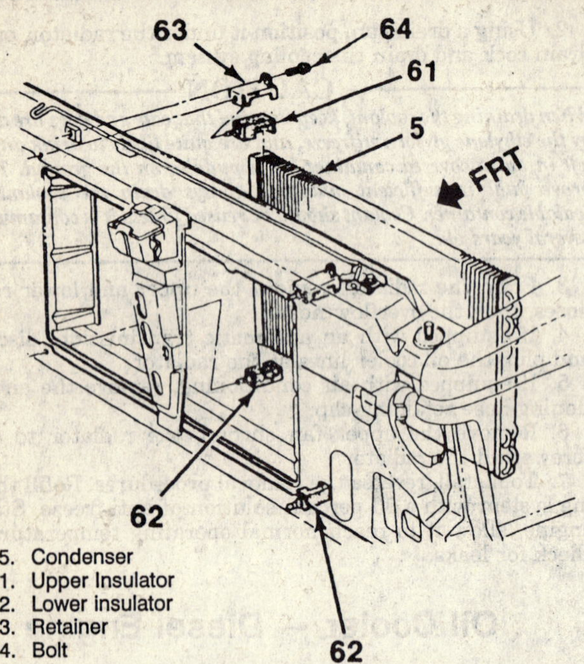

Exploded view of the air conditioner condenser

7. Remove the condenser retainers and lines. Remove the condenser.
8. Installation is the reverse of removal. Recharge the air conditioning system and fill the cooling system.

Engine Clutch Fan

DIAGNOSIS

Start the engine and listen for fan noise. Fan noise is usually evident during the first few minutes after start-up and when the clutch is engaged for maximum cooling (during idle). If fan noise is excessive, the fan cannot be rotated by hand or there is a rough grating feel as the fan is turned, replace the clutch.

Check a loose fan assembly for wear and replace as necessary. Under certain conditions, the fan may flex up to ¼ in. This is not cause for replacement.

The fan clutch is not affected by small fluid leaks which may occur in the area around the bearing assembly. If leakage appears excessive, replace the fan clutch.

If the fan clutch free-wheels with no drag (revolves more than 5 times when spun by hand), replace the clutch.

REMOVAL AND INSTALLATION

NOTE: Do not use or repair a damaged fan assembly. An unbalanced fan assembly could fly apart and cause personal injury or property damage. Replace damaged assemblies with new ones.

1. Remove the upper radiator shroud.
2. Remove the fan attaching nuts and remove the fan and clutch assembly from the engine.
3. Remove clutch from the fan by removing the attaching nuts.
4. To install, reverse the removal procedures. Torque bolts to the following torque:
   - 2.5L and 2.8L clutch-to-fan bolts: 9 ft. lbs.
   - 4.3L clutch-to-fan bolts: 25 ft. lbs.
   - All others clutch-to-fan bolts: 11–16 ft. lbs.
   - Fan-to-pulley nuts: 27–40 ft. lbs.

Water Pump

DIAGNOSIS

Check the water pump operation by running the engine while squeezing the upper radiator hose. When the engine warms (thermostat opens) a pressure surge should be felt. Check for a plugged vent hole at the pump snout.

REMOVAL AND INSTALLATION

1.9L Engine

1. Disconnect the negative battery terminal.
2. Raise and support the front of the vehicle on jackstands, then remove the lower fan shroud.
3. Position a drain pan under the radiator, open the drain cock and drain the coolant.

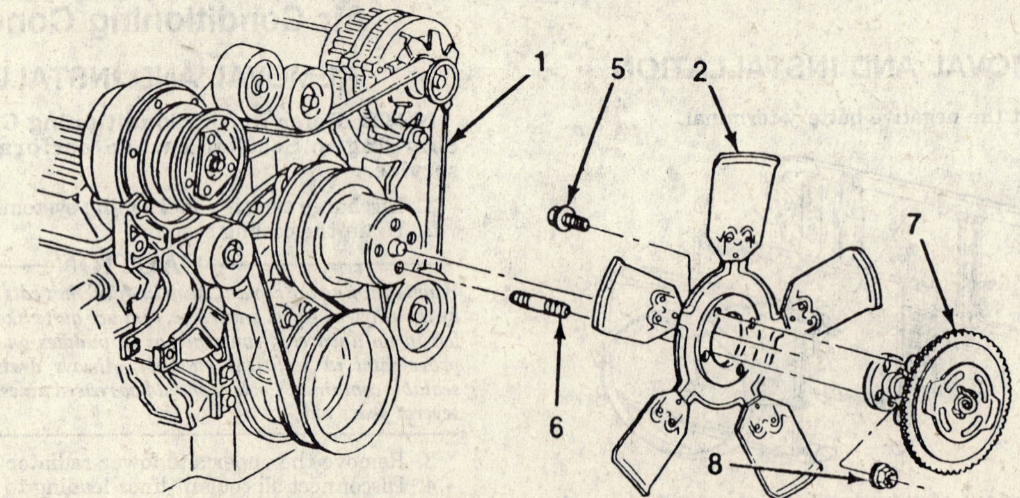

Exploded view of a fan clutch assembly — 4.3L engine

CAUTION

When draining the coolant, keep in mind that cats and dogs are attracted by the ethylene glycol antifreeze, and are quite likely to drink any that is left in an uncovered container or in puddles on the ground. This will prove fatal in sufficient quantity. Always drain the coolant into a sealable container. Coolant should be reused unless it is contaminated or several years old.

4. If not equipped with air conditioning, remove the fan-to-water pump nuts and the fan from the vehicle.
5. If equipped with air conditioning, perform the following procedures:
   a. Loosen the air pump and alternator adjusting bolts, pivot them toward the engine and remove the drive belt(s).
   b. Remove the fan-to-water pump nuts and the fan (with the fan and air pump drive pulley) from the vehicle.
   c. Remove the fan set plate/pulley-to-water pump bolts, then remove the set plate and the pulley.
6. Remove the water pump-to-engine bolts and the water pump from the engine.
7. Using a putty knife, clean the gasket mounting surfaces.
8. To install, use a new gasket, if equipped, RTV sealant, if necessary, and reverse the removal procedures. Refill the cooling system with a 50 percent solution of anti-freeze. Start the engine, allow it to reach normal operating temperatures and check for leaks.

2.0L Engine

1. Disconnect the negative battery terminal.
2. Position a drain pan under the radiator, open the drain cock and drain the coolant.

CAUTION

When draining the coolant, keep in mind that cats and dogs are attracted by the ethylene glycol antifreeze, and are quite likely to drink any that is left in an uncovered container or in puddles on the ground. This will prove fatal in sufficient quantity. Always drain the coolant into a sealable container. Coolant should be reused unless it is contaminated or several years old.

3. Remove the upper fan shroud and all of the necessary drive belts.
4. Disconnect the radiator and heater hoses from the water pump.
5. Remove the water pump-to-engine bolts and the water pump from the vehicle.
6. Using a putty knife, clean the gasket mounting surfaces.
7. To install, use a new gasket, if equipped, RTV sealant, if necessary, and reverse the removal procedures. Refill the cooling system with a 50 percent solution of anti-freeze. Start the engine, allow it to reach normal operating temperatures and check for leaks.

2.2L Diesel Engine

1. Disconnect the negative battery terminal.
2. At the fan shroud, disconnect the power steering reservoir. Remove the upper fan shroud.
3. Position a drain pan under the radiator, open the drain cock and drain the coolant.

CAUTION

When draining the coolant, keep in mind that cats and dogs are attracted by the ethylene glycol antifreeze, and are quite likely to drink any that is left in an uncovered container or in puddles on the ground. This will prove fatal in sufficient quantity. Always drain the coolant into a sealable container. Coolant should be reused unless it is contaminated or several years old.

4. Loosen the drive belts, the fan and the air conditioning compressor (move it aside).
5. Disconnect the front center radiator pipe.
6. From the right side of the water pump, disconnect the radiator and heater hoses.
7. Disconnect the PCV valve from the rocker cover. Remove the air cleaner and the heater pipe from the intake manifold.
8. Disconnect the heater hose from the left side of the water pump, then the alternator brace.
9. Remove the water pump-to-engine bolts and the water pump from the engine.
10. Using a putty knife, clean the gasket mounting surfaces.
11. To install, use a new gasket, RTV sealant, if necessary, and reverse the removal procedures. Torque the water pump-to-engine bolts to 10–17 ft. lbs. Refill the cooling system with a 50 percent solution of anti-freeze. Start the engine, allow it to reach normal operating temperatures and check for leaks.

2.5L Engine

1. Disconnect the negative battery terminal.
2. Place a catch pan under the radiator, open the drain cock and drain the cooling system.

CAUTION

When draining the coolant, keep in mind that cats and dogs are attracted by the ethylene glycol antifreeze, and are quite likely to drink any that is left in an uncovered container or in puddles on the ground. This will prove fatal in sufficient quantity. Always drain the coolant into a sealable container. Coolant should be reused unless it is contaminated or several years old.

3. At the front of the engine, loosen the accessory drive belt adjustments and remove the drive belts.
4. Remove the upper fan shroud. Remove the fan/clutch assembly-to-water pump bolts and the fan/clutch assembly from the water pump pulley.
5. Remove the drive belt pulley from the water pump.

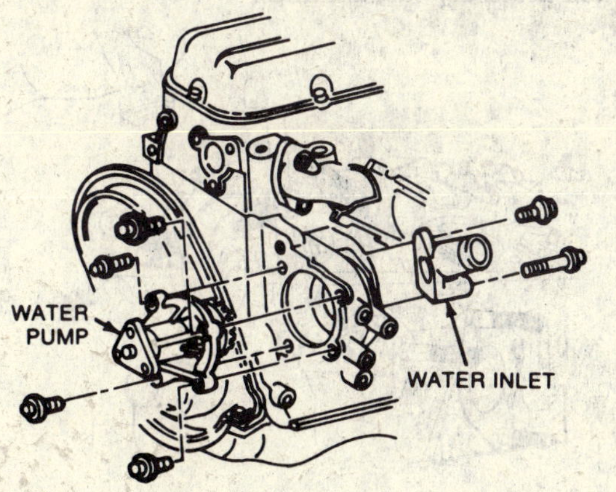

Exploded view of the water pump assembly — 2.0L engine

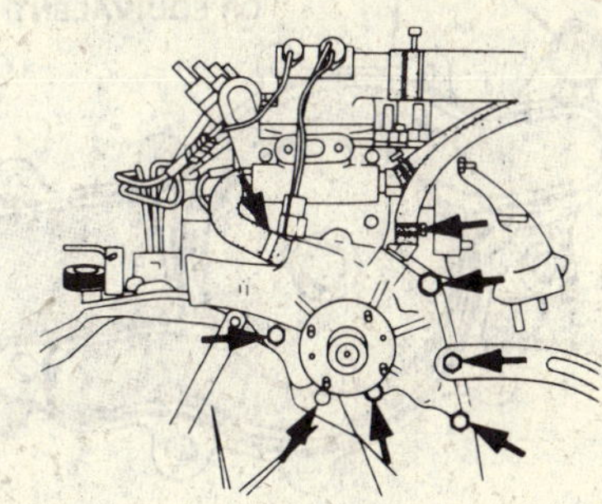

Exploded view of the water pump assembly — 1.9L diesel engine

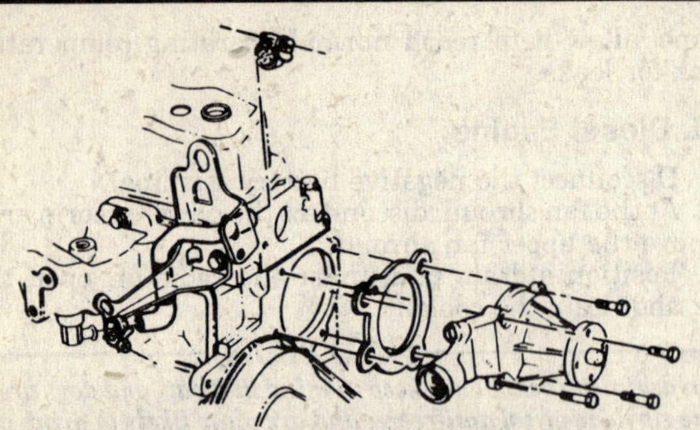

Exploded view of the water pump assembly — 2.5L engine

6. Remove the clamps and the hoses from the water pump.
7. Remove the water pump-to-engine bolts and the water pump from the engine.
8. Using a putty knife, clean the gasket mounting surfaces.
9. To install, use new gasket(s), coat the bolt threads with sealant and reverse the removal procedures. Torque the water pump-to-engine bolts to 22 ft. lbs. Refill the cooling system with a 50 percent solution of anti-freeze. Start the engine, allow it to reach normal operating temperatures and check for leaks.

2.8L and 4.3L Engines

1. Disconnect the negative battery terminal.
2. Position a drain pan under the radiator, open the drain cock and drain the coolant from the engine.

CAUTION

When draining the coolant, keep in mind that cats and dogs are attracted by the ethylene glycol antifreeze, and are quite likely to drink any that is left in an uncovered container or in puddles on the ground. This will prove fatal in sufficient quantity. Always drain the coolant into a sealable container. Coolant should be reused unless it is contaminated or several years old.

Exploded view of the water pump assembly — 2.8L and 4.3L engines

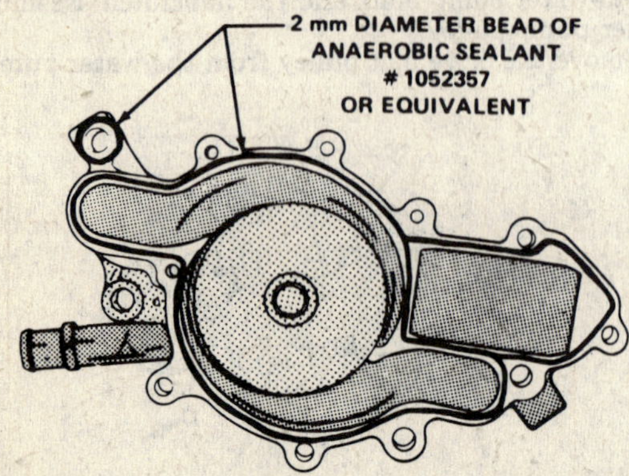

Applying sealant to the water pump assembly — V6 engines

3. Disconnect the radiator and heater hoses from the water pump.
4. At the front of the engine, loosen the accessory drive belt adjustments and remove the drive belts.
5. Remove the upper fan shroud. Remove the fan/clutch assembly-to-water pump bolts and the fan/clutch assembly from the water pump pulley.
6. Remove the water pump-to-engine bolts and the water pump from the engine.
7. Using a putty knife, clean the gasket mounting surfaces.
8. To install, use a new gaskets, RTV sealant, if necessary, and reverse the removal procedures. Torque the water pump-to-engine bolts to 22 ft. lbs. Refill the cooling system with a 50 percent solution of anti-freeze. Start the engine, allow it to reach normal operating temperatures and check for leaks.

NOTE: Before installing the water pump, place a $^{3}/_{32}$ in. (2mm) bead of sealer on the water pump mating surface. Coat the bolt threads with pipe compound and mount the pump on the engine.

Cylinder Head

REMOVAL AND INSTALLATION

1.9L Engine

1. Refer to the Rocker Arm Cover, Removal and Installation procedures in this section and remove the rocker arm cover.
2. From the rear of the cylinder head, remove EGR pipe clamp bolt.
3. Raise and support the front of the vehicle on jackstands.
4. Disconnect the exhaust pipe from the exhaust manifold, then lower the vehicle.
5. Position a drain pan under the radiator, open the drain cock and drain the coolant from the engine.

CAUTION

When draining the coolant, keep in mind that cats and dogs are attracted by the ethylene glycol antifreeze, and are quite likely to drink any that is left in an uncovered container or in puddles on the ground. This will prove fatal in sufficient quantity. Always drain the coolant into a sealable container. Coolant should be reused unless it is contaminated or several years old.

6. From the intake manifold and the front of the cylinder head, disconnect the heater hoses.
7. If equipped with an air conditioning compressor and/or a power steering pump, disconnect them and lay them aside.
8. From the carburetor, disconnect the accelerator linkage, the fuel line, all necessary electrical connections, the spark plug wires and necessary vacuum lines.

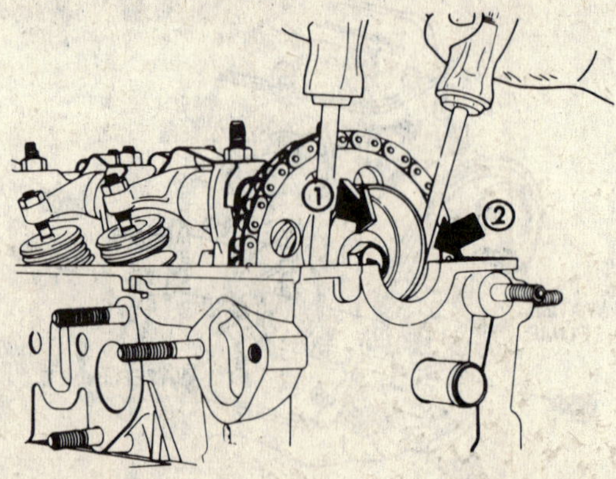

Using 2 prybars to lock the automatic adjuster into position — 1.9L engine

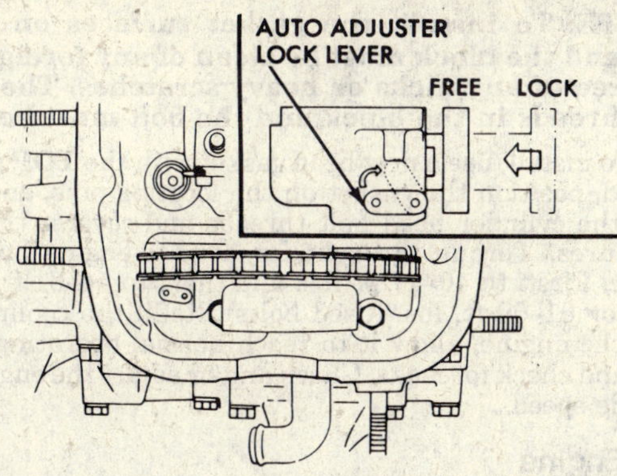

Locking the timing chain adjuster — 1.9L engine

9. Rotate the camshaft until the No. 4 cylinder is in the firing position. Remove the distributor cap and mark rotor-to-housing relationship, then remove the distributor.

10. Disconnect the fuel lines from the fuel pump and remove it.

11. Using 2 prybars, depress the adjuster lock lever to lock the automatic adjuster shoe in its fully retracted position.

12. From the camshaft, remove timing sprocket-to-camshaft bolt, the sprocket and the fuel pump drive cam. Keep the sprocket on the chain damper and tensioner—do not remove the sprocket from the chain.

13. Disconnect the AIR hose and check valve from the air manifold.

14. Remove the cylinder head-to-timing cover bolts.

15. Using the extension bar wrench tool J-24239-01 or equivalent, remove cylinder head-to-engine bolts; remove the bolts in a progressional sequence, beginning with the outer bolts and working inward.

16. Using an assistant, remove the cylinder head, intake and exhaust manifold as an assembly.

17. Using a putty knife, clean the gasket mounting surfaces.

NOTE: The gasket surfaces on both the head and block must be clean of any foreign matter and free of nicks or heavy scratches. The cylinder bolt threads in the block and thread on the bolts must be cleaned (dirt will affect the bolt torque).

18. To install, place the new gasket over dowel pins with **TOP** side of gasket up.

NOTE: Be sure to lubricate the cylinder head bolts with engine oil before installing them.

19. To complete the installation, reverse the removal procedures. Torque the cylinder head-to-engine bolts, a little at a time, in the sequence to 61 ft. lbs. and then retighten to 72 ft. lbs. Refill the cooling system. Start the engine, allow it to reach normal operating temperatures and check for leaks. Check and/ or adjust the engine timing and idle speed.

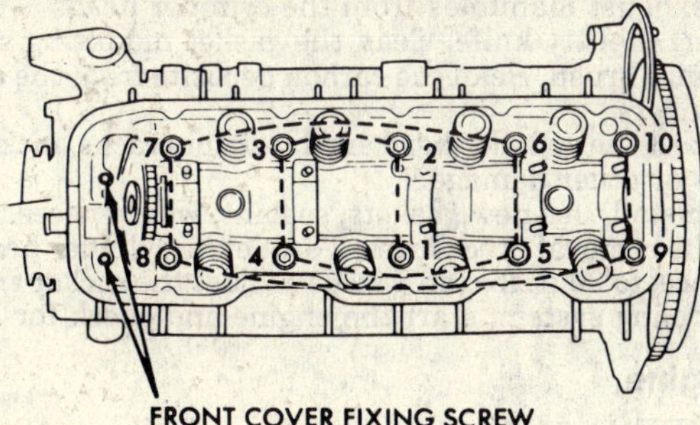

Cylinder head bolt torquing sequence — 1.9L engine

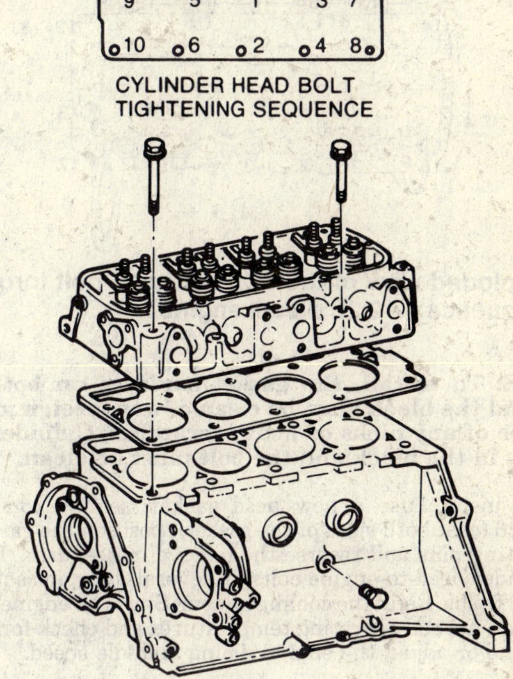

Exploded view of the cylinder head and bolt torquing sequence — 2.0L engine

2.0L Engine

NOTE: The engine should be overnight cold before removing the cylinder head.

1. Disconnect the negative battery terminal.

2. Position a drain pan under the radiator, open the drain cock and drain the coolant from the engine.

CAUTION

When draining the coolant, keep in mind that cats and dogs are attracted by the ethylene glycol antifreeze, and are quite likely to drink any that is left in an uncovered container or in puddles on the ground. This will prove fatal in sufficient quantity. Always drain the coolant into a sealable container. Coolant should be reused unless it is contaminated or several years old.

3. Remove the air cleaner, then raise and support the front of the vehicle on jackstands.

4. Remove the exhaust shield, then disconnect the exhaust pipe from the exhaust manifold. Lower the vehicle.

5. Disconnect the accelerator linkage, the necessary electrical wiring connectors and the vacuum lines.

6. From the top-front of the engine, remove the fuel vapor canister harness (steel) pipes.

7. Remove the distributor cap, then mark the rotor-to-distributor housing and the distributor housing-to-engine.

8. Remove the rocker arm cover, the rocker arms and the pushrods.

9. Remove the upper radiator hose, the heater hose, the upper fan shroud and the fan.

10. Remove the AIR management valve, the air pump and the upper AIR bracket.

11. Remove the fuel line from the fuel pump. Disconnect the wire from the rear of the cylinder head.

12. Remove the cylinder head-to-engine bolts and the cylinder head.

13. Using a putty knife, clean the gasket mounting surfaces.

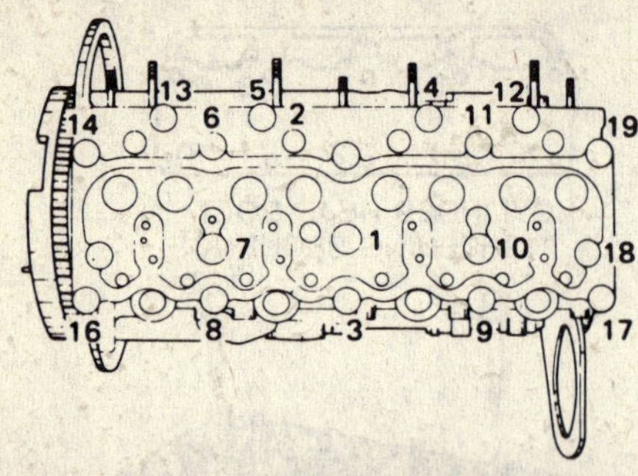

Exploded view of the cylinder head bolt torque sequence — 2.2L diesel engine

NOTE: To install, the gasket surfaces on both the head and the block must be clean of any foreign matter and free of any nicks or heavy scratches. Cylinder bolt threads in the block and the bolt must be clean.

14. To install, use a new head gasket, sealing compound 10520026 (coat both sides of the gasket), position the gasket on the locating pins and reverse the removal procedures. Torque the cylinder head-to-engine bolts (in several steps, in sequence) to 65–75 ft. lbs. Refill the cooling system. Start the engine, allow it to reach normal operating temperatures and check for leaks. Check and/or adjust the engine timing and idle speed.

2.2L Engine

NOTE: The injection timing must be reset after this procedure. See Section 5 for details and special tools required.

1. Disconnect the negative battery terminal.
2. Position a drain pan under the radiator, open the drain cock and drain the coolant from the engine.

CAUTION

When draining the coolant, keep in mind that cats and dogs are attracted by the ethylene glycol antifreeze, and are quite likely to drink any that is left in an uncovered container or in puddles on the ground. This will prove fatal in sufficient quantity. Always drain the coolant into a sealable container. Coolant should be reused unless it is contaminated or several years old.

3. Remove the rocker arm cover, the rocker arm shaft and the pushrods.
4. From the cylinder head, remove the upper radiator hose and the heater hose.
5. Disconnect the heater tube and remove the exhaust pipe from the exhaust manifold.
6. Remove the vacuum pump and the air conditioning compressor, if equipped, move it aside.
7. Disconnect the heater hose/bracket, the necessary electrical wiring connectors. Disconnect the PCV valve hose from the pipe and move it aside.
8. Disconnect the dipstick tube bracket and dipstick, the breather pipe and the oil jet pipe.
9. Disconnect the fuel injection lines and cover them with protective caps.
10. Remove the air conditioning bracket and disconnect the return hose.
11. Remove the cylinder head-to-engine bolts and the cylinder head from the vehicle.
12. Using a putty knife, clean the gasket mounting surfaces. Inspect the cylinder head for distortion, cracks and/or damage.

NOTE: To install, the gasket surfaces on both the head and the block must be clean of any foreign matter and free of any nicks or heavy scratches. The cylinder bolt threads in the block and the bolt must be clean.

13. To install, use a new head gasket with the **TOP** side facing upward, position the gasket on the locating pins, apply engine oil to the cylinder head bolt threads and reverse the removal procedures. Torque the cylinder head-to-engine bolts, in sequence: First, to 40–47 ft. lbs. and then, to 54–61 ft. lbs. (new bolts) or 61–69 ft. lbs. (used bolts). Refill the cooling system. Start the engine, allow it to reach normal operating temperatures and check for leaks. Check and/or adjust the engine timing and idle speed.

2.5L Engine

NOTE: Before disassembling the engine, make sure it is overnight cold.

CAUTION

Relieve the pressure on the fuel system before disconnecting any fuel line connection.

1. Remove the rocker arm cover.
2. Place a catch pan under the radiator, open the drain cock and drain the cooling system.

CAUTION

When draining the coolant, keep in mind that cats and dogs are attracted by the ethylene glycol antifreeze, and are quite likely to drink any that is left in an uncovered container or in puddles on the ground. This will prove fatal in sufficient quantity. Always drain the coolant into a sealable container. Coolant should be reused unless it is contaminated or several years old.

3. Disconnect the accelerator, the cruise control and the TVS cables, if equipped.
4. From the intake manifold, remove the water pump bypass and heater hoses.
5. From the alternator, remove the front and rear braces, then move it aside.
6. Disconnect the air conditioning compressor brackets and move the compressor aside.
7. Remove the thermostat housing-to-cylinder head bolts and the housing from the engine.
8. Remove the ground cable and any necessary electrical connectors from the cylinder head. Disconnect the wires from the spark plugs and the oxygen sensor. Disconnect and remove the ignition coil from the intake manifold and the cylinder head.
9. Remove the vacuum lines and fuel hoses from the intake manifold and the TBI unit.
10. Disconnect the exhaust pipe from the exhaust manifold.
11. Remove the rocker arm nuts, the washers, the rocker arms and the pushrods from the cylinder head.
12. Remove the cylinder head-to-engine bolts and the cylinder head from the engine (with the manifolds attached), then place the assembly on a workbench. If necessary, remove the intake and the exhaust manifolds from the cylinder head.
13. Using a putty knife, clean the gasket mounting surfaces. Using a wire brush, clean the carbon deposits from the combustion chambers.
14. Inspect the cylinder head and block for cracks, nicks, heavy scratches or other damage.
15. To install, use new gaskets, sealant, where necessary, and reverse the removal procedures. Torque the cylinder head bolts, in sequence, to 90 ft. lbs., in 3 steps. Adjust the rocker arms. Refill the cooling system, start the engine and check for leaks.

2.8L Engine

LEFT SIDE

1. Remove the intake manifold.

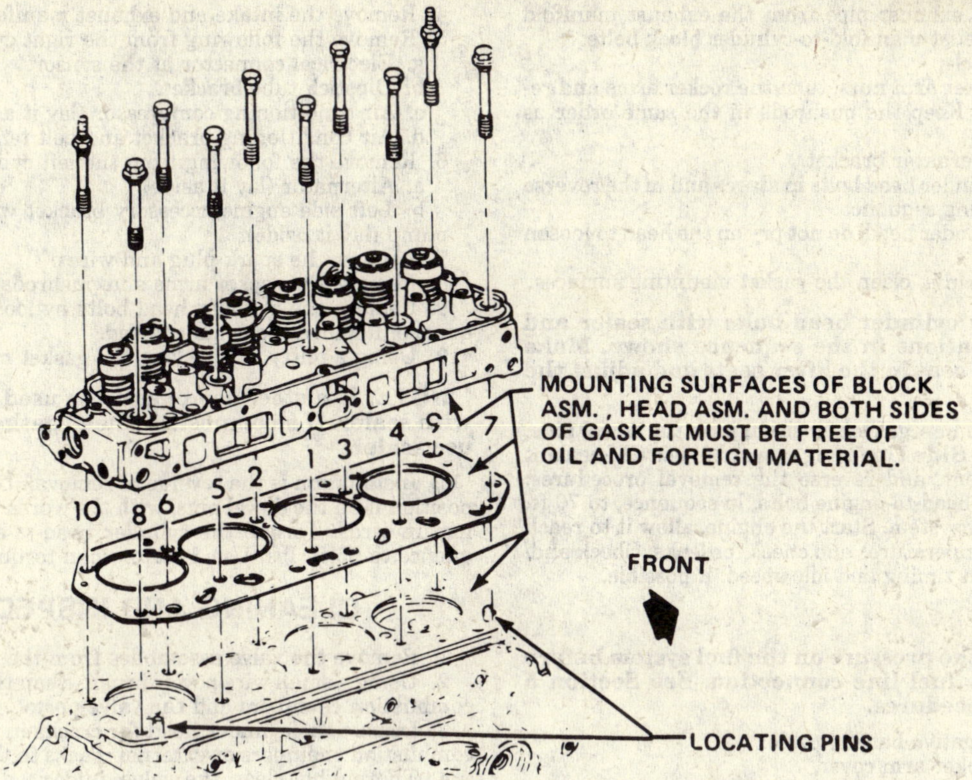

Exploded view of the cylinder head bolt torque sequence — 2.5L engine

2. Raise and support the front of the vehicle on jackstands.
3. Position a drain pan under the radiator, open the drain cock and drain the coolant from the block.

CAUTION

When draining the coolant, keep in mind that cats and dogs are attracted by the ethylene glycol antifreeze, and are quite likely to drink any that is left in an uncovered container or in puddles on the ground. This will prove fatal in sufficient quantity. Always drain the coolant into a sealable container. Coolant should be reused unless it is contaminated or several years old.

4. Disconnect the exhaust pipe from the exhaust manifold and remove the exhaust manifold-to-cylinder block bolts.
5. Remove the dipstick tube from the engine.
6. Lower the vehicle.
7. Loosen the rocker arm nuts, turn the rocker arms and remove the pushrods. Keep the pushrods in the same order as removed.
8. Remove the cylinder head bolts in stages and in the reverse order of the tightening sequence.
9. Remove the cylinder head; do not pry on the head to loosen it.
10. Using a putty knife, clean the gasket mounting surfaces.

NOTE: Coat the cylinder head bolts with sealer and torque to specifications in the sequence shown. Make sure the pushrods seat in the lifter seats and adjust the valves.

11. To install, use a new gasket (position it on the dowel pins, with the words **This Side Up** facing upwards), use GM sealant 1052080 or equivalent and reverse the removal procedures. Torque the cylinder head-to-engine bolts, in sequence, to 70 ft. lbs. Refill the cooling system. Start the engine, allow it to reach normal operating temperatures and check for leaks. Check and/or adjust the ignition timing and idle speed, if possible.

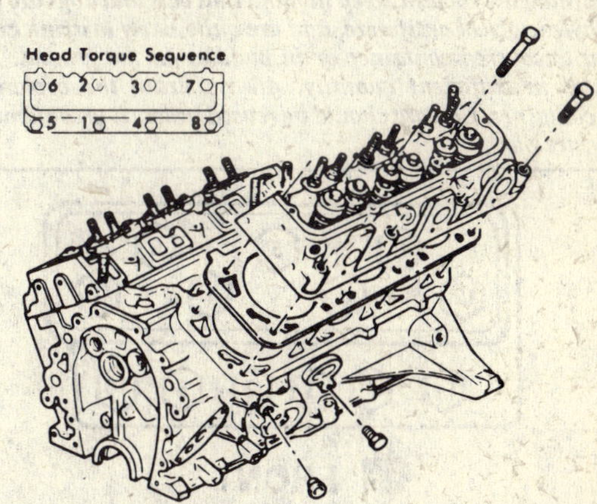

Exploded view of the cylinder head and bolt torque sequence — 2.8L engine

RIGHT SIDE

1. Remove the intake manifold.
2. Raise and support the front of the vehicle on jackstands.
3. Position a drain pan under the radiator, open the drain cock and drain the coolant from the block.

CAUTION

When draining the coolant, keep in mind that cats and dogs are attracted by the ethylene glycol antifreeze, and are quite likely to drink any that is left in an uncovered container or in puddles on the ground. This will prove fatal in sufficient quantity. Always drain the coolant into a sealable container. Coolant should be reused unless it is contaminated or several years old.

4. Disconnect the exhaust pipe from the exhaust manifold and remove the exhaust manifold-to-cylinder block bolts.
5. Lower the vehicle.
6. Loosen the rocker arm nuts, turn the rocker arms and remove the pushrods. Keep the pushrods in the same order as removed.
7. Remove the alternator bracket.
8. Remove the cylinder head bolts in stages and in the reverse order of the tightening sequence.
9. Remove the cylinder head; do not pry on the head to loosen it.
10. Using a putty knife, clean the gasket mounting surfaces.

NOTE: Coat the cylinder head bolts with sealer and torque to specifications in the sequence shown. Make sure the pushrods seat in the lifter seats and adjust the valves.

11. To install, use a new gasket (position it on the dowel pins, with the words **This Side Up** facing upwards), use GM sealant 1052080 or equivalent, and reverse the removal procedures. Torque the cylinder head-to-engine bolts, in sequence, to 70 ft. lbs. Refill the cooling system. Start the engine, allow it to reach normal operating temperatures and check for leaks. Check and/or adjust the ignition timing and idle speed, if possible.

4.3L Engine

NOTE: Relieve the pressure on the fuel system before disconnecting any fuel line connection. See Section 5 for the proper procedures.

1. Remove the negative battery cable.
2. Remove the rocker arm cover.
3. Drain the cooling system.

CAUTION

When draining the coolant, keep in mind that cats and dogs are attracted by the ethylene glycol antifreeze, and are quite likely to drink any that is left in an uncovered container or in puddles on the ground. This will prove fatal in sufficient quantity. Always drain the coolant into a sealable container. Coolant should be reused unless it is contaminated or several years old.

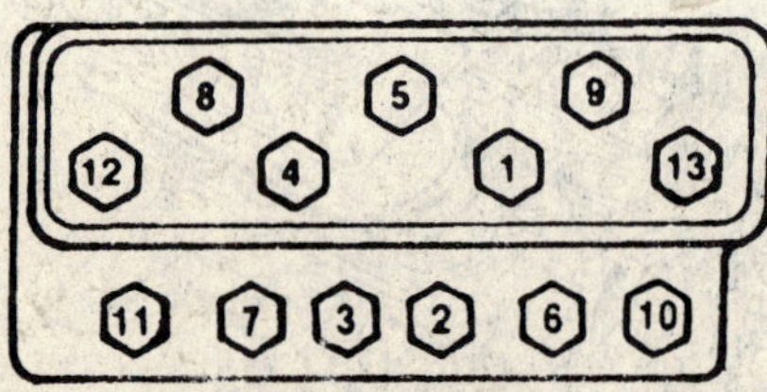

View of the cylinder head bolt torque sequence — 4.3L engine

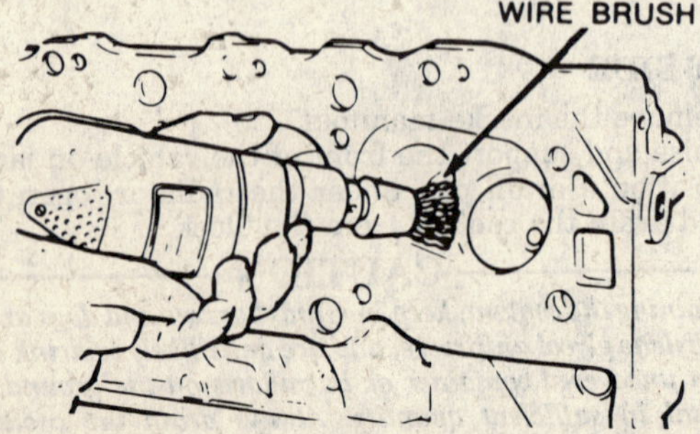

Remove the carbon from the cylinder head with a wire brush and electric drill

4. Remove the intake and exhaust manifolds.
5. Remove the following from the right cylinder head:
   a. Electrical connector at the sensor.
   b. Dipstick tube bracket.
   c. Air conditioning compressor (lay it aside).
   d. Air conditioning bracket and belt tensioner.
6. Remove the following from the left cylinder head:
   a. Alternator (lay it aside).
   b. Left side engine accessory bracket with power steering pump (lay it aside).
7. Remove the spark plug and wires.
8. Remove the rocker arms and pushrods.
9. Remove the cylinder head bolts by loosening them in sequence. Remove the cylinder head.
10. Using a putty knife, clean the gasket mounting surfaces.

NOTE: If a steel head gasket is used, coat both sides with sealer. If a composition head gasket is used, do not use sealer.

11. Installation is the reverse of removal. Using a new gasket, position it on the dowel pins, with the words **This Side Up** facing upwards. Torque the cylinder head-to-engine bolts in sequence to 65 ft. lbs. Use 3 steps when torquing.

CLEANING AND INSPECTION

1. Remove the valve assemblies from the cylinder head.
2. Using a small wire power brush, clean the carbon from the combustion chambers and the valve ports.
3. Inspect the cylinder head for cracks in the exhaust ports, combustion chambers or external cracks to the water chamber.
4. Thoroughly clean the valve guides using a suitable wire bore brush.

NOTE: Excessive valve stem-to-bore clearance will cause excessive oil consumption and may cause valve breakage. Insufficient clearance will result in noisy and sticky functioning of the valve and disturb engine smoothness.

5. Measure the valve stem clearance as follows:
   a. Clamp a dial indicator on one side of the cylinder head rocker arm cover gasket rail.
   b. Locate the indicator so movement of the valve stem from side to side (crosswise to the head) will cause a direct movement of the indicator stem. The indicator stem must contact the side of the valve stem just above the valve guide.
   c. Prop the valve head about $^1/_{16}$ in. (1.6mm) off the valve seat.

Measuring valve stem clearance with a dial gauge

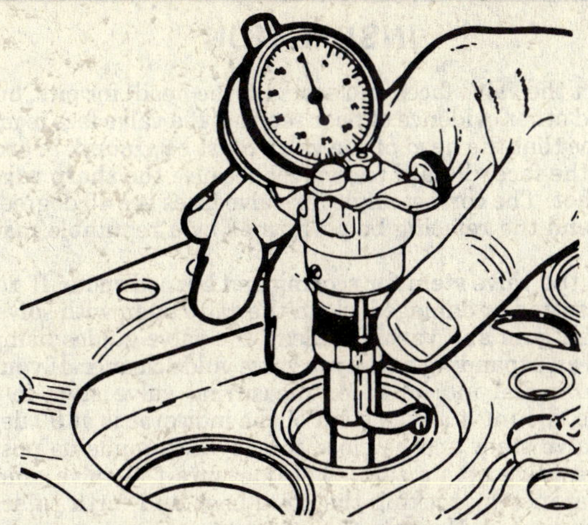

Checking the valve seat concentricity with a run-out gauge

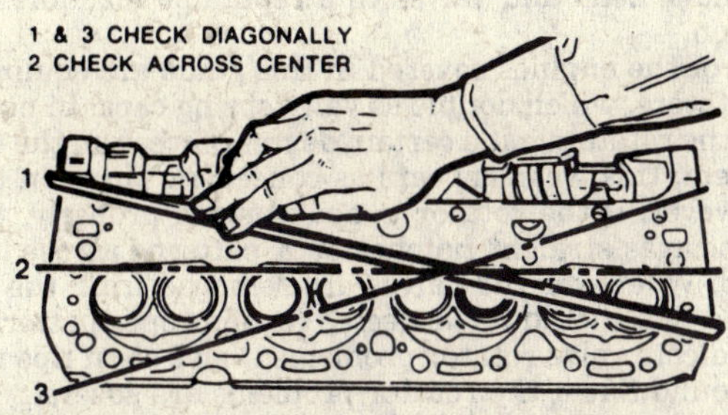

Checking the cylinder head for warpage

d. Move the stem of the valve from side to side using light pressure to obtain a clearance reading. If the clearance exceeds specifications, it will be necessary to ream (for oversize valves) or knurl (raise the bore for original valves) the valve guides.

6. Inspect the rocker arm studs for wear or damage.
7. Install a dial micrometer into the valve guide and check the valve seat forconcentricity.

RESURFACING

1. Using a straightedge, check the cylinder head for warpage.
2. If warpage exceeds 0.003 in. in a 6 in. span, or 0.006 in. over the total length, the cylinder head must be resurfaced. Resurfacing can be performed at most machine shops.

NOTE: When resurfacing the cylinder head(s), the intake manifold mounting position is altered and must be corrected by machining a proportionate amount from the intake manifold flange.

Valves

REMOVAL AND INSTALLATION

Cylinder Head Removed

NOTE: The following procedures requires the use of a valve spring compressor tool J-15062 or equivalent.

1. Remove the cylinder head.
2. Remove the rocker arm assemblies or the rocker arm nuts, the ball washers and the rocker arms, if not previously done.

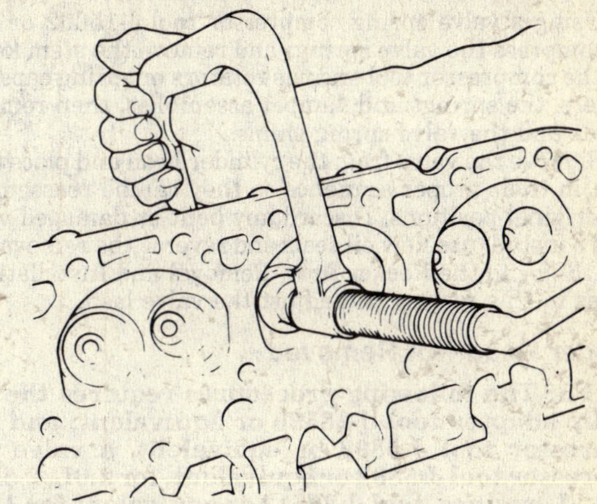

Compression valve spring tool – typical

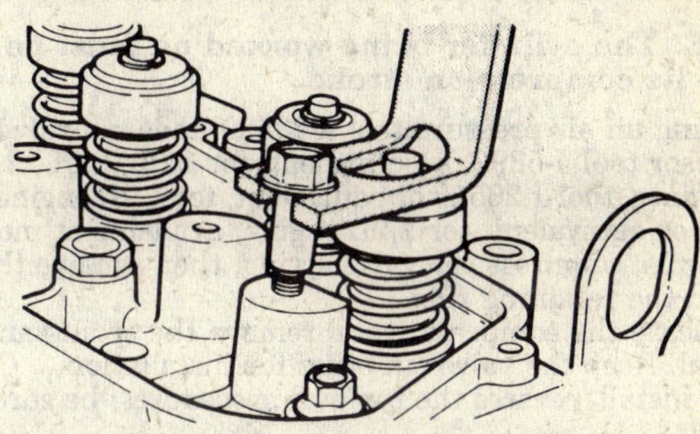

Using tool J-5892 to remove the valve keepers – 2.0L, 2.5L, 2.8L and 4.3L engines

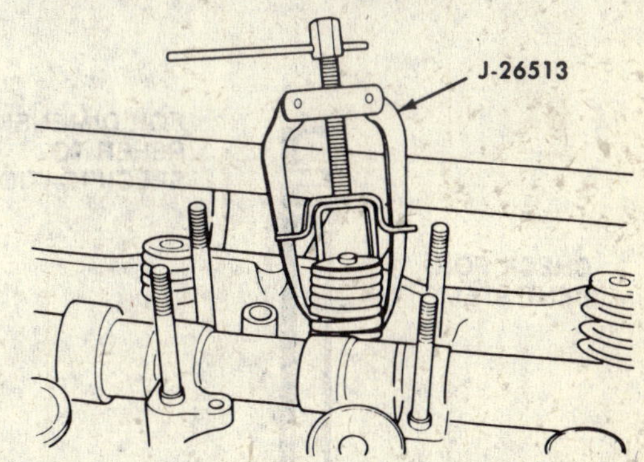

Using tool J-26513 to remove the valve keepers – 1.9L engine

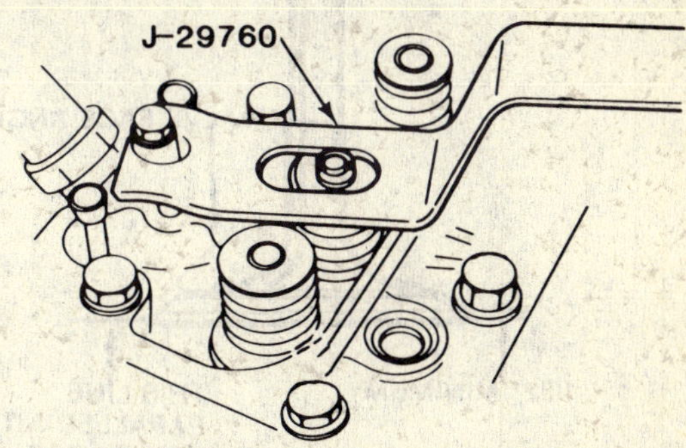

Using tool J-29760 to remove the valve keepers – 2.2L engine

3. Using a valve spring compressor tool J-15062 or equivalent, compress the valve springs and remove the stem keys. Release the compressor tool and the rotators or spring caps, the oil shedders, the springs and damper assemblies, then remove the oil seals and the valve spring shims.

4. Remove the valve from the cylinder head and place them in a rack in their proper sequence so they can be reassembled in their original positions. Discard any bent or damaged valves.

5. To install, use new oil seals and reverse the removal procedures. Refer to the Rocker Arm, Removal and Installation procedures in this section and adjust the valve lash.

Cylinder Head Not Removed

NOTE: The following procedures requires the use of GM air adapter tool J-23590 or equivalent, and spring compressor tool J-5892 or equivalent, a valve spring compressor tool J-5892 or equivalent, for 2.0L, 2.5L, 2.8L and 4.3L engines, tool J-26513 or equivalent for 1.9L engine or tool J-29760 or equivalent, for 2.2L engine.

1. Remove the spark plug (in the cylinder being worked on).

NOTE: The cylinder being worked on must be at the TDC of its compression stroke.

2. Using an air pressure tool J-23590 and/or a valve spring compressor tool J-5892 or equivalent, for 2.0L, 2.5L, 2.8L and 4.3L engines, tool J-26513 or equivalent, for 1.9L engine or tool J-29760 or equivalent, for 2.2L engine, available at most auto parts stores, compress the valve spring, then remove the valve keys and the retaining ring.

3. Release the compressor and remove the spring and valve stem seal. Keep the valves in order for installation.

4. To install, reverse the removal procedures; be sure to use new seals.

NOTE: Keep all parts in order so they may be assembled in their original locations.

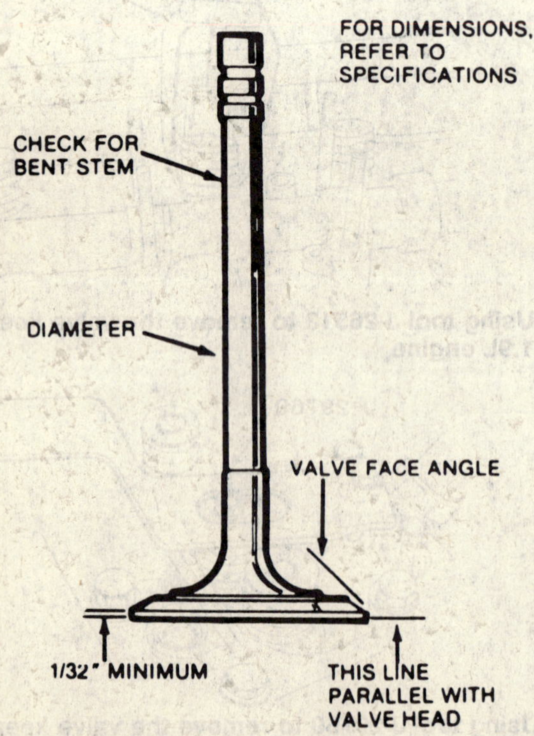

Critical valve dimensions

INSPECTION

Inspect the valve faces and seats (in the head) for pits, burned spots and other evidence of poor seating. If a valve face is in such bad shape that the head of the valve must be ground, in order to true up the face, discard the valve, because the sharp edge will run too hot. The correct angle for valve faces are 45 degrees. We recommend the refacing be performed by a reputable machine shop.

Check the valve stem for scoring and burned spots. If not noticeably scored or damaged, clean the valve stem with solvent to remove all gum and varnish. Clean the valve guides using solvent and an expanding wire-type valve guide cleaner. If you have access to a dial indicator for measuring valve stem-to-guide clearance, mount it so the stem of the indicator is at 90 degrees to the valve stem and as close to the valve guide as possible. Move the valve off its seat, then measure the valve guide-to-stem clearance by rocking the stem back and forth to actuate the dial indicator. Measure the valve stem diameter using a micrometer and compare to specifications to determine whether the stem or guide wear is responsible for the excess clearance. If a dial indicator and micrometer are not available to you, take the cylinder head and valves to a reputable machine shop for inspection.

Some of the engines covered in this guide are equipped with valve rotators, which double as valve spring caps. In normal operation the rotators put a certain degree of wear on the tip of the valve stem; this wear appears as concentric rings on the stem tip. However, if the rotator is not working properly, the wear may appear as straight notches or **X** patterns across the valve stem tip. Whenever the valves are removed from the cylinder head, the tips should be inspected for improper pattern, which could indicate valve rotator problems. Valve stem tips will have to be ground flat if the rotator problems are severe.

REFACING

NOTE: All valve grinding operations should be performed by a qualified machine shop; only the valve lapping operation is recommended to be performed by the inexperienced mechanic.

Valve Lapping

When valve faces and seats have been refaced and/or recut, or if they are determined to be in good condition, the valves MUST BE lapped in to ensure efficient sealing when the valve closes against the seat.

1. Invert the cylinder head so the combustion chambers are facing upward.

2. Lightly lubricate the valve stems with clean engine oil and coat the valve seats with valve grinding compound. Install the valves in the cylinder head as numbered.

3. Attach the suction cup of a valve lapping tool to a valve head. ***You will probably have to moisten the cup to securely attach the tool to the valve.***

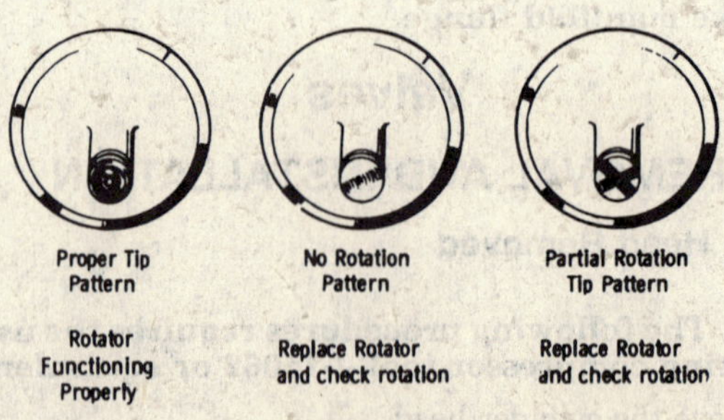

View of the valve stem wear patterns

Lapping the valves by hand

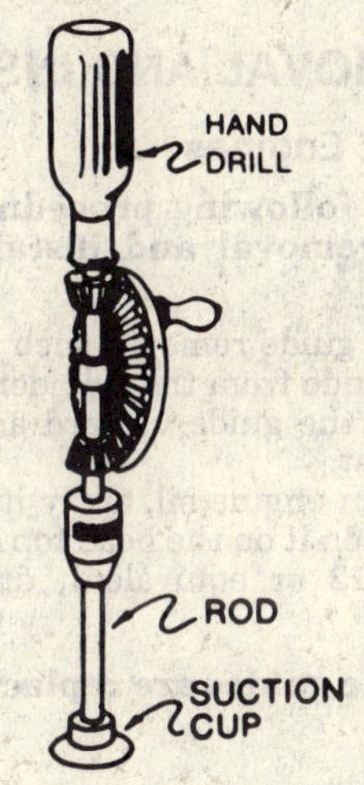

Home made valve lapping tool

4. Rotate the tool between the palms, changing position and lifting the tool often to prevent grooving. Lap the valve until a smooth polished seat is evident (you may have to add a bit more compound after some lapping is done).

5. Remove the valve and tool, then remove ALL traces of the grinding compound with a solvent-soaked rag or rinse the head with solvent.

NOTE: Valve lapping can also be done by fastening a suction cup to a piece of drill rod in a hand egg-beater type drill. Proceed as above, using the drill as a lapping tool. Due to the higher speeds involved when using the hand drill, care must be exercised to avoid grooving the seat. Lift the tool and change direction of rotation often.

Valve Springs

REMOVAL AND INSTALLATION

If the cylinder head is removed from the engine, refer to the Valve, Removal and Installation procedures in this section and remove the valve spring.

NOTE: The following procedures requires the use of GM air adapter tool J-23590 or equivalent, and spring compressor tool J-5892 for 2.0L, 2.5L, 2.8L and 4.3L engines, tool J-26513 for 1.9L engine, tool J-29760 or equivalent for 2.2L diesel engine.

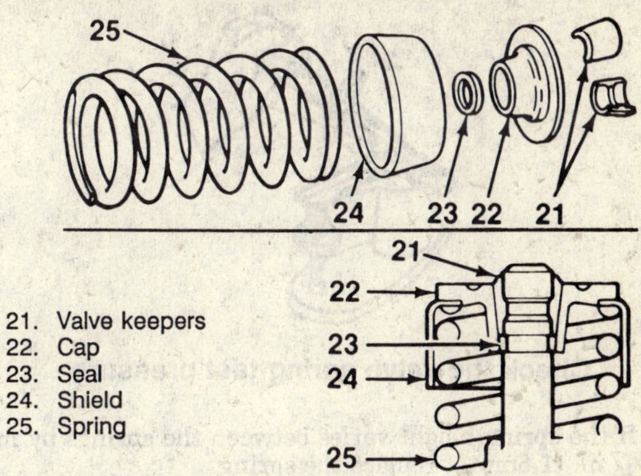

Exploded view of the valve assembly

1. Remove the rocker arm nuts/bolts and the rocker arms.
2. Remove the spark plugs from the cylinders being worked on.
3. To remove the valve keepers, perform the following procedures:
   a. Using the GM air adapter tool J-23590 or equivalent, install it into the spark plug hole.
   b. Apply compressed air to the cylinder to hold the valves in place.
   c. Install a rocker arm nut/bolt into the cylinder head.
   d. Using the GM spring compressor tool J-5892 for 2.0L, 2.5L, 2.8L and 4.3L engines, tool J-26513 for 1.9L engine, tool J-29760 or equivalent for 2.2L diesel engine, compress the valve spring and remove the valve keepers.

   e. Carefully release the spring pressure and remove the compressor tool.
4. Remove the valve cap, the shield and the spring.
5. Remove the O-ring seal and valve stem seal.
6. Inspect the valve spring, replace as necessary.
7. Lubricate the parts with engine oil, then install a new O-ring seal and valve stem seal onto each valve stem.
8. To complete the installation, adjust the valves and reverse the removal procedures. Start the engine, then check and/or adjust the timing.

INSPECTION

1. Position the valve spring on a flat, clean surface next to a square.

2. Measure the height of the spring and rotate it against the engine of the square to measure the distortion (out-of-round-

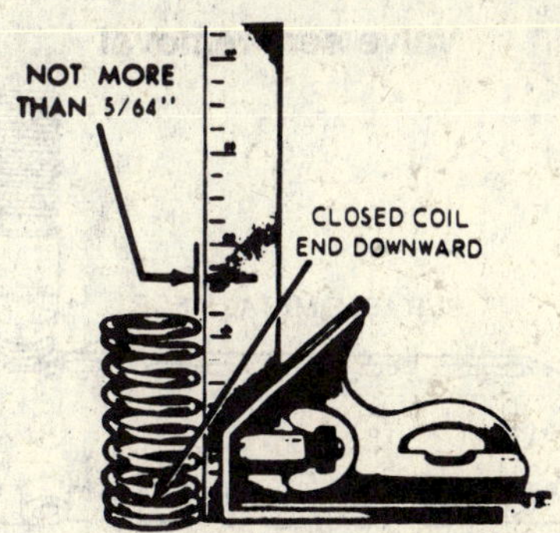

Check the valve spring free length and squareness

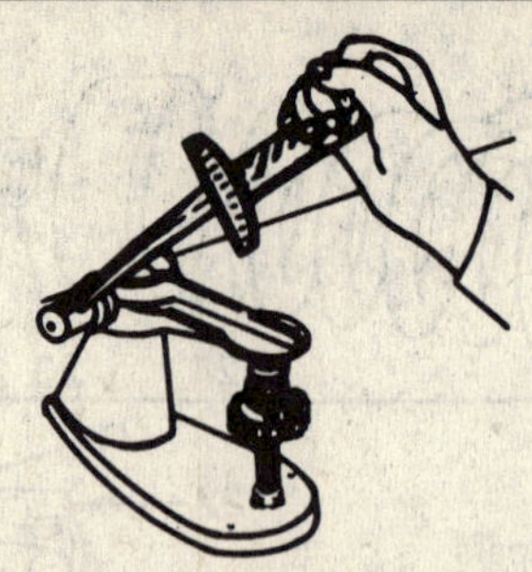

Check the valve spring test pressure

ness). If the spring height varies between the springs by more than 1/16 in. (1.6mm) , replace the spring.

3. Using a valve spring tester, check the spring pressure at the installed and compressed height.

Valve Seats

REMOVAL AND INSTALLATION

1.9L and 2.2L Engines

NOTE: The following procedures requires the use of an arc welder, a wire brush, a slide hammer puller, dry ice and an arbor press.

1. Weld pieces of welding rod to several points around the seat, then allow the head to cool for about 5 minutes.
2. Using a slide hammer puller, remove the valve seats attached to the welding rods.
3. Using a wire brush, clean the valve seat recess carefully.
4. Place the new valve seat in dry ice while heating the recess in the head with steam. Take about 5 minutes for this procedure. Perform the heating and cooling simultaneously.
5. Using protective gloves, insert the valve seat into the cylinder head recess. The seat depth below the combustion chamber face should be 0.0031–0.0047 in. (0.08–0.12mm).

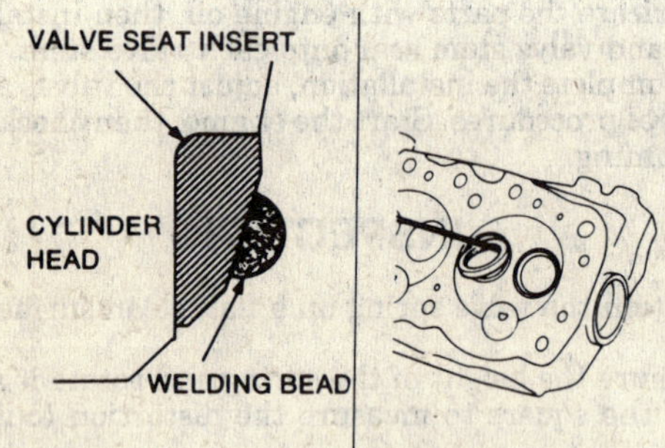

Valve seat removal

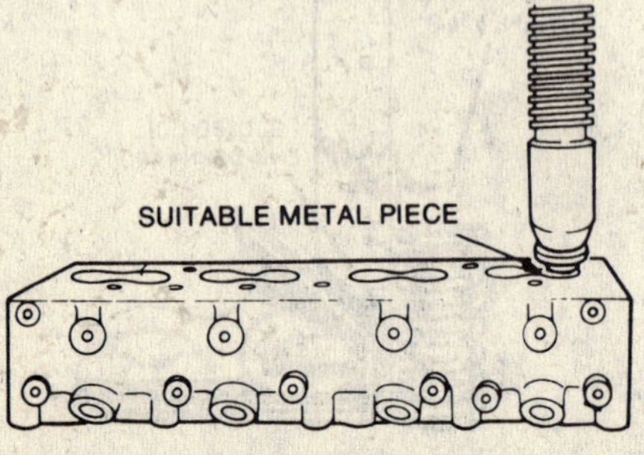

Valve seat installation using a press

6. Cut the valve seat to the angle shown in the valve specifications chart. Valve seat contact width should be 0.0472–0.0630 in. (1.2–1.6mm).
7. Polish the seat using lapping compound and a suction type lapper.
8. Smear the seat and the face of a correctly ground and cleaned valve with a dye such as Prussian blue. Turn the valve against the seat several times, remove the valve and check that the dye shows and even contact.

2.0L, 2.5L, 2.8L and 4.3L Engines

The valve seats used on these engines are an integral part of the cylinder head and are not replaceable; they should be refaced, cleaned and lapped, only. See the valve specifications chart for proper seat angle.

Valve Guides

REMOVAL AND INSTALLATION

1.9L and 2.2L Engines

NOTE: The following procedures requires the use of valve guide removal and installation tool J-26512 or equivalent.

1. Insert the guide remover such as tool J-26512 or equivalent, into the guide from the cylinder head's combustion chamber side. Drive the guide upward and out. Remove the lower valve spring seat.
2. Using clean engine oil, apply it to the outside of the new guide and position it on the head top side. Using opposite side of the tool J-26512 or equivalent, drive the guide in until it bottoms.

NOTE: If the guides are replaced, the valves should be replaced also.

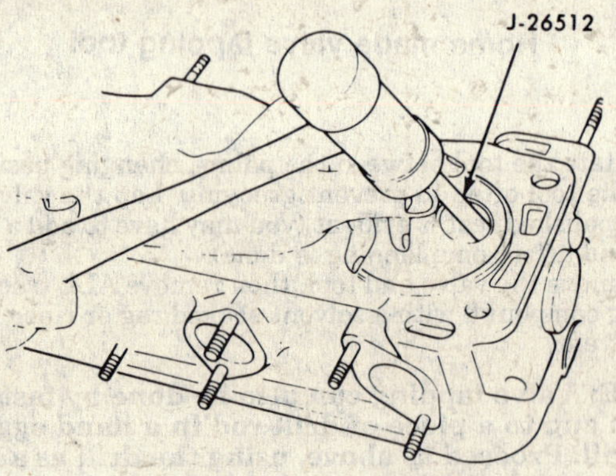

Remove the valve guides

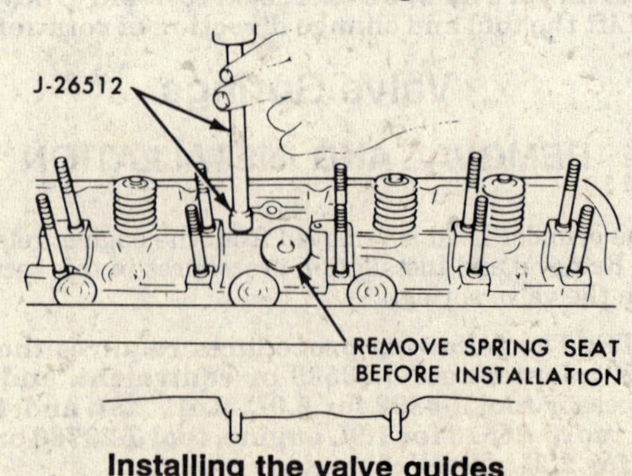

Installing the valve guides

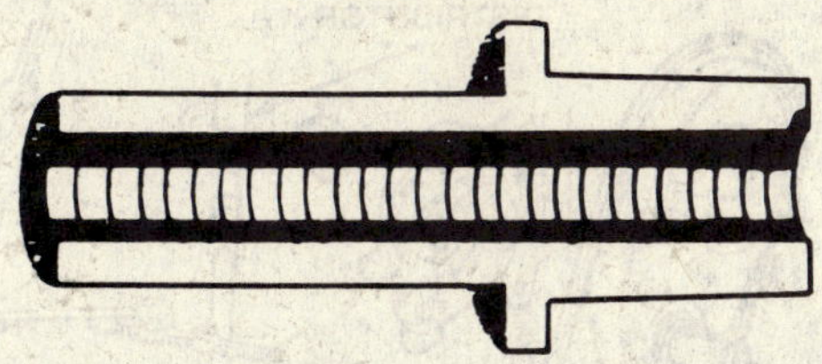

Sectional view of a knurled valve guide

3. The guide should protrude 0.4724 in. (12mm) above the head surface. Grind the end of the guide to achieve this height. Make certain that the guide has bottomed before grinding.

2.0L, 2.5L, 2.8L and 4.3L Engines

The valve guides are not replaceable. The guides should be reamed to accommodate valves with oversized stems. Oversized stems are available in 0.089mm, 0.394mm and 0.775mm.

KNURLING

Valve guides which are not excessively worn or distorted may, in some cases, be knurled. knurling is a process in which metal is displaced and raised, thereby reducing clearance. Knurling also provides excellent oil control.

This procedure should only be performed by a qualified machine shop.

Valve Lifter

REMOVAL AND INSTALLATION

2.0L Engine

1. Remove the rocker arm covers.
2. Loosen the rocker arms and remove the pushrods and guide plates.
3. Using Valve Lifter Removal tool J-29834 or equivalent, remove the valve lifters.

NOTE: Keep all components in order. If reusing components, install them into their original positions.

4. For proper rotation during engine operation, the lifter bottom must be convex. Check the lifter bottom for proper shape using a straightedge. If the lifter bottom is not convex, replace the lifter. Chances are if lifters are in need of replacement, so is the camshaft.
5. Using the valve lifter tool, install the lifters into the block.
6. Installation is the reverse of removal. Adjust the valve lash.

2.2L Diesel Engine

NOTE: The diesel engine uses solid type lifters.

1. Remove the rocker arm cover and side cover.
2. Remove the rocker arm shaft assembly.
3. Remove the pushrods.
4. Remove the hydraulic lifters using an appropriate lifter removal tool.
5. Installation is the reverse of removal.
6. Adjust the valve lash.

2.5L Engine

1. Remove the rocker arm and pushrod covers.

NOTE: Keep all components in order. If reusing components, install them into their original positions. If a new hydraulic lifter is being installed, all sealer coating inside the lifter must be removed.

2. Remove the pushrods.
3. Remove the lifter studs and retainers.
4. Remove the lifter guides and lifters.
5. Inspect the lifter and lifter bore for wear and scuffing. Examine the roller for freedom of movement and/or flat spots on the roller surface.
6. Installation is the reverse of removal.

2.8L Engine

Some engines have both standard size and 0.010 in. (0.25mm) oversize valve lifters. The cylinder block will be marked with a white paint mark and 0.25mm O.S. stamp where the oversize lifters are used. If lifters replacement is necessary, use new lifters with a narrow flat along the lower ¾ of the body length. This provides additional oil to the cam lobe and lifter surfaces.

NOTE: This procedure requires the use of a Hydraulic Lifter Remover tool J-9290-1.

1. Remove the rocker arm covers.
2. Remove the intake manifold.
3. Remove the rocker arm nuts and balls.
4. Remove the rocker arms and pushrods.

NOTE: Keep all components in order. If reusing components, install them into their original positions.

5. Using the Hydraulic Lifter Remover tool, remove the lifters.
6. For proper rotation during engine operation, the lifter bottom must be convex. Check the lifter bottom for proper shape using a straightedge. If the lifter bottom is not convex, replace the lifter. Chances are if lifters are in need of replacement, so is the camshaft.
7. Lubricate and install the lifters.
8. Installation is the reverse of removal.
9. Adjust the valve lash.

4.3L Engine

1. Remove the rocker arm cover.
2. Remove the intake manifold.

NOTE: Keep all components in order. If reusing components, install them into their original positions.

3. Remove the rocker arms and pushrods.
4. Remove the hydraulic lifter retainer bolts, retainers and restrictors.
5. Inspect the lifter and lifter bore for wear and scuffing. Examine the roller for freedom of movement and/or flat spots on the roller surface.
6. Installation is the reverse of removal.
7. Adjust the valve lash.

Oil Pan

REMOVAL AND INSTALLATION

1.9L Engine

NOTE: On 4WD, the engine must be removed before removing the oil pan.

1. Disconnect the negative battery terminal.
2. Raise and support the vehicle on jack stands.
3. Position a catch pan under the oil pan, remove the drain plug and drain the oil.

CAUTION

The EPA warns that prolonged contact with used engine oil may cause a number of skin disorders, including cancer! You should make every effort to minimize your exposure to used engine oil. Protective gloves should be worn when changing the oil. Wash your hands and any other exposed skin areas as soon as possible after exposure to used engine oil. Soap and water, or waterless hand cleaner should be used.

4. If equipped, remove the front splash shield.
5. Remove the front crossmember, if necessary.
6. Disconnect the relay rod from the idler arm and lower the relay rod.
7. Remove the left side bellhousing bracket and the vacuum line from the oil pan.
8. Remove the oil pan-to-engine bolts and the pan.

NOTE: It may be necessary to remove the motor mounts and raise the engine in order to remove the oil pan.

9. Using a putty knife, clean the gasket mounting surfaces.
10. To install, use a new gasket, seals, RTV sealant, if necessary, and reverse the removal procedures. Torque the oil pan-to-engine bolts to 43 inch lbs.

2.0L Engine

1. Disconnect the negative battery terminal.
2. Position a catch pan under the oil pan, remove the drain plug and drain the crankcase.

CAUTION

The EPA warns that prolonged contact with used engine oil may cause a number of skin disorders, including cancer! You should make every effort to minimize your exposure to used engine oil. Protective gloves should be worn when changing the oil. Wash your hands and any other exposed skin areas as soon as possible after exposure to used engine oil. Soap and water, or waterless hand cleaner should be used.

3. Raise and support the front of the vehicle on jackstands.
4. If equipped with air conditioning, remove the air conditioning compressor brace.
5. Remove the exhaust shield and disconnect the exhaust pipe from the exhaust manifold.
6. Remove the starter motor (position it out of the way) and the flywheel cover.
7. Remove the oil pan-to-engine bolts and the oil pan from the vehicle.
8. Using a putty knife, clean the gasket mounting surfaces. Make sure the sealing surfaces on the pan, cylinder block and front cover are clean and free of oil.
9. To install, use a new gasket, RTV sealant, apply an ⅛ in. bead to the oil pan sealing surface, a new oil pan rear seal and reverse the removal procedures. Torque the oil pan-to-engine bolts to 9–13 ft. lbs. Refill the crankcase with clean engine oil. Start the engine and check for leaks.

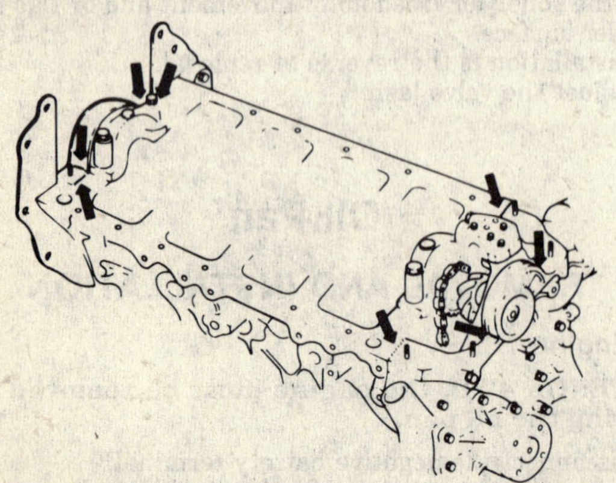

Oil pan sealant location — 1.9L engine

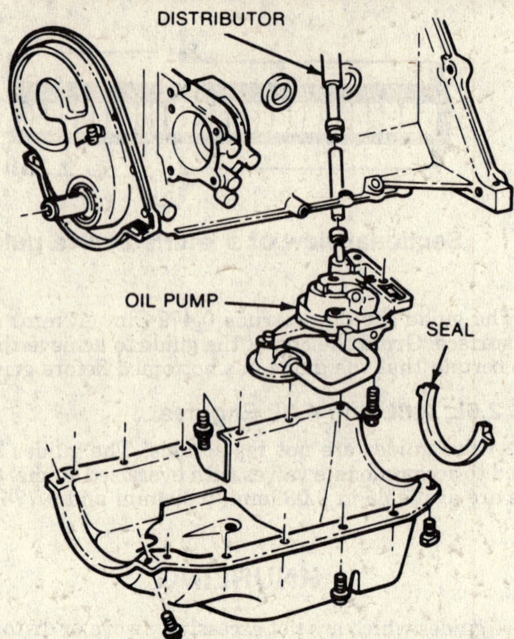

Exploded view of the oil pan — 2.0L engine

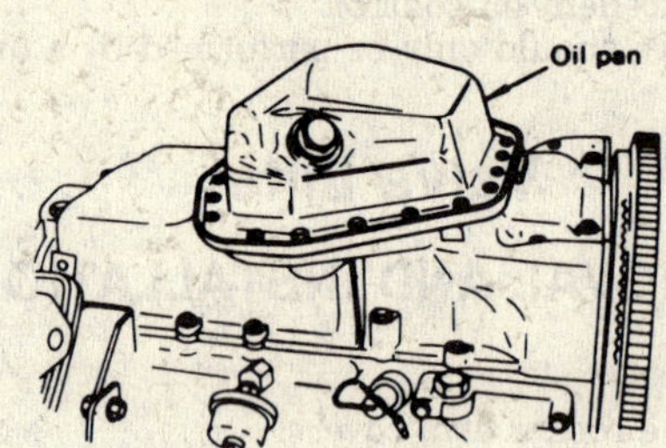

View of the oil pan — 2.2L diesel engine

2.2L Diesel Engine

1. Refer to the Engine, Removal and Installation procedures in this section and remove the engine and secure it to a workstand.
2. Remove the oil pan-to-crankcase bolts, the crankcase-to-engine bolts and the oil pans from the engine.
3. Using a putty knife, clean the gasket mounting surfaces.
4. Make sure the sealing surfaces on the pan, the cylinder block and the crankcase are clean and free of oil.
5. To install, use a new gasket, RTV sealant, apply an ⅛ in. bead to the oil pan sealing surface, and reverse the removal procedures. Torque the oil pan-to-crankcase bolts to 5–9 ft. lbs. and/or the crankcase-to-engine bolts to 15 ft. lbs. Refill the crankcase with clean engine oil. Start the engine and check for leaks.

2.5L Engine

1. Disconnect the negative battery terminal.
2. Raise and support the front of the vehicle on jackstands.
3. Position a catch pan under the crankcase and drain the oil from the engine.

CAUTION

The EPA warns that prolonged contact with used engine oil may cause a number of skin disorders, including cancer! You should make every effort to minimize your exposure to used engine oil. Protective gloves should be worn when changing the oil. Wash your hands and any other exposed skin areas as soon as possible after exposure to used engine oil. Soap and water, or waterless hand cleaner should be used.

4. Remove the strut rods. Remove the flywheel/torque convertor dust cover from the bellhousing.
5. Disconnect the electrical connectors from the starter, then remove the starter-to-engine bolts, the brace and the starter from the vehicle.
6. Disconnect the exhaust pipe(s) from the exhaust manifold(s) and the exhaust pipe-to-catalytic converter hanger(s).
7. If necessary, remove the engine mount through bolts, then using an engine lifting device, raise the engine (enough) in order to make room for the oil pan removal.
8. Remove the oil pan-to-engine bolts and the oil pan from the engine.
9. Using a putty knife, clean the gasket mounting surfaces. Using solvent, clean the excess oil from the mounting surfaces.
10. Apply a $^3/_{16}$ in. (4.7mm) bead of RTV sealant to the oil pan flange (keep the bead inside the bolt holes), the rear main bearing, the timing gear cover and the engine block sealing surface. Refill the crankcase with fresh oil. Start the engine, establish normal operating temperatures and check for leaks.

2.8L and 4.3L Engines

2WD MODELS

1. Remove the engine and secure it to a workstand.
2. Remove the oil pan-to-engine bolts and the pan.
3. Using a putty knife, clean the gasket mounting surfaces. Make sure the sealing surfaces are free of oil and old RTV material.

NOTE: The oil pan does not use a preformed gasket; it is sealed with RTV gasket material.

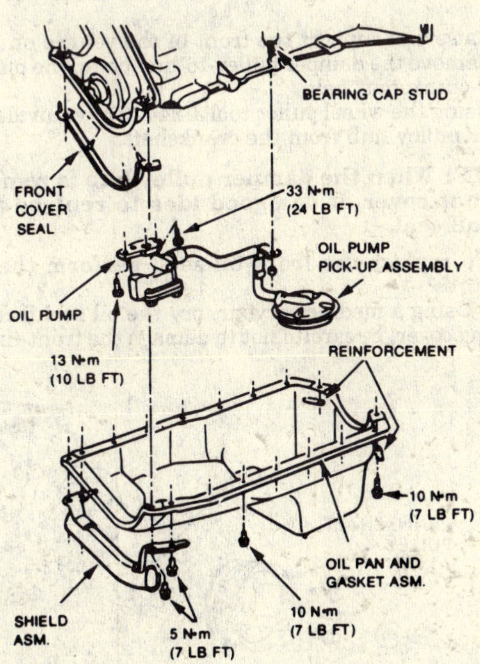

Exploded view of the oil pan and oil pump assembly — 2.5L engine

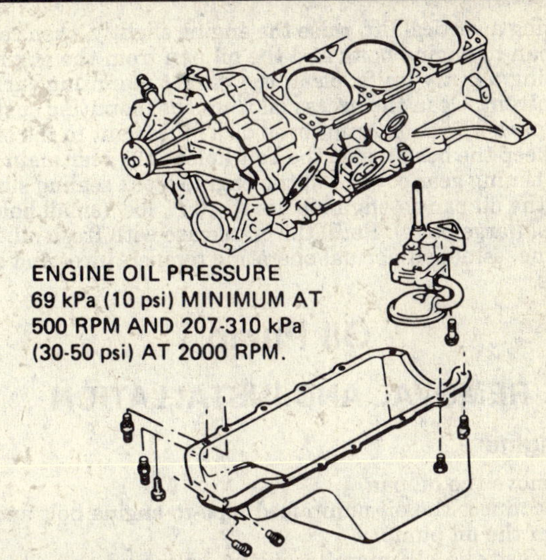

Exploded view of the oil pan and oil pump assembly — 2.8L and 4.3L engines

4. Using RTV sealant, run an ⅛ in. bead of sealer along the entire sealing surface of the pan.
5. Position the pan on the engine and finger tighten the bolts. Torque the smaller bolts to 10 ft. lbs.; the larger bolts to 22 ft. lbs. Refill the crankcase with clean engine oil. Start the engine and check for leaks.

4WD MODELS

1. Disconnect the negative battery terminal.
2. Remove the dipstick.
3. Raise and support the front of the vehicle on jackstands.
4. Remove the drive belt splash pan, the front axle shield and the transfer case shield.
5. Remove the brake line clips from the crossmember and the 2nd crossmember from the vehicle.
6. If equipped with an automatic transmission, remove the hanger bolt and the exhaust pipe clamp from the catalytic converter, then disconnect the exhaust pipes from the exhaust manifolds and move the exhaust pipe rearward.
7. From the front drive pinion, remove the drive shaft-to-drive pinion nuts/bolts and the drive shaft from the vehicle.
8. Remove the flywheel cover-to-engine braces and the engine-to-chassis braces.
9. Remove the flywheel cover, the starter-to-engine bolts and the starter (lay it aside).
10. Remove the steering shock absorber from the frame bracket. Using a scribing tool, mark the position of the idler arm-to-chassis, then remove the steering gear-to-chassis bolts, the steering gear, the idler arm-to-chassis bolts and the idler arm from the vehicle.
11. Remove the front differential-to-bracket bolts from the sides of the chassis, then pull the steering gear and linkage forward.
12. Remove the motor mount through bolts.
13. Position a catch pan under the oil pan, remove the drain plug and drain the crankcase.

CAUTION

The EPA warns that prolonged contact with used engine oil may cause a number of skin disorders, including cancer! You should make every effort to minimize your exposure to used engine oil. Protective gloves should be worn when changing the oil. Wash your hands and any other exposed skin areas as soon as possible after exposure to used engine oil. Soap and water, or waterless hand cleaner should be used.

14. Using a vertical lift, raise the engine slightly, then remove the oil pan-to-engine bolts and the oil pan from the engine.
15. Using a putty knife, clean the gasket mounting surfaces. Using solvent, clean the excess oil from the mounting surfaces.
16. Apply a $^3/_{16}$ in. (4.7mm) bead of RTV sealant to the oil pan flange (keep the bead inside the bolt holes), the rear main bearing, the timing gear cover and the engine block sealing surface. Torque the oil pan-to-engine bolts to 10 ft. lbs. (small bolts) or 22 ft. lbs. (large bolts). Refill the crankcase with fresh oil. Start the engine, establish normal operating temperatures and check for leaks.

Oil Pump

REMOVAL AND INSTALLATION

1.9L Engine

1. Remove the oil pan.
2. Disconnect the oil pump feed pipe-to-engine bolt and the pipe from the oil pump.
3. Remove the oil pump-to engine bolts and the oil pump from the engine.
4. To install, reverse the removal procedures.

2.0L Engine

1. Remove the oil pan.
2. Remove the oil pump-to-engine bolts and carefully lower the oil pump.

NOTE: To ensure immediate oil pressure upon start-up, the oil pump gear cavity should be (primed) packed with petroleum jelly.

3. To install, reverse the removal procedures. Torque the oil pump-to-engine bolts to 26–35 ft. lbs.

2.2L Diesel Engine

1. Refer to the Oil Pan, Removal and Installation procedures in this section, then remove the crankcase-to-engine bolts and the crankcase together with the oil pan.

NOTE: Pry off the crankcase by fitting a screwdriver into the slots in the crankcase.

2. Remove the oil pipe sleeve nut.
3. Remove the oil pump-to-engine bolts and the oil pump with oil pipe from the engine.
4. To install, reverse the removal procedures and leave the joints semi-tight.
5. Fully tighten the oil pump fixing bolts and then the oil pipe joints.
6. To complete the installation, reverse the removal procedures.

2.5L Engine

1. Remove the oil pan.
2. Remove the oil pump-to-rear main bearing cap bolts, the pump and the extension shaft.
3. To install, assemble the oil pump and the extension shaft into the rear main bearing cap; be sure to align the slot (on top of the extension shaft) with the drive tang (on the lower end of the distributor driveshaft).
4. Torque the oil pump-to-bearing cap bolts to 22 ft. lbs. Refill the crankcase with fresh oil. Start the engine, establish normal operating temperatures and check for leaks.

2.8L and 4.3L Engine

1. Remove the oil pan.
2. Remove the oil pump-to-engine bolts and oil pump from the vehicle.
3. To install, reverse the removal procedures. Torque the oil pump-to-engine bolts to 26–35 ft. lbs. for 2.8L engine or 65 ft. lbs. for 4.3L engine.

Crankshaft Damper and Oil Seal

REMOVAL AND INSTALLATION

1.9L Engine

1. Disconnect the negative battery terminal.
2. Using a catch pan, place it under the radiator and drain the cooling system.

CAUTION

When draining the coolant, keep in mind that cats and dogs are attracted by the ethylene glycol antifreeze, and are quite likely to drink any that is left in an uncovered container or in puddles on the ground. This will prove fatal in sufficient quantity. Always drain the coolant into a sealable container. Coolant should be reused unless it is contaminated or several years old.

3. Remove the cooling fan-to-engine bolts and the fan from the engine.
4. Remove the upper and lower radiator hoses from the engine.
5. Remove the radiator-to-chassis screws and the radiator from the vehicle.
6. Remove the alternator and air conditioning compressor drive belts.
7. Remove the crankshaft pulley center bolt and the pulley/hub assembly from the crankshaft.
8. To install, reverse the removal procedures. Torque the crankshaft pulley center bolt to 87 ft. lbs. Adjust the drive belts.

2.0L Engine

NOTE: The following procedure requires the use of the wheel puller tool J-24420 or equivalent, and the oil sealer installation tool J-23042 or equivalent.

1. Disconnect the negative battery terminal.
2. Remove the accessory drive belts from the crankshaft pulley.
3. Raise and support the front of the vehicle on jackstands.
4. Remove the damper pulley-to-hub bolts, the pulley and the hub-to-crankshaft bolt.
5. Using the wheel puller tool J-24420 or equivalent, pull the damper pulley hub from the crankshaft.

NOTE: When the damper pulley hub is removed from the front cover, it is a good idea to replace the crankshaft oil seal.

6. To replace the front oil seal, perform the following procedures:
    a. Using a medium prybar, pry the oil seal from the front timing cover; be careful not to damage the front timing cover.

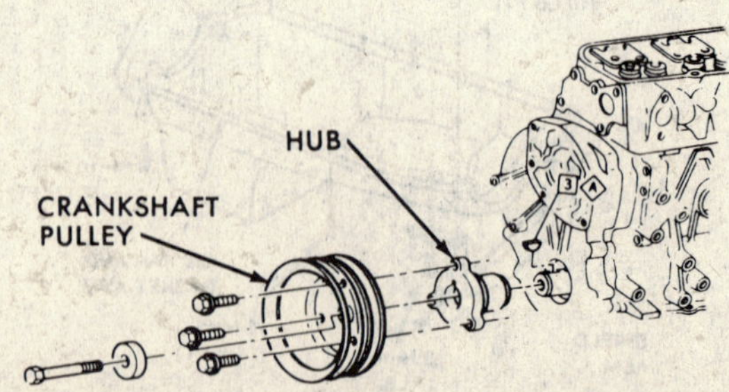

Exploded view of the damper pulley and hub assembly — 2.0L engine

b. Using a new oil seal and the oil sealer installation tool J-23042 or equivalent, lubricate the seal lips with engine oil and drive the new seal into the timing cover, until it seats.

7. To complete the installation, reverse the removal procedures. Torque the hub-to-crankshaft bolt to 66–88 ft. lbs. and the damper pulley-to-hub bolts to 29–44 ft. lbs. Adjust the drive belts.

2.2L Diesel Engine

1. Disconnect the negative battery terminal.

NOTE: If there is not enough room, it may be necessary to drain the cooling system and remove the radiator to provide enough room for the crankshaft pulley removal.

2. Loosen the accessory drive belt adjustments and remove the drive belts from the crankshaft pulley.
3. Remove the crankshaft pulley-to-crankshaft pulley center and the crankshaft pulley from the engine.

NOTE: To replace the front oil seal, it will be necessary to remove the timing belt and the crankshaft timing pulley.

4. To install, reverse the removal procedures. Install and adjust the drive belt tensions.

2.5L Engine

NOTE: The following procedure requires the use of the GM seal installer/centering tool J-34995 or equivalent.

1. Disconnect the negative battery terminal.
2. If equipped, remove the upper fan shroud. Loosen and remove the accessory-to-damper pulley drive belts.
3. Remove the damper pulley/hub assembly-to-crankshaft bolt and washer, then the pulley/hub assembly from the crankshaft.

NOTE: The damper pulley is connected to the damper pulley hub by 3 bolts; if necessary, remove the pulley-to-hub bolts and separate the pulley from the hub. When it becomes necessary to remove the damper pulley/hub assembly, always replace the front oil seal with a new one.

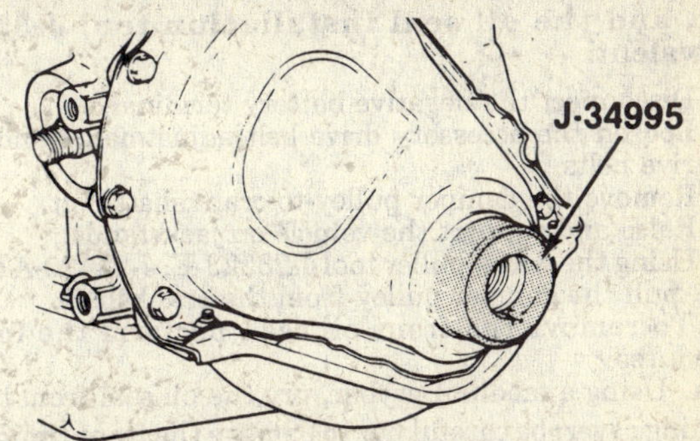

Using tool No. J-34995 to replace the front oil seal — 2.5L engine

4. Inspect the damper hub (oil seal surface) for rust or burrs; remove the roughness with fine emery cloth.

NOTE: When installing the damper pulley hub to the crankshaft, be careful not to damage the front oil seal.

5. To replace the timing cover oil seal, perform the following procedures:
   a. Using a medium prybar, pry the oil seal from the timing cover.
   b. Using the GM seal installer/centering tool J-34995 or equivalent, install the new oil seal into the timing cover, then remove the tool from the timing cover.
6. To install the damper hub, lubricate the it with engine oil, align it onto the keyway and reverse the removal procedures. Torque the damper pulley hub-to-crankshaft bolt to 160 ft. lbs. Install the drive belts and adjust the belt tension.

2.8L and 4.3L Engines

NOTE: The following procedure requires the use of the wheel puller tool J-23523-E, J-24420-A or equivalent, the torsional damper installer tool J-29113 or equiva-

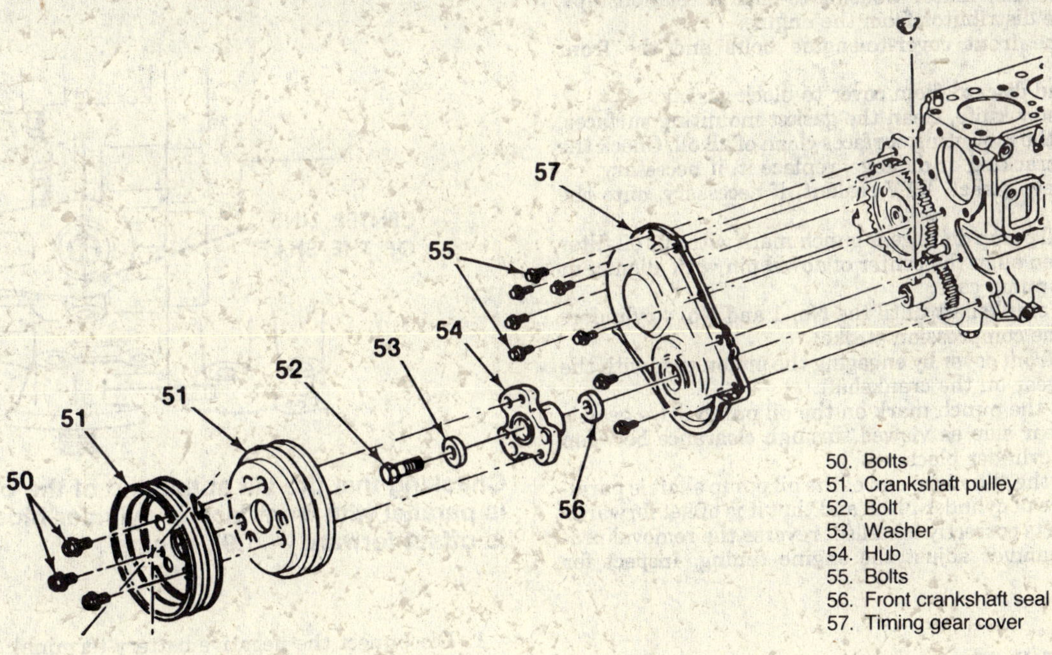

Exploded view of the crankshaft pulley assembly, the timing cover and the timing sprockets — 2.5L enigne

lent, and the oil seal installation tool J-35468 or equivalent.

1. Disconnect the negative battery terminal.
2. Loosen the accessory drive belt adjustments and remove the drive belts.
3. Remove the damper pulley-to-crankshaft bolt.
4. Raise and support the vehicle on jackstands.
5. Using the wheel puller tool J-23523-E, J-24420-A or equivalent, pull the damper pulley from the crankshaft.
6. To remove the front oil seal, perform the following procedures:
   a. Using a medium prybar, pry the oil seal from the front timing cover; be careful not to damage the front timing cover.
   b. Using engine oil, lubricate the new seal.
   c. Using the oil seal Installation tool J-35468 or equivalent, position it onto the timing cover and drive it into position, until it seats.
7. To complete the installation, reverse the removal procedures. Torque the damper pulley-to-crankshaft bolt to 70 ft. lbs. Adjust the drive belt tensions.

Timing (Front) Covers

REMOVAL AND INSTALLATION

1.9L Engine

1. Remove the cylinder head and the oil pan from the engine.
2. Remove the oil pickup tube from the oil pump.
3. Remove the harmonic balancer from the crankshaft.
4. Remove AIR pump drive belt.
5. If equipped with air conditioning, remove the compressor and move it aside, then remove compressor mounting brackets. If equipped with power steering, remove the power steering pump, the bracket and move it aside.

CAUTION

Do not remove any refrigerant lines from the air conditioning compressor.

6. Remove the distributor cap. Mark the rotor-to-distributor housing and the distributor housing-to-engine relationships, then remove the distributor from the engine.
7. Remove the front cover-to-engine bolts and the front cover.
8. Remove and discard from cover to block gasket.
9. Using a putty knife, clean the gasket mounting surfaces. Be sure to wipe the mounting surfaces clean of all oil. Check the front cover for cracking or damage, replace it, if necessary.
10. Install a new gasket, RTV sealant, if necessary, onto the cylinder block.
11. Align the oil pump drive gear punch mark with the oil filter side of cover; then align the center of dowel pin with alignment mark on the oil pump case.
12. Rotate the crankshaft until the No. 1 and No. 4 cylinders are at TDC of the compression stroke.
13. Install the front cover by engaging the pinion gear with the oil pump drive gear on the crankshaft.
14. Check that the punch mark on the oil pump drive gear is turned to the rear side as viewed through clearance between front cover and cylinder block.
15. Check that the slit at the end of the oil pump shaft is parallel with front face of cylinder block and that it is offset forward.
16. With all parts correctly installed, reverse the removal procedures. Check and/or adjust the engine timing. Inspect for leaks.

2.0L Engine

NOTE: The following procedure requires the use of the centering tool J-23042 or equivalent.

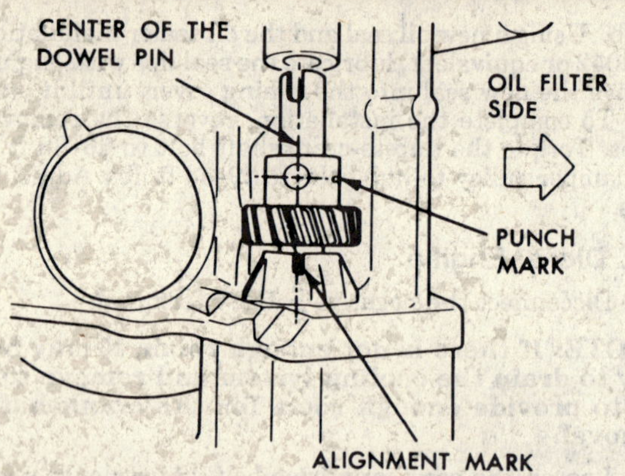

Aligning the oil pump drive gear mark with the oil filter side of cover and the center of dowel pin with the mark on the oil pump case — 1.9L engine

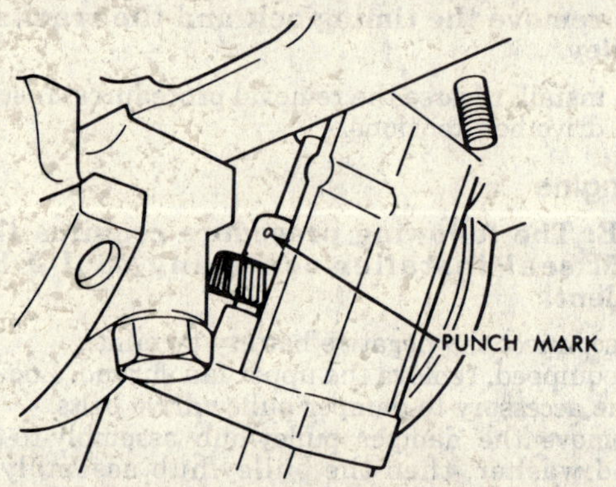

Checking that the punch mark on the oil pump drive gear is turned to the rear side as viewed through clearance between front cover and cylinder block — 1.9L engine

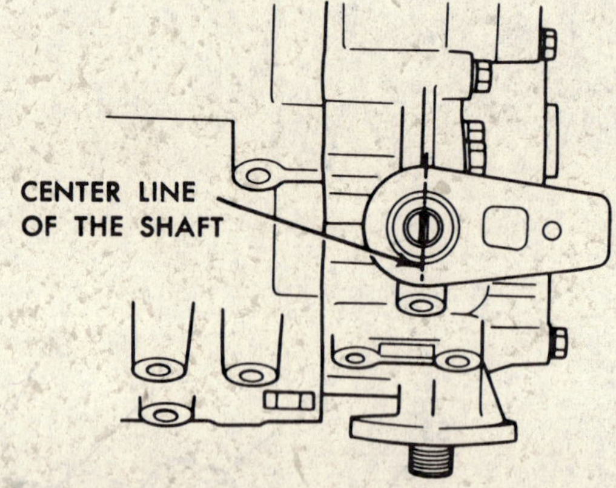

Checking that the slit at the end of the oil pump shaft is parallel with front face of cylinder block and that it is offset forward — 1.9L engine

1. Disconnect the negative battery terminal.
2. Position a catch pan under the radiator, open the drain cock and drain the cooling system.

CAUTION

When draining the coolant, keep in mind that cats and dogs are attracted by the ethylene glycol antifreeze, and are quite likely to drink any that is left in an uncovered container or in puddles on the ground. This will prove fatal in sufficient quantity. Always drain the coolant into a sealable container. Coolant should be reused unless it is contaminated or several years old.

3. Remove the upper fan shroud.
4. Loosen the accessory drive belt adjusters and remove the drive belts from the crankshaft pulley.
5. Remove the cooling fan-to-water pump bolts and the pulley.
6. Remove the radiator hose and the heater hose from the water pump. Remove the water pump-to-engine bolts and the water pump from the engine.
7. Remove the crankshaft pulley-to-hub bolt and the pulley from the crankshaft.
8. Using the puller tool J-24420 or equivalent, pull the hub assembly from the crankshaft.
9. Remove the front cover-to-engine bolts and the cover from the engine.
10. Using a putty knife, clean the gasket mounting surfaces. Using solvent, clean the oil and grease from the gasket mounting surfaces.
11. The oil seal may be replaced with the cover removed or installed on the engine, by performing the following procedures:
    a. Using a medium prybar, pry the oil seal from the front cover; be careful not to distort the seal mating surface.
    b. Using engine oil, lubricate the new oil seal.
    c. Install the new seal so the open side (helical side) is towards the engine.
    d. Using the installation tool J-23042 or equivalent, drive the new seal into the front cover until it seats.
12. To complete the installation, apply an 1⁄8 in. bead of RTV sealant to the front cover and reverse the removal procedures. Torque the hub-to-crankshaft bolt to 66–88 ft. lbs. and the damper pulley-to-hub bolts to 29–44 ft. lbs. Adjust the drive belts.

NOTE: When applying RTV sealant to the front cover, be sure to keep it out of the bolt holes. The sealant must be wet to the touch when the bolts are torqued down.

2.2L Diesel Engine

1. Disconnect the negative battery terminal.

NOTE: If there is not enough room, it may be necessary to drain the cooling system and remove the radiator to provide room for the crankshaft pulley removal.

2. Loosen the accessory drive belt adjustments and remove the drive belts from the crankshaft pulley.
3. Remove the crankshaft pulley-to-crankshaft pulley center and the crankshaft pulley from the engine.

NOTE: To replace the front oil seal, it will be necessary to remove the timing belt and the crankshaft timing pulley.

4. Remove the front cover housing-to-engine bolts and the covers.
5. To install, reverse the removal procedures. Install and adjust the drive belt tensions. If the radiator was removed, refill the cooling system.

2.5L Engine

NOTE: The following procedure requires the use of the GM seal installer/centering tool J-34995 or equivalent.

1. Refer to the Crankshaft Pulley, Damper and Oil Seal, Removal and Installation procedures in this section and remove the damper from the crankshaft.
2. Remove the fan and the pulley. Remove the alternator and the brackets from the front of the engine.
3. Position a catch pan under the radiator, open the drain cock and drain the cooling system.

CAUTION

When draining the coolant, keep in mind that cats and dogs are attracted by the ethylene glycol antifreeze, and are quite likely to drink any that is left in an uncovered container or in puddles on the ground. This will prove fatal in sufficient quantity. Always drain the coolant into a sealable container. Coolant should be reused unless it is contaminated or several years old.

4. Remove the lower radiator hose clamp at the water pump.
5. Remove the timing cover-to-oil pan bolts, the timing cover-to-engine bolts and the timing cover from the engine.
6. Using a medium prybar, pry the oil seal from the timing cover.
7. Using a putty knife, clean the gasket mounting surfaces. Clean the surface with solvent to remove all traces of oil and grease.

NOTE: The timing cover can become distorted very easily, so be careful when cleaning the gasket surface.

8. Apply engine oil to the lips of the new oil seal. Using the GM seal installer/centering tool J-34995 or equivalent, install the new oil seal into the timing cover; leave the tool installed in the timing cover.
9. Using RTV sealant or equivalent, apply a 1⁄4 in. (6mm) wide bead to the timing cover mounting surface and a 3⁄8 in. (9.5mm) wide bead to the oil pan at the timing cover sealing surface.
10. Install the timing cover onto the engine and partially tighten the bolts.
11. First, torque the timing cover-to-engine bolts to 90 inch lbs.; secondly, torque the timing cover-to-oil pan bolts to 90 inch lbs. Remove the seal installer/centering tool J-34995 or equivalent, from the timing cover.
12. To complete the installation, reverse the removal procedures. Torque the damper pulley hub-to-crankshaft bolt to 160 ft. lbs. Adjust the drive belt(s) tension. Refill the cooling system and the power steering reservoir, if equipped.

2.8L Engine

NOTE: The following procedure requires the use of the GM seal installer/centering tool J-34995 or equivalent.

CAUTION

The engines use a harmonic balancer. Breakage may occur if the balancer is hammered back onto the crankshaft; a press or special installation tool is necessary.

1. Remove the water pump.
2. If equipped with air conditioning, remove the compressor and move it aside; do not remove any of the air conditioning lines.
3. Using a wheel puller, remove the harmonic balancer.

NOTE: The outer ring (weight) of the harmonic balancer is bonded to the hub with rubber. The balancer must be removed with a puller which acts on the inner hub only. Pulling on the outer portion of the balancer will break the rubber bond or destroy the tuning of the torsional damper.

4. Disconnect the lower radiator hose and heater hose.
5. Remove timing gear cover attaching screw, the cover and the gasket.
6. Using a putty knife, clean the gasket mounting surfaces on the front cover and block.

7. Apply a continuous $^3/_{32}$ in. (2mm) bead of sealant 1052357 or equivalent, to front cover sealing surface and around coolant passage parts and central bolt holes. Apply a bead of silicone sealer to the oil pan-to-cylinder block joint.
8. Using the GM seal installer/centering tool J-34995 or equivalent, position it in the crankcase snout hole in the front cover, then install the front cover.
9. Install the front cover bolts finger tight, remove the centering tools and tighten the cover bolts. Install the harmonic balancer, the pulley, the water pump, the drive belts, the radiator and all other parts. Adjust the drive belt(s) tension. Refill the cooling system and the power steering reservoir, if equipped.

4.3L Engine

1. Remove the torsional damper center bolts and remove the damper with suitable puller.

NOTE: The outer ring (weight) of the torsional damper is bonded to the hub with rubber. The damper must be removed with a puller which acts on the inner hub only. Pulling on the outer portion of the damper will break the rubber bond or destroy the tuning of the unit.

2. Drain the cooling system.

CAUTION

When draining the coolant, keep in mind that cats and dogs are attracted by the ethylene glycol antifreeze, and are quite likely to drink any that is left in an uncovered container or in puddles on the ground. This will prove fatal in sufficient quantity. Always drain the coolant into a sealable container. Coolant should be reused unless it is contaminated or several years old.

3. Remove the water pump.
4. Remove the oil pan.
5. Remove the upper radiator hose, air conditioner compressor (lay it aside) and right side engine accessory bracket.
6. Remove the front cover bolts and front cover.
7. If the front cover seal is to be replaced, it may be pryed front the front cover with a prybar. Use tool J-35468 to install the seal.
8. Clean all sealing surfaces and install a new gasket to the front cover. Use sealant to hold it in place.
9. Install the front cover and tighten the bolts to 10 ft. lbs.
10. Installation is the reverse of removal.

Timing Chains, Sprockets and Tensioners

REMOVAL AND INSTALLATION

1.9L Engine

NOTE: The following procedure requires the use of the wheel puller tool J-25031 or equivalent, and timing sprocket installation tool J-26587 or equivalent.

1. Remove the timing cover.
2. At the shoe automatic adjuster, depress the adjuster lock lever to lock the shoe in the fully retracted position.
3. Remove timing chain from crankshaft sprocket.

NOTE: To remove the timing chain, it may be necessary to remove the camshaft sprocket. Before removing the timing chain, be sure to align the timing marks.

4. Check the timing sprockets for wear or damage. If crankshaft sprocket must be replaced, remove the sprocket and the pinion gear from crankshaft using the puller tool J-25031 or equivalent.
5. Check timing chain for wear or damage; replace as necessary. Measure distance (L) with chain stretched with a pull of approximately 22 lbs. (98N). Standard (L) valve is 15 in. (381mm); replace chain of (L) is greater than 15.16 in. (385mm).

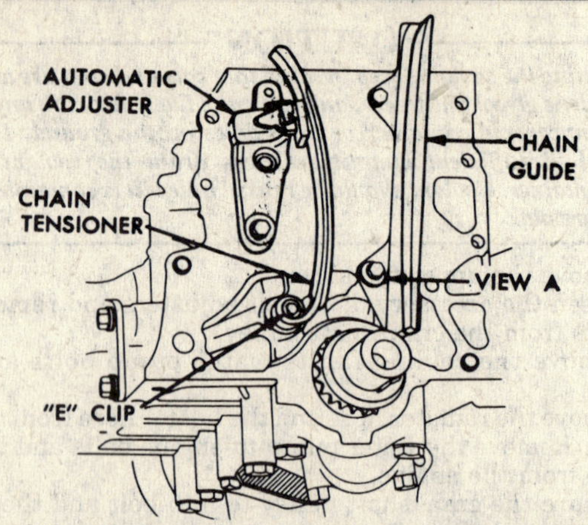

View of the timing chain guide and tensioner — 1.9L engine

6. Remove the automatic chain adjuster-to-engine bolt and the adjuster.
7. To check the operation of the automatic chain adjuster, push the shoe inwards, if it becomes locked, the adjuster is working properly. The adjuster assembly must be replaced if rack teeth are found to be worn excessively.
8. To remove the chain tensioner, remove the E-clip and the tensioner. Check the tensioner for wear or damage; if necessary, replace it.
9. Inspect the tensioner pin for wear or damage. If replacement is necessary, remove the pin from the cylinder block using a pair of locking pliers. Lubricate the NEW pin tensioner with clean engine oil. Start the pin into block, then place the tensioner over the appropriate pin. Position the E-clip onto the pin, then (using a hammer) tap it into the block until clip just clears tensioner. Check the tensioner and adjuster for freedom of rotation on the pins.
10. Inspect the guide for wear or damage and plugged lower oil jet. If replacement or cleaning is necessary, remove the guide bolts, the guide and the oil jet. Install a new guide and upper attaching bolt. Install the lower oil jet and bolt, so the oil port is pointed toward crankshaft.
11. Install the timing sprocket and the pinion gear (groove side

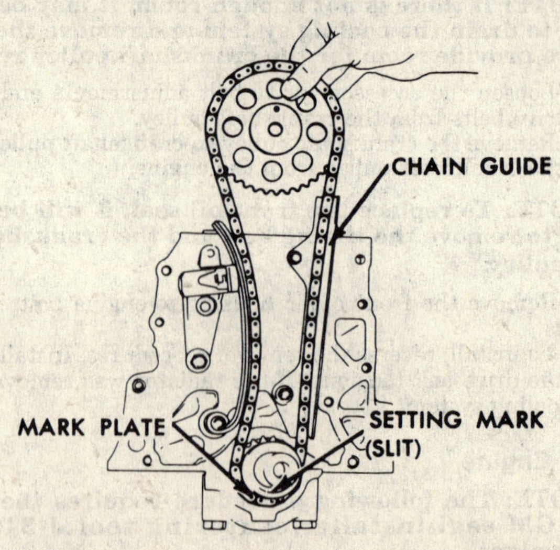

Alignment of the timing chain — 1.9L engine

toward the front cover). Align the key groove with crankshaft key, then drive it into position using installing tool J-26587 or equivalent.

12. Turn the crankshaft so key is turned toward the cylinder head side (No. 1 and No. 4 pistons at TDC).

13. Install the timing chain, align the timing chain mark plate with the mark on the crankshaft timing sprocket. The side of the chain with the mark plate is on the front side and the side of chain with the most linkes between mark plates is on the chain guide side. Keep the timing chain engaged with the camshaft timing sprocket until the camshaft timing sprocket is installed on the camshaft.

14. Install the camshaft timing sprocket so it's marked side faces forward and it's triangular mark aligns with the chain mark plate.

15. Install the automatic chain adjuster.

16. Release the lock by depressing the shoe on adjuster by hand, and check to make certain the chain is properly tensioned when the lock is released.

17. Install from cover assembly as outlined previously.

2.0L Engine

NOTE: The following procedure requires the use of the spring compressor tool J-33875 or equivalent, the gear puller tool J-22888-20 or equivalvent.

1. Refer to the Timing (Front) Cover, Removal and Installation procedures in this section and remove the timing cover.
2. Rotate the crankshaft to position the No. 4 piston on TDC of the compression stroke; the marks on the camshaft and crankshaft sprockets are in alignment.
3. Loosen the timing chain tensioner nut, as far as possible, without actually removing it.
4. Remove the camshaft sprocket-to-camshaft bolts and the sprocket; remove the timing chain with the sprocket. If the sprocket does not slide from the camshaft easily, a light blow with a soft mallet at the lower edge of the sprocket will dislodge it.
5. Using the gear puller tool J-22888-20 or equivalvent, remove the crankshaft sprocket.
6. Using a putty knife, clean the gasket mounting surfaces. Inspect the timing chain and the sprocket teeth for wear and/or damage; replace the parts, if necessary.
7. To install, press the crankshaft sprocket back onto the crankshaft, position the timing chain over the camshaft sprocket and then around the crankshaft sprocket. Make sure that the marks on the 2 sprockets are aligned. Lubricate the thrust surface with Molykote® or equivalent.
8. Align the dowel in the camshaft with the dowel hole in the sprocket and then install the sprocket onto the camshaft. Torque the camshaft sprocket-to-camshaft bolts to 27–33 ft. lbs.
9. Lubricate the timing chain with clean engine oil. Using the spring compressor tool J-33875 or equivalent, position the tangs under the sliding block and pull the tool to compress the spring. Tighten the chain tensioner.
10. To complete the installation, reverse the removal procedures.

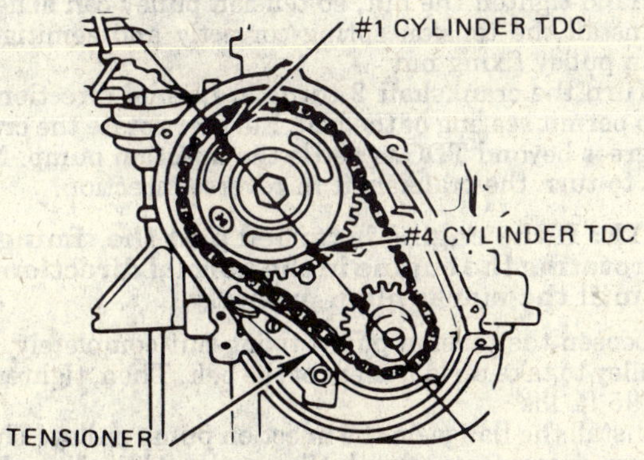

Alignment of the timing chain – 2.0L enigne

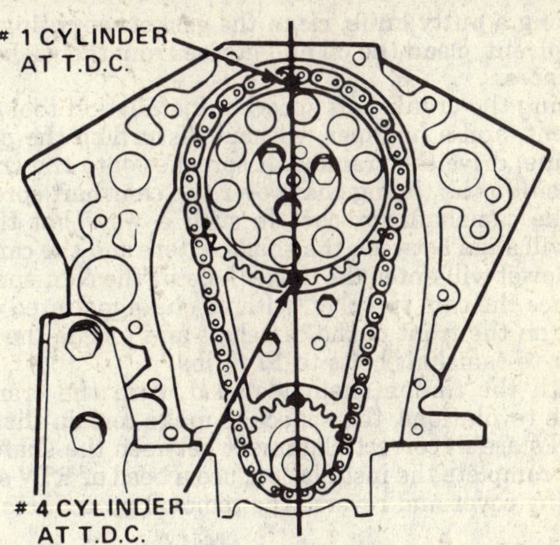

Alignment of the timing chain – 2.8L and 4.3L engines

Removing the crankshaft sprocket – 2.8L and 4.3L engines

2.8L and 4.3L Engines

NOTE: The following procedure requires the use of the crankshaft sprocket removal tool J-5825 or equivalent, and the crankshaft sprocket installation tool J-5590 or equivalent.

1. Remove the timing cover.
2. Rotate the crankshaft until the No. 4 cylinder is on the TDC of its compression stroke and the camshaft sprocket mark (No. 4 cylinder) aligns with the mark on the crankshaft sprocket (facing each other) and in line with the shaft centers.
3. Remove the camshaft sprocket-to-camshaft bolts and the camshaft sprocket (with timing chain). If camshaft is difficult to remove, use a plastic mallet to bump the sprocket from the camshaft.

NOTE: The camshaft sprocket (located by a dowel) is lightly pressed onto the camshaft and will come off readily. The chain comes off with the camshaft sprocket.

4. Using the crankshaft sprocket removal tool J-5825 or equivalent, remove the timing sprocket from the crankshaft.
5. Inspect the timing chain and the timing sprockets for wear or damage, replace the damaged parts, if necessary.

6. Using a putty knife, clean the gasket mounting surfaces. Using solvent, clean the oil and grease from the gasket mounting surfaces.
7. Using the crankshaft sprocket installation tool J-5590 or equivalent, and a hammer, without disturbing the position of the engine, drive the crankshaft sprocket onto the crankshaft.
8. Position the timing chain over the camshaft sprocket. Arrange the camshaft sprocket in such a way that the timing marks will align between the shaft centers and the camshaft locating dowel will enter the dowel hole in the cam sprocket.
9. Place the cam sprocket, with its chain mounted over it, in position on the front of the camshaft and torque the camshaft sprocket-to-camshaft bolts to 17 ft. lbs.
10. With the timing chain installed, turn the crankshaft 2 complete revolutions, then check to make certain that the timing marks are in correct alignment between the shaft centers.
11. To complete the installation, use a bead of RTV sealant on the timing cover and reverse the removal procedures.

Timing Belt

REMOVAL AND INSTALLATION

2.2L Diesel Engine

NOTE: The following procedure requires the use of the belt tension gauge tool J-29771 or equivalent.

1. Remove the front cover.
2. From the injection pump timing pulley, remove the flange-to-pulley screws and the flange.
3. Remove the timing belt tension pulley spring.

NOTE: When removing tension spring, avoid using excess force or distortion of spring will result.

4. Remove the timing belt tension pulley-to-engine fixing nut, then the tension pulley and tension center.
5. Remove the timing belt. Avoid twisting or kinking the belt and keep it free from water, oil, dust and other foreign matter.

NOTE: No attempt should be made to readjust belt tension. If the belt has been loosened through service of the timing system, it should be replaced with a new one.

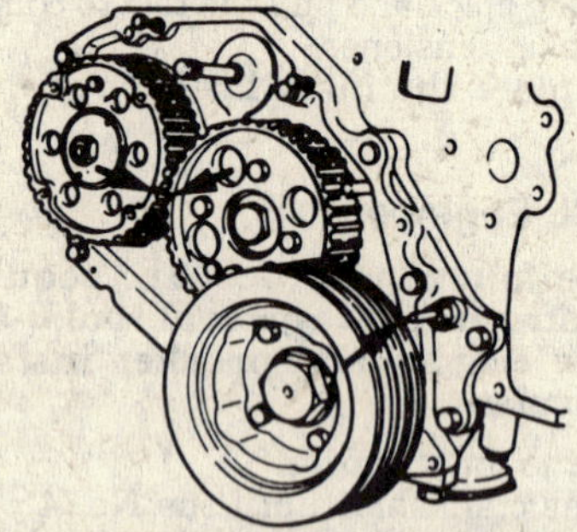

Aligning the timing marks — 2.2L diesel engine

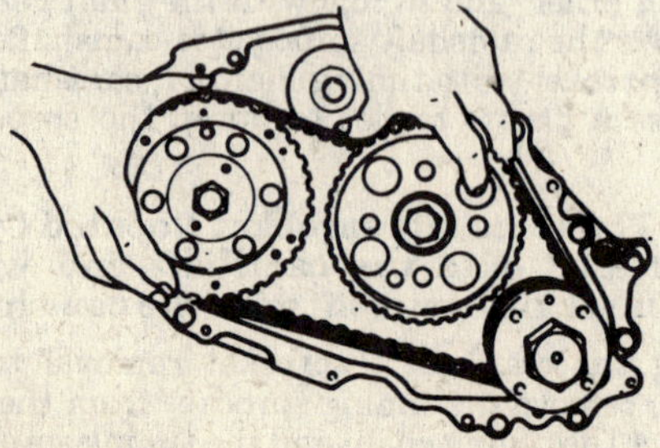

Installing the timing belt — 2.2L diesel engine

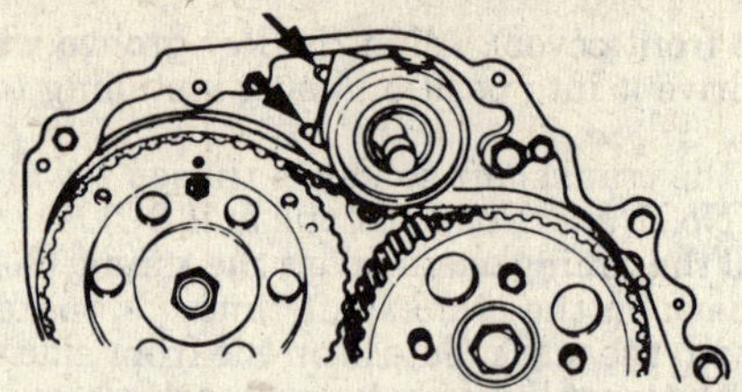

Aligning the tension pulley to make proper contact with the 2 housing pins — 2.2L diesel engine

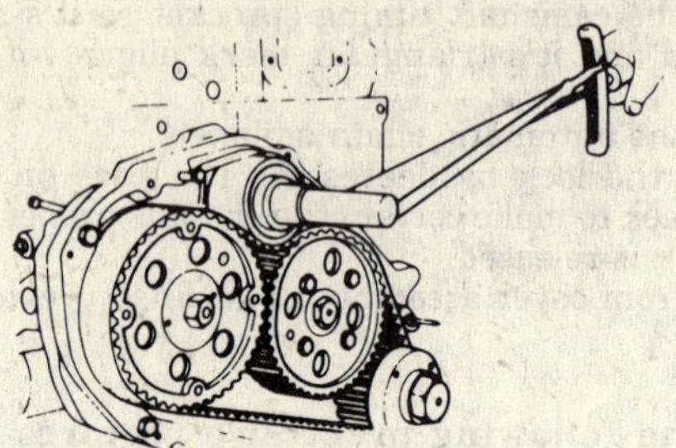

Torquing the tension pulley — 2.2L diesel engine

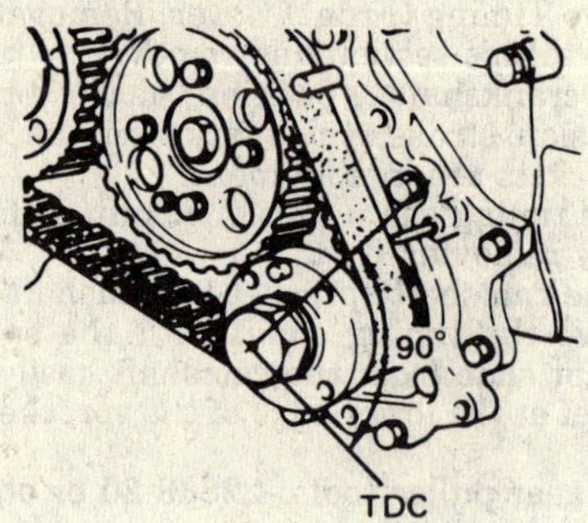

Bringing the No. 1 cylinder to TDC — 2.2L diesel engine

6. Check that the setting marks on the crank pulley, injection pump timing pulley, and camshaft pulley are in alignment, then install the timing belt in sequence of crankshaft timing pulley, camshaft timing pulley and injection pump timing pulley.
7. Make an adjustment, so slackness of the belt is taken up by the tension pulley. When installing the timing belt, care should be taken so as not to damage the belt.
8. Install the tension center and tension pulley, making certain the end of the tension center is in proper contact with 2 pins on the timing pulley housing.
9. Hand-tighten the nut, so tension pulley can slide freely.
10. Install the tension spring correctly and semitighten the tension pulley fixing nut.
11. Turn the crankshaft 2 turns in normal direction of rotation to permit seating of the belt. Further rotate the crankshaft 90 degrees beyond TDC to settle the injection pump. Never attempt to turn the crankshaft in reverse direction.

NOTE: If the engine is turned past the timing marks, keep rotating the engine in the normal direction of rotation until the marks align properly.

12. Loosen the tension pulley fixing nut completely, allowing the pulley to take up looseness of the belt. Then, tighten the nut to 78–95 ft. lbs.
13. Install the flange on the injection pump pulley. The hole in the outer circumference of the flange should be aligned with the timing mark **triangle** on the injection pump pulley.

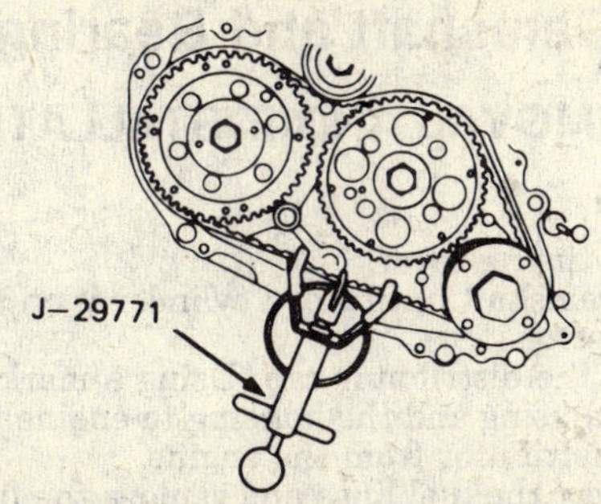

Using tool J-29771 to check the belt tension – 2.2L diesel engine

14. Turn the crankshaft 2 (clockwise) turns to position the No. 1 cylinder on to TDC of it's compression stroke, then check that the **triangle** mark on the timing pulley is in alignment with the hole in the flange.
15. The belt tension should be checked at a point between the injection pump pulley and crankshaft pulley using tool J-29771 or equivalent, to 33–55 lbs. as read on the scale.
16. To complete the installation, adjust valve clearances and reverse the removal procedures. Check the injection timing.

Timing Gears

REMOVAL AND INSTALLATION

2.5L Engine

The timing gear is pressed onto the camshaft. To remove or install the timing gear, an arbor press must be used.

NOTE: The following procedure requires the use of an arbor press, a press plate, the GM gear removal tool J-971 or equivalent, the GM gear installation tool J-21474-13, J-21795-1 or equivalent.

1. Remove the camshaft from the engine.
2. Using an arbor press, a press plate and the GM gear removal tool J-971 or equivalent, press the timing gear from the camshaft.

NOTE: When pressing the timing gear from the camshaft, be certain that the position of the press plate does not contact the woodruff key.

3. To assembly, position the press plate to support the camshaft at the back of the front journal. Place the gear spacer ring and the thrust plate over the end of the camshaft, then install the woodruff key. Press the timing gear onto the camshaft, until it bottoms against the gear spacer ring.

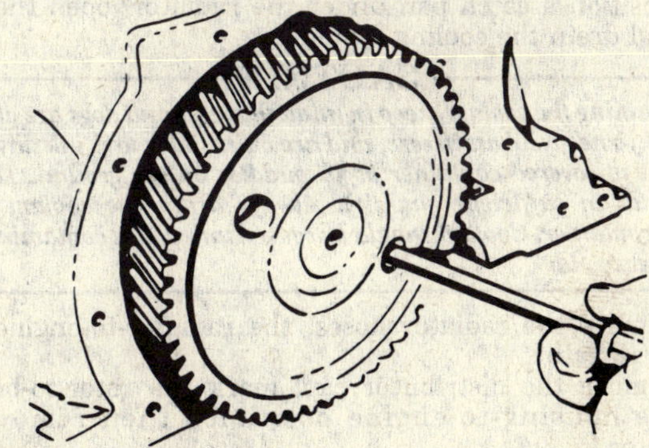

Removing the camshaft thrust plate-to-engine screws – 2.5L engine

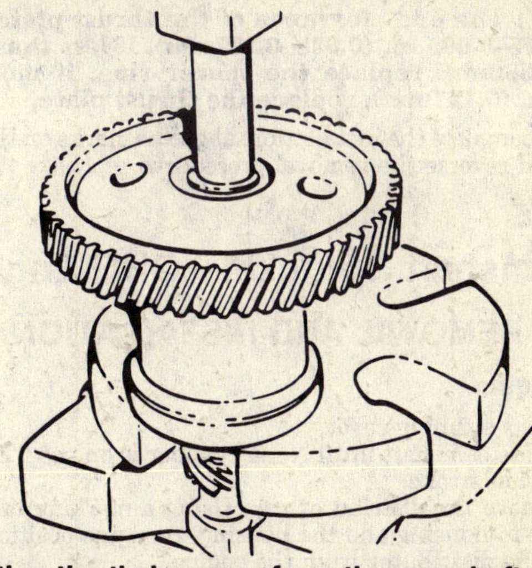

Separating the timing gear from the camshaft – 2.5L engine

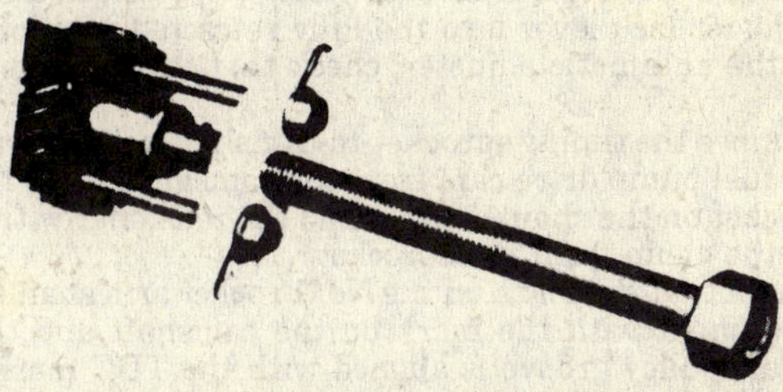

Removing the timing gear from the crankshaft – 2.5L engine

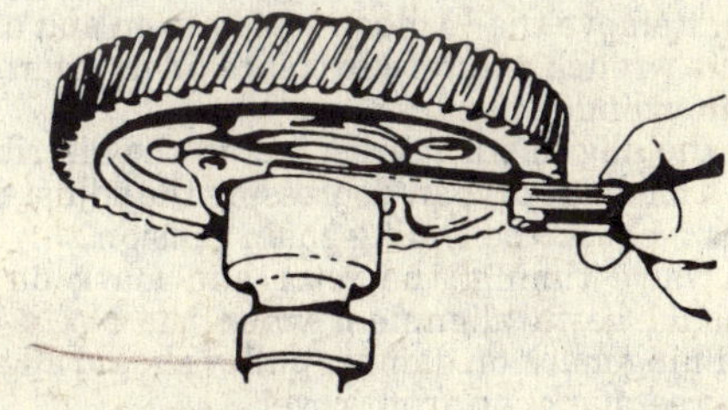

Using a feeler gauge to check the thrust plate clearance – 2.5L engine

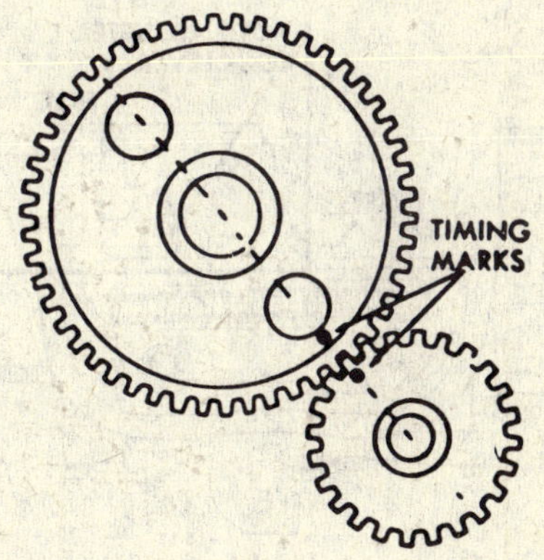

View of the timing marks – 2.5L engine

NOTE: The end clearance of the thrust plate should be 0.0015–0.005 in. (0.038–0.127mm). If less than 0.0015 in. (0.038mm), replace the spacer ring; if more than 0.005 in. (0.127mm), replace the thrust plate.

4. To complete the installation, align the marks on the timing gears and reverse the removal procedures.

Camshaft Sprocket – OHC Engine

REMOVAL AND INSTALLATION

1.9L Engine

1. Remove timing cover.
2. Rotate camshaft until No. 4 cylinder is on the TDC of it's compression stroke.
3. Remove the distributor cap. Using a marking tool, mark the rotor-to-housing and the housing-to-engine positions, then remove the distributor from the engine.
4. Disconnect the fuel lines and remove the fuel pump from the engine.
5. Using a screwdriver or equivalent, depress the automatic shoe adjuster lock lever into the fully retracted position. After locking the automatic adjuster, check that the chain is in free state.
6. Remove the timing sprocket-to-camshaft bolt, the sprocket and the fuel pump drive cam from the camshaft. Keep the timing sprocket on the chain damper and the tensioner without removing the chain from the sprocket.
7. Check that the mark on the No. 1 rocker arm shaft bracket is in alignment with the mark on the camshaft and that the crankshaft pulley groove is aligned with the TDC mark (0 degree) on the front cover.
8. Assemble the timing sprocket to the camshaft by aligning it with the pin on the camshaft; use care not to remove the chain from the sprocket.
9. Install the fuel pump drive cam, the sprocket retaining bolt and washer. Remove the ½ moon seal in from end of head; then install torque wrench and torque bolt to 58 ft. lbs; replace the ½ moon seal in cylinder head.
10. Using the alignment marks, install the distributor.
11. Using a medium prybar, depressing the adjuster shoe to release the lock, check the timing chain tension.
12. Check valve timing, the rotor and mark on distributor housing should be in alignment when the No. 4 cylinder on TDC. The timing mark on damper pulley should align with TDC mark (0 degree mark) on front cover.
13. To complete the installation, reverse the removal procedures.

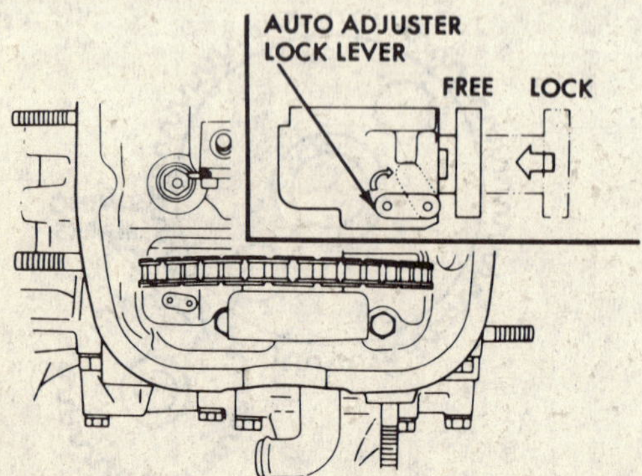

Locking the timing chain adapter – 1.9L engine

Camshaft and Bearings

REMOVAL AND INSTALLATION

1.9L Engine

1. Remove timing cover.
2. Rotate camshaft until No. 4 cylinder is on the TDC of it's compression stroke.
3. Remove the distributor cap. Using a marking tool, mark the rotor-to-housing and the housing-to-engine positions, then remove the distributor from the engine.
4. Disconnect the fuel lines and remove the fuel pump from the engine.
5. Using a screwdriver or equivalent, depress the automatic shoe adjuster lock lever into the fully retracted position. After locking the automatic adjuster, check that the chain is in free state.
6. Remove the timing sprocket-to-camshaft bolt, the sprocket and the fuel pump drive cam from the camshaft. Keep the timing sprocket on the chain damper and the tensioner without removing the chain from the sprocket.
7. Remove rocker arm, the shaft and the bracket assembly, the remove the camshaft assembly.
8. Using set of V-blocks and a dial indicator, inspect the camshaft for damage and/or wear; replace it, if necessary.
9. Using a generous amount of clean engine oil, lubricate the camshaft and journals.
10. Install the camshaft, the rocker arm, the shaft and the bracket assembly.
11. Check that the mark on the No. 1 rocker arm shaft bracket is in alignment with the mark on the camshaft and that the crankshaft pulley groove is aligned with the TDC mark (0 degree) on the front cover.
12. Assemble the timing sprocket to the camshaft by aligning it with the pin on the camshaft; use care not to remove the chain from the sprocket.
13. Install the fuel pump drive cam, the sprocket retaining bolt and washer. Remove the ½ moon seal in from end of head; then install torque wrench and torque bolt to 58 ft. lbs; replace the ½ moon seal in cylinder head.
14. Using the alignment marks, install the distributor.
15. Using a medium prybar, depressing the adjuster shoe to release the lock, check the timing chain tension.
16. Check valve timing, the rotor and mark on distributor housing should be in alignment when the No. 4 cylinder on TDC. The timing mark on damper pulley should align with TDC mark (0 degree mark) on front cover.
17. To complete the installation, reverse the removal procedures. Adjust the drive belts. Refill the cooling system.

2.0L Engine

1. Remove the timing chain and the rocker arm assemblies.
2. Position a catch pan under the radiator, open the drain cock and drain the cooling system.

CAUTION

When draining the coolant, keep in mind that cats and dogs are attracted by the ethylene glycol antifreeze, and are quite likely to drink any that is left in an uncovered container or in puddles on the ground. This will prove fatal in sufficient quantity. Always drain the coolant into a sealable container. Coolant should be reused unless it is contaminated or several years old.

3. Remove the radiator hoses, the radiator-to-engine bolts and the radiator.
4. Remove the distributor cap, mark the rotor-to-housing and the housing-to-engine positions, then remove the distributor.
5. Raise and support the front of the vehicle on jackstands.
6. Disconnect the fuel lines and remove the fuel pump.

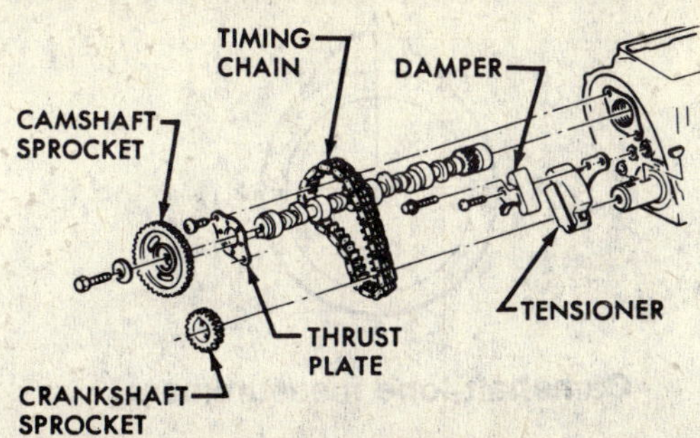

Exploded view of the timing chain and camshaft assemblies – 2.0L engine

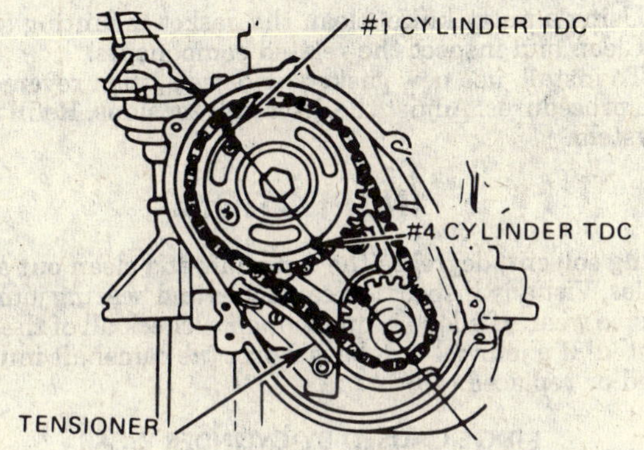

View of the timing marks – 2.0L engine

7. Lower the vehicle.
8. Remove the rocker arm studs and the pushrod guides.
9. Remove the valve lifters.

NOTE: When removing the pushrods and the valve lifters, keep them in order.

10. From the front of the engine, carefully pull the camshaft from the block, being sure the camshaft lobes do not contact the bearings.
11. Using set of V-blocks and a dial indicator, inspect the camshaft for damage, wear and/or out-of-round – 0.0009 in. (0.0228mm) max; replace it, if necessary.

NOTE: If installing a new camshaft, be sure to coat the lobes with GM part 1051396 or equivalent.

12. Using a putty knife, clean the gasket mounting surfaces.
13. To install, lubricate the camshaft journals with clean engine oil and reverse the removal procedures. Lubricate the lobes with Molykote® or the equivalent. Install the camshaft into the engine, being extremely careful not to contact the bearings with the cam lobes. Adjust the valve lash after installing the engine. Adjust the drive belts. Refill the cooling system.

2.2L Diesel Engine

NOTE: The following procedure requires the use of the camshaft bearing removal/installation tool J-29764 or equivalent.

1. Remove the engine from the vehicle and mount it on a workstand.
2. Disconnect the PCV hoses from the rocker arm cover.
3. Remove the rocker arm cover, the rocker arm shaft and the pushrods.
4. Remove the upper timing housing cover. Turn the crankshaft to align the timing marks, then install a holding bolt into the injection pump gear.
5. Remove the crankshaft damper pulley and the lower timing housing cover.
6. Remove the injection pump timing gear flange, the timing belt tension spring and the pulley, then remove the timing belt.
7. Remove the camshaft sprocket, the hub and the camshaft oil seal retainer.
8. Remove the oil pump and the valve lifters.
9. From the front of the engine, pull the camshaft forward to remove it; be careful not to damage the camshaft bearings.
10. Using the camshaft bearing removal/installation tool J-29764 or equivalent, remove the camshaft bearings.
11. Inspect the inner bearing faces for damage. Using an inside micrometer, measure the inside diameter of the camshaft bearings; if bearing clearance is greater than 0.0047 in. (0.12mm), replace the bearing(s).
12. Using the camshaft bearing removal/installation tool J-29764 or equivalent, install the camshaft bearings into the engine block; be sure to align the oil ports in the bearings with those in the cylinder body.
13. To complete the installation, reverse the removal procedures.

2.5L Engine

1. Remove the pushrods and the valve lifters from the engine.

NOTE: When removing the pushrods and the valve lifters, be sure to keep them in order for reassembly purposes.

2. Place a catch pan under the radiator, open the drain cock and drain the cooling system.

CAUTION

When draining the coolant, keep in mind that cats and dogs are attracted by the ethylene glycol antifreeze, and are quite likely to drink any that is left in an uncovered container or in puddles on the ground. This will prove fatal in sufficient quantity. Always drain the coolant into a sealable container. Coolant should be reused unless it is contaminated or several years old.

3. Remove the power steering reservoir from the fan shroud, then the upper fan shroud, the radiator. Remove the grille, the headlight bezel and the bumper filler panel.
4. Remove the accessory drive belts, the cooling fan and the water pump pulley.
5. If equipped with air conditioning, disconnect the condenser baffles and the condenser, then raise the condenser and block it aside.
6. Remove the crankshaft drive belt pulley and the damper hub. Remove the timing gear cover-to-engine bolts and the cover.
7. Label and disconnect the distributor electrical connectors, then the hold-down bolt and the distributor from the engine. Remove the oil pump driveshaft.
8. Label and disconnect the vacuum lines from the intake manifold and the thermostat housing, then remove the Exhaust Gas Recirculation (EGR) valve from the intake manifold.
9. Remove the camshaft thrust plate-to-engine bolts. While

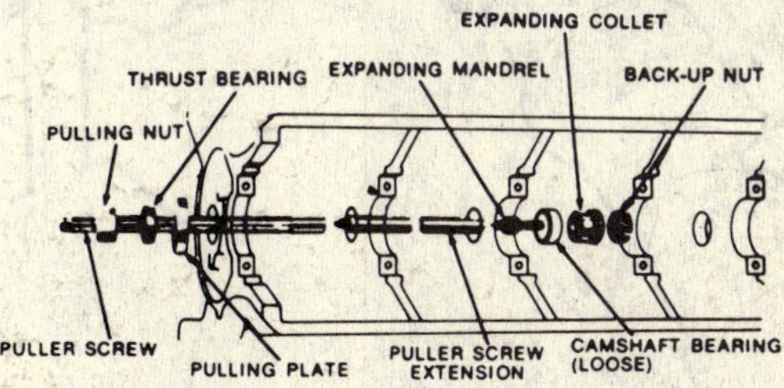

Camshaft bearing removal and installation tool – OHV engines only

supporting the camshaft (to prevent damaging the bearing or lobe surfaces), remove it from the front of the engine.

10. Inspect the camshaft for scratches, pitting and/or wear on the bearing and lobe surfaces. Check the timing gear teeth for damage.

11. To install, lubricate all of the parts with engine oil and reverse the removal procedures. Torque the camshaft thrust plate-to-engine bolts to 90 inch lbs. Refill the cooling system, start the engine, allow it to reach operating temperatures and check for leaks.

2.8L and 4.3L Engines

1. Remove the intake manifold, the timing chain and the sprocket.
2. Remove the radiator-to-vehicle bolts and the radiator from the vehicle.
3. Remove the rocker arm covers, the rocker arm assemblies, the pushrods and the valve lifters.

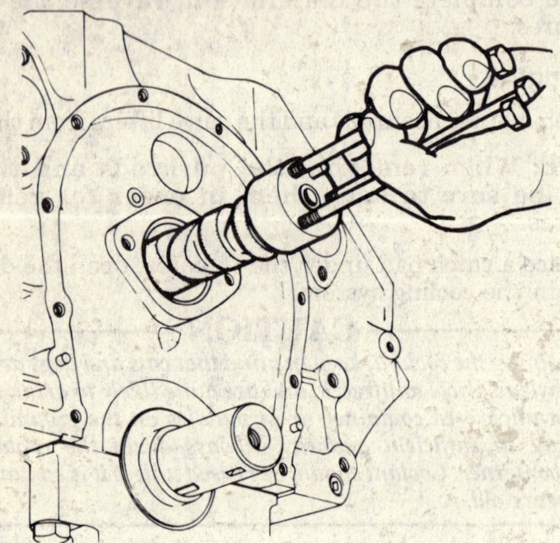

Using 3 long bolts to replace the camshaft – 2.8L and 4.3L engines

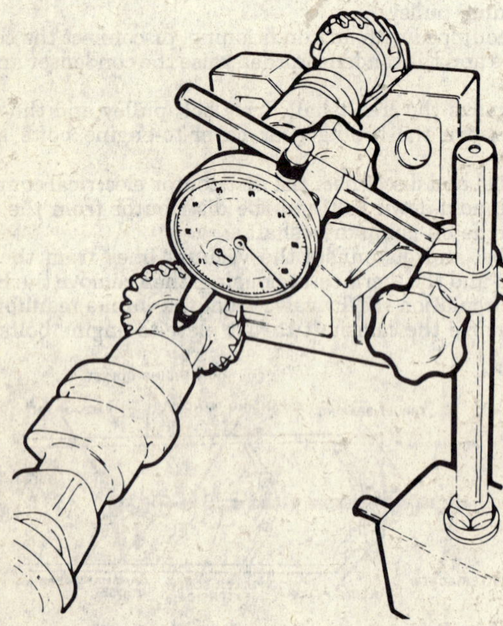

Check the camshaft for straightness

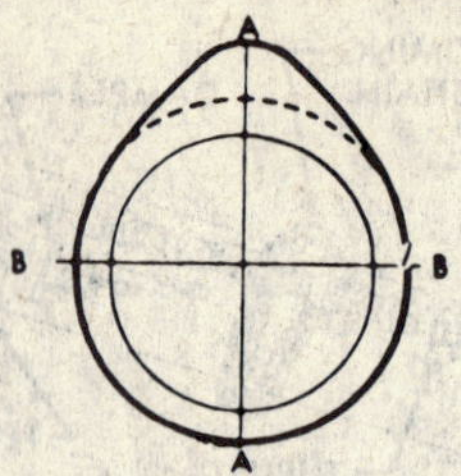

Camshaft lobe measurement

4. Using 3 long bolts, install them into the threaded holes in the end of the camshaft. Grasping the 3 bolts, pull the camshaft from the front of the engine block; be careful not to damage the bearing surfaces.
5. Using a putty knife, clean the gasket mounting surfaces.
6. Clean and inspect the related components.
7. To install, use new gaskets and seals, then reverse the removal procedures. Adjust the drive belt tensions. Refill the cooling system.

INSPECTION

Using solvent, degrease the camshaft and clean out all of the oil holes. Visually inspect the cam lobes and bearing journals for excessive wear. If a lobe is questionable, check all of the lobes as indicated. If a journal or lobe is worn, the camshaft must be reground or replaced.

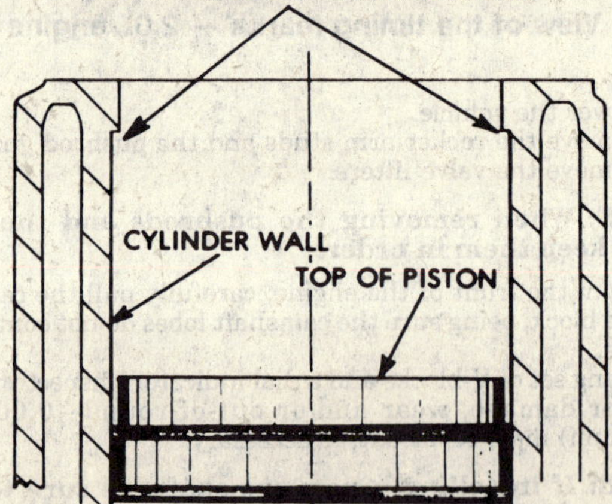

The ridge must be removed before the pistons are removed

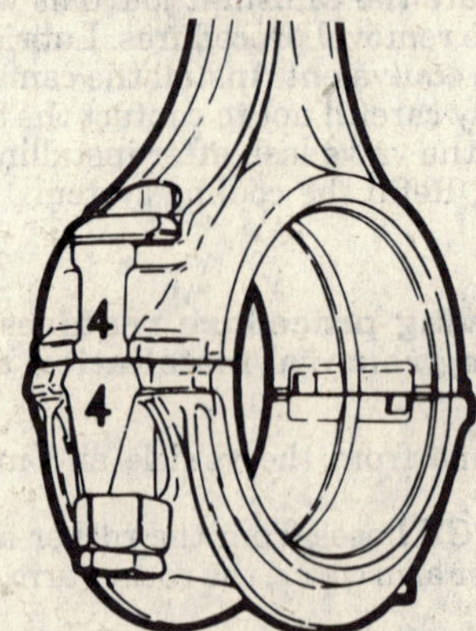

Match the connecting rods to their cylinders with a number stamp

NOTE: If a journal is worn, there is a good chance that the bushings are worn and need replacement.

If the lobes and journals appear intact, place the front and rear journals in V-blocks and rest a dial indicator on the center journal. Rotate the camshaft to check the straightness. If deviation exceeds 0.001 in. (0.0254mm), replace the camshaft.

Check the camshaft lobes with a micrometer, by measuring the lobes from the nose to the base and again at 90 degrees, see illustration. The lobe lift is determined by subtracting the second measurement from the first. If all of the exhaust and intake lobes are not identical, the camshaft must be reground or replace.

Pistons and Connecting Rods

REMOVAL

1. Remove the engine from the vehicle.
2. Remove the intake manifold and the cylinder head(s).
3. Remove the oil pan and the oil pump assembly.
4. Stamp the cylinder number on the machined surfaces of the bolt bosses of the connecting rod and cap for identification when reinstalling. If the pistons are to be removed from the connecting rod, mark the cylinder number on the piston with a silver pencil or quick drying paint for proper cylinder identification and cap to rod location.

NOTE: The cylinders on a 4-cylinder engine are numbered 1–2–3–4 (front-to-rear); on the V6 (2.8L) engine, are numbered 1–3–5 (front-to-rear) on the right side and 2–4–6 (front-to-rear) on the left side.

5. Examine the cylinder bore above the ring travel. If a ridge exists, remove it with a ridge reamer before attempting to remove the piston and rod assembly.
6. Remove the connecting rod bearing cap and bearing.
7. Install a ⅜ in. rubber guide hose over the rod bolt threads; this will prevent damage to the bearing journal and rod bolt threads.
8. Remove the rod and piston assembly through the top of the cylinder bore; remove the other rod and piston assemblies in the same manner.
9. Clean and inspect the engine block, the crankshaft, the pistons and the connecting rods.

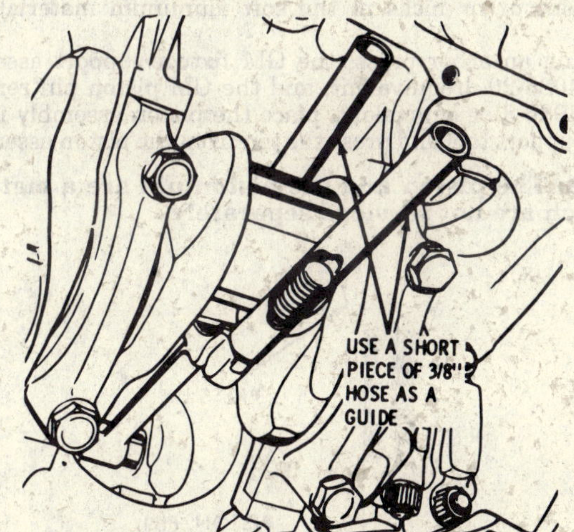

Cut rubber hose for connecting rod bolt guides

Carefully tap the piston and rod assembly out with a wooden hammer handle

CLEANING AND INSPECTION

Using a piston ring expanding tool, remove the piston rings from the pistons; any other method (screwdriver blades, pliers, etc.) usually results in the rings being bent, scratched or distorted and/or the piston itself being damaged.

Pistons

Clean the varnish from the piston skirts and pins with a cleaning solvent. Do not wire brush any part of the piston. Clean the ring grooves with a groove cleaner and make sure the oil ring holes and slots are clean.

Inspect the piston for cracked ring lands, scuffed or damaged skirts, eroded areas at the top of the piston. Replace the pistons that are damaged or show signs of excessive wear.

Inspect the grooves for nicks of burrs that might cause the rings to hang up.

Measure the piston skirt, across the center line of the piston pin, and check the piston clearance.

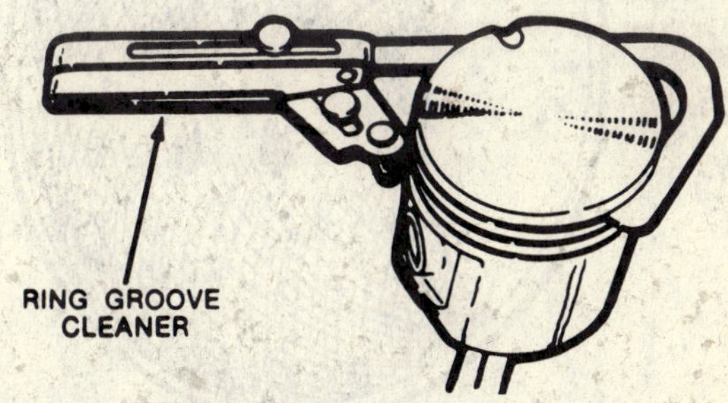

Cleaning the piston rings grooves using a ring groove cleaner

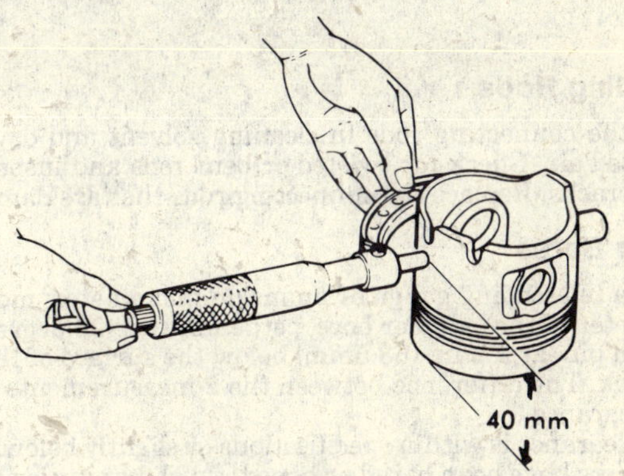

Measuring the piston diameter

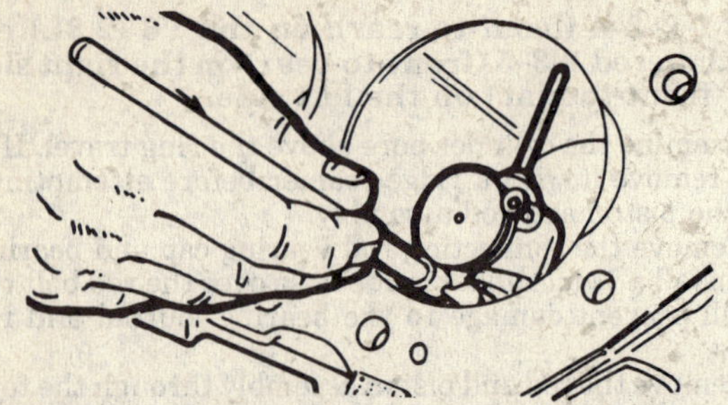

Measuring the cylinder bore with a dial gauge

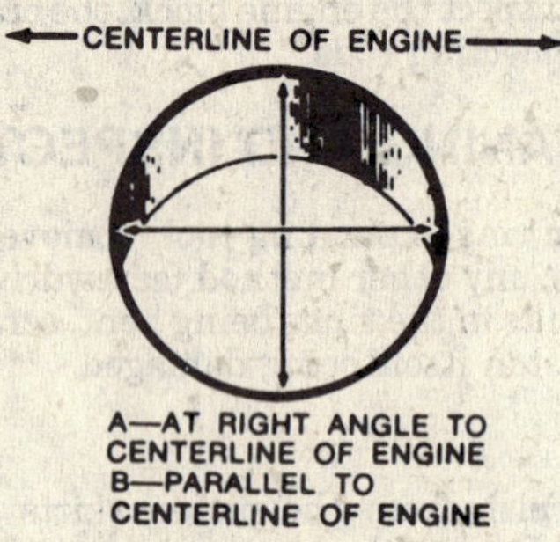

Cylinder bore measuring points

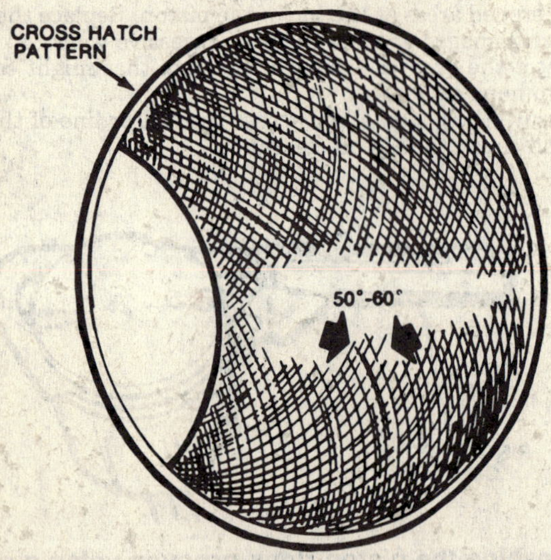

Cylinder bore cross-hatching after honing

Connecting Rods

Wash the connecting rods in cleaning solvent and dry with compressed air. Check for twisted or bent rods and inspect for nicks or cracks. Replace the connecting rods that are damaged.

Cylinder Bores

Using a telescoping gauge or an inside micrometer, measure the diameter of the cylinder bore, perpendicular (90 degrees) to the piston pin, at 2½ in. (63.5mm) below the surface of the cylinder block. The difference between the 2 measurements is the piston clearance.

If the clearance is within specifications or slightly below, after the cylinders have been bored or honed, finish honing is all that is necessary, If the clearance is excessive, try to obtain a slightly larger piston to bring the clearance within specifications. If this is not possible obtain the first oversize piston and hone the cylinder or, if necessary, bore the cylinder to size. Generally, if the cylinder bore is tapered more than 0.005 in. (0.127mm) or is out-of-round more than 0.003 in. (0.0762mm), it is advisable to rebore for the smallest possible oversize piston and rings. After measuring, mark the pistons with a felt-tip pen for reference and for assembly.

NOTE: Boring of the cylinder block should be performed by a reputable machine shop with the proper equipment. In some cases, clean-up honing can be done with the cylinder block in the vehicle, but most excessive honing and all cylinder boring must be done with the block stripped and removed from the vehicle.

PISTON PIN REPLACEMENT

All Engines—Except 2.2L Diesel

NOTE: The following procedure requires the use of the GM fixture/support assembly tool J-24086-20 or equivalent, the GM piston pin removal tool J-24086-8 or equivalent, and the GM piston pin installation tool J-24086-9 or equivalent.

Use care at all times when handling and servicing the connecting rods and pistons. To prevent possible damage to these units, do not clamp the rod or piston in a vise since they may become distorted. Do not allow the pistons to strike one another, against hard objects or bench surfaces, since distortion of the piston contour or nicks in the soft aluminum material may result.

1. Using an arbor press, the GM fixture/support assembly tool J-24086-20 orequivalent, and the GM piston pin removal tool J-24086-8 or equivalent, place the piston assembly in the fixture/support tool and press the pin from the piston assembly.

NOTE: The piston and the piston pin are a matched set which are not serviced separately.

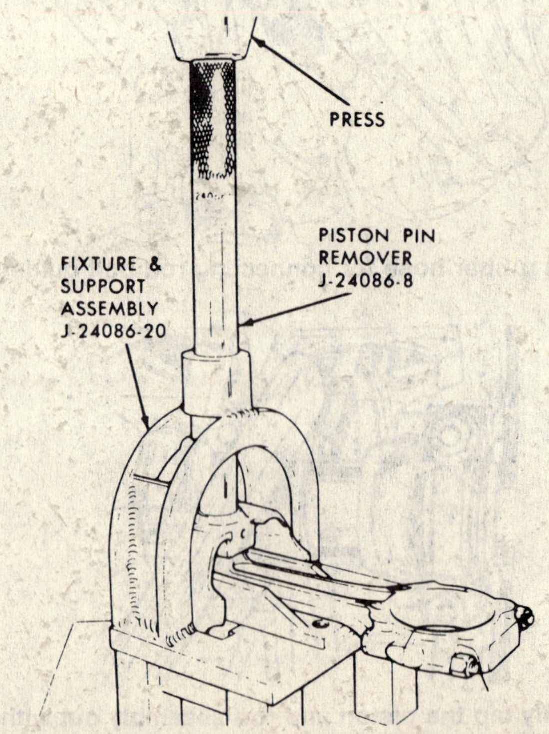

Removing the piston pin from the piston assembly

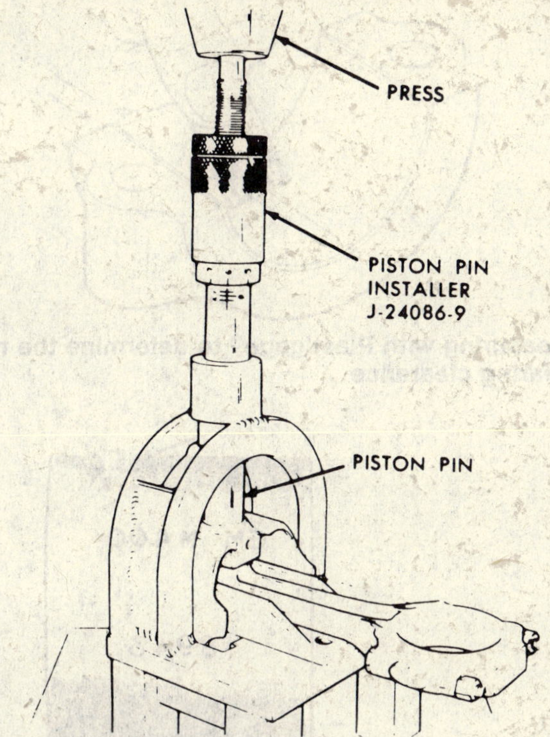

Installing the piston pin into the piston assembly

2. Using solvent, wash the varnish and oil from the parts, then inspect the parts for scuffing or wear.
3. Using a micrometer, measure the diameter of the piston pin. Using a inside micrometer or a dial bore gauge, measure the diameter of the piston bore.

NOTE: If the piston pin-to-piston clearance is in excess of 0.001 in. (0.0254mm), replace the piston and piston pin assembly.

4. Before installation, lubricate the piston pin and the piston bore with engine oil.
5. To install the piston pin into the piston assembly, use an arbor press, the GM fixture/support assembly tool J-24086-20 or equivalent, and the GM piston pin installation tool J-24086-9 or equivalent, then press the piston pin into the piston/connecting rod assembly.

NOTE: When installing the piston pin into the piston/connecting rod assembly and the installation tool bottoms onto the support assembly, do not exceed 5000 lbs. of pressure for structural damage may occur to the tool.

6. After installing the piston pin, make sure that the piston has freedom of movement with the piston pin. The piston/connecting rod assembly is ready for installation into the engine block.

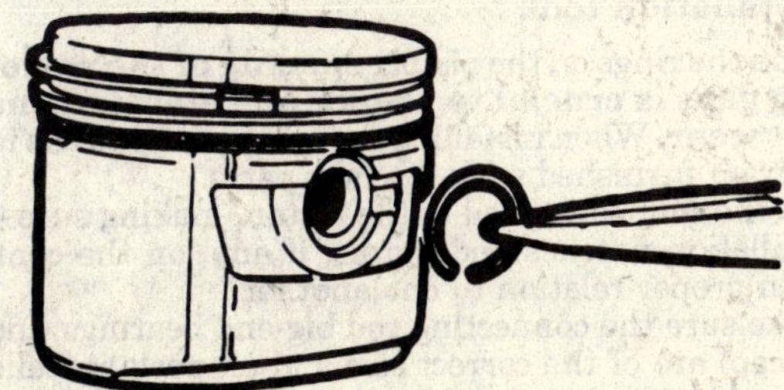
Replacing the piston pin snapring — 2.2L diesel engine only

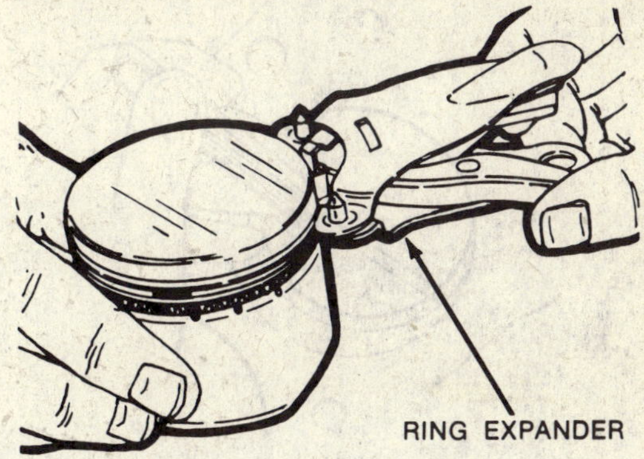

Removing the piston rings

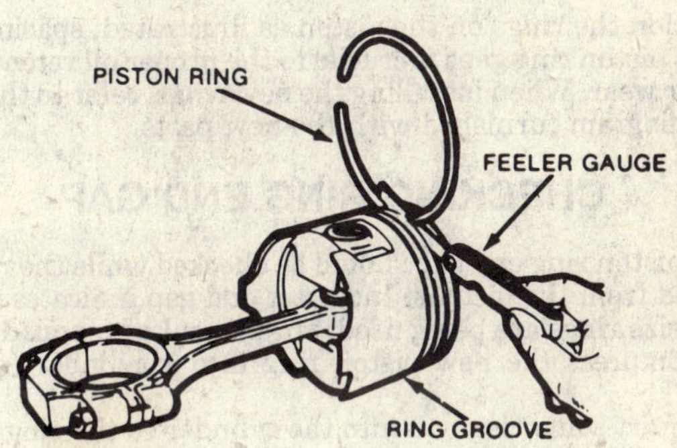

Checking the ring side clearance

2.2L Diesel Engine

1. Using a pair of snapring pliers, remove the piston pin snapring from the piston.
2. Slide the piston pin from the connecting rod and piston assembly.

NOTE: When separating the piston from the connecting rod, be sure to mark them for reassembly purposes.

3. Clean and inspect the piston and the connnecting rod bearing surfaces for damage and/or wear; if necessary, replace the damaged part.
4. To install, lubricate the piston pin and bearing surfaces with clean engine oil, then reverse the removal procedures.

PISTON RING REPLACEMENT AND SIDE CLEARANCE MEASUREMENT

Check the pistons to see that the ring grooves and oil return holes have been properly cleaned. Slide a piston ring into its groove and check the side clearance with a feeler gauge. Make sure the feeler gauge is inserted between the ring and its lower land (lower edge of the groove), because any wear that occurs forms a step at the inner portion of the lower land. If the piston grooves have been worn to the extent that relatively high steps exist on the lower land, the piston should be replaced, because these will interfere with the operation of the new rings and ring clearances will be excessive. Piston rings are not furnished in oversize widths to compensate for ring groove wear.

Install the rings on the piston, bottom ring first, using a piston ring expander. There is a high risk of breaking or distorting the rings and/or scratching the piston, if the rings are installed by hand or other means.

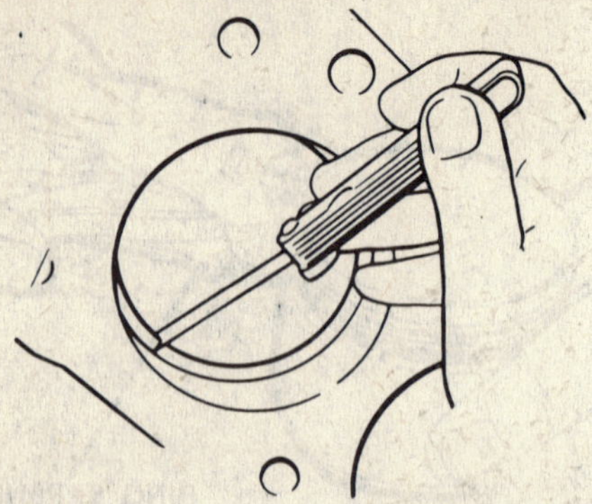

Checking the piston ring end gap

Position the rings on the piston as illustrated; spacing of the various piston ring gaps is crucial to the proper oil retention and cylinder wear. When installing the new rings, refer to the installation diagram furnished with the new parts.

CHECKING RING END GAP

The piston ring end gap should be checked while the rings are removed from the pistons. Incorrect end gap indicates that the wrong size rings are being used; **ring breakage could result.**

1. Compress the new piston ring into a cylinder (one at a time).
2. Squirt some clean oil into the cylinder so the ring and the top 2 in. (51mm) of the cylinder wall are coated.
3. Using an inverted piston, push the ring approximately 1 in. (25.4mm) below the top of the cylinder.
4. Using a feeler gauge, measure the ring gap and compare it to the Ring Gap chart in this Section. Carefully remove the ring from the cylinder.

CONNECTING ROD BEARING REPLACEMENT

Replacement bearings are available in standard size and undersize (for reground crankshafts). Connecting rod-to-crankshaft bearing clearance is checked using Plastigage® at either the top or the bottom of each crank journal. The Plastigage® has a range of 0.001–0.003 in. (0.0254–0.0762mm).

1. Remove the rod cap with the bearing shell. Completely clean the bearing shell and the crank journal, blow any oil from the oil hole in the crankshaft; place the Plastigage® lengthwise along the bottom center of the lower bearing shell, then install the cap with the shell and torque the bolt or nuts to specification. Do not turn the crankshaft with the Plastigage® on the bearing.
2. Remove the bearing cap with the shell. The flattened Plastigage® will be found sticking to either the bearing shell or the crank journal. Do not remove it yet.
3. Use the scale printed on the Plastigage® envelope to measure the flattened material at its widest point. The number within the scale which most closely corresponds to the width of the Plastigage® indicates the bearing clearance in thousandths of an inch.
4. Check the specifications chart in this Section for the desired clearance. It is advisable to install a new bearing if the clearance exceeds 0.003 in. (0.0762mm); however, if the bearing is in good condition and is not being checked because of bearing noise, bearing replacement is not necessary.
5. If you are installing new bearings, try a standard size, then each undersize in order until one is found that is within the specified limits when checked for clearance with Plastigage®; each undersize shell has its size stamped on it.

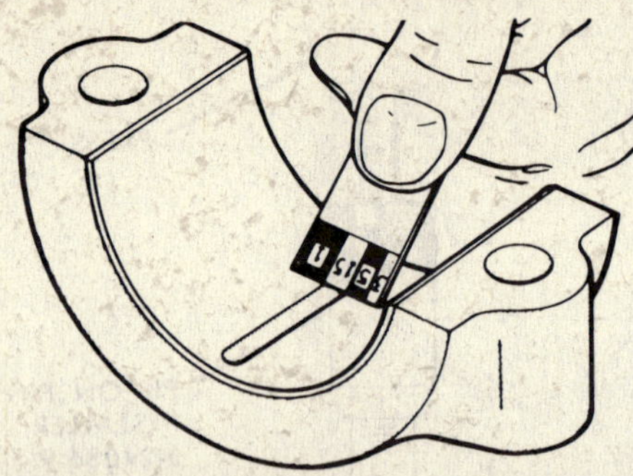

Measuring with Plastigage® to determine the main bearing clearance

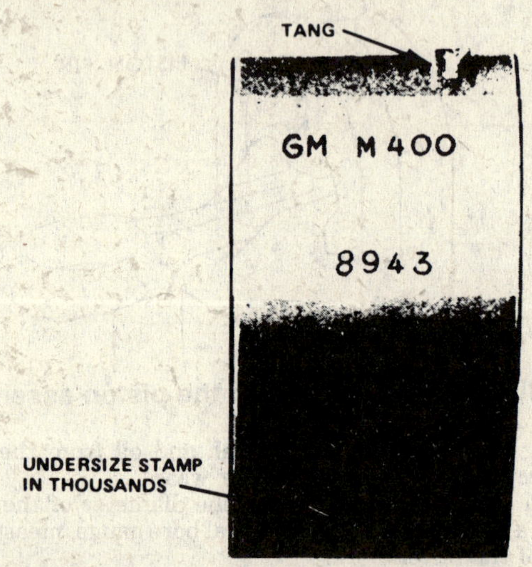

Undersize marks are stamped on the bearing shells. The tang fits in the notch on the rod and cap

6. When the proper size shell is found, clean off the Plastigage®, oil the bearing thoroughly, reinstall the cap with its shell and torque the rod bolt nuts to specifications.

NOTE: With the proper bearing selected and the nuts torqued, it should be possible to move the connecting rod back and forth freely on the crank journal as allowed by the specified connecting rod end clearance. If the rod cannot be moved, either the rod bearing is too far undersize or the rod is misaligned.

INSTALLATION

NOTE: The following procedure requires the use of the ring compressor tool J-8037 or equivalent, and the ring installation tool.

Position the rings on the piston; **spacing of the various piston ring gaps is crucial to proper oil retention and even cylinder wear.** When installing new rings, refer to the installation diagram furnished with the new parts.

Install the connecting rod to the piston, making sure the piston installation notches and marks, if any, on the connecting rod are in proper relation to one another.

1. Make sure the connecting rod big-end bearings (including the end cap) are of the correct size and properly installed.
2. Fit rubber hoses over the connecting rod bolts to protect the crankshaft journals, as in the Piston Removal procedure. Lubricate the connecting rod bearings with clean engine oil.

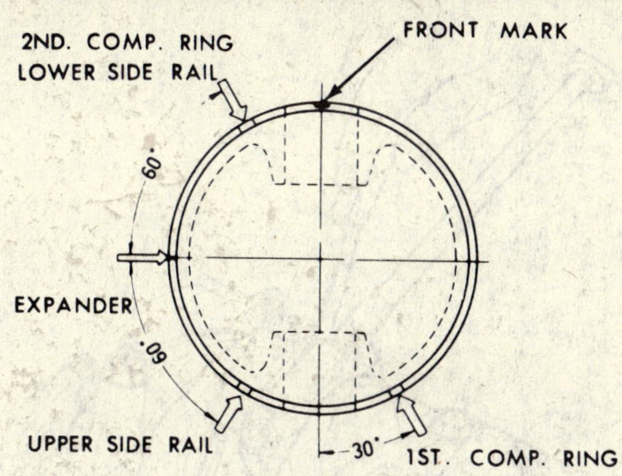

Piston ring positioning — 1.9L engine

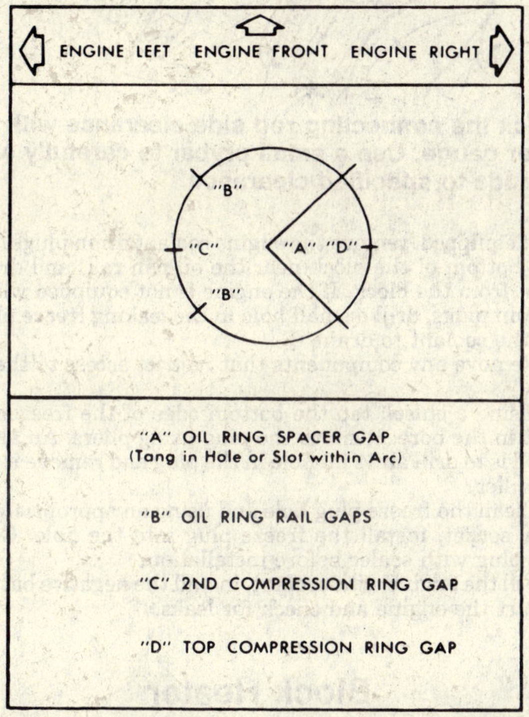

Piston ring spacing — 2.0L and 2.5L engines

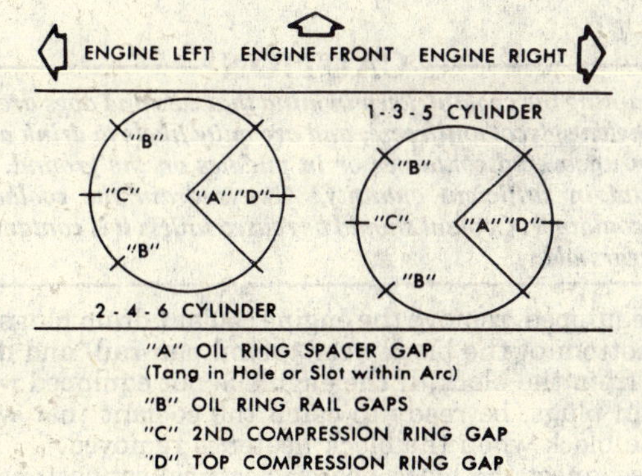

Piston ring positioning — 2.8L and 4.3L engines

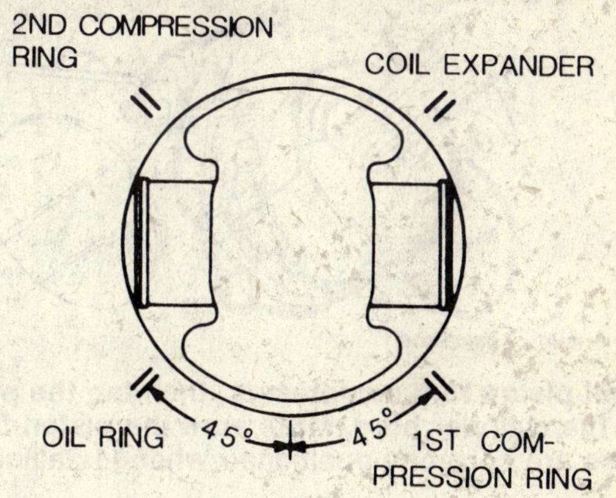

Piston ring positioning — 2.2L diesel engine

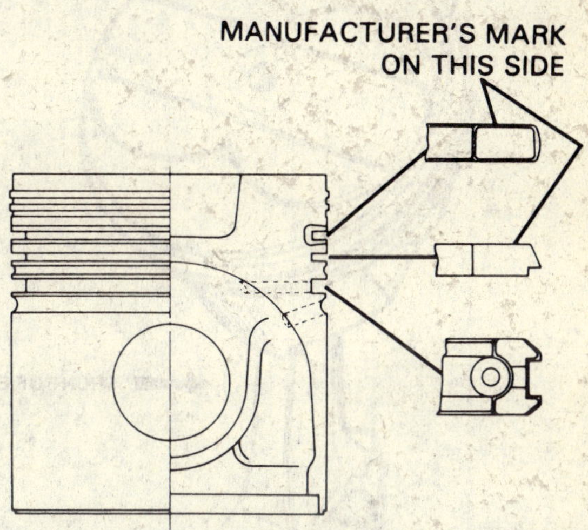

Installing the rings onto the piston — typical

3. Using the ring compressor tool J-8037 or equivalent, compress the rings around the piston head. Insert the piston assembly into the cylinder, so the notch (on top of the piston) faces the front of the engine.

4. Working under the engine, coat each crank journal with clean oil. Using a hammer handle, drive the connecting rod/piston assembly into the cylinder bore. Align the connecting rod (with bearing shell) onto the crankshaft journal.

5. Remove the rubber hoses from the studs. Install the bearing cap (with bearing shell) onto the connecting rod and the cap nuts. Torque the connecting rod cap nuts to 43 ft. lbs. for 1.9L engine, 36 ft. lbs. for 2.0L engine, 62 ft. lbs. for 2.2L engine, 32 ft. lbs. for 2.5L engine or 39 ft. lbs. for 2.8L and 4.3L engines.

NOTE: When more than one connecting rod/piston assembly are being installed, the connecting rod cap nuts should only be tightened enough to keep each rod in position until the all have been installed. This will ease the installation of the remaining piston assemblies.

6. Check the clearance between the sides of the connecting rods and the crankshaft using a feeler gauge. Spread the rods slightly with a small prybar to insert the feeler gauge. If the clearance is below the minimum tolerance, the rod may be machined to provide adequate clearance. If the clearance is excessive, substitute an unworn rod and recheck. If clearance is still outside specifications, the crankshaft must be welded and reground or replaced.

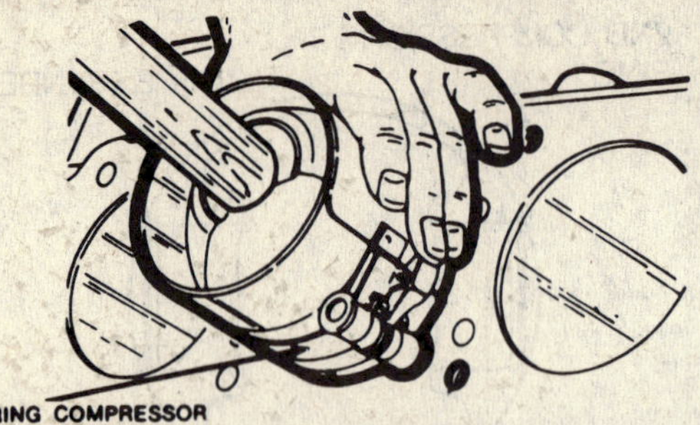

Install piston ring compressor, then tap the piston into the cylinder bore. Make sure the piston front marks are correctly positioned when installing

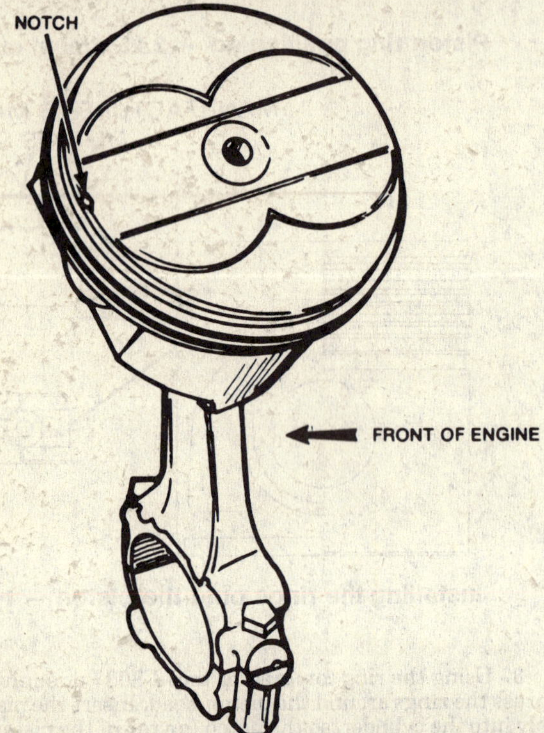

Install the pistons with the notch facing the front of the engine

7. To complete the installation, reverse the removal procedures. Refill the cooling system. Refill the engine crankcase. Start the engine, allow it to reach normal operating temperatures and check for leaks.

Freeze Plugs

REMOVAL AND INSTALLATION

1. Remove the negative battery cable.
2. Drain the cooling system.

CAUTION

When draining the coolant, keep in mind that cats and dogs are attracted by the ethylene glycol antifreeze, and are quite likely to drink any that is left in an uncovered container or in puddles on the ground. This will prove fatal in sufficient quantity. Always drain the coolant into a sealable container. Coolant should be reused unless it is contaminated or several years old.

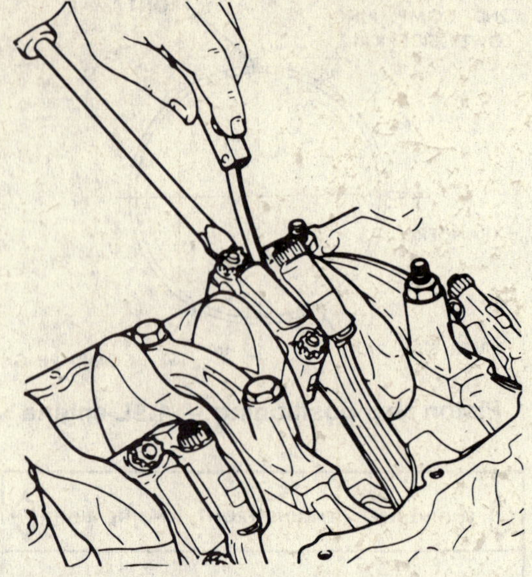

Check the connecting rod side clearance with a feeler gauge. Use a small prybar to carefully spread the rods to specified clearance

3. If equipped, remove the engine coolant drain plugs (located at the bottom of the block near the oil pan rail) and drain the coolant from the block. If the engine is not equipped with coolant drain plugs, drill a small hole in the leaking freeze plug and allow the coolant to drain.
4. Remove any components that restrict access to the freeze plug.
5. Using a chisel, tap the bottom edge of the freeze plug to cock it in the bore. Remove the plug using pliers. An alternate method is to drill an ⅛ in. hole in the plug and remove it using a dent puller.
6. Clean the freeze plug hole and using an appropriate driver tool or socket, install the freeze plug into the hole. Coat the freeze plug with sealer before installation.
7. Fill the engine with coolant, install the negative battery cable, start the engine and check for leaks.

Block Heater

REMOVAL AND INSTALLATION

1. Remove the negative battery cable.
2. Drain the cooling system.

CAUTION

When draining the coolant, keep in mind that cats and dogs are attracted by the ethylene glycol antifreeze, and are quite likely to drink any that is left in an uncovered container or in puddles on the ground. This will prove fatal in sufficient quantity. Always drain the coolant into a sealable container. Coolant should be reused unless it is contaminated or several years old.

3. If equipped, remove the engine coolant drain plugs (located at the bottom of the block near the oil pan rail) and drain the coolant from the block. If the engine is not equipped with coolant drain plugs, be ready to catch the coolant that will drain from the block when the block heater is removed.
4. Disconnect the block heater electrical connector.
5. Loosen the block heater retaining screw and remove the block heater from the engine.

6. Coat the block heater O-ring with engine oil and clean the block heater hole of rust.
7. Install the block heater and tighten the retaining screw.
8. Fill the engine with coolant, install the negative battery cable, start the engine and check for leaks.

Rear Main Oil Seal

REPLACEMENT

1.9L Engine

NOTE: The following procedure requires the use of the seal installer tool J-22928-A or equivalent

1. Disconnect the negative battery terminal.
2. Raise and support the front of the vehicle on jackstands.
3. Position a catch pan under the oil pan, remove the drain plug and drain the crankcase. Remove the oil pan-to-engine bolts and the oil pan from the engine.

CAUTION

The EPA warns that prolonged contact with used engine oil may cause a number of skin disorders, including cancer! You should make every effort to minimize your exposure to used engine oil. Protective gloves should be worn when changing the oil. Wash your hands and any other exposed skin areas as soon as possible after exposure to used engine oil. Soap and water, or waterless hand cleaner should be used.

4. Remove driveshaft from the differential and slide it from the transmission. Remove the torque converter-to-flywheel bolts for automatic transmission, the transmission-to-engine bolts, the crossmember and the transmission.

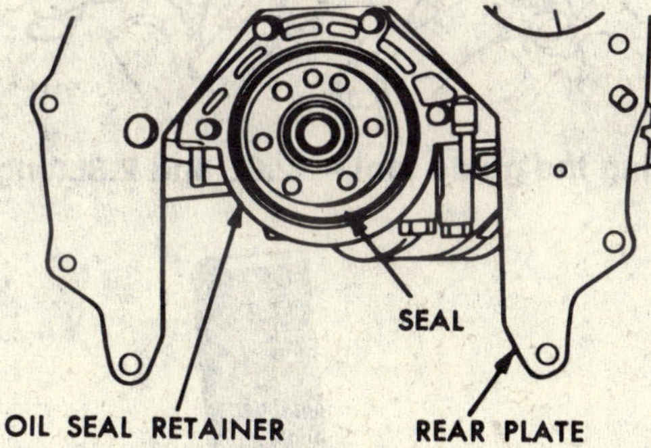

View of the rear main oil seal — 1.9L engine

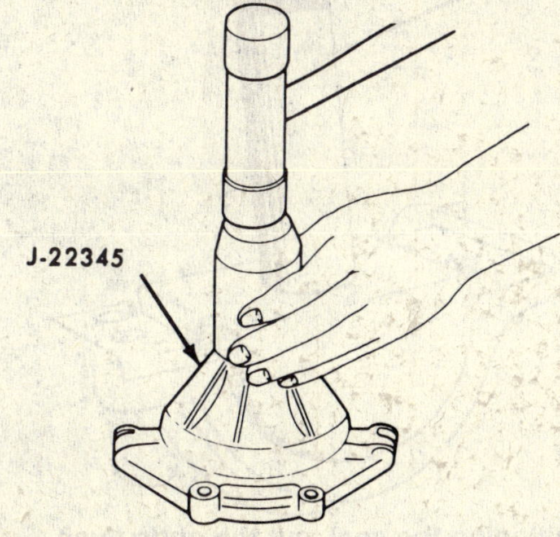

Installing the rear main oil seal — 1.9L engine

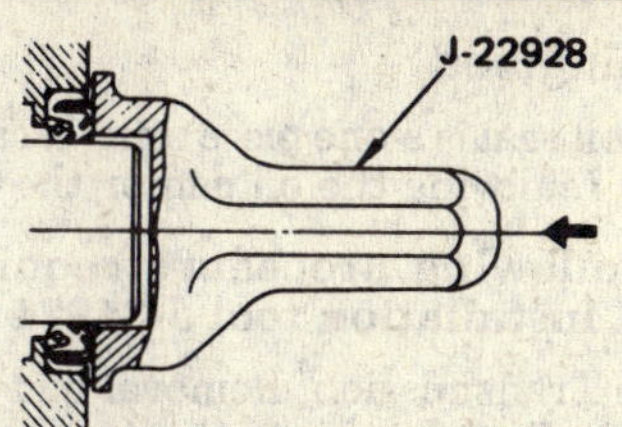

Installing the rear main oil seal — 2.2L diesel engine

CAUTION

Before removing the transmission, be sure to secure the engine.

NOTE: On manual transmissions, remove the clutch assembly.

5. Unbolt the starter and support it out of the way.
6. Remove the flywheel-to-crankshaft bolts and the flywheel.
7. Remove the rear main seal retainer from the engine.
8. Using a medium prybar, remove the rear main oil seal from the retainer and discard it.
9. To install, lubricate the seal lips, fill the space between the seal and the crankshaft with grease. Using the seal installer tool J-22928-A or equivalent, drive the new rear main oil seal into it's housing.
10. To complete the installation, reverse the removal procedures. Refill the crankcase.

2.2L Diesel Engine

NOTE: The following procedure requires the use of the seal installation tool J-22928 or equivalent.

1. Refer to the Engine, Removal and Installation procedures in this section and remove the engine from the vehicle.
2. Remove the flywheel-to-crankshaft bolts and the flywheel.
3. Using a medium prybar, pry the rear main seal from the rear of the engine.
4. Using clean engine oil, lubricate the lips of the new seal.
5. Using the seal installation tool J-22928 or equivalent, drive the new seal into the rear of the engine until it seats.
6. To complete the installation, reverse the removal procedures.

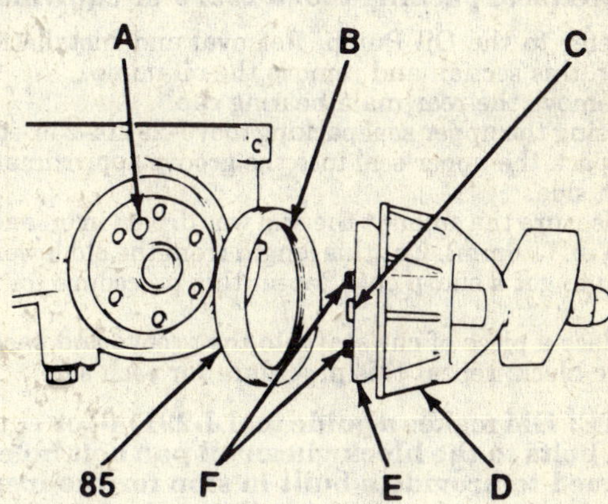

A. Alignment hole in crankshaft
B. Dust lip
C. Dowel pin
D. Collar
E. Mandrel
F. Screws
85. Crankshaft rear oil seal

Installing the rear main oil seal — 2.5L and 4.3L engines

2.5L and 4.3L Engines

The rear main oil seal is a one piece unit. It can be removed or installed without removing the oil pan or the crankshaft.

NOTE: The following procedure requires the use of the GM oil seal installation tool J-34924 or equivalent.

1. Refer to the Transmission, Removal and Installation procedures in Section 7 and remove the transmission from the vehicle.
2. If equipped with a manual transmission, remove the clutch assembly, the flywheel-to-crankshaft bolts and the flywheel from the crankshaft.
3. Using a small prybar, pry the oil seal from the rear of the crankshaft.

NOTE: When removing the oil seal, be careful not to damage the crankshaft sealing surface.

4. To install the new oil seal into the rear retainer, perform the following procedures:
   a. Using new engine oil, lubricate the inner and outer diameter of the seal.
   b. Using the GM oil seal installation tool J-34924 or equivalent, install the new oil seal onto it, position the assembly against the crankshaft.
   c. Align the dowel with the alignment hole in the crankshaft and thread the attaching screws into the tapped holes in the crankshaft.
   d. Using a screwdriver, tighten the screws securely; this will ensure that the seal is installed squarely over the crankshaft.
   e. Turn the handle until it bottoms and remove the installation tool.
5. To complete the installation, install the flywheel, the clutch assembly and the transmission. Torque the flywheel-to-crankshaft bolts to 55 ft. lbs. and the bellhousing-to-engine bolts to 46 ft. lbs.

2.0L and 2.8L Engines

NOTE: The following procedure requires the use of the upper seal packing tool J-29114-2 or equivalent, and the lower seal packing tool J-29590 or equivalent.

1. Refer to the Oil Pump, Removal and Installation procedures in this section and remove the oil pump.
2. Remove the rear main bearing cap.
3. Using the upper seal packing tool J-29114-2 or equivalent, gently pack the upper seal into the groove approximately ¼ in. on each side.
4. Measure the amount the seal was driven in on one side and add $^1/_{16}$ in. (1.6mm). Cut this length from the old lower cap seal. Be sure to get a sharp cut. Repeat this procedure for the other side.
5. Place a piece of cut seal into the groove and pack the seal into the block; repeat this procedure for each side.

NOTE: GM makes a guide tool J-29114-l or equivalent, which bolts to the block via an oil pan bolt hole and are machined to provide a built-in stop for the installation of the short cut pieces. Using the packing tool, work the short pieces of seal onto the guide tool, then pack them into the block.

6. Install a new lower seal in the rear main cap.
7. Install a piece of Platigage® or equivalent, on the bearing journal. Install the rear cap and tighten to 70 ft. lbs. Remove the cap and check for gauge for bearing clearance. If out of specification, the ends of the seal may be frayed or not flush, preventing the cap from proper seating. Correct as required.
8. Clean the journal, and apply a thin film of sealer to the

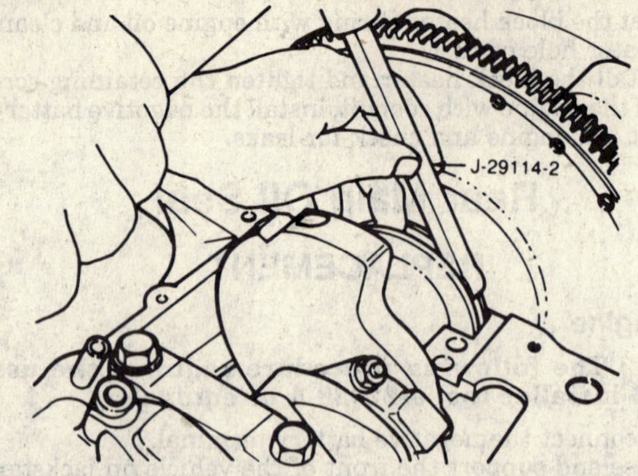

Using the packing tool — 2.0L and 2.8L engines

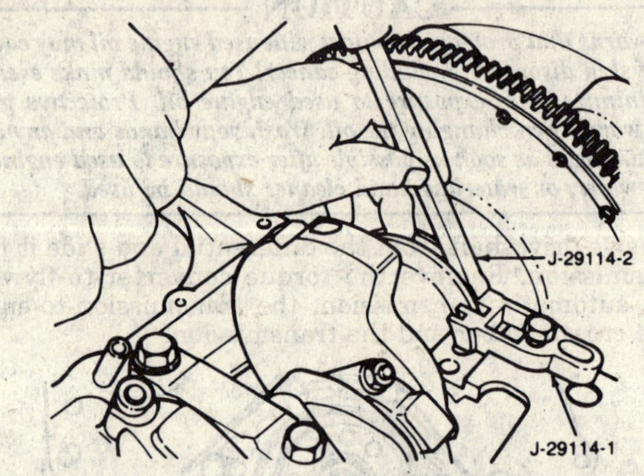

Using the guide tool — 2.0L and 2.8L engines

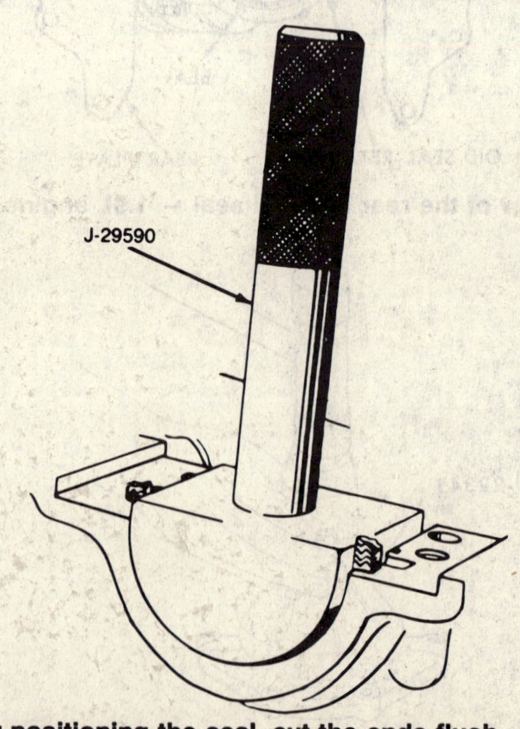

After positioning the seal, cut the ends flush — 2.0L and 2.8L engines

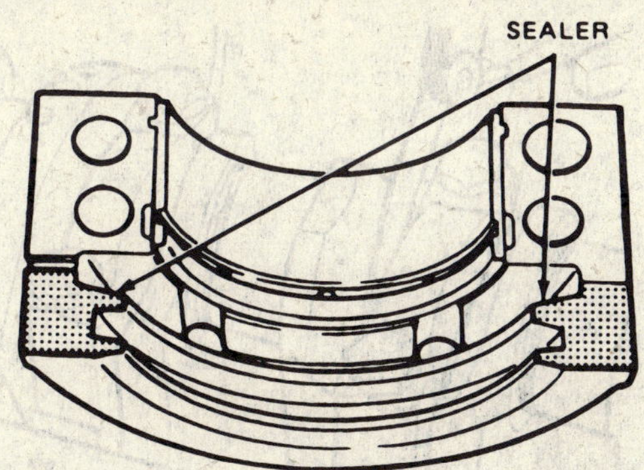

Applying sealer to the rear main cap — 2.0L and 2.8L engines

mating surfaces of the cap and tighten to 70 ft. lbs. Install the pan and pump.

9. Clean the journal, and apply a thin film of sealer to the mating surfaces of the cap and block. Do not allow any sealer to get onto the journal or bearing. Install the bearing cap and tighten to 70 ft. lbs.

10. To complete the installation, reverse the removal procedures.

Crankshaft and Main Bearings

REMOVAL AND INSTALLATION

NOTE: The following procedure requires the use of the main bearing removal/installation tool J-8080, a fabricated cotter pin or equivalent.

1. Refer to the Engine, Removal and Installation procedures in this section and remove the engine from the vehicle.

NOTE: If removing the crankshaft from the 1.9L engine, it will be necessary to remove the timing sprocket from the rocker arm shaft to disconnect the timing chain from the crankshaft sprocket.

2. If equipped with a flywheel, remove it and mount the engine onto a workstand.
3. Disconnect the spark plug wires from the plugs, then remove the spark plugs.
4. Remove the drive belt pulley from the damper pulley/hub, the damper pulley/hub-to-crankshaft bolt, the damper pulley/hub from the crankshaft and the timing cover from the engine.

NOTE: After removing the damper pulley/hub from the crankshaft, be sure to remove the woodruff key from the crankshaft. When removing the damper pulley/hub from the crankshaft, the oil seal should be replaced.

5. Rotate the crankshaft, until the timing marks on the timing gears or sprockets align with each other, then remove the timing gear or sprocket from the crankshaft.

NOTE: After removing the timing gear or sprocket from the crankshaft, be sure to remove the woodruff key from the crankshaft.

6. Place a catch pan under the engine, remove the oil pan plug and drain the oil into the pan. Invert the engine and remove the oil pan from the engine.

CAUTION

The EPA warns that prolonged contact with used engine oil may cause a number of skin disorders, including cancer! You should make every effort to minimize your exposure to used engine oil. Protective gloves should be worn when changing the oil. Wash your hands and any other exposed skin areas as soon as possible after exposure to used engine oil. Soap and water, or waterless hand cleaner should be used.

7. On the 2.0L, 2.2L (diesel), 2.8L and 4.3L engines, it will be necessary to remove the oil pump.
8. Inspect the connecting rods and bearing caps for identification marks (numbers); if there are none, mark them for reassembly purposes.
9. Remove the connecting rod nuts and caps, then store them in the order of removal. Be sure to place short pieces of rubber hose on the connecting rod studs to prevent damaging the crankshaft bearing surfaces.

NOTE: When installing the rubber hoses onto the connecting rod studs, position the long tool so it may be used to push the connecting rod up into the bore.

10. Check the main bearing caps for identification marks, if not identified, mark them. Remove the main bearing caps and store them in order, for reassembly purposes; the caps must be reinstalled in their original position.
11. Remove the crankshaft, the main bearing inserts and the rear main oil seal, the rear main oil seal/retainer or the rear main oil shell sections.

NOTE: When removing the bearing shells, it is recommended to replace them with new ones.

12. Using solvent, clean all of the parts for inspection purposes. If necessary, replace any part that may be questionable.
13. To install, use new bearing shell inserts and check the bearing clearances using the Plastigage® method.

NOTE: If necessary, deliver the crankshaft to an automotive machine shop, have the crankshaft journals ground and new bearing shells matched.

14. Lubricate all of the parts and oil seals with clean engine oil.
15. Using a feeler gauge and a medium prybar, move the crankshaft forward-and-rearward, then the feeler gauge to check the crankshaft end play.
16. To complete the installation, use new gaskets (sealant if necessary) and reverse the removal procedures. Torque the main bearing cap-to-engine bolts to 70 ft. lbs. for all

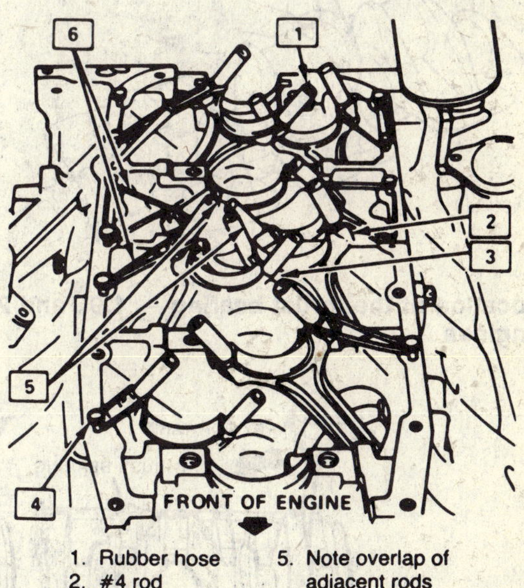

Support the connecting rods with rubber bands and install rubber rod bolt caps when the crankshaft is removed — V6 engines

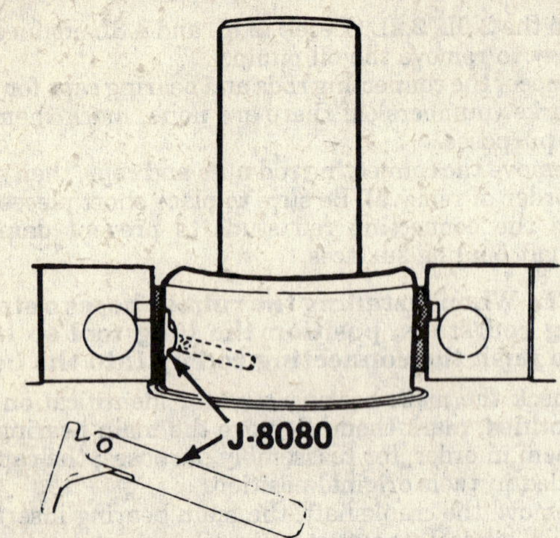

Using the main bearing removal/installation tool No. J-8080

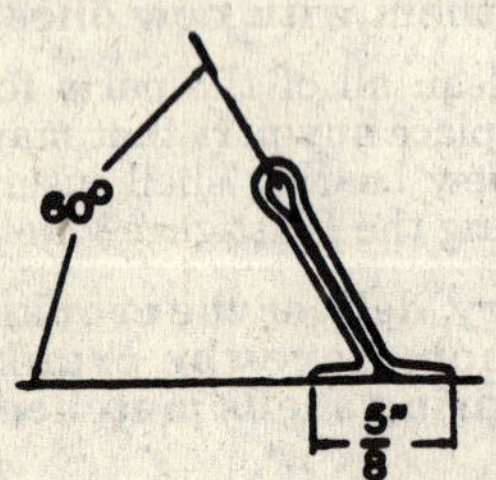

Fabricate a roll-out pin as illustrated, if necessary

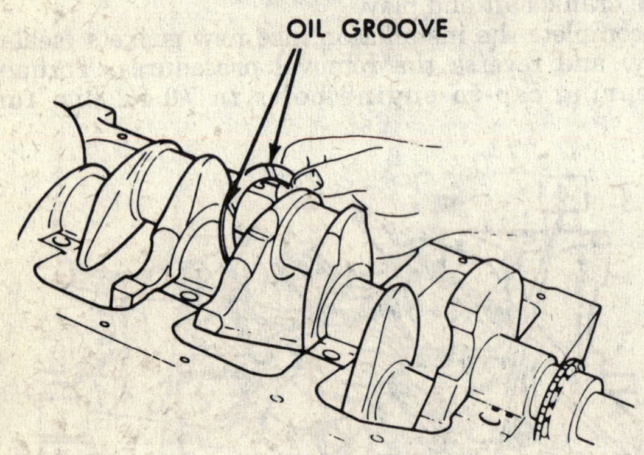

Location of the thrust bearing — 1.9L and 2.2L engines

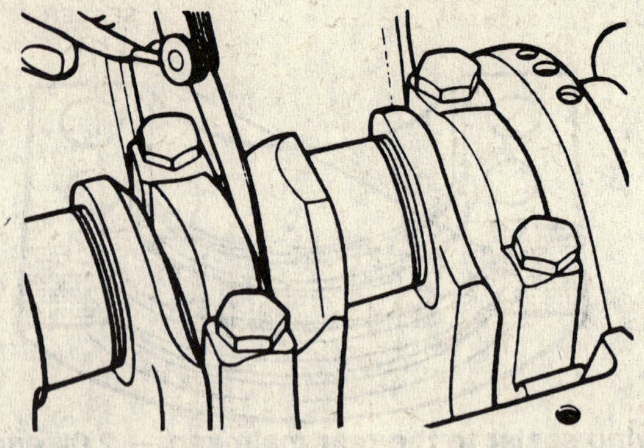

Use a feeler gauge to check the crankshaft endplay during assembly

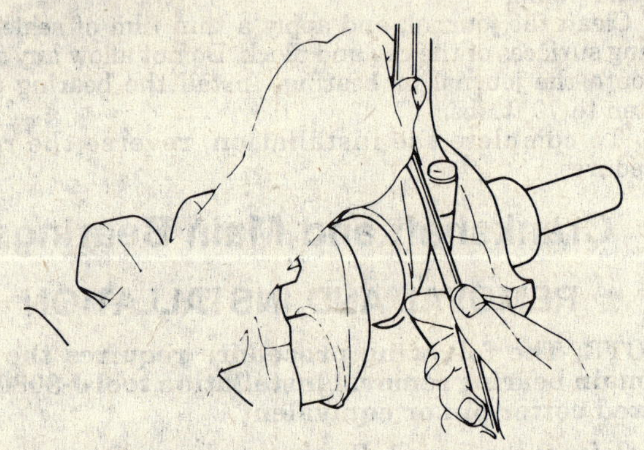

Measuring conneting rod side clearance

engines,except 2.2L diesel or 124 ft. lbs. for 2.2L diesel engine. Refill the cooling system (with the saved coolant) and the crankcase (with new oil). Start the engine, allow it to reach normal operating temperatures and check for leaks.

CLEANING AND INSPECTION

NOTE: The following procedure requires the use of a set of V-blocks, a dial indicator, an outside micrometer, an inside micrometer and Plastigage®.

1. Remove the bearing cap and wipe the oil from the crankshaft journal and outer/inner surfaces of the bearing shell.
2. To inspect the crankshaft bearing journals, perform the following procedures:
   a. Using a set of V-blocks and a dial indicator, inspect the main bearing journals for runnout; if necessary, regrind the bearing journals.
   b. Using an outside micrometer, measure the main bearing

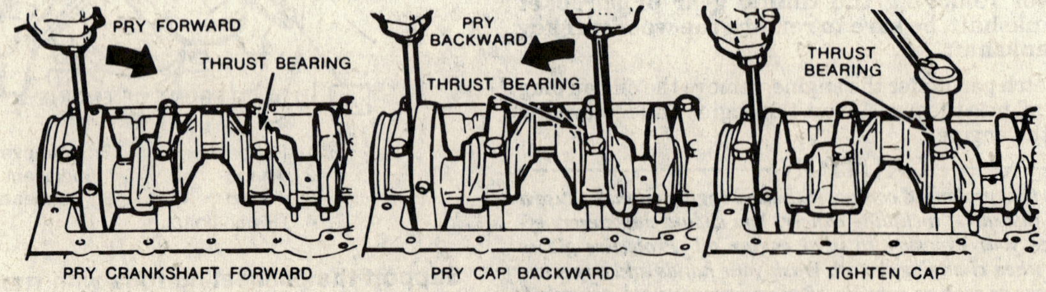

Aligning the thrust bearings and torquing the main bearing caps

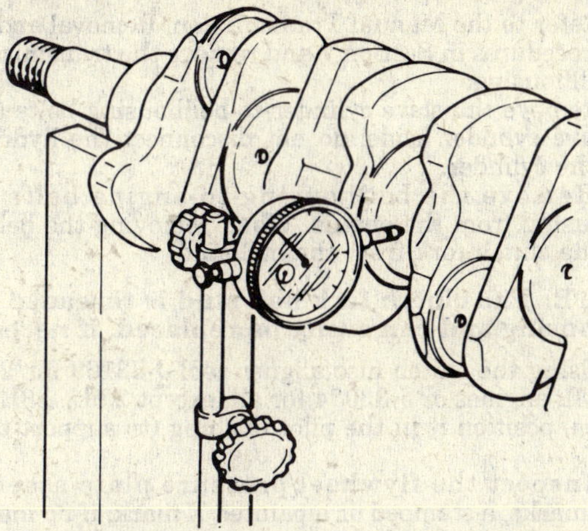
Checking crankshaft journal runout

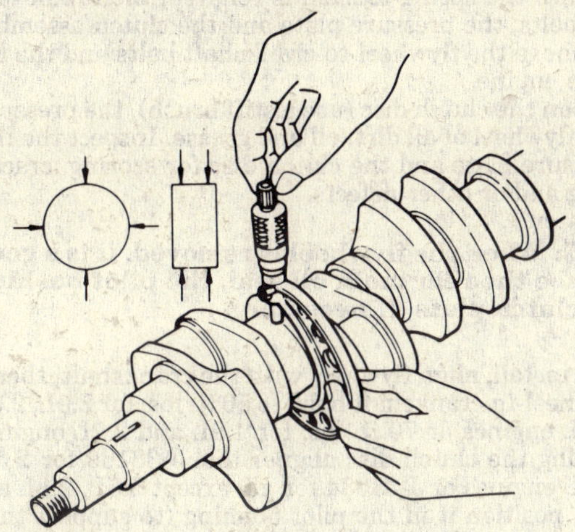
checking main bearing journal diameter

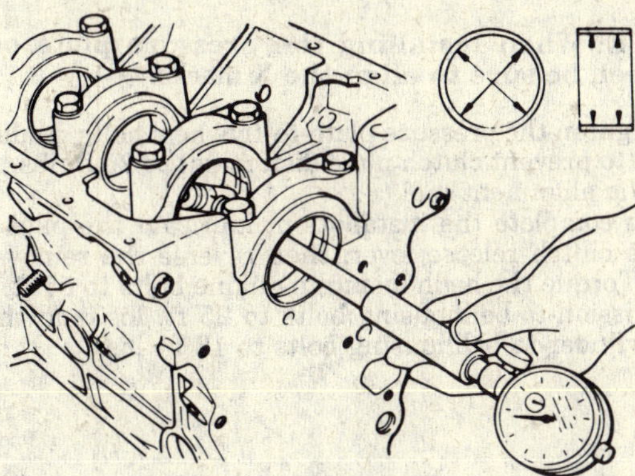
Measuring the main bearing diameter

journals for diameter and out-of-round conditions; if necessary, regrind the bearing journals.

c. Install the main bearing caps and torque the nuts/bolts to specifications. Using an inside micrometer, inspect the main bearing journals in the engine block; if necessary, rebore the bearing seats in the engine block.

3. To inspect the main bearing surfaces, using the Plastigage® method, perform the following procedures:

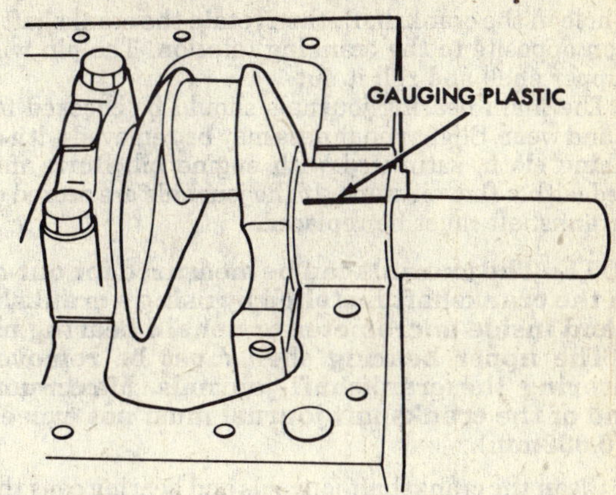

Measuring Plastigage® after bearing cap removal

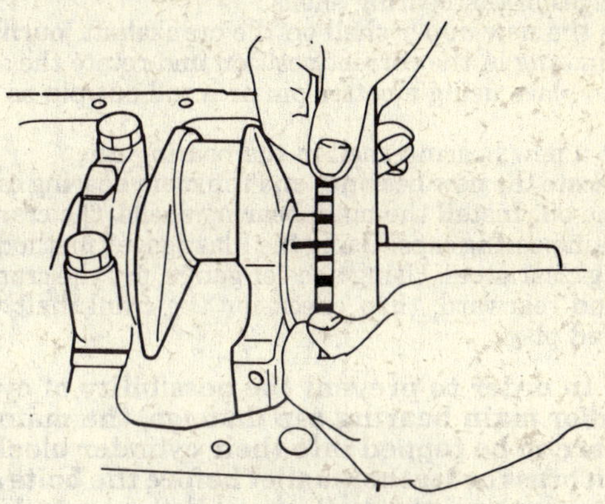
Using Plastigage®

a. Using a piece of Plastigage® material, position it in the center of the main bearing surface(s).

b. Install the main bearing cap(s) and torque the cap nuts/bolts to specifications.

NOTE: When the Plastigage® material is installed on the bearing surfaces, do not rotate the crankshaft.

c. Remove the bearing caps and determine the bearing clearance by comparing the width of the flattened Plastigage® material at its widest point with the graduations on the gauging material conatainer.

NOTE: The number within the graduation on the envelope indicates the clearance in millimeters or thousandths of an inch. If the clearance is greater than allowed. Replace both bearing shells as a set. Recheck the clearance after replacing the shells. Refer to the Main Bearing Replacement in this section.

MAIN BEARING REPLACEMENT

Main bearing clearances must be corrected by the use of selective upper and lower shells. Under no circumstances should the use of shims behind the shells to compensate for wear be attempted. To install the main bearing shells, proceed as follows:

1. Refer to the Oil Pan, Removal and Installation procedures in this section and remove the oil pan.
2. Loosen all of the main bearing cap bolts.
3. Remove the bearing cap bolts, the caps and the lower bearing shell.
4. Insert a flattened cotter pin or a roll out pin in the oil pas-

sage hole in the crankshaft, then rotate the crankshaft in the direction opposite to the cranking rotation. The pin will contact the upper shell and roll it out.

5. The main bearing journals should be checked for roughness and wear. Slight roughness may be removed with a fine grit polishing cloth, saturated with engine oil. Burrs may be removed with a fine oil stone. If the journals are scored or ridged, the crankshaft must be replaced.

NOTE: The journals can be measured for out-of-round with the crankshaft installed by using a crankshaft caliper and inside micrometer or a main bearing micrometer. The upper bearing shell must be removed when measuring the crankshaft journals. Maximum out-of-round of the crankshaft journal must not exceed 0.0015 in. (0.038mm).

6. Clean the crankshaft journals and bearing caps thoroughly before installing the new main bearings.
7. Apply special lubricant, GM 1050169 or equivalent, to the thrust flanges of the bearing shells.
8. Place the new upper shell on the crankshaft journal with the locating tang in the correct position and rotate the shaft to turn it into place using a cotter pin or a roll out pin as during removal.
9. Place a new bearing shell in the bearing cap.
10. Lubricate the new bearings and the main bearing cap bolts with engine oil. Install the main bearing shells, the crankshaft and the main bearing caps. Using the Plastigage® method, check the bearing clearances. Using a feeler gauge, pry the crankshaft forward and rearward, then check for the crankshaft (thrust bearing) end play.

NOTE: In order to prevent the possibility of cylinder block and/or main bearing cap damage, the main bearing caps are to be tapped into their cylinder block cavity, using a brass or leather mallet before the bolts are installed. Do not use the bolts to pull the main bearing caps into their seats. Failure to observe this procedure may damage the cylinder block or bearing cap.

11. To complete the installation, use new oil seals, gaskets (sealant, if necessary) and reverse the removal procedures. Torque the main bearing cap-to-engine bolts to 70 ft. lbs. for all, engines – except 2.2L diesel or 124 ft. lbs. for 2.2L diesel engine.

Flywheel

The flywheel and the ring gear are machined from one piece of metal and cannot be separated.

REMOVAL AND INSTALLATION

NOTE: The following procedure requires the use of the clutch disc aligner tool J-33169 for 2.5L and 2.8L engines or J-33034 for all, except 2.5L and 2.8L engines.

1. Refer to the Manual Transmission, Removal and Installation procedures in Section 7 and remove the transmission from the bellhousing.
2. Remove the slave cylinder-to-bellhousing bolts and move the slave cylinder aside; do not disconnect the hydraulic line from the cylinder.
3. Remove the bellhousing-to-engine bolts and the bellhousing from the engine. When removing the bellhousing, slide the clutch fork from the ball stud.

NOTE: The clutch fork ball stud is threaded into the bellhousing and can easily be replaced, if necessary.

4. Using the clutch disc aligner tool J-33169 for 2.5L, 2.8L and 4.3L engines or J-33034 for all, except 2.5L, 2.8L and 4.3L engines, position it in the pilot bushing (to support the clutch disc).
5. Inspect the flywheel/pressure plate assembly for matchmarks, a stamped or a painted **X** mark; if no mark exists, mark the flywheel and the pressure plate.
6. Loosen the clutch-to-flywheel bolts, evenly (one turn at a time), until the spring tension is relieved, then remove the retaining bolts, the pressure plate and the clutch assembly.
7. Remove the flywheel-to-crankshaft bolts and the flywheel from the engine.
8. Clean the clutch disc (use a stiff brush), the pressure plate and the flywheel of all dirt, oil and grease. Inspect the flywheel, the pressure plate and the clutch disc for scoring, cracks, heat checking and/or other defects.

NOTE: When the flywheel is removed, it is a good idea to replace the rear main oil seal, the pilot bushing and/or the clutch plate, if necessary.

9. To install, align flywheel with the crankshaft, then torque the flywheel-to-crankshaft bolts to 50 ft. lbs. for 2.0L, 2.5L, 2.8L and 4.3L engines or 70 ft. lbs. for 1.9L and 2.2L engines.
10. Using the clutch disc aligner tool J-33169 for 2.5L, 2.8L and 4.3L engines or J-33034 for all, except 2.5L, 2.8L and 4.3L engines, position it in the pilot bushing (to support the clutch disc), then assemble the clutch disc (the damper springs facing the transmission), the pressure plate and the retaining bolts onto the flywheel.

NOTE: When installing the pressure plate onto the flywheel, be sure to align the X marks.

11. Tighten the pressure plate-to-flywheel bolts gradually and evenly (to prevent clutch plate distortion) to 20 ft. lbs., then remove the alignment tool.
12. To complete the installation, lubricate the pilot bushing and the clutch release lever, then reverse the removal procedures. Torque the bellhousing-to-engine bolts to 55 ft. lbs., the transmission-to-bellhousing bolts to 25 ft. lbs. and the clutch slave cylinder-to-bellhousing bolts to 13 ft. lbs.

EXHAUST SYSTEM

Two types of pipe connections are used on the exhaust system, they are: the ball joint (to allow angular movement for alignment purposes) and the slip joint. Gaskets are used with the ball joint type connections.

The system is supported by free hanging rubber mountings which permit some movement of the exhaust system but do not allow the transfer of noise and vibration into the passenger compartment. Any noise vibrations or rattles in the exhaust system are usually caused by misalignment of the parts.

CAUTION

Before performing any operation on the exhaust system, be sure to allow it to cool down.

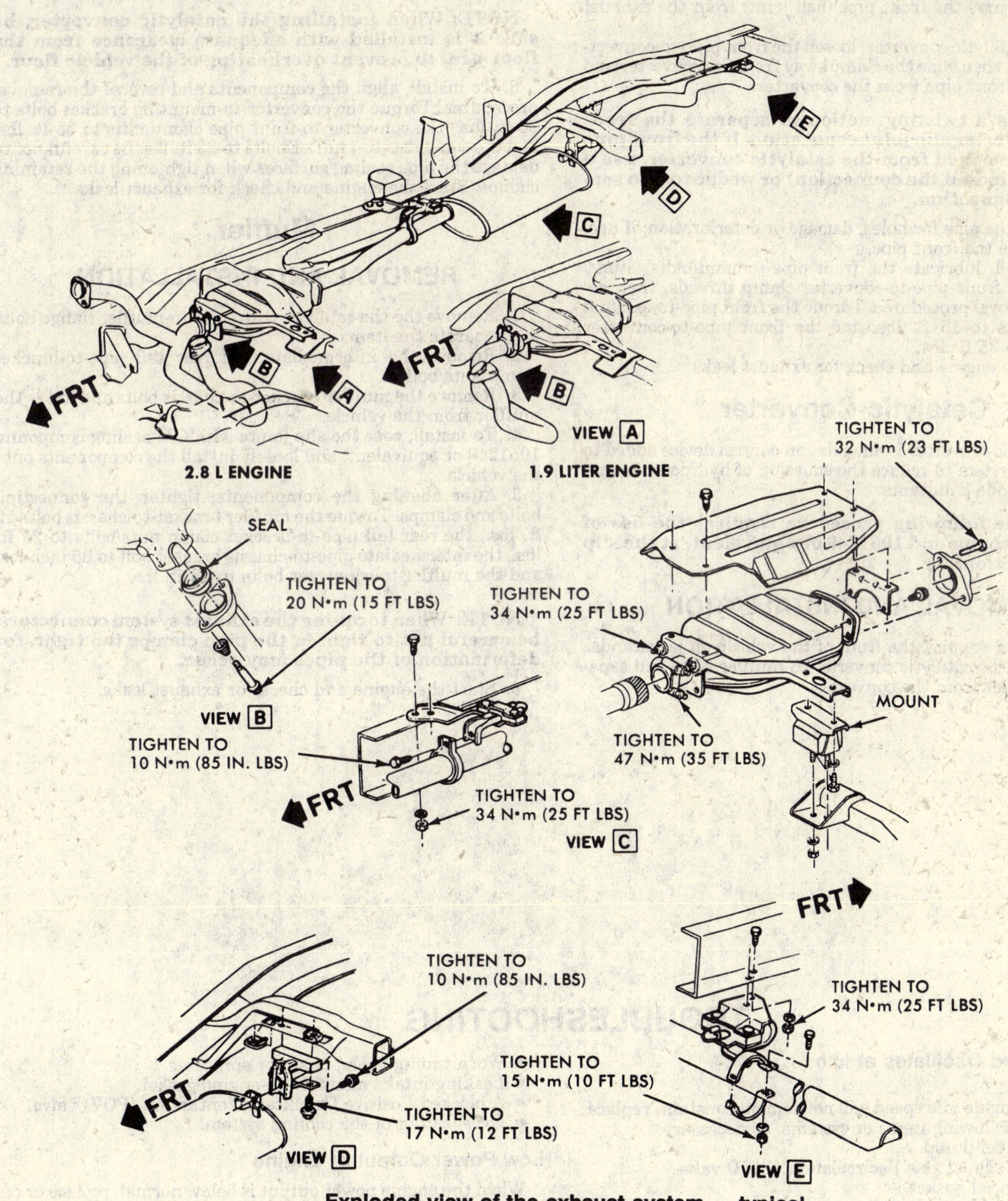

Exploded view of the exhaust system — typical

Front Pipe

REMOVAL AND INSTALLATION

NOTE: The following procedure requires the use of GM sealing compound 1051249 or equivalent, at the slip joint connection.

1. Raise and support the front of the vehicle on jackstands.
2. Remove the front pipe(s)-to-manifold(s) nuts and separate (pry, if necessary) the front pipe (ball joint) from the exhaust manifold(s).
3. At the catalytic converter, loosen the front pipe-to-converter clamp nuts, then slide the clamp away from the converter and separate the front pipe from the converter.

NOTE: Use a twisting motion to separate the front pipe-to-converter slip joint connection. If the front pipe cannot be removed from the catalytic converter, use a hammer (to loosen the connection) or wedge tool to separate the connection.

4. Inspect the pipe for holes, damage or deterioration; if necessary, replace the front pipe.
5. To install, lubricate the front pipe-to-manifold(s) studs/nuts and the front pipe-to-converter clamp threads, then reverse the removal procedures. Torque the front pipe-to-exhaust manifold bolts to 15 ft. lbs. and the front pipe-to-converter clamp nuts to 35 ft. lbs.
6. Start the engine and check for exhaust leaks.

Catalytic Converter

The catalytic converter is an emission control device added to the exhaust system to reduce the emission of hydrocarbon and carbon monoxide pollutants.

NOTE: The following procedure requires the use of GM sealing compound 1051249 or equivalent, at the slip joint connection.

REMOVAL AND INSTALLATION

1. Raise and support the front of the vehicle on jackstands.
2. Remove the catalytic converter-to-muffler bolts and separate the muffler from the converter.

NOTE: The connection between the converter and the muffler is a ball joint type, which can be easily separated.

3. Remove the catalytic converter-to-front pipe clamp nuts and move the clamp forward.
4. Remove the converter-to-mounting bracket bolts, then twist the converter to separate it from the front pipe.
5. Inspect the condition of the catalytic converter for physical damage, replace it, if necessary.

NOTE: When installing the catalytic converter, be sure it is installed with adequate clearance from the floor pan, to prevent overheating of the vehicle floor.

6. To install, align the components and reverse the removal procedures. Torque the converter-to-mounting bracket bolts to 25 ft. lbs., the converter-to-front pipe clamp nuts to 35 ft. lbs. and the converter-to-muffler bolts to 23 ft. lbs. Be careful not to damage the pipe sealing surfaces when tightening the retaining clamps. Start the engine and check for exhaust leaks.

Muffler

REMOVAL AND INSTALLATION

1. Remove the the catalytic converter-to-muffler flange bolts and separate the items.
2. Remove the intermediate and rear tail pipe-to-bracket clamp nuts/bolts.
3. Remove the muffler bracket-to-chassis bolts and lower the muffler from the vehicle.
4. To install, coat the slip joints with GM sealing compound 1051249 or equivalent, and loosely install the components onto the vehicle.
5. After aligning the components, tighten the connecting bolts and clamps. Torque the muffler bracket-to-chassis bolts 12 ft. lbs., the rear tail pipe-to-bracket clamp nuts/bolts to 25 ft. lbs., the intermediate pipe-to-chassis bracket bolt to 85 inch lbs. and the muffler-to-converter bolts to 23 ft. lbs.

NOTE: When torquing the exhaust system connectors, be careful not to tighten the pipe clamps too tight, for deformation of the pipes may occur.

6. Start the engine and check for exhaust leaks.

TROUBLESHOOTING

Engine Speed Oscillates at Idle

When the engine idle speed will not remain constant, replace or repair the following items or systems, as necessary:

- A faulty fuel pump.
- A leaky Exhaust Gas Recirculation (EGR) valve.
- A blown head gasket.
- A worn camshaft.
- Worn timing gears, chain or sprockets.
- Leaking intake manifold-to-engine gasket.
- A blocked Positive Crankcase Ventilation (PCV) valve.
- Overheating of the cooling system.

Low Power Output of Engine

When the engine power output is below normal, replace or repair the following items or systems, as necessary:

- Overheating of the cooling system.
- Leaks in the vacuum system.
- Leaking of the fuel pump or hoses.
- Unadjusted valve timing.
- A blown head gasket.
- A slipping clutch disc or unadjustment pedal.
- Excessive piston-to-bore clearance.
- Worn piston rings.
- A worn camshaft.
- Sticking valve(s) or weak valve spring(s).
- A poorly operating diverter valve.
- A faulty pressure regulator valve for automatic transmission.
- Low fluid level for automatic transmission.

Poor High Speed Operation

When the engine cannot maintain high speed operations, replace or repair the following items or systems, as necessary:

- A faulty fuel pump producing low fuel volume.
- A restriction in the intake manifold.
- A worn distributor shaft.
- Unadjusted valve timing.
- Leaking valves or worn valve springs.

Poor Acceleration

When the engine experiences poor acceleration characteristics, replace or repair the following items or systems, as necessary:

- Incorrect ignition timing.
- Poorly seated valves.
- Improperly adjusted accelerator pump stroke (carburetor equipped).
- Worn accelerator pump diaphragm or piston (carburetor equipped).

Backfire – Intake Manifold

When the engine backfires through the intake manifold, replace or repair the following items or systems, as necessary:

- Incorrect ignition timing.
- Incorrect operation of the choke (carburetor equipped).
- Choke setting (initial clearance) too large (carburetor equipped).
- Defective Exhaust Gas Recirculation (EGR) valve.
- A very lean air/fuel mixture (carburetor equipped).

Backfire – Exhaust Manifold

When the engine backfires through the exhaust manifold, replace or repair the following items or systems, as necessary:

- Leaks in the vacuum hose system.
- Leaks in the exhaust sytem.
- Faulty choke adjustments or operation (carburetor equipped).
- Faulty vacuum diverter valve.

Engine Detonation (Dieseling)

When the engine operates beyond the controlled limits, replace or repair the following items or systems, as necessary:

- Faulty ignition electrical system components.
- The ignition timing may be too far advanced.
- Inoperative Exhaust Gas Recirculation (EGR) valve.
- Inoperative Positive Crankcase Ventilation (PCV) valve.
- Faulty or loose spark plugs.
- Clogged fuel delivery system.
- Sticking, leaking or broken valves.
- Excessive deposits in the combustion chambers.
- Leaks in the vacuum system.

Excessive Oil Leakage

When large amounts of oil are noticed under the engine after each operation, replace or repair the following items or systems, as necessary:

- Damaged or broken oil filter gasket.
- Leaking oil pressure sending switch.
- Worn rear main oil seal gasket.
- Worn front main oil seal gasket.
- Damaged or broken fuel pump gasket (mechanical pump).
- Damaged or loose valve cover gasket.
- Damaged oil pan gasket or bent oil pan.
- Improperly seated oil pan drain plug.
- Broken timing chain cover gasket.
- Blocked camshaft bearing drain hole.

Heavy Oil Consumption

When the engine is burning large amounts of oil, replace or repair the following items or systems, as necessary:

- The engine oil level may be to high.
- The engine oil may be to thin.
- Wrong size of piston rings.
- Clogged piston ring grooves or oil return slots.
- Insufficient tension of the piston rings.
- Piston rings may be sticking in the grooves.
- Excessively worn piston ring grooves.
- Reversed (upsidedown) compression rings.
- Non-staggered piston ring gaps.
- Improper Positive Crankcase Ventilation (PCV) valve operation.
- Damaged valve O-ring seals.
- Restricted oil drain back holes.
- Worn valve stem or guides.
- Damaged valve stem oil deflectors.
- Too long intake gasket dowels.
- Mismatched rail and expander of the oil ring.
- Excessive clearance of the main and connecting rods.
- Scored or worn cylinder walls.

Negative Oil Pressure

When the engine presents no oil pressure, replace or repair the following items or systems, as necessary:

- Low oil level in the crankcase.
- Broken oil pressure gauge or sender.
- Blocked oil pump passages.
- Blocked oil pickup screen or tube.
- Malfunctioning oil pump.
- Sticking oil pressure relief valve.
- Leakage of the internal oil passages.
- Worn (loose) camshaft bearings.

Low Oil Pressure

When the engine presents low oil pressure, replace or repair the following items or systems, as necessary:

- Low oil level in the crankcase.
- Blocked oil pickup screen or tube.
- Malfunctioning or excessive clearance of the oil pump.
- Sticking oil pressure relief valve.
- Very thin engine oil.
- Worn (loose) main, rod or camshaft bearings.

High Oil Pressure

When the engine presents high oil pressure, replace or repair the following items or systems, as necessary:

- Sticking (closed) oil pressure relief valve.
- Wrong grade of oil.
- Faulty oil pressure gauge or sender.

Knocking Main Bearings

When the main bearings are constantly making noise, replace or repair the following items or systems, as necessary:

- Oval shaped crankshaft journals.
- Loose torque converter or flywheel mounting bolts.
- Loose damper pulley hub.
- Excessive clearance of the main bearings.
- Excessive belt tension.
- Low oil supply to the main bearings.
- Extreme crankshaft end play.

Knocking Connecting Rods

When the connecting rod bearings are constantly making noise, replace or repair the following items or systems, as necessary:

- Misaligned connecting rod or cap.
- Missing bearing shell or excessive bearing clearance.
- Incorrectly torqued connecting rod bolts.
- Connecting rod journal of the crankshaft is out-of-round.

Knocking Pistons and Rings

When the pistons and/rings are constantly making noise, replace or repair the following items or systems, as necessary:

- Misaligned connecting rods.
- Out-of-round or tapered cylinder bore.
- Loose or tight ring side clearance.
- Build-up of carbon on the piston(s).
- Piston-to-cylinder bore clearance is excessive.
- Broken piston rings.
- Loose or seized piston pin(s).

Knocking Valve Train

When the valve train is constantly making noise, replace or repair the following items or systems, as necessary:

- Retighten any loose rocker arms.
- Remove any dirt or chips in the valve lifters.
- Excessive valve stem-to-guide clearance.
- Remove restrictions from valve lifter oil holes.
- Incorrect valve lifter may be installed in the engine.
- Valve lock(s) may be missing.
- Valve lifter check ball may be faulty.
- Valve lifter leak down may be excessive.
- Rocker arm nut may be reversed (installed upsidedown).
- Camshaft lobes may be excessively worn.
- Bent or worn pushrods.
- Excessively worn bridged pivots or rocker arms.
- Cocked or broken valve springs.
- Bent valve(s).
- Worn valve lifter face(s).
- Damaged lifter plunger or pushrod seat.

Knocking Valves

When the valves are constantly noisy, replace or repair the following items or systems, as necessary:

- Unadjusted valve lash.
- Valve springs may be broken.
- Pushrods may be bent.
- Camshaft lobes may be excessively worn.
- Dirty or worn valve lifters.
- Valve guides may be worn.
- Valve seat or face runout may be excessive.
- Loose rocker arm studs.

4 Emission Controls

QUICK REFERENCE INDEX

GENERAL INDEX

EMISSION CONTROLS

Crankcase Ventilation System

OPERATION

The crankcase vapors are drawn into the intake manifold to be burned in the combustion chambers, instead of merely venting the crankcase vapors into the atmosphere. An added benefit to engines equipped with this system is that the engine oil will tend to stay cleaner for a longer period of time; therefore, if you notice that the oil in your engine becomes dirty very easily, check the functioning of the PCV valve. Engines which use a PCV system are calibrated to run richer, to compensate for the added air which accompanies the crankcase vapors to be combustion chambers. If the PCV valve or line is clogged, the engine idle will tend to be rough due to excessively rich mixture. Maintenance is covered in Section 1.

On the 1.9L engine, the blow by gases are forced back into the intake manifold through a closed loop system which consists of a baffle plate and an orfice mounted in the intake mainfold.

SERVICE

NOTE: Inspect the PCV system hose(s) and connections at each tune-up and replace any deteriorated hoses. Check the PCV valve at every tune-up and replace it at 30,000 mile intervals.

1. Remove the PCV valve from the rocker arm cover.
2. Operate the engine at idle speed.

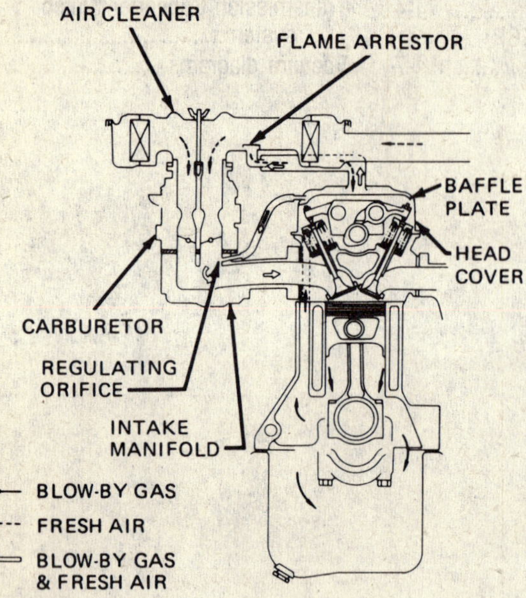

View of the positive crankcase ventilation system – 1.9L engine

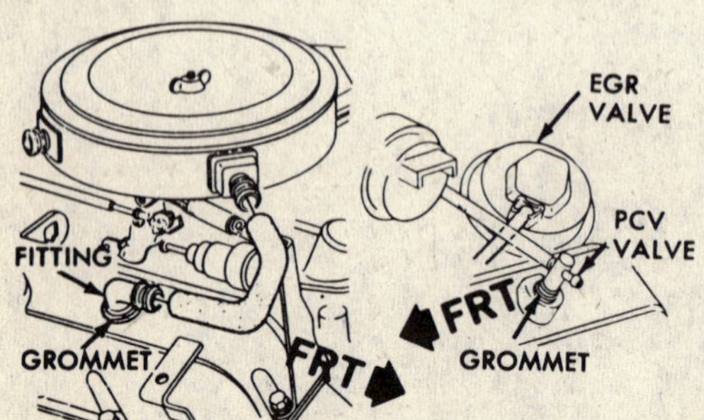

Exploded view of the positive Crankcase ventilation (PCV) valve – 2.8L engine

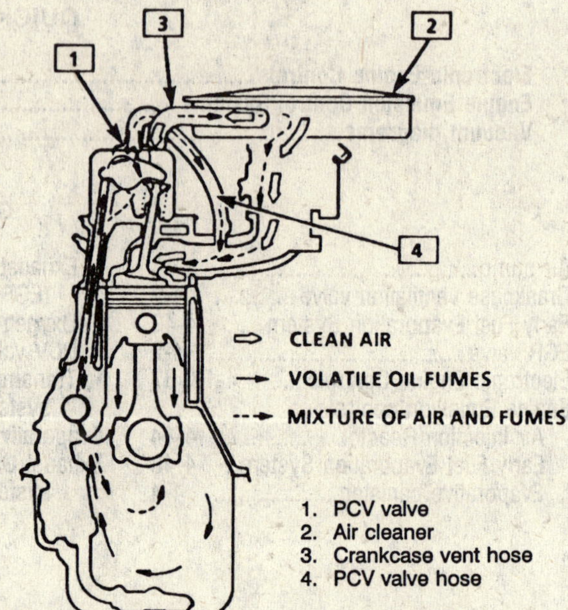

View of the PCV flow – 4 cylinder engines

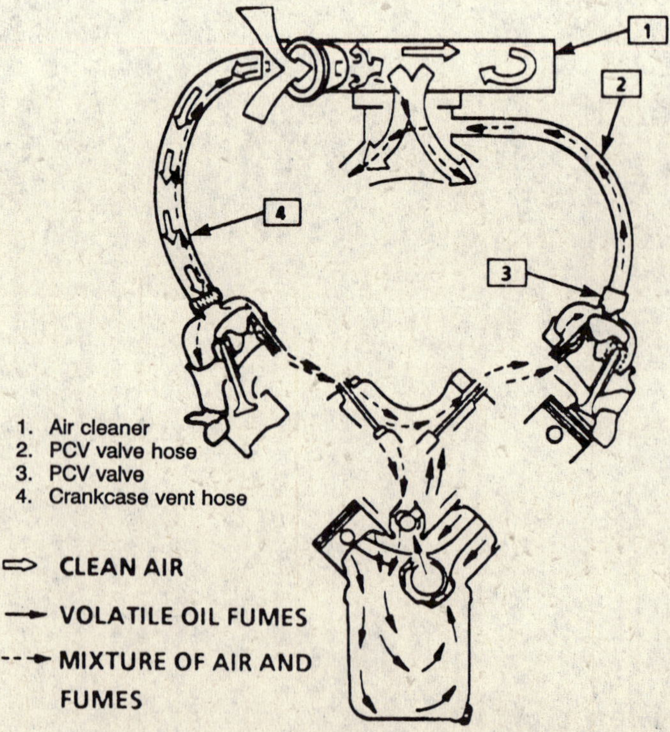

View of the PCV flow – V6 engines

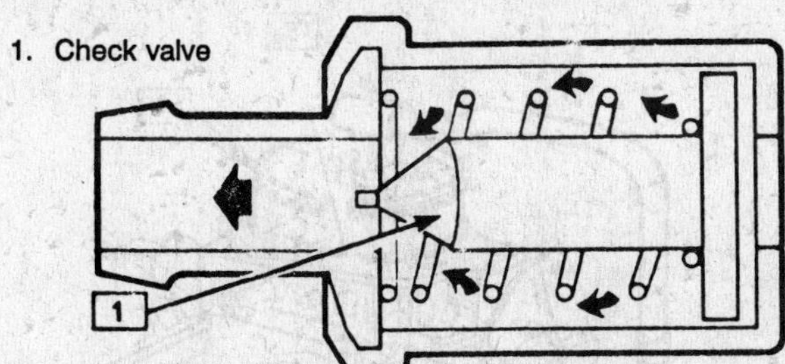

Cross-sectional view of a PCV valve

3. Place your thumb over the end of the valve to check for vacuum. If no vacuum exists, check the valve, the hoses or the manifold port for a plugged condition.

4. Remove the valve from the hose(s), then shake it and listen for a rattling of the check needle (inside the valve); the rattle means the valve is working. If no rattle is heard, replace the valve.

REMOVAL AND INSTALLATION

1. Pull the PCV valve from the rocker arm cover grommet.
2. Remove the hose(s) from the PCV valve.
3. Shake the valve to make sure it is not plugged.

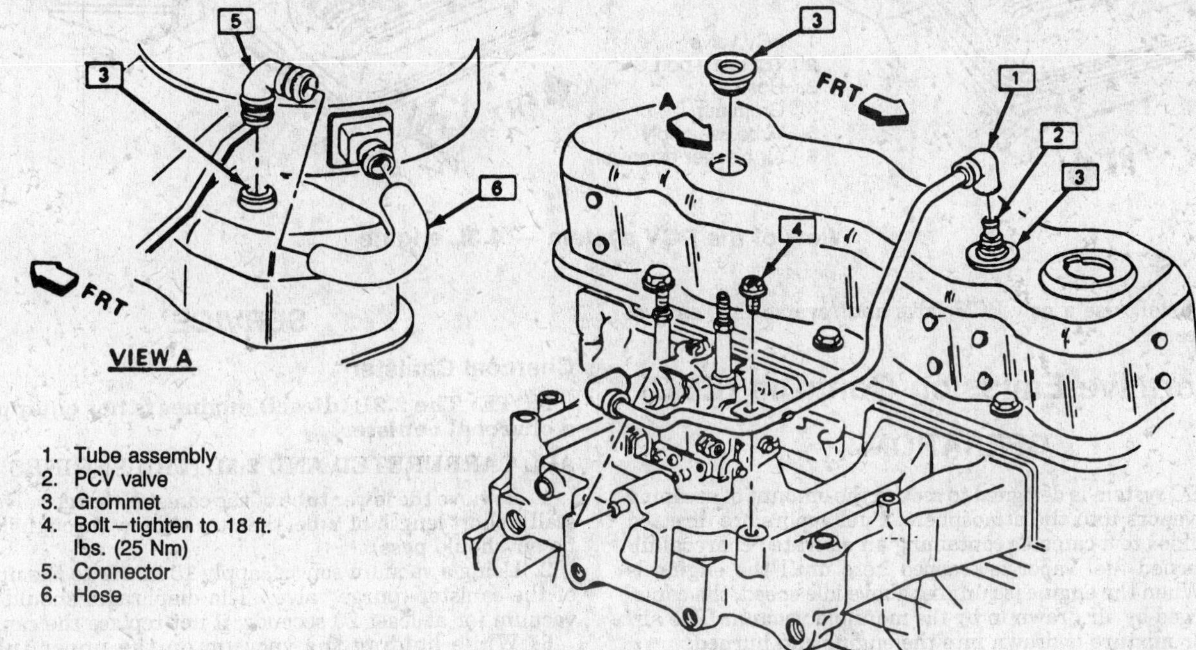

View of the PCV system — 2.5L engine

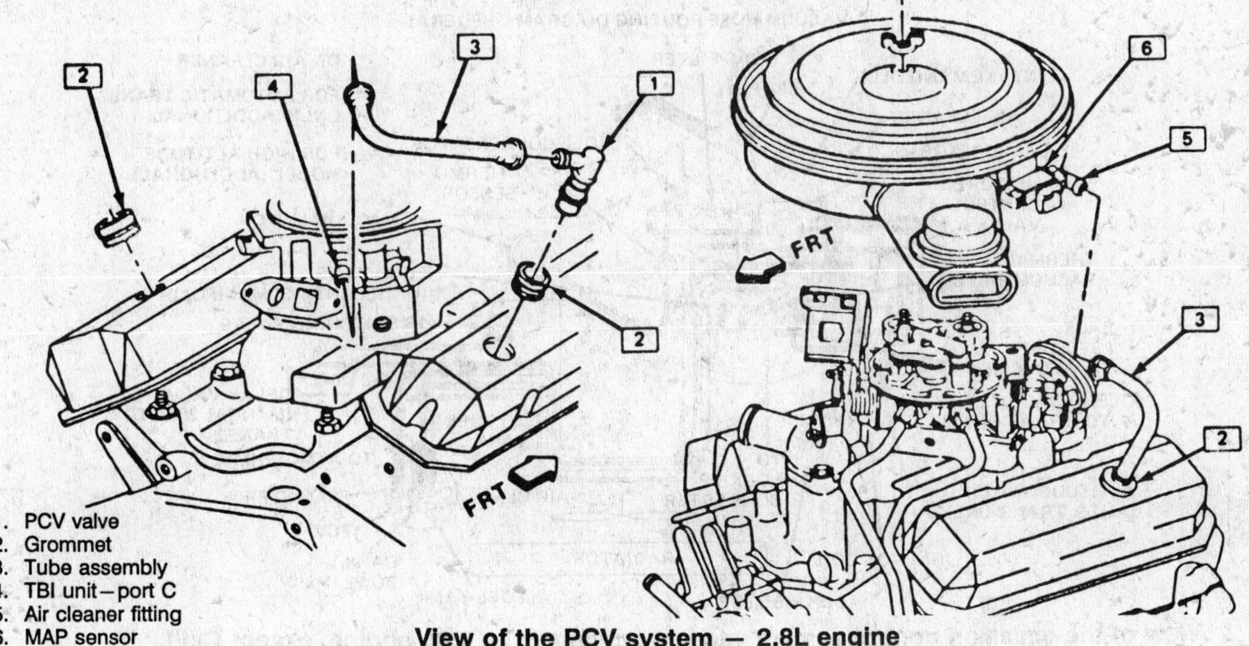

View of the PCV system — 2.8L engine

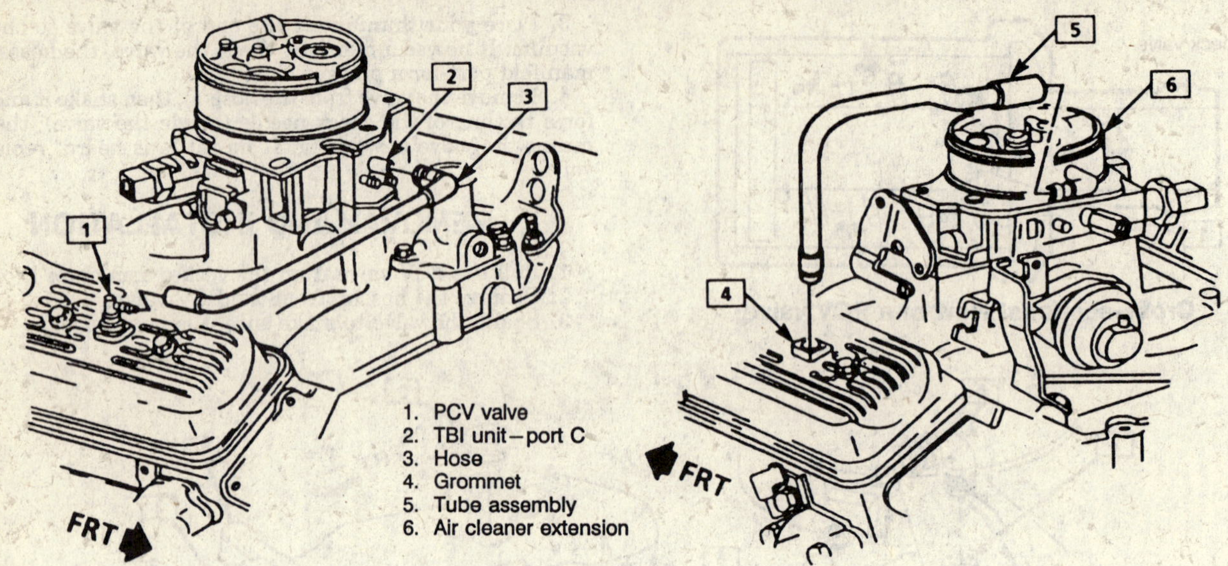

View of the PCV system — 4.3L engine

4. To install, use a new PCV valve and reverse the removal procedures.

Evaporative Emission Controls (EEC)

OPERATION

The EEC system is designed to reduce the amount of escaping gasoline vapors into the atmosphere. Fuel vapors are directed through lines to a canister containing an activated charcoal filter; unburned fuel vapor is trapped here until the engine is started. When the engine is running above idle speed, the canister is purged by air drawn in by the manifold vacuum. The air/fuel vapor mixture is drawn into the engine and burned.

SERVICE

Charcoal Canister

NOTE: The 2.2L (diesel) engines is not equipped with a charcoal canister.

ALL CARBURETED AND 2.5L (TBI) ENGINES

1. Remove the lower tube of the canister (purge valve) and install a short length of tube, then try to blow through it (little or no air should pass).
2. Using a vacuum source, apply 15 in. Hg to the upper tube of the canister (purge valve). The diaphragm should hold the vacuum for at least 20 seconds, if not replace the canister.
3. While holding the vacuum on the upper tube, blow

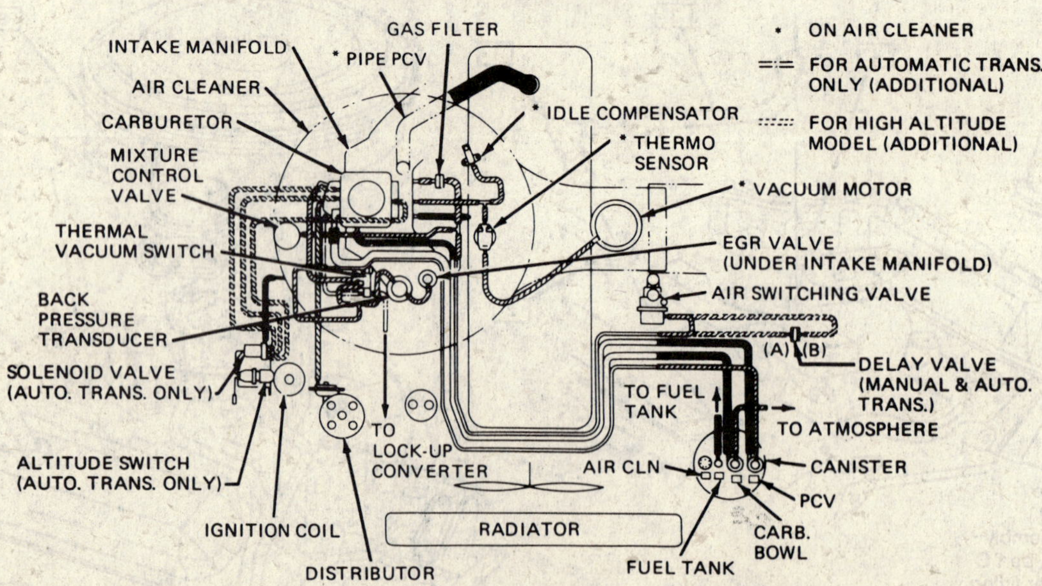

View of the emission control system vacuum schematic — 1.9L engine, except Calif.

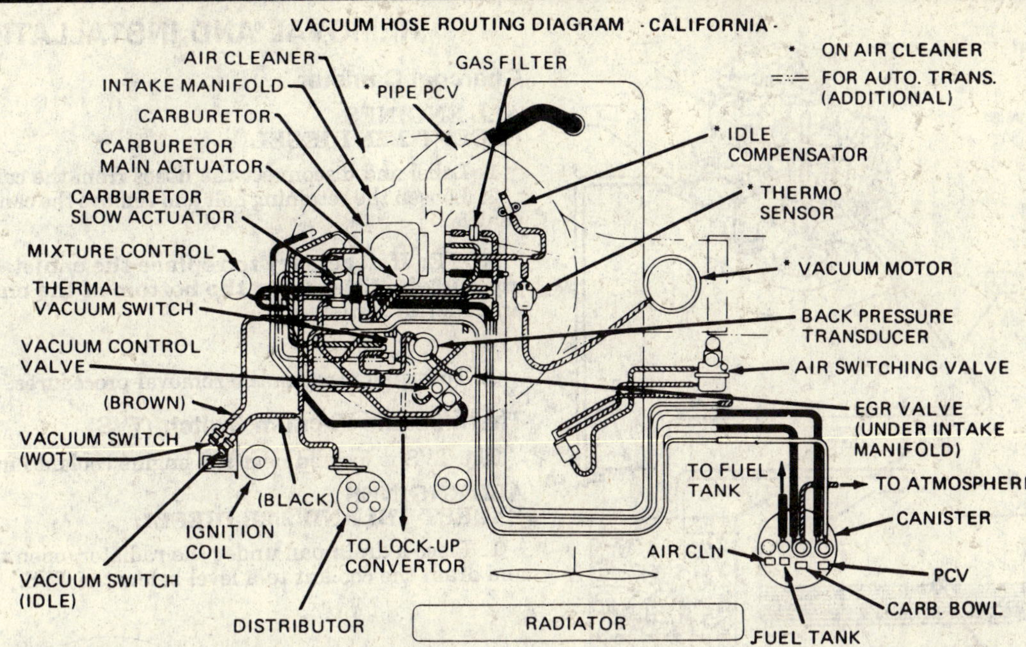

View of the emission control system vacuum schematic — 1.9L engine Calif.

through the lower tube (air should now pass); if not, replace the canister.

Thermostatic Vacuum Switch (TVS)

NOTE: The number stamped on the base of the switch (valve) is the calibration temperature.

CARBURETED ENGINES

1. If the TVS is hot, allow it to cool to a level below the calibration temperature.
2. Make sure the switch is in good condition.
3. Using a vacuum gauge, connect it to the output ports of the TVS and check the vacuum readings.

NOTE: A leakage of up to 2 in. Hg vacuum/2 min. is allowable and does not mean that the valve is defective.

4. Using boiling water, heat the TVS to a level above the calibration temperature; the valve should open, if not, replace it.

1. Carburetor
2. Top view of canister
3. Fuel tank
4. Canister
5. TVS
6. PVC
7. Carburetor bowl vent line
8. Fuel tank vapor line
9. Ported vacuum line
10. Fuel vapor purge line
11. Canister purge valve
12. Control vacuum tube (ported vac)
13. Purge tube (PCV)
14. Canister vent
15. Vapor vent valve
16. Vapor from carburetor tube
17. Control vacuum tube (manifold vac)
18. Sealed fuel tank cap
19. Fuel tank vapor line restriction

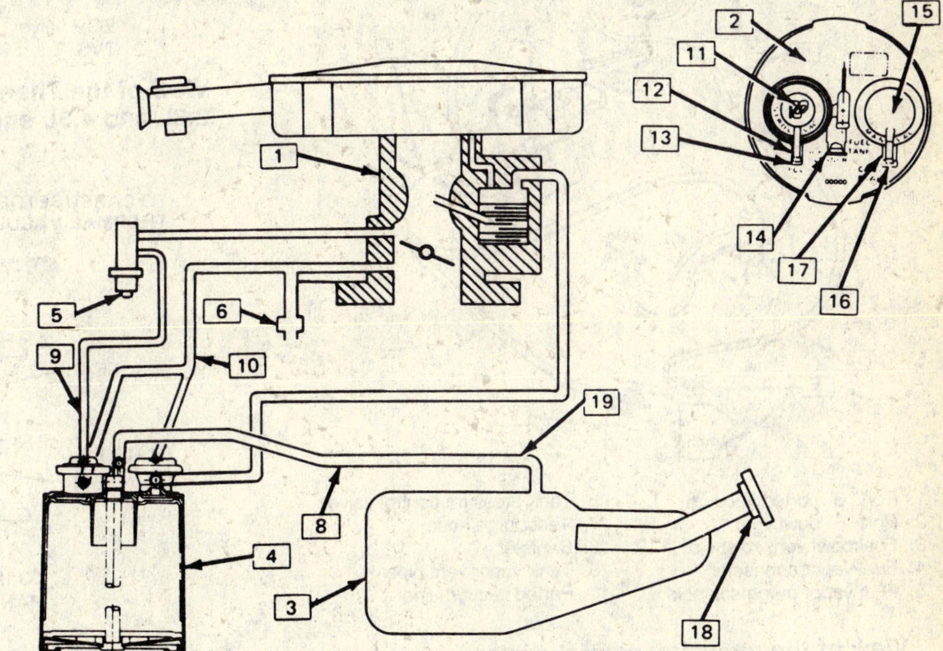

View of the emission control system vacuum schematic — 2.0L, 2.8L and 4.3L engines

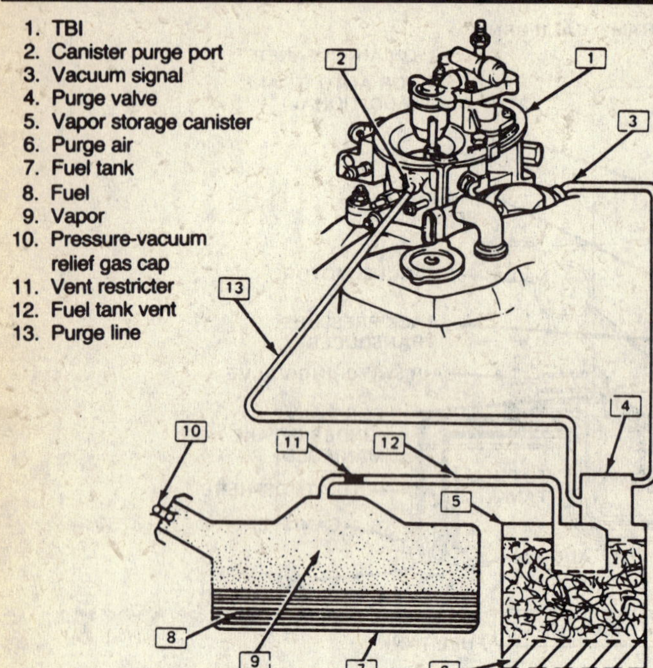

View of the emission control system vacuum schematic — 2.5L engine

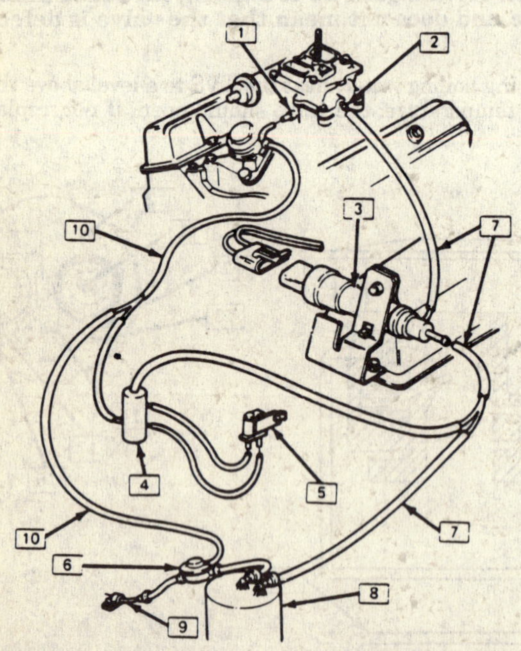

View of the emission control system vacuum schematic — 2.8L and 4.3L engines

REMOVAL AND INSTALLATION

Charcoal Canister

ALL ENGINES
EXCEPT 2.2L DIESEL

1. Label and disconnect the hoses from the canister.
2. Loosen the retaining bolt and remove the canister from the vehicle.

NOTE: If necessary to replace the canister filter, simply pull the filter from the bottom of the charcoal filter and install a new one.

3. To install, reverse the removal procedures.

Thermostatic Vacuum Switch (TVS)

The TVS is located near the engine coolant outlet housing.

ALL ENGINES
EXCEPT TBI AND 2.2L DIESEL

1. Place a drain pan under the radiator, open the drain cock and drain the coolant to a level below the TVS.

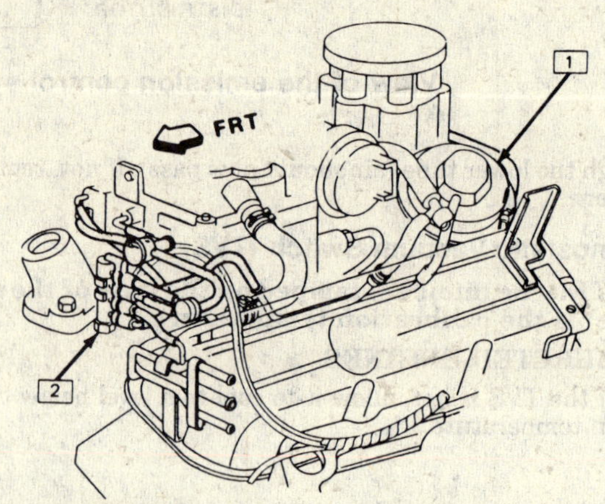

View of the Thermostatic Vacuum Switch (TVS) — 2.8L and 4.3L engines

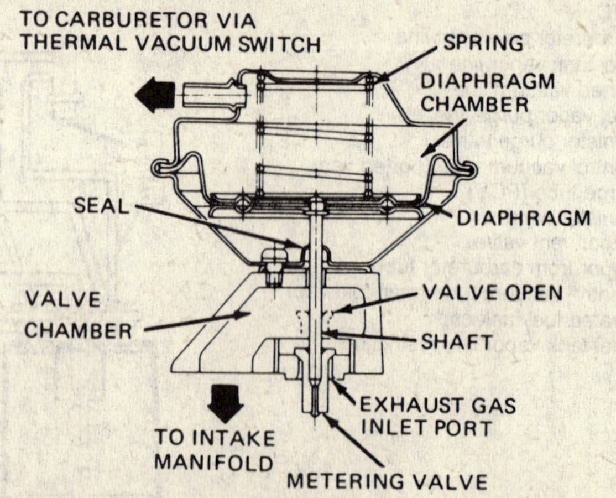

Cross-sectional view of the Exhaust Gas Recycling (EGR) valve — 1.9L engine

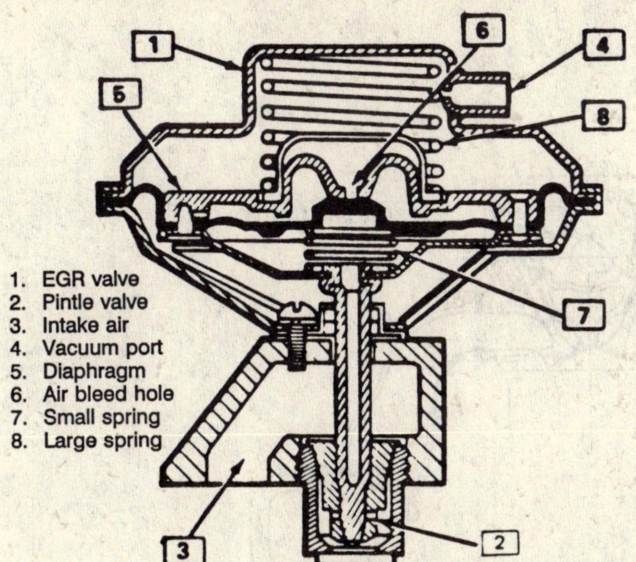

Cross-sectional view of the Exhaust Gas Recycling (EGR) valve with negative backpressure — 2.5L engine

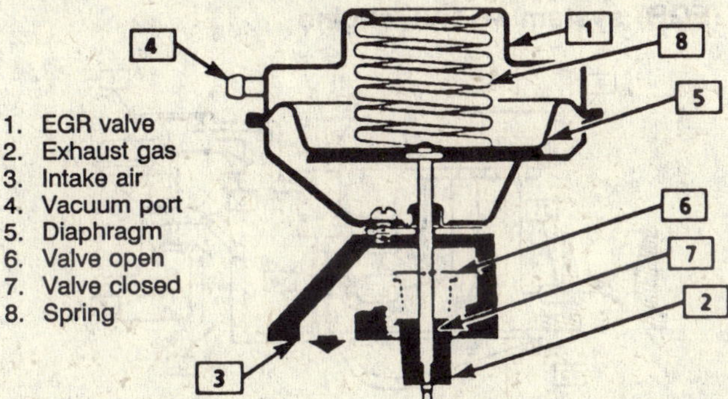

Cross-sectional view of the Exhaust Gas Recycling (EGR) valve — 2.8L and 4.3L engines

CAUTION

When draining the coolant, keep in mind that cats and dogs are attracted by the ethylene glycol antifreeze, and are quite likely to drink any that is left in an uncovered container or in puddles on the ground. This will prove fatal in sufficient quantity. Always drain the coolant into a sealable container. Coolant should be reused unless it is contaminated or several years old.

2. Disconnect the vacuum hoses from the TVS.
3. Using a wrench, remove the TVS from the engine.
4. Inspect and test the TVS; if defective, replace it.
5. Using soft setting sealant, apply it to the TVS threads and reverse the removal procedures. Torque the TVS-to-engine to 120 inch lbs. Reconnect the vacuum hoses. Refill the cooling system.

NOTE: When applying sealant, be sure the sensor end of the TVS does not become covered.

Exhaust Gas Recirculation (EGR) System

The EGR valves are mounted on the intake manifold and is connected, through a pipe to the exhaust manifold.

OPERATION

All engines are equipped with an exhaust gas recirculation (EGR) system. This system consists of a metering valve, a vacuum line to the intake manifold and cast-in exhaust gas passages in the intake manifold.

On the 1.9L engine, the vacuum diaphragm of the EGR valve is connected to a signal port at the carburetor flange through a Back Pressure Transducer (BPT) which is responsive to the exhaust pressure to modulate the vacuum signal and a thermal vacuum valve which operates for the EGR cold override.

On the 2.5L engine, the EGR is controlled by manifold vacuum which accordingly opens and closes to admit exhaust gases into the fuel/air mixture. The exhaust gases lower the combustion temperature and reduce the amount of oxides of nitrogen (NOx) produced. The valve is closed at idle between the two extreme throttle positions.

On the 2.0L and 2.8L carbureted engines, the vacuum to the EGR valve is controlled by a Thermal Vacuum Switch (TVS). On the 2.8L and 4.3L(TBI) engines, the vacuum to the EGR valve is controlled by EGR solenoid (controlled by the ECM). Vacuum to the EGR valve is restricted until the engine is hot. This prevents the stalling and lumpy idle conditions which would result if the EGR occurred when the engine was cold.

SERVICE

EGR Valve

1. Check hose routing (Refer to Vehicle Emission Control Information Label).
2. Check the EGR valve signal tube orifice for obstructions.
3. Connect a vacuum gauge between EGR valve and carburetor, then check the vacuum; the engine must be at operating temperature of 195°F (90°C). With the engine running at approximately 3000 rpm there should be at least 5 in. Hg vacuum.
4. Check the EGR solenoid for correct operation.
5. To check the valve, perform the following procedures:
   a. Depress the valve diaphragm.
   b. With the diaphragm still depressed hold finger over source tube and release the diaphragm.
   c. Check the diaphragm and seat for movement. The valve is good if it takes over 20 seconds for the diaphragm to move to the seated position (valve closed).
   d. Replace the EGR valve if it takes less than 20 seconds to move to the seated position.

EGR Solenoid

2.8L AND 4.3L TBI ENGINES

1. Disconnect the electrical connector from the solenoid.
2. Using an ohmmeter, measure the solenoid's resistance, it should be more than 20Ω. If less than 20Ω, replace the solenoid and/or possibly the ECM.

Thermostatic Vacuum Switch (TVS)

If the thermostatic vacuum switch is not working, a Code 32 will store in the ECM memory and a "Service Engine Soon" lamp will light on the instrument panel.

1. Remove the TVS from the engine.
2. Using a vacuum gauge, connect it to one of the hose connections and apply 10 in. Hg vacuum.

NOTE: A vacuum drop of 2 in. Hg vacuum/2 minutes is allowable.

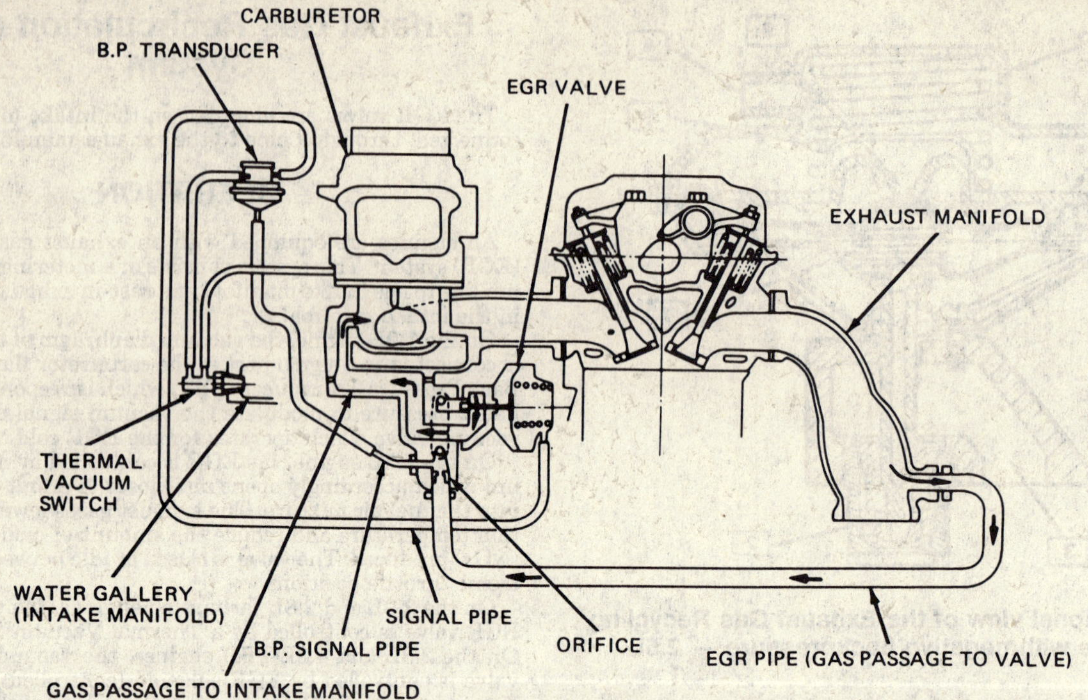

View of the Exhaust Gas Recycling (EGR) system — 1.9L engine

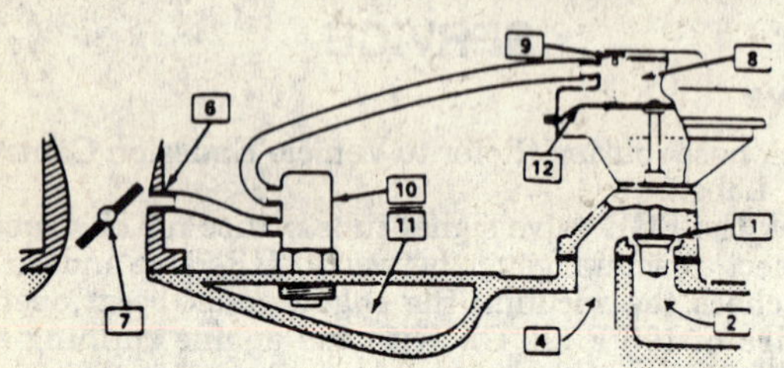

1. EGR valve
2. Exhaust gas
4. Intake flow
6. Vacuum port
7. Throttle valve
8. Vacuum chamber
9. Valve return spring
10. Thermal vacuum switch
11. Coolant
12. Diaphragm

View of the Termostatic Vacuum Switch (TVS) controlled EGR system — 2.8L engine

3. Place the tip of the switch in boiling water. When the switch reaches 195°F (91°C), the valve should open and the vacuum will drop; if not, replace the switch.

RESETTING ECM

To clear the codes stored in the ECM, turn the ignition **OFF** and disconnect the negative battery terminal or the ECM B fuse for 10 seconds.

EGR VALVE CLEANING

NOTE: Do not wash valve assembly in solvents or degreaser — permanent damage to valve diaphragm may result. Also, sand blasting of the valve is recommended since this can affect the operation of the valve.

1. Remove the EGR valve-to-intake manifold bolts and the valve, discard the gasket.
2. With a wire brush, buff the exhaust deposits from the mounting surface and around the valve.
3. Depress the valve diaphragm and look at the valve seating area through the valve outlet for cleanliness. If the valve and/or seat are not completely clean, repeat Step 2.
4. Look for exhaust deposits in the valve outlet. Remove the deposit build-up with a small scraper.
5. Clean the mounting surfaces of the intake manifold and the valve assembly, then using a new gasket install the valve assembly to the intake manifold. Torque the bolts to 35 inch lbs. (4 Nm) for 2.5L engine or 18 inch lbs. (2 Nm) for 2.8L and 4.3L engines.
6. Connect the vacuum hoses.

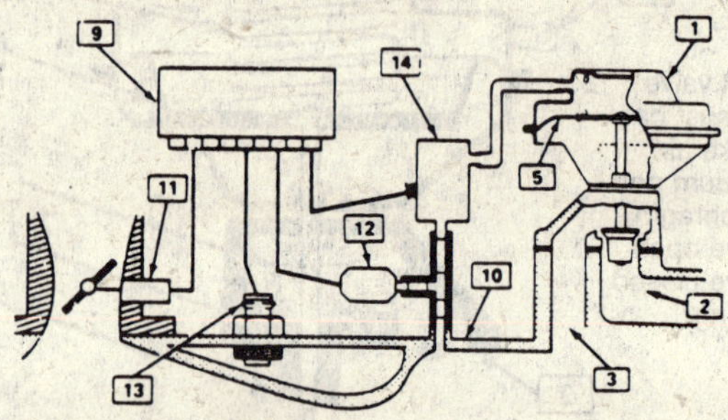

1. EGR valve
2. Exhaust gas
3. Intake air
5. Diaphragm
9. Electronic control module
10. Manifold vacuum
11. Throttle position sensor
12. Manifold pressure sensor
13. Coolant temperature sensor
14. EGR control solenoid

View of the Electronic Control Module (ECM) controlled EGR system — 2.8L and 4.3L TBI engines

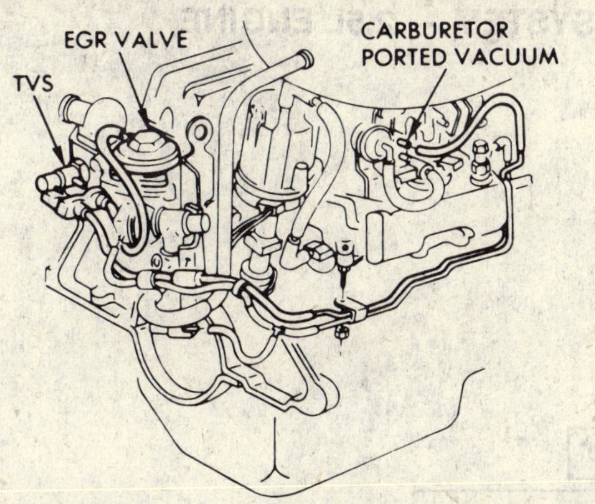

View of the Exhaust Gas Recirculation (EGR) system — 2.0L engine

REMOVAL AND INSTALLATION

EGR Valve

1. Remove the air cleaner.
2. Detach the vacuum hose from the EGR valve.
3. On the 2.8L and 4.3L TBI engines, disconnect the temperature switch from the EGR valve.
4. Remove the EGR valve-to-intake manifold bolts and the valve from the manifold.
5. To install, use a new gasket and reverse the removal procedures. Torque the EGR valve-to-manifold bolts to 18 ft. lbs. (25 Nm) for 2.5L and 2.8L engines or 15 ft. lbs. (20 Nm) for 4.3L engine.

EGR Solenoid

2.8L TBI ENGINE

1. Disconnect the negative battery cable from the battery.
2. Remove the air cleaner.

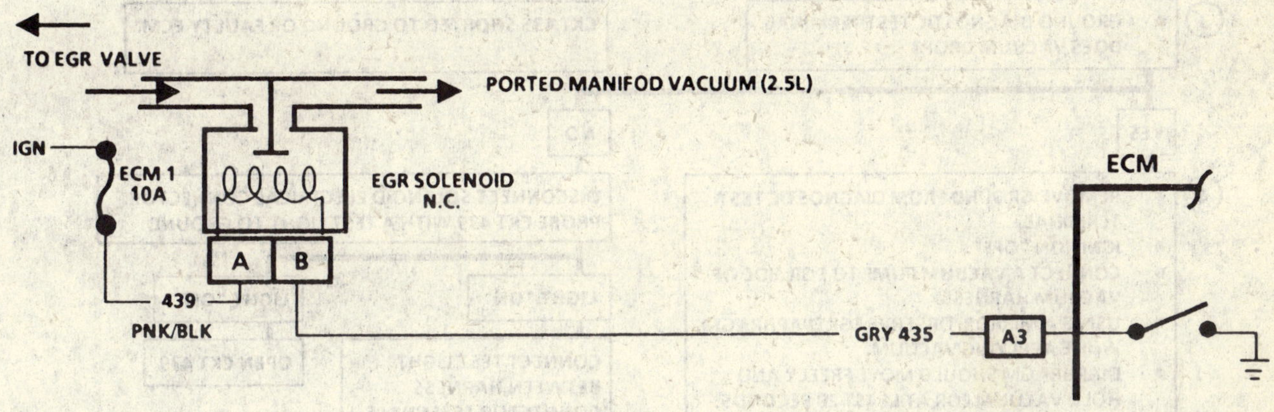

EGR system electrical and vacuum schematic — 2.5L engine

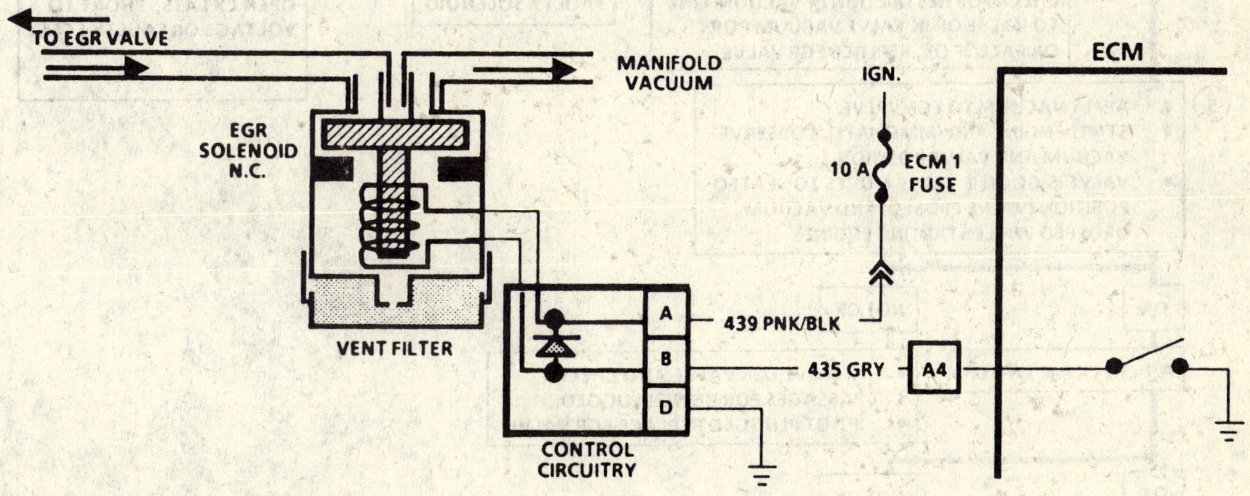

EGR system electrical and vacuum schematic — 2.8L and 4.3L engines

TROUBLESHOOTING THE EGR SYSTEM – 2.5L ENGINE

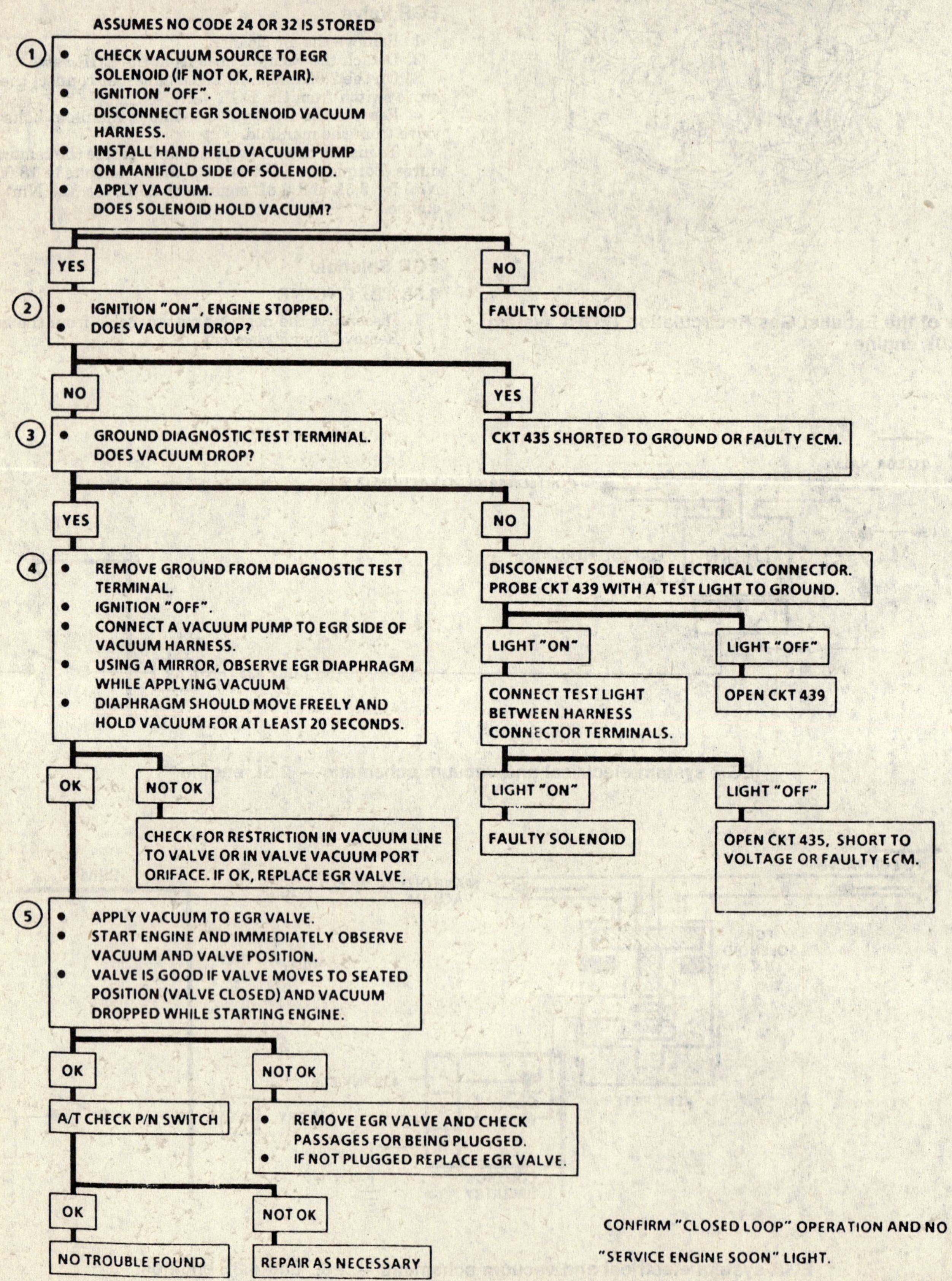

TROUBLESHOOTING THE EGR SYSTEM – 2.8L AND 4.3L

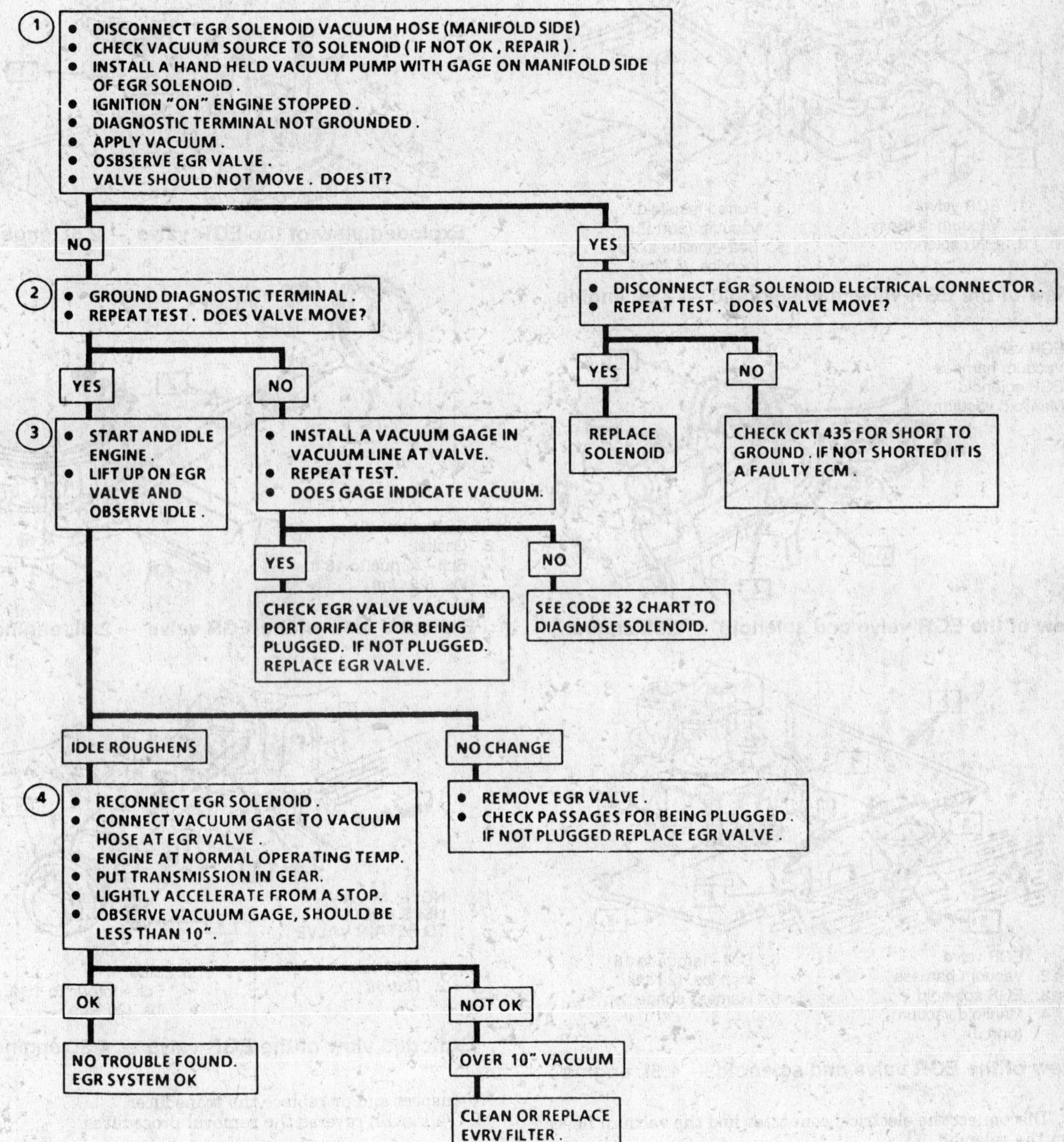

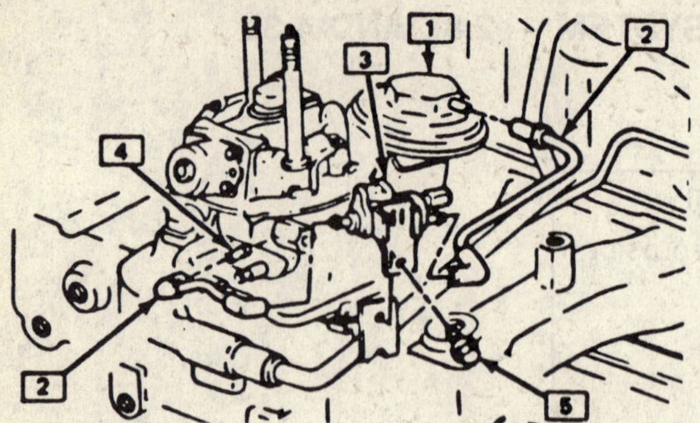

1. EGR valve
2. Vacuum harness
3. EGR solenoid
4. Ported manifold vacuum (port F)
5. Bolt—torque to 35 inch lbs. (4 Nm)

View of the EGR valve and solenoid – 2.5L engine

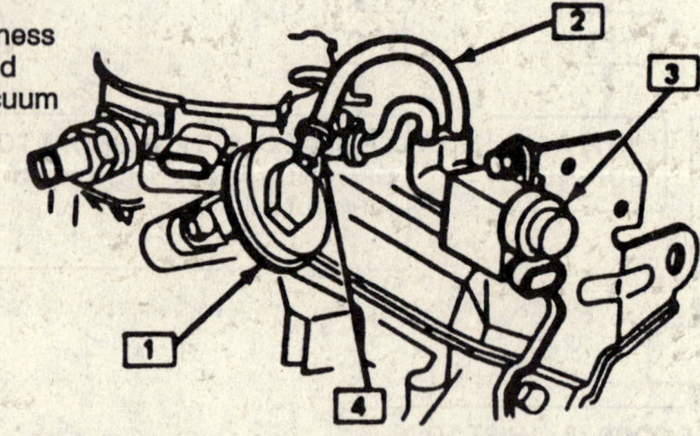

1. EGR valve
2. Vacuum harness
3. EGR solenoid
4. Manifold vacuum

View of the EGR valve and solenoid – 2.8L engine

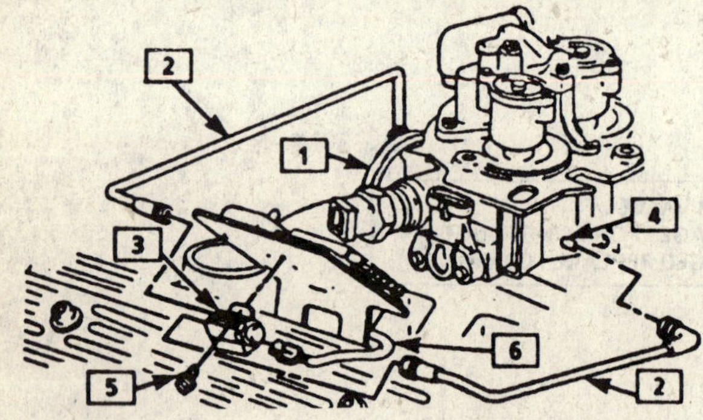

1. EGR valve
2. Vacuum harness
3. EGR solenoid
4. Manifold vacuum (port J)
5. Bolt—torque to 18 inch lbs. (2 Nm)
6. Harness connector

View of the EGR valve and solenoid – 4.3L engine

3. Disconnect the electrical connector and the vacuum hoses from the solenoid.
4. Remove the mounting nut and the solenoid.
5. To install, reverse the removal procedures. Torque the solenoid mounting nut to 17 ft. lbs. (24 Nm).

Back Pressure Transducer

1. Remove the back pressure transducer from the clamp bracket.
2. Remove the hoses from the transducer.

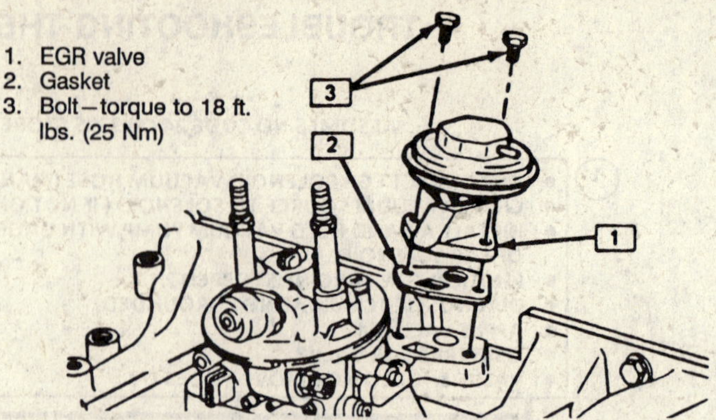

1. EGR valve
2. Gasket
3. Bolt—torque to 18 ft. lbs. (25 Nm)

Exploded view of the EGR valve – 2.5L engine

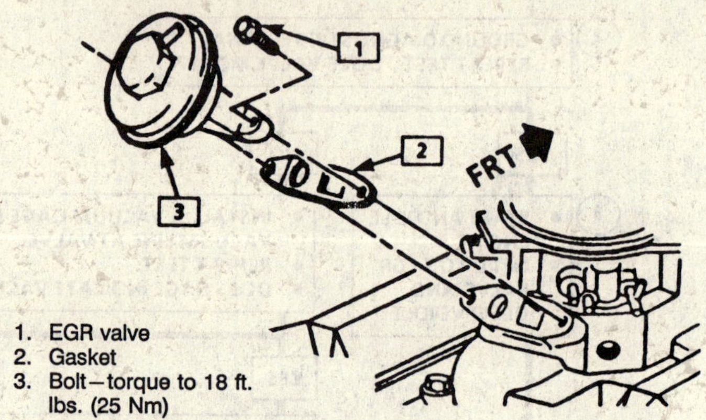

1. EGR valve
2. Gasket
3. Bolt—torque to 18 ft. lbs. (25 Nm)

Exploded view of the EGR valve – 2.8L engine

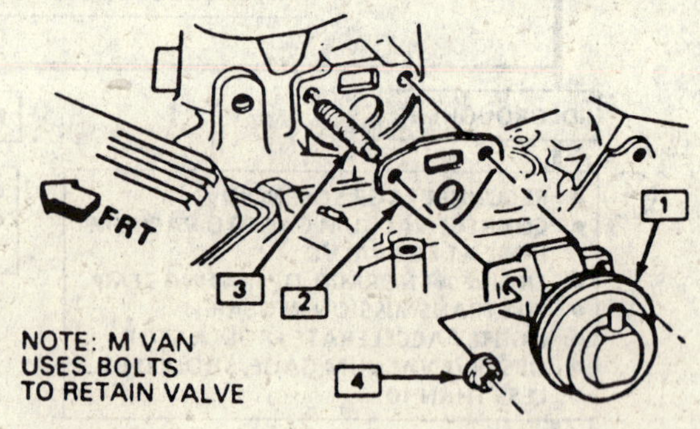

1. EGR valve
2. Gasket
3. Stud
4. Bolt—torque to 15 ft. lbs. (20 Nm)

Exploded view of the EGR valve – 4.3L engine

3. Inspect and/or replace the transducer.
4. To install, reverse the removal procedures.

Thermostatic Air Cleaner (THERMAC)

OPERATION

This system is designed to improve driveability and exhaust emissions when the engine is cold. Components added to the basic air cleaner assembly include a temperature sensor (connected to a manifold vacuum source), a vacuum diaphragm motor

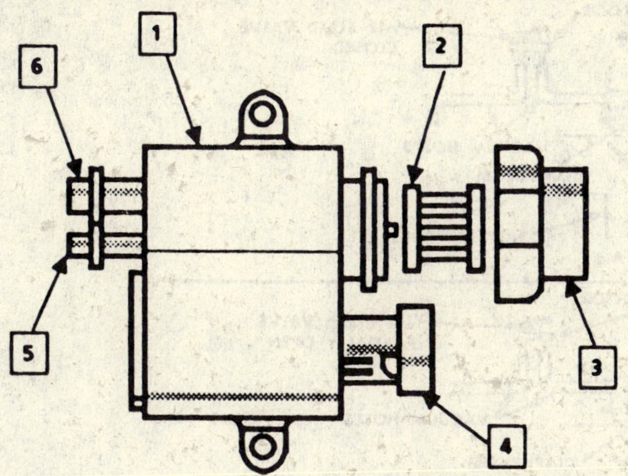

1. EGR control solenoid assembly
2. Filter
3. Cover
4. Electrical connector
5. Vacuum connector from source
6. Vacuum connector to EGR valve

Exploded view of the EGR control solenoid (EVRV) – 2.8L and 4.3L engines

1. EGR control solenoid assembly
2. Electrical connector
3. Vacuum connector from source
4. Vacuum connector to EGR valve
5. Vent

Exploded view of the EGR control solenoid – 2.5L engine

(connected to the temperature sensor) and an inlet damper door (installed in the air cleaner inlet snorkel). Additional components of the system include a hot idle compensator (1.9L) and a hot air duct running from the heat source to the underside of the air cleaner snorkel.

When the engine is cold, the temperature sensor allows vacuum to pass through to the vacuum diaphragm motor. The vacuum acting on the vacuum motor causes the motor to close the damper door, which prohibits the introduction of cold, outside air to the air cleaner. The intake vacuum then pulls hot air, generated by the exhaust manifold, through the hot air duct and into the air cleaner. This heated air supply helps to more effectively vaporize the fuel mixture entering the engine. As the engine warms, the temperature sensor bleeds off vacuum to the vacuum motor, allowing the damper door to gradually open.

The usual problems with this system are leaking vacuum lines (which prevent proper operation of the sensor and/or motor); torn or rusted through hot air ducts and/or rusted through heat stoves (either condition will allow the introduction of too much cold air to the air cleaner). Visually check and replace these items as necessary. Should the system still fail to operate properly, disconnect the vacuum line from the vacuum motor and apply at least 7 in. Hg vacuum directly to the motor from an outside vacuum source; the damper door should close. If the door does not close, either the vacuum motor is defective or the damper door and/or linkage is binding. If the door closes, but then gradually opens (with a steady vacuum source), the vacuum motor is defective.

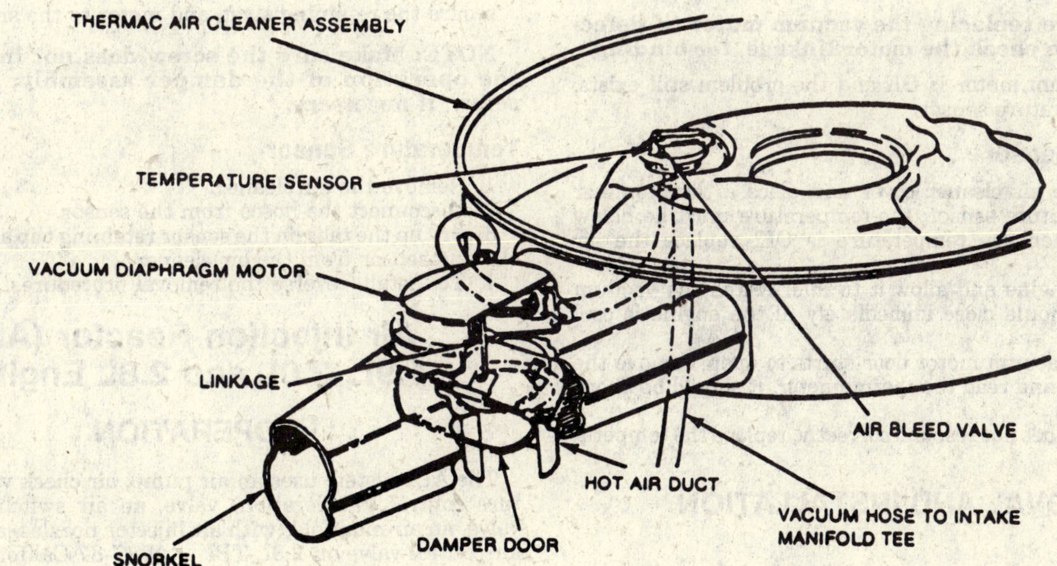

View of a thermostatic air cleaner – typical

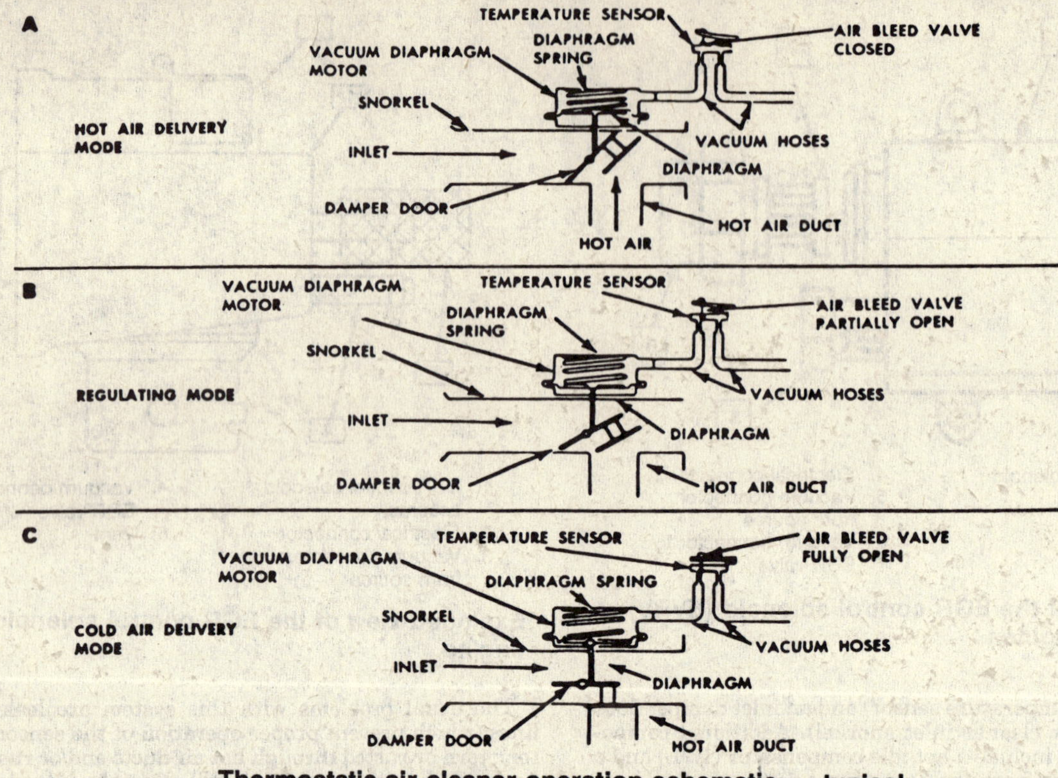

Thermostatic air cleaner operation schematic — typical

SERVICE

Vacuum Motor

1. With the engine Off, disconnect the hose from the vacuum diaphragm motor.
2. Using a vacuum source, apply 7 in. Hg vacuum to the vacuum motor; the door should close and block off the outside air, completely.
3. Bend the vacuum hose (to trap the vacuum in the motor) and make sure the door stays closed; if not, replace the vacuum motor.

NOTE: Before replacing the vacuum motor (if defective), be sure to check the motor linkage, for binding.

4. If the vacuum motor is OK and the problem still exists, check the temperature sensor.

Temperature Sensor

1. Remove the air cleaner cover and place a thermometer near the temperature sensor; the temperature must be below 86°F (30°C). When the temperature is OK, replace the air cleaner.
2. Start the engine and allow it to idle. Watch the vacuum motor door, it should close immediately (if the engine is cool enough).
3. When the vacuum motor door starts to open, remove the air cleaner cover and read the thermometer, it should be about 131°F (55°C).
4. If the door does not respond correctly, replace the temperature sensor.

REMOVAL AND INSTALLATION

Vacuum Motor

1. Remove the air cleaner.
2. Disconnect the vacuum hose from the motor.
3. Using a ⅛ in. drill bit, drill out the spot welds, then enlarge as necessary to remove the retaining strap.
4. Remove the retaining strap.
5. Lift up the motor and cock it to one side to unhook the motor linkage at the control damper assembly.
6. Install the new vacuum motor as follows:
   a. Using a $^{7}/_{64}$ in. drill bit, drill a hole in the snorkel tube at the center of the vacuum motor retaining strap.
   b. Insert the vacuum motor linkage into the control damper assembly.
   c. Use the motor retaining strap and a sheet metal screw to secure the retaining strap and motor to the snorkel tube.

NOTE: Make sure the screw does not interfere with the operation of the damper assembly; shorten the screw, if necessary.

Temperature Sensor

1. Remove the air cleaner.
2. Disconnect the hoses from the sensor.
3. Pry up the tabs on the sensor retaining clip and remove the clip and sensor from the air cleaner.
4. To install, reverse the removal procedures.

Air Injection Reactor (AIR) 1.9L, 2.0L and 2.8L Engines

OPERATION

The AIR system uses an air pump, air check valve(s), a mixture control (deceleration) valve, an air switching (diverter) valve, an air manifold (with air injector nozzles) and an electric air control valve on 2.8L TBI — 1986–87 California.

On the Federal, 1.9L engine models, the air switching (diverter) valve, directs the air flow from the AIR pump to the exhaust

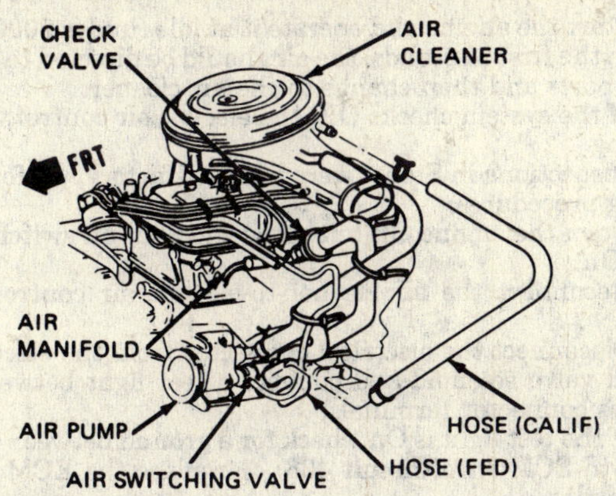

Exploded view of the Air Injection Reaction (AIR) system — 1.9L engine

manifolds (during normal operation) and away from the exhaust manifolds (during engine deceleration).

On the 1.9L engine for California and the 2.8L TBI engine models, the Electronic Control Module (ECM) operates the electric air control valve which directs the air flow to the engine exhaust manifold ports or the the air cleaner. When the engine is cold or in wide-open throttle, the ECM energizes the solenoid to direct the air flow into the exhaust manifold check valves. When the engine warms, operating at high speeds or deceleration, the ECM de-energizes the electric air control valve, changing the air flow from the exhaust manifold to the air cleaner. The diversion of the air flow to the air cleaner acts as a silencer.

A check valve(s) prevents back flow of the exhaust gases into the air pump, if there is an exhaust backfire or pump drive belt failure.

The deceleration valve (if equipped) helps to prevent backfiring during periods of high vacuum (deceleration) by allowing large quantities of air to flow into the intake manifold.

SERVICE

Air Injection Pump

Accelerate the engine to approximately 1500 rpm and observe the air flow from hose(s). If the air flow increases as the engine is accelerated, the pump is operating satisfactorily. If the air flow does not increase or is not present, proceed as follows:

1. Check for proper drive belt tension. The Air Management System is not completely noiseless. Under normal conditions, noise rises in pitch as the engine speed increases. To determine if excessive noise is the present, operate the engine with the pump drive belt removed. If excessive noise does not exist with the belt removed, proceed as follows:
2. Check for a seized Air Injection Pump. Do not oil the air pump.
3. Check the hoses, the pipes and all connections for leaks and proper routing.
4. Check the air control valve.
5. Check air injection pump for proper mounting and bolt torque.
6. Repair irregularities in these components, as necessary.
7. If no irregularities exist and the air injection pump noise is still excessive, replace the pump.

Check Valves

1. The check valve should be inspected whenever the hose is disconnected from the check valve or whenever check valve failure is suspected (A pump that had become inoperative and had shown indications of having exhaust gases in the pump would indicate check valve failure).

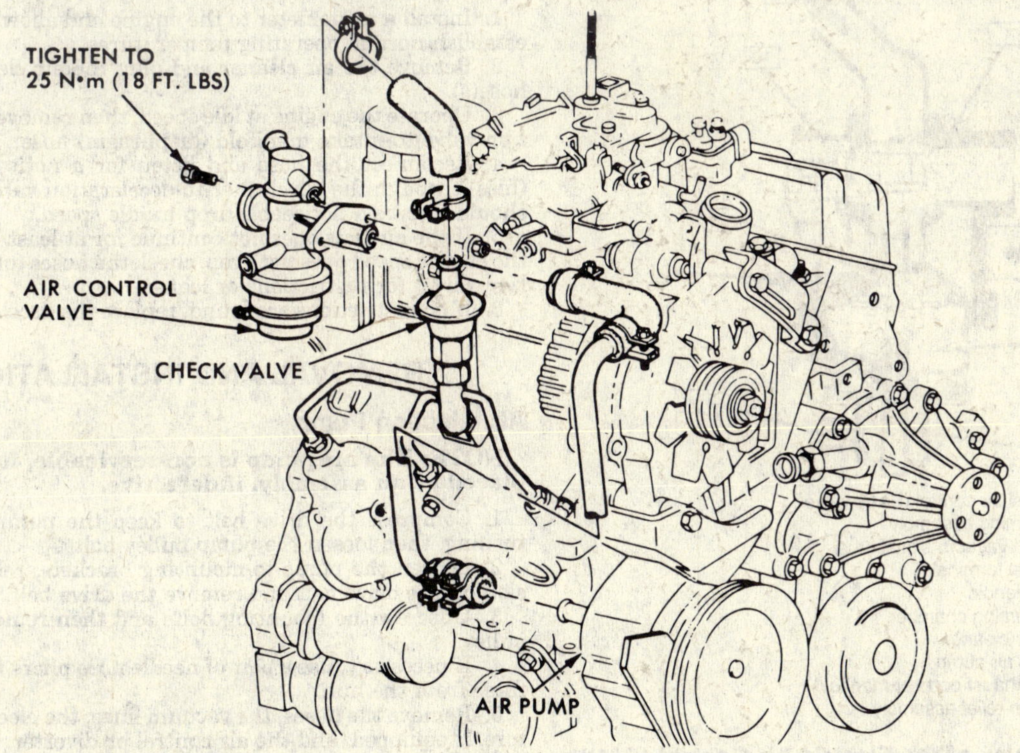

Exploded view of the Air Injection Reaction (AIR) system — 2.8L engine

2. Blow through the check valve (toward the cylinder head) then attempt to suck back through check valve. The flow should only be in one direction (toward the exhaust manifold). Replace the valve which does not function correctly.

Air Hoses and Injection Pipes

1. Inspect all hoses for deterioration or holes.
2. Inspect all air injection pipes for cracks of holes.
3. Check all hose and pipe connections.
4. Check pipe and hose routing; interference may cause wear.
5. If a leak is suspected on the pressure side of the system or any hose has been disconnected on the pressure-side, the connection should be checked for leaks with a soapy water solution.
6. If a hose, manifold and/or pipe assembly replacement is required, note the routing, then replace the item as required.
7. When installing the new item, be sure to connect the hoses correctly.

Air Switching (Diverter) Valve (ASV)

The diverter valve will act like the electric air control valve, except, that it is not controlled by an ECM. Air is directed to the exhaust ports, unless there is a sudden rise of manifold vacuum due to throttle deceleration.

If the air switching valve is normal, the secondary air continues to blow out from the valve for a few seconds when the accelerator pedal is depressed all the way to floor and released quickly. If the secondary air continues to blow out for more than 5 seconds, replace the air switching valve.

Electric Air Control Valve
2.8L TBI Engine

1. Perform the following inspection checks:
   a. The engine coolant must be at operating temperatures.
   b. Disconnect the air cleaner-to-electric air control valve hose.

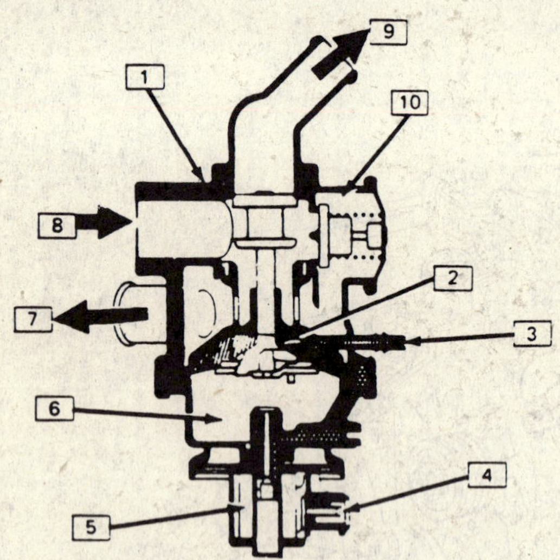

1. Electrical air control (EAC) valve
2. Decel timing assembly
3. Manifold vacuum signal tube
4. Electrical terminal
5. EAC solenoid
6. Decel Timing chamber
7. Air to air cleaner
8. Air from air pump
9. Air to exhaust ports or manifold
10. Pressure relief assembly

Cross-sectional view of the Electric Air Control (EAC) valve — 2.8L TBI engine

   c. Start the engine and operate it at idle (under 2000 rpm). Within the first 5 seconds, the air should be directed to the exhaust ports and then change to the air cleaner.
   d. If the system checks OK, the electric air control valve is working.
2. If inspections in Step 1 were not satisfactory, perform the following procedures:
   a. Turn the engine Off but allow the ignition switch to remain On.
   b. Reconnect the air cleaner-to-electric air control valve hose.
   c. Disconnect the electrical connector from the electric air control valve solenoid and connect a test light between the harness connector terminals.
   d. If the test light is On, check for a ground between the solenoid-to-ECM wire(Circuit 436) or replace the ECM (if not grounded).
3. If the test light is Off, perform the following procedures:
   a. Using a jumper wire, connect it between the ECM diagnostic (C2) terminal and ground.
   b. If the test light turns On, replace the electric air control valve.
   c. Remove the jumper wire.
4. If the test light still remains Off, perform the following procedures:
   a. Connect one probe of the test light to terminal **A** of the solenoid's connector and the other probe to a ground.
   b. If the light still remains Off, check for a blown fuse or an broken ignition (pink) wire.
5. If the light turns On, check for the following problems:
   a. A broken solenoid-to-ECM (Circuit 436) wire or check the solenoid's resistance of the air control valve.
   b. If the resistance of the solenoid is above 20Ω, replace the ECM.
   c. If the resistance of the solenoid is below 20Ω, replace the electric air control valve and the ECM.

Mixture Control (Deceleration) Valve

1. Install a tachometer to the engine and allow the engine to establish normal operating temperatures.
2. Remove the air cleaner and plug the air cleaner vacuum hose(s).
3. Operate the engine at idle speed, then remove the deceleration valve-to-intake manifold (diaphragm) hose.
4. Reconnect the hose and listen for a noticeable air flow (hiss) through the air cleaner-to-deceleration valve hose; there should also be a noticeable drop in idle speed.
5. If the air flow does not continue for at least one second or the engine speed does not drop, check the hoses (of the deceleration valve) for restrictions or leaks.
6. If no restrictions are found, replace the deceleration valve.

REMOVAL AND INSTALLATION

Air Injection Pump

NOTE: The air pump is non-servicable, it must be replaced as an assembly, if defective.

1. Compress the drive belt to keep the pump pulley from turning, then loosen the pump pulley bolts.
2. Loosen the pump-to-mounting brackets, release the tension on the drive belt and remove the drive belt.
3. Unscrew the mounting bolts and then remove the pump pulley.
4. If necessary, use a pair of needle nose pliers to pull the fan filter from the hub.
5. Remove the hoses, the vacuum lines, the electrical connectors, if equipped, and the air control or diverter valve.
6. Unscrew the pump mounting bolts and then remove the pump.

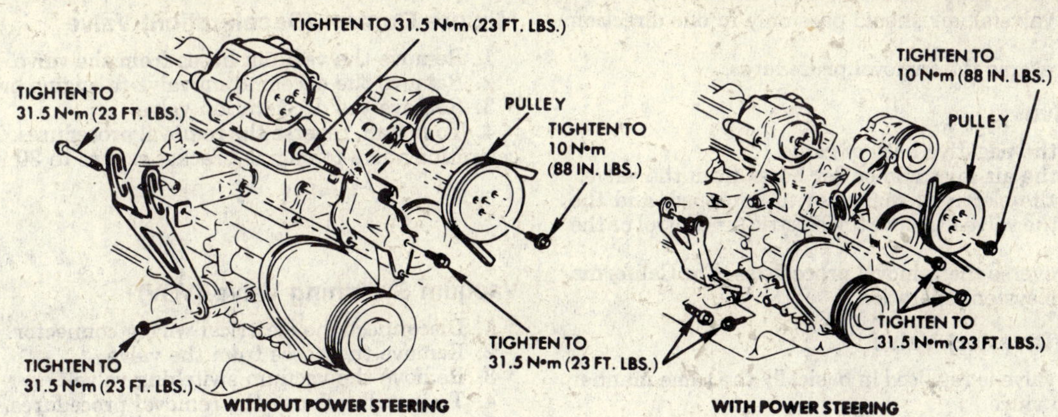

Exploded view of the air pump assembly – 2.0L engine

7. To install, reverse the removal procedures. Torque the pump pulley bolts to 90 inch lbs. and the pump-to-bracket nuts/bolts to 25 ft. lbs. Adjust the drive belt tension after installation.

Air Pump Drive Belt Adjustment and Replacement

1. Inspect the drive belt for wear, cracks or deterioration.
2. Loosen the pump adjustment and the pivot bolts.
3. Replace the drive belt, if necessary.
4. Move the air pump until the drive belt is at proper tension, then retighten bolts.
5. Check the drive belt tension using a belt tension gauge.

Air Pump Pulley Replacement

1. Hold the pump pulley from turning by compressing the drive belt, then loosen the pump pulley bolts.
2. Loosen the pump through bolt and the adjusting bolt.
3. Remove the drive belt, the pump pulley and the pulley spacer.
4. Install the pump pulley and spacer with the retaining bolts hand tight.
5. Install the drive belt and adjust to proper tension.
6. Hold the pump pulley from turning by compressing the drive belt, then torque the pump pulley bolts to 24 ft. lbs.
7. Recheck drive belt tension and adjust it, if necessary.

Air Pump Filter Fan Replacement

Before starting this operation, note the following:

- Do not allow any filter fragments to enter the air pump intake hole.
- Do not remove the filter fan by inserting a screwdriver between pump and filter fan. Air damage to the sealing lip pump will result.
- Do not remove the metal drive hub from the filter fan.
- It is seldom possible to remove the filter fan without destroying it.

1. Remove the drive belt, the pump pulley and spacer.
2. Insert needle nose pliers and pull the filter fan from hub.
3. Position a new filter fan onto the pump hub.
4. Position the spacer and the pump pulley against the centrifugal filter fan.
5. Install the pump pulley bolts and torque them equally to 80 inch lbs. This will compress the centrifugal filter fan into the pump hole. Do not drive the filter fan on with a hammer.

A slight amount of interference with the housing bore is normal. After a new filter fan has been installed, it may squeal upon initial operation or until O.D. sealing lip has worn in. This may require a short period of pump operation at various engine speeds.

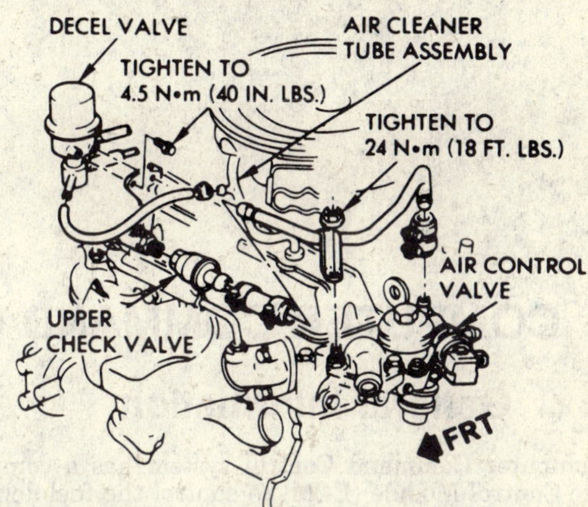

Exploded view of the upper check valve and hoses – 2.0L engine

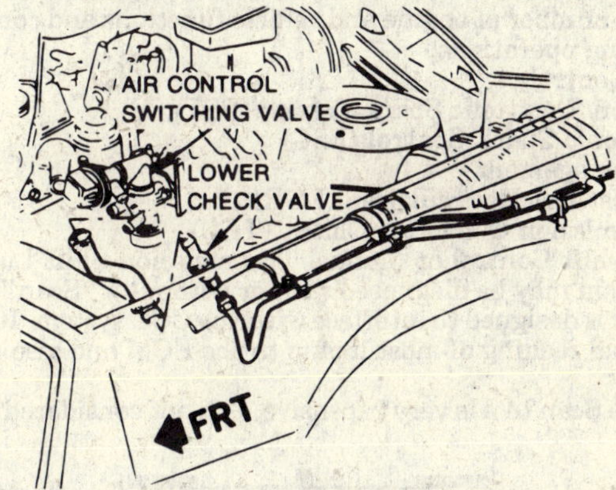

Exploded view of the lower check valve and hoses – 2.0L engine

6. To complete the installation, replace the pump drive belt and adjust it.

Check Valve(s)

1. Remove the clamp(s) and disconnect the hose from the valve(s).
2. Unscrew the valve(s) from the air injection pipe(s).

3. To test the valve(s), air should pass only in one direction only.
4. To install, reverse the removal procedures.

Air Control Valve

1. Disconnect the negative battery cable.
2. Disconnect the air inlet and outlet hoses from the valve.
3. Disconnect the electrical connector, if equipped, and the vacuum hoses at the valve. Remove the electric air control or the diverter valve.
4. To install, reverse the removal procedures. For California models, check the system operation.

Air Switching (Diverter) Valve

The switching valve is replaced in basically the same manner as the air control valve.

Mixture Control (Deceleration) Valve

1. Remove the vacuum hoses from the valve.
2. Remove the deceleration valve-to-engine bracket screws.
3. Remove the deceleration valve.
4. To install, reverse the removal procedures. Torque the deceleration valve-to-engine bracket screws to 30 inch lbs.

Vacuum Switching Valve (VSV)

1. Disconnect the electrical wiring connector.
2. Remove the hoses from the valve.
3. Remove the vacuum switching valve.
4. To install, reverse the removal procedures.

COMPUTER COMMAND CONTROL (CCC or C³) SYSTEM

General Information

The Computer Command Control system has a computer Electronic Control Module (ECM) to control the fuel delivery, ignition timing, some emission control systems and engagement of the transmission converter clutch, downshift control or the manual transmission shaft light.

The system, through the electronic control module (ECM), monitors a number of engine and vehicle functions and controls the following operations:

- Fuel Control
- Ignition/Electronic Spark Timing (EST)
- Electronic Spark Control (ESC)
- Air Management
- Exhaust Gas Recirculation (EGR)
- Transmission Converter Clutch (TCC)
- Downshift Control or Manual Transmission Shift Light

The system may be diagnosed with or without a "Scan" tool. A Scan tool is designed to interface with the CCC system. It supplies a visual reading of most inputs to the ECM and also some outputs.

Since the Scan tool is very expensive, it is not considered to be practical for the home mechanic. All diagnostic procedures in this section are for use when a Scan tool is not available.

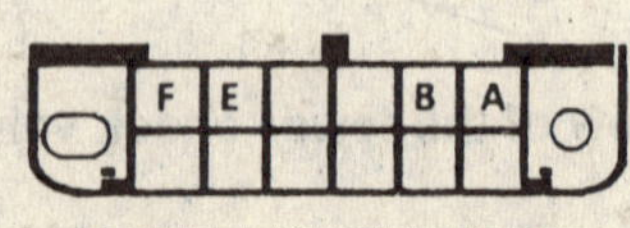

View of the ALDL connector

ALDL Connector

The Assembly Line Diagnostic Link (ALDL) is wired to the ECM and is located under the instrument panel in the passenger compartment.

The connector has terminals that are used to diagnose the system with jumper wires. The following terminals are used:

A – The terminal provides a ground circuit to other terminals.

B – The terminal is the "diagnostic terminal" for the ECM. When grounded to terminal **A** with the key **ON** and the engine **OFF**, the SERVICE ENGINE SOON light will enter the Diagnostic Mode and flash codes. With the engine running, the SERVICE ENGINE SOON light will flash a Field Service Mode to determine of the system is in Closed Loop or Open Loop operation.

C – The terminal, on some air management systems is wired to the ground side of the electric air control valve. It can be used to diagnose the Air Management System.

E – The terminal is the serial data line on all engines except the 2.5L and is used by the Scan tool to read various system data information.

F – The terminal is used to diagnose the TCC system and is wired to the ground side of the TCC solenoid.

M – The terminal is the serial data line for the 2.5L engine and is used by the Scan tool to read various system data information.

A wiring harness connects the ECM to various sensors, solenoids, relays and the ALDL connector. The ECM is located in the passenger compartment, usually behind the right side kick panel.

DIAGNOSIS

The Computer Command Control System has a diagnostic system built into the ECM to indicate a failed circuit. An amber SERVICE ENGINE SOON light on the instrument panel will illuminate if a problem has been detected when the engine and vehicle are running. The light is also used for a bulb and system check.

The system requires a tachometer, test light, ohmmeter, digital voltmeter, vacuum gage and jumper wires for diagnosis.

Bulb Check

With the ignition **ON** and the engine **OFF**, the lamp should be illuminated, which indicates that the ECM has completed the circuit to turn ON the light. If the SERVICE ENGINE SOON light is not illuminated, refer to Chart-A1 for diagnosis.

When the engine is started, the light will turn OFF. If the light remains ON, refer to System Check.

Code System

The ECM self-diagnosis system detects system failure and aids in finding the circuit at fault. If a sensor reading is not what the ECM thinks it should be the ECM will illuminate the SERVICE ENGINE SOON light on the instrument panel and will store a Fault Code in memory. The code will which circuit the trouble is in. A circuit consists of a sensor, the wiring and connectors to it and the ECM.

An Intermittent Code is one which does not reset itself and is not present while you are working on the vehicle; this is often caused by a loose connection.

A Hard Code is one which is present when you are working on the vehicle and the condition still exists while working on the vehicle.

System Check

The system check provides a starting point and a method to determine if:

- The SERVICE ENGINE SOON light illuminates.
- The diagnostic system is working (Code 12).
- Any fault codes are present in memory.
- The fuel system is operating normally (Field Service Mode).

DIAGNOSTIC MODE

If the diagnostic terminal **B** is grounded with the ignition **ON** and the engine **OFF**, the system will enter the Diagnostic Mode.

With the key **ON** and the engine **OFF**, jumper ALDL terminals **B** to **A** with a jumper tool or paper clip. The SERVICE ENGINE SOON light will flash Code 12 to indicate that the diagnostic system is working. Code 12 consists of one flash, followed by a pause and then 2 flashes. The code will repeat three times and will continue to repeat if no other codes are stored. If Code 12 does not display, refer to Chart-A2.

Any additional codes stored in memory will begin to flash after Code 12. Each code stored will flash 3 times. At the end of the cycle Code 12 will flash again, indicating a completed cycle. If a code is displayed, a code chart is used to diagnose the problem. The chart will determine if the problem still exists (hard failure) or if it is an intermittent problem.

FIELD SERVICE MODE

If the diagnostic terminal is grounded with the engine running, the system will enter the Field Service Mode. In this mode, the SERVICE ENGINE SOON light will show whether the system is in the Open Loop or Closed Loop and if the fuel system is operating normally.

If the engine cranks but will not start, refer to Chart-A3 for further diagnostic procedures.

With the diagnostic terminal grounded and the engine at normal operating temperature, turn the engine at 1400–1600 rpm for 2 minutes and note the light.

- The fuel system is operating normally and the system is in a Closed Loop operation if the light is flashing at a rate of once per second.
- The system is in Open Loop operation if the light flashes at a rate of 2.5 times per second.

Open Loop indicates that the oxygen sensor has not reached normal operating temperature and the sensor voltage signal is not usable to the ECM. Signal voltage should be at a constant between 0.35–0.55 volts.

The system will flash Open Loop from 30 seconds to 2 minutes after the engine starts or until the oxygen sensor reaches normal operating temperature. If the system fails to go Closed Loop, refer to Code 13.

- A SERVICE ENGINE SOON light that is OFF most of the time indicates that the exhaust is lean. The oxygen sensor signal voltage will be less than 0.35 volts and steady. See Code 44 for diagnosis.
- A SERVICE ENGINE SOON light that is ON most of the time indicates that the exhaust is rich. The oxygen sensor signal voltage will be above 0.55 volts and steady. See Code 45 for diagnosis.

NOTE: The ECM Closed Loop timer is bypassed and new trouble codes can not be stored while the system is in the field service mode.

Clearing Codes

When the ECM sets a code, the SERVICE ENGINE SOON light will illuminate and a code will be stored in memory. If the problem is intermittent, the light will go out after 10 seconds, when the fault goes away. However, the code will stay in the ECM memory for 50 starts or until the battery voltage to the ECM is disconnected. Removing battery voltage for 30 seconds will clear all stored codes.

Codes should be cleared after repairs have been completed. Also, some diagnostic charts will tell you to clear the codes before using the chart. This allows the ECM to set the code while going through the chart, which will help to find the cause of the problem more quickly.

TROUBLESHOOTING THE CODE IDENTIFICATION CHART

The "SERVICE ENGINE SOON" light will only be "ON" if the malfunction exists under the conditions listed below. If the malfunction clears, the light will go out and the code will be stored in the ECM. Any codes stored will be erased if no problem reoccurs within 50 engine starts.

CODE AND CIRCUIT	PROBABLE CAUSE
Code 13 - O_2 Sensor Open Oxygen Sensor Circuit	Indicates that the oxygen sensor circuit or sensor was open for one minute while off idle.
Code 14 - Coolant Sensor High Temperature Indication	Sets if the sensor or signal line becomes grounded for 3 seconds.
Code 15 - Coolant Sensor Low Temperature Indication	Sets if the sensor, connections, or wires open for 3 seconds.
Code 21 - TPS Signal Voltage High	TPS voltage greater than 2.5 volts for 3 seconds with less than 1200 RPM.
Code 22 - TPS Signal Voltage Low	A shorted to ground or open signal circuit will set code in 3 seconds.
Code 23 - MAT Low Temperature Indication	Sets if the sensor, connections, or wires open for 3 seconds.
Code 24 - VSS No Vehicle Speed Indication	No vehicle speed present during a road load decel.
Code 25 - MAT High Temperature Indication	Sets if the sensor or signal line becomes grounded for 3 seconds.
Code 32 - EGR	Vacuum switch shorted to ground on start up OR Switch not closed after the ECM has commanded EGR for a specified period of time. OR EGR solenoid circuit open for a specified period of time.
Code 33 - MAP Sensor Low Vacuum	MAP sensor output to high for 5 seconds or an Open signal circuit.
Code 34 - MAP Sensor High Vacuum	Low or no output from sensor with engine running.
Code 35 - IAC	IAC error
Code 42 - EST	ECM has seen an open or grounded EST or Bypass circuit.
Code 43 - ESC	Signal to the ECM has remained low for too long or the system has failed a functional check.
Code 44 Lean Exhaust Indication	Sets if oxygen sensor voltage remains below .2 volts for about 20 seconds.
Code 45 Rich Exhaust Indication	Sets if oxygen sensor voltage remains above .7 volts for about 1 minute.
Code 51	Faulty MEM-CAL, PROM, or ECM.
Code 52	Fuel CALPAK missing or faulty.
Code 53	System overvoltage. Indicates a basic generator problem.
Code 54 - Fuel Pump Low voltage	Sets when the fuel pump voltage is less than 2 volts when reference pulses are being received.
Code 55	Faulty ECM

CODE 13 – TROUBLESHOOTING THE OXYGEN SENSOR CIRCUIT

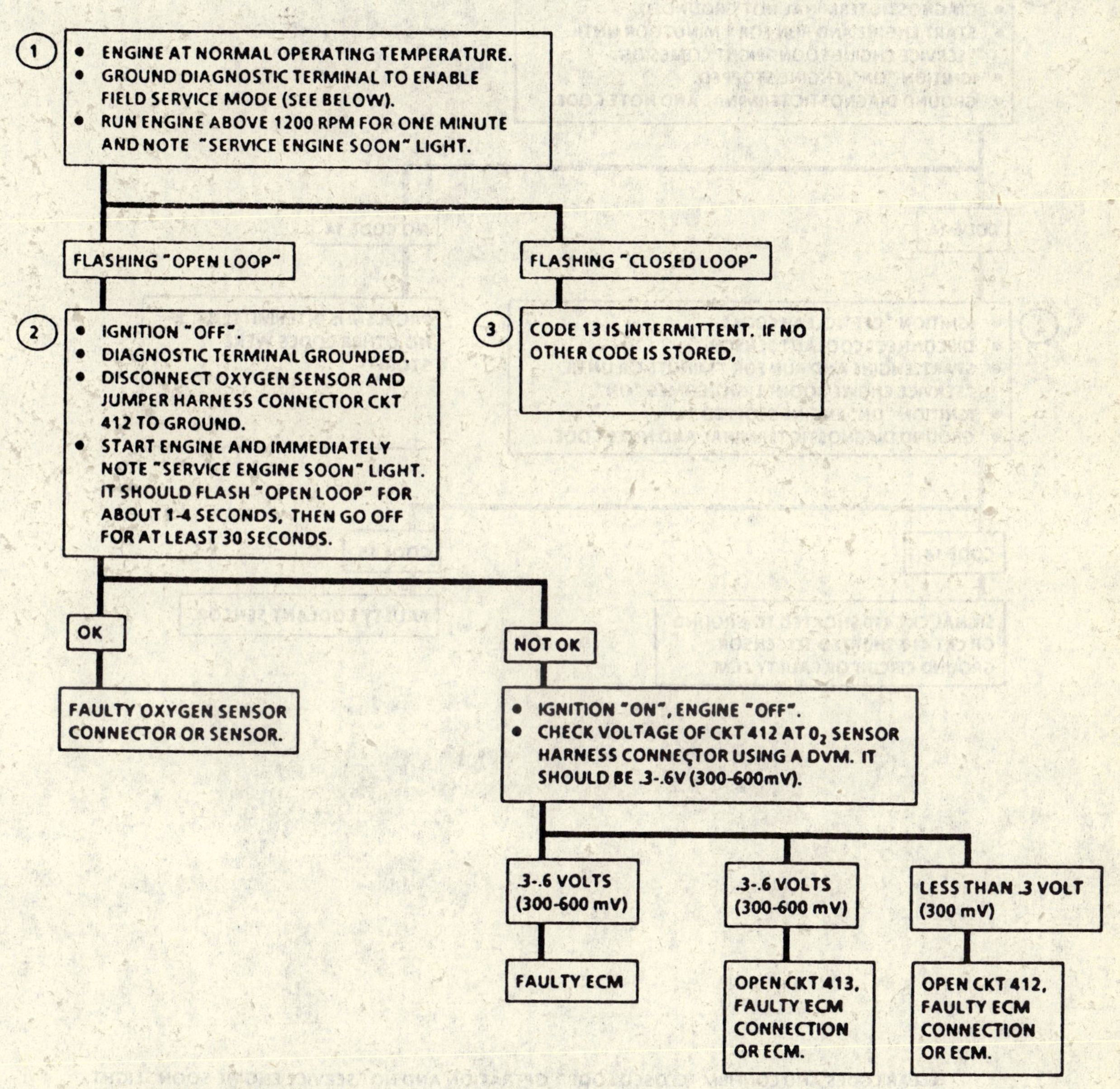

FIELD SERVICE MODE:
ENGINE RUNNING, DIAGNOSTIC TERMINAL GROUNDED.
"OPEN LOOP": "SERVICE ENGINE SOON" LIGHT FLASHES AT A RATE OF 2 TIMES PER SECOND.
"CLOSED LOOP": "SERVICE ENGINE SOON" LIGHT FLASHES AT A RATE OF 1 TIME PER SECOND.

CLEAR CODES AND CONFIRM "CLOSED LOOP" OPERATION AND NO "SERVICE ENGINE SOON" LIGHT.

CODE 14 – TROUBLESHOOTING THE COOLANT TEMPERATURE SENSOR LOW VOLTAGE CIRCUIT

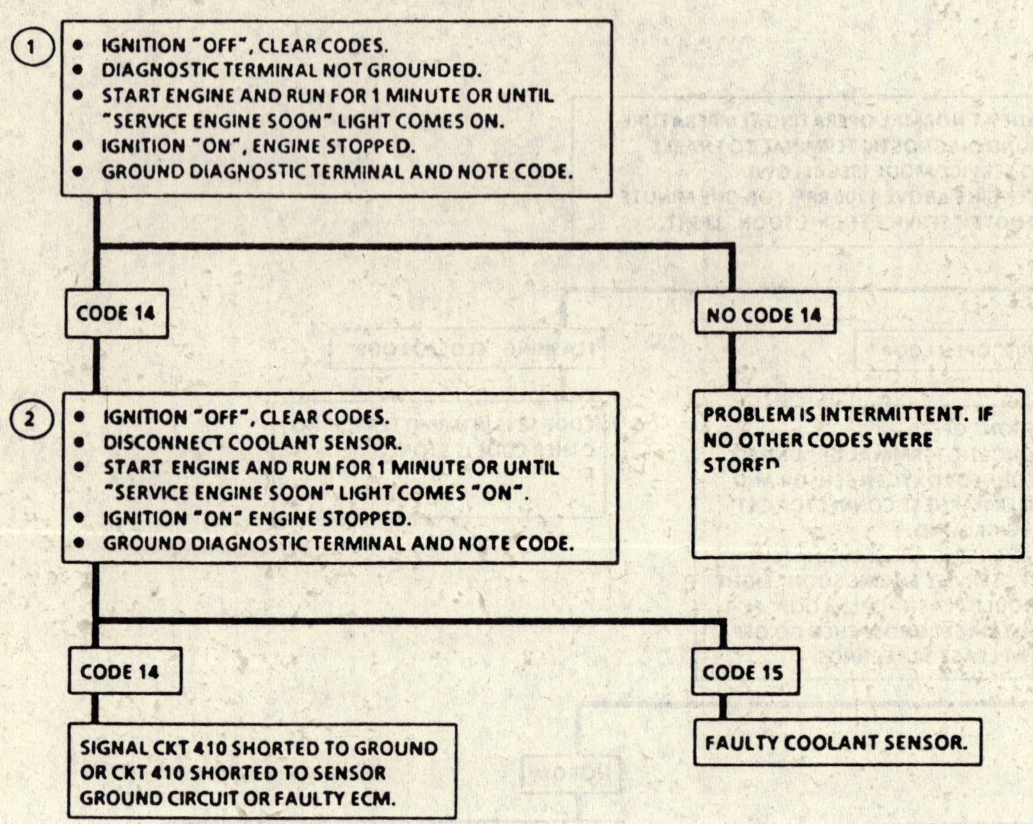

CLEAR CODES AND CONFIRM "CLOSED LOOP" OPERATION AND NO "SERVICE ENGINE SOON" LIGHT.

CODE 15 – TROUBLESHOOTING THE COOLANT TENPERATURE SENSOR HIGH VOLTAGE CIRCUIT

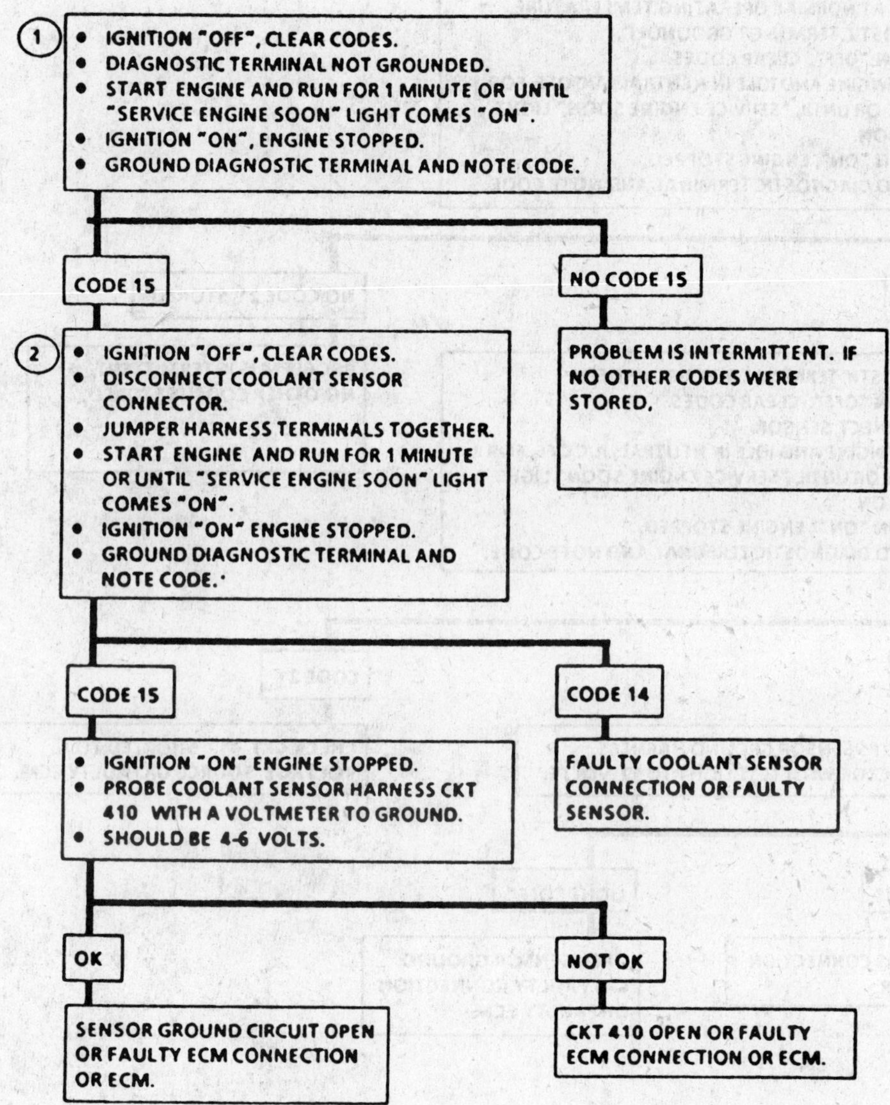

CLEAR CODES AND CONFIRM "CLOSED LOOP" OPERATION AND NO "SERVICE ENGINE SOON" LIGHT.

CODE 21 – TROUBLESHOOTING THE THROTTLE POSITION SENSOR (TPS) HIGH VOLTAGE CIRCUIT

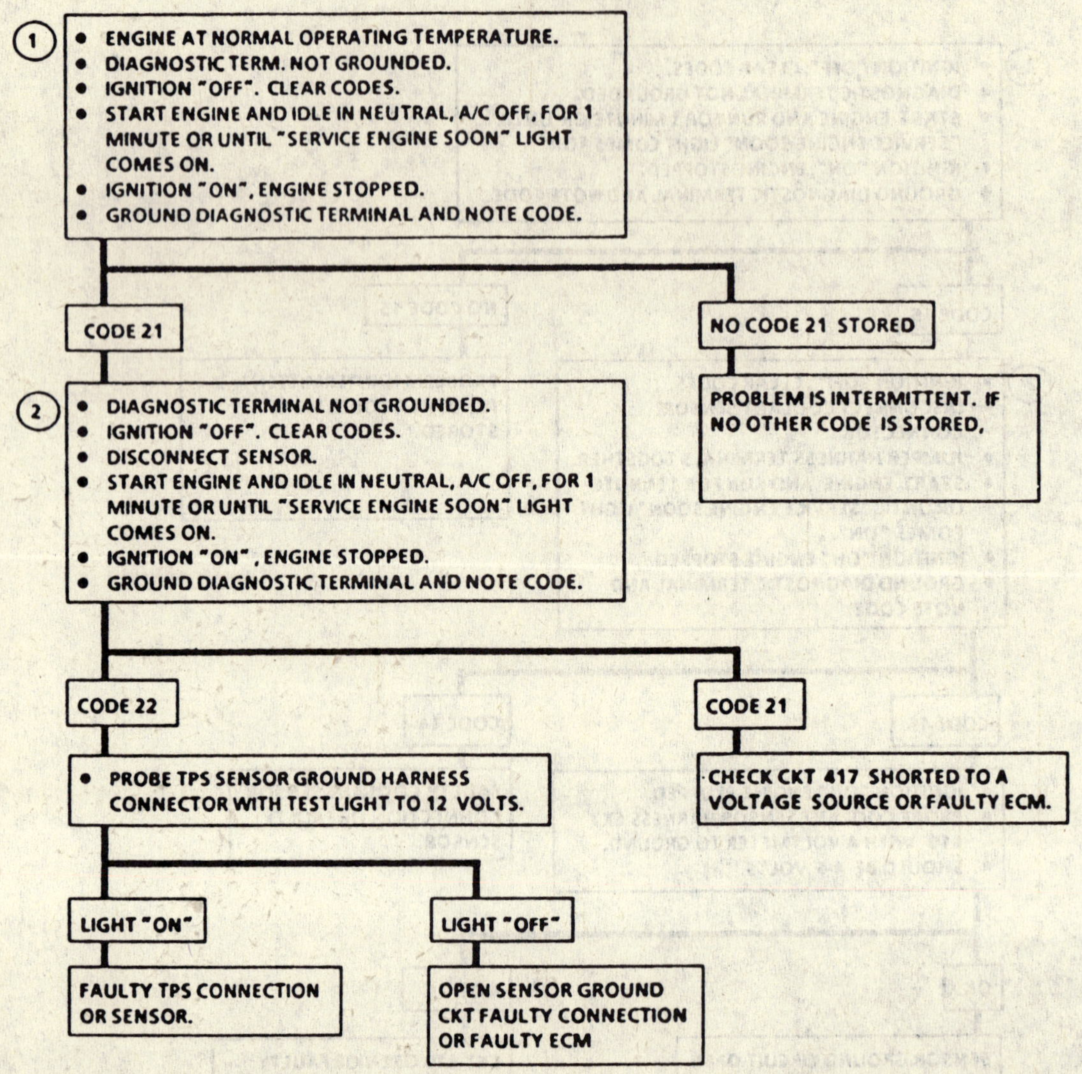

CLEAR CODES AND CONFIRM "CLOSED LOOP" OPERATION AND NO "SERVICE ENGINE SOON" LIGHT.

CODE 22 – TROUBLESHOOTING THE THROTTLE POSITION SENSOR (TPS) LOW VOLTAGE CIRCUIT

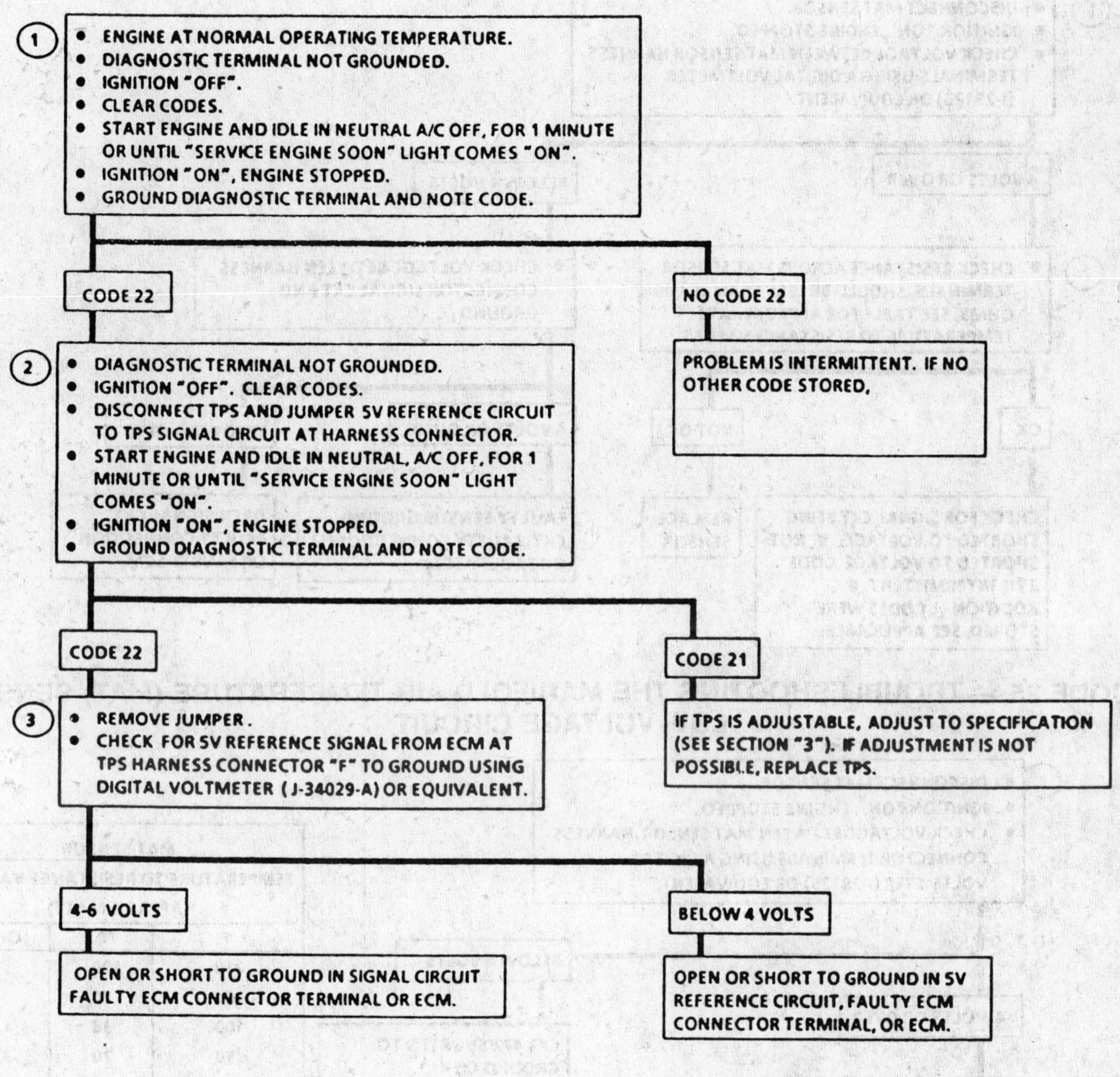

CLEAR CODES AND CONFIRM "CLOSED LOOP" OPERATION AND NO "SERVICE ENGINE SOON" LIGHT.

CODE 23 – TROUBLESHOOTING THE MANIFOLD AIR TEMPERATURE (MAT) SENSOR HIGH VOLTAGE CIRCUIT

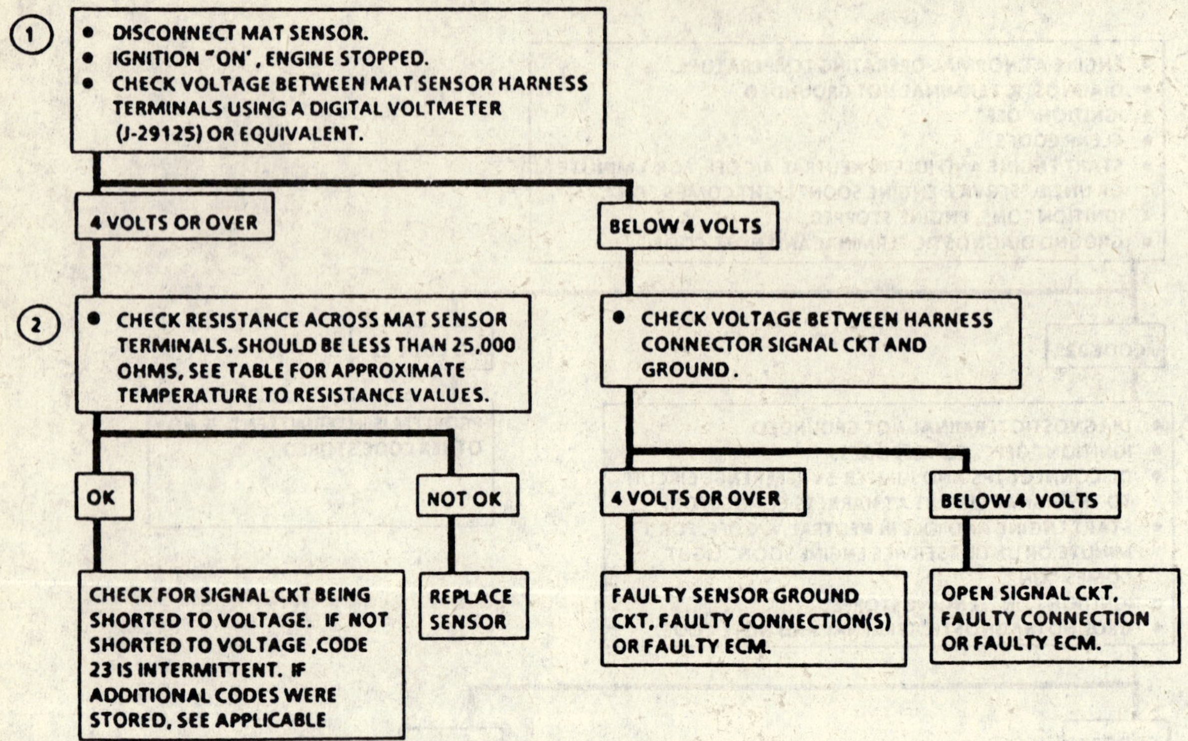

CODE 25 – TROUBLESHOOTING THE MANIFOLD AIR TEMPERATURE (MAT) SENSOR LOW VOLTAGE CIRCUIT

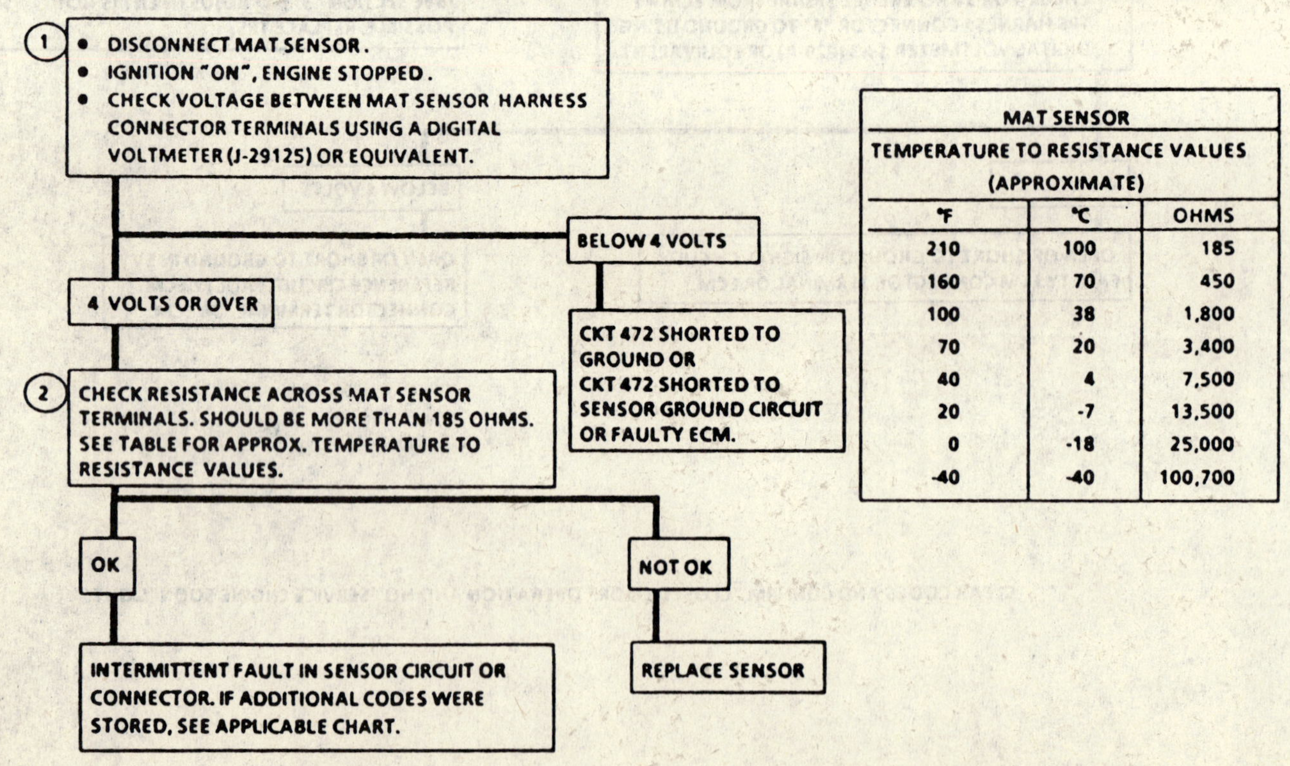

MAT SENSOR TEMPERATURE TO RESISTANCE VALUES (APPROXIMATE)

°F	°C	OHMS
210	100	185
160	70	450
100	38	1,800
70	20	3,400
40	4	7,500
20	-7	13,500
0	-18	25,000
-40	-40	100,700

CODE 32 – TROUBLESHOOTING THE VEHICLE SPEED SENSOR (VSS) CIRCUIT

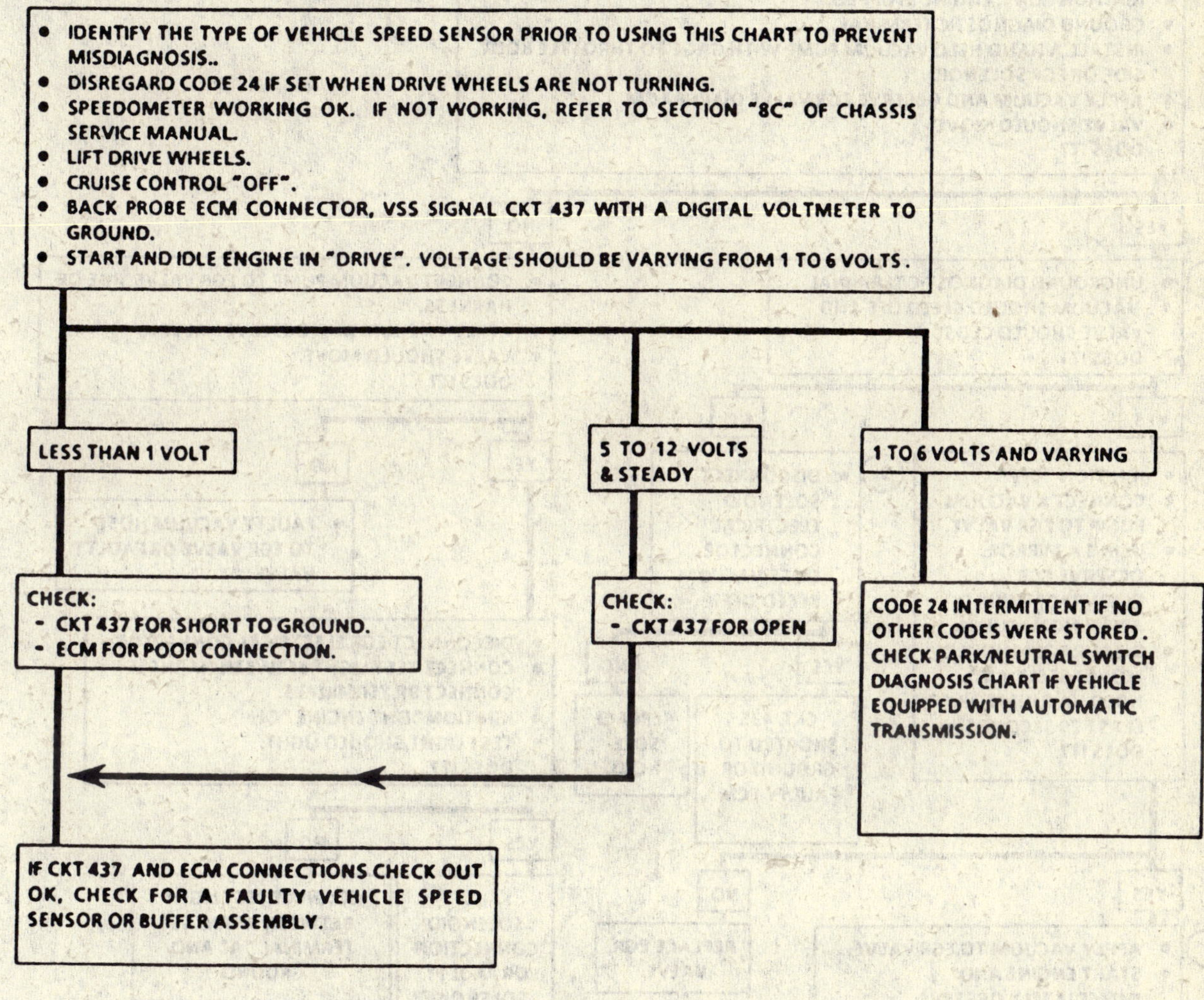

CLEAR CODES AND CONFIRM "CLOSED LOOP" OPERATION AND NO "SERVICE ENGINE SOON" LIGHT.

CODE 32 – TROUBLESHOOTING THE EXHAUST GAS RECIRCULATION (EGR) SYSTEM CIRCUIT

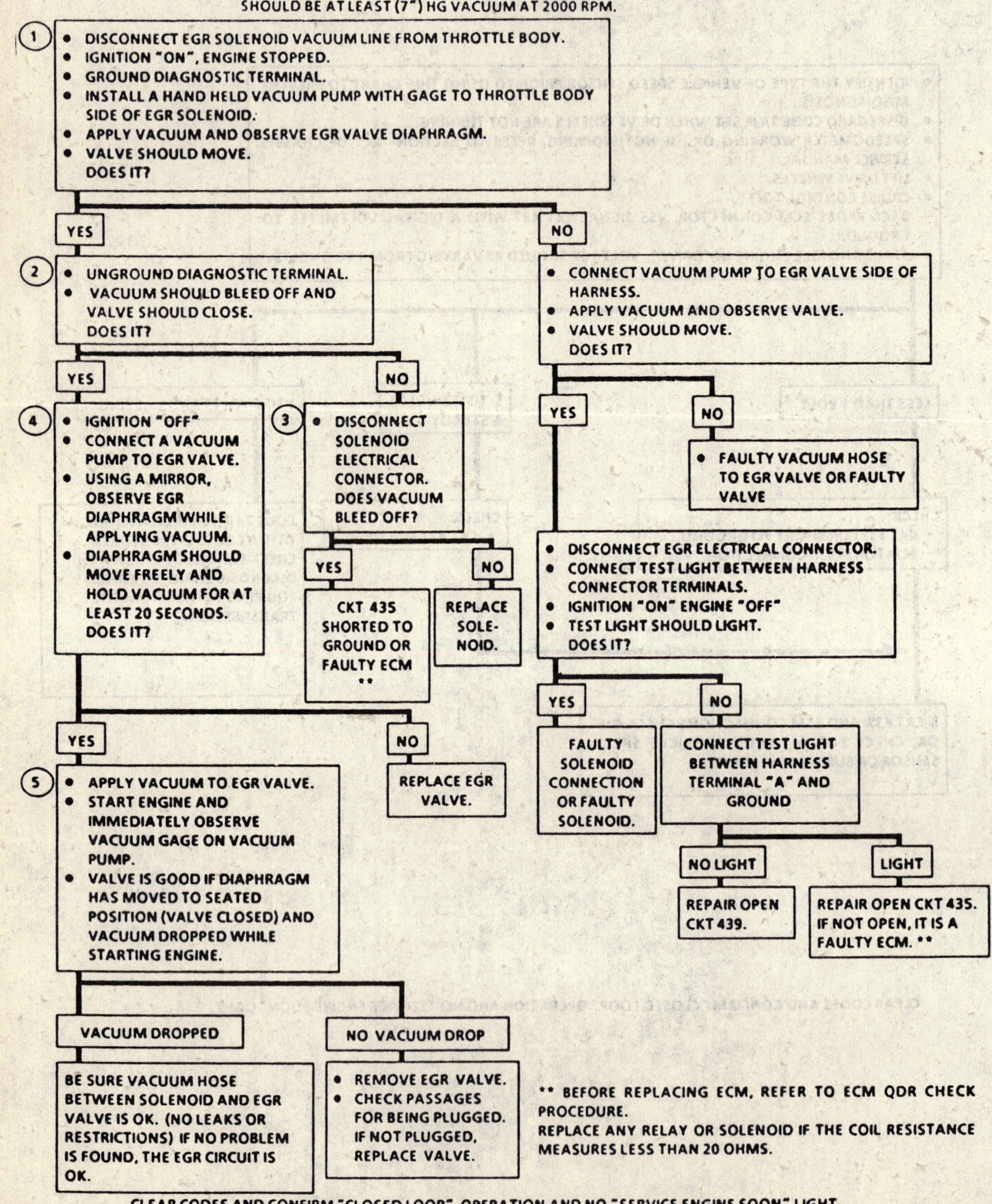

CODE 33 – TROUBLESHOOTING THE MANIFOLD AIR PRESSURE (MAP) SENSOR HIGH VOLTAGE CIRCUIT

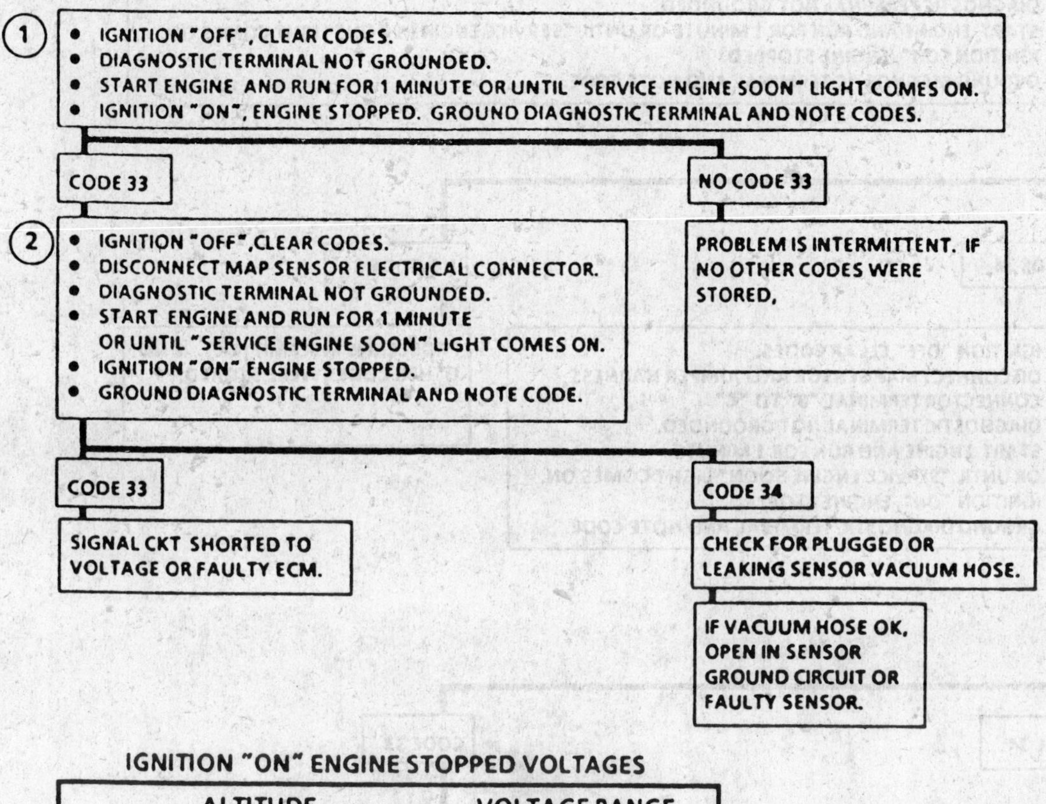

IGNITION "ON" ENGINE STOPPED VOLTAGES

ALTITUDE Meters	ALTITUDE Feet	VOLTAGE RANGE
Below 305	Below 1,000	3.8---5.5V
305--- 610	1,000--2,000	3.6---5.3V
610--- 914	2,000--3,000	3.5---5.1V
914--1219	3,000--4,000	3.3---5.0V
1219--1524	4,000--5,000	3.2---4.8V
1524--1829	5,000--6,000	3.0---4.6V
1829--2133	6,000--7,000	2.9---4.5V
2133--2438	7,000--8,000	2.8---4.3V
2438--2743	8,000--9,000	2.6---4.2V
2743--3048	9,000--10,000	2.5---4.0V

LOW ALTITUDE = HIGH PRESSURE = HIGH VOLTAGE

CLEAR CODES AND CONFIRM "CLOSED LOOP" OPERATION AND NO "SERVICE ENGINE SOON" LIGHT.

CODE 34 – TROUBLESHOOTING THE MANIFOLD AIR PRESSURE (MAP) SENSOR LOW VOLTAGE CIRCUIT

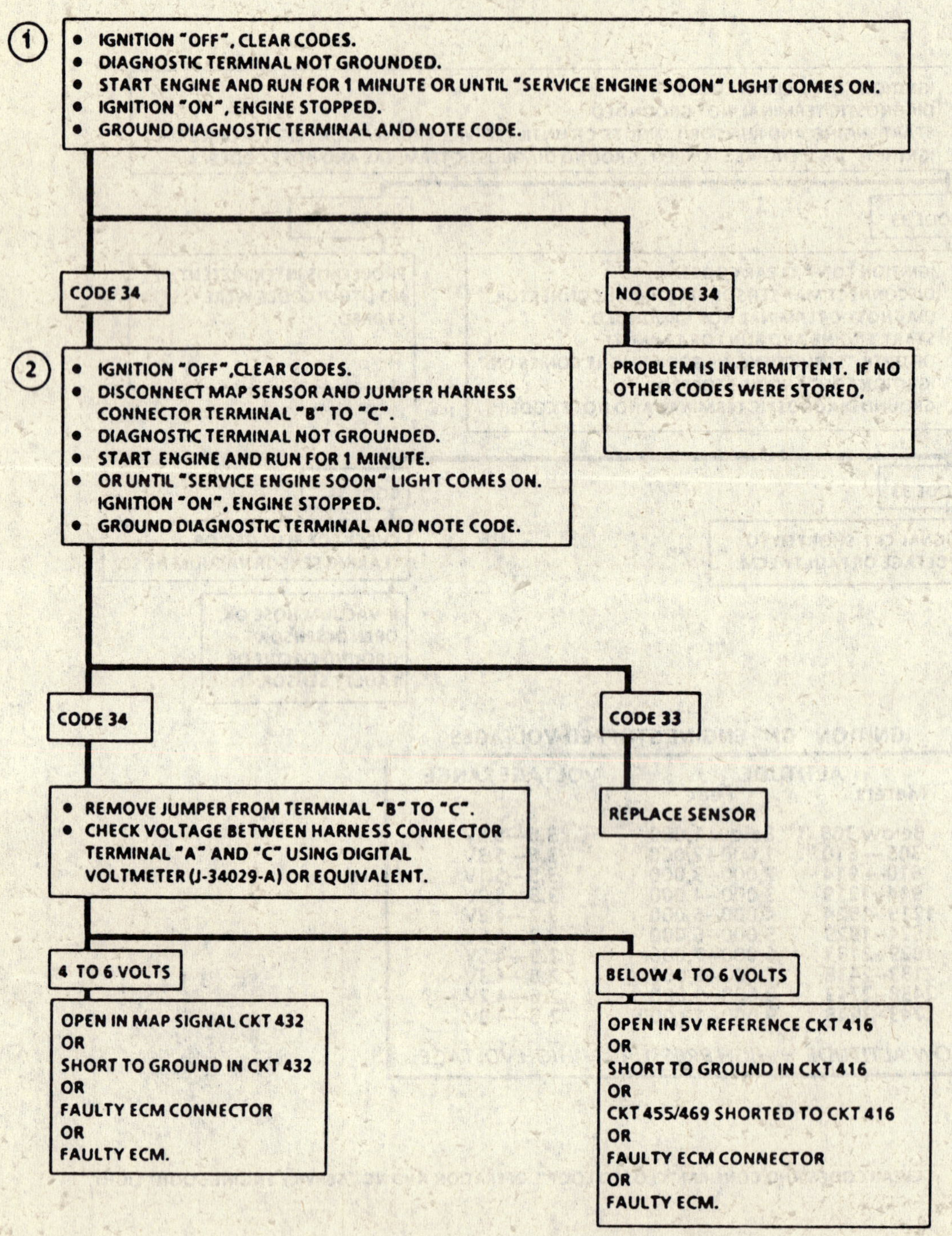

CLEAR CODES AND CONFIRM "CLOSED LOOP" OPERATION AND NO "SERVICE ENGINE SOON" LIGHT.

CODE 35 – TROUBLESHOOTING THE IDLE AIR CONTROL (IAC) SYSTEM – 2.5L ENGINE

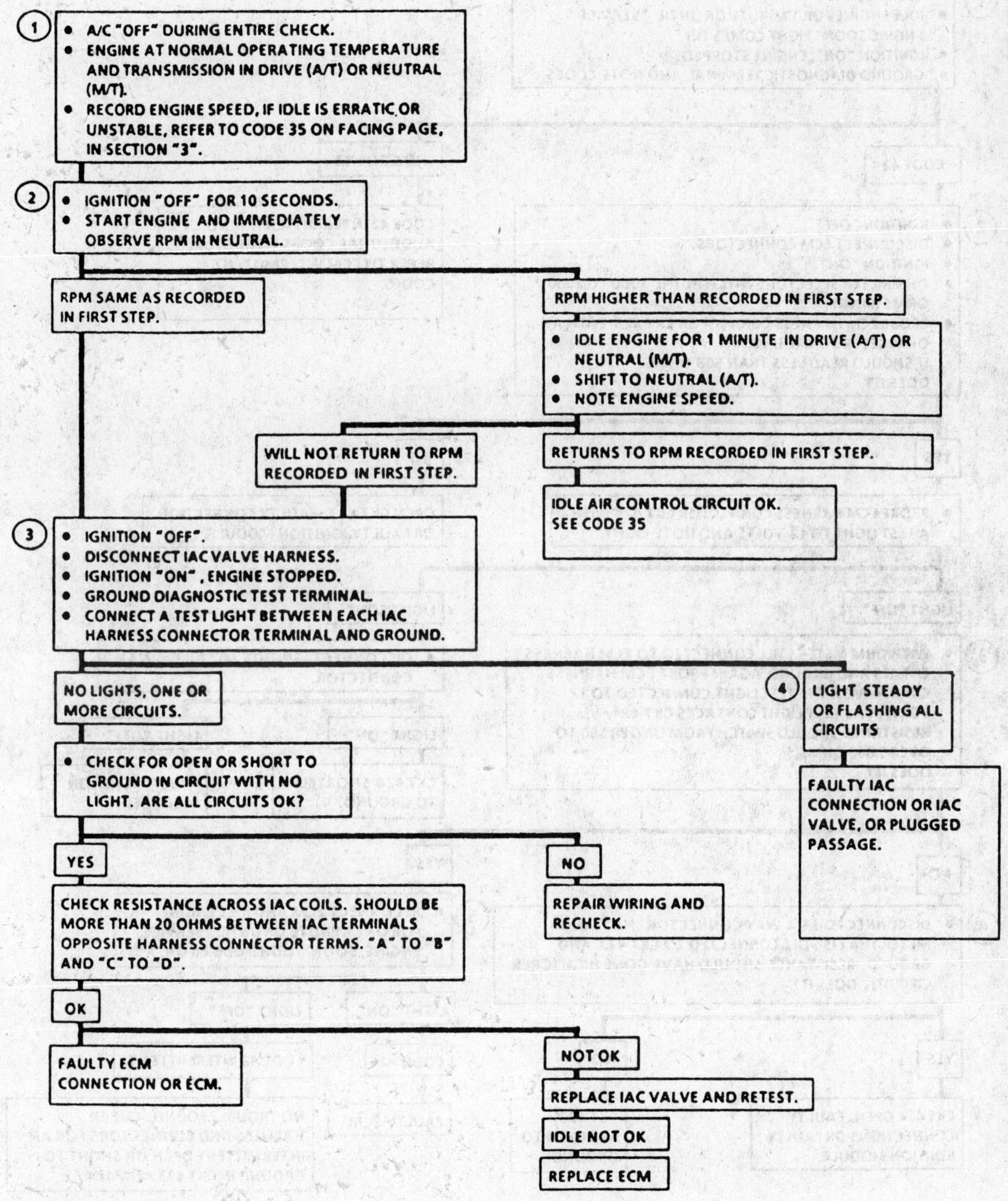

CLEAR CODES, CONFIRM "CLOSED LOOP" OPERATION, NO "SERVICE ENGINE SOON" LIGHT.

CODE 42 – TROUBLESHOOTING THE ELECTRONIC SPARK TIMING (EST) CIRCUIT

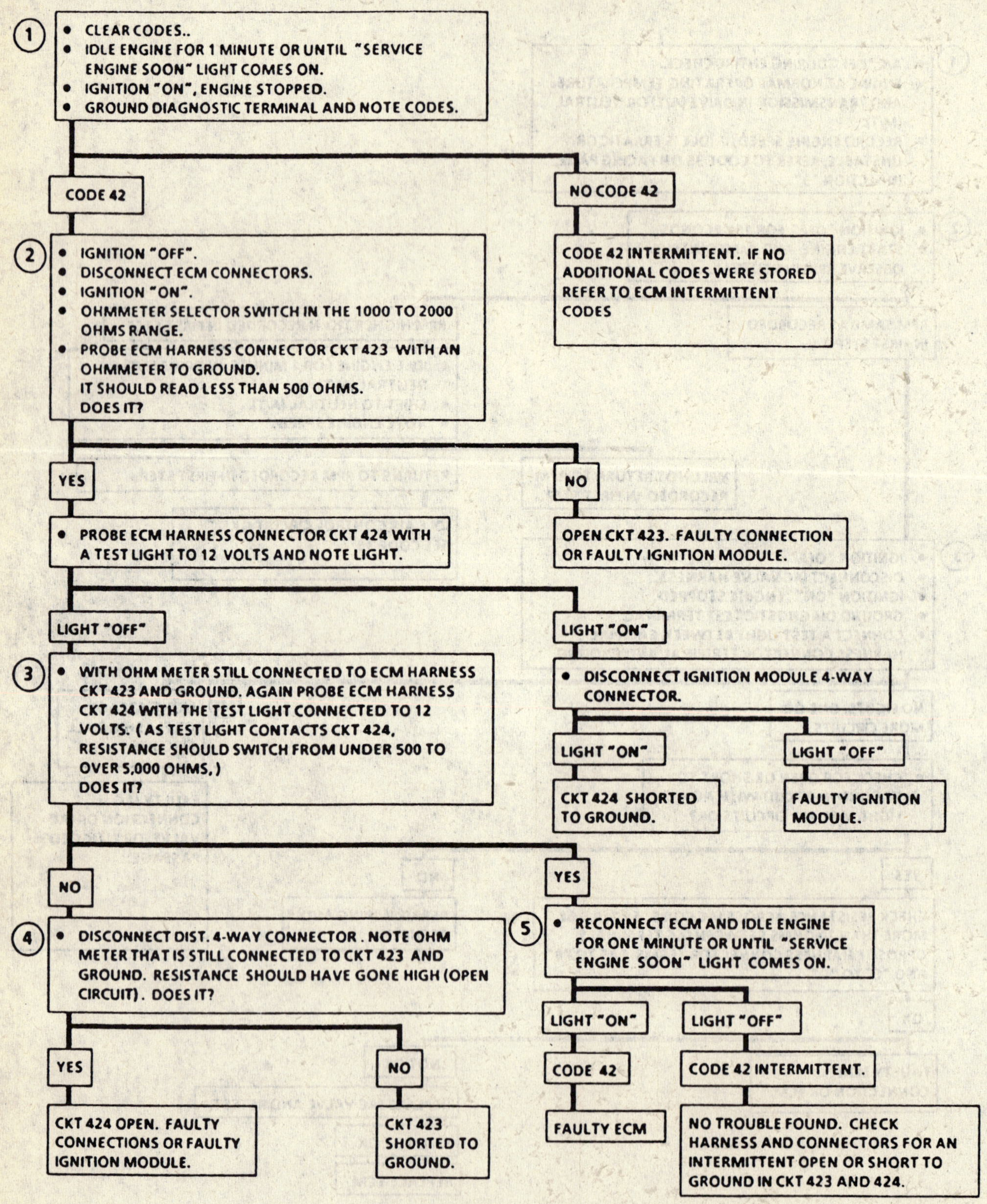

CODE 43 – TROUBLESHOOTING THE ELECTRONIC SPARK CONTROL (ESC) SYSTEM – 2.8L and 4.3L ENGINES

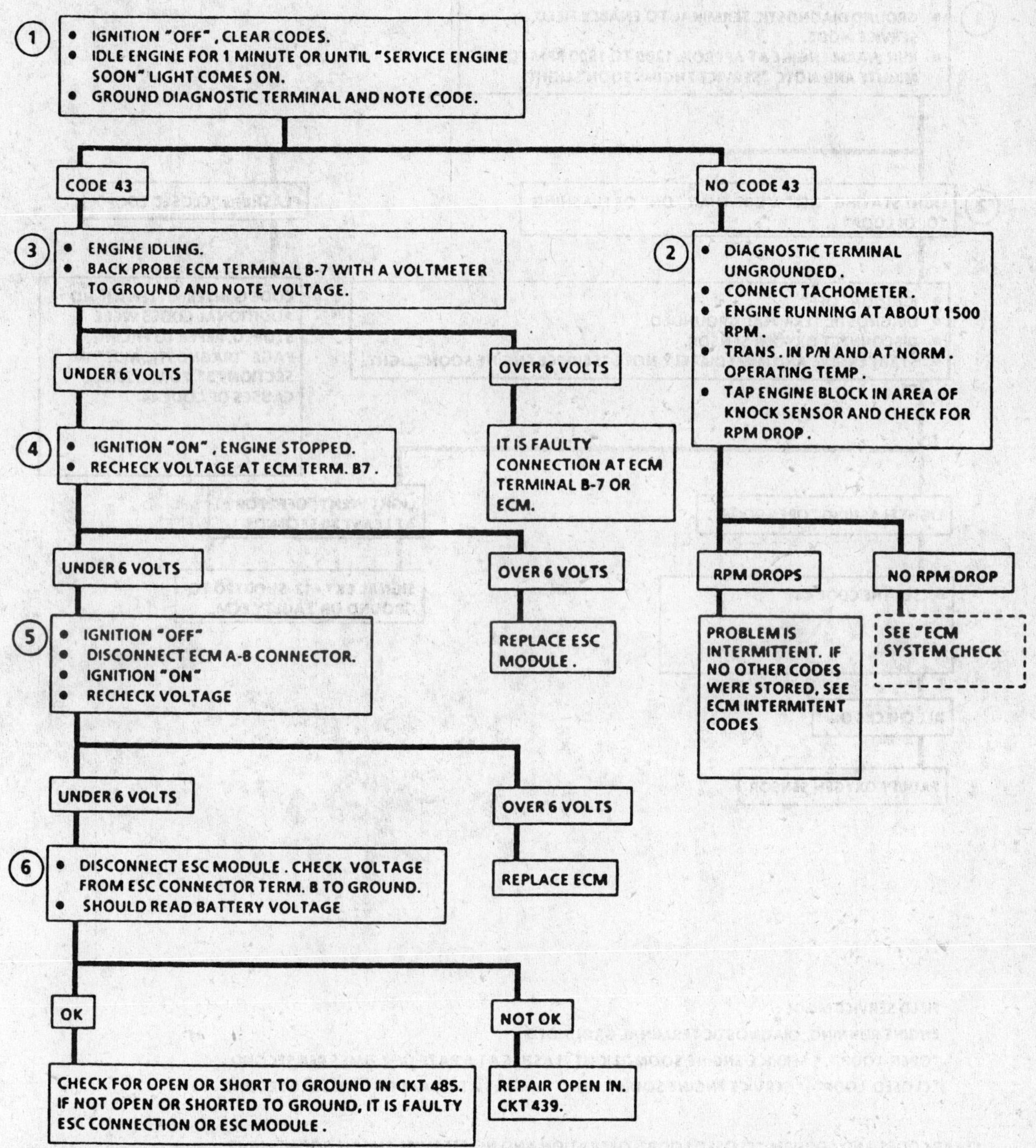

CLEAR CODES AND CONFIRM "CLOSED LOOP" OPERATION AND NO "SERVICE ENGINE SOON" LIGHT.

CODE 44 – TROUBLESHOOTING THE OXYGEN SENSOR CIRCUIT – LEAN EXHAUST INDICATED

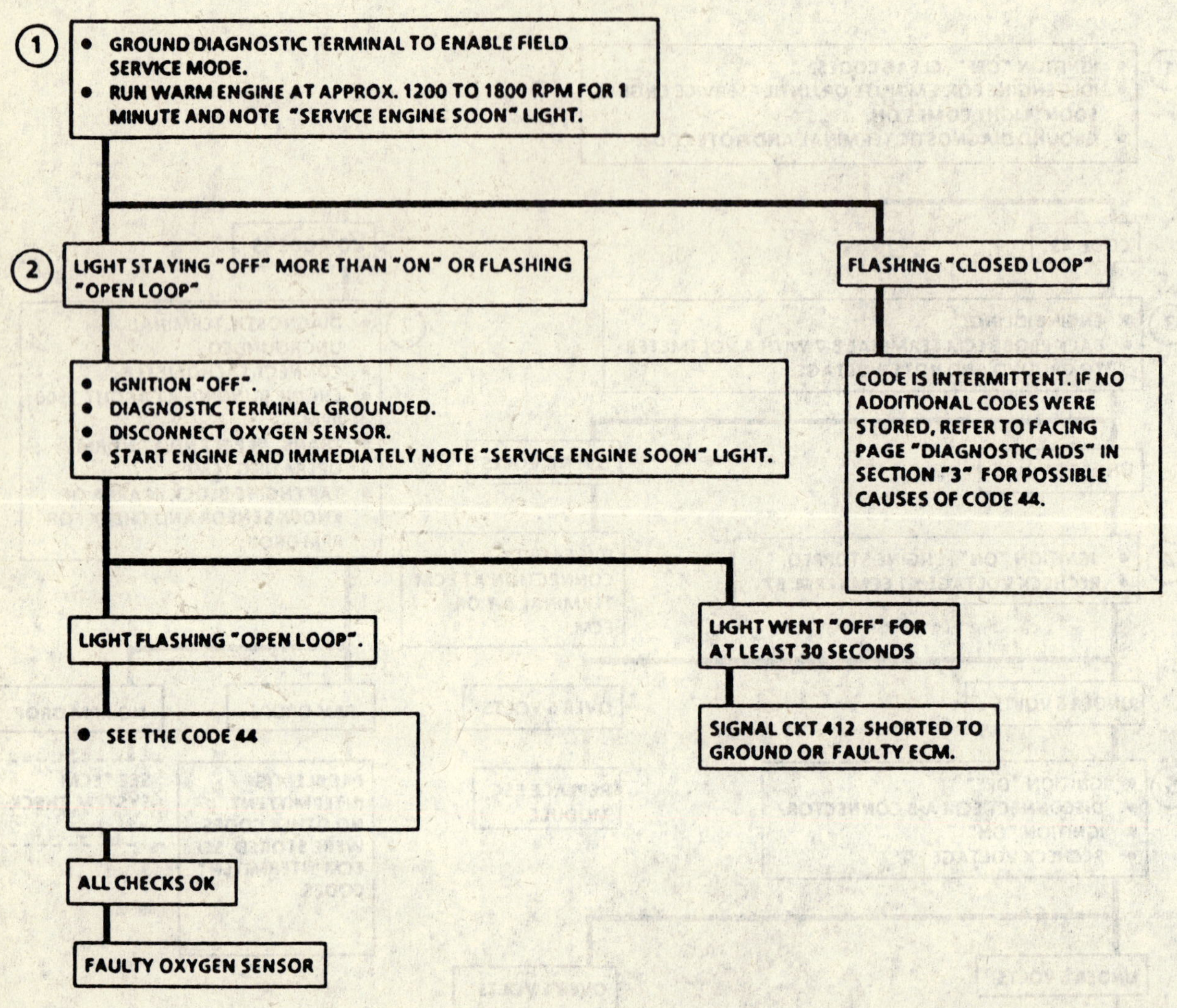

FIELD SERVICE MODE :

ENGINE RUNNING , DIAGNOSTIC TERMINAL GROUNDED .

"OPEN LOOP" , " SERVICE ENGINE SOON " LIGHT FLASHES AT A RATE OF 2 TIMES PER SECOND .

"CLOSED LOOP" , " SERVICE ENGINE SOON " LIGHT FLASHES AT A RATE OF 1 TIME PER SECOND .

CLEAR CODES AND CONFIRM "CLOSED LOOP" OPERATION AND NO "SERVICE ENGINE SOON" LIGHT.

CODE 45 – TROUBLESHOOTING THE OXYGEN SENSOR CIRCUIT – RICH EXHAUST INDICATED

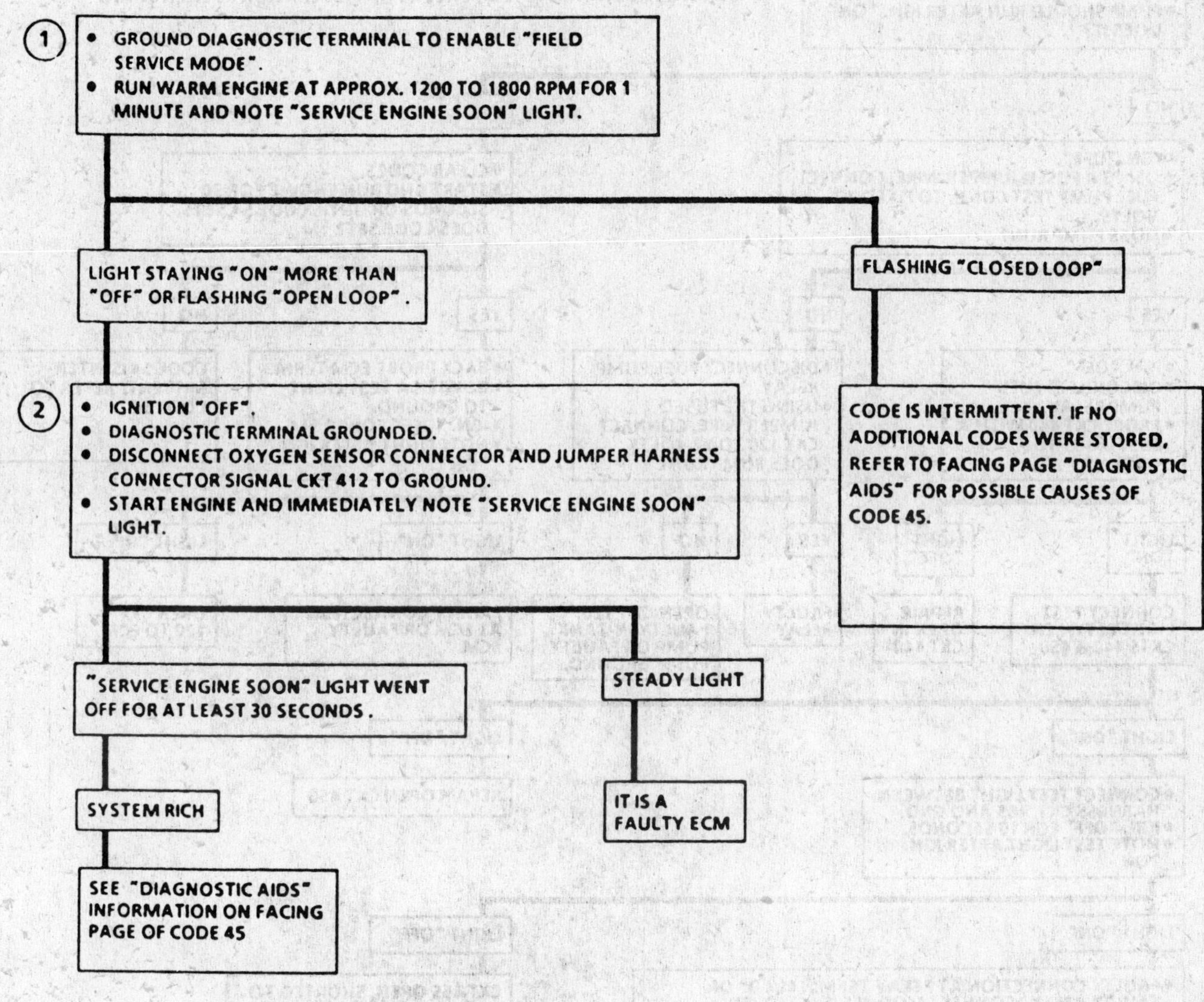

FIELD SERVICE MODE;

- ENGINE RUNNING, DIAGNOSTIC TERMINAL GROUNDED.
- "OPEN LOOP", "SERVICE ENGINE SOON" LIGHT FLASHES AT A RATE OF 2.5 TIMES PER SECOND.
- "CLOSED LOOP", "SERVICE ENGINE SOON" LIGHT FLASHES AT A RATE OF 1 TIME PER SECOND.

CLEAR CODES AND CONFIRM "CLOSED LOOP" OPERATION AND NO "SERVICE ENGINE SOON" LIGHT.

CODE 54 – TROUBLESHOOTING THE FUEL PUMP CIRCUIT – LOW VOLTAGE INDICATED

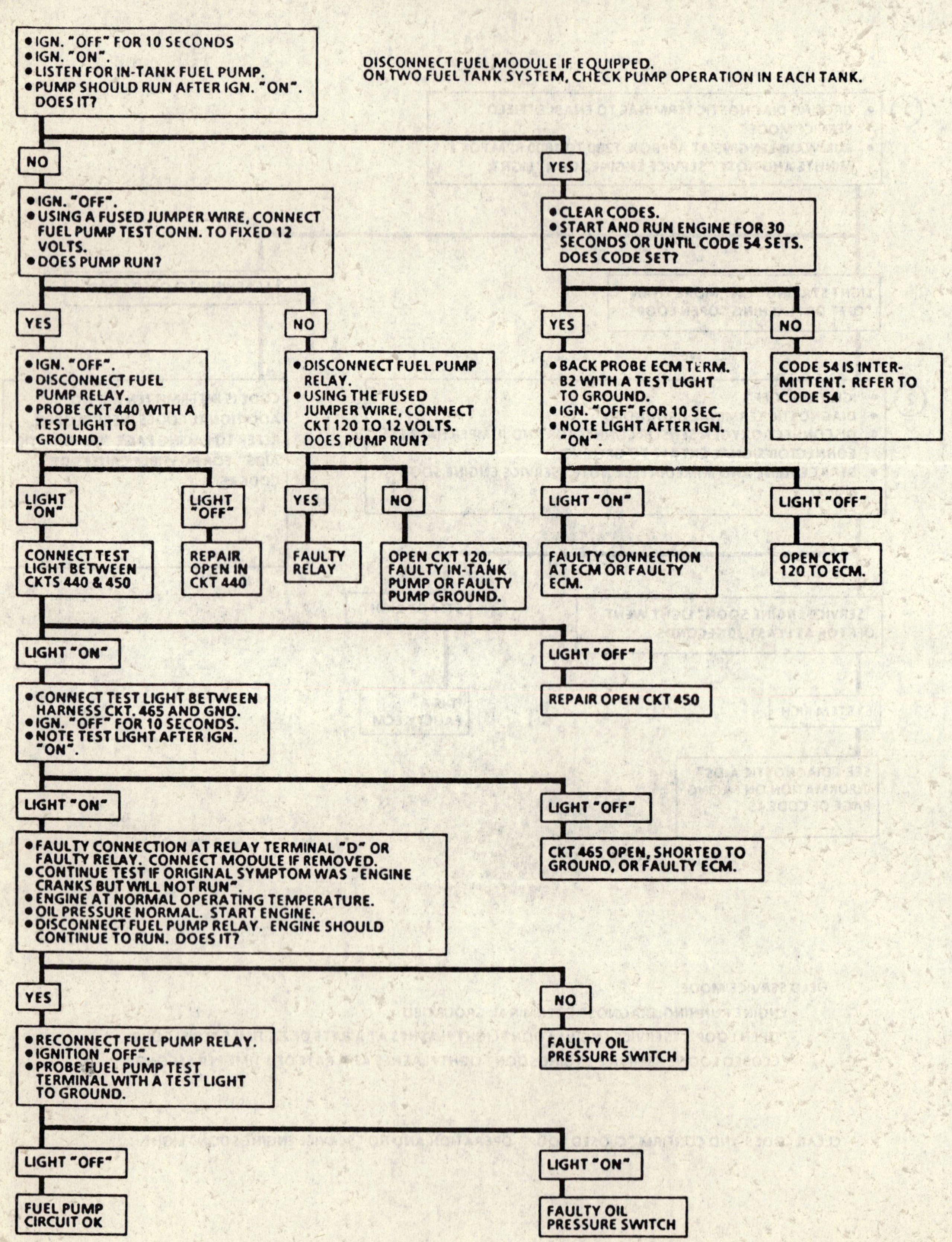

CODE 51 – TROUBLESHOOTING A FAULTY MEM-CAL – EXCEPT 2.5L ENGINE

CHECK THAT ALL PINS ARE FULLY INSERTED IN THE SOCKET. IF OK, REPLACE PROM, CLEAR MEMORY, AND RECHECK. IF CODE 51 REAPPEARS, REPLACE ECM.

CODE 52 – TROUBLESHOOTING A FUEL CALPAK MISSING – EXCEPT 2.5L ENGINE

CHECK FOR MISSING CALPAK AND THAT ALL PIN ARE FULLY INSERTED IN THE SOCKET - IF OK, REPLACE ECM.

CODE 53 – TROUBLESHOOTING A SYSTEM OVERVOLTAGE – EXCEPT 2.5L ENGINE

THIS CODE INDICATES THERE IS A BASIC GENERATOR PROBLEM.

- CODE 53 WILL SET IF VOLTAGE AT ECM TERMINAL B1 IS GREATER THAN 17.1 VOLTS FOR 2 SECONDS.
- CHECK AND REPAIR CHARGING SYSTEM.

CODE 55 – ALL ENGINES – EXCEPT 2.5L ENGINE

BE SURE ECM GROUNDS ARE OK AND THAT MEM-CAL IS PROPERLY LATCHED. IF OK REPLACE ELECTRONIC CONTROL MODULE (ECM).

CLEAR CODES AND CONFIRM "CLOSED LOOP" OPERATION AND NO "SERVICE ENGINE SOON" LIGHT.

ELECTRONIC ENGINE CONTROLS

Electronic Spark Timing (EST) System

The EST system does not have vacuum or mechanical spark advance mechanisms, as these functions are controlled electronically by the distributor module assembly and the ECM of the computer emissions system.

The purpose of the EST system is to precisely adjust the spark timing according to specific engine operating conditions, as sensed by the various monitoring devices of the computer emissions system.

Because the EST system is directly tied into the computer emissions system, service, testing and repair should be performed by a qualified, professional technician.

For further EST system information, refer to the Electronic Spark Control (ESC) System in this section.

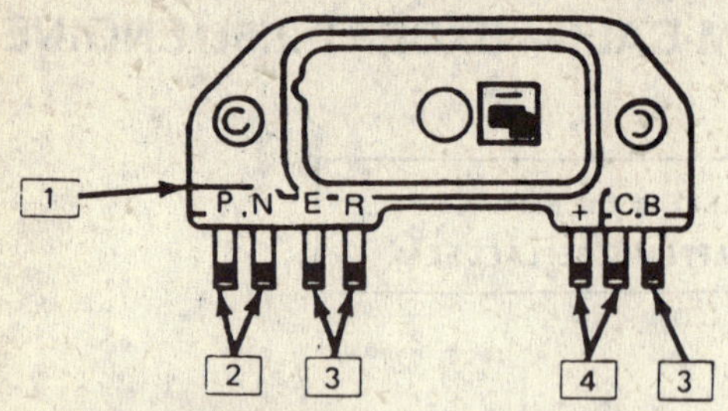

1. Distributor HEI module
2. Ignition coil terminals
3. EST terminals
4. Pick-up coil terminals

Description of the ignition control module terminals – 2.5L and 2.8L TBI engine

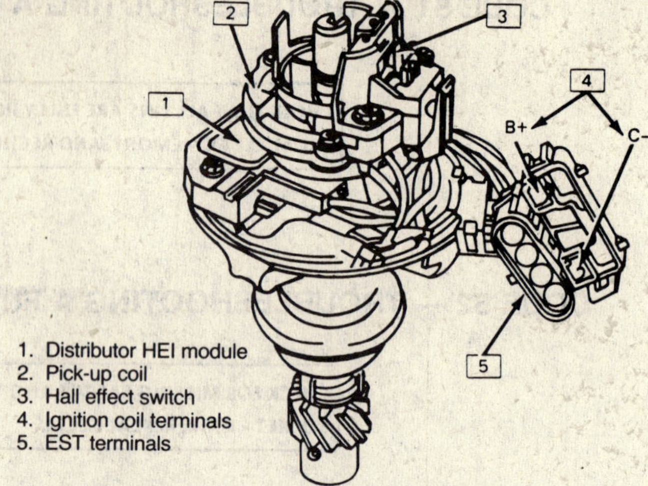

1. Distributor HEI module
2. Pick-up coil
3. Hall effect switch
4. Ignition coil terminals
5. EST terminals

Description of the distributor terminals – 2.5L TBI engine

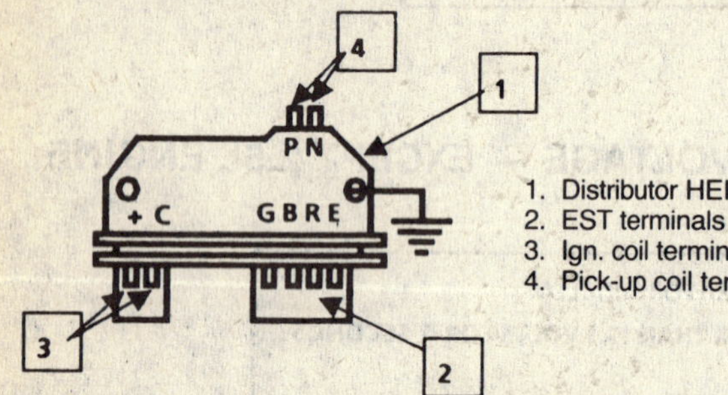

1. Distributor HEI module
2. EST terminals
3. Ign. coil terminals
4. Pick-up coil terminals

Description of the ignition control module terminals – 4.3L TBI engine

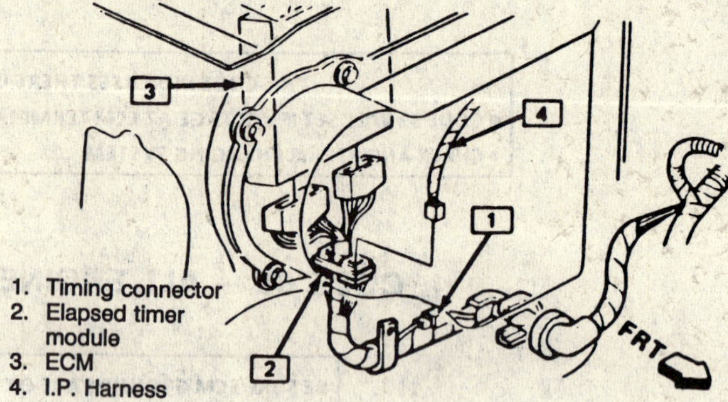

1. Timing connector
2. Elapsed timer module
3. ECM
4. I.P. Harness

Location of the timing connectors – 2.8L and 4.3L engines

Electronic Spark Control (ESC) System

OPERATION

Since varying octane levels of gasoline can cause detonation (spark knock) in an engine, causing piston and ring rattle or vibration, the ESC system has been added to the engine to remedy the knocking situation by retarding the spark timing by as much as 20 degrees; this allows the engine to maximize the spark advance to improve the fuel economy and driveability.

A sensor is mounted on the left side of the block (near the cylinders) to detect the knock and send the information to the Electronic Spark Control (ESC) module. The ESC module sends a signal to the Electronic Control Module (ECM) which adjusts the Electronic Spark Timing (EST) to reduce the spark knock. If

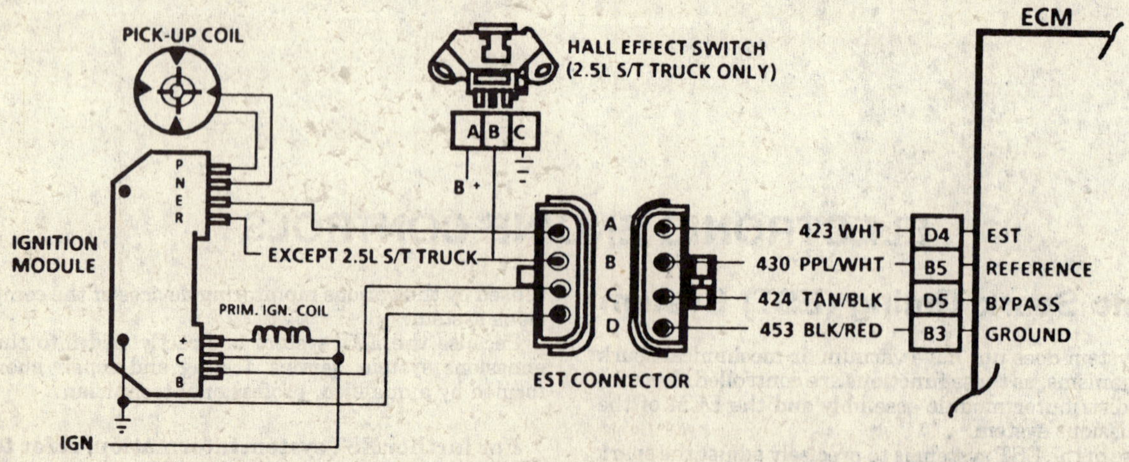

Electronic Spark Timing (EST) schematic – 2.5L and 2.8L engines

TROUBLESHOOTING THE ELECTRONIC SPARK TIMING (EST) SYSTEM – 2.5L AND 2.8L ENGINES

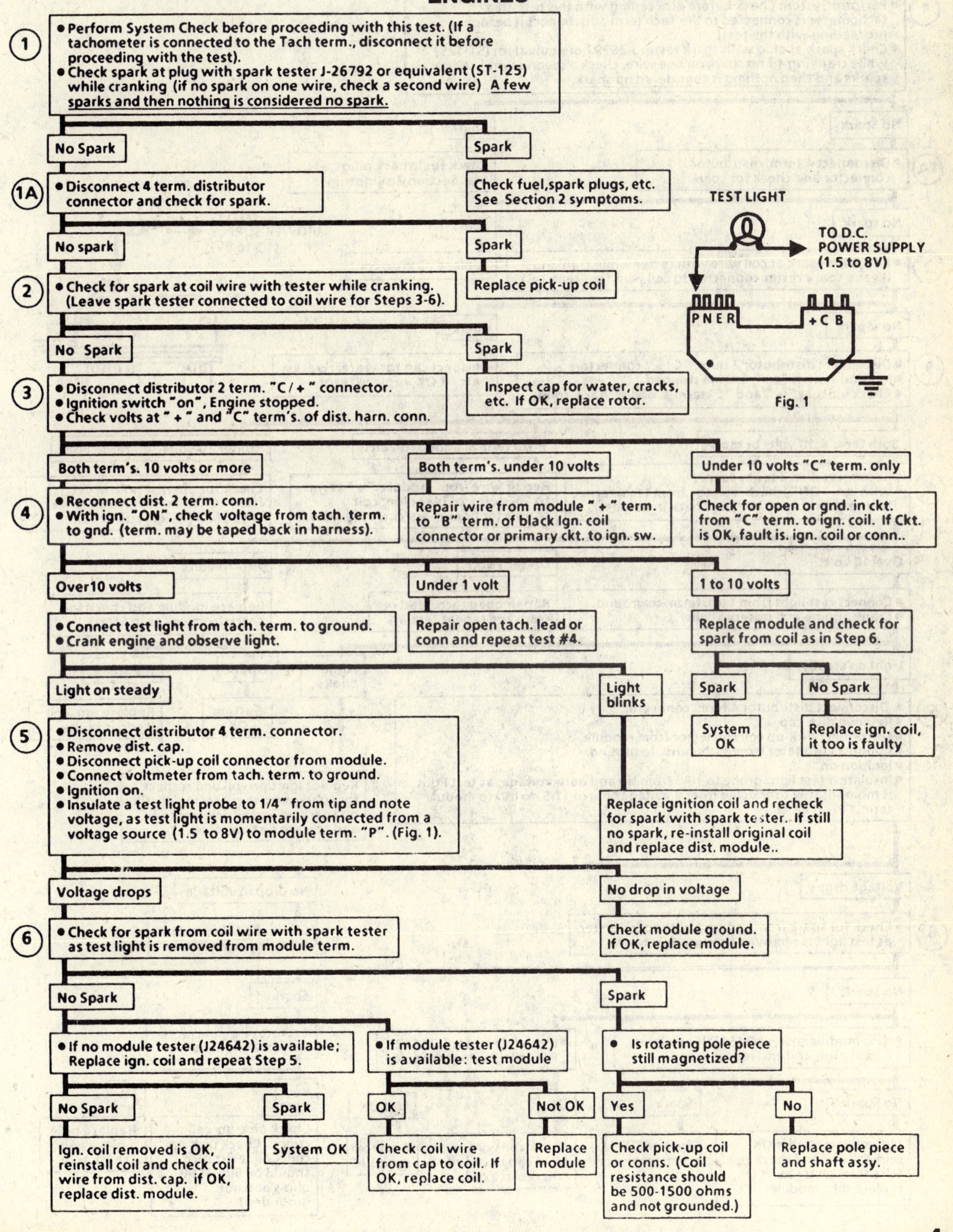

Fig. 1

TROUBLESHOOTING THE ELECTRONIC SPARK TIMING (EST) SYSTEM – 4.3L ENGINE

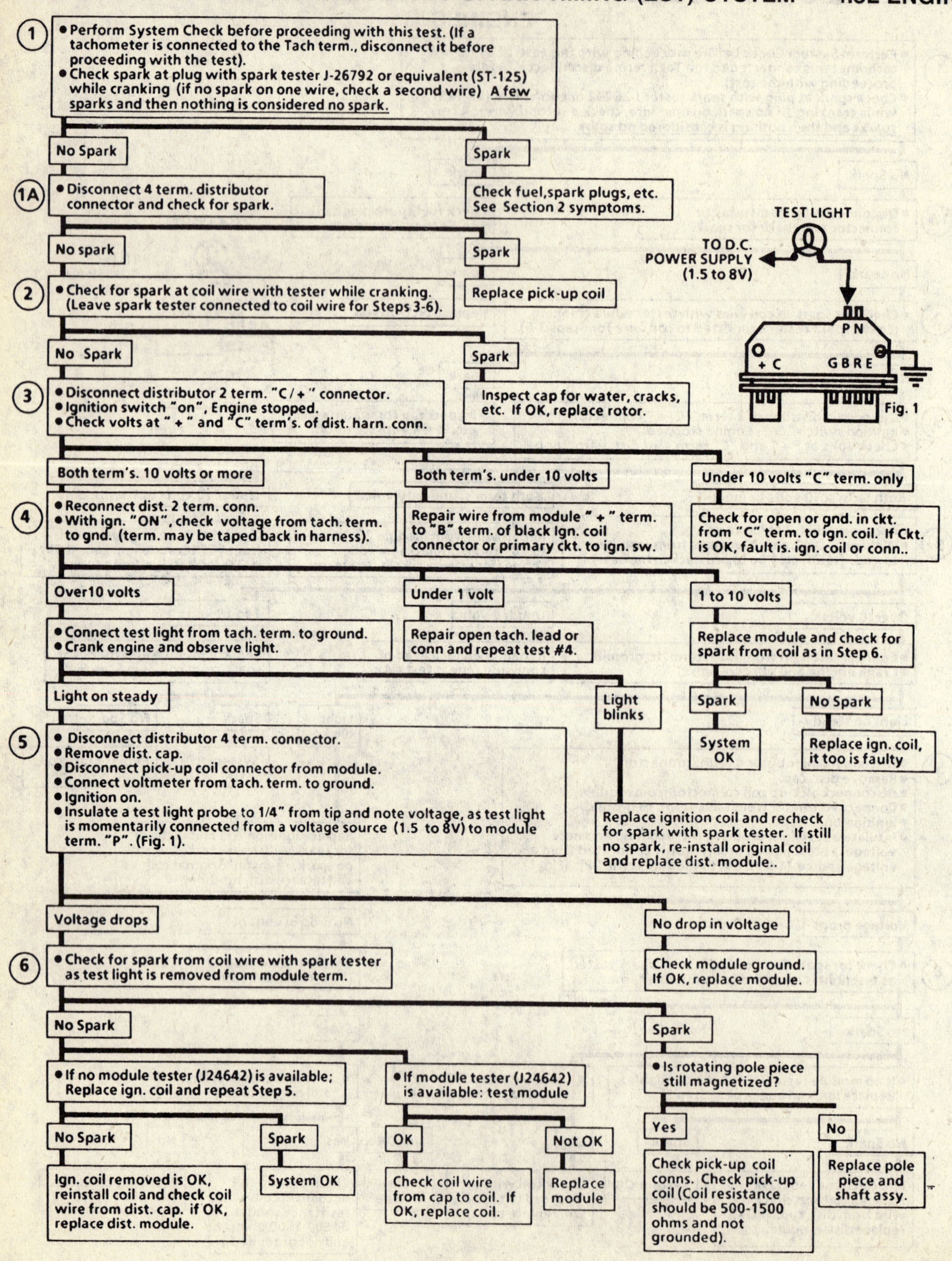

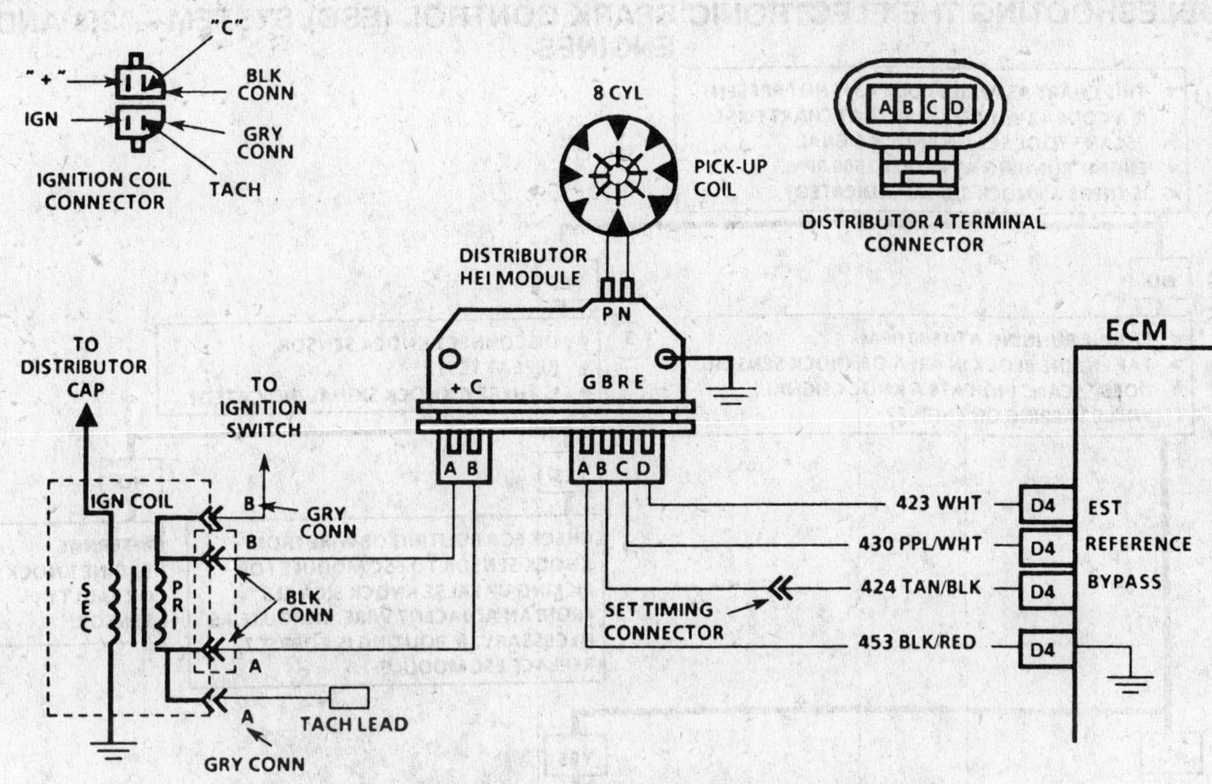

Electronic Spark Timing (EST) schematic — 4.3L engine

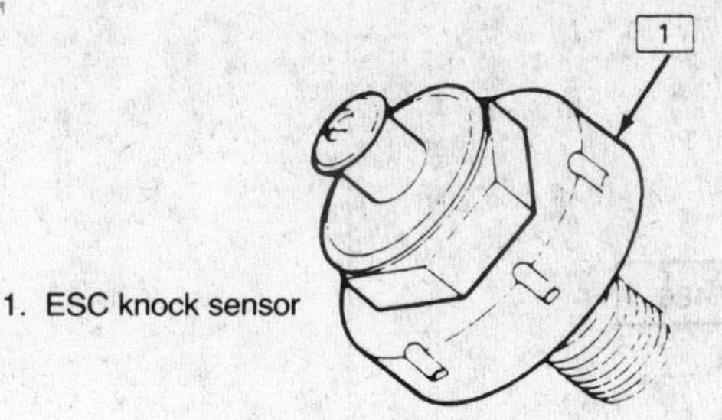

1. ESC knock sensor

View of the knock sensor — 2.8L and 4.3L engines

no signal is received from the ESC sensor, the ECM provides normal spark advance.

Loss of the signal, through a bad ESC sensor, ESC module or a poor ground, will cause the engine to operate sluggishly and cause a Code 43 (to be set).

SERVICE

1. With the engine operating at 1500 rpm, the transmission in Neutral or Park, tap on the engine block in the area of the knock sensor, the engine rpm should drop.

NOTE: If the speed does not drop, the timing is not retarding or it is retarded all of the time.

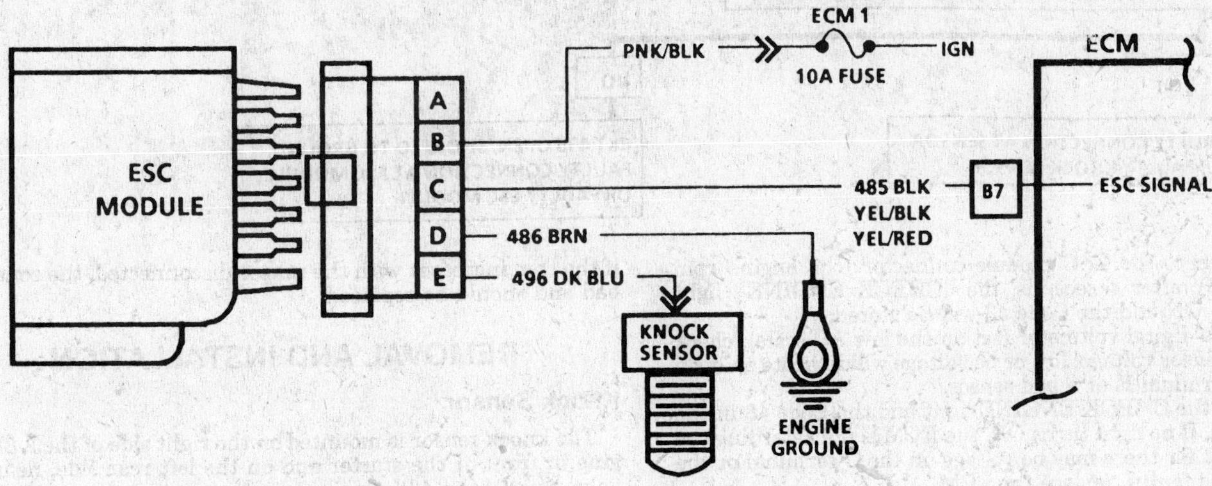

Electronic Spark Control (ESC) system schematic — 2.8L and 4.3L engines

TROUBLESHOOTING THE ELECTRONIC SPARK CONTROL (ESC) SYSTEM — 2.8 AND 4.3L ENGINES

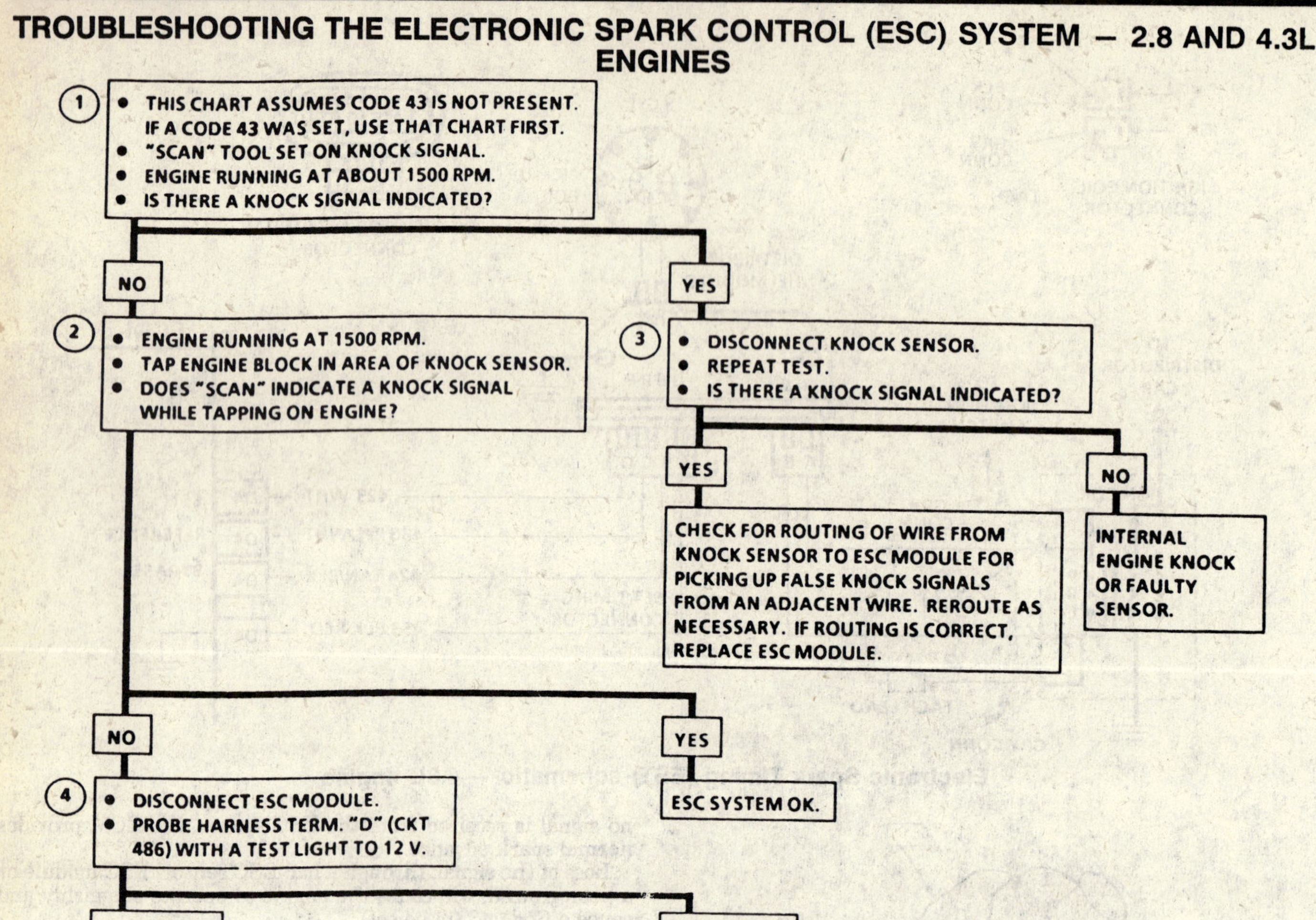

2. Disconnect the ESC module connector (the engine rpm should drop); after 4 seconds, the "CHECK ENGINE" light should turn ON and the Code 43 will be stored.
3. Using a digital voltmeter (set on the low AC scale), check the knock sensor voltage; low or no voltage will indicate an open circuit at terminal E or a bad sensor.
4. Check the CHECK ENGINE light and the Code 43 in the ESC system. If no light turns ON, the ECM is not retarding the engine spark for there may be voltage on the C terminal or the ECM may be faulty, replace the ECM.
5. Disconnect the electrical connector from the knock sensor; if the rpm increases with the sensor disconnected, the sensor is bad and should be replaced.

REMOVAL AND INSTALLATION

Knock Sensor

The knock sensor is mounted on the right side of the 2.8L engine in front of the starter and on the left rear side, near the valve cove of the 4.3L engine.

1. Disconnect the negative battery terminal from the battery.

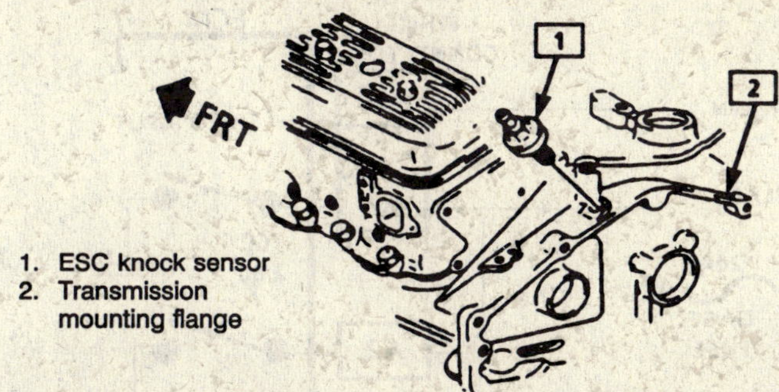

Exploded view of the electronic spark control knock sensor — 4.3L engine

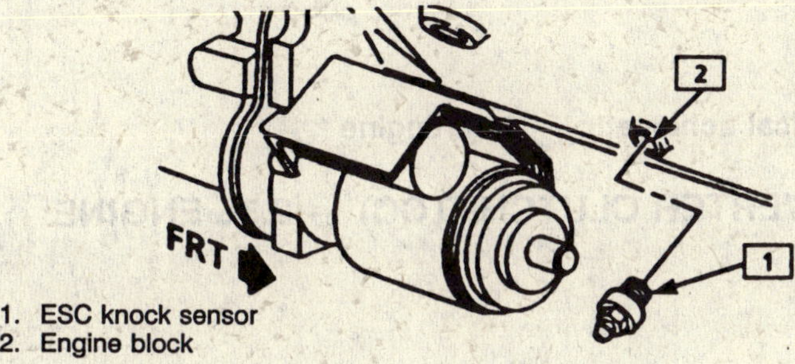

Exploded view of the electronic spark control knock sensor — 2.8L engine

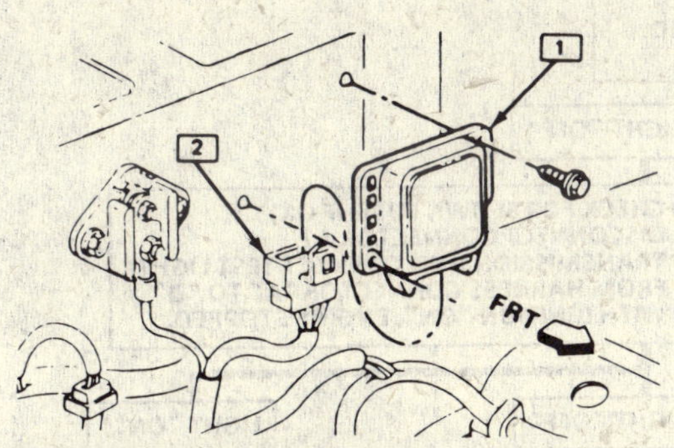

Exploded view of the Electronic Spark Control (ESC) module — 2.8L and 4.3L engines

2. Disconnect the electrical harness connector from the knock sensor.
3. Remove the knock sensor from the engine block.
4. To install, apply teflon tape to the threads and reverse the removal procedures.

ESC Module

The ESC module is located at the top-rear of the engine.

1. Disconnect the electrical harness connector from the ESC module.
2. Remove the mounting screws and the ESC module from the vehicle.
3. To install, reverse the removal procedures.

Transmission Converter Clutch (TCC) System

All vehicles equipped with an automatic transmission use the TCC system. The ECM controls the converter by means of a solenoid mounted in the outdrive housing of the transmission. When the vehicle speed reaches a certain level, the ECM energizes the solenoid and allows the torque converter to mechanically couple the transmission to the engine. When the operating conditions indicate that the transmission should operate as a normal fluid coupled transmission, the ECM will de-energize the solenoid. Depressing the brake pedal will also return the transmission to normal automatic operation.

The ECM monitors the following sensors to control the transmission converter clutch operation.

- Throttle Position Sensor (TPS) — Acceleration and deceleration conditions are used to the clutch.
- Coolant Temperature Sensor — The engine MUST BE warmed before the clutch can be applied.
- Pulse Switch — During a 4-to-3 downshift condition, the clutch switch is opened momentarily.
- Brake Switch — Depressing the brake pedal will de-energize the clutch system.

Early Fuel Evaporation System Carbureted Engines

OPERATION

The early fuel evaporation system provides a rapid heating source to the engine induction system during cold driveaway conditions, thus, providing quick fuel evaporation and more uniform fuel distribution. When reducing the length of carburetor choking time, the exhaust emissions are also reduced.

The system consists of a ceramic heater grid (located between the carburetor and the intake manifold) and a temperature switch (non-ECM models) or a relay (ECM models) which activates the heater during cold operation. The relay, located under the right fender, is operated by the ECM.

As the coolant temperature increases, the temperature switch (non-ECM models) or the relay (ECM models) turns Off the current to the ceramic heater, allowing the engine to operate on it's own.

NOTE: Operational checks should be made at normal maintenance intervals.

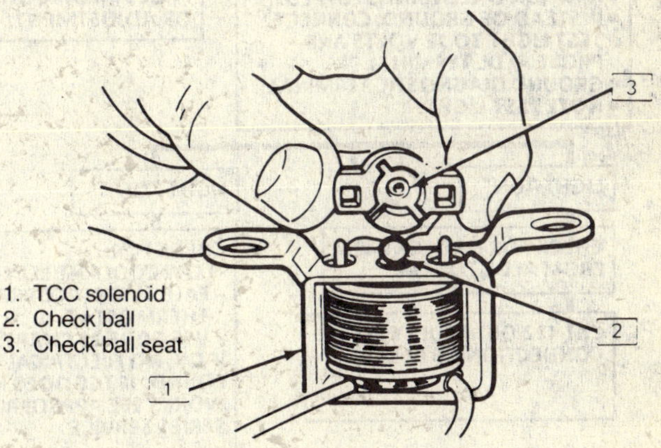

Exploded view of the Transmission Converter Clutch (TCC) solenoid

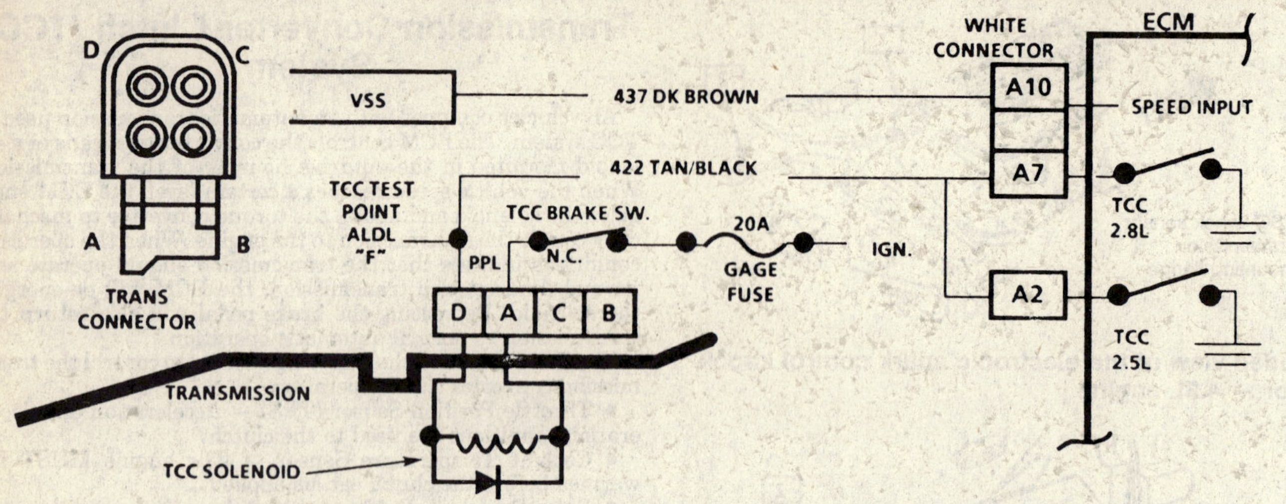

Torque Converter Clutch (TCC) electrical schematic — 2.5L engine

TROUBLESHOOTING THE TORQUE CONVERTER CLUTCH (TCC) — 2.5L ENGINE

USE A "SCAN" TOOL TO CHECK THE FOLLOWING AND CORRECT IF NECESSARY:
- COOLANT TEMPERATURE
- TPS
- VSS
- CODES - IF 24 IS PRESENT, SEE CODE CHART 24. ALSO, PERFORM MECHANICAL CHECKS, SUCH AS LINKAGE, OIL LEVEL, ETC., BEFORE USING THIS CHART.

(1)
- ENGINE AT NORMAL OPERATING TEMPERATURE AND "CLOSED LOOP".
- CONNECT TEST LIGHT FROM TCC TEST POINT, ALDL TERM "F" AND GROUND.
- NOTE LIGHT.

LIGHT "ON"

TEST LIGHT SHOULD GO OUT AS BRAKE PEDAL IS DEPRESSED.

OK

(2)
- IGNITION ON. ENGINE STOPPED.
- INSTEAD OF GROUND. CONNECT TEST LIGHT TO 12 VOLTS AND PROBE ALDL TERMINAL "F".
- GROUND DIAGNOSTIC TERMINAL
- NOTE TEST LIGHT.

LIGHT "ON"

CHECK FOR OPEN CKT 422 FROM ALDL TO ECM.

CKT 422 OK. FAULTY ECM CONNECTION OR ECM.

LIGHT "OFF"

CHECK FOR:
- LOW COOLANT LEVEL.
- FAULTY OR INCORRECT THERMOSTAT.
- VSS CODE 24 CHART.

IF OK, NO ELECTRICAL TROUBLE FOUND. IF TCC DOES NOT WORK, SEE APPROPRIATE SERIES SERVICE

NOT OK

FAULTY BRAKE SWITCH OR ADJUSTMENT.

LIGHT "OFF"

(3)
- CHECK FOR BLOWN FUSE. IF OK, DISCONNECT CONNECTOR AT TRANSMISSION AND CONNECT TEST LIGHT FROM HARNESS CONNECTOR "A" TO "D" WITH IGNITION "ON", ENGINE STOPPED.

LIGHT "OFF"

- CONNECT A TEST LIGHT FROM TERM "A" TO GROUND.

LIGHT "OFF"

REPAIR OPEN IN TCC BRAKE SWITCH CIRCUIT OR ADJ. SWITCH.

LIGHT "ON"

- GROUND TCC TEST POINT AND AGAIN CONNECT TEST LIGHT BETWEEN HARNESS CONNECTOR TERMS "A" AND "D".

LIGHT "ON"

FAULTY:
- TRANSMISSION TCC CONNECTION
- TCC SOLENOID.

LIGHT "OFF"

REPAIR OPEN IN WIRE FROM TRANSMISSION TO ALDL TEST POINT, TERM "F".

LIGHT "ON"

CHECK FOR SHORT TO GROUND IN CKT 422. IF NOT GROUNDED. REPLACE ECM.

CLEAR CODES AND CONFIRM "CLOSED LOOP" OPERATION AND NO "SERVICE ENGINE SOON" LIGHT.

TROUBLESHOOTING THE TORQUE CONVERTER CLUTCH (TCC) – 4.3L ENGINE

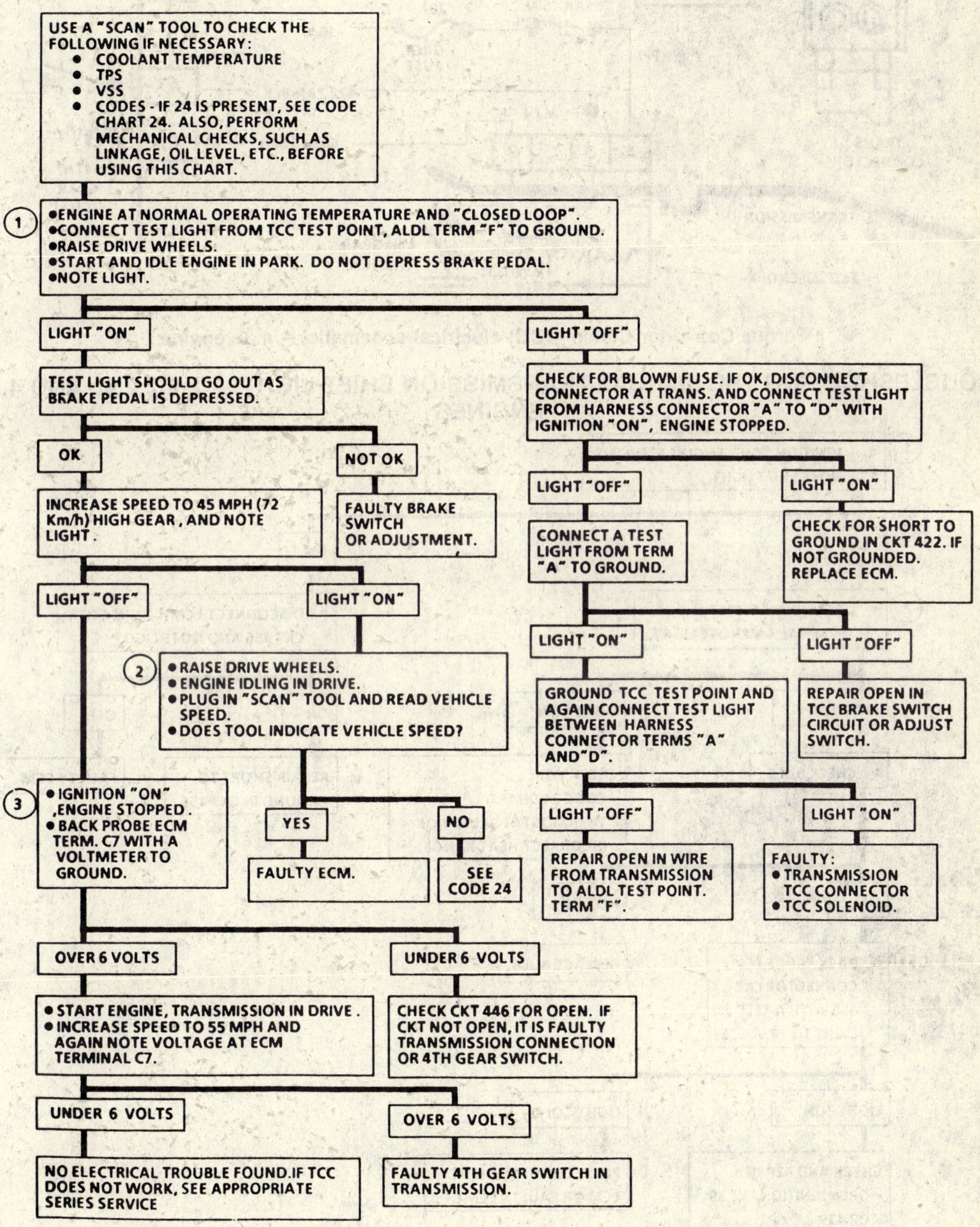

CLEAR CODES AND CONFIRM "CLOSED LOOP" OPERATION AND NO "SERVICE ENGINE SOON" LIGHT.

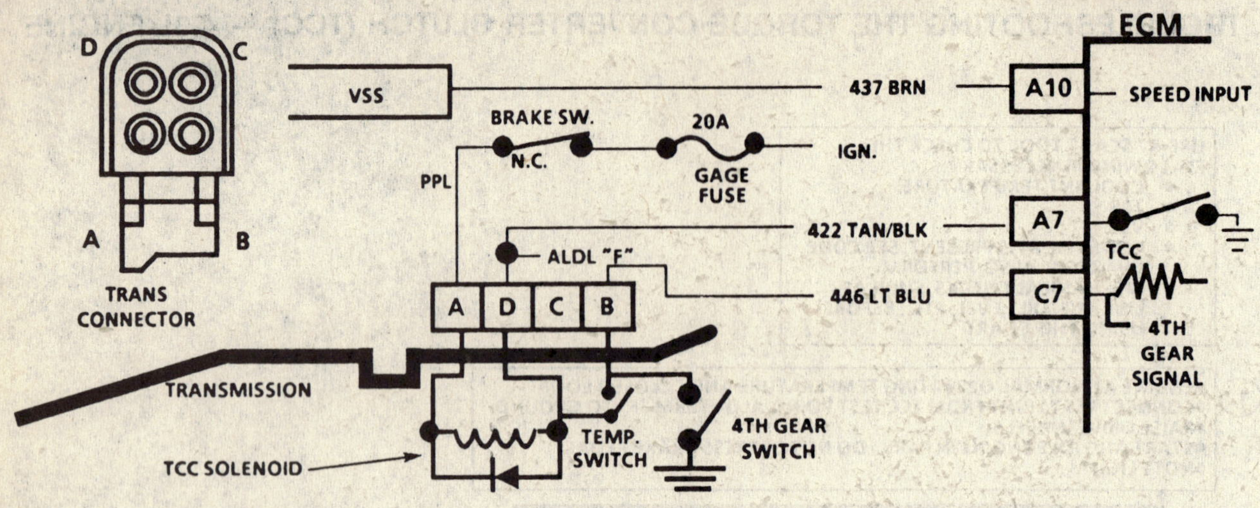

Torque Converter Clutch (TCC) electrical schematic – 4.3L engine

TROUBLESHOOTING THE MANUAL TRANSMISSION SHIFT LIGHT – 2.5L, 2.8L AND 4.3L ENGINES

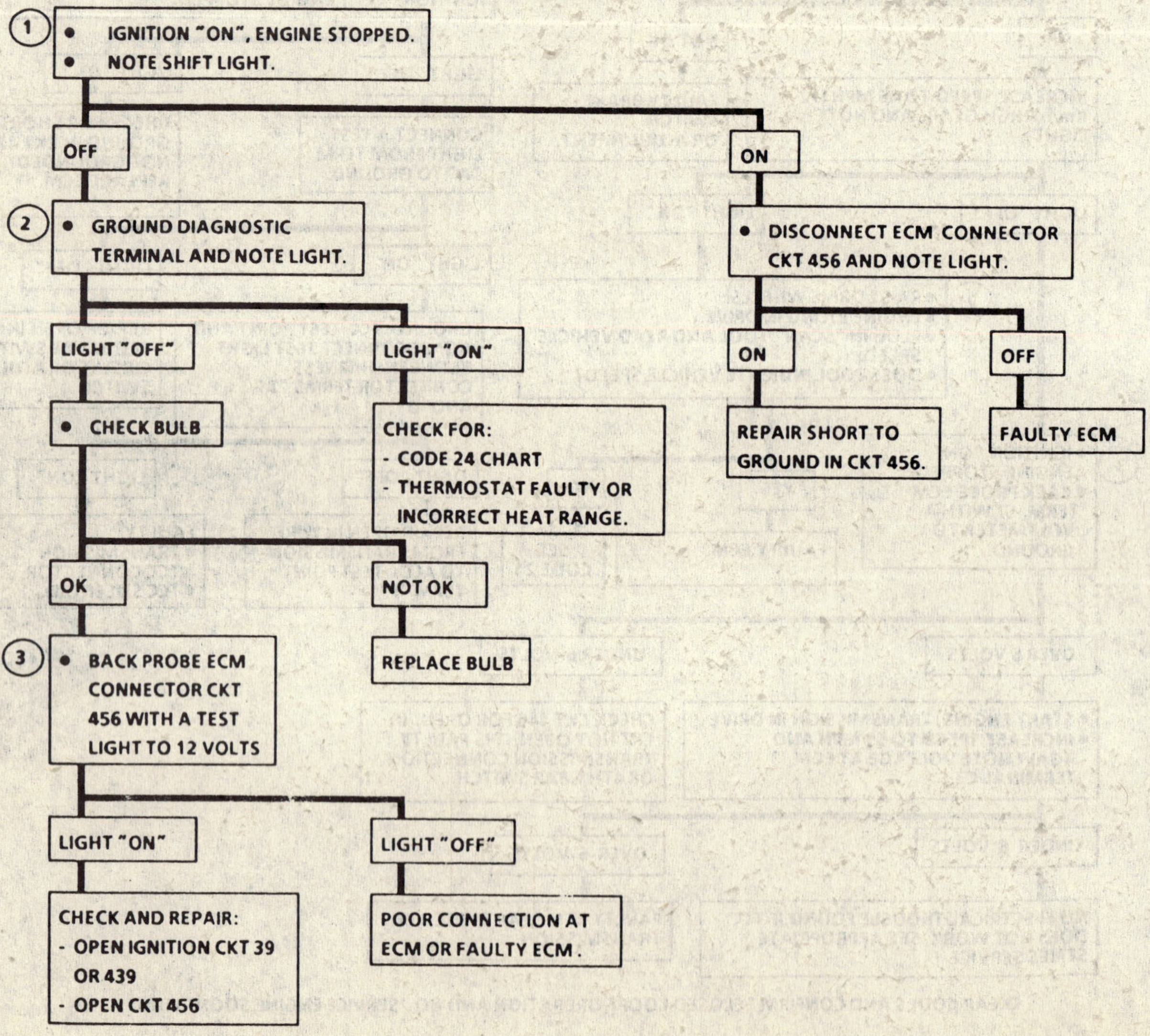

(1)
- IGNITION "ON", ENGINE STOPPED.
- NOTE SHIFT LIGHT.

OFF:

(2)
- GROUND DIAGNOSTIC TERMINAL AND NOTE LIGHT.

LIGHT "OFF":
- CHECK BULB

OK:

(3)
- BACK PROBE ECM CONNECTOR CKT 456 WITH A TEST LIGHT TO 12 VOLTS

LIGHT "ON": CHECK AND REPAIR:
- OPEN IGNITION CKT 39 OR 439
- OPEN CKT 456

LIGHT "OFF": POOR CONNECTION AT ECM OR FAULTY ECM.

NOT OK: REPLACE BULB

LIGHT "ON": CHECK FOR:
- CODE 24 CHART
- THERMOSTAT FAULTY OR INCORRECT HEAT RANGE.

ON:
- DISCONNECT ECM CONNECTOR CKT 456 AND NOTE LIGHT.

ON: REPAIR SHORT TO GROUND IN CKT 456.

OFF: FAULTY ECM

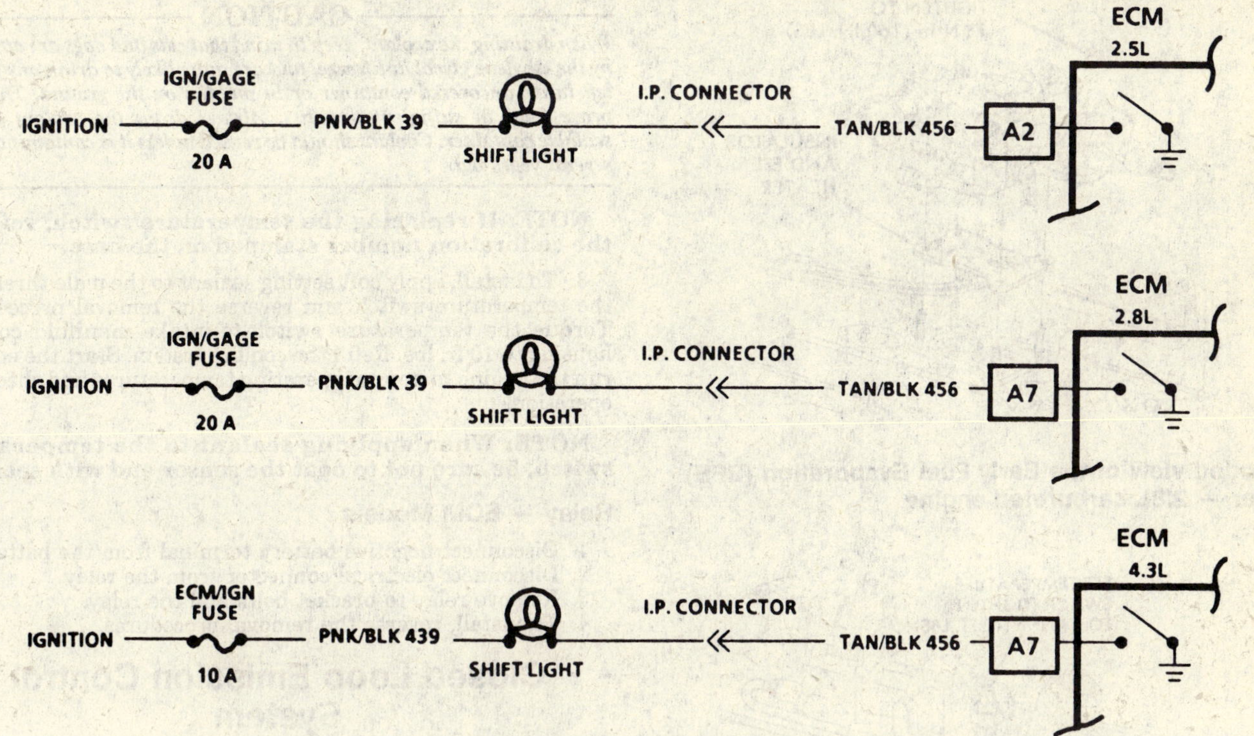

View of the manual transmissio shift light schematic — 2.5L, 2.8L and 4.3L engines

SERVICE

Temperature Switch

1. Disconnect the electrical connector from temperature switch.
2. Connect a 12 volt test lamp across the connector terminals.
3. If the lamp glows when the ignition switch is **ON** and engine **OFF**, the EFE heater is good.
4. If the lamp does not glow, reconnect the heater switch connector. With the engine temperature below 140°F (60°C), measure the voltage across the EFE heater by inserting the test probes into the rear of the connector body (black wire is Negative). The voltage should be approximately 11–13 volts.
5. If the voltage is not 11–13 volts across the heater terminals, check the black wire voltage-to-ground. If the voltage is not 0 volts, the black (ground) wire is an open circuit; repair it.
6. If the voltage is 0 volts, check the voltage-to-vehicle ground from each heater switch terminal — the voltage should be 11–13 volts at each switch terminal.
7. If 11–13 volts is measured at one switch terminal but low or 0 volts at the other, inspect the connector for deformed terminals and repair, as required.
8. If the connector is making proper contact, replace heater switch.
9. If the voltage is not 11–13 volts at both switch terminals, inspect the wiring circuit between the heater switch and the ignition switch, then repair, as required.
10. Start the engine and allow it to warm up to above 170°F (76.7°C). Check the voltage across the EFE heater terminals. The voltage should be 0 volts. If the voltage is not 0 volts, replace the temperature switch.

REMOVAL AND INSTALLATION

EFE Heater

1. Remove the air cleaner.
2. Disconnect all electrical, vacuum and fuel connections from carburetor.
3. Disconnect the EFE Heater electrical connector.
4. Remove the carburetor-to-intake mainfold nuts/bolts and the carburetor.
5. Remove the EFE Heater isolator assembly.
6. To intall, reverse the removal procedures.
7. Start the engine and check for leaks.

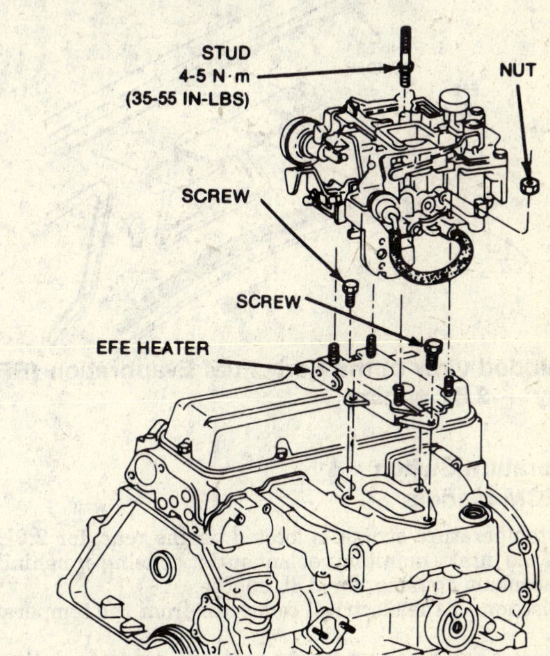

Exploded view of the Early Fuel Evaporation (EFE) system — 2.0L engine

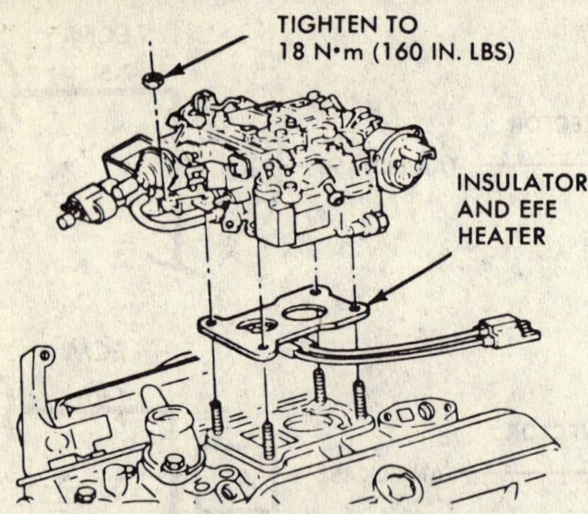

Exploded view of the Early Fuel Evaporation (EFE) heater — 2.8L carbureted engine

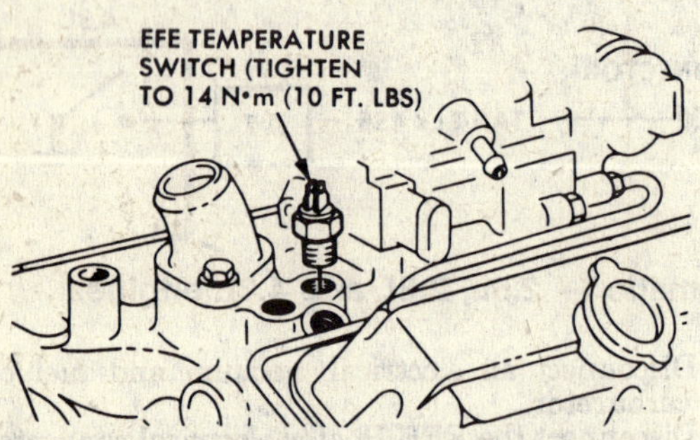

Exploded view of the Early Fuel Evaporation (EFE) temperature switch — 2.8L carbureted engine

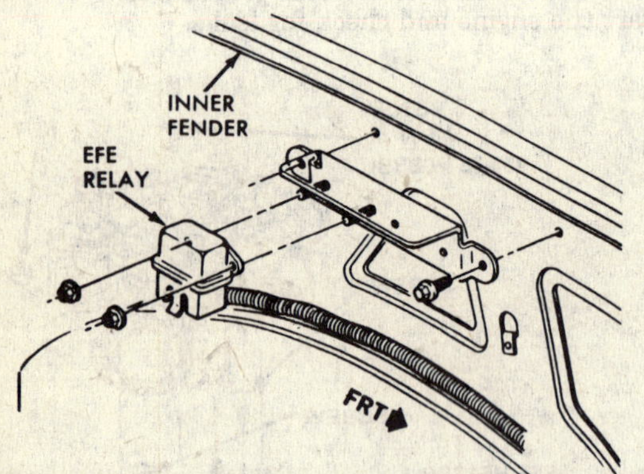

Exploded view of the Early Fuel Evaporation (EFE) relay — 2.8L engine

Temperature Switch
Non-ECM Models

The temperature switch is located on the rear, for 2.0L engine, of the intake manifold coolant outlet housing or behind the engine coolant housing, for 2.8L engine.

1. Disconnect the electrical connector from the temperature switch.
2. Place a catch pan under the radiator, open the drain cock and drain the coolant to a level below the intake manifold coolant housing.

CAUTION

When draining the coolant, keep in mind that cats and dogs are attracted by the ethylene glycol antifreeze, and are quite likely to drink any that is left in an uncovered container or in puddles on the ground. This will prove fatal in sufficient quantity. Always drain the coolant into a sealable container. Coolant should be reused unless it is contaminated or several years old.

NOTE: If replacing the temperature switch, refer to the calibration number stamped on the base.

3. To install, apply soft setting sealant to the male threads of the temperature switch and reverse the removal procedures. Torque the temperature switch-to-intake manifold coolant housing to 10 ft. lbs. Refill the cooling system. Start the engine, run the engine to normal operating temperatures and check the operation.

NOTE: When applying sealant to the temperature switch, be sure not to coat the sensor end with sealant.

Relay — ECM Models

1. Disconnect negative battery terminal from the battery.
2. Disconnect electrical connector from the relay.
3. Remove relay-to-bracket bolts and the relay.
4. To install, reverse the removal procedures.

Closed Loop Emission Control System

NOTE: When troubleshooting the system, always check the electrical and vacuum connectors which may be the source of a problem before testing or replacing a component.

VACUUM CONTROLLER REPLACEMENT

1. Disconnect the electrical connector.
2. Disconnect the vacuum hoses from the vacuum regulator and solenoid.
3. Remove the vacuum controller.
4. To install, reverse the removal procedures.

IDLE AND WIDE OPEN THROTTLE (WOT) VACUUM SWITCH REPLACEMENT

1. Disconnect the electrical harness connector.
2. Disconnect the vacuum hoses from the sensors.
3. Remove the idle and the WOT vacuum switch.
4. To install, reverse the removal procedures.

Oxygen Sensor

The oxygen sensor protrudes into the exhaust stream and monitors the oxygen content of the exhaust gases. The difference between the oxygen content of the exhaust gases and that of the outside air generates a voltage signal to the ECM. The ECM monitors this voltage and depending upon the value of the signal received, issues a command to adjust for a rich or a lean condition.

No attempt should ever be made to measure the voltage output of the sensor. The current drain of any conventional voltmeter would be such that it would permanently damage the sensor. No jumpers, test leads or any other electrical connections should ever be made to the sensor. Use these tools only on the ECM side of the wiring harness connector after disconnecting it from the sensor.

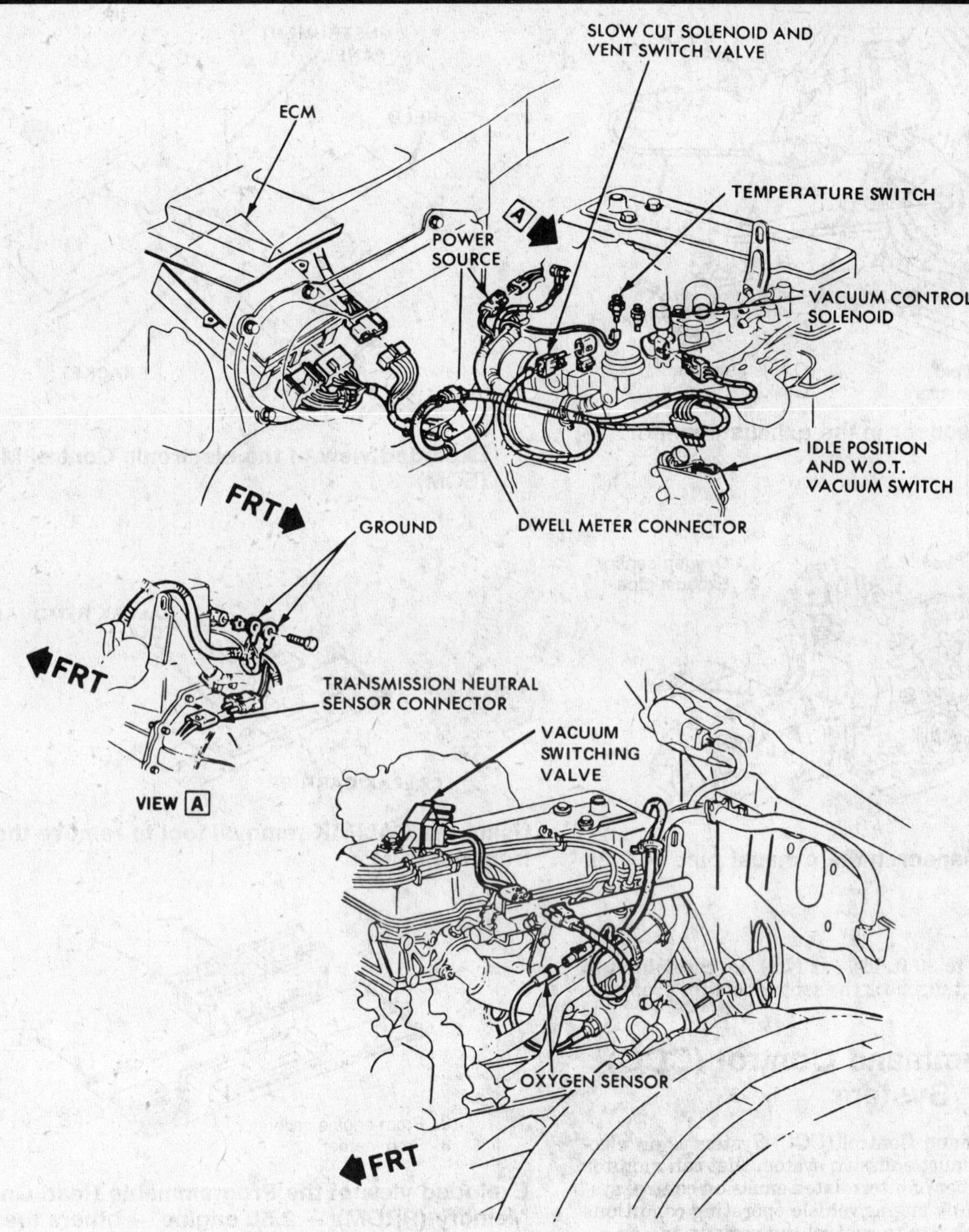

Closed loop emission system compartment components — 1.9L engine

REMOVAL AND INSTALLATION

The oxygen sensor must be replaced every 30,000 miles (48,000 km). The sensor may be difficult to remove when the engine temperature is below 120°F (48°C). Excessive removal force may damage the threads in the exhaust manifold or pipe; follow the removal procedure carefully.

1. Locate the oxygen sensor.

NOTE: It protrudes from the exhaust manifold on the left side for 4 cylinder engines, the right side for 2.8L engine – 1982–85, the left exhaust pipe for 2.8L engine – 1986–87, Federal, the right exhaust pipe for 2.8L engine – 1986–87, Calif. or the exhaust pipe for 2.8L engine – 1988 and 4.3L engines.

2. Disconnect the electrical connector from the oxygen sensor.
3. Spray a commercial solvent onto the sensor threads and allow it to soak in for at least five minutes.
4. Carefully unscrew and remove the sensor.
5. To install, first coat the new sensor's threads with GM Anti-Sieze Compound No. 5613695 or equivalent. This is not a conventional anti-seize paste. The use of a regular compound may electrically insulate the sensor, rendering it inoperative. You must coat the threads with an electrically conductive anti-seize compound.

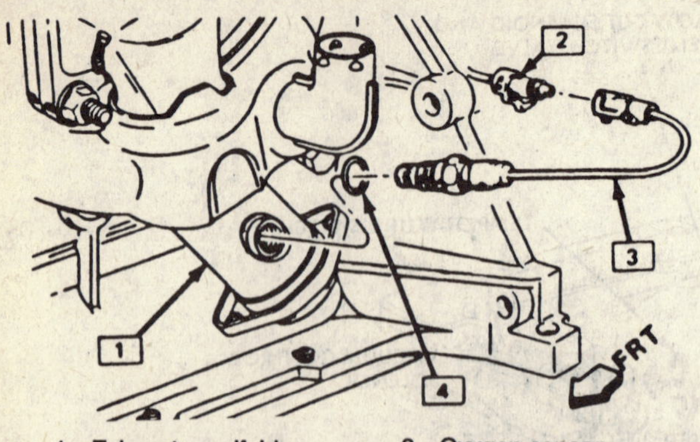

1. Exhaust manifold
2. Electrical connector
3. Oxygen sensor
4. Gasket

Location of the O_2 sensor in the exhaust manifold – 2.5L engine

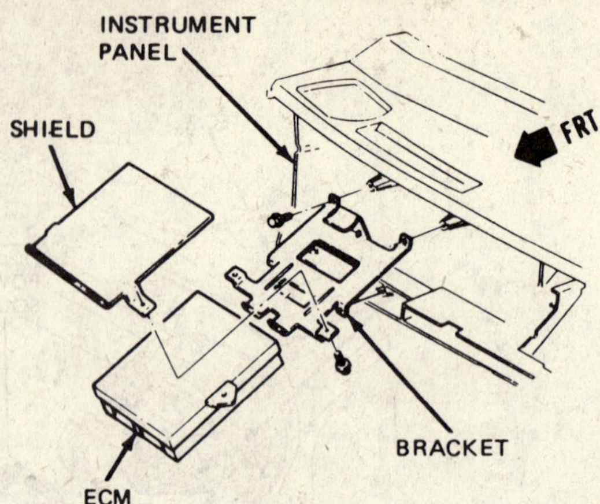

Exploded view of the electronic Control Module (ECM)

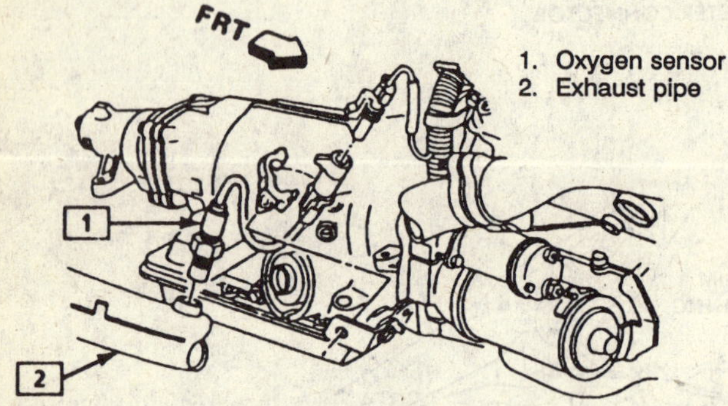

1. Oxygen sensor
2. Exhaust pipe

Location of the O_2 sensor in the exhaust pipe – 2.8L and 4.3L engines

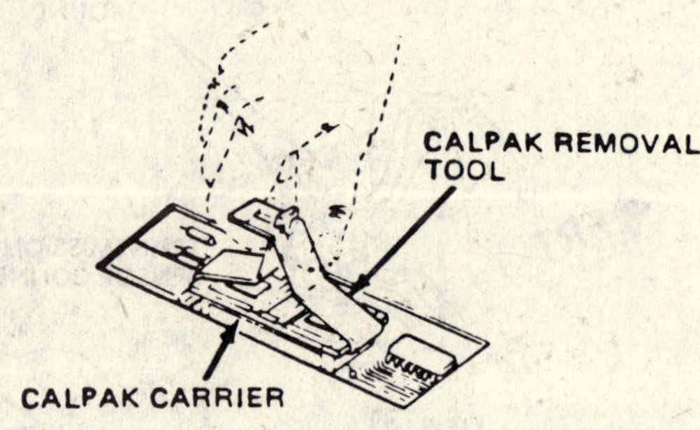

Using the CALPAK removal tool to remove the PROM from the ECM

6. Torque the sensor to 30 ft. lbs. (42 Nm). Be careful not to damage the electrical pigtail; check the sensor boot for proper fit and installation.

Computer Command Control (CCC) System

The Computer Command Control (CCC) System is an electronically controlled exhaust emission system that can monitor and control a large number of interrelated emission control systems. It can monitor many engine/vehicle operating conditions and then use the information to control the various engine related systems. The system is thereby making constant adjustments to maintain good vehicle performance under all normal driving conditions while at the same time allowing the catalytic converter to effectively control the emissions of HC, CO and NOx.

OPERATION

Electronic Control Module (ECM)

The Electronic Control Module (ECM) is the control center of the fuel control system. It constantly monitors various information from the sensors and controls the systems that affect the vehicle performance. The ECM has two parts: A Controller (the ECM without the PROM) and a separate calibrator (the PROM). The ECM is located on the right-side of instrument panel, accessible form the engine compartment.

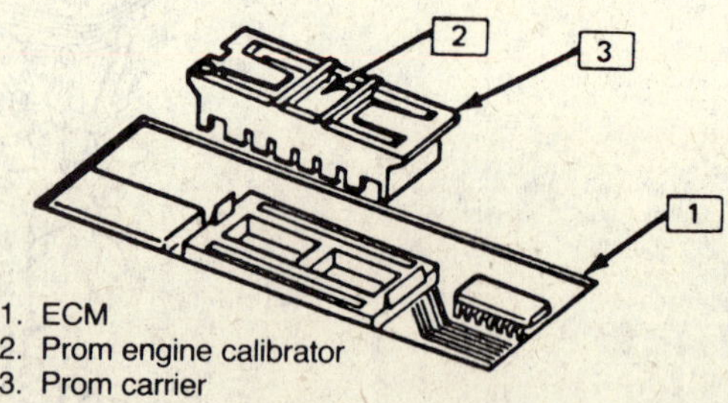

1. ECM
2. Prom engine calibrator
3. Prom carrier

Exploded view of the Programmable Read Only Memory (PROM) – 2.5L engine – others are similar

Programmable Read Only Memory (PROM)

To allow the controller to be used in many different vehicles, a device called a Calibrator or Programmable Read Only Memory (PROM) is used. The PROM which is located inside the ECM, stores information such as: the vehicle's weight, engine, transmission, axle ratio and many other specifications. Since the PROM stores specific information, it is important that the correct one be used in the right vehicle.

NOTE: Due to the intricacy of the system, it is advised to have a qualified mechanic perform any testing, adjusting or replacement of the system components.

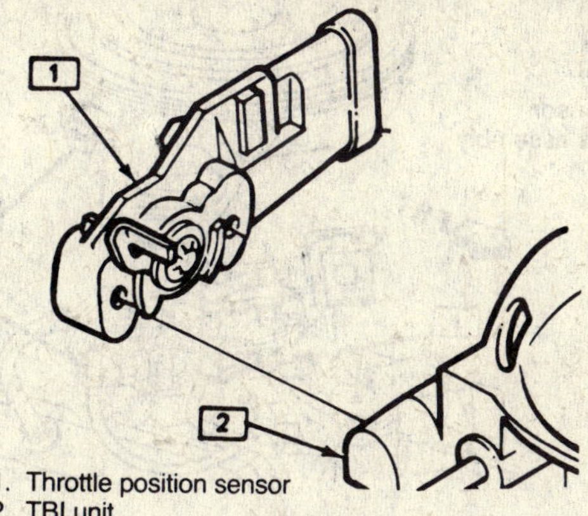

1. Throttle position sensor
2. TBI unit

Exploded view of the Throttle Position Sensor (TPS) – 2.5L engine

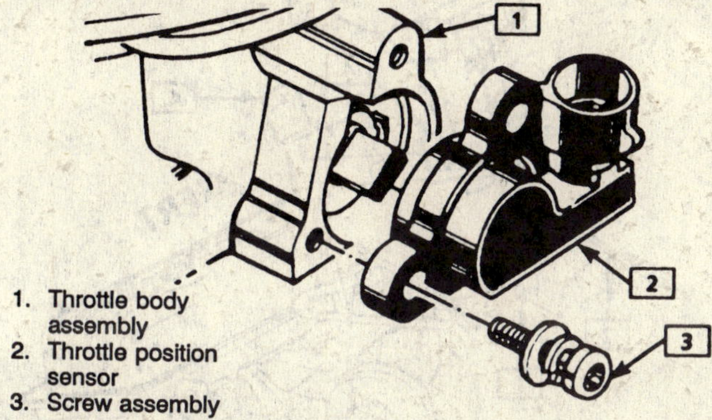

1. Throttle body assembly
2. Throttle position sensor
3. Screw assembly

Exploded view of the Throttle Position Sensor (TPS) – 700 Throttle Body Injection (TBI)

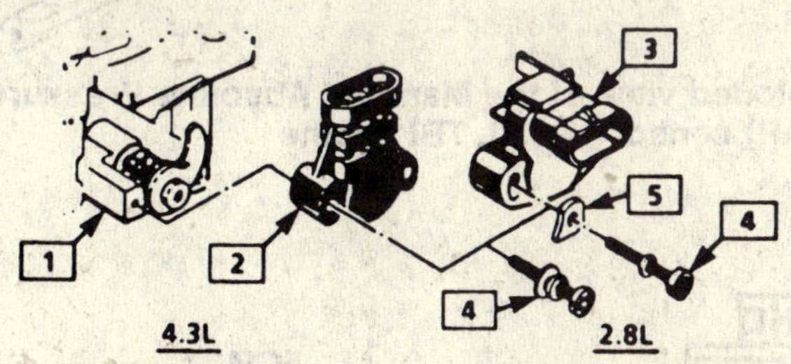

1. Throttle Body assembly
2. Throttle position sensor–non-adjustment
3. Throttle position sensor–adjustment
4. Screw assembly
5. Retainer

Exploded view of the Throttle Position Sensor (TPS) – 220 Throttle Body Injection (TBI) – 2.8L and 4.3L engines

Throttle Position Sensor (TPS)

The throttle position sensor is mounted on the throttle body or carburetor and is used to supply throttle position information to the ECM. The ECM memory stores an average of operating conditions with the ideal air/fuel ratios for each of these conditions. When the ECM receives a signal that indicates throttle position change, it immediately shifts to the last remembered set of operating conditions that resulted in an ideal air/fuel ratio control. The memory is continually being updated during normal operations.

SERVICE

The throttle position sensor is non-adjustable but a test should be performed only when throttle body parts have been replaced or AFTER the minimum idle speed has been adjusted.

NOTE: The following procedure requires the use of the Digital Voltmeter tool J-29125-A or equivalent.

1. Using the Digital Voltmeter tool J-29125-A or equivalent, set it on the 0–5.0 volts scale, then connect the probes to the center terminal **B** and the outside terminal **C** for 2.5L engine or **A** for 2.8L engine.

NOTE: To attach probes to the TPS electrical connector, disconnect the TPS electrical connector, install thin wires into the sockets and reconnect the connector.

2. Turn the ignition switch On (engine stopped).
3. The output voltage should be 1.25 volts. If the voltage is more that 1.25 volts, replace the TPS.
4. Remove the voltmeter and the jumper wires.

REMOVAL AND INSTALLATION

1. Remove the air cleaner.
2. Disconnect the electrical connector from the Throttle Position Sensor (TPS).
3. Remove the TPS mounting screws, the lockwashers and the retainers.
4. Remove the TPS sensor.
5. To install, make sure the throttle valve is in the closed position, then install the TPS sensor.

NOTE: Make sure the TPS pickup lever is located above the tang on the throttle actuator lever.

6. To complete the installation, lubricate the mounting screws with Loctite® (thread locking compound) No. 262 or equivalent, then reverse the removal procedures.

Manifold Pressure Sensor (MAP)

The manifold pressure sensors, used only on fuel injected engines, are located on the air cleaner side.

OPERATION

The manifold pressure sensor measures the pressure (load and speed) changes in the intake manifold, then converts these changes into voltage output. The voltage changes are sent to the ECM, which analyzes the information to alter the fuel delivery and the ignition timing.

At closed throttle, the MAP sensor produces relatively low MAP output, while at wide-open throttle, it would produce high output. When the pressure inside the intake manifold is equal to the outside pressure, the MAP sensor will produce high output voltage.

NOTE: The manifold absolute pressure is opposite what would measure on a vacuum gauge.

This sensor is also used to measure the barometric pressure (under certain conditions) to adjust for differences in altitude.

The failure of the MAP sensor circuit should set a Code 33 or 34.

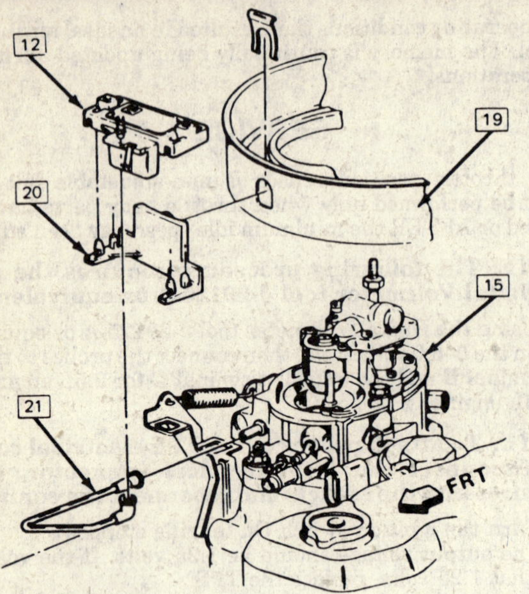

12. Map sensor
15. TBI unit
19. Air cleaner asm.
20. Map sensor mounting bracket
21. Map sensor tube

Exploded view of the Manifold Absolute Pressure (MAP) sensor – 2.5L TBI engine – others are sililar

SERVICE

NOTE: The following procedure requires the use of a Voltmeter and a Vacuum pump.

1. Turn the ignition switch On (engine stopped).
2. Using a voltmeter, set it on the 0–10.0 volts scale, then attach the probes to the MAP sensor terminals A and B. Compare the acquired voltage to the voltage/altitude chart for the correct

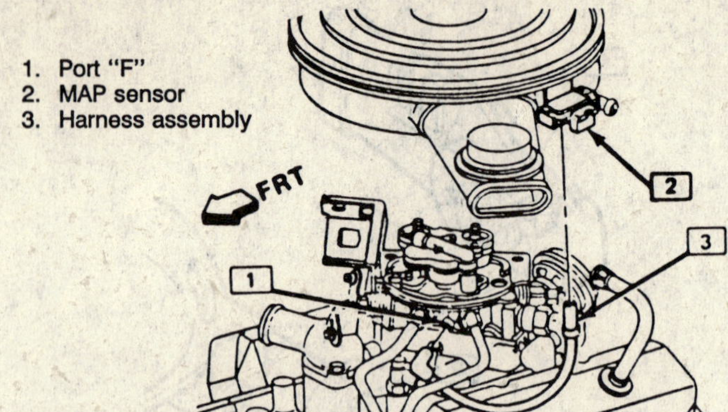

1. Port "F"
2. MAP sensor
3. Harness assembly

Exploded view of the Manifold Absolute Pressure (MAP) sensor – 2.8L TBI engine

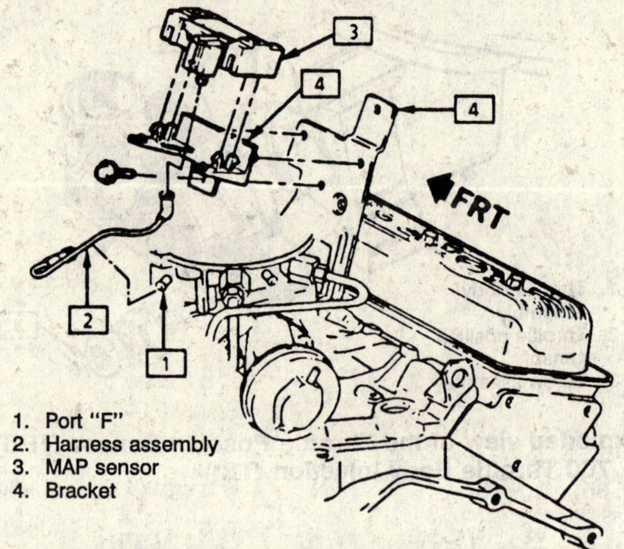

1. Port "F"
2. Harness assembly
3. MAP sensor
4. Bracket

Exploded view of the Manifold Absolute Pressure (MAP) sensor – 4.3L TBI engine

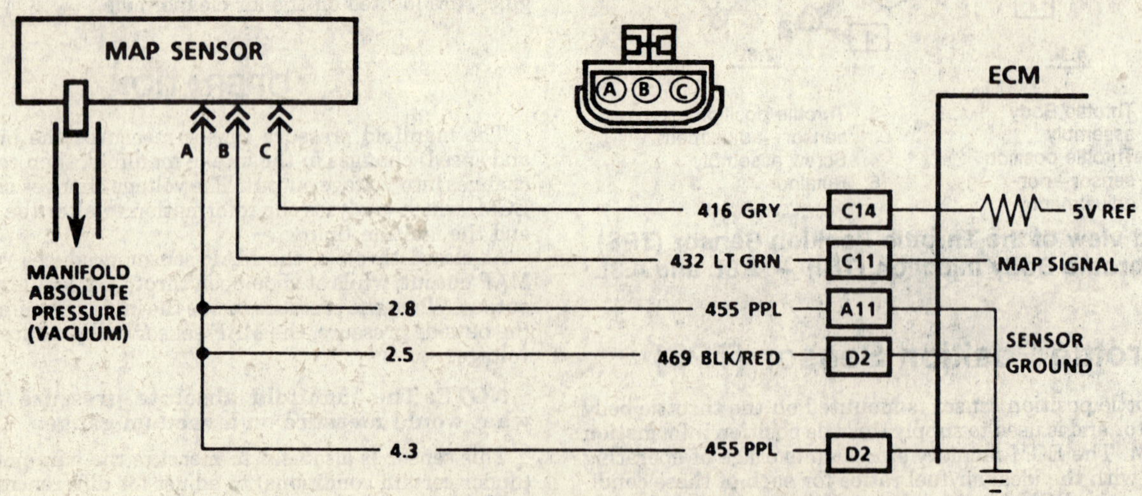

Schematic of the Manifold Absolute Pressure (MAP) system

values; if not correct, replace the sensor.

3. Using a vacuum pump, apply 10 in. Hg vacuum to the MAP sensor and note the change; it should be 1.2–2.3 volts less than the initial voltage, if not, replace the sensor.

4. If no trouble is found, check the vacuum hose for leakage or restriction. If replacing the hose, be sure to use one specifically for MAP sensor use.

REMOVAL AND INSTALLATION

1. Remove the sensor-to-throttle body vacuum hose.
2. Disconnect the sensor's electrical connector.
3. Remove the MAP sensor from the air cleaner mounting bracket.
4. To install, reverse the removal procedures.

TROUBLESHOOTING THE MANIFOLD ABSOLUTE PRESSURE (MAP) SYSTEM

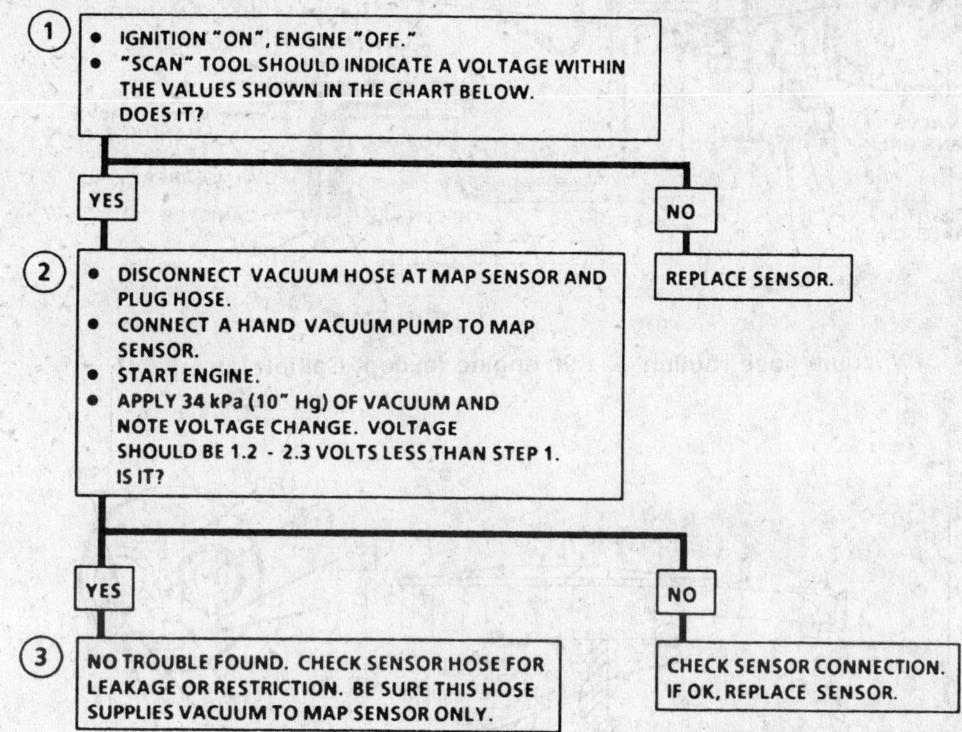

MAP SENSOR VOLTAGE VS. ALTITUDE
WITH IGNITION "ON" AND ENGINE "OFF"

ALTITUDE		VOLTAGE RANGE
Meters	Feet	
305--- 610	1,000--2,000	3.6---5.2V
610--- 914	2,000--3,000	3.5---5.1V
914--1219	3,000--4,000	3.3---5.0V
1219--1524	4,000--5,000	3.2---4.8V
1524--1829	5,000--6,000	3.0---4.6V
1829--2133	6,000--7,000	2.9---4.5V
2133--2438	7,000--8,000	2.8---4.3V
2438--2743	8,000--9,000	2.6---4.2V
2743--3048	9,000--10,000	2.5---4.0V

LOW ALTITUDE = HIGH PRESSURE = HIGH VOLTAGE

CLEAR CODES AND CONFIRM "CLOSED LOOP" OPERATION AND NO "SERVICE ENGINE SOON" LIGHT.

VACUUM DIAGRAMS

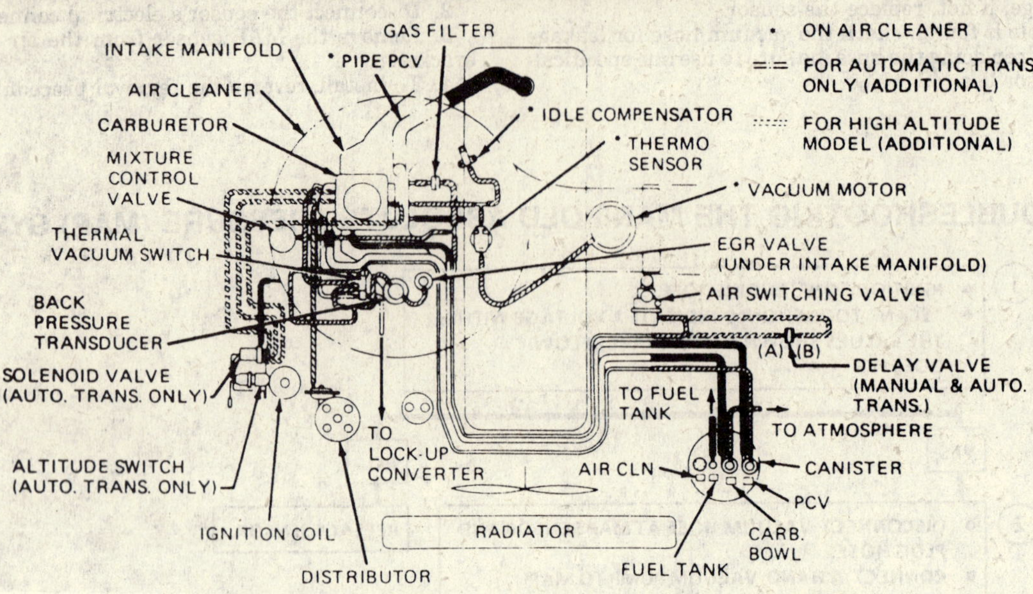

Vacuum hose routing — 1.9L engine (except California)

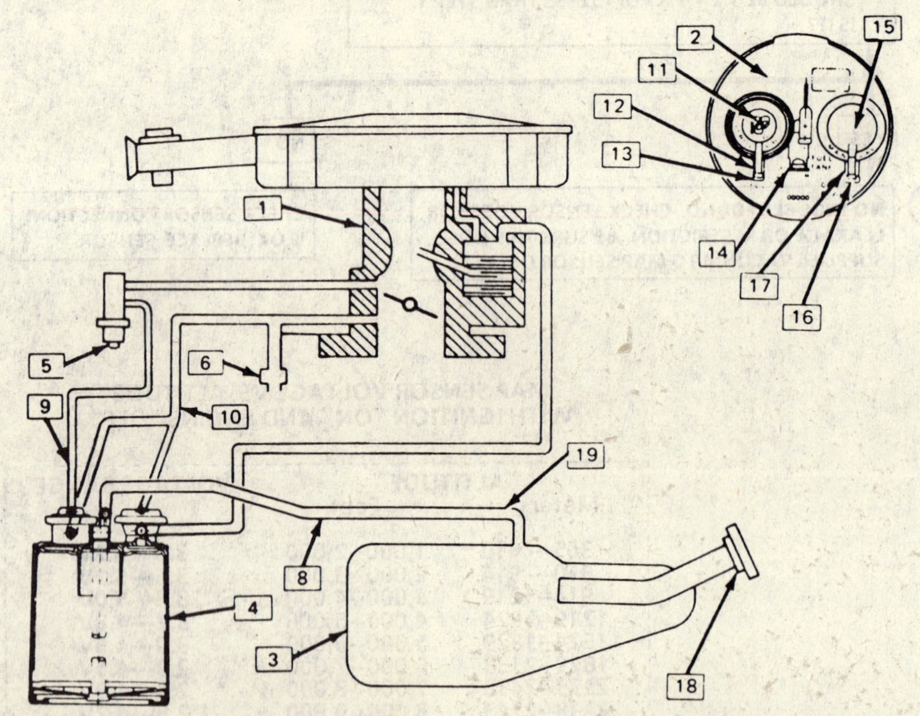

1. Carburetor
2. Top view of canister
3. Fuel tank
4. Canister
5. TVS
6. PVC
7. Carburetor bowl vent line
8. Fuel tank vapor line
9. Ported vacuum line
10. Fuel vapor purge line
11. Canister purge valve
12. Control vacuum tube (ported vac)
13. Purge tube (PCV)
14. Canister vent
15. Vapor vent valve
16. Vapor from carburetor tube
17. Control vacuum tube (manifold vac)
18. Sealed fuel tank cap
19. Fuel tank vapor line restriction

Emissions control system schematic — 2.0L and 2.8L carbureted engines

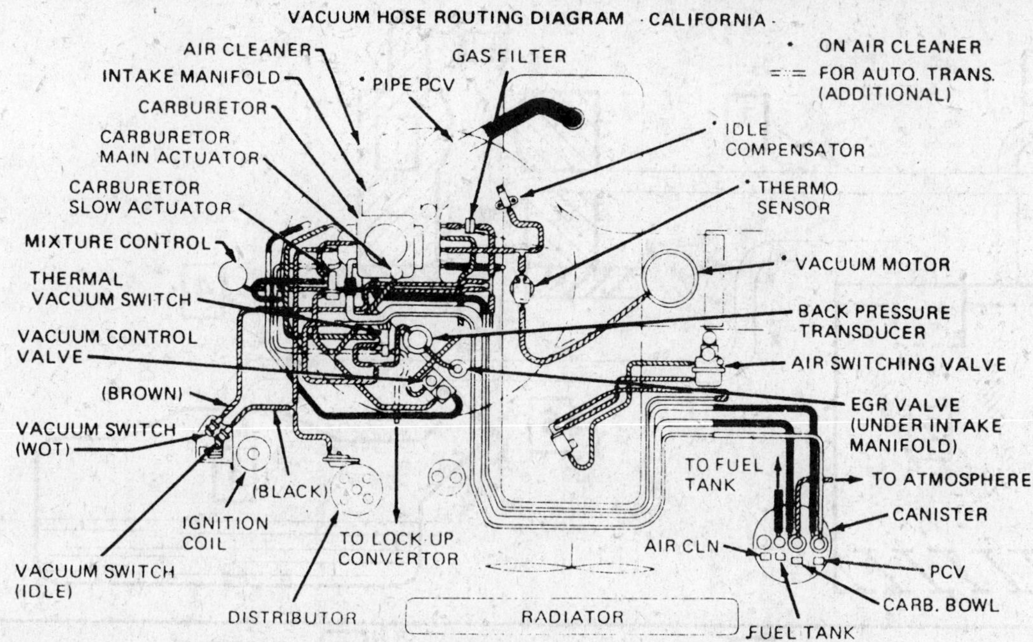

Vacuum hose routing — 1.9L engine (California)

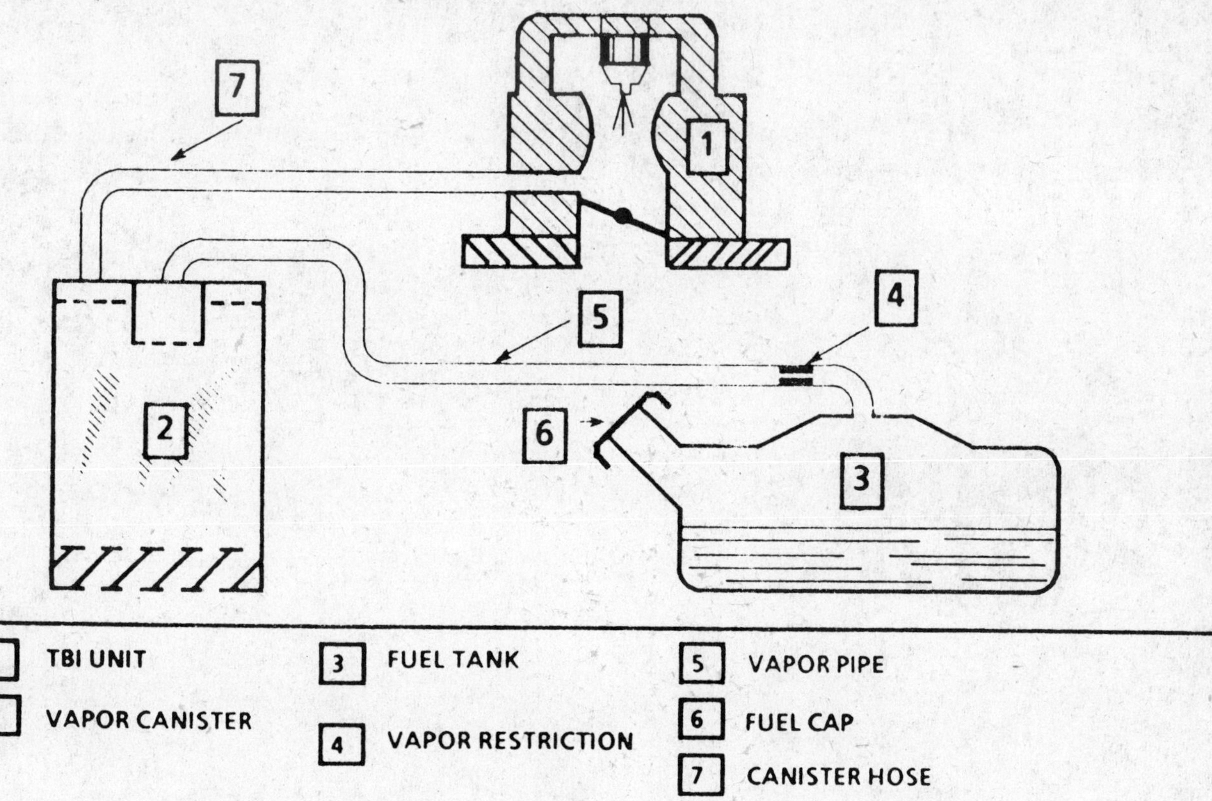

1	TBI UNIT	3	FUEL TANK	5	VAPOR PIPE
2	VAPOR CANISTER	4	VAPOR RESTRICTION	6	FUEL CAP
				7	CANISTER HOSE

Emissions control system schematic — 2.5L and 4.3L TBI engine

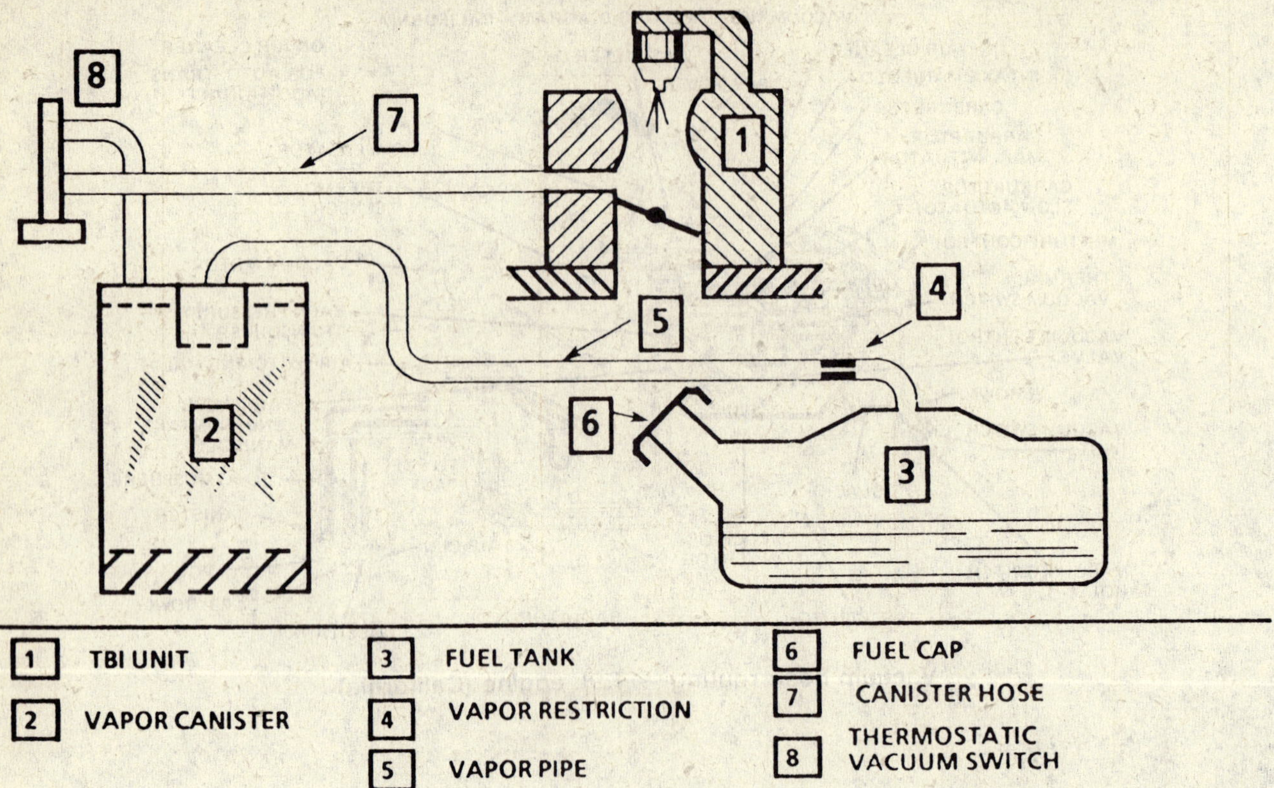

Emissions control system schematic — 2.8L TBI engine

Fuel System

QUICK REFERENCE INDEX

GENERAL INDEX

CARBURETED FUEL SYSTEM

Mechanical Fuel Pump

All engine use a mechanical fuel pump, driven off the camshaft and located on the engine block.

REMOVAL AND INSTALLATION

1.9L and 2.0L Engines

The fuel pump is located near the front right side of the engine.
1. Disconnect the negative battery terminal from the battery.
2. Remove the distributor.
3. Disconnect the fuel hoses from the fuel pump.
4. Remove the engine lifting hook.
5. Remove the fuel pump-to-engine bolts and the fuel pump, then discard the gasket.

NOTE: Before installing the fuel pump, rotate the crankshaft so the cam lobe is on the down stroke.

6. To install, use a new gasket, RTV sealant and reverse the removal procedures. Torque the fuel pump-to-engine bolts to 15 ft. lbs. Check and/or adjust the timing.

2.8L Engine

The fuel pump is located near the front left side of the engine.
1. Disconnect the negative battery terminal from the battery.
2. Disconnect the fuel hoses the from pump.
3. Remove the fuel pump-to-engine bolts and the fuel pump from the engine, then discard the gasket.

NOTE: Before installing the fuel pump, rotate the crankshaft so the cam lobe is on the down stroke.

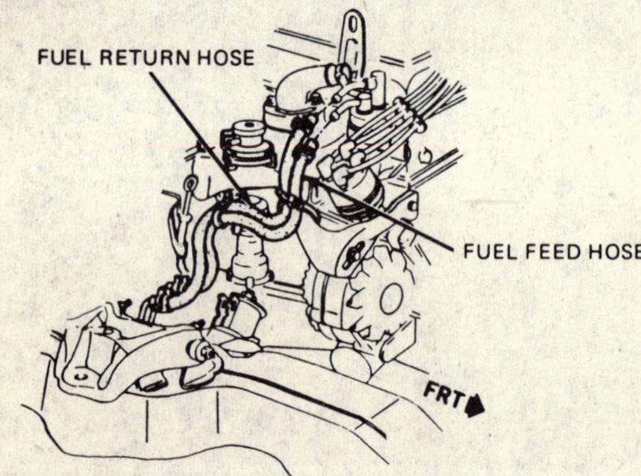

View of the fuel pump and hoses — 1.9L and 2.0L engines

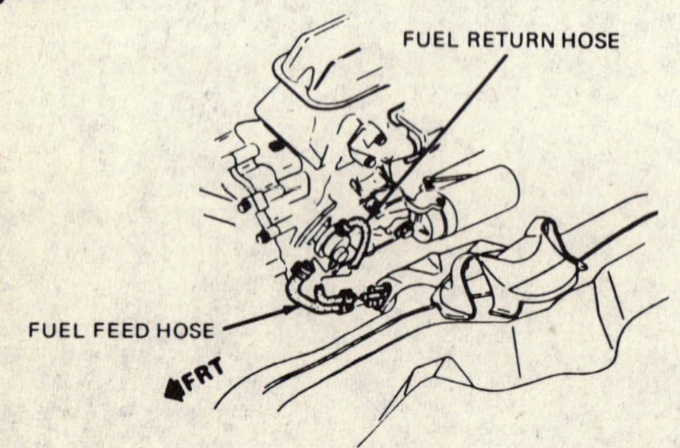

View of the fuel pump and hoses — 2.8L engine

4. To install, use a new gasket, RTV sealant and reverse the removal procedures. Torque the fuel pump-to-engine bolts to 15 ft. lbs.

TESTING

To determine if the pump is in good condition, tests for both volume and pressure should be performed. The tests are made with the pump installed, and the engine at normal operating temperature and idle speed. Never replace a fuel pump without first performing these simple tests.

Be sure the fuel filter has been changed at the specified interval. If in doubt, install a new filter first.

Pressure Test

1. Disconnect the fuel line from the carburetor and connect a fuel pump pressure gauge.
2. Start the engine and check the pressure with the engine at idle. If the pump has a vapor return hose, squeeze it off so an accurate reading can be obtained. Pressure should not be below 4.5 psi.
3. If the pressure is incorrect, replace the pump. It if is OK, perform the volume test.

Volume Test

1. Disconnect the fuel line from the carburetor and connect a fuel pump pressure gauge.
2. Place the fuel line into a graduated container.
3. Run the engine at idle until one pint of gasoline has been pumped. One pint should be delivered in 30 seconds or less. There is normally enough fuel in the carburetor float bowl to perform this test, but refill it, if necessary.
4. If the delivery rate is below the minimum, check the lines for restrictions or leaks, then replace the pump.

Carburetor

ADJUSTMENTS

NOTE: Refer to the "Idle Speed and Mixture Adjustment" procedures in Section 2 and adjust the idle speed and fuel mixture.

1.9L Engine

FLOAT LEVEL

The fuel level is normal if it is seen to be within the mark on the float bowl window. If not, Remove the top of the carburetor and bend the float seat to regulate the level.

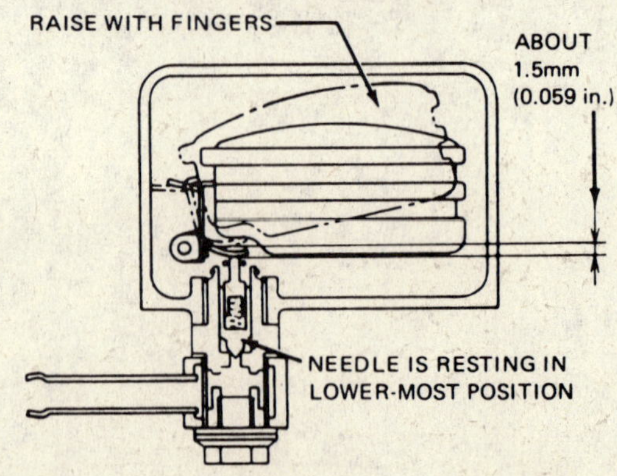

Adjusting the float level — 1.9L engine

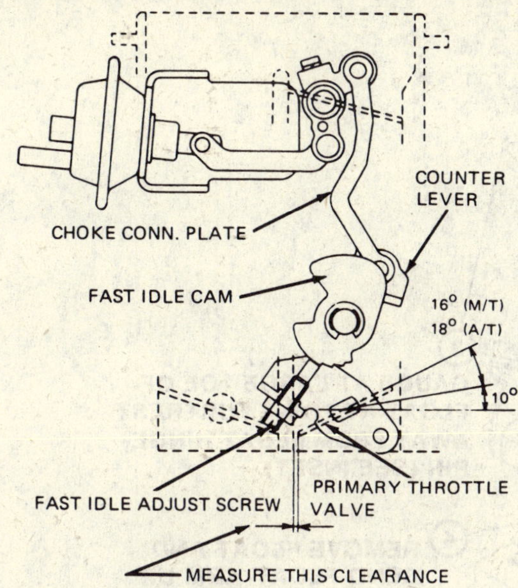

Adjusting the primary throttle valve — 1.9L engine

PRIMARY THROTTLE VALVE

When the choke plate is completely closed, the primary throttle valve should be opened by the fast idle screw to an angle of 16 degrees for manual transmission or 18 degrees for automatic transmission. To check this adjustment, perform the following procedures:

1. Close the choke plate completely, then measure between the throttle plate and the air horn wall; the clearance should be 0.050–0.059 in. (1.27–1.49mm) for manual transmission or 0.059–0.069 in. (1.49–1.75mm) for automatic transmission.

NOTE: The measurement should be made at the center point of the choke plate.

2. If necessary, adjust the opening by turning the fast idle screw.

THROTTLE LINKAGE

1. Turn the primary throttle valve plate until the adjustment plate is in contact with the kickdown lever. This is a primary throttle plate opening of about 47 degrees.
2. Measure the clearance between the center point of the primary throttle plate and the air horn wall; the clearance should be 0.24–0.30 in. (6.1–7.6mm), if not, bend the kickdown lever tab.

KICKDOWN LEVER ADJUSTMENT

1. Turn the primary throttle lever until the plate is completely closed. Back off the throttle adjustment screw, if necessary.
2. Loosen the locknut on the kickdown lever screw and turn the screw until it just contacts the return plate, then tighten the locknut.

2.0L and 2.8L Engines

FLOAT LEVEL

1. With the engine Cold, remove the top of the carburetor.
2. While holding a finger lightly but firmly, on the float retainer, press down lightly on the float tab to seat the needle valve.
3. Measure the distance between the float bowl gasket surface and the point on the float farthest from the needle valve.
4. If the measurement is not correct, remove the float and bend the tab.

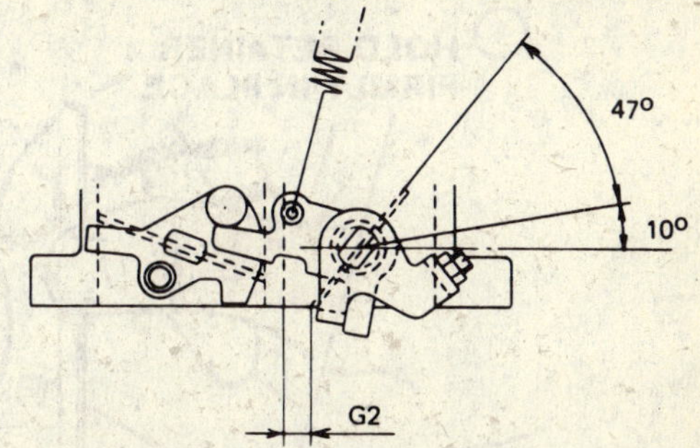

Adjusting the throttle linkage — 1.9L engine

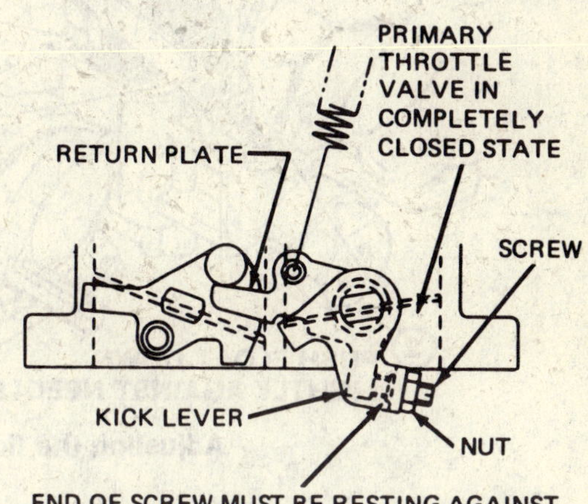

Adjusting the kickdown lever — 1.9L engine

PUMP

1. With the throttle plate in the Closed position and the fast idle screw off the steps of the fast idle cam, measure the distance from the air horn casting to the top of the pump stem.
2. To adjust, remove the retaining screw, the washer and the pump lever. Bend the end of the lever to correct the stem height. Do not twist the lever or bend it sideways.
3. Install the lever, washer and screw, then check the adjustment. When correct, open and close the throttle a few times to check the linkage movement and alignment.

FAST IDLE

1. Set the ignition timing and curb idle speed, then disconnect and plug the hoses as directed on the emission control decal.
2. Position the fast idle screw on the highest step of the fast idle cam.
3. Start the engine and adjust the engine speed to specification with the fast idle screw.

CHOKE COIL LEVER

NOTE: The following procedure requires the use of the Choke Valve Angle Gauge tool J-26701 or BT-7704 or equivalent.

1. Remove the 3 retaining screws, the choke cover and coil. On models with a riveted choke cover, drill out the 3 rivets, then remove the cover and the choke coil.

NOTE: A choke stat cover retainer kit is required for reassembly.

2. Place the fast idle screw on the high step of the fast idle cam.

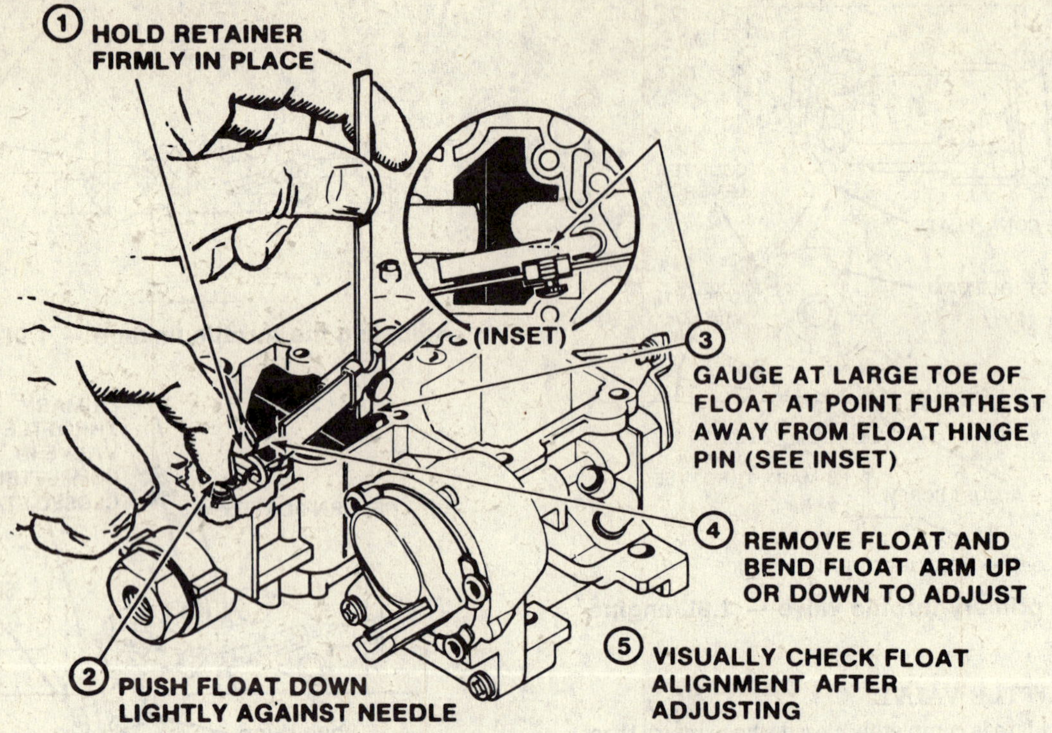

Adjusting the float level — 2.0L and 2.8L engines

3. Close the choke plate by pushing in on the intermediate choke lever.
4. Insert a drill or plug gauge, of the specified size, into the hole in the choke housing. The choke lever in the housing should be up against the side of the gauge.
5. If the lever does not just touch the gauge, bend the intermediate choke rod to adjust.

FAST IDLE CAM (CHOKE ROD)

NOTE: The following procedure requires the use of the Choke Valve Angle Gauge tool J-26701 or BT-7704 or equivalent.

1. First, adjust the choke coil lever and fast idle speed.
2. Rotate the degree scale until it is zeroed.

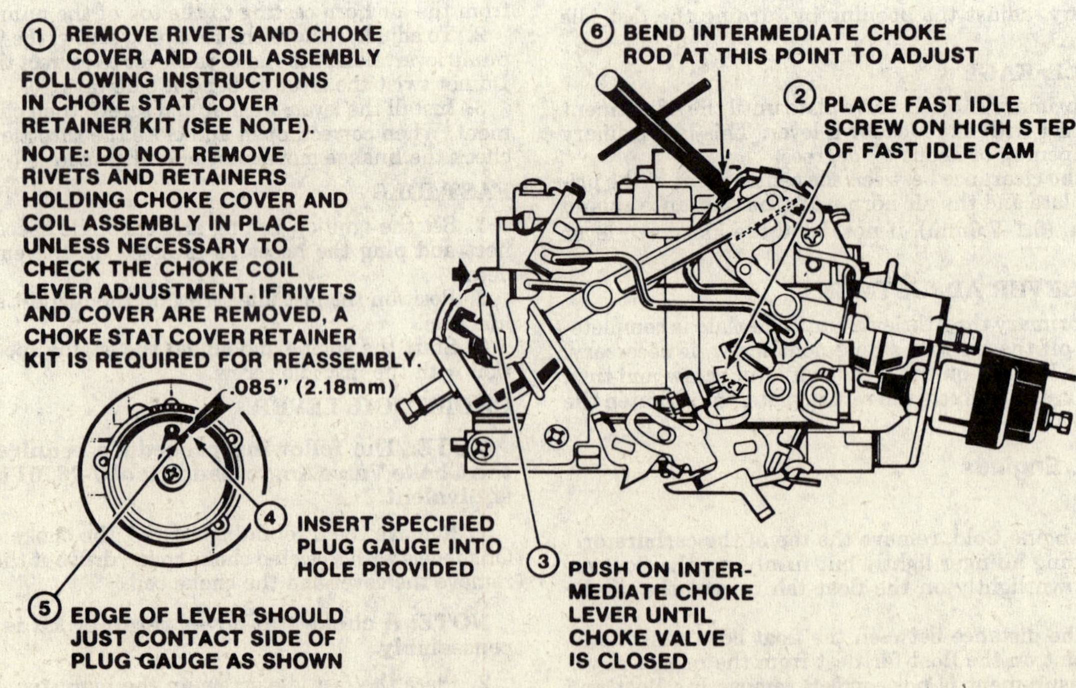

Adjusting the choke coil lever — 2.0L and 2.8L engines

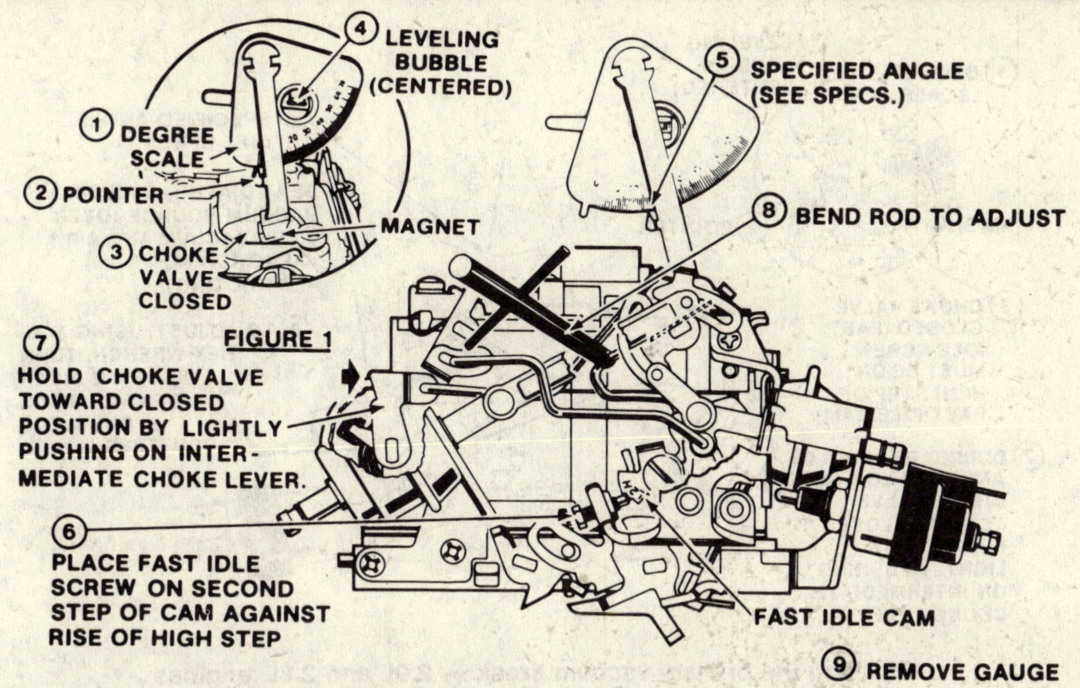

Adjusting the choke rod — 2.0L and 2.8L engines

3. Close the choke and install the degree scale onto the choke plate. Center the leveling bubble.
4. Rotate the scale so the specified degree is opposite the scale pointer.
5. Place the fast idle screw on the second step of the cam (against the high step). Close the choke by pushing in the intermediate lever.
6. Push on the vacuum break lever, to Open the choke, until the lever is against the rear tang on the choke lever.
7. Bend the fast idle cam rod at the U to adjust the angle to specifications.

AIR VALVE ROD

NOTE: The following procedure requires the use of the Choke Valve Angle Gauge tool J-26701 or BT-7704 or equivalent.

9›

1. Align the 0 degree mark with the pointer on an angle gauge.
2. Close the air valve and place a magnet on top of it.
3. Rotate the bubble until it is centered.

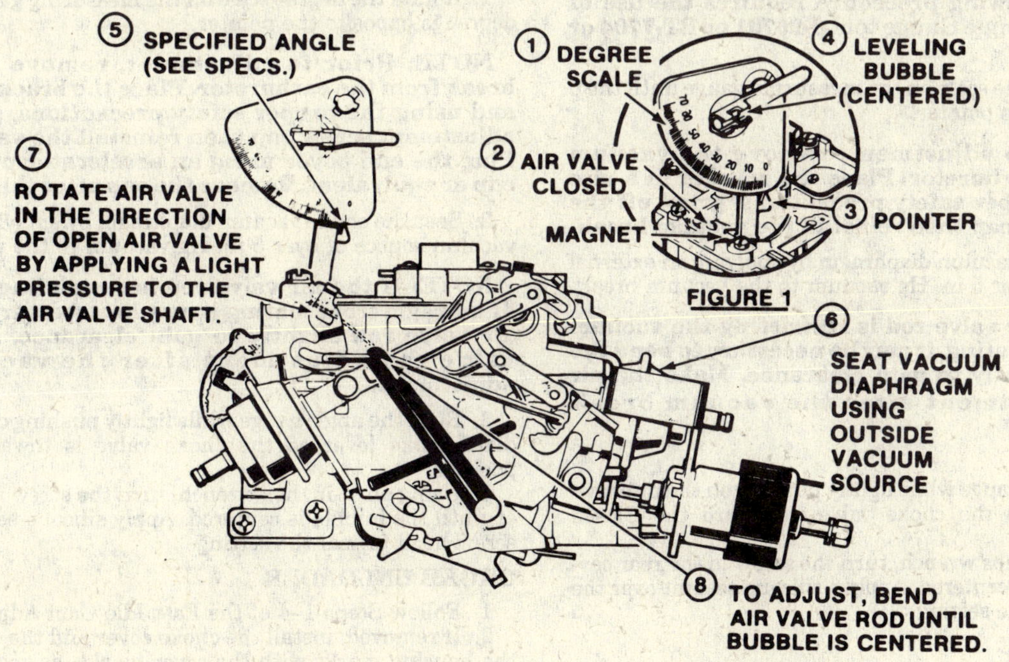

Adjusting the air valve rod — 2.0L and 2.8L engines

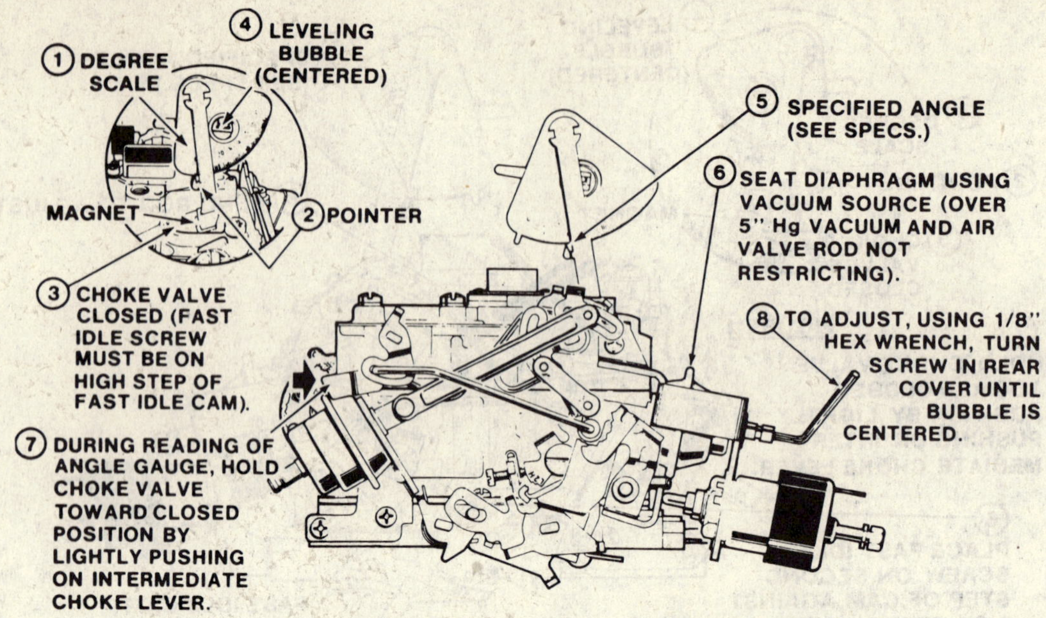

Adjusting the primary vacuum break — 2.0L and 2.8L engines

4. Rotate the degree scale until the specified degree mark is aligned with the pointer.
5. Seat the vacuum diaphragm using an external vacuum source.
6. On 4 cylinder models plug the end cover. Unplug after adjustment.
7. Apply a light pressure to the air valve shaft in the direction to open the air valve until all the slack is removed between the air link and plunger slot.
8. Bend the air valve link until the bubble is centered.

PRIMARY SIDE VACUUM BREAK

NOTE: The following procedure requires the use of the Choke Valve Angle Gauge tool J-26701 or BT-7704 or equivalent.

1. Rotate the degree scale on the measuring gauge until the 0 degree is opposite the pointer.

NOTE: Prior to adjustment, remove the vacuum break from the carburetor. Place the bracket in a vise and using the proper safety precautions, grind off the adjustment screw cap then reinstall the vacuum break.

2. Seat the choke vacuum diaphragm by applying an external vacuum source of over 5 in. Hg vacuum to the vacuum break.

NOTE: If the air valve rod is restricting the vacuum diaphragm from seating, it may be necessary to bend the air valve rod slightly to gain clearance. Make the air valve rod adjustment after the vacuum break adjustment.

3. Read the angle gauge while lightly pushing on the intermediate choke lever so the choke valve is toward the Closed position.
4. Using an ⅛ in. hex wrench, turn the screw in the rear cover until the bubble is centered. Apply a silicone sealant over the screw head to seal the setting.

ELECTRIC CHOKE

This procedure is only for those carburetors with choke covers retained by screws. Riveted choke covers are preset and nonadjustable.

1. Loosen the 3 retaining screws.
2. Place the fast idle screw on the high step of the cam.
3. Rotate the choke cover to align the cover mark with the specified housing mark.

SECONDARY VACUUM BREAK

NOTE: The following procedure requires the use of the Choke Valve Angle Gauge tool J-26701, BT-7704 or equivalent.

1. Rotate the degree scale on the measuring gauge until the 0 degree is opposite the pointer.

NOTE: Prior to adjustment, remove the vacuum break from the carburetor. Place the bracket in the vise and using the proper safety precautions, grind off the adjustment screw cap then reinstall the vacuum break. Plug the end cover using an accelerator pump plunger cup or equivalent. Remove the cup after the adjustment.

2. Seat the choke vacuum diaphragm by applying an external vacuum source of over 5 in. Hg vacuum to the vacuum break.

NOTE: If the air valve rod is restricting the vacuum diaphragm from seating it may be necessary to bend the air valve rod slightly to gain clearance. Make an air valve rod adjustment after the vacuum break adjustment.

3. Read the angle gauge while lightly pushing on the intermediate choke lever so the choke valve is toward the Closed position.
4. Using an ⅛ in. hex wrench, turn the screw in the rear cover until the bubble is centered. Apply silicone sealant over the screw head to seal the setting.

CHOKE UNLOADER

1. Follow Steps 1–4 of the Fast Idle Cam Adjustment.
2. If removed, install the choke cover and the coil, then align the housing marks with the cover marks, as specified.
3. Hold the primary throttle valve Wide Open.

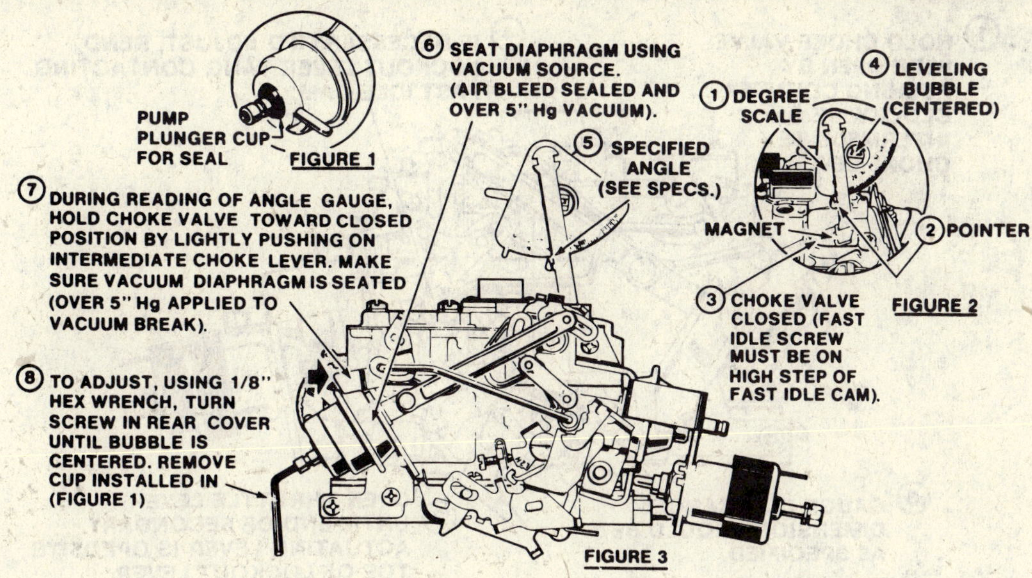

Adjusting the secondary vacuum break – 2.0L and 2.8L engines

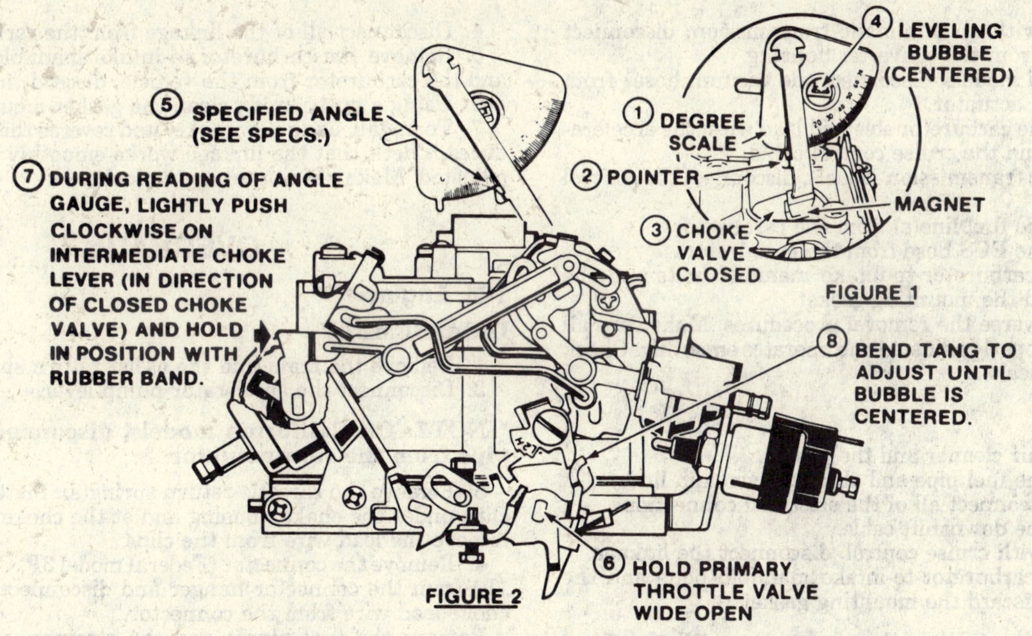

Adjusting the choke unloader – 2.0L and 2.8L engines

4. If the engine is Warm, push inward on the intermediate choke lever to close the choke valve.
5. Bend the unloader tang until the bubble is centered.

SECONDARY LOCKOUT

1. Place the choke in the Wide Open position by pushing outward on the intermediate choke lever.
2. Open the throttle valve until the end of the secondary actuating lever is opposite the toe of the lockout lever.
3. Gauge the clearance between the lockout lever and secondary lever, as specified.
4. To adjust, bend the lockout lever where it contacts the fast idle cam.

REMOVAL AND INSTALLATION

1.9L Engine

1. Remove the PCV valve from the rocker arm cover.
2. Disconnect the ECS hose from the air cleaner.
3. Disconnect the AIR hose from the pump.
4. On California models, disconnect the air hose from the slow carburetor.
5. Unbolt the air cleaner, lift it slightly, disconnect the hoses and remove the unit.
6. Disconnect the rubber piping from the TVS switch.
7. Disconnect the vacuum advance hose, if equipped, from the distributor.

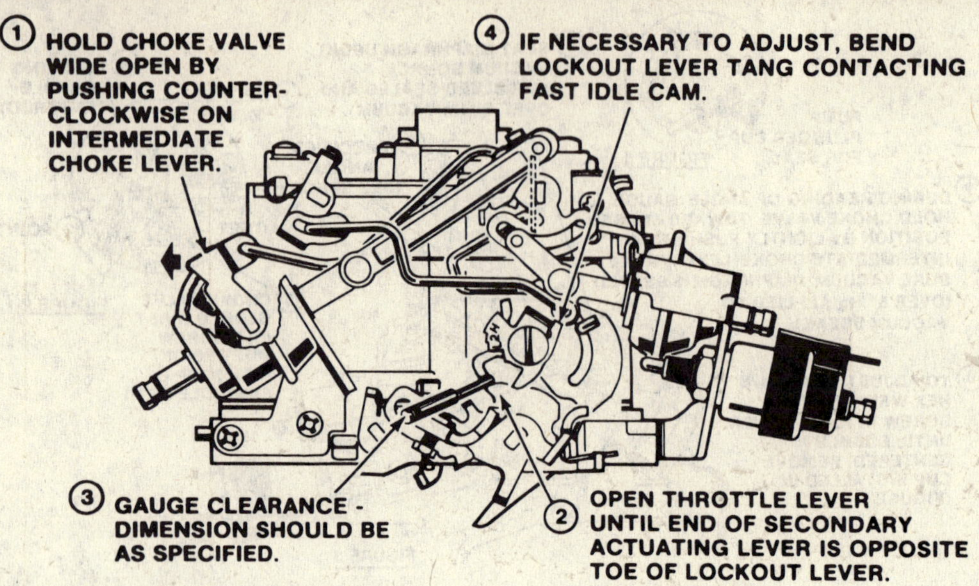

Adjusting the secondary lockout — 1.9L engine

8. If equipped with an automatic transmission, disconnect the vacuum hose from the converter housing.
9. On California models, disconnect the vacuum hoses from the slow and main actuator.
10. Disconnect the carburetor solenoid lead wire, the accelerator control cable and the cruise control cable.
11. On automatic transmission models, disconnect the control cable.
12. Disconnect the fuel line(s) from the carburetor.
13. Disconnect the ECS hose from the carburetor.
14. Remove the carburetor-to-intake manifold bolts and the carburetor; discard the mounting gasket.
15. To install, reverse the removal procedures. Make sure all of the linkage is properly adjusted and operates smoothly. Check that there are no leaks.

2.0L Engine

1. Remove the air cleaner and the gasket.
2. Disconnect the fuel pipe and all of the vacuum lines.
3. Label and disconnect all of the electrical connections.
4. Disconnect the downshift cable.
5. If equipped with cruise control, disconnect the linkage.
6. Remove the carburetor-to-intake manifold bolts and the carburetor, then discard the mounting gasket.

NOTE: Before installing the carburetor, fill the float bowl with gasoline to reduce the battery strain and the possibility of backfiring when the engine is started again.

7. Inspect the EFE heater for damage. Using a putty knife, clean the gasket mounting surfaces. Be sure the throttle body and EFE mating surfaces are clean.
8. To install, use a new gasket and the carburetor; tighten the nuts alternately.
9. To complete the installation, reverse the removal procedures.

2.8L Engine

1. Remove the air cleaner.
2. Disconnect the fuel and vacuum lines from the carburetor.
3. Disconnect all of the electrical connectors from the carburetor.
4. Disconnect all of the linkage from the carburetor.
5. Remove the carburetor-to-intake manifold nuts or bolts and the carburetor from the vehicle; discard the gasket.
6. Using a putty knife, clean the gasket mounting surfaces.
7. To install, use a new gasket and reverse the removal procedures. Check that the linkage works smoothly and is properly adjusted. Make sure there are no leaks.

OVERHAUL

1.9L Engine

DISASSEMBLY

1. Remove the main and the assist return spring.
2. Disconnect the accelerator pump lever.

NOTE: On California models, disconnect the rubber pipe from the slow-actuator.

3. Remove the throttle return spring(s). Flatten the harness clips under the choke housing and at the choke chamber, then remove the lead wire from the clips.
4. Remove the connector (Federal model 3P, California model 1P) from the connector hanger and disconnect the automatic choke lead wire from the connector.

Remove the fuel nipple and the strainer; remove strainer carefully to avoid distorting it.

5. Disconnect the switch vent valve lead wire from the connector.
6. Disconnect the choke connecting rod from the counter lever by removing the circuit clip.
7. Disconnect the automatic choke vacuum hose from the float chamber. Remove the choke chamber assembly-to-float chamber screws and the choke chamber assembly.
8. Remove the circuit clip between the diaphragm and the secondary throttle lever. Loosen the 3 diaphragm chamber attaching screws, then remove the diaphragm assembly.
9. Separate the float chamber assembly from the throttle chamber assembly.
10. Remove the slow-actuator, the accelerating pump plunger assembly and the float needle valve assembly.
11. On Federal models, remove the retaining level gauge cover screws, the level gauge and the float, be careful not to damage the rubber seal or lose the float collar.

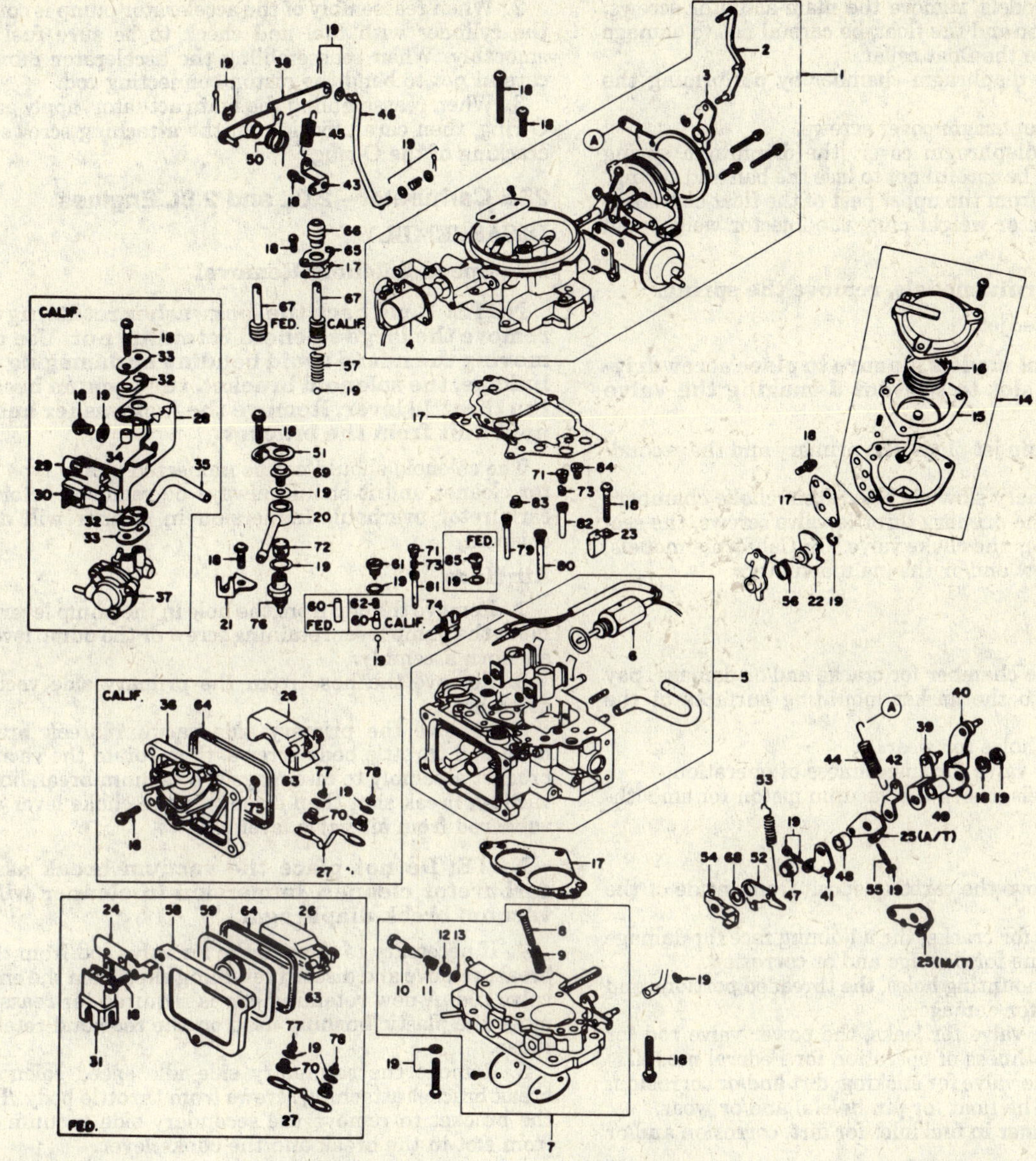

1. Chamber asm., choke
2. Plate, choke, connecting
3. Lever, counter, choke
4. Valve, solenoid, sw. vent.
5. Chamger asm., float
6. Valve, solenoid, slow cut
7. Chamber asm., throttle
8. Screw, throttle adj.
9. Spring, throttle adj.
10. Screw, idle adj.
11. Spring, idle adj.
12. Washer, idle adj.
13. Seal, rubber, idle adj.
14. Chamber asm., diaphragm
15. Diaphragm
16. Spring, diaphragm
17. Gasket kit
18. Screw & washer kit (A)
19. Screw & washer kit (B)
20. Nipple, fuel
21. Plate, stopping
22. Cam, fast idle
23. Holder, lead wire
24. Hanger, connector
25. Lever, fast idj.
26. Float, fuel
27. Plate, lock, drain plug
28. Hanger, connector
29. Connector
30. Connector
31. Connector
32. Rubber, mounting
33. Plate, mt. rubber
34. Collar, mt. rubber
35. Hose, rubber
36. Actuator, main
37. Actuator, slow
38. Lever, pump
39. Lever, accele
40. Lever, cruise
41. Lever, kick
42. Hanger, spring "A"
43. Hanger, spring "B"
44. Spring, main
45. Spring, assist
46. Rod, pump
47. Sleeve
48. Collar, shaft "A"
49. Collar, shaft "B"
50. Spring, pump lever
51. Lever, lock
52. Plate, return
53. Spring, throttle, "S"
54. Lever, adj.
55. Screw, fast idle
56. Spring, cam
57. Spring, piston return
58. Cover, level gauge
59. Gauge, level
60. Weight, injector
61. Screw, pump set
62. Spring, injector
63. Collar, "C"
64. Seal, rubber
65. Plate, cyl.
66. Cover, dust
67. Piston
68. Washer, throttle shaft
69. Screw, nipple set
70. Plug, drain fuel
71. Plug, taper
72. Filter
73. Spring, slow jet
74. Connector, lead wire
75. O-ring
76. Valve, needle
77. Jet, main, "P"
78. Jet, main, "S"
79. Bleed, air main. "P"
80. Bleed, air main, "S"
81. Jet, slow, "P"
82. Jet, slow, "S"
83. Bleed, air, slow, "P"
84. Bleed, air, slow, "S"
85. Valve, power

Exploded view of the carburetor — 1.9L engine

12. On California models, remove the main-actuator screws, then the main-actuator and the float, be careful not to damage the rubber seal or lose the float collar.
13. Disassemble the diaphragm chamber by performing the following procedures:
 a. Remove the diaphragm cover screws.
 b. Separate the diaphragm cover, the diaphragm spring and the diaphragm; be careful not to lose the ball and spring.
14. Remove the jets from the upper part of the float chamber.
15. Remove the injector weight plug, the injector weight and the check ball.

NOTE: On California models, remove the spring.

16. Remove the power jet.

NOTE: On Federal models, be sure to place screwdriver properly in the slot to prevent damaging the valve rod.

17. Remove the 2 main jet plugs, the primary and the secondary main jets.
18. Remove the primary slow air bleed from choke chamber.
19. Do not remove the primary throttle valve screws, the secondary throttle valve or the choke valve. On California models, do not remove the slow and/or the main actuators.

INSPECTION

Choke Chamber

1. Inspect the choke chamber for cracks and/or damage, pay particular attention to the gasket mounting surfaces of the chamber.
2. Check the shaft holes for wear.
3. Check the choke valve for smoothness of operation.
4. On Federal models, check the vacuum piston for smoothness of operation.

Float Chamber

1. Inspect and remove the carbon deposit from inside of the body.
2. Inspect the body for cracks, the adjoining face for damage and the thread portions for damage and/or corrosion.
3. Inspect the jets mounting holes, the threaded portions and the screwdriver slots for damage.
4. Check the power valve for leaks, the power valve rod for bending and for smoothness of operation for Federal model.
5. Inspect the needle valve for sticking, dirt and/or corrosion.
6. Carefully check the float for pin hole(s) and/or wear.
7. Inspect fuel strainer in fuel inlet for dirt, corrosion and/or damage.
8. Inspect the accelerator pump plunger for damage and/or distortion. Also check for pump plunger for smooth movement within the cylinder.
9. Check the accelerating pump rubber boot for damage.

Throttle Chamber

1. Check the slow port, the idle port and others for clogging.
2. Check the primary and secondary throttle valve for the presence of carbon deposits and/or wear.
3. Check the throttle valve shaft holes for wear.
4. Check idle mixture adjusting screw seating face for step wear and the threaded portion for damage.
5. Check the diaphragm for deterioration and/or damage.

Solenoid

Inspect for looseness of attaching parts and/or damage of wiring harness connector.

ASSEMBLY

To assemble the carburetor, reverse the disassembly procedures.

1. On Federal models, be careful not to bend valve rod when installing the power jet valve.
2. When reassembly of the accelerator pump is completed, fill the cylinder with fuel and check to be sure fuel is injected smoothly. When reassembling the accelerator pump parts be careful not to bend the piston connecting rod.
3. When reassembling the main actuator, apply grease to the O-ring, then carefully tighten the attaching screws to prevent cracking of the O-ring.

2SE Carburetor—2.0L and 2.8L Engines

DISASSEMBLY

Idle Speed Solenoid Removal

NOTE: Bend back the lockwasher retaining taps; then remove the large solenoid retaining nut. Use care in removing the nut to avoid bending or damaging the choke linkage, the solenoid bracket, the vacuum break unit or the throttle lever. Remove the lockwasher and the solenoid unit from the bracket.

The solenoid should not be immersed in any type of carburetor cleaner and it should always be removed before complete carburetor overhaul. Immersion in cleaner will damage the solenoid.

Air Horn

1. Remove the clip from the hole in the pump lever. Do not remove the pump lever retaining screw or the pump lever from the air horn assembly.
2. Remove the hose from the primary side vacuum break assembly.
3. Remove the primary side vacuum break bracket-to-air horn and throttle body screws, then rotate the vacuum break/bracket assembly to disengage the vacuum break link from the vacuum break slot, then disengage the choke lever and the air valve rod from air valve lever slot.

NOTE: Do not place the vacuum break assembly in carburetor cleaner. Immersion in cleaner will damage vacuum break diaphragm.

4. If necessary to remove the air valve rod from the vacuum break, remove and discard retaining clips from the end of the air valve rod. A new retaining clip is required for reassembly. Remove the plastic bushing used on the rods and retain for later reuse.
5. Remove the secondary side idle speed solenoid-vacuum break bracket attaching screws from throttle body. Then rotate the bracket to remove the secondary side vacuum break link from slot in the break and the choke lever.

NOTE: Do not place the vacuum break assembly and solenoid in carburetor cleaner. Immersion in cleaner will damage the vacuum break diaphragm.

6. Remove and discard the retaining clip from the intermediate choke rod at the choke lever. A new retaining clip is required for reassembly. Remove the choke rod and the plastic bushing from the choke lever, then save the the bushing for later use.
7. Remove and retain the hot idle compensator valve small screws, if used. Remove the valve and seal from the air horn; discard the seal. The hot idle compensator valve must be removed to gain access to the short air horn-to-bowl screw.
8. Remove the air horn-to-fuel bowl screws and lockwashers. Remove the vent and the screen assembly.
9. Rotate the fast idle cam to the full UP position and remove the air horn assembly by tilting it to disengage the fast idle cam and pump rod from the hole in the pump lever. If the pump plunger remains with the air horn, remove it. The air horn gasket should remain on the float bowl for removal later.

Do not remove the fast idle cam screw and the cam from the float bowl. These parts are not serviced separately and are to remain permanently in place. The new service replacement float

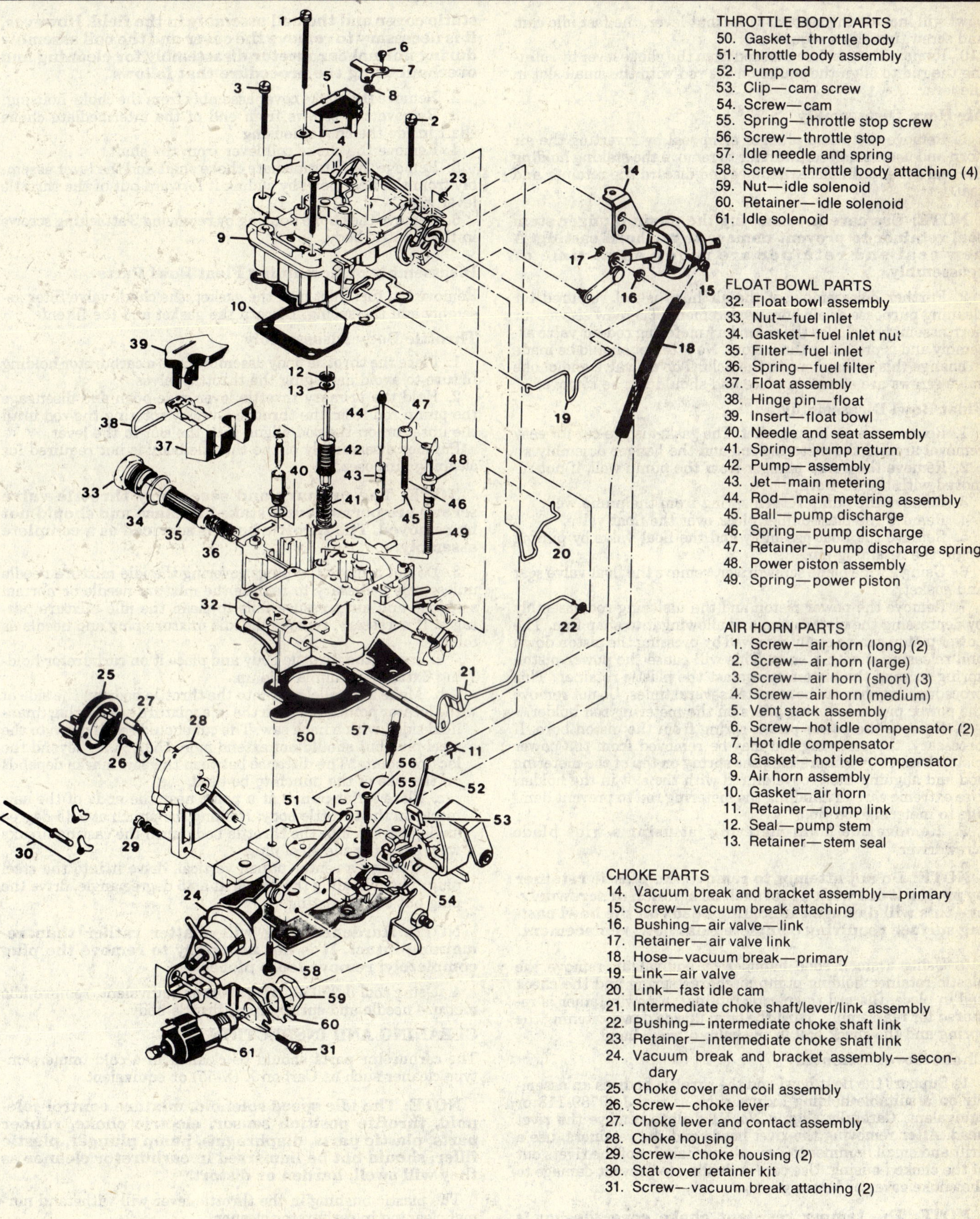

Exploded view of the 2SE carburetor – 2.0L and 2.8L engines

bowl will include the secondary lockout lever, the fast idle cam and screw, install as required.

10. Remove the fast idle cam rod from the choke lever by rotating the rod to align the squirt on the rod with the small slot in the lever.

Air Horn Disassembly

1. Remove the pump plunger stem seal by inverting the air horn and use a small screwdriver to remove the staking holding the seal retainer in place. Remove and discard the retainer and seal.

NOTE: Use care in removing the pump plunger stem seal retainer to prevent damage to air horn casting. A new seal and retainer are required at time of reassembly.

2. Further disassembly of the air horn is not required for cleaning purposes or air horn replacement. The new service air horn assembly includes the secondary metering rod-air valve assembly and is pre-set at the factory. No attempt should be made to change this adjustment in the field. The air valve and choke valve screws are staked in place and should not be removed.

Float Bowl Disassembly

1. Remove the air horn gasket. The gasket is pre-cut for easy removal around the metering rod and the hanger assembly.
2. Remove the pump plunger from the pump well, if not removed with the air horn.
3. Remove the pump return spring from the pump well.
4. Remove the plastic filler block over the float valve.
5. Remove the float assembly and the float valve by pulling up on the retaining pin.
6. Using a wide blade screwdriver, remove the float valve seat and gasket.
7. Remove the power piston and the metering rod assembly by depressing the piston stem and allowing it to snap free. The power piston can be easily removed by pressing the piston down and releasing it with a snap. This will cause the power piston spring to snap the piston up against the plastic retainer. This procedure may have to be repeated several times. Do not remove the power piston by using pliers on the metering rod holder.
8. Remove the power piston spring from the piston bore. If necessary, the metering rod may be removed from the power piston hanger by compressing the spring on top of the metering rod and aligning the groove on rod with the slot in the holder. Use extreme care in handling the metering rod to prevent damage to metering rod tip.
9. Remove the main metering jet using a wide blade screwdriver.

NOTE: Do not attempt to remove the plastic retainer by prying it out with a tool such as a punch or screwdriver—this will damage the sealing beads on the bowl casting surface requiring complete float bowl replacement.

10. Using a small slide hammer or equivalent, remove the plastic retainer holding pump discharge spring and the check ball in place. Discard the plastic retainer; a new retainer is required for reassembly. Turn the bowl upside down catching the spring and the check ball in the palm of your hand.

Choke Cover Removal

1. Support the float bowl and the throttle body as an assembly on a suitable holding fixture such as tool J-09789-118 or equivalent. Carefully align a No. 21 drill to remove the rivet head. After removing the rivet heads and the retainers, use a drift and small hammer to drive the remainder of the rivets out of the choke housing. Use care in drilling to prevent damage to the choke cover or housing.

NOTE: The tamper resistant choke cover design is used to discourage readjustment of the choke thermostatic cover and the coil assembly in the field. However, it is necessary to remove the cover and the coil assembly during normal carburetor disassembly for cleaning and overhaul using the procedure that follows.

2. Remove the choke cover assembly from the choke housing.
3. Remove the screws from end of the intermediate choke shaft inside the choke housing.
4. Remove the choke coil lever from the shaft.
5. Remove the intermediate choke shaft and the lever assembly from the float bowl by sliding it forward out of the throttle lever side.
6. Remove the choke housing by removing 2 attaching screws in the throttle body.

Disassembly of Remaining Float Bowl Parts

Remove the fuel inlet nut, the gasket, the check valve/filter assembly and the spring. Discard the gasket and the filter.

Throttle Body Disassembly

1. Place the throttle body assembly onto a carburetor holding fixture to avoid damaging the throttle valves.
2. Hold the primary throttle lever wide-open and disengage the pump rod from the throttle lever by rotating the rod until the upset on on the rod aligns with the slot in the lever.

Further disassembly of the throttle body is not required for cleaning purposes.

NOTE: The primary and secondary throttle valve screws are permanently staked in place and should not be removed. The throttle body is serviced as a complete assembly.

3. Do not remove the plugs covering the idle mixture needle unless it is necessary to replace the mixture needle or normal soakings and air pressure fails to clean the idle mixture passages. If necessary, remove the idle mixture plug and needle as follows:
   a. Invert the throttle body and place it on carburetor holding fixture—manifold side up.
   b. Make 2 parallel cuts into the throttle body on the side of the locator points, beneath the idle mixture needle plug (manifold side), with a hack saw. The cut should reach down to the steel plug but should not extend more than ⅛ in. beyond the locator points. The distance between the saw marks depends on the size of the punch to be used.
   c. Place a flat punch at a point near the ends of the saw marks in the throttle body. Holding the punch at a 45 degree angle, drive it into the throttle body until the casting breaks way, exposing the steel plug.
   d. Holding a center punch vertical, drive it into the steel plug. Then, holding the punch at a 45 degree angle, drive the plug out of the casting.

NOTE: Hardened plug will shatter rather than remaining intact. It is not necessary to remove the plug completely; remove loose pieces.

4. Using tool J-29030, BT-7610B or equivalent, remove idle mixture needle and spring from throttle body.

CLEANING AND INSPECTION

The carburetor parts should be cleaned in a cold immersion-type cleaner such as Carbon X (X-55) or equivalent.

NOTE: The idle speed solenoid, mixture control solenoid, throttle position sensor, electric choke, rubber parts, plastic parts, diaphragms, pump plunger, plastic filler, should not be immersed in carburetor cleaner as they will swell, harden or distort.

The plastic bushing in the throttle lever will withstand normal cleaning in carburetor cleaner.

1. Thoroughly clean all metal parts and blow dry with com-

pressed air. Make sure all fuel passages and metering parts are free of burrs and dirt. Do not pass drills or wires through jets and passages.

2. Inspect upper and lower surface of carburetor casting for damage.

3. Inspect holes in levers for excessive wear or out of round conditions. If worn, levers should be replaced. Inspect plastic bushings for damage and excessive wear. Replace as required.

4. Check, repair or replace parts if the following problems are encountered:

A. Flooding

1. Inspect float valve and seat for dirt, deep wear grooves, scores and proper seating.
2. Inspect float valve pull clip for proper installation. Be careful not to bend pull clip.
3. Inspect float, float arms and hinge pin for distortion, binds and burrs. Check density of material in the float; if heavier than normal, replace float.
4. Clean or replace fuel inlet filter and check valve assembly.

B. Hesitation

1. Inspect pump plunger and cup for cracks, scores or cup excessive wear. A used pump cup will shrink when dry. If dried out, soak in fuel for 8 hours before testing.
2. Inspect pump duration and return springs for being weak or distorted.
3. Check all pump passages and jet for dirt, improper seating of discharge check ball and scores in pump well. Check condition of pump discharge check ball spring, then replace as necessary.
4. Check pump linkage for excessive wear; repair or replace, as necessary.

C. Hard Starting—Poor Cold Operation

1. Check choke valve and linkage for excessive wear, binds or distortion.
2. Inspect choke vacuum diaphragms for leaks.
3. Replace carburetor fuel filter.
4. Inspect float valve for sticking, dirt, etc.
5. Also check items under "Flooding".

D. Poor Performance—Poor Gas Mileage

1. Clean all fuel and vacuum passages in the castings.
2. Check the choke valve for freedom of movement.
3. Check the Mixture Control Solenoid for sticking, binding or leaking as follows:
   a. Connect one end of a jumper wire to either terminal of the solenoid connector and the other end to the positive (+) terminal of a 12V battery source.
   b. Connect a jumper wire to the other terminal of the solenoid connector and the other end to a known good ground.
   c. With the rubber seal, retainer and the spacer removed from the end of the solenoid stem, attach a hose from a hand vacuum pump.
   d. With the solenoid fully energized (lean position), apply 25 in. Hg vacuum and time the leak-down rate should not exceed 5 in. Hg vacuum in 5 seconds. If leakage exceeds that amount, replace the solenoid.
   e. To check the solenoid for sticking in the down position, remove the jumper lead from the 12V source and observe hand vacuum pump reading. The reading should go to 0 in less than 1 second.
4. Inspect the metering jet for dirt, loose parts or damage.

NOTE: Do not attempt to readjust the mixture screw located inside the metering jet. The screw is factory adjusted and a change can upset the fuel system calibration. No attempt should be made to change this adjustment in the field except as the result of a Computer Command Control system performance check.

5. Check the air valve and the secondary metering rod for binding conditions. If the air valve or metering rod is damaged or the metering rod adjustment is changed from the factory setting, the air horn assembly must be replaced. Also check the air valve spring for proper installation (tension against the air valve shaft pin).

E. Rough Idle

1. Inspect gasket and gasket mating surfaces on castings for nicks, burrs or damage to the sealing beads.
2. Check operation and sealing of mixture control solenoid.
3. Clean all idle fuel passages.
4. If removed, inspect idle mixture needle for ridges, burrs or being bent.
5. Check the throttle lever and valves for bind, nicks and other damage.
6. Check all diaphragms for possible ruptures or leaks.

NOTE: When cleaning plastic parts, only use low volatile cleaning solvent—never in gasoline.

ASSEMBLY

Throttle Body Assembly

1. Holding the primary throttle lever wide open, install lower end of pump rod in throttle lever by aligning the squirt on rod with the slot in the lever. The end of the rod should point outward toward the throttle lever.
2. If removed, install idle mixture needle and spring using the tool J-29030-B or equivalent. Lightly seat needle and then back out 3 turns as a preliminary idle mixture adjustment. Final idle mixture adjustment must be made on the vehicle. Refer to the "On-Vehicle Service" section for idle mixture adjustment procedures.

Float Bowl Assembly

1. Install new throttle body to bowl insulator gasket over 2 locating dowels on the bowl.

NOTE: If a new float bowl assembly is used, stamp or engrave the model number on the new float bowl.

2. Rotate the fast idle cam so the steps face fast idle screw on throttle lever when properly installed, install the throttle body making certain the throttle body is properly located over dowels on float bowl; then install the throttle body-to-bowl screws and lockwashers, then tighten evenly and securely.

Inspect the linkage to insure lockout tang is located properly to engage slot in the secondary lockout lever and that linkage moves freely and does not bind.

3. Place the carburetor on a proper fixture tool J-9789-118 or equivalent.

4. Install fuel inlet filter spring, new filter assembly, new gasket and inlet nut, then torque the nut to 18 ft. lbs.

When installing a service replacement filter, make sure the filter is the type that includes a check valve to meet U.S. Motor Vehicle Safety Standards (MVSS). When properly installed, the hole in filter faces the inlet nut.

NOTE: Ribs on closed end of filter element prevent filter from being installed incorrectly unless forced. Tightening beyond specified torque can damage the nylon gasket and cause fuel leakage.

5. Install the choke housing onto the throttle body, making sure raised boss and locating lug on rear of housing fit into recesses in float bowl casting. Install the choke housing attaching screws and lockwashers onto the throttle body, then tighten the screws evenly and securely.

6. Install the intermediate choke shaft assembly into the float bowl by pushing the shaft through from throttle lever side.

7. With the intermediate choke lever in the UP (12 o'clock) position, install the choke coil lever inside the choke housing onto the flats on the intermediate choke shaft. The choke coil lever is properly aligned when the coil pick-up tang is in the UP

position. Install the choke coil lever retaining screw into the end of intermediate choke shaft and tighten securely.

8. Install the pump discharge steel check ball, spring and plastic retainer into the float bowl. Tap lightly into place until the top of the retainer is flush with bowl casting surface.

9. Using a wide-blade screwdriver, install the main metering jet and the float valve seat (with gasket) into the bottom of the float bowl. Tighten and seat securely.

10. To make the adjustment easier, carefully bend float arm upward at the notch in arm before assembly.

11. Install the float valve onto the float arm by sliding the float lever under the pull clip. Correct installation of the pull clip is to hook the clip over the edge of the float on the float arm facing the float pontoon.

12. Install the float hinge pin into float arm with the end of the loop of the pin facing the pump well. Then, install the float assembly by aligning the valve in the seat and the float hinge pin into the locating channels in float bowl.

13. To adjust the float level, perform the following procedures:

   a. Hold the float hinge pin firmly in place and push down lightly on the float arm at outer end against the top of the float valve.

   b. Using an adjustable "T" scale, measure from top of float bowl casting surface (air horn gasket removed) to top of float at the toe.

   c. Bend the float arm, as necessary, for proper adjustment, by pushing on pontoon; see adjustment chart for specifications.

   d. Visually check the float alignment after adjustment.

14. Install the plastic filler block over the float valve pressing downward until properly seated (flush with the bowl casting surface).

15. Install the Throttle Position Sensor return spring into the bottom of the float bowl well.

16. Install the Throttle Position Sensor (TPS) and connector assembly in the float bowl by aligning the groove in the electrical connector with the "V" in the float bowl casting, push down on the connector and sensor assembly so the connector wires and sensor are located below the bowl casting surface.

NOTE: Care must be taken when installing the throttle position sensor to assure that the electrical integrity is maintained. Make sure the wires between the connector and the sensor assembly are not pinched or insulation broken upon final assembly. Accidental electrical grounding of the TPS must be avoided.

17. Install the air horn gasket onto the float bowl by locating the gasket over the 2 dowel locating pins on the bowl.

18. Install the pump return spring into the pump well.

19. Install the pump plunger assembly into the pump well.

Air Horn Assembly

1. Install the new pump plunger stem seal and retainer into the air horn casting. Lightly stake the seal retainer in 3 places, choosing locations different from the original stakings.

2. Install the new Throttle Position Sensor (TPS) actuator plunger seal and retainer into the air horn casting. Lightly stake the seal retainer in 3 places, choosing location different from the original stakings.

3. Install the vent/screen assembly by installing the 2 small attaching screws; tighten securely.

4. Inspect the air valve shaft pin for lubrication, apply a liberal quantity of lithium base grease to the air valve shaft pin. Make sure to lubricate the pin surface contact by windup spring.

5. Install the fast idle cam rod into the lower hole of the choke lever, aligning the squirt on the rod with small slot in lever.

6. Install the TPS plunger through seal in the air horn until about ½ of the plunger extends above the surface of the air horn casing. The seal pressure should hold the plunger in place during the air horn installation on the float bowl.

Air Horn to Bowl Installation

1. Rotate the fast idle cam to the the full UP position and tilt the air horn assembly to engage the lower end of the fast idle cam rod in the slot of the fast idle cam and install the pump rod end into hole of the pump lever. Then, holding down on the pump plunger assembly, carefully lower the air horn assembly onto the float bowl, guiding the pump plunger stem through the hole in the air horn casting. Do not force the air horn assembly onto the bowl but rather lightly lower it into place.

2. Install the vent and screen assembly over the vent stack in the air horn. Then, install the air horn-to-bowl screws and the lockwashers—tighten evenly and securely.

3. Install new the retainer clip through the hole in end of the pump rod.

4. Install the new seal in the recess of the air horn, then install the hot idle compensator valve and retain it with the small screws; tighten the screws securely.

5. Install the plastic bushing in the upper hole in the vacuum break and choke lever, making sure the small end of the bushing faces the retaining clip when installed. With the inner coil lever and the intermediate choke lever at the 12 o'clock position, install the intermediate choke rod into the bushing; retain it with needlenose pliers. Make sure the clip has full contact on the rod but is not seated tightly against the bushing. The rod-to-bushing clearance should be 0.030 in. (0.762mm).

6. Install the idle speed solenoid, the lockwasher and the retaining nut on the secondary side vacuum break; tighten the nut securely. Then, bend back 2 retaining tabs on the lockwasher to fit slots in the bracket.

7. Rotate the secondary side vacuum break and the bracket assembly, then insert the end ("T" pin) of the vacuum break link into the upper slot of the vacuum break and the choke lever. Install the bracket onto the throttle body and the countersunk screws; tighten the screws securely.

8. If the air valve rod has been removed from primary side vacuum break plunger, install the plastic bushings in the hole in the primary side vacuum break plunger, making sure the small end of the bushing faces the retaining clip when installed. Then, insert the end of the air valve rod through the bushing. Retain with the new clip, by it pressing the clip in place using needlenose pliers. Make sure the clip has full contact on the rod but is not sealed tightly against the bushing. The rod-to-bushing clearance should be 0.030 in. (0.762mm).

9. Rotate the primary side vacuum break assembly and the bracket, then insert the end of the air valve rod into the slot of the air valve lever and the end of the "T" pin of the vacuum break link into the lower slot of the vacuum break and choke lever. Position the bracket over the locating lug on the air horn and install the (2) countersunk screws and tighten securely.

10. Reinstall the hose onto the primary side vacuum break assembly and the throttle body tube.

11. Perform the choke coil lever adjustment procedure as specified in the carburetor adjustment section.

12. Install the choke cover and the coil assembly in the choke housing, aligning the notch in cover with raised casting projection on the housing cover flange. Make sure the choke coil lever is located inside the "trapped stat" coil tang when installing the choke cover and the coil assembly.

The ground contact for the electric choke is provided by a metal plate located at the rear of the choke cover assembly. Do not install a choke cover gasket between the electric choke assembly and the choke housing.

A choke cover retainer kit is required to attach choke cover to choke housing. Install the proper retainers and rivets contained in the kit, using a suitable blind rivet installation tool.

E2SE Carburetor—2.0L and 2.8L Engines

DISSASSEMBLY

Secondary Vacuum Break Removal

Remove the secondary vacuum break/bracket assembly-to-throttle body screws. Then, rotate the assembly to disengage the vacuum break link ("T" Pin) from the choke lever slot.

Do not immerse the idle speed solenoid or the vacuum break units in any type of carburetor cleaner. These items must always be removed before complete cleaning or damage to the components will result.

Air Horn Removal

1. Remove the clip from the hole in the pump rod.

NOTE: Do not remove the pump lever retaining screw or the pump lever from the air horn assembly.

2. Remove and discard the retaining clip from the intermediate choke link at the choke lever. A new retaining clip is required for reassembly. Remove the choke link and the plastic bushing from the choke lever, then save the bushing for later reuse.
3. Remove the mixture control solenoid-to-air horn screws; then, using a slight twisting motion, carefully lift the solenoid out of the air horn. Remove and discard the solenoid gasket.
4. Remove the seal retainer and the rubber seal from the end of the solenoid stem, being careful not to damage or nick end of the solenoid stem. Discard the seal and retainer. Retain the spacer for use at time of reassembly.
5. Remove the air horn-to-fuel bowl screws and lockwashers.
6. Rotate the fast idle cam to the full UP position and remove the air horn assembly by tilting to disengage the fast idle cam rod from the slot in the fast idle cam and the pump rod from the pump lever hole. If the pump plunger comes out of the float bowl with the air horn removal, remove the pump plunger from the air horn. The air horn gasket should remain on the float bowl for removal later. Do not remove the fast idle cam screw and the cam from the float bowl. These parts are not serviced separately and are to remain permanently in place as installed by the factory. The new service replacement float bowl will include the secondary lockout lever, the fast idle cam and screw installed as required.
7. Remove the fast idle cam link from the choke lever by rotating the rod to align the upset on the link with the small slot in the lever.

Air Horn Disassembly

1. Remove the Throttle Position Sensor (TPS) plunger by pushing it downward through the air horn seal.

NOTE: Use your fingers only to remove the plunger to prevent damage to the sealing surface of the plunger.

2. Remove the TPS seal by inverting the air horn and use a small screwdriver to remove the staking, holding the seal retainer in place. Remove and discard the retainer and seal.
3. Remove the pump plunger stem seal by inverting the air horn and using a small screwdriver to remove the staking, holding the seal retainer in place. Remove and discard the retainer and seal.

NOTE: Use care in removing the TPS plunger seal retainer and the pump plunger stem seal retainer to prevent damage to the air horn casting. New seals and retainers are required for reassembly.

4. Remove the vent/screen assembly by removing the 2 small attaching screws.
5. Further disassembly of the air horn is not required for cleaning purposes or air horn replacement. A new service air horn assembly includes the secondary metering rod-air valve assembly with adjustments pre-set to factory specifications. No attempt should be made to change the air valve settings. The air valve and the choke valve attaching screws are staked in place and are not removable. A new service air horn assembly will also include a TPS adjustment screw (refer to "on Vehicle Service," section or proper adjustment procedure for the TPS). The new service air horn assembly will also have the thermostatic pump bypass assembly installed, this temperature sensitive device is pressed permanently into place and is not serviceable, separately.

Float Bowl Disassembly

1. Remove the air horn gasket.
2. Remove the pump plunger from the pump well, if not removed with the air horn.
3. Remove the pump return spring from the pump well.
4. Push up from the bottom on the electrical connector and remove the Throttle Position Sensor (TPS) and the connector assembly from the float bowl. Remove the spring from the bottom of TPS well in the bowl.

NOTE: Use care in removing the sensor and connector assembly to prevent damage to this critical electrical part.

5. Remove the plastic filler block over the float valve.
6. Remove the float assembly and the float valve by pulling up the hinge pin (hold the float valve clip in place with your finger while tilting the float to clear the bowl vapor purge tube).
7. Using a removal tool or a wide-blade screwdriver, remove the float valve seat (with gasket) and the extended metering jet from the float bowl.

NOTE: Do not remove or change the adjustment of the small calibration screw located deep inside the metering jet during routine servicing. The adjustment screw is pre-set at the factory and no attempt should be made to change this adjustment in the field except as the result of a Computer Command Control system performance check.

8. Using a small slidehammer or equivalent, remove the plastic retainer holding the pump discharge spring and check ball in place. Discard the plastic retainer; a new retainer is required for reassembly.

NOTE: Do not attempt to remove the plastic retainer by prying it out with a tool such as a punch or screwdriver as this will damage the sealing beads on the bowl casting surface and require complete float bowl replacement.

Turn the fuel bowl upside down catching the pump discharge spring and the check ball in palm of your hand. Return the bowl to the upright position.

9. Remove the fuel inlet nut, the gasket, the check valve filter assembly and the spring.

Choke Disassembly

A tamper resistant choke cover design is used to discourage readjustment of the choke thermostatic coil assembly in the field. However, it is necessary to remove the cover and coil assembly during normal carburetor disassembly for cleaning and overhaul using the following procedures:

1. Support the float bowl and the throttle body as an assembly on a suitable holding fixture.
2. Carefully align a No. 21 drill (0.159 in.) on the rivet head and drill only enough to remove the rivet head. After removing the rivet heads and retainers, use a drift and a small hammer to drive the remainder of the rivets out of the choke housing.

NOTE: Use care in drilling to prevent damage to the choke cover or housing.

3. Remove the screw from the end of the intermediate choke shaft inside the choke housing.
4. Remove the choke coil lever from the end of the shaft.
5. Remove the intermediate choke shaft assembly from the float bowl by sliding the shaft rearward and out of the throttle lever side.
6. Remove the choke housing by removing the 2 attaching screws.

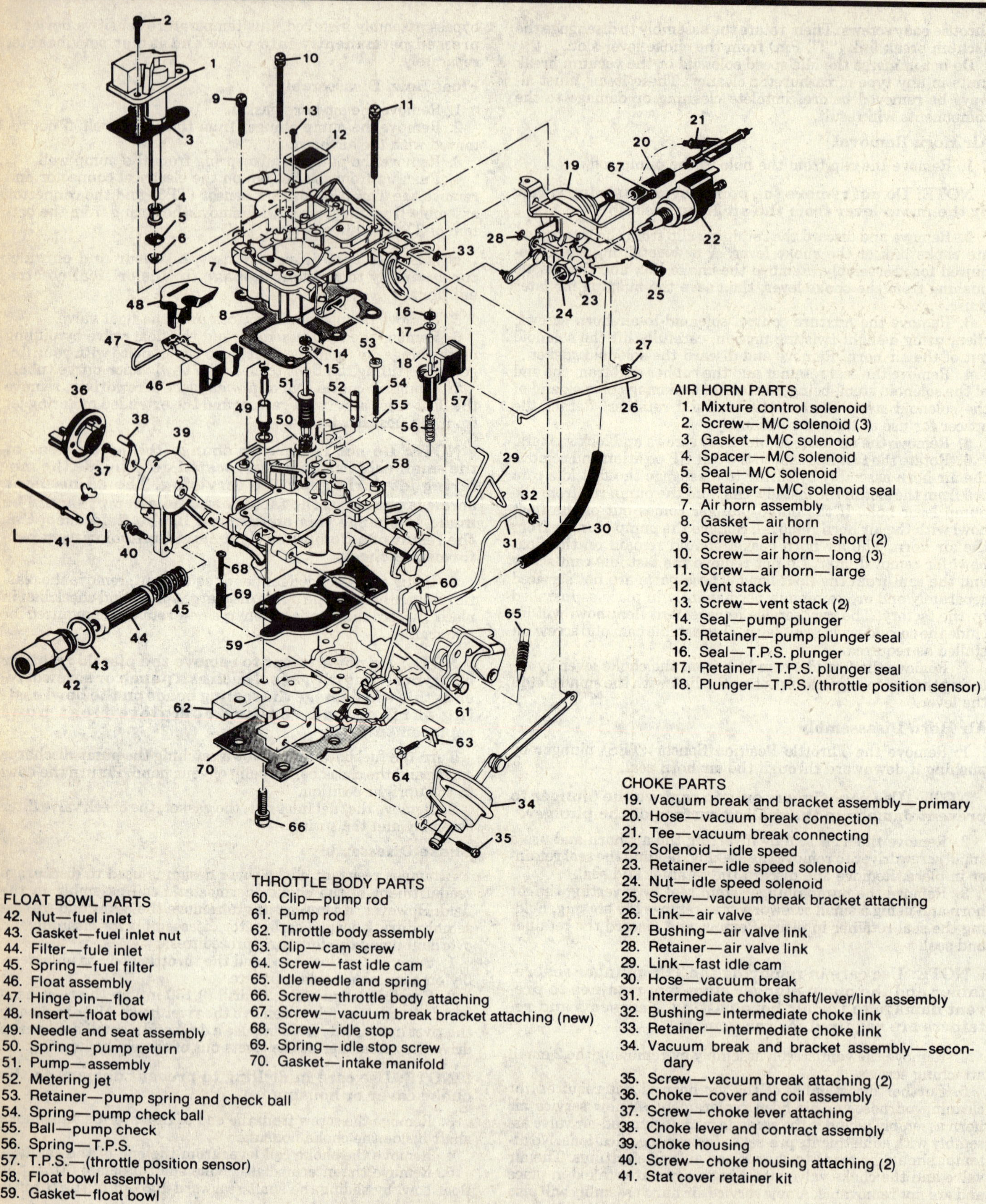

Exploded view of the E2SE carburetor – 2.0L and 2.8L engines

Throttle Body Removal

1. Remove the throttle body-to-bowl screws and the throttle body assembly from the float bowl.
2. Remove the throttle body gasket.

Throttle Body Disassembly

1. Place the throttle body assembly on the carburetor holding fixture to avoid damaging the throttle valves.
2. Hold the primary throttle lever wide-open and disengage the pump rod from the throttle lever by rotating the rod until the upset on the rod aligns with slot in the lever.

Further disassembly of the throttle body is not required for cleaning purposes.

NOTE: The primary and secondary throttle valve screws are permanently staked in place and should not be removed. The throttle body is serviced as a complete assembly.

3. Do not remove the plugs covering the idle mixture needle unless it is necessary to replace the mixture needle or normal soakings and air pressure fails to clean the idle mixture passages. If necessary, remove the idle mixture plug and needle as follows:
    a. Invert the throttle body and place it on a suitable holding fixture—manifold side up.
    b. Make 2 parallel cuts into the throttle body on either side of the locator point beneath the idle mixture needle plug (manifold side) with a hacksaw. The cuts should reach down to the steel plug but should not extend more than ⅛ in. beyond the locator point. The distance between the saw marks depends on the size of the punch to be used.
    c. Place a flat punch at a point near the ends of the saw marks in the throttle body. Holding the punch at a 45 degree angle, drive it into the throttle body until the casting breaks away, exposing the steel plug.
    d. Holding a center punch vertical, drive it into the steel plug. Then holding the punch at a 45 degree angle, drive the plug out of the casting.

NOTE: The hardened plug will break rather than remaining intact. It is not necessary to remove the plug whole; instead, remove loose pieces to allow use of Idle Mixture Adjusting tool J-29030, BT-7610B or equivalent.

4. Using the tool J-29030, BT-7610B or equivalent, remove the idle mixture needle and spring from the throttle body.

CLEANING AND INSPECTION

The carburetor parts should be cleaned in a cold immersion-type cleaner such as Carbon X (X-55) or equivalent.

NOTE: The idle speed solenoid, the mixture control solenoid, the throttle position sensor, the electric choke, the rubber parts, the plastic parts, the diaphragms, the pump plunger, the plastic filler block, should not be immersed in carburetor cleaner as they will harden, swell or distort.

The plastic bushing in the throttle elver will withstand normal cleaning in the carburetor cleaner.

1. Thoroughly clean all of the metal parts and blow dry with shop air. Make sure all the fuel passages and metering parts are free of burrs and dirt. Do not pass the drills or wires through the jets and passages.
2. Inspect the upper and lower surface of the carburetor castings for damage.
3. Inspect the holes in the levers for excessive wear or out of round conditions. If worn, the levers should be replaced. Inspect the plastic bushings in the levers for damage and excessive wear, replace as required.
4. Check, repair or replace parts, if the following problems are encountered:

A. Flooding

1. Inspect the float valve and seat for dirt, deep wear grooves, scores and improper sealing.
2. Inspect the float valve pull clip for proper installation; be careful not to bend the pull clip.
3. Inspect the float, the float arms and the hinge pin for distortion, binds, and burrs. Check the density of the material in the float; if heavier than normal, replace the float.
4. Clean or replace the fuel inlet filter and check the valve assembly.

B. Hesitation

1. Inspect the pump plunger for cracks, scores, or cup excessive wear. A used pump cup will shrink when dry. If dried out, soak in fuel for 8 hours before testing.
2. Inspect the pump duration and return springs for weakness or distortion.
3. Check the pump passages and the jet(s) for dirt, improper seating of the discharge checkball or the temperature bypass disc and/or scores in the pump well. Check the condition of the pump discharge check ball spring, replace as necessary.
4. Check the pump linkage for excessive wear; repair or replace as necessary.

C. Hard Starting—Poor Cold Operation

1. Check the choke valve and linkage for excessive wear, binds or distortion.
2. Test the vacuum break diaphragm(s) for leaks.
3. Clean or replace the fuel filter.
4. Inspect the float valve for sticking, dirt, etc.
5. Also check the items under "Flooding."

D. Poor Performance—Poor Gas Mileage

1. Clean all fuel and vacuum passages in the castings.
2. Check the choke valve for freedom of movement.
3. Check the Mixture Control Solenoid for sticking, binding or leaking as follows:
    a. Connect 1 end of a jumper wire to either terminal of the solenoid connector and the other end to the positive (+) terminal of a 12-volt battery source.
    b. Connect a jumper wire to the other terminal of the solenoid connector and the other end to a known good ground.
    c. With the rubber seal, retainer and spacer removed from the end of the solenoid stem, attach a hose from a hand vacuum pump.
    d. With the solenoid fully energized (lean position), apply 25 in. Hg vacuum and time the leak-down rate from 20–15 in. Hg vacuum in 5 seconds. If the leakage exceeds that amount, replace the solenoid.
    e. To check the solenoid for sticking in the down position, remove the jumper lead to a 12V source and observe the hand vacuum pump reading; the reading should go to 0 in less than 1 second.
4. Inspect the metering jet for dirt, loose parts or damage.

NOTE: Do not attempt to readjust the mixture screw located inside the metering jet. The screw is factory adjusted and a change can upset the fuel system calibration. No attempt should be made to change this adjustment in the field except as the result of a Computer Command Control system performance check.

5. Check the air valve and secondary metering rod for binding conditions. If the air valve or metering rod is damaged or the metering rod adjustment is changed from the factory setting, the air horn assembly must be replaced. Also check the air valve lever spring for proper installation (tension against the air valve shaft pin).

E. Rough Idle

1. Inspect the gasket and gasket mating surfaces on the casting for nicks, burrs or damage to the sealing beads.

2. Check the operation and sealing of the mixture control solenoid.
3. Clean all of the idle field passages.
4. If removed, inspect the idle mixture needle for ridges, burrs or being bent.
5. Check the throttle lever and valves for binds, nicks or other damage.
6. Check all of the diaphragms for possible ruptures or leaks.

ASSEMBLY

Throttle Body Assembly

1. Holding the primary throttle lever wide-open, install the lower end of the pump rod in the throttle lever by aligning the squirt on the rod with the slot in the lever. End of the rod should point outward toward the throttle lever.
2. If removed, install the idle mixture needle and spring using tool J-029030 or equivalent. Lightly seat the needle and then back out 3 turns as a preliminary idle mixture adjustment. Final idle mixture adjustment must be made on-vehicle. Refer to the "On-Vehicle Service" section for the idle mixture adjustment procedures.

Float Bowl Assembly

1. Install a new throttle-to-bowl gasket over the 2 locating dowels on the bowl.

NOTE: If a new float bowl assembly is used, stamp or engrave the model number on the new float bowl.

2. Rotate the fast idle cam so the steps face fast the idle screw on the throttle lever when properly installed, install the throttle body making certain the throttle body is properly located over the dowels on the float bowl; then install the throttle body-to-bowl screws and lockwashers, then tighten evenly and securely.

Inspect the linkage to insure the lockout tang is located properly to engage the slot in the secondary lockout lever and that the linkage moves freely and does not bind.

3. Place the carburetor on suitable holding fixture.
4. Install the fuel inlet filter spring, the filter assembly, a new gasket and inlet nut, then tighten the nut to 18 ft. lbs.

When installing a service replacement filter, make sure the filter is the type that includes the check valve to need U.S. Motor Vehicle Safety Standards (MVSS).

When properly installed, the hole (check valve end) in the filter faces toward the inlet nut.

NOTE: Tightening beyond the specified torque can damage the nylon gasket to cause a fuel leak.

5. Install the choke housing on the throttle body, making sure the raised boss and locating lug on the rear of the housing fit into the recesses in the float bowl casting. Install the choke housing attaching screws and lockwashers, then tighten the screws evenly and securely.
6. Install the immediate choke shaft assembly in the float bowl by pushing the shaft through from the throttle lever side.
7. With the intermediate choke lever in the UP (12 o'clock) position, install the choke coil lever inside the choke housing onto flats on the intermediate choke shaft. The choke coil lever is properly aligned when the coil pick-up tang is in the UP position. Install the choke coil lever retaining screws into the end of the intermediate choke shaft and tighten securely.
8. Install the pump discharge check ball, the spring and a new plastic retainer in the float bowl. Tap lightly into place until the top of retainer is flush with the bowl casting surface.
9. Using a wide-blade screwdriver, install the float valve seat (with gasket) and the metering jet; tighten securely.
10. To make the adjustment easier, carefully bend the float arm upward at the notch in the arm before assembly.
11. Install the float valve onto the float arm by sliding the float lever under the pull clip. The correct installation of the pull clip is to hook the clip over the edge of the float on the float arm facing the float pontoon.
12. Install the float hinge pin into the float arm with the end of loop of pin facing the pump well. Then, install the float assembly by aligning the valve in the seat and the float hinge pin into locating channels in the float bowl.
13. To adjust the float level, perform the following procedures:
    a. Hold the float hinge pin firmly in place and push down lightly on the arm at the outer end against the top of the float valve.
    b. Using adjustment "T" scale, measure from the top of the float bowl casting surface (air horn gasket removed) to the top of the float at the toe.
    c. Bend the float arm, as necessary, for proper adjustment by pushing on the pontoon (see Adjustment Chart for specifications).
    d. Visually check the float alignment after adjustment.
14. Install the plastic filler block over the float valve by pressing downward until properly seated (flush with the bowl casting surface).
15. Install the Throttle Position Sensor (TPS) return spring in the bottom of the well in the float bowl.
16. Install the Throttle Position Sensor (TPS) and the connector assembly in the float bowl by aligning the groove in the electrical connector with the "V" in the float bowl casting, push down on the connector and sensor assembly so the connector wires and sensor are located below the bowl casting surface.

NOTE: Care must be taken when installing the throttle position sensor to assure that the electrical integrity is maintained. Make sure the wires between the connector and sensor assembly are not pinched or the insulation broken upon final assembly. Accidental electrical grounding of the TPS must be avoided.

17. Install the air horn gasket on the float bowl, locating the gasket over the 2 dowel locating pins on the bowl.
18. Install the pump return spring and plunger in the pump well.

Air Horn Assembly

1. Install the new pump plunger stem seal and retainer in the air horn casting. Lightly stake the seal retainer in 3 places, choosing locations different from the original stakings.
2. Install new Throttle Position Sensor (TPS) actuator plunger seal and retainer in the air horn casting. Lightly stake the seal retainer in 3 places, choosing locations different from the original stakings.
3. Install the vent/screen assembly by installing the 2 small attaching screws; tighten securely.
4. Inspect the air valve shaft pin for lubrication, apply a liberal quantity of lithium base grease to the air valve shaft pin. Make sure to lubricate the pin surface contacted by the windup spring.
5. Install the fast idle cam rod in lower hole of the choke lever, aligning the squirt on the rod with small slot in the lever.
6. Install the TPS plunger through seal in the air horn until

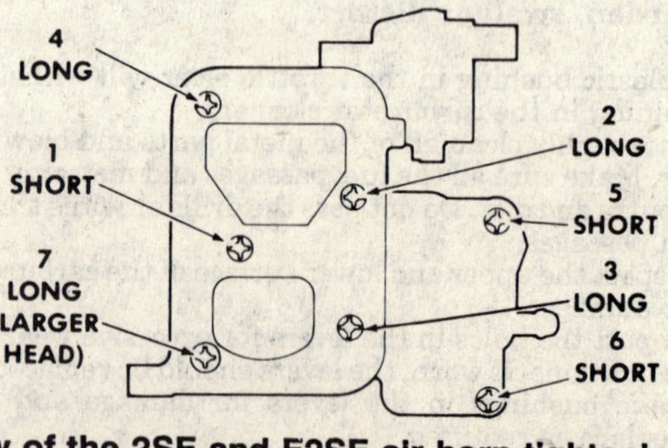

View of the 2SE and E2SE air horn tightening sequence

about ½ of the plunger extends above the surface of the air horn casting. Seal pressure should hold the plunger in place during the air horn installation on the float bowl.

Air Horn to Bowl Installation

1. Rotate the fast idle cam to the full UP position and tilt the air horn assembly to engage the lower end of the fast idle cam rod in the slot in the fast idle cam and install the pump rod end into hole in the pump lever; check the intermediate choke rod for position, then, holding down on the the pump plunger assembly, carefully lower the air horn assembly onto the float bowl, guiding the pump plunger stem through the seal in the air horn casting.

Do not force the air horn assembly onto the bowl but rather lightly lower it into place. Make sure the TPS actuator plunger engages the sensor plunger in the bowl by checking the plunger movement.

2. Install the air horn-to-bowl screws and lockwashers, tighten evenly and securely.

3. Install a new retainer clip through the hole in the end of the pump rod extending through the pump lever, making sure the clip is securely locked in place.

4. If not tested previously, test the mixture control solenoid for sticking, binding or leaking, following the steps noted in the cleaning and inspection procedure. Then, install the spacer and new rubber seal on the mixture control solenoid stem making sure the seal is up against the spacer. Then, using a $^3/_{16}$ in. socket and light hammer, carefully drive a new retainer on the stem. Drive the retainer onto the stem only far enough to retain the rubber seal on the stem leaving a slight clearance between the retainer and seal to allow for seal expansion.

5. Prior to installing the mixture control solenoid, lightly coat the rubber seal on the end of the solenoid stem with a silicone grease or light engine oil. Using a new mounting gasket, install the mixture control solenoid on the air horn, carefully aligning the solenoid stem with recess in bottom of the bowl. Use a slight twisting motion of the solenoid during installation to ensure the rubber seal on stem is guided into the recess in the bottom of the bowl, to prevent distortion or damage to the rubber seal. Install the solenoid attaching screws and tighten securely.

6. Install the plastic bushing in the hole in the choke lever, making sure the small end of bushing faces the retaining clip, when installed. With the inner coil lever and intermediate choke lever at the 12 o'clock position, install the intermediate choke rod in the bushing. Retain the rod with new clip, pressing the clip securely in place with needle nose pliers. Make sure the clip has full contact on the rod but is not seated tightly against the bushing. The rod-to-bushing clearance should be 0.030 in. (0.762mm).

7. Install the secondary vacuum break assembly. Rotate the assembly and insert the end ("T" Pin) of the vacuum break link into the upper slot of the choke lever. Attach the bracket-to-throttle body with countersunk screws and tighten the screws securely.

8. If the air valve rod has been removed from the primary side vacuum break plunger, install a plastic bushing in the hole in the primary side vacuum break plunger, making sure the small end of the bushing faces the retaining clip when installed. Then insert the end of the air valve rod through the bushing. Retain with a new clip, pressing the clip into place using needlenose pliers. Make sure the clip has full contact on the rod but is not seated tightly against the bushing. The rod-to-bushing clearance should be 0.030 in. (0.762mm).

9. Rotate the primary side vacuum break assembly (with the idle speed solenoid and bracket), then insert the end of the air valve rod into the slot of the air valve lever and end ("T" Pin) of the vacuum break link into the lower slot of the choke lever. Connect the primary vacuum break hose-to-tube on the throttle body and tube on the vacuum break unit. Position the bracket over the locating lug on the air horn and install the 2 countersunk screws on the air horn and screw with lockwasher in the throttle body; tighten the screws securely.

10. Perform the choke coil lever adjustment procedure as specified in carburetor adjustment section.

11. Install the choke cover and coil assembly in the choke housing, aligning the notch in the cover with the raised casting projection on the housing cover flange. Make sure the coil pick-up tang engages the inside choke coil lever.

The tang on the thermostatic coil is the "trapped stat" design. This means that the coil tang is formed so it will completely encircle the coil pick-up lever. Make sure the coil pick-up lever is located inside the coil tang when installing the choke cover and coil assembly.

NOTE: The ground contact for the electric choke is provided by a metal plate located at the rear of the choke cover assembly. Do not install a choke cover gasket between the electric choke assembly and the choke housing. A choke cover retainer kit is required to attach the choke cover-to-choke housing. Install the proper retainers and rivets contained in kit, using a blind rivet installation tool.

Carburetor Specifications

Type DCH340 4-1950cc Engine

Primary Throttle Plate Gap (in.)	Primary Main Jet Number	Secondary Main Jet Number	Primary Slow Jet Number	Secondary Slow Jet Number	Power Jet Number	Primary Main Air Bleed Number	Secondary Main Air Bleed Number	Slow Air Bleed Number
.050–.059 (MT) .059–.069 (AT)	114 Fed. 85 Cal.	170	50 Fed. 54 Cal.	100	50	120 Fed. 110 Cal.	70 Fed. 90 Cal.	150 Fed. 130 Cal.

Type E2SE 6-2800 (California)

Carb. Number	Float Level (in.)	Fast Idle Cam (deg.)	Primary Vacuum Break (deg.)	Air Valve Rod (deg.)	Secondary Vacuum Break (deg.)	Choke Unloader (deg.)
17082356	13/32	22	25	1	30	30
17082357	13/32	22	25	1	32	30
17082358	13/32	22	25	1	30	30
17082359	13/32	22	25	1	32	30
17072683	9/32	28	25	1	35	45
17074812	9/32	28	25	1	35	45
17084356	9/32	22	25	1	30	30
17084357	9/32	22	25	1	30	30
17084358	9/32	22	25	1	30	30
17084359	9/32	22	25	1	30	30
17084368	1/8	22	25	1	30	30
17084370	1/8	22	25	1	30	30
17084430	11/32	15	26	1	38	42
17084431	11/32	15	26	1	38	42
17084434	11/32	15	26	1	38	42
17084435	11/32	15	26	1	38	42
17084452	5/32	28	25	1	35	45
17084453	5/32	28	25	1	35	45
17084455	5/32	28	25	1	35	45
17084456	5/32	28	25	1	35	45
17084458	5/32	28	25	1	35	45
17084532	5/32	28	25	1	35	45
17084534	5/32	28	25	1	35	45
17084535	5/32	28	25	1	35	45
17084537	5/32	28	25	1	35	45
17084538	5/32	28	25	1	35	45
17084540	5/32	28	25	1	35	45
17084542	1/8	28	25	1	35	45
17084632	9/32	28	25	1	35	45
17084633	9/32	28	25	1	35	45
17084635	9/32	28	25	1	35	45
17084636	9/32	28	25	1	35	45

Type 2SE 4-2000 6-2800 (excluding California)

Carb. Number	Float Level (in.)	Fast Idle Cam. (deg.)	Primary Vacuum Break (deg.)	Air Valve Rod (deg.)	Secondary Vacuum Break (deg.)	Choke Unloader (deg.)
17082348	7/16	22	26	1	32	40
17082349	7/16	22	28	1	32	40
17082350	7/16	22	26	1	32	40
17082351	7/16	22	28	1	32	40
17082353	7/16	22	28	1	35	30
17082355	7/16	22	28	1	35	30
17083348	7/16	22	30	1	32	40
17083349	7/16	22	30	1	32	40
17083350	7/16	22	30	1	32	40
17083351	7/16	22	30	1	32	40
17083352	7/16	22	30	1	35	40
17083353	7/16	22	30	1	35	40
17083354	7/16	22	30	1	35	40
17083355	7/16	22	30	1	35	40
17083360	7/16	22	30	1	32	40
17083361	7/16	22	28	1	32	40
17083362	7/16	22	30	1	32	40
17083363	7/16	22	28	1	32	40
17083364	7/16	22	30	1	35	40
17083365	7/16	22	30	1	35	40
17083366	7/16	22	30	1	35	40
17083367	7/16	22	30	1	35	40
17083390	13/32	28	30	1	35	38
17083391	13/32	28	30	1	35	38
17083392	13/32	28	30	1	35	38
17083393	13/32	28	30	1	35	38
17083394	13/32	28	30	1	35	38
17083395	13/32	28	30	1	35	38
17083396	13/32	28	30	1	35	38
17083397	13/32	28	30	1	35	38
17084410	11/32	15	23	1	38	42
17084412	11/32	15	23	1	38	42
17084425	11/32	15	26	1	36	40
17084427	11/32	15	26	1	36	40
17084560	11/32	15	24	1	34	38
17084562	11/32	15	24	1	34	38
17084569	11/32	15	24	1	34	38

GASOLINE FUEL INJECTION SYSTEM

NOTE: This book contains simple testing and service procedures for for your vehicle's fuel injection system.

Electric Fuel Pump

The electric fuel pump is attached to the fuel sending unit, located in the fuel tank.

REMOVAL AND INSTALLATION

NOTE: The following procedure requires the use of the GM Fuel Gauge Sending Unit Retaining Cam tool J-24187 or equivalent, a brass drift and a hammer.

1. If the 2.8L TBI or 4.3L TBI engine has been in use, turn the ignition switch Off and allow the system time to reduce the fuel pressure.
2. To relieve the fuel pressure on the 2.5L TBI engine, perform the following procedures:
   a. From the fuse block, located in the passenger compartment, remove the fuel pump fuse.
   b. Start the engine and allow it to Run until the fuel, in the system is used up.
   c. After the engine stops, crank the engine a few times to make sure all of the fuel is removed from the system.
3. Disconnect the negative battery terminal from the battery.

NOTE: Be sure to keep a Class B (dry chemical) fire extinguisher nearby.

CAUTION

Due to the possibility of fire or explosion, never drain or store gasoline in an open container.

4. Using a hand pump or a siphon hose, drain the gasoline into an approved container.
5. Raise and support the vehicle on jackstands.
6. Support the fuel tank and remove the fuel tank-to-vehicle straps.
7. Lower the tank slightly, then remove the sender unit wires, the hoses and the ground strap.
8. Remove the fuel tank from the vehicle.
9. Using the GM Fuel Gauge Sending Unit Retaining Cam tool J-24187 (or equivalent) or a brass drift and a hammer, remove the cam locking ring (fuel sending unit) counterclockwise, then lift the sending unit from the fuel tank.

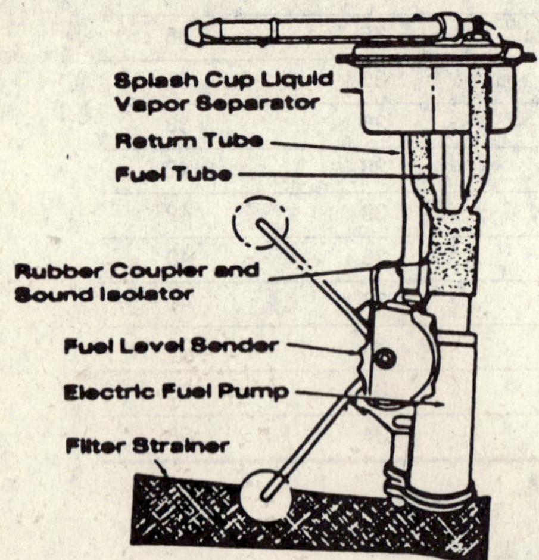

View of the TBI fuel pump — typical

10. Remove the fuel pump from the fuel sending unit, by performing the following procedures:
    a. Pull the fuel pump up into the mounting tube, while pulling outward (away) from the bottom support.

NOTE: When removing the fuel pump from the sending unit, be careful not to damage the rubber insulator and the strainer.

    b. When the pump assembly is clear of the bottom support, pull it out of the rubber connector.
11. Inspect the fuel pump hose and bottom sound insulator for signs of deterioration, then replace it, if necessary.
12. Push the fuel pump onto the sending tube.
13. Using a new sending unit-to-fuel tank O-ring, install the sending unit into the fuel tank.

NOTE: When installing the sending unit, be careful not to fold or twist the fuel strainer, for it will restrict the fuel flow.

14. Using the GM Fuel Gauge Sending Unit Retaining Cam tool J-24187 (or equivalent) or a brass drift and a hammer, turn the sending unit-to-fuel tank locking ring clockwise.
15. To install the fuel tank, align the insulator strips and reverse the removal procedures. Torque the inner fuel tank strap-to-vehicle bolts to 26 ft. lbs. and the outer fuel tank strap-to-vehicle nuts/bolts to 26 ft. lbs.

TESTING AND ADJUSTMENTS

Flow Test

1. Remove the fuel pump-to-throttle body line from the throttle body.
2. Place the fuel line in a clean container.
3. Turn the ignition switch On; approximately ½ pint of the fuel should be delivered in 15 seconds.
4. If the fuel flow is below minimum, inspect the fuel system for restrictions; if no restrictions are found, replace the fuel pump.

Pressure Test

NOTE: The following procedure requires the use of a GM Fuel Pressure Gauge tool J-29658-A or equivalent.

1. If equipped with an EFI equipped engine, refer to the "Fuel Pressure Relief" procedures in this section and relieve the fuel pressure.
2. Remove the air cleaner, then disconnect and plug the THERMAC vacuum port on the throttle body unit.
3. Place a rag (to catch excess fuel) under the fuel line-to-

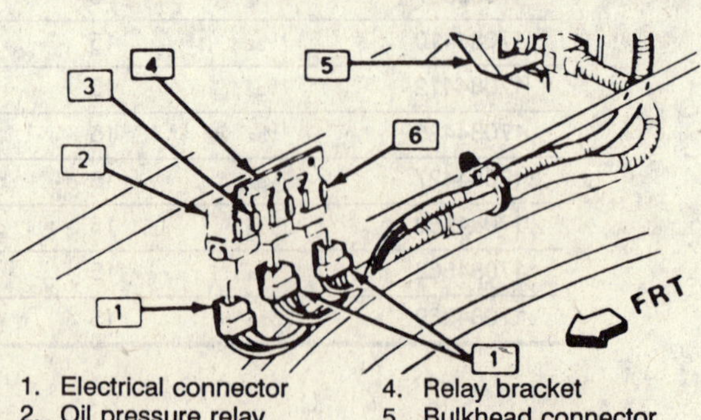

1. Electrical connector
2. Oil pressure relay
3. A/C relay
4. Relay bracket
5. Bulkhead connector
6. Fuel pump relay

View of the fuel pump relay — all 1983–90 TBI engines

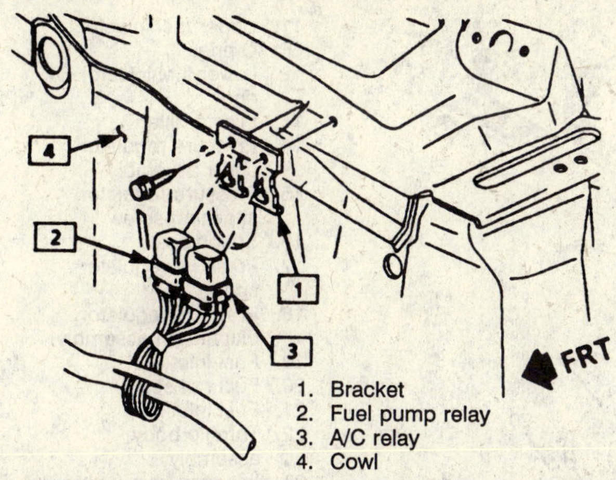

View of the fuel pump relay – 4.3L TBI engine for 1991

throttle body connection. Disconnect the fuel line from the throttle body.

NOTE: When disconnecting the fuel line, use a back-up wrench to hold the fuel nut on the throttle body.

4. Using a GM Fuel Pressure Gauge tool J-29658-A or equivalent, install it into the fuel line.
5. Start the engine and observe the fuel pressure, it should be 9–13 psi.

NOTE: If the fuel pressure does not meet specifications, inspect the fuel system for restrictions or replace the fuel pump.

6. Turn the engine **OFF**, relieve the fuel pressure and remove the GM Fuel Pressure Gauge tool J-29658-A or equivalent.
7. Install a new fuel line-to-throttle body O-ring and reverse the removal procedures. Unplug from the THERMAC vacuum port. Start the engine and check for fuel leaks.

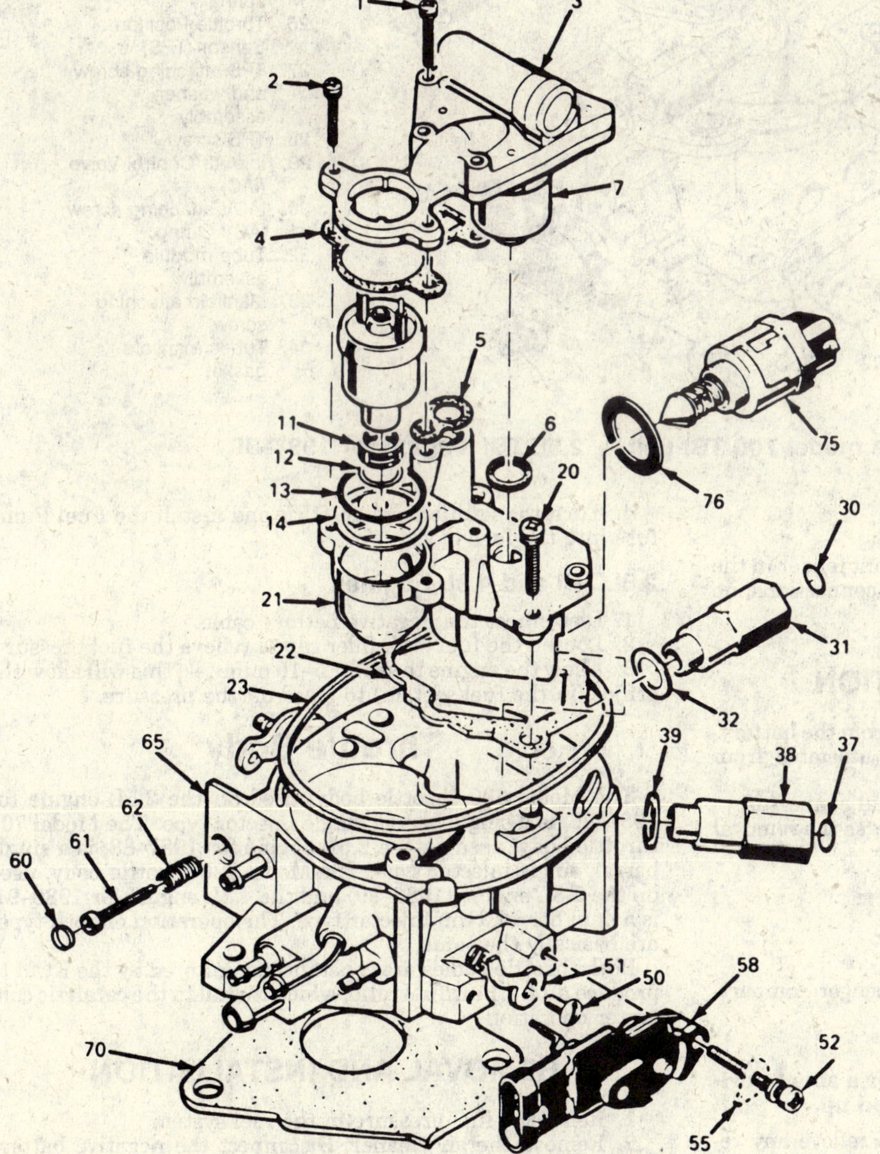

Exploded view of the model 300 TBI unit – 2.5L TBI engine for 1985–86

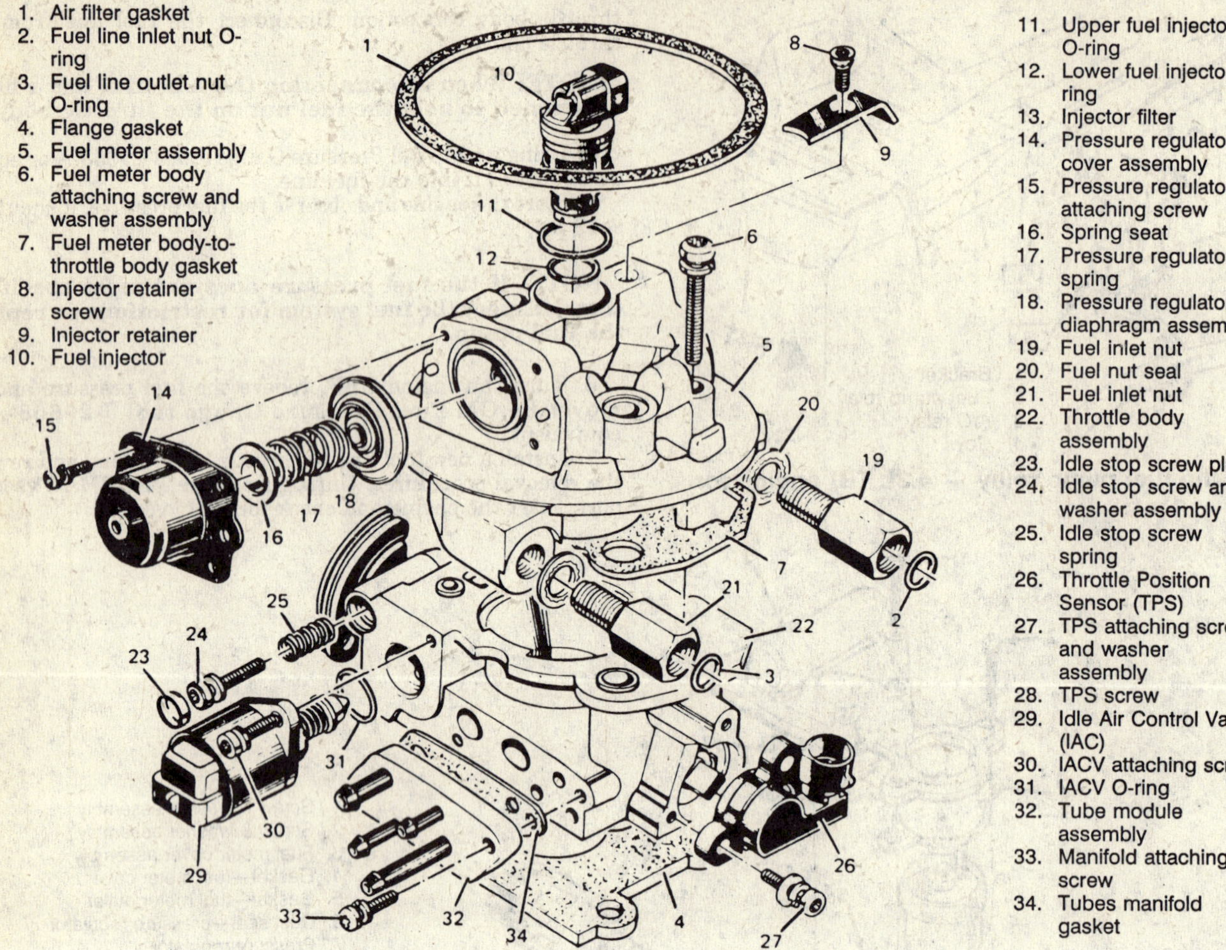

1. Air filter gasket
2. Fuel line inlet nut O-ring
3. Fuel line outlet nut O-ring
4. Flange gasket
5. Fuel meter assembly
6. Fuel meter body attaching screw and washer assembly
7. Fuel meter body-to-throttle body gasket
8. Injector retainer screw
9. Injector retainer
10. Fuel injector
11. Upper fuel injector O-ring
12. Lower fuel injector O-ring
13. Injector filter
14. Pressure regulator cover assembly
15. Pressure regulator attaching screw
16. Spring seat
17. Pressure regulator spring
18. Pressure regulator diaphragm assembly
19. Fuel inlet nut
20. Fuel nut seal
21. Fuel inlet nut
22. Throttle body assembly
23. Idle stop screw plug
24. Idle stop screw and washer assembly
25. Idle stop screw spring
26. Throttle Position Sensor (TPS)
27. TPS attaching screw and washer assembly
28. TPS screw
29. Idle Air Control Valve (IAC)
30. IACV attaching screw
31. IACV O-ring
32. Tube module assembly
33. Manifold attaching screw
34. Tubes manifold gasket

Exploded view of the model 700 TBI unit — 2.5L TBI engine for 1987–89

Fuel Pump Relay

The fuel pump relay is mounted on the left-front fender in the engine compartment. Check for loose electrical connections; no other service is possible, except replacement.

REMOVAL AND INSTALLATION

1. Disconnect the negative battery terminal from the battery.
2. Disconnect the relay/electrical connector assembly from the bracket.
3. Pull the fuel pump relay from the electrical connector.
4. If necessary, use a new fuel pump and reverse the removal procedures.

FUEL PRESSURE RELIEF

2.5L TBI Engine

1. From the fuse block, located in the passenger compartment, remove the fuse labeled, Fuel Pump.
2. Start the engine.

NOTE: The engine will start and run, for a short period of time, until the remaining fuel is used up.

3. Engage the starter, a few more times, to relieve any remaining pressure.
4. Turn the ignition switch **OFF** and install the Fuel Pump fuse into the fuse block.

2.8L TBI and 4.3L Engines

1. Disconnect the negative battery cable.
2. Loosen the fuel tank filler cap to relieve the fuel pressure.
3. Allow the engine to set for 5–10 minutes; this will allow the orifice (in the fuel system) to bleed off the pressure.

Throttle Body

The Model 300 throttle body, used on the 2.5L engine for 1985–86, is a single barrel, single injector type. The Model 700 throttle body, used on the 2.5L engine for 1987–88, is a single barrel, single injector type. The Model 220 throttle body, used on the 2.8L engine (1986–89) and the 4.3L engine for 1988–91, is a dual barrel, twin injector type. The operation of both types are basically the same.

Both throttle bodies are constantly monitored by the ECM to produce a 14.7:1 air/fuel ratio, which is vital to the catalytic converter operation.

REMOVAL AND INSTALLATION

1. Relief the fuel pressure in the fuel system.
2. Remove the air cleaner. Disconnect the negative battery cable from the battery.

1. Screw assembly—fuel meter cover attaching—long
2. Screw assembly—fuel meter cover attaching—short
3. Fuel meter cover assembly
4. Gasket—fuel meter cover
5. Gasket—fuel meter outlet
6. Seal—pressure regulator
7. Pressure regulator
10. Injector—fuel
11. Filter—fuel injector inlet
12. O-ring—fuel injector—lower
13. O-ring—fuel injector—upper
14. Washer—fuel injector
20. Screw assembly—fuel meter body—throttle body attaching
21. Fuel meter body assembly
22. Gasket—throttle body to fuel meter body
23. Gasket—air filter
30. O-ring—fuel return line
31. Nut—fuel outlet
37. O-ring—fuel inlet line
38. Nut—fuel inlet
40. Gasket—fuel outlet nut
41. Gasket—fuel inlet nut
50. Screw—TPS lever attaching
51. Lever—TPS
52. Screw assembly—TPS attaching
55. Retainer—TPS attachingscrew
58. Sensor—throttle position (TPS)
60. Plug—idle stop screw
61. Screw assembly—idle stop
62. Spring—idle stop screw
65. Throttle body assembly
70. Gasket—flange
75. Valve assembly—idle air control (IAC)
76. Gasket—idle air control valve assembly

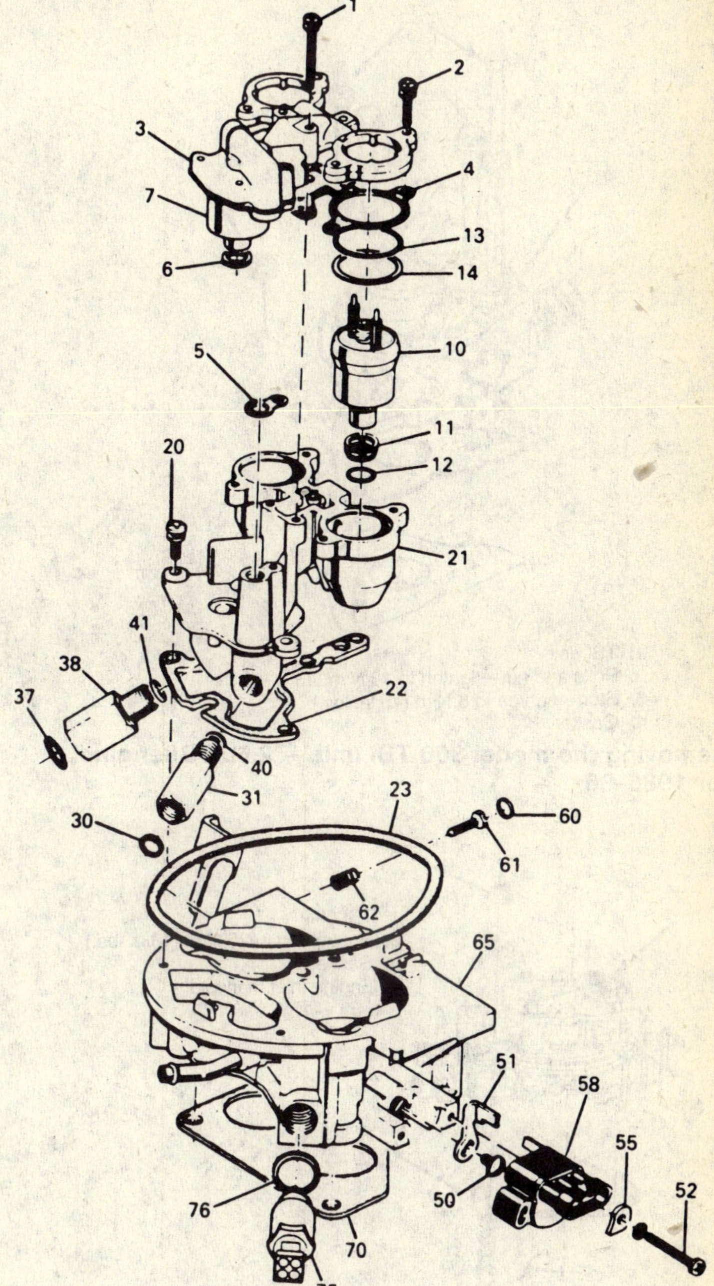

Exploded view of the model 220 TBI unit – 2.8L TBI and 4.3L engines

3. Disconnect the electrical connectors from the idle air control valve, the throttle position sensor and the fuel injector(s).
4. Remove the throttle return spring(s), the cruise control, if equipped, and the throttle linkage.
5. Label and disconnect the vacuum hoses from the throttle body.
6. Place a rag (to catch the excess fuel) under the fuel line-to-throttle body connection, then disconnect the fuel line from the throttle body.
7. Remove the attaching hardware, the throttle body-to-intake manifold bolts, the throttle body and the gasket.

NOTE: Be sure to place a cloth in the intake manifold to prevent dirt from entering the engine.

8. Using a putty knife, if necessary, clean the gasket mounting surfaces.
9. To install, use a new gasket and reverse the removal procedures. Torque the throttle body-to-intake manifold nuts/bolts to 13 ft. lbs. (18 Nm) for 2.5L and 4.3L engines or 18 ft. lbs. (25 Nm) for 2.8L engine. Depress the accelerator pedal to the floor and release it, to see if the pedal returns freely. Turn the ignition switch On and check for fuel leaks.

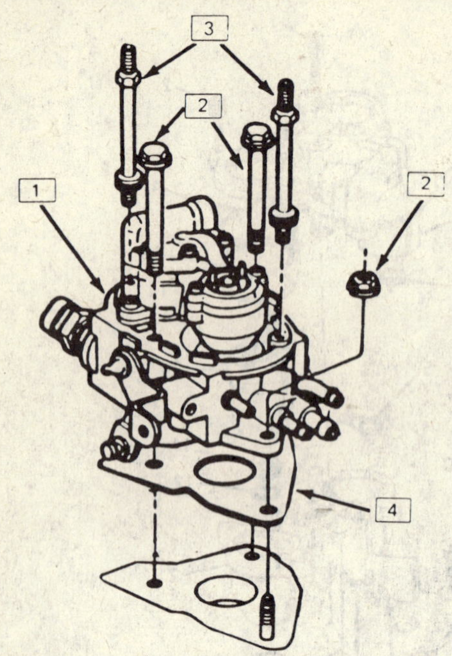

1. TBI unit
2. Bolts and nut—tighten to 18 N·m (13 ft. lbs.)
3. Stud—tighten to 5 N·m (45 in. lbs.)
4. Gasket

Removing the model 300 TBI unit – 2.5L TBI engine for 1985–86

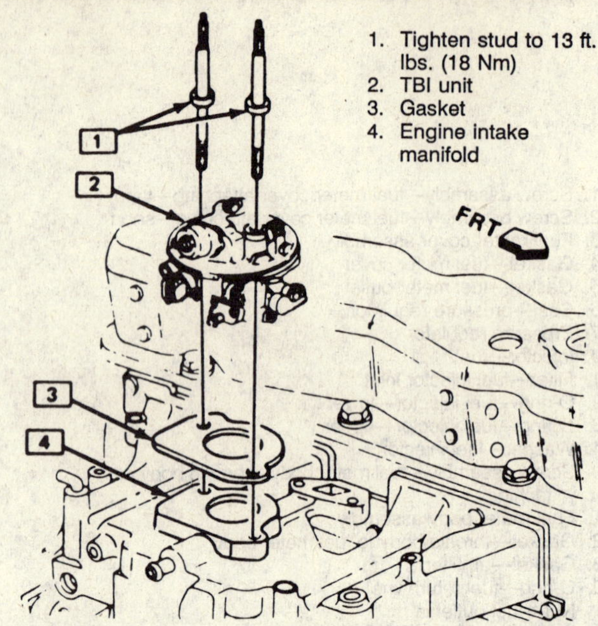

1. Tighten stud to 13 ft. lbs. (18 Nm)
2. TBI unit
3. Gasket
4. Engine intake manifold

Removing the model 700 TBI unit – 2.5L TBI engine for 1987–89

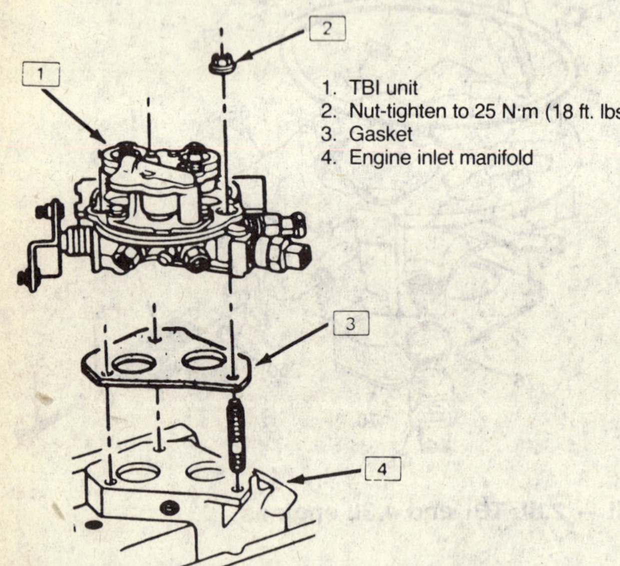

1. TBI unit
2. Nut-tighten to 25 N·m (18 ft. lbs.)
3. Gasket
4. Engine inlet manifold

Removing the model 220 TBI unit – 2.8L TBI engine for 1986–89

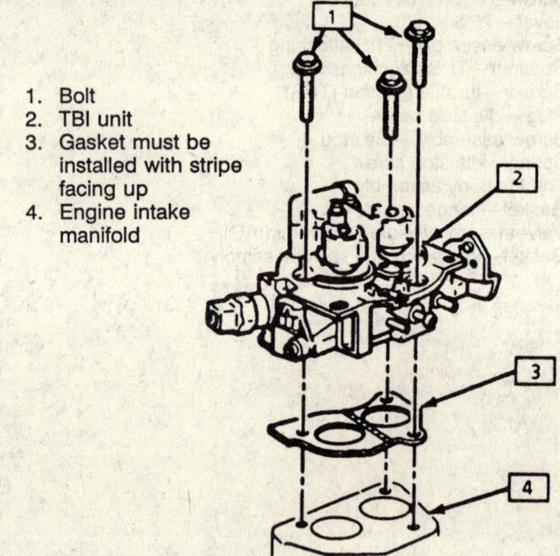

1. Bolt
2. TBI unit
3. Gasket must be installed with stripe facing up
4. Engine intake manifold

Removing the model 220 TBI unit – 4.3L TBI engine

INJECTOR REPLACEMENT

Model 300 for 2.5L TBI Engine (1985–86) and Model 220 for 2.8L and 4.3L TBI Engines

NOTE: When removing the injector(s), be careful not to damage the electrical connector pins (on top of the injector), the injector fuel filter and the nozzle. The fuel injector is serviced as a complete assembly only, it is an electrical component and should not be immersed in any kind of cleaner.

1. Remove the air cleaner. Disconnect the negative battery terminal.
2. Relieve the fuel pressure.
3. At the injector connector, squeeze the 2 tabs together and pull it straight up.
4. Remove the fuel meter cover and leave the cover gasket in place.
5. Using a small prybar or tool J-26868, carefully lift the injector until it is free from the fuel meter body.
6. Remove the small O-ring form the nozzle end of the injector. Carefully rotate the injector's fuel filter back-and-forth to remove it from the base of the injector.

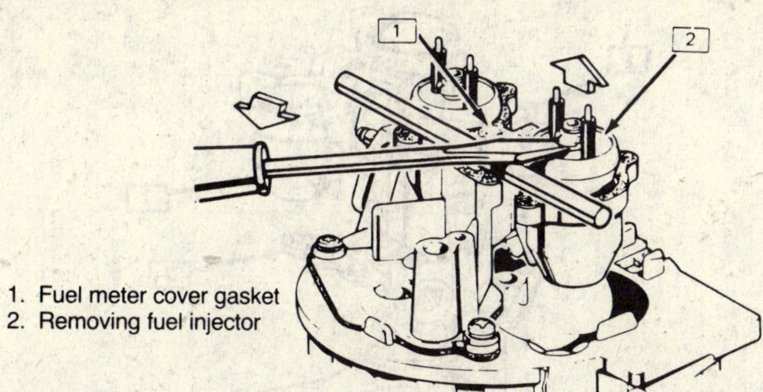

Removing the fuel injector from the Model 220 throttle body – 2.8L and 4.3L TBI engines – 2.5L TBI engine for 1985–86 is similar

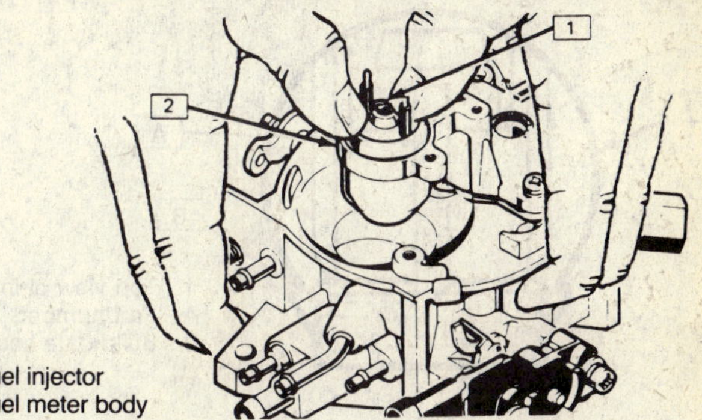

Installing the Model 300 fuel injector – 2.5L TBI engine for 1985–86 – 2.8L and 4.3L TBI engines are similar

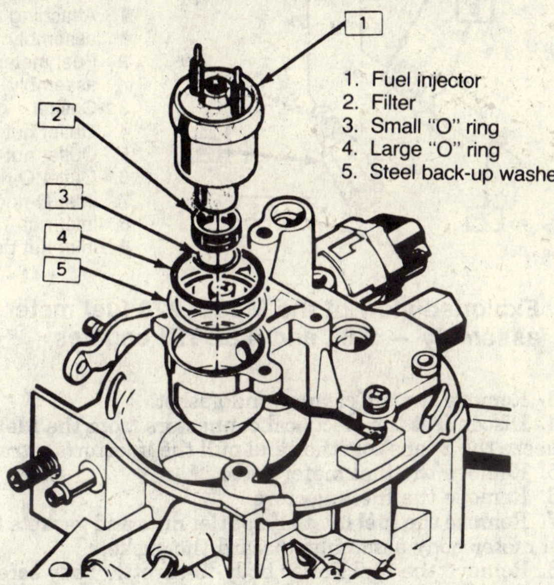

Exploded view of the Model 300 fuel injector – 2.5L TBI engine for 1985–86 – 2.8L and 4.3L TBI engines are similar

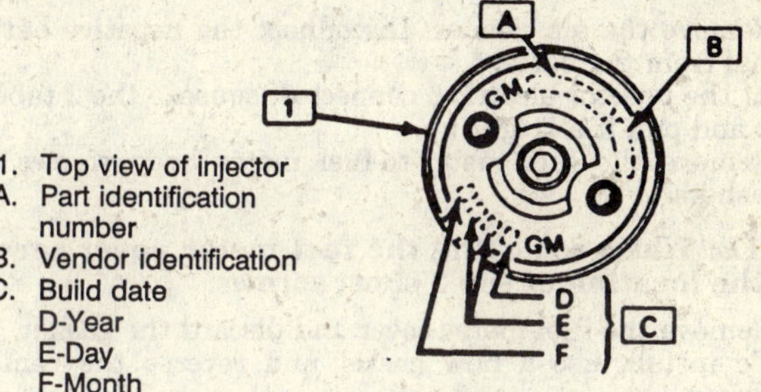

View of the Model 220 fuel injector part number location – 2.8L and 4.3L TBI engines

7. Discard the fuel meter cover gasket.
8. Remove the large O-ring and back-up washer from the top of the counterbore of the fuel meter body injector cavity.
9. To install, lubricate the O-rings with automatic transmission fluid and push it into the fuel injector cavity. To complete the installation, reverse the removal procedures. Start the engine and check for fuel leaks.

Model 700 for 2.5L TBI Engine (1987–89)

1. Relieve the fuel pressure in the system.
2. Disconnect the negative battery cable.
3. Remove the air cleaner and gasket; discard the gasket.
4. Disconnect the electrical connector from the fuel injector.
5. Remove the injector retainer screw and the retainer.
6. Using a small prybar and a fulcrum, place the prybar under the ridge opposite the fuel injector and pry it carefully from the housing.
7. Remove the upper and lower O-rings from the fuel injector and/or cavity; discard them.

To install:

8. Inspect the fuel injector for dirt and/or other contaminants. If necessary, replace the fuel injector with an identical part.
9. Using new O-rings, lubricate them with automatic transmission fluid and install them onto the fuel injector; make sure the upper O-ring is in the groove and the lower 1 is flush against the filter.
10. Install the injector by pushing it straight into the fuel injector cavity.

NOTE: Be sure the electrical connector end, of the injector, is facing in the general direction to the cut-out in the fuel meter body for the wire grommet.

11. Apply thread locking compound to the retainer screw and install the injector retainer. Torque the screw to 27 inch lbs. (3.0 Nm).
12. With the engine **OFF**, turn the ignition switch **ON** and check for fuel leaks.
13. Install the air cleaner with a new gasket.

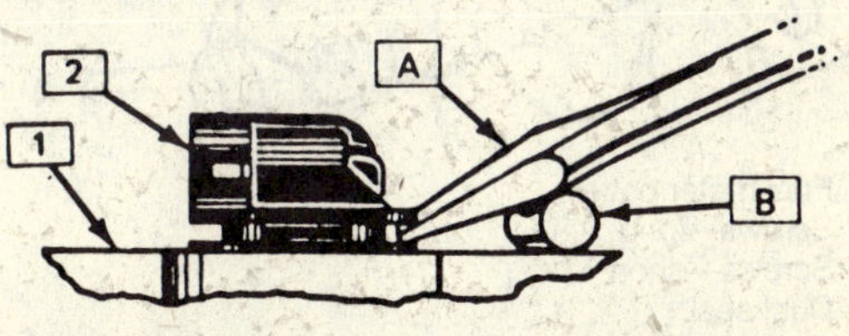

Removing the fuel injector from the Model 700 throttle body – 2.5L TBI engine for 1987–89

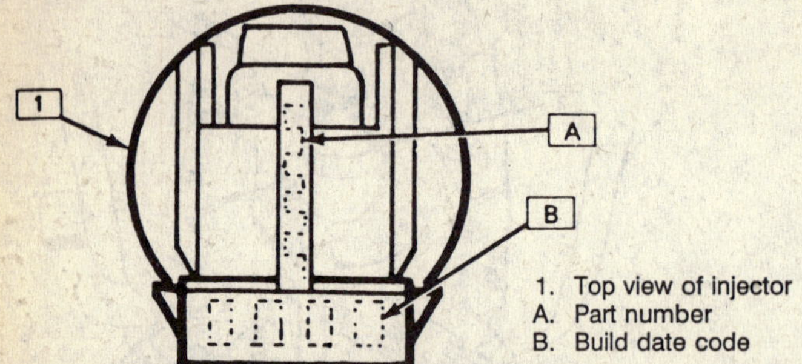

View of the Model 700 fuel injector part number — 2.5L TBI engine for 1987–89

FUEL METER COVER REPLACEMENT

1. Remove the air cleaner. Disconnect the negative battery terminal from the battery.
2. At the injector electrical connector, squeeze the 2 tabs together and pull it straight up.
3. Remove the fuel meter-to-fuel meter body screws and lockwashers.

NOTE: When removing the fuel meter cover screws, note the location of the 2 short screws.

4. Remove the fuel meter cover and discard the gasket.
5. To install, use a new gasket and reverse the removal procedures.

FUEL INJECTOR ASSEMBLY—MODEL 220

1. Relieve the fuel pressure from the fuel system.
2. Disconnect the negative battery cable.

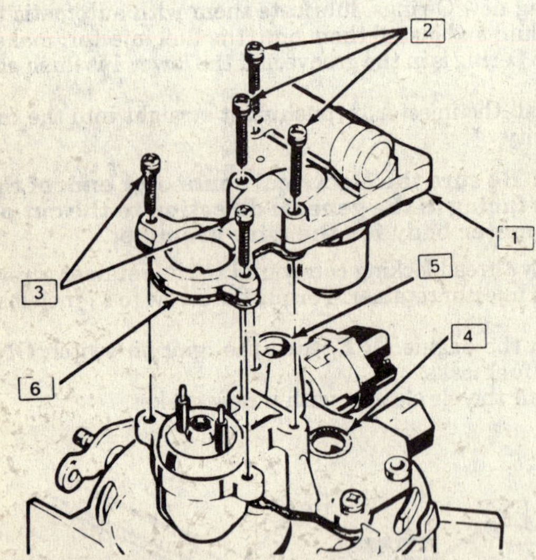

Exploded view of the Model 300 fuel meter cover — 2.5L TBI engine for 1985–86 — 2.8L and 4.3L TBI engines are similar

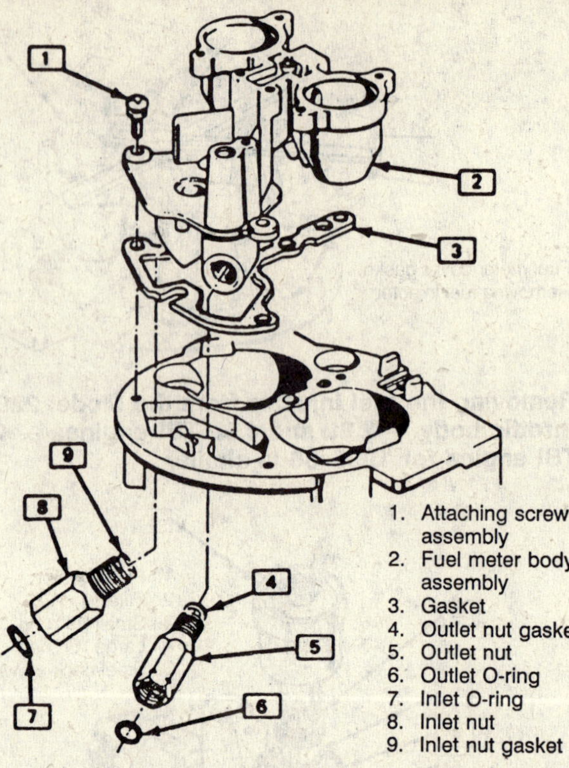

Exploded view of the Model 220 fuel meter body assembly — 2.8L and 4.3L TBI engines

3. Remove the air cleaner and gasket.
4. Disconnect the electrical connectors from the fuel meters, squeeze the 2 tabs together and pull the injector(s) straight up.
5. Remove the fuel meter cover.
6. Remove the fuel injectors.
7. Remove the fuel inlet and outlet nuts and gaskets from the fuel meter body assembly; discard the gaskets.
8. Remove the fuel meter body-to-throttle body screws.
9. Remove the fuel meter body from the throttle body and discard the gasket.
10. Using a new fuel meter assembly-to-throttle body gasket, lubricate the screws with locking compound and torque the fuel meter assembly screws to 30 inch lbs. (4.0 Nm).
11. Using new gaskets, install the fuel meter inlet and outlet nuts and torque to the outlet nut to 21 ft. lbs. (29 Nm) and the inlet nut to 30 ft. lbs. (40 Nm).
12. Using new O-rings and a back-up wrench, install the fuel inlet and outlet lines; torque the fuel lines to 17 ft. lbs. (23 Nm).
13. Using new fuel injector O-rings, lubricate them with automatic transmission fluid; install them into the fuel injector body assembly.
14. Install the fuel meter cover assembly.
15. Coat the screws with locking compound and torque the screws to 27 inch lbs. (3.0 Nm).
16. Connect the electrical connectors to the fuel injectors. Connect the negative battery cable.
17. With the engine **OFF**, turn the ignition switch **ON** and check for fuel leaks.

PRESSURE REGULATOR ASSEMBLY MODEL 700 TBI UNIT

NOTE: To prevent leaks, the pressure regulator diaphragm assembly must be replaced whenever the cover is removed.

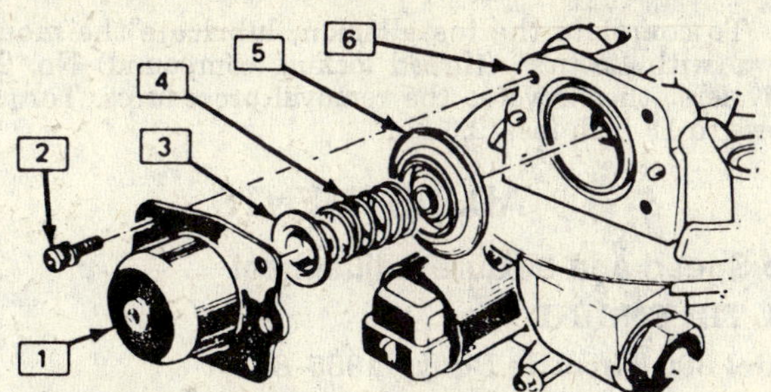

1. Pressure regulator cover
2. Screw assembly
3. Spring seat
4. Spring
5. Diaphragm
6. Fuel meter assembly

Exploded view of the pressure regulator assembly — Model 700 2.5L TBI engine

1. Relieve the fuel pressure from the fuel system.
2. Disconnect the negative battery cable.
3. While keeping the pressure regulator spring compressed, remove the pressure regulator-to-throttle body screws.

CAUTION

The pressure regulator contains a large spring under heavy compression pressure. Use care when removing the screw to prevent personal injury.

4. Remove the pressure regulator cover assembly.
5. Remove the pressure regulator spring.
6. Remove the spring seat.
7. Remove the pressure regulator diaphragm assemlby.

To install:

8. Inspect the pressure regulator seat in the fuel meter body for pitting, nicks or irregularities; use a magnifying glass, if necessary. If any problelm exists, replace the whole fuel body.
9. Using a new pressure regulator diaphragm, make sure it is seated in the groove in the fuel meter body.
10. Install the regulator spring seat and spring into the cover assembly.
11. Install the cover assembly of the diaphragm, while aligning the mounting holes; be careful not to misalign the pressure regulator, for leaks may exists.
12. While maintaining the regulator spring pressure, coat the screws with locking compound and install. Torque the screws to 22 inch lbs. (2.5 Nm).
13. With the engine **OFF** and the engine **ON**; check for fuel leaks.
14. To complete the installation, reverse the removal procedures.

IDLE AIR CONTROL (IAC) VALVE REPLACEMENT

Model 220 and 300 Throttle Bodys

1. Remove the air cleaner. Disconnect the negative battery terminal from the battery.
2. Disconnect the electrical connector from the Idle Air Control (IAC) valve.
3. Remove the idle air control valve and discard the O-ring.

NOTE: Before installing a new idle air control valve, measure the distance that the valve extends (from the motor housing to the end of the cone); the distance should be no greater than 1⅛ in. (28mm). If it extends to far, damage will occur to the valve when it is installed.

4. To install, use a new gasket, lubricate it with automatic transmission fluid and reverse the removal procedures. Torque the IAC to 13 ft. lbs. (18 Nm). Start the engine and allow it to reach normal operating temperatures; then, turn it **OFF**.

NOTE: The ECM will reset the idle Air Control (IAC) valve after the engine has normal operating temperatures.

Model 700 Throttle Body

1. Remove the air cleaner. Disconnect the negative battery terminal from the battery.
2. Disconnect the electrical connector from the Idle Air Control (IAC) valve.
3. Remove the idle air control valve and discard the O-ring.

NOTE: Before installing a new idle air control valve, measure the distance that the valve extends (from the motor housing to the end of the cone); the distance should be no greater than 1⅛ in. (28mm). If it extends to far, damage will occur to the valve when it is installed.

4. To install, use a new gasket, lubricate it with automatic transmission fluid and reverse the removal procedures. Torque the IAC to 28 inch lbs. (3.2 Nm). Start the engine and allow it to reach normal operating temperatures; then, turn it **OFF**.

NOTE: The ECM will reset the idle Air Control (IAC) valve after the engine has normal operating temperatures.

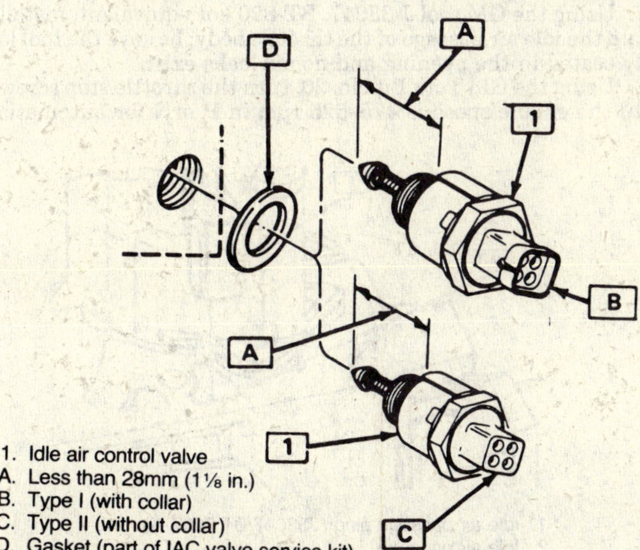

1. Idle air control valve
A. Less than 28mm (1⅛ in.)
B. Type I (with collar)
C. Type II (without collar)
D. Gasket (part of IAC valve service kit)

Exploded view of the Idle Air Control (IAC) valves — Model 220 and Model 300 throttle bodies

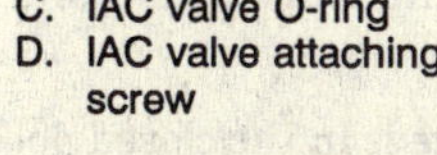

A. Distance of pintle extension
B. Diameter of pintle
C. IAC valve O-ring
D. IAC valve attaching screw

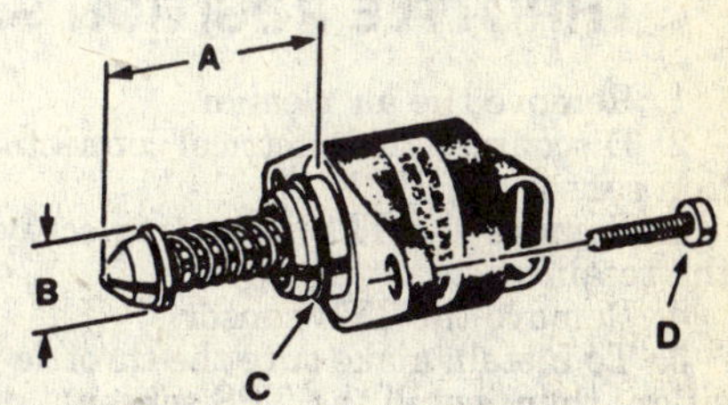

Exploded view of the Idle Air Control (IAC) valves — Model 700 throttle body

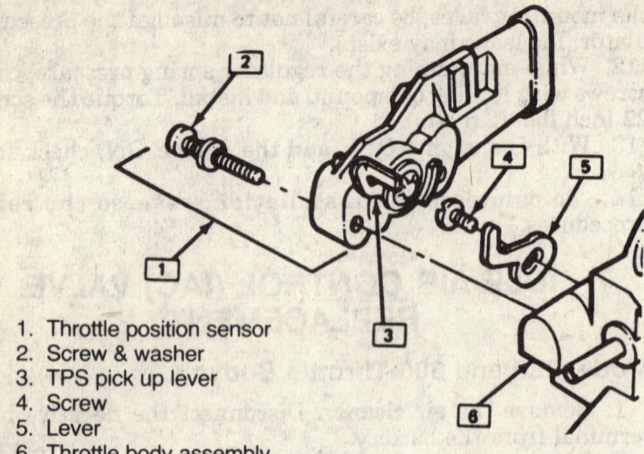

1. Throttle position sensor
2. Screw & washer
3. TPS pick up lever
4. Screw
5. Lever
6. Throttle body assembly

Exploded view of the Throttle Position Sensor (TPS) – Model 300 throttle body

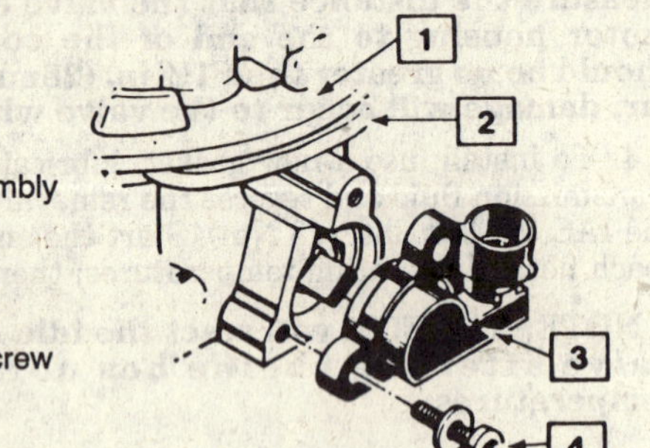

1. Fuel meter assembly
2. Throttle body assembly
3. Throttle position sensor
4. TPS attaching screw and washer assembly

Exploded view of the Throttle Position Sensor (TPS) – Model 700 throttle body

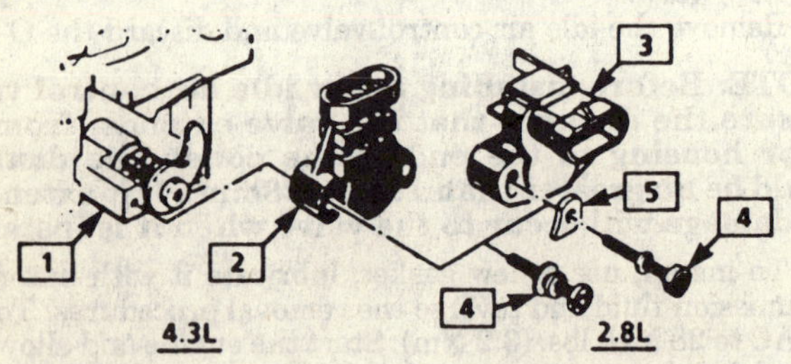

1. Throttle body assembly
2. Throttle position sensor–non-adjustable
3. Throttle position sensor–adjustable
4. Screw assembly
5. Retainer

THROTTLE POSITION SENSOR (TPS)

1. Remove the air cleaner.
2. Disconnect the electrical connector from the throttle position sensor (TPS).
3. Remove the TPS mounting screws, the lockwashers and the retainers.
4. Remove the TPS sensor.
5. To install, make sure the throttle valve is in the closed position, then install the TPS sensor.

NOTE: Make sure the the TPS pickup lever is located above the tang on the throttle actuator lever.

6. To complete the installation, lubricate the mounting screws with Loctite® (thread locking compound) No. 262 or equivalent, then reverse the removal procedures. Torque the screws to 18 inch lbs. (2.0 Nm).

ADJUSTMENTS

Idle Speed and Mixture Adjustment

2.5L TBI ENGINE

Model 300 Throttle Body–1985–86

NOTE: The following procedures require the use a tachometer, GM tool J-33047, BT-8207 or equivalent, GM Torx Bit No. 20, silicone sealant, a $^5/_{32}$ in. drill bit, a prick punch and a $^1/_{16}$ in. pin punch.

The throttle stop screw, used in regulating the minimum idle speed, is adjusted at the factory and is not necessary to perform. This adjustment should be performed only when the throttle body has been replaced.

NOTE: The replacement of the complete throttle body assembly will have the minimum idle adjusted at the factory.

1. Remove the air cleaner and the gasket. Be sure to plug the THERMAC vacuum port (air cleaner vacuum line-to-throttle body) on the throttle body.
2. Remove the throttle valve cable from the throttle control bracket to provide access to the minimum air adjustment screw.
3. Using the manufacturer's instructions, connect a tachometer to the engine.
4. Remove the electrical connector from the Idle Air Control (IAC) valve, located on the throttle body.
5. If necessary to remove the throttle stop screw cover, perform the following procedures:
   a. Using a prick punch, mark the housing at the top over the center line of the throttle stop screw.
   b. Using a $^5/_{32}$ in. drill bit, drill (on an angle) a hole through the casting to the hardened cover.
   c. Using a $^1/_{16}$ in. pin punch, place it through the hole and drive out the cover to expose the throttle stop screw.
6. Place the transmission in **P** for automatic transmission or Neutral for manual transmission, start the engine and allow the idle speed to stabilize.
7. Using the GM tool J-33047, BT-8207 or equivalent, install it into the idle air passage of the throttle body; be sure the tool is fully seated in the opening and no air leaks exist.
8. Using the GM Torx Bit No. 20, turn the throttle stop screw until the engine speed is 475–525 rpm in **P** or**N** for automatic

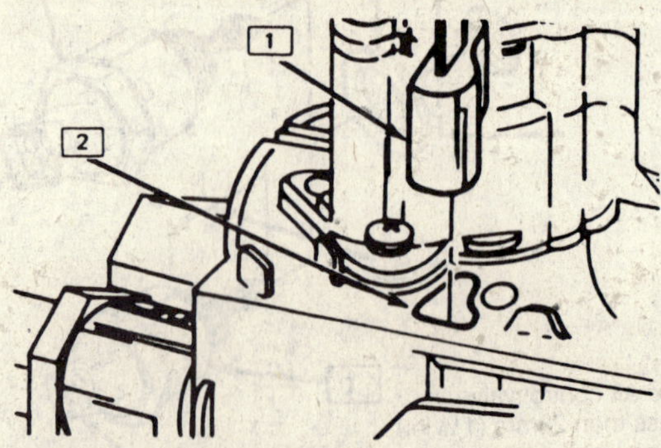

1. Idle air passage plug (J33047/BT 8207-A)
2. Idle air passage

Plug the passage of the throttle body as shown – 2.5L TBI engine

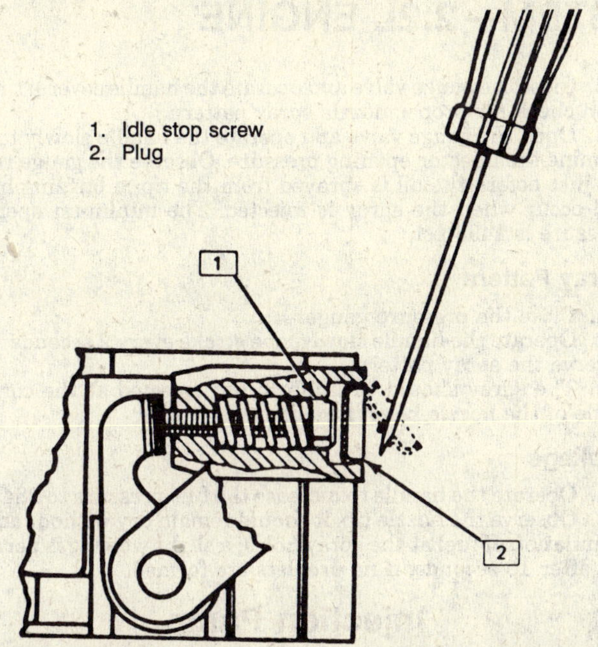

Unpluging the idle stop screw plug — Model 220 throttle body

transmission or 750–800 rpm in Neutral for manual transmission.

9. With the idle speed adjusted, stop the engine, remove the tool J-33047, BT-8207 or equivalent, from the throttle body.
10. Reconnect the Idle Air Control (IAC) electrical connector.
11. Using silicone sealant or equivalent, cover the throttle stop screw.
12. Reinstall the gasket and the air cleaner assembly.

Model 700 Throttle Body—1987–89

1. Remove the air cleaner and discard the gasket.
2. Plug any vacuum line ports, as necessary.
3. With the IAC connected, ground the diagnostic terminal (ALDL connector).
4. Turn the ignition switch to the **START** position; do not start the engine. This allows the IAC valve pintle to extend and seat in the throttle body.
5. With the ignition switch **ON**, disconnect the IAC valve electrical connector.
6. Remove the ground from the diagnostic terminal and start the engine.
7. Remove the plug, by first piercing it with an awl, then apply leverage to remove it.
8. Adjust the idle stop screw to obtain 650 rpm ± 25 rpm in Neutral.
9. Turn the ignition switch **OFF** and reconnect the IAC valve electrical connector.
10. Unplug any plugged vacuum line ports and install the air cleaner and a new gasket.

2.8L TBI AND 4.3L ENGINES

NOTE: The following procedure requires the use of a tachometer, a prick punch, a $^5/_{32}$ in. drill bit, a $^1/_{16}$ in. pin punch, a grounding wire and silicone sealant.

1. Remove the air cleaner and the gasket.
2. If necessary to remove the throttle stop screw cover, perform the following procedures:
   a. Using a prick punch, mark the housing at the top over the center line of the throttle stop screw.
   b. Using a $^5/_{32}$ in. drill bit, drill (on an angle) a hole through the casting to the hardened cover.
   c. Using a $^1/_{16}$ in. pin punch, place it through the hole and drive out the cover to expose the throttle stop screw.

NOTE: The following adjustment should be performed only when the throttle body assembly has been replaced; the engine should be at normal operating temperatures before making this adjustment.

3. With the Idle Air Control (IAC) connected, ground the diagnostic terminal of the Assembly Line Communications Link (ALCL) connector.

NOTE: The Assembly Line Communications Link (ALCL) connector is located in the engine compartment on the left side firewall.

4. Turn the ignition switch **ON** but do not start the engine. Wait 30 seconds, this will allow the IAC valve pintle to extend and seat in the throttle body.
5. With the ignition switch turned **ON**, disconnect the Idle Air Control (IAC) valve electrical connector.
6. Remove the ground from the Diagnostic Terminal ALCL connector and start the engine.
7. Adjust the idle stop screw to obtain 700 rpm ± 25 rpm for the 2.8L engine, to 600–650 rpm, in Neutral, for manual transmission for 4.3L engine or 500–550 rpm, in **D** for automatic transmission for 4.3L engine.
8. Turn the ignition switch **OFF** and reconnect the IAC valve electrical connector.
9. Using silicone sealant or equivalent, cover the throttle stop screw.
10. Reinstall the gasket and the air cleaner assembly.

Throttle Position Sensor (TPS)

2.5L AND 2.8L TBI ENGINES

The throttle position sensor is non-adjustable but a test should be performed only when throttle body parts have been replaced or AFTER the minimum idle speed has been adjusted.

NOTE: The following procedure requires the use of the Digital Voltmeter tool J-29125-A or equivalent.

1. Using the Digital Voltmeter tool J-29125-A or equivalent, set it on the 0–5.0V scale, then connect the probes to the center terminal **B** and the outside terminal **C**.

NOTE: To attach probes to the TPS electrical connector, disconnect the TPS electrical connector, install thin wires into the sockets and reconnect the connector.

2. Turn the ignition **ON** (engine stopped).
3. On the 2.5L TBI engine, the output voltage should be 1.25V. If the voltage is more that 1.25V, replace the TPS.
4. On the 2.8L TBI engine, the output voltage should be 0.420–0.450V; if not, rotate the TPS to obtain the correct voltage.
5. Remove the voltmeter and the jumper wires.

DIESEL ENGINE FUEL SYSTEM – 2.2L ENGINE

CAUTION

The following procedures should not be attempted unless all tools necessary to adjust the injection pump timing are available.

Fuel Injectors

The primary function of the nozzles is to distribute the fuel in the combustion chamber, which effects the combustion efficiency and engine performance.

REMOVAL AND INSTALLATION

1. Disconnect the negative battery terminal from the battery.
2. From the fuel injector nozzle(s), disconnect the fuel return line(s).
3. From the fuel injector nozzle(s), disconnect the fuel injection line(s).
4. Remove the fuel injector nozzle(s) from the engine.
5. Inspect and test the fuel injector nozzle(s).
6. To install, reverse the removal procedures.

TESTING

NOTE: The following procedure requires the use of a reliable pressure tester and Calibrating Oil SAE J9670 or equivalent (70°F).

CAUTION

Do not use diesel fuel; it is unstable with the respect to corrosion inhibition and may cause skin problems.

Opening Pressure

1. Using a reliable pressure tester, connect the test line to a fuel nozzle and tighten the fittings.

CAUTION

Exercise extreme care, when using the pressure tester, not to damage the gauge with excessive pressure during the test procedure. When testing the nozzle(s), be sure not to position your hands or arms near the nozzle tip. The atomized high pressure fuel spray has enough penetrating power to puncture the flesh and destroy tissue and may also cause blood poisoning. The nozzle tip should always be enclosed in a transparent receptacle, to contain the spray.

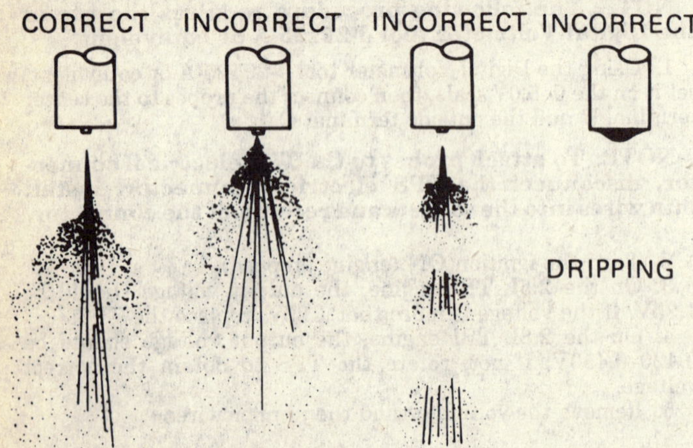

Description of the fuel nozzle spray pattern – 2.2L Diesel engine

2. Close the gauge valve and operate the handle several times, then check for proper nozzle spray pattern.
3. Open the gauge valve and operate the handle slowly to determine the injector opening pressure. Observe the gauge reading just before the oil is sprayed from the tip; a buzzing noise will occur when the spray is injected. The minimum opening pressure is 1493 psi.

Spray Pattern

1. Close the pressure gauge.
2. Operate the handle slowly, one stroke every 2 seconds, and observe the spray pattern.
3. The spray should be uniform and injected at the correct angle of the nozzle being tested.

Leakage

1. Operate the handle to increase the fuel pressure to 284 psi.
2. Observe the nozzle tip, it should remain dry without an accumulation of fuel at the spray holes; a slight wetting is permitted after 10 seconds, if no droplets are formed.

Injection Pump

REMOVAL AND INSTALLATION

1. Raise the hood. Relieve the fuel pressure in the fuel system.
2. Disconnect the negative battery terminal from the battery. Remove the battery.
3. Remove the undercover.
4. Place a drain pan under the radiator, open the drain cock and on the cylinder block, then drain the cooling system.
5. Disconnect the upper water hose from the engine side.
6. Loosen the compressor drive belt by moving the power steering oil pump or idler, if equipped.
7. Remove the cooling fan and the fan shroud.
8. Disconnect the lower water hose from the engine side.
9. Remove the air conditioner compressor, if equipped.
10. Remove the fan belt, the crankshaft pulley and the timing pulley housing covers.
11. Remove the tension spring and the fixing bolt, then remove the tension center and pulley.
12. Remove the timing belt, the engine control cable and the wiring harness of the fuel cut solenoid.
13. Remove the fuel hoses and the injection pipes. Using a wrench to hold the delivery holder, loosen the sleeve nuts on the injection pump side.
14. Install a 6mm bolt (with pitch of 1.25) into threaded hole in the timing pulley housing through the hole in pulley to prevent turning of the pulley.
15. Remove the bolt fixing the injection pump timing pulley, then remove the pulley using pulley puller.

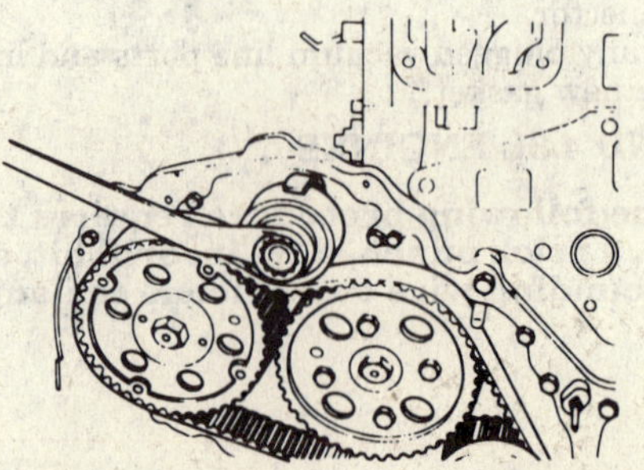

Loosening the tension pulley – 2.2L Diesel engine

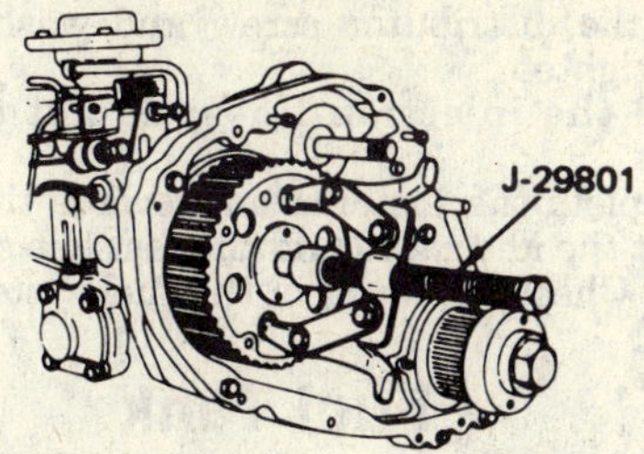

Removing the timing pulley — 2.2L Diesel engine

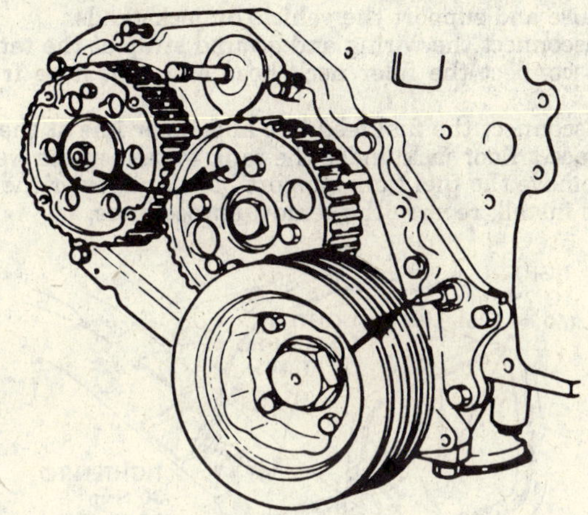

Correct timing mark alignment at TDC — 2.2L Diesel engine

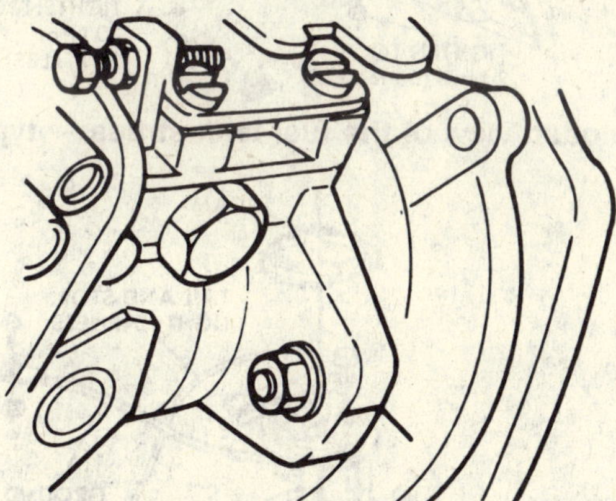

Injection pump and flange alignment — 2.2L Diesel engine

16. Remove injection pump flange fixing nuts and rear bracket bolts, then remove the injection pump.

To Install:

17. Install the injection pump by aligning the notched line on the flange with the line on the front bracket.
18. Install the injection pump timing pulley by aligning it with the key groove, then torque the bolts to 42–52 ft. lbs.
19. Position the piston of the No. 1 cylinder to TDC of the compression stoke and align marks on the timing pulleys.
20. Refer to the "Timing Belt, Installation" procedures in Section 3, then install and adjust the timing belt.
21. Check the injection timing.
22. To complete the installation, reverse the removal procedures.

TESTING AND ADJUSTMENT

NOTE: The following procedure requires the use of the Static Timing Gauge tool J-29763 or equivalent.

1. Check that notched line on the injection pump flange is in alignment with notched line on the injection pump front bracket.

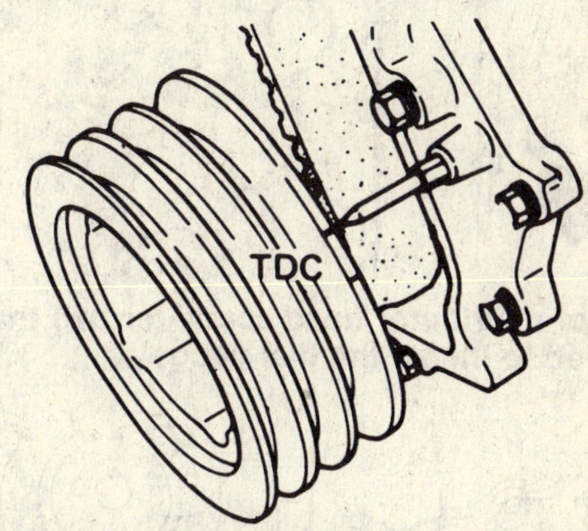

View of the No. 1 piston at TDC — 2.2L Diesel engine

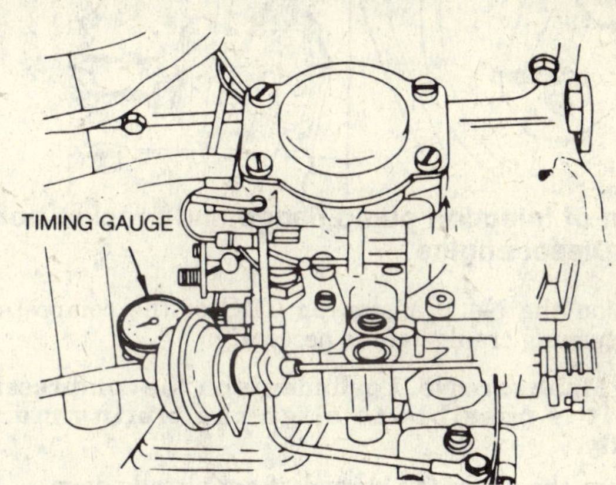

Injection timing dial gauge installed in injection pump — 2.2L Diesel engine

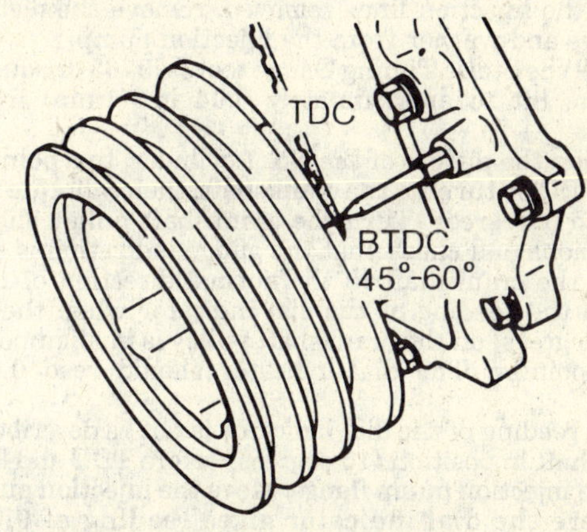

Bring the No. 1 piston to 45–60 degrees BTDC and then zero the dial gauge before adjusting the injection timing — 2.2L Diesel engine

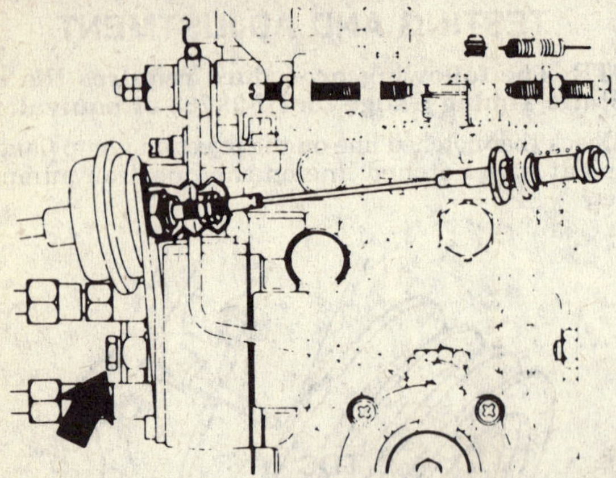

Location of distributor head screw (arrow) that must be removed to install the dial gauge

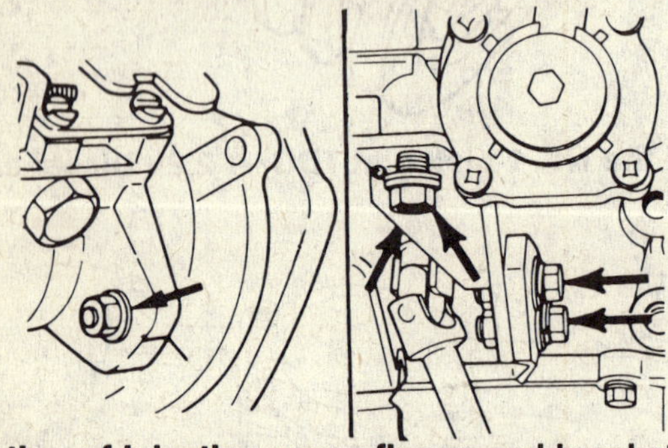

Location of injection pump flange and bracket bolts – 2.2L Diesel engine

2. Position the No. 1 piston on TDC of the compression stroke by turning crankshaft as necessary.

NOTE: Make sure No. 1 cylinder is on the compression stroke; it is possible to align the timing marks incorrectly.

3. Remove the upper fan shroud, if not already done.
4. With the upper cover removed, check that the timing belt is properly tensioned and that the timing marks are properly aligned. If the marks are not aligned properly, the timing belt will have to be removed and readjusted.
5. With the injection lines removed, remove the distributor head screws and washer from the injection pump.
6. Install the Static Timing Gauge tool J-29763 or equivalent, and set the lift to approximately 0.04 in. (1mm) from the plunger.
7. Position the piston, of the No. 1 cylinder, to a point 45–60 degrees BTDC by turning the crankshaft, then calibrate the dial indicator to 0 degrees. Turn the crankshaft pulley slightly in both directions and check that the gauge indication is stable.
8. Turn the crankshaft in the normal direction of rotation and record the reading of the dial indicator when the timing mark (15 degrees) on the crankshaft pulley is in alignment with the TDC pointer. The dial indicator should read 0.020 in. (0.5mm).
9. If the reading of the dial indicator is not as described, hold the crankshaft in position (15 degrees) before TDC and loosen 2 nuts on the injection pump flange. Move the injection pump to a point where the dial indicator gives reading of 0.020 in. (0.5mm), then tighten pump flange nuts.
10. Recheck the dial indicator reading and readjust the injection pump as necessary. Remove the dial indicator from the pump.
11. Install the distributor screw and washer into injection pump, then tighten.
12. Install the injection lines; do not overtighten the connections.
13. To complete the installation, reverse the removal procedures. Adjust the idle speed and the fast idle speed as described in Section 2. Check for leaks in the fuel system and correct, if necessary.

Fuel Tank

REMOVAL AND INSTALLATION

1. Drain the tank.
2. Raise and support the vehicle on jackstands.
3. Disconnect the wiring and ground strap at the tank.
4. Disconnect the filler neck hose and vent hose from the tank.
5. Disconnect the fuel feed line and vapor line at the tank.
6. Place a floor jack under the tank to take up its weight.
7. Remove the fuel tank support bolts and lower the tank.
8. To install, reverse the removal procedures.

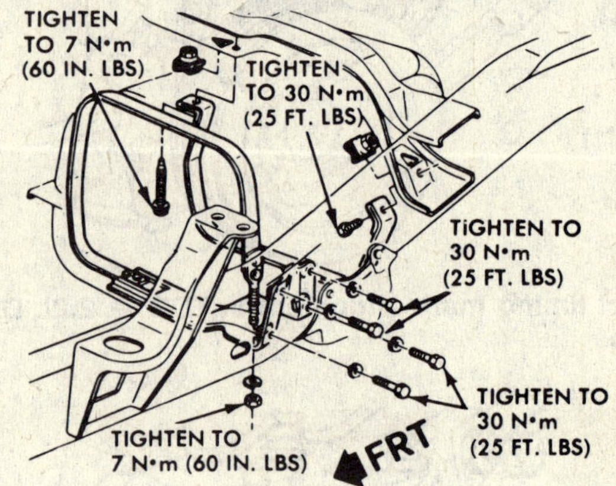

Exploded view of the fuel tank straps – typical

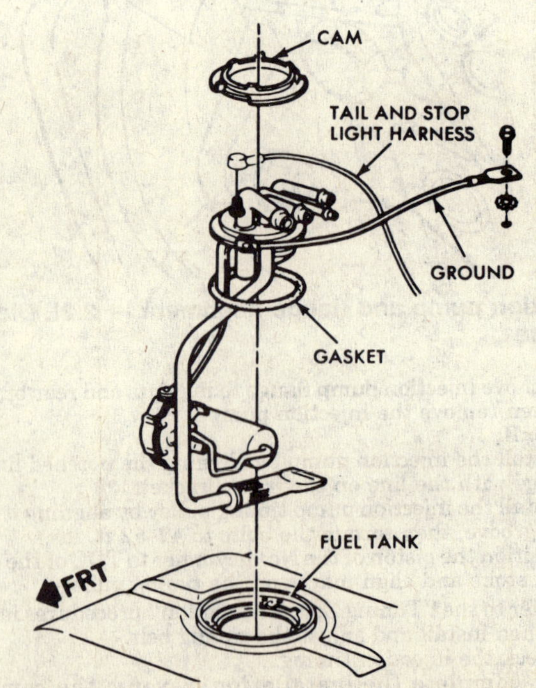

Exploded view of the fuel meter assembly – typical

6 Chassis Electrical

QUICK REFERENCE INDEX

GENERAL INDEX

6 CHASSIS ELECTRICAL

UNDERSTANDING AND TROUBLESHOOTING ELECTRICAL SYSTEMS

At the rate which both import and domestic manufacturers are incorporating electronic control systems into their production lines, it won't be long before every new vehicle is equipped with one or more on-board computer, like the unit installed on your truck. These electronic components (with no moving parts) should theoretically last the life of the vehicle, provided nothing external happens to damage the circuits or memory chips.

While it is true that electronic components should never wear out, in the real world malfunctions do occur. It is also true that any computer-based system is extremely sensitive to electrical voltages and cannot tolerate careless or haphazard testing or service procedures. An inexperienced individual can literally do major damage looking for a minor problem by using the wrong kind of test equipment or connecting test leads or connectors with the ignition switch ON. When selecting test equipment, make sure the manufacturers instructions state that the tester is compatible with whatever type of electronic control system is being serviced. Read all instructions carefully and double check all test points before installing probes or making any test connections.

The following section outlines basic diagnosis techniques for dealing with computerized automotive control systems. Along with a general explanation of the various types of test equipment available to aid in servicing modern electronic automotive systems, basic repair techniques for wiring harnesses and connectors is given. Read the basic information before attempting any repairs or testing on any computerized system, to provide the background of information necessary to avoid the most common and obvious mistakes that can cost both time and money. Although the replacement and testing procedures are simple in themselves, the systems are not, and unless one has a thorough understanding of all components and their function within a particular computerized control system, the logical test sequence these systems demand cannot be followed. Minor malfunctions can make a big difference, so it is important to know how each component affects the operation of the overall electronic system to find the ultimate cause of a problem without replacing good components unnecessarily. It is not enough to use the correct test equipment; the test equipment must be used correctly.

Safety Precautions

CAUTION

Whenever working on or around any computer based microprocessor control system, always observe these general precautions to prevent the possibility of personal injury or damage to electronic components.

- Never install or remove battery cables with the key ON or the engine running. Jumper cables should be connected with the key OFF to avoid power surges that can damage electronic control units. Engines equipped with computer controlled systems should avoid both giving and getting jump starts due to the possibility of serious damage to components from arcing in the engine compartment when connections are made with the ignition ON.
- Always remove the battery cables before charging the battery. Never use a high output charger on an installed battery or attempt to use any type of "hot shot" (24 volt) starting aid.
- Exercise care when inserting test probes into connectors to insure good connections without damaging the connector or spreading the pins. Always probe connectors from the rear (wire) side, NOT the pin side, to avoid accidental shorting of terminals during test procedures.
- Never remove or attach wiring harness connectors with the ignition switch ON, especially to an electronic control unit.
- Do not drop any components during service procedures and never apply 12 volts directly to any component (like a solenoid or relay) unless instructed specifically to do so. Some component electrical windings are designed to safely handle only 4 or 5 volts and can be destroyed in seconds if 12 volts are applied directly to the connector.
- Remove the electronic control unit if the vehicle is to be placed in an environment where temperatures exceed approximately 176°F (80°C), such as a paint spray booth or when arc or gas welding near the control unit location in the car.

ORGANIZED TROUBLESHOOTING

When diagnosing a specific problem, organized troubleshooting is a must. The complexity of a modern automobile demands that you approach any problem in a logical, organized manner. There are certain troubleshooting techniques that are standard:

1. Establish when the problem occurs. Does the problem appear only under certain conditions? Were there any noises, odors, or other unusual symptoms?
2. Isolate the problem area. To do this, make some simple tests and observations; then eliminate the systems that are working properly. Check for obvious problems such as broken wires, dirty connections or split or disconnected vacuum hoses. Always check the obvious before assuming something complicated is the cause.
3. Test for problems systematically to determine the cause once the problem area is isolated. Are all the components functioning properly? Is there power going to electrical switches and motors? Is there vacuum at vacuum switches and/or actuators? Is there a mechanical problem such as bent linkage or loose mounting screws? Doing careful, systematic checks will often turn up most causes on the first inspection without wasting time checking components that have little or no relationship to the problem.
4. Test all repairs after the work is done to make sure that the problem is fixed. Some causes can be traced to more than one component, so a careful verification of repair work is important to pick up additional malfunctions that may cause a problem to reappear or a different problem to arise. A blown fuse, for example, is a simple problem that may require more than another fuse to repair. If you don't look for a problem that caused a fuse to blow, for example, a shorted wire may go undetected.

Experience has shown that most problems tend to be the result of a fairly simple and obvious cause, such as loose or corroded connectors or air leaks in the intake system; making careful inspection of components during testing essential to quick and accurate troubleshooting. Special, hand held computerized testers designed specifically for diagnosing the system are available from a variety of after market sources, as well as from the vehicle manufacturer, but care should be taken that any test equipment being used is designed to diagnose that particular computer controlled system accurately without damaging the control unit (ECU) or components being tested.

NOTE: Pinpointing the exact cause of trouble in an electrical system can sometimes only be accomplished by the use of special test equipment. The following describes commonly used test equipment and explains how to put it to best use in diagnosis. In addition to the information covered below, the manufacturer's instructions booklet provided with the tester should be read and clearly understood before attempting any test procedures.

TEST EQUIPMENT

Jumper Wires

Jumper wires are simple, yet extremely valuable, pieces of test equipment. Jumper wires are merely wires that are used to bypass sections of a circuit. The simplest type of jumper wire is merely a length of multistrand wire with an alligator clip at each end. Jumper wires are usually fabricated from lengths of standard automotive wire and whatever type of connector (alligator clip, spade connector or pin connector) that is required for the particular vehicle being tested. The well equipped tool box will have several different styles of jumper wires in several different lengths. Some jumper wires are made with three or more terminals coming from a common splice for special purpose testing. In cramped, hard-to-reach areas it is advisable to have insulated boots over the jumper wire terminals in order to prevent accidental grounding, sparks, and possible fire, especially when testing fuel system components.

Jumper wires are used primarily to locate open electrical circuits, on either the ground (−) side of the circuit or on the hot (+) side. If an electrical component fails to operate, connect the jumper wire between the component and a good ground. If the component operates only with the jumper installed, the ground circuit is open. If the ground circuit is good, but the component does not operate, the circuit between the power feed and component is open. You can sometimes connect the jumper wire directly from the battery to the hot terminal of the component, but first make sure the component uses 12 volts in operation. Some electrical components, such as fuel injectors, are designed to operate on about 4 volts and running 12 volts directly to the injector terminals can burn out the wiring. By inserting an inline fuse holder between a set of test leads, a fused jumper wire can be used for bypassing open circuits. Use a 5 amp fuse to provide protection against voltage spikes. When in doubt, use a voltmeter to check the voltage input to the component and measure how much voltage is being applied normally. By moving the jumper wire successively back from the lamp toward the power source, you can isolate the area of the circuit where the open is located. When the component stops functioning, or the power is cut off, the open is in the segment of wire between the jumper and the point previously tested.

CAUTION

Never use jumpers made from wire that is of lighter gauge than used in the circuit under test. If the jumper wire is of too small gauge, it may overheat and possibly melt. Never use jumpers to bypass high resistance loads (such as motors) in a circuit. Bypassing resistances, in effect, creates a short circuit which may, in turn, cause damage and fire. Never use a jumper for anything other than temporary bypassing of components in a circuit.

12 Volt Test Light

The 12 volt test light is used to check circuits and components while electrical current is flowing through them. It is used for voltage and ground tests. Twelve volt test lights come in different styles but all have three main parts; a ground clip, a probe, and a light. The most commonly used 12 volt test lights have pick-type probes. To use a 12 volt test light, connect the ground clip to a good ground and probe wherever necessary with the pick. The pick should be sharp so that it can penetrate wire insulation to make contact with the wire, without making a large hole in the insulation. The wrap-around light is handy in hard to reach areas or where it is difficult to support a wire to push a probe pick into it. To use the wrap around light, hook the wire to probed with the hook and pull the trigger. A small pick will be forced through the wire insulation into the wire core.

CAUTION

Do not use a test light to probe electronic ignition spark plug or coil wires. Never use a pick-type test light to probe wiring on computer controlled systems unless specifically instructed to do so. Any wire insulation that is pierced by the test light probe should be taped and sealed with silicone after testing.

Like the jumper wire, the 12 volt test light is used to isolate opens in circuits. But, whereas the jumper wire is used to bypass the open to operate the load, the 12 volt test light is used to locate the presence of voltage in a circuit. If the test light glows, you know that there is power up to that point; if the 12 volt test light does not glow when its probe is inserted into the wire or connector, you know that there is an open circuit (no power). Move the test light in successive steps back toward the power source until the light in the handle does glow. When it does glow, the open is between the probe and point previously probed.

NOTE: The test light does not detect that 12 volts (or any particular amount of voltage) is present; it only detects that some voltage is present. It is advisable before using the test light to touch its terminals across the battery posts to make sure the light is operating properly.

Self-Powered Test Light

The self-powered test light usually contains a 1.5 volt penlight battery. One type of self-powered test light is similar in design to the 12 volt test light. This type has both the battery and the light in the handle and pick-type probe tip. The second type has the light toward the open tip, so that the light illuminates the contact point. The self-powered test light is dual purpose piece of test equipment. It can be used to test for either open or short circuits when power is isolated from the circuit (continuity test). A powered test light should not be used on any computer controlled system or component unless specifically instructed to do so. Many engine sensors can be destroyed by even this small amount of voltage applied directly to the terminals.

Open Circuit Testing

To use the self-powered test light to check for open circuits, first isolate the circuit from the vehicle's 12 volt power source by disconnecting the battery or wiring harness connector. Connect the test light ground clip to a good ground and probe sections of the circuit sequentially with the test light. (start from either end of the circuit). If the light is out, the open is between the probe and the circuit ground. If the light is on, the open is between the probe and end of the circuit toward the power source.

Short Circuit Testing

By isolating the circuit both from power and from ground, and using a self-powered test light, you can check for shorts to ground in the circuit. Isolate the circuit from power and ground. Connect the test light ground clip to a good ground and probe any easy-to-reach test point in the circuit. If the light comes on, there is a short somewhere in the circuit. To isolate the short, probe a test point at either end of the isolated circuit (the light should be on). Leave the test light probe connected and open connectors, switches, remove parts, etc., sequentially, until the light goes out. When the light goes out, the short is between the last circuit component opened and the previous circuit opened.

NOTE: The 1.5 volt battery in the test light does not provide much current. A weak battery may not provide enough power to illuminate the test light even when a complete circuit is made (especially if there are high resistances in the circuit). Always make sure that the test battery is strong. To check the battery, briefly touch the ground clip to the probe; if the light glows brightly the

battery is strong enough for testing. Never use a self-powered test light to perform checks for opens or shorts when power is applied to the electrical system under test. The 12 volt vehicle power will quickly burn out the 1.5 volt light bulb in the test light.

Voltmeter

A voltmeter is used to measure voltage at any point in a circuit, or to measure the voltage drop across any part of a circuit. It can also be used to check continuity in a wire or circuit by indicating current flow from one end to the other. Voltmeters usually have various scales on the meter dial and a selector switch to allow the selection of different voltages. The voltmeter has a positive and a negative lead. To avoid damage to the meter, always connect the negative lead to the negative (–) side of circuit (to ground or nearest the ground side of the circuit) and connect the positive lead to the positive (+) side of the circuit (to the power source or the nearest power source). Note that the negative voltmeter lead will always be black and that the positive voltmeter will always be some color other than black (usually red). Depending on how the voltmeter is connected into the circuit, it has several uses.

A voltmeter can be connected either in parallel or in series with a circuit and it has a very high resistance to current flow. When connected in parallel, only a small amount of current will flow through the voltmeter current path; the rest will flow through the normal circuit current path and the circuit will work normally. When the voltmeter is connected in series with a circuit, only a small amount of current can flow through the circuit. The circuit will not work properly, but the voltmeter reading will show if the circuit is complete or not.

Available Voltage Measurement

Set the voltmeter selector switch to the 20V position and connect the meter negative lead to the negative post of the battery. Connect the positive meter lead to the positive post of the battery and turn the ignition switch ON to provide a load. Read the voltage on the meter or digital display. A well charged battery should register over 12 volts. If the meter reads below 11.5 volts, the battery power may be insufficient to operate the electrical system properly. This test determines voltage available from the battery and should be the first step in any electrical trouble diagnosis procedure. Many electrical problems, especially on computer controlled systems, can be caused by a low state of charge in the battery. Excessive corrosion at the battery cable terminals can cause a poor contact that will prevent proper charging and full battery current flow.

Normal battery voltage is 12 volts when fully charged. When the battery is supplying current to one or more circuits it is said to be "under load". When everything is off the electrical system is under a "no-load" condition. A fully charged battery may show about 12.5 volts at no load; will drop to 12 volts under medium load; and will drop even lower under heavy load. If the battery is partially discharged the voltage decrease under heavy load may be excessive, even though the battery shows 12 volts or more at no load. When allowed to discharge further, the battery's available voltage under load will decrease more severely. For this reason, it is important that the battery be fully charged during all testing procedures to avoid errors in diagnosis and incorrect test results.

Voltage Drop

When current flows through a resistance, the voltage beyond the resistance is reduced (the larger the current, the greater the reduction in voltage). When no current is flowing, there is no voltage drop because there is no current flow. All points in the circuit which are connected to the power source are at the same voltage as the power source. The total voltage drop always equals the total source voltage. In a long circuit with many connectors, a series of small, unwanted voltage drops due to corrosion at the connectors can add up to a total loss of voltage which impairs the operation of the normal loads in the circuit.

INDIRECT COMPUTATION OF VOLTAGE DROPS

1. Set the voltmeter selector switch to the 20 volt position.
2. Connect the meter negative lead to a good ground.
3. Probe all resistances in the circuit with the positive meter lead.
4. Operate the circuit in all modes and observe the voltage readings.

DIRECT MEASUREMENT OF VOLTAGE DROPS

1. Set the voltmeter switch to the 20 volt position.
2. Connect the voltmeter negative lead to the ground side of the resistance load to be measured.
3. Connect the positive lead to the positive side of the resistance or load to be measured.
4. Read the voltage drop directly on the 20 volt scale.

Too high a voltage indicates too high a resistance. If, for example, a blower motor runs too slowly, you can determine if there is too high a resistance in the resistor pack. By taking voltage drop readings in all parts of the circuit, you can isolate the problem. Too low a voltage drop indicates too low a resistance. If, for example, a blower motor runs too fast in the MED and/or LOW position, the problem can be isolated in the resistor pack by taking voltage drop readings in all parts of the circuit to locate a possibly shorted resistor. The maximum allowable voltage drop under load is critical, especially if there is more than one high resistance problem in a circuit because all voltage drops are cumulative. A small drop is normal due to the resistance of the conductors.

HIGH RESISTANCE TESTING

1. Set the voltmeter selector switch to the 4 volt position.
2. Connect the voltmeter positive lead to the positive post of the battery.
3. Turn on the headlights and heater blower to provide a load.
4. Probe various points in the circuit with the negative voltmeter lead.
5. Read the voltage drop on the 4 volt scale. Some average maximum allowable voltage drops are:

FUSE PANEL – 7 volts
IGNITION SWITCH – 5 volts
HEADLIGHT SWITCH – 7 volts
IGNITION COIL (+) – 5 volts
ANY OTHER LOAD – 1.3 volts

NOTE: Voltage drops are all measured while a load is operating; without current flow, there will be no voltage drop.

Ohmmeter

The ohmmeter is designed to read resistance (ohms) in a circuit or component. Although there are several different styles of ohmmeters, all will usually have a selector switch which permits the measurement of different ranges of resistance (usually the selector switch allows the multiplication of the meter reading by 10, 100, 1000, and 10,000). A calibration knob allows the meter to be set at zero for accurate measurement. Since all ohmmeters are powered by an internal battery (usually 9 volts), the ohmmeter can be used as a self-powered test light. When the ohmmeter is connected, current from the ohmmeter flows through the circuit or component being tested. Since the ohmmeter's internal resistance and voltage are known values, the amount of current flow through the meter depends on the resistance of the circuit or component being tested.

The ohmmeter can be used to perform continuity test for opens or shorts (either by observation of the meter needle or as a self-powered test light), and to read actual resistance in a circuit. It should be noted that the ohmmeter is used to check the resistance of a component or wire while there is no voltage applied to the circuit. Current flow from an outside voltage source (such as the vehicle battery) can damage the ohmmeter, so the circuit or component should be isolated from the vehicle electrical system before any testing is done. Since the ohmmeter uses its own voltage source, either lead can be connected to any test point.

NOTE: When checking diodes or other solid state components, the ohmmeter leads can only be connected one way in order to measure current flow in a single direction. Make sure the positive (+) and negative (-) terminal connections are as described in the test procedures to verify the one-way diode operation.

In using the meter for making continuity checks, do not be concerned with the actual resistance readings. Zero resistance, or any resistance readings, indicate continuity in the circuit. Infinite resistance indicates an open in the circuit. A high resistance reading where there should be none indicates a problem in the circuit. Checks for short circuits are made in the same manner as checks for open circuits except that the circuit must be isolated from both power and normal ground. Infinite resistance indicates no continuity to ground, while zero resistance indicates a dead short to ground.

RESISTANCE MEASUREMENT

The batteries in an ohmmeter will weaken with age and temperature, so the ohmmeter must be calibrated or "zeroed" before taking measurements. To zero the meter, place the selector switch in its lowest range and touch the two ohmmeter leads together. Turn the calibration knob until the meter needle is exactly on zero.

NOTE: All analog (needle) type ohmmeters must be zeroed before use, but some digital ohmmeter models are automatically calibrated when the switch is turned on. Self-calibrating digital ohmmeters do not have an adjusting knob, but its a good idea to check for a zero readout before use by touching the leads together. All computer controlled systems require the use of a digital ohmmeter with at least 10 megohms impedance for testing. Before any test procedures are attempted, make sure the ohmmeter used is compatible with the electrical system or damage to the on-board computer could result.

To measure resistance, first isolate the circuit from the vehicle power source by disconnecting the battery cables or the harness connector. Make sure the key is OFF when disconnecting any components or the battery. Where necessary, also isolate at least one side of the circuit to be checked to avoid reading parallel resistances. Parallel circuit resistances will always give a lower reading than the actual resistance of either of the branches. When measuring the resistance of parallel circuits, the total resistance will always be lower than the smallest resistance in the circuit. Connect the meter leads to both sides of the circuit (wire or component) and read the actual measured ohms on the meter scale. Make sure the selector switch is set to the proper ohm scale for the circuit being tested to avoid misreading the ohmmeter test value.

CAUTION

Never use an ohmmeter with power applied to the circuit. Like the self-powered test light, the ohmmeter is designed to operate on its own power supply. The normal 12 volt automotive electrical system current could damage the meter.

Ammeters

An ammeter measures the amount of current flowing through a circuit in units called amperes or amps. Amperes are units of electron flow which indicate how fast the electrons are flowing through the circuit. Since Ohms Law dictates that current flow in a circuit is equal to the circuit voltage divided by the total circuit resistance, increasing voltage also increases the current level (amps). Likewise, any decrease in resistance will increase the amount of amps in a circuit. At normal operating voltage, most circuits have a characteristic amount of amperes, called "current draw" which can be measured using an ammeter. By referring to a specified current draw rating, measuring the amperes, and comparing the two values, one can determine what is happening within the circuit to aid in diagnosis. An open circuit, for example, will not allow any current to flow so the ammeter reading will be zero. More current flows through a heavily loaded circuit or when the charging system is operating.

An ammeter is always connected in series with the circuit being tested. All of the current that normally flows through the circuit must also flow through the ammeter; if there is any other path for the current to follow, the ammeter reading will not be accurate. The ammeter itself has very little resistance to current flow and therefore will not affect the circuit, but it will measure current draw only when the circuit is closed and electricity is flowing. Excessive current draw can blow fuses and drain the battery, while a reduced current draw can cause motors to run slowly, lights to dim and other components to not operate properly. The ammeter can help diagnose these conditions by locating the cause of the high or low reading.

Multimeters

Different combinations of test meters can be built into a single unit designed for specific tests. Some of the more common combination test devices are known as Volt/Amp testers, Tach/Dwell meters, or Digital Multimeters. The Volt/Amp tester is used for charging system, starting system or battery tests and consists of a voltmeter, an ammeter and a variable resistance carbon pile. The voltmeter will usually have at least two ranges for use with 6, 12 and 24 volt systems. The ammeter also has more than one range for testing various levels of battery loads and starter current draw and the carbon pile can be adjusted to offer different amounts of resistance. The Volt/Amp tester has heavy leads to carry large amounts of current and many later models have an inductive ammeter pickup that clamps around the wire to simplify test connections. On some models, the ammeter also has a zero-center scale to allow testing of charging and starting systems without switching leads or polarity. A digital multimeter is a voltmeter, ammeter and ohmmeter combined in an instrument which gives a digital readout. These are often used when testing solid state circuits because of their high input impedance (usually 10 megohms or more).

The tach/dwell meter combines a tachometer and a dwell (cam angle) meter and is a specialized kind of voltmeter. The tachometer scale is marked to show engine speed in rpm and the dwell scale is marked to show degrees of distributor shaft rotation. In most electronic ignition systems, dwell is determined by the control unit, but the dwell meter can also be used to check the duty cycle (operation) of some electronic engine control systems. Some tach/dwell meters are powered by an internal battery, while others take their power from the car battery in use. The battery powered testers usually require calibration much like an ohmmeter before testing.

Special Test Equipment

A variety of diagnostic tools are available to help troubleshoot and repair computerized engine control systems. The most sophisticated of these devices are the console type engine analyzers that usually occupy a garage service bay, but there are several types of aftermarket electronic testers available that will allow quick circuit tests of the engine control system by plugging directly into a special connector located in the engine compartment or under the dashboard. Several tool and equipment manufacturers offer simple, hand held testers that measure various circuit voltage levels on command to check all system components for proper operation. Although these testers usually cost about $300–500, consider that the average computer control unit (or ECM) can cost just as much and the money saved by not replacing perfectly good sensors or components in an attempt to correct a problem could justify the purchase price of a special diagnostic tester the first time it's used.

These computerized testers can allow quick and easy test measurements while the engine is operating or while the car is being driven. In addition, the on-board computer memory can be read to access any stored trouble codes; in effect allowing the computer to tell you where it hurts and aid trouble diagnosis by pinpointing exactly which circuit or component is malfunctioning. In the same manner, repairs can be tested to make sure the problem has been corrected. The biggest advantage these special testers have is their relatively easy hookups that minimize or eliminate the chances of making the wrong connections and getting false voltage readings or damaging the computer accidentally.

NOTE: It should be remembered that these testers check voltage levels in circuits; they don't detect mechanical problems or failed components if the circuit voltage falls within the preprogrammed limits stored in the tester PROM unit. Also, most of the hand held testers are designed to work only on one or two systems made by a specific manufacturer.

A variety of after market testers are available to help diagnose different computerized control systems. Owatonna Tool Company (OTC), for example, markets a device called the OTC Monitor which plugs directly into the assembly line diagnostic link (ALDL). The OTC tester makes diagnosis a simple matter of pressing the correct buttons and, by changing the internal PROM or inserting a different diagnosis cartridge, it will work on any model from full size to subcompact, over a wide range of years. An adapter is supplied with the tester to allow connection to all types of ALDL links, regardless of the number of pin terminals used. By inserting an updated PROM into the OTC tester, it can be easily updated to diagnose any new modifications of computerized control systems.

Wiring Harnesses

The average automobile contains about ½ mile of wiring, with hundreds of individual connections. To protect the many wires from damage and to keep them from becoming a confusing tangle, they are organized into bundles, enclosed in plastic or taped together and called wire harnesses. Different wiring harnesses serve different parts of the vehicle. Individual wires are color coded to help trace them through a harness where sections are hidden from view.

A loose or corroded connection or a replacement wire that is too small for the circuit will add extra resistance and an additional voltage drop to the circuit. A ten percent voltage drop can result in slow or erratic motor operation, for example, even though the circuit is complete. Automotive wiring or circuit conductors can be in any one of three forms:

1. Single strand wire
2. Multistrand wire
3. Printed circuitry

Single strand wire has a solid metal core and is usually used inside such components as alternators, motors, relays and other devices. Multistrand wire has a core made of many small strands of wire twisted together into a single conductor. Most of the wiring in an automotive electrical system is made up of multistrand wire, either as a single conductor or grouped together in a harness. All wiring is color coded on the insulator, either as a solid color or as a colored wire with an identification stripe. A printed circuit is a thin film of copper or other conductor that is printed on an insulator backing. Occasionally, a printed circuit is sandwiched between two sheets of plastic for more protection and flexibility. A complete printed circuit, consisting of conductors, insulating material and connectors for lamps or other components is called a printed circuit board. Printed circuitry is used in place of individual wires or harnesses in places where space is limited, such as behind instrument panels.

Wire Gauge

Since computer controlled automotive electrical systems are very sensitive to changes in resistance, the selection of properly sized wires is critical when systems are repaired. The wire gauge number is an expression of the cross section area of the conductor. The most common system for expressing wire size is the American Wire Gauge (AWG) system.

Wire cross section area is measured in circular mils. A mil is 1/000" (0.001"); a circular mil is the area of a circle one mil in diameter. For example, a conductor ¼" in diameter is 0.250 in. or 250 mils. The circular mil cross section area of the wire is 250 squared (250") or 62,500 circular mils. Imported car models usually use metric wire gauge designations, which is simply the cross section area of the conductor in square millimeters (mm).

Gauge numbers are assigned to conductors of various cross section areas. As gauge number increases, area decreases and the conductor becomes smaller. A 5 gauge conductor is smaller than a 1 gauge conductor and a 10 gauge is smaller than a 5 gauge. As the cross section area of a conductor decreases, resistance increases and so does the gauge number. A conductor with a higher gauge number will carry less current than a conductor with a lower gauge number.

NOTE: Gauge wire size refers to the size of the conductor, not the size of the complete wire. It is possible to have two wires of the same gauge with different diameters because one may have thicker insulation than the other.

12 volt automotive electrical systems generally use 10, 12, 14, 16 and 18 gauge wire. Main power distribution circuits and larger accessories usually use 10 and 12 gauge wire. Battery cables are usually 4 or 6 gauge, although 1 and 2 gauge wires are occasionally used. Wire length must also be considered when making repairs to a circuit. As conductor length increases, so does resistance. An 18 gauge wire, for example, can carry a 10 amp load for 10 feet without excessive voltage drop; however if a 15 foot wire is required for the same 10 amp load, it must be a 16 gauge wire.

An electrical schematic shows the electrical current paths when a circuit is operating properly. It is essential to understand how a circuit works before trying to figure out why it doesn't. Schematics break the entire electrical system down into individual circuits and show only one particular circuit. In a schematic, no attempt is made to represent wiring and components as they physically appear on the vehicle; switches and other components are shown as simply as possible. Face views of harness connectors show the cavity or terminal locations in all multi-pin connectors to help locate test points.

If you need to backprobe a connector while it is on the component, the order of the terminals must be mentally reversed. The wire color code can help in this situation, as well as a keyway, lock tab or other reference mark.

NOTE: Wiring diagrams are not included in this book. As trucks have become more complex and available with longer option lists, wiring diagrams have grown in size and complexity. It has become almost impossible to provide a readable reproduction of a wiring diagram in a book this size. Information on ordering wiring diagrams from the vehicle manufacturer can be found in the owner's manual.

WIRING REPAIR

Soldering is a quick, efficient method of joining metals permanently. Everyone who has the occasion to make wiring repairs should know how to solder. Electrical connections that are soldered are far less likely to come apart and will conduct electricity much better than connections that are only "pig-tailed" together. The most popular (and preferred) method of soldering is with an electrical soldering gun. Soldering irons are available in many sizes and wattage ratings. Irons with higher wattage ratings deliver higher temperatures and recover lost heat faster. A small soldering iron rated for no more than 50 watts is recommended, especially on electrical systems where excess heat can damage the components being soldered.

There are three ingredients necessary for successful soldering; proper flux, good solder and sufficient heat. A soldering flux is necessary to clean the metal of tarnish, prepare it for soldering and to enable the solder to spread into tiny crevices. When soldering, always use a resin flux or resin core solder which is non-corrosive and will not attract moisture once the job is finished. Other types of flux (acid core) will leave a residue that will attract moisture and cause the wires to corrode. Tin is a unique metal with a low melting point. In a molten state, it dissolves and alloys easily with many metals. Solder is made by mixing tin with lead. The most common proportions are 40/60, 50/50 and 60/40, with the percentage of tin listed first. Low priced solders usually contain less tin, making them very difficult for a beginner to use because more heat is required to melt the solder. A common solder is 40/60 which is well suited for all-around general use, but 60/40 melts easier, has more tin for a better joint and is preferred for electrical work.

Soldering Techniques

Successful soldering requires that the metals to be joined be heated to a temperature that will melt the solder—usually 360–460°F (182–238°C). Contrary to popular belief, the purpose of the soldering iron is not to melt the solder itself, but to heat the parts being soldered to a temperature high enough to melt the solder when it is touched to the work. Melting flux-cored solder on the soldering iron will usually destroy the effectiveness of the flux.

NOTE: Soldering tips are made of copper for good heat conductivity, but must be "tinned" regularly for quick transference of heat to the project and to prevent the solder from sticking to the iron. To "tin" the iron, simply heat it and touch the flux-cored solder to the tip; the solder will flow over the hot tip. Wipe the excess off with a clean rag, but be careful as the iron will be hot.

After some use, the tip may become pitted. If so, simply dress the tip smooth with a smooth file and "tin" the tip again. An old saying holds that "metals well cleaned are half soldered." Flux-cored solder will remove oxides but rust, bits of insulation and oil or grease must be removed with a wire brush or emery cloth. For maximum strength in soldered parts, the joint must start off clean and tight. Weak joints will result in gaps too wide for the solder to bridge.

If a separate soldering flux is used, it should be brushed or swabbed on only those areas that are to be soldered. Most solders contain a core of flux and separate fluxing is unnecessary. Hold the work to be soldered firmly. It is best to solder on a wooden board, because a metal vise will only rob the piece to be soldered of heat and make it difficult to melt the solder. Hold the soldering tip with the broadest face against the work to be soldered. Apply solder under the tip close to the work, using enough solder to give a heavy film between the iron and the piece being soldered, while moving slowly and making sure the solder melts properly. Keep the work level or the solder will run to the lowest part and favor the thicker parts, because these require more heat to melt the solder. If the soldering tip overheats (the solder coating on the face of the tip burns up), it should be retinned. Once the soldering is completed, let the soldered joint stand until cool. Tape and seal all soldered wire splices after the repair has cooled.

Wire Harness and Connectors

The on-board computer (ECM) wire harness electrically connects the control unit to the various solenoids, switches and sensors used by the control system. Most connectors in the engine compartment or otherwise exposed to the elements are protected against moisture and dirt which could create oxidation and deposits on the terminals. This protection is important because of the very low voltage and current levels used by the computer and sensors. All connectors have a lock which secures the male and female terminals together, with a secondary lock holding the seal and terminal into the connector. Both terminal locks must be released when disconnecting ECM connectors.

These special connectors are weather-proof and all repairs require the use of a special terminal and the tool required to service it. This tool is used to remove the pin and sleeve terminals. If removal is attempted with an ordinary pick, there is a good chance that the terminal will be bent or deformed. Unlike standard blade type terminals, these terminals cannot be straightened once they are bent. Make certain that the connectors are properly seated and all of the sealing rings in place when connecting leads. On some models, a hinge-type flap provides a backup or secondary locking feature for the terminals. Most secondary locks are used to improve the connector reliability by retaining the terminals if the small terminal lock tangs are not positioned properly.

Molded-on connectors require complete replacement of the connection. This means splicing a new connector assembly into the harness. All splices in on-board computer systems should be soldered to insure proper contact. Use care when probing the connections or replacing terminals in them as it is possible to short between opposite terminals. If this happens to the wrong terminal pair, it is possible to damage certain components. Always use jumper wires between connectors for circuit checking and never probe through weatherproof seals.

Open circuits are often difficult to locate by sight because corrosion or terminal misalignment are hidden by the connectors. Merely wiggling a connector on a sensor or in the wiring harness may correct the open circuit condition. This should always be considered when an open circuit or a failed sensor is indicated. Intermittent problems may also be caused by oxidized or loose connections. When using a circuit tester for diagnosis, always probe connections from the wire side. Be careful not to damage sealed connectors with test probes.

All wiring harnesses should be replaced with identical parts, using the same gauge wire and connectors. When signal wires are spliced into a harness, use wire with high temperature insulation only. With the low voltage and current levels found in the system, it is important that the best possible connection at all wire splices be made by soldering the splices together. It is seldom necessary to replace a complete harness. If replacement is necessary, pay close attention to insure proper harness routing. Secure the harness with suitable plastic wire clamps to prevent vibrations from causing the harness to wear in spots or contact any hot components.

NOTE: Weatherproof connectors cannot be replaced with standard connectors. Instructions are provided with replacement connector and terminal packages. Some wire harnesses have mounting indicators (usually pieces of colored tape) to mark where the harness is to be secured.

In making wiring repairs, it's important that you always replace damaged wires with wires that are the same gauge as the wire being replaced. The heavier the wire, the smaller the gauge number. Wires are color-coded to aid in identification and whenever possible the same color coded wire should be used for replacement. A wire stripping and crimping tool is necessary to install solderless terminal connectors. Test all crimps by pulling on the wires; it should not be possible to pull the wires out of a good crimp.

Wires which are open, exposed or otherwise damaged are repaired by simple splicing. Where possible, if the wiring harness is accessible and the damaged place in the wire can be located, it is best to open the harness and check for all possible damage. In an inaccessible harness, the wire must be bypassed with a new insert, usually taped to the outside of the old harness.

When replacing fusible links, be sure to use fusible link wire, NOT ordinary automotive wire. Make sure the fusible segment is of the same gauge and construction as the one being replaced and double the stripped end when crimping the terminal connector for a good contact. The melted (open) fusible link segment of the wiring harness should be cut off as close to the harness as possible, then a new segment spliced in as described. In the case of a damaged fusible link that feeds two harness wires, the harness connections should be replaced with two fusible link wires so that each circuit will have its own separate protection.

NOTE: Most of the problems caused in the wiring harness are due to bad ground connections. Always check all vehicle ground connections for corrosion or looseness before performing any power feed checks to eliminate the chance of a bad ground affecting the circuit.

Repairing Hard Shell Connectors

Unlike molded connectors, the terminal contacts in hard shell connectors can be replaced. Weatherproof hard-shell connectors with the leads molded into the shell have non-replaceable terminal ends. Replacement usually involves the use of a special terminal removal tool that depress the locking tangs (barbs) on the connector terminal and allow the connector to be removed from the rear of the shell. The connector shell should be replaced if it shows any evidence of burning, melting, cracks, or breaks. Replace individual terminals that are burnt, corroded, distorted or loose.

NOTE: The insulation crimp must be tight to prevent the insulation from sliding back on the wire when the wire is pulled. The insulation must be visibly compressed under the crimp tabs, and the ends of the crimp should be turned in for a firm grip on the insulation.

The wire crimp must be made with all wire strands inside the crimp. The terminal must be fully compressed on the wire strands with the ends of the crimp tabs turned in to make a firm grip on the wire. Check all connections with an ohmmeter to insure a good contact. There should be no measurable resistance between the wire and the terminal when connected.

Mechanical Test Equipment

Vacuum Gauge

Most gauges are graduated in inches of mercury (in.Hg), although a device called a manometer reads vacuum in inches of water (in. H2O). The normal vacuum reading usually varies between 18 and 22 in.Hg at sea level. To test engine vacuum, the vacuum gauge must be connected to a source of manifold vacuum. Many engines have a plug in the intake manifold which can be removed and replaced with an adapter fitting. Connect the vacuum gauge to the fitting with a suitable rubber hose or, if no manifold plug is available, connect the vacuum gauge to any device using manifold vacuum, such as EGR valves, etc. The vacuum gauge can be used to determine if enough vacuum is reaching a component to allow its actuation.

Hand Vacuum Pump

Small, hand-held vacuum pumps come in a variety of designs. Most have a built-in vacuum gauge and allow the component to be tested without removing it from the vehicle. Operate the pump lever or plunger to apply the correct amount of vacuum required for the test specified in the diagnosis routines. The level of vacuum in inches of Mercury (in.Hg) is indicated on the pump gauge. For some testing, an additional vacuum gauge may be necessary.

Intake manifold vacuum is used to operate various systems and devices on late model vehicles. To correctly diagnose and solve problems in vacuum control systems, a vacuum source is necessary for testing. In some cases, vacuum can be taken from the intake manifold when the engine is running, but vacuum is normally provided by a hand vacuum pump. These hand vacuum pumps have a built-in vacuum gauge that allow testing while the device is still attached to the component. For some tests, an additional vacuum gauge may be necessary.

HEATING AND AIR CONDITIONING

SYSTEM DESCRIPTION

The heater and air conditioning systems are controlled manually. The manual system controls can be cable-actuated or actuated through a vacuum switching valve and vacuum actuators.

The heating system provides heating, ventilation and defrosting for the windshield and, on some vehicles, the side windows. The heater core is a heat exchanger supplied with coolant from the engine cooling system. Temperature is controlled by the temperature valve which moves an air door that directs air flow through the heater core for more heat or bypasses the heater core for less heat.

The mode doors may be cable operated or controlled by vacuum actuators. On the vacuum controlled system, the mode selector on the control panel directs engine vacuum to the actuators. The position of the mode doors determines whe ther air flows from the floor, panel, defrost or panel and defrost ducts (bi-level mode).

The basic air conditioning refrigerant system used on these vehicles is called Cycling Clutch Orifice Tube (CCOT). On CCOT systems, the compressor cycles on and off according to

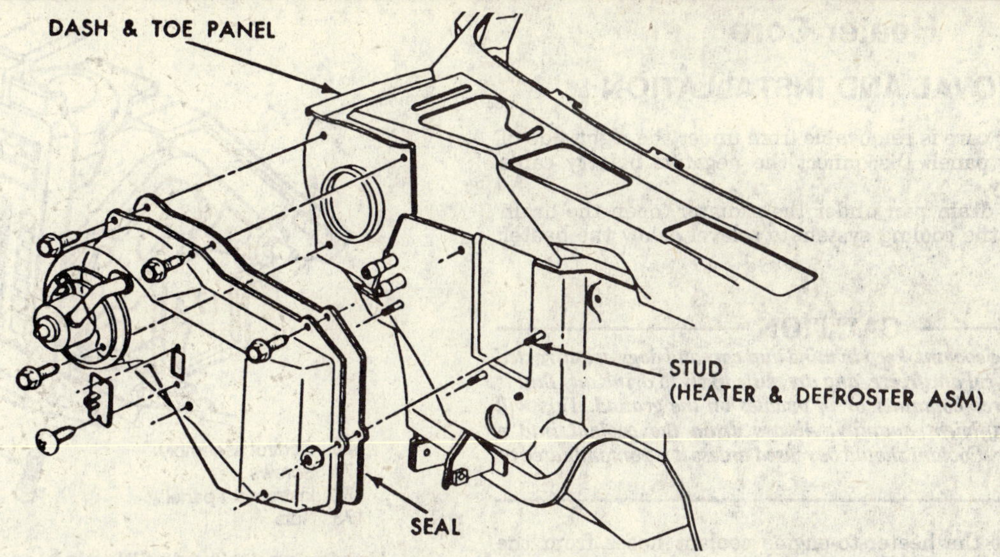

The blower motor can be removed from the heater case

system demands. The compressor driveshaft is driven by the serpentine belt when the electro-magnetic clutch is engaged. System pressure is controlled by the pressure cycling switch. The HR-6 compressor is a fixed displacement axial compressor consisting of 3 double-ended pistons actuated by a swash plate shaft assembly. The R-4 compressor uses a 4 cylinder radial opposed design.

Blower Motor

REMOVAL AND INSTALLATION

1. Disconnect the negative battery cable from the battery.

2. Disconnect the electrical connectors from the blower motor.

NOTE: On some earlier models equipped with air conditioning, it may be necessary to remove the air conditioning vacuum tank and move it aside.

3. Remove the blower motor-to-case screws, then lift the blower motor from the case.
4. To install, reverse the removal procedures. Torque the blower motor-to-case screws to 18 ft. lbs.

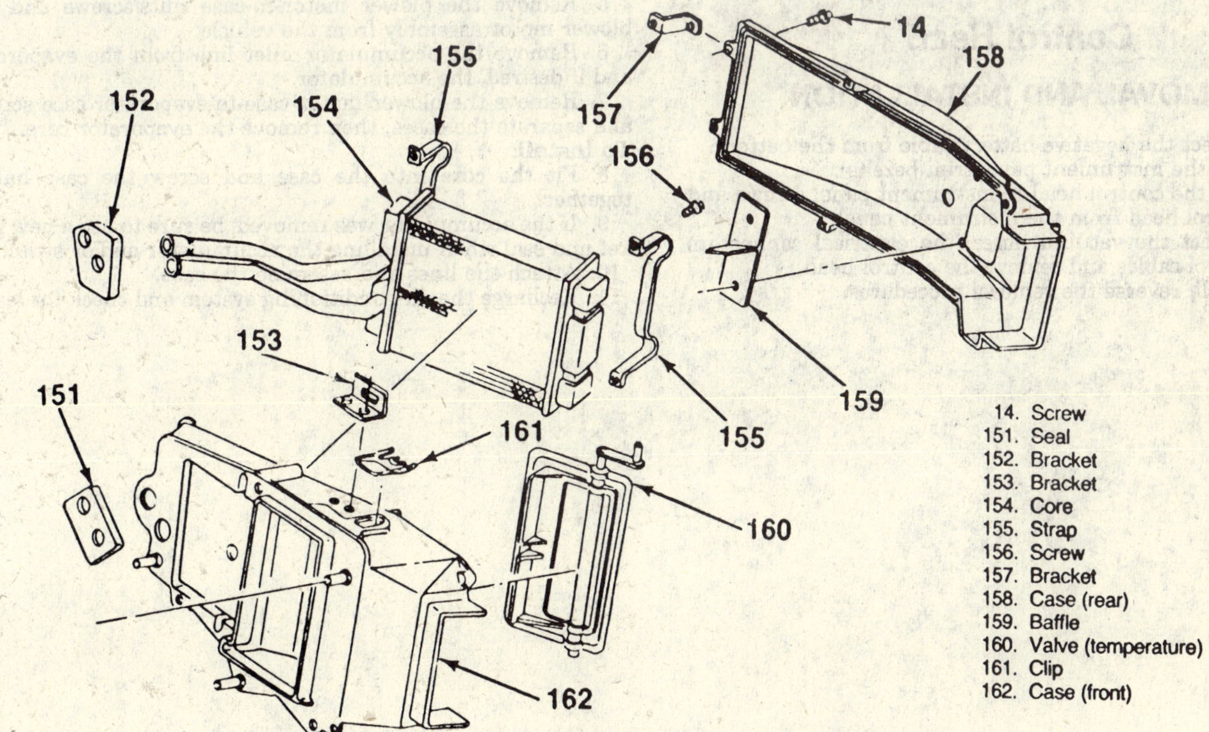

Heater core is removed from under the right side dashboard

Heater Core

REMOVAL AND INSTALLATION

1. The heater core is removable from under the right-side of the instrument panel. Disconnect the negative battery cable from the battery.
2. Position a drain pan under the radiator, open the drain cock and drain the cooling system to a level below the heater core.

CAUTION

When draining the coolant, keep in mind that cats and dogs are attracted by the ethylene glycol antifreeze, and are quite likely to drink any that is left in an uncovered container or in puddles on the ground. This will prove fatal in sufficient quantity. Always drain the coolant into a sealable container. Coolant should be reused unless it is contaminated or several years old.

3. Disconnect the heater-to-engine coolant hoses from the core tubes on the fire wall, in the engine compartment.

NOTE: Plug the heater core tubes to avoid spilling coolant in the passenger compartment during removal.

4. Remove the heater core cover-to-cowl screws and the cover from the vehicle.
5. Remove the brackets from each end of the heater core and lift out the heater core.
6. To install, position the heater core and secure the brackets.
7. Make sure the temperature valve is properly positioned and install the cover. Torque the rear cover-to-case screws to 27 inch lbs.
8. Connect the hoses, refill the cooling system and the start the engine to check for leaks.

Control Head

REMOVAL AND INSTALLATION

1. Disconnect the negative battery cable from the battery.
2. Remove the instrument panel trim bezel(s).
3. Remove the control head-to-instrument panel screws and pull the control head from the instrument panel.
4. Disconnect the vacuum hoses, the electrical connectors and the control cables and remove the control head.
5. To install, reverse the removal procedures.

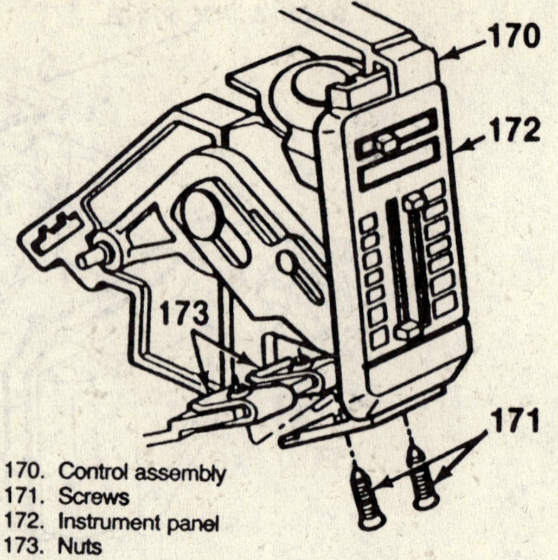

Heater and air conditioning controls removal

Evaporator Core and Accumulator

REMOVAL AND INSTALLATION

1. The evaporator core with the accumulator can be removed separately or as a unit from under the hood. Refer to "Discharging the Air Conditioning System" in Section 1 and discharge the air conditioning system.
2. Disconnect the negative battery cable from the battery.
3. Disconnect the electrical connectors from the resistor and the blower motor.
4. Remove the inlet line from the air conditioning evaporator.
5. Remove the blower motor-to-case nuts/screws and the blower motor assembly from the vehicle.
6. Remove the accumulator inlet line from the evaporator and if desired, the accumulator.
7. Remove the blower motor case-to-evaporator case screws and separate the cases, then remove the evaporator core.

To install:

8. Fit the core into the case and screw the case halves together.
9. If the accumulator was removed, be sure to use a new gasket and seal when installing the accumulator and/or switch.
10. Attach the lines and assemble the case.
11. Recharge the air conditioning system and check for leaks.

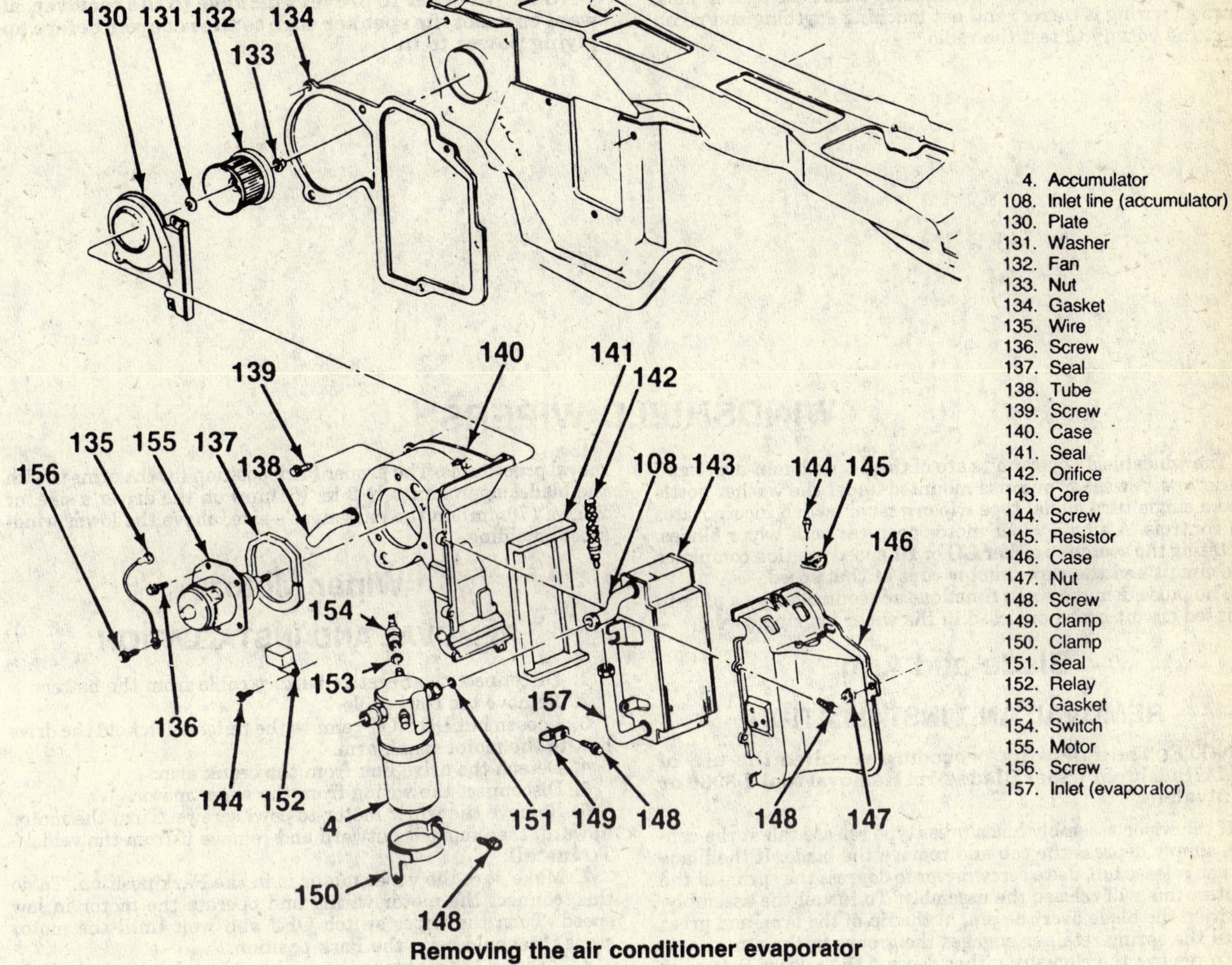

Removing the air conditioner evaporator

RADIO

REMOVAL AND INSTALLATION

1. Disconnect the negative battery cable from the battery.
2. Remove the ash tray and any necessary wires.
3. Remove the instrument panel center bezel and the support clip nuts.
4. Remove the radio bracket-to-instrument panel bracket screws and pull the radio forward.
5. Disconnect the antenna, the clock connector, the speaker connectors and any electrical wires, then remove the radio.

CAUTION

DO NOT let the antenna cable touch the clock connector! It is very important when changing speakers or performing any radio work to avoid pinching the wires. A short circuit-to-ground from any radio wire will cause damage to the output circuit in the radio.

6. To install, reconnect the clock, speaker and power wires, then the antenna.
7. Slide the radio into place and secure it with the bracket

screws. Before installing the remianing dash board parts, make sure all wiring is correct and not touching anything and reconnect the battery to test the radio.

NOTE: In order to prevent damage to the receiver, always connect the speaker wire to the receiver before applying power to it.

WINDSHIELD WIPERS

The windshield wiper units are of the 2-speed, non-depressed park type. A washer pump is mounted under the washer bottle and a single turn signal type wiper/washer switch incorporates all controls. A single wiper motor operates both wiper blades. Rotating the switch to either **LO** or **HI** speed position completes the circuit and the wiper motor runs at that speed.

The pulse/demand wash functions are controlled by a plug-in printed circuit board enclosed in the wiper housing cover.

Blade and Arm

REMOVAL AND INSTALLATION

NOTE: The following procedure requires the use of GM Windshield Wiper Blade/Arm Removal tool J-8966 or equivalent.

If the wiper assembly has a press type release tab at the center, simply depress the tab and remove the blade. If the blade has no release tab, use a screwdriver to depress the spring at the center; this will release the assembly. To install the assembly, position the blade over the pin, at the tip of the arm, and press until the spring retainer engages the groove in the pin.

To remove the element, either depress the release button or squeeze the spring type retainer clip, at the outer end, together and slide the blade element out. To install, slide the new element in until it latches.

1. Remove the wiper arm as described above. If equipped, disconnect the washer hose from the arm.
2. To install, operate the wiper motor (momentarily) to position the pivot shafts into the Park position and reverse the removal procedures. The proper Park position for the arms is with the blades approximately 2 in. (51mm) on the driver's side, or 2¾ in. (70mm) on the passenger's-side, above the lower windshield molding.

Using the GM wiper arm removal tool J-8966

Wiper Motor

REMOVAL AND INSTALLATION

1. Disconnect the negative battery cable from the battery.
2. Remove the cowl grille.
3. Loosen but DO NOT remove the nuts which hold the drive link to the motor crank arm.
4. Detach the drive link from the crank arm.
5. Disconnect the wiring from the wiper motor.
6. Remove the wiper motor-to-cowl screws. Turn the motor upward, then move it outward and remove it from the vehicle.

To install:

7. Make sure the wiper motor is in the Park position. To do this, connect the motor wiring and operate the motor in low speed. Turn the wiper switch OFF and wait until the motor stops. It should be in the Park position.
8. Position the motor to the cowl and loosely attach the linkage. Torque the wiper motor-to-cowl screws to 50–75 inch lbs.
9. Place the wiper arms into the Park position and secure the linkage to the motor. Test the system before installing the remaining body parts.

Wiper Linkage

REMOVAL AND INSTALLATION

1. Disconnect the negative battery cable from the battery.
2. Using the GM Windshield Wiper Blade/Arm Removal tool J-8966 or equivalent, remove the wiper arms.
3. Remove the cowl grille.
4. Remove the wiper linkage-to-motor clamp.
5. Remove the wiper linkage-to-cowl panel screws.
6. To install, reverse the removal procedures. Torque the wiper linkage-to-panel screws to 50–80 inch lbs.

Rear Wiper Motor

REMOVAL AND INSTALLATION

1. Disconnect the negative battery cable from the battery.
2. Remove the screws to remove the plastic cover from the rear wiper motor.

1. Arm, windshield wiper
2. Blade
   insert
3. Nozzle
4. Spacer, nozzle
5. Nut, type R stamped (M16)
6. Transmission, left hand
   transmission, right hand
7. Lever
8. Module
9. Lens, pulse switch
10. Knob, pulse switch
11. Nut, pulse module retaining
12. Reserovir
13. Bolt, (M6 × 1 × 25)
14. Hose, (5/32" ID)
15. Strap
16. Connector
17. Motor assembly
18. Bolt (M5 × .8 × 28)
19. Screw, (M6.3 × 1.69 × 20)
20. Pump

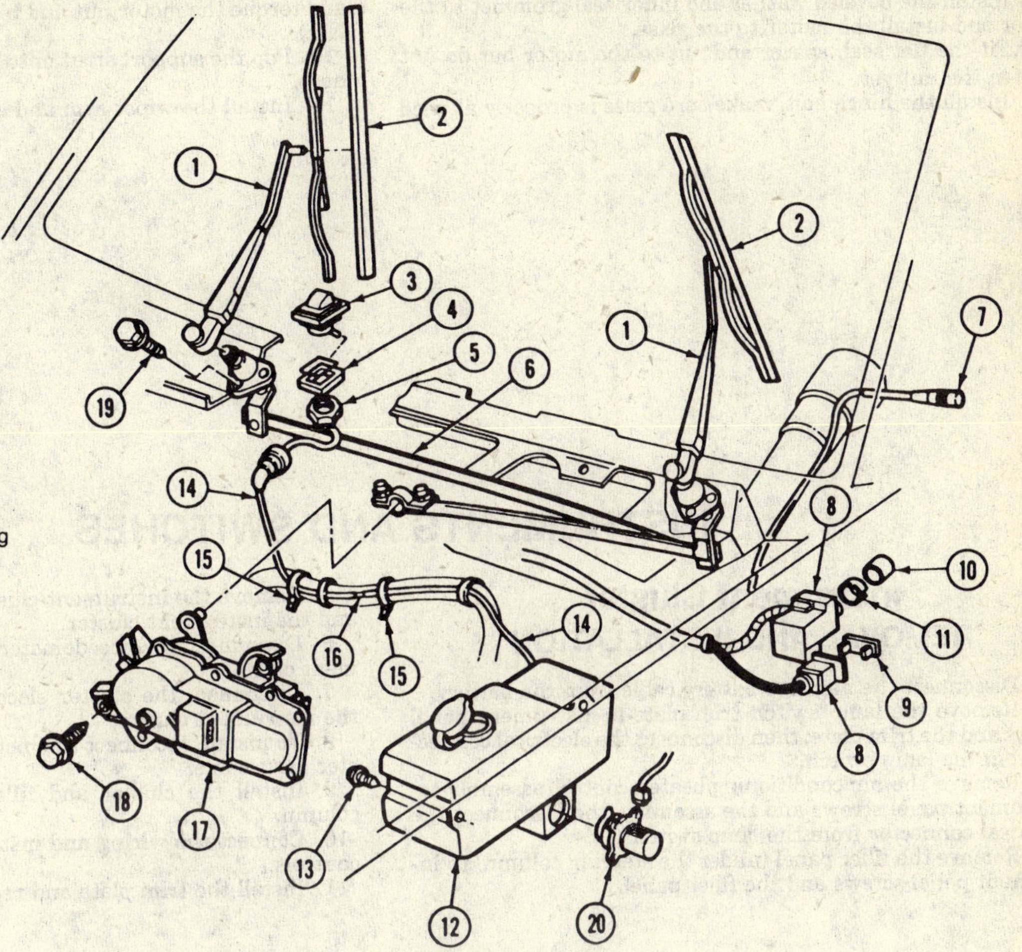

Windshield wiper and washer system

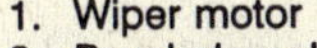

1. Wiper motor
2. Beveled washer
3. Inner seal grommet
4. Flat seal
5. Spacer
6. Nut
7. Hinge assembly
8. Wiper arm assembly
9. Cover
10. Retainer screws
11. Motor/hinge bolt
12. End gate glass

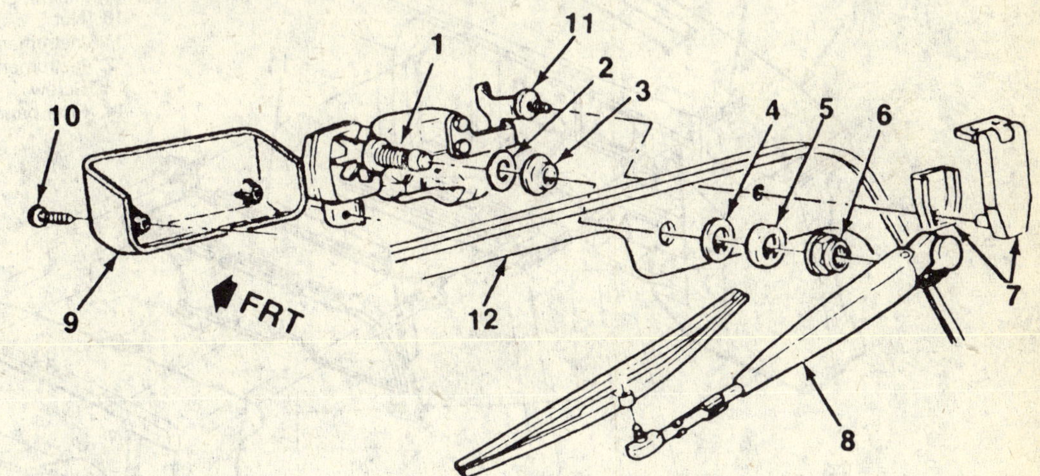

Rear wiper motor assembly: a hinge bolt also holds the motor

3. To remove the rear wiper arm, insert a 1/8 inch (3mm) drift pin through the hole in the arm hinge. This will depress the detent and the arm should pull right off.

4. Carefully pry off the support arm socket from the ball on the glass and support the glass.

5. One of the wiper motor bolts also holds the hinge to the glass. Make sure the glass is properly supported and unbolt the motor to remove it.

To install:

6. When installing the motor, replace all rubber sealing parts.

7. Install the beveled washer and inner seal grommet to the motor and install the motor to the glass.
8. Fit the flat seal, spacer and nut to the motor but do not tighten the nut yet.
9. Install the hinge bolt, make sure glass is properly aligned and torque the motor nut and hinge bolt both to 54 inch lbs. (6 Nm).
10. Pop the support strut onto the ball and attach the washer hose.
11. Install the wiper arm and cover.

INSTRUMENTS AND SWITCHES

Instrument Cluster

REMOVAL AND INSTALLATION

1. Disconnect the negative battery cable from the battery.
2. Remove the lamp switch trim plate-to-instrument panel screws and the trim plate, then disconnect the electrical connector from the lamp switch.
3. Remove the air conditioning/heater control assembly-to-instrument panel screws and the assembly, the disconnect the electrical connector from the lamp switch.
4. Remove the filler panel (under the steering column) to instrument panel screws and the filler panel.
5. Remove the instrument cluster-to-instrument panel nuts and the instrument cluster.
6. Disconnect the speedometer drive cable from the instrument cluster.
7. Disconnect the cluster electrical connectors and remove the instrument cluster.
8. To install, reconnect the instrument wiring and speedometer drive cable.
9. Install the cluster and filler panel under the steering column.
10. Connect the wiring and install the air conditioner/heater controls.
11. Install the trim plate and reconnect the battery.

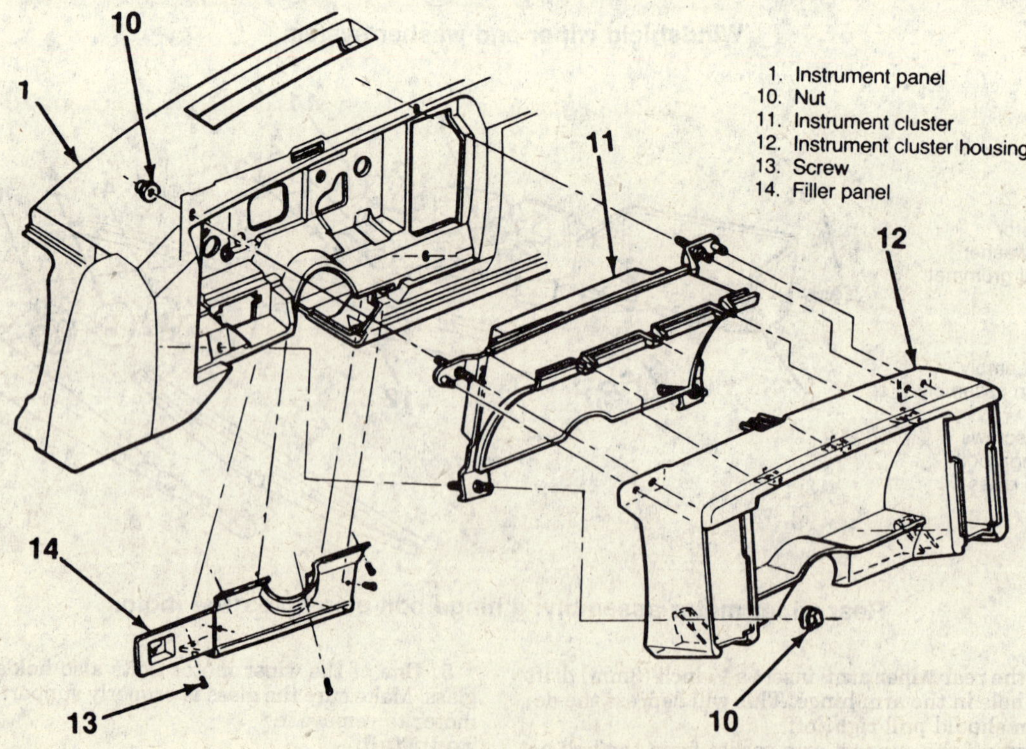

Instrument panel removal

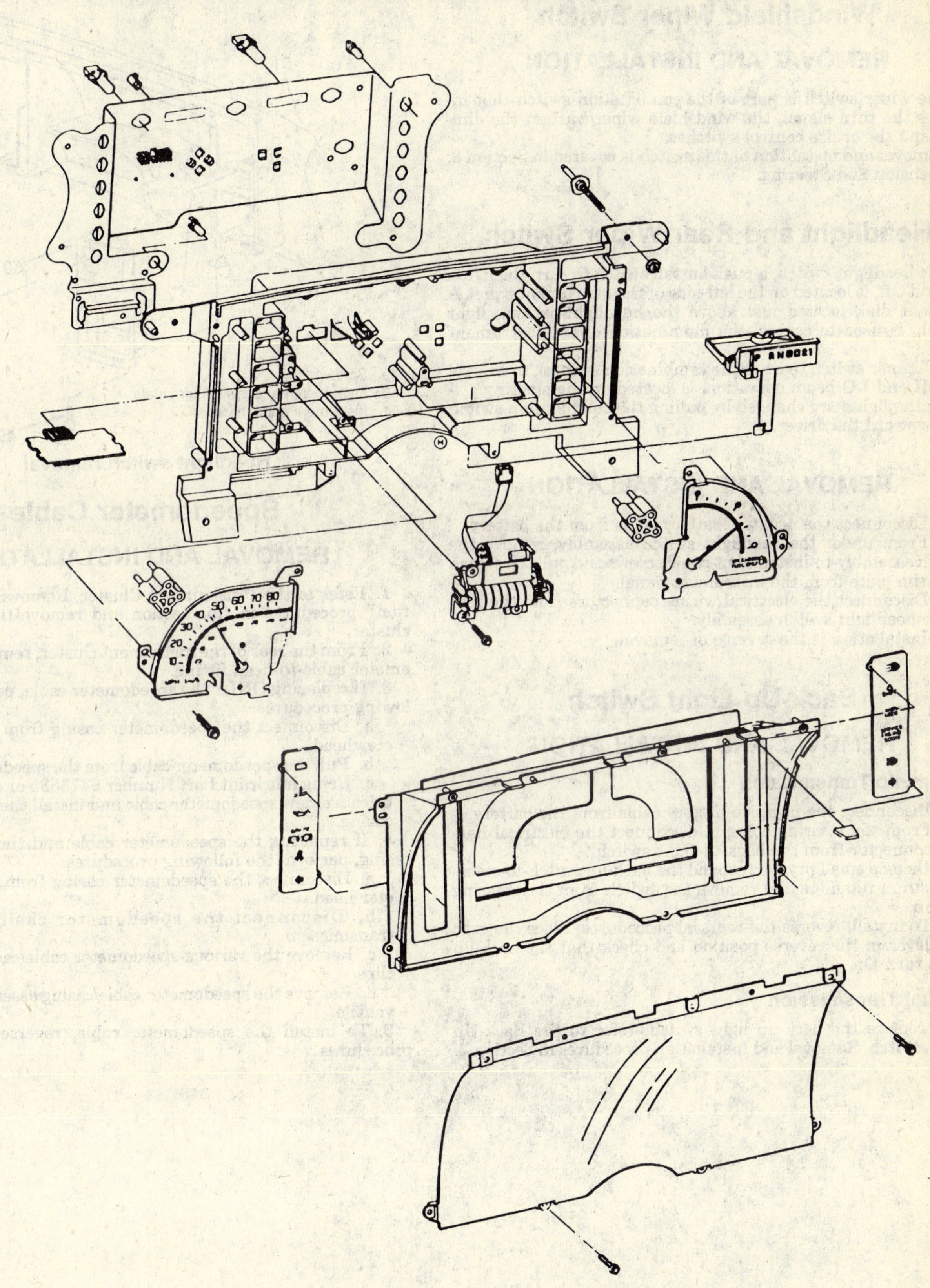

Instrument panel components

Windshield Wiper Switch

REMOVAL AND INSTALLATION

The wiper switch is part of the combination switch that includes the turn signal, the windshield wiper/washer, the dimmer and the cruise control switches.

Removal and installtion of this switch is covered in Section 8, Suspension and Steering.

Headlight and Rear Wiper Switch

The headlight switch, a push button switch to turn the lights On and Off, is located on the left-side of the instrument panel. A rheostat dial, located just above the headlight/parking light switch, is used to control the illumination of the instrument panel.

A dimmer switch (part of the combination switch), to control the **HI** and **LO** beam operation, is located on the steering column; the lights are changed by pulling the combination switch lever toward the driver.

REMOVAL AND INSTALLATION

1. Disconnect the negative battery cable from the battery.
2. From under the headlight switch assembly, remove the switch assembly-to-instrument panel screws and pull the switch and trim plate from the instrument panel.
3. Disconnect the electrical wiring connectors from the rear of the headlight switch assembly.
4. Installation is the reverse of removal.

Back-Up Light Switch

REMOVAL AND INSTALLATION

Automatic Transmission

1. Disconnect the negative battery cable from the battery.
2. From the steering column, disconnect the electrical harness connector from the back-up light switch.
3. Using a small pry bar, expand the back-up switch-to-steering column retainers and remove the switch from the steering column.
4. To install, reverse the removal procedures. Place the gear shift lever in the reverse position and check that the back-up lights turn On.

Manual Transmission

To replace the back-up light switch, refer to the Back-Up Light Switch, Removal and Installation procedures in Section 7.

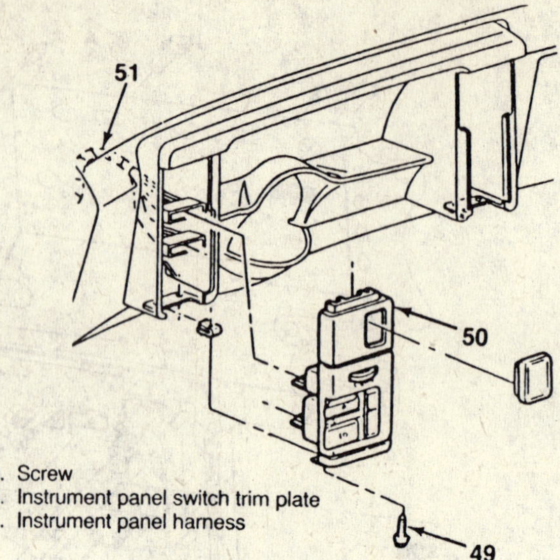

Headlight switch removal

Speedometer Cable

REMOVAL AND INSTALLATION

1. Refer to the "Instrument Cluster, Removal and Installation" procedures in this section and remove the instrument cluster.
2. From the rear of the instrument cluster, remove the speedometer cable-to-head fitting.
3. If replacing ONLY the speedometer cable, perform the following procedures:
   a. Disconnect the speedometer casing from the speedometer head.
   b. Pull the speedometer cable from the speedometer casing.
   c. Using lubricant Part Number 6478535 or equivalent, lubricate a new speedometer cable and install the cable into the casing.
4. If replacing the speedometer cable and the speedometer casing, perform the following procedures:
   a. Disconnect the speedometer casing from the speedometer head.
   b. Disconnect the speedometer casing from the transmission.
   c. Remove the various speedometer cable/casing retaining clips.
   d. Remove the speedometer cable/casing assembly from the vehicle.
5. To install the speedometer cable, reverse the removal procedures.

LIGHTING

Headlights

REMOVAL AND INSTALLATION

1. Disconnect the negative battery cable from the battery.
2. Remove the headlight-to-fender bezel and the retaining spring.
3. Rotate the headlight to the right and remove it from the adjusters.
4. Disconnect the electrical harness connector from the rear of the headlight and remove the headlight from the vehicle.
5. To install, reverse the removal procedures.

Signal and Marker Lights

REMOVAL AND INSTALLATION

Front Turn Signal/Marker Lights

1. Disconnect the negative battery cable from the battery.
2. Remove the headlight bezel-to-fender screws and the bezel; allow the bezel to hang by the turn signal/marker light wires.
3. At the rear of the headlight bezel, turn the turn signal/marker bulb socket ¼ turn and remove it from the headlight bezel.
4. Remove the bulb from the turn signal/marker bulb socket; if necessary, replace the bulb.

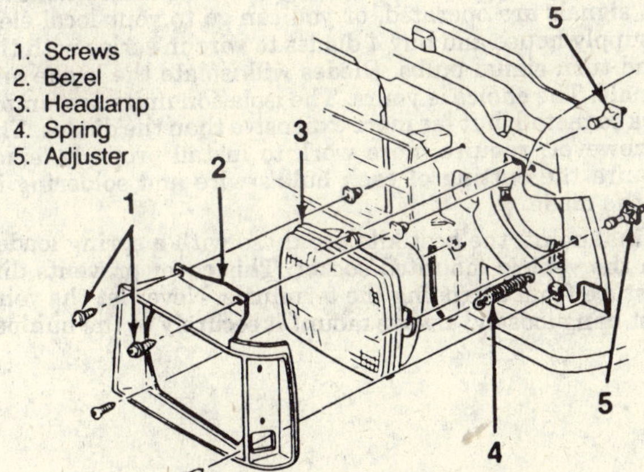

Headlight and adjuster assembly

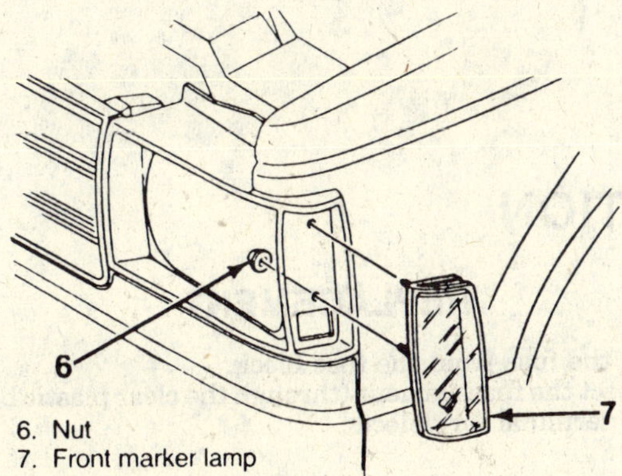

Front turn signal/marker light assembly

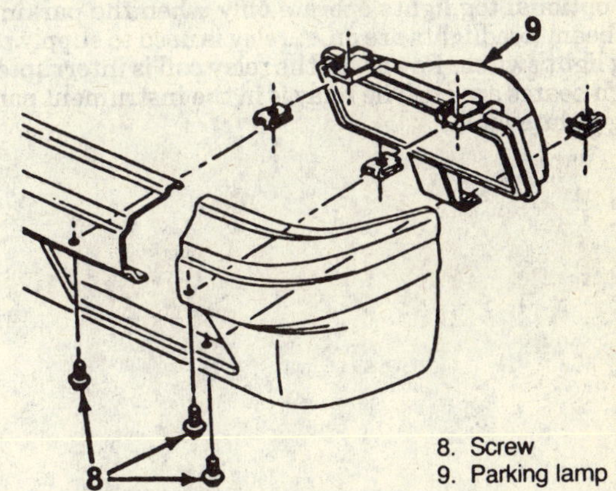

Front parking light assembly

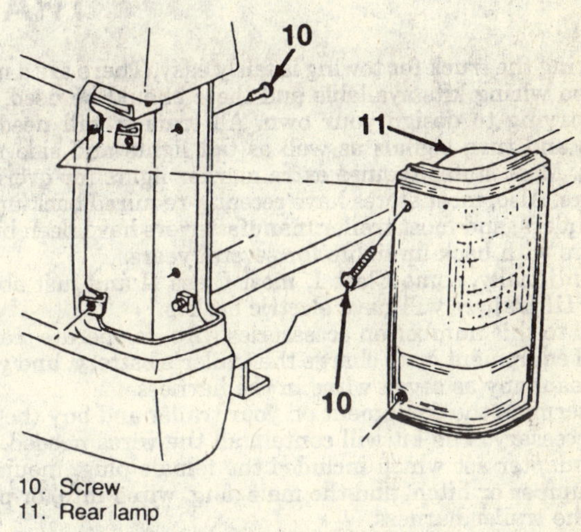

Remove the rear lens to access the bulbs

5. To install, use a new bulb, if necessary, and reverse the removal procedures. Check the turn signal/marker light operations.

Parking Lights

1. Disconnect the negative battery cable from the battery.
2. At the rear of the front bumper, turn the bulb socket ¼ turn and remove the socket from the parking brake housing.
3. Remove the bulb from the socket; if necessary, replace the bulb.
4. To install, reverse the removal procedures. Check the parking light operations.

Rear Turn Signal, Brake and Parking Lights

1. Disconnect the negative battery cable from the battery.
2. Remove the rear turn signal/brake/parking lamp-to-vehicle screws and the lamp housing from the vehicle.
3. Turn the bulb socket ¼ turn and remove the socket from the lamp housing.
4. Remove the bulb from the bulb socket; if necessary, replace the bulb.
5. To install, reverse the removal procedures. Check the turn signal/brake/parking light operations.

Fog Lights

The optional fog lights operate only when the parking lights or low beam headlights are on. A relay is used to supply power to the fog light switch. Power for the relay coil is interrupted when the high beams are on. The relay is in the instrument panel near the fog light switch.

REMOVAL AND INSTALLATION

1. Disconnect the negative battery cable from the battery.
2. Remove the fog light retaining screws and pull the light away from the air dam.
3. Disconnect the wiring and remove the light. Installation is the reverse of removal. The lights cannot be aimed.

TRAILER WIRING

Wiring the truck for towing is fairly easy. There are a number of good wiring kits available and these should be used, rather than trying to design your own. All trailers will need brake lights and turn signals as well as tail lights and side marker lights. Most states require extra marker lights for overly wide trailers. Also, most states have recently required back-up lights for trailers, and most trailer manufacturers have been building trailers with back-up lights for several years.

Additionally, some Class I, most Class II and just about all Class III trailers will have electric brakes.

Add to this number an accessories wire, to operate trailer internal equipment or to charge the trailer's battery, and you can have as many as seven wires in the harness.

Determine the equipment on your trailer and buy the wiring kit necessary. The kit will contain all the wires needed, plus a plug adapter set which included the female plug, mounted on the bumper or hitch, and the male plug, wired into, or plugged into the trailer harness.

When installing the kit, follow the manufacturer's instructions. The color coding of the wires is standard throughout the industry.

One point to note: some domestic vehicles, and most imported vehicles, have separate turn signals. On most domestic vehicles, the brake lights and rear turn signals operate with the same bulb. For those vehicles with separate turn signals, you can purchase an isolation unit so the brake lights won't blink whenever the turn signals are operated, or you can go to your local electronics supply house and buy 4 diodes to wire in series with the brake and turn signal bulbs. Diodes will isolate the brake and turn signals. The choice is yours. The isolation units are simple and quick to install, but far more expensive than the diodes. The diodes, however, require more work to install properly, since they require the cutting of each bulb's wire and soldering in place of the diode.

One, final point, the best kits are those with a spring loaded cover on the vehicle mounted socket. This cover prevents dirt and moisture from corroding the terminals. Never let the vehicle socket hang loosely; always mount it securely to the bumper

CIRCUIT PROTECTION

Fuses

The fuses are of the miniaturized (compact) size and are located on a fuse block, they provide increased circuit protection and reliability. Access to the fuse block is gained through a swing-down unit at the far left-side of the dash panel. Each fuse receptacle is marked as to the circuit it protects and the correct amperage of the fuse.

REPLACEMENT

1. Pull the fuse from the fuse block.
2. Inspect the fuse element (through the clear plastic body) to the blade terminal for defects.

NOTE: When replacing the fuse, do not use one of a higher amperage.

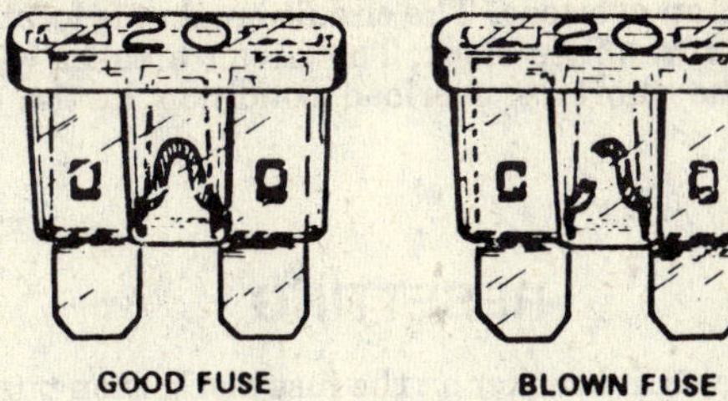

Miniature fuses used in all models

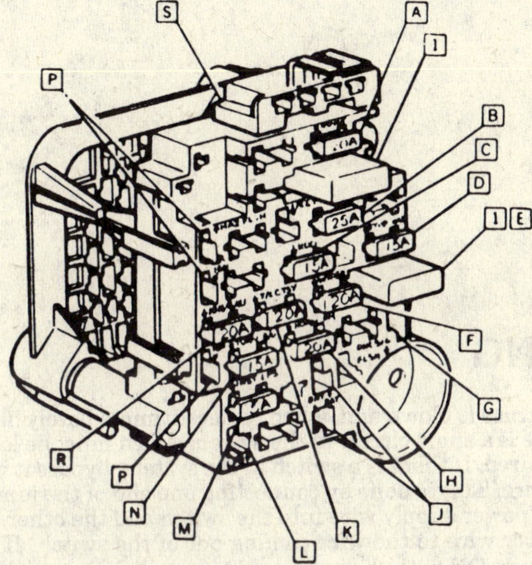

1 Circuit breaker
A Fuse—choke
B Fuse—heater or air condition
C Fuse—radio
D Fuse—stop, hazard lamps
E Power accessory
F Fuse—windshield wiper
G Receptacle—power door locks
H Fuse—horn
J Receptacle—clock, courtesy lamp, dome lamp, I/P compt lamp & hdlp wrng buzzer
K Fuse—tail & ctsy lamps
L Receptacle—headlamp on warning
M Fuse—instrument panel lamps
N Fuse—turn & back up lamps
P Receptacle—cruise control & auto trans
R Fuse—ignition & gauges
S Connector—seat belt warning buzzer & timer

Fuse block is marked with amperage and circuit identification

3. To install, reverse the removal procedures.

Convenience Center

The Convenience Center is a swing-down unit located on the underside of the instrument panel, near the steering column. The swing-down feature provides central location and easy access to buzzers, relays and flasher units. All units are serviced by plug-in replacement.

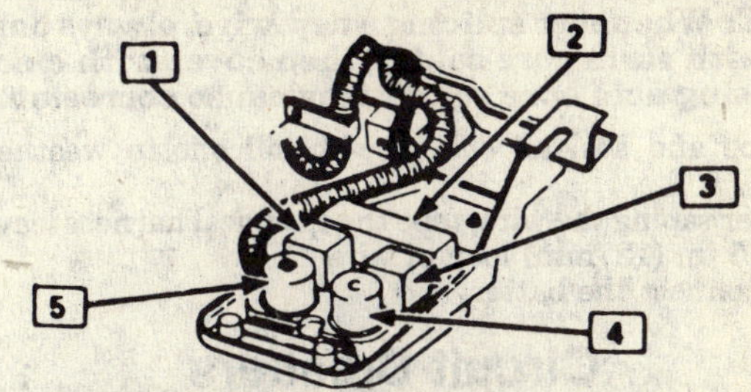

1. Horn relay
2. Seat belt-ignition key-headlight buzzer
3. Choke relay (vacant w/EFI)
4. Hazard flasher
5. Signal flasher

Convenience center holds most of the relays

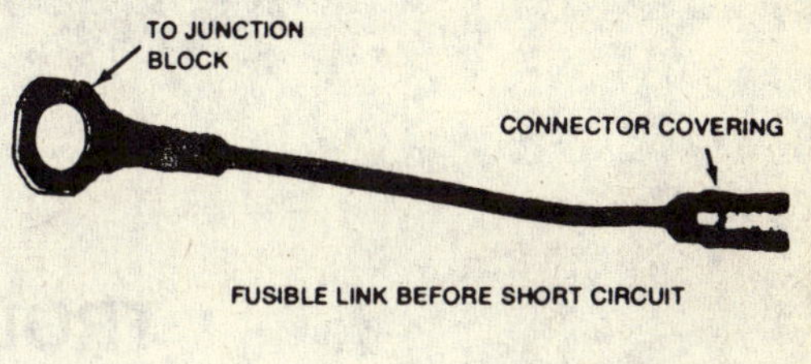

Fusible links before and after a short circuit

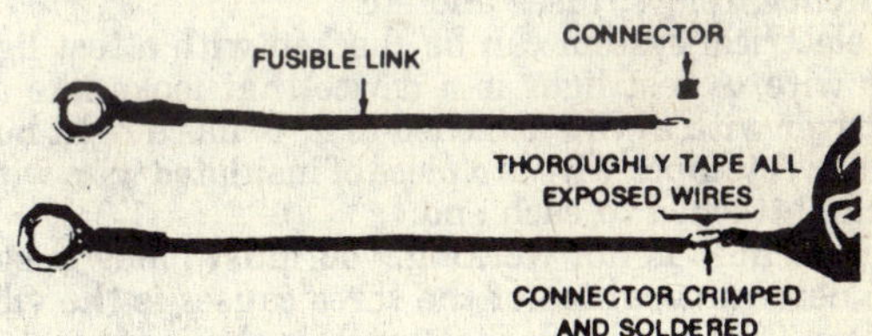

New fusible links are spliced to the wire

Fusible Links

In addition to fuses, the wiring harness incorporates fusible links (in the battery feed circuits) to protect the wiring. Fusible links are 4 in. (102mm) sections of copper wire, 4 gauges smaller than the circuit(s) they are protecting, designed to melt under electrical overload. There are 4 different gauge sizes used. The fusible links are color coded so they may be installed in their original positions.

REPLACEMENT

1. Disconnect the negative battery cable from the battery.
2. Locate the burned out link.
3. Strip away the melted insulation and cut the burned link ends from the wire.
4. Strip the wire back ½ in. (13mm) to allow soldering of the new link.
5. Using a new fusible link 4 gauges smaller than the protected circuit, approx. 10 in. (254mm) long, solder it into the circuit.

NOTE: Whenever splicing a new wire, always bond the splice with rosin core solder, then cover with electrical tape. Using acid core solder may cause corrosion.

6. Tape and seal all splices with silicone to weatherproof repairs.
7. After taping the wire, tape the electrical harness leaving an exposed 5 in. (127mm) loop of wire.
8. Reconnect the battery.

Circuit Breakers

A circuit breaker is an electrical switch which breaks the circuit in case of an overload. The circuit breaker is located on the lower center of the fuse block. The circuit breaker will remain open until the short or overload condition in the circuit is corrected.

RESETTING

Locate the circuit breaker on the fuse block, then push the circuit breaker in until it locks. If the circuit breaker kicks itself Off again, locate and correct the problem in the electrical circuit.

TROUBLESHOOTING

Electrical problems generally fall into one of three areas:
1. The component that is not functioning is not receiving current.
2. The component itself is not functioning.
3. The component is not properly grounded. Problems that fall into the first category are by far the most complicated. It is the current supply system to the component which contains all the switches, relays, fuses and etc.

The electrical system can be checked with a test light and a jumper wire. A test light is a device that looks like a pointed screwdriver with a wire attached to it. It has a light bulb inside its handle. A jumper wire is a piece of insulated wire with an alligator clip attached to each end.

If a light bulb is not working, you must follow a systematic plan to determine which of the three causes is the villain.
1. Turn On the switch that controls the inoperable bulb.
2. Disconnect the power supply wire from the bulb.
3. Attach the ground wire on the test light to a good metal ground.
4. Touch the probe end of the test light to the end of the power supply wire that was disconnected from the bulb. If the bulb is receiving current, the test light will turn ON.

NOTE: If the bulb is one which works only when the ignition key is turned ON (turn signal), make sure the key is turned On.

If the test light does not turn ON, then the problem is in the circuit between the battery and the bulb. As mentioned before, this includes all the switches, fuses and relays in the system. The problem is an open circuit between the battery and the bulb. If the fuse is blown and, when replaced, immediately blows again, there is a short circuit in the system which must be located and repaired. If there is a switch in the system, bypass it with a jumper wire. This is done by connecting one end of the jumper wire to the power supply wire into the switch and the other end of the jumper wire to the wire coming out of the switch. If the test light turns ON with the jumper wire installed, the switch or whatever was bypassed is defective.

NOTE: Never substitute the jumper wire for the bulb, as the bulb is the component required to use the power from the power source.

5. If the bulb in the test light turns On, the current is getting to the bulb that is not working in the vehicle. This eliminates the first of the three possible causes. Connect the power supply wire and connect a jumper wire from the bulb to a good metal ground. Do this with the switch which controls the bulb turned On and also the ignition switch turned ON, if it is required for the light to work. If the bulb works with the jumper wire installed, then it has a bad ground. This is usually caused by the metal area on which the bulb mounts to the vehicle being coated with some type of foreign matter or rust.
6. If neither test located the source of the trouble, then the light bulb itself is defective.

The above test procedures can be applied to any of the components of the chassis electrical system by substituting the component that is not working for the light bulb. Remember that for any electrical system to work, all connections must be clean and tight.

Troubleshooting Basic Turn Signal and Flasher Problems

Most problems in the turn signals or flasher system can be reduced to defective flashers or bulbs, which are easily replaced. Occasionally, problems in the turn signals are traced to the switch in the steering column, which will require professional service.

F = Front R = Rear ● = Lights off ○ = Lights on

Problem		Solution
Turn signals light, but do not flash	F F / R R	• Replace the flasher
No turn signals light on either side	F F / R R	• Check the fuse. Replace if defective. • Check the flasher by substitution • Check for open circuit, short circuit or poor ground
Both turn signals on one side don't work	F F / R R	• Check for bad bulbs • Check for bad ground in both housings
One turn signal light on one side doesn't work	F F / R R	• Check and/or replace bulb • Check for corrosion in socket. Clean contacts. • Check for poor ground at socket
Turn signal flashes too fast or too slow	F F / R R	• Check any bulb on the side flashing too fast. A heavy-duty bulb is probably installed in place of a regular bulb. • Check the bulb flashing too slow. A standard bulb was probably installed in place of a heavy-duty bulb. • Check for loose connections or corrosion at the bulb socket
Indicator lights don't work in either direction		• Check if the turn signals are working • Check the dash indicator lights • Check the flasher by substitution

Troubleshooting Basic Turn Signal and Flasher Problems

Most problems in the turn signals or flasher system can be reduced to defective flashers or bulbs, which are easily replaced. Occasionally, problems in the turn signals are traced to the switch in the steering column, which will require professional service.

F = Front R = Rear • = Lights off o = Lights on

Problem		Solution
One indicator light doesn't light	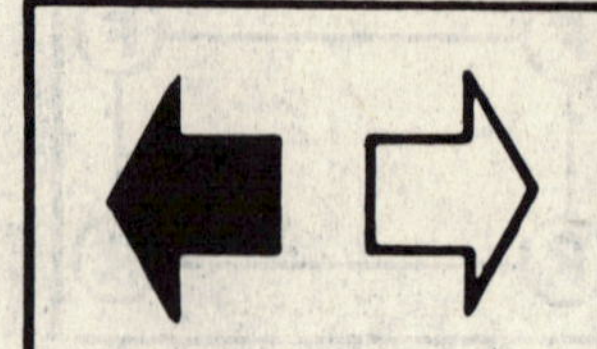	• On systems with 1 dash indicator: See if the lights work on the same side. Often the filaments have been reversed in systems combining stoplights with taillights and turn signals. Check the flasher by substitution • On systems with 2 indicators: Check the bulbs on the same side Check the indicator light bulb Check the flasher by substitution

Troubleshooting Basic Lighting Problems

Problem	Cause	Solution
Lights		
One or more lights don't work, but others do	• Defective bulb(s) • Blown fuse(s) • Dirty fuse clips or light sockets • Poor ground circuit	• Replace bulb(s) • Replace fuse(s) • Clean connections • Run ground wire from light socket housing to car frame
Lights burn out quickly	• Incorrect voltage regulator setting or defective regulator • Poor battery/alternator connections	• Replace voltage regulator • Check battery/alternator connections
Lights go dim	• Low/discharged battery • Alternator not charging • Corroded sockets or connections • Low voltage output	• Check battery • Check drive belt tension; repair or replace alternator • Clean bulb and socket contacts and connections • Replace voltage regulator
Lights flicker	• Loose connection • Poor ground • Circuit breaker operating (short circuit)	• Tighten all connections • Run ground wire from light housing to car frame • Check connections and look for bare wires
Lights "flare"—Some flare is normal on acceleration—if excessive, see "Lights Burn Out Quickly"	• High voltage setting	• Replace voltage regulator

Troubleshooting Basic Lighting Problems

Problem	Cause	Solution
Lights glare—approaching drivers are blinded	• Lights adjusted too high • Rear springs or shocks sagging • Rear tires soft	• Have headlights aimed • Check rear springs/shocks • Check/correct rear tire pressure
Turn Signals		
Turn signals don't work in either direction	• Blown fuse • Defective flasher • Loose connection	• Replace fuse • Replace flasher • Check/tighten all connections
Right (or left) turn signal only won't work	• Bulb burned out • Right (or left) indicator bulb burned out • Short circuit	• Replace bulb • Check/replace indicator bulb • Check/repair wiring
Flasher rate too slow or too fast	• Incorrect wattage bulb • Incorrect flasher	• Flasher bulb • Replace flasher (use a variable load flasher if you pull a trailer)
Indicator lights do not flash (burn steadily)	• Burned out bulb • Defective flasher	• Replace bulb • Replace flasher
Indicator lights do not light at all	• Burned out indicator bulb • Defective flasher	• Replace indicator bulb • Replace flasher

Troubleshooting Basic Dash Gauge Problems

Problem	Cause	Solution
Coolant Temperature Gauge		
Gauge reads erratically or not at all	• Loose or dirty connections • Defective sending unit • Defective gauge	• Clean/tighten connections • Bi-metal gauge: remove the wire from the sending unit. Ground the wire for an instant. If the gauge registers, replace the sending unit. • Magnetic gauge: disconnect the wire at the sending unit. With ignition ON gauge should register COLD. Ground the wire; gauge should register HOT.
Ammeter Gauge—Turn Headlights ON (do not start engine). Note reaction		
Ammeter shows charge Ammeter shows discharge Ammeter does not move	• Connections reversed on gauge • Ammeter is OK • Loose connections or faulty wiring • Defective gauge	• Reinstall connections • Nothing • Check/correct wiring • Replace gauge

Troubleshooting Basic Dash Gauge Problems

Problem	Cause	Solution
Oil Pressure Gauge		
Gauge does not register or is inaccurate	• On mechanical gauge, Bourdon tube may be bent or kinked	• Check tube for kinks or bends preventing oil from reaching the gauge
	• Low oil pressure	• Remove sending unit. Idle the engine briefly. If no oil flows from sending unit hole, problem is in engine.
	• Defective gauge	• Remove the wire from the sending unit and ground it for an instant with the ignition ON. A good gauge will go to the top of the scale.
	• Defective wiring	• Check the wiring to the gauge. If it's OK and the gauge doesn't register when grounded, replace the gauge.
	• Defective sending unit	• If the wiring is OK and the gauge functions when grounded, replace the sending unit
All Gauges		
All gauges do not operate	• Blown fuse • Defective instrument regulator	• Replace fuse • Replace instrument voltage regulator
All gauges read low or erratically	• Defective or dirty instrument voltage regulator	• Clean contacts or replace
All gauges pegged	• Loss of ground between instrument voltage regulator and car • Defective instrument regulator	• Check ground • Replace regulator
Warning Lights		
Light(s) do not come on when ignition is ON, but engine is not started	• Defective bulb • Defective wire	• Replace bulb • Check wire from light to sending unit
	• Defective sending unit	• Disconnect the wire from the sending unit and ground it. Replace the sending unit if the light comes on with the ignition ON.
Light comes on with engine running	• Problem in individual system • Defective sending unit	• Check system • Check sending unit (see above)

Troubleshooting the Heater

Problem	Cause	Solution
Blower motor will not turn at any speed	• Blown fuse • Loose connection • Defective ground • Faulty switch • Faulty motor • Faulty resistor	• Replace fuse • Inspect and tighten • Clean and tighten • Replace switch • Replace motor • Replace resistor
Blower motor turns at one speed only	• Faulty switch • Faulty resistor	• Replace switch • Replace resistor
Blower motor turns but does not circulate air	• Intake blocked • Fan not secured to the motor shaft	• Clean intake • Tighten security
Heater will not heat	• Coolant does not reach proper temperature • Heater core blocked internally • Heater core air-bound • Blend-air door not in proper position	• Check and replace thermostat if necessary • Flush or replace core if necessary • Purge air from core • Adjust cable
Heater will not defrost	• Control cable adjustment incorrect • Defroster hose damaged	• Adjust control cable • Replace defroster hose

Troubleshooting Basic Windshield Wiper Problems

Problem	Cause	Solution
Electric Wipers		
Wipers do not operate— Wiper motor heats up or hums	• Internal motor defect • Bent or damaged linkage • Arms improperly installed on linking pivots	• Replace motor • Repair or replace linkage • Position linkage in park and reinstall wiper arms
Wipers do not operate— No current to motor	• Fuse or circuit breaker blown • Loose, open or broken wiring • Defective switch • Defective or corroded terminals • No ground circuit for motor or switch	• Replace fuse or circuit breaker • Repair wiring and connections • Replace switch • Replace or clean terminals • Repair ground circuits
Wipers do not operate— Motor runs	• Linkage disconnected or broken	• Connect wiper linkage or replace broken linkage
Vacuum Wipers		
Wipers do not operate	• Control switch or cable inoperative • Loss of engine vacuum to wiper motor (broken hoses, low engine vacuum, defective vacuum/fuel pump) • Linkage broken or disconnected • Defective wiper motor	• Repair or replace switch or cable • Check vacuum lines, engine vacuum and fuel pump • Repair linkage • Replace wiper motor
Wipers stop on engine acceleration	• Leaking vacuum hoses • Dry windshield • Oversize wiper blades • Defective vacuum/fuel pump	• Repair or replace hoses • Wet windshield with washers • Replace with proper size wiper blades • Replace pump

WIRING DIAGRAMS

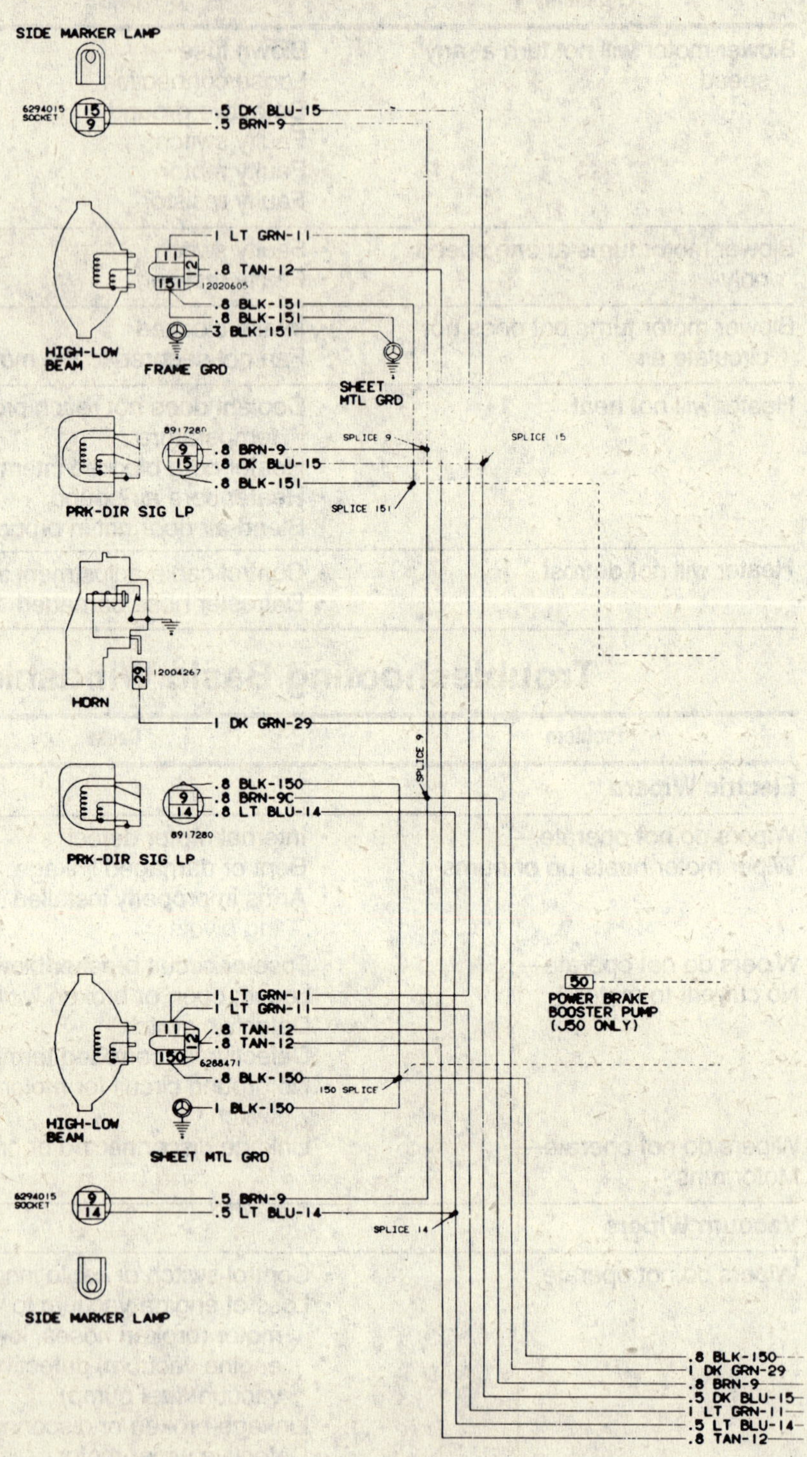

1982-85

32 BLK
3 BLK
BATTERY
.8 WHT-121
.8 RED/WHT-440
.8 PNK/BLK-39
REF 3C HARN
3 PNK-3
3 PNK-3
.5 DK GRN-35
10 AMP
3 RED-2
JUNCTION BLOCK
DIST
TO DIST CAP
COOLENT TEMP
CHOKE HEATER
EFE TEMP SW
.8 LT BLU-78
3 PNK/BLK-903
3 PNK/BLK-913
1 PNK
1 BLK
VACUUM PUMP (J50 ONLY)
OIL PRESS
TO POS BAT CABLE (J50 ONLY)
SHEET METAL GRD
4 STRAP
ENG GRD
3 BLK-150
.8 TAN-31
1 BRN-25
3 RED-2
3 PNK-3
1 BRN-25
.8 LT BLU-78
.8 PNK/WHT-350
EFE RELAY
SPLICE 50
BOOSTER SWITCH (J50 ONLY)
L4 ENG
CALIFORNIA
RPO MV9 EXT OR MANUAL BACKUP EXT
.8 LT GRN-924
.8 DK BLU-975
.8 BLK-150
1 DK GRN-29
.8 BRN-9A
.5 DK BLU-15
1 LT GRN-11
.5 LT BLU-14
.8 TAN-12

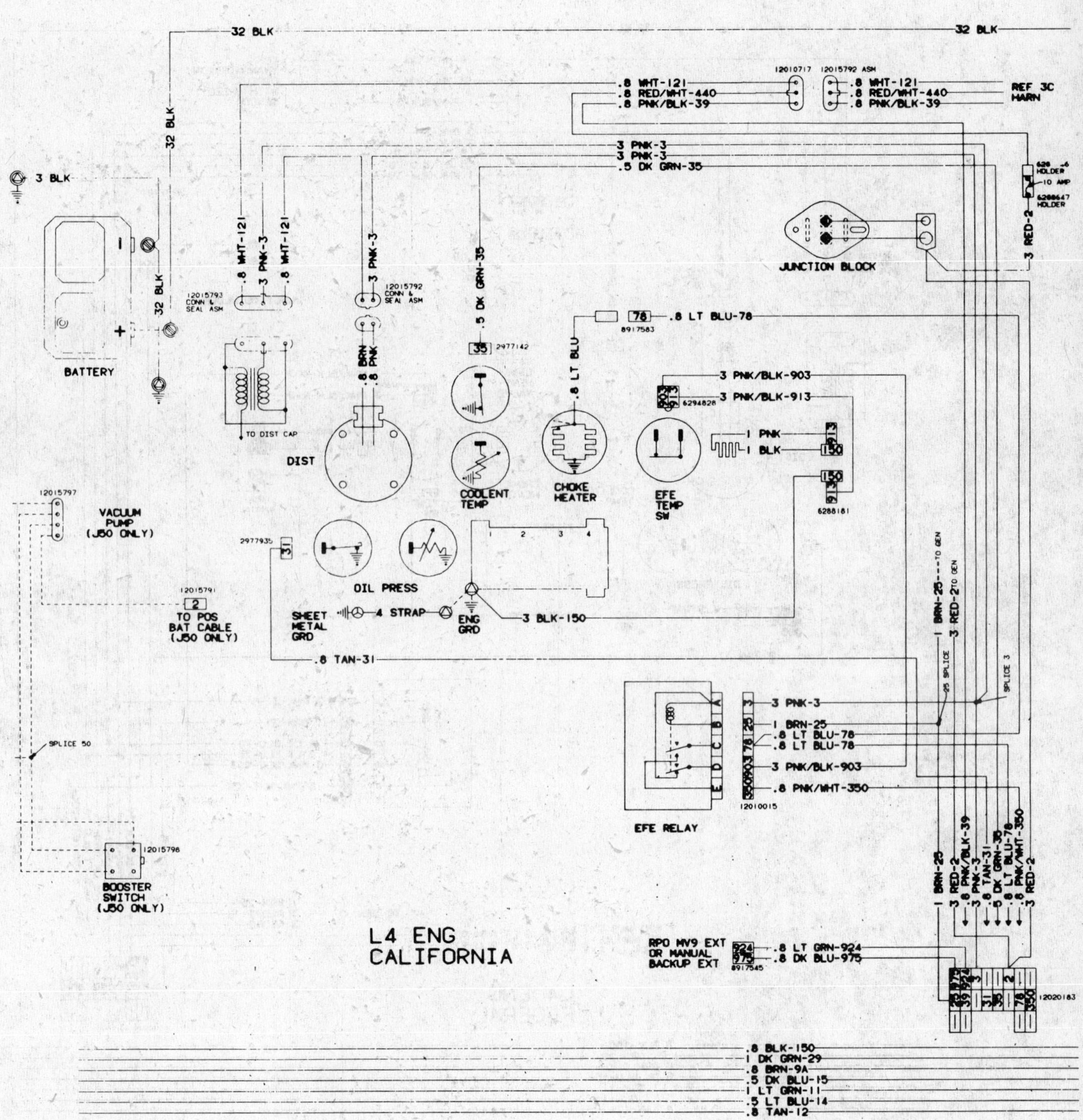

1982-85

32 BLK
.8 WHT-121
.8 PPL-904
1 PNK/BLK-39
REF TRANSMISSION CIRCUIT WITH SPEED SENSOR
3 PNK-3
3 PNK-3
.5 DK GRN-35
.8 LT BLU 78
1 PNK/BLK-39
39 SPLICE
SLOW CUT SOL
JUNCTION BLOCK
CARB VENT VALVE
DIST
TO DIST CAP
COOLENT TEMP
CHOKE HEATER
EFE TEMP SW
3 PNK/BLK-903
3 PNK/BLK-913
1 PNK
1 BLK
OIL PRESS
SHEET METAL GRD
4 STRAP
ENG GRD
3 BLK-150
.8 TAN-31
3 PNK-3
1 BRN-25
.8 LT BLU-78
.8 LT BLU-78
3 PNK/BLK-903
.8 PNK/WHT-350
SPLICE 25
SPLICE 3
TO GEN
1 BRN-25
3 RED-2
3 RED-2
RPO MV9 EXT OR MANUAL BACK UP EXT
.8 LT GRN-924
.8 LT BLU-975
L4 ENG FEDERAL
.8 BLK-150
1 DK GRN-29
.8 BRN-9
.5 DK BLU-15
1 LT GRN-11
.5 LT BLU-14
.8 TAN-12

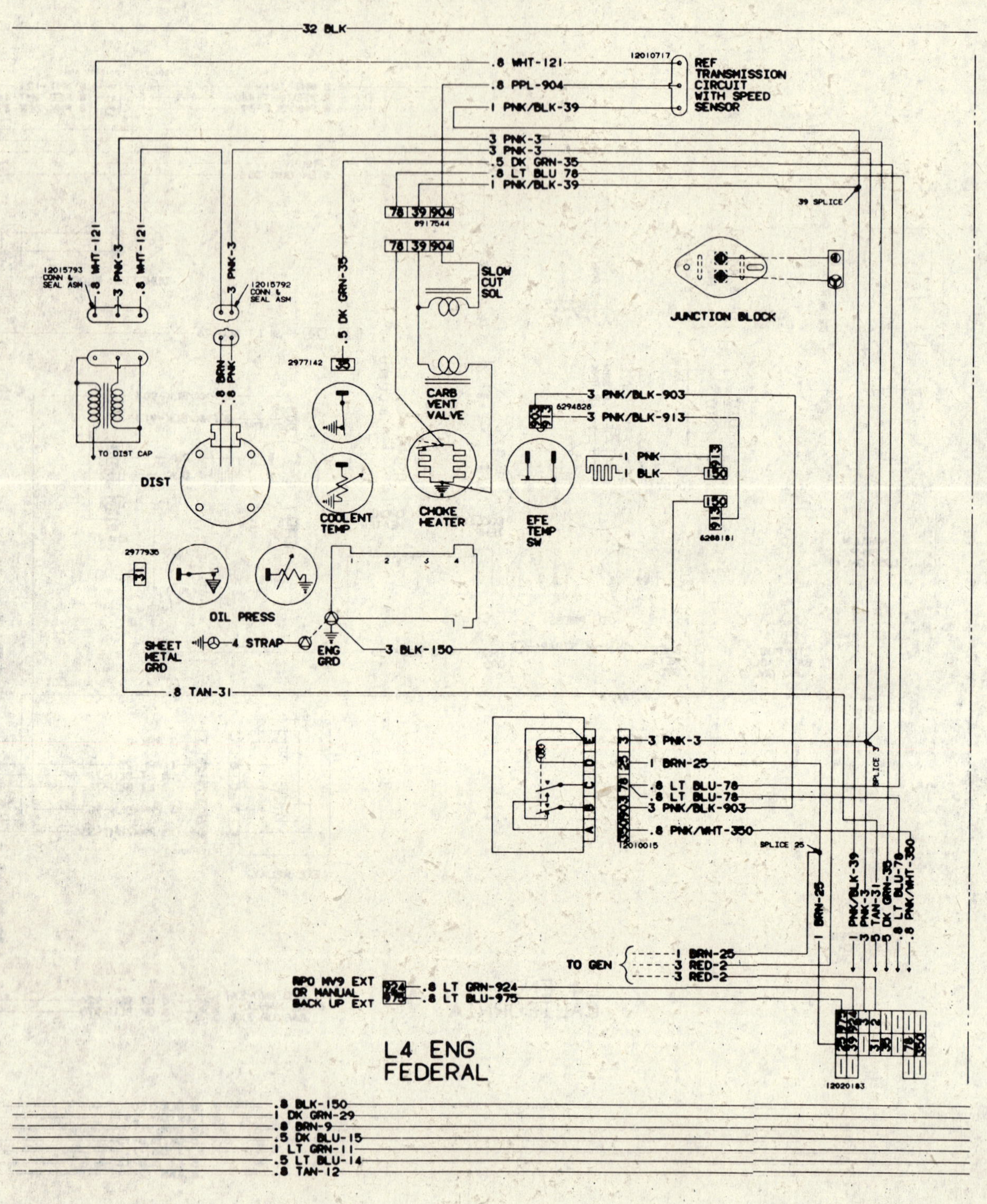

1982-85

32 BLK
3 RED-2
6288646 HOLDER
10 AMP
6288647 HOLDER
.8 RED/WHT-440
12010973
12010973 CONN SEAL ASM
JUNCTION BLOCK
.8 GRN-440
.8 PNK/BLK-439
.8 PNK/BLK-439
REF 3C HARN
TO DIST CAP
1 BRN
1 PNK
REF 3C HARN
PICKUP COIL
8917651
PNK-3
OIL PRESS
4 STRAP
SHEET METAL GRD
2977935
6288704
COOLANT TEMP
AC EXT HARN
12015987
.8 BLK/GRN-966
CHOKE HEATER
12010031
SPLICE 3
3 PNK-3
2977253
8900420
THROTTLE KICKER SOLENOID
2962953
.8 BLK-150
12015978
.5 DK GRN-35
.5 TAN-31
.8 LT BLU-78
.8 LT BLU-78
3 PNK-3
1 BRN-25
25 SPLICE
.8 PNK/WHT-350
12010015
.8 DK BLU-987
12015271
.8 PNK/BLK-39
1 BRN-25
3 PNK-3
.5 TAN-31
.5 DK GRN-35
.8 LT BLU-78
.8 PNK/WHT-350
TO GEN
1 BRN-25
3 RED-2
3 RED-2
RPO MV9 EXT OR MANUAL BACK UP EXT
.8 LT GRN-924
.8 LT BLU-975
12020183
V6 ENG
CALIFORNIA
.8 BLK-150
1 DK GRN-29
.8 BRN-9
.5 DK BLU-15
1 LT GRN-11
.5 LT BLU-14
.8 TAN-12

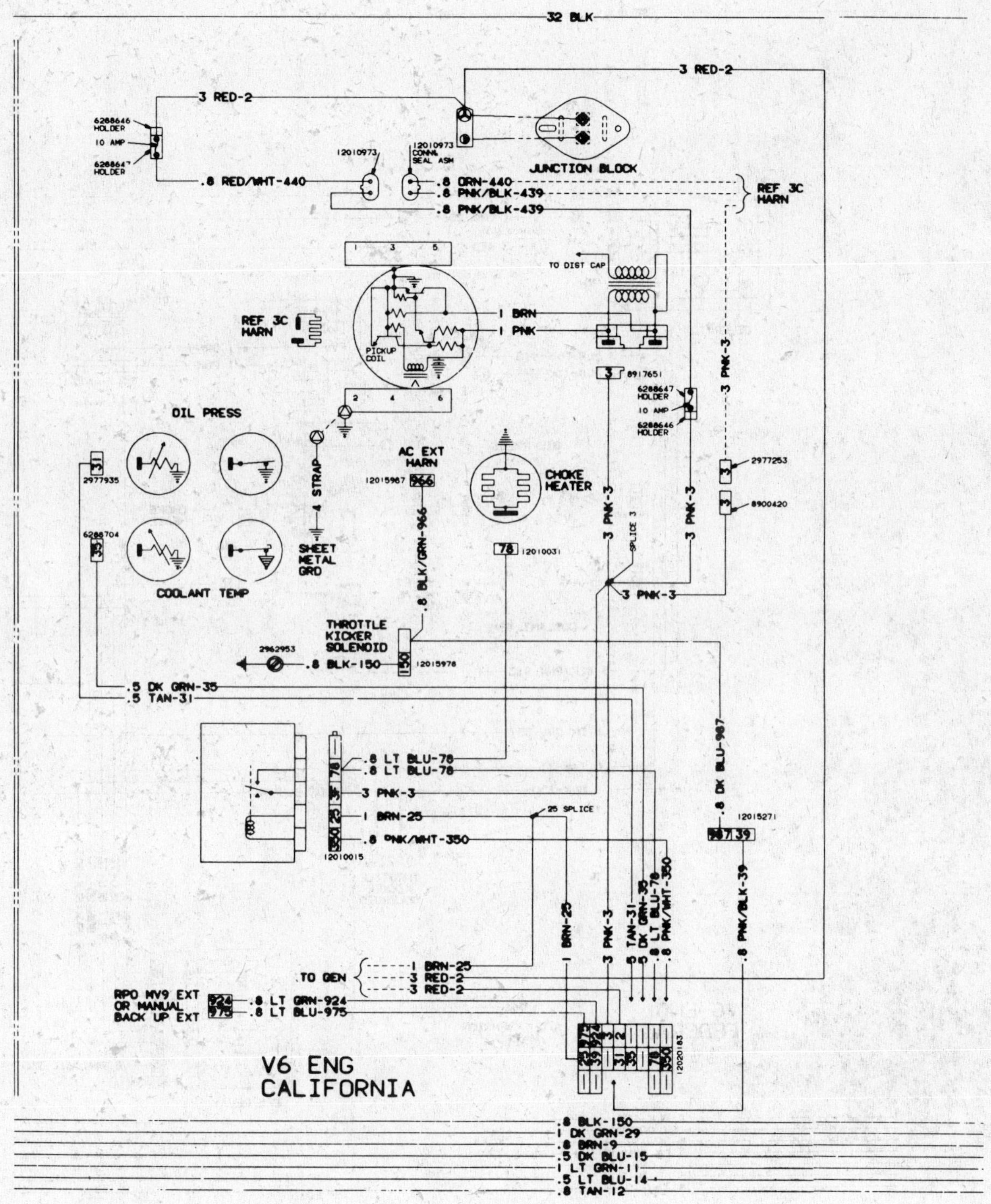

1982-85

32 BLK
6294493
3 RED/WHT-2
1 BRN-25
2984033 BOOT
3 RED-2
BAT
FOR M6 OR #12 STUD
GENERATOR
TO DIST CAP
COIL
6288181
3 BLK/PNK-913
3 BLK-150
EFE HEATER
1 BRN
1 PNK
PICKUP COIL
8917651
OIL PRESS
2977935
4 STRAP
EFE TEMP SW
CHOKE HEATER
3 PNK-3
6288704
SHEET METAL GRD
2973872
12010031
SPLICE 3
COOLANT TEMP
3 BLK/PNK-913
.5 DK GRN-35
.5 TAN-31
.8 BLK-150
.8 DK BLU-987
12015978
THROTTLE KICKER SOLENOID
3 PNK-3
.8 LT BLU-78
.8 LT BLU-78
1 BRN-25
3 PNK/BLK-903
V6 ENG
FEDERAL
12015987
A/C EXTENSION HARNESS
.8 PNK/WHT-350
12010015
EFE RELAY
.8 BLK-150
1 DK GRN-29
.8 BRN-9
.5 DK BLU-15
1 LT GRN-11
.5 LT BLU-14
.8 TAN-12

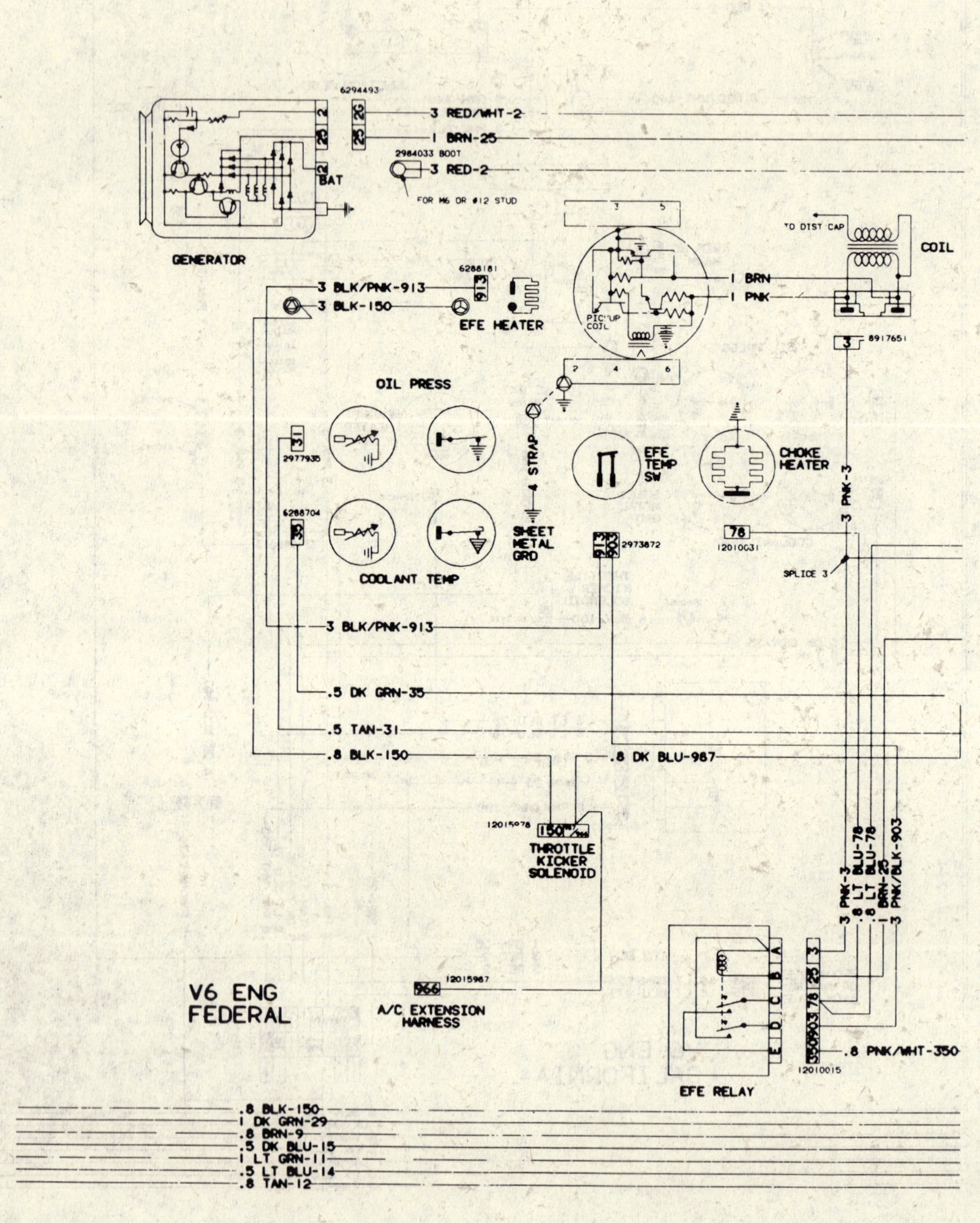

1982-85

FUSABLE LINK
L4 ONLY
1 RED-2 THERMO HW
1 RED-2 THERMO HW
STARTER MOTOR
SOL
SPLICE 2
BLOWER MOTOR
6288317
2 ORG-52
2977976
2 ORG-52
2 LT BLU-72
2 YEL-51
3 RED-2
SPLICE 2
JUNCTION BLOCK
.8 RED
4 AMP FUSE
.8 ORG
UNDER HOOD LAMP
1 BRN-25
.8 PPL-92
.8 GRA-91
.8 ORN-98
.8 WHT-93
12015664
PARK CONTACTS
WIPER MOTOR
3 RED/WHT-2
3 PPL-6
3 RED-2
.8 LT BLU-78
3 PNK-3
RPO MV9 EXT OR MANUAL BACK UP EXT
P917545
.8 LT GRN-924
.8 DK BLU-975
SPLICE 25
1 BRN-25
12020183
.8 GRA-91
12015271
.8 PNK/BLK-39
.5 DK GRN-35
.8 WHT-93
.8 ORN-98
.5 TAN-31
.8 PPL-92
.8 PNK/WHT-350
8917261
WASHER PUMP
.8 BLK-150
.8 PNK-94
.8 TAN/WHT-33
1 DK GRN-29
.8 BRN-9
.5 DK BLU-15
1 LT GRN-11
.5 LT BLU-14
.8 TAN-12
12020099
12020100
BRAKE PRESS WARNING SWITCH
FRONT OF DASH
.8 BLK-150
1 DK GRN-29
.8 BRN-9
.5 DK BLU-15
1 LT GRN-11
.5 LT BLU-14
.8 TAN-12
.8 PNK-30
.8 BRN-9
.8 DK GRN-19
.8 YEL-18
.8 LT GRN-24

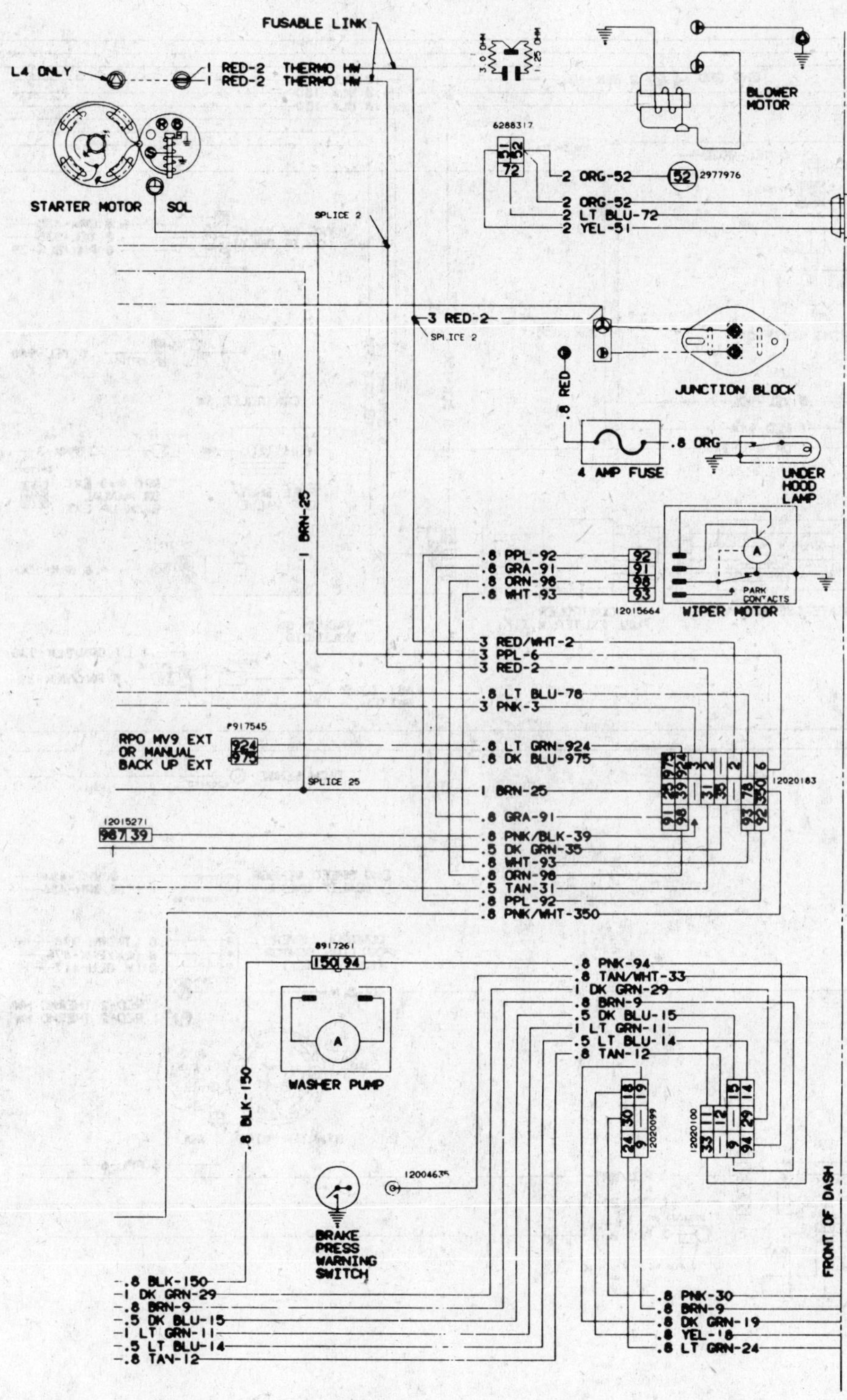

1982-85

RELAY 1
RELAY 2
1 PPL-6
1 PPL-6
1 BLK/GRN-942
.5 BKL-150
.5 BKL-150
ENG GRD
2 BLK-150
.8 BLK-150
.8 BLK-150
.8 BLK-150
150 SPLICE
5 YEL-902
5 YEL-902B
902 SPLICE
5 NAT/WHT-904
5 RED-2
5 RED-2
2 RED-2 THERMO HW
32 BLK
BATTERY
DROPPING RESISTOR
VAC SW VALVE (CALIF ONLY)
.8 GRA-435
.8 YEL-535
.8 PNK/BLK-39
CONTROLER SW
.5 YEL-948
5 YEL-902
1 RED-944
1 DK GRN-946
SENSING RESISTOR
GLOW PLUGS
OIL PRESS
COOLANT TEMP
.8 BLK-150
.8 BRN/WHT-141
.8 YEL/BLK-508
FUEL SHUT-OFF VALVE
3 PNK-3
RPO MV9 EXT OR MANUAL BACK UP EXT
HEATER&SENSOR ASSM
CONTROLER FUEL FILTER W.I.F.
.8 BLK-150
VACUUM SW SOLENOID
.8 LT GRN/BLK-936
FAST IDLE SWITCH
.8 PNK/BLK-39
.5 DK GRN-35
.8 TAN-31
TACH SENSE
ENG SPEED SENSOR (CALIF ONLY)
.8 WHT-484
.8 BRN-486
CONTROL LEVER POSITION SENSOR (CALIF ONLY)
.8 LT GRN-974
.8 BLK/PNK-476
.8 DK BLU-417
32 BLK
1 RED-2 THERMO HW
1 RED-2 THERMO HW
STARTER MOTOR
SOL
3 PPL-6
3 RED/WHT-2
1 BRN-25
3 RED-2
BAT
GENERATOR

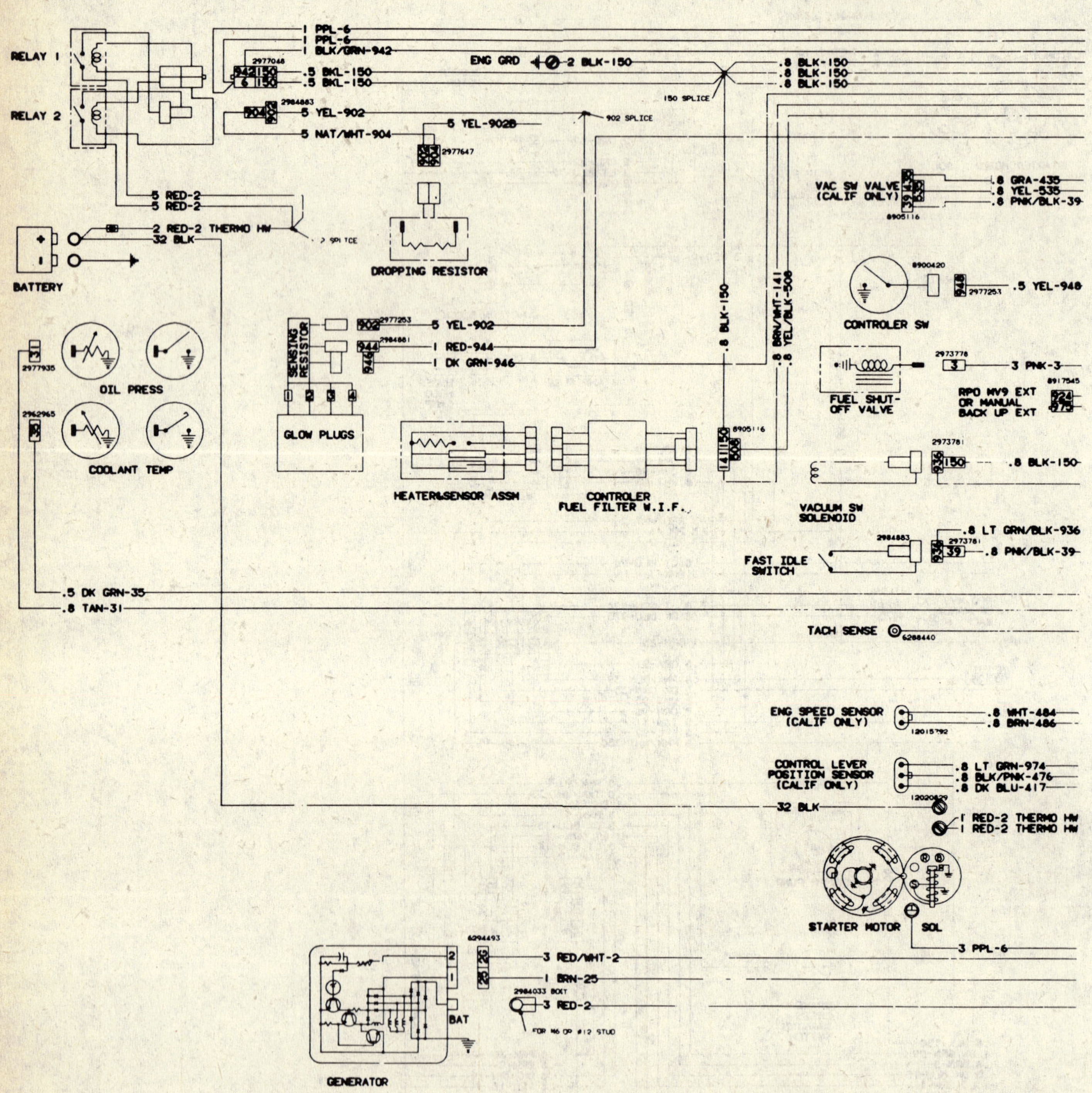

1982-85

3 RED-2C(SXL)
.8 BLK/PNK-476
.8 WHT-484
.5 YEL-948
1 PPL-6
.5 BLK-150
1 BLK/GRN-942
1 DK GRN-946
.8 BRN/WHT-141
.5 TAN/BLK-33
.8 GRA-435
.8 DK BLU-417
.8 BRN-486
.8 YEL/BLK-508
.8 PNK/BLK-39
.8 LT GRN-974
1 RED-944
.8 YEL-535
.8 BLK-150
12004275
LOW VACUUM WARNING SW
.8 PNK/BLK-39
.8 PPL-92
.8 GRA-91
.8 ORN-98
.8 NAT/WHT-93
12015664
PARK CONTACTS
WIPER MOTOR
2 SPLICE
6 SPLICE
.5 BLK-6 THERMO HW
3 RED/WHT-2
3 RED-2
3 PNK-3
.8 LT GRN-924
.8 DK BLU-975
12020183
39 SPLICE
1 BRN-25
.8 GRA-91
.8 PNK/BLK-39
.8 ORN-98
.8 NAT/WHT-93
.5 DK GRN-35
.8 TAN-31
.8 PPL-92
.8 WHT-121
FRONT OF DASH
3 PPL-6
2 SPLICE

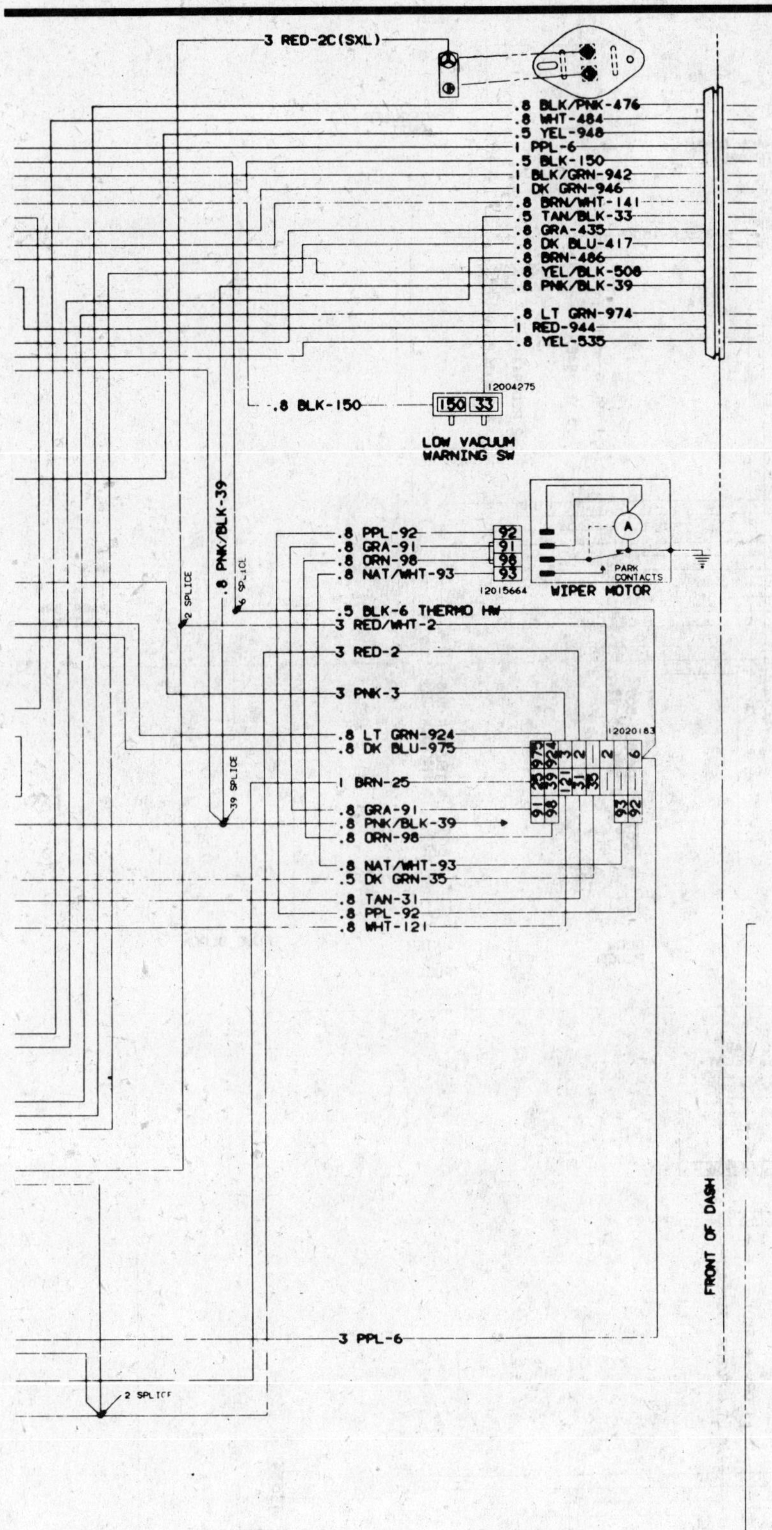

1982-85

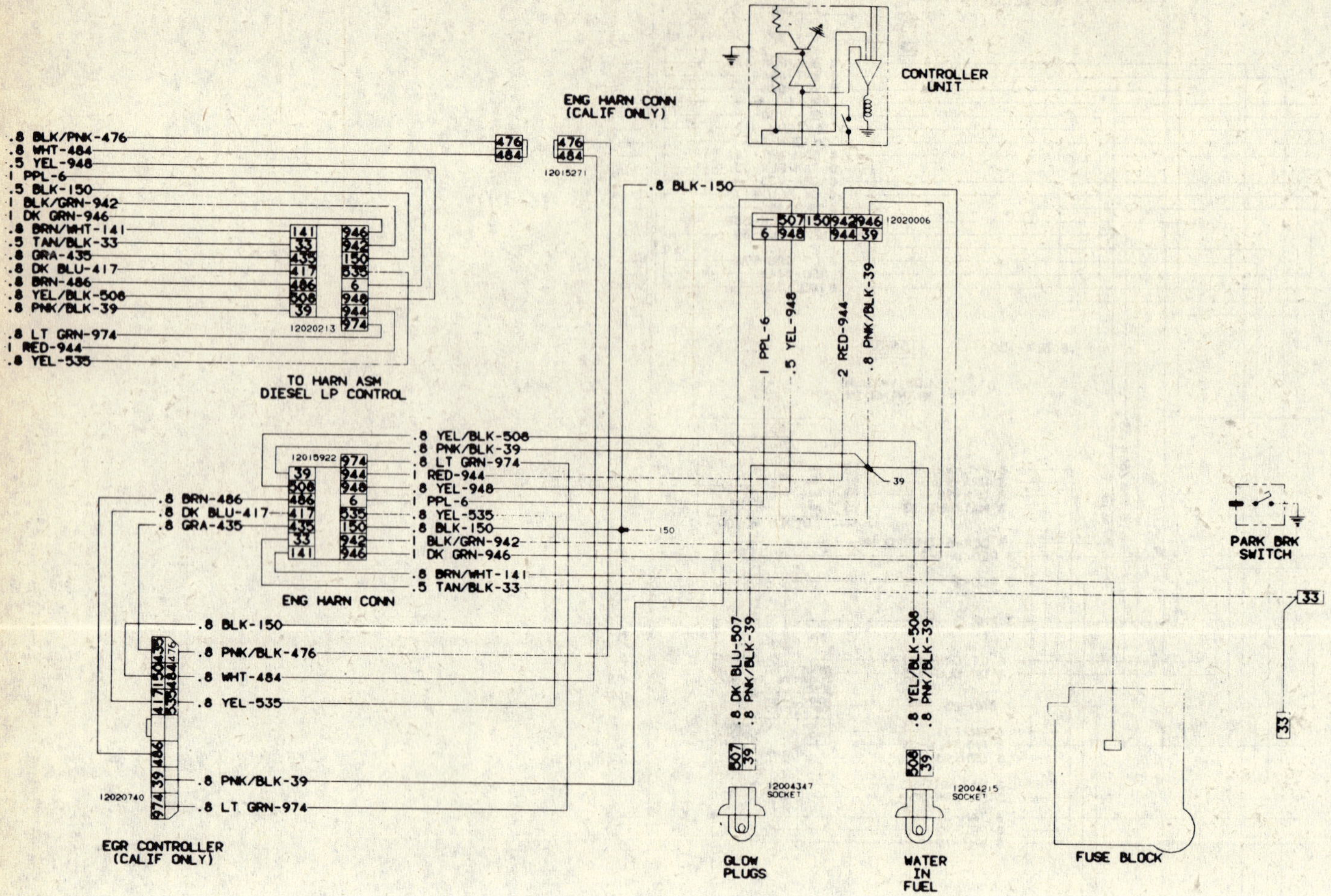

CONTROLLER UNIT
ENG HARN CONN (CALIF ONLY)
12015271
.8 BLK/PNK-476
.8 WHT-484
.5 YEL-948
1 PPL-6
.5 BLK-150
1 BLK/GRN-942
1 DK GRN-946
.8 BRN/WHT-141
.5 TAN/BLK-33
.8 GRA-435
.8 DK BLU-417
.8 BRN-486
.8 YEL/BLK-508
.8 PNK/BLK-39
.8 LT GRN-974
1 RED-944
.8 YEL-535
12020213
TO HARN ASM DIESEL LP CONTROL
.8 BLK-150
12020006
1 PPL-6
.5 YEL-948
2 RED-944
.8 PNK/BLK-39
12015922
.8 BRN-486
.8 DK BLU-417
.8 GRA-435
.8 YEL/BLK-508
.8 PNK/BLK-39
.8 LT GRN-974
1 RED-944
.8 YEL-948
1 PPL-6
.8 YEL-535
.8 BLK-150
1 BLK/GRN-942
1 DK GRN-946
.8 BRN/WHT-141
.5 TAN/BLK-33
ENG HARN CONN
.8 BLK-150
.8 PNK/BLK-476
.8 WHT-484
.8 YEL-535
.8 PNK/BLK-39
.8 LT GRN-974
12020740
EGR CONTROLLER (CALIF ONLY)
.8 DK BLU-507
.8 PNK/BLK-39
12004347 SOCKET
GLOW PLUGS
.8 YEL/BLK-508
.8 PNK/BLK-39
12004215 SOCKET
WATER IN FUEL
PARK BRK SWITCH
FUSE BLOCK

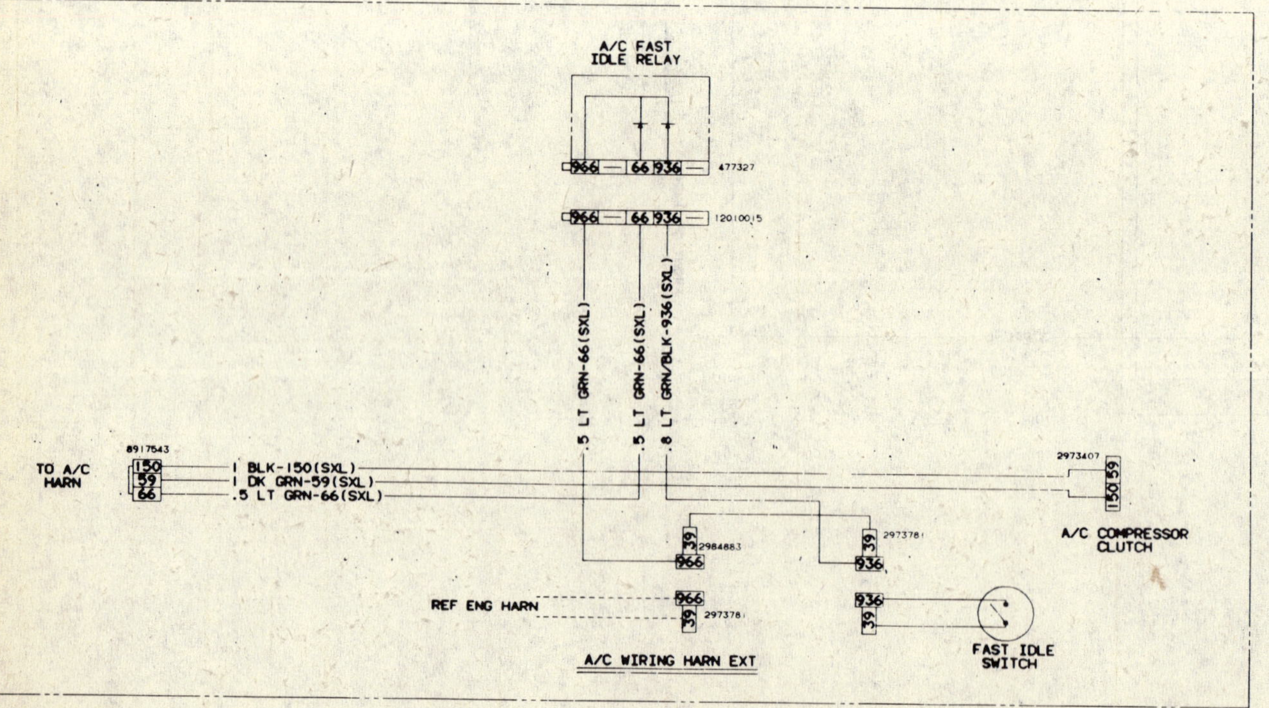

1982-85

INST CLUSTER (BASE)
12004215 SOCKET
AC &/OR HEATER CONTROL ASSY LP
TERM OPT NAME
1 RPO AU3/A33
2 RPO LR1
3 RPO U35
4 RPO CD4
5 RPO TR9
6
BUS BAR GRD
FUEL
TEMP
GEN
OIL
R TURN
L TURN
SEAT BELT
HIGH BEAM
BRK
CHOKE
ILLUM
2 ORG-52
2 LT BLU-72
2 YEL-51
OFF
HI
HEATER BLOWER SW
2 BRN-50
.8 LT BLU-78
3 PPL-6
3 RED-2
.5 DK GRN-35
3 RED-2
3 PNK-3
3 RED-2
3 PNK-3
.8 LT GRN/BLK-924
REF RPO MV9 OR B/U LAMP CIRCUIT
8900826
.8 DK BLU-975
.5 BRN-25 (W/O GAGES)
130 (W/GAGES-TO IGN SW)
.8 PNK/BLK-39
.5 TAN-31
.5 LT BLU-14
.5 DK BLU-15
.5LT GRN-11
.5 TAN/WHT-33
1 DK GRN-29
.8 PNK/WHT-350
.5 DK BLU-15
.5 LT BLU-14
.8 BRN-9
.8 TAN-12
1 LT GRN-11
.8 WHT-93
.8 BRN-9
.5 TAN/WHT-33
.8 BRN-9
.8 ORN-98
.8 GRA-91
.8 WHT-93
.8 PPL-92
.8 PNK-94
12004060
8905800
8905214
.8 ORN/BLK-240
.8 WHT/BLK-156C
.8 WHT/BLK-156
.8 ORN/BLK-240
.8 ORN/BLK-240
.8 WHT/BLK-156
.5 PNK-30
.8 LT GRN-24
.8 YEL-18
.8 BRN-9
.8 DK GRN-19
.8 ORN-240
.8 WHT-156
.8 ORN-240
.8 WHT-156
.8 PNK-30
.8 LT GRN-24
.8 YEL-18
.8 BRN-9
.8 DK GRN-19

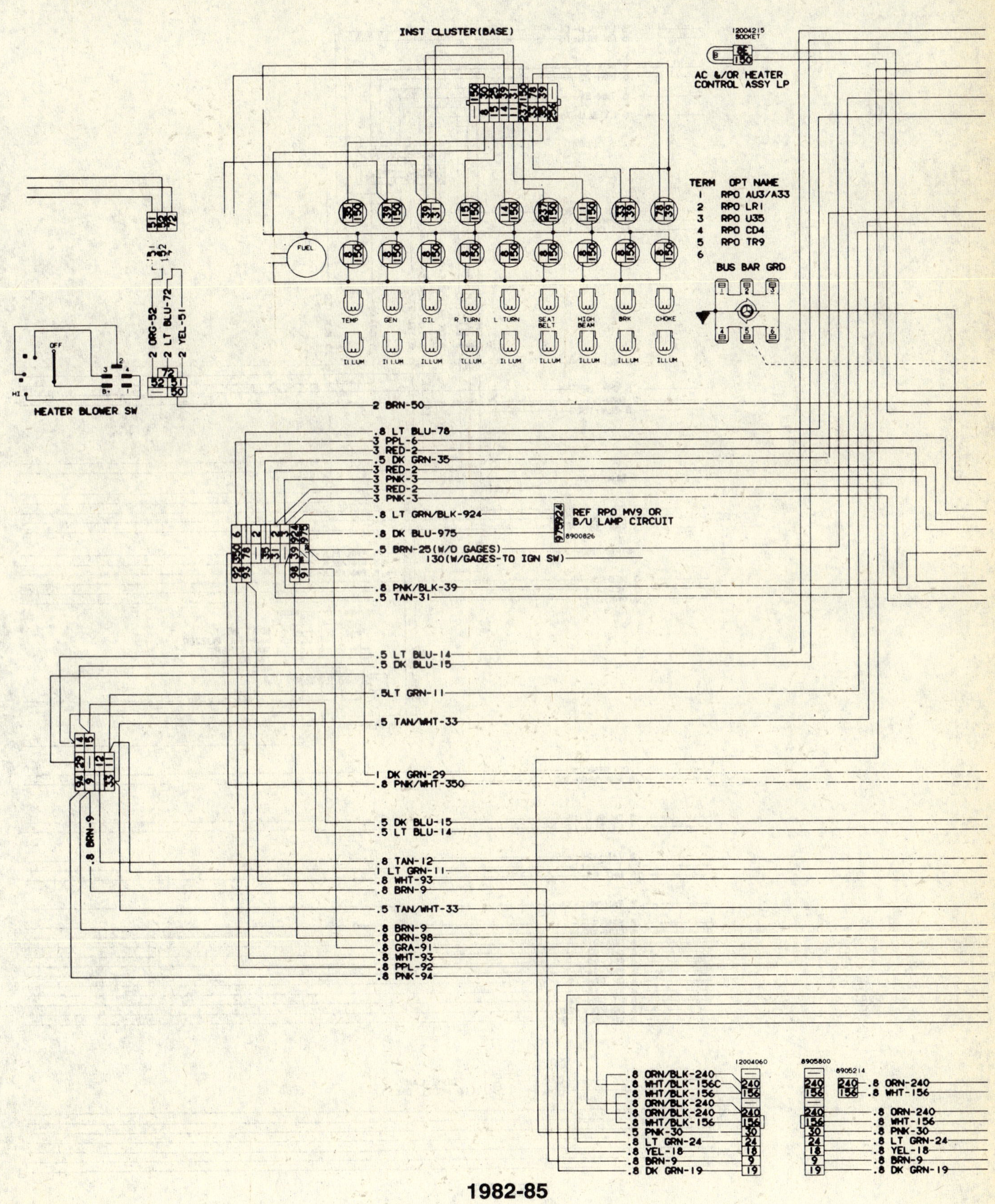

1982-85

.5 LT BLU-14
.5 DK BLU-15
.5 PNK-30
.5 BRN-25
.5 TAN-31
.8 LT BLU-78
.5 DK GRN-35
.5 TAN/WHT-33
.5LT GRN-11
.8 PNK/BLK-39
.8 PNK/BLK-39
.8 BLK-150
.8 DK BLU/WHT-236
.5 TAN/WHT-33
.8 YEL-237
.5 GRA-8
.8 BLK-150
.8 BLK-150
.5 GRA-8E
2 BRN-50
.8 BLK-150G
3 BLK-150A
SPLICE 150
3 PPL-6
3 RED-2G
3 PNK-3B
.8 PNK/BLK-39
.8 PNK/BLK-39
.8 PNK/BLK-39
.8 PNK/BLK-39
3 RED-2A
3 RED-2F
3 PNK-3A
HTR
BUZZER
SEAT BELT WARNING BUZZER AND TIMER (ALSO SEE RPO T63)
8917102
.8 YEL-237
.8 PNK/BLK-39
.8 BLK-150
1 DK GRN-29
.8 PNK/WHT-350
.5 DK BLU-15
.5 LT BLU-14
.8 TAN-12
1 LT GRN-11
.8 WHT-93
.5 TAN/WHT-33
.8 BRN-9
.8 ORN-98
.8 GRA-91
.8 WHT-93
.8 PPL-92
.8 PNK-94
.8 DK GRN-19
.8 YEL-18
.8 LT GRN-24
.8 ORN/BLK-240
.8 WHT/BLK-156
12015654 LAMP BODY
240
156
DOME LAMP (16 MODEL ONLY)

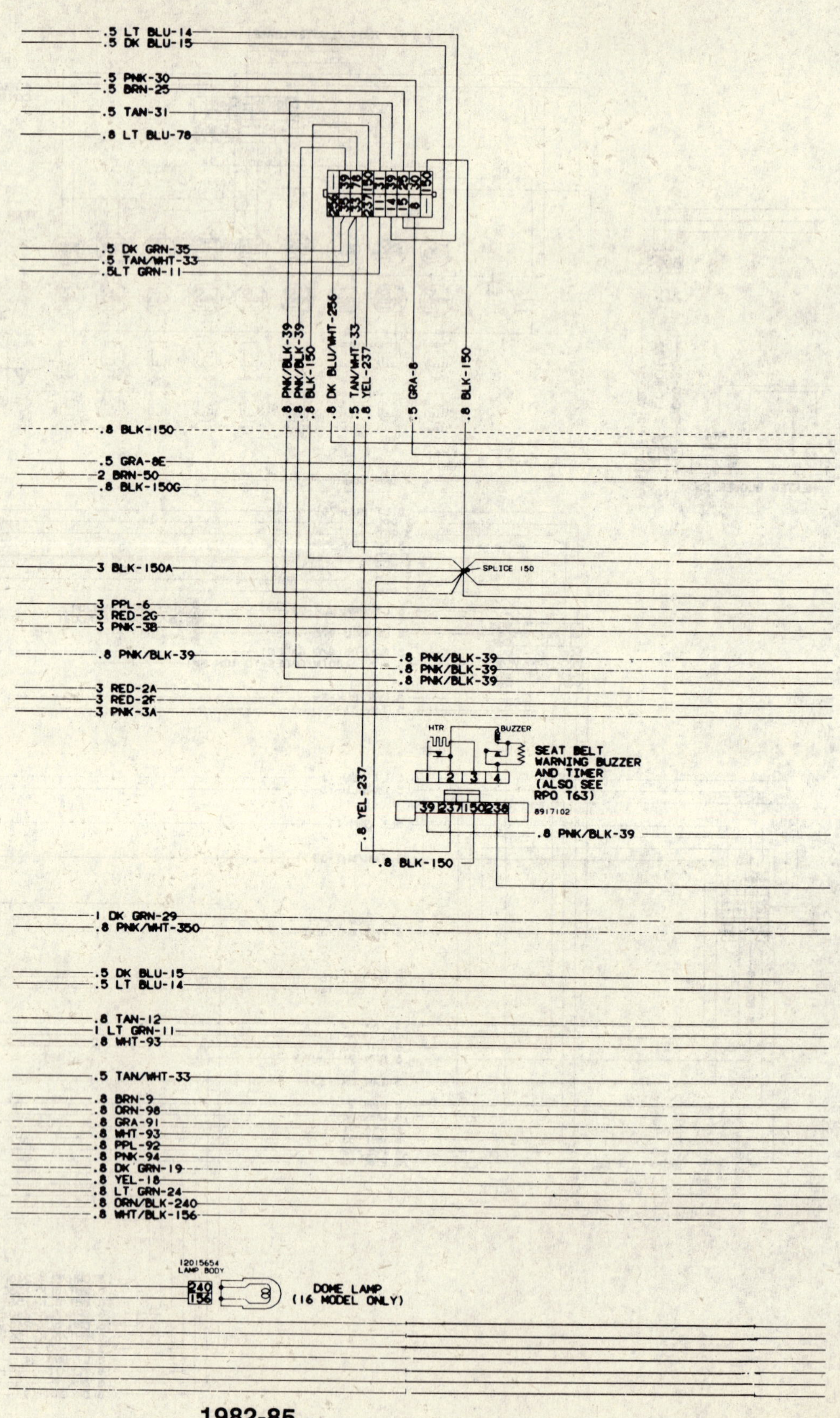

1982-85

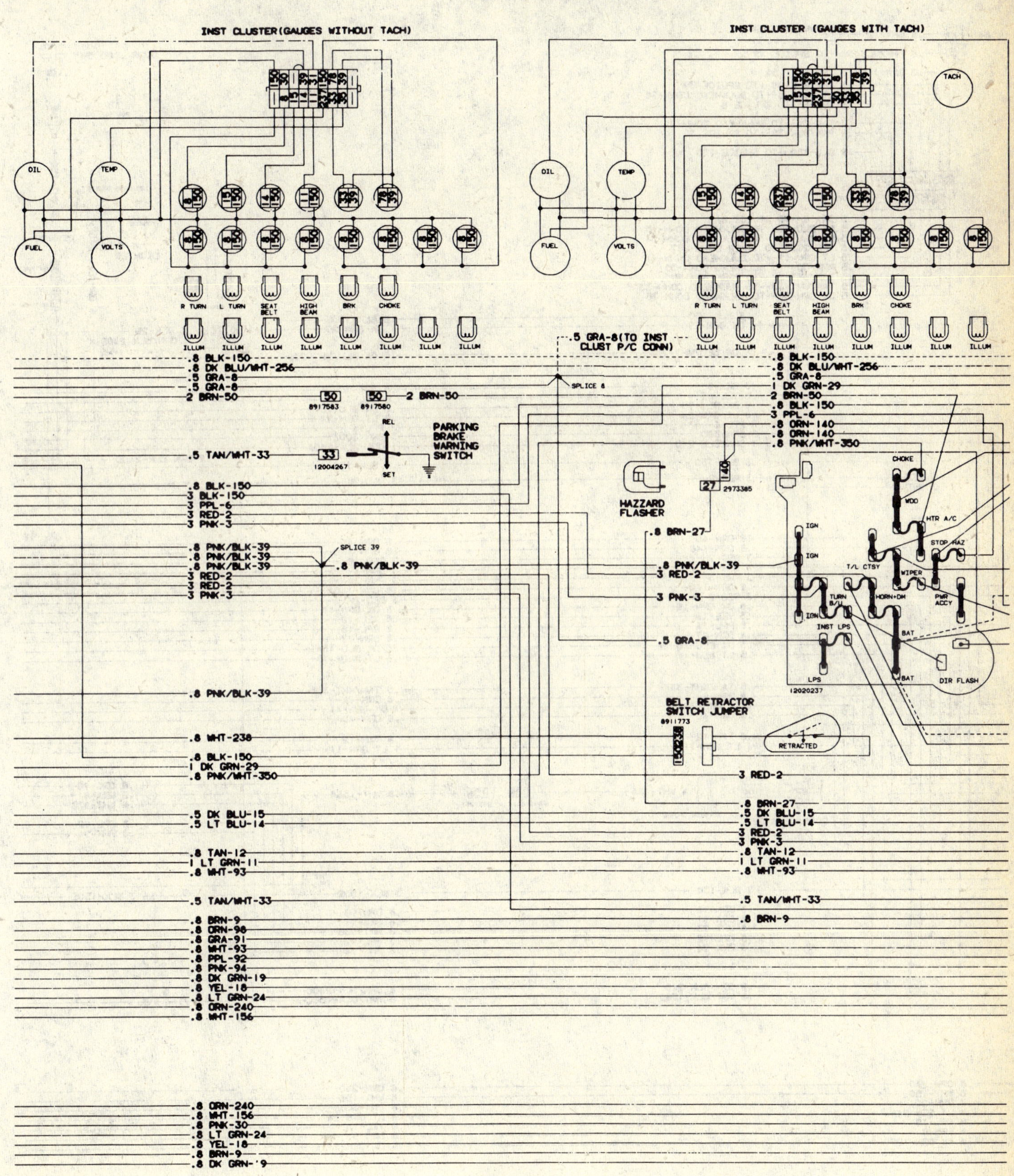

1982-85

2965164
.8 WHT-121
TACH FILTER
8917583
.8 PNK/BLK-39--TO SPLICE 39
.8 BLK-150--TO SPLICE 150
.8 PNK/BLK-39--TO SPLICE 39
.8 LT BLU-78--TO BULKHEAD CONN-78
.8 GRA-8--TO SPLICE-8
.5 TAN-31--TO BULKHEAD CONN-31
.8 PNK/BLK-39--TO SPLICE 39
.8 BLK-150--TO SPLICE 150
8911075
.5 GRA-8--TO SPLICE 8
.5 DK BLU-15--TO BULKHEAD CONN-15
.5 LT BLU-14--TO BULKHEAD CONN-14
.8 YEL-237--TO TIMER CONN-237
.5 LT GRN-11--TO BULKHEAD CONN-11
.5 PNK-30--TO BULKHEAD CONN-30
.5 TAN/WHT-33--TO PARK BRK SW
.5 TAN/WHT-33--TO BULKHEAD CONN-33
.5 DK GRN-35--TO BULKHEAD CONN-35
DOOR JAMB SW
2965508 TERM
.8 WHT-156
12015958 GROMMET
240
LIGHTER
HORN
RELAY
.8 ORN/BLK 240F
2977253
9800420
.8 BLK-150
1 DK GRN-29
.8 BLK-150F
1 DK GRN-29
.5 BLK-28
.8 ORN/BLK 240B
2984164
SPLICE 240
.8 DK BLU/WHT-256
.8 DK BLU/WHT-256
.5 GRA-8
.5 YEL-43
.8 DK BLU-75
.8 LT GRN-24
3 PPL-6
3 ORN-300
1 ORN/BLK-240
.5 GRA-8C
.5 YEL-43
.8 DK BLU-75
.8 LT GRN-24
3 PPL-6
3 ORN-300Z
1 ORN/BLK-240A
.8 BLK-150
.8 BLK 150
.8 ORN/BLK-240C
3 RED-2
3 RED-2
3 RED-2
SPLICE 2
3 RED-2E
.8 ORN-40
.8 ORN-140
3 RED-2
3 BRN-4
3 PNK-3
.8 ORN-140
3 RED-2
.8 DK GRN-19
.8 YEL-18
.8 PPL-16
.8 BRN-27
.5 DK BLU-15
.5 LT BLU-14
.8 ORN-40
.8 ORN-140
3 RED-2C
3 BRN-4
3 PNK-3A
.8 ORN-140A
3 RED-2F
.8 DK GRN-19
.8 YEL-18
.8 PPL-16
.8 BRN-27
.5 DK BLU-15A
.5 LT BLU-14A
.5 TAN/WHT-33
.8 BRN-9
1 DK GRN-44
.8 ORN-40
.5 TAN/WHT-33B
.8 BRN-9A
1 DK GRN-44
.8 ORN-40A
.8 TAN-12
1 LT GRN-11
.8 TAN-12
1 LT GRN-11A
2984369 TERM
156
.8 WHT-156
DOOR JAMB SW
12015958 GROMMET
8900423
2977253
.8 WHT-156A
.8 ORG-98
.8 GRA-91
.8 WHT-93B
.8 PPL-92
.8 PNK-94
3 BLK-150
3 BLK-150E
3 BLK-150E
.8 ORN-98
.8 GRA-91
.8 WHT-93
.8 PPL-92
.8 PNK-94
.8 ORN-98
.8 GRA-91
.8 WHT-93B
.8 PPL-92
.8 PNK-94
.8 ORN/BLK-240
.8 WHT/BLK-156
.8 ORN/BLK-240C
.8 WHT/BLK-156C
.8 ORN-240
.8 WHT-156
.8 PNK-30
.8 LT GRN-24
.8 YEL-18
.8 BRN-9
.8 DK GRN-19
.8 ORN-240
.8 WHT-156
.8 PNK-30
.8 LT GRN-24
.8 YEL-18
.8 BRN-9
.8 DK GRN-19

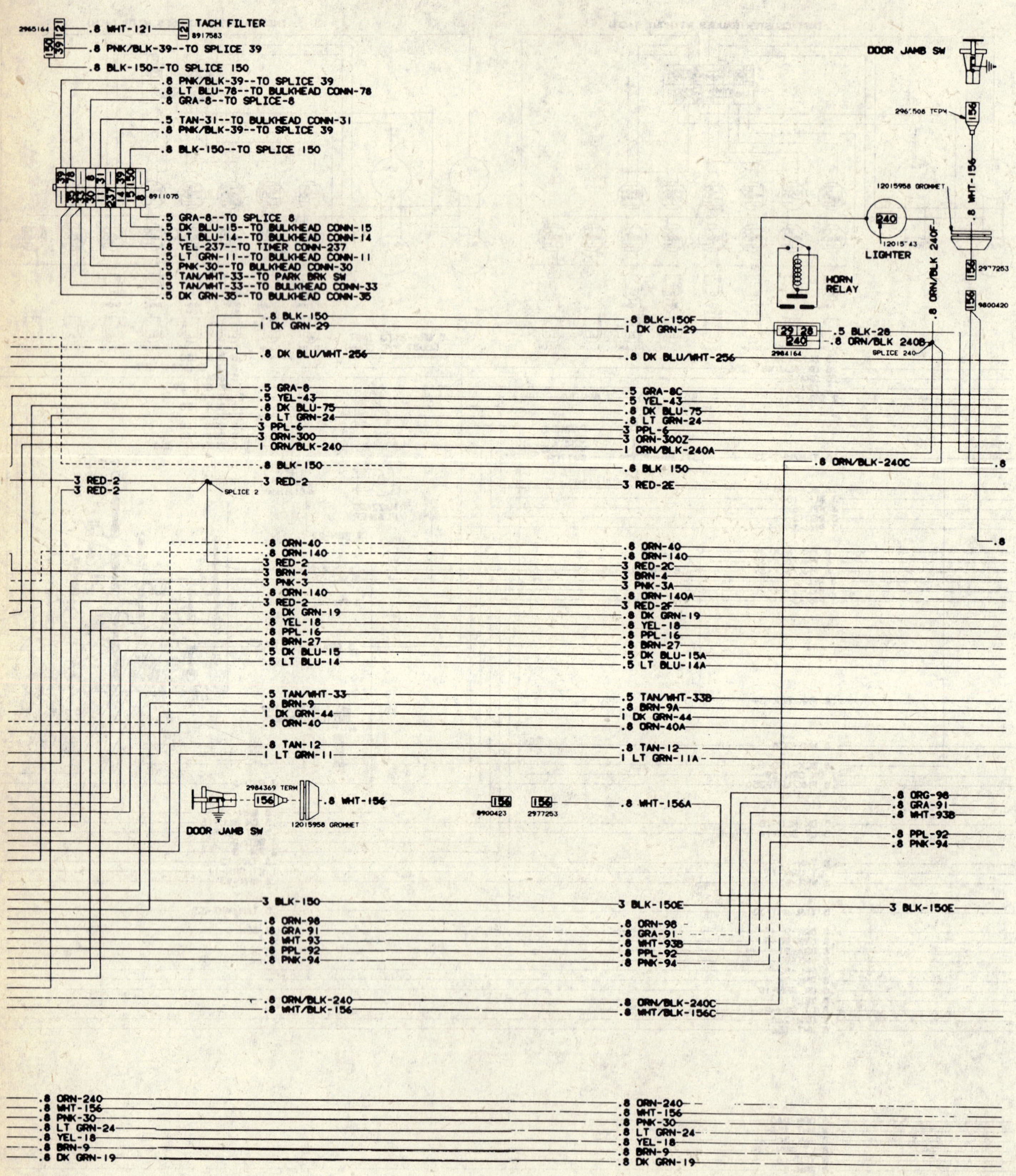

1982-85

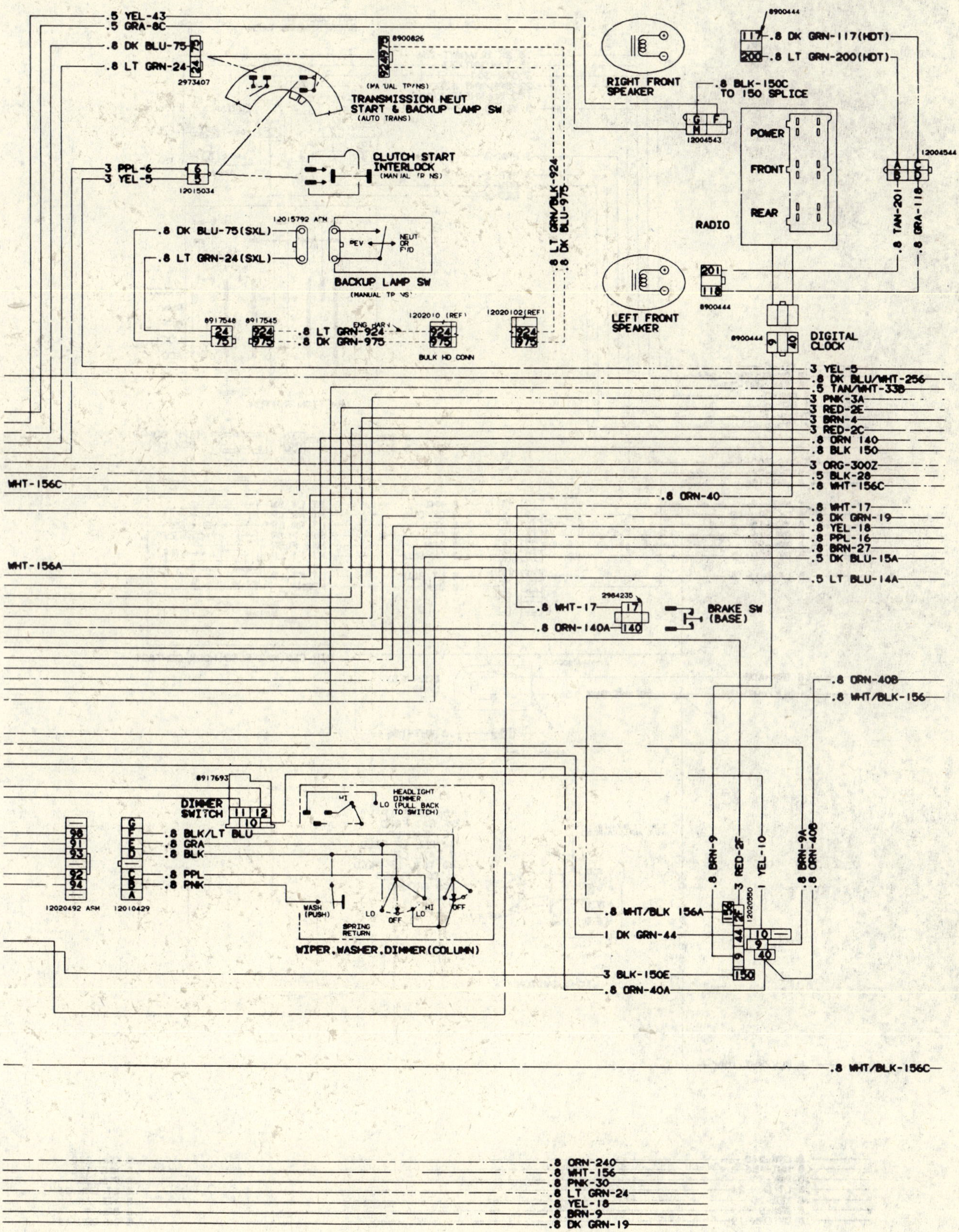

.5 YEL-43
.5 GRA-8C
.8 DK BLU-75
.8 LT GRN-24
2973407
8900826
(MANUAL TRANS)
TRANSMISSION NEUT START & BACKUP LAMP SW
(AUTO TRANS)
3 PPL-6
3 YEL-5
12015034
CLUTCH START INTERLOCK
(MANUAL TRANS)
12015792 ASM
.8 DK BLU-75(SXL)
.8 LT GRN-24(SXL)
REV
NEUT OR P/D
BACKUP LAMP SW
(MANUAL TRANS)
8917548
8917545
.8 LT GRN-924
.8 DK GRN-975
ENG HARN
12020010 (REF)
12020102(REF)
BULK HD CONN
.8 LT GRN/BLK-924
.8 DK BLU-975
RIGHT FRONT SPEAKER
.8 BLK-150C TO 150 SPLICE
12004543
POWER
FRONT
REAR
RADIO
LEFT FRONT SPEAKER
8900444
.8 DK GRN-117(HDT)
.8 LT GRN-200(HDT)
12004544
.8 TAN-201
.8 GRA-118
DIGITAL CLOCK
3 YEL-5
.8 DK BLU/WHT-256
.5 TAN/WHT-33B
3 PNK-3A
3 RED-2E
3 BRN-4
3 RED-2C
.8 ORN 140
.8 BLK 150
3 ORG-300Z
.5 BLK-28
.8 WHT-156C
WHT-156C
.8 ORN-40
.8 WHT-17
.8 DK GRN-19
.8 YEL-18
.8 PPL-16
.8 BRN-27
.5 DK BLU-15A
WHT-156A
.5 LT BLU-14A
2984235
.8 WHT-17
.8 ORN-140A
BRAKE SW (BASE)
.8 ORN-40B
.8 WHT/BLK-156
8917693
DIMMER SWITCH
HEADLIGHT DIMMER (PULL BACK TO SWITCH)
.8 BLK/LT BLU
.8 GRA
.8 BLK
.8 PPL
.8 PNK
12020492 ASM
12010429
WASH (PUSH)
SPRING RETURN
LO
OFF
HI
WIPER, WASHER, DIMMER (COLUMN)
.8 BRN-9
3 RED-2F
1 YEL-10
.8 BRN-9A
.8 ORN-40B
12020550
.8 WHT/BLK 156A
1 DK GRN-44
3 BLK-150E
.8 ORN-40A
.8 WHT/BLK-156C

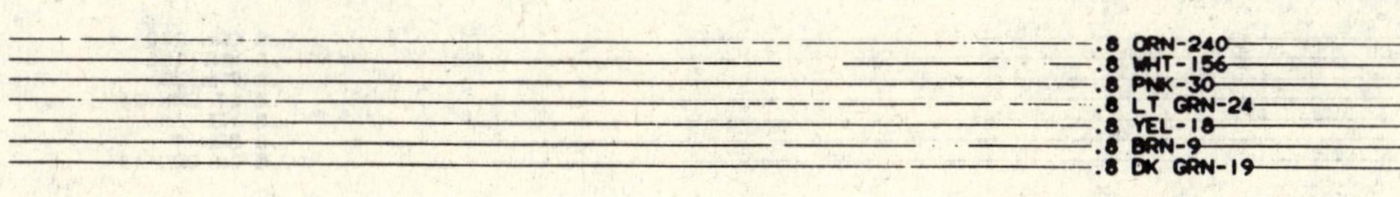

1982-85

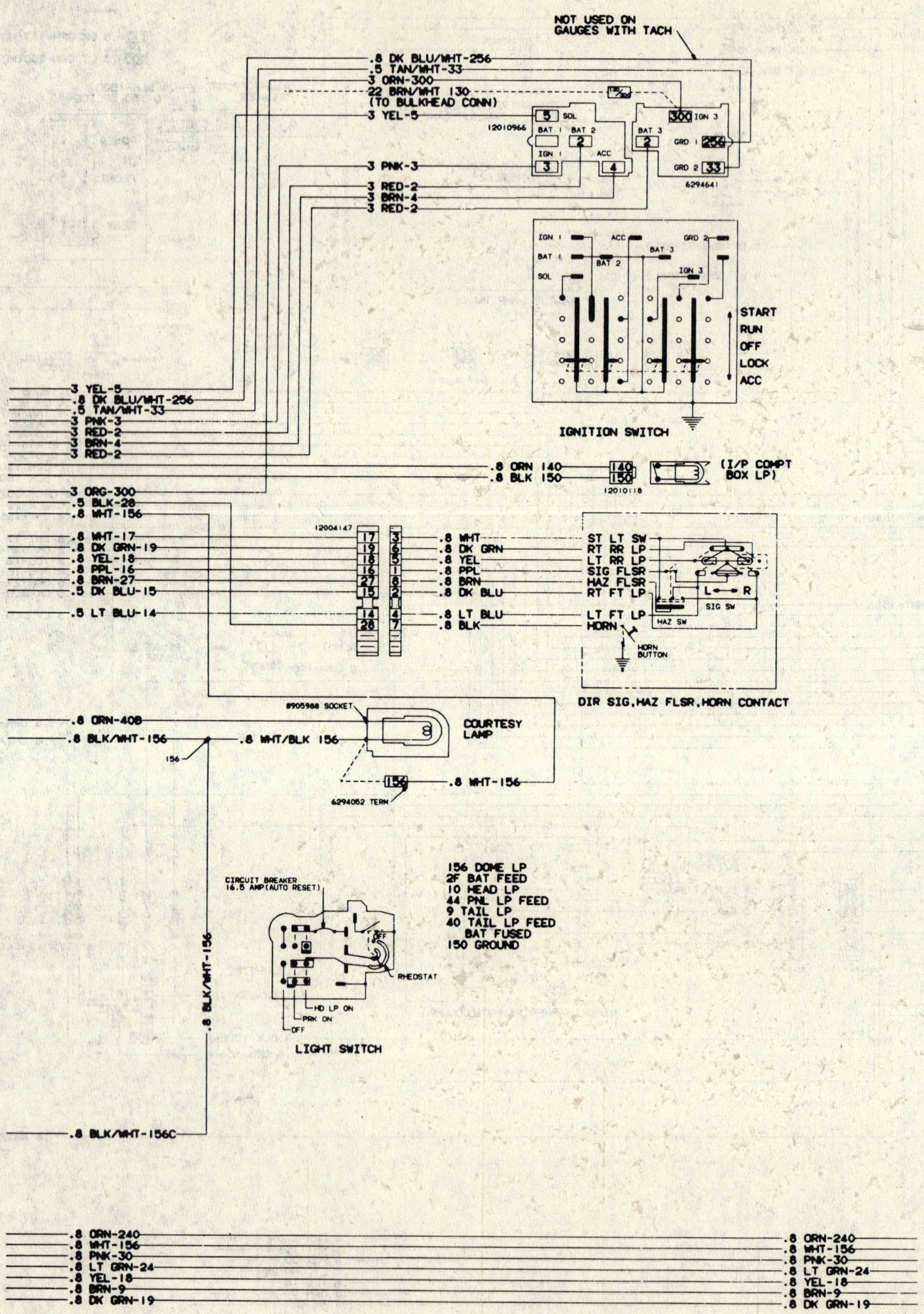

NOT USED ON GAUGES WITH TACH

.8 DK BLU/WHT-256
.5 TAN/WHT-33
3 ORN-300
22 BRN/WHT 130
(TO BULKHEAD CONN)
3 YEL-5
3 PNK-3
3 RED-2
3 BRN-4
3 RED-2

12010966
5 SOL
BAT 1
BAT 2
2
IGN 1
3
ACC
4

300 IGN 3
BAT 3
2
GRD 1 256
GRD 2 33
6294641

IGN 1
ACC
GRD 2
BAT 1
BAT 2
BAT 3
SOL
IGN 3
START
RUN
OFF
LOCK
ACC

IGNITION SWITCH

3 YEL-5
.8 DK BLU/WHT-256
.5 TAN/WHT-33
3 PNK-3
3 RED-2
3 BRN-4
3 RED-2

.8 ORN 140
.8 BLK 150
140
150
12010118
(I/P COMPT BOX LP)

3 ORG-300
.5 BLK-28
.8 WHT-156

12004147
.8 WHT-17
.8 DK GRN-19
.8 YEL-18
.8 PPL-16
.8 BRN-27
.5 DK BLU-15
.5 LT BLU-14

17 3
19 6
18 5
16 1
27 8
15 2
14 4
28 7

.8 WHT
.8 DK GRN
.8 YEL
.8 PPL
.8 BRN
.8 DK BLU
.8 LT BLU
.8 BLK

ST LT SW
RT RR LP
LT RR LP
SIG FLSR
HAZ FLSR
RT FT LP
LT FT LP
HORN
L R
SIG SW
HAZ SW
HORN BUTTON

DIR SIG, HAZ FLSR, HORN CONTACT

8905988 SOCKET
.8 ORN-40B
.8 BLK/WHT-156
156
.8 WHT/BLK 156
COURTESY LAMP
156
.8 WHT-156
6294082 TERM

CIRCUIT BREAKER 16.5 AMP (AUTO RESET)
OFF
RHEOSTAT
HD LP ON
PRK ON
OFF

LIGHT SWITCH

156 DOME LP
2F BAT FEED
10 HEAD LP
44 PNL LP FEED
9 TAIL LP
40 TAIL LP FEED
BAT FUSED
150 GROUND

.8 BLK/WHT-156

.8 BLK/WHT-156C

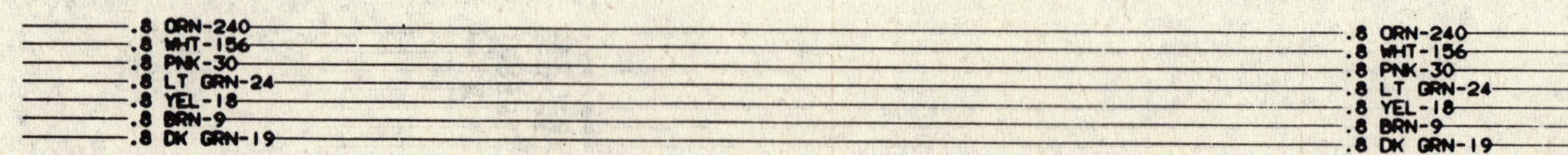

1982-85

FRAME GRD
.8 BLK-150A
.8 BRN-9
6294015 SOCKET
SPLICE 9
2989576 GROMMET
2984378
6288191
.8 BLK-150
.8 YEL-18
.8 BRN-9
.8 BLK-150
SPLICE 150
8917818 SOCKET
TAIL STOP & DIR
.8 LT GRN-24
.8 BLK-150
12010804 SOCKET
B/U LAMP
.8 DK GRN-19
.8 LT GRN-24
.8 BRN-9
GRD
.8 BLK-150
RT DOME LP SW
.8 WHT-156
.8 WHT-156
2973407
FUEL METER
FRAME GRD
LICENSE LAMP
.8 BRN-9
2977107
REAR DOME LAMP
.8 ORN-240
8900863
.8 PNK-30
.8 LT GRN-24
.8 PNK-30
.8 WHT-156
.8 ORN-240
.8 DK GRN-19
.8 BRN-9
8900441
.8 YEL-18
.8 LT GRN 24
8900440
.8 BLK-150
.8 LT GRN-24
.8 BLK-150
.8 BRN-9
.8 YEL-18
.8 BLK-150
.8 BRN-9
6294015 SOCKET
B/U LAMP
TAIL STOP & DIR

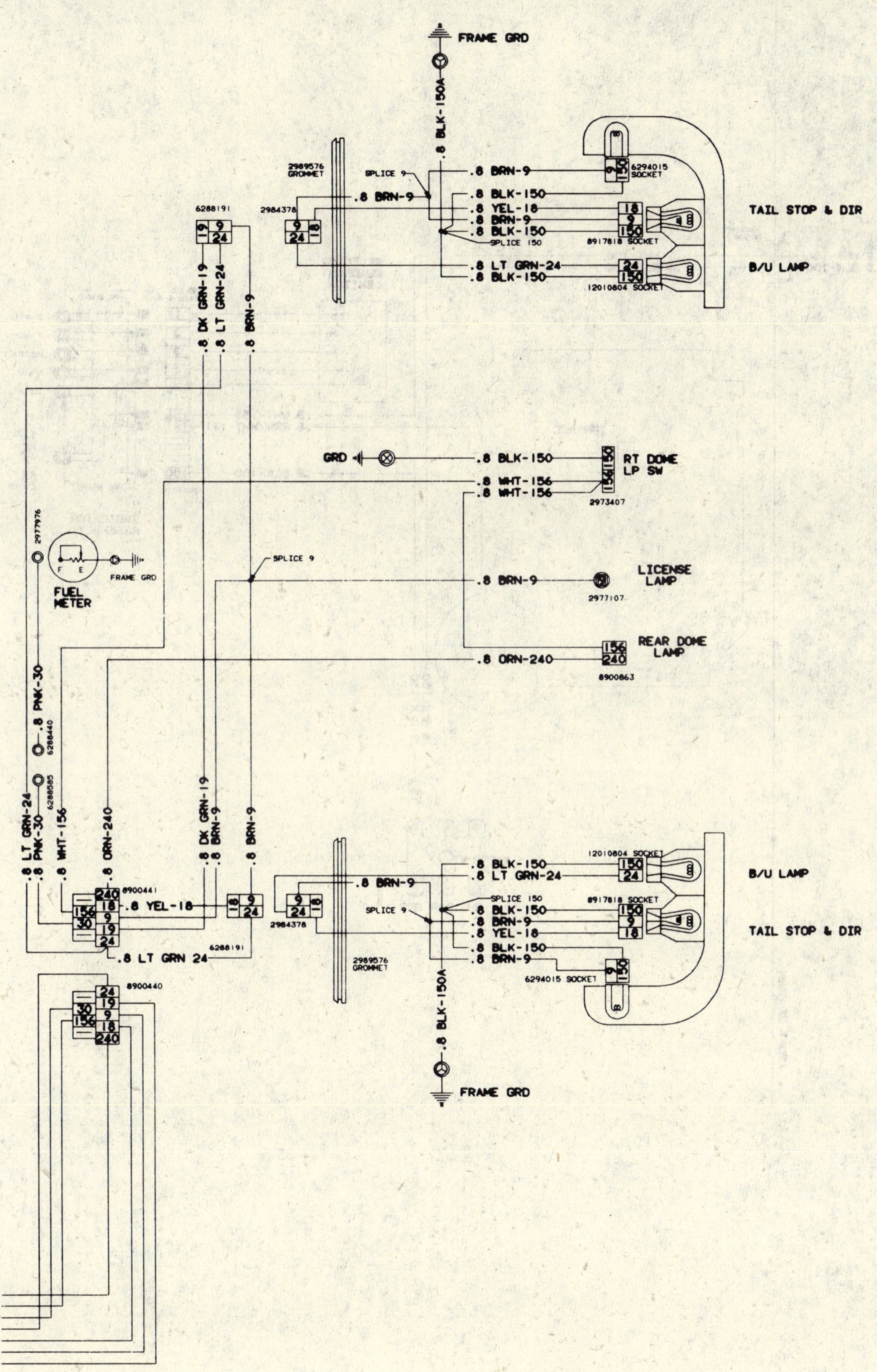

1982-85

FRONT AXLE SW
12015792
.8 WHT-156
.8 BLK 150
12010973
12015792
.8 WHT-156
.8 BLK 150
12015957 GROMMET
.5 WHT-156
.8 BLK 150
SELECTOR QUADRANT SWITCH
MOLEX 6422-6-4
PC BOARD
2 WHEEL
4 HIGH
NEUTRAL
4 LOW
ILLUM
IGN ACC
.5 WHT-156
.8 BRN/WHT-141
.8 BLK-150
12034018
PC BOARD
FRONT & REAR AXLE DISPLAY
INDICATOR ASSEMBLY
.8 BLK 150
.8 BLK-150
12004267
BUS BAR GRD
FRONT OF DASH

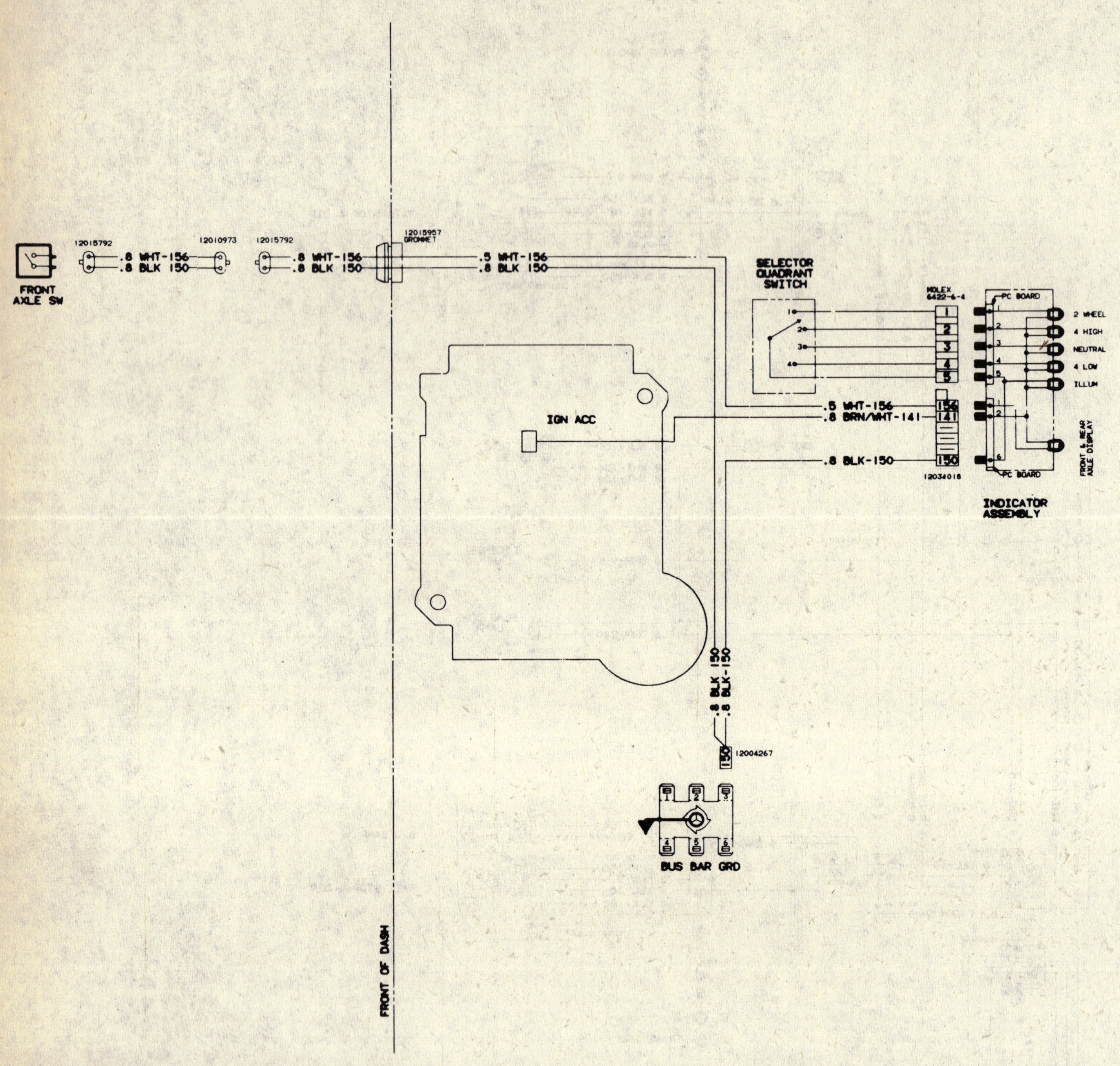

1982-85

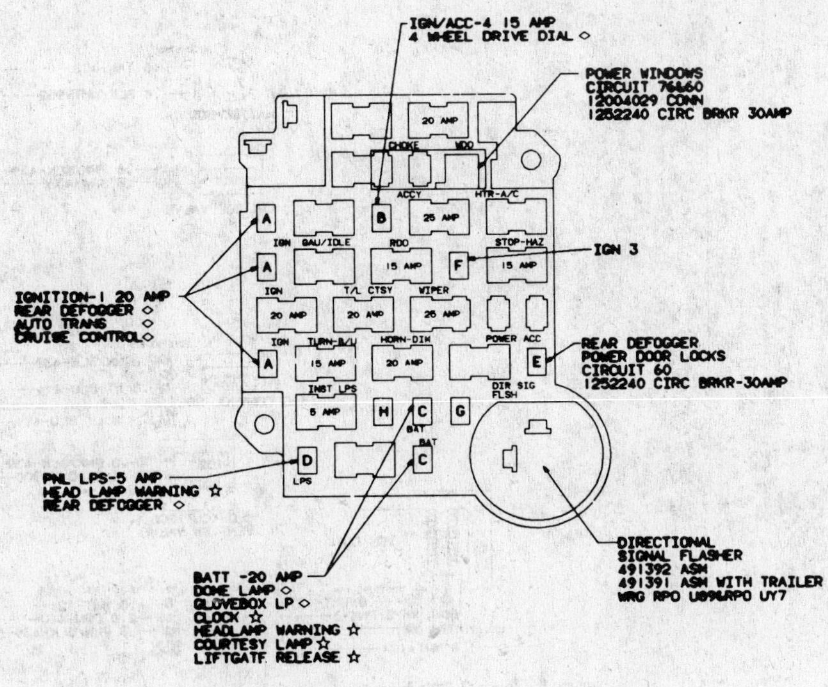

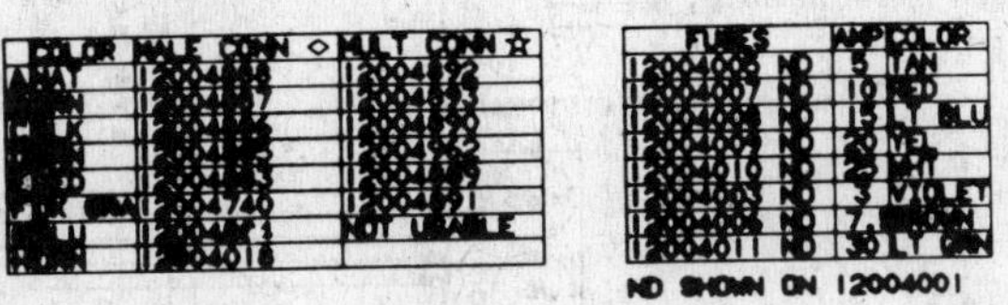

COLOR	MALE CONN ◇	MULT CONN ☆
[illegible]	[illegible]	[illegible]
[illegible]	[illegible]	[illegible]
[illegible]	[illegible]	[illegible]
[illegible]	[illegible]	[illegible]
[illegible]	[illegible]	[illegible]
[illegible]	[illegible]	[illegible]
[illegible]	[illegible]	[illegible]
[illegible]	[illegible]	NOT USABLE
[illegible]	[illegible]	

FUSES		AMP	COLOR
[illegible]	ND	5	TAN
[illegible]	ND	10	RED
[illegible]	ND	15	LT BLU
[illegible]	ND	20	YEL
[illegible]	ND	25	WHT
[illegible]	ND	3	VIOLET
[illegible]	ND	7.5	[illegible]
12004011	ND	30	LT GRN

ND SHOWN ON 12004001

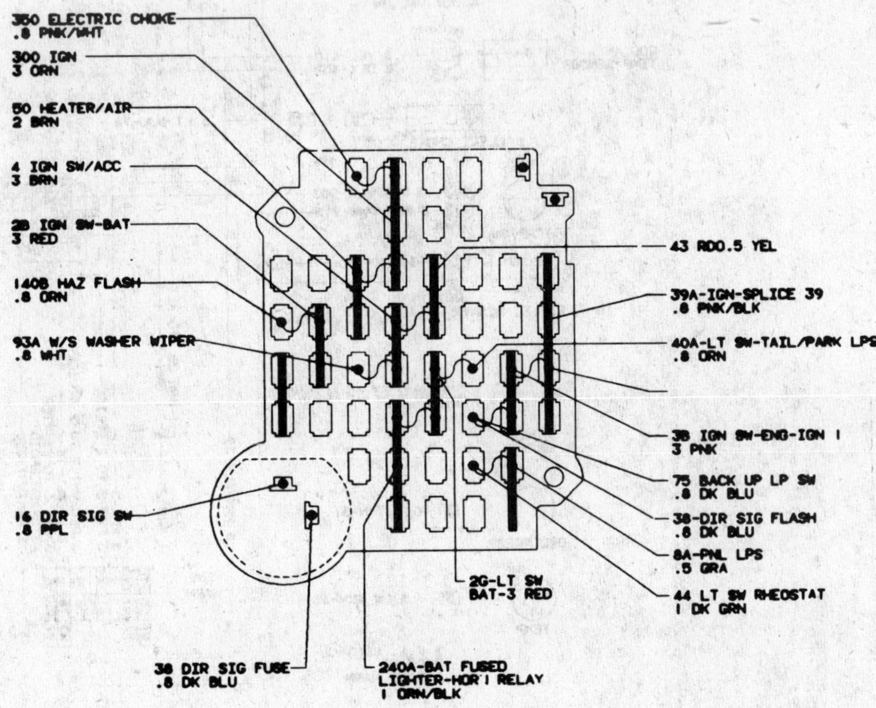

1982-85

12015792
.8 TAN-472
.8 BLK/WHT-952
MAT SENSOR
12015792 ASM
.8 PNK/BLK-439
.8 BRN-436
AIR SOL VALVE
12015793 ASM
.8PNK/BLK-439
.8 LT BLU-411
VAC CONTROL SOL
12015256
DIAGNOSIS
.8 LT BLU-411
.8 PNK/BLK-439
.8 DK/BLU-900
12015792 ASM
SLOW CUT SOL & VENT SW VALVE
IGN COIL
12015793 ASM
.8 WHT-121
3 PNK-3
12010717
.8 WHT-121
12010973
12015793 ASM
.8 WHT-121
2.0 ORN-440
.8 PNK/BLK-439
SPEED SENSOR
12015792 ASM
3 PNK-3
12010973
DISTRIBUTOR
412
12015791
OXYGEN SENSOR
.8 PNK/BLK-39
3 PNK-3
3 PNK-3
12015797
CLOSED
OPEN
2J(BATT JUNCTION BLK)
.8 GRA/RED-902
.8 DK GRN-904
.8 LT GRN-415
.8 GRA-901
.8 YEL-410
IDLE POSITION & WOT VAC SW
12020407 GROMMET
COOLANT TEMP SENSOR
12015008
410
452
.8 YEL-410
.8 BLK-452
78
78
8917583
.8 LT BLU-78
ELECT CHOKE
12010015
3 PNK/BLK-903
3 BLK/PNK-913
6294826
TEMP SW
EFE RELAY
150
3 BLK-150
6288181
E.F.E. HEATER
1 BRN 25 TO ALT
1 BRN-25
2&42F GO TO SEPARATE #2 SPLICES WHICH GO TO THE BATT TERM ON STARTER MOTOR
3 PNK-3
3 RED 2 TO 2 SPLICE
3 RED/WHT 2 TO 2 SPLICE
.8 LT BLU-78
3 PPL 6 TO STARTER MOTOR SOLENOID
.8 PNK/WHT-350
FRT OF DASH
31
.8 TAN-31
2977935
OIL PRESS
.8 PNK/BLK-39
1 BRN-25
ENG HARN
35
.5 DK GRN-35
2977142
TEMP
12020183
E.F.E. CONTROL PART OF ENGINE HARN

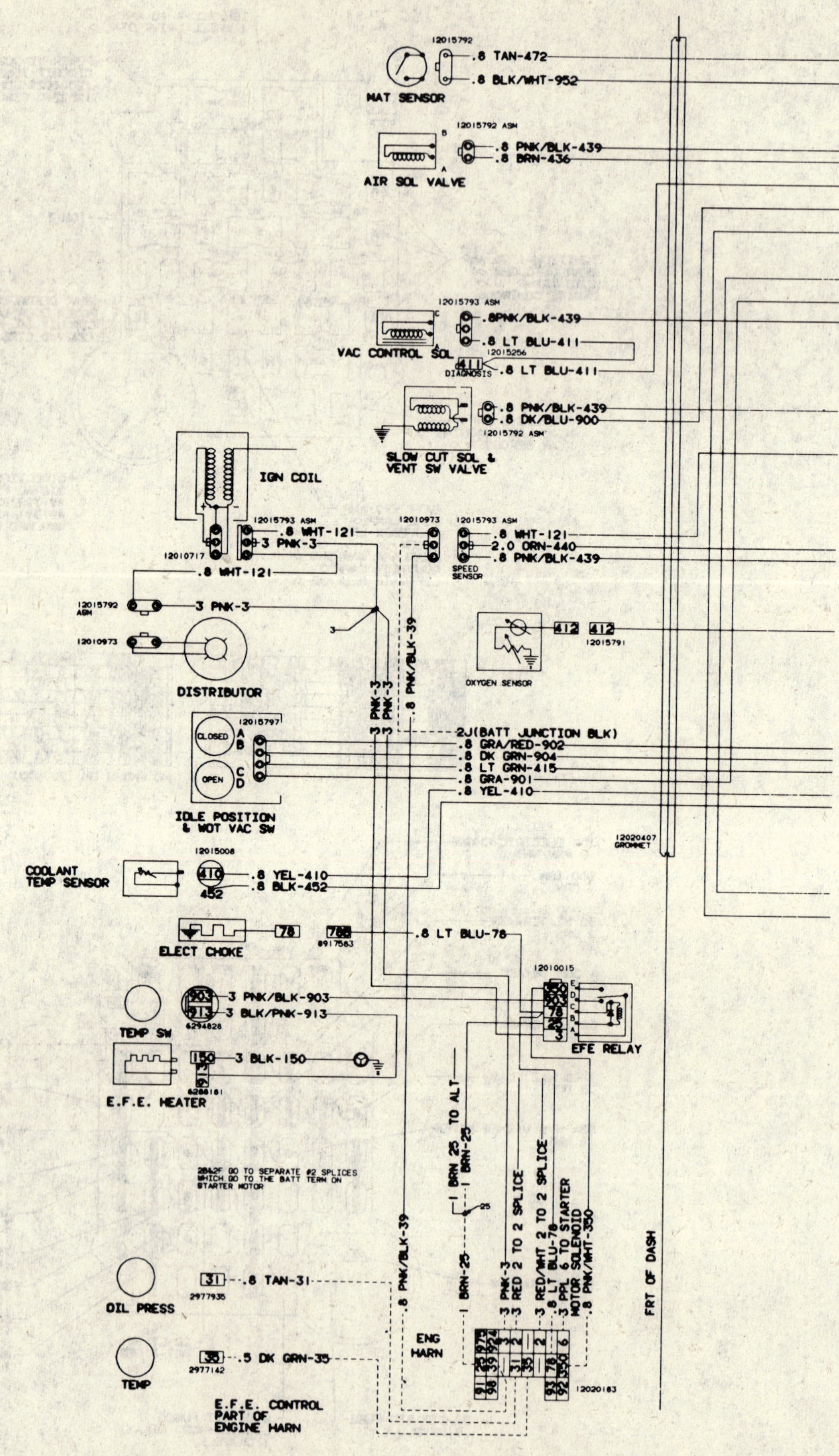

1982-85

ELECTRONIC CONTROL MODULE
A VAC CONTROL SOL
B CARB FUEL CUT SOL
C MALFUNCTION LIGHT
D IGN
E WOT SW GRD
F BATTERY
G POWER GRD
H NOT USED
I AIR SOL
J TACH INPUT
K IDLE SW GRD
L CASE GRD
M CONTROL GRD
1 OXYGEN SENSOR INPUT
2 COOLANT TEMP SENSOR INPUT
3 NOT USED
4 NOT USED
5 BAROMETRIC SW INPUT
6 IDLE POSITION SW INPUT
7 WOT POSITION SW INPUT
8 DIAGNOSTIC ENABLE ALDL
9 INLET AIR & BARO SW GRD
10 OXYGEN SENSOR GRD
11 COOLANT TEMP SENSOR GRD
12 NOT USED
13 AIR INLET TEMP INPUT
14 NOT USED
15 NOT USED
16 NOT USED
17 NOT USED
SPLICE 436
.8 LT BLU-411
.8 DK/BLU-900
.8 WHT/DK GRN-487
1 PNK/BLK-139
.5 GRA-901
.8 ORN-440B
12033796
ENG GRD
1 BLK/WHT-150
.5 TAN-413
SENSOR GRD
.5 PPL-412
12020816
.5 BLK-452
.5 BLK/WHT-952
BARO SW
12015792
GRA/BLK-433
BLK/WHT-952
.8 PNK/BLK-39
.8 YEL-489
.8 BLK-150
.8 WHT/DK GRN-487
LAMP DRIVER
GRD
.8 BRN-436
.5 GRA/BLK-433
.8 BLK/WHT-952
2 ORN-440
1 PNK/BLK-139
.5 WHT/BLK-451
12015416
12015922
SPLICE 139
ENG CHK LP
12004215 SOCKET
2 PNK/BLK-139
12010632
ECM RELAY
2 ORN-440
.8 BLK/WHT-451
.8 BRN-436
ALDL TEST CONN
12020043

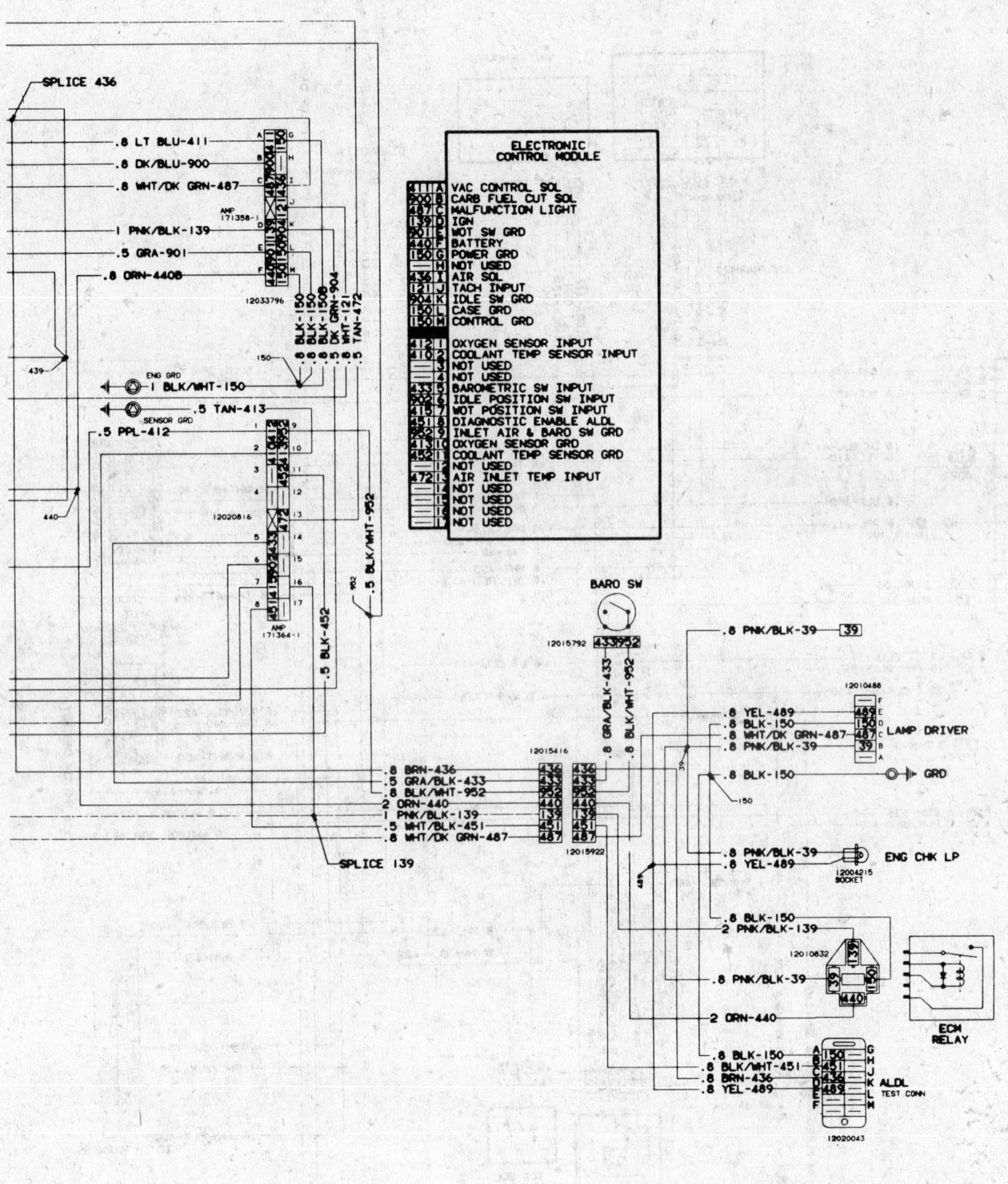

1982-85

EST
HEI REF
EST SIG COND
VAC SENSOR
DIAGNOSIS
FRT OF DASH
ENG/HARN
THROTTLE POSITION SENSOR
COOLANT TEMP SENSOR
OXYGEN SENSOR
EFE HTR
AIR FUEL CARB SOL
TO ENG HARN
IGN I FEED
AIR DIVERT
.8 GRA-416
.8 BLK-452
.8 DK BLU-417
.8 YEL-410
.8 PPL-412
3 BLK-150
3 PNK-3
.8 LT BLU-411
.8 PNK/BLK-439
I BLK/WHT-450
.8 ORN-440
.5 BRN-436
.5 PNK/BLK-439
I PNK/BLK-439
.8 LT GRN 432
.8 WHT/BLK-451
.8 GRA/RED-445
.8 PPL/WHT-430
.8 TAN-424
.8 WHT-423
.8 BLK/RED-453
.8 TAN-413
NOTE
CONN CAVITYS DESIGNATED 999 ARE DUMMYS OR NON-FUNCTIONAL CIRCUITS
.8 TAN/BLK-422
.8 BLK/WHT-450
.8 BRN-436
1.0 PNK/BLK-439
.8 WHT/DK GRN 487
.8 PPL-420
.8 TAN/BLK-422
.8WHT/BLK-451
I PNK/BLK-439
.8 TAN/BLK-422B
TO IP HARNESS
EFE RELAY
TCC SOL (AUTO ONLY)
RED 10A FUSED
PNK/BLK
ENG HARN

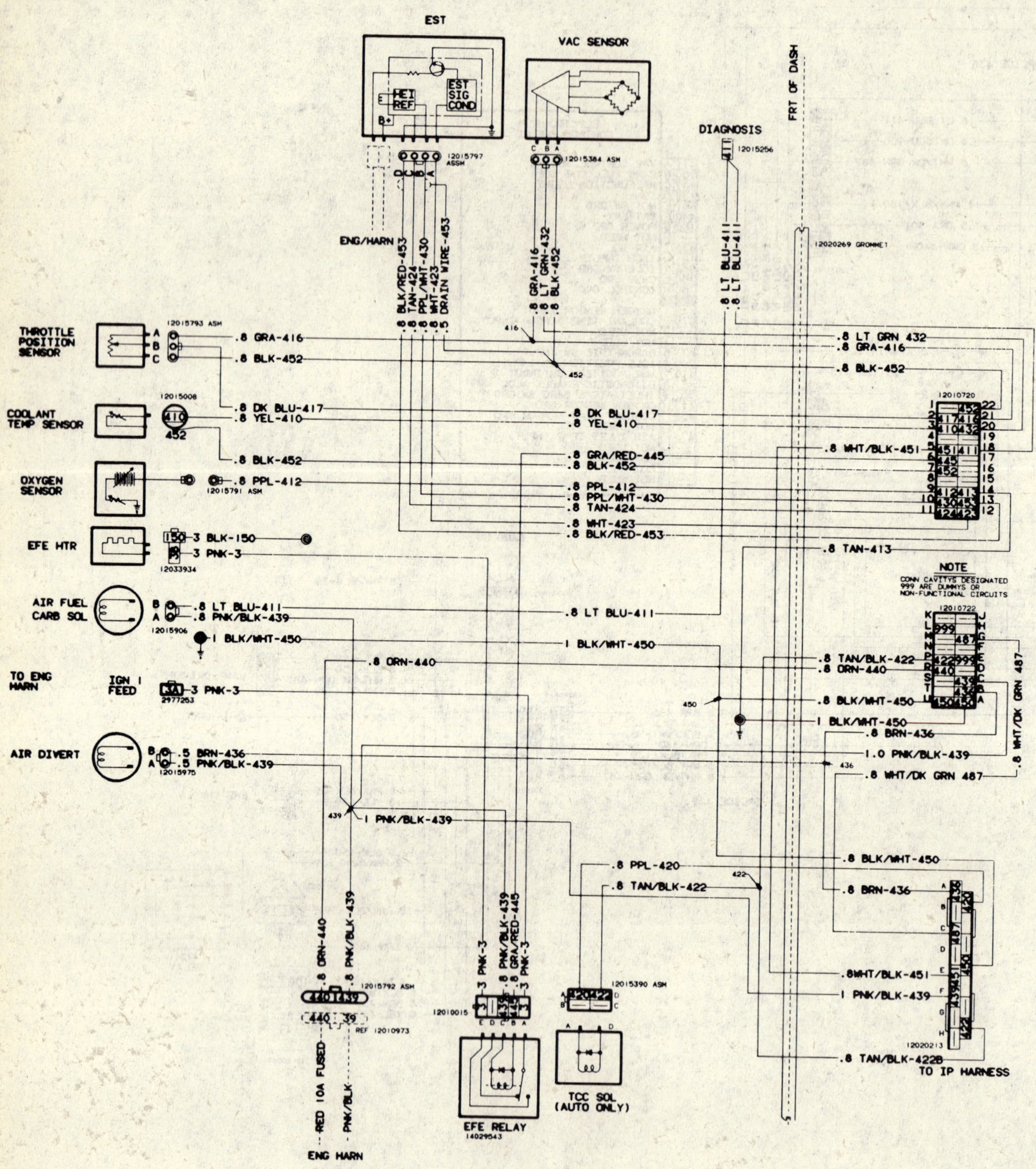

1982-85

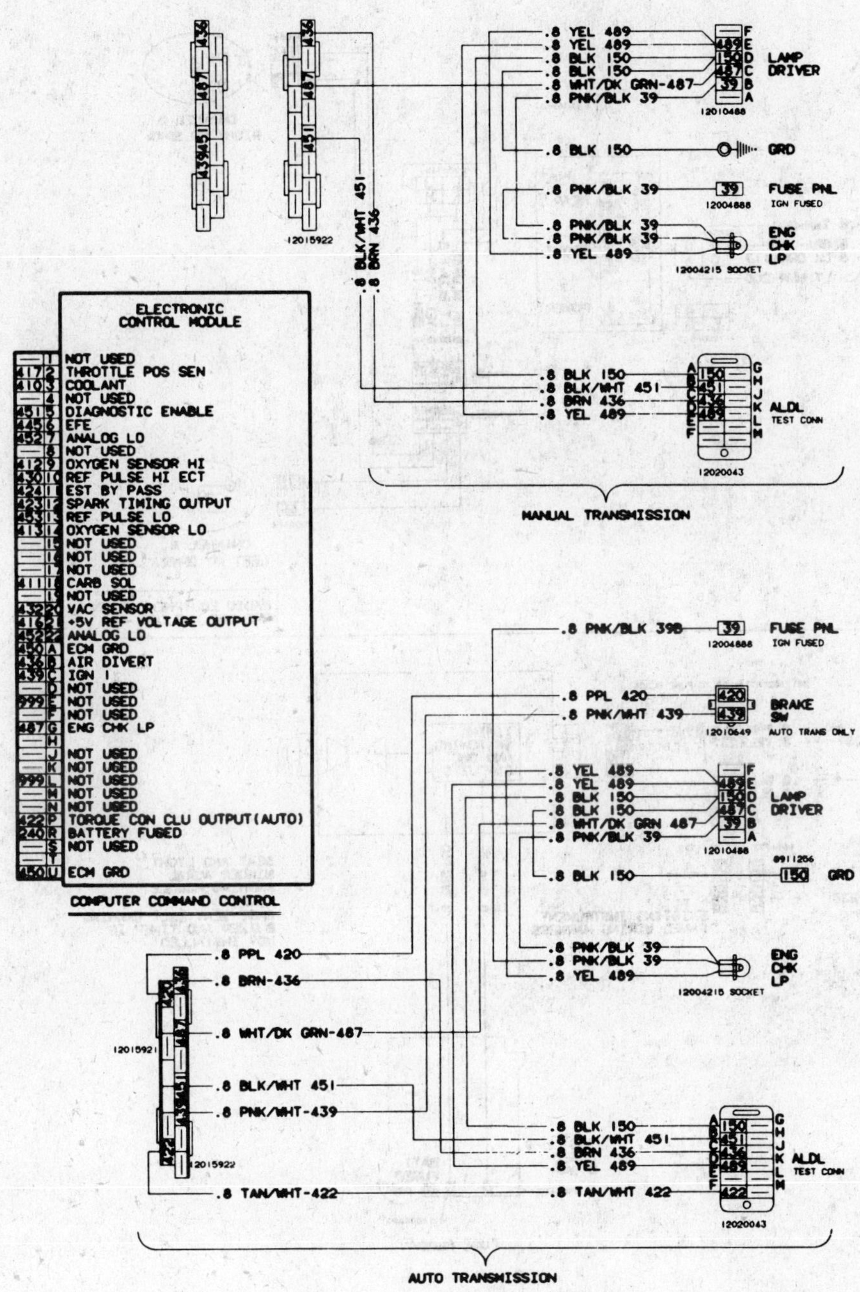

ELECTRONIC CONTROL MODULE
NOT USED
THROTTLE POS SEN
COOLANT
NOT USED
DIAGNOSTIC ENABLE
EFE
ANALOG LO
NOT USED
OXYGEN SENSOR HI
REF PULSE HI ECT
EST BY PASS
SPARK TIMING OUTPUT
REF PULSE LO
OXYGEN SENSOR LO
NOT USED
NOT USED
NOT USED
CARB SOL
NOT USED
VAC SENSOR
+5V REF VOLTAGE OUTPUT
ANALOG LO
ECM GRD
AIR DIVERT
IGN I
NOT USED
NOT USED
NOT USED
ENG CHK LP
NOT USED
NOT USED
NOT USED
NOT USED
NOT USED
TORQUE CON CLU OUTPUT (AUTO)
BATTERY FUSED
NOT USED
ECM GRD
COMPUTER COMMAND CONTROL
12015922
.8 BLK/WHT 451
.8 BRN 436
.8 YEL 489
.8 BLK 150
.8 WHT/DK GRN-487
.8 PNK/BLK 39
12010486
LAMP DRIVER
GRD
FUSE PNL
IGN FUSED
12004886
ENG CHK LP
12004215 SOCKET
ALDL
TEST CONN
12020043
MANUAL TRANSMISSION
.8 PNK/BLK 39B
.8 PPL 420
.8 PNK/WHT 439
BRAKE SW
AUTO TRANS ONLY
12010649
8911206
.8 BRN-436
.8 PNK/WHT-439
.8 TAN/WHT-422
.8 TAN/WHT 422
12015921
AUTO TRANSMISSION

1982-85

CHANNEL B
RIGHT FRONT
SPEAKER
CHANNEL B
RIGHT RR SPKR
ANTENNA
REAR
FRONT
POWER
.8 TAN-201
.8 GRA-118
.8 DK GRN-117
.8 LT GRN-200
.8 DK BLU-46
.8 LT BLU-115
.8 YEL-199
.8 BRN-116
CHANNEL A
LEFT FRONT
SPEAKER
CHANNEL A
LEFT RR SPKR
RADIO EQUIPMENT STEREO
RPO UM2,UN3,U58
SPLICE 39 (IGN 1 FUSED)
TO INST CLUSTER CONN 237
(SEAT BELT WARNING LAMP)
SPLICE 150 (GROUND CIRCUIT)
.8 PNK/BLK-39
.8 YEL-237
.8 BLK-150
.8 BLK-150
TIMING
SWITCHING
AND OSC
CIRCUITS
EXTENDED
RETRACTED
SEAT BELT
RETRACTOR SW
.8 BLK-150
.8 WHT-238
EXISTING INSTRUMENT
PANEL WIRING HARNESS
.8 GRA-8
.8 ORG-40
SEAT AND LIGHT
MINDER AURAL
WARNING MODULE
NOTE:
BASE SEAT BELT WARNING
BUZZER AND TIMER IS
NOT INSTALLED
INST LPS
FUSED
5 AMP
BATT
FUSED
20 AMP
FUSE BLOCK
HEADLAMP WARNING BUZZER
RPO T63

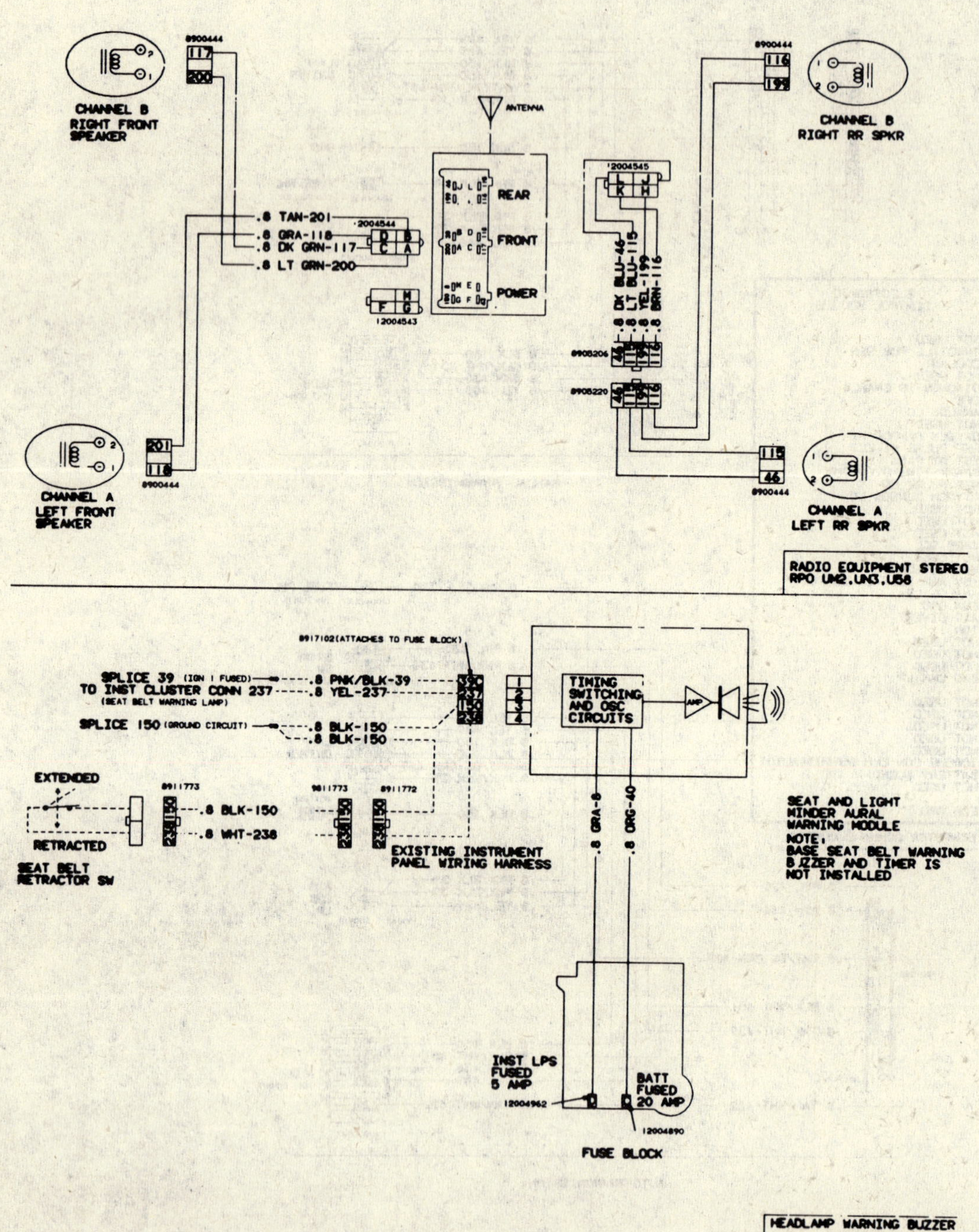

1982-85

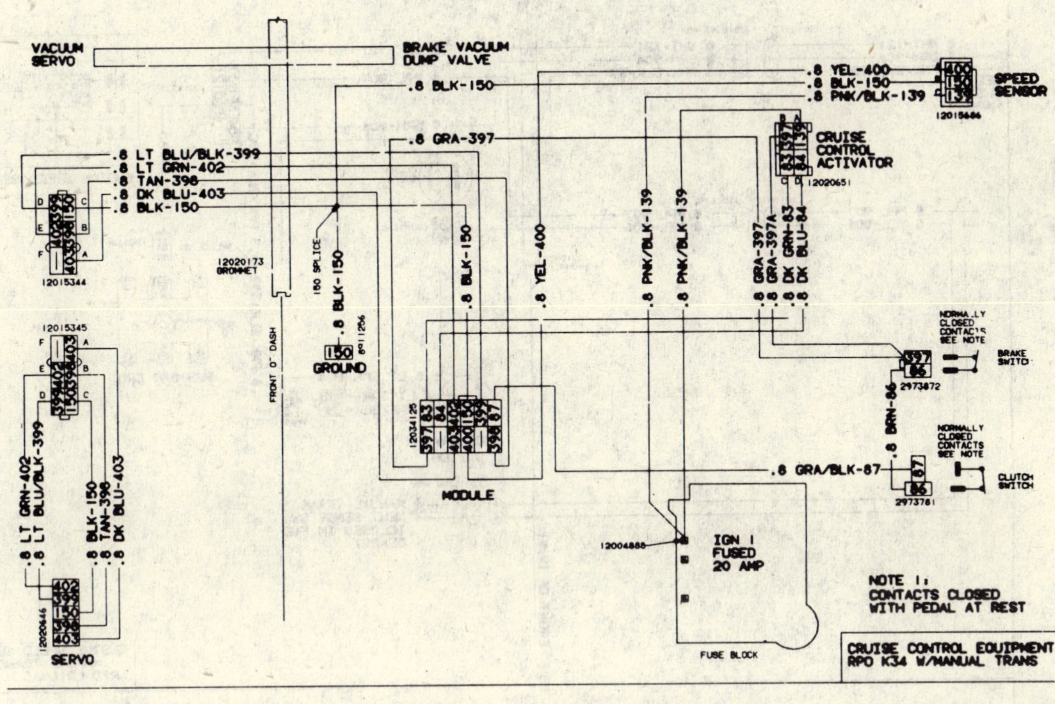

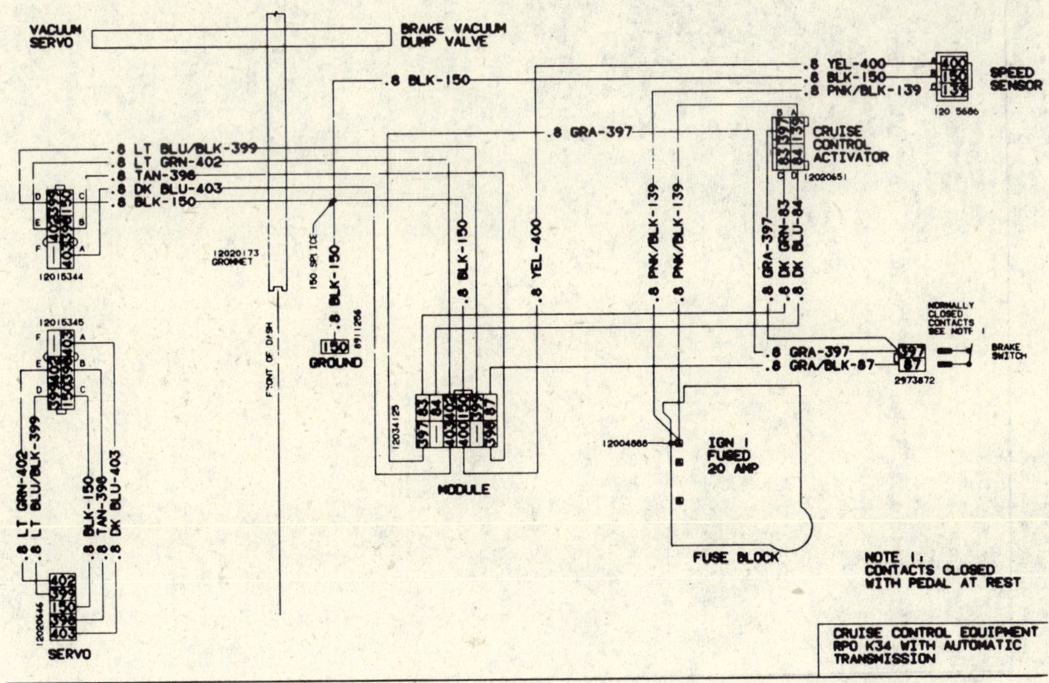

VACUUM SERVO
BRAKE VACUUM DUMP VALVE
.8 BLK-150
.8 YEL-400
.8 BLK-150
.8 PNK/BLK-139
SPEED SENSOR
12015686
.8 GRA-397
CRUISE CONTROL ACTIVATOR
12020651
.8 LT BLU/BLK-399
.8 LT GRN-402
.8 TAN-398
.8 DK BLU-403
.8 BLK-150
12015344
12020173 GROMMET
150 SPLICE
.8 BLK-150
GROUND
FRONT O' DASH
.8 BLK-150
.8 YEL-400
.8 PNK/BLK-139
.8 PNK/BLK-139
.8 GRA-397
.8 GRA-397A
.8 DK GRN-83
.8 DK BLU-84
NORMALLY CLOSED CONTACTS SEE NOTE
BRAKE SWITCH
2973872
.8 BRN-86
NORMALLY CLOSED CONTACTS SEE NOTE
CLUTCH SWITCH
2973781
.8 GRA/BLK-87
12015345
12034125
MODULE
12004888
IGN I FUSED 20 AMP
FUSE BLOCK
NOTE I: CONTACTS CLOSED WITH PEDAL AT REST
.8 LT GRN-402
.8 LT BLU/BLK-399
.8 BLK-150
.8 TAN-398
.8 DK BLU-403
12020446
SERVO
CRUISE CONTROL EQUIPMENT RPO K34 W/MANUAL TRANS

VACUUM SERVO
BRAKE VACUUM DUMP VALVE
.8 BLK-150
.8 YEL-400
.8 BLK-150
.8 PNK/BLK-139
SPEED SENSOR
120 5686
.8 GRA-397
CRUISE CONTROL ACTIVATOR
12020651
.8 LT BLU/BLK-399
.8 LT GRN-402
.8 TAN-398
.8 DK BLU-403
.8 BLK-150
12015344
12020173 GROMMET
150 SPLICE
.8 BLK-150
GROUND
FRONT OF DASH
.8 BLK-150
.8 YEL-400
.8 PNK/BLK-139
.8 PNK/BLK-139
.8 GRA-397
.8 DK GRN-83
.8 DK BLU-84
NORMALLY CLOSED CONTACTS SEE NOTE I
BRAKE SWITCH
.8 GRA-397
.8 GRA/BLK-87
2973872
12015345
12034125
MODULE
12004888
IGN I FUSED 20 AMP
FUSE BLOCK
NOTE I: CONTACTS CLOSED WITH PEDAL AT REST
.8 LT GRN-402
.8 LT BLU/BLK-399
.8 BLK-150
.8 TAN-398
.8 DK BLU-403
12020446
SERVO
CRUISE CONTROL EQUIPMENT RPO K34 WITH AUTOMATIC TRANSMISSION

1982-85

.8 WHT-121
.8 BRN-904
.8 PNK/BLK-39
REF
ENG
HARN
12010717
12015793 ASM
.8 PPL 907
12015737
.8 BLK-150
ENGINE SPEED SENSOR
CLUTCH SWITCH
.8 PNK/BLK-39C
12010973
12015792
.8 YEL-906
12015340
12015958 GROMMET
SPLICE 39
12004267
.8 PNK/BLK-39B
BUS BAR GRD
.8 LT GRN-905
1 LT GRN
1 PNK/BLK
8911773
ACCELERATOR SWITCH
12015792 ASM
MANUAL TRANS NEUT SENSE SW (CLOSED IN FWD GEARS)
FRONT OF DASH
ENGINE SPEED SENSOR
MANUAL TRANS
RPO LR1&NA5

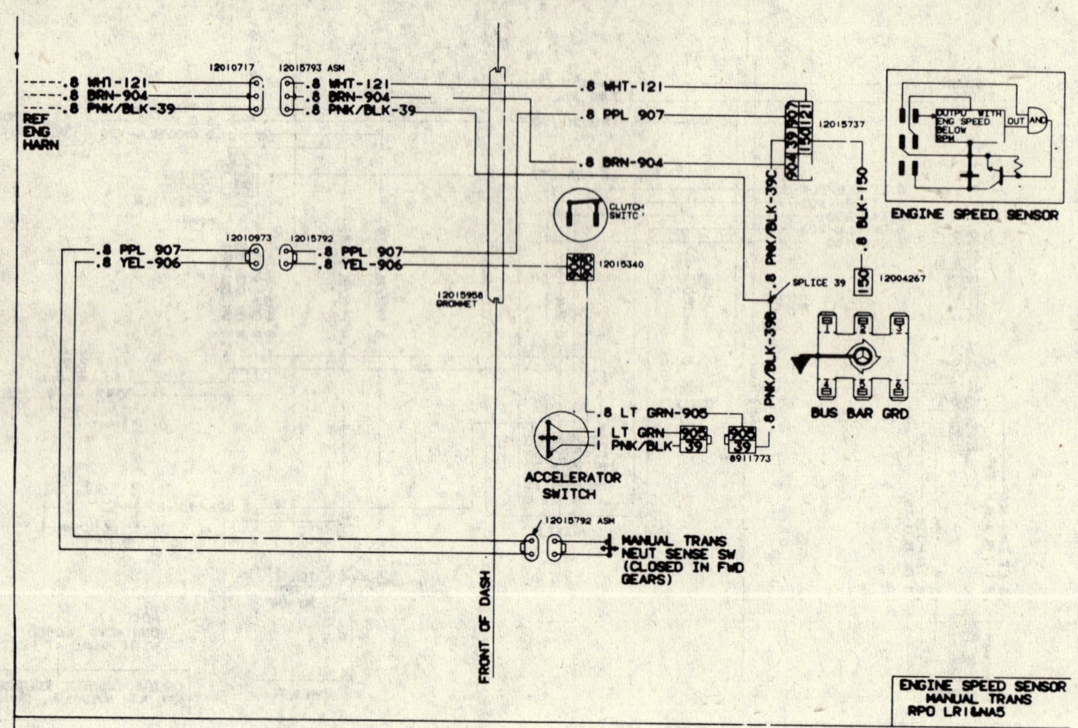

1982-85

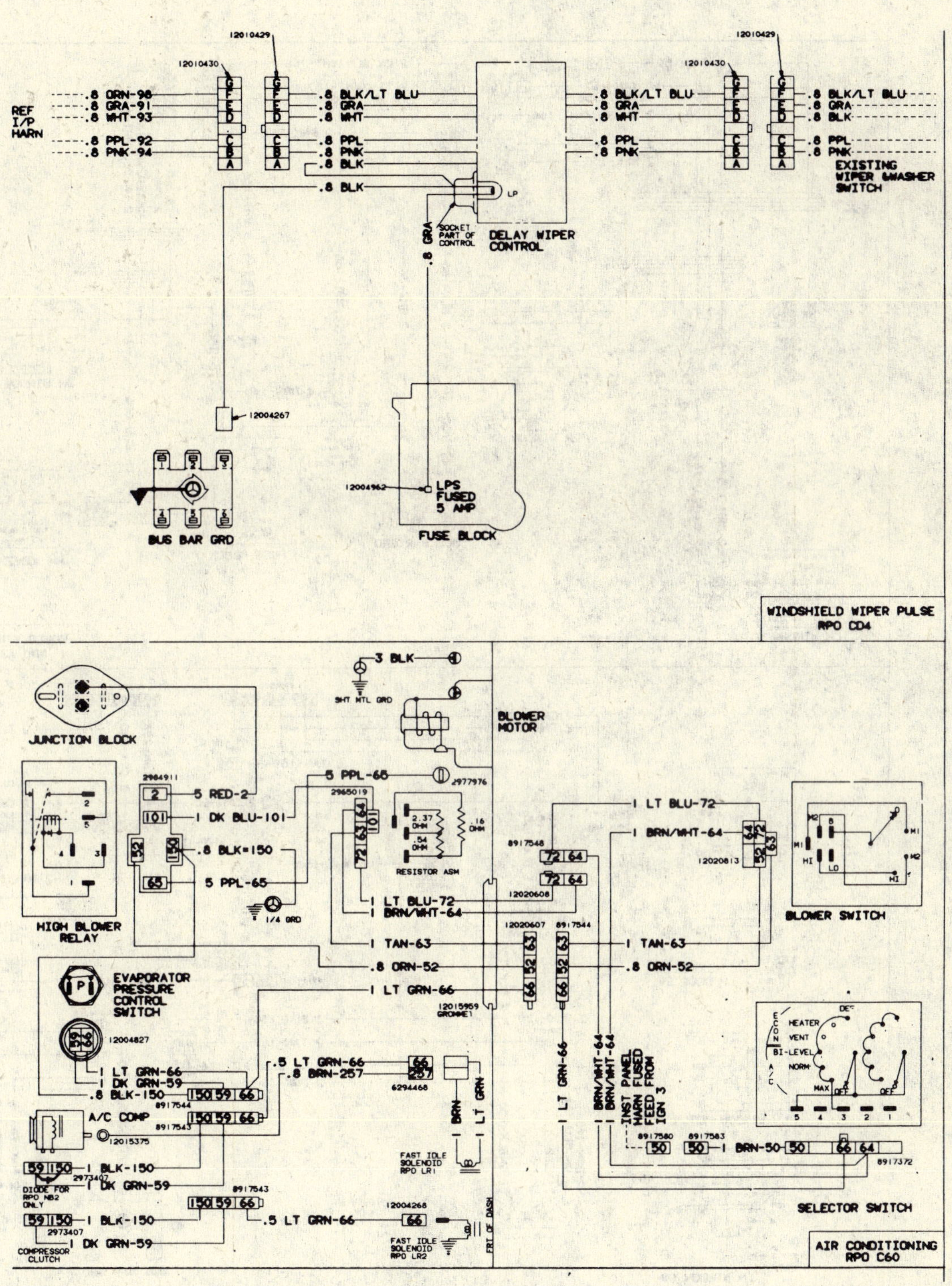
REF I/P HARN
.8 ORN-98
.8 GRA-91
.8 WHT-93
.8 PPL-92
.8 PNK-94
.8 BLK/LT BLU
.8 GRA
.8 WHT
.8 PPL
.8 PNK
.8 BLK
SOCKET PART OF CONTROL
DELAY WIPER CONTROL
EXISTING WIPER &WASHER SWITCH
BUS BAR GRD
LPS FUSED 5 AMP
FUSE BLOCK
WINDSHIELD WIPER PULSE RPO CD4
JUNCTION BLOCK
3 BLK
SHT MTL GRD
BLOWER MOTOR
HIGH BLOWER RELAY
5 RED-2
1 DK BLU-101
.8 BLK-150
5 PPL-65
5 PPL-68
RESISTOR ASM
1/4 GRD
1 LT BLU-72
1 BRN/WHT-64
1 TAN-63
.8 ORN-52
1 LT GRN-66
BLOWER SWITCH
EVAPORATOR PRESSURE CONTROL SWITCH
1 LT GRN-66
1 DK GRN-59
.8 BLK-150
.5 LT GRN-66
.8 BRN-257
A/C COMP
1 BLK-150
1 DK GRN-59
DIODE FOR RPO NB2 ONLY
COMPRESSOR CLUTCH
FAST IDLE SOLENOID RPO LR1
FAST IDLE SOLENOID RPO LR2
FRT OF DASH
INST PANEL HARN FUSED FEED FROM IGN 3
1 BRN-50
HEATER
VENT
BI-LEVEL
NORM
MAX
OFF
SELECTOR SWITCH
AIR CONDITIONING RPO C60

POWER WINDOWS
RPO A31
LH WINDOW MOTOR
LH WINDOW SW
RH WINDOW SW
BUS BAR GRD
FUSE BLOCK
LH LOCK MOTOR
LH DOOR SW
LEFT DOOR

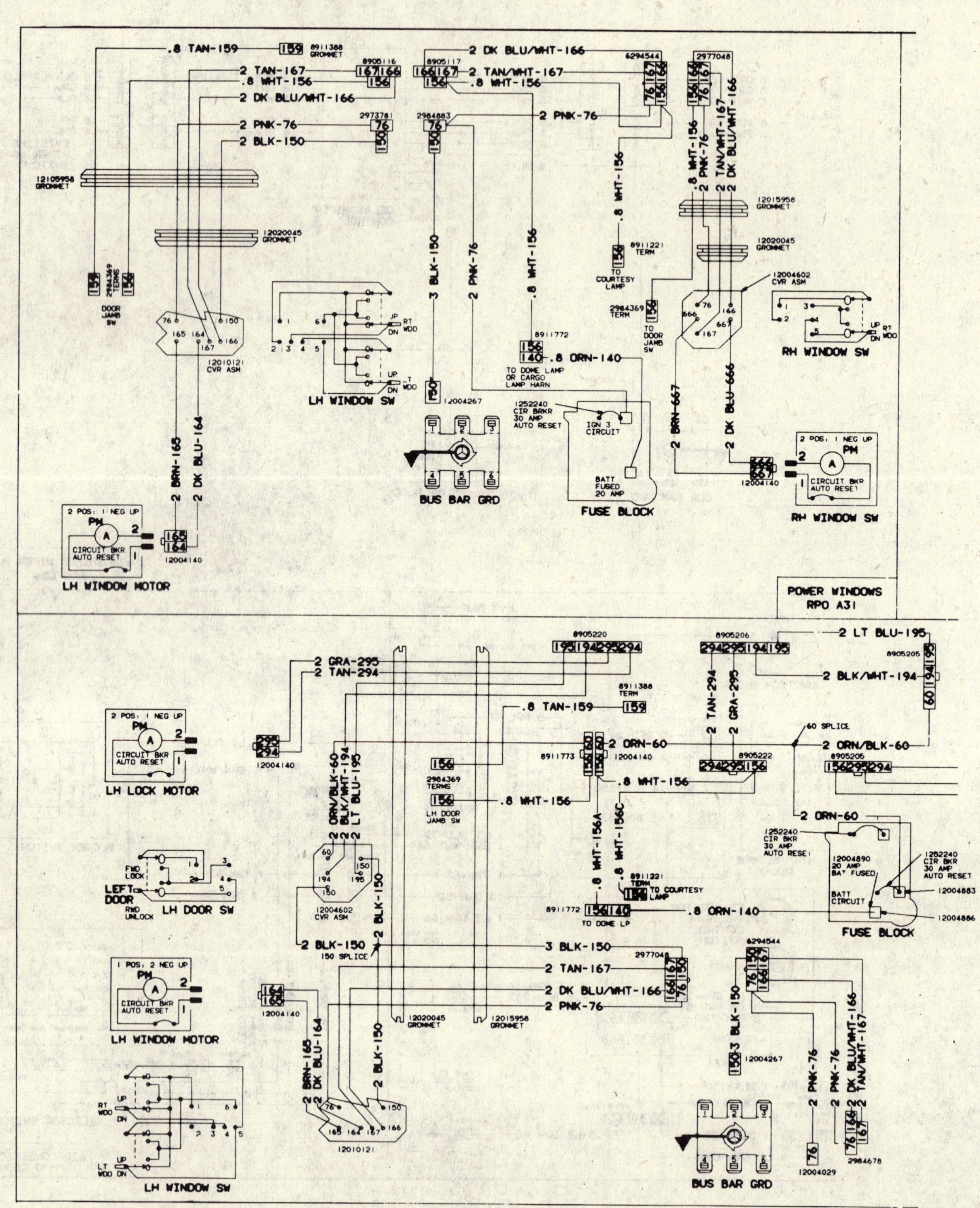

1982-85

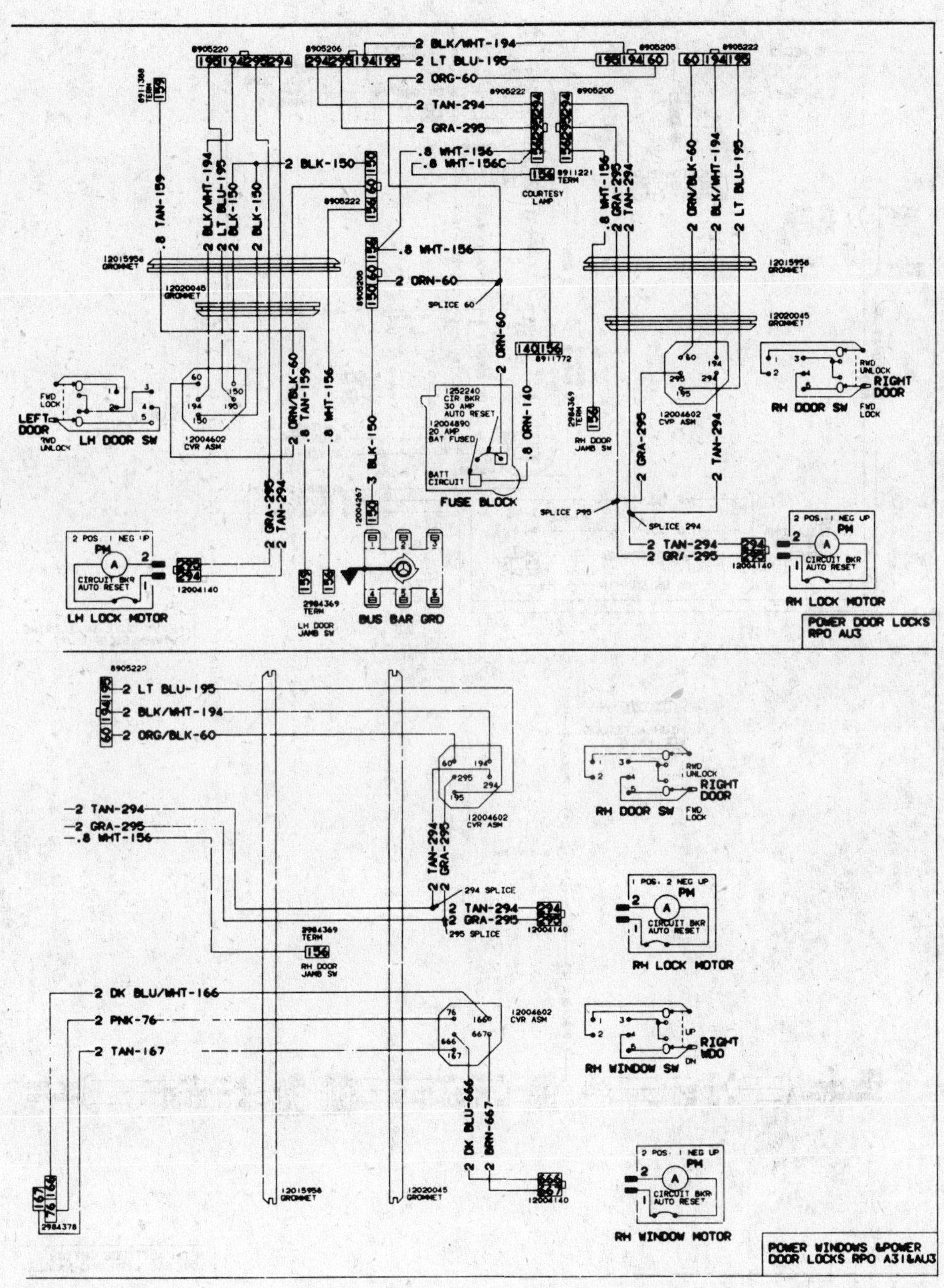
2 BLK/WHT-194
2 LT BLU-195
2 ORG-60
2 TAN-294
2 GRA-295
.8 WHT-156
.8 WHT-156C
2 BLK-150
COURTESY LAMP
.8 TAN-159
.8 WHT-156
2 ORN-60
SPLICE 60
12015958 GROMMET
12020045 GROMMET
LEFT DOOR
LH DOOR SW
12004602 CVR ASM
2 ORN/BLK-60
2 BLK/WHT-194
2 LT BLU-195
RH DOOR SW
RIGHT DOOR
FWD LOCK
RWD UNLOCK
1252240 CIR BKR 30 AMP AUTO RESET
12004890 20 AMP BAT FUSED
BATT CIRCUIT
FUSE BLOCK
.8 ORN-140
3 BLK-150
2 GRA-295
2 TAN-294
SPLICE 295
SPLICE 294
RH DOOR JAMB SW
LH DOOR JAMB SW
2984369 TERM
BUS BAR GRD
2 POS. 1 NEG UP
PM
CIRCUIT BKR AUTO RESET
LH LOCK MOTOR
RH LOCK MOTOR
POWER DOOR LOCKS RPO AU3
2 ORG/BLK-60
294 SPLICE
295 SPLICE
2 DK BLU/WHT-166
2 PNK-76
2 TAN-167
2 DK BLU-666
2 BRN-667
RH WINDOW SW
RIGHT WDO
RH WINDOW MOTOR
POWER WINDOWS &POWER DOOR LOCKS RPO A31&AU3

.5 RED-2
JUNCTION BLOCK
REF ENG WRG
BATTERY CIRCUIT
30 AMP
IN LINE
FUSE
5291294 HOLDER
8290791 CAP
9426331 FUSE
3 DK BLU-47
5 RED-2
.8 LT GRN-24
.8 LT GRN-24
.8 DK GRN-19
.8 YEL-18
.8 BRN-9
REF
TAIL COMB
LAMP
HARNESS
6288565
6288566
.8 BRN-9
.8 LT GRN-24
.8 DK GRN-19
.8 YEL-18
SPLICE 9
SPLICE 24
SPLICE 19
SPLICE 18
SHEET
METAL
GROUND
2 WHT-22
REF TO
TRAILER
.8 BRN-9
5 RED-2
3 DK BLU-47
REF
TAIL COMB
LAMP EXT
HARNESS
HEAVY DUTY TRAILERING
HARNESS RPO UY7
HIGH ALTITUDE
SOL VALVE
1 PNK/BLK
12015791 ASM
1 PNK/BLK-39
REF
WIRE FROM
CARBURETOR
.8 PPL
1 PNK/BLK
.8 LT BLU
.8 PPL-904
1 PNK/BLK-39
.8 LT BLU-78
8917544
8917543
REF ENG
HARNESS
HIGH ALTITUDE OPTION
RPO NA6 WITH RPO NA5&LR1

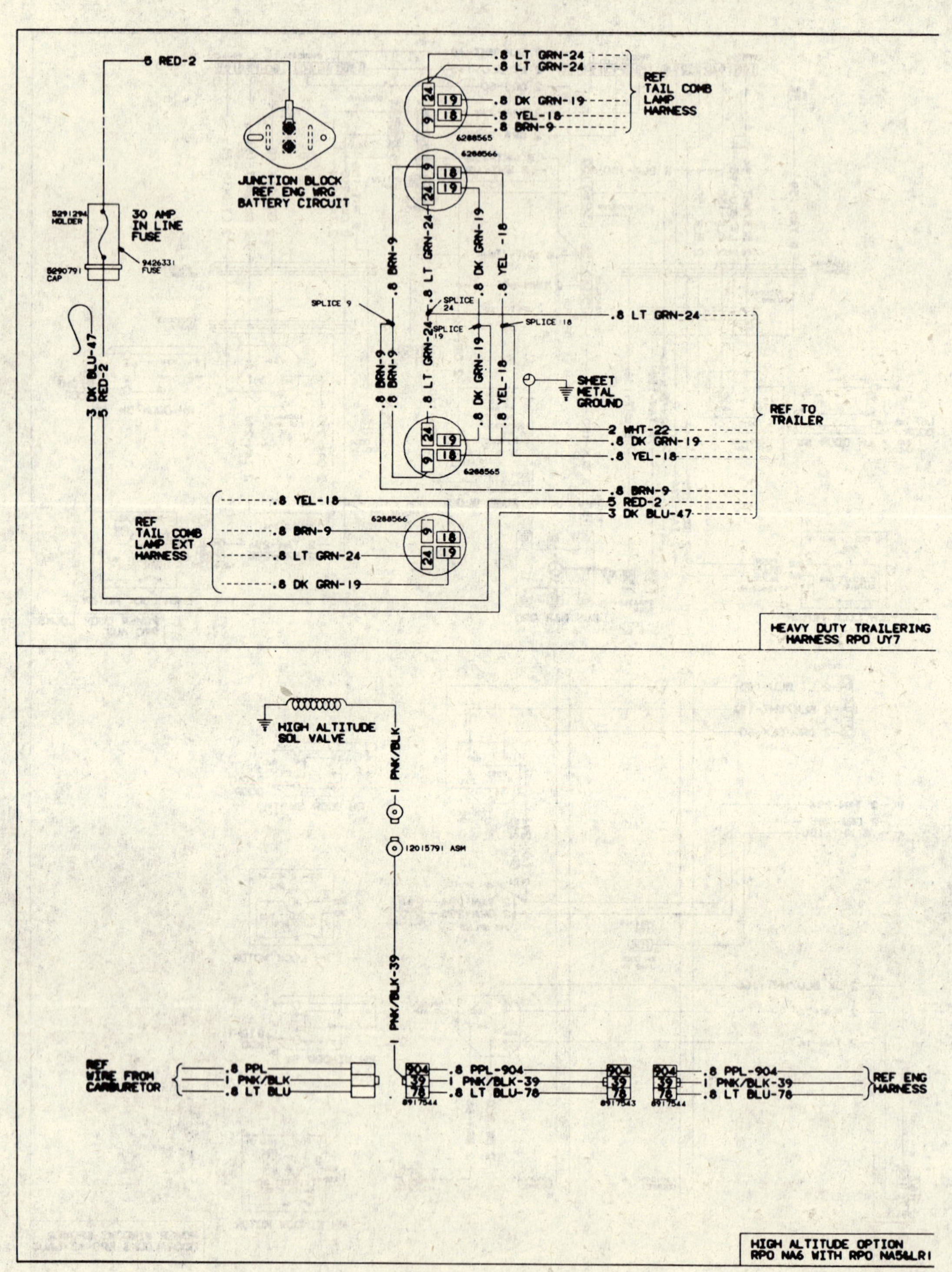

1982-85

DIST
12015792 ASM
3 PNK-3
.8 WHT-121
SPLICE 121
12010973
12015376
1 WHT-121
REF ENG HARN
8917580
8917583
.8 WHT
FILTER AS BELOW
8917649
COIL
TO DIST CAP
BRN
PNK
TO DISTRIBUTOR
SHEET METAL GROUND
TACH FILTER
12015957 GROMMET
.8 BLK-150
SPLICE 150
.8 PNK/BLK-39
SPLICE 39
FRONT OF DASH
0-5000 RPM
INSTRUMENT CLUSTER
TACHOMETER RPO U16
LOW VACUUM SWITCH
8911772
.8 LT GRN-384
.8 LT BLU-383
8917546
8917545
.8 LT GRN-924
.8 DK BLU/BLK-975
ENG HARN
I/P HARN
12020101 BULKHEAD&CONN ENG REF ENG WIRING
12020102 BULKHEAD CONN I/P REF I/P WIRING
8900838
.8 PNK/BLK-139
ALDL TEST
8900826
2973407
LOCK
N/C CONTACTS
BRAKE SWITCH
12010649
.8 PNK BLK-139
12004888
IGN FUSED 20 AMP
FUSE BLOCK
12015260
CONVERTER LOCK SOL
CLOSED ABOVE 26 MPH
RPO MV9(THM 200)
AUTOMATIC TRANSMISSION RPO MV9 W/O RPO LR2 & NB2

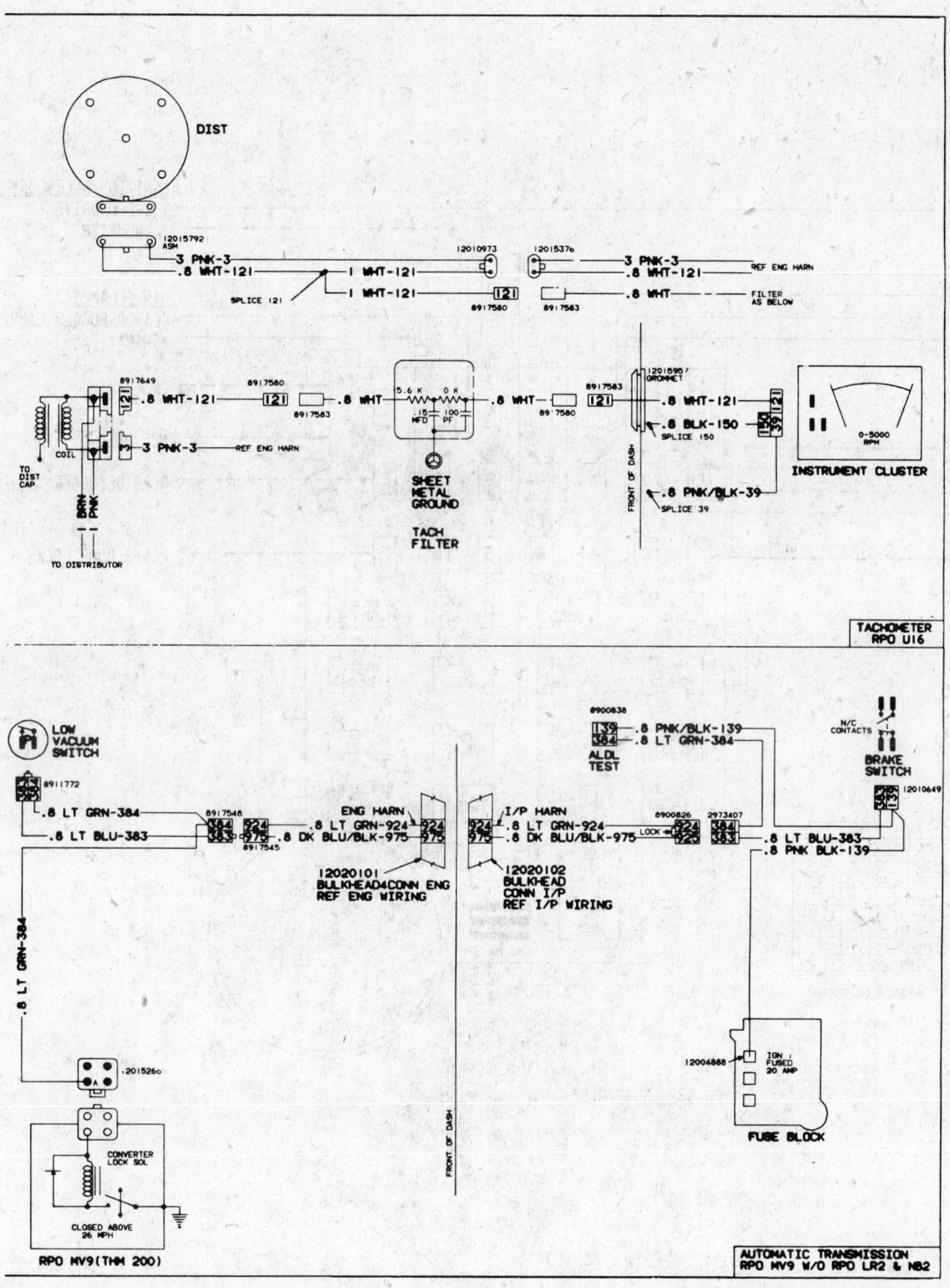

1982-85

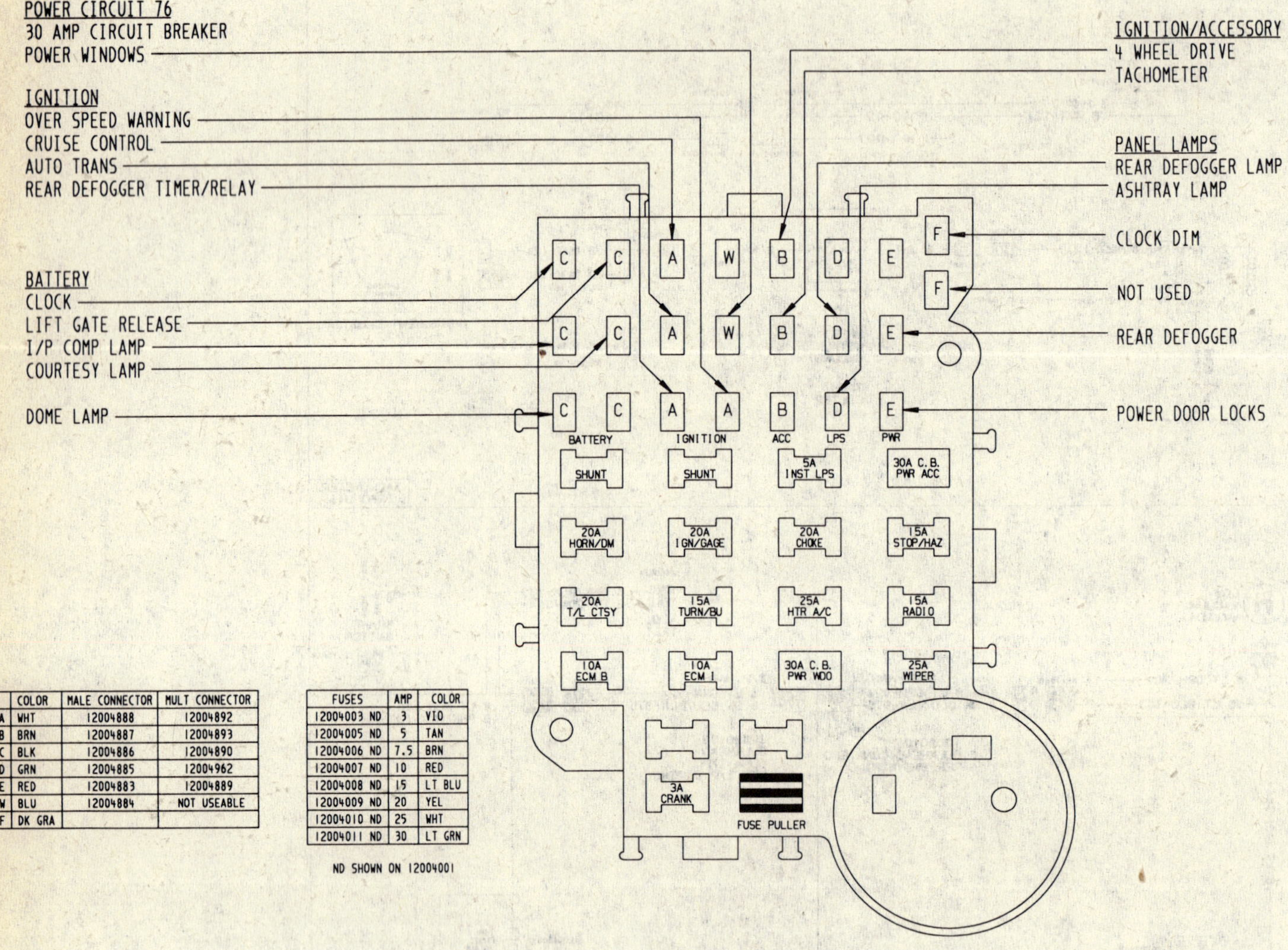

	COLOR	MALE CONNECTOR	MULT CONNECTOR
A	WHT	12004888	12004892
B	BRN	12004887	12004893
C	BLK	12004886	12004890
D	GRN	12004885	12004962
E	RED	12004883	12004889
W	BLU	12004884	NOT USEABLE
F	DK GRA		

FUSES	AMP	COLOR
12004003 ND	3	VIO
12004005 ND	5	TAN
12004006 ND	7.5	BRN
12004007 ND	10	RED
12004008 ND	15	LT BLU
12004009 ND	20	YEL
12004010 ND	25	WHT
12004011 ND	30	LT GRN

ND SHOWN ON 12004001

12052632 FUSE BLOCK

1986-87

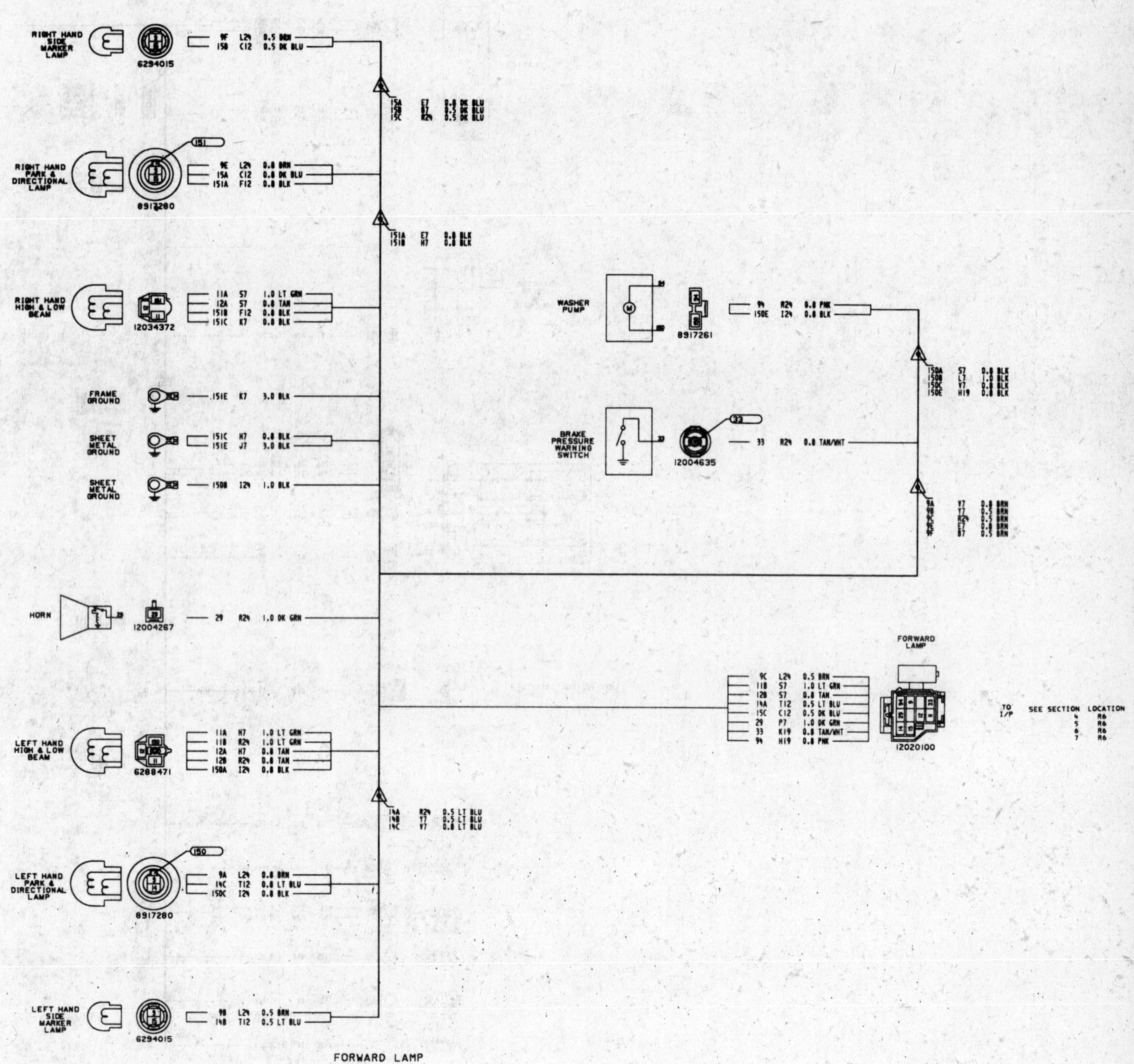

FORWARD LAMP

1986-87

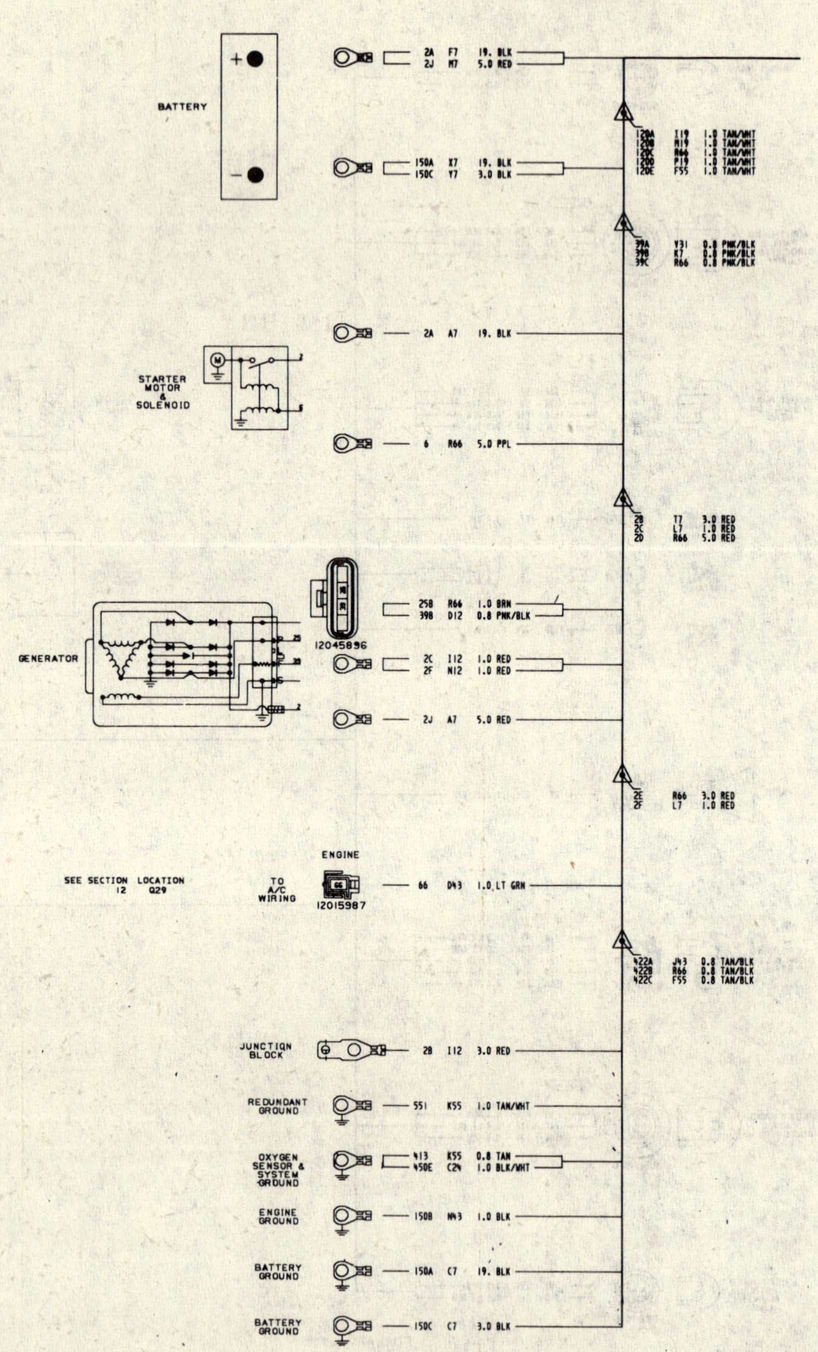

BATTERY
STARTER MOTOR & SOLENOID
GENERATOR
12045896
ENGINE
SEE SECTION 12 LOCATION Q29
TO A/C WIRING
12015987
JUNCTION BLOCK
REDUNDANT GROUND
OXYGEN SENSOR & SYSTEM GROUND
ENGINE GROUND
BATTERY GROUND
BATTERY GROUND

1986-87

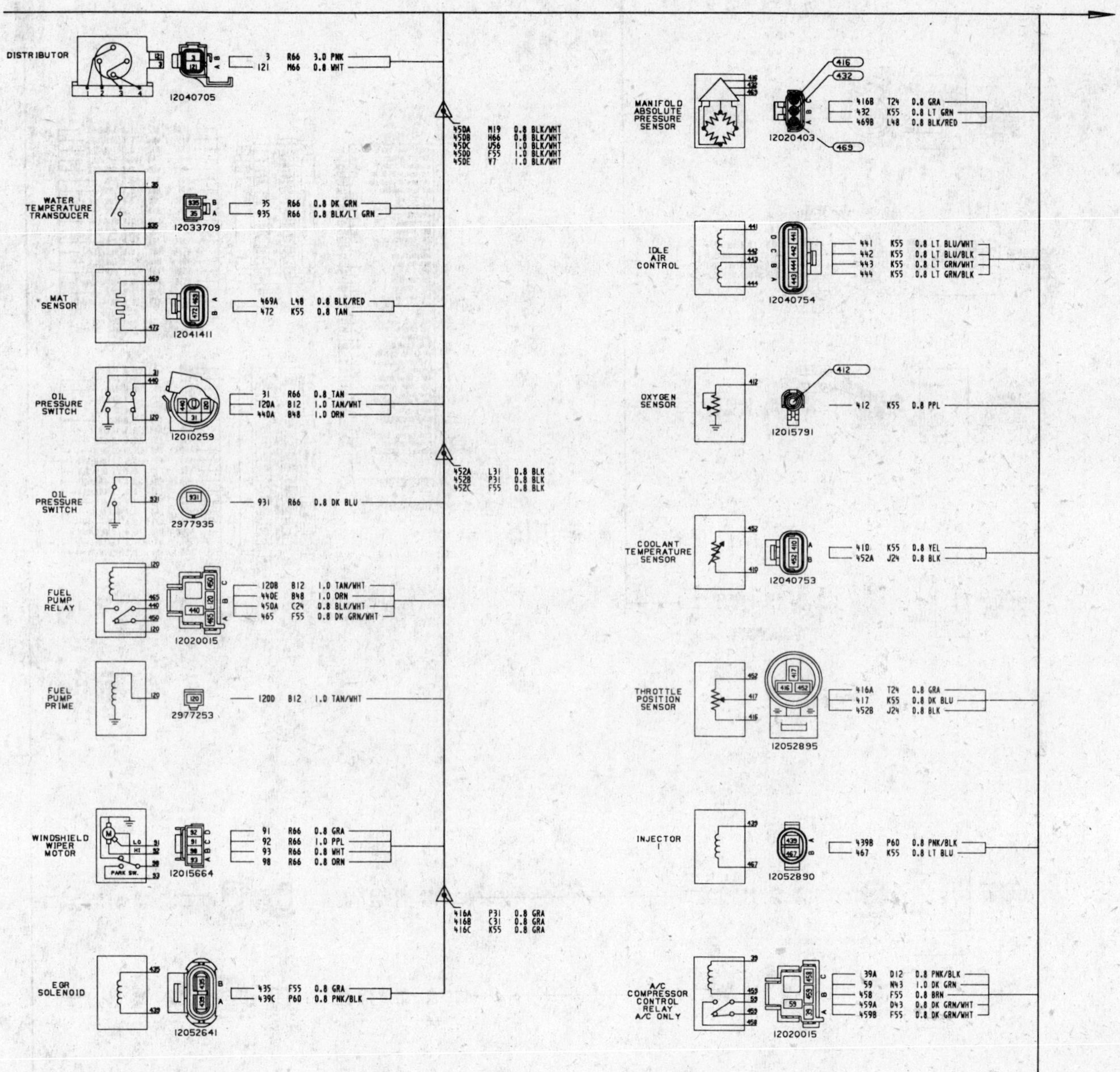

ENGINE HARNESS
LN8 L4 W/TBI

1986-87

440A I19 1.0 ORN
440B R66 1.0 ORN
440C F55 1.0 ORN
440D K55 1.0 DK BLU
440E M19 1.0 ORN
GROMMET
A/C LOW PRESSURE SWITCH A/C ONLY
12041137
66 Q7 1.0 LT GRN
459A V31 0.8 DK GRN/WHT
ELECTRONIC SPARK TIMING
E.S.T. SIGNAL
E.S.T. BYPASS
E.S.T. REF. PULSE HI
E.S.T. REF. PULSE LO
12020832
453
424
430
423
423 K55 0.8 WHT
424 K55 0.8 TAN/BLK
430 F55 0.8 PPL/WHT
453 F55 0.8 RED/BLK
TORQUE CONVERTER CLUTCH SOLENOID AUTO. TRANS.
12015390
420
422
420 R66 0.8 PPL
422A R12 0.8 TAN/BLK
469A G19 0.8 BLK/RED
469B C31 0.8 BLK/RED
469C K55 0.8 BLK/RED
A/C COMPRESSOR CLUTCH A/C ONLY
2973407
59 V31 1.0 DK GRN
150B W7 1.0 BLK
WIRE 151 JUMPERED IN CONNECTOR
ECM
FUEL PUMP FEED
DIRECT GROUND
COOLANT TEMP
OXYGEN SENSOR HI
OXYGEN SENSOR LO
5V REF SENSOR
T.P.S.
SYSTEM CHECK LP
ECM TO TCC
EST SIGNAL
EST BYPASS
EST REF PULSE HI
M.A.P.
PK/NEUT. SW
EGR SOLENOID
VSS
12V IGNITION
12V BATTERY
IAC COIL A HI
IAC COIL A LO
IAC COIL B HI
IAC COIL B LO
GROUND
DIAG ENABLE
LO LEVEL GROUND
EST REF PULSE LO
UPSHIFT LP
FUEL PUMP RELAY
A/C COMP. RELAY
ECC DATA
FUEL PUMP RELAY
INJ A DRIVE
M.A.P. RETURN
MAT SIGNAL
ECM TO PWR STEER
ENGINE GROUND
CRANK
120 151 410 412 413 416 417 419 422 423 424 430 432 434 435 437 439 440 441 442 443 444 450 451 452 453 456 458 459 461 465 467 469 472 495 551 806
12020753
120E B12 1.0 TAN/WHT
419 H66 0.8 BRN/WHT
422C R12 0.8 TAN/BLK
430 G43 0.8 PPL/WHT
434 H66 0.8 ORN/BLK
435 Y19 0.8 GRA
437 H66 0.8 BRN
439D P60 0.8 PNK/BLK
440C B48 1.0 ORN
450D C24 1.0 BLK/WHT
451 H66 0.8 WHT/BLK
452C J24 0.8 BLK
453 G43 0.8 RED/BLK
456 R66 0.8 TAN/BLK
458 V31 0.8 BRN
459B V31 0.8 DK GRN/WHT
461 H66 0.8 ORN
465 M19 0.8 DK GRN/WHT
× WIRE 422 FOR AUTO. TRANS.
WIRE 456 FOR MANUAL TRANS.
12020754
410 L31 0.8 YEL
412 I31 0.8 PPL
413 V7 0.8 TAN
416C T24 0.8 GRA
417 P31 0.8 DK BLU
423 G43 0.8 WHT
424 G43 0.8 TAN/BLK
432 C31 0.8 LT GRN
440D B48 1.0 DK BLU
441 F31 0.8 LT BLU/WHT
442 F31 0.8 LT BLU/BLK
443 F31 0.8 LT GRN/WHT
444 F31 0.8 LT GRN/BLK
467 S31 0.8 LT BLU
469C L48 0.8 BLK/RED
472 G19 0.8 TAN
495A U56 0.8 LT BLU/ORN
551 U7 1.0 TAN/WHT
806 R66 0.8 PPL/WHT
439A R66 1.0 PNK/BLK
439B S31 0.8 PNK/BLK
439C Y19 0.8 PNK/BLK
439D F55 0.8 PNK/BLK
POWER STEERING PRESSURE SWITCH
12020599
450F U55 0.8 BLK/WHT
495B U55 0.8 LT BLU/ORN
450F U43 0.8 BLK/WHT
495B U43 0.8 LT BLU/ORN
12015199
12015271
450C C24 1.0 BLK/WHT
495A K55 0.8 LT BLU/ORN
BACK-UP LAMP SWITCH MAN. TRANS.
75
24
12015792
24 W55 0.8 LT GRN
75 W55 0.8 DK BLU
24 W43 0.8 LT GRN
75 W43 0.8 DK BLU
8917548
8917545
924 R66 0.8 LT GRN/BLK
975 R66 0.8 DK BLU
ENGINE HARNESS
LN8 L4 W/TBI

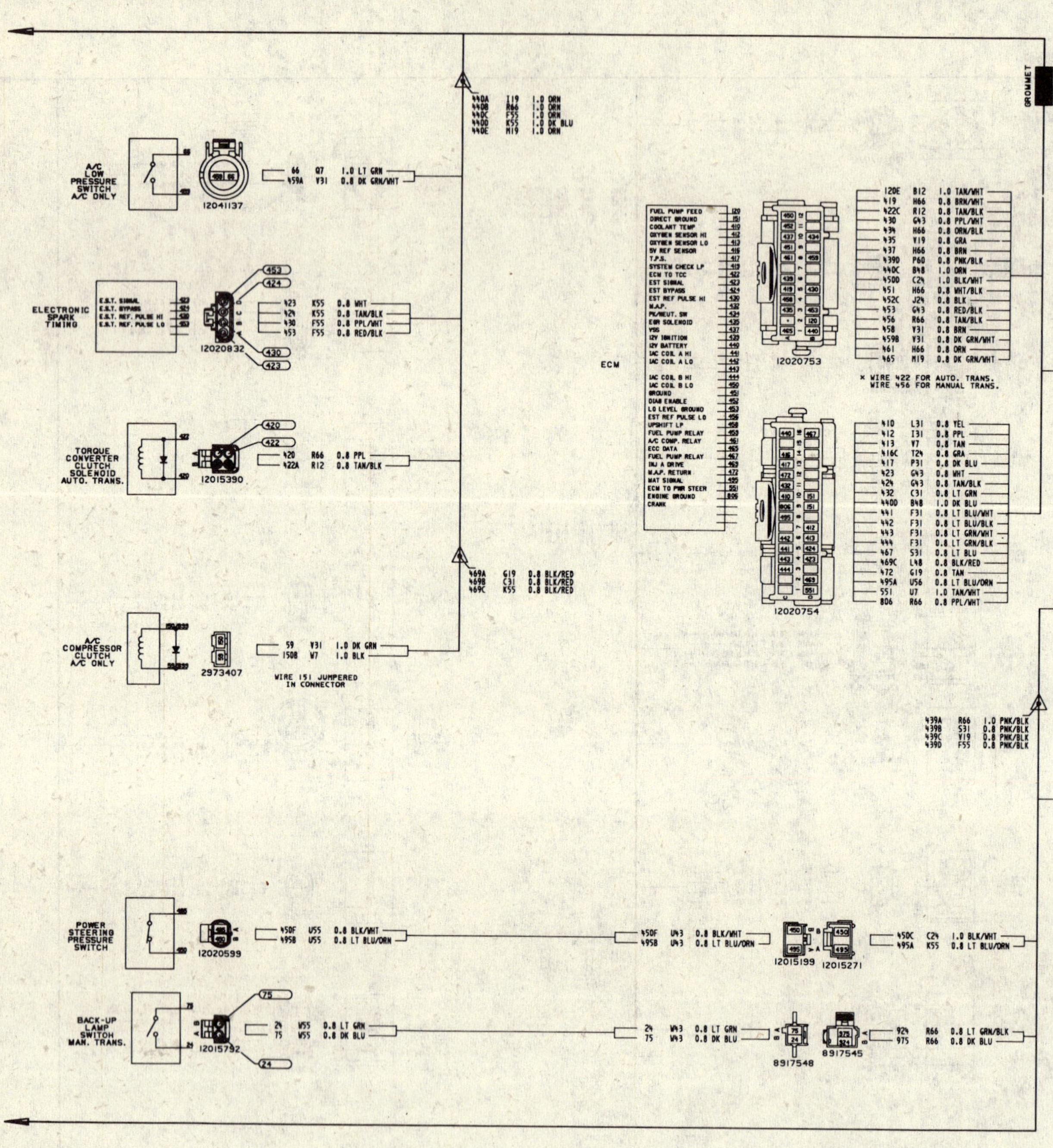

1986-87

ENGINE
419 F55 0.8 BRN/WHT
434 F55 0.8 ORN/BLK
437 F55 0.8 BRN
450B C24 0.8 BLK/WHT
451 F55 0.8 WHT/BLK
461 F55 0.8 ORN
12045688
WIRE 434 FOR AUTO TRANS ONLY
TO I/P
:E SECTION LOCATION
4 H7
5 H7
6
7 H7
ENGINE
121 B19 0.8 WHT
8917580
TO TACHOMETER FILTER
SEE SECTION LOCATION
8 M31
2D I12 5.0 RED
2E N12 3.0 RED
3 B19 3.0 PNK
6 H7 5.0 PPL
25B K7 1.0 BRN
31 I19 0.8 TAN
35 E19 0.8 DK GRN
39C D12 0.8 PNK/BLK
91 S19 0.8 GRA
92 S19 1.0 PPL
93 S19 0.8 WHT
98 S19 0.8 ORN
120C B12 1.0 TAN/WHT
420 J43 0.8 PPL
422B R12 0.8 TAN/BLK
439A P60 1.0 PNK/BLK
440B B48 1.0 ORN
456 F55 0.8 TAN/BLK
806 K55 0.8 PPL/WHT
924 W56 0.8 LT GRN/BLK
931 K19 0.8 DK BLU
935 E19 0.8 BLK/LT GRN
975 W56 0.8 DK BLU
ENGINE
12020183
TO I/P
SEE SECTION LOCATION
4 R6
5 R6
6 R6
7 R6
WIRE 935 IN THE SAME CAVITY AS WIRE 931
× WIRE 935 MAN. TRANS. WIRE 420 AUTO. TRANS.
×× WIRE 924 MAN. TRANS. WIRE 422 AUTO. TRANS.

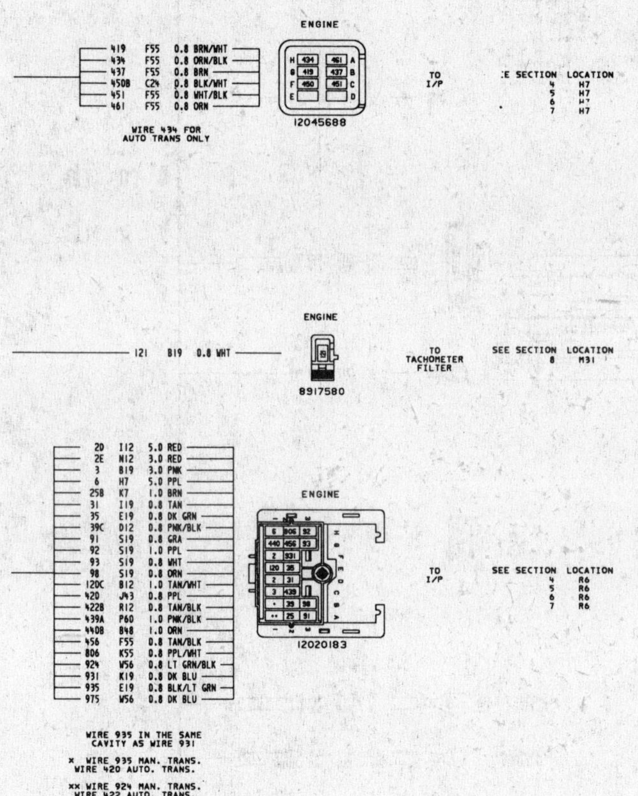

1986-87

BATTERY
2A F7 19. BLK
150A W7 19. BLK
150B X7 3.0 BLK
440A E19 1.0 ORN
440B R66 1.0 ORN
440C K55 0.8 ORN
440D F55 0.8 ORN
440E C55 0.8 ORN
440F Q19 1.0 ORN
2B FUSIBLE LINK
2A A7 19. BLK
2B I12 1.0 RED
STARTER MOTOR & SOLENOID
6 R66 3.0 PPL
2B F7 1.0 RED
2C T7 3.0 RED
2E R66 3.0 RED
2F M7 1.0 RED
GENERATOR
12045896
25A S12 0.8 BRN
39B H24 0.8 PNK/BLK
2F FUSIBLE LINK
2F J12 1.0 RED
SEE SECTION 11 LOCATION Q29
ENGINE
TO A/C WIRING
12015271
59A L43 1.0 DK GRN
59B F55 1.0 DK GRN
150 N43 1.0 BLK
25A K7 0.8 BRN
25B R66 0.8 BRN
JUNCTION BLOCK
2C I12 3.0 RED
2D R66 3.0 RED
REDUNDANT GROUND
151B N19 0.8 BLK
551 K55 1.0 TAN/WHT
OXYGEN SENSOR & SYSTEM GROUND
413 K55 0.5 TAN
450F B24 1.0 BLK/WHT
BATTERY GROUND
150A C7 19. BLK
BATTERY GROUND
150B C7 3.0 BLK

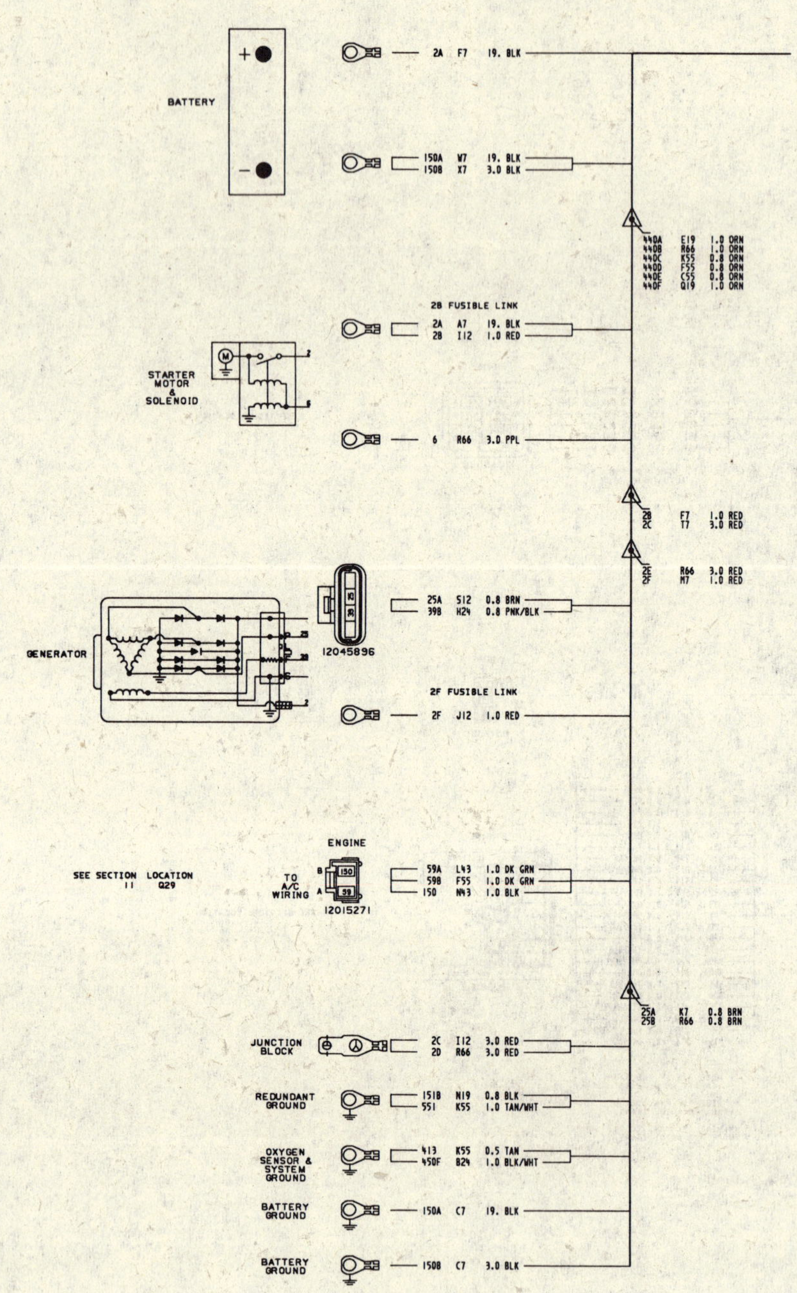

1986-87

OIL PRESSURE SENDER
6288920
31A M24 0.5 TAN
151A N19 0.8 BLK
901 N19 0.8 BRN
OIL PRESSURE SENDER
12004275
120A P60 1.0 TAN/WHT
440A D12 1.0 ORN
OIL PRESSURE SENDER
2977935
31B M24 0.5 TAN
DISTRIBUTOR
12040705
3 R66 3.0 PNK
121 M66 0.8 WHT
WATER TEMPERATURE SWITCH SENSOR
12033709
35 R66 0.5 DK GRN
935 R66 0.5 GRN/WHT
OIL PRESSURE RELAY
12020266
39A H24 0.8 PNK/BLK
151A C19 0.8 BLK
151B U7 0.8 BLK
901 C19 0.8 BRN
931 R66 0.8 YEL
FUEL PUMP RELAY
12020015
120B P60 1.0 TAN/WHT
120E T19 1.0 TAN/WHT
440F D12 1.0 ORN
450A B24 1.0 BLK/WHT
465 F55 0.8 DK GRN/WHT
FUEL PUMP PRIME
2977253
120E Q19 1.0 TAN/WHT
WINDSHIELD WIPER MOTOR
PARK SW.
12015664
91 R66 0.8 GRA
92 R66 0.8 PPL
93 R66 0.8 WHT
98 R66 0.8 ORN
450A Q19 1.0 BLK/WHT
450B H66 0.8 BLK/WHT
450C C55 1.0 BLK/WHT
450D F55 1.0 BLK/WHT
450E H43 0.8 BLK/WHT
450F V7 1.0 BLK/WHT
486 C31 1.0 BRN
39A N19 0.8 PNK/BLK
39B K7 0.8 PNK/BLK
39C L43 0.8 PNK/BLK
39D R66 0.8 PNK/BLK
31A C19 0.5 TAN
31B G19 0.5 TAN
31C R66 0.5 TAN
452A S31 0.8 BLK
452B U31 0.5 BLK
452C K55 0.5 BLK
HALF FUNCTION ELECTRONIC PARK CONTROL
IGNITION SWITCH
E.S.C. SIGNAL
E.S.C. DIST. GRD.
DETONATION SENSOR
12020646
439D M48 0.8 PNK/BLK
485 F55 0.8 BLK
486 B24 1.0 BRN
496 F31 0.8 DK BLU
ENGINE KNOCK SENSOR
12015375
496 C31 0.8 DK BLU
MANIFOLD ABSOLUTE PRESSURE SENSOR
12020403
416B E48 0.5 GRA
432 K55 0.8 LT GRN
455 F55 0.8 PPL
IDLE AIR CONTROL SOLENOID
12015798
441 K55 0.8 LT BLU/WHT
442 K55 0.8 LT BLU/BLK
443 K55 0.8 LT GRN/WHT
444 K55 0.8 LT GRN/BLK
OXYGEN SENSOR
12015791
412 K55 0.5 PPL
ELECTRONIC SPARK TIMING
E.S.T. SIGNAL
E.S.T. BYPASS
E.S.T. REF. PULSE HI
E.S.T. REF. PULSE LO
12015797
423 K55 0.5 WHT
424A J66 0.8 TAN/BLK
430 F55 0.5 PPL/WHT
453 F55 0.8 RED/BLK
COOLANT TEMPERATURE SENSOR
12040753
410 K55 0.8 YEL
452A R24 0.8 BLK
THROTTLE POSITION SENSOR
12015793
416A E48 0.5 GRA
417 K55 0.5 DK BLU
452B R24 0.5 BLK
AIR CONTROL SOLENOID
12015975
429 K55 0.8 PNK/BLK
436A B60 0.8 PNK/BLK
439F M48 0.8 PNK/BLK
WIRE 429 NA5/NA6 ONLY
WIRE 436 NB2 ONLY
ENGINE HARNESS
C60 &
NB2-(CALIFORNIA) &
NA5/NA6-(FEDERAL)

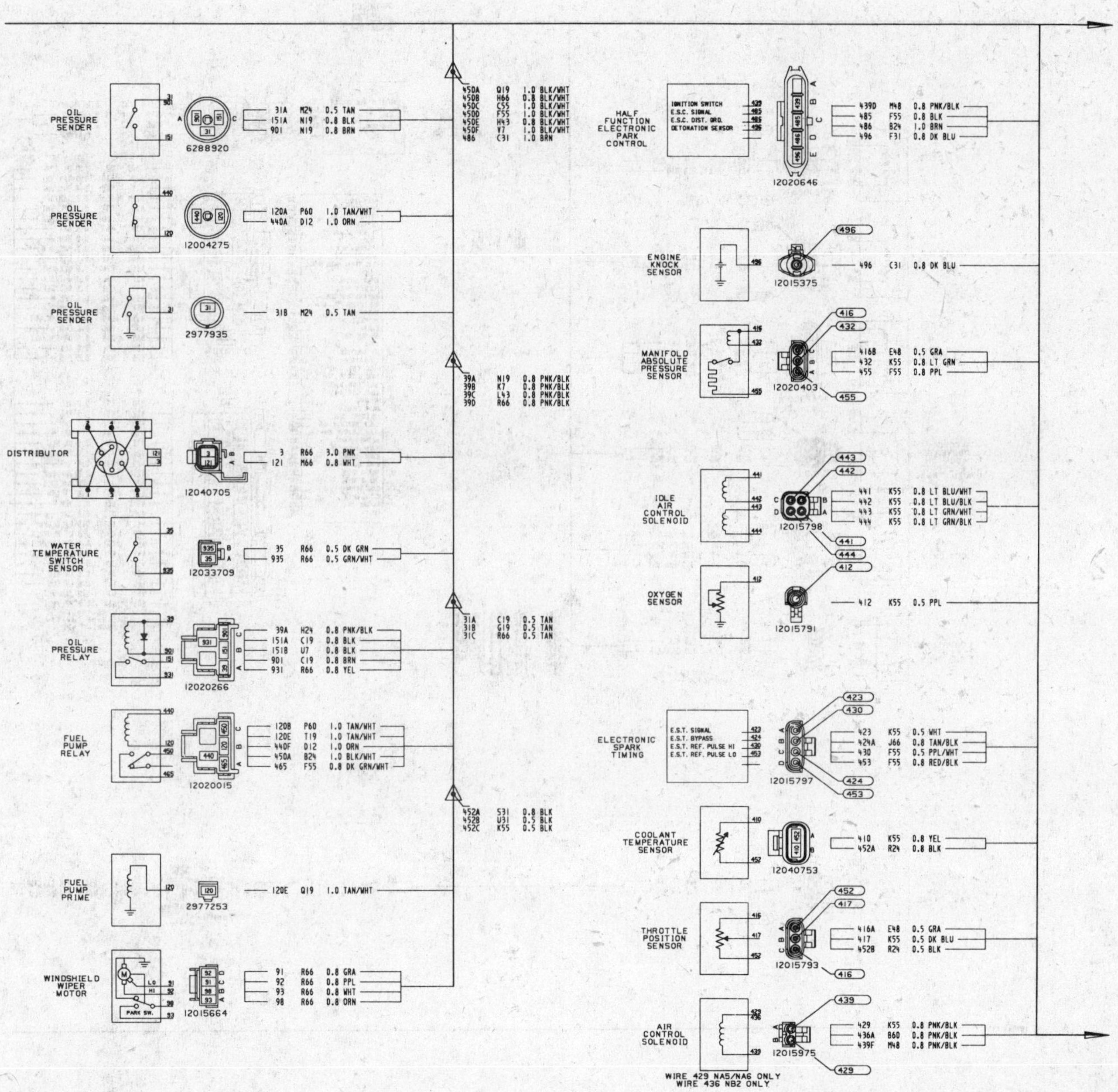

1986-87

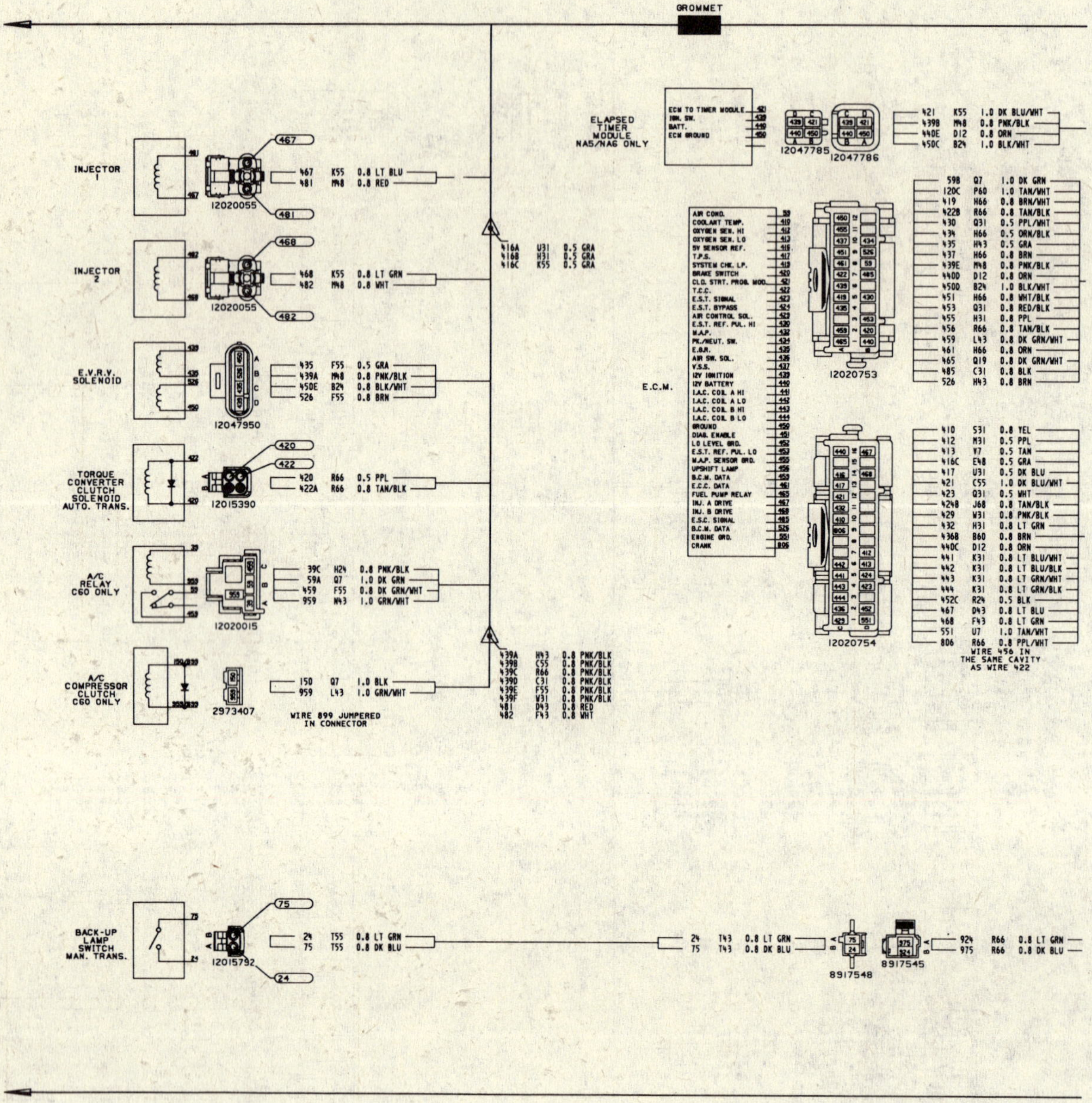

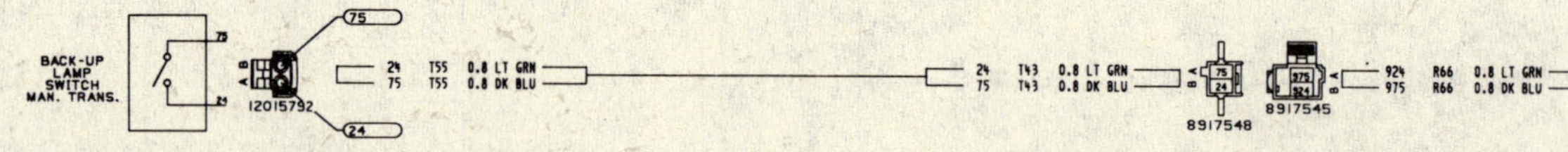

ENGINE HARNESS
C60 &
NB2-(CALIFORNIA)
NA5/NA6-(FEDERAL)

1986-87

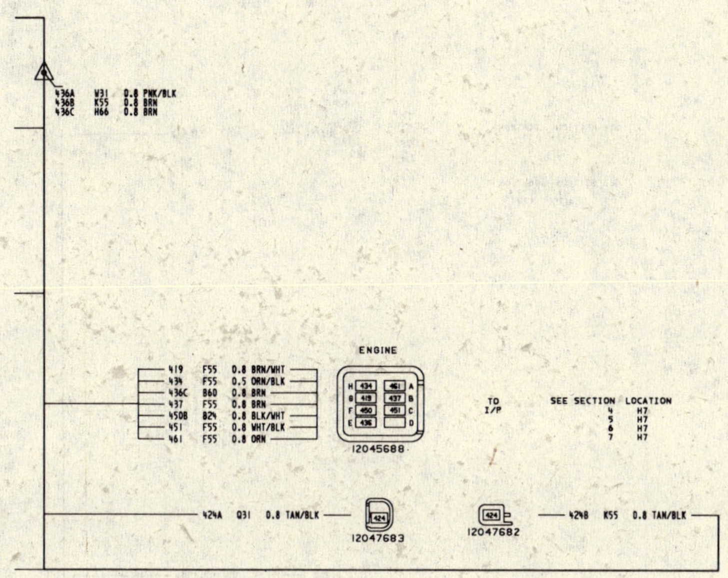

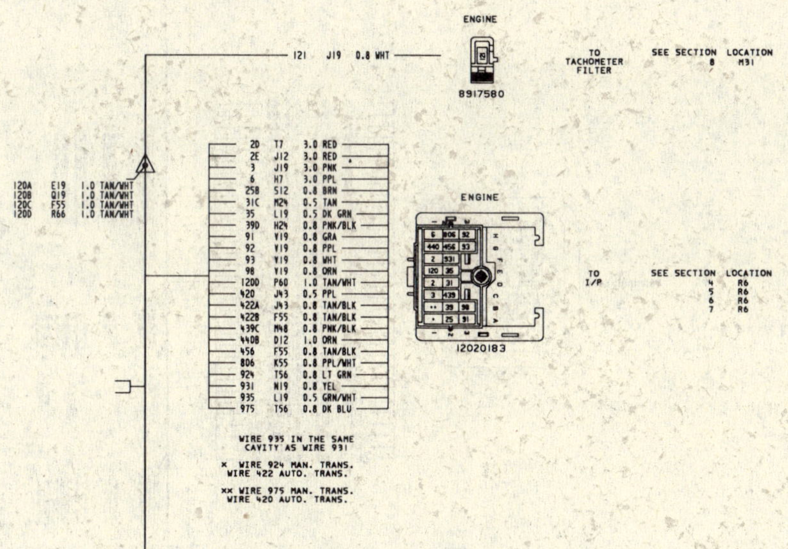

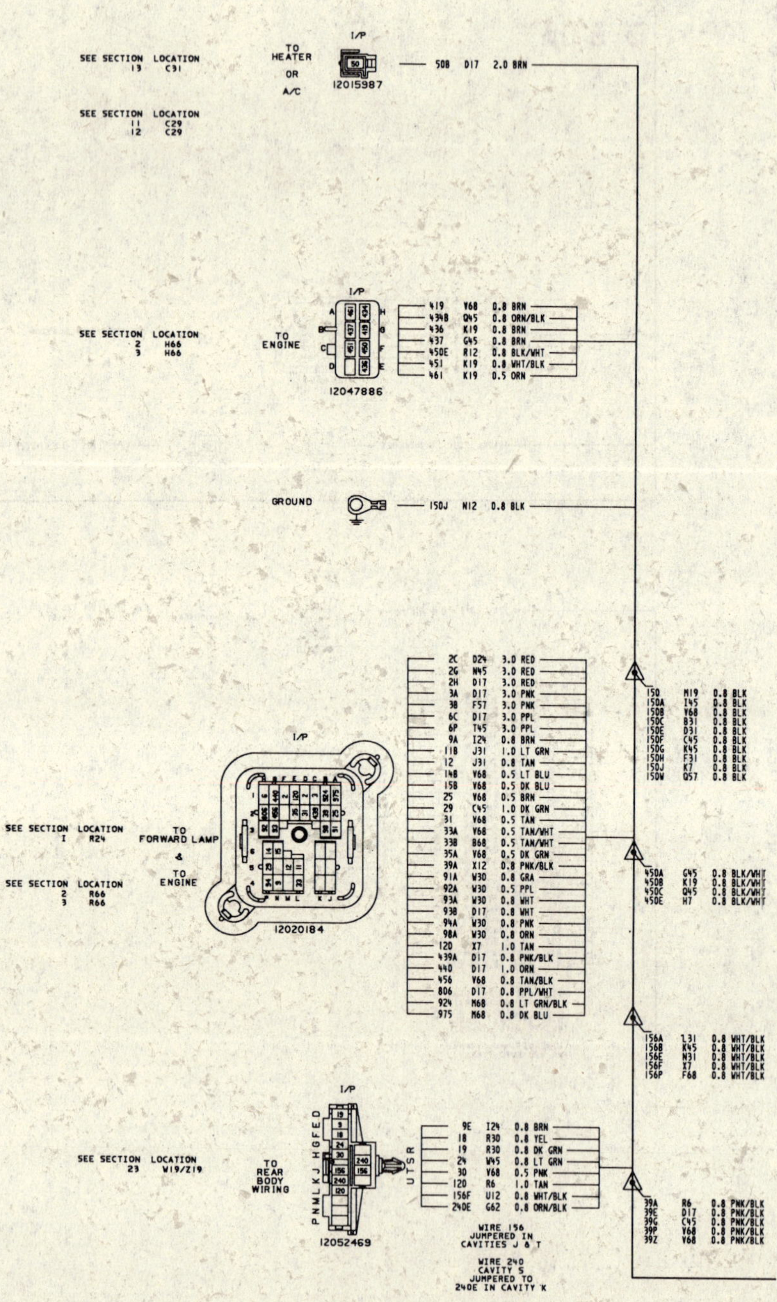
SEE SECTION 13 LOCATION C31
TO HEATER OR A/C
I/P
12015987
508 D17 2.0 BRN
SEE SECTION 11 12 LOCATION C29 C29
SEE SECTION 2 3 LOCATION H66 H66
TO ENGINE
I/P
12047886
419 Y68 0.8 BRN
434B Q45 0.8 ORN/BLK
436 K19 0.8 BRN
437 G45 0.8 BRN
450E R12 0.8 BLK/WHT
451 K19 0.8 WHT/BLK
461 K19 0.5 ORN
GROUND
150J N12 0.8 BLK
SEE SECTION 1 LOCATION R24
TO FORWARD LAMP & TO ENGINE
SEE SECTION 2 3 LOCATION R66 R66
I/P
12020184
SEE SECTION 23 LOCATION W19/Z19
TO REAR BODY WIRING
I/P
12052469
9E I24 0.8 BRN
18 R30 0.8 YEL
19 R30 0.8 DK GRN
24 W45 0.8 LT GRN
30 Y68 0.5 PNK
120 R6 1.0 TAN
156F U12 0.8 WHT/BLK
240E G62 0.8 ORN/BLK
WIRE 156 JUMPERED IN CAVITIES J & T
WIRE 240 CAVITY S JUMPERED TO 240E IN CAVITY K

SEAT BELT RETRACTOR
8911773
CIGARETTE LIGHTER
12041296
ASH TRAY LAMP
12015892
STOP LAMP SWITCH
2984235
DIMMER SWITCH
8917693
RIGHT HAND I/P COURTESY LAMP
12047677
LEFT HAND I/P COURTESY LAMP
12047677
12004147
12020492
SEE FUSE BLOCK DETAILS
WIRES 76 & 38 JUMPERED IN FUSE BLOCK
A.L.D.L.
12020219
I/P COMPARTMENT BOX LAMP
12010118
DIRECTIONAL SIGNAL SWITCH
KEY WARNING BUZZER
HORN
12004148
DIRECTIONAL SIGNAL ASSEMBLY
WIPER WASHER SWITCH
12010429
WINDSHIELD WIPER ASSEMBLY
INSTRUMENT PANEL
BLAZER ONLY

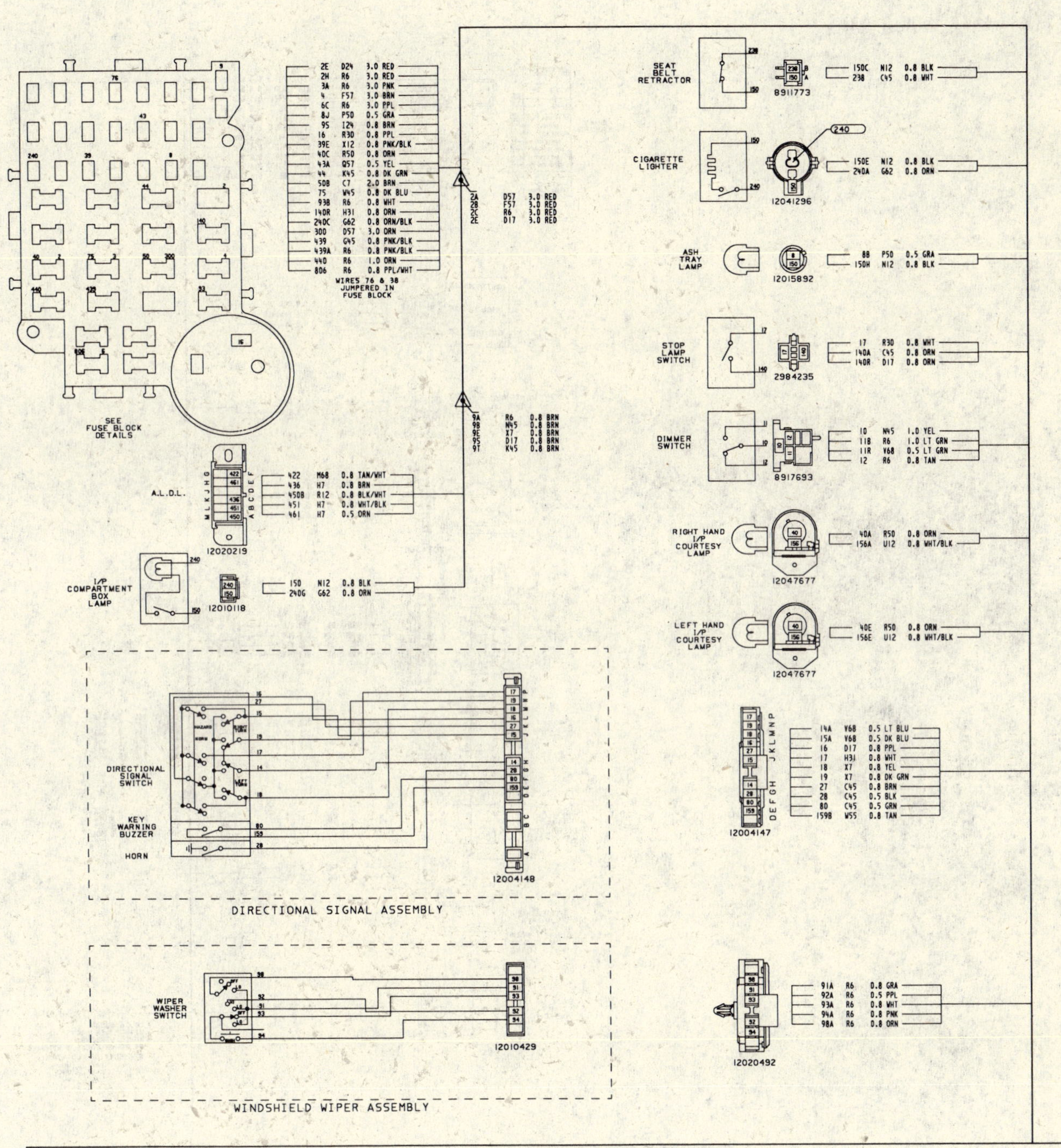

1986-87

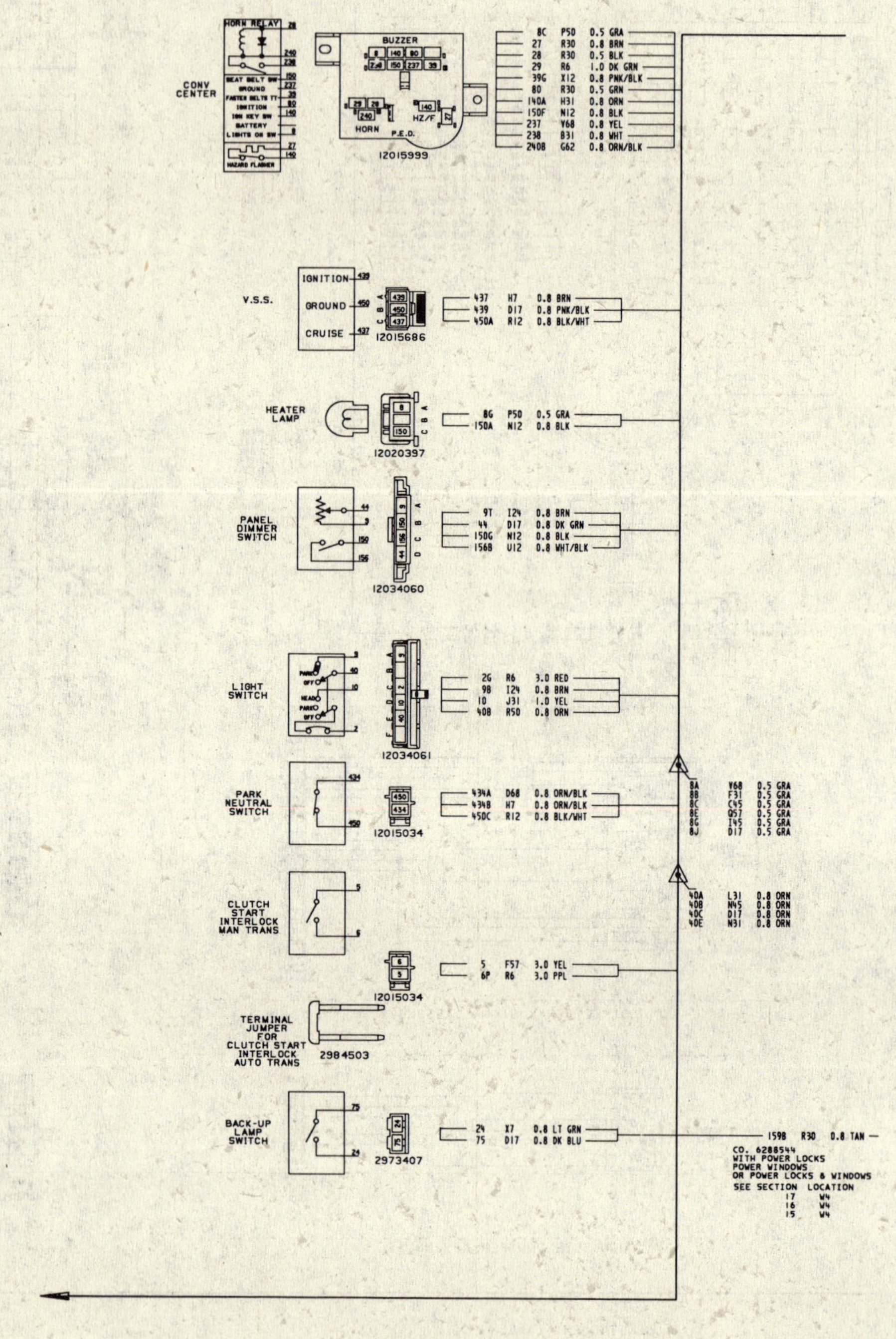

1986-87

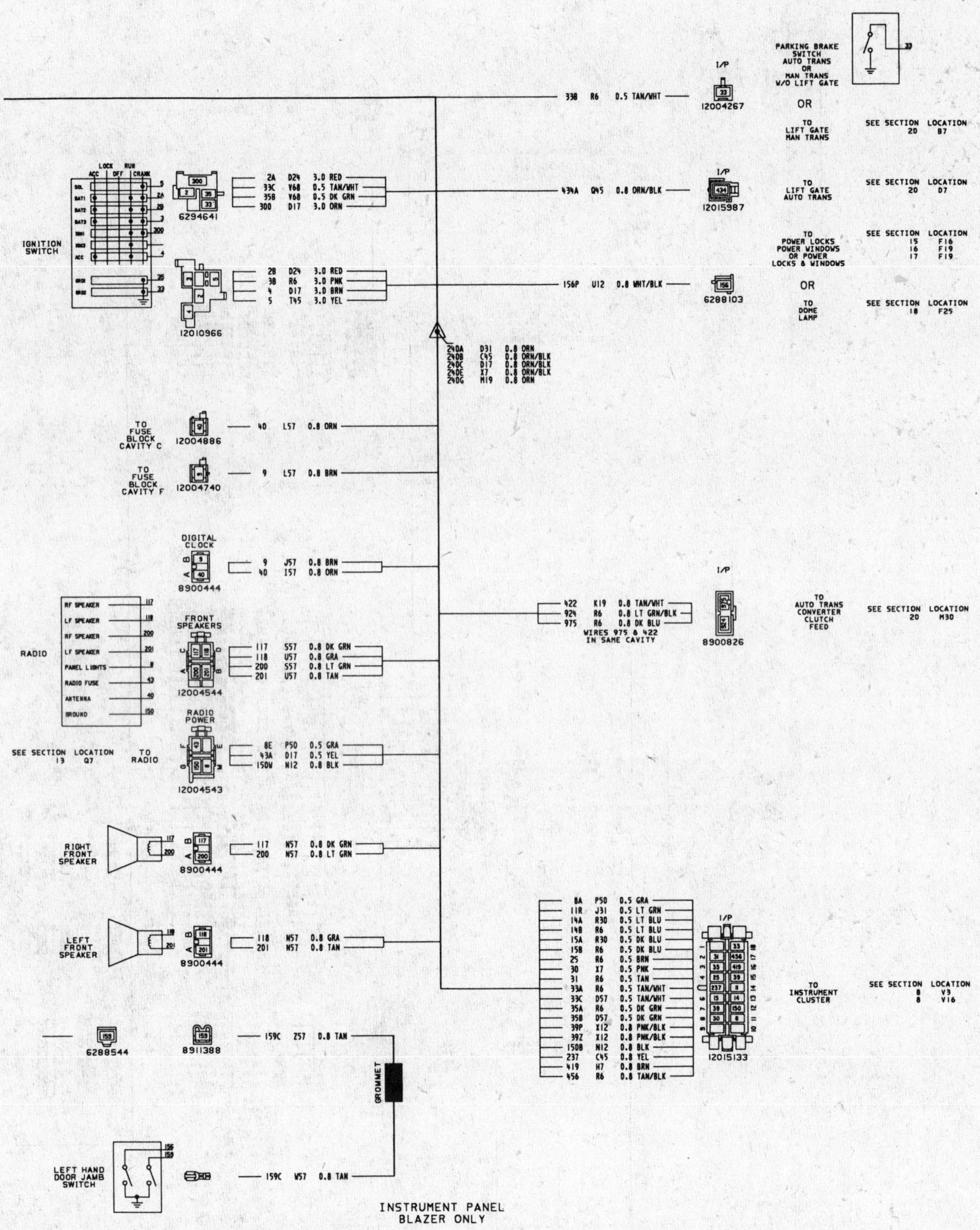

INSTRUMENT PANEL
BLAZER ONLY

1986-87

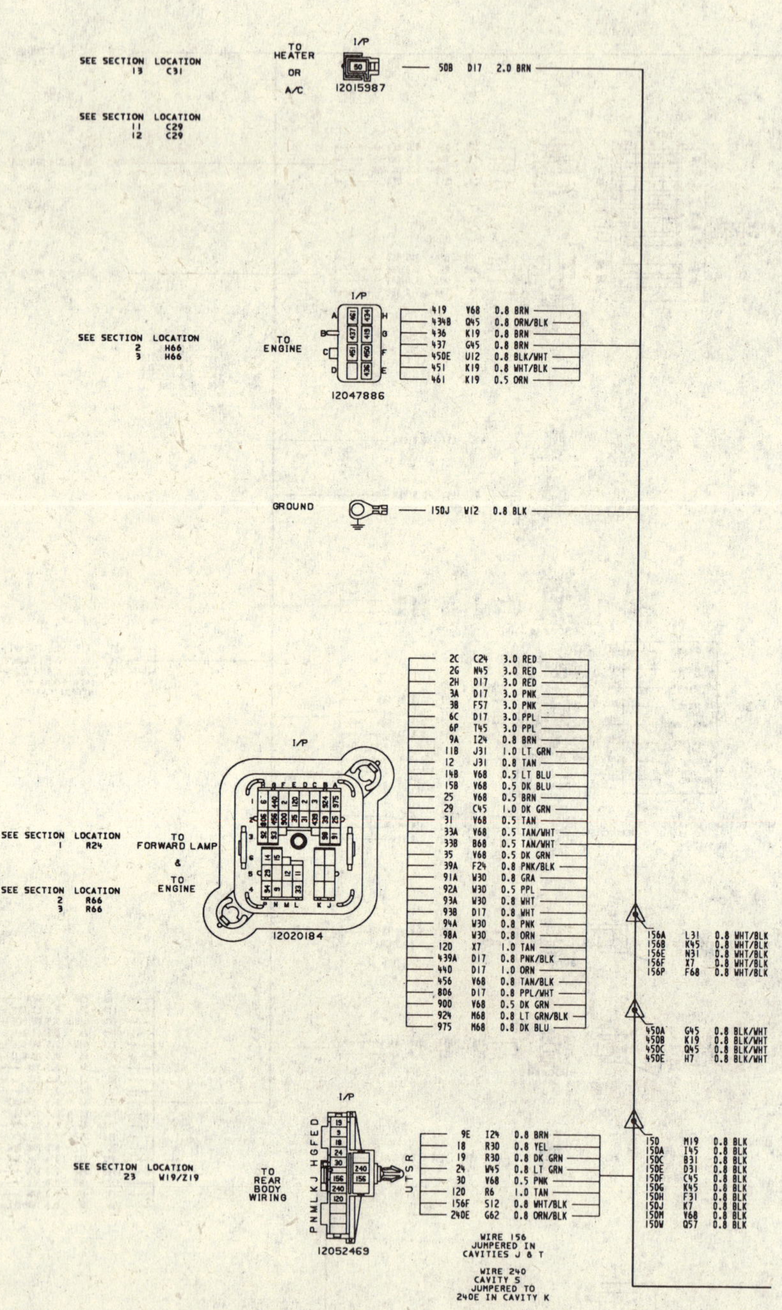

1986-87

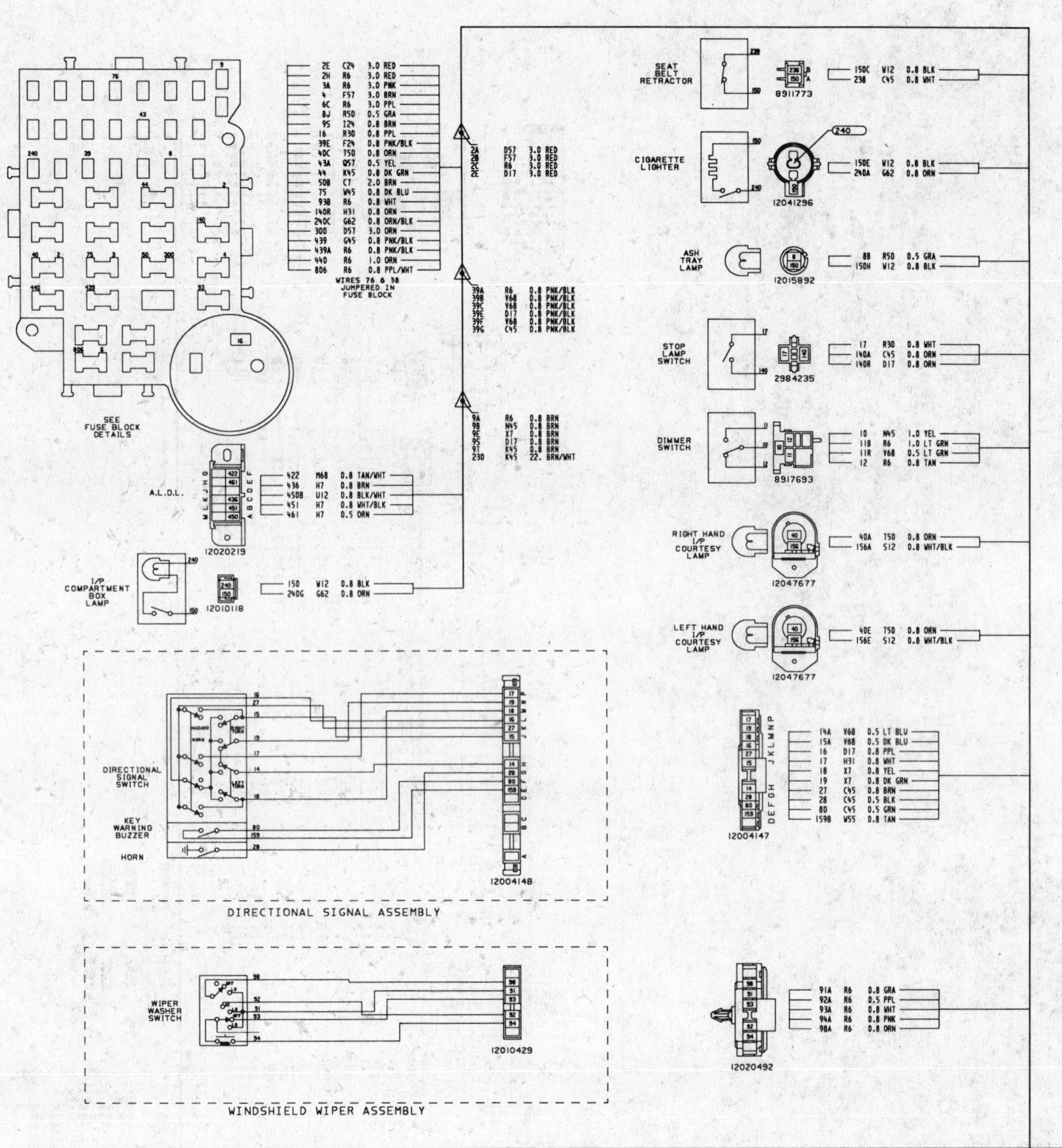

INSTRUMENT PANEL BLAZER WITH GAGES

1986-87

HORN RELAY
CONV CENTER
SEAT BELT SW
GROUND
FASTEN BELTS TT
IGNITION
IGN KEY SW
BATTERY
LIGHTS ON SW
HAZARD FLASHER
BUZZER
HORN
HZ/F
P.E.D.
12015999
8C R50 0.5 GRA
27 R30 0.8 BRN
28 R30 0.5 BLK
29 R6 1.0 DK GRN
39G F24 0.8 PNK/BLK
80 R30 0.5 GRN
140A H31 0.8 ORN
150F V12 0.8 BLK
237 Y68 0.8 YEL
238 B31 0.8 WHT
240B G62 0.8 ORN/BLK
WIRE 140 JUMPERED TO 140A IN CONNECTOR
V.S.S.
IGNITION
GROUND
CRUISE
12015686
437 H7 0.8 BRN
439 D17 0.8 PNK/BLK
450A U12 0.8 BLK/WHT
HEATER LAMP
12020397
8G R50 0.5 GRA
150A V12 0.8 BLK
PANEL DIMMER SWITCH
12034060
9T I24 0.8 BRN
44 D17 0.8 DK GRN
150G V12 0.8 BLK
156B S12 0.8 WHT/BLK
230 I24 22. BRN/WHT
WIRES 230 & 44 IN CAVITY D
LIGHT SWITCH
PARK
OFF
HEAD
12034061
2G R6 3.0 RED
9B I24 0.8 BRN
10 J31 1.0 YEL
40B T50 0.8 ORN
PARK NEUTRAL SWITCH
12015034
434A D68 0.8 ORN/BLK
434B H7 0.8 ORN/BLK
450C U12 0.8 BLK/WHT
CLUTCH START INTERLOCK MAN TRANS
12015034
5 F57 3.0 YEL
6P R6 3.0 PPL
TERMINAL JUMPER FOR CLUTCH START INTERLOCK AUTO TRANS
2984503
8A V68 0.5 GRA
8B F31 0.5 GRA
8C C45 0.5 GRA
8E Q57 0.5 GRA
8G I45 0.5 GRA
8J D17 0.5 GRA
40A L31 0.8 ORN
40B N45 0.8 ORN
40C D17 0.8 ORN
40E N31 0.8 ORN
BACK-UP LAMP SWITCH
2973407
24 X7 0.8 LT GRN
75 D17 0.8 DK BLU
159B R30 0.8 TAN
CO.6288544
WITH POWER LOCKS
POWER WINDOWS
OR POWER LOCKS & WINDOWS
SEE SECTION LOCATION
17 W4
16 W4
15 W4

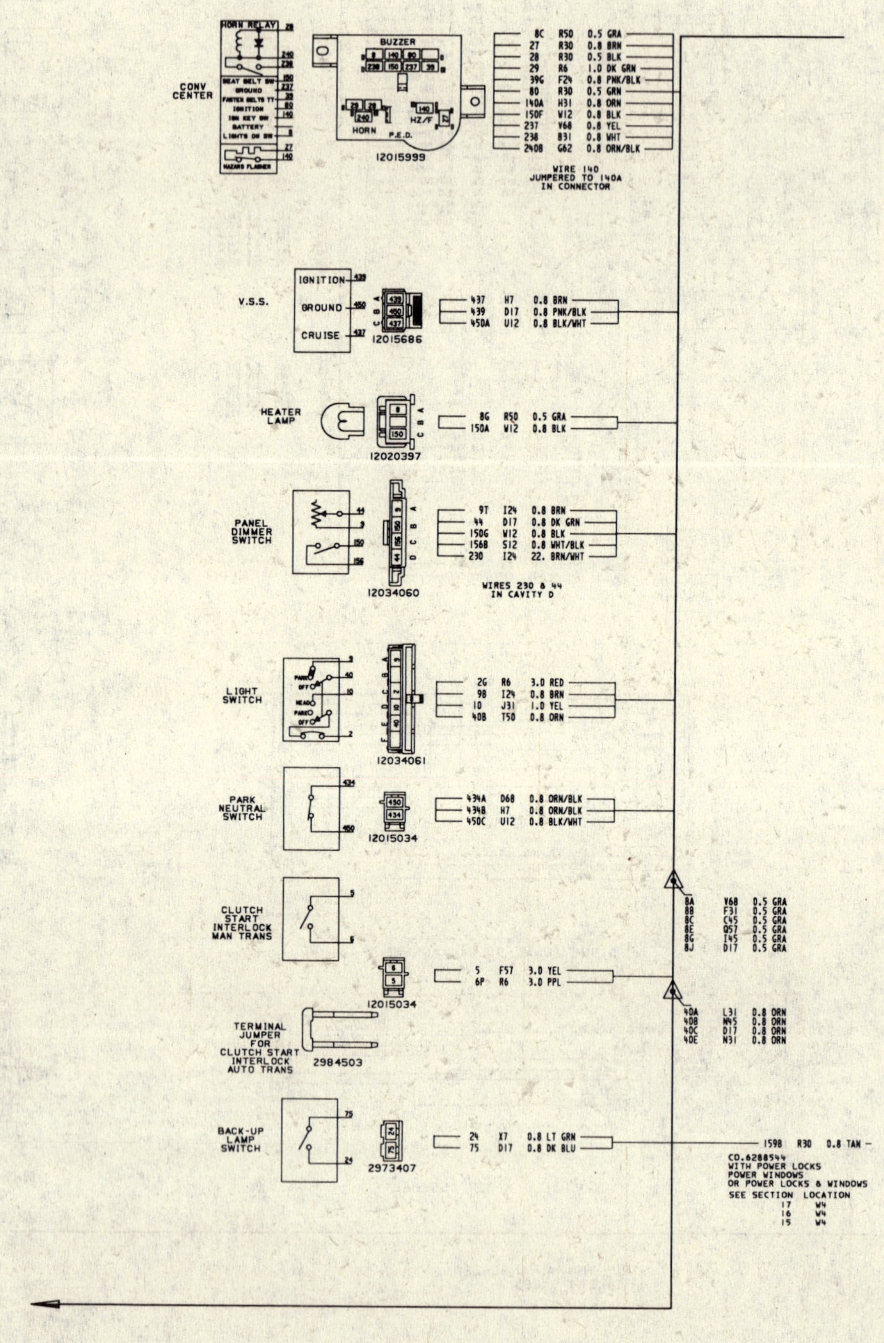

1986-87

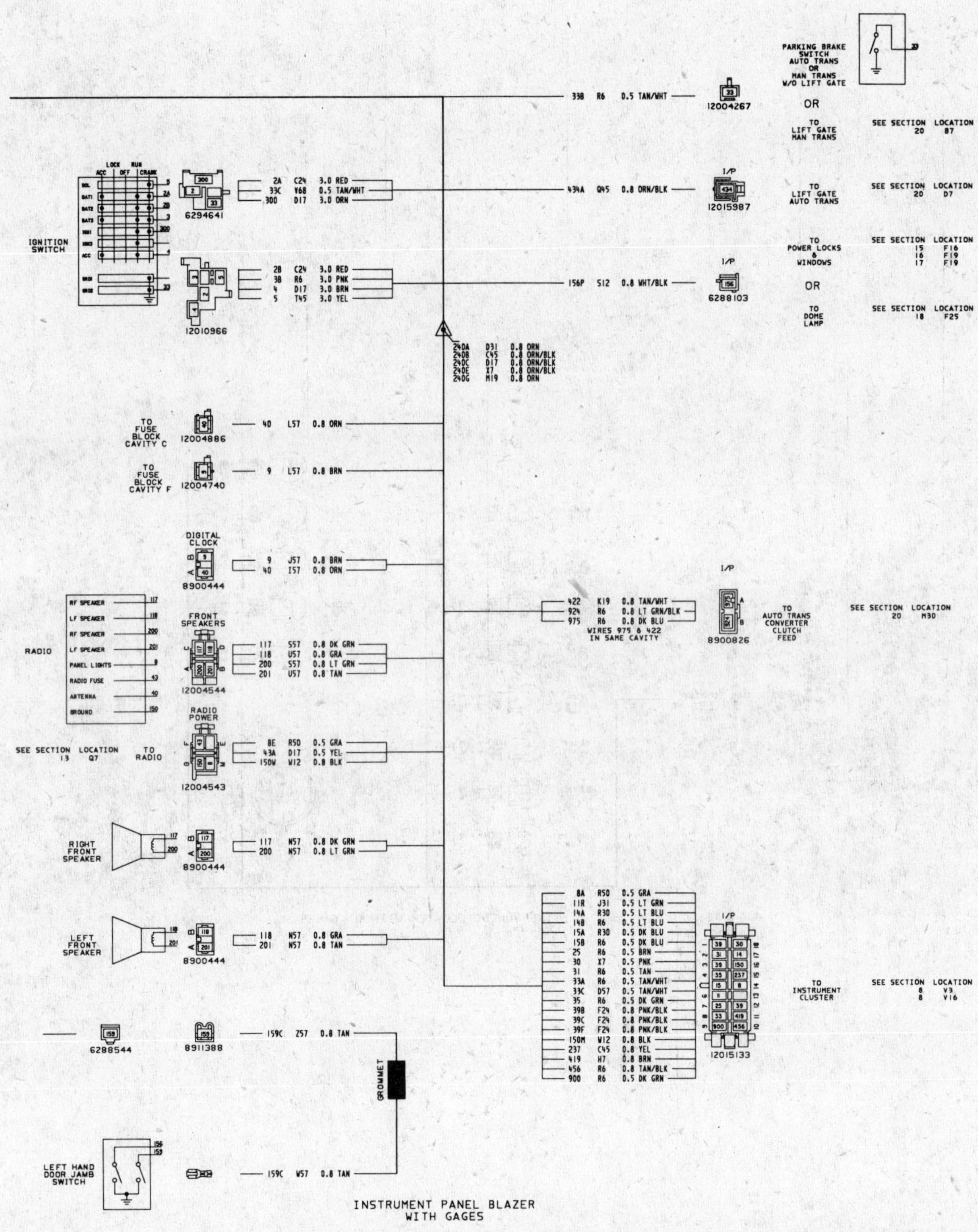

INSTRUMENT PANEL BLAZER WITH GAGES

1986-87

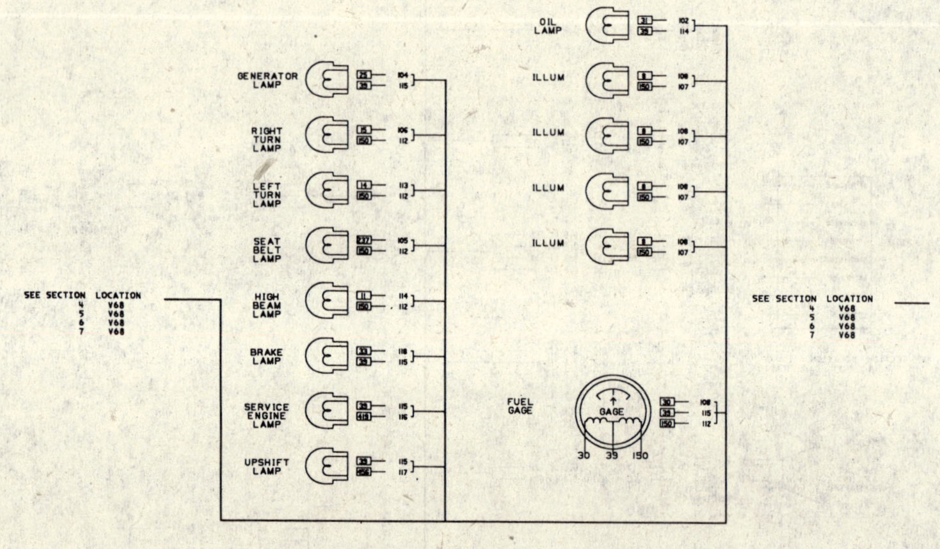

INSTRUMENT CLUSTER WITHOUT GAGES

1986-87

GENERATOR LAMP
RIGHT TURN LAMP
LEFT TURN LAMP
SEAT BELT LAMP
HIGH BEAM LAMP
BRAKE LAMP
SERVICE ENGINE LAMP
UPSHIFT LAMP
CHECK GAGES LAMP
ILLUM
ILLUM
VOLT METER
METER
FUEL GAGE
GAGE
OIL GAGE
GAGE
TEMP GAGE
GAGE
× 39 CIRCUIT
CAVITY 112 W/TACH
CAVITY 101 W/O TACH
INSTRIMENT CLUSTER WITH GAGES
SEE SECTION LOCATION
2 M66
3 M66
TO ENGINE
TACH
8917583
121C U31 0.8 WHT
GROMMET
TO FUSE BLOCK CAVITY B
TACH
12004887
41 U31 0.8 BRN/WHT
INSTRUMENT CLUSTER
2965164
41 R31 0.8 BRN/WHT
121C M31 0.8 WHT
150 X31 0.8 BLK
BUS BAR GROUND
12004267
150 U31 0.8 BLK
TACHOMETER
U16

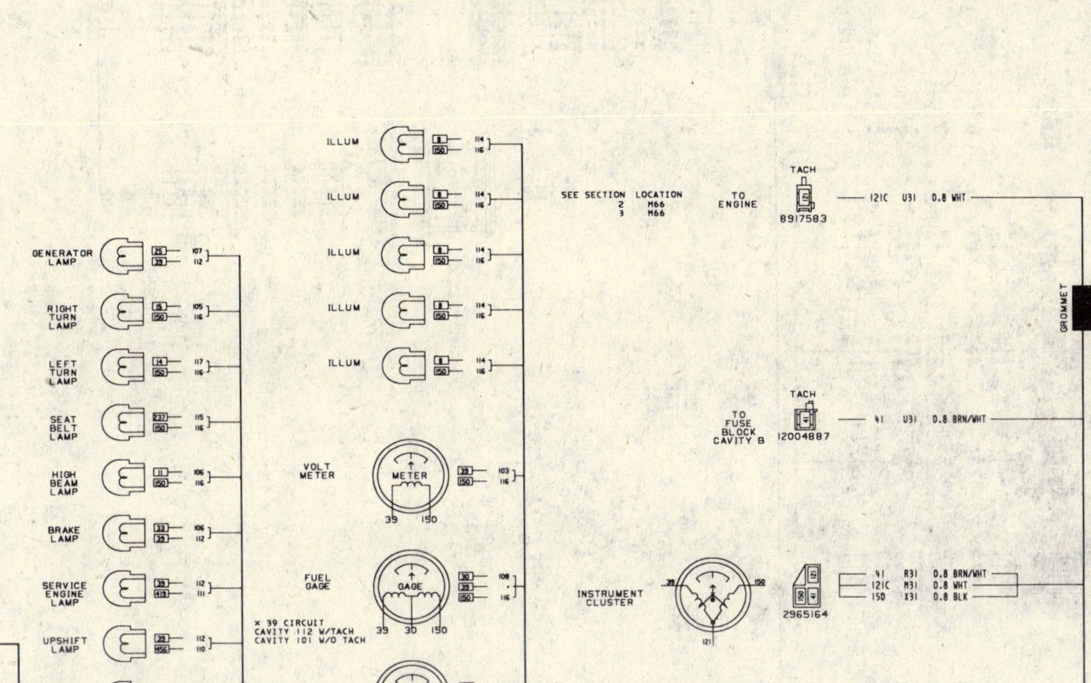

1986-87

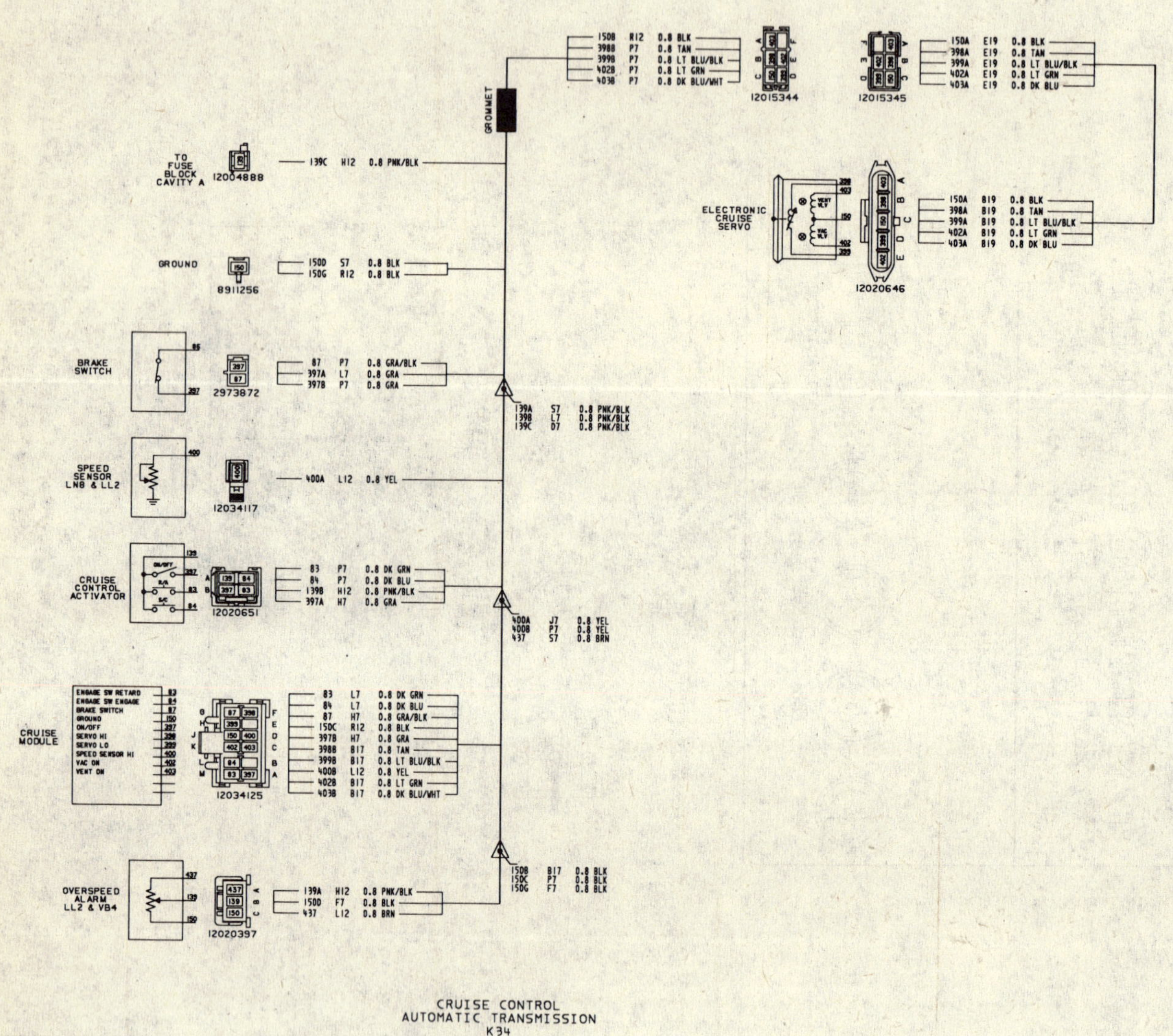

CRUISE CONTROL
AUTOMATIC TRANSMISSION
K34

1986-87

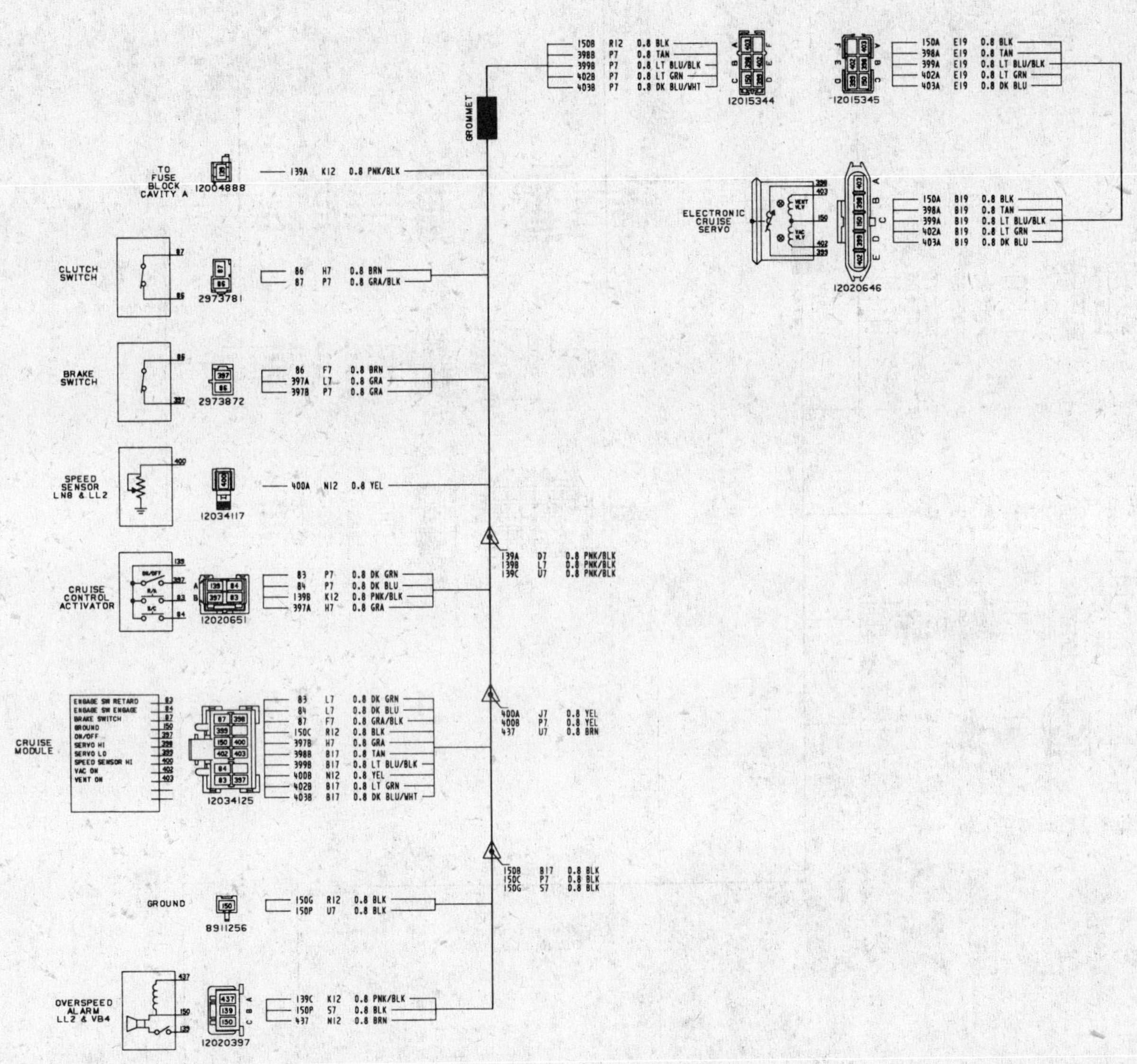

CRUISE CONTROL
MANUAL TRANSMISSION
K34

1986-87

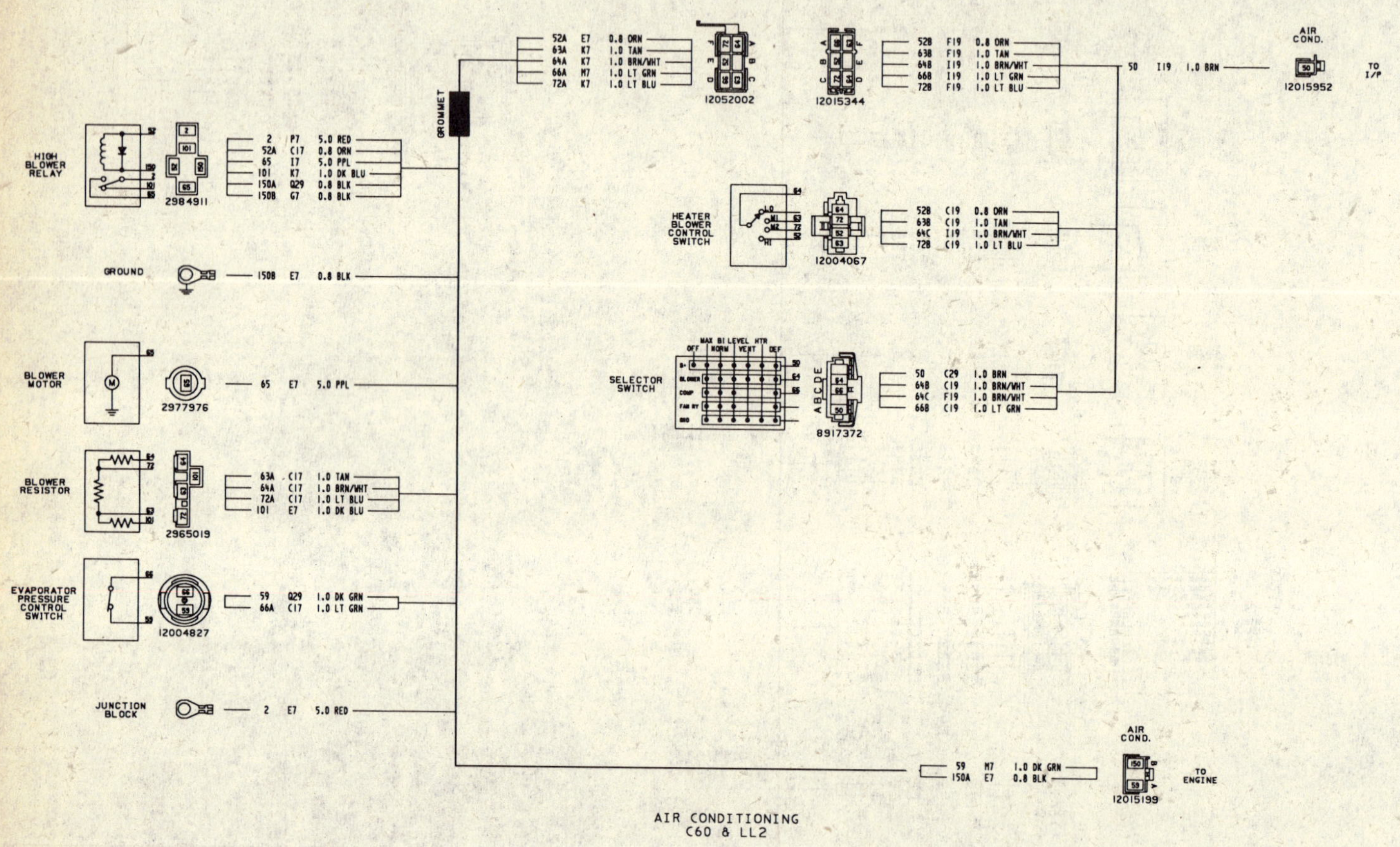

AIR CONDITIONING
C60 & LL2

1986-87

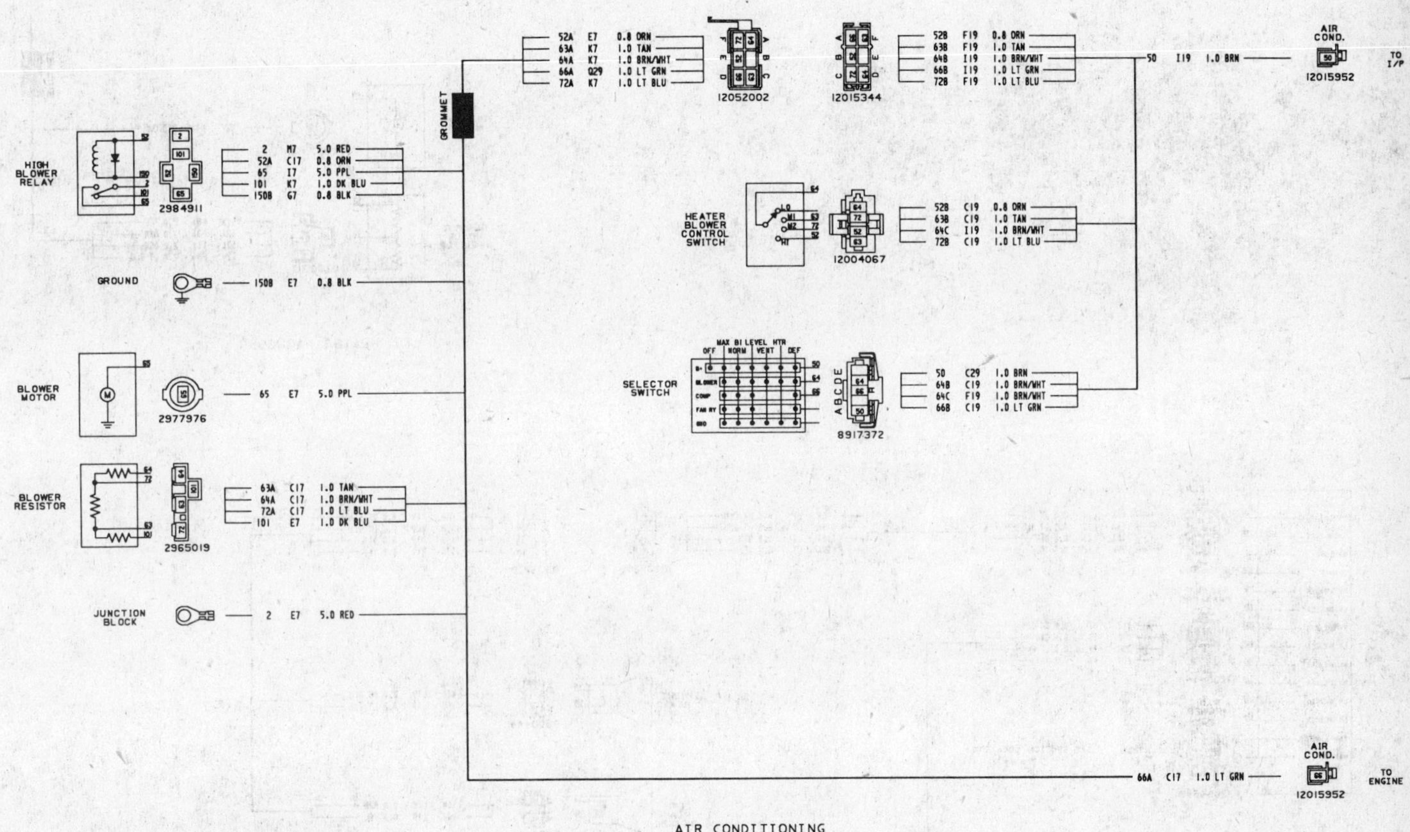

AIR CONDITIONING
C60 & LN8

1986-87

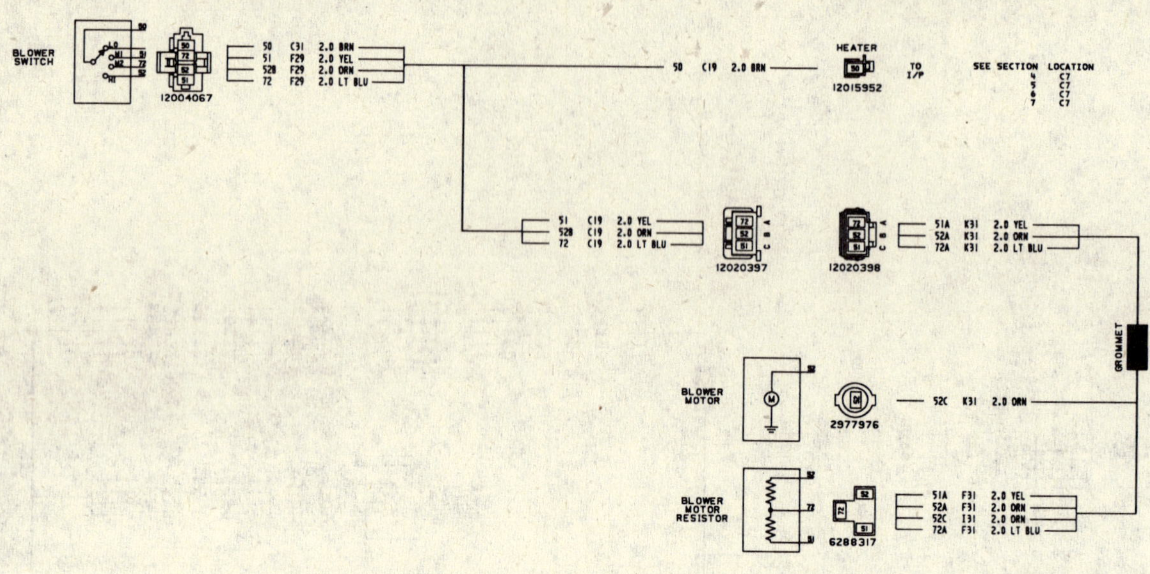

HEATER HARNESS

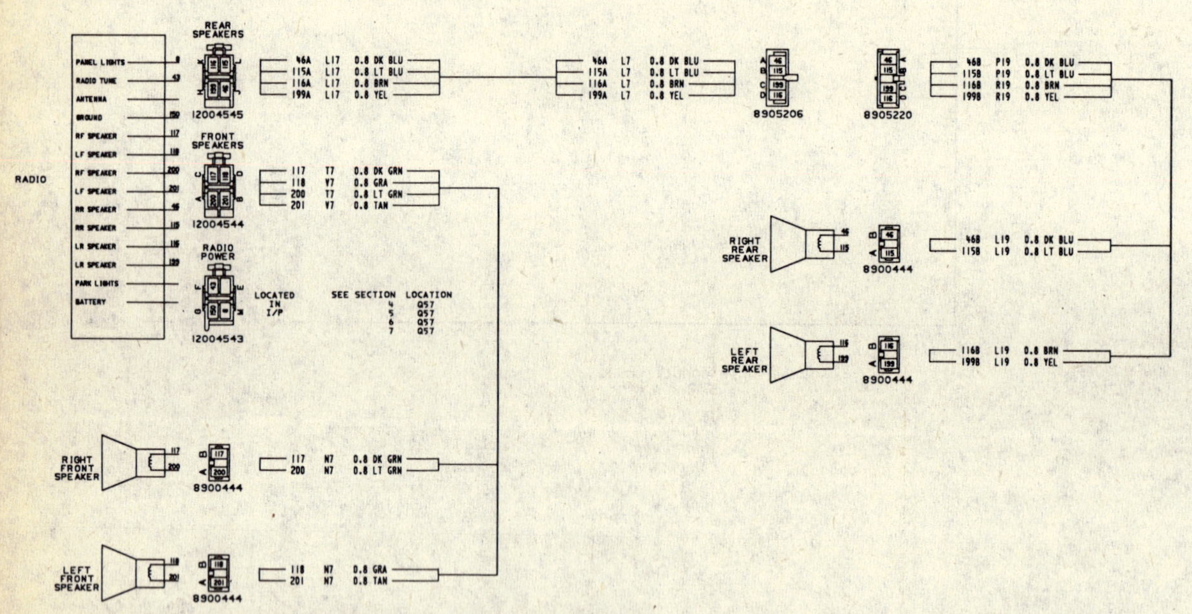

RADIO EQUIPMENT STEREO
UM2 UM3 U58

1986-87

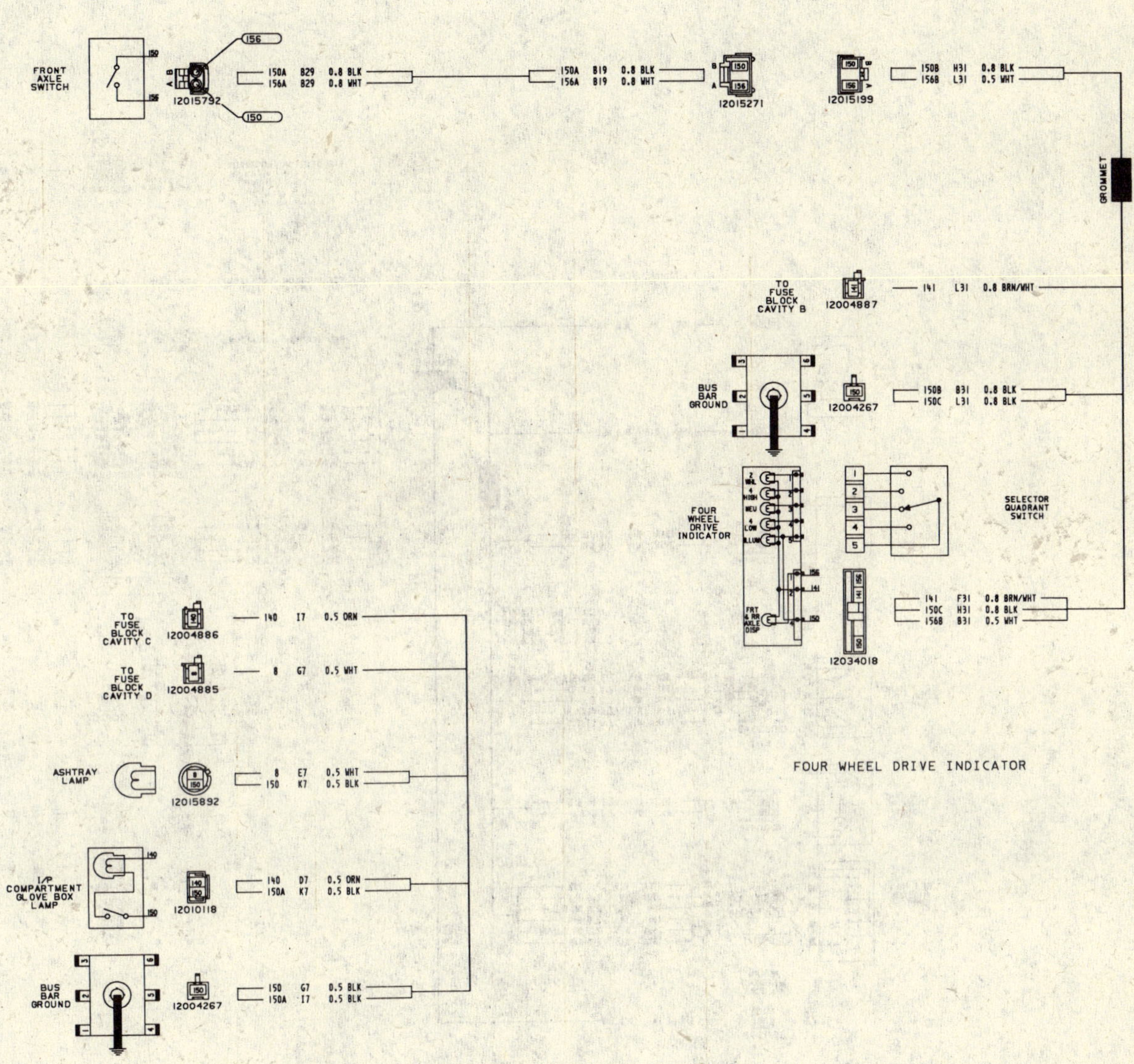

FOUR WHEEL DRIVE INDICATOR

ASHTRAY LAMP & I/P COMPARTMENT LAMP TR9

1986-87

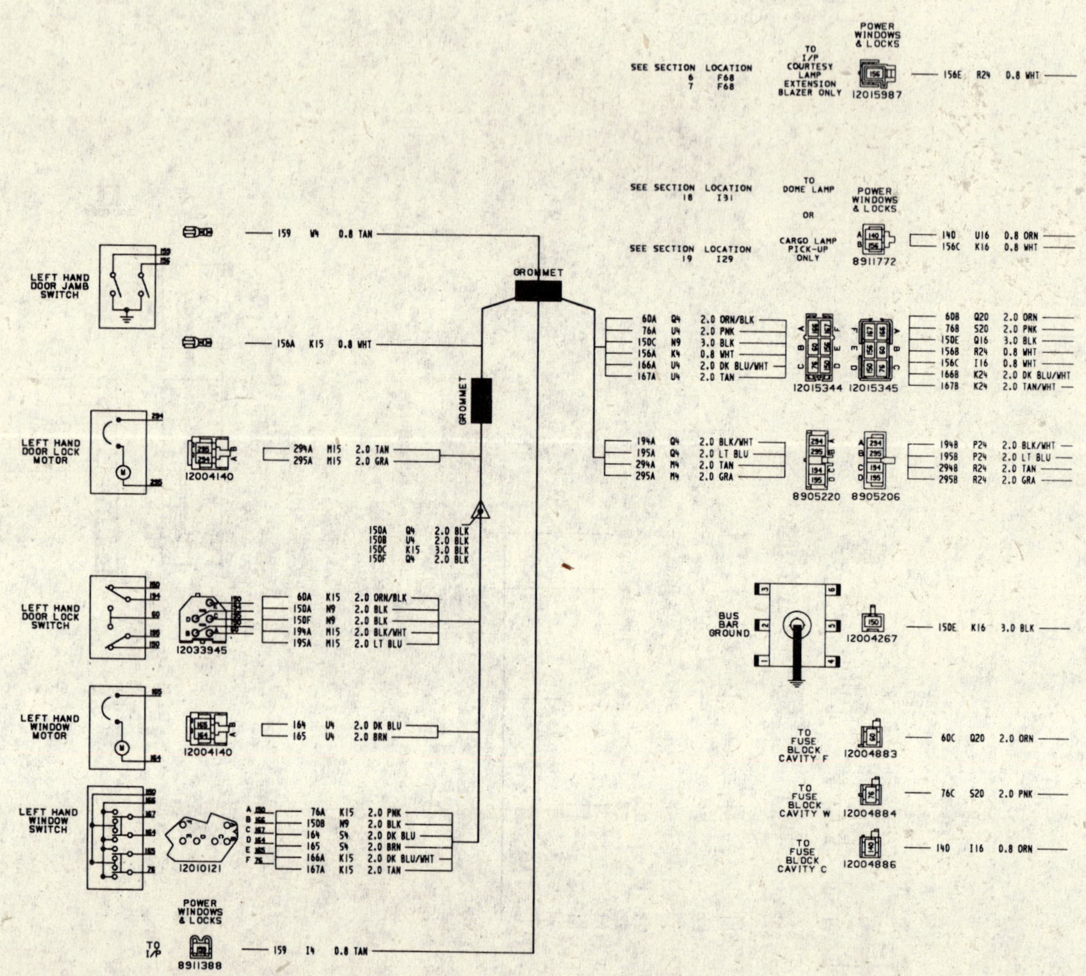

POWER WINDOWS
&
POWER LOCKS
A31 & AU3

1986-87

RIGHT HAND WINDOW MOTOR
12004140
666 H30 2.0 DK BLU
667 H30 2.0 BRN
RIGHT HAND WINDOW SWITCH
12034136
76F K25 2.0 PNK
166C K25 2.0 DK BLU/WHT
167C K25 2.0 TAN
666 F30 2.0 DK BLU
667 F30 2.0 BRN
76E S20 2.0 PNK
166B K16 2.0 DK BLU/WHT
167B K16 2.0 TAN/WHT
12020398 12020397
76F H30 2.0 PNK
166C H30 2.0 DK BLU/WHT
167C H30 2.0 TAN
GROMMET
GROMMET
60B K16 2.0 ORN
60C S16 2.0 ORN
60E P24 2.0 ORN
60E Q20 2.0 ORN
194B M16 2.0 BLK/WHT
195B M16 2.0 LT BLU
8905205 8905222
60F W30 2.0 ORN/BLK
194C W30 2.0 BLK/WHT
195C W30 2.0 LT BLU
156B K16 0.8 WHT
156E F16 0.8 WHT
294B M16 2.0 TAN
295B M16 2.0 GRA
8905222 8905205
156F T30 0.8 WHT
294C Q37 2.0 TAN
295C S37 2.0 GRA
294C R25 2.0 TAN
294E W30 2.0 TAN
294F Y30 2.0 TAN
76B K16 2.0 PNK
76C T16 2.0 PNK
76E K24 2.0 PNK
295C R25 2.0 GRA
295E W30 2.0 GRA
295F Y30 2.0 GRA
RIGHT HAND DOOR JAMB SWITCH
156F R25 0.8 WHT
RIGHT HAND DOOR LOCK SWITCH
12033945
60F P25 2.0 ORN/BLK
194C P25 2.0 BLK/WHT
195C P25 2.0 LT BLU
294E Q37 2.0 TAN
295E S37 2.0 GRA
RIGHT HAND DOOR LOCK MOTOR
12004140
294F Q37 2.0 TAN
295F S37 2.0 GRA

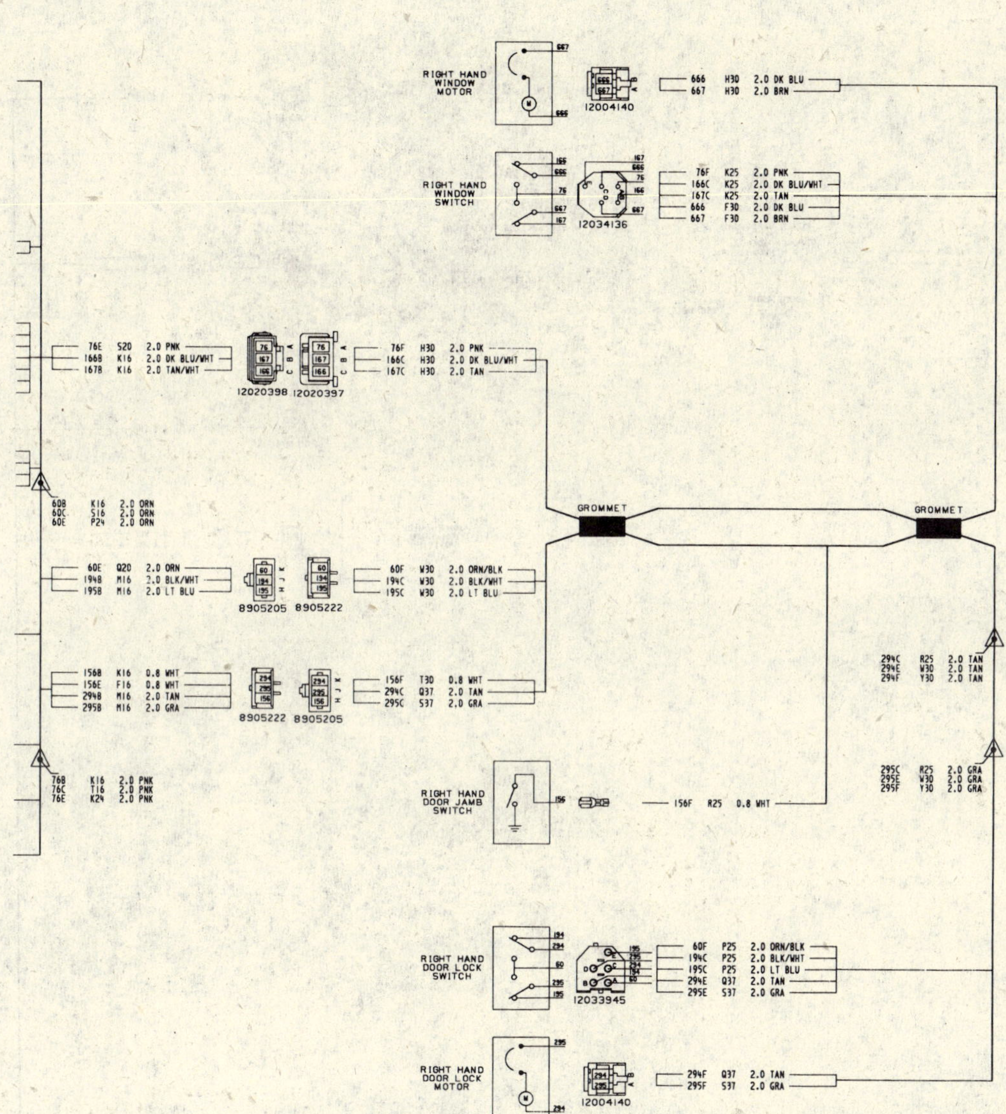

1986-87

DOME LAMP
140A I17 0.8 ORN
156A I17 0.8 WHT
140A H7 0.8 ORN
156A J7 0.8 WHT
DOME LAMP
8911773
TO POWER LOCKS OR POWER WINDOWS OR POWER LOCKS & WINDOWS
OR
TO DOME LAMP EXT. POWER FEED
SEE SECTION LOCATION
17 I19
16 I19
15 I16
SEE SECTION LOCATION
18 I25
SEE SECTION LOCATION
6 F68
7 F68
COURTESY LAMP
TO I/P
12015987
156E N27 0.8 WHT
SEE SECTION LOCATION
19 I29
SEE SECTION LOCATION
18 I17
TO CARGO LAMP
OR
TO DOME LAMP EXT.
DOME LAMP
8911772
140B L27 0.8 ORN
156B I32 0.8 WHT
156B I27 0.8 WHT
156C Z27 0.8 WHT
156D N27 0.8 WHT
TO FUSE BLOCK CAVITY C
12004886
140B I27 0.8 ORN
RIGHT HAND DOOR JAMB SWITCH
8900420
156D I32 0.8 WHT
156E F27 0.8 WHT
DOME LAMP
(91 ST000(03)
SEE SECTION LOCATION
4 Z57
5 Z57
6 Z57
7 Z57
TO LEFT HAND DOOR JAMB SWITCH I/P
DOME LAMP
2977253
156C I32 0.8 WHT

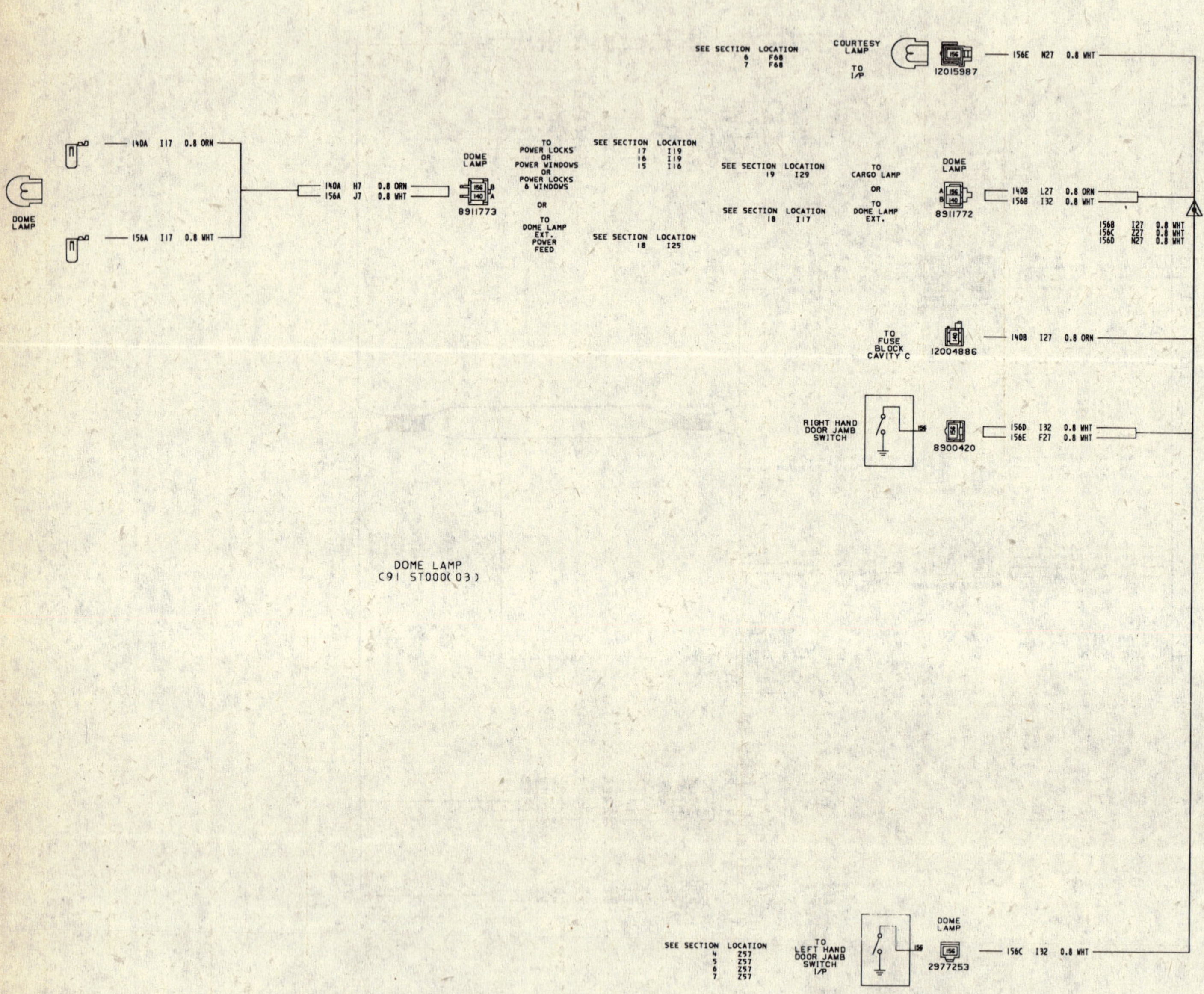

1986-87

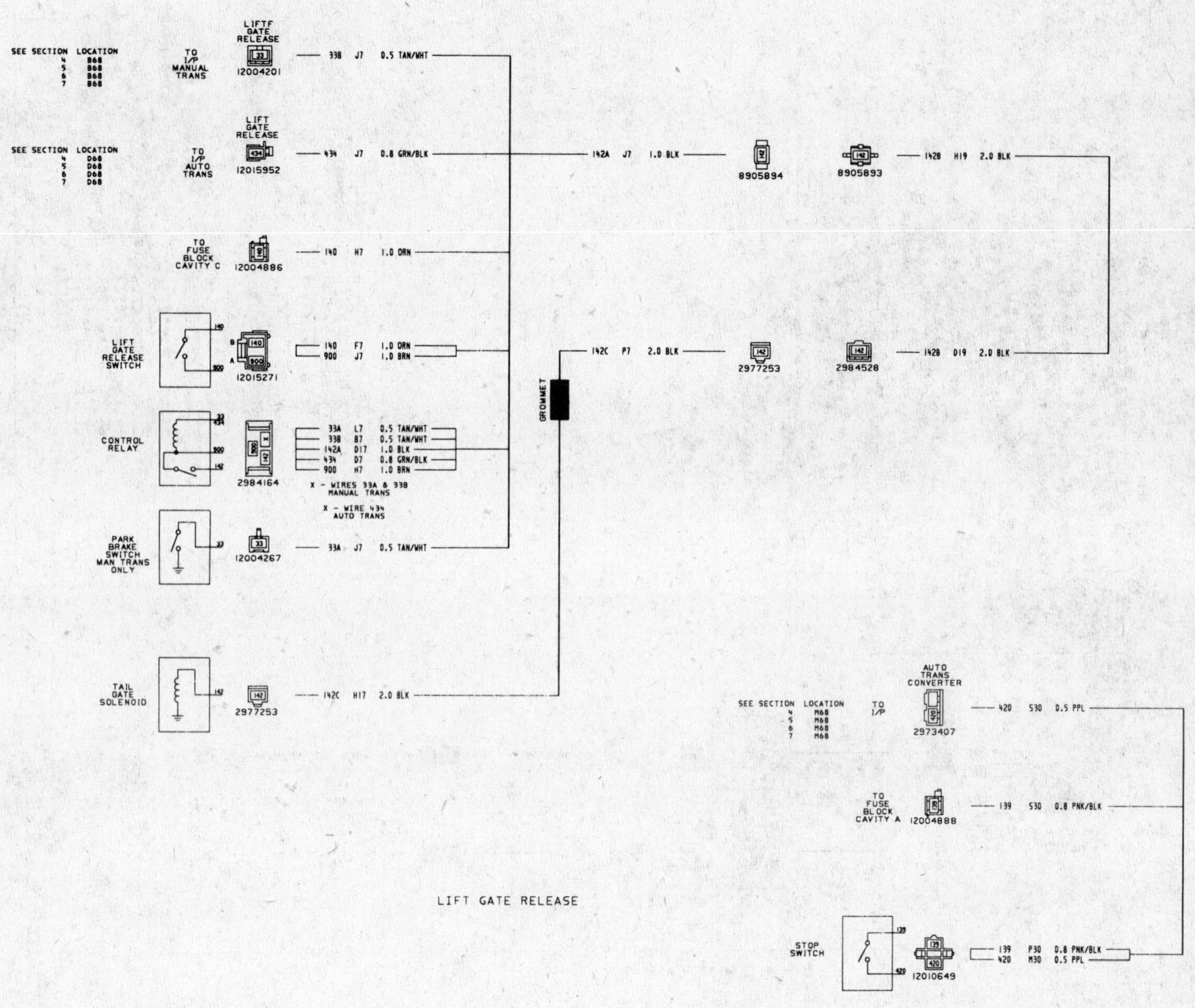

LIFT GATE RELEASE

AUTOMATIC TRANSMISSION CONVERTER CLUTCH FEED
MD8

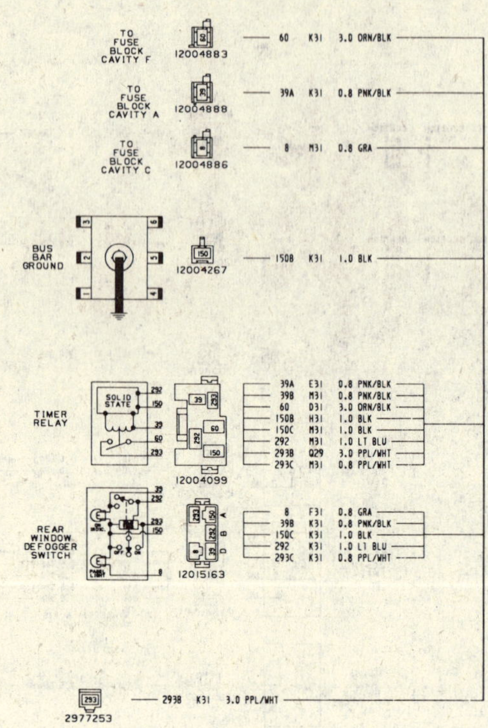

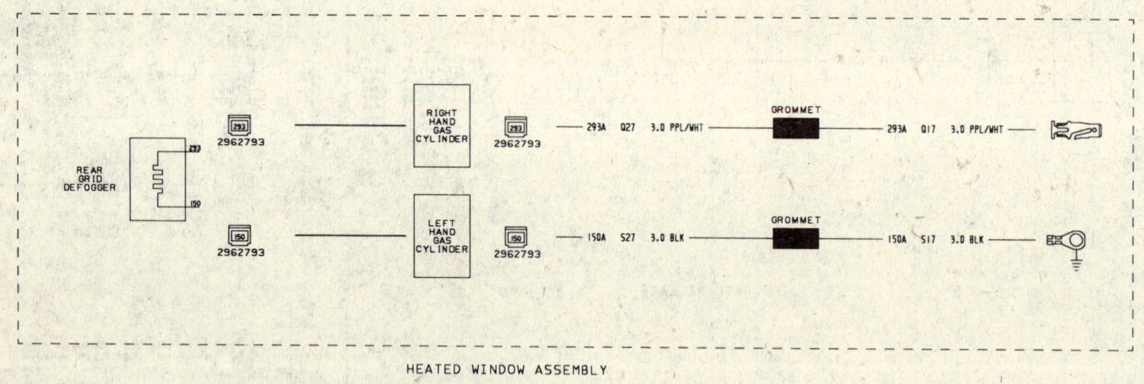

HEATED LIFT GATE WINDOW
C49

1986-87

RIGHT HAND BACK-UP LAMP
12010804
RIGHT HAND TAIL STOP & DIRECTIONAL LAMP
8917818
RIGHT HAND SIDE MARKER LAMP
6294015
GROUND
LEFT HAND BACK-UP LAMP
12010804
LEFT HAND TAIL STOP & DIRECTIONAL LAMP
8917818
LEFT HAND SIDE MARKER LAMP
6294015
GROUND
GROMMET
12020397
12020398
REAR DOME LAMP & SWITCH
12015937
GROUND
LICENSE LAMP
2977107
FUEL PUMP & SENSOR
12010973
TAIL LIC. PARK MARKER
STOP DIR. LAMP LH
STOP DIR. LAMP RH
TRAILER DIR. GROUND
BACK UP LAMP
TO TRAILER
8900440
8900441
REAR LAMP BLAZER
12034337
TO I/P
SEE SECTION 6 7
LOCATION X7 X7
DOME LAMP
12015645
REAR BODY BLAZER
12034338

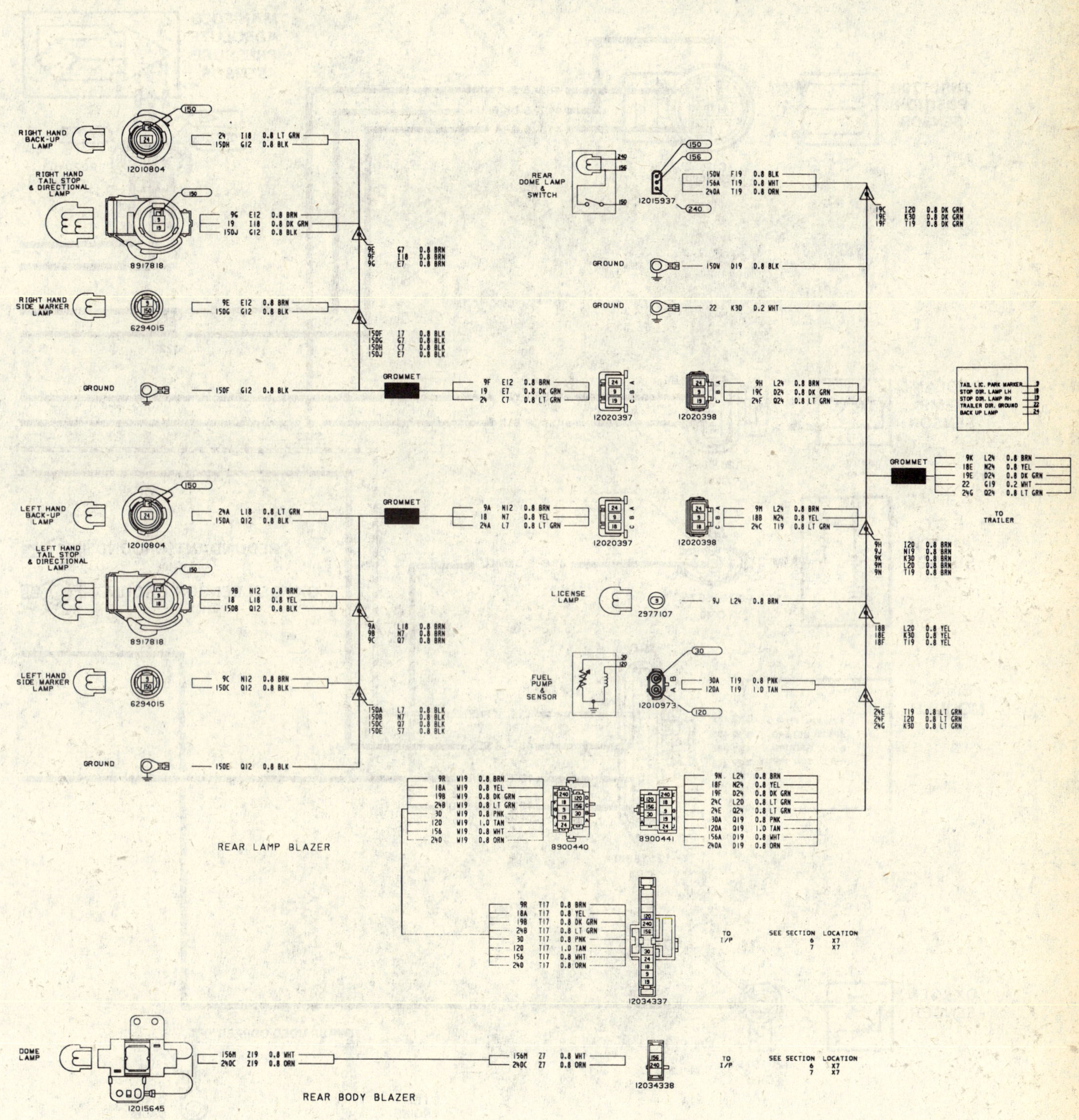

1986-87

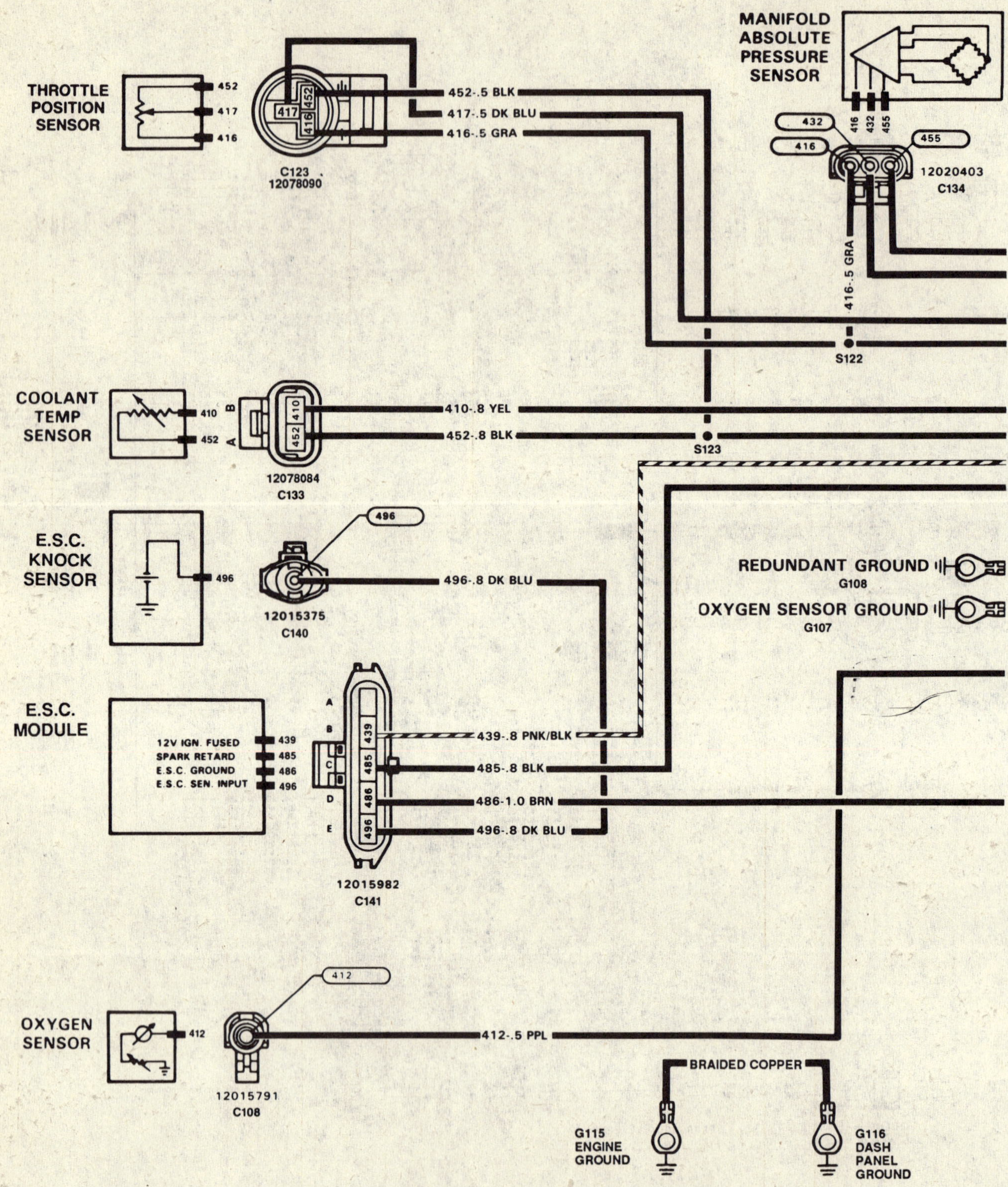

100 ELECTRONIC CONTROL MODULE - INPUTS - 2.8L (173 CID) ENGINE

1988-91

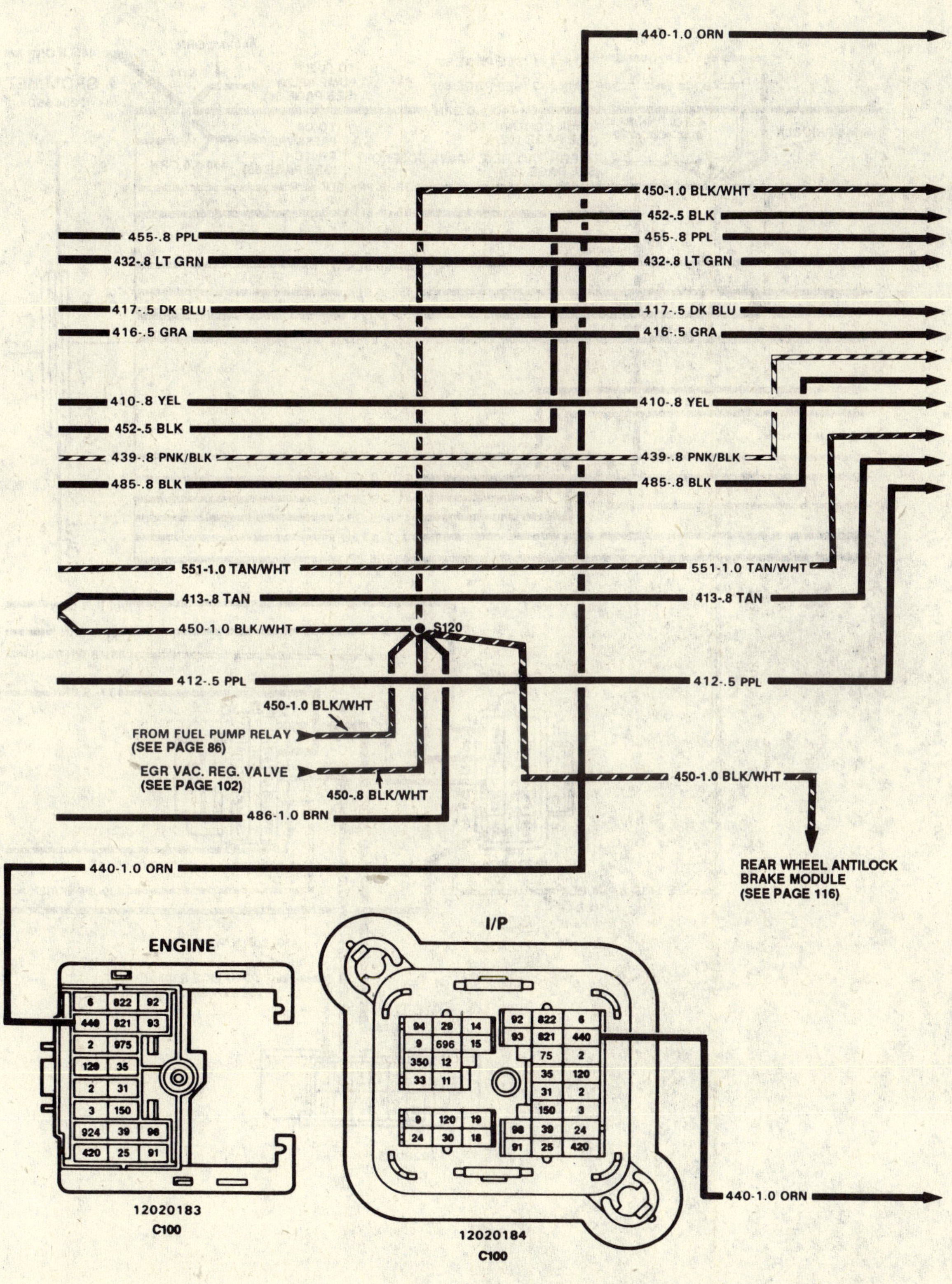
440-1.0 ORN
450-1.0 BLK/WHT
452-.5 BLK
455-.8 PPL
455-.8 PPL
432-.8 LT GRN
432-.8 LT GRN
417-.5 DK BLU
417-.5 DK BLU
416-.5 GRA
416-.5 GRA
410-.8 YEL
410-.8 YEL
452-.5 BLK
439-.8 PNK/BLK
439-.8 PNK/BLK
485-.8 BLK
485-.8 BLK
551-1.0 TAN/WHT
551-1.0 TAN/WHT
413-.8 TAN
413-.8 TAN
450-1.0 BLK/WHT
S120
412-.5 PPL
412-.5 PPL
450-1.0 BLK/WHT
FROM FUEL PUMP RELAY
(SEE PAGE 86)
EGR VAC. REG. VALVE
(SEE PAGE 102)
450-.8 BLK/WHT
450-1.0 BLK/WHT
486-1.0 BRN
REAR WHEEL ANTILOCK
BRAKE MODULE
(SEE PAGE 116)
440-1.0 ORN
ENGINE
I/P
12020183
C100
12020184
C100
440-1.0 ORN
1988-91

481-.8 RED
TO INJ #1 (SEE PAGE 86)
482-.8 WHT
TO INJ #2 (SEE PAGE 86)
440-1.0 ORN
TO FUEL PUMP RELAY (SEE PAGE 86)
S114
440-.8 ORN
GROMMET 12066507
439-.8 PNK/BLK
TO AIR CONTROL SOL (SEE PAGE 102)
TO EGR VAC. REG. VALVE SOLENOID (SEE PAGE 102)
TO OIL PRESSURE SWITCH (SEE PAGE 86)
S116
485-.8 BLK
450-1.0 BLK/WHT
452-.5 BLK
455-.8 PPL
432-.8 LT GRN
551-1.0 TAN/WHT
410-.8 YEL
417-.5 DK BLU
416-.5 GRA
413-.8 TAN
412-.5 PPL
COWL
461-.8 ORN
437-.8 BRN
451-.8 WHT/BLK
ENGINE
I/P
12064770
12064764
C101
461-.5 ORN
451-.8 WHT/BLK
450-.8 BLK/WHT
TO SPLICE S306 (SEE PAGE 21)
A.L.D.L.
12020043
C308
440-1.0 ORN

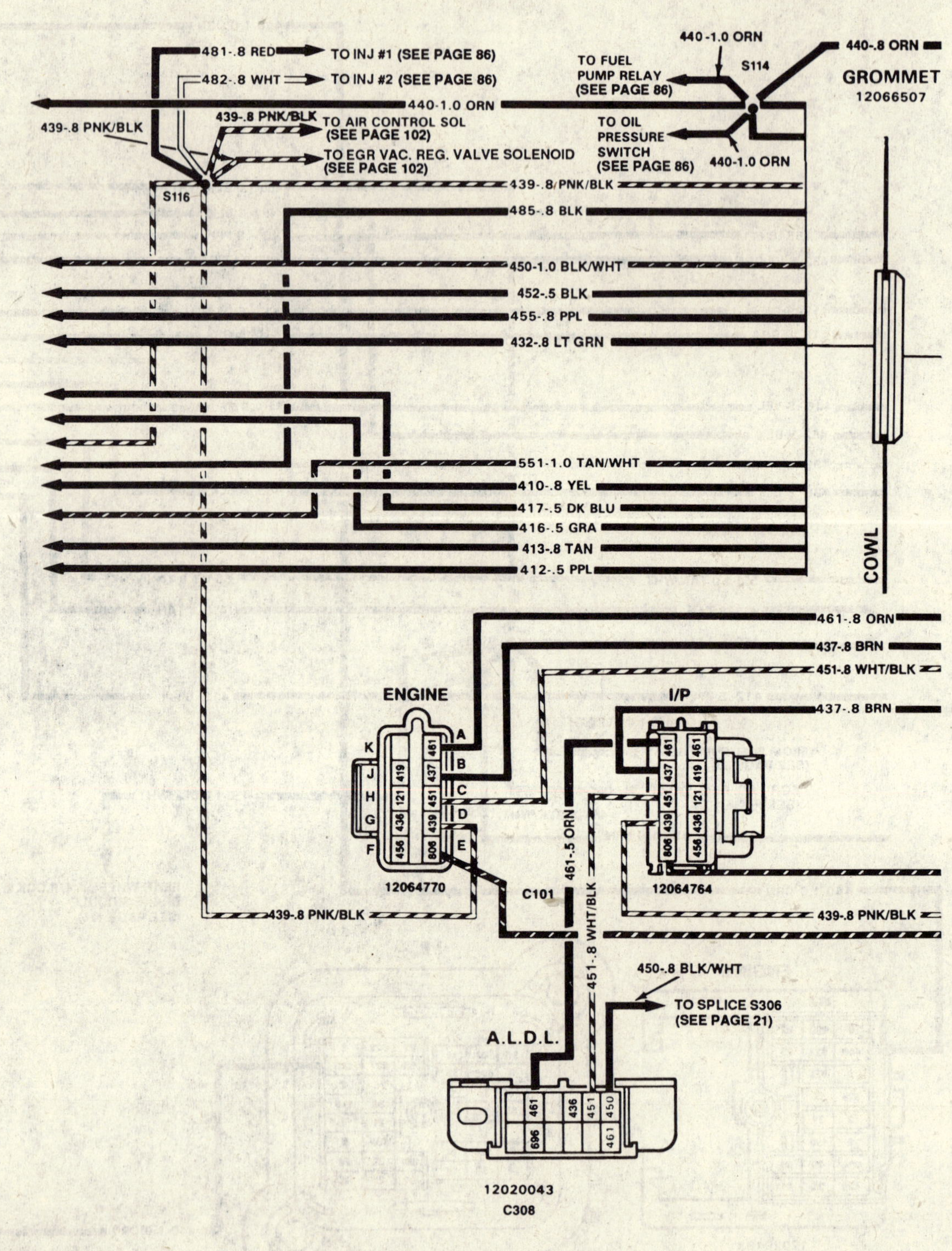

1988-91

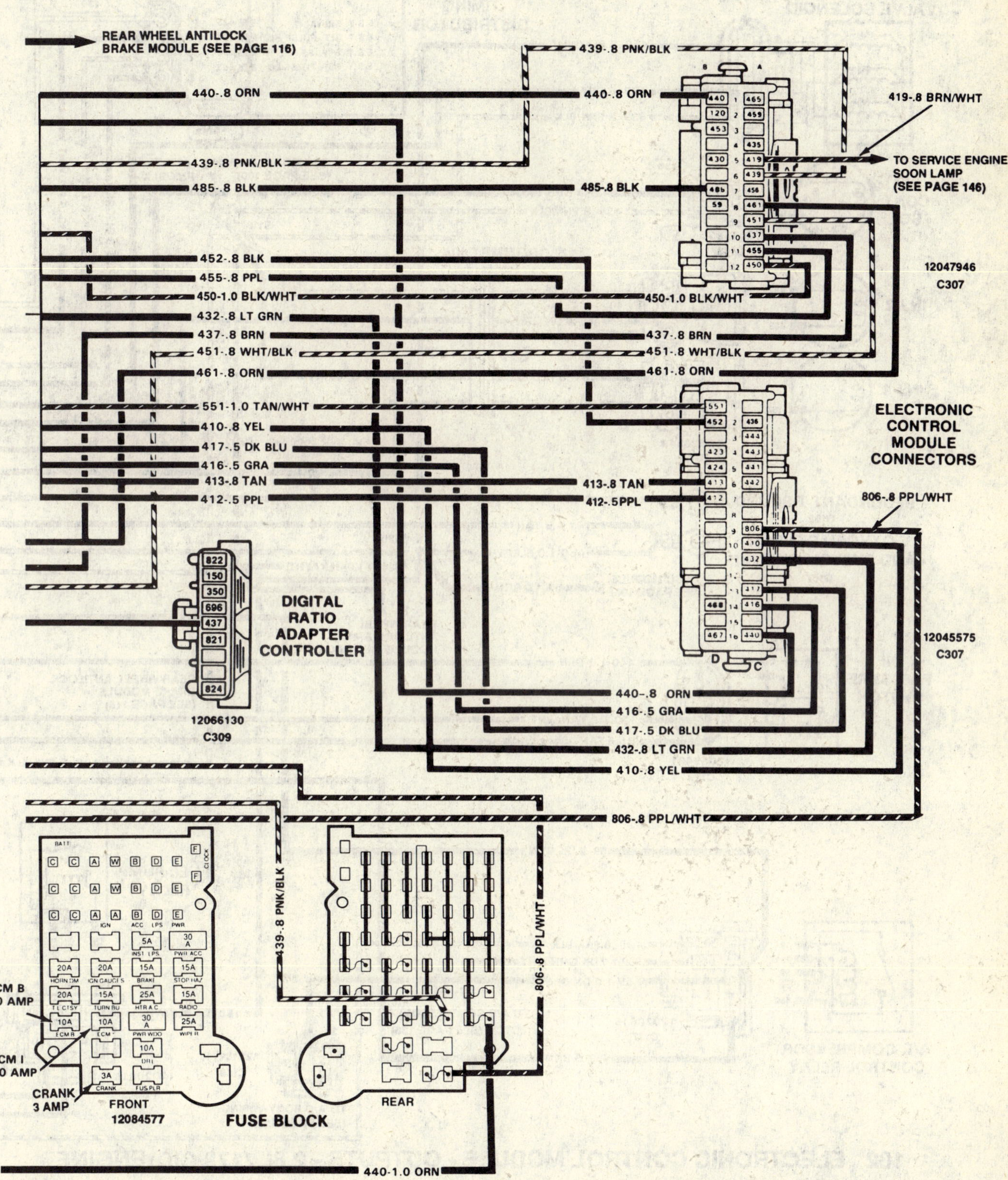

ELECTRONIC CONTROL MODULE - INPUTS - 2.8L (173 CID) ENGINE 101
1988-91

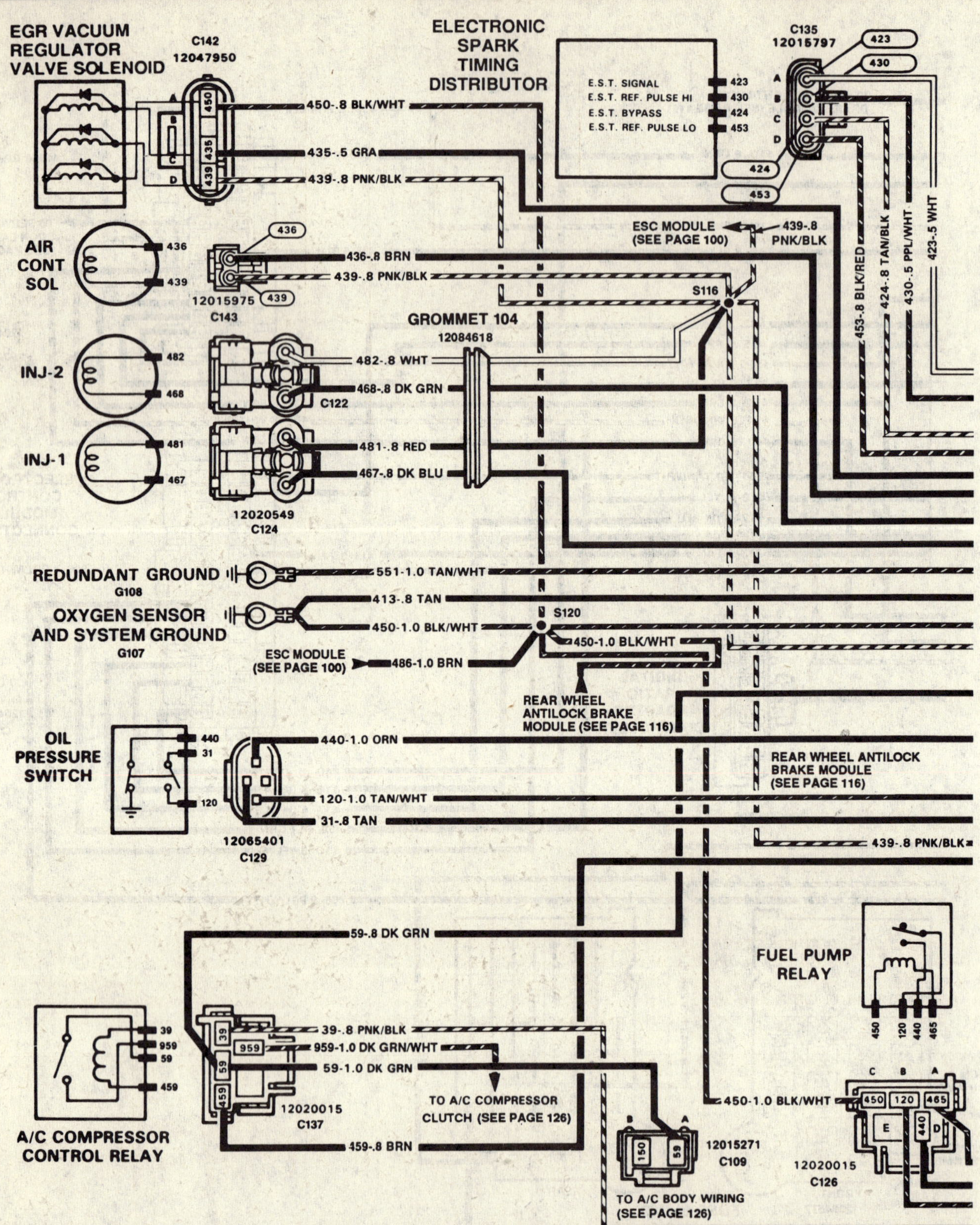

102 ELECTRONIC CONTROL MODULE - OUTPUTS - 2.8L (173 CID) ENGINE

1988-91

IDLE AIR
CONTROL—
INJ. ACTUATOR
441
442
443
444
A
D
12015798
C125
444-.8 LT GRN/BLK
443-.8 LT GRN/WHT
442-.8 LT BLU/BLK
441-.8 LT BLU/WHT
423-.5 WHT
430-.5 PPL/WHT
424-.8 TAN/BLK
453-.8 BLK/RED
435-.8 GRA
435-.5 GRA
436-.8 BRN
468-.8 DK GRN
467-.8 DK BLU
551-1.0 TAN/WHT
413-.8 TAN
450-1.0 BLK/WHT
439-.8 PNK/BLK
120-.8 TAN/WHT
59-.8 DK GRN
S114
440-.8 ORN
440-1.0 ORN
120-1.0 TAN/WHT
31-.8 TAN
459-.8 BRN
465-.8 DK GRN/WHT
465-.8 DK GRN/WHT
440-1.0 ORN
120-1.0 TAN/WHT
120-.8 TAN/WHT
FUEL
PUMP
PRIME
120
2977253
C128
S115
39-.8 PNK/BLK

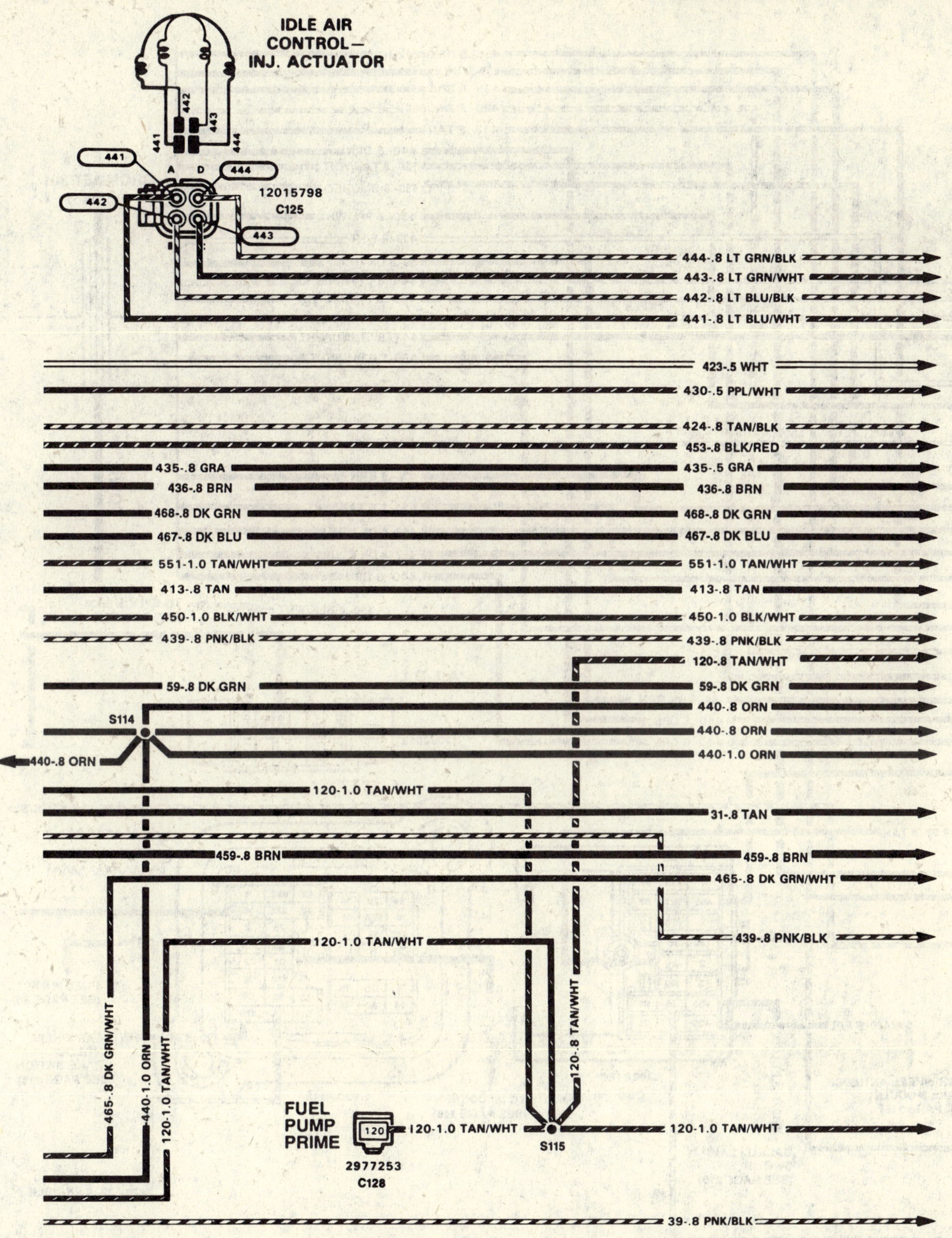

1988-91

465-.8 DK GRN/WHT
459-.8 BRN
435-.5 GRA
439-.8 PNK/BLK
413-.8 TAN
440-.8 ORN
120-.8 TAN/WHT
453-.8 BLK/RED
430-.5 PPL/WHT
423-.5 WHT
59-.8 DK GRN
444-.8 LT GRN/BLK
443-.8 LT GRN/WHT
442-.8 LT BLU/BLK
441-.8 LT BLU/WHT
450-1.0 BLK/WHT
GROMMET 301
12066507
COWL
424-.8 TAN/BLK
436-.8 BRN
551-1.0 TAN/WHT
468-.8 DK GRN
467-.8 DK BLU
440-.8 ORN
450-.8 BLK/WHT
TO SPLICE S306
(SEE PAGE 21)
436-.8 BRN
A.L.D.L.
59-.8 DK GRN
440-.8 ORN
440-.8 ORN
12020043
C308
439-.8 PNK/BLK
31-.8 TAN
HOT AT ALL TIMES
120-1.0 TAN
FUEL PUMP
(SEE PAGE 86)
420-.8 PPL
REAR WHEEL ANTILOCK
BRAKE MODULE
(SEE PAGE 116)
924-.8 LT GRN
BACKUP LAMP
SWITCH
(SEE PAGE 210)
12020183
C100
31-.5 TAN
TO I/P CONN
(SEE PAGE 146)
12020184
420-.8 PPL
REAR WHEEL
ANTILOCK
BRAKE SWITCH
(SEE PAGE 116)
39-.8 PNK/BLK
39-.8 PNK/BLK

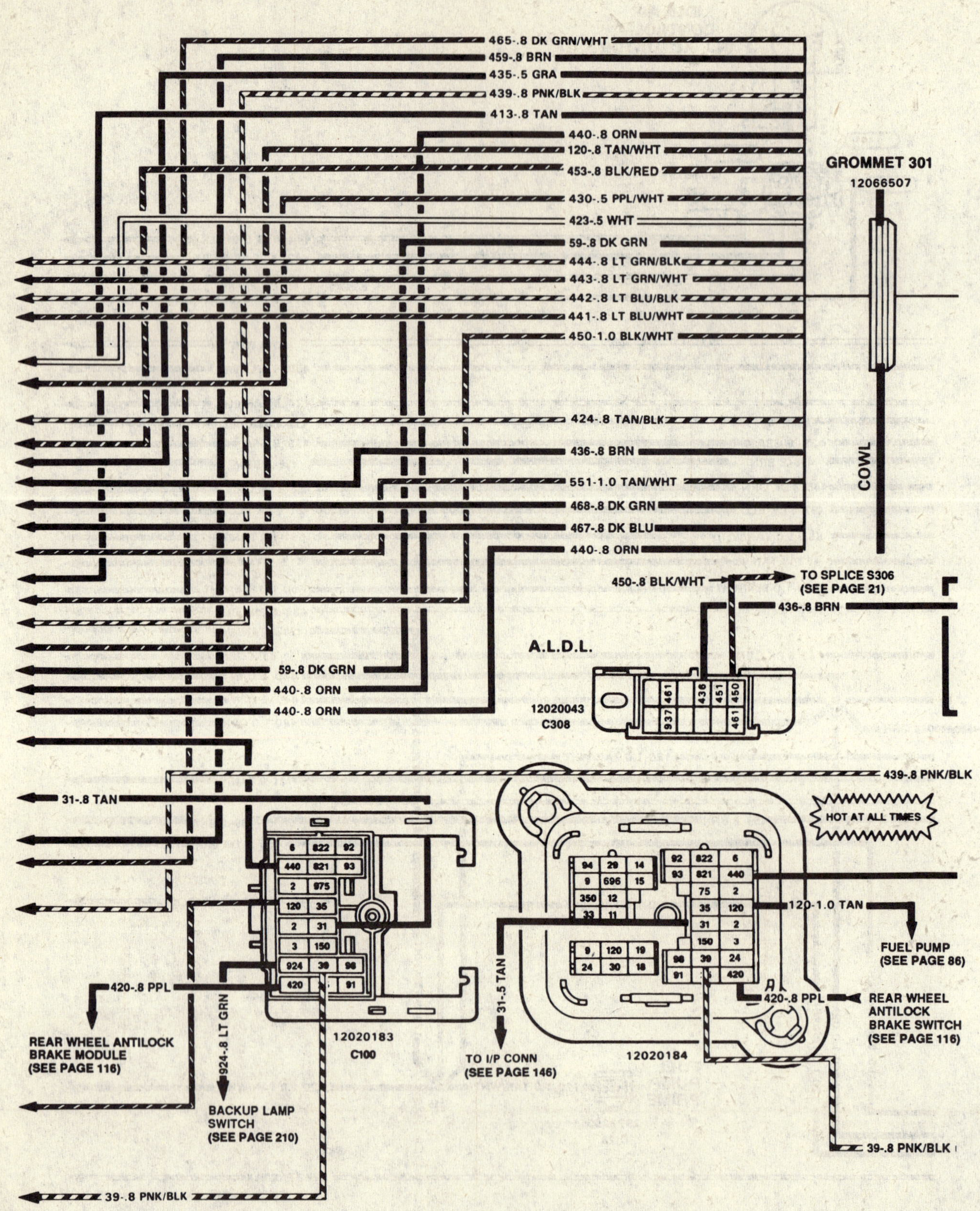

1988-91

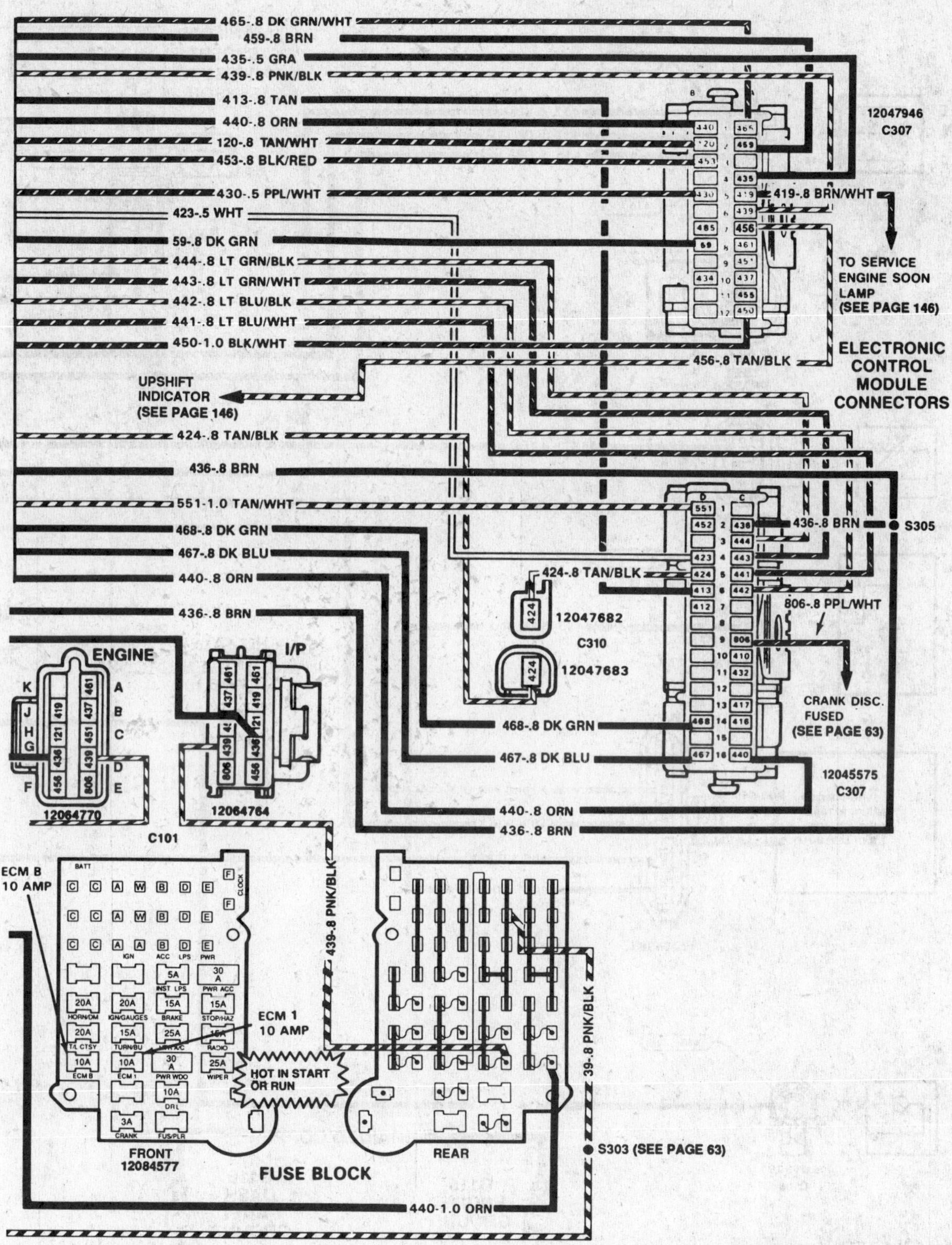

ELECTRONIC CONTROL MODULE - OUTPUTS - 2.8L (173 CID) ENGINE 103

1988-91

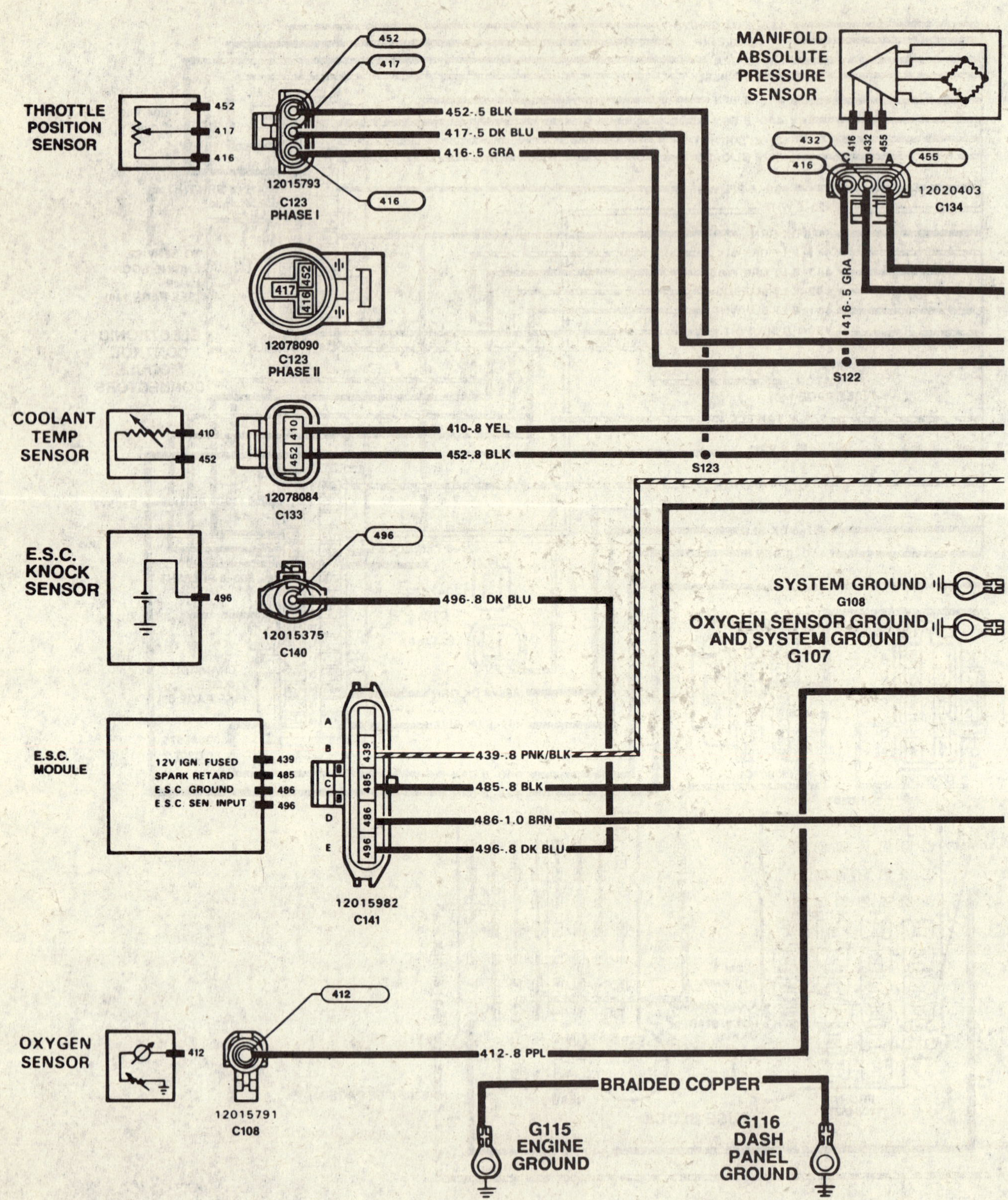

106 ELECTRONIC CONTROL MODULE - INPUTS - 4.3L (262 CID) ENGINE

1988-91

440-1.0 ORN
450-1.0 BLK/WHT
452-.8 BLK
455-.8 PPL
455-.8 PPL
432-.8 LT GRN
432-.8 LT GRN
417-.5 DK BLU
417-.5 DK BLU
416-.5 GRA
416-.5 GRA
410-.8 YEL
410-.8 YEL
452-.8 BLK
439-.8 PNK/BLK
439-.8 PNK/BLK
485-.8 BLK
485-.8 BLK
551 1.0 TAN/WHT
551-1.0 TAN/WHT
413-.8 TAN
413-.8 TAN
450-1.0 BLK/WHT
S120
412-.8 PPL
412-.8 PPL
450-1.0 BLK/WHT
FUEL PUMP RELAY
(SEE PAGE 89)
EGR VACUUM
REGULATOR VALVE SOL
(SEE PAGE 108)
450-.8 BLK/WHT
486-1.0 BRN
450-1.0 BLK/WHT
440-1.0 ORN
REAR WHEEL ANTILOCK
BRAKE MODULE
(SEE PAGE 116)
4-WHEEL ANTILOCK
BRAKE MODULE
(SEE PAGE 114)
ENGINE
I/P
12020183
C100
12020184
C100
440-1.0 ORN

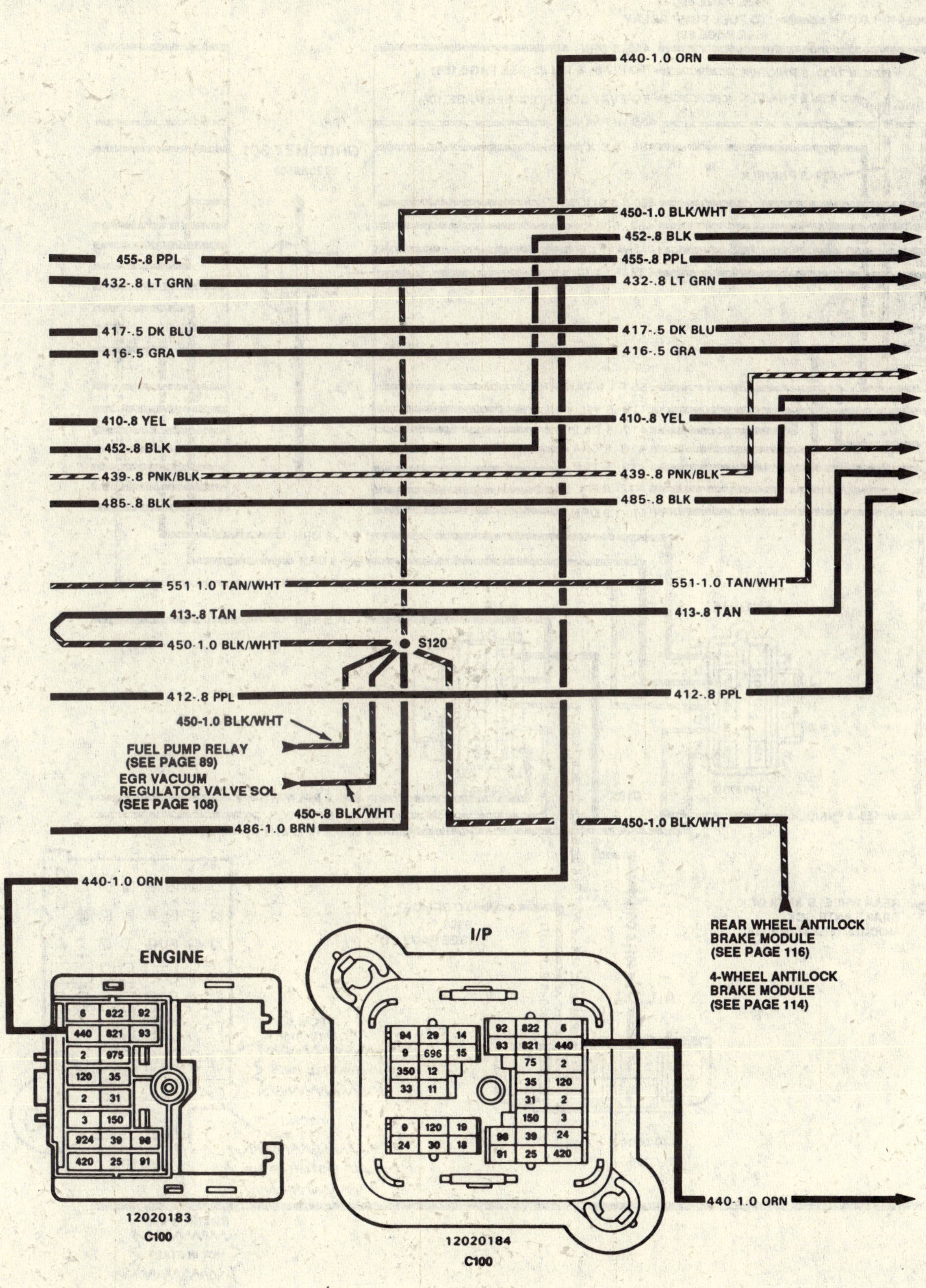

1988-91

440-.8 ORN
TO OIL PRESS. SW. (SEE PAGE 89)
440-1.0 ORN
TO FUEL PUMP RELAY (SEE PAGE 89)
S114
440-1.0 ORN
440-.8 ORN
439-.8 PNK/BLK
TO INJ #1 & INJ #2 (SEE PAGE 108)
S116
439-.8 PNK/BLK
TO EVRV SOLENOID (SEE PAGE 108)
439-.8 PNK/BLK
485-.8 BLK
439-.8 PNK/BLK
GROMMET 301
12066507
450-1.0 BLK/WHT
452-.5 BLK
455-.8 PPL
432-.8 LT GRN
551-1.0 TAN/WHT
410-.5 YEL
417-.5 DK BLU
416-.5 GRA
413-.5 TAN
412-.8 PPL
440-1.0 ORN
461-.8 ORN
437-.8 BRN
451-.8 WHT/BLK
437-.5 BRN
ENGINE
I/P
12064770
C101
12064764
440-.8 ORN
439-.8 PNK/BLK
806-.8 PPL/WHT
439-.8 PNK/BLK
806-.8 PPL/WHT
REAR WHEELS ANTILOCK BRAKE ANTILOCK MODULE (SEE PAGE 116)
461-.5 ORN
451-.8 WHT/BLK
450-.8 BLK/WHT
TO SPLICE S306 (SEE PAGE 21)
A.L.D.L.
12020043
C308
ECM B 10 AMP
HOT AT ALL TIMES
ECM I 10 AMP
HOT IN START OR RUN
FRONT
12084577
CRANK 3 AMP
HOT IN START
440-1.0 ORN

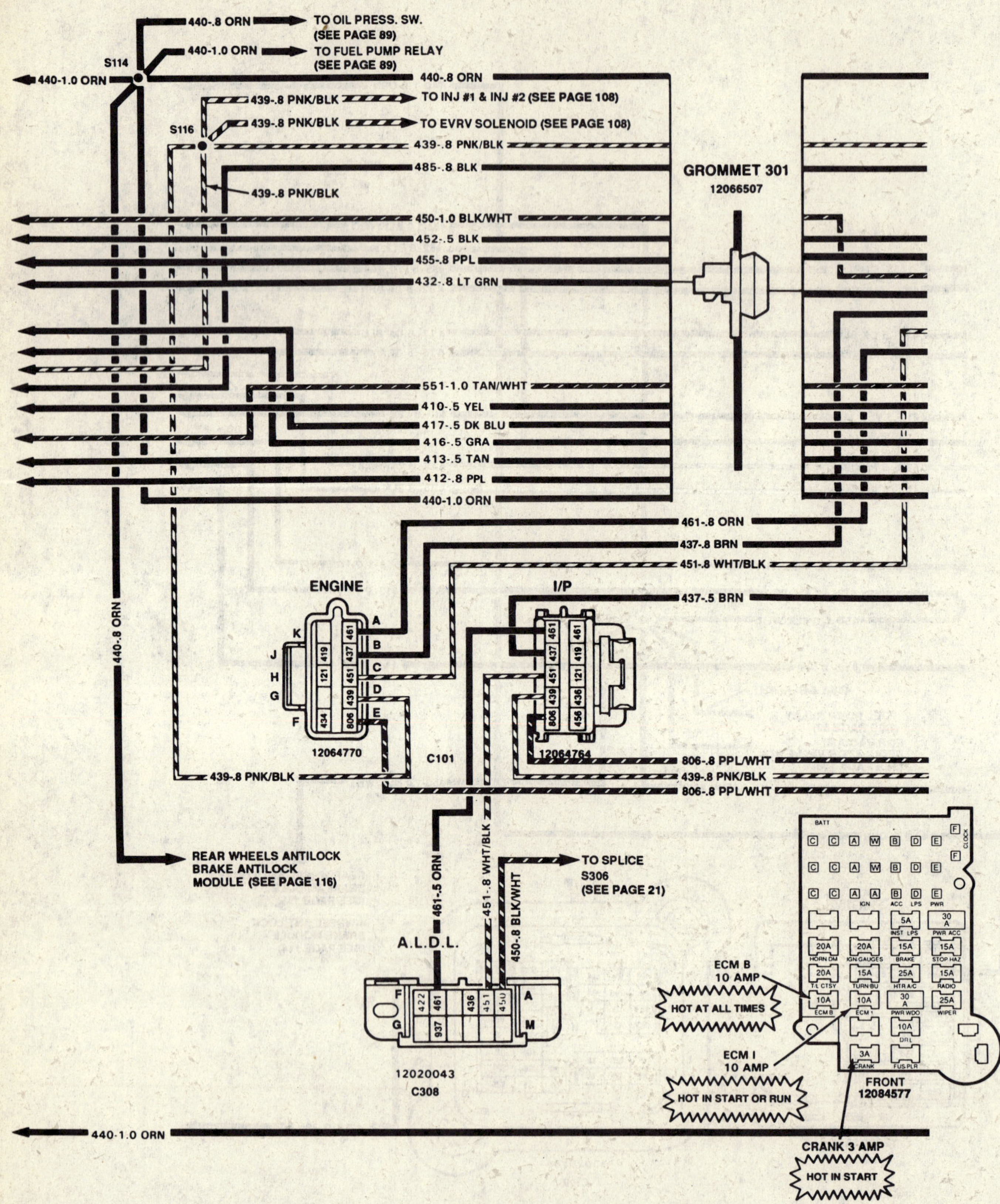

1988-91

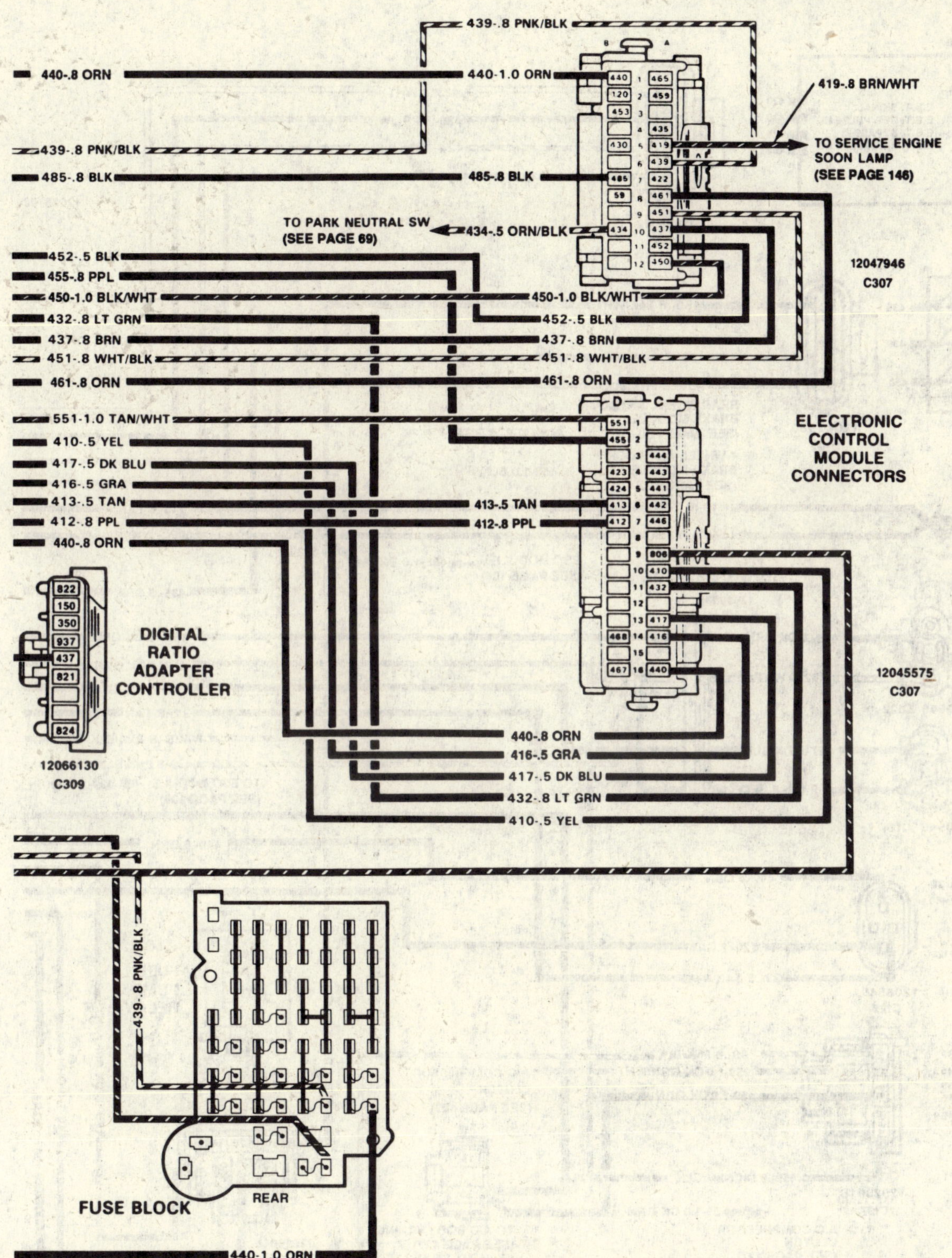

ELECTRONIC CONTROL MODULE - INPUTS - 4.3L (262 CID) ENGINE 107

1988-91

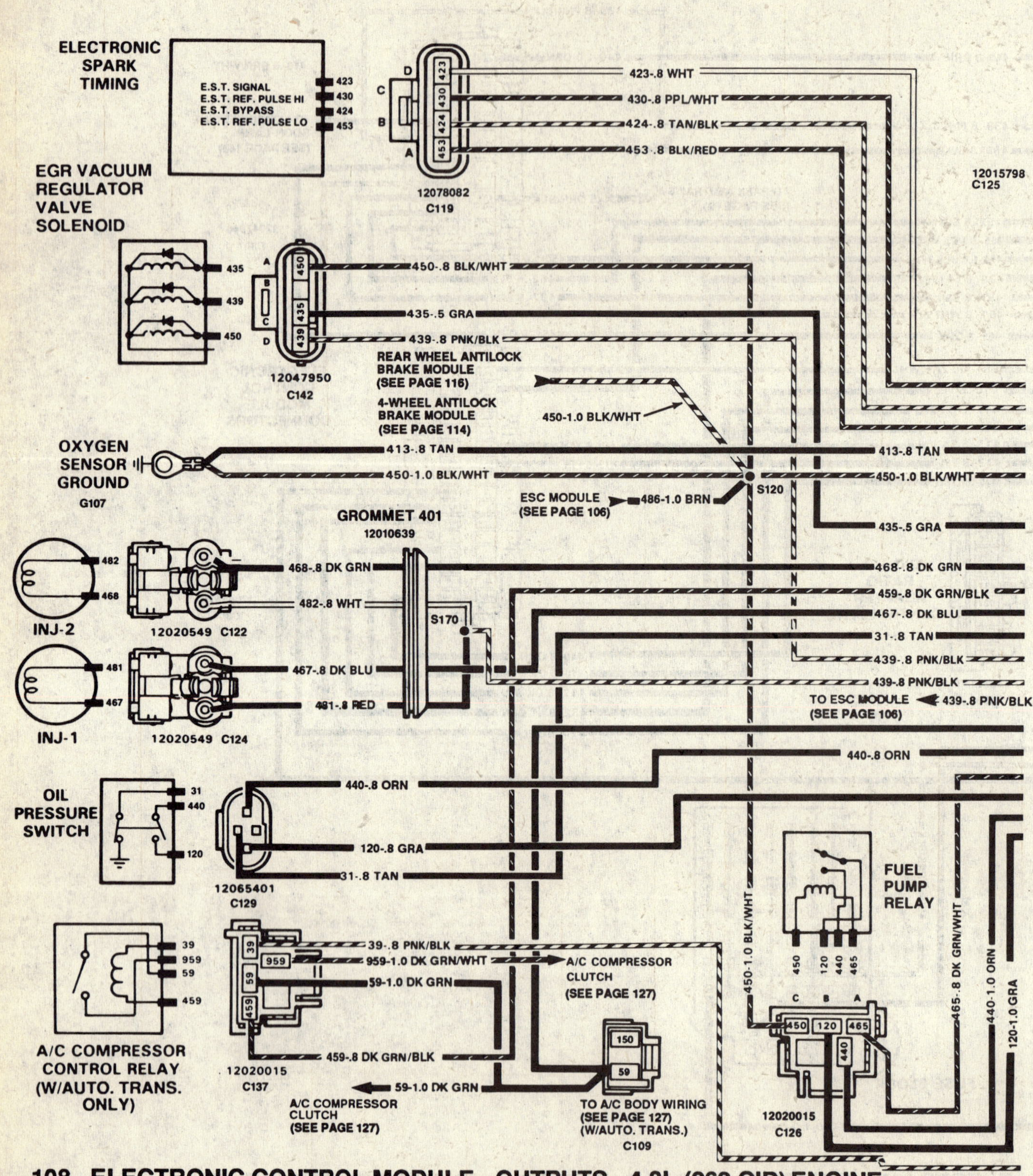

108 ELECTRONIC CONTROL MODULE - OUTPUTS - 4.3L (262 CID) ENGINE

1988-91

IDLE AIR
CONTROL–
INJ. ACTUATOR
441
442
443
444
446
422
420
12010503
C139
CLOSES WITH
INC. TEMP
OPENS IN
4TH GEAR
OPENS ON
4-3 SHIFT
TRANSMISSION
CONVERTER CLUTCH
SOLENOID
(AUTO. TRANS. ONLY)
446-.8 LT BLU
422-.8 TAN/BLK
420-.5 PPL
446-.8 LT BLU
444-.8 LT GRN/BLK
443-.8 LT GRN/WHT
442-.8 LT BLU/BLK
441-.8 LT BLU/WHT
423-.8 WHT
430-.8 PPL/WHT
424-.8 TAN/BLK
453-.8 BLK/RED
413-.8 TAN
450-1.0 BLK/WHT
435-.5 GRA
439-.8 PNK/BLK
468-.8 DK GRN
459-.8 DK GRN/BLK
467-.8 DK BLU
31-.8 TAN
59-.8 DK GRN
S116
59-.8 DK GRN
120-.8 GRA
440-.8 ORN
465-.8 DK GRN/WHT
120-.8 GRA
440-1.0 ORN
120-1.0 GRA
439-.8 PNK/BLK
422-.8 TAN/BLK
120-.8 GRA
120-.8 GRA
120-1.0 GRA
FUEL
PUMP
PRIME
120
120-1.0 GRA
S115
2977253
C128
39-.8 PNK/BLK

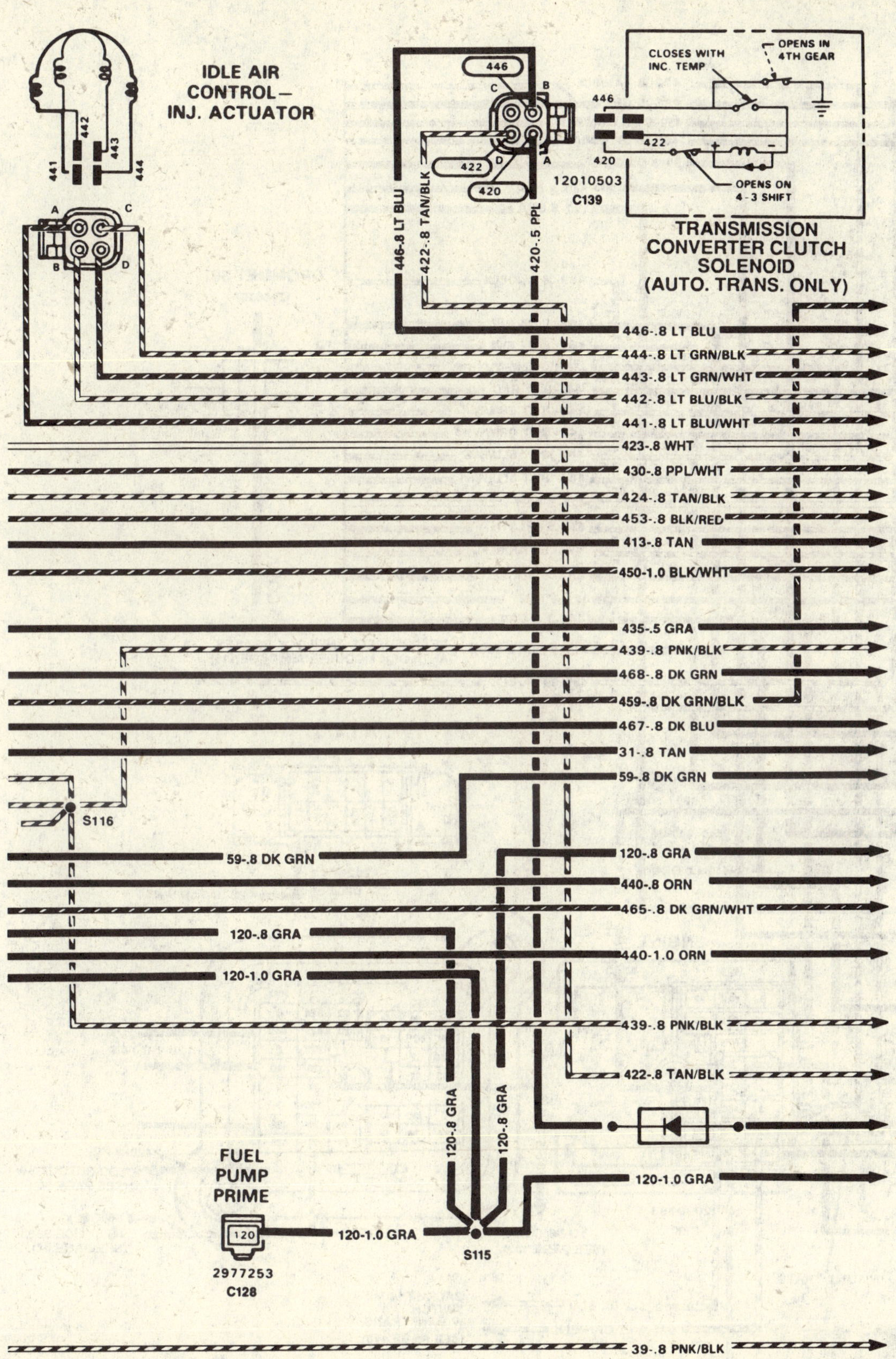

1988-91

422-.8 TAN/BLK
435-.5 GRA
459-.8 DK GRN/BLK
465-.8 DK GRN/WHT
59-.8 DK GRN
440-.8 ORN
120-.8 GRA
439-.8 PNK/BLK
GROMMET 301
12066507
468-.8 DK GRN
467-.8 DK BLU
450-1.0 BLK/WHT
446-.8 LT BLU
444-.8 LT GRN/BLK
443-.8 LT GRN/WHT
442-.8 LT BLU/BLK
441-.8 LT BLU/WHT
423-.5 WHT
430-.5 PPL/WHT
424-.8 TAN/BLK
453-.8 BLK/RED
413-.8 TAN
COWL
S114
440-1.0 ORN
440-.8 ORN
REAR WHEELS ANTILOCK BRAKES
ANTILOCK MODULE (SEE PAGE 116)
439-.8 PNK/BLK
A.L.D.L.
M
A
G
F
12020043
C308
422-.8 TAN/WHT
I/P
440-.8 ORN
440-1.0 ORN
31-.8 TAN
ENGINE
440-1.0 ORN
422-.8 TAN/BLK
420-.5 PPL
120-1.0 GRA
W/AUTO. TRANS.
2020183
C100
31-.5 TAN
TO I/P CONN
(SEE PAGE 142)
12020184
120-1.0 TAN
420-.8 PPL
TCC CUTOUT SW
(SEE PAGE 66)
39-.8 PNK/BLK
TO SPLICE S303
(SEE PAGE 64)
975-.8 DK BLU
924-.8 LT GRN/BLK
BACKUP LAMP
SWITCH
W/MAN. TRANS.
(SEE PAGE 170)
39-.8 PNK/BLK

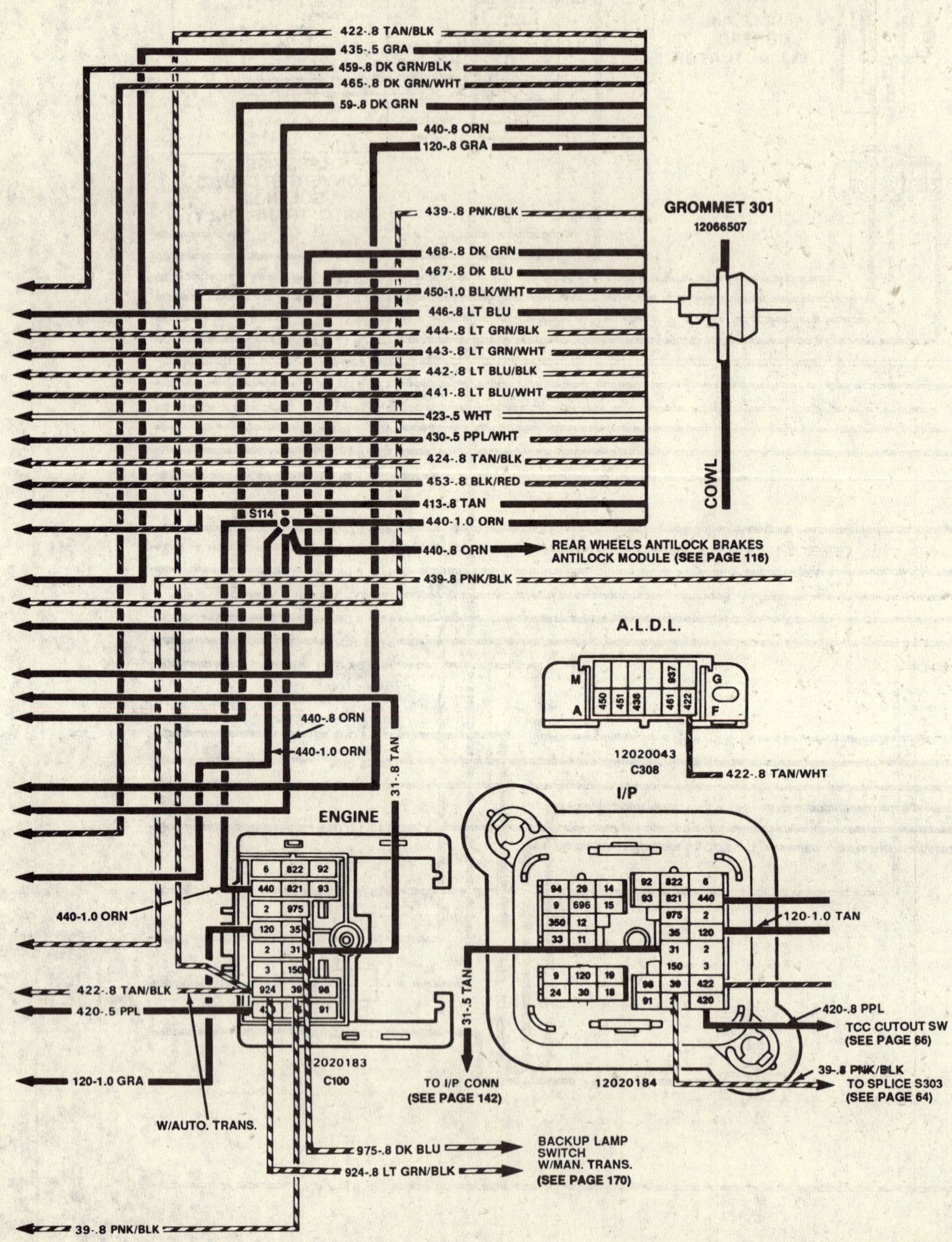

1988-91

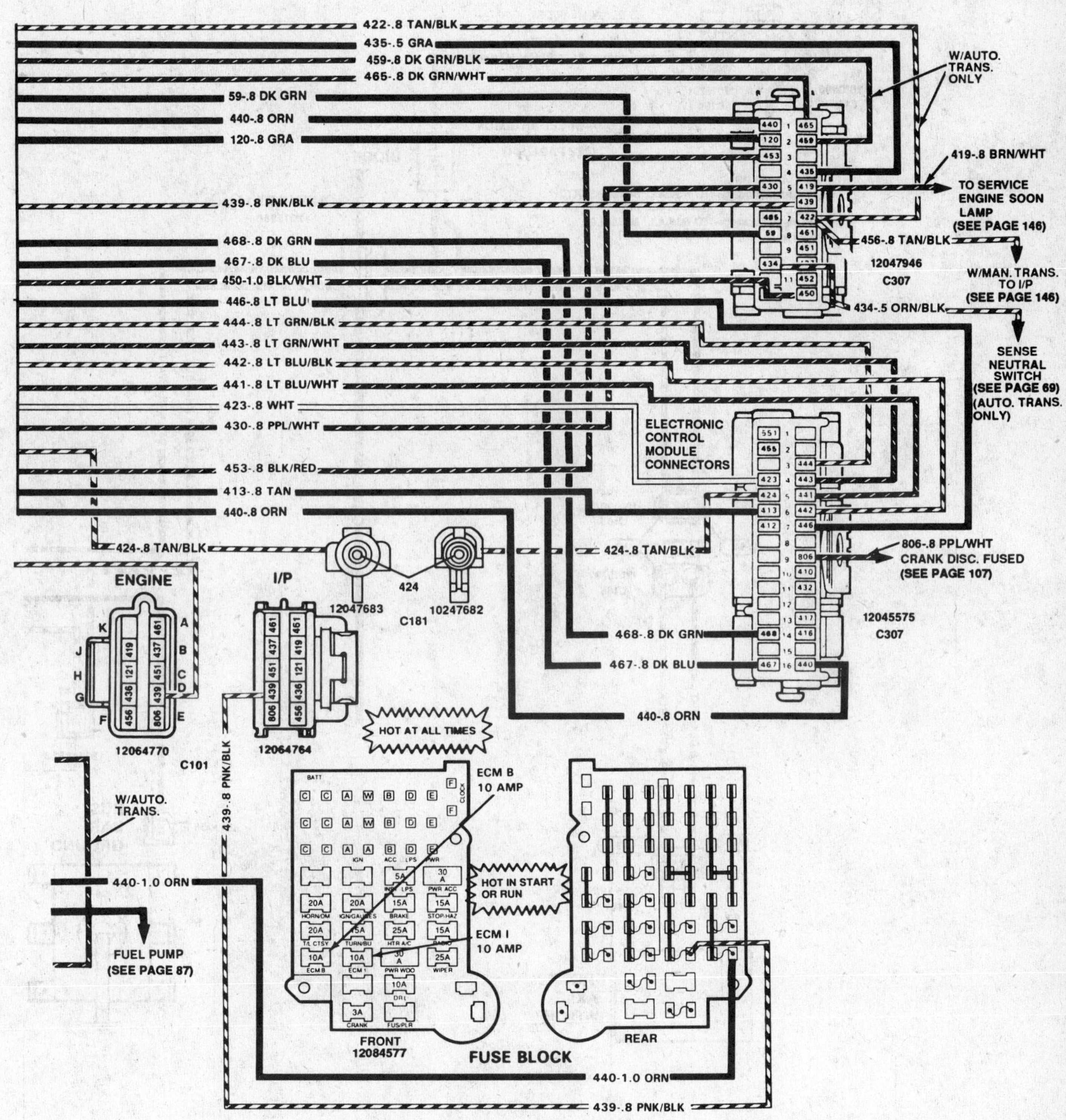

ELECTRONIC CONTROL MODULE - OUTPUTS - 4.3L (262 CID) ENGINE 109

1988-91

941
12010996
C159
12015791
C159
.8 BLK/WHT W/DRL
941-.8 BLK/WHT
941-.8 BLK/WHT
941-.8 BRN
4-WHEEL ANTILOCK
BRAKE MODULE
(SEE PAGE 114)
IN-LINE
DIODE
420-.8 PPL
TO R.W.A.L. BRAKE SWITCH
(SEE PAGE 116)
S171
TO R.W.A.L. MODULE
(SEE PAGE 116)
420-.8 PPL
GROMMET 101
12015958
941-.8 BLK/WHT
39-.8 PNK/BLK
39-.8 PNK/BLK
941-.8 BLK/WHT
COWL
12010973
C165
941
39
12015792
C165
941-.8 BLK/WHT
39-.8 PNK/BLK
941
39
12015792
C166
941
141
FRONT
AXLE
SWITCH
150-.8 BLK
39
120048888
8911256
150
BUS
BAR
GROUND
3
6
2
5
1
4

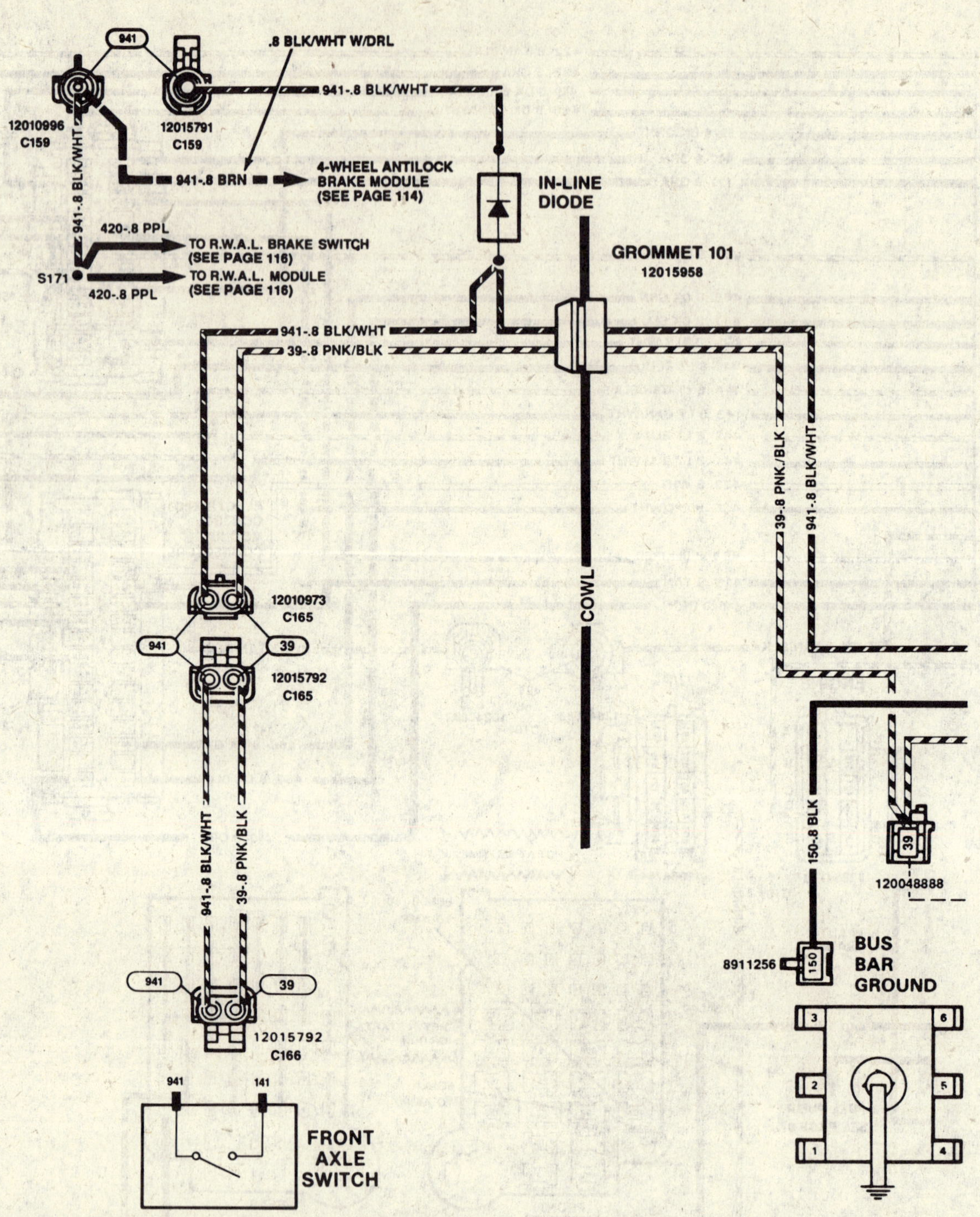

1988-91

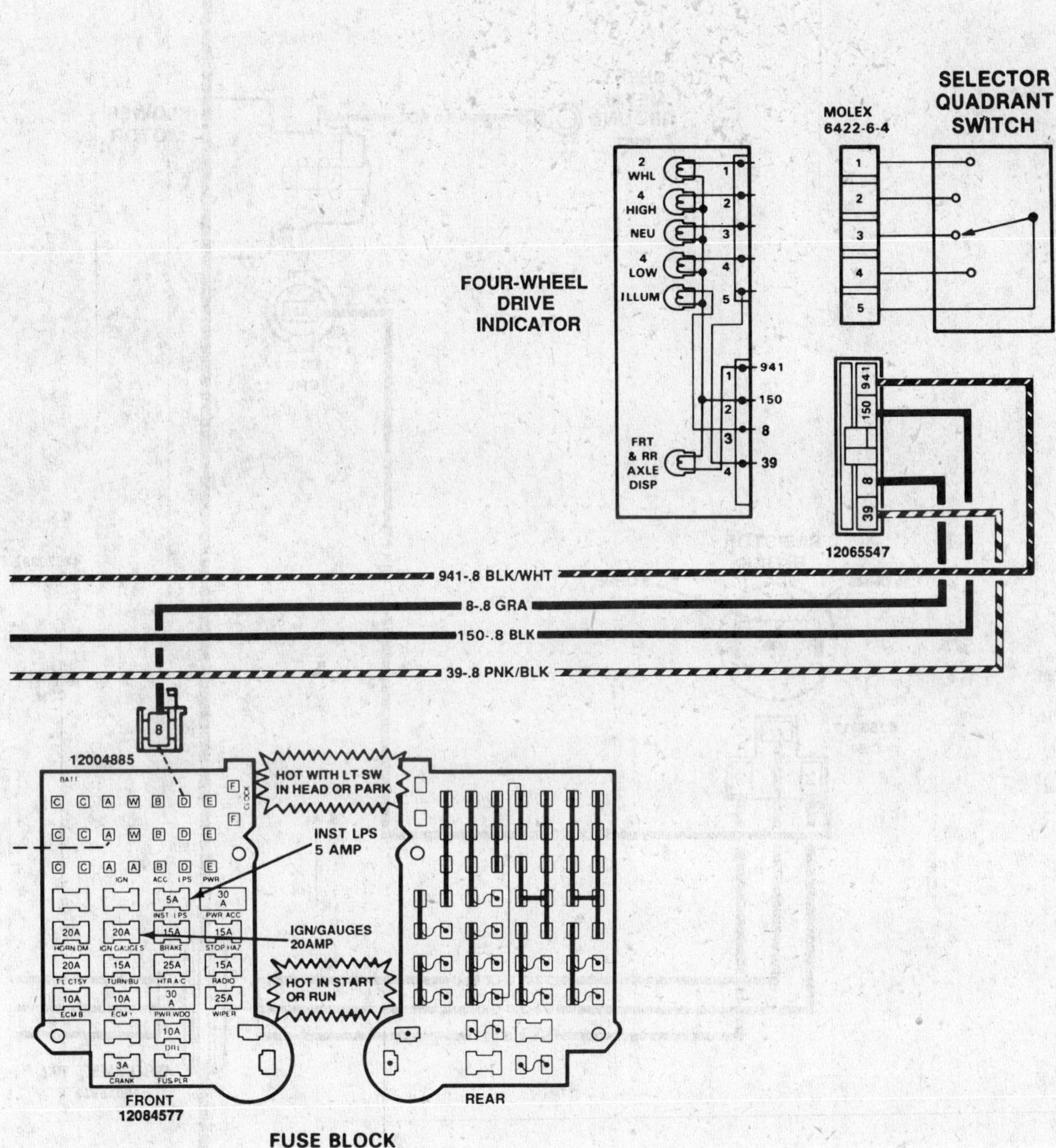

FOUR-WHEEL DRIVE INDICATOR 111

1988-91

SHEET
METAL
GROUND
G103
3.0 BLK
152
BLOWER
MOTOR
52
52
2977976
C146
52-2.0 ORN
12020397
C318
12033963
C318
RESISTOR
BLOCK
1.25 OHMS
3 OHMS
52
72
51
6288317
C150
72
52
51
52-2.0 ORN
72-2.0 LT BLU
52-2.0 ORN
51-2.0 YEL
GROMMET 102
12015959

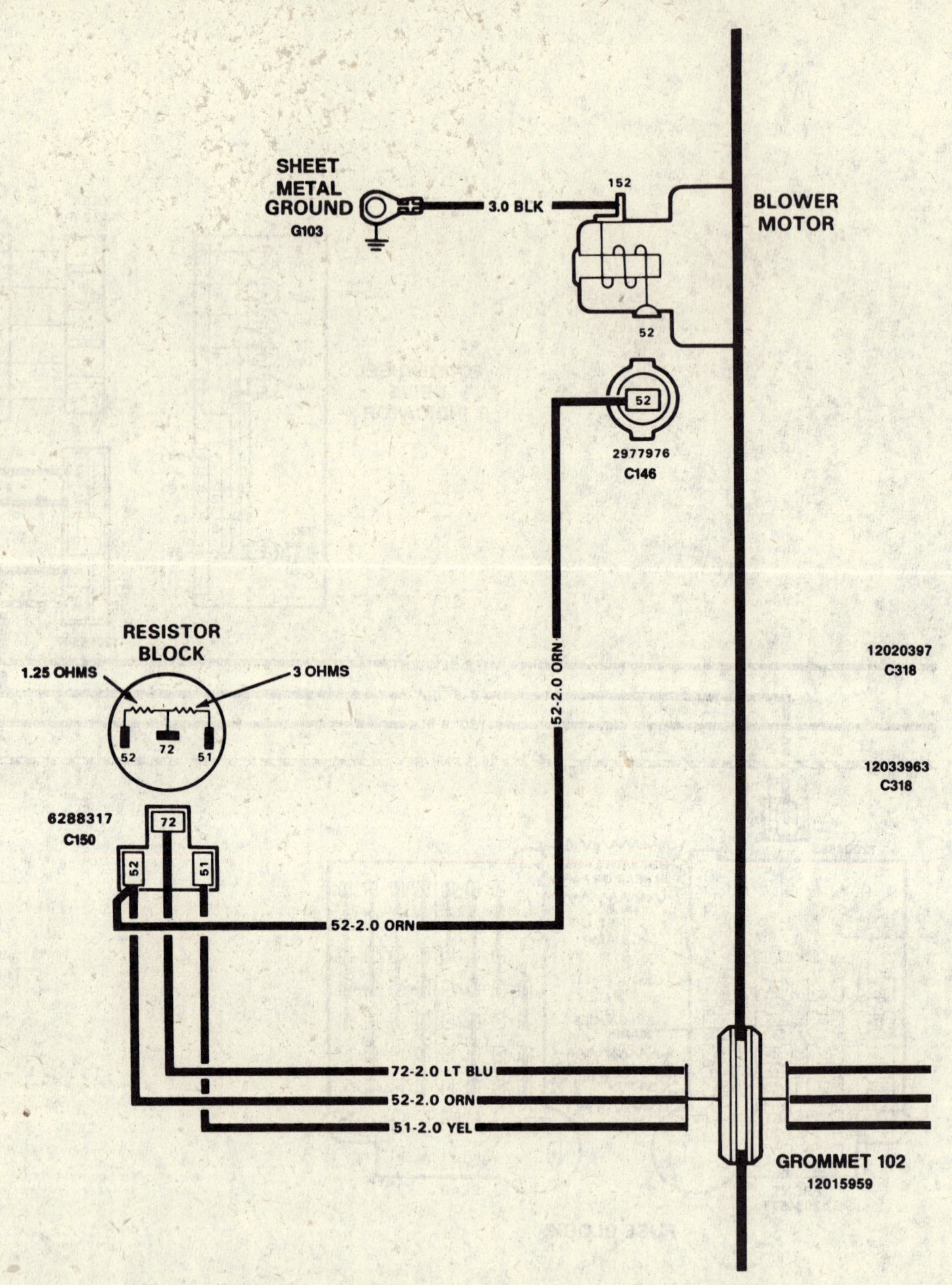

1988-91

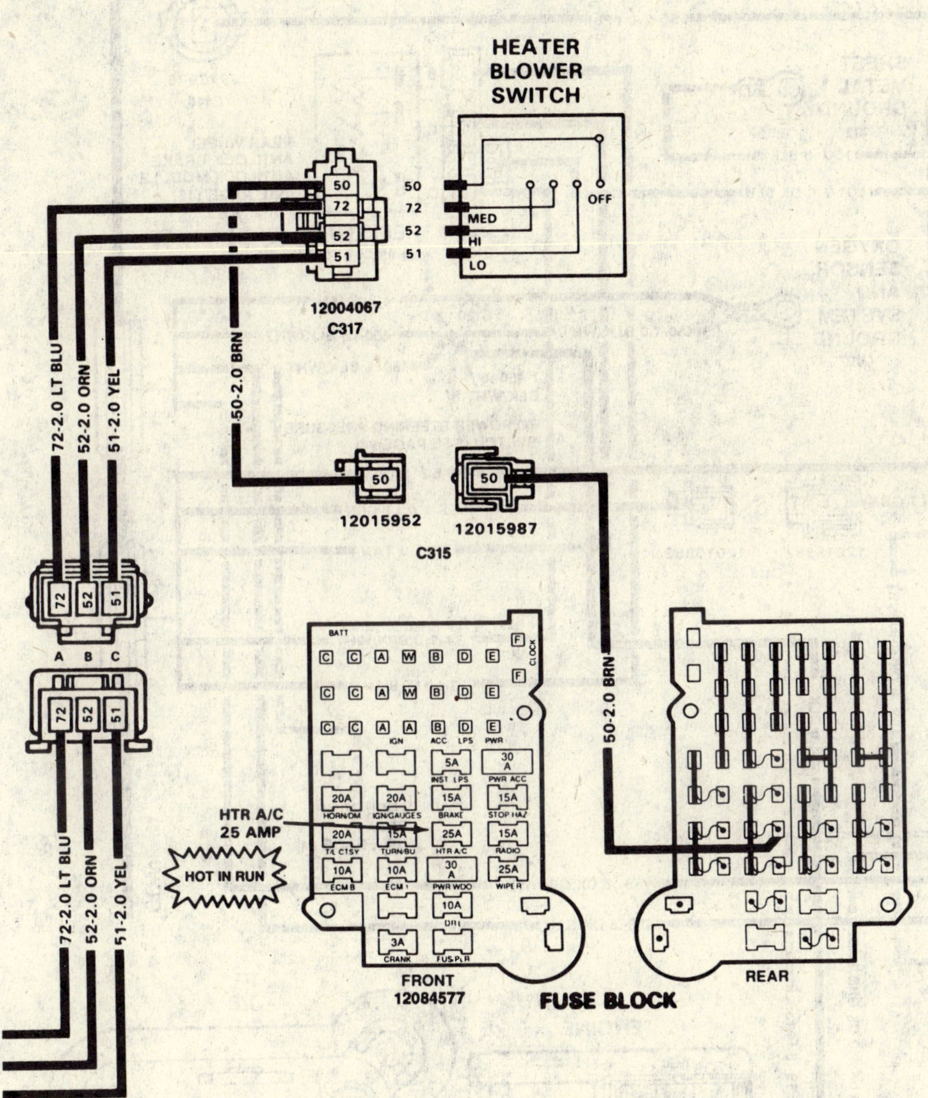

HEATER (C42) 121

1988-91

JUNCTION BLOCK
HI BLOWER RELAY
SHEET METAL GROUND G103
3.0 BLK
BLOWER MOTOR
65-5.0 PPL
2-5.0 RED
SHEET METAL GROUND G102
150-.8 BLK
101-1.0 DK BLU
2984911 C148
2977976 C146
2965019 C147
RESISTOR
REAR WHEEL ANTILOCK BRAKE ANTILOCK MODULE (SEE PAGE 116)
OXYGEN SENSOR AND SYSTEM GROUND G107
450-1.0 BLK/WHT
413-.8 TAN
S120
450-.8 BLK/WHT
TO POWER STEERING PRESSURE SWITCH (SEE PAGE 94)
A/C LOW PRESSURE SW (PART OF COMPRESSOR ASM)
66-.8 LT GRN
12078086 C138
12015987 C116
12015952
52-.8 ORN
66-1.0 LT GRN
63-1.0 TAN
64-1.0 BRN/WHT
72-1.0 LT BLU
459-.8 DK GRN/WHT
150-1.0 BLK
A/C COMPRESSOR CONTROL RELAY
FUEL PUMP RELAY (SEE PAGE 84)
458-.8 DK BLU
COWL
12020015 C137
COMPRESSOR
8917476
59-1.0 DK GRN
39-.8 PNK/BLK
ENGINE
I/P
150-1.0 BLK
2973407
DIODE
12020183 C100
12020184 C100

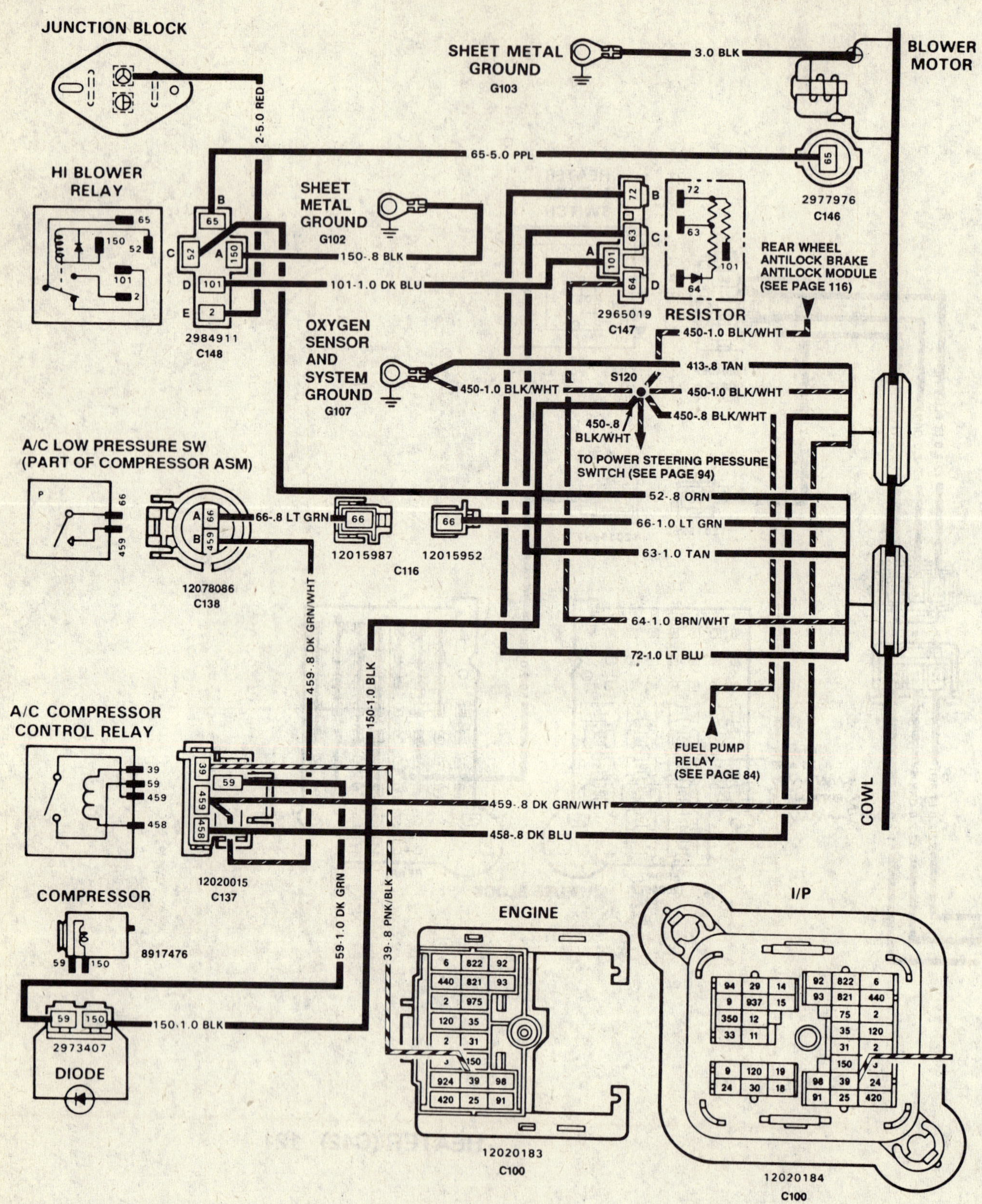

1988-91

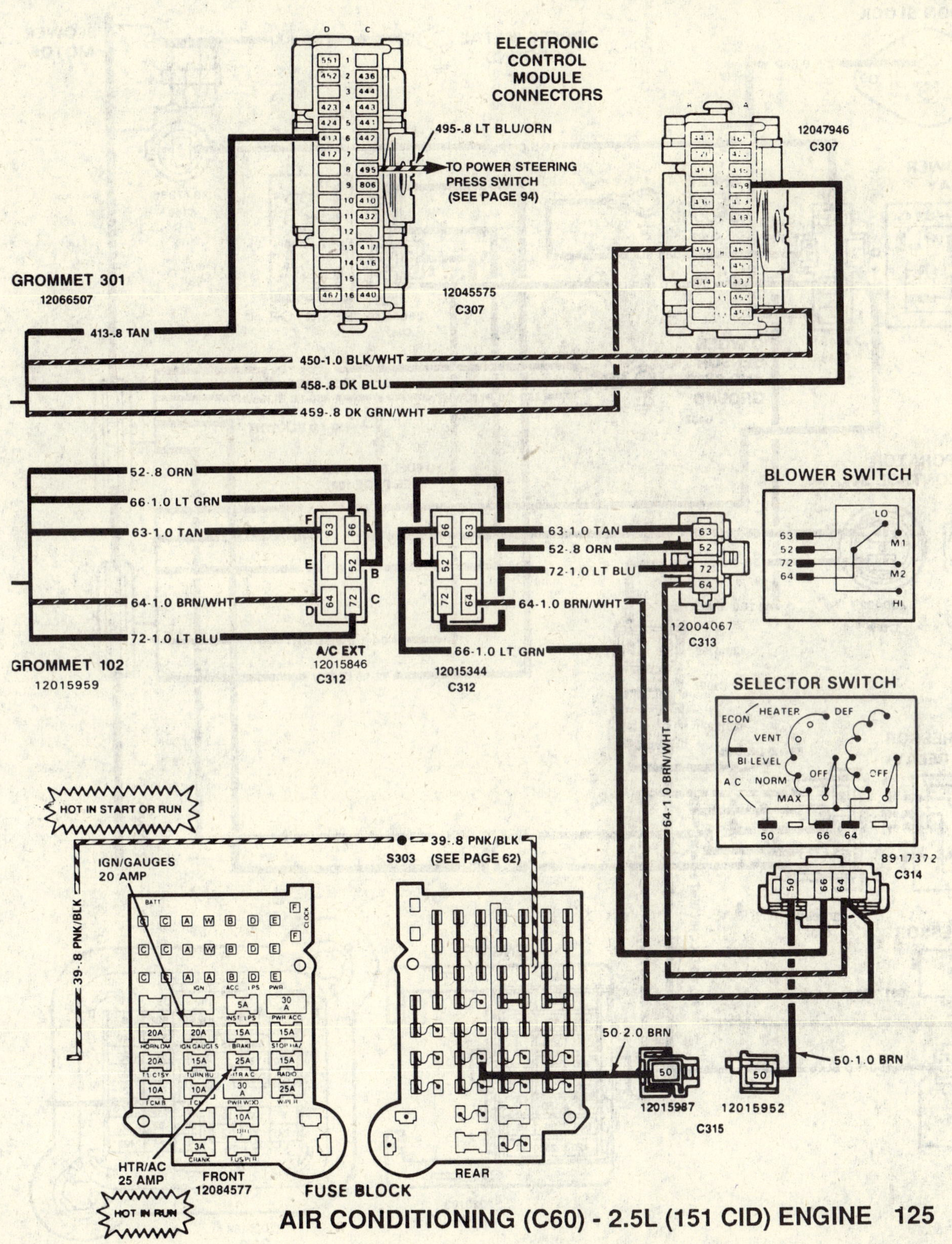

AIR CONDITIONING (C60) - 2.5L (151 CID) ENGINE 125

1988-91

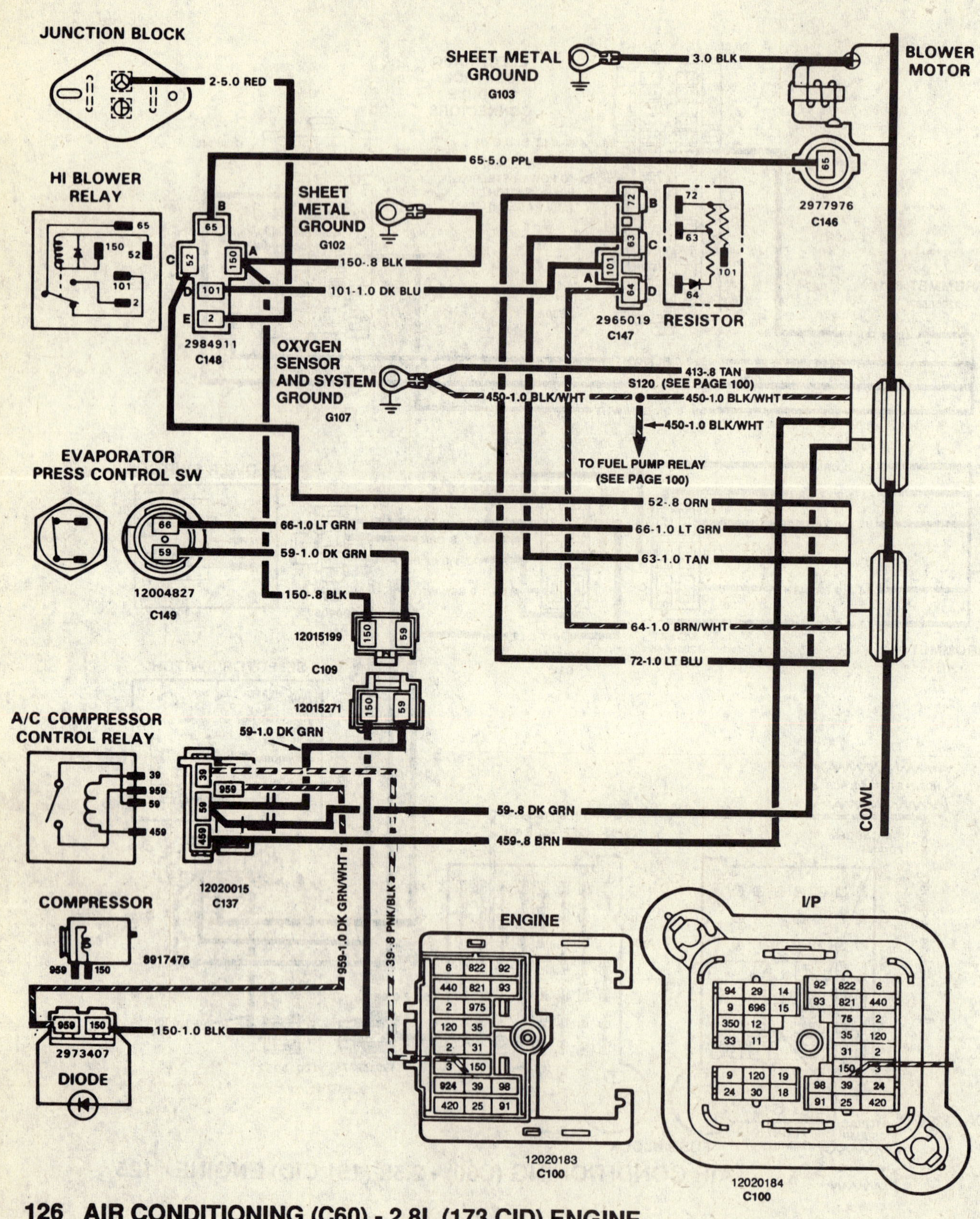

126 AIR CONDITIONING (C60) - 2.8L (173 CID) ENGINE

1988-91

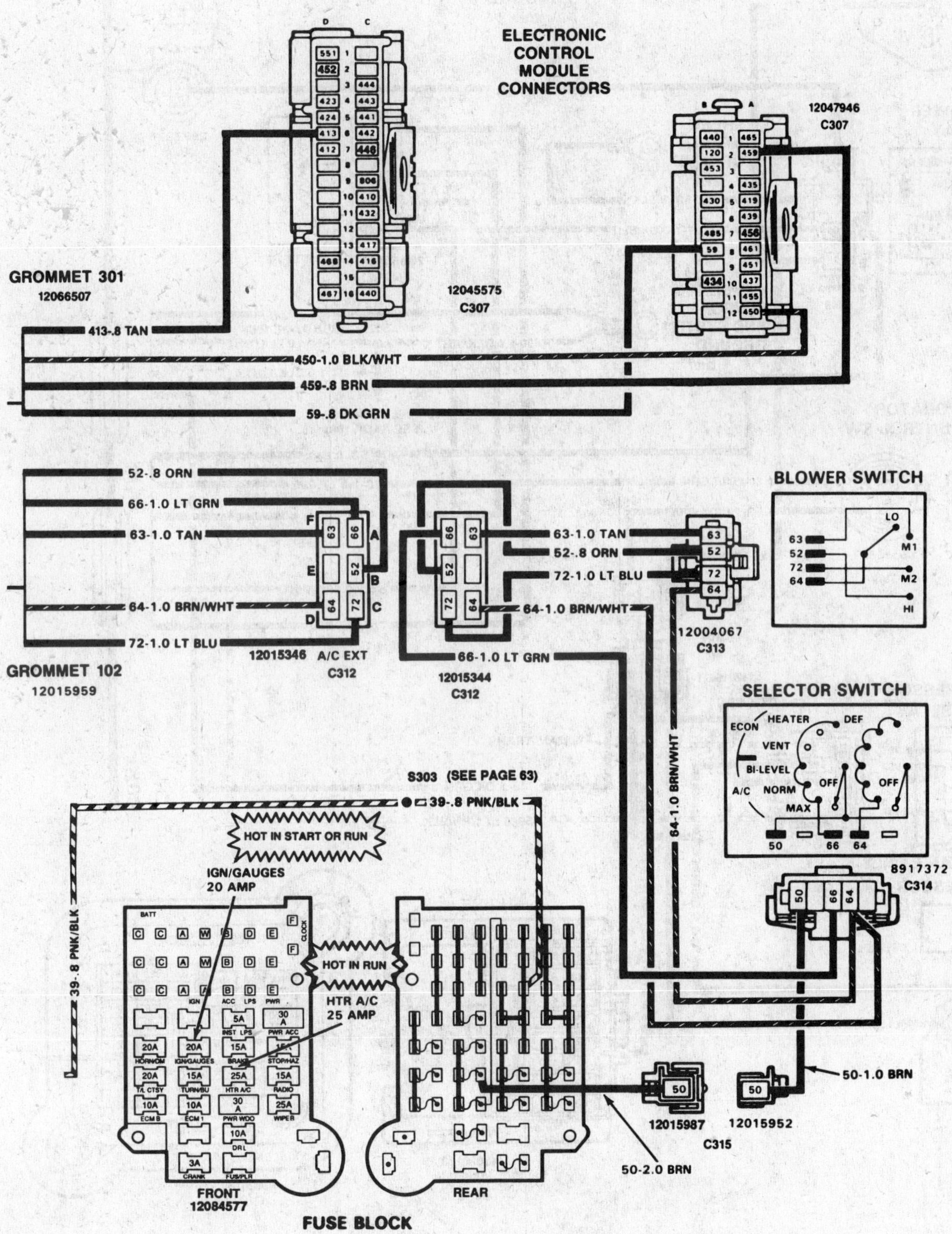

ELECTRONIC CONTROL MODULE CONNECTORS
12045575
C307
12047946
C307
GROMMET 301
12066507
413-.8 TAN
450-1.0 BLK/WHT
459-.8 BRN
59-.8 DK GRN
52-.8 ORN
66-1.0 LT GRN
63-1.0 TAN
64-1.0 BRN/WHT
72-1.0 LT BLU
GROMMET 102
12015959
12015346 A/C EXT
C312
12015344
C312
BLOWER SWITCH
LO
M1
M2
HI
12004067
C313
SELECTOR SWITCH
ECON
HEATER
DEF
VENT
BI-LEVEL
A/C
NORM
MAX
OFF
8917372
C314
S303 (SEE PAGE 63)
39-.8 PNK/BLK
HOT IN START OR RUN
IGN/GAUGES
20 AMP
HOT IN RUN
HTR A/C
25 AMP
50-1.0 BRN
50-2.0 BRN
12015987
12015952
C315
FRONT
12084577
REAR
FUSE BLOCK

JUNCTION BLOCK
2-5.0 RED
HI BLOWER RELAY
65
150
52
101
2
SHEET METAL GROUND
G103
3.0 BLK
BLOWER MOTOR
65-5.0 PPL
2977976
C146
SHEET METAL GROUND
G102
150-.8 BLK
101-1.0 DK BLU
2984911
C148
2965019
C147
RESISTOR
72
63
64
OXYGEN SENSOR AND SYSTEM GROUND
G107
413-.8 TAN
(SEE PAGE 108)
S120
450-1.0 BLK/WHT
TO FUEL PUMP RELAY
(SEE PAGE 108)
EVAPORATOR PRESS CONTROL SW
52-.8 ORN
66-1.0 LT GRN
59-1.0 DK GRN
63-1.0 TAN
12004827
C149
150-.8 BLK
12015199
C109
12015271
64-1.0 BRN/WHT
72-1.0 LT BLU
A/C COMPRESSOR CONTROL RELAY
39
959
59
459
W/MAN. TRANS.
59-.8 DK GRN
459-.8 LT GRN/BLK
COWL
W/AUTO. TRANS. ONLY
12020015
C137
COMPRESSOR
8917476
59-1.0 DK GRN
39-.8 PNK/BLK
150-1.0 BLK
2973407
DIODE
ENGINE
I/P
12020183
C100
12020184
C100

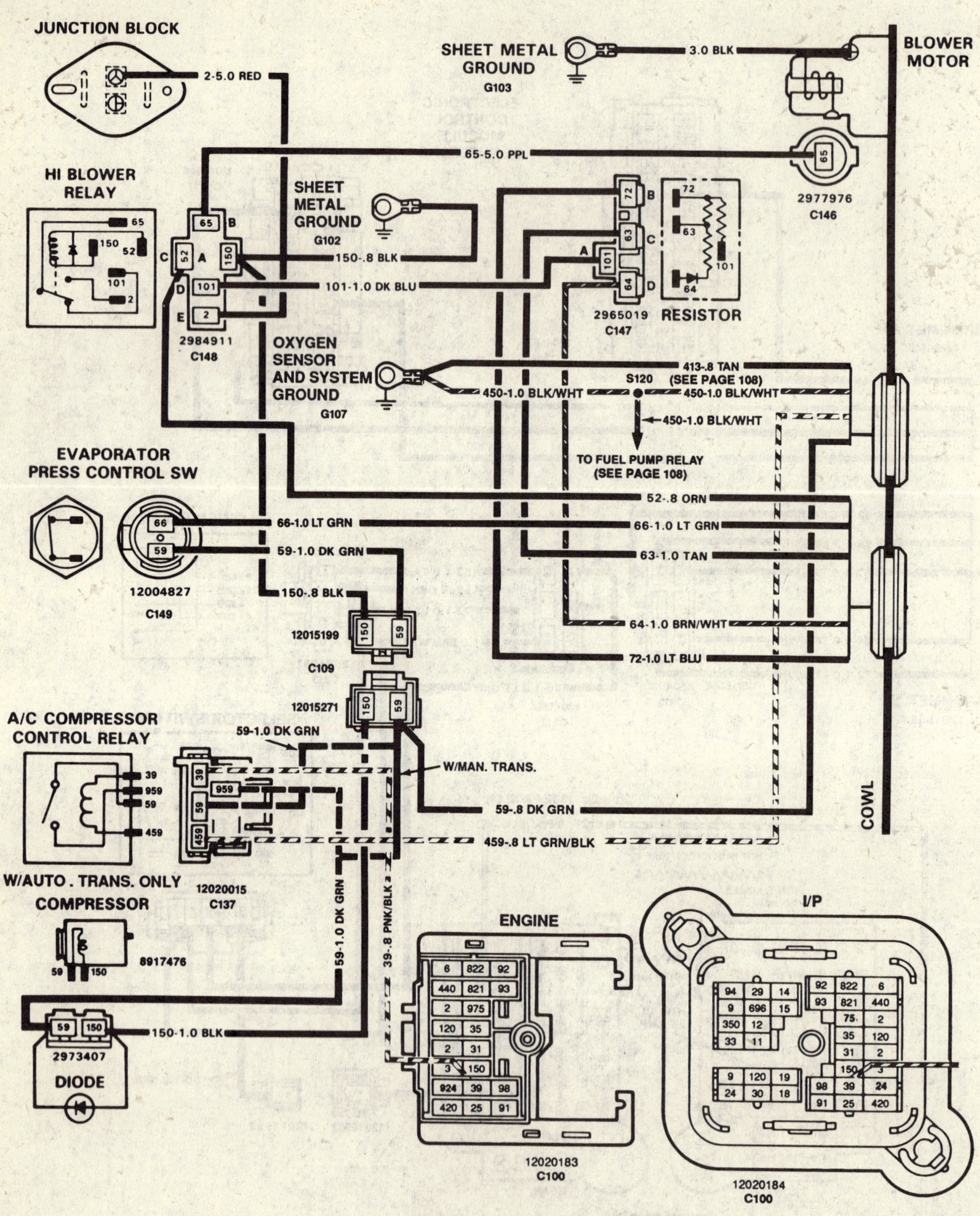

1988-91

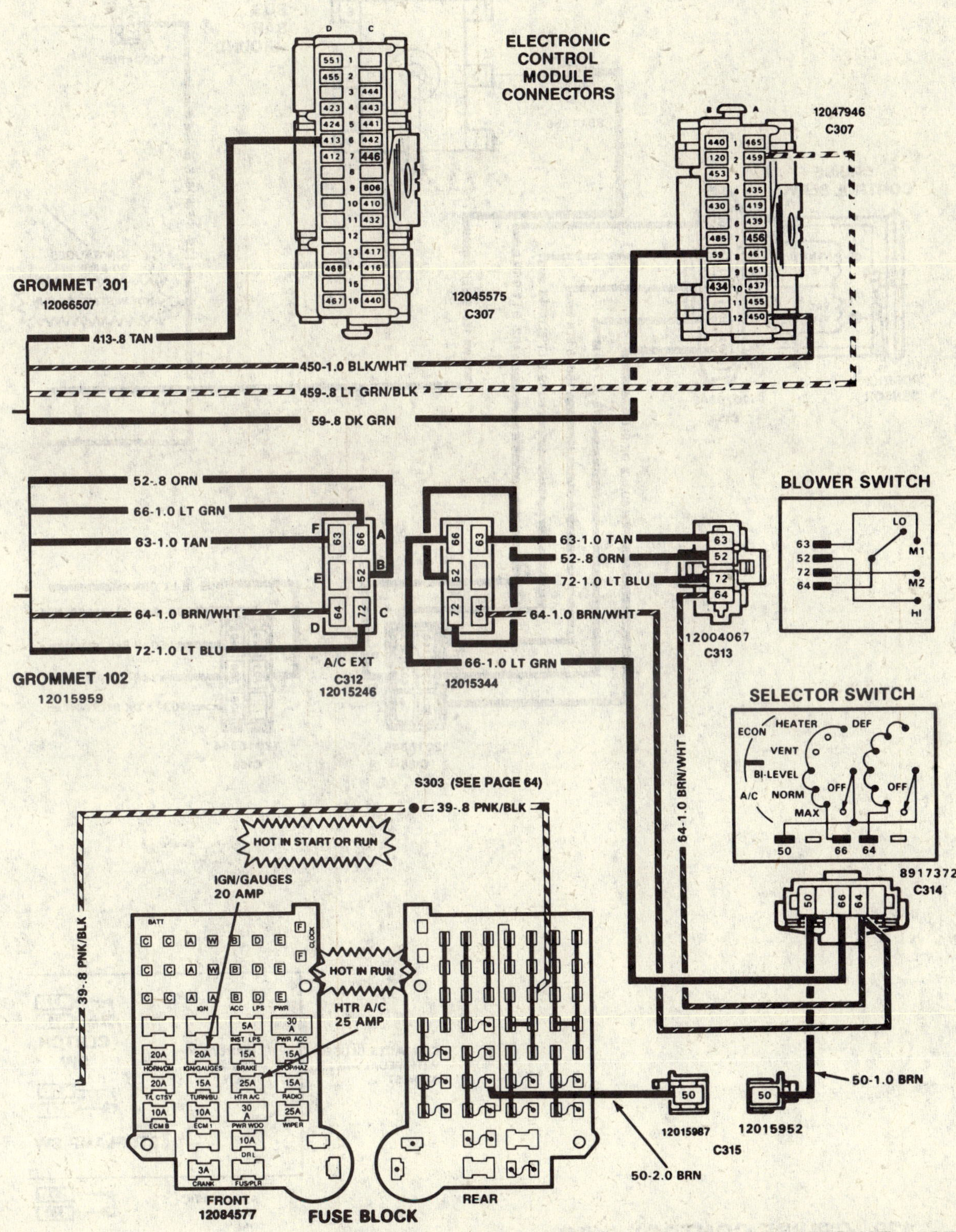

AIR CONDITIONING (C60) - 4.3L (262 CID) ENGINE 127

1988-91

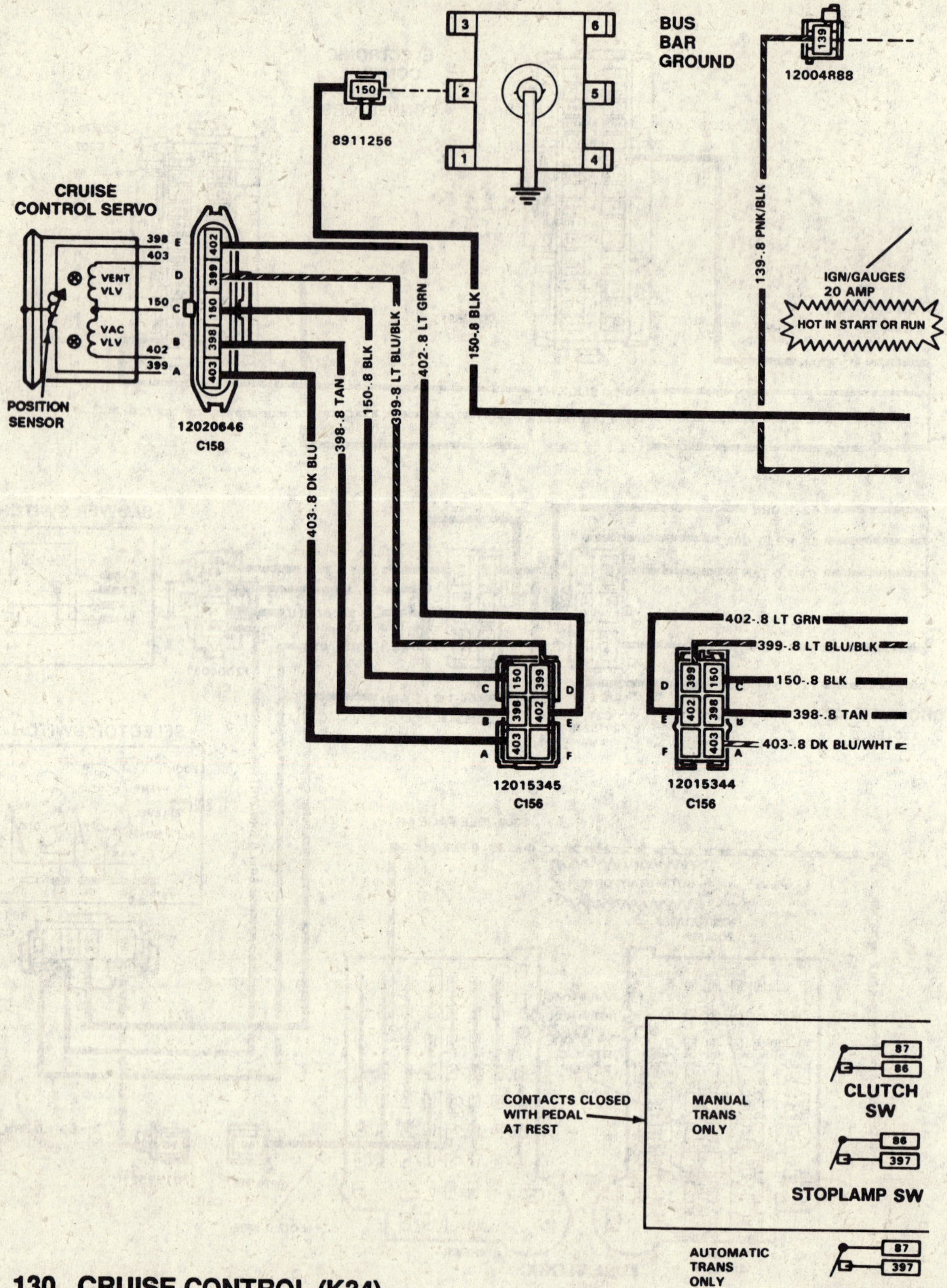

BUS BAR GROUND

8911256

12004R88

CRUISE CONTROL SERVO

VENT VLV

VAC VLV

POSITION SENSOR

12020646 C158

139-.8 PNK/BLK

IGN/GAUGES 20 AMP

HOT IN START OR RUN

403-.8 DK BLU

398-.8 TAN

150-.8 BLK

399-8 LT BLU/BLK

402-.8 LT GRN

150-.8 BLK

402-.8 LT GRN

399-.8 LT BLU/BLK

150-.8 BLK

398-.8 TAN

403-.8 DK BLU/WHT

12015345 C156

12015344 C156

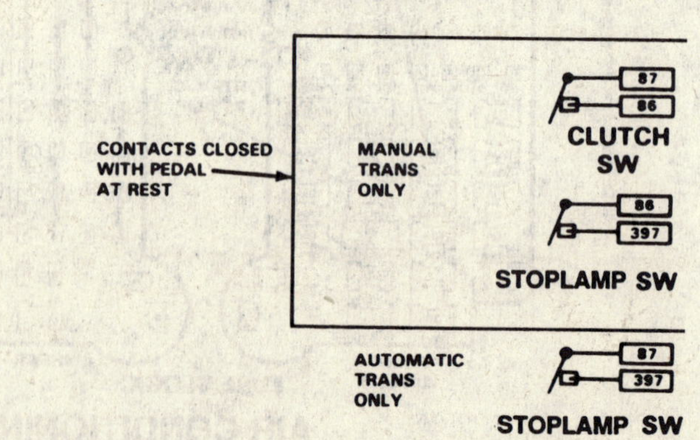

130 CRUISE CONTROL (K34)

1988-91

BATT
CLOCK
IGN
ACC
LPS
PWR
5A
30 A
INST LPS
PWR ACC
20A
HORN DM
20A
IGN GAUGES
15A
BRAKE
15A
STOP HAZ
20A
T/L CTSY
15A
TURN BU
25A
HTR A/C
15A
RADIO
10A
ECM B
10A
ECM I
30 A
PWR WDO
25A
WIPER
10A
DRL
3A
CRANK
FUS/PLR
FRONT
12084577
FUSE BLOCK
REAR

CRUISE CONTROL MODULE
12034125
C342
S313
150-.8 BLK
150-.8 BLK
402-.8 LT GRN
397-.8 GRA
403-.8 DK BLU/WHT
398-.8 TAN
399-.8 LT BLU/BLK
139-.8 PNK/BLK
GROMMET 103
12020173
COWL
403 SERVO VENT VALVE
402 SERVO VACUUM VALVE
400 SPEED SENSOR INPUT
399 SERVO POSITION INPUT
398 SERVO POSITION INPUT
397 ON/OFF SIGNAL
150 GROUND
87 BRAKE CLUTCH INPUT
84 RESUME/ACCEL SIGNAL
83 SET/COAST SIGNAL
84-.8 DK BLU
83-.8 DK GRN
CRUISE CONTROL SWITCH
S/C
R/A
ON/OFF
397-.8 GRA
87-.8 GRA/BLK
400-.8 YEL
397-.8 GRA
12020651
C341
400-.8 YEL
12066189
C363
DIGITAL RATIO ADAPTER CONTROLLER (SEE PAGE 118)
C344
87-.8 GRA/BLK
86-.8 BRN
2973781
C343
86-.8 BRN
397-.8 GRA
397-.8 GRA
12015197
C343
87-.8 GRA/BLK
397-.8 GRA
397-.8 GRA
12015197

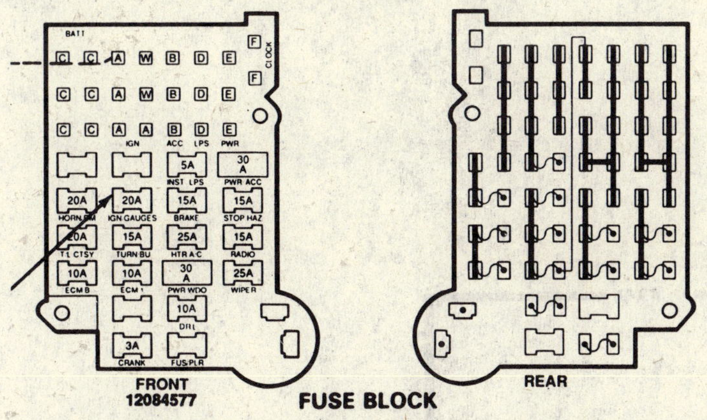

1988-91

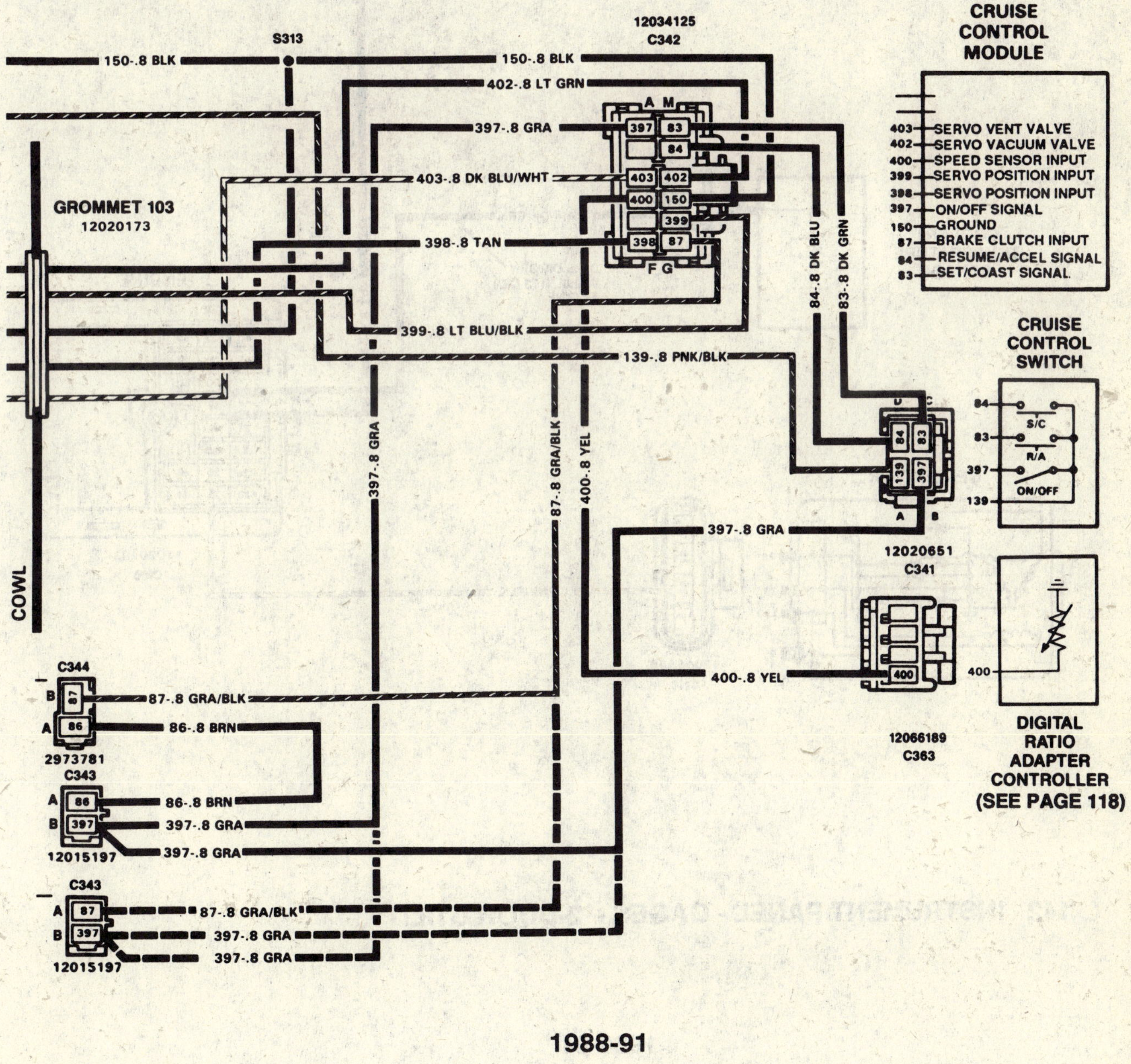

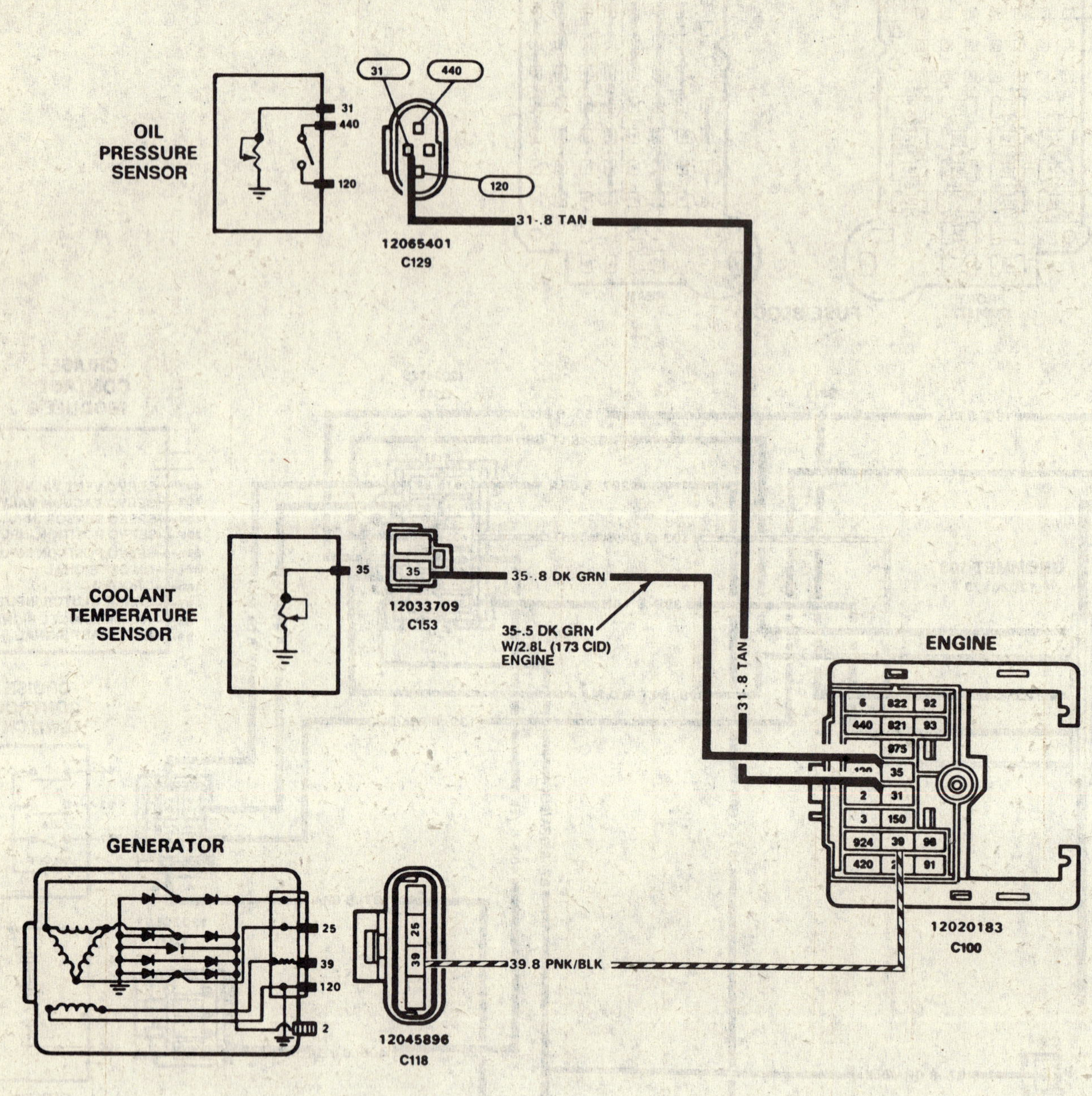

142 INSTRUMENT PANEL - GAGES - 2-DOOR UTILITY

1988-91

HOT WITH LT SW IN HEAD OR PARK
INST LPS 5 AMP
FRONT
12084577
FUSE BLOCK
REAR
I/P
REAR BODY
12020099
C112
12020184
C100
39-.8 PNK/BLK
39-.8 PNK/BLK
25-.5 BRN
35-.5 DK GRN
31-.5 TAN
30-.5 PNK
30-.8 PNK
30-.8 PNK

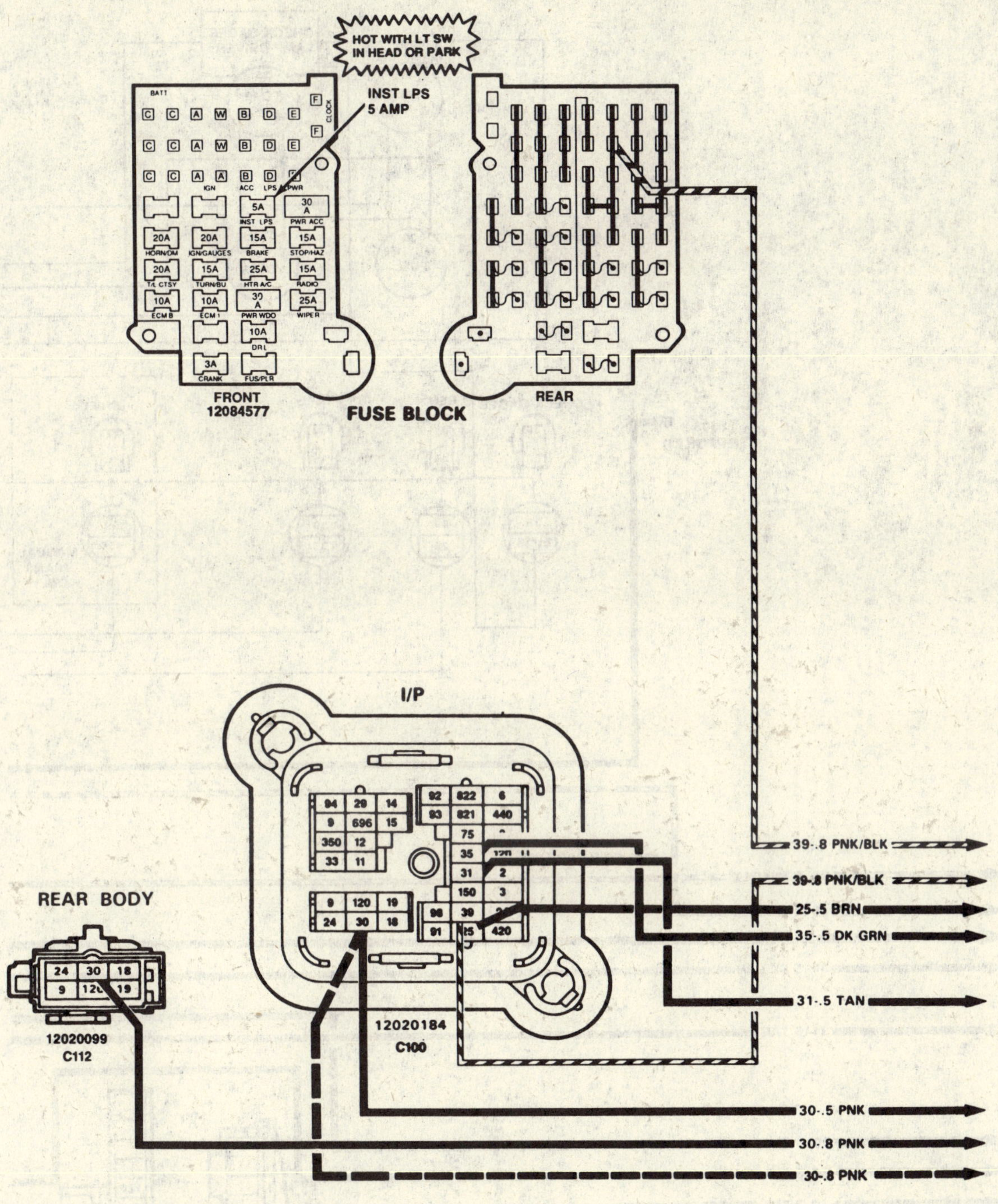

1988-91

CHECK GAGES LAMP DRIVER
31
OIL
39
150
35
TEMP
39
150
30
39
150
FUEL
150
VOLTS
CHECK GAGES
GEN
BRAKE
SHIFT
S306
(SEE PAGE 21)
39
31/35
39
25
39
33
39
456
MANUAL TRANS ONLY
S303 (SEE PAGE 62)
39-.8 PNK/BLK
39-.8 PNK/BLK
25-.5 BRN
35-.5 DK GRN
31-.5 TAN
30-.5 PNK
30-.8 PNK
30-.8 PNK
120
240
156
156
240
30
24
18
9
19
120
240
156
30
24
18
9
19
12052469
C404
12034337
C404

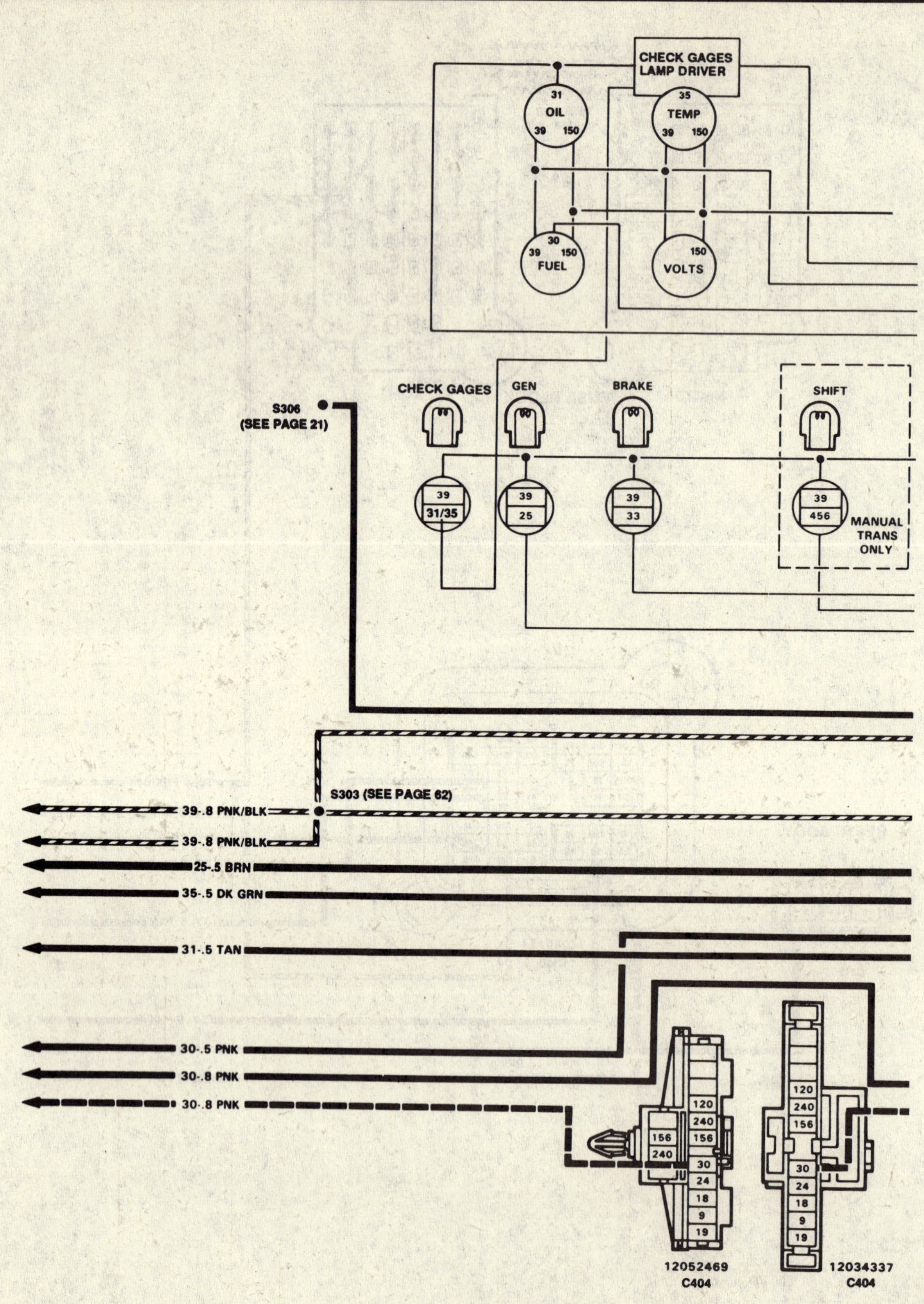

1988-91

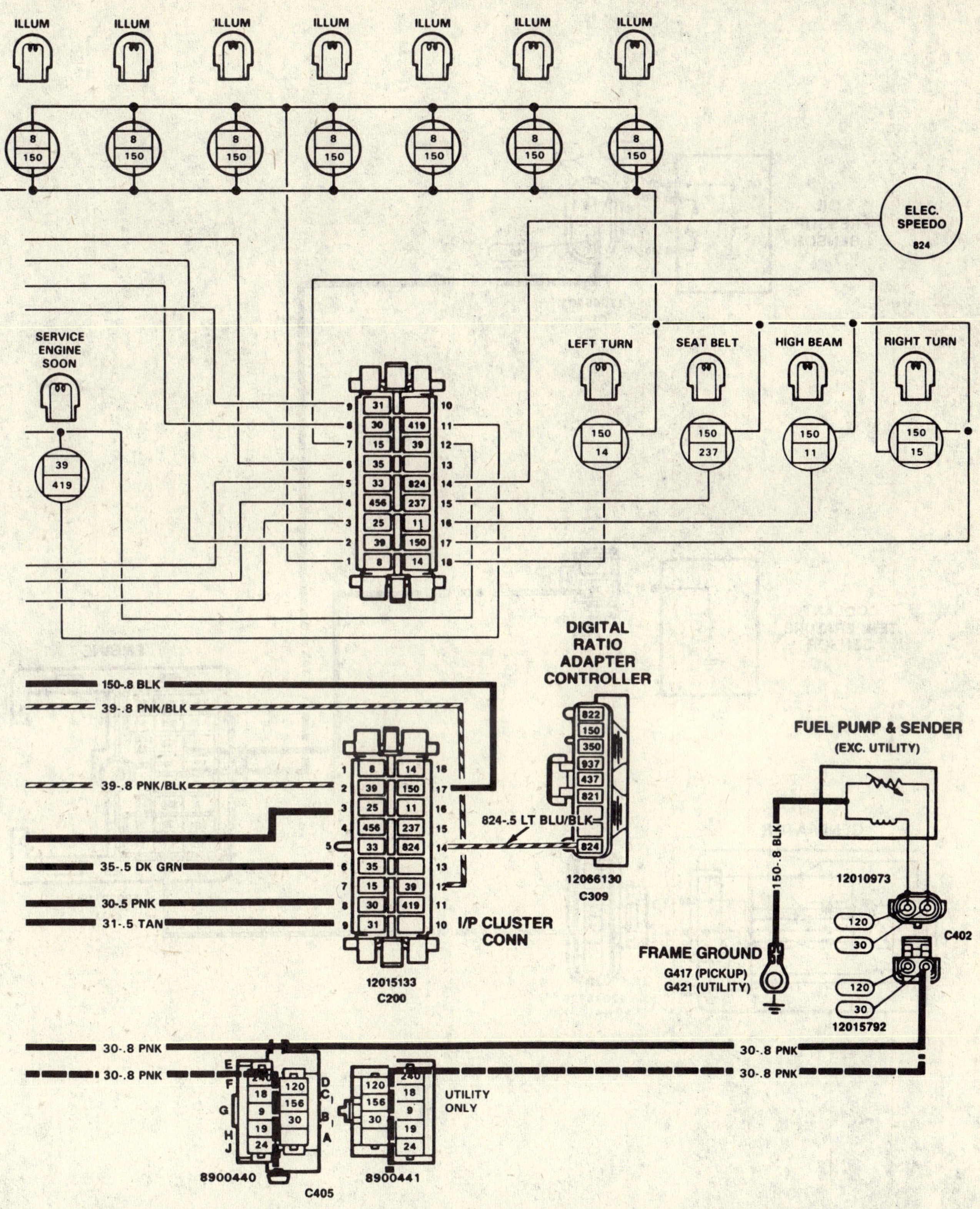

INSTRUMENT PANEL - GAGES - 2-DOOR UTILITY 143

1988-91

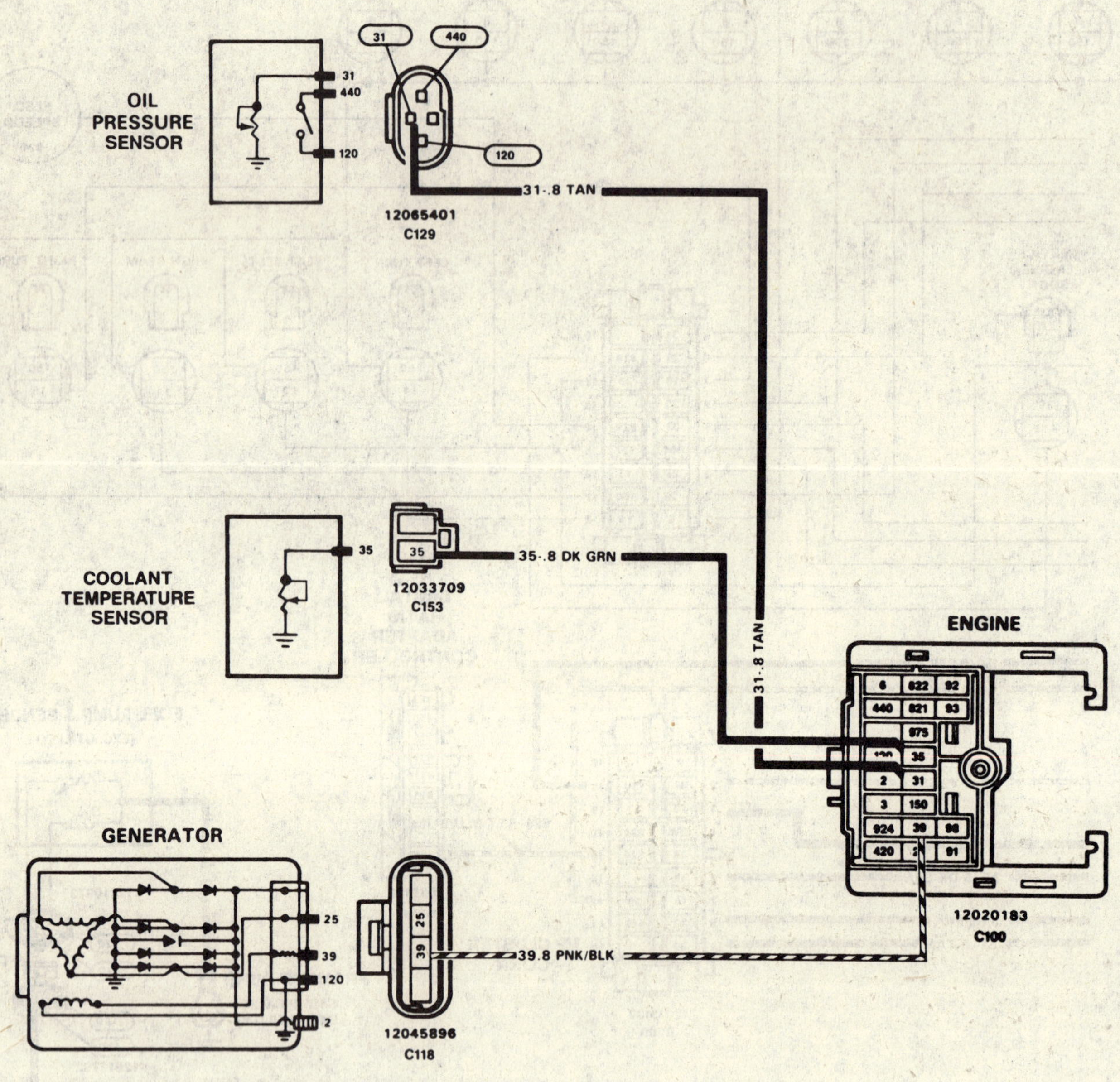

144 INSTRUMENT PANEL - GAGES - 4-DOOR UTILITY

1988-91

HOT WITH LT SW IN HEAD OR PARK
INST LPS 5 AMPS
FRONT
12064577
08900320
P
D
12004060
REAR
FUSE BLOCK
I/P
12020184
C100
30-.8 PNK
30-.5 PNK
39-.8 PNK/BLK
39-.8 PNK/BLK
25-.5 BRN
35-.5 DK GRN
31-.5 TAN
30-.8 PNK

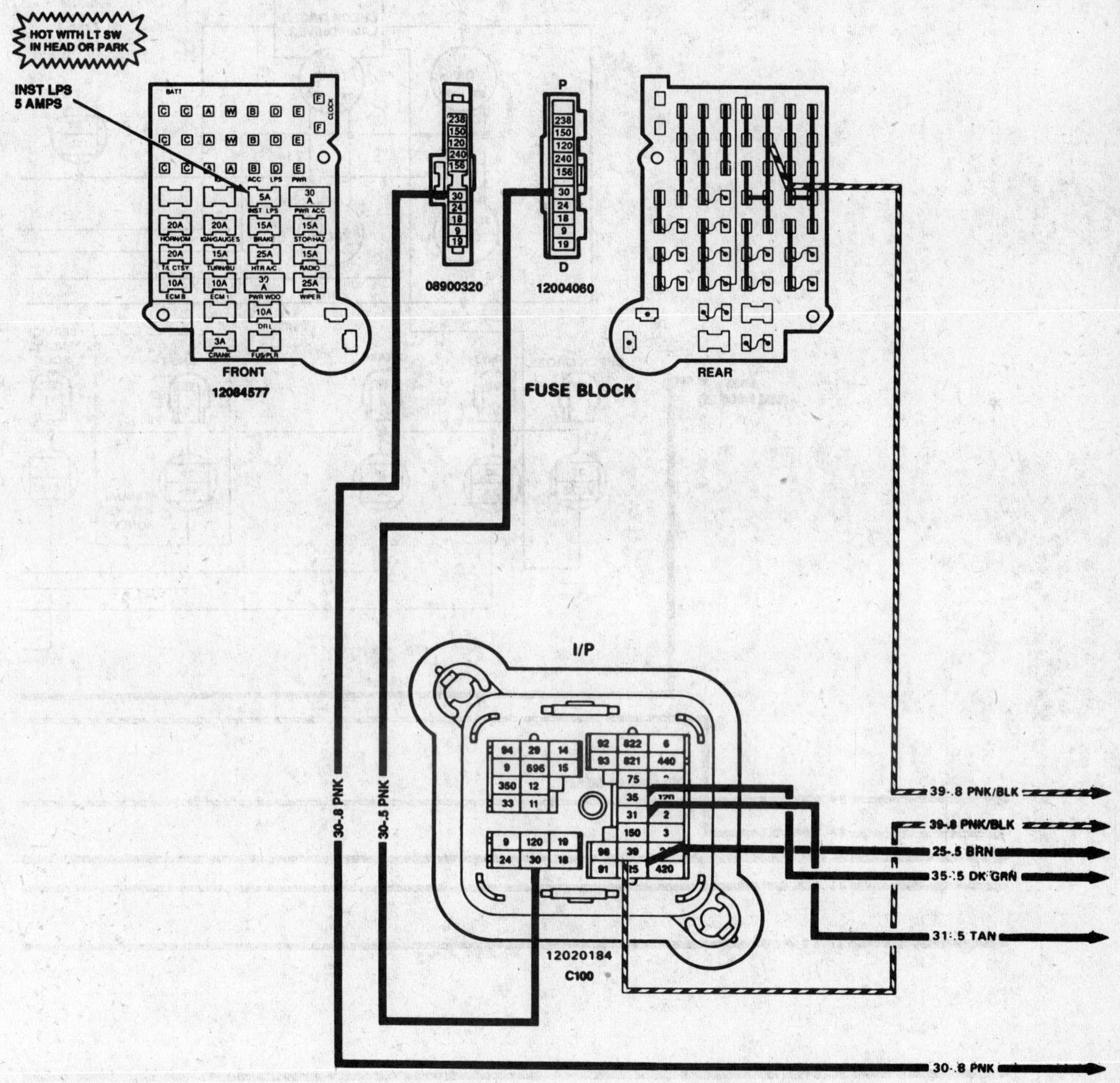

1988-91

CHECK GAGES
LAMP DRIVER
ILLUM
31
OIL
39 150
35
TEMP
39 150
8
150
30
39 150
FUEL
150
VOLTS
SERVICE
ENGINE
SOON
CHECK GAGES
GEN
BRAKE
SHIFT
S306
(SEE PAGE 21)
39
31/35
39
25
39
33
39
456
MANUAL
TRANS
ONLY
39
419
S303 (SEE PAGE 64)
39-.8 PNK/BLK
39-.8 PNK/BLK
25-.5 BRN
35-.5 DK GRN
31-.5 TAN
30-.8 PNK

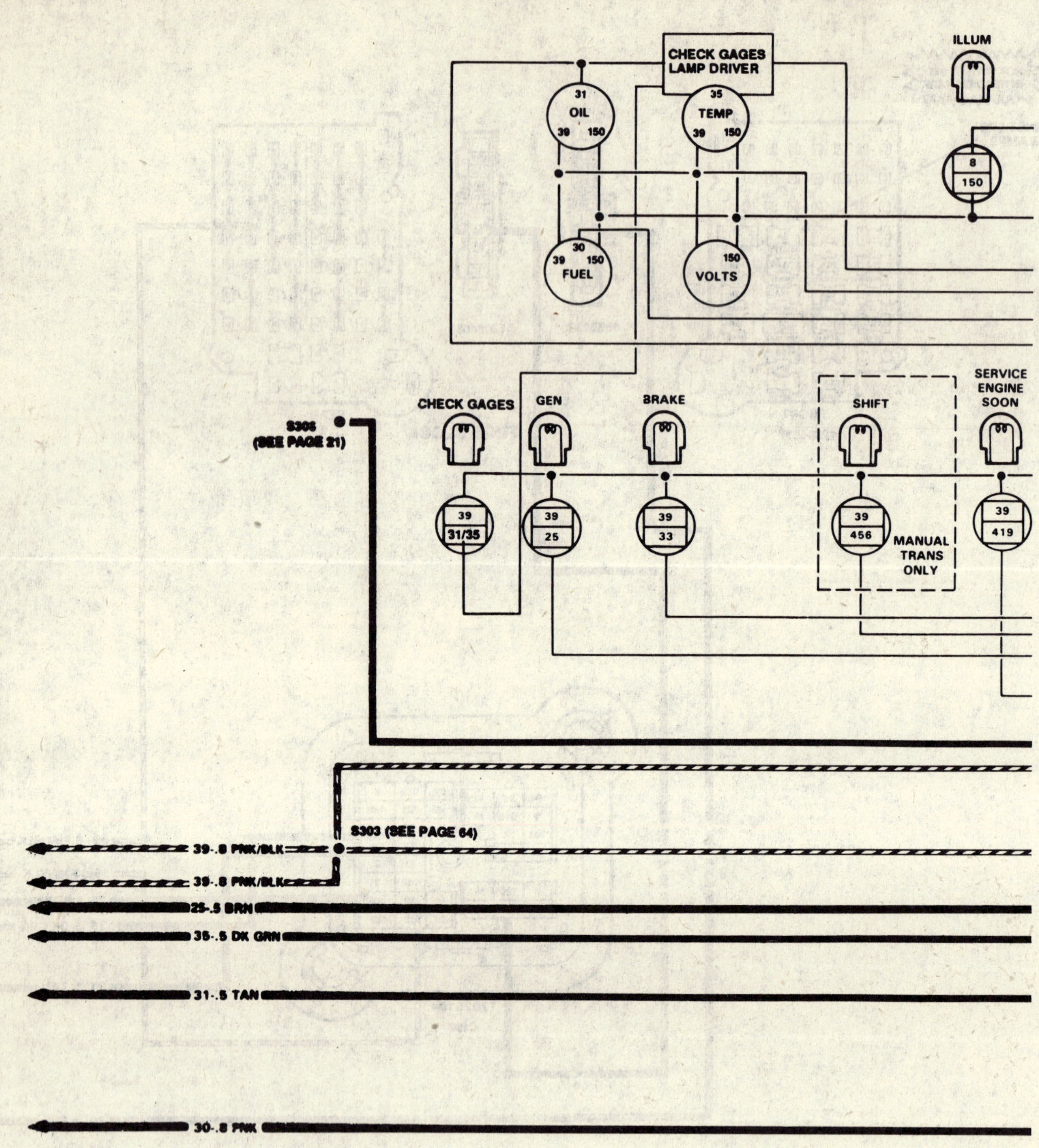

1988-91

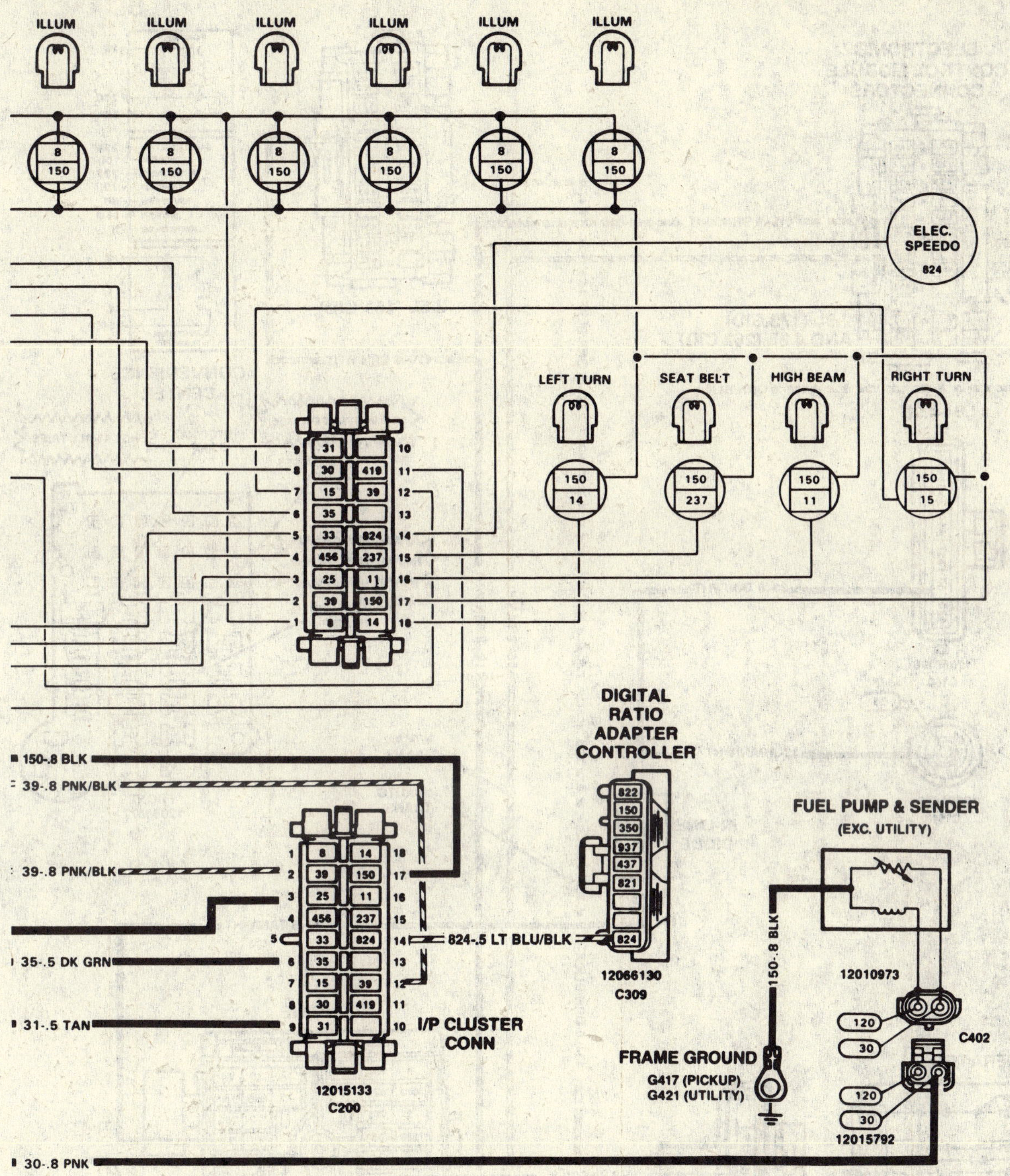

INSTRUMENT PANEL - GAGES - GAGES I/P - 4-DOOR UTILITY 145

1988-91

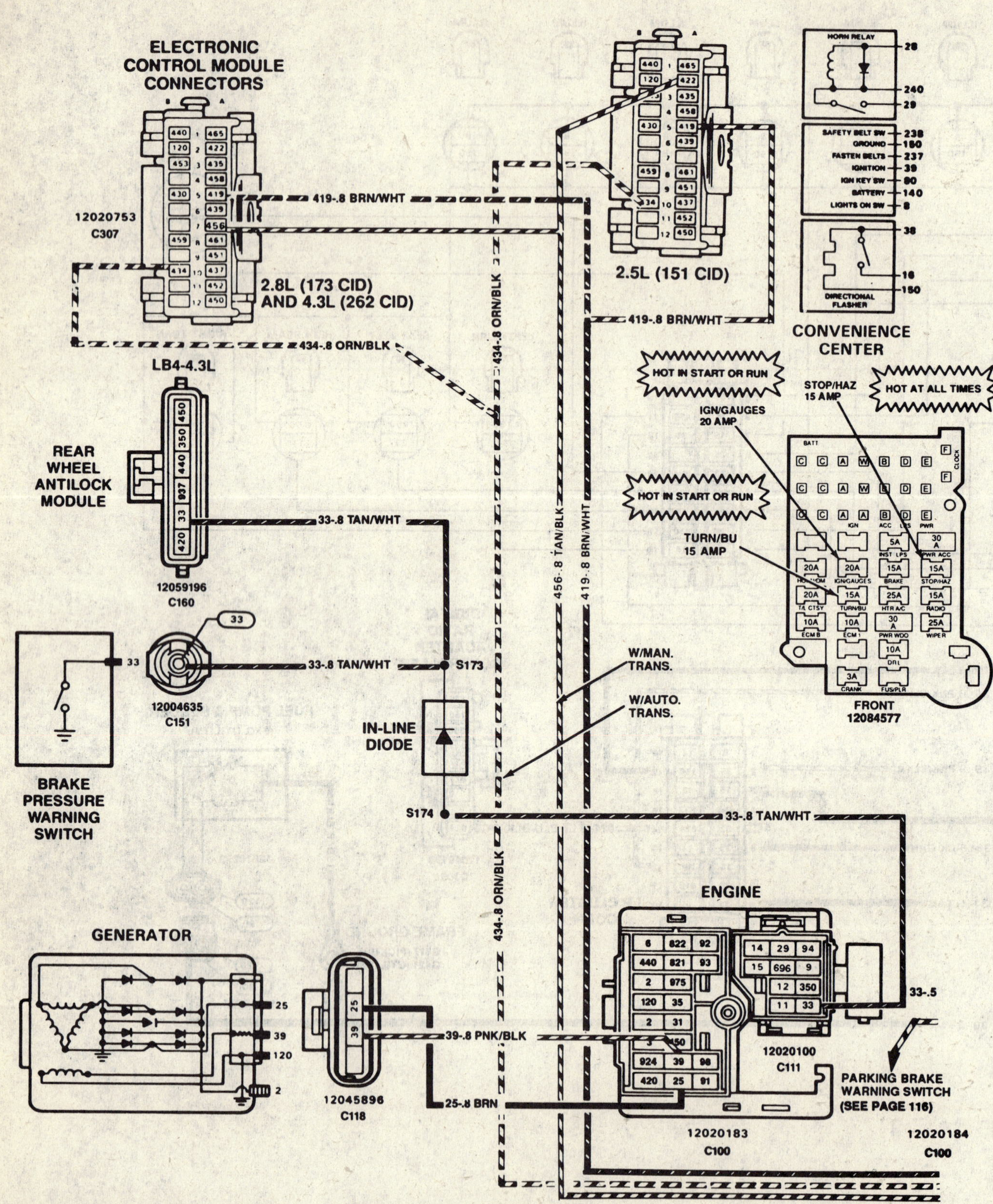

146 INSTRUMENT PANEL - INDICATOR LAMPS - GAGES I/P - 2-DOOR UTILITY

1988-91

140-.8 ORN
BUZZER
HORN
HZ/F
P.E.D.
12015999
140-.8 ORN
TO STOP
LAMP SW
(SEE PAGE 216)
12033699
C370
140-.8 ORN
FUSE BLOCK
REAR
38-.8 DK BLU
16-.8 PPL
27-.8 BRN
39-.8 PNK/BLK
16-.8 PPL
237-.8 YEL
150-.8 BLK
15-.5 DK BLU
14-.5 LT BLU
12004147
C305
12004148
C305
(STEERING COL SWITCHES)
LEFT
RIGHT
TURN SIGNAL
HORN
KEY
NORMALLY
OPEN
SWITCHES
HAZARD
DIRECTIONAL
SIGNAL SW
39-.8 PNK/BLK
39-.8 PNK/BLK
39-.8 PNK/BLK
150-.8 BLK
25-.5 BRN
237-.8 YEL
15-.5 DK BLU
33-.5 TAN/WHT
I/P
TAN/WHT
39-.8 PNK/BLK
11-.8 LT GRN
11-1.0 LT GRN
35-.5 DK GKRN
31-.5 TAN
14-.5 LT BLU
ENGINE
I/P
PARK NEUTRAL SWITCH
(SEE PAGE 69)
419-.8 BRN/WHT
434-.8 ORN/BLK
456-.8 TAN/BLK
419-.8 BRN/WHT
434-.8 ORN/BLK
456-.8 TAN/BLK
C101
12064770
12064764

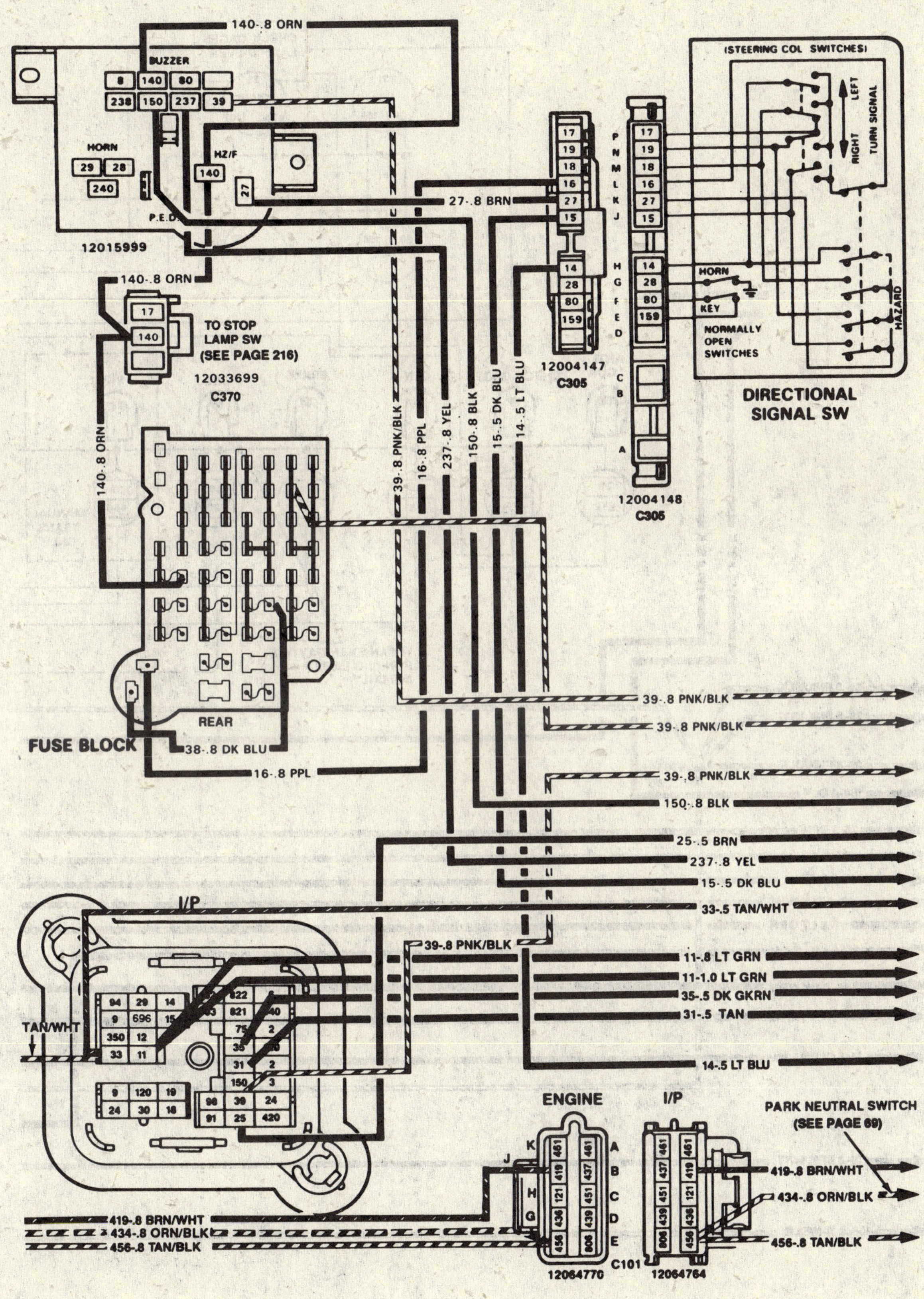

1988-91

CHECK GAGES
LAMP DRIVER
31
OIL
39 150
35
TEMP
39 150
30
39 150
FUEL
150
VOLTS
S306 (SEE PAGE 21)
ANTI
LOCK
CHECK GAGES
GEN
BRAKE
DRL
SHIFT
39
852
39
31/35
39
25
39
33
39
592
39
456
MANUAL
TRANS
ONLY
150-.8 BLK
150-.8 BLK
W/CANADIAN DAYTIME
RUNNING LAMPS
Z49 ONLY
39-.8 PNK/BLK
39-.8 PNK/BLK
39-.8 PNK/BLK
S303
150-.8 BLK
25-.5 BRN
237-.8 YEL
15-.5 DK BLU
33-.5 TAN/WHT
11-.8 LT GRN
11-1.0 LT GRN
35-.5 DK GRN
31-.5 TAN
14-.5 LT BLU
419-.8 BRN/WHT
456-.8 TAN/BLK

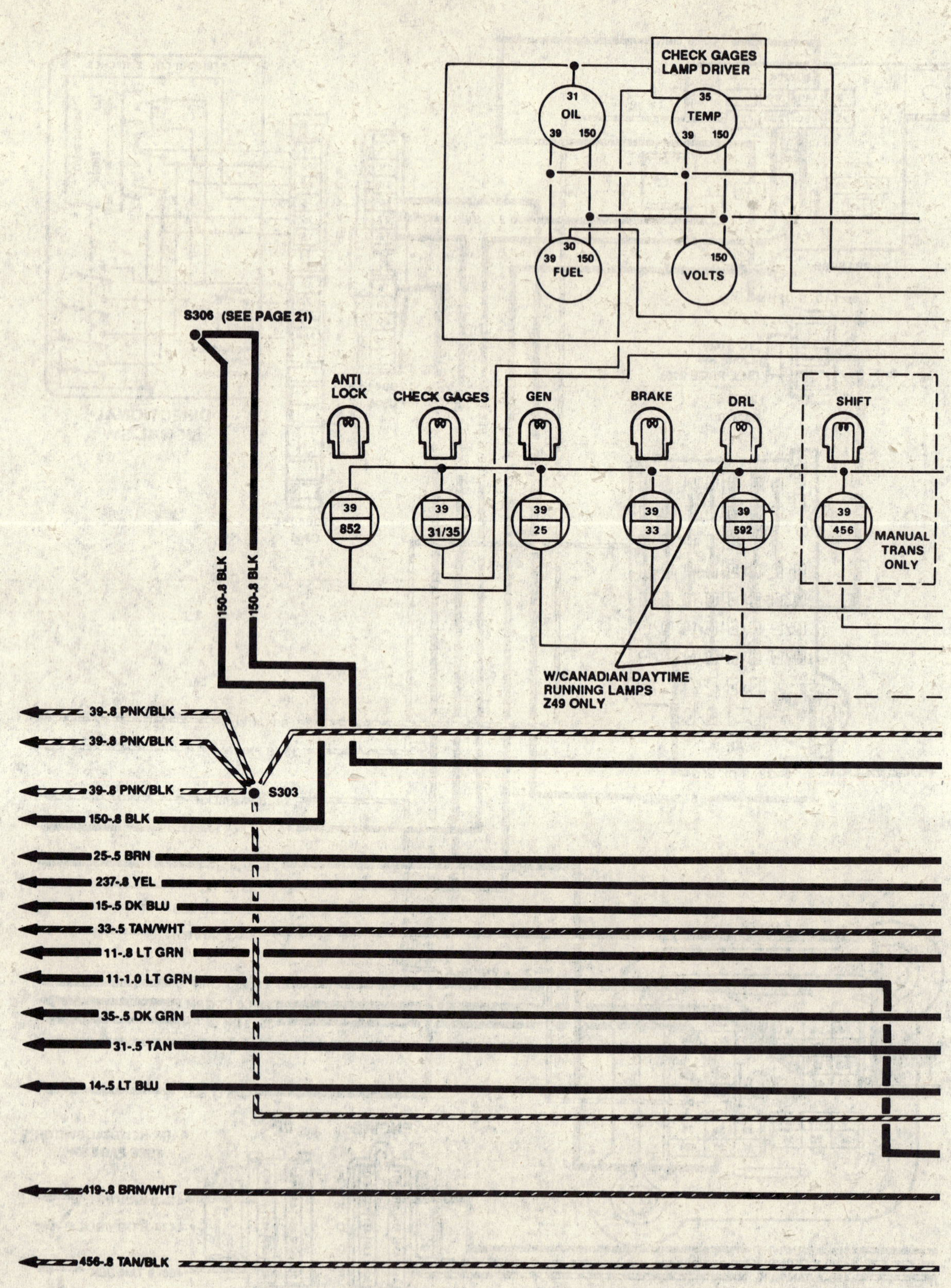

1988-91

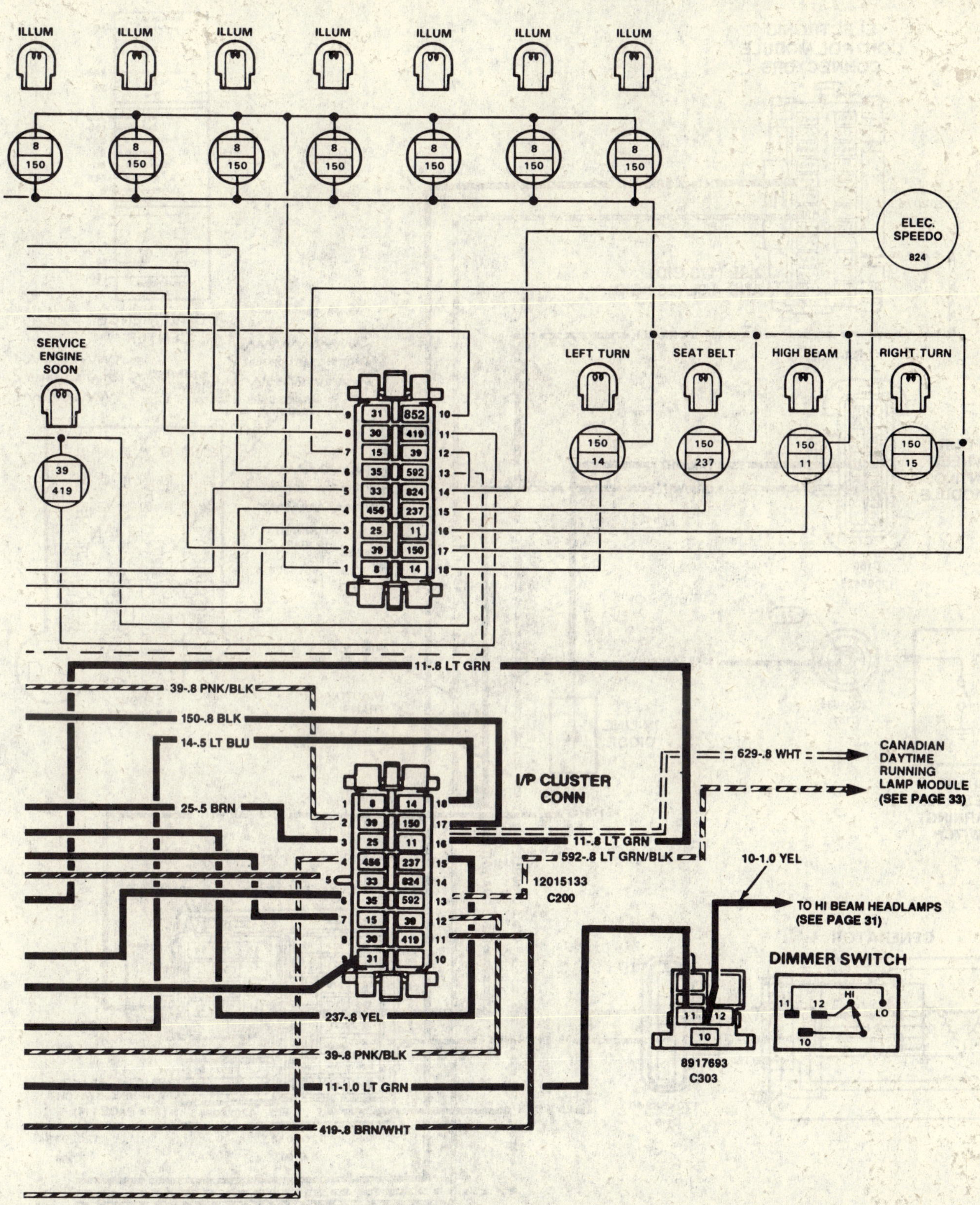

INSTRUMENT PANEL - INDICATOR LAMPS - GAGES I/P - 2-DOOR UTILITY 147

1988-91

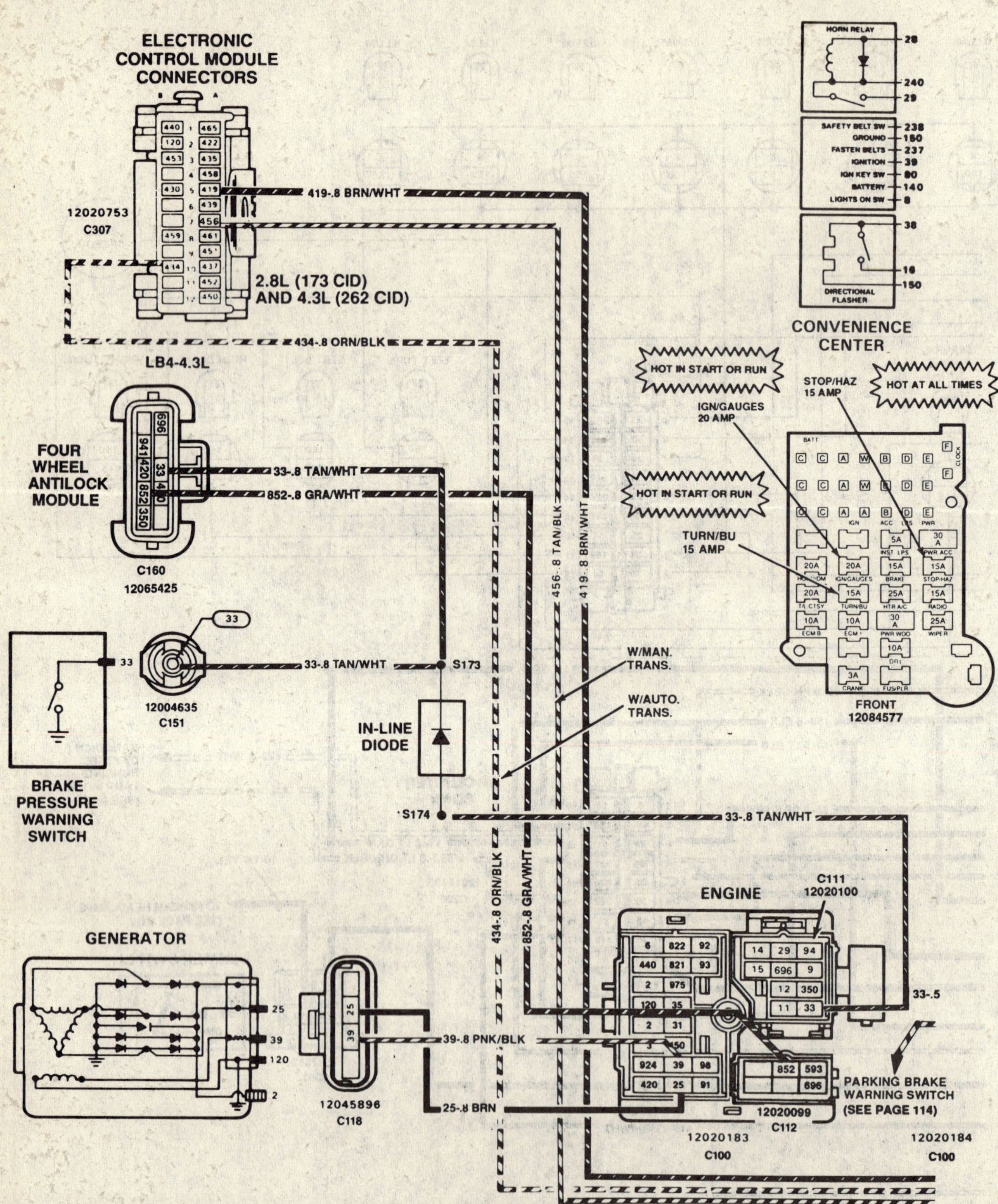

148 INSTRUMENT PANEL - INDICATOR LAMPS - GAGES I/P - 4- DOOR UTILITY

1988-91

140-.8 ORN
BUZZER
8
140
80
238
150
237
39
HORN
29
28
240
HZ/F
140
27
P.E.D.
12015999
140-.8 ORN
17
140
TO STOP LAMP SW (SEE PAGE 219)
12033699
C370
140-.8 ORN
REAR
FUSE BLOCK
38-.8 DK BLU
16-.8 PPL
27-.8 BRN
39-.8 PNK/BLK
16-.8 PPL
237-.8 YEL
150-.8 BLK
15-.5 DK BLU
14-.5 LT BLU
12004147
C305
12004148
C305
(STEERING COL SWITCHES)
LEFT
RIGHT
TURN SIGNAL
HORN
KEY
NORMALLY OPEN SWITCHES
HAZARD
DIRECTIONAL SIGNAL SW
39-.8 PNK/BLK
39-.8 PNK/BLK
39-.8 PNK/BLK
150-.8 BLK
25-.5 BRN
237-.8 YEL
15-.5 DK BLU
33-.5 TAN/WHT
I/P
39-.8 PNK/BLK
11-.8 LT GRN
11-1.0 LT GRN
35-.5 DK GKRN
31-.5 TAN
TAN/WHT
14-.5 LT BLU
852-.5 GRA/WHT
ENGINE
I/P
PARK NEUTRAL SWITCH (SEE PAGE 69)
419-.8 BRN/WHT
434-.8 ORN/BLK
456-.8 TAN/BLK
419-.8 BRN/WHT
434-.8 ORN/BLK
456-.8 TAN/BLK
C101
12064770
12064764

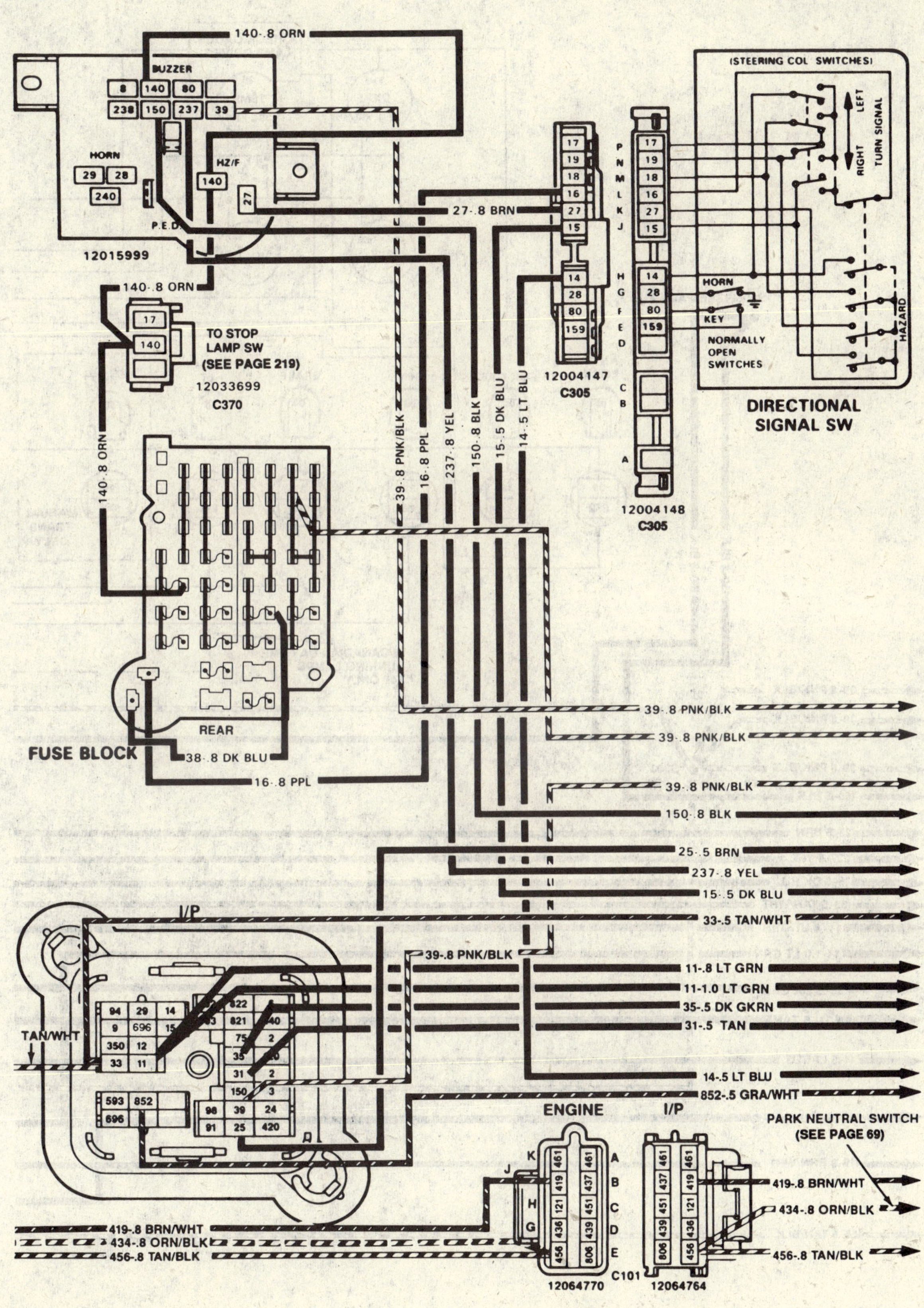

1988-91

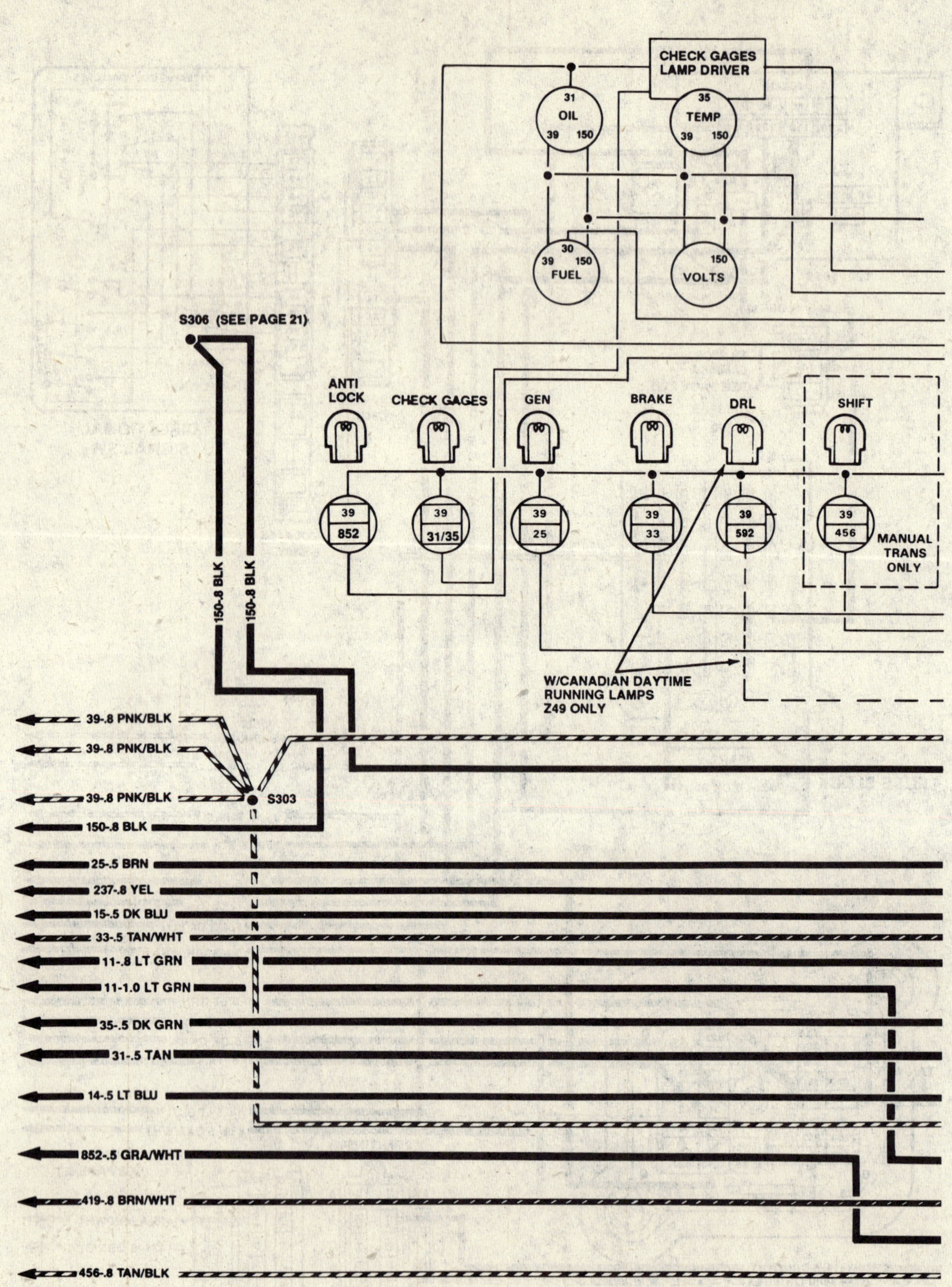

1988-91

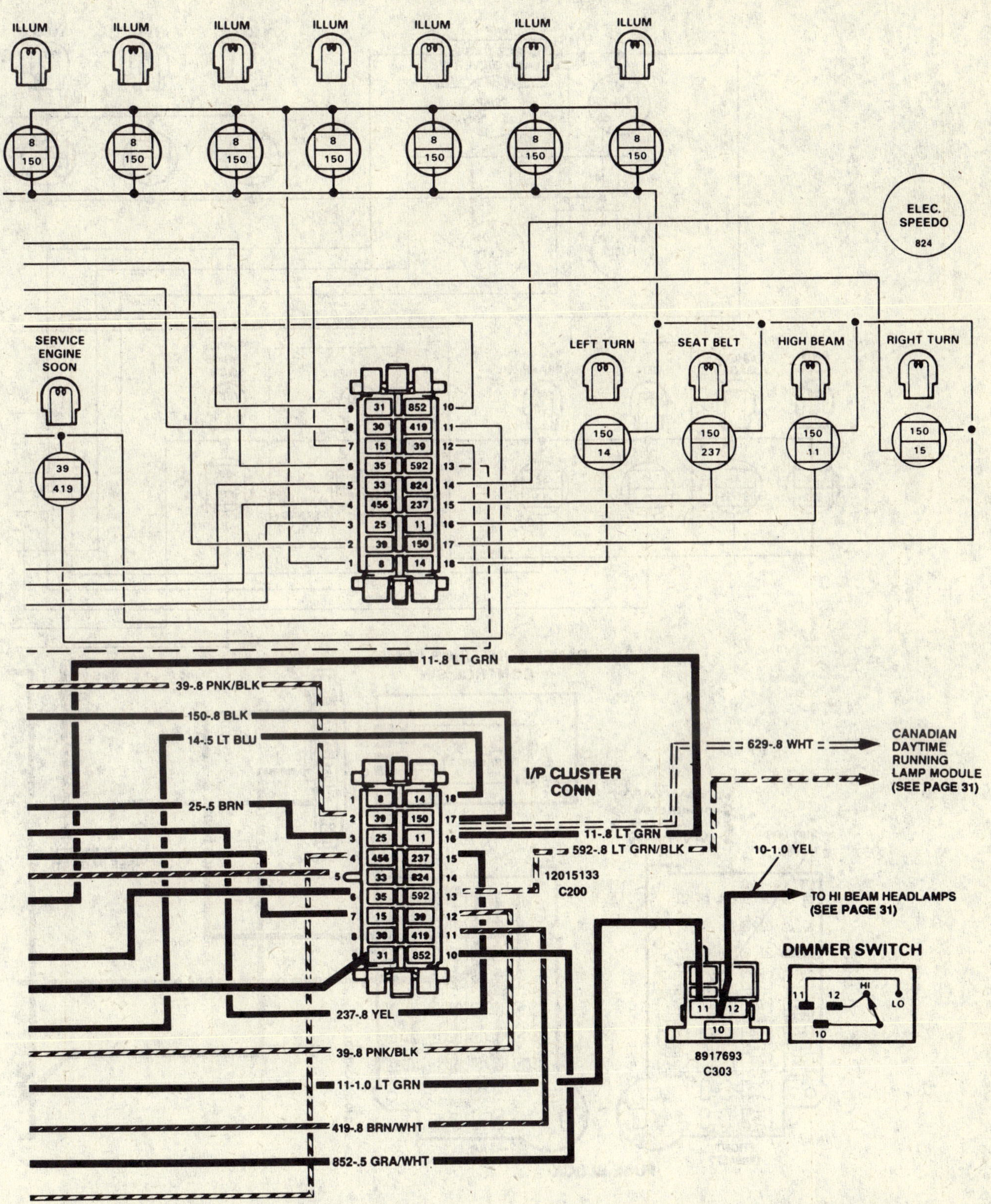

INSTRUMENT PANEL - INDICATOR LAMPS - GAGES I/P - 4-DOOR UTILITY 149

1988-91

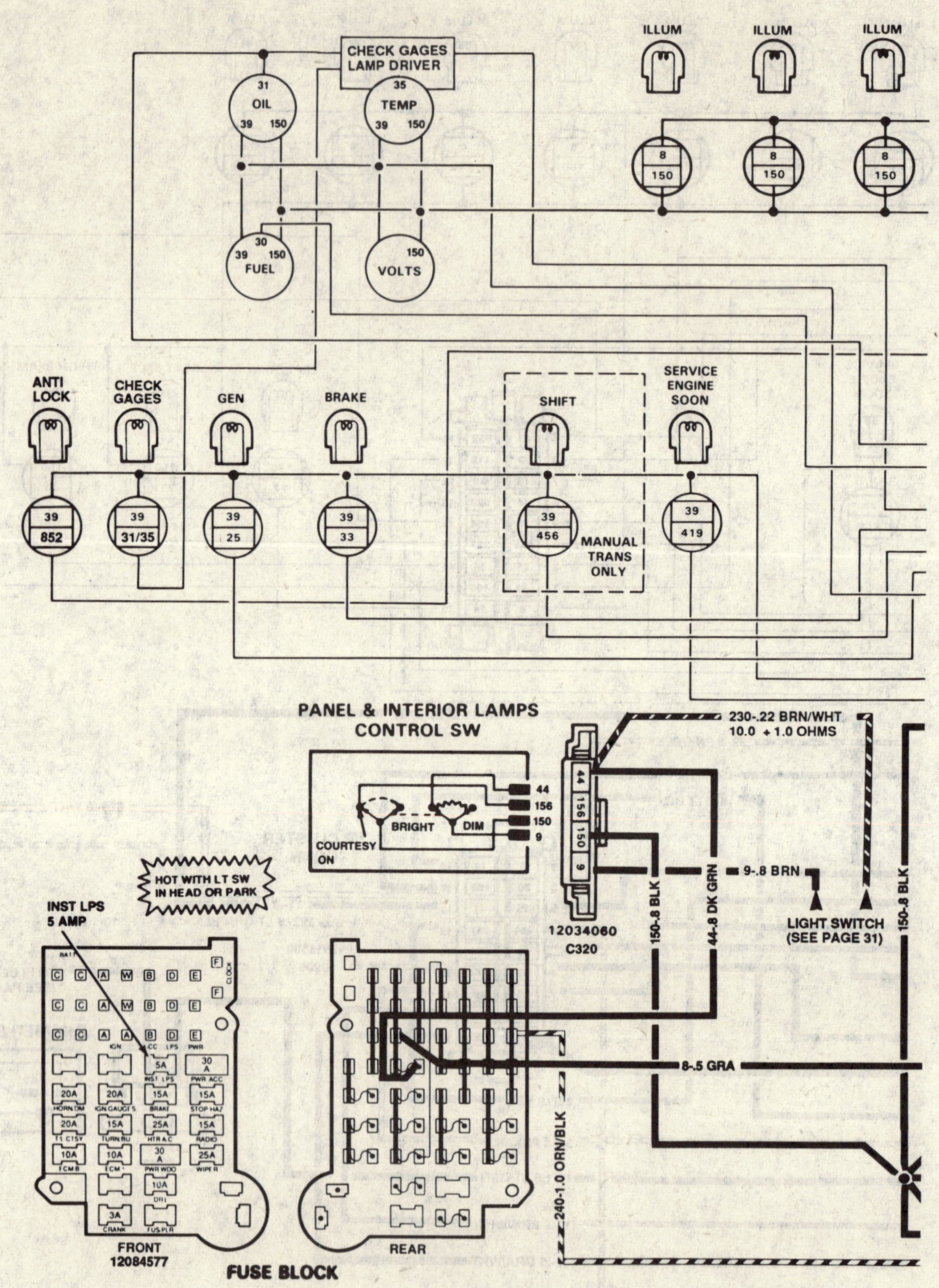

150 INSTRUMENT PANEL - ILLUMINATION LAMPS - GAGES I/P

1988-91

ILLUM
ILLUM
ILLUM
ILLUM
ELEC. SPEEDO
824
BUZZER
HORN
HZ/F
P.E.D.
12015999
LEFT TURN
SEAT BELT
HIGH BEAM
RIGHT TURN
8-.5 GRA
240-.8 ORN/BLK
240-.8 ORN/BLK
ASH TRAY LAMP (W/UTILITY VEHICLES ONLY)
CIGARETTE LIGHTER
RADIO POWER
HEATER LAMP
I/P CLUSTER CONN
12015133
C200
12004543
C350
12020397
C323
12089063
C322
12041296
C321
S307
8-.5 GRA
8-.5 GRA
8-.5 GRA
8-.5 GRA
150-.8 BLK
S306 (SEE PAGE 21)
150-.8 BLK
150-.5 BLK
150-.8 BLK
150-.8 BLK
240-1.0 ORN/BLK
W/UTILITY VEHICLES
W/PICKUP VEHICLES
240-.8 ORN/BLK
240-1.0 ORN/BLK
240-1.0 ORN/BLK
S302
240-1.0 ORN/BLK
240-.8 ORN/BLK
240-.8 ORN/BLK
CONVENIENCE CENTER (SEE PAGE 59)
UTILITY I/P COMP BOX LAMP (SEE PAGE 174)
UTILITY DOME LAMPS (SEE PAGE 170)
W/UTILITY VEHICLES

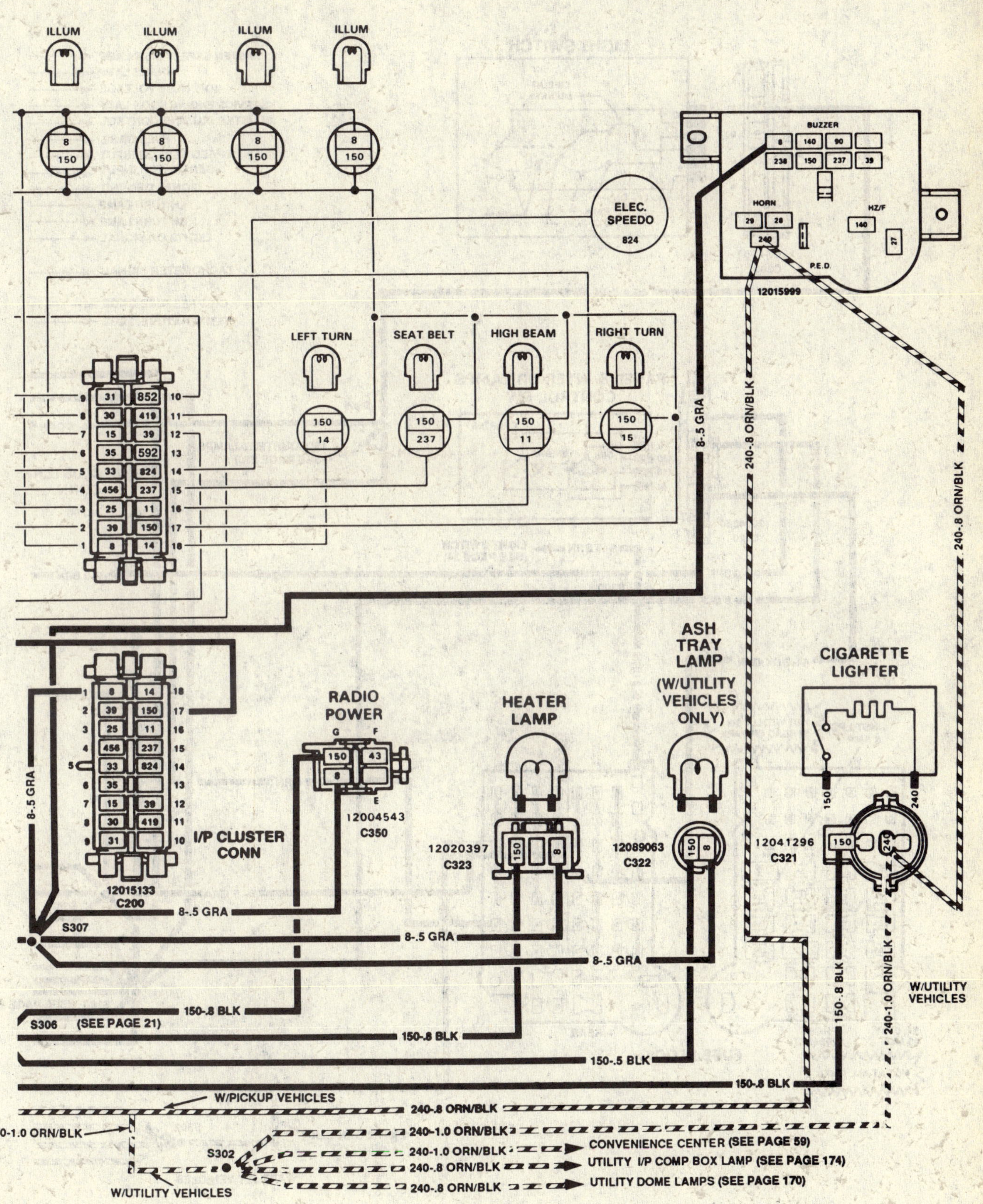

1988-91

LIGHT SWITCH
CIRCUIT BREAKER
HD LP – ON
PARK
HD LP – OFF
OFF
PARK
12034061
C302
40-.8 ORN
17
FASTEN SAFETY BELT LAMP
BRAKE LAMP
IGN. NO. 1 VOLTAGE
SERVICE ENGINE SOON LAMP
CLUSTER DIMMING CONTROL
FUEL GAGE
SPEED SENSOR INPUT
GENERATOR INPUT
SIGNAL GROUND
LH TURN LAMP
RH TURN LAMP
LIGHTS ON SIGNAL
TACHOMETER SIGNAL
OIL PRESSURE GAGE
TEMPERATURE GAGE
PANEL & INTERIOR LAMPS CONTROL SW
COURTESY ON
DIM
BRIGHT
12034060
C320
S308
40-.5 ORN
40-.8 ORN
I/P COURTESY LAMPS (SEE PAGE 170)
I/P CLUSTER CONN
C200
9-.8 BRN
LIGHT SWITCH (SEE PAGE 31)
9-.8 BRN
S300
150-.8 BLK
150-.5 BLK
44-.8 DK GRN
8-.5 GRA
INST LPS 5 AMP
HOT WITH LT SW IN HEAD OR PARK
40-.8 ORN
8-.5 GRA
S307
S306 (SEE PAGE 21)
T/L CTSY 20 AMP
FRONT 12084577
REAR
FUSE BLOCK
HOT AT ALL TIMES
W/PICKUP VEHICLES
240-1.0 ORN/BLK
240-1.0 ORN/BLK
S302
W/UTILITY VEHICLES

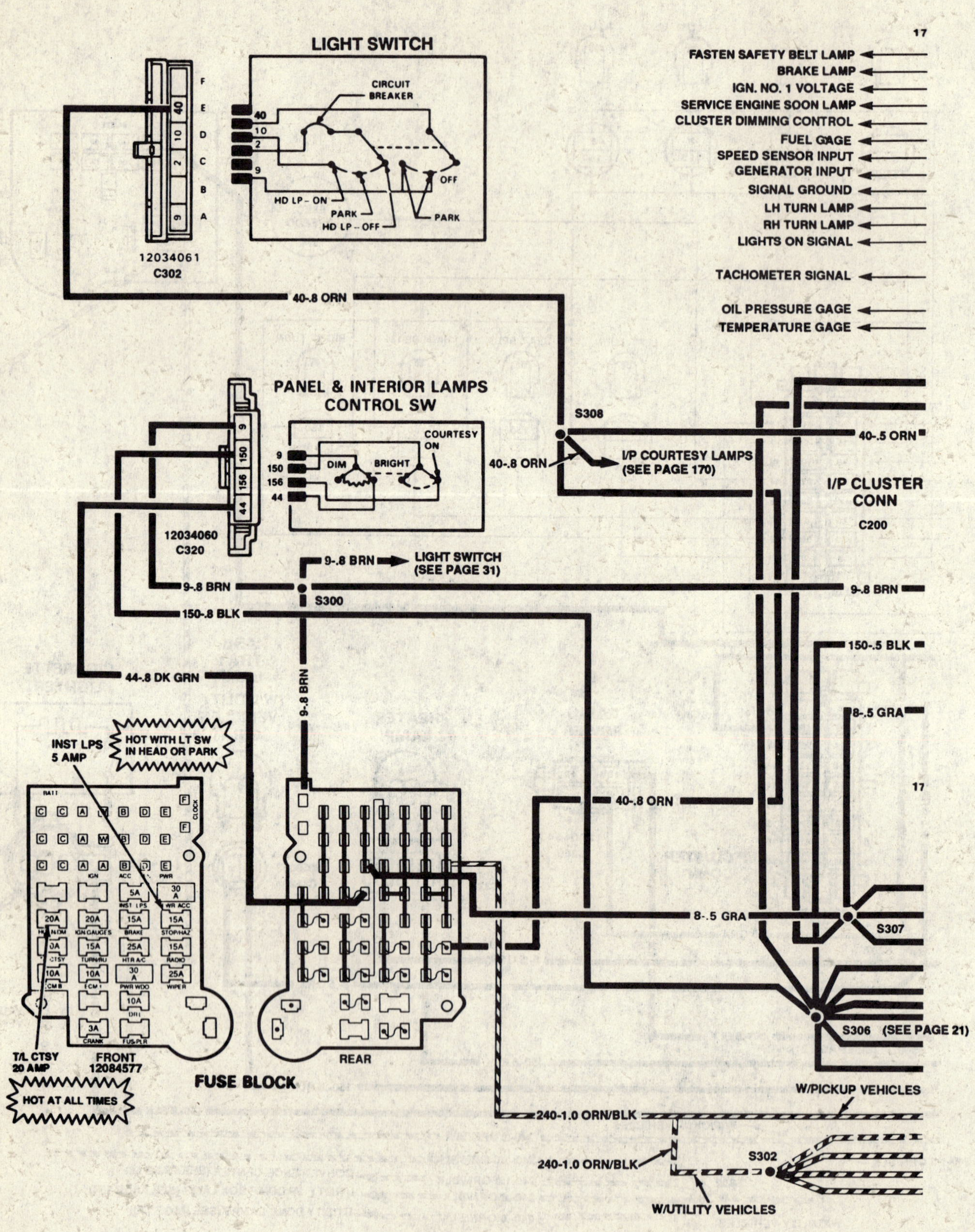

1988-91

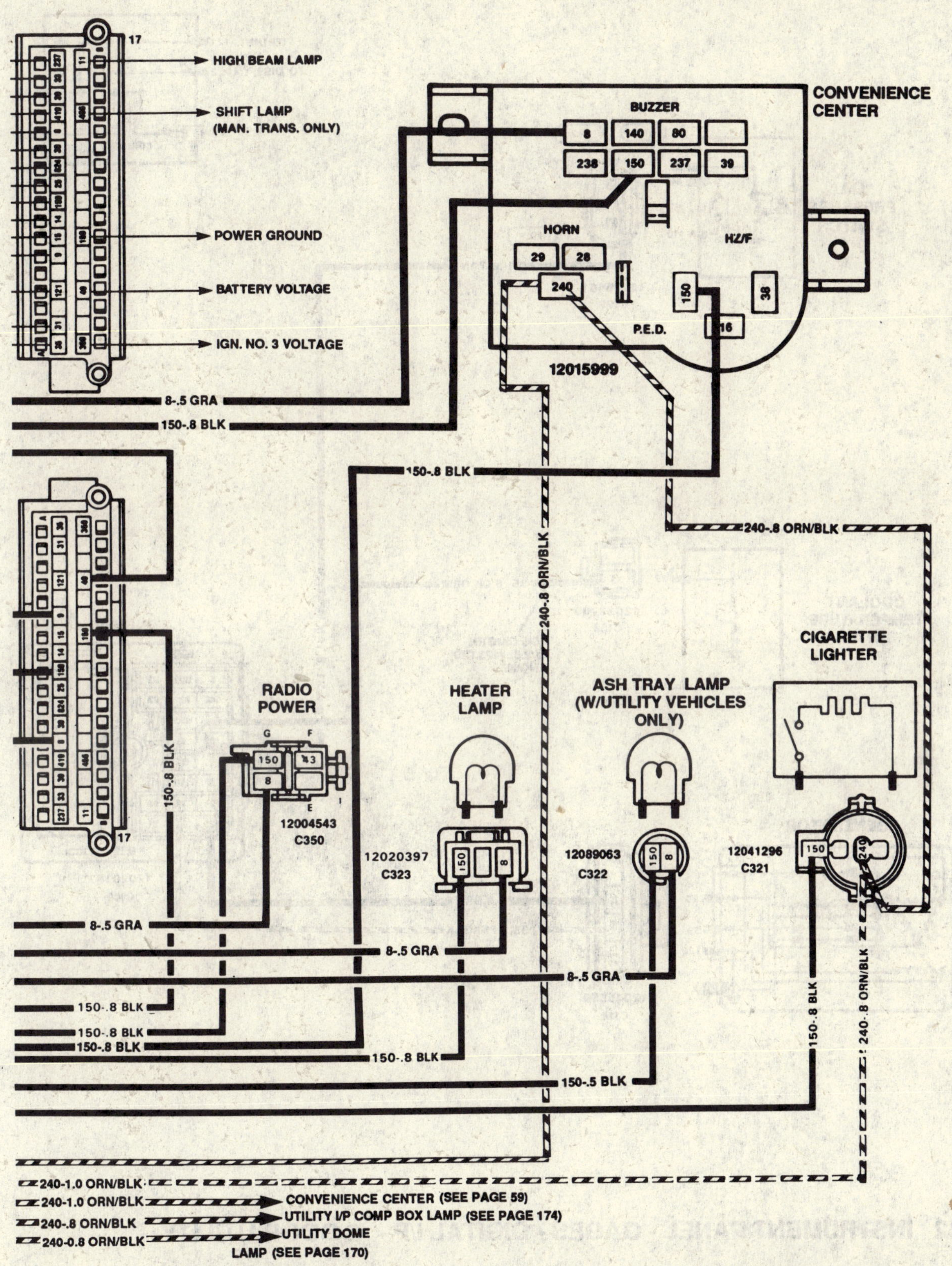

INSTRUMENT PANEL - ILLUMINATION LAMPS - DIGITAL I/P 151

1988-91

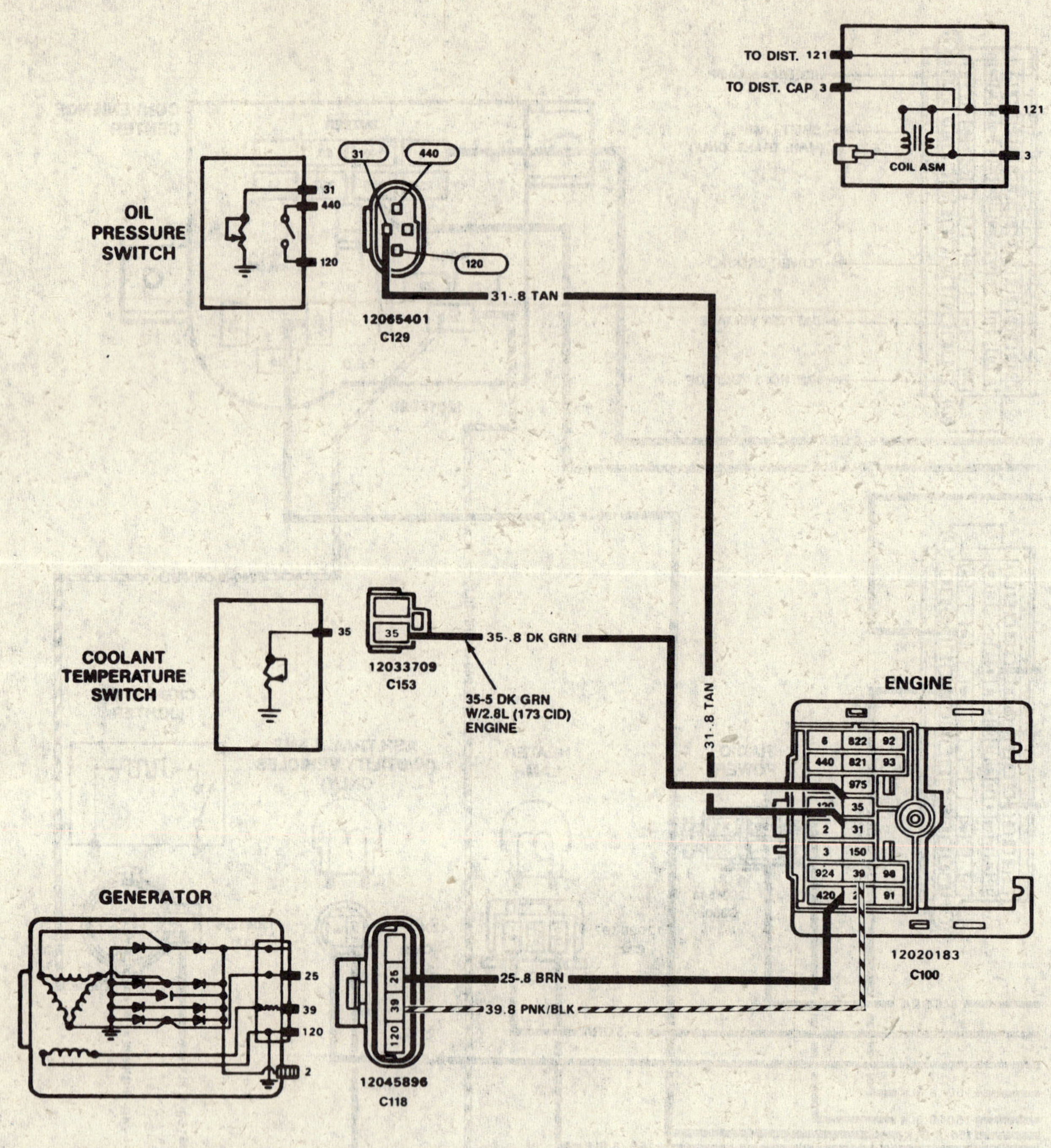

152 INSTRUMENT PANEL - GAGES - DIGITAL I/P - 2-DOOR UTILITY

1988-91

GROMMET 301
12066507
ENGINE
I/P
121-.8 WHT
121-.8 WHT
121-.8 WHT
C120
12064770
12064764
C101
HOT IN START OR RUN
IGN/GAGES
20 AMP
FRONT
12084577
FUSE BLOCK
REAR
I/P
39-.8 PNK/BLK
39-.8 PNK/BLK
31-.5 TAN
35-.5 DK GRN
25-.5 BRN
REAR BODY
12020099
C112
12020184
C100
PICKUP
30-.5 PNK
30-.8 PNK
30-.8 PNK
UTILITY

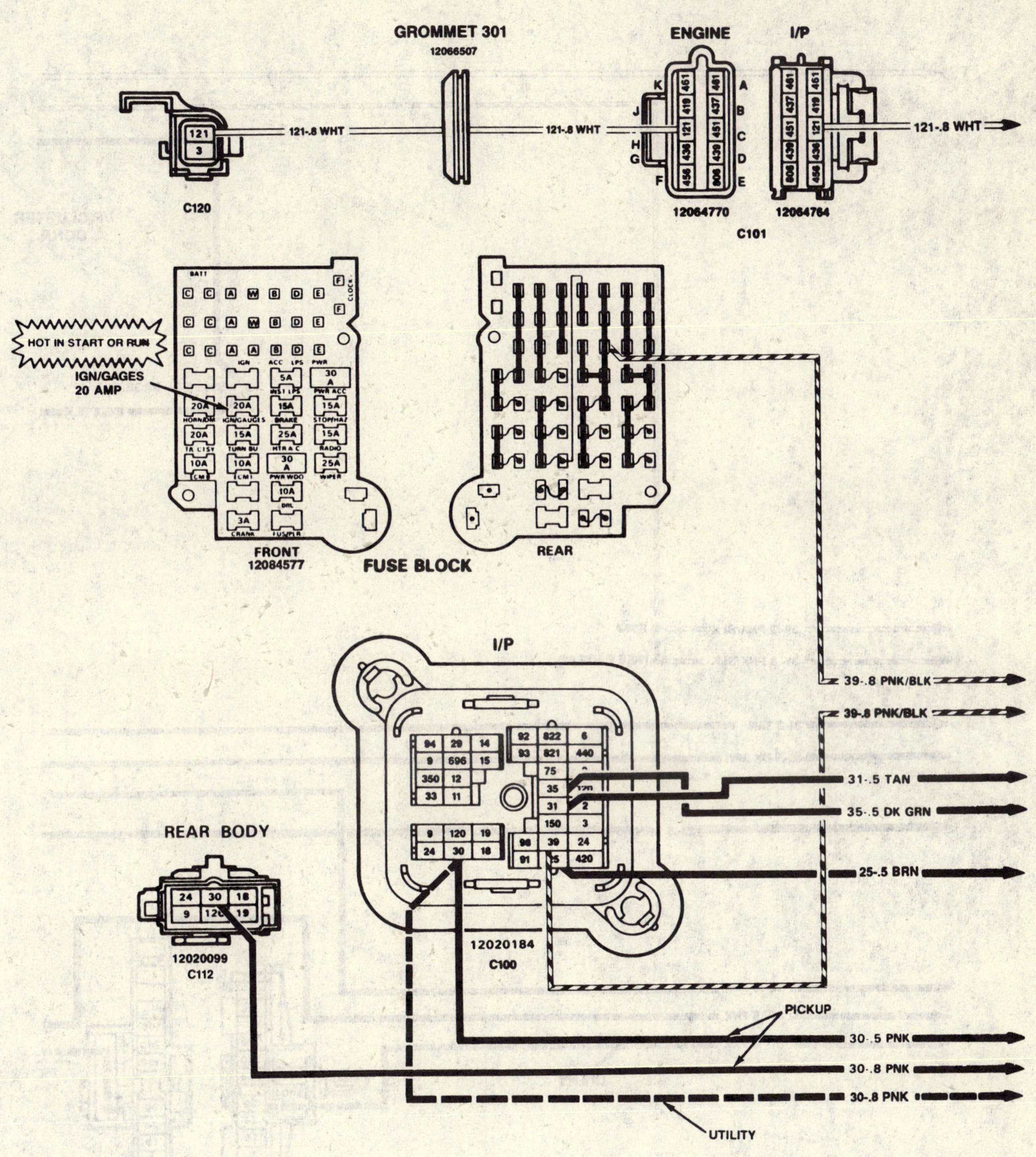

1988-91

121-.8 WHT
I/P CLUSTER
CONN
S306 (SEE PAGE 19)
150-.8 BLK
39-.8 PNK/BLK
S303
39-.8 PNK/BLK
(SEE PAGE 62)
31-.5 TAN
35-.5 DK GRN
25-.5 BRN
30-.5 PNK
30-.8 PNK
30-.8 PNK
UTILITY
120
240
156
156
240
30
24
18
9
19
120
240
156
30
24
18
9
19
12052469
C404
12034337
C404

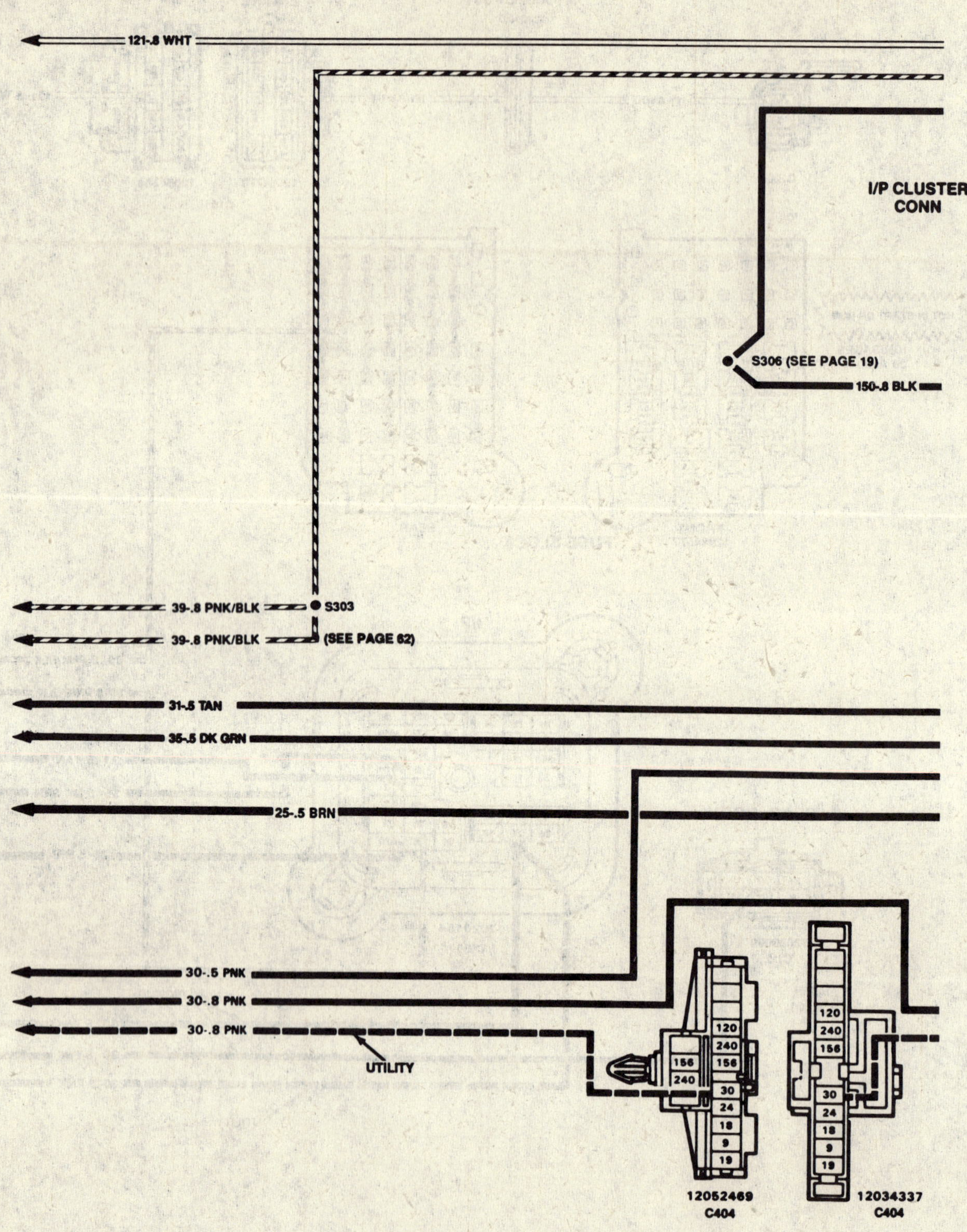

1988-91

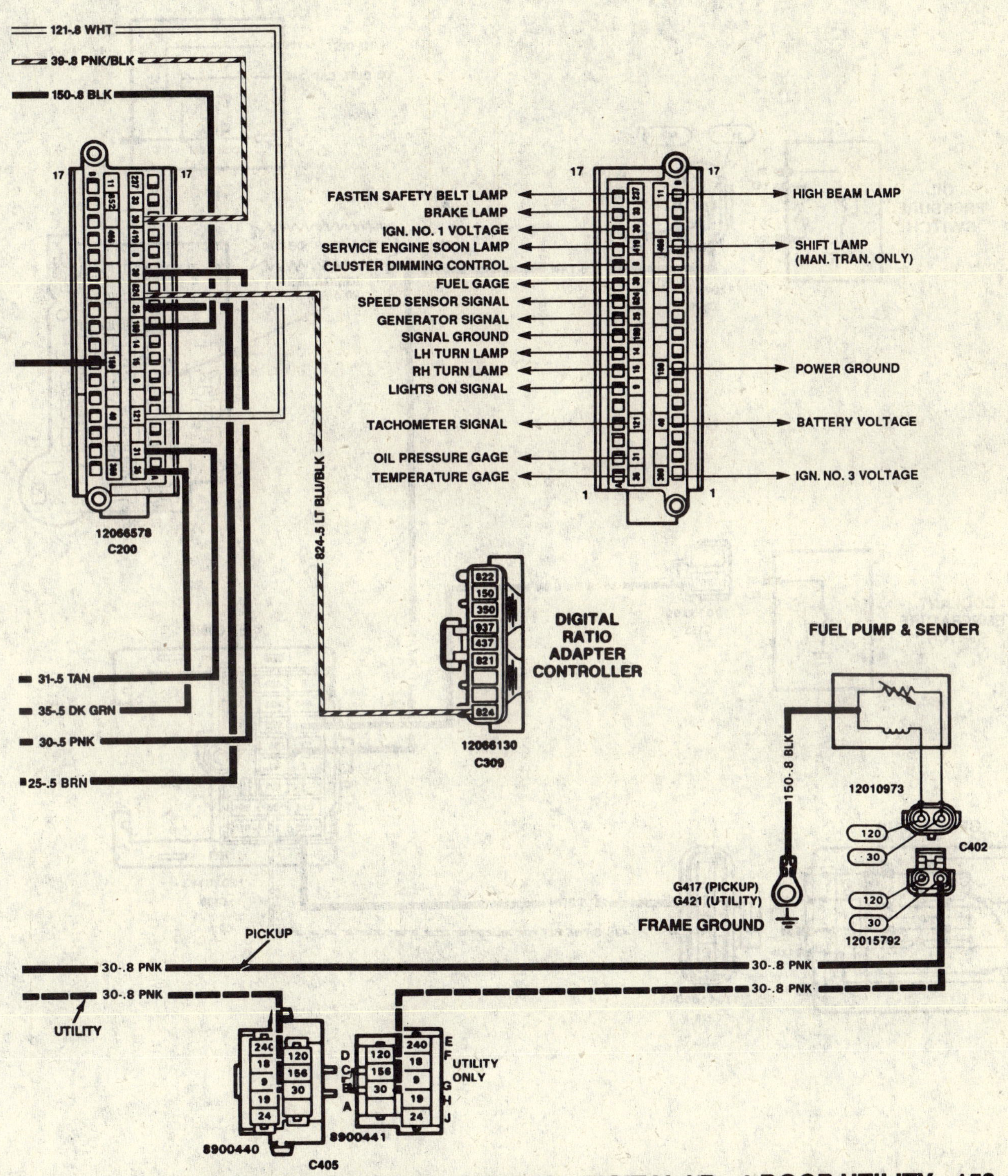

INSTRUMENT PANEL - GAGES - DIGITAL I/P - 4-DOOR UTILITY 153

1988-91

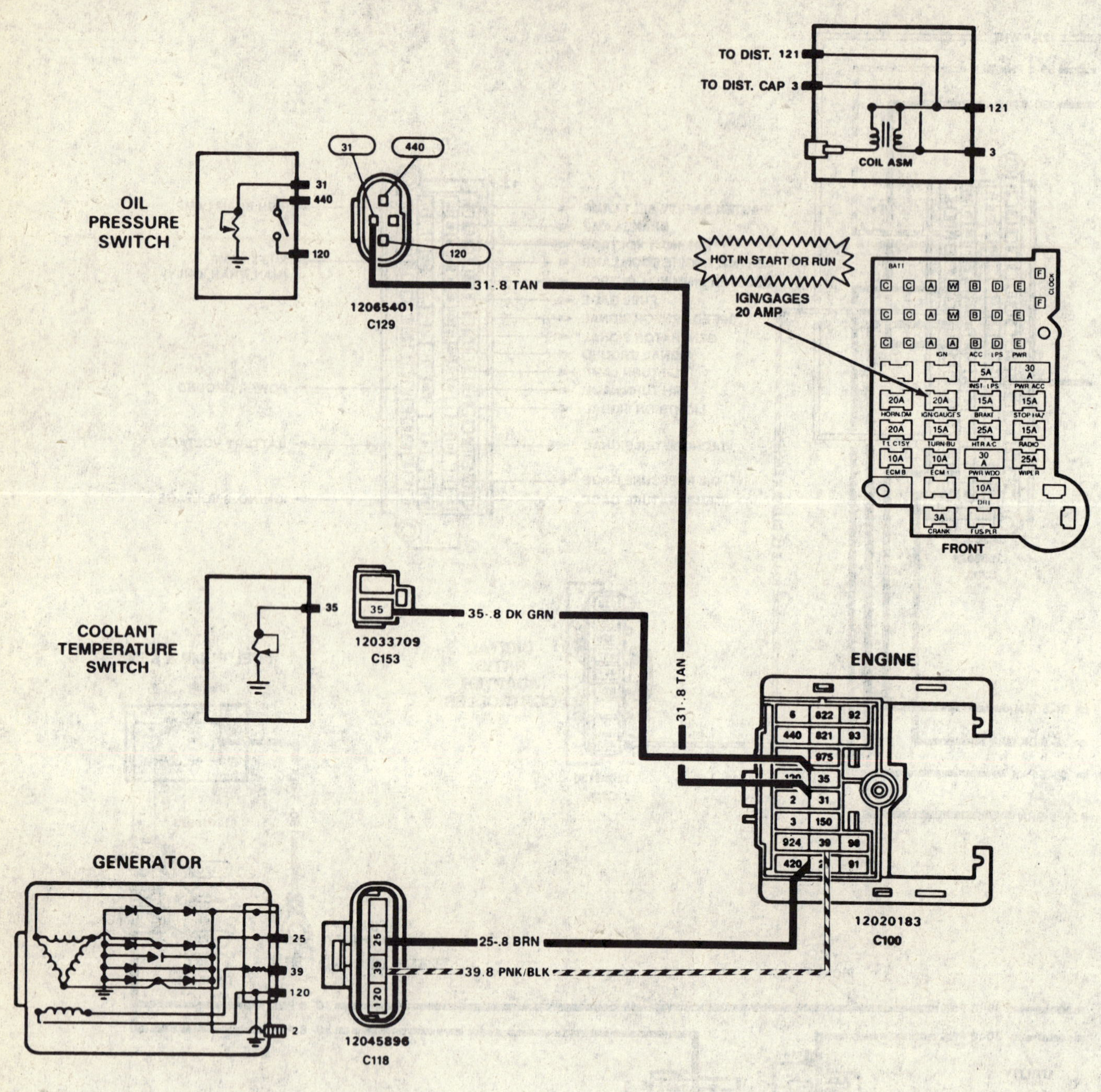

154 INSTRUMENT PANEL - GAGES - DIGITAL I/P - 4-DOOR UTILITY

1988-91

GROMMET 301
12066507
121-.8 WHT
121-.8 WHT
C120
ENGINE
I/P
12064770
12064764
C101
121-.8 WHT
08900320
12004060
FUSE BLOCK
REAR
I/P
12020184
C100
30-.8 PNK
30-.5 PNK
39-.8 PNK/BLK
39-.8 PNK/BLK
31-.5 TAN
35-.5 DK GRN
25-.5 BRN
30-.5 PNK
30-.8 PNK

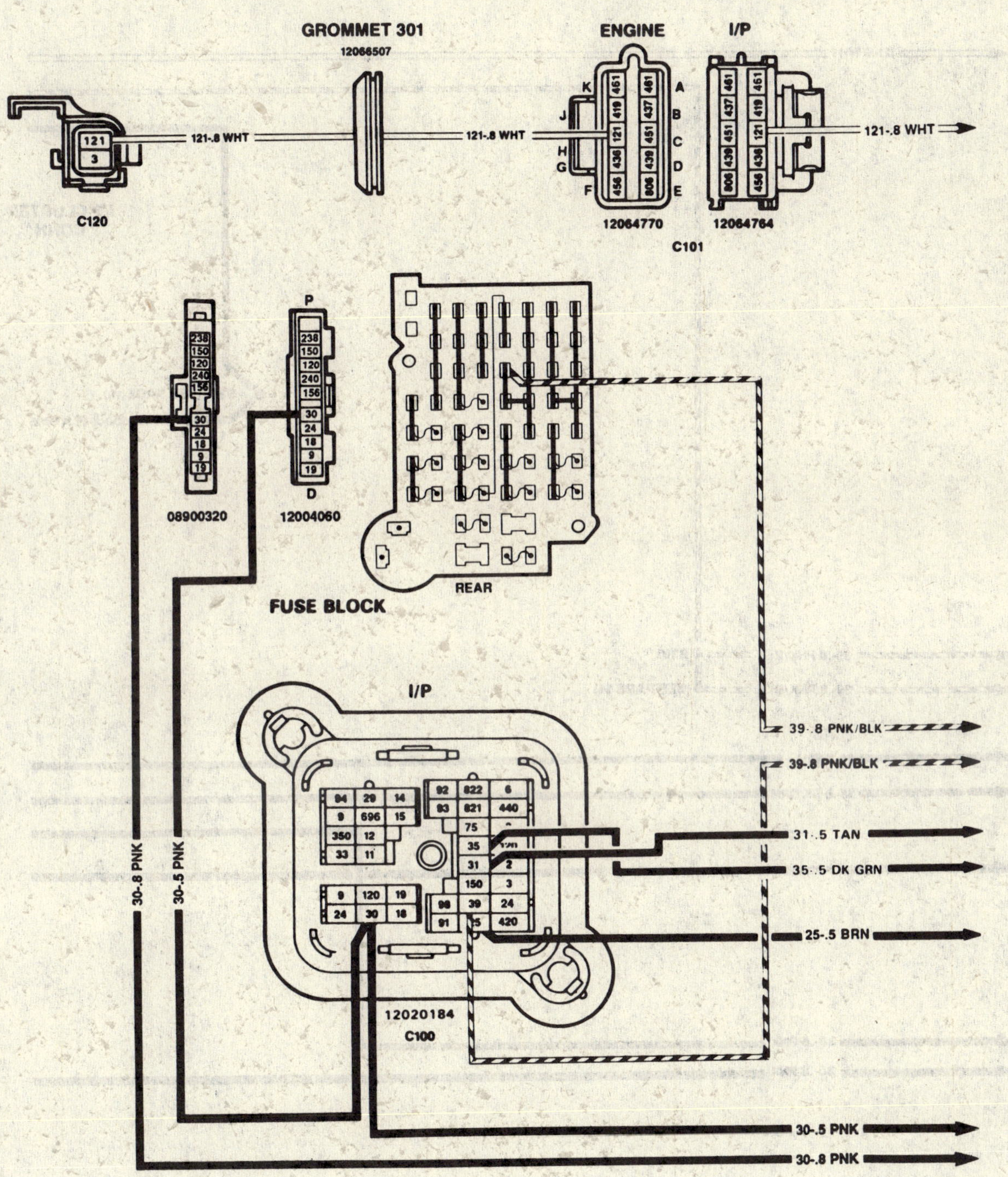

1988-91

121-.8 WHT
I/P CLUSTER CONN
S306 (SEE PAGE 19)
150-.8 BLK
39-.8 PNK/BLK
S303
39-.8 PNK/BLK
(SEE PAGE 64)
31-.5 TAN
35-.5 DK GRN
25-.5 BRN
30-.5 PNK
30-.8 PNK

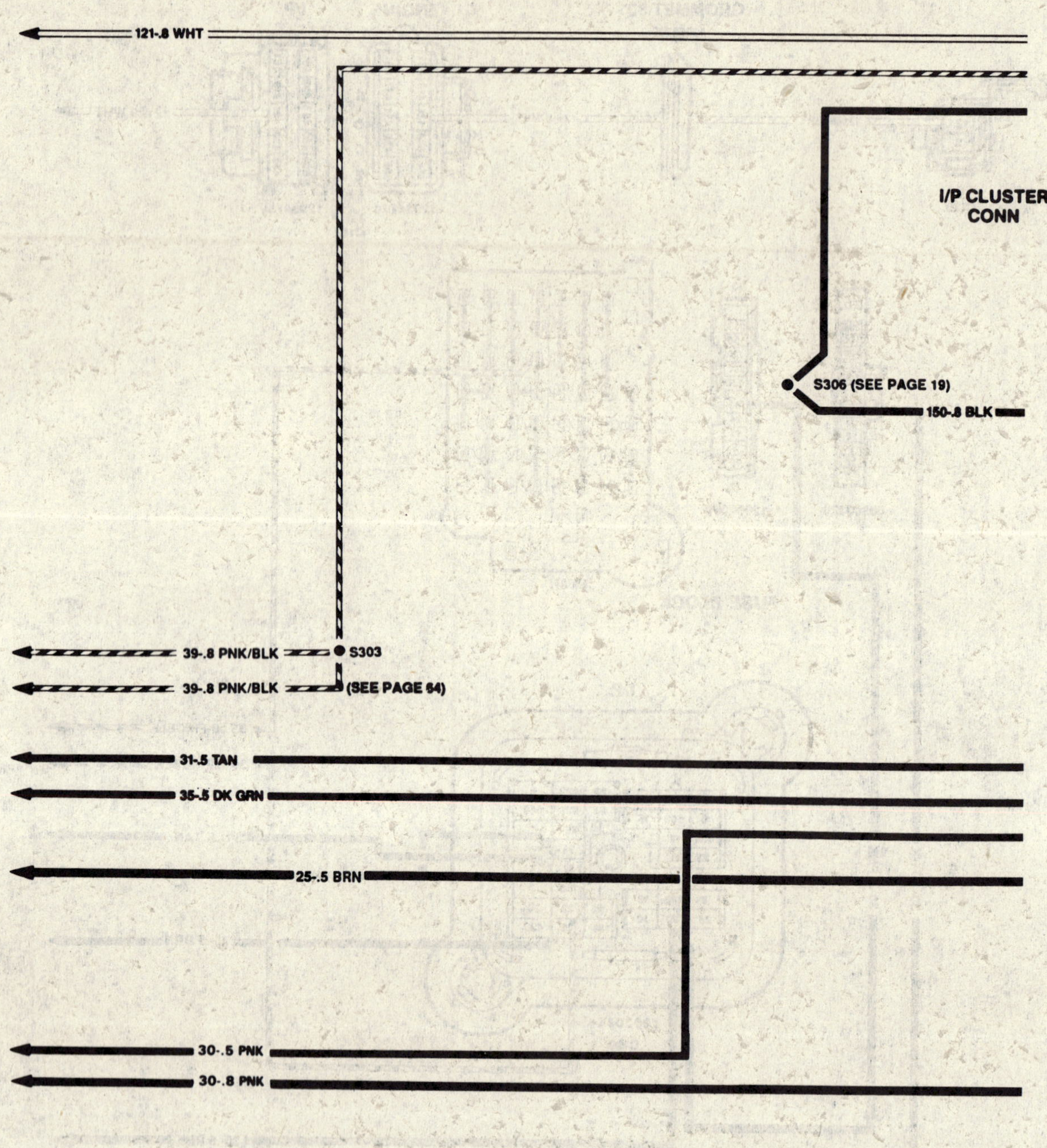

1988-91

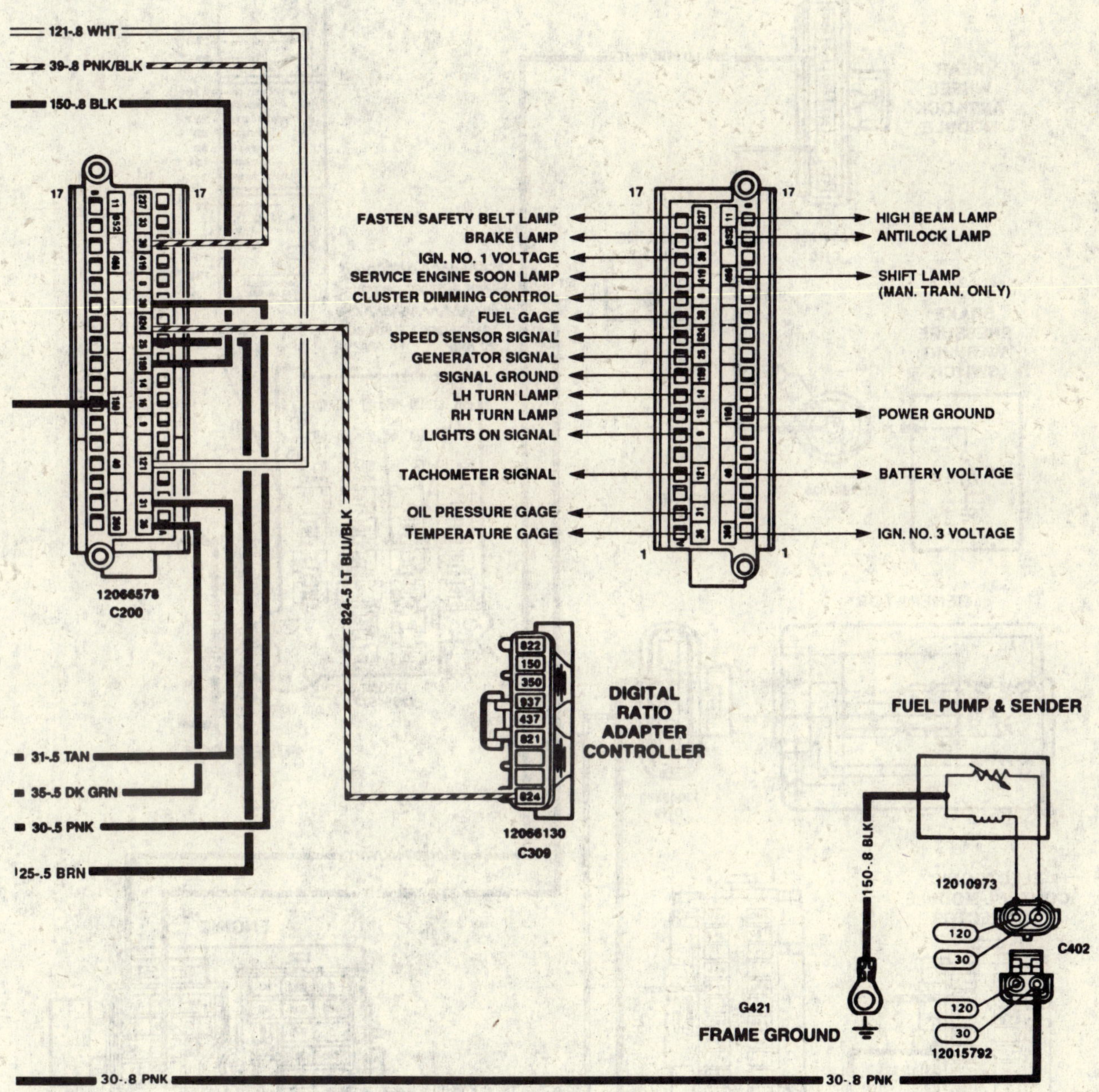

INSTRUMENT PANEL - GAGES - DIGITAL I/P - 4-DOOR UTILITY 155

1988-91

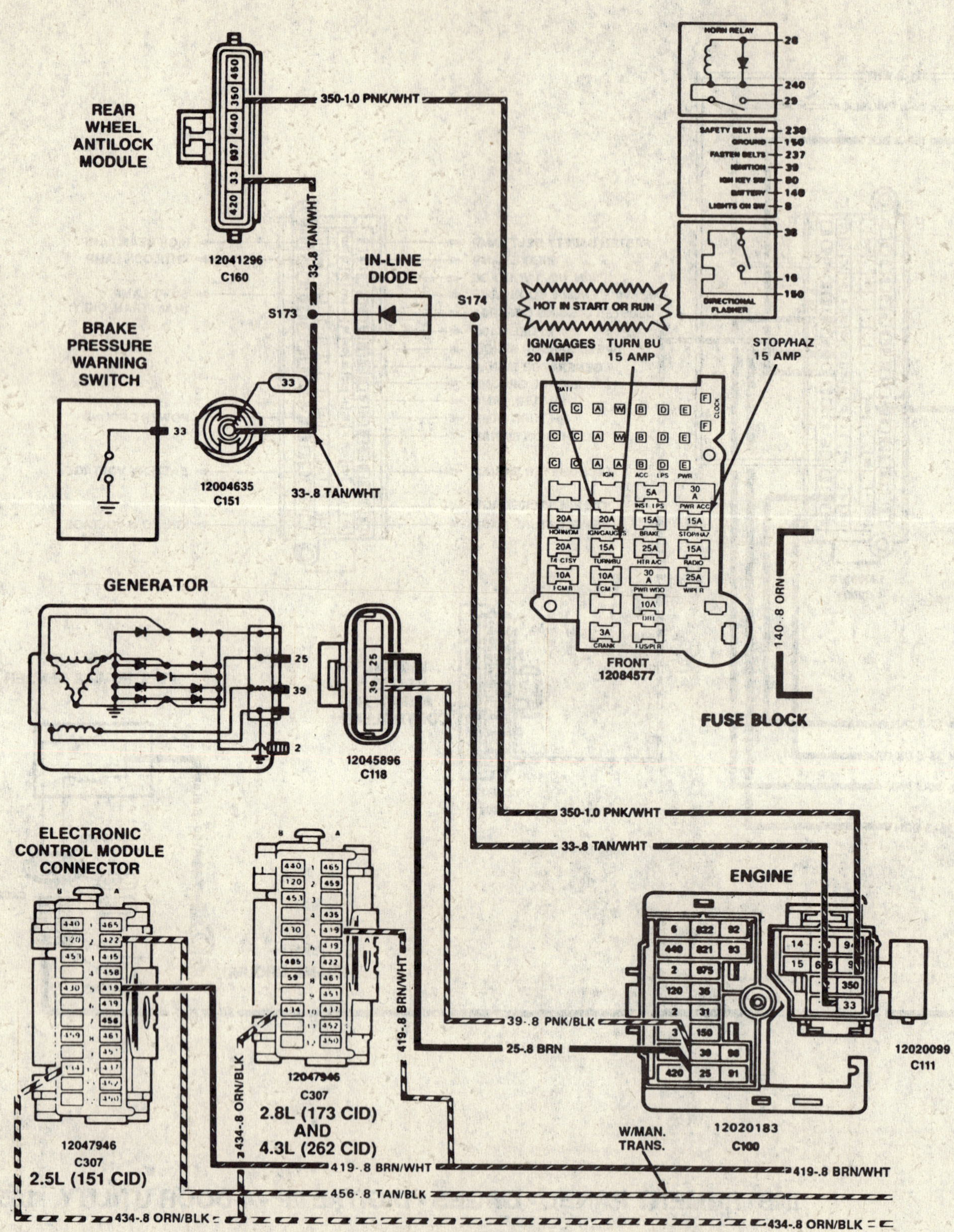

156 INSTRUMENT PANEL - INDICATOR LAMPS - DIGITAL I/P - 2-DOOR UTILITY

1988-91

CONVENIENCE CENTER
140-.8 ORN
BUZZER
39-.8 PNK/BLK
237-.5 YEL
HORN
T/S
16-.8 PPL
27-.8 BRN
12066631
(STEERING COL SWITCHES)
LEFT
RIGHT
TURN SIGNAL
HORN
KEY
NORMALLY OPEN SWITCHES
HAZARD
12004147
C305
12004148
C305
DIRECTIONAL SIGNAL SW
HOT AT ALL TIMES
38-.8 DK BLU
15-.5 DK BLU
14-.5 LT BLU
39-.8 PNK/BLK
27-.8 BRN
REAR
140-.8 ORN
14-.5 LT BLU
15-.5 DK BLU
39-.8 PNK/BLK
S303 (SEE PAGE 62)
150-.8 BLK
150-.8 BLK
237-.5 YEL
40-.8 ORN
I/P
350-.5 PNK/WHT
33-.5 TAN/WHT
11-.5 LT GRN
11-1.0 LT GRN
35-.5 DK GRN
31-.5 TAN
39-.8 PNK/BLK
25-.5 BRN
25-.5 BRN
ENGINE
I/P
419-.8 BRN/WHT
434-.8 ORN/BLK
PARK NEUTRAL SWITCH (SEE PAGE 69)
456-.8 TAN/BLK
12020184
C100
12064770
12064764
C101
W/AUTO. TRANS.

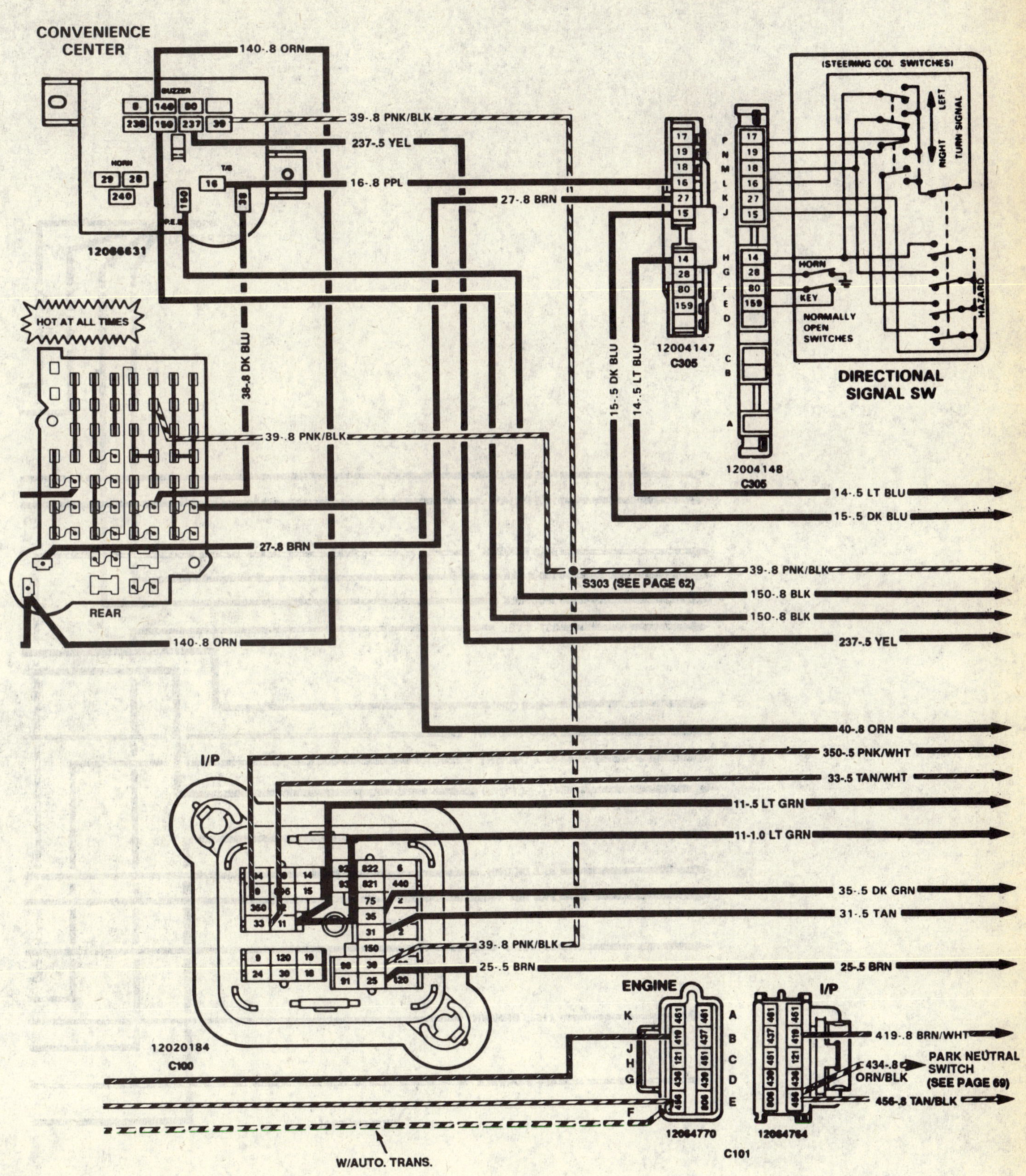

1988-91

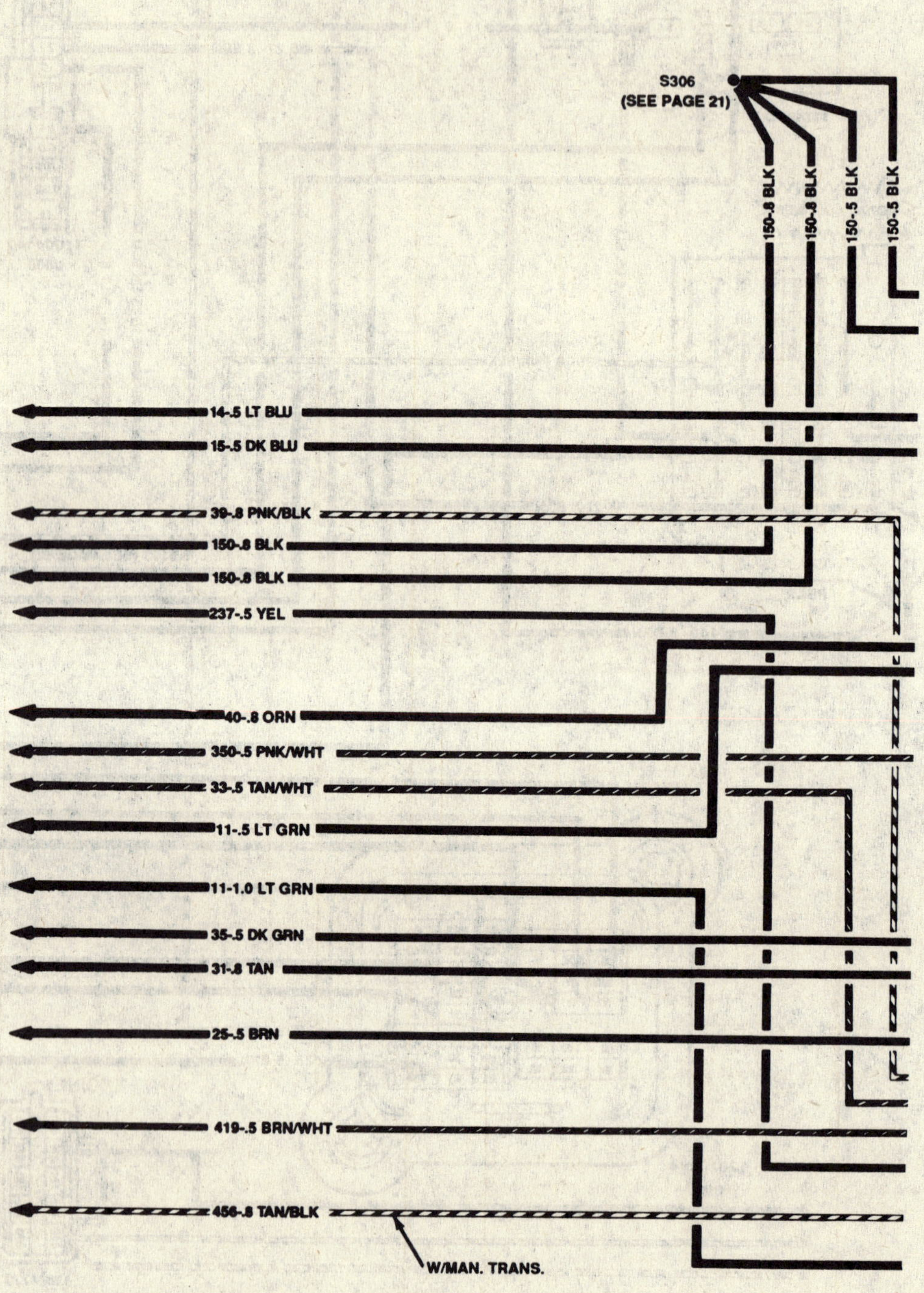

1988-91

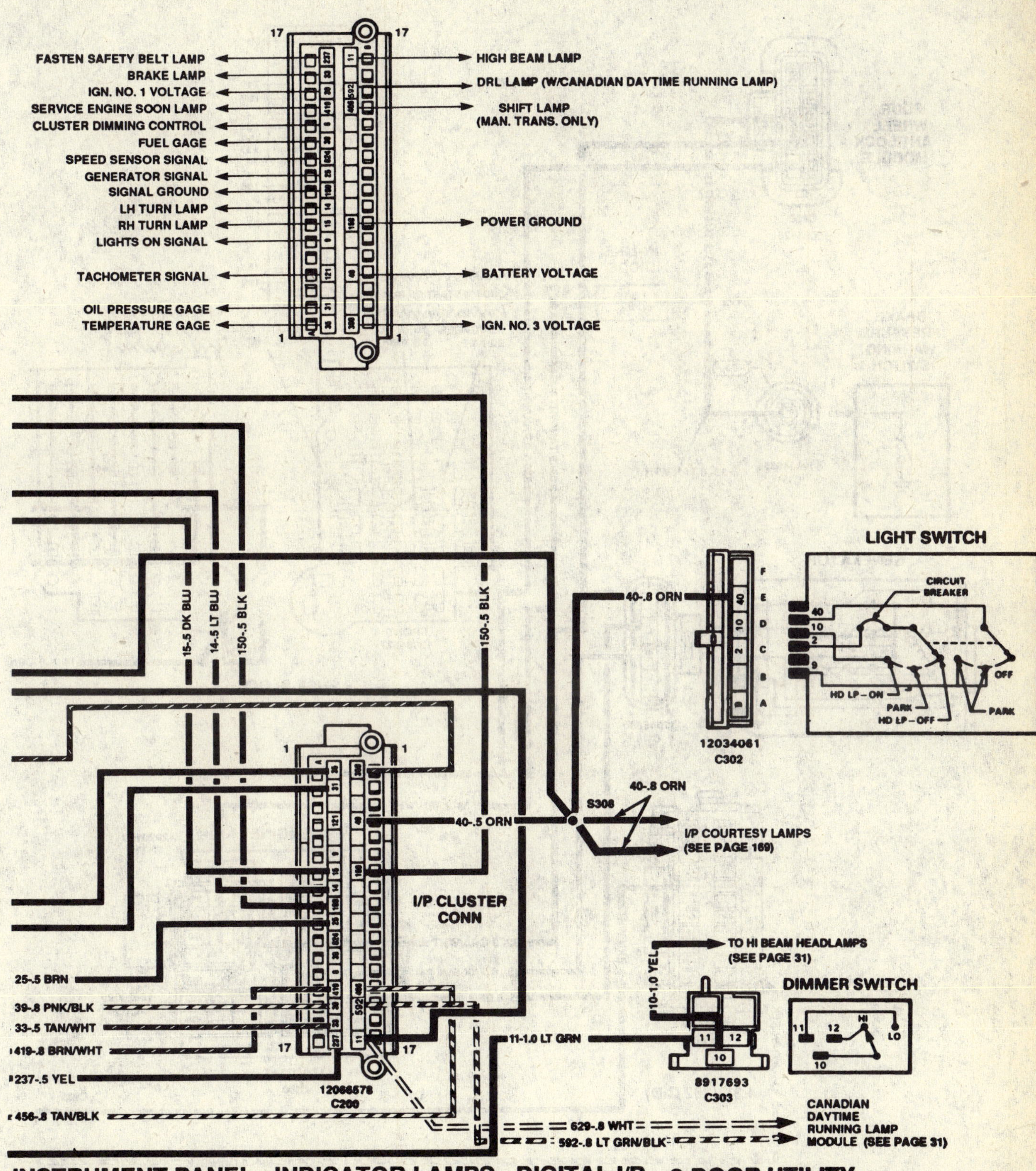

INSTRUMENT PANEL - INDICATOR LAMPS - DIGITAL I/P - 2-DOOR UTILITY

1988-91

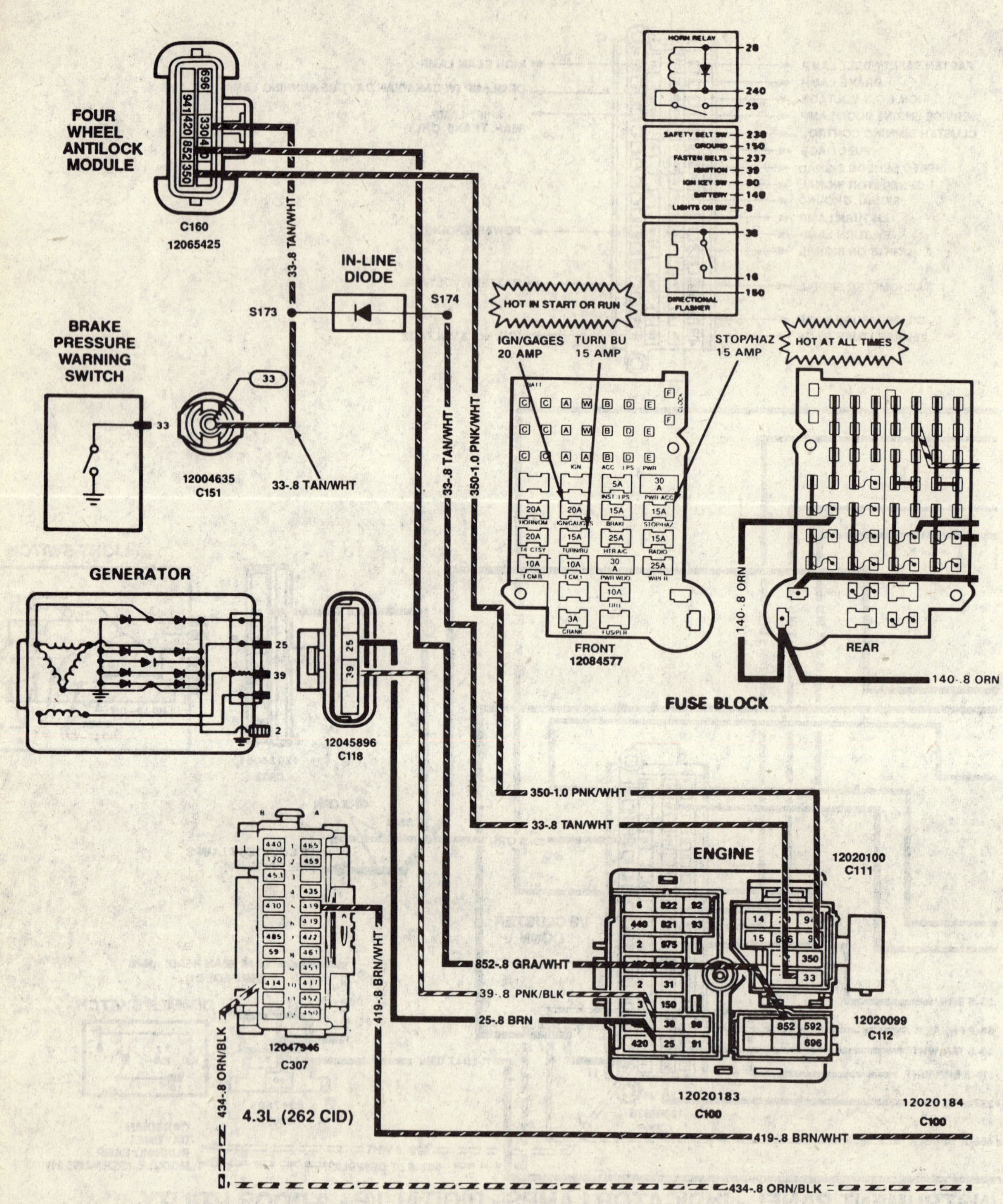

158 INSTRUMENT PANEL - INDICATOR LAMPS - DIGITAL I/P - 4- DOOR UTILITY

1988-91

CONVENIENCE CENTER
140-.8 ORN
BUZZER
HORN
T/S
12066631
39-.8 PNK/BLK
237-.5 YEL
16-.8 PPL
27-.8 BRN
(STEERING COL SWITCHES)
LEFT
RIGHT
TURN SIGNAL
HORN
KEY
NORMALLY OPEN SWITCHES
HAZARD
DIRECTIONAL SIGNAL SW
12004147
C305
12004148
C305
38-.8 DK BLU
15-.5 DK BLU
14-.5 LT BLU
14-.5 LT BLU
15-.5 DK BLU
852-.5 GRA/WHT
S303 (SEE PAGE 64)
39-.8 PNK/BLK
150-.8 BLK
150-.8 BLK
237-.5 YEL
40-.8 ORN
I/P
350-.5 PNK/WHT
33-.5 TAN/WHT
11-.5 LT GRN
11-1.0 LT GRN
35-.5 DK GRN
31-.5 TAN
39-.8 PNK/BLK
25-.5 BRN
25-.5 BRN
ENGINE
I/P
419-.8 BRN/WHT
434-.8 ORN/BLK
PARK NEUTRAL SWITCH (SEE PAGE 69)
456-.8 TAN/BLK
12064770
12064764
C101
W/AUTO. TRANS.

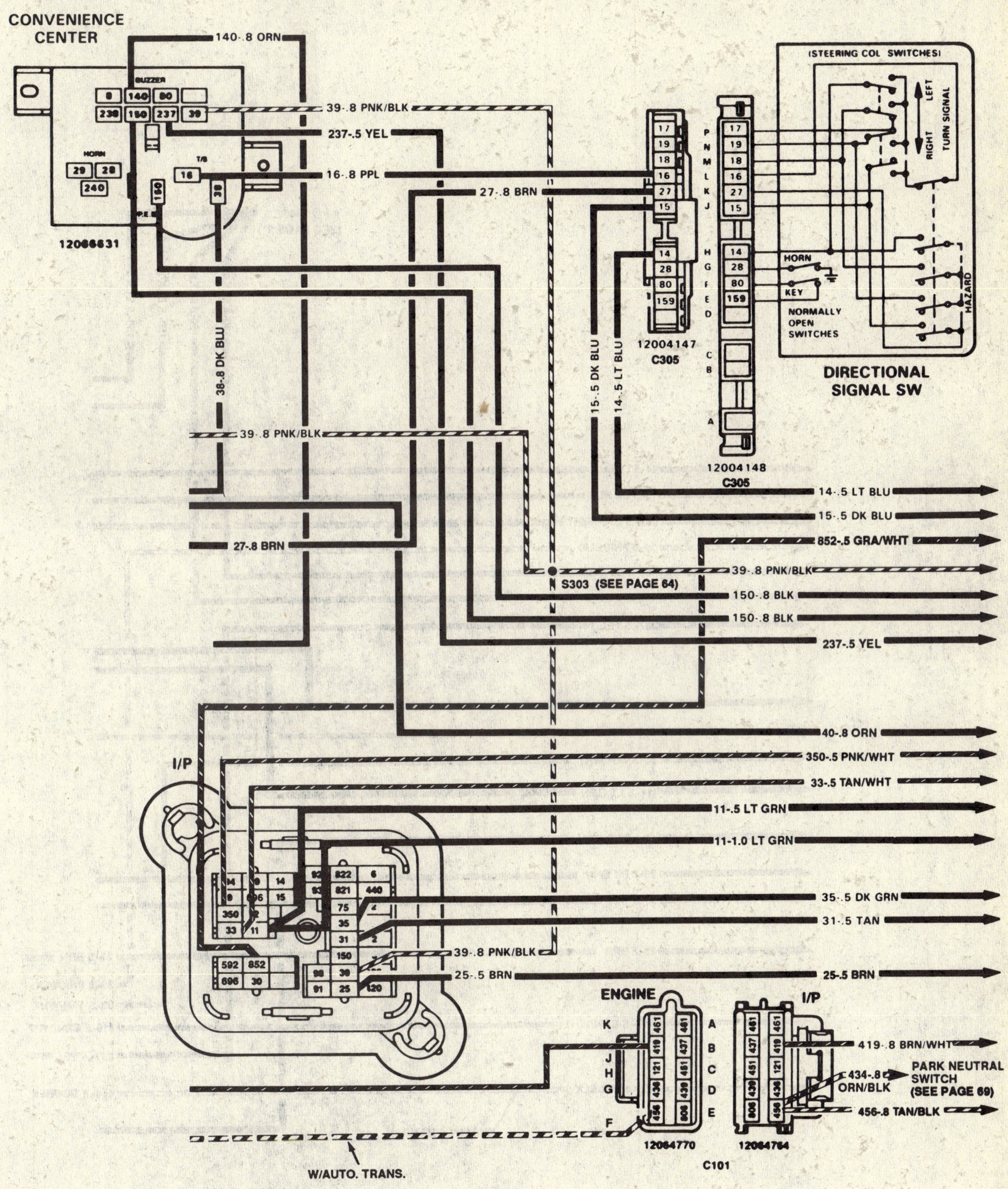

1988-91

S306
(SEE PAGE 21)
150-.8 BLK
150-.8 BLK
150-.5 BLK
150-.5 BLK
14-.5 LT BLU
15-.5 DK BLU
852-.5 GRA/WHT
39-.8 PNK/BLK
150-.8 BLK
150-.8 BLK
237-.5 YEL
40-.8 ORN
350-.5 PNK/WHT
33-.5 TAN/WHT
11-.5 LT GRN
11-1.0 LT GRN
35-.5 DK GRN
31-.8 TAN
25-.5 BRN
25-.5 BRN
39-.8 PNK/BLK
33-.5 TAN/WHT
419-.5 BRN/WHT
419-.8 BRN/WHT
237-.5 YEL
456-.8 TAN/BLK
456-.8 TAN/BLK
W/MAN. TRANS.

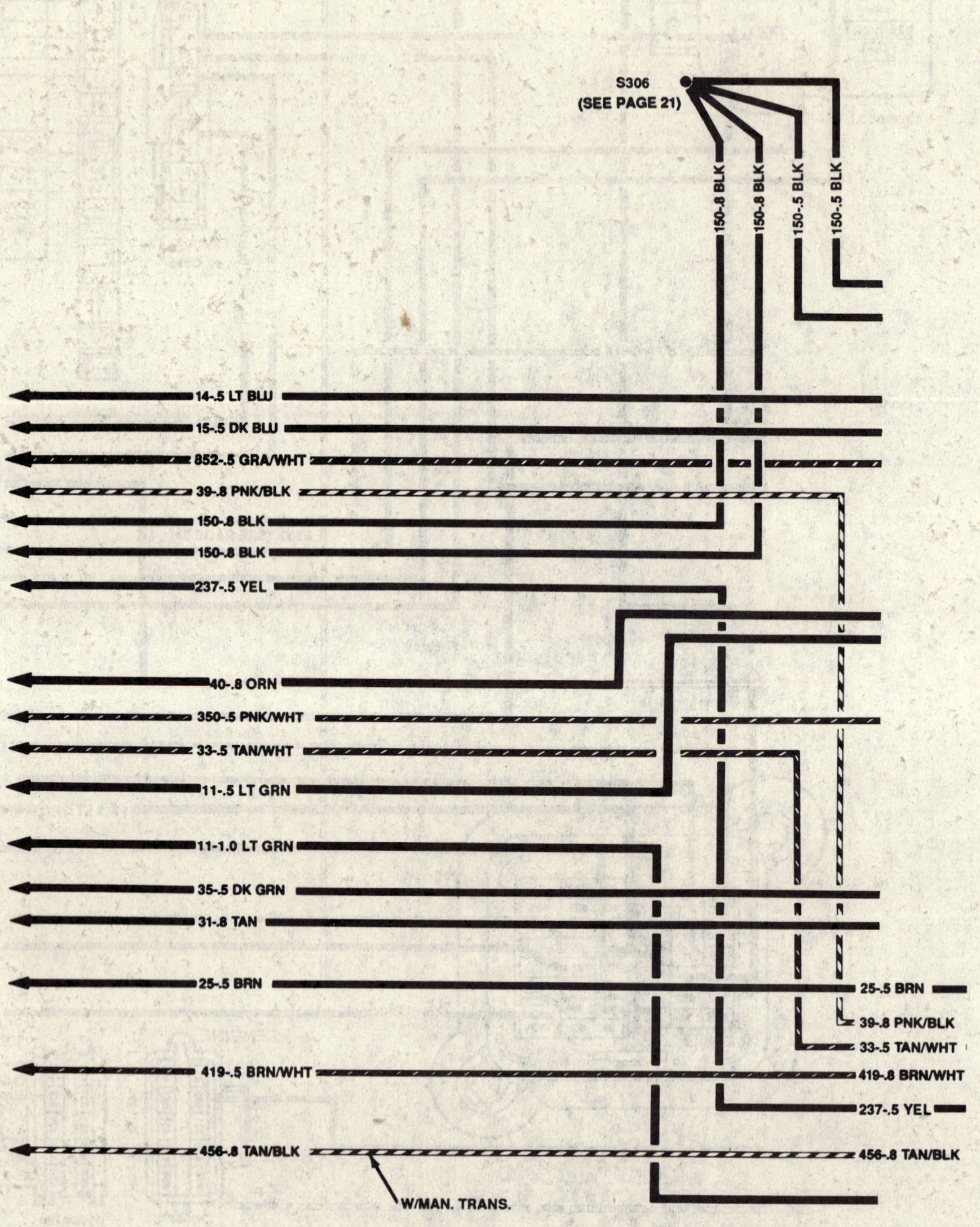

1988-91

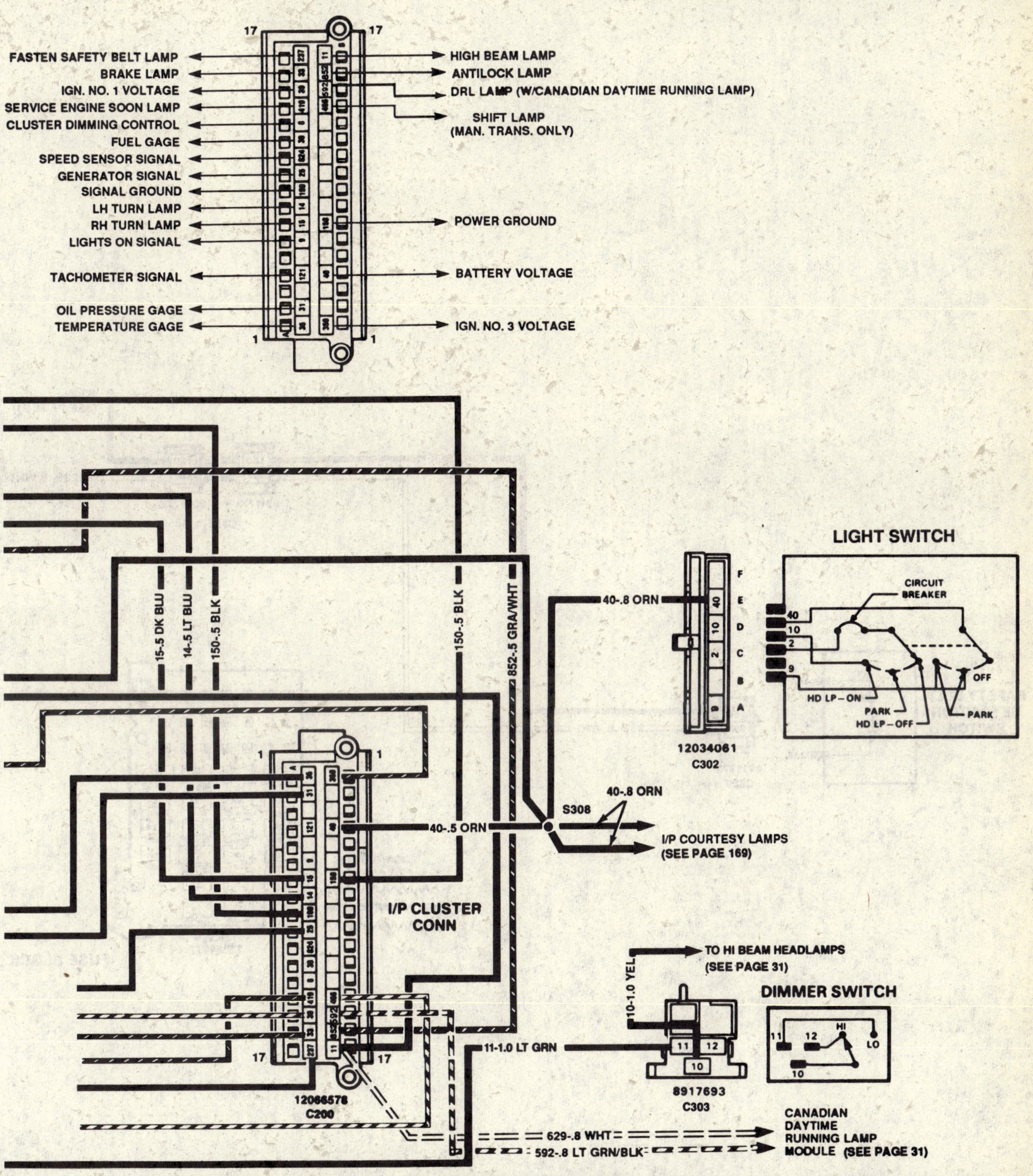

INSTRUMENT PANEL - INDICATOR LAMPS - DIGITAL I/P - 4-DOOR UTILITY 159

1988-91

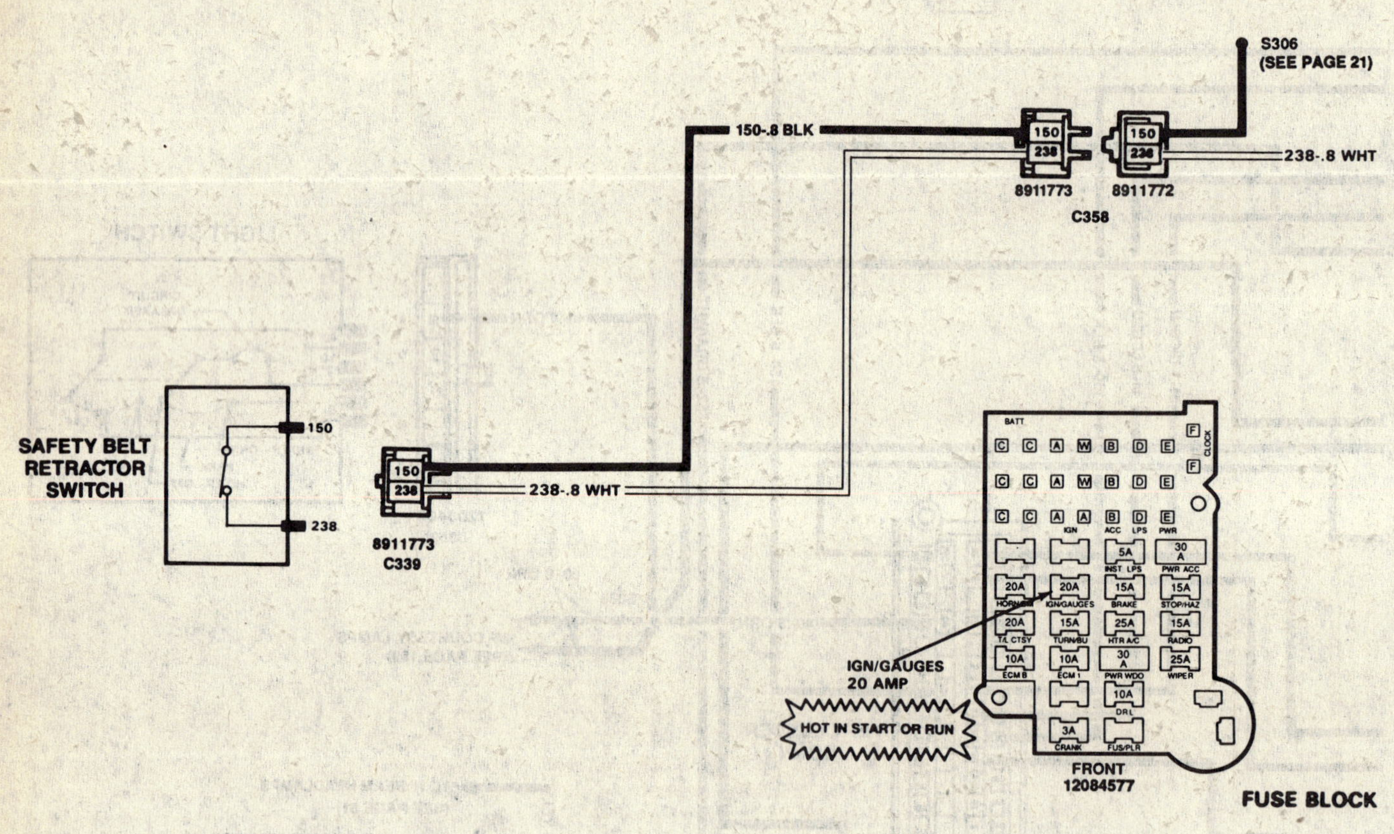

1988-91

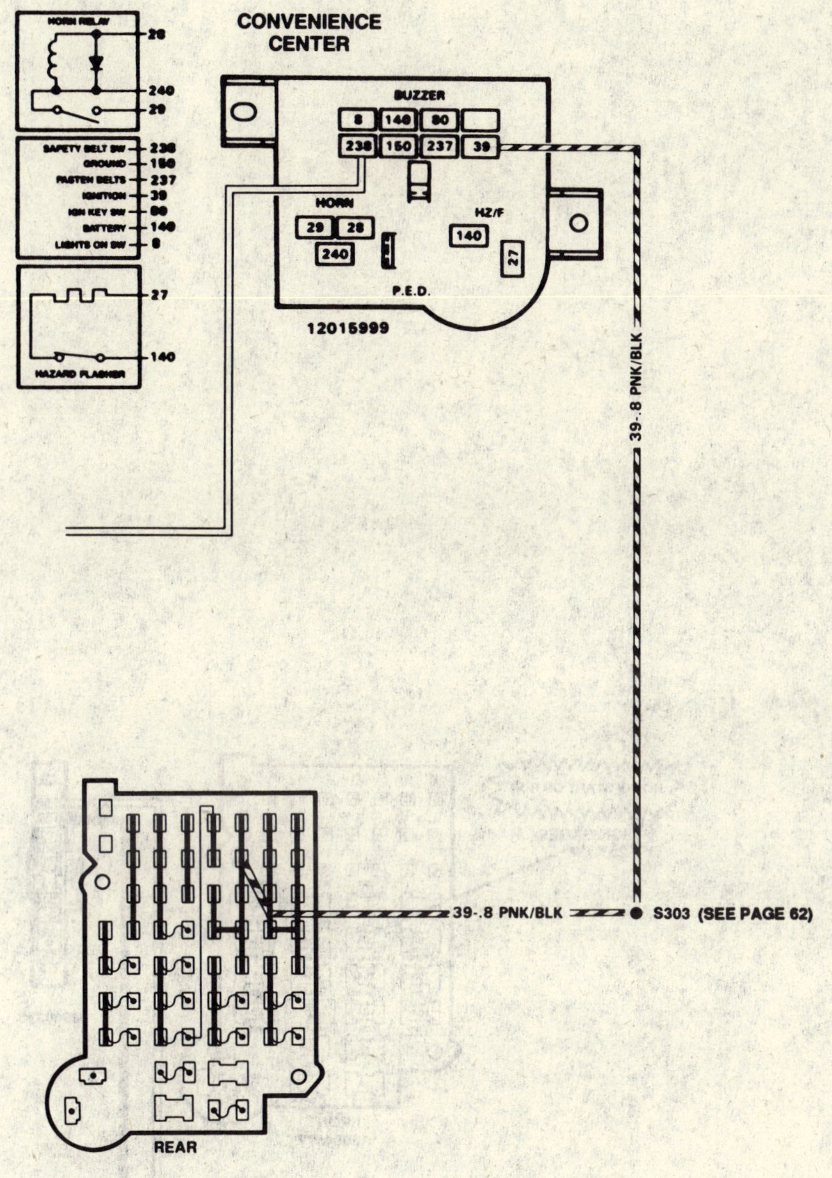

SAFETY BELT WARNING BUZZER - 2-DOOR UTILITY 163

1988-91

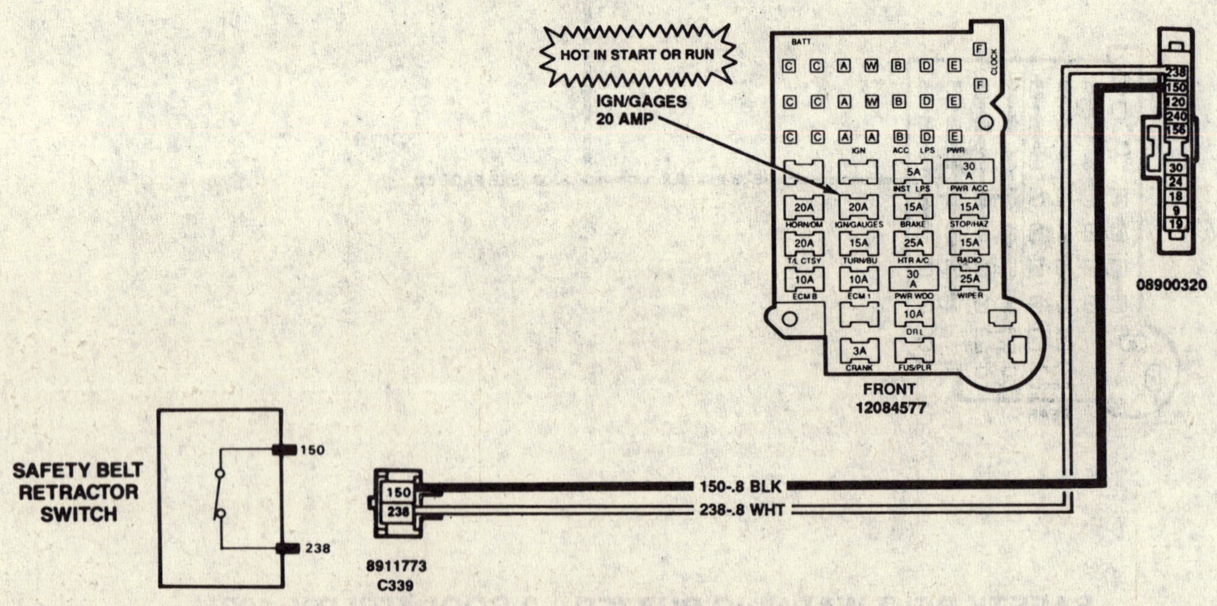

164 SAFETY BELT WARNING BUZZER - 4-DOOR UTILITY

1988-91

CONVENIENCE CENTER
HORN RELAY
28
240
29
SAFETY BELT SW — 238
GROUND — 150
FASTEN BELTS — 237
IGNITION — 39
IGN KEY SW — 80
BATTERY — 140
LIGHTS ON SW — 8
27
140
HAZARD FLASHER
BUZZER
8
140
80
238
150
237
39
HORN
29
28
240
HZ/F
140
27
P.E.D.
12015999
S306
(SEE PAGE 21)
238-.8 WHT
39-.8 PNK/BLK
P
238
150
120
240
156
30
24
18
9
19
D
12004060
C442
39-.8 PNK/BLK
S383 (SEE PAGE 64)
REAR
FUSE BLOCK

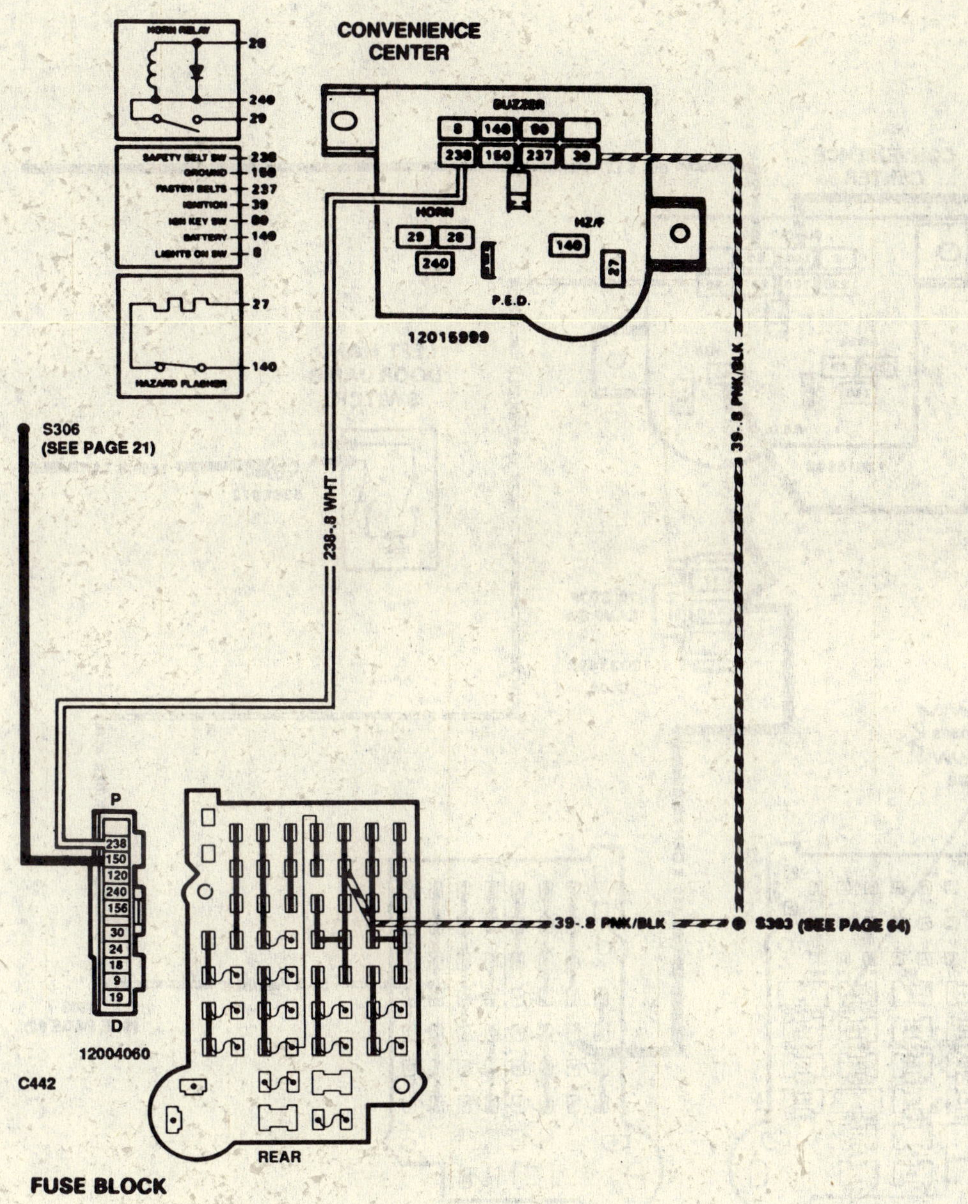

1988-91

CONVENIENCE
CENTER
80-.5 LT GRN
BUZZER
8
140
80
238
150
237
39
HORN
29
28
240
HZ/F
140
27
P.E.D.
12015999
140-.8 ORN
140-.8 ORN
39-.8 PNK/BLK
LEFT HAND
DOOR JAMB
SWITCH
156
159
159-.8 TAN
6288872
17
140
TO STOP
LAMP SW
12033699
C304
HOT AT ALL TIMES
STOP/HAZ
15 AMP
140-.8 ORN
39-.8 PNK/BLK
39-.8 PNK/BLK
S303
(SEE PAGE 62)
IGN/GAGES
20 AMP
HOT IN START OR RUN
FRONT
12084577
FUSE BLOCK
REAR

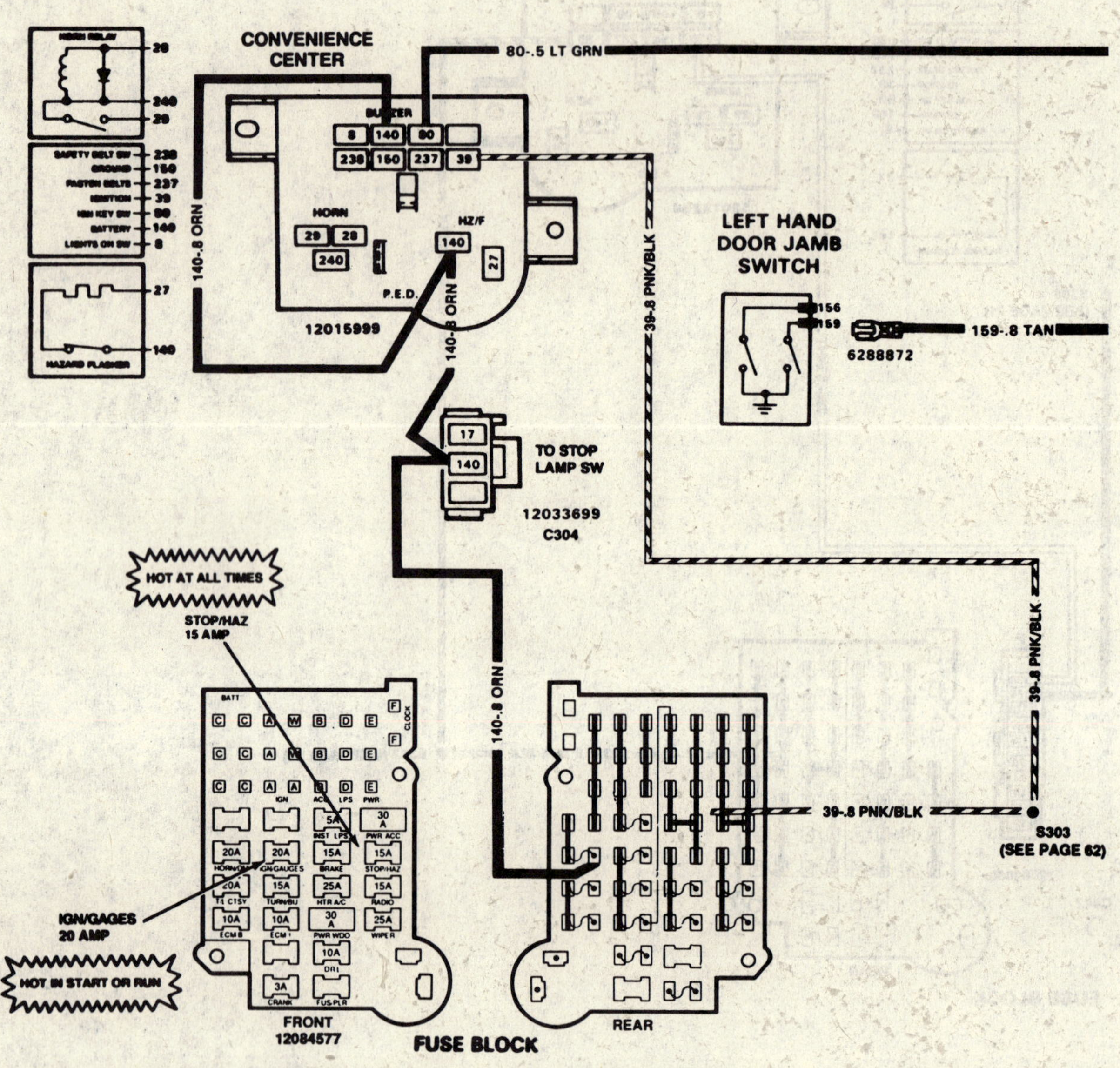

1988-91

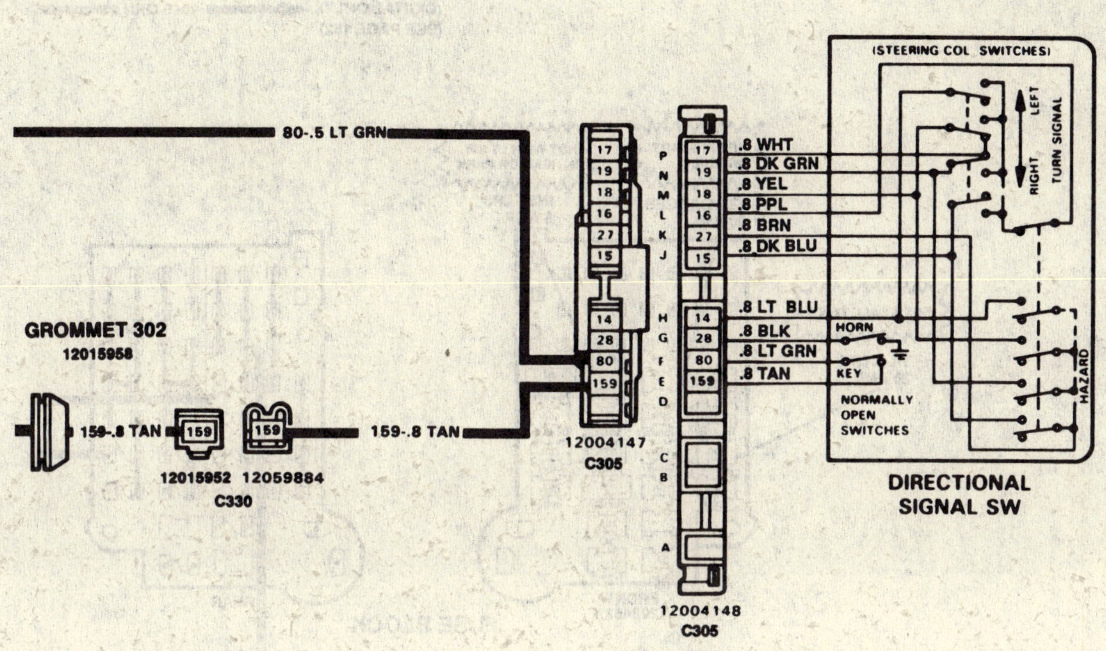

KEY-IN WARNING BUZZER 165

1988-91

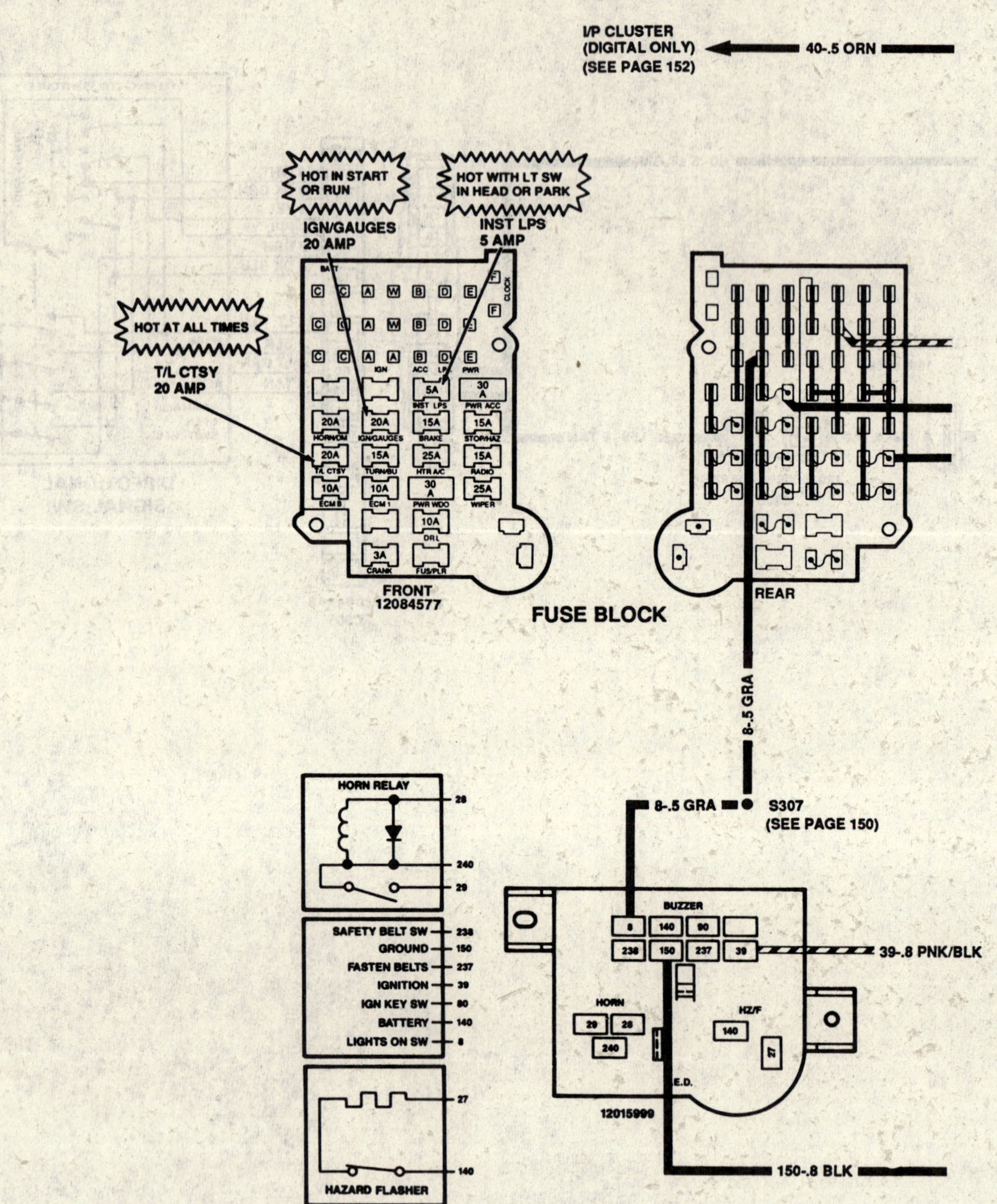

166 LAMPS-ON WARNING BUZZER

1988-91

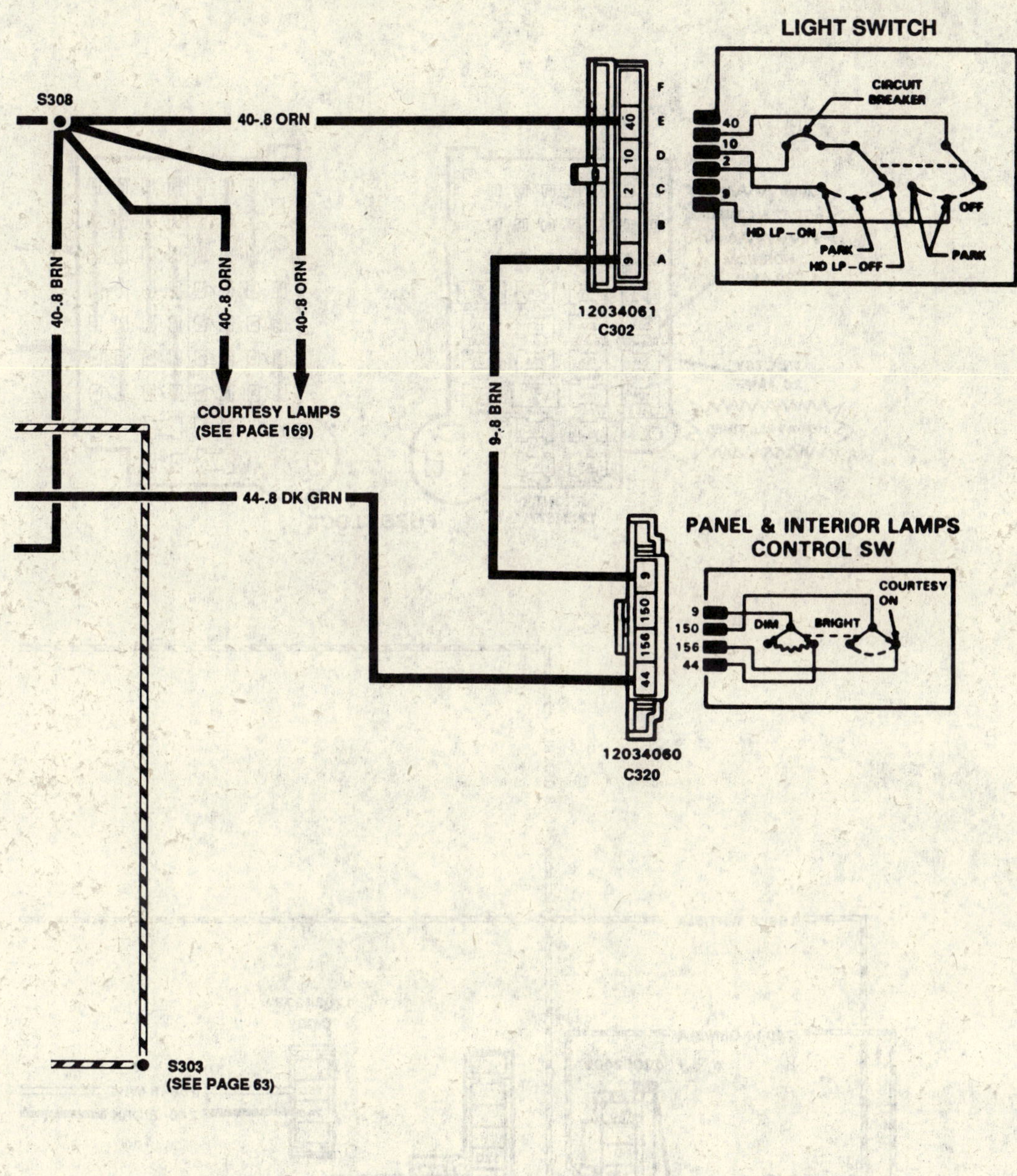

LIGHT SWITCH
S308
40-.8 ORN
F
E
D
C
B
A
40
10
2
9
CIRCUIT BREAKER
OFF
HD LP—ON
PARK
HD LP—OFF
PARK
40-.8 BRN
40-.8 ORN
40-.8 ORN
12034061
C302
9-.8 BRN
COURTESY LAMPS
(SEE PAGE 169)
44-.8 DK GRN
PANEL & INTERIOR LAMPS
CONTROL SW
COURTESY ON
DIM
BRIGHT
150
156
44
12034060
C320
S303
(SEE PAGE 63)
FROM S306
(SEE PAGE 21)

1988-91

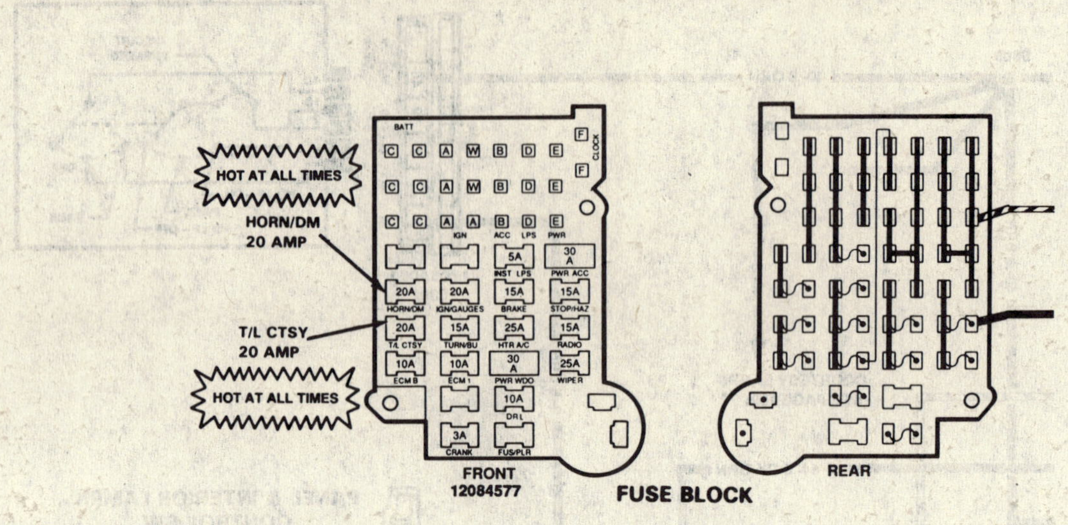

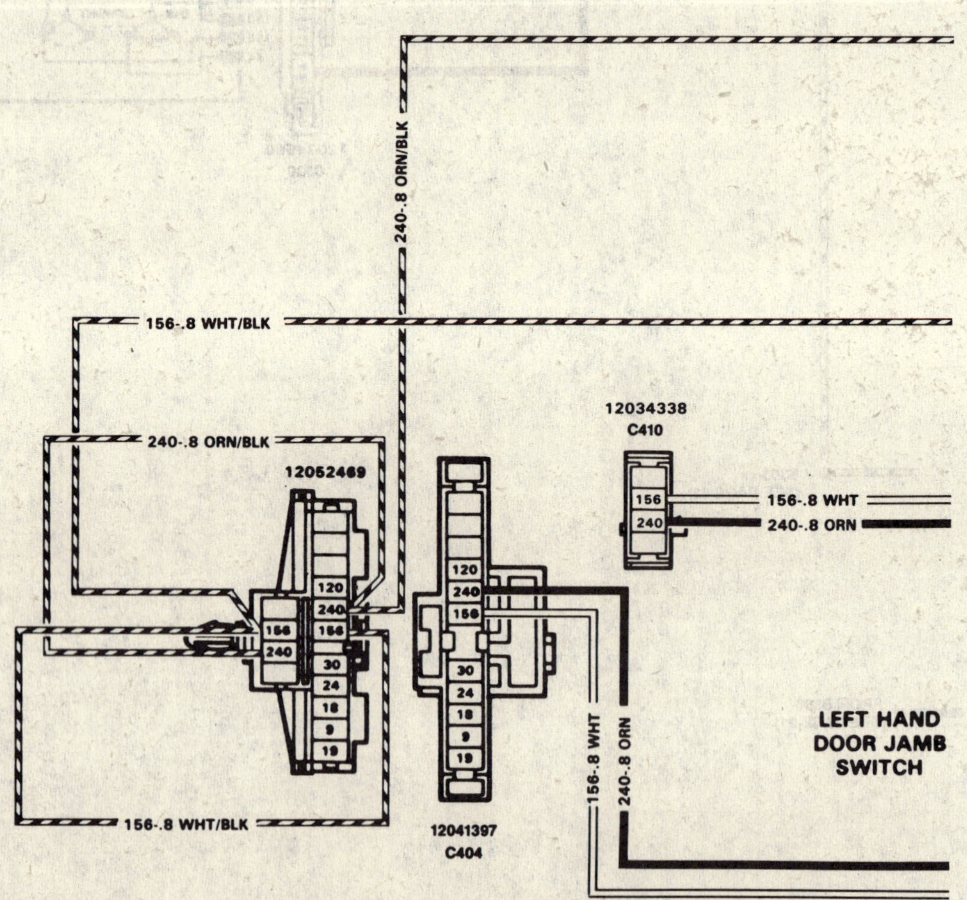

170 DOME AND COURTESY LAMPS - 2-DOOR UTILITY - W/O POWER WINDOWS AND DOOR LOCKS

1988-91

RIGHT HAND
DOOR JAMB
SWITCH
156
6288872
156-.8 WHT
GROMMET 303
12015958
C334
W/POWER WINDOWS AND DOOR LOCKS
(SEE PAGE 184)
156
12047682
156
12047683
C326
156-.8 WHT
40-.8 ORN
240-.8 ORN/BLK
240-.8 ORN/BLK
LIGHTER
(SEE PAGE 150)
S302
240-1.0 ORN/BLK
CONV CENTER
(SEE PAGE 59)
240-.8 ORN/BLK
I/P COMPT BOX LP
(SEE PAGE 174)
156-.8 WHT/BLK
12048498
DOME
LAMP
KEY-IN WARNING BUZZER
(SEE PAGE 165)
159-.8 TAN
C330
12065652
12059884
159-.8 TAN
159
159
159-.8 TAN
156-.8 WHT
159
156
6288872
156-.8 WHT
156
156
156-.8 WHT
C333
W/POWER WINDOWS
AND DOOR LOCKS
(SEE PAGE 184)
12047683
12047682
C327
GROMMET 302
12015958
240-.8 ORN
156-.8 WHT

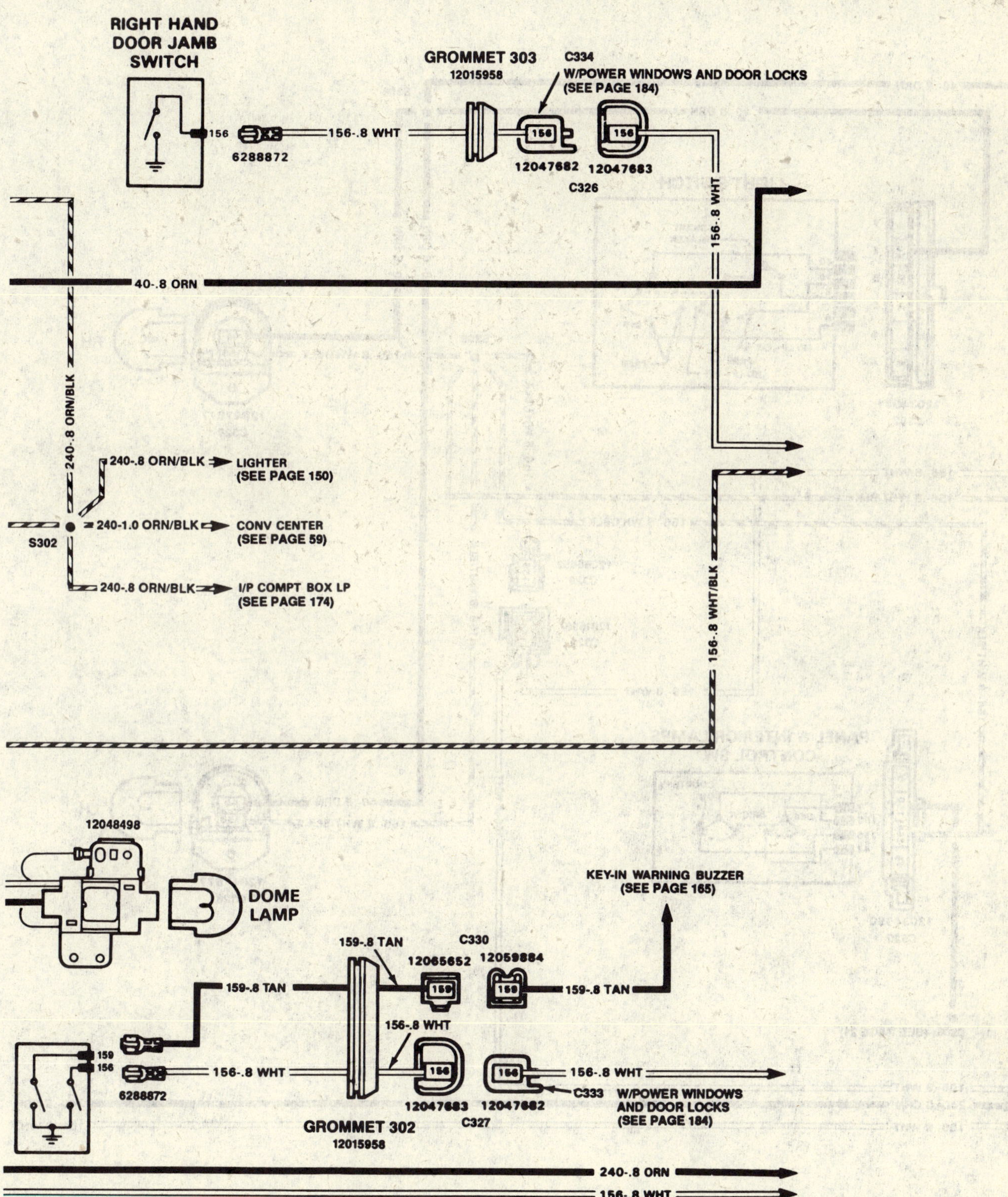

1988-91

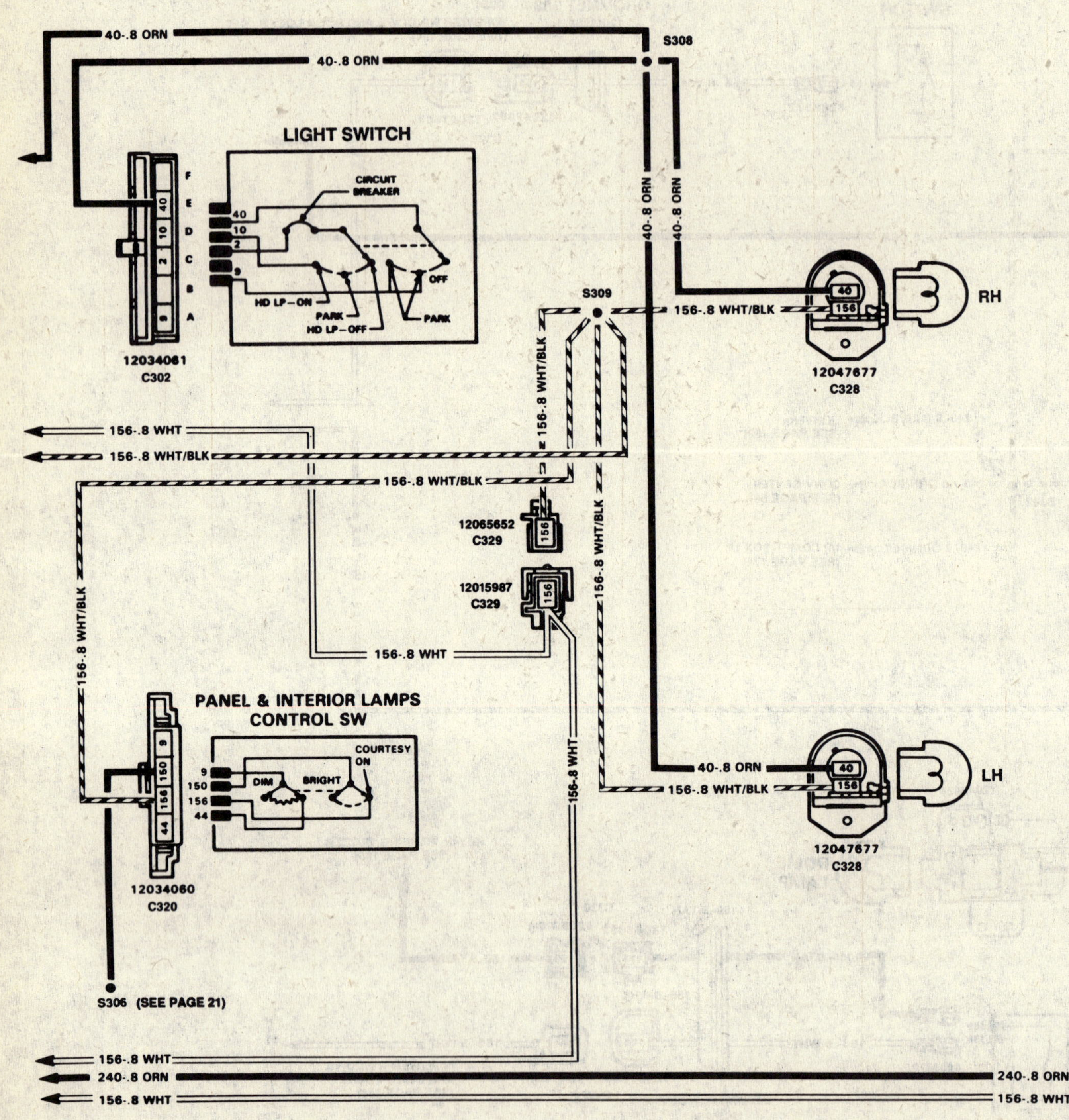

DOME AND COURTESY LAMPS - 2-DOOR UTILITY -

1988-91

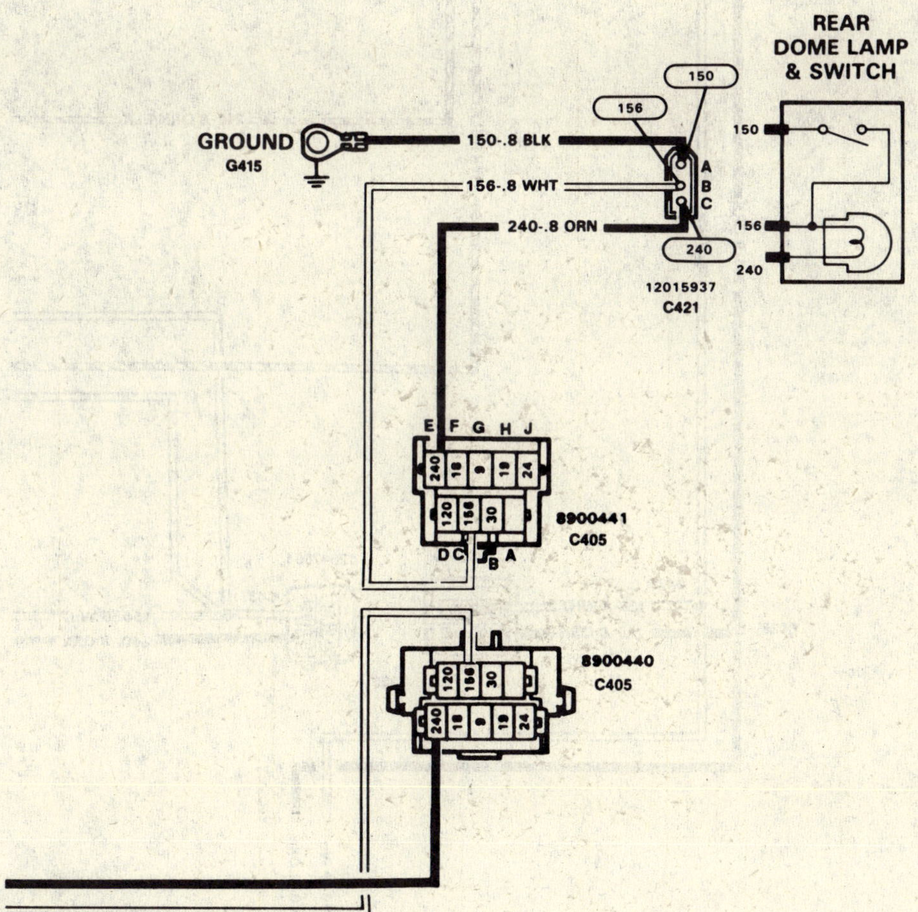

W/O POWER WINDOWS AND DOOR LOCKS 171

1988-91

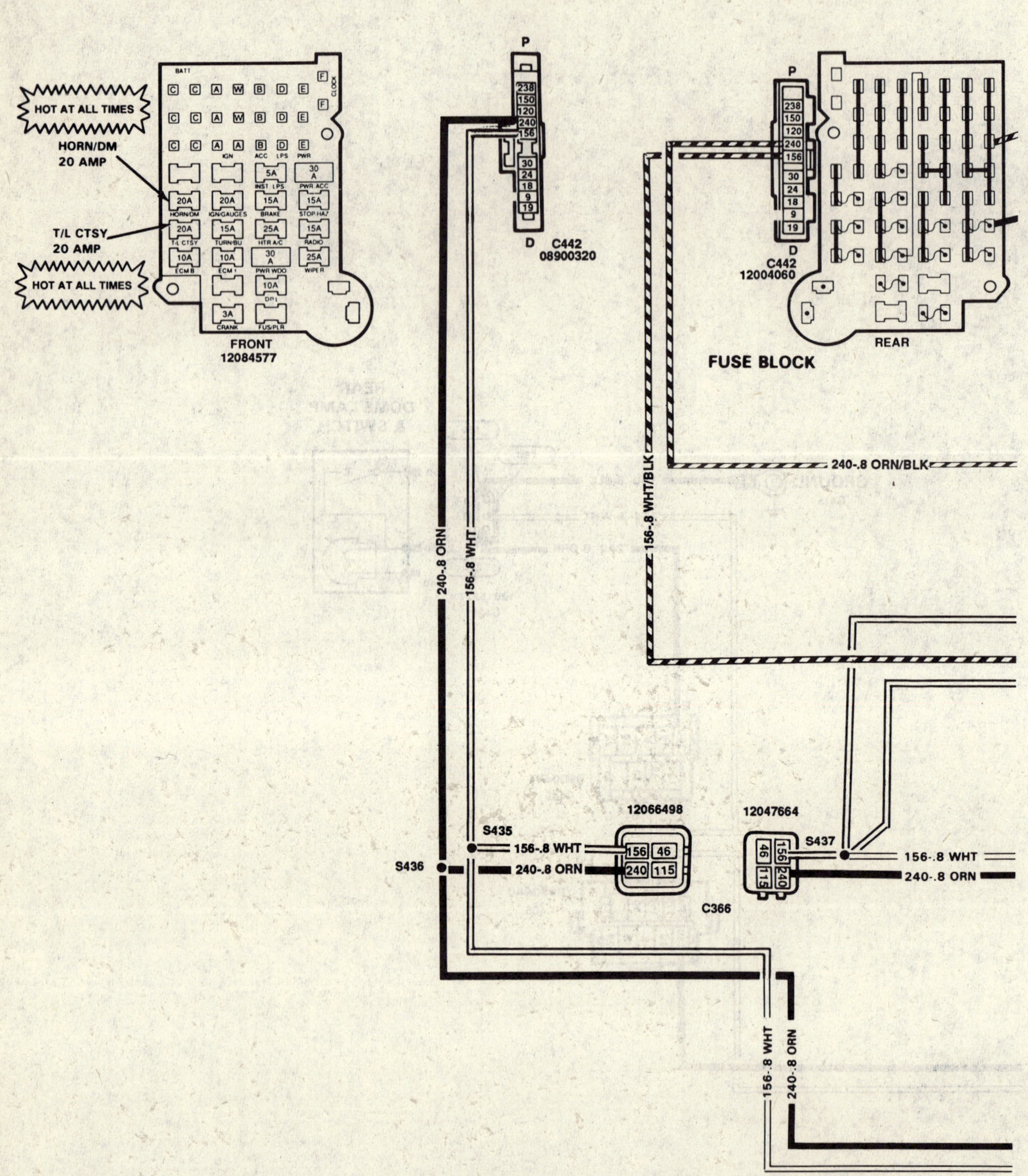

172 DOME AND COURTESY LAMPS - 4-DOOR UTILITY - W/O POWER WINDOWS AND

1988-91

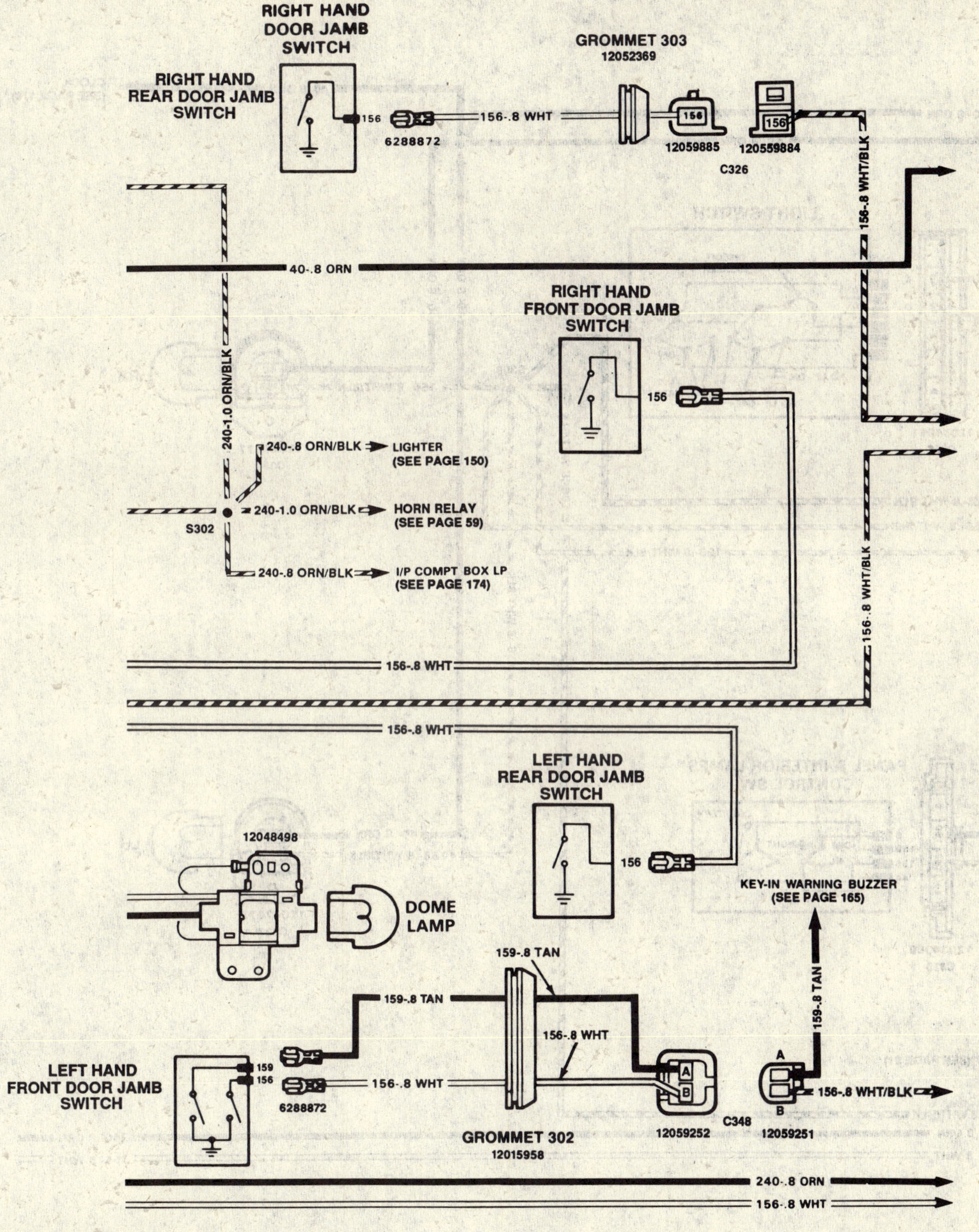

DOOR LOCKS

1988-91

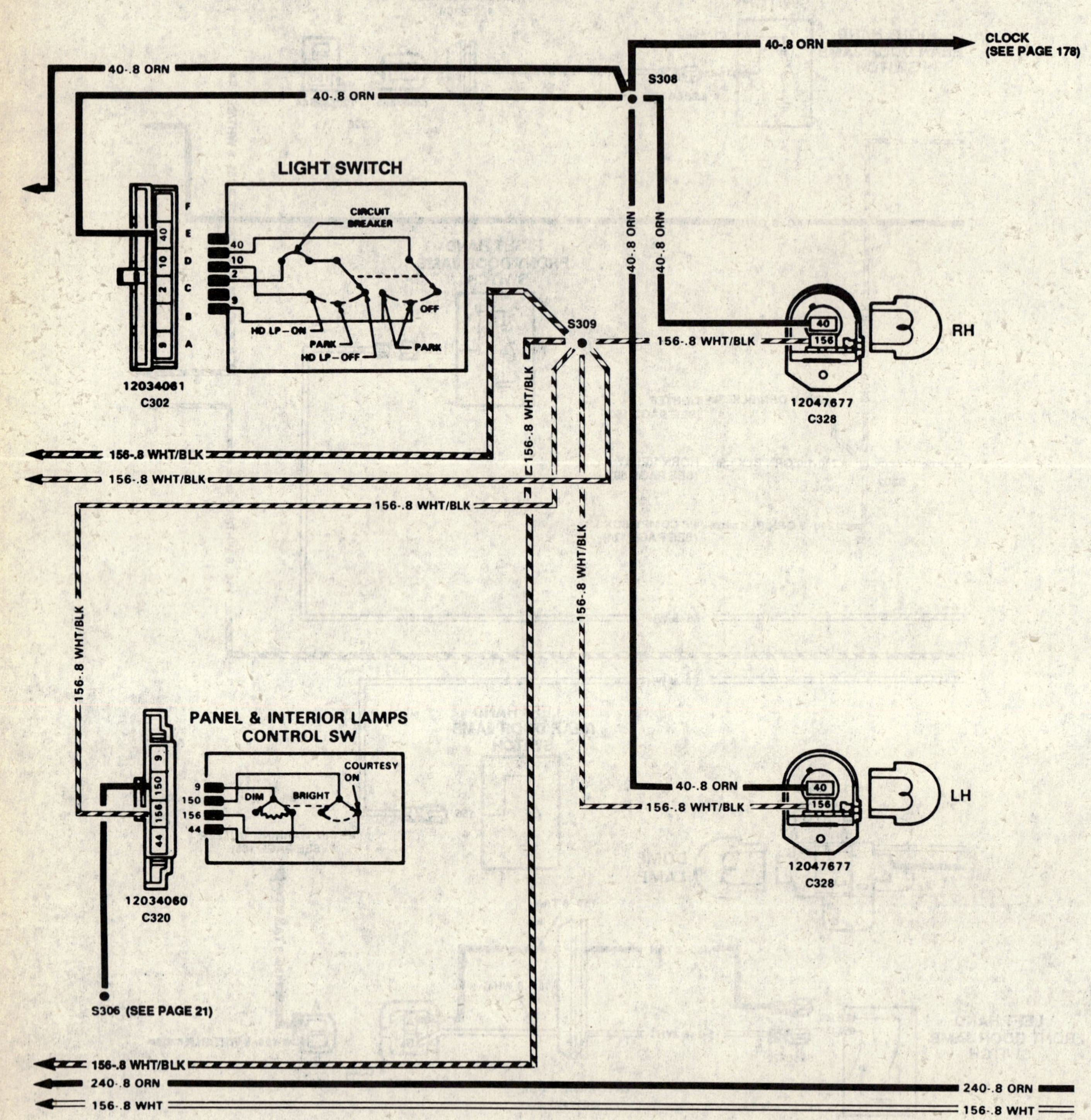

DOME AND COURTESY LAMPS -

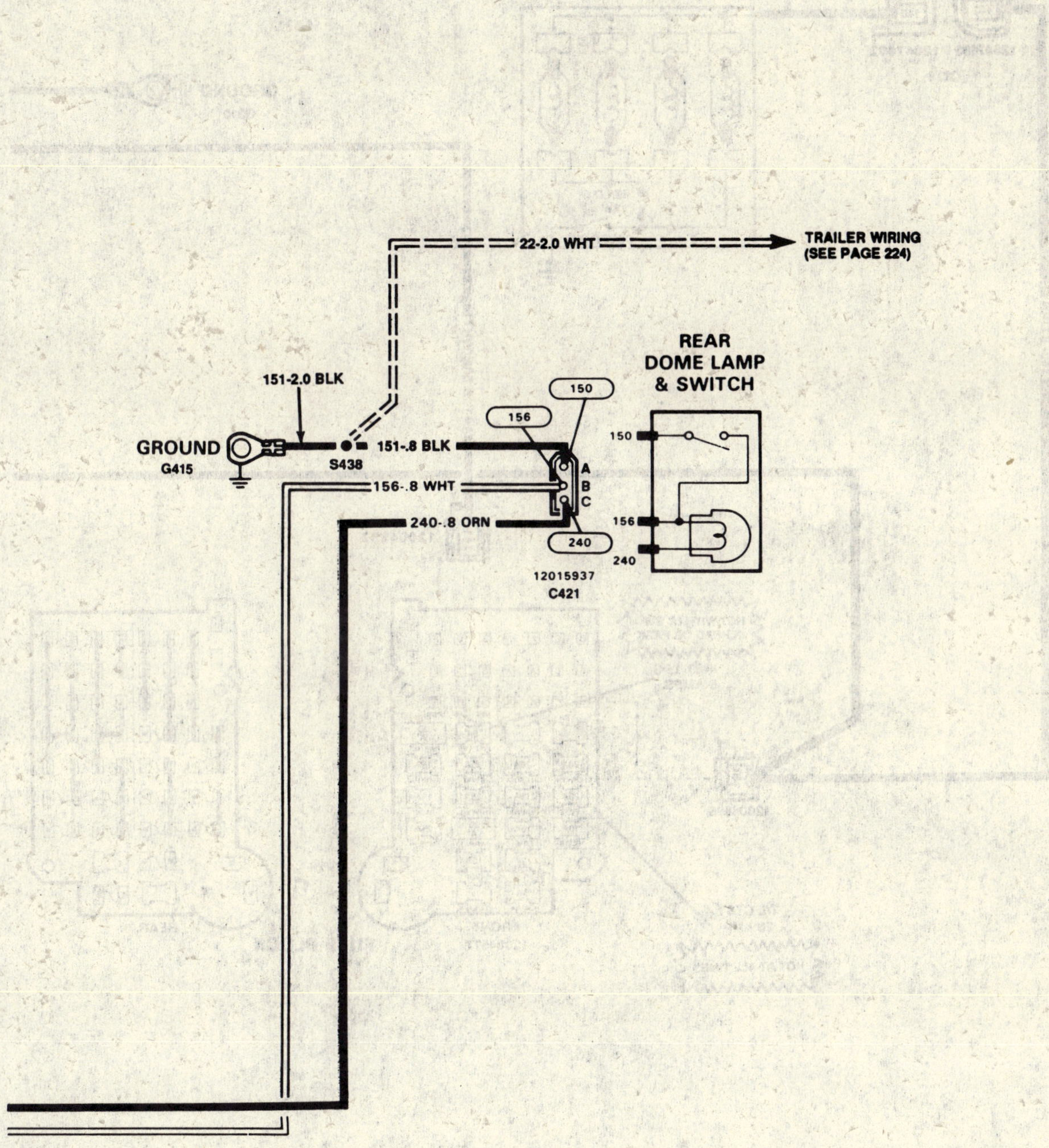

4-DOOR UTILITY - W/O POWER WINDOWS AND DOOR LOCKS 173

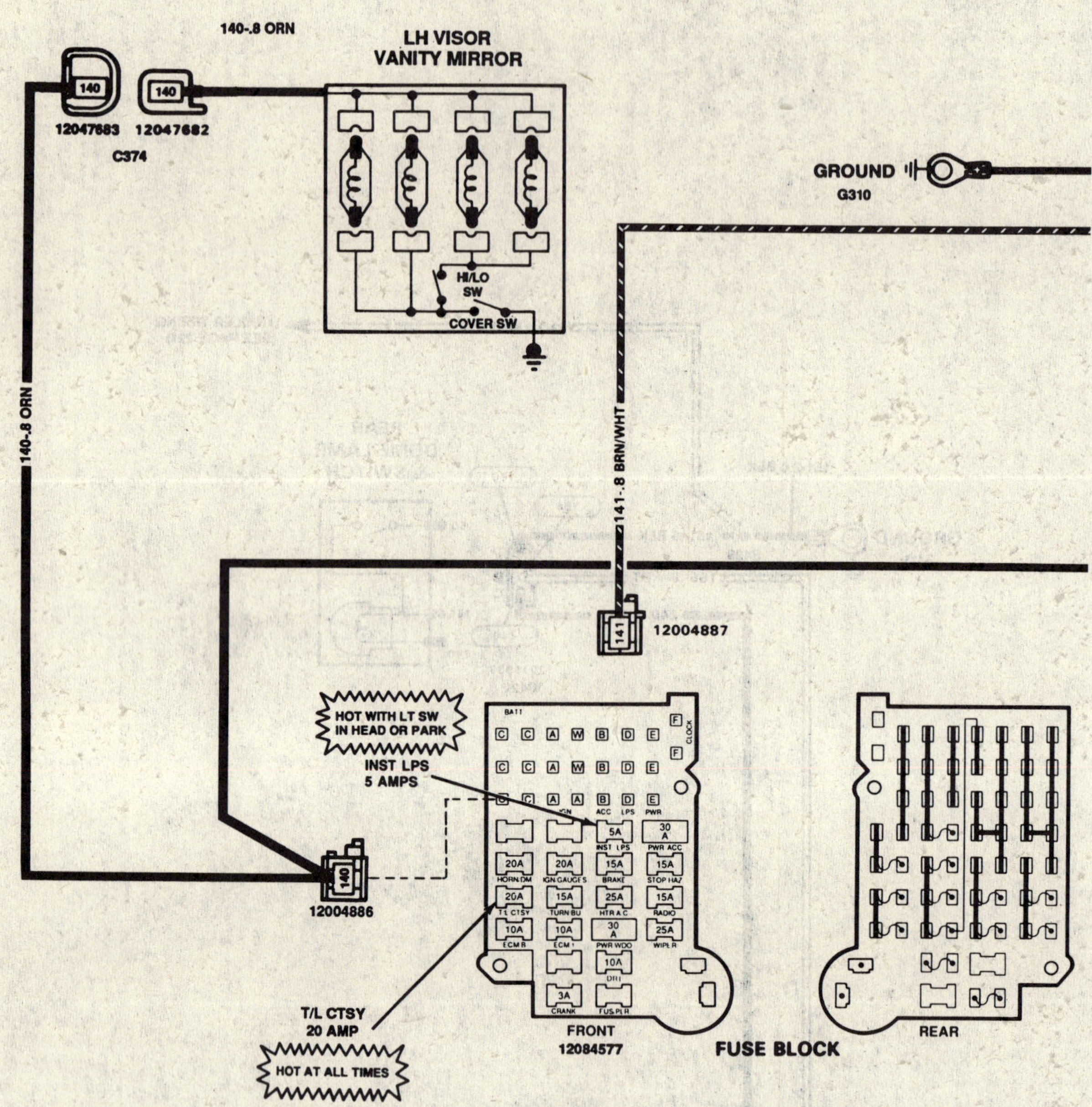

LIGHTED

1988-91

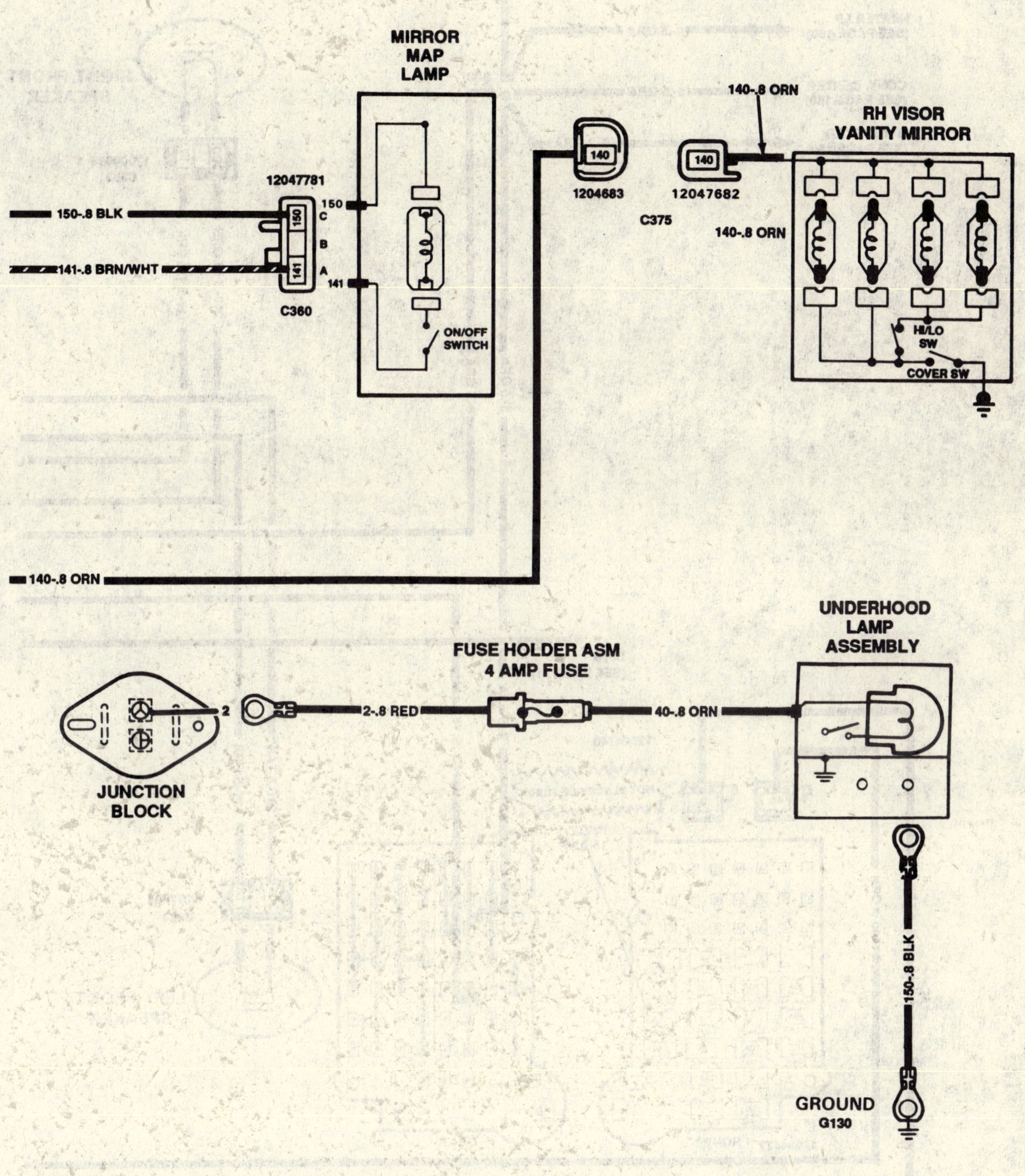

VANITY MIRROR W/REARVIEW MIRROR MAP LAMP/ UNDERHOOD LAMP 175

1988-91

ASHTRAY LP (SEE PAGE 150)
8-.5 GRA
HEATER LP (SEE PAGE 150)
8-.5 GRA
CONV. CENTER (SEE PAGE 150)
8-.5 GRA
I/P CLUSTER (SEE PAGE 150)
8-.5 GRA
S307
RIGHT FRONT SPEAKER
A
B
200
117
12004886
C353
200-.5 LT GRN
117-.5 DK GRN
8-.5 GRA
8-.5 GRA
S306 (SEE PAGE 21)
8-.5 GRA
43-.5 YEL
201-.5 TAN
118-.5 GRA
12004740
40
9
HOT IN ACCY OR RUN
RADIO 15 AMP
9-.8 BRN
40-.8 ORN
201
118
12077887
C354
B
A
LEFT FRONT SPEAKER
12084577 FRONT
REAR

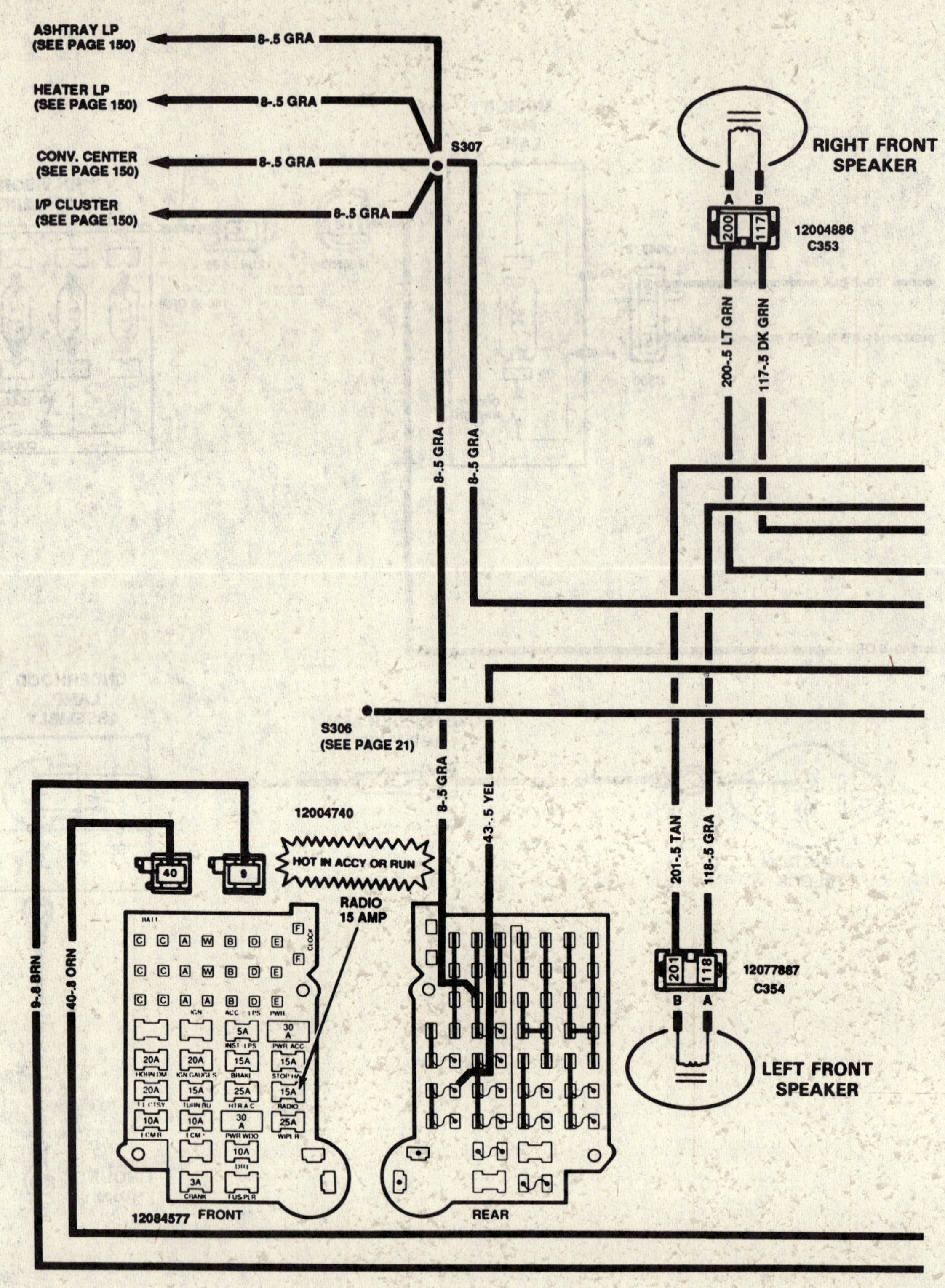

1988-91

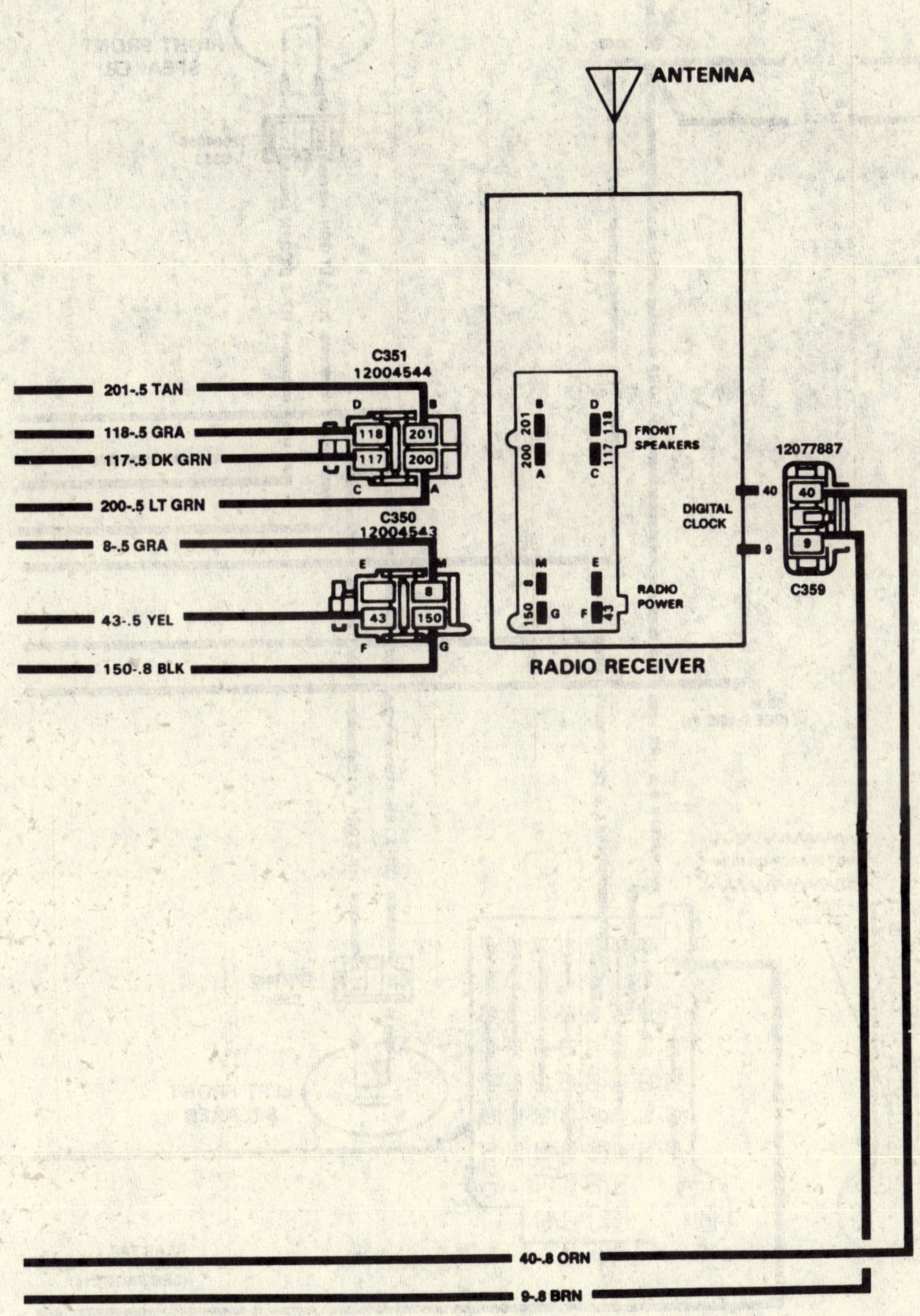

RADIO EQUIPMENT AND CLOCK - MONAURAL - 2-DOOR UTILITY 177

1988-91

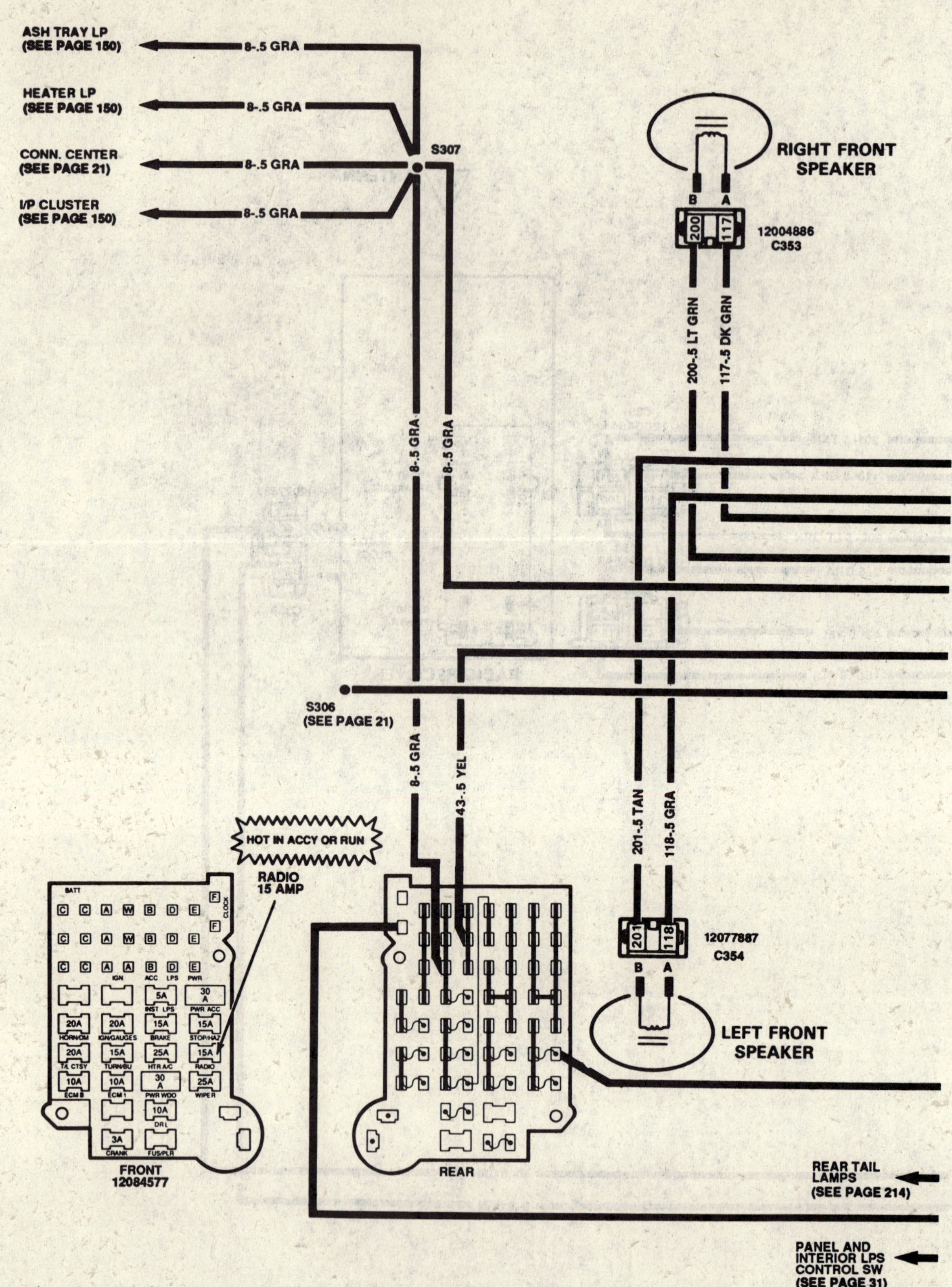

178 RADIO EQUIPMENT AND CLOCK - STEREO - 4-DOOR UTILITY

1988-91

F
E
D
C
B
A
40
10
2
9
CIRCUIT BREAKER
OFF
HD LP–ON
PARK
HD LP–OFF
PARK
12034061
C302
LIGHT SWITCH
40-.8 ORN
9-.8 BRN
201-.5 TAN
118-.5 GRA
117-.5 DK GRN
200-.5 LT GRN
8-.5 GRA
43-.5 YEL
150-.8 BLK
I/P COURTESY LPS (SEE PAGE 172)
40-.8 ORN
40-.8 ORN
40-.8 ORN
S308
40-.8 ORN
9-.8 BRN
9-.8 BRN
9-.8 BRN
S300
9-.8 BRN
DIGITAL CLUSTER (SEE PAGE 31)
9-.8 BRN
230-.22 BRN/WHT 10.0 ± 1.0 OHMS (WITH GAGES ONLY) OPTIONS YC2/Z53
PANEL AND INTERIOR LAMPS CONTROL SWITCH (SEE PAGE 31)

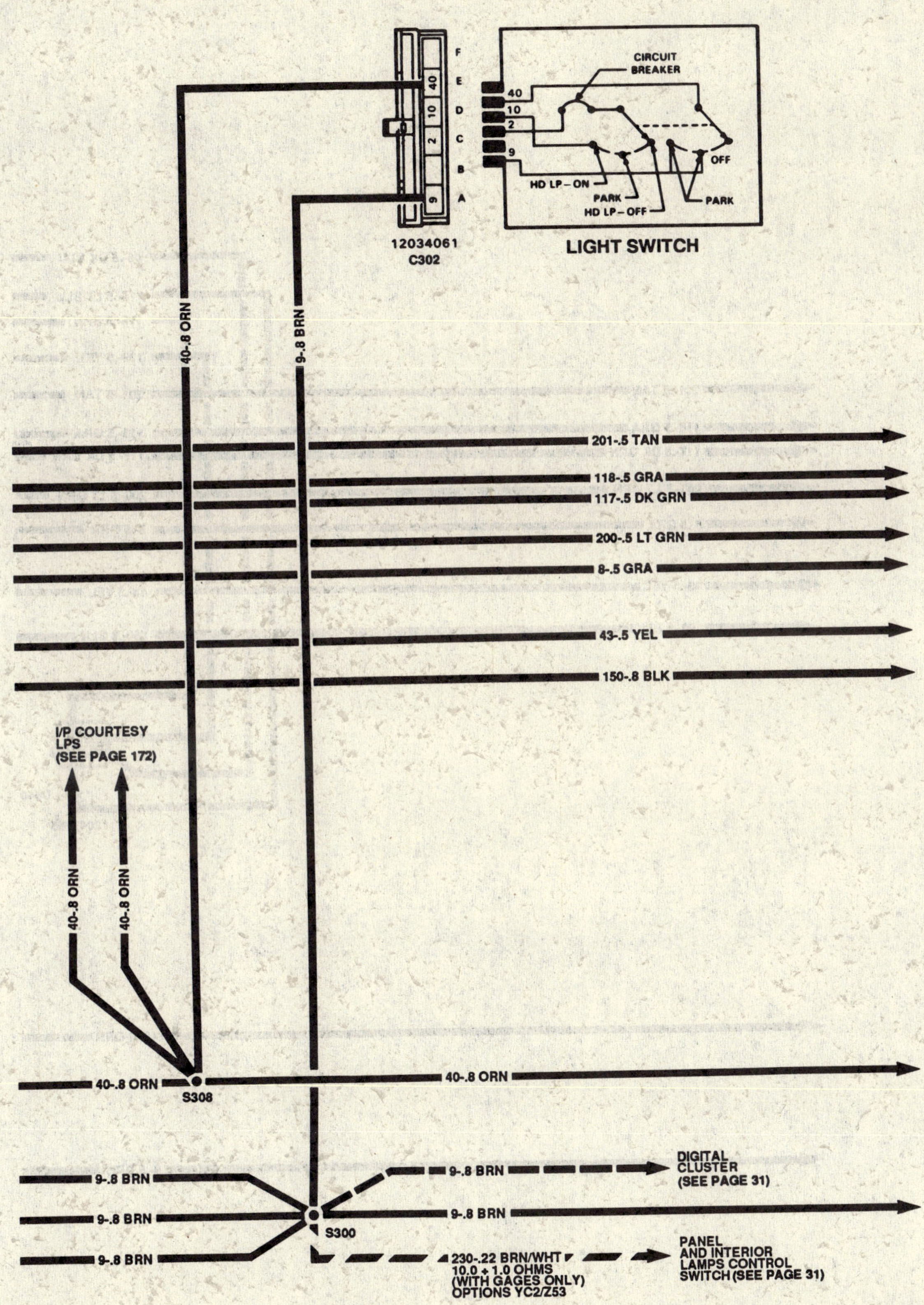

1988-91

46-.5 DK BLU
115-.5 LT BLU
116-.5 BRN
199-.5 YEL
201-.5 TAN
201-.5 TAN
118-.5 GRA
118-.5 GRA
117-.5 DK GRN
117-.5 DK GRN
200-.5 LT GRN
200-.5 LT GRN
8-.5 GRA
8-.5 GRA
43-.5 YEL
43-.5 YEL
150-.8 BLK
150-.8 BLK
199
116
46
115
C340
12047785
40-.8 ORN
9-.8 BRN

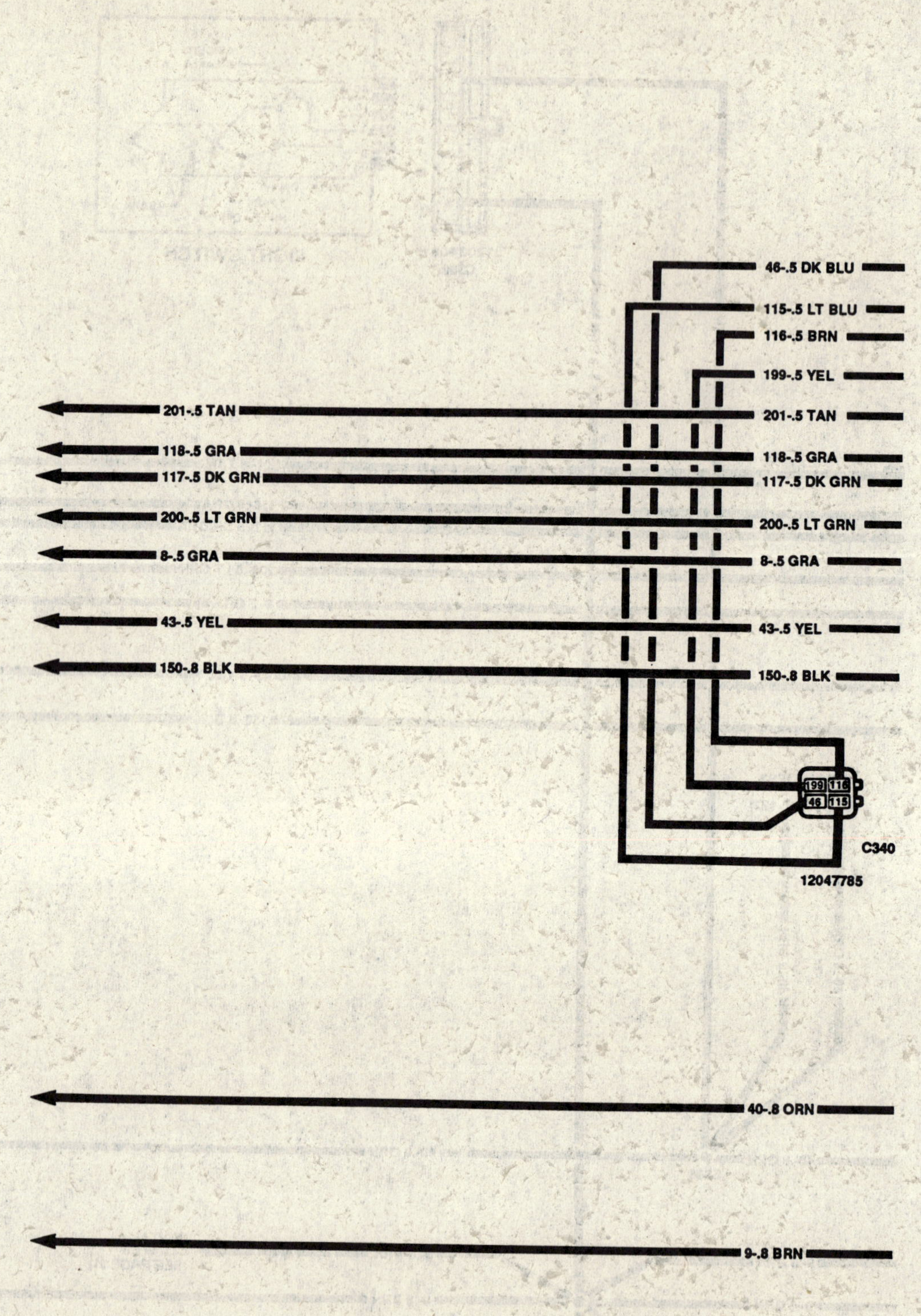

1988-91

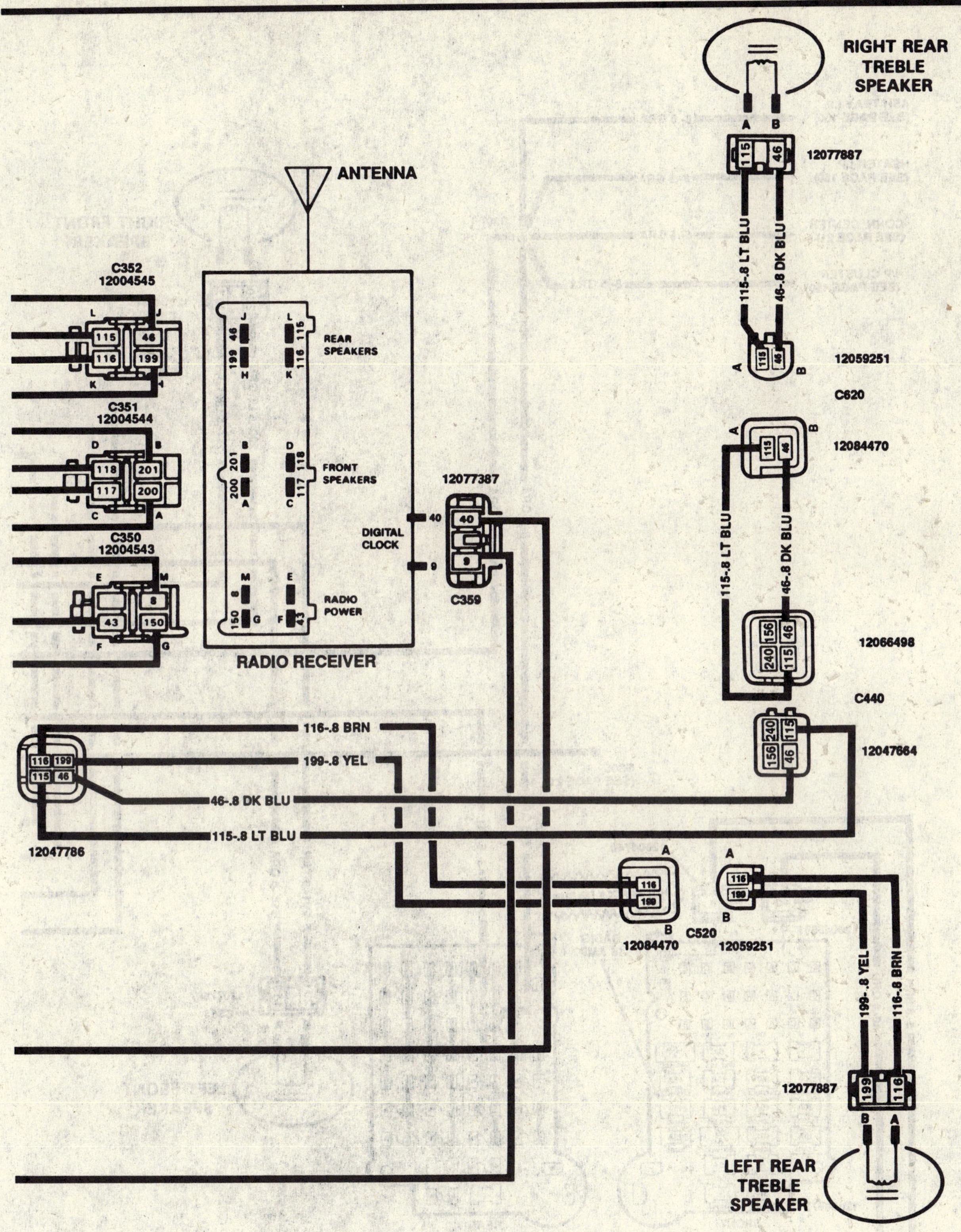

RADIO EQUIPMENT AND CLOCK - STEREO - 4-DOOR UTILITY 179

1988-91

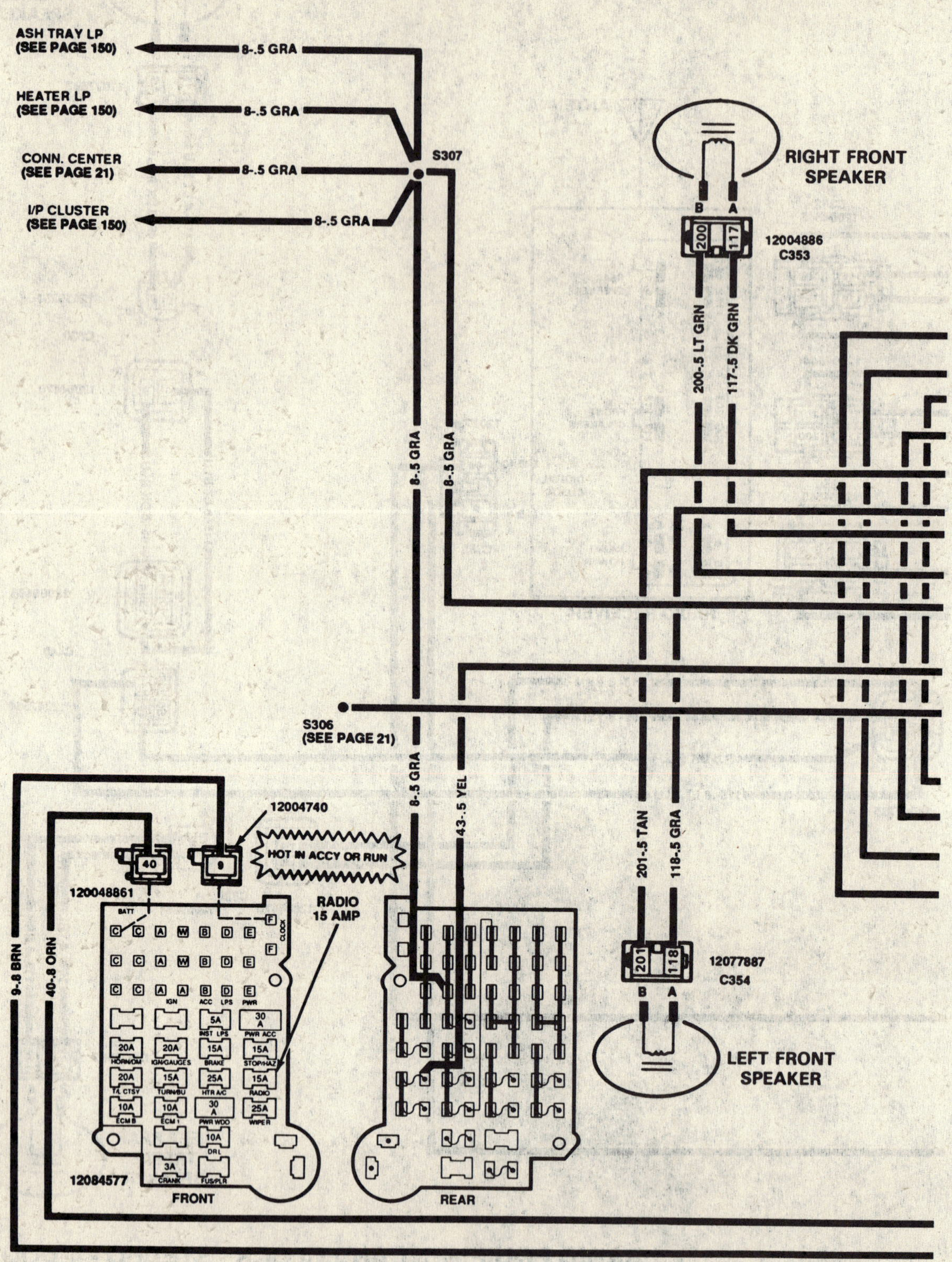

180 RADIO EQUIPMENT AND CLOCK - STEREO - 2-DOOR UTILITY
1988-91

RIGHT REAR
TREBLE
SPEAKER
A B
115 46
12077887
ANTENNA
C352
12004545
46-.5 DK BLU
115-.5 LT BLU
116-.5 BRN
199-.5 YEL
115 46
116 199
REAR
SPEAKERS
115-.8 LT BLU
46-.8 DK BLU
C351
12004544
201-.5 TAN
201-.5 TAN
117-.5 DK GRN
200-.5 LT GRN
118 201
117 200
FRONT
SPEAKERS
12077887
40
9
DIGITAL
CLOCK
C359
C350
12004543
8-.5 GRA
43-.5 YEL
150-.8 BLK
8
43 150
RADIO
POWER
RADIO RECEIVER
116-.8 BRN
199-.8 YEL
115-.8 LT BLU
46-.8 DK BLU
8905206
8905220
C357
W/PICKUP
VEHICLES ONLY
12077887
199 116
B A
LEFT REAR
TREBLE
SPEAKER
40-.8 ORN
9-.8 BRN

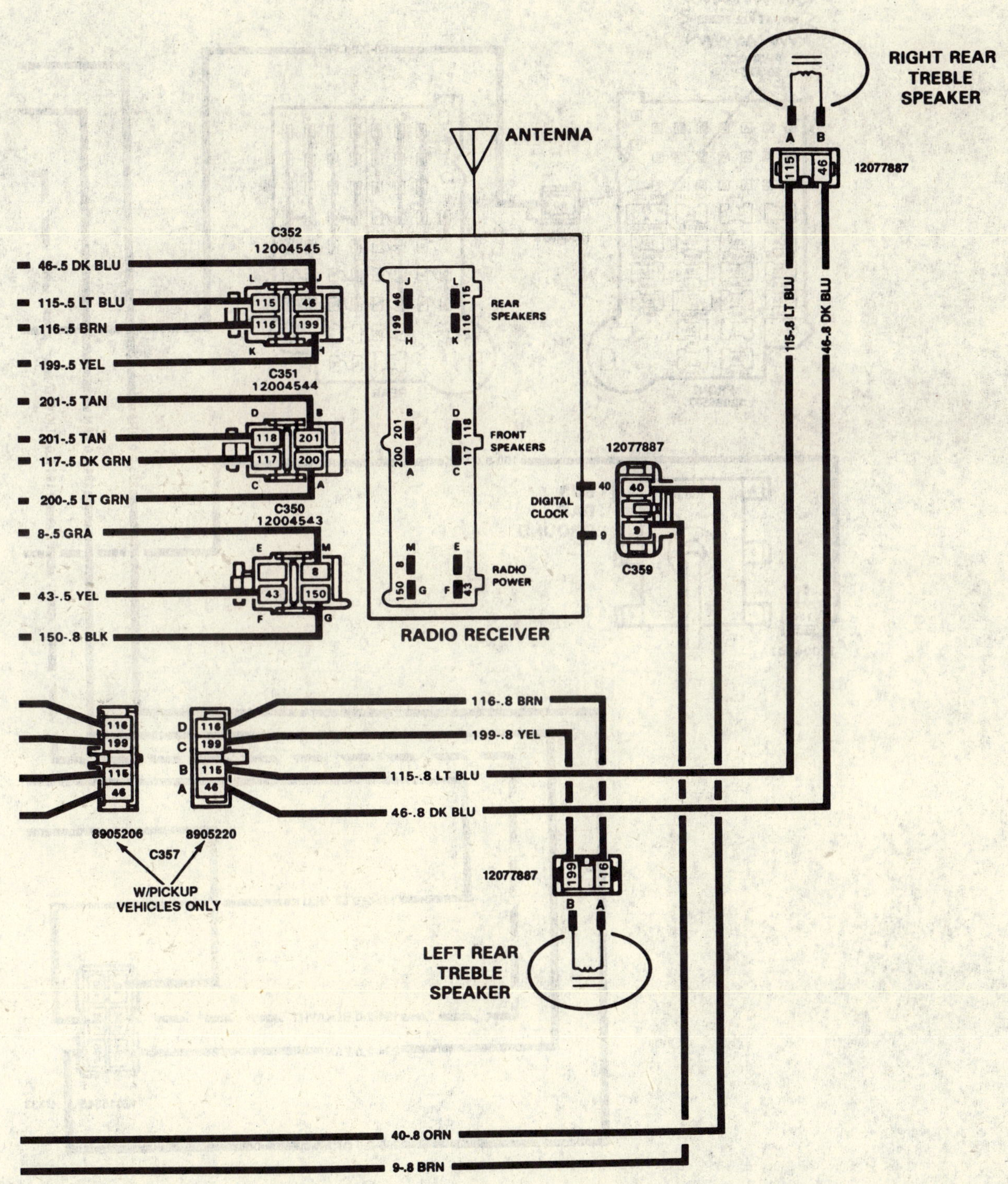

1988-91

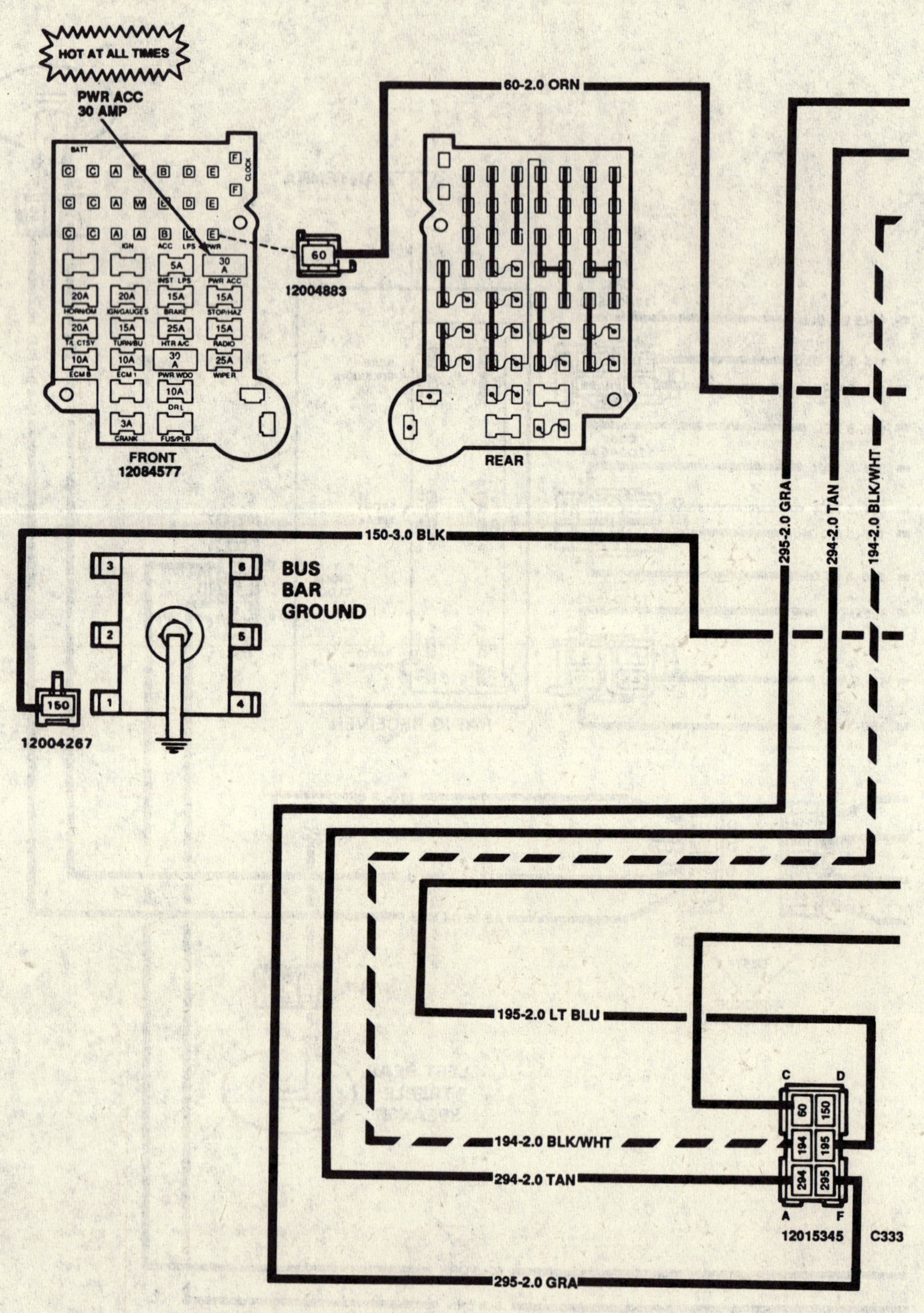

182 POWER DOOR LOCKS (AU3) - 4-DOOR UTILITY

1988-91

295-2.0 GRA
294-2.0 TAN
194-2.0 BLK/WHT
195-2.0 LT BLU
60-2.0 ORN
S311
195-2.0 LT BLU
60-2.0 ORN
150-3.0 BLK
LH POWER WINDOW SWITCH (SEE PAGE 190)
S320
150-3.0 BLK
12033945
C502
150
194
195
150
60
RWD UNLOCK
150
195
194
60
150
FWD LOCK
195-2.0 LT BLU
194-2.0 BLK/WHT
60-2.0 ORN/BLK
UNLOCK
LOCK
L.H. DOOR LOCK SWITCH
12034136
GROMMET 304
12015958
195-2.0 LT BLU
60-2.0 ORN/BLK
194-2.0 BLK/WHT
L.H. DOOR LOCK MOTOR
D
C
150
60
195
194
295
294
F
A
12015344
294-2.0 TAN
295-2.0 GRA
294-2.0 TAN
CIRCUIT BREAKER
B
2
295
294
1
M
A
12004140
C503
GROMMET 500
12020045
295-2.0 GRA

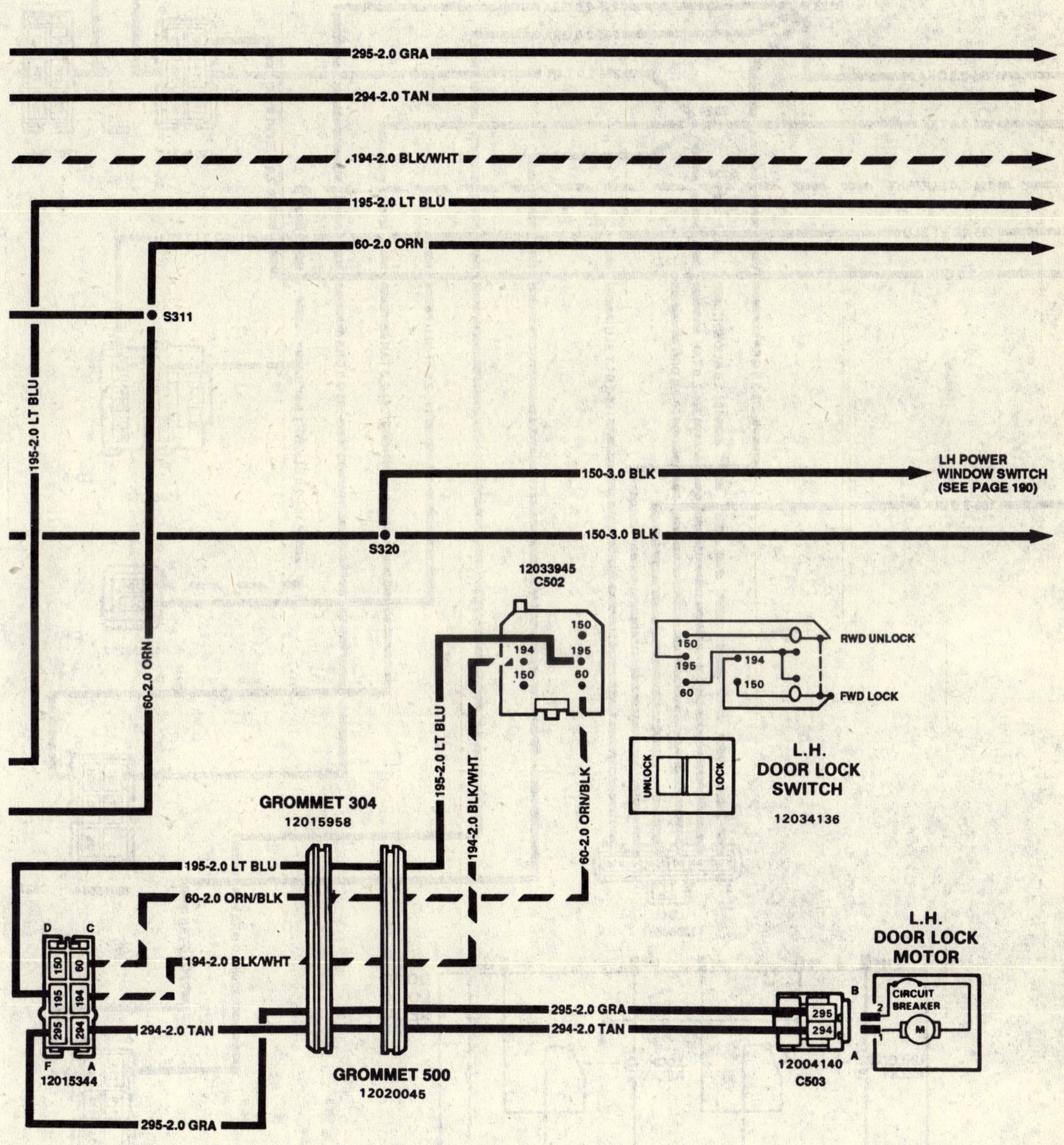

1988-91

S323
295-2.0 GRA
295-2.0 GRA
295-2.0 GRA
295-2.0 GRA
294-2.0 TAN
S324
294-2.0 TAN
S235
194-2.0 BLK/WHT
S236
195-2.0 LT BLU
195-2.0 LT BLU
S237
60-2.0 ORN
60-2.0 ORN/BLK
C334
12015345
12015344
C345
12064762
194-2.0 BLK/WHT
C341
12059252
150-3.0 BLK
295-2.0 GRA
194-2.0 BLK/WHT
294-2.0 TAN
60-2.0 ORN
195-2.0 LT BLU
195-2.0 LT BLU
294-2.0 TAN
295-2.0 GRA
C345
12059561
C627
12045544
295-2.0 GRA
294-2.0 TAN
C527
12045544
DOOR
LOCK
RELAY
UNLOCK
RELAY
LOCK
RELAY

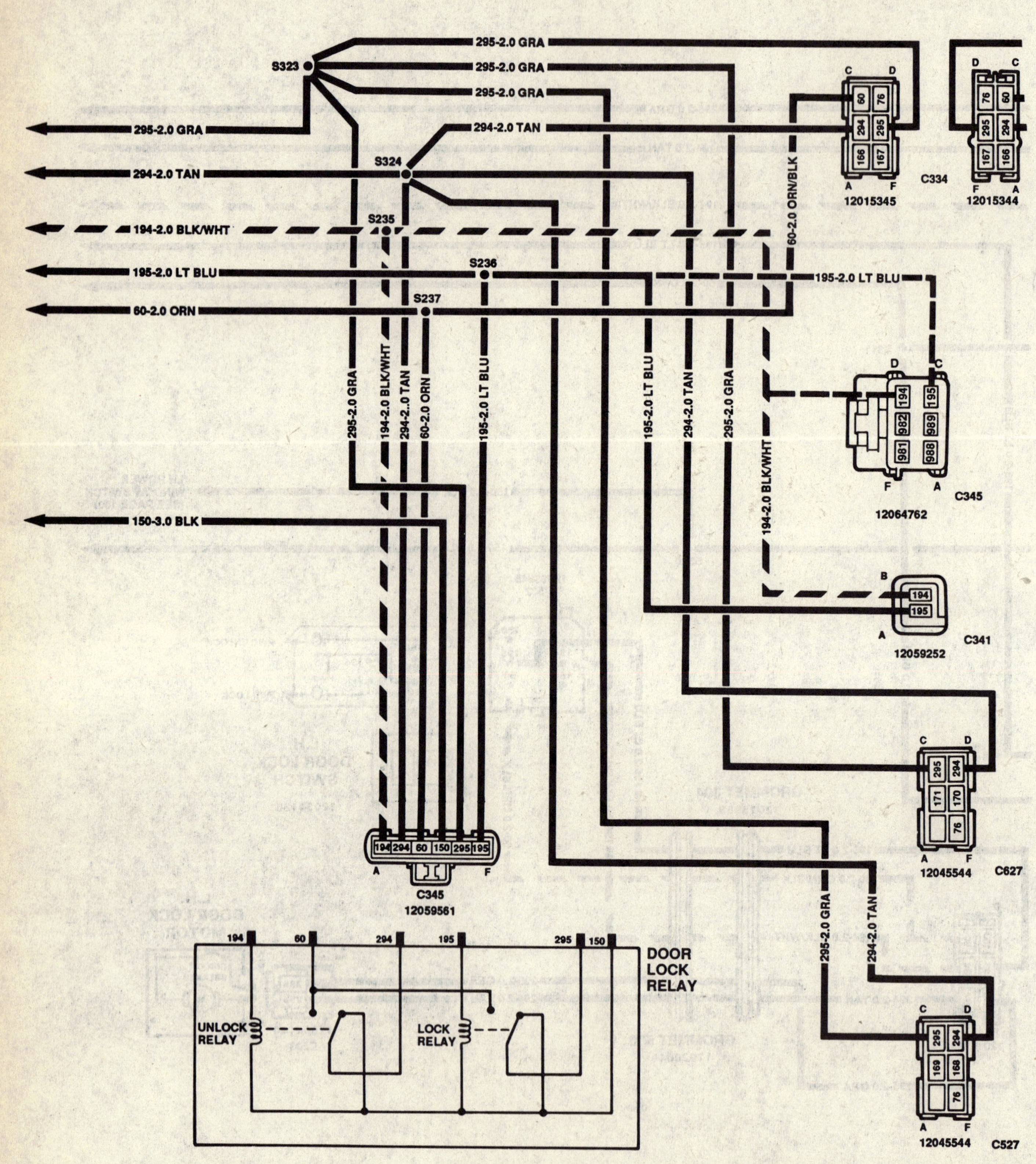

1988-91

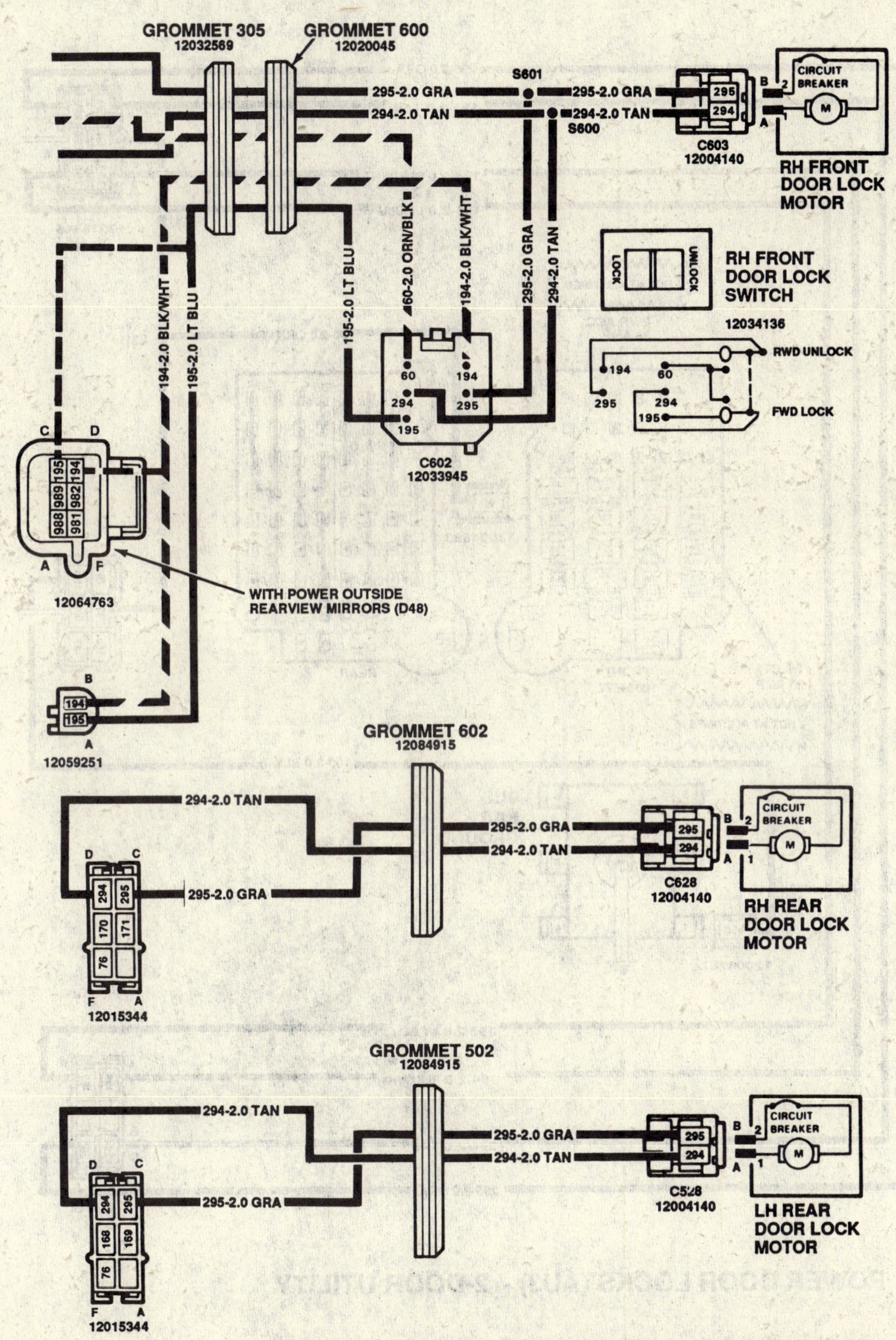

POWER DOOR LOCKS (AU3) - 4-DOOR UTILITY 183

1988-91

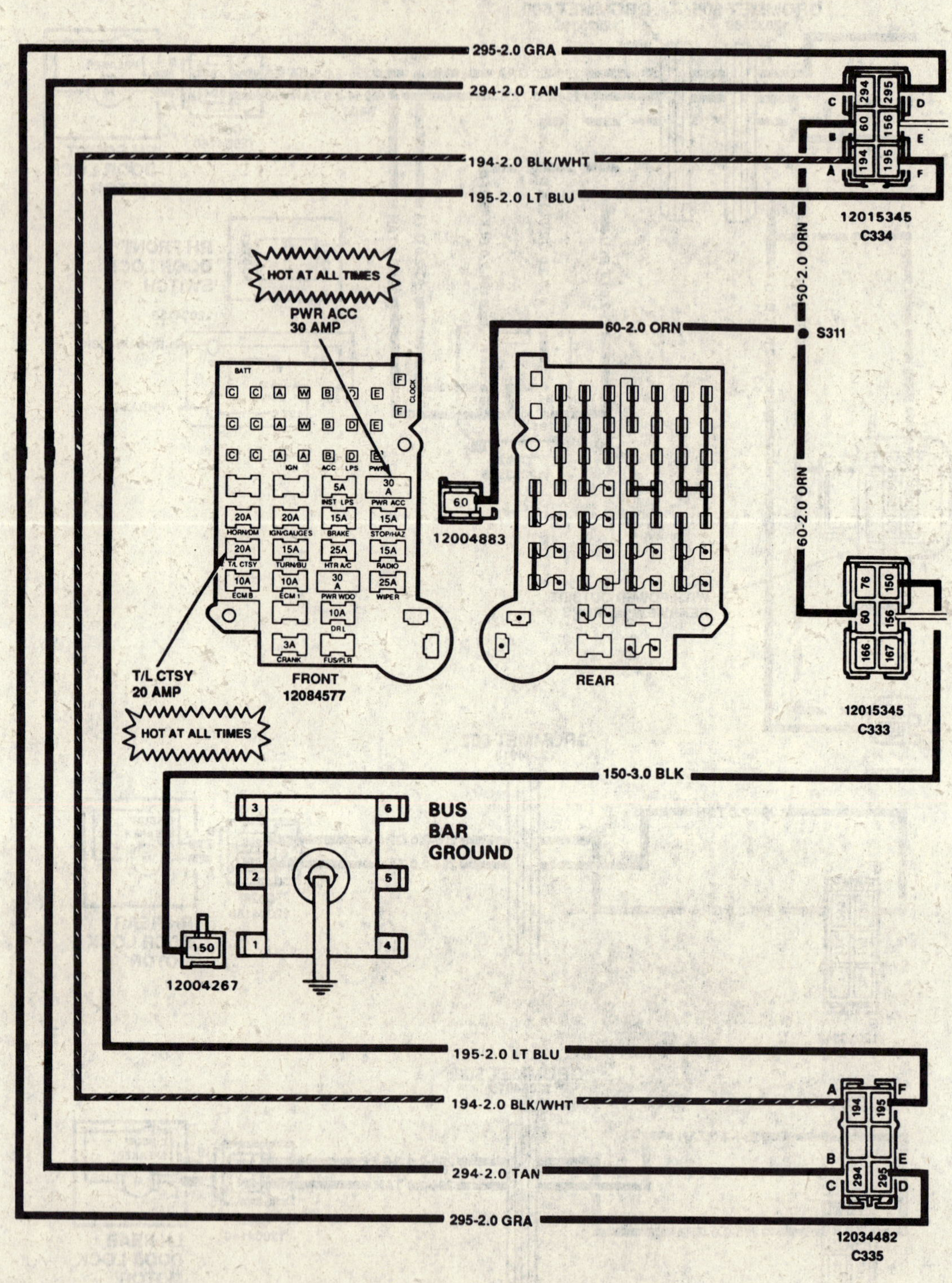

184 POWER DOOR LOCKS (AU3) - 2-DOOR UTILITY

1988-91

GROMMET 600
12020045
295-2.0 GRA
294-2.0 TAN
S601
S600
12004140
C603
CIRCUIT BREAKER
R.H. DOOR LOCK MOTOR
12015344
C334
156-.8 WHT
GROMMET 305
12052369
195-2.0 LT BLU
60-2.0 ORN/BLK
194-2.0 BLK/WHT
295-2.0 GRA
294-2.0 TAN
UNLOCK
LOCK
R.H. DOOR LOCK SWITCH
12034136
RWD UNLOCK
FWD LOCK
PANEL AND INTERIOR LAMPS CONTROL SWITCH (SEE PAGE 171)
156-.8 WHT
12033945
C602
RIGHT HAND DOOR JAMB SWITCH (SEE PAGE 167)
12015344
C333
60-2.0 ORN/BLK
150-3.0 BLK
12033945
C502
150-2.0 BLK
POWER WINDOWS (SEE PAGE 189)
S500
150-2.0 BLK
FWD LOCK
UNLOCK
LOCK
L.H. DOOR LOCK SWITCH
12034136
LEFT HAND INTERIOR DOOR JAMB SWITCH (SEE PAGE 167)
GROMMET 304
12015958
150-3.0 BLK
195-2.0 LT BLU
194-2.0 BLK/WHT
60-2.0 ORN/BLK
L.H. DOOR LOCK MOTOR
12034481
C335
GROMMET 500
12020045
295-2.0 GRA
294-2.0 TAN
12004140
C503

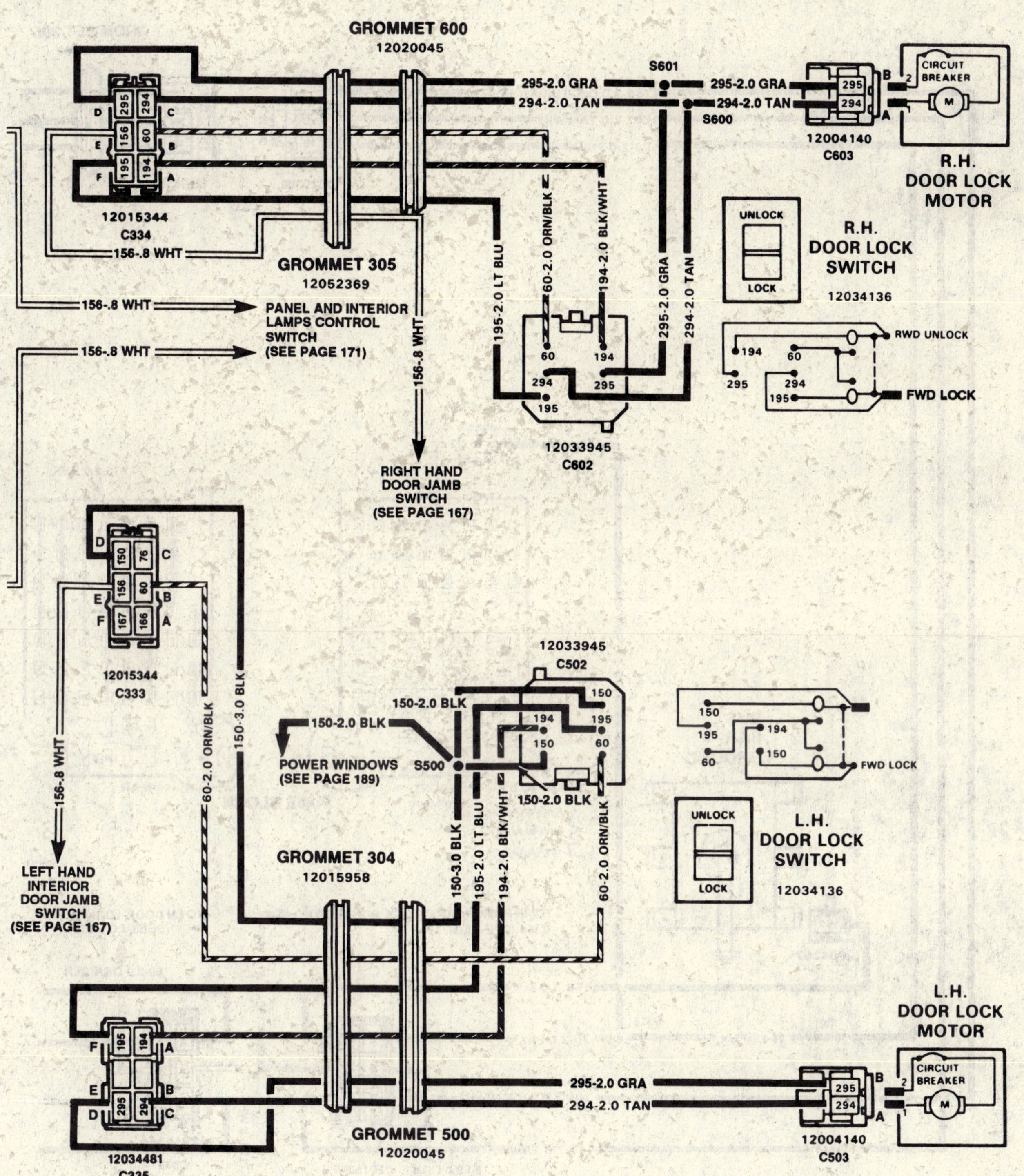

1988-91

GROMMET 305
12052369
166-2.0 DK BLU/WHT
167-2.0 TAN/WHT
76-2.0 PNK
12020398
12020397
C332
12004884
76-2.0 PNK
FRONT
12084577
FUSE BLOCK
REAR
PWR WDO
30 AMP (C.B.)
HOT IN RUN
BUS
BAR
GROUND
12004267
150-3.0 BLK
S314
76-2.0 PNK
166-2.0 DK BLU/WHT
167-2.0 TAN/WHT
TO RH POWER DOOR LOCK CONNECTOR
C334 (SEE PAGE 184)
156-.8 WHT
TO LH DOOR LOCK SWITCH
(SEE PAGE 184)
60-2.0 ORN/BLK
60-2.0 ORN
12015345
C333
12015344
C333
TO SPLICE S311
(SEE PAGE 184)
TO LH DOOR JAMB SWITCH
(SEE PAGE 184)

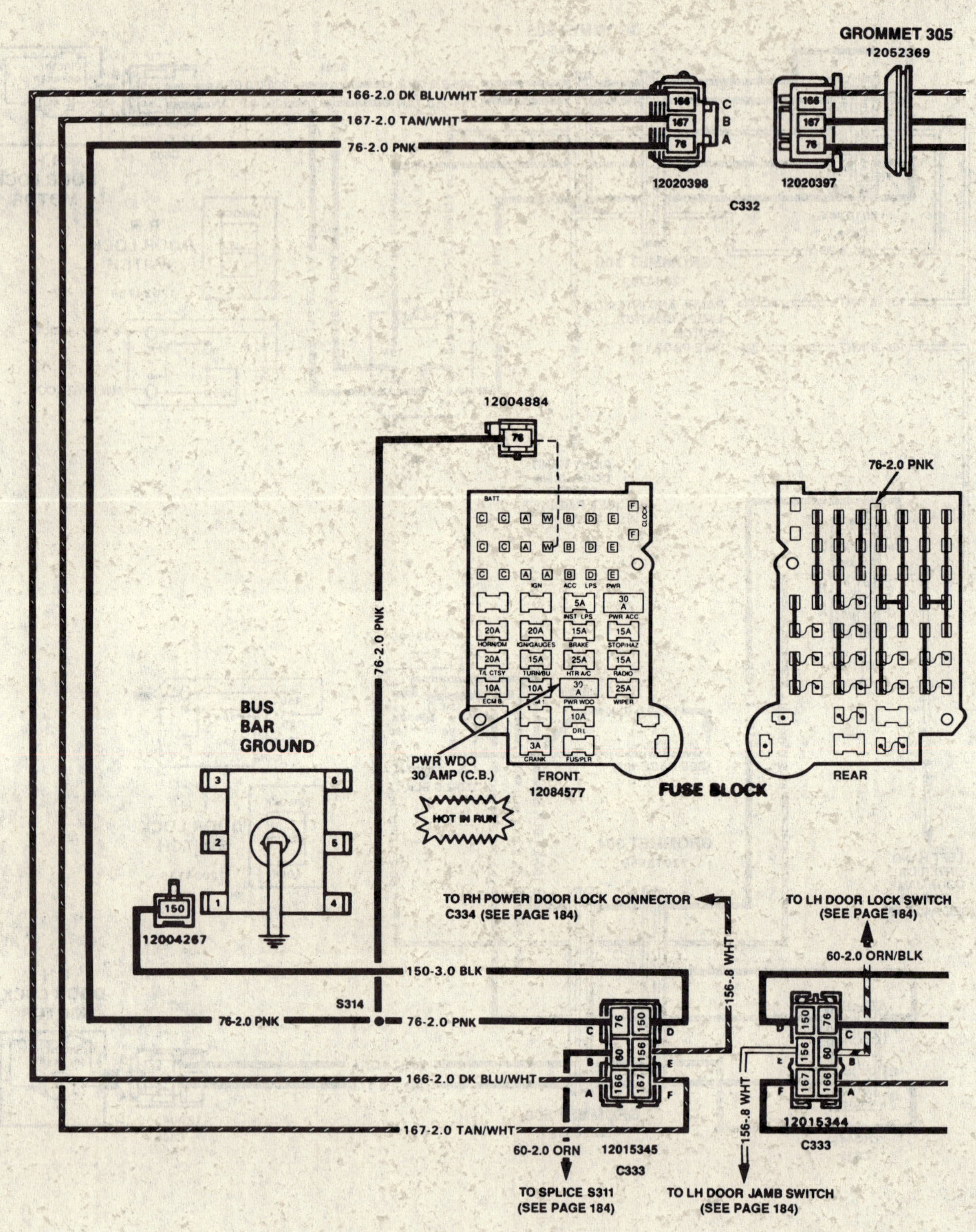

1988-91

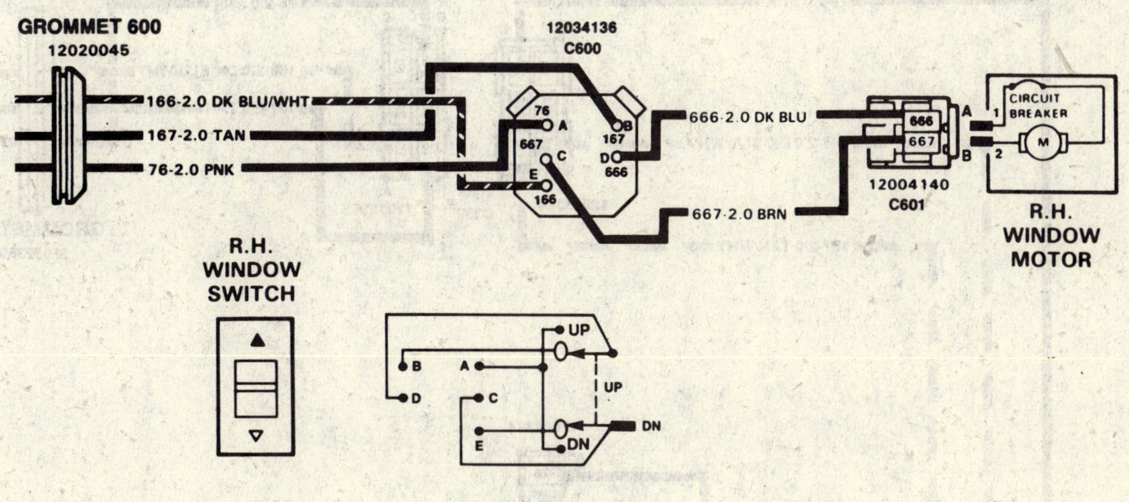

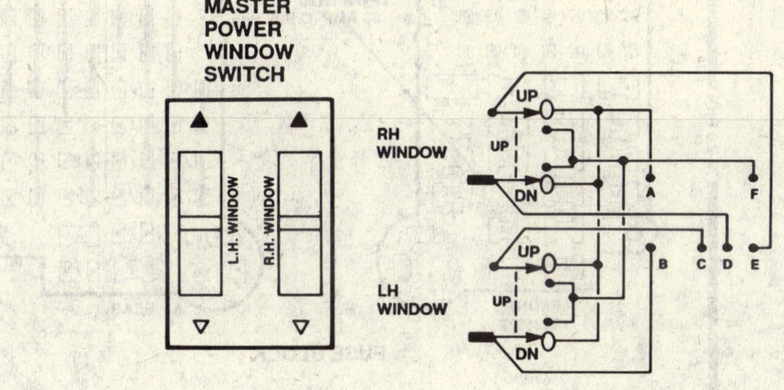

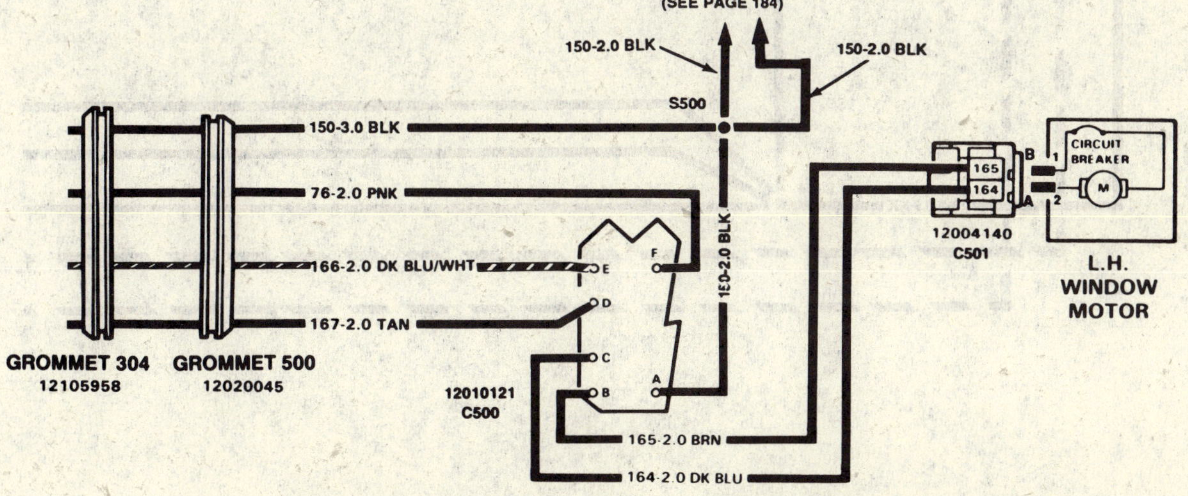

POWER WINDOWS (A31) - 2-DOOR UTILITY 189

1988-91

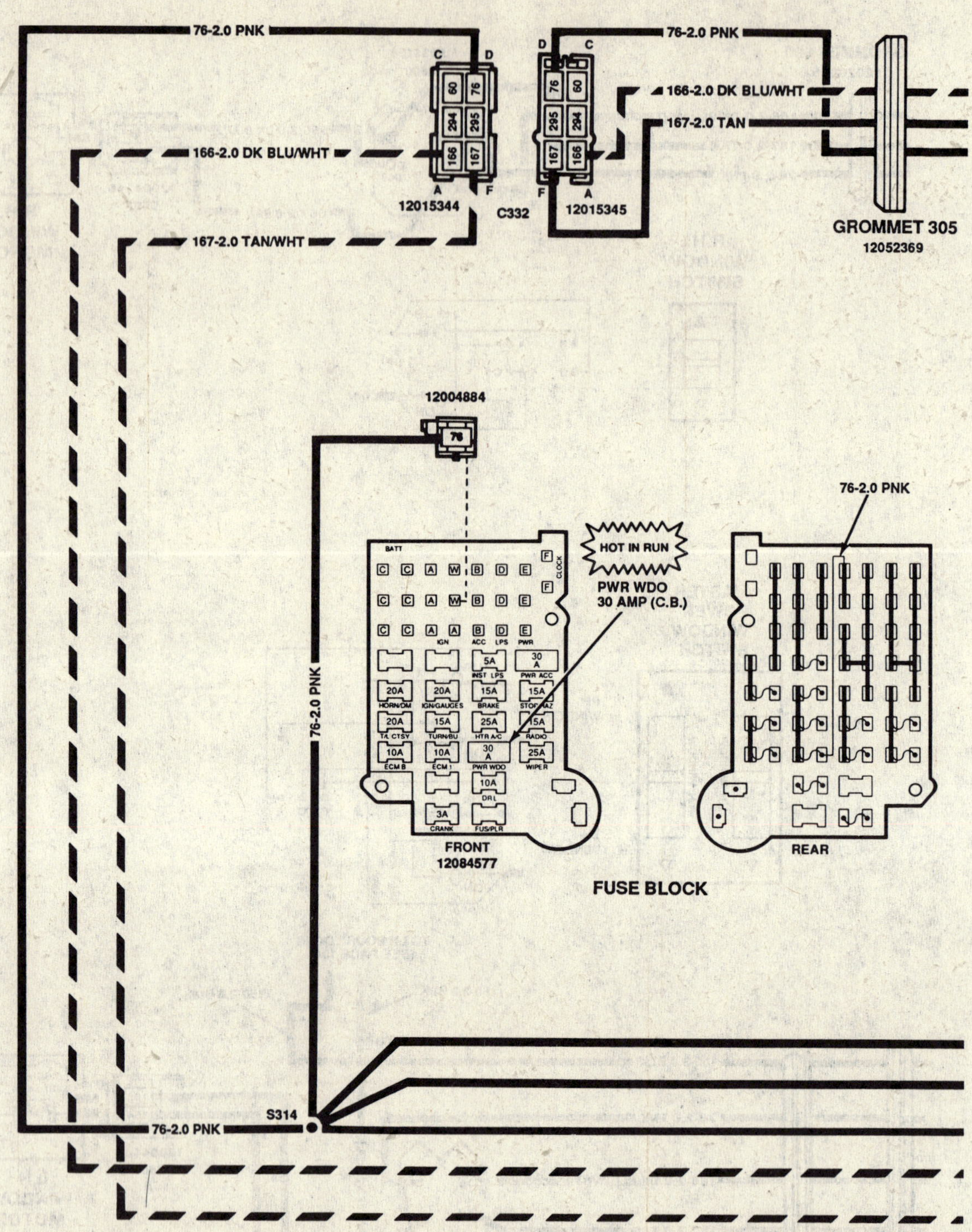

190 POWER WINDOWS (A31) - 4-DOOR UTILITY

1988-91

12034136
C600
166-2.0 DK BLU/WHT
167-2.0 TAN
76-2.0 PNK
667-2.0 BRN
666-2.0 DK BLU
12004140
C601
CIRCUIT BREAKER
RH FRONT WINDOW MOTOR
GROMMET 600
12020045
RH FRONT AND REAR WINDOW SWITCHES
RH REAR WINDOW
LH REAR WINDOW
RH FRONT WINDOW
LH FRONT WINDOW
MASTER POWER WINDOW SWITCH
76-2.0 PNK
76-2.0 PNK
76-2.0 PNK
166-2.0 DK BLU/WHT
167-2.0 TAN/WHT

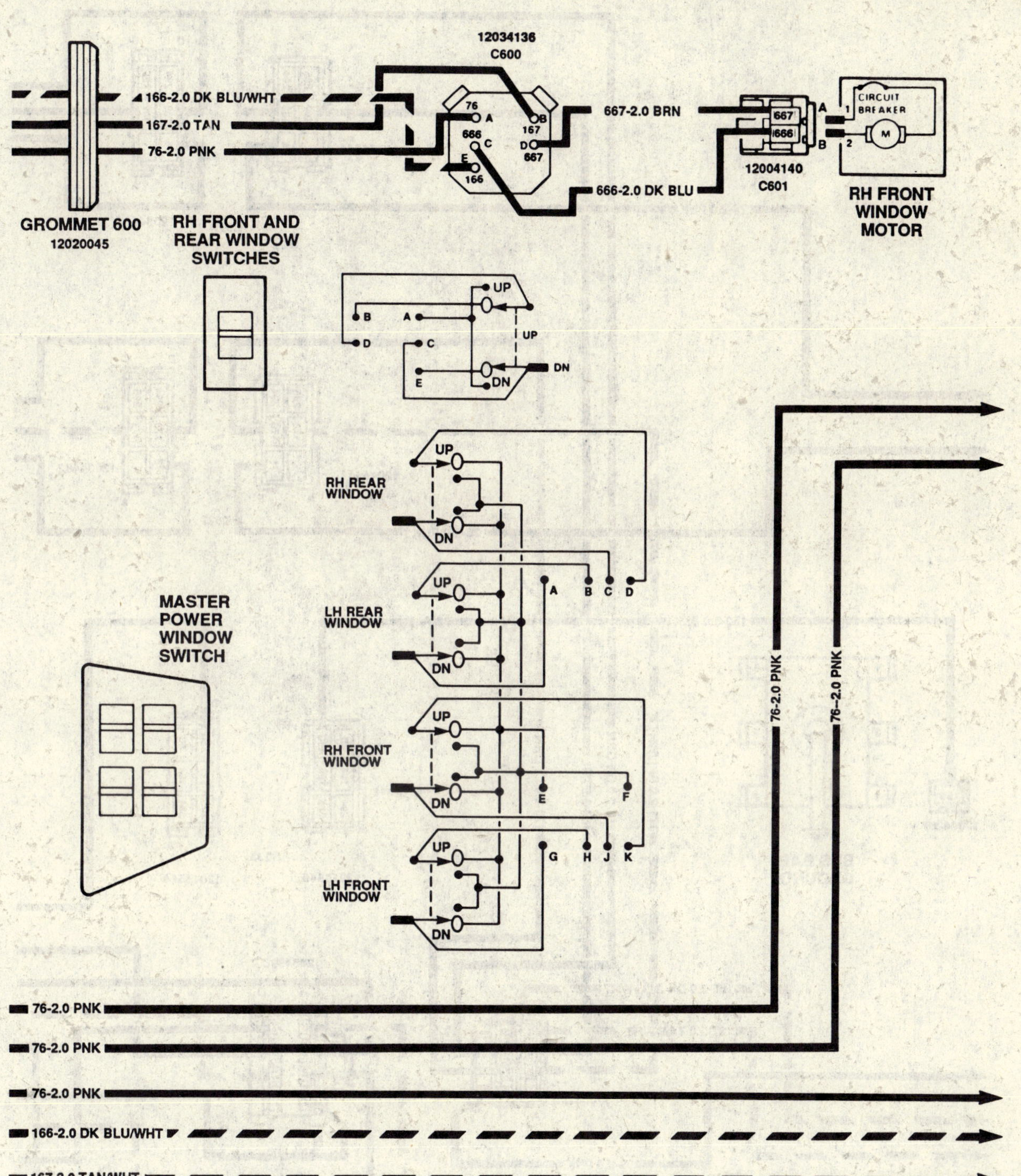

1988-91

C
D
295
294
169
158
76
12045544
A
F
C527
D
C
294
295
158
169
76
F
A
12034482
76-2.0 PNK
C
D
295
294
171
170
76
12045544
A
F
C627
D
C
294
295
170
171
76
12034482
F
A
76-2.0 PNK
150-3.0 BLK
150
12004267
BUS BAR
GROUND
171-2.0 PPL/WHT
168-2.0 DK GRN
169-2.0 PPL
170-2.0 LT GRN
C
D
60
150
194
195
294
295
A
F
12015545
C333
D
C
150
60
195
194
295
294
F
A
12015544
166-2.0 DK BLU/WHT
167-2.0 TAN/WHT
D
E
12066195
A
H
76-2.0 PNK
12064998
E
D
H
A
C343

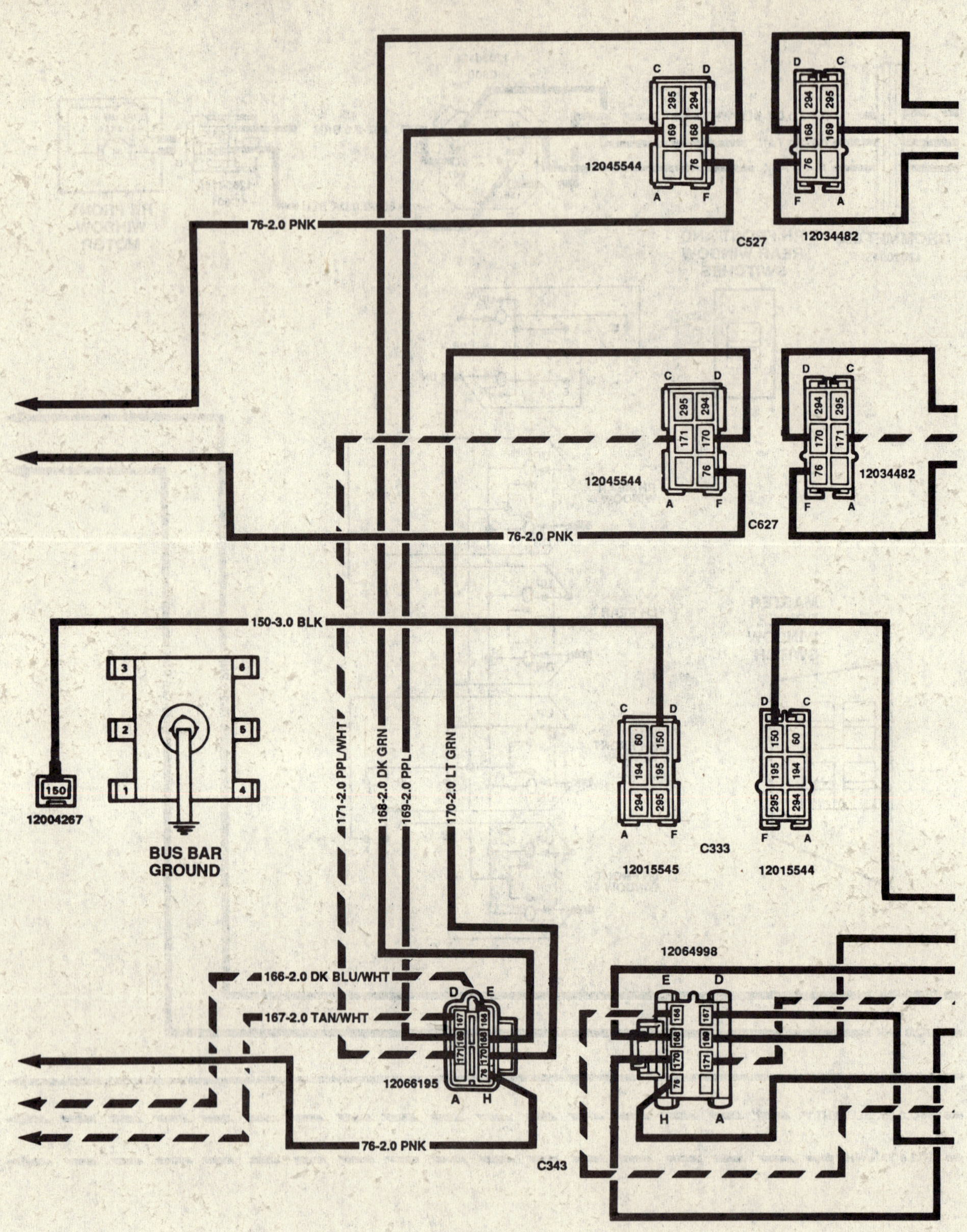

1988-91

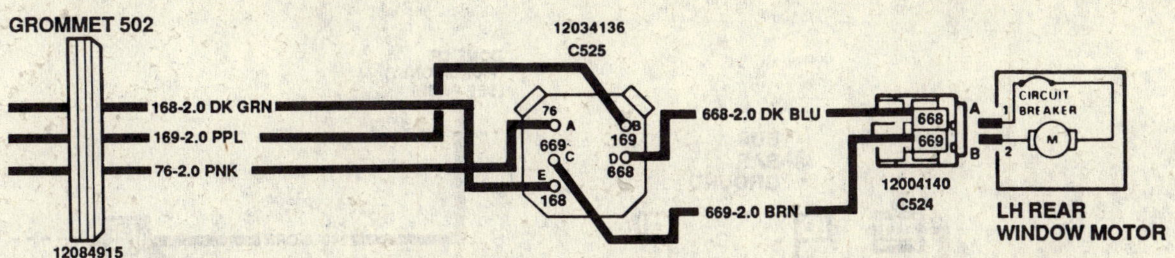

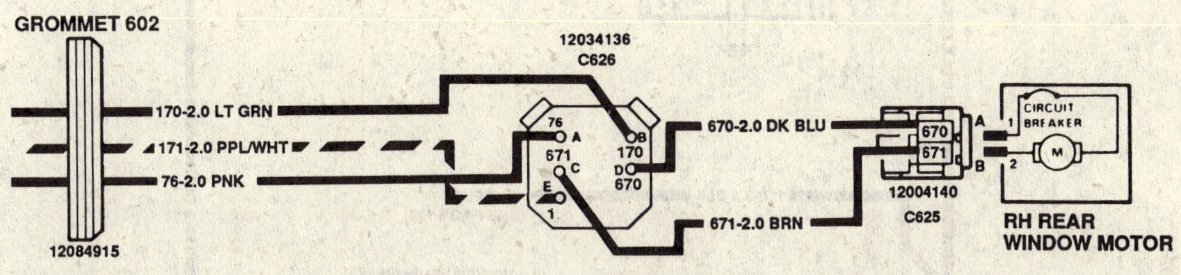

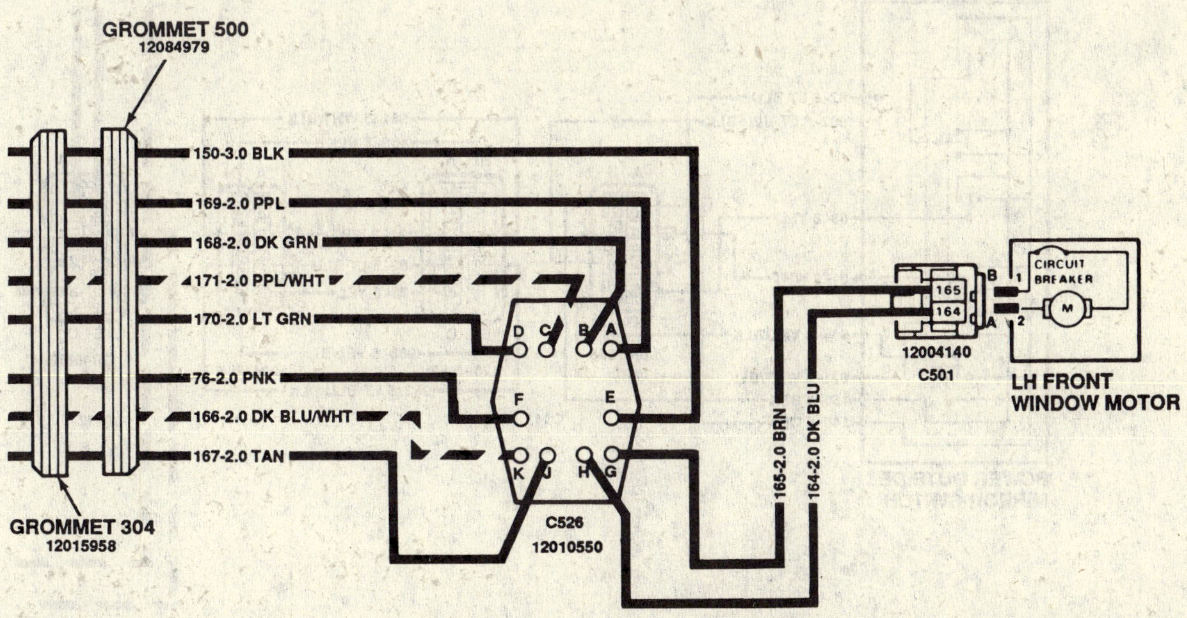

POWER WINDOWS (A31) - 4-DOOR UTILITY 191

1988-91

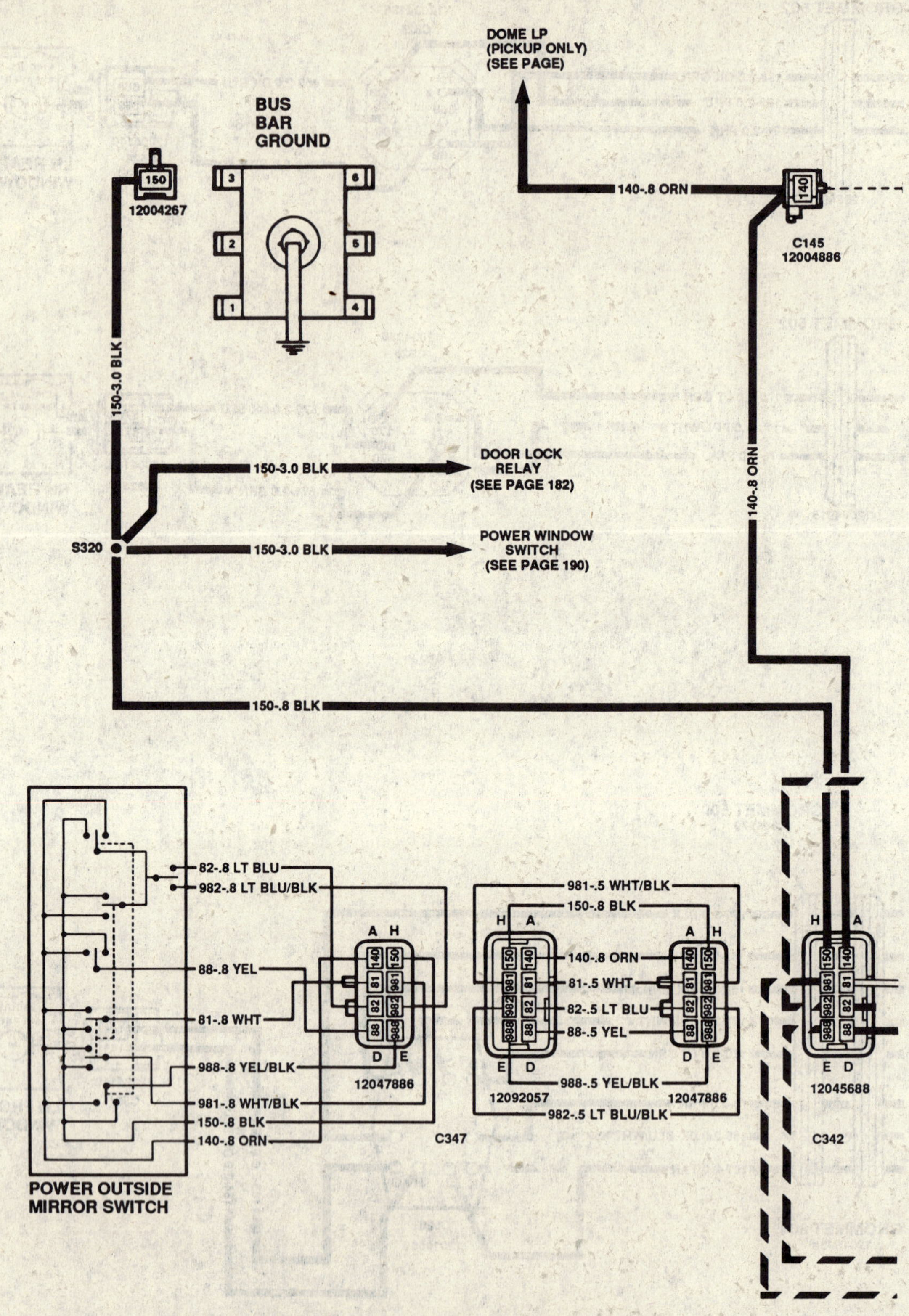

194 POWER OUTSIDE REARVIEW MIRRORS (D48)

1988-91

76-2.0 PNK
HOT IN RUN
PWR WDO
30 AMP (C.B.)
BATT
CLOCK
IGN
ACC
LPS
PWR
5A
INST LPS
30 A
PWR ACC
20A
HORN/DM
20A
IGN/GAUGES
15A
BRAKE
15A
STOP/HAZ
20A
T/L CTSY
15A
TURN/BU
25A
HTR A/C
15A
RADIO
10A
ECM B
10A
ECM I
30 A
PWR WDO
25A
WIPER
10A
DRL
3A
CRANK
FUS/PLR
FRONT
12084577
REAR

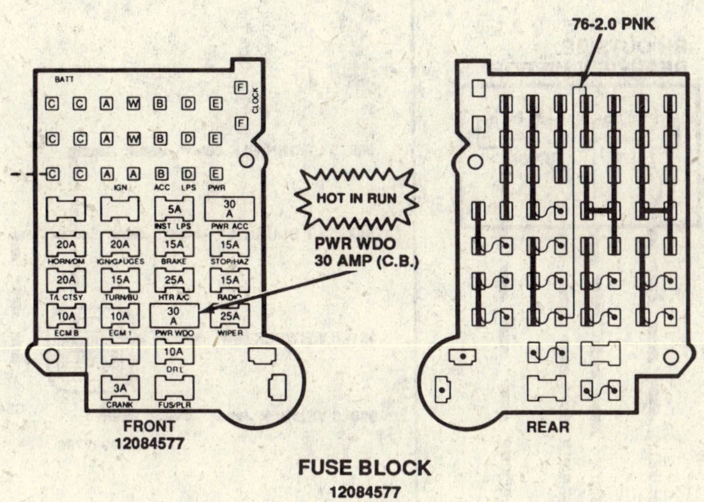

FUSE BLOCK
12084577

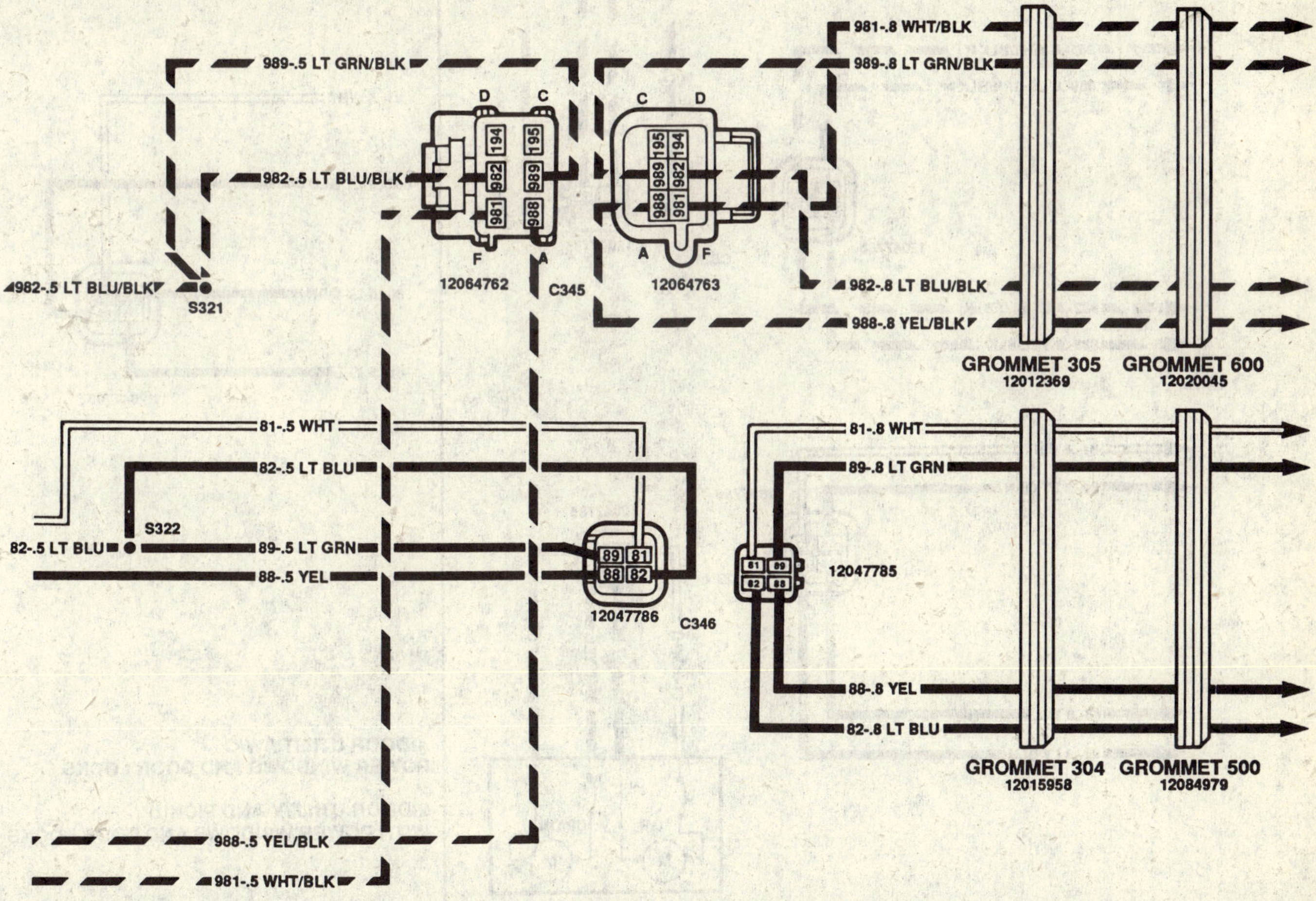

981-.8 WHT/BLK
989-.5 LT GRN/BLK
989-.8 LT GRN/BLK
D
C
C
D
194
195
195
194
982
989
989
982
981
988
988
981
982-.5 LT BLU/BLK
982-.5 LT BLU/BLK
S321
F
A
A
F
12064762
C345
12064763
982-.8 LT BLU/BLK
988-.8 YEL/BLK
GROMMET 305
12012369
GROMMET 600
12020045
81-.5 WHT
81-.8 WHT
82-.5 LT BLU
89-.8 LT GRN
S322
82-.5 LT BLU
89-.5 LT GRN
88-.5 YEL
89
81
88
82
12047786
C346
81
89
82
88
12047785
88-.8 YEL
82-.8 LT BLU
GROMMET 304
12015958
GROMMET 500
12084979
988-.5 YEL/BLK
981-.5 WHT/BLK

1988-91

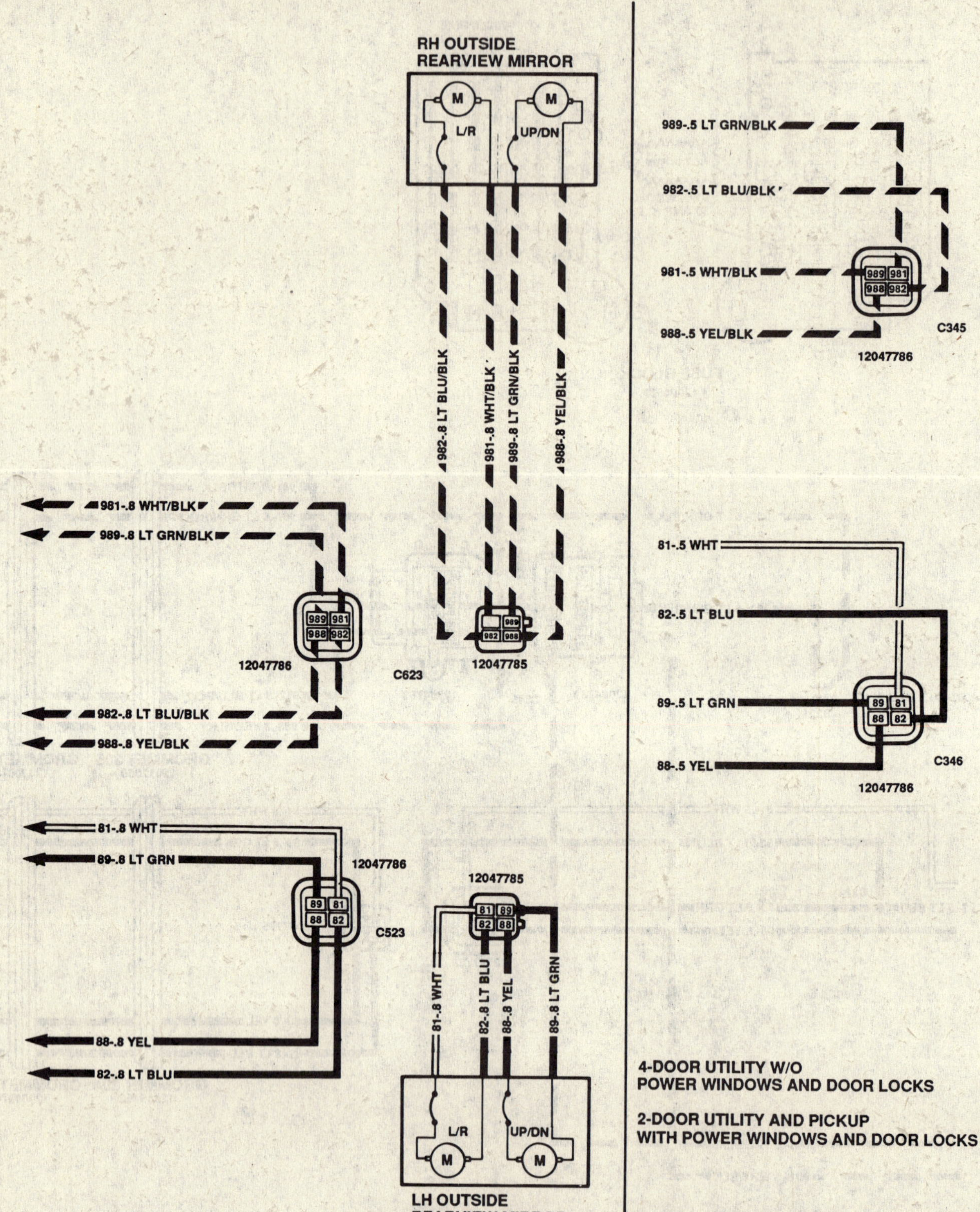

4-DOOR UTILITY W/O POWER WINDOWS AND DOOR LOCKS

2-DOOR UTILITY AND PICKUP WITH POWER WINDOWS AND DOOR LOCKS

1988-91

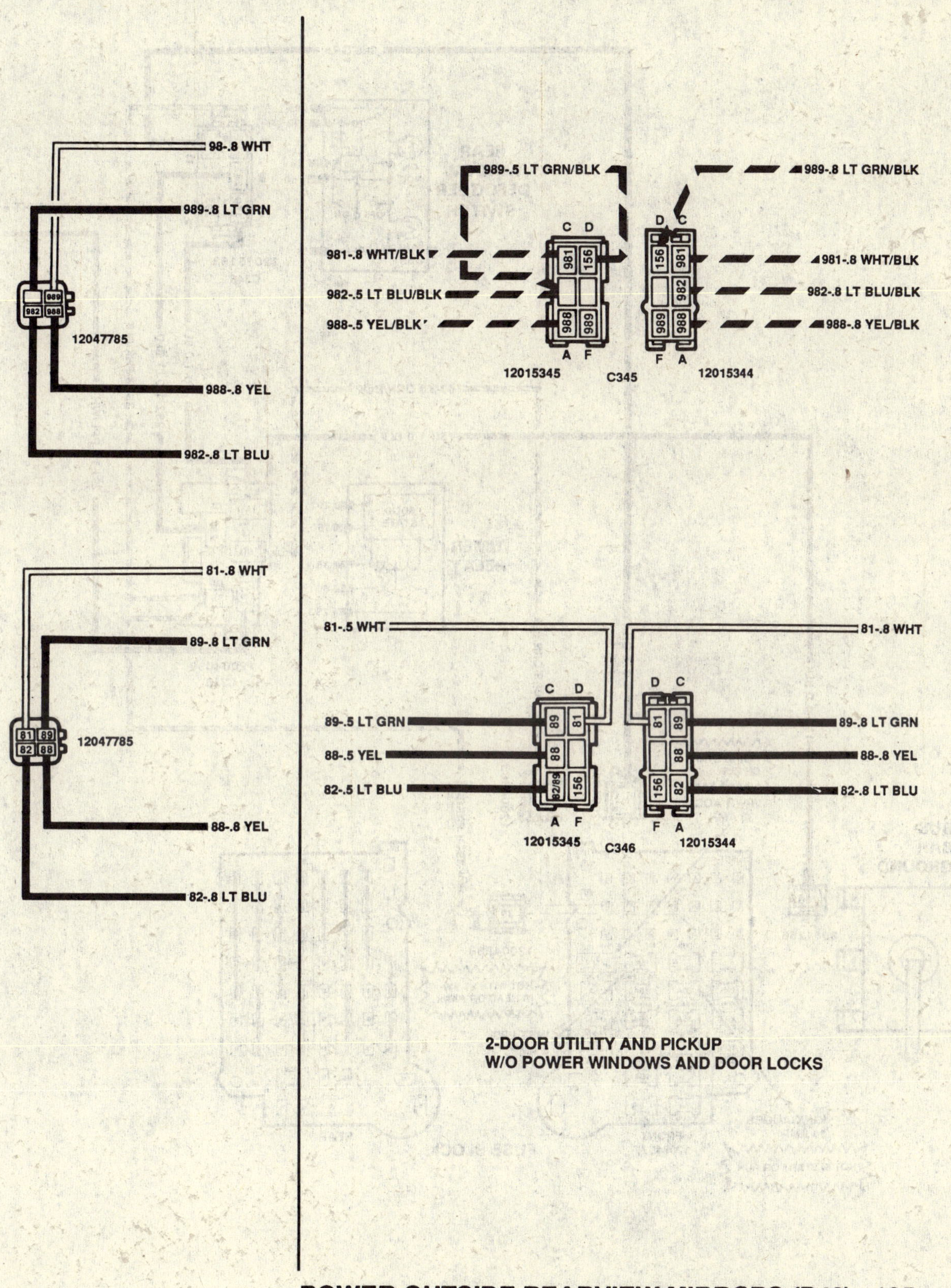

POWER OUTSIDE REARVIEW MIRRORS (D48) 195

1988-91

8-.8 GRA
REAR WINDOW DEFOGGER SWITCH
ON INDC.
OFF
ON
PANEL LIGHT
293
292
39
150
8
D
C
B
A
P
12015163
C345
293-.8 PPL/WHT
150-1.0 BLK
292-1.0 LT BLU
39-.8 PNK/BLK
293-5.0 PPL/WHT
60-3.0 ORN/BLK
TIMER RELAY
SOLID STATE
60
E
12004099
C346
8-.8 GRA
60-.3 ORN/BLK
HOT IN START OR RUN
PWR ACC 30 AMP
12004885
12004883
BUS BAR GROUND
8911256
12004888
HOT WITH LT SW IN HEAD OR PARK
INST LPS 5 AMP
IGN/GAUGES 20 AMP
HOT IN START OR RUN
FRONT 12084577
FUSE BLOCK
REAR

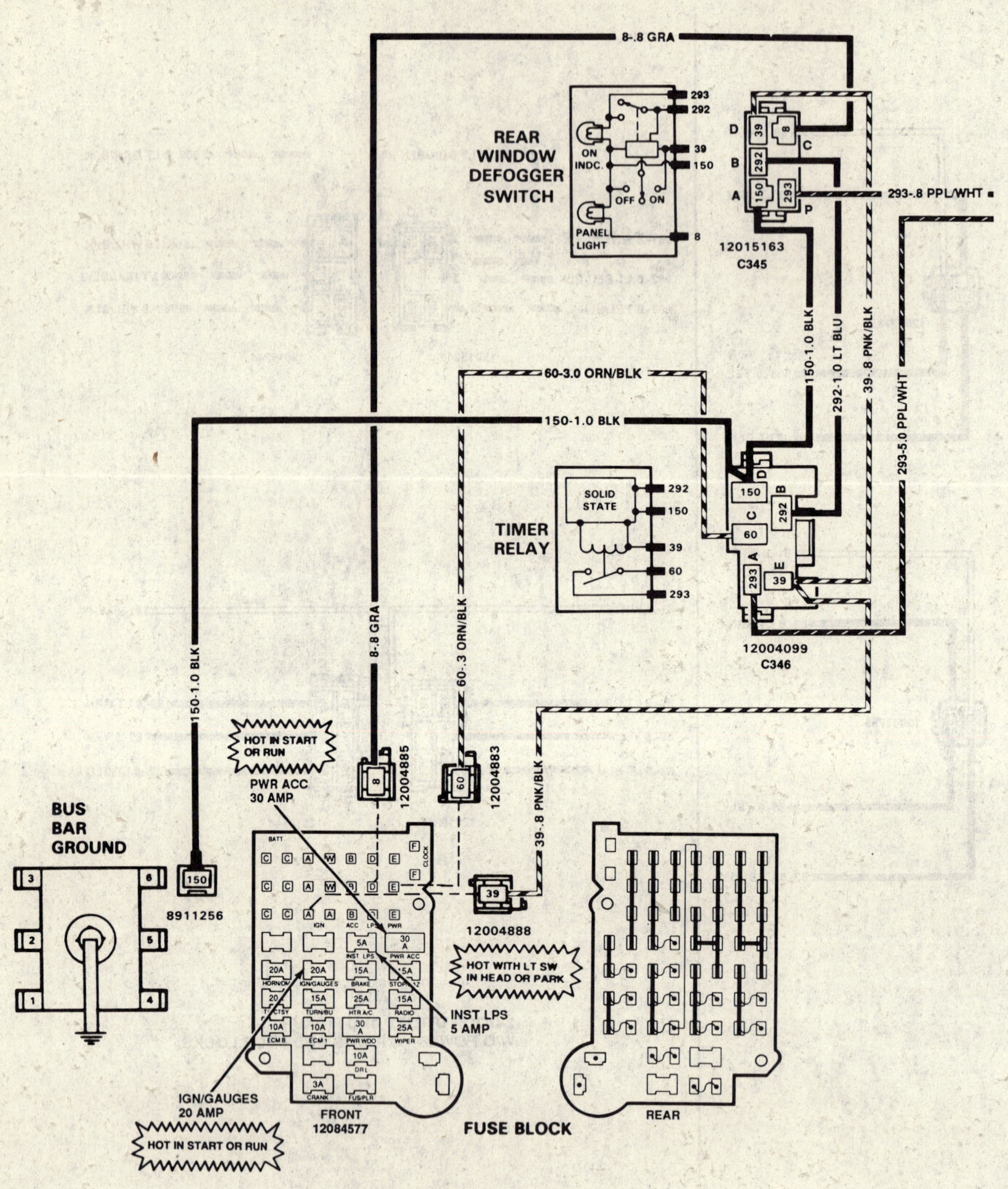

1988-91

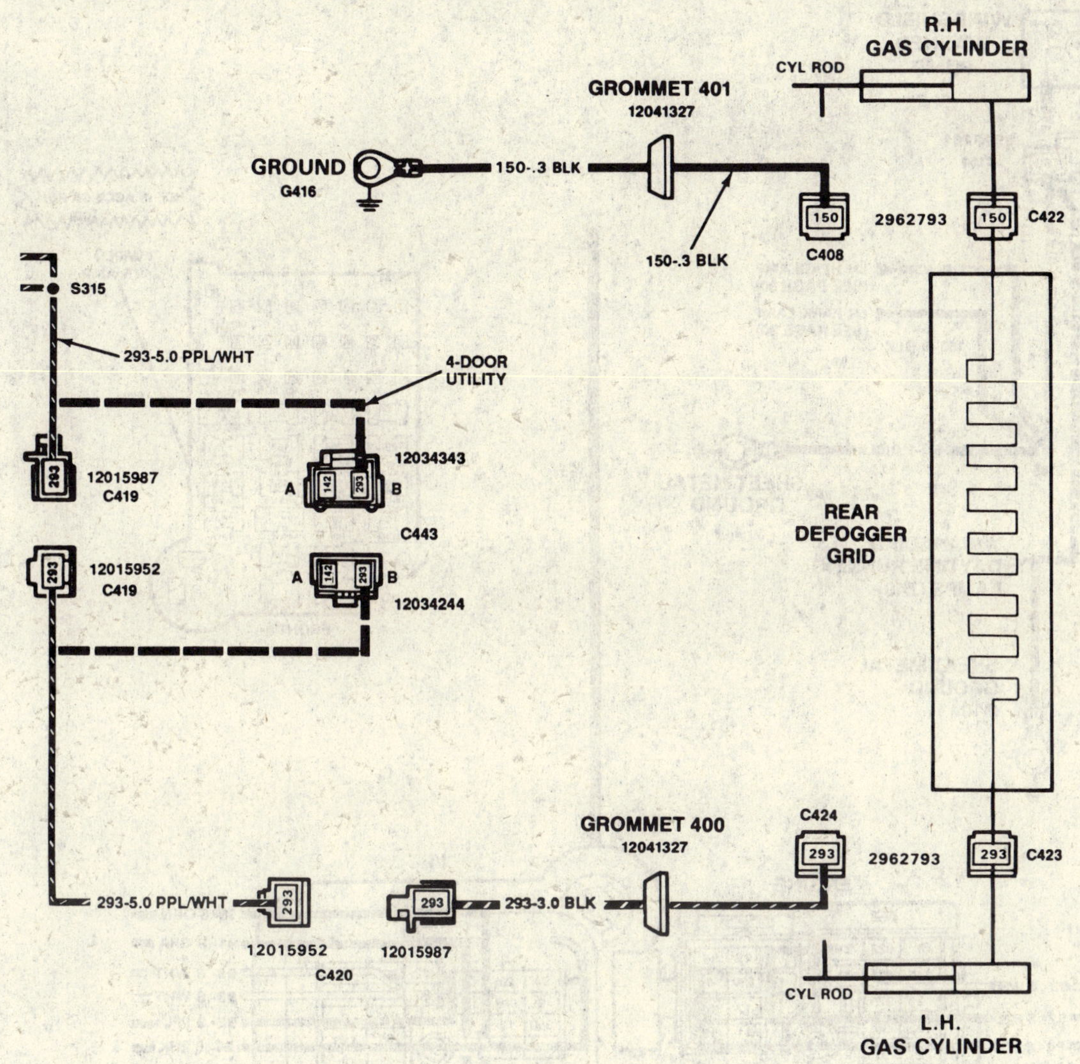

REAR DEFOGGER (C49) 197

1988-91

WINDSHIELD WASHER PUMP
8917261
C154
150-.8 BLK
LH HEADLAMP (SEE PAGE 30)
LH PARK LAMP (SEE PAGE 30)
150-.8 BLK
150-1.0 BLK
S165
SHEET METAL GROUND
G104
WIPER MOTOR
W/CANADIAN DAYTIME RUNNING LAMPS (Z49)
SHEET METAL GROUND
G104
12015664
C155
HOT IN ACCY OR RUN
WIPER 25 AMP
FRONT
12084577
ENGINE
1.0 PPL W/2.5L (151 CID) ENGINE
93-.8 WHT
92-.8 PPL
94-.8 PNK
98-.8 ORN
91-.8 GRA
12020100
C111
12020183
C100
I/P
98-.8 ORN
91-.8 GRA
93-.8 WHT
93-.8 WHT
92-.8 PPL
94-.8 PNK
12020184
C100

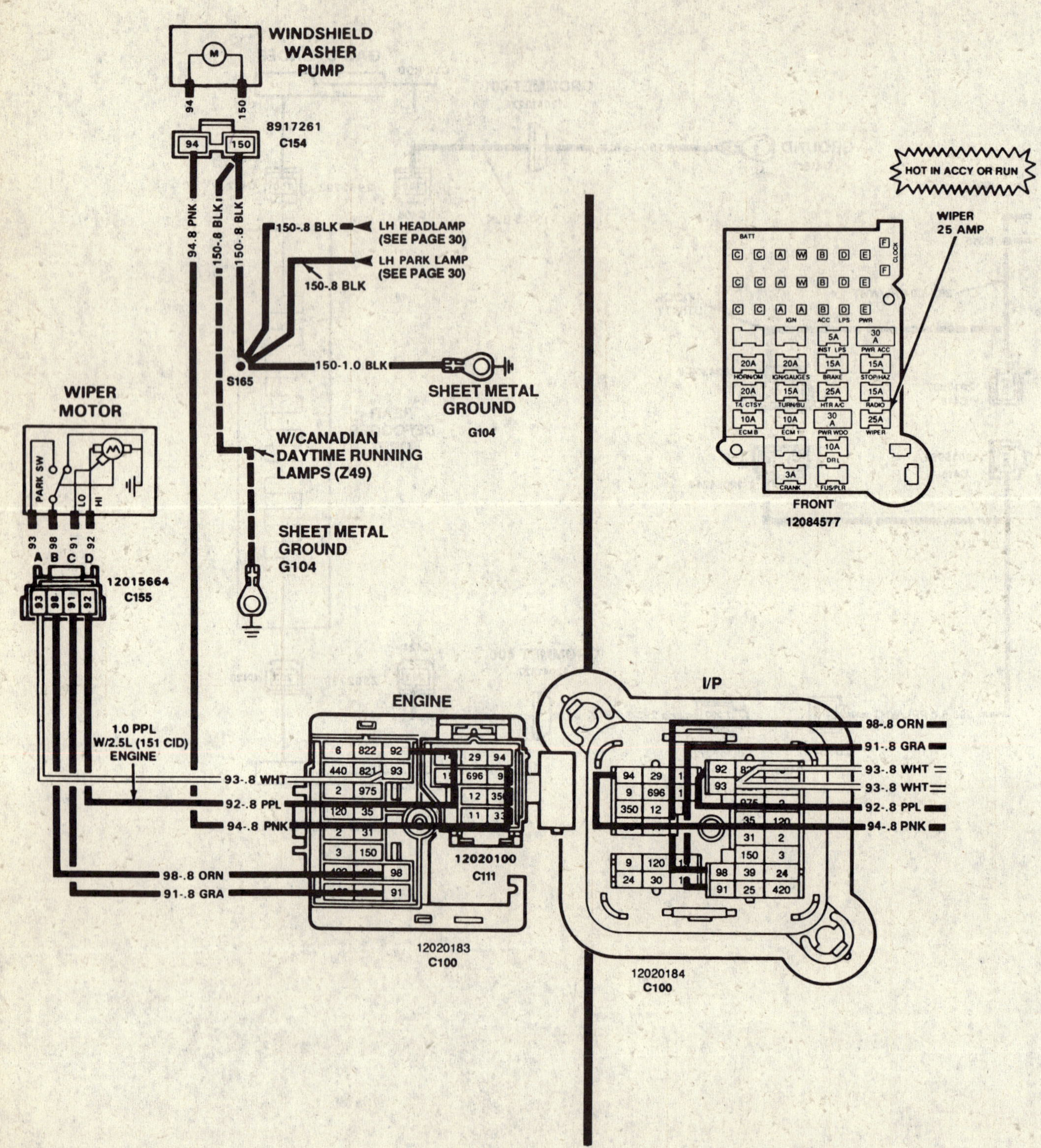

1988-91

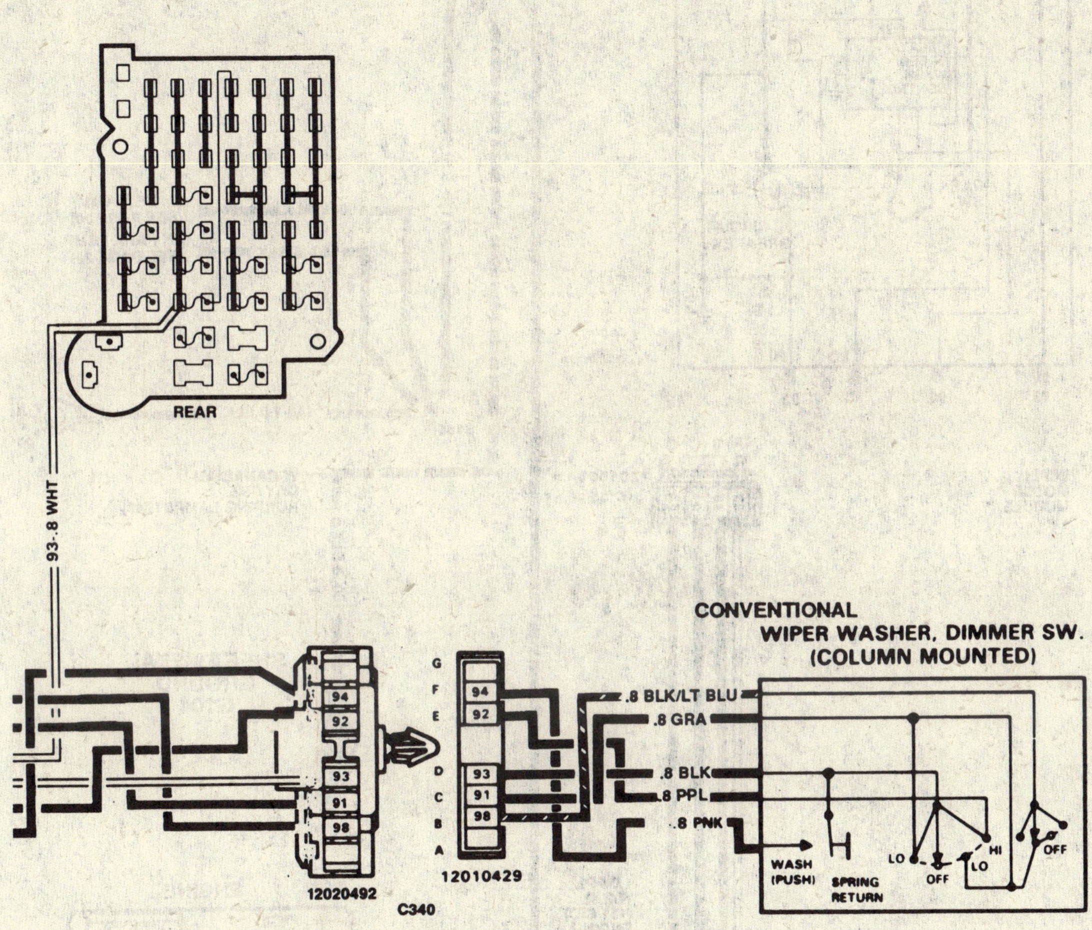

CONVENTIONAL WIPER/WASHER 201

1988-91

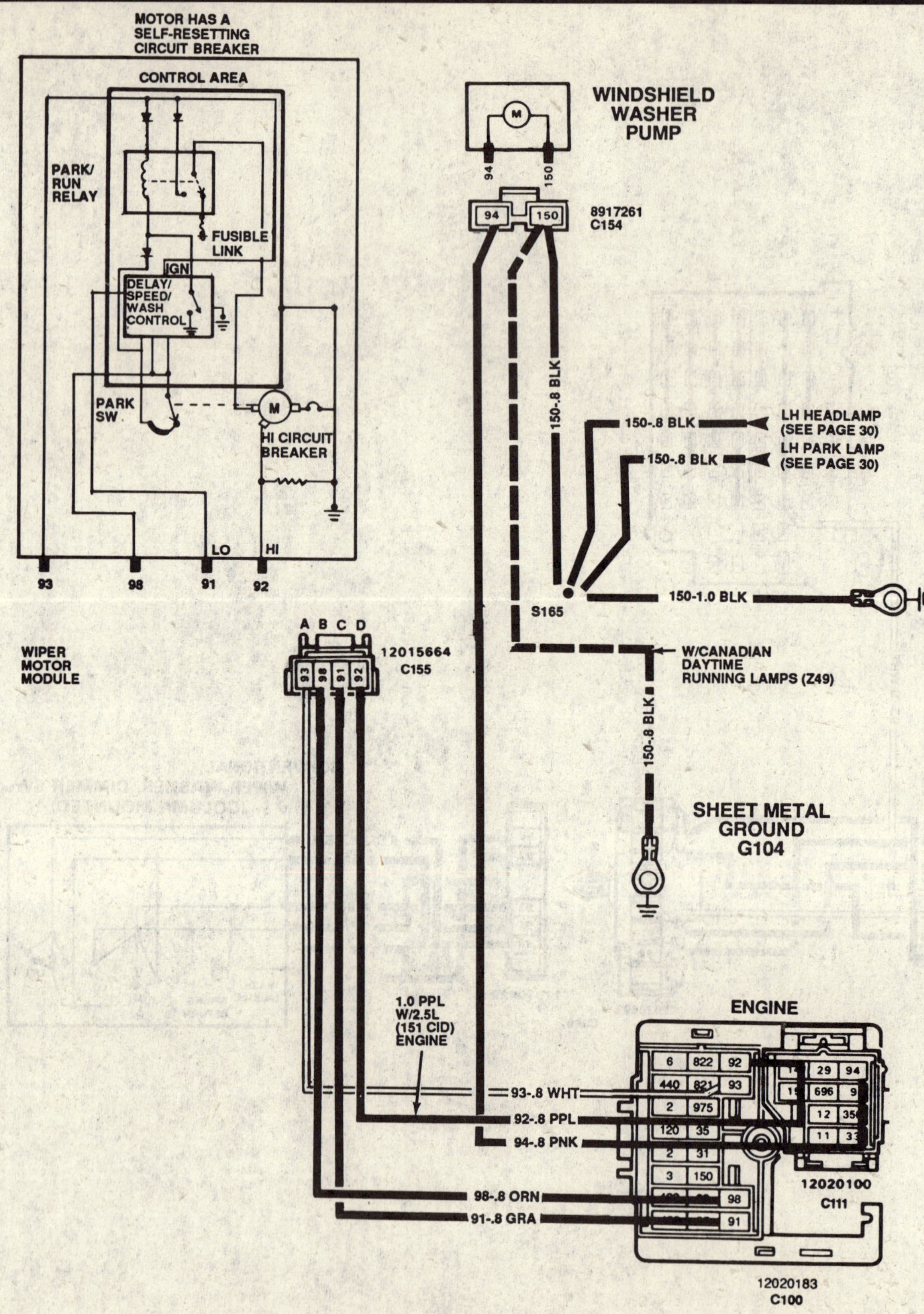

202 PULSE WIPER/WASHER

1988-91

HOT IN ACCY OR RUN
WIPER 25 AMP
BATT
CLOCK
IGN
ACC
LPS
PWR
5A
30 A
INST LPS
PWR ACC
20A
20A
15A
15A
HORN/DM
IGN/GAUGES
BRAKE
STOP/HAZ
20A
15A
25A
15A
T/L CTSY
TURN/BU
HTR A/C
RADIO
10A
10A
30 A
25A
ECM B
ECM 1
PWR WDO
WIPER
10A
DRL
3A
CRANK
FUS/PLR
FRONT
12084577
REAR
SHEET METAL
GROUND
G104
93-.8 WHT
I/P
93-.8 WHT
98-.8 GRN
91-.8 GRA
93-.8 WHT
92-.8 PPL
94-.8 PNK
12020184
C100
12020492
C340
12010429
.8 BLK/LT BLU
.8 GRA
.8 BLK
.8 PPL
.8 PNK
PULSE WIPER/WASHER SW.
(COLUMN MOUNTED)
MIST
OFF
HI
LO
PULSE
WASH
(PULSE)

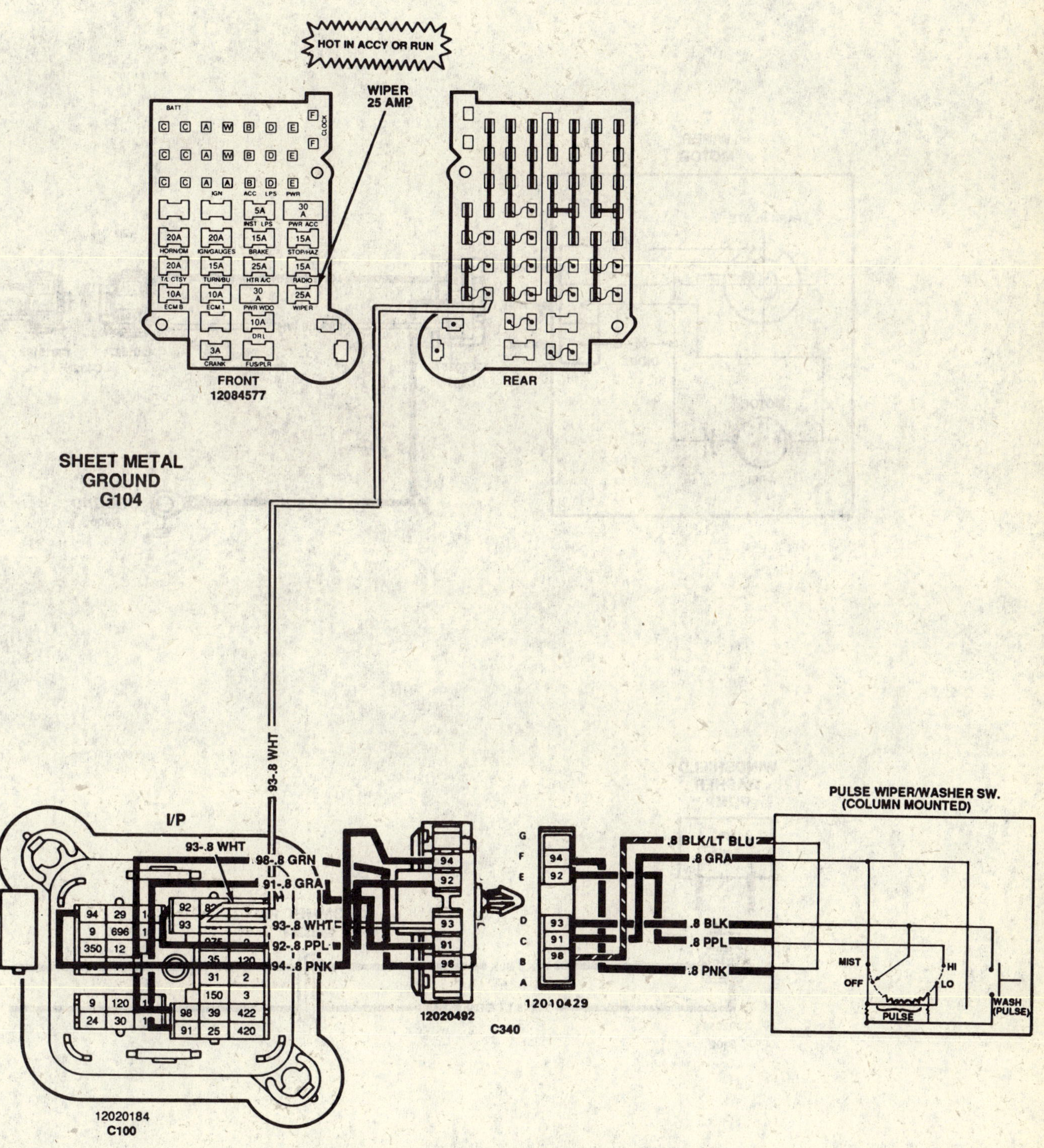

1988-91

WIPER MOTOR
PARK PLATE
141 A
150B
393C
DIODE
MOTOR
ARM
141
150
393
12020397
C901
141-1.0 BRN
393-1.0 WHT
141
393
B
141
393
12015271
12015199
C432
150-.8 BLK
GROUND
G900

WINDSHIELD WASHER PUMP
392
150
B A
392
150
12020599
C162
150-.8 BLK
392-.8 LT GRN
GROMMET 100
12015958

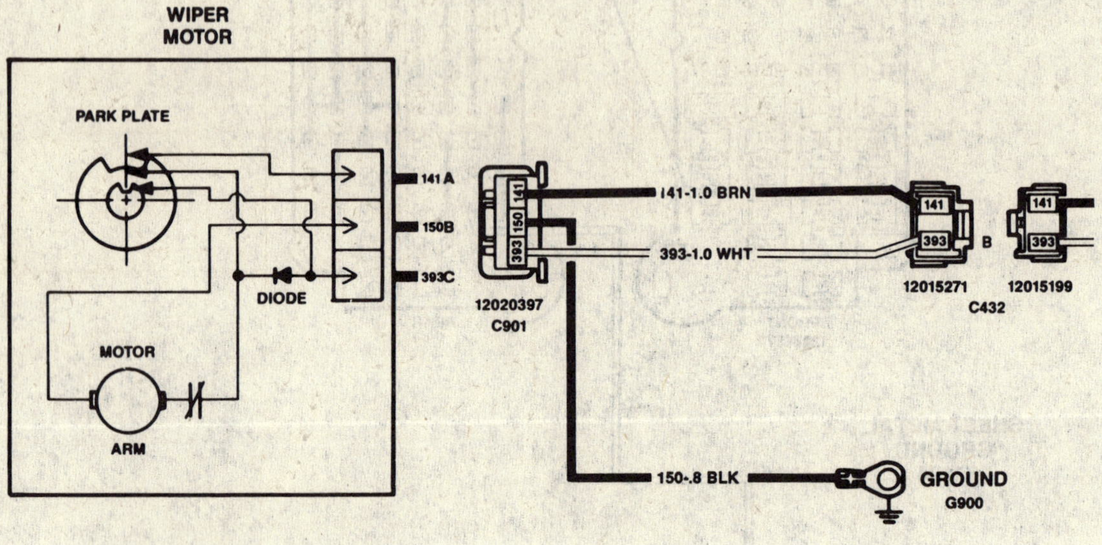

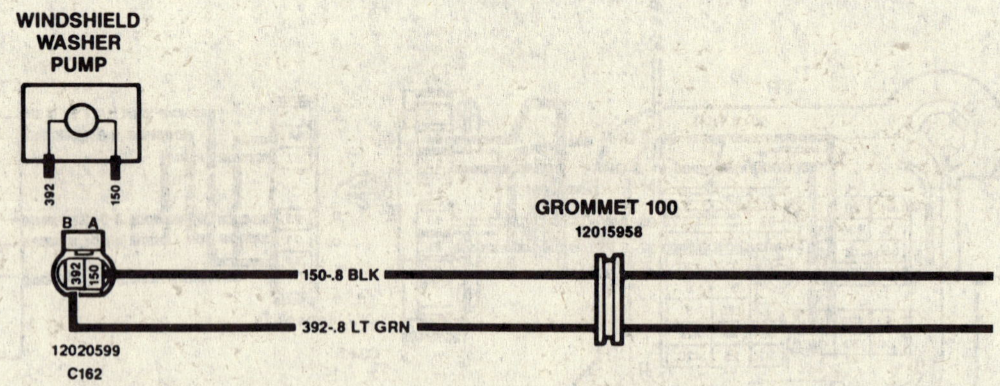

1988-91

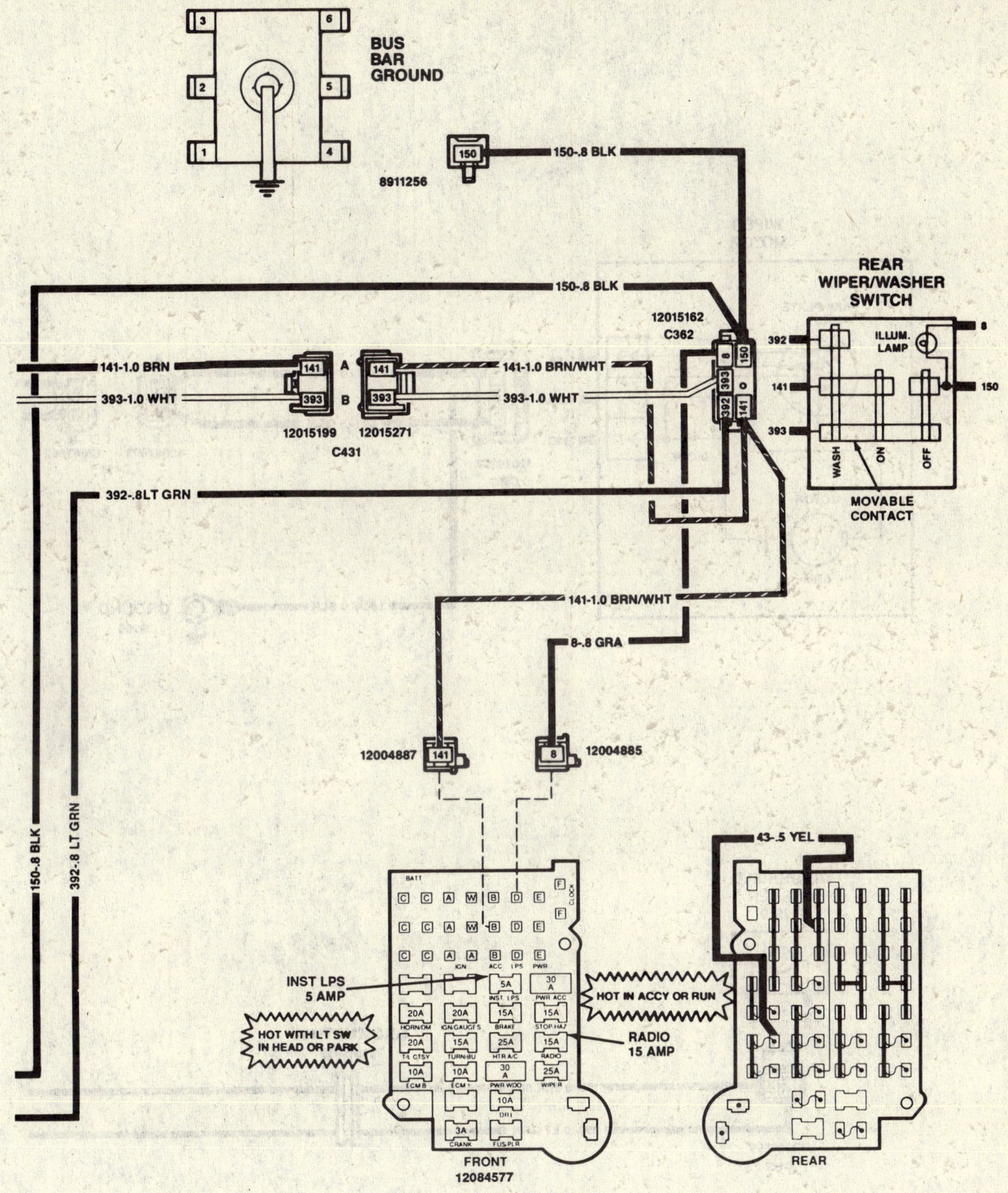

REAR WIPER/WASHER (C25) - 2-DOOR UTILITY 203

1988-91

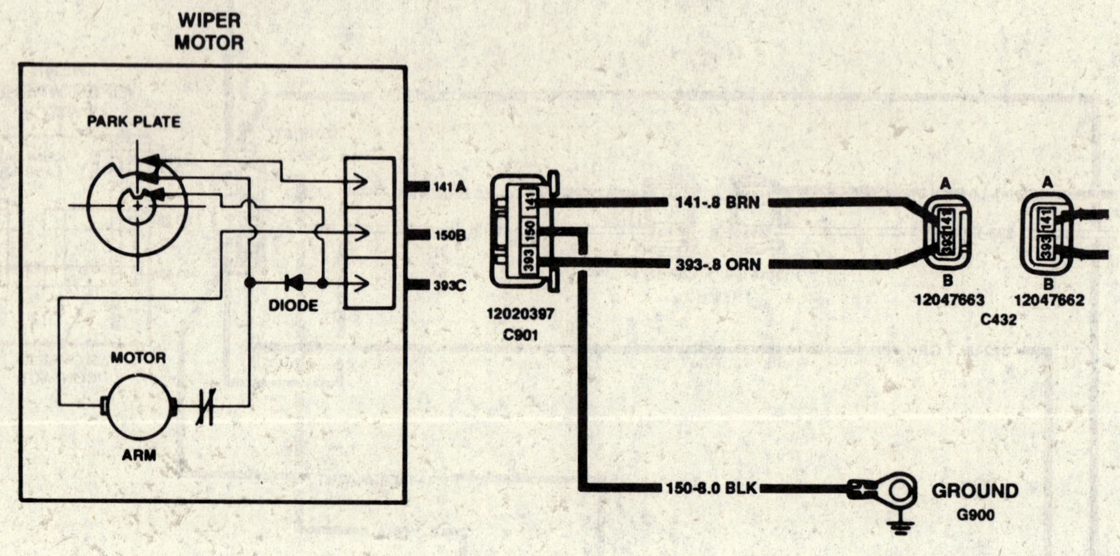

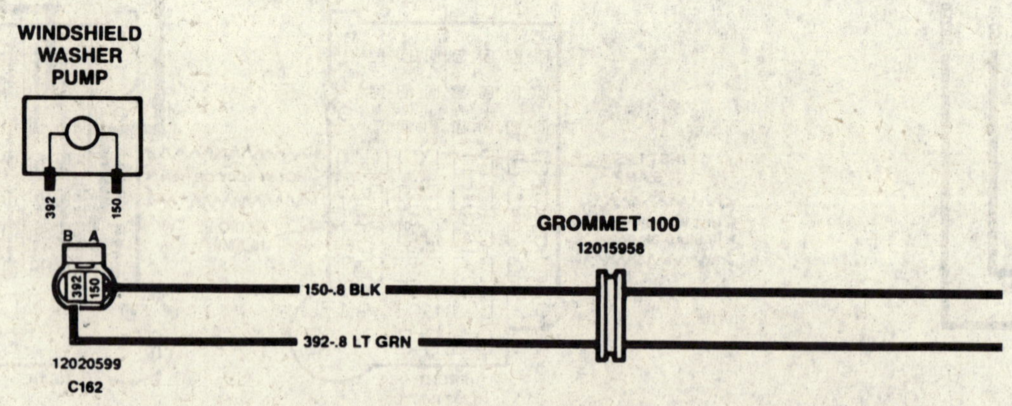

204 REAR WIPER/WASHER (C25) - 4-DOOR UTILITY

1988-91

BUS
BAR
GROUND
150
8911256
150-.8 BLK
150-.8 BLK
REAR
WIPER/WASHER
SWITCH
12015162
C362
141-.8 BRN
393-.8 ORN
392-.8LT GRN
392
141
393
8
150
ILLUM.
LAMP
WASH
ON
OFF
MOVABLE
CONTACT
141-1.0 BRN/WHT
8-.8 GRA
12004887
141
8
12004885
150-.8 BLK
392-.8 LT GRN
43-.5 YEL
INST LPS
5 AMP
HOT IN ACCY OR RUN
HOT WITH LT SW
IN HEAD OR PARK
RADIO
15 AMP
FRONT
12084577
REAR

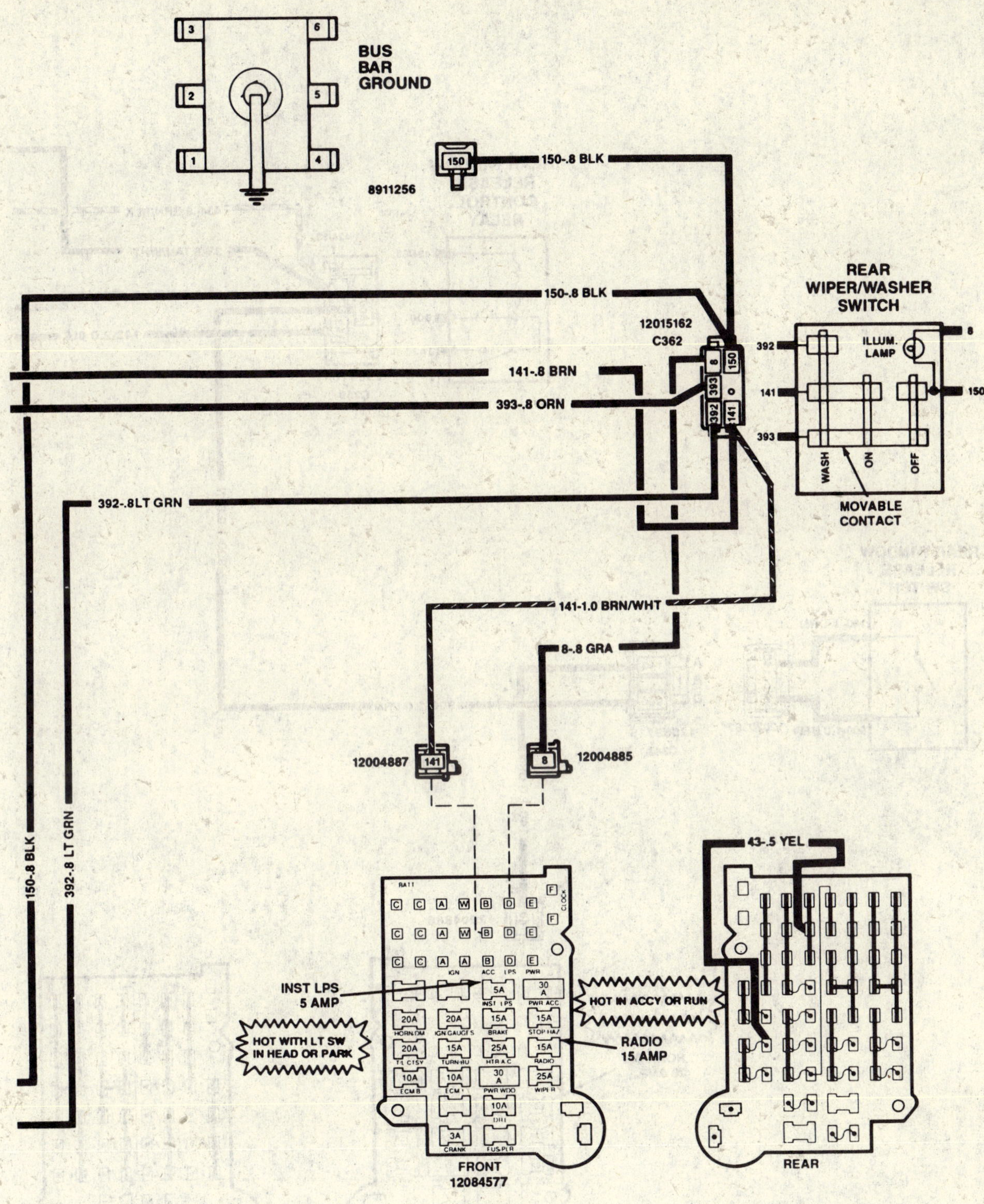

1988-91

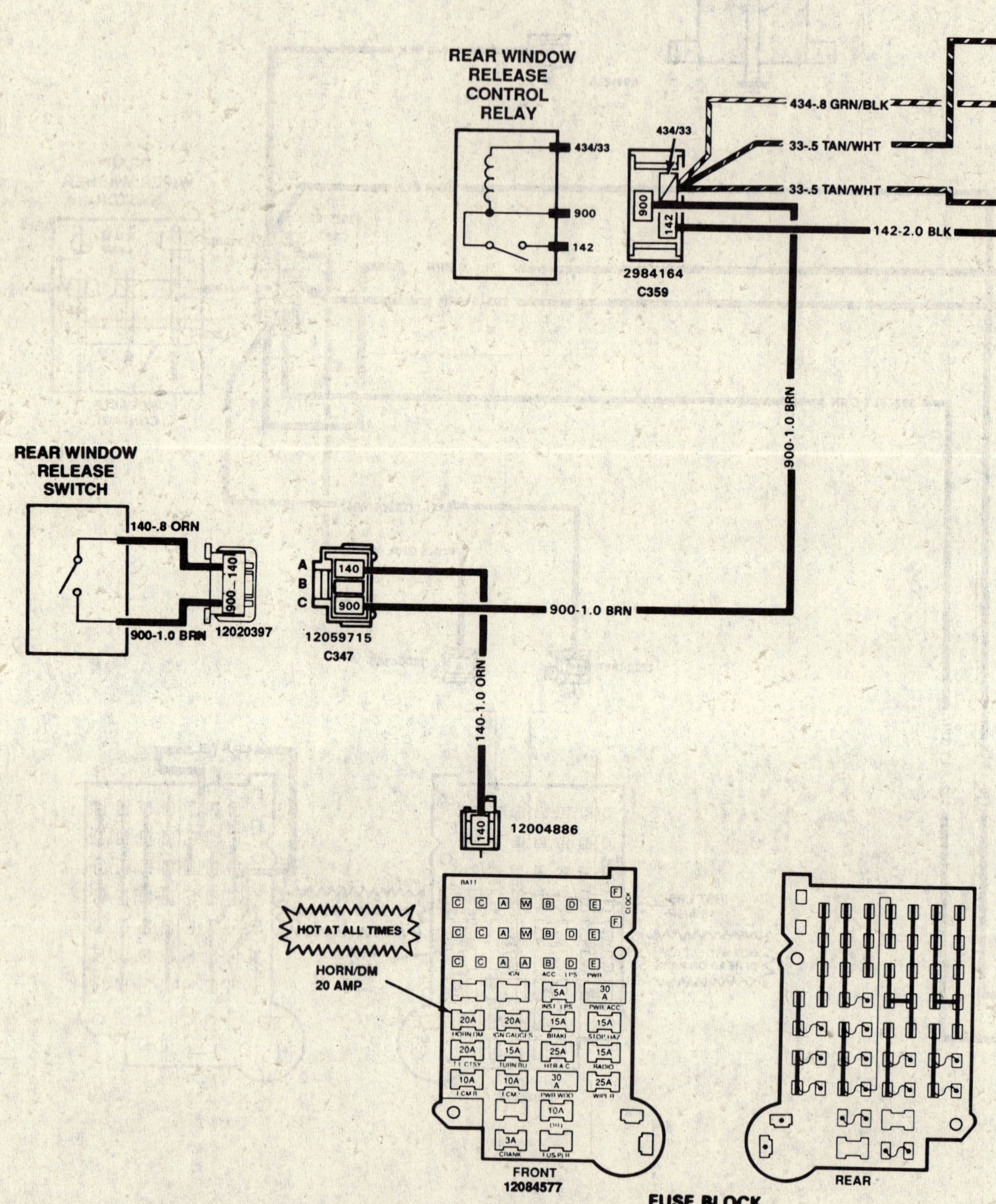

206 REAR WINDOW RELEASE (AU6) - 2-DOOR UTILITY

1988-91

33-.5 TAN/WHT
PARKING BRAKE SW (SEE PAGE 116)
33-.5 TAN/WHT
I/P CLUSTER (SEE PAGE 116)
PRK NEUTRAL SW (AUTO. TRANS.) (SEE PAGE 69)
33
12004201
12004267
C376
W/AUTO. TRANS.
434
434-.8 GRN/BLK
C376
142
12015952
12015987
C418
142-2.0 BLK
12059885
C460
12059884
142-2.0 BLK
GROMMET 900
20040276
142-2.0 BLK
REL
SET
33
12004267
C319
PARKING BRAKE WARNING SWITCH
REAR WINDOW RELEASE SOLENOID
142
2977253
C900

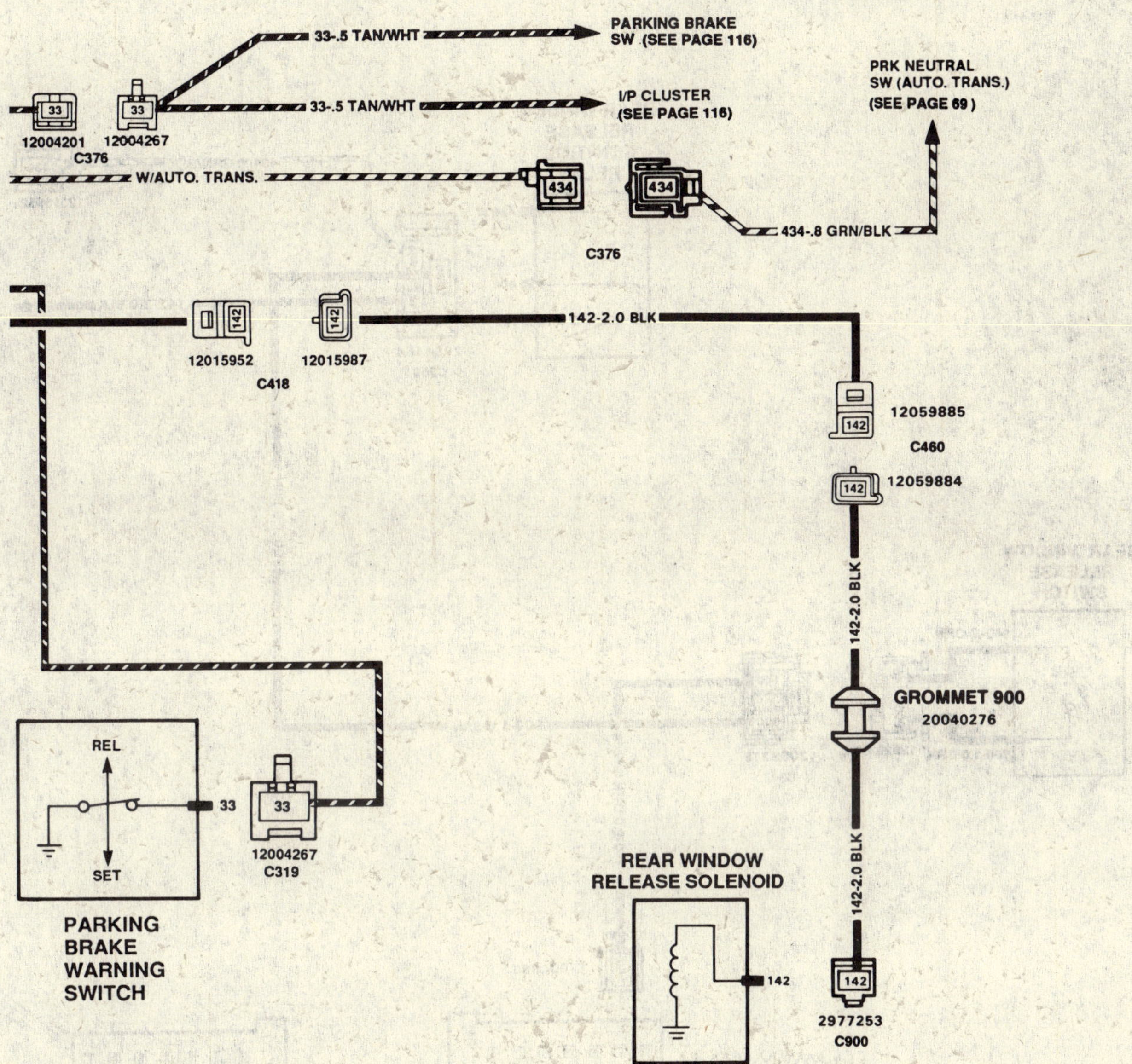

1988-91

REAR WINDOW RELEASE CONTROL RELAY
434/33
900
142
434
900
142
2984164
C359
434-.8 GRN/BLK
434
12015952
142-2.0 BLK
900-1.0 BRN
REAR WINDOW RELEASE SWITCH
140-.8 ORN
900-1.0 BRN
140
900
12020397
A
B
C
140
900
12059715
C347
900-1.0 BRN
140-2.0 ORN
140
12004886
HOT AT ALL TIMES
HORN/DM 20 AMP
FRONT 12084577
REAR
FUSE BLOCK

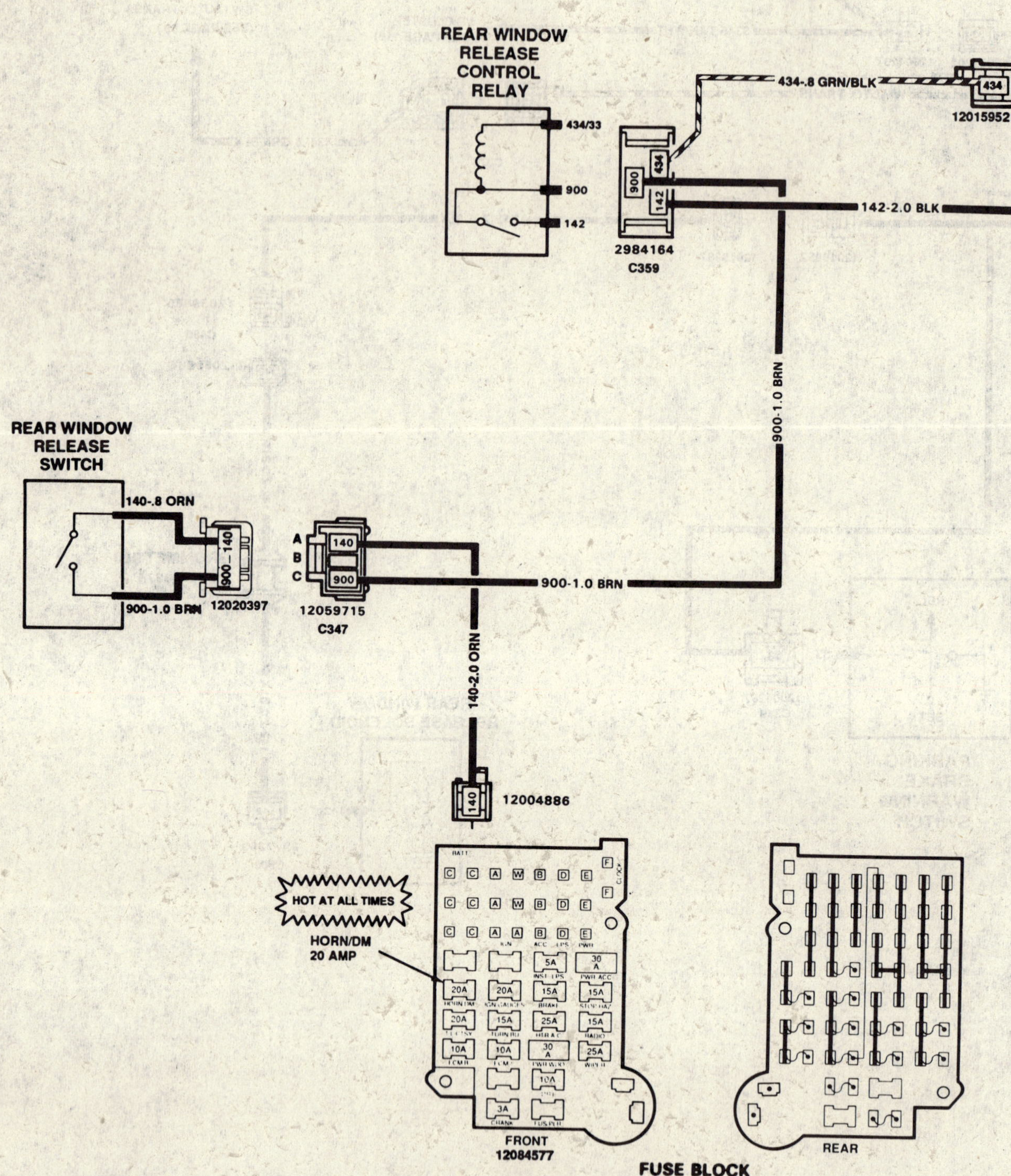

1988-91

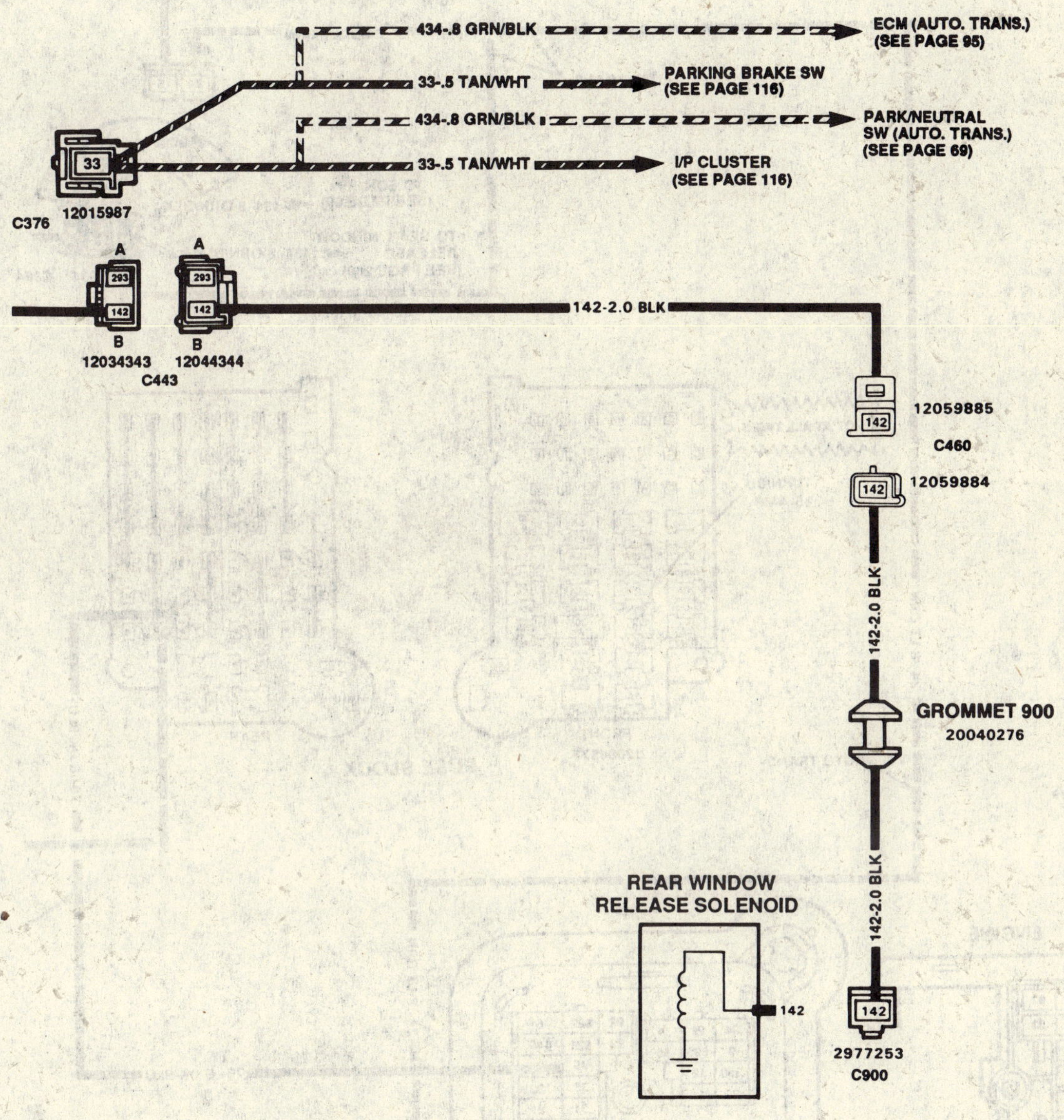

REAR WINDOW RELEASE (AU6) - 4-DOOR UTILITY 207

1988-91

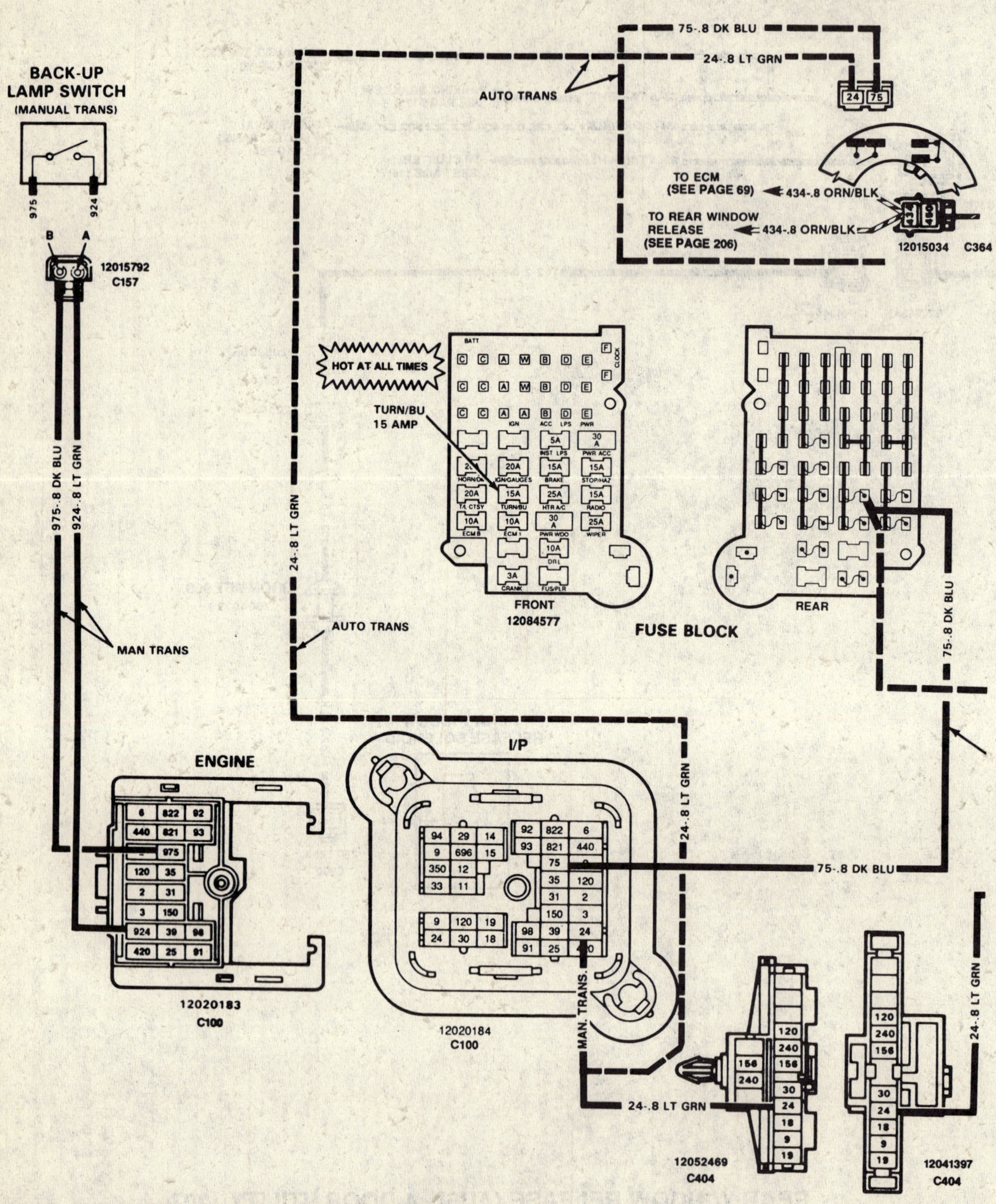

210 BACKUP LAMPS - 2-DOOR UTILITY

1988-91

R.H. SIDE MARKER LAMP (SEE PAGE 42)
FRAME GROUND
G418
150-.8 BLK
150-.8 BLK
2973407
C349
TRANSMISSION NEUTRAL SENSE & BACK UP LAMP SW
(AUTO TRANS)
S418
R.H. TAIL, STOP, & DIR. LAMP
150-.8 BLK
(SEE PAGE 213)
450-.8 BLK/WHT
TO SPLICE S306 (SEE PAGE 21)
GROMMET 402
2989576
150-.8 BLK
R.H. BACKUP LAMP
150
24
9
18
A
B
C
12047676
12020397
C406
12010804
C424
24-.8 LT GRN
24-.8 LT GRN
75-.8 DK BLU
AUTO TRANS
MAN TRANS
24-.8 LT GRN
GROMMET 403
2989576
L.H. BACKUP LAMP
240
18
9
19
24
120
156
30
D
C
B
A
E
F
G
J
24-.8 LT GRN
8900440
C405
8900441
C405
12047676
12020397
C417
12010804
C426
150-.8 BLK
150-.8 BLK
24-.8 LT GRN
FRAME GROUND
G419
150-.8 BLK
S419
L.H. TAIL, STOP, & DIR. LAMP
(SEE PAGE 213)
150-.8 BLK
L.H. SIDE MARKER LAMP
(SEE PAGE 42)

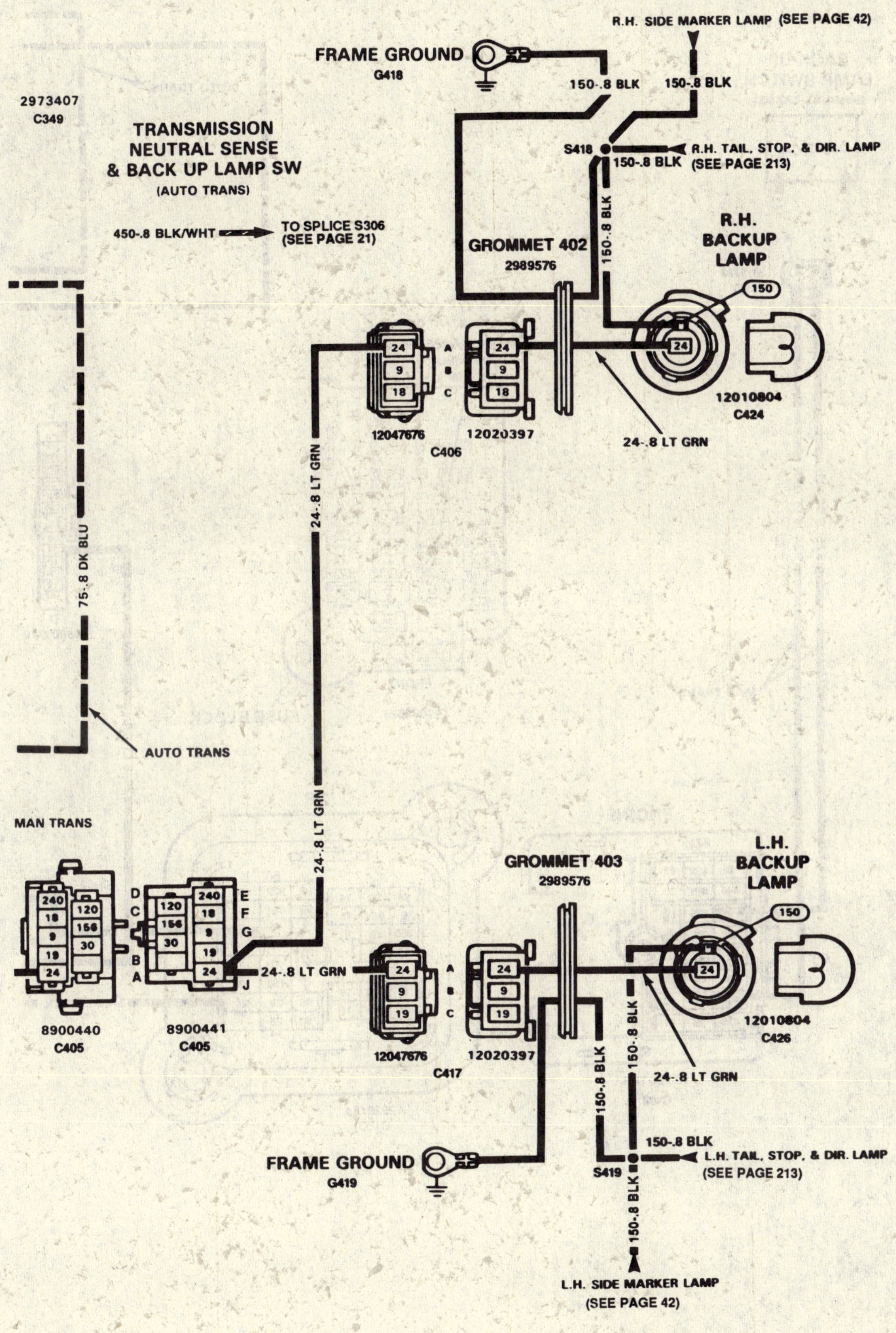

1988-91

BACK-UP
LAMP SWITCH
(MANUAL TRANS)
975
924
B
A
12015792
C157
975-.8 DK BLU
924-.8 LT GRN
MAN TRANS
AUTO TRANS
24-.8 LT GRN
HOT IN START OR RUN
TURN/BU
15 AMP
FRONT
12084577
FUSE BLOCK
P
D
08900320
ENGINE
12020183
C100
I/P
12020184
C100

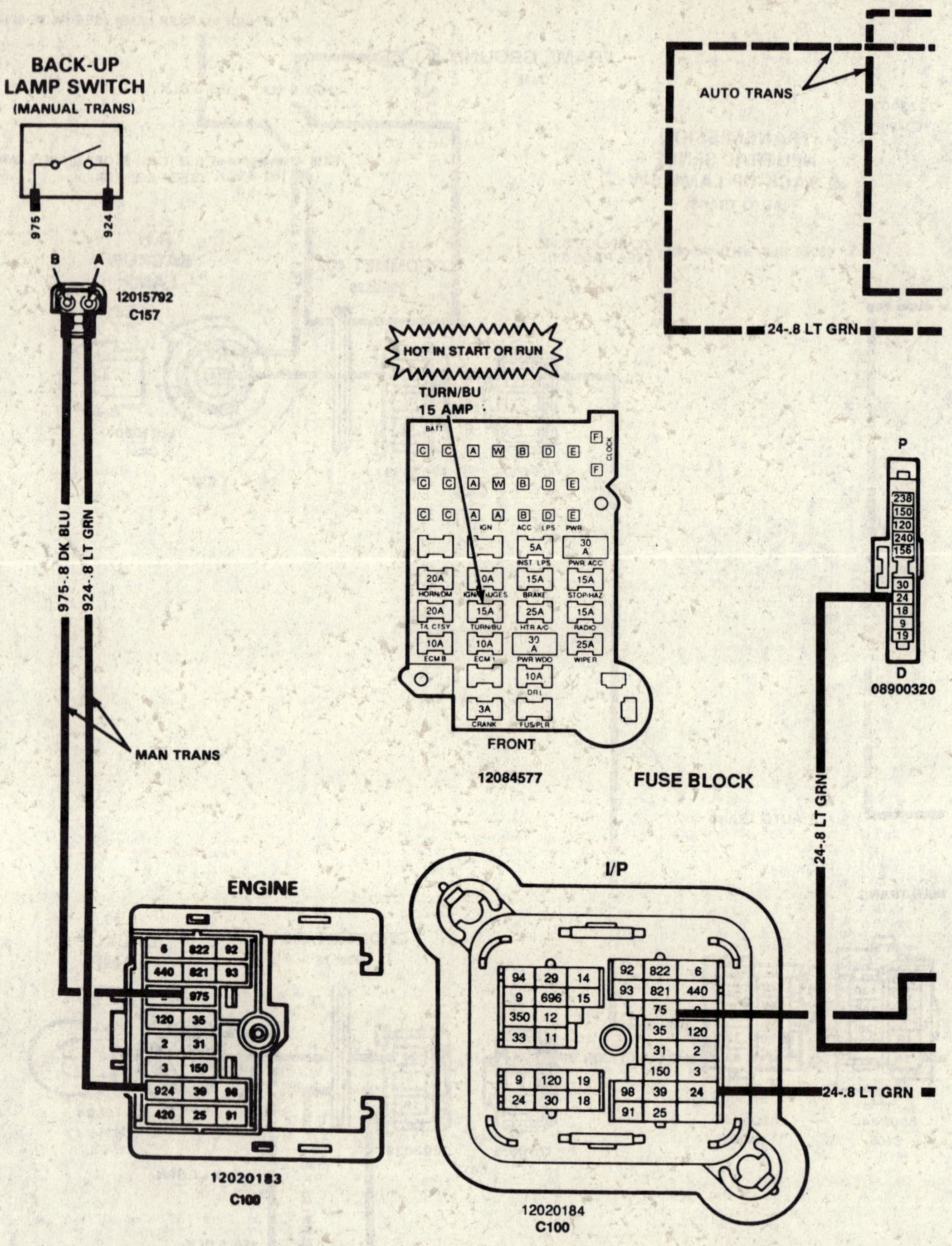

1988-91

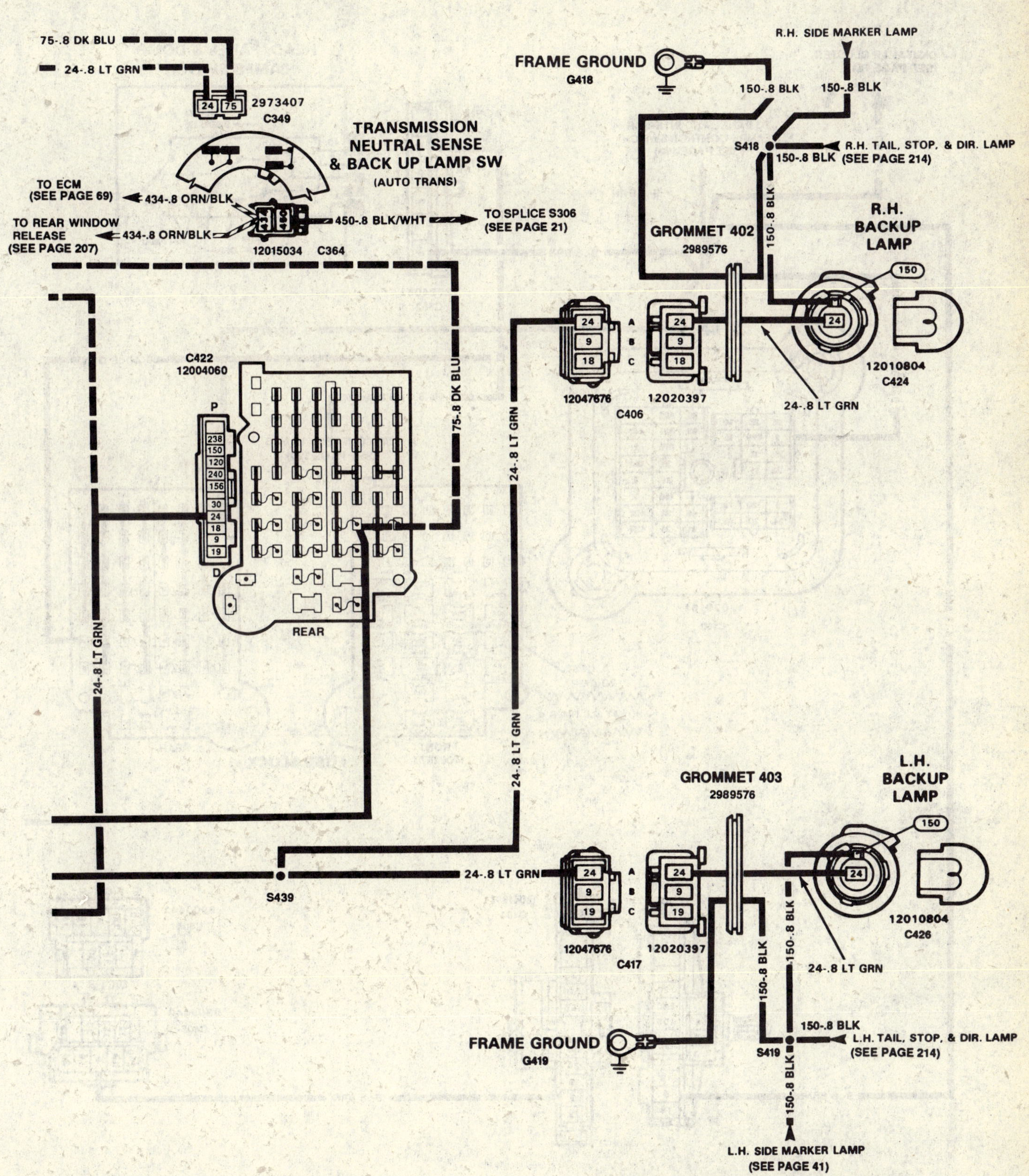

BACKUP LAMPS - 4-DOOR UTILITY 211

1988-91

DIGITAL I/P CLUSTER
(SEE PAGE 151)
TO PANEL AND INTERIOR LAMPS CONTROL SWITCH (SEE PAGE 150)
HEAD, PANEL & DOME LAMPS SWITCH
CIRCUIT BREAKER
HD LP-ON
PARK
HD LP-OFF
OFF
PARK
9-.5 BRN
9-.8 BRN
40-.8 ORN
S300
S308
I/P
12034061
C302
12020184
C100
I/P COURTESY LAMPS (SEE PAGE 170)
T/L CTSY 20 AMP
HOT AT ALL TIMES
FRONT
12084577
FUSE BLOCK
REAR
12052469
C404
12041397
C404
8900441
C405
8900440
C405

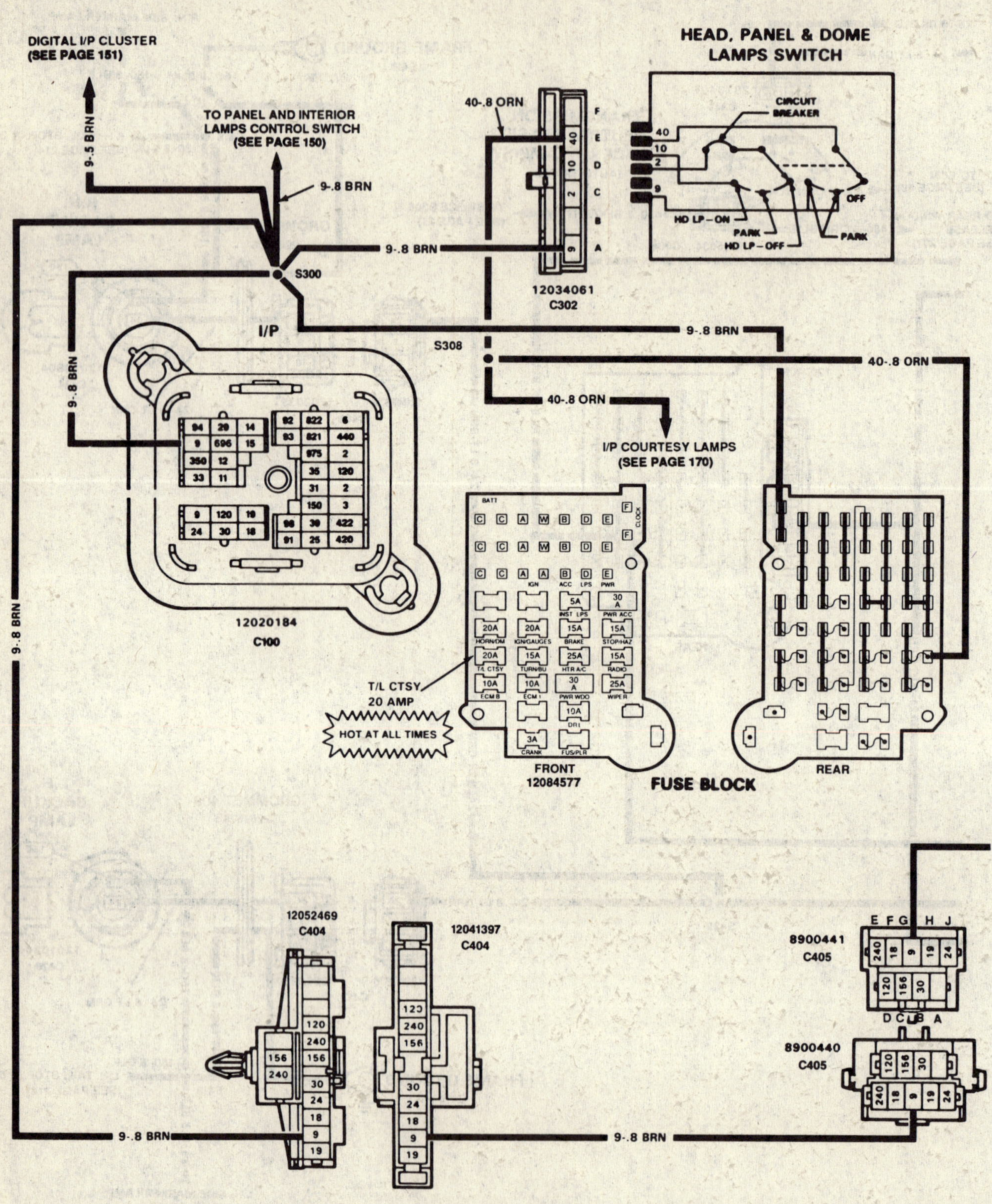

1988-91

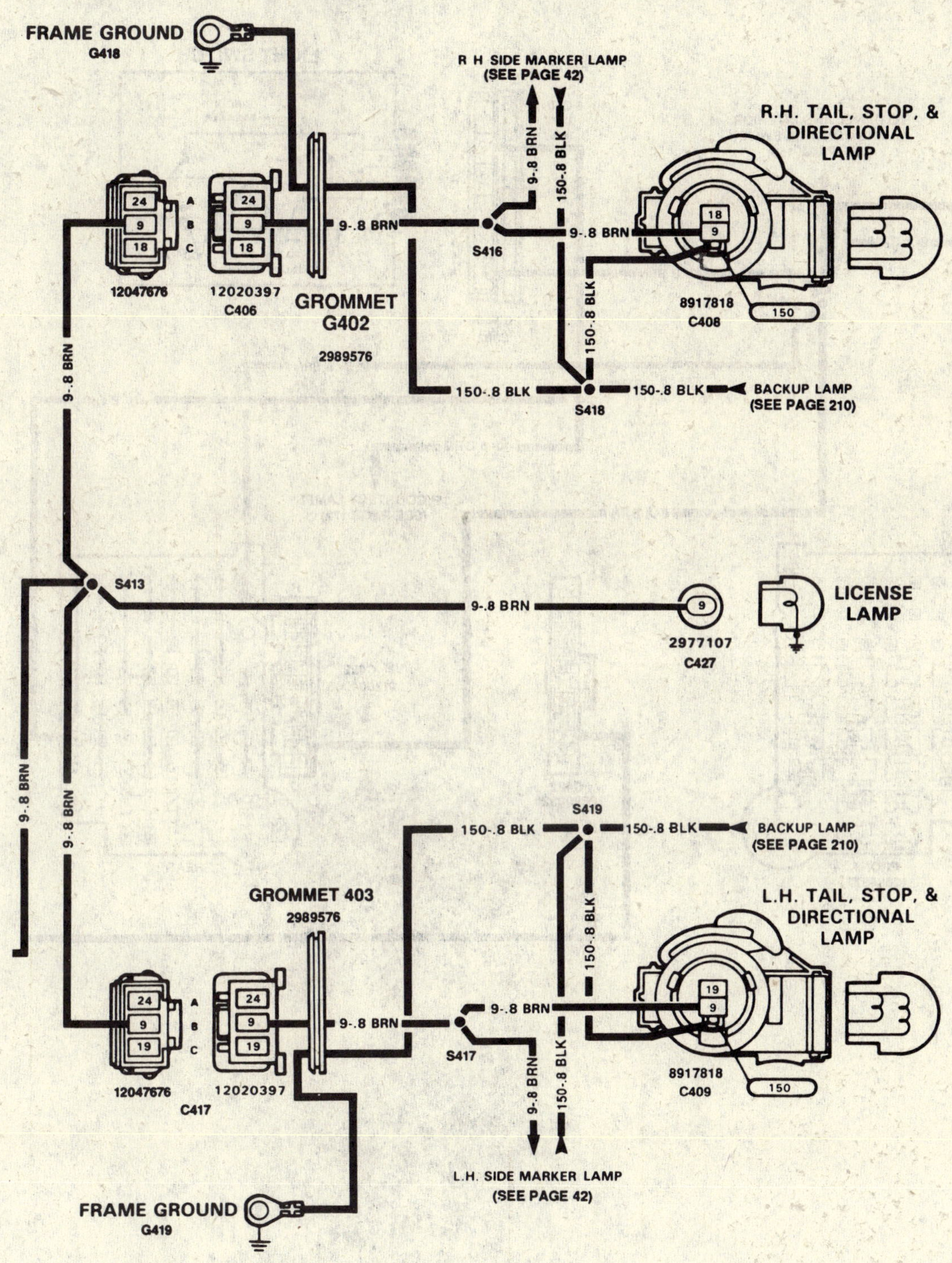

TAIL LAMPS - 2-DOOR UTILITY 213

1988-91

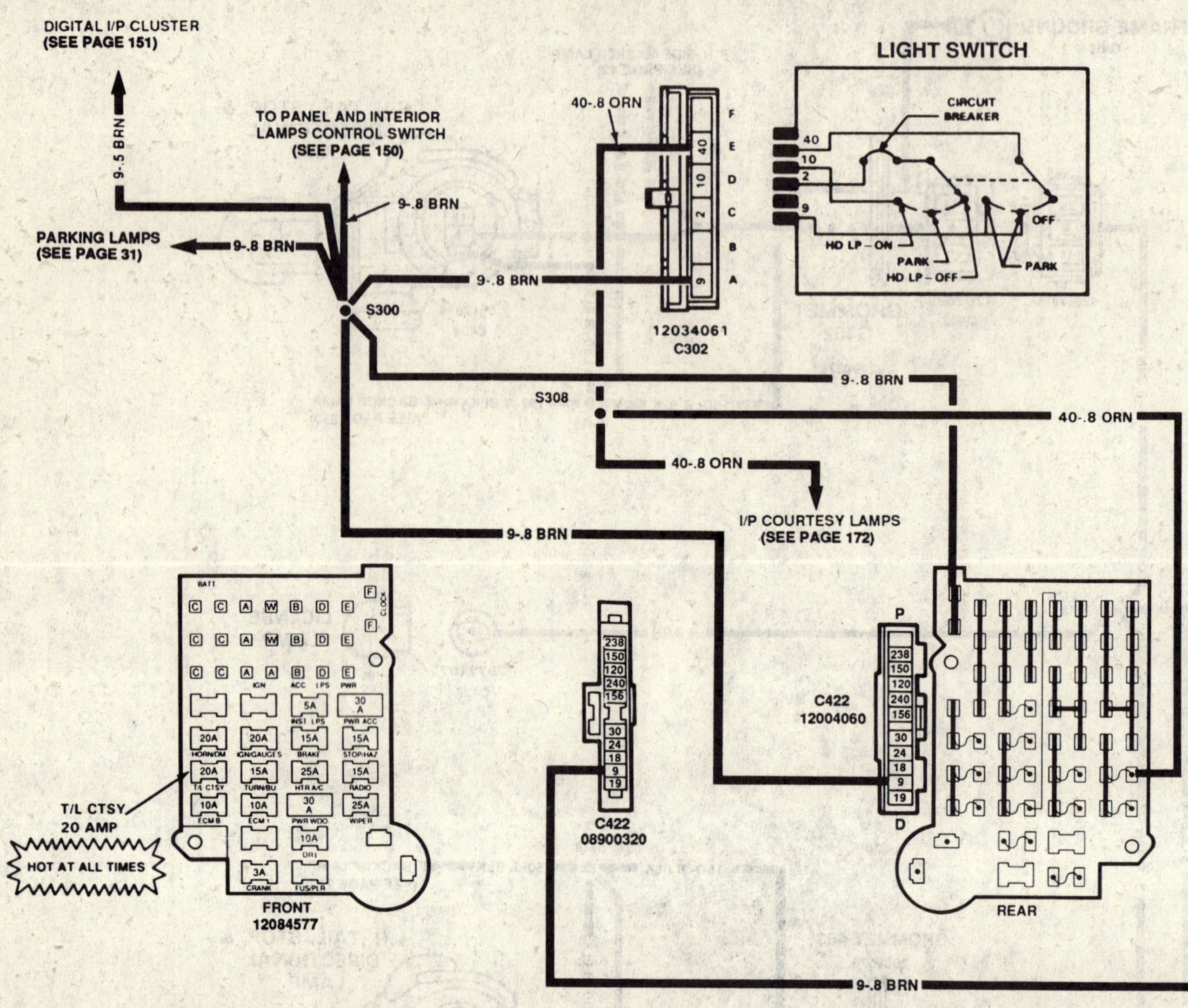

214 TAIL LAMPS - 4-DOOR UTILITY

1988-91

FRAME GROUND
G418
R H SIDE MARKER LAMP
(SEE PAGE 28)
R.H. TAIL, STOP, &
DIRECTIONAL
LAMP
9-.8 BRN
150-.8 BLK
24
9
18
A
B
C
12047676
12020397
C406
GROMMET
G402
2989576
S416
8917818
C408
150
S418
BACKUP LAMP
(SEE PAGE 211)
S413
LICENSE
LAMP
2977107
C427
S419
GROMMET 403
2989576
L.H. TAIL, STOP, &
DIRECTIONAL
LAMP
19
S417
C417
8917818
C409
L.H. SIDE MARKER LAMP
(SEE PAGE 41)
FRAME GROUND
G419

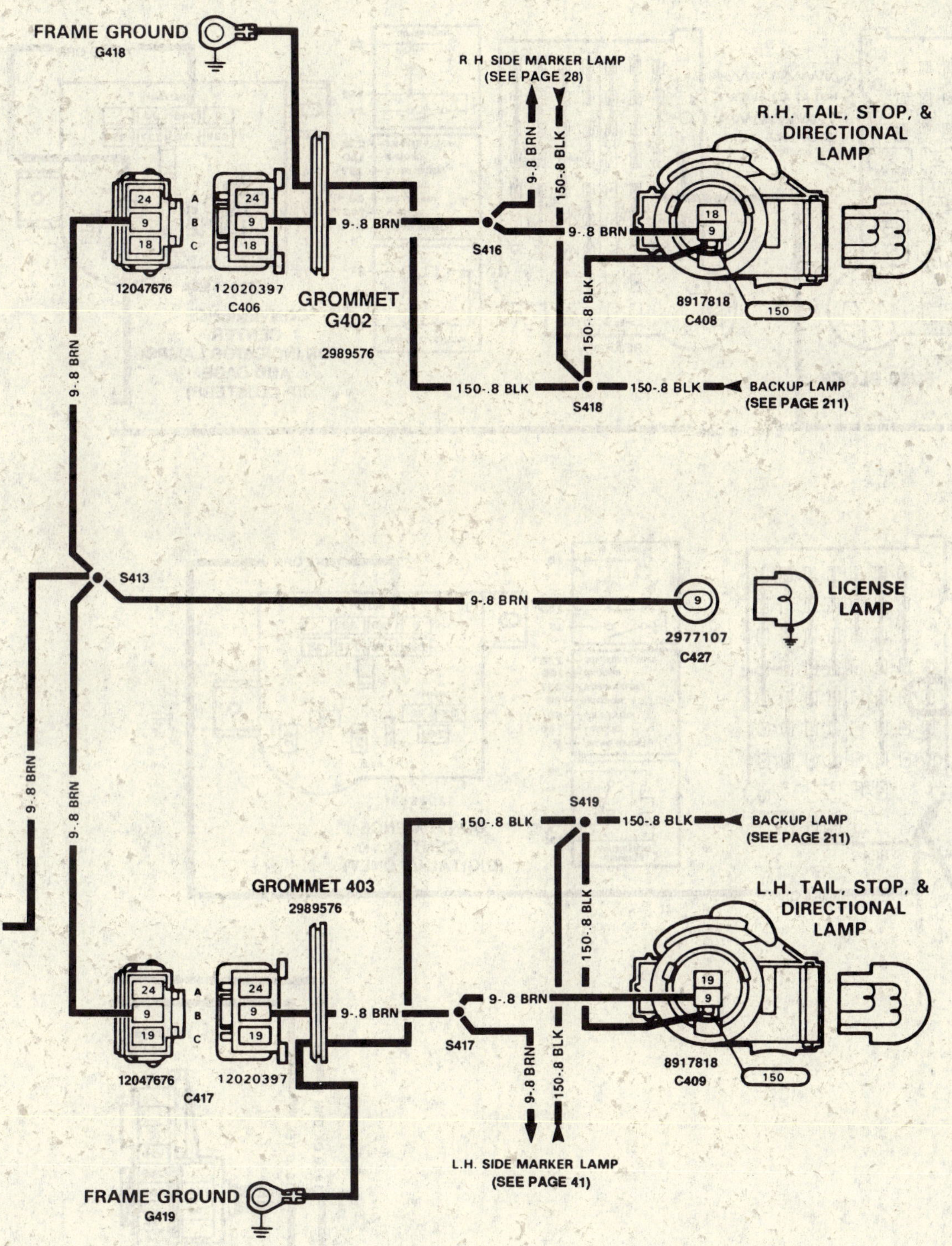

1988-91

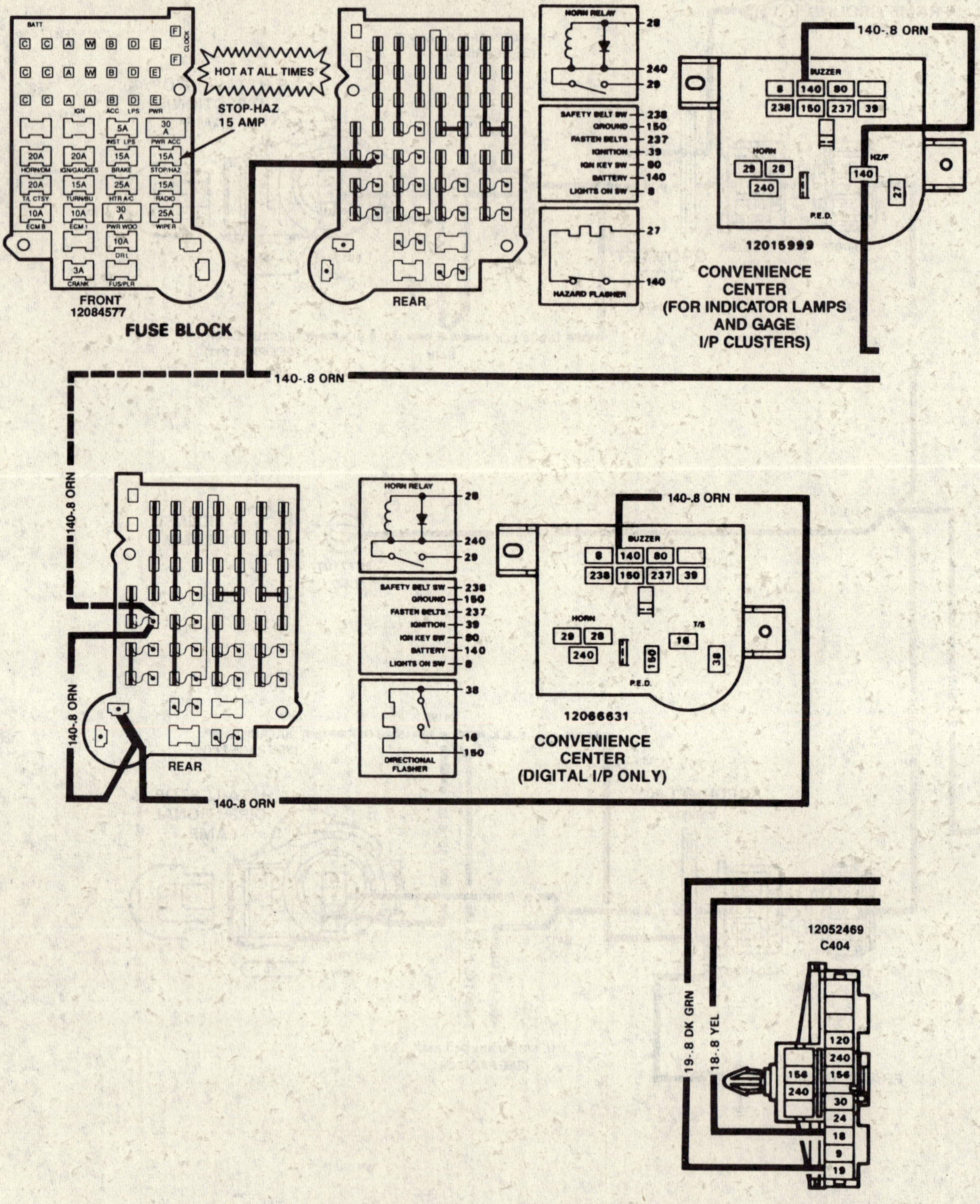

HOT AT ALL TIMES

STOP-HAZ 15 AMP

FRONT 12084577

REAR

FUSE BLOCK

HORN RELAY

HAZARD FLASHER

140-.8 ORN

BUZZER

HORN

HZ/F

P.E.D.

12015999

CONVENIENCE CENTER (FOR INDICATOR LAMPS AND GAGE I/P CLUSTERS)

140-.8 ORN

140-.8 ORN

REAR

HORN RELAY

DIRECTIONAL FLASHER

140-.8 ORN

BUZZER

HORN

T/S

P.E.D.

12066631

CONVENIENCE CENTER (DIGITAL I/P ONLY)

140-.8 ORN

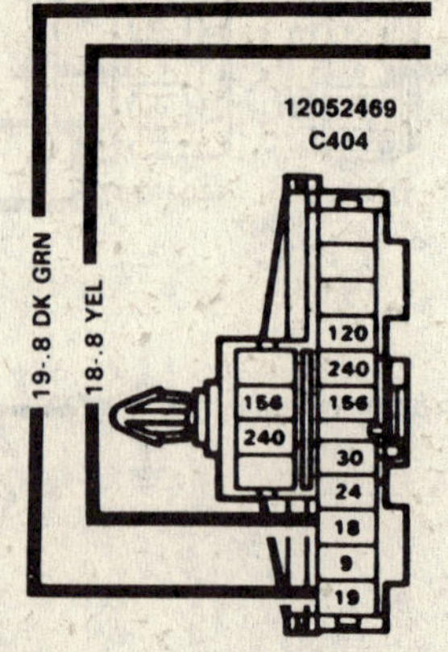

216 STOP LAMPS - 2-DOOR UTILITY

1988-91

17-.8 WHT
STOPLAMP
SWITCH
C370
17
C
B
140
A
140-.8 ORN
140-.8 ORN
12033699
17
140

19-.8 DK GRN
18-.8 YEL
12041397
C404
120
240
156
30
24
18
9
19
18-.8 YEL
19-.8 DK GRN

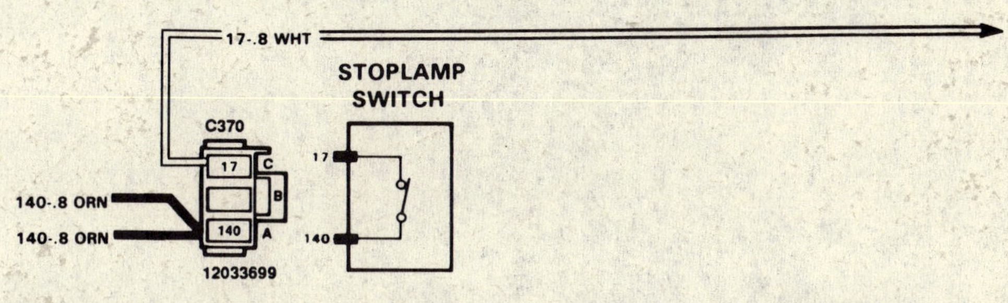

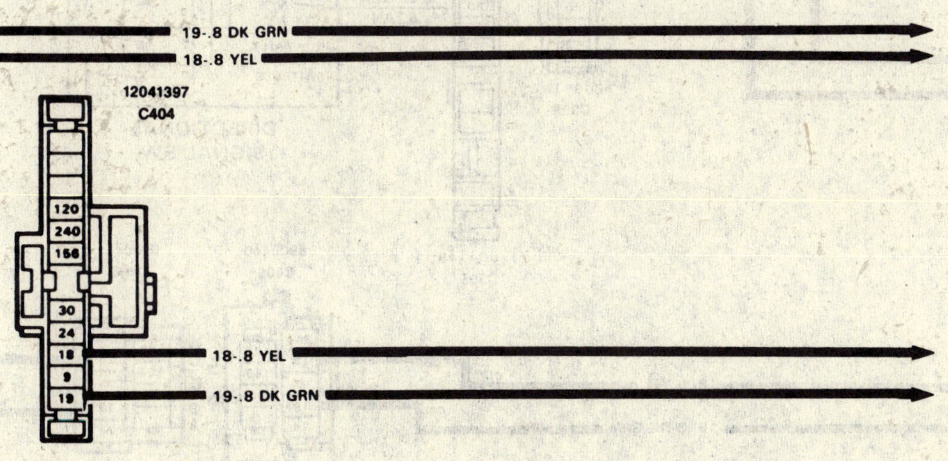

1988-91

17-.8 WHT
19-.8 DK GRN
18-.8 YEL
12004147
C305
P
N
M
L
K
J
H
G
F
E
D
C
B
A
.8 WHT
.8 DK GRN
.8 YEL
.8 PPL
.8 BRN
.8 DK BLU
.8 LT BLU
.8 BLK
.8 LT GRN
.8 TAN
12004148
C305
(STEERING COL SWITCHES)
LEFT
RIGHT
TURN SIGNAL
HORN
KEY
NORMALLY OPEN SWITCHES
HAZARD
DIRECTIONAL SIGNAL SW
8900440
C405
8900441
C405
18-.8 YEL
19-.8 DK GRN

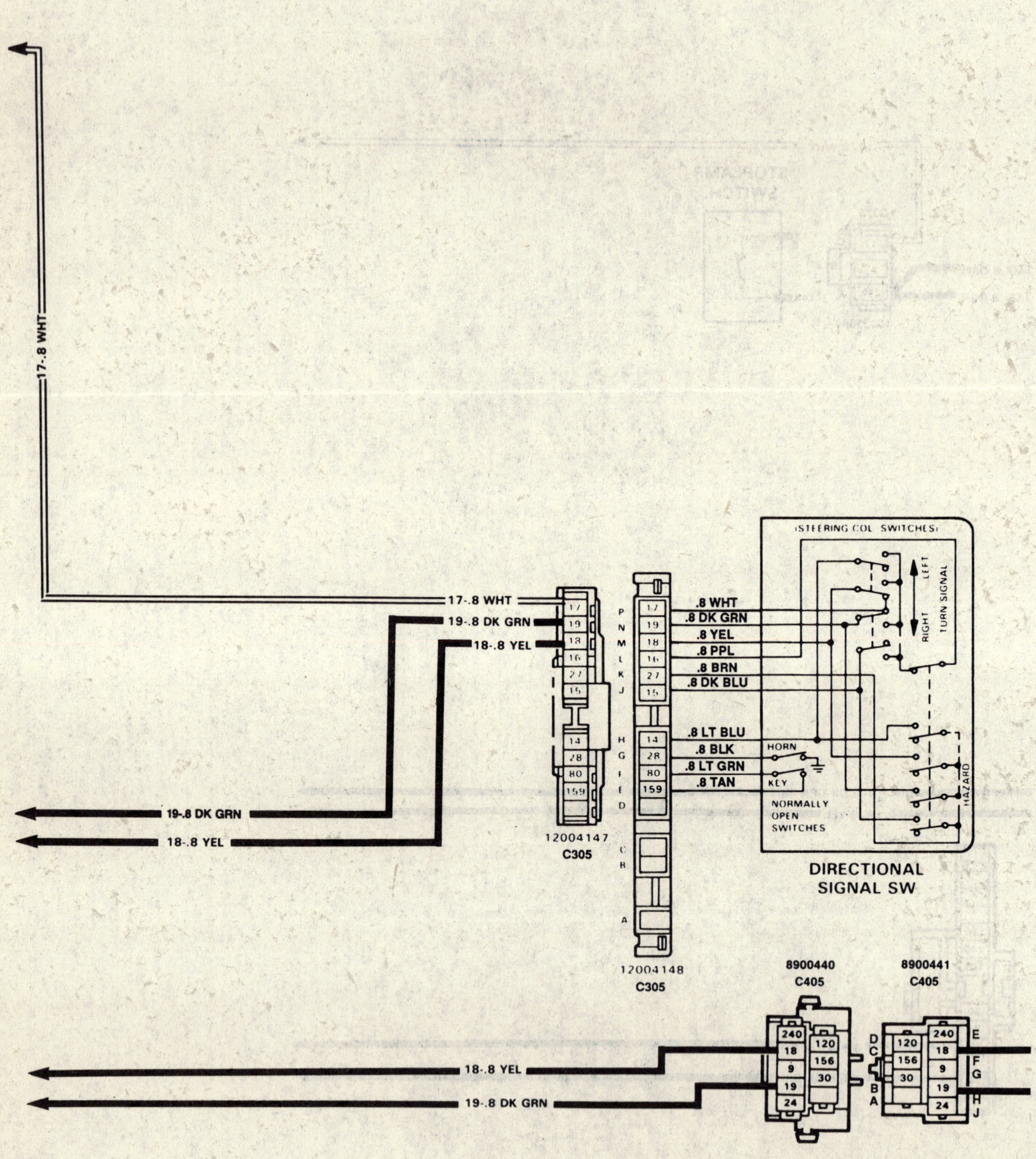

1988-91

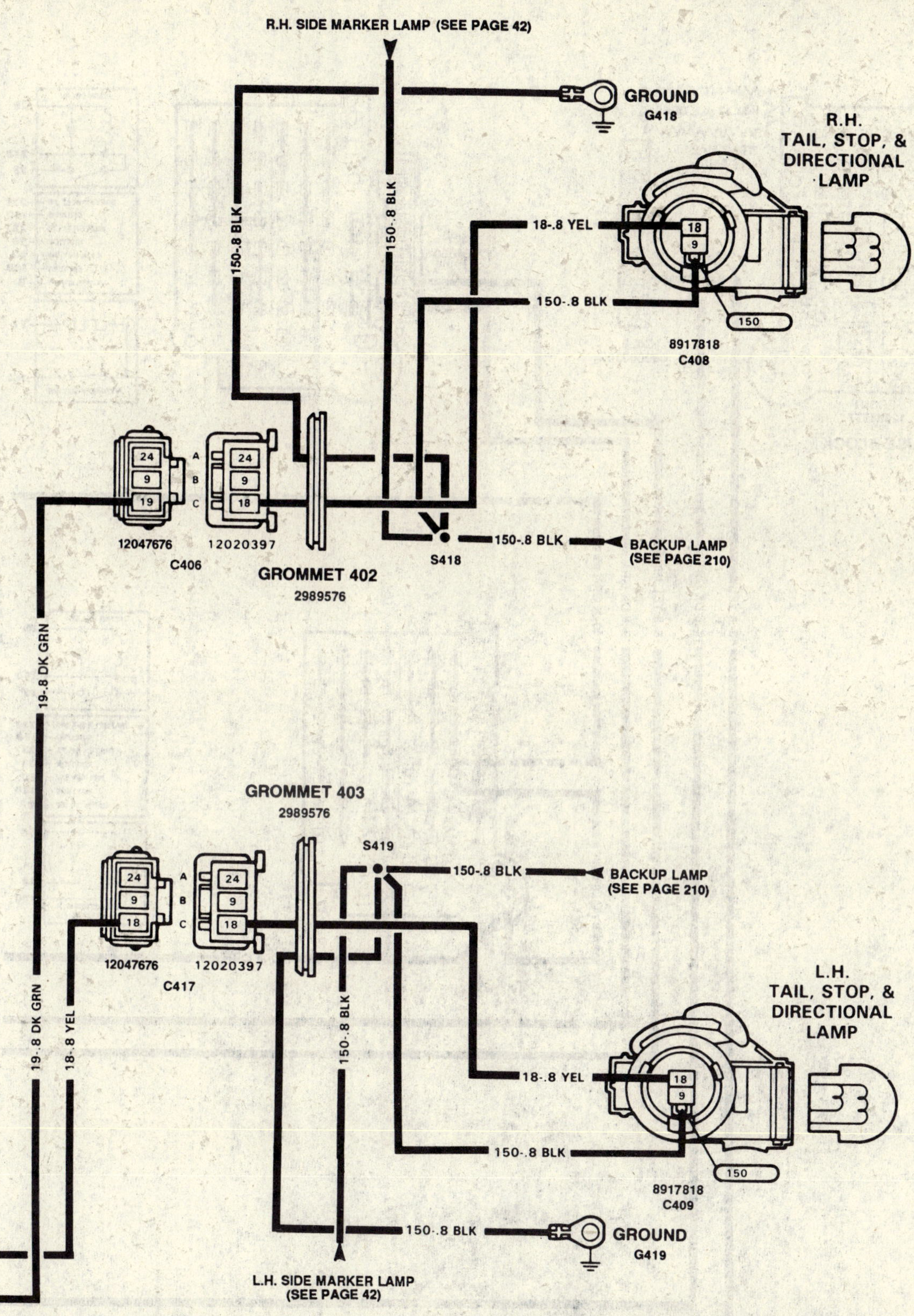

STOP LAMPS - 2-DOOR UTILITY 217

1988-91

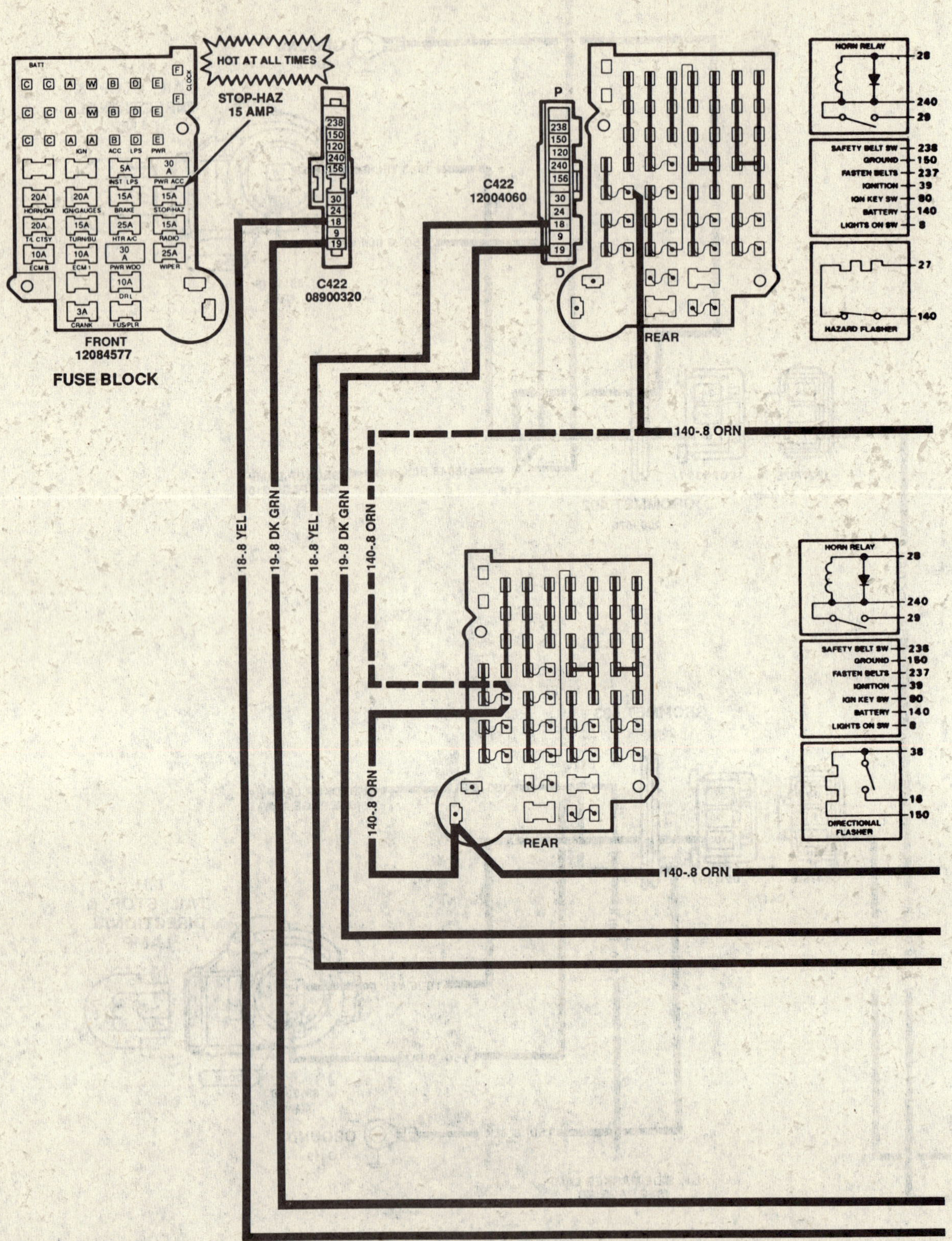

218 STOP LAMPS - 4-DOOR UTILITY

1988-91

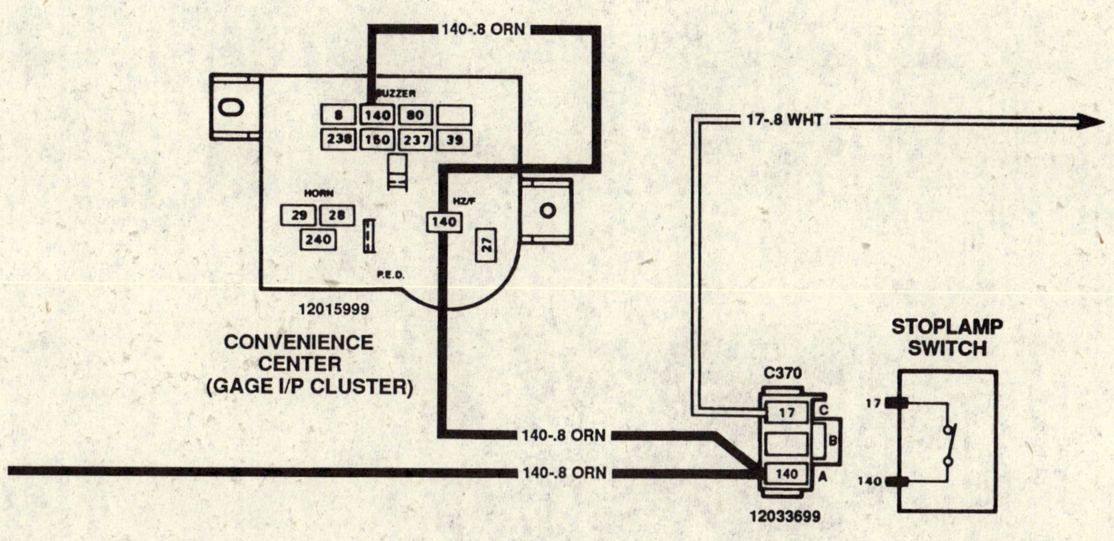

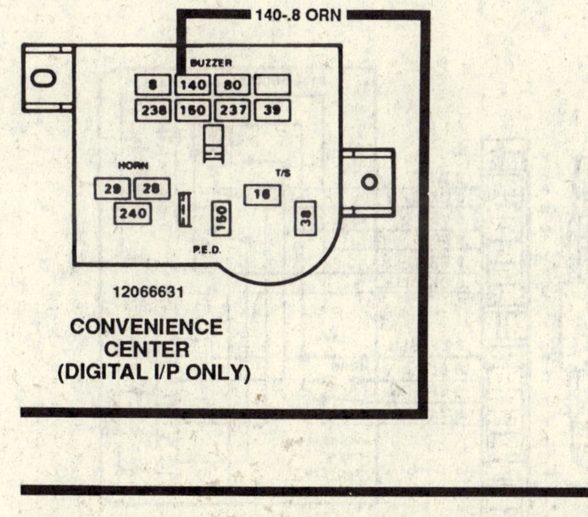

19-.8 DK GRN
18-.8 YEL

19-.8 DK GRN
18-.8 YEL

1988-91

17-.8 WHT
17-.8 WHT
19-.8 DK GRN
18-.8 YEL
19-.8 DK GRN
18-.8 YEL
12004147
C305
12004148
C305
.8 WHT
.8 DK GRN
.8 YEL
.8 PPL
.8 BRN
.8 DK BLU
.8 LT BLU
.8 BLK
.8 LT GRN
.8 TAN
(STEERING COL SWITCHES)
LEFT
RIGHT
TURN SIGNAL
HORN
KEY
NORMALLY
OPEN
SWITCHES
HAZARD
DIRECTIONAL
SIGNAL SW
19-.8 DK GRN
18-.8 YEL

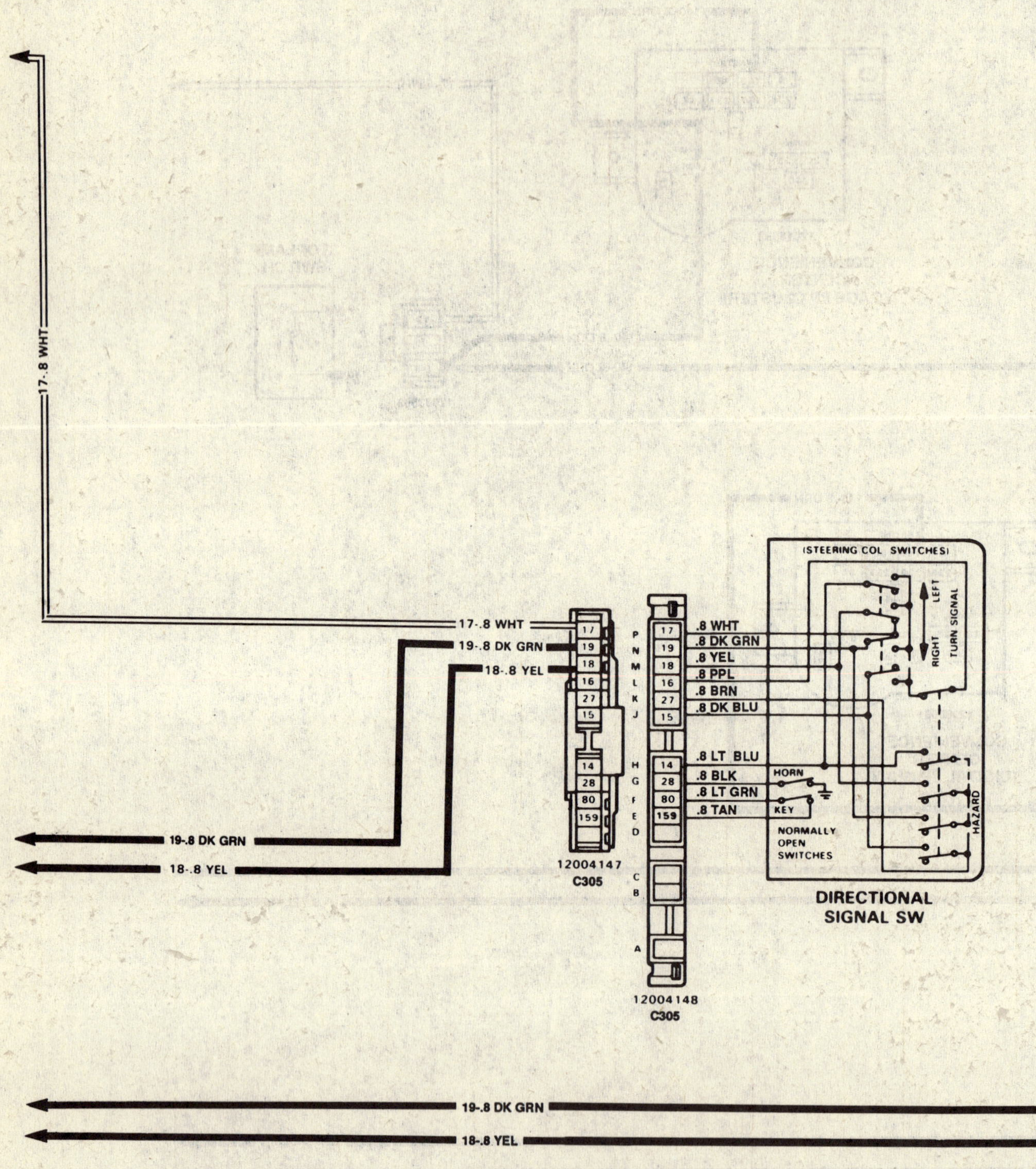

1988-91

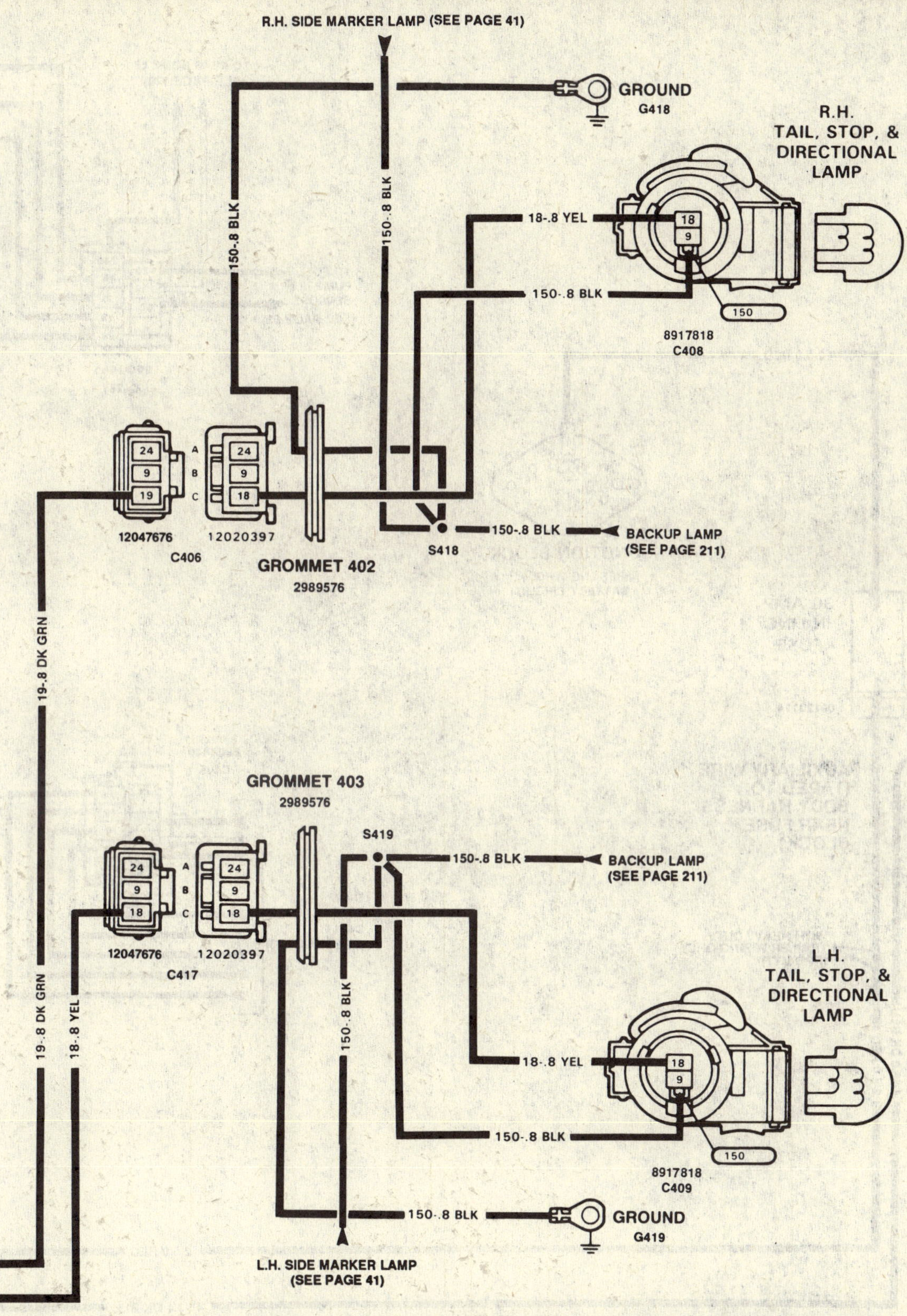

STOP LAMPS - 4-DOOR UTILITY 219

1988-91

TO REAR DOME LP
(SEE PAGE 170)
TO FUEL
PUMP
SENSORS
(SEE PAGE 83)
120
156
30
240
18
9
19
24
8900441
C428
2-5.0 RED
JUNCTION BLOCK
(REF ENG WRG
BATTERY CIRCUIT)
30 AMP
IN LINE
FUSE
00120114
AUXILIARY WIRE
(TAPED TO
BODY HARNESS
NEAR FUSE
BLOCK)
8900440
C405
24
19
9
18
240
30
156
120
FROM
CONNECTOR
C404
(SEE PAGE 213)
WITH HEAVY DUTY
TRAILER WIRING ONLY
(RPO UY7)
47-3.0 DK BLU
2-5.0 RED
2-5.0 RED
47-3.0 DK BLU

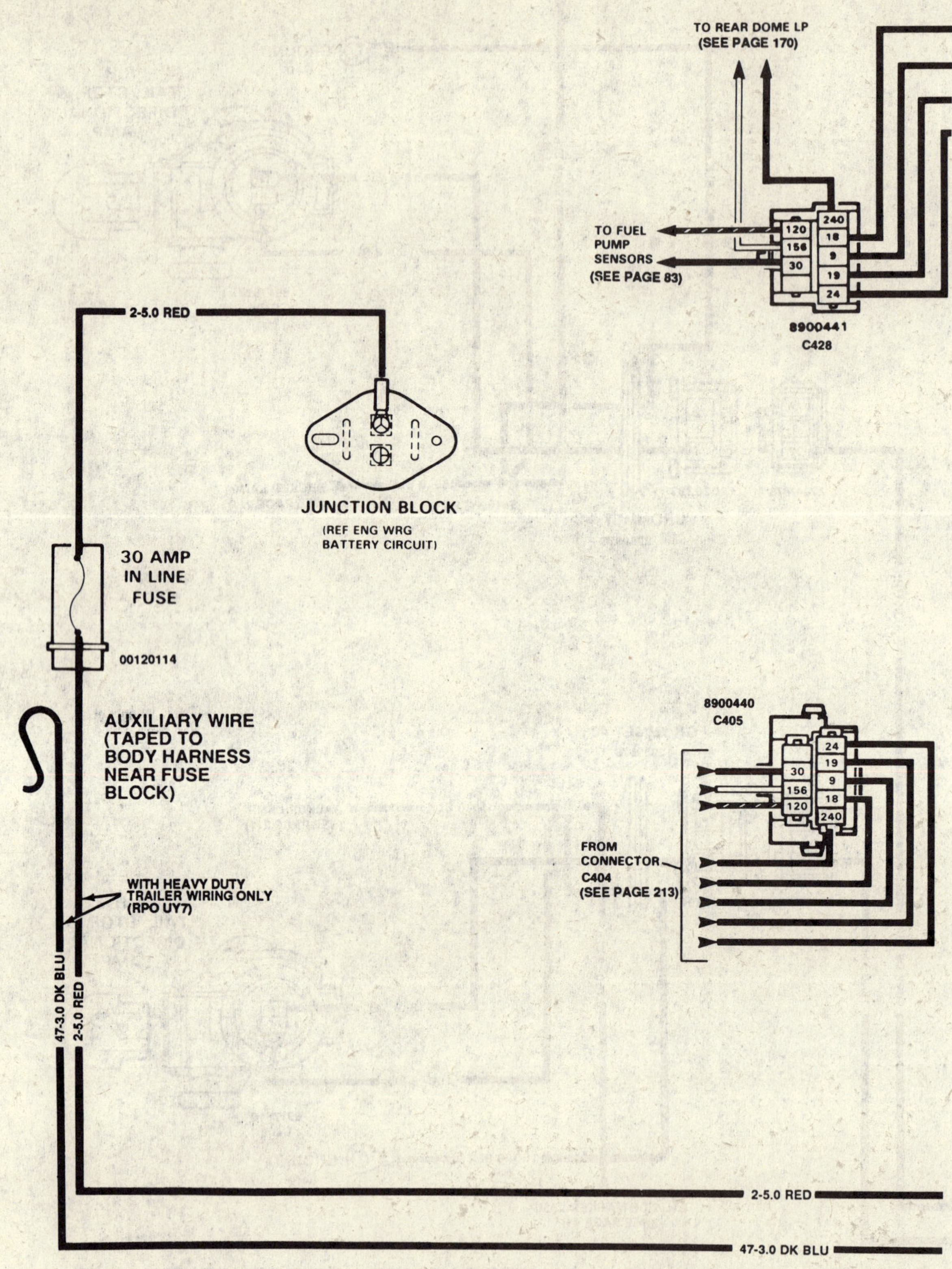

1988-91

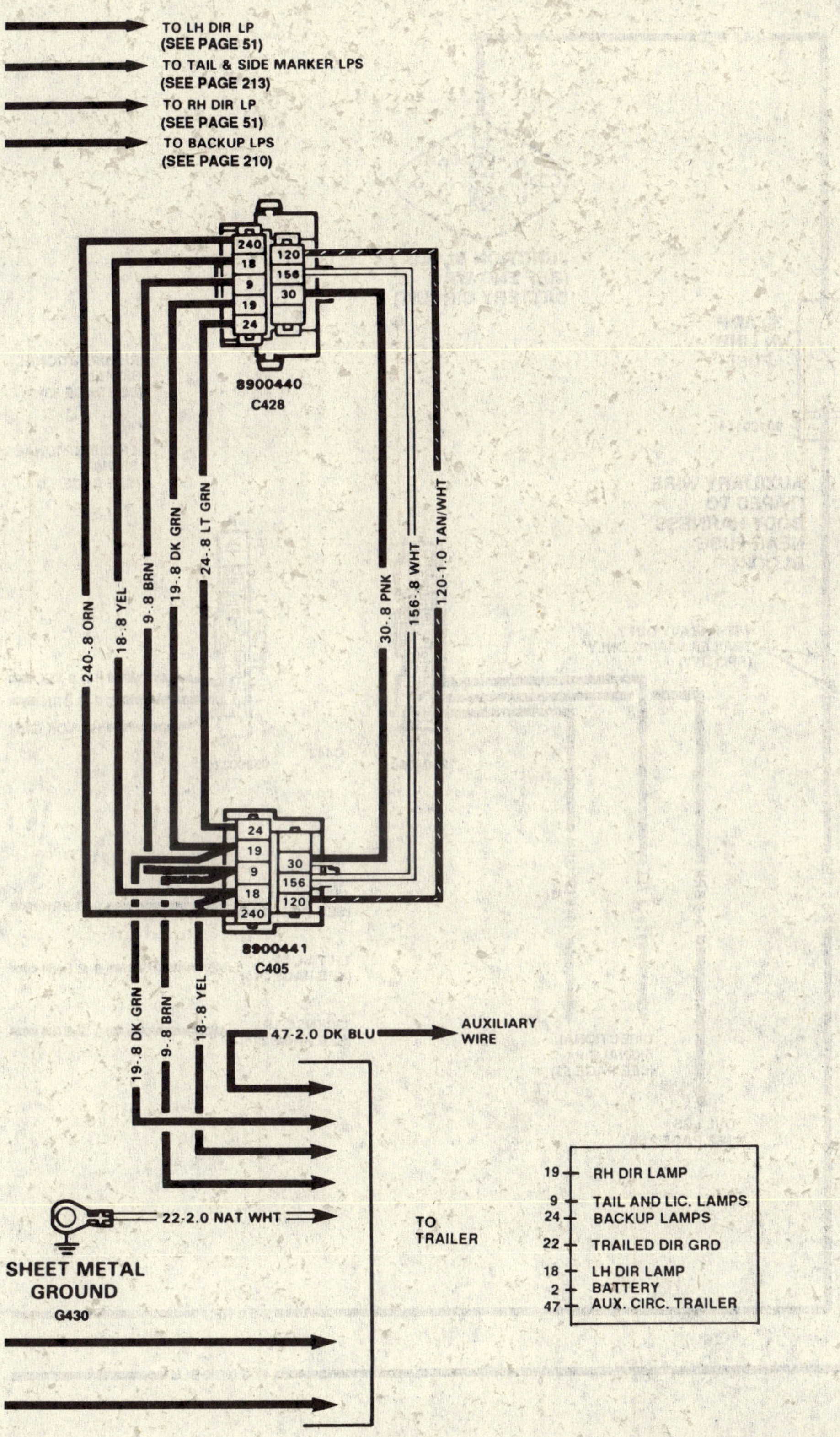

TRAILER WIRING (U86) - 2-DOOR UTILITY 223

1988-91

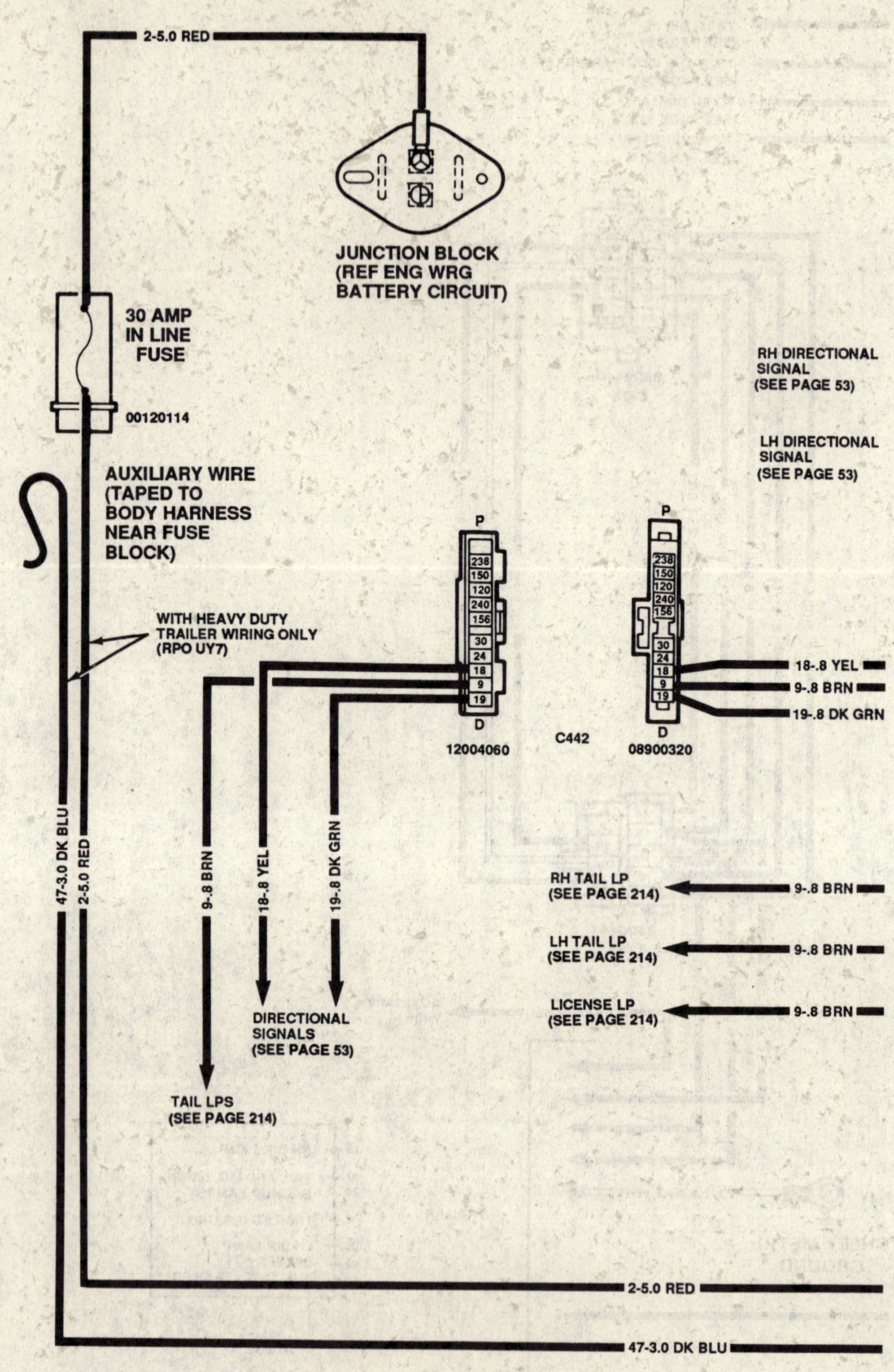

224 TRAILER WIRING (U86) - 4-DOOR UTILITY

1988-91

AUXILIARY WIRE
47-2.0 DK BLU
19-.8 DK GRN
18-.8 YEL
S442
S441
S440
19-.8 DK GRN
18-.8 YEL
9-.8 BRN
22-2.0 WHT
TO TRAILER
AUX. CKT TRAILER 47
RH DIR LAMP 19
LH DIR LAMP 18
TAIL LIGHTS 9
TRAILER DIRECT GRD 22
BACK-UP LP 24
REAR DOME LP (SEE PAGE)
151-.8 BLK
151-2.0 BLK
G415
S438
SHEET METAL GROUND

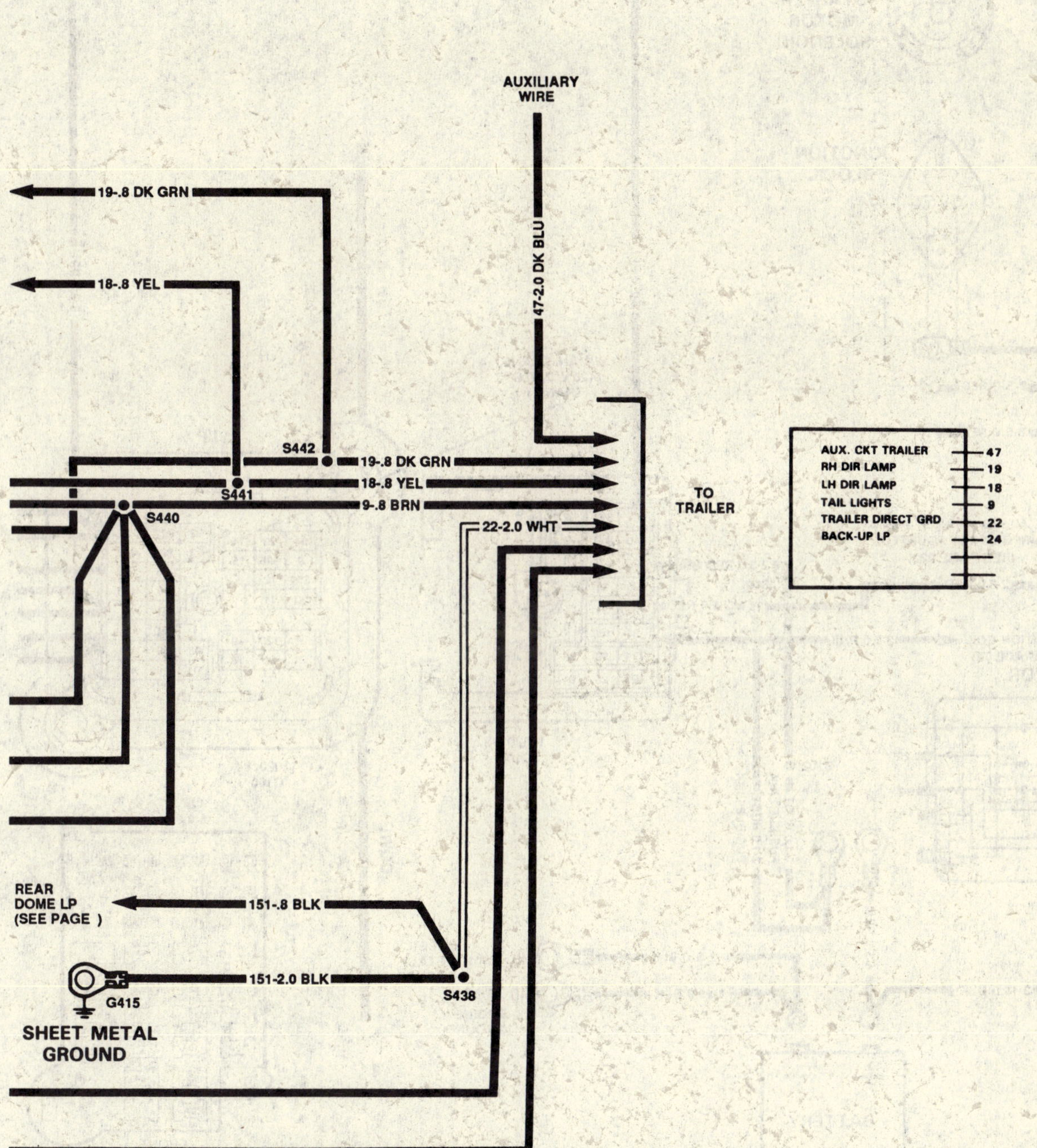

1988-91

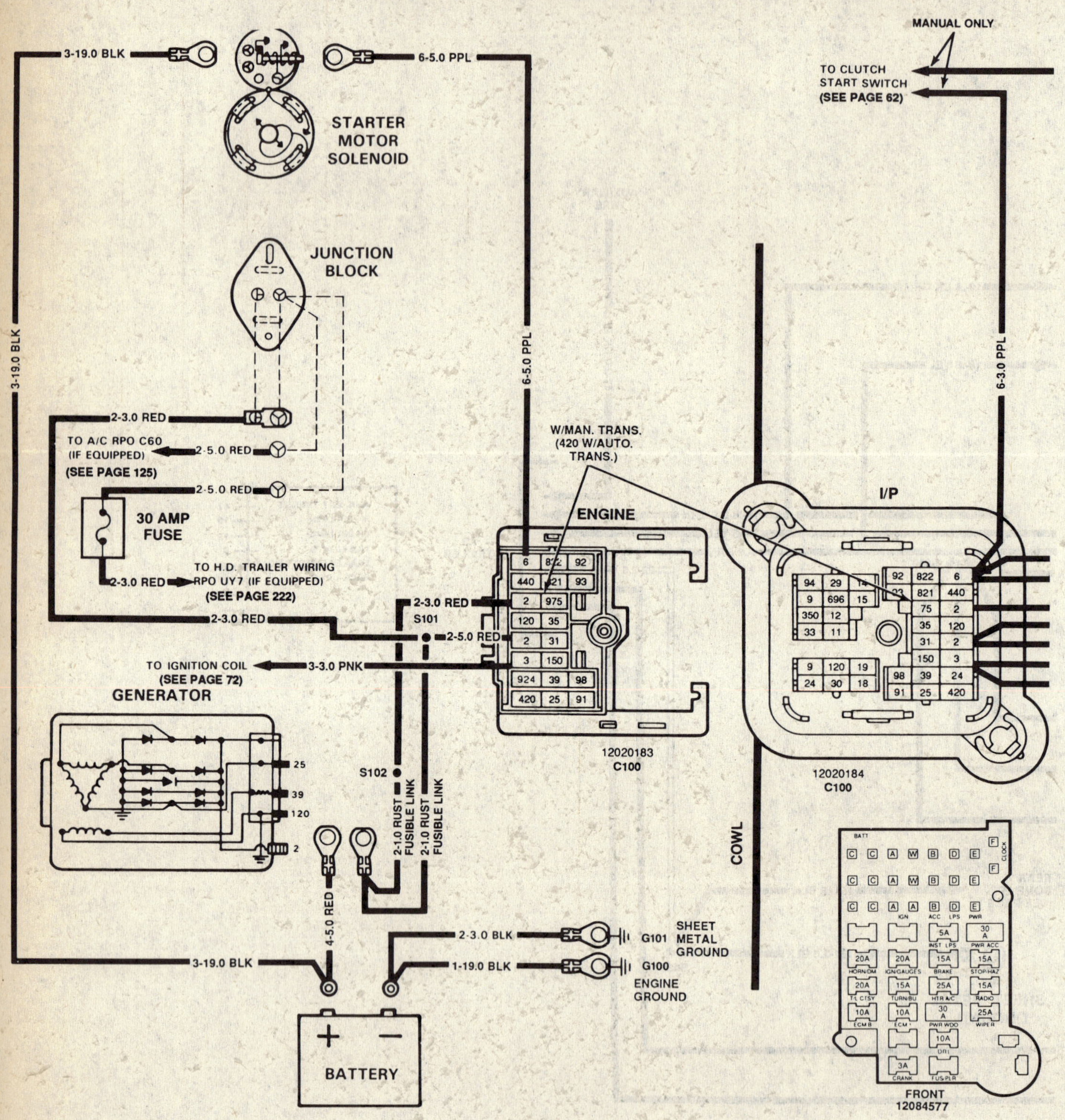

16 POWER DISTRIBUTION - 2.5L (151 CID) ENGINE

1988-91

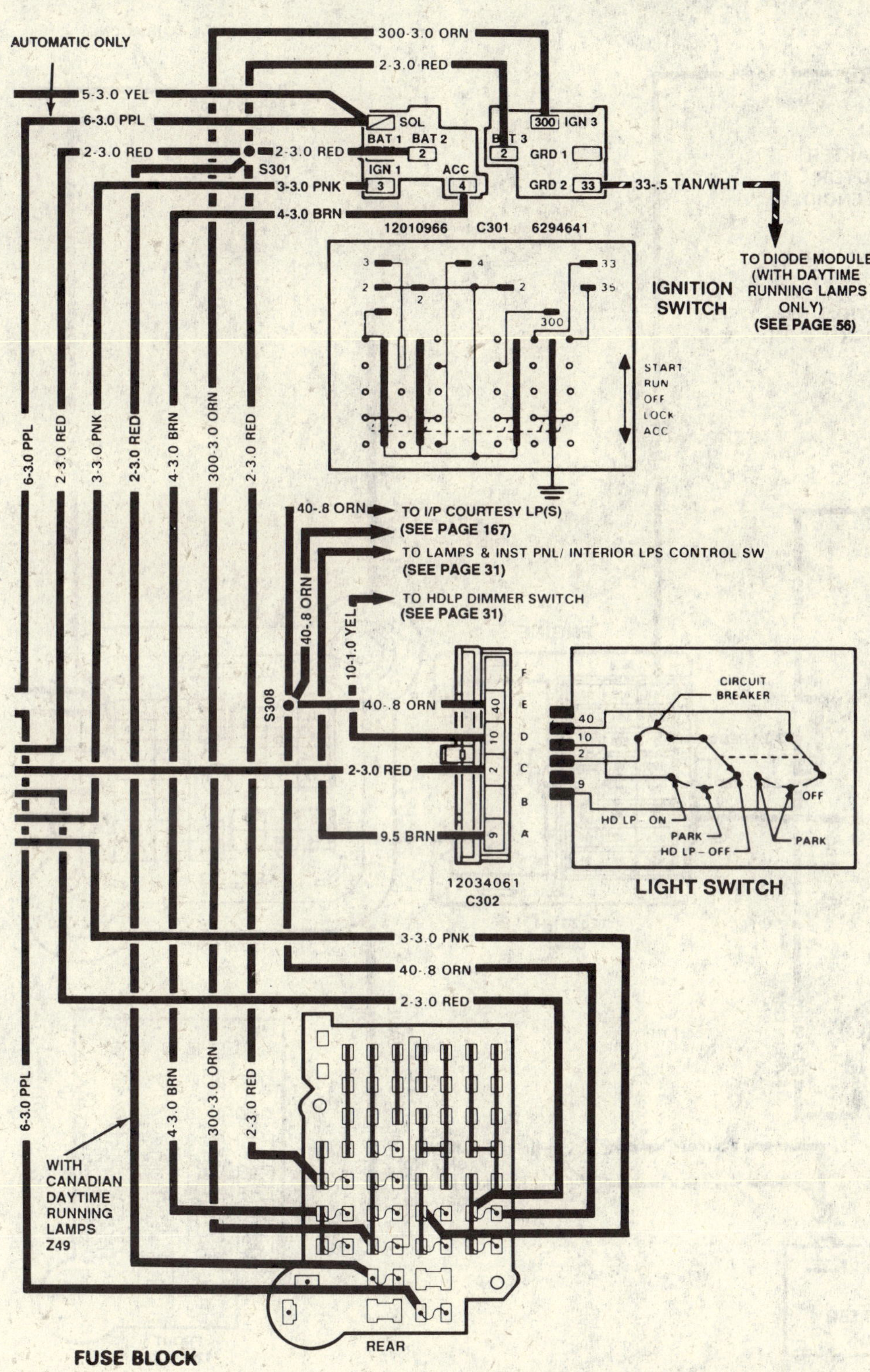
AUTOMATIC ONLY
300-3.0 ORN
2-3.0 RED
5-3.0 YEL
6-3.0 PPL
2-3.0 RED
S301
3-3.0 PNK
4-3.0 BRN
SOL
BAT 1
BAT 2
IGN 1
ACC
IGN 3
BAT 3
GRD 1
GRD 2
33-.5 TAN/WHT
12010966
C301
6294641
TO DIODE MODULE (WITH DAYTIME RUNNING LAMPS ONLY) (SEE PAGE 56)
IGNITION SWITCH
START
RUN
OFF
LOCK
ACC
40-.8 ORN
TO I/P COURTESY LP(S) (SEE PAGE 167)
TO LAMPS & INST PNL/ INTERIOR LPS CONTROL SW (SEE PAGE 31)
TO HDLP DIMMER SWITCH (SEE PAGE 31)
10-1.0 YEL
S308
9.5 BRN
12034061
C302
CIRCUIT BREAKER
HD LP - ON
PARK
HD LP - OFF
OFF
LIGHT SWITCH
WITH CANADIAN DAYTIME RUNNING LAMPS Z49
FUSE BLOCK
REAR

1-19.0 BLK
6-3.0 PPL
STARTER MOTOR SOLENOID
2-1.0 RUST FUSIBLE LINK
S103
JUNCTION BLOCK
1-19.0 BLK
2-3.0 RED
TO A/C RPO C60 (IF EQUIPPED) (SEE PAGE 126)
2-5.0 RED
2-5.0 RED
30 AMP FUSE
2-3.0RED
TO H.D. TRAILER WIRING RPO UY7 (IF EQUIPPED) (SEE PAGE 222)
2-3.0 RED
2-3.0 RED
2-3.0 RED
TO IGNITION COIL (SEE PAGE 74)
3-3.0 PNK
GENERATOR
25
39
120
2
S101
2-1.0 RUST FUSIBLE LINK
2-5.0 BLK/RED
1-19.0 BLK
2-3.0 BLK
G101 SHEET METAL GROUND
1-19.0 BLK
G100 ENGINE GROUND
BATTERY
ENGINE
12020183
C100
COWL
MANUAL ONLY
TO CLUTCH START SWITCH (SEE PAGE 63)
6-3.0 PPL
I/P
12020184
C100
FRONT
12084577

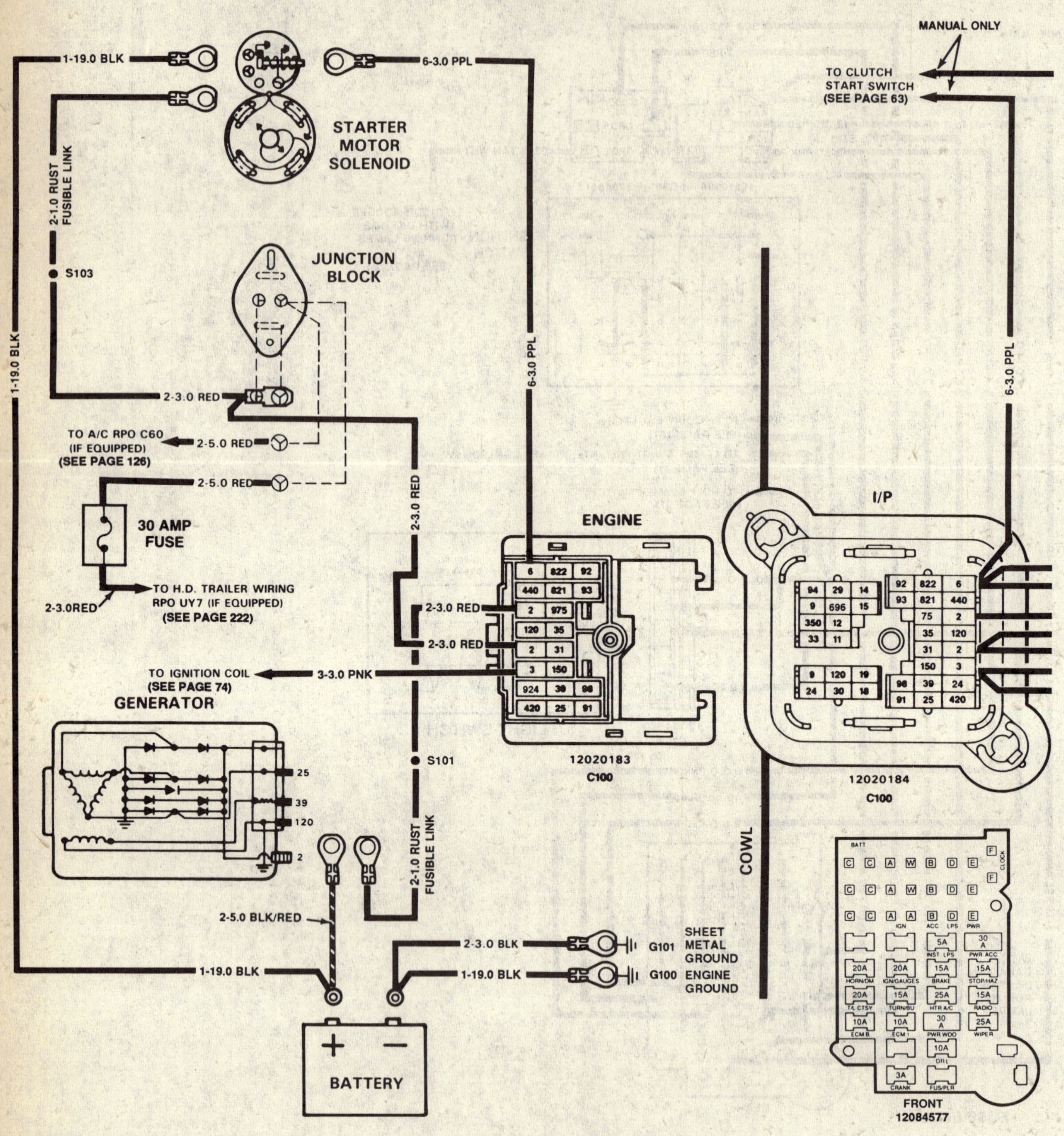

1988-91

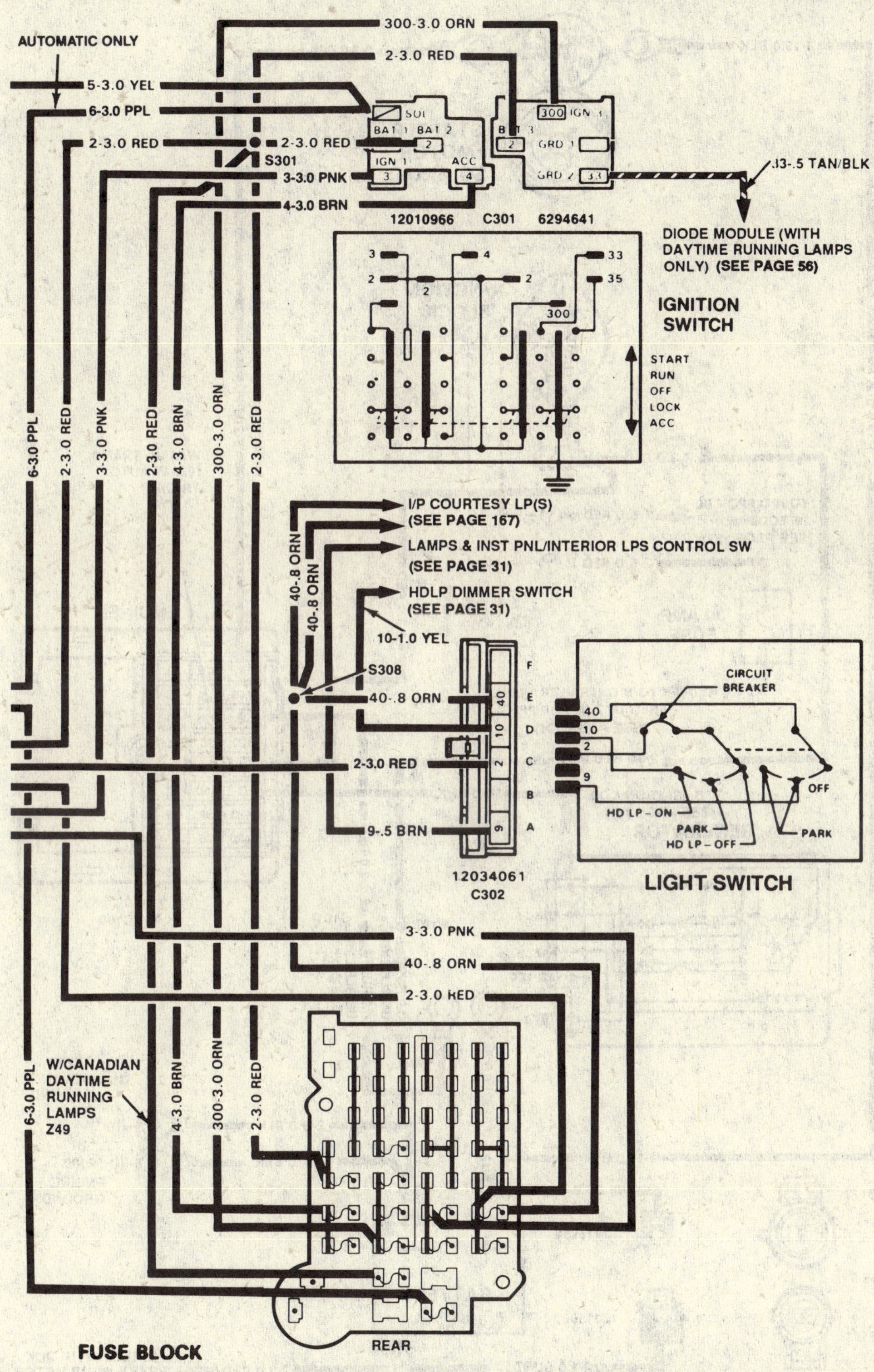

POWER DISTRIBUTION - 2.8L (173 CID) ENGINE 17

1988-91

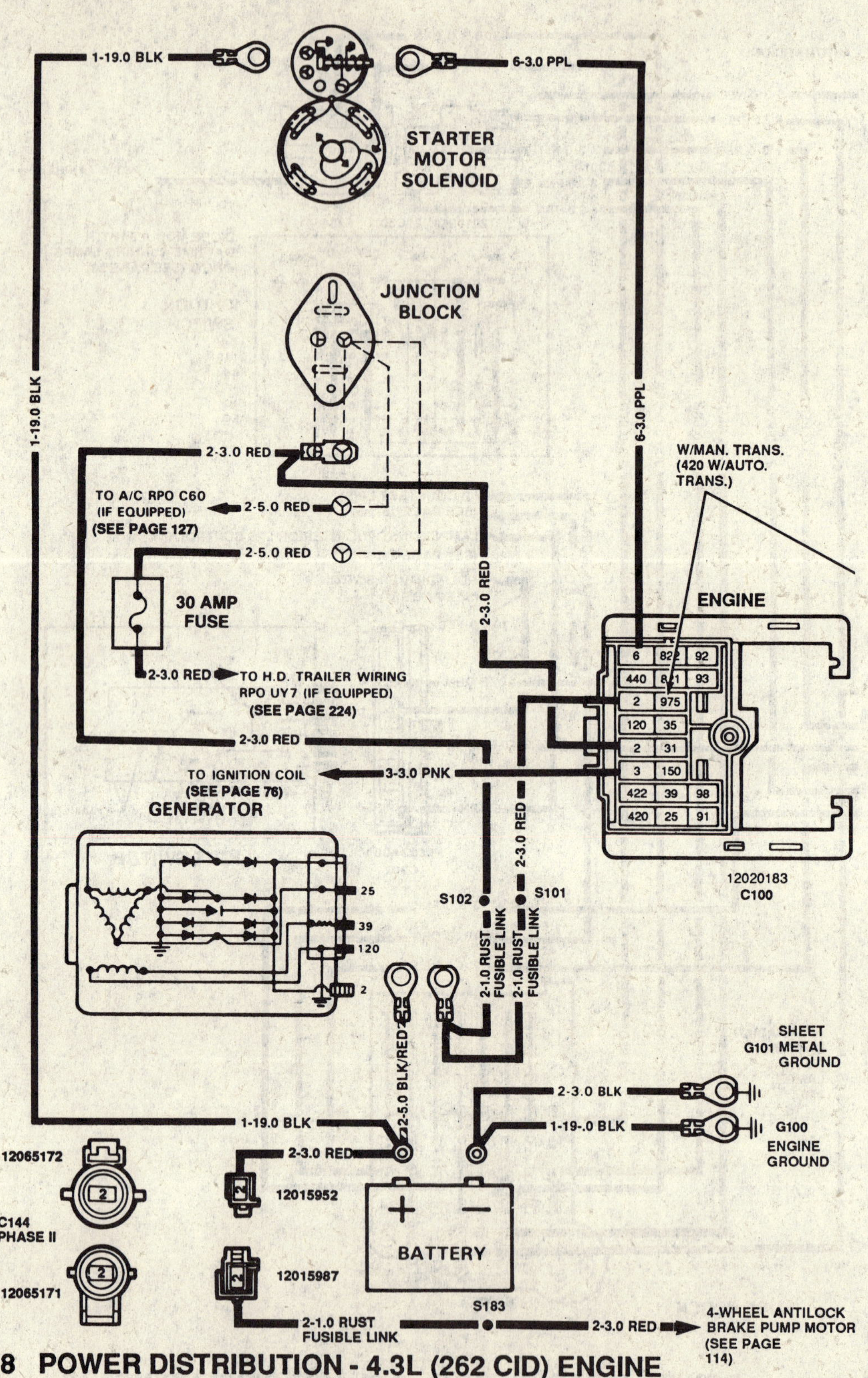

18 POWER DISTRIBUTION - 4.3L (262 CID) ENGINE

1988-91

MANUAL ONLY
AUTOMATIC ONLY
TO CLUTCH START SWITCH (SEE PAGE 64)
300-3.0 ORN
2-3.0 RED
5-3.0 YEL
6-3.0 PPL
2-3.0 RED
S301
3-3.0 PNK
4-3.0 BRN
SOL
BAT 1
BAT 2
IGN 1
ACC
IGN 3
BAT 3
GRD 1
GRD 2
33-.5 TAN/BLK
12010966
C301
6294641
TO DIODE MODULE (WITH DAYTIME RUNNING LAMPS ONLY) (SEE PAGE 56, 57)
IGNITION SWITCH
START
RUN
OFF
LOCK
ACC
40-.8 BRN
TO I/P COURTESY LP(S) (SEE PAGE 167)
TO LAMPS & INST PNL/ INTERIOR LPS CONTROL SW (SEE PAGE 30)
TO HDLP DIMMER SWITCH (SEE PAGE 30)
10-1.0 YEL
S308
40-.8 ORN
2-3.0 RED
9-.5 BRN
12034061
C302
CIRCUIT BREAKER
HD LP - ON
PARK
HD LP - OFF
OFF
LIGHT SWITCH
I/P
12020184
C100
COWL
3-3.0 PNK
40-.8 ORN
2-3.0 RED
WITH CANADIAN DAYTIME RUNNING LAMPS Z49
FRONT
12084577
FUSE BLOCK
REAR

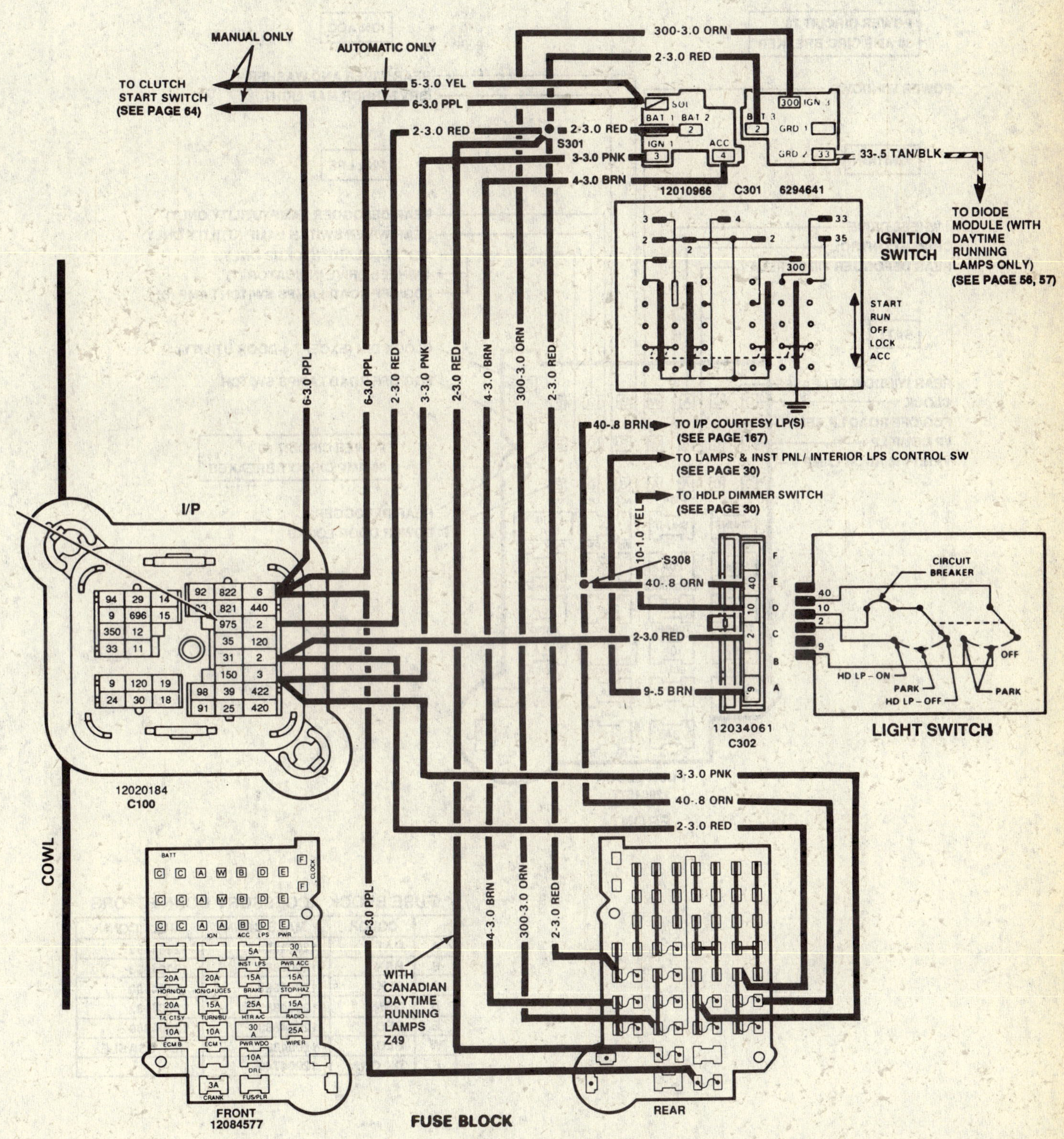

1988-91

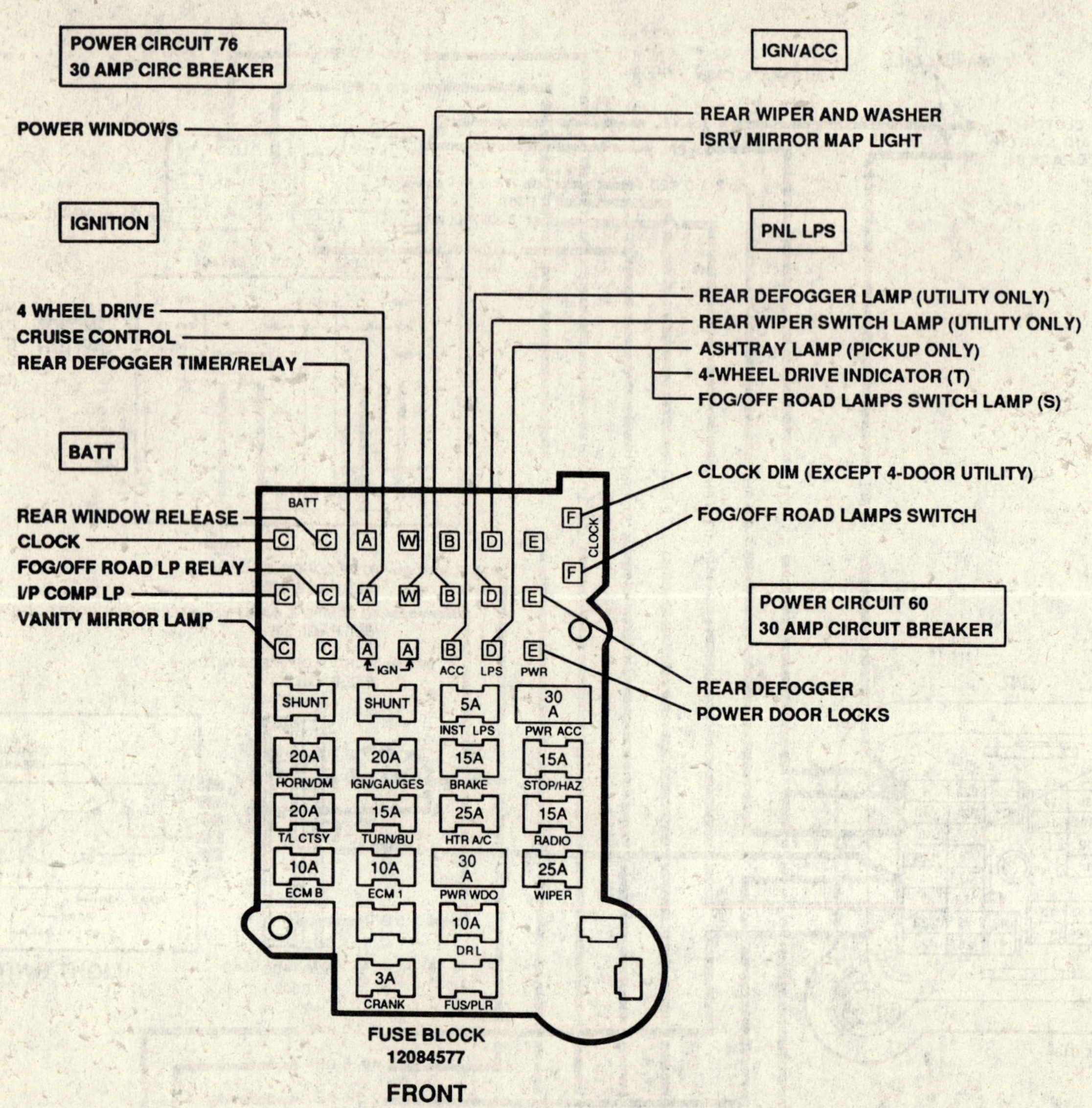

FUSE BLOCK
12084577

FRONT

FUSE BLOCK ACCESSORY CONNECTORS

	COLOR	MALE CONN	MULT CONN
A	NAT	12004888	12004892
B	BRN	12004887	12004893
C	BLK	12004886	12004890
D	GRN	12004885	12004962
E	RED	12004883	12004889
W	BLU	12004884	NOT USABLE
F	DK GRA	12004740	

1988-91

CAUTION: Determine if non-cycling circuit breakers are hot before removing them. Hot non-cycling circuit breakers can cause personal injury.

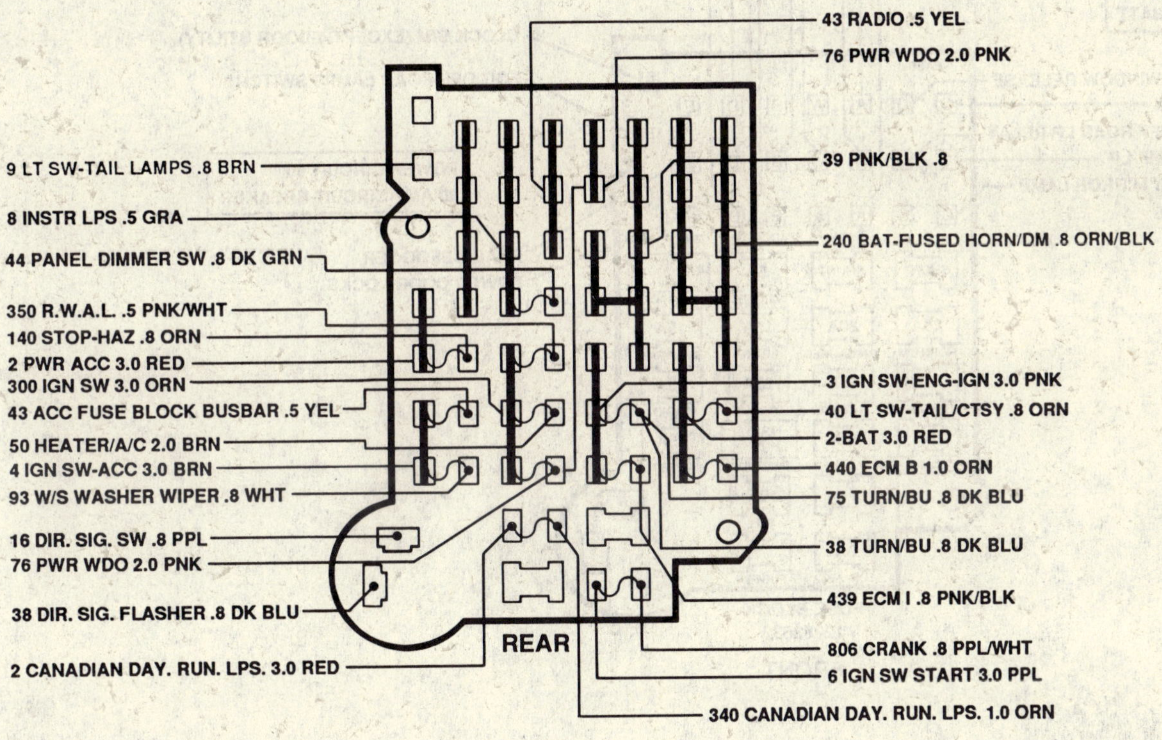

FUSE INFORMATION

FUSES	AMP	COLOR
12004005	5	TAN
12004007	10	RED
12004008	15	LT BLU
12004009	20	YEL
12004010	25	WHT
12004003	3	VIOLET
12004006	7.5	BROWN
12004011	30	LT GRN

POWER DISTRIBUTION - FUSE BLOCK W/GAGES I/P 19

1988-91

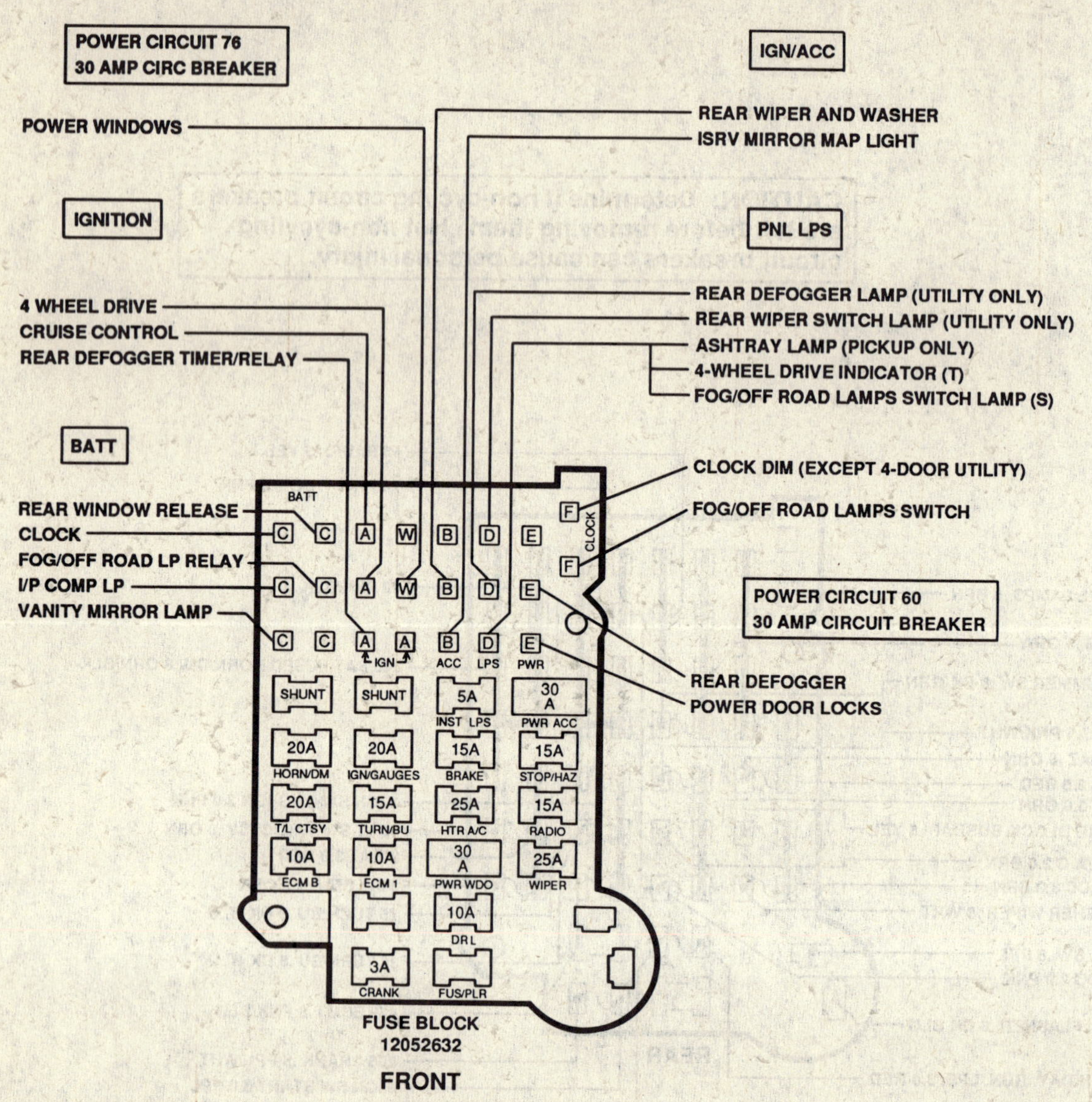

FUSE BLOCK ACCESSORY CONNECTORS

	COLOR	MALE CONN	MULT CONN
A	NAT	12004888	12004892
B	BRN	12004887	12004893
C	BLK	12004886	12004890
D	GRN	12004885	12004962
E	RED	12004883	12004889
W	BLU	12004884	NOT USABLE
F	DK GRA	12004740	

20 POWER DISTRIBUTION - FUSE BLOCK W/DIGITAL I/P

1988-91

CAUTION: Determine if non-cycling circuit breakers are hot before removing them. Hot non-cycling circuit breakers can cause personal injury.

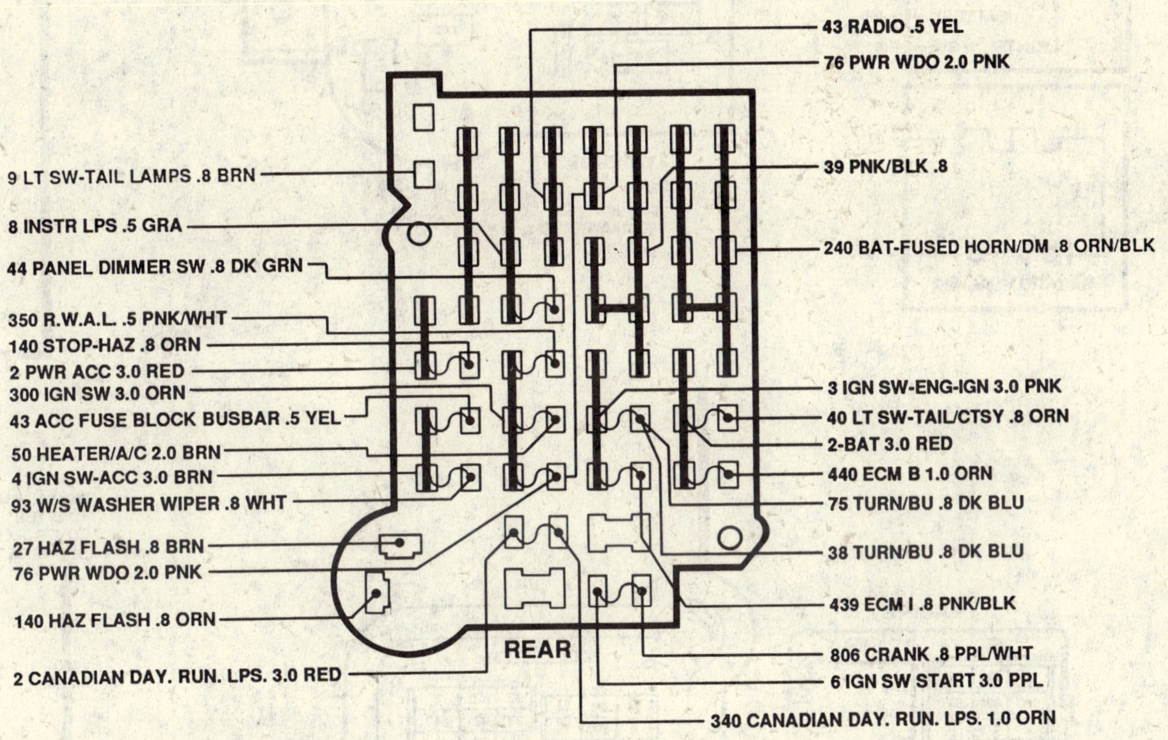

FUSE INFORMATION

FUSES	AMP	COLOR
12004005	5	TAN
12004007	10	RED
12004008	15	LT BLU
12004009	20	YEL
12004010	25	WHT
12004003	3	VIOLET
12004006	7.5	BROWN
12004011	30	LT GRN

1988-91

HORN RELAY
28
240
29
SAFETY BELT SW 238
GROUND 150
FASTEN BELTS 237
IGNITION 39
IGN KEY SW 80
BATTERY 140
LIGHTS ON SW 8
27
140
HAZARD FLASHER
BUZZER
8 140 80
238 150 237 39
HORN
29 28
240
HZ/F
140
27
P.E.D.
12015999
GAGES
I/P CLUSTER (Z53)
DIGITAL RATIO ADAPTER CONTROLLER (SEE PAGE 118)
150 .5 BLK
ENGINE
6 822 92
440 821 93
2 975
120 35
2 31
3 150
924 39 98
420 25 91
150 3.0 BLK
G140 ENGINE GROUND
12020183 C100
I/P
94 29 14
9 696 15
350 12
33 11
92 822 6
93 821 440
75 2
35 120
31 2
150 3
9 120 19
24 30 18
98 39 24
91 25 420
150-3.0 BLK
12020184 C100
COWL
450 .8 BLK/WHT
A.L.D.L. TEST CONNECTOR (SEE PAGE 97)
150 .8 BLK
I/P COMPT BOX LAMP (UTILITY ONLY) (SEE PAGE 174)

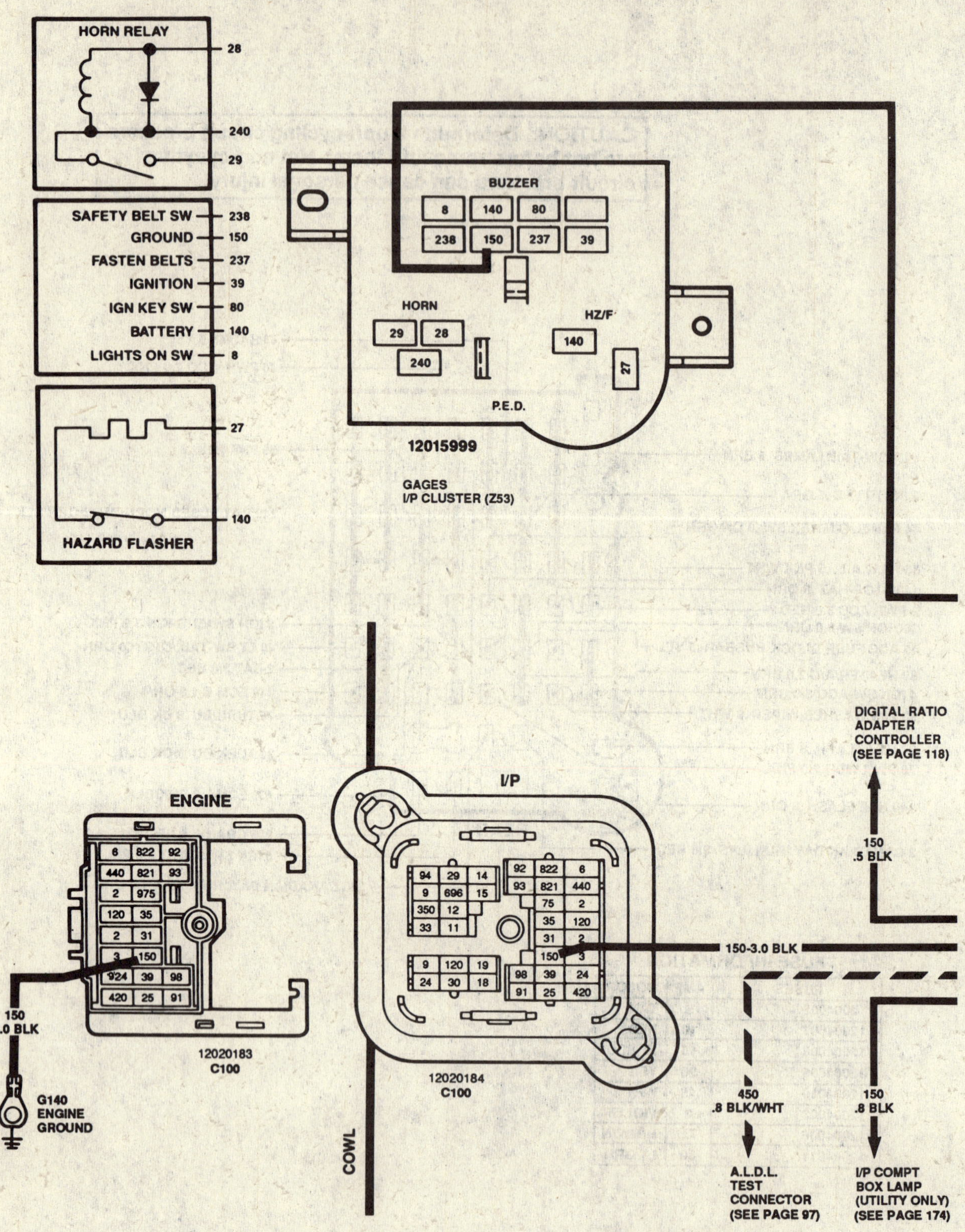

1988-91

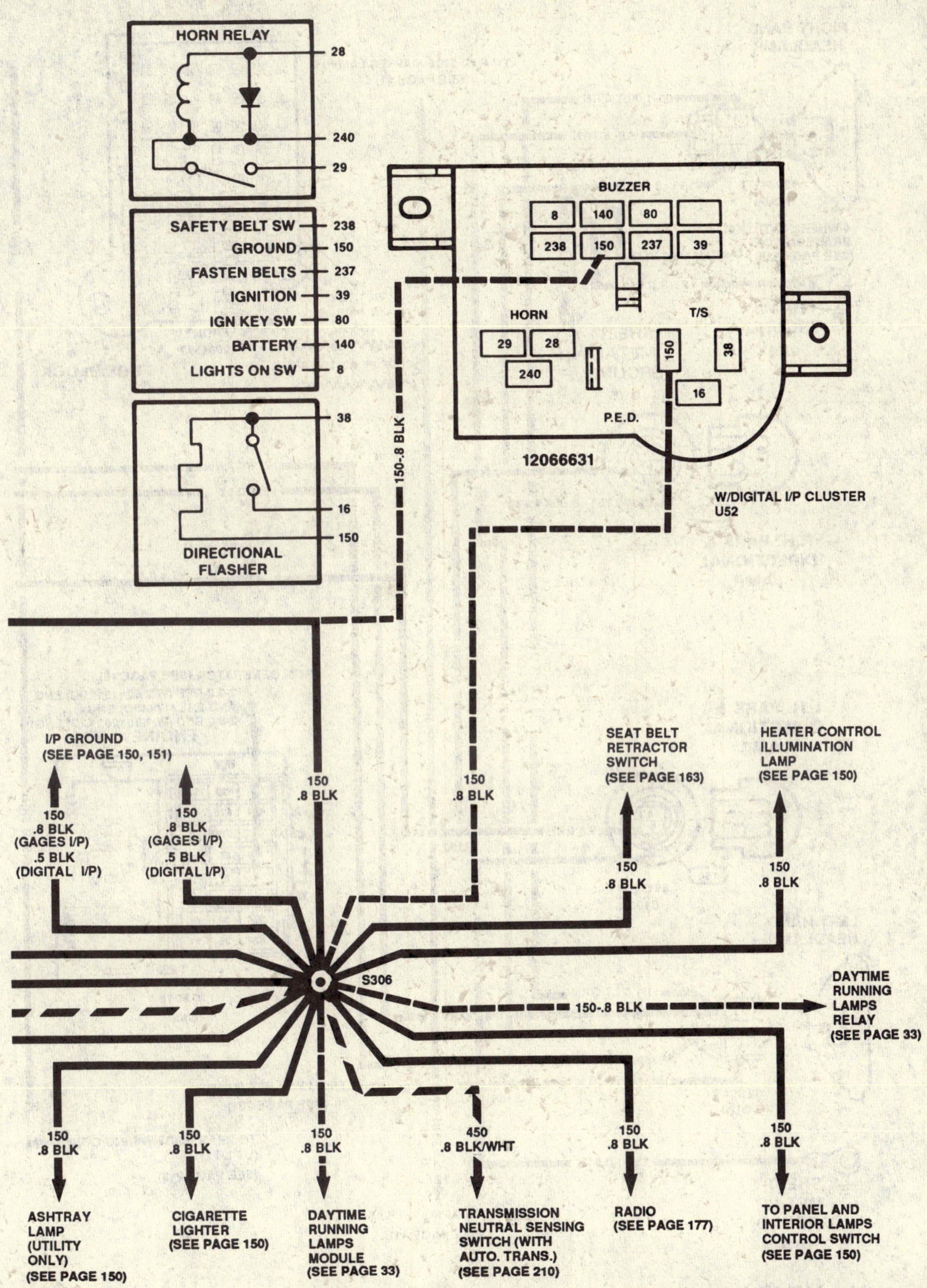

POWER DISTRIBUTION - CONVENIENCE CENTER 21

1988-91

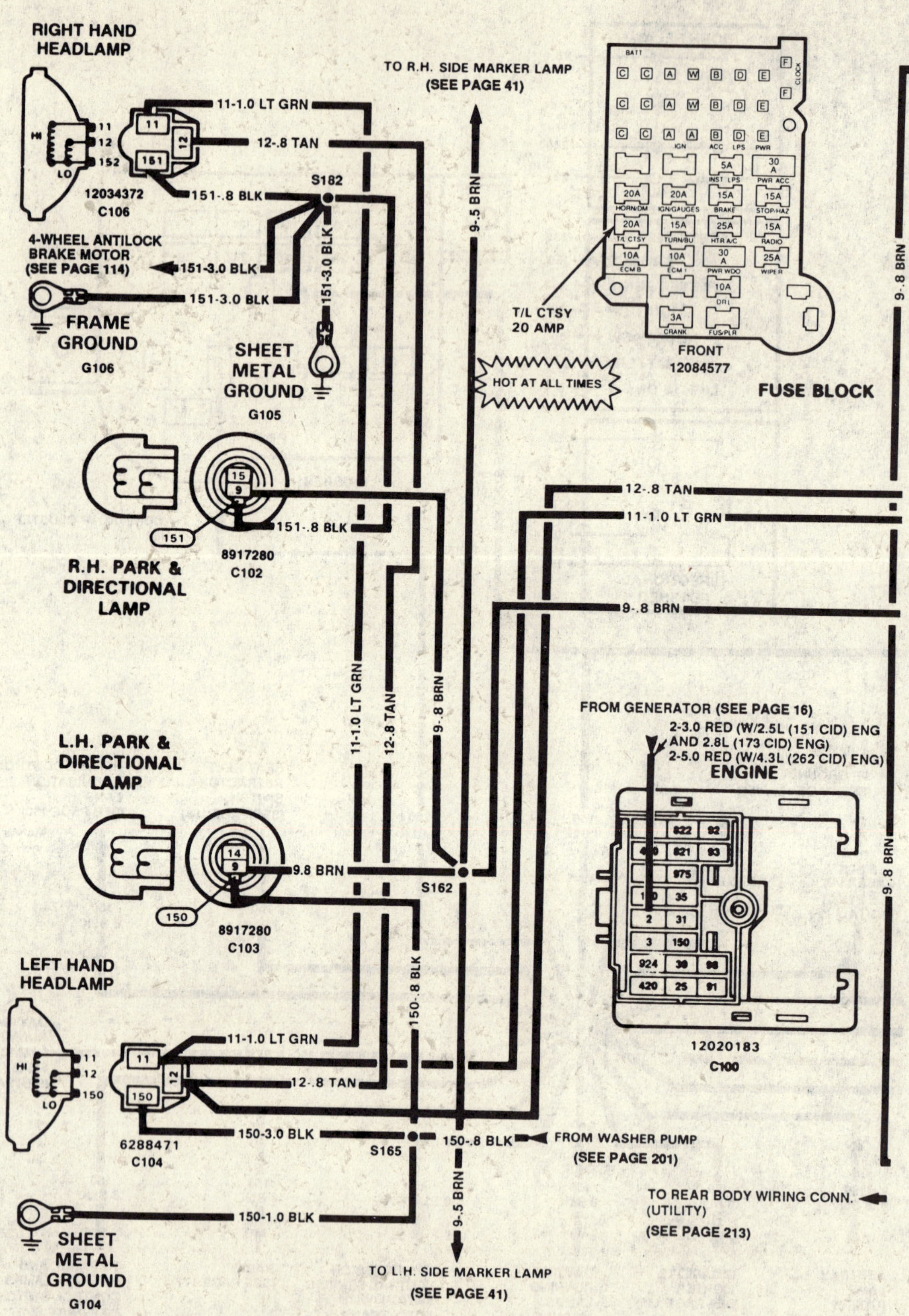

30 HEADLAMPS AND PARKING LAMPS - W/O CANADIAN DAYTIME

1988-91

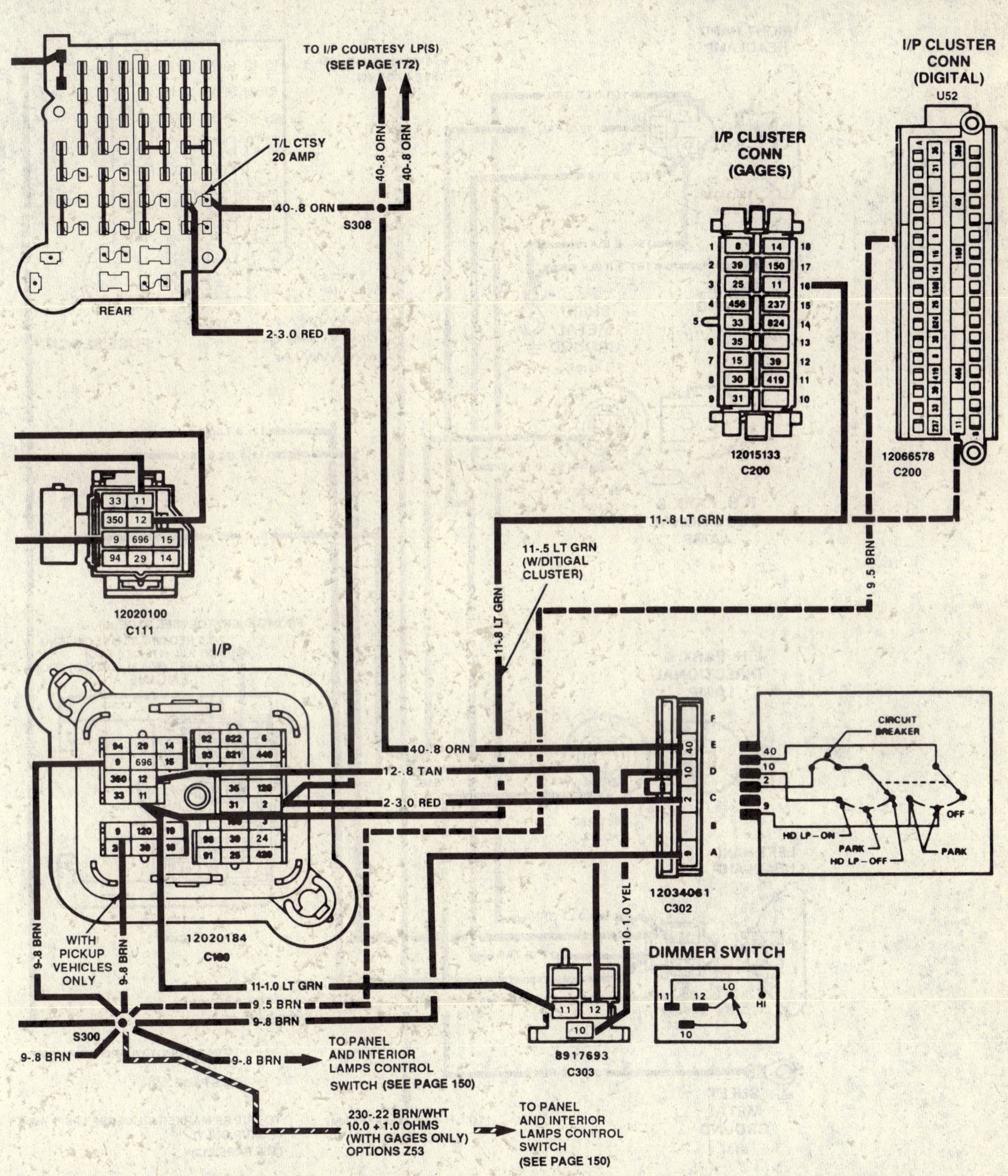

RUNNING LAMPS Z49 - 4-DOOR UTILITY

1988-91

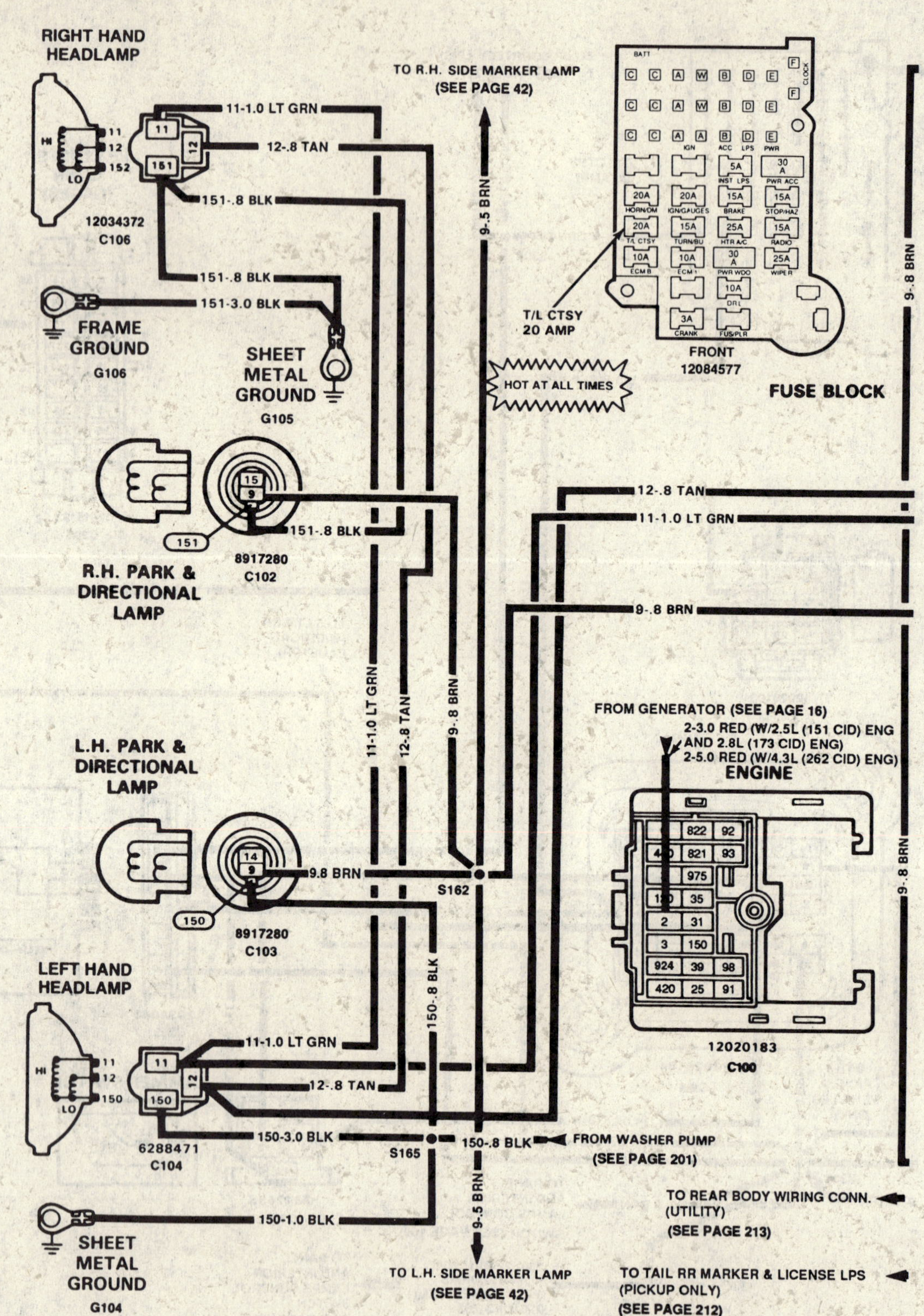

HEADLAMPS AND PARKING LAMPS

1988-91

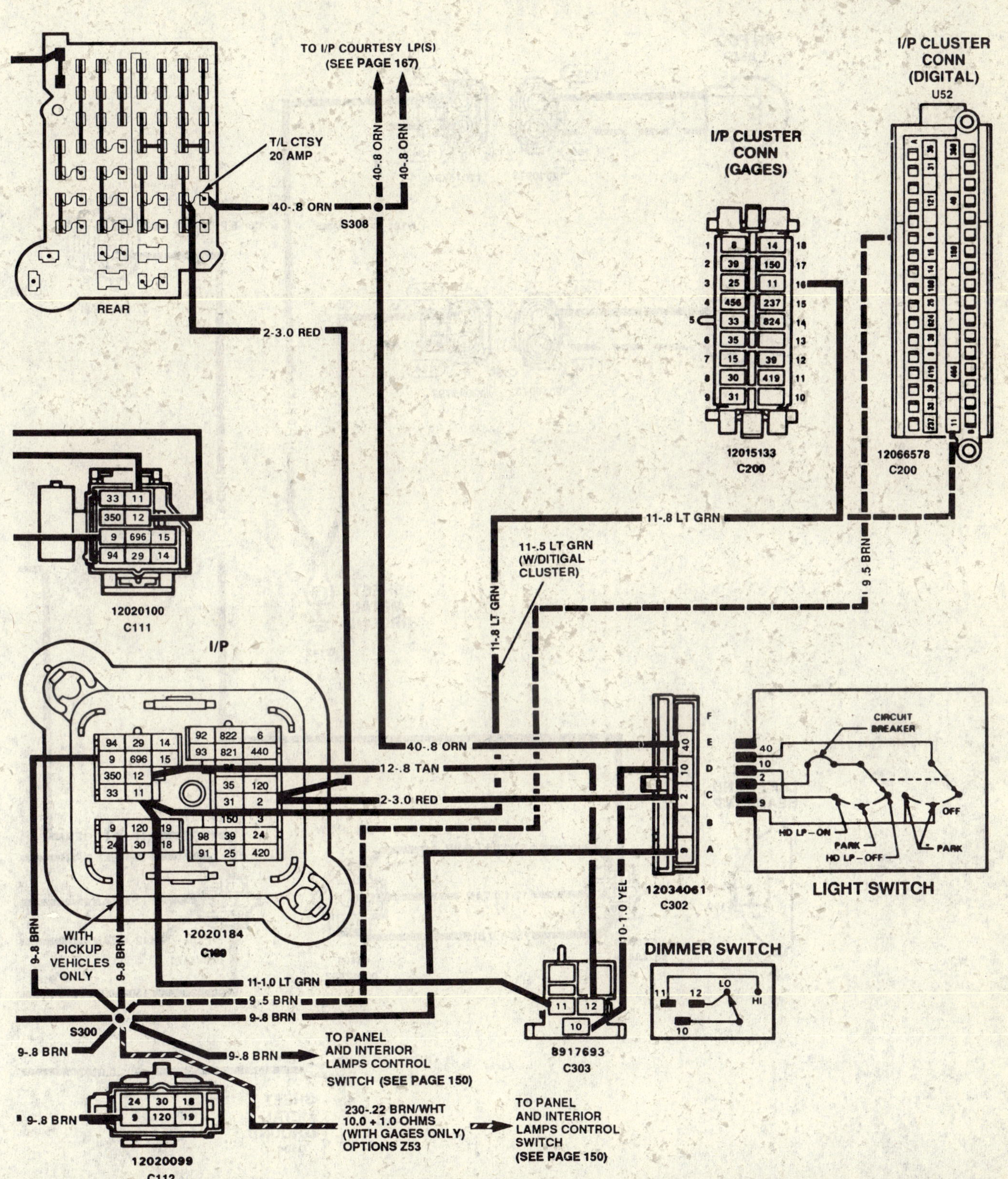

- W/O CANADIAN DAYTIME RUNNING LAMPS Z49 - PICKUP AND 2-DOOR UTILITY 31

1988-91

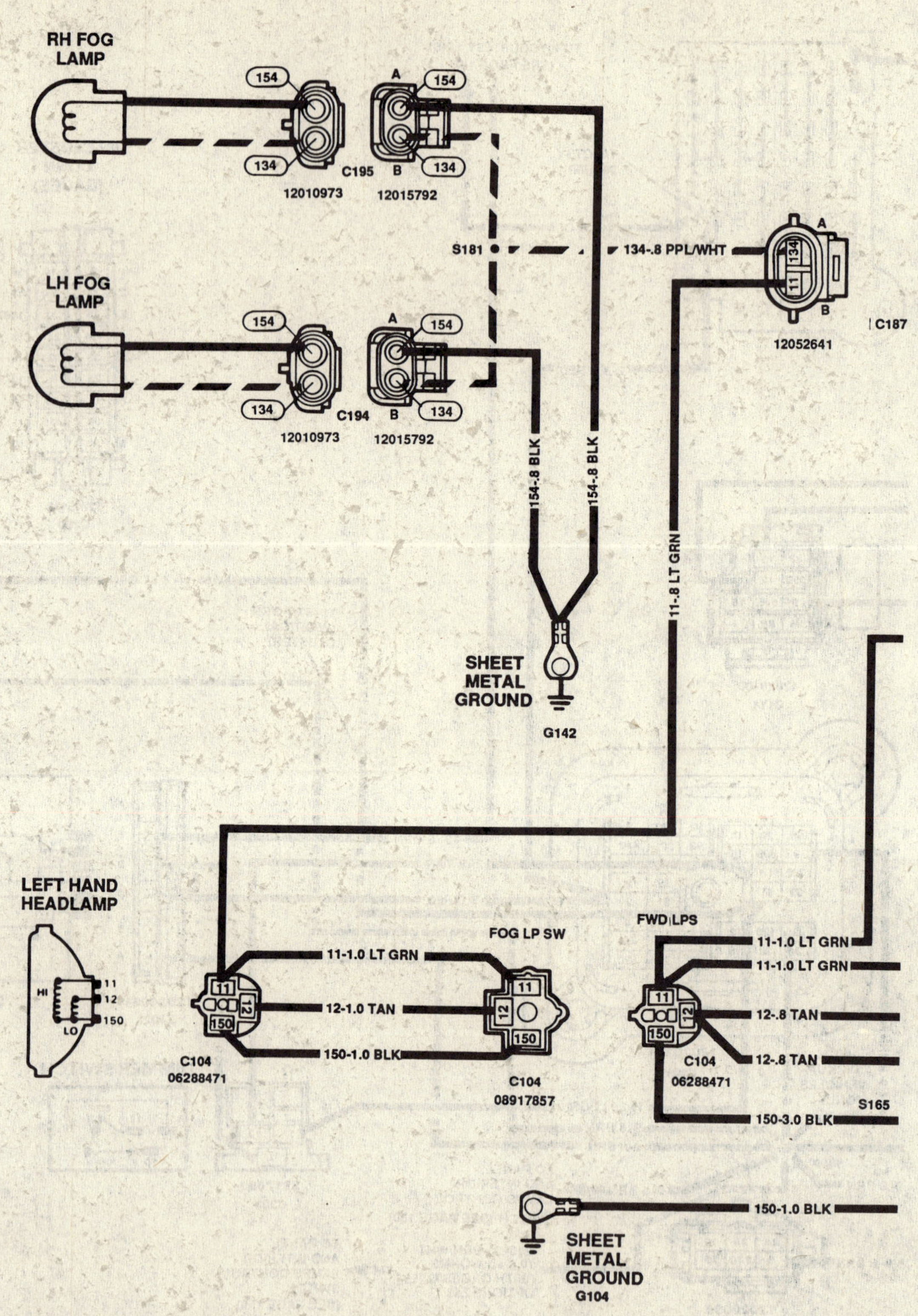

36 FOG LAMPS (ANL) - W/O CANADIAN DAYTIME RUNNING LAMPS Z49

1988-91

8-.8 GRA
9-.8 BRN
GROMMET 132
12015998
A
134
11
B
134-.8 PPL/WHT
11-.8 LT GRN
12052647
40-.8 ORN
11-.8 LT GRN
C189
12034003
34-.8 PPL
FOG LAMP
RELAY
134-.8 PPL/WHT
134-.8 PPL/WHT
12-.8 TAN
11-1.0 LT GRN
A
H
D
E
12092057
150-.8 BLK
C186
12045688
RH HEADLAMP
(SEE PAGE 30)
RH HEADLAMP
(SEE PAGE 30)
150-.8 BLK
FROM WASHER PUMP
(SEE PAGE 201)
150-.8 BLK
LH FRONT
PARK LAMP
(SEE PAGE 30)
150-.8 BLK
34-.8 PPL
9-.8 BRN
134-.8 PPL/WHT
8-.8 GRA
FOG
LAMPS
ON
INDICATOR
ILLUM.
LAMP
BUS
BAR
GROUND
C190
12004267

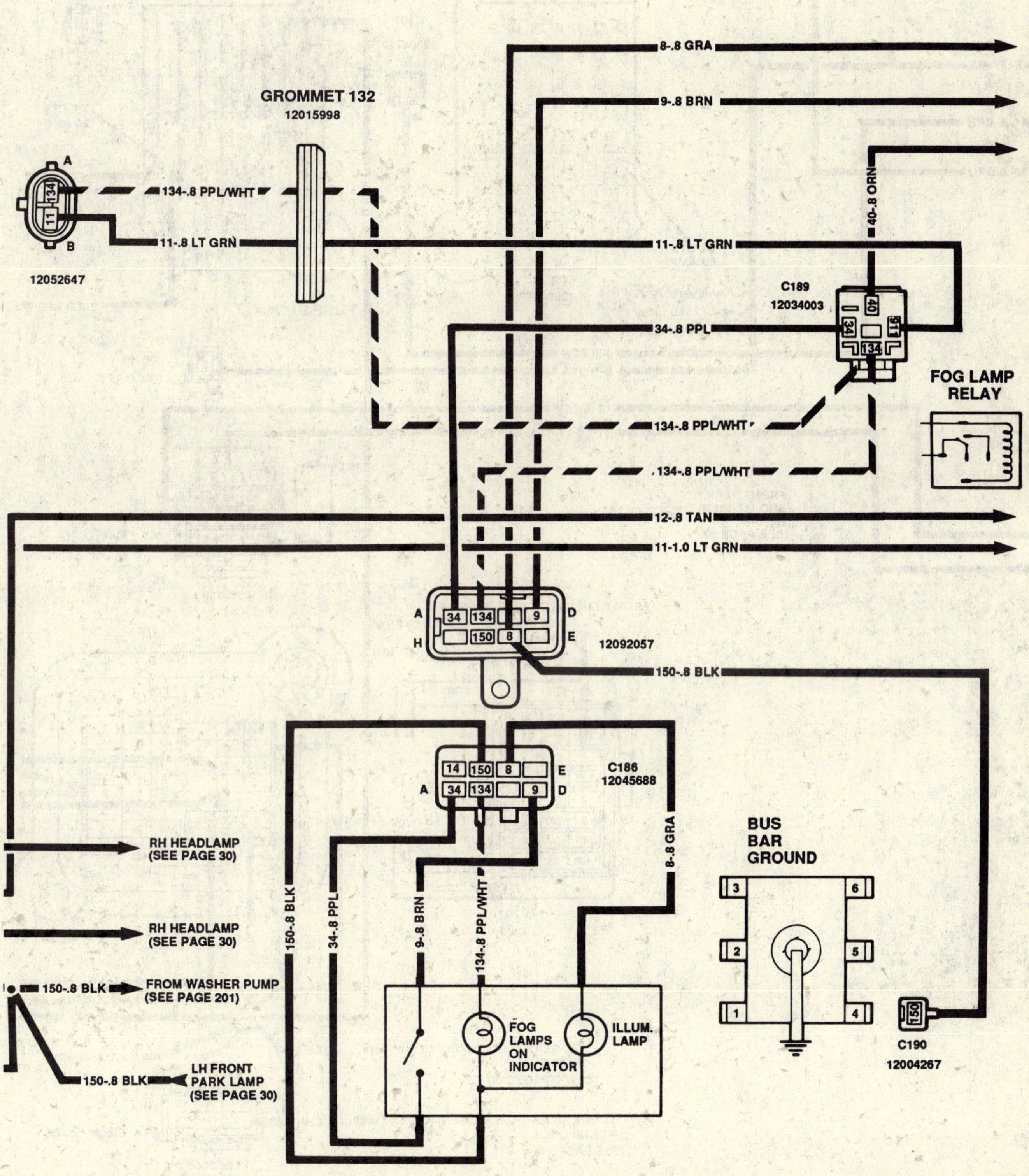

1988-91

8-.8 GRA
9-.8 BRN
40-.8 ORN
T/L CTSY
20 AMP
FRONT
12084577
HOT AT ALL TIMES
C192
12004740
C193
12004886
T/L CTSY
20 AMP
40-.8 ORN
REAR
FUSE BLOCK
2-3.0 RED
9-.8 BRN
8-.8 GRA
C191
12004885
12-.8 TAN
11-1.0 LT GRN
FRONT PARK
AND MARKER
LAMPS
(SEE PAGE 30)
12020100
C111
FROM GENERATOR (SEE PAGE 16)
2-3.0 RED (W/2.5L (151 CID) ENG
AND 2.8L (173 CID) ENG)
2-5.0 RED (W/4.3L (262 CID) ENG)
ENGINE
I/P
12020183
C100
WITH
PICKUP
VEHICLES
ONLY
12020184
C100
11-1.0 LT GRN
9 .5 BRN
9-.8 BRN
S300
TO REAR BODY WIRING CONN.
(UTILITY)
(SEE PAGE 213)
9-.8 BRN
TO TAIL RR MARKER & LICENSE LPS
(PICKUP ONLY)
(SEE PAGE 212)
12020099
C112

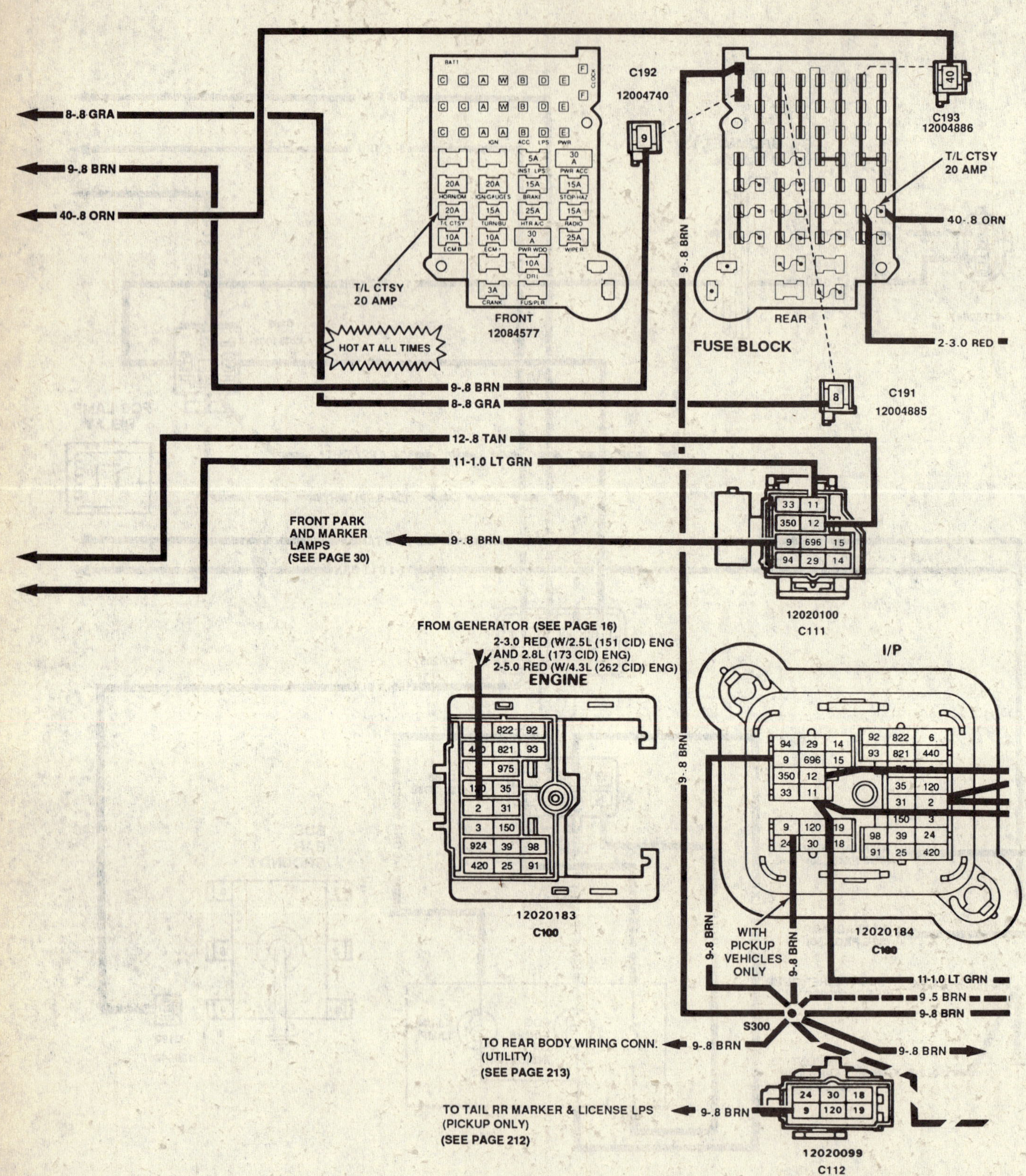

1988-91

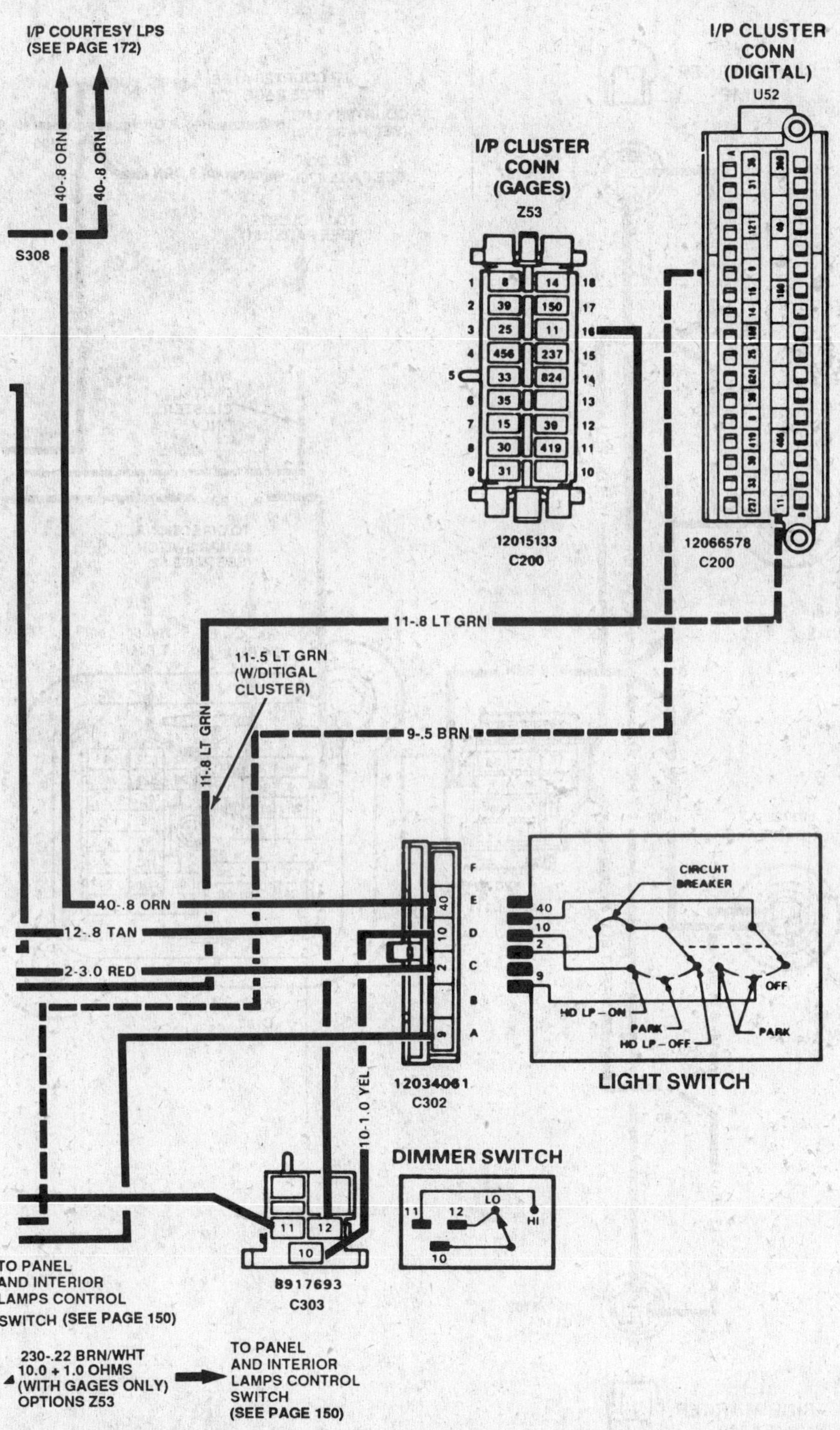

FOG LAMPS (ANL) - W/O CANADIAN DAYTIME RUNNING LAMPS Z49 37

1988-91

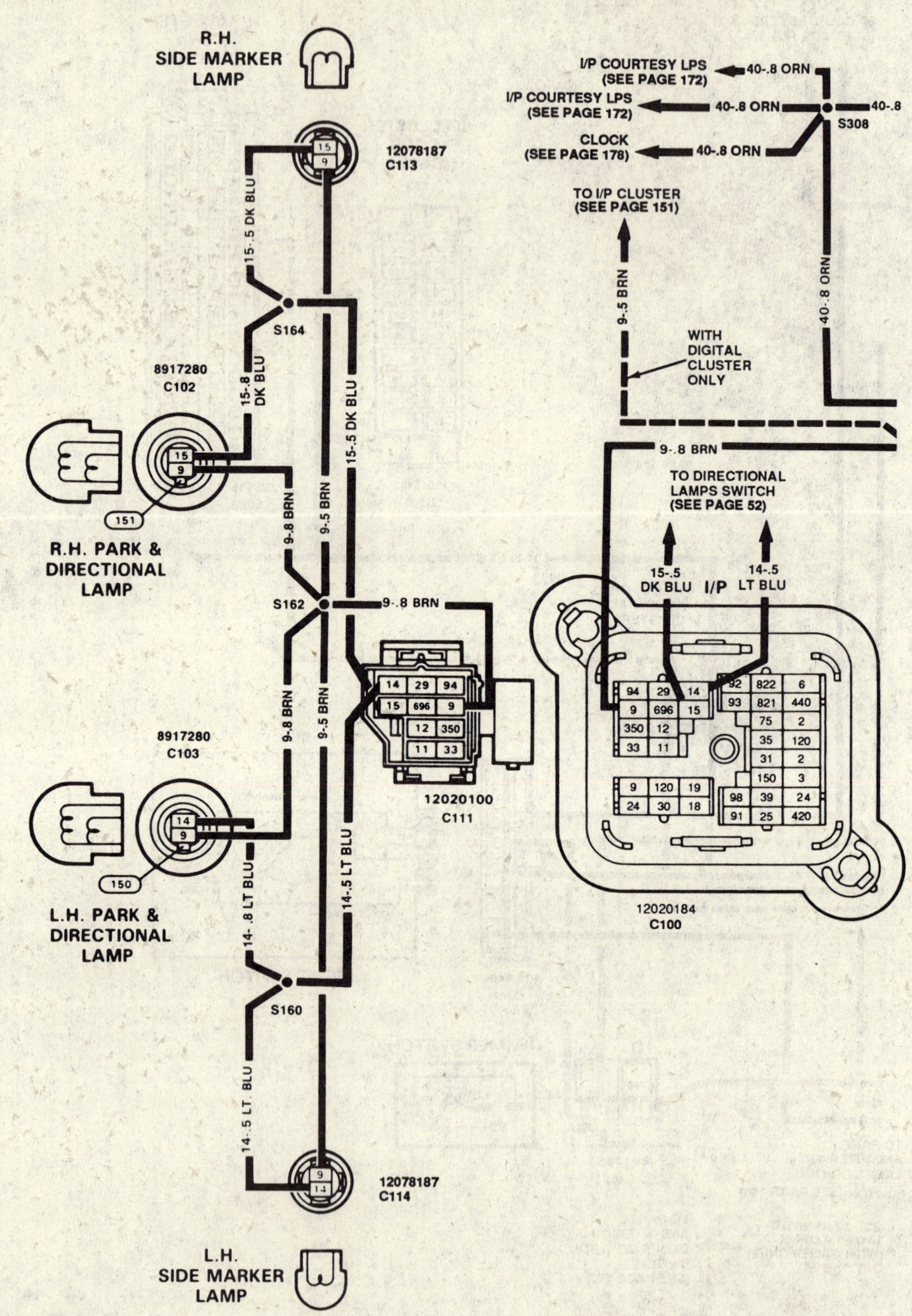

40 MARKER LAMPS - 4-DOOR UTILITY
1988-91

LIGHT SWITCH
CIRCUIT BREAKER
HD LP – ON
PARK
HD LP – OFF
OFF
PARK
ORN
12034061
C302
9-.8 BRN
PANEL AND INTERIOR LAMPS CONTROL SWITCH (SEE PAGE 150)
230-.22 BRN/WHT
10.0 + 1.0 OHMS
(WITH GAGE OPTIONS YC2/Z53)
PANEL AND INTERIOR LAMPS CONTROL SWITCH (SEE PAGE 150)
40-.8 ORN
S300
C442
08900320
C442
12004060
T/L CTSY
20 AMP
HOT AT ALL TIMES
FRONT
12084577
FUSE BLOCK
REAR

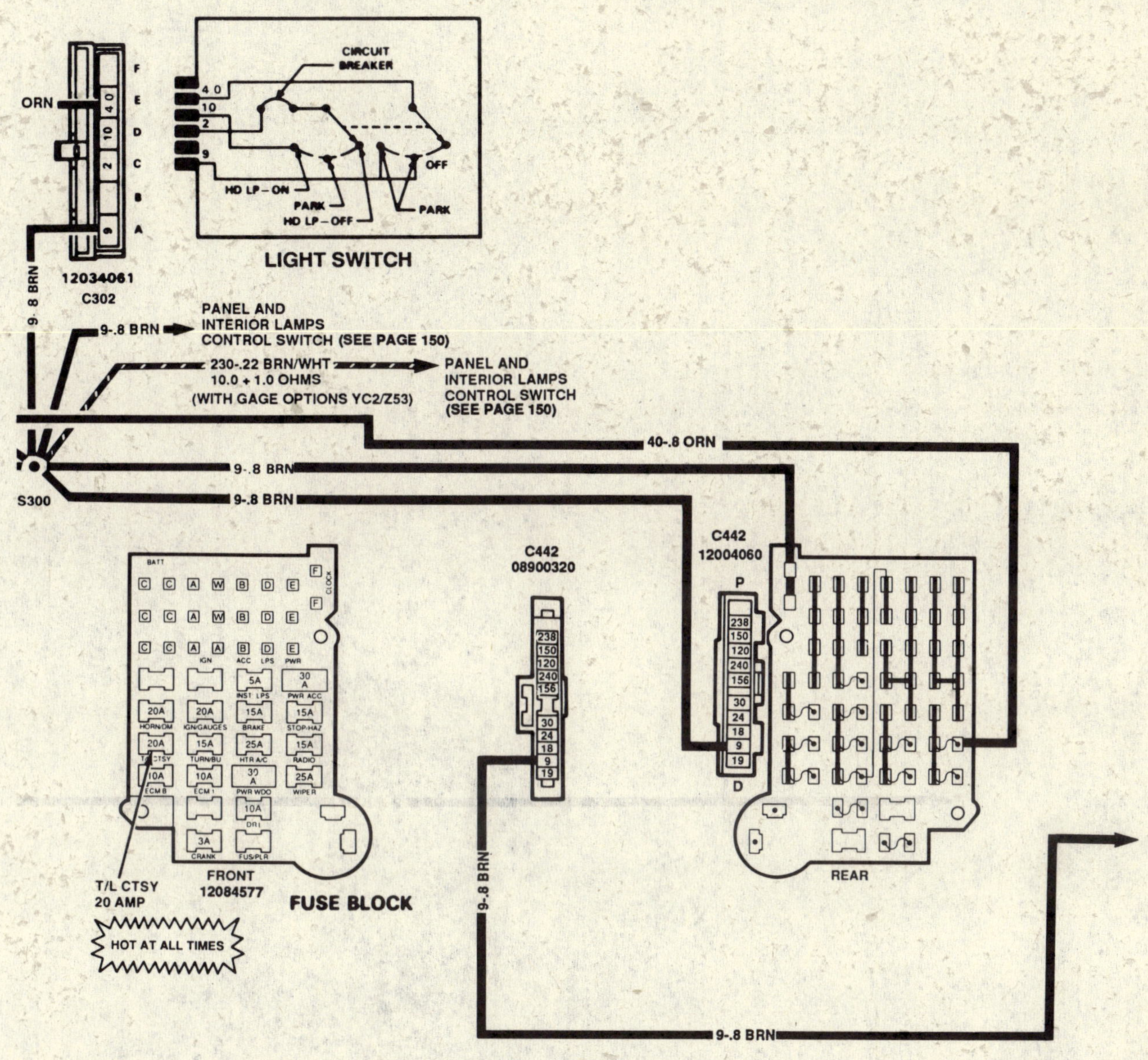

1988-91

1988-91

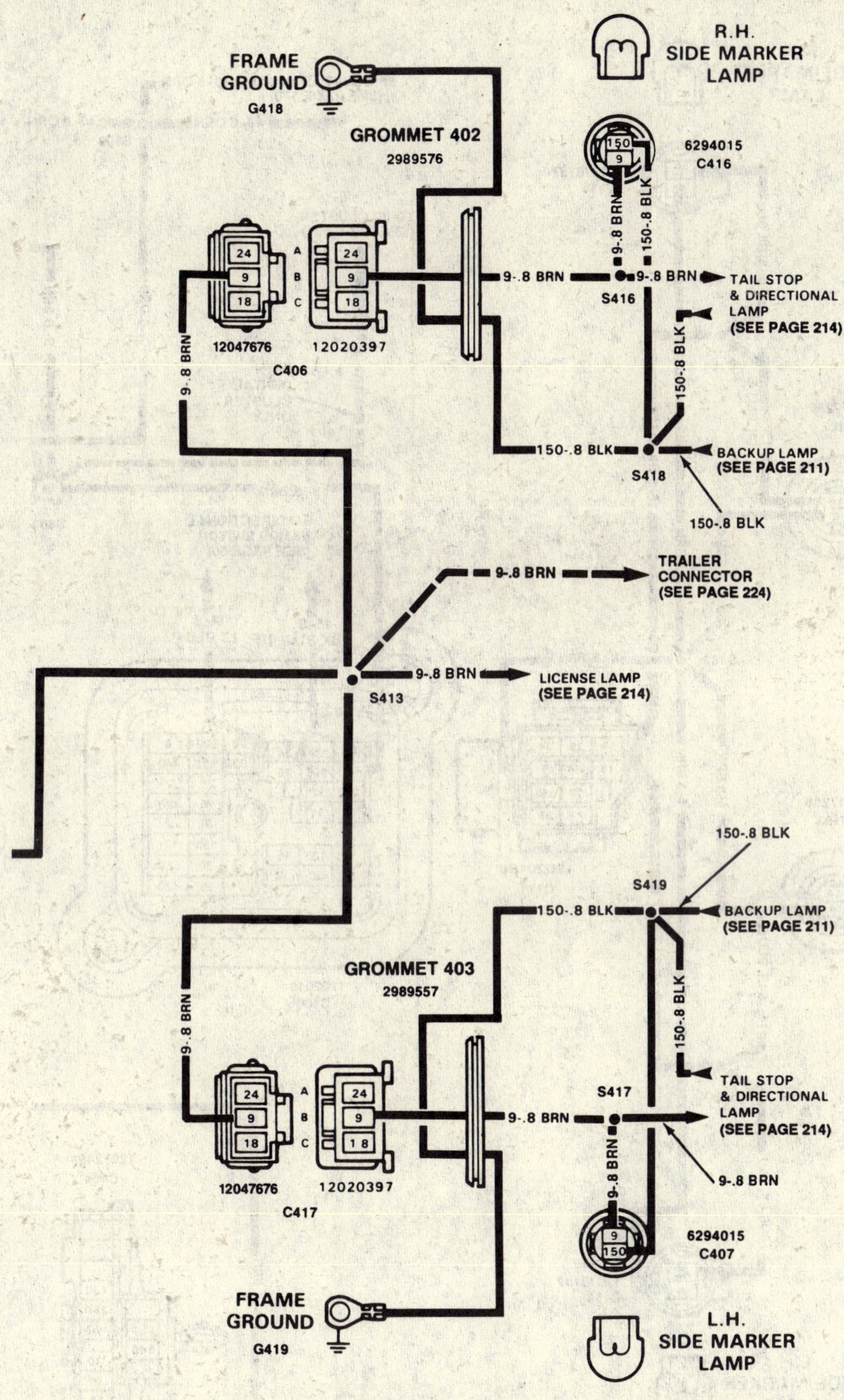

MARKER LAMPS - 4-DOOR UTILITY 41

1988-91

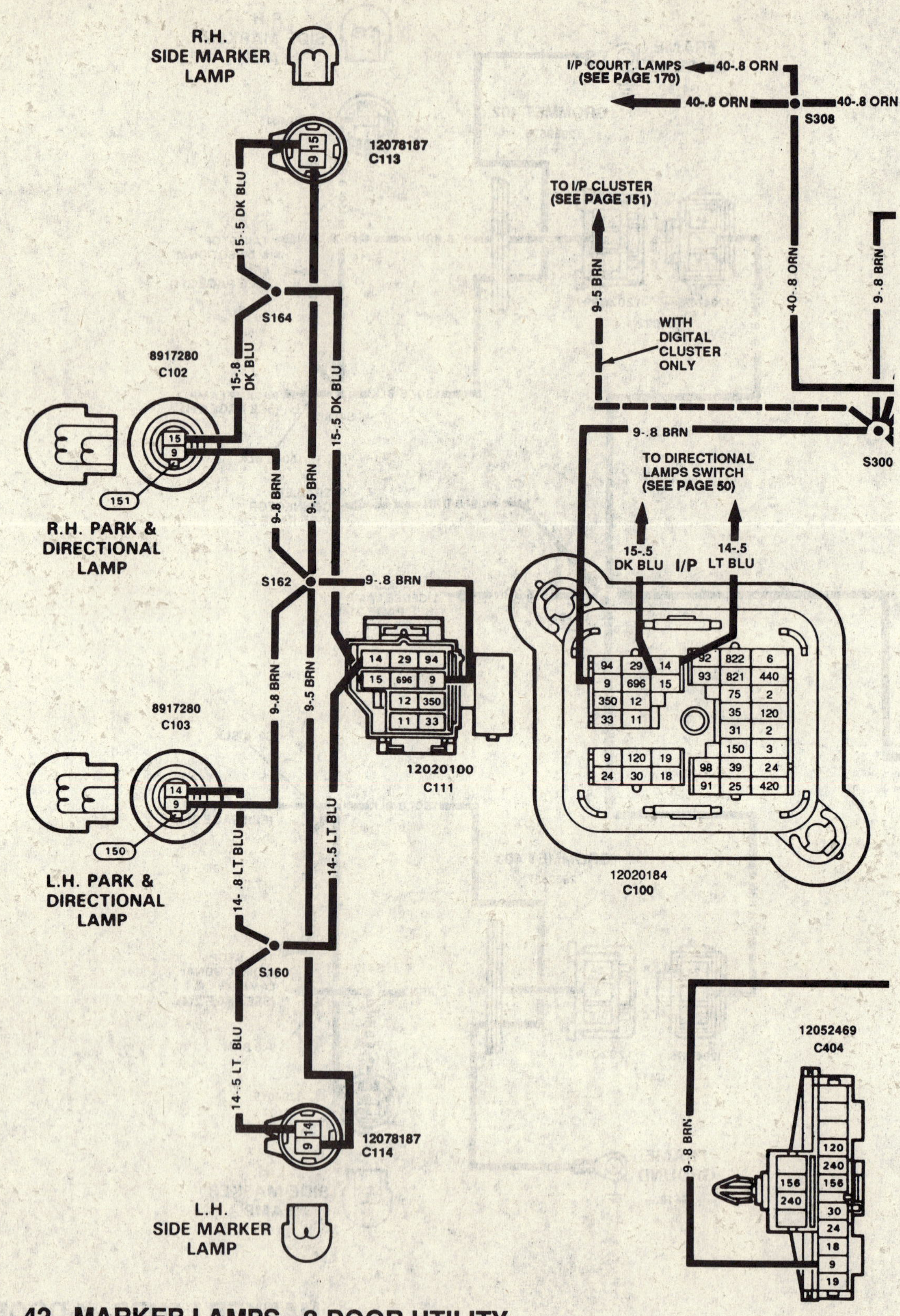

42 MARKER LAMPS - 2-DOOR UTILITY

1988-91

LIGHT SWITCH
CIRCUIT BREAKER
HD LP-ON
PARK
HD LP-OFF
OFF
PARK
12034061
C302
9-.8 BRN
PANEL AND INTERIOR LAMPS CONTROL SWITCH (SEE PAGE 150)
230-.22 BRN/WHT
10.0 + 1.0 OHMS
(WITH GAGE OPTIONS YC2/Z53)
PANEL AND INTERIOR LAMPS CONTROL SWITCH (SEE PAGE 150)
40-.8 ORN
T/L CTSY 20 AMP
HOT AT ALL TIMES
FRONT
12084577
FUSE BLOCK
REAR
FRAME GROUND
G418
GROMMET 402
2989576
12047676
12020397
C406
R.H. SIDE MARKER LAMP
6294015
C416
S416
TAIL STOP & DIRECTIONAL LAMP (SEE PAGE 213)
150-.8 BLK
S418
BACKUP LAMP (SEE PAGE 210)
S413
LICENSE LAMP (SEE PAGE 213)
S419
BACKUP LAMP (SEE PAGE 213)
GROMMET 403
2989557
S417
TAIL STOP & DIRECTIONAL LAMP (SEE PAGE 210)
C417
6294015
C407
FRAME GROUND
G419
L.H. SIDE MARKER LAMP
12034337
C404
8900441
C405
8900440
C405

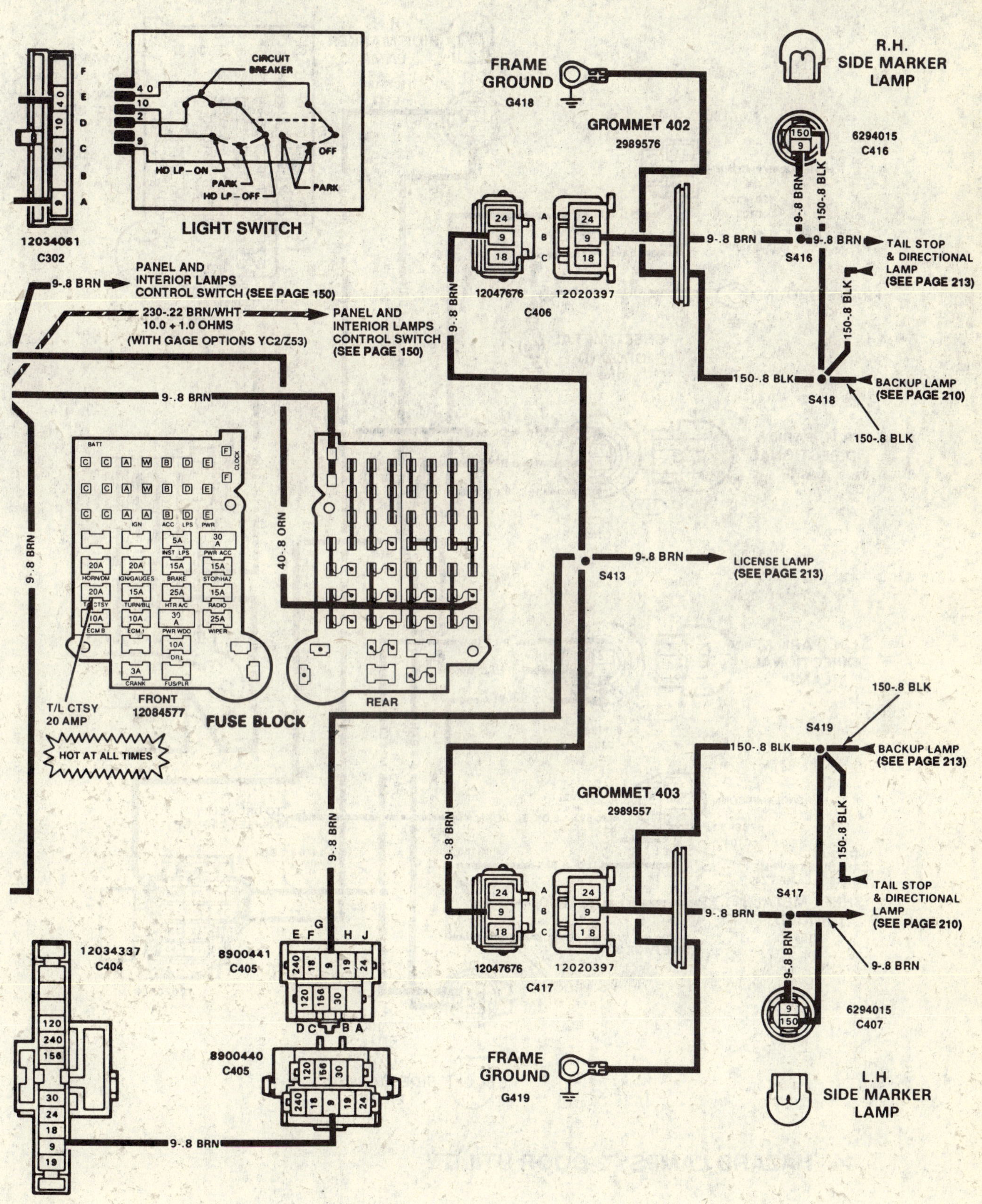

1988-91

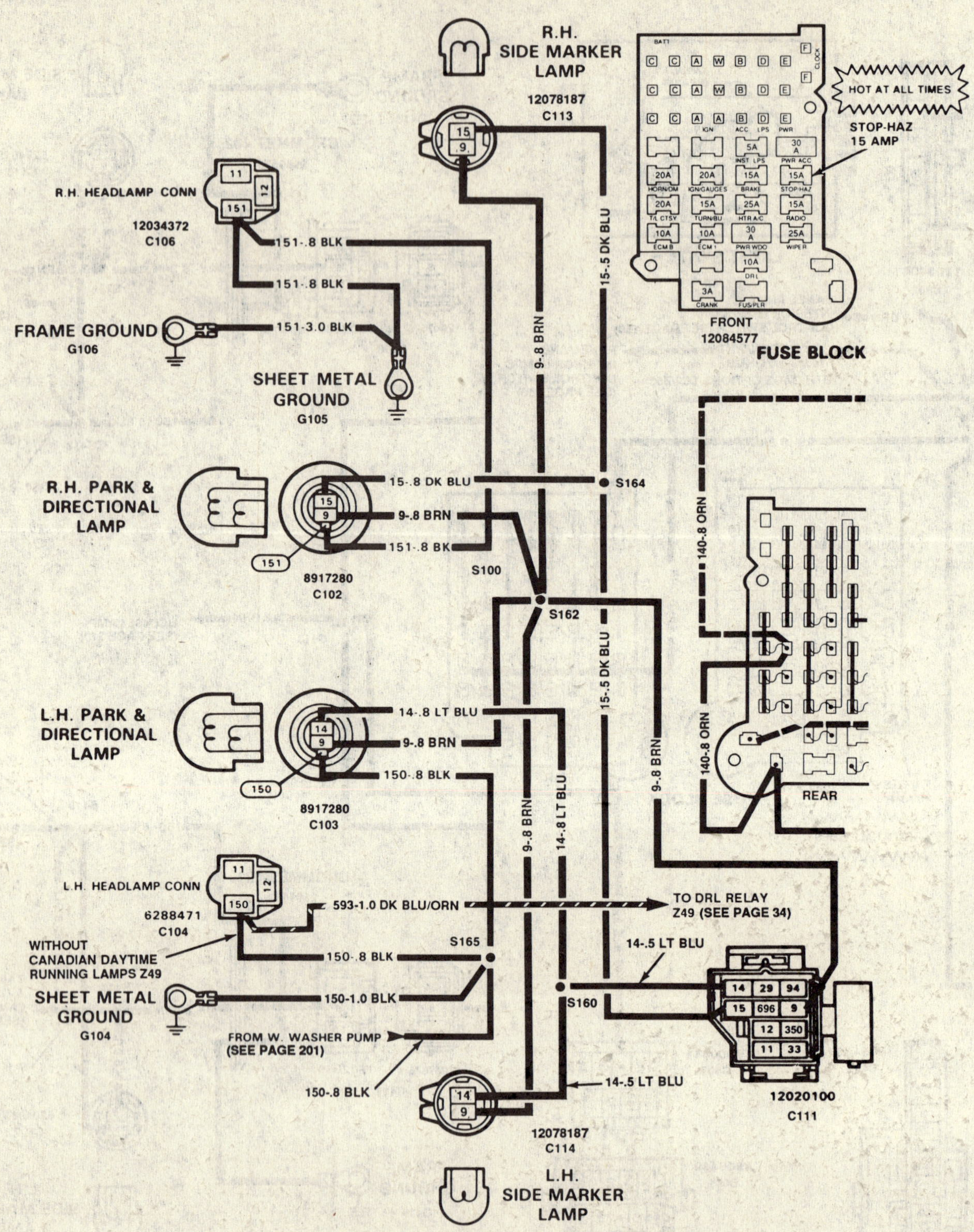

44 HAZARD LAMPS - 2-DOOR UTILITY

1988-91

HORN RELAY
SAFETY BELT SW
GROUND
FASTEN BELTS
IGNITION
IGN KEY SW
BATTERY
LIGHTS ON SW
HAZARD FLASHER
REAR
140-.8 ORN
BUZZER
HORN
HZ/F
P.E.D.
12015999
CONVENIENCE CENTER (FOR GAGE I/P CLUSTERS)
27-.8 BRN
17-.8 WHT
STOPLAMP SWITCH
C370
12033699
DIRECTIONAL FLASHER
T/S
12066631
CONVENIENCE CENTER (DIGITAL I/P ONLY)
I/P
14-.5 LT BLU
15-.5 DK BLU
19-.8 DK GRN
18-.8 YEL
12052469
C404
12041397
C404
9-.8 BRN
12020184
C100
LIGHT SWITCH (SEE PAGE 33)

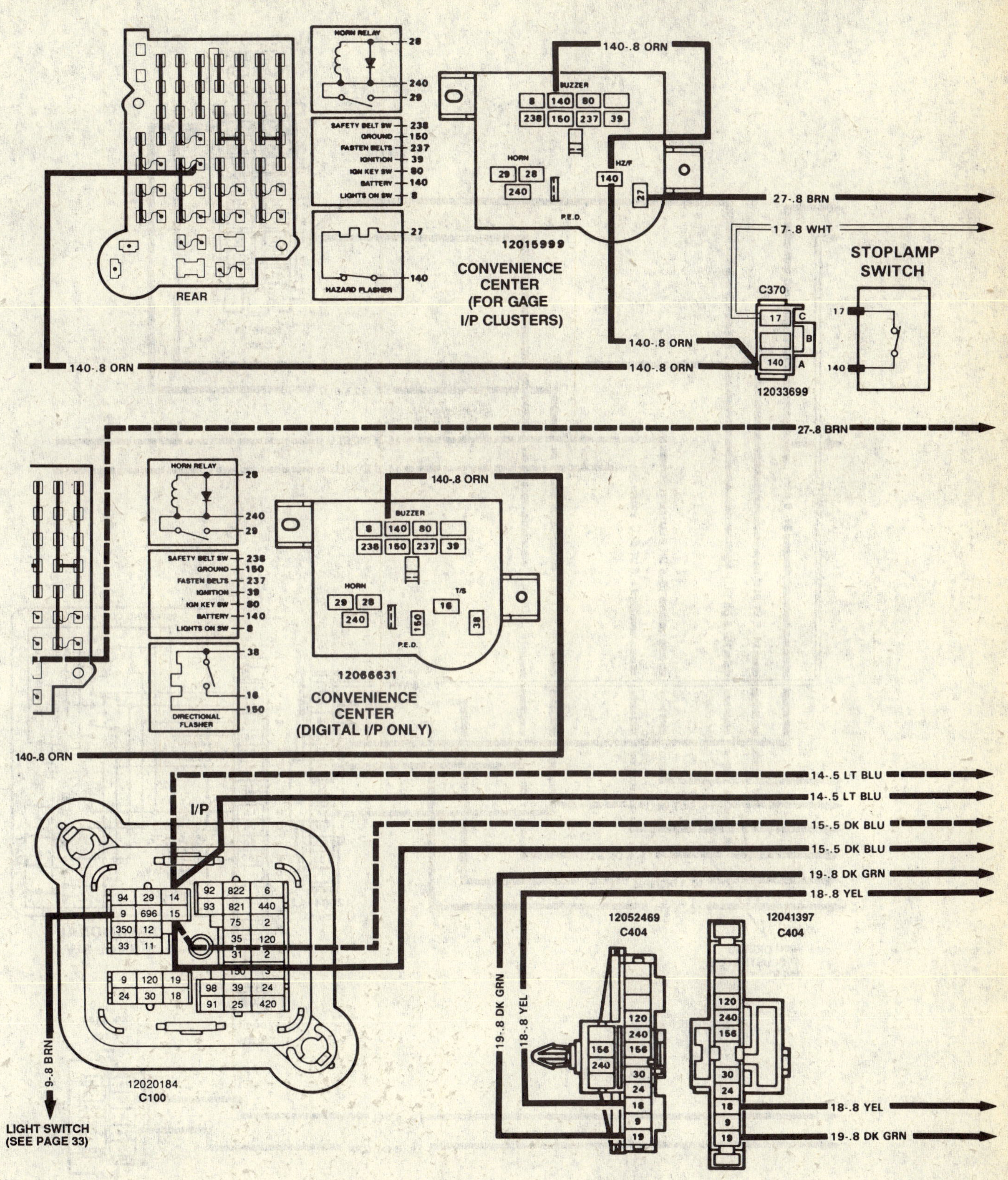

1988-91

I/P CLUSTER
CONN
(GAGES)
12015133
C200
14-.5 LT BLU
14-.5 LT BLU
15-.5 DK BLU
14-.5 LT BLU
17-.8 WHT
27-.8 BRN
14-.5 LT BLU
15-.5 DK BLU
15-.5 DK BLU
14-.5 LT BLU
14-.5 LT BLU
15-.5 DK BLU
17-.8 WHT
19-.8 DK GRN
18-.8 YEL
14-.5 LT BLU
15-.5 DK BLU
19-.8 DK GRN
18-.8 YEL
WITH DIGITAL
I/P CLUSTER U52
ONLY
12004147
C305
12004148
C305
(STEERING COL SWITCHES)
LEFT
RIGHT
TURN SIGNAL
.8 WHT
.8 DK GRN
.8 YEL
.8 PPL
.8 BRN
.8 DK BLU
.8 LT BLU
HORN
.8 BLK
.8 LT GRN
KEY
.8 TAN
NORMALLY
OPEN
SWITCHES
HAZARD
DIRECTIONAL
SIGNAL SW
8900440
C405
18-.8 YEL
19-.8 DK GRN

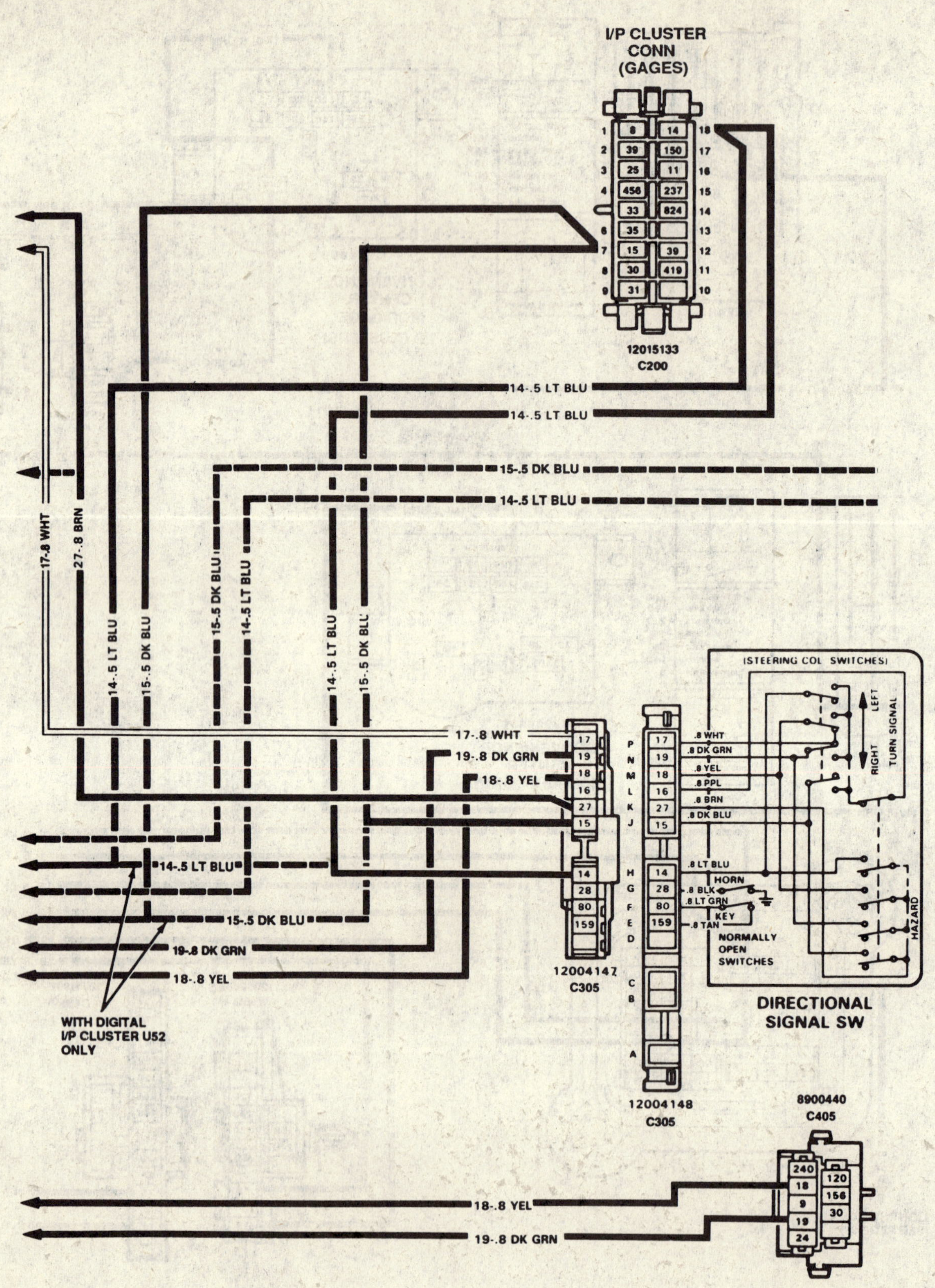

1988-91

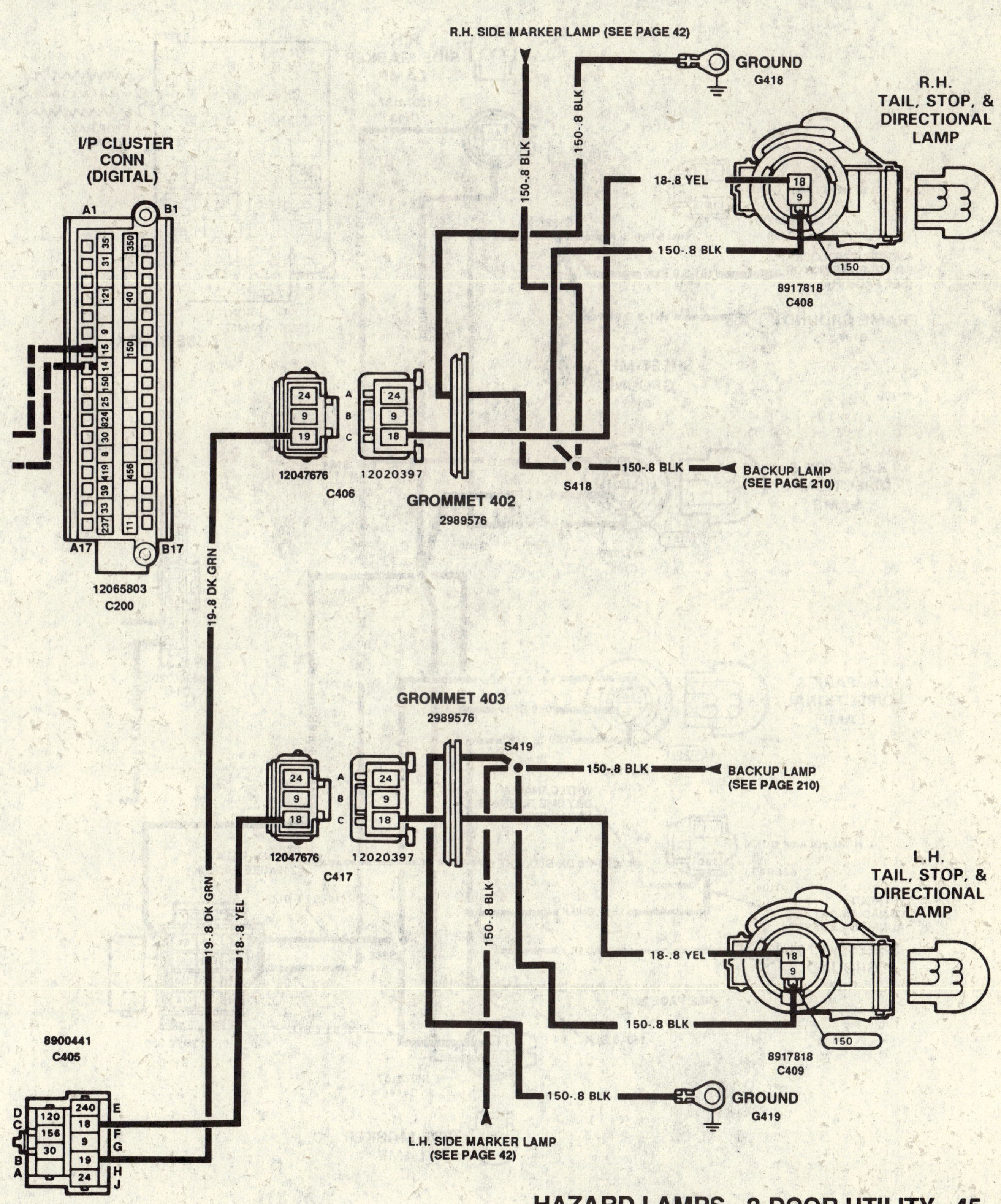

HAZARD LAMPS - 2-DOOR UTILITY 45

1988-91

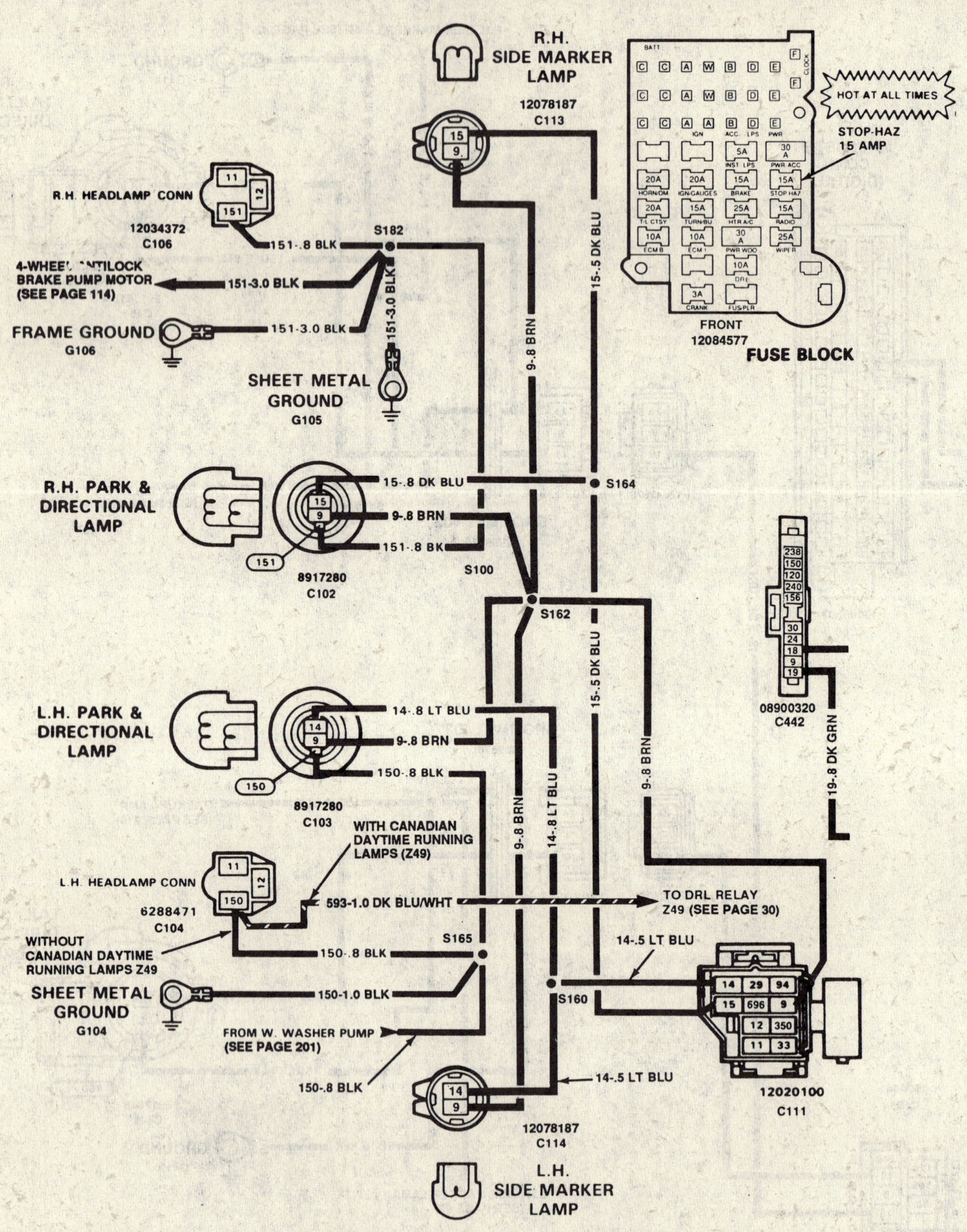

46 HAZARD LAMPS - 4-DOOR UTILITY
1988-91

C442
12004060
P
D
REAR
HORN RELAY
SAFETY BELT SW
GROUND
FASTEN BELTS
IGNITION
IGN KEY SW
BATTERY
LIGHTS ON SW
HAZARD FLASHER
BUZZER
HORN
HZ/F
P.E.D.
12015999
CONVENIENCE CENTER (FOR GAGE I/P CLUSTERS)
140-.8 ORN
27-.8 BRN
18-.8 YEL
19-.8 DK GRN
DIRECTIONAL FLASHER
T/S
12066631
CONVENIENCE CENTER (DIGITAL I/P ONLY)
I/P
12020184
C100
9-.8 BRN
LIGHT SWITCH (SEE PAGE 30)
14-.5 LT BLU
15-.5 DK BLU

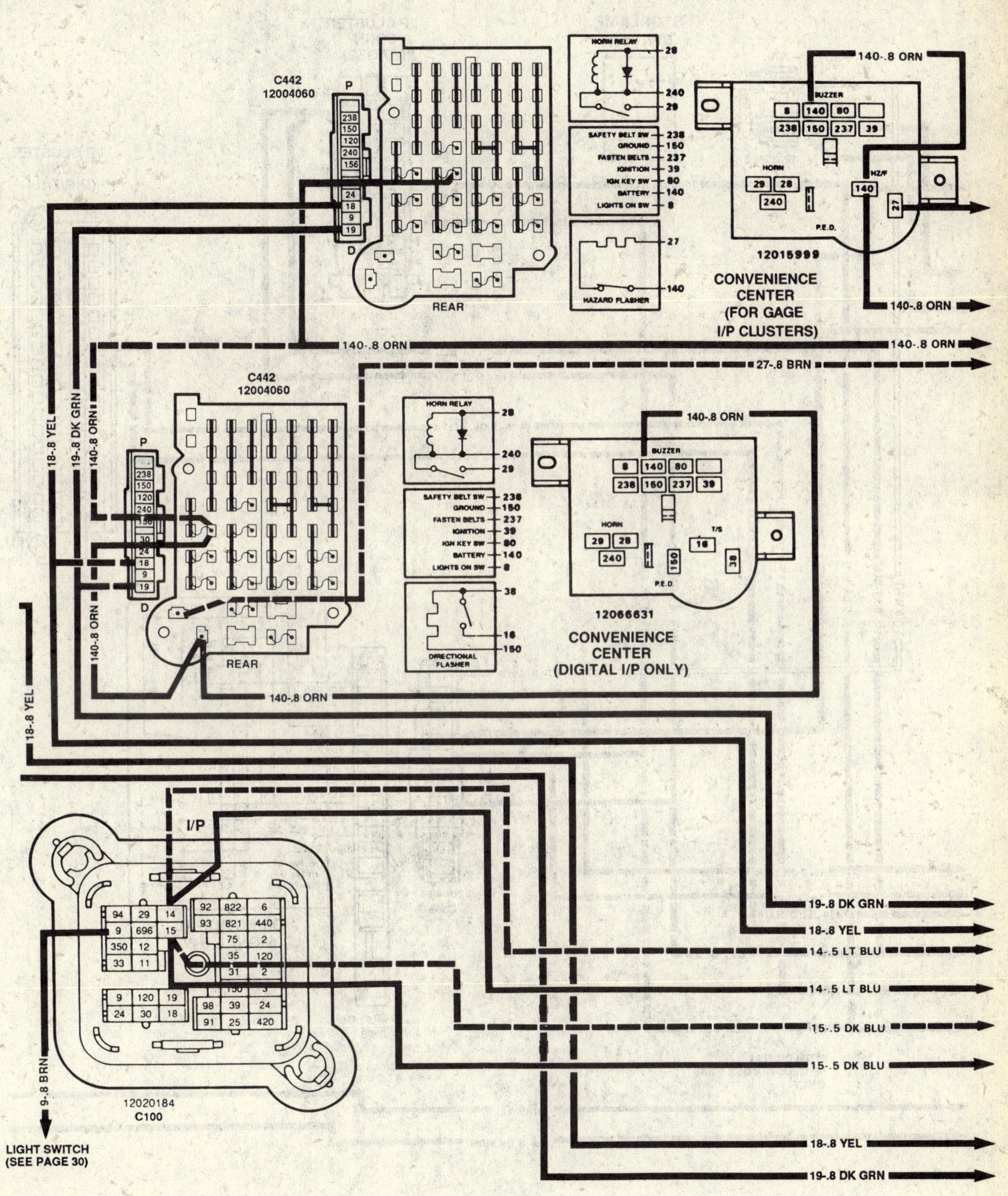

1988-91

STOPLAMP SWITCH
I/P CLUSTER CONN (GAGES)
C370
12033699
140-.8 ORN
15-.5 DK BLU
12015133
C200
I/P CLUSTER CONN (DIGITAL)
A1
B1
A17
B17
12065803
C200
14-.5 LT BLU
17-.8 WHT
27-.8 BRN
19-.8 DK GRN
18-.8 YEL
12004147
C305
12004148
C305
(STEERING COL SWITCHES)
LEFT
RIGHT
TURN SIGNAL
HAZARD
HORN
KEY
NORMALLY OPEN SWITCHES
DIRECTIONAL SIGNAL SW
WITH DIGITAL I/P CLUSTER U52 ONLY

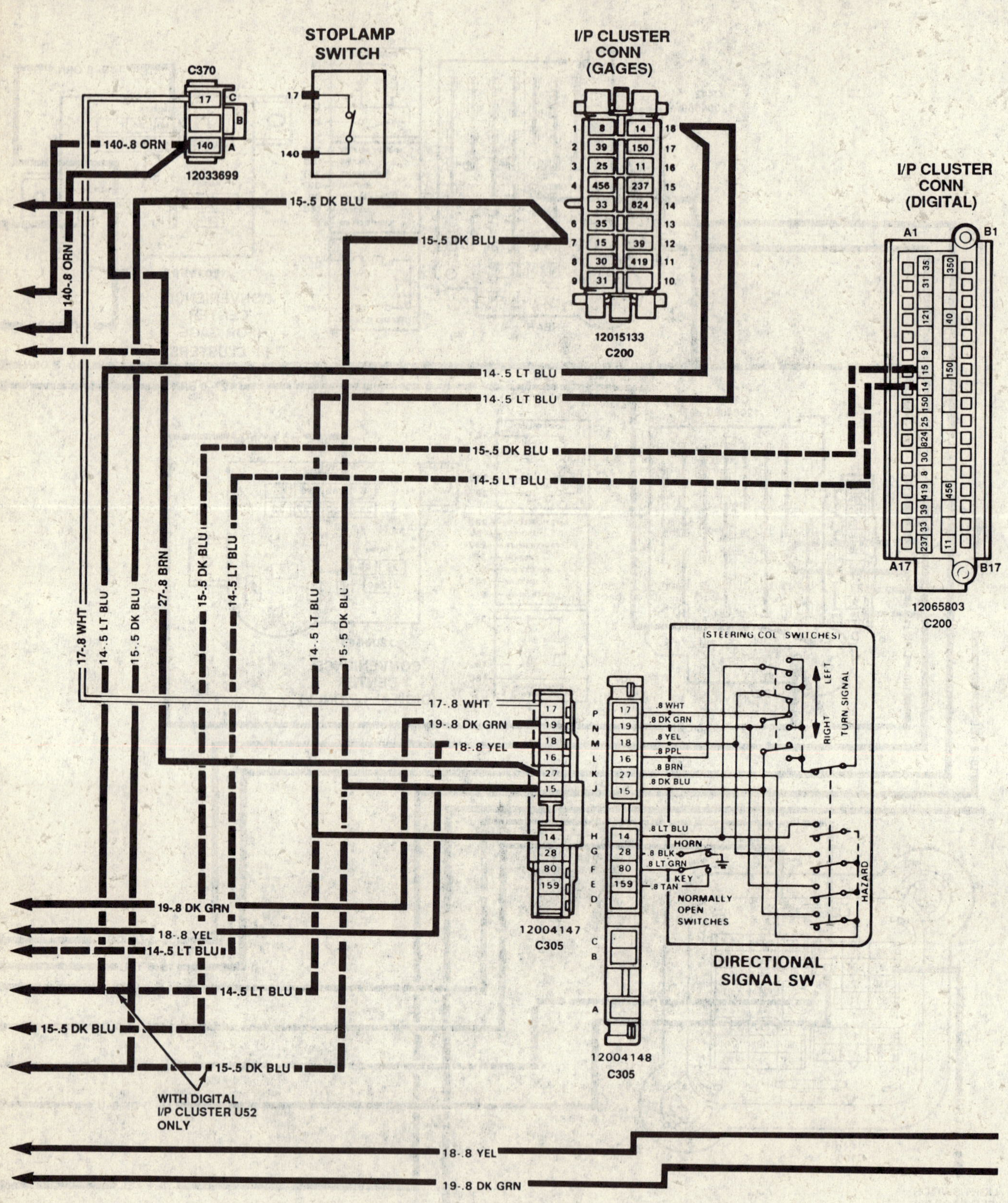

1988-91

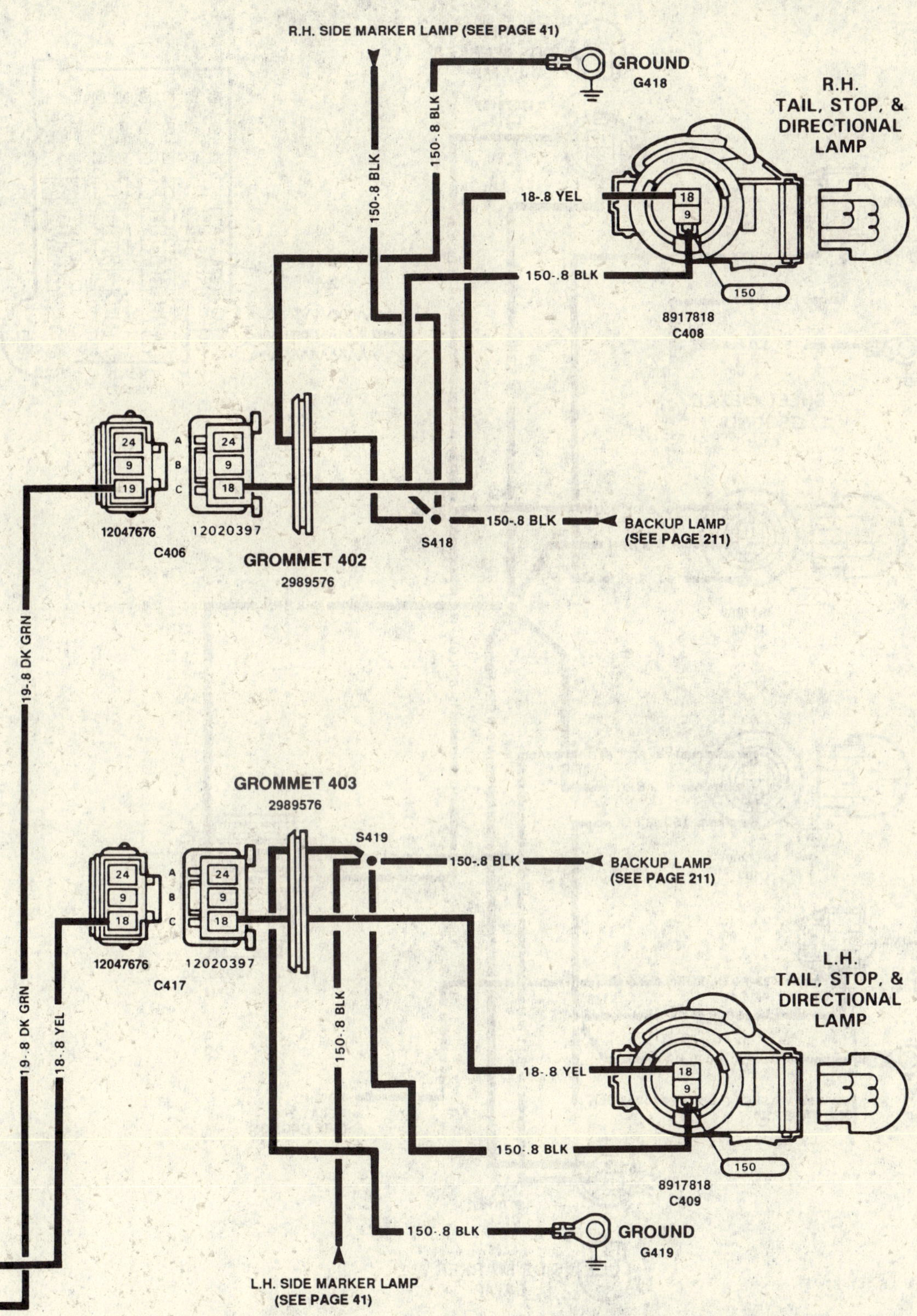

HAZARD LAMPS - 4-DOOR UTILITY 47

1988-91

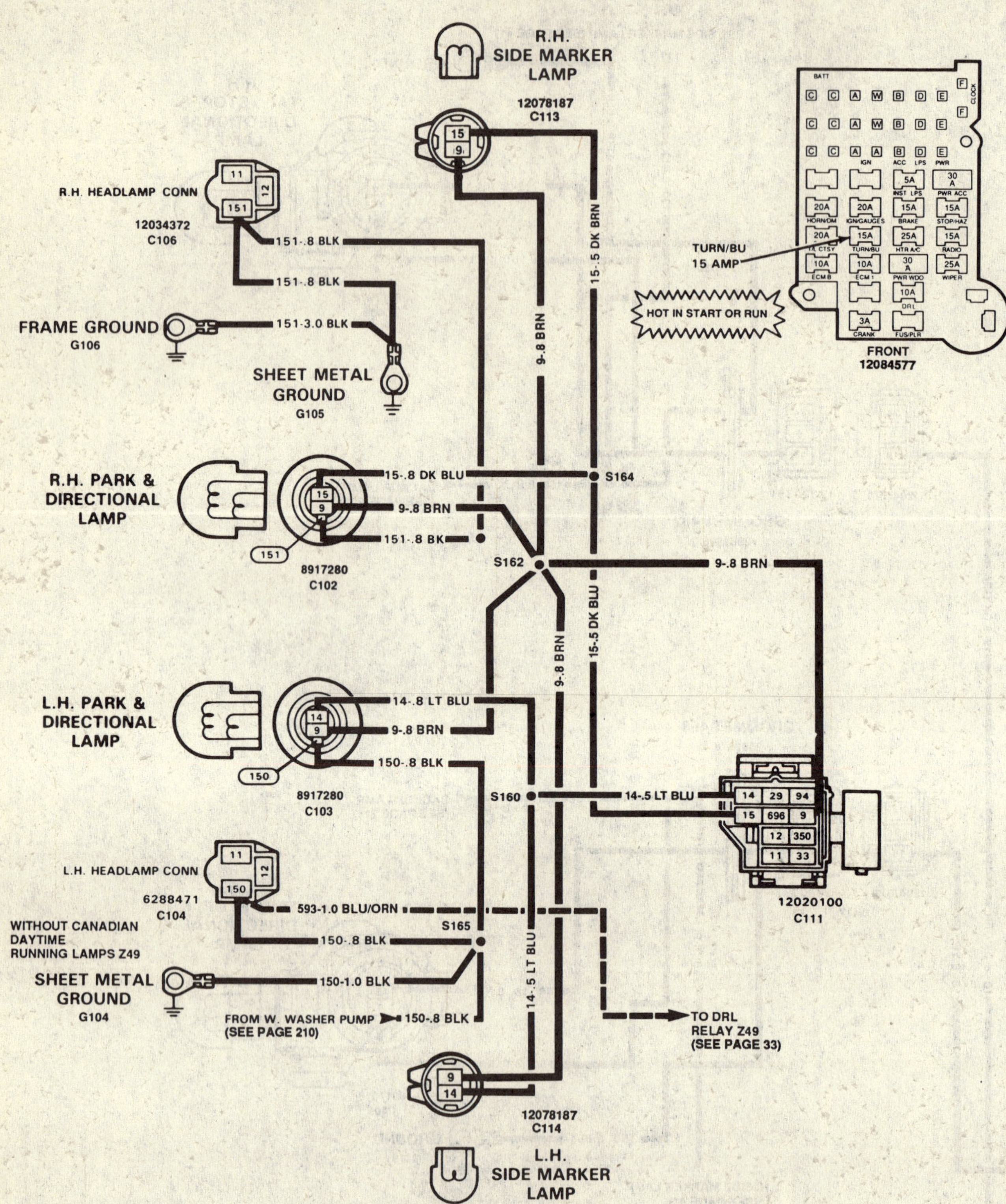

50 DIRECTIONAL LAMPS - 2-DOOR UTILITY

1988-91

BACKUP LPS
(SEE PAGE 201)
75-.8 DK BLU
HORN RELAY
28
240
29
SAFETY BELT SW 238
GROUND 150
FASTEN BELTS 237
IGNITION 39
IGN KEY SW 80
BATTERY 140
LIGHTS ON SW 8
38
16
150
DIRECTIONAL FLASHER
CONVENIENCE CENTER
BUZZER
HORN
T/S
P.E.
12066631
REAR
FUSE BLOCK
38-.8 DK BLU
16-.8 PPL
WITH DIGITAL I/P CLUSTER U52
16-.8 PPL
150-.5 BLK
ENGINE GROUND G140 (SEE PAGE 21)
150-3.0 BLK
S306
LIGHT SWITCH (SEE PAGE 33)
9-.8 BRN
I/P
14-.5 LT BLU
15-.5 DK BLU
12020184
C100
19-.8 DK GRN
18-.8 YEL
12052469
12034337
C404

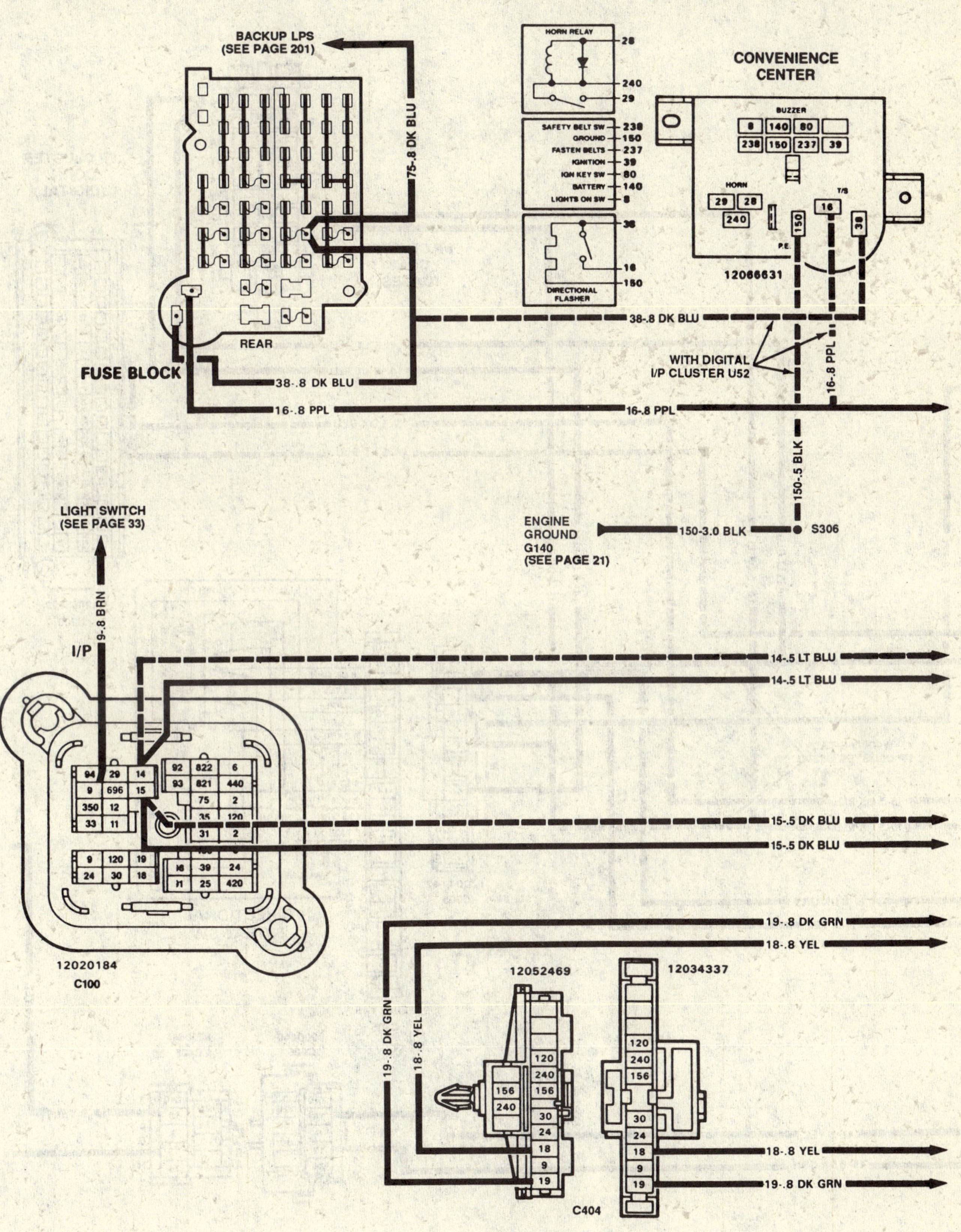

1988-91

I/P CLUSTER
CONN
(GAGES)
12015133
C200
I/P CLUSTER
CONN
(DIGITAL)
12065803
C200
14-.5 LT BLU
14-.5 LT BLU
15-.5 DK BLU
14-.5 LT BLU
16-.8 PPL
14-.5 LT BLU
15-.5 DK BLU
WITH DIGITAL
I/P CLUSTER U52
ONLY
15-.5 DK BLU
15-.5 DK BLU
19-.8 DK GRN
18-.8 YEL
12004147
C305
12004148
C305
(STEERING COL SWITCHES)
.8 WHT
.8 DK GRN
.8 YEL
.8 PPL
.8 BRN
.8 DK BLU
.8 LT BLU
.8 BLK HORN
.8 LT GRN
.8 TAN KEY
NORMALLY
OPEN
SWITCHES
LEFT
RIGHT
TURN SIGNAL
HAZARD
DIRECTIONAL
SIGNAL SW
8900440
C405
8900441
C405
18-.8 YEL
19-.8 DK GRN
18-.8 YEL
18-.8 YEL

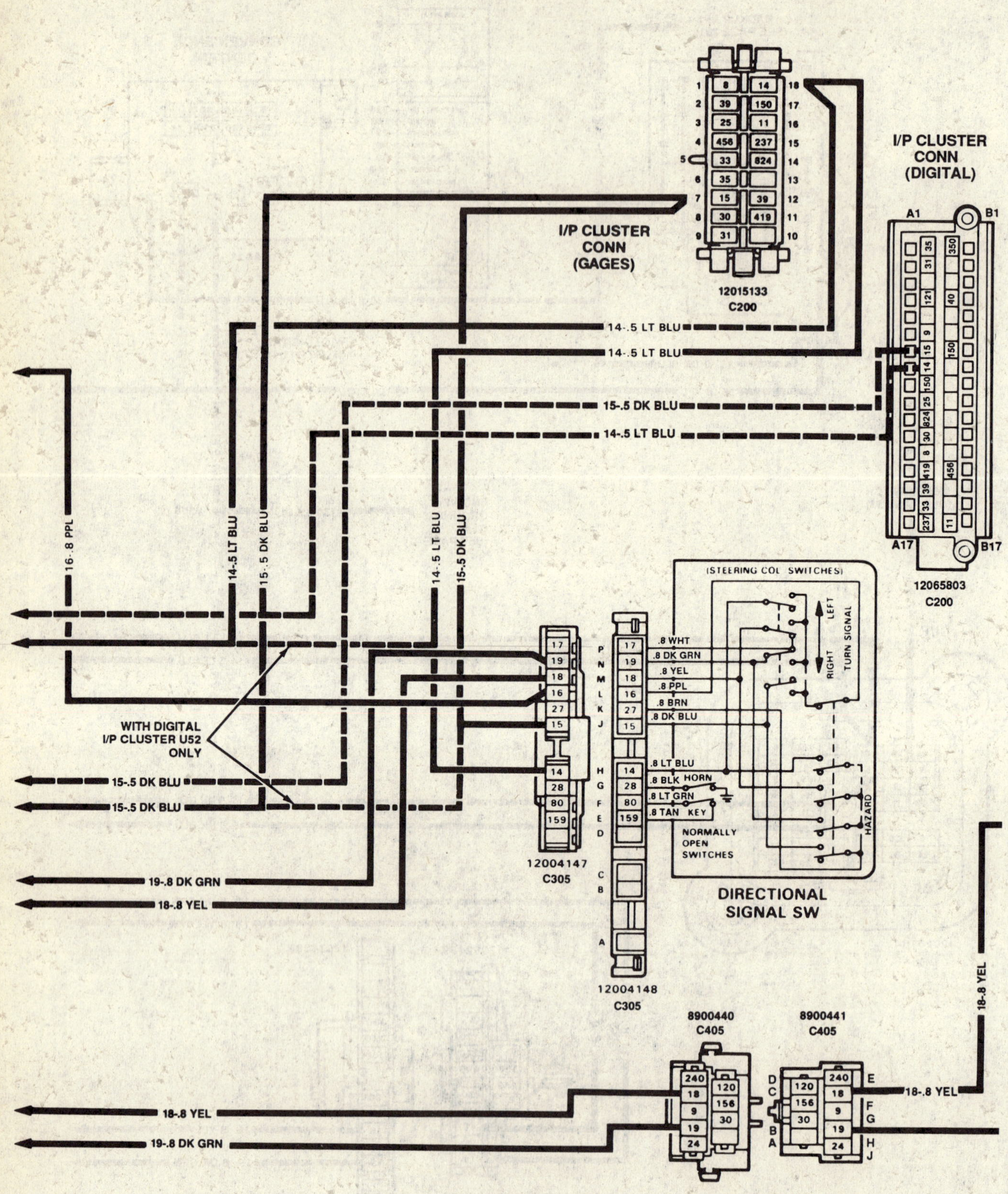

1988-91

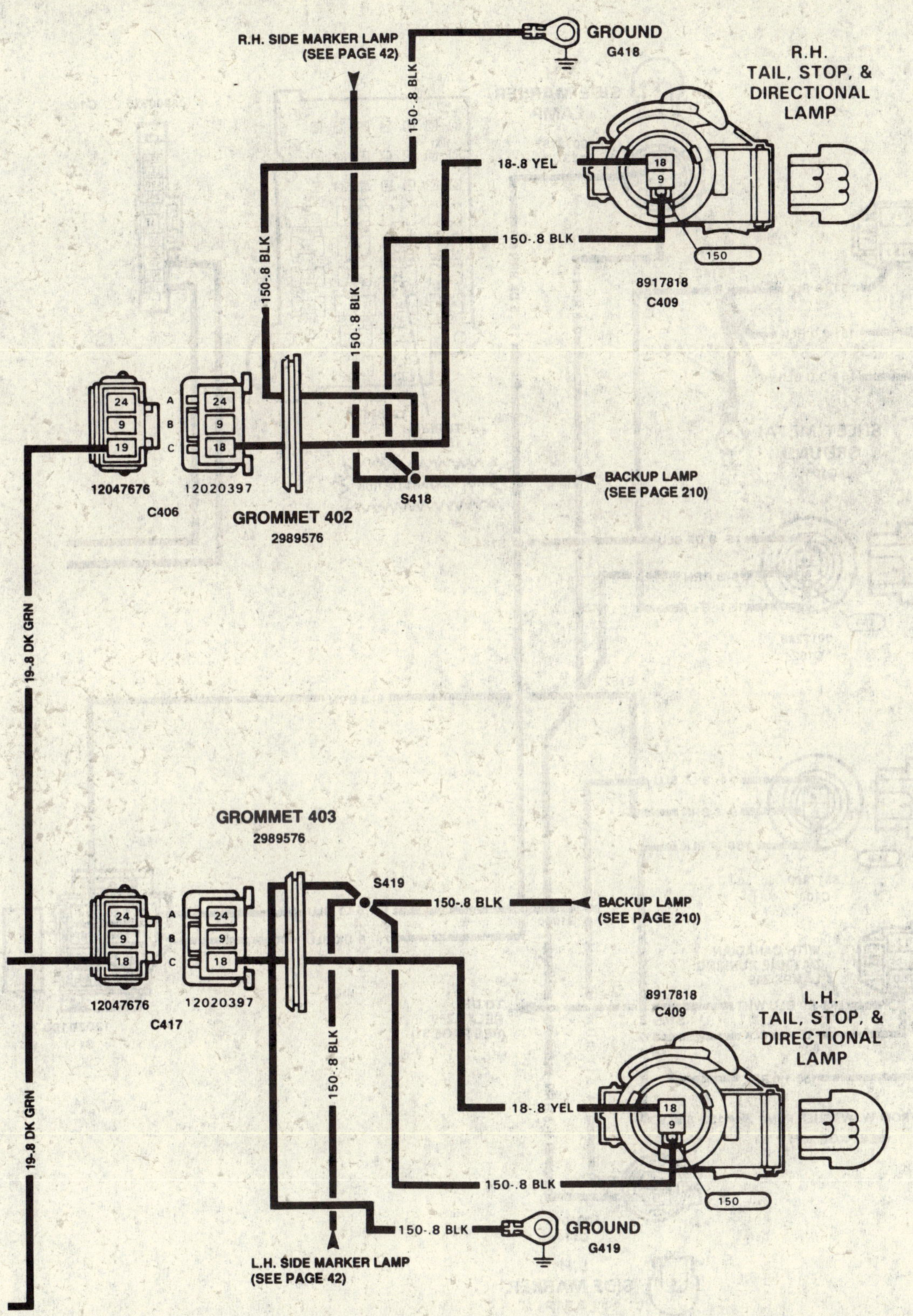

DIRECTIONAL LAMPS - 2-DOOR UTILITY 51

1988-91

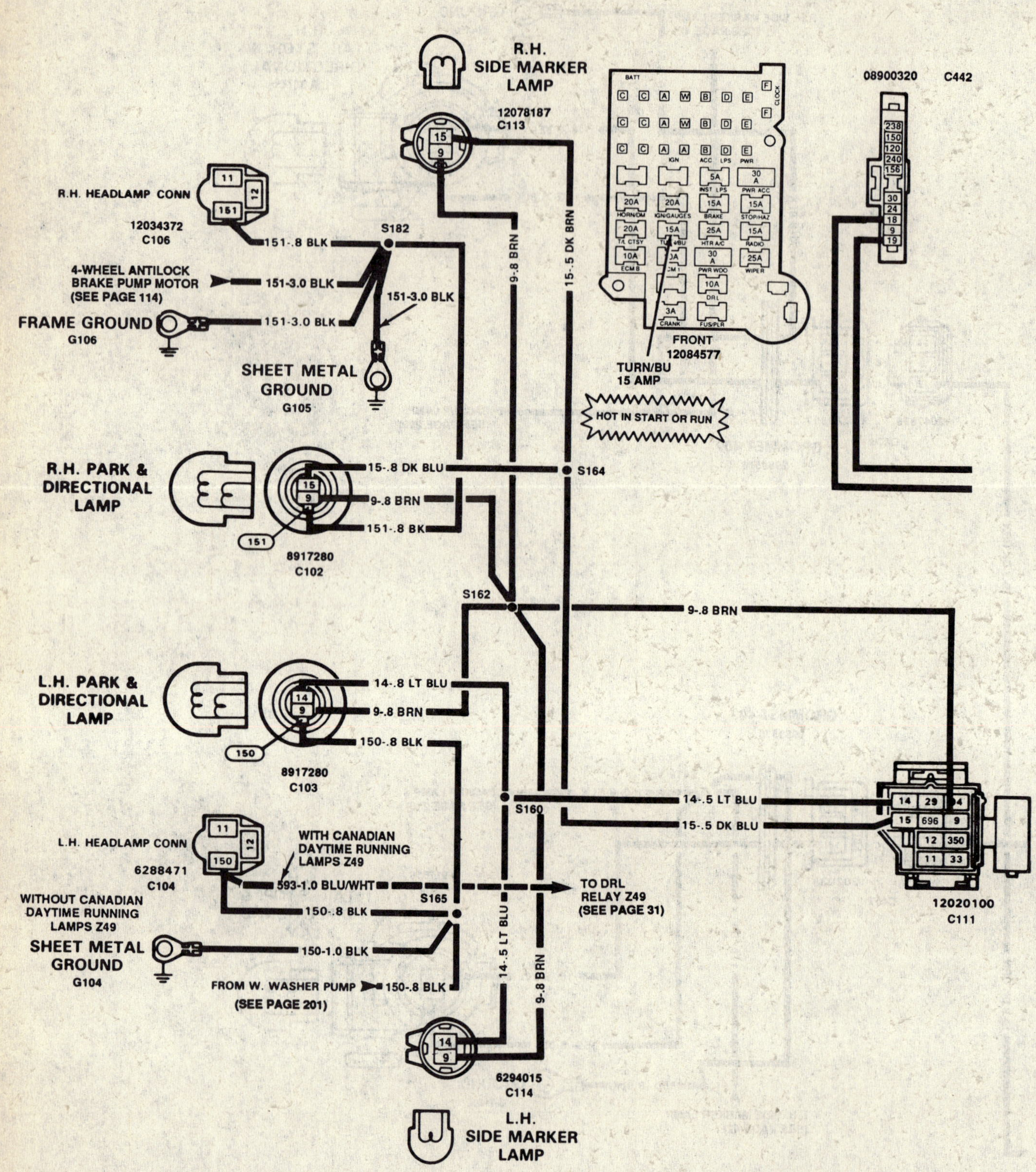

52 DIRECTIONAL LAMPS - 4-DOOR UTILITY

1988-91

BACKUP LPS
(SEE PAGE 211)
12004060
P
238
150
120
240
156
30
24
18
9
19
D
REAR
75-.8 DK BLU
HORN RELAY
28
240
29
SAFETY BELT SW 238
GROUND 150
FASTEN BELTS 237
IGNITION 39
IGN KEY SW 80
BATTERY 140
LIGHTS ON SW 8
38
16
150
DIRECTIONAL FLASHER
CONVENIENCE CENTER
BUZZER
8 140 80
238 150 237 39
HORN
29 28
240
T/S
16
150
38
P.E.
12066631
38-.8 DK BLU
W/DIGITAL I/P CLUSTER U52
16-.8 PPL
38-.8 DK BLU
16-.8 PPL
16-.8 PPL
19-.8 DK GRN
18-.8 YEL
19-.8 DK GRN
18-.8 YEL
S306 (SEE PAGE 19)
ENGINE GROUND G140 (SEE PAGE 21)
LIGHT SWITCH (SEE PAGE 31)
9-.8 BRN
I/P
14-.5 LT BLU
14-.5 LT BLU
94 29 14
9 696 15
350 12
33 11
92 822 6
93 821 440
75 2
35 120
31 2
150 3
9 120 19
24 30 18
98 39 24
91 25 420
15 .5 DK BLU
15-.5 DK BLU
12020184
C100
19-.8 DK GRN
18-.8 YEL
19-.8 DK GRN
18-.8 YEL

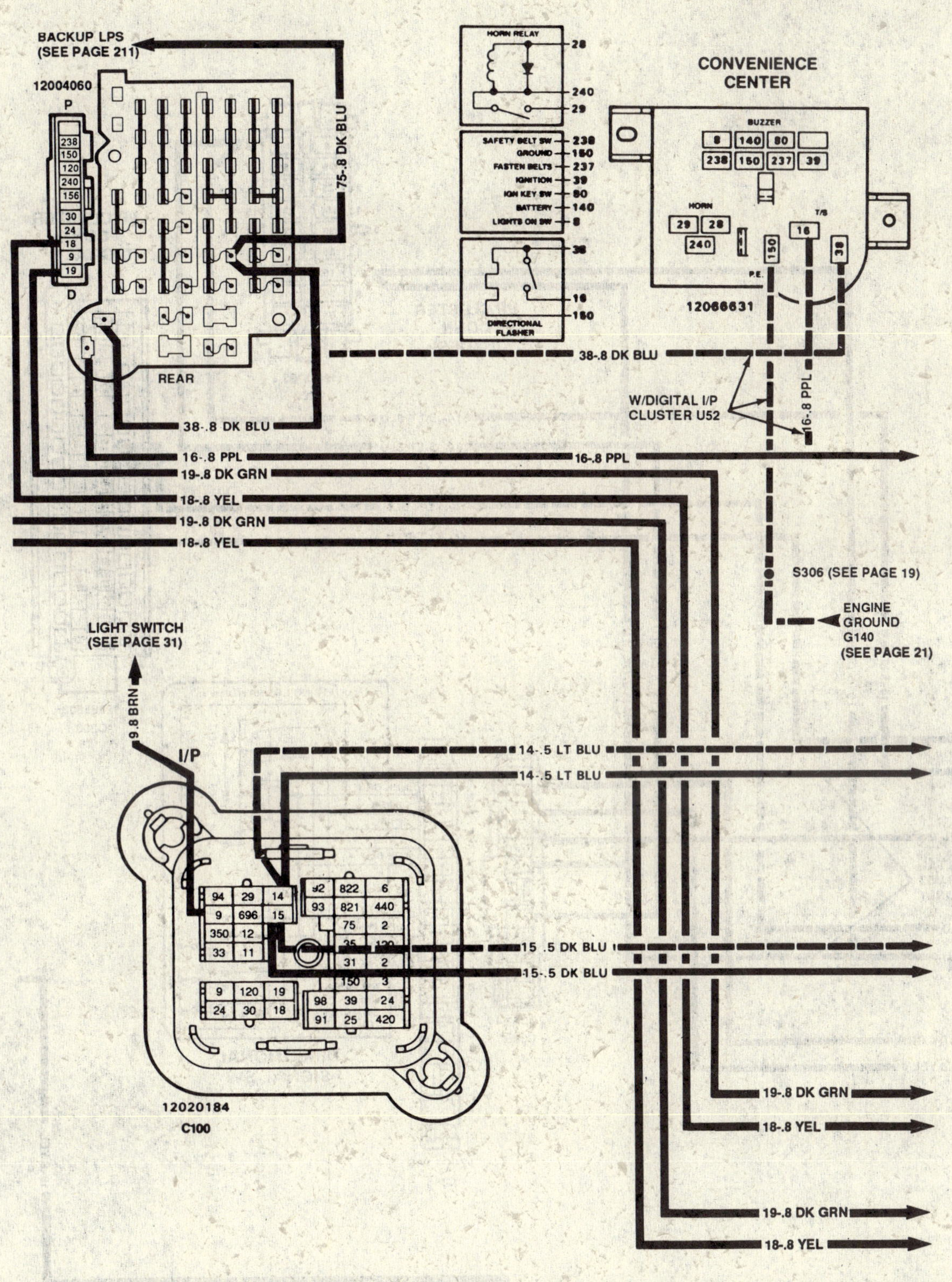

1988-91

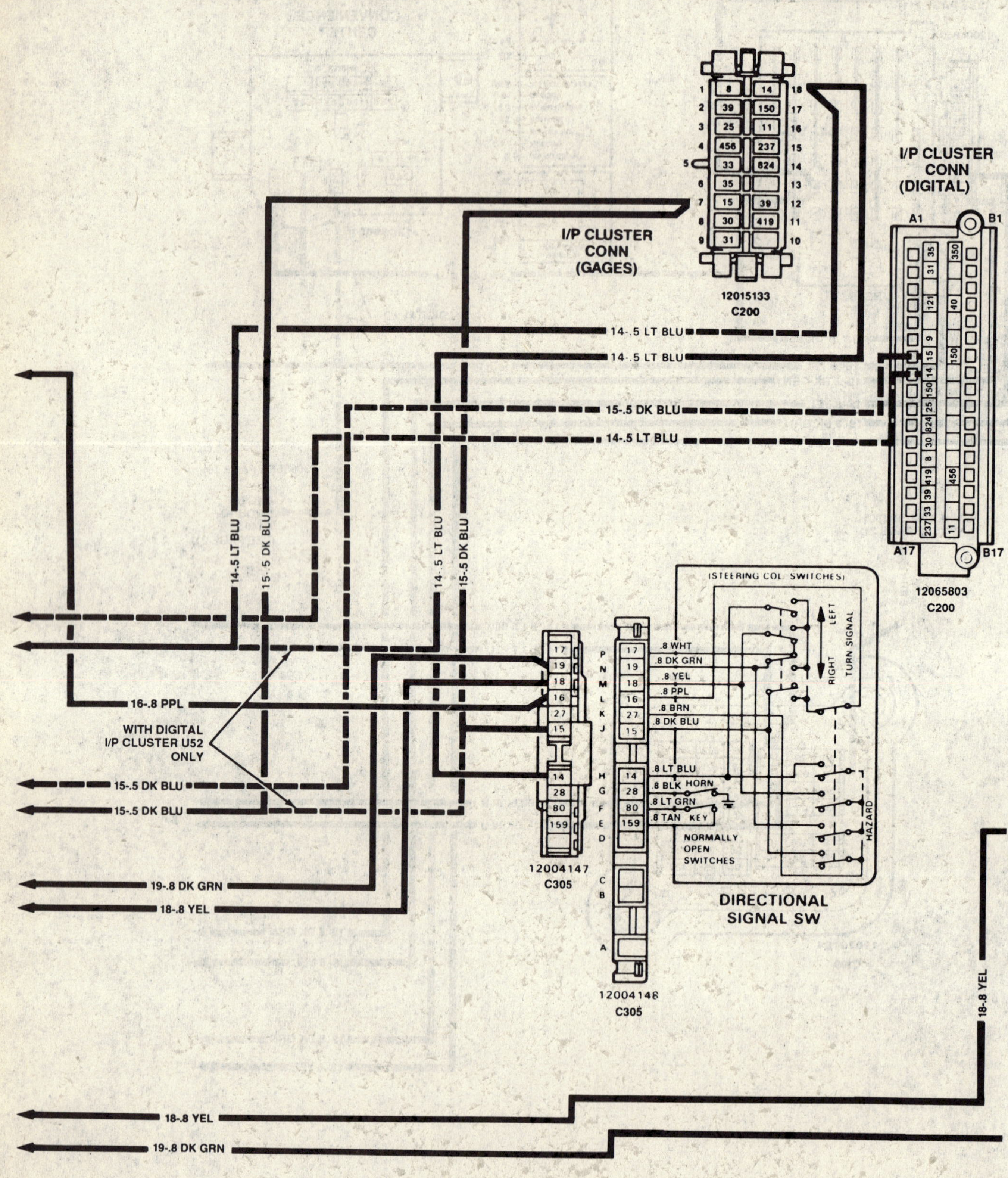

1988-91

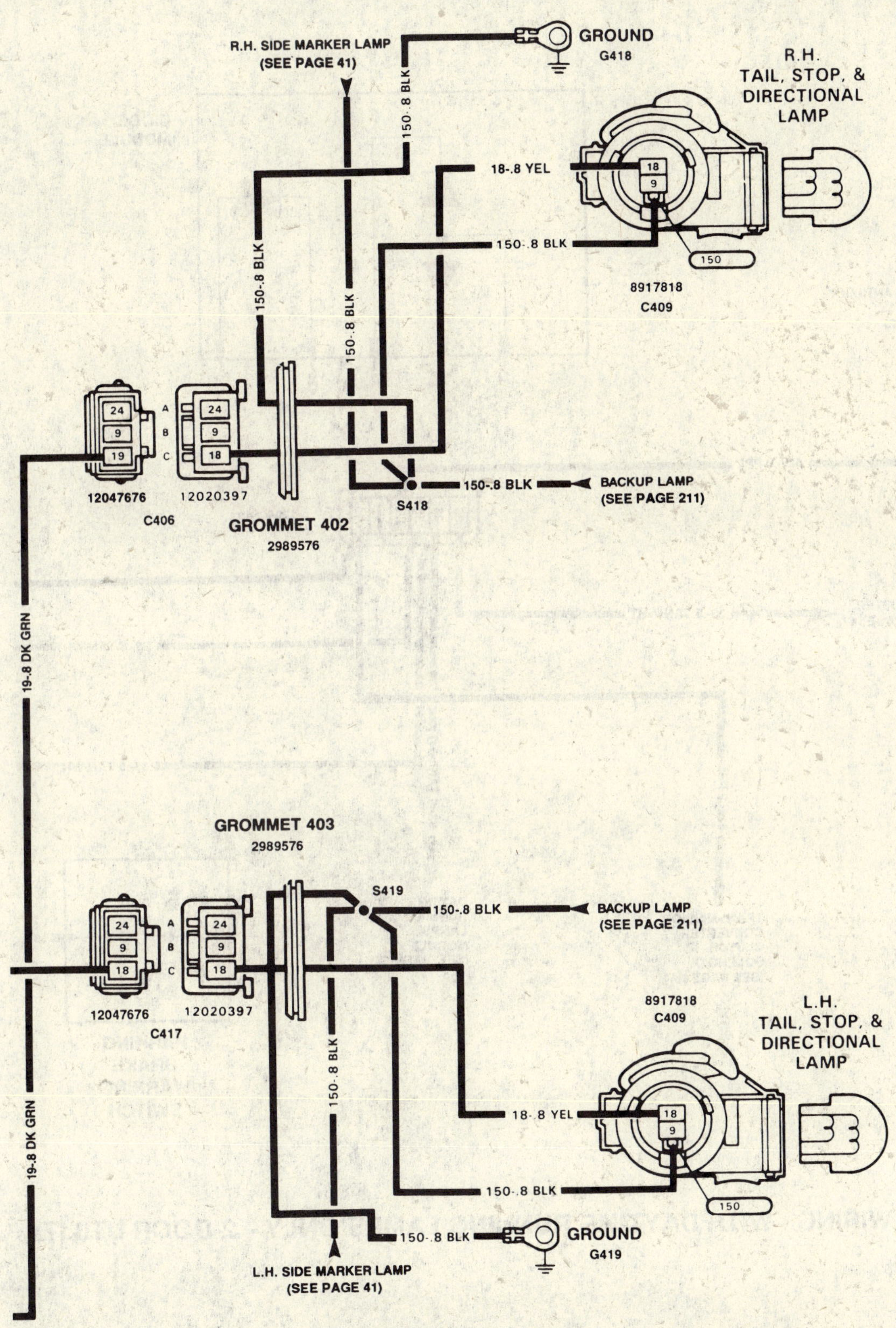

DIRECTIONAL LAMPS - 4-DOOR UTILITY 53

1988-91

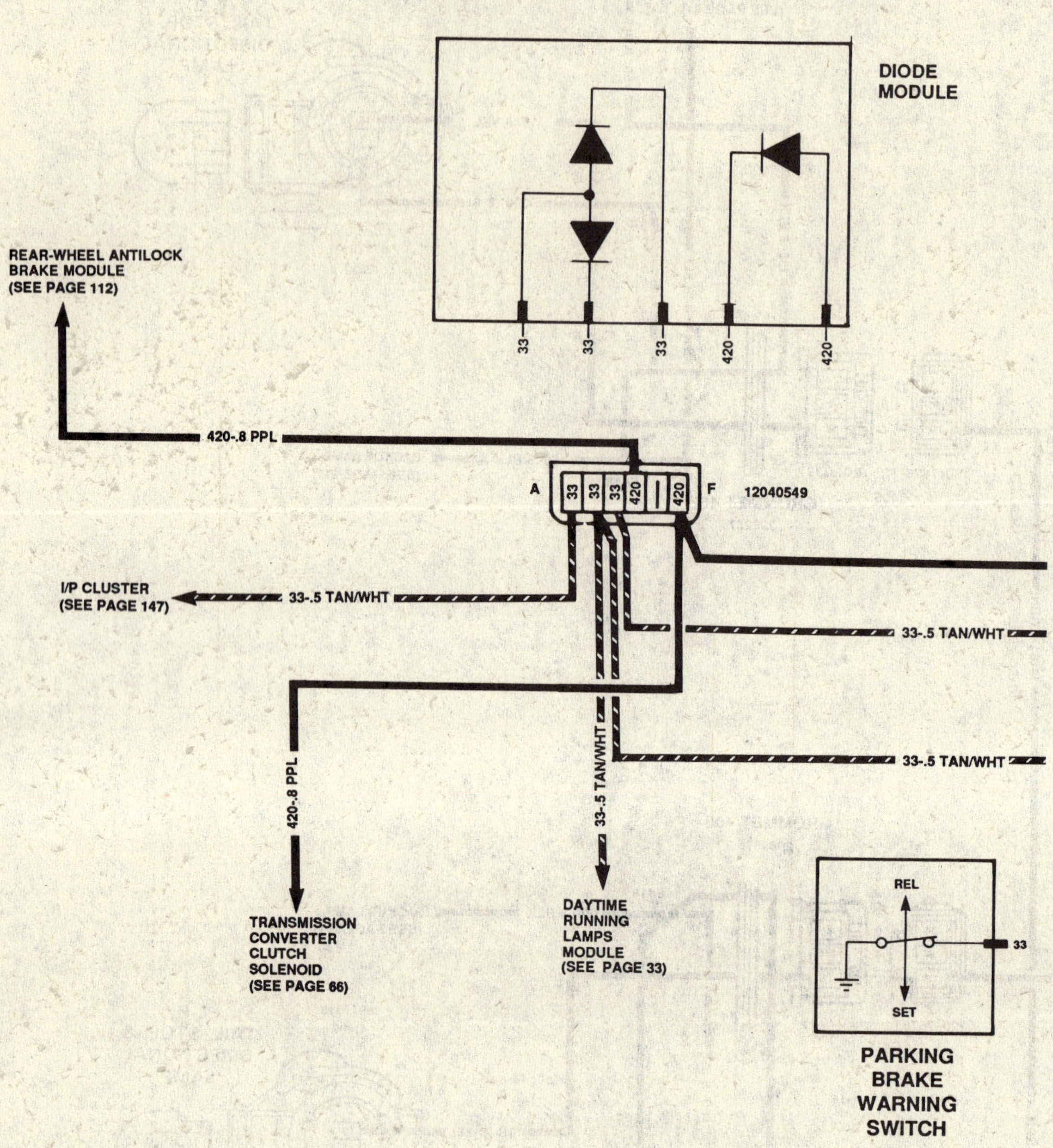

56 DIODE MODULE WIRING - WITH DAYTIME RUNNING LAMPS ONLY - 2-DOOR UTILITY

1988-91

420-.8 PPL
T.C.C.
STOPLAMP
SWITCH
(SEE PAGE 113)
BRAKE PRESSURE
WARNING SW
(SEE PAGE 112)
REAR-WHEEL ANTILOCK
BRAKE MODULE
(SEE PAGE 112)
33
12004267
C319
33-.5 TAN/WHT
IGNITION
SWITCH
(SEE PAGE 73)

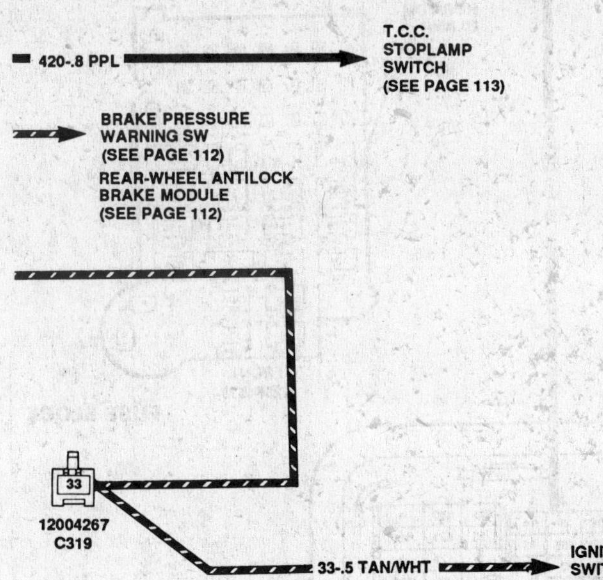

1988-91

HORN
29
29
12004267
C117
COWL
29-1.0 DK GRN
29-1.0 DK GRN
HOT AT ALL TIMES
HORN/DM
20 AMP
BATT
CLOCK
IGN
ACC
LPS
PWR
5A
30 A
INST LPS
PWR ACC
20A
HORN/DM
20A
IGN/GAUGES
15A
BRAKE
15A
STOP/HAZ
20A
T/L CTSY
15A
TURN/BU
25A
HTR A/C
15A
RADIO
10A
ECM B
10A
ECM 1
30 A
PWR WDO
25A
WIPER
10A
DRL
3A
CRANK
FUS/PLR
FRONT
12084577
FUSE BLOCK
I/P
14 29 94
15 636 9
12 350
11 33
12020100
C111
94 29 14
9 636 15
350 12
33 11
92 822 6
93 821 440
75 2
35 120
31 2
150 3
9 120 19
24 30 18
98 39 24
91 25 420
12020184
C100

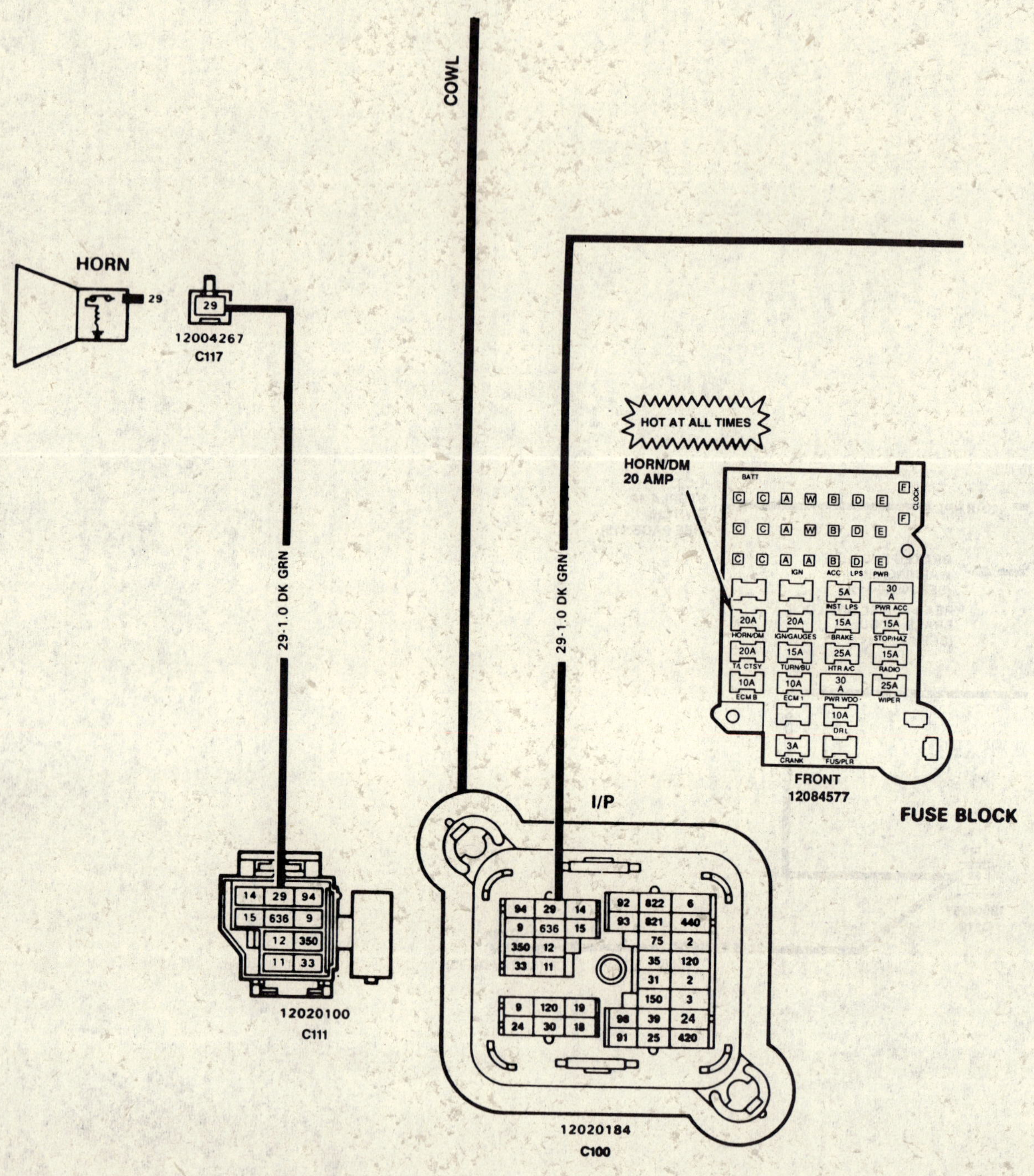

1988-91

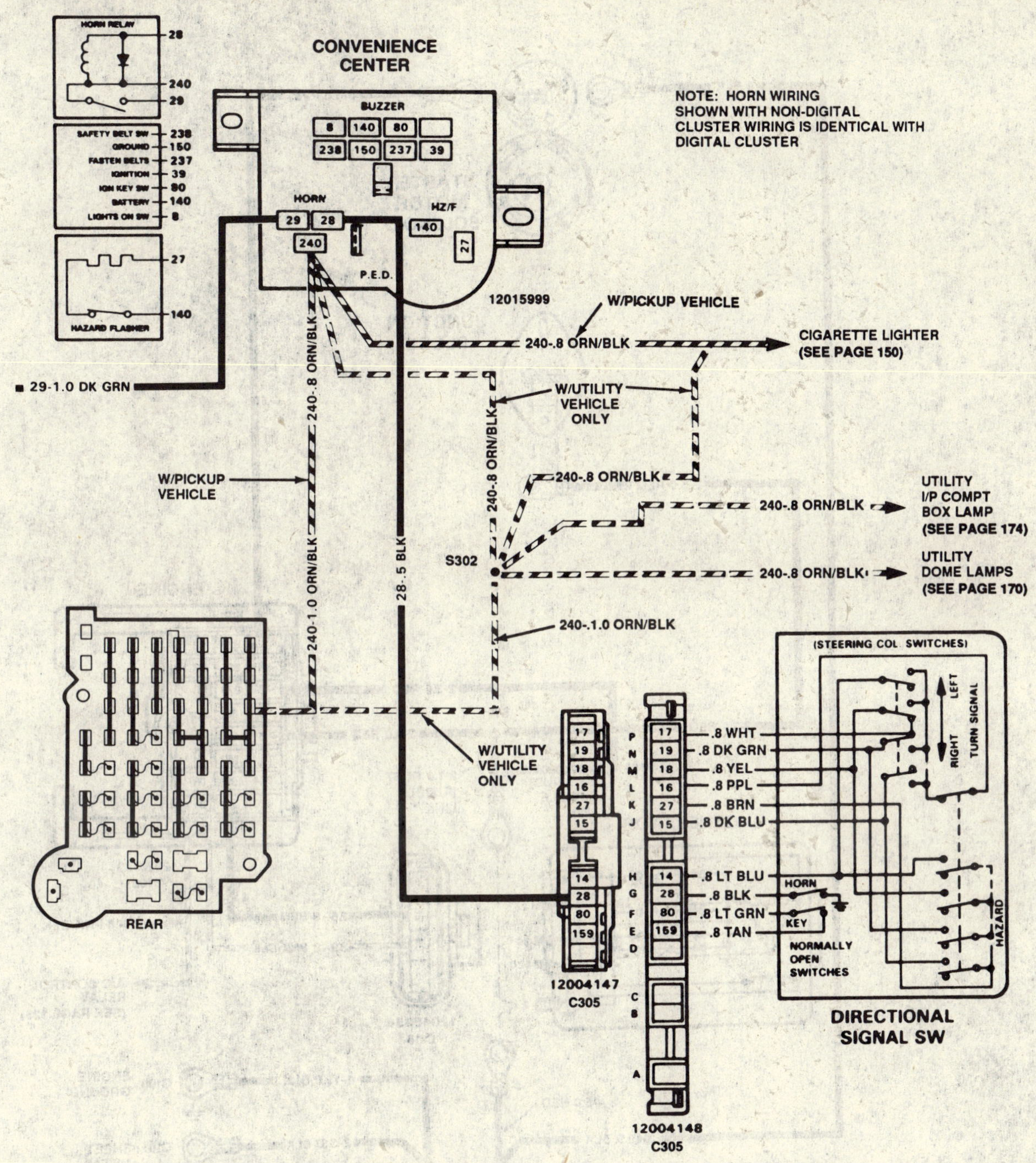

HORN 59

1988-91

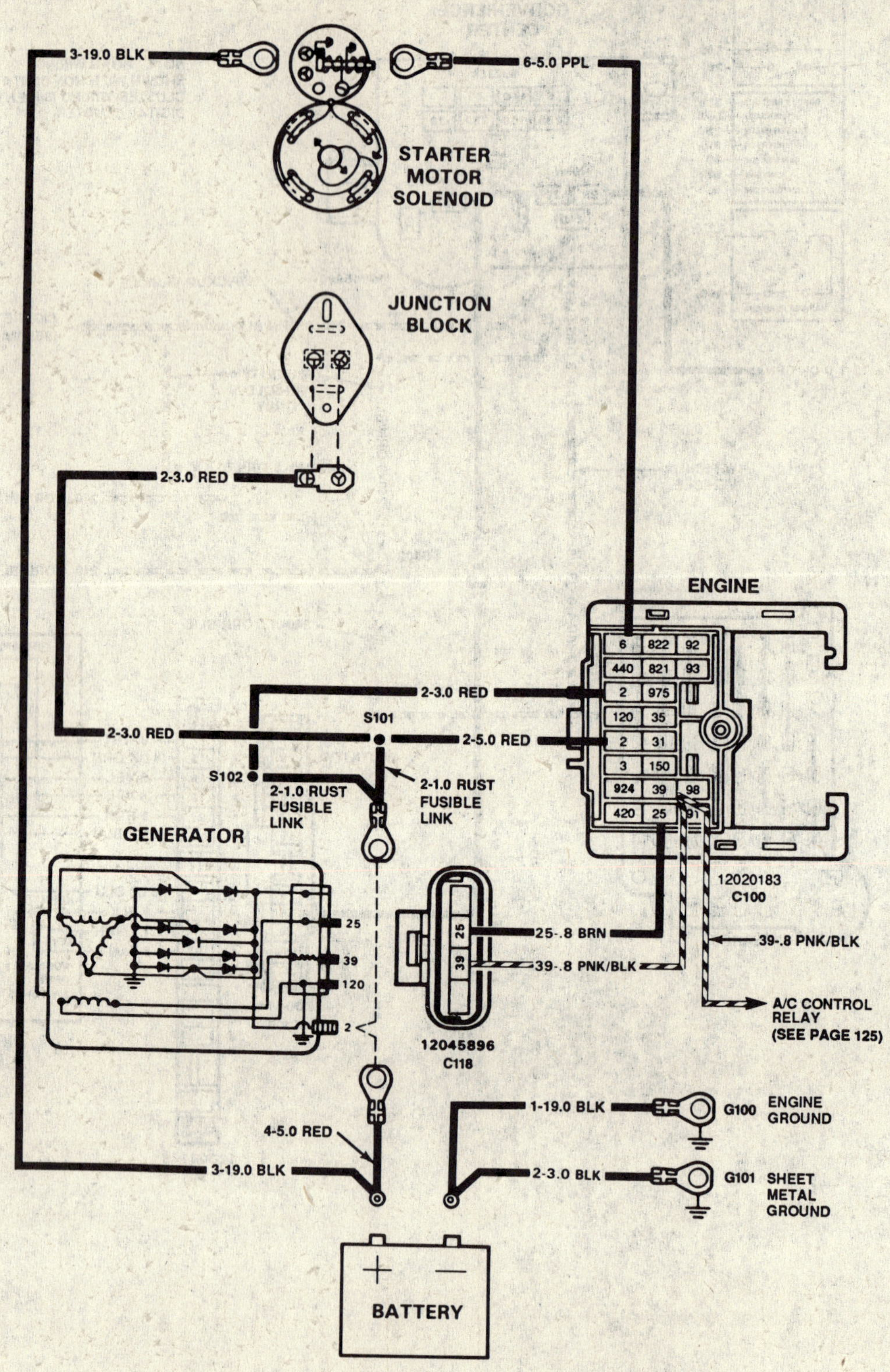

62 STARTING AND CHARGING - 2.5L (151 CID) ENGINE

1988-91

W/MAN. TRANS.
39-.8 PNK/BLK
BRAKE SWITCH (SEE PAGE 68)
W/AUTO. TRANS.
CONVENIENCE CENTER (SEE PAGE 21)
STOPLAMP SWITCH (SEE PAGE 68)
I/P CLUSTER (SEE PAGE 142)
DAYTIME RUNNING LAMPS RELAY (SEE PAGE 33)
I/P
S303
6-3.0 PPL
S301
2-3.0 RED
TO LIGHT SW (SEE PAGE 31)
5-3.0 YEL
MANUAL ONLY
12033711
12010966
6294641
C303
12020184
C100
CLUTCH START SWITCH
8917948
C306
25-.5 BRN
CHARGING SYSTEM INDICATORS (SEE PAGE 146)
IGNITION SWITCH
START
RUN
OFF
LOCK
ACC
COWL
CRANK 3 AMP
HOT IN START
FRONT
12084577
FUSE BLOCK
REAR
906-.8 PPL/WHT
TO ECM (SEE PAGE 95)

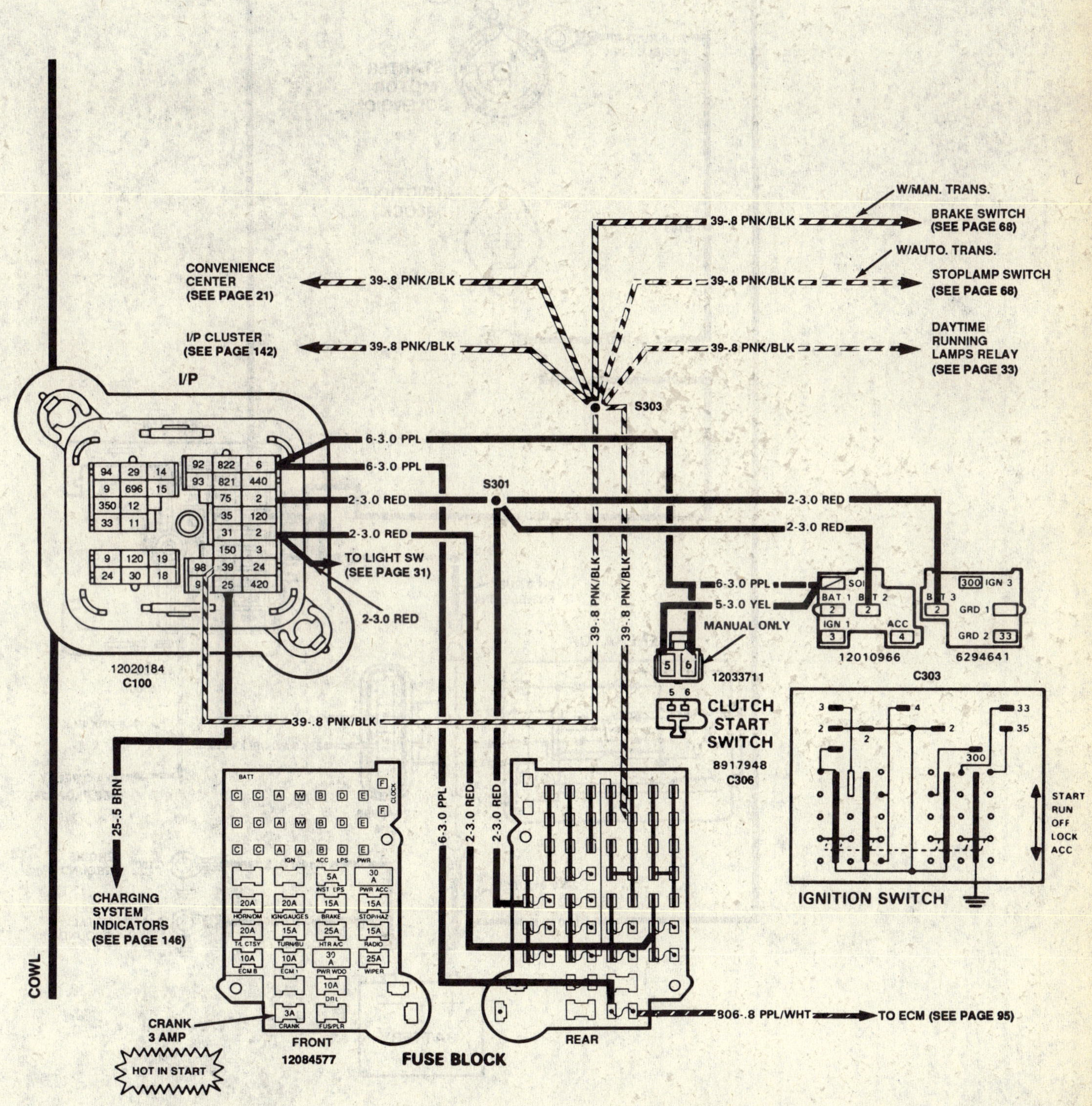

1988-91

1-19.0 BLK
6-3.0 PPL
2-1.0 RUST
FUSIBLE LINK
STARTER
MOTOR
SOLENOID
JUNCTION
BLOCK
S103
2-3.0 RED
ENGINE
2-3.0 RED
S101
2-3.0 RED
2-1.0 RUST
FUSIBLE LINK
GENERATOR
25
39
120
2
12020183
C100
25-.8 BRN
39-.8 PNK/BLK
39-.8 PNK/BLK
TO A/C RELAY
(SEE PAGE 126)
12045896
C118
1-19.0 BLK
G100
ENGINE
GROUND
2-5.0 BLK/RED
2-3.0 BLK
G101
SHEET
METAL
GROUND
1-19.0 BLK
BATTERY

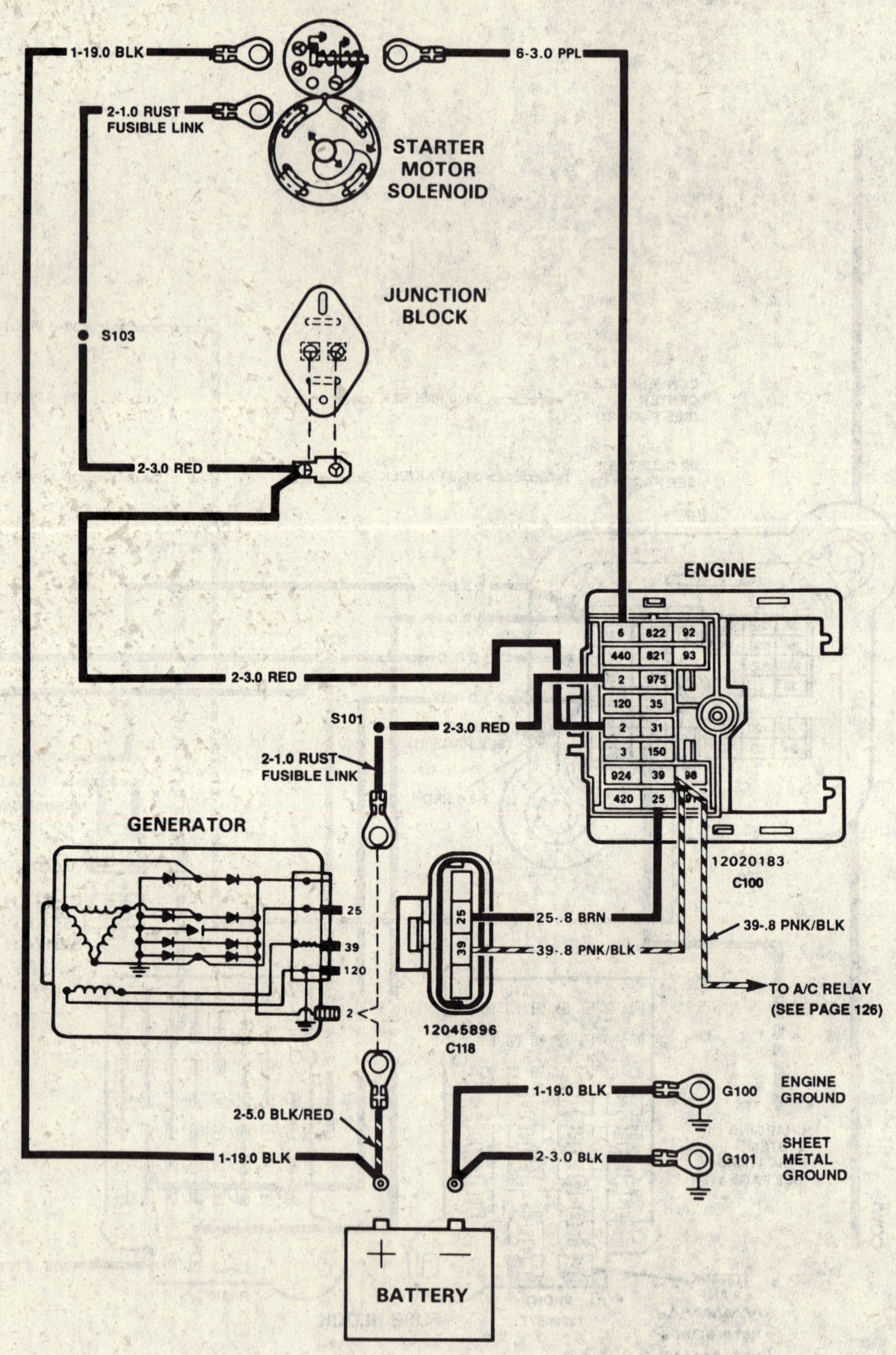

1988-91

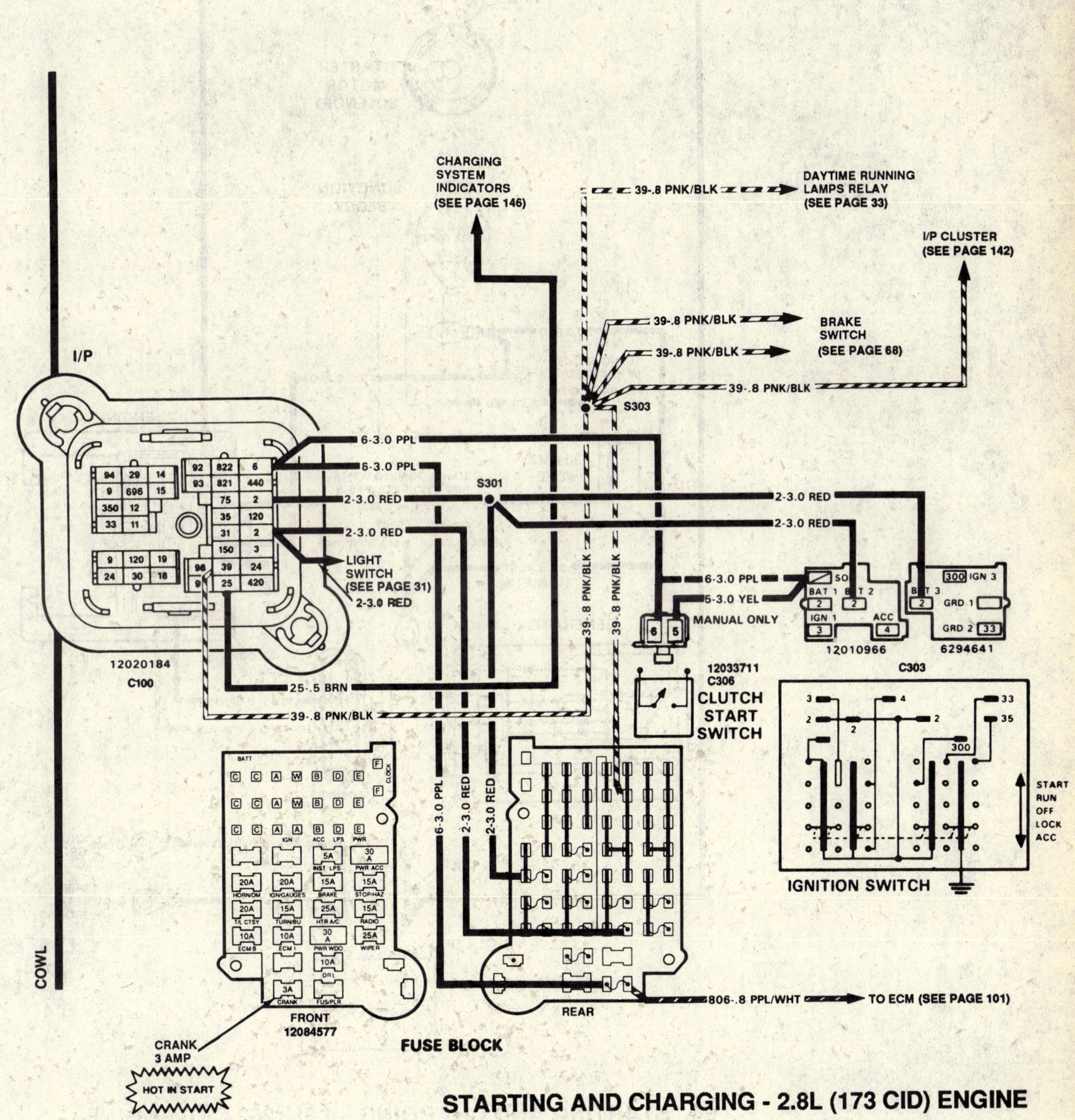

STARTING AND CHARGING - 2.8L (173 CID) ENGINE

1988-91

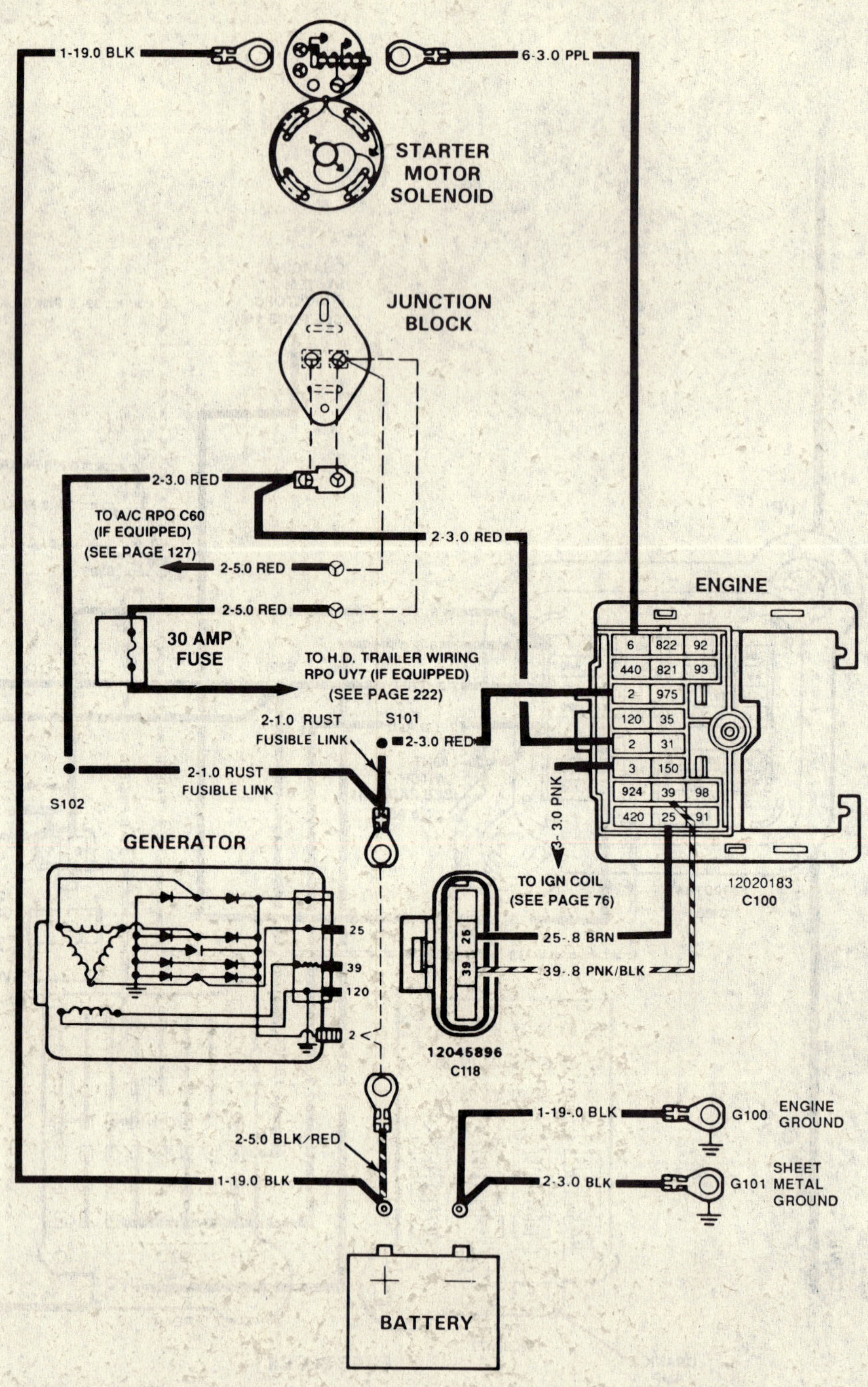

64 STARTING AND CHARGING - 4.3L (262 CID) ENGINE

1988-91

W/MAN. TRANS. BRAKE SWITCH (SEE PAGE 66)
39-.8 PNK/BLK
W/AUTO. TRANS. STOPLAMP SWITCH (SEE PAGE 66)
DAYTIME RUNNING LAMPS RELAY (SEE PAGE 33)
CONVENIENCE CENTER (SEE PAGE 21)
I/P CLUSTER (SEE PAGE 117)
I/P
S303
S301
6-3.0 PPL
2-3.0 RED
5-3.0 YEL
TO LIGHT SW (SEE PAGE 31)
MANUAL ONLY
12010966
6294641
C303
12020184
C100
CLUTCH START SWITCH
8917948
C306
25-.5 BRN
CHARGING SYSTEM INDICATORS (SEE PAGE 146)
HOT IN START
CRANK 3 AMP
START
RUN
OFF
LOCK
ACC
IGNITION SWITCH
806-.8 PPL/WHT
TO ECM (SEE PAGE 107)
FRONT
12084577
FUSE BLOCK
REAR
COWL

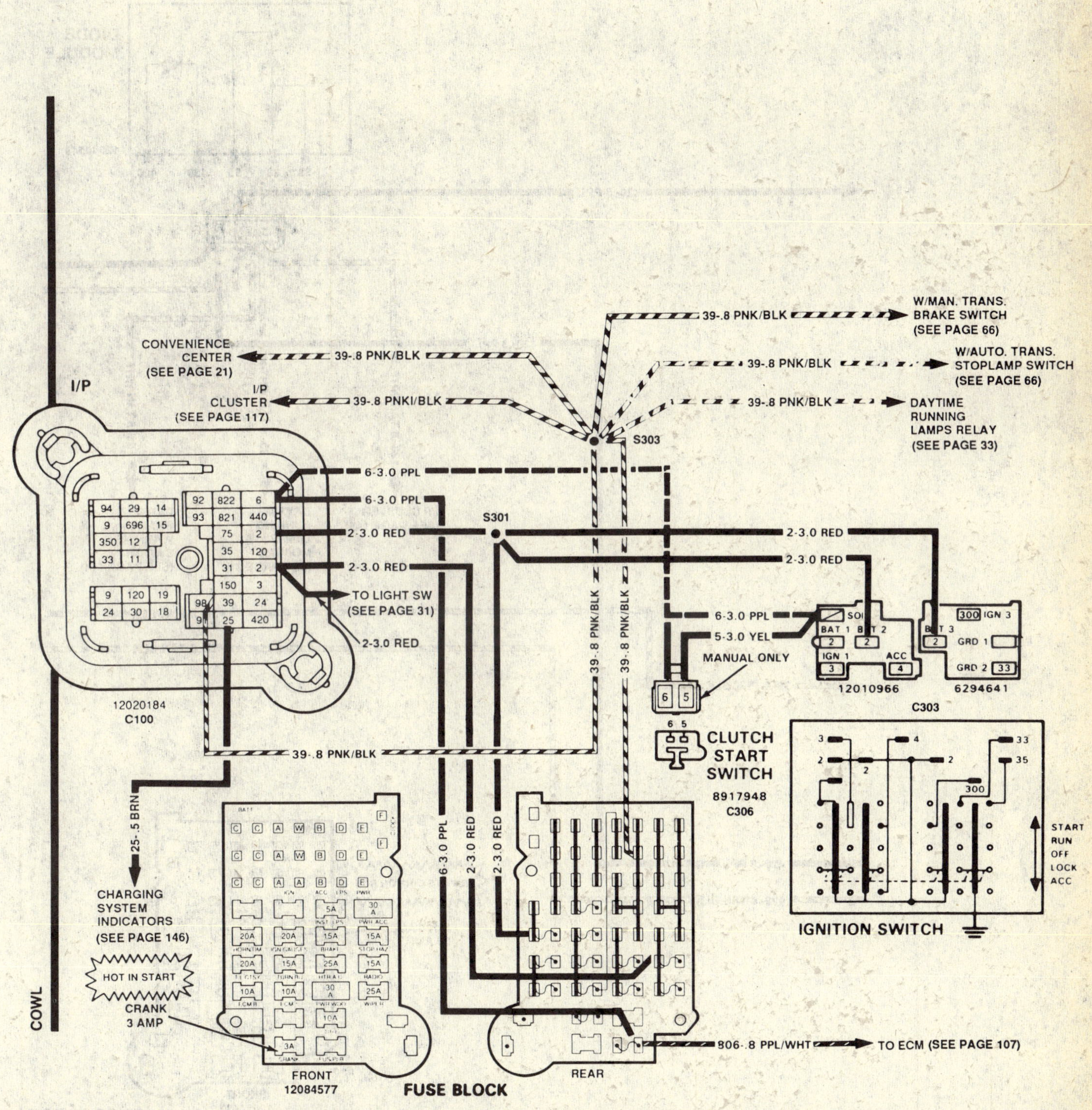

1988-91

DIODE
MODULE
12040549
33
33
33
420
420
420-.8 PPL
A
33
33
33
420
420
F
420-.8 PPL
33-.5 TAN/WHT
33-.5 TAN/WHT
33-.5 TAN/WHT
I/P CLUSTER
(SEE PAGE 146)
DAYTIME
RUNNING
LAMPS
MODULE
(SEE PAGE 31)
PARKING
BRAKE
WARNING
SWITCH
(SEE PAGE 114)
39-.8 PNK/BLK
422-.8 TAN/BLK
39-.8 PNK/BLK
420-.8 PPL
422-.8 TAN/BLK
HOT IN START OR RUN
IGN/GAGES
20 AMP
BATT
CLOCK
IGN
ACC
LPS
PWR
5A
INST LPS
30 A
PWR ACC
20A
HORN/DM
20A
IGN/GAUGES
15A
BRAKE
15A
STOP/HAZ
20A
T/L CTSY
15A
TURN/BU
25A
HTR A/C
15A
RADIO
10A
ECM B
10A
ECM 1
30 A
PWR WDO
25A
WIPER
10A
DRL
3A
CRANK
FUS/PLR
FRONT
12084577
FUSE BLOCK

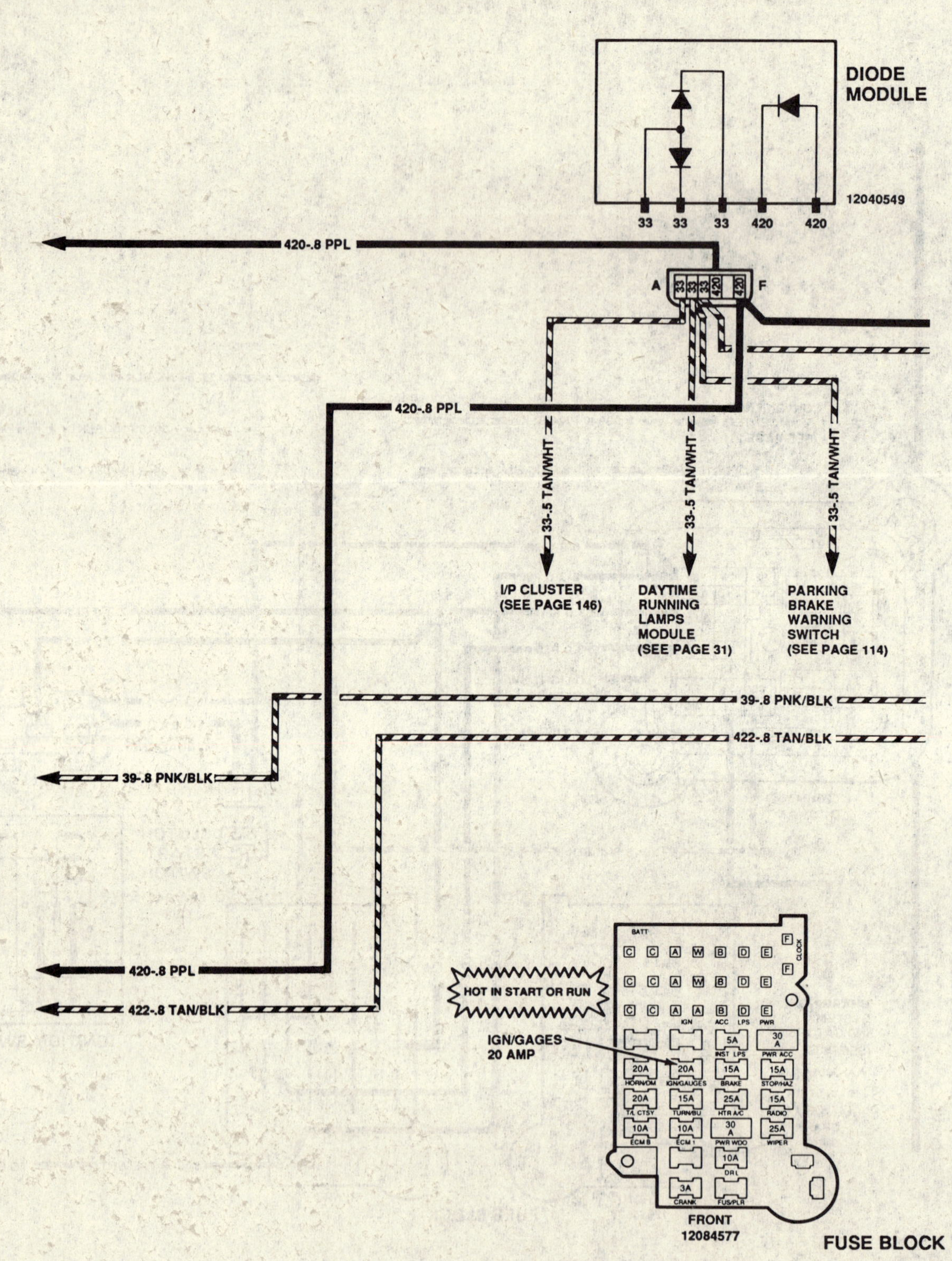

1988-91

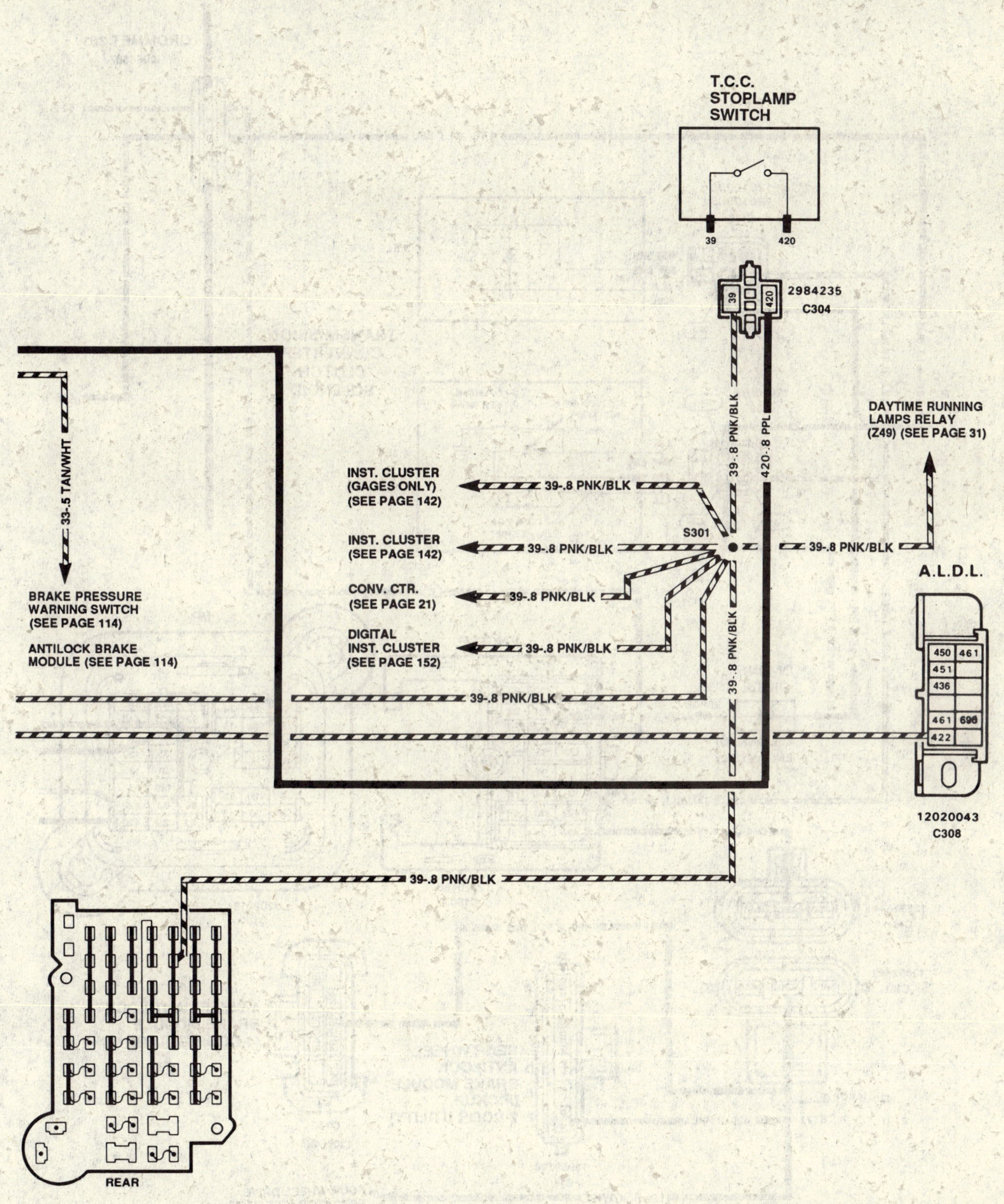

TCC DETENT SOLENOID - W/CANADIAN DAYTIME RUNNING LAMPS Z49 67

1988-91

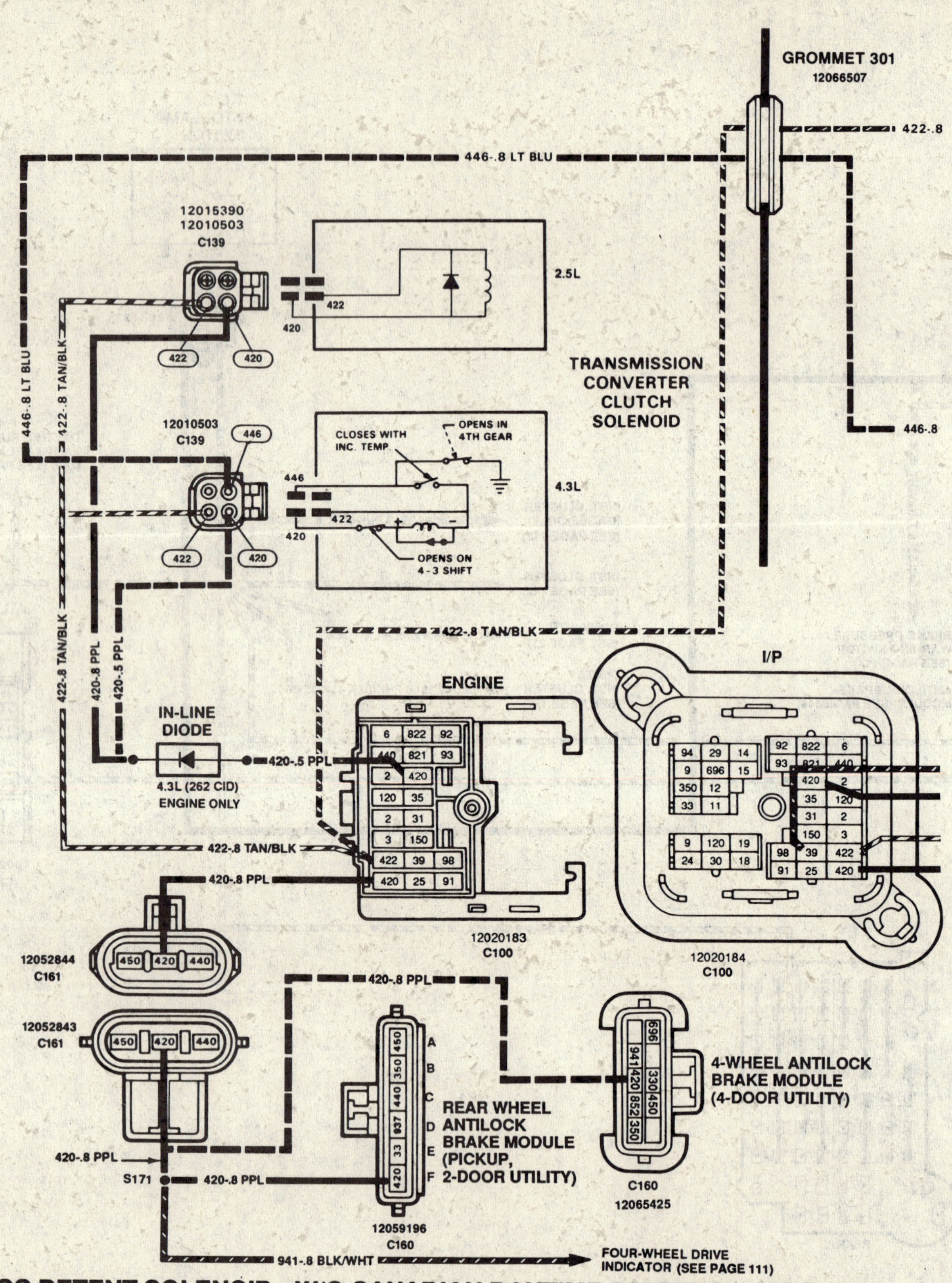

68 TCC DETENT SOLENOID - W/O CANADIAN DAYTIME RUNNING LAMPS Z49

1988-91

TAN/WHT
12047946
C307
2.5L (151 CID)
12047946
C307
4.3L (262 CID)
T.C.C.
STOPLAMP
SWITCH
39
420
2984235
C304
LT BLU
4.3L (262 CID)
12045575
C307
ELECTRONIC
CONTROL MODULE
CONNECTORS
INST. CLUSTER
(GAUGES ONLY)
(SEE PAGE 146)
39-.8 PNK/BLK
INST. CLUSTER
(SEE PAGE 146)
CONV. CTR.
(SEE PAGE 21)
S 303
DIGITAL
INST. CLUSTER
(SEE PAGE 151)
39-.8 PNK/BLK
420-.8 PPL
A.L.D.L.
W/AUTO.
TRANS.
420-.8 PPL
422-.8 TAN/BLK
420-.8 PPL
RESISTOR 1 WATT
12020043
C308
HOT IN START OR RUN
IGN/GAGES
20 AMP
FRONT
12084577
FUSE BLOCK
REAR

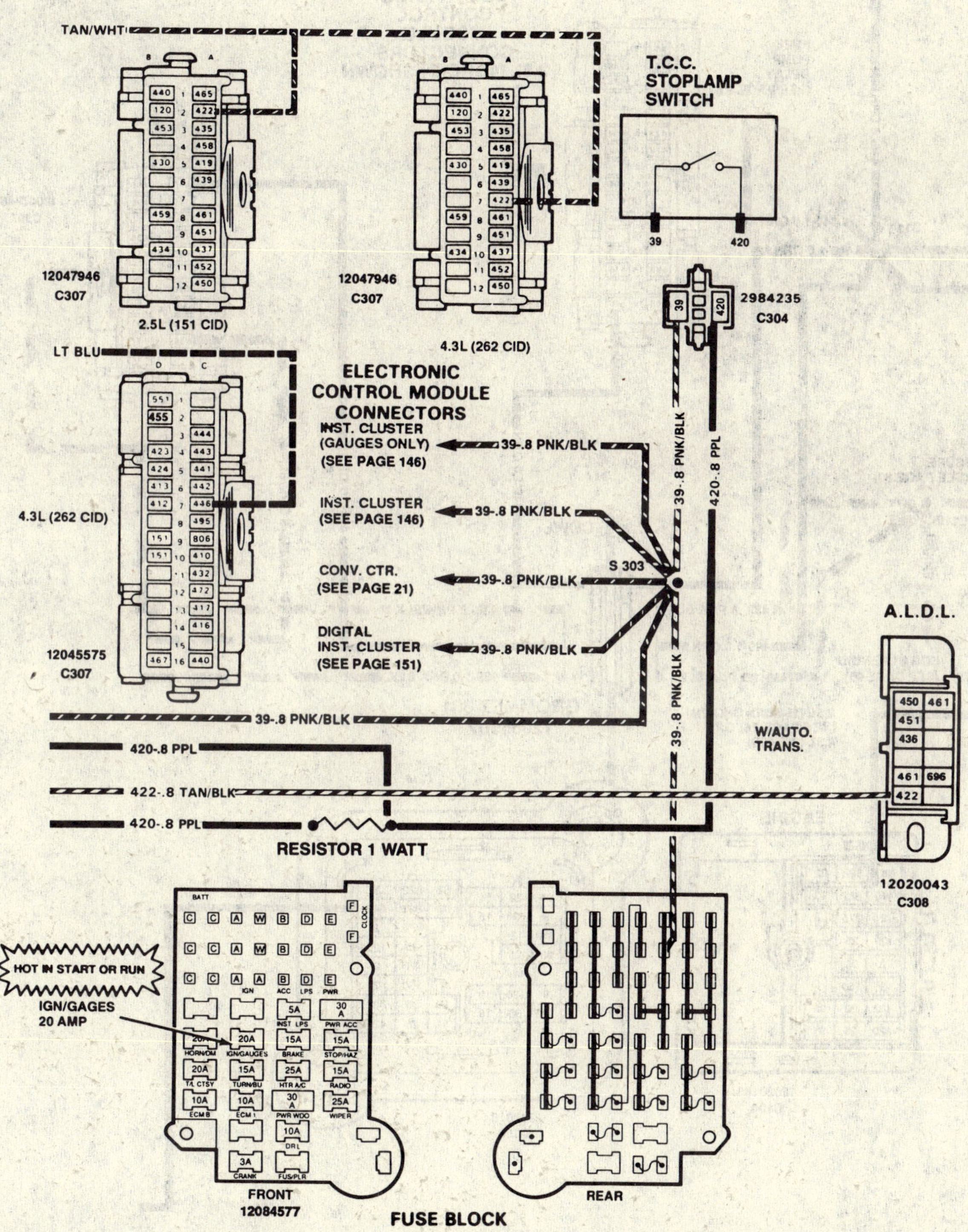

1988-91

REAR WHEEL ANTILOCK
BRAKES ANTILOCK MODULE
(SEE PAGE 116)
FUEL
PUMP
RELAY
(SEE PAGE 83)
ELECTRONIC
CONTROL
MODULE
CONNECTORS
2.5L (151 CID) SHOWN
12045575
C307
12047946
C307
440-.8 ORN
S114
440-1.0 ORN
440-1.0 ORN
440-1.0 ORN
440-1.0 ORN
OIL PRESSURE
SWITCH (SEE PAGE 83)
S116
439-.8 PNK/BLK
439 .8 PNK/BLK
INJECTOR
(SEE PAGE 79)
EGR SOLENOID
(SEE PAGE 96)
439 .8 PNK/BLK
440-1.0 ORN
439 1.0 PNK/BLK
440 1.0 ORN
COWL
439-.8 PNK/BLK
439-1.0 PNK/BLK
440-1.0 ORN
434-.8 ORN/BLK
GROMMET 301
12066507
2.5L (151 CID) SHOWN
(SEE PAGE 76) OR
4.3L (262 CID)
ENGINE
I/P
12020183
C100
12020184
C100

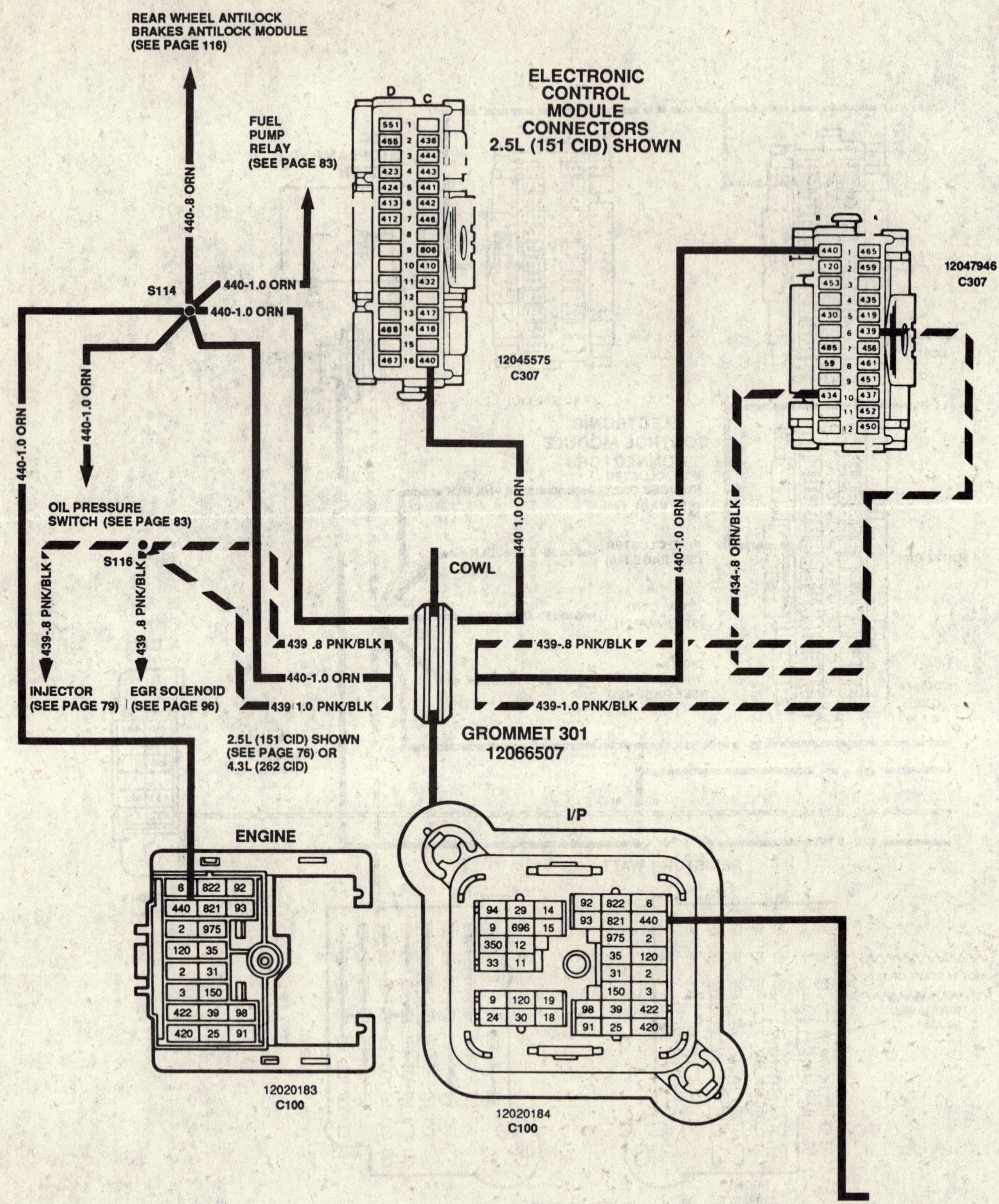

1988-91

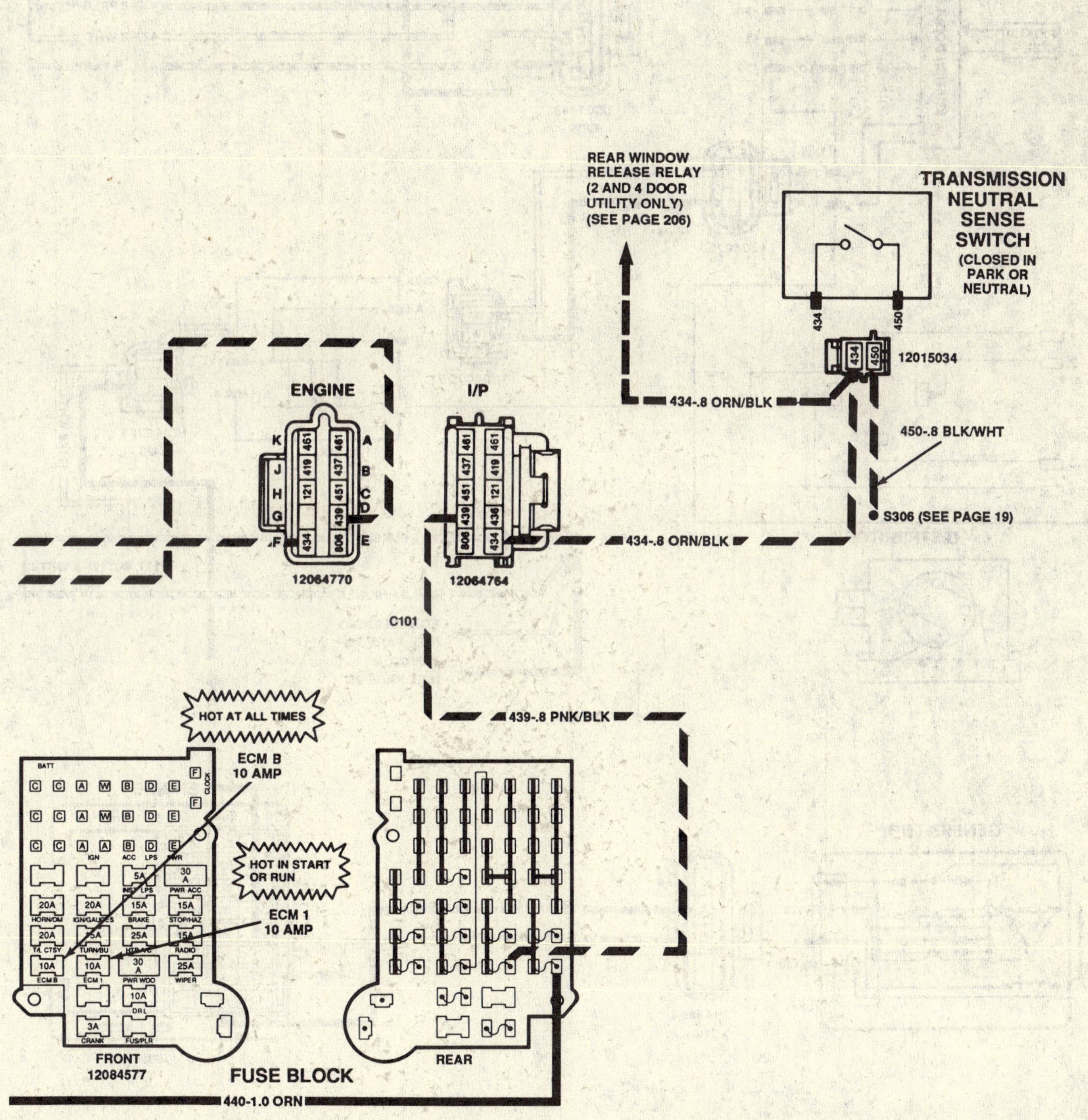

PARK NEUTRAL SWITCH - AUTO. TRANS ONLY 69

1988-91

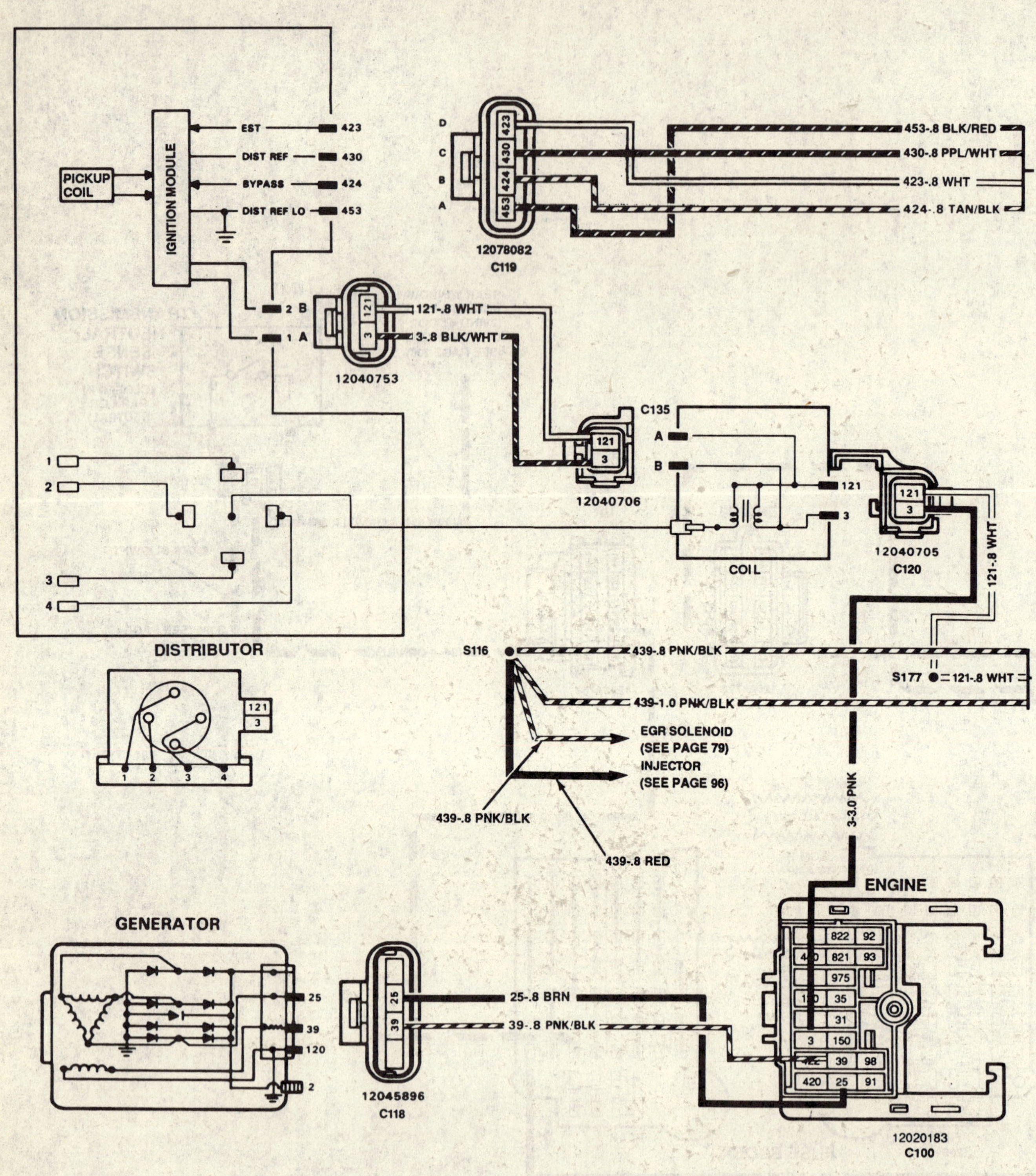

72 IGNITION - 2.5L (151 CID) ENGINE

1988-91

GROMMET 301
12066507
453-.8 BLK/RED
430-.8 PPL/WHT
423-.8 WHT
424-.8 TAN/BLK
12047946
C307
439-.8 PNK/BLK
ELECTRONIC
CONTROL
MODULE
CONNECTORS
COWL
12045575
C307
ENGINE
I/P
121-.5 WHT
439-.8 PNK/BLK
12064770
12064764
C101
GROMMET
301
I/P
3-3.0 PNK
3-3.0 PNK
39-.8 PNK/BLK
25-.8 BRN
12020184
C100

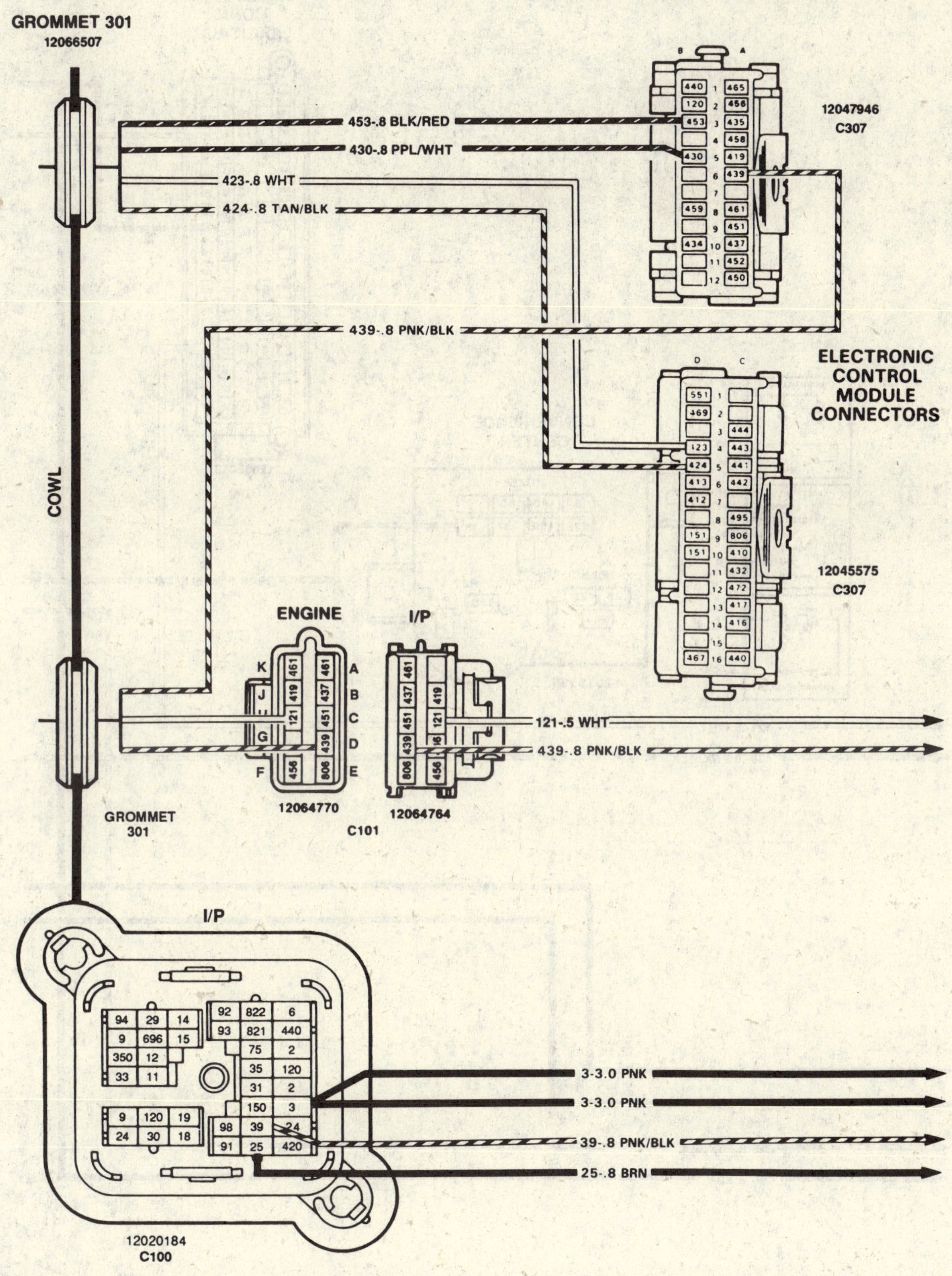

1988-91

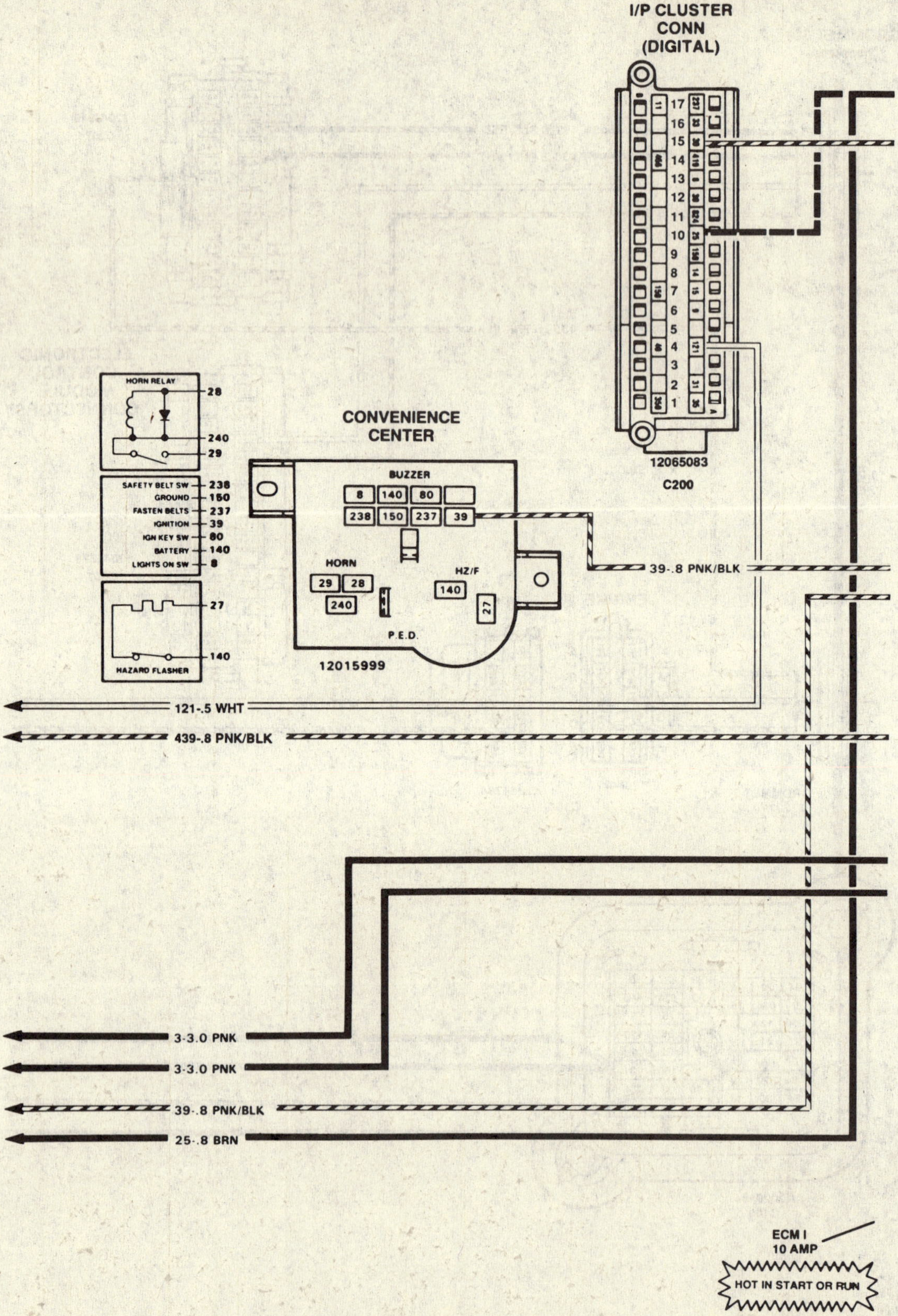

I/P CLUSTER CONN (DIGITAL)

12065083

C200

CONVENIENCE CENTER

BUZZER

HORN

HZ/F

P.E.D.

12015999

HORN RELAY — 28, 240, 29

SAFETY BELT SW — 238
GROUND — 150
FASTEN BELTS — 237
IGNITION — 39
IGN KEY SW — 80
BATTERY — 140
LIGHTS ON SW — 8

HAZARD FLASHER — 27, 140

39-.8 PNK/BLK

121-.5 WHT

439-.8 PNK/BLK

3-3.0 PNK

3-3.0 PNK

39-.8 PNK/BLK

25-.8 BRN

ECM I
10 AMP

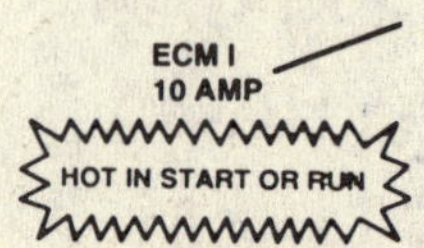

1988-91

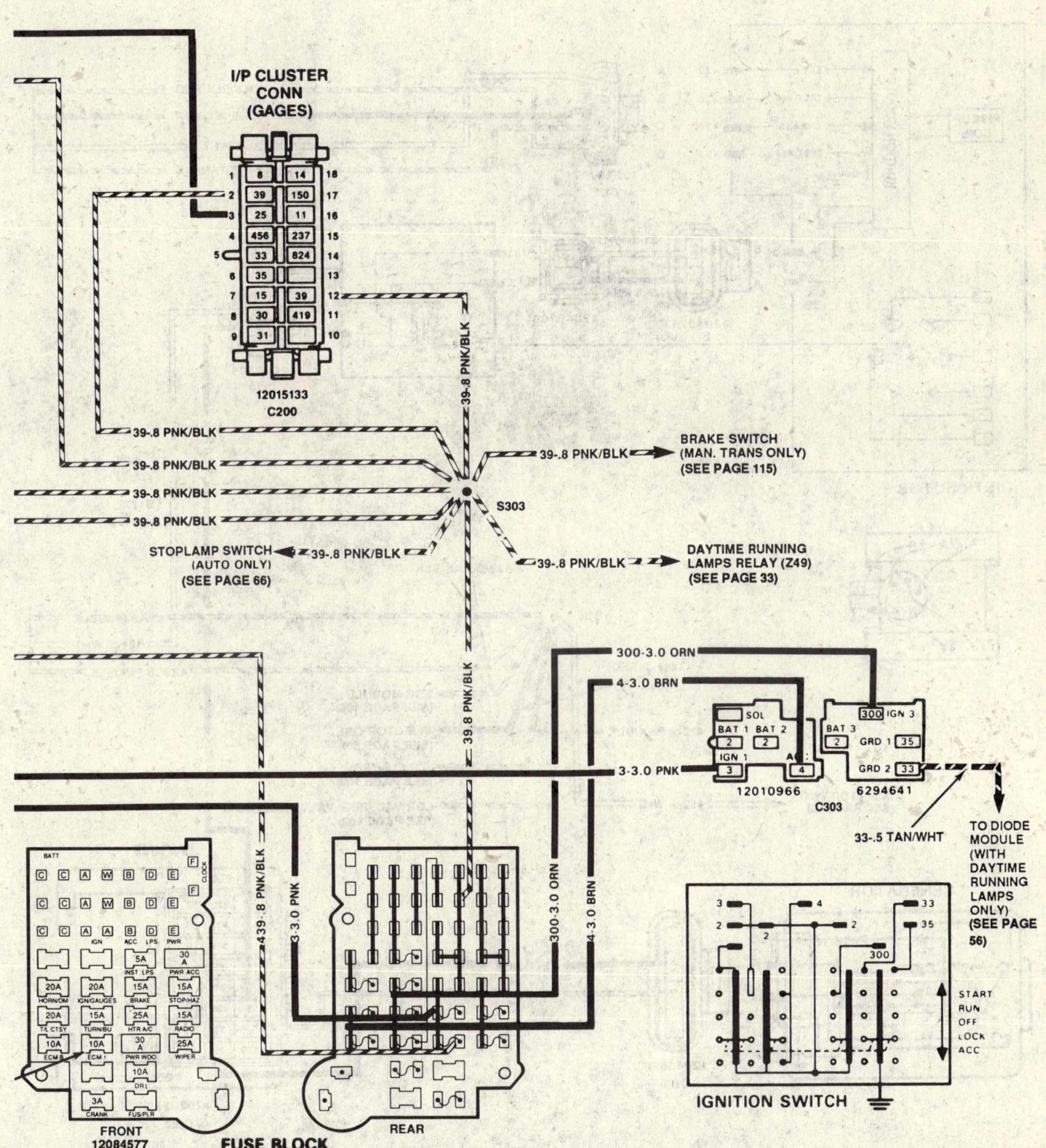

IGNITION - 2.5L (151 CID) ENGINE 73

1988-91

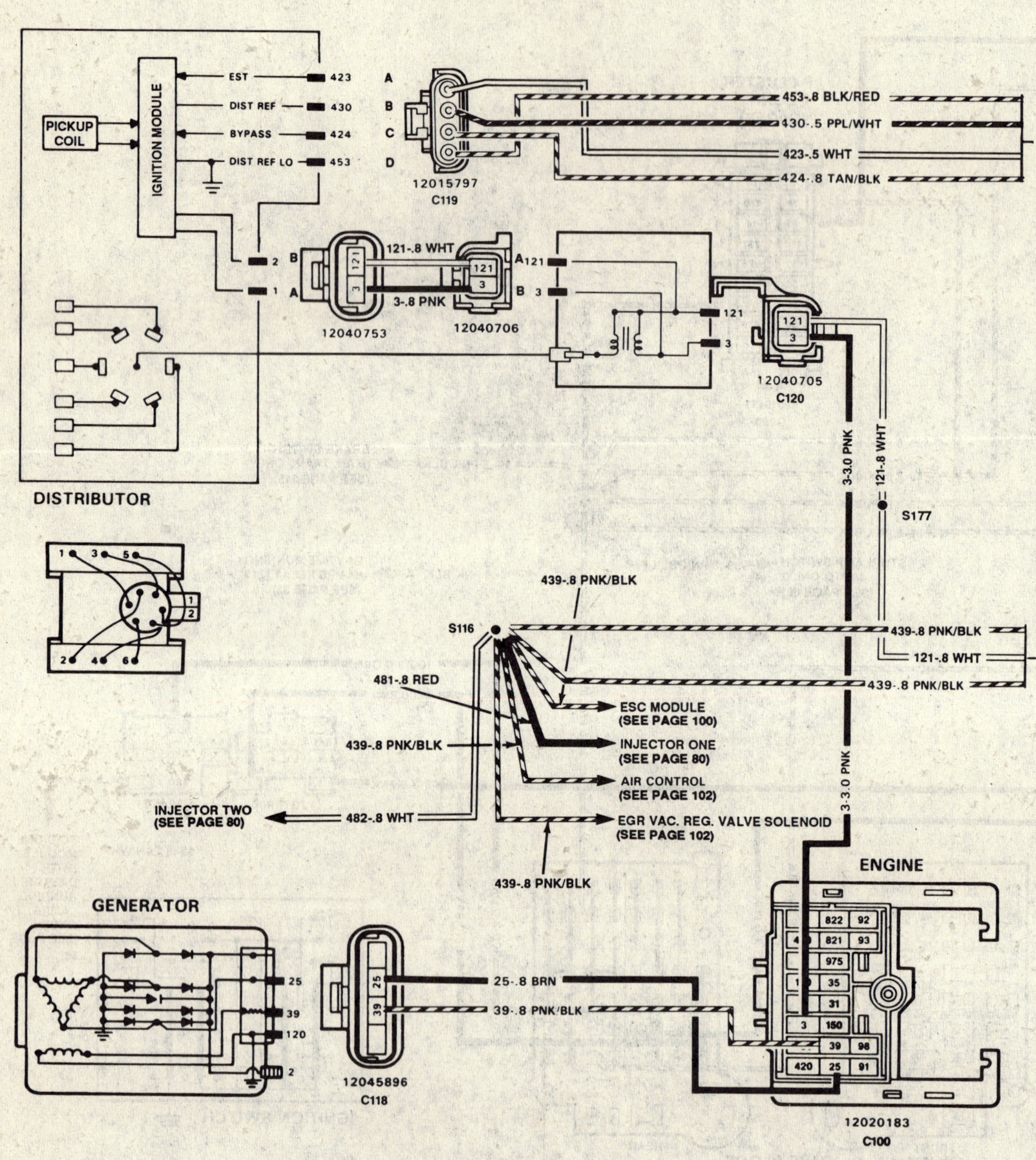

74 IGNITION - 2.8L (173 CID) ENGINE

1988-91

GROMMET 301
12066507
453-.8 BLK/RED
430-.5 PPL/WHT
423-.5 WHT
424-.8 TAN/BLK
439-.8 PNK/BLK
12047946
C307
ELECTRONIC CONTROL MODULE CONNECTORS
12045575
C307
COWL
ENGINE
I/P
12064770
C101
12064764
121-.5 WHT
439-.8 PNK/BLK
W/DIGITAL I/P ONLY
I/P
3-3.0 PNK
3-3.0 PNK
39-.8 PNK/BLK
25-.8 BRN
12020184
C100

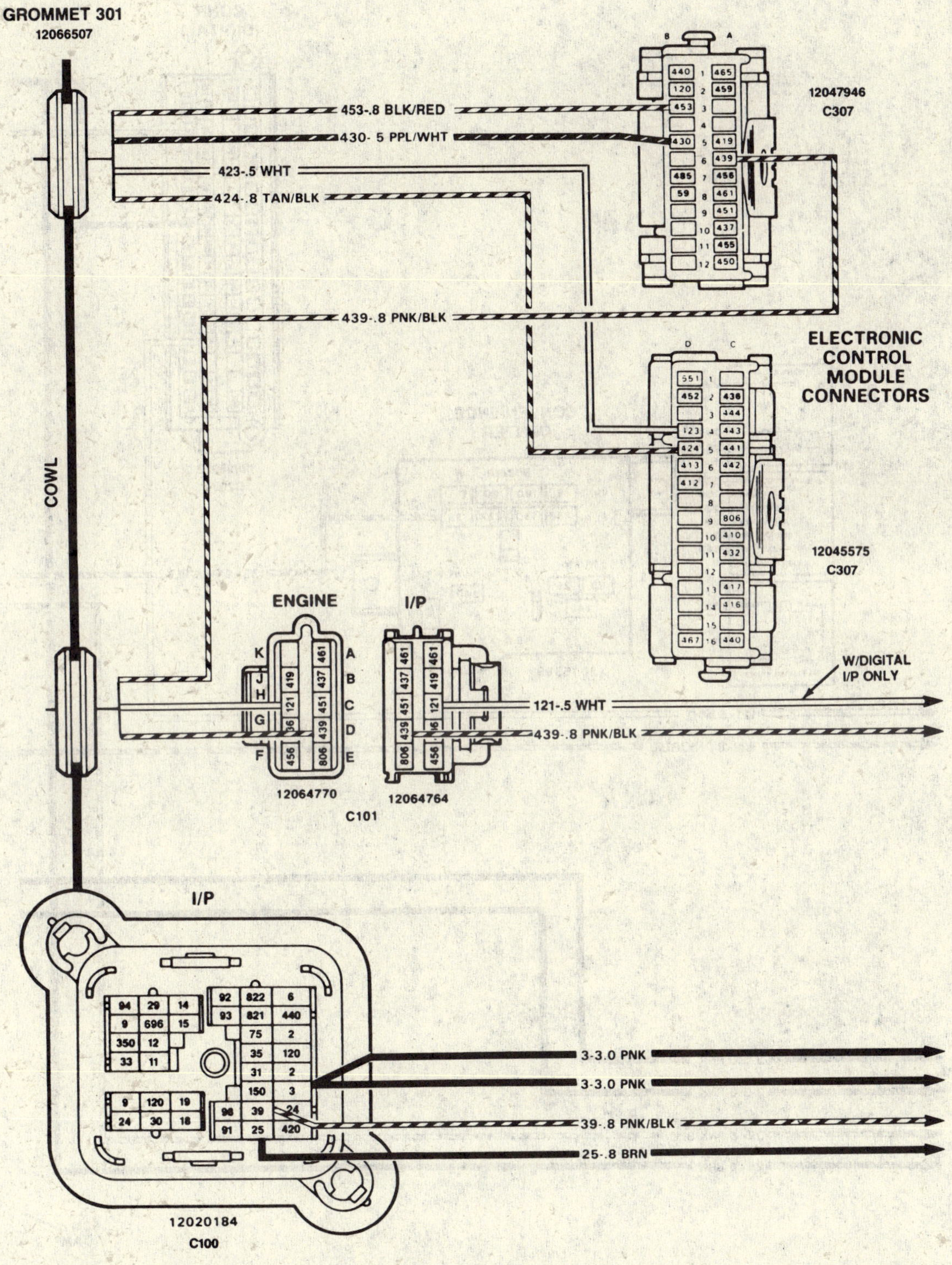

1988-91

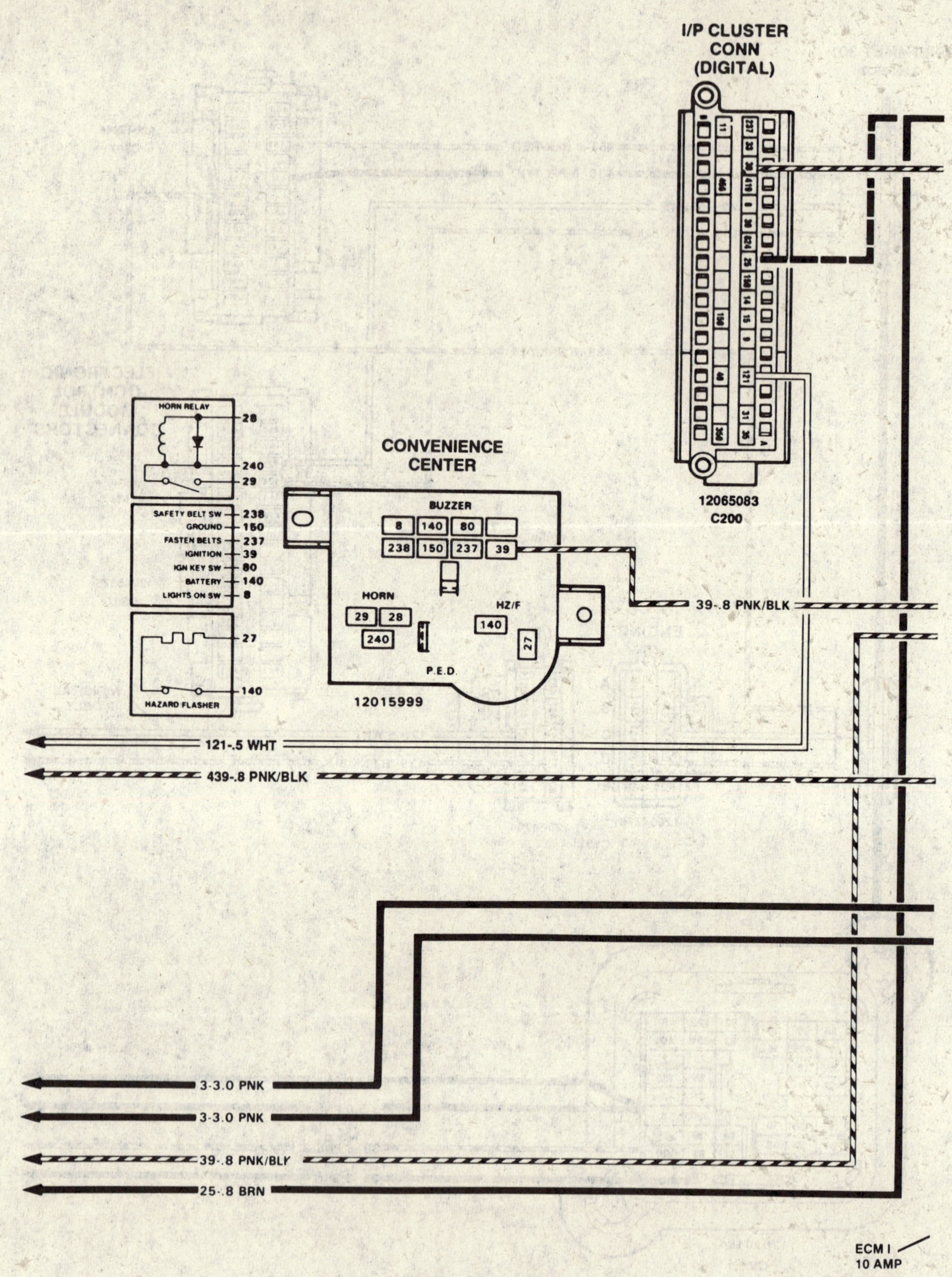

1988-91

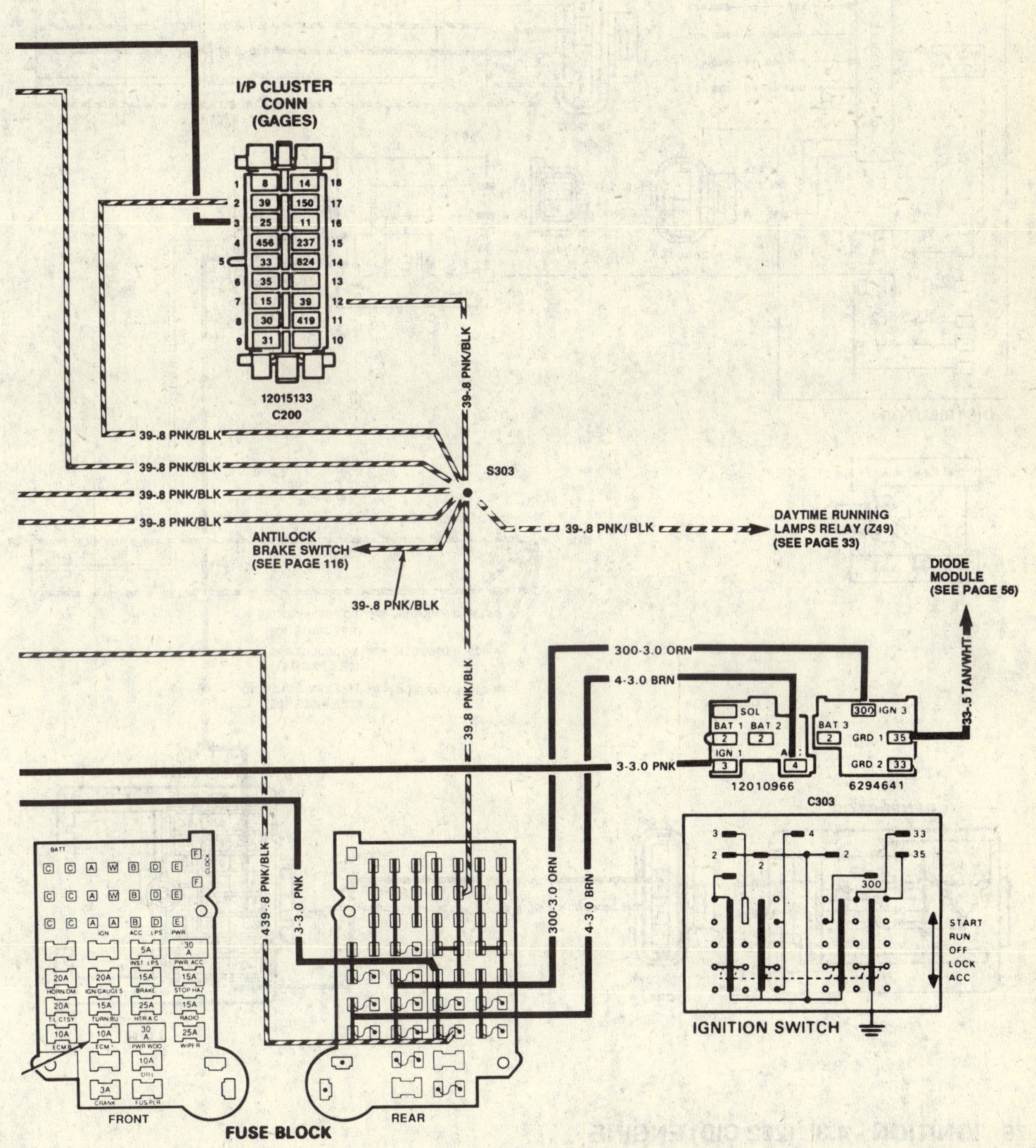

IGNITION - 2.8L (173 CID) ENGINE 75

1988-91

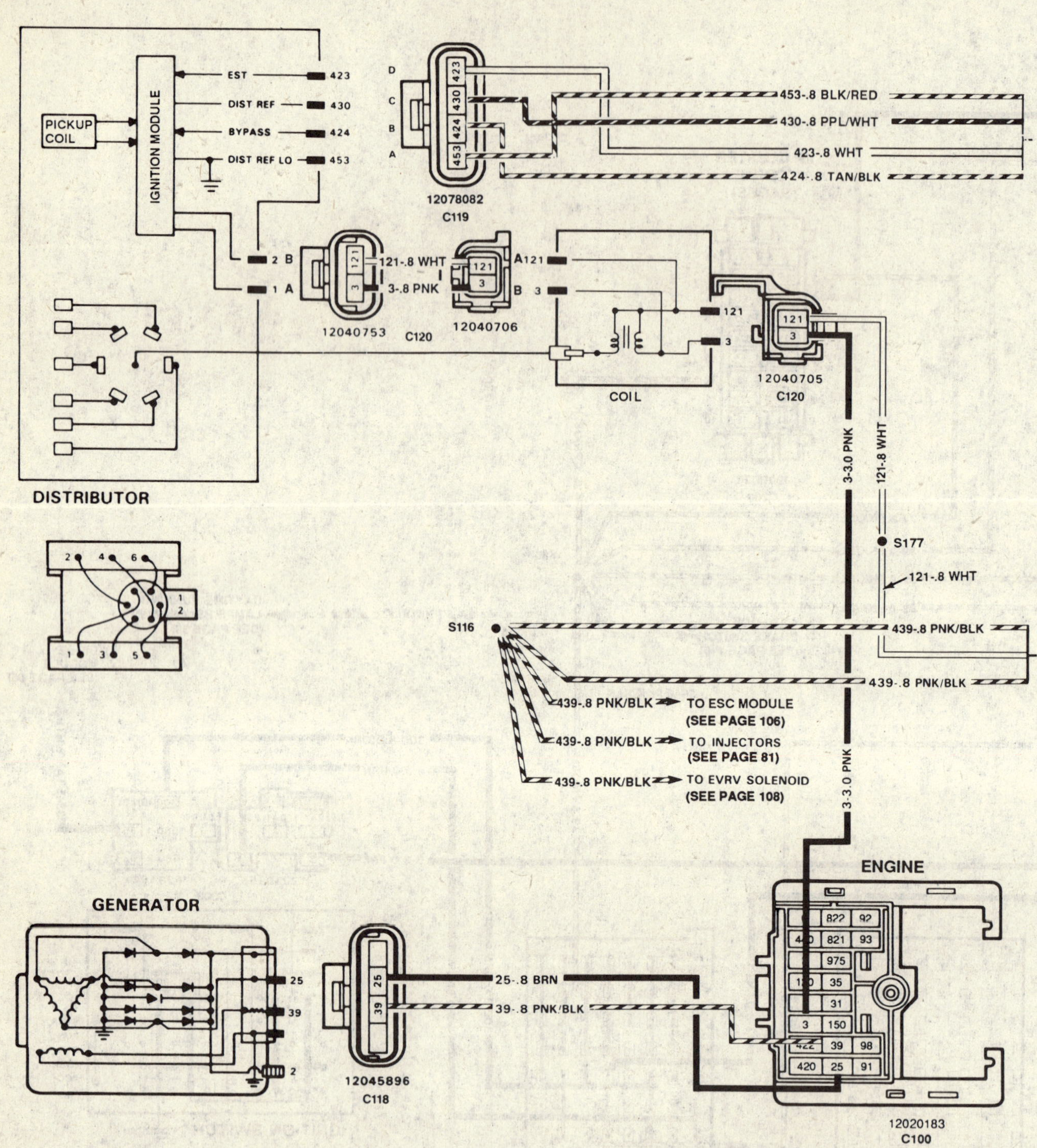

76 IGNITION - 4.3L (262 CID) ENGINE

1988-91

GROMMET 301
12066507
453-.8 BLK/RED
430-.8 PPL/WHT
423-.8 WHT
424-.8 TAN/BLK
439-.8 PNK/BLK
12047946
C307
ELECTRONIC
CONTROL
MODULE
CONNECTORS
COWL
12047683
C181
12047682
424-.8 TAN/BLK
SET TIMING
CONNECTOR
12045575
C307
ENGINE
I/P
GROMMET 301
12064770
C101
12064764
121-.5 WHT
439-.8 PNK/BLK
I/P
3-3.0 PNK
3-3.0 PNK
39-.8 PNK/BLK
25-.8 BRN
12020184
C100

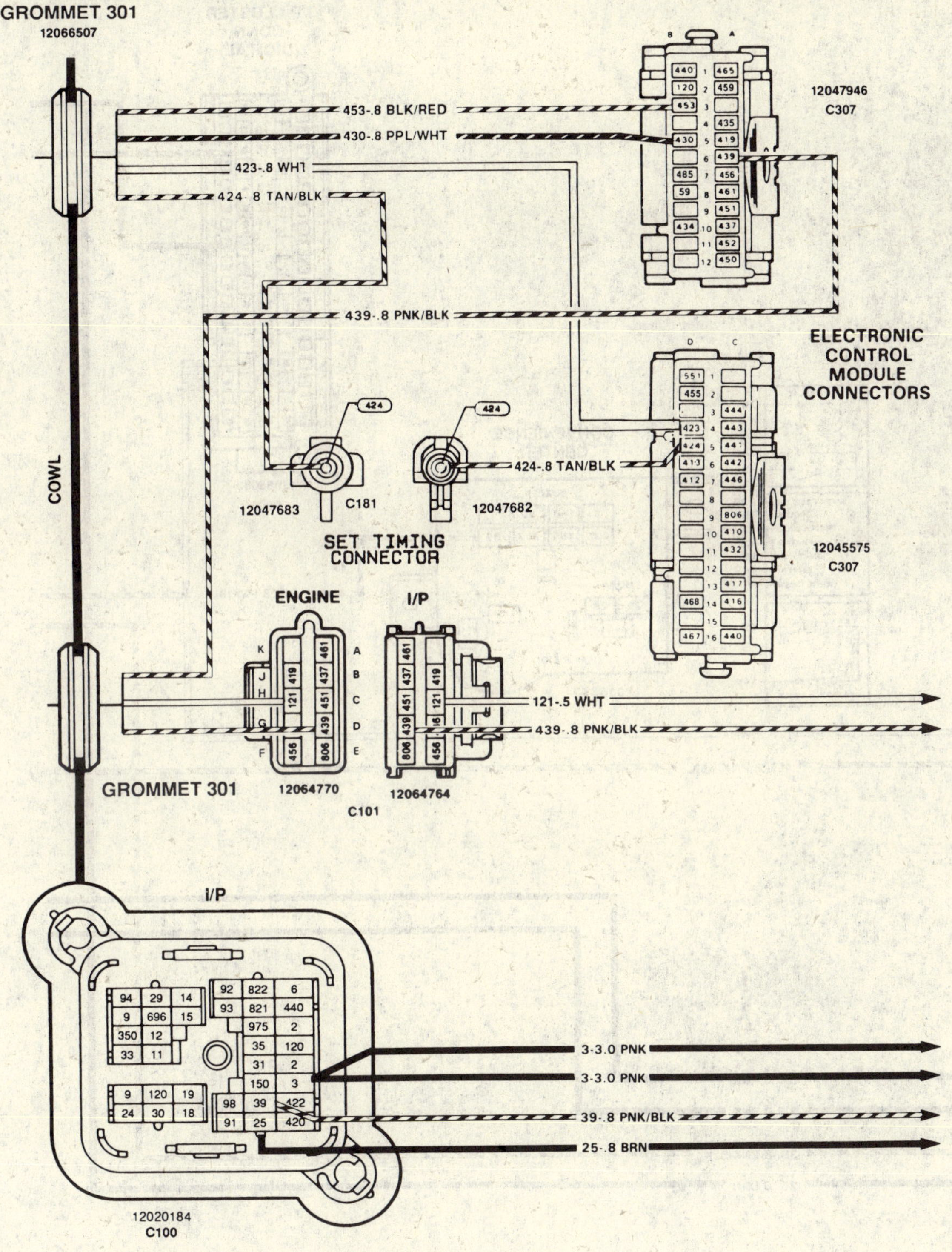

1988-91

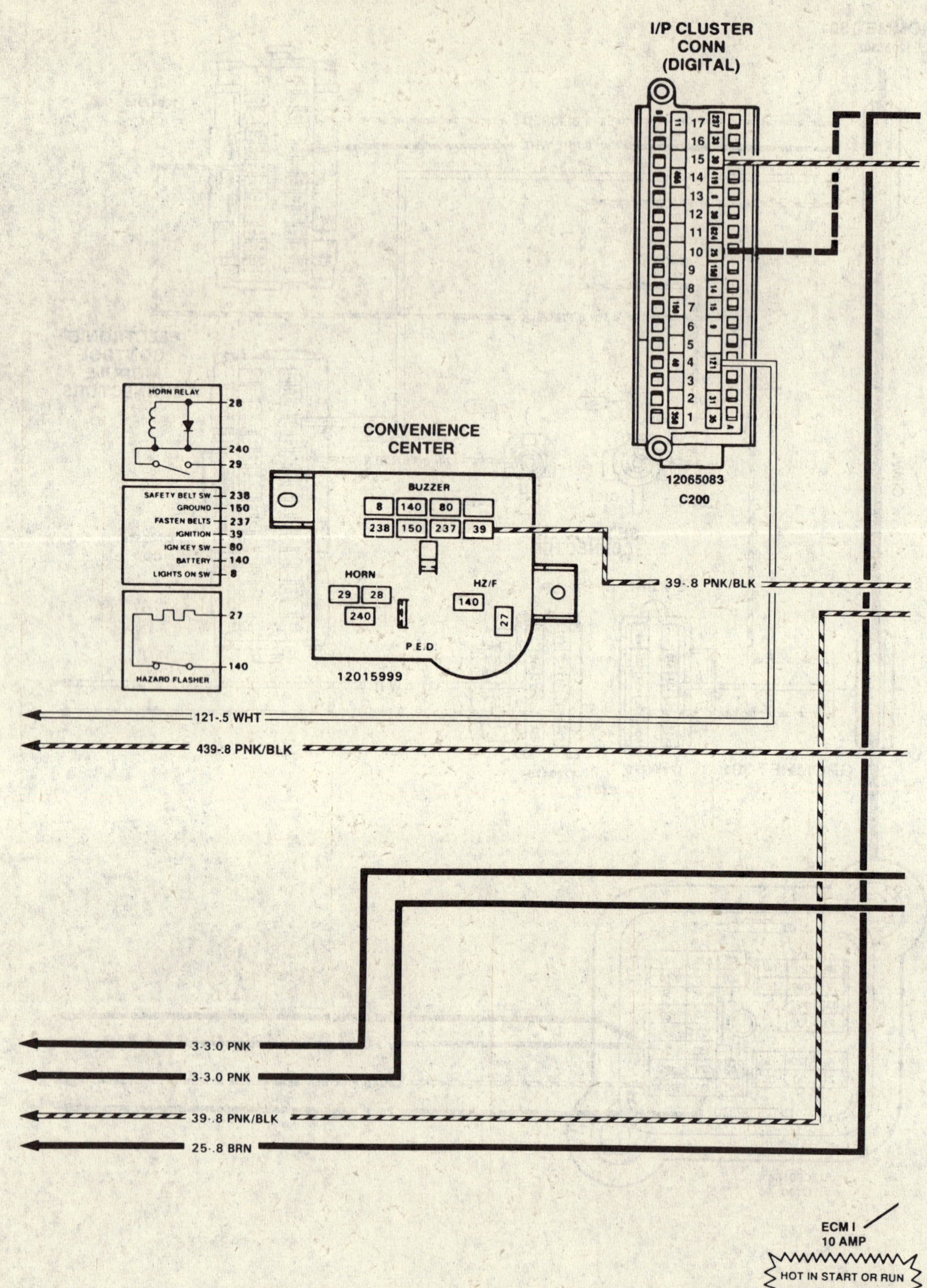

1988-91

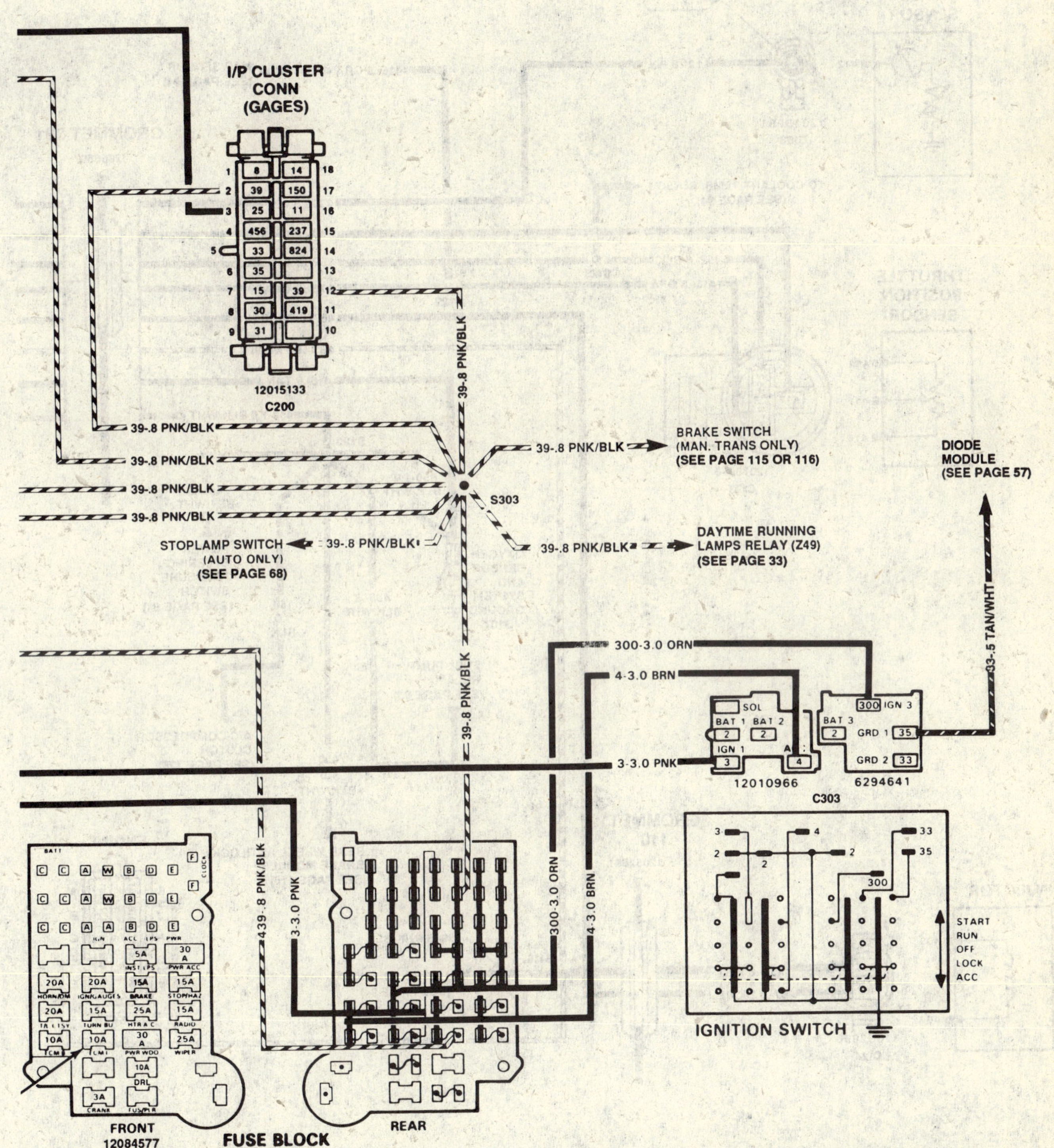

IGNITION - 4.3L (262 CID) ENGINE 77

1988-91

OXYGEN SENSOR
412
12015791
C108
412-.8 PPL
416-.8 GRA
MAP SENSOR (SEE PAGE 94)
GROMMET 301
12066507
452 .8 BLK
TO COOLANT TEMP. SENSOR (SEE PAGE 94)
412-.8 PPL
417-.8 DK BLU
452-.8 BLK
S123
416-.8 GRA
S122
467-.8 DK BLU
439-.8 PNK/BLK
413-.8 TAN
450-1.0 BLK/WHT
THROTTLE POSITION SENSOR
452
417
416
12078090
C123
S120
450-1.0 BLK/WHT
450-.8 BLK/WHT
COWL
POWER STEERING PRESSURE SWITCH (SEE PAGE 94)
OXYGEN SENSOR AND SYSTEM GROUND G107
450-.8 BLK/WHT
150 1.0 BLK
FUEL PUMP RELAY (SEE PAGE 83)
A/C COMPRESSOR CLUTCH (SEE PAGE 125)
450 1.0 BLK/WHT
REAR WHEEL ANTILOCK BRAKE MODULE (SEE PAGE 116)
GROMMET 110
12052891
ENGINE
INJECTOR
439
467
A
B
439-.8 RED
467-.8 DK BLU
12052890
C124
S116
439-.8 PNK/BLK
TO EGR SOLENOID (SEE PAGE 94)
439-.8 PNK/BLK
12064770
C101

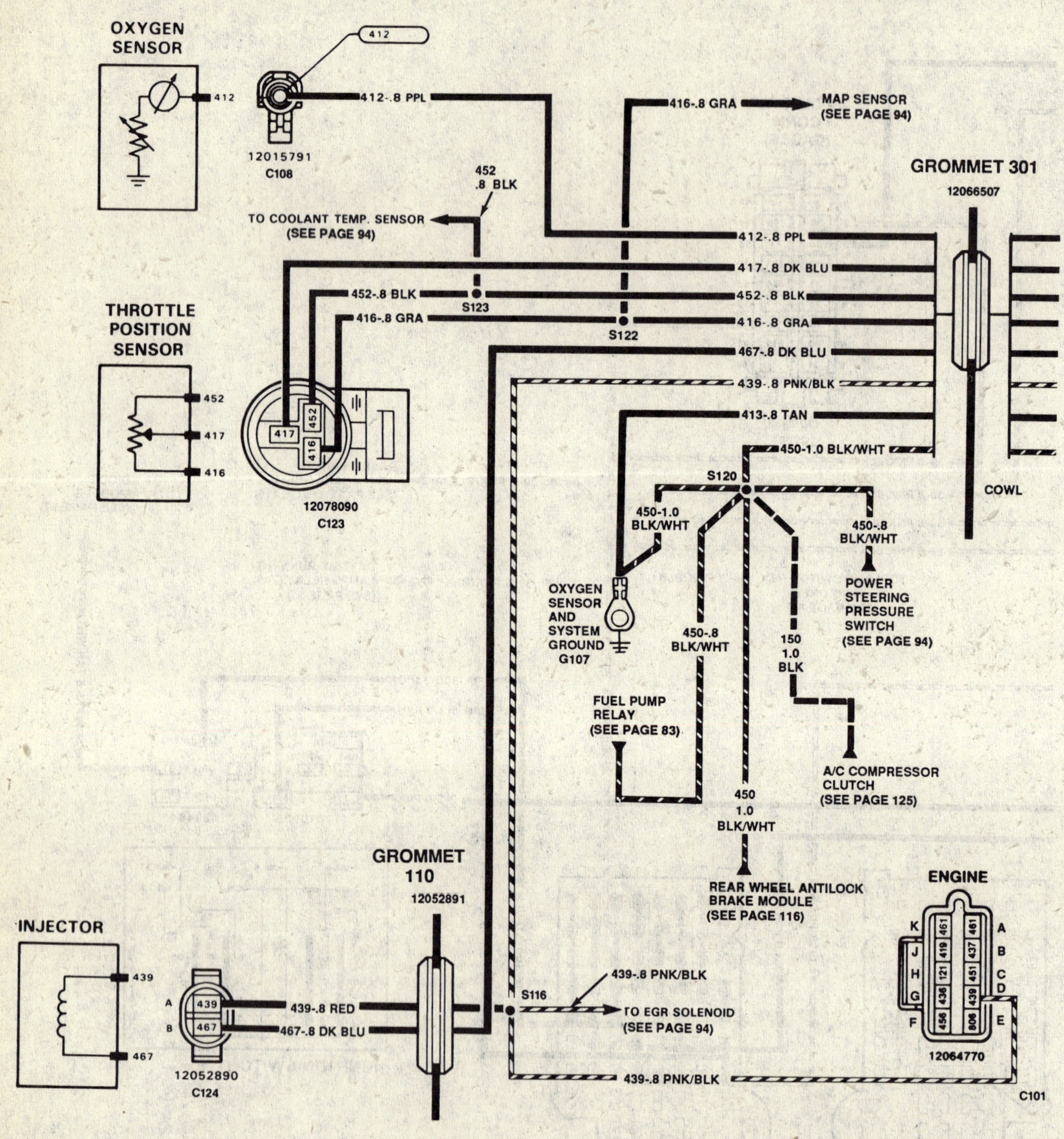

1988-91

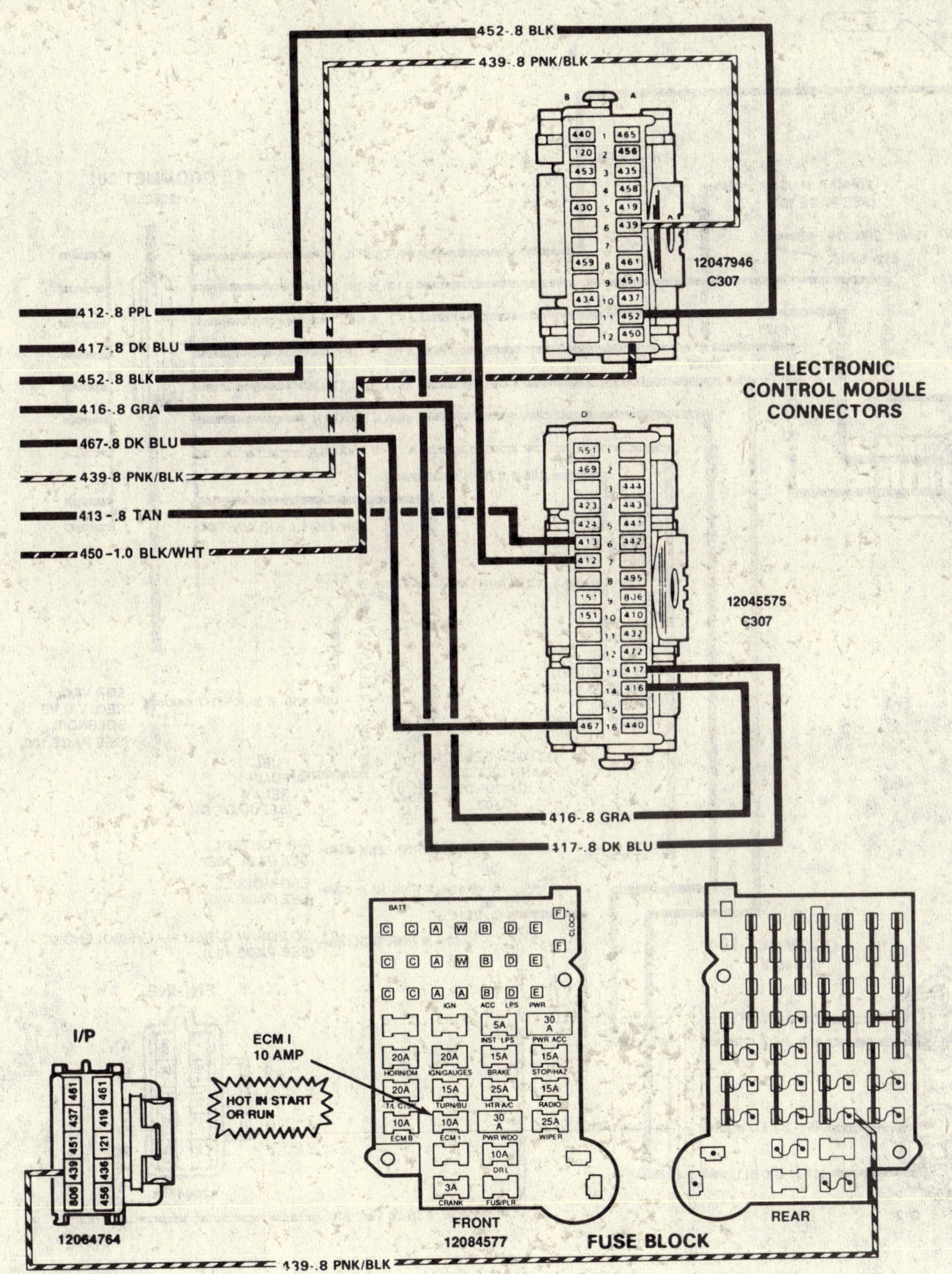

THROTTLE BODY INJECTION - 2.5L (151 CID) ENGINE 79

1988-91

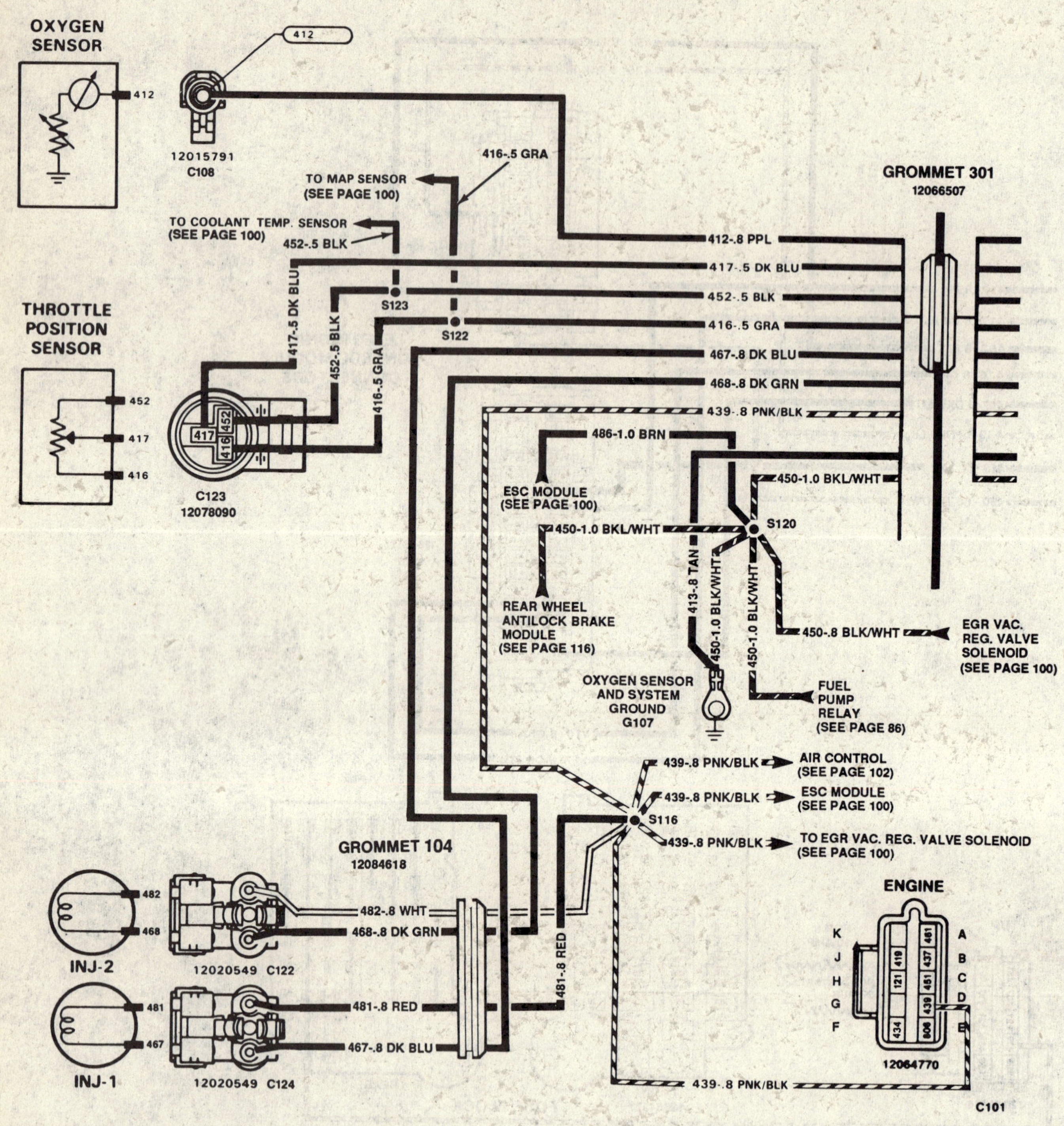

80 THROTTLE BODY INJECTION - 2.8L (173 CID) ENGINE

1988-91

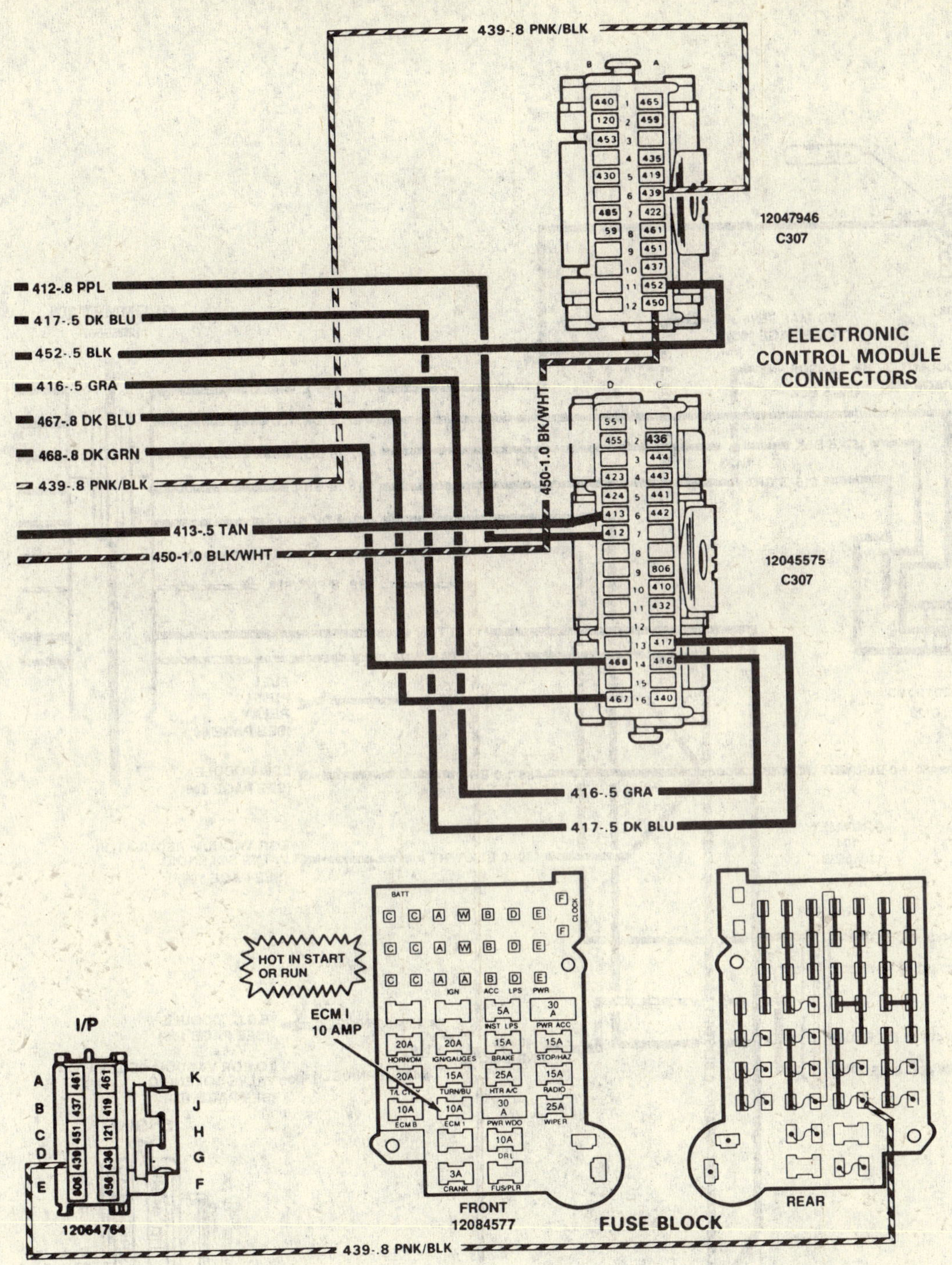

439-.8 PNK/BLK
12047946
C307
412-.8 PPL
417-.5 DK BLU
452-.5 BLK
416-.5 GRA
467-.8 DK BLU
468-.8 DK GRN
439-.8 PNK/BLK
ELECTRONIC CONTROL MODULE CONNECTORS
450-1.0 BK/WHT
413-.5 TAN
450-1.0 BLK/WHT
12045575
C307
416-.5 GRA
417-.5 DK BLU
HOT IN START OR RUN
ECM I 10 AMP
I/P
12064764
FRONT
12084577
FUSE BLOCK
REAR
439-.8 PNK/BLK

OXYGEN SENSOR
412
12015791
C108
TO MAP SENSOR (SEE PAGE 106)
416-.5 GRA
TO COOLANT TEMP. SENSOR (SEE PAGE 106)
452-.5 BLK
GROMMET 301
12066507
412-.8 PPL
417-.5 DK BLU
452-.5 BLK
S123
416-.5 GRA
S122
THROTTLE POSITION SENSOR
452
417
416
A
B
C
467-.8 DK BLU
468-.8 DK GRN
439-.8 PNK/BLK
413-.8 TAN
450-1.0 BLK/WHT
12015793
C123
450-1.0 BLK/WHT
FUEL PUMP RELAY (SEE PAGE 89)
REAR WHEEL ANTILOCK BRAKE MODULE (SEE PAGE 116)
4-WHEEL ANTILOCK BRAKE MODULE (SEE PAGE 114)
450-1.0 BLK/WHT
486-1.0 BRN
ESC MODULE (SEE PAGE 106)
GROMMET 104 12010639
450-.8 BLK/WHT
EGR VACUUM REGULATOR VALVE SOLENOID (SEE PAGE 108)
INJ-2
482
468
12084618
468-.8 DK GRN
482-.8 WHT
S170
481
467
467-.8 DK BLU
481-.8 RED
INJ-1
450-1.0 BLK/WHT
439-.8 PNK/BLK
S116
439-.8 PNK/BLK
E.S.C. MODULE (SEE PAGE 106)
439-.8 PNK/BLK
TO EGR VACUUM REGULATOR VALVE SOLENOID (SEE PAGE 108)
ENGINE
K J H G F
A B C D E
461 419 121 434
461 437 451 439 806
12064770
G107
OXYGEN SENSOR AND SYSTEM GROUND
439-.8 PNK/BLK
C101

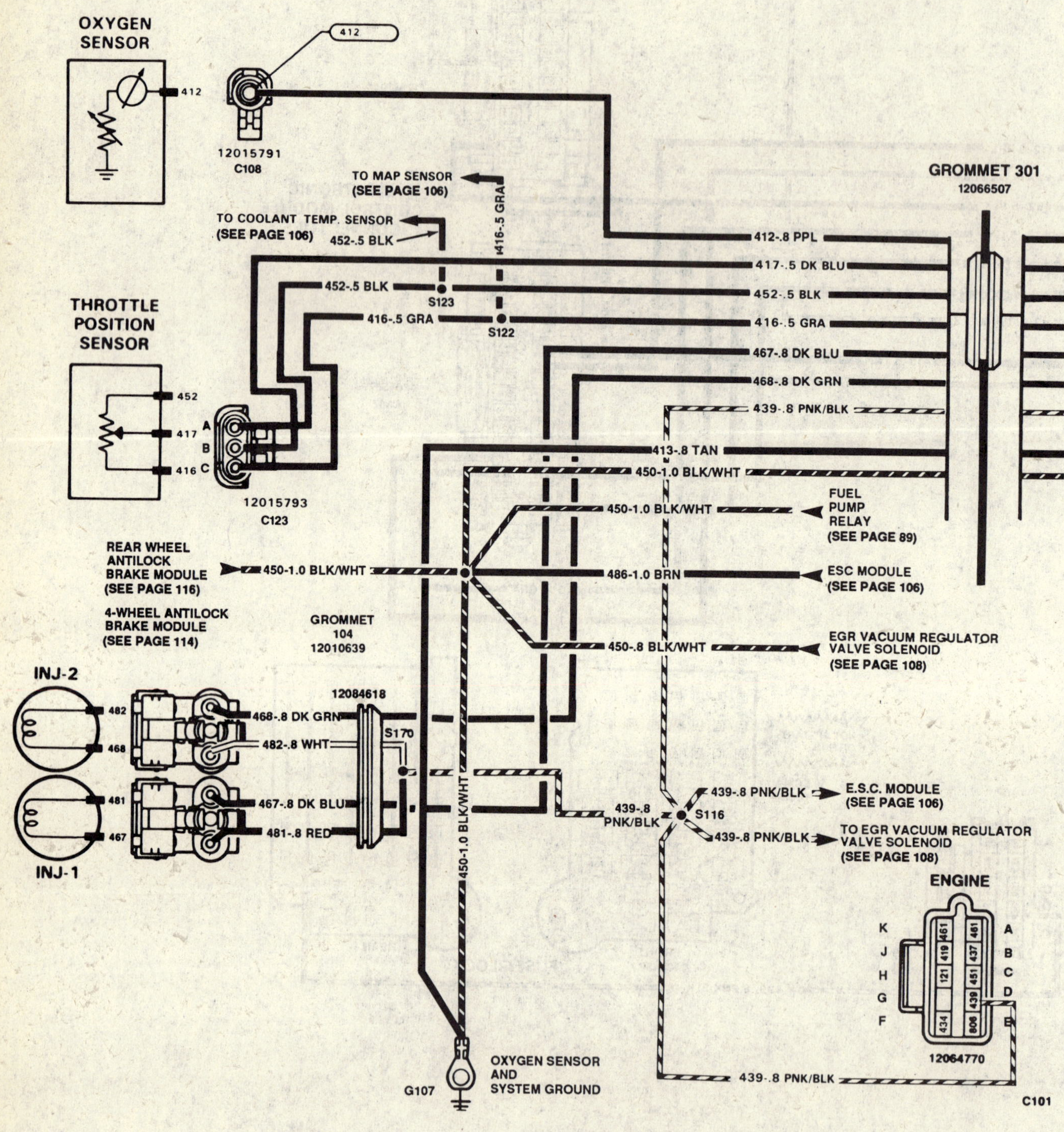

1988-91

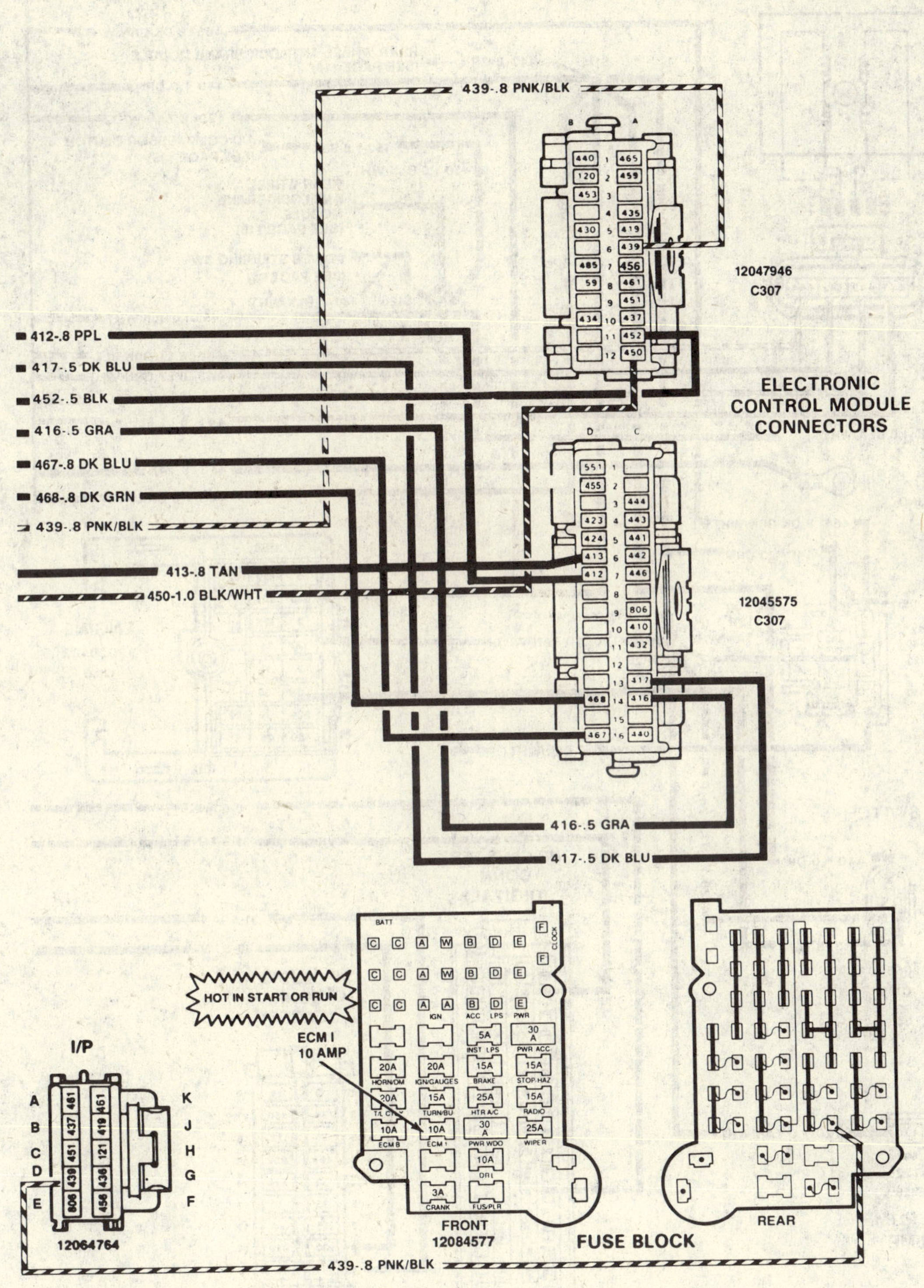

THROTTLE BODY INJECTION - 4.3L (262 CID) ENGINE 81
1988-91

IDLE AIR
CONTROL
12078082
C125
465-.8 DK GRN/WHT
S114
440-.8 ORN
REAR WHEEL ANTILOCK BRAKE MODULE
(SEE PAGE 116)
440-1.0 ORN
120-.8 TAN/WHT
150-1.0 BLK
A/C COMPRESSOR CLUTCH
(SEE PAGE 125)
450-1.0 BLK/WHT
REAR WHEEL
ANTILOCK BRAKE
MODULE
(SEE PAGE 116)
POWER STEERING SW
(SEE PAGE 94)
S120
450-.8 BLK/WHT
450-1.0 BLK WHT
444-.8 LT GRN/BLK
443-.8 LT GRN/WHT
442-.8 LT BLU/BLK
441-.8 LT BLU/WHT
413-.8 TAN
OXYGEN SENSOR
GROUND
AND SYSTEM GROUND
G107
465-.8 DK GRN/WHT
440-1.0 ORN
FUEL PUMP
RELAY
12020015
C126
120-1.0
TAN/WHT
120-.8 TAN/WHT
120-1.0 TAN/WHT
S126
ENGINE
12020183
C100
450-.8 BLK/WHT
OIL PRESSURE SWITCH
440-1.0 ORN
31.8 TAN
12065401
C129
120-1.0 TAN/WHT
30-.5 PNK
31-.5 TAN
I/P CLUSTER
CONN
(DIGITAL)
I/P CLUSTER
CONN
(GAGES)
2977253
C128
FUEL PUMP
PRIME
12066578
C200
12015133
C200

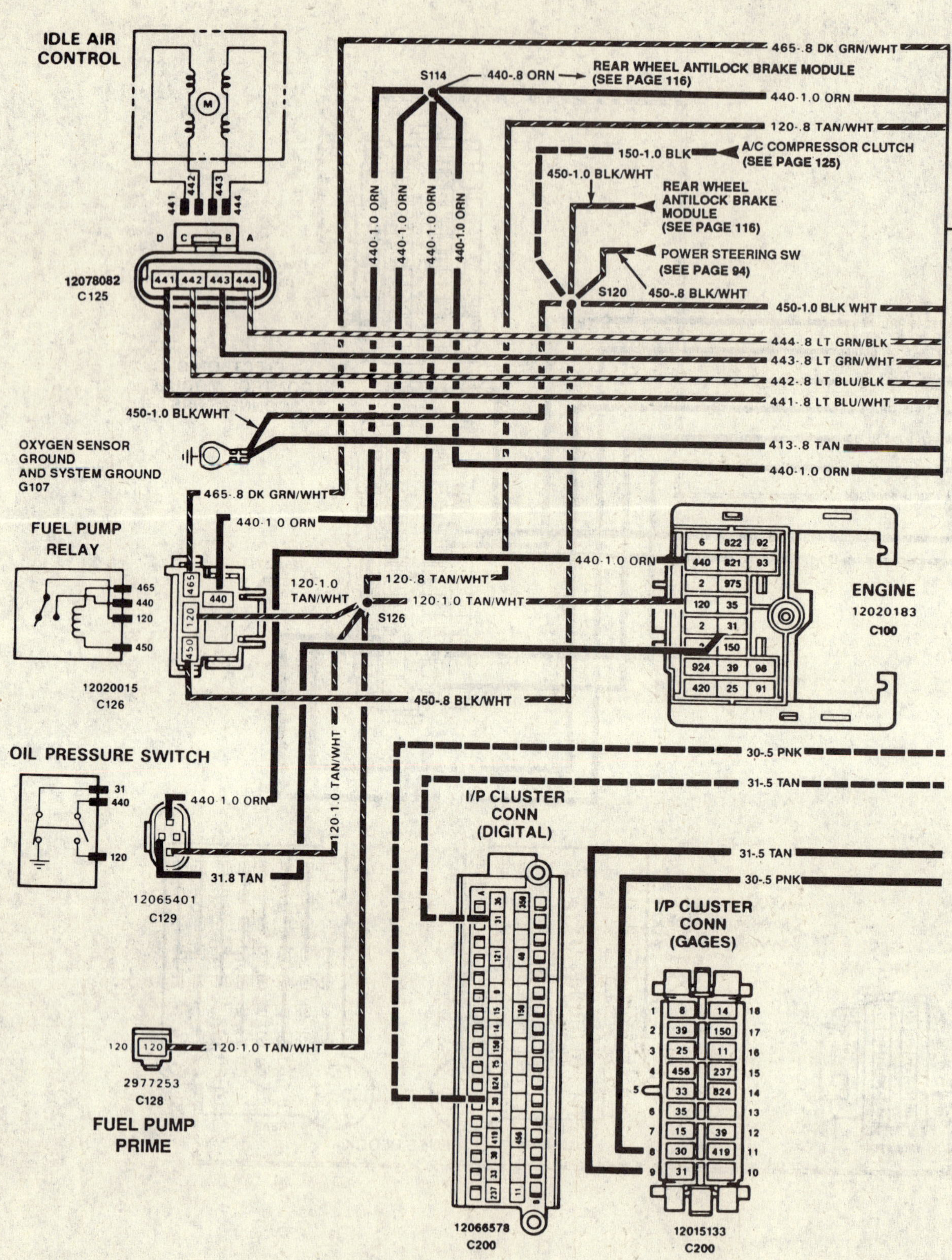

1988-91

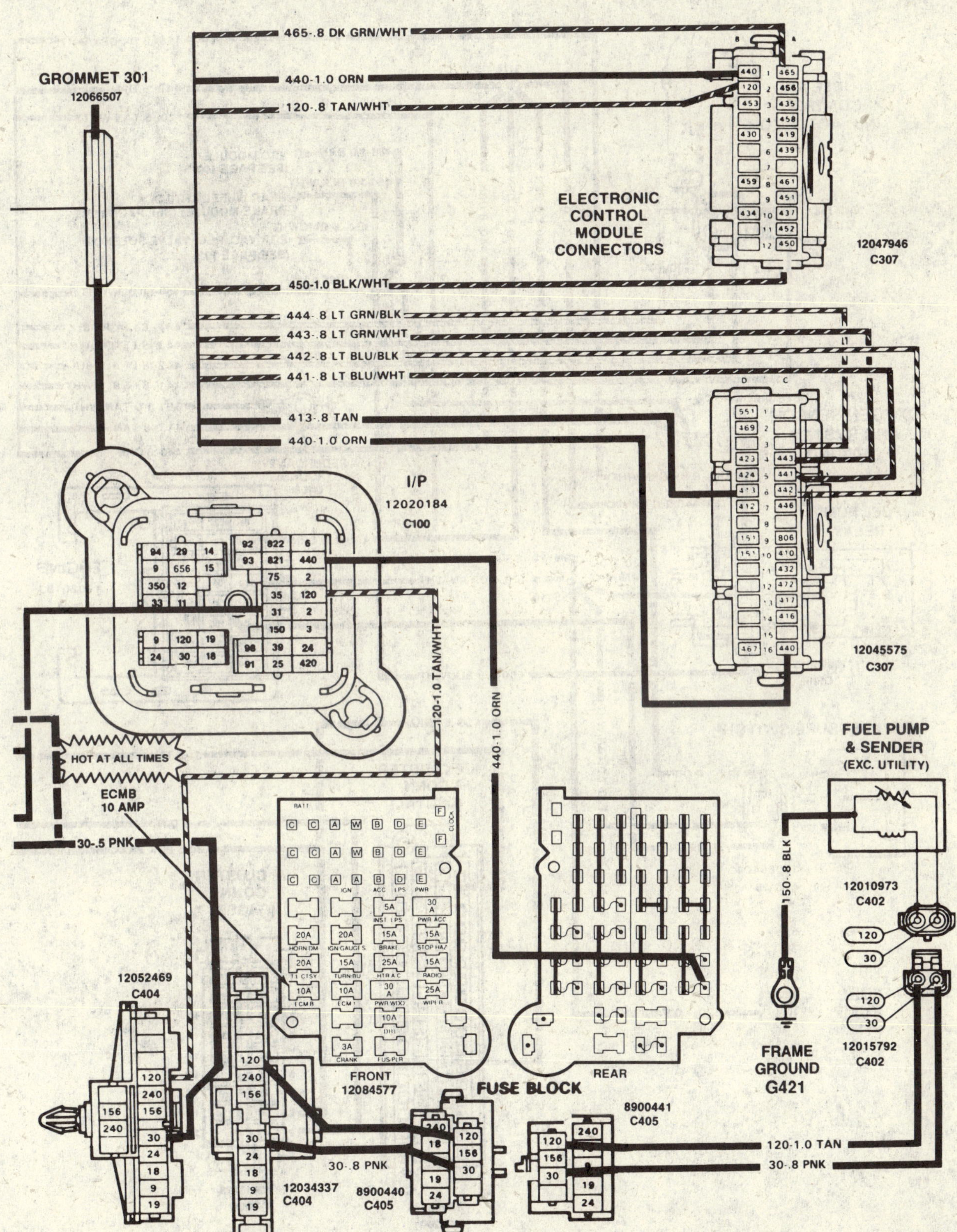

FUEL CONTROL AND IDLE AIR CONTORL - 2.5L (151 CID) ENGINE - 2-DOOR UTILITY 83
1988-91

IDLE AIR CONTROL – INJ. ACTUATOR
12015798
C125
465-.8 DK GRN/WHT
S114
440-.8 ORN
120-.8 TAN/WHT
486-1.0 BRN
ESC MODULE (SEE PAGE 100)
450-1.0 BLK/WHT
REAR WHEEL ANTILOCK BRAKE MODULE (SEE PAGE 116)
450-.8 BLK/WHT
EGR VAC. REG. VALVE SOLENOID (SEE PAGE 102)
S120
450-1.0 BLK/WHT
444-.8 LT GRN/BLK
443-.8 LT GRN/WHT
442-.8 LT BLU/BLK
441-.8 LT BLU/WHT
551-1.0 TAN/WHT
413-.8 TAN
440-.8 ORN
OXYGEN SENSOR AND SYSTEM GROUND
G107
REDUNDANT GROUND
G108
FUEL PUMP RELAY
12020015
C126
465-.8 DK GRN/WHT
440-1.0 ORN
120-1.0 TAN/WHT
S115
450-1.0 BLK/WHT
ENGINE
12020183
C100
OIL PRESSURE SWITCH
12065401
C129
31-.8 TAN
30-.5 PNK
31-.5 TAN
I/P CLUSTER CONN (DIGITAL)
I/P CLUSTER CONN (GAGES)
FUEL PUMP PRIME
2977253
C128
12065083
C200
12015133
C200

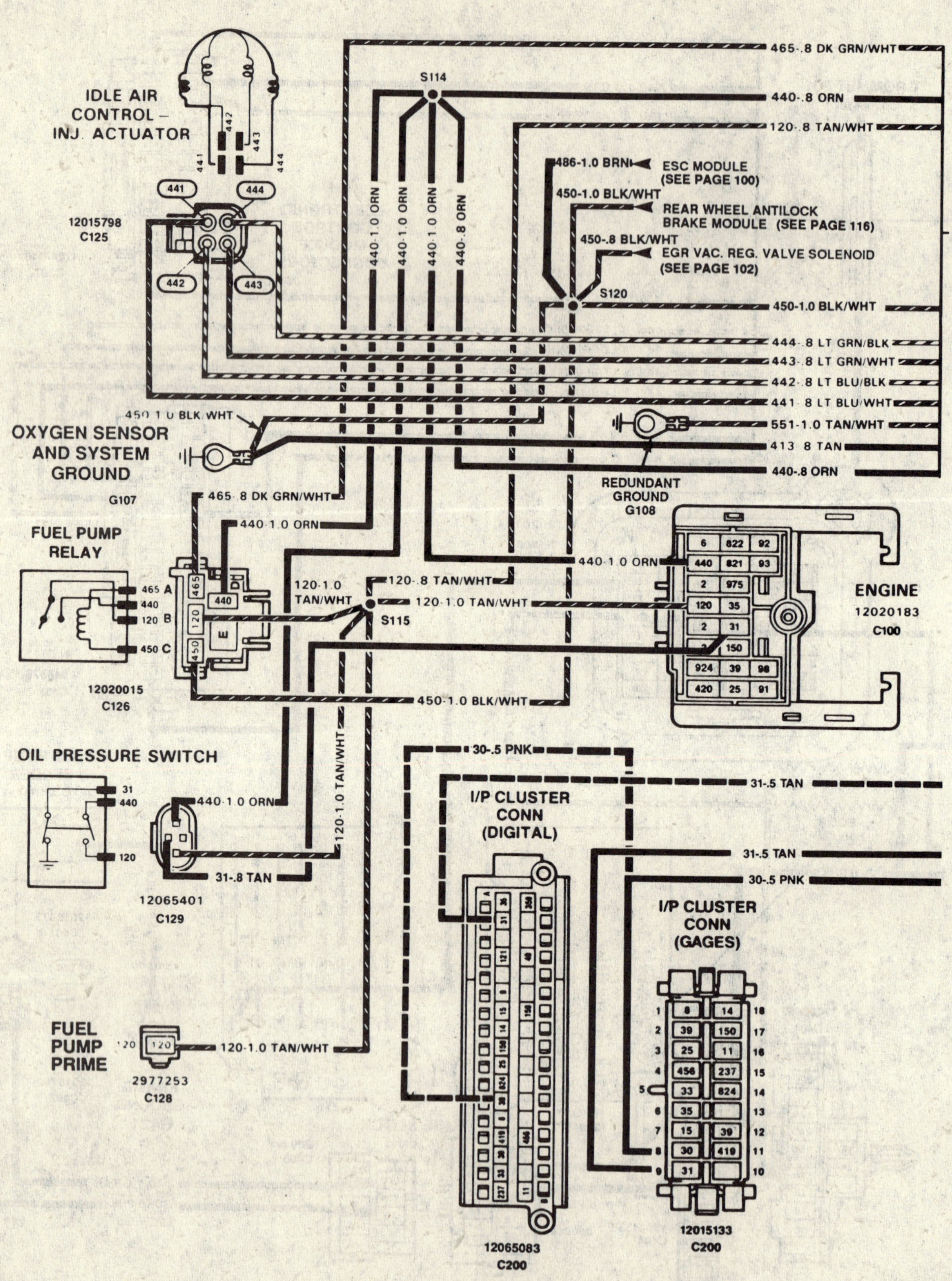

1988-91

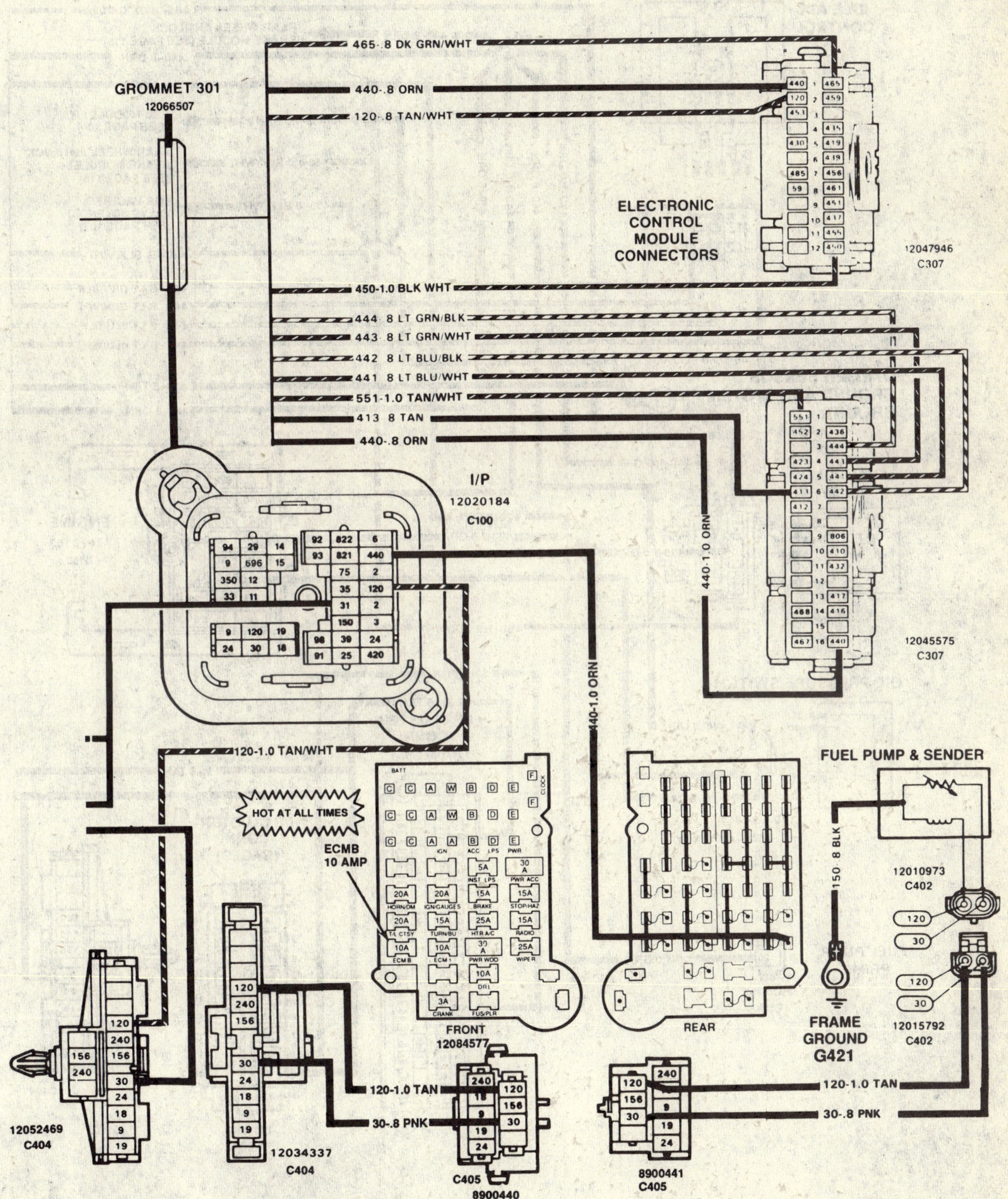

FUEL CONTROL AND IDLE AIR CONTROL - 2.8L (173 CID) ENGINE - 2- DOOR UTILITY 85
1988-91

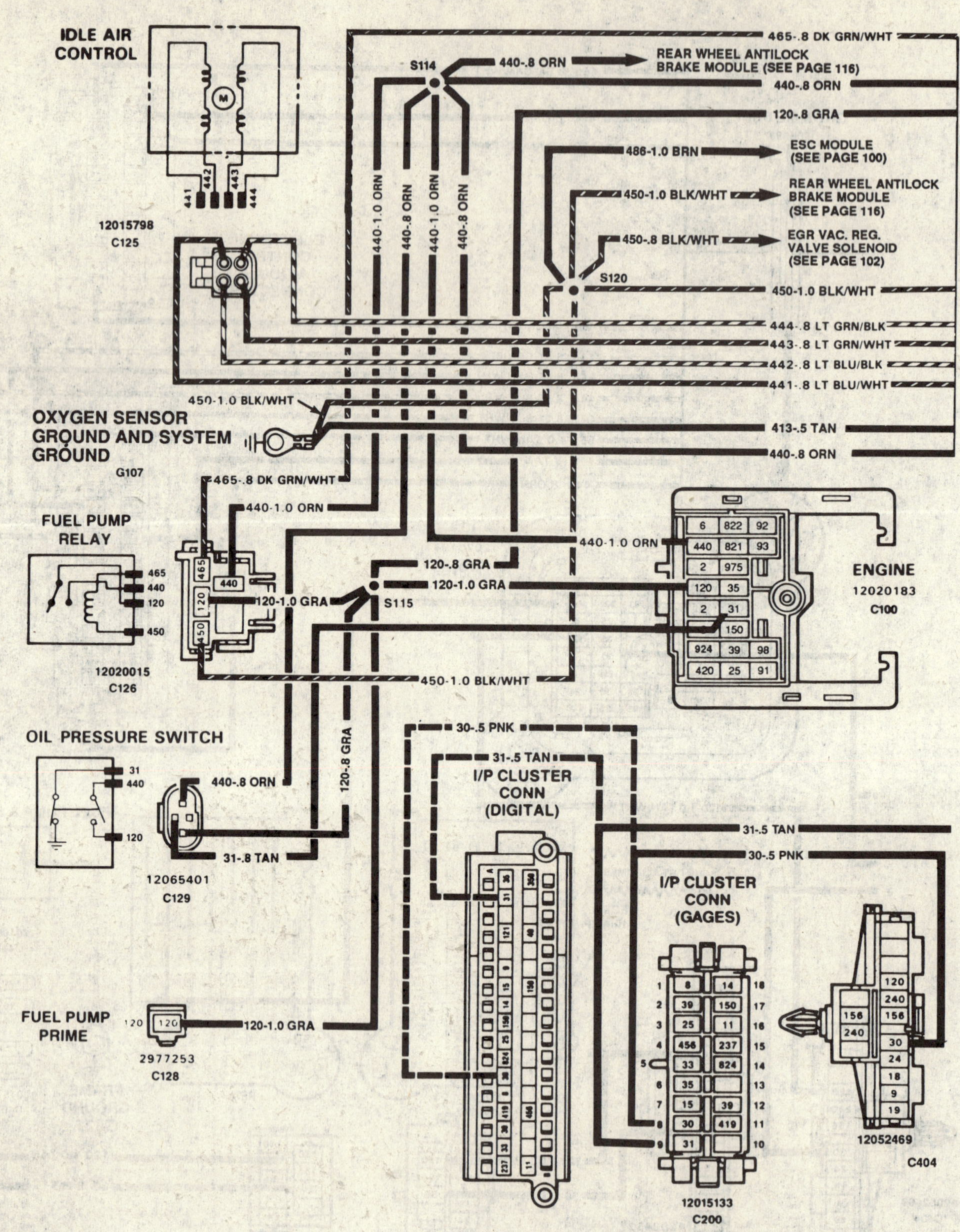
IDLE AIR CONTROL
441
442
443
444
12015798
C125
465-.8 DK GRN/WHT
S114
440-.8 ORN
REAR WHEEL ANTILOCK BRAKE MODULE (SEE PAGE 116)
440-.8 ORN
120-.8 GRA
486-1.0 BRN
ESC MODULE (SEE PAGE 100)
450-1.0 BLK/WHT
REAR WHEEL ANTILOCK BRAKE MODULE (SEE PAGE 116)
450-.8 BLK/WHT
EGR VAC. REG. VALVE SOLENOID (SEE PAGE 102)
S120
450-1.0 BLK/WHT
440-1.0 ORN
440-.8 ORN
444-.8 LT GRN/BLK
443-.8 LT GRN/WHT
442-.8 LT BLU/BLK
441-.8 LT BLU/WHT
OXYGEN SENSOR GROUND AND SYSTEM GROUND
G107
413-.5 TAN
440-.8 ORN
FUEL PUMP RELAY
465
440
120
450
12020015
C126
465-.8 DK GRN/WHT
440-1.0 ORN
120-1.0 GRA
120-.8 GRA
120-1.0 GRA
S115
440-1.0 ORN
450-1.0 BLK/WHT
ENGINE
12020183
C100
OIL PRESSURE SWITCH
31
440
120
440-.8 ORN
31-.8 TAN
120-.8 GRA
12065401
C129
FUEL PUMP PRIME
120
2977253
C128
120-1.0 GRA
30-.5 PNK
31-.5 TAN
I/P CLUSTER CONN (DIGITAL)
31-.5 TAN
30-.5 PNK
I/P CLUSTER CONN (GAGES)
12015133
C200
12052469
C404

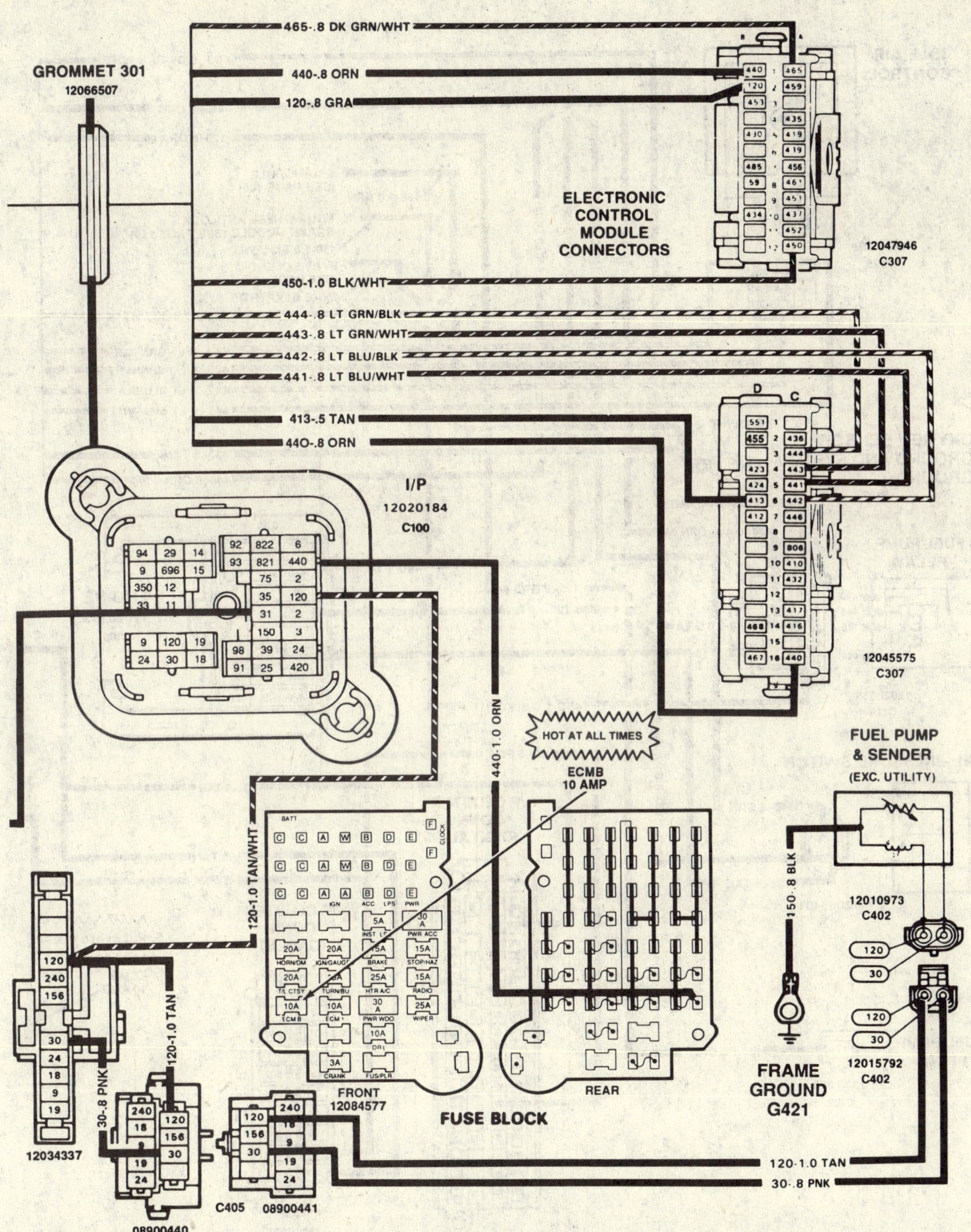

FUEL CONTROL AND IDLE AIR CONTROL - 4.3L (262 CID) ENGINE - 2-DOOR UTILITY 87

1988-91

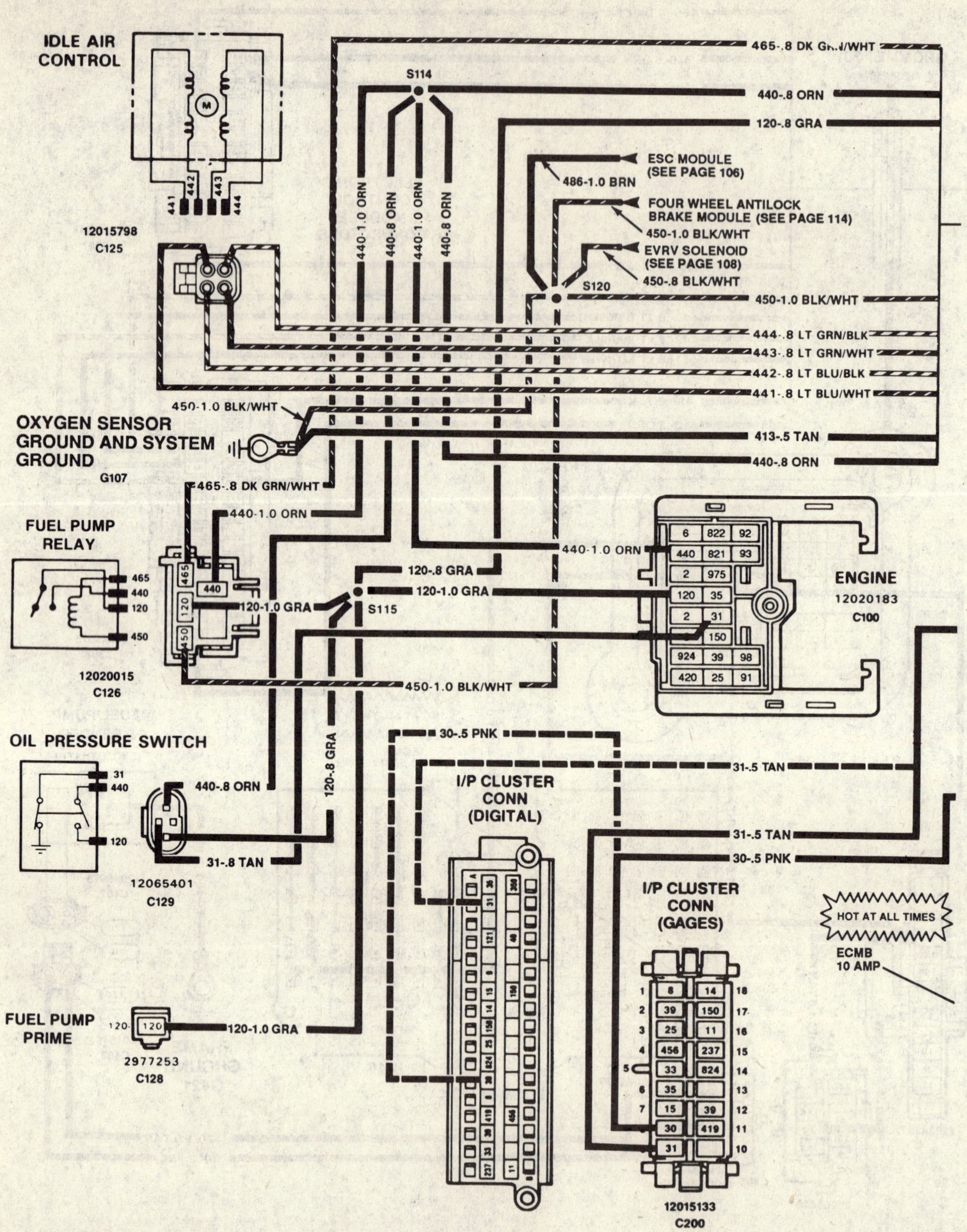

88 FUEL CONTROL AND IDLE AIR CONTROL - 4.3L (262 CID) ENGINE - 4-DOOR

1988-91

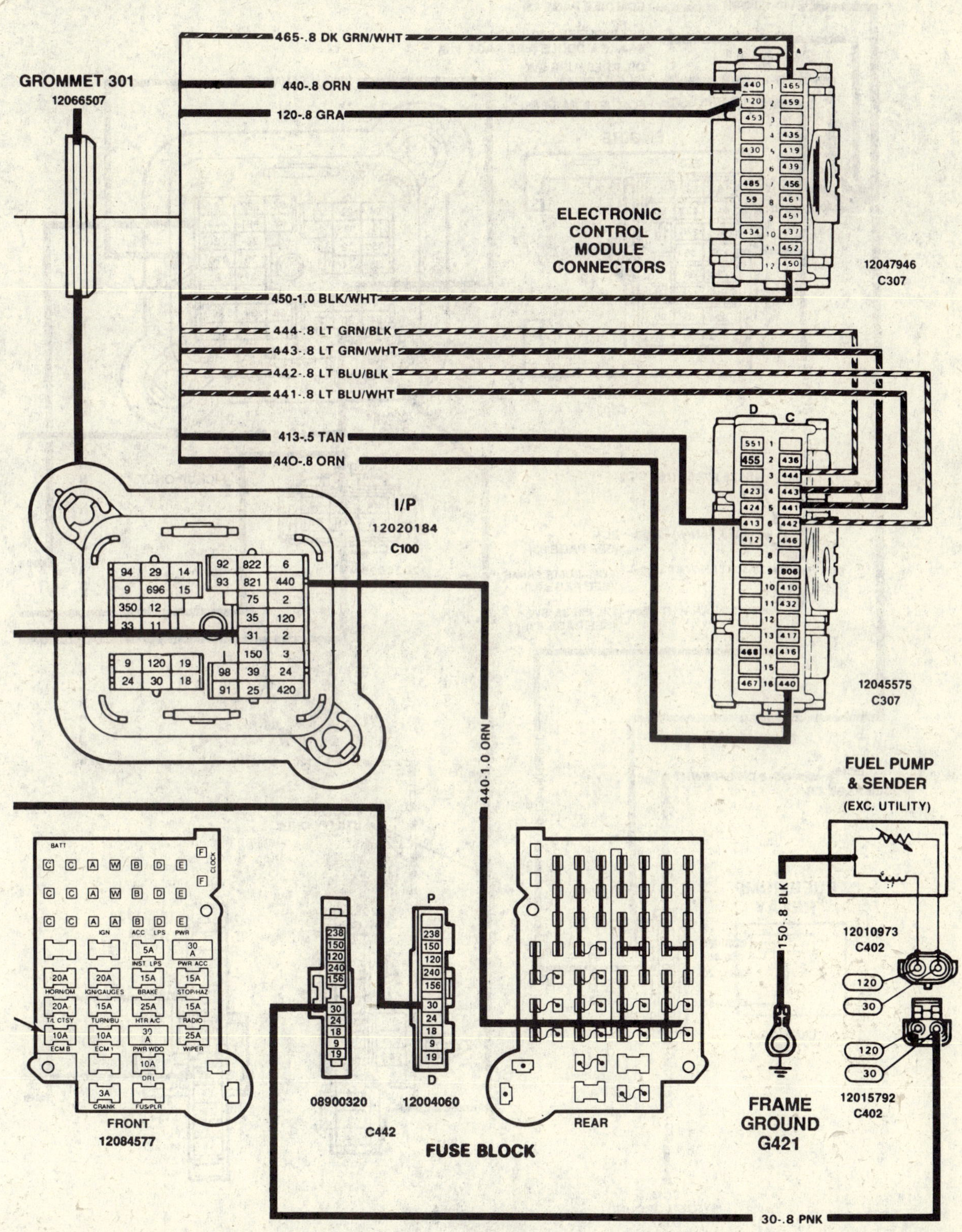

UTILITY

1988-91

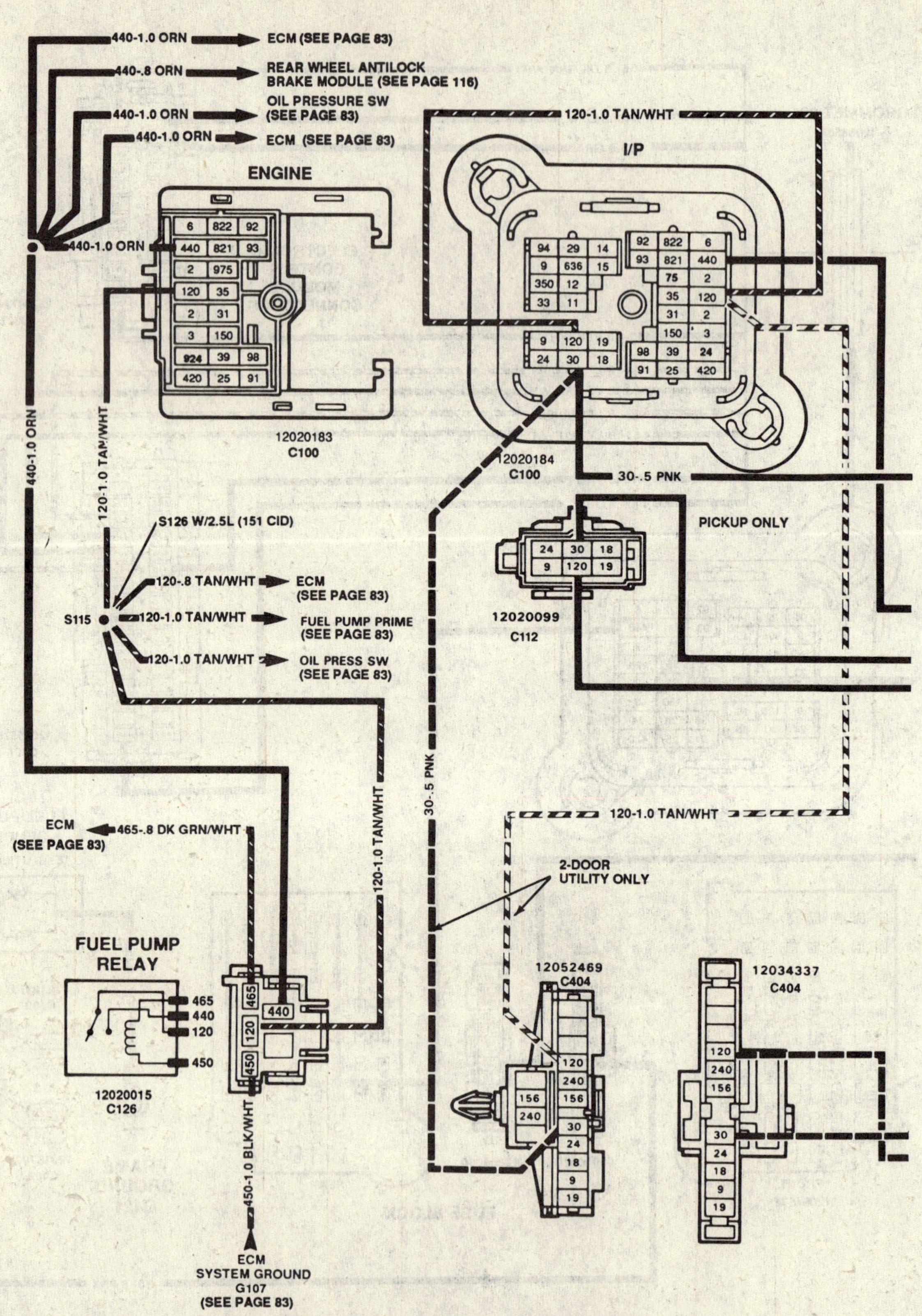

90 FUEL SENSOR - PICKUP AND 2-DOOR UTILITY

1988-91

I/P CLUSTER CONN (GAGES)
12015133
C200
I/P CLUSTER CONN (DIGITAL)
12066578
C200
FUEL PUMP & SENSOR
150-.8 BLK
12010973
C402
12015792
C402
120
30
FRAME GROUND
G417 (PICKUP)
G421 (UTILITY)
30-.5 PNK
440-1.0 ORN
30-.8 PNK
120-1.0 TAN
UTILITY ONLY
ECMB 10 AMP
FRONT
12084577
REAR
HOT AT ALL TIMES
FUSE BLOCK
8900440
8900441
C405

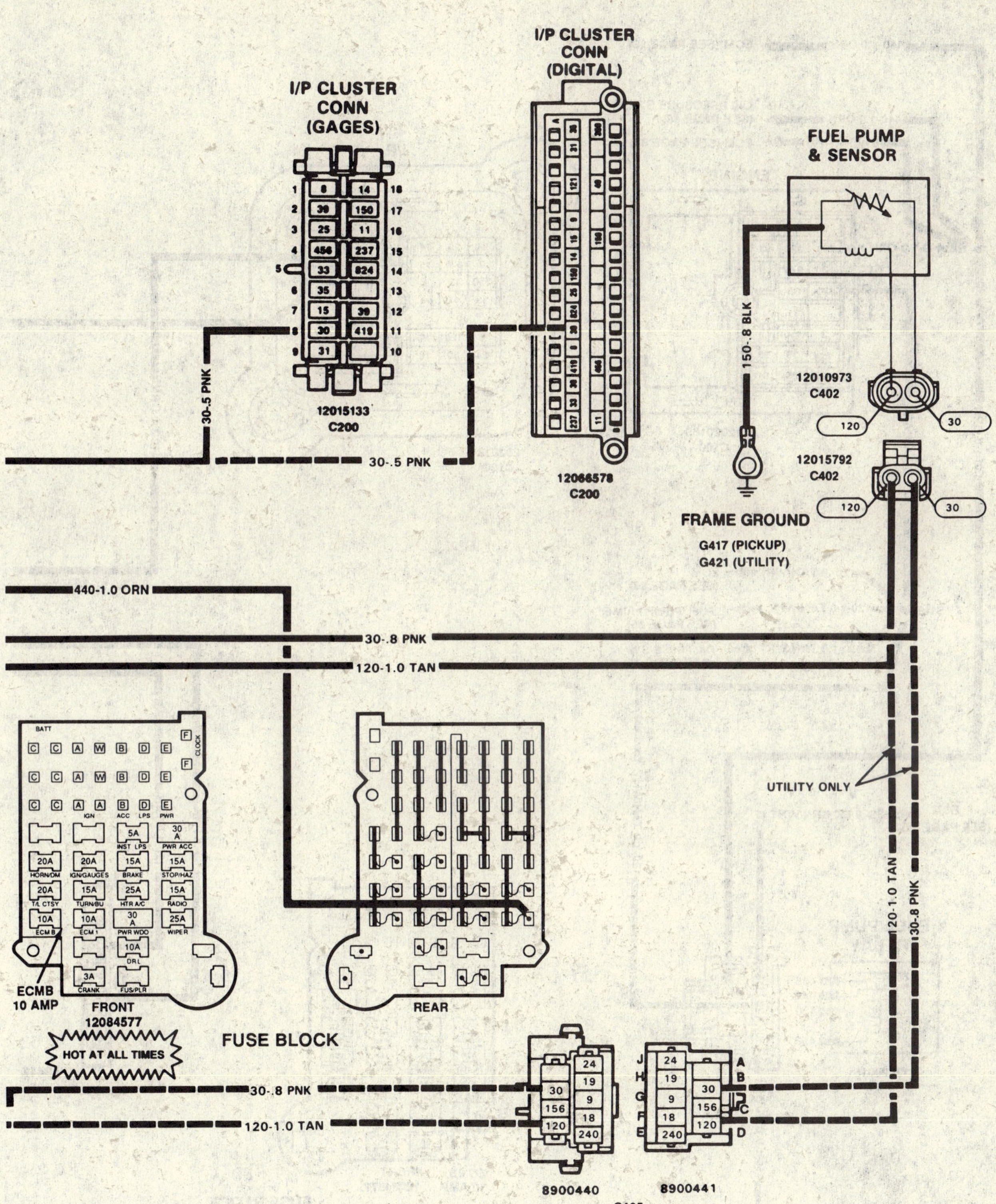

1988-91

440-1.0 ORN
ECM (SEE PAGE 88)
440-1.0 ORN
OIL PRESSURE SW
(SEE PAGE 88)
440-1.0 ORN
ECM (SEE PAGE 88)
ENGINE
440-1.0 ORN
12020183
C100
I/P
12020184
C100
440-1.0 ORN
120-1.0 TAN/WHT
440-1.0 ORN
120-.8 TAN/WHT
ECM
(SEE PAGE 88)
S115
120-1.0 TAN/WHT
FUEL PUMP PRIME
(SEE PAGE 88)
120-1.0 TAN/WHT
OIL PRESS SW
(SEE PAGE 88)
ECM
(SEE PAGE 88)
465-.8 DK GRN/WHT
120-1.0 TAN/WHT
FUEL PUMP
RELAY
12020015
C126
450-1.0 BLK/WHT
ECM
SYSTEM GROUND
G107
(SEE PAGE 88)
30-.8 PNK
120-1.0 TAN
C442
08900320
ECMB
10 AMP
FRONT
12084577
FUSE BLOCK
HOT AT ALL TIMES

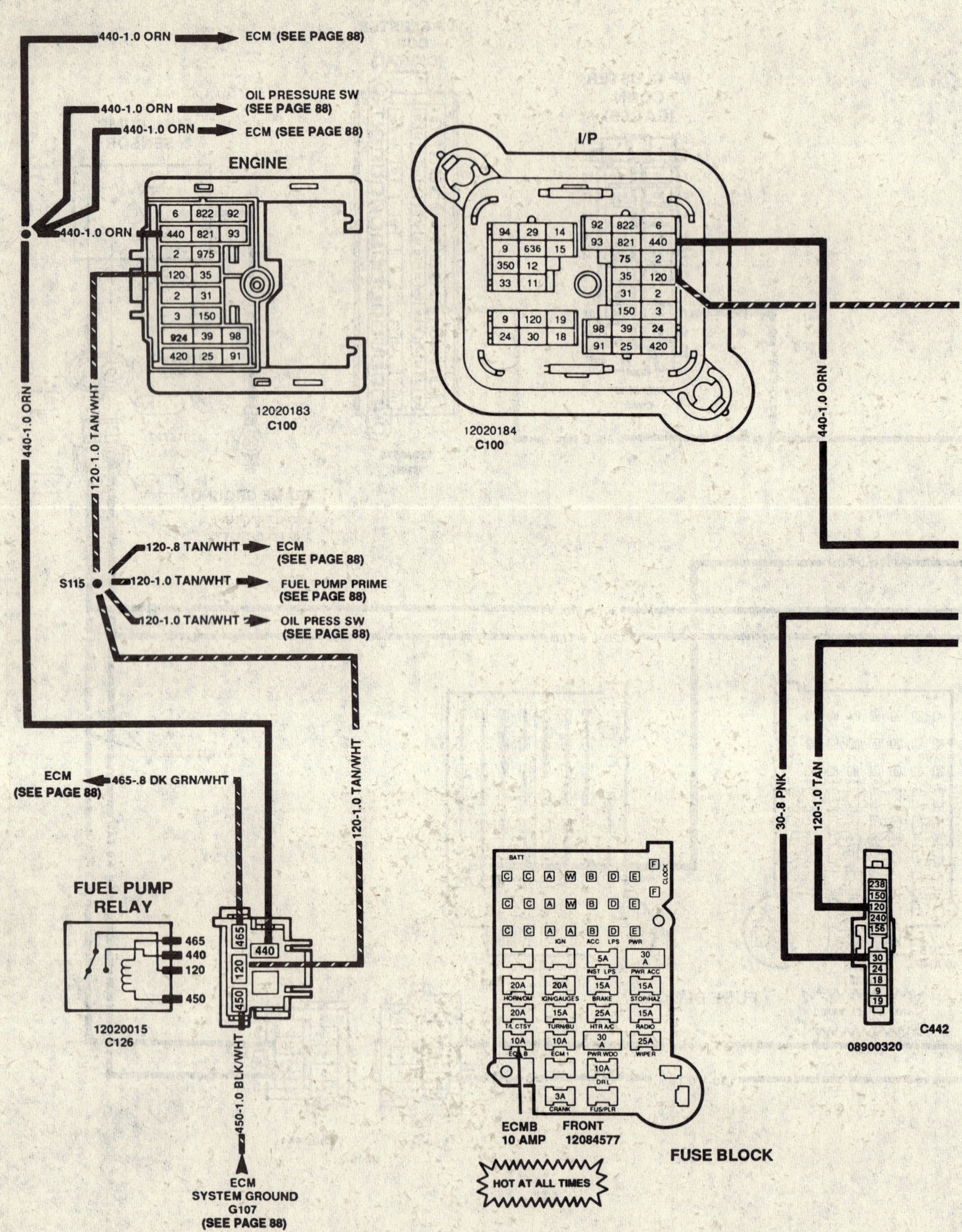

1988-91

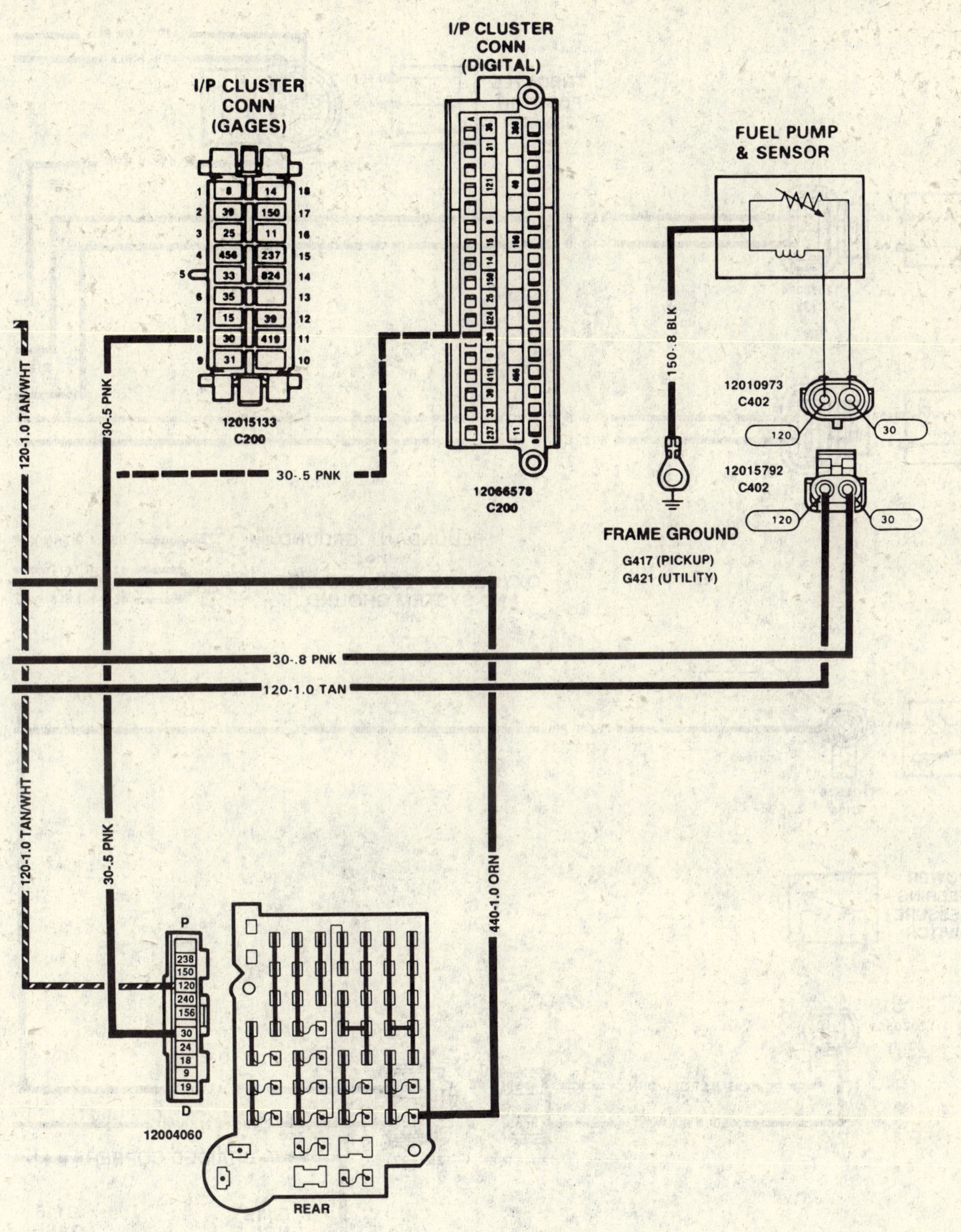

FUEL SENSOR - 4-DOOR UTILITY 91

1988-91

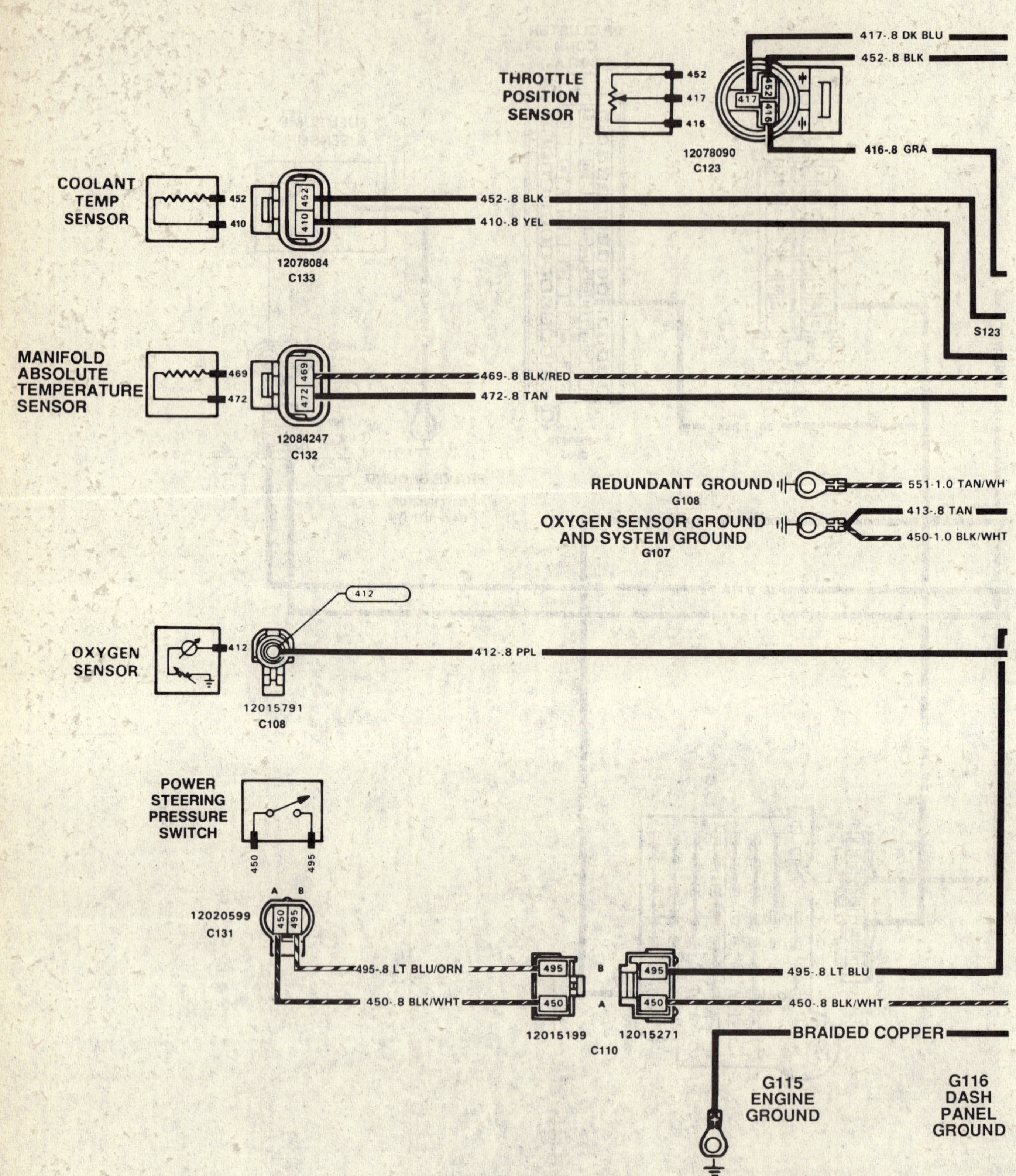

94 ELECTRONIC CONTROL MODULE - INPUTS - 2.5L (151 CID) ENGINE

1988-91

MANIFOLD ABSOLUTE PRESSURE SENSOR
416
432
469
12020403
C134
416-.8 GRA
469-.8 BLK/RED
432-.8 LT GRN
S122
416-.8 GRA
417-.8 DK BLU
452-.8 BLK
410-.8 YEL
S169
469-.8 BLK/RED
472-.8 TAN
452-.8 BLK
469-.8 BLK/RED
472-.8 TAN
413-.8 TAN
450-.8 BLK/WHT
412-.8 PPL
432-.8 LT GRN
416-.8 GRA
417-.8 DK BLU
495-.8 LT BLU
410-.8 YEL
551-1.0 TAN/WHT
450-1.0 BLK/WHT
FROM FUEL PUMP RELAY (SEE PAGE 83)
S120
150-1.0 BLK
A/C COMPRESSOR CLUTCH (SEE PAGE 125)
450-1.0 BLK/WHT
450-.8 BLK/WHT
495-.8 LT BLU
412-.8 PPL
450-.8 BLK/WHT
REAR WHEEL ANTILOCK BRAKE MODULE (SEE PAGE 116)
440-1.0 ORN
440-1.0 ORN
ENGINE
I/P
440-1.0 ORN
12020183
C100
12020184
C100

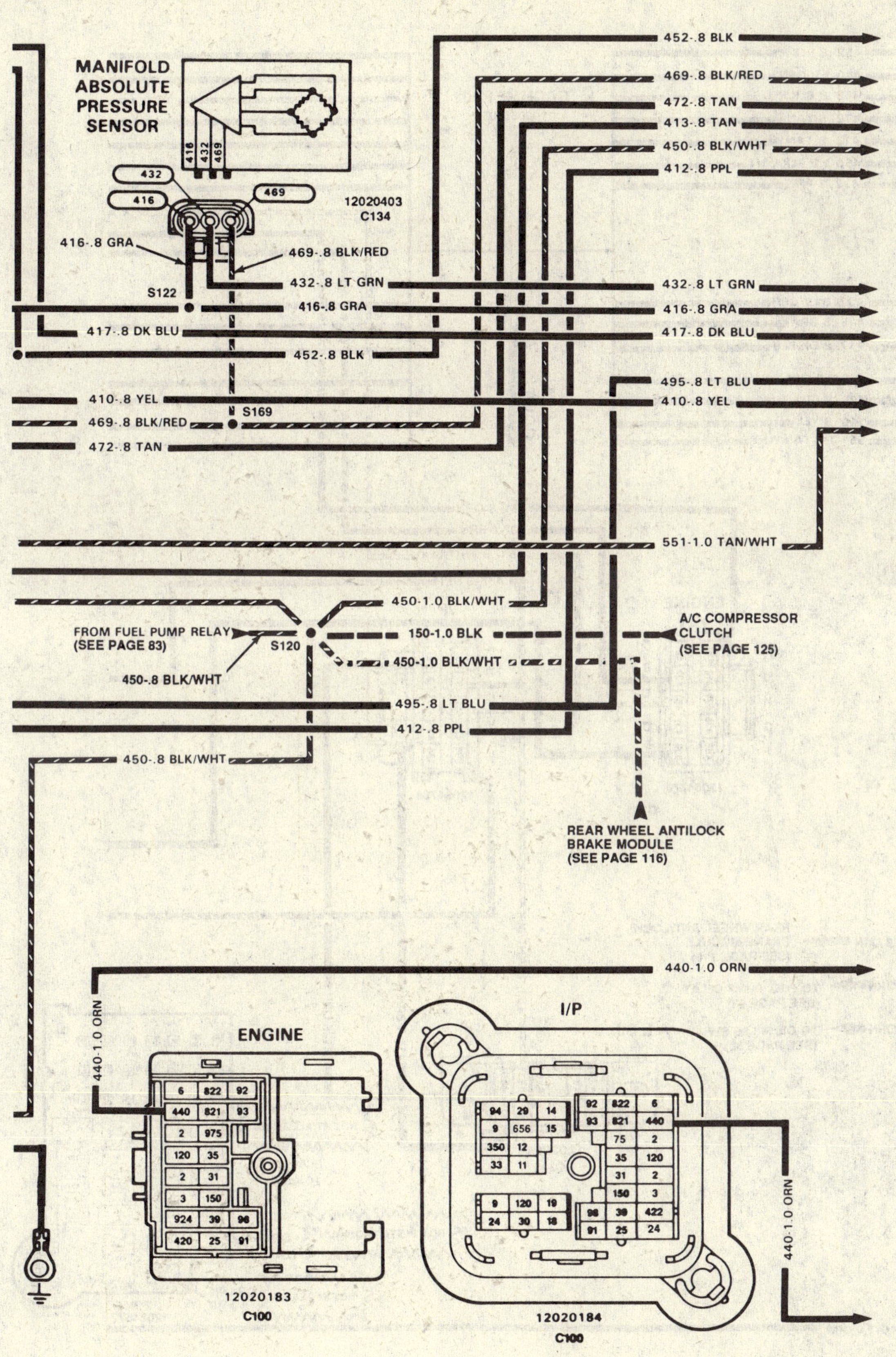

1988-91

452-.8 BLK
440-1.0 ORN
469-.8 BLK/RED
472-.8 TAN
413-.8 TAN
450-1.0 BLK/WHT
412-.8 PPL
GROMMET 301
12066507
432-.8 LT GRN
416-.8 GRA
417-.8 DK BLU
440-1.0 ORN
495-.8 LT BLU
410-.8 YEL
551-1.0 TAN/WHT
COWL
461-.8 ORN
437-.8 BRN
451-.8 WHT/BLK
437-.5 BRN
ENGINE
I/P
12064770
C101
12064764
440-1.0 ORN
440-1.0 ORN
440-.8 ORN
REAR WHEEL ANTILOCK BRAKE MODULE (SEE PAGE 116)
440-1.0 ORN
TO FUEL PUMP RELAY (SEE PAGE 83)
S114
440-1.0 ORN
TO OIL PRESS SW (SEE PAGE 83)
440-1.0 ORN
A.L.D.L.
451-.8 WHT/BLK
436-.8 BRN
461-.5 ORN
12020043
C308
HOT AT ALL TIMES
ECM B 10 AMP
HOT IN START OR RUN
ECM I 10 AMP
HOT IN START
CRANK 3 AMP
FRONT
12084577
440-1.0 ORN

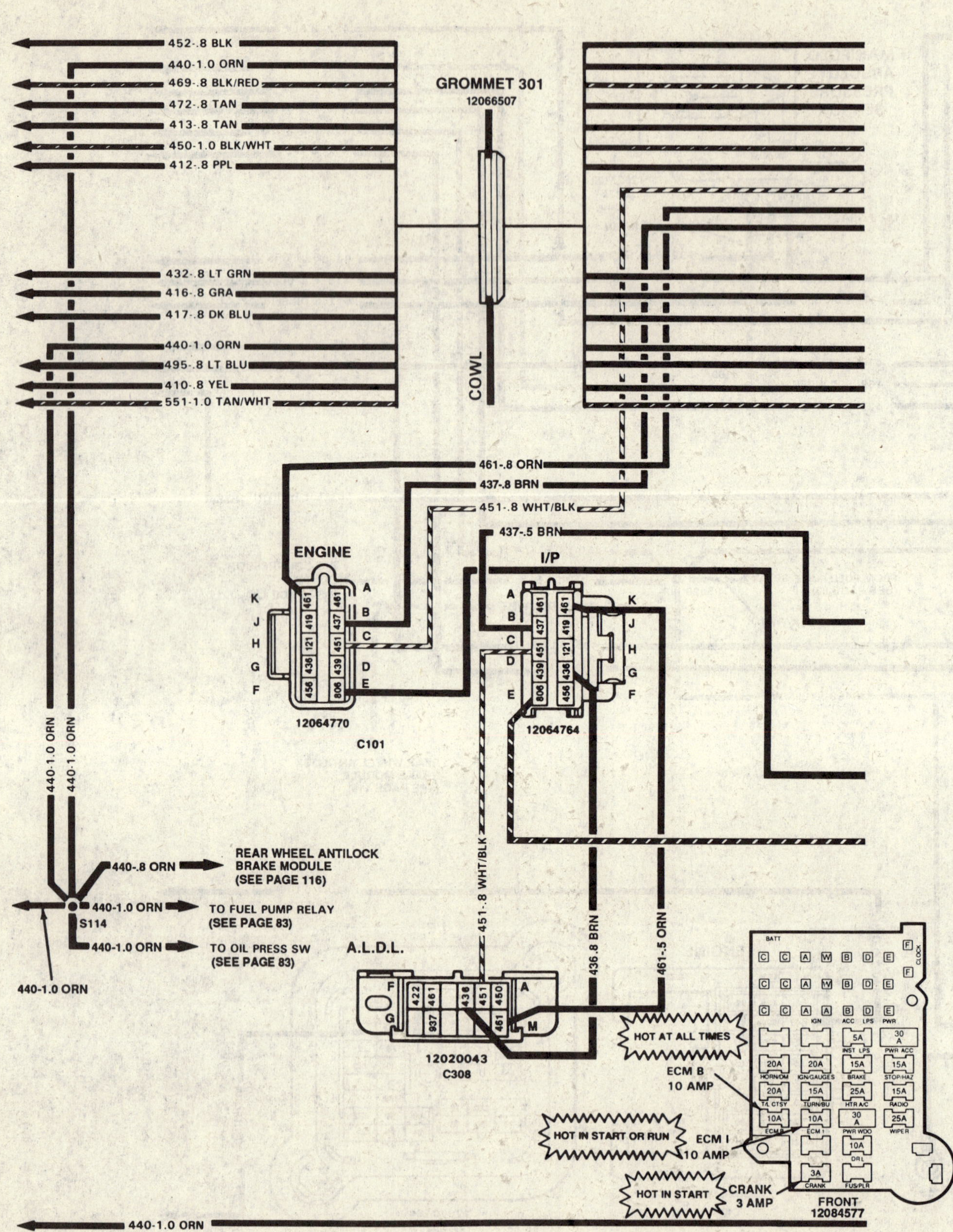

1988-91

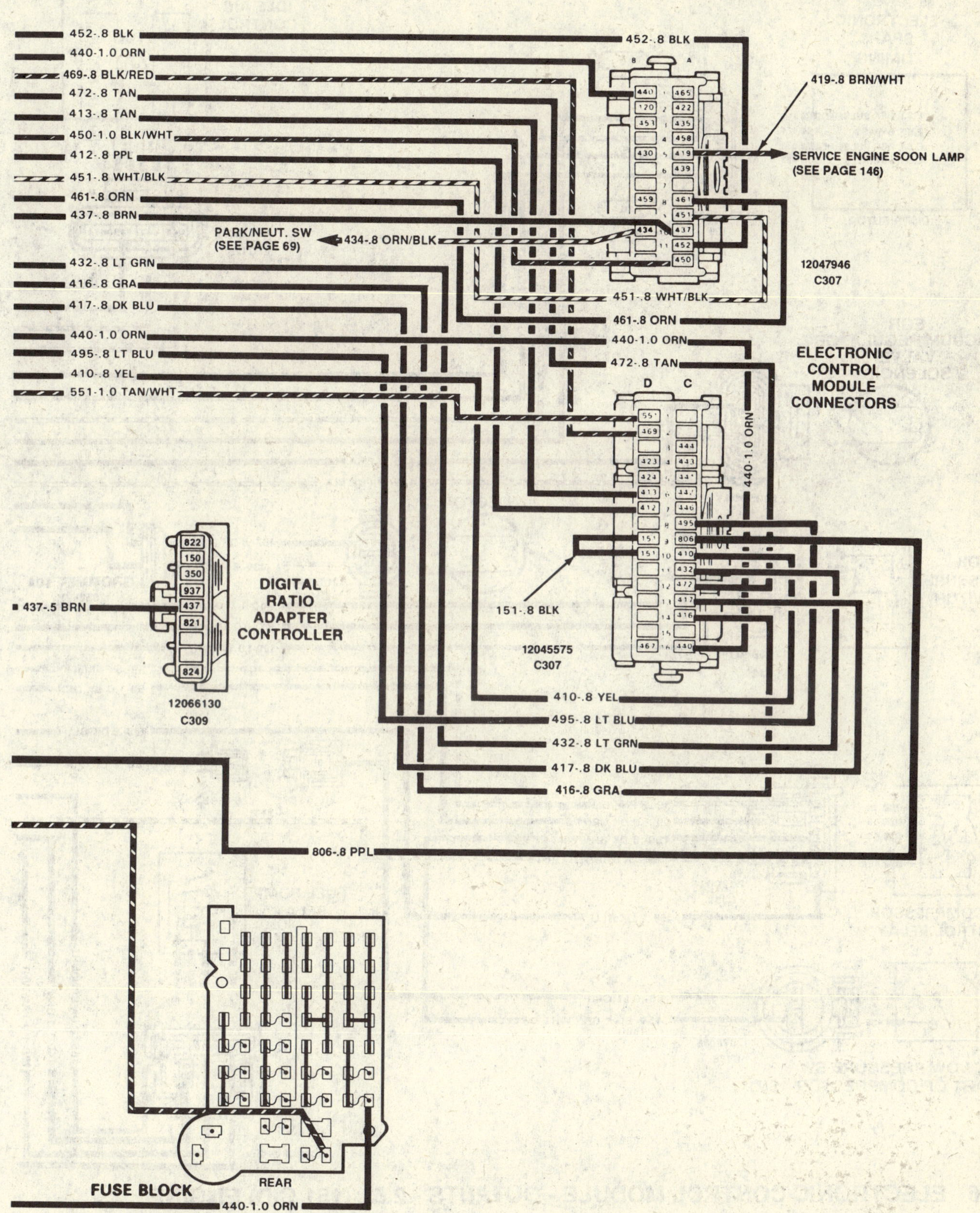

ELECTRONIC CONTROL MODULE - INPUTS - 2.5L (151 CID) ENGINE 95

1988-91

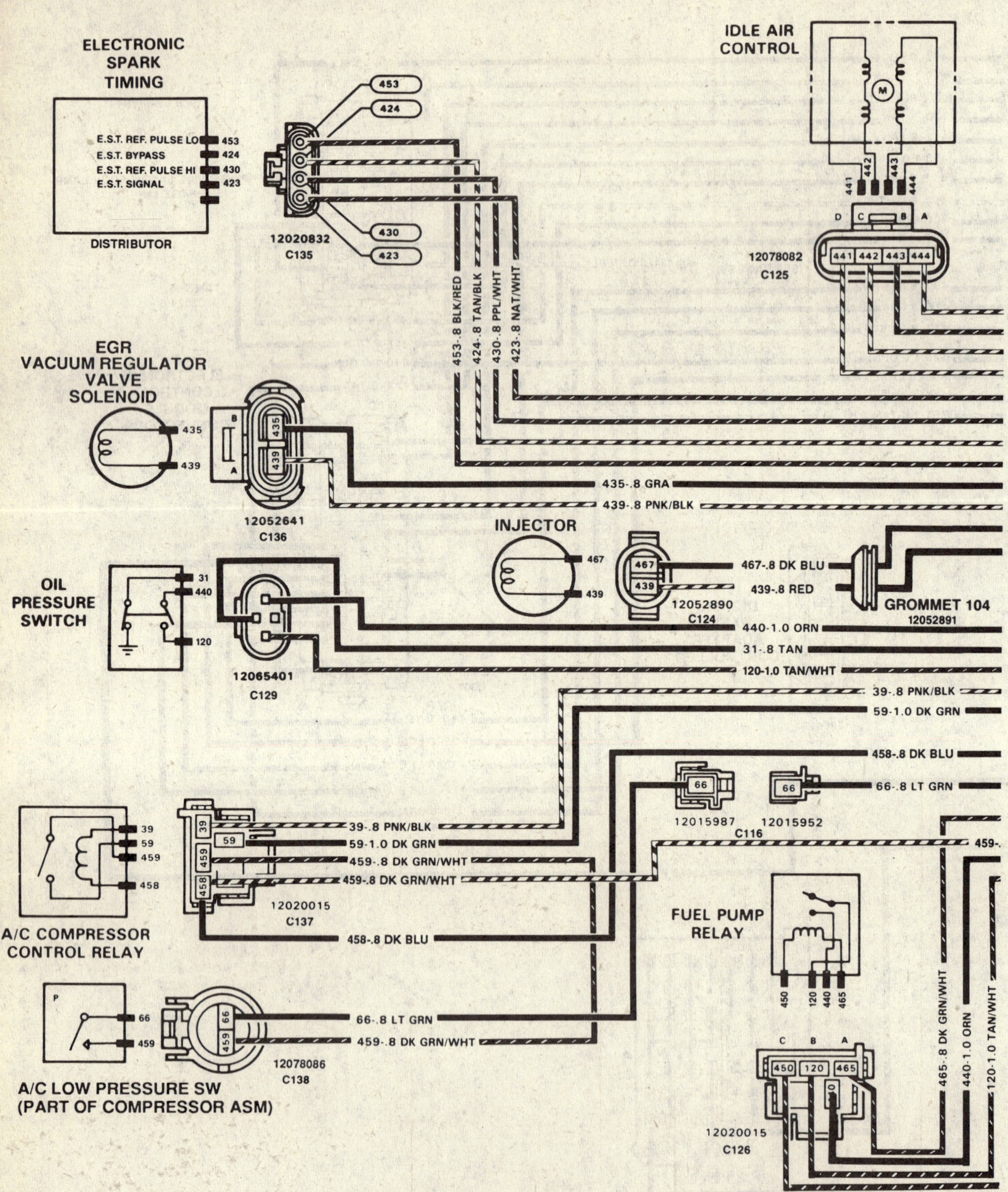

96 ELECTRONIC CONTROL MODULE - OUTPUTS - 2.5L (151 CID) ENGINE

1988-91

TRANSMISSION
CONVERTER
CLUTCH
SOLENOID
(W/AUTO.TRANS.)
422
420
422
420
A B
12015390
C139
422-.8 TAN/BLK
420-.8 PPL
120-.8 TAN/WHT
420-.8 PPL
444-.8 LT GRN/BLK
443-.8 LT GRN/WHT
442-.8 LT BLU/BLK
441-.8 LT BLU/WHT
423-.8 NAT/WHT
430-.8 PPL/WHT
424-.8 TAN/BLK
453-.8 BLK/RED
435-.8 GRA
439-.8 PNK/BLK
467-.8 DK BLU
439-.8 RED
440-1.0 ORN
31-.8 TAN
39-.8 PNK/BLK
TO A/C COMPRESSOR
CLUTCH (SEE PAGE 125)
458-.8 DK BLU
422-.8 TAN/BLK
TO A/C SELECTOR SW
(SEE PAGE 125)
465-.8 DK GRN/WHT
8 DK GRN/WHT
459-.8 DK GRN/WHT
440-1.0 ORN
120-1.0 TAN/WHT
450-.8 BLK/WHT
120-1.0 TAN/WHT
120-1.0 TAN/WHT
450-.8 BLK/WHT
FUEL
PUMP
PRIME
120
120-1.0 TAN/WHT
S126
120-1.0 TAN/WHT
2977253
C128

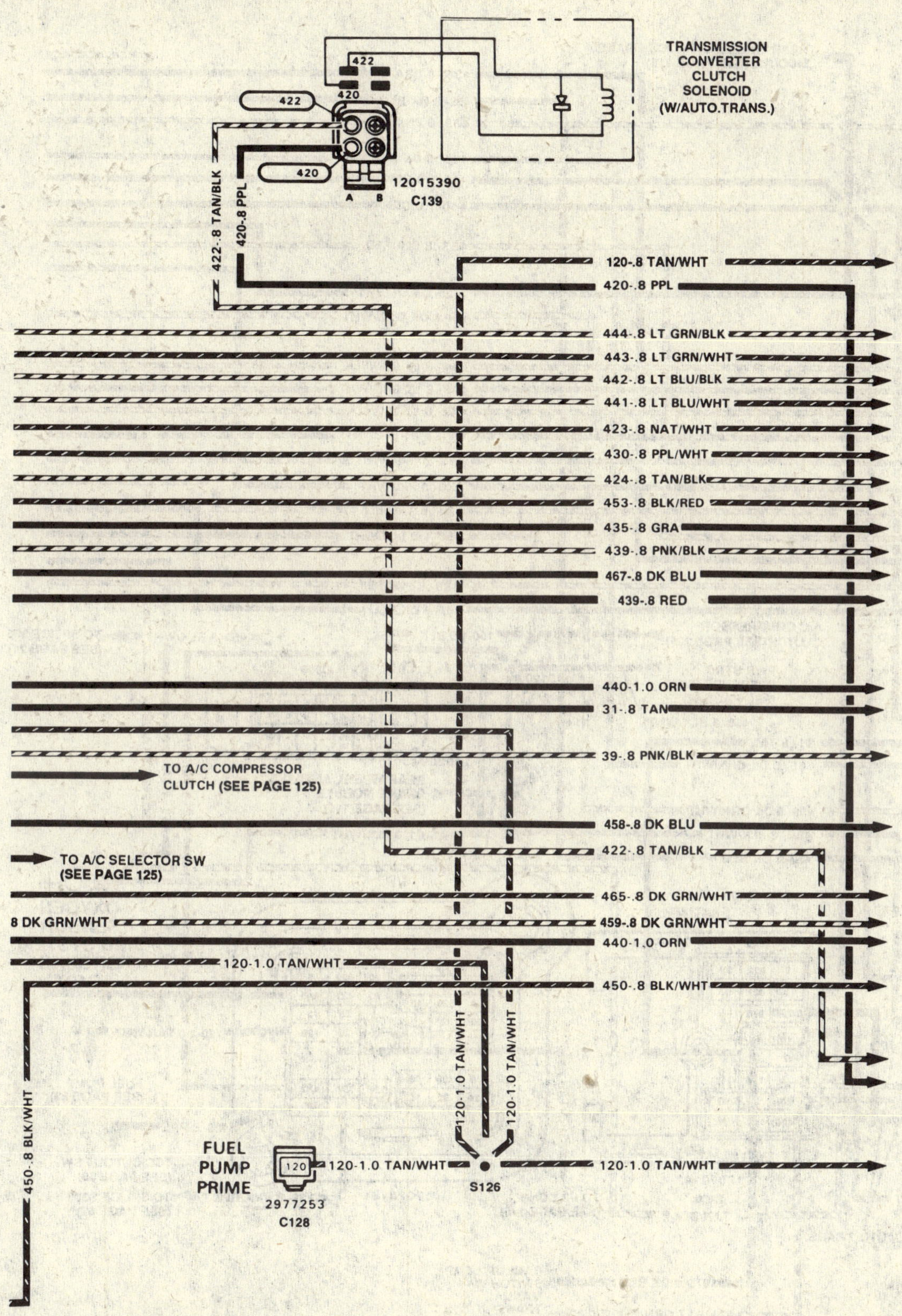

1988-91

REAR WHEEL ANTILOCK BRAKE MODULE (SEE PAGE 116)
S116
S114
440-.8 ORN
439-.8 PNK/BLK
439-.8 RED
435-.8 GRA
458-.8 DK BLU
465-.8 DK GRN/WHT
440-1.0 ORN
453-.8 BLK/RED
120-.8 TAN/WHT
459-.8 DK GRN/WHT
444-.8 LT GRN/BLK
443-.8 LT GRN/WHT
442-.8 LT BLU/BLK
441-.8 LT BLU/WHT
423-.8 NAT/WHT
430-.8 PPL/WHT
424-.8 TAN/BLK
450-1.0 BLK/WHT
467-.8 DK BLU
A/C COMPRESSOR CLUTCH(SEE PAGE 125)
150-1.0 BLK
450-.8 BLK/WHT
TO SPLICE 306 (SEE PAGE 21)
A.L.D.L.
C308
PWR STRG PRESSURE SW (SEE PAGE 94)
S120
31-.8 TAN
12020043
REAR WHEEL ANTILOCK BRAKE MODULE (SEE PAGE 116)
450-1.0 BKK/WHT
I/P
422-.8 TAN/WHT
413-.8 TAN
422-.8 TAN/BLK
OXYGEN SENSOR AND SYSTEM GROUND G107
ENGINE
120-1.0 TAN/WHT
FUEL PUMP (SEE PAGE 83)
31-.5 TAN
420-.8 PPL
TCC CUTOUT SW. (SEE PAGE 66)
12020183
C100
TO I/P CONN (SEE PAGE 146)
12020184
39-.8 PNK/BLK
TO SPLICE S303 (SEE PAGE 62)
W/AUTO. TRANS.
975-.8 DK BLU
924-.8 LT GRN/BLK
BACKUP LAMP SWITCH W/ MANUAL TRANS. (SEE PAGE 210)

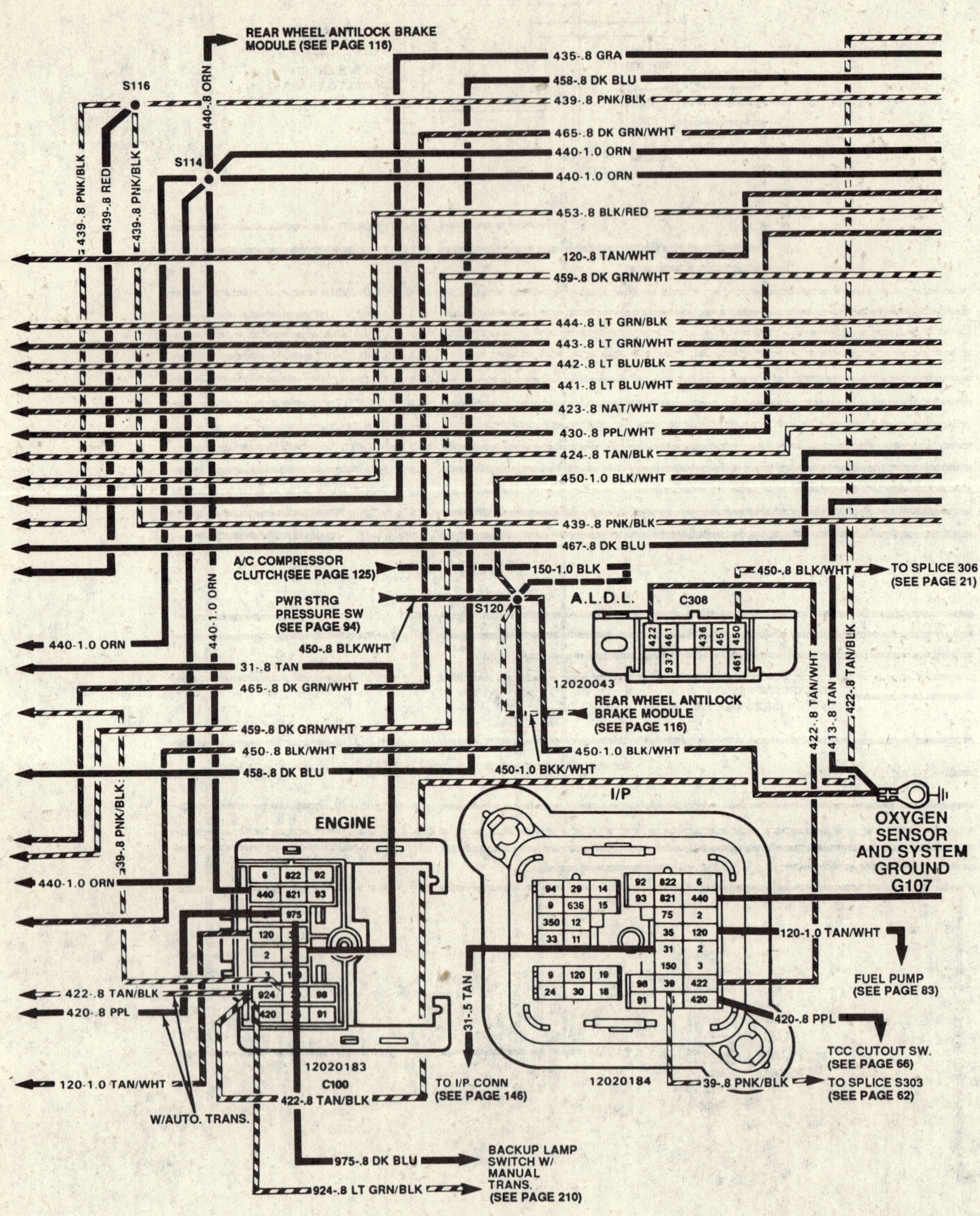

1988-91

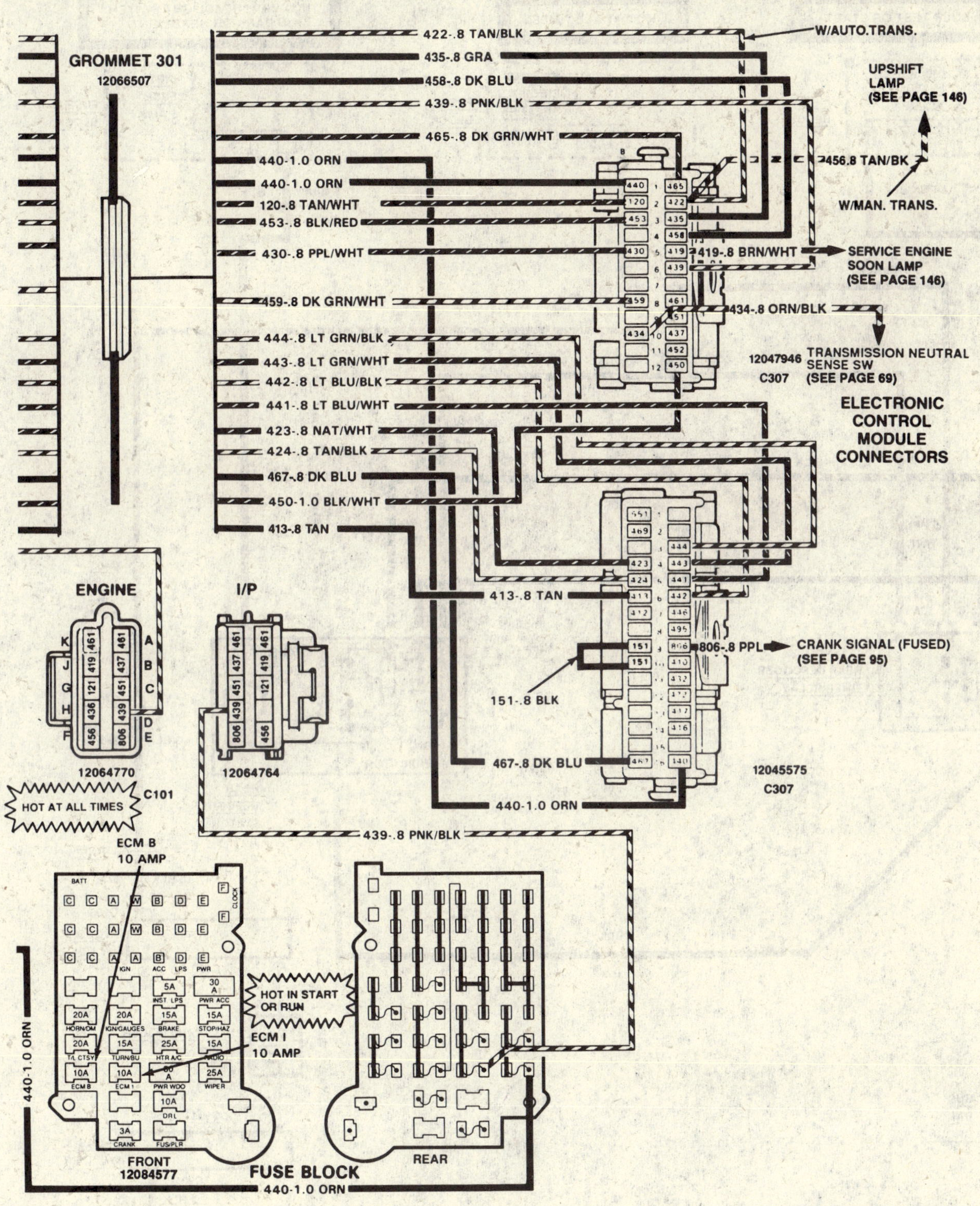

ELECTRONIC CONTROL MODULE - OUTPUTS - 2.5L (151 CID) ENGINE 97

1988-91

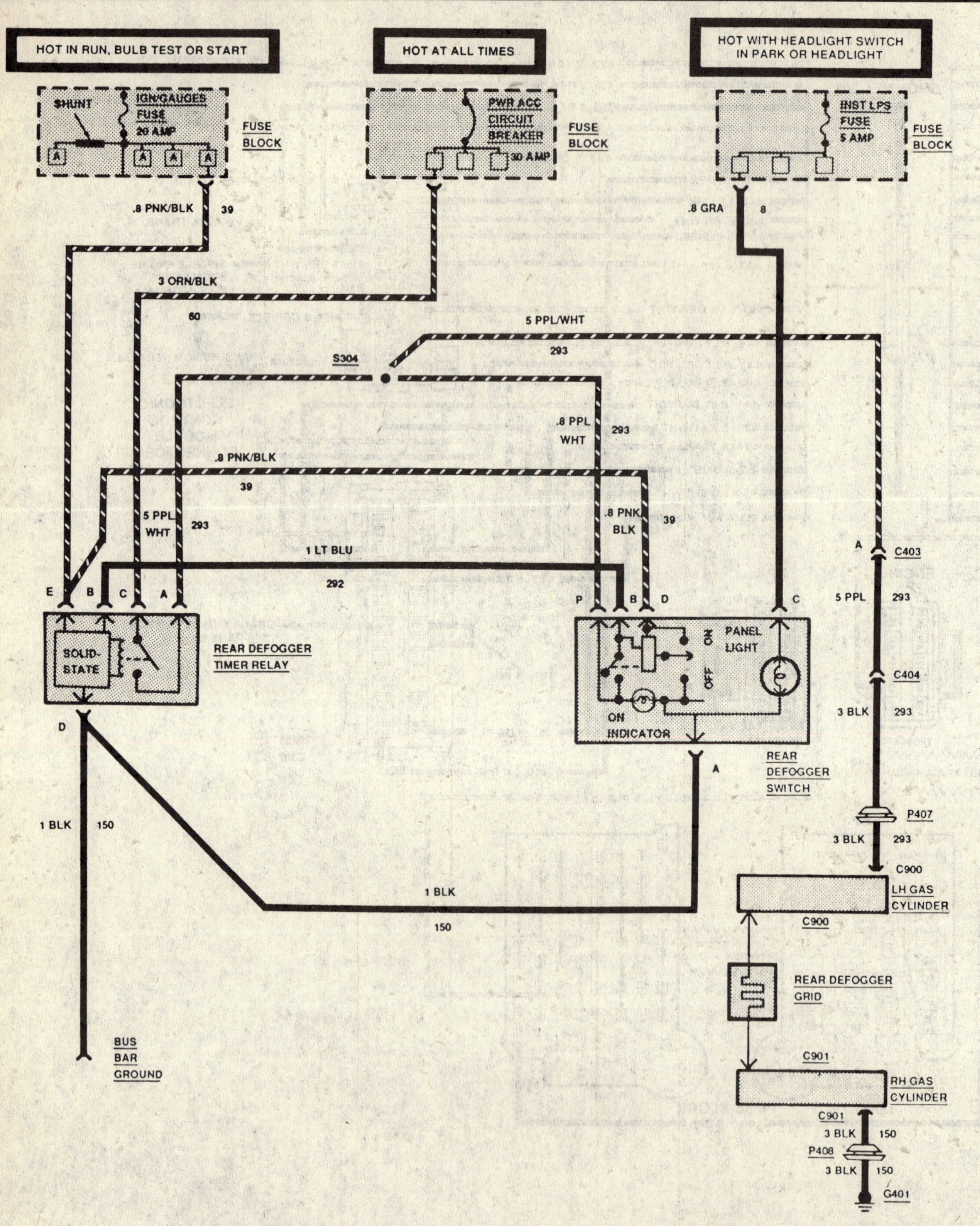

Electrical schematic of the Rear Defogger—Bravada

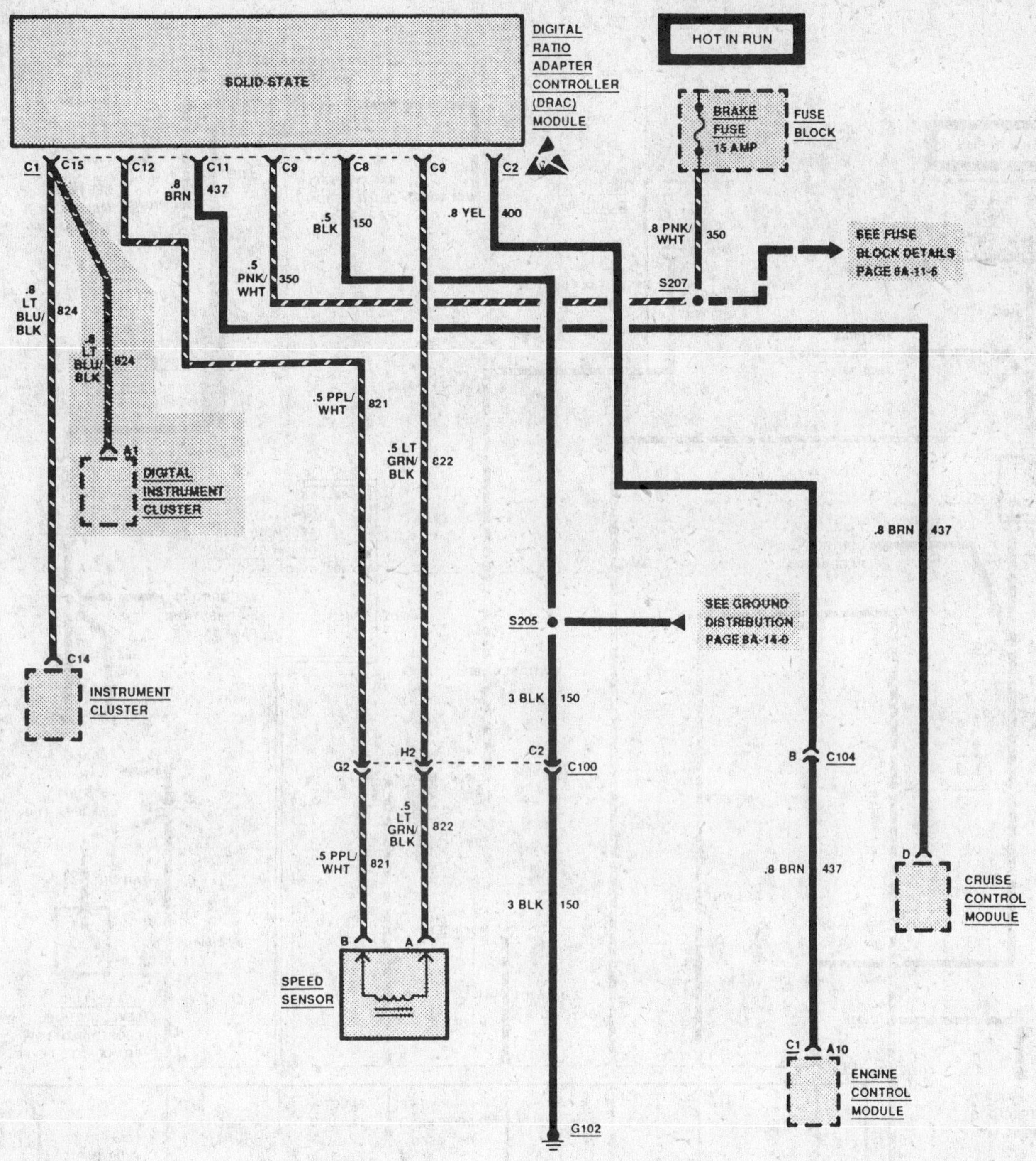

ECM CONNECTOR IDENTIFICATION
C1 · BLACK · 24 WAY
C2 · BLACK · 32 WAY

Electrical schematic of the Digital Ratio Adapter Controller (DRAC) module—Bravada

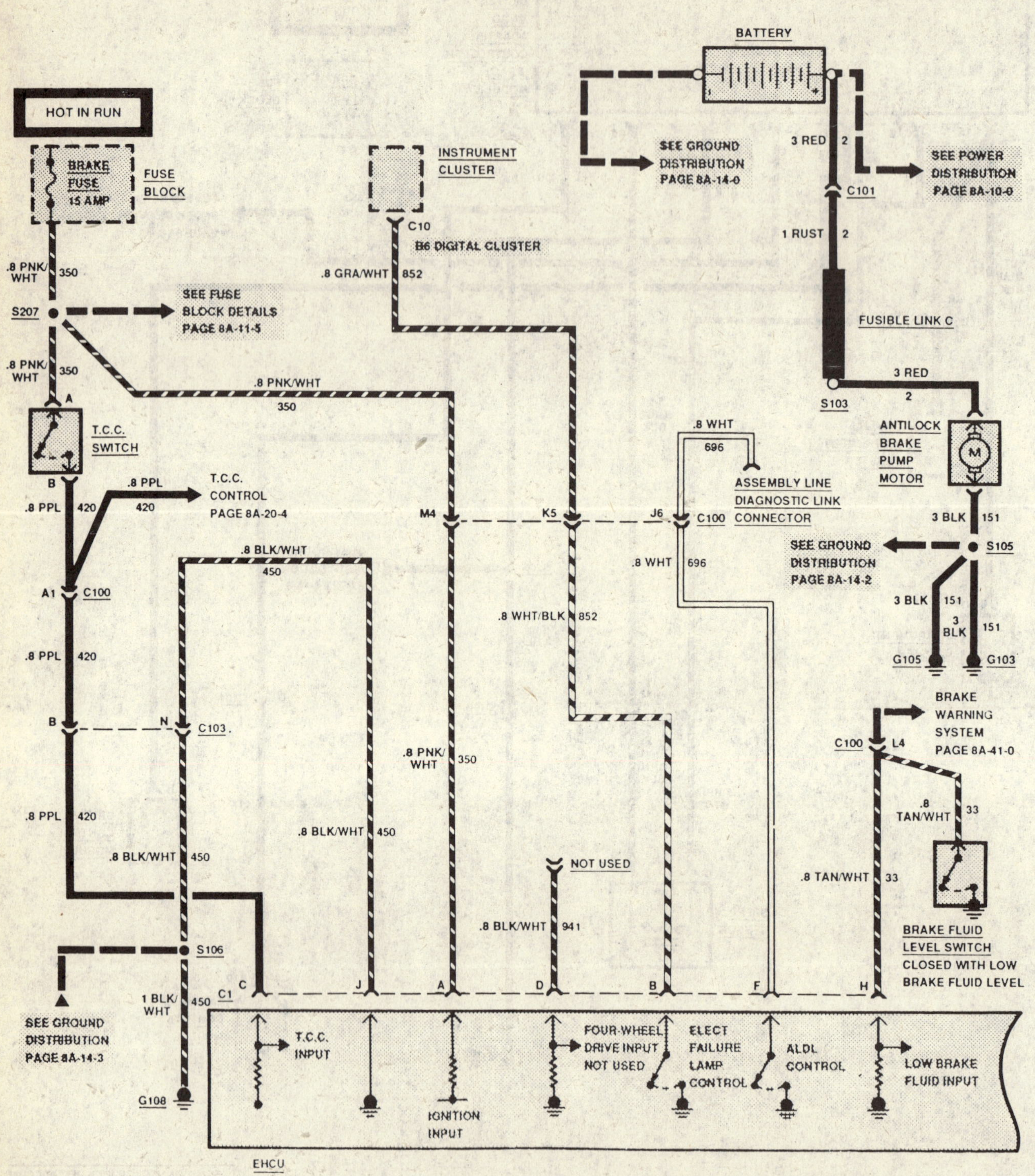

Electrical schematic of the Four-Wheel Antilock Brake System—Bravada

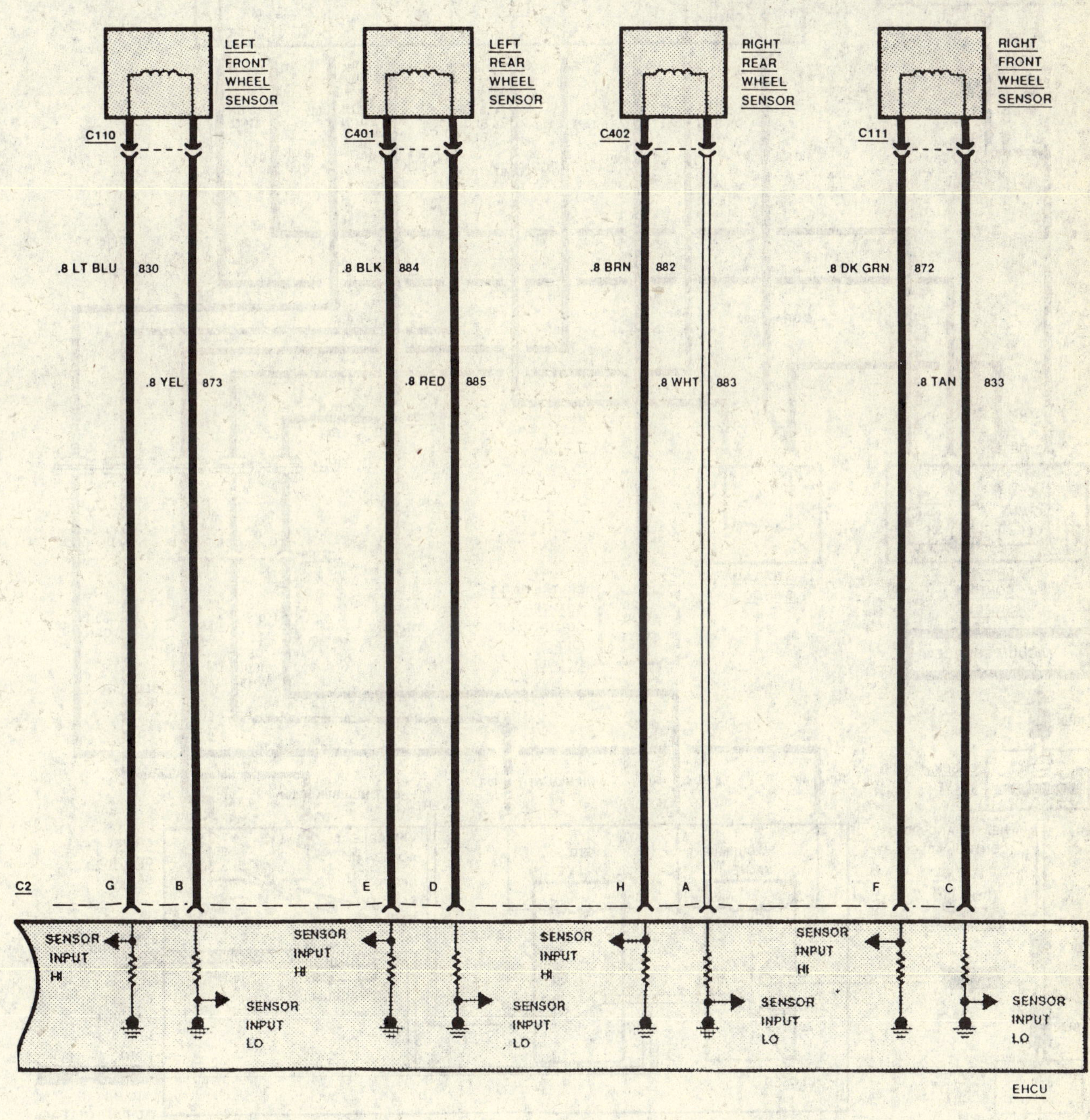

Electrical schematic of the Four-Wheel Antilock Brake System—Bravada, cont.

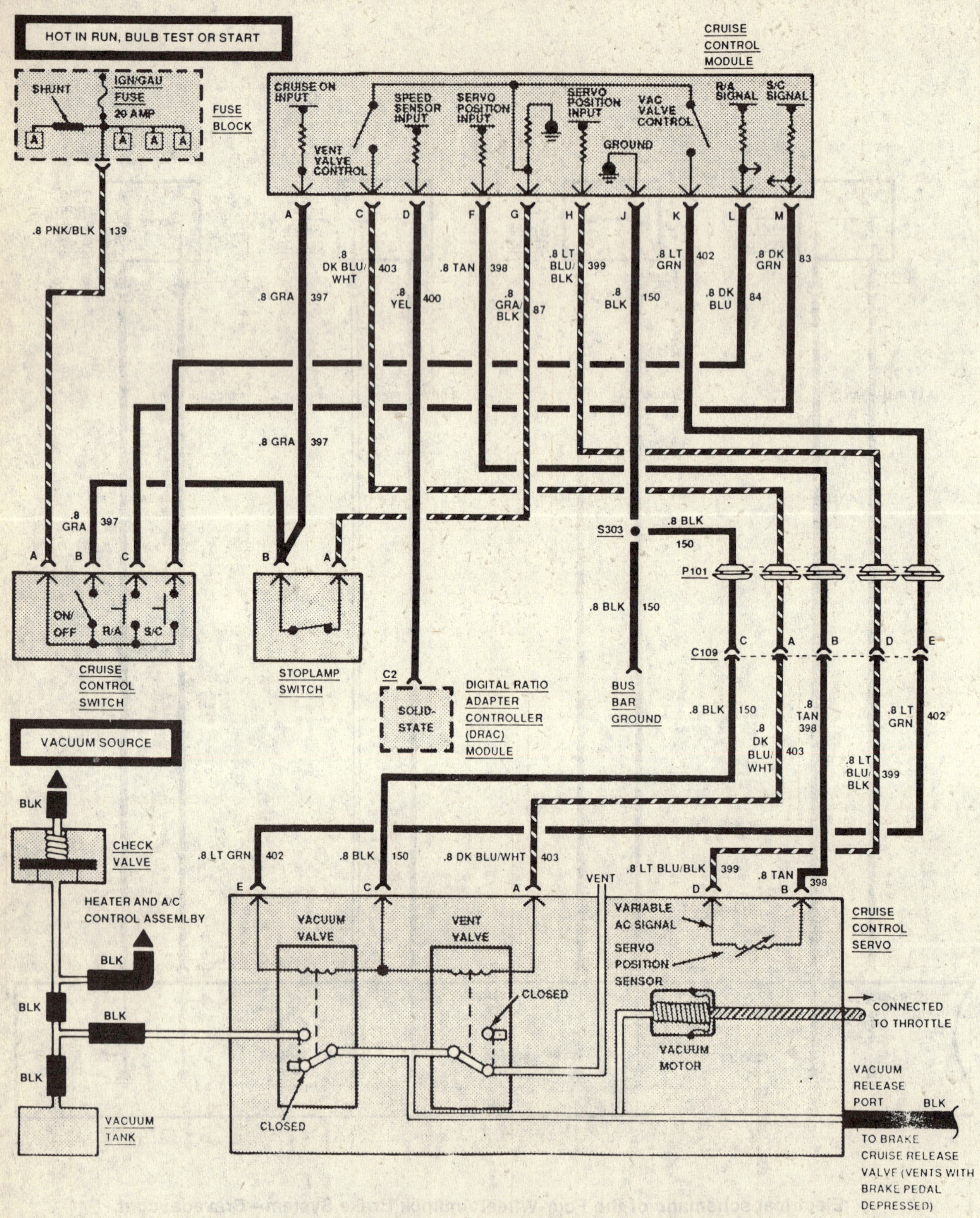

Electrical schematic of the Cruise Control—Bravada

7 Drive Train

QUICK REFERENCE INDEX

GENERAL INDEX

Troubleshooting the Manual Transmission and Transfer Case

Problem	Cause	Solution
Transmission shifts hard	• Clutch adjustment incorrect • Clutch linkage or cable binding • Shift rail binding • Internal bind in transmission caused by shift forks, selector plates, or synchronizer assemblies • Clutch housing misalignment • Incorrect lubricant • Block rings and/or cone seats worn	• Adjust clutch • Lubricate or repair as necessary • Check for mispositioned selector arm roll pin, loose cover bolts, worn shift rail bores, worn shift rail, distorted oil seal, or extension housing not aligned with case. Repair as necessary. • Remove, dissemble and inspect transmission. Replace worn or damaged components as necessary. • Check runout at rear face of clutch housing • Drain and refill transmission • Blocking ring to gear clutch tooth face clearance must be 0.030 inch or greater. If clearance is correct it may still be necessary to inspect blocking rings and cone seats for excessive wear. Repair as necessary.
Gear clash when shifting from one gear to another	• Clutch adjustment incorrect • Clutch linkage or cable binding • Clutch housing misalignment • Lubricant level low or incorrect lubricant • Gearshift components, or synchronizer assemblies worn or damaged	• Adjust clutch • Lubricate or repair as necessary • Check runout at rear of clutch housing • Drain and refill transmission and check for lubricant leaks if level was low. Repair as necessary. • Remove, disassemble and inspect transmission. Replace worn or damaged components as necessary.
Transmission noisy	• Lubricant level low or incorrect lubricant • Clutch housing-to-engine, or transmission-to-clutch housing bolts loose • Dirt, chips, foreign material in transmission • Gearshift mechanism, transmission gears, or bearing components worn or damaged • Clutch housing misalignment	• Drain and refill transmission. If lubricant level was low, check for leaks and repair as necessary. • Check and correct bolt torque as necessary • Drain, flush, and refill transmission • Remove, disassemble and inspect transmission. Replace worn or damaged components as necessary. • Check runout at rear face of clutch housing

Troubleshooting the Manual Transmission and Transfer Case (cont.)

Problem	Cause	Solution
Jumps out of gear	• Clutch housing misalignment	• Check runout at rear face of clutch housing
	• Gearshift lever loose	• Check lever for worn fork. Tighten loose attaching bolts.
	• Offset lever nylon insert worn or lever attaching nut loose	• Remove gearshift lever and check for loose offset lever nut or worn insert. Repair or replace as necessary.
	• Gearshift mechanism, shift forks, selector plates, interlock plate, selector arm, shift rail, detent plugs, springs or shift cover worn or damaged	• Remove, disassemble and inspect transmission cover assembly. Replace worn or damaged components as necessary.
	• Clutch shaft or roller bearings worn or damaged	• Replace clutch shaft or roller bearings as necessary
Jumps out of gear (cont.)	• Gear teeth worn or tapered, synchronizer assemblies worn or damaged, excessive end play caused by worn thrust washers or output shaft gears	• Remove, disassemble, and inspect transmission. Replace worn or damaged components as necessary.
	• Pilot bushing worn	• Replace pilot bushing
Will not shift into one gear	• Gearshift selector plates, interlock plate, or selector arm, worn, damaged, or incorrectly assembled	• Remove, disassemble, and inspect transmission cover assembly. Repair or replace components as necessary.
	• Shift rail detent plunger worn, spring broken, or plug loose	• Tighten plug or replace worn or damaged components as necessary
	• Gearshift lever worn or damaged	• Replace gearshift lever
	• Synchronizer sleeves or hubs, damaged or worn	• Remove, disassemble and inspect transmission. Replace worn or damaged components.
Locked in one gear—cannot be shifted out	• Shift rail(s) worn or broken, shifter fork bent, setscrew loose, center detent plug missing or worn	• Inspect and replace worn or damaged parts
	• Broken gear teeth on countershaft gear, clutch shaft, or reverse idler gear	• Inspect and replace damaged part
	Gearshift lever broken or worn, shift mechanism in cover incorrectly assembled or broken, worn damaged gear train components	• Disassemble transmission. Replace damaged parts or assemble correctly.

Troubleshooting the Manual Transmission and Transfer Case (cont.)

Problem	Cause	Solution
Transfer case difficult to shift or will not shift into desired range	• Vehicle speed too great to permit shifting	• Stop vehicle and shift into desired range. Or reduce speed to 3–4 km/h (2–3 mph) before attempting to shift.
	• If vehicle was operated for extended period in 4H mode on dry paved surface, driveline torque load may cause difficult shifting	• Stop vehicle, shift transmission to neutral, shift transfer case to 2H mode and operate vehicle in 2H on dry paved surfaces
	• Transfer case external shift linkage binding	• Lubricate or repair or replace linkage, or tighten loose components as necessary
	• Insufficient or incorrect lubricant	• Drain and refill to edge of fill hole
	• Internal components binding, worn, or damaged	• Disassemble unit and replace worn or damaged components as necessary
Transfer case noisy in all drive modes	• Insufficient or incorrect lubricant	• Drain and refill to edge of fill hole Check for leaks and repair if necessary. Note: If unit is still noisy after drain and refill, disassembly and inspection may be required to locate source of noise.
Noisy in—or jumps out of four wheel drive low range	• Transfer case not completely engaged in 4L position	• Stop vehicle, shift transfer case in Neutral, then shift back into 4L position
	• Shift linkage loose or binding	• Tighten, lubricate, or repair linkage as necessary
	• Shift fork cracked, inserts worn, or fork is binding on shift rail	• Disassemble unit and repair as necessary
Lubricant leaking from output shaft seals or from vent	• Transfer case overfilled • Vent closed or restricted	• Drain to correct level • Clear or replace vent if necessary
Lubricant leaking from output shaft seals or from vent (cont.)	• Output shaft seals damaged or installed incorrectly	• Replace seals. Be sure seal lip faces interior of case when installed. Also be sure yoke seal surfaces are not scored or nicked. Remove scores, nicks with fine sandpaper or replace yoke(s) if necessary.
Abnormal tire wear	• Extended operation on dry hard surface (paved) roads in 4H range	• Operate in 2H on hard surface (paved) roads

MANUAL TRANSMISSION

Identification

Manual transmissions are officially identified by using the following descriptions:

a. The number of forward gears.

b. The measured distance between the center lines of the mainshaft and the countergear.

The 4-speed (77.5mm) transmission is a fully synchronized unit with blocker ring synchronizers and a sliding mesh reverse gear. It is contained in an aluminum alloy case with an integral clutch housing, a center support and an extension housing, which houses some of the gears, bearings and shafts. The shift lever is mounted on top of the extension housing. Tis transmission is used with the 2.8L 6-cylinder and the 1.9L 4-cylinder engines. The easiest way to identify the 77.5mm transmission is that the gear box and bell housing are one casting.

The 4-speed (77mm) and 5-speed (77mm) model transmissions are fully synchronized units with blocker ring synchronizers and a sliding mesh reverse gear. They have the more familiar aluminum gear box type of transmission case that houses the various gears, bearings and shafts. The floor-mounted gearshift lever assembly is located on top of the extension housing. The ML2 model is used with the 2.5L 4-cylinder engine; the ML3 model is used with the V6 engine. The easiest way to identify 77mm transmissions is that the gear box can be removed from the bell housing.

Adjustments

CLUTCH SWITCH

A clutch switch is located under the instrument panel and attached to the top of the clutch pedal. Its function is to prevent starter operation unless the clutch pedal is depressed. On some vehicles, the switch must be adjusted for reliable starter operation.

1. Remove the lower steering column-to-instrument panel cover.
2. Disconnect the electrical connector from the clutch switch.
3. Be sure to leave any carpets and floor mats in place when making the adjustment.
4. At the clutch switch, move the slider (A) rearward (towards the clutch switch) on the clutch switch shaft (B).
5. Push the clutch pedal to the floor. A clicking noise will be heard as the switch adjusts itself.

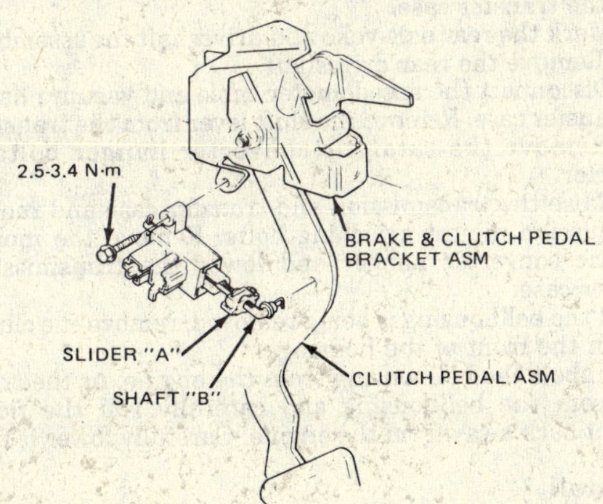

On some models the clutch safety start switch is adjustable

6. Release the clutch pedal; the adjustment is complete.
7. Reconnect the switch and test it.

Shift Lever

REMOVAL AND INSTALLATION

1. With the transmission in Neutral, loosen the lock nut under the shift knob and unscrew the knob from the lever.
2. Unscrew and remove the shifter boot.
3, On 1984–91 models, there is another lock nut which can be loosened to remove upper portion of the lever.
4. Remove the bolts to remove the shift lever from the housing assembly.
5. When reassembling, lightly lubricate the shifter with moly grease and use a new gasket or silicone sealer. Torque the bolts to 10 ft. lbs. (13 Nm).

Back-Up Light Switch

REMOVAL AND INSTALLATION

1. Disconnect the negative battery terminal from the battery.
2. At the left-rear of the transmission, the back-up light switch is threaded into the transmission case. The speed sensor is held in with a separate bracket. Disconnect the electrical connector from the back-up light switch.
3. Remove the back-up light switch from the transmission.
4. To install, reverse the removal procedures. Place the gear shift lever in the reverse position and check the back-up lights work.

Extension Housing Seal

REMOVAL AND INSTALLATION

2-Wheel Drive

This seal controls transmission oil leakage around the driveshaft. Continued failure of this seal usually indicates a worn output shaft bushing. If so, there will be signs of the same wear on the driveshaft where it contacts the seal and bushing. The seal is available and is fairly simple to install, with the proper tool.

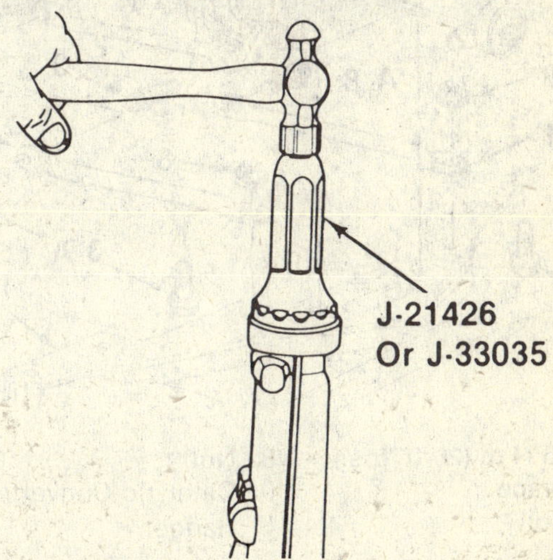

Using an oil seal installation tool on the extension housing seal

1. Raise and safely support rear of the vehicle to minimumize transmission oil loss when the driveshaft is removed.
2. Unbolt the driveshaft from the differential and center support bearing, if equipped. Wrap tape around the bearing cups to keep them in place on the universal joint and slide the shaft out of the transmission.
3. Use a small pry tool to carefully pry out the old seal. Be carefull not to insert the tool too far into the housing or the bushing will be damaged.
4. Use an oil seal installation tool to evenly drive the new seal into the housing. Make sure the tool only contacts the outer metal portion of the seal.
5. Install the driveshaft. Torque the universal bearing cup retainer bolts to 15 ft. lbs. Torque the center bearing bolts to 25 ft. lbs.

Transmission

REMOVAL AND INSTALLATION

2-Wheel Drive

1. Disconnect the negative battery terminal from the battery.
2. If the bell housing is being removed with the transmission (77.5mm 4-speed) remove the starter. The 77mm 4- and 5-speed can be removed without removing the bellhousing.
3. Shift the transmission into Neutral. Remove the shift lever boot-to-console screws and slide the boot up the shift lever.
4. Remove the shift lever.
5. Raise and safely support the truck on jackstands. Remove the drain plug and drain the oil. Dispose of old oil properly at a reclaimation center, such as a gas station or parts retailer.
6. Disconnect the speedometer cable and/or the electrical wiring connectors from the transmission.
7. Remove the driveshaft(s). Refer to the Driveline section if necessary.
8. Disconnect the exhaust pipe-to-exhaust manifold nuts and separate the exhaust pipe from the manifold.
9. On the 1982–83 models, disconnect the clutch cable from the clutch lever. On the 1984–91 models, remove the clutch slave cylinder from the clutch release lever. It can be secured out of the way without disconnecting the hydraulic line.
10. Position a floor jack under the transmission and support the transmission. Secure the jack to the transmission so it won't slip

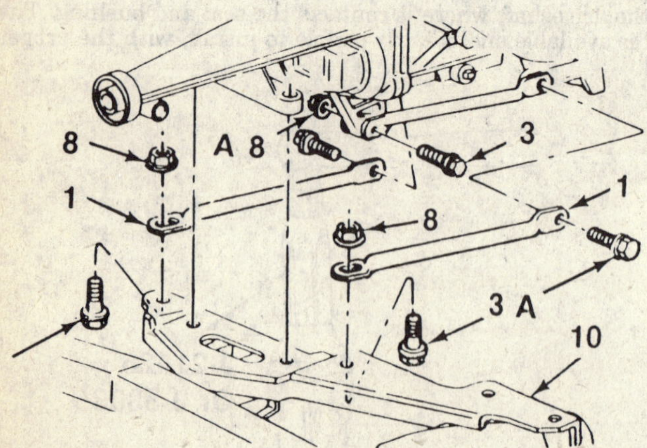

A. 35 N·m (26 ft. lbs.)
1. Brace
3. Bolt
8. Nut
10. Catalytic Converter Hanger

Catalytic converter hanger assembly under transmission

11. Remove the transmission-to-crossmember mount bolts.
12. Remove the catalytic converter-to-chassis hanger bolts.
13. Remove the crossmember-to-chassis bolts and the crossmember from the vehicle.
14. If the bellhousing is being removed, remove the clutch cover from the front of the housing.
15. Unbolt the bellhousing from the engine, or the transmission from the bellhousing and carefully roll the floor jack straight back away from the engine. Carefully lower it from the vehicle.

To install

16. Lightly coat the input shaft spline with high temperature or molyebdenum grease. Don't use too much or the clutch disc will be ruined.
17. If the clutch was removed, make sure it is properly aligned or it will be impossible to install the transmission.
18. Put the transmission into high gear.
19. With the transmission properly placed behind the engine, turn the output shaft slowly to engage the splines of the input shaft into the clutch while pushing the transmission forward into place. Don't force it, the transmission will easily fall into place when everything is properly aligned.
20. On 4-cylinder engines with the 77.5mm transmission, torque the bellhousing-to-engine bolts to 25 ft. lbs. On all others, torque all the bolts to 55 ft. lbs.
21. Install the cross member and torque the bolts to 25 ft. lbs.
22. Install the support braces and catalyst hanger and torque the nuts and bolts to 35 ft. lbs.
23. Install the clutch inspection cover and starter.
24. On 1984–91 models, install the slave cylinder and if necessary, attach the hydraulic line and bleed the system.
25. On earlier models, attach the clutch cable and push the pedal to test its operation.
26. Install the shift lever and boot.
27. Reassemble the exhaust system.
28. Install the driveshaft and refill the transmission with the proper oil.
20. Connect the wiring for the back-up lights and speed sensor, or the speedometer cable.
30. Lower the vehicle to the ground and reconnect the battery.

4-Wheel Drive

1. Shift the transfer case into **4H**.
2. Disconnect the negative battery cable.
3. Raise and support the vehicle safely. Remove the skid plate.
4. Drain the lubricant from the transfer case.
5. Mark the transfer case front output shaft yoke and driveshaft for assembly reference. Disconnect the front driveshaft from the transfer case.
6. Mark the rear axle yoke and driveshaft for assembly reference. Remove the rear driveshaft.
7. Disconnect the speedometer cable and vacuum harness at the transfer case. Remove the shift lever from the transfer case.
8. Remove the catalytic converter hanger bolts at the converter.
9. Raise the transmission and transfer case and remove the transmission mount attaching bolts. Remove the mount and catalytic converter hanger and lower the transmission and transfer case.
10. If the bellhousing is being removed, remove the clutch cover from the front of the housing.
11. Unbolt the bellhousing from the engine, or the transmission from the bellhousing and carefully roll the floor jack straight back away from the engine. Carefully lower it from the vehicle.

To install

12. Lightly coat the input shaft spline with high temperature or molyebdenum grease. Don't use too much or the clutch disc will be ruined.

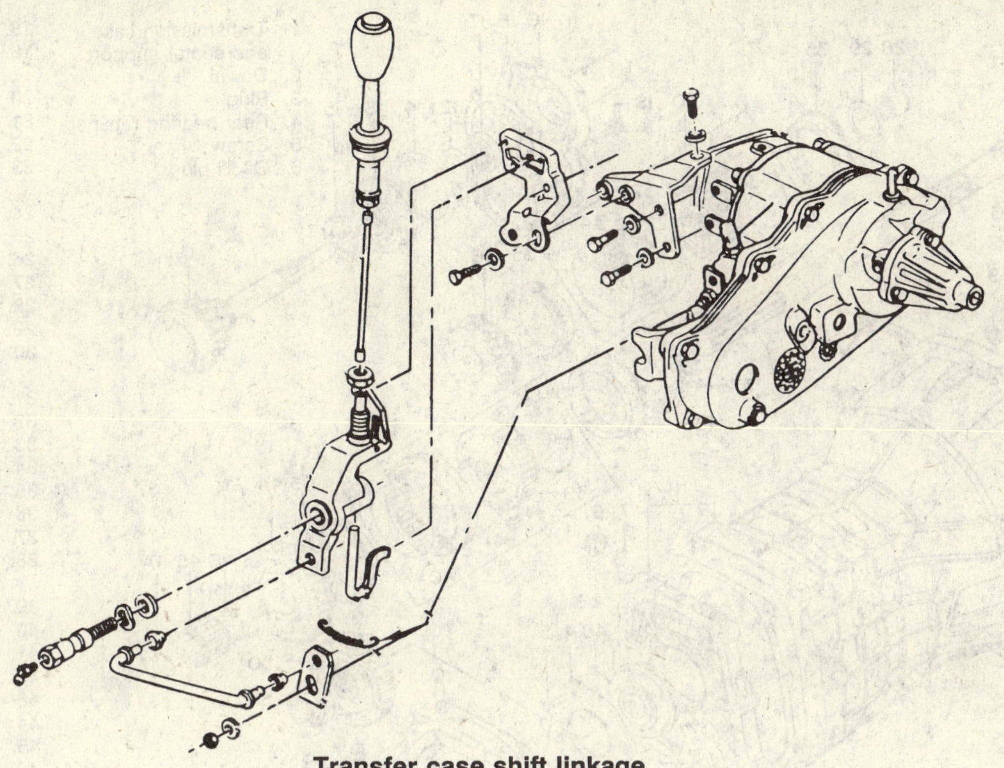

Transfer case shift linkage

13. If the clutch was removed, make sure it is properly aligned or it will be impossible to install the transmission.
14. Put the transmission into high gear.
15. With the transmission properly placed behind the engine, turn the output shaft slowly to engage the splines of the input shaft into the clutch while pushing the transmission forward into place. Don't force it, the transmission will easily fall into place when everything is properly aligned.
16. On 4-cylinder engines with the 77.5mm transmission, torque the bellhousing-to-engine bolts to 25 ft. lbs. On all others, torque all the bolts to 55 ft. lbs.
17. Install the cross member and torque the bolts to 25 ft. lbs.
18. Install the support braces and catalyst hanger and torque the nuts and bolts to 35 ft. lbs.
19. Install the clutch inspection cover and starter.
20. On 1984–91 models, install the slave cylinder and if necessary, attach the hydraulic line and bleed the system.
21. On earlier models, attach the clutch cable and push the pedal to test its operation.
22. Install the transmission shift lever and transfer case shift linkage.
23. Reassemble the exhaust system.
24. Install the driveshafts. Note the alignment marks and make sure the
shafts are installed the same way.
25. Refill the transmission and transfer case with the proper fluids.
26. Connect the wiring for the back-up lights and speed sensor, or the speedometer cable. Connect the transfer case vacuum lines.
27. Lower the vehicle to the ground and reconnect the battery.

77.5mm 4-Speed Overhaul

Cleanliness is an important factor in the overhaul of the transmission. Before attempting any disassembly operation, the exterior of the transmission should be thoroughly cleaned. During inspection and reassembly, all parts should be thoroughly cleaned and then air dried. Wiping cloths or rags should not be used to dry parts. All oil passages should be blown out and checked to make sure that they are not obstructed. All parts should be inspected to determine which parts are to be replaced.

DISASSEMBLY

1. Throughly clean the exterior of the transmission.
2. In the bell housing, disconnect the retaining clips and remove the clutch release bearing, fork and boot.
3. If not already done, drain the oil. Remove the bolts to remove the front bearing retainer. Remove the ball stud, if equipped.
4. Remove the speedometer drive and back-up light switch.
5. Remove the shift cover and gasket.
6. Remove the rear extension housing and gasket.
7. Remove the speedometer drive gear from the mainshaft.
8. Support the shift rods with a block of wood. Using a punch, carefully drive the pin from the reverse shift block.
9. Remove the reverse block retaining bolts. Remove the reverse shifter shaft, shift block, shift fork and reverse gear as an assembly.
10. Remove the retaining rings from the counter shaft and drive gear shaft bearings.
11. Remove the center support assembly fron the transmission case. Be careful not to hit the front end drive gear shaft while removing the center support, or the shaft will fall out.
12. Support the shift shafts and drive out the pins holding the forks.
13. Loosen the bolts and remove the plate, gasket and springs.
14. Bring the shifter shafts into neutral position and remove the reverse shifter shaft, then the 1st/2nd shaft, then the 3rd/4th shaft in that order. Be careful not to loose the interlock pins and detent balls.
15. Remove the 3 detent balls and 2 interlock pins. Remove the shift forks.

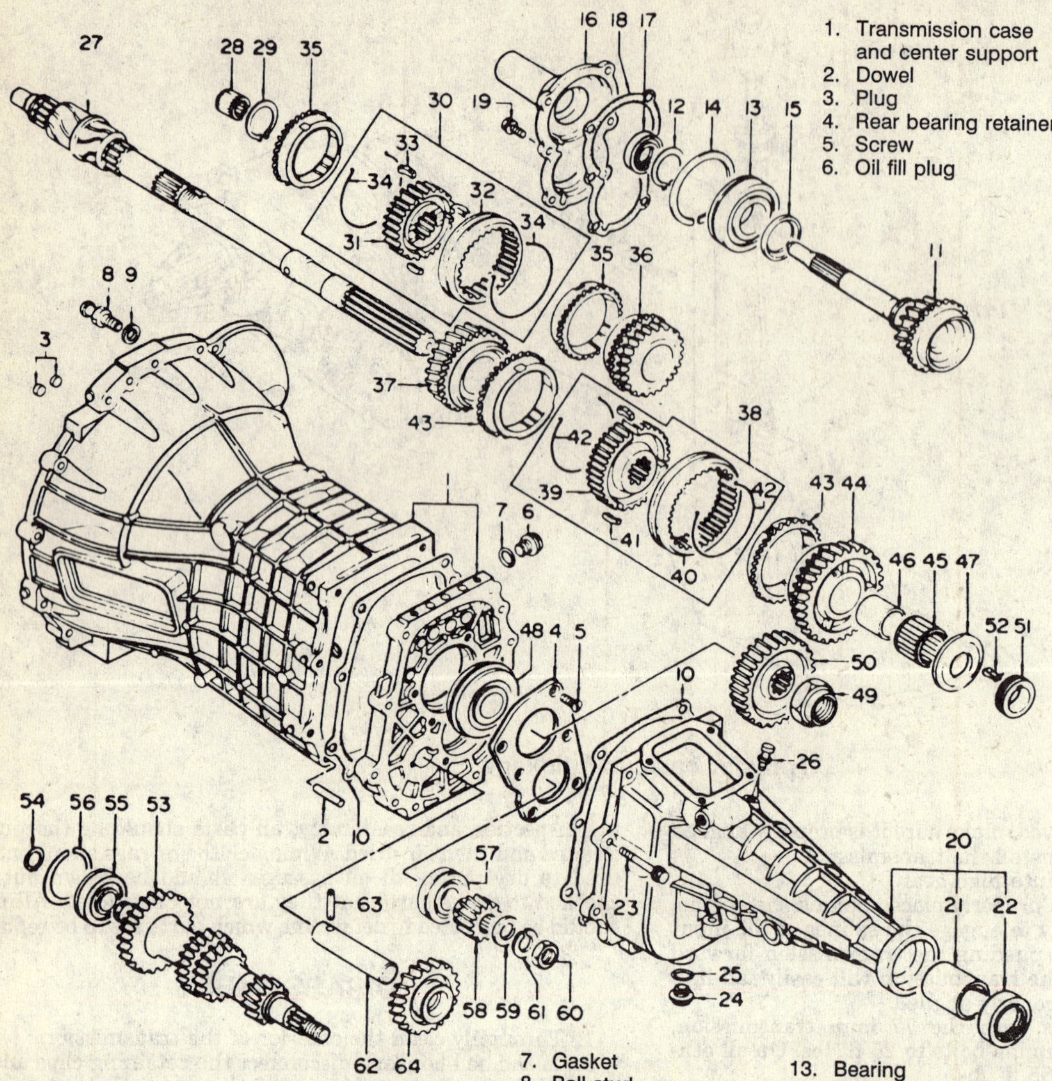

1. Transmission case and center support
2. Dowel
3. Plug
4. Rear bearing retainer
5. Screw
6. Oil fill plug
7. Gasket
8. Ball stud
9. Washer
10. Gasket
11. Drive gear/input shaft
12. Retainer ring
13. Bearing
14. Retainer ring
15. Spacer
16. Front bearing retainer
17. Oil seal
18. Gasket
19. Bolt and spring washer
20. Extension housing
21. Bushing
22. Rear oil seal
23. Bolt, plain washer and spring washer
24. Oil drain plug
25. Gasket
26. Ventilator
27. Mainshaft
28. Needle roller bearing
29. Retainer ring
30. 3rd/4th gear synchronizer
31. Clutch hub
32. Sleeve
33. Insert
34. Spring
35. Blocker ring
36. 3rd gear
37. 2nd gear
38. 1st/2nd gear synchronizer
39. Clutch hub
40. Sleeve
41. Insert
42. Spring
43. Blocker ring
44. 1st gear
45. Needle roller bearing
46. Bearing collar
47. Thrust washer
48. Bearing
49. Nut
50. Reverse gear
51. Speedometer drive gear
52. Clip
53. Counter shaft
54. Retainer ring
55. Bearing
56. Retainer ring
57. Bearing
58. Reverse gear
59. Plain washer
60. Nut
61. Spring washer
62. Reverse idler shaft
63. Spring pin
64. Reverse idler gear

Exploded view of the 77.5mm four speed transmission

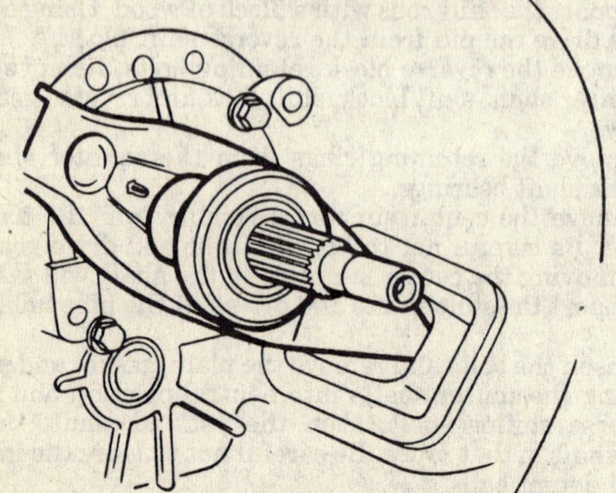

Remove the clutch release bearing and fork

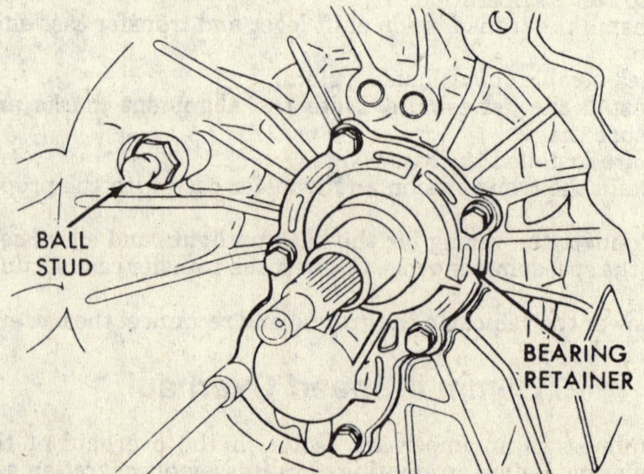

Remove the ball stud and bearing retainer

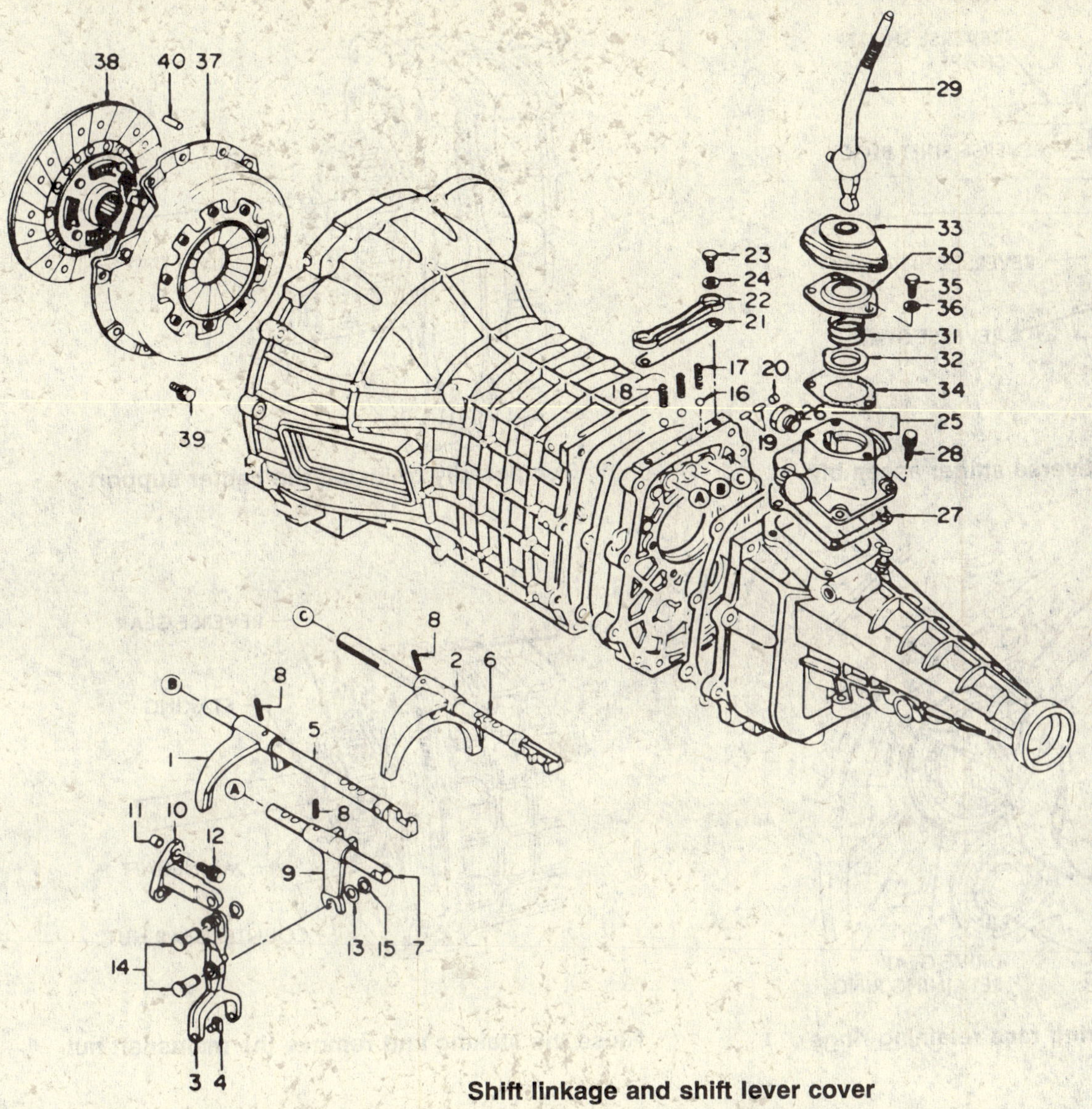

1. 3rd/4th shift fork
2. 1st/2nd shift fork
3. Reverse shift fork
4. Reverse shift piece
5. 3rd/4th shifter shaft
6. 1st/2nd shifter shaft
7. Reverse shifter shaft
8. Spring pin
9. Reverse shift block
10. Reverse block
11. Dowel
12. Bolt and spring washer
13. Plain washer
14. Joint pin
15. Retainer ring
16. Detent ball
17. Detent spring
18. Reverse detent spring
19. Interlock pin
20. Plug
21. Gasket
22. Detent spring plate
23. Bolt
24. Washer
25. Gearshift quadrant
27. Gasket
28. Bolt, plain washer and spring washer
29. Gearshift lever
30. Cover
31. Spring
32. Cage
33. Dust cover
34. Gasket
35. Bolt
36. Spring washer
37. Clutch pressure plate
38. Clutch disc
39. Bolt and spring washer
40. Pin

Shift linkage and shift lever cover

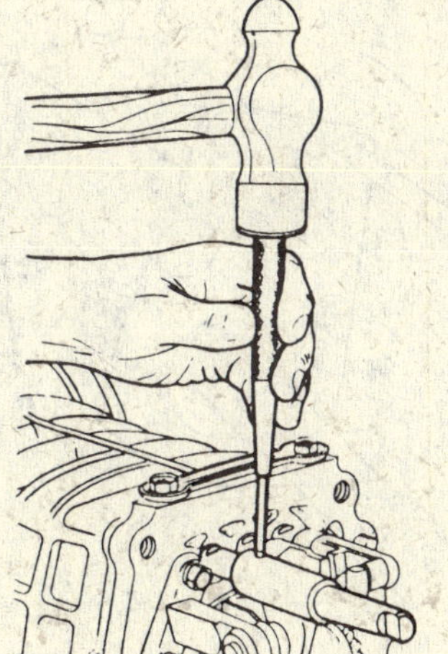

Carefully drive out the reverse shift block pin

16. Engage the synchronizers to prevent the mainshaft from turning. Temporarily install the center support section onto the transmission case.
17. Use a punch to raise the staking on the mainshaft rear nut, then remove the nut. The reverse gear can now be removed fron the mainshaft.
18. Remove the nut and reverse counter gear from the counter shaft.
19. Remove the center support section from the transmission.
20. Set the synchronizers in neutral and remove the rear bearing retainer.
21. Carefully move the counter shaft back and forth to push the outer bearing race out far enough to be able to pry it out.
22. Remove the race, then remove the countershaft.
23. To remove the mainshaft, install special tool J-22912-01 or an equivilant gear puller on the rear face of 2nd gear. Press the mainshaft out of the center support, being careful not to loose the sychronizers and bearings as the shaft is slid out.
24. Remove the snapring from the other end of the mainshaft. Install the gear puller onto 3rd gear and press the shaft out of the gear.

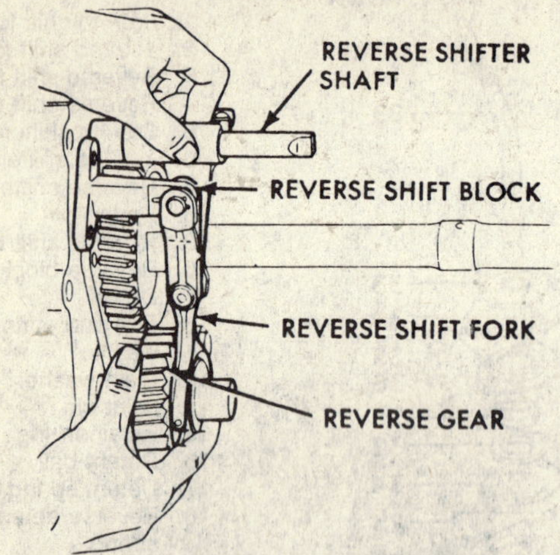

Remove the reverse shifter assembly

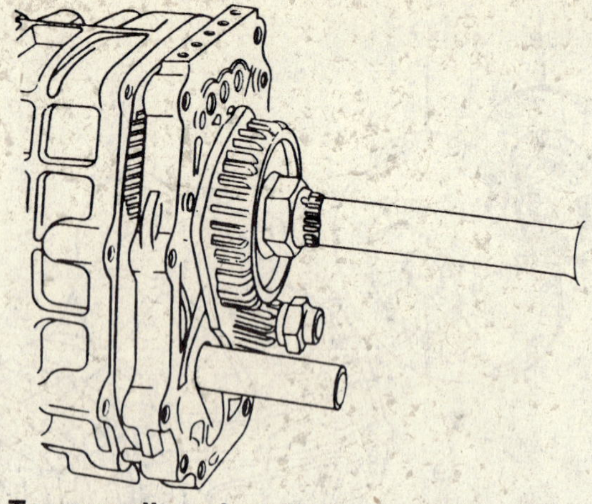

Temporarily re-install the center support

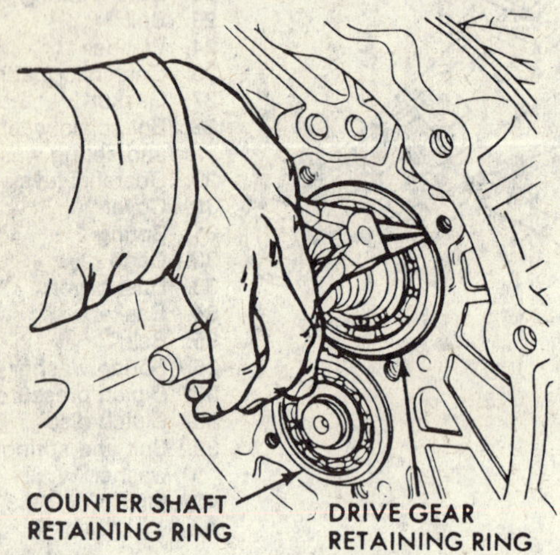

Remove the bearing race retaining rings

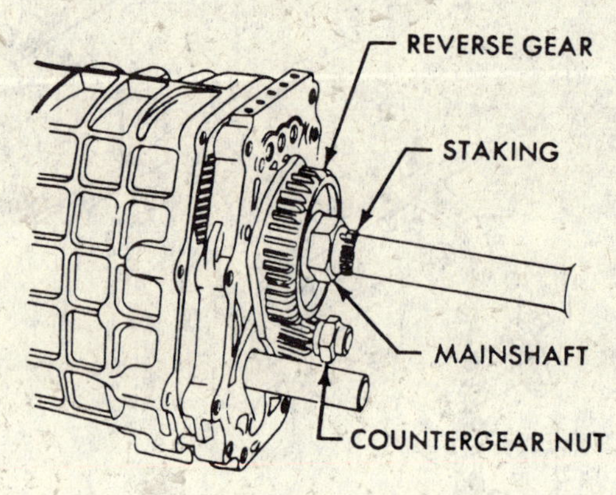

Raise the staking and remove the mainshaft nut

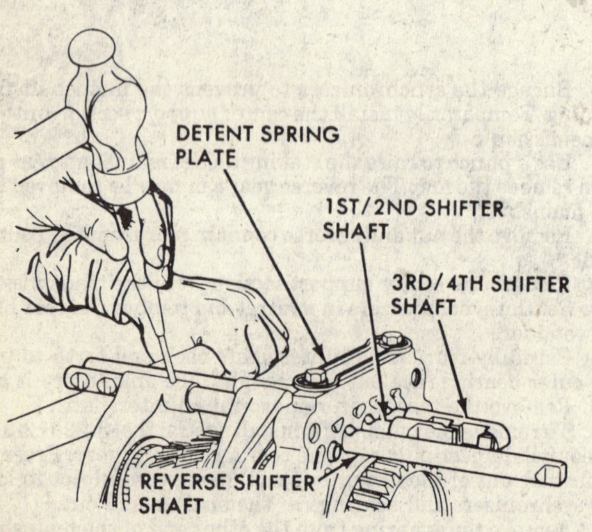

Support the rails and drive the pins out

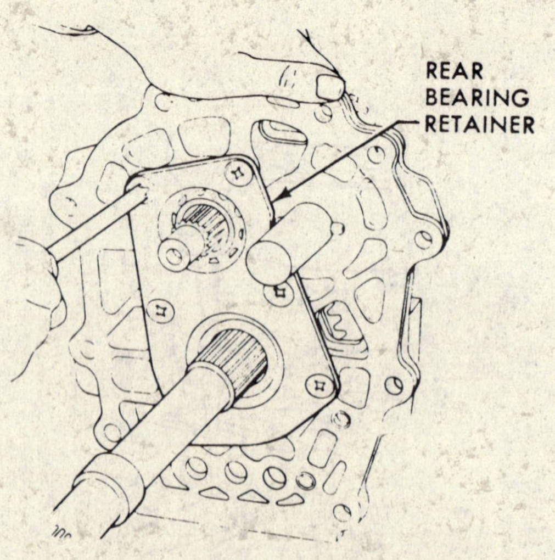

Remove the rear bearing retainer

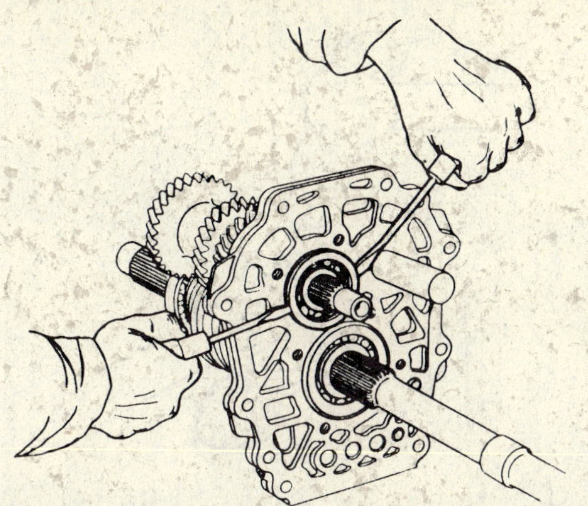

Carefully pry the bearing race out of the center support

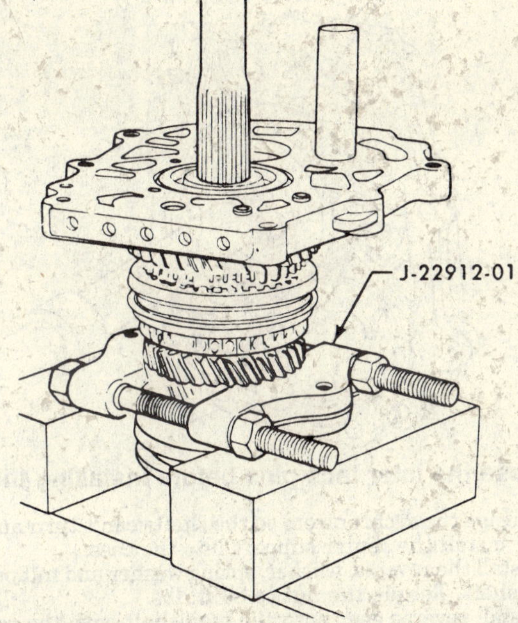

The mainshaft must be pressed out of the center support

INSPECTION

Throughly clean all parts and the case. Carefully inspect the case for signs of cracking or burrs, especially near the bearing areas. If the front bearing oil seal has been leaking, check the shaft for rust or wear in the seal area. While the transmission is apart, it is usually advisable to change the shaft seals at both ends. Clean and blow dry the bearings. Do not spin the bearings with air, this will cause damage to the bearing or to your hands. Inspect the bearings for signs of wear, then lightly oil them and slowly rotate, feeling for any roughness that may not be visible. Closely inspect the gears for uneven or heavy wear patterns, chips or cracks. If a gear shows enough wear or damage to warrent replacement, make sure the countershaft is still usable. Synchronizer hubs and sleeves must be replaced as an assembly, but the springs and keys may be replaced separately.

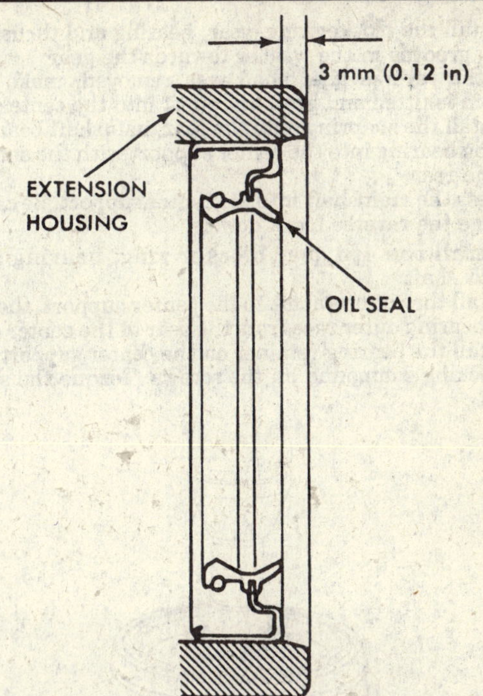

Installation of rear extension housing oil seal

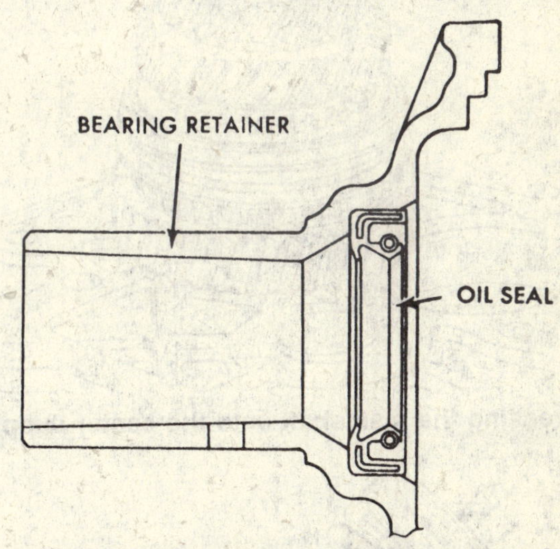

Installation of front bearing retainer oil seal

ASSEMBLY

25. To assemble the mainshaft, install 3rd gear and the 3rd gear blocker ring onto the shaft.
26. When installing the 3rd/4th synchronizer onto the shaft, make sure the hub is supported on the press blocks while pressing the shaft.
27. Install the retaining ring to the front of the mainshaft.
28. Install the 2nd gear and blocker ring to the mainshaft.
29. Press the 1st/2nd sychronizer assembly onto the shaft, making sure to press against the sychronizer hub.
30. Press the 1st gear bearing collar to the mainshaft using a suitable spacer.

31. Install the blocker ring, gear, bearing and thrust washer, with the grooves in the washer towards the gear.
32. If the reverse idler shaft was removed, make sure the spring pin is fitted and press the shaft into the center support.
33. Install the snapring onto the rear mainshaft bearing, then install the bearing into the center support with the snapring towards the rear.
34. Press the mainshaft into the center support. Be careful not to damage the reverse block dowels.
35. Install the 4th gear blocker ring, bearing and 4th gear/input shaft.
36. Install the countershaft to the center support, then install the rear bearing outer race from the rear of the center support.
37. Install the bearing retainer on the center support, using a thread locking compound on the screws. Torque the screws to 15 ft. lbs.

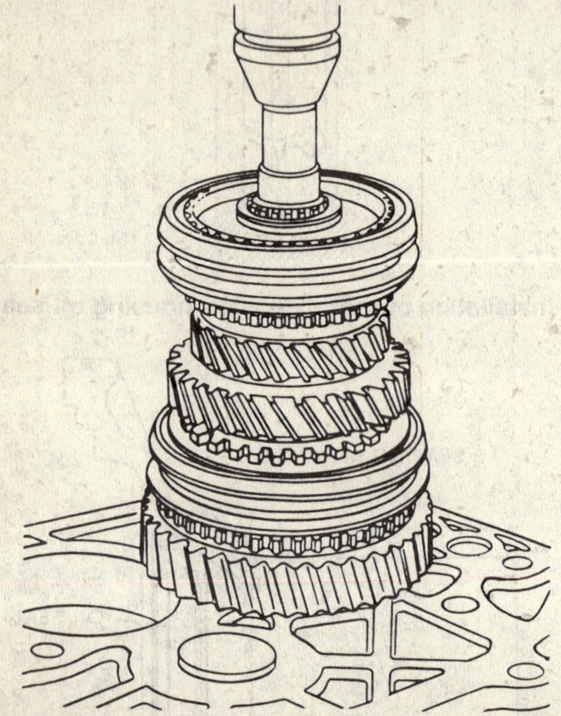

Pressing the mainshaft onto the center support

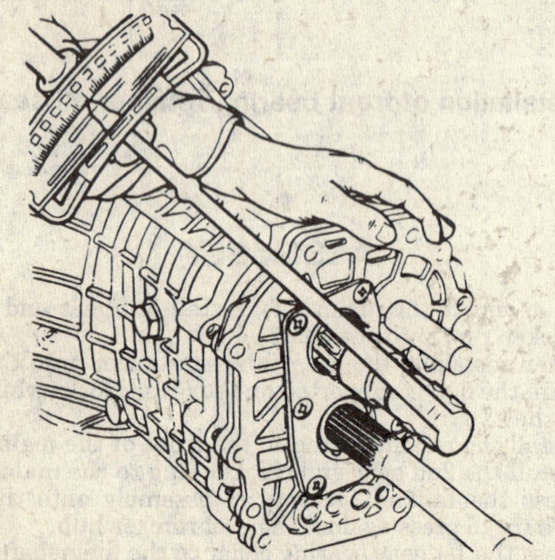

Use a torque wrench when installing the shaft nuts

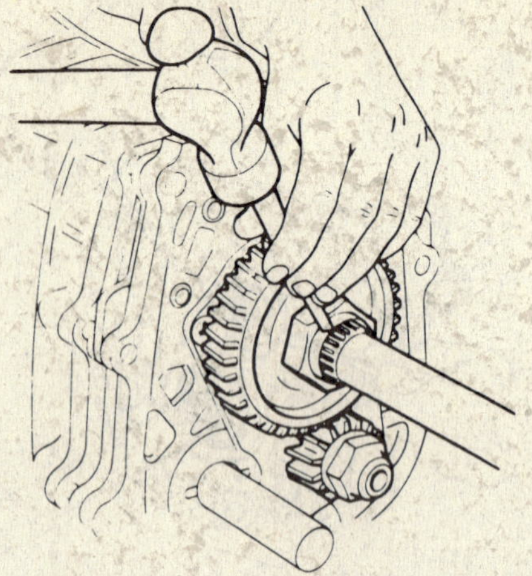

Stake the mainshaft nut in place

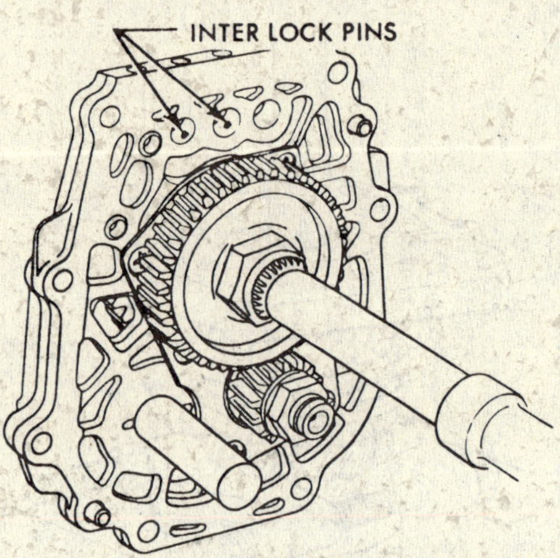

Grease the inter lock pins before installing them

38. Engage the sychronizers so the shafts can't turn and temporarily install the center support into the case.
39. Install the reverse, washer, spring washer and nut onto the countershaft. Torque the nut to 80 ft. lbs.
40. Install reverse gear onto the mainshaft with the rounded edge of the teeth towards the rear. Install the nut, torque it to 95 ft. lbs. and stake the nut in place.
41. Remove the center support. Grease and install the 2 inter lock pins.
42. Lay the shift forks onto the synchronizers. Carefully slide the 3rd/4th shift shaft through the center support, then through the fork. Install the 1st/2nd shaft, then the reverse shaft.
43. Support the shafts on a block of wood and carefully drive the spring pins into the forks.
44. Drop the detent balls into their holes, put in a few drops of oil and install the springs. The reverse spring is the shorter one.
45. Install the gasket and detent spring retainer plate and torque the bolts to 15 ft. lbs.
46. Install the gasket and carefully install the center support onto the case. Install the retaining rings on the bearing races in the bell housing.
47. Assemble the reverse shift block, reverse block and reverse shift fork using the pins and snaprings.
48. Install the shift block assembly to the reverse shift fork, then insert the shift fork into the groove in the reverse idler gear.

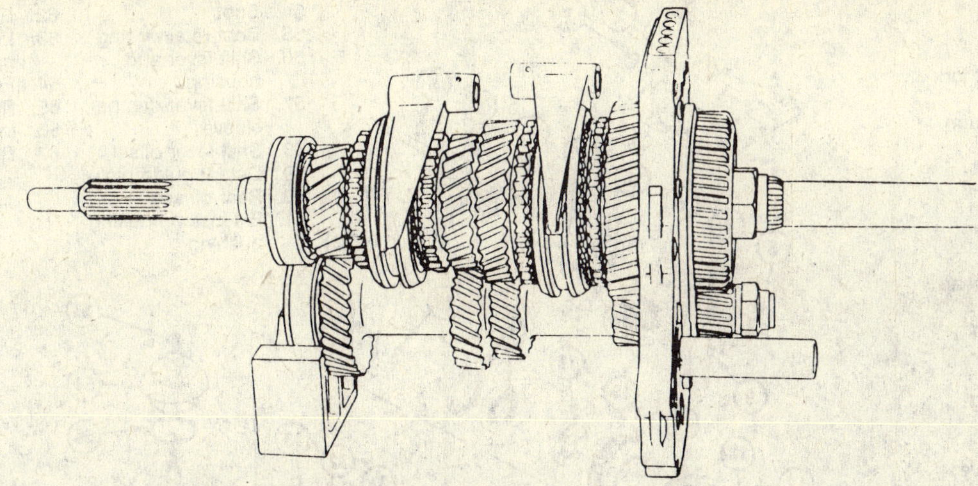

Lay the forks on the synchronizers in the proper direction

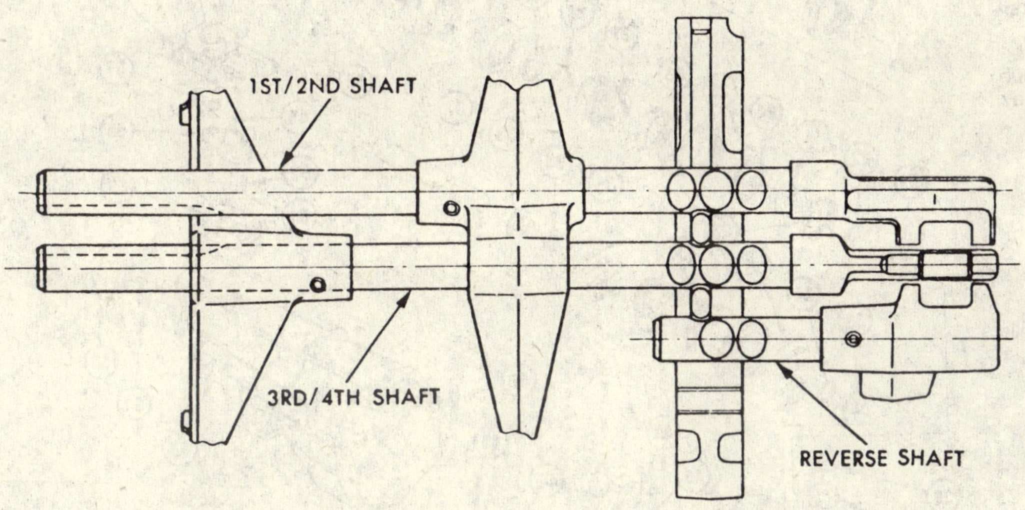

Make sure the shafts are in neutral when installing the pins

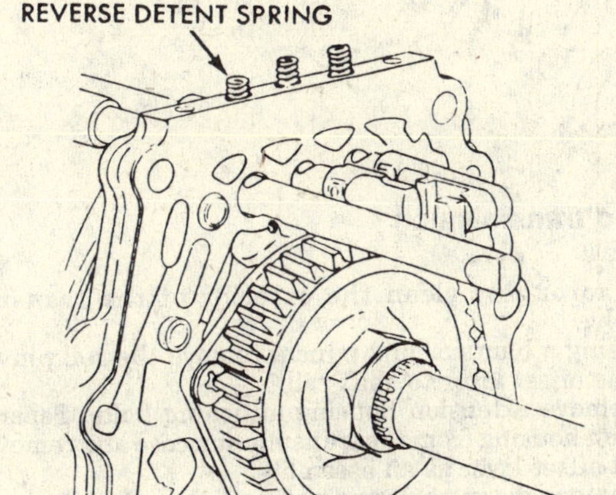

The reverse detent spring is the short one

49. Install the assembly to the shafts and torque the reverse block bolts to 15 ft. lbs.
50. Install the speedometer drive gear.
51. Using a new gasket, install the extension housing and torque the bolts to 30 ft. lbs.
52. Temporarily install the shift lever. Turn the input shaft while shifting the gears to make sure everything works smoothly.
53. When installing the front bearing retainer, the bolts must be sealed with a gasket sealer.
54. Install the clutch release parts. Torque the ball stud to 30 ft. lbs. (40 Nm).
55. The gear shift lever must be removed to install the transmission. When installing it in the vehicle, use a new gasket and torque the bolts to 15 ft. lbs. (20Nm).

77MM 4-Speed Overhaul

Cleanliness is an important factor in the overhaul of the transmission. Before attempting any disassembly operation, the

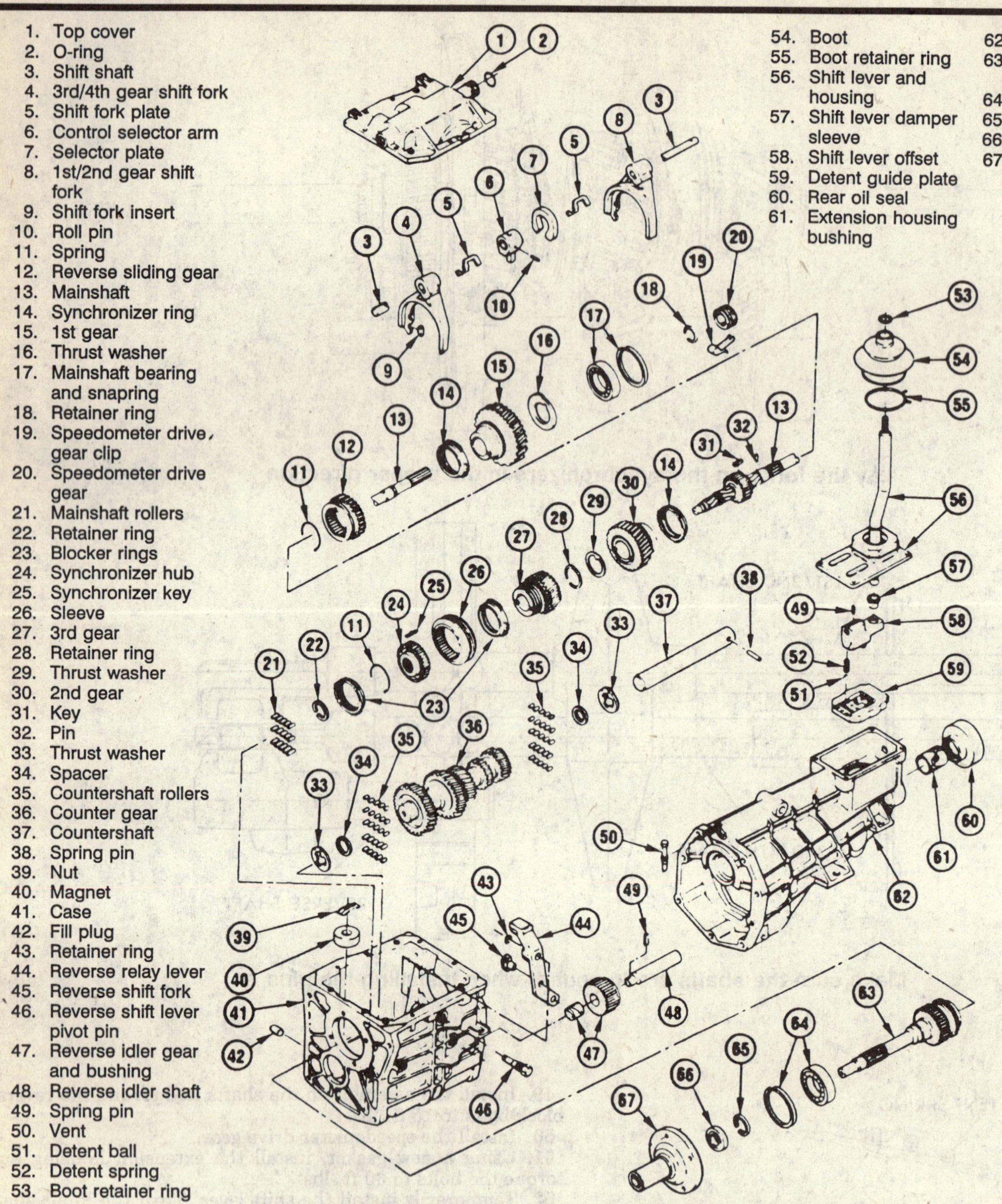

Exploded view of 77mm 4 speed transmission

exterior of the transmission should be thoroughly cleaned. During inspection and reassembly, all parts should be thoroughly cleaned and then air dried. Wiping cloths or rags should not be used to dry parts. All oil passages should be blown out and checked to make sure that they are not obstructed. All parts should be inspected to determine which parts are to be replaced.

DISASSEMBLY

1. Remove drain plug and drain lubricant from transmission.
2. Thoroughly clean the exterior of the transmission assembly.
3. Using a hammer and punch, remove the roll pin that retains the offset lever to shift rail.
4. Remove extension housing attaching bolts. Separate the extension housing from the transmission case and remove housing and offset lever as an assembly.
5. Remove detent ball and spring from offset lever and remove roll pin from extension housing or offset lever.
6. Remove transmission shift cover attaching bolts. Pry the shift cover loose and remove cover from transmission case.

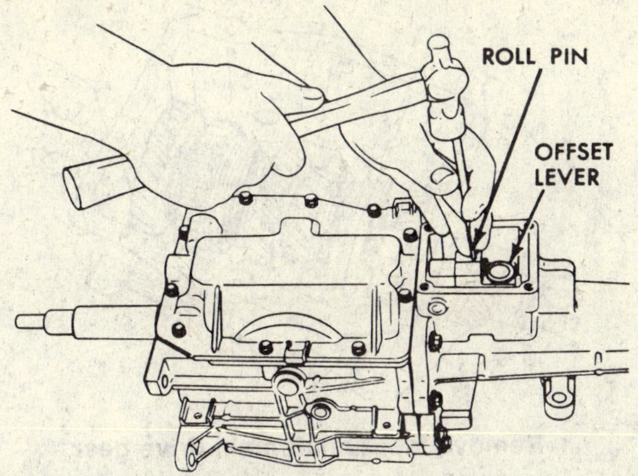

Removing offset lever roll pin

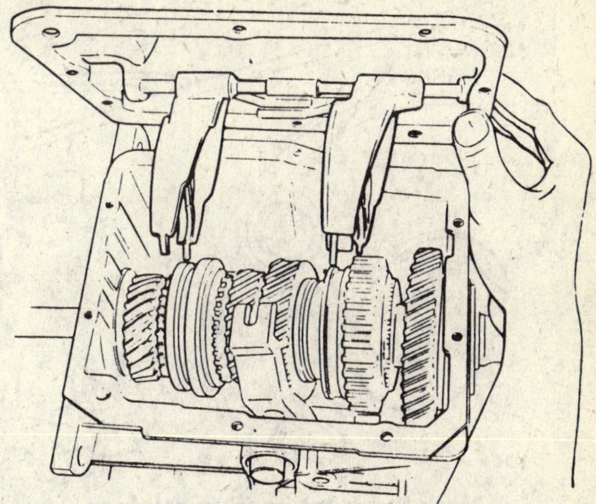
Remove top cover and shift forks

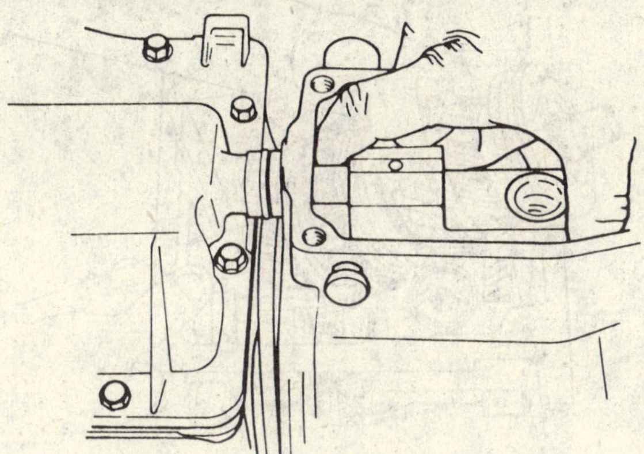
Remove the extension housing

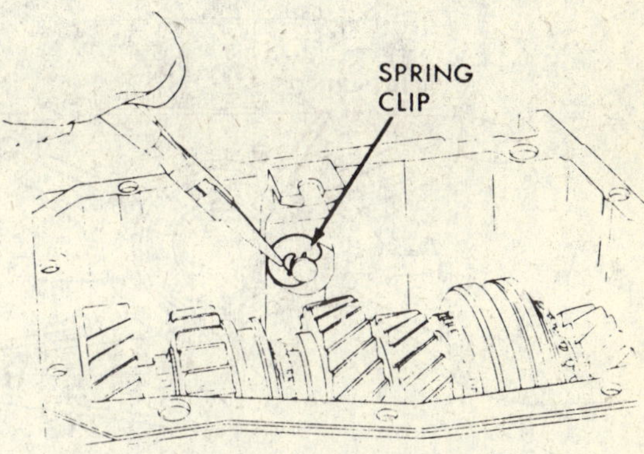

Remove reverse lever retainer clip

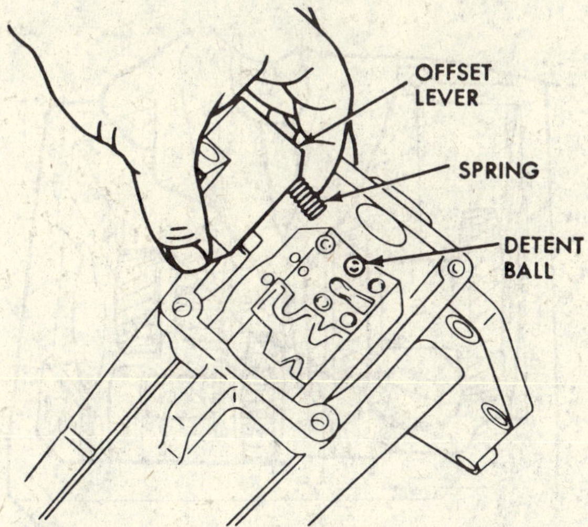

Lift out offset lever, detent ball and spring

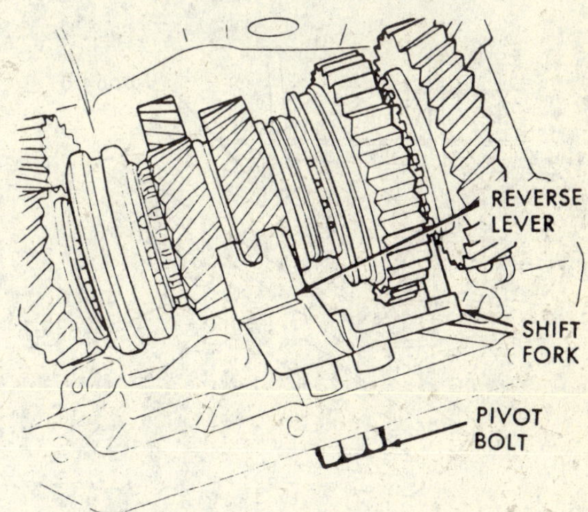

Remove reverse lever and shift fork

7. Remove clip that retains reverse lever to reverse lever pivot bolt.
8. Remove reverse lever pivot bolt and remove reverse lever and fork as an assembly.
9. Using a hammer and punch, mark position of front bearing cap to transmission case. Remove front bearing cap bolts and remove bearing cap.
10. Remove small retaining and large locating snaprings from front drive gear bearing.
11. Install bearing puller J-22912-01 or equivalent, on front bearing and puller J-8433-1 or equivalent, with 2 bolts on end of drive gear and remove and discard bearing. A new bearing must be used when assembling the transmission.
12. Remove retaining and locating snaprings from rear bear-

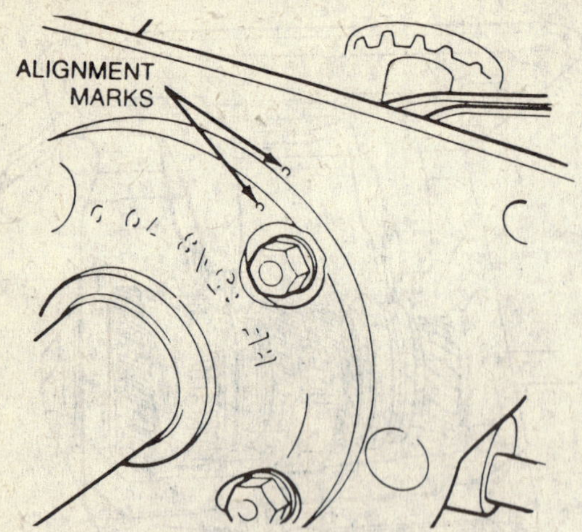

Mark the front bearing retainer

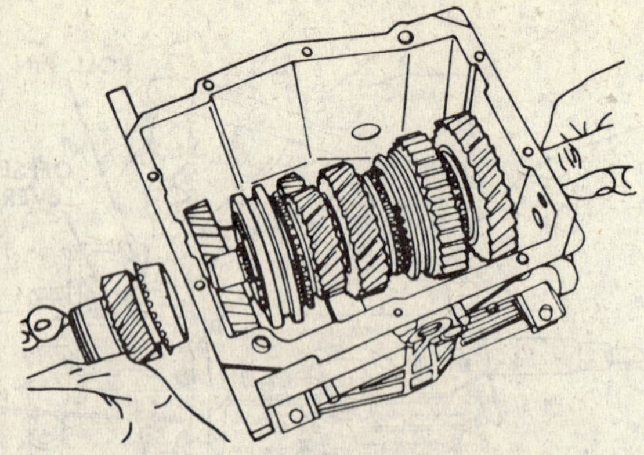

Remove input shaft/main drive gear

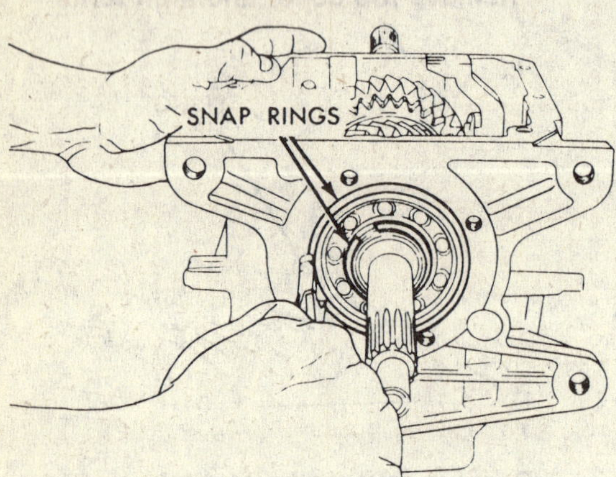

Remove snaprings from both bearings

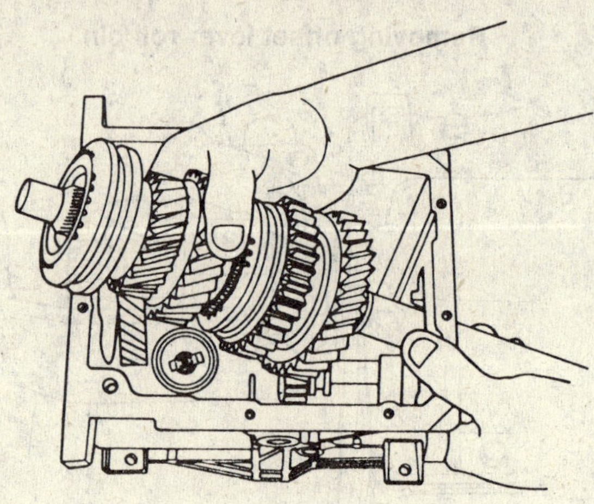

Lift the mainshaft out

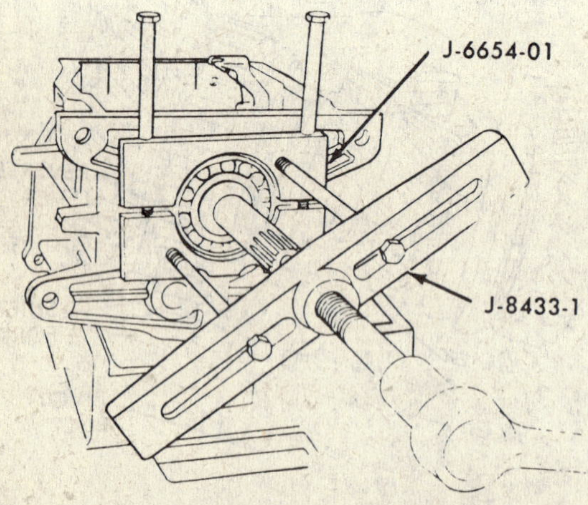

Bearings must be replaced

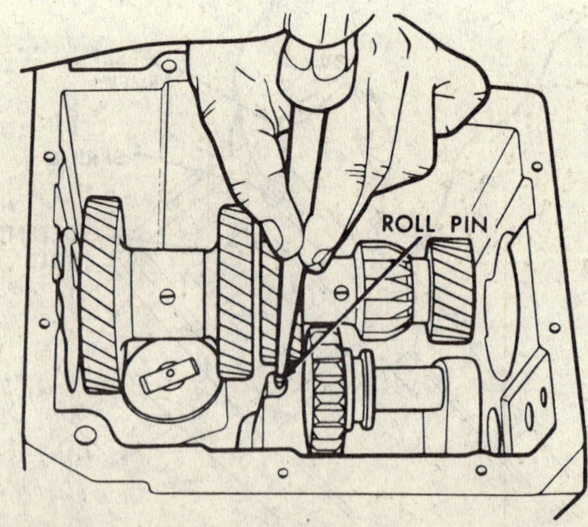

Remove roll pin from reverse idler shaft

ing and mainshaft. Install puller J–22912–01 or equivalent, on bearing and puller J–8433–1 or equivalent, with 2 bolts (J–33171 or equivalent) on end of mainshaft and remove and discard used bearing. A new bearing must be used when assembling transmission.

13. Remove drive gear from mainshaft and transmission case.

14. Remove mainshaft from transmission case by tipping mainshaft down at the rear and lifting shaft out through shift cover opening.

15. Using a hammer and punch, remove roll pin retaining reverse idler gear shaft in transmission case. Remove idler gear and shaft from case.

16. Remove countershaft from rear of case using loading tool J–26624. Remove countershaft gear and loading tool as an assembly from case along with thrust washers.

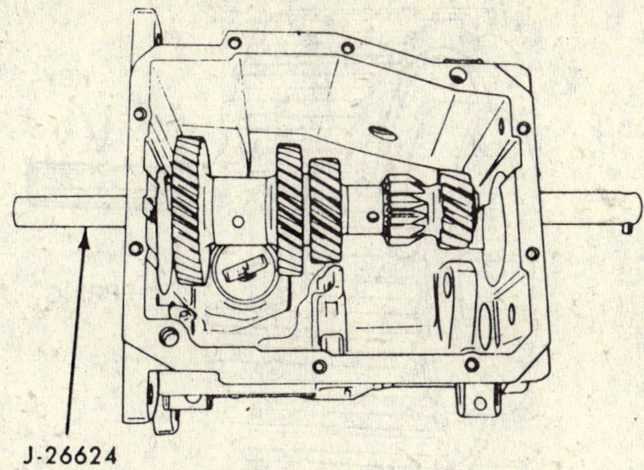

Use alignment tool to remove countershaft

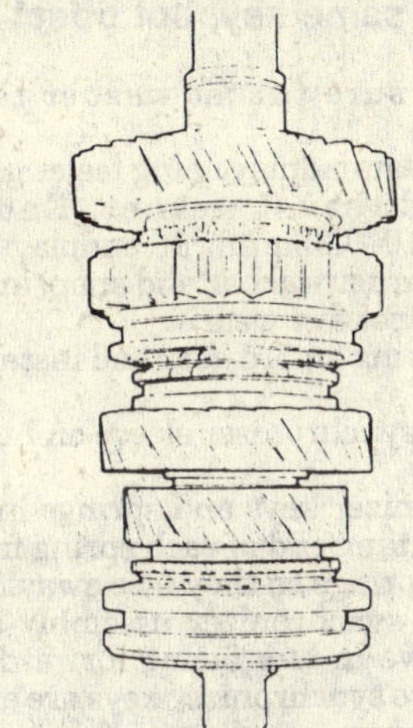

Mainshaft assembly

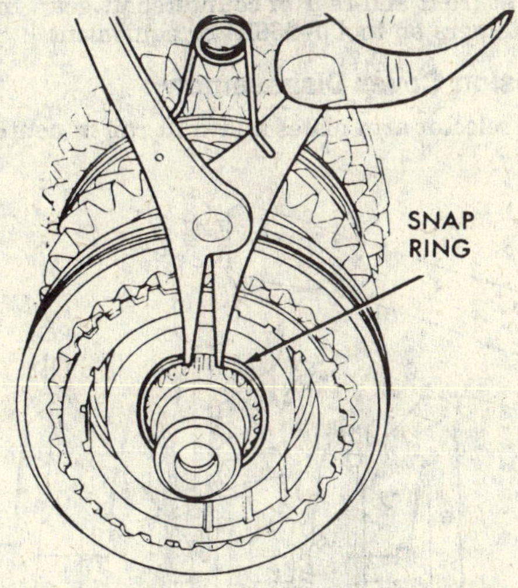

Remove 3dr/4th synchronizer snapring

Mainshaft Disassembly

1. Scribe an alignment mark on 3rd/4th synchronizer hub and sleeve for reassembly. Remove retaining snapring and remove 3rd/4th synchronizer assembly from mainshaft.

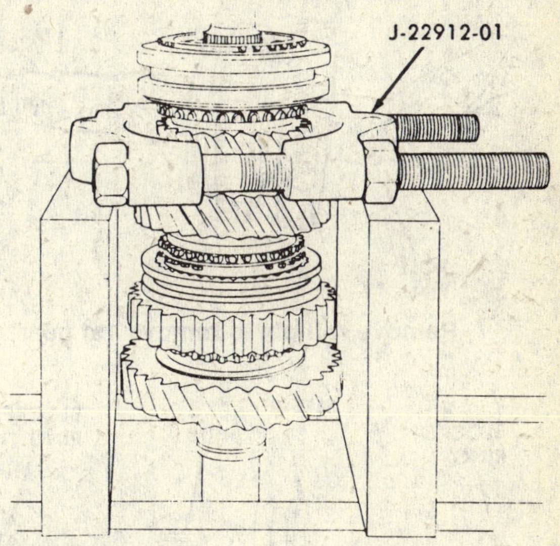

The tool must contact the gear

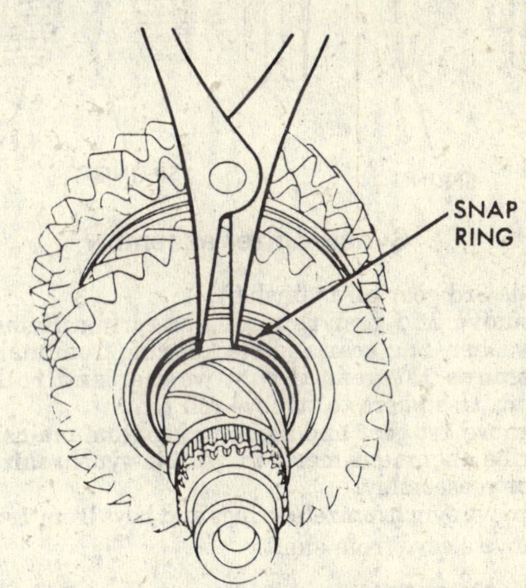

Remove 2nd gear snapring

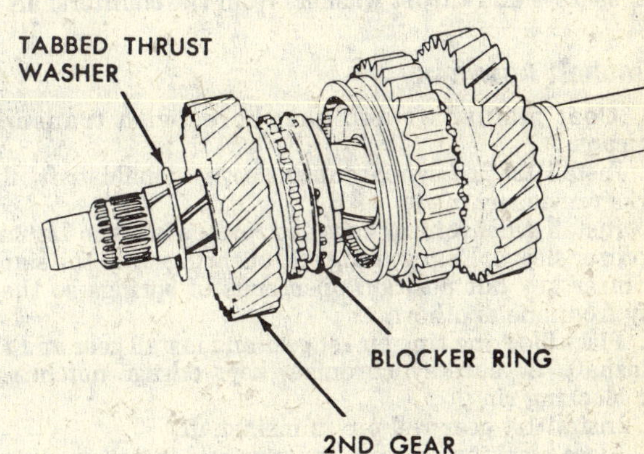

Remove 2nd gear and blocker ring

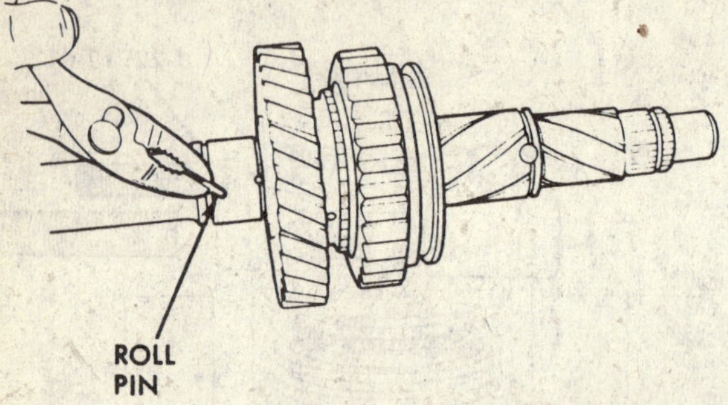

Remove roll pin to remove 1st gear

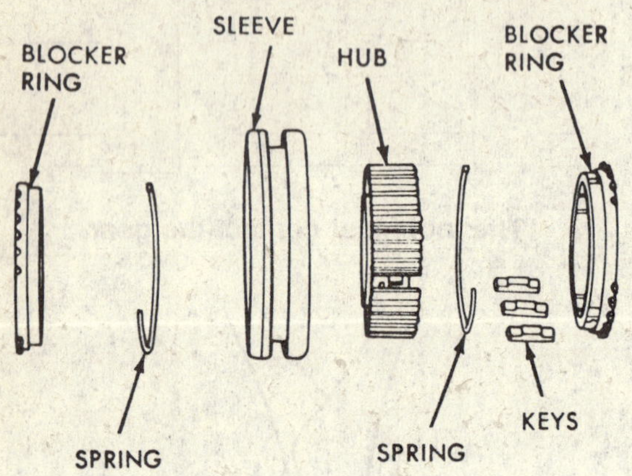

Synchronizer assembly

2. Slide 3rd gear off mainshaft.
3. Remove 2nd gear retaining snapring. Remove tabbed thrust washer, 2nd gear and blocker ring from mainshaft.
4. Remove 1st gear thrust washer and roll pin from mainshaft. Use pliers to remove roll pin.
5. Remove 1st gear and blocker ring from mainshaft.
6. Scribe alignment mark on 1st/2nd synchronizer hub and sleeve for reassembly.
7. Remove synchronizer springs and keys from 1st/2nd sleeve and remove sleeve from shaft.

NOTE: Do not attempt to remove the 1st/2nd hub from the mainshaft. The hub and mainshaft are assembled and machined as a unit.

8. Remove loading tool J-26624 or equivalent, roller bearings, spacers and thrust washers from the countershaft gear.

Mainshaft Assembly

1. Coat mainshaft and gear bores with transmission lubricant.
2. Install 1st/2nd synchronizer sleeve on mainshaft, aligning marks previously made.
3. Install synchronizer keys and springs into the 1st/2nd synchronizer sleeve. Engage tang end of springs into the same synchronizer key but position open ends of springs so they face away from one another.
4. Place blocking ring on 1st gear and install gear and ring on mainshaft. Be sure synchronizer keys engage notches in 1st gear blocking ring.
5. Install 1st gear roll pin in mainshaft.
6. Place blocking ring on 2nd gear and install gear and ring on mainshaft. Be sure synchronizer keys engage notches in 2nd gear blocking ring. Install 2nd gear thrust washer and snapring

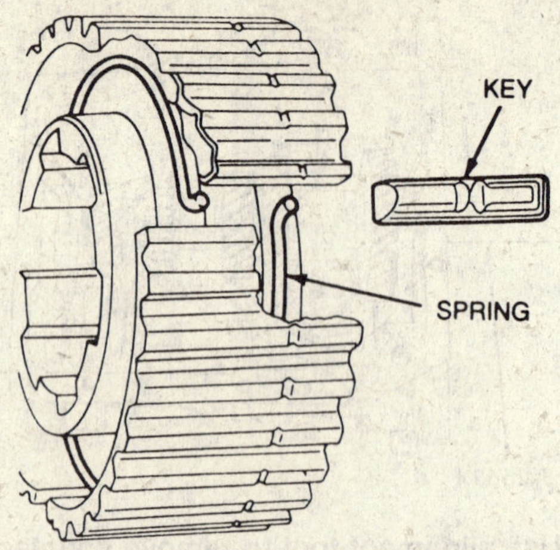

Put tangs into same key, but offset the openings

on mainshaft. Be sure thrust washer tab is engaged in mainshaft notch.
7. Measure 2nd gear endplay using feeler gauge. Insert gauge between gear and thrust washer. Endplay should be 0.004–0.014 in. (0.10–0.35mm). If endplay is over 0.014 in. (0.35mm), replace thrust washer and snapring and inspect synchronizer hub for excessive wear.
8. Place blocking ring on 3rd gear and install gear and ring on mainshft.
9. Install 3rd/4th synchronizer sleeve on hub, aligning marks previously made.
10. Install synchronizer keys and springs in 3rd/4th synchronizer sleeve. Engage tang end of each spring in same key but position open ends of springs so they face away from one another.
11. Install 3rd/4th synchronizer assembly on the mainshaft with machined groove in hub facing forward. Install snapring on mainshaft. Be sure synchronizer keys are engaged in notches in 3rd gear blocker ring.
12. Install tool J-26624 or equivalent, into countershaft gear. Using a light weight grease, lubricate roller bearings and install into bores at front and rear of countershaft gear. Install roller bearing retainers on tool J-26624 or equivalent.

Transmission Cover Disassembly

1. Place selector arm plates and shift rail in neutral position (centered).

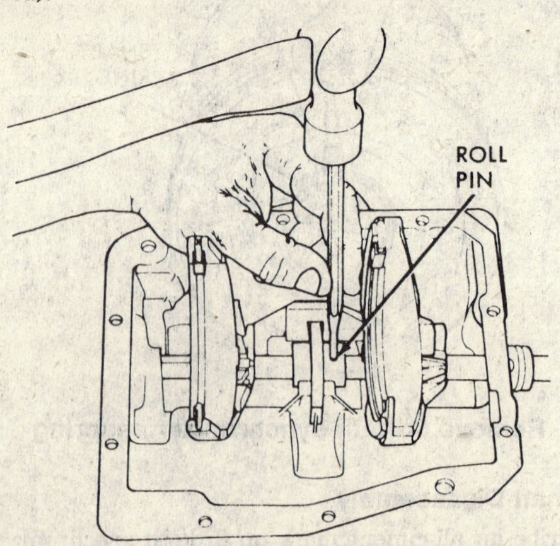

Remove roll pin to disassemble the shift forks

2. Rotate shift rail until selector arm disengages from selector arm plates and roll pin is accessible.
3. Remove selector arm roll pin using a pin punch and hammer.
4. Remove shift rail, shift forks, selector arm plates, selector arm, interlock plate and roll pin.
5. Remove shift cover to extension housing O-ring seal using a suitable tool.
6. Remove nylon inserts and selector arm plates from shift forks. Note position of inserts and plates for assembly reference.

Inspection

1. Inspect the shift rail for wear.
2. Inspect the shift forks and selector arm for wear.
3. Inspect the selector arm plates and interlock plate for wear.

Cover Assembly

1. Install nylon inserts and selector arm plates in shift forks.
2. If removed, install shift rail plug. Coat edges of plug with sealer before installing.
3. Coat shift rail and rail bores with light weight grease and insert shift rail in cover. Install rail until flush with inside edge of cover.
4. Place 1st/2nd shift fork in cover with fork offset facing rear of cover and push shift rail through fork. The 1st/2nd shift fork is the larger of the 2 forks.
5. Position selector arm and C-shaped interlock plate in cover and insert shift rail through arm. Widest part of interlock plate must face away from cover and selector arm roll pin hole must face downward and toward rear of cover.
6. Position 3rd/4th shift fork in cover with fork offset facing rear of cover. The 3rd/4th shift fork selector arm plate must be under 1st/2nd shift for selector arm plate.
7. Push shift rail through 3rd/4th shift fork and into front bore in cover.
8. Rotate shift rail until selector arm plate at forward end of rail faces away from, but is parallel to cover.
9. Align roll pin holes in selector arm and shift rail and install roll pin. Roll pin must be flush with surface of selector arm to prevent pin from contacting selector arm plates during shifts.
10. Install a new shift cover to extension housing O-ring seal. Coat O-ring seal with transmission lubricant.

TRANSMISSION ASSEMBLY

1. Coat countershaft gear thrust washers with petroleum jelly and position washer in case.
2. Position countershaft gear in case and install countershaft from rear of case. Be sure that thrust washers stay in place during installation of countershaft and gear.
3. Position reverse idler gear in case with shift lever groove facing rear of case and install reverse idler shaft from rear of case. Install roll pin in shaft and center pin in shaft.
4. Install mainshaft assembly into the case. Do not disturb position of synchronizer assemblies during installation.
5. Install 4th gear blocking ring in 3rd/4th synchronizer sleeve. Be sure synchronizer keys engaged in notches in blocker ring.
6. Install input shaft/drive gear into case and engage with mainshaft.
7. Position mainshaft 1st gear against the rear of the case. Using a new bearing, start front bearing onto input shaft/drive gear. Align bearing with bearing bore in case and drive bearing onto drive gear and into case using tool J–25234 or equivalent.
8. Install front bearing retaining and locating snaprings.
9. Apply a ⅛ in. (3mm) diameter bead of RTV sealant, No. 732 or equivalent, on case mating surface of front bearing cap. Install bearing cap aligning marks previously made. Apply non-hardening sealer on attaching bolts and install bolts. Torque bolts to 15 ft. lbs. (20 Nm).

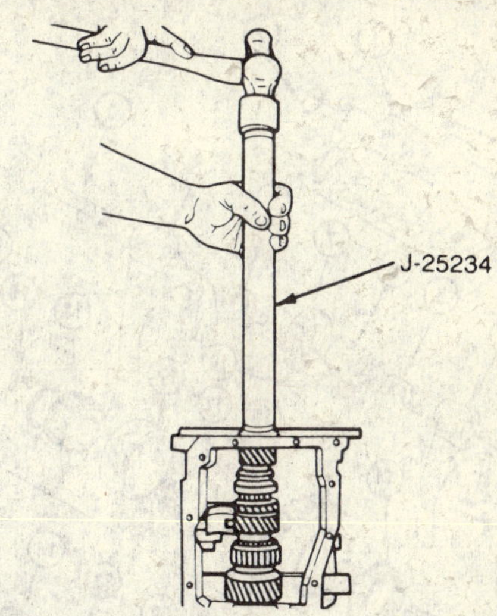

The bearing is driven onto the shaft

10. Install 1st gear thrust washer with oil grove facing 1st gear on mainshaft, aligning slot in washer with 1st gear roll pin.
11. Using a new bearing, position rear bearing on mainshaft. Align bearing with bearing bore in case and drive bearing into case using tool J–25234 or equivalent.
12. Install locating and retaining snaprings on rear bearing.
13. Install speedometer gear and retaining clip on mainshaft.
14. Apply non-hardening sealer to threads of reverse lever pivot bolt and start bolt into case. Engage reverse lever fork in the reverse idler gear and reverse lever on pivot bolt. Torque bolt to 20 ft. lbs. (27 Nm) and install retaining clip.
15. Rotate drive gear and mainshaft gear. If blocker rings tend to stick on gears, release the rings by gently prying them off the cones.
16. Apply a ⅛ in. (3mm) diameter bead or RTV sealant, No. 732 or equivalent, on the cover mating surface of transmission. Place reverse lever in neutral and position cover on case.
17. Install 2 dowel type bolts first to align cover on case. Install remaining cover bolts and torque to 10 ft. lbs. (13 Nm). The offset lever to shift rail roll pin hole must be in the vertical position after cover installation.
18. Apply a ⅛ in. (3mm) diameter bead of RTV sealant, No. 732 or equivalent, on the extension housing to transmission case mating surface.
19. Place extension housing over mainshaft to a position where shift rail is in shift cover opening.
20. Install detent spring in offset lever. Place ball in neutral guide plate detent position. Apply pressure on the offset lever, slide offset lever onto shift rail and seat extension housing to transmission case.
21. Install extension housing retaining bolts. Torque bolts to 25 ft. lbs. (30 Nm).
22. Align hole in offset lever and shift rail and install roll pin.
23. Temporarily install the shift lever. Rotate the input shaft while shifting gears to make sure the unit works.

77mm 5-Speed Overhaul

Cleanliness is an important factor in the overhaul of the transmission. Before attempting any disassembly operation, the exterior of the transmission should be thoroughly cleaned to prevent the possibility of dirt entering the transmission internal mechanism. During inspection and reassembly, all parts should be thoroughly cleaned with cleaning fluid and then air dried. Wiping cloths or rags should not be used to dry parts. All oil pas-

Exploded view of 77mm 5 speed transmission

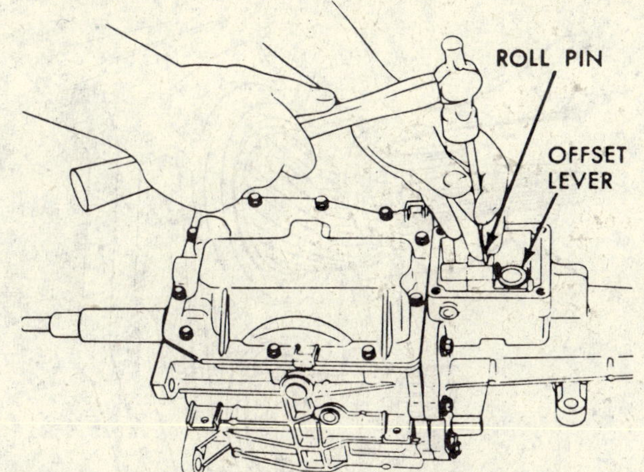

Remove offset lever roll pin only

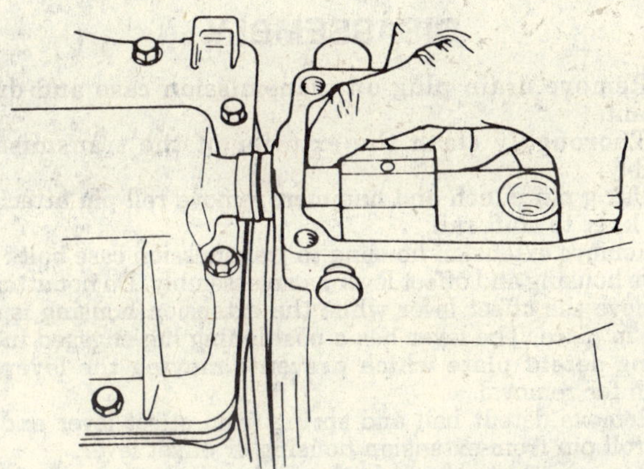
Remove extension housing

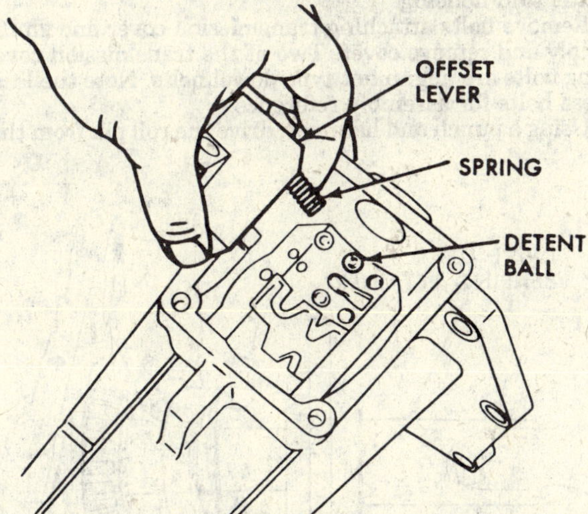

Remove detent spring and ball

sages should be blown out and checked to make sure that they are not obstructed. Small passages should be checked with tag wire. All parts should be inspected to determine which parts are to be replaced.

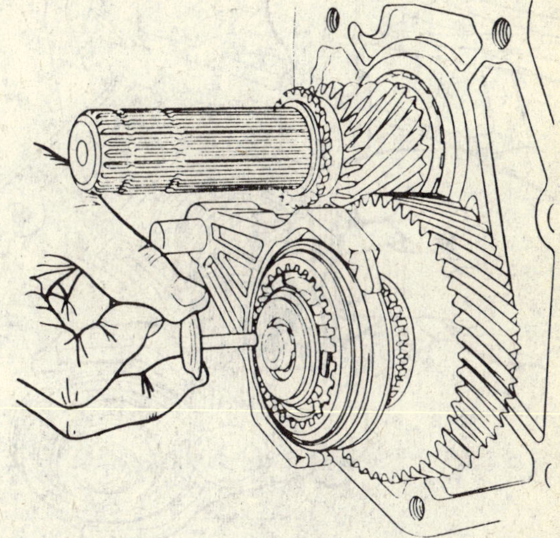
Plastic funnel on rear of the countershaft

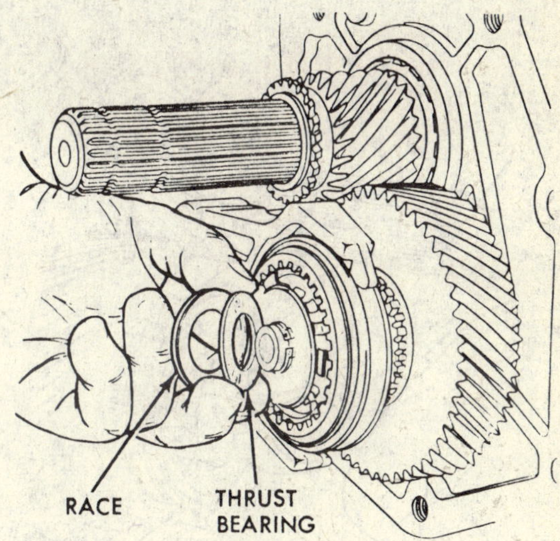

Remove the thrust bearing and race

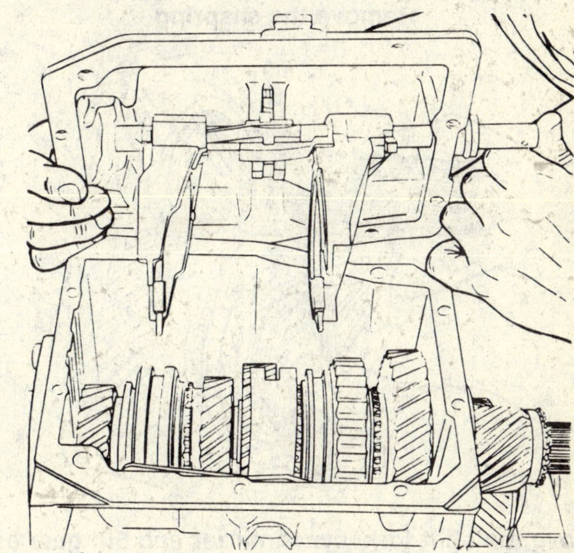
Remove the top cover, note where the dowel bolts go

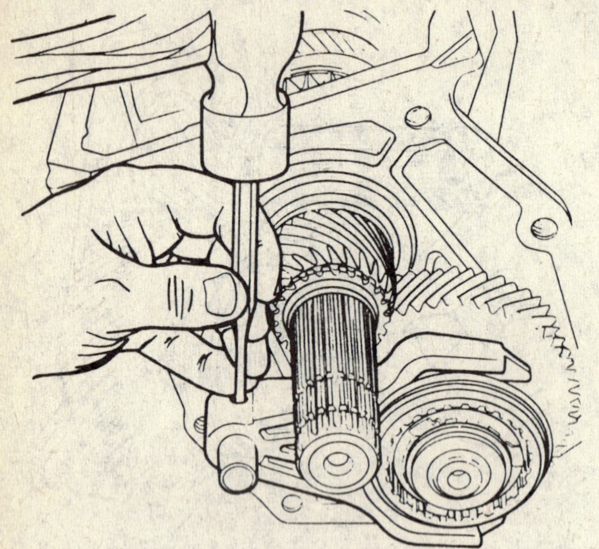
Support the shaft and drive out the 5th gear shift fork roll pin

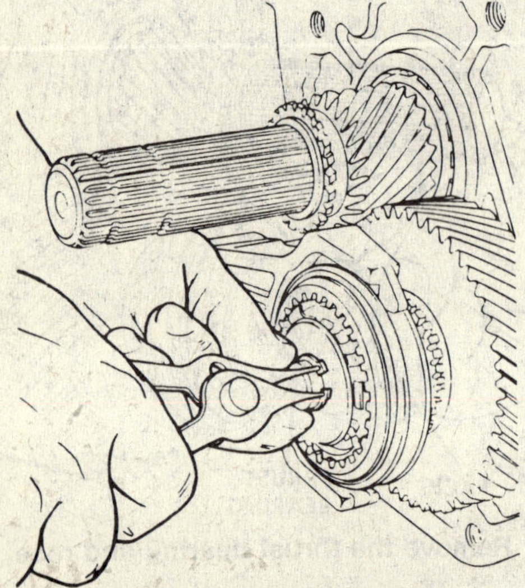
Remove the snapring

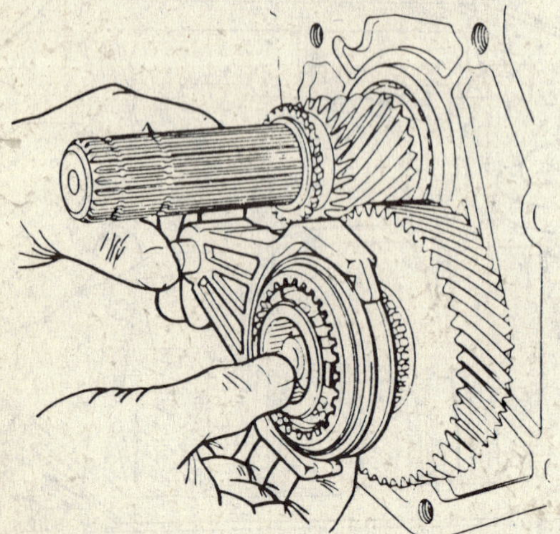
Remove the shift fork, synchronizer and 5th gear as an assembly

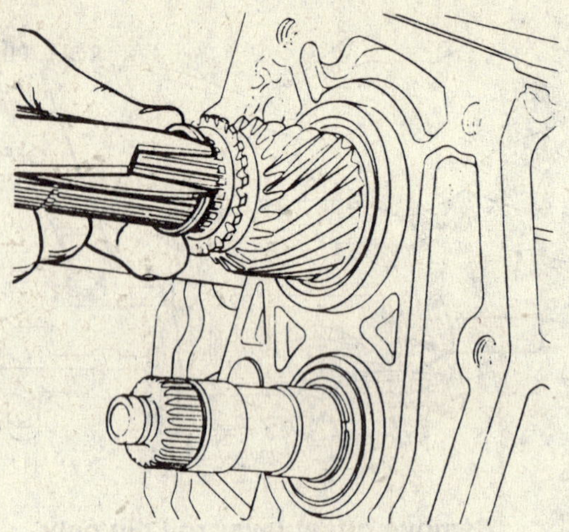
Snapring for 5th gear driven gear

DISASSEMBLY

1. Remove drain plug on transmission case and drain lubricant.
2. Thoroughly clean the exterior of the transmission assembly.
3. Using pin punch and hammer, remove roll pin attaching offset lever to shift rail.
4. Remove extension housing to transmission case bolts and remove housing and offset lever as an assembly. Do not attempt to remove the offset lever while the extension housing is still bolted in place. The lever has a positioning lug engaged in the housing detent plate which prevents moving the lever far enough for removal.
5. Remove detent ball and spring from offset lever and remove roll pin from extension housing or offset lever.
6. Remove plastic funnel, thrust bearing race and thrust bearing from rear of countershaft. The countershaft rear thrust bearing, bearing washer and plastic funnel may be found inside the extension housing.
7. Remove bolts attaching transmission cover and shift fork assembly and remove cover. Two of the transmission cover attaching bolts are alignment-type dowel bolts. Note the location of these bolts for assembly reference.
8. Using a punch and hammer, drive the roll pin from the 5th

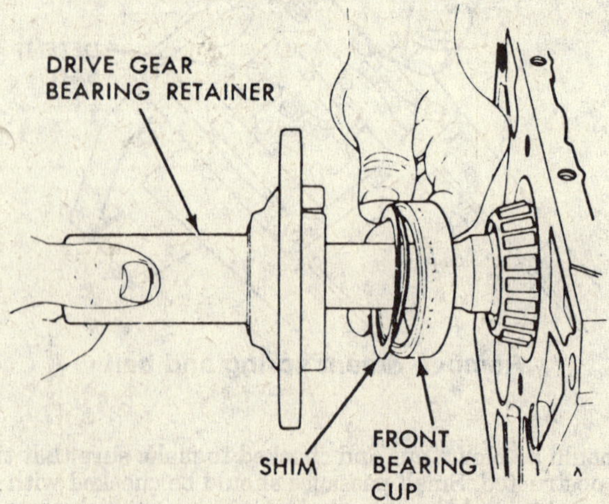

Keep the cap, shims and race together

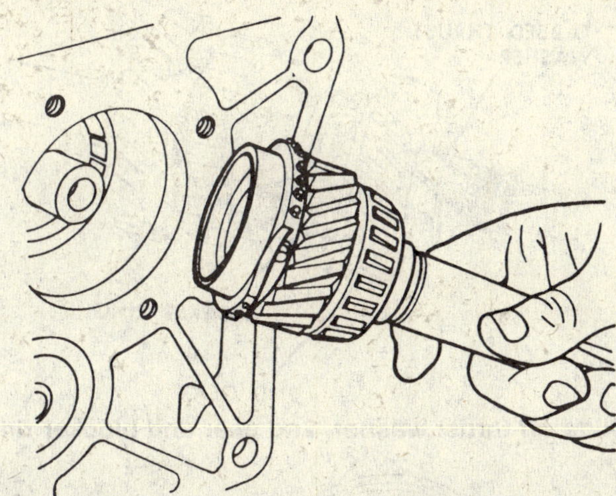
When flat surface faces countershaft, gear can be removed

gearshift fork while supporting the end of the shaft with a block of wood.

9. Remove 5th synchronizer gear snapring, shift fork, 5th gear synchronizer sleeve, blocking ring and 5th speed drive gear from rear of countershaft.
10. Remove snapring from 5th speed driven gear.
11. Using a hammer and punch, mark both bearing cap and case for assembly reference.
12. Remove front bearing cap bolts and remove front bearing cap. Remove front bearing race and endplay shims from front bearing cap.
13. Rotate drive gear until flat surface faces counter shaft and remove drive gear from transmission case.
14. Remove reverse lever C-clip and pivot bolt.
15. Remove mainshaft rear bearing race and then tilt mainshaft assembly upward and remove assembly from transmission case.
16. Unhook overcenter link spring from front of transmission case.
17. Rotate 5th gear/reverse shift rail to disengage rail from reverse lever assembly. Remove shift rail from rear of transmission case.
18. Remove reverse lever and fork assembly from transmission case.
19. Using hammer and punch, drive roll pin from forward end of reverse idler shaft and remove reverse idler shaft, rubber O-ring and gear from the transmission case.
20. Remove rear countershaft snapring and spacer.
21. Insert a brass drift through drive gear opening in front of

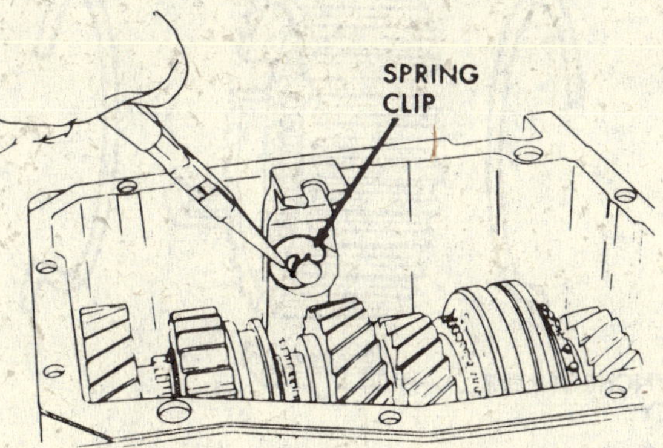

Remove reverse lever spring clip

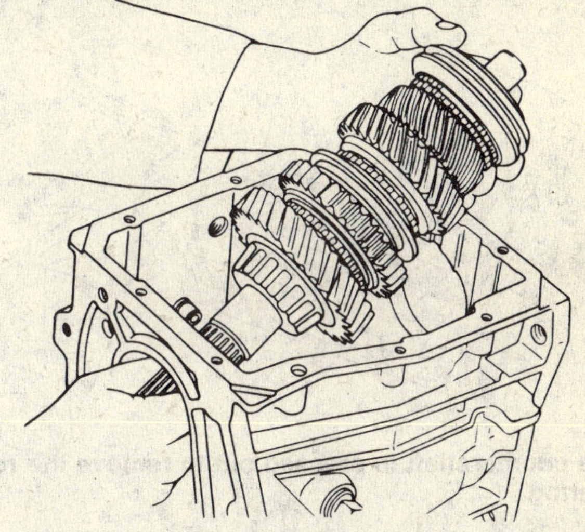
Lift out the main shaft

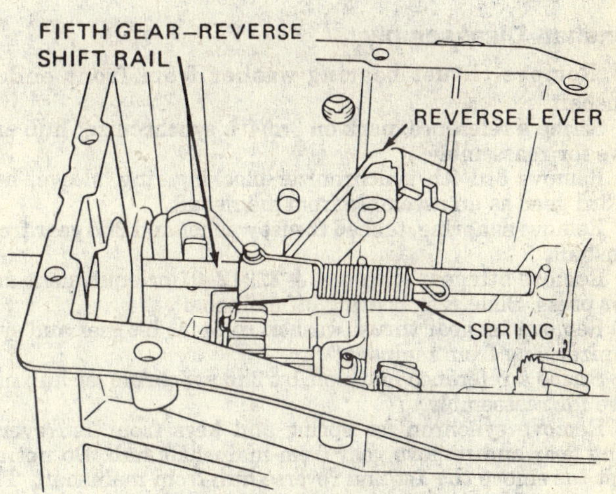

5th/reverse shift rail

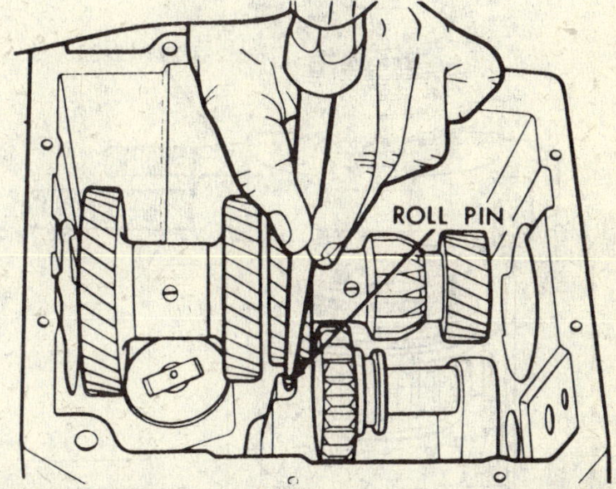

Drive out the roll pin from reverse idler shaft

transmission case and, using an arbor press, carefully press countershaft rearward to remove rear countershaft bearing.
22. Move countershaft assembly rearward, tilt countershaft upward and remove from case. Remove countershaft front thrust washer and rear bearing spacer.

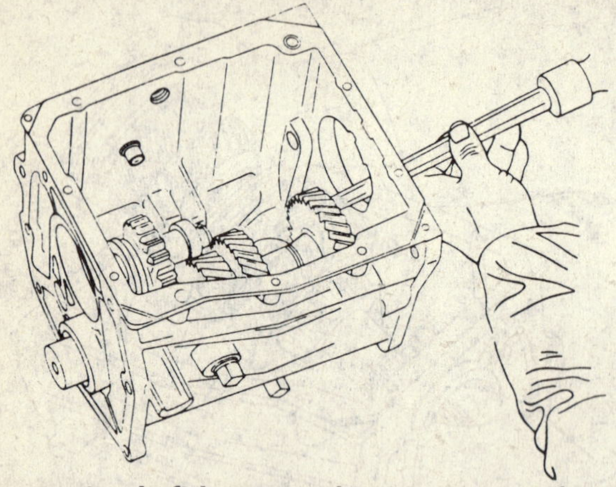

The countershaft is pressed out to remove the rear bearing

23. Remove countershaft front bearing from transmission case using an arbor press.

Mainshaft Disassembly

1. Remove thrust bearing washer from front end of mainshaft.
2. Scribe a reference mark on 3rd/4th synchronizer hub and sleeve for reassembly.
3. Remove 3rd/4th synchronizer blocking ring, sleeve, hub and 3rd gear as an assembly from mainshaft.
4. Remove snapring, tabbed thrust washer and 2nd gear from mainshaft.
5. Remove 5th gear with tool J-22912-01 or equivalent and arbor press. Slide rear bearing off mainshaft.
6. Remove 1st gear thrust washer, roll pin, 1st gear and synchronizer ring from mainshaft.
7. Scribe a reference mark on 1st/2nd synchronizer hub and sleeve for reassembly.
8. Remove synchronizer spring and keys from 1st/reverse sliding gear and remove gear from mainshaft hub. Do not attempt to remove the 1st/2nd reverse hub from mainshaft. The hub and shaft are assembled and machined as a matched set.

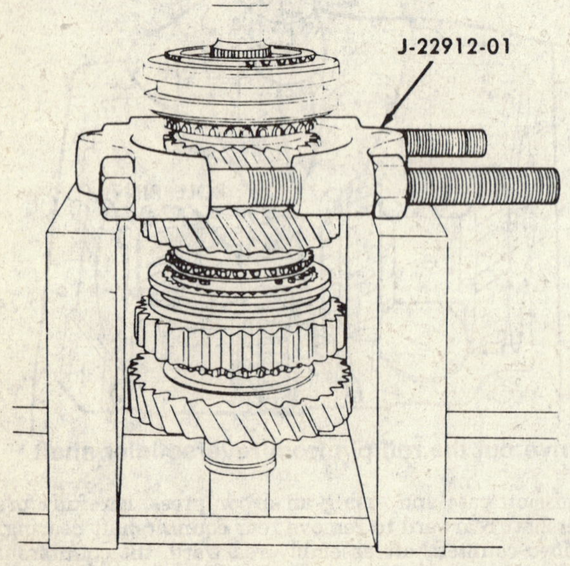

Removing 3dr/4th synchronizer with a press

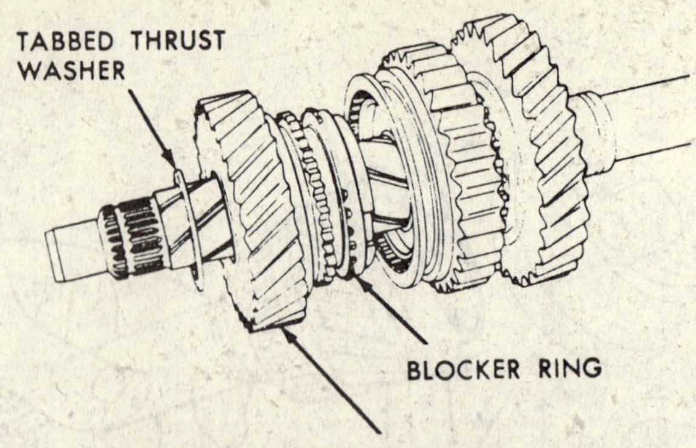

Slide off thrust washer, 2nd gear and blocker ring

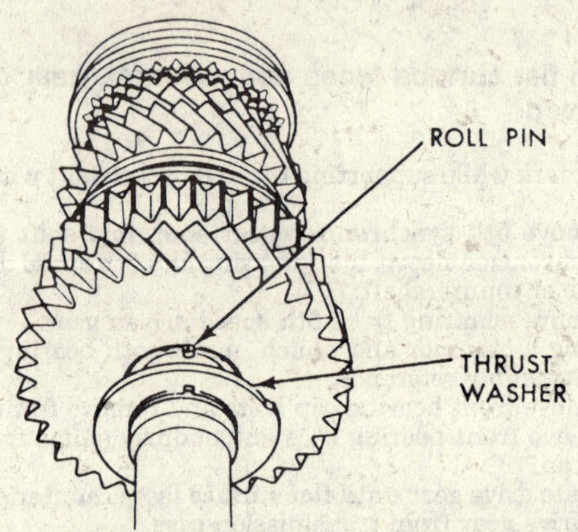

First gear thrust washer and roll pin

Mainshaft Assembly

1. Coat mainshaft and gear bores with transmission lubricant.
2. Install 1st/2nd synchronizer sleeve on mainshaft hub aligning marks made at disasssembly.
3. Install 1st/2nd synchronizer keys and springs. Engage tang end of each spring in same synchronizer key but position open end of springs opposite of each other.

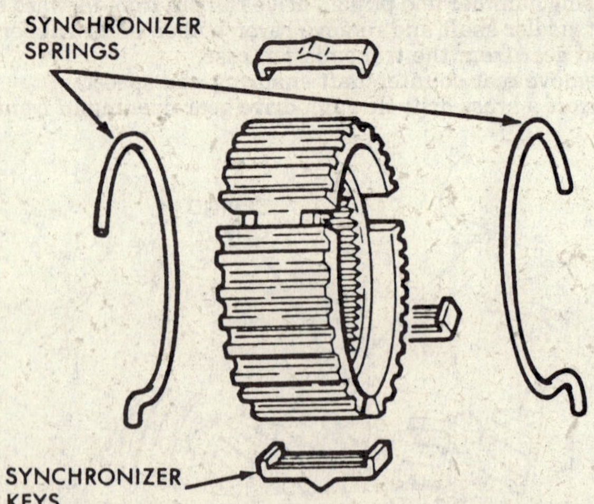

Install synchronizer spring tangs into the same key with the springs facing opposite directions

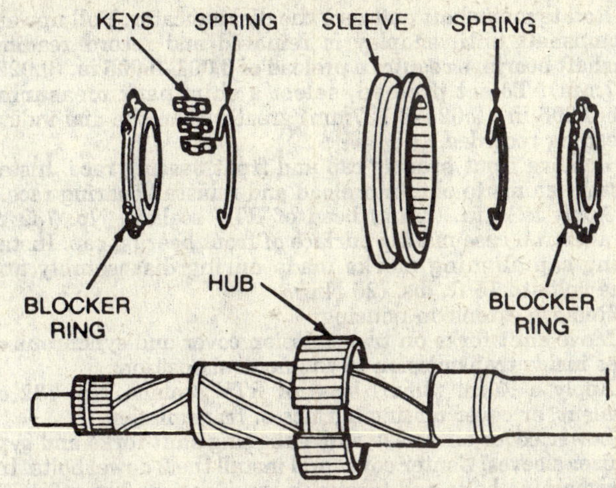

First/2nd gear synchronizer assembly, others similar

4. Install blocker ring and 2nd gear on mainshaft. Install tabbed thrust washer and 2nd gear retaining snapring on mainshaft. Be sure washer tab is properly seated in mainshaft notch.
5. Install blocker ring and 1st gear on mainshaft. Install 1st gear roll pin and then 1st gear thrust washer.
6. Slide rear bearing on mainshaft.
7. Install 5th speed gear on mainshaft using tool J–22912–01 or equivalent and arbor press. Install snapring on mainshaft.
8. Install 3rd gear, 3rd/4th synchronizer assembly and thrust bearing on mainshaft. Synchronizer hub offset must face forward.

Transmission Cover Disassembly

1. Place selector arm plates and shift rail in neutral position (centered).
2. Rotate shift rail until selector arm disengages from selector arm plates and roll pin is accessible.
3. Remove selector arm roll pin using a pin punch and hammer.
4. Remove shift rail, shift forks, selector arm plates, selector arm, interlock plate and roll pin.
5. Remove shift cover to extension housing O-ring seal using a suitable tool.
6. Remove nylon inserts and selector arm plates from shift forks. Note position of inserts and plates for assembly reference.

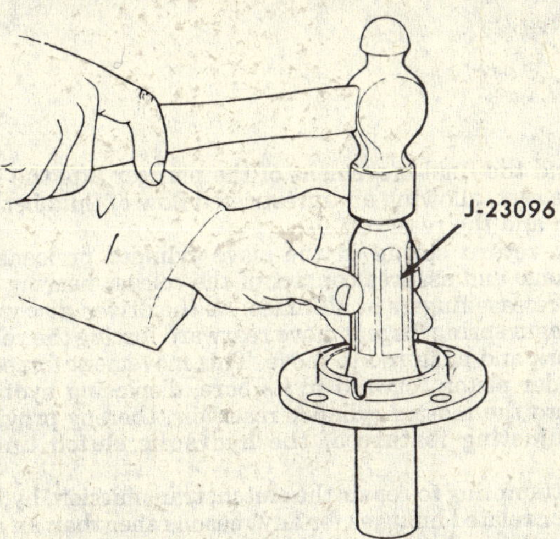

Exploded view of transmission cover

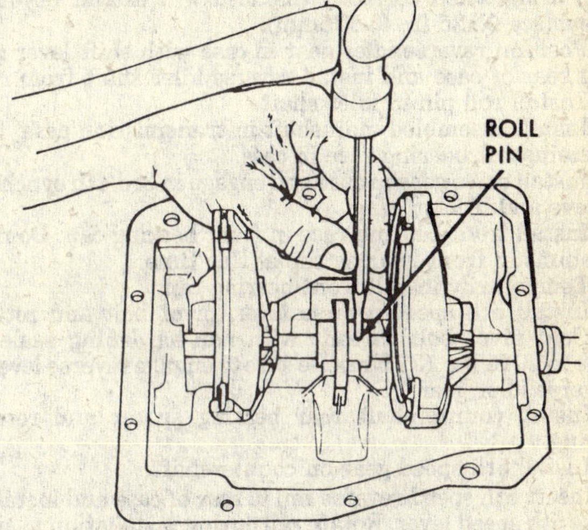

Remove selector arm roll pin

Inspection

1. Inspect the shift rail for wear.
2. Inspect the shift forks and selector arm for wear.
3. Inspect the selector arm plates and interlock plate for wear.

Cover Assembly

1. Install nylon inserts and selector arm plates in shift forks.
2. If removed, install shift rail plug. Coat edges of plug with sealer before installing.
3. Coat shift rail and rail bores with light weight grease and insert shift rail in cover. Install rail until flush with inside edge of cover.
4. Place 1st/2nd shift fork in cover with fork offset facing rear of cover and push shift rail through fork. The 1st/2nd shift fork is the larger of the 2 forks.
5. Position selector arm and C-shaped interlock plate in cover and insert shift rail through arm. Widest part of interlock plate must face away from cover and selector arm roll pin hole must face downward and toward rear of cover.
6. Position 3rd/4th shift fork in cover with fork offset facing rear of cover. The 3rd/4th shift fork selector arm plate must be under 1st/2nd shift for selector arm plate.
7. Push shift rail through 3rd/4th shift fork and into front bore in cover.
8. Rotate shift rail until selector arm plate at forward end of rail faces away from, but is parallel to cover.
9. Align roll pin holes in selector arm and shift rail and install roll pin. Roll pin must be flush with surface of selector arm to prevent pin from contacting selector arm plates during shifts.
10. Install a new shift cover to extension housing O-ring seal. Coat O-ring seal with transmission lubricant.

TRANSMISSION ASSEMBLY

1. Coat countershaft front bearing bore with Loctite® 601, or equivalent and install front countershaft bearing flush with facing of case using an arbor press.
2. Coat countershaft tabbed thrust washer with grease and install washer so tab engages depression in case.
3. Tip transmission case on end and install countershaft in front bearing bore.
4. Install countershaft rear bearing spacer. Coat countershaft rear bearing with grease and install bearing using tool J–29895 or equivalent and sleeve J–33032, or its equivalent.

The bearing when correctly installed will extend beyond the case surface 0.125 in. (3.175mm).

5. Position reverse idler gear in case with shift lever groove facing rear of case and install reverse idler shaft from rear of case. Install roll pin in idler shaft.

6. Install assembled mainshaft in transmission case. Install rear mainshaft bearing race in case.

7. Install drive gear in case and engage in 3rd/4th synchronizer sleeve and blocker ring.

8. Install front bearing race in front bearing cap. Do not install shims in front bearing cap at this time.

9. Temporarily install front bearing cap.

10. Install 5th speed/reverse lever, pivot bolt and retaining clip. Coat pivot bolt threads with non-hardening sealer and torque to 20 ft. lbs. (27 Nm). Be sure to engage reverse lever fork in reverse idler gear.

11. Install countershaft rear bearing spacer and retaining snapring.

12. Install 5th speed gear on countershaft.

13. Insert 5th speed/reverse rail in rear of case and install into reverse 5th speed lever. Rotate rail during installation to simplify engagement with lever. Connect spring to front of case.

14. Position 5th gear shift fork on 5th gear synchronizer assembly and install synchronizer on countershaft and shift fork on shift rail. Make sure roll pin hole in shift fork and shift rail are aligned.

15. Support 5th gear shift rail and fork on a block of wood and install roll pin.

16. Install thrust race against 5th speed synchronizer hub and install snapring. Install thrust bearing against race on countershaft. Coat both bearing and race with petroleum jelly.

17. Install lipped thrust race over needle-type thrust bearing and install plastic funnel into hole in end of countershaft gear.

18. Temporarily install extension housing and attaching bolts. Turn transmission case on end and mount a dial indicator on extension housing with indicator on the end of mainshaft.

19. Rotate mainshaft and zero the dial indicator. Pull upward on mainshaft until endplay is removed and record reading. Mainshaft bearings require a preload of 0.001–0.005 in. (0.025–0.127mm). To set preload, select a shim pack measuring 0.001–0.005 in. (0.025–0.127mm) greater than the dial indicator reading recorded.

20. Remove front bearing cap and front bearing race. Install necessary shims to obtain preload and reinstall bearing race.

21. Apply a ⅛ in. (3mm) bead of RTV sealant, No. 732 or equivalent, on case mating surface of front bearing cap. Install bearing cap aligning marks made during disassembly and torque bolts to 15 ft. lbs. (20 Nm).

22. Remove extension housing.

23. Move shift forks on transmission cover and synchronizer sleeves inside transmission to the neutral position.

24. Apply a ⅛ in. (3mm) bead of RTV sealant, No. 732 or equivalent, or cover mating surface of transmission.

25. Lower cover onto case while aligning shift forks and synchronizer sleeves. Center cover and install the 2 dowel bolts. Install remaining bolts and torque to specification. The offset lever to shift rail roll pin hole must be in the vertical position after cover installation.

26. Apply a ⅛ in. (3mm) bead of RTV sealant, No. 732 or equivalent, on extension housing to transmission case mating surface.

27. Install extension housing over mainshaft and shift rail to a position where shift rail just enters shift cover opening.

28. Install detent spring into offset lever and place steel ball in neutral guide plate detent. Position offset lever on steel ball and apply pressure on offset lever and at the time seat extension housing against transmission case.

29. Install extension housing bolts and torque to 25 ft. lbs. (30 Nm).

30. Align and install roll pin in offset lever and shift rail.

31. Temporarily install the shift lever. Rotate the input shaft while shifting gears to make sure the unit works.

CLUTCH

The 1984–91 trucks use a hydraulic clutch system which consists of a master and a slave cylinder. When pressure is applied to the clutch pedal (pedal depressed), the push rod contacts the plunger and pushes it up the bore of the master cylinder. In the first $\frac{1}{32}$ in. (0.8mm) of movement, the center valve seal closes the port to the fluid reservoir tank and as the plunger continues to move up the bore of the cylinder, the fluid is forced through the outlet line to the slave cylinder mounted on the clutch housing. As fluid is pushed down the pipe from the master cylinder, this in turn forces the piston in the slave cylinder outward. A push rod is connected to the slave cylinder and rides in the pocket of the clutch fork. As the slave cylinder piston moves rearward the push rod forces the clutch fork and the release bearing to disengage the pressure plate from the clutch disc. On the return stroke (pedal released), the plunger moves back as a result of the return pressure of the clutch. Fluid returns to the master cylinder and the final movement of the plunger lifts the valve seal off the seat, allowing an unrestricted flow of fluid between the system and the reservoir.

A piston return spring in the slave cylinder preloads the clutch linkage and assures contact of the release bearing with the clutch release fingers at all times. As the driven disc wears, the diaphragm spring fingers move rearward forcing the release bearing, fork and push rod to move. This movement forces the slave cylinder piston forward in its bore, displacing hydraulic fluid up into the master cylinder reservoir, thereby providing the self-adjusting feature of the hydraulic clutch linkage system.

Before attempting to repair the clutch, transmission, hydraulic system or related linkages for any reason other than an obvious failure, the problem and probable cause should be identified. A large percentage of clutch and manual transmission

Troubleshooting Basic Clutch Problems

Problem	Cause
Excessive clutch noise	Throwout bearing noises are more audible at the lower end of pedal travel. The usual causes are: • Riding the clutch • Too little pedal free-play • Lack of bearing lubrication A bad clutch shaft pilot bearing will make a high pitched squeal, when the clutch is disengaged and the transmission is in gear or within the first 2" of pedal travel. The bearing must be replaced. Noise from the clutch linkage is a clicking or snapping that can be heard or felt as the pedal is moved completely up or down. This usually requires lubrication. Transmitted engine noises are amplified by the clutch housing and heard in the passenger compartment. They are usually the result of insufficient pedal free-play and can be changed by manipulating the clutch pedal.
Clutch slips (the car does not move as it should when the clutch is engaged)	This is usually most noticeable when pulling away from a standing start. A severe test is to start the engine, apply the brakes, shift into high gear and SLOWLY release the clutch pedal. A healthy clutch will stall the engine. If it slips it may be due to: • A worn pressure plate or clutch plate • Oil soaked clutch plate • Insufficient pedal free-play
Clutch drags or fails to release	The clutch disc and some transmission gears spin briefly after clutch disengagement. Under normal conditions in average temperatures, 3 seconds is maximum spin-time. Failure to release properly can be caused by: • Too light transmission lubricant or low lubricant level • Improperly adjusted clutch linkage
Low clutch life	Low clutch life is usually a result of poor driving habits or heavy duty use. Riding the clutch, pulling heavy loads, holding the car on a grade with the clutch instead of the brakes and rapid clutch engagement all contribute to low clutch life.

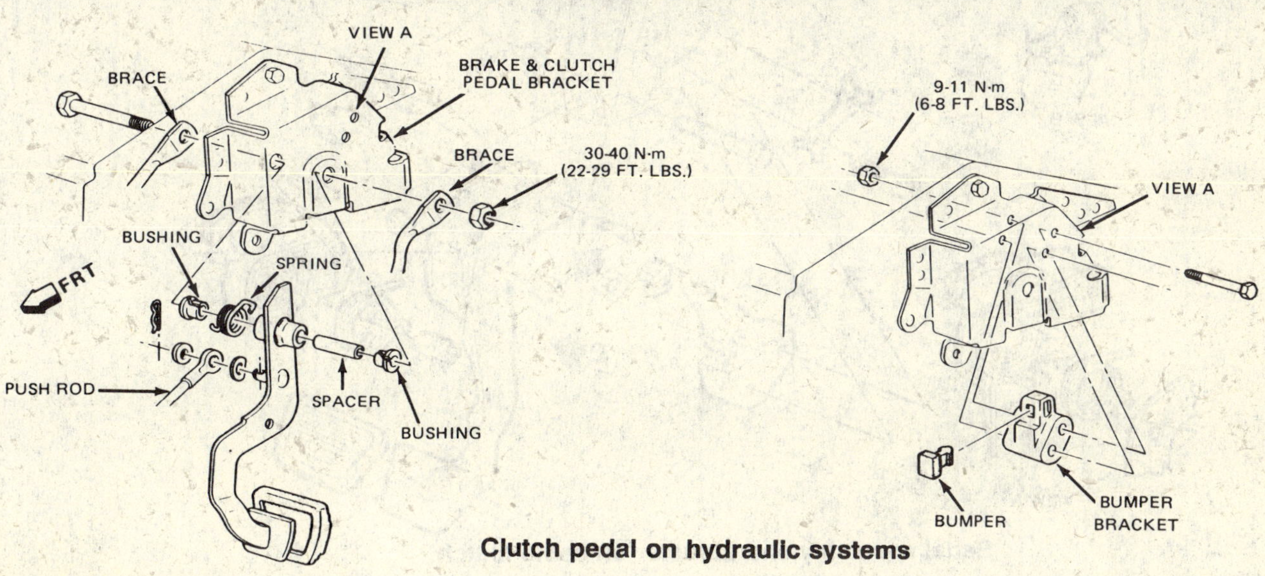

Clutch pedal on hydraulic systems

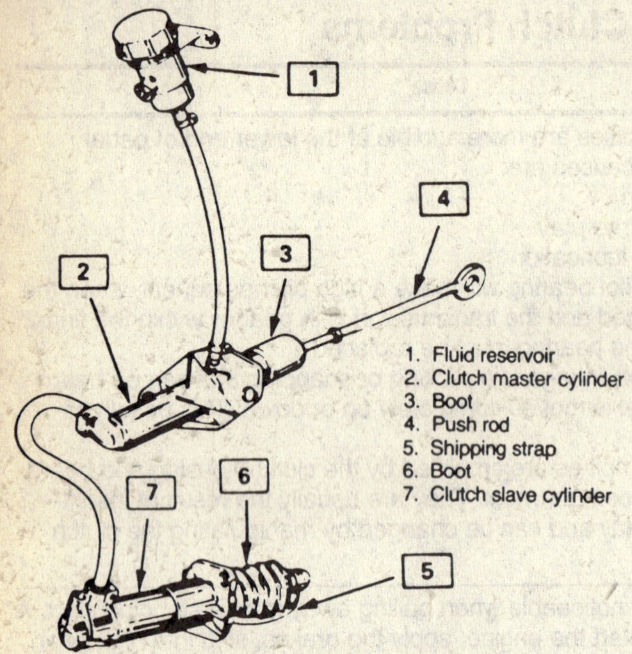

Hydraulic clutch system

problems are manifested by shifting difficulties such as high shift effort, gear clash and grinding or transmission blockout. When any of these problems occur, a careful analysis of these difficulties should be made, then the basic checks and adjustments performed before removing the clutch or transmission for repairs. Run the engine at a normal idle with the transmission in Neutral (clutch engaged). Disengage the clutch, wait about 10 seconds and shift the transmission into Reverse (no grinding noise should be heard). A grinding noise indicates incorrect clutch travel, lost motion, clutch misalignment or internal problems such as failed dampers, facings, cushion springs, diaphragm spring fingers, pressure plate drive straps, pivot rings or etc.

Adjustment

Since the hydraulic system provides automatic clutch adjustment, no adjustment of the clutch linkage or pedal height is required.

CLUTCH CABLE – 1982–83

1. Lift up on the pedal to allow the self adjuster to adjust the cable length.
2. Depress the pedal several times to set the pawl into mesh with the detent teeth.
3. Check the linkage for lost motion caused by loose or worn swivels, mounting brackets or a damaged cable.

Clutch Plate and Pressure Plate

REMOVAL AND INSTALLATION

CAUTION

The clutch plate contains asbestos, which has been determined to be a cancer causing agent. Never clean the clutch surfaces with compressed air! Avoid inhaling any dust from any clutch surface! When cleaning clutch surfaces, use a commercially available brake cleaning fluid.

1. Refer to the "Transmission, Removal and Installation" procedures in this section and remove the transmission.

NOTE: If equipped with a clutch cable (1982–83), disconnect the cable from the clutch lever and move it aside. If equipped with a hydraulic clutch system (1984–91), disconnect the slave cylinder from the clutch release fork and move it aside.

2. If the bellhousing was not removed with the transmission, remove it.
3. Remove the clutch fork from the ball stud and the dust boot.
4. Using the Clutch Alignment tool No. J-33169 (V6) or J-33034 (4-cyl), insert it into the crankshaft pilot bearing to support the clutch assembly.

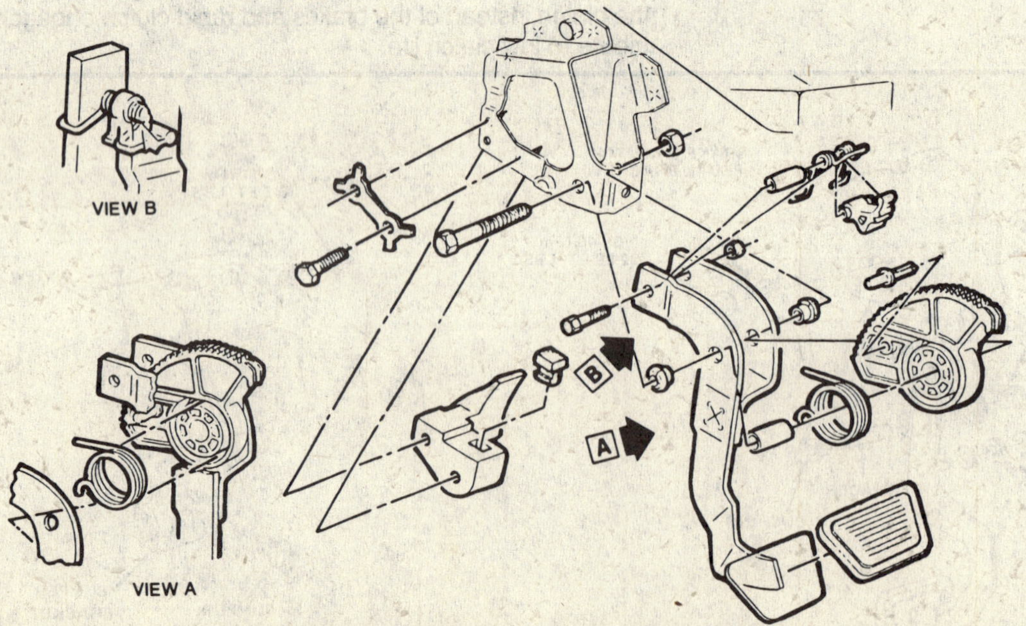

Pedal assembly and adjuster on cable clutch

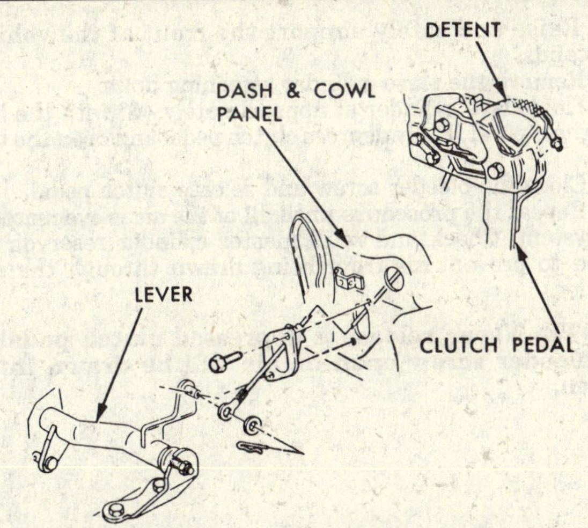

Clutch alignment tool is required to assembly clutch

5. Check for an "X" or other painted mark on the pressure plate and flywheel. If there isn't a mark, mark the assembly for installation purposes.
6. Loosen the pressure plate-to-flywheel bolts, evenly and alternately, a little at a time, until the spring tension is released. Remove the pressure plate and the driven clutch plate.
7. Check the flywheel for cracks, wear, scoring or other damage. Check the pilot bearing for wear. Replace it by removing it with a slide-type bearing puller and driving in a new one with a wood or plastic hammer.
8. To install, use the clutch assembly alignment tool and reverse the removal procedures. The raised hub of the driven plate faces the transmission. Align the mating marks and torque the pressure plate-to-flywheel bolts (evenly and alternately) to 20 ft. lbs.

NOTE: If equipped with a clutch cable (1982–83), install and/or adjust the clutch cable.

Master Cylinder

The clutch master cylinder is located in the engine compartment, on the left-side of the firewall, above the steering column.

REMOVAL AND INSTALLATION

1. Disconnect negative battery terminal from the battery.
2. Remove hush panel from under the dash.
3. Disconnect push rod from clutch pedal.
4. Disconnect hydraulic line from the clutch master cylinder.
5. Remove the master cylinder-to-cowl brace nuts. Remove master cylinder and overhaul (if necessary).
6. Using a putty knife, clean the master cylinder and cowl mounting surfaces.
7. To install, reverse the removal procedures. Torque the master cylinder-to-cowl brace nuts to 10–15 ft. lbs. (14–20 Nm). Fill master cylinder with new hydraulic fluid conforming to Dot 3 specifications. Bleed and check the hydraulic clutch system for leaks.

OVERHAUL

1. Remove the filler cap and drain fluid from the master cylinder.
2. Remove the reservoir and seal from the master cylinder. Pull back the dust cover and remove the snapring.
3. Remove the push rod assembly. Using a block of wood, tap the master cylinder on it to eject the plunger assembly from the cylinder bore.
4. Remove the seal (carefully) from the front of the plunger assembly, ensuring no damage occurs to the plunger surfaces.
5. From the rear of the plunger assembly, remove the spring, the support, the seal and the shim.
6. Using clean brake fluid, clean all of the parts.
7. Inspect the cylinder bore and the plunger for ridges, pitting and/or scratches, the dust cover for wear and cracking; replace the parts if any of the conditions exist.
8. To install, use new seals, lubricate all of the parts in clean brake fluid, fit the plunger seal to the plunger and reverse the removal procedures.
9. Insert the plunger assembly, valve end leading into the cylinder bore (easing the entrance of the plunger seal).
10. Position the push rod assembly into the cylinder bore, then install a new snapring to retain the push rod. Install dust cover onto the master cylinder. Lubricate the inside of the dust cover with Girling® Rubber Grease or equivalent.

NOTE: Be careful not to use any lubricant that will deteriorate rubber dust covers or seals.

Slave Cylinder

The slave cylinder is located on the left side of the bellhousing and controls the clutch release fork operation.

REMOVAL AND INSTALLATION

1. Disconnect the negative battery cable.
2. Raise and safely support the front of the vehicle on jackstands.
3. Disconnect the hydraulic line from clutch master cylinder. Remove the hydraulic line-to-chassis screw and the clip from the chassis.

NOTE: Be sure to plug the line opening to keep dirt and moisture out of the system.

4. Remove the slave cylinder-to-bellhousing nuts.
5. Remove the push rod and the slave cylinder from the vehicle, then overhaul it (if necessary).
6. To install, reverse the removal procedures. Lubricate leading end of the slave cylinder with Girling® Rubber Lube or equivalent. Torque the slave cylinder-to-bellhousing nuts to 10–15 ft. lbs. (14–20 Nm). Fill the master cylinder with new brake fluid conforming to Dot 3 specifications. Bleed the hydraulic system.

OVERHAUL

1. Remove the shield, the pushrod and dust cover from the slave cylinder, then inspect the cover for damage or deterioration.
2. Remove the snapring from the end of the cylinder bore.
3. Using a block of wood, tap the slave cylinder on it to eject the plunger, then remove the seal and the spring.
4. Using clean brake fluid, clean all of the parts.
5. Inspect the cylinder bore and the plunger for ridges, pitting and/or scratches, the dust cover for wear and cracking; replace the parts if any of the conditions exist.
6. To install, use new seals and lubricate all of the parts in clean brake fluid. Install the spring, the plunger seal and the plunger into the cylinder bore, then install a new snapring.
7. Lubricate the inside of the dust cover with Girling® Rubber Grease or equivalent, then install it into the slave cylinder.

NOTE: Be careful not to use any lubricant that will deteriorate the rubber dust covers or seals.

BLEEDING THE HYDRAULIC CLUTCH

Bleeding air from the hydraulic clutch system is necessary whenever any part of the system has been disconnected or the fluid level (in the reservoir) has been allowed to fall so low, that air has been drawn into the master cylinder.

1. Fill master cylinder reservoir with new brake fluid conforming to Dot 3 specifications.

CAUTION

Never, under any circumstances, use fluid which has been bled from a system to fill the reservoir as it may be aerated, have too much moisture content and possibly be contaminated.

2. Raise and safely support the front of the vehicle on jackstands.
3. Remove the slave cylinder attaching bolts.
4. Hold slave cylinder at approximately 45° with the bleeder at highest point. Fully depress clutch pedal and open the bleeder screw.
5. Close the bleeder screw and release clutch pedal.
6. Repeat the procedure until all of the air is evacuated from the system. Check and refill master cylinder reservoir as required to prevent air from being drawn through the master cylinder.

NOTE: Never release a depressed clutch pedal with the bleeder screw open or air will be drawn into the system.

AUTOMATIC TRANSMISSION

Identification

The Turbo Hydra-Matic (THM) 180C and 200C transmission is a fully automatic transmission which provides 3 forward gears and a reverse gear.

The Turbo Hydra-Matic (THM) 700-R4 and 4L60 transmission is a fully automatic transmission which provides 4 forward gears and a reverse gear. The oil pressure and shifting points are controlled by the throttle opening, via a Throttle Valve (TV) cable.

Troubleshooting Basic Automatic Transmission Problems

Problem	Cause	Solution
Fluid leakage	• Defective pan gasket	• Replace gasket or tighten pan bolts
	• Loose filler tube	• Tighten tube nut
	• Loose extension housing to transmission case	• Tighten bolts
	• Converter housing area leakage	• Have transmission checked professionally
Fluid flows out the oil filler tube	• High fluid level	• Check and correct fluid level
	• Breather vent clogged	• Open breather vent
	• Clogged oil filter or screen	• Replace filter or clean screen (change fluid also)
	• Internal fluid leakage	• Have transmission checked professionally

Troubleshooting Basic Automatic Transmission Problems

Problem	Cause	Solution
Transmission overheats (this is usually accompanied by a strong burned odor to the fluid)	• Low fluid level • Fluid cooler lines clogged • Heavy pulling or hauling with insufficient cooling • Faulty oil pump, internal slippage	• Check and correct fluid level • Drain and refill transmission. If this doesn't cure the problem, have cooler lines cleared or replaced. • Install a transmission oil cooler • Have transmission checked professionally
Buzzing or whining noise	• Low fluid level • Defective torque converter, scored gears	• Check and correct fluid level • Have transmission checked professionally
No forward or reverse gears or slippage in one or more gears	• Low fluid level • Defective vacuum or linkage controls, internal clutch or band failure	• Check and correct fluid level • Have unit checked professionally
Delayed or erratic shift	• Low fluid level • Broken vacuum lines • Internal malfunction	• Check and correct fluid level • Repair or replace lines • Have transmission checked professionally

Lockup Torque Converter Service Diagnosis

Problem	Cause	Solution
No lockup	• Faulty oil pump • Sticking governor valve • Valve body malfunction (a) Stuck switch valve (b) Stuck lockup valve (c) Stuck fail-safe valve • Failed locking clutch • Leaking turbine hub seal • Faulty input shaft or seal ring	• Replace oil pump • Repair or replace as necessary • Repair or replace valve body or its internal components as necessary • Replace torque converter • Replace torque converter • Repair or replace as necessary
Will not unlock	• Sticking governor valve • Valve body malfunction (a) Stuck switch valve (b) Stuck lockup valve (c) Stuck fail-safe valve	• Repair or replace as necessary • Repair or replace valve body or its internal components as necessary
Stays locked up at too low a speed in direct	• Sticking governor valve • Valve body malfunction (a) Stuck switch valve (b) Stuck lockup valve (c) Stuck fail-safe valve	• Repair or replace as necessary • Repair or replace valve body or its internal components as necessary
Locks up or drags in low or second	• Faulty oil pump • Valve body malfunction (a) Stuck switch valve (b) Stuck fail-safe valve	• Replace oil pump • Repair or replace valve body or its internal components as necessary

Lockup Torque Converter Service Diagnosis

Problem	Cause	Solution
Sluggish or stalls in reverse	• Faulty oil pump • Plugged cooler, cooler lines or fittings • Valve body malfunction (a) Stuck switch valve (b) Faulty input shaft or seal ring	• Replace oil pump as necessary • Flush or replace cooler and flush lines and fittings • Repair or replace valve body or its internal components as necessary
Loud chatter during lockup engagement (cold)	• Faulty torque converter • Failed locking clutch • Leaking turbine hub seal	• Replace torque converter • Replace torque converter • Replace torque converter
Vibration or shudder during lockup engagement	• Faulty oil pump • Valve body malfunction • Faulty torque converter • Engine needs tune-up	• Repair or replace oil pump as necessary • Repair or replace valve body or its internal components as necessary • Replace torque converter • Tune engine
Vibration after lockup engagement	• Faulty torque converter • Exhaust system strikes underbody • Engine needs tune-up • Throttle linkage misadjusted	• Replace torque converter • Align exhaust system • Tune engine • Adjust throttle linkage
Vibration when revved in neutral Overheating: oil blows out of dip stick tube or pump seal	• Torque converter out of balance • Plugged cooler, cooler lines or fittings • Stuck switch valve	• Replace torque converter • Flush or replace cooler and flush lines and fittings • Repair switch valve in valve body or replace valve body
Shudder after lockup engagement	• Faulty oil pump • Plugged cooler, cooler lines or fittings • Valve body malfunction • Faulty torque converter • Fail locking clutch • Exhaust system strikes underbody • Engine needs tune-up • Throttle linkage misadjusted	• Replace oil pump • Flush or replace cooler and flush lines and fittings • Repair or replace valve body or its internal components as necessary • Replace torque converter • Replace torque converter • Align exhaust system • Tune engine • Adjust throttle linkage

Transmission Fluid Indications

The appearance and odor of the transmission fluid can give valuable clues to the overall condition of the transmission. Always note the appearance of the fluid when you check the fluid level or change the fluid. Rub a small amount of fluid between your fingers to feel for grit and smell the fluid on the dipstick.

If the fluid appears:	It indicates:
Clear and red colored	• Normal operation
Discolored (extremely dark red or brownish) or smells burned	• Band or clutch pack failure, usually caused by an overheated transmission. Hauling very heavy loads with insufficient power or failure to change the fluid, often result in overheating. Do not confuse this appearance with newer fluids that have a darker red color and a strong odor (though not a burned odor).
Foamy or aerated (light in color and full of bubbles)	• The level is too high (gear train is churning oil) • An internal air leak (air is mixing with the fluid). Have the transmission checked professionally.
Solid residue in the fluid	• Defective bands, clutch pack or bearings. Bits of band material or metal abrasives are clinging to the dipstick. Have the transmission checked professionally.
Varnish coating on the dipstick	• The transmission fluid is overheating

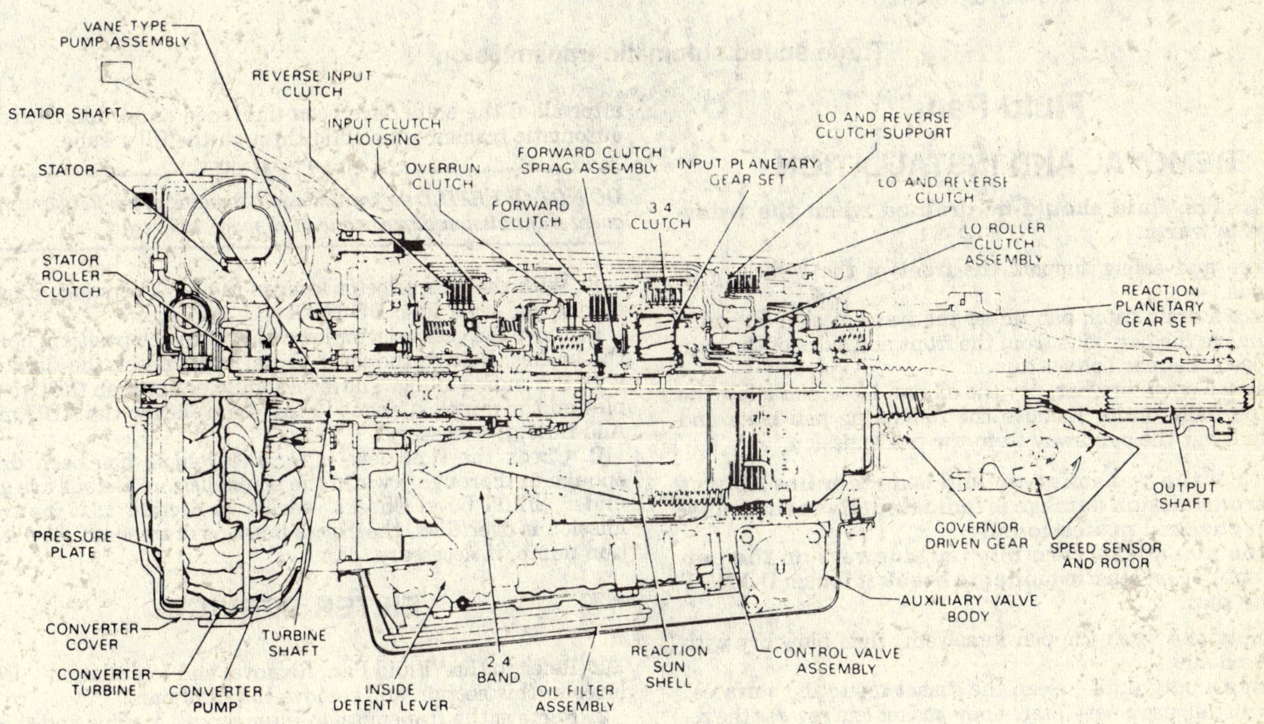

Four speed automatic transmission

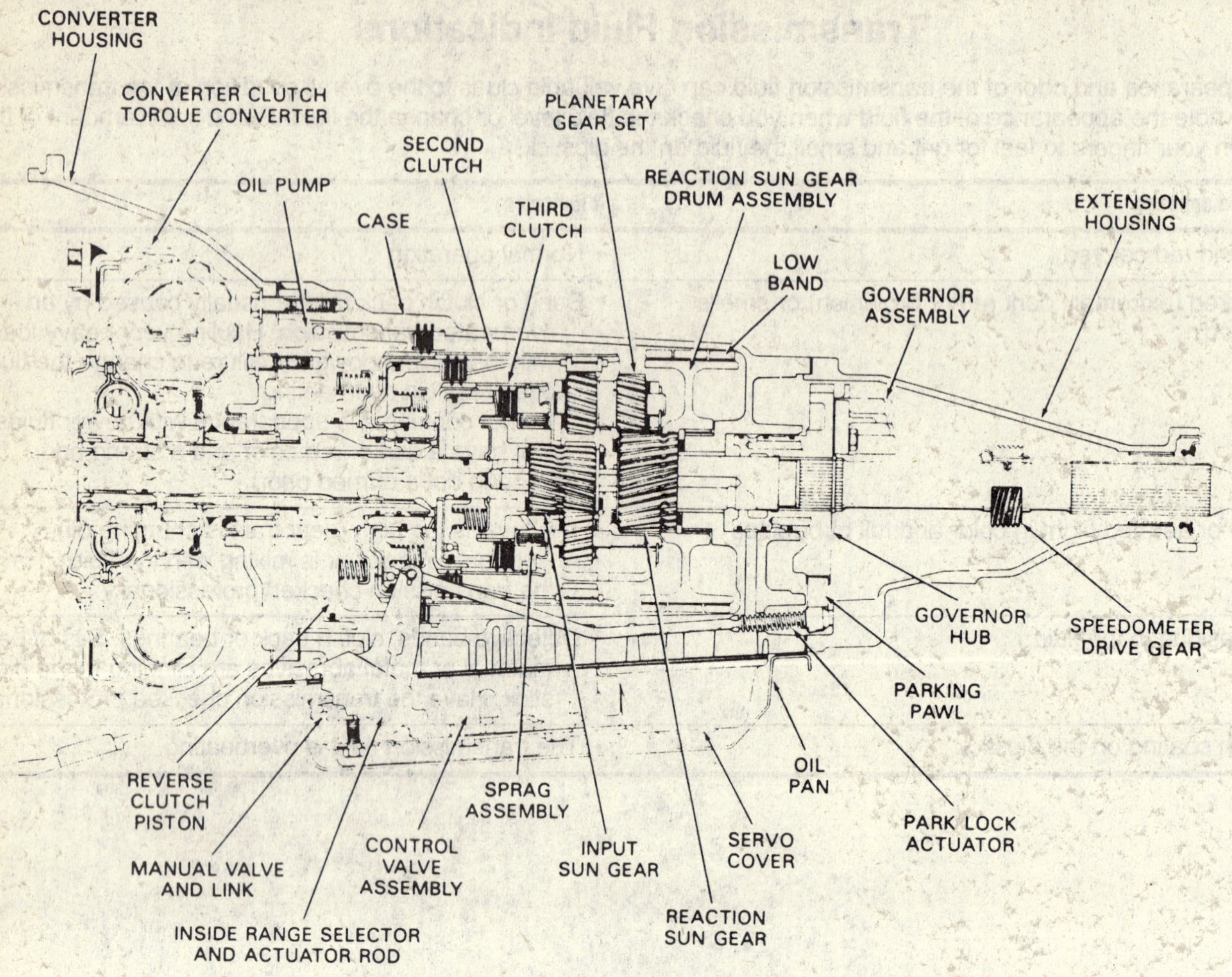

Three speed automatic transmission

Fluid Pan

REMOVAL AND INSTALLATION

NOTE: The fluid should be drained when the transmission is warm.

1. Raise and safely support the front of the vehicle with jackstands.
2. Place a drain catch pan under the transmission oil pan.
3. Remove the pan bolts from the front and sides of the pan, then loosen the rear bolts 4 turns.
4. Using a small pry bar, pry the oil pan loose and allow the pan to partially drain. Remove the remaining pan bolts and carefully lower the pan away from the transmission.

NOTE: If the transmission fluid is dark or has a burnt smell, transmission damage is indicated. Have the transmission checked professionally.

If the pan sticks, carefully tap sideways on the pan with a rubber or plastic mallet to break it loose; DO NOT dent the pan.

5. Empty and wash the pan in solvent, then blow dry with compressed air.
6. Using a putty knife, clean the gasket mounting surfaces.
7. To install, use a new filter, a new gasket and reverse the removal procedures. Torque the pan-to-transmission bolts to 12–14 ft. lbs. (in a criss-cross pattern). Recheck the bolt torque after all of the bolts have been tightened once. Add Dexron®II automatic transmission fluid through the filler tube.

CAUTION

DO NOT OVERFILL the transmission; foaming of the fluid and subsequent transmission damage due to slippage will result.

8. With the gear selector lever in the Park position, start the engine and let it idle; DO NOT race the engine.
9. Move the gear selector lever through each position, holding the brakes. Return the lever to Park and check the fluid level with the engine idling. The level should be between the two dimples on the dipstick, about ¼ in. (6mm) below the ADD mark. Add fluid, if necessary.
10. Check the fluid level after the vehicle has been driven enough to thoroughly warm the transmission. Details are given under "Fluid Level Checks" earlier in Section 1. If the transmission is overfilled, the excess must be drained off. Use a suction pump, if necessary.

FILTER SERVICE

1. Refer to the "Fluid Pan, Removal and Installation" procedures in this section and remove the fluid pan.
2. Remove the transmission filter screws or clips and the filter from the valve body. The filter may have either a fibrous or screen filtering element and is retained by one or two fasteners.

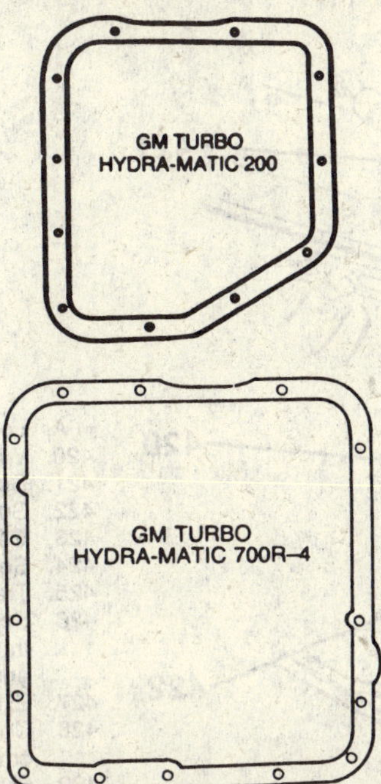

Three speed and four speed transmission pans

NOTE: If the transmission uses a filter having a fully exposed screen, it may be cleaned and reused.

3. To install, use a new filter, a new gasket and reverse the removal procedures. Torque the pan-to-transmission bolts to 12–14 ft. lbs. (in a criss-cross pattern). Recheck the bolt torque after all of the bolts have been tightened once. Add Dexron®II automatic transmission fluid through the filler tube.

Adjustments

SHIFT LINKAGE

The shift linkage should be adjusted so that the engine will start when the transmission is in the Park and Neutral positions.

1. Firmly apply the parking brake and chock the rear wheels.
2. Raise and safely support the front of the vehicle on jackstands.
3. At the left-side of the transmission, loosen the shift rod swivel-to-equalizer lever nut.
4. Rotate the transmission shift lever clockwise (forward) to the last detent (Park) position, then turn it counterclockwise (rearward) to the rear of the 2nd detent (Neutral) position.
5. At the steering column, place the gear selector lever into the Neutral position.

NOTE: When positioning the gear selector lever, DO NOT use the steering column indicator to find the Neutral position.

6. Tightly, hold the shifting rod (swivel) against the equalizer lever, then torque the adjusting nut to 11 ft. lbs.
7. Using the gear selector lever (on the steering column), place it in the Park position and check the adjustment. Move the gear selector lever into the various positions; the engine must start in the Park and the Neutral positions.

NOTE: If the engine will not start in the Neutral and/or Park positions, refer to Back-Up Light Switch adjustment procedures in Section 5 and adjust the switch.

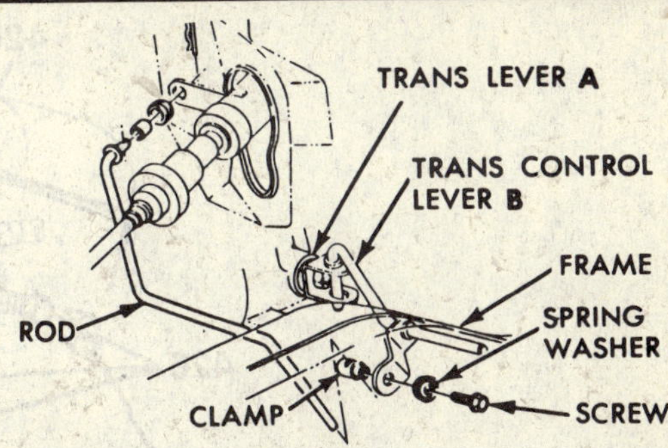

Transmission shift linkage adjustment

CAUTION

With the gear selector lever in the Park position, the parking pawl should engage the rear internal gear lugs or output ring gear lugs to prevent the vehicle from rolling and causing personal injury.

8. Align the gear selector lever indicator, if necessary. Lower the vehicle and release the parking brake.

THROTTLE VALVE (TV) CABLE

If the TV cable is broken, sticking, misadjusted or using an incorrect part for the model, the vehicle may exhibit various malfunctions, such as: delayed or full throttle shifts.

Preliminary Checks

1. Inspect and/or correct the transmission fluid level.
2. Make sure that the brakes are not dragging and that the engine is operating correctly.
3. Make sure that the cable is connected at both ends.
4. Make sure that the correct cable is installed.

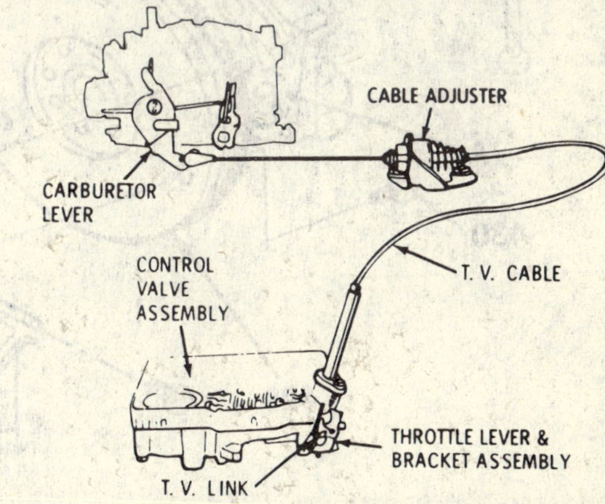

Throttle valve (TV) cable

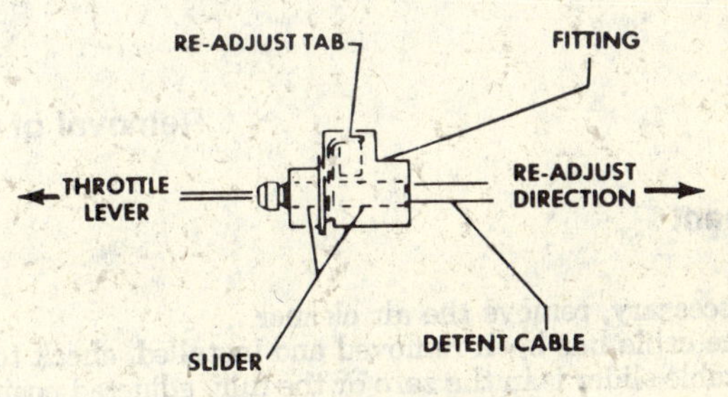

TV cable adjustment

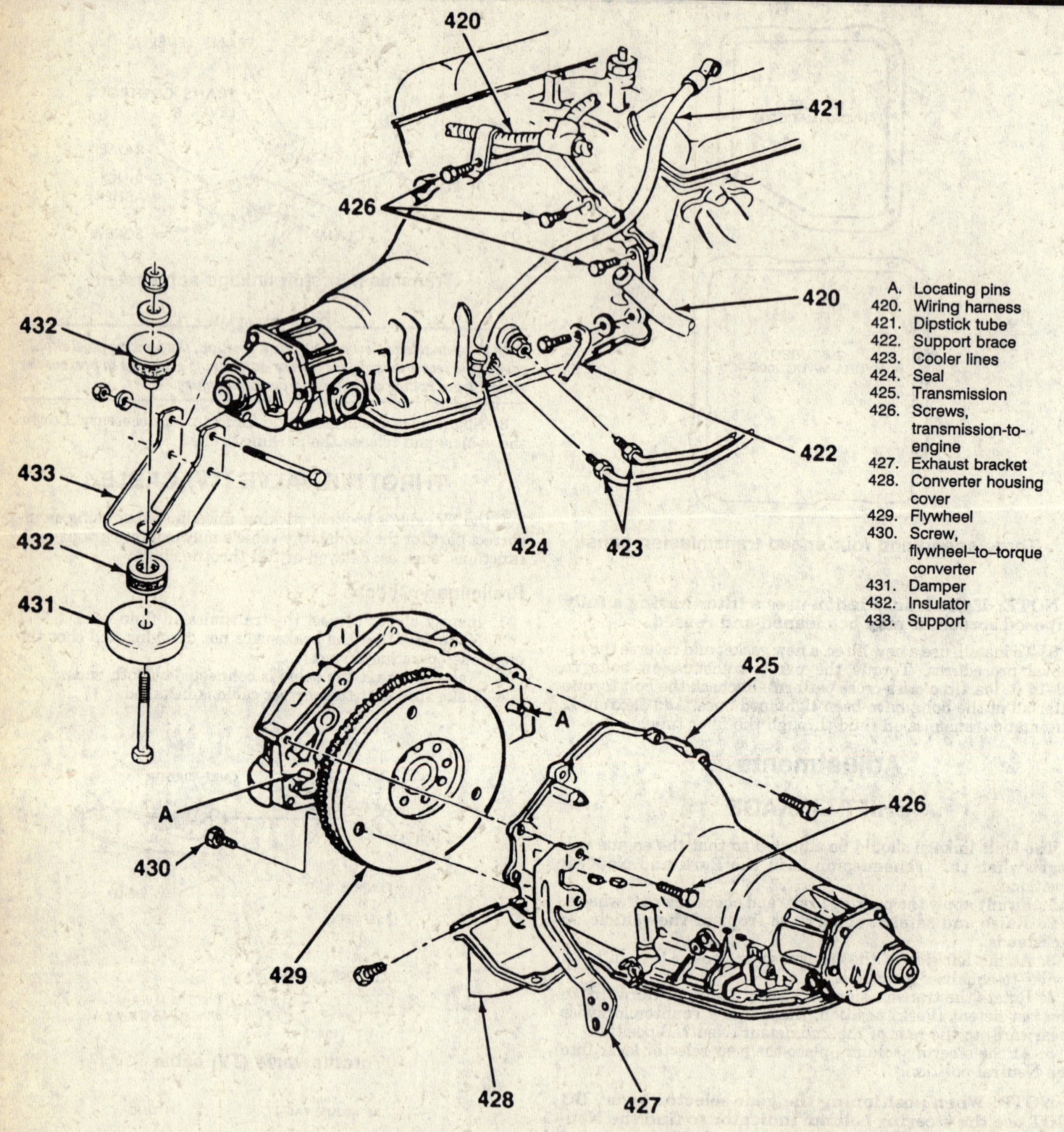

Removal of automatic transmission

Adjustment

1. If necessary, remove the air cleaner.
2. If the cable has been removed and installed, check to see that the cable slider is in the zero or the fully adjusted position; if not, perform the following procedures:
   a. Depress and hold the readjust tab.
   b. Move the slider back through the fitting (away from the throttle lever) until it stops against the fitting.
   c. Release the readjust tab.
3. Rotate the throttle lever to the Full Throttle Stop position to obtain a minimum of 1 click.
4. Release the throttle lever.

Neutral Safety Switch

The Neutral Safety Switch is a part of the Back-Up Light Switch. For the replacement or adjustment procedures, refer to the "Back-Up Light Switch, Removal and Installation" procedures in Section 6, Chassis Electrical.

Back-Up Light Switch

NOTE: The back-up light switch is located on the steering column. To replace the back-up light switch, refer to the "Back-Up Light Switch, Removal and Installation" procedures in Section 6, Chassis Electrical.

Transmission

REMOVAL AND INSTALLATION

NOTE: The following procedure requires the use of the Torque Converter Holding Strap tool No. J-21366 or equivalent.

1. Disconnect the negative battery terminal from the battery.
2. Remove the air cleaner assembly.
3. Disconnect the Throttle Valve (TV) cable from the throttle linkage.

NOTE: If equipped with a 4-cyl engine, remove the upper starter bolt.

4. Raise and safely support the truck on jackstands.
5. Remove the driveshaft-to-differential bolts, the slide the driveshaft from the transmission (2WD) or transfer case (4WD).
6. Disconnect the speedometer cable, the dipstick tube (and seal), the shift linkage and the electrical wiring connectors from the transmission.
7. Remove the transmission-to-catalytic converter support brackets and the engine–to–transmission support brackets, if equipped.
8. Remove the transmission-to-crossmember nuts/bolts, slide the crossmember rearward and remove it from the vehicle.
9. Remove the torque converter cover, then match-mark the torque converter-to-flywheel.
10. Remove the torque converter-to-flywheel bolts. Using the Converter Holding Strap tool No. J-21366 or equivalent, secure the torque converter to the transmission.
11. Using a transmission jack, position and secure it to the underside of the transmission, then to take up its weight.
12. Remove the transmission-to-engine mount bolts and the mounts from the vehicle.
13. Lower the transmission slightly to gain access to the fluid cooler lines, then disconnect and cap the fluid lines.
14. Disconnect the Throttle Valve (TV) cable from the transmission.
15. Position a floor jack or jackstand under the engine and support it.
16. Remove the transmission-to-engine bolts and then the transmission from the engine; pull the transmission rearward to disengage it and lower it from the truck.

NOTE: When removing the transmission, be careful not to allow the transmission to hang from the pilot shaft, for it could become bent.

To install:

17. Carefully position the transmission behind the engine and push it foreward to engage the pilot shaft.
18. Install the transmission–to–engine bolts. On 4–cylinder engines, torque the bolts to 25 ft. lbs. (30 Nm). On V6 engines, torque the bolts to 55 ft. lbs. (75 Nm).
19. Connect the fluid coolant lines and the TV cable.
20. Install the transmission mount bolts and torque to 25 ft. lbs. Make sure the torque converter turns freely by hand.
21. Install the crossmember bolts and torque to 25 ft. lbs. (35 Nm).
23. Install all the converter–to–flywheel bolts finger tight, then torque to 35 ft. lbs. (50 Nm). Install the converter cover.
24. Install the transmission–to–engine bracket bolts, if equipped and torque to 41 ft. lbs. (55 Nm) at the transmission end and 52 ft. lbs. (70 Nm) at the engine end.
25. Install the catalyst support bracket and torque to 50 Ft. lbs. (68 Nm).
26. Install the dipstick tube, speedometer cable and wiring.
27. Attach and adjust the shift linkage as required.
28. Install the driveshaft(s). Torque the shaft bearing cap retainer bolts on both 2WD and 4WD shafts to 17 ft. lbs. (23 Nm). On two piece shafts, torque the center bearing mount bolts to 25 ft. lbs. (39 Nm).
29. On 4-cylinder engines, install the starter bolt.
30. Lower the vehicle and connect the TV cable. Adjust as necessary.
31. Refill the transmission with fluid and check as described in Filter Service.

TRANSFER CASE

Identification

An identification tag, which is attached to the rear half of the case, gives the model number, low range reduction ratio and assembly number. The vehicles use one of three units: the New Process 207, New Process 231 or on Bravada, the Borg Warner 4472.

The Model 207 transfer case is an aluminum case, chain drive, 4 position unit providing 4WD High and Low ranges, a 2WD High range and a Neutral position. The 207 is a part-time 4WD

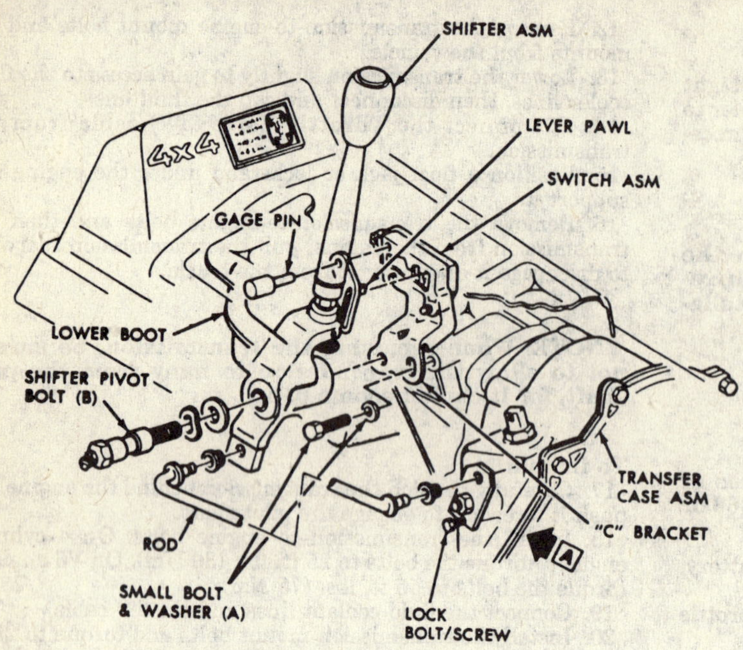

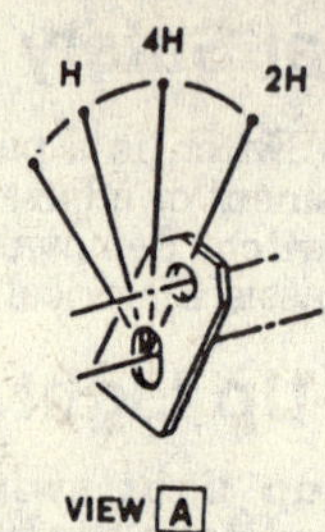

ADJUSTMENT PROCEDURE

1. Loosen bolt (A) and pivot bolt (B).
2. Shift transfer case shifter to 4 Hi.
3. Remove console and raise boot up shifter.
4. Install a gage pin 8mm or 5/16 drill bit through shifter into bracket (C).
5. Install a bolt at the transfer case shift lever as shown in View A. This will lock the transfer case in 4 Hi.
6. Tighten bolt (A) to 34-48 N•m (25-35 FT. LBS.) next tighten pivot bolt (B) to 120-140 N•m (88-103 FT. LBS.).
7. Remove the bolt at the transfer case lever and the gage pin at the shifter.
8. Install shifter boot retaining screws and install console.

Shift lever adjustment on Model 207 and 231 transfer case

unit. Range positions are selected by a floor mounted shift lever. Dexron® II automatic transmission fluid, or equavalent, is the recommended lubricant.

The Model 231 is a part-time transfer case with a bulit in low range gear reduction system. A front axle disconnect mechanism is used for 2-wheel drive operation. The 231 has three operating ranges — 2-wheel drive High and 4-wheel drive High and Low, plus Neutral. The 4-wheel drive operating ranges are undifferentiated. Dexron® II automatic transmission fluid, or equivalent, is used as a lubricant.

The Model 4472 used on the Bravada is an all-wheel drive system. It has a two piece aluminum case and a chain driven viscous clutch that in turn drives a planetary gear set. The gear set splits the torque ⅓ to the front and ⅔ to the rear. This system is engaged full time, there is no neutral or high/low range and no control lever or switch. The clutch pack is sealed and not servicable.

Adjustment

SHIFT LEVER

Model 207 and 231

1. Loosen the switch-to-transfer case bolt and the shift lever-to-transfer case pivot bolt.
2. Using the shift lever, shift the transfer case to the 4WD High position.
3. Remove the console and slide the upper boot Up the shift lever.
4. Loosen the lower transfer case shift lever-to-transfer case lock bolt.
5. Using a $^{3}/_{16}$ in. (5mm) drill bit, insert it through the shift lever and into the switch bracket.
6. Install the lower transfer case shift lever-to-transfer case lock bolt to lock the lever into position; this will lock the transfer case into 4WD High position.
7. Torque the switch bracket bolt to 30 ft. lbs. and the shifter pivot bolt to 96 ft. lbs.
8. Remove the lower transfer case shift lever-to-transfer case lock bolt, which was installed to lock the lever.
9. Remove the drill bit and check the shifting action.

Transfer Case

REMOVAL AND INSTALLATION

1. Disconnect the negative battery cable from the battery.
2. Shift the transfer case into the 4WD High range.
3. Raise and safely support the vehicle on jackstands.
4. From under the transmission/transfer case assembly, remove the skid plate bolts and the skid plate.
5. Remove the front/rear driveshaft-to-transfer case nuts/bolts and lower the driveshafts from the transfer case.
6. Remove the speedometer cable, the vacuum harness and/or the electrical connectors from the transmission.
7. Remove console cover from the console; slide the upper boot up the shift lever and remove the shift boot.
8. Remove the shift lever-to-transfer case bolt and shift lever from the case.
9. Remove the catalytic converter hanger-to-catalytic converter bolts.
10. Remove the transmission/transfer case assembly mount-to-crossmember bolts.
11. Using a transmission jack, secure it to the transmission/transfer case assembly, then raise the assembly.
12. Remove the crossmember-to-chassis bolts and the crossmember from the vehicle.
13. Lower the transmission/transfer case assembly, then remove transfer case-to-transmission bolts, the transfer case from the adapter (A/T) or extension housing (M/T).

To install:

14. Use a new transfer case-to-transmission gasket and mount the unit to the transmission. Torque the bolts to 23 ft. lbs. (31 Nm), or 38 ft. lbs. (52 Nm) on Bravada.
15. Lower the transmission enough to install the shift lever bracket bolts, if removed.

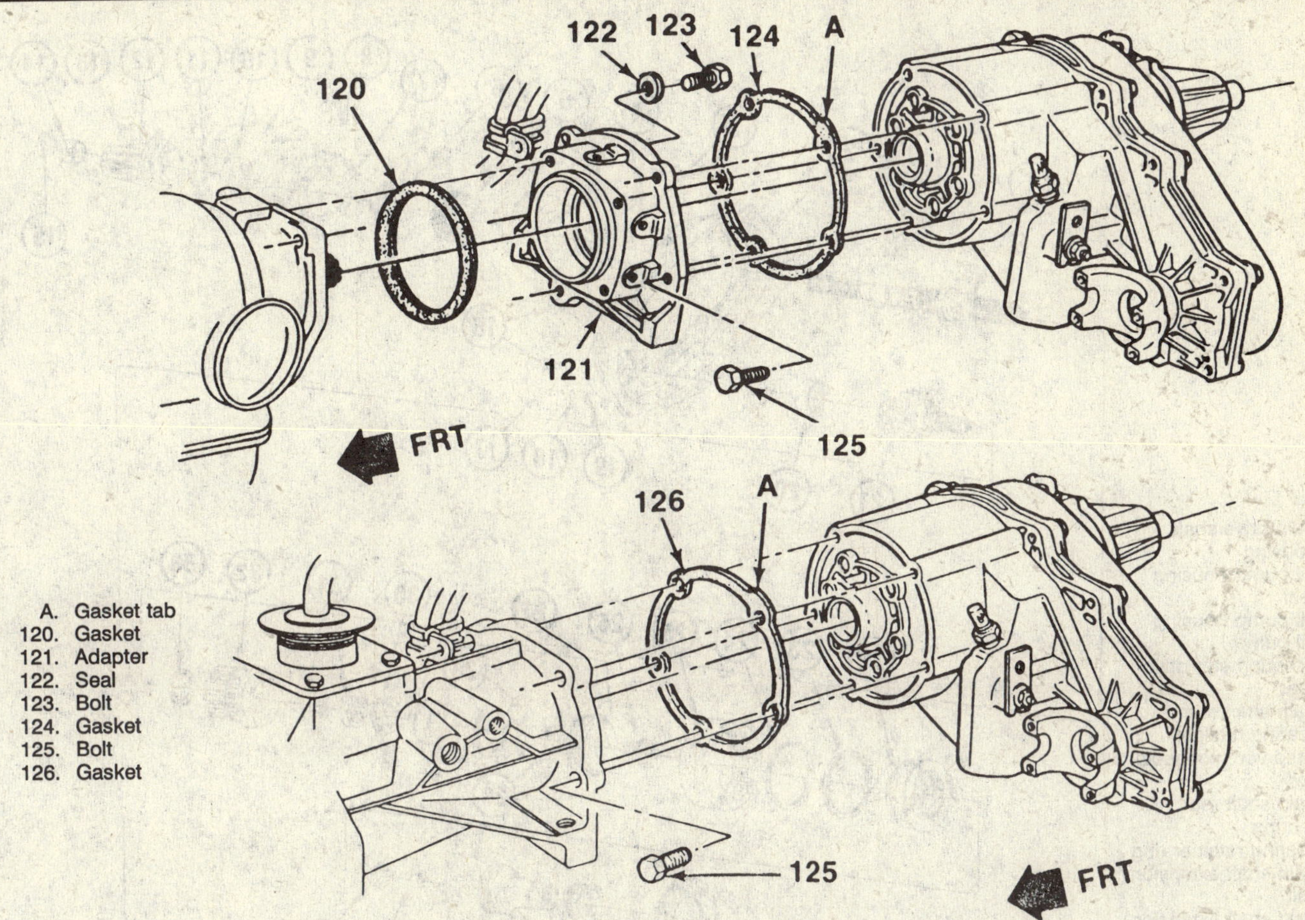

Removing transfer case from manual and automatic transmission

16. Raise the transmission to install the catalytic converter hanger and crossmember. Torque the crossmember and the converter hanger–to–transmission bolts to 22 ft. lbs. (30 Nm). Torque the converter bolts to 40 ft. lbs. (53 Nm).
17. Install the driveshafts and torque the bearing cap retainer bolts to 15 ft. lbs. (20 Nm).
18. Connect the speedometer cable and shift linkage. Adjust as required.
19. Install the skid plate if equipped, fill the transfer case with Dextron II transmission fluid and road test the vehicle.

New Process 207 Overhaul

CASE DISASSEMBLY

1. Remove fill and drain plugs.
2. Remove front yoke. Discard yoke seal washer and yoke nut.
3. Turn transfer case on end and position front case on wood blocks.
4. Shift transfer case to 4-Low.
5. Remove extension housing attaching bolts. Using a hammer, tap the shoulder on the extension housing to break sealer loose.
6. Remove the snapring for the rear bearing from the main shaft and discard.
7. Remove the rear retainer attaching bolts. Using a hammer, tap the shoulder on the retainer to break sealer loose.
8. Remove the rear retainer and pump housing from the transfer case.
9. Remove the pump seal from the pump housing and discard.
10. Remove the speedometer drive gear from the main shaft.
11. Remove the pump gear from the main shaft.
12. Remove the bolts attaching the rear case to the front case and remove rear case. To separate the case, insert a pry bar into the slots cast into the case ends and pry upward. DO NOT attempt to wedge the case halves apart at any point on the mating surfaces.
13. Remove the front output shaft and drive chain as an assembly. It may be necessary to raise the main shaft slightly for the output shaft to clear the case.
14. Pull up on the mode fork rail until rail clears range fork and rotate mode fork and rail and remove from transfer case.
15. Pull up on the main shaft until it separates from the planetary assembly. Remove the main shaft from the transfer case.
16. Remove the planetary assembly with the range fork from the transfer case.
17. Remove the planetary thrust washer, input gear thrust bearing and front thrust washer from the transfer case.
18. Remove the shift sector detent spring and retaining bolt.
19. Remove the shift sector, shaft and spacer from the transfer case.
20. Remove the locking plate retaining bolts and lock plate from the transfer case.
21. Remove the input gear pilot bearing using J-29369-1 or equivalent with a slide hammer.

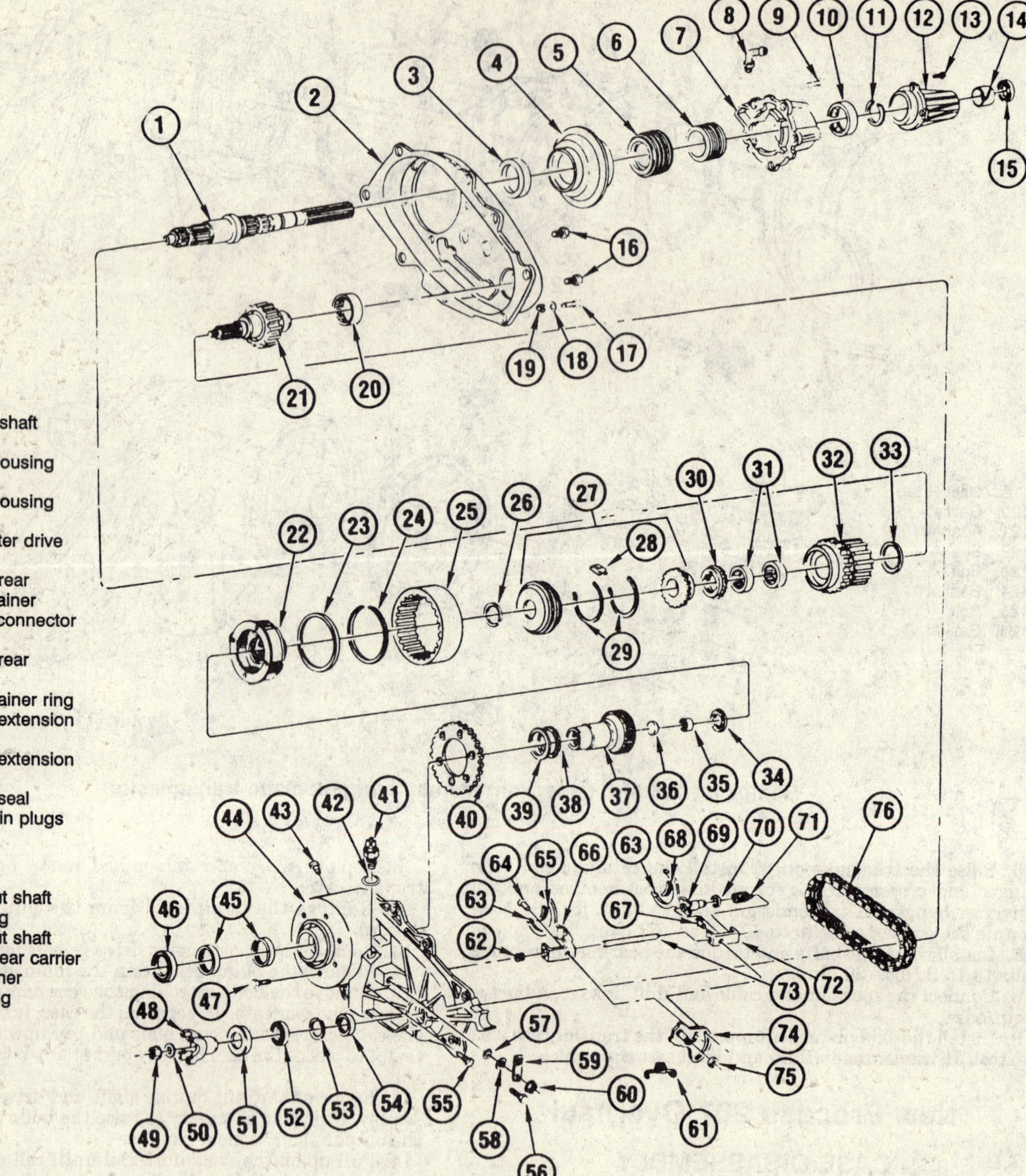

1. Main drive shaft
2. Housing
3. Oil pump housing seal
4. Oil pump housing
5. Oil pump
6. Speedometer drive gear
7. Main shaft rear bearing retainer
8. Case vent connector
9. Bolt
10. Main shaft rear bearing
11. Bearing retainer ring
12. Main shaft extension
13. Bolt
14. Main shaft extension bushing
15. Main shaft seal
16. Fill and drain plugs
17. Bolt
18. Washer
19. Dowel
20. Front output shaft pilot bearing
21. Front output shaft
22. Planetary gear carrier
23. Thrust washer
24. Retainer ring

Exploded view of New Process transfer case

22. Remove the front output shaft seal, input shaft seal and the rear extension seal using a brass drift.
23. Using J-33841 with J-8092 or equivalent, press the 2 caged roller bearings for the front input shaft gear from the transfer case.
24. Using J-29369-2 with J-33367 or a slide hammer, remove the rear bearing for the front output shaft.
25. Using a hammer and drift, remove the rear main shaft bearing from the rear retainer.
26. Using an awl, remove the snapring retaining the front out-

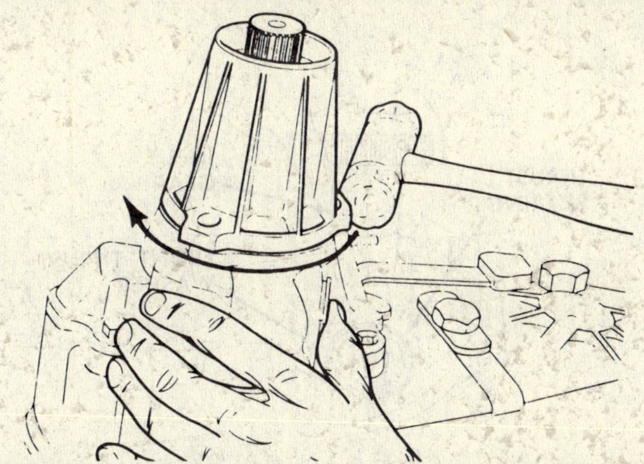
Tap the extension housing sideways to break the seal

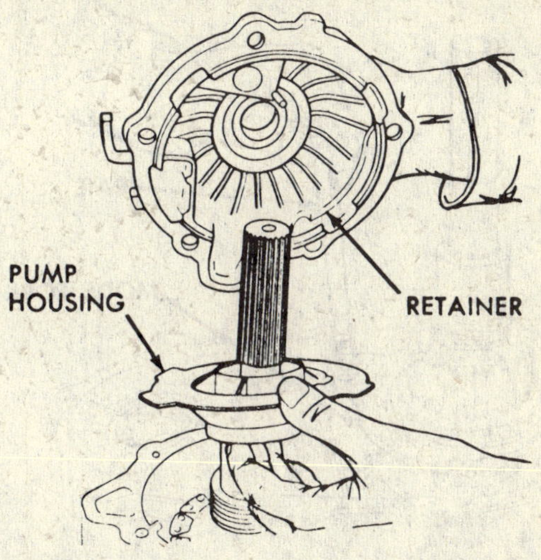

Remove the pump housing and retainer

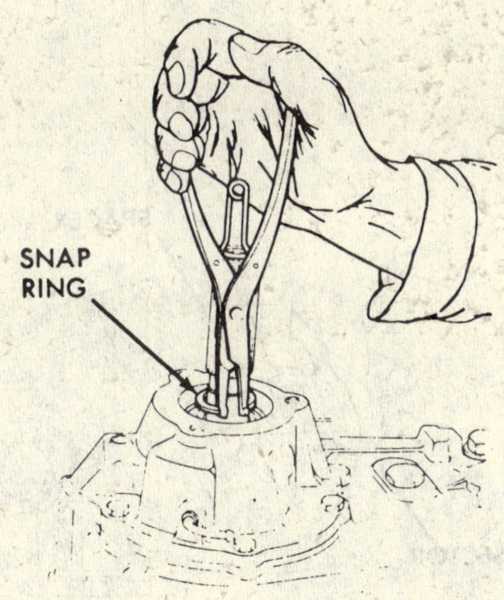

Rear bearing retainer snapring

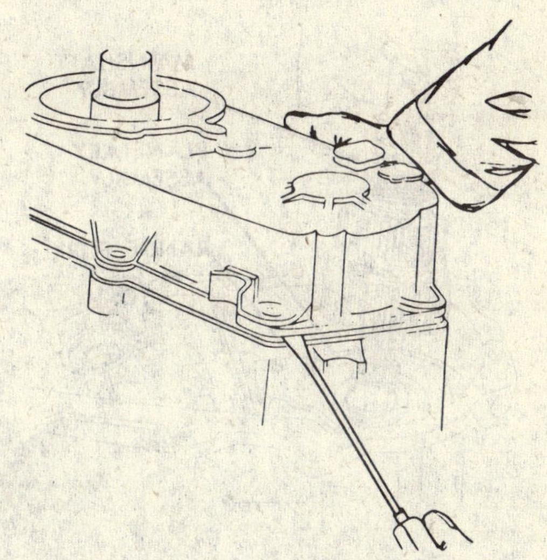
Carefully pry the case apart at the slots

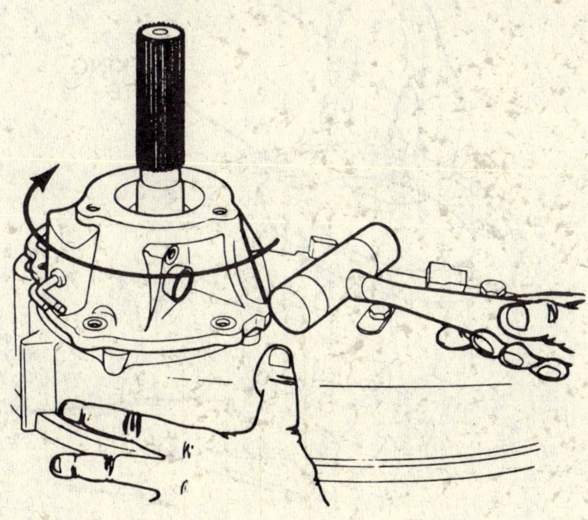
Tap the retainer housing to break the seal

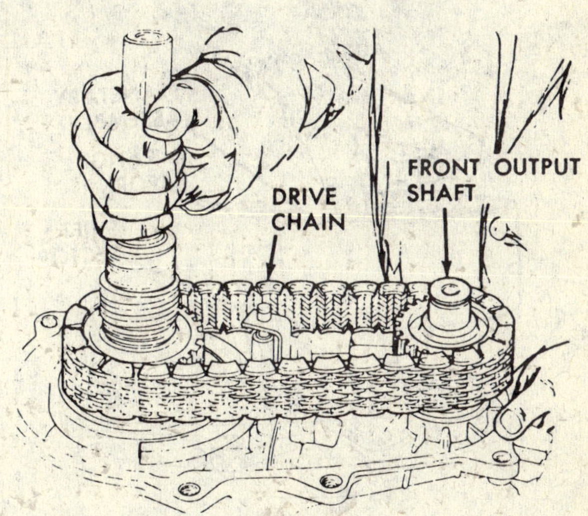

Raise the mainshaft slightly to remove the output shaft and chain

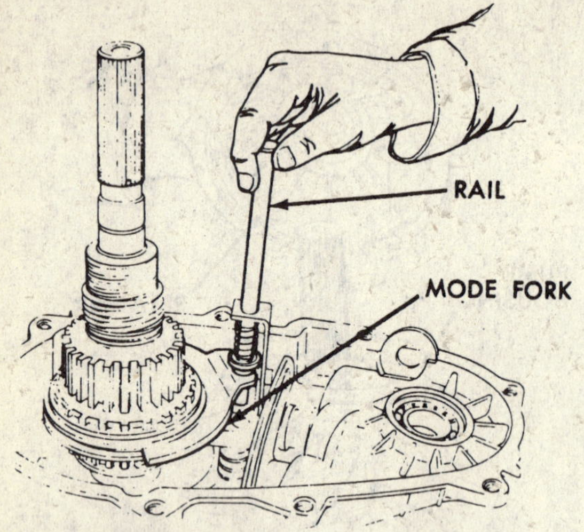

Remove the rail and mode fork

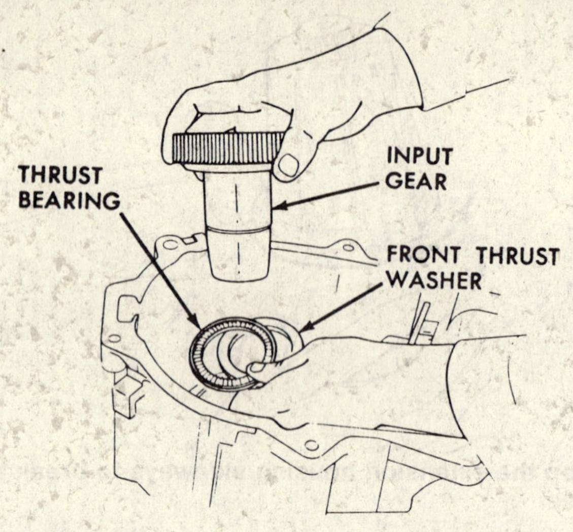

Lift out the input gear and thrust bearing

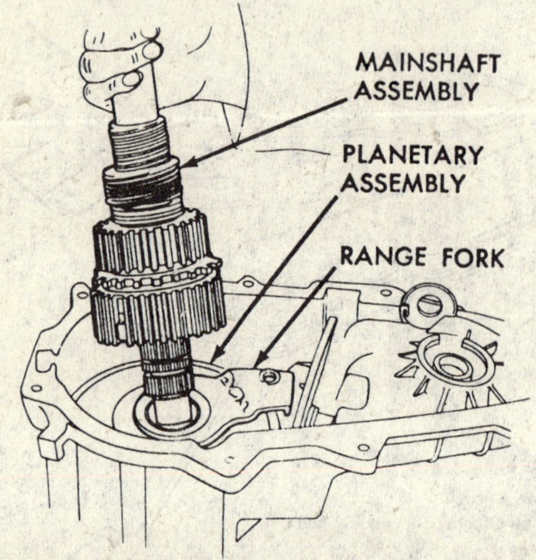

Remove the mainshaft

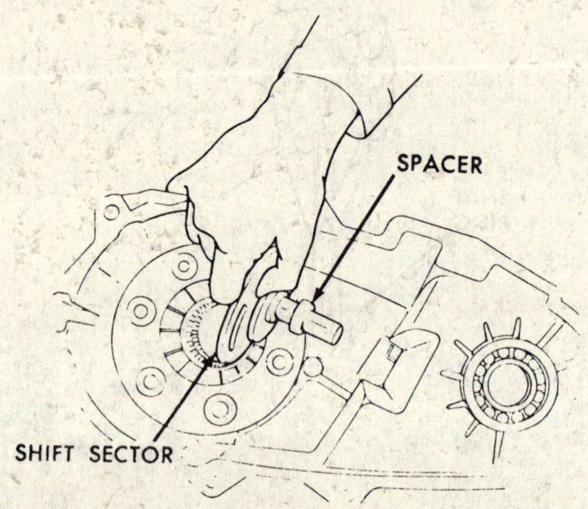

Remove the shift selector

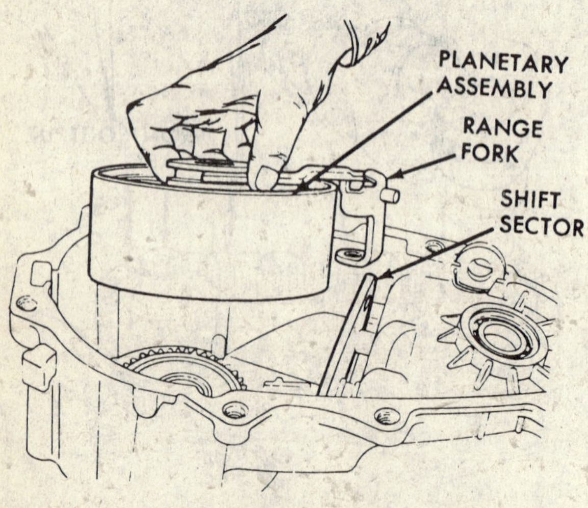

Lift out the planetary assembly

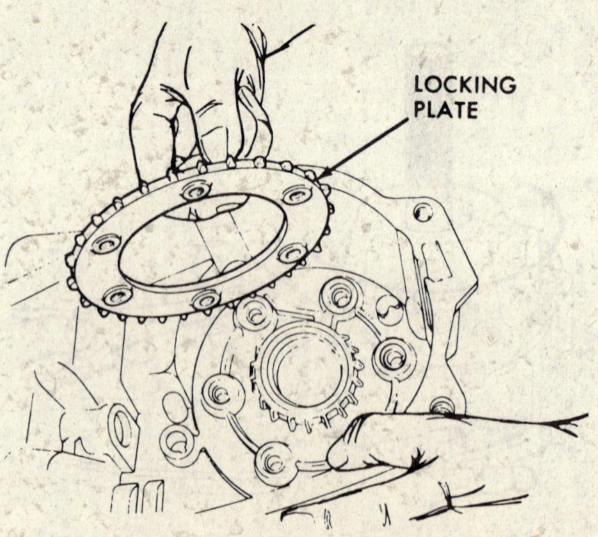

Remove the locking plate

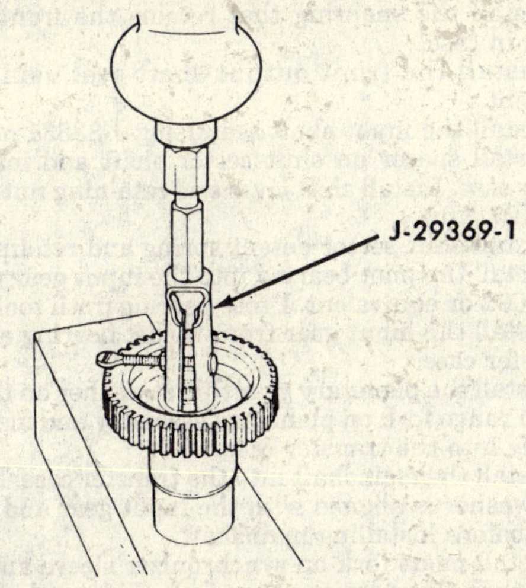

A special tool is required to remove the pilot bearing

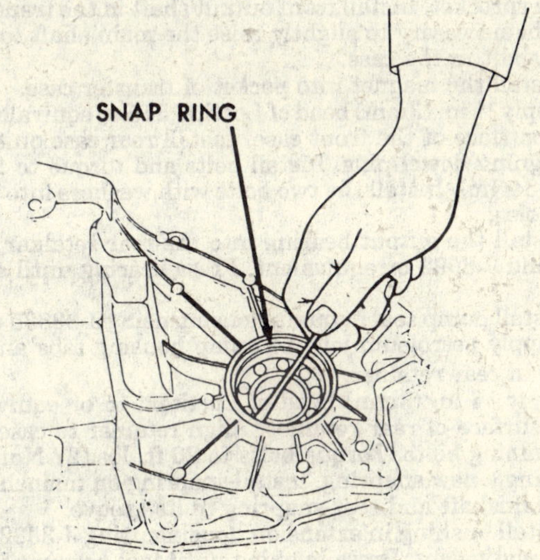

Pry out the snapring to remove the output shaft bearing

put shaft bearing. Using a hammer and drift, remove the bearing from the case.

27. Remove the bushing from the extension housing using J-33839 with J-8092 or equivalent. Press bushing from the extension housing.

MAINSHAFT DISASSEMBLY

1. Remove the speedometer gear.
2. Carefully pry off the pump gear from the mainshaft.
3. Remove the snapring retaining the synchronizer hub from the mainshaft.
4. Using a brass hammer, tap the synchronizer hub from mainshaft.
5. Remove the drive sprocket.
6. Using J-33826 and J-8092 or equivalent, press 2 caged roller bearings from the drive sprocket.
7. Remove synchronizer keys and retaining rings from the synchronizer hub.
8. Clean and inspect all parts. Replace any parts if they show evidence of excessive wear, distortion or damage.

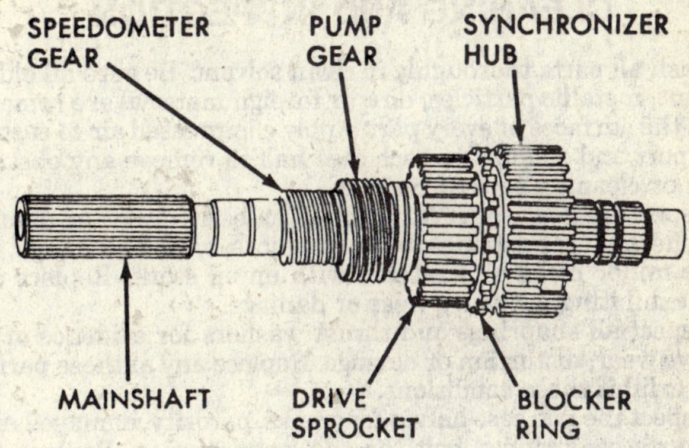

Mainshaft assembly

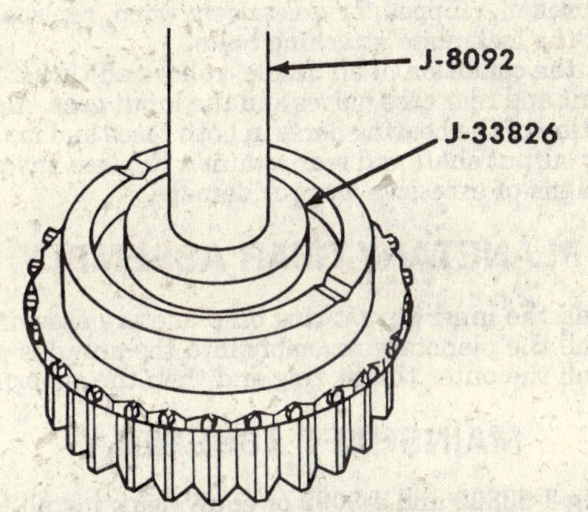

The drive sprocket must be pressed off

PLANETARY GEAR DISASSEMBLY

1. Remove the snapring retaining the planetary gear in the annulus gear.
2. Remove outer thrust ring and discard.
3. Remove planetary assembly from the annulus gear.
4. Remove inner thrust ring from the planetary assembly and discard.
5. Clean and inspect parts. Replace any parts if they show evidence of excessive wear, distortion or damage.

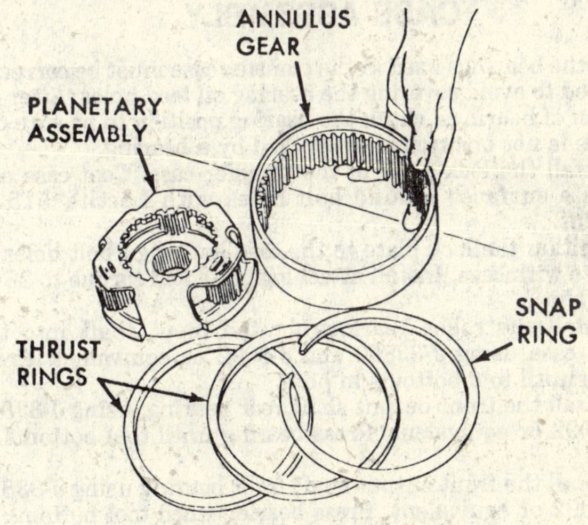

Planetary gear assembly

CLEANING AND INSPECTION

Wash all parts thoroughly in clean solvent. Be sure all old lubricant, metallic particles, dirt, or foreign material are removed from the surfaces of every part. Apply compressed air to each oil feed port and channel in each case half to remove any obstructions or cleaning solvent residue.

Inspect all gear teeth for signs of excessive wear or damage and check all gear splines for burrs, nicks, wear or damage. Remove minor nicks or scratches with an oil stone. Replace any part exhibiting excessive wear or damage.

Inspect all snaprings and thrust washers for evidence of excessive wear, distortion or damage. Replace any of these parts if they exhibit these conditions.

Inspect the two case halves for cracks, porosity, damaged mating surfaces, stripped bolt threads, or distortion. Replace any part that exhibits these conditions. Inspect the low range lock plate in the front case. If the lock plate teeth or the plate hub is cracked, broken, chipped, or excessively worn, replace the lock plate and the lock plate attaching bolts.

Inspect the condition of all needle, roller and thrust bearings in the front and rear case halves and the input gear. Also, check the condition of the bearing bores in both cases and in the input gear, rear output shaft and rear retainer. Replace any part that exhibits signs of excessive wear or damage.

PLANETARY GEAR ASSEMBLY

1. Install the inner thrust ring on planetary assembly.
2. Install the planetary assembly into the annulus gear.
3. Install the outer thrust ring and then the snapring.

MAINSHAFT ASSEMBLY

1. Using J-33828 and J-8092 or equivalent, install the front drive sprocket bearing. Press bearing until tool bottoms out. Bearing should be flush with front surface. Reverse tool on J-8092 or equivalent and press rear bearing into sprocket until tool bottoms out. The rear bearing should be recessed after installation.
2. Install thrust washer on the mainshaft.
3. Install drive sprocket on the mainshaft.
4. Install blocker ring and synchronizer hub on the mainshaft. Seat hub on main shaft and install a new snapring to retain.
5. Install pump gear on the mainshaft. Tap the gear with a hammer to seat on mainshaft.
6. Install speedometer gear on the mainshaft.

CASE ASSEMBLY

All of the bearings used in the transfer case must be correctly positioned to avoid covering the bearing oil feed holes. After installation of bearings, check the bearing position to be sure the feed hole is not obstructed or blocked by a bearing.

1. Install the lock plate in the transfer case. Coat case and lock plate surfaces around bolt holes with Loctite®515 or equivalent.
2. Position the lock plate to the case and align bolt holes in lock plate with case. Install attaching bolts and torque to 25 ft. lbs. (34 Nm).
3. Install the roller bearings for the input shaft into the transfer case using J-33830 and J-8092 or equivalent. Press bearings until tool bottoms in bore.
4. Install the front output shaft rear bearing, using J-33832 and J-8092 or equivalent. Press bearing until tool bottoms in case.
5. Install the front output shaft front bearing using J-33833 and J-8092 or equivalent. Press bearing until tool bottoms in bore.
6. Install the snapring that retains the front output shaft bearing in case.
7. Install the front output shaft seal using J-33834 or equivalent.
8. Install the input shaft seal using J-33831 or equivalent.
9. Install spacer on shift sector shaft and install sector in transfer case. Install shift lever and retaining nut. Torque to 20 ft. lbs. (27 Nm).
10. Install shift sector detent spring and retaining bolt.
11. Install the pilot bearing into the input gear using J-33829 and J-8092 or equivalent. Press bearing until tool bottoms out.
12. Install the input gear front thrust bearing and input gear in transfer case.
13. Install the planetary gear thrust washer on the input gear. Position range fork on planetary assembly and install planetary assembly into the transfer case.
14. Install the mainshaft into the transfer case. Make sure the thrust washer is aligned with the input gear and planetary assembly before installing mainshaft.
15. Install mode fork on synchronizer sleeve and rotate until mode fork is aligned with range fork. Slide mode fork rail down through range fork until rail is seated in bore of transfer case.
16. Position drive chain on front output shaft and install chain on drive sprocket. Install front output shaft in the transfer case. It may be necessary to slightly raise the main shaft to seat the output shaft in the case.
17. Install the magnet into pocket of transfer case.
18. Apply ⅛ in. (3mm) bead of Loctite®515 or equivalent to the mating surface of the front case. Install rear case on the front case aligning dowel pins. Install bolts and torque to 20–25 ft. lbs.(27–34Nm). Install the two bolts with washers into the dowel pin holes.
19. Install the output bearing into the rear retainer using J-33833 and J-8092 or equivalent. Press bearing until seated in bore.
20. Install pump seal in pump housing using J-33835 or equivalent. Apply petroleum jelly to pump housing tabs and install housing in rear retainer.
21. Apply ⅛ in. (3mm) bead of Loctite®515 or equivalent to mating surface of rear retainer. Align retainer to case and install retaining bolts. Torque bolts to 20 ft. lbs.(27 Nm).
22. Using a new snapring, install snapring on mainshaft. Pull up on mainshaft and seat snapring in its groove.
23. Install bushing in extension housing using J-33826 and J-8092 or equivalent. Press bushing until tool bottoms in bore.
24. Install a new seal in the extension housing using J-33843 or equivalent.
25. Apply ⅛ in. (3mm) bead of Loctite®515 or equivalent to mating surface of extension housing. Align extension housing to the rear retainer and install attaching bolts. Torque bolts to specification 25 ft. lbs. (34 Nm).
26. Install front yoke on output shaft. Install a new yoke seal washer with a new nut and torque to 90–130 ft. lbs. (122–176 Nm).
27. Install drain and fill plugs.

New Process 231 Overhaul

DISASSEMBLY

1. Remove the transfer case from the vehicle and clean it before disassembly.
2. Remove the attaching nuts from the front and rear output yokes. Remove the yokes and sealing washers.
3. Move the range lever to 4-LOW. Remove the bolts and tap the extension housing off of the rear retainer.

NOTE: To avoid damaging the sealing surfaces of the extension housing, DO NOT attempt to pry or wedge the housing off the retainer.

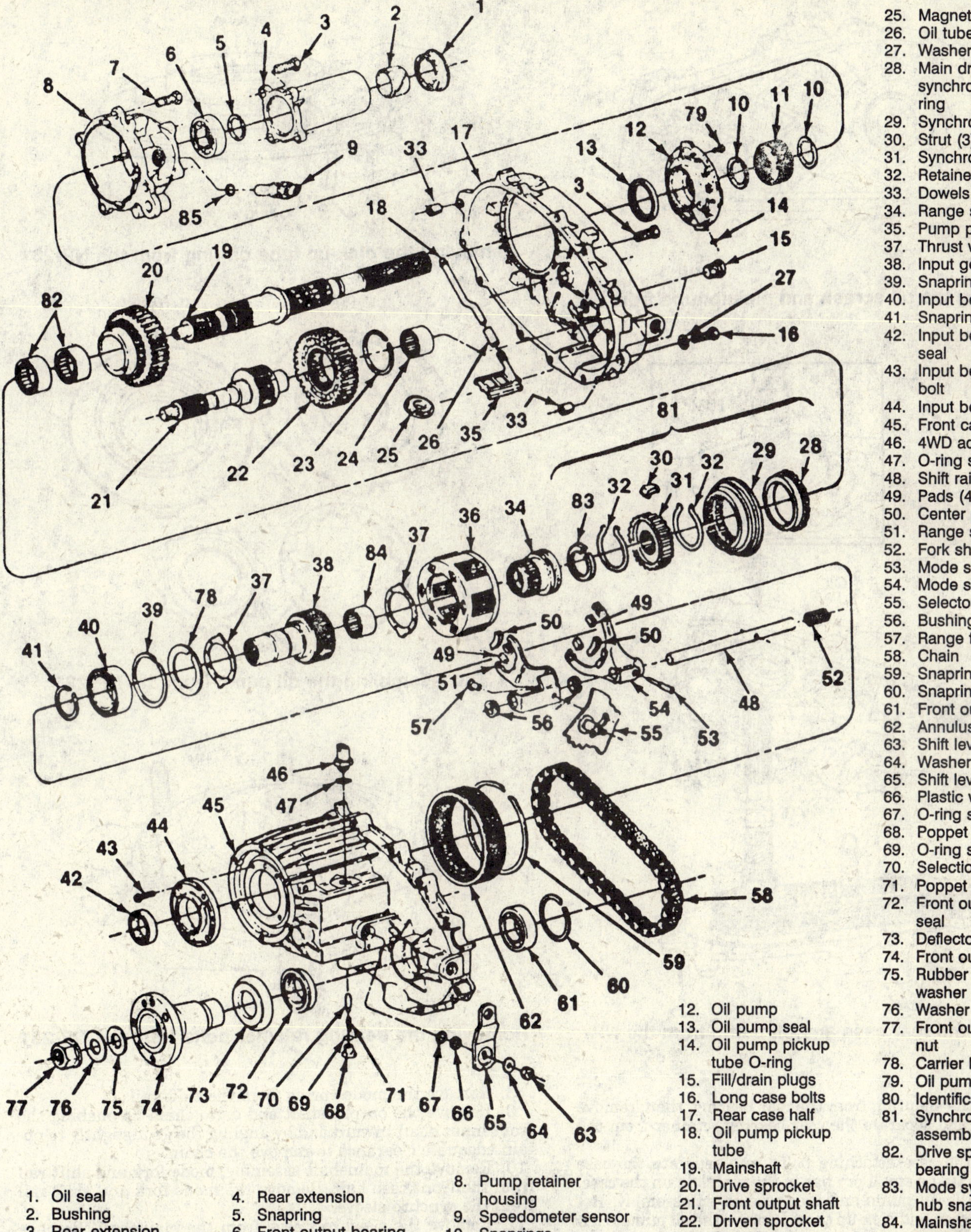

1. Oil seal
2. Bushing
3. Rear extension housing/case bolts
4. Rear extension
5. Snapring
6. Front output bearing
7. Pump retainer housing bolts
8. Pump retainer housing
9. Speedometer sensor
10. Snaprings
11. Speedometer tone wheel
12. Oil pump
13. Oil pump seal
14. Oil pump pickup tube O-ring
15. Fill/drain plugs
16. Long case bolts
17. Rear case half
18. Oil pump pickup tube
19. Mainshaft
20. Drive sprocket
21. Front output shaft
22. Driven sprocket
23. Snapring
24. Front output rear bearing
25. Magnet
26. Oil tube connector
27. Washer
28. Main drive synchronizer stop ring
29. Synchronizer sleeve
30. Strut (3)
31. Synchronizer hub
32. Retainer springs
33. Dowels
34. Range shift hub
35. Pump pickup screen
37. Thrust washers (2)
38. Input gear
39. Snapring
40. Input bearing
41. Snapring
42. Input bearing retainer seal
43. Input bearing retainer bolt
44. Input bearing retainer
45. Front case half
46. 4WD actuator switch
47. O-ring seal
48. Shift rail
49. Pads (4)
50. Center pads (2)
51. Range shift fork
52. Fork shift spring
53. Mode shift fork pin
54. Mode shift fork
55. Selector with shaft
56. Bushings (2)
57. Range fork pin
58. Chain
59. Snapring
60. Snapring
61. Front output bearing
62. Annulus gear
63. Shift lever nut
64. Washer
65. Shift lever
66. Plastic washer
67. O-ring seal
68. Poppet screw
69. O-ring seal
70. Selection plunger
71. Poppet spring
72. Front output shaft seal
73. Deflector
74. Front output flange
75. Rubber sealing washer
76. Washer
77. Front output flange nut
78. Carrier lockring
79. Oil pump screw
80. Identification tag
81. Synchronizer assembly
82. Drive sprocket bearing
83. Mode synchronizer hub snapring
84. Mainshaft pilot bearing
85. Speedometer sensor O-ring seal

Exploded view of New Process 241 transfer case

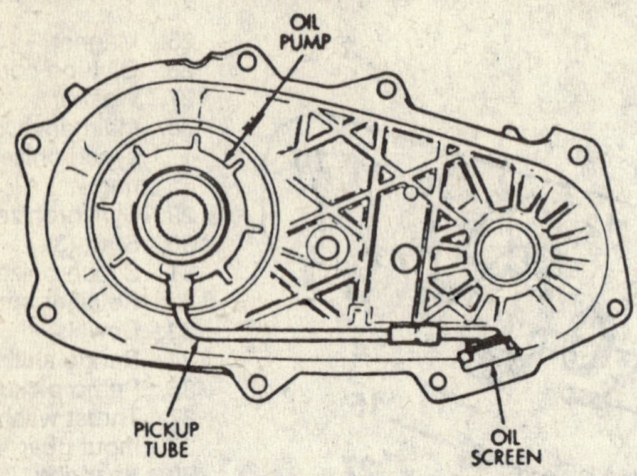

Removing the oil screen and pickup tube from the NP-231

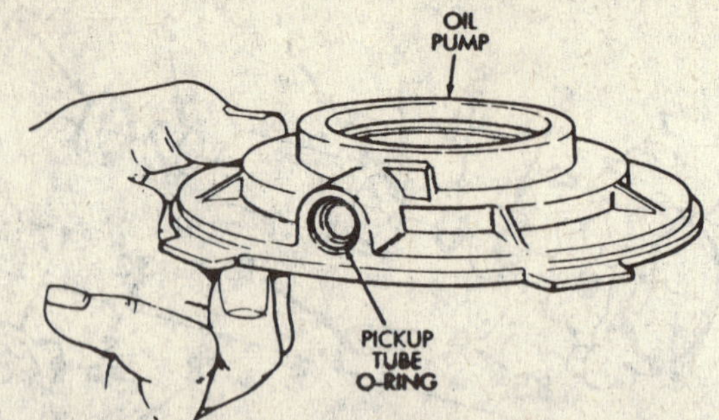

Removing the pick-up tube oil ring from the NP-231

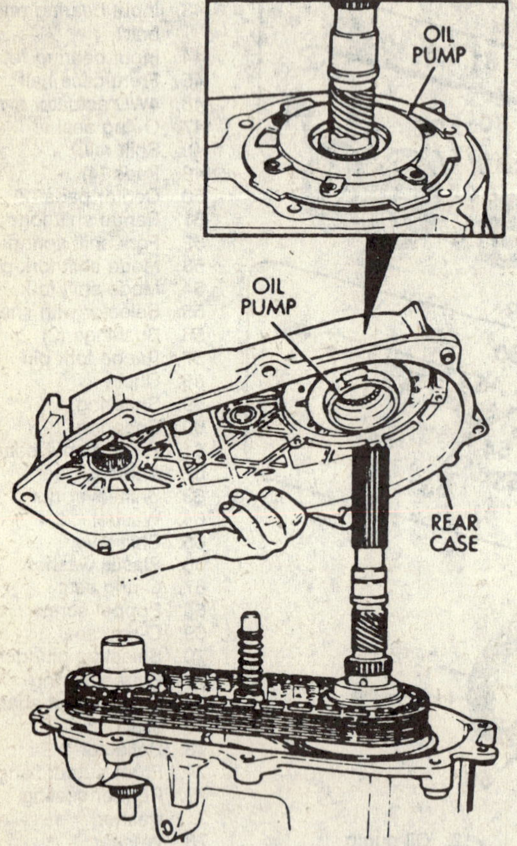

Removing the rear case and oil pump from the NP-231

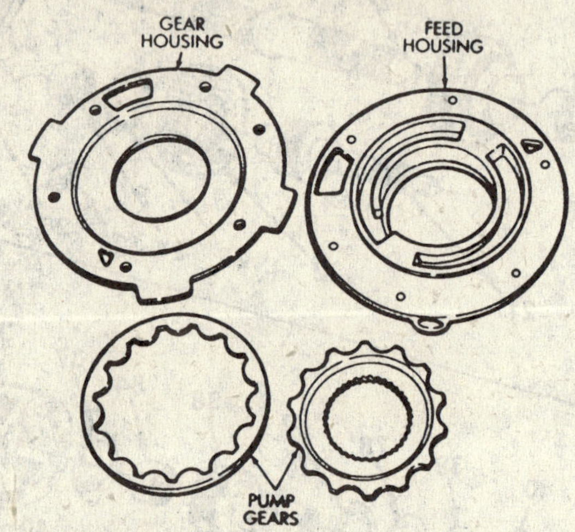

Disassembling the oil pump from the NP-231

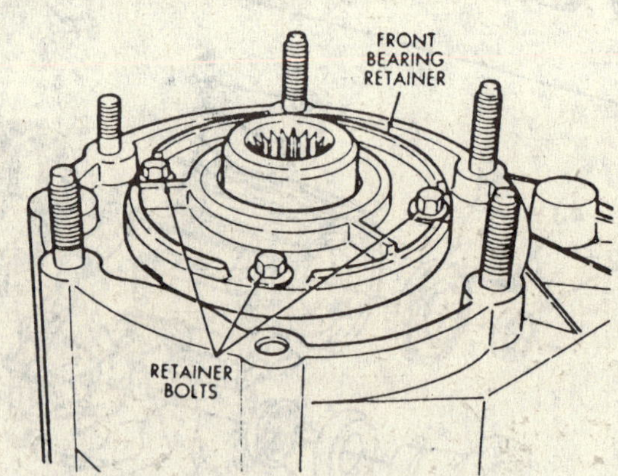

Removing the bearing retainer bolts from the NP-231

4. Remove the snapring from the rear bearing, then, remove the four bolts and separate the rear bearing retainer from the rear case half.

5. Remove the case attaching bolts, and separate the case halves by inserting a small pry bar in the pry slots on the case.

6. Remove the oil pump and rear case as an assembly. Remove the oil screen and pick-up tube. Remove the oil pump from the rear case. Remove the pickup tube O-ring.

7. Mark the position of the oil pump housings for referance. Separate the two halves of the pump. Remove the feed housing from the gear housing. Note the position of the pump gears and remove.

8. Remove the mode spring from the shift rail.

9. Remove the output shaft and drive chain by pushing the front input shaft inward and by angling the gear slightly to obtain adequate clearance to remove the chain.

10. Remove the mainshaft assembly, mode fork and shift rail from the front case half. Remove the mode fork and shift rail from the synchro sleeve.

11. Remove the synchro sleeve from the mainshaft. Remove the synchro hub snapring and stop ring.

12. Remove the drive sprocket. Slide the range fork pin out of the shift sector and remove the range fork and shift hub.

13. Remove the transger case range lever from the sector shaft. Remove the sector shaft, shaft bushing and O-ring.

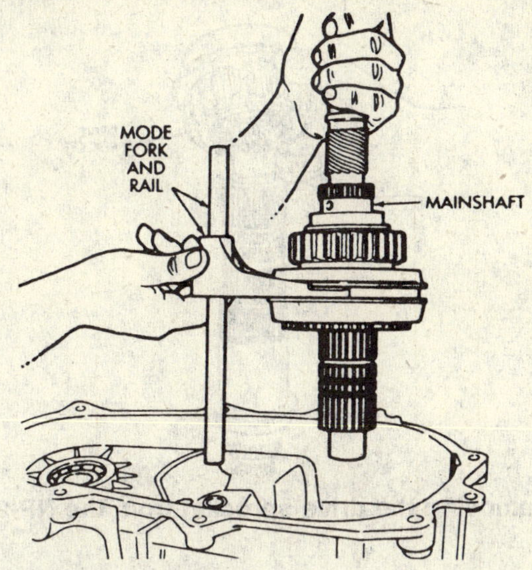

Removing the mainshaft, mode fork and shift rail from the NP-231

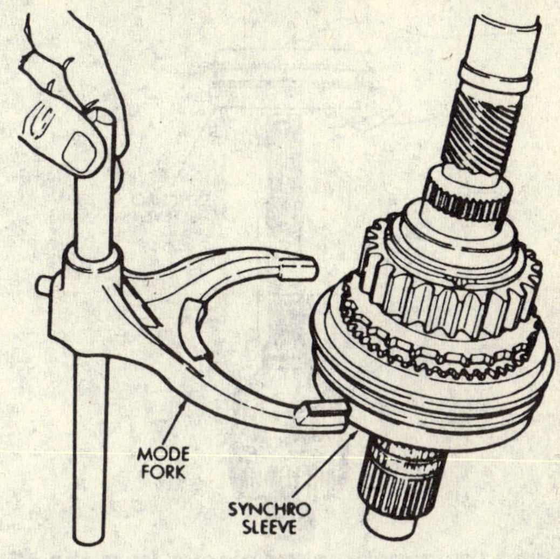

Removing the mode fork from the NP-231

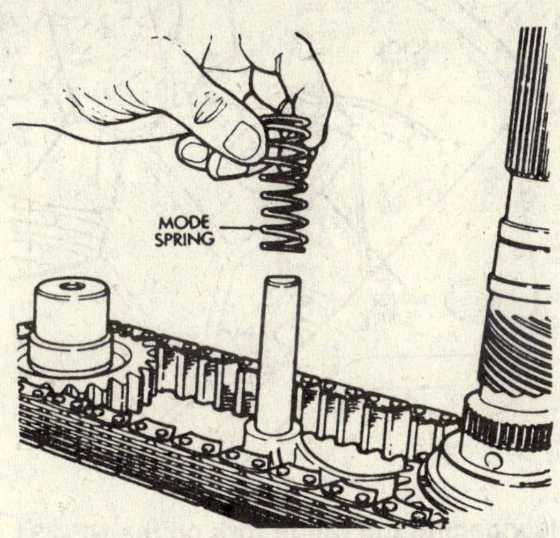

Removing the mode spring from the NP-231

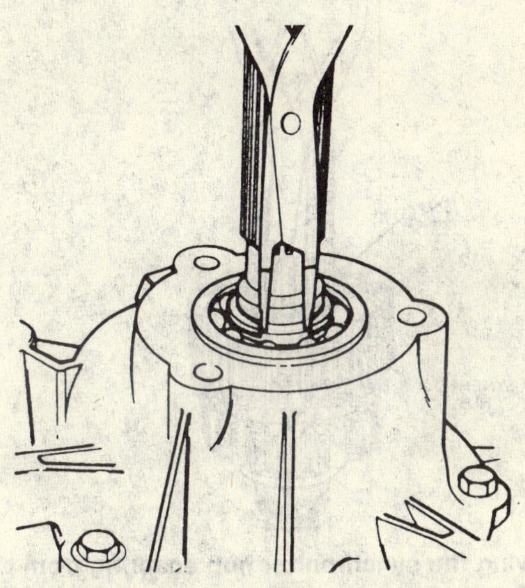

Removing the rear bushing snapring from the NP-231

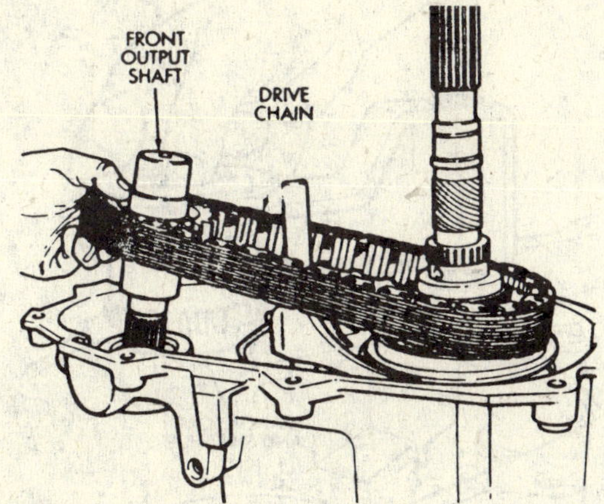

Removing the front output shaft and drive chain from the NP-231

14. Remove the shift detent pin, spring and plug.
15. Turn the case over and remove the front bearing retainer bolts. Remove the bearing retainer.
16. Remove the input gear snapring. Press input/low range gear assembly out of input gear bearing using the appropriate tools.
17. Remove low range gear snapring. Remove retainer, thrust washers and input gear from low range gear.
18. Remove oil seals from rear retainer, rear extension housing, oil pump feed housing and case halves. Remove magnet from front case.
19. Remove speedometer gear, seals and adaptor.
20. Remove output shaft snapring, oil seal and bearing.

CLEANING & INSPECTION

1. Wash all components thoroughly in clean solvent. Ensure that all lubricant, metallic particles, dirt, and foreign material are removed from the surfaces of every component.

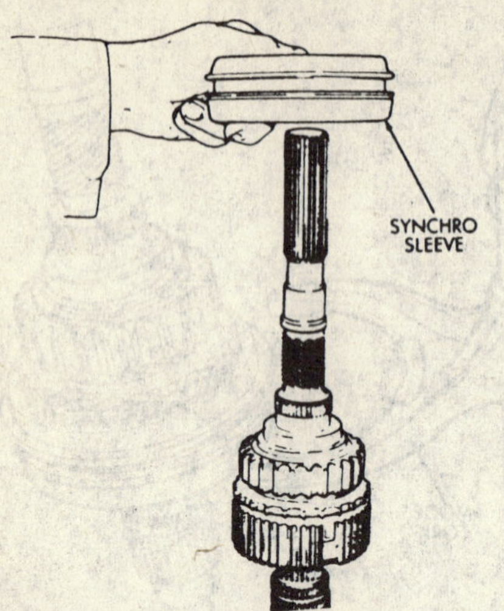

Removing the synchronizer sleeve from the NP-231

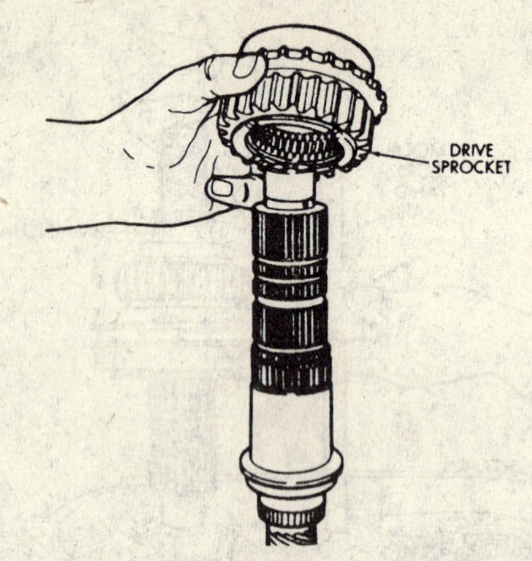

Removing the drive sprocket from the NP-231

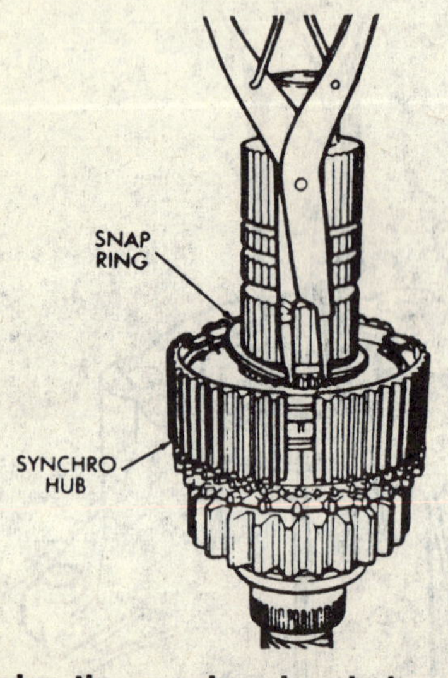

Removing the synchronizer hub snapring from the NP-231

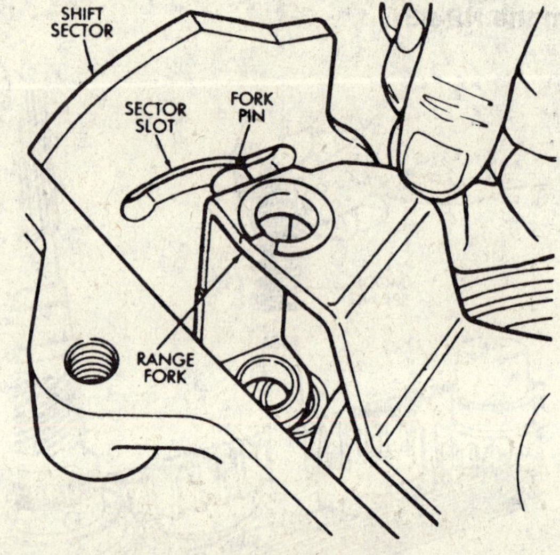

Disengaging the range fork on the NP-231

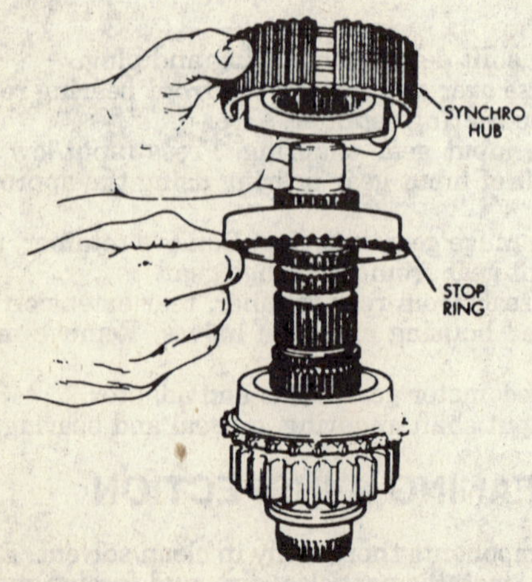

Removing the hub and stop ring from the NP-231

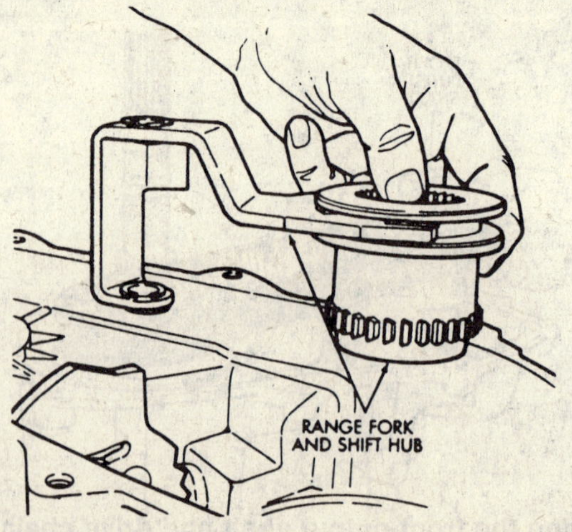

Removing the range fork and hub from the NP-231

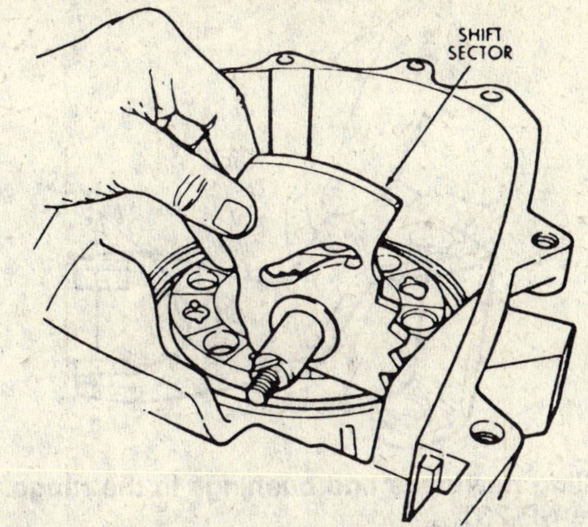

Removing the shift selector from the NP-231

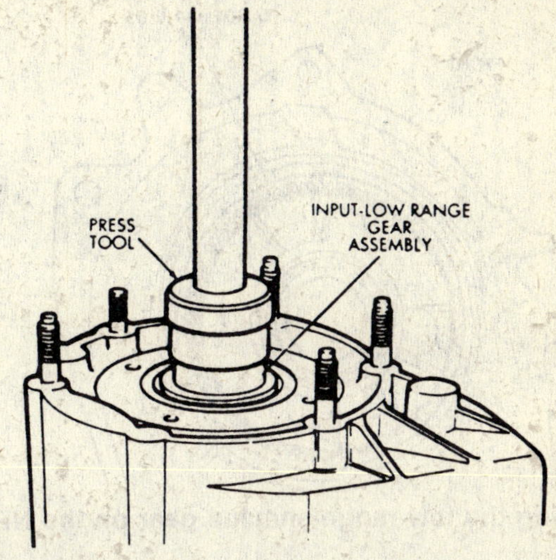

Removing the input/low range gear assembly from the NP-231

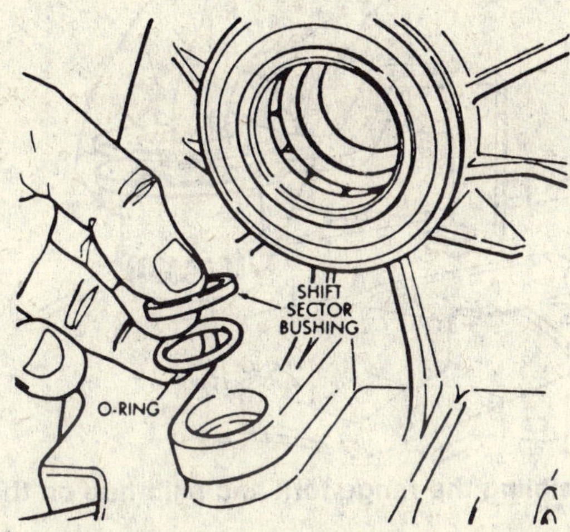

Removing the selector shaft bushing and O-ring from the NP-231

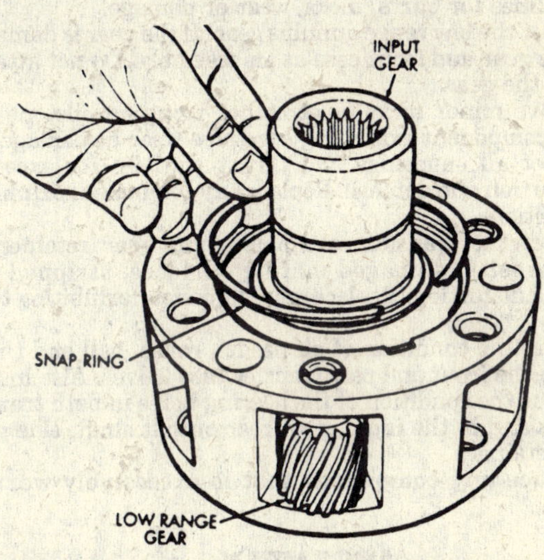

Removing the low range gear snapring from the NP-231

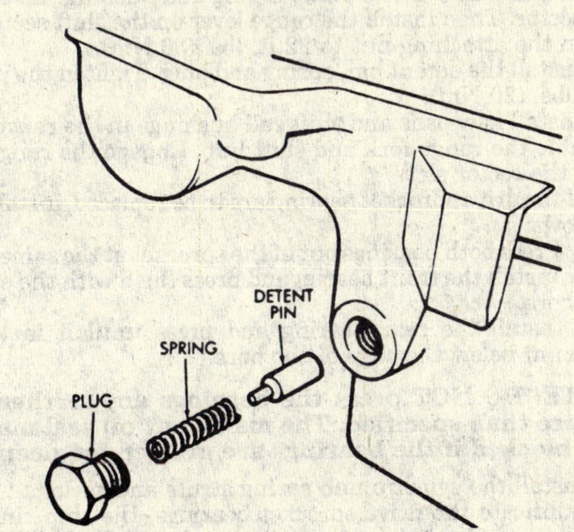

Removing the detent pin, spring and plug from the NP-231

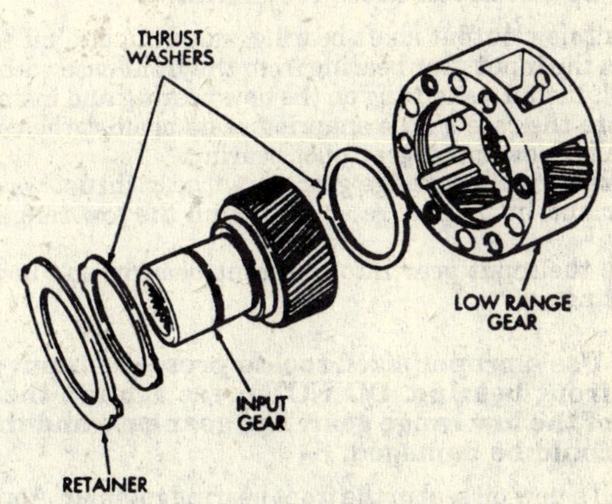

Disassembling the input/low range gear from the NP-231

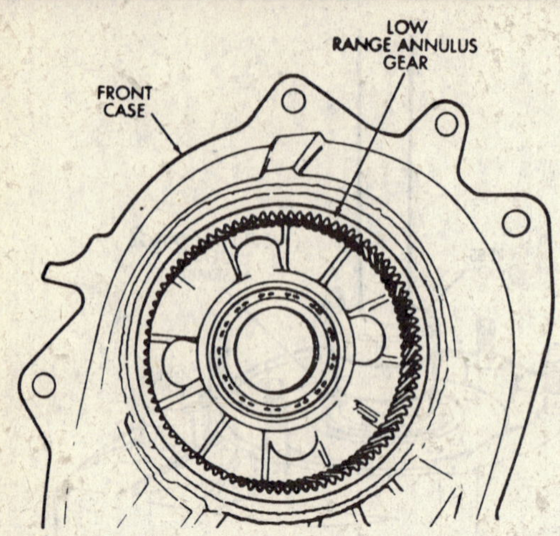

Inspecting the low range annulus gear on the NP-231

2. Apply compressed air to each oil supply port and channel in each transfer case half to remove any obstructions or cleaning solvent residue.
3. Inspect all gear teeth for excessive wear or damage. Inspect all gear splines for burrs, nicks, wear or damage.
4. Inspect the low range annulus gear. If the gear is damaged, replace the gear and front case as an assembly. Do not attempt to remove the gear.
5. Remove minor nicks or scratches using an oilstone. Replace any component exhibiting excessive wear or damage.
6. Inspect all snaprings and thrust washers for excessive wear, distortion and damage. Replace any component exhibiting these conditions.
7. Inspect the transfer case halves and rear retainer for cracks, porosity, damaged mating surfaces, stripped bolt threads and distortion. Replace any component exhibiting these conditions.
8. Inspect the condition of all needle, roller, ball and thrust bearings in the front and rear transfer case halves. Also inspect to determine the condition of the bearing bores in both transfer case halves and in the input gear, rear output shaft, side gear, and rear retainer.
9. Replace any component that is excessively worn or damaged.

ASSEMBLY

NOTE: The bearing bores in various transfer case components contain oil feed holes. Ensure replacement bearings do not block these feed holes.

1. Install new output shaft bearing, snapring and oil seal.
2. Press the input gear bearing from the front case with a remover tool. Install a snapring on the new bearing and install the bearing into the case so the snapring seats against the case.
3. Install a new input gear pilot bearing.
4. Assemble the low range gear, input gear thrust washers, input gear and input gear retainer. Install the low range gear snapring.
5. Press the input gear into the front bearing and install a new snapring.

NOTE: Use a proper sized tool to press the input gear into the front bearing. DO NOT press against the end surfaces of the low range gear. The gear case and thrust washers could be damaged.

6. Install a new oil seal in the front bearing retainer. Apply an ⅛ in. (3mm) bead of RTV sealer to the front bearing retainter sealing surfaces.

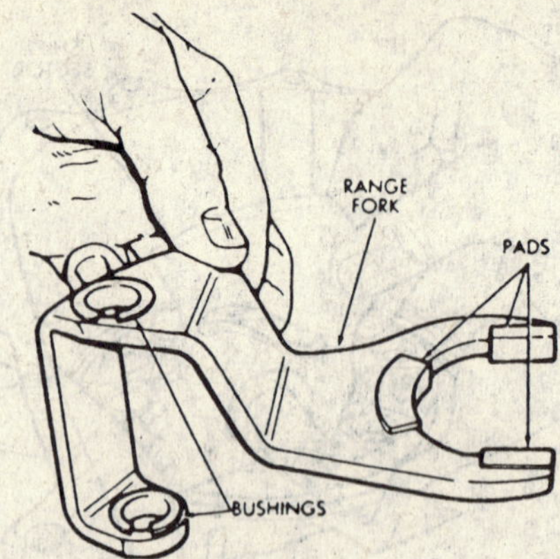

Installing new pads and bushings in the range fork on the NP-231

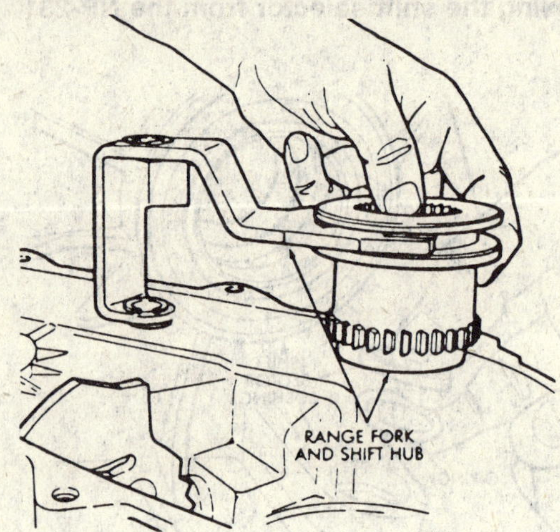

Assembling the range fork and shift hub on the NP-231

7. Install the front bearing retainer on the front case and tighten the bolts to 16 ft. lbs.(23 Nm).
8. Install a new sector shaft O-ring and bushing. Install the shift sector. Then install the range lever on the shift sector and tighten the attaching nut to 22 ft. lbs. (30 Nm).
9. Install the detent pin, spring and plug. Tighten the plug to 15 ft. lbs. (20 Nm).
10. Install new pads and shift rail bushings in the range fork. Assemble the range fork and shift hub. Engage the range fork pin in the sector slot.
11. If the drive sprocket bearing are to be replaced, install then as follows:
    a. Press both bearings out of the sprocket at the same time.
    b. Install the front bearingand press flush with the edge of the bore.
    c. Install the rear bearing and press until it is $^1/_{16}$ in. (1.6mm) below the edge of the bore.

NOTE: DO NOT press the bearings any farther into the bore than specified. The mainshaft oil seal may become blocked if the bearings are pressed too deeply.

12. Install the synchro hub spring struts and spring.
13. Lubricate the drive sprocket bearings, the stop ring and the synchro hub with automatic transmission fluid and install on the mainshaft. Be sure to seat the hub struts on the stop ting lugs.

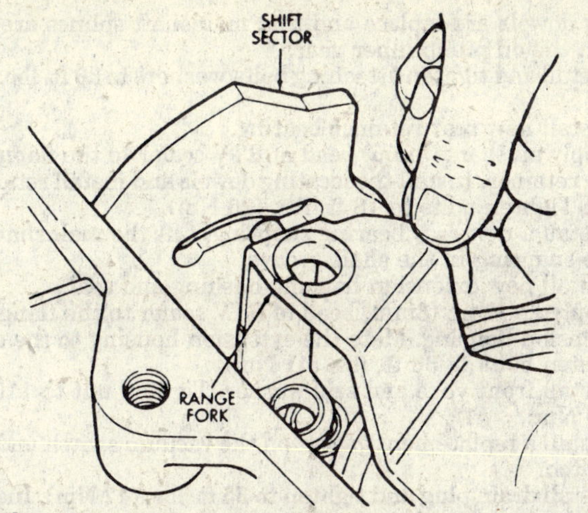

Seating the range fork in the selector on the NP-231

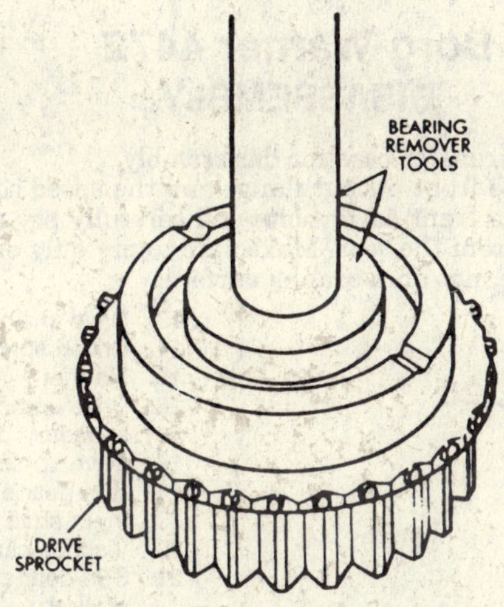

Removing the drive sprocket bearings on the NP-231

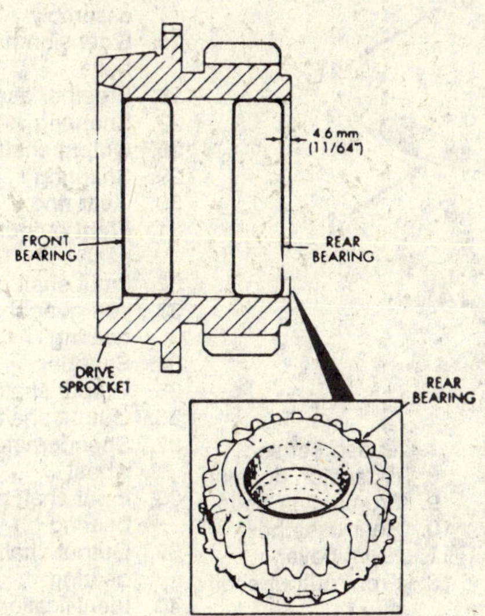

Installing the drive sprocket bearings on the NP-231

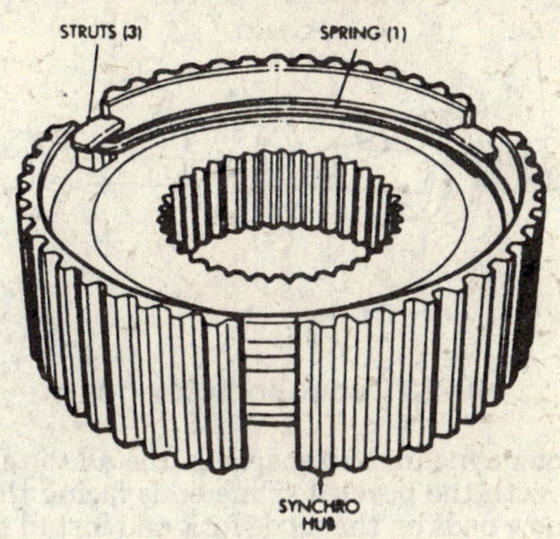

Installing the synchronizer hub, spring and struts on the NP-231

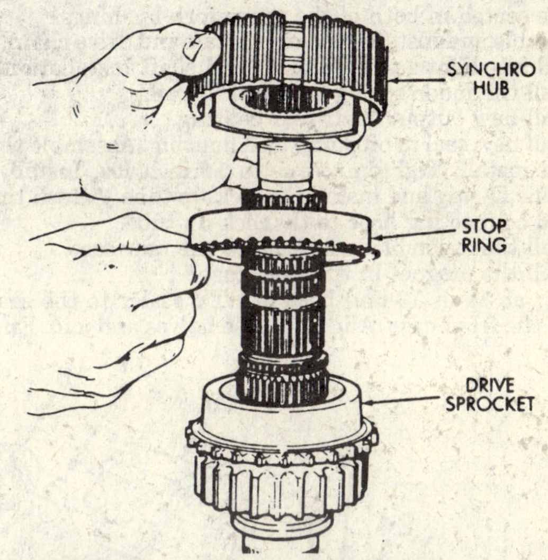

Installing the drive sprocket, stop ring and synchronizer hub on the NP-231

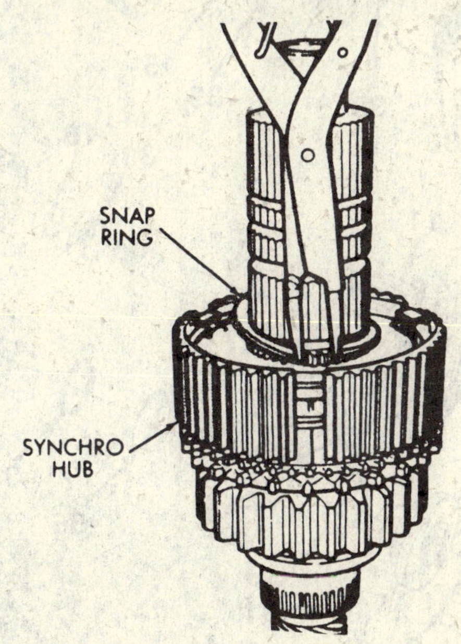

Installing the synchronizer hub snapring on the NP-231

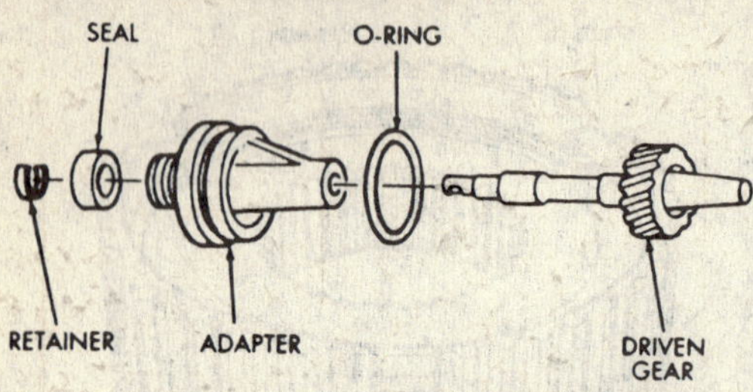

NP-231 speedometer gears

14. Install new synchro hub snapring. Install the sleeve on the synchro hub with the beveled spline ends facing the stop ring.
15. Install new pads on the mode fork and install the shift rail in the fork.
16. Engage the mode fork in the synchro sleeve. Install the mode fork mainshaft assembly in the case. Be sure the mode fork rail is seated in both of the range fork bushings.
17. Assemble and install the output shaft and drive chain. Lift the mainshaft slightle to ease chain and shaft installation.
18. Install the mode spring on the shift rail.
19. Install new output shaft rear bearing.
20. Install new seal in oil pump feed housing. Assemble the oil pump and install. Tighten screws to 14 inch lbs. Install new pick-up tube O-ring and install the pick-up tube. Attach the oil screen and connecting hose to the pick-up tube.
21. Install the assembled oil pump in the rear case.
22. Install the magnet in the from case.
23. Apply an ⅛ in. (3mm) bead of RTV sealer to the sealing surface of the front case. Align the case halves and join. Ensure locating dowels are inplace and that mainshaft splines are engaged in the oil pump inner gear.
24. Install and tighten attaching bolts/washers to 30 ft. lbs. (41 Nm).
25. Install new rear retainer bearing.
26. Apply an ⅛ in. (3mm) bead of RTV sealer to the flange of the rear retainer. Install the locating dowels and install retainer on case. Tighten bolts to 18 ft. lbs. (25 Nm).
27. Install a new rear bearing snapring. Lift the mainshaft to seat the snapring in the shaft groove.
28. Install new extension housing bushing and seal.
29. Apply an ⅛ in. (3mm) bead of RTV sealer to the flange of the extension housing. Mate the extension housing to the case and tighten bolts to 30 ft. lbs. (41 Nm).
30. Install front yoke and seal washer. Tighten nut to 110 ft. lbs. 150 Nm).
31. Install a replacement gasket on the vacuum switch and install switch.
32. Install drain plug and tighten to 35 ft. lbs. (47 Nm). Install speedometer gear, seals and adaptor.
33. Fill the case with lubricant and install fill plug. Tighten fill plug to 35 ft. lbs. (47 Nm).

Borg-Warner 4472

DISASSEMBLY

1. Clean the transfer case for disassembly.
2. Remove the front output flange and the speed sensor.
3. Remove the front cover bolts and carefully pry the front case half away from the rear. Make sure to pry only on the pry tabs on the case, not on a sealing surface.

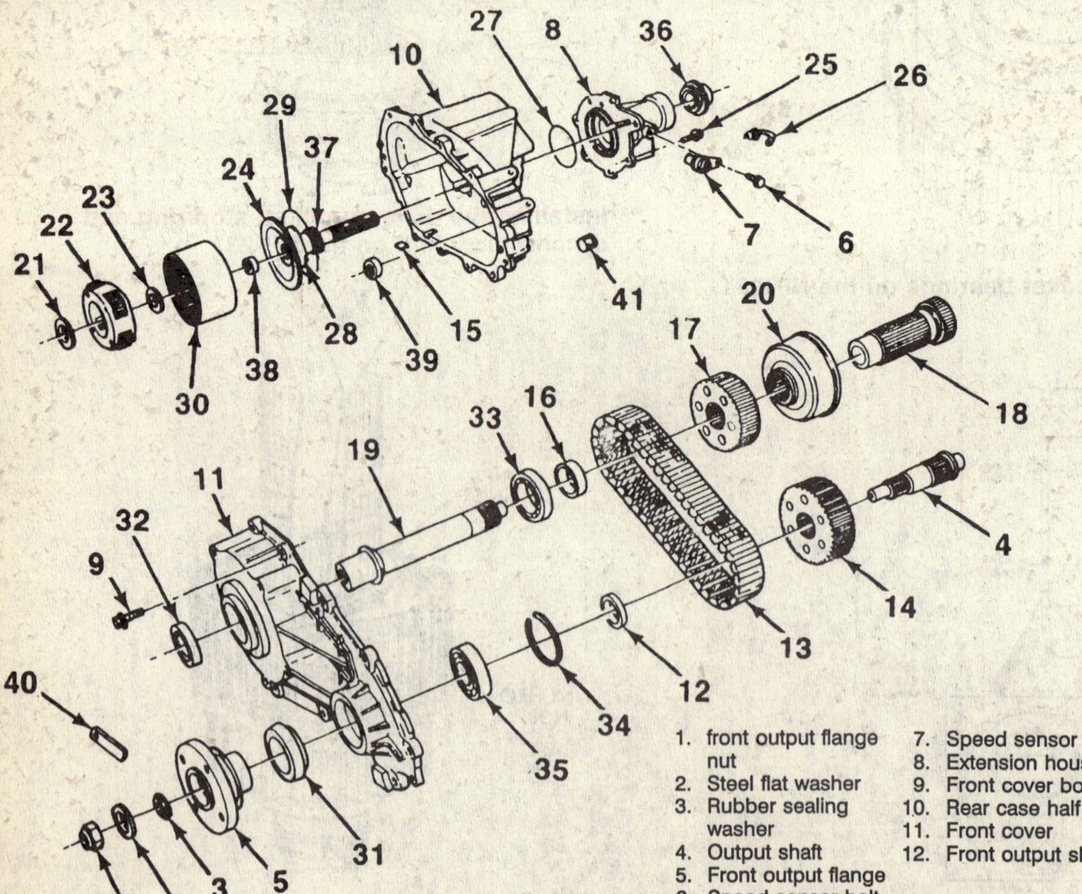

1. front output flange nut
2. Steel flat washer
3. Rubber sealing washer
4. Output shaft
5. Front output flange
6. Speed sensor bolt
7. Speed sensor
8. Extension housing
9. Front cover bolts
10. Rear case half
11. Front cover
12. Front output shaft
13. Drive chain
14. Driven sprocket
15. Magnet
16. Drive sprocket spacer
17. Drive sprocket
18. Sun gear shaft
19. Input shaft
20. Viscous clutch
21. Sun gear shaft thrust washer
22. Planet gear carrier assembly
23. Thrust washer
24. Output shaft assembly
25. Extension housing bolts
26. Breather assembly
27. Snapring
28. Output shaft bearing
29. Snapring
30. Gear ring
31. Front output shaft oil seal
32. Input shaft oil seal
33. sun gear shaft bearing
34. Snapring
35. Output shaft bearing
36. Output shaft oil seal
37. Speedometer tone wheel
38. Input shaft pilot bearing
39. Output shaft rear bearing
40. Identification tag
41. Drain/fill plug

Exploded view of Borg-Warner 4472 transfer case

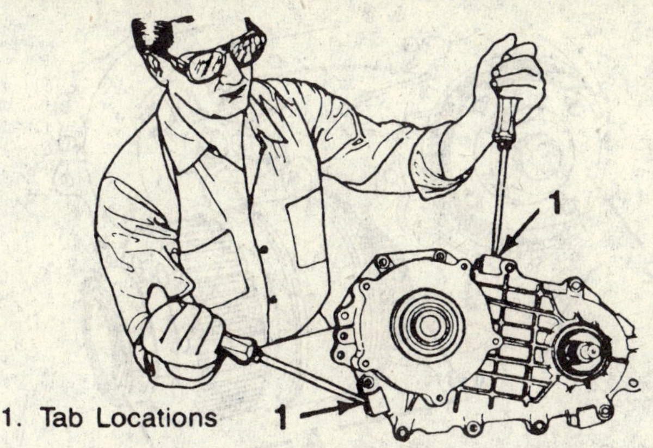

Pry the case apart only at the pry tabs

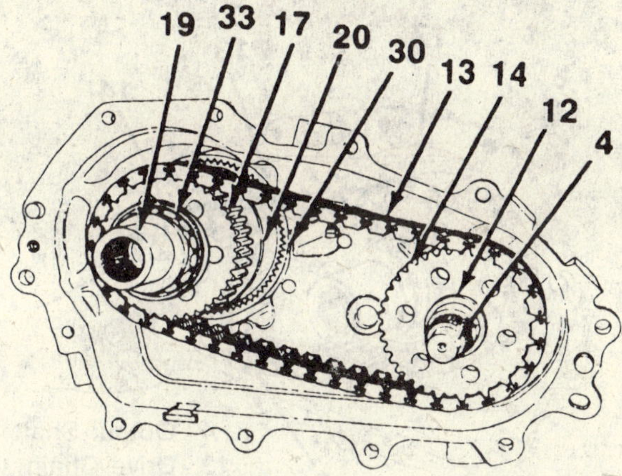

4. Front Output Shaft
12. Front Output Shaft Spacer
13. Drive Chain
14. Driven Sprocket
17. Drive Sprocket
19. Input Shaft
20. Viscous Clutch
30. Gear Ring
33. Sun Gear Shaft Bearing

Inside the rear case half

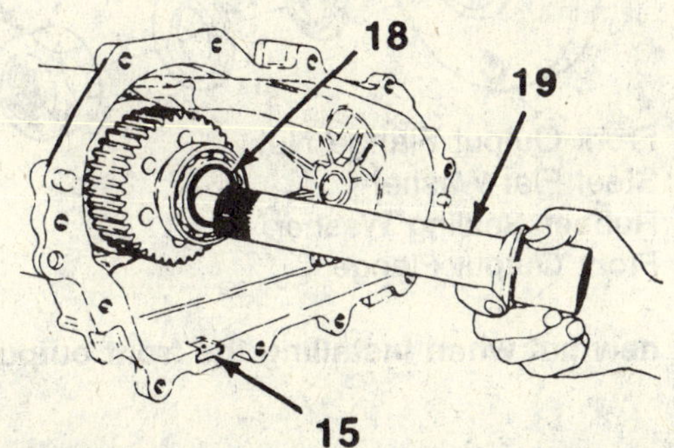

15. Magnet
18. Sun Gear Shaft
19. Input Shaft

Slide out the input shaft

4. Lift the front output shaft, sprocket and drive chain out as a unit. It may be necessary to lift the input shaft to disengage the chain.
5. Remove the magnet from the rear case half.
6. Slide the input shaft out of the sun gear shaft.
7. Remove the sun gear shaft, viscous clutch and drive sprocket as an assembly. The spacer and bearing should come with it.
8. Remove the planetary gear carrier and thrust washer from the output shaft.
9. To remove the extension housing, turn the rear case half over and support the output shaft assembly so it is not hanging in the case.
10.Remove the output shaft snapring and the ring gear snapring to remove the output shaft from the case and from the ring gear.

INSPECTION

Carefully inspect all bearings for signs of wear or lack of lubrication. Be sure to inspect the pilot bearings in the output shaft, replace as necessary. Check gear teeth and the chain for excessive wear. Inspect the shaft splines for uneven wear patterns and check the oil scoop on the output shaft for cracks. Carefully check the case for signs of damage to the mating surfaces or cracks, especially at the bearing areas. All seals should be replaced before assembling the transfer case.

ASSEMBLY

1. Install the clutch, drive sprocket with spacer, and sun gear shaft bearing onto the sun gear shaft.
2. Install the output shaft assembly into the gear ring and install the snapring.
3. Install the output shaft bearing to the front cover and install the snapring.
4. Install the output shaft assembly and gear ring through the rear case half and secure it with the snapring.
5. With the case turned over and the output shaft supported, apply a ⅛ in. (3mm) bead of Loctite®51580 gasket eliminator or equivalent silicone sealer to the extension housing sealing surface.
6. Install the extension housing and torque the bolts to 35 ft. lbs. (47 Nm).

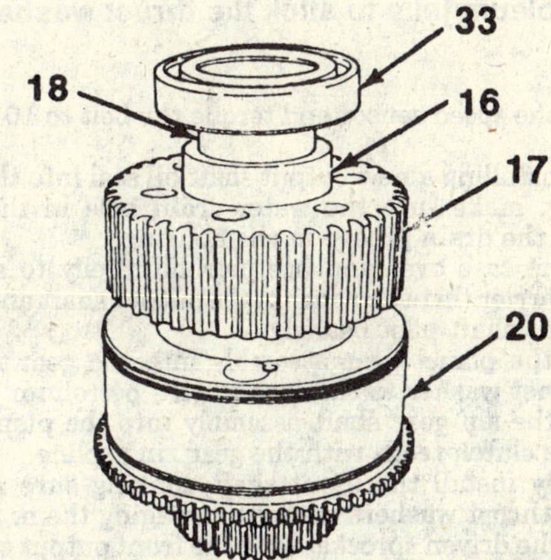

16. Drive Sprocket Spacer
17. Drive Sprocket
18. Sun Gear Shaft
20. Viscous Clutch
33. Sun Gear Shaft Bearing

Assemble the sun gear shaft components

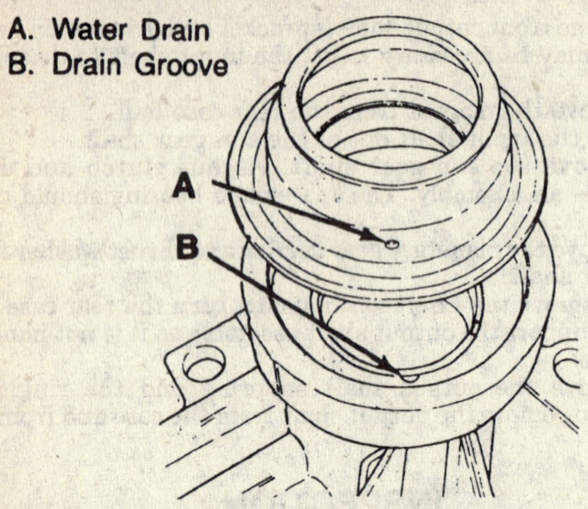

Align the oil seal water drain with the groove in the case

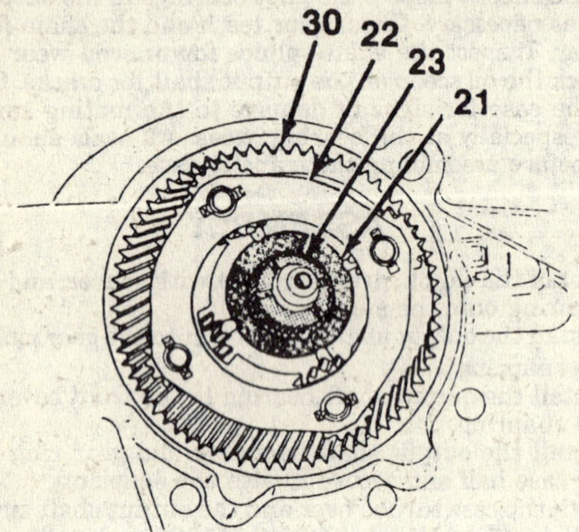

21. Sun Gear Shaft Thust Washer
22. Planet Carrier Assembly
23. Planet Carrier Assembly Thrust Washer
30. Gear Ring

Use petroleum jelly to stick the thrust washer in place

7. Install the speed sensor and torque the bolt to 10 inch lbs. (1 Nm).
8. When installing a new output shaft oil seal into the extension housing, make sure the water drain hole in the seal is aligned with the drain groove in the housing.
9. Turn the case over and use petrolium jelly to stick the planet gear carrier thrust washer to the output shaft and align it with the input shaft pilot bearing.
10. Install the planet gear assembly into the gear ring and stick the thrust washer to the carrier with petrolium jelly.
11. Install the sin gear shaft assembly into the planet gears and align the clutch teeth with the gear ring spline.
12. Carefully install the input shaft, making sure it passes through the thrust washers without damaging them.
13. Install the driven sprocket onto the front output shaft and install the chain onto the sprocket.
14. Install the the drive chain over the drive sprocket and install front output shaft.
15. Install the front ouput shaft spacer and the magnet.
16. Apply a ⅛ in. (3mm) bead of silicone gasket eliminator to the rear case half and assemble the case halves. Torque the bolts to 35 ft. lbs. (47 Nm).
17. With new input and output shaft seals installed, install the front output flange using a new nut. Torque the nut to 80 ft. lbs. (108 Nm).

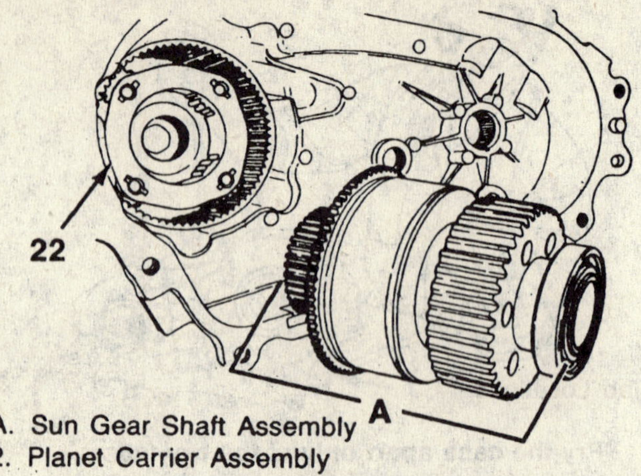

A. Sun Gear Shaft Assembly
22. Planet Carrier Assembly

Install the sun gear shaft assembly

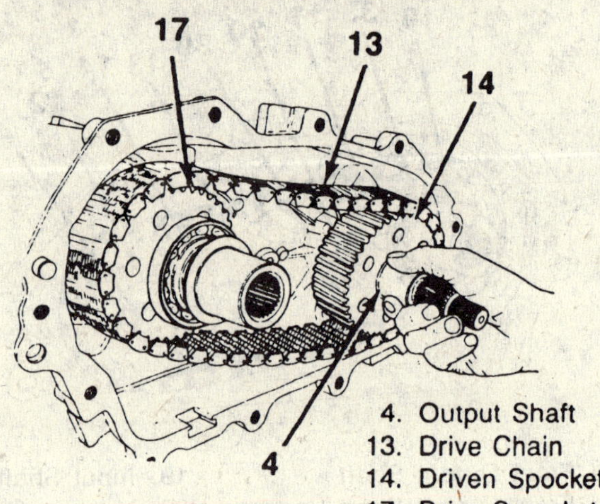

4. Output Shaft
13. Drive Chain
14. Driven Spocket
17. Drive Sprocket

Install the drive chain

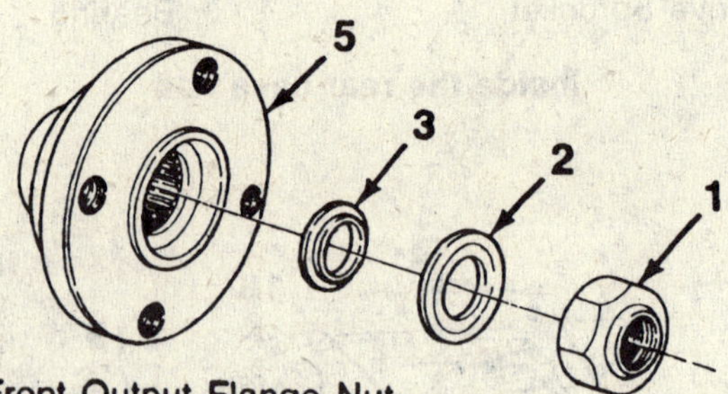

1. Front Output Flange Nut
2. Steel Flat Washer
3. Rubber Sealing Washer
5. Front Output Flange

Use a new nut when installing the front output flange

DRIVELINE

On all models, conventional, open type driveshafts are used. Located at either end of the driveshaft is a universal joint (U-joint), which allows the driveshaft to move up and down to match the motion of the rear axle.

Since the truck can be obtained in 2WD and 4WD, three types of driveshafts may be employed. On the 2WD model, a one-piece driveshaft is used. On some 4WD models is a two-piece rear driveshaft with a center bearing, and the front shaft is a two piece telescope type with internal splines.

On the front of the one-piece driveshaft (2WD) or the two-piece driveshaft (4WD), the U-joints connect the driveshaft to a slip-jointed yoke. This yoke is internally splined and allows the driveshaft to move in and out on the transmission splines.

On the rear of the one-piece driveshaft (2WD) or the two-piece

DRIVELINE

Troubleshooting Basic Driveshaft and Rear Axle Problems

When abnormal vibrations or noises are detected in the driveshaft area, this chart can be used to help diagnose possible causes. Remember that other components such as wheels, tires, rear axle and suspension can also produce similar conditions.

BASIC DRIVESHAFT PROBLEMS

Problem	Cause	Solution
Shudder as car accelerates from stop or low speed	• Loose U-joint • Defective center bearing	• Replace U-joint • Replace center bearing
Loud clunk in driveshaft when shifting gears	• Worn U-joints	• Replace U-joints
Roughness or vibration at any speed	• Out-of-balance, bent or dented driveshaft • Worn U-joints • U-joint clamp bolts loose	• Balance or replace driveshaft • Replace U-joints • Tighten U-joint clamp bolts
Squeaking noise at low speeds	• Lack of U-joint lubrication	• Lubricate U-joint; if problem persists, replace U-joint
Knock or clicking noise	• U-joint or driveshaft hitting frame tunnel • Worn CV joint	• Correct overloaded condition • Replace CV joint

BASIC REAR AXLE PROBLEMS

First, determine when the noise is most noticeable.

Drive Noise—Produced under vehicle acceleration.

Coast Noise—Produced while the car coast with a closed throttle.

Float Noise—Occurs while maintaining constant car speed (just enough to keep speed constant) on a level road.

Road Noise

Brick or rough surfaced concrete roads produce noises that seem to come from the rear axle. Road noise is usually identical in Drive or Coast and driving on a different type of road will tell whether the road is the problem.

Tire Noise

Tire noises are often mistaken for rear axle problems. Snow treads or unevenly worn tires produce vibrations seeming to originate elsewhere. Temporarily inflating the tire to 40 lbs will significantly alter tire noise, but will have no effect on rear axle noises (which normally cease below about 30 mph).

Engine/Transmission Noise

Determine at what speed the noise is more pronounced, then stop the car in a quiet place. With the transmission in Neutral, run the engine through speeds corresponding to road speeds where the noise was noticed. Noises produced with the car standing still are coming from the engine or transmission.

Front Wheel Bearings

While holding the car speed steady, lightly apply the foot brake; this will often decease bearing noise, as some of the load is taken from the bearing.

Rear Axle Noises

Eliminating other possible sources can narrow the cause to the rear axle, which normally produces noise from worn gears or bearings. Gear noises tend to peak in a narrow speed range, while bearing noises will usually vary in pitch with engine speeds.

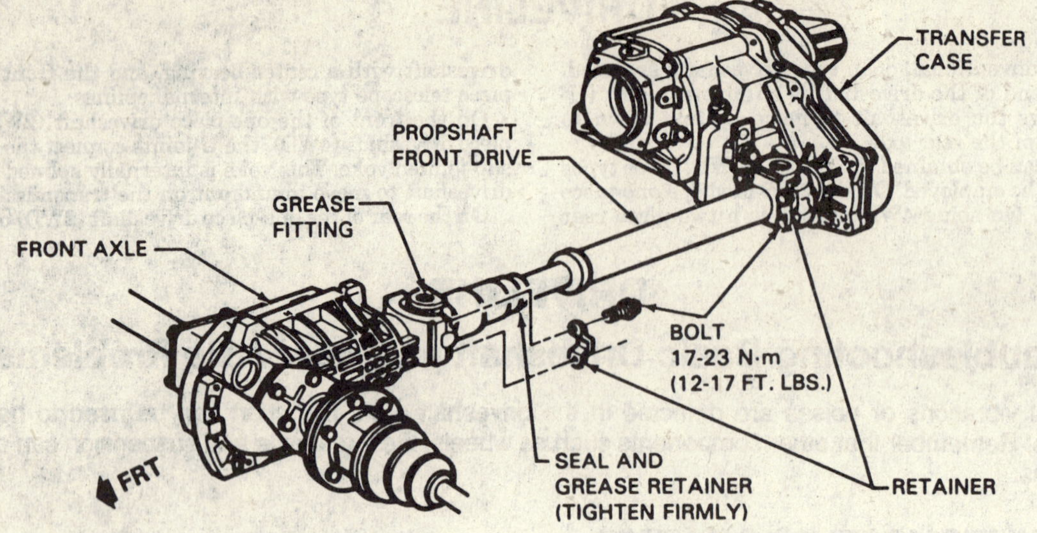

Front drive shaft assembly on Blazer and Jimmy; Bravada similar

driveshaft (4WD), the U-joint is clamped to the rear axle pinion. It is attached to the rear axle pinion by use of bolted straps.

On the front driveshaft (4WD), the U-joints are secured to the transfer case and the front differential by the use of bolted straps. Located in the center of the driveshaft is a slip-joint, which allows the driveshaft to move in and out on its own splines.

On production U-joints, nylon is injected through a small hole in the yoke during manufacture and flows along a circular groove between the U-joint and the yoke, creating a non-metallic snapring.

Bad U-joints, requiring replacement, will produce a clunking sound when the vehicle is put into gear and when the transmission shifts from gear-to-gear. This is due to worn needle bearings or scored trunnion ends. U-joints require no periodic maintenance and therefore have no lubrication fittings.

Front driveshaft and U-Joints

REMOVAL AND INSTALLATION

Blazer and Jimmy

NOTE: DO NOT pound on the original driveshaft ears or the injected nylon U-joints may fracture.

1. Raise and safely support the front of the truck on jackstands.
2. Mark the relationship of the driveshaft to the front axle and the transfer case flanges.
3. Remove the driveshaft-to-retainer bolts and the retainers.
4. Collapse the driveshaft so it may be disengaged from the transfer case flange.
5. Move the driveshaft rearward (between the transfer case and the chassis) to disengage it from the front axle.

NOTE: Use care when handling the driveshaft to avoid dropping the U-joint cap assemblies.

6. Using tape, wrap it around the loose caps (if necessary) to hold them in place.
7. To install, use the alignment marks and reverse the removal procedures. Torque the retainer-to-transfer case/front axle bolts to 12–17 ft. lbs.

Bravada

1. Raise and safely support the front of the vehicle.
2. Mark the position of the driveshaft flanges to the transfer case and front axle flanges.
3. Unbolt the flanges and lower the driveshaft out of the truck.
4. When installing, make sure the match marks line up properly. Torque the front axle flange bolts to 53 ft. lbs. (72 Nm). Torque the transfer case flange bolts to 92 ft. lbs. (125 Nm).

U-JOINT OVERHAUL

A universal type U-joint is used: it uses an internal snapring (production is plastic injected).

NOTE: The following procedure requires the use of an Arbor Press, the GM Cross Press tool No. J-9522-3 or equivalent, the GM Spacer tool No. J-9522-5 or equivalent, and a 1⅛ in. (29mm) socket.

1. While supporting the driveshaft, in the horizontal position, position it so that the lower ear of the front universal joint's shaft yoke is supported on a 1⅛ in. (29mm) socket.

NOTE: DO NOT clamp the driveshaft tube in a vise, for the tube may become damaged.

2. Using the GM Cross Press tool No. J-9522-3 or equivalent, place it on the horizontal bearing cups and press the lower bearing cup out of the yoke ear; the pressing action will shear the plastic retaining ring from the lower bearing cup. If the bearing cup was not completely removed, insert the GM Spacer tool No. J-9522-5 or equivalent, onto the universal joint, then complete the pressing procedure to remove the joint.
3. Rotate the driveshaft and shear the plastic retainer from the opposite side of the yoke.
4. Disengage the slip yoke from the driveshaft.
5. To remove the universal joint from the slip yoke, perform the procedures used in Steps 1–4.

NOTE: When the front universal joint has been disassembled, it must be discarded and replaced with a service kit joint, for the production joint is not equipped with bearing retainer grooves on the bearing cups.

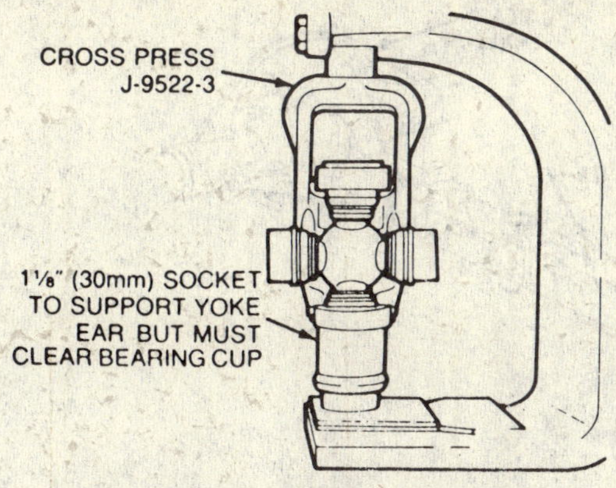

Pressing out the old U-joint

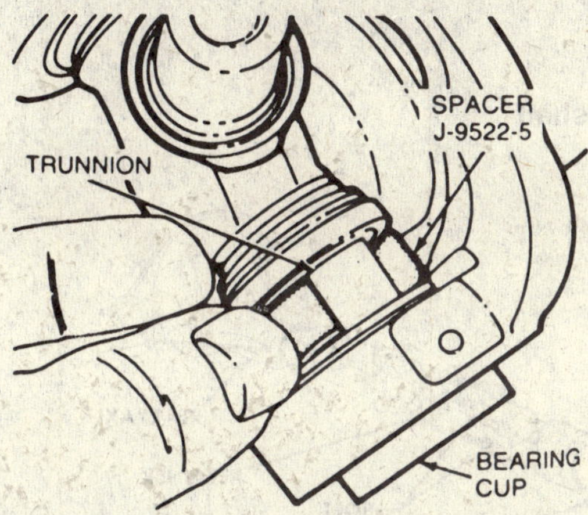

Spacer tool used to push the cup out all the way

6. Clean (remove any remaining plastic particles) and inspect the slip yoke and driveshaft for damage, wear or burrs.

NOTE: The universal joint service kit includes: A pregreased cross assembly, four bearing cups with seals, needle rollers, washers, four bearing retainers and grease. Make sure that the bearing cup seals are installed to hold the needle bearings in place for handling.

7. To install, position one bearing cup assembly part way into the yoke ear (turn the ear to the bottom), insert the bearing cross (into the yoke) so that the trunnion seats freely into the bearing cup. Turn the yoke 180° and install the other bearing cup assembly.

NOTE: When installing the bearing cup assemblies, make sure the trunnions are started straight and true into the bearing cups.

8. Using the arbor press, press the bearing cups onto the cross trunnion, until they seat.

NOTE: While installing the bearing cups, twist the cross trunnion to work it into the bearings. If there seems to be a hangup, stop the pressing and recheck the needle roller alignment.

9. Once the bearing cup retainer grooves have cleared the inside of the yoke, stop the pressing and install the snaprings.
10. If the other bearing cup retainer groove has not cleared the inside of the yoke, use a hammer to aid in the seating procedure.
11. To install the yoke/universal assembly to the driveshaft, perform the Steps 7–10 of this procedure.

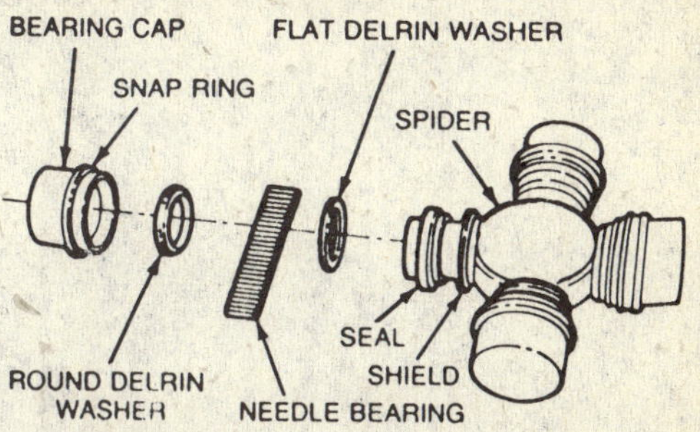

Internal snapring U-joint assembly

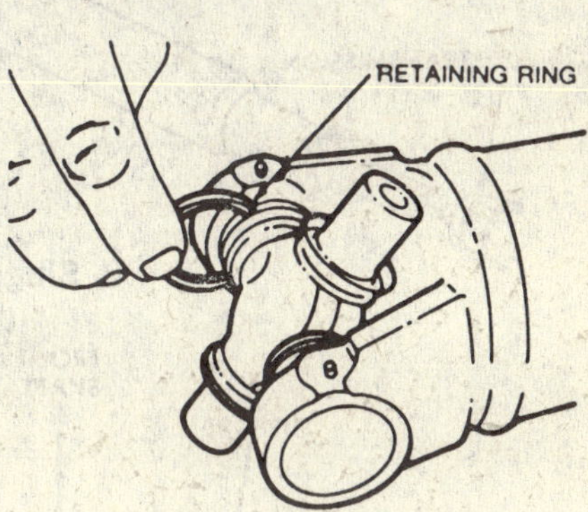

Installing the snapring

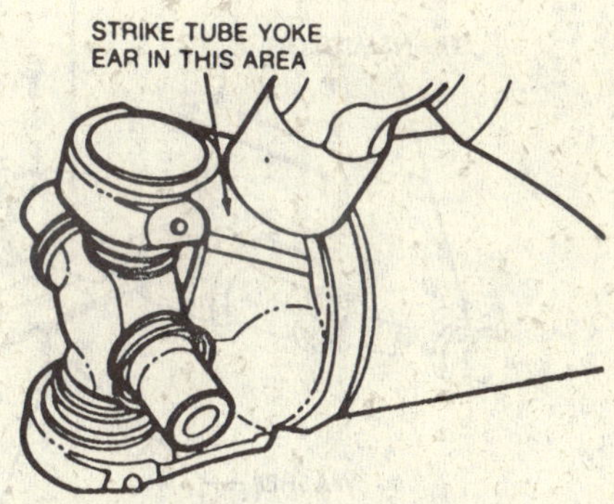

Seating the snapring

Rear Driveshaft and U-Joints

REMOVAL AND INSTALLATION

NOTE: DO NOT pound on the original propeller shaft yoke ears for the injected nylon joints may fracture.

1. Raise and safely support the rear of the vehicle on jackstands.
2. Mark relationship of the driveshaft-to-pinion flange and disconnect the rear universal joint by removing retainers. If the bearing cups are loose, tape them together to prevent dropping and loss of bearing rollers.
3. If equipped with a one-piece driveshaft, perform the following procedures:
   a. Slide the driveshaft forward to disengage it from the rear axle flange.
   b. Move the driveshaft rearward to disengage it from the transmission slip-joint, passing it under the axle housing.
4. If equipped with a two-piece driveshaft, perform the following procedures:

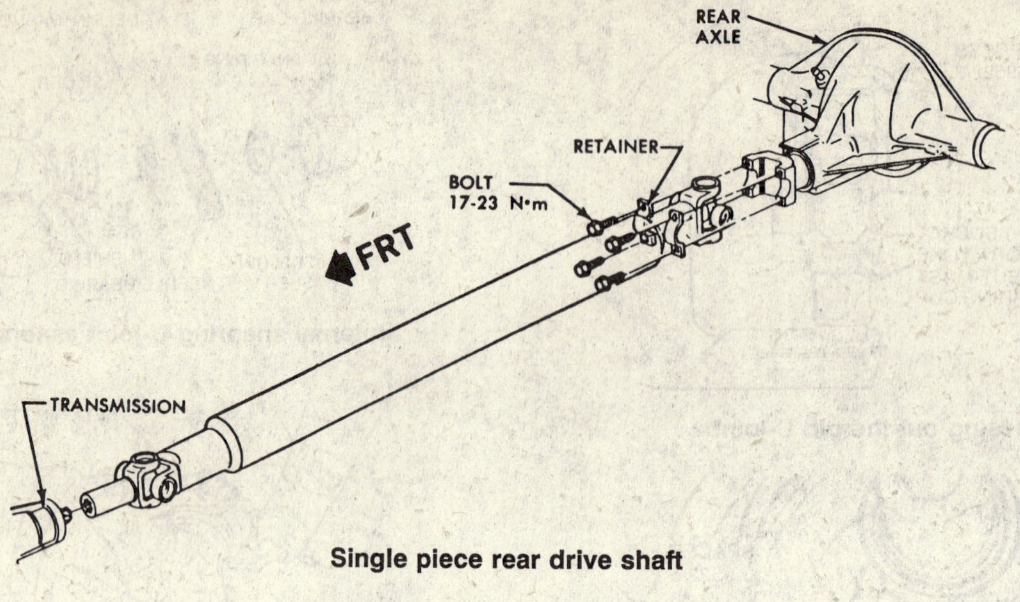

Single piece rear drive shaft

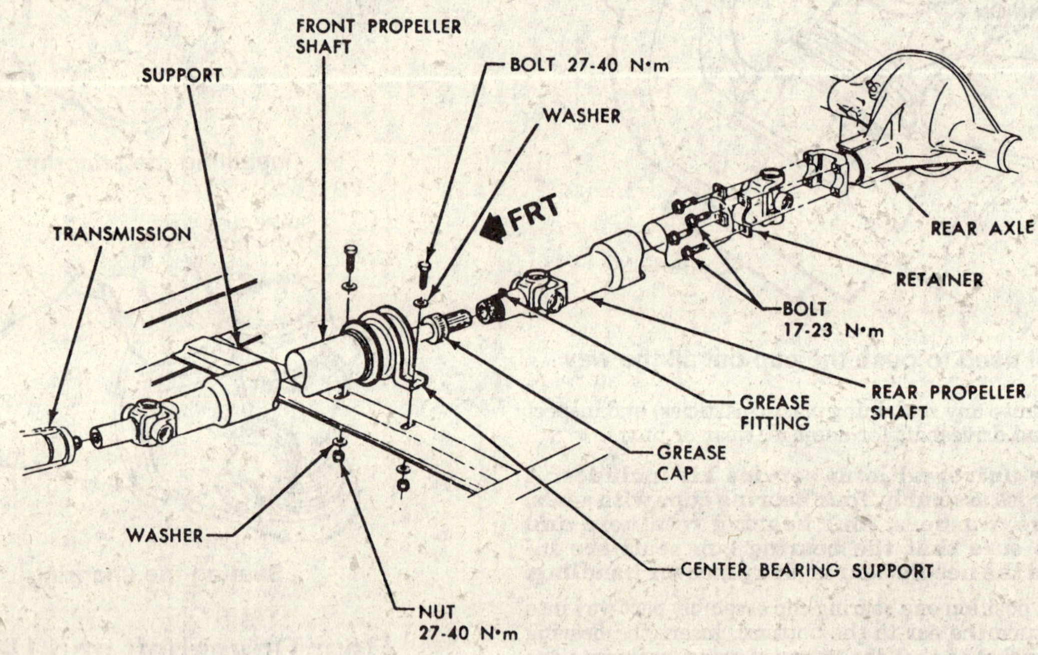

Two-piece rear drive shaft

a. Slide the driveshaft forward to disengage it from the rear axle flange.

b. Slide the driveshaft rearward to disengage it from slip-joint of the front half-shaft, passing it under the axle housing.

c. Remove the center bearing-to-support nuts and bolts.

d. Slide the front half-shaft rearward to disengage it from the transfer case slip-joint.

NOTE: DO NOT allow the driveshaft to drop or allow the universal joints to bend to extreme angles, as this might fracture injected joint internally. Support propeller shaft during removal.

5. Inspect the slip-joint splines for damage, burrs or wear, for this will damage the transmission seal. Apply engine oil to all splined propeller shaft yokes.

6. DO NOT use a hammer to force the driveshaft into place. Check for burrs on transmission output shaft spline, twisted slip yoke splines or possibly the wrong U-joint. Make sure the splines agree in number and fit. To prevent trunnion seal damage, DO NOT place any tool between yoke and splines.

7. If installing a one-piece driveshaft, perform the following procedures:

a. Slide driveshaft into the transmission.

b. Align the rear universal joint-to-rear axle pinion flange, make sure the bearings are properly seated in the pinion flange yoke.

c. Install the rear driveshaft-to-pinion fasteners. Torque the fasteners to 15 ft. lbs. (20 Nm).

8. If installing a two-piece drivehaft, perform the following procedures:

a. Install the front half-shaft into the transmission and bolt the center bearing-to-support. Torque the center bearing to support nuts and bolts to 25 ft. lbs. (34 Nm).

NOTE: The front half-shaft yoke must be bottomed out in the transmission (fully forward) before installation to the support.

b. Rotate the shaft so that the front U-joint trunnion is in the correct position.

NOTE: Before installing the rear driveshaft, align the U-joint trunnions (a "key" in the output spline of the front half-shaft will align with a missing spline in the rear yoke).

c. Attach the rear U-joint to axle. Torque the retainers to 15 ft. lbs. (20 Nm).

9. Road test the vehicle.

Center Support Bearing

REMOVAL AND INSTALLATION

1. Refer to the "Rear Driveshaft, Removal and Installation" procedures in this section and remove the driveshaft.
2. Remove the strap retaining the rubber cushion from the bearing support.
3. Pull the support bracket from the rubber cushion and the cushion from the bearing.
4. Press the bearing assembly from half-shaft.
5. To assemble the bearing support, perform the following procedures:

a. If removed, install the inner deflector onto the half-shaft and prick punch the deflector at 2 opposite points to make sure it is tight on the shaft.

b. Fill the space between the inner dust shield and bearing with lithium soap grease.

c. Start the bearing and slinger assembly straight onto the shaft journal. Support the half-shaft and using a length of pipe over the splined end of the shaft, press the bearing and inner slinger against the shoulder of the half-shaft.

d. Install the bearing retainer, the rubber cushion onto bearing, the bracket onto the cushion and the retaining strap.

6. To install driveshaft, reverse the removal procedures. Torque the center bearing-to-support nuts/bolts to 20–30 ft. lbs. and the driveshaft-to-pinion retainer bolts to 12–17 ft. lbs.

NOISE DIAGNOSIS

The Noise Is	Most Probably Produced By
• Identical under Drive or Coast	• Road surface, tires or front wheel bearings
• Different depending on road surface	• Road surface or tires
• Lower as the car speed is lowered	• Tires
• Similar with car standing or moving	• Engine or transmission
• A vibration	• Unbalanced tires, rear wheel bearing, unbalanced driveshaft or worn U-joint
• A knock or click about every 2 tire revolutions	• Rear wheel bearing
• Most pronounced on turns	• Damaged differential gears
• A steady low-pitched whirring or scraping, starting at low speeds	• Damaged or worn pinion bearing
• A chattering vibration on turns	• Wrong differential lubricant or worn clutch plates (limited slip rear axle)
• Noticed only in Drive, Coast or Float conditions	• Worn ring gear and/or pinion gear

REAR AXLE

Identification

The rear axle identification code and manufacturer's code must be known before attempting to adjust or repair axle shafts or rear axle case assembly. Rear axle ratio, differential type, manufacturer, and build date information is stamped on the right axle tube on the forward side. Any reports made on rear axle assemblies must include the full code letters and build date numbers.

Determining Axle Ratio

An axle ratio is obtained by dividing the number of teeth on the drive pinion gear into the number of teeth on the ring gear. For instance, on a 4.11:1 ratio, the driveshaft will turn 4.11 times for every turn of the rear wheels.

The most accurate way to determine the axle ratio is to drain the differential, remove the cover and count the number of teeth on the ring and the pinion.

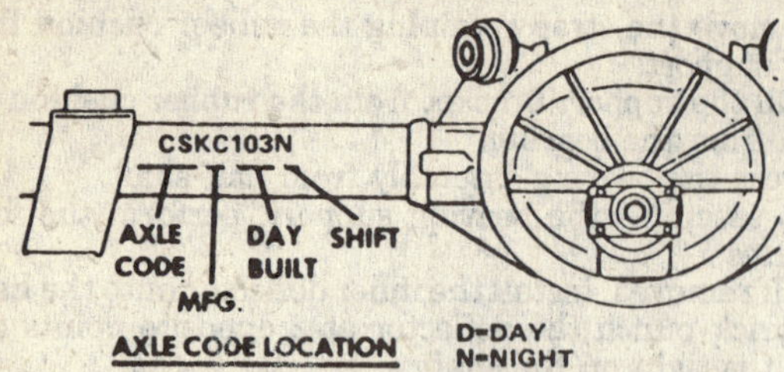

Axle data on the rear axle housing

An easier method is raise and safely support the rear of the vehicle on jackstands. Make a chalk mark on the rear wheel and the driveshaft. Block the front wheels and put the transmission in Neutral. Turn the rear wheel one complete revolution and count the number of turns made by the driveshaft. The number of driveshaft rotations is the axle ratio. More accuracy can be obtained by going more than one tire revolution and dividing the result by the number of tire rotations.

The axle ratio is also identified by the axle serial number prefix on the axle; the axle ratios are listed in the dealer's parts books according to the prefix number.

Axle Shaft, Bearing and Seal

REMOVAL AND INSTALLATION

NOTE: The following procedures requires the use of the GM Slide Hammer tool No. J-2619 or equivalent, the GM Adapter tool No. J-2619-4 or equivalent, the GM Axle Bearing Puller tool No. J-22813-01 or equivalent, the GM Axle Shaft Seal Installer tool No. J-33782, J-23771 or equivalent and the Axle Shaft Bearing Installer tool No. J-34974, J-23765 or equivalent.

1. Raise and support the rear of the vehicle on jackstands.
2. Remove the rear wheel assemblies and the brake drums.

CAUTION

Brake shoes contain asbestos, which has been determined to be a cancer causing agent. Never clean the brake surfaces with compressed air! Avoid inhaling any dust from any brake surface! When cleaning brake surfaces, use a commercially available brake cleaning fluid.

3. Using a wire brush, clean the dirt/rust from around the rear axle cover.
4. Place a catch pan under the differential, then remove the drain plug (if equipped) or rear axle cover and drain the oil.
5. At the differential, remove the rear pinion shaft lock bolt and the pinion shaft.
6. Push the axle shaft inward and remove the C-lock from the button end of the axle shaft.
7. Remove the axle shaft from the axle housing, be careful not to damage the oil seal.
8. Using a putty knife, clean the gasket mounting surfaces.

NOTE: It is recommended, when the axle shaft is removed, to replace the oil seal.

9. To replace the oil seal, perform the following procedures:
   a. Using a medium pry bar, pry the oil seal from the end of the rear axle housing; DO NOT damage the housing oil seal surface.
   b. Clean and inspect the axle tube housing.
   c. Using the GM Axle Shaft Seal Installer tool No. J-33782, J-23771 or equivalent, drive the new seal into the housing until it is flush with the axle tube.
   d. Using gear oil, lubricate the new seal lips.
10. If replacing the wheel bearing, perform the following procedures:

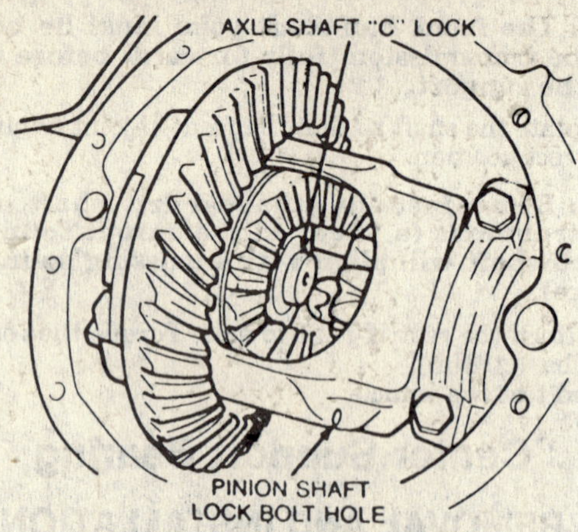

Removing the axle shaft C–lock

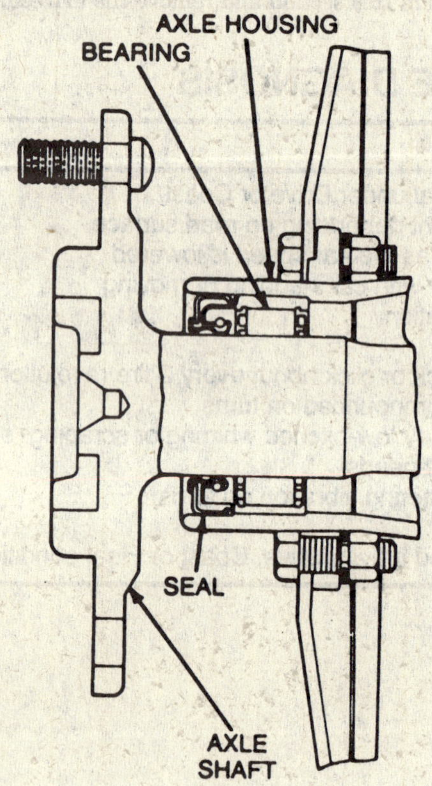

Axle bearing and seal

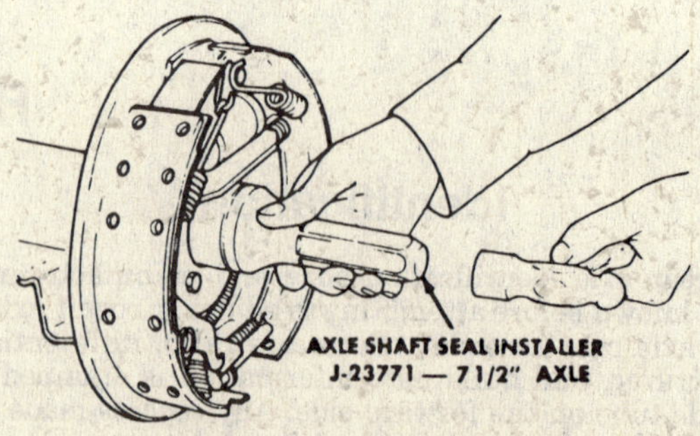

Installing the axle seal

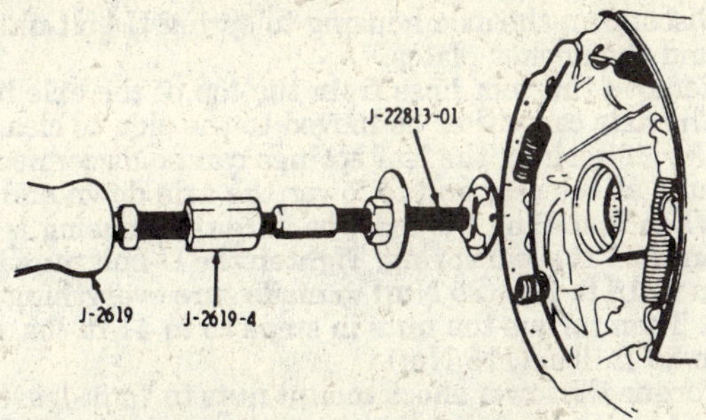

Removing the axle bearing

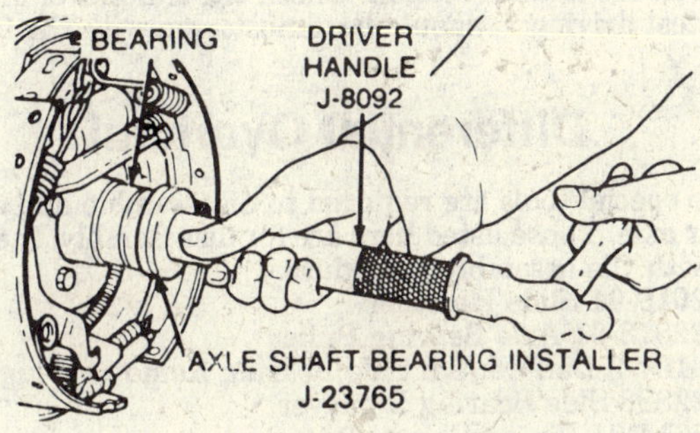

Installing the axle bearing

a. Using the GM Slide Hammer tool No. J-2619 or equivalent, the GM Adapter tool No. J-2619-4 or equivalent and the GM Axle Bearing Puller tool No. J-22813-01 or equivalent, install the tool assembly so that the tangs engage the outer race of the bearing.

b. Using the action of the slide hammer, pull the wheel bearing from the axle housing.

c. Using solvent, throughly clean the wheel bearing, then blow dry with compressed air. Inspect the wheel bearing for excessive wear or damage. If it feels rough, replace it.

d. With a new or the reused bearing, place a blob of heavy grease in the palm of your hand, then work the bearing into the grease until it is thoroughly lubricated.

e. Using the Axle Shaft Bearing Installer tool No. J-34974, J-23765 or equivalent, drive the bearing into the axle housing until it bottoms against the seat. Install a new seal.

11. To install, slide the axle shaft into the rear axle housing and engage the splines of the axle shaft with the splines of the rear axle side gear, then install the C-lock retainer on the axle shaft button end. After the C-lock is installed, pull the axle shaft outward to seat the C-lock retainer in the counterbore of the side gears.

NOTE: When installing the axle shaft(s), be careful not to cut the oil seal lips.

12. Install the pinion shaft through the case and the pinions, then install a new pinion shaft lock bolt. Torque the new lock bolt to 25 ft. lbs. (34 Nm).

13. To complete the installation, use a new rear axle cover gasket and reverse the removal procedures. Torque the carrier cover-to-rear axle housing bolts to 20 ft. lbs. (27 Nm). Refill the housing with SAE-80W or SAE-80W-90 GL-5 oil to a level ⅜ in. (10mm) below the filler plug hole.

NOTE: When adding oil to the rear axle, be aware that some locking differentials require the use of a special gear lubricant additive GM No. Seal Replacement

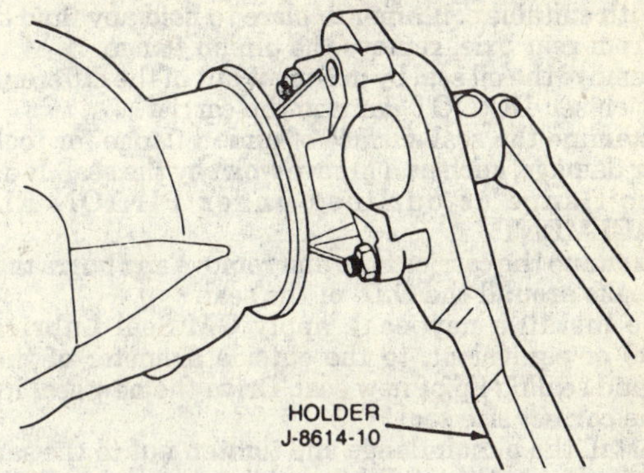

Special tools used to remove the pinion nut

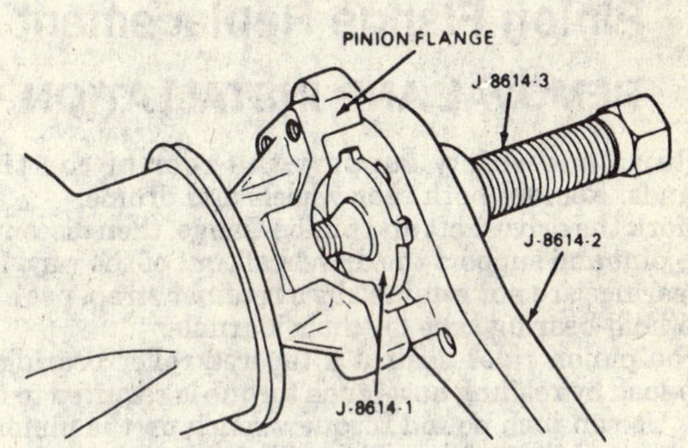

Puller used to remove pinion flange

Pinion Oil Seal Replacement

REMOVAL AND INSTALLATION

NOTE: The following procedure requires the use of the Pinion Holding tool No. J-8614-10 or equivalent, the Pinion Flange Removal tool No. J-8614-1, J-8614-2, J-8614-3 or equivalent, and the Pinion Oil Seal Installation tool No. J-23911 or equivalent.

1. Mark the driveshaft and pinion flange so they can be reassembled in the same position.

2. Disconnect the driveshaft from rear axle pinion flange and support the shaft up in body tunnel by wiring the driveshaft to the exhaust pipe. If the U-joint bearings are not retained by a retainer strap, use a piece of tape to hold bearings on their journals.

3. Mark the position of the pinion flange, the pinion shaft and nut so the proper pinion bearing pre-load can be maintained.

4. Using the Pinion Holding tool No. J-8614-10 or equivalent, the Pinion Flange Removal tool No. J-8614-1, J-8614-2, J-8614-3 or equivalent, remove the pinion flange nut and washer.

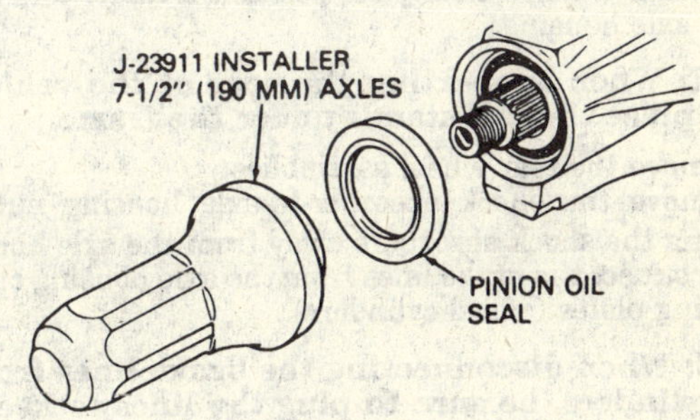

Installing pinion oil seal

5. With suitable container in place to hold any fluid that may drain from rear axle, remove the pinion flange.
6. Remove the oil seal by driving it out of the differential with a blunt chisel; DO NOT damage the carrier.
7. Examine the seal surface of pinion flange for tool marks, nicks or damage, such as a groove worn by the seal. If damaged, replace flange as outlined under PINION FLANGE REPLACEMENT.
8. Examine the carrier bore and remove any burrs that might cause leaks around the O.D. of the seal.
9. To install a new seal, apply GM Seal Lubricant No. 1050169 or equivalent, to the outside diameter of the pinion flange and sealing lip of new seal. Drive the new seal into place with the correct size tool.
10. Install the pinion flange and tighten nut to the same position as marked in Step 4. While holding the pinion flange tighten the nut $^1/_{16}$ in. (1.5mm) beyond the alignment marks.

Pinion Flange Replacement

REMOVAL AND INSTALLATION

1. Raise and safely support the rear of the truck on jackstands. Remove both rear wheels and drums.
2. Mark the driveshaft and pinion flange, then disconnect the rear U-joint and support the driveshaft out of the way. If the U-joint bearings are not retained by a retainer strap, use a piece of tape to hold bearing caps on their journals.
3. The pinion rides against a tapered roller bearing. Check the pre-load by reading how much torque is required to turn the pinion. Use an inch pound torque wrench on the pinion flange nut and record the reading. This will give combined pinion bearing, carrier bearing, axle bearing and seal pre-load.
4. Remove pinion flange nut and washer.
5. With a suitable container in place to hold any fluid that may drain from the rear axle, remove the pinion flange.
6. Apply the GM Seal lubricant No. 1050169 or equivalent, to the outside diameter of the new pinion flange, then install the pinion flange, washer and pinion flange nut finger tight.
7. While holding the pinion flange, tighten the nut a little at a time and turn the drive pinion several revolutions after each tightening to set the rollers. Check the pre-load of bearings each time with an inch pound torque wrench until pre-load is 3–5 inch lbs. more than the reading obtained in Step 3.
8. Install the driveshaft-to-rear axle pinion flange and torque the retainer bolts to 15 ft. lbs. (20 Nm).
9. To complete the installation, reverse the removal procedures. Check and/or add correct lubricant as necessary.

Axle Housing

REMOVAL AND INSTALLATION

1. Refer to the "Driveshaft, Removal and Installation" procedures in this section and disconnect the driveshaft from the rear axle housing; the driveshaft may either be removed or supported on a wire. Using a floor jack, position it under and support the rear axle housing.

NOTE: When supporting the rear of the vehicle, be sure to place the jackstands under the frame.

2. Remove the rear wheel assemblies.
3. Remove the shock absorber-to-axle housing nuts/bolts, then swing the shock absorbers away from the axle housing.
4. Disconnect the brake lines from the axle housing clips and the backing plates (wheel cylinders).

NOTE: When disconnecting the brake lines from the wheel cylinders, be sure to plug the lines to keep dirt from entering the lines.

5. Disconnect the axle housing-to-spring U-bolt nuts, the U-bolts and the anchor plates.
6. Remove the vent hose from the top of the axle housing.
7. The axle can either be moved to the side to clear the leaf spring or, if desired, the leaf springs can be disconnected from the frame at the rear end to lower the axle down and back.
8. When installing the axle, be sure the housing is properly positioned on the leaf spring. Tighten the U-bolt nuts in a cross pattern to 18 ft. lbs. (25 Nm) to made sure everything is evenly seated. Then torque the nuts in stepa to to 41 ft. lbs. (55 Nm), then to 85 ft. lbs. (115 Nm).
9. Torque the lower shock mount nuts to 74 ft. lbs. (100 Nm) and the U-joint-to-pinion flange retainer bolts to 15 ft. lbs. (20 Nm).
10. Reconnect the rear brake lines and bleed the system as described in the Brakes section. Check the fluid level in the axle before test driving: it should be almost even with the filler plug hole.

Differential Overhaul

Some special tools are required to disassemble and assemble the rear axle. Those listed here are for disassembly, the rest are listed with the assembly procedure.

- J-2619-01 Slide Hammer
- J-22813-01 Axle Bearing Puller
- J-8107-2 Defferential Side Bearing Remover Plug
- J-22888 Side Bearing Remover
- J-8614-01 Pinion Flange Remover
- J-25320 Rear Pinion Bearing Remover

Before disassembly, there are some things to check. First drain the oil and examine it. If there is heavy gear or bearing wear in the axle, usually the oil takes on a metal-flake appearence from the worn metal being suspended in the oil. Also check the backlash, described later in this procedure. This information can be useful in determining the cause of axle problems and in deciding on the shim packs to be used for assembly.

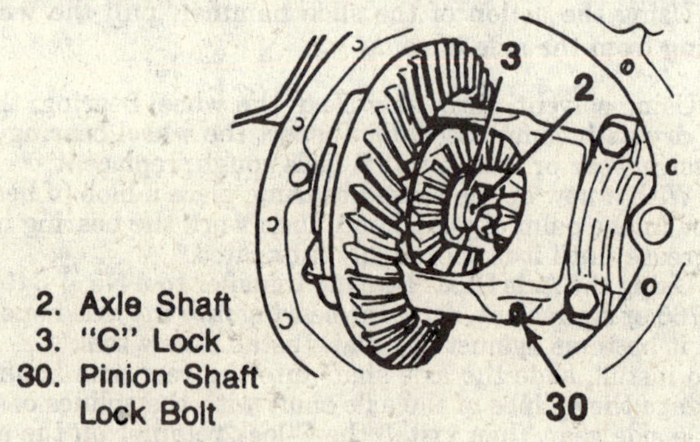

Removing the pinion shaft lock bolt

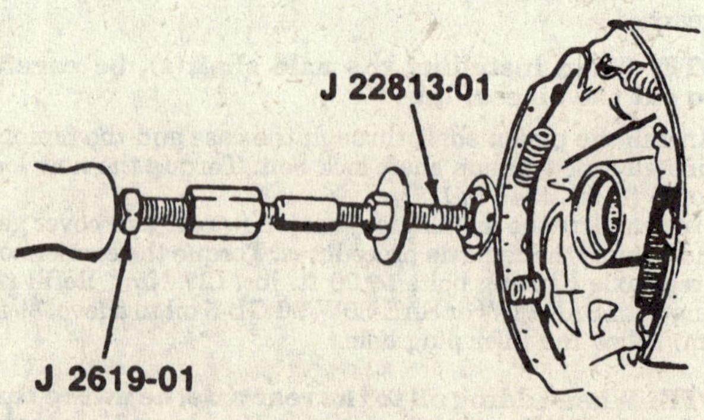

Removing the axle bearing with the proper tool

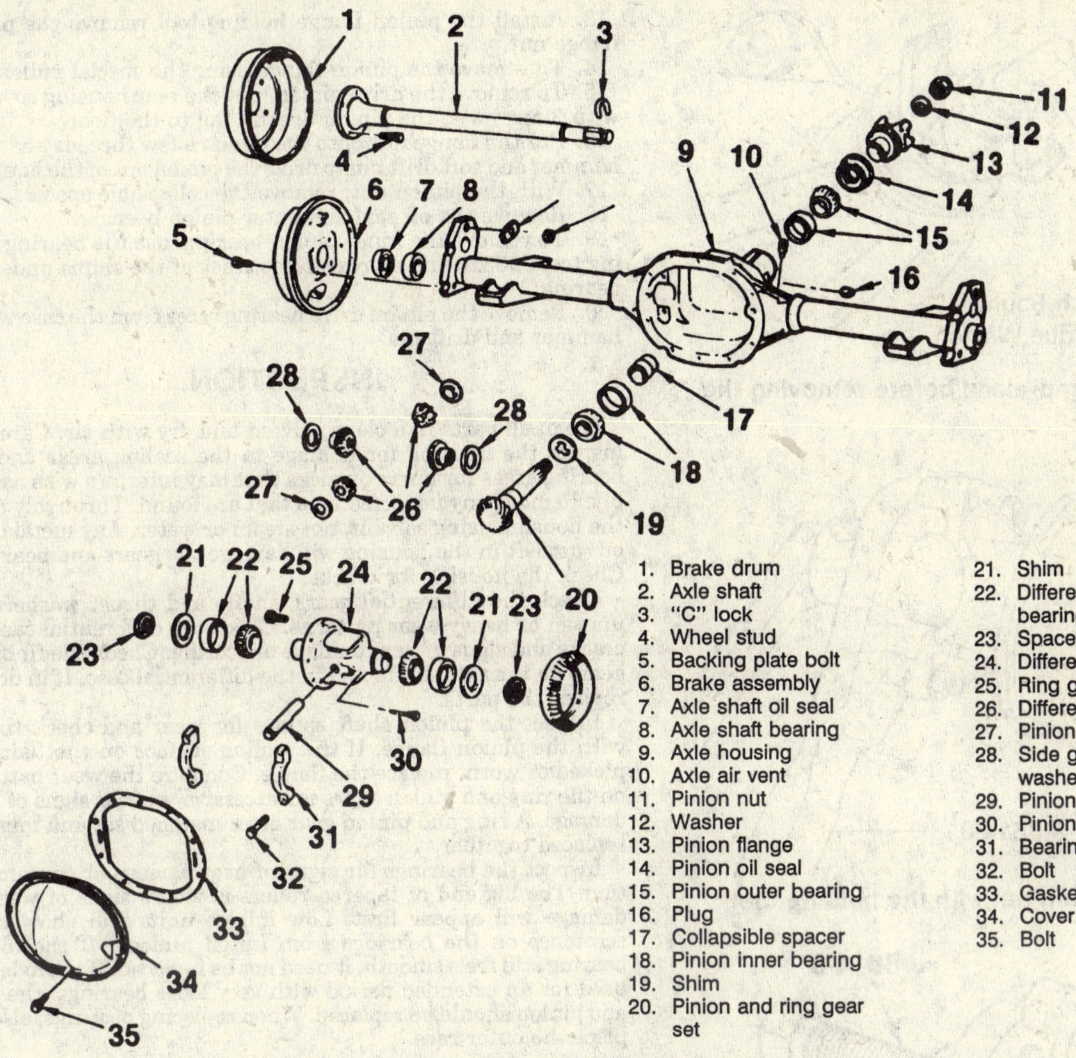

1. Brake drum
2. Axle shaft
3. "C" lock
4. Wheel stud
5. Backing plate bolt
6. Brake assembly
7. Axle shaft oil seal
8. Axle shaft bearing
9. Axle housing
10. Axle air vent
11. Pinion nut
12. Washer
13. Pinion flange
14. Pinion oil seal
15. Pinion outer bearing
16. Plug
17. Collapsible spacer
18. Pinion inner bearing
19. Shim
20. Pinion and ring gear set
21. Shim
22. Differential side bearing
23. Spacer
24. Differential case
25. Ring gear bolt
26. Differential gears
27. Pinion thrust washers
28. Side gear thrust washers
29. Pinion shaft
30. Pinion shaft lock bolt
31. Bearing cap
32. Bolt
33. Gasket
34. Cover
35. Bolt

Exploded view of rear axle

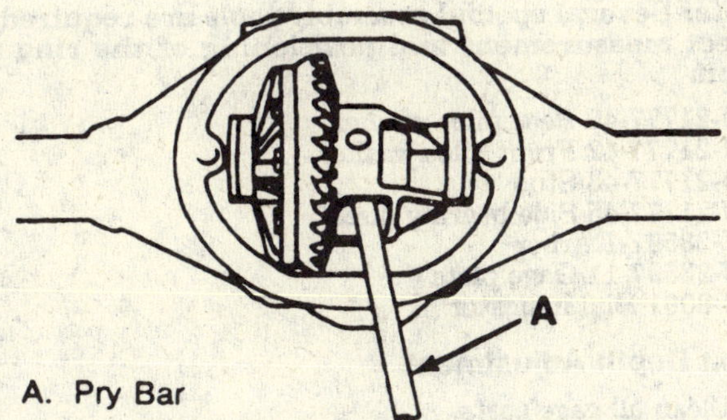

Insert the pry bar through the differential window

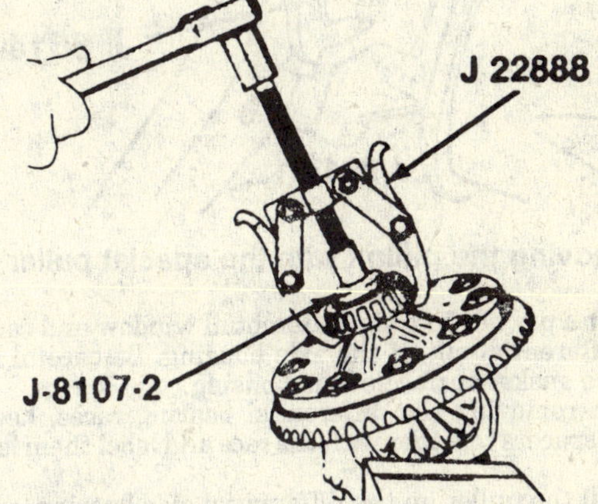

Use a puller to remove the differential side bearings

1. With the axle properly supported and the brake backplates removed, remove the rear cover.
2. Remove the pinion shaft lock bolt, pinion shaft and C locks from the button end of the axles shafts.
3. Remove the axle shafts and carefully pry out the oil seal from each end of the housing.
4. Use the bearing removal tools to remove the axle bearings. Make sure the tool engages the outer race of the bearing.
5. Roll the pinion gears out of the case with their thrust washers. Label their position.
6. Remove the side gears and thrust washers and label their position.
7. Mark the differential bearing caps left and right and remove them.

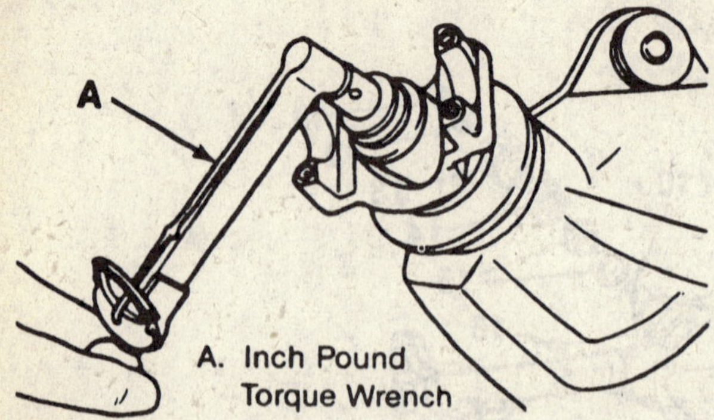

Check the bearing preload before removing the pinion

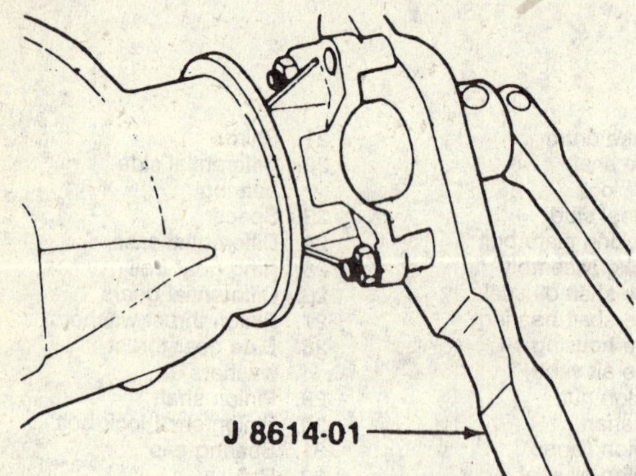

Removing the pinion nut with the holding tool

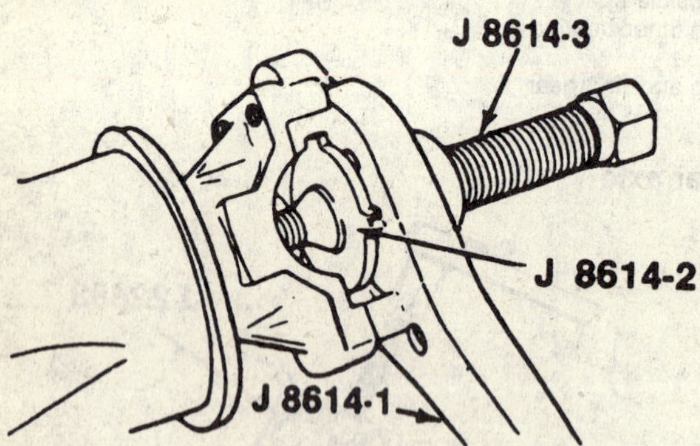

Removing the pinion with the special puller

8. Insert a pry bar into the differential window and carefully pry the differential out of the axle housing. Be careful not to damage the gasket surface of the housing.
9. When removing the differential bearing races, keep the shims and spacers together with the race and label them left and right.
10. Install the puller on the differential side bearing, making sure the jaws contact the inner race of the bearing, not the cage. Remove the bearings.
11. Remove the ring gear from the differential case. The 10 bolts are left hand thread. DO NOT pry the gear off, this will damage the gear and the case.
12. Before removing the drive pinion, use an inch pound torque wrench to see how much torque is required to turn the pinion. This checks the bearing preload.
13. Install the pinion flange holding tool remove the pinion flange nut.
14. To remove the pinion flange using the special puller.
15. To remove the drive pinion, put the rear housing cover on with 2 screws so the pinion doesn't fall to the floor.
16. Put the flange nut onto the pinion a few threads and use a hammer and soft drift pin to drive the pinion out of the housing.
17. With the pinion out, remove the collapsible spacer.
18. Remove the oil seal and outer pinion bearing.
19. To remove the inner pinion bearing, use the bearing pulling tool J25320 and a press. Keep track of the shims under the bearing.
20. Remove the pinion drive bearing races from the case with a hammer and drift pin.

INSPECTION

Clean all parts in a clean solvent and dry with air. Carefully inspect the housing for damage to the sealing areas and the bearing areas for burrs or nicks that may interfere with assembly. Remove any imperfections that are found. Throughly clean the housing using solvent, not steam or water. Any metal chips or rust left in the housing will damage the gears and bearings. Check the housing for cracks.

Check the differential gears, shafts and thrust washers for uneven or heavy wear patterns. Check the differential case for cracks and signs of heat damage or scoring. Check the fit of the gears on the axle shafts and in the differential case. If in doubt, replace the parts.

Inspect the pinion shaft splines for wear and check the fit with the pinion flange. If the sealing surface on the flange is nicked or worn, replace the flange. Compare the wear patterns on the ring and pinion gears for excessive wear or signs of heat damage. A ring and pinion gear are a matched set and must be replaced together.

Inspect the bearings for signs of heat damage or contamination. The big end of tapered rollers is where signs of wear or damage will appear first. Low milage units will show some scratches on the bearings from initial preload. If the (oiled) bearing still feels smooth, it need not be replaced. If the axle was used for an extended period with very loose bearings, the ring and pinion should be replaced. When replacing bearings, also replace the outer race.

ASSEMBLY

Note: Several special assembly tools are required for correct measurement and positioning of the ring and pinion.

- J-21777-40 Rear pilot washer
- J-21777-42 Front pilot washer
- J-21777-43 Stud
- J-21777-45 Side bearing discs
- J-23597-1 Arbor
- J-23597-11 Gage plate
- J-8001 Dial indicator

Pinion Depth Adjustment

1. Clean all gage parts.
2. Lubricate the front and rear pinion bearings with gear oil.
3. With the outer races installed into the axle housing, place the bearings into the outer races and secure them in place with the pilot washers and stud assembly tool and gage plate as shown.
4. Torque the J 21777-43 stud assembly to 20 inch lbs. (2.2 Nm).
5. Rotate the gage plate and bearings several revolutions to seat the bearings.
6. Retorque the stud assembly.
7. Install the arbor, side bearing disks and dial indicator as shown.

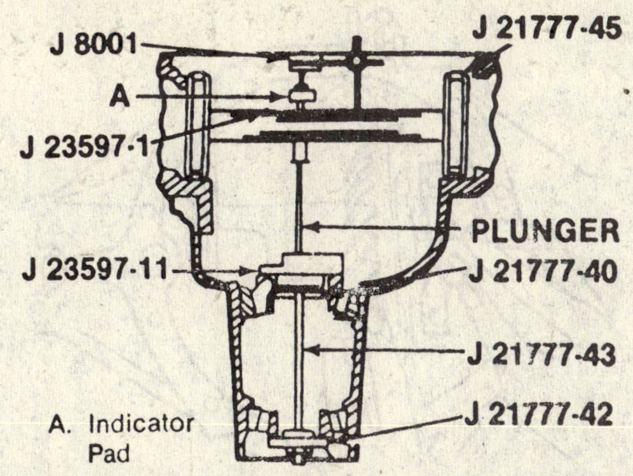

Secure the bearings in place with the adjustment tools

8. Install the side bearing caps and finger tighten the bolts.
9. Rotate the gage plate until the gaging areas are parallel with the disks.
10. Position the gage plate shaft assembly in the carrier so that the dial indicator rod is centered on the gage area of the gage block.
11. Set the dial indicator at zero and preload the dial to about ¾ turn of the needle.
12. Rotate the gage shaft to find the high point and zero the dial.
13. Rotate the gage shaft until the dial indicator rod does not touch the gage block.
14. Record the actual number on the dial indicator, not the number which represents how far the needle traveled. This is the nominal pinion setting. Example: If the indicator moved left 0.067 in. (1.7mm) to a reading of 0.033 in. (0.84mm), record the reading of 0.033 in. (0.84mm), not the travel of 0.067 in. (1.7mm). At this point the indicator should be in the 0.020–0.050 in. (0.50–1.27mm) range.
15. Check the pinion face for a pinion adjustment mark. This mark is the best running position for the pinion from the nominal setting.
16. Remove the measuring tools and install the pinion shim according to the measurements taken.

Differential Assembly

1. Lubricate all parts with gear oil.
2. Install the side gear thrust washers to the side gears.
3. Install the side gears into the same side that they were removed from.

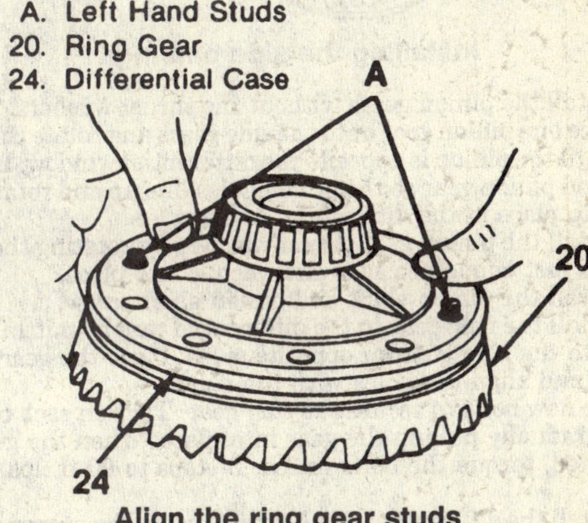

Align the ring gear studs

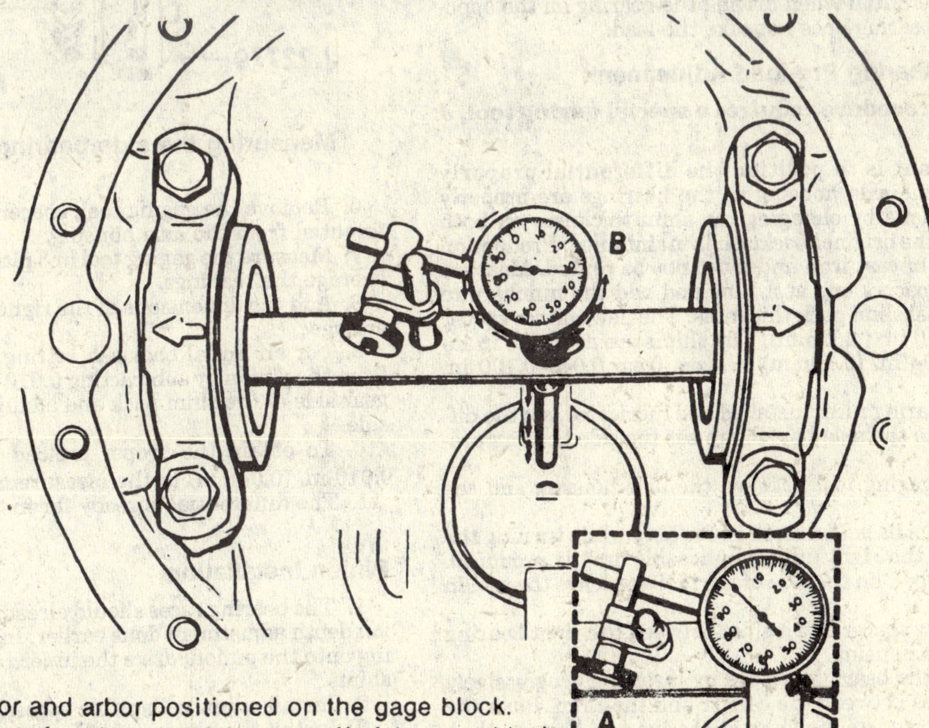

A. Dial indicator and arbor positioned on the gage block.
B. Measurement after the arbor is moved off of the gage block.

Checking nominal pinion depth

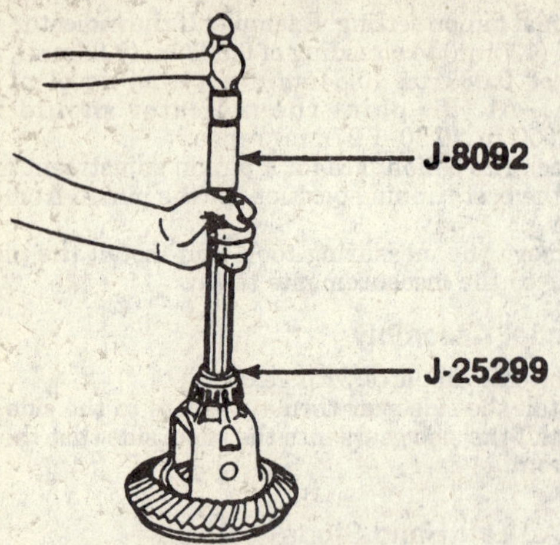

Installing the side bearings

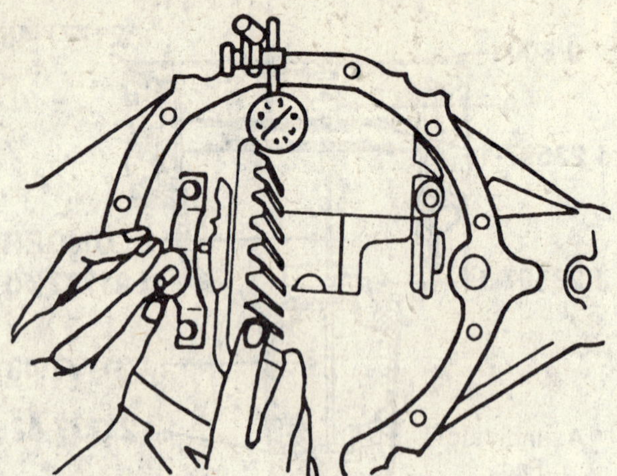

Install the side bearing gaging tool

4. Install the pinion gears without the thrust washers. To do this, place one pinion gear onto the side gears ang rotate the side gears until the pinion is opposite the differential window. Install the second pinion gear so the pinion holes line up and rotate the gears into place in the differential housing.
5. Install the pinion gear thrust washers by rotating the pinion gears just enough to slide the washer into place.
6. Install the pinion shaft and pinion shaft screw.
7. Install the ring gear to the differential case by putting two studs into the ring gear on opposite sides. Place the gear onto the case and align the holes with the studs.
8. Use new bolts to secure the ring gear. Tighten each one in stages, gradually pulling the gear into place. When the gear is fully seated, torque the bolts in 2 or 3 steps to 90 ft. lbs. (120 Nm).
9. Install the differential side bearings using the proper tools. Support the differential when driving the bearing on the opposite side so the bearing does not take the load.

Setting Side Bearing Pre-load Adjustment

Note: This procedure requires a special gaging tool, J 22779.

The adjustment is to position the differential properly side–to–side in the axle housing so the bearings are properly loaded. This is done by changing the shim thickness on both sides equally so the original backlash is maintained. Production shims are made of cast iron and must not be reused. Measure the shims and spacers one at a time and add the numbers to optain the original shim pack thickness. The new service spacer thickness is 0.170 in. (4.32mm). The shims are available in increments of 0.004 in. (0.10mm) in sizes from 0.040–0.100 in. (1.0–2.5mm).

1. With the bearing races installed and lubricated, set the differential case into the axle housing to set the side bearing preload adjustment.
2. Insert the gaging tool between the axle housing and the left bearing cup.
3. Move the tool back and forth in the bore while turning the adjusting nut to the right until a noticeable drag is produced. Tighten the lock bolt on the side of the tool and leave the tool in place.
4. Install a new spacer and a shim between the right bearing race and the axle housing.
5. Determine the bearing preload by inserting progressively larger feeler gages between the carrier and the shim. Push the gage down so it contacts the shim at the top and bottom, then contacts the axle housing. The point just before additional drag begins is the correct feeler gage thickness. This is the zero setting without preload.

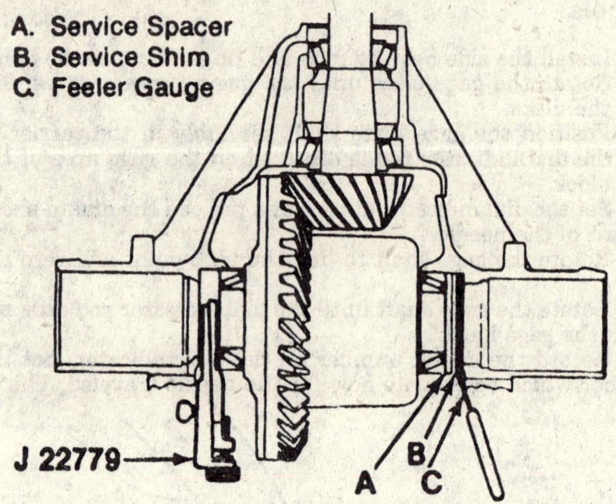

Measuring the side bearing shim requirements

6. Remove the gaging tool, spacer, shim, feeler gage and differential from the axle housing.
7. Measure the gaging tool in 3 places using a micrometer and average the readings.
8. Add the dimensions of the right side spacer, shim and feeler gage.
9. For an initial backlash setting, move the ring gear away from the pinion by subtracting 0.010 in. (0.04mm) from the ring gear side of the shim pack and adding the same to the opposite side.
10. To obtain the proper preload on the side bearings, add 0.010 in. (0.04mm) to the measurement of each shim pack.
11. The differential is ready for installation.

Pinion Installation

1. The bearing races should already be installed from the pinion depth adjustment done earlier. Install the pinion inner bearing onto the pinion; drive the inner race until it is seated on the shims.
2. Install a new collapsible spacer.
3. Install the pinion into the axle housing.
4. While holding the pinion in place, carefully drive the outer bearing onto the pinion shaft.
5. Install a new pinion oil seal.

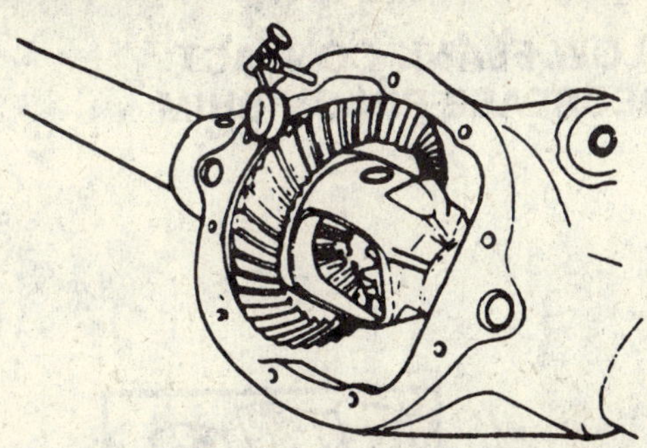

Dial indicator on the heel of a ring gear tooth

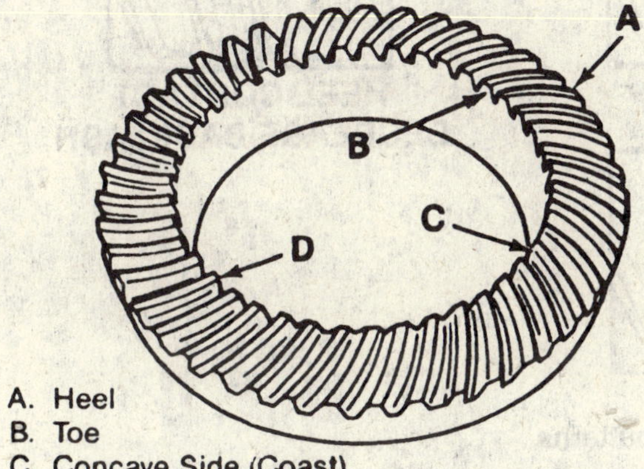

A. Heel
B. Toe
C. Concave Side (Coast)
D. Convex Side (Drive)

Ring gear tooth nomenclature

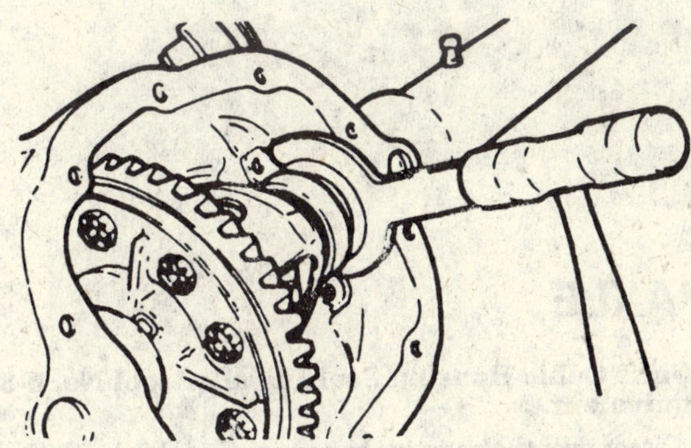

Installing the final differential bearing shim pack

6. Install the pinion flange by tapping it with a soft mallet until enough threads show to start the nut.
7. Install the flange holding tool and install the washer and a new nut. DO NOT tighten the nut. The bearing preload must be adjusted.

Pinion Bearing Preload Adjustment

1. Tighten the pinion nut just until the end play is taken out.
2. Remove the holding tool and use an inch pound torque wrench to determine how much torque is required to turn the pinion. This is bearing preload. Some of the resistance to turning the pinion shaft comes from the seal, so make sure it is properly lubricated. Turn the pinion several times to seat the bearings before taking a reading.
3. The preload should be 24–32 inch lbs. (2.7–3.6 Nm) on new bearings. On used bearings the preload should be 8–12 inch lbs. (1.0–1.4 Nm).
4. If the preload is low, tighten the nut in small increments and check the preload again. If the preload is exceded, the collapsible spacer must be replaced.
5. Once the proload is correct, install the differential and set the backlash.

Backlash Adjustment

1. With the side bearing preload properly adjusted and the differential installed, install the bearing caps and torque the bolts to 55 ft. lbs. (75 Nm). Rotate the pinion and differential several times to seat the bearings.
2. Install a dial indicator to the axle housing. A unit with a magnetic base is acceptable.
3. Touch the stem to the heel of a tooth on the ring gear. That's the outer edge of the convex or drive side.
4. Hold the pinion fast and rock the ring gear to see how much play there is between the gear teeth; backlash. Record the reading and check 3 or 4 more places around the ring gear.
5. The readings should all be within 0.002 in. (0.05mm). If the readings vary more than this, check for burrs, a distorted case flange or uneven torque of the ring gear bolts.
6. The correct backlash is 0.005–0.009 in. (0.13–0.23mm) for new gear sets.
7. To adjust backlash, remove shim thickness from one side of the differential and add the same amount to the other side. This moves the ring gear to one side while maintaining the side bearing preload. Moving 0.002 in. (0.05mm) of shim changes the backlash by 0.001 in. (0.03mm).
8. When the backlash is correctly adjusted, remove the side bearing caps and shim packs.
9. Add 0.004 in. (0.10mm) of shim to the left side shim pack and install it. Install the left bearing cap but do not tighten the bolts yet.
10. Add 0.004 in. (0.10mm) of shim to the right side shim pack and drive the shim pack into place. Install the bearing cap and torque the bolts to 55 ft. lbs. (75 Nm).
11. Recheck the backlash and adjust as needed.

Final Assembly

1. Install new axle bearings and oil them with gear oil.
2. Install new axle seals and oil the lips with gear oil.
3. Install the axle shafts and edgage the splines with the side gears in the differential.
4. Install the C locks on the end of the shafts. Pull out on the shafts to seat the C locks in the side gears.
5. Install the pinion shaft into the differential gears and install the lock bolt. DO NOT over tighten the lock bolt. Torque it to 25 ft. lbs. (34 Nm).
6. Install the rear cover with a new gasket and torque the bolts to 20 ft. lbs. (27 Nm). Refill with lubricant.

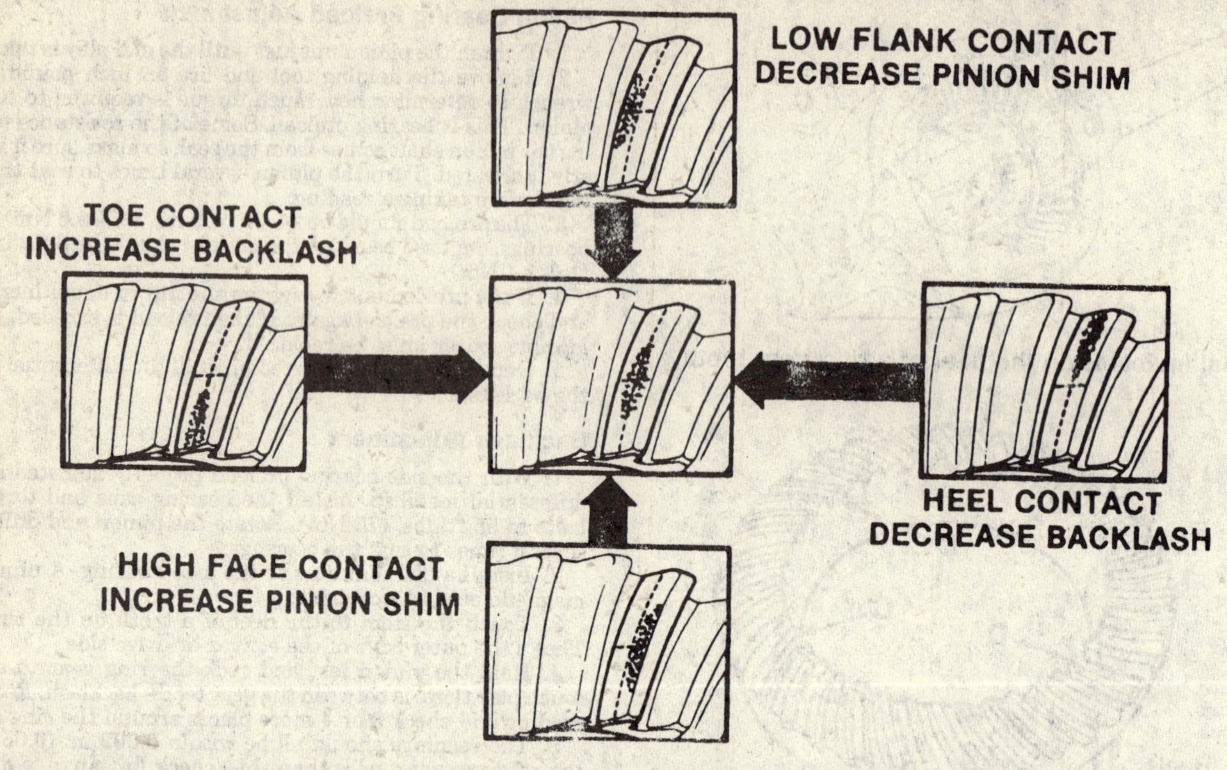

Ring gear tooth wear patterns

FRONT DRIVE AXLE

Identification

The front axle assembly, used on the 4WD models, utilizes a central disconnect type front axle/transfer case system which allows shifting in and out of 4WD when the vehicle is moving under most driving conditions. The axle has an aluminum carrier which includes a vacuum activated center lock feature.

The drive axles employ completely flexible assemblies which consist of inner and outer constant velocity (CV) joints connected by an axle shaft. The inner CV joint is a "tri-pot" design, which is completely flexible and can move in and out. The outer CV joint is a "Rzeppa" design which is also flexible but cannot move in or out.

Axle Tube and Shaft Assembly

REMOVAL AND INSTALLATION

NOTE: The following procedure requires the use of the Shift Cable Housing Seal Installer tool No. J-33799 or equivalent.

1. Disconnect the negative battery terminal from the battery.
2. Disconnect the shift cable from the vacuum actuator by disengaging the locking spring. Then push the actuator diaphragm in to release the cable.
3. Unlock the steering wheel at steering column so the linkage is free to move.
4. Raise and safely support the front of the truck on jackstands.

NOTE: If a twin post hoist is used, place the jackstands under frame and lower front post hoist.

5. Remove the front wheel assemblies, the engine drive belt shield and the front axle skid plate (if equipped).
6. Place a support under right-side lower control arm and disconnect right-side upper ball joint, then remove the support so the control arm will hang free.

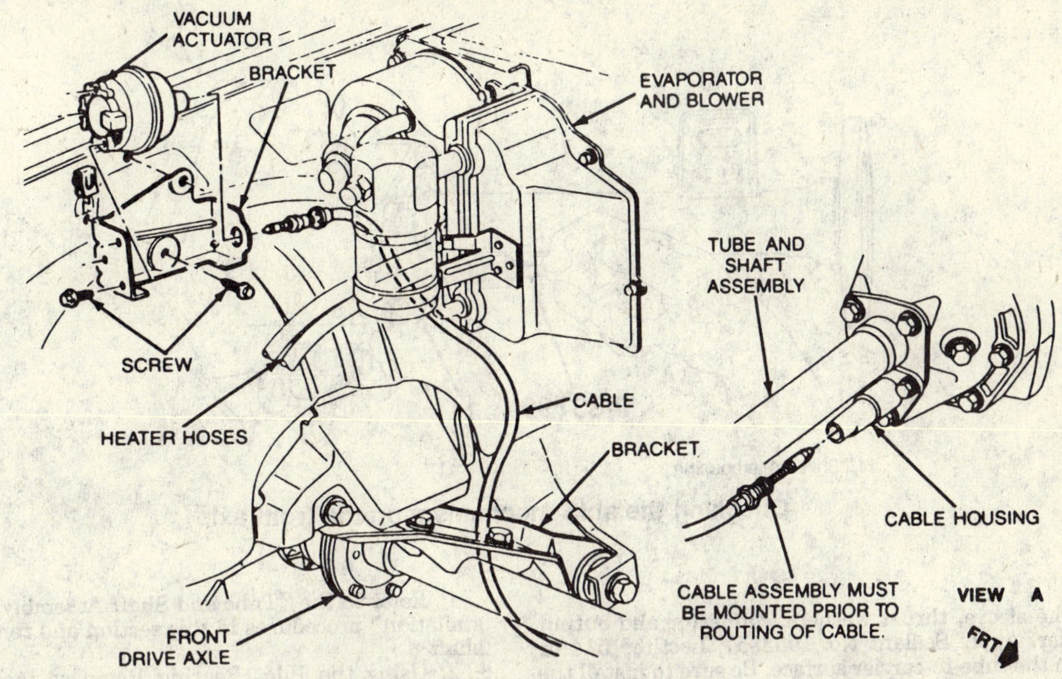

Disconnect the vacuum actuator

NOTE: To keep the axle from turning, insert a drift through the opening in the top of the brake caliper, into the corresponding vane of the brake rotor.

7. Remove the right-side drive axle shaft-to-tube assembly bolts and separate the drive axle from the tube assembly, then remove the drift from the brake caliper and rotor.
8. Disconnect the four wheel drive indicator lamp electrical connector from the switch.
9. Remove the three bolts securing the cable and switch housing-to-carrier and pull the housing away to gain access to the cable locking spring. DO NOT unscrew the cable coupling nut unless the cable is being replaced.
10. Disconnect the cable from the shift fork shaft by lifting spring over slot in shift fork.
11. Remove the two bolts securing the tube bracket to the frame.
12. Remove the remaining upper bolts securing the tube assembly to the carrier.
13. Remove the tube assembly by working around the drive axle. Be careful not to allow the sleeve, thrust washers, connector and output shaft to fall out of carrier or be damaged when removing the tube.

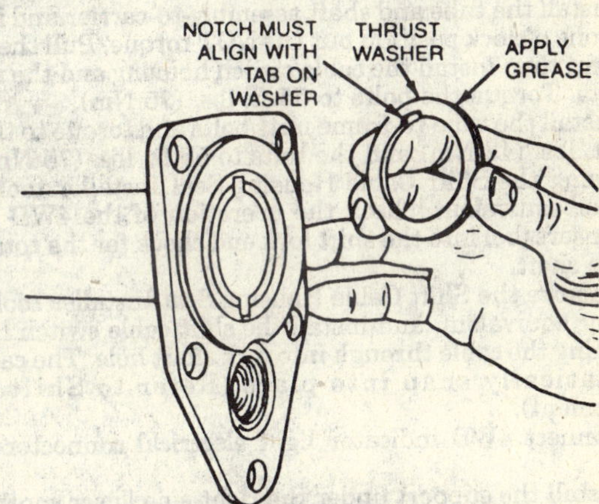

Thrust washer

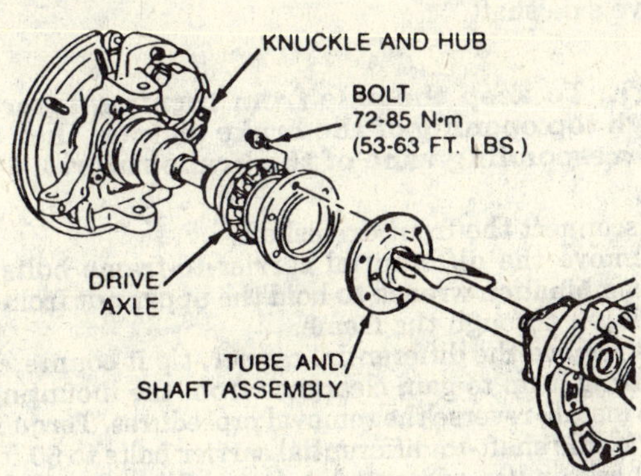

Remove the drive axle bolts

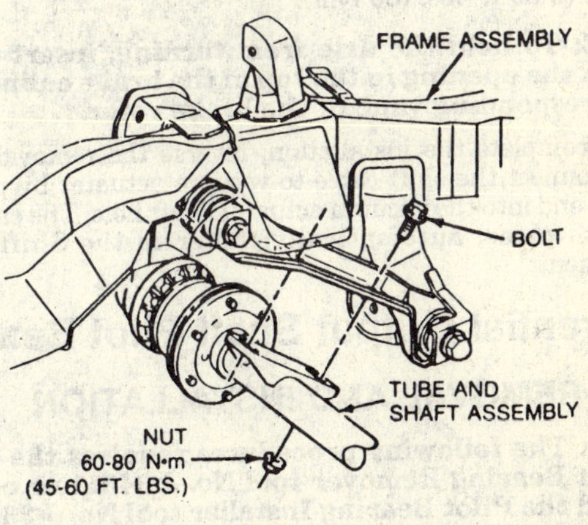

Tube-to-frame attachment

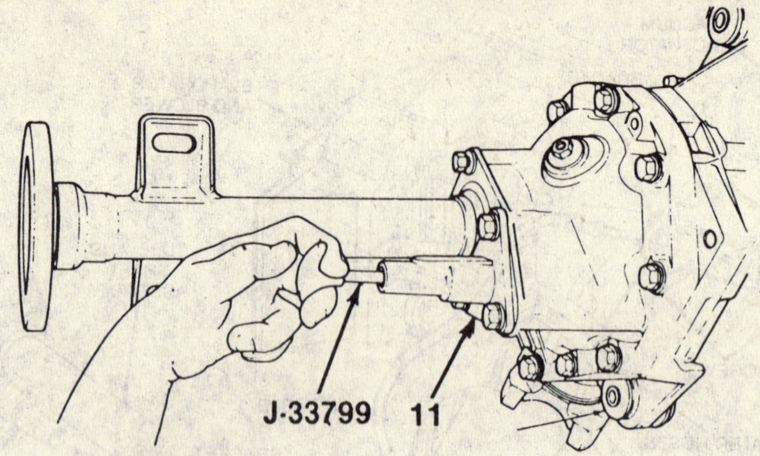

11. Shift cable housing

Checking the shift mechanism on the front axle

To install:

14. Install the sleeve, thrust washers, connector and output shaft in carrier. Apply Sealant No. 1052357, Loctite® 514 or equivalent, on the tube-to-carrier surface. Be sure to install the thrust washer. Apply grease to the washer to hold it in place during assembly.

15. Install the tube and shaft assembly-to-carrier and install a bolt at one o'clock position but DO NOT torque. Pull the assembly down, then install the cable/switch housing and the remaining bolts. Torque the bolts to 55 ft. lbs. (75 Nm).

16. Install the tube-to-frame nuts/bolts and torque to the bolts to 36 ft. lbs. (48 Nm) and the nuts to 55 ft. lbs. (75 Nm).

17. Using the Shift Cable Housing Seal Installer tool No. J-33799 or equivalent, check the operation of the 4WD mechanism. Insert tool into the shift fork and check for the rotation of the axle shaft.

18. Remove the Shift Cable Housing Seal Installer tool No. J-33799 or equivalent, and install the shift cable switch housing by pushing the cable through into fork shaft hole. The cable will automatically snap into place (Refer to Shift Cable Replacement).

19. Connect 4WD indicator light electrical connector to the switch.

20. Install the support under the right-side lower control arm to raise arm and connect upper ball joint.

21. Install right-side drive axle-to-axle tube by installing one bolt first, then, rotate the axle to install remaining bolts. Torque the bolts to 60 ft. lbs. (80 Nm).

NOTE: To hold the axle from turning, insert a drift through the opening in the top of the brake caliper into the corresponding vane of the brake rotor.

22. To complete the installation, reverse the removal procedures. Connect the shift cable-to-vacuum actuator by pushing the cable end into the vacuum actuator shaft hole. The cable will snap into place, automatically; Refer to the Shift Cable Replacement.

Differential Output Shaft Pilot Bearing

REMOVAL AND INSTALLATION

NOTE: The following procedures requires the use of the Pilot Bearing Remover tool No. J-34011 or equivalent, and the Pilot Bearing Installer tool No. J-33842 or equivalent.

1. Refer to the "Tube and Shaft Assembly, Removal and Installation" procedures in this section and remove the tube and shaft.
2. Using the Pilot Bearing Remover tool No. J-34011 or equivalent, remove the pilot bearing.
3. Using axle fluid, lubricate the new bearing.
4. Using the Pilot Bearing Installer tool No. J-33842 or equivalent, install the new pilot bearing.

Differential Carrier

REMOVAL AND INSTALLATION

1. Raise and safely support the front of the truck on jackstands.

NOTE: If a twin post hoist is used, place jackstands under the frame and lower front post.

2. Refer to the "Tube and Shaft Assembly, Removal and Installation" procedures in this section and remove the tube and shaft assembly.
3. Remove the stabilizer-to-frame bolts.
4. Using a scribing tool, mark the location of the steering idler arm-to-frame, then remove the steering arm-to-frame bolts.
5. Push the steering linkage towards the front of the truck.
6. Remove the axle vent hose from the carrier fitting.
7. Remove the left-side drive axle shaft-to-carrier bolts and the drive axle shaft.

NOTE: To keep the axle from turning, insert a drift through top opening of the brake caliper, then through the corresponding vane of the brake rotor.

8. Disconnect the front driveshaft.
9. Remove the differential carrier-to-frame bolts; use an 18mm combination wrench to hold the upper nut from turning, by holding it through the frame.
10. To remove the differential carrier, tip it counterclockwise while lifting it up to gain clearance from the mounting ears.
11. To install, reverse the removal procedures. Torque the left-side drive axle shaft-to-differential carrier bolts to 60 ft. lbs. (80 Nm). Check and/or add axle lubricant, fill to level of fill plug hole. Lower vehicle, test drive and recheck the lubricant.

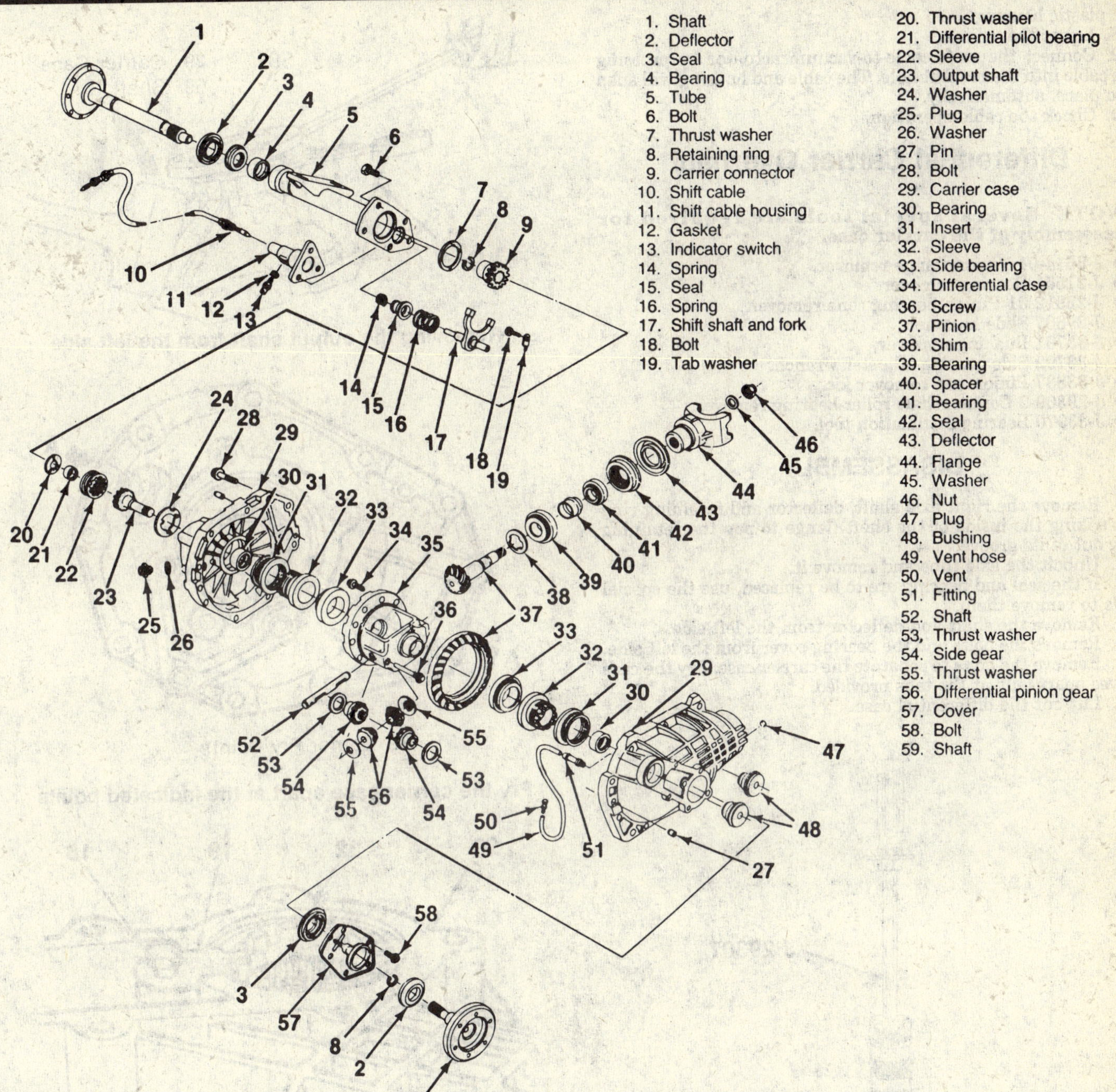

Exploded view of front drive axle

Shift Cable

REMOVAL AND INSTALLATION

1. Disengage the shift cable from the vacuum actuator by disengaging the locking spring, then, push the actuator diaphragm in to release the cable. Using a pair of pliers, squeeze the two cable locking fingers, then pull the cable out of the bracket hole.
2. Raise and safely support the front of the truck on jackstands, then remove cable/switch housing-to-carrier bolts and pull housing away to gain access to the cable locking spring. Disconnect the cable from the shift fork shaft by lifting the spring over shift fork slot.
3. Unscrew the cable from the housing.
4. Remove the cable from the truck.
5. To install the cable, observe the proper routing.
6. Install the cable/switch housing-to-carrier bolts. Torque the bolts to 36 ft. lbs. (48 Nm).
7. Guide the cable through the switch housing into the fork shaft hole and push the cable inward; the cable will automatically snap into place. Start turning the coupling nut by hand, to avoid cross threading, then torque the nut to 71–106 inch lbs. DO NOT overtorque the nut as this will cause thread damage to

the plastic housing.
8. Lower the vehicle.
9. Connect the shift cable-to-vacuum actuator by pressing the cable into the bracket hole. The cable and housing will snap into place, automatically.
10. Check the cable operation.

Differential Carrier Overhaul

NOTE: Several special tools are required for dissassembly of the carrier case.

- J-8614-01 Pinion flange remover.
- J-21551 Bearing remover.
- J-22912-01 Pinion bearing cone remover.
- J-29307 Slide hammer.
- J-33791 Bushing remover.
- J-33792 Side bearing adjuster wrench.
- J-33837 Pinion cup remover kit.
- J-29369-2 Countershaft roller bearing remover.
- J-33970 Bearing installation tool.

DISASSEMBLY

1. Remove the right axle shaft, deflector and retaining ring by striking the inside of the shaft flange to pop the retaining ring out of its groove.
2. Unbolt the axle tube and remove it.
3. If the seal and bearing are to be replaced, use the special tools to remove them.
4. Remove the shaft and deflector from the left side.
5. Remove the bolts and the bearing cover from the left side.
6. Remove the bolts to separate the carrier case. Pry the case halves apart only at the tabs provided.
7. Lift out the differential case.

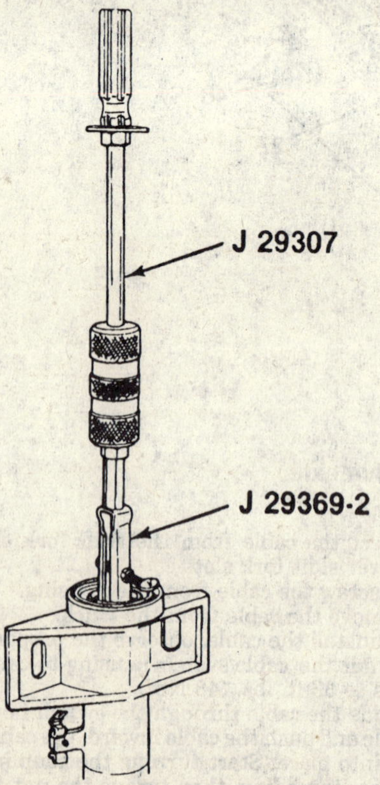

Removing the right side axle tube seal and bearing

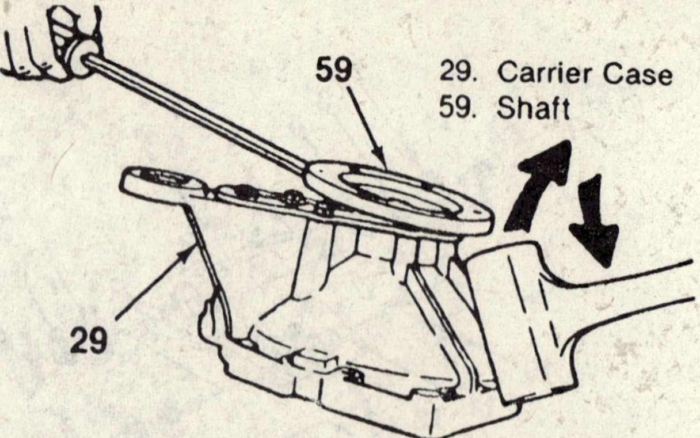

Removing the output shaft from the left side

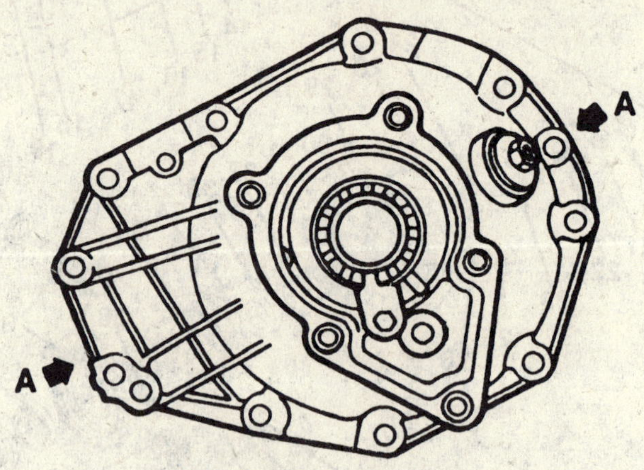

Pry the carrier case apart at the indicated points

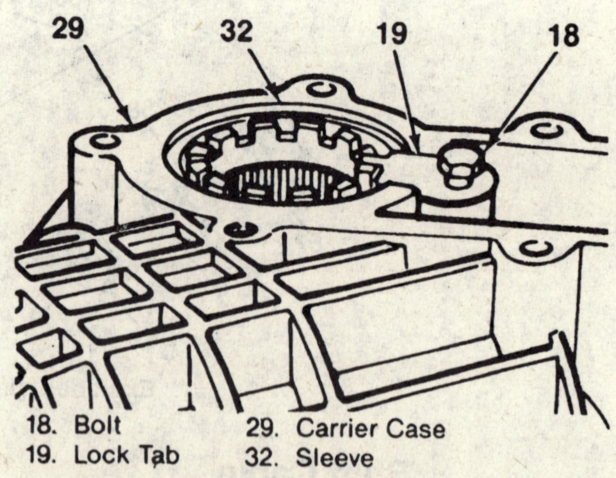

Remove the lock tabs

8. Remove the bolts and lock tabs from the side bearing adjuster sleeves.
9. Remove the bearing cups and sleeves from the case using the special tool.
10. Remove the input flange nut and washer and use the special puller to remove the flange.
11. Remove the pinion and use a press to remove the pinion bearing.

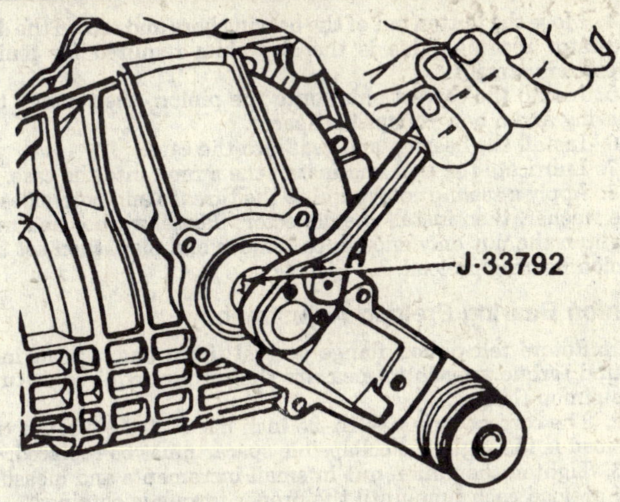

Removing the side bearing cup

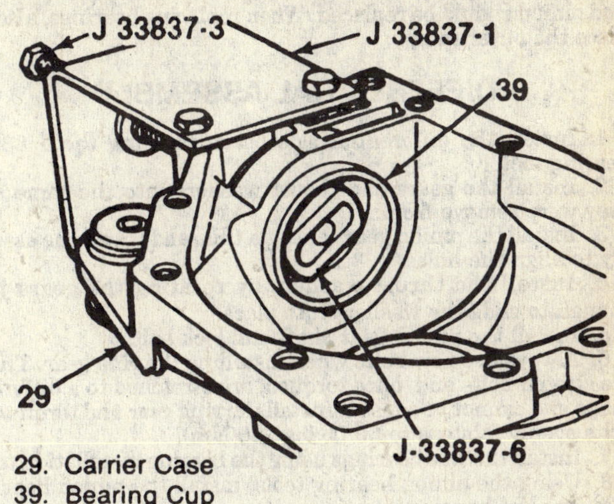

Removing the pinion bearing race from the case

12. To remove the bearing race from the case, attach the special tools as shown. Thread the J 33837-3 screw into the puller and turn the screw to draw the parts out of the case.
13. Remove the bolt and shaft from the differential case to remove the pinion gears and thrust washers. Label the gears and washers for installation.
14. Remove the differential side gears and thrust washers. Label the gears and washers for installation.
15. Unbolt the ring gear and carefully drive it off with a brass drift pin.
16. Using the special puller, remove the side bearings from the differential.

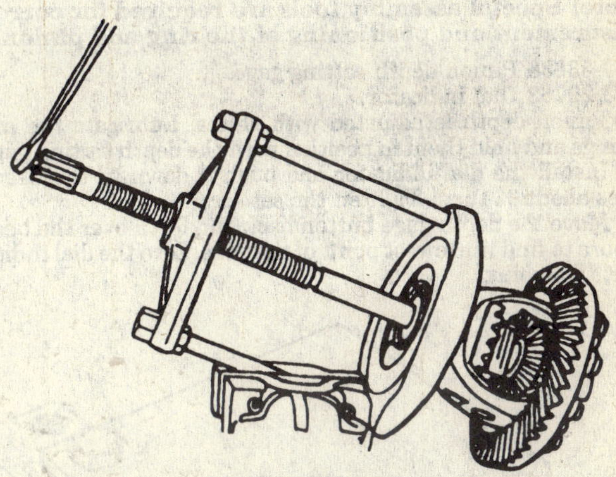

Removing the differential side bearings

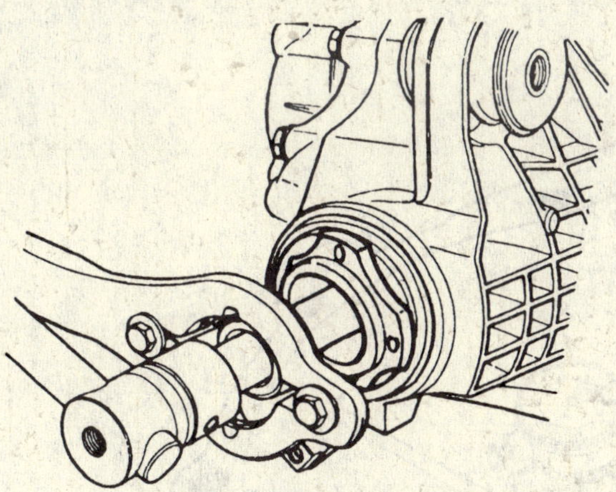

Removing the pinion nut

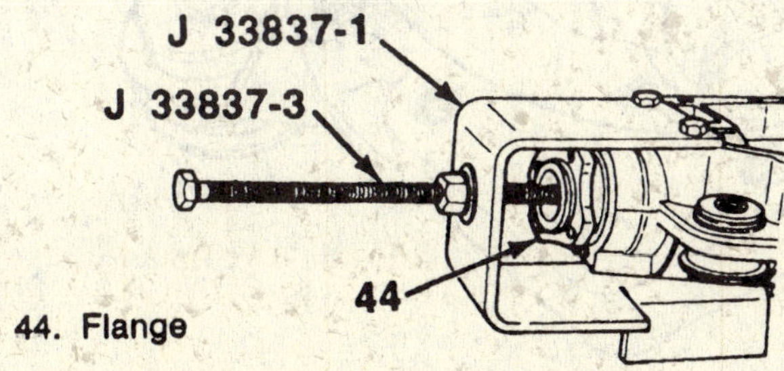

Removing the pinion flange

INSPECTION

Clean all parts in a clean solvent and dry with air. Carefully inspect the housing for damage to the sealing areas and the bearing areas for burrs or nicks that may interfere with assembly. Remove any imperfections that are found. Throughly clean the housing using solvent, not steam or water. Any metal chips or rust left in the housing will damage the gears and bearings. Check the housing for cracks.

Check the differential gears, shafts and thrust washers for uneven or heavy wear patterns. Check the differential case for cracks and signs of heat damage or scoring. Check the fit of the gears on the axle shafts and in the differential case. If in doubt, replace the parts.

Inspect the pinion shaft splines for wear and check the fit with the pinion flange. If the sealing surface on the flange is nicked or worn, replace the flange. Compare the wear patterns on the ring and pinion gears for excessive wear or signs of heat damage. A ring and pinion gear are a matched set and must be replaced together.

Inspect the bearings for signs of heat damage or contamination. The big end of tapered rollers is where signs of wear or damage will appear first. Low milage units will show some scratches on the bearings from initial preload. If the (oiled) bearing still feels smooth, it need not be replaced. If the axle was used for an extended period with very loose bearings, the ring and pinion should be replaced. When replacing bearings, also replace the outer race.

DIFFERENTIAL ASSEMBLY

1. Install the differential side bearings using the J 33970 bearing tool.
2. Install the gears and thrust washers into the same side they were remove from.
3. Install the pinion gears one at a time and rotate the assembly to align the holes.
4. Install the thrust washers by rotating the gears just enough to slide the washers into place.
5. Install the pinion gear shaft and lock bolt.
6. Always use new bolts when installing the ring gear. These are stretch bolts and, once torqued, are stretched to a different shape and cannot be reused. Install the ring gear and torque the bolts evenly in steps to 60 ft. lbs. (80 Nm).
7. Install the side bearings using the bearing installation tool.
8. Using the pinion bearing tools, install the pinion bearing race into the housing.

Pinion Depth Adjustment

Note: Special assembly tools are required for correct measurement and positioning of the ring and pinion.

- J-33838 Pinion depth setting gage.
- J-29763 Dial indicator.

1. Pinion depth is adjusted with shims. Lubricate the axle bearings and hold them in position with the depth setting gage.
2. Install the dial indicator and push it down til the needle moves about ¾ turn. Tighten the set screw.
3. Move the depth gage button back and forth over the bearing bore to find the lowest point of the bore. Zero the dial indicator at this point.
4. Move the button out of the bearing bore and record the dial indicator reading. This is the size shim required for pinion depth adjustment.
5. Install the correct shim onto the pinion, then install the bearing and a new collapsible spacer.
6. Install the bearing and seal into the case.
7. Lubricate the seal and install the pinion into the case.
8. Apply a sealing compound to the threads and both sides of the washer, then install the deflector, flange, washer and nut. Tighten the nut only enough to remove end play, then set the pinion bearing preload.

Pinion Bearing Preload Adjustment

1. Rotate teh pinion flange seversl times and use an inch pound torque wrench to measure the torque required to turn the pinion flange.
2. The correct torque is 15–25 inch lbs. (1.7–2.8 Nm). If the preload is too high, the collapsible spacer must be replaced.
3. Tighten the pinion nut in small increments and measure the preload each time until the proper torque is obtained.

Backlash Adjustment

Note: Special tools are required for this adjustment:

- J-33792 Side bearing adjusting wrench.
- J-34047 Dial indicator adapter.
- J-25025-1 Dial indicator stand.
- J-8001-1 Dial indicator clamp

1. With the bearings and adjusting sleeves installed into the case, install the differential into the case with the pinion.
2. Temporarily assemble the case halves. If they don't make full contact, back out the right hand adjusting sleeve.
3. Torque the case bolts to 37 ft. lbs. (50 Nm).
4. Torque the right, then the left bearing sleeve to 100 ft. lbs. (140 Nm) using the side bearing adjusting wrench.

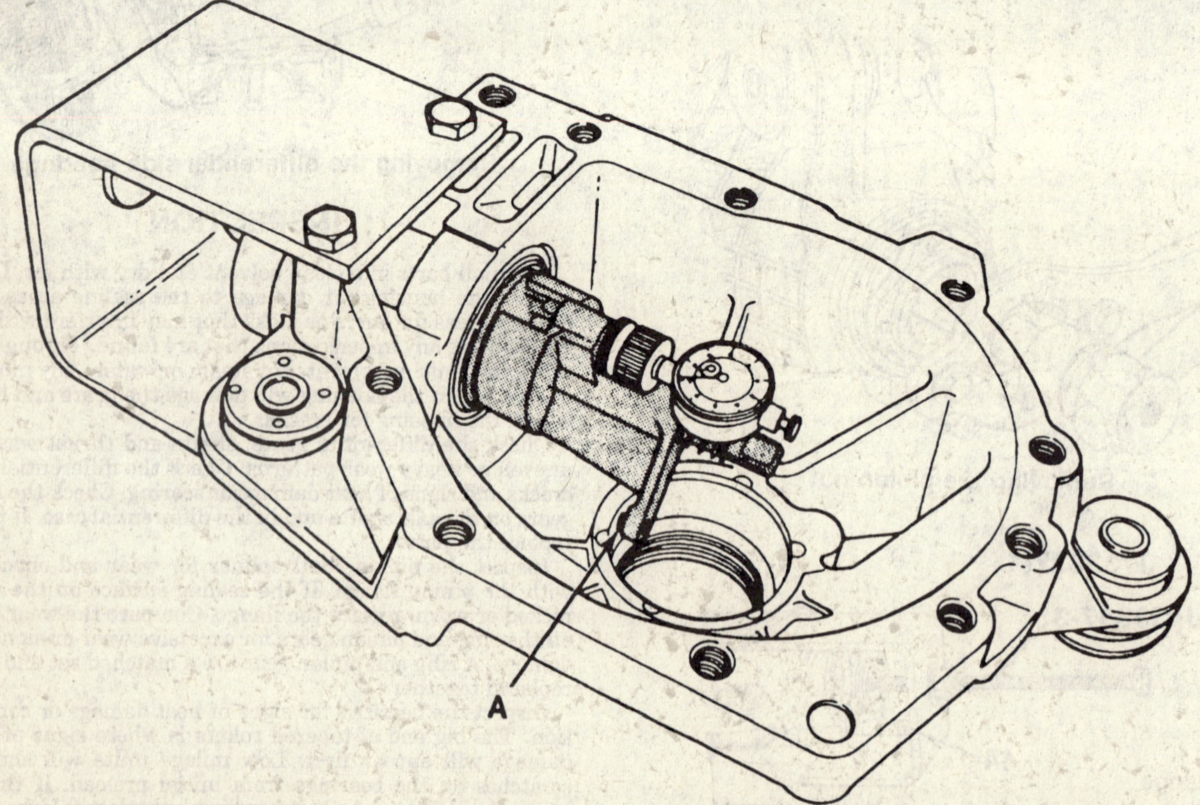

Install the pinion depth setting gage and dial indicator with the button A in the bore

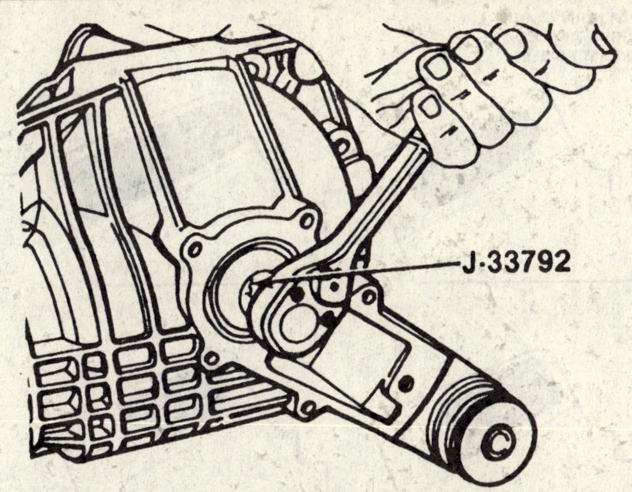

Installing the adjusting sleeve

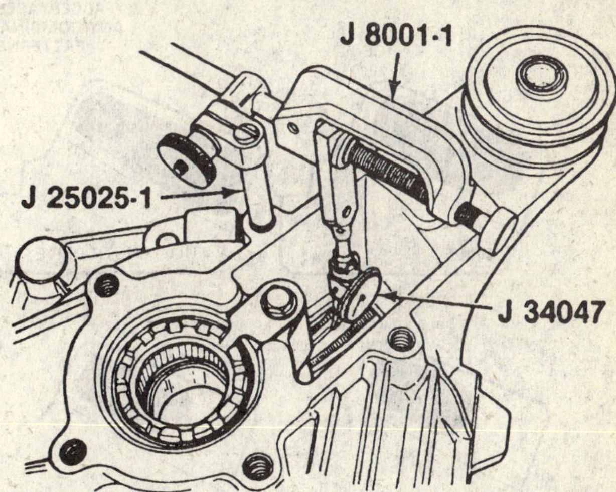

Touch the stem to the heel of a ring gear tooth

5. Mark the position of the sleeves to the case so the notches can be counted during adjustment.
6. Turn the right sleeve OUT 2 notches, and the left sleeve IN 1 notch.
7. Rotate the pinion several times to seat the bearings.
8. Install the dial indicator tools and place the stem of the indicator at the heel end of a tooth on the ring gear.
9. Hold the pinion steady and measure the gear backlash. Take measurements at 3 or 4 places on the ring gear.
10. The backlash should be within 0.002 in. (0.05mm) at all points. If the readings vary more than this, check for a distorted case flange, uneven bolting of the case or ring gear or improper seating of the ring gear on the differential.
11. Backlash should be 0.006 ± 0.003 in. (0.16 ± 0.08mm).
12. To adjust backlash, turn both sleeves the same number of notches: one side IN, the other side OUT. To increase backlash, move the left sleeve IN, to decrease, move the left side OUT. Always be sure to move both sleeves the same number of notches. If you loose count, go back to step 4.
13. When the backlash is correct, mark the position of the adjusting sleeves for final assembly.

Final Assembly

1. Remove the case bolts and remove the right side case half. Make sure the sealing surfaces are clean and dry and apply a bead of silicone sealer.
2. Assemble the case and torque the bolts to 35 ft. lbs. (47 Nm).
3. Make sure the adjusting sleeves are in the correct position and install the sleeve locks and bolts. Torque the bolts to 70 inch lbs. (8 Nm).
4. Install the left side seal to the bore cover, making sure the bore area is properly supported when installing the seal.
5. Apply a silicone sealer and install the cover. Torque the bolts to 18 ft. lbs. (25 Nm).
6. With the retaining ring on the left output shaft, install the deflector and output shaft. Tap the shaft into place.
7. If it was removed, install the bearing into the right side axle shaft housing with a new seal.
8. Use a silicone sealer to seal the axle tube to the housing and install the tube. Torque the bolts to 35 ft. lbs. (48 Nm).
9. Install the right axle shaft by tapping into place with a soft face mallet.

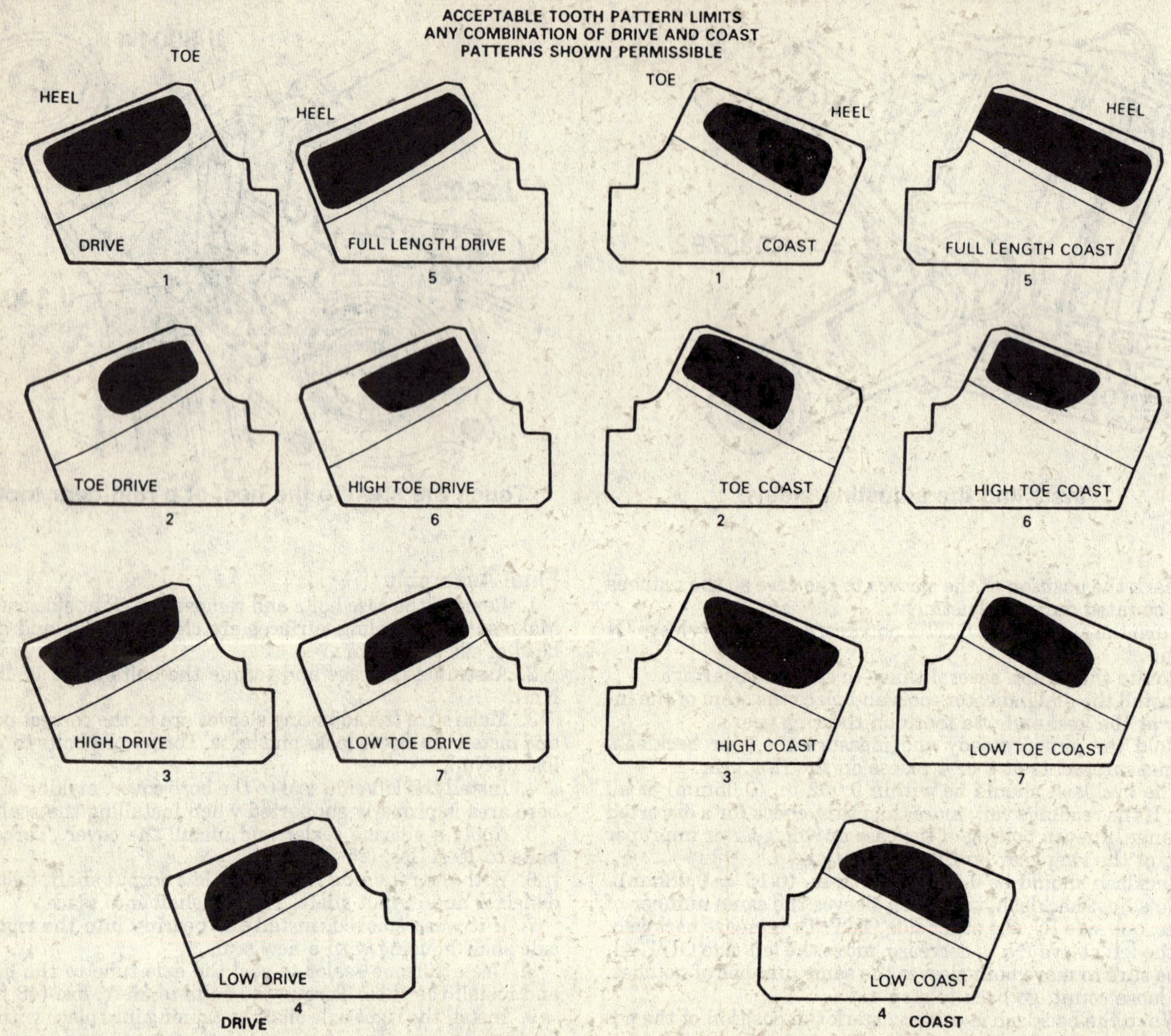

Acceptable gear tooth pattern limits

8 Suspension and Steering

QUICK REFERENCE INDEX

GENERAL INDEX

Troubleshooting Basic Steering and Suspension Problems

Problem	Cause	Solution
Hard steering (steering wheel is hard to turn)	• Low or uneven tire pressure • Loose power steering pump drive belt • Low or incorrect power steering fluid • Incorrect front end alignment • Defective power steering pump • Bent or poorly lubricated front end parts	• Inflate tires to correct pressure • Adjust belt • Add fluid as necessary • Have front end alignment checked/adjusted • Check pump • Lubricate and/or replace defective parts
Loose steering (too much play in the steering wheel)	• Loose wheel bearings • Loose or worn steering linkage • Faulty shocks • Worn ball joints	• Adjust wheel bearings • Replace worn parts • Replace shocks • Replace ball joints
Car veers or wanders (car pulls to one side with hands off the steering wheel)	• Incorrect tire pressure • Improper front end alignment • Loose wheel bearings • Loose or bent front end components • Faulty shocks	• Inflate tires to correct pressure • Have front end alignment checked/adjusted • Adjust wheel bearings • Replace worn components • Replace shocks
Wheel oscillation or vibration transmitted through steering wheel	• Improper tire pressures • Tires out of balance • Loose wheel bearings • Improper front end alignment • Worn or bent front end components	• Inflate tires to correct pressure • Have tires balanced • Adjust wheel bearings • Have front end alignment checked/adjusted • Replace worn parts
Uneven tire wear	• Incorrect tire pressure • Front end out of alignment • Tires out of balance	• Inflate tires to correct pressure • Have front end alignment checked/adjusted • Have tires balanced

WHEELS

2- and 4-Wheel Drive

REMOVAL AND INSTALLATION

These vehicles use a variety of wheel styles, but from the factory they are all one piece rims with 5 bolt holes in a 4¾ in. (120.65mm) bolt circle. Standard sizes are 14 × 6 in. (152.4mm) and 15 × 7 in. (177.8mm). A space saver spare for emergency use only comes in a 16 × 4 in. (101.6mm) size.

1. When removing a wheel, loosen all the lug nuts with the wheel on the ground, then raise and safely support the vehicle.
2. If the wheel is stuck or rusted on the hub, make all the lug nuts finger tight, then back each one off 2 turns. Put the truck back on the ground and rock it side to side. Get another person to help if necessary. This is far safer than hitting a stuck wheel with the vehicle on a jack or lift.
3. When installing a wheel, tighten the lug nuts in a rotation, skipping every other one. If the nuts are numbered 1 through 5 in a circle, the tigntening sequence will be 1–3–5–2–4.
4. Always use a torque wrench to avoid uneven tightening, which will distort the brake drum or disc. On steel wheels, torque the nuts to 73 ft. lbs. (100Nm). On aluminum alloy wheels, torque the nuts to 90 ft. lbs. (120Nm).

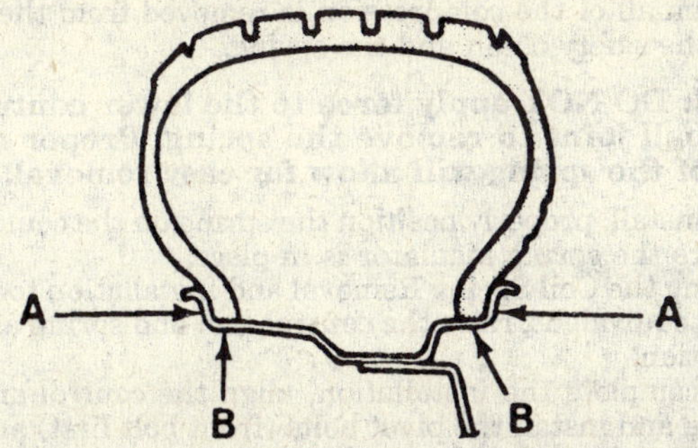

Use a dial indicator to measure radial and lateral runout with or without the tire on the rim

INSPECTION

Wheels can be distorted or bent and not effect dry road handling to a noticable degree. Out of round wheels will show up as uneven tire wear, or will make it difficult to balance the tire. Runout can be checked with the wheel on or off the truck, with the tire on or off the rim, but off is better.

1. If the tire is on the wheel, set a dial indicator to touch the wheel in position "A" in the illustration to measure lateral runout.
2. To measure radial runout, set the dial indicator to position "B".
3. If the tire is not on the wheel, use the same positions on the inside of the rim. This is usually more accurate and easier to get a clean surface for the indicator stem.
4. For steel wheels, the radial runout limit is 1mm (0.040 in.), the lateral runout limit is 1.1mm (0.045 in.).
5. For aluminum alloy wheels, the limit for both runout directions is 0.8mm (0.030 in.).

Wheel Lug Studs

REMOVAL AND INSTALLATION

2-Wheel Drive Front Wheels

1. Raise and safely support the vehicle and remove the wheel.
2. Remove the brake pads and caliper. Refer to the section on brakes if necessary.
3. Remove the outer wheel bearing and lift the rotor off the axle. Refer to **Front Wheel Bearings** later in this section, if necessary.

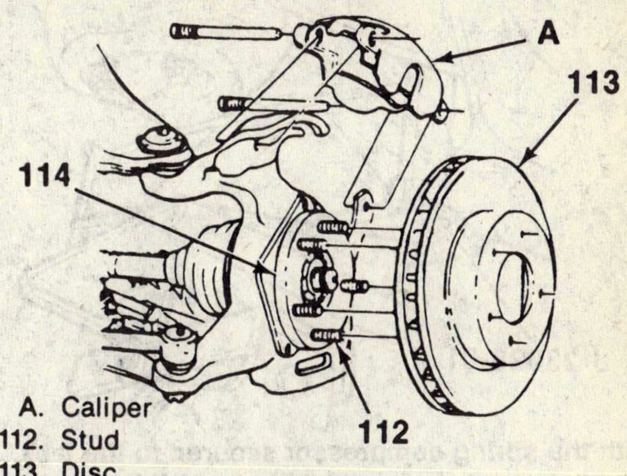

A. Caliper
112. Stud
113. Disc
114. Hub and Bearing Assembly

Pressing the old stud off

4. Properly support the rotor and press the stud out.
5. Clean the stud hole with a wire brush and start the new stud with a hammer and drift pin. Do not use any lubricant or thread sealer.
6. Finish installing the stud with the press.
7. Install the rotor, adjust the wheel bearing and install the brake caliper and pads.

4-Wheel Drive Front
2- and 4-Wheel Drive Rear

1. Raise and safely support the vehicle and remove the wheel.
2. On front wheels, remove the brake, caliper and rotor. On rear wheels, remove the brake drum. Refer to the section on brakes if necessary.
3. Do not hammer the wheel stud to remove it. This will ruin the wheel bearing. Use the stud press tool J6627A or equivalvent to press the stud out of the hub.
4. Clean the hole with a wire brush and start the new stud into the hole. Do not use any lubricant or thread sealer.
5. Stack 4 or 5 washers onto the stud and then put the nut on. Tighten the nut to draw the stud into place.It should be easy to feel when the stud is seated.
6. Reinstall the rotor and caliper or drum and use a torque wrench when installing the wheel.

FRONT SUSPENSION

Coil Spring—2WD

REMOVAL

NOTE: The following procedure requires the use of the Coil Spring Removal and Installation tool No. J-23028 or equivalent.

1. Raise and safely support the front of the vehicle so that the front wheels hang free.
2. Remove the shock absorber-to-lower control arm bolts,

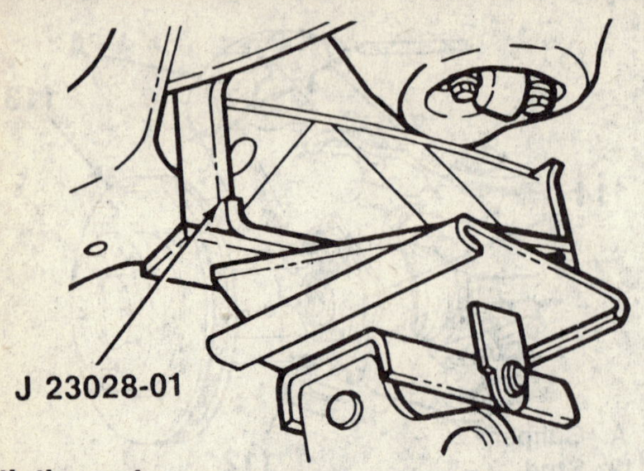

With the spring compressor secured to the jack, lift the control arm to take the tension off the spring

then push the shock up through the control arm and into the spring.

3. Using the Coil Spring Removal and Installation tool No. J-23028 or equivalent, secured to the end of a jack, cradle the inner control arm bushings.

4. Remove the stabilizer bar link from the lower control arm.

5. To remove the lower control arm pivot bolts, perform the following procedures:

a. Raise the jack to remove the tension from the lower control arm pivot bolts.

b. Install a chain around the spring and through the control arm as a safety measure.

c. Remove the lower control arm-to-frame pivot nuts and bolts—remove the rear pivot bolt first.

d. Lower the control arm by slowly lowering the jack.

6. When all of the compression is removed from the spring, remove the safety chain and the spring.

NOTE: DO NOT apply force to the lower control arm and/or ball joint to remove the spring. Proper maneuvering of the spring will allow for easy removal.

7. To install, properly position the spring on the control arm, make sure the spring insulator is in place.

8. Using the Coil Spring Removal and Installation tool No. J-23028 or equivalent, raise the control arm and spring assembly into position.

9. To complete the installation, align the control arm with the frame and install the pivot bolts (front bolt first) and nuts, then reverse the removal procedures. Torque the lower control arm-to-frame pivot nuts/bolts to 45 ft. lbs., the stabilizer bar-to-lower control arm link to 13 ft. lbs. and the shock absorber-to-lower control arm bolts to 20 ft. lbs. Road test the vehicle.

Torsion Bar—4WD

REMOVAL AND INSTALLATION

NOTE: The following procedure requires the use of the Torsion Bar Unloader tool No. J-22517-C or equivalent.

1. Raise and safely support the front of the vehicle on jackstands.

2. Using the Torsion Bar Unloader tool No. J-22517-C or equivalent, attach it and apply pressure (to relax the tension) to the torsion bar adjusting arm screw; remove the adjusting screw by counting the number of turns necessary to remove the screw.

3. Remove the torsion support-to-insulator nut/bolt, the support insulator-to-frame nuts/bolts, the insulator retainer and the insulator from the support.

4. Slide the torsion bar(s) forward into the control arm(s) to clear the support.

37. Coil spring
40. Lower control arm
42. Upper control arm
66. Upper ball joint
67. Nut
68. Cotter pin
69. Lower ball joint
70. Bolt
71. Nut
72. Bolt
73. Insulator
74. Bumper
75. Bushing
76. Bushing
77. Bolt
78. Nut
79. Shaft
80. Nut
81. Shim
82. Nut
83. Retainer
84. Bushing

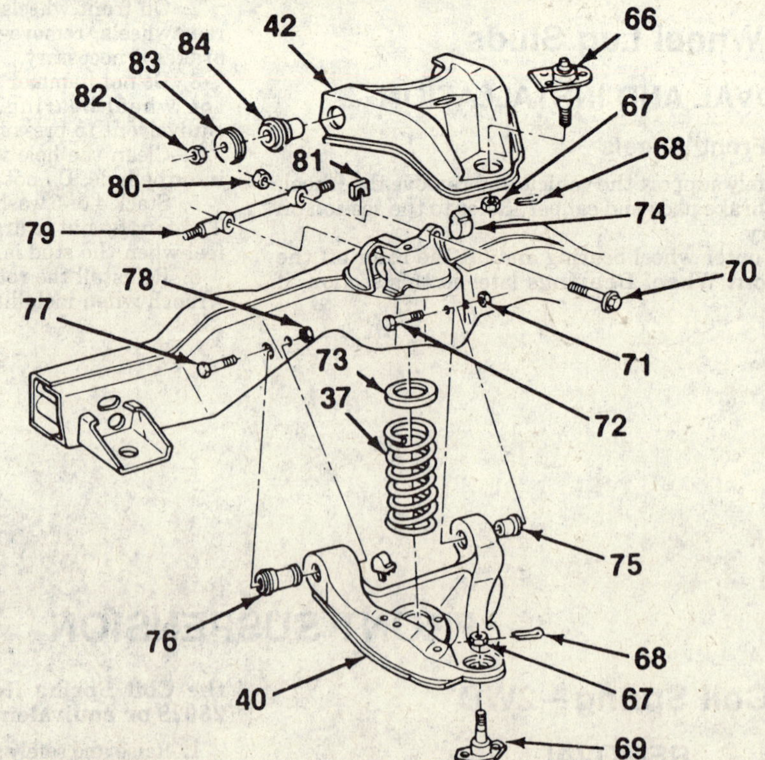

Front control arms and components on 2WD

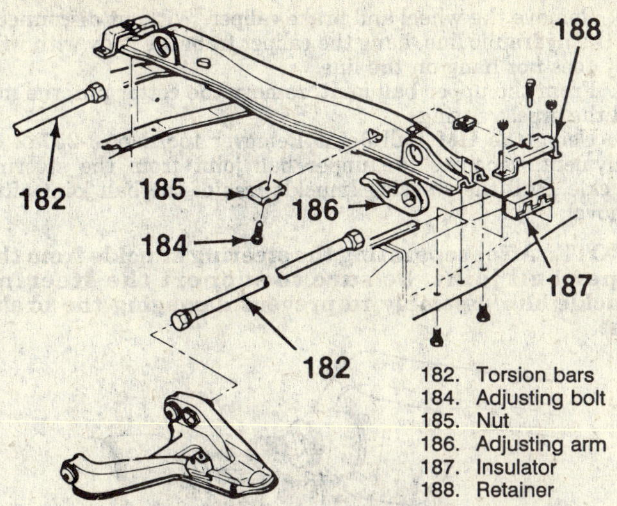

Torsion bar front suspension on 4WD

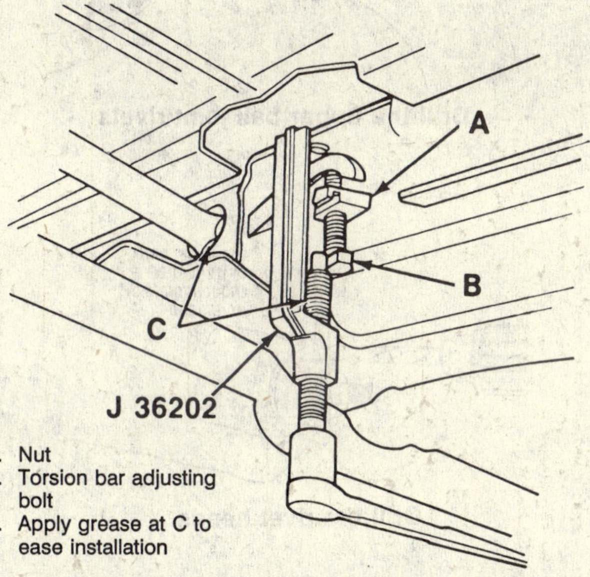

Using the torsion bar unloader tool

5. Remove the adjusting arm, the adjusting arm screw and the nut from the support.
6. Remove the torsion bar from the control arm and the support.
7. To install the support insulator, reverse the removal procedures. Torque the insulator-to-frame nuts/bolts to 26 ft. lbs. and the torsion support-to-insulator nut/bolt to 25 ft. lbs.
8. To install the torsion bar, perform the following procedures:
   a. Slide the torsion bar into the lower control arm.
   b. Raise and slide the torsion bar into the adjusting arm.

NOTE: Be sure the torsion bar clearance at the support is 6mm (0.236 in.).

   c. Using the Torsion Bar Unloader tool No. J-22517-C or equivalent, install it to the adjusting arm, then turn the adjusting arm screw the same number of turns which were necessary to remove it.
   d. After the adjustment is complete, remove the Torsion Bar Unloader tool No. J-22517-C or equivalent.

9. Lower the truck. Refer to the "Front End Alignment" in this section and adjust the final "Z" trim height.

Shock Absorbers

REMOVAL AND INSTALLATION

2WD Models

1. Raise and safely support the front of the truck.
2. Using an open end wrench, hold the shock absorber upper stem from turning, then remove the upper stem retaining nut, the retainer and rubber grommet.
3. Remove the shock absorber-to-lower control arm bolts and lower the shock absorber assembly from the bottom of the control arm.
4. Inspect and test the shock absorber; replace it, if necessary.
5. To install the shock absorber, fully extend the shock absorber stem, then push it up through the lower control arm and spring, so that the upper stem passes through the mounting hole in the upper control arm frame bracket.
6. Torque the upper shock absorber nut to 8 ft. lbs. If desired, use the old nut as a jam nut. Be careful not to crush the rubber bushing.
7. Torque the shock absorber-to-lower control arm bolts to 20 ft. lbs.

4WD Models

1. Raise and safely support the front of the truck.
2. Remove the shock absorber-to-lower control arm nut and bolt, then collapse the shock absorber.
3. Remove the upper shock absorber-to-frame nut and bolt.
4. Inspect and test the shock absorber; replace it, if necessary.
5. To install, reverse the removal procedures. Torque the upper and lower mounting bolts to 54 ft. lbs.

TESTING

Visually inspect the shock absorber. If there is evidence of leakage and the shock absorber is covered with oil, the shock is defective and should be replaced.

If there is no sign of excessive leakage (a small amount of weeping is normal) bounce the truck at one corner by pressing down on the bumper and releasing it. When you have the truck bouncing as much as you can, release the bumper. The truck should stop bouncing after the first rebound. If the bouncing continues past the center point of the bounce more than once, the shock absorbers are worn and should be replaced.

Upper Ball Joint

INSPECTION

NOTE: Before performing this inspection, make sure that the wheel bearings are adjusted correctly and that the control arm bushings are in good condition.

1. Raise and safely support the front of the vehicle by placing jackstands under each lower control arm as close as possible to each lower ball joint. Make sure that the vehicle is stable and the control arm bumpers are not contacting the frame.
2. Using a dial indicator, position it so that it contacts the wheel rim.
3. To measure the horizontal deflection, perform the following procedures:
   a. Grasp the tire (top and bottom), then pull outward on the top and push inward on the bottom; record the reading on the dial indicator.

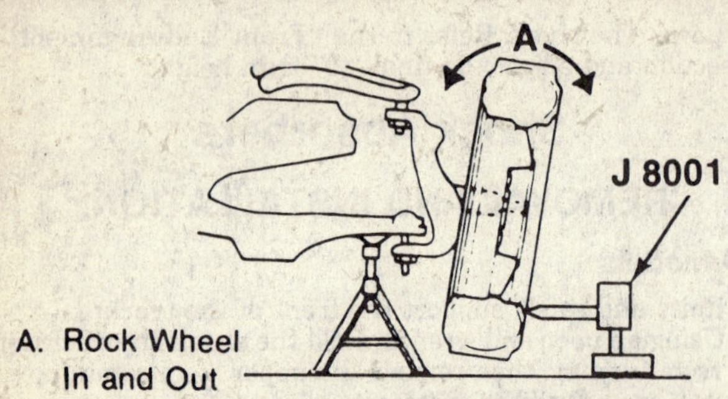

Using a dial indicator to determine ball joint ware

b. Grasp the tire (top and bottom), then pull outward on the bottom and push inward on the top; record the reading on the dial indicator.

c. If the difference in the dial indicator reading is more than 3mm (0.12 in.), or if the rubber seal is cut or appears damaged, the ball joint must be replaced.

REMOVAL AND INSTALLATION

NOTE: The following procedure requires the use of the GM Ball Joint Remover tool No. J-23742 or equivalent.

1. Raise and safely support the front of the vehicle by placing jackstands under the frame, not the lower control arms.
2. Place the floor jack under the lower control arm spring seat and raise it slightly to retain the spring and the lower control arm in position.

CAUTION

With the ball joint nut removed, the floor jack is holding the lower control arm in place against the coil spring. Make sure the jack is firmly engaged with the spring seat and cannot move, or personal injury could result.

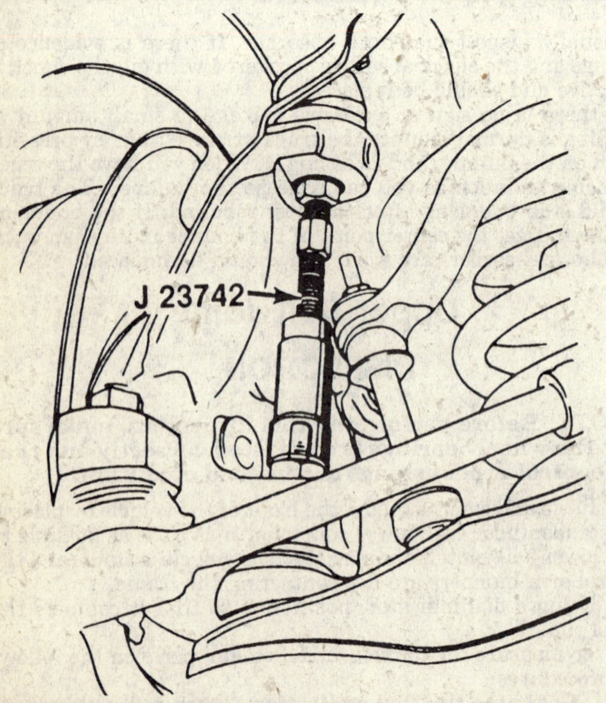

Use a ball joint removal tool to press the upper joint out of the steering knuckle

3. Remove the wheel and brake caliper. Without disconnecting the hydraulic line, hang the caliper from the body with wire so it does not hang on the line.
5. From the upper ball joint, remove the cotter pin, the nut and the grease fitting.
6. Using the GM Ball Joint Remover tool No. J-23742 or equivalent, separate the upper ball joint from the steering knuckle. Pull the steering knuckle free of the ball joint after removal.

NOTE: After separating the steering knuckle from the upper ball joint, be sure to support the steering knuckle/hub assembly to prevent damaging the brake hose.

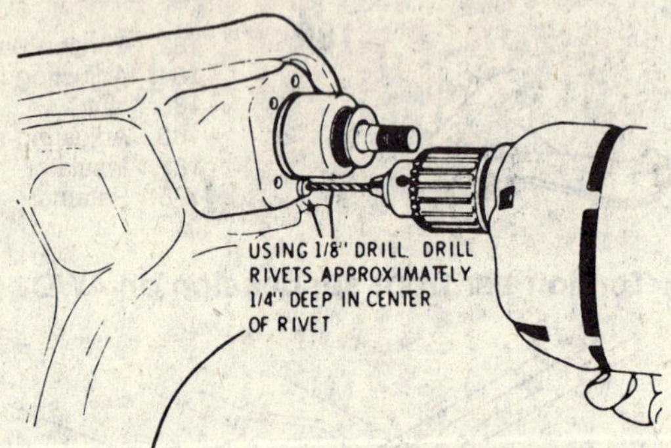

Drill the upper ball joint rivets

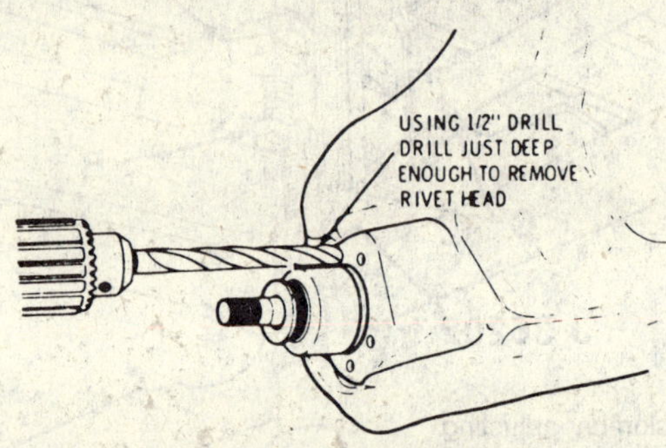

Drill the rivet heads

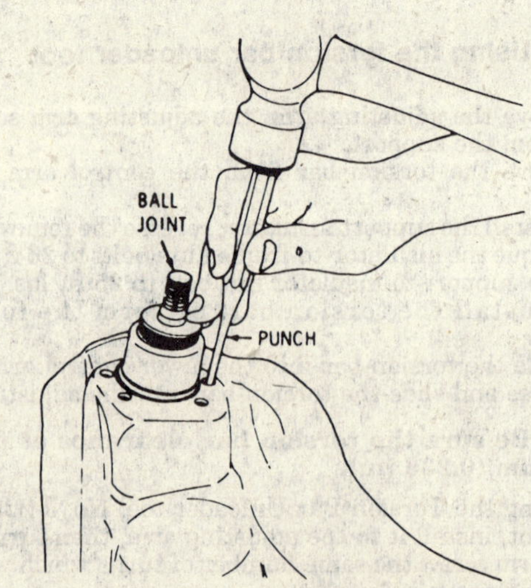

Punch the rivets out to remove the ball joint

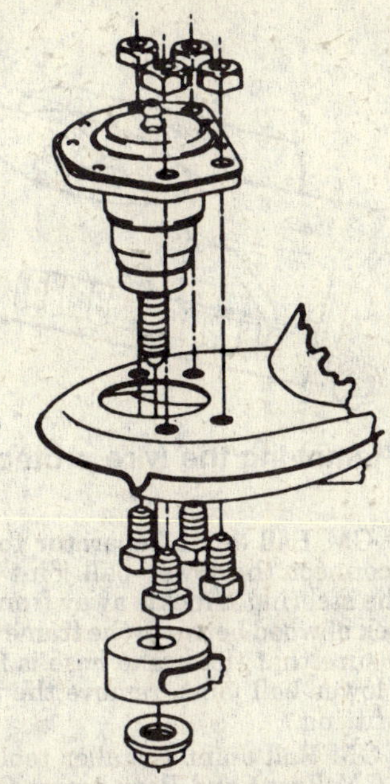

Install the new joint down onto the bolts, nuts touching the joint

7. To remove the upper ball joint from the upper control arm, perform the following procedures:
   a. Using a ⅛ in. (3mm) drill bit, drill a ¼ in. (6mm) deep hole into each rivet.
   b. Using a ½ in. (13mm) drill bit, drill off the rivet heads.
   c. Using a pin punch and the hammer, drive the rivets from the upper ball joint-to-upper control arm assembly and remove the upper ball joint.

8. Clean and inspect the steering knuckle hole. Replace the steering knuckle if the hole is out of round.

To install:

9. When installing the new joint, put the bolts up through the control arm and install the joint down onto the bolts. Torque the nuts to 17 ft. lbs.
10. To complete the installation, seat the upper ball joint into the steering knuckle and install the nut. Torque the upper ball joint-to-steering knuckle nut to 65 ft. lbs. and install a new cotter pin.

NOTE: When installing the cotter pin, never loosen the castle nut to expose the cotter pin hole.

11. Use a grease gun to lubricate the upper ball joint.
12. Install the brake caliper and pads and the wheel. When a ball joint is replaced, a front end alignment is strongly recommended.

Lower Ball Joint

INSPECTION

NOTE: Before performing this inspection, make sure that the wheel bearings are adjusted correctly and that the control arm bushings are in good condition.

Visually check the wear indicator, the small nub that the grease fitting screws into. If it is flush or inside the ball joint cover surface, replace the ball joint. If the rubber grease seal is broken, the ball joint must be replaced.

REMOVAL AND INSTALLATION

NOTE: The following procedure requires the use of the GM Ball Joint Separator tool No. J-23742 or equivalent, the GM Front and Rear Lower Control Arm Bushing Installer tool No. J-21474-13 or equivalent, the GM Ball Joint Installer tool No. J-9519-9 or equivalent, the

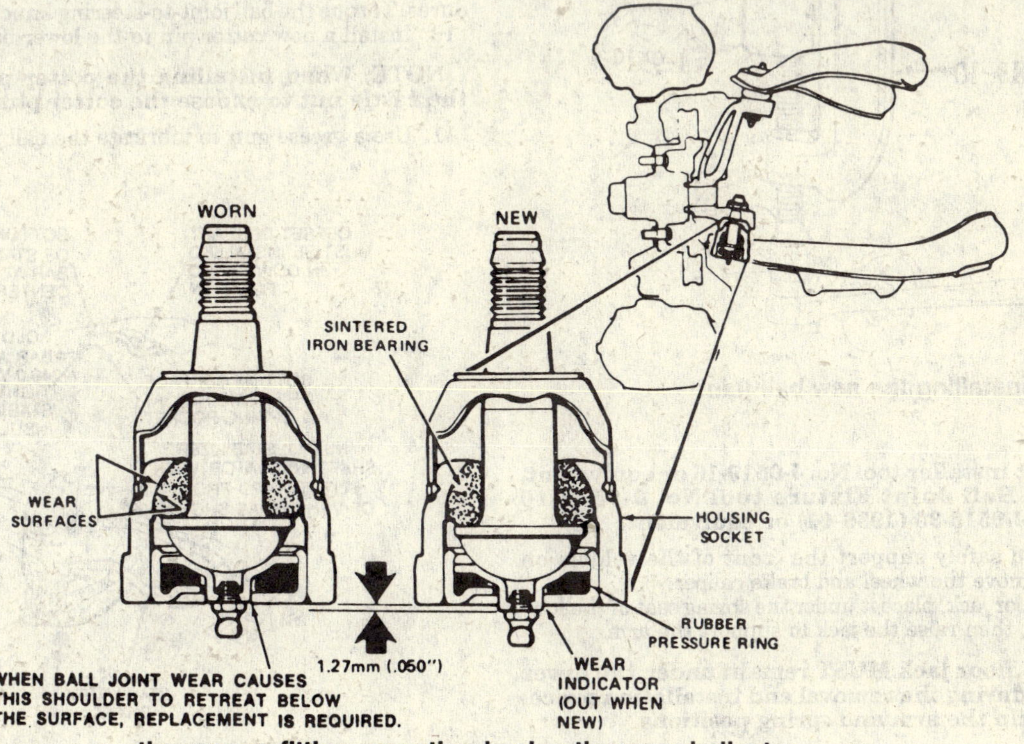

the grease fitting mounting is also the wear indicator

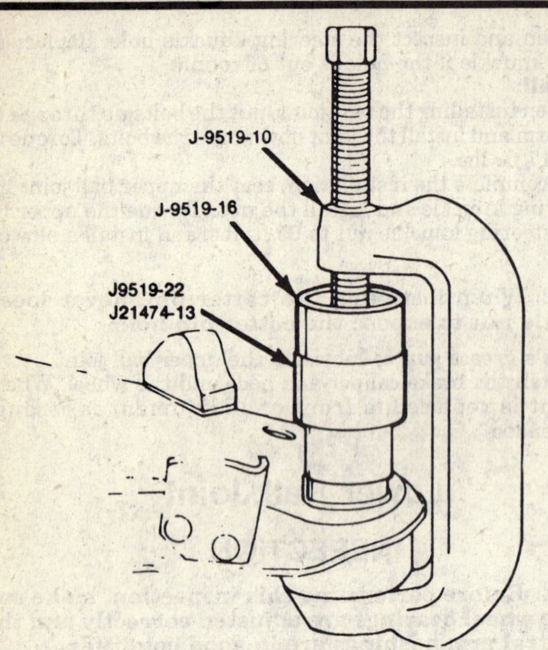

Pressing the lower ball joint out of the control arm

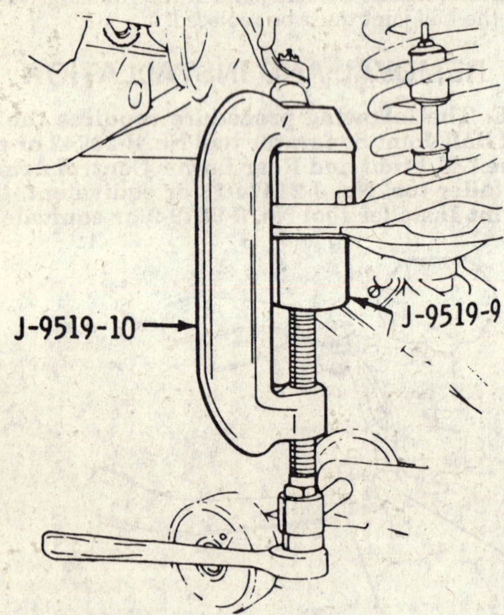

Installing the new ball joint

GM Ball Joint Installer tool No. J-9519-16 or equivalent, and the GM Ball Joint Fixture tool No. J-9519-10 (1982–85) or J-9519-30 (1986–91) or equivalent.

1. Raise and safely support the front of the vehicle on jackstands. Remove the wheel and brake caliper.
2. Using a floor jack, place it under the spring seat of the lower control arm, then raise the jack to support the arm.

NOTE: The floor jack MUST remain under the lower control arm, during the removal and installation procedures, to retain the arm and spring positions.

3. Remove the cotter pin (discard it) and the ball joint nut.

Removing the wire protector

4. Using the GM Ball Joint Separator tool No. J-23742 or equivalent, disconnect the lower ball joint from the steering knuckle. Pull the steering knuckle away from the lower control arm, place a block of wood between the frame and the upper control arm; make sure that the brake hose is free of tension.
5. From the lower ball joint, remove the rubber grease seal and the grease fitting.
6. Using the GM Ball Joint Installer tool No. J-9519-16 or equivalent, the GM Front and Rear Lower Control Arm Bushing Installer tool No. J-21474-13 or equivalent, and the GM Ball Joint Fixture tool No. J-9519-10 (1982–85) or J-9519-30 (1986–91) or equivalent, remove the lower ball joint from the lower control arm.
7. To install, position the new lower ball joint into the lower control arm. Using the GM Ball Joint Installer tool No. J-9519-9 or equivalent, and the GM Ball Joint Fixture tool No. J-9519-10 (1982–85) or J-9519-30 (1986–91) or equivalent, press the new lower ball joint into the lower control arm.
8. Install the grease fitting and the grease seal onto the lower ball joint; the grease seal MUST BE fully seated on the ball joint and the grease purge hole MUST face inboard.
9. To complete the installation, reverse the removal procedures. Torque the ball joint-to-steering knuckle nut to 90 ft. lbs.
10. Install a new cotter pin to the lower ball joint stud.

NOTE: When installing the cotter pin, never loosen the castle nut to expose the cotter pin hole.

11. Use a grease gun to lubricate the ball joint.

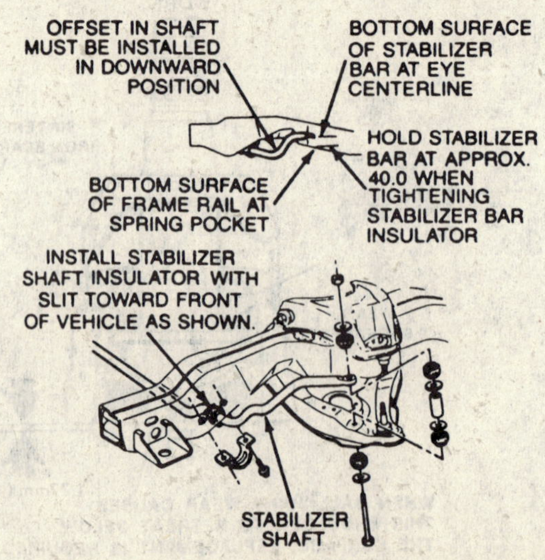

Front stabilizer bar mounting on 2WD

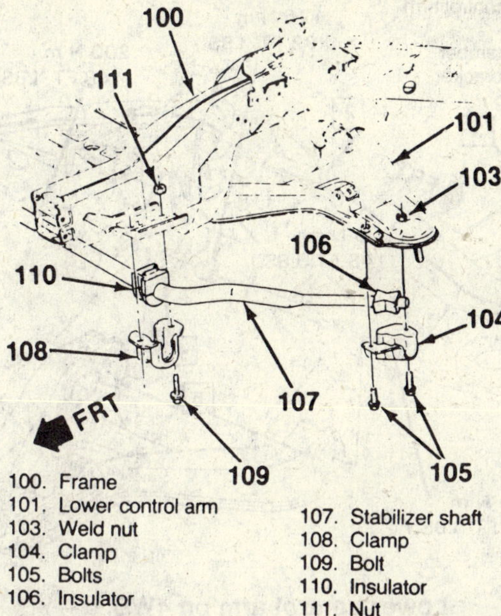

Front stabilizer bar mounting on 4WD

12. Install the brake caliper and pads and the wheel. When a ball joint is replaced, a front end alignment is strongly recommended.

Stabilizer Bar

REMOVAL AND INSTALLATION

1. Raise and safely support the front of the vehicle on jackstands. Remove the wheels.
2. Disconnect the stabilizer bar link nuts from the lower control arms.
3. Remove the stabilizer bar-to-frame clamps.
4. Remove the stabilizer bar from the vehicle.
5. To install, reverse the removal procedures. Torque the stabilizer bar link-to-lower control arm nuts/bolts to 13 ft. lbs. (2WD) or 24 ft. lbs. (4WD) and the stabilizer retainer-to-frame nuts/bolts to 24 ft. lbs. (2WD) or 35 ft. lbs. (4WD).

Upper Control Arm

REMOVAL AND INSTALLATION

NOTE: The following procedure requires the use of the GM Ball Joint Remover tool No. J-23742 or equivalent.

1. Raise and safely support the front of the vehicle by placing jackstands under the frame.

NOTE: Allow the floor jack to remain under the lower control arm seat, to retain the spring and the lower control arm position.

2. Remove the wheels and brake caliper. Hang the caliper from the body with wire to avoid straining the hydraulic line.
3. From the upper ball joint, remove the cotter pin and the ball joint-to-upper control arm nut.
4. Using the GM Ball Joint Remover tool No. J-23742 or equivalent, separate the upper ball joint from the steering knuckle/hub assembly. Pull the steering knuckle free of the ball joint after removal.

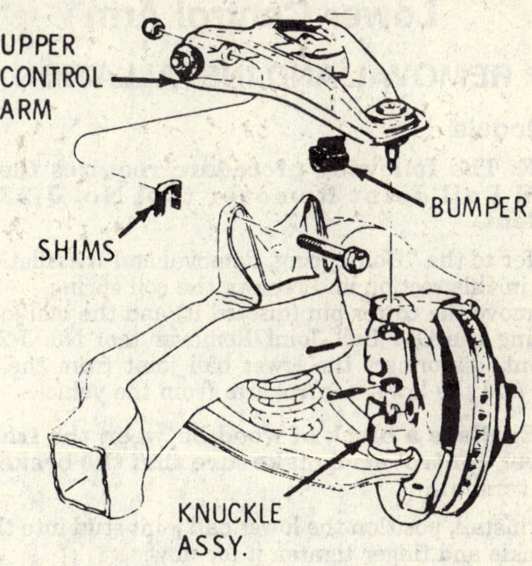

Upper control arm removal

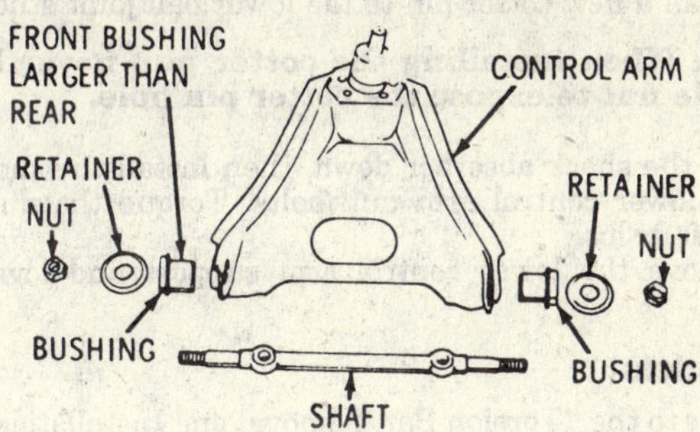

Upper control arm components

NOTE: After separating the steering knuckle from the upper ball joint, be sure to support steering knuckle/hub assembly to prevent damaging the brake hose.

5. Remove the upper control arm-to-frame nuts and bolts, then lift and remove the upper control arm from the vehicle.

NOTE: On 2WD, tape the shims together and identify them so that they can be re-installed in the same place.

6. Clean and inspect the steering knuckle hole. Replace the steering knuckle, if any out of roundness is noted.

To install

7. Attach the upper control arm to the frame, insert the shims in their proper positions, and torque the upper control arm bolts to 45 ft. lbs. (2WD) or 70 ft. lbs. (4WD).
8. Seat the upper ball joint into the steering knuckle, install the nut and torque it to 61 ft. lbs.
9. Install a new cotter pin to the upper ball joint stud.

NOTE: When installing the cotter pin, never loosen the castle nut to expose the cotter pin hole.

10. Use a grease gun to lubricate the upper ball joint.
11. Install the brake caliper and pads and the wheel. On 4WD, when a control arm is removed, a front end alignment is escential.

Lower Control Arm

REMOVAL AND INSTALLATION

2WD Models

NOTE: The following procedure requires the use of the GM Ball Joint Remover tool No. J-23742 or equivalent.

1. Refer to the "Coil Spring, Removal and Installation" procedures in this section and remove the coil spring.
2. Remove the cotter pin (discard it) and the ball joint nut.
3. Using the GM Ball Joint Remover tool No. J-23742 or equivalent, disconnect the lower ball joint from the steering knuckle and the lower control arm from the vehicle.

NOTE: Place a block of wood between the frame and the upper control arm; make sure that the brake hose is free of tension.

4. To install, position the lower ball joint stud into the steering knuckle and finger tignten it for now.
5. Install the control arm bolts, making sure the bolt goes in from the front of the vehicle. Torque the front nut and bolt to 94 ft. lbs., and the rear nut and bolt to 66 ft. lbs. Torque the ball joint-to-steering knuckle nut to 81 ft. lbs.
6. Install a new cotter pin to the lower ball joint stud.

NOTE: When installing the cotter pin, never loosen the castle nut to expose the cotter pin hole.

7. Pull the shock absorber down, then install the shock absorber-to-lower control arm nuts/bolts. Torque the nuts and bolts to 20 ft. lbs.
9. Remove the lower control arm support and lower the vehicle.

4WD Models

1. Refer to the "Torsion Bar, Removal and Installation" procedures in this section, then remove the torsion bar and support assembly.
2. Remove the stabilizer bar-to-lower control arm nuts/bolts.
3. Remove the shock absorber-to-lower control arm nuts/bolts and push the shock absorber upward.
4. Remove the lower control arm-to-frame nuts/bolts and the lower control arm from the truck.

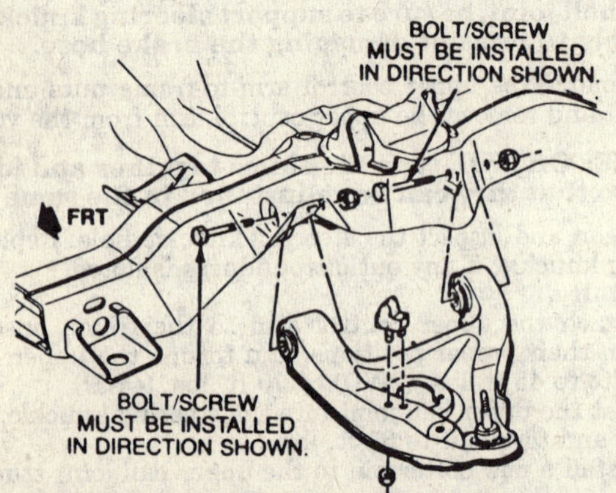

Lower control arm installation on 2WD

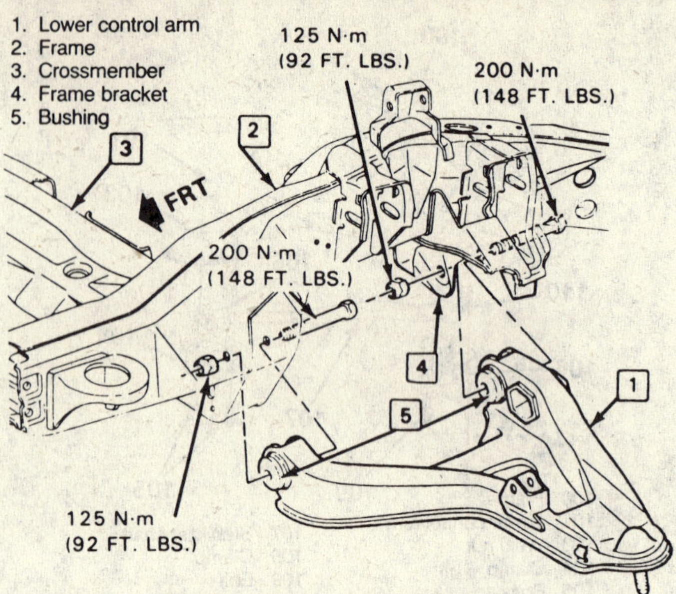

Lower control arm on 4WD

5. To install, reverse the removal procedures. Torque the lower control arm-to-frame bolts to 148 ft. lbs., the lower control arm-to-frame nuts to 92 ft. lbs., the shock absorber-to-lower control arm nut/bolt to 54 ft. lbs., the stabilizer bar-to-lower control arm nuts/bolts to 24 ft. lbs. and the lower control arm ball joint-to-steering knuckle nut to 83 ft. lbs.

Steering Knuckle and Spindle

REMOVAL AND INSTALLATION

2WD Model

NOTE: The following procedure requires the use of the GM Tie Rod End Puller tool J-6627 or equivalent, and the GM Ball Joint Remover tool No. J-23742 or equivalent.

1. Siphon some brake fluid from the brake master cylinder.
2. Raise and safely support the front of the vehicle on jackstands. Remove the wheels.

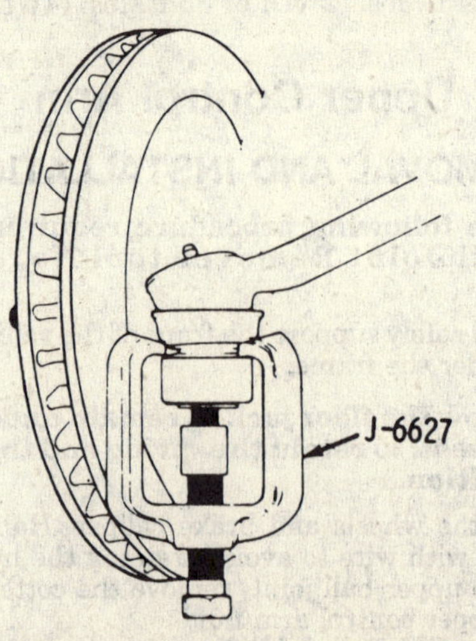

Removing the tie rod end from the steering knuckle

NOTE: When supporting the vehicle on jackstands, DO NOT place the jackstands under the lower control arms. Place them under the frame.

3. Remove the brake caliper from the steering knuckle and hang it from the body on a wire.
4. Remove the grease cup, the cotter pin, the castle nut and the hub–and–rotor assembly.
5. Remove the splash shield-to-steering knuckle bolts and the shield.
6. At the tie rod end-to-steering knuckle stud, remove the cotter pin and the nut. Using the GM Tie Rod End Puller tool J-6627 or equivalent, separate the tie rod end from the steering knuckle.
7. Using a floor jack, place it under the spring seat of the lower control arm and support the arm.
8. From the upper and lower ball joint studs, remove the cotter pins and the nuts.
9. Using the GM Ball Joint Remover tool No. J-23742 or equivalent, separate the upper ball joint from the steering knuckle.
10. Raise the upper control arm to separate it from the steering knuckle.
11. Using the GM Ball Joint Remover tool No. J-23742 or equivalent, separate the lower ball joint from the steering knuckle, then lift the steering knuckle from the lower control arm.
12. Clean and inspect the steering knuckle and spindle for signs of wear or damage; if necessary, replace the steering knuckle.
13. To install the steering knuckle, position it onto the lower ball joint stud, then lift the upper control arm to insert the upper ball joint stud into the steering knuckle. Torque the upper ball joint-to-steering knuckle nut to 65 ft. lbs. and the lower ball joint-to-steering knuckle nut to 90 ft. lbs. Remove the floor jack from under the lower control arm.
14. Install a new cotter pin into the upper and lower ball joint studs.

NOTE: When installing the cotter pin, never loosen the castle nut to expose the cotter pin hole.

15. To complete the installation, reverse the removal procedures. Torque the tie rod end-to-steering knuckle nut to 40 ft. lbs., the splash shield-to-steering knuckle bolts to 10 ft. lbs. Check and/or adjust the wheel bearing and the front end alignment.
16. Remove the jackstands and lower the vehicle. Refill the brake master cylinder.

4WD Model

NOTE: The following procedure requires the use of the Universal Steering Linkage Puller tool No. J-24319-01 or equivalent, the Axle Shaft Boot Seal Protector tool No. J-28712 or equivalent, the Ball Joint Separator tool No. J-34026 or equivalent, and the Steering Knuckle Seal Installation tool No. J-28574 or equivalent.

1. Refer to the "Torsion Bar, Removal and Installation" procedures in this section and relieve the torsion bar pressure.
2. Raise and support the front of the truck on jackstands; place the jackstands under the frame.
3. Remove the wheel and tire.
4. Using the Axle Shaft Boot Seal Protector tool No. J-28712 or equivalent, attach it to the tripot axle joint.
5. Remove the disc brake caliper-to-steering knuckle bolts, lift the brake caliper and support it (out of the way) on a wire.
6. Remove the brake disc from the wheel hub.
7. At the wheel hub, remove the cotter pin, the retainer, the castle nut, the thrust washer.
8. From the tie-rod-to-steering knuckle assembly, remove the cotter pin and the castle nut.
9. Using the Universal Steering Linkage Puller tool No. J-24319-01 or equivalent, tie-rod from the steering knuckle.
10. Remove the hub/bearing assembly-to-steering knuckle bolts and the hub/bearing assembly from the steering knuckle.
11. From the upper and lower ball joints, remove the cotter pin(s) and back off the castle nut(s).
12. Using the Ball Joint Separator tool No. J-34026 or equivalent, disconnect the ball joints from the steering knuckle. Remove the ball joint nut(s) and separate the ball joint(s) from the steering knuckle.

NOTE: When removing the steering knuckle from the wheel hub, be careful not to damage the splined surface of the half shaft.

13. Remove the spacer and the seal from the steering knuckle.
14. Clean and inspect the parts for nicks, scores and/or damage, then replace them as necessary.
15. Using the Steering Knuckle Seal Installation tool No. J-28574 or equivalent, install a new seal into the steering knuckle.
16. Install the spacer, then the upper and lower ball joints to the steering knuckle. Torque the upper ball joint-to-steering knuckle nut to 61 ft. lbs. and the lower ball joint-to-steering knuckle nut to 83 ft. lbs. DO NOT loosen the nut for the cotter pin installation, simply turn the nut a $\frac{1}{6}$ turn further; bend the pin ends against the nut flats.
17. Install the wheel hub/bearing assembly-to-steering knuckle, be careful to align the threads and splines carefully. Torque the hub/bearing assembly-to-steering knuckle bolts to 86 ft. lbs.
18. Install the tie-rod end-to-steering knuckle, then torque the tie-rod end nut to 35 ft. lbs. Install the cotter pin and bend the ends against the nut flats.
19. To complete the installation, reverse the removal procedures. Before torquing the wheel hub/bearing, put the vehicle

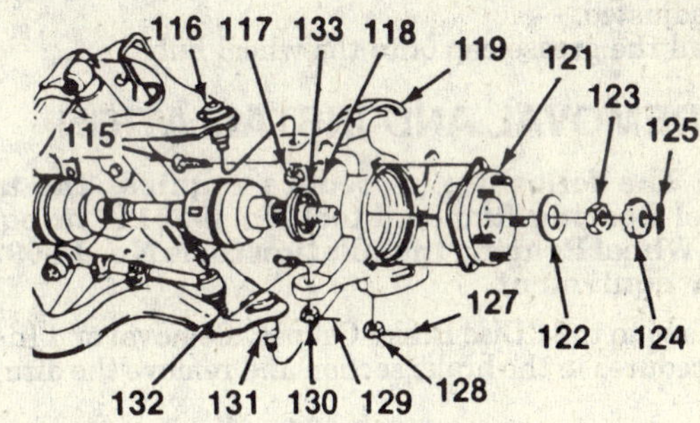

115. Bolt
116. Upper control arm ball joint
117. Nut
118. Pin
119. Knuckle
121. Hub and bearing assembly
122. Washer
123. Nut
124. Retainer
125. Pin
127. Pin
128. Nut
129. Pin
130. Nut
131. Lower control arm ball joint
132. Tie rod end
133. Seal

Steering knuckle and hub assembly on 4WD

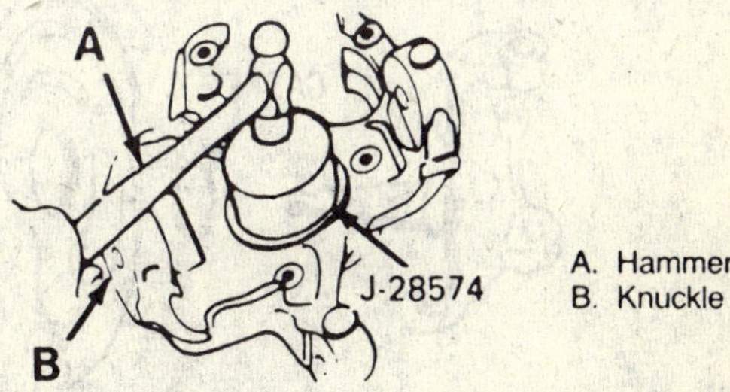

A. Hammer
B. Knuckle

Installing the new steering knuckle seal on 4WD

on the ground. The torque is high enough to cause the truck to fall off the jack stands. Torque the wheel hub/bearing assembly-to-half shaft nut to 181 ft. lbs. Check and/or adjust the front end alignment.

2-Wheel Drive Front Wheel Bearings

The proper functioning of the front suspension cannot be maintained unless the front wheel taper roller bearings are correctly adjusted. The cones must be a slip fit on the spindle and the inside diameter should be lubricated to insure that the cones will creep. The spindle nut must be a free-running fit on threads.

ADJUSTMENT

1. Raise and support the front of the vehicle on jackstands, then remove the grease cap from the hub.
2. Remove the cotter pin from axle spindle and spindle nut.
3. Tighten the spindle nut to 12 ft. lbs. while turning the wheel assembly forward by hand to fully seat the bearings. This will remove any grease or burrs which could cause excessive wheel bearing play later.
4. Back off the nut to the "just loose" position.
5. Hand tighten the spindle nut. Loosen the spindle nut until either hole in the spindle aligns with a slot in the nut; not more than ½ flat.
6. Install a new cotter pin; bend the ends against nut flat, cut off extra length to ensure ends will not interfere with the grease cap.
7. Measure the looseness in the wheel hub assembly. There will be from 0.03–0.13mm (0.001–0.005 in.) end play when properly adjusted.
8. Install the grease cap onto the wheel hub.

REMOVAL AND INSTALLATION

NOTE: The following procedure requires the use of the Wheel Bearing Removal tool No. J-29117 or equivalent, the Wheel Bearing Installation tools No. J-8092 and J-8850 or equivalent.

1. Remove to the "Disc Brake Caliper, Removal and Installation" procedures in the brake section and remove the disc brake caliper.

CAUTION

Brake shoes and pads contain asbestos, which has been determined to be a cancer causing agent. Never clean the brake surfaces with compressed air! Avoid inhaling any dust from any brake surface! When cleaning brake surfaces, use a commercially available brake cleaning fluid.

2. Remove the grease cup from wheel hub.
3. Remove the cotter pin, the castle nut and the thrust washer from the spindle.
4. Carefully pull wheel hub assembly from the spindle.
5. Remove the outer wheel bearing from the wheel hub. The inner wheel bearing will remain in the hub and may be removed after prying out the inner wheel bearing grease seal; discard the seal.
6. Using the Wheel Bearing Removal tool No. J-29117 or equivalent, remove the inner and outer wheel bearing races from the wheel hub.
7. Clean all of the parts in clean solvent and air dry.
8. Inspect the bearings for cracks, worn or pitted rollers.
9. Inspect the bearing races for cracks, scores or a brinelled condition.
10. If the the outer races were removed, use the Wheel Bearing Installation tools No. J-8092 and J-8850 or equivalent, drive or press the races into the hub.
11. Clean off any grease in the hub/spindle and thoroughly clean out any grease in the bearings. Use clean solvent and a small brush, with no loose bristles, to clean out all old grease. DO NOT spin the bearing with compressed air while drying it or the bearing may be damaged.
12. Use an approved high temperature front wheel bearing grease.

NOTE: DO NOT mix greases as mixing may change the grease properties and result in poor performance.

13. Apply a thin film of grease to the spindle at the outer bear-

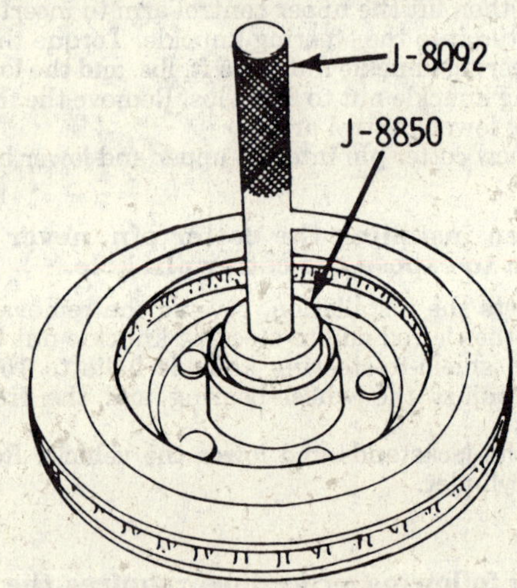

Installing inner bearing race

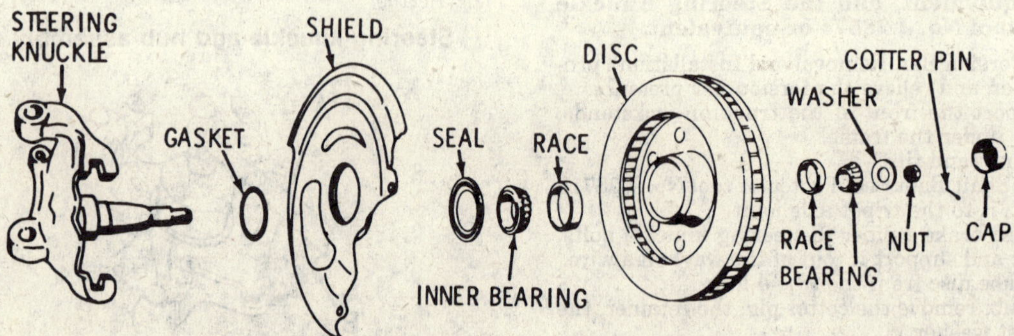

Front hub and wheel bearings, 2WD

ing seat and at the inner bearing seat, the shoulder and the seal seat.

14. Put a small quantity of grease inboard of each bearing cup in the hub. This can be applied with your finger, forming a dam to provide extra grease availability to the bearing and to keep thinned grease from flowing out of the bearing.

15. Fill the bearing cone and roller assemblies full of grease.

NOTE: A preferred method for doing this is with a cone type grease machine that forces grease into the bearing. If a cone greaser is not available, the bearings can be packed by hand. If hand packing is used, it is extremely important to work the grease thoroughly into the bearings between the rollers, cone and the cage. Failure to do this could result in premature bearing failure.

16. Place the inner bearing cone and roller assembly in the hub. Then using your finger, put an additional quantity of grease outboard of the bearing.

17. Install a new grease seal using a flat plate until the seal is flush with the hub. Lubricate the seal lip with a thin layer of grease.

18. Carefully install the hub and rotor assembly. Place the outer bearing cone and roller assembly in the outer bearing cup. Install the washer and nut and initially tighten the nut to 12 ft. lbs. while turning the wheel assembly forward by hand. Put an additional quantity of grease outboard the bearing. This provides extra grease availability to the bearing.

19. Check and/or adjust the wheel bearing.

4-Wheel Drive Front Wheel Bearings

The wheel bearing is installed in the wheel hub assembly and is serviced by replacement only.

Refer to the "Steering Knuckle, Removal and Installation" procedures in this section and replace the wheel hub assembly.

Front End Alignment

CASTER

Caster is the tilting of the front steering axis either forward or backward from the vertical. A backward tilt is said to be positive (+) and a forward tilt is said to be negative (−).

CAMBER

Camber is the inward or outward tilting of the front wheels from the vertical. When the wheels tilt outward at the top, the camber is said to be positive (+). When the wheels tilt inward at the top, the camber is said to be negative (−). The amount of tilt is measured in degrees from the vertical and this measurement is called the camber angle.

TOE-IN

Toe-in is the turning in of the front wheels. The actual amount of toe-in is normally only a fraction of a degree. The purpose of toe-in is to ensure parallel rolling of the front wheels. Excessive toe-in or toe-out will cause tire wear.

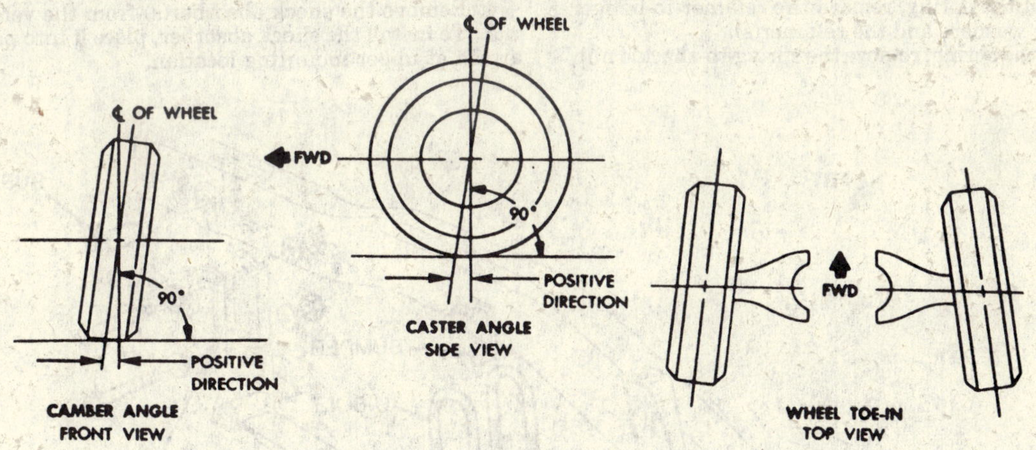

Camber, caster and toe are adjusted in degrees

Wheel Alignment Specifications

Toe-in		Camber		Caster	
Range (in.)	Preferred (in.)	Range (deg.)	Preferred (deg.)	Range (deg.)	Preferred (deg.)
1/16–3/32P	1/16P	5/16–13/16P	13/16P	1 1/2–2 1/2P	2P

REAR SUSPENSION

The rear suspension system consists of several major components: The double acting shock absorbers, variable rate multi-leaf springs and various attachment parts. The multi-leaf springs are connected to the frame by a hanger assembly with integral bushings in the front and a shackle assembly with integral bushings in the rear. The shackle assembly, in response to different road and payload conditions, allows the leaf spring to "change its length". The rear axle is connected to both the leaf springs and the shock absorbers by various attaching parts.

Leaf Springs

REMOVAL AND INSTALLATION

NOTE: The following procedure requires the use of two sets of jackstands.

1. Raise and safely support the rear frame of the vehicle on jackstands. support the rear axle with the second set of jackstands.

NOTE: When supporting the rear of the vehicle, support the axle and the body separately to relieve the load on the rear spring.

2. Remove the wheel and tire assembly.
3. At the rear of the spring, loosen (DO NOT remove) the shackle-to-frame bolt and the shackle-to-spring bolt.
4. Remove the shock absorber.
5. Remove the axle U-bolt-to-anchor plate nuts, the lower plate-to-anchor plate nuts, the U-bolts and the lower plate, then jack up the axle on that side only just enough to lift off of the spring.
6. At the front of the spring, remove the retainer-to-hanger assembly nuts, the washers and the retainer(s).
7. At the rear of the spring, remove the spring-to-shackle nut, washer and bolt. Remove the spring from the vehicle.

To install:

8. When installing a new spring, it is usually easier to put the rear end up first. Put the bolts through one of the shackle plates, hang the shackle on the frame, hang the spring on the shackle and put on the other shackle plate. Install the nuts finger tight.
9. It should be possible to move the spring enough on the shackle to line up the holes for the front mounting bolt. Install the washers and nut finger tight.
10. Lower the axle to rest on the spring and install the U-bolts and anchor plates. Torque the nuts in a cross pattern first to 18 ft. lbs., then to 85 ft. lbs. It is important that the U-bolts are tigntened evenly.
11. Raise the axle so there is about 6.75 inches (171mm) between the axle housing and the frame of the truck. Measure from the housing between the U-bolts to the metal part of the rubber bump stop on the frame.
12. Torque the front spring mounting bolt and the rear shackle bolts to 92 ft. lbs. Install the shock absorber and wheel.

Shock Absorbers

REMOVAL AND INSTALLATION

1. Raise and support the rear of the truck on jackstands; support the rear axle.
2. At the upper mounting location, disconnect shock absorber bolts.
3. At the lower mounting location, remove the nut and washer.
4. Remove the shock absorber(s) from the vehicle.
5. To install the shock absorber, place it into position and reattach at upper mounting location.

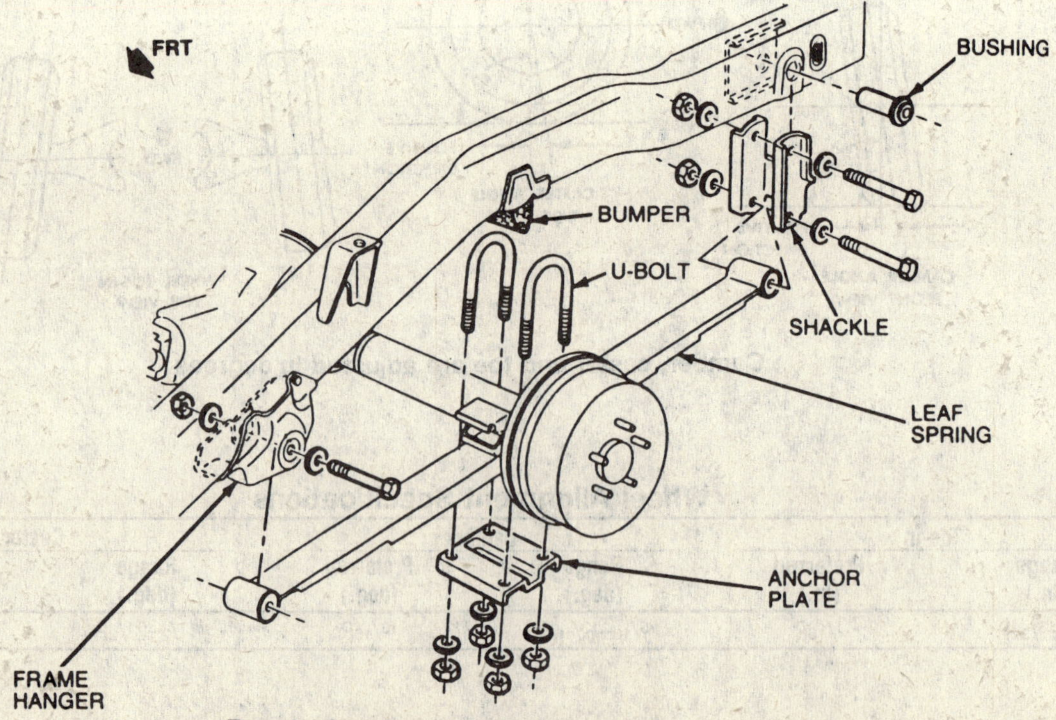

Rear leaf spring and axle attachment

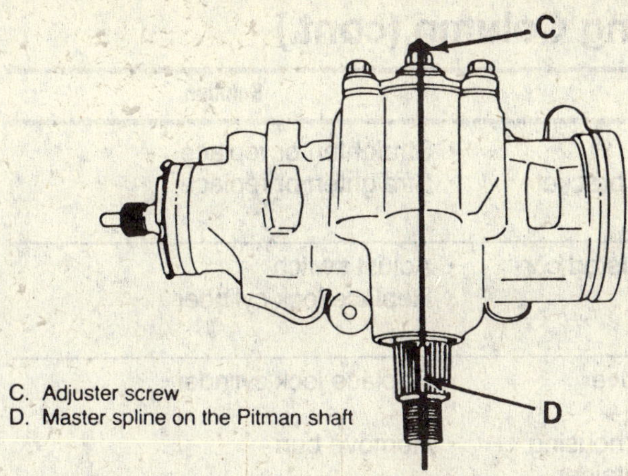

Align the pitman arm shaft master spline

6. Align the lower-end of the shock absorber with the anchor plate stud and install the washer and nut.
7. Torque the shock absorber-to-body bolts to 15 ft. lbs. and the shock absorber-to-axle nut to 50 ft. lbs.
8. Lower vehicle and remove from hoist.

TESTING

Visually inspect the shock absorber. If there is evidence of leakage and the shock absorber is covered with oil, the shock is defective and should be replaced.

If there is no sign of excessive leakage (a small amount of weeping is normal) bounce the truck at one corner by pressing down on the bumper and releasing it. When you have the truck bouncing as much as you can, release the bumper. The truck should stop bouncing after the first rebound. If the bouncing continues past the center point of the bounce more than once, the shock absorbers are worn and should be replaced.

STEERING

The steering box (manual or power) consists of a recirculating balls, which transmits force from the worm gear to the sector gear. A relay type steering linkage is used with a pitman arm connected to one end of the relay rod. The relay rod is supported by two idler arms; the idler arms pivot on a support which is attached to the frame. The relay rod is connected to the steering

Troubleshooting the Steering Column

Problem	Cause	Solution
Will not lock	• Lockbolt spring broken or defective	• Replace lock bolt spring
High effort (required to turn ignition key and lock cylinder)	• Lock cylinder defective • Ignition switch defective • Rack preload spring broken or deformed • Burr on lock sector, lock rack, housing, support or remote rod coupling • Bent sector shaft • Defective lock rack • Remote rod bent, deformed • Ignition switch mounting bracket bent • Distorted coupling slot in lock rack (tilt column)	• Replace lock cylinder • Replace ignition switch • Replace preload spring • Remove burr • Replace shaft • Replace lock rack • Replace rod • Straighten or replace • Replace lock rack

Troubleshooting the Steering Column (cont.)

Problem	Cause	Solution
Will stick in "start"	• Remote rod deformed • Ignition switch mounting bracket bent	• Straighten or replace • Straighten or replace
Key cannot be removed in "off-lock"	• Ignition switch is not adjusted correctly • Defective lock cylinder	• Adjust switch • Replace lock cylinder
Lock cylinder can be removed without depressing retainer	• Lock cylinder with defective retainer • Burr over retainer slot in housing cover or on cylinder retainer	• Replace lock cylinder • Remove burr
High effort on lock cylinder between "off" and "off-lock"	• Distorted lock rack • Burr on tang of shift gate (automatic column) • Gearshift linkage not adjusted	• Replace lock rack • Remove burr • Adjust linkage
Noise in column	• One click when in "off-lock" position and the steering wheel is moved (all except automatic column) • Coupling bolts not tightened • Lack of grease on bearings or bearing surfaces • Upper shaft bearing worn or broken • Lower shaft bearing worn or broken • Column not correctly aligned • Coupling pulled apart • Broken coupling lower joint • Steering shaft snap ring not seated • Shroud loose on shift bowl. Housing loose on jacket—will be noticed with ignition in "off-lock" and when torque is applied to steering wheel.	• Normal—lock bolt is seating • Tighten pinch bolts • Lubricate with chassis grease • Replace bearing assembly • Replace bearing. Check shaft and replace if scored. • Align column • Replace coupling • Repair or replace joint and align column • Replace ring. Check for proper seating in groove. • Position shroud over lugs on shift bowl. Tighten mounting screws.
High steering shaft effort	• Column misaligned • Defective upper or lower bearing • Tight steering shaft universal joint • Flash on I.D. of shift tube at plastic joint (tilt column only) • Upper or lower bearing seized	• Align column • Replace as required • Repair or replace • Replace shift tube • Replace bearings
Lash in mounted column assembly	• Column mounting bracket bolts loose • Broken weld nuts on column jacket • Column capsule bracket sheared	• Tighten bolts • Replace column jacket • Replace bracket assembly

Troubleshooting the Steering Column (cont.)

Problem	Cause	Solution
Lash in mounted column assembly (cont.)	• Column bracket to column jacket mounting bolts loose	• Tighten to specified torque
	• Loose lock shoes in housing (tilt column only)	• Replace shoes
	• Loose pivot pins (tilt column only)	• Replace pivot pins and support
	• Loose lock shoe pin (tilt column only)	• Replace pin and housing
	• Loose support screws (tilt column only)	• Tighten screws
Housing loose (tilt column only)	• Excessive clearance between holes in support or housing and pivot pin diameters	• Replace pivot pins and support
	• Housing support-screws loose	• Tighten screws
Steering wheel loose—every other tilt position (tilt column only)	• Loose fit between lock shoe and lock shoe pivot pin	• Replace lock shoes and pivot pin
Steering column not locking in any tilt position (tilt column only)	• Lock shoe seized on pivot pin	• Replace lock shoes and pin
	• Lock shoe grooves have burrs or are filled with foreign material	• Clean or replace lock shoes
	• Lock shoe springs weak or broken	• Replace springs
Noise when tilting column (tilt column only)	• Upper tilt bumpers worn	• Replace tilt bumper
	• Tilt spring rubbing in housing	• Lubricate with chassis grease
One click when in "off-lock" position and the steering wheel is moved	• Seating of lock bolt	• None. Click is normal characteristic sound produced by lock bolt as it seats.
High shift effort (automatic and tilt column only)	• Column not correctly aligned	• Align column
	• Lower bearing not aligned correctly	• Assemble correctly
	• Lack of grease on seal or lower bearing areas	• Lubricate with chassis grease
Improper transmission shifting—automatic and tilt column only	• Sheared shift tube joint	• Replace shift tube
	• Improper transmission gearshift linkage adjustment	• Adjust linkage
	• Loose lower shift lever	• Replace shift tube

arms by two adjustable tie rods. The trucks are equipped with a collapsible steering column designed to collapse on impact, thereby reducing possible chest injuries during accidents. When making any repairs to the steering column or steering wheel, excessive pressure or force capable of collapsing the column must be avoided. The ignition lock, ignition switch and an antitheft system are built into each column.

On the automatic transmission, the ignition key cannot be removed unless the shift lever is in the Park position and the ignition switch in the Lock position. Placing the key in the Lock position activates a rod within the column which locks the steering wheel and shift lever.

Steering Wheel

REMOVAL AND INSTALLATION

NOTE: The following procedure requires the use of the GM Steering Wheel Puller tool No. J-1859-03 or equivalent.

1. Disconnect the negative battery cable from the battery.
2. Position the steering wheel so that it is in the horizontal position and the front wheel are straight.
3. If equipped with a horn cap, pry the cap from the center of

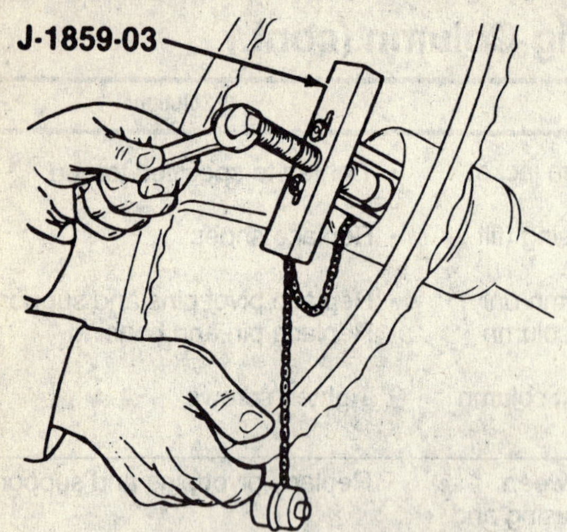

Using a steering wheel puller

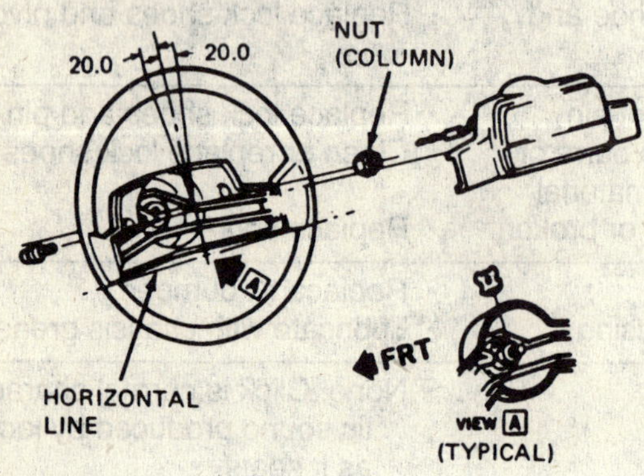

Make sure the wheel is properly aligned when installing it

the steering wheel. If equipped with a steering wheel shroud, remove the screw from the rear of the steering wheel and remove the shroud.

NOTE: If the horn cap or shroud is equipped with an electrical connector, disconnect it.

4. Remove the steering wheel-to-steering shaft retainer (snapring) and nut.

NOTE: Since the steering column is designed to collapse upon impact, it is recommended NEVER to hammer on it.

5. Matchmark the relationship of the steering wheel to the steering shaft.
6. Using the GM Steering Wheel Puller tool No. J-1859-03 or equivalent, press the steering wheel from the steering column.

NOTE: Before installing the steering wheel, be sure that the turn signal switch is in the Neutral position. DO NOT misalign the steering wheel more than 1 in. (25mm) from the horizontal centerline.

7. To install the steering wheel, align the matchmarks and push it onto the steering shaft splines, torque the steering wheel-to-steering shaft nut to 30 ft. lbs. Install the horn cap or pad.

Combination Switch

The combination switch is a combination of the turn signal, the windshield wiper/washer, the dimmer and the cruise control switches.

REMOVAL AND INSTALLATION

NOTE: The following procedure requires the use of the GM Lock Plate Compressor tool No. J-23653 or equivalent.

1. Disconnect the negative battery cable. Refer to the "Steering Wheel, Removal and Installation" procedures in this section and remove the steering wheel.
2. If necessary, remove the steering column-to-lower instrument panel cover. Disconnect the electrical harness connector from the steering column jacket (under the dash).
3. Using a screwdriver, insert into the slots between the steering shaft lock plate cover and the steering column housing, then pry upward to remove the cover from the lock plate.
4. Using the GM Lock Plate Compressor tool No. J-23653-A or equivalent, screw the center shaft onto the steering shaft (as far as it will go), then screw the center post nut clockwise until the lock plate is compressed.
5. Pry the snapring from the steering shaft slot.

NOTE: If the steering column is being disassembled on a bench, the steering shaft will slide out of the mast jacket when the snapring is removed.

6. Remove the GM Lock Plate Compressor tool No. J-23653 or equivalent, and the lock plate.
7. Remove the multi-function lever-to-switch screw and the lever.
8. To remove the hazard warning switch, press the knob inward and unscrew it.
9. Remove the combination switch assembly-to-steering column screws.
10. Lift the combination switch assembly from the steering column, then slide the electrical connector through the column housing and the protector.

NOTE: If the steering column is the tilting type, position the steering housing into the Low position.

11. To remove the harness cover, pull it toward the lower end of the column; be careful not to damage the wires.
12. To remove the wire protector, grab the protector's tab with a pair of pliers, then pull the protector downward, out of the steering column.

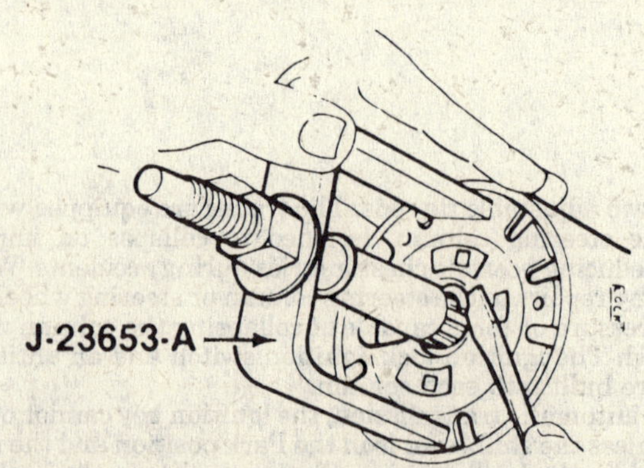

Removing the steering column lock plate with the compressor tool installed

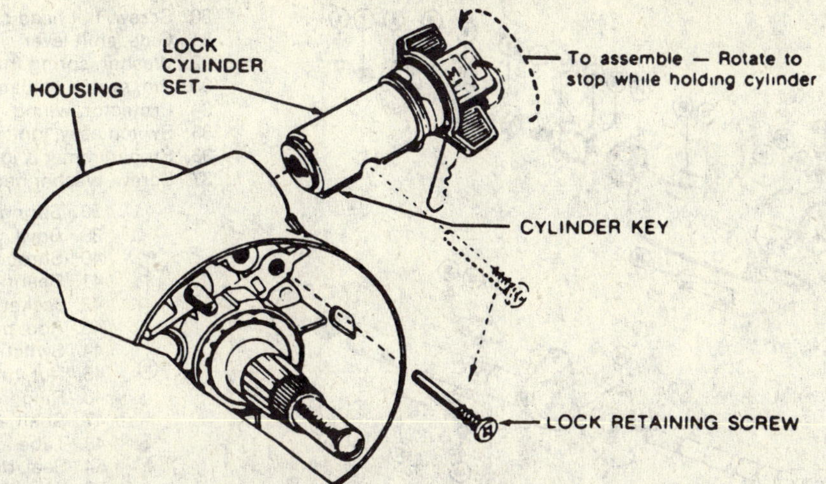

Ignition lock cylinder replacement

NOTE: When assembling the steering column, use only fasteners of the correct length; overlength fasteners could prevent a portion of the assembly from compressing under impact.

To install:

13. To install the combination switch electrical connector, perform the following procedures:
   a. On the non-tilt columns, be sure that the electrical connector is on the protector, then feed it and the cover down through the housing and under the mounting bracket.
   b. On the tilt columns, feed the electrical connector down through the housing and under the mounting bracket, then install the cover onto the housing.
14. Install the clip on the electrical connector to the clip on the jacket, the combination switch-to-steering column mounting screws, the lower instrument trim panel, the turn signal lever/screws and the hazard warning knob.

NOTE: With the multi-function lever installed, place it into the Neutral position. With the hazard warning knob installed, pull it Outward.

15. Onto the upper end of the steering shaft, install the washer, the upper bearing preload spring, the canceling cam, the lock plate and a new retaining ring (snapring). Using the GM Lock Plate Compressor tool No. J-23653 or equivalent, compress the lock plate and slide the new retaining ring into the steering shaft groove.
16. To complete the installation, reverse the removal procedures. Torque the multi-function switch-to-steering column screws to 35 inch lbs. and the steering wheel nut to 30 ft. lbs.

Ignition Switch

The ignition switch, for anti-theft reasons, is located inside the channel section of the brake pedal support and is completely inaccessible without first lowering the steering column. The switch is actuated by a rod and rack assembly. A gear on the end of the lock cylinder engages the toothed upper end of the actuator rod.

REMOVAL AND INSTALLATION

1. Remove the lower instrument panel-to-steering column cover. Remove the steering column-to-dash bolts and lower the steering column; be sure to properly support it.
2. Place the ignition switch in the Locked position.

NOTE: If the lock cylinder was removed, the actuating rod should be pulled up until it stops, then moved down one detent; the switch is now in the Lock position.

3. Remove the two ignition switch-to-steering column screws and the switch assembly.
4. Before installing the ignition switch, place it in the Locked position, then make sure that the lock cylinder and actuating rod are in the Locked position (1st detent from the top).
5. Install the activating rod into the ignition switch and assemble the switch onto the steering column. Torque the ignition switch-to-steering column screws to 35 inch lbs.

NOTE: When installing the ignition switch, use only the specified screws since overlength screws could impair the collapsibility of the column.

6. To complete the installation, install the steering column and the lower instrument panel cover. Torque the steering column-to-instrument bolts to 22 ft. lbs.

Ignition Lock Cylinder

REMOVAL AND INSTALLATION

1. Disconnect the negative battery cable. Refer to the "Combination Switch, Removal and Installation" procedures in this section and remove the combination switch.
2. Place the lock cylinder in the **Run** position.
3. Remove the buzzer switch, the lock cylinder screw and the lock cylinder.

CAUTION

If the screw is dropped upon removal, it could fall into the steering column, requiring complete disassembly to retrieve the screw.

4. To install, rotate the lock cylinder clockwise to align the cylinder key with the keyway in the housing.
5. Push the lock cylinder all the way in.
6. Install the cylinder lock-to-housing screw. Tighten the screw to 14 inch lbs.

Steering Column

REMOVAL AND INSTALLATION

NOTE: The following procedure requires the use of the Steering Column Holding Fixture tool No. J-23074 or equivalent.

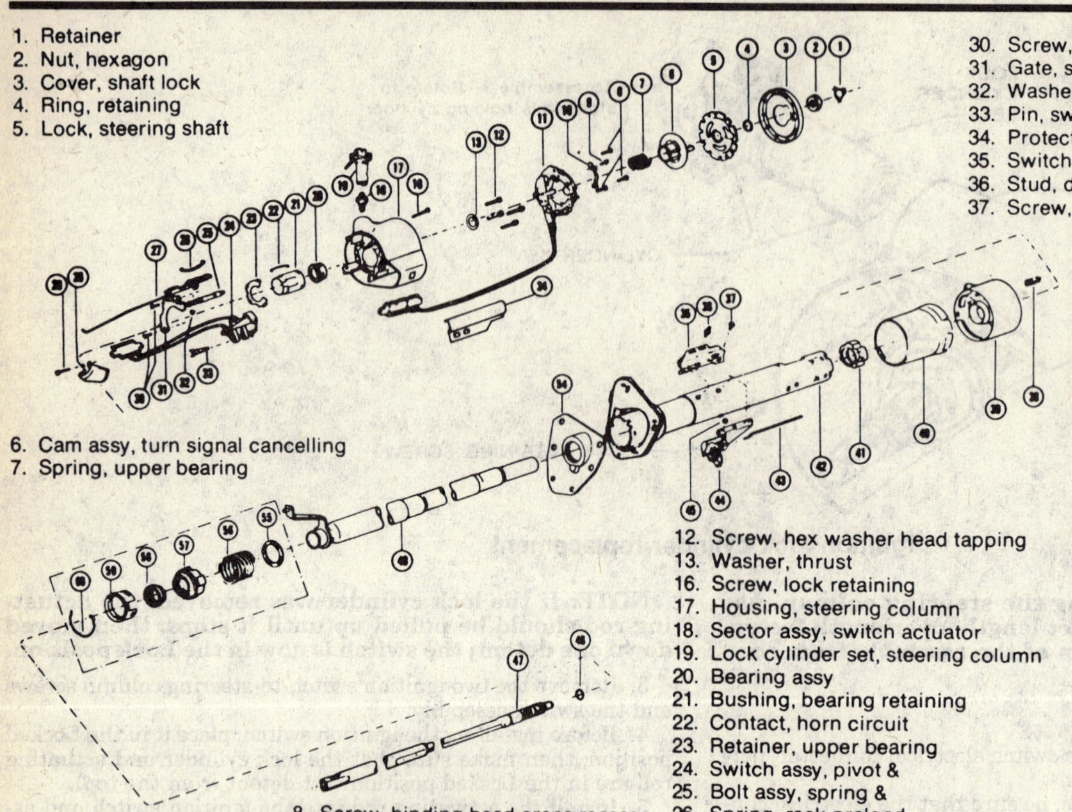

Standard steering column components

1. Disconnect the negative battery cable. Refer to the "Steering Wheel, Removal and Installation" procedures in this section and remove the steering wheel.
2. Disconnect the negative battery terminal from the battery.
3. If equipped with a column shift, disconnect the transmission control linkage from the column shift tube levers.
4. From inside the engine compartment, remove the intermediate shaft-to-steering column shaft (pot-joint) bolt.

NOTE: Before separating the intermediate shaft from the steering column shaft, mark the relationship of the two shafts.

5. Remove the lower instrument panel-to-steering column cover, the steering column bracket-to-dash nuts/bolts (support the steering column) and the steering column-to-firewall cover (if necessary).
6. From under the dash, disconnect the electrical harness connectors from the steering column.

NOTE: Some models are equipped with a back-up light switch and a neutral/start switch, be sure to disconnect the electrical connectors from them.

7. Remove the steering column from the vehicle.

NOTE: If equipped with a column shifter, rotate the steering column so that the shift lever clears the dash opening.

8. To install, align the matchmarks of the steering column shaft and the intermediate shaft, tighten the fasteners finger tight and reverse the removal procedures.
9. Torque the intermediate shaft-to-steering column shaft (pot-joint) pinch bolt to 30 ft. lbs., the steering column bracket-to-dash nuts to 25 ft. lbs. and the steering column-to-firewall screws to 7 ft. lbs.

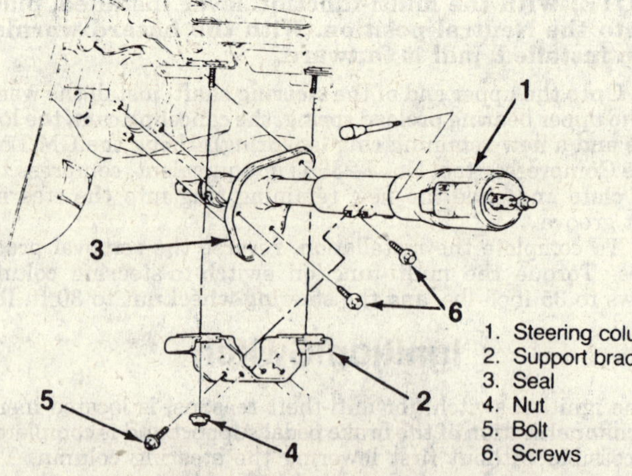

Steering column removal

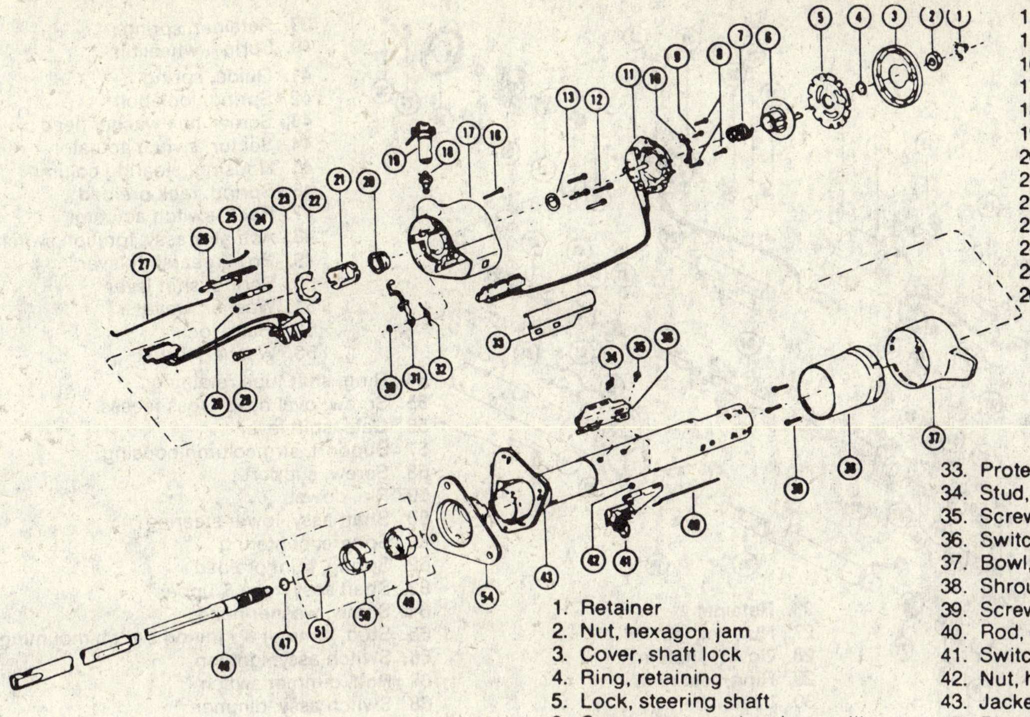

1. Retainer
2. Nut, hexagon jam
3. Cover, shaft lock
4. Ring, retaining
5. Lock, steering shaft
6. Cam assy, turn signal cancelling
7. Spring, upper bearing
8. Screw, binding head cross recess
9. Screw, round washer head
10. Arm assy, switch actuator
11. Switch assy, turn signal
12. Screw, hex washer head tapping
13. Washer, thrust
16. Screw, lock retaining
17. Housing, steering column
18. Sector assy, switch actuator
19. Lock cylinder set, steering column
20. Bearing assy
21. Bushing, bearing retaining
22. Retainer, upper bearing
23. Switch assy, pivot &
24. Bolt assy, spring &
25. Spring, rack preload
26. Rack, switch actuator
27. Rod, switch actuator
28. Washer, spring thrust
29. Pin, switch actuator pivot
30. Washer, wave
31. Lever, key release
32. Spring, key release
33. Protector, wiring
34. Stud, dimmer and ignition switch mounting
35. Screw, washer head
36. Switch assy, ignition
37. Bowl, floor shift
38. Shroud, shift bowl
39. Screw, binding head cross recess
40. Rod, dimmer switch actuator
41. Switch assy, dimmer
42. Nut, hexagon
43. Jacket assy, steering column
47. Ring, retaining
48. Shaft assy, steering
49. Bushing assy. steering shaft
50. Retainer, bearing adapter
51. Clip, lower bearing adapter
54. Bracket assy, column dash

Key release standard steering column components

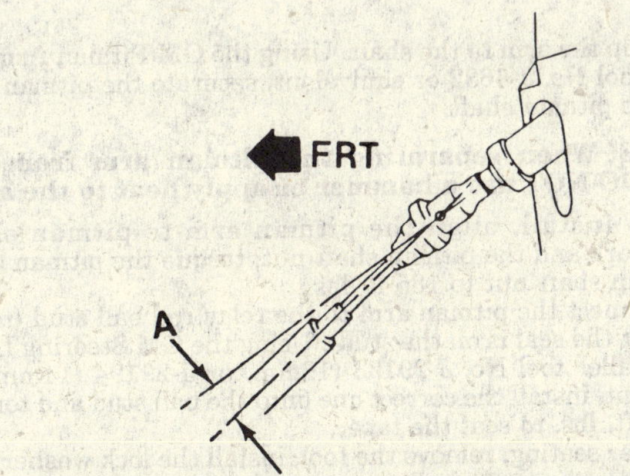

Pot joint angle not to exceed 12.5 degrees

10. Reconnect the electrical harness-to-steering column connectors. Reinstall the steering wheel and the negative battery terminal.

NOTE: If equipped with steering column shifter, reconnect the transmission-to-steering column linkage.

Steering Linkage

The steering linkage consists of: a forward mounted linkage, crimp nuts at the inner pivots, castellated nuts at the steering knuckle arm, an idler arm, a steering gear pitman arm, a relay rod and a steering damper (manual steering). Grease fittings are equipped with each joint, for durability.

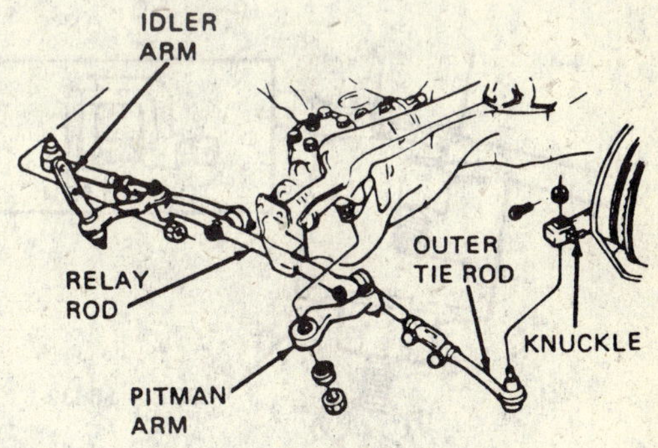

Steering linkage

REMOVAL AND INSTALLATION

Pitman Arm

NOTE: The following procedure requires the use of the GM Steering Linkage Puller tool No. J-24319-01 or equivalent, the GM Pitman Arm Remover tool No. J-

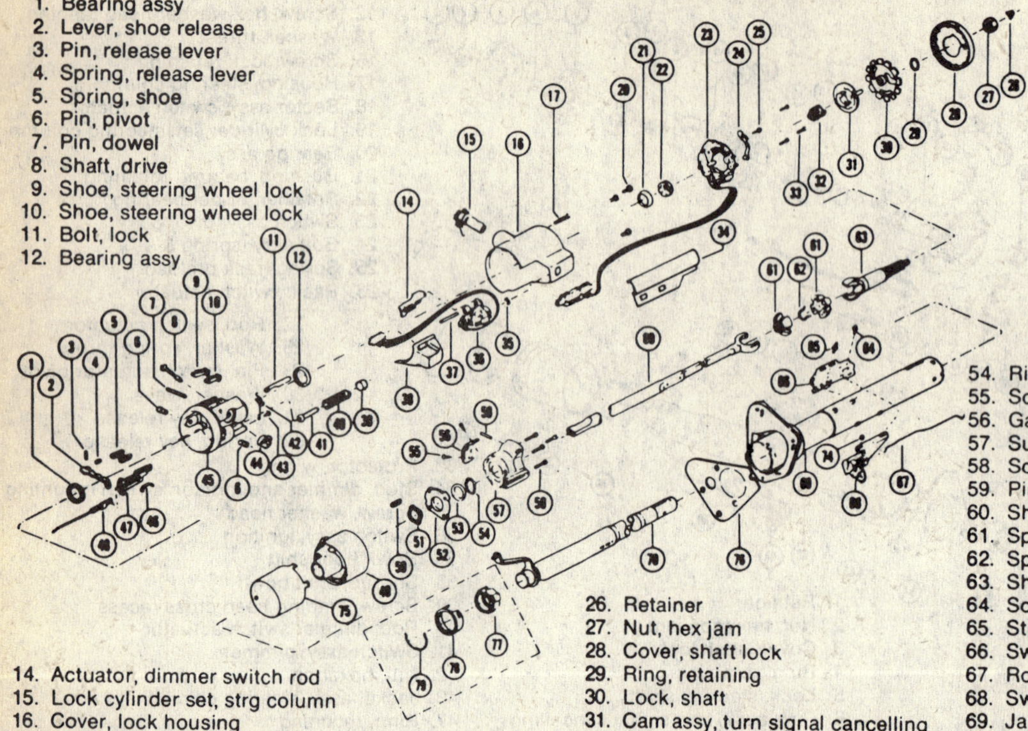

1. Bearing assy
2. Lever, shoe release
3. Pin, release lever
4. Spring, release lever
5. Spring, shoe
6. Pin, pivot
7. Pin, dowel
8. Shaft, drive
9. Shoe, steering wheel lock
10. Shoe, steering wheel lock
11. Bolt, lock
12. Bearing assy
14. Actuator, dimmer switch rod
15. Lock cylinder set, strg column
16. Cover, lock housing
17. Screw, lock retaining
20. Screw, pan head cross recess
21. Race, inner
22. Seat, upper bearing inner race
23. Switch assy, turn signal
24. Arm assy, signal switch
25. Screw, round washer head
26. Retainer
27. Nut, hex jam
28. Cover, shaft lock
29. Ring, retaining
30. Lock, shaft
31. Cam assy, turn signal cancelling
32. Spring, upper bearing
33. Screw, binding head cross recess
34. Protector, wiring
35. Spring, pin preload
36. Switch assy, pivot &
37. Pin, switch actuator pivot
38. Cap, column housing cover end
39. Retainer, spring
40. Spring, wheel tilt
41. Guide, spring
42. Spring, lock bolt
43. Screw, hex washer head
44. Sector, switch actuator
45. Housing, steering column
46. Spring, rack preload
47. Rack, switch actuator
48. Actuator assy, ignition switch
49. Bowl, gearshift lever
50. Spring, shift lever
51. Washer, wave
52. Plate, lock
53. Washer, thrust
54. Ring, shift tube retaining
55. Screw, oval head cross recess
56. Gate, shift lever
57. Support, strg column housing
58. Screw, support
59. Pin, dowel
60. Shaft assy, lower steering
61. Sphere, centering
62. Spring, joint preload
63. Shaft assy, race & upper
64. Screw, washer head
65. Stud, dimmer & ignition switch mounting
66. Switch assy, ignition
67. Rod, dimmer switch
68. Switch assy, dimmer
69. Jacket assy, steering column
70. Tube assy, shift
74. Nut, hexagon
75. Shroud, gearshift bowl
76. Seal, dash
77. Bushing assy, steering shaft
78. Retainer, bearing adapter
79. Clip, lower bearing adapter

Tilt steering column components

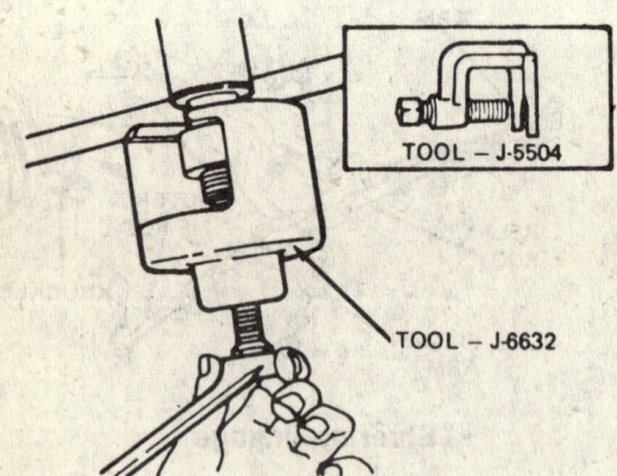

Pitman arm removal using the proper tool

6632 or equivalent, and the GM Steering Linkage Installer tool No. J-29193 (12mm) or J-29194 (14mm) or equivalent.

1. Raise and safely support the front frame of the vehicle on jackstands.
2. Disconnect the nut from the pitman arm ball joint stud.
3. Using the GM Steering Linkage Puller tool No. J-24319-01 or equivalent, separate the relay rod from the pitman arm. Pull down on the relay rod and separate it from the stud.
4. Remove the pitman arm-to-pitman shaft nut, mark the relationship the arm to the shaft. Using the GM Pitman Arm Remover tool No. J-6632 or equivalent, separate the pitman arm from the pitman shaft.

NOTE: When separating the pitman arm from the shaft, DO NOT use a hammer or apply heat to the arm.

5. To install, align the pitman arm-to-pitman shaft matchmark and the pitman shaft nut; torque the pitman arm-to-pitman shaft nut to 185 ft. lbs.
6. Connect the pitman arm to the relay rod ball stud (make sure that the seal is on the stud). Using the GM Steering Linkage Installer tool No. J-29193 (12mm) or J-29194 (14mm) or equivalent, install the correct one onto the ball stud and torque it to 40 ft. lbs. to seat the taper.
7. After seating, remove the tool, install the lock washer and nut and torque to 60 ft. lbs.

Idler Arm

NOTE: The following procedure requires the use of the GM Steering Linkage Puller tool No. J-24319-01 or equivalent, the GM Steering Linkage Installer tool No. J-29193 (12mm) or J-29194 (14mm) or equivalent, and a spring scale.

1. Raise and safely support the front frame of the vehicle on jackstands.

NOTE: Jerking the right wheel assembly back and forth is not an acceptable testing procedure; there is no control on the amount of force being applied to the idler

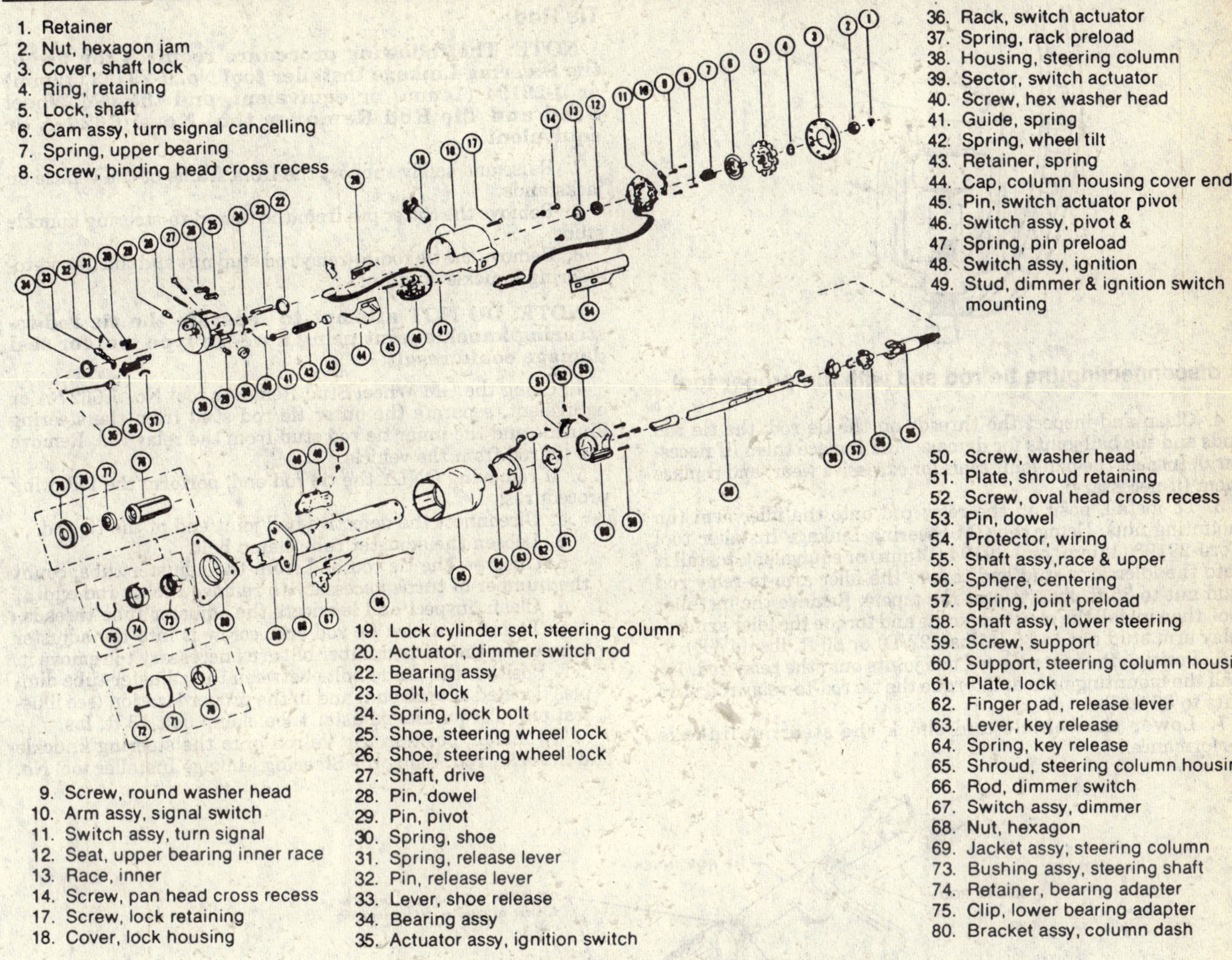

Tilt steering column with key release components

arm. Before suspecting idler arm shimmying complaints, check the wheels for imbalance, runout, force variation and/or road surface irregularities.

2. To inspect for a defective idler arm, perform the following procedures:
   a. Position the wheels in the straight ahead position.
   b. Using a spring scale, position it near the relay rod end of the idler arm, then exert 25 lbs. of force upward and then downward.
   c. Measure the distance between the upward and downward directions that the idler arm moves. The allowable deflection is ⅛ in. (3mm) for each direction; a total difference of ¼ in. (6mm); if the idler arm deflection is beyond the allowable limits, replace it.
3. Remove the idler arm-to-frame bolts and the idler arm-to-relay rod ball joint nut.
4. Using the GM Steering Linkage Puller tool No. J-24319-01 or equivalent, separate the relay rod from the ball joint stud.
5. Inspect and/or replace (if necessary) the idler arm.
6. Install the idler arm-to-frame bolts and torque them to 60 ft. lbs.
7. Connect the relay rod to the idler arm ball joint stud. Using the GM Steering Linkage Installer tool No. J-29193 (12mm) or J-29194 (14mm) or equivalent, seat (torque) the relay rod-to-idler arm ball joint stud to 40 ft. lbs., then remove the tool.
8. Install the idler arm-to-relay rod stud nut and torque it to 35 ft. lbs. (2WD) or 60 ft. lbs. (4WD).
9. Lower the vehicle. Check and/or adjust the toe-in.

Relay Rod

NOTE: The following procedure requires the use of the GM Steering Linkage Puller tool No. J-24319-01 or equivalent, and the GM Steering Linkage Installer tool No. J-29193 (12mm) or J-29194 (14mm) or equivalent.

1. Refer to the "Tie Rod, Removal and Installation" procedures in this section and disconnect the inner tie rod ends from the relay rod.
2. Remove the idler arm stud-to-relay rod nut.
3. Using the GM Steering Linkage Puller tool No. J-24319-01 or equivalent, disconnect the relay rod from the idler arm, then remove the relay rod from the vehicle.

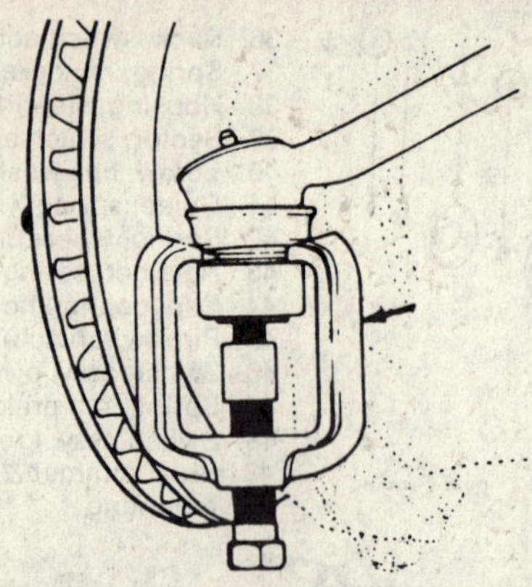

disconnecting the tie rod end with the proper tool

4. Clean and inspect the threads on the tie rod, the tie rod ends and the ball joints for damage, and replace them (if necessary). Inspect the ball joint seals for excessive wear, and replace them (if necessary).

5. To install, position the relay rod onto the idler arm (no mounting nut). Using the GM Steering Linkage Installer tool No. J-29193 (12mm) or J-29194 (14mm) or equivalent, install it onto the idler arm stud and torque the idler arm-to-relay rod stud nut to 35 ft. lbs. (to seat the taper). Remove the installer tool, then install the mounting nuts and torque the idler arm-to-relay arm stud nut to 35 ft. lbs. (2WD) or 60 ft. lbs. (4WD).

6. Position the inner tie rod ball joints onto the relay rod. Install the mounting nuts and torque the tie rod-to-relay rod stud nuts to 35 ft. lbs.

7. Lower the vehicle and check the steering linkage performance.

Tie Rod

NOTE: The following procedure requires the use of the Steering Linkage Installer tool No. J-29193 (12mm) or J-29194 (14mm) or equivalent, and the GM Wheel Stud and Tie Rod Remover tool No. J-6627-A or equivalent.

1. Raise and safely support the front frame of the vehicle on jackstands.
2. Remove the cotter pin from the tie rod-to-steering knuckle stud.
3. Remove the tie rod-to-relay rod stud nut and the tie rod-to-steering knuckle stud nut.

NOTE: DO NOT attempt to separate the tie rod-to-steering knuckle joint using a wedge type tool for seal damage could result.

4. Using the GM Wheel Stud Remover tool No. J-6627-A or equivalent, separate the outer tie rod stud from the steering knuckle and the inner tie rod stud from the relay rod. Remove the tie rod from the vehicle.
5. If removing ONLY the tie rod end, perform the following procedures:
   a. Disconnect the defective ball joint end of the tie rod.
   b. Loosen the adjuster tube clamp bolt.
   c. Unscrew the tie rod end from the adjuster tube; count the number of turns necessary to remove the tie rod end.
   d. Clean, inspect and lubricate the adjuster tube threads.
   e. To install a new tie rod end, screw it into the adjuster tube using the same number of turns necessary to remove it.
   f. Position the clamp bolts between the adjuster tube dimples (located at each end) and in the proper location (see illustration). Torque the adjuster tube clamp bolt 13 ft. lbs.
6. To install, position the tie rod onto the steering knuckle and the relay rod. Using the Steering Linkage Installer tool No.

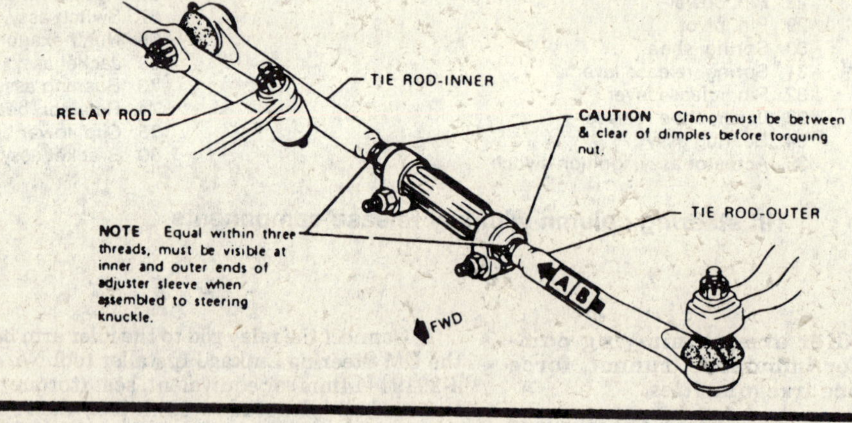

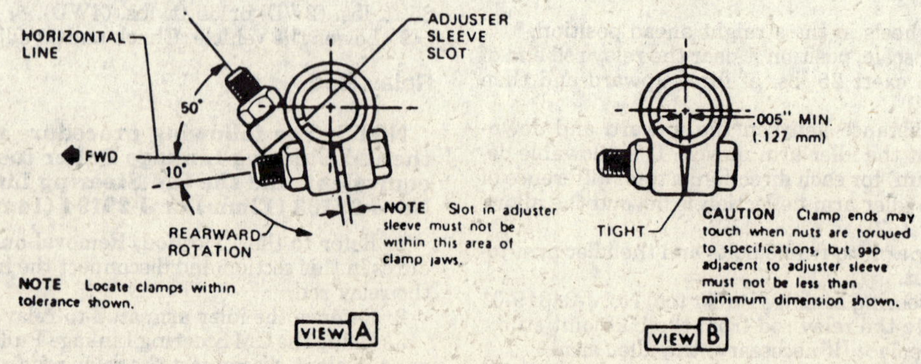

Tie rod clamp and sleeve positioning

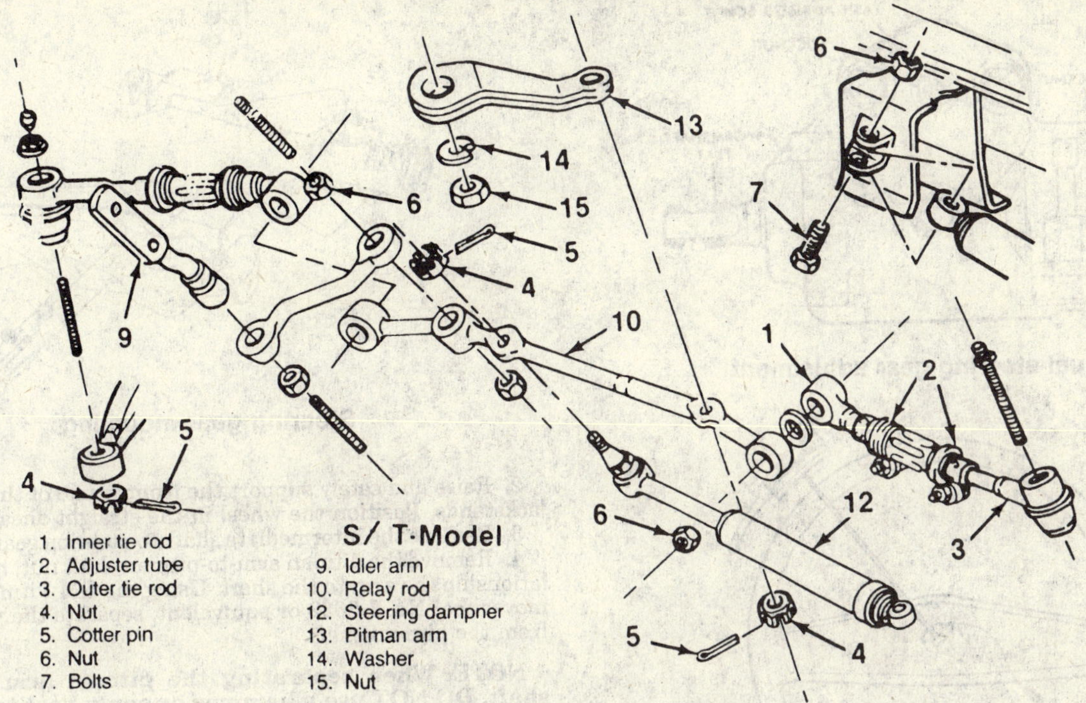

Steering linkage with damper

J-29193 (12mm) or J-29194 (14mm) or equivalent, install them onto the studs and torque them to 35 ft. lbs. (to seat the tapers). After seating the tapers, remove the tool.

7. At the tie rod-to-steering knuckle stud, tighten the nut until the castle nut slot aligns with the hole in the stud, then install a new cotter pin.

8. Lower the vehicle and check the steering linkage performance.

Damper Assembly

The damper assembly is used to the remove steering wheel vibration and vehicle wonder; not all vehicles are equipped with it.

NOTE: The following procedure requires the use of the Steering Linkage Puller tool No. J-24319-01 or equivalent.

1. Raise and safely support the front frame of the vehicle on jackstands.
2. Remove the damper assembly-to-relay rod cotter pin and nut.
3. Using the Steering Linkage Puller tool No. J-24319-01 or equivalent, separate the damper assembly from the relay rod.
4. Remove the damper assembly-to-bracket nut/bolt and the damper assembly from the vehicle.
5. If necessary, use a new damper assembly and reverse the removal procedures. Torque the damper assembly-to-bracket nut/bolt to 26 ft. lbs. and the damper assembly-to-relay rod nut to 45 ft. lbs. Align the castle nut slot with the hole in the ball joint stud and install a new cotter pin.

Manual Steering Gear

The recirculating ball type manual steering gear is manufactured by Saginaw and is equipped with a mechanical ratio of 24:1.

ADJUSTMENTS

NOTE: The following procedure requires the use the GM Steering Linkage Puller tool No. J-6632 or equivalent, and a 0–50 inch lbs. torque wrench.

1. Disconnect the negative battery cable from the battery.
2. Raise and safely support the front frame of the vehicle on jackstands.

NOTE: Before adjustments are made to the steering gear, be sure to check the front end alignment, the shock absorbers, the wheel balance and the tire pressure.

3. Remove the pitman arm-to-pitman shaft nut and matchmark the pitman arm to the pitman shaft. Using the GM Steering Linkage Puller tool No. J-6632 or equivalent, remove the pitman arm from the pitman shaft.
4. Loosen the steering gear adjuster plug locknut and back-off the adjuster plug ¼ turn.
5. From the steering wheel, remove the horn cap or cover.
6. Gently, turn the steering wheel (in one direction) to the stop; then, turn it back ½ turn.

NOTE: When the steering linkage is disconnected from the steering gear, DO NOT turn the steering wheel hard against the stops for damage to the ball guides may result.

7. Using a torque wrench (0–50 inch lbs.), position it onto the steering wheel nut, then measure and record the bearing drag. To measure the bearing drag, use the torque wrench to rotate the steering wheel 90°.
8. Using a torque wrench (0–50 inch lbs.), tighten the adjuster plug (on the steering gear) to obtain a thrust bearing preload of 5–8 inch lbs. After the thrust bearing preload is obtained, torque the adjuster plug locknut to 25 ft. lbs.

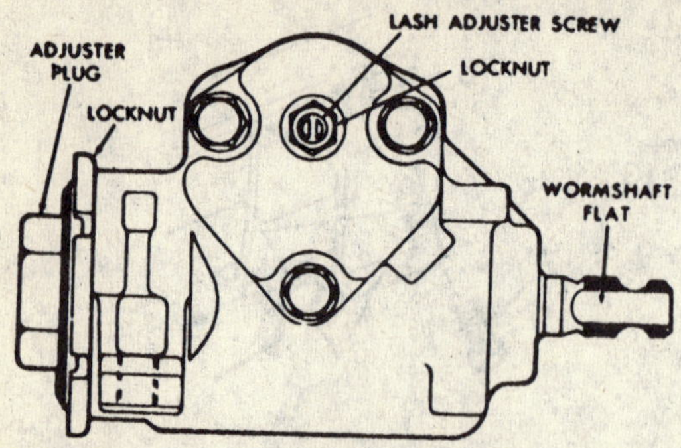

Manual steering gear adjustment

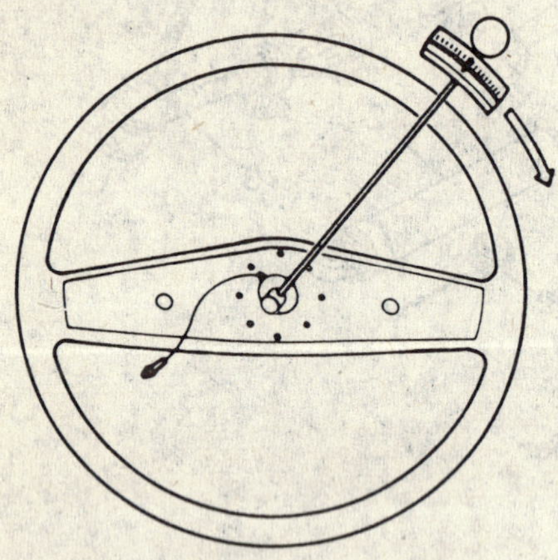

Measure steering wheel rotation effort

NOTE: If the steering gear feels lumpy (after adjustment), suspect damage to the bearings, probably due to the improper adjustment or severe impact.

9. To adjust the overcenter preload, perform the following procedures:
   a. Turn the steering wheel, from one stop all the way to the other stop, counting the number of turns. Turn the steering wheel back exactly ½ way, to the center position.
   b. Turn the overcenter adjusting screw clockwise, until the lash is removed between the ball nut and the pitman shaft sector teeth, then tighten the locknut.
   c. Using a torque wrench (0–50 inch lbs.), check the highest force necessary to turn the steering wheel through the center position; the usable torque is 4–10 inch lbs.
   d. If necessary, loosen the locknut and readjust the overcenter adjusting screw to obtain the proper torque. Retorque the locknut to 25 ft. lbs. and recheck the steering wheel torque through the center of travel.

NOTE: If the maximum is too high, turn the overcenter adjuster screw counterclockwise, then torque the adjuster lock nut in the clockwise motion to achieve the proper torque.

10. To install, realign the pitman arm-to-pitman shaft, torque the pitman shaft nut to 185 ft. lbs.

REMOVAL AND INSTALLATION

NOTE: The following procedure requires the use of the GM Pitman Arm Remover tool No. J-6632 or equivalent.

1. Disconnect the negative battery cable from the battery.

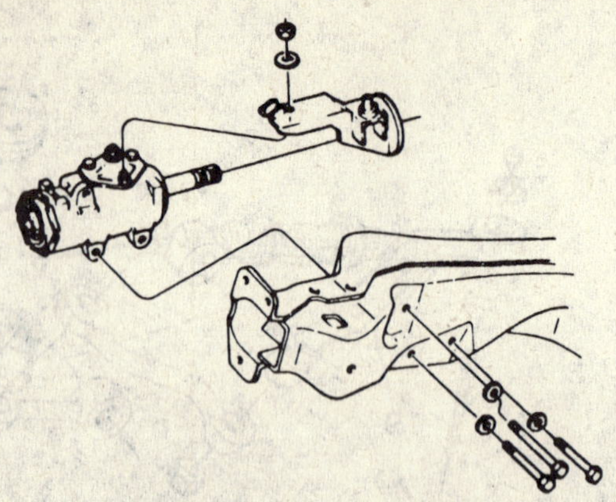

Steering gear mounting

2. Raise and safely support the front frame of the vehicle on jackstands. Position the wheel in the straight ahead direction.
3. Remove the intermediate shaft-to-steering gear pinch bolt.
4. Remove the pitman arm-to-pitman shaft nut, mark the relationship the arm to the shaft. Using the GM Pitman Arm Remover tool No. J-6632 or equivalent, separate the pitman arm from the pitman shaft.

NOTE: When separating the pitman arm from the shaft, DO NOT use a hammer or apply heat to the arm.

5. Remove the steering gear-to-frame bolts and the gear from the vehicle.

NOTE: When installing the steering gear, be sure that the intermediate shaft bottoms on the worm shaft, so that the pinch bolt passes through the undercut on the worm shaft. Check and/or adjust the alignment of the pitman arm-to-pitman shaft.

6. To install, align the matchmarks and reverse the removal procedures. Torque the steering gear-to-frame bolts to 60 ft. lbs., the pitman arm-to-pitman shaft nut to 185 ft. lbs. and the intermediate steering shaft-to-steering gear bolt to 30 ft. lbs.

Power Steering Gear

The recirculating ball type power steering gear is basically the same as the manual steering gear, except that it uses a hydraulic assist on the rack piston.

The power steering gear control valve directs the power steering fluid to either side of the rack piston, which rides up and down the worm shaft. The steering rack converts the hydraulic pressure into mechanical force. Should the vehicle loose the hydraulic pressure, it can still be controlled mechanically.

ADJUSTMENTS

NOTE: To perform adjustments to the power steering gear, it is recommended to remove the power steering gear from the vehicle and place it in a vise. Before adjustments are performed to the system, be sure to check problems relating to hydraulic pressures and performance.

Worm Bearing Preload

NOTE: The following procedure requires the use of the GM Adjustable Spanner Wrench tool No. J-7624 or equivalent.

1. Refer to the "Power Steering Gear, Removal and Installation" procedures in this section, remove the steering gear from the vehicle and position it in a vise.

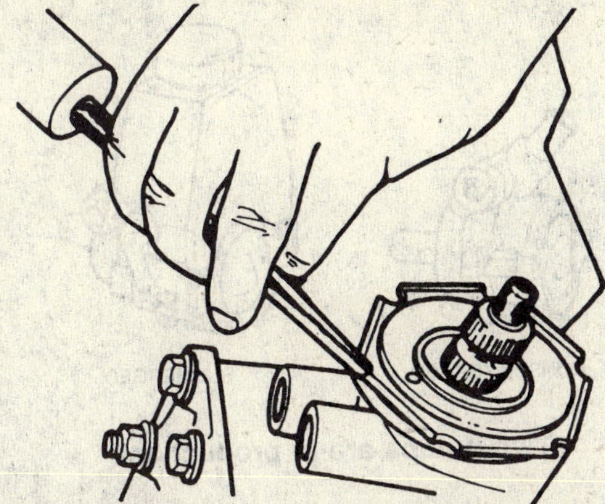

Removing the adjuster plug lock nut from the power steering gear

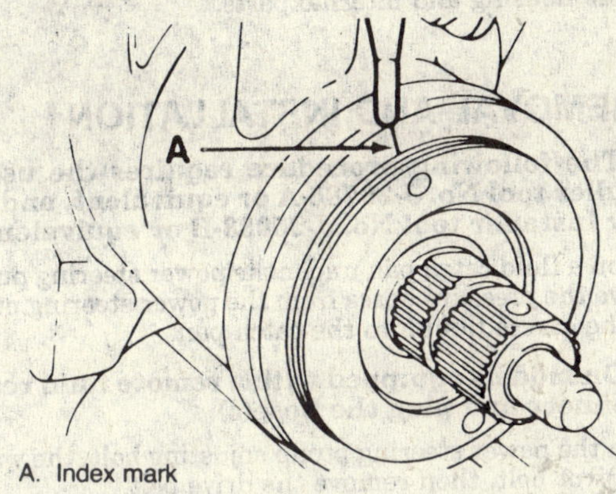

A. Index mark

Marking the housing with the adjuster plug hole

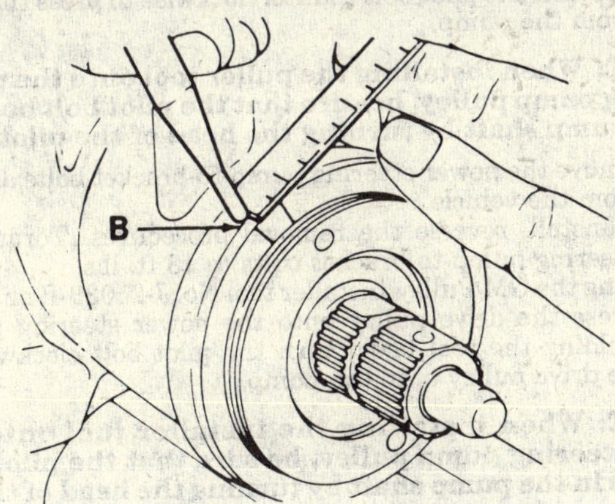

Make the second index mark

2. Using a hammer and a brass punch, drive the adjuster plug lock nut counterclockwise and remove it from the end of the steering gear.
3. Using the GM Adjustable Spanner Wrench tool No. J-7624 or equivalent, turn the adjuster plug inward, until it firmly bottoms in the housing with a torque of 20 ft. lbs.
4. Using a scribing tool, place a matchmark (on the housing) next to the one of the spanner wrench holes in the adjuster plug.

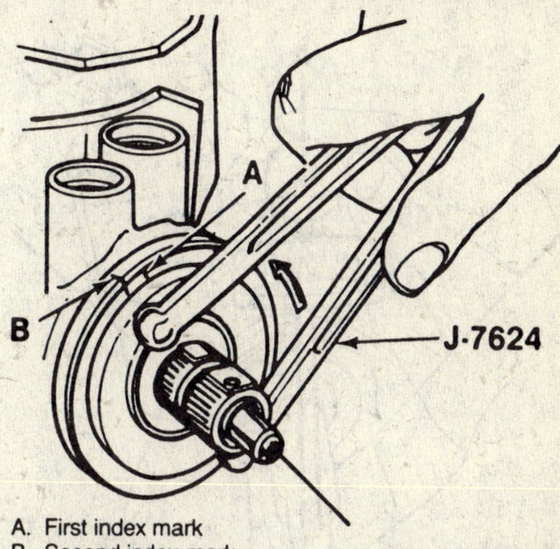

A. First index mark
B. Second index mark

Using the spanner to align the adjuster plug with the second mark

5. Using a ruler, measure ½ in. (13mm) counterclockwise from the scribed mark (on the housing) and place another mark.
6. Using the GM Adjustable Spanner Wrench tool No. J-7624 or equivalent, turn the adjuster plug (counterclockwise) until the hole in the adjuster plug aligns with the 2nd scribed mark.
7. While holding the adjuster plug in alignment, install and tighten the adjuster plug lock nut.
8. Perform the overcenter preload adjustment.

Overcenter Preload

1. Refer to the "Power Steering Gear, Removal and Installation" procedures in this section, remove the steering gear from the vehicle and position it in a vise.
2. Rotate the stud shaft from stop-to-stop and count the number of turns necessary.
3. Starting from one stop, turn the stub shaft back ½ the number of turns (center of the gear).

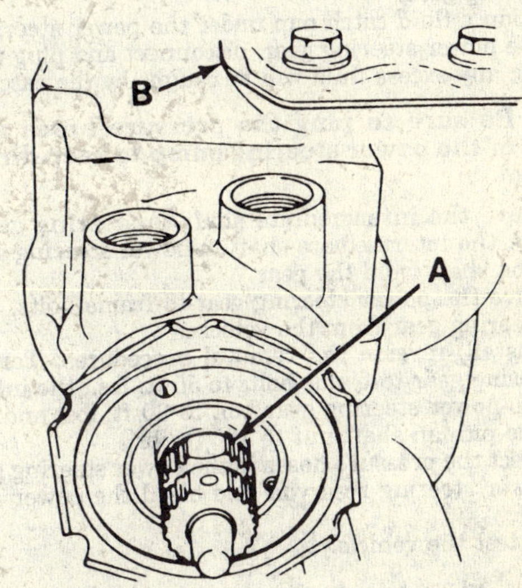

A. Stub shaft flat
B. Side cover

Aligning the stub shaft with the side cover

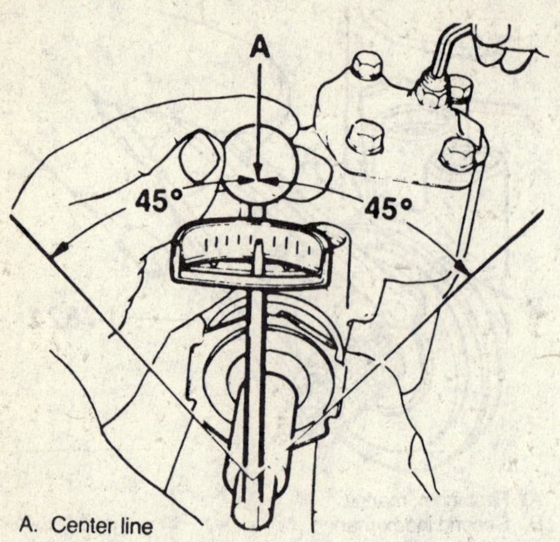

Reading over center rotation torque

NOTE: With the stub gear centered, the flat on top of the shaft should face upward and be parallel with the side cover; the master spline on the pitman shaft should be in line with the adjuster screw.

4. Loosen the pitman shaft adjuster screw locknut and turn the adjuster screw counterclockwise until it is fully extended, then turn it clockwise one full turn.
5. Using a torque wrench (0–50 inch lbs.), position it onto the stub shaft, rotate it 45° (to each side) and record the highest drag measured near or on the center.
6. Turn the adjuster screw inward until the torque on the stub shaft is 6–10 inch lbs. greater than the initial reading.
7. Install the adjuster screw jam nut and torque it to 20 ft. lbs. Reinstall the power steering gear into the vehicle.

REMOVAL AND INSTALLATION

1. Refer to the "Pitman Arm, Removal and Installation" procedures in this section and disconnect the pitman arm from the power steering gear.
2. Position a fluid catch pan under the power steering gear.
3. At the power steering gear, disconnect and plug the pressure hoses; any excess fluid will be caught by the catch pan.

NOTE: Be sure to plug the pressure hoses and the openings of the power steering pump to keep dirt out of the system.

4. Remove the intermediate shaft-to-steering gear bolt. Matchmark the intermediate shaft-to-power steering gear and separate the shaft from the gear.
5. Remove the power steering gear-to-frame bolts, washers and the steering gear from the vehicle.
6. To install, reverse the removal procedures. Torque the power steering gear-to-frame bolts to 55 ft. lbs., the intermediate shaft-to-power steering gear bolt to 30 ft. lbs. and the pitman arm-to-pitman shaft nut to 185 ft. lbs.
7. Connect the pressure hoses to the power steering gear, refill the power steering reservoir and bleed the power steering system.
8. Road test the vehicle.

Power Steering Pump

Two types of power steering pumps are offered, they are: The submerged and the non-submerged. The submerged pump has a housing and internal parts which are inside the reservoir and operate submerged in oil. The non-submerged pump functions the same as the submerged pump except the reservoir is separate from the housing and internal parts.

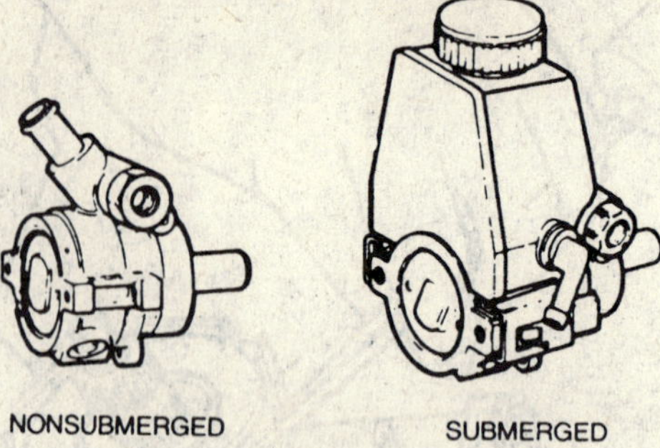

Two pumps are in production

REMOVAL AND INSTALLATION

NOTE: The following procedure requires the use of the GM Puller tool No. J-29785-A or equivalent, and the GM Pulley Installer tool No. J-25033-B or equivalent.

1. Position a fluid catch pan under the power steering pump.
2. Remove the pressure hoses from the power steering pump and drain the excess fluid into the catch pan.

NOTE: On models equipped with a remote fluid reservoir, disconnect and plug the hose(s).

3. Loosen the power steering pump adjusting bolt, the washer and the pivot bolt, then remove the drive belt.
4. Using the GM Puller tool No. J-29785-A or equivalent, install it onto the power steering pump pulley. While holding the tool body, turn the pilot bolt counterclockwise to press the drive pulley from the pump.

NOTE: When installing the puller tool onto the power steering pump pulley, be sure that the pilot bolt bottoms in the pump shaft by turning the head of the pilot bolt.

5. Remove the power steering pump-to-bracket bolts and the pump from the vehicle.
6. To install, reverse the removal procedures. Torque the power steering pump-to-bracket bolts to 18 ft. lbs.
7. Using the GM Pulley Installer tool No. J-25033-B or equivalent, press the drive pulley onto the power steering pump. While holding the tool body, turn the pilot bolt clockwise to press the drive pulley onto the pump.

NOTE: When installing the installer tool onto the power steering pump pulley, be sure that the pilot bolt bottoms in the pump shaft by turning the head of the pilot bolt.

8. Hand tighten the pivot bolt, the adjusting bolt and the washer.
9. Install the drive belt and adjust the drive belt tension. Torque the mounting bolts and nut to 36 ft. lbs. (submerged type) or 20 ft. lbs. (nonsubmerged type). Install the pressure hoses (to the pump), refill the power steering reservoir and bleed the system.

NOTE: Be sure to secure any hoses which may get in the way or rub other components.

10. Test drive the vehicle.

SYSTEM BLEEDING

1. Run the engine until the power steering fluid reaches normal operating temperature, approximately 170°F (76°C), then shut the engine Off. Remove the reservoir filler cap and check the oil level.
2. If the oil level is low, add power steering fluid to proper level and replace the filler cap. When adding or making a complete fluid change, always use GM No. 1050017 or equivalent, power steering fluid. DO NOT use transmission fluid.
3. Start the engine and turn the wheels in both directions (to the stops) several times. Stop the engine and add power steering fluid to the level indicated on the reservoir.

NOTE: Maintain the fluid level just above the internal pump casting. Fluid with air in it will have a light tan or milky appearance. This air must be eliminated from the fluid before normal steering action can be obtained.

4. Return the wheels to the center position and continue to run it for 2–3 minutes, then shut the engine Off.
5. Road test the vehicle to make sure the steering functions normally and is free from noise.
6. Allow the vehicle to stand for 2–3 hours, then recheck the power steering fluid.

Troubleshooting the Ignition Switch

Problem	Cause	Solution
Ignition switch electrically inoperative	• Loose or defective switch connector • Feed wire open (fusible link) • Defective ignition switch	• Tighten or replace connector • Repair or replace • Replace ignition switch
Engine will not crank	• Ignition switch not adjusted properly	• Adjust switch
Ignition switch wil not actuate mechanically	• Defective ignition switch • Defective lock sector • Defective remote rod	• Replace switch • Replace lock sector • Replace remote rod
Ignition switch cannot be adjusted correctly	• Remote rod deformed	• Repair, straighten or replace

Troubleshooting the Turn Signal Switch

Problem	Cause	Solution
Turn signal will not cancel	• Loose switch mounting screws • Switch or anchor bosses broken • Broken, missing or out of position detent, or cancelling spring	• Tighten screws • Replace switch • Reposition springs or replace switch as required
Turn signal difficult to operate	• Turn signal lever loose • Switch yoke broken or distorted • Loose or misplaced springs • Foreign parts and/or materials in switch • Switch mounted loosely	• Tighten mounting screws • Replace switch • Reposition springs or replace switch • Remove foreign parts and/or material • Tighten mounting screws
Turn signal will not indicate lane change	• Broken lane change pressure pad or spring hanger • Broken, missing or misplaced lane change spring • Jammed wires	• Replace switch • Replace or reposition as required • Loosen mounting screws, reposition wires and retighten screws

Troubleshooting the Turn Signal Switch (cont.)

Problem	Cause	Solution
Turn signal will not stay in turn position	• Foreign material or loose parts impeding movement of switch yoke • Defective switch	• Remove material and/or parts • Replace switch
Hazard switch cannot be pulled out	• Foreign material between hazard support cancelling leg and yoke	• Remove foreign material. No foreign material impeding function of hazard switch—replace turn signal switch.
No turn signal lights	• Inoperative turn signal flasher • Defective or blown fuse • Loose chassis to column harness connector • Disconnect column to chassis connector. Connect new switch to chassis and operate switch by hand. If vehicle lights now operate normally, signal switch is inoperative • If vehicle lights do not operate, check chassis wiring for opens, grounds, etc.	• Replace turn signal flasher • Replace fuse • Connect securely • Replace signal switch • Repair chassis wiring as required
Instrument panel turn indicator lights on but not flashing	• Burned out or damaged front or rear turn signal bulb • If vehicle lights do not operate, check light sockets for high resistance connections, the chassis wiring for opens, grounds, etc. • Inoperative flasher • Loose chassis to column harness connection • Inoperative turn signal switch • To determine if turn signal switch is defective, substitute new switch into circuit and operate switch by hand. If the vehicle's lights operate normally, signal switch is inoperative.	• Replace bulb • Repair chassis wiring as required • Replace flasher • Connect securely • Replace turn signal switch • Replace turn signal switch
Stop light not on when turn indicated	• Loose column to chassis connection • Disconnect column to chassis connector. Connect new switch into system without removing old.	• Connect securely • Replace signal switch

Troubleshooting the Turn Signal Switch (cont.)

Problem	Cause	Solution
Stop light not on when turn indicated (cont.)	Operate switch by hand. If brake lights work with switch in the turn position, signal switch is defective. • If brake lights do not work, check connector to stop light sockets for grounds, opens, etc.	 • Repair connector to stop light circuits using service manual as guide
Turn indicator panel lights not flashing	• Burned out bulbs • High resistance to ground at bulb socket • Opens, ground in wiring harness from front turn signal bulb socket to indicator lights	• Replace bulbs • Replace socket • Locate and repair as required
Turn signal lights flash very slowly	• High resistance ground at light sockets • Incorrect capacity turn signal flasher or bulb • If flashing rate is still extremely slow, check chassis wiring harness from the connector to light sockets for high resistance • Loose chassis to column harness connection • Disconnect column to chassis connector. Connect new switch into system without removing old. Operate switch by hand. If flashing occurs at normal rate, the signal switch is defective.	• Repair high resistance grounds at light sockets • Replace turn signal flasher or bulb • Locate and repair as required • Connect securely • Replace turn signal switch
Hazard signal lights will not flash—turn signal functions normally	• Blow fuse • Inoperative hazard warning flasher • Loose chassis-to-column harness connection • Disconnect column to chassis connector. Connect new switch into system without removing old. Depress the hazard warning lights. If they now work normally, turn signal switch is defective. • If lights do not flash, check wiring harness "K" lead for open between hazard flasher and connector. If open, fuse block is defective	• Replace fuse • Replace hazard warning flasher in fuse panel • Conect securely • Replace turn signal switch • Repair or replace brown wire or connector as required

Troubleshooting the Manual Steering Gear

Problem	Cause	Solution
Hard or erratic steering	• Incorrect tire pressure	• Inflate tires to recommended pressures
	• Insufficient or incorrect lubrication	• Lubricate as required (refer to Maintenance Section)
	• Suspension, or steering linkage parts damaged or misaligned	• Repair or replace parts as necessary
	• Improper front wheel alignment	• Adjust incorrect wheel alignment angles
	• Incorrect steering gear adjustment	• Adjust steering gear
	• Sagging springs	• Replace springs
Play or looseness in steering	• Steering wheel loose	• Inspect shaft spines and repair as necessary. Tighten attaching nut and stake in place.
	• Steering linkage or attaching parts loose or worn	• Tighten, adjust, or replace faulty components
	• Pitman arm loose	• Inspect shaft splines and repair as necessary. Tighten attaching nut and stake in place
	• Steering gear attaching bolts loose	• Tighten bolts
	• Loose or worn wheel bearings	• Adjust or replace bearings
	• Steering gear adjustment incorrect or parts badly worn	• Adjust gear or replace defective parts
Wheel shimmy or tramp	• Improper tire pressure	• Inflate tires to recommended pressures
	• Wheels, tires, or brake rotors out-of-balance or out-of-round	• Inspect and replace or balance parts
	• Inoperative, worn, or loose shock absorbers or mounting parts	• Repair or replace shocks or mountings
	• Loose or worn steering or suspension parts	• Tighten or replace as necessary
	• Loose or worn wheel bearings	• Adjust or replace bearings
	• Incorrect steering gear adjustments	• Adjust steering gear
	• Incorrect front wheel alignment	• Correct front wheel alignment
Tire wear	• Improper tire pressure	• Inflate tires to recommended pressures
	• Failure to rotate tires	• Rotate tires
	• Brakes grabbing	• Adjust or repair brakes
	• Incorrect front wheel alignment	• Align incorrect angles
	• Broken or damaged steering and suspension parts	• Repair or replace defective parts
	• Wheel runout	• Replace faulty wheel
	• Excessive speed on turns	• Make driver aware of conditions

Troubleshooting the Manual Steering Gear

Problem	Cause	Solution
Vehicle leads to one side	• Improper tire pressures	• Inflate tires to recommended pressures
	• Front tires with uneven tread depth, wear pattern, or different cord design (i.e., one bias ply and one belted or radial tire on front wheels)	• Install tires of same cord construction and reasonably even tread depth, design, and wear pattern
	• Incorrect front wheel alignment	• Align incorrect angles
	• Brakes dragging	• Adjust or repair brakes
	• Pulling due to uneven tire construction	• Replace faulty tire

Troubleshooting the Power Steering Gear

Problem	Cause	Solution
Hissing noise in steering gear	• There is some noise in all power steering systems. One of the most common is a hissing sound most evident at standstill parking. There is no relationship between this noise and performance of the steering. Hiss may be expected when steering wheel is at end of travel or when slowly turning at standstill.	• Slight hiss is normal and in no way affects steering. Do not replace valve unless hiss is extremely objectionable. A replacement valve will also exhibit slight noise and is not always a cure. Investigate clearance around flexible coupling rivets. Be sure steering shaft and gear are aligned so flexible coupling rotates in a flat plane and is not distorted as shaft rotates. Any metal-to-metal contacts through flexible coupling will transmit valve hiss into passenger compartment through the steering column.
Rattle or chuckle noise in steering gear	• Gear loose on frame	• Check gear-to-frame mounting screws.
	• Steering linkage looseness	• Check linkage pivot points for wear. Replace if necessary.
	• Pressure hose touching other parts of car	• Adjust hose position. Do not bend tubing by hand.
	• Loose pitman shaft over center adjustment **NOTE:** A slight rattle may occur on turns because of increased clearance off the "high point." This is normal and clearance must not be reduced below specified limits to eliminate this slight rattle.	• Adjust to specifications
	• Loose pitman arm	• Tighten pitman arm nut to specifications

Troubleshooting the Power Steering Gear (cont.)

Problem	Cause	Solution
Squawk noise in steering gear when turning or recovering from a turn	• Damper O-ring on valve spool cut	• Replace damper O-ring
Poor return of steering wheel to center	• Tires not properly inflated • Lack of lubrication in linkage and ball joints • Lower coupling flange rubbing against steering gear adjuster plug • Steering gear to column misalignment • Improper front wheel alignment • Steering linkage binding • Ball joints binding • Steering wheel rubbing against housing • Tight or frozen steering shaft bearings • Sticking or plugged valve spool • Steering gear adjustments over specifications • Kink in return hose	• Inflate to specified pressure • Lube linkage and ball joints • Loosen pinch bolt and assemble properly • Align steering column • Check and adjust as necessary • Replace pivots • Replace ball joints • Align housing • Replace bearings • Remove and clean or replace valve • Check adjustment with gear out of car. Adjust as required. • Replace hose
Car leads to one side or the other (keep in mind road condition and wind. Test car in both directions on flat road)	• Front end misaligned • Unbalanced steering gear valve **NOTE:** If this is cause, steering effort will be very light in direction of lead and normal or heavier in opposite direction	• Adjust to specifications • Replace valve
Momentary increase in effort when turning wheel fast to right or left	• Low oil level • Pump belt slipping • High internal leakage	• Add power steering fluid as required • Tighten or replace belt • Check pump pressure. (See pressure test)
Steering wheel surges or jerks when turning with engine running especially during parking	• Low oil level • Loose pump belt • Steering linkage hitting engine oil pan at full turn • Insufficient pump pressure • Pump flow control valve sticking	• Fill as required • Adjust tension to specification • Correct clearance • Check pump pressure. (See pressure test). Replace relief valve if defective. • Inspect for varnish or damage, replace if necessary

Troubleshooting the Power Steering Gear (cont.)

Problem	Cause	Solution
Excessive wheel kickback or loose steering	• Air in system	• Add oil to pump reservoir and bleed by operating steering. Check hose connectors for proper torque and adjust as required.
	• Steering gear loose on frame	• Tighten attaching screws to specified torque
	• Steering linkage joints worn enough to be loose	• Replace loose pivots
	• Worn poppet valve	• Replace poppet valve
	• Loose thrust bearing preload adjustment	• Adjust to specification with gear out of vehicle
	• Excessive overcenter lash	• Adjust to specification with gear out of car
Hard steering or lack of assist	• Loose pump belt	• Adjust belt tension to specification
	• Low oil level **NOTE:** Low oil level will also result in excessive pump noise	• Fill to proper level. If excessively low, check all lines and joints for evidence of external leakage. Tighten loose connectors.
	• Steering gear to column misalignment	• Align steering column
	• Lower coupling flange rubbing against steering gear adjuster plug	• Loosen pinch bolt and assemble properly
	• Tires not properly inflated	• Inflate to recommended pressure
Foamy milky power steering fluid, low fluid level and possible low pressure	• Air in the fluid, and loss of fluid due to internal pump leakage causing overflow	• Check for leak and correct. Bleed system. Extremely cold temperatures will cause system aeriation should the oil level be low. If oil level is correct and pump still foams, remove pump from vehicle and separate reservoir from housing. Check welsh plug and housing for cracks. If plug is loose or housing is cracked, replace housing.
Low pressure due to steering pump	• Flow control valve stuck or inoperative	• Remove burrs or dirt or replace. Flush system.
	• Pressure plate not flat against cam ring	• Correct
Low pressure due to steering gear	• Pressure loss in cylinder due to worn piston ring or badly worn housing bore	• Remove gear from car for disassembly and inspection of ring and housing bore
	• Leakage at valve rings, valve body-to-worn seal	• Remove gear from car for disassembly and replace seals

Troubleshooting the Power Steering Pump

Problem	Cause	Solution
Chirp noise in steering pump	• Loose belt	• Adjust belt tension to specification
Belt squeal (particularly noticeable at full wheel travel and stand still parking)	• Loose belt	• Adjust belt tension to specification
Growl noise in steering pump	• Excessive back pressure in hoses or steering gear caused by restriction	• Locate restriction and correct. Replace part if necessary.
Growl noise in steering pump (particularly noticeable at stand still parking)	• Scored pressure plates, thrust plate or rotor • Extreme wear of cam ring	• Replace parts and flush system • Replace parts
Groan noise in steering pump	• Low oil level • Air in the oil. Poor pressure hose connection.	• Fill reservoir to proper level • Tighten connector to specified torque. Bleed system by operating steering from right to left—full turn.
Rattle noise in steering pump	• Vanes not installed properly • Vanes sticking in rotor slots	• Install properly • Free up by removing burrs, varnish, or dirt
Swish noise in steering pump	• Defective flow control valve	• Replace part
Whine noise in steering pump	• Pump shaft bearing scored	• Replace housing and shaft. Flush system.
Hard steering or lack of assist	• Loose pump belt • Low oil level in reservoir **NOTE:** Low oil level will also result in excessive pump noise • Steering gear to column misalignment • Lower coupling flange rubbing against steering gear adjuster plug • Tires not properly inflated	• Adjust belt tension to specification • Fill to proper level. If excessively low, check all lines and joints for evidence of external leakage. Tighten loose connectors. • Align steering column • Loosen pinch bolt and assemble properly • Inflate to recommended pressure
Foaming milky power steering fluid, low fluid level and possible low pressure	• Air in the fluid, and loss of fluid due to internal pump leakage causing overflow	• Check for leaks and correct. Bleed system. Extremely cold temperatures will cause system aeriation should the oil level be low. If oil level is correct and pump still foams, remove pump from vehicle and separate reservoir from body. Check welsh plug and body for cracks. If plug is loose or body is cracked, replace body.

Troubleshooting the Power Steering Pump (cont.)

Problem	Cause	Solution
Low pump pressure	• Flow control valve stuck or inoperative • Pressure plate not flat against cam ring	• Remove burrs or dirt or replace. Flush system. • Correct
Momentary increase in effort when turning wheel fast to right or left	• Low oil level in pump • Pump belt slipping • High internal leakage	• Add power steering fluid as required • Tighten or replace belt • Check pump pressure. (See pressure test)
Steering wheel surges or jerks when turning with engine running especially during parking	• Low oil level • Loose pump belt • Steering linkage hitting engine oil pan at full turn • Insufficient pump pressure	• Fill as required • Adjust tension to specification • Correct clearance • Check pump pressure. (See pressure test). Replace flow control valve if defective.
Steering wheel surges or jerks when turning with engine running especially during parking (cont.)	• Sticking flow control valve	• Inspect for varnish or damage, replace if necessary
Excessive wheel kickback or loose steering	• Air in system	• Add oil to pump reservoir and bleed by operating steering. Check hose connectors for proper torque and adjust as required.
Low pump pressure	• Extreme wear of cam ring • Scored pressure plate, thrust plate, or rotor • Vanes not installed properly • Vanes sticking in rotor slots • Cracked or broken thrust or pressure plate	• Replace parts. Flush system. • Replace parts. Flush system. • Install properly • Freeup by removing burrs, varnish, or dirt • Replace part

Troubleshooting Basic Turn Signal and Flasher Problems

Most problems in the turn signals or flasher system can be reduced to defective flashers or bulbs, which are easily replaced. Occasionally, problems in the turn signals are traced to the switch in the steering column, which will require professional service.

F = Front   R = Rear   ● = Lights off   ○ = Lights on

Problem		Solution
Turn signals light, but do not flash	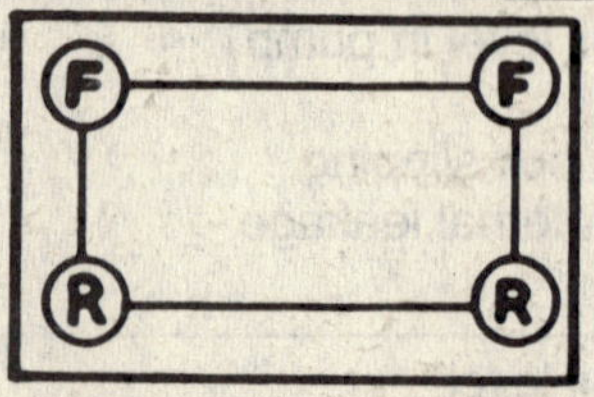 F F / R R (all lights on)	• Replace the flasher
No turn signals light on either side	 F F / R R (all lights off)	• Check the fuse. Replace if defective. • Check the flasher by substitution • Check for open circuit, short circuit or poor ground
Both turn signals on one side don't work	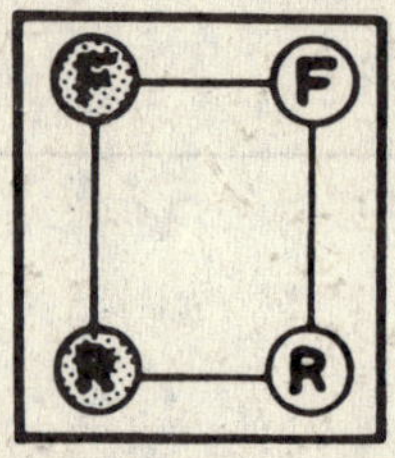 F F / R R (left side off)	• Check for bad bulbs • Check for bad ground in both housings
One turn signal light on one side doesn't work	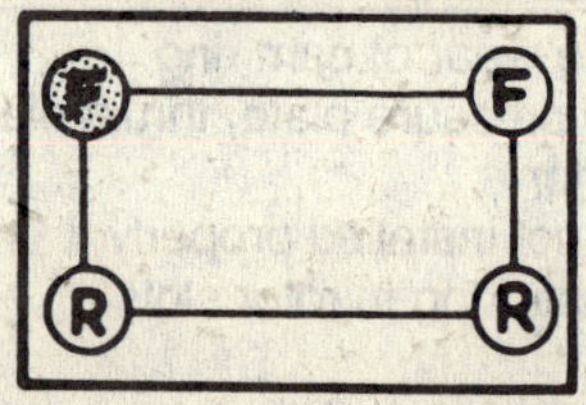 F F / R R (left front off)	• Check and/or replace bulb • Check for corrosion in socket. Clean contacts. • Check for poor ground at socket
Turn signal flashes too fast or too slow	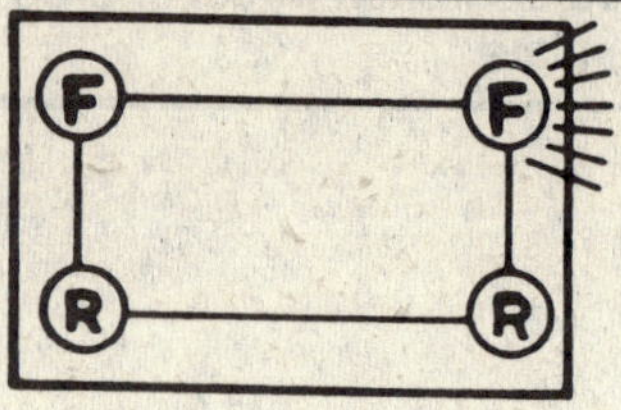 F F / R R	• Check any bulb on the side flashing too fast. A heavy-duty bulb is probably installed in place of a regular bulb. • Check the bulb flashing too slow. A standard bulb was probably installed in place of a heavy-duty bulb. • Check for loose connections or corrosion at the bulb socket
Indicator lights don't work in either direction		• Check if the turn signals are working • Check the dash indicator lights • Check the flasher by substitution

9 Brakes

QUICK REFERENCE INDEX

GENERAL INDEX

Troubleshooting the Brake System

Problem	Cause	Solution
Low brake pedal (excessive pedal travel required for braking action.)	• Excessive clearance between rear linings and drums caused by inoperative automatic adjusters	• Make 10 to 15 alternate forward and reverse brake stops to adjust brakes. If brake pedal does not come up, repair or replace adjuster parts as necessary.
	• Worn rear brakelining	• Inspect and replace lining if worn beyond minimum thickness specification
	• Bent, distorted brakeshoes, front or rear	• Replace brakeshoes in axle sets
	• Air in hydraulic system	• Remove air from system. Refer to Brake Bleeding.
Low brake pedal (pedal may go to floor with steady pressure applied.)	• Fluid leak in hydraulic system	• Fill master cylinder to fill line; have helper apply brakes and check calipers, wheel cylinders, differential valve tubes, hoses and fittings for leaks. Repair or replace as necessary.
	• Air in hydraulic system	• Remove air from system. Refer to Brake Bleeding.
	• Incorrect or non-recommended brake fluid (fluid evaporates at below normal temp).	• Flush hydraulic system with clean brake fluid. Refill with correct-type fluid.
	• Master cylinder piston seals worn, or master cylinder bore is scored, worn or corroded	• Repair or replace master cylinder
Low brake pedal (pedal goes to floor on first application—o.k. on subsequent applications.)	• Disc brake pads sticking on abutment surfaces of anchor plate. Caused by a build-up of dirt, rust, or corrosion on abutment surfaces	• Clean abutment surfaces
Fading brake pedal (pedal height decreases with steady pressure applied.)	• Fluid leak in hydraulic system	• Fill master cylinder reservoirs to fill mark, have helper apply brakes, check calipers, wheel cylinders, differential valve, tubes, hoses, and fittings for fluid leaks. Repair or replace parts as necessary.
	• Master cylinder piston seals worn, or master cylinder bore is scored, worn or corroded	• Repair or replace master cylinder

Troubleshooting the Brake System (cont.)

Problem	Cause	Solution
Decreasing brake pedal travel (pedal travel required for braking action decreases and may be accompanied by a hard pedal.)	• Caliper or wheel cylinder pistons sticking or seized	• Repair or replace the calipers, or wheel cylinders
	• Master cylinder compensator ports blocked (preventing fluid return to reservoirs) or pistons sticking or seized in master cylinder bore	• Repair or replace the master cylinder
	• Power brake unit binding internally	• Test unit according to the following procedure: (a) Shift transmission into neutral and start engine (b) Increase engine speed to 1500 rpm, close throttle and fully depress brake pedal (c) Slow release brake pedal and stop engine (d) Have helper remove vacuum check valve and hose from power unit. Observe for backward movement of brake pedal. (e) If the pedal moves backward, the power unit has an internal bind—replace power unit
Grabbing brakes (severe reaction to brake pedal pressure.)	• Brakelining(s) contaminated by grease or brake fluid	• Determine and correct cause of contamination and replace brakeshoes in axle sets
	• Parking brake cables incorrectly adjusted or seized	• Adjust cables. Replace seized cables.
	• Incorrect brakelining or lining loose on brakeshoes	• Replace brakeshoes in axle sets
	• Caliper anchor plate bolts loose	• Tighten bolts
	• Rear brakeshoes binding on support plate ledges	• Clean and lubricate ledges. Replace support plate(s) if ledges are deeply grooved. Do not attempt to smooth ledges by grinding.
	• Incorrect or missing power brake reaction disc	• Install correct disc
	• Rear brake support plates loose	• Tighten mounting bolts
Spongy brake pedal (pedal has abnormally soft, springy, spongy feel when depressed.)	• Air in hydraulic system	• Remove air from system. Refer to Brake Bleeding.
	• Brakeshoes bent or distorted	• Replace brakeshoes
	• Brakelining not yet seated with drums and rotors	• Burnish brakes
	• Rear drum brakes not properly adjusted	• Adjust brakes

Troubleshooting the Brake System (cont.)

Problem	Cause	Solution
Hard brake pedal (excessive pedal pressure required to stop vehicle. May be accompanied by brake fade.)	• Loose or leaking power brake unit vacuum hose	• Tighten connections or replace leaking hose
	• Incorrect or poor quality brake-lining	• Replace with lining in axle sets
	• Bent, broken, distorted brakeshoes	• Replace brakeshoes
	• Calipers binding or dragging on mounting pins. Rear brakeshoes dragging on support plate.	• Replace mounting pins and bushings. Clean rust or burrs from rear brake support plate ledges and lubricate ledges with molydisulfide grease. **NOTE:** If ledges are deeply grooved or scored, do not attempt to sand or grind them smooth—replace support plate.
	• Caliper, wheel cylinder, or master cylinder pistons sticking or seized	• Repair or replace parts as necessary
	• Power brake unit vacuum check valve malfunction	• Test valve according to the following procedure: (a) Start engine, increase engine speed to 1500 rpm, close throttle and immediately stop engine (b) Wait at least 90 seconds then depress brake pedal (c) If brakes are not vacuum assisted for 2 or more applications, check valve is faulty
	• Power brake unit has internal bind	• Test unit according to the following procedure: (a) With engine stopped, apply brakes several times to exhaust all vacuum in system (b) Shift transmission into neutral, depress brake pedal and start engine (c) If pedal height decreases with foot pressure and less pressure is required to hold pedal in applied position, power unit vacuum system is operating normally. Test power unit. If power unit exhibits a bind condition, replace the power unit.

Troubleshooting the Brake System (cont.)

Problem	Cause	Solution
Hard brake pedal (excessive pedal pressure required to stop vehicle. May be accompanied by brake fade.)	• Master cylinder compensator ports (at bottom of reservoirs) blocked by dirt, scale, rust, or have small burrs (blocked ports prevent fluid return to reservoirs).	• Repair or replace master cylinder **CAUTION:** Do not attempt to clean blocked ports with wire, pencils, or similar implements. Use compressed air only.
	• Brake hoses, tubes, fittings clogged or restricted	• Use compressed air to check or unclog parts. Replace any damaged parts.
	• Brake fluid contaminated with improper fluids (motor oil, transmission fluid, causing rubber components to swell and stick in bores	• Replace all rubber components, combination valve and hoses. Flush entire brake system with DOT 3 brake fluid or equivalent.
	• Low engine vacuum	• Adjust or repair engine
Dragging brakes (slow or incomplete release of brakes)	• Brake pedal binding at pivot	• Loosen and lubricate
	• Power brake unit has internal bind	• Inspect for internal bind. Replace unit if internal bind exists.
	• Parking brake cables incorrrectly adjusted or seized	• Adjust cables. Replace seized cables.
	• Rear brakeshoe return springs weak or broken	• Replace return springs. Replace brakeshoe if necessary in axle sets.
	• Automatic adjusters malfunctioning	• Repair or replace adjuster parts as required
	• Caliper, wheel cylinder or master cylinder pistons sticking or seized	• Repair or replace parts as necessary
	• Master cylinder compensating ports blocked (fluid does not return to reservoirs).	• Use compressed air to clear ports. Do not use wire, pencils, or similar objects to open blocked ports.
Vehicle moves to one side when brakes are applied	• Incorrect front tire pressure	• Inflate to recommended cold (reduced load) inflation pressure
	• Worn or damaged wheel bearings	• Replace worn or damaged bearings
	• Brakelining on one side contaminated	• Determine and correct cause of contamination and replace brakelining in axle sets
	• Brakeshoes on one side bent, distorted, or lining loose on shoe	• Replace brakeshoes in axle sets
	• Support plate bent or loose on one side	• Tighten or replace support plate
	• Brakelining not yet seated with drums or rotors	• Burnish brakelining
	• Caliper anchor plate loose on one side	• Tighten anchor plate bolts
	• Caliper piston sticking or seized	• Repair or replace caliper
	• Brakelinings water soaked	• Drive vehicle with brakes lightly applied to dry linings
	• Loose suspension component attaching or mounting bolts	• Tighten suspension bolts. Replace worn suspension components.
	• Brake combination valve failure	• Replace combination valve

Troubleshooting the Brake System (cont.)

Problem	Cause	Solution
Chatter or shudder when brakes are applied (pedal pulsation and roughness may also occur.)	• Brakeshoes distorted, bent, contaminated, or worn	• Replace brakeshoes in axle sets
	• Caliper anchor plate or support plate loose	• Tighten mounting bolts
	• Excessive thickness variation of rotor(s)	• Refinish or replace rotors in axle sets
Noisy brakes (squealing, clicking, scraping sound when brakes are applied.)	• Bent, broken, distorted brakeshoes	• Replace brakeshoes in axle sets
	• Excessive rust on outer edge of rotor braking surface	• Remove rust
Noisy brakes (squealing, clicking, scraping sound when brakes are applied.) (cont.)	• Brakelining worn out—shoes contacting drum of rotor	• Replace brakeshoes and lining in axle sets. Refinish or replace drums or rotors.
	• Broken or loose holdown or return springs	• Replace parts as necessary
	• Rough or dry drum brake support plate ledges	• Lubricate support plate ledges
	• Cracked, grooved, or scored rotor(s) or drum(s)	• Replace rotor(s) or drum(s). Replace brakeshoes and lining in axle sets if necessary.
	• Incorrect brakelining and/or shoes (front or rear).	• Install specified shoe and lining assemblies
Pulsating brake pedal	• Out of round drums or excessive lateral runout in disc brake rotor(s)	• Refinish or replace drums, re-index rotors or replace

BRAKE SYSTEM

The trucks are equipped with independent front and rear brake systems. The systems consist of a power booster, a master cylinder, a combination valve, front disc and rear drum assemblies.

The master cylinder, mounted on the left firewall or power booster, consists of two fluid reservoirs, a primary (rear) cylinder, a secondary (front) cylinder and springs. The reservoirs, being independent of one another, are contained within the same housing; fluid cannot pass from one to the other. The rear reservoir supplies fluid to the front brakes while the front reservoir supplies fluid to the rear brakes.

During operation, fluid drains from the reservoirs to the master cylinder. When the brake pedal is applied, fluid from the master cylinder is sent to the combination valve (mounted on a bracket, directly under the master cylinder), here it is monitored and proportionally distributed to the front or rear brake systems. Should a loss of pressure occur in one system, the other system will provide enough braking pressure to stop the vehicle. Also, should a loss of pressure in one system occur, the differential warning switch (located on the combination valve) will turn ON the brake warning light (located on the dash board).

As the fluid enters each brake caliper or wheel cylinder, the pistons are forced outward. The outward movement of the pistons force the brake pads against a round flat disc or the brake shoes against a round metal drum. The brake lining attached to the pads or shoes comes in contact with the revolving disc or drum, causing friction, which brings the wheel to a stop.

In time, the brake linings wear down. If not replaced, their metal support plates (bonded type) or rivet heads (riveted type) will come in contact with the disc or drum; damage to the disc or drum will occur. Never use brake pads or shoes with a lining thickness less than $\frac{1}{32}$ in. (0.8mm).

Most manufacturers provide a wear sensor, a piece of spring steel, attached to the rear edge of the inner brake pad. When the pad wears to the replacement thickness, the sensor will contact the disc and produce a high pitched squeal.

Adjustments

FRONT DISC BRAKES

Disc brakes are not adjustable. They are, in effect, self adjusting.

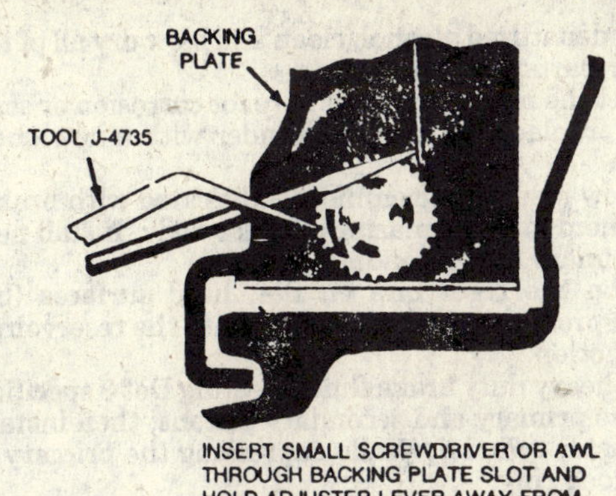

Adjusting the rear brake by turning the star wheel

ADJUSTMENT OF REAR BRAKES

Normal adjustments of the rear drum brakes are automatic and are made during the reverse applications of the brakes. ONLY, if the lining has been renewed, should the following procedure be performed.

NOTE: The following procedure requires the use of the GM Brake Adjustment tool No. J-4735 or equivalent.

1. Raise and safely support the rear of the vehicle on jackstands.
2. Using a punch and a hammer, at the rear of the backing plate, knock out the lanced metal area near the starwheel assembly.

NOTE: When knocking out the lanced metal area from the backing plate, the wheels must be removed and all of the metal pieces discarded.

3. Using the GM Brake Adjustment tool No. J-4735 or equivalent, insert it into the slot and engage the lowest possible tooth on the starwheel. Move the end of the brake tool downward to move the starwheel upward and expand the adjusting screw. Repeat this operation until the brakes just lock the wheel.
4. Insert a small screwdriver or piece of firm wire (coathanger wire) into the adjusting slot and push the automatic adjuster lever out and free of the starwheel on the adjusting screw.
5. While holding the adjusting lever out of the way, engage the topmost tooth possible on the starwheel (with the brake tool). Move the end of the adjusting tool upward to move the adjusting screw starwheel downward and contact the adjusting screw. Back off the adjusting screw starwheel until the wheel spins freely with a minimum of drag. Keep track of the number of turns the starwheel is backed off.
6. Repeat this operation for the other side. When backing off the brakes on the other side, the adjusting lever must be backed off the same number of turns to prevent side-to-side brake pull.

NOTE: Backing off the starwheel 12 notches (clicks) is usually enough to eliminate brake drag.

7. Repeat this operation on the other side of the rear brake system.
8. After the brakes are adjusted, install a rubber hole cover into the backing plate slot. To complete the brake adjustment operation, make several stops while backing the truck to equalize the adjustment.
9. Road test the vehicle.

BRAKE PEDAL TRAVEL

The brake pedal travel is the distance the pedal moves toward the floor from the fully released position. Inspection should be made with 100 lbs. pressure on the brake pedal, when the brake system is Cold. The brake pedal travel should be 4¾ in. (120mm) for manual, or 2½ in. (61mm) for power.

NOTE: If equipped with power brakes, be sure to pump the brake pedal at least 3 times with the engine Off, before making the brake pedal check.

1. From under the dash, remove the pushrod-to-pedal clevis pin and separate the pushrod from the brake pedal.
2. Loosen the pushrod adjuster lock nut, then adjust the pushrod.
3. After the correct travel is established, reverse the removal procedure.

Brake Light Switch

REMOVAL AND INSTALLATION

1. Disconnect the negative battery cable from the battery.
2. Disconnect the electrical connector from the brake light switch.
3. Turn the brake light switch retainer (to align the key with the bracket slot), then remove the switch with the retainer.
4. To install, reverse the removal procedures. Adjust the brake light switch.

ADJUSTMENT

1. Depress the brake pedal and press the brake light switch inward until it seats firmly against the clip.

NOTE: As the switch is being pushed into the clip, audible clicks can be heard.

2. Release the brake pedal, then pull it back against the pedal stop until the audible click can no longer be heard.
3. The brake light switch will operate when the pedal is depressed 0.53 in. (13mm) from the fully released position.

Master Cylinder

REMOVAL AND INSTALLATION

1. Apply the parking brakes and block the wheels.

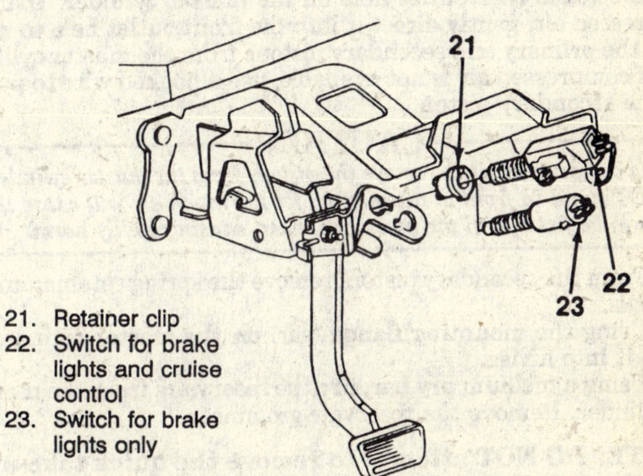

Installing and adjusting the brake light switch

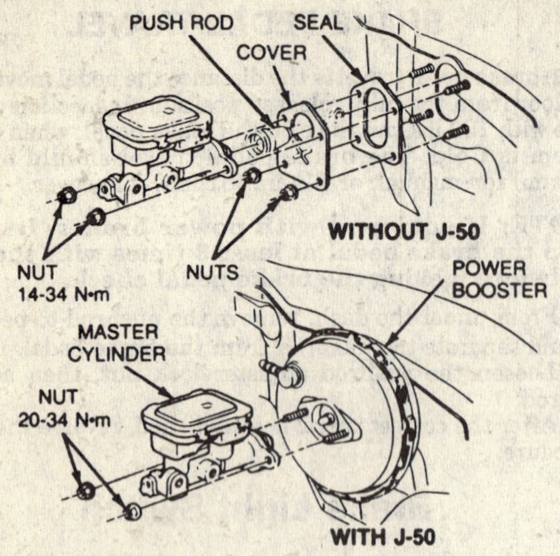

Master cylinder mounting with standard and power brakes

2. Use a line wrench to disconnect and plug the hydraulic lines from the master cylinder.
3. If equipped with a manual brake system, disconnect the pushrod from the brake pedal.
4. Remove the master cylinder-to-bracket (manual) or vacuum booster (power) nuts, then separate the combination valve/bracket from the master cylinder.
5. Remove the master cylinder, the gasket and the rubber boot from the vehicle.
6. To install, bench bleed the master cylinder and reverse the removal procedures. Torque the master cylinder mounting nuts to 20 ft. lbs.
7. Refill the master cylinder with clean brake fluid, bleed the brake system and check the brake pedal travel.

NOTE: If equipped with manual brakes, be sure to reconnect the pushrod to the brake pedal.

OVERHAUL

1. Refer to the "Master Cylinder, Removal and Installation" procedures in this section and remove the master cylinder from the vehicle.
2. At the rear of the master cylinder, depress the primary piston and remove the lock ring.
3. Block the rear outlet hole on the master cylinder. Using compressed air, gently direct it into the front outlet hole to remove the primary and secondary pistons from the master cylinder. If compressed air is not available, use a hooked wire to pull out the secondary piston.

CAUTION

If using compressed air to remove the pistons from the master cylinder, DO NOT stand in front of the pistons, for too much air will cause the pistons to be fired from the master cylinder, causing bodily harm.

4. From the secondary piston, remove the spring retainer and the seals.
5. Using the mounting flange (ear) on the master cylinder, clamp it into a vise.
6. Using a medium pry bar, pry the reservoirs from the master cylinder. Remove the reservoir grommets.

NOTE: DO NOT attempt to remove the quick take-up valve from the master cylinder body; the valve is not serviceable separately.

7. Using denatured alcohol, clean and blow dry all of the master cylinder parts.
8. Inspect the master cylinder bore for corrosion or scratches; if damaged, replace the master cylinder with a new one.

To install:

9. Use new reservoir grommets (lubricated with brake fluid) and press them into the master cylinder body. Install new seals onto the primary and secondary pistons.
10. Position the reservoirs on flat, hard surfaces (block of wood), then press the master cylinder onto the reservoirs, using a rocking motion.
11. Using heavy duty brake fluid, meeting Dot 3 specifications, lubricate the primary and secondary pistons, then install them into the master cylinder. While depressing the primary piston, install the lock ring.
12. Install new diaphragms onto the reservoir covers.
13. Install the master cylinder on the vehicle, fill with new brake fluid and bleed the brakes.

Power Brake Booster

The power brake booster is a tandem vacuum suspended unit, equipped with a single or dual function vacuum switch that activates a brake warning light should low booster vacuum be present. Under normal operation, vacuum is present on both sides of the diaphragms. When the brakes are applied, atmospheric air is admitted to one side of the diaphragms to provide power assistance.

REMOVAL AND INSTALLATION

1. Apply the parking brake and block the wheels.
2. Remove the master cylinder-to-power brake booster nuts and move the master cylinder out of the way; if necessary, support the master cylinder on a wire.

NOTE: When removing the master cylinder from the power brake booster, it is not necessary to disconnect the hydraulic lines.

3. Disconnect the vacuum hose from the power brake booster.
4. From under the dash, disconnect the pushrod from the brake pedal.
5. From under the dash, remove the power brake booster-to-cowl nuts.
6. From the engine compartment, remove the power brake booster and the gasket from the vehicle.
7. To install, use a new gaskets and reverse the removal procedures. Torque the power brake booster-to-cowl nuts to 15 ft. lbs. and the master cylinder-to-power brake booster nuts to 20 ft. lbs. Start the engine and check the brake system operation.

Combination Valve

The combination valve is located in the engine compartment, directly under the master cylinder. It consists of three sections: the metering valve, the warning switch and the proportioning valve.

The metering section limits the pressure to the front disc brakes until a predetermined front input pressure is reached, enough to overcome the rear shoe retractor springs. Under 3 psi, there is no restriction of the inlet pressures; the pressures are allowed to equalize during the no brake period.

The proportioning section controls the outlet pressure to the rear brakes after a predetermined rear input pressure has been reached; this feature is provided for vehicles with light loads, to help prevent rear wheel lock-up. The by-pass feature of this valve assures full system pressure to the rear brakes in the event of a front brake system malfunction. Also, full front pressure is retained if the rear system malfunctions.

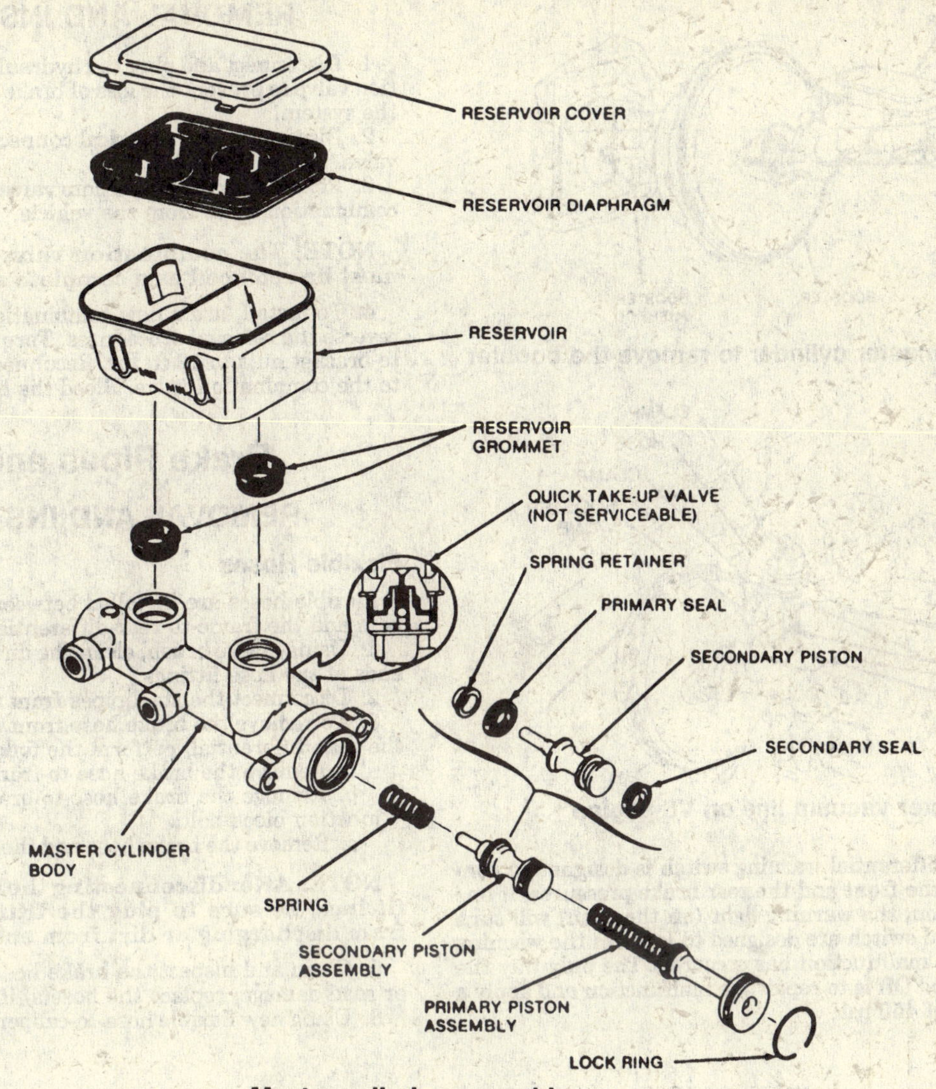

Master cylinder assembly

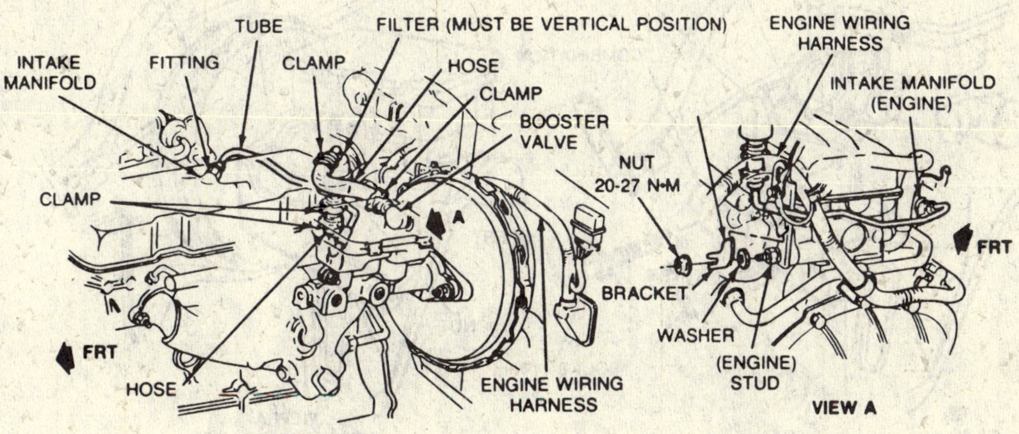

Booster vacuum lines on 4-cylinder engine

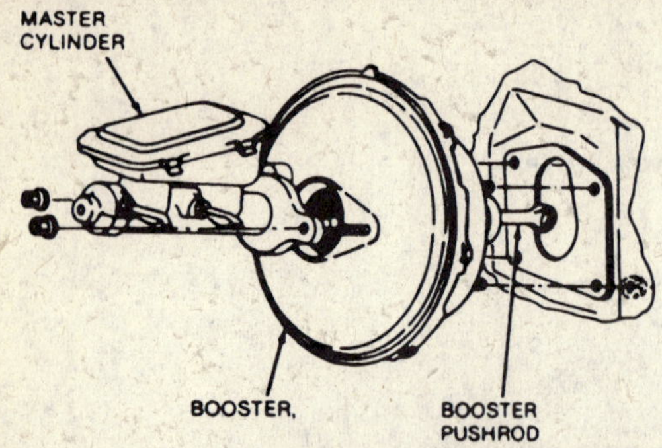

Remove the master cylinder to remove the booster

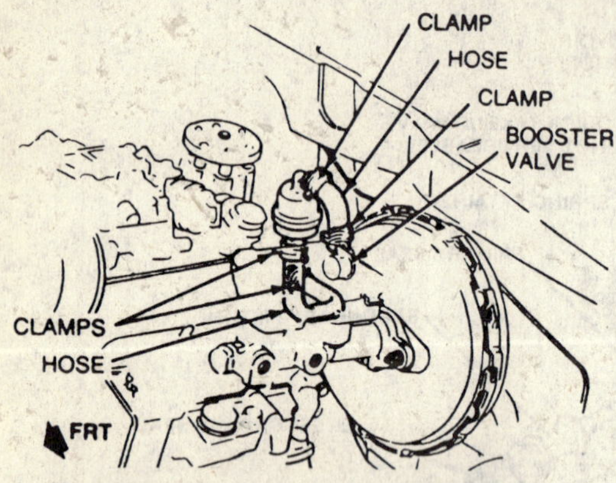

Booster vacuum line on V6 engine

The pressure differential warning switch is designed to constantly compare the front and the rear brake pressures; if one should malfunction, the warning light (on the dash) will turn On. The valve and switch are designed to lock On the warning position once the malfunction has occurred. The only way the light can be turned Off is to repair the malfunction and apply a brake line force of 450 psi.

REMOVAL AND INSTALLATION

1. Disconnect and plug the hydraulic lines from the combination valve to prevent the loss of brake fluid or dirt from entering the system.
2. Disconnect the electrical connector from the combination valve.
3. Remove the combination valve-to-bracket nuts and the combination valve from the vehicle.

NOTE: The combination valve is not repairable and must be replaced as a complete assembly.

4. To install, use a new combination valve (if defective) and reverse the removal procedures. Torque the combination valve-to-bracket nuts to 12 ft. lbs. Reconnect the electrical connector to the combination valve. Bleed the brake system.

Brake Pipes and Hoses

REMOVAL AND INSTALLATION

Flexible Hoses

Flexible hoses are installed between the frame-to-front calipers and the frame-to-rear differential.

1. Using a wire brush, clean the dirt and/or grease from both ends of the hose fittings.
2. Disconnect the steel pipes from the flexible hose.
3. To remove the brake hose from the front brake caliper or the rear differential, perform the following procedures:
   a. Remove the brake hose-to-frame bracket retaining clip.
   b. Remove the brake hose-to-brake caliper or differential junction block bolt.
   c. Remove the brake hose and the gaskets from the vehicle.

NOTE: After disconnecting the brake hose(s) from the fittings, be sure to plug the fittings to keep the fluid from discharging or dirt from entering the system.

5. Clean and inspect the brake hose(s) for cracking, chafing or road damage; replace the hose(s) if any signs are observed.
6. Using new flexible hose-to-caliper gaskets, install the flexi-

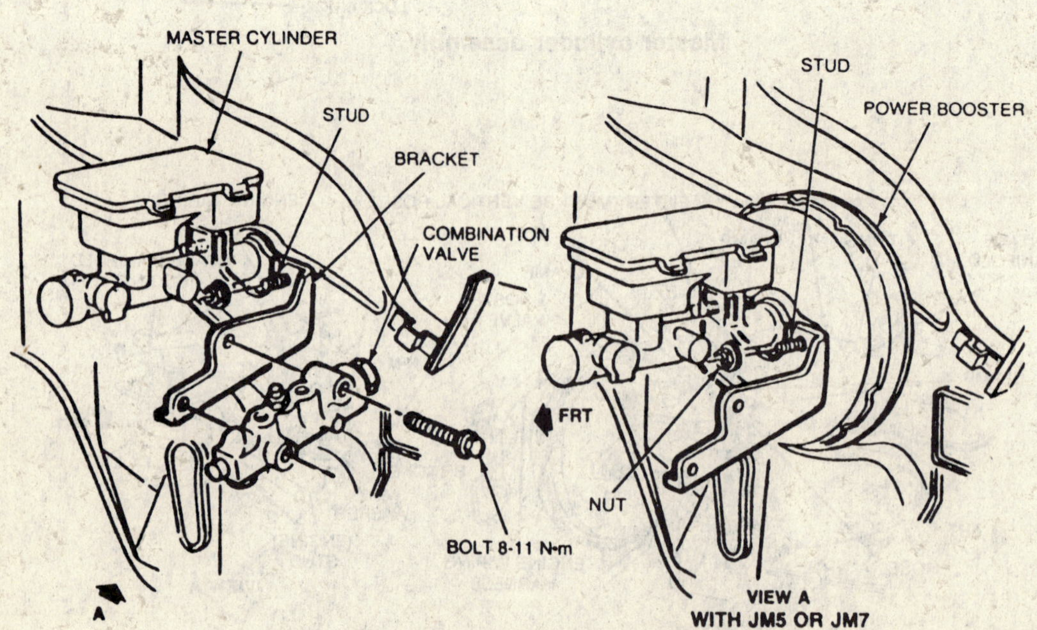

Removing combination valve

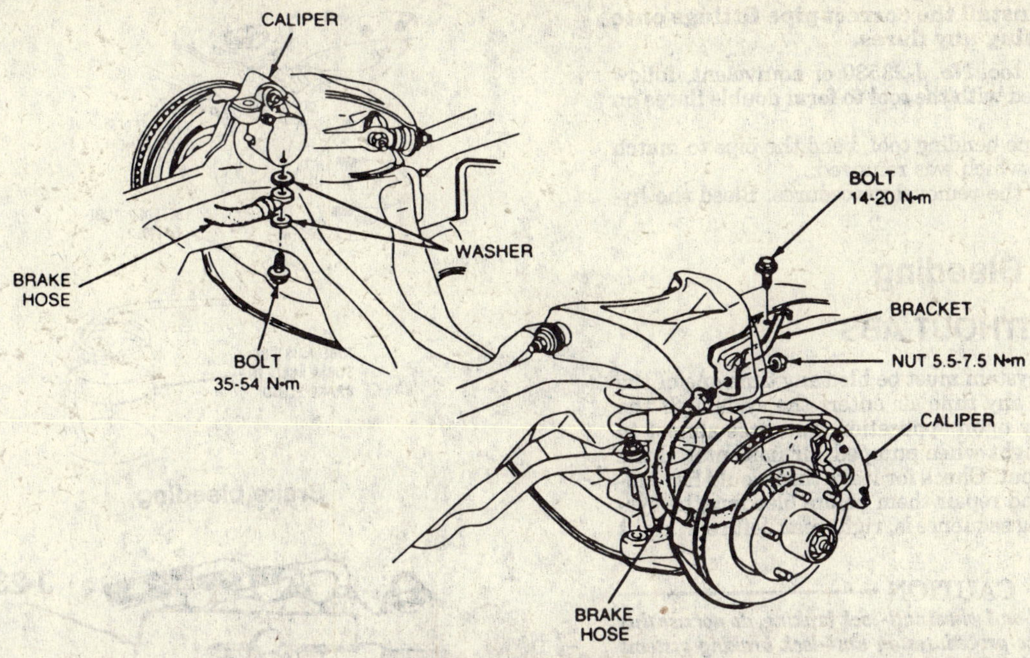

Front brake hose removal, 4WD

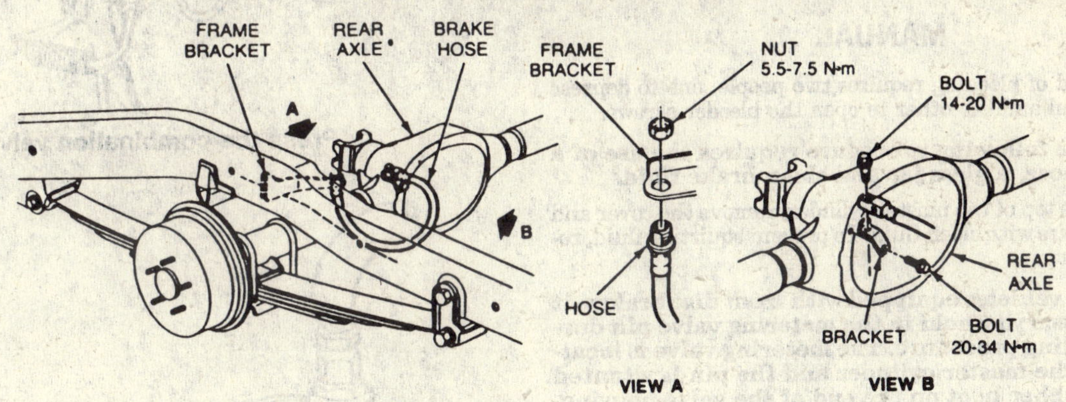

Rear brake line removal

ble hose(s) and reverse the removal procedures. Torque the flexible hose(s)-to-front caliper bolt(s) to 32 ft. lbs. and all other brake pipe fittings to 13 ft. lbs. Bleed the brake system.

NOTE: Be sure that the hoses do not make contact with any of the suspension components.

Steel Pipes

When replacing the steel brake pipes, always use steel piping which is designed to withstand high pressure, resist corrosion and is of the same size.

CAUTION

Never use copper tubing, for it is subject to fatigue, cracking, and/or corrosion, which will result in brake line failure.

NOTE: The following procedure requires the use of the GM Tube Cutter tool No. J-23533 or equivalent, and the GM Flaring tool No. J-23530 or equivalent.

1. Disconnect the steel brake pipe(s) from the flexible hose connections or the rear wheel cylinders; be sure to remove any retaining clips.

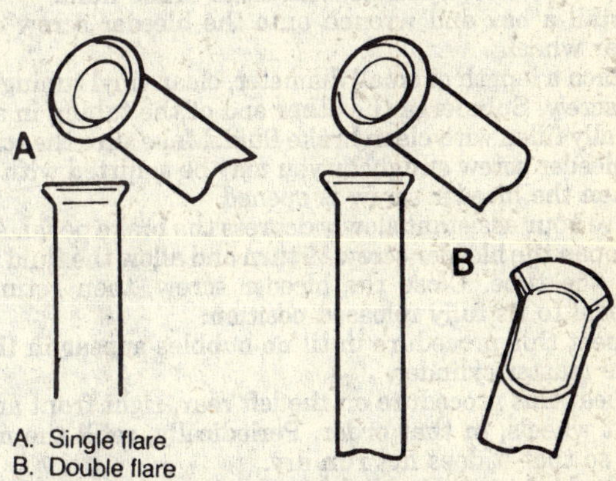

Single flare (A) and double flare (B) tubing ends

2. Remove the steel brake pipe from the vehicle.
3. Using new steel pipe (same size) and the GM Tube Cutter tool No. J-23533 or equivalent, cut the pipe to length; be sure to add ⅛ in. (3mm) for each flare.

NOTE: Be sure to install the correct pipe fittings onto the tube before forming any flares.

4. Using the Flaring tool No. J-23530 or equivalent, follow the instructions equipped with the tool to form double flares on the ends of the pipes.
5. Using the small pipe bending tool, bend the pipe to match the contour of the pipe which was removed.
6. To install, reverse the removal procedures. Bleed the hydraulic system.

Bleeding

WITHOUT ABS

The hydraulic brake system must be bled any time one of the lines is disconnected or any time air enters the system. If the brake pedal feels spongy upon application, and goes almost to the floor but regains height when pumped, air has entered the system. It must be bled out. Check for leaks that would have allowed the entry of air and repair them before bleeding the system. The correct bleeding sequence is; right rear, left rear, right front and left front.

CAUTION

If the vehicle has rear wheel or 4 wheel anti–lock braking, do not use this procedure. Improper service procedures on anti–lock braking systems can cause serious personal injury. Refer to the ABS service procedures.

MANUAL

This method of bleeding requires two people, one to depress the brake pedal and the other to open the bleeder screws.

NOTE: The following procedure requires the use of a clear vinyl hose, a glass jar and clean brake fluid.

1. Clean the top of the master cylinder, remove the cover and fill the reservoirs with clean fluid. To prevent squirting fluid, replace the cover.

NOTE: On vehicles equipped with front disc brakes, it will be necessary to hold in the metering valve pin during the bleeding procedure. The metering valve is located beneath the master cylinder and the pin is situated under the rubber boot on the end of the valve housing. This may be tapped in or held by an assistant.

2. Fill the master cylinder with clean brake fluid.
3. Install a box end wrench onto the bleeder screw on the right rear wheel.
4. Attach a length of small diameter, clear vinyl tubing to the bleeder screw. Submerge the other end of the tubing in a glass jar partially filled with clean brake fluid. Make sure the tube fits on the bleeder screw snugly or you may be squirted with brake fluid when the bleeder screw is opened.
5. Have your assistant slowly depress the brake pedal. As this is done, open the bleeder screw ½ turn and allow the fluid to run through the tube. Close the bleeder screw, then return the brake pedal to its fully released position.
6. Repeat this procedure until no bubbles appear in the jar. Refill the master cylinder.
7. Repeat this procedure on the left rear, right front and the left front wheels, in that order. Periodically, refill the master cylinder so that it does not run dry.
8. If the brake warning light is On, depress the brake pedal firmly. If there is no air in the system, the dash light will turn Off.

PRESSURE

NOTE: The following procedure requires the use of

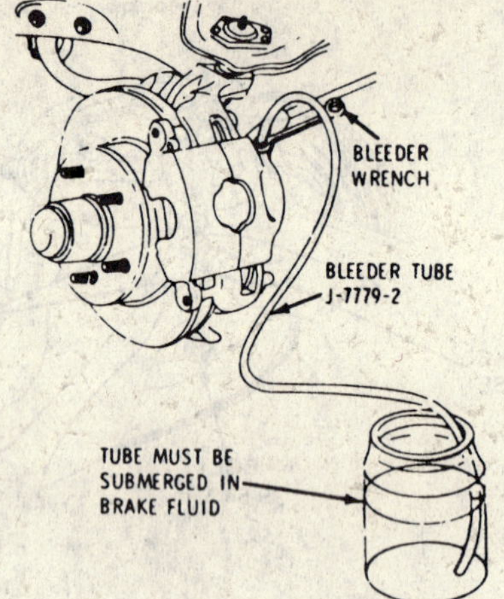

Brake bleeding

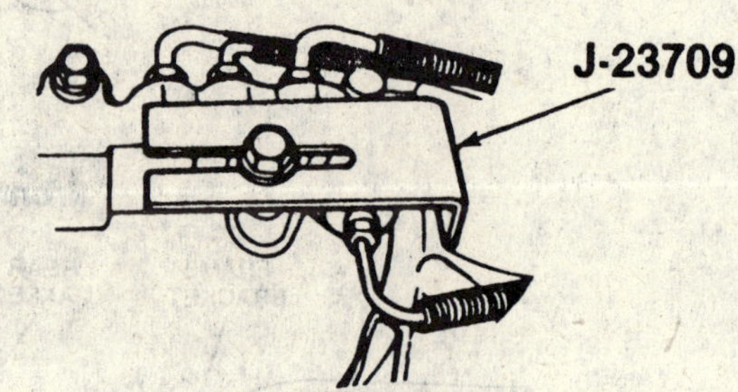

Press the combination valve

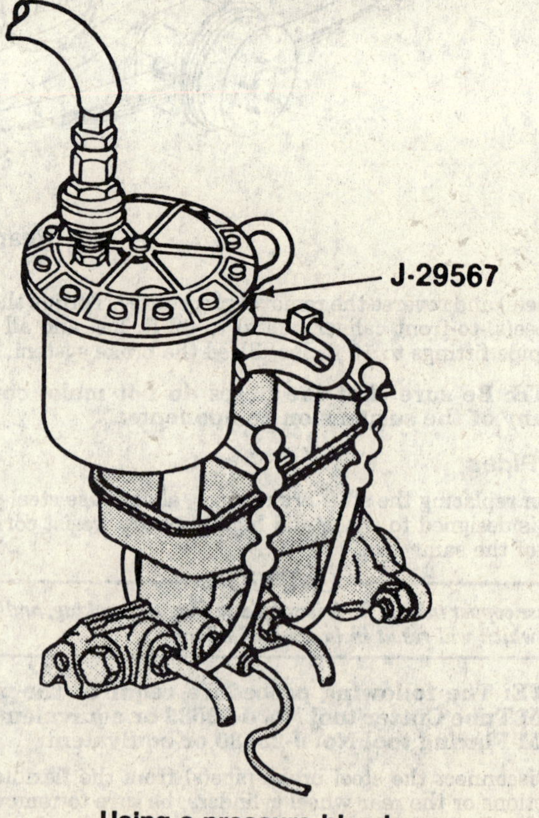

Using a pressure bleeder

the GM Brake Bleeder Adapter tool No. J-29567 or equivalent, and the GM Combination Valve Depressor tool No. J-23709 or equivalent.

1. Using the GM Brake Bleeder Adapter tool No. J-29567 or equivalent, fill the pressure tank to at least ⅓ full of brake fluid. Using compressed air, charge the pressure tank to 20–25 psi., then install it onto the master cylinder.
2. Using the GM Combination Valve Depressor tool No. J-35856 or equivalent, install it onto the combination valve to hold the valve open during the bleeding operation.
3. Bleed each wheel cylinder or caliper in the following sequence: right rear, left rear, right front and left front.
4. Connect a hose from the bleeder tank to the adapter at the master cylinder, then open the tank valve.
5. Attach a clear vinyl hose to the brake bleeder screw, then immerse the opposite end into a container partially filled with clean brake fluid.
6. Open the bleeder screw ¾ turn and allow the fluid to flow until no air bubbles are seen in the fluid, then close the bleeder screw.
7. Repeat the bleeding process to each wheel.
8. Inspect the brake pedal for sponginess and if necessary, repeat the entire bleeding procedure.
9. Remove the depressor tool from the combination valve and the bleeder adapter from the master cylinder.
10. Refill the master cylinder to the proper level with brake fluid.

FRONT DISC BRAKES

CAUTION

Brake shoes contain asbestos, which has been determined to be a cancer causing agent. Never clean the brake surfaces with compressed air! Avoid inhaling any dust from any brake surface! When cleaning brake surfaces, use a commercially available brake cleaning fluid.

Brake Pads

INSPECTION

Brake pads should be inspected once a year or at 7,500 miles, which ever occurs first. Check both ends of the outboard shoe, looking in at each end of the caliper; then check the lining thickness on the inboard shoe, looking down through the inspection hole. The lining should be more than 0.032 in. (0.8mm) thick above the rivet (so that the lining is thicker than the metal backing). Keep in mind that any applicable state inspection standards that are more stringent, take precedence. All four pads must be replaced if one shows excessive wear.

NOTE: All models have a wear indicator that makes a noise when the linings wear to a degree where replacement is necessary. The spring clip is an integral part of the inboard shoe and lining. When the brake pad reaches a certain degree of wear, the clip will contact the rotor and produce a warning noise.

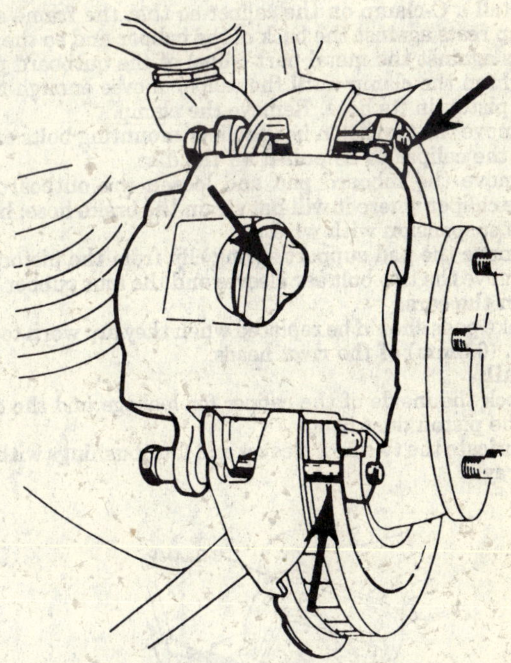

Inspecting front brake pads

REMOVAL AND INSTALLATION

NOTE The following procedure requires the use of a C-clamp and adjustable pliers.

1. If the fluid reservoir is full, siphon off about ⅔ of the brake fluid from the master cylinder reservoirs.

CAUTION

The insertion of thicker replacement pads will push the piston back into its bore and will cause a full master cylinder reservoir to overflow, possibly causing paint damage. In addition to siphoning off fluid, it would be wise to keep the reservoir cover on during pad replacement.

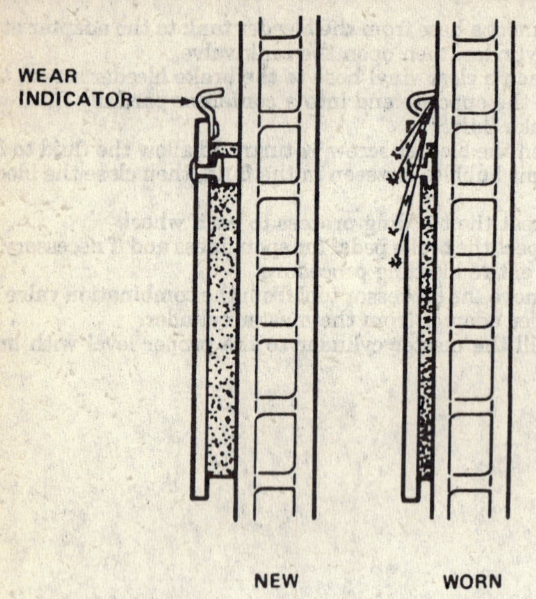

Brake wear indicators

2. Raise and safely support the front of the vehicle on jackstands. Remove the wheels.

NOTE: When replacing the pads on just one wheel, uneven braking will result; always replace the pads on both wheels.

3. Install a C-clamp on the caliper so that the frame side of the clamp rests against the back of the caliper and so the screw end rests against the metal part (shoe) of the outboard pad.
4. Tighten the clamp until the caliper moves enough to bottom the piston in its bore. Remove the clamp.
5. Remove the two Allen head caliper mounting bolts enough to allow the caliper to be pulled off the disc.
6. Remove the inboard pad and loosen the outboard pad. Place the caliper where it will not strain the brake hose; hang it from the suspension with wire.
7. Remove the pad support spring clip from the piston.
8. Remove the two bolt ear sleeves and the four rubber bushings from the ears.
9. Brake pads should be replaced when they are worn to within $^1/_{32}$ in. (0.8mm) of the rivet heads.

To install:

10. Check the inside of the caliper for leakage and the condition of the piston dust boot.
11. Lubricate the two new sleeves and four bushings with a silicone spray.

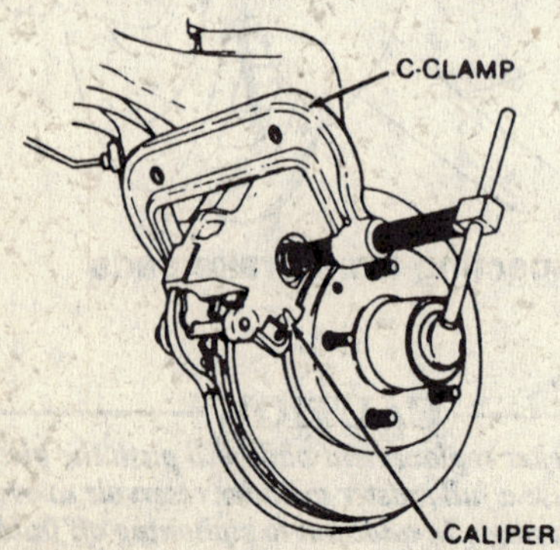

Use a C-clamp to bottom the piston

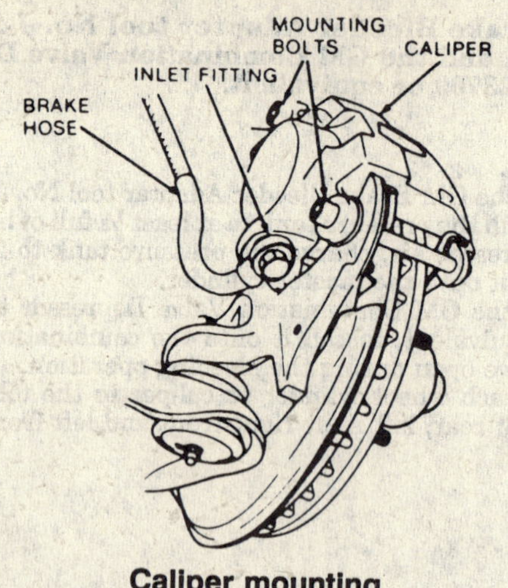

Caliper mounting

Hang the caliper with wire

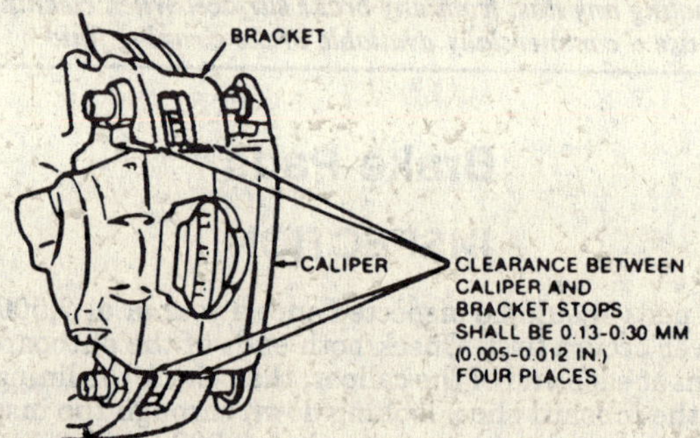

Checking the caliper-to-bracket stop clearance

12. Install the bushings in each caliper ear. Install the two sleeves in the two inboard ears.
13. Install the pad support spring clip and the old pad into the center of the piston. You will then push this pad down to get the piston flat against the caliper. This part of the job is a hassle and requires an assistant. While the assistant holds the caliper and loosens the bleeder valve to relieve the pressure, obtain a medium pry bar and try to force the old pad inward, making the piston flush with the caliper surface. When it is flush, close the bleeder valve so that no air gets into the system.

NOTE: Make sure that the wear sensor is facing toward the rear of the caliper.

14. Place the outboard pad in the caliper with its top ears over the caliper ears and the bottom tab engaged in the caliper cutout.
15. After both pads are installed, lift the caliper and place the

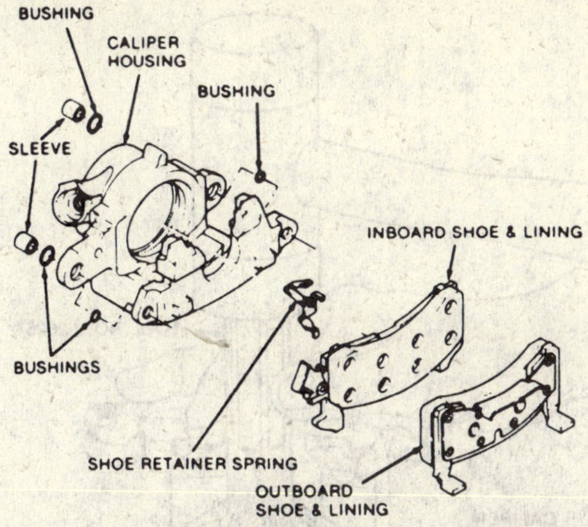

Removing pads from the caliper

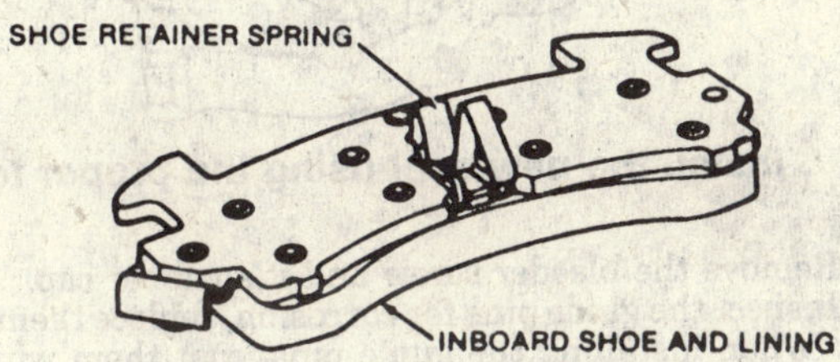

Installing the shoe retaining spring

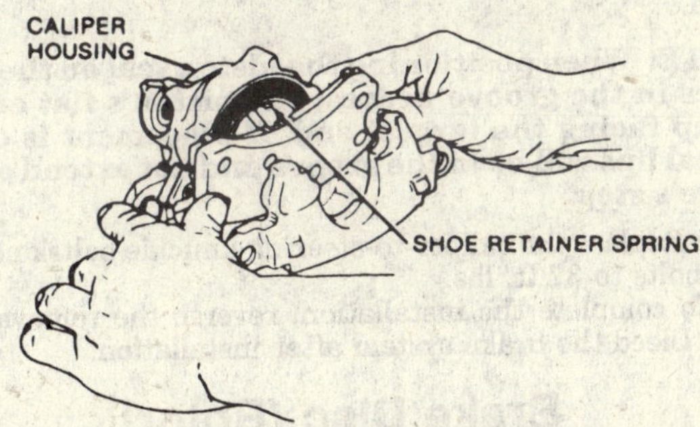

Installing the pads in the caliper

bottom edge of the outboard pad on the outer edge of the disc to make sure that there is no clearance between the tab on the bottom of the shoes and the caliper abutment.

16. Place the caliper over the disc, lining up the hole in the caliper ears with the hole in the mounting bracket. Make sure that the brake hose is not kinked.

17. Start the caliper-to-mounting bracket bolts through the sleeves in the inboard caliper ears and through the mounting bracket, making sure that the ends of the bolts pass under the retaining ears of the inboard shoe.

18. Push the mounting bolts through to engage the holes in the outboard shoes and the outboard caliper ears and then thread them into the mounting bracket.

19. Torque the mounting bolts to 37 ft. lbs. Pump the brake pedal to seat the linings against the rotors.

20. Using a pair of channel lock pliers, place them on the notch on the caliper housing, bend the caliper upper ears until no clearance exists between the shoe and the caliper housing.

21. Install the wheels, lower the vehicle and refill the master cylinder reservoirs with brake fluid. Pump the brake pedal to make sure that it is firm. If it is not, bleed the brakes.

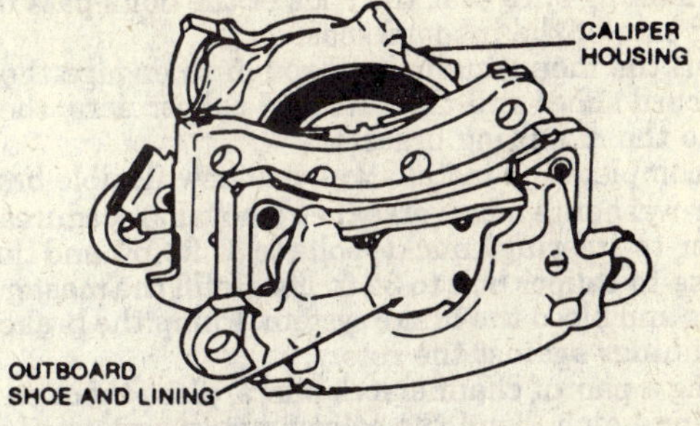

Position of pad in caliper

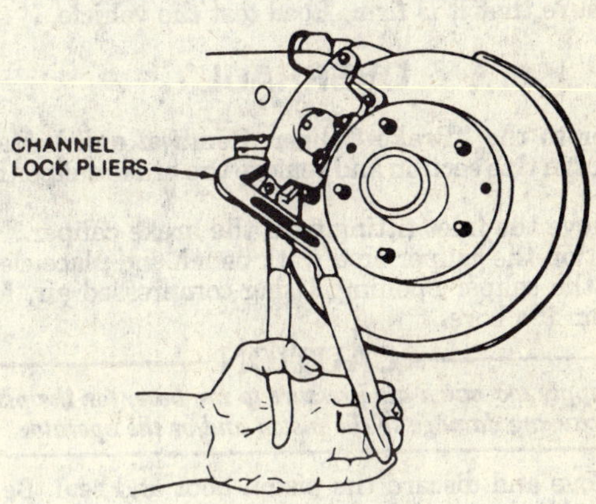

Seating the caliper

Brake Caliper

REMOVAL AND INSTALLATION

1. Refer to the "Brake Pads, Removal and Installation" procedures in this section and remove the brake caliper from the steering knuckle.
2. Disconnect the flexible brake hose-to-caliper bolt, discard the pressure fitting washers, then remove the brake caliper from the vehicle and place it on a work bench.
3. To inspect the caliper assembly, perform the following procedures:
   a. Check the inside of the caliper assembly for signs of leakage; if necessary, replace or rebuild the caliper.
   b. Check the mounting bolts and sleeves for signs of corrosion; if necessary, replace the bolts.

NOTE: If the mounting bolts have signs of corrosion, DO NOT attempt to polish away the corrosion.

4. To install, use new caliper bushings and sleeves, use Delco® Silicone Lube or equivalent to lubricate the mounting bolts and new brake pads (if necessary).
5. After both pads are installed, lift the caliper and place the bottom edge of the outboard pad on the outer edge of the disc to make sure that there is no clearance between the tab on the bottom of the shoes and the caliper abutment.
6. Place the caliper over the disc, lining up the hole in the caliper ears with the hole in the mounting bracket.
7. Start the caliper-to-mounting bracket bolts through the sleeves in the inboard caliper ears and through the mounting

bracket, making sure that the ends of the bolts pass under the retaining ears of the inboard shoe.

8. Push the mounting bolts through to engage the holes in the outboard shoes and the outboard caliper ears, then thread them into the mounting bracket.

9. To complete the installation, use new flexible brake hose-to-caliper washers and reverse the removal procedures. Torque the caliper-to-steering knuckle bolts to 37 ft. lbs. and the flexible brake hose-to-caliper bolt to 32 ft. lbs. Refill the master cylinder reservoirs and bleed the brake system. Pump the brake pedal to seat the linings against the rotors.

10. Using a pair of channel lock pliers, place them on the caliper housing notch, bend the caliper upper ears until no clearance exists between the shoe and the caliper housing.

11. Install the wheels, lower the vehicle. Pump the brake pedal to make sure that it is firm. Road test the vehicle.

OVERHAUL

1. Refer to the "Brake Caliper, Removal and Installation" procedures in this section and remove the brake caliper from the vehicle.

2. Remove the inlet fitting from the brake caliper.

3. Position the caliper on a work bench and place clean shop cloths in the caliper opening. Using compressed air, force the piston from it's bore.

CAUTION

DO NOT apply too much air pressure to the bore, for the piston may jump out, causing damage to the piston and/or the operator.

4. Remove and discard the piston boot and seal. Be careful not to scratch the bore.

5. Clean all of the parts with non-mineral based solvent and blow dry with compressed air. Replace the rubber parts with those in the brake service kit.

6. Inspect the piston and the caliper bore for damage or corrosion. Replace the caliper and/or the piston (if necessary).

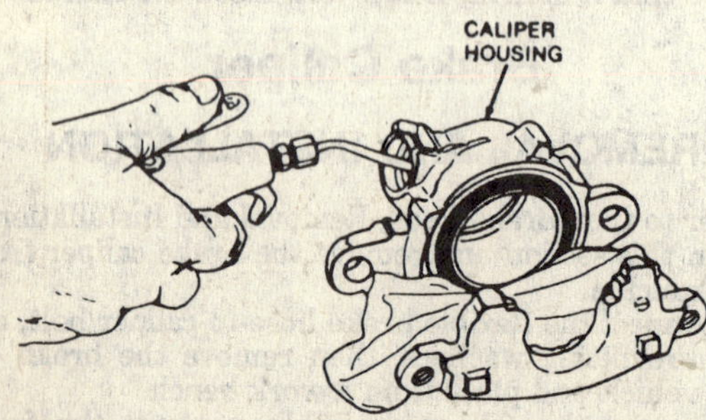

Use a clean rag to catch the piston as it is blown out of the bore

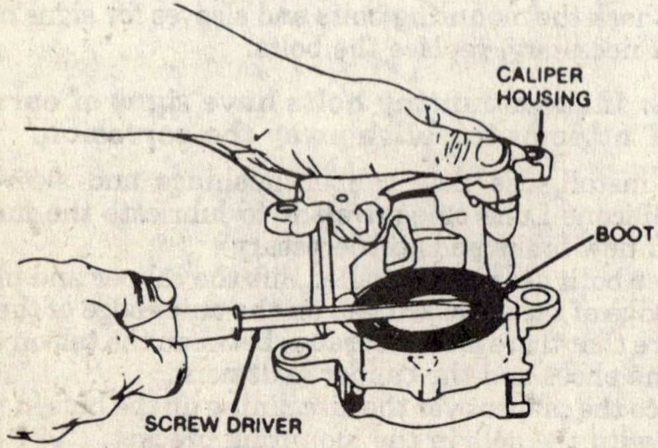

Remove the dust boot and piston seal

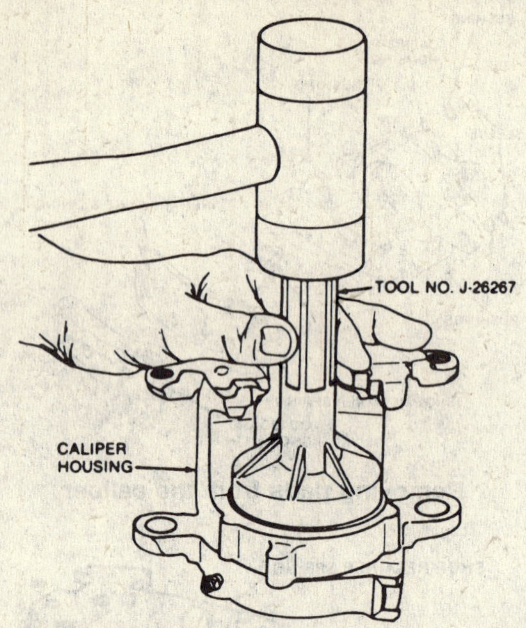

Install the new seal using the proper tool

7. Remove the bleeder screw and it's rubber cap.

8. Inspect the guide pins for corrosion, replace them (if necessary). When installing the guide pins, coat them with silicone grease.

9. To install, perform the following procedures:

a. Lubricate the piston, caliper and seal with clean brake fluid.

NOTE: When positioning the piston seal on the piston, it goes in the groove nearest the piston's flat end with the lap facing the largest end. If placement is correct, the seal lips will be in the groove and not extend over the groove's step.

b. Replace the caliper-to-steering knuckle bolts and torque the bolts to 37 ft. lbs.

10. To complete the installation, reverse the removal procedures. Bleed the brake system after installation.

Brake Disc (Rotor)

REMOVAL AND INSTALLATION

2WD Model

1. Siphon some brake fluid from the brake master cylinder.

2. Raise and safely support the front of the vehicle on jackstands. Remove the wheels.

3. Remove the brake caliper from the steering knuckle and hang it on a wire.

4. Remove the grease cup, the cotter pin, the castle nut and the hub assembly.

5. Inspect the brake discs for signs of wear or damage; if necessary, replace the brake disc.

6. To install the brake disc, reverse the removal procedures. Check and/or adjust the wheel bearing and the front end alignment.

7. Remove the jackstands and lower the vehicle. Refill the brake master cylinder.

4WD Model

1. Refer to the "Torsion Bar, Removal and Installation" procedures in Section 7 and relieve the torsion bar pressure.

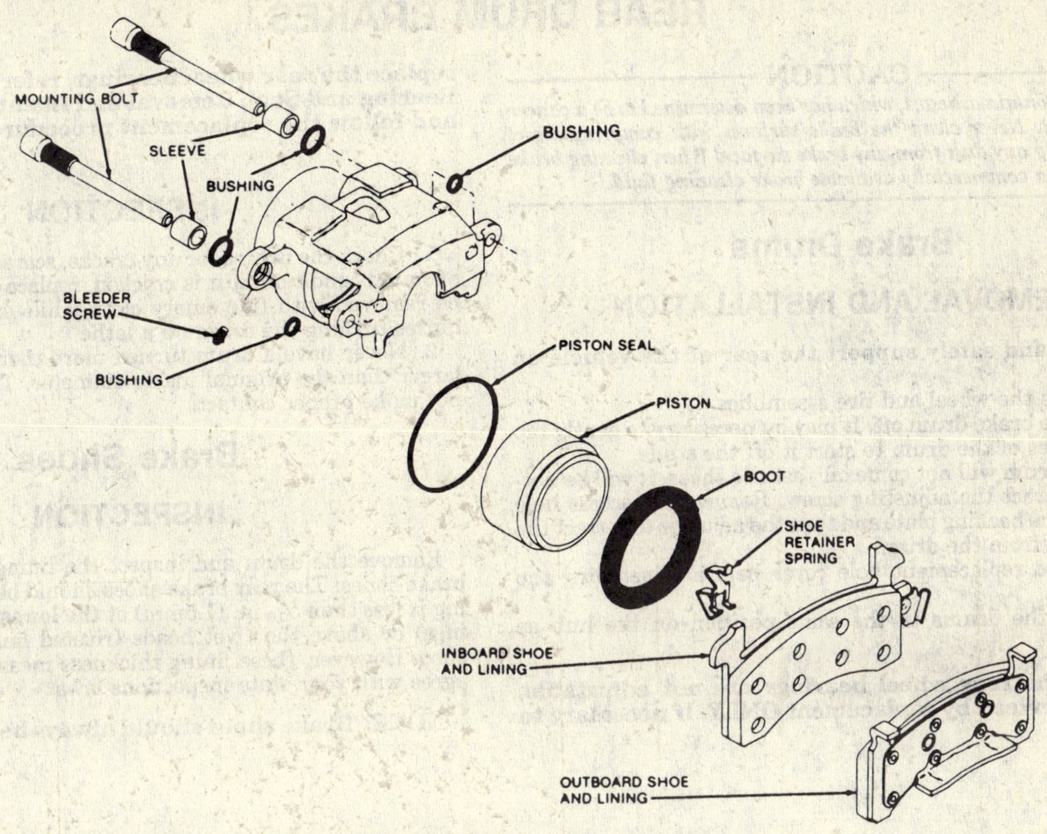

Caliper assembly

2. Raise and safely support the front of the truck on jackstands; place the jackstands under the frame.
3. Remove the wheel and tire assembly.
4. Remove the disc brake caliper-to-steering knuckle bolts, lift the brake caliper and support it (out of the way) on a wire.
5. Remove the brake disc from the wheel hub.

NOTE: When removing the steering knuckle from the wheel hub, be careful not to damage the splined surface of the half shaft.

6. Inspect the disc for nicks, scores and/or damage, then replace it if necessary.
7. To install, reverse the removal procedures. Check and/or adjust the front end alignment.

INSPECTION

1. Raise and safely support the front of the vehicle on jackstands. Remove the wheels.
2. To check the disc runout, perform the following procedures:
   a. Using a dial indicator, secure and position it so that the button contacts the disc about 1 in. (25.4mm) from the outer edge.
   b. Rotate the disc. The lateral reading should not exceed 0.004 in. (0.1mm). If the reading is excessive, recondition or replace the disc.
3. To check the disc parallelism, perform the following procedures:
   a. Using a micrometer, check the disc thickness at 4 locations around the disc, at the same distance from the edge.
   b. The thickness should not vary more than 0.0005 in. (0.0127mm). If the readings are excessive, recondition or replace the disc.
4. The surface finish must be relatively smooth to avoid pulling and erratic performance, also, to extend the lining life. Light rotor surface scoring of up to 0.015 in. (0.38mm) in depth, can be tolerated. If the scoring depths are excessive, refinish or replace the rotor.

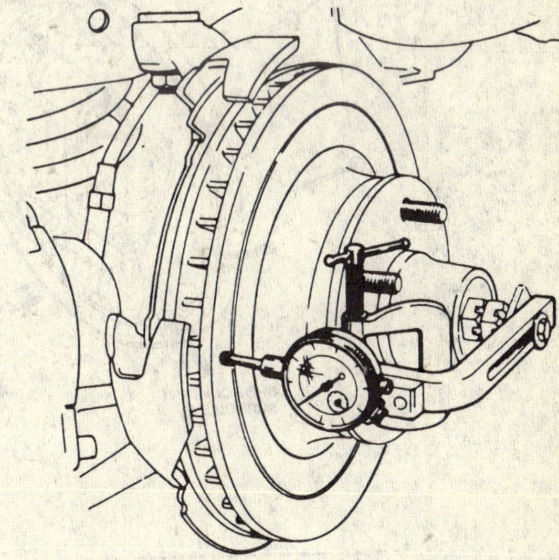

Use a dial indicator to check disc run-out

REAR DRUM BRAKES

CAUTION

Brake shoes contain asbestos, which has been determined to be a cancer causing agent. Never clean the brake surfaces with compressed air! Avoid inhaling any dust from any brake surface! When cleaning brake surfaces, use a commercially available brake cleaning fluid.

Brake Drums

REMOVAL AND INSTALLATION

1. Raise and safely support the rear of the vehicle on jackstands.
2. Remove the wheel and tire assemblies.
3. Pull the brake drum off. It may by necessary to gently tap the rear edges of the drum to start it off the studs.
4. If the drum will not come off past the shoes, it will be necessary to retract the adjusting screw. Remove the access hole cover from the backing plate and turn the adjuster to retract the linings away from the drum.
5. Install a replacement hole cover before reinstalling the drum.
6. Install the drums in the same position on the hub as removed.

NOTE: The rear wheel bearings are not adjustable, they are serviced by replacement ONLY. If necessary to replace the rear wheel bearings, refer to the Axle Shaft, Bearing and Seal, Removal and Installation procedures and follow the replacement procedures.

INSPECTION

1. Check the drums for any cracks, scores, grooves or an out-of-round condition; if it is cracked, replace it. Slight scores can be removed with fine emery cloth while extensive scoring requires turning the drum on a lathe.
2. Never have a drum turned more than 0.060 in. (1.5mm) larger than the original inside diameter. The brake shoes will not make proper contact.

Brake Shoes

INSPECTION

Remove the drum and inspect the lining thickness of both brake shoes. The rear brake shoes should be replaced if the lining is less than $^1/_{16}$ in. (1.5mm) at the lowest point (bonded linings) or above the rivet heads (riveted linings) on the brake shoe. However, these lining thickness measurements may disagree with your state inspections laws.

NOTE: Brake shoes should always be replaced in sets.

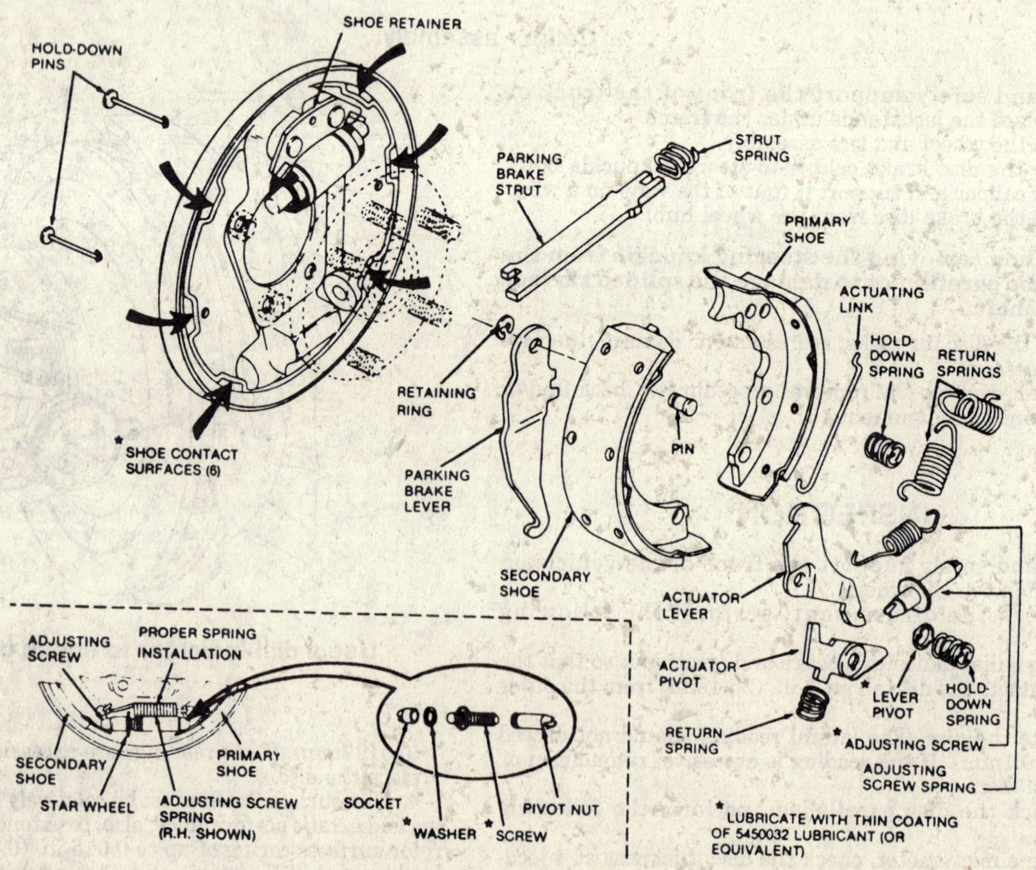

Drum brake assembly with self adjuster

REMOVAL AND INSTALLATION

NOTE: The following procedure requires the use of the GM Brake Spring Pliers tool No. J-8057 or equivalent.

1. Raise and safely support the rear of the vehicle on jackstands.
2. Slacken the parking brake cable.
3. Remove the rear wheels and the brake drum.
4. Using the GM Brake Spring Pliers tool No. J-8057 or equivalent, disconnect the brake shoe return springs, the actuator pullback spring, the holddown pins/springs and the actuator assembly.

NOTE: Special brake spring tools are available from the auto supply stores, which will ease the replacement of the spring and anchor pin, but the job may still be performed with common hand tools.

5. Disconnect the adjusting mechanism and spring, then remove the primary shoe. The primary shoe has a shorter lining than the secondary and is mounted at the front of the wheel.
6. Disconnect the parking brake lever from the secondary shoe and remove the shoe.
7. Clean and inspect all of the brake parts.
8. Check the wheel cylinders for seal condition and leaking.
9. Inspect the wheel bearing for leakage and replace, if necessary.
10. Inspect the replacement shoes for nicks or burrs, lightly lubricate the backing plate contact points, the brake cable, the levers and adjusting screws with brake grease, then reassemble them.
11. Make sure that the right and left hand adjusting screws are not mixed. You can prevent this by working on one side at a time. This will also provide you with a reference for reassembly. The star wheel should be nearest to the secondary shoe when correctly installed.
12. To complete the installation, reverse the removal procedures. When completed, make an initial adjustment as previously described.

Wheel Cylinders

REMOVAL AND INSTALLATION

1. Refer to the "Brake Shoe, Removal and Installation" procedures in this section and remove the brake shoe assembly from the backing plate.
2. Clean away all of the dirt, crud and foreign material from around the wheel cylinder. It is important that dirt be kept away from the brake line when the cylinder is disconnected.
3. Disconnect and plug the hydraulic line at the wheel cylinder.
4. Remove the wheel cylinder-to-backing plate bolts and the wheel cylinder from the backing plate.

NOTE: If the wheel cylinder is sticking, use a hammer and a punch to drive the wheel cylinder from the backing plate.

5. To install, reverse the removal procedures. Torque the wheel cylinder-to-backing plate bolts to 160 inch lbs. Adjust and bleed the rear brake system.

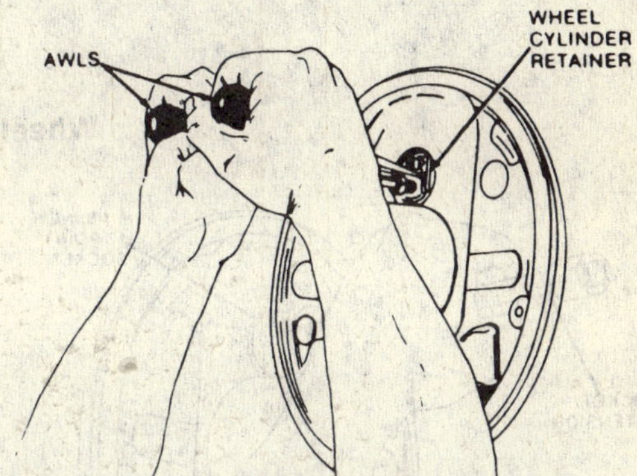

Removing the wheel cylinder retainer

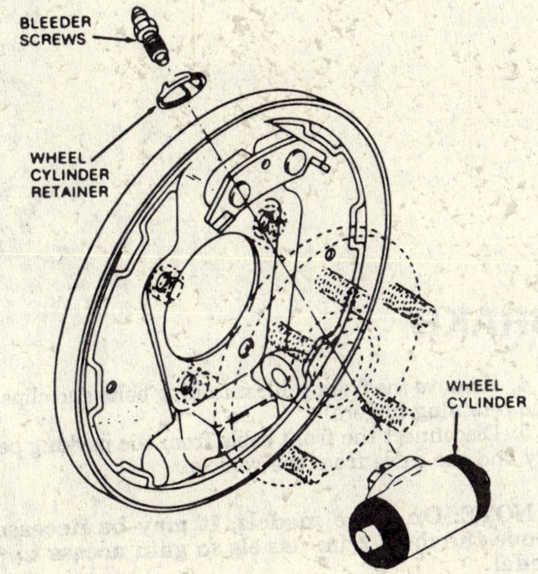

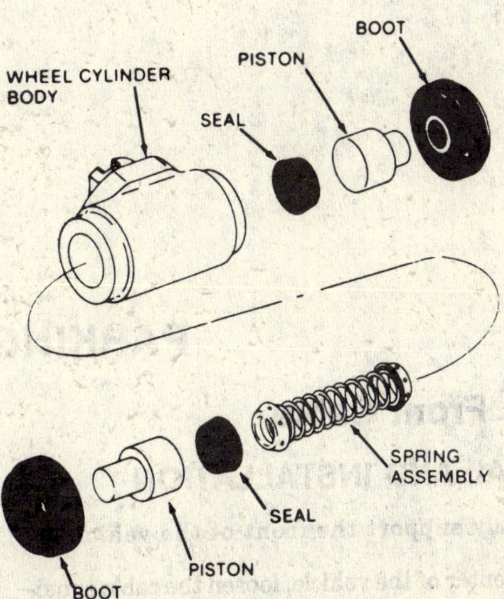

Wheel cylinder attachment

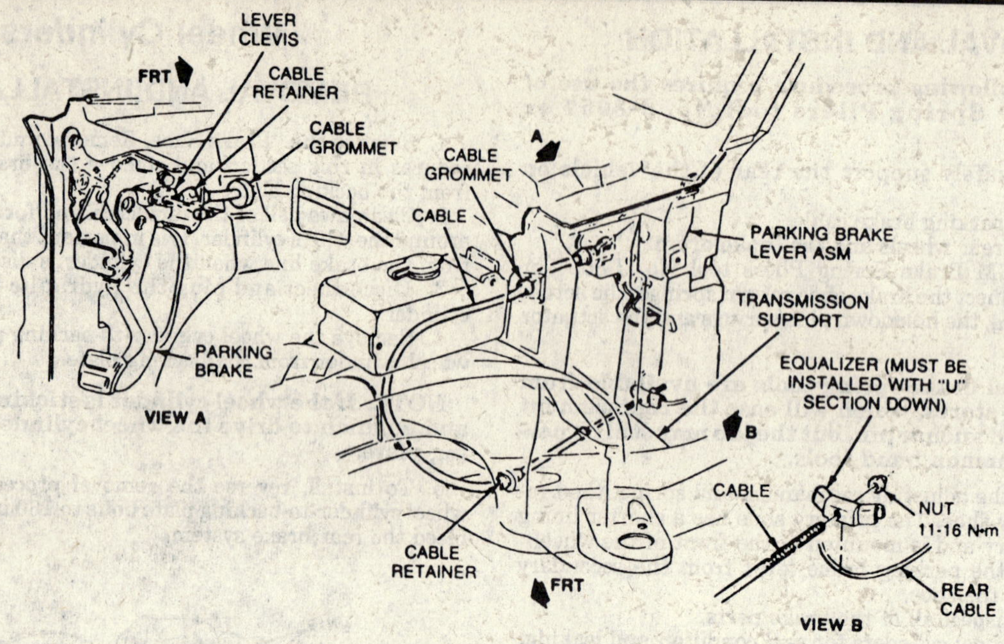

Wheel cylinder components

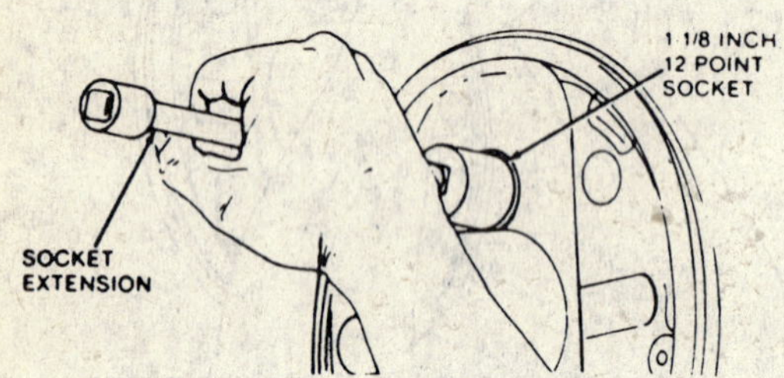

Installing the wheel cylinder retainer

OVERHAUL

1. Remove the boots, pistons, seals and spring.
2. Dry the bore and pistons, then check for wear, scoring, pitting or corrosion. GM does not recommend honing of the bore. If light corrosion exists it may be removed with crocus cloth. If crocus cloth does not do the job, replace the cylinder.
3. To assemble, use new seals/boots, coat all of the parts with clean silicone brake fluid and reverse the removal procedures.

PARKING BRAKE

Front Cable

REMOVAL AND INSTALLATION

1. Raise and safely support the front of the vehicle on jackstands.
2. Under the left center of the vehicle, loosen the cable equalizer assembly.
3. Separate the front cable connector from the equalizer cable.
4. Remove the front cable retaining bolts and clips, then bend the retaining fingers.
5. Disconnect the front cable from the parking pedal assembly and the cable from the vehicle.

NOTE: On some models, it may be necessary to remove the dash trim panels to gain access to the brake pedal.

6. To install the front cable, attach a piece of wire to the ca-

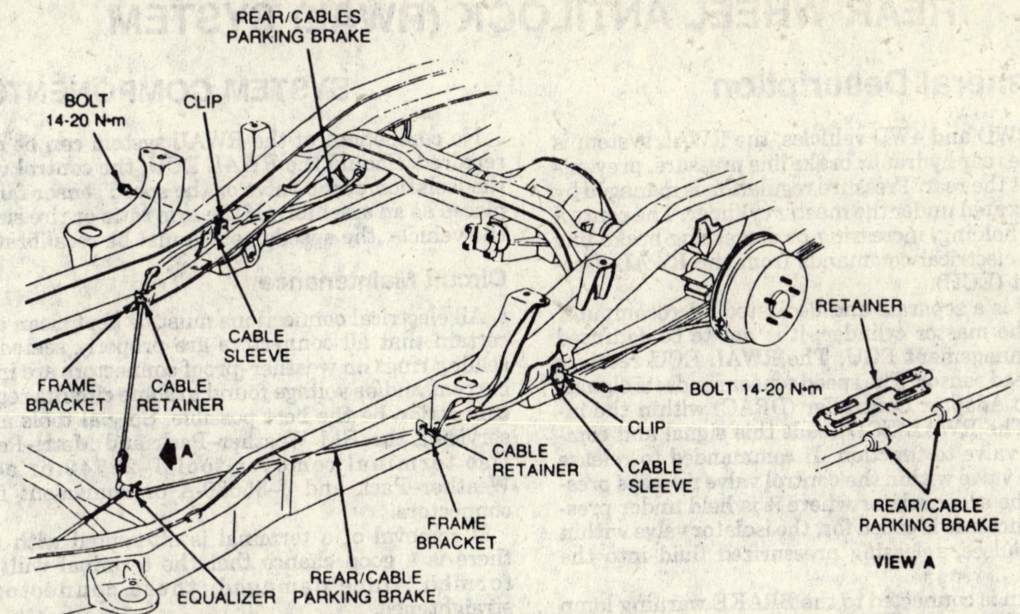

Equalizer and rear cable

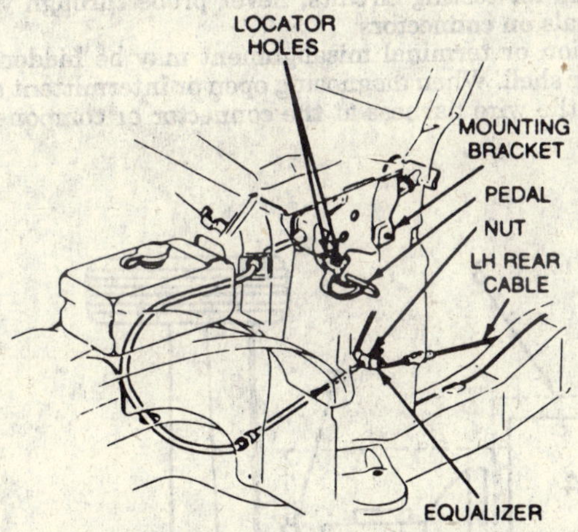

Parking brake adjustment

ble, fish it through the cowl and reverse the removal procedures. Adjust the parking brake.

7. Lower the vehicle and check the parking brake operation.

Rear Cable

REMOVAL AND INSTALLATION

Left and Right Rear Cables

1. Raise and safely support the rear of the vehicle on jackstands.
2. Under the left center of the vehicle, loosen the cable equalizer assembly.
3. Separate the front cable connector from the equalizer cable.
4. Refer to the "Brake Shoe, Removal and Installation" procedures in this section and remove the brake shoes.
5. At the backing plate, bend the cable retaining fingers.
6. Disconnect the rear cable from the secondary brake shoe and the cable from the vehicle.
7. To install the rear cable, reverse the removal procedures. Adjust the parking brake.

NOTE: When installing the rear parking brake cables, make sure that the retaining fingers are completely through the backing plate.

8. Before lowering the vehicle, check the parking brake operation.

ADJUSTMENT

NOTE: Before adjusting the parking brakes, check the condition of the service brakes; replace any necessary parts.

1. Block the front wheels.
2. Raise and safely support the rear of the vehicle on jackstands.
3. Under the left center of the vehicle, loosen the equalizer.
4. On the 2WD model, position the parking brake pedal (ratchet) on the 8th click (1982–84) or 2nd click (1985–91); on the 4WD model, position the parking brake pedal (ratchet) on the 10th click (1983–84) or the 3rd click (1985–91).
5. Turn the cable equalizer until the rear wheel drags (when turned by hand).
6. Tighten the equalizer lock nut.
7. Release the parking brake pedal, then test it; the correct adjustment to specifications.

REAR WHEEL ANTILOCK (RWAL) SYSTEM

General Description

Found on both 2WD and 4WD vehicles, the RWAL system is designed to regulate rear hydraulic brake line pressure, preventing wheel lock-up at the rear. Pressure regulation is managed by the control valve, located under the master cylinder. The control valve is capable of holding, increasing or decreasing brake line pressure based on electrical commands from the RWAL Electronic Control Unit (ECU).

The RWAL ECU is a separate and dedicated microcomputer mounted next to the master cylinder; it is not to be confused with the engine management ECU. The RWAL ECU receives signals from the speed sensor. The speed sensor sends its signals to the Digital Ratio Adapter Controller (DRAC) within the instrument cluster. The RWAL ECU reads this signal and commands the control valve to function. If commanded to release pressure, the dump valve within the control valve releases pressurized fluid into the accumulator where it is held under pressure. If a pressure increase is called for, the isolator valve within the control valve pulses, releasing pressurized fluid into the system.

The RWAL system is connected to the BRAKE warning lamp on the instrument cluster. A RWAL self-check and a bulb test are performed every time the ignition switch is turned to **ON**. The BRAKE warning lamp should illuminate for about 2 seconds and then go off. Problems within the RWAL system will be indicated by the BRAKE warning lamp staying illuminated.

If a fault is detected within the system, the RWAL ECU will assign a fault code and store the code in memory. The code may be read to aid in diagnosis.

SYSTEM COMPONENTS

No component of the RWAL system can be disassembled or repaired. Should the RWAL ECU, the control valve containing the isolation/dump valve or the speed sensor fail, it must be replaced as an assembly. If the axle ratio or tire size is changed on the vehicle, the speedometer must be recalibrated.

Circuit Maintenance

All electrical connections must be kept clean and tight. Make certain that all connectors are properly seated and all of the sealing rings on weather–proof connectors are in place. The low current and/or voltage found in some circuits require that every connection be the best possible. Special tools are required for servicing the GM Weather–Pack and Metri–Pack connectors. Use terminal remover tool J–28742 or equivalent for Weather–Pack and J–35689-A or equivalent for Metri–Pack connectors.

If removal of a terminal is attempted with a regular pick, there is a good chance that the terminal will be bent or deformed. Once damaged, these connectors cannot be straightened.

Use care when probing the connections or replacing terminals; it is possible to short between adjacent terminals, causing component damage. Always use jumper wires between circuit connectors for testing circuits; never probe through weather–proof seals on connectors.

Oxidation or terminal misalignment may be hidden by the connector shell. When diagnosing open or intermittent circuits, wiggling the wire harness at the connector or component may

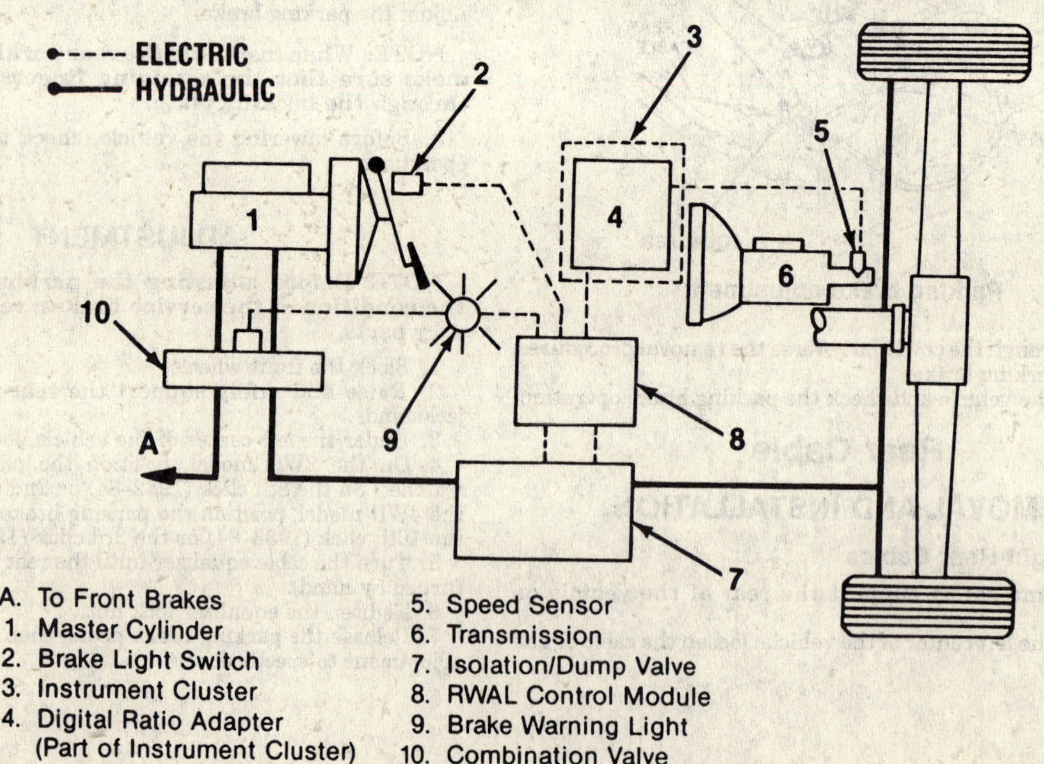

A. To Front Brakes
1. Master Cylinder
2. Brake Light Switch
3. Instrument Cluster
4. Digital Ratio Adapter (Part of Instrument Cluster)
5. Speed Sensor
6. Transmission
7. Isolation/Dump Valve
8. RWAL Control Module
9. Brake Warning Light
10. Combination Valve

Rear wheel anti-lock system wiring diagram

reveal or correct the condition. When the location of the fault is identified, the connector should be separated and the problem corrected. Never disconnect a harness connector with the ignition **ON**.

NOTE: When working with the RWAL ECU connectors, do not touch the connections or pins with the fingers. Do not allow the connectors or pins to contact brake fluid; internal damage to the RWAL ECU will occur.

Diagnosis and Testing

SYSTEM PRECAUTIONS

- If the vehicle is equipped with airbag (SIR) system, always properly disable the system before commencing work on the ABS system.
- Certain components within the RWAL system are not intended to be serviced or repaired. Only those components with removal and installation procedures should be serviced.
- Do not use rubber hoses or other parts not specifically specified for the RWAL system. When using repair kits, replace all parts included in the kit. Partial or incorrect repair may lead to functional problems.
- Lubricate rubber parts with clean, fresh brake fluid to ease assembly. Do not use lubricated shop air to clean parts; damage to rubber components may result.
- Use only brake fluid from an unopened container. Use of suspect or contaminated brake fluid can reduce system performance and/or durability.
- A clean repair area is essential. Perform repairs after components have been thoroughly cleaned; use only denatured alcohol to clean components. Do not allow components to come into contact with any substance containing mineral oil; this includes used shop rags.
- The RWAL ECU is a microprocessor similar to other computer units in the vehicle. Insure that the ignition switch is **OFF** before removing or installing controller harnesses. Avoid static electricity discharge at or near the controller.
- Never disconnect any electrical connection with the ignition switch **ON** unless instructed to do so in a test.
- Always wear a grounded wrist strap when servicing any control module or component labeled with a Electrostatic Discharge (ESD) symbol.
- Avoid touching module connector pins.
- Leave new components and modules in the shipping package until ready to install them.
- To avoid static discharge, always touch a vehicle ground after sliding across a vehicle seat or walking across carpeted or vinyl floors.
- Never allow welding cables to lie on, near or across any vehicle electrical wiring. When doing any electric welding on the vehicle, disconnect the negative battery cable and all ECUs connectors.
- Do not allow extension cords for power tools or droplights to lie on, near or across any vehicle electrical wiring.

PRELIMINARY DIAGNOSIS

Before reading trouble codes, perform the Diagnostic Circuit Check according to the chart. This test will aid in separating RWAL system problems from common problems in the hydraulic brake system. The diagnostic circuit check will direct the reading of trouble codes as necessary.

READING TROUBLE CODES

The RWAL ECU will assign a code to the first fault found in the system. If there is more than 1 fault, only the first recognized code will the stored and transmitted.

Trouble codes are read by connecting a jumper wire from pin H on ALDL to pin A; the fault code will be displayed through the flashing of the BRAKE warning lamp on the dash. The terminals must be connected for about 20 seconds before the display begins. The display will begin with 1 long flash followed by shorter ones—count the long flash as part of the display.

NOTE: Sometimes the first display sequence will be inaccurate or short; subsequent displays will be accurate.

DIAGNOSTIC CIRCUIT CHECK

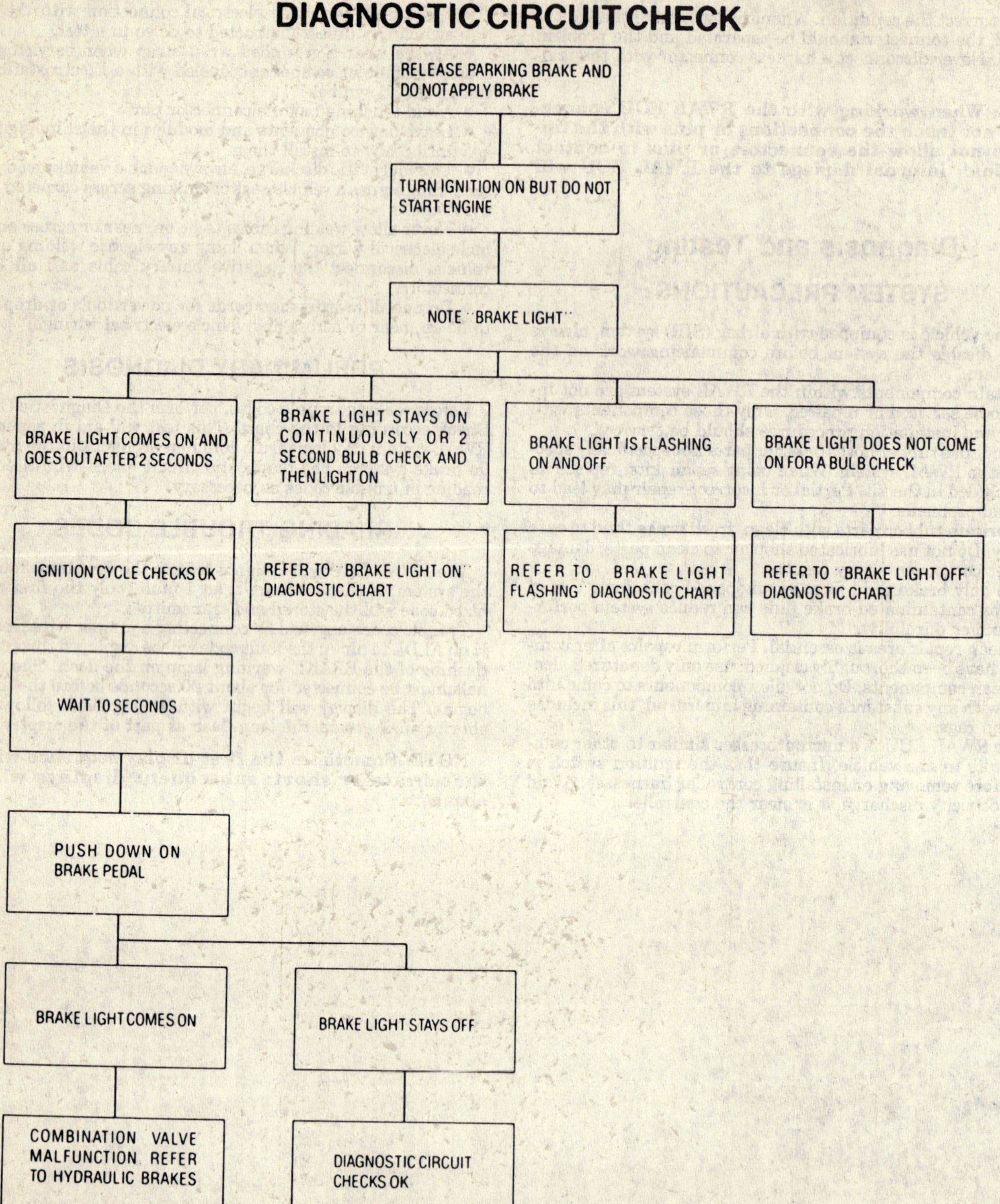

BRAKE LIGHT ON — PART 1

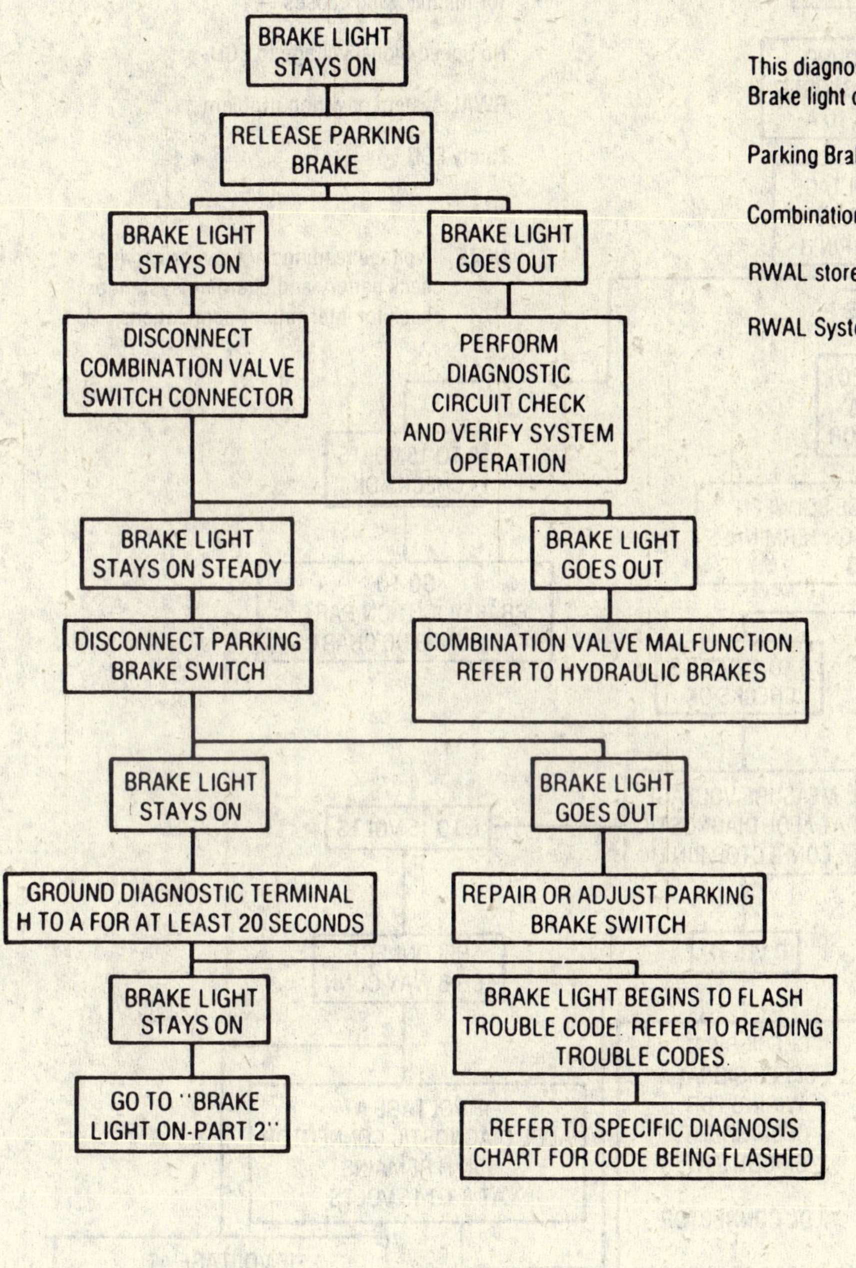

This diagnostic chart checks for the Brake light on for the following causes —

Parking Brake on or switch problem

Combination Valve Switch closed

RWAL stored diagnostic code

RWAL System problem

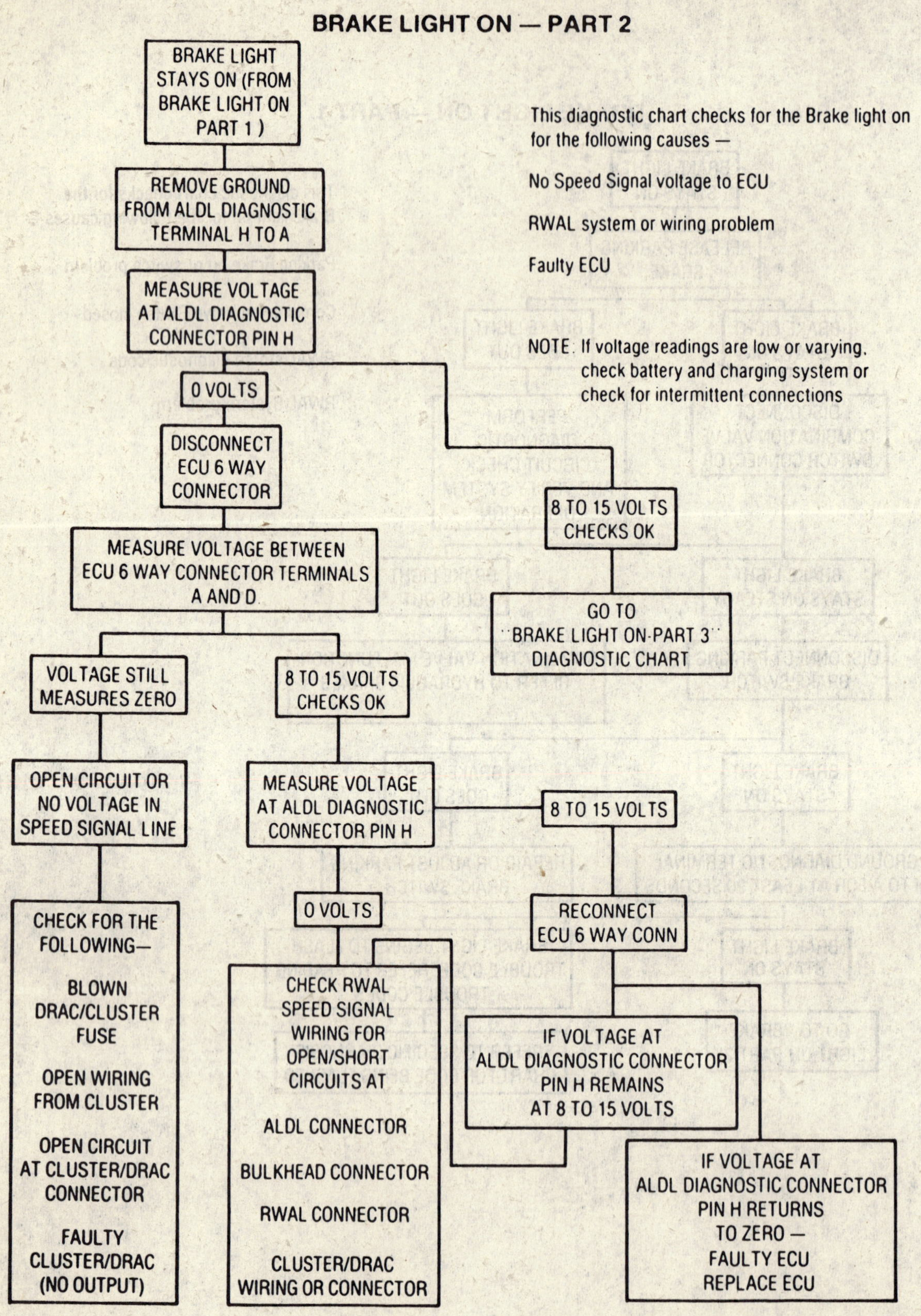
BRAKE LIGHT ON — PART 2
BRAKE LIGHT STAYS ON (FROM BRAKE LIGHT ON PART 1)
REMOVE GROUND FROM ALDL DIAGNOSTIC TERMINAL H TO A
MEASURE VOLTAGE AT ALDL DIAGNOSTIC CONNECTOR PIN H
0 VOLTS
DISCONNECT ECU 6 WAY CONNECTOR
MEASURE VOLTAGE BETWEEN ECU 6 WAY CONNECTOR TERMINALS A AND D
VOLTAGE STILL MEASURES ZERO
OPEN CIRCUIT OR NO VOLTAGE IN SPEED SIGNAL LINE
CHECK FOR THE FOLLOWING—
BLOWN DRAC/CLUSTER FUSE
OPEN WIRING FROM CLUSTER
OPEN CIRCUIT AT CLUSTER/DRAC CONNECTOR
FAULTY CLUSTER/DRAC (NO OUTPUT)
8 TO 15 VOLTS CHECKS OK
MEASURE VOLTAGE AT ALDL DIAGNOSTIC CONNECTOR PIN H
0 VOLTS
CHECK RWAL SPEED SIGNAL WIRING FOR OPEN/SHORT CIRCUITS AT
ALDL CONNECTOR
BULKHEAD CONNECTOR
RWAL CONNECTOR
CLUSTER/DRAC WIRING OR CONNECTOR
8 TO 15 VOLTS
RECONNECT ECU 6 WAY CONN
IF VOLTAGE AT ALDL DIAGNOSTIC CONNECTOR PIN H REMAINS AT 8 TO 15 VOLTS
IF VOLTAGE AT ALDL DIAGNOSTIC CONNECTOR PIN H RETURNS TO ZERO — FAULTY ECU REPLACE ECU
8 TO 15 VOLTS CHECKS OK
GO TO "BRAKE LIGHT ON-PART 3" DIAGNOSTIC CHART
This diagnostic chart checks for the Brake light on for the following causes —
No Speed Signal voltage to ECU
RWAL system or wiring problem
Faulty ECU
NOTE: If voltage readings are low or varying, check battery and charging system or check for intermittent connections

BRAKE LIGHT ON — PART 3

8 TO 15 VOLTS CHECKS OK (FROM "BRAKE LIGHT" ON-PART 3)

DISCONNECT ECU 6 WAY CONNECTOR

MEASURE VOLTAGE BETWEEN ECU CONNECTOR TERMINALS A AND D.

- 0 VOLTS
  - THE BRAKE LIGHT IS ON BECAUSE THE ECU DOES NOT SEE ANY VOLTAGE ON THE SPEED SIGNAL LINE

    CHECK FOR THE FOLLOWING—

    BLOWN FUSE FOR CLUSTER/DRAC

    OPEN OR SHORT IN WIRING FROM CLUSTER/DRAC TO ECU

    OPEN OR SHORT IN WIRING TO CLUSTER/DRAC IGNITION FEED
- 8 TO 15 VOLTS
  - MEASURE VOLTAGE BETWEEN ECU 6 WAY CONNECTOR TERMINALS B AND C. THIS CHECKS THE BATTERY AND IGNITION VOLTAGE FEEDS TO THE ECU
    - IF BOTH PINS MEASURE 8 TO 15 VOLTS
      - RECONNECT ECU 6 WAY CONNECTOR

        IF LIGHT REMAINS ON, REPLACE THE ECU

        IF LIGHT GOES OUT

        CHECK FOR WIRING PROBLEM — SHORT CIRCUIT IN

        ECU 6 WAY CONNECTOR OR HARNESS
    - IF EITHER PIN MEASURES 0 VOLTS
      - CHECK FOR THE FOLLOWING —

        BLOWN FUSE IN

        RWAL BATTERY VOLTAGE FEED CIRCUIT

        RWAL IGNITION VOLTAGE FEED CIRCUIT

        OPEN CIRCUIT IN RWAL BATTERY VOLTAGE OR IGNITION VOLTAGE FEED

        CHECK WIRING CONNECTORS AND TERMINATIONS

This diagnostic chart checks for the Brake light on for the following causes —

No Battery voltage feed to ECU

No Ignition voltage feed to ECU

NOTE: The RWAL system is designed to turn the Brake light on if the ignition is on and there is no battery or ignition voltage feed to the ECU.

Faulty ECU

NOTE: If voltage readings are low or varying, check battery and charging system or check for intermittent connections

BRAKE LIGHT FLASHING

This diagnostic chart checks for the Brake light flashing for the following causes -

Intermittent Speed Signal voltage tothe ECU

RWAL system problem (stored code)

NOTE: If voltage readings are low or varying, check battery and charging system or check for intermittent connections

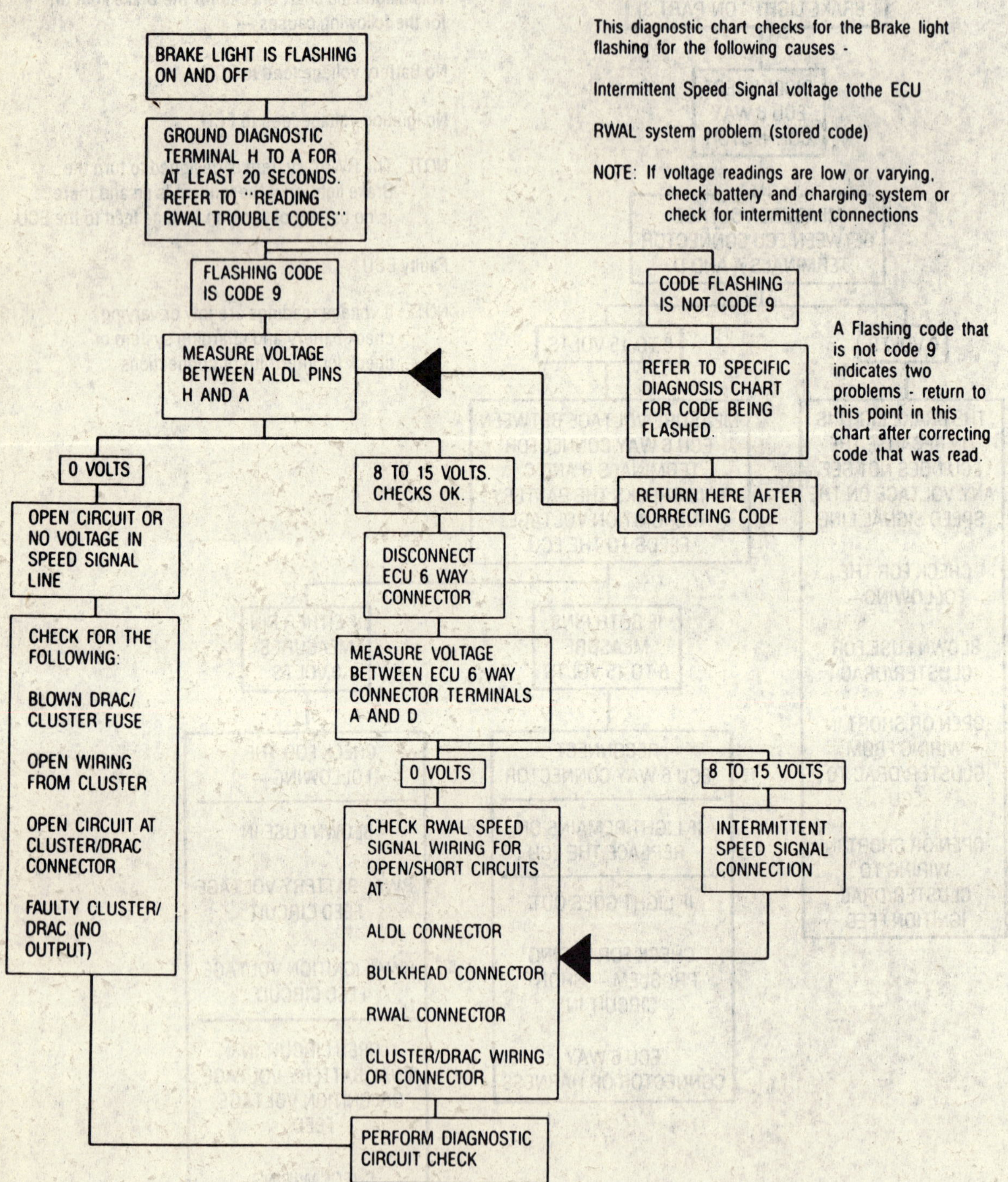

BRAKE LIGHT OFF

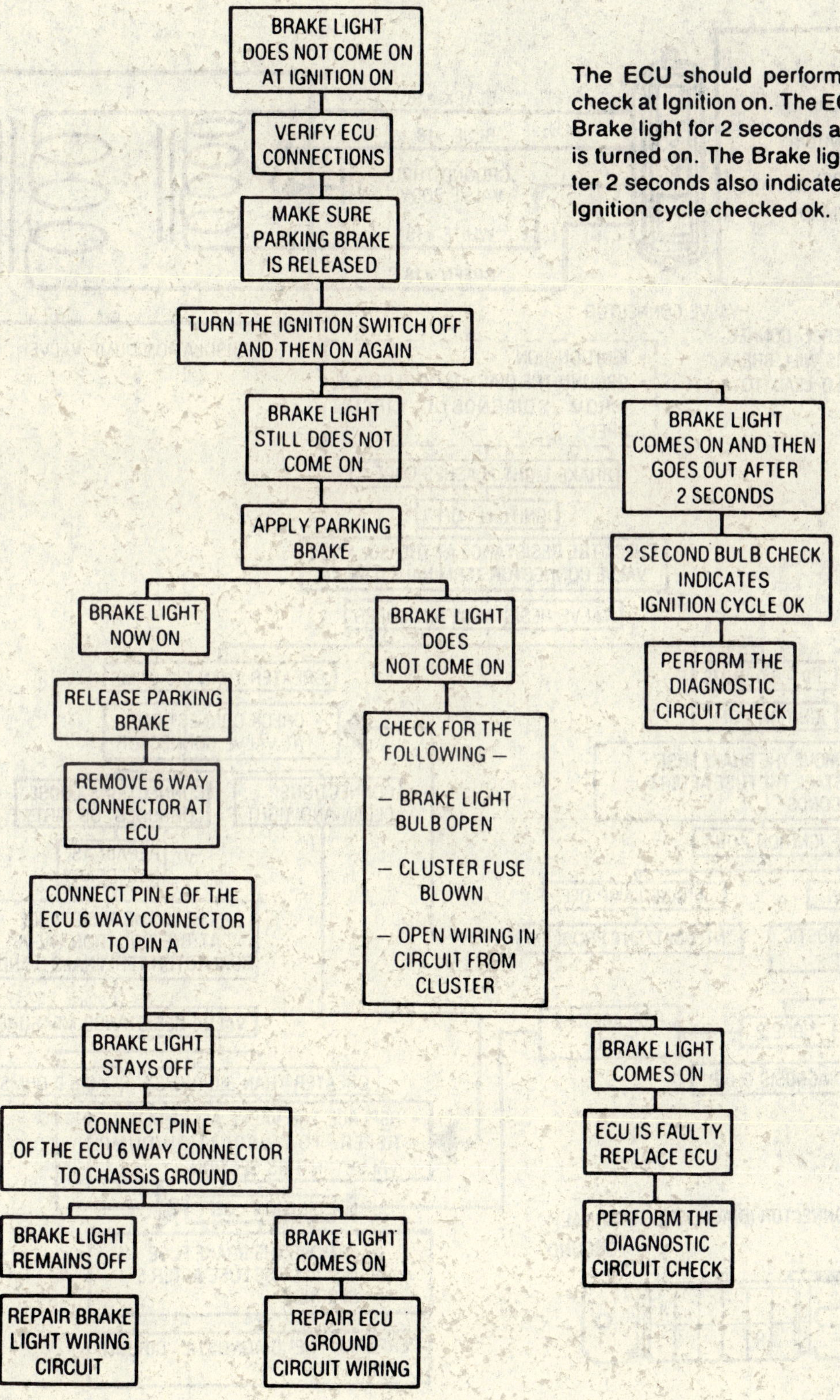

The ECU should perform a Brake light check at Ignition on. The ECU turns on the Brake light for 2 seconds after the ignition is turned on. The Brake light going out after 2 seconds also indicates that the ECU Ignition cycle checked ok.

CODE 2
OPEN ISOLATION VALVE OR MALFUNCTIONING ECU

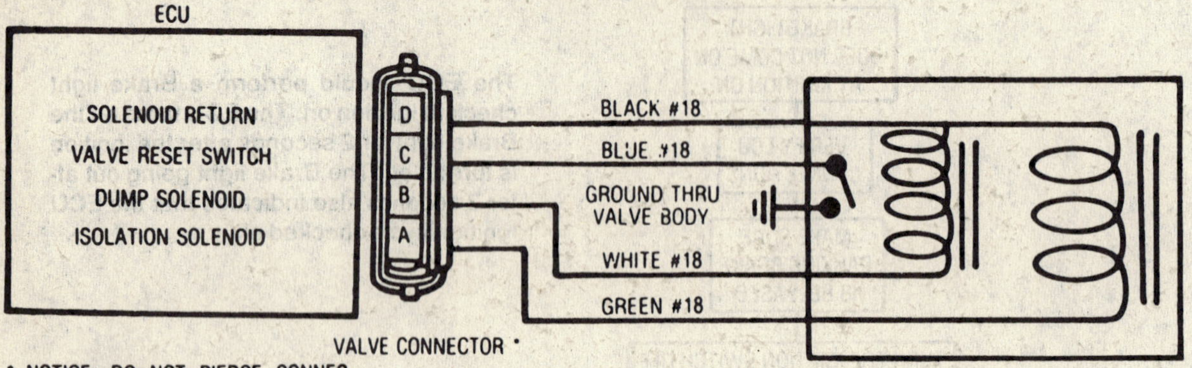

ECU
SOLENOID RETURN — D — BLACK #18
VALVE RESET SWITCH — C — BLUE #18
DUMP SOLENOID — B — GROUND THRU VALVE BODY
ISOLATION SOLENOID — A — WHITE #18
GREEN #18

VALVE CONNECTOR *

ISOLATION/DUMP VALVE

* NOTICE: DO NOT PIERCE CONNECTORS, OR WIRES. THIS WILL BREAK THE SEAL AND COULD LEAD TO A POOR CONNECTION.

- IGNITION "ON"
- GROUND THE DIAGNOSTIC TERMINAL (FROM "DIAGNOSTIC CIRCUIT CHECK")

BRAKE LIGHT FLASHES CODE 2

IGNITION "OFF"

CHECK THE RESISTANCE AT THE ISOLATION VALVE CONNECTOR TERMINALS D AND A

VALVE RESISTANCE MEASURES

3.0 - 6.0 OHMS

IGNITION "OFF"

- REMOVE THE BRAKE FUSE
- INSTALL THE FUSE AFTER 5 SECONDS

IGNITION "ON"

BRAKE LAMP ON → GROUND THE DIAGNOSTIC TERMINAL H
- CODE 7 → REFER TO CODE 7 DIAGNOSIS CHART
- CODE 2 → REPLACE THE E.C.U. → IGNITION "OFF"

BRAKE LAMP OFF → INTERMITTENT PROBLEM → CHECK CONNECTIONS AT VALVE CONNECTOR

GREATER THAN 6.0 OHMS

- CHECK CONNECTIONS AT VALVE CONNECTOR

CONNECTIONS CLEAN AND TIGHT → REPLACE THE VALVE ASSEMBLY

CONNECTIONS LOOSE, CORRODED, OR DIRTY

REPAIR AS NECESSARY

CHECK THE RESISTANCE AT THE ISOLATION VALVE CONNECTOR TERMINALS D AND A

VALVE RESISTANCE MEASURES

GREATER THAN 6.0 OHMS →
- REPLACE THE VALVE ASSEMBLY
- REFER TO "ISOLATION/DUMP VALVE" IN THIS SECTION

3.0-6.0 OHMS → IGNITION "OFF"

IGNITION "OFF"

- REMOVE THE BRAKE FUSE
- INSTALL THE FUSE AFTER 5 SECONDS

PERFORM THE DIAGNOSTIC CIRCUIT CHECK

ALDL CONNECTOR (DIAGNOSTIC TERMINAL)

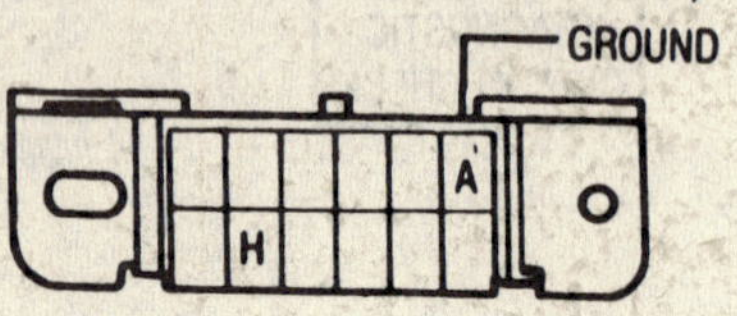

GROUND
A
H

CODE 3
OPEN DUMP VALVE OR MALFUNCTIONING ECU

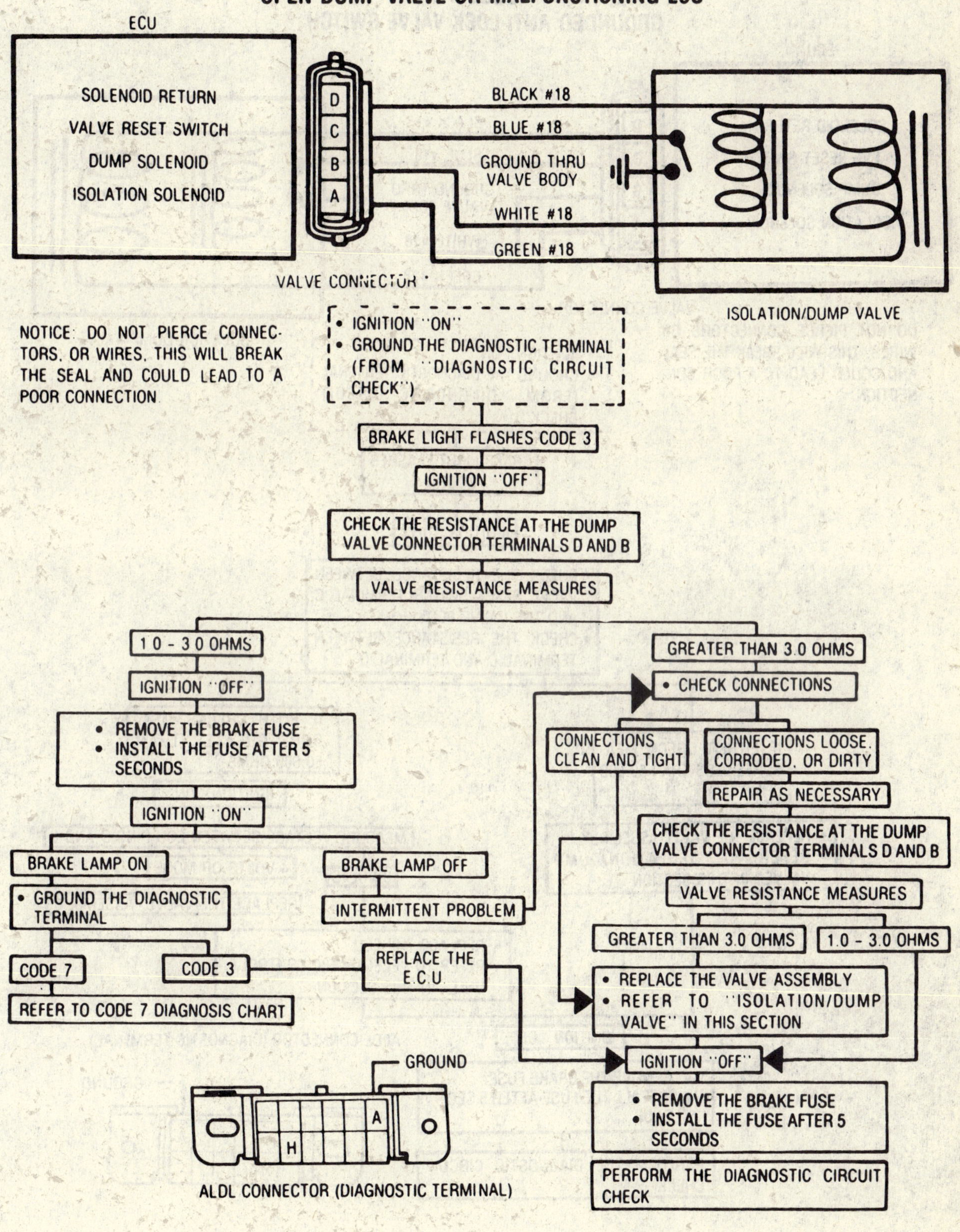

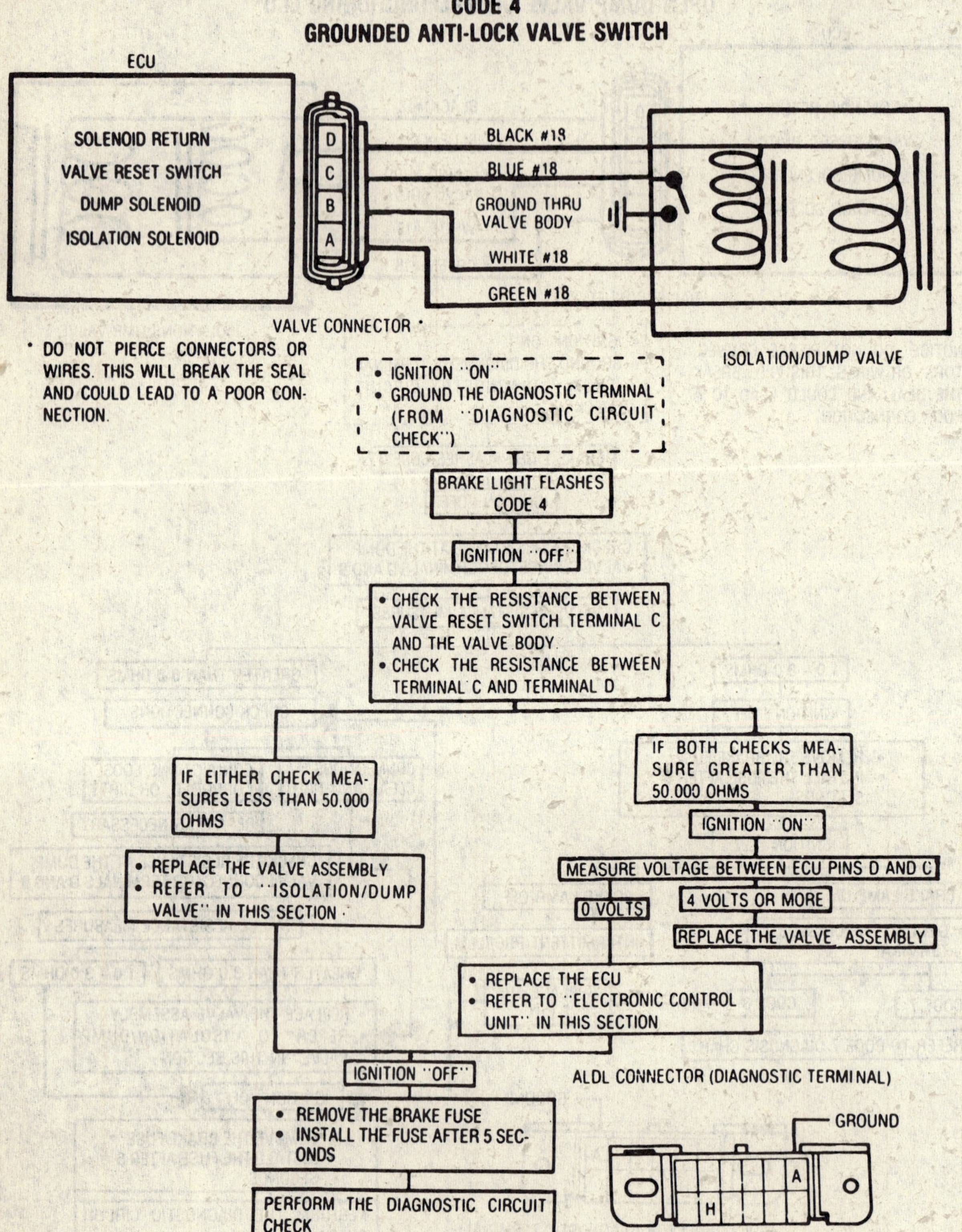
CODE 4
GROUNDED ANTI-LOCK VALVE SWITCH
ECU
SOLENOID RETURN
VALVE RESET SWITCH
DUMP SOLENOID
ISOLATION SOLENOID
D
C
B
A
BLACK #18
BLUE #18
GROUND THRU VALVE BODY
WHITE #18
GREEN #18
VALVE CONNECTOR *
ISOLATION/DUMP VALVE
* DO NOT PIERCE CONNECTORS OR WIRES. THIS WILL BREAK THE SEAL AND COULD LEAD TO A POOR CONNECTION.
• IGNITION "ON"
• GROUND THE DIAGNOSTIC TERMINAL (FROM "DIAGNOSTIC CIRCUIT CHECK")
BRAKE LIGHT FLASHES CODE 4
IGNITION "OFF"
• CHECK THE RESISTANCE BETWEEN VALVE RESET SWITCH TERMINAL C AND THE VALVE BODY
• CHECK THE RESISTANCE BETWEEN TERMINAL C AND TERMINAL D
IF EITHER CHECK MEASURES LESS THAN 50,000 OHMS
IF BOTH CHECKS MEASURE GREATER THAN 50,000 OHMS
• REPLACE THE VALVE ASSEMBLY
• REFER TO "ISOLATION/DUMP VALVE" IN THIS SECTION
IGNITION "ON"
MEASURE VOLTAGE BETWEEN ECU PINS D AND C
0 VOLTS
4 VOLTS OR MORE
REPLACE THE VALVE ASSEMBLY
• REPLACE THE ECU
• REFER TO "ELECTRONIC CONTROL UNIT" IN THIS SECTION
IGNITION "OFF"
• REMOVE THE BRAKE FUSE
• INSTALL THE FUSE AFTER 5 SECONDS
PERFORM THE DIAGNOSTIC CIRCUIT CHECK
ALDL CONNECTOR (DIAGNOSTIC TERMINAL)
GROUND
A
H

CODE 5
EXCESSIVE ACTUATIONS OF THE DUMP VALVE DURING AN ANTILOCK STOP

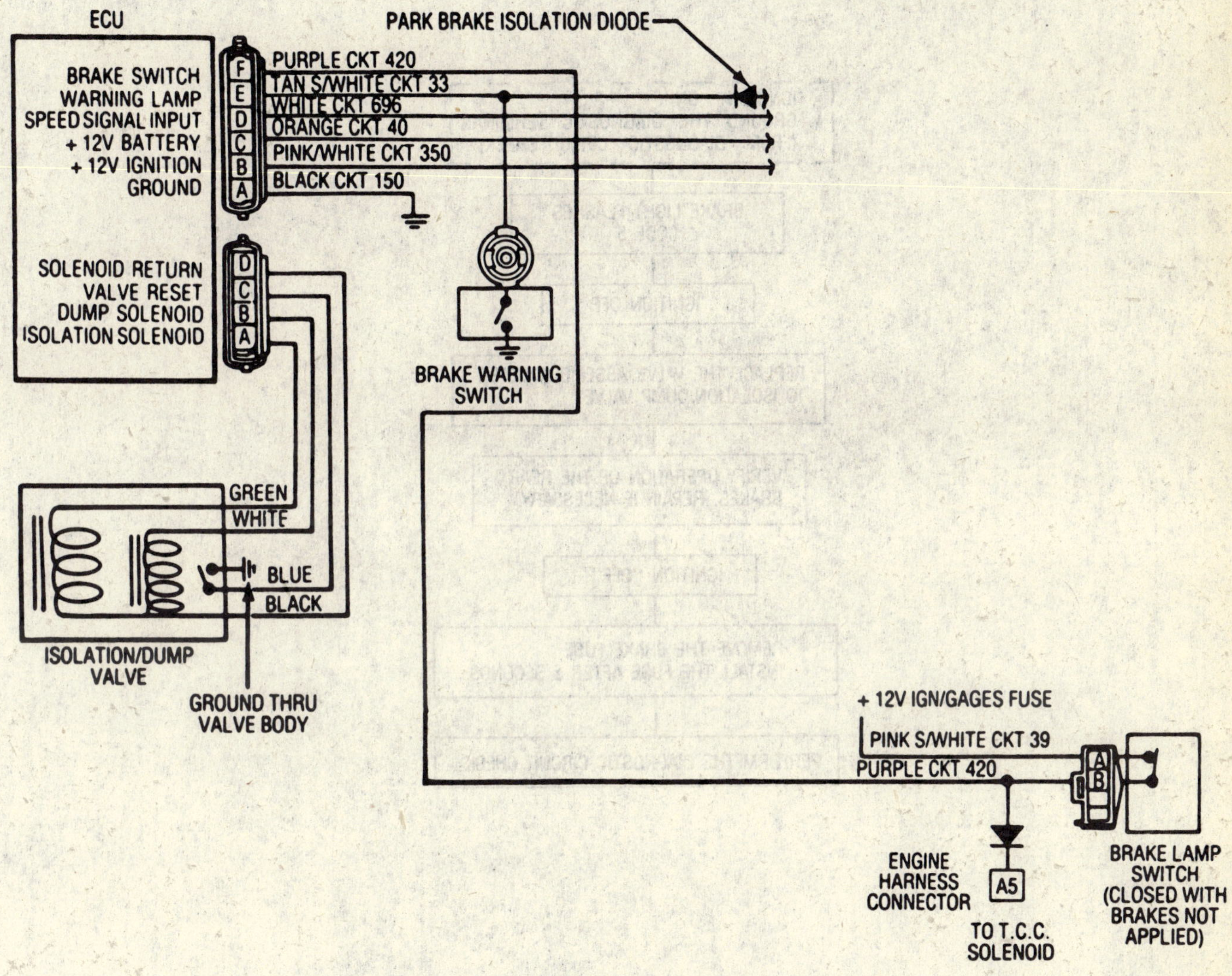

CODE 5
EXCESSIVE ACTUATIONS OF THE DUMP VALVE DURING AN ANTI-LOCK STOP

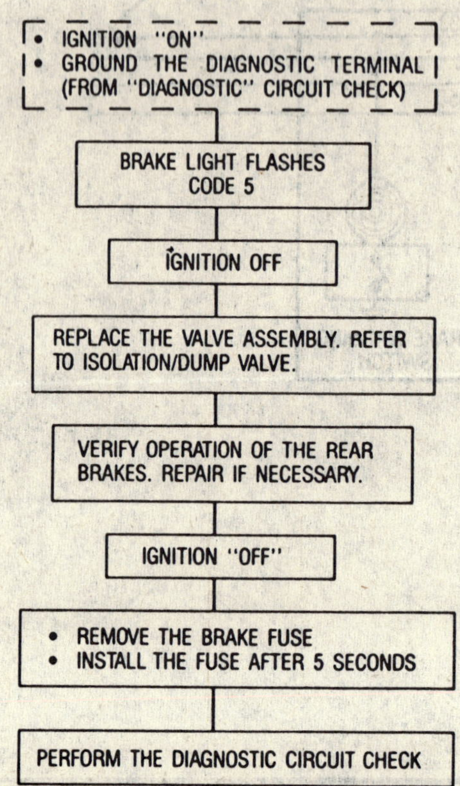

ALDL CONNECTOR (DIAGNOSTIC TERMINAL)

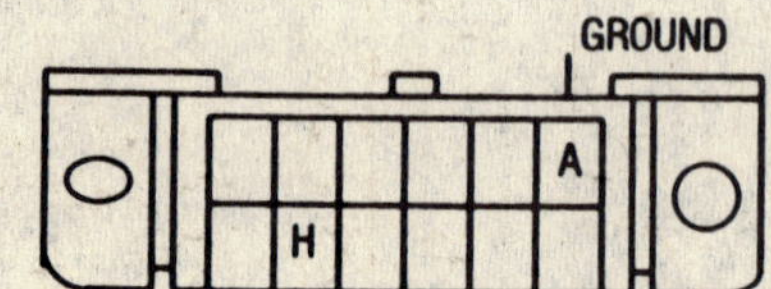

CODE 6
ERRATIC SPEED SIGNAL

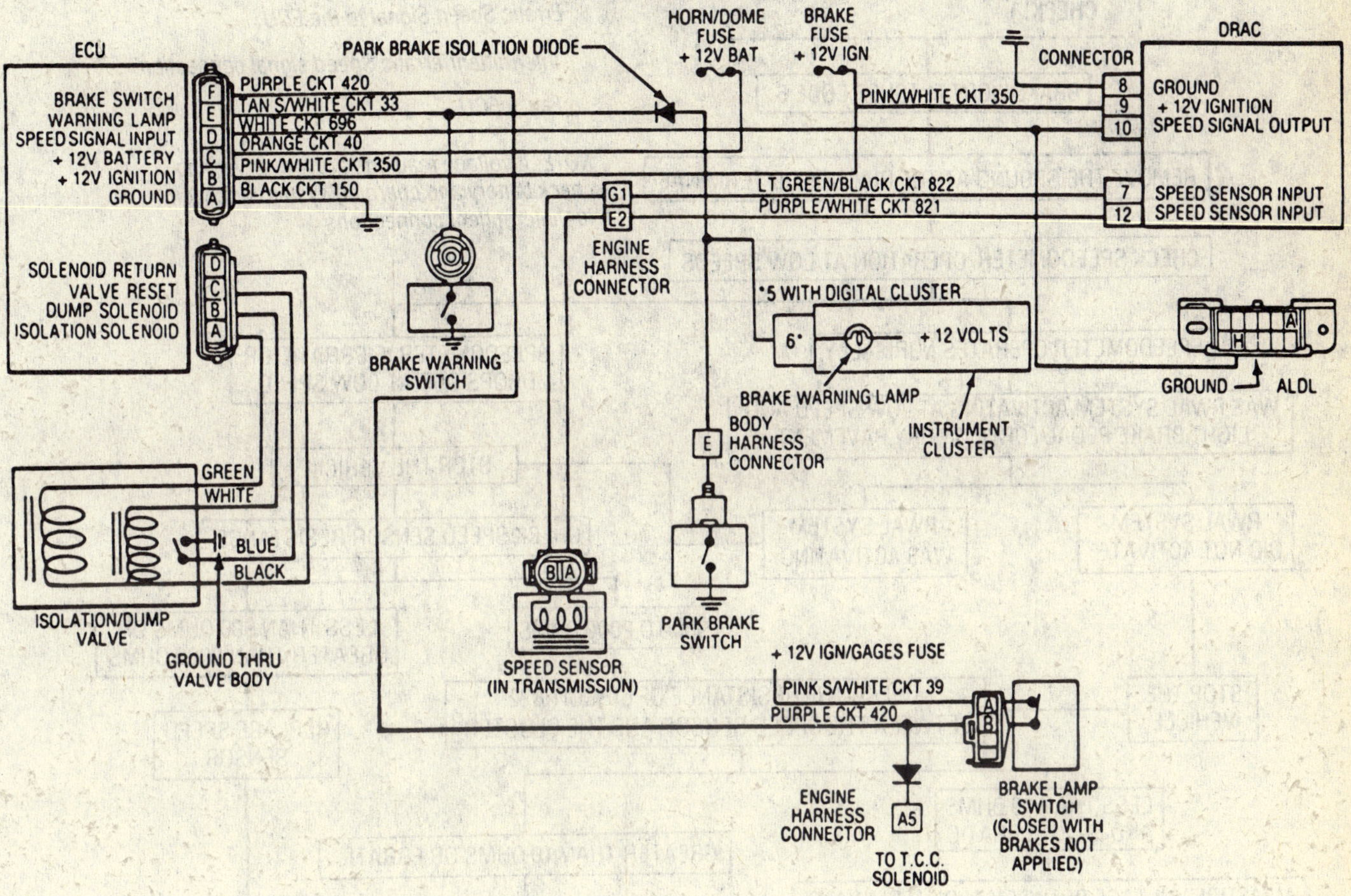

ECU
BRAKE SWITCH
WARNING LAMP
SPEED SIGNAL INPUT
+ 12V BATTERY
+ 12V IGNITION
GROUND
F E D C B A
PURPLE CKT 420
TAN S/WHITE CKT 33
WHITE CKT 696
ORANGE CKT 40
PINK/WHITE CKT 350
BLACK CKT 150
SOLENOID RETURN
VALVE RESET
DUMP SOLENOID
ISOLATION SOLENOID
D C B A
PARK BRAKE ISOLATION DIODE
HORN/DOME FUSE + 12V BAT
BRAKE FUSE + 12V IGN
CONNECTOR
DRAC
8 GROUND
9 + 12V IGNITION
10 SPEED SIGNAL OUTPUT
PINK/WHITE CKT 350
LT GREEN/BLACK CKT 822
PURPLE/WHITE CKT 821
7 SPEED SENSOR INPUT
12 SPEED SENSOR INPUT
G1
E2
ENGINE HARNESS CONNECTOR
BRAKE WARNING SWITCH
*5 WITH DIGITAL CLUSTER
6*
+ 12 VOLTS
BRAKE WARNING LAMP
INSTRUMENT CLUSTER
GROUND
ALDL
A
H
BODY HARNESS CONNECTOR
E
GREEN
WHITE
BLUE
BLACK
ISOLATION/DUMP VALVE
GROUND THRU VALVE BODY
B A
SPEED SENSOR (IN TRANSMISSION)
PARK BRAKE SWITCH
+ 12V IGN/GAGES FUSE
PINK S/WHITE CKT 39
PURPLE CKT 420
A B
ENGINE HARNESS CONNECTOR
A5
TO T.C.C. SOLENOID
BRAKE LAMP SWITCH (CLOSED WITH BRAKES NOT APPLIED)

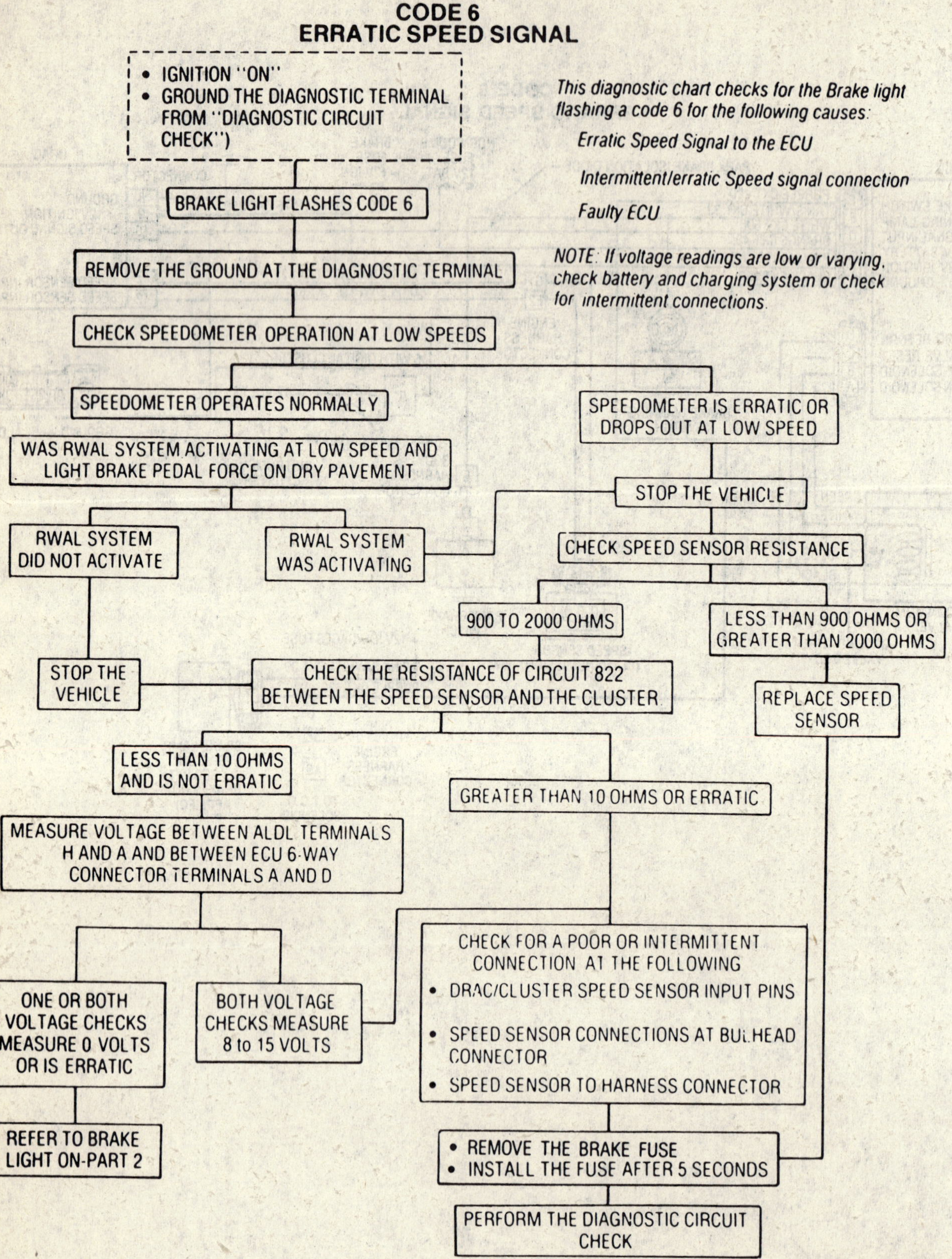

This diagnostic chart checks for the Brake light flashing a code 6 for the following causes:

Erratic Speed Signal to the ECU

Intermittent/erratic Speed signal connection

Faulty ECU

NOTE: If voltage readings are low or varying, check battery and charging system or check for intermittent connections.

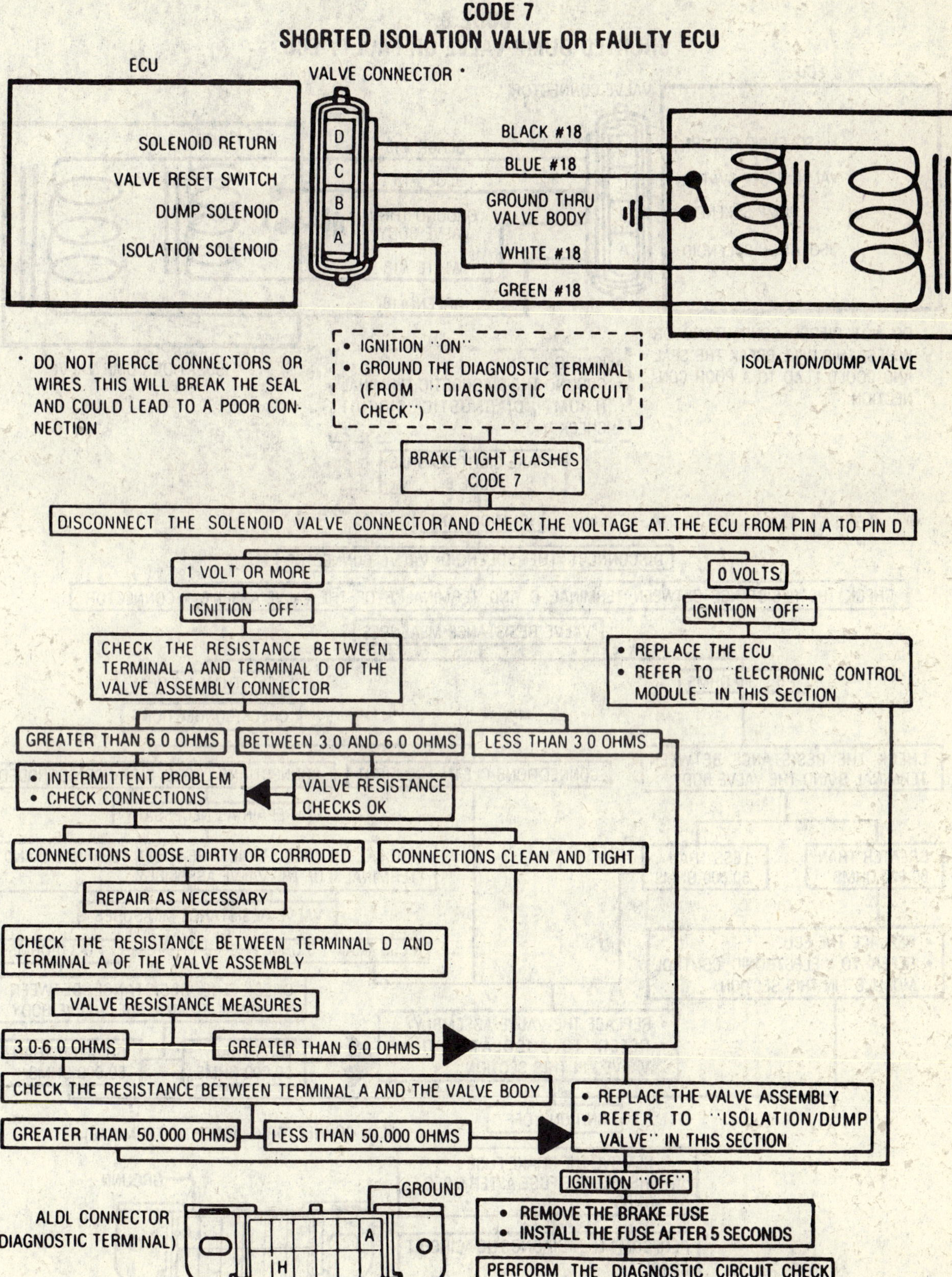
CODE 7
SHORTED ISOLATION VALVE OR FAULTY ECU
ECU
VALVE CONNECTOR *
SOLENOID RETURN
VALVE RESET SWITCH
DUMP SOLENOID
ISOLATION SOLENOID
D
C
B
A
BLACK #18
BLUE #18
GROUND THRU VALVE BODY
WHITE #18
GREEN #18
ISOLATION/DUMP VALVE
* DO NOT PIERCE CONNECTORS OR WIRES. THIS WILL BREAK THE SEAL AND COULD LEAD TO A POOR CONNECTION
• IGNITION "ON"
• GROUND THE DIAGNOSTIC TERMINAL (FROM "DIAGNOSTIC CIRCUIT CHECK")
BRAKE LIGHT FLASHES CODE 7
DISCONNECT THE SOLENOID VALVE CONNECTOR AND CHECK THE VOLTAGE AT THE ECU FROM PIN A TO PIN D
1 VOLT OR MORE
0 VOLTS
IGNITION "OFF"
IGNITION "OFF"
CHECK THE RESISTANCE BETWEEN TERMINAL A AND TERMINAL D OF THE VALVE ASSEMBLY CONNECTOR
• REPLACE THE ECU
• REFER TO "ELECTRONIC CONTROL MODULE" IN THIS SECTION
GREATER THAN 6.0 OHMS
BETWEEN 3.0 AND 6.0 OHMS
LESS THAN 3.0 OHMS
• INTERMITTENT PROBLEM
• CHECK CONNECTIONS
VALVE RESISTANCE CHECKS OK
CONNECTIONS LOOSE, DIRTY OR CORRODED
CONNECTIONS CLEAN AND TIGHT
REPAIR AS NECESSARY
CHECK THE RESISTANCE BETWEEN TERMINAL D AND TERMINAL A OF THE VALVE ASSEMBLY
VALVE RESISTANCE MEASURES
3.0-6.0 OHMS
GREATER THAN 6.0 OHMS
CHECK THE RESISTANCE BETWEEN TERMINAL A AND THE VALVE BODY
• REPLACE THE VALVE ASSEMBLY
• REFER TO "ISOLATION/DUMP VALVE" IN THIS SECTION
GREATER THAN 50,000 OHMS
LESS THAN 50,000 OHMS
IGNITION "OFF"
• REMOVE THE BRAKE FUSE
• INSTALL THE FUSE AFTER 5 SECONDS
PERFORM THE DIAGNOSTIC CIRCUIT CHECK
GROUND
ALDL CONNECTOR
DIAGNOSTIC TERMINAL)
A
H

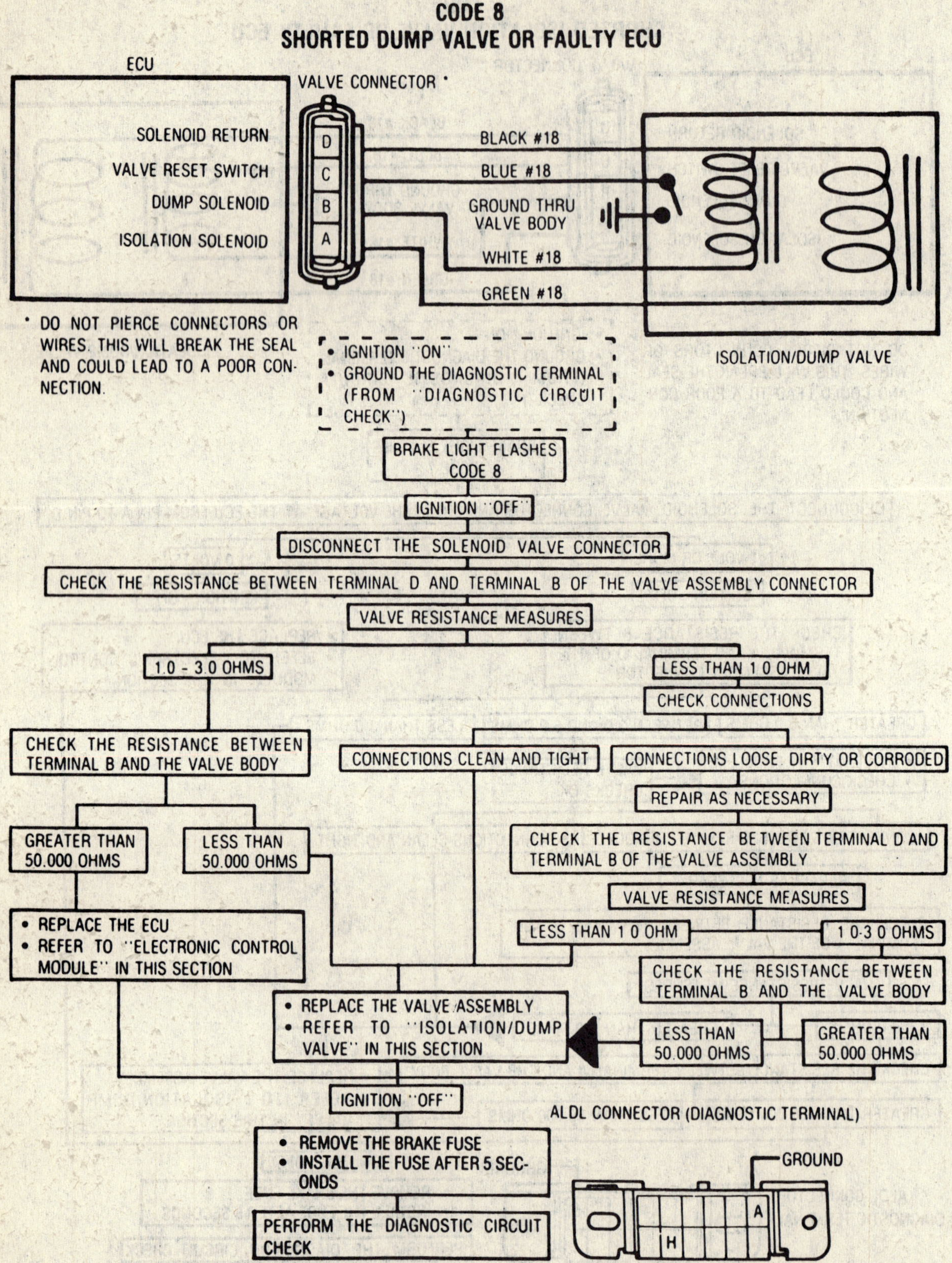
CODE 8
SHORTED DUMP VALVE OR FAULTY ECU
ECU
SOLENOID RETURN
VALVE RESET SWITCH
DUMP SOLENOID
ISOLATION SOLENOID
VALVE CONNECTOR *
D
C
B
A
BLACK #18
BLUE #18
GROUND THRU VALVE BODY
WHITE #18
GREEN #18
ISOLATION/DUMP VALVE
* DO NOT PIERCE CONNECTORS OR WIRES. THIS WILL BREAK THE SEAL AND COULD LEAD TO A POOR CONNECTION.
• IGNITION "ON"
• GROUND THE DIAGNOSTIC TERMINAL (FROM "DIAGNOSTIC CIRCUIT CHECK")
BRAKE LIGHT FLASHES CODE 8
IGNITION "OFF"
DISCONNECT THE SOLENOID VALVE CONNECTOR
CHECK THE RESISTANCE BETWEEN TERMINAL D AND TERMINAL B OF THE VALVE ASSEMBLY CONNECTOR
VALVE RESISTANCE MEASURES
1.0 - 3.0 OHMS
LESS THAN 1.0 OHM
CHECK CONNECTIONS
CHECK THE RESISTANCE BETWEEN TERMINAL B AND THE VALVE BODY
CONNECTIONS CLEAN AND TIGHT
CONNECTIONS LOOSE, DIRTY OR CORRODED
REPAIR AS NECESSARY
GREATER THAN 50,000 OHMS
LESS THAN 50,000 OHMS
CHECK THE RESISTANCE BETWEEN TERMINAL D AND TERMINAL B OF THE VALVE ASSEMBLY
VALVE RESISTANCE MEASURES
LESS THAN 1.0 OHM
1.0-3.0 OHMS
• REPLACE THE ECU
• REFER TO "ELECTRONIC CONTROL MODULE" IN THIS SECTION
CHECK THE RESISTANCE BETWEEN TERMINAL B AND THE VALVE BODY
• REPLACE THE VALVE ASSEMBLY
• REFER TO "ISOLATION/DUMP VALVE" IN THIS SECTION
LESS THAN 50,000 OHMS
GREATER THAN 50,000 OHMS
IGNITION "OFF"
ALDL CONNECTOR (DIAGNOSTIC TERMINAL)
GROUND
A
H
• REMOVE THE BRAKE FUSE
• INSTALL THE FUSE AFTER 5 SECONDS
PERFORM THE DIAGNOSTIC CIRCUIT CHECK

CODE 9
OPEN CIRCUIT TO THE SPEED SIGNAL

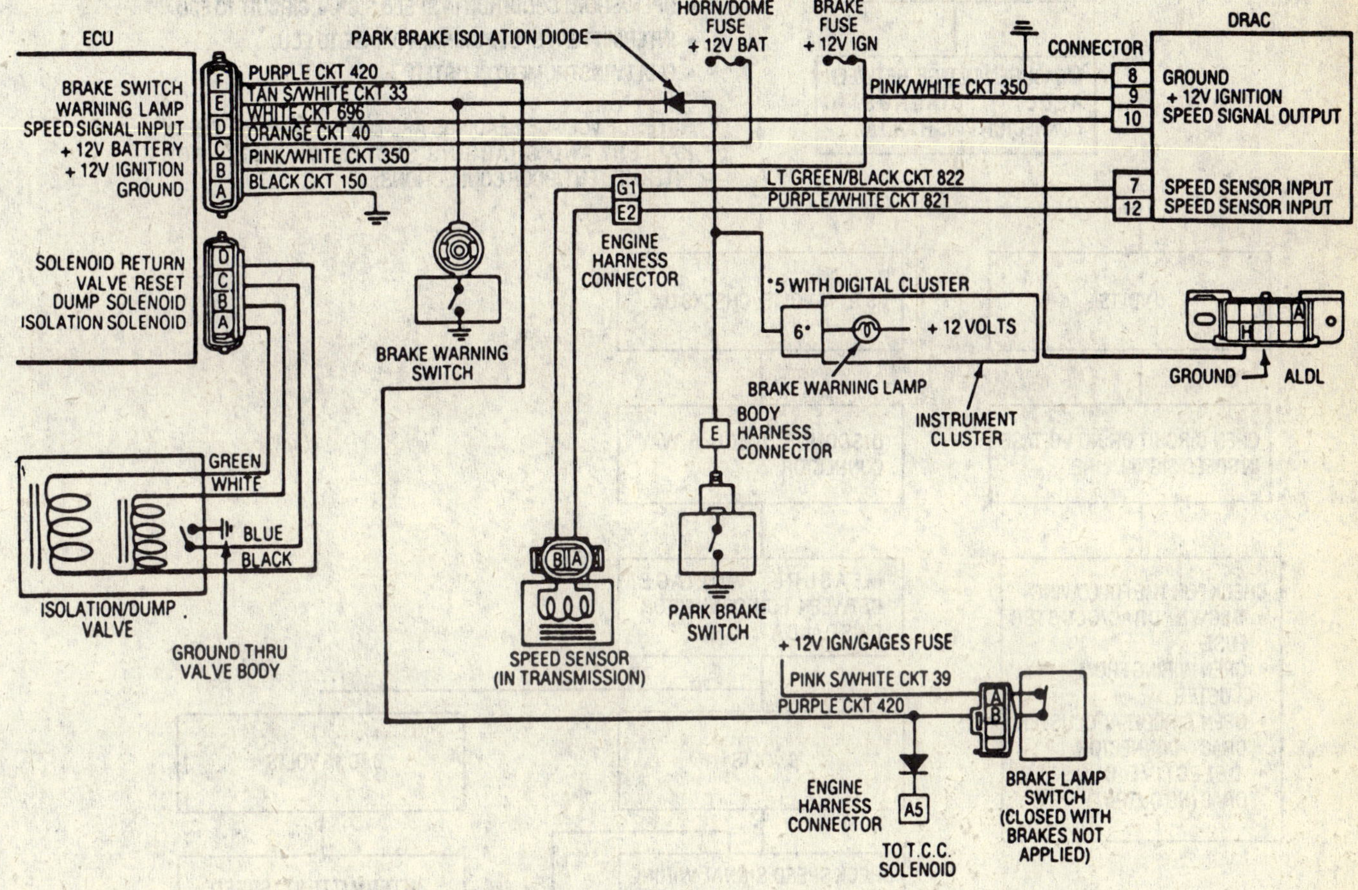

CODE 9
OPEN CIRCUIT TO THE SPEED SIGNAL

THIS DIAGNOSTIC CHART CHECKS FOR THE BRAKE LIGHT FLASHING FOR THE FOLLOWING CAUSES -

- OPEN/SHORT CONDITION IN SPEED SIGNAL CIRCUIT TO ECU
- INTERMITTENT SPEED SIGNAL VOLTAGE TO ECU
- FAULTY INSTRUMENT CLUSTER

NOTE: IF VOLTAGE READINGS ARE LOW OR VARYING, CHECK BATTERY AND CHARGING SYSTEM OR CHECK FOR INTERMITTENT/POOR CONNECTIONS.

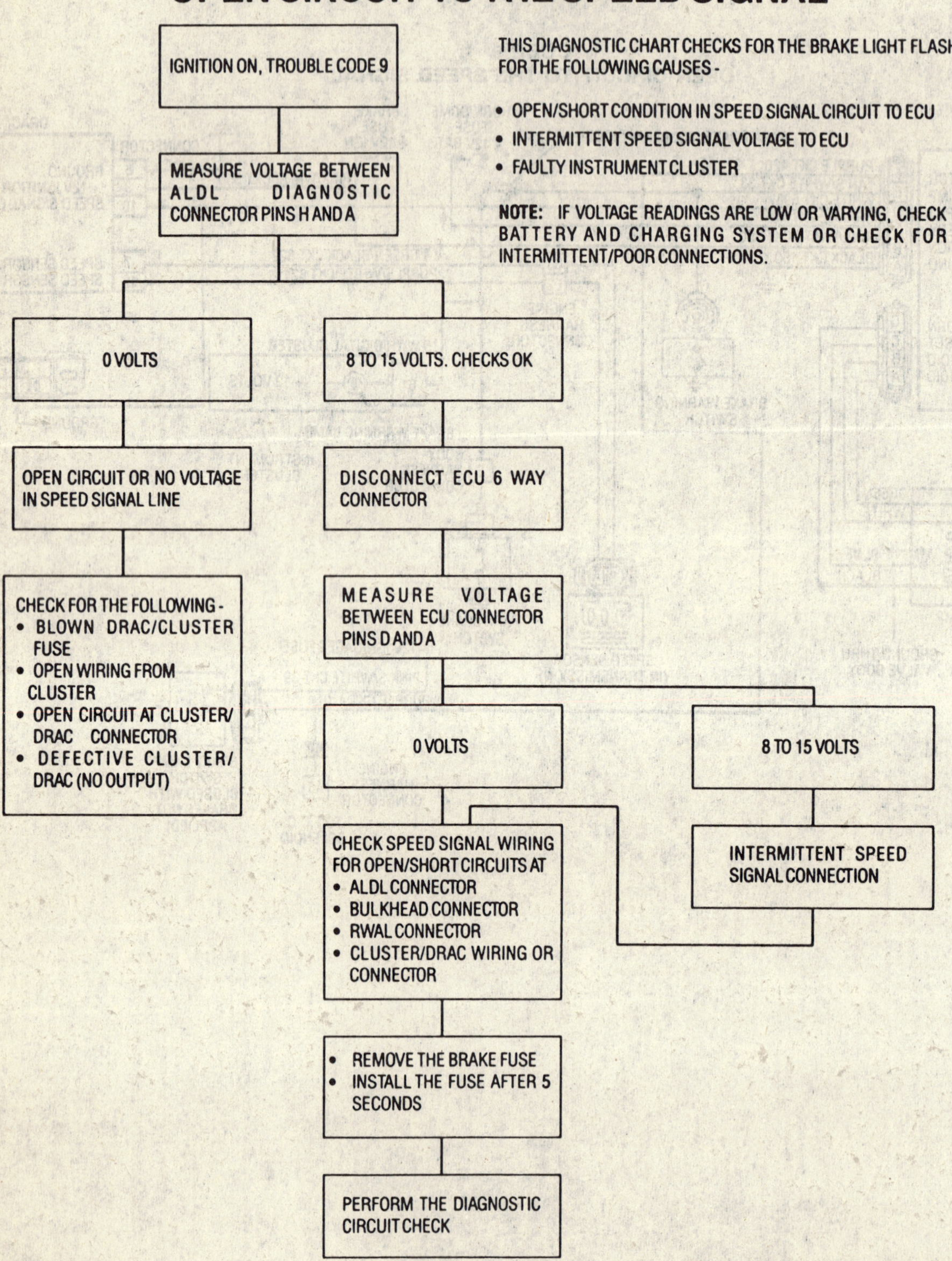

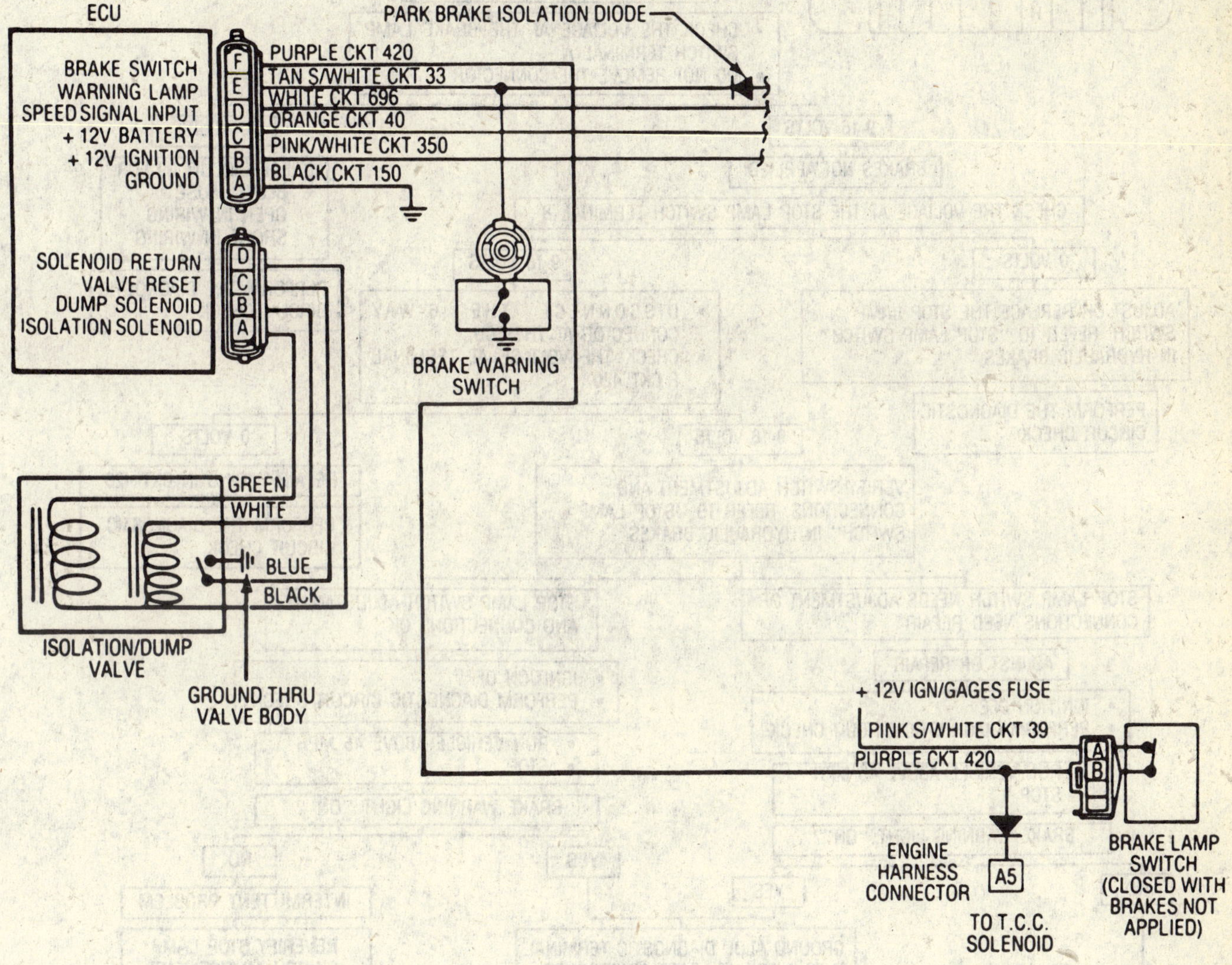
CODE 10
BRAKE LAMP SWITCH CIRCUIT
ECU
BRAKE SWITCH
WARNING LAMP
SPEED SIGNAL INPUT
+ 12V BATTERY
+ 12V IGNITION
GROUND
F
E
D
C
B
A
PURPLE CKT 420
TAN S/WHITE CKT 33
WHITE CKT 696
ORANGE CKT 40
PINK/WHITE CKT 350
BLACK CKT 150
PARK BRAKE ISOLATION DIODE
SOLENOID RETURN
VALVE RESET
DUMP SOLENOID
ISOLATION SOLENOID
D
C
B
A
BRAKE WARNING
SWITCH
GREEN
WHITE
BLUE
BLACK
ISOLATION/DUMP
VALVE
GROUND THRU
VALVE BODY
+ 12V IGN/GAGES FUSE
PINK S/WHITE CKT 39
PURPLE CKT 420
A
B
ENGINE
HARNESS
CONNECTOR
A5
TO T.C.C.
SOLENOID
BRAKE LAMP
SWITCH
(CLOSED WITH
BRAKES NOT
APPLIED)

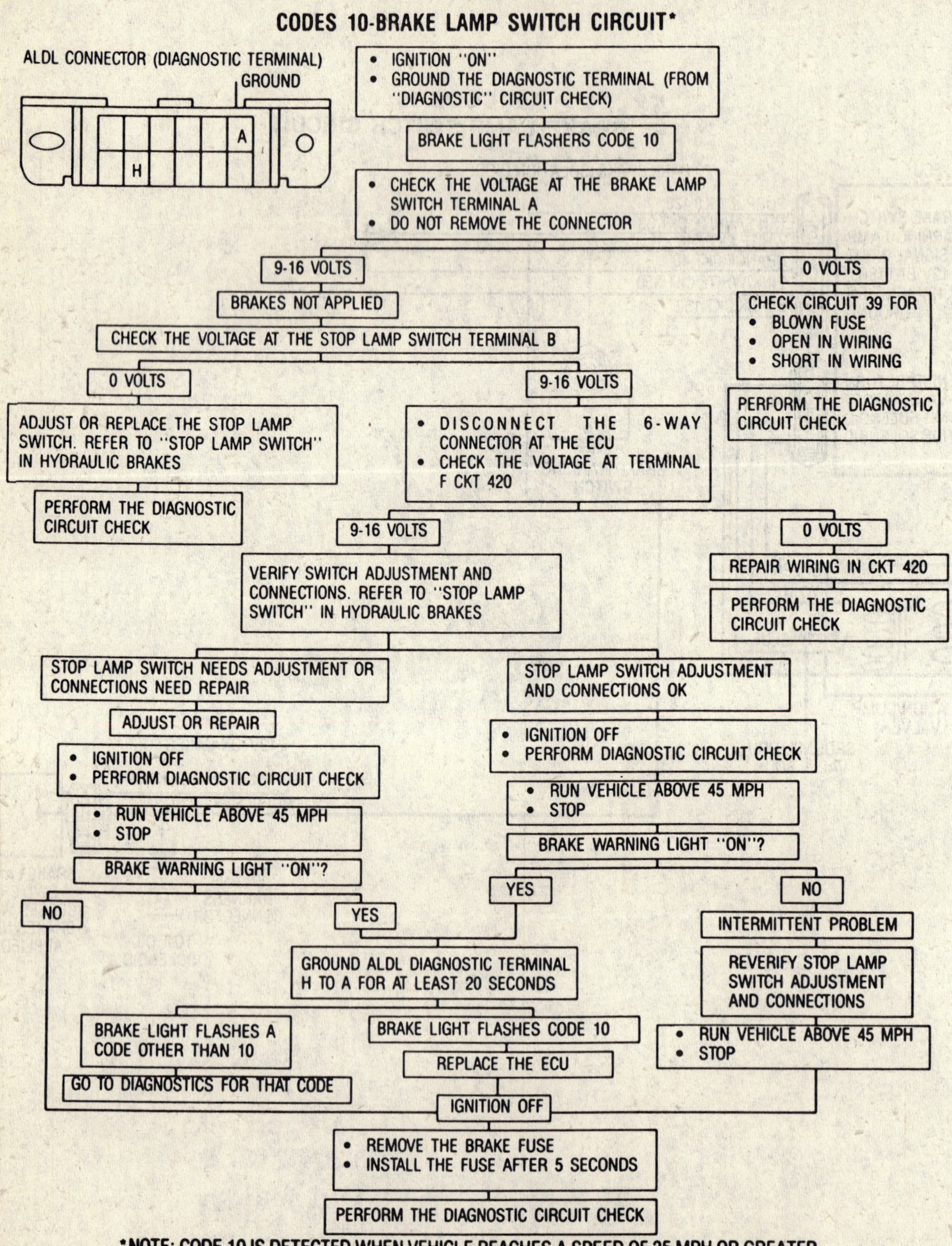
CODES 10-BRAKE LAMP SWITCH CIRCUIT*
ALDL CONNECTOR (DIAGNOSTIC TERMINAL)
GROUND
A
H
• IGNITION "ON"
• GROUND THE DIAGNOSTIC TERMINAL (FROM "DIAGNOSTIC" CIRCUIT CHECK)
BRAKE LIGHT FLASHERS CODE 10
• CHECK THE VOLTAGE AT THE BRAKE LAMP SWITCH TERMINAL A
• DO NOT REMOVE THE CONNECTOR
9-16 VOLTS
0 VOLTS
BRAKES NOT APPLIED
CHECK CIRCUIT 39 FOR
• BLOWN FUSE
• OPEN IN WIRING
• SHORT IN WIRING
CHECK THE VOLTAGE AT THE STOP LAMP SWITCH TERMINAL B
PERFORM THE DIAGNOSTIC CIRCUIT CHECK
0 VOLTS
9-16 VOLTS
ADJUST OR REPLACE THE STOP LAMP SWITCH. REFER TO "STOP LAMP SWITCH" IN HYDRAULIC BRAKES
• DISCONNECT THE 6-WAY CONNECTOR AT THE ECU
• CHECK THE VOLTAGE AT TERMINAL F CKT 420
PERFORM THE DIAGNOSTIC CIRCUIT CHECK
9-16 VOLTS
0 VOLTS
VERIFY SWITCH ADJUSTMENT AND CONNECTIONS. REFER TO "STOP LAMP SWITCH" IN HYDRAULIC BRAKES
REPAIR WIRING IN CKT 420
PERFORM THE DIAGNOSTIC CIRCUIT CHECK
STOP LAMP SWITCH NEEDS ADJUSTMENT OR CONNECTIONS NEED REPAIR
STOP LAMP SWITCH ADJUSTMENT AND CONNECTIONS OK
ADJUST OR REPAIR
• IGNITION OFF
• PERFORM DIAGNOSTIC CIRCUIT CHECK
• IGNITION OFF
• PERFORM DIAGNOSTIC CIRCUIT CHECK
• RUN VEHICLE ABOVE 45 MPH
• STOP
• RUN VEHICLE ABOVE 45 MPH
• STOP
BRAKE WARNING LIGHT "ON"?
BRAKE WARNING LIGHT "ON"?
YES
NO
NO
YES
INTERMITTENT PROBLEM
REVERIFY STOP LAMP SWITCH ADJUSTMENT AND CONNECTIONS
GROUND ALDL DIAGNOSTIC TERMINAL H TO A FOR AT LEAST 20 SECONDS
• RUN VEHICLE ABOVE 45 MPH
• STOP
BRAKE LIGHT FLASHES A CODE OTHER THAN 10
BRAKE LIGHT FLASHES CODE 10
REPLACE THE ECU
GO TO DIAGNOSTICS FOR THAT CODE
IGNITION OFF
• REMOVE THE BRAKE FUSE
• INSTALL THE FUSE AFTER 5 SECONDS
PERFORM THE DIAGNOSTIC CIRCUIT CHECK
*NOTE: CODE 10 IS DETECTED WHEN VEHICLE REACHES A SPEED OF 35 MPH OR GREATER

CODES 1, 11 AND 12
ELECTRONIC CONTROL UNIT MALFUNCTION

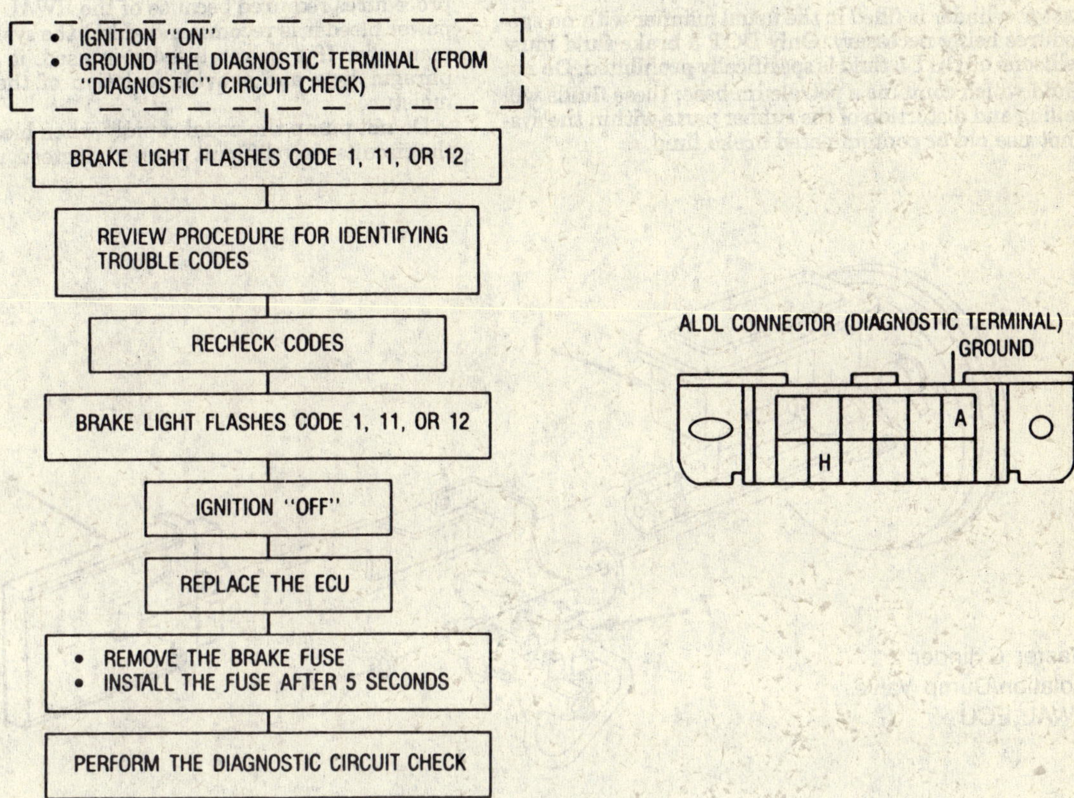

CODE 13, 14, AND 15
ELECTRONIC CONTROL UNIT MALFUNCTION

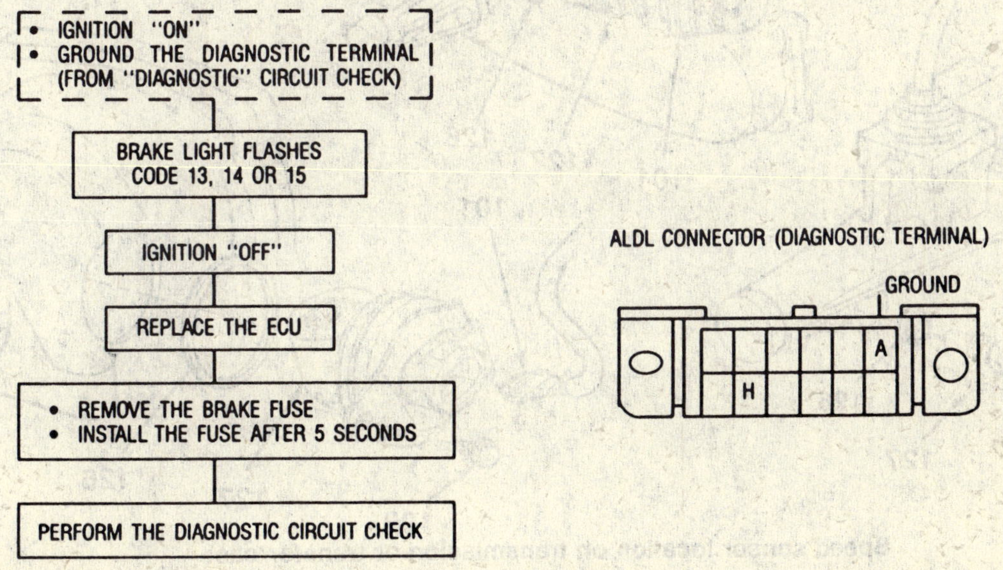

Component Replacement

SYSTEM FILLING

The master cylinder is filled in the usual manner with no special procedures being necessary. Only DOT 3 brake fluid must be used; silicone or DOT 5 fluid is specifically prohibited. Do not use any fluid which contains a petroleum base; these fluids will cause swelling and distortion of the rubber parts within the system. Do not use old or contaminated brake fluid.

SYSTEM BLEEDING

The brake system is bled in the usual manner with no special procedures required because of the RWAL system. The use of a power bleeder is recommended but the system may also be bled manually. If a power bleeder is used, it must be of the diaphragm type and provide isolation of the fluid from air and moisture.

Do not pump the pedal rapidly when bleeding; this can make the circuits very difficult to bleed. Instead, press the brake pedal

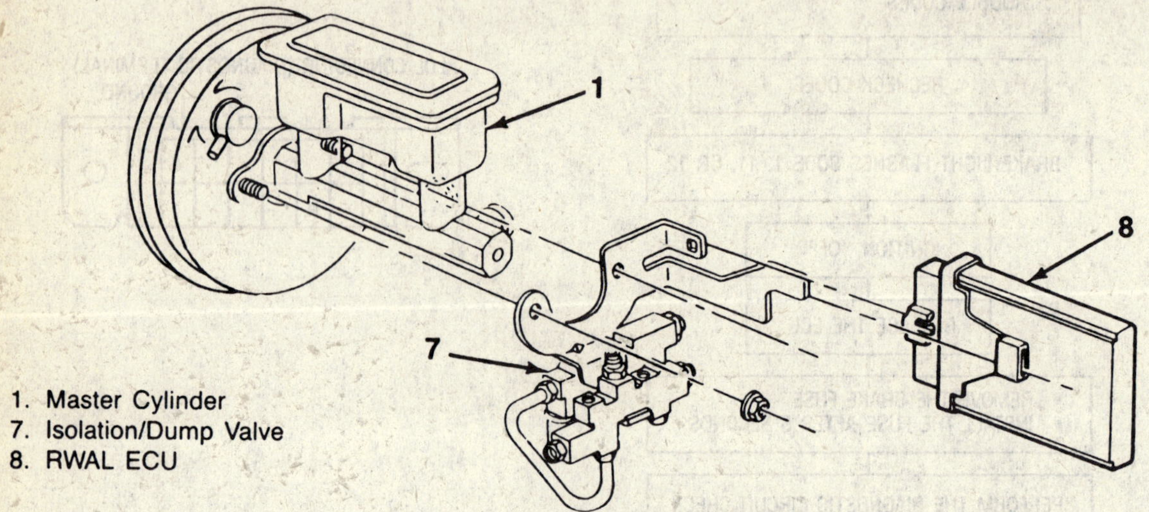

Rear wheel anti-lock control unit

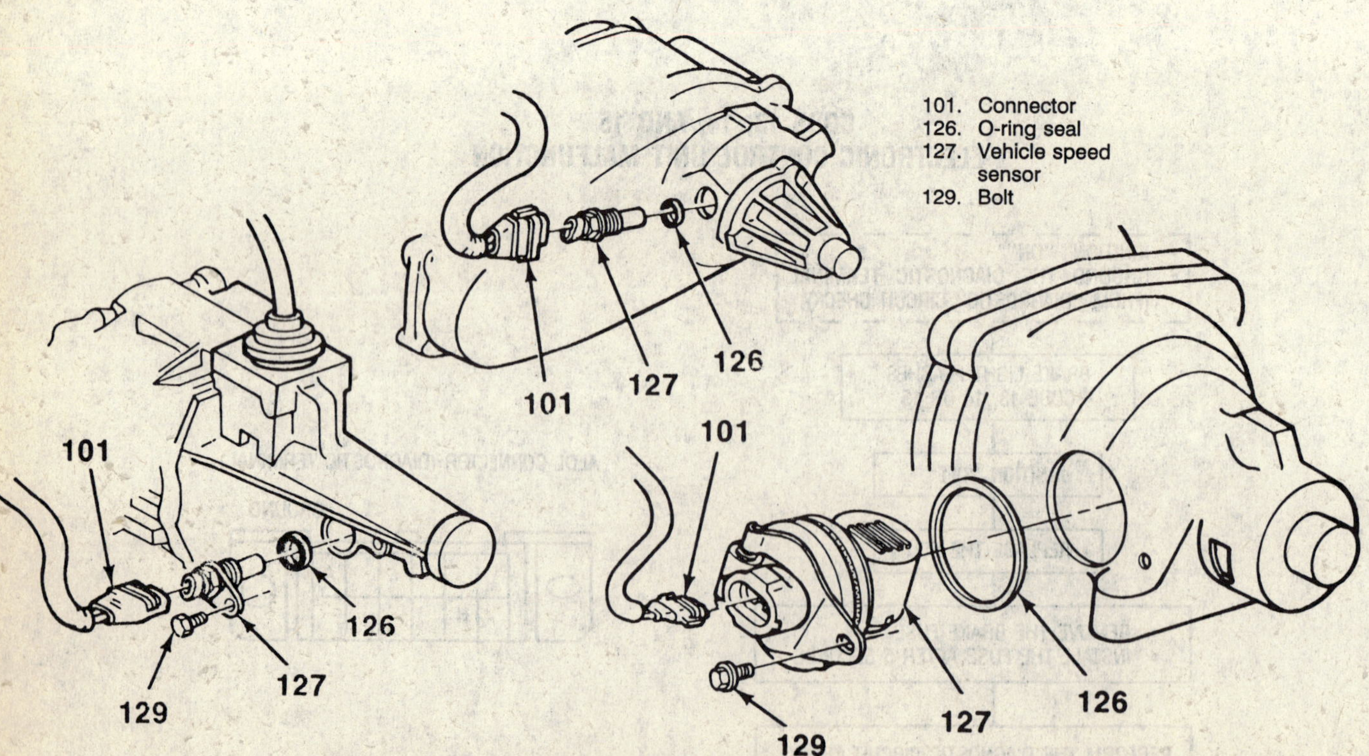

Speed sensor location on transmission or transfer case

slowly 1 time and hold it down while bleeding takes place. Tighten the bleeder screw, release the pedal and wait 15 seconds before repeating the sequence. Because of the length of the brake lines and other factors, it may take 10 or more repetitions of the sequence to bleed each line properly. When necessary to bleed all 4 wheels, the correct order is right rear, left rear, right front and left front.

CAUTION

Do not move the vehicle until a firm brake pedal is achieved. Failure to properly bleed the system may cause impaired braking and the possibility of injury and/or property damage

RWAL ELECTRONIC CONTROL UNIT (ECU)

REMOVAL AND INSTALLATION

The RWAL ECU is a non-serviceable unit. It must be replaced when diagnosis indicates a malfunction.

1. Turn the ignition switch **OFF**.
2. Disconnect the wiring harness to the ECU.
3. Gently pry the tab at the rear of the ECU; remove the control unit toward the front of the vehicle.

NOTE: Do not touch the electrical connectors or pins; do not allow them to contact brake fluid. If contaminated with brake fluid, clean them with water followed by isopropyl alcohol.

4. Install the RWAL ECU by sliding it into the bracket until the tab locks into the hole.
5. Connect the wiring harness to the ECU.

ISOLATION/DUMP VALVE (CONTROL VALVE)

REMOVAL AND INSTALLATION

1. Disconnect the brake line fittings at the valve. Protect surrounding paintwork from spillage.
2. Remove the bolts holding the valve to the bracket.
3. Disconnect the bottom connector from the RWAL ECU. Do not allow the isolation/dump valve to hang by the wiring.

NOTE: Do not touch the electrical connectors or pins; do not allow them to contact brake fluid. If contaminated with brake fluid, clean them with water followed by isopropyl alcohol.

4. Remove the valve from the vehicle.

To install:

5. Place the valve in position and install the retaining bolts. Tighten the bolts to 21 ft. lbs. (29 Nm).
6. Connect the electrical connector to the RWAL ECU.
7. Install the brake lines; tighten the fittings to 18 ft. lbs. (24 Nm)
8. Bleed the brake system at all 4 wheels.

SPEED SENSOR

REMOVAL AND INSTALLATION

The speed sensor is not serviceable and must replaced if malfunctioning. The sensor is located in the left rear of the transmission case on 2wd vehicles and on the transfer case of 4wd vehicles.

The speed sensor may be tested with an ohmmeter; the correct resistance is 900–2000 ohms. To remove the speed sensor:

1. Disconnect the electrical connector from the speed sensor.
2. Remove the sensor retaining bolt if one is used.
3. Remove the speed sensor; have a container handy to catch transmission fluid when the sensor is removed.
4. Recover the O-ring used to seal the sensor; inspect it for damage or deterioration.

To install:

5. When installing, coat the new O-ring with a thin film of transmission fluid.
6. Install the O-ring and speed sensor.
7. If a retaining bolt is used, tighten the bolt to 8 ft. lbs. (11 Nm) in automatic transmissions or 9 ft. lbs. (12 Nm) for all other transmissions.
8. If the sensor is a screw-in unit, tighten it to 32 ft. lbs. (43 Nm).
9. Connect the wire harness to the sensor.

4-WHEEL ANTILOCK SYSTEM

General Description

The 4 wheel anti-lock system is designed to reduce brake lock-up during severe brake application. The electro–hydraulic control unit (EHCU) valve—located under the master cylinder—controls the hydraulic pressure within the brake lines.

The control valve is made up of 2 types of valves. Each front wheel and the combined rear wheels are served by a dedicated isolation valve and a dump valve. The isolation valves maintain pressure within their respective circuits; the dump valves release pressure within each circuit as commanded by the EHCU. The valves are controlled by a micro-computer within the EHCU valve.

SYSTEM OPERATION

In a severe brake application, the EHCU valve will allow pressure to increase within the system, maintain or isolate pressure within the system or release pressure through the dump valves into the accumulators.

The EHCU valve operates by receiving signals from the speed sensors which are located at each wheel and from the brake lamp switch. The speed sensors connect directly to the EHCU valve through an 8 pin connector.

The system is connected to the ANTILOCK warning lamp on the dashboard. The warning lamp will illuminate for about 2 seconds every time the vehicle is started. The warning lamp will

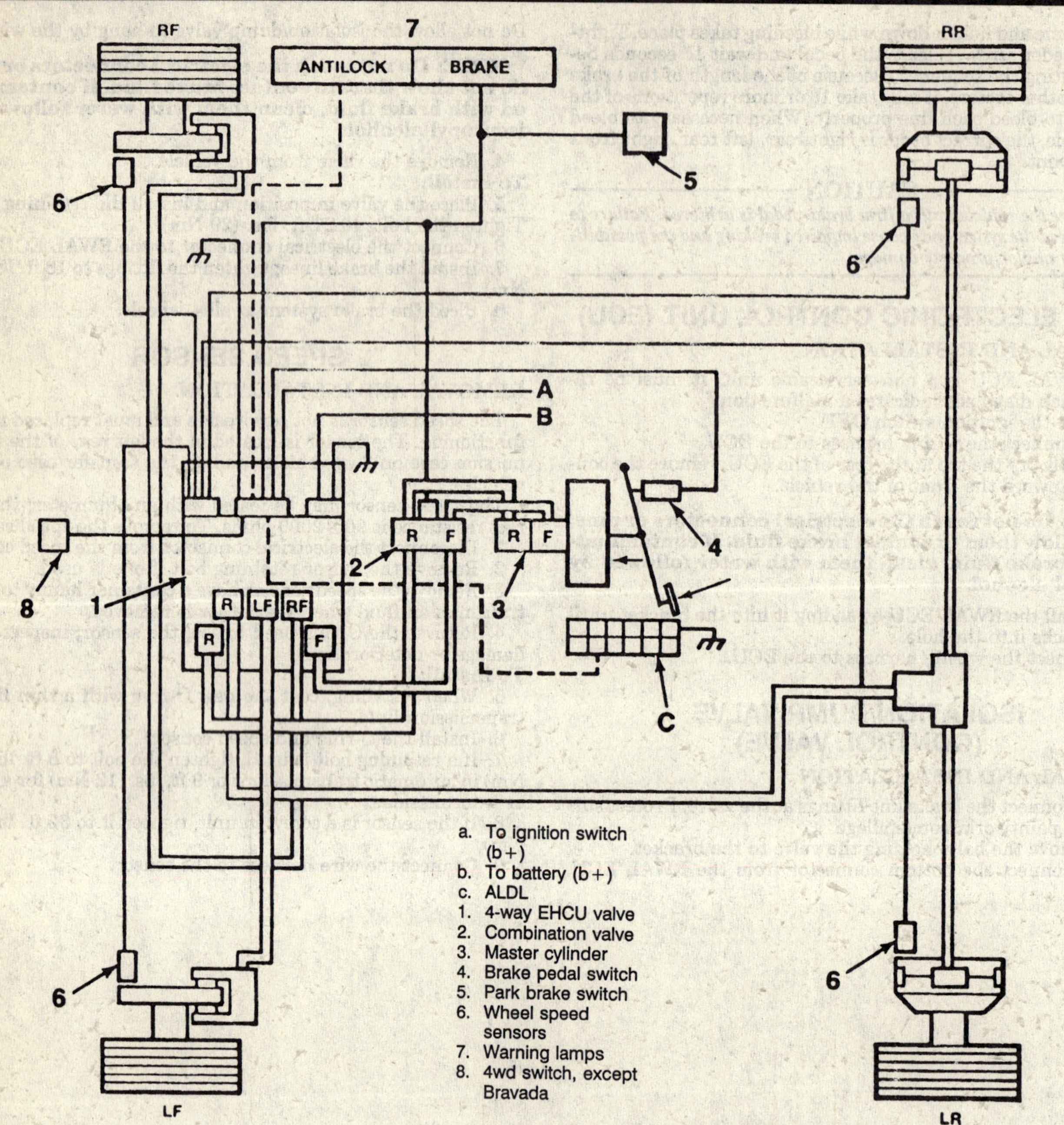

Four wheel anti-lock brake system

illuminate if the micro-computer detects a problem within the anti-lock system during vehicle operation.

SYSTEM COMPONENTS

EHCU Valve

The EHCU valve is mounted underneath the master cylinder and combination valve. The valve is not serviceable and must be replaced if malfunctioning.

Front Wheel Speed Sensors

On both 2- and 4-WD vehicles, the front wheel speed sensors are permanently mounted to the brake rotor splash shield. If the sensor fails, the rotor and splash shield must be removed. On four-wheel drive vehicles, the hub and bearing assembly must also be removed for access.

Rear Wheel Speed Sensors

The rear wheel speed sensors are held by 2 bolts at each rear wheel. The brake drum and primary brake shoe must be removed for access.

Diagnosis and Testing

PRELIMINARY DIAGNOSIS

System diagnosis begins with the diagnostic circuit check as given in the chart. If the chart is used correctly, it will aid in

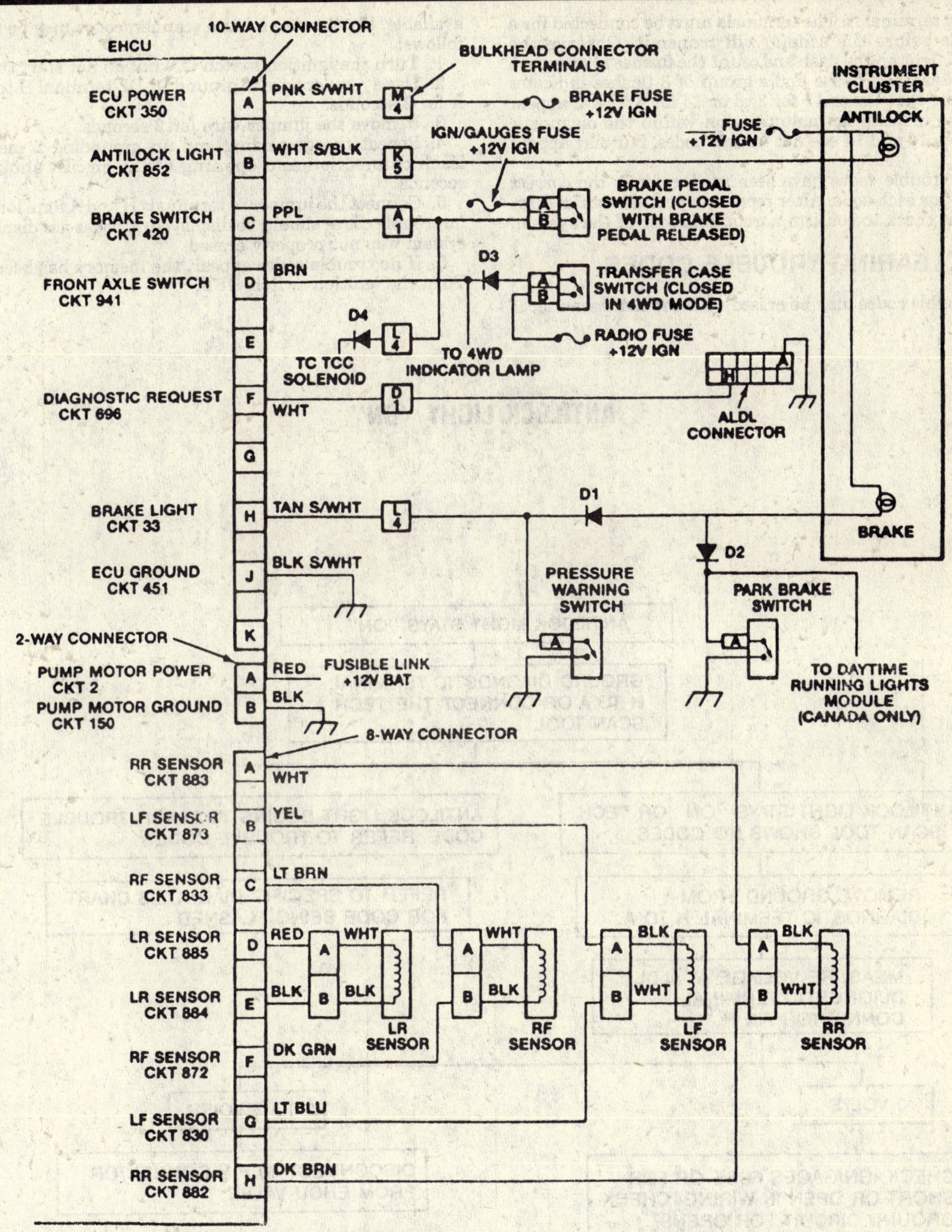

Four wheel anti-lock wiring diagram: Front axle switch connection "D" not present on Bravada

elimination of simple, non–system problems such as blown fuses or failed bulbs. The chart will prompt the reading of codes at the proper point in the diagnosis.

READING TROUBLE CODES

Stored trouble codes are transmitted through the flashing of the amber ANTILOCK dash warning light. The system may be put into diagnostic mode with a jumper wire, however the use of the Tech 1 hand scanning tool or its equivalent is highly recommended. The scanner will allow performance of specific system tests called for by the trouble tree for each code.

To read trouble codes without the use of a hand scanner, use a jumper wire to connect terminal H on the ALDL to either body ground or to terminal A. The terminals must be connected for a few seconds before the code(s) will transmit. Observe the ANTILOCK light on the dash and count the flashes in groups: a group of 4 flashes, a pause and a group of 3 flashes indicates Code 43. Note that Codes 12 for 2wd or 14 for 4wd will appear frequently to indicate normal operation within the diagnostic circuit. Codes 12 and 14 are not trouble codes, but may appear with them.

After the trouble codes have been read, refer to the correct trouble tree for each code. After repairs, repeat the initial diagnostic circuit check to confirm normal behavior of the system.

CLEARING TROUBLE CODES

Stored trouble codes may be erased with the hand scanner if available. If not using a hand scanner, codes may be cleared as follows:

1. Turn the ignition switch **ON** but do not start the engine.
2. Use a jumper wire to ground ALDL terminal H to terminal A for 2 seconds.
3. Remove the jumper wire for 2 seconds.
4. Repeat the grounding and un-grounding 2 more times. Each connection and opening of the circuit should last 2 seconds.
5. Connect the jumper to terminals H and A for a longer time; no trouble codes should be displayed. If codes are displayed, the system was not properly erased.
6. If no trouble codes appear, the memory has been cleared. Turn the ignition switch **OFF**.

ANTILOCK LIGHT "ON"

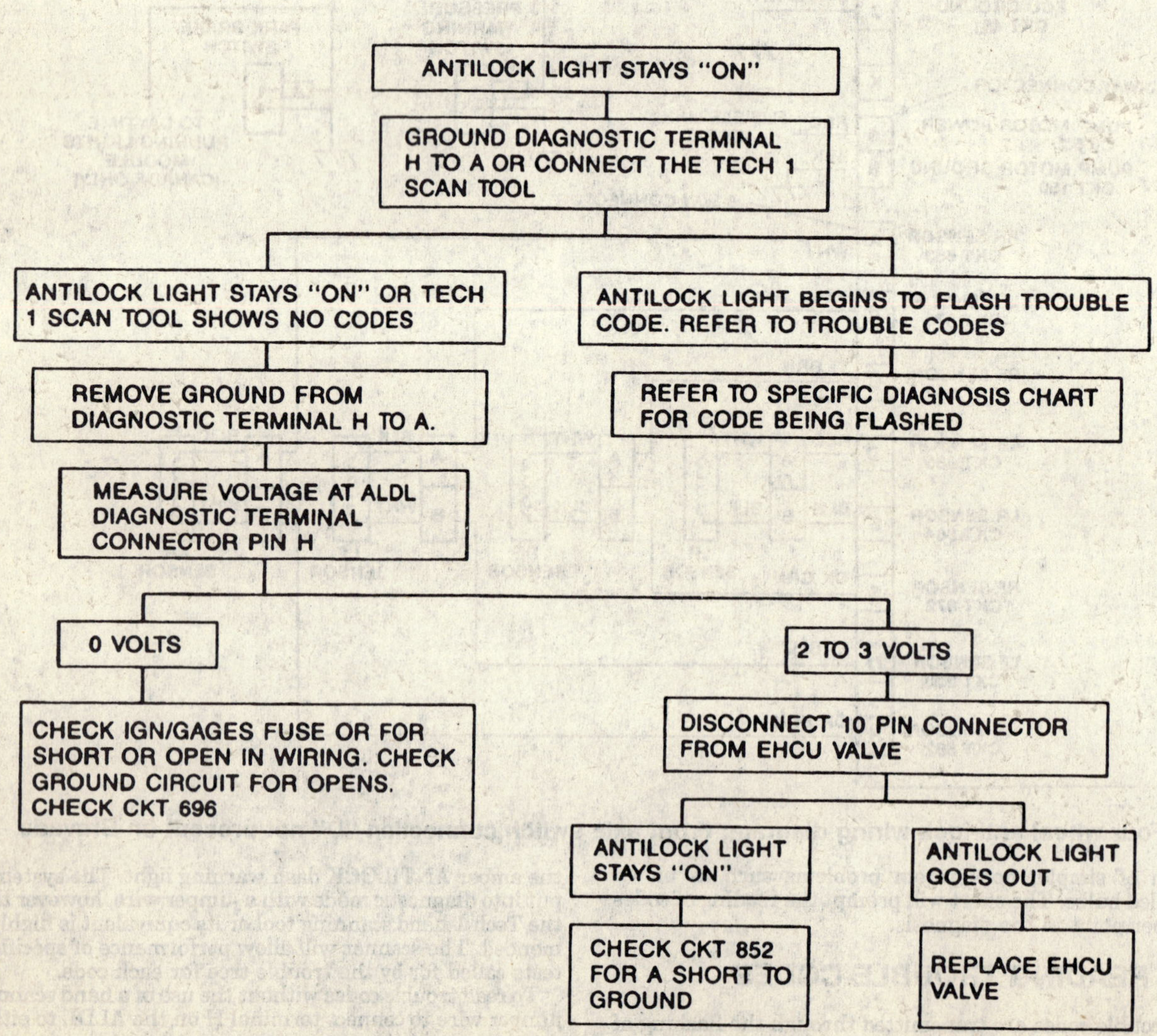

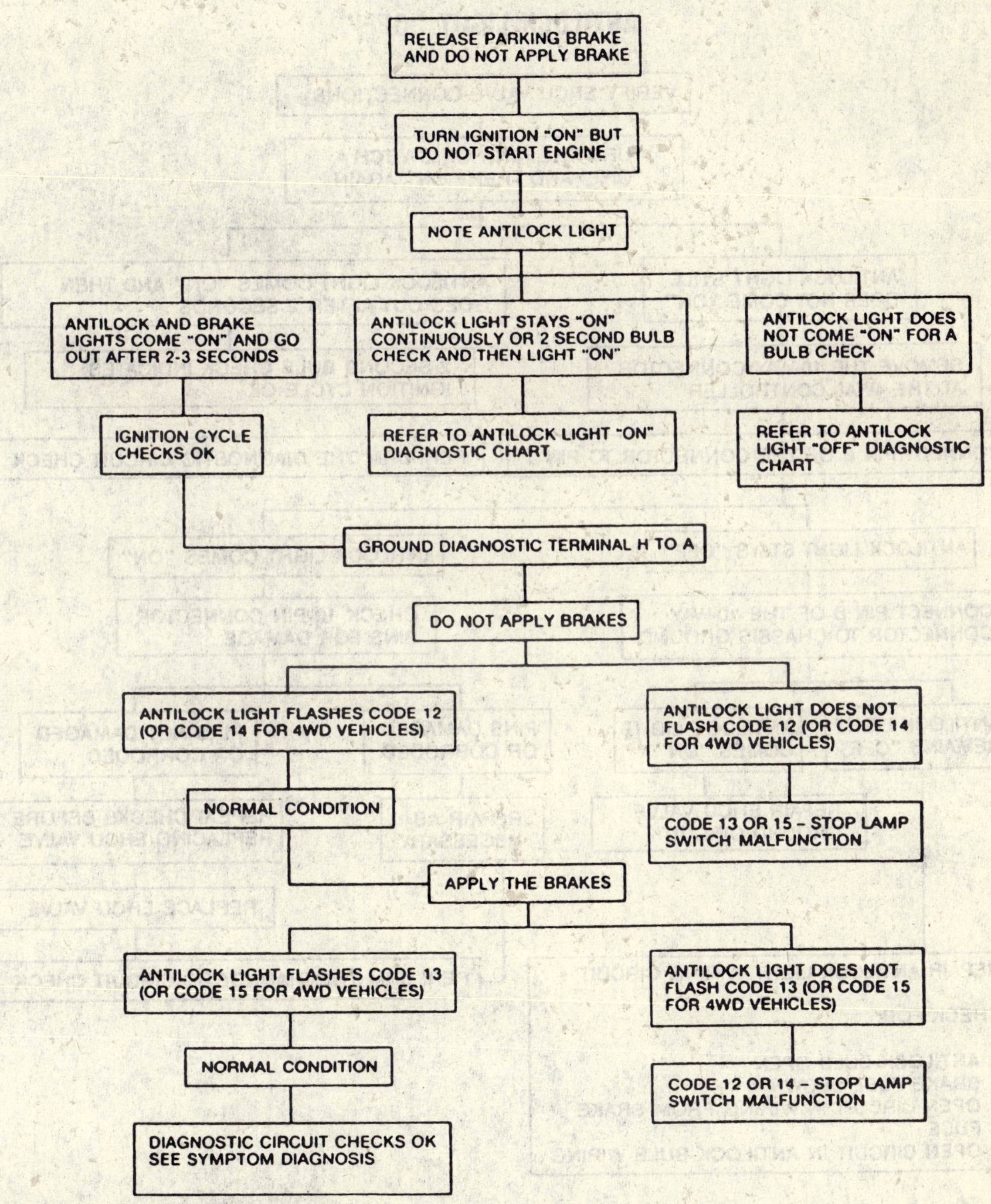
DIAGNOSTIC CIRCUIT CHECK
RELEASE PARKING BRAKE AND DO NOT APPLY BRAKE
TURN IGNITION "ON" BUT DO NOT START ENGINE
NOTE ANTILOCK LIGHT
ANTILOCK AND BRAKE LIGHTS COME "ON" AND GO OUT AFTER 2-3 SECONDS
ANTILOCK LIGHT STAYS "ON" CONTINUOUSLY OR 2 SECOND BULB CHECK AND THEN LIGHT "ON"
ANTILOCK LIGHT DOES NOT COME "ON" FOR A BULB CHECK
IGNITION CYCLE CHECKS OK
REFER TO ANTILOCK LIGHT "ON" DIAGNOSTIC CHART
REFER TO ANTILOCK LIGHT "OFF" DIAGNOSTIC CHART
GROUND DIAGNOSTIC TERMINAL H TO A
DO NOT APPLY BRAKES
ANTILOCK LIGHT FLASHES CODE 12 (OR CODE 14 FOR 4WD VEHICLES)
ANTILOCK LIGHT DOES NOT FLASH CODE 12 (OR CODE 14 FOR 4WD VEHICLES)
NORMAL CONDITION
CODE 13 OR 15 - STOP LAMP SWITCH MALFUNCTION
APPLY THE BRAKES
ANTILOCK LIGHT FLASHES CODE 13 (OR CODE 15 FOR 4WD VEHICLES)
ANTILOCK LIGHT DOES NOT FLASH CODE 13 (OR CODE 15 FOR 4WD VEHICLES)
NORMAL CONDITION
CODE 12 OR 14 - STOP LAMP SWITCH MALFUNCTION
DIAGNOSTIC CIRCUIT CHECKS OK SEE SYMPTOM DIAGNOSIS

ANTILOCK LIGHT "OFF"

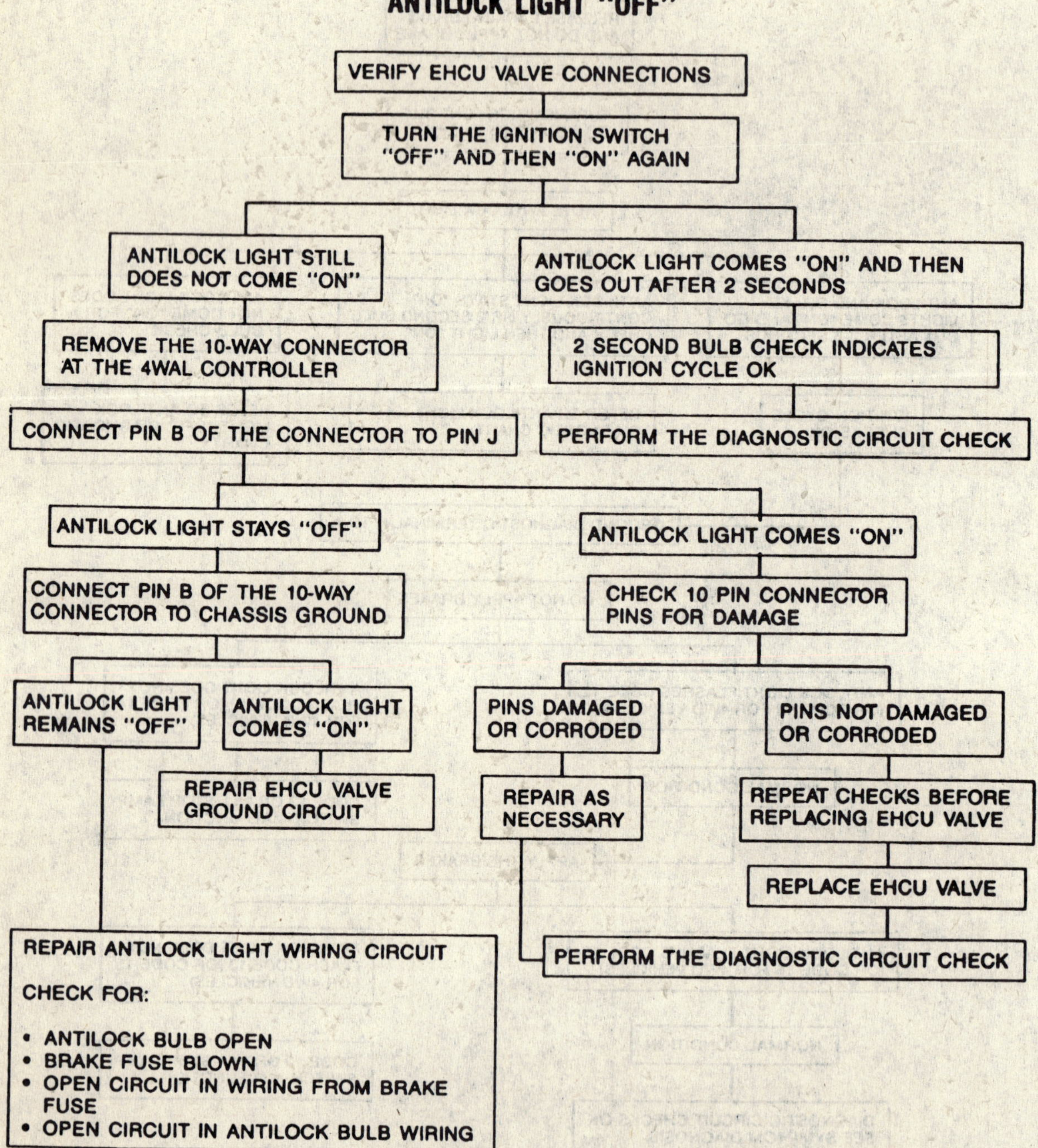

CODE 21
RIGHT FRONT SPEED SENSOR OR CIRCUIT OPEN

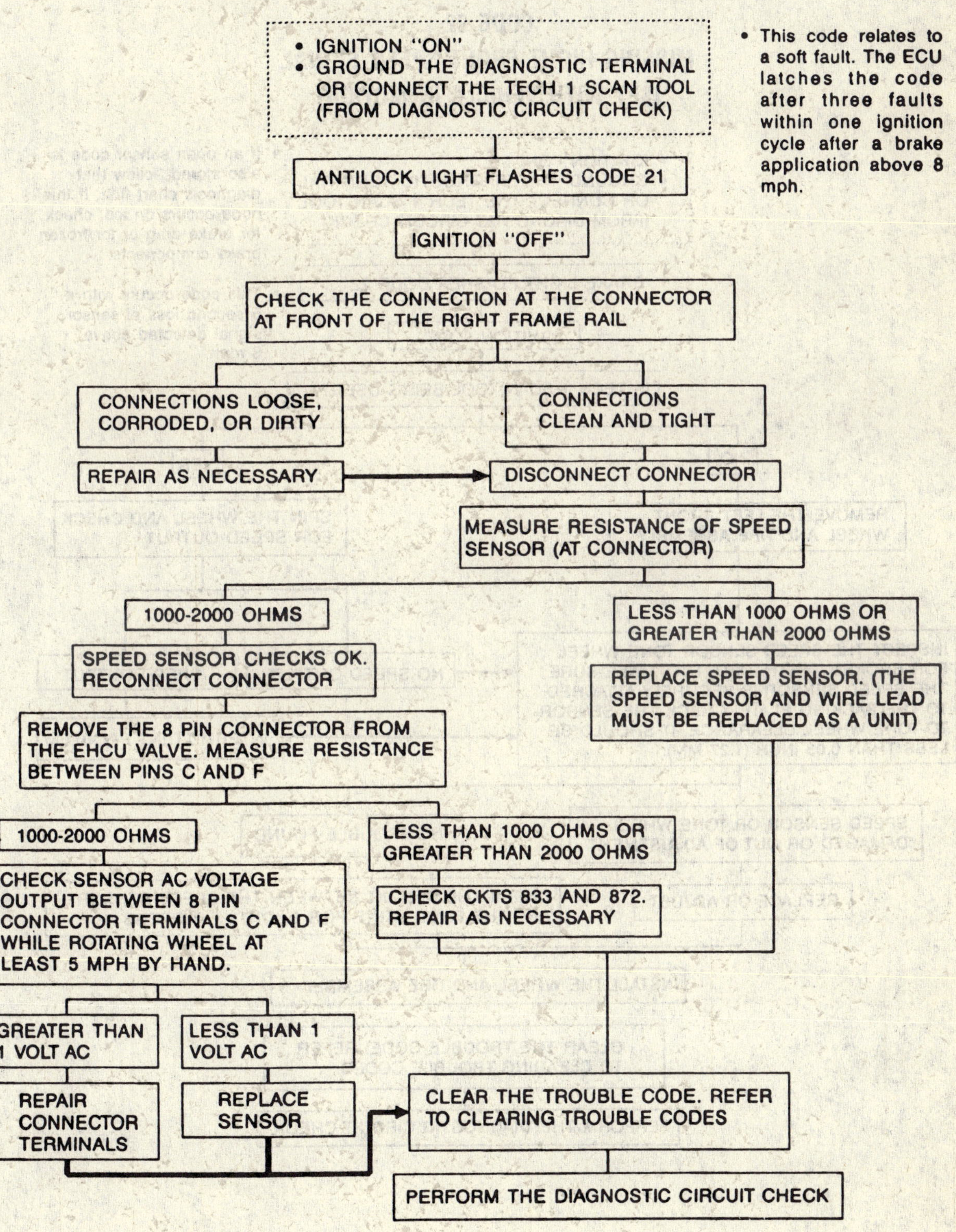

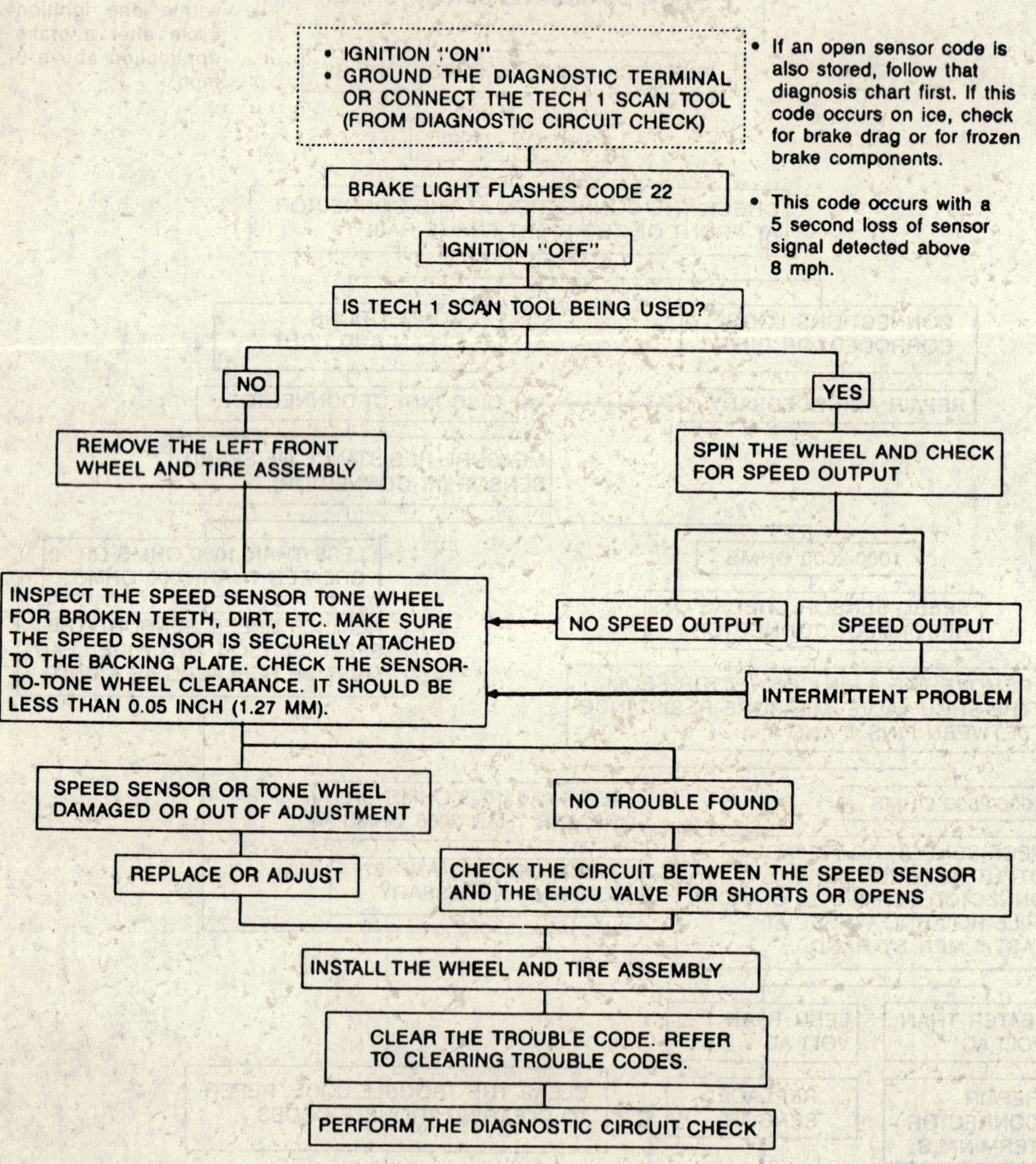
CODE 22
MISSING RIGHT FRONT SPEED SIGNAL
(SET WITH VEHICLE IN MOTION)
• IGNITION "ON"
• GROUND THE DIAGNOSTIC TERMINAL OR CONNECT THE TECH 1 SCAN TOOL (FROM DIAGNOSTIC CIRCUIT CHECK)
• If an open sensor code is also stored, follow that diagnosis chart first. If this code occurs on ice, check for brake drag or for frozen brake components.
• This code occurs with a 5 second loss of sensor signal detected above 8 mph.
BRAKE LIGHT FLASHES CODE 22
IGNITION "OFF"
IS TECH 1 SCAN TOOL BEING USED?
NO
YES
REMOVE THE LEFT FRONT WHEEL AND TIRE ASSEMBLY
SPIN THE WHEEL AND CHECK FOR SPEED OUTPUT
INSPECT THE SPEED SENSOR TONE WHEEL FOR BROKEN TEETH, DIRT, ETC. MAKE SURE THE SPEED SENSOR IS SECURELY ATTACHED TO THE BACKING PLATE. CHECK THE SENSOR-TO-TONE WHEEL CLEARANCE. IT SHOULD BE LESS THAN 0.05 INCH (1.27 MM).
NO SPEED OUTPUT
SPEED OUTPUT
INTERMITTENT PROBLEM
SPEED SENSOR OR TONE WHEEL DAMAGED OR OUT OF ADJUSTMENT
NO TROUBLE FOUND
REPLACE OR ADJUST
CHECK THE CIRCUIT BETWEEN THE SPEED SENSOR AND THE EHCU VALVE FOR SHORTS OR OPENS
INSTALL THE WHEEL AND TIRE ASSEMBLY
CLEAR THE TROUBLE CODE. REFER TO CLEARING TROUBLE CODES.
PERFORM THE DIAGNOSTIC CIRCUIT CHECK

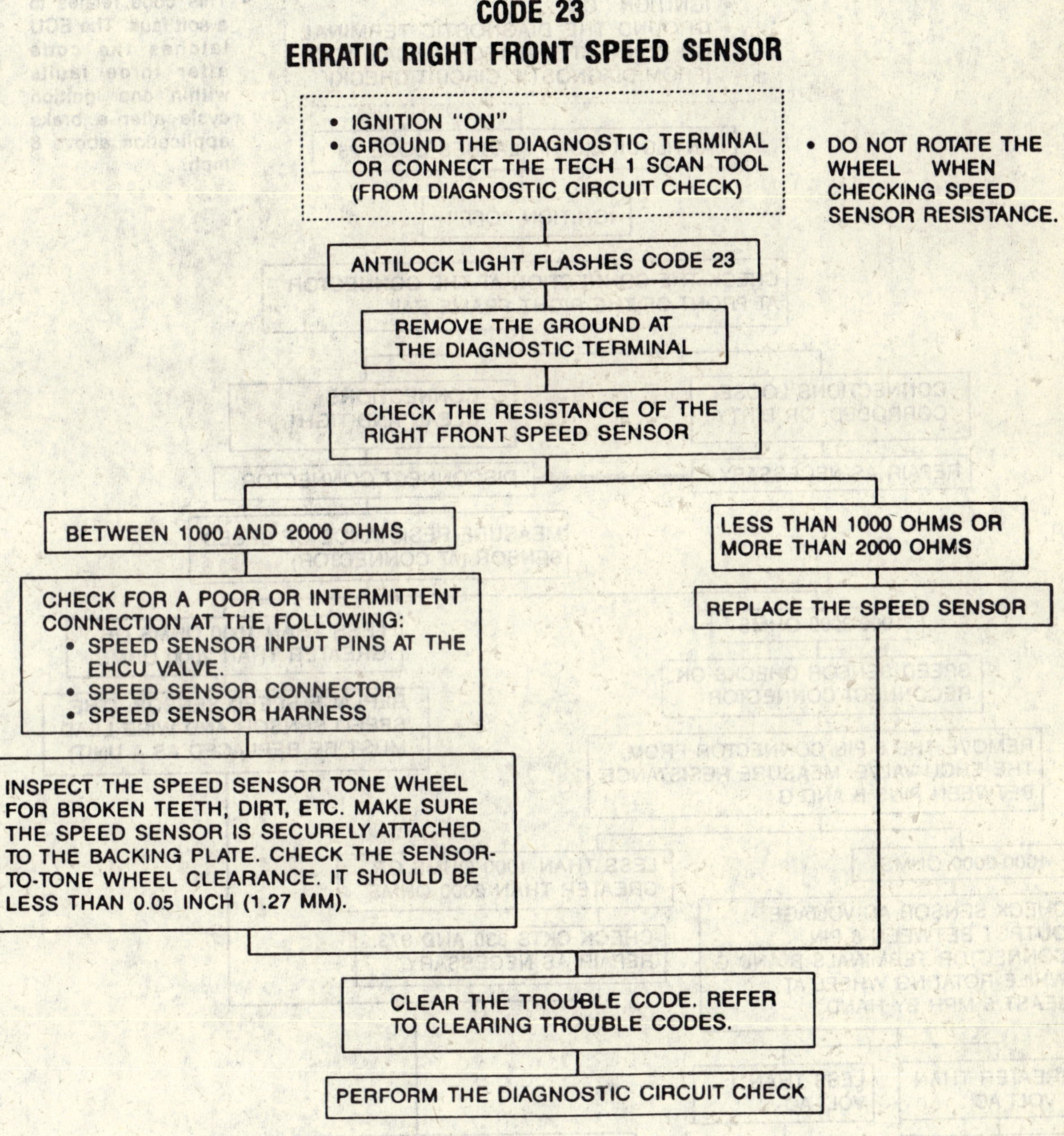
CODE 23
ERRATIC RIGHT FRONT SPEED SENSOR
• IGNITION "ON"
• GROUND THE DIAGNOSTIC TERMINAL OR CONNECT THE TECH 1 SCAN TOOL (FROM DIAGNOSTIC CIRCUIT CHECK)
• DO NOT ROTATE THE WHEEL WHEN CHECKING SPEED SENSOR RESISTANCE.
ANTILOCK LIGHT FLASHES CODE 23
REMOVE THE GROUND AT THE DIAGNOSTIC TERMINAL
CHECK THE RESISTANCE OF THE RIGHT FRONT SPEED SENSOR
BETWEEN 1000 AND 2000 OHMS
LESS THAN 1000 OHMS OR MORE THAN 2000 OHMS
CHECK FOR A POOR OR INTERMITTENT CONNECTION AT THE FOLLOWING:
• SPEED SENSOR INPUT PINS AT THE EHCU VALVE.
• SPEED SENSOR CONNECTOR
• SPEED SENSOR HARNESS
REPLACE THE SPEED SENSOR
INSPECT THE SPEED SENSOR TONE WHEEL FOR BROKEN TEETH, DIRT, ETC. MAKE SURE THE SPEED SENSOR IS SECURELY ATTACHED TO THE BACKING PLATE. CHECK THE SENSOR-TO-TONE WHEEL CLEARANCE. IT SHOULD BE LESS THAN 0.05 INCH (1.27 MM).
CLEAR THE TROUBLE CODE. REFER TO CLEARING TROUBLE CODES.
PERFORM THE DIAGNOSTIC CIRCUIT CHECK

CODE 25
LEFT FRONT SPEED SENSOR OR CIRCUIT OPEN

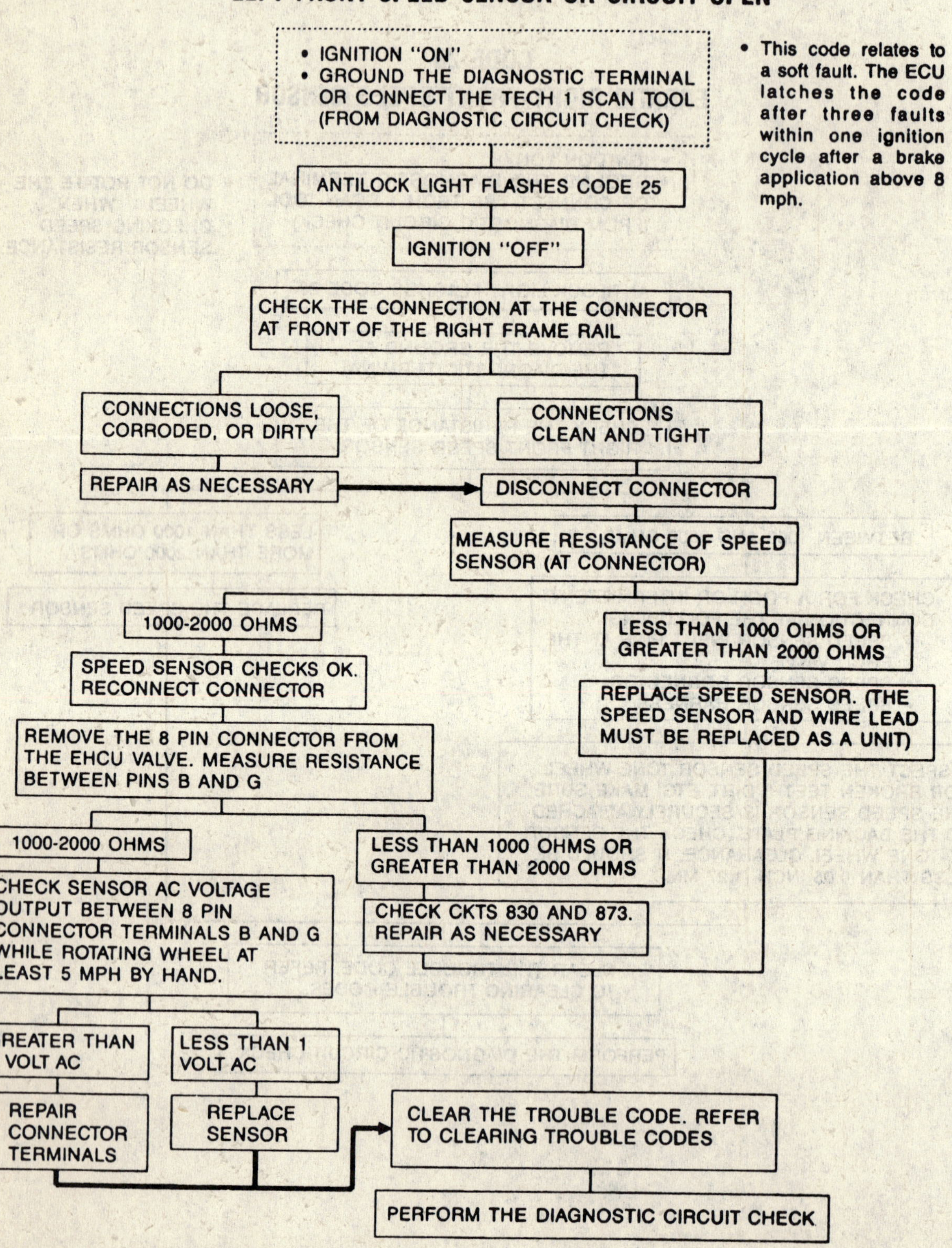

CODE 26
MISSING LEFT FRONT SPEED SIGNAL
(SET WITH VEHICLE IN MOTION)

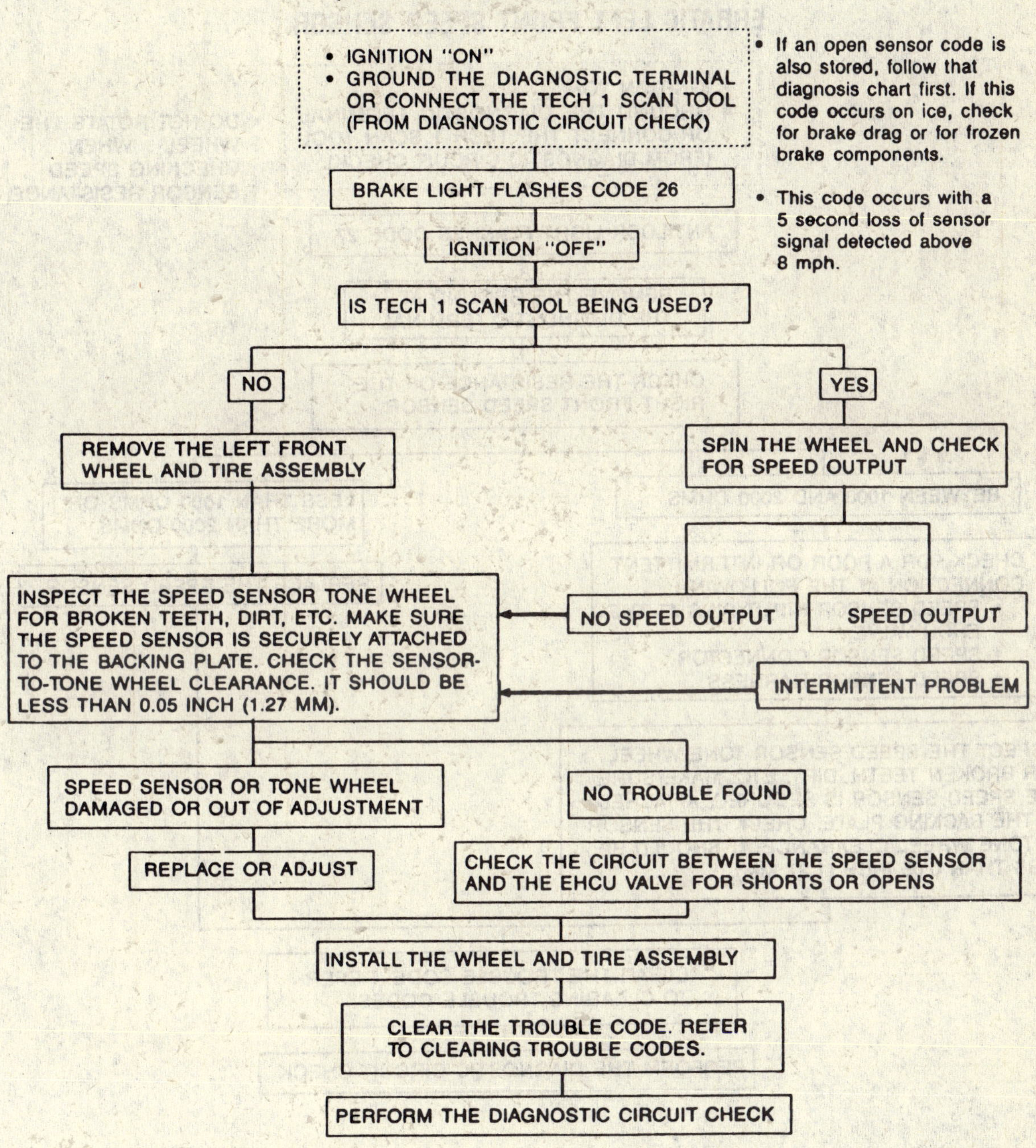

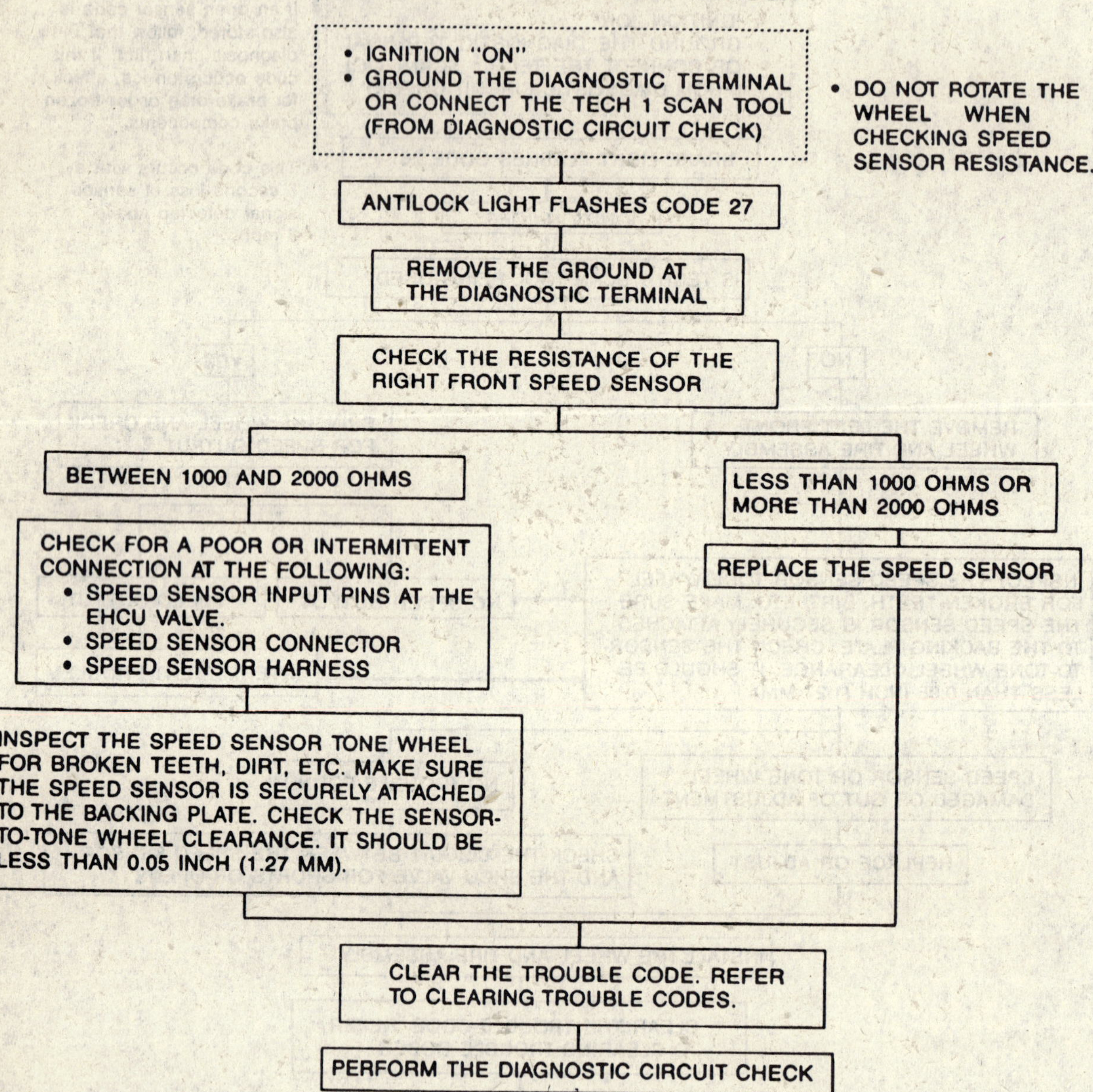
CODE 27
ERRATIC LEFT FRONT SPEED SENSOR
• IGNITION "ON"
• GROUND THE DIAGNOSTIC TERMINAL OR CONNECT THE TECH 1 SCAN TOOL (FROM DIAGNOSTIC CIRCUIT CHECK)
• DO NOT ROTATE THE WHEEL WHEN CHECKING SPEED SENSOR RESISTANCE.
ANTILOCK LIGHT FLASHES CODE 27
REMOVE THE GROUND AT THE DIAGNOSTIC TERMINAL
CHECK THE RESISTANCE OF THE RIGHT FRONT SPEED SENSOR
BETWEEN 1000 AND 2000 OHMS
LESS THAN 1000 OHMS OR MORE THAN 2000 OHMS
CHECK FOR A POOR OR INTERMITTENT CONNECTION AT THE FOLLOWING:
• SPEED SENSOR INPUT PINS AT THE EHCU VALVE.
• SPEED SENSOR CONNECTOR
• SPEED SENSOR HARNESS
REPLACE THE SPEED SENSOR
INSPECT THE SPEED SENSOR TONE WHEEL FOR BROKEN TEETH, DIRT, ETC. MAKE SURE THE SPEED SENSOR IS SECURELY ATTACHED TO THE BACKING PLATE. CHECK THE SENSOR-TO-TONE WHEEL CLEARANCE. IT SHOULD BE LESS THAN 0.05 INCH (1.27 MM).
CLEAR THE TROUBLE CODE. REFER TO CLEARING TROUBLE CODES.
PERFORM THE DIAGNOSTIC CIRCUIT CHECK

CODE 28
ERRATIC SPEED SENSOR SIGNAL
TWO DROP-OUTS ABOVE 20 MPH

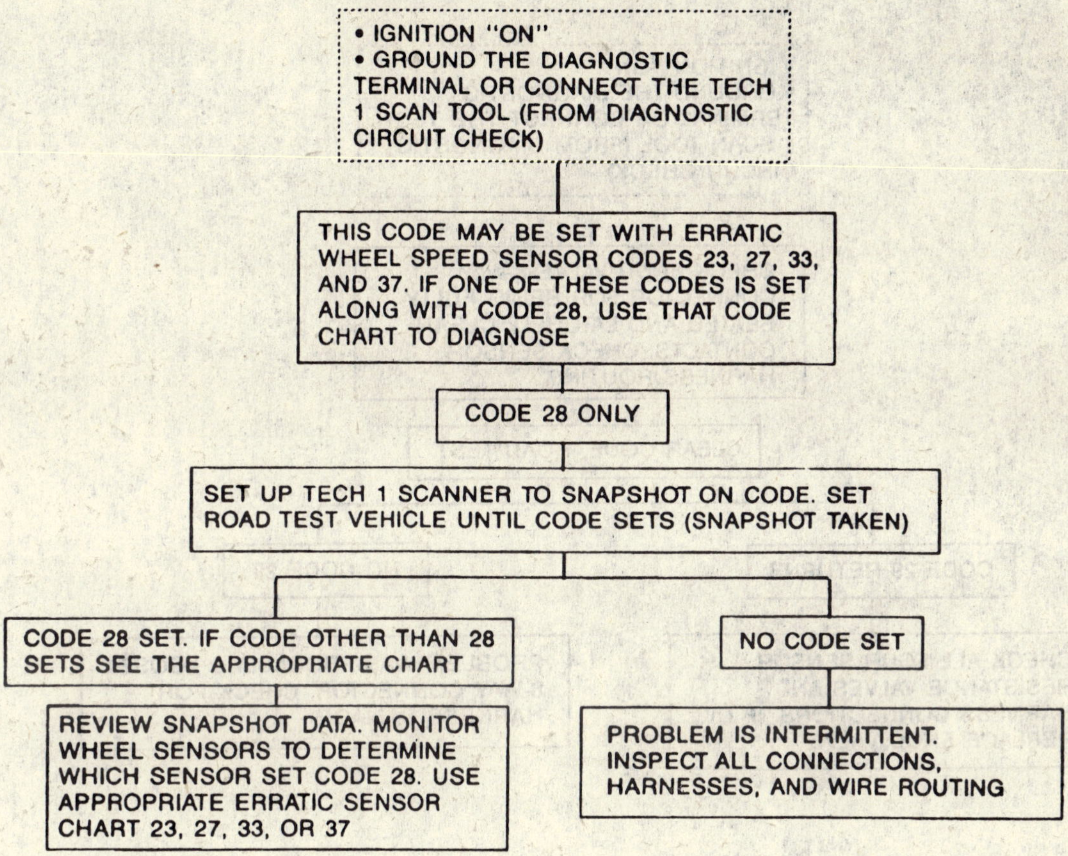

• IGNITION "ON"
• GROUND THE DIAGNOSTIC TERMINAL OR CONNECT THE TECH 1 SCAN TOOL (FROM DIAGNOSTIC CIRCUIT CHECK)

THIS CODE MAY BE SET WITH ERRATIC WHEEL SPEED SENSOR CODES 23, 27, 33, AND 37. IF ONE OF THESE CODES IS SET ALONG WITH CODE 28, USE THAT CODE CHART TO DIAGNOSE

CODE 28 ONLY

SET UP TECH 1 SCANNER TO SNAPSHOT ON CODE. SET ROAD TEST VEHICLE UNTIL CODE SETS (SNAPSHOT TAKEN)

CODE 28 SET. IF CODE OTHER THAN 28 SETS SEE THE APPROPRIATE CHART

REVIEW SNAPSHOT DATA. MONITOR WHEEL SENSORS TO DETERMINE WHICH SENSOR SET CODE 28. USE APPROPRIATE ERRATIC SENSOR CHART 23, 27, 33, OR 37

NO CODE SET

PROBLEM IS INTERMITTENT. INSPECT ALL CONNECTIONS, HARNESSES, AND WIRE ROUTING

CODE 29
SIMULTANEOUS DROP-OUT OF ALL FOUR SENSORS AT SPEEDS ABOVE 8 MPH

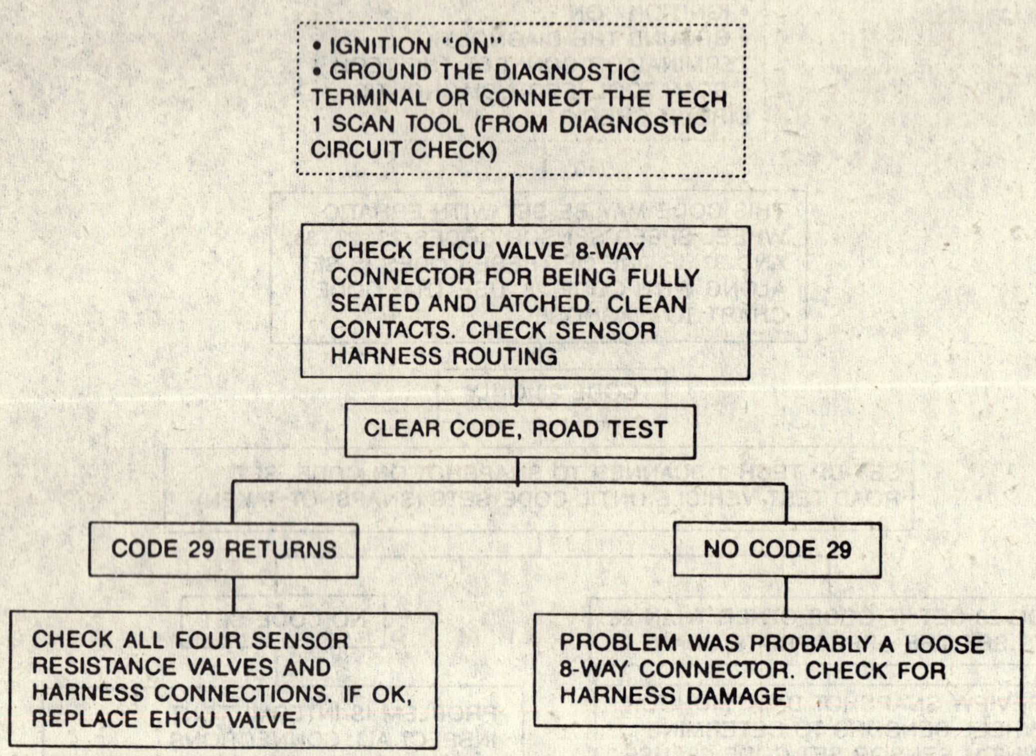

CODE 31
RIGHT REAR SPEED SENSOR OR CIRCUIT OPEN

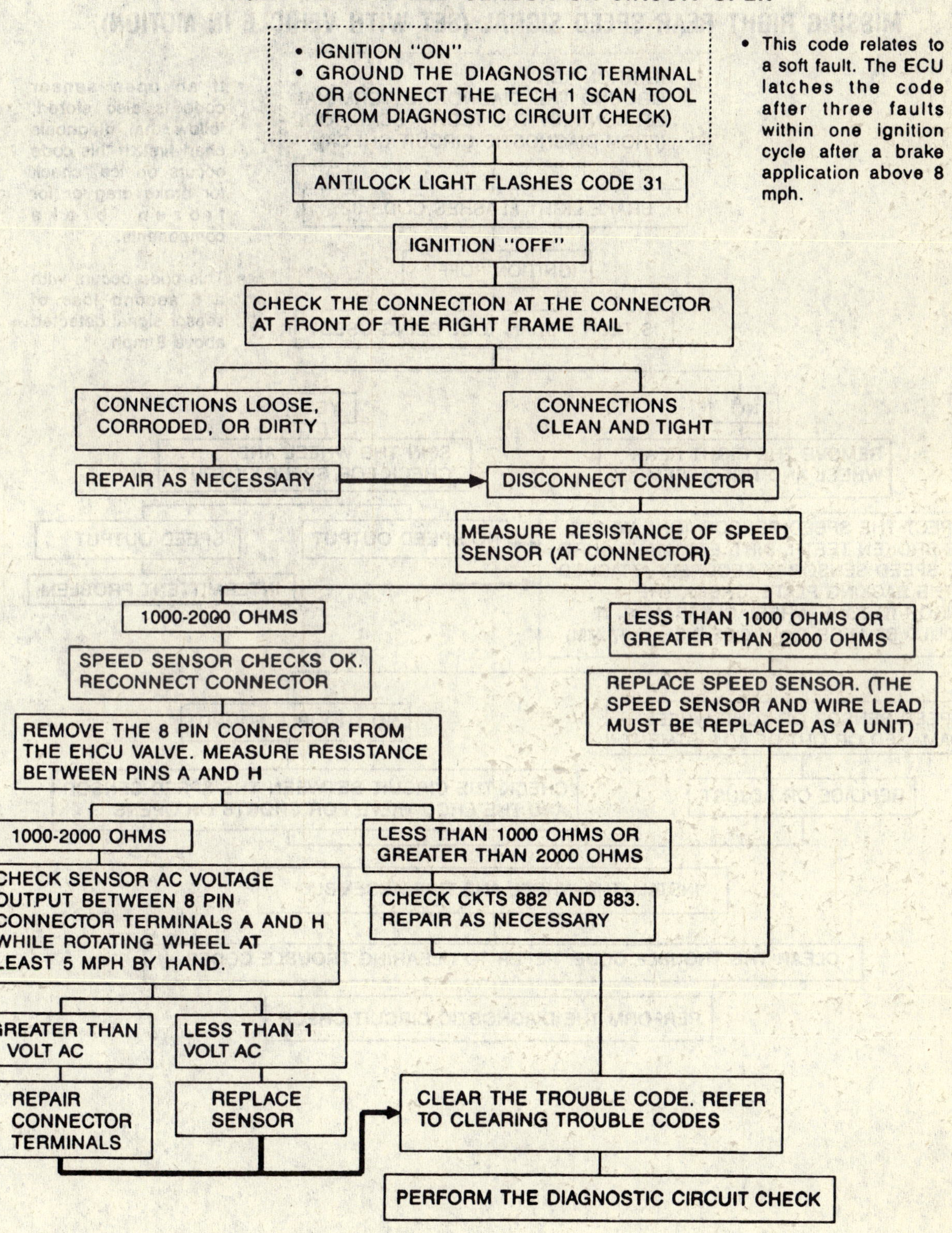

• This code relates to a soft fault. The ECU latches the code after three faults within one ignition cycle after a brake application above 8 mph.

CODE 32
MISSING RIGHT REAR SPEED SIGNAL (SET WITH VEHICLE IN MOTION)

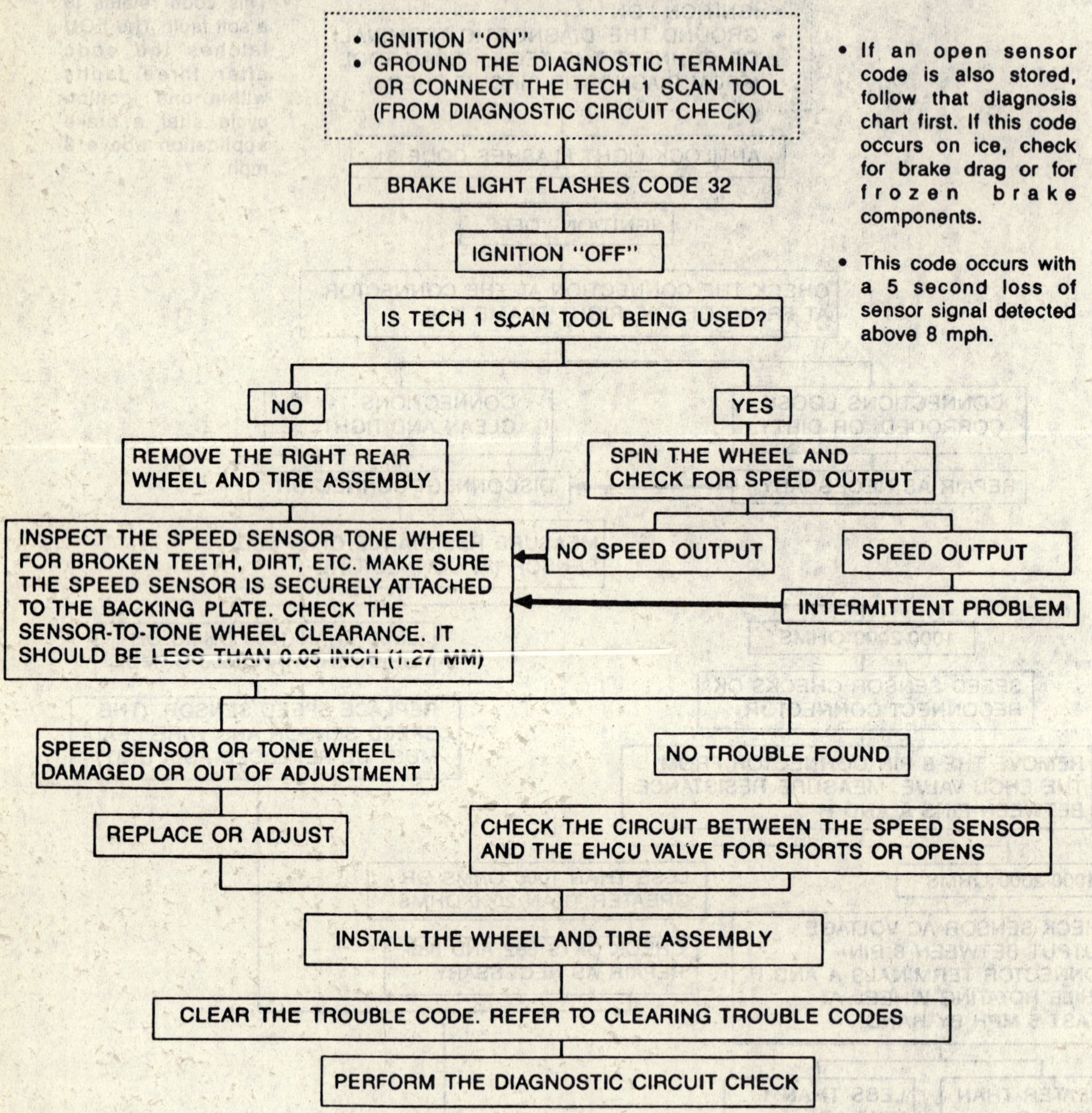

- If an open sensor code is also stored, follow that diagnosis chart first. If this code occurs on ice, check for brake drag or for frozen brake components.
- This code occurs with a 5 second loss of sensor signal detected above 8 mph.

CODE 33
ERRATIC RIGHT REAR SPEED SENSOR

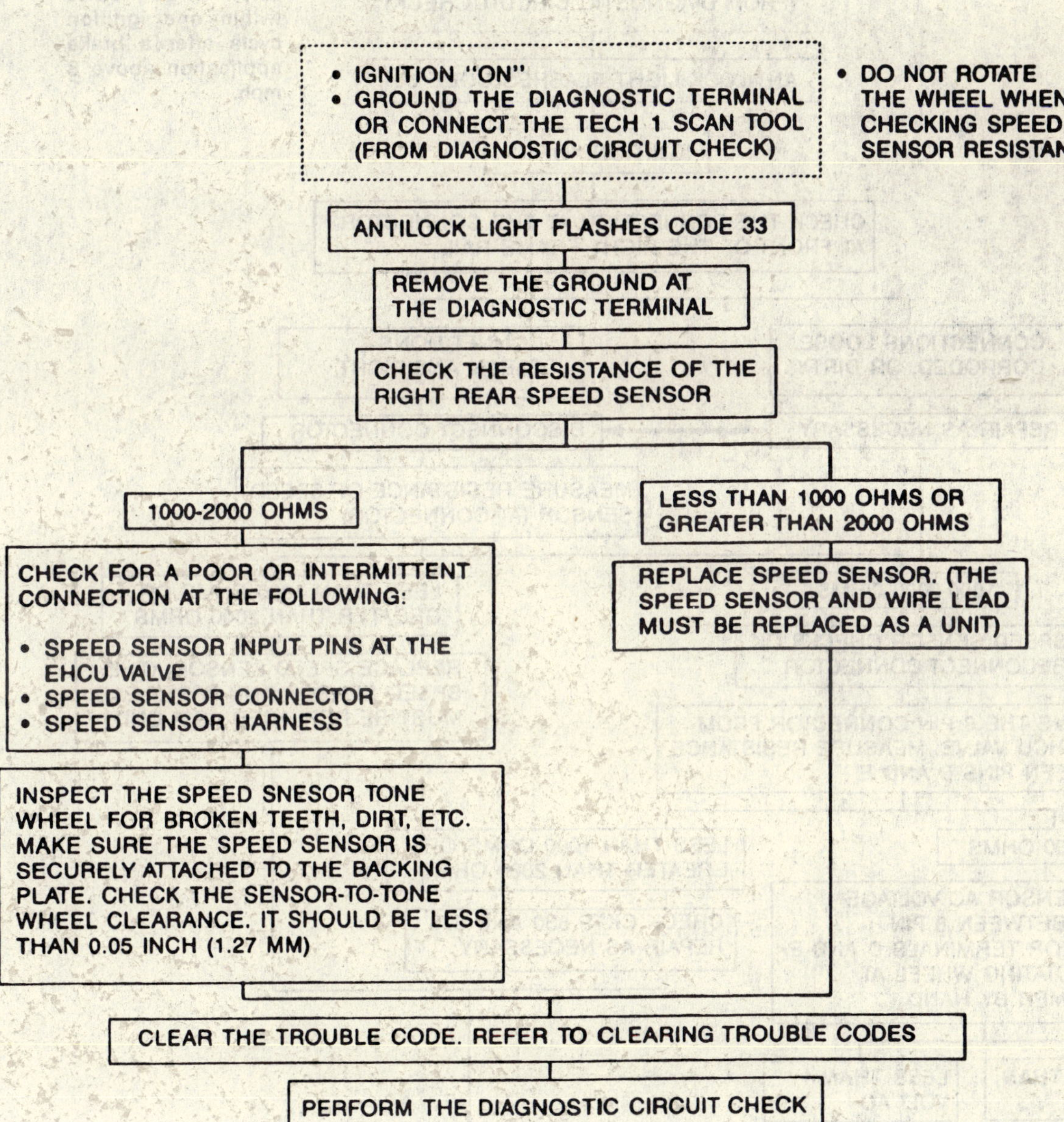

CODE 35
LEFT REAR SPEED SENSOR OR CIRCUIT OPEN

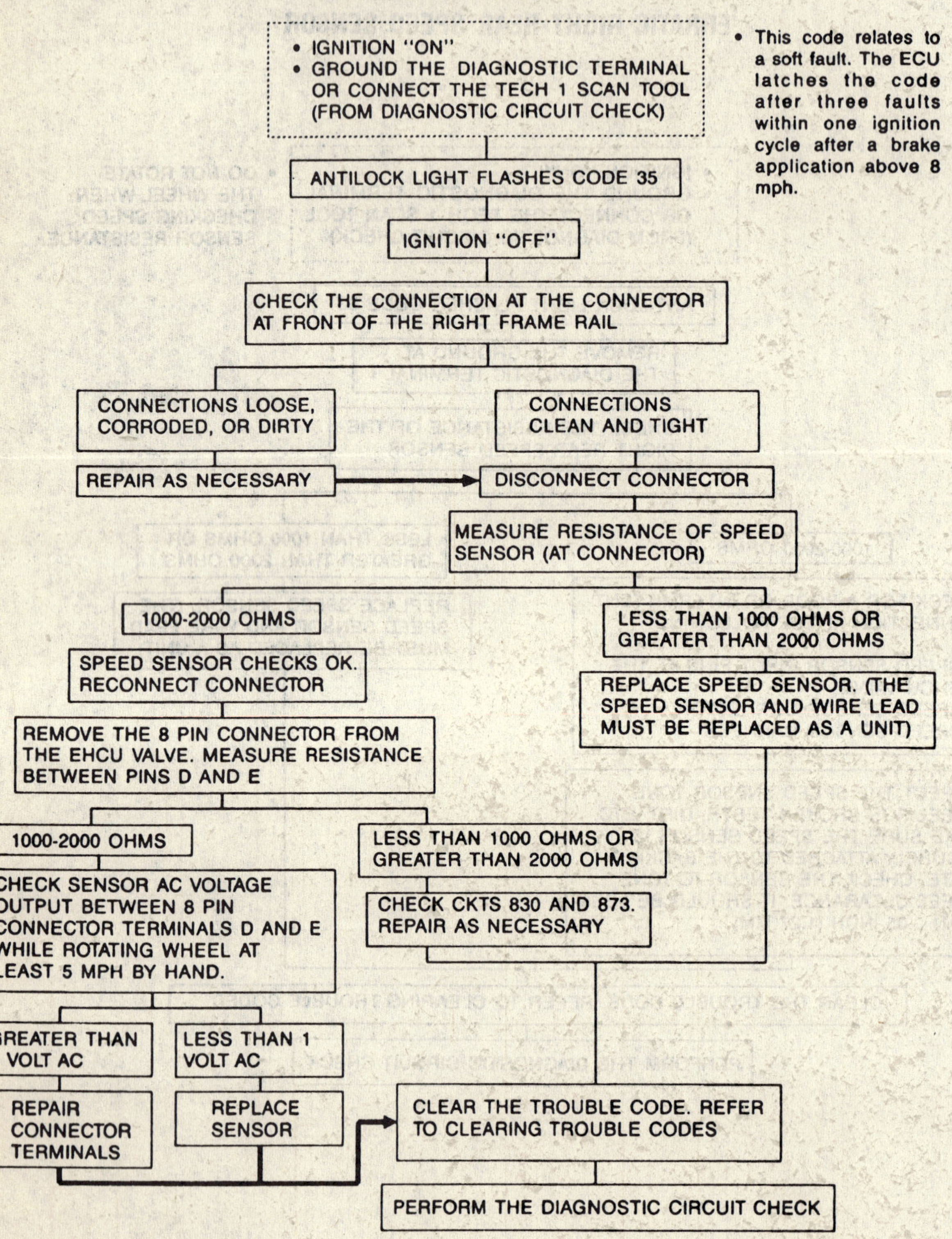

• This code relates to a soft fault. The ECU latches the code after three faults within one ignition cycle after a brake application above 8 mph.

CODE 36

MISSING LEFT REAR SPEED SIGNAL (SET WITH VEHICLE IN MOTION)

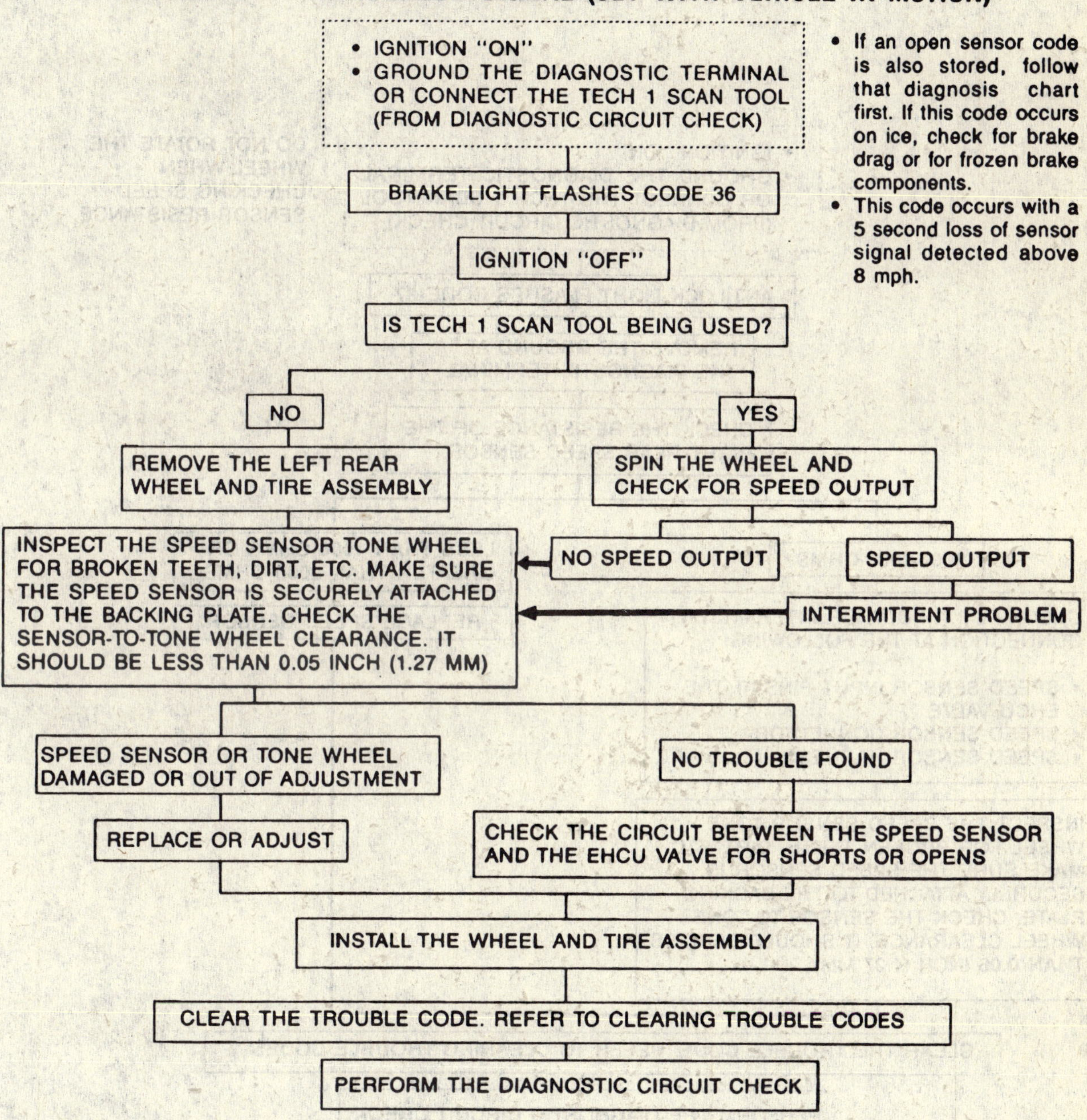

- If an open sensor code is also stored, follow that diagnosis chart first. If this code occurs on ice, check for brake drag or for frozen brake components.
- This code occurs with a 5 second loss of sensor signal detected above 8 mph.

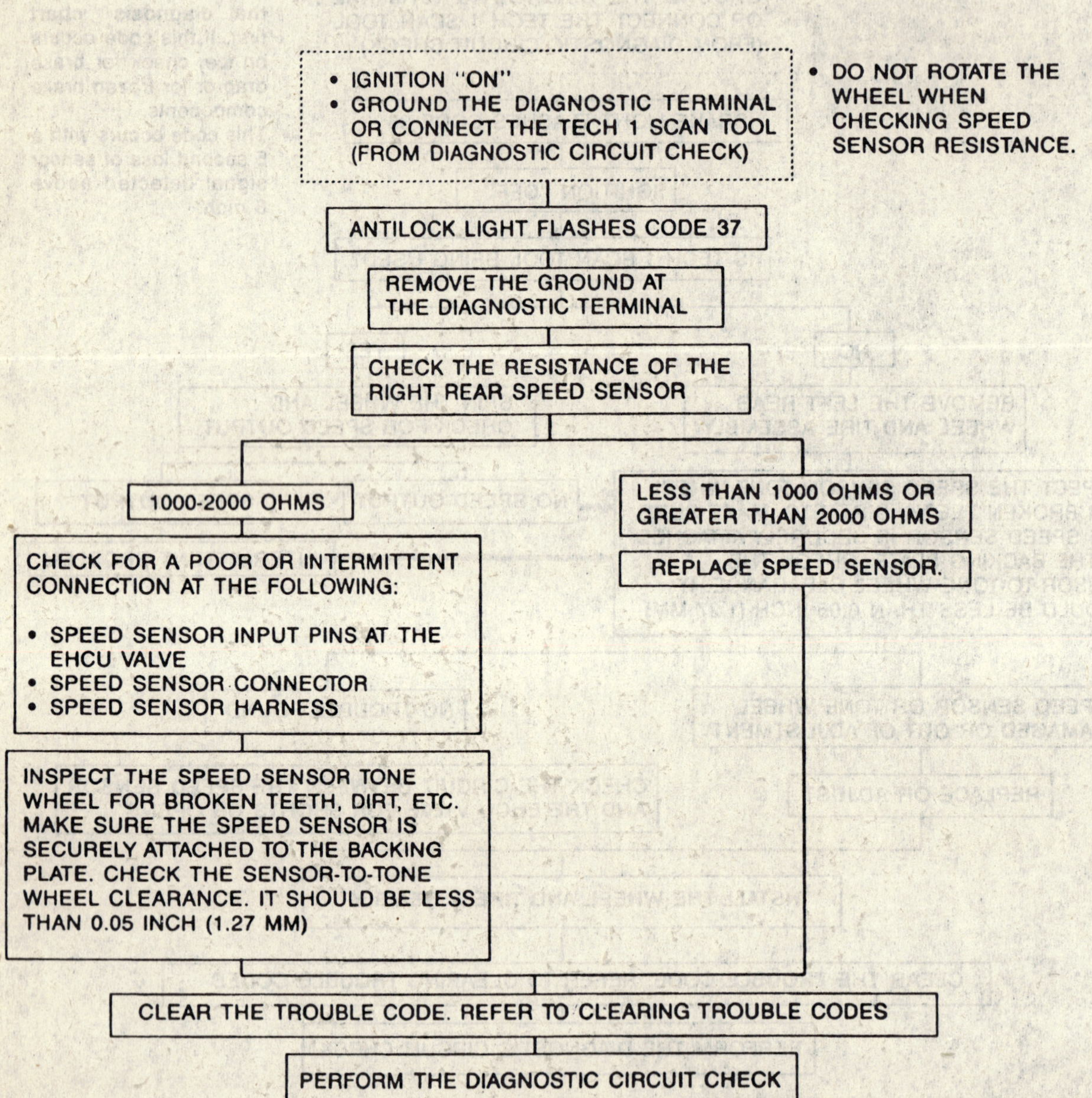
CODE 37
ERRATIC LEFT REAR SPEED SENSOR
• IGNITION "ON"
• GROUND THE DIAGNOSTIC TERMINAL OR CONNECT THE TECH 1 SCAN TOOL (FROM DIAGNOSTIC CIRCUIT CHECK)
• DO NOT ROTATE THE WHEEL WHEN CHECKING SPEED SENSOR RESISTANCE.
ANTILOCK LIGHT FLASHES CODE 37
REMOVE THE GROUND AT THE DIAGNOSTIC TERMINAL
CHECK THE RESISTANCE OF THE RIGHT REAR SPEED SENSOR
1000-2000 OHMS
LESS THAN 1000 OHMS OR GREATER THAN 2000 OHMS
REPLACE SPEED SENSOR.
CHECK FOR A POOR OR INTERMITTENT CONNECTION AT THE FOLLOWING:
• SPEED SENSOR INPUT PINS AT THE EHCU VALVE
• SPEED SENSOR CONNECTOR
• SPEED SENSOR HARNESS
INSPECT THE SPEED SENSOR TONE WHEEL FOR BROKEN TEETH, DIRT, ETC. MAKE SURE THE SPEED SENSOR IS SECURELY ATTACHED TO THE BACKING PLATE. CHECK THE SENSOR-TO-TONE WHEEL CLEARANCE. IT SHOULD BE LESS THAN 0.05 INCH (1.27 MM)
CLEAR THE TROUBLE CODE. REFER TO CLEARING TROUBLE CODES
PERFORM THE DIAGNOSTIC CIRCUIT CHECK

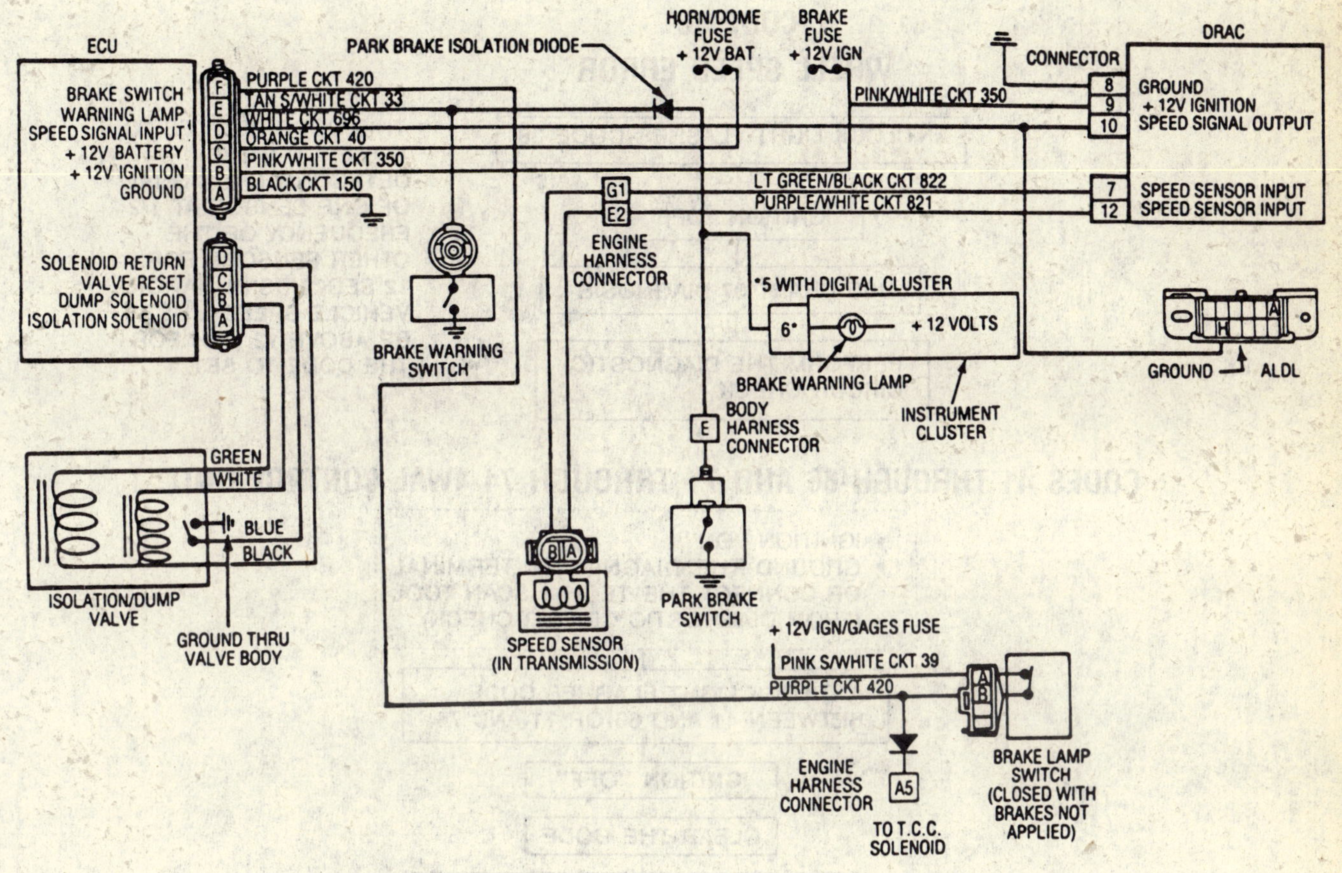

Rear wheel anti-lock wiring diagram

CODE 38
WHEEL SPEED ERROR

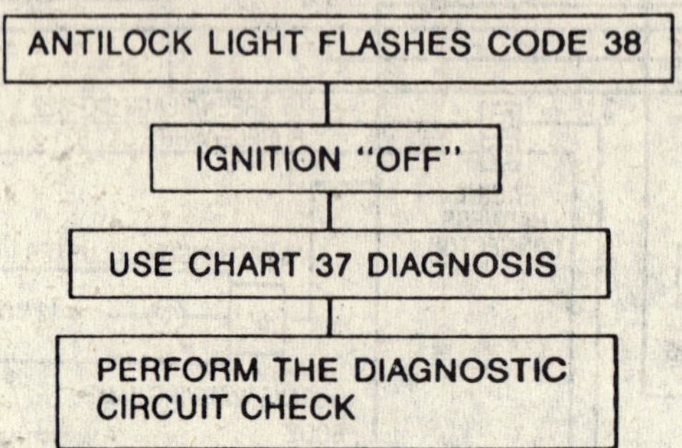

- THIS CODE RELATES TO THE EHCU VALVE DETECTING THE SIGNAL OF ONE SENSOR AT 1/2 FREQUENCY OF THE OTHER SENSORS FOR 12 SECONDS DURATION. VEHICLE SPEED MUST BE ABOVE 12 MPH FOR THE CODE TO SET.

CODES 41 THROUGH 66 AND 71 THROUGH 74 4WAL CONTROL UNIT*

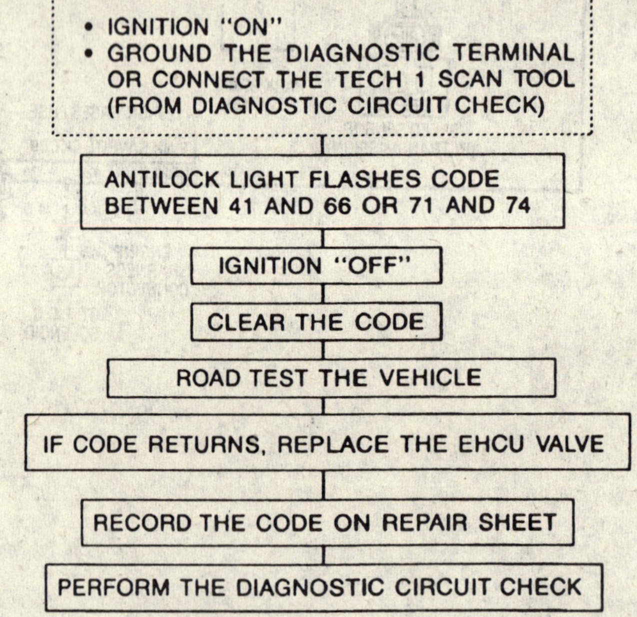

*Code 65 may set during service, due to erratic grounding of ALDL terminal H.

CODE 67
OPEN MOTOR CIRCUIT OR SHORTED ECU OUTPUT

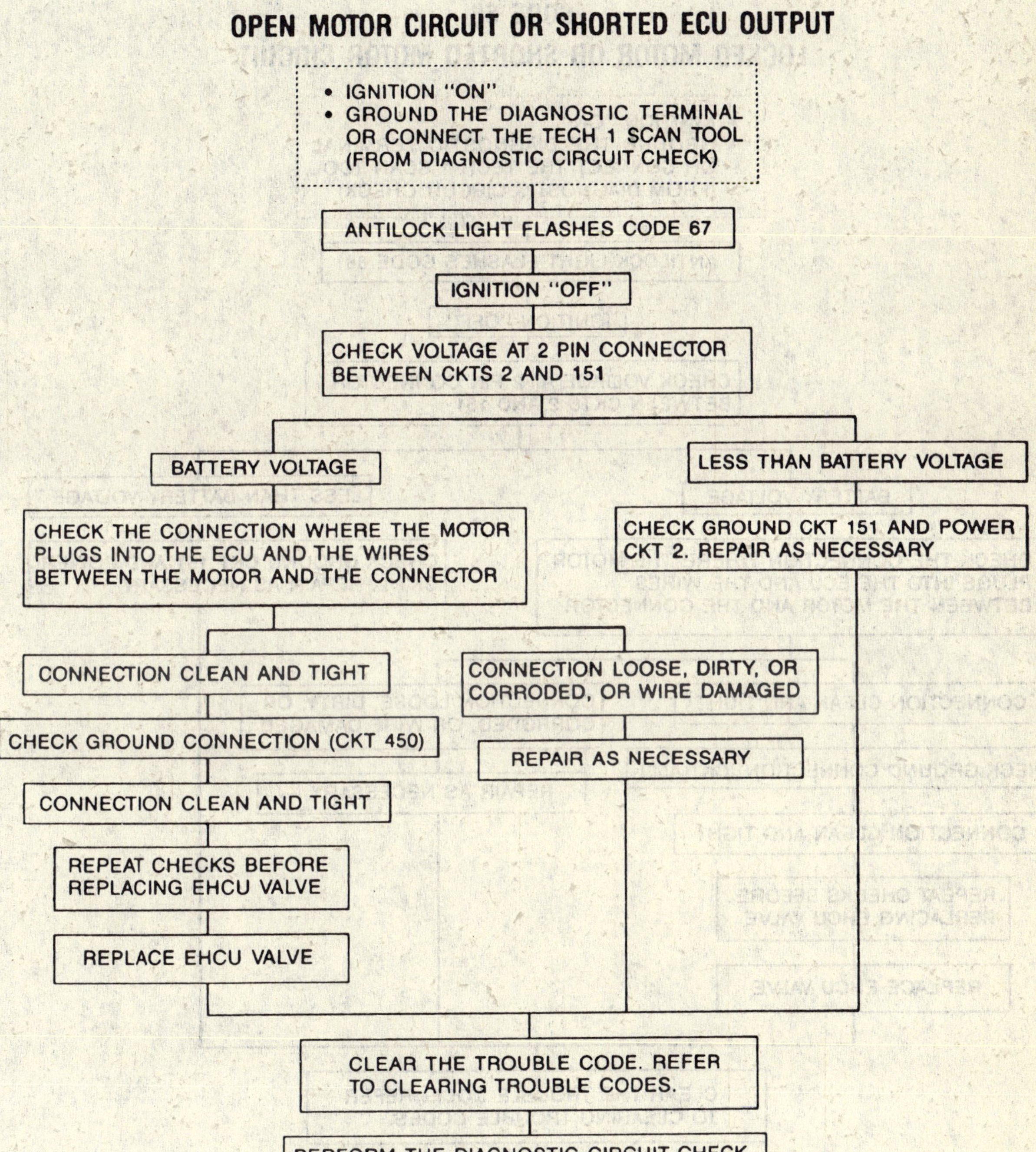

CODE 68
LOCKED MOTOR OR SHORTED MOTOR CIRCUIT

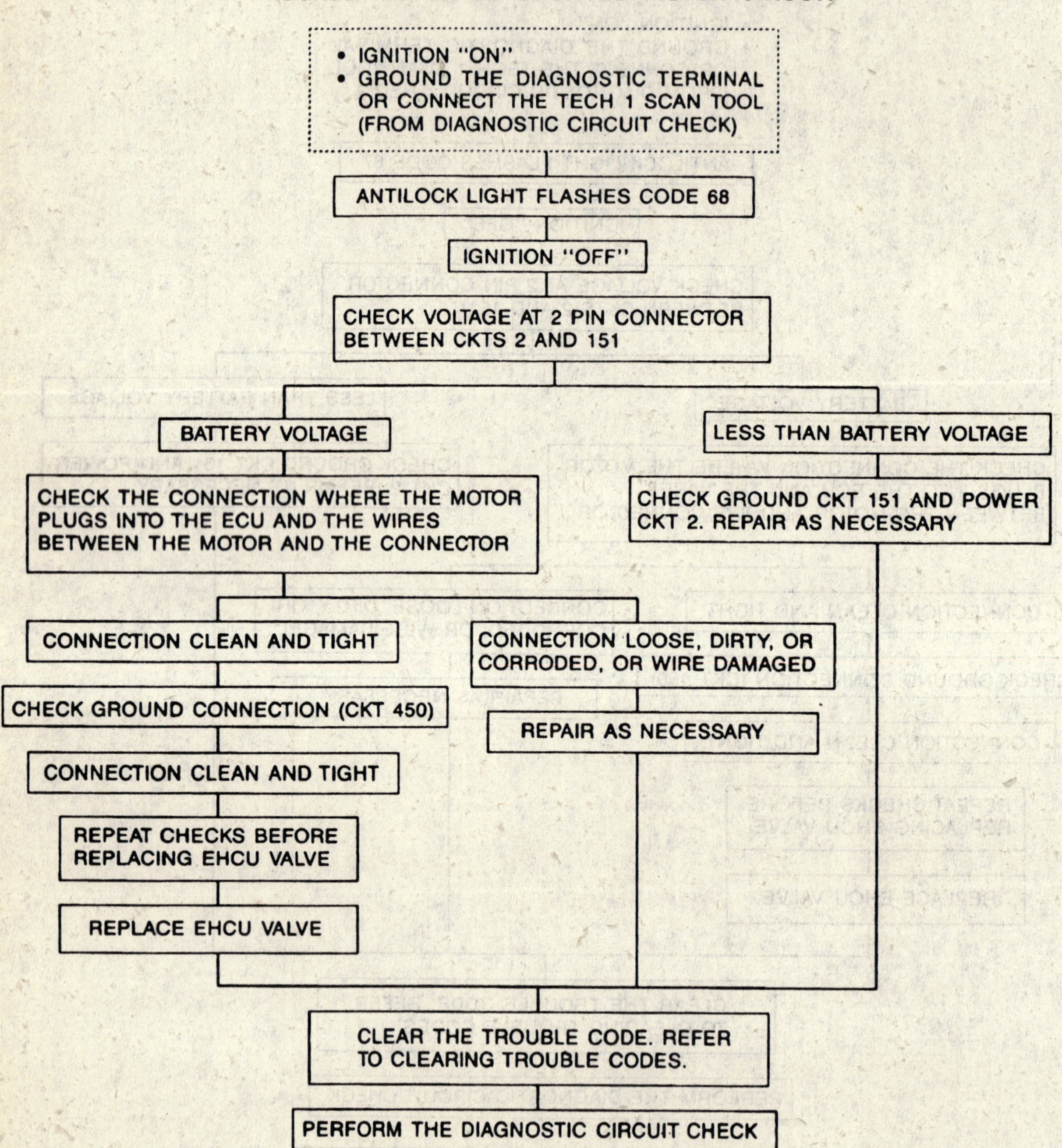

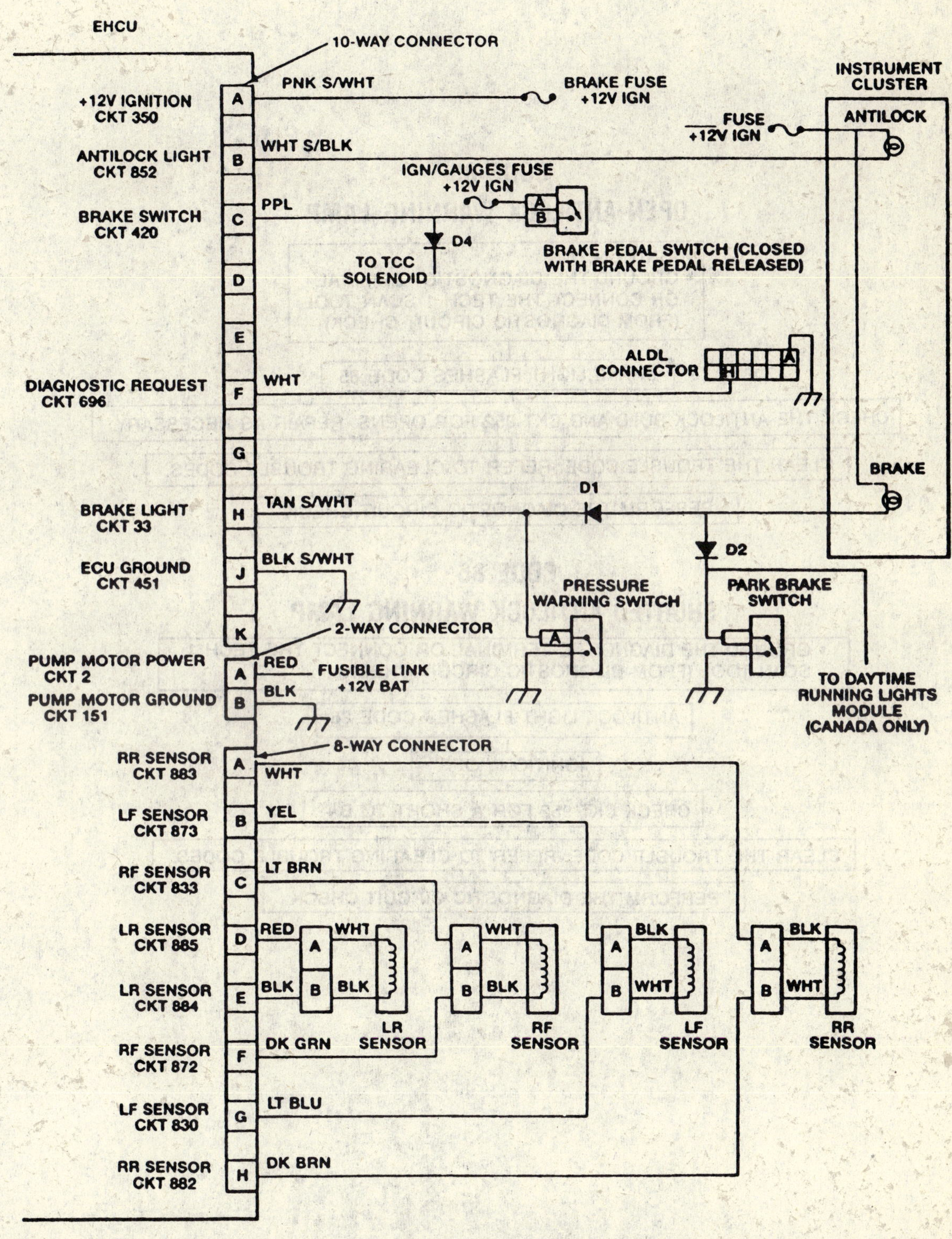

Four Wheel Antilock Wiring Diagram

CODE 85
OPEN ANTILOCK WARNING LAMP

- IGNITION "ON"
- GROUND THE DIAGNOSTIC TERMINAL OR CONNECT THE TECH 1 SCAN TOOL (FROM DIAGNOSTIC CIRCUIT CHECK)

BRAKE LIGHT FLASHES CODE 85

CHECK THE ANTILOCK BULB AND CKT 952 FOR OPENS. REPAIR AS NECESSARY.

CLEAR THE TROUBLE CODE. REFER TO CLEARING TROUBLE CODES.

PERFORM THE DIAGNOSTIC CIRCUIT CHECK

CODE 86
SHORTED ANTILOCK WARNING LAMP

- GROUND THE DIAGNOSTIC TERMINAL OR CONNECT THE TECH 1 SCAN TOOL (FROM DIAGNOSTIC CIRCUIT CHECK)

ANTILOCK LIGHT FLASHES CODE 86

IGNITION "OFF"

CHECK CKT 952 FOR A SHORT TO B+

CLEAR THE TROUBLE CODE. REFER TO CLEARING TROUBLE CODES.

PERFORM THE DIAGNOSTIC CIRCUIT CHECK

CODE 81
BRAKE SWITCH CIRCUIT SHORTED OR OPEN

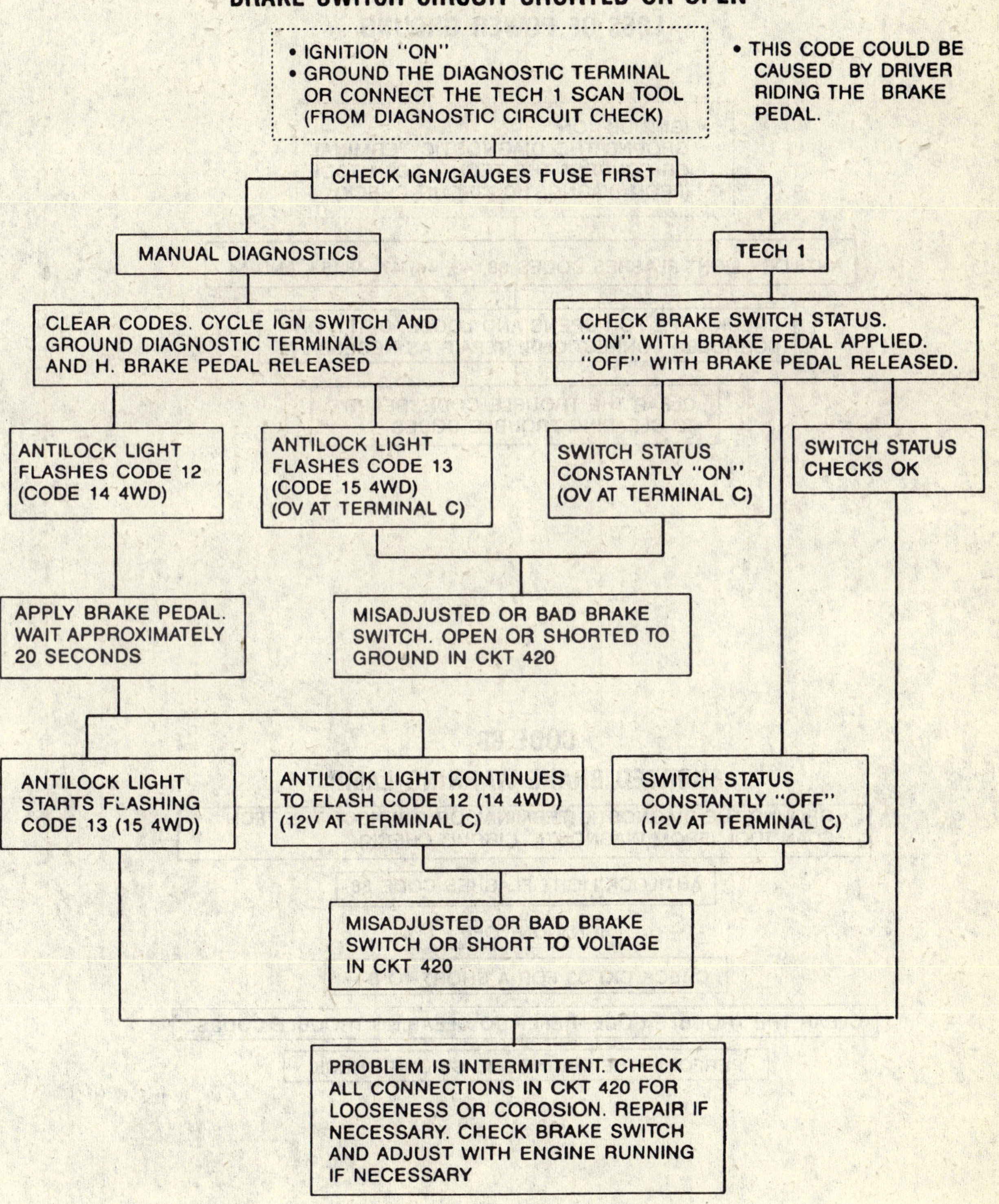

CODES 68, 43, 44, 47, 48, 53, AND 54
LOSS OF POWER GROUND

- IGNITION "ON"
- GROUND THE DIAGNOSTIC TERMINAL OR CONNECT THE TECH 1 SCAN TOOL (FROM DIAGNOSTIC CIRCUIT CHECK)

ANTILOCK LIGHT FLASHES CODES 68, 43, 44, 47, 48, 53, AND 54

CHECK CKT 2 FOR OPENS AND LOOSE, DIRTY, OR CORRODED CONNECTIONS. REPAIR AS NECESSARY

CLEAR THE TROUBLE CODE. REFER TO CLEARING TROUBLE CODES

CODE 88
SHORTED BRAKE WARNING LAMP

- GROUND THE DIAGNOSTIC TERMINAL OR CONNECT THE TECH 1 SCAN TOOL (FROM DIAGNOSTIC CIRCUIT CHECK)

ANTILOCK LIGHT FLASHES CODE 88

IGNITION "OFF"

CHECK CKT 33 FOR A SHORT TO B+

CLEAR THE TROUBLE CODE. REFER TO CLEARING TROUBLE CODES.

PERFORM THE DIAGNOSTIC CIRCUIT CHECK

BRAKE PEDAL PULSES (NO CODE CONDITION)

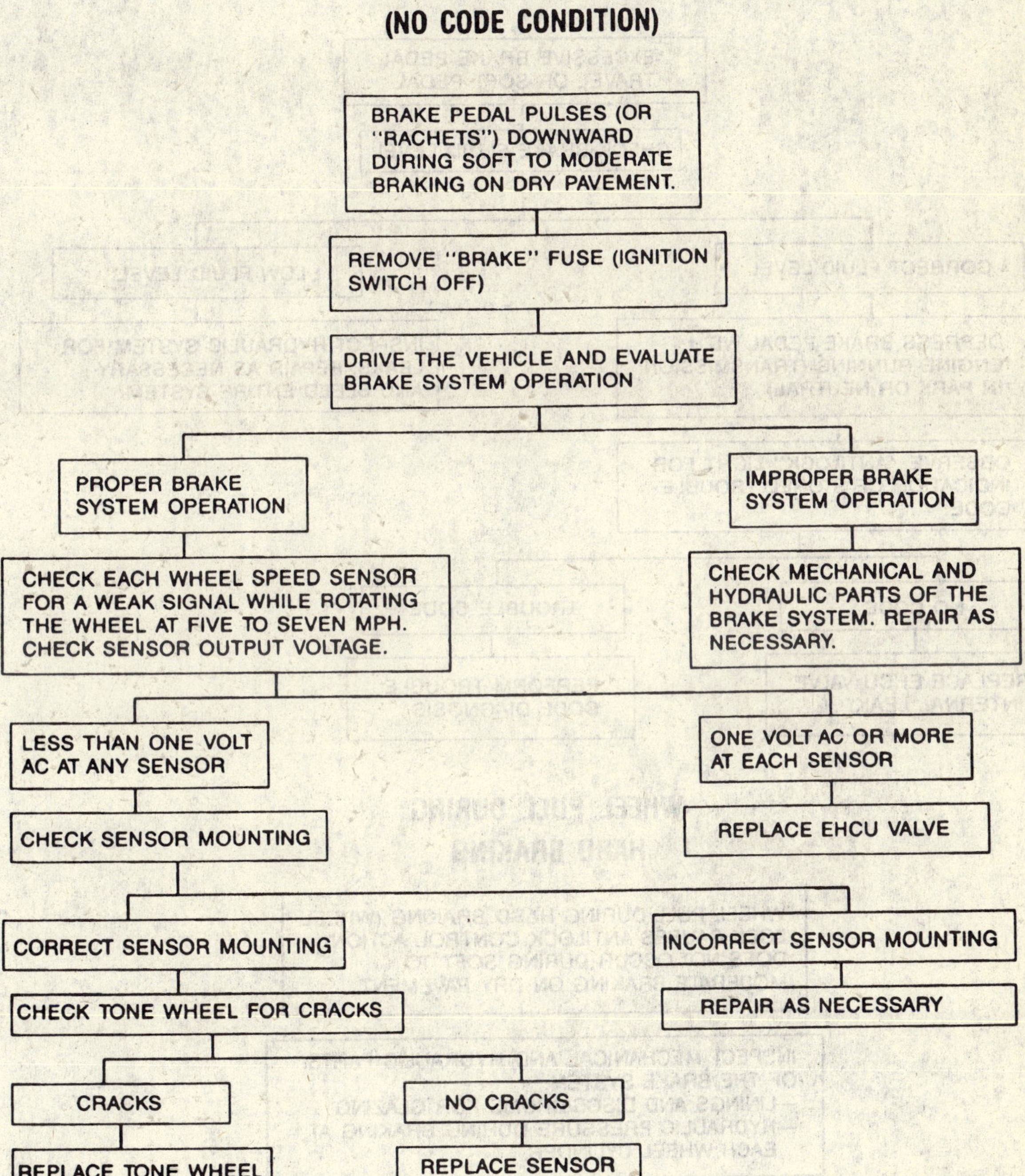

EXCESSIVE BRAKE PEDAL TRAVEL OR SOFT PEDAL

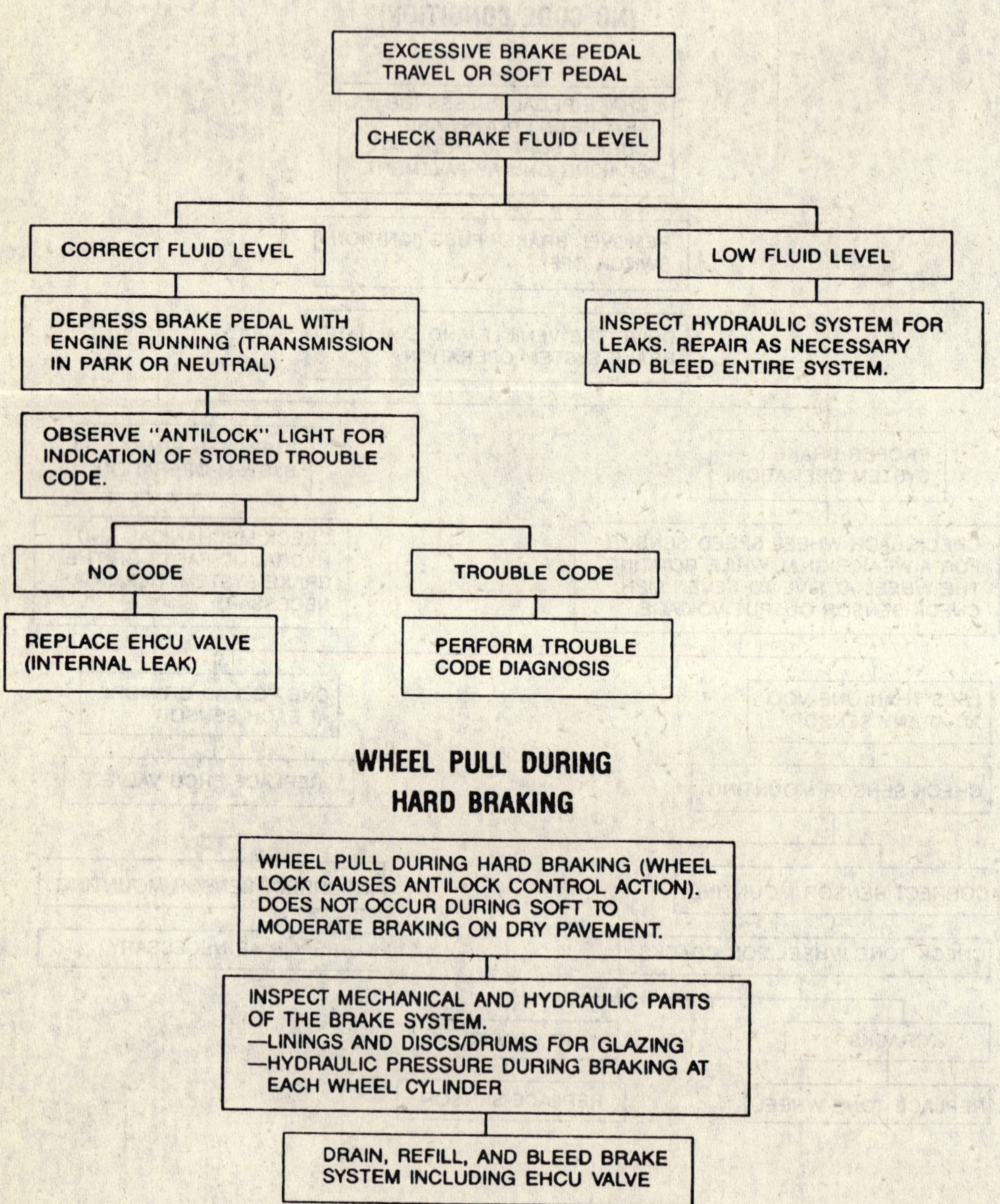

WHEEL PULL DURING HARD BRAKING

Component Replacement

SYSTEM FILLING

The master cylinder reservoirs must be kept properly filled to prevent air from entering the system. No special procedures are required because of the 4 wheel anti-lock brakes.

When adding fluid, use only DOT 3 fluid. The use of DOT 5 or silicone fluids is specifically prohibited. Use of improper or contaminated fluid may cause the fluid to boil or cause the rubber components in the system to deteriorate. Never use any fluid with a petroleum base or any fluid which has been exposed to water or moisture.

SYSTEM BLEEDING

Bleeding the system is also done in the usual fashion. The vacuum booster reserve should be released by pumping the pedal several times before beginning bleeding procedures. Bleeding may be done manually or with a pressure bleeder; if a pressure bleeder is used, it must contain a diaphragm to separate the air supply from the brake fluid.

When it is necessary to bleed all wheels, the correct order is right rear, left rear, right front and left front. The EHCU valve is not routinely bled; it only requires bleeding after replacement.

EHCU VALVE

REMOVAL AND INSTALLATION

1. Remove the intermediate steering shaft from the steering column.
2. Disconnect the brake lines from the bottom of the combination valve.
3. Label and remove the electrical connectors from the combination valve.
4. Remove the master cylinder and combination valve assembly.
5. Label and disconnect the wiring connectors from the EHCU valve.
6. Remove the nuts and bolt holding the EHCU valve bracket to the firewall. Remove the valve and bracket assembly as a unit.
7. Separate the EHCU valve from the bracket on the workbench.

NOTE: The EHCU valve is not serviceable. Do not attempt to disassemble or repair the unit.

To Install:

8. Place the EHCU valve on the bracket and install the 6 screws. Tighten these screws only to 60 inch lbs. (7 Nm); overtightening may result in excessive noise transfer from the EHCU valve to the interior.
9. Install the valve and bracket assembly into the vehicle. Install the nuts and bolt. Tighten the bolt to 33 ft. lbs. (45 Nm) and the nuts to 20 ft. lbs. (27 Nm).
10. Connect the wiring connectors to the EHCU valve.
11. Connect the brake lines to the EHCU valve. Tighten the lines to 16 ft. lbs. (25 Nm).
12. Install the master cylinder and combination valve assembly.
13. Connect the wiring connector to the combination valve.
14. Install the brake lines to the bottom of the combination valve and tighten the lines to 15 ft. lbs. (20 Nm).
15. Install the intermediate shaft to the steering column.
16. Bleed the brake system at the calipers and wheel cylinders.
17. Bleed the EHCU valve.

Bleeding

The EHCU valve should be bled only after replacement. It should not be necessary to bleed the valve during normal brake bleeding operations. The valve should be bled after the calipers and wheel cylinders have been bled. Use the 2 bleed screws on the EHCU valve to bleed the unit.

NOTE: There are also 2 bleeders on the front of the unit that look like normal brake bleeders. These are NOT the correct ports for bleeding the EHCU valve and should not be loosened.

Bleeding the EHCU valve requires the use of a combination valve depressor such as tool J–35856 or its equivalent. To bleed the EHCU valve:

1. Make sure the ignition switch is ‹cf35›OFF‹cf33› or false trouble codes will be set. Install the combination valve depressor on the left high pressure accumulator bleed stem of the EHCU valve.
2. Slowly depress the brake pedal 1 time and hold in the depressed position.
3. Loosen the left bleeder screw ¼–½ turn to purge the air from the EHCU valve.
4. Tighten the bleeder screw to 60 inch lbs. (7 Nm) and slowly release the pedal.
5. Wait 15 seconds, then repeat the bleeding sequence including the 15 second wait until all air is purged from the unit. Correct final torque on the bleeder is 60 inch lbs. (7 Nm).
6. Install the combination valve depressor on the right high pressure accumulator bleed stem and repeat the bleeding sequence.
7. Remove the valve depressor tools.

FRONT WHEEL SPEED SENSOR

REMOVAL AND INSTALLATION

1. Elevate and safely support the vehicle.
2. Remove the tire and wheel.
3. Remove the brake caliper.
4. Remove the hub and rotor assembly (2WD). On 4WD vehicles, remove the rotor first, then the hub and bearing assembly.
5. Disconnect the wheel speed sensor wire connector.
6. Release the sensor wire from the clip on the upper control arm.
7. On 2WD vehicles, remove the bolts holding the splash shield to the knuckle.
8. Remove the splash shield and sensor assembly from the knuckle.

To Install:

9. To install, position the splash shield and sensor assembly on the knuckle.
10. On 2WD vehicles, install the retaining bolts and tighten them to 11 ft. lbs. (15 Nm).
11. Place the sensor wire into the clip on the upper control arm.
12. Connect the sensor wire to the harness connector.
13. On 4WD vehicles, install the hub and bearing assembly followed by the brake rotor.
14. On 2WD vehicles, install the hub and rotor assembly.
15. Install the brake caliper.
16. Install the tire and wheel. Lower the vehicle to the ground.

REAR WHEEL SPEED SENSORS

REMOVAL AND INSTALLATION

1. Elevate and safely support the vehicle.
2. Remove the wheel and tire.
3. Remove the brake drum.
4. Remove the primary brake shoe.
5. Disconnect the sensor wiring at the connector.
6. Remove the sensor wire from the rear axle clips.

7. Remove the 2 bolts holding the sensor.
8. Remove the speed sensor by tracking the wire through the hole in the backing plate.

To Install:

9. To install, route the wire through the hole in the backing plate and fit the sensor into position.
10. Install the 2 bolts and tighten them to 26 ft. lbs. (35 Nm).
11. Secure the sensor wire within the rear axle clips.
12. Connect the sensor wiring to the harness connector.
13. Install the primary brake shoe.
14. Install the brake drum.
15. Install the wheel and tire assembly.
16. Lower the vehicle to the ground.

BRAKE SPECIFICATIONS

(All specifications in inches)

Years	Model	Master Cyl. Bore	Brake Disc Original Thickness	Brake Disc Minimum Thickness	Brake Disc Maximum Run-out	Brake Drum Orig. Inside Dia.	Brake Drum Max. Wear Limit	Brake Drum Maximum Machine O/S	Wheel Cyl. or Caliper Bore Front	Wheel Cyl. or Caliper Bore Rear
1982–91	All	0.945	1.03	0.965 ①	0.004	9.50	9.59	9.56	—	0.874

① Do not reface if rotor thickness is less than 0.980.

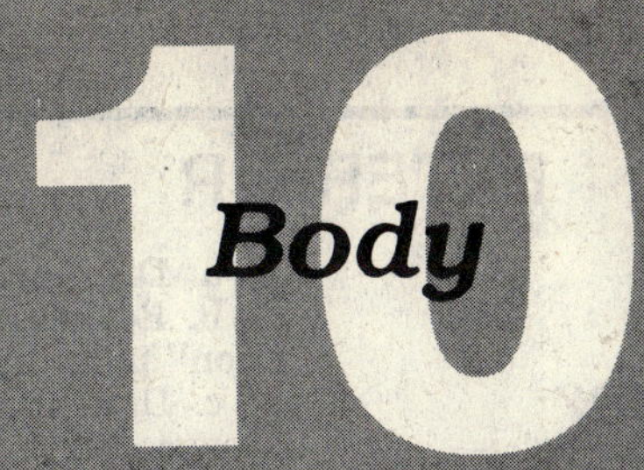

10 Body

QUICK REFERENCE INDEX

GENERAL INDEX

EXTERIOR

Doors

REMOVAL AND INSTALLATION

NOTE: The following procedure requires the use of the GM Door Hinge Spring Compressor tool No. J-28625-A or equivalent.

1. If equipped with power door components, perform the following procedures:

a. Disconnect the negative battery cable from the battery.
b. Refer to the "Door Trim Panel, Removal and Installation" procedures in this section and remove the door panel.
c. Disconnect the electrical harness connector from the power door lock motor and/or the power window regulator.
d. Remove the electrical harness from the door.

CAUTION

Before removing the hinge spring from the door, be sure to cover it (to keep it from flying); it could cause personal injury!

Hood, Trunk Lid, Hatch Lid, Glass and Doors

Problem	Possible Cause	Correction
HOOD/TRUNK/HATCH LID		
Improper closure.	• Striker and latch not properly aligned.	• Adjust the alignment.
Difficulty locking and unlocking.	• Striker and latch not properly aligned.	• Adjust the alignment.
Uneven clearance with body panels.	• Incorrectly installed hood or trunk lid.	• Adjust the alignment.
WINDOW/WINDSHIELD GLASS		
Water leak through windshield	• Defective seal. • Defective body flange.	• Fill sealant • Correct.
Water leak through door window glass.	• Incorrect window glass installation. • Gap at upper window frame.	• Adjust position. • Adjust position.
Water leak through quarter window.	• Defective seal. • Defective body flange.	• Replace seal. • Correct.
Water leak through rear window.	• Defective seal. • Defective body flange.	• Replace seal. • Correct.
FRONT/REAR DOORS		
Door window malfunction.	• Incorrect window glass installation. • Damaged or faulty regulator.	• Adjust position. • Correct or replace.
Water leak through door edge.	• Cracked or faulty weatherstrip.	• Replace.
Water leak from door center.	• Drain hole clogged. • Inadequate waterproof skeet contact or damage.	• Remove foreign objects. • Correct or replace.
Door hard to open.	• Incorrect latch or striker adjustment.	• Adjust.
Door does not open or close completely.	• Incorrect door installation. • Defective door check strap. • Door check strap and hinge require grease.	• Adjust position. • Correct or replace. • Apply grease.
Uneven gap between door and body.	• Incorrect door installation.	• Adjust position.
Wind noise around door.	• Improperly installed weatherstrip. • Improper clearance between door glass and door weatherstrip. • Deformed door.	• Repair or replace. • Adjust. • Repair or replace.

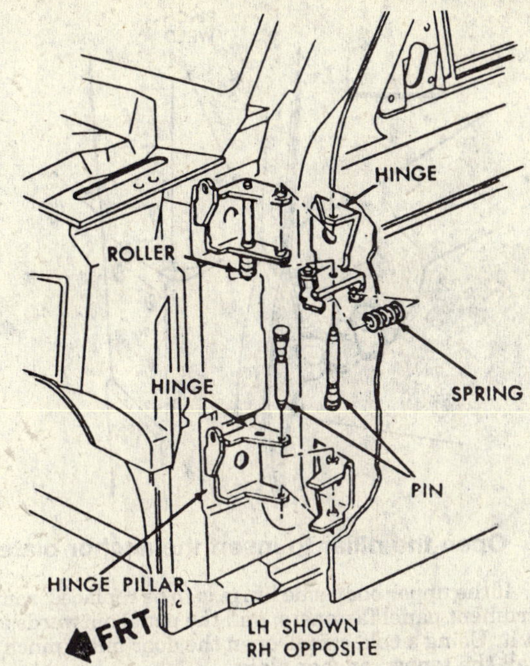

Remove the hinge pins to remove the door

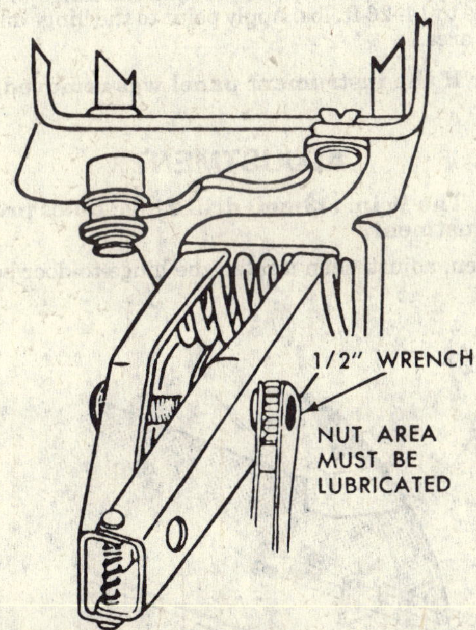

When using the spring compressor tool, be careful the spring doesn't fly out and cause damage or injury

2. Using the GM Door Hinge Spring Compressor tool No. J-28625-A or equivalent, compress the door hinge spring and remove it.
3. To remove the door hinge pin clips, spread the clips and move them above the recess on the pin; when the pin is removed, the clip will ride on the pin and fall free of it.
4. Using a soft-head hammer and a pair of locking pliers, remove the lower pin from the door hinge; then, install a bolt (in the lower pin hole) to hold the door in place until the upper hinge pin is removed.
5. Remove the upper door hinge pin and support the door, then remove the bolt from the lower hinge pin hole and the door from the truck.
6. To install the door, position it on the hinges and insert a bolt through the lower hinge pin hole.
7. Using a new hinge pin clip, install the upper hinge pin.
8. Remove the bolt from the lower hinge pin hole. Using a new hinge pin, install it into the lower hinge pin holes.
9. Using the GM Door Hinge Spring Compressor tool No. J-28625-A or equivalent, compress the door hinge spring and install it into the door hinge.
10. If equipped with power door components, reconnect the electrical harness connector(s), install the door panel and the reconnect the negative battery terminal.

ADJUSTMENTS

Factory installed hinges are welded in place, so no adjustment of the system is necessary or recommended.

Door Hinges

NOTE: The following procedure requires the use of an ⅛ in. (3mm) drill bit, ½ in. (13mm) drill bit, a center punch, a cold chisel, a portable body grinder, a putty knife and a scribing tool.

REMOVAL AND INSTALLATION

1. Refer to the "Door, Removal and Installation" procedures in this section and remove the door(s), then place the door on a padded workbench.
2. Using a putty knife, remove the sealant from the around the edge of the hinge.
3. Using a scribing tool, outline the position of the hinge(s) on the door and the body pillar.
4. Using a center punch, mark the center position of the hinge-to-door and the hinge-to-body pillar welds.
5. Using a ⅛ in. (3mm) drill bit, drill a pilot hole completely through each weld.

NOTE: When drilling the holes through the hinge welds, DO NOT drill through the door or the body pillar.

6. Using a ½ in. (13mm) drill bit, drill a hole through the hinge base, following the ⅛ in. (3mm) pilot hole.
7. Using a cold chisel and a hammer, separate the hinge from the door and/or the body pillar. Using a portable grinder, clean off any welds remaining on the door or the body pillar.
8. To fasten the replacement hinge(s) to the door and/or body pillar, perform the following procedures:
    a. Align the replacement hinge, with the scribe lines, previously made.
    b. Using a center punch and the new hinge as a template, mark the location of each bolt hole.
    c. Using a ½ in. (13mm) drill bit, drill holes (using the center marks) through the door and body pillar.

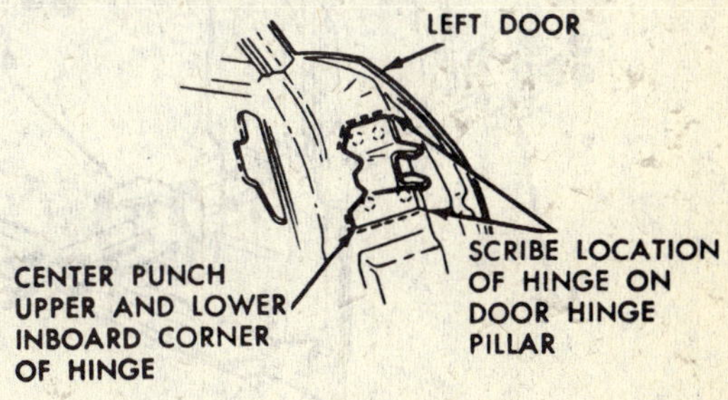

Mark the position of the hinge for correct location

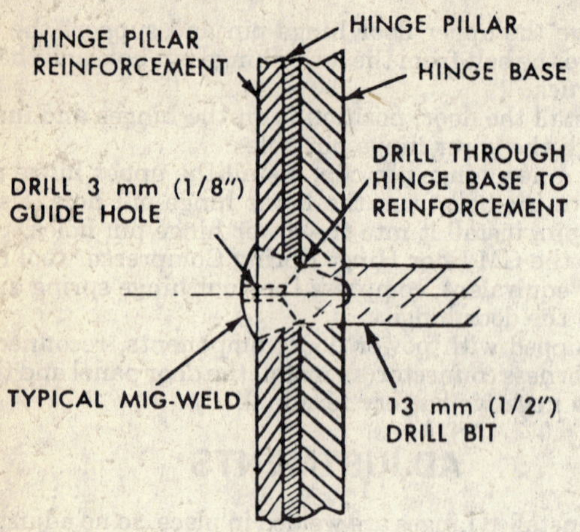

Use a drill to remove the welds

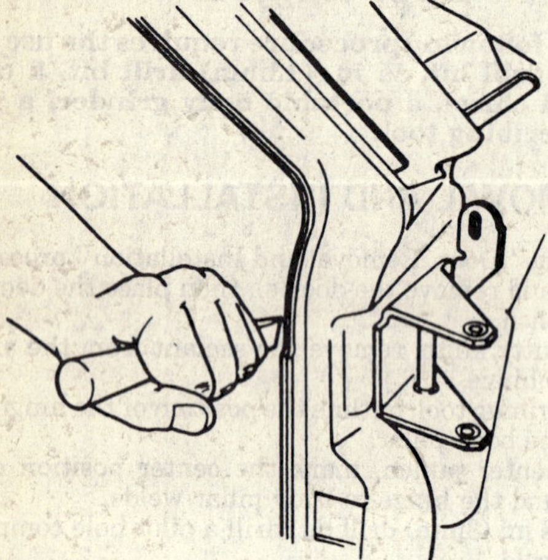

Use a cold chisel to open the door pillar weld

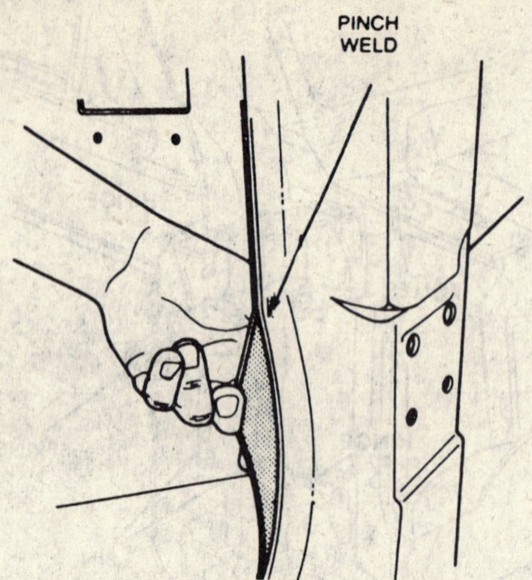

Open the pillar to insert the anchor plate

d. If the upper body-side hinge is to be replaced, remove the instrument panel fasteners, pull the panel outwards and support it. Using a cold chisel, open the door pillar pinch weld to install the tapped anchor plate.

9. To install, use medium body sealant (apply it to the hinge-to-door or body pillar surface), the hinge-to-door/body pillar bolts and tapped anchor plate. Torque the hinge-to-door/body pillar bolts to 14–26 ft. lbs. Apply paint to the hinge and the surrounding area.

NOTE: If the instrument panel was removed, replace it.

ADJUSTMENT

NOTE: The ½ in. (13mm) drill hinge holes provide for some adjustment.

1. Loosen, adjust, then tighten the hinge-to-door/body pillar

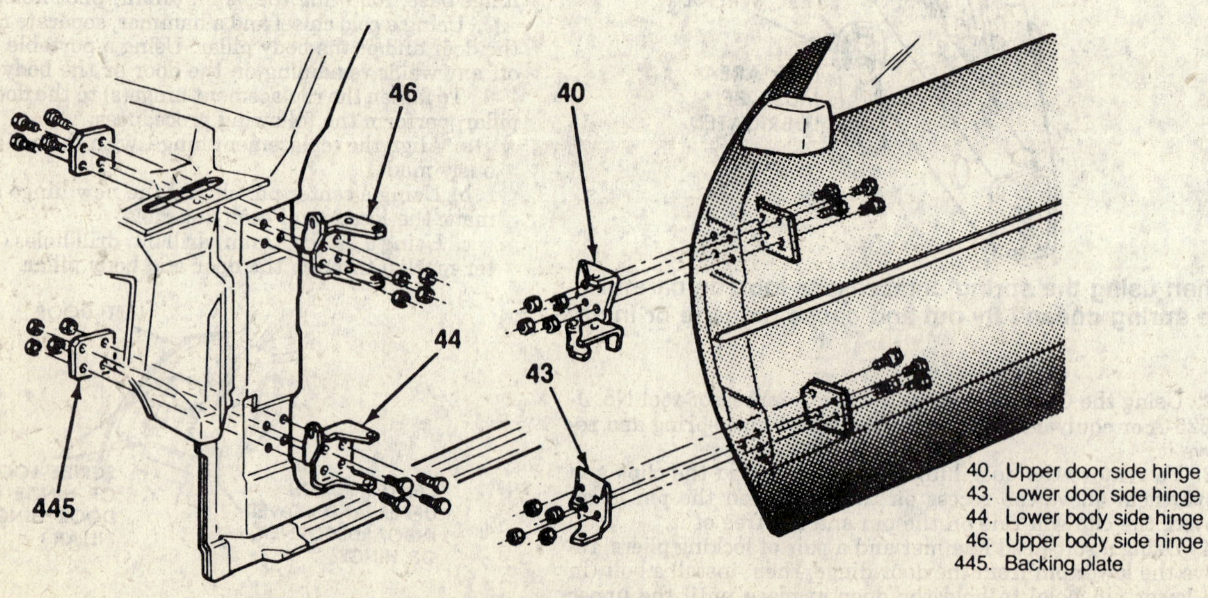

Doors with replacement hinges can be adjusted

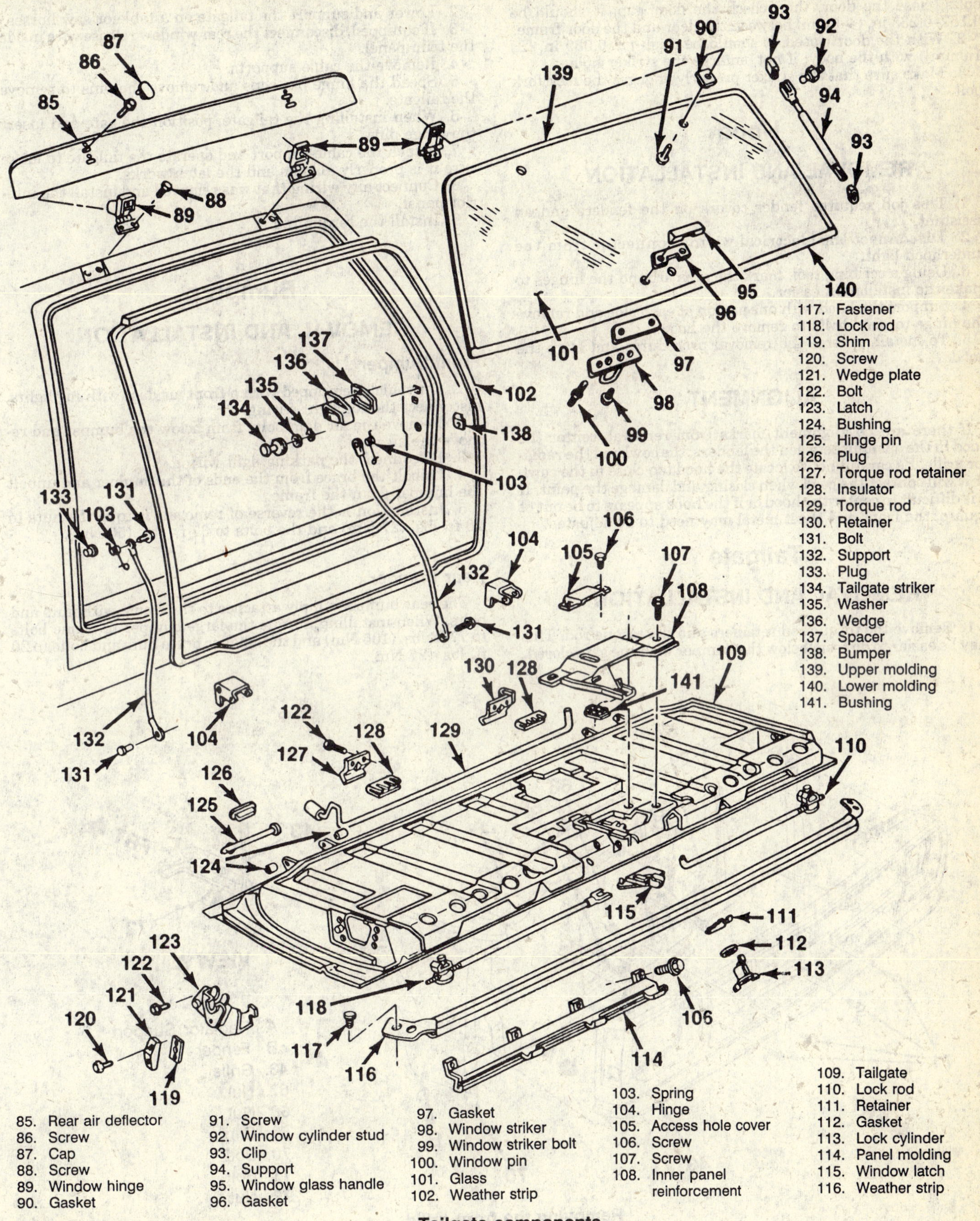

Tailgate components

bolts; close the door, then check the door gap, it should be 0.157–0.235 in. (4–6mm) between the door and the door frame.

2. With the door closed, it should be flush (± 0.039 in. [± 1.0mm]) with the body; if not, enlarge the striker hole.

3. Make sure that the striker properly engages the lock fork bolt.

Hood

REMOVAL AND INSTALLATION

1. This job requires fender covers on the fenders and an assistant.

2. Disconnect the electrical wiring connector from the underhood light.

3. Using a scribing tool, mark the area around the hinges to make the installation easier.

4. Support the hood with one preson at each side and remove the hinge-to-hood bolts to remove the hood.

5. To install, reverse the removal procedures and align the hood.

ALIGNMENT

If there are no alignment marks from removal, center the hood in the opening between the fenders, the cowl and the radiator grille. Be careful not to locate the hood too close to the cowl, or it will contact the cowl when closing and damage the paint. If it is difficult to center the hood or if the hood appears to be out of square, the front end sheet metal may need to be adjusted.

Tailgate

REMOVAL AND INSTALLATION

1. Remove the torque rod retainers and the torque rod. This may be easier to do from below the bumper with the gate closed.

2. Lower and support the tailgate on a table or saw horses.

3. If equipped, disconnect the rear window release wire inside the trim panel.

4. Remove the cable supports.

5. Spead the hinge pin clips and remove the pins to remove the tailgate.

6. When installing the tailgate, position the gate and insert the hinge pins.

7. Attach the cable support and operate the tailgate to make sure it is properly aligned and the latch works.

8. Connect any wiring that was removed and install the interior panel.

9. Install the torque rod.

Bumpers

REMOVAL AND INSTALLATION

Front Bumper

1. On vehicles equipped with a front air dam with fog lights, disconnect the fog light wiring.

2. Remove the air dam bolts from below the bumper and remove the air dam.

3. Disconnect the parking light wiring.

4. Unbolt the brace from the ends of the bumper and unbolt the bumper from the frame.

5. Installation is the reverse of removal. Torque the nuts to 20 ft. lbs. (27 Nm) and the bolts to 37 ft. lbs. (50 Nm).

Rear Bumper

The rear bumper simply attaches to the frame with nuts and bolts. When installing, torque the large bumper-to-frame bolts to 77 ft. lbs. (105 Nm) and the smaller brace nuts and bolts to 20 ft. lbs. (27 Nm).

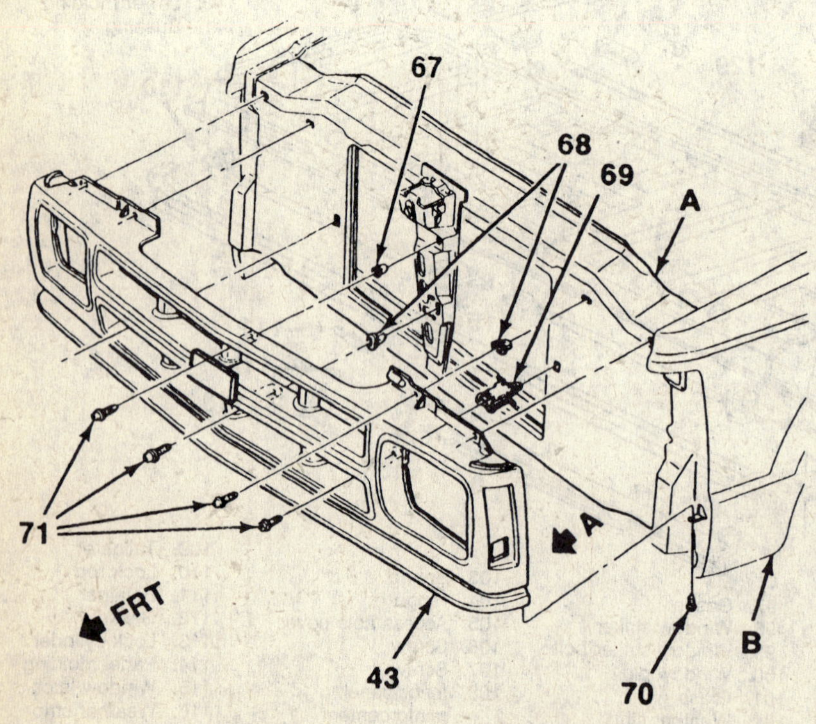

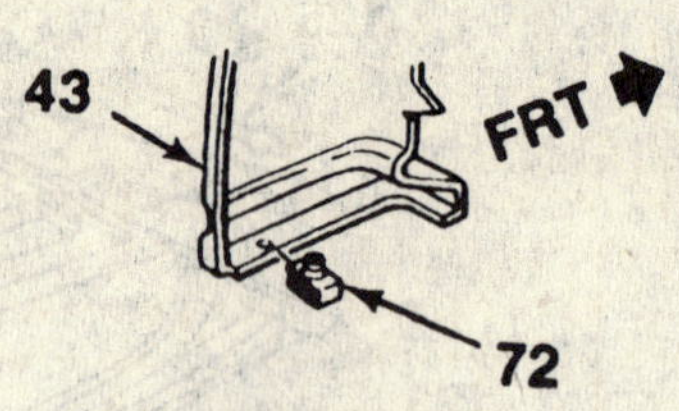

A. Radiator Support
B. Fender
43. Grille
67. Nut
68. Nut
69. Clip
70. Bolt
71. Bolt
72. Nut

Removing the front grille

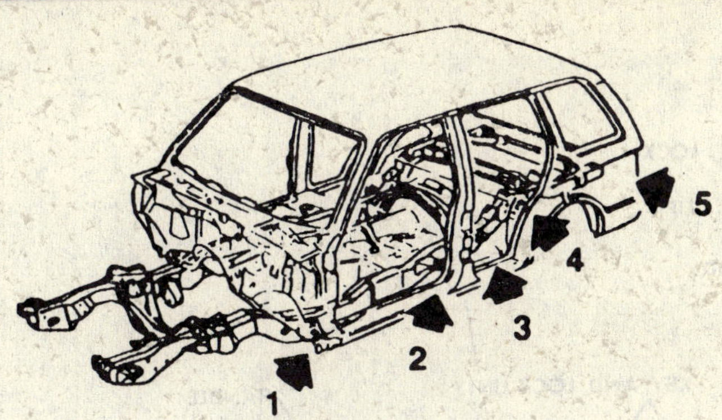

Body mount locations

Radiator Grille

REMOVAL AND INSTALLTION

1. Remove the grille-to-fender bolts.
2. Remove the grille-to-radiator support bolts.
3. Remove the grille, being careful not to loose the clips.
4. Installation is the reverse of removal.

Front Fenders

REMOVAL AND INSTALLATION

1. Raise the hood and remove the battery and battery tray.
2. Remove the front grille and head lights.
3. Remove the bumper.
4. Remove the washer fluid and coolant bottles.
5. Remove the wiper arms and cowl vent grille to access the rear bolts.
6. Remove the bolts and lift the fender off the vehicle.
7. When installing the fender, connect all wiring before connecting the battery.

Body Mounts

When replacing body mounts, it is important to properly support body, loosen all mounts on that side and lower the frame away from the body. Shims are available in 0.50 and 0.110 inch sizes (1.5 and 3.0mm). No shim stack should exceed 0.240 in. (6.0mm). Torque body mount bolts to 52 ft. lbs. (70 Nm).

INTERIOR

Door Panels

REMOVAL AND INSTALLATION

1. Remove the door handle bezel-to-door screws and the bezel from the door.
2. Using the Window Handle Spring Removal tool No. J-9886 or equivalent, remove the window handle spring clip and the door handle.

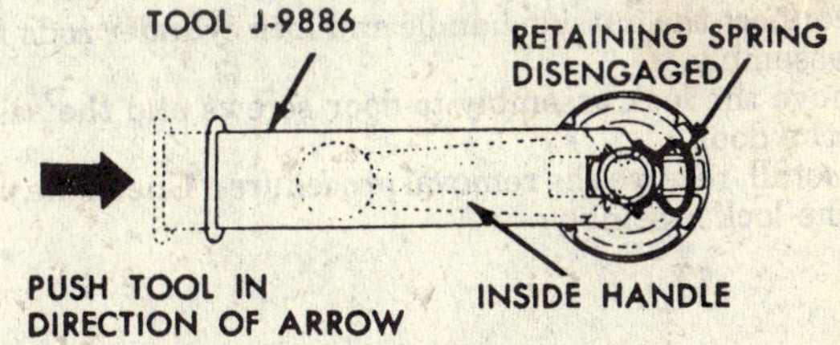

Use the special tool to remove the window handle

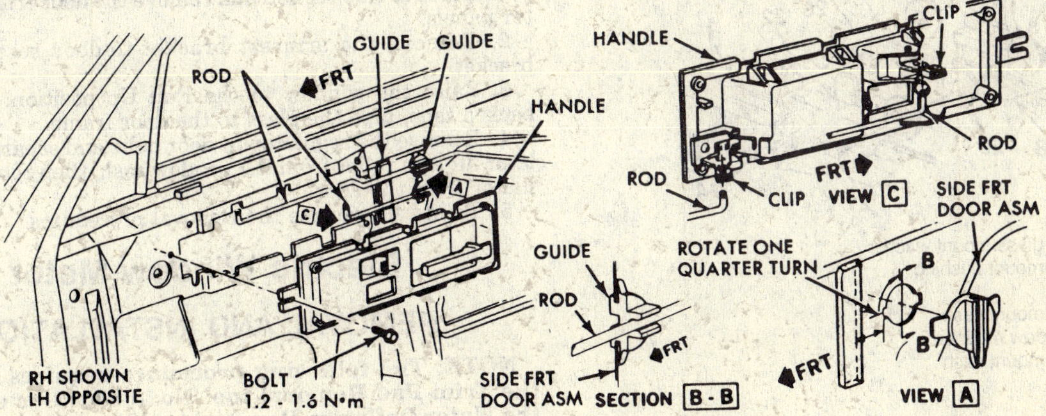

Removing the outside door handle

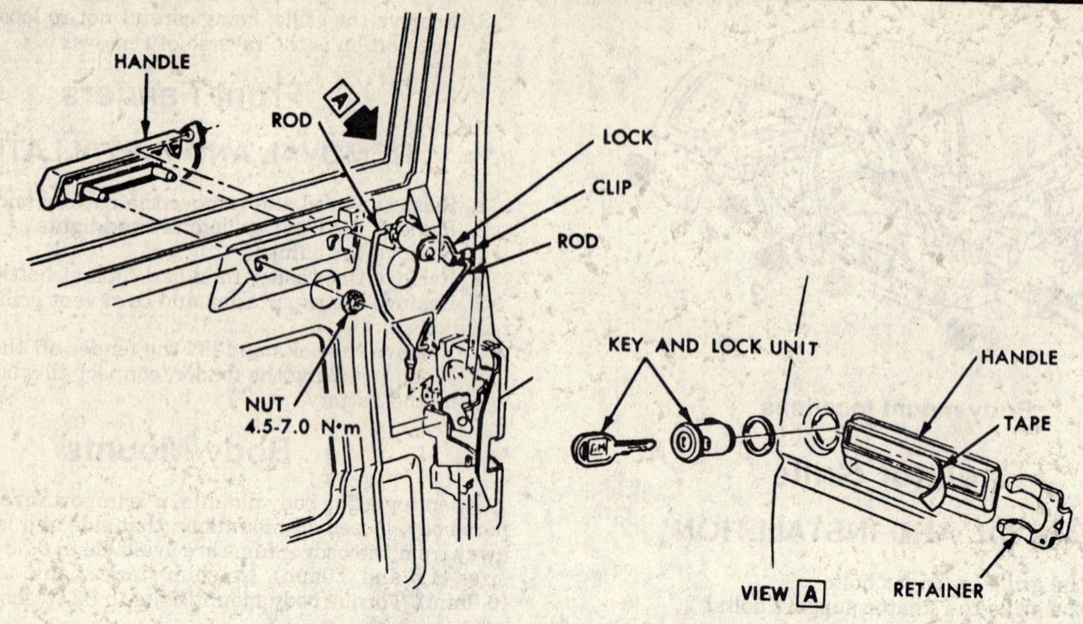

Door lock rods and lock cylinder

3. Remove the armrest-to-door screws and the armrest.
4. Remove the door trim panel-to-door screws and carefully pry the panel fasteners from the door to remove the panel. Installation is the reverse of removal.

Door Locks

REMOVAL AND INSTALLATION

Door Lock Assembly

1. Remove the door trim panel and insulator panel.
2. Remove the lock rod and the lever rod from the inner door handle housing.
3. Disconnect the outside handle and lock cylinder rods from the lock assembly.
4. Remove the lock assembly-to-door screws and the assembly from the door.
5. To install, reverse the removal procedures. Check the operation of the lock assembly.

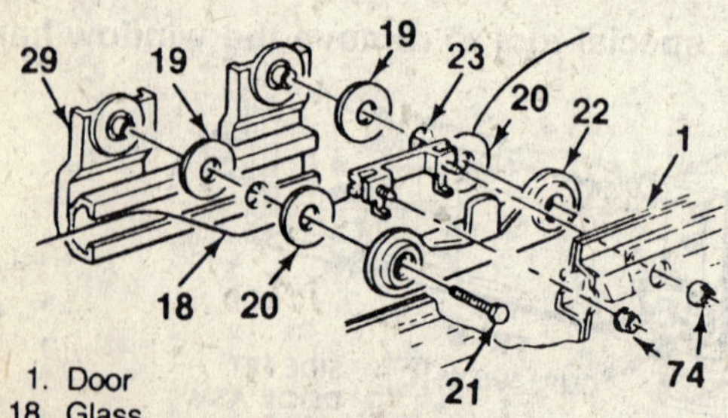

1. Door
18. Glass
19. Window glass mount washer
20. Window mount bushing
21. Bolt
22. Window mount sash
23. Side window retainer
29. Window mount sash
74. Nut

Window regulator and sash parts

Door Glass and Regulator

REMOVAL AND INSTALLATION

CAUTION

Always wear heavy gloves when handling glass to minimize the risk of injury!

Door Glass

1. Refer to the "Door Trim Panel, Removal and Installation" procedures in this section and remove the door trim panel and the insulator panel.
2. Remove the arm rest bracket.
3. Lower the window until it and the sash channel can be seen in the door panel opening, then remove the sash assembly-to-window bolts.
4. Remove the sash assembly and the window from the door.
5. To install, reverse the removal procedures. Lightly lubricate the window in the sash with baby powder.

Door Regulator

1. Refer to the "Door Trim Panel, Removal and Installation" procedures in this section and remove the door trim and insulator panels.
2. Remove the armrest bracket-to-door screws and the bracket.
3. Raise the window to the Full Up position. Using cloth backed tape, tape the glass to the door frame.
4. Remove the regulator-to-door bolts and separate the regulator lift arm roller from the window sash, then remove the regulator from the door.
5. To install, reverse the removal procedures.

Electric Window Motor

REMOVAL AND INSTALLATION

NOTE: The following procedure requires the use of the Trim Pad Removal tool No. J-24595 or equivalent, the Water Deflector Removal tool No. J-21104 or equivalent, the Rivet Installation tool No. J-29022 or equiva-

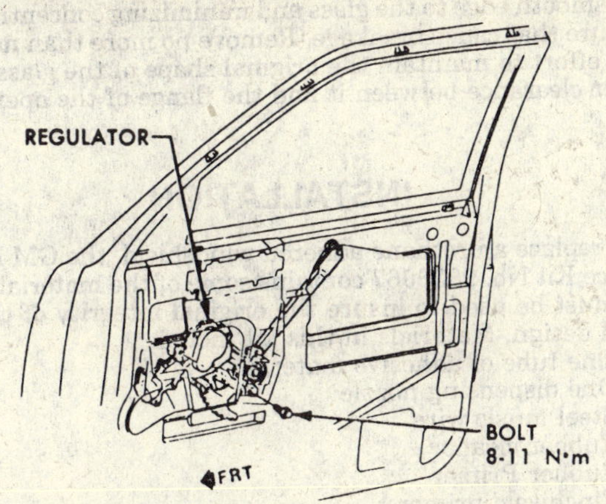

Use a bolt to secure the sector gear on the electric window regulator

lent, the Window Regulator Clip Removal tool No. J-9886-01 or equivalent, and $^3/_{16}$ in. rivets.

1. Refer to the "Door Trim Panel, Removal and Installation" procedures in this section and remove the door trim panel.
2. Disconnect the negative battery terminal from the battery.
3. Remove the armrest bracket-to-door screws and the bracket.
4. Using the Water Deflector Removal tool No. J-21104 or equivalent, remove the water deflector from the door.
5. Raise the window to the Full Up position. Using cloth backed tape, tape the glass to the door frame.
6. Disconnect the electrical wiring connector from the window regulator motor.
7. Separate the regulator lift arm roller from the window sash.

CAUTION

The sector gear must be locked into position. The lift arm is balanced by a spring that is now under tension and could cause injury if the sector gear is not properly secured!

8. If removing the window regulator motor from the door, perform the following procedure:
   a. Drill a hole through the regulator sector gear and backplate, then install a bolt/nut to lock the sector gear in position.
   b. Using a $^3/_{16}$ in. (5mm) drill bit, drill out the motor-to-door rivets.
   c. Remove the motor from the door.

To install:

9. Using the Rivet Installation tool No. J-29022 or equivalent, rivet the window regulator motor to the door.
10. After the motor is riveted to the door, remove the nut/bolt from the sector gear.
11. Install the lift arm to the window mount.
12. Connect the wiring and battery and test the window before installing the water deflector and trim panel.

Windshield

NOTE: Bonded windshields require special tools and special removal procedures to be performed to ensure the windshield will be removed without being broken. For this reason we recommend that you refer all removal and installation to a qualified technician.

CAUTION

Always wear heavy gloves when handling glass to reduce the risk of injury.

When replacing a cracked windshield, it is important that the cause of the crack be determined and the condition corrected, before a new glass is installed. The cause of the crack may be an obstruction or a high spot somewhere around the flange of the opening; cracking may not occur until pressure from the high spot or obstruction becomes particularly high due to winds, extremes of temperature or rough terrain.

When a windshield is broken, the glass may have already have fallen or been removed from the weatherstrip. Often, however, it is necessary to remove a cracked or otherwise imperfect windshield that is still intact. In this case, it is a good practice to crisscross the glass with strips of masking tape before removing the it; this will help hold the glass together and minimize the risk of injury.

If a crack extends to the edge of the glass, mark the point where the crack meets the weather strip. (Use a piece of chalk to mark the point on the cab, next to the weatherstrip.) Later, examining the window flange for a cause of the crack which started at the point marked.

The higher the temperature of the work area, the more pliable the weather strip will be. The more pliable the weather strip, the more easily the windshield can be removed.

There are two methods of windshield removal, depending on the method of windshield replacement chosen. When using the short method of installation, it is important to cut the glass from the urethane adhesive as close to the glass as possible. This is due to the fact that the urethane adhesive will be used to provide a base for the replacement windshield.

When using the extended method of windshield replacement, all the urethane adhesive must be removed from the pinchweld flange so, the process of cutting the window from the adhesive is less critical.

REMOVAL AND INSTALLATION

NOTE: The following procedure requires the use of the Urethane Glass Sealant Remover (hot knife) tool No. J-24709-1 or equivalent, the Glass Sealant Remover Knife tool No. J-24402-A or equivalent.

1. Place the protective covering around the area where the glass will be removed.

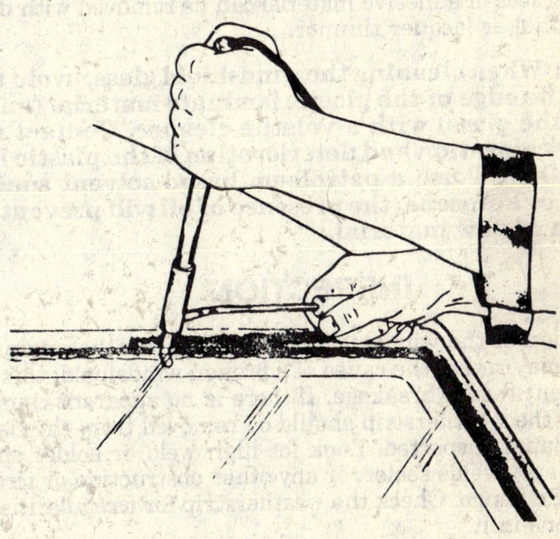

Using a hot knife to remove the windshield seal

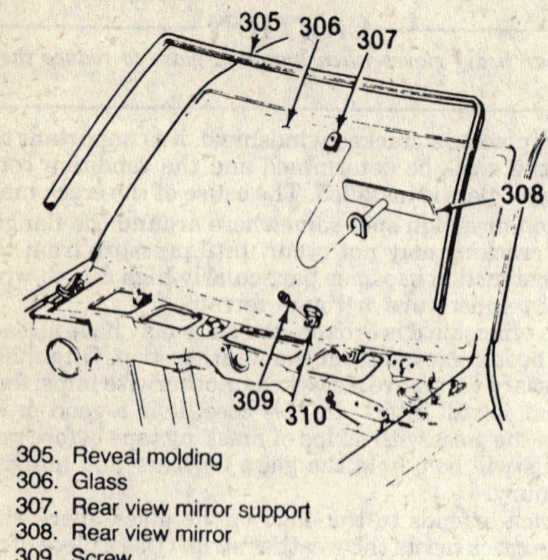

305. Reveal molding
306. Glass
307. Rear view mirror support
308. Rear view mirror
309. Screw
310. Support

Windshield installation

2. Remove the windshield wiper arms, the cowl vent grille, the windshield supports, the rear view mirror and the interior garnish moldings.

NOTE: If equipped with a radio antenna, embedded in the windshield, disconnect the electrical connector from the windshield.

3. Remove the exterior reveal molding from the urethane adhesive by prying one end of the molding from the adhesive. Pull the free end of the molding away from the windshield or the pinchweld flange until the molding is completely free of the windshield.

4. Using the Urethane Glass Sealant Remover (hot knife) tool No. J-24709-1 or equivalent, and the Glass Sealant Remover Knife tool No. J-24402-A or equivalent, cut the windshield from the urethane adhesive. If the short method of glass replacement is to be used, keep the knife as close to the glass as possible in order to leave a base for the replacement glass.

5. With the help of an assistant, remove the glass.

6. If the original glass is to be reinstalled, place it on a protected bench or a holding or holding fixture. Remove any remaining adhesive with a razor blade or a sharp scraper. Any remaining traces of adhesive material can be removed with denatured alcohol or lacquer thinner.

NOTE: When cleaning the windshield glass, avoid contacting the edge of the plastic laminate material (on the edge of the glass) with a volatile cleaner. Contact may cause discoloration and deterioration of the plastic laminate. DO NOT use a petroleum based solvent such as gasoline or kerosene; the presence of oil will prevent the adhesion of new material.

INSPECTION

Inspection of the windshield opening, the weather strip and the glass may reveal the cause of a broken windshield; this can help prevent future breakage. If there is no apparent cause of breakage, the weatherstrip should be removed from the flange and the flange inspected. Look for high weld or solder spots, hardened spot welds sealer, or any other obstruction or irregularity in the flange. Check the weatherstrip for irregularities or obstructions in it.

Check the windshield to be installed to make sure that it does not have chipped edges. Chipped edges can be ground off, restoring a smooth edge to the glass and minimizing concentrations of pressure that cause breakage. Remove no more than necessary, in an effort to maintain the original shape of the glass and the proper clearance between it and the flange of the opening.

INSTALLATION

To replace a urethane adhered windshield, the GM Adhesive Service Kit No. 9636067 contains some of the materials needed and must be used to insure the original integrity of the windshield design. Materials in this kit include:

- One tube of adhesive material
- One dispensing nozzle
- Steel music wire
- Rubber cleaner
- Rubber Primer
- Pinchweld primer
- Blackout primer
- Filler strip (for use on windshield installations of vehicles equipped with an embedded windshield antenna)
- Primer applicators

Other materials required for windshield installation which are not included in the service kit, are:

- GM rubber lubricant No. 1051717
- Alcohol for cleaning the edge of the glass
- Adhesive dispensing gun No. J-24811 or equivalent
- A commercial type razor knife
- Two rubber support spacers

Short Method

1. Using masking tape, apply the tape across the windshield pillar-to-windshield opening, then cut the tape and remove the windshield.

2. Using an alcohol dampened cloth, clean the metal flange surrounding the windshield opening. Allow the alcohol to air dry.

3. Using the pinchweld primer, found in the service kit, apply it to the pinchweld area. DO NOT let any of the primer touch the exposed paint for damage to the finish may occur; allow five minutes for the primer to dry.

4. Cut the tip of the adhesive cartridge approximately $^3/_{16}$ in. (5mm) from the end of the tip.

5. Apply the adhesive first in and around the spacer blocks. Apply a smooth continuous bead of adhesive into the gap between the glass edge and the sheet metal. Use a flat bladed tool to paddle the material into position if necessary. Be sure that the adhesive contacts the entire edge of the glass and extends to fill the gap between the glass and the solidified urethane base.

6. With the aid of a helper, position the windshield on the filler strips against the two support spacers.

NOTE: The vehicle should not be driven and should remain at room temperature for six hours to allow the adhesive to cure.

7. Spray a mist of water onto the urethane. Water will assist in the curing process. Dry the area where the reveal molding will contact the body and glass.

8. Install new reveal moldings. Remove the protective tape covering the butyl adhesive on the underside of the molding. Push the molding caps onto each end of one of the reveal moldings. Press the lip of the molding into the urethane adhesive while holding it against the edge of the windshield. Take care to seat the molding in the corners. The lip must fully contact the adhesive and the gap must be entirely covered by the crown of the molding. Slide the molding caps onto the adjacent moldings. Use tape to hold the molding in position until the adhesive cures.

9. Install the wiper arms and the interior garnish moldings.

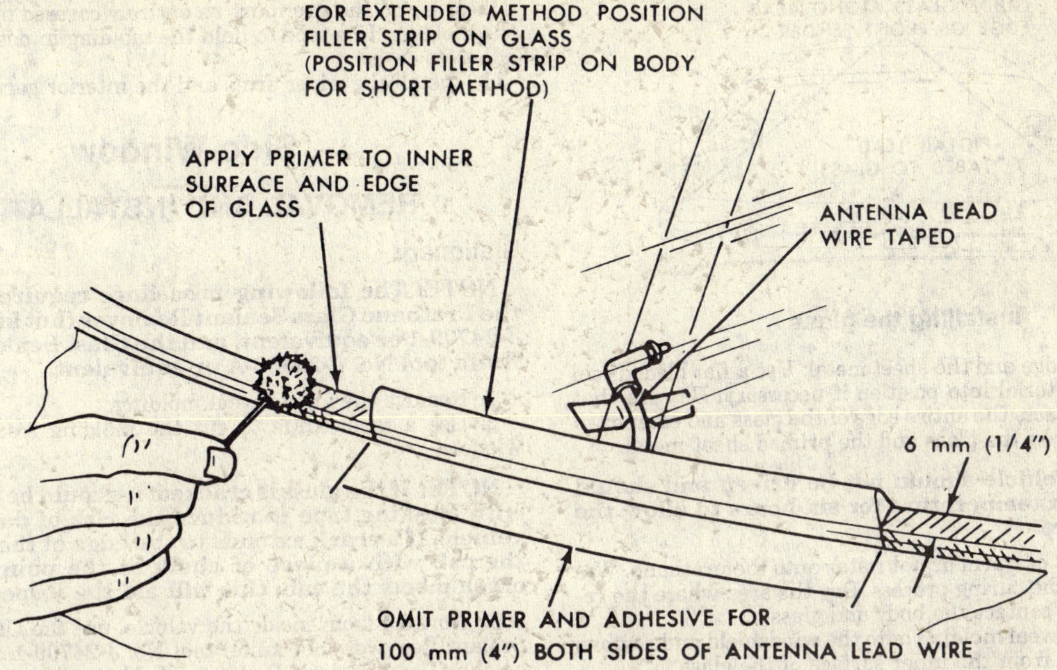

Apply primer to the windshield

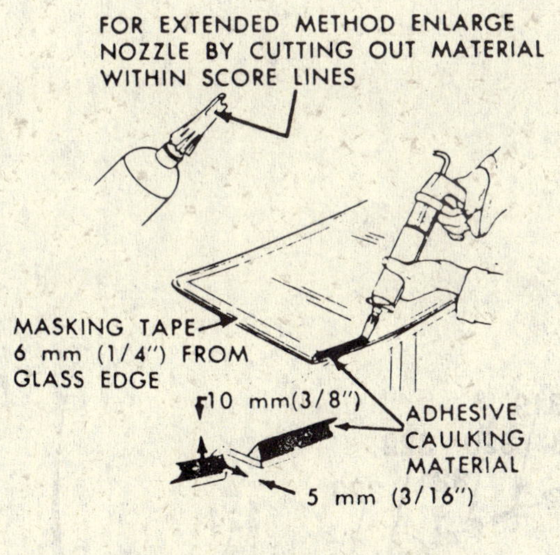

Apply sealant to the glass

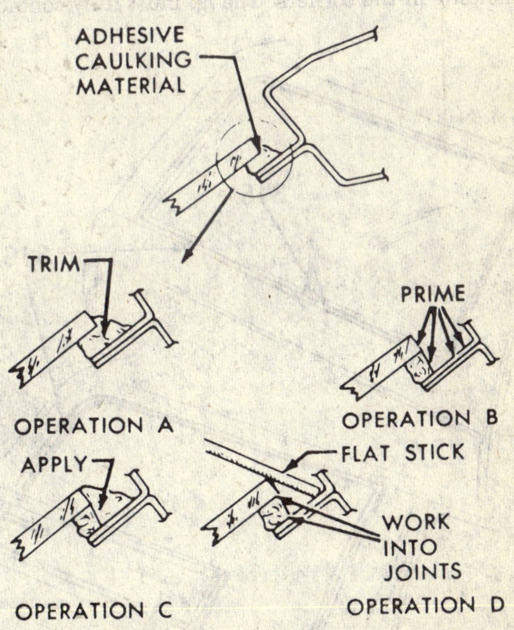

Trim the sealant so the reveal molding will fit properly

NOTE: The vehicle should not be driven and should remain at room temperature for six hours to allow the adhesive to cure.

Extended Method

1. Using the GM Strip Filler No. 20146247 or equivalent, install the sealing strip onto the pinchweld flange. The joint of the molding should be located at the bottom center of the molding.
2. Using masking tape, apply the tape across the windshield pillar-to-windshield opening, then cut the tape and remove the windshield.
3. Using an alcohol dampened cloth, clean the metal flange surrounding the windshield opening. Allow the alcohol to air dry.
4. Using the pinchweld primer, found in the service kit, apply it to the pinchweld area. DO NOT let any of the primer touch the exposed paint for damage to the finish may occur; allow five minutes for the primer to dry.
5. With the aid of an assistant, position the windshield on the filler strips against the two support spacers.
6. Cut the tip of the adhesive cartridge approximately ⅜ in. (10mm) from the end of the tip.
7. Apply the adhesive first in and around the spacer blocks. Apply a smooth continuous bead of adhesive into the gap be-

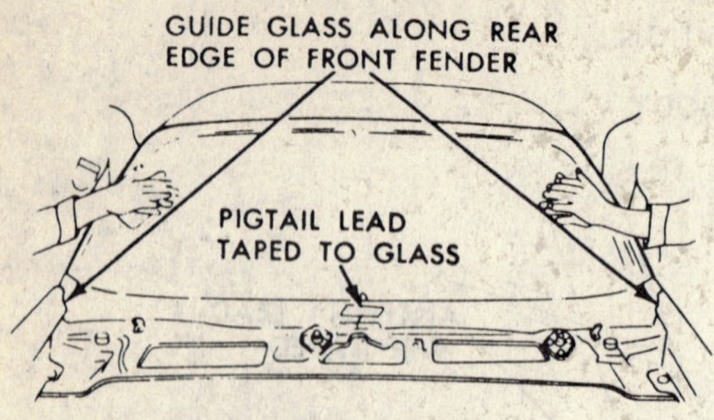

Installing the glass

tween the glass edge and the sheet metal. Use a flat bladed tool to paddle the material into position if necessary. Be sure that the adhesive contacts the entire edge of the glass and extends to fill the gap between the glass and the primed sheet metal.

NOTE: The vehicle should not be driven and should remain at room temperature for six hours to allow the adhesive to cure.

8. Spray a mist of warm or hot water onto the urethane. Water will assist in the curing process. Dry the area where the reveal molding will contact the body and glass.
9. Install the reveal molding onto the windshield and remove the masking tape from the inner surface of the glass.
10. Press the lip of the molding into the urethane adhesive while holding it against the edge of the windshield. Take care to seat the molding in the corners. The lip must fully contact the adhesive and the gap must be entirely covered by the crown of the molding. Use tape to hold the molding in position until the adhesive cures.
11. Install the wiper arms and the interior garnish moldings.

Side Window

REMOVAL AND INSTALLATION

Stationary

NOTE: The following procedure requires the use of the Urethane Glass Sealant Remover (hot knife) tool No. J-24709-1 or equivalent, and the Glass Sealant Remover Knife tool No. J-24402-A or equivalent.

1. Remove the vinyl reveal molding.
2. Use a razor knife to cut the molding from around the window.

NOTE: If the glass is cracked, it should be crisscrossed with masking tape to reduce the risk of damage to the vehicle. If a crack extends to the edge of the glass, mark the cab with a piece of chalk at the point where the crack meets the cab; this will aid the inspection later.

3. Working from inside the vehicle, use the Urethane Glass Sealant Remover (hot knife) tool No. J-24709-1 or equivalent, or the Glass Sealant Remover Knife tool No. J-24402-A or equivalent, separate the window glass and molding.
4. Remove the molding and the glass from the window frame.
5. Using a scraper or a chisel, remove the adhesive from the

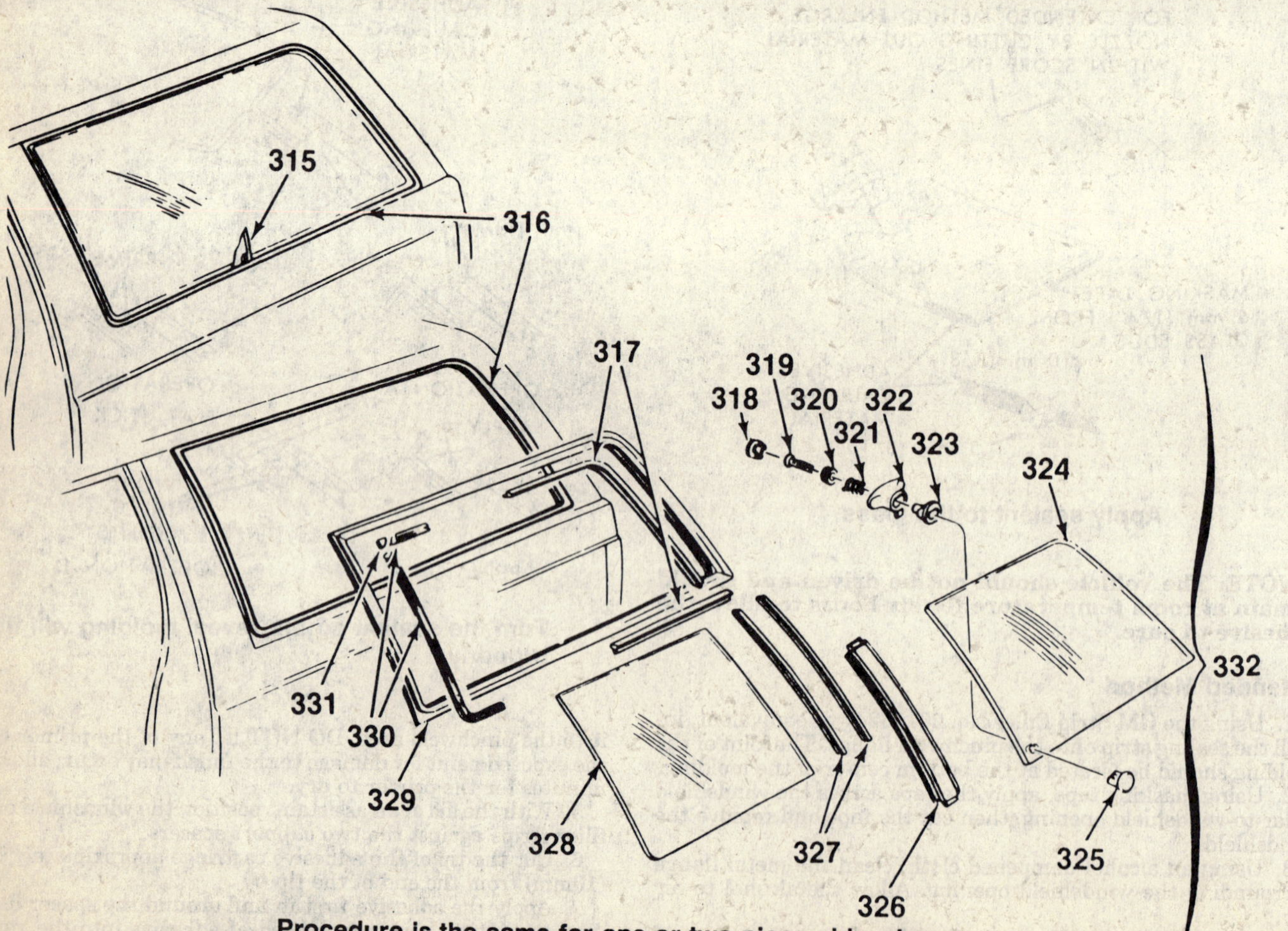

Procedure is the same for one or two piece side glass

pinchweld flange; be sure to remove all of the mounds or loose adhesive.

6. Using alcohol and a clean cloth, clean the pinchweld flange. Allow the alcohol to air dry.

7. Using the pinchweld primer, found in the service kit, apply it to the pinchweld area. DO NOT let any of the primer touch the exposed paint for damage to the finish may occur; allow five minutes for the primer to dry.

8. Apply a smooth continuous bead of adhesive around the molding edge. Be sure that the adhesive contacts the entire edge of the molding and extends to fill the gap between the glass and the primed sheet metal.

9. Using hand pressure, press the glass/molding assembly onto the pinchweld flange. Using retaining clips, secure the glass/molding assembly to the pinchweld.

10. Spray a mist of warm or hot water onto the urethane. Water will assist in the curing process. Dry the area where the reveal molding will contact the body and glass.

Seats

REMOVAL AND INSTALLATION

Front

1. Remove the cover screws and covers from the seat tracks.
2. Remove the nuts and lift the seat and track from the vehicle.
3. When installing, torque the track retaining nuts to 24 ft. lbs. (32 Nm).

Rear

1. Remove the front support cover screws and covers.
2. Remove the front support bracket bolts and fold the seat forward.
3. Support the seat and remove the center support bracket nuts. Remove the seat.
4. When installing, torque the nuts to 28 ft. lbs. (38 Nm).

Seat Belts

REMOVAL AND INSTALLATION

Front Belts

1. Remove the cover from the door pillar anchor plate and unbolt the plate.
2. Remove the cover from the floor mounted retractor assembly bolt and unbolt the assembly from the floor.
3. When unbolting the buckle assembly from the driver side, don't forget to disconnect the wire for the warning buzzer.
4. Inspect the belts for damage or wear, especially at the retractor. If any belt is frayed or worn, replace both halves of the

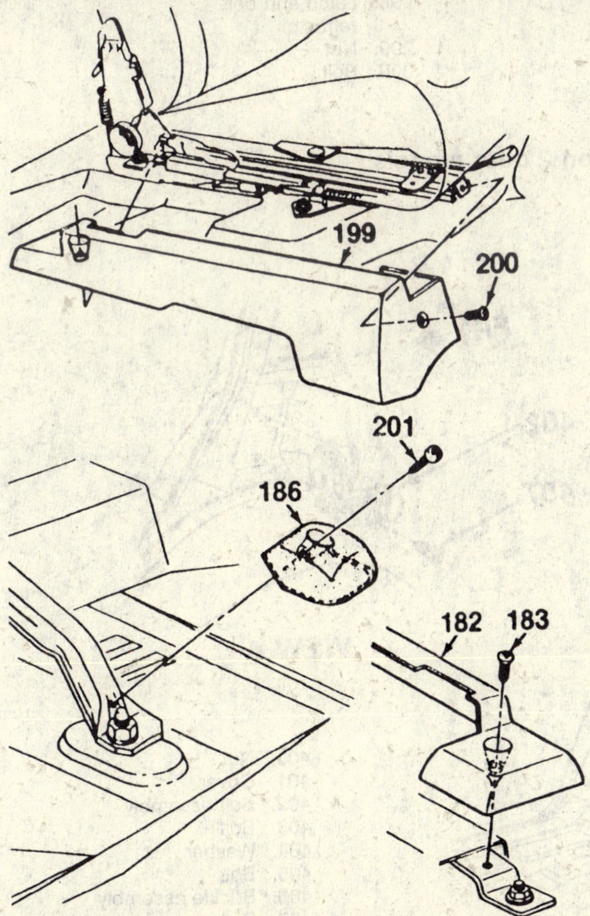

182. Cover 183. Screw 186. Cover 199. Cover 200. Screw 201. Screw

Front seat track comes out with the seat

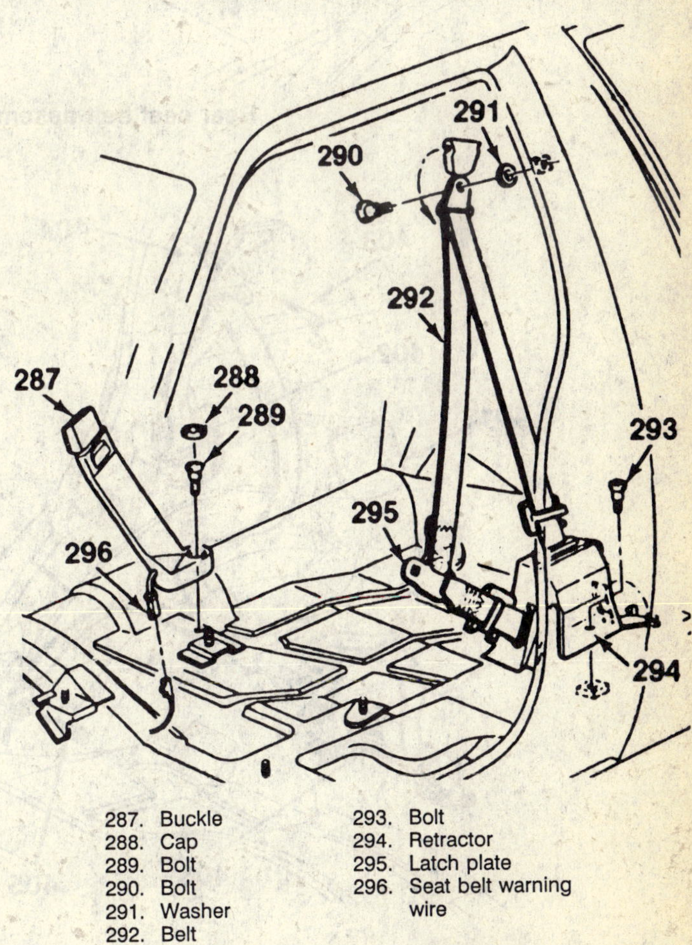

287. Buckle
288. Cap
289. Bolt
290. Bolt
291. Washer
292. Belt
293. Bolt
294. Retractor
295. Latch plate
296. Seat belt warning wire

Front seat belt assembly

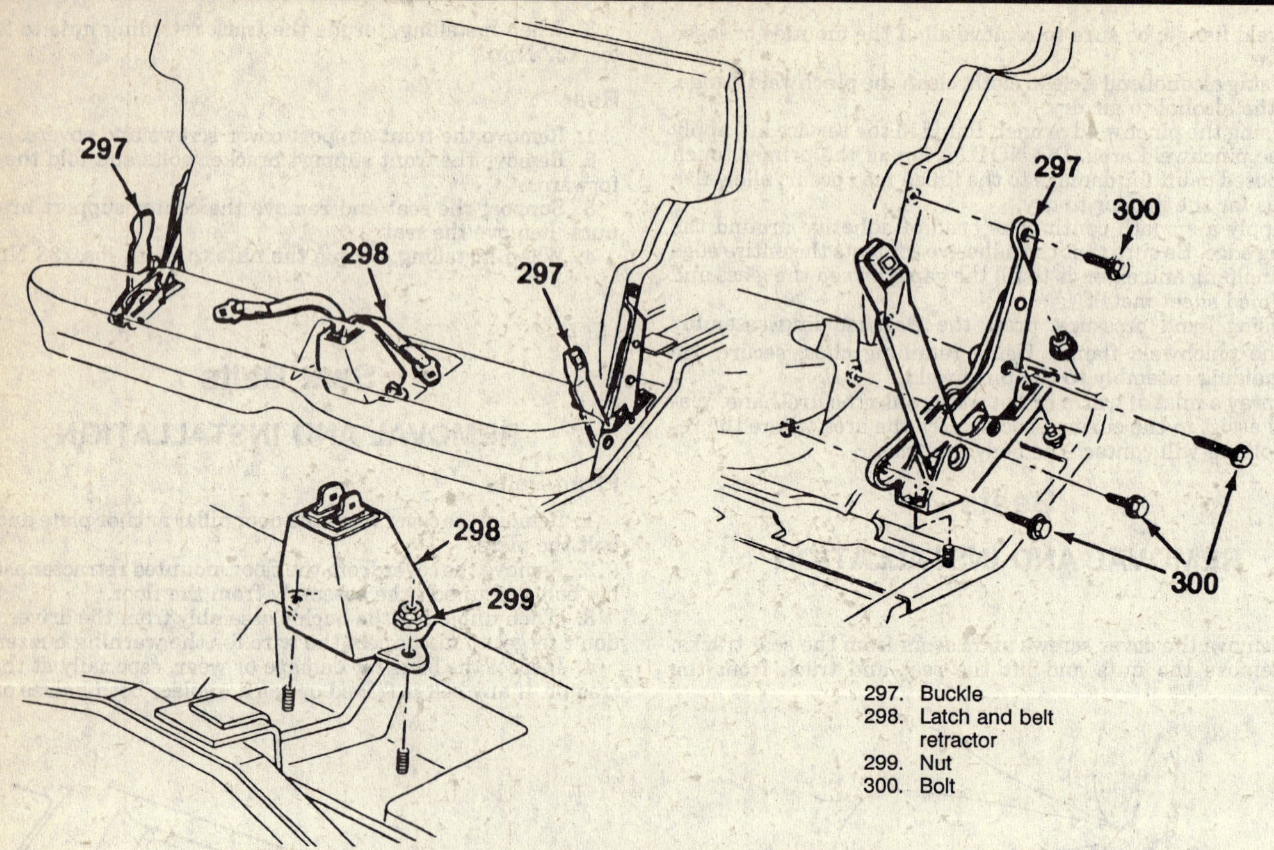

Rear seat belt assembly on 2 door models

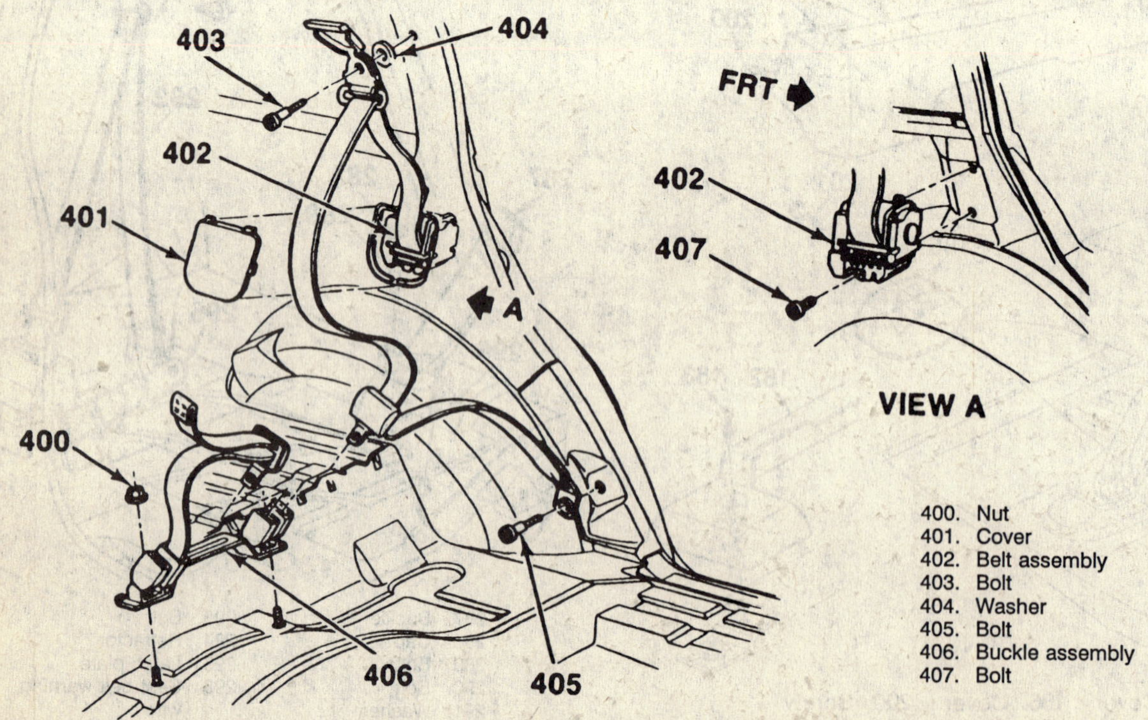

Rear seat belt assembly on 4 door models

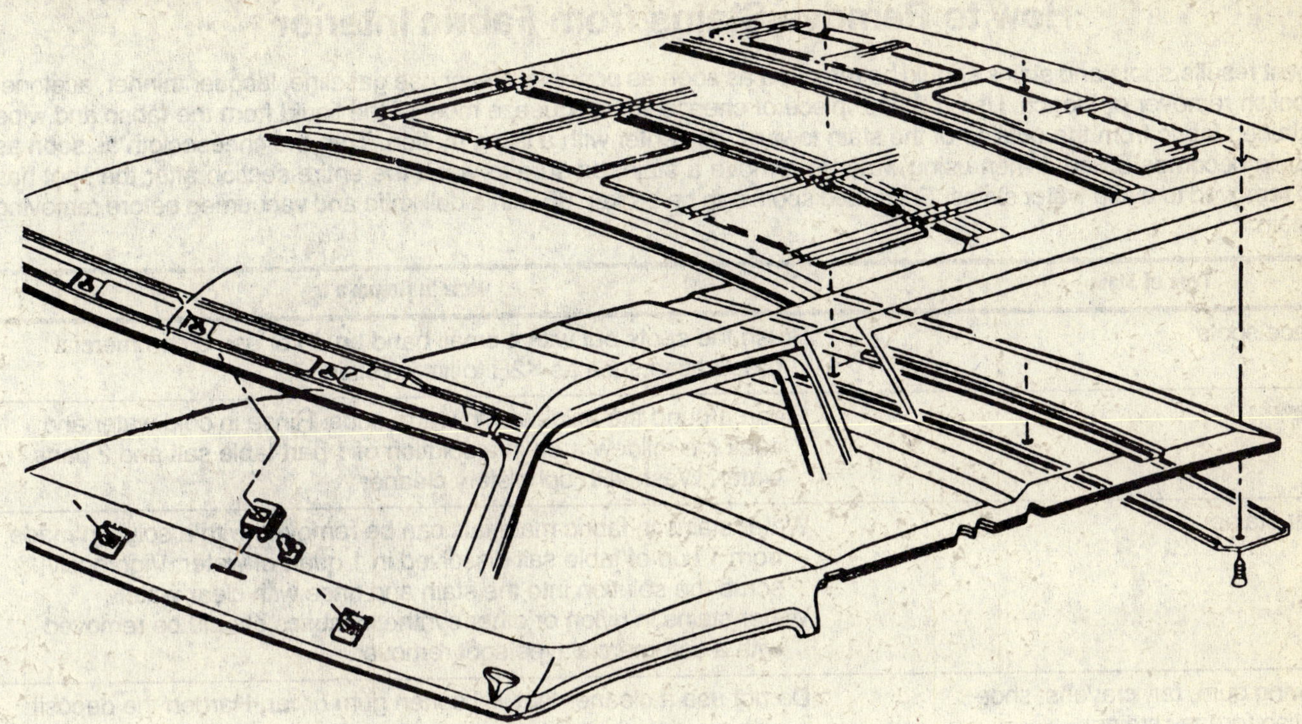

The entire headliner comes out as one piece

belt as a set. If the retractor will not lock when tilted, replace the belt as a set.

5. Installation is the reverse of removal. Torque the mounting bolts to 39 ft. lbs. (53 Nm).

Rear Belts

1. Remove the rear seat.
2. Unbolt the retractor from the pillar and the belt from the body panel.
3. Remove the nuts to remove the buckle assembly.
4. Inspect the belts for damage or wear, especially at the retractor. If any belt is frayed or worn, replace both halves of the belt as a set. If the retractor will not lock when tilted, replace the belt as a set.
5. Installation is the reverse of removal. Torque the mounting bolts to 35 ft. lbs. (48 Nm) and the nuts to 28 ft. lbs. (38 Nm).

Headliner

REMOVAL AND INSTALLATION

1. Remove the rear-quarter trim panel garnish molding.
2. Remove the right and left rear-quarter trim upper moldings.
3. Remove the right and left windshield garnish molding.
4. Remove the right and left sunshades.
5. To remove the headliner, perform the following procedures:
   a. Grasp the headliner at the right and left-sides, near the front of the cab.
   b. While pulling down on the headliner, shift it from side-to-side, to disengage the front from the roof.
   c. Remove the headliner from the cab.
6. To install, reverse the removal procedures.

How to Remove Stains from Fabric Interior

For best results, spots and stains should be removed as soon as possible. Never use gasoline, lacquer thinner, acetone, nail polish remover or bleach. Use a 3′ x 3″ piece of cheesecloth. Squeeze most of the liquid from the fabric and wipe the stained fabric from the outside of the stain toward the center with a lifting motion. Turn the cheesecloth as soon as one side becomes soiled. When using water to remove a stain, be sure to wash the entire section after the spot has been removed to avoid water stains. Encrusted spots can be broken up with a dull knife and vacuumed before removing the stain.

Type of Stain	How to Remove It
Surface spots	Brush the spots out with a small hand brush or use a commercial preparation such as K2R to lift the stain.
Mildew	Clean around the mildew with warm suds. Rinse in cold water and soak the mildew area in a solution of 1 part table salt and 2 parts water. Wash with upholstery cleaner.
Water stains	Water stains in fabric materials can be removed with a solution made from 1 cup of table salt dissolved in 1 quart of water. Vigorously scrub the solution into the stain and rinse with clear water. Water stains in nylon or other synthetic fabrics should be removed with a commercial type spot remover.
Chewing gum, tar, crayons, shoe polish (greasy stains)	Do not use a cleaner that will soften gum or tar. Harden the deposit with an ice cube and scrape away as much as possible with a dull knife. Moisten the remainder with cleaning fluid and scrub clean.
Ice cream, candy	Most candy has a sugar base and can be removed with a cloth wrung out in warm water. Oily candy, after cleaning with warm water, should be cleaned with upholstery cleaner. Rinse with warm water and clean the remainder with cleaning fluid.
Wine, alcohol, egg, milk, soft drink (non-greasy stains)	Do not use soap. Scrub the stain with a cloth wrung out in warm water. Remove the remainder with cleaning fluid.
Grease, oil, lipstick, butter and related stains	Use a spot remover to avoid leaving a ring. Work from the outisde of the stain to the center and dry with a clean cloth when the spot is gone.
Headliners (cloth)	Mix a solution of warm water and foam upholstery cleaner to give thick suds. Use only foam—liquid may streak or spot. Clean the entire headliner in one operation using a circular motion with a natural sponge.
Headliner (vinyl)	Use a vinyl cleaner with a sponge and wipe clean with a dry cloth.
Seats and door panels	Mix 1 pint upholstery cleaner in 1 gallon of water. Do not soak the fabric around the buttons.
Leather or vinyl fabric	Use a multi-purpose cleaner full strength and a stiff brush. Let stand 2 minutes and scrub thoroughly. Wipe with a clean, soft rag.
Nylon or synthetic fabrics	For normal stains, use the same procedures you would for washing cloth upholstery. If the fabric is extremely dirty, use a multi-purpose cleaner full strength with a stiff scrub brush. Scrub thoroughly in all directions and wipe with a cotton towel or soft rag.

Glossary

AIR/FUEL RATIO: The ratio of air to gasoline by weight in the fuel mixture drawn into the engine.

AIR INJECTION: One method of reducing harmful exhaust emissions by injecting air into each of the exhaust ports of an engine. The fresh air entering the hot exhaust manifold causes any remaining fuel to be burned before it can exit the tailpipe.

ALTERNATOR: A device used for converting mechanical energy into electrical energy.

AMMETER: An instrument, calibrated in amperes, used to measure the flow of an electrical current in a circuit. Ammeters are always connected in series with the circuit being tested.

AMPERE: The rate of flow of electrical current present when one volt of electrical pressure is applied against one ohm of electrical resistance.

ANALOG COMPUTER: Any microprocessor that uses similar (analogous) electrical signals to make its calculations.

ARMATURE: A laminated, soft iron core wrapped by a wire that converts electrical energy to mechanical energy as in a motor or relay. When rotated in a magnetic field, it changes mechanical energy into electrical energy as in a generator.

ATMOSPHERIC PRESSURE: The pressure on the Earth's surface caused by the weight of the air in the atmosphere. At sea level, this pressure is 14.7 psi at 32°F (101 kPa at 0°C).

ATOMIZATION: The breaking down of a liquid into a fine mist that can be suspended in air.

AXIAL PLAY: Movement parallel to a shaft or bearing bore.

BACKFIRE: The sudden combustion of gases in the intake or exhaust system that results in a loud explosion.

BACKLASH: The clearance or play between two parts, such as meshed gears.

BACKPRESSURE: Restrictions in the exhaust system that slow the exit of exhaust gases from the combustion chamber.

BAKELITE: A heat resistant, plastic insulator material commonly used in printed circuit boards and transistorized components.

BALL BEARING: A bearing made up of hardened inner and outer races between which hardened steel balls roll.

BALLAST RESISTOR: A resistor in the primary ignition circuit that lowers voltage after the engine is started to reduce wear on ignition components.

BEARING: A friction reducing, supportive device usually located between a stationary part and a moving part.

BIMETAL TEMPERATURE SENSOR: Any sensor or switch made of two dissimilar types of metal that bend when heated or cooled due to the different expansion rates of the alloys. These types of sensors usually function as an on/off switch.

BLOWBY: Combustion gases, composed of water vapor and unburned fuel, that leak past the piston rings into the crankcase during normal engine operation. These gases are removed by the PCV system to prevent the buildup of harmful acids in the crankcase.

BRAKE PAD: A brake shoe and lining assembly used with disc brakes.

BRAKE SHOE: The backing for the brake lining. The term is, however, usually applied to the assembly of the brake backing and lining.

BUSHING: A liner, usually removable, for a bearing; an anti-friction liner used in place of a bearing.

BYPASS: System used to bypass ballast resistor during engine cranking to increase voltage supplied to the coil.

CALIPER: A hydraulically activated device in a disc brake system, which is mounted straddling the brake rotor (disc). The caliper contains at least one piston and two brake pads. Hydraulic pressure on the piston(s) forces the pads against the rotor.

CAMSHAFT: A shaft in the engine on which are the lobes (cams) which operate the valves. The camshaft is driven by the crankshaft, via a belt, chain or gears, at one half the crankshaft speed.

CAPACITOR: A device which stores an electrical charge.

CARBON MONOXIDE (CO): A colorless, odorless gas given off as a normal byproduct of combustion. It is poisonous and extremely dangerous in confined areas, building up slowly to toxic levels without warning if adequate ventilation is not available.

CARBURETOR: A device, usually mounted on the intake manifold of an engine, which mixes the air and fuel in the proper proportion to allow even combustion.

CATALYTIC CONVERTER: A device installed in the exhaust system, like a muffler, that converts harmful byproducts of combustion into carbon dioxide and water vapor by means of a heat-producing chemical reaction.

CENTRIFUGAL ADVANCE: A mechanical method of advancing the spark timing by using flyweights in the distributor that react to centrifugal force generated by the distributor shaft rotation.

CHECK VALVE: Any one-way valve installed to permit the flow of air, fuel or vacuum in one direction only.

GLOSSARY

CHOKE: A device, usually a moveable valve, placed in the intake path of a carburetor to restrict the flow of air.

CIRCUIT: Any unbroken path through which an electrical current can flow. Also used to describe fuel flow in some instances.

CIRCUIT BREAKER: A switch which protects an electrical circuit from overload by opening the circuit when the current flow exceeds a predetermined level. Some circuit breakers must be reset manually, while most reset automatically

COIL (IGNITION): A transformer in the ignition circuit which steps up the voltage provided to the spark plugs.

COMBINATION MANIFOLD: An assembly which includes both the intake and exhaust manifolds in one casting.

COMBINATION VALVE: A device used in some fuel systems that routes fuel vapors to a charcoal storage canister instead of venting them into the atmosphere. The valve relieves fuel tank pressure and allows fresh air into the tank as the fuel level drops to prevent a vapor lock situation.

COMPRESSION RATIO: The comparison of the total volume of the cylinder and combustion chamber with the piston at BDC and the piston at TDC.

CONDENSER: 1. An electrical device which acts to store an electrical charge, preventing voltage surges.
2. A radiator-like device in the air conditioning system in which refrigerant gas condenses into a liquid, giving off heat.

CONDUCTOR: Any material through which an electrical current can be transmitted easily.

CONTINUITY: Continuous or complete circuit. Can be checked with an ohmmeter.

COUNTERSHAFT: An intermediate shaft which is rotated by a mainshaft and transmits, in turn, that rotation to a working part.

CRANKCASE: The lower part of an engine in which the crankshaft and related parts operate.

CRANKSHAFT: The main driving shaft of an engine which receives reciprocating motion from the pistons and converts it to rotary motion.

CYLINDER: In an engine, the round hole in the engine block in which the piston(s) ride.

CYLINDER BLOCK: The main structural member of an engine in which is found the cylinders, crankshaft and other principal parts.

CYLINDER HEAD: The detachable portion of the engine, fastened, usually, to the top of the cylinder block, containing all or most of the combustion chambers. On overhead valve engines, it contains the valves and their operating parts. On overhead cam engines, it contains the camshaft as well.

DEAD CENTER: The extreme top or bottom of the piston stroke.

DETONATION: An unwanted explosion of the air/fuel mixture in the combustion chamber caused by excess heat and compression, advanced timing, or an overly lean mixture. Also referred to as "ping".

DIAPHRAGM: A thin, flexible wall separating two cavities, such as in a vacuum advance unit.

DIESELING: A condition in which hot spots in the combustion chamber cause the engine to run on after the key is turned off.

DIFFERENTIAL: A geared assembly which allows the transmission of motion between drive axles, giving one axle the ability to turn faster than the other.

DIODE: An electrical device that will allow current to flow in one direction only.

DISC BRAKE: A hydraulic braking assembly consisting of a brake disc, or rotor, mounted on an axle, and a caliper assembly containing, usually two brake pads which are activated by hydraulic pressure. The pads are forced against the sides of the disc, creating friction which slows the vehicle.

DISTRIBUTOR: A mechanically driven device on an engine which is responsible for electrically firing the spark plug at a predetermined point of the piston stroke.

DOWEL PIN: A pin, inserted in mating holes in two different parts allowing those parts to maintain a fixed relationship.

DRUM BRAKE: A braking system which consists of two brake shoes and one or two wheel cylinders, mounted on a fixed backing plate, and a brake drum, mounted on an axle, which revolves around the assembly. Hydraulic action applied to the wheel cylinders forces the shoes outward against the drum, creating friction, slowing the vehicle.

DWELL: The rate, measured in degrees of shaft rotation, at which an electrical circuit cycles on and off.

ELECTRONIC CONTROL UNIT (ECU): Ignition module, module, amplifier or igniter. See Module for definition.

ELECTRONIC IGNITION: A system in which the timing and firing of the spark plugs is controlled by an electronic control unit, usually called a module. These systems have no points or condenser.

ENDPLAY: The measured amount of axial movement in a shaft.

ENGINE: A device that converts heat into mechanical energy.

EXHAUST MANIFOLD: A set of cast passages or pipes which conduct exhaust gases from the engine.

FEELER GAUGE: A blade, usually metal, of precisely predetermined thickness, used to measure the clearance between two parts. These blades usually are available in sets of assorted thicknesses.

F-Head: An engine configuration in which the intake valves are in the cylinder head, while the camshaft and exhaust valves are located in the cylinder block. The camshaft operates the intake valves via lifters and pushrods, while it operates the exhaust valves directly.

FIRING ORDER: The order in which combustion occurs in the cylinders of an engine. Also the order in which spark is distributed to the plugs by the distributor.

FLATHEAD: An engine configuration in which the camshaft and all the valves are located in the cylinder block.

FLOODING: The presence of too much fuel in the intake manifold and combustion chamber which prevents the air/fuel mixture from firing, thereby causing a no-start situation.

FLYWHEEL: A disc shaped part bolted to the rear end of the crankshaft. Around the outer perimeter is affixed the ring gear. The starter drive engages the ring gear, turning the flywheel, which rotates the crankshaft, imparting the initial starting motion to the engine.

FOOT POUND (ft.lb. or sometimes, ft. lbs.): The amount of energy or work needed to raise an item weighing one pound, a distance of one foot.

FUSE: A protective device in a circuit which prevents circuit overload by breaking the circuit when a specific amperage is present. The device is constructed around a strip or wire of a lower amperage rating than the circuit it is designed to protect. When an amperage higher than that stamped on the fuse is present in the circuit, the strip or wire melts, opening the circuit.

GEAR RATIO: The ratio between the number of teeth on meshing gears.

GENERATOR: A device which converts mechanical energy into electrical energy.

HEAT RANGE: The measure of a spark plug's ability to dissipate heat from its firing end. The higher the heat range, the hotter the plug fires.

HUB: The center part of a wheel or gear.

HYDROCARBON (HC): Any chemical compound made up of hydrogen and carbon. A major pollutant formed by the engine as a byproduct of combustion.

HYDROMETER: An instrument used to measure the specific gravity of a solution.

INCH POUND (in.lb. or sometimes, in. lbs.): One twelfth of a foot pound.

INDUCTION: A means of transferring electrical energy in the form of a magnetic field. Principle used in the ignition coil to increase voltage.

INJECTION PUMP: A device, usually mechanically operated, which meters and delivers fuel under pressure to the fuel injector.

INJECTOR: A device which receives metered fuel under relatively low pressure and is activated to inject the fuel into the engine under relatively high pressure at a predetermined time.

INPUT SHAFT: The shaft to which torque is applied, usually carrying the driving gear or gears.

INTAKE MANIFOLD: A casting of passages or pipes used to conduct air or a fuel/air mixture to the cylinders.

JOURNAL: The bearing surface within which a shaft operates.

KEY: A small block usually fitted in a notch between a shaft and a hub to prevent slippage of the two parts.

MANIFOLD: A casting of passages or set of pipes which connect the cylinders to an inlet or outlet source.

MANIFOLD VACUUM: Low pressure in an engine intake manifold formed just below the throttle plates. Manifold vacuum is highest at idle and drops under acceleration.

MASTER CYLINDER: The primary fluid pressurizing device in a hydraulic system. In automotive use, it is found in brake and hydraulic clutch systems and is pedal activated, either directly or, in a power brake system, through the power booster.

MODULE: Electronic control unit, amplifier or igniter of solid state or integrated design which controls the current flow in the ignition primary circuit based on input from the pick-up coil. When the module opens the primary circuit, the high secondary voltage is induced in the coil.

NEEDLE BEARING: A bearing which consists of a number (usually a large number) of long, thin rollers.

OHM: (Ω) The unit used to measure the resistance of conductor to electrical flow. One ohm is the amount of resistance that limits current flow to one ampere in a circuit with one volt of pressure.

OHMMETER: An instrument used for measuring the resistance, in ohms, in an electrical circuit.

OUTPUT SHAFT: The shaft which transmits torque from a device, such as a transmission.

OVERDRIVE: A gear assembly which produces more shaft revolutions than that transmitted to it.

OVERHEAD CAMSHAFT (OHC): An engine configuration in which the camshaft is mounted on top of the cylinder head and operates the valve either directly or by means of rocker arms.

OVERHEAD VALVE (OHV): An engine configuration in which all of the valves are located in the cylinder head and the camshaft is located in the cylinder block. The camshaft operates the valves via lifters and pushrods.

OXIDES OF NITROGEN (NOx): Chemical compounds of nitrogen produced as a byproduct of combustion. They combine with hydrocarbons to produce smog.

OXYGEN SENSOR: Used with the feedback system to sense the presence of oxygen in the exhaust gas and signal the computer which can reference the voltage signal to an air/fuel ratio.

PINION: The smaller of two meshing gears.

PISTON RING: An open ended ring which fits into a groove on the outer diameter of the piston. Its chief function is to form a seal between the piston and cylinder wall. Most automotive pistons have three rings: two for compression sealing; one for oil sealing.

PRELOAD: A predetermined load placed on a bearing during assembly or by adjustment.

PRIMARY CIRCUIT: Is the low voltage side of the ignition system which consists of the ignition switch, ballast resistor or resistance wire, bypass, coil, electronic control unit and pick-up coil as well as the connecting wires and harnesses.

PRESS FIT: The mating of two parts under pressure, due to the inner diameter of one being smaller than the outer diameter of the other, or vice versa; an interference fit.

RACE: The surface on the inner or outer ring of a bearing on which the balls, needles or rollers move.

REGULATOR: A device which maintains the amperage and/or voltage levels of a circuit at predetermined values.

RELAY: A switch which automatically opens and/or closes a circuit.

RESISTANCE: The opposition to the flow of current through a circuit or electrical device, and is measured in ohms. Resistance is equal to the voltage divided by the amperage.

RESISTOR: A device, usually made of wire, which offers a preset amount of resistance in an electrical circuit.

RING GEAR: The name given to a ring-shaped gear attached to a differential case, or affixed to a flywheel or as part a planetary gear set.

ROLLER BEARING: A bearing made up of hardened inner and outer races between which hardened steel rollers move.

ROTOR: 1. The disc-shaped part of a disc brake assembly, upon which the brake pads bear; also called, brake disc.
2. The device mounted atop the distributor shaft, which passes current to the distributor cap tower contacts.

SECONDARY CIRCUIT: The high voltage side of the ignition system, usually above 20,000 volts. The secondary includes the ignition coil, coil wire, distributor cap and rotor, spark plug wires and spark plugs.

SENDING UNIT: A mechanical, electrical, hydraulic or electromagnetic device which transmits information to a gauge.

SENSOR: Any device designed to measure engine operating conditions or ambient pressures and temperatures. Usually electronic in nature and designed to send a voltage signal to an on-board computer, some sensors may operate as a simple on/off switch or they may provide a variable voltage signal (like a potentiometer) as conditions or measured parameters change.

SHIM: Spacers of precise, predetermined thickness used between parts to establish a proper working relationship.

SLAVE CYLINDER: In automotive use, a device in the hydraulic clutch system which is activated by hydraulic force, disengaging the clutch.

SOLENOID: A coil used to produce a magnetic field, the effect of which is produce work.

SPARK PLUG: A device screwed into the combustion chamber of a spark ignition engine. The basic construction is a conductive core inside of a ceramic insulator, mounted in an outer conductive base. An electrical charge from the spark plug wire travels along the conductive core and jumps a preset air gap to a grounding point or points at the end of the conductive base. The resultant spark ignites the fuel/air mixture in the combustion chamber.

SPLINES: Ridges machined or cast onto the outer diameter of a shaft or inner diameter of a bore to enable parts to mate without rotation.

TACHOMETER: A device used to measure the rotary speed of an engine, shaft, gear, etc., usually in rotations per minute.

THERMOSTAT: A valve, located in the cooling system of an engine, which is closed when cold and opens gradually in response to engine heating, controlling the temperature of the coolant and rate of coolant flow.

TOP DEAD CENTER (TDC): The point at which the piston reaches the top of its travel on the compression stroke.

TORQUE: The twisting force applied to an object.

TORQUE CONVERTER: A turbine used to transmit power from a driving member to a driven member via hydraulic action, providing changes in drive ratio and torque. In automotive use, it links the driveplate at the rear of the engine to the automatic transmission.

TRANSDUCER: A device used to change a force into an electrical signal.

TRANSISTOR: A semi-conductor component which can be actuated by a small voltage to perform an electrical switching function.

TUNE-UP: A regular maintenance function, usually associated with the replacement and adjustment of parts and components in the electrical and fuel systems of a vehicle for the purpose of attaining optimum performance.

TURBOCHARGER: An exhaust driven pump which compresses intake air and forces it into the combustion chambers at higher than atmospheric pressures. The increased air pressure allows more fuel to be burned and results in increased horsepower being produced.

VACUUM ADVANCE: A device which advances the ignition timing in response to increased engine vacuum.

VACUUM GAUGE: An instrument used to measure the presence of vacuum in a chamber.

VALVE: A device which control the pressure, direction of flow or rate of flow of a liquid or gas.

VALVE CLEARANCE: The measured gap between the end of the valve stem and the rocker arm, cam lobe or follower that activates the valve.

VISCOSITY: The rating of a liquid's internal resistance to flow.

VOLTMETER: An instrument used for measuring electrical force in units called volts. Voltmeters are always connected parallel with the circuit being tested.

WHEEL CYLINDER: Found in the automotive drum brake assembly, it is a device, actuated by hydraulic pressure, which, through internal pistons, pushes the brake shoes outward against the drums.